WEST

ILLINOIS VEHICLE CODE

CHAPTER 625 ILLINOIS COMPILED STATUTES

2003

Using the Classification and Numbering System of the Official Illinois Compiled Statutes, text complete through end of the 2002 Regular and Special Sessions of the 92nd General Assembly.

INDEX

THOMSON
WEST

Mat #40069995

ISBN 0–314–10351–1

PRINTED ON 10% POST CONSUMER RECYCLED PAPER

PREFACE

The text of The Illinois Vehicle Code is to date as amended through the end of the 2002 Regular and Special Sessions of the 92nd General Assembly.

The Vehicle Code Index was prepared and brought to date by the publisher.

THE PUBLISHER

April, 2003

Internet Access
Contact the West Editorial Department directly with your questions and suggestions by e-mail at editor@westgroup.com.
Visit West's home page on the World Wide Web at http://www.westgroup.com.

*

COORDINATED RESEARCH IN ILLINOIS FROM WEST GROUP

WEST'S ILLINOIS PRACTICE SERIES*

Illinois Business Organizations

Illinois Civil Litigation Guide

Illinois Civil Procedure Before Trial

Illinois Civil Trial Procedure

Illinois Civil Discovery

Illinois Criminal Practice and Procedure

Illinois Uniform Commercial Code Forms

Illinois Uniform Commercial Code With Illinois Code Comments

West's Illinois Practice Series (CD–ROM)

JURY INSTRUCTIONS

Illinois Pattern Jury Instructions—IPI—Civil (Westlaw)

Illinois Pattern Jury Instructions—IPI—Criminal (Westlaw)

Illinois Non–Pattern Jury Instructions, 3d*

ILLINOIS FORMS

West's Illinois Forms—Business Organizations

West's Illinois Forms—Civil Practice

Callaghan's Illinois Civil Practice Forms* (CD–ROM, Westlaw)

West's Illinois Forms—Debtor–Creditor Relations

West's Illinois Forms—Domestic Relations

Federal Estate Tax Returns: Illinois Form 700

Illinois Forms (CD–ROM)

Callaghan's Illinois Legal Forms*

Illinois Forms—Legal and Business* (CD–ROM, Westlaw)

Personal Injury Forms*

West's Illinois Forms—Probate and Administration of Estates

West's Illinois Forms—Real Estate Transactions

West's Illinois Forms—Wills and Trusts

COORDINATED RESEARCH

West's Smith–Hurd Illinois Compiled Statutes Annotated*
(CD–ROM, Westlaw)

Illinois Compiled Statutes, State Bar Association Edition*

Illinois Legislative Service

Illinois Administrative Code (CD–ROM)

Illinois Appellate Practice Manual*

Nichols Illinois Civil Practice Deskbook (Westlaw)

Nichols Illinois Civil Practice With Forms, ADR Handbook (Westlaw)

Illinois Corporate Practice Manual

Illinois Counseling the Older Client, 2d

Illinois Court Rules and Procedure—Volume I—State

Illinois Court Rules and Procedure—Volume II—Federal

Illinois Court Rules and Procedure—Volume III—Circuit Courts

Illinois Criminal Law and Procedure

Illinois Damages Awards, Personal Injury & Intentional Torts

Illinois Decisions* (CD–ROM, Westlaw)

Illinois Decisions, Smith–Hurd Illinois Compiled Statutes
Unannotated (CD–ROM)

Illinois Digest (1st & 2d)*

Estate Planning and Administration in Illinois*

Illinois Evidence Manual, 3d

Illinois Family Laws and Court Rules

Illinois Practice of Family Law

Illinois Insurance Laws

Illinois Law and Practice (CD–ROM, Westlaw)

Illinois Law Finder

The Law of Medical Practice in Illinois, 2d

Illinois Lawyers Manual, 3d

Illinois Leave to Appeal Table

Illinois Official Reports (Appellate or Supreme)

Illinois Personal Injury

Illinois Practice Guide Personal Injury, 2d

Illinois Probate Act and Related Laws

Horner Probate Practice and Estates*

Illinois Real Estate Practice Guide, 2d

Illinois Real Property Service*

Illinois Tort Law and Practice, 2d*

COORDINATED RESEARCH

Trial Handbooks for Illinois Lawyers, 7th (Civil, Criminal and Criminal Sentencing), 8th (Criminal), and (Homicide)

Illinois Vehicle Code

WESTCheck® and WESTMATE®

WEST*fax*®

WESTLAW

WIN®

West CD–ROM Libraries™

WESTLAW AND WEST BOOKS
The Ultimate Research System

---

* Also available in non-print form (e.g., CD–ROM or disk depending on product)

For more information about any of these Illinois practice resources, please call your West Representative or **1–800–328–9352**.

NEED RESEARCH HELP?

You can get quality research results with free help—call the West Reference Attorneys when you have questions concerning WESTLAW or West Publications at 1–800–733–2889.

NEED A NEW CASE TODAY?

You can get copies of new court cases faxed to you today—office, courthouse or hotel, anywhere a fax machine is available. Call West*fax* at 1–800–562–2329.

INTERNET ACCESS

Contact the West Editorial Department directly with your questions and suggestions by e-mail at editor@westgroup.com. Visit West's home page on the World Wide Web at http://www.westgroup.com.

*

TABLE OF CONTENTS

Chapter 625. Vehicle Code

For analysis of subheadings and sections, see beginning of each Act

TABLE OF CONTENTS

CHAPTER 625

VEHICLES

ACT 5. ILLINOIS VEHICLE CODE

CHAPTER 1. TITLE AND DEFINITIONS

5/1-100. Short Title

§ 1-100. Short Title. This Act may be cited as the Illinois Vehicle Code.

Portions of this Act may likewise be cited by a short title as follows:

Chapters 2, 3, 4 and 5: the Illinois Vehicle Title & Registration Law.[1]

Chapter 6: the Illinois Driver Licensing Law.[2]

Chapter 7: the Illinois Safety and Family Financial Responsibility Law.[3]

Chapter 11: the Illinois Rules of the Road.[4]

Chapter 12: the Illinois Vehicle Equipment Law.[5]

Chapter 13: the Illinois Vehicle Inspection Law.[6]

Chapter 14: the Illinois Vehicle Equipment Safety Compact.[7]

Chapter 15: the Illinois Size and Weight Law.[8]

Chapter 17: the Illinois Highway Safety Law.[9]

Chapter 18a: the Illinois Commercial Relocation of Trespassing Vehicles Law.[10]

Chapter 18b: the Illinois Motor Carrier Safety Law.[11]

Chapter 18c: the Illinois Commercial Transportation Law.[12]

P.A. 76-1586, § 101, eff. July 1, 1970. Amended by P.A. 80-1459, § 2, eff. Jan. 1, 1979; P.A. 84-796, § 1, eff. Jan. 1, 1986; P.A. 84-1025, § 2, eff. Jan. 1, 1986; P.A. 85-553, § 2, eff. Sept. 18, 1987; P.A. 86-611, § 1, eff. Sept. 1, 1989; P.A. 86-1475, Art. 4, § 4-49, eff. Jan. 10, 1991; P.A. 89-92, § 10, eff. July 1, 1996.

Formerly Ill.Rev.Stat.1991, ch. 95 ½, ¶ 1-100.

1 625 ILCS 5/2-101 et seq., 5/3-100 et seq., 5/4-100 et seq., 5/5-100 et seq.

2 625 ILCS 5/6-100 et seq.

3 625 ILCS 5/7-100 et seq.

4 625 ILCS 5/11-100 et seq.

5 625 ILCS 5/12-100 et seq.

6 625 ILCS 5/13-100 et seq.

7 Former Ill.Rev.Stat. ch. 95½, ¶ 15-100 et seq. (repealed).

8 625 ILCS 5/15-100 et seq.

9 625 ILCS 5/17-101; Former Ill.Rev.Stat. ch. 95½, ¶ 17-102 et seq. (repealed).

10 625 ILCS 5/18a-100 et seq.

11 625 ILCS 5/18b-100.

12 625 ILCS 5/18c-1101 et seq.

Title of Act:

An Act in relation to the regulation of vehicles and of commercial transportation. P.A. 76-1586, eff. July 1, 1970. Title amended by P.A. 84-796, § 2, approved Sept. 21, 1985, eff. Jan. 1, 1986.

5/1-101. Definition of words and phrases

§ 1-101. Definition of words and phrases. The following words and phrases when used in this Code shall, for the purpose of this Code, have the meanings respectively ascribed to them in this Chapter, except when the context otherwise requires and except where another definition set forth in another Chapter of this Code and applicable to that Chapter or a designated part thereof is applicable.

P.A. 76-1586, § 1-101, eff. July 1, 1970. Amended by P.A. 83-831, § 1, eff. Jan. 1, 1984.

Formerly Ill.Rev.Stat.1991, ch. 95 ½, ¶ 1-101.

5/1-101.05. Abandoned vehicle

§ 1-101.05. Abandoned vehicle. For the purposes of Chapter 4,[1] "abandoned vehicle" means any vehicle in a state of disrepair rendering the vehicle incapable of being driven in its condition or any vehicle that has not been moved or used for 7 consecutive days or more and is apparently deserted.

P.A. 76-1586, § 1-101.05, added by P.A. 90-89, § 15, eff. Jan. 1, 1998.

1 625 ILCS 5/4-100 et seq.

5/1-101.1. Act

§ 1-101.1. Act. The word "Act" as used in this Code shall, unless the context otherwise clearly indicates, mean "The Illinois Vehicle Code".[1]

P.A. 76-1586, § 1-101.1, added by P.A. 82-123, § 1, eff. Jan. 1, 1982.

Formerly Ill.Rev.Stat.1991, ch. 95 ½, ¶ 1-101.1.

1 625 ILCS 5/1-100 et seq.

5/1-101.1a. Administrative decision

§ 1-101.1a. Administrative decision. The term "administrative decision" is defined as in Section 3-101 of the Code of Civil Procedure.[1]

P.A. 76-1586, § 1-101.1a, added by P.A. 90-89, § 15, eff. Jan. 1, 1998.

1 735 ILCS 5/3-101.

5/1-101.2. Affirmation

§ 1-101.2. Affirmation. A signed statement to the effect that the information provided by the signer is true and correct. The affirmation shall subject any person who shall knowingly affirm falsely, in matter material to any issue or point in question, to the penalties inflicted by law on persons convicted of perjury under Section 32-2 of the Criminal Code of 1961.[1]

P.A. 76-1586, § 1-101.2, added by P.A. 83-1473, § 1, eff. Jan. 1, 1985.

Formerly Ill.Rev.Stat.1991, ch. 95 ½, ¶ 1-101.2.

1 720 ILCS 5/32-2.

5/1-101.3. § 1-101.3. Repealed by P.A. 90-89, § 20, eff. Jan. 1, 1998

5/1-101.5. Agency

§ 1-101.5. Agency. For the purposes of Chapter 13B,[1] "Agency" means the Illinois Environmental Protection Agency.

P.A. 76-1586, § 1-101.5, added by P.A. 90-89, § 15, eff. Jan. 1, 1998.

1 625 ILCS 5/13B-1 et seq.

5/1-101.6. Agricultural movements

§ 1-101.6. Agricultural movements. The operation of a motor vehicle or combination of vehicles controlled and operated by a private motor carrier of property that is using the vehicle to transport nonhazardous or hazardous agricultural crop production fertilizers or agricultural chemicals from a local source of supply to farm or field, from one farm or field to another, or from farm or field back to the local source of supply.

P.A. 76-1586, § 1-101.6, added by P.A. 90-89, § 15, eff. Jan. 1, 1998.

5/1-101.8. All-terrain vehicle

§ 1-101.8. All-terrain vehicle. Any motorized off-highway device designed to travel primarily off-highway, 50 inches or less in width, having a manufacturer's dry weight of 900 pounds or less, traveling on 3 or more low-pressure tires, designed with a seat or saddle for operator use, and handlebars or steering wheel for steering control, except equipment such as lawnmowers.

P.A. 76-1586, § 1-102.02, added by P.A. 85-830, § 1, eff. Sept. 24, 1987. Renumbered § 1-101.8 and amended by P.A. 90-89, § 15, eff. Jan. 1, 1998. Amended by P.A. 92-812, § 5, eff. Aug. 21, 2002.

Formerly Ill.Rev.Stat.1991, ch. 95 ½, ¶ 1-102.02.

5/1-102. Alley

§ 1-102. Alley. A public way within a block, generally giving access to the rear of lots or buildings and not used for general traffic circulation.

P.A. 76-1586, § 1-102, eff. July 1, 1970.

Formerly Ill.Rev.Stat.1991, ch. 95 ½, ¶ 1-102.

5/1-102.01. Ambulance

§ 1-102.01. Ambulance. Any publicly or privately owned vehicle which is specifically designed, constructed or modified and equipped, and is intended to be used for, and is maintained or operated for the emergency transportation of persons who are sick, injured, wounded or otherwise incapacitated or helpless.

P.A. 76-1586, § 1-102.01, added by P.A. 82-433, § 1, eff. Sept. 8, 1981.

Formerly Ill.Rev.Stat.1991, ch. 95 ½, ¶ 1-102.01.

Section 3 of P.A. 82-433 approved Sept. 8, 1981, provided:

"This Act takes effect upon its becoming a law, except that the provisions relating to safety tests and proof of financial responsibility for medical transport vehicles apply only to applications for and the issuance of registration plates which are required to be displayed on January 1, 1982 or thereafter."

5/1–102.02. § 1–102.02. Renumbered as § 1–101.8 by P.A. 90–89, § 15, eff. Jan. 1, 1998

5/1–102.1. Antique vehicle

§ 1–102.1. Antique vehicle. A motor vehicle that is more than 25 years of age or a bona fide replica thereof and which is driven on the highways only going to and returning from an antique auto show or an exhibition, or for servicing or demonstration, or a fire-fighting vehicle more than 20 years old which is not used as fire-fighting equipment but is used only for the purpose of exhibition of demonstration.

P.A. 76–1586, § 1–102.1, added by P.A. 77–217, § 1, eff. Jan. 1, 1972. Amended by P.A. 78–667, § 1, eff. July 1, 1974.

Formerly Ill.Rev.Stat.1991, ch. 95 ½, ¶ 1–102.1.

5/1–102.2. Apportionable semitrailer

§ 1–102.2. Apportionable semitrailer. Through March 31, 1996, an apportionable semitrailer is a semitrailer that is paying annual fees to a foreign jurisdiction under the provisions of the International Registration Plan. Beginning April 1, 1996, an apportionable semitrailer is a semitrailer used in interstate commerce and registered with an apportioned power fleet.

P.A. 76–1586, § 1–102.2, added by P.A. 87–1040, § 1, eff. Sept. 11, 1992. Amended by P.A. 89–245, § 5, eff. Jan. 1, 1996.

Formerly Ill.Rev.Stat., ch. 95½, ¶ 1–102.2.

5/1–102.3. Apportionable trailer

§ 1–102.3. Apportionable trailer. A trailer involved in interstate commerce.

P.A. 76–1586, § 1–102.3, added by P.A. 87–1040, § 1, eff. Sept. 11, 1992.

Formerly Ill.Rev.Stat., ch. 95½, ¶ 1–102.3.

5/1–103. Approved driver education course

§ 1–103. Approved driver education course. (a) Any course of driver education approved by the State Board of Education, offered by public or private schools maintaining grades 9 through 12, and meeting at least the minimum requirements of the "Driver Education Act", as now or hereafter amended,[1] or (b) any course of driver education offered by a school licensed to give driver education instructions under this Act which meets at least the minimum educational requirements of the "Driver Education Act", as now or hereafter amended, and is approved by the State Board of Education or (c) any course of driver education given in another State to an Illinois resident attending school in such State and approved by the State administrator of the Driver Education Program of such other State.

P.A. 76–1586, § 1–103, eff. July 1, 1970. Amended by P.A. 76–2120, § 1, eff. July 1, 1970; P.A. 81–1508, § 8, eff. Sept. 25, 1980.

Formerly Ill.Rev.Stat.1991, ch. 95 ½, ¶ 1–103.

1 105 ILCS 5/27–24 et seq.

5/1–104. § 1–104. Repealed by P.A. 90–89, § 20, eff. Jan. 1, 1998

5/1–104.1. Article

§ 1–104.1. Article. The word "Article" as used in this Code shall, unless the context otherwise clearly indicates, mean an Article of a Chapter of "The Illinois Vehicle Code".[1]

P.A. 76–1586, § 1–104.1, added by P.A. 82–123, § 1, eff. Jan. 1, 1982.

Formerly Ill.Rev.Stat.1991, ch. 95 ½, ¶ 1–104.1.

1 625 ILCS 5/1–100 et seq.

5/1–105. Authorized emergency vehicle

§ 1–105. Authorized emergency vehicle.

Emergency vehicles of municipal departments or public service corporations as are designated or authorized by proper local authorities; police vehicles; vehicles of the fire department; ambulances; vehicles of the Illinois Emergency Management Agency; and vehicles of the Department of Nuclear Safety.

P.A. 76–1586, § 1–105, eff. July 1, 1970. Amended by P.A. 92–138, § 5, eff. July 24, 2001.

Formerly Ill.Rev.Stat.1991, ch. 95 ½, ¶ 1–105.

5/1–105.3. Automotive parts recycler

§ 1–105.3. Automotive parts recycler. A person who is in the business of acquiring previously owned vehicles and vehicle parts for the primary purpose of disposing of parts of vehicles in a manner other than that described in the definition of a "scrap processor" in this Code.

P.A. 76–1586, § 1–105.3, added by P.A. 90–89, § 15, eff. Jan. 1, 1998.

5/1–105.5. Automated red light enforcement system

§ 1–105.5. Automated red light enforcement system. A system in a municipality with a population of 1,000,000 or more operated by a governmental agency, in cooperation with a law enforcement agency, that photographically records a motor vehicle's response to a traffic control signal with a red light indication and is designed to obtain a clear photograph of the vehicle and the vehicle's license plate when the motor vehicle is involved in a motor vehicle accident, leaving the scene of a motor vehicle accident, or reckless driving that results in bodily injury.

P.A. 76–1586, § 1–105.5, added by P.A. 90–86, § 5, eff. July 10, 1997.

5/1–105.6. Axle load

§ 1–105.6. Axle load. The total load transmitted to the road by all wheels whose centers may be included between 2 parallel transverse vertical planes 40 inches apart extending across the full width of the vehicle.

P.A. 76–1586, § 1–105.6, added by P.A. 90–89, § 15, eff. Jan. 1, 1998.

5/1–106. Bicycle

§ 1–106. Bicycle. Every device propelled by human power upon which any person may ride, having two tandem wheels except scooters and similar devices.

P.A. 76–1586, § 1–106, eff. July 1, 1970. Amended by P.A. 85–951, § 1, eff. July 1, 1988.

Formerly Ill.Rev.Stat.1991, ch. 95 ½, ¶ 1–106.

5/1–106.5. Bumper

§ 1–106.5. Bumper. Any device or system of devices protruding from and attached to the front and rear of a motor vehicle that has been designed to be used to absorb the impact of a collision. For the purposes of this Code, a bumper also includes a device or system of devices similar in design to those with which new motor vehicles are equipped.

P.A. 76-1586, § 1-106.5, added by P.A. 90-89, § 15, eff. Jan. 1, 1998. Amended by P.A. 92-61, § 5, eff. Jan. 1, 2002.

5/1-107. Bus

§ 1-107. Bus. Every motor vehicle, other than a commuter van, designed for carrying more than 10 persons.

P.A. 76-1586, § 1-107, eff. July 1, 1970. Amended by P.A. 80-529, § 1, eff. Jan. 1, 1979; P.A. 82-1011, § 2, eff. Sept. 17, 1982.

Formerly Ill.Rev.Stat.1991, ch. 95 ½, ¶ 1-107.

5/1-108. Business district

§ 1-108. Business district. The territory contiguous to and including a highway when within any 600 feet along such highway there are buildings in use for business or industrial purposes, including but not limited to hotels, banks, or office buildings, railroad stations and public buildings which occupy at least 300 feet of frontage on one side or 300 feet collectively on both sides of the highway.

P.A. 76-1586, § 1-108, eff. July 1, 1970.

Formerly Ill.Rev.Stat.1991, ch. 95 ½, ¶ 1-108.

5/1-109. § 1-109. Repealed by P.A. 81-969, § 2

The repeal was effective at the "start of the 1981 registration year."

5/1-109.01. Camping trailer

§ 1-109.01. Camping trailer. A trailer, not used commercially, constructed with partial side walls which fold for towing and unfold to provide temporary living quarters for recreational camping or travel use and of a size or weight not requiring an overdimension permit when towed on a highway.

P.A. 76-1586, § 1-109.01, added by P.A. 81-969, § 1, eff. Jan. 1, 1980.

Formerly Ill.Rev.Stat.1991, ch. 95 ½, ¶ 1-109.01.

Section 3 of P.A. 81-969, approved Sept. 22, 1979, provided:

"This amendatory Act takes effect at the start of the 1981 registration year."

Effective date of P.A. 81-969: Section 3 of P.A. 81-969, approved Sept. 22, 1979, provided the Act would take effect at the start of the 1981 registration year.

5/1-110. Cancellation of driver's license

§ 1-110. Cancellation of driver's license. The annulment or termination by formal action of the Secretary of a person's driver's license because of some error or defect in the license or because the licensee is no longer entitled to such license, but, with the exception of Sections 6-107, 6-108 and 6-201, the cancellation of a license is without prejudice and application for a new license may be made at any time after such cancellation.

P.A. 76-1586, § 1-110, eff. July 1, 1970. Amended by P.A. 86-1450, § 2, eff. July 1, 1991.

Formerly Ill.Rev.Stat.1991, ch. 95 ½, ¶ 1-110.

5/1-110.1. § 1-110.1. Renumbered as § 1-111.1b by P.A. 90-89, § 15, eff. Jan. 1, 1998

Another § 1-110.1 was renumbered § 1-110.2 by P.A. 83-1528, Art. II, § 24, eff. Jan. 17, 1985.

5/1-110.2. Certificate of purchase

§ 1-110.2. Certificate of purchase. A bill of sale given to a licensee making an acquisition of a vehicle under Sections 4-208 and 4-209 of this Code.

P.A. 76-1586, § 1-110.1, added by P.A. 83-1473, § 1, eff. Jan. 1, 1985. Renumbered § 1-110.2 and amended by P.A. 83-1528, Art. II, § 24, eff. Jan. 17, 1985.

Formerly Ill.Rev.Stat.1991, ch. 95 ½, ¶ 1-110.2.

P.A. 83-1528, the Second 1984 Revisory Act, provides in Art. II, for the nonsubstantive revision or renumbering or repeal of sections of certain Acts of the 83rd General Assembly and for the correction of misspelled words and technical errors in Acts of the 83rd General Assembly.

5/1-110a. § 1-110a. Renumbered as § 1-111.1c by P.A. 90-89, § 15, eff. Jan. 1, 1998

5/1-111. § 1-111. Repealed by P.A. 90-89, § 20, eff. Jan. 1, 1998

5/1-111.1. Chapter

§ 1-111.1. Chapter. The word "Chapter" as used in this Code shall, unless the context otherwise clearly indicates, mean a Chapter of "The Illinois Vehicle Code".[1]

P.A. 76-1586, § 1-111.1, added by P.A. 82-123, § 1, eff. Jan. 1, 1982.

Formerly Ill.Rev.Stat.1991, ch. 95 ½, ¶ 1-111.1.

[1] 625 ILCS 5/1-100 et seq.

5/1-111.1a. Charitable vehicle

§ 1-111.1a. Charitable vehicle.

(a) Any vehicle that is exclusively owned and operated by a religious or charitable not-for-profit organization and is used primarily in conducting the official activities of such organization.

(b) This definition does not include:

(1) a bus operated by a public utility, municipal corporation or common carrier authorized to conduct local or interurban transportation of passengers when such bus is on a regularly scheduled route for the transportation of other fare paying passengers or furnishing charter service for the transportation of groups on special trips or in connection with special events and not over a regular or customary religious organization bus route;

(2) a school bus as defined in Section 1-182 of this Code; or

(3) a First Division vehicle, other than one designed for transporting not less than 7 nor more than 10 passengers, as defined in Section 1-217 of this Code; except that for purposes of determining the number of persons a vehicle is designed to carry, in any vehicle equipped with one or more wheelchair tiedowns, each wheelchair tiedown shall be counted as 4 persons.

P.A. 76-1586, § 1-171.01, added by P.A. 79-798, § 1, eff. July 1, 1976. Amended by P.A. 81-509, § 1, eff. Jan. 1, 1980; P.A. 82-1011, § 2, eff. Sept. 17, 1982; P.A. 83-743, § 1, eff. Jan. 1, 1984; P.A. 87-1025, § 1, eff. Jan. 1, 1993. Renumbered § 1-111.1a and amended by P.A. 90-89, § 15, eff. Jan. 1, 1998. Amended by P.A. 91-64, § 5, eff. Jan. 1, 2000.

Formerly Ill.Rev.Stat.1991, ch. 95 ½, ¶ 1-171.01.

5/1-111.1b. Chassis

§ 1-111.1b. Chassis. Every frame or supportive element of a vehicle whether or not a manufacturer's identification number, serial number, or other identifying numbers are present on said part.

P.A. 76-1586, § 1-110.1, added by P.A. 83-831, § 1, eff. Jan. 1, 1984. Renumbered § 1-111.1b and amended by P.A. 90-89, § 15, eff. Jan. 1, 1998.

Formerly Ill.Rev.Stat.1991, ch. 95 ½, ¶ 1-110.1.

5/1-111.1c. Chassis manufacturer

§ 1-111.1c. Chassis manufacturer. A person who manufactures and produces the frame upon which is mounted the body of a motor vehicle.

P.A. 76-1586, § 1-110a, added by P.A. 86-971, § 1, eff. Jan. 1, 1991. Renumbered § 1-111.1c and amended by P.A. 90-89, § 15, eff. Jan. 1, 1998.

Formerly Ill.Rev.Stat.1991, ch. 95 ½, ¶ 1-110a.

5/1-111.2. Code

§ 1-111.2. Code. The word "Code" as used in this Act shall, unless the context otherwise clearly indicates, mean "The Illinois Vehicle Code".[1]

P.A. 76-1586, § 1-111.2, added by P.A. 82-123, § 1, eff. Jan. 1, 1982.

Formerly Ill.Rev.Stat.1991, ch. 95 ½, ¶ 1-111.2.

1 625 ILCS 5/1-100 et seq.

5/1-111.3. Collection costs

§ 1-111.3. Collection costs. Collection costs consist of reasonable costs incurred in locating the owner, lienholder, or other legally entitled persons, and demanding payment, together with court costs and reasonable attorney's fees as determined by the court.

P.A. 76-1586, § 1-111.3, added by P.A. 89-433, § 5, eff. Dec. 15, 1995.

Another § 1-111.3, defining "component part", was enacted by P.A. 83-831, and was repealed by P.A. 83-1473, § 2, eff. Jan. 1, 1985.

5/1-111.4. Commerce

§ 1-111.4. Commerce. Trade, commerce, or transportation.

P.A. 76-1586, § 1-111.4, added by P.A. 90-89, § 15, eff. Jan. 1, 1998.

5/1-111.5. Commercial driver instruction permit

§ 1-111.5. Commercial driver instruction permit. A permit issued pursuant to Section 6-508 of this Code.

P.A. 76-1586, § 1-111.5, added by P.A. 90-89, § 15, eff. Jan. 1, 1998.

5/1-111.6. Commercial driver's license (CDL)

§ 1-111.6. Commercial driver's license (CDL). A driver's license issued by a state to a person that authorizes that person to drive a certain class of commercial motor vehicle or vehicles.

P.A. 76-1586, § 1-111.6, added by P.A. 90-89, § 15, eff. Jan. 1, 1998.

5/1-111.7. Commercial driver license information system (CDLIS)

§ 1-111.7. Commercial driver license information system (CDLIS). The information system established, pursuant to the Commercial Motor Vehicle Safety Act of 1986 (CMVSA) (49 U.S.C. 2701 et seq.), to serve as a clearinghouse for locating information related to the licensing and identification of commercial motor vehicle drivers.

P.A. 76-1586, § 1-111.7, added by P.A. 90-89, § 15, eff. Jan. 1, 1998.

5/1-111.8. Commercial vehicle

§ 1-111.8. Commercial vehicle. Any vehicle operated for the transportation of persons or property in the furtherance of any commercial or industrial enterprise, For-Hire or Not-For-Hire, but not including a commuter van, a vehicle used in a ridesharing arrangement when being used for that purpose, or a recreational vehicle not being used commercially.

P.A. 76-1586, § 1-114, eff. July 1, 1970. Amended by P.A. 76-1909, § 1; P.A. 80-529, § 1, eff. Jan. 1, 1979; P.A. 81-1452, § 1, eff. Jan. 1, 1981; P.A. 83-1091, § 1, eff. July 1, 1984. Renumbered § 1-111.8 and amended by P.A. 90-89, § 15, eff. Jan. 1, 1998.

Formerly Ill.Rev.Stat.1991, ch. 95 ½, ¶ 1-114.

5/1-111.9. Commuter van

§ 1-111.9. Commuter van. A motor vehicle designed for the transportation of not less than 7 nor more than 16 passengers, which is: (1) used in a ridesharing arrangement; or (2) owned or leased by or on behalf of a company or an employee organization and operated on a non-profit basis with the primary purpose of transporting employees of the company between the employees' homes and the company's place of business or a public transportation station and in which the operating, administrative, maintenance and reasonable depreciation costs are paid principally by the persons utilizing the commuter van.

P.A. 76-1586, § 1-114.1, added by P.A. 80-529, § 1, eff. Jan. 1, 1979. Amended by P.A. 81-492, § 1, eff. Jan. 1, 1980; P.A. 83-1091, § 1, eff. July 1, 1984; P.A. 84-603, § 1, eff. Jan. 1, 1986. Renumbered § 1-111.9 and amended by P.A. 90-89, § 15, eff. Jan. 1, 1998.

Formerly Ill.Rev.Stat.1991, ch. 95 ½, ¶ 1-114.1.

5/1-112. Controlled access highway

§ 1-112. Controlled access highway. Every highway, street or roadway in respect to which owners or occupants of abutting lands and other persons have no legal right of access to or from the same except at such points only and in such manner as may be determined by the public authority having jurisdiction over such highway, street or roadway.

P.A. 76-1586, § 1-112, eff. July 1, 1970.

Formerly Ill.Rev.Stat.1991, ch. 95 ½, ¶ 1-112.

5/1-112.1. Conversion

§ 1-112.1. Conversion. A motor vehicle, other than a motor home, which has been modified by a person other than the manufacturer of the chassis of the motor vehicle and which has not been the subject of a retail sale.

P.A. 76-1586, § 1-112.1, added by P.A. 86-971, § 1, eff. Jan. 1, 1991.

Formerly Ill.Rev.Stat.1991, ch. 95 ½, ¶ 1-112.1.

5/1-112.2. Converter or second stage manufacturer

§ 1-112.2. Converter or second stage manufacturer. A person who prior to the retail sale of a motor vehicle, assembles, installs or affixes a body, cab, or special equipment to a chassis, or who adds, subtracts from, or modifies a previously assembled or manufactured motor vehicle.

P.A. 76-1586, § 1-112.2, added by P.A. 86-971, § 1, eff. Jan. 1, 1991. Amended by P.A. 90-89, § 15, eff. Jan. 1, 1998.

Formerly Ill.Rev.Stat.1991, ch. 95 ½, ¶ 1-112.2.

5/1-112.3. Converter Dolly

§ 1-112.3. Converter Dolly. A vehicle consisting of a chassis equipped with one or more axles, a fifth wheel or an equivalent mechanism, and draw bar, the attachment of which converts a semitrailer to a full trailer.

P.A. 76-1586, § 1-112.3, added by P.A. 87-1203, § 1, eff. Sept. 25, 1992.

Formerly Ill.Rev.Stat., ch. 95½, ¶ 1-112.3.

5/1-112.5. Counterfeit

§ 1-112.5. Counterfeit. To copy or imitate, without legal authority, with the intent of deceiving or defrauding.

P.A. 76-1586, § 1-114.2, added by P.A. 83-1473, § 1, eff. Jan. 1, 1985. Renumbered § 1-112.5 and amended by P.A. 90-89, § 15, eff. Jan. 1, 1998.

Formerly Ill.Rev.Stat.1991, ch. 95 ½, ¶ 1-114.2.

5/1-112.7. Court

§ 1-112.7. Court. A court of law, traffic tribunal, or circuit court of Illinois, including a judge of a court of law, traffic tribunal, or circuit court of Illinois.

P.A. 76-1586, § 1-112.7, added by P.A. 90-89, § 15, eff. Jan. 1, 1998.

5/1-113. Crosswalk

§ 1-113. Crosswalk. (a) That part of a roadway at an intersection included within the connections of the lateral lines of the sidewalks on opposite sides of the highway measured from the curbs or, in the absence of curbs, from the edges of the traversable roadway, and in the absence of a sidewalk on one side of the highway, that part of the highway included within the extension of the lateral line of the existing sidewalk to the side of the highway without the sidewalk, with such extension forming a right angle to the centerline of the highway;

(b) Any portion of a roadway at an intersection or elsewhere distinctly indicated for pedestrian crossing by lines or other markings on the surface placed in accordance with the provisions in the Manual adopted by the Department of Transportation as authorized in Section 11-301.

P.A. 76-1586, § 1-113, eff. July 1, 1970. Amended by P.A. 76-2121, § 1, eff. July 1, 1970; P.A. 83-831, § 1, eff. Jan. 1, 1984.

Formerly Ill.Rev.Stat.1991, ch. 95 ½, ¶ 1-113.

5/1-113.1. Custom vehicle

§ 1-113.1. Custom vehicle. A motor vehicle that is at least 25 years of age and of a model year after 1948 or a vehicle that has been certified by an inspector of the National Street Rod Association, on a form prescribed by the Secretary of State, to be a custom vehicle manufactured to resemble a vehicle at least 25 years of age and of a model year after 1948 and has been altered from the manufacturer's original design or has a body constructed from non-original materials and which is maintained for occasional transportation, exhibitions, club activities, parades, tours, and similar uses and which is not used for general daily transportation.

P.A. 76-1586, § 1-113.1, added by P.A. 92-668, § 5, eff. Jan. 1, 2003.

5/1-114. § 1-114. Renumbered § 1-111.8 and amended by P.A. 90-89, § 15, eff. Jan. 1, 1998

5/1-114.1. § 1-114.1. Renumbered § 1-111.9 and amended by P.A. 90-89, § 15, eff. Jan. 1, 1998

5/1-114.2. § 1-114.2. Renumbered § 1-112.5 and amended by P.A. 90-89, § 15, eff. Jan. 1, 1998

5/1-115. Dealer

§ 1-115. Dealer. Every person engaged in the business of acquiring or disposing of vehicles or their essential parts and who has an established place of business for such purpose.

P.A. 76-1586, § 1-115, eff. July 1, 1970. Amended by P.A. 83-1473, § 1, eff. Jan. 1, 1985.

Formerly Ill.Rev.Stat.1991, ch. 95 ½, ¶ 1-115.

5/1-115.05. Department

§ 1-115.05. Department. The Department of Transportation of the State of Illinois, acting directly or through its duly authorized officers and agents, except that in Chapter 5 [1] and Articles X and XI of Chapter 3 of this Code,[2] "Department" means the Department of Revenue of the State of Illinois.

P.A. 76-1586, § 1-115.05, added by P.A. 90-89, § 15, eff. Jan. 1, 1998.

1 625 ILCS 5/1-100 et seq.

2 625 ILCS 5/3-1001 et seq. and 5/3-2001 et seq.

5/1-115.07. Derelict vehicle

§ 1-115.07. Derelict vehicle. Any inoperable, unregistered, discarded motor vehicle, regardless of title, having lost its character as a substantial property and left unattended without justification on the owner's land contrary to the public policy expressed in Section 4-301 of this Code.

P.A. 76-1586, § 1-115.07, added by P.A. 90-89, § 15, eff. Jan. 1, 1998.

5/1-115.1. Disposition of vehicle or vehicle part

§ 1-115.1. Disposition of vehicle or vehicle part. The purchase, exchange, transfer, sale, assignment or other change of ownership or possession or the junking or wrecking of a vehicle or vehicle part.

P.A. 76-1586, § 1-115.1, added by P.A. 83-1473, § 1, eff. Jan. 1, 1985.

Formerly Ill.Rev.Stat.1991, ch. 95 ½, ¶ 1-115.1.

5/1-115.3. Disqualification

§ 1-115.3. Disqualification. A withdrawal of the privilege to drive a commercial motor vehicle.

P.A. 76-1586, § 1-115.3, added by P.A. 90-89, § 15, eff. Jan. 1, 1998.

5/1-115.5. Domicile

§ 1-115.5. Domicile. A true, fixed, and permanent legal home of a person or the place to which the person intends to return even though the person may reside elsewhere. As a further explanation, "A person may have more than one residence but only one domicile".

P.A. 76-1586, § 1-115.5, added by P.A. 90-89, § 15, eff. Jan. 1, 1998.

5/1-115.6. Domiciliary

§ 1-115.6. Domiciliary. A person who is domiciled.

P.A. 76-1586, § 1-115.6, added by P.A. 90-89, § 15, eff. Jan. 1, 1998.

5/1-115.8. Drive

§ 1-115.8. Drive. To drive, operate, or be in physical control of a motor vehicle.

P.A. 76-1586, § 1-115.8, added by P.A. 90-89, § 15, eff. Jan. 1, 1998.

5/1-116. Driver

§ 1-116. Driver. Every person who drives or is in actual physical control of a vehicle.

P.A. 76-1586, § 1-116, eff. July 1, 1970.

Formerly Ill.Rev.Stat.1991, ch. 95 ½, ¶ 1-116.

5/1-116.1. Driver's license

§ 1-116.1. Driver's license. Any license to operate a motor vehicle issued under the laws of this State.

P.A. 76-1586, § 1-116.1, added by P.A. 84-1394, § 5, eff. Sept. 18, 1986.

Formerly Ill.Rev.Stat.1991, ch. 95 ½, ¶ 1-116.1.

5/1-117. Driver License Compact

§ 1-117. Driver License Compact. The Driver License Compact set forth in Chapter 6 of this Act.[1]

P.A. 76-1586, § 1-117, eff. July 1, 1970.

Formerly Ill.Rev.Stat.1991, ch. 95 ½, ¶ 1-117.

1 625 ILCS 5/6-700 et seq.

5/1-117.5. Driver's license or permit making implement

§ 1-117.5. Driver's license or permit making implement. Any implement specially designed or primarily used in the manufacture, assembly, or authentication of an official driver's license or permit issued by the Secretary of State or other official driver's license agency in another jurisdiction. These implements include, but are not limited to, cameras used for creating driver's license captured images, camera cards, or driver's license or permit laminates.

P.A. 76-1586, § 1-117.5, added by P.A. 90-89, § 15, eff. Jan. 1, 1998.

5/1-117.7. Electric personal assistive mobility device

Text of section added effective June 1, 2003

§ 1-117.7. Electric personal assistive mobility device. A self-balancing 2 non-tandem wheeled device designed to transport only one person with an electric propulsion system that limits the maximum speed of the device to 15 miles per hour or less.

P.A. 76-1586, § 1-117.7, added by P.A. 92-868, § 5, eff. June 1, 2003.

5/1-118. Essential Parts

§ 1-118. Essential Parts. All integral and body parts of a vehicle of a type required to be registered hereunder, the removal, alteration or substitution of which would tend to conceal the identity of the vehicle or substantially alter its appearance, model, type or mode of operation. "Essential parts" includes the following: vehicle hulks, shells, chassis, frames, front end assemblies (which may consist of headlight, grill, fenders and hood), front clip (front end assembly with cowl attached), rear clip (which may consist of quarter panels, fenders, floor and top), doors, hatchbacks, fenders, cabs, cab clips, cowls, hoods, trunk lids, deck lids, T-tops, sunroofs, moon roofs, astro roofs, transmissions of vehicles of the second division, seats, aluminum wheels, engines and similar parts. Essential parts shall also include stereo radios, cassette radios, compact disc radios, cassette/compact disc radios and compact disc players and compact disc changers which are either installed in dash or trunk-mounted.

An essential part which does not have affixed to it an identification number as defined in Section 1-129 adopts the identification number of the vehicle to which such part is affixed, installed or mounted.

P.A. 76-1586, § 1-118, eff. July 1, 1970. Amended by P.A. 83-1473, § 1, eff. Jan. 1, 1985; P.A. 86-1179, § 2, eff. Aug. 17, 1990; P.A. 86-1209, § 1, eff. Jan. 1, 1991; P.A. 87-435, Art. 2, § 2-19, eff. Sept. 10, 1991.

Formerly Ill.Rev.Stat.1991, ch. 95 ½, ¶ 1-118.

P.A. 87-435, the First 1991 Revisory Act, provides in Article 2 for the revision and renumbering of certain Sections of Acts which have been added or amended by more than one Act of the 86th General Assembly; incorporates amendments to repealed Acts into successor laws passed by the same General Assembly; corrects errors, revises cross-references and deletes obsolete text in such Sections contained in Public Acts through P.A. 86-1490.

5/1-119. Explosives

§ 1-119. Explosives. Any chemical compound or mechanical mixture that is commonly used or intended for the purpose of producing an explosion and which contains any oxidizing and combustive units or other ingredients in such proportions, quantities or packing that an ignition by fire, by friction, by concussion, by percussion or by detonator of any part of the compound or mixture may cause such a sudden generation of highly heated gases that the resultant gaseous pressures are capable of producing destructive effects on contiguous objects or of destroying life or limb.

P.A. 76-1586, § 1-119, eff. July 1, 1970.

Formerly Ill.Rev.Stat.1991, ch. 95 ½, ¶ 1-119.

5/1-119.3. Expressway

§ 1-119.3. Expressway. A freeway with full control access and with grade separations at intersections.

P.A. 76-1586, § 1-119.3, added by P.A. 90-89, § 15, eff. Jan. 1, 1998.

5/1-119.6. Farm to market agricultural transportation

§ 1-119.6. Farm to market agricultural transportation. The operation of a motor vehicle controlled and operated by a farmer who is a private motor carrier of property, who is using the vehicle to transport agricultural products to or from a farm operated by the farmer or to transport farm machinery or farm supplies to or from a farm operated by the farmer, and who is not using the commercial vehicle to transport hazardous materials of a type or quantity that requires the vehicle to be placarded in accordance with the Illinois Hazardous Materials Transportation Act.[1]

P.A. 76–1586, § 1–119.6, added by P.A. 90–89, § 15, eff. Jan. 1, 1998.

1 430 ILCS 30/1 et seq.

5/1–120. Farm tractor

§ 1–120. Farm tractor. Every motor vehicle designed and used primarily as a farm implement for drawing wagons, plows, mowing machines and other implements of husbandry, and every implement of husbandry which is self propelled, excluding all-terrain vehicles and off-highway motorcycles as defined in this Code.

P.A. 76–1586, § 1–120, eff. July 1, 1970. Amended by P.A. 85–830, § 1, eff. Sept. 24, 1987; P.A. 85–1010, § 1, eff. March 2, 1988.

Formerly Ill.Rev.Stat.1991, ch. 95 ½, ¶ 1–120.

P.A. 85–1010 incorporated the amendment by P.A. 85–830.

5/1–120.5. Fifth wheel assembly

§ 1–120.5. Fifth wheel assembly. A coupling device connecting 2 or more vehicles operating in combination. The lower half of a fifth wheel assembly mounted on a truck tractor or converter dolly must be secured to the frame of that vehicle with properly designed brackets, mounting plates, or angles and properly tightened bolts of adequate size and grade or devices that provide equivalent security. The installation shall not cause cracking, warping, or deformation of the frame. The installation shall include a device for positively preventing the lower half of the fifth wheel assembly from shifting on the frame to which it is attached.

The upper half of a fifth wheel assembly must be fastened to the motor vehicle with at least the same security required for the installation of the lower half on a truck tractor or converter dolly.

Every fifth wheel assembly shall have a locking mechanism. The locking mechanism and any adapter used in conjunction with it must prevent separation of the upper and lower halves of the fifth wheel assembly unless a positive manual release is activated. The release may be located so that the driver can operate it from the cab. If a motor vehicle has a fifth wheel assembly designed and constructed to be readily separable, the fifth wheel assembly locking devices shall apply automatically on coupling.

The lower half of a fifth wheel assembly shall be located so that, regardless of the condition of loading, the relationship between the kingpin and the rear axle or axles of the towing motor vehicle will properly distribute the gross weight of both the towed and towing vehicles on the axles of those vehicles, will not unduly interfere with the steering, braking, and other maneuvering of the towing vehicle, and will not otherwise contribute to unsafe operation of the vehicles comprising the combination. The upper half of a fifth wheel assembly shall be located so that the weight of the vehicles is properly distributed on their axles and the combination of vehicles will operate safely during normal operation.

P.A. 76–1586, § 1–120.5, added by P.A. 90–89, § 15, eff. Jan. 1, 1998.

5/1–121. Flammable liquid

§ 1–121. Flammable liquid. Any liquid which has a flash point of 70 degrees Fahrenheit, or less, as determined by a tagliabue or equivalent closed-cup test device.

P.A. 76–1586, § 1–121, eff. July 1, 1970. Amended by P.A. 91–357, § 231, eff. July 29, 1999.

Formerly Ill.Rev.Stat.1991, ch. 95 ½, ¶ 1–121.

5/1–122. Fleet

§ 1–122. Fleet. 1 or more commercial motor vehicles.

P.A. 76–1586, § 1–122, eff. July 1, 1970. Amended by P.A. 79–1041, § 1, eff. Jan. 1, 1976.

Formerly Ill.Rev.Stat.1991, ch. 95 ½, ¶ 1–122.

5/1–122.1. Fleet safety vehicle

§ 1–122.1. Fleet safety vehicle. Any motor vehicle which is used to supervise operations of vehicles of the second division on the highway so as to promote safety and legal operations of such second division vehicle.

P.A. 76–1586, § 1–122.1, added by P.A. 79–870, § 1, eff. Oct. 1, 1975.

Formerly Ill.Rev.Stat.1991, ch. 95 ½, ¶ 1–122.1.

5/1–122.5. For-hire

§ 1–122.5. For-hire. The operation of a vehicle for compensation and subject to federal regulation by the Interstate Commerce Commission or to state regulation by the Illinois Commerce Commission and those vehicles governed by Chapters 8 and 9 under this Code[1] and regulated by the Secretary of State.

P.A. 76–1586, § 1–124, eff. July 1, 1970. Amended by P.A. 86–880, § 1, eff. Jan. 1, 1990. Renumbered § 1–122.5 and amended by P.A. 90–89, § 15, eff. Jan. 1, 1998.

Formerly Ill.Rev.Stat.1991, ch. 95 ½, ¶ 1–124.

1 625 ILCS 5/8–100 et seq. and 5/9–100 et seq.

5/1–122.7. For-profit ridesharing arrangement

§ 1–122.7. For-profit ridesharing arrangement. The transportation by motor vehicle of not more than 16 persons, including the driver, for which a fee is charged in accordance with Section 6 of the Ridesharing Arrangements Act.[1]

P.A. 76–1586, § 1–122.7, added by P.A. 90–89, § 15, eff. Jan. 1, 1998.

1 625 ILCS 30/6 et seq.

5/1–123. Foreign vehicle

§ 1–123. Foreign vehicle. Every vehicle of a type required to be registered hereunder brought into this State from another State, territory or country other than in the ordinary course of business by or through a manufacturer or dealer and not registered in this State.

P.A. 76–1586, § 1–123, eff. July 1, 1970.

Formerly Ill.Rev.Stat.1991, ch. 95 ½, ¶ 1–123.

5/1–123.1. § 1–123.1. Repealed by P.A. 90–89, § 20, eff. Jan. 1, 1998

5/1–123.3. Frame

§ 1–123.3. Frame. The main longitudinal structural members of the chassis of the vehicle or, for vehicles with unitized body construction, the lowest main longitudinal structural members of the body of the vehicle.

P.A. 76-1586, § 1-123.3, added by P.A. 90-89, § 15, eff. Jan. 1, 1998.

5/1-123.4. Fraudulent driver's license or permit

§ 1-123.4. Fraudulent driver's license or permit. Any license or permit that purports to be an official driver's license or permit for which a computerized number and file have not been created by the Secretary of State or other official driver's license agency in another jurisdiction.

P.A. 76-1586, § 1-123.4, added by P.A. 90-89, § 15, eff. Jan. 1, 1998.

5/1-123.5. Freeway

§ 1-123.5. Freeway. A highway or street especially designed for through traffic and to, from, or over which owners of or persons having an interest in abutting land or other persons have no right or easement or only a limited right or easement of access, crossing, light, air, or view by reason of the fact that the property abuts upon the highway or street or for any other reason.

P.A. 76-1586, § 1-123.5, added by P.A. 90-89, § 15, eff. Jan. 1, 1998.

5/1-123.7. Garbage

§ 1-123.7. Garbage. Any material or load consisting of waste from the facilities of the generator of the waste when transported for disposal or to a permitted recycling or waste processing facility when the generator receives no direct or indirect compensation from anyone for the material or load and when transported by a truck specially equipped with a selfcompactor or an industrial roll-off hoist and roll-off container.

P.A. 76-1586, § 1-123.7, added by P.A. 90-89, § 15, eff. Jan. 1, 1998.

5/1-124. § 1-124. Renumbered as § 1-122.5 by P.A. 90-89, § 15, eff. Jan. 1, 1998

5/1-124.1. Grey Market Vehicle

§ 1-124.1. Grey Market Vehicle. A vehicle not originally manufactured in compliance with U.S. emission or safety standards.

P.A. 76-1586, § 1-124.1, added by P.A. 85-951, § 1, eff. July 1, 1988. Amended by P.A. 86-444, § 1, eff. Jan. 1, 1990.

Formerly Ill.Rev.Stat.1991, ch. 95 ½, ¶ 1-124.1.

5/1-124.5. Gross Vehicle Weight Rating (GVWR)

§ 1-124.5. Gross Vehicle Weight Rating (GVWR). The value specified by the manufacturer or manufacturers as the maximum loaded weight of a single vehicle. The GVWR of a combination of vehicles (commonly referred to as the "Gross Combination Weight Rating" or GCWR) is the GVWR of the power unit plus the GVWR of the towed unit or units. In the absence of a value specified by the manufacturer, GCWR is determined by adding the GVWR of the power unit and the total weight of the towed unit and any load on the unit.

P.A. 76-1586, § 1-124.5, added by P.A. 90-89, § 15, eff. Jan. 1, 1998.

5/1-125. Gross weight

§ 1-125. Gross weight. The weight of a vehicle whether operated singly or in combination without load plus the weight of the load thereon.

P.A. 76-1586, § 1-125, eff. July 1, 1970.

Formerly Ill.Rev.Stat.1991, ch. 95 ½, ¶ 1-125.

5/1-125.7. Headset receiver

§ 1-125.7. Headset receiver. Any device, other than a hearing aid, designed to be worn on a person's head that enables the wearer to hear or receive electronic communications.

P.A. 76-1586, § 1-125.7, added by P.A. 90-89, § 15, eff. Jan. 1, 1998.

5/1-126. Highway

§ 1-126. Highway.

The entire width between the boundary lines of every way publicly maintained when any part thereof is open to the use of the public for purposes of vehicular travel or located on public school property.

P.A. 76-1586, § 1-126, eff. July 1, 1970. Amended by P.A. 92-780, § 5, eff. Aug. 6, 2002.

Formerly Ill.Rev.Stat.1991, ch. 95 ½, ¶ 1-126.

5/1-126.1. Highway Designations

§ 1-126.1. Highway Designations. The Department of Transportation may designate streets or highways in the system of State highways as follows:

(a) Class I highways include interstate highways, expressways, tollways, and other highways deemed appropriate by the department.

(b) Class II highways include major arterials not built to interstate highway standards that have at least 11 feet lane widths.

(c) Class III highways include those State highways that have lane widths of less than 11 feet.

(d) Non-designated highways are highways in the system of State highways not designated as Class I, II, or III, or local highways which are part of any county, township, municipal, or district road system. Local authorities also may designate Class II or Class III highways within their systems of highways.

P.A. 76-1586, § 1-126.1, added by P.A. 92-417, § 5, eff. Jan. 1, 2002.

5/1-127. § 1-127. Repealed by P.A. 81-969, § 2

5/1-128. House trailer

§ 1-128. House trailer. (a) A trailer or semitrailer equipped and used for living quarters or for human habitation (temporarily or permanently) rather than for the transportation of freight, goods, wares and merchandise; or

(b) A house trailer or a semitrailer which is used commercially (temporarily or permanently), that is, for the advertising, sales, display or promotion of merchandise or services, or for any other commercial purpose except the transportation of property for hire or the transportation of property for distribution by a private carrier.

P.A. 76-1586, § 1-128, eff. July 1, 1970. Amended by P.A. 81-969, § 1, eff. Jan. 1, 1980.

Formerly Ill.Rev.Stat.1991, ch. 95 ½, ¶ 1-128.

Section 3 of P.A. 81-969, approved Sept. 22, 1979, provided:

"This amendatory Act takes effect at the start of the 1981 registration year."

5/1-129. Identification Number

§ 1-129. Identification Number. The numbers and letters, if any, on a vehicle or essential part, affixed by its manufacturer, the Illinois Secretary of State or the Illinois Department of State Police for the purpose of identifying the vehicle or essential part, or which is required to be affixed to the vehicle or part by federal or state law.

P.A. 76-1586, § 1-129, eff. July 1, 1970. Amended by P.A. 84-1302, § 1, eff. Jan. 1, 1987; P.A. 84-1304, § 1, eff. Jan. 1, 1987.

Formerly Ill.Rev.Stat.1991, ch. 95 ½, ¶ 1-129.

The amendments by P.A. 84-1302 and P.A. 84-1304 were identical.

5/1-129.1. Ignition interlock device

§ 1-129.1. Ignition interlock device. A device installed in a motor vehicle that prevents the vehicle from starting until the device has determined by an analysis of the driver's breath that the driver's blood alcohol is below a certain preset level.

P.A. 76-1586, § 1-129.1, added by P.A. 91-127, § 5, eff. Jan. 1, 2000.

5/1-130. Implement of husbandry

§ 1-130. Implement of husbandry. Every vehicle designed and adapted exclusively for agricultural, horticultural, or livestock raising operations, including farm wagons, wagon trailers or like vehicles used in connection therewith, or for lifting or carrying an implement of husbandry provided that no farm wagon, wagon trailer or like vehicle having a gross weight of more than 36,000 pounds, shall be included hereunder.

P.A. 76-1586, § 1-130, eff. July 1, 1970. Amended by P.A. 81-327, § 1, eff. Jan. 1, 1980.

Formerly Ill.Rev.Stat.1991, ch. 95 ½, ¶ 1-130.

5/1-131. Improved highway

§ 1-131. Improved highway. Any roadway of concrete, brick, asphalt, macadam and crushed stone or gravel.

P.A. 76-1586, § 1-131, eff. July 1, 1970.

Formerly Ill.Rev.Stat.1991, ch. 95 ½, ¶ 1-131.

5/1-132. Intersection

§ 1-132. Intersection. The area embraced within the prolongation or connection of the lateral curb lines, or, if none, then the lateral boundary lines of the roadways of two highways which join one another at, or approximately at, right angles or the area within which vehicles traveling upon different roadways joining at any other angle may come in conflict.

(b)[1] Where a highway includes two roadways 40 feet or more apart, then every crossing of each roadway of such divided highway by an intersecting highway shall be regarded as a separate intersection.

(c) The junction of an alley with a street or highway does not constitute an intersection.

P.A. 76-1586, § 1-132, eff. July 1, 1970. Amended by P.A. 77-321, § 1, eff. Jan. 1, 1972.

Formerly Ill.Rev.Stat.1991, ch. 95 ½, ¶ 1-132.

[1] No "(a)" in enrolled bill.

5/1-133. Interstate or interstate commerce

§ 1-133. Interstate or interstate commerce. Transportation between 2 or more States or transportation originating in one State and passing into or through other States for delivery in another State, and which is not intrastate.

P.A. 76-1586, § 1-133, eff. July 1, 1970.

Formerly Ill.Rev.Stat.1991, ch. 95 ½, ¶ 1-133.

5/1-133.05. Interstate carrier of property

§ 1-133.05. Interstate carrier of property. Any person who is engaged in the transportation of property only by motor vehicle in whole or in part in interstate or foreign commerce in this State either with or without authority issued from the Interstate Commerce Commission.

P.A. 76-1586, § 1-133.05, added by P.A. 90-89, § 15, eff. Jan. 1, 1998.

5/1-133.1. Interstate highway

§ 1-133.1. Interstate highway. Any highway which is now, or shall hereafter be, a part of the national system of interstate and defense highways within this State.

P.A. 76-1586, § 1-133.1, added by P.A. 85-830, § 1, eff. Sept. 24, 1987.

Formerly Ill.Rev.Stat.1991, ch. 95 ½, ¶ 1-133.1.

5/1-134. Intrastate or intrastate commerce

§ 1-134. Intrastate or intrastate commerce. Transportation originating at any point or place within this State and destined to any other point or place within this State, irrespective of the route, highway or highways traversed, and including transportation which passes into or through another State before delivery is made within this State, and including any act of transportation which includes or completes a pickup within Illinois for delivery within Illinois.

P.A. 76-1586, § 1-134, eff. July 1, 1970.

Formerly Ill.Rev.Stat.1991, ch. 95 ½, ¶ 1-134.

5/1-134.1. Junk vehicle

§ 1-134.1. Junk vehicle. A junk vehicle is a vehicle which has been or is being disassembled, crushed, compressed, flattened, destroyed or otherwise reduced to a state in which it no longer can be returned to an operable state.

P.A. 76-1586, § 1-134.1, added by P.A. 83-1473, § 1, eff. Jan. 1, 1985.

Formerly Ill.Rev.Stat.1991, ch. 95 ½, ¶ 1-134.1.

5/1-135. Lane-control signal

§ 1-135. Lane-control signal. An official traffic control device consisting of an electrically controlled and illuminated signal of a square or rectangular design and employing distinctive colors or symbols used to control the direction of vehicular flow on the particular lane to which the indication applies.

P.A. 76-1586, § 1-135, eff. July 1, 1970. Amended by P.A. 76-2122, § 1, eff. July 1, 1970.

Formerly Ill.Rev.Stat.1991, ch. 95 ½, ¶ 1-135.

5/1-136. Laned roadway

§ 1-136. Laned roadway. A roadway which is divided into two or more clearly marked lanes for vehicular traffic.

P.A. 76-1586, § 1-136, eff. July 1, 1970.

Formerly Ill.Rev.Stat.1991, ch. 95 ½, ¶ 1-136.

5/1-136.5. Law enforcement agency

§ 1-136.5. Law enforcement agency. Every governmental enforcement agency or officer having authority to enforce the provisions of this Act or applicable local vehicle ordinances.

P.A. 76-1586, § 1-136.5, added by P.A. 90-89, § 15, eff. Jan. 1, 1998.

5/1-137. Lease

§ 1-137. Lease. A written document vesting exclusive possession, use, control and responsibility of the lessee during the periods the vehicle is operated by or for the lessee for a specific period of time.

P.A. 76-1586, § 1-137, eff. July 1, 1970. Amended by P.A. 81-501, § 1, eff. Jan. 1, 1980.

Formerly Ill.Rev.Stat.1991, ch. 95 ½, ¶ 1-137.

5/1-138. License to drive

§ 1-138. License to drive. Any driver's license or any other license or permit to operate a motor vehicle issued under the laws of this State including:

1. Any temporary license or instruction permit;

2. The privilege of any person to drive a motor vehicle whether or not such person holds a valid license or permit.

3. Any nonresident's driving privilege as defined herein.

P.A. 76-1586, § 1-138, eff. July 1, 1970.

Formerly Ill.Rev.Stat.1991, ch. 95 ½, ¶ 1-138.

5/1-138.1. Licensee

§ 1-138.1. Licensee. A person licensed or required to be licensed under Sections 5-101, 5-102, 5-201 and 5-301 of this Code.

P.A. 76-1586, § 1-138.1, added by P.A. 83-1473, § 1, eff. Jan. 1, 1985.

Formerly Ill.Rev.Stat.1991, ch. 95 ½, ¶ 1-138.1.

5/1-139. Lienholder

§ 1-139. Lienholder. A person holding a security interest in a vehicle.

P.A. 76-1586, § 1-139, eff. July 1, 1970.

Formerly Ill.Rev.Stat.1991, ch. 95 ½, ¶ 1-139.

5/1-139.1. Limousine

§ 1-139.1. Limousine. Any privately owned first division vehicle intended to be used for the transportation of persons for-hire when the payment is not based on a meter charge, but is prearranged for a designated destination.

P.A. 76-1586, § 1-139.1, added by P.A. 88-415, § 10, eff. Aug. 20, 1993.

5/1-140. Local authorities

§ 1-140. Local authorities. Every county, municipal and other local board or body having authority to enact laws relating to traffic under the constitution and laws of this State.

P.A. 76-1586, § 1-140, eff. July 1, 1970.

Formerly Ill.Rev.Stat.1991, ch. 95 ½, ¶ 1-140.

5/1-140.5. Local mass transit system

§ 1-140.5. Local mass transit system. An organized system providing passenger transportation over regular routes within a designated municipality or area.

P.A. 76-1586, § 1-140.5, added by P.A. 90-89, § 15, eff. Jan. 1, 1998.

5/1-141. Mail

§ 1-141. Mail. To deposit in the United States mail properly addressed and with postage prepaid.

P.A. 76-1586, § 1-141, eff. July 1, 1970.

Formerly Ill.Rev.Stat.1991, ch. 95 ½, ¶ 1-141.

5/1-142. Manufacturer

§ 1-142. Manufacturer. Every person engaged in the business of manufacturing and assembling vehicles or reconstructed vehicles, or engine and driveline components for vehicles.

P.A. 76-1586, § 1-142, eff. July 1, 1970. Amended by P.A. 76-1798, § 1, eff. July 1, 1970.

Formerly Ill.Rev.Stat.1991, ch. 95 ½, ¶ 1-142.

5/1-142.01. Materially altered vehicle

§ 1-142.01. Materially altered vehicle. Any vehicle which has been modified, rebuilt, repaired, reconstructed, restored or specially constructed.

P.A. 76-1586, § 1-142.01, added by P.A. 83-1473, § 1, eff. Jan. 1, 1985.

Formerly Ill.Rev.Stat.1991, ch. 95 ½, ¶ 1-142.01.

5/1-142.05. Maxi-cube vehicle

§ 1-142.05. Maxi-cube vehicle. A combination of vehicles consisting of a truck-tractor, upon which is mounted a separable cargo carrying semi-trailer, and a trailing unit that is attached by a pintle hook or similar connection, with the separable cargo carrying semi-trailer designed so as to be loaded and unloaded through the trailing unit, except that the entire combination shall not exceed 65 feet in length and that neither the semi-trailer nor the trailing unit in the combination shall by itself exceed 34 feet in length.

P.A. 76-1586, § 1-142.05, added by P.A. 90-89, § 15, eff. Jan. 1, 1998.

5/1-142.1. Medical Carrier

§ 1-142.1. Medical Carrier. Any publicly or privately owned vehicle which is specifically designed, constructed or modified and equipped, and is intended to be used for, and is maintained or operated for the nonemergency transportation of persons for compensation for the purpose of obtaining medical services.

P.A. 76-1586, § 1-142.1, added by P.A. 82-433, § 1, eff. Sept. 8, 1981.

Formerly Ill.Rev.Stat.1991, ch. 95 ½, ¶ 1-142.1.

Section 3 of P.A. 82-433 approved Sept. 8, 1981, provided:

"This Act takes effect upon its becoming a law, except that the provisions relating to safety tests and proof of financial responsibility for medical transport vehicles apply only to applications for and the issuance of registration plates which are required to be displayed on January 1, 1982 or thereafter."

5/1-142.1a. § 1-142.1a. Repealed by P.A. 92-703, § 15, eff. July 19, 2002

5/1-142.1b. Medical limitation or condition

§ 1-142.1b. Medical limitation or condition. A scientifically recognized condition that may medically impair a person's physical or mental health to the extent the person is unable to safely operate a motor vehicle.

P.A. 76-1586, § 1-142.1b, added by P.A. 90-89, § 15, eff. Jan. 1, 1998.

5/1-142.2. Medical transport vehicle

§ 1-142.2. Medical transport vehicle. Includes ambulances, medical carriers, and rescue vehicles.

P.A. 76-1586, § 1-142.2, added by P.A. 82-433, § 1, eff. Sept. 8, 1981.

Formerly Ill.Rev.Stat.1991, ch. 95 ½, ¶ 1-142.2.

Effective date of P.A. 82-433, see Historical and Statutory Notes following 625 ILCS 5/1-102.01.

5/1-143, 5/1-144. §§ 1-143, 1-144. Repealed by P.A. 90-89, § 20, eff. Jan. 1, 1998

5/1-144.05. Model year

§ 1-144.05. Model year. The year of manufacture of a vehicle based upon the annual production period of the vehicle as designated by the manufacturer and indicated on the title and registration of the vehicle. If the manufacturer does not designate a production period for the vehicle, then "model year" means the calendar year of manufacture.

P.A. 76-1586, § 1-144.05, added by P.A. 90-89, § 15, eff. Jan. 1, 1998.

5/1-144.1. Modified vehicle

§ 1-144.1. Modified vehicle. Every vehicle of a type required to be registered under this Code altered by the addition, deletion, or modification of the body, chassis, component or essential parts, new or used.

P.A. 76-1586, § 1-144.1, added by P.A. 83-831, § 1, eff. Jan. 1, 1984.

Formerly Ill.Rev.Stat.1991, ch. 95 ½, ¶ 1-144.1.

5/1-145. Motor carrier

§ 1-145. Motor carrier. An operator of For-Hire vehicles pursuant to the Illinois Motor Carrier of Property Law.[1]

P.A. 76-1586, § 1-145, eff. July 1, 1970.

Formerly Ill.Rev.Stat.1991, ch. 95 ½, ¶ 1-145.

[1] Former Ill.Rev.Stat. ch. 95½, ¶ 18-100 et seq. (repealed).

5/1-145.001. Motor driven cycle

§ 1-145.001. Motor driven cycle. Every motorcycle and every motor scooter with less than 150 cubic centimeter piston displacement including motorized pedalcycles.

P.A. 76-1586, § 1-148, eff. July 1, 1970. Amended by P.A. 80-262, § 1, eff. Aug. 20, 1977. Renumbered § 1-145.001 and amended by P.A. 90-89, § 15, eff. Jan. 1, 1998.

Formerly Ill.Rev.Stat.1991, ch. 95 ½, ¶ 1-148.

5/1-145.01. Motor home, mini motor home or van camper

§ 1-145.01. Motor home, mini motor home or van camper. A self-contained motor vehicle, not used commercially, designed or permanently converted to provide living quarters for recreational, camping or travel use, with direct walk through access to the living quarters from the driver's seat. Such vehicles must include at least four of the following:

a) A cooking facility with an on-board fuel source;

b) A gas or electric refrigerator;

c) A toilet with exterior evacuation;

d) A heating or air conditioning system with an on-board power or fuel source separate from the vehicle engine;

e) A potable water supply system that includes at least a sink, a faucet, and a water tank with an exterior service supply connection;

f) A 110-125 volt electric power supply.

P.A. 76-1586, § 1-145.01, added by P.A. 81-969, § 1, eff. Jan. 1, 1980. Amended by P.A. 86-971, § 1, eff. Jan. 1, 1991.

Formerly Ill.Rev.Stat.1991, ch. 95 ½, ¶ 1-145.01.

Section 3 of P.A. 81-969, approved Sept. 22, 1979, provided:

"This amendatory Act takes effect at the start of the 1981 registration year."

5/1-146. Motor vehicle

§ 1-146. Motor vehicle. Every vehicle which is self-propelled and every vehicle which is propelled by electric power obtained from overhead trolley wires, but not operated upon rails, except for vehicles moved solely by human power and motorized wheelchairs. For this Act, motor vehicles are divided into two divisions:

First Division: Those motor vehicles which are designed for the carrying of not more than 10 persons.

Second Division: Those motor vehicles which are designed for carrying more than 10 persons, those motor vehicles designed or used for living quarters, those motor vehicles which are designed for pulling or carrying freight, cargo or implements of husbandry, and those motor vehicles of the First Division remodelled for use and used as motor vehicles of the Second Division.

P.A. 76-1586, § 1-146, eff. July 1, 1970. Amended by P.A. 84-672, § 1, eff. Sept. 20, 1985; P.A. 85-1010, § 1, eff. March 2, 1988.

Formerly Ill.Rev.Stat.1991, ch. 95 ½, ¶ 1-146.

5/1-147. Motorcycle

§ 1-147. Motorcycle. Every motor vehicle having a seat or saddle for the use of the rider and designed to travel on not more than 3 wheels in contact with the ground, but excluding a tractor.

P.A. 76-1586, § 1-147, eff. July 1, 1970. Amended by P.A. 80-262, § 1, eff. Aug. 20, 1977.

Formerly Ill.Rev.Stat.1991, ch. 95 ½, ¶ 1-147.

5/1-148. § 1-148. Renumbered as § 1-145.001 by P.A. 90-89, § 15, eff. Jan. 1, 1998

5/1-148.1. § 1-148.1. Renumbered as § 1-148.3b by P.A. 90-89, § 15, eff. Jan. 1, 1998

5/1-148.2. Motorized Pedalcycle

§ 1-148.2. Motorized Pedalcycle. A motorized pedalcycle is a motor-driven cycle whose speed attainable in one mile is 30 mph or less, which is equipped with a motor that produces 2 brake horsepower or less. If an internal combustion engine is used, the displacement shall not exceed 50 cubic centimeter displacement and the power drive system shall not require the operator to shift gears.

P.A. 76-1586, § 1-148.2, added by P.A. 80-262, § 1, eff. Aug. 20, 1977. Amended by P.A. 83-820, § 1, eff. Jan. 1, 1984.

Formerly Ill.Rev.Stat.1991, ch. 95 ½, ¶ 1-148.2.

5/1-148.3. Motorized wheelchair

§ 1-148.3. Motorized wheelchair. Any self-propelled vehicle, including a three-wheeled vehicle, designed for and used by a person with disabilities, that is incapable of a speed in excess of 8 miles per hour on level ground.

P.A. 76-1586, § 1-148.3, added by P.A. 84-672, § 1, eff. Sept. 20, 1985. Amended by P.A. 88-685, § 5, eff. Jan. 24, 1995.

Formerly Ill.Rev.Stat.1991, ch. 95 ½, ¶ 1-148.3.

5/1-148.3a. Muffler

§ 1-148.3a. Muffler. A device consisting of a series of chambers or baffle plates or other mechanical design for the purpose of receiving exhaust gas from an internal combustion engine or turbine wheels for the purpose of receiving exhaust gas from a diesel engine, all of which are effective in reducing noise.

P.A. 76-1586, § 1-148.3a, added by P.A. 90-89, § 15, eff. Jan. 1, 1998.

5/1-148.3b. Multipurpose passenger vehicle

§ 1-148.3b. Multipurpose passenger vehicle. A motor vehicle with motive power, except a trailer, designed to carry 10 persons or less that is constructed either on a truck chassis or with special features for occasional off-road operation.

P.A. 76-1586, § 1-148.1, added by P.A. 78-343, § 1, eff. Jan. 1, 1974. Renumbered § 1-148.3b and amended by P.A. 90-89, § 15, eff. Jan. 1, 1998.

Formerly Ill.Rev.Stat.1991, ch. 95 ½, ¶ 1-148.1.

5/1-148.4. New Vehicle

§ 1-148.4. New Vehicle. A new vehicle which has not been previously sold to any person except a franchised distributor or franchised new vehicle dealer.

P.A. 76-1586, § 1-148.4, added by P.A. 86-444, § 1, eff. Jan. 1, 1990.

Formerly Ill.Rev.Stat.1991, ch. 95 ½, ¶ 1-148.4.

5/1-148.5. News media

§ 1-148.5. News media. A newspaper or other periodical issued at regular intervals whether in print or electronic format, a news service whether in print or electronic format, a radio station, a television station, a television network, a community antenna television service, or a person or corporation engaged in making news reels or other motion picture news for public showing.

P.A. 76-1586, § 1-148.5, added by P.A. 90-144, § 15, eff. July 23, 1997. Amended by P.A. 92-335, § 30, eff. Aug. 10, 2001.

5/1-148.6. Noncommercial vehicle

§ 1-148.6. Noncommercial vehicle. Any vehicle that is not a commercial vehicle.

P.A. 76-1586, § 1-151, eff. July 1, 1970. Renumbered § 1-148.6 and amended by P.A. 90-89, § 15, eff. Jan. 1, 1998.

Formerly Ill.Rev.Stat.1991, ch. 95 ½, ¶ 1-151.

5/1-148.8. Nondivisible load or vehicle

§ 1-148.8. Nondivisible load or vehicle. A load or vehicle that when separated into smaller loads or vehicles further dismantling would:

(1) Compromise the intended use of the load or vehicle or make it unable to perform the function for which it was intended.

(2) Destroy the value of the load or vehicle or make it unusable for its intended purpose.

(3) Require more than 8 work hours to dismantle using appropriate equipment. The applicant for a nondivisible load has the burden of proof as to the number of work hours required to dismantle the load.

P.A. 76-1586, § 1-148.8, added by P.A. 90-89, § 15, eff. Jan. 1, 1998.

5/1-149. Nonresident

§ 1-149. Nonresident. Every person who is not a resident of this State.

P.A. 76-1586, § 1-149, eff. July 1, 1970.

Formerly Ill.Rev.Stat.1991, ch. 95 ½, ¶ 1-149.

5/1-150. Nonresident's driving privilege

§ 1-150. Nonresident's driving privilege. The privilege conferred upon a nonresident by the laws of this State pertaining to the operation by such person of a motor vehicle, or the use of a vehicle owned by such person, in this State.

P.A. 76-1586, § 1-150, eff. July 1, 1970.

Formerly Ill.Rev.Stat.1991, ch. 95 ½, ¶ 1-150.

5/1-151. § 1-151. Renumbered as § 1-148.6 by P.A. 90-89, § 15, eff. Jan. 1, 1998

5/1-152. § 1-152. Repealed by P.A. 79-1041, § 2, eff. Jan. 1, 1976

5/1-153. Not-for-hire

§ 1-153. Not-for-hire. Operation of a commercial vehicle in furtherance of any commercial or industrial enterprise but not For-Hire.

P.A. 76-1586, § 1-153, eff. July 1, 1970.

Formerly Ill.Rev.Stat.1991, ch. 95 ½, ¶ 1-153.

5/1-153.1. Off-highway motorcycle

§ 1-153.1. Off-highway motorcycle. Any motorized device designed to travel primarily off-highway on 2 wheels, having a seat or saddle for the use of the operator, upon or by which any person, persons or property may be transported or drawn.

P.A. 76-1586, § 1-153.1, added by P.A. 85-830, § 1, eff. Sept. 24, 1987.

Formerly Ill.Rev.Stat.1991, ch. 95 ½, ¶ 1-153.1.

5/1-154. Official traffic-control devices

§ 1-154. Official traffic-control devices. All signs, signals, markings, and devices which conform with the State Manual and not inconsistent with this Act placed or erected by authority of a public body or official having jurisdiction, for the purpose of regulating, warning, or guiding traffic.

P.A. 76-1586, § 1-154, eff. July 1, 1970.

Formerly Ill.Rev.Stat.1991, ch. 95 ½, ¶ 1-154.

5/1–154.1. Operate

§ 1–154.1. Operate. To ride in or on, other than as a passenger, use or control in any manner the operation of any device or vehicle whether motorized or propelled by human power.

P.A. 76–1586, § 1–154.1, added by P.A. 85–830, § 1, eff. Sept. 24, 1987.

Formerly Ill.Rev.Stat.1991, ch. 95 ½, ¶ 1–154.1.

5/1–154.2. Operator

§ 1–154.2. Operator. Every person who operates or is in actual physical control of any device or vehicle whether motorized or propelled by human power.

P.A. 76–1586, § 1–154.2, added by P.A. 85–830, § 1, eff. Sept. 24, 1987.

Formerly Ill.Rev.Stat.1991, ch. 95 ½, ¶ 1–154.2.

5/1–154.4. Organ transport vehicle

§ 1–154.4. Organ transport vehicle. A motor vehicle of the second division equipped and used exclusively for the transportation of organs for human transplant or the transportation of members of the surgical team performing the organ harvesting or transplant operations. Vehicles defined in this Section shall be owned or operated by a company that has a contractual agreement with a federally designated organ procurement organization for the purposes stated in this Section.

P.A. 76–1586, § 1–154.4, added by P.A. 90–347, § 5, eff. Jan. 1, 1998.

5/1–154.5. Out-of-service order

§ 1–154.5. Out-of-service order. A temporary prohibition against driving a commercial motor vehicle.

P.A. 76–1586, § 1–154.5, added by P.A. 90–89, § 15, eff. Jan. 1, 1998.

5/1–154.7. Out-of-state salvage vehicle buyer

§ 1–154.7. Out-of-state salvage vehicle buyer. A person who is licensed in another state for the primary purpose of acquiring salvage vehicles and who is issued an out-of-state salvage vehicle buyer's identification card in this State for the sole purpose of acquiring salvage vehicles and taking them out of state.

P.A. 76–1586, § 1–154.7, added by P.A. 90–89, § 15, eff. Jan. 1, 1998.

5/1–155. Owner

§ 1–155. Owner. A person who holds legal title of a vehicle, or in the event a vehicle is the subject of an agreement for the conditional sale or lease thereof with the right of purchase upon performance of the conditions stated in the agreement and with an immediate right of possession vested in the conditional vendee or lessee, or in the event a mortgagor of such vehicle is entitled to possession, then such conditional vendee or lessee or mortgagor shall be deemed the owner for the purpose of this Code.

P.A. 76–1586, § 1–155, eff. July 1, 1970. Amended by P.A. 85–1201, § 1, eff. July 1, 1989.

Formerly Ill.Rev.Stat.1991, ch. 95 ½, ¶ 1–155.

5/1–155.5. Owner-operator

§ 1–155.5. Owner-operator. A commercial motor vehicle lessor who leases the commercial motor vehicle, with driver, to a lessee.

P.A. 76–1586, § 1–155.5, added by P.A. 90–89, § 15, eff. Jan. 1, 1998.

5/1–156. Park or parking

§ 1–156. Park or parking. Means the standing of a vehicle, whether occupied or not, otherwise than when temporarily and actually engaged in loading or unloading merchandise or passengers.

P.A. 76–1586, § 1–156, eff. July 1, 1970.

Formerly Ill.Rev.Stat.1991, ch. 95 ½, ¶ 1–156.

5/1–156.5. Park district

§ 1–156.5. Park district. Any park district formed under the Park District Code [1] or any Submerged Land Park District as that term is defined in subsection (c) of Section 1–3 of the Park District Code.[2]

P.A. 76–1586, § 1–156.5, added by P.A. 90–89, § 15, eff. Jan. 1, 1998.

1 70 ILCS 1205/1–1 et seq.

2 70 ILCS 1205/1–3.

5/1–157. Passenger car

§ 1–157. Passenger car. A motor vehicle of the First Division including a multipurpose passenger vehicle, that is designed for carrying not more than 10 persons.

P.A. 76–1586, § 1–157, eff. July 1, 1970. Amended by P.A. 78–343, § 1, eff. Jan. 1, 1974.

Formerly Ill.Rev.Stat.1991, ch. 95 ½, ¶ 1–157.

5/1–158. Pedestrian

§ 1–158. Pedestrian.

Any person afoot, including a person with a physical, hearing, or visual disability.

P.A. 76–1586, § 1–158, eff. July 1, 1970. Amended by P.A. 88–685, § 5, eff. Jan. 24, 1995.

Formerly Ill.Rev.Stat.1991, ch. 95 ½, ¶ 1–158.

5/1–158.5. Penalties and offenses—definitions

§ 1–158.5. Penalties and offenses-definitions. The following words and phrases when used in this Act, shall for the purposes of this Act, have the meanings ascribed to them in Article V of the "Unified Code of Corrections", as now or hereafter amended: [1]

Business Offense;

Conviction;

Court;

Felony;

Class 1 Felony;

Class 2 Felony;

Class 3 Felony;

Class 4 Felony;

Imprisonment;

Judgment;

Misdemeanor;

Class A Misdemeanor;

Class B Misdemeanor;

Class C Misdemeanor;

Offense;

Petty Offense;

Sentence.

P.A. 76-1586, § 1-300, added by P.A. 78-142, § 1, eff. Oct. 1, 1973. Renumbered § 1-158.5 and amended by P.A. 90-89, § 15, eff. Jan. 1, 1998.

Formerly Ill.Rev.Stat.1991, ch. 95 ½, ¶ 1-300.

[1] 730 ILCS 5/5-1-1 et seq.

5/1-159. Person

§ 1-159. Person. Every natural person, firm, copartnership, association or corporation.

P.A. 76-1586, § 1-159, eff. July 1, 1970.

Formerly Ill.Rev.Stat.1991, ch. 95 ½, ¶ 1-159.

5/1-159.1. Person with disabilities

§ 1-159.1. Person with disabilities. A natural person who, as determined by a licensed physician: (1) cannot walk without the use of, or assistance from, a brace, cane, crutch, another person, prosthetic device, wheelchair, or other assistive device; (2) is restricted by lung disease to such an extent that his or her forced (respiratory) expiratory volume for one second, when measured by spirometry, is less than one liter, or the arterial oxygen tension is less than 60 mm/hg on room air at rest; (3) uses portable oxygen; (4) has a cardiac condition to the extent that the person's functional limitations are classified in severity as Class III or Class IV, according to standards set by the American Heart Association; (5) is severely limited in the person's ability to walk due to an arthritic, neurological, or orthopedic condition; or (6) cannot walk 200 feet without stopping to rest because of one of the above 5 conditions.

P.A. 76-1586, § 1-159.1, added by P.A. 78-321, § 1, eff. Oct. 1, 1973. Amended by P.A. 83-1058, § 1, eff. July 1, 1984; P.A. 88-685, § 5, eff. Jan. 24, 1995; P.A. 92-411, § 5, eff. Jan. 1, 2002.

Formerly Ill.Rev.Stat.1991, ch. 95 ½, ¶ 1-159.1.

5/1-159.2. Personally identifying information

§ 1-159.2. Personally identifying information. Information that identifies an individual, including his or her photograph, social security number, driver identification number, name, address (but not the 5 digit zip code), telephone number, and medical or disability information, but "personally identifying information" does not include information on vehicular accidents, driving violations, and driver's status.

P.A. 76-1586, § 1-159.2, added by P.A. 92-32, § 10, eff. July 1, 2001.

5/1-159.3. Photograph

§ 1-159.3. Photograph. Any color photograph or digitally produced and captured image of an applicant for a driver's license or permit.

P.A. 76-1586, § 1-159.3, added by P.A. 90-191, § 10, eff. Jan. 1, 1998.

5/1-160. Pneumatic tire

§ 1-160. Pneumatic tire. Every tire in which compressed air is designed to support the load.

P.A. 76-1586, § 1-160, eff. July 1, 1970.

Formerly Ill.Rev.Stat.1991, ch. 95 ½, ¶ 1-160.

5/1-161. Pole trailer

§ 1-161. Pole trailer. Every vehicle without motive power designed to be drawn by another vehicle and attached to the towing vehicle by means of a reach or pole, or by being boomed or otherwise secured to the towing vehicle, and ordinarily used for transporting long or irregularly shaped loads such as poles, pipes or structural members capable, generally, of sustaining themselves as beams between the supporting connections.

P.A. 76-1586, § 1-161, eff. July 1, 1970.

Formerly Ill.Rev.Stat.1991, ch. 95 ½, ¶ 1-161.

5/1-162. Police officer

§ 1-162. Police officer. Every officer authorized to direct or regulate traffic or to make arrests and issue citations for violations of traffic regulations.

P.A. 76-1586, § 1-162, eff. July 1, 1970. Amended by P.A. 90-89, § 15, eff. Jan. 1, 1998.

Formerly Ill.Rev.Stat.1991, ch. 95 ½, ¶ 1-162.

5/1-162.5. Principal place of business

§ 1-162.5. Principal place of business. The place where any person transacts his principal business, or where he makes up and approves his payroll, maintains a central file of records and maintains his principal executive offices. In the event that not all of these functions are performed in one place, then that place where a majority of such functions are performed or the place where such person does in fact principally transact and control his business affairs.

P.A. 76-1586, § 1-164, eff. July 1, 1970. Renumbered § 1-162.5 and amended by P.A. 90-89, § 15, eff. Jan. 1, 1998.

Formerly Ill.Rev.Stat.1991, ch. 95 ½, ¶ 1-164.

5/1-163. Private road or driveway

§ 1-163. Private road or driveway. Every way or place in private ownership and used for vehicular travel by the owner and those having express or implied permission from the owner, but not by other persons.

P.A. 76-1586, § 1-163, eff. July 1, 1970.

Formerly Ill.Rev.Stat.1991, ch. 95 ½, ¶ 1-163.

5/1-164. § 1-164. Renumbered as § 1-162.5 by P.A. 90-89, § 15, eff. Jan. 1, 1998

5/1-164.1. Probationary license to drive

§ 1-164.1. Probationary license to drive. A conditional license granting full driving privileges during a period of suspension.

P.A. 76-1586, § 1-164.1, added by P.A. 84-1394, § 5, eff. Sept. 18, 1986. Amended by P.A. 86-549, § 1, eff. Jan. 1, 1990.

Formerly Ill.Rev.Stat.1991, ch. 95 ½, ¶ 1-164.1.

5/1-164.2. Processing costs

§ 1-164.2. Processing costs. Processing costs consist of fees paid to the Secretary of State for a record search to determine the name and address of the last registered owner, lienholder, and other legally entitled persons, plus the cost of sending certified mail notice to those persons.

P.A. 76-1586, § 1-164.2, added by P.A. 89-433, § 5, eff. Dec. 15, 1995.

5/1-164.5. Proof of financial responsibility

§ 1-164.5. Proof of financial responsibility. Proof of ability to respond in damages for any liability thereafter incurred resulting from the ownership, maintenance, use or operation of a motor vehicle for bodily injury to or death of any person in the amount of $20,000, and subject to this limit for any one person injured or killed, in the amount of $40,000 for bodily injury to or death of 2 or more persons in any one accident, and for damage to property in the amount of $15,000 resulting from any one accident. This proof in these amounts shall be furnished for each motor vehicle registered by every person required to furnish this proof.

P.A. 76-1586, § 1-164.5, added by P.A. 90-89, § 15, eff. Jan. 1, 1998.

5/1-164.7. Public utility

§ 1-164.7. Public utility. Each firm lawfully licensed and engaged in any of the following: the transmission of telegraphic or telephonic messages; the production, storage, transmission, distribution, sale, delivery, or furnishing of heat, cold, light, power, electricity, gas, or water; the disposal of sewage; the conveyance of oil or gas by pipeline; the drilling of water wells; or the installation or repair of facilities for any of these foregoing activities.

P.A. 76-1586, § 1-164.7, added by P.A. 90-89, § 15, eff. Jan. 1, 1998.

5/1-165. § 1-165. Repealed by P.A. 81-969, § 2

The repeal was effective at the "start of the 1981 registration year."

5/1-166. Railroad

§ 1-166. Railroad. A carrier of persons or property upon cars, other than streetcars, operated upon stationary rails.

P.A. 76-1586, § 1-166, eff. July 1, 1970.

Formerly Ill.Rev.Stat.1991, ch. 95 ½, ¶ 1-166.

5/1-166.1. Railroad-highway grade crossing

§ 1-166.1. Railroad-highway grade crossing. The intersection of stationary rails owned or used in the operation of a railroad corporation across a highway.

P.A. 76-1586, § 1-166.1, added by P.A. 78-314, § 1, eff. Oct. 1, 1973.

Formerly Ill.Rev.Stat.1991, ch. 95 ½, ¶ 1-166.1.

5/1-167. Railroad sign or signal

§ 1-167. Railroad sign or signal. Any sign, signal or device, other than an official traffic control signal or device, erected in accordance with the laws governing same and intended to give notice of the presence of railroad tracks or the approach of a railroad train.

P.A. 76-1586, § 1-167, eff. July 1, 1970. Amended by P.A. 76-2124, § 1, eff. July 1, 1970; P.A. 83-831, § 1, eff. Jan. 1, 1984.

Formerly Ill.Rev.Stat.1991, ch. 95 ½, ¶ 1-167.

5/1-168. Railroad train

§ 1-168. Railroad train. A steam engine, electric or other motor, with or without cars coupled thereto, operated upon rails, except streetcars.

P.A. 76-1586, § 1-168, eff. July 1, 1970.

Formerly Ill.Rev.Stat.1991, ch. 95 ½, ¶ 1-168.

5/1-168.05. Rebuilder

§ 1-168.05. Rebuilder. A person who is in the business of returning a vehicle for which a salvage certificate has been previously issued back to its original or operating condition.

P.A. 76-1586, § 1-168.05, added by P.A. 90-89, § 15, eff. Jan. 1, 1998.

5/1-168.1. Rebuilt vehicle

§ 1-168.1. Rebuilt vehicle. A vehicle for which a salvage certificate has been issued and which subsequently has been put back into its original or operating condition by a licensed rebuilder and which has met all the requirements of a salvage vehicle inspection.

P.A. 76-1586, § 1-168.1, added by P.A. 83-1473, § 1, eff. Jan. 1, 1985. Amended by P.A. 85-951, § 1, eff. July 1, 1988.

Formerly Ill.Rev.Stat.1991, ch. 95 ½, ¶ 1-168.1.

5/1-168.5. Recognized repair technician

§ 1-168.5. Recognized repair technician. A person professionally engaged in vehicle repair, employed by a going concern whose purpose is vehicle repair, or possessing nationally recognized certification for emission-related diagnosis and repair.

P.A. 76-1586, § 1-168.5, added by P.A. 90-89, § 15, eff. Jan. 1, 1998.

5/1-169. Recreational vehicle

§ 1-169. Recreational vehicle. Every camping trailer, motor home, mini motor home, travel trailer, truck camper or van camper used primarily for recreational purposes and not used commercially nor owned by a commercial business.

P.A. 76-1586, § 1-169, eff. July 1, 1970. Amended by P.A. 78-343, § 1, eff. Jan. 1, 1974; P.A. 81-969, § 1, eff. Jan. 4, 1980; P.A. 84-986, § 1, eff. Sept. 25, 1985.

Formerly Ill.Rev.Stat.1991, ch. 95 ½, ¶ 1-169.

Section 3 of P.A. 81-969, approved Sept. 22, 1979, provided:

"This amendatory Act takes effect at the start of the 1981 registration year."

5/1-169.5. Refuse

§ 1-169.5. Refuse. Any material or load consisting of waste from the facilities of the generator of the waste when transported for disposal or to a permitted recycling or waste processing facility when the generator receives no direct or indirect compensation from anyone for the material or load and when transported by a truck specially equipped with a selfcompactor or an industrial roll-off hoist and roll-off container.

P.A. 76-1586, § 1-169.5, added by P.A. 90-89, § 15, eff. Jan. 1, 1998.

5/1-170. § 1-170. Repealed by P.A. 85-951, § 2, eff. July 1, 1988

5/1-171. Registration—Registration Sticker

§ 1-171. Registration—Registration Sticker. Registration. The registration certificate or certificates, registration plates and registration stickers issued under the laws of this State pertaining to the registration of vehicles.

Registration Sticker or Stickers. A device or devices to be attached to a rear registration plate that will renew the registration and registration plate or plates for a pre-determined period not to exceed one registration year except as provided in subsection (1) of Section 3-414 of this Code. Should the Secretary of State determine it is advisable to require a registration sticker to be attached to a front registration plate, he may require such action and provide the necessary additional sticker. Such determination shall be publicly announced at least 30 days in advance of a new annual registration year.

P.A. 76-1586, § 1-171, eff. July 1, 1970. Amended by P.A. 80-230, § 1, eff. Oct. 1, 1977; P.A. 80-1185, § 1, eff. March 8, 1978.

Formerly Ill.Rev.Stat.1991, ch. 95 ½, ¶ 1-171.

5/1-171.01. § 1-171.01. Renumbered as § 1-111.1a by P.A. 90-89, § 15, eff. Jan. 1, 1998

5/1-171.01a. Remittance agent

§ 1-171.01a. Remittance agent. For the purposes of Article IX of Chapter 3,[1] the term "remittance agent" means any person who holds himself or herself out to the public as being engaged in or who engages in accepting money for remittance to the State of Illinois or any of its instrumentalities or political subdivisions, or to any of their officials, for the payment of vehicle taxes or vehicle license or registration fees regardless of when the money is accepted from the public or remitted to the State, whether or not the person renders any other service in connection with the making of any such remittance or is engaged in any other endeavor. The term "remittance agent" does not include any licensed dealer in motor vehicles who accepts money for remittance to the State of Illinois for the payment of vehicle taxes or vehicle licenses or registration fees as an incident to his or her business as a motor vehicle dealer.

P.A. 76-1586, § 1-171.01a, added by P.A. 90-89, § 15, eff. Jan. 1, 1998.

1 625 ILCS 5/3-900 et seq.

5/1-171.01b. Remittee

§ 1-171.01b. Remittee. The State of Illinois location where the remittance agent brings the money and application he or she receives from the general public (remitter) to be processed by the State of Illinois.

P.A. 76-1586, § 1-171.01b, added by P.A. 90-89, § 15, eff. Jan. 1, 1998.

5/1-171.01c. Remitter

§ 1-171.01c. Remitter. Any person who gives money to a remittance agent to submit to the State of Illinois and its licensing and taxing agencies for the payment of vehicle taxes or vehicle license and registration fees.

P.A. 76-1586, § 1-171.01c, added by P.A. 90-89, § 15, eff. Jan. 1, 1998.

5/1-171.02. Repaired vehicle

§ 1-171.02. Repaired vehicle. A vehicle other than a rebuilt vehicle which has been put back into its original or operating condition by restoring, mending, straightening, replacing, altering or painting its essential parts by a licensed repairer.

P.A. 76-1586, § 1-171.02, added by P.A. 83-1473, § 1, eff. Jan. 1, 1985.

Formerly Ill.Rev.Stat.1991, ch. 95 ½, ¶ 1-171.02.

5/1-171.04. Replica trolley

§ 1-171.04. Replica trolley. A motor vehicle that is a replica of or is specifically designed to resemble a cable car or an antique trolley car, except that the vehicle is not operated on rails.

P.A. 76-1586, § 1-171.04, added by P.A. 89-687, § 5, eff. June 1, 1997.

5/1-171.3. Repairer

§ 1-171.3. Repairer. A person who is in the business of returning a vehicle other than a vehicle for which a salvage certificate has been issued back to its original or operating condition by restoring, mending, straightening, replacing, altering, or painting its essential parts.

P.A. 76-1586, § 1-171.3, added by P.A. 90-89, § 15, eff. Jan. 1, 1998.

5/1-171.6. Rescue squad

§ 1-171.6. Rescue squad. A voluntary association of individuals or a fire department dedicated to saving lives through the rescue of persons entrapped in wrecked vehicles or other hazardous circumstances and associated with some unit of government.

P.A. 76-1586, § 1-222, added by P.A. 79-537, § 1, eff. Oct. 1, 1975. Renumbered § 1-171.6 and amended by P.A. 90-89, § 15, eff. Jan. 1, 1998.

Formerly Ill.Rev.Stat.1991, ch. 95 ½, ¶ 1-222.

5/1-171.8. Rescue vehicle

§ 1-171.8. Rescue vehicle. Any publicly or privately owned vehicle which is specifically designed, configured, and equipped for the performance of access and extrication of persons from hazardous or life-endangering situations, as well as for the emergency transportation of persons who are sick, injured, wounded or otherwise incapacitated or helpless.

P.A. 76-1586, § 1-224, added by P.A. 82-433, § 1, eff. Sept. 8, 1981. Renumbered § 1-171.8 and amended by P.A. 90-89, § 15, eff. Jan. 1, 1998.

Formerly Ill.Rev.Stat.1991, ch. 95 ½, ¶ 1-224.

Section 3 of P.A. 82-433 approved Sept. 8, 1981, provided:

"This Act takes effect upon its becoming a law, except that the provisions relating to safety tests and proof of financial responsibility for medical transport vehicles apply only to applications for and the issuance of registration plates which are required to be displayed on January 1, 1982 or thereafter."

5/1-172. Residence district

§ 1-172. Residence district. The territory contiguous to and including a highway not comprising a business district when the property on such highway for a distance of 300 feet or more is in the main improved with residences or residences and buildings in use for business.

For purposes of establishing maximum speed limits, a residence district shall be at least a quarter of a mile long with residences or residences and buildings in use for businesses spaced no more than 300 feet apart.

P.A. 76-1586, § 1-172, eff. July 1, 1970. Amended by P.A. 81-875, § 1, eff. Jan. 1, 1980.

Formerly Ill.Rev.Stat.1991, ch. 95 ½, ¶ 1-172.

5/1-173. Resident

§ 1-173. Resident. (a) Every natural person who resides in this state shall be deemed a resident of this State.

(b) In the case of a firm, copartnership or association, if the principal place of business of such firm, copartnership or association is located in the State of Illinois, then such firm, copartnership or association shall be deemed a resident of the State of Illinois.

(c) In the case of a corporation, if the corporation was incorporated under the laws of the State of Illinois or if the principal place of business of such corporation is in the State of Illinois, then such corporation shall be deemed a resident of the State of Illinois.

P.A. 76-1586, § 1-173, eff. July 1, 1970.

Formerly Ill.Rev.Stat.1991, ch. 95 ½, ¶ 1-173.

5/1-173.1. Restricted Driving Permit

§ 1-173.1. Restricted Driving Permit. A restricted driving permit is that document which grants and specifies limited privileges to drivers of motor vehicles who have had their full driving privileges suspended, revoked or cancelled. The restricted driving permit is valid only when in the immediate possession of the driver to whom it is issued.

P.A. 76-1586, § 1-173.1, added by P.A. 81-1400, § 1, eff. Aug. 25, 1980.

Formerly Ill.Rev.Stat.1991, ch. 95 ½, ¶ 1-173.1.

5/1-174. Retail sale

§ 1-174. Retail sale. The act or attempted act of selling vehicles or otherwise disposing of a vehicle to a person for use as a consumer.

P.A. 76-1586, § 1-174, eff. July 1, 1970.

Formerly Ill.Rev.Stat.1991, ch. 95 ½, ¶ 1-174.

5/1-175. § 1-175. Repealed by P.A. 90-89, § 20, eff. Jan. 1, 1998

5/1-176. Revocation of driver's license

§ 1-176. Revocation of driver's license. The termination by formal action of the Secretary of a person's license or privilege to operate a motor vehicle on the public highways, which termination shall not be subject to renewal or restoration except that an application for a new license may be presented and acted upon by the Secretary after the expiration of at least one year after the date of revocation.

P.A. 76-1586, § 1-176, eff. July 1, 1970.

Formerly Ill.Rev.Stat.1991, ch. 95 ½, ¶ 1-176.

5/1-176.1. Ridesharing arrangement

§ 1-176.1. Ridesharing arrangement. The transportation by motor vehicle of not more than 16 persons, including the driver, (1) for purposes incidental to another purpose of the driver, for which no fee is charged or paid except to reimburse the driver or owner of the vehicle for his or her operating expenses on a nonprofit basis or (2) when these persons are traveling between their homes and their places of employment, or places reasonably convenient thereto, for which (i) no fee is charged or paid except to reimburse the driver or owner of the vehicle for his or her operating expenses on a nonprofit basis or (ii) a fee is charged in accordance with the provisions of Section 6 of the Ridesharing Arrangements Act.[1]

P.A. 76-1586, § 1-176.1, added by P.A. 81-1452, § 1, eff. Jan. 1, 1981. Amended by P.A. 83-1091, § 1, eff. July 1, 1984; P.A. 90-89, § 15, eff. Jan. 1, 1998.

Formerly Ill.Rev.Stat.1991, ch. 95 ½, ¶ 1-176.1.

1 625 ILCS 30/1 et seq.

5/1-177. Right-of-way

§ 1-177. Right-of-way. The right of one vehicle or pedestrian to proceed in a lawful manner in preference to another vehicle or pedestrian approaching under such circumstances of direction, speed and proximity as to give rise to danger of collision unless one grants precedence to the other.

P.A. 76-1586, § 1-177, eff. July 1, 1970.

Formerly Ill.Rev.Stat.1991, ch. 95 ½, ¶ 1-177.

5/1-178. Road tractor

§ 1-178. Road tractor. Every motor vehicle designed and used for drawing other vehicles and not so constructed as to carry any load thereon either independently or any part of the weight of a vehicle or load so drawn.

P.A. 76-1586, § 1-178, eff. July 1, 1970.

Formerly Ill.Rev.Stat.1991, ch. 95 ½, ¶ 1-178.

5/1-179. Roadway

§ 1-179. Roadway. That portion of a highway improved, designed or ordinarily used for vehicular travel, exclusive of the berm or shoulder. In the event a highway includes two or more separate roadways the term "roadway" as used herein shall refer to any such roadway separately but not to all such roadways collectively.

P.A. 76-1586, § 1-179, eff. July 1, 1970.

Formerly Ill.Rev.Stat.1991, ch. 95 ½, ¶ 1-179.

5/1-179.5. Rooftop

§ 1-179.5. Rooftop. The major uppermost portion of a bus body that is flat in a fore and aft direction.

P.A. 76-1586, § 1-179.5, added by P.A. 90-89, § 15, eff. Jan. 1, 1998.

5/1-180. Rural mail delivery vehicle

§ 1-180. Rural mail delivery vehicle. Every vehicle used to deliver U. S. mail on a rural mail delivery route.

P.A. 76-1586, § 1-180, eff. July 1, 1970.

Formerly Ill.Rev.Stat.1991, ch. 95 ½, ¶ 1-180.

5/1-180.5. Safety glazing material

§ 1-180.5. Safety glazing material. Any glazing material so constructed, treated, or combined with other materials as to reduce substantially, in comparison with ordinary sheet glass or plate glass, the likelihood of injury to persons by objects from exterior sources or by these safety glazing materials when they may be cracked or broken.

P.A. 76-1586, § 1-180.5, added by P.A. 90-89, § 15, eff. Jan. 1, 1998.

5/1-181. Safety zone

§ 1-181. Safety zone. The area or space officially set apart within a roadway for the exclusive use of pedestrians and which is protected or is so marked or indicated by adequate signs as to be plainly visible at all times while set apart as a safety zone.

P.A. 76-1586, § 1-181, eff. July 1, 1970.

Formerly Ill.Rev.Stat.1991, ch. 95 ½, ¶ 1-181.

5/1-182. School bus

§ 1-182. School bus.

(a) "School bus" means every motor vehicle, except as provided in paragraph (b) of this Section, owned or operated by or for any of the following entities for the transportation of persons regularly enrolled as students in grade 12 or below in connection with any activity of such entity:

Any public or private primary or secondary school;

Any primary or secondary school operated by a religious institution; or

Any public, private or religious nursery school.

(b) This definition shall not include the following:

1. A bus operated by a public utility, municipal corporation or common carrier authorized to conduct local or interurban transportation of passengers when such bus is not traveling a specific school bus route but is:

On a regularly scheduled route for the transportation of other fare paying passengers;

Furnishing charter service for the transportation of groups on field trips or other special trips or in connection with other special events; or

Being used for shuttle service between attendance centers or other educational facilities.

2. A motor vehicle of the First Division.

3. A motor vehicle designed for the transportation of not less than 7 nor more than 16 persons that is operated by or for a public or private primary or secondary school, including any primary or secondary school operated by a religious institution, for the purpose of transporting not more than 15 students to and from interscholastic athletic or other interscholastic or school sponsored activities.

P.A. 76-1586, § 1-182, eff. July 1, 1970. Amended by P.A. 78-1244, § 1, eff. Sept. 5, 1974; P.A. 79-63, § 1, eff. June 26, 1975; P.A. 79-798, § 1, eff. July 1, 1976; P.A. 79-1454, § 44, eff. Aug. 31, 1976; P.A. 80-1034, § 1, eff. Oct. 1, 1977; P.A. 81-509, § 1, eff. Jan. 1, 1980; P.A. 82-1011, § 2, eff. Sept. 17, 1982; P.A. 83-299, § 1, eff. Jan. 1, 1984; P.A. 89-132, § 10, eff. July 14, 1995.

Formerly Ill.Rev.Stat.1991, ch. 95 ½, ¶ 1-182.

5/1-182.3. Scrap processor

§ 1-182.3. Scrap processor. A person who purchases a vehicle, junk vehicle, or vehicle cowl for processing into a form other than a vehicle, junk vehicle, or vehicle cowl for remelting purposes only, who from a fixed location utilizes machinery and equipment for processing or manufacturing ferrous or nonferrous metallic scrap into prepared grades, and whose principal product is metallic scrap and who records the purchases on a weight ticket.

P.A. 76-1586, § 1-182.3, added by P.A. 90-89, § 15, eff. Jan. 1, 1998.

5/1-182.6. Seat safety belts

§ 1-182.6. Seat safety belts. A set of belts or a harness meeting the specifications established by the Department of Transportation and installed in such manner as to prevent or materially reduce the movement of the person using the belts or harness in the event of collision or upset of the vehicle.

P.A. 76-1586, § 1-182.6, added by P.A. 90-89, § 15, eff. Jan. 1, 1998.

5/1-182.8. Second stage manufacturer or converter

§ 1-182.8. Second stage manufacturer or converter. A person who prior to the retail sale of a motor vehicle, assembles, installs or affixes a body, cab, or special equipment to a chassis, or who adds, subtracts from, or modifies a previously assembled or manufactured motor vehicle.

P.A. 76-1586, § 1-182.8, added by P.A. 90-89, § 15, eff. Jan. 1, 1998.

5/1-183. Secretary

§ 1-183. Secretary. The Illinois Secretary of State or his or her designee.

P.A. 76-1586, § 1-183, eff. July 1, 1970. Amended by P.A. 90-89, § 15, eff. Jan. 1, 1998.

Formerly Ill.Rev.Stat.1991, ch. 95 ½, ¶ 1-183.

5/1-184. Secretary of State

§ 1-184. Secretary of State. The Secretary of State of Illinois.

P.A. 76-1586, § 1-184, eff. July 1, 1970.

Formerly Ill.Rev.Stat.1991, ch. 95 ½, ¶ 1-184.

5/1-185. Security agreement

§ 1-185. Security agreement. A written agreement which reserves or creates a security interest.

P.A. 76-1586, § 1-185, eff. July 1, 1970.

Formerly Ill.Rev.Stat.1991, ch. 95 ½, ¶ 1-185.

5/1-186. Security interest

§ 1-186. Security interest. An interest in a vehicle reserved or created by agreement and which secures payment or performance of an obligation. The term includes the interest of a lessor under a lease intended as security. A security interest is "perfected" when it is valid against third parties generally, subject only to specific statutory exceptions.

P.A. 76-1586, § 1-186, eff. July 1, 1970.

Formerly Ill.Rev.Stat.1991, ch. 95 ½, ¶ 1-186.

5/1-186.5. Selling price

§ 1-186.5. Selling price. The consideration received for a motor vehicle subject to the tax imposed by Section 3-1001 valued in money, whether received in money or otherwise, including cash, credits, service, or property. In the case of gifts or transfers without reasonable consideration, "selling price" shall be deemed to be the fair market value as determined by the Department of Revenue.

P.A. 76-1586, § 1-186.5, added by P.A. 90-89, § 15, eff. Jan. 1, 1998.

5/1-187. Semitrailer

§ 1-187. Semitrailer. Every vehicle without motive power, other than a pole trailer, designed for carrying persons or property and for being drawn by a motor vehicle and so constructed that some part of its weight and that of its load rests upon or is carried by another vehicle.

P.A. 76-1586, § 1-187, eff. July 1, 1970.

Formerly Ill.Rev.Stat.1991, ch. 95 ½, ¶ 1-187.

5/1-187.001. Serious traffic violation

§ 1-187.001. Serious traffic violation.

(a) A conviction when operating a motor vehicle for:

(1) a violation of subsection (a) of Section 11–402, relating to a motor vehicle accident involving damage to a vehicle;

(2) a violation of Section 11–403, relating to failure to stop and exchange information after a motor vehicle collision, property damage only;

(3) a violation of subsection (a) of Section 11–502, relating to illegal transportation, possession, or carrying of alcoholic liquor within the passenger area of any vehicle;

(4) a violation of Section 6–101 relating to operating a motor vehicle without a valid license or permit;

(5) a violation of Section 11–403, relating to failure to stop and exchange information or give aid after a motor vehicle collision involving personal injury or death;

(6) a violation relating to excessive speeding, involving a single speeding charge of 30 miles per hour or more above the legal speed limit;

(7) a violation relating to reckless driving;

(8) a violation of subsection (d) of Section 11–707, relating to passing in a no-passing zone;

(9) a violation of subsection (b) of Section 11–1402, relating to limitations on backing upon a controlled access highway;

(10) a violation of subsection (b) of Section 11–707, relating to driving on the left side of a roadway in a no-passing zone;

(11) a violation of subsection (e) of Section 11–1002, relating to failure to yield the right-of-way to a pedestrian at an intersection;

(12) a violation of Section 11–1008, relating to failure to yield to a pedestrian on a sidewalk; or

(13) a violation of Section 11–1201, relating to failure to stop for an approaching railroad train or signals; or

(b) Any other similar violation of a law or local ordinance of any state relating to motor vehicle traffic control, other than a parking violation.

(c) A violation of any of these defined serious traffic offenses shall not preclude the defendant from being eligible to receive an order of court supervision under Section 5–6–1 of the Unified Code of Corrections.[1]

P.A. 76–1586, § 1–187.001, added by P.A. 90–369, § 5, eff. Jan. 1, 1998.

1 730 ILCS 5/5–6–1.

5/1–187.01. Servicing of vehicles

§ 1–187.01. Servicing of vehicles. The altering or maintaining of the parts of a vehicle other than its essential parts. Regarding engines and transmissions, however, repair or replacement of parts, which does not result in the removal of all or any part of the identification number shall be deemed servicing of the vehicle.

P.A. 76–1586, § 1–187.01, added by P.A. 84–1302, § 1, eff. Jan. 1, 1987; P.A. 84–1304, § 1, eff. Jan. 1, 1987.

Formerly Ill.Rev.Stat.1991, ch. 95 ½, ¶ 1–187.01.

P.A. 84–1302 and P.A. 84–1304 enacted identical text.

5/1–187.1. Shoulder

§ 1–187.1. Shoulder. That portion of the highway adjacent to the roadway for accommodating stopped vehicles or for emergency use.

P.A. 76–1586, § 1–187.1, added by P.A. 84–873, § 1, eff. Jan. 1, 1986.

Formerly Ill.Rev.Stat.1991, ch. 95 ½, ¶ 1–187.1.

5/1–188. Sidewalk

§ 1–188. Sidewalk. That portion of a street between the curb lines, or the lateral lines of a roadway, and the adjacent property lines, intended for use of pedestrians.

P.A. 76–1586, § 1–188, eff. July 1, 1970.

Formerly Ill.Rev.Stat.1991, ch. 95 ½, ¶ 1–188.

5/1–188.2. Signature

§ 1–188.2. Signature. The name of a person as written by that person and captured in a manner acceptable to the Secretary of State.

P.A. 76–1586, § 1–188.2, added by P.A. 90–191, § 10, eff. Jan. 1, 1998.

5/1–189. Situs or base of vehicle

§ 1–189. Situs or base of vehicle. The place where a vehicle is principally garaged, or from whence it is principally dispatched, or where the movements of such vehicle usually originate.

P.A. 76–1586, § 1–189, eff. July 1, 1970.

Formerly Ill.Rev.Stat.1991, ch. 95 ½, ¶ 1–189.

5/1–190. Solid tire

§ 1–190. Solid tire. Every tire of rubber or other resilient material which does not depend upon compressed air for the support of the load.

P.A. 76–1586, § 1–190, eff. July 1, 1970.

Formerly Ill.Rev.Stat.1991, ch. 95 ½, ¶ 1–190.

5/1–190.05. Special hauling vehicle

§ 1–190.05. Special hauling vehicle. A vehicle or combination of vehicles transporting asphalt or concrete in the plastic state or a vehicle or combination of vehicles that is subject to the weight limitations in subsections (a) and (b) of Section 15–111 for which the owner of the vehicle or combination of vehicles has elected to pay, in addition to the registration fees stated in subsection (a) or (c) of Section 3–815 or Section 3–818, $100 to the Secretary of State for each registration year.

P.A. 76–1586, § 1–190.05, added by P.A. 90–89, § 15, eff. Jan. 1, 1998.

5/1–190.1. Special license plate

§ 1–190.1. Special license plate. Registration plates issued by the Secretary of State that by statute require, in addition to the applicable registration fee, an additional fee that is to be deposited into the Secretary of State Special License Plate Fund.

P.A. 76–1586, § 1–190.1, added by P.A. 89–282, § 10, eff. Aug. 10, 1995.

5/1–191. Special mobile equipment

§ 1–191. Special mobile equipment. Every vehicle not designed or used primarily for the transportation of persons or property and only incidentally operated or moved over a highway, including but not limited to: street sweepers, ditch digging apparatus, well boring apparatus and road construction and maintenance machinery such as asphalt spreaders, bituminous mixers, bucket loaders, tractors other than truck tractors, ditchers, levelling graders, finishing machines, motor graders, road rollers, scarifiers, earth moving carryalls and scrapers, power shovels and drag lines, and self-propelled cranes and earth moving equipment. The term does not include house trailers, dump trucks, truck mounted transit mixers, cranes or shovels, or other vehicles designed for the transportation of persons or property to which machinery has been attached.

P.A. 76-1586, § 1-191, eff. July 1, 1970. Amended by P.A. 85-951, § 1, eff. July 1, 1988.

Formerly Ill.Rev.Stat.1991, ch. 95 ½, ¶ 1-191.

5/1-192. Specially constructed vehicle

§ 1-192. Specially constructed vehicle. Every vehicle of a type required to be registered hereunder that: (a) has been materially altered from its original construction by the removal, addition or substitution of essential parts; or (b) was not originally constructed under a distinctive name by a generally recognized manufacturer of vehicles.

P.A. 76-1586, § 1-192, eff. July 1, 1970. Amended by P.A. 83-1473, § 1, eff. Jan. 1, 1985; P.A. 85-951, § 1, eff. July 1, 1988.

Formerly Ill.Rev.Stat.1991, ch. 95 ½, ¶ 1-192.

5/1-193. Speed-change lane

§ 1-193. Speed-change lane. An auxiliary lane, including tapered areas, primarily for the acceleration or deceleration of vehicles entering or leaving the through traffic lanes.

P.A. 76-1586, § 1-193, eff. July 1, 1970.

Formerly Ill.Rev.Stat.1991, ch. 95 ½, ¶ 1-193.

5/1-194. Stand or standing

§ 1-194. Stand or standing. Means the halting of a vehicle, whether occupied or not, otherwise than when temporarily and actually engaged in receiving or discharging passengers.

P.A. 76-1586, § 1-194, eff. July 1, 1970.

Formerly Ill.Rev.Stat.1991, ch. 95 ½, ¶ 1-194.

5/1-195. State

§ 1-195. State. A state, territory or possession of the United States, the District of Columbia, the Commonwealth of Puerto Rico or a province of the Dominion of Canada.

P.A. 76-1586, § 1-195, eff. July 1, 1970.

Formerly Ill.Rev.Stat.1991, ch. 95 ½, ¶ 1-195.

5/1-196. State highways

§ 1-196. State highways. Defined in the "Illinois Highway Code" as the same may from time to time be amended.[1]

P.A. 76-1586, § 1-196, eff. July 1, 1970.

Formerly Ill.Rev.Stat.1991, ch. 95 ½, ¶ 1-196.

[1] 605 ILCS 5/1-101 et seq.

5/1-197. State Police

§ 1-197. State Police. The Illinois State Police.

P.A. 76-1586, § 1-197, eff. July 1, 1970.

Formerly Ill.Rev.Stat.1991, ch. 95 ½, ¶ 1-197.

5/1-197.5. Statutory summary alcohol or other drug related suspension of driver's privileges

§ 1-197.5. Statutory summary alcohol or other drug related suspension of driver's privileges. The withdrawal by the circuit court of a person's license or privilege to operate a motor vehicle on the public highways for the periods provided in Section 6-208.1. Reinstatement after the suspension period shall occur after all appropriate fees have been paid, unless the court notifies the Secretary of State that the person should be disqualified. The bases for this withdrawal of driving privileges shall be the individual's refusal to submit to or failure to complete a chemical test or tests following an arrest for the offense of driving under the influence of alcohol, other drugs, or intoxicating compounds, or any combination thereof, or submission to such a test or tests indicating an alcohol concentration of 0.08 or more as provided in Section 11-501.1 of this Code.

P.A. 76-1586, § 1-203.1, added by P.A. 84-272, § 7, eff. Jan. 1, 1986. Amended by P.A. 84-1394, § 5, eff. Sept. 18, 1986; P.A. 90-43, § 5, eff. July 2, 1997. Renumbered § 1-197.5 and amended by P.A. 90-89, § 15, eff. Jan. 1, 1998. Amended by P.A. 90-655, § 153, eff. July 30, 1998; P.A. 92-834, § 5, eff. Aug. 22, 2002.

Formerly Ill.Rev.Stat.1991, ch. 95 ½, ¶ 1-203.1.

P.A. 90-655, the First 1998 General Revisory Act, amended various Acts to delete obsolete text, to correct patent and technical errors, to revise cross references, to resolve multiple actions in the 89th and 90th General Assemblies and to make certain technical corrections in P.A. 89-708 through P.A. 90-566.

5/1-198. Stinger-steered semitrailer

§ 1-198. Stinger-steered semitrailer. Every semitrailer which has its kingpin on a projection to the front of the structure of such semitrailer and is combined with the 5th wheel of the truck tractor at a point not less than two feet to the rear of the center of the rearmost axle of such tractor.

P.A. 76-1586, § 1-198, eff. July 1, 1970.

Formerly Ill.Rev.Stat.1991, ch. 95 ½, ¶ 1-198.

5/1-199. Stop

§ 1-199. Stop. When required means complete cessation from movement.

P.A. 76-1586, § 1-199, eff. July 1, 1970.

Formerly Ill.Rev.Stat.1991, ch. 95 ½, ¶ 1-199.

5/1-200. Stop or stopping

§ 1-200. Stop or stopping. Means any halting even momentarily of a vehicle, whether occupied or not, except when necessary to avoid conflict with other traffic or in compliance with the directions of a police officer or traffic-control sign or signal.

P.A. 76-1586, § 1-200, eff. July 1, 1970. Amended by P.A. 76-2125, § 1, eff. July 1, 1970.

Formerly Ill.Rev.Stat.1991, ch. 95 ½, ¶ 1-200.

5/1-201. Street

§ 1-201. Street. The entire width between boundary lines of every way publicly maintained, when any part thereof is open to the use of the public for purposes of vehicular travel.

P.A. 76-1586, § 1-201, eff. July 1, 1970. Amended by P.A. 90-655, § 153, eff. July 30, 1998.

Formerly Ill.Rev.Stat.1991, ch. 95 ½, ¶ 1-201.

5/1-202. Streetcar

§ 1-202. Streetcar. A car other than a railroad train for transporting persons or property and operated upon rails principally within a municipality.

P.A. 76-1586, § 1-202, eff. July 1, 1970.

Formerly Ill.Rev.Stat.1991, ch. 95 ½, ¶ 1-202.

5/1-202.1. Street rod

§ 1-202.1. Street rod. A motor vehicle that is a 1948 or older vehicle or a vehicle that has been certified by an inspector of the National Street Rod Association, on a form prescribed by the Secretary of State, to be a street rod that was manufactured after 1948 to resemble a vehicle that was manufactured before 1949 and has been altered from the manufacturer's original design or has a body constructed from non-original materials and which is maintained for occasional transportation, exhibitions, club activities, parades, tours, and similar uses and which is not used for general daily transportation.

P.A. 76-1586, § 1-202.1, added by P.A. 92-668, § 5, eff. Jan. 1, 2003.

5/1-202.5. Strobe lamp

§ 1-202.5. Strobe lamp. A vehicular signaling device that generates flashes of light by inducing intermittent flows of electricity through a gas.

P.A. 76-1586, § 1-202.5, added by P.A. 90-89, § 15, eff. Jan. 1, 1998.

5/1-203. Suburban district

§ 1-203. Suburban district. That portion of any city, village or incorporated town other than the business and residence districts.

P.A. 76-1586, § 1-203, eff. July 1, 1970.

Formerly Ill.Rev.Stat.1991, ch. 95 ½, ¶ 1-203.

5/1-203.1. § 1-203.1. Renumbered as § 1-197.5 by P.A. 90-89, § 15, eff. Jan. 1, 1998

5/1-204. Suspension of driver's license

§ 1-204. Suspension of driver's license. The temporary withdrawal by formal action of the Secretary of a person's license or privilege to operate a motor vehicle on the public highways, for a period specifically designated by the Secretary.

P.A. 76-1586, § 1-204, eff. July 1, 1970.

Formerly Ill.Rev.Stat.1991, ch. 95 ½, ¶ 1-204.

5/1-204.05. Suspension system

§ 1-204.05. Suspension system. The system of devices consisting of but not limited to springs, spring shackles, shock absorbers, torsion bars, a frame, or any other supporting members used to attach the body of a motor vehicle to its axles.

P.A. 76-1586, § 1-204.05, added by P.A. 90-89, § 15, eff. Jan. 1, 1998.

5/1-204.1. Sworn report

§ 1-204.1. Sworn report. A confirmation of correctness and truth by an affidavit, oath, deposition or a verification by certification executed pursuant to Section 1-109 of the Code of Civil Procedure.[1]

P.A. 76-1586, § 1-204.1, added by P.A. 85-992, § 1, eff. Jan. 5, 1988.

Formerly Ill.Rev.Stat.1991, ch. 95 ½, ¶ 1-204.1.

[1] 735 ILCS 5/1-109.

5/1-204.3. Tandem axles

§ 1-204.3. Tandem axles. Any 2 or more single axles whose centers are more than 40 inches and not more than 96 inches apart, measured to the nearest inch between extreme axles in the series, except as provided in Section 15-111 for special hauling vehicles.

P.A. 76-1586, § 1-204.3, added by P.A. 90-89, § 15, eff. Jan. 1, 1998.

5/1-204.4. Tank vehicle

§ 1-204.4. Tank vehicle. Any commercial motor vehicle that is designed to transport any liquid or gaseous material within a tank that is either permanently or temporarily attached to the vehicle or the chassis. Those vehicles include, but are not limited to, cargo tanks and portable tanks, as defined in 49 C.F.R. Part 171. However, for the purposes of Article V of Chapter 6 of this Code,[1] this definition does not include portable tanks having a rated capacity of less than 1,000 gallons.

P.A. 76-1586, § 1-204.4, added by P.A. 90-89, § 15, eff. Jan. 1, 1998.

[1] 625 ILCS 5/6-500 et seq.

5/1-205. Through highway

§ 1-205. Through highway. Every highway or portion thereof on which vehicular traffic is given preferential right of way, and at the entrances to which vehicular traffic from intersecting highways is required by law to yield right of way to vehicles on such through highway in obedience to either a stop sign or a yield sign, when such signs are erected as provided in this Act.

P.A. 76-1586, § 1-205, eff. July 1, 1970.

Formerly Ill.Rev.Stat.1991, ch. 95 ½, ¶ 1-205.

5/1-205.01. Tollroad or toll highway

§ 1-205.01. Tollroad or toll highway. All highways under the jurisdiction of the Illinois State Toll Highway Authority.

P.A. 76-1586, § 1-205.01, added by P.A. 85-830, § 1, eff. Sept. 24, 1987. Amended by P.A. 90-89, § 15, eff. Jan. 1, 1998.

Formerly Ill.Rev.Stat.1991, ch. 95 ½, ¶ 1-205.01.

5/1-205.1. Tow-Truck

§ 1-205.1. Tow-Truck. Every truck designed or altered and equipped for and used to push, tow, carry upon, or draw vehicles by means of a crane, hoist, towbar, towline or auxiliary axle, or carried upon to render assistance to disabled vehicles, except for any truck tractor temporarily converted to a tow truck by means of a portable wrecker unit attached to the fifth wheel of the truck tractor and used only by the owner to tow a disabled vehicle also owned by him or her and never used for hire.

P.A. 76-1586, § 1-205.1, added by P.A. 78-324, § 1, eff. Jan. 1, 1974. Amended by P.A. 83-1473, § 1, eff. Jan. 1, 1985; P.A. 89-245, § 5, eff. Jan. 1, 1996; P.A. 90-89, § 15, eff. Jan. 1, 1998.

Formerly Ill.Rev.Stat.1991, ch. 95 ½, ¶ 1-205.1.

5/1-205.2. Tower

§ 1-205.2. Tower. A person who owns or operates a tow-truck or a wrecker.

P.A. 76-1586, § 1-205.2, added by P.A. 83-1473, § 1, eff. Jan. 1, 1985.

Formerly Ill.Rev.Stat.1991, ch. 95 ½, ¶ 1-205.2.

5/1-206. Trackless trolley coach

§ 1-206. Trackless trolley coach. Every motor vehicle which is propelled by electric power obtained from overhead trolley wires but not operated upon rails.

P.A. 76-1586, § 1-206, eff. July 1, 1970.

Formerly Ill.Rev.Stat.1991, ch. 95 ½, ¶ 1-206.

5/1-207. Traffic

§ 1-207. Traffic. Pedestrians, ridden or herded animals, vehicles, streetcars and other conveyances either singly or together while using any highway for purposes of travel.

P.A. 76-1586, § 1-207, eff. July 1, 1970.

Formerly Ill.Rev.Stat.1991, ch. 95 ½, ¶ 1-207.

5/1-208. Traffic control signal

§ 1-208. Traffic control signal. Any official traffic control device other than a railroad sign or signal, whether manually, electrically or mechanically operated, by which traffic is alternately directed to stop and permitted to proceed.

P.A. 76-1586, § 1-208, eff. July 1, 1970. Amended by P.A. 76-2126, § 1, eff. July 1, 1970; P.A. 83-831, § 1, eff. Jan. 1, 1984.

Formerly Ill.Rev.Stat.1991, ch. 95 ½, ¶ 1-208.

5/1-209. Trailer

§ 1-209. Trailer. Every vehicle without motive power in operation, other than a pole trailer, designed for carrying persons or property and for being drawn by a motor vehicle and so constructed that no part of its weight rests upon the towing vehicle.

P.A. 76-1586, § 1-209, eff. July 1, 1970. Amended by P.A. 76-1798, § 1, eff. July 1, 1970.

Formerly Ill.Rev.Stat.1991, ch. 95 ½, ¶ 1-209.

5/1-209.5. Transportation

§ 1-209.5. Transportation. The actual movement of property or passengers by motor vehicle, together with loading, unloading, and any other accessorial or ancillary service provided by the carrier in connection with movement by motor vehicle.

P.A. 76-1586, § 1-209.5, added by P.A. 90-89, § 15, eff. Jan. 1, 1998.

5/1-210. Transporter

§ 1-210. Transporter. Every person engaged in the driveaway or towaway business of transporting vehicles, not his own, by driving, either singly or by the towbar, saddle mount or full mount methods or any combinations thereof or by drawing or towing house trailers, semitrailers or trailers, including their coupling devices, and using the public highways of this State therefor.

P.A. 76-1586, § 1-210, eff. July 1, 1970. Amended by P.A. 78-858, § 1, eff. Jan. 1, 1974.

Formerly Ill.Rev.Stat.1991, ch. 95 ½, ¶ 1-210.

5/1-210.01. Travel trailer

§ 1-210.01. Travel trailer. A trailer, not used commercially, designed to provide living quarters for recreational, camping or travel use, and of a size or weight not requiring an overdimension permit when towed on a highway.

P.A. 76-1586, § 1-210.01, added by P.A. 81-969, § 1, eff. Jan. 1, 1980.

Formerly Ill.Rev.Stat.1991, ch. 95 ½, ¶ 1-210.01.

5/1-211. Truck

§ 1-211. Truck. Every motor vehicle designed, used, or maintained primarily for the transportation of property.

P.A. 76-1586, § 1-211, eff. July 1, 1970. Amended by P.A. 86-1005, § 3, eff. Dec. 28, 1989; P.A. 88-476, § 2, eff. July 1, 1994.

Formerly Ill.Rev.Stat.1991, ch. 95 ½, ¶ 1-211.

5/1-211.01. Truck camper

§ 1-211.01. Truck camper. A truck, not used commercially, when equipped with a portable unit designed to be loaded onto the bed which is constructed to provide temporary living quarters for recreational, travel, or camping use.

P.A. 76-1586, § 1-211.01, added by P.A. 81-969, eff. Jan. 1, 1980. Amended by P.A. 91-357, § 231, eff. July 29, 1999.

Formerly Ill.Rev.Stat.1991, ch. 95 ½, ¶ 1-211.01.

5/1-211.1. § 1-211.1. Renumbered as § 1-212.5 by P.A. 90-89, § 15, eff. Jan. 1, 1998

5/1-212. Truck tractor

§ 1-212. Truck tractor. Every motor vehicle designed and used primarily for drawing other vehicles and not so constructed as to carry a load other than a part of the weight of the vehicle and load so drawn.

P.A. 76-1586, § 1-212, eff. July 1, 1970.

Formerly Ill.Rev.Stat.1991, ch. 95 ½, ¶ 1-212.

5/1-212.5. Truckster

§ 1-212.5. Truckster. Every motor vehicle or motorcycle with 3 wheels designed, used or maintained primarily for the transportation of property.

P.A. 76-1586, § 1-211.1, added by P.A. 77-1633, § 1, eff. Sept. 23, 1971. Renumbered § 1-212.5 and amended by P.A. 90-89, § 15, eff. Jan. 1, 1998.

Formerly Ill.Rev.Stat.1991, ch. 95 ½, ¶ 1-211.1.

5/1-213. § 1-213. Repealed by P.A. 90-89, § 20, eff. Jan. 1, 1998

5/1-213.4. Type I school bus

§ 1-213.4. Type I school bus. A school bus with a Gross Vehicle Weight Rating more than 10,000 pounds.

P.A. 76-1586, § 1-213.4, added by P.A. 90-89, § 15, eff. Jan. 1, 1998.

5/1-213.5. Type II school bus

§ 1-213.5. Type II school bus. A school bus with a Gross Vehicle Weight Rating of 10,000 pounds or less.

P.A. 76-1586, § 1-213.5, added by P.A. 90-89, § 15, eff. Jan. 1, 1998.

5/1-214. Urban district

§ 1-214. Urban district. The territory contiguous to and including any street which is built up with structures devoted to business, industry or dwelling houses situated at intervals of less than 100 feet for a distance of a quarter of a mile or more.

P.A. 76-1586, § 1-214, eff. July 1, 1970.

Formerly Ill.Rev.Stat.1991, ch. 95 ½, ¶ 1-214.

5/1-214.1. § 1-214.1. Renumbered as § 1-214.8 by P.A. 90-89, § 15, eff. Jan. 1, 1998

5/1-214.8. Urban area

§ 1-214.8. Urban area. An urban area is any incorporated or unincorporated area developed primarily for residential and/or business purposes.

P.A. 76-1586, § 1-214.1, added by P.A. 77-58, § 1, eff. July 1, 1971. Renumbered § 1-214.8 and amended by P.A. 90-89, § 15, eff. Jan. 1, 1998.

Formerly Ill.Rev.Stat.1991, ch. 95 ½, ¶ 1-214.1.

5/1-215. Used car dealer

§ 1-215. Used car dealer. Every person engaged in the business of buying, selling or exchanging used motor vehicles and who has an established place of business for such purpose in this State.

P.A. 76-1586, § 1-215, eff. July 1, 1970.

Formerly Ill.Rev.Stat.1991, ch. 95 ½, ¶ 1-215.

5/1-216. Used motor vehicle

§ 1-216. Used motor vehicle. Every motor vehicle which has been sold, bargained, exchanged, given away, or title transferred from the person who first acquired it from the manufacturer or importer, dealer, or agent of the manufacturer or importer and so used as to have become what is commonly known as "second hand" within the ordinary meaning thereof: Provided, that a new motor vehicle shall not be considered as a "used motor vehicle" until it has been placed in a bona fide consumer use, notwithstanding the number of transfers of such motor vehicle. The term "bona fide consumer use" means actual operation by an owner who acquired the vehicle for use in business or for pleasure purposes and who has been granted a Certificate of Title on such motor vehicle and has registered such motor vehicle, all in accordance with the laws of the residence of the owner.

P.A. 76-1586, § 1-216, eff. July 1, 1970.

Formerly Ill.Rev.Stat.1991, ch. 95 ½, ¶ 1-216.

5/1-217. Vehicle

§ 1-217. Vehicle. Every device, in, upon or by which any person or property is or may be transported or drawn upon a highway or requiring a certificate of title under Section 3-101(d) of this Code, except devices moved by human power, devices used exclusively upon stationary rails or tracks and snowmobiles as defined in the Snowmobile Registration and Safety Act.[1]

For the purposes of this Code, unless otherwise prescribed, a device shall be considered to be a vehicle until such time it either comes within the definition of a junk vehicle, as defined under this Code, or a junking certificate is issued for it.

For this Code, vehicles are divided into 2 divisions:

First Division: Those motor vehicles which are designed for the carrying of not more than 10 persons.

Second Division: Those vehicles which are designed for carrying more than 10 persons, those designed or used for living quarters and those vehicles which are designed for pulling or carrying property, freight or cargo, those motor vehicles of the First Division remodelled for use and used as motor vehicles of the Second Division, and those motor vehicles of the First Division used and registered as school buses.

P.A. 76-1586, § 1-217, eff. July 1, 1970. Amended by P.A. 76-1798, § 1, eff. July 1, 1970; P.A. 77-68, § 1, eff. Jan. 1, 1972; P.A. 77-1313, § 1, eff. Aug. 27, 1971; P.A. 77-2829, § 40, eff. Dec. 22, 1972; P.A. 78-255, § 61, eff. Oct. 1, 1973; P.A. 78-343, § 1, eff. Jan. 1, 1974; P.A. 78-1297, § 58, eff. March 4, 1975; P.A. 83-1473, § 1, eff. Jan. 1, 1985; P.A. 92-812, § 5, eff. Aug. 21, 2002.

Formerly Ill.Rev.Stat.1991, ch. 95 ½, ¶ 1-217.

[1] 625 ILCS 40/1-1 et seq.

5/1-217.1. Vehicle cowl

§ 1-217.1. Vehicle cowl. The portion of the vehicle that separates the front compartment from the rear compartment, commonly referred to as the firewall, to which a vehicle identification number is normally attached.

P.A. 76-1586, § 1-217.1, added by P.A. 85-1204, § 1, eff. Aug. 26, 1988.

Formerly Ill.Rev.Stat.1991, ch. 95 ½, ¶ 1-217.1.

5/1-218. § 1-218. Repealed by P.A. 90-89, § 20, eff. Jan. 1, 1998

5/1-218.1. Vehicle shell

§ 1-218.1. Vehicle shell. Every sheet metal part of a vehicle whether or not attached to a chassis or part of a chassis. For the purposes of this definition the term vehicle shell shall include the terms, shell, vehicle hulk, body, vehicle body.

P.A. 76-1586, § 1-218.1, added by P.A. 83-831, § 1, eff. Jan. 1, 1984.

Formerly Ill.Rev.Stat.1991, ch. 95 ½, ¶ 1-218.1.

5/1-218.5. Verified evidence

§ 1-218.5. Verified evidence. A document that is confirmed or substantiated by a sworn report or any public record received from a court of competent jurisdiction.

P.A. 76-1586, § 1-218.5, added by P.A. 90-89, § 15, eff. Jan. 1, 1998.

5/1-219. § 1-219. Repealed by P.A. 90-89, § 20, eff. Jan. 1, 1998

5/1-221. § 1-221. Repealed by P.A. 90-89, § 20, eff. Jan. 1, 1998

5/1-222. § 1-222. Renumbered as § 1-171.6 by P.A. 90-89, § 15, eff. Jan. 1, 1998

5/1-223. § 1-223. Repealed by P.A. 90-89, § 20, eff. Jan. 1, 1998

5/1-224. § 1-224. Renumbered as § 1-171.8 by P.A. 90-89, § 15, eff. Jan. 1, 1998

5/1-226 to 5/1-229. §§ 1-226 to 1-229. Repealed by P.A. 83-831, § 2, eff. Jan. 1, 1984

5/1–300. § 1–300. Renumbered as § 1–158.5 by P.A. 90–89, § 15, eff. Jan. 1, 1998

CHAPTER 2. THE SECRETARY OF STATE

Section

5/2–101. Administration vested in Secretary of State

§ 2–101. Administration vested in Secretary of State. The Secretary of State is hereby vested with powers and duties and jurisdiction of administering Chapters 2, 3, 4, 5, 6, 7, 8 and 9 of The Illinois Vehicle Code.[1]

P.A. 76–1586, § 2–101, eff. July 1, 1970.

Formerly Ill.Rev.Stat.1991, ch. 95 ½, ¶ 2–101.

[1] 625 ILCS 5/2–101 et seq. to 5/9–110 et seq.

5/2–102. Organization of administration

§ 2–102. Organization of administration. The Secretary of State shall organize the work of the administration of the portion of this Act delegated to him in such manner as he may deem necessary to carry out those provisions of this Act.

P.A. 76–1586, § 2–102, eff. July 1, 1970.

Formerly Ill.Rev.Stat.1991, ch. 95 ½, ¶ 2–102.

5/2–103. Secretary of State to appoint subordinates

§ 2–103. Secretary of State to appoint subordinates. The Secretary of State shall appoint such subordinate officers, clerks, investigators, and other employees as may be necessary to carry out the provisions of this Act.

P.A. 76–1586, § 2–103, eff. July 1, 1970. Amended by P.A. 82–783, Art. IV, § 25, eff. July 13, 1982.

Formerly Ill.Rev.Stat.1991, ch. 95 ½, ¶ 2–103.

5/2–104. Powers and duties of the Secretary of State

§ 2–104. Powers and duties of the Secretary of State. (a) The administration of Chapters 2, 3, 4, 5, 6, 7, 8 and 9 of this Act [1] is vested in the Secretary of State, who is charged with the duty of observing, administering and enforcing the provisions of this Act.

(b) The Secretary may from time to time make, amend, and rescind such rules and regulations as may be necessary in the public interest to carry out the provisions of this Act, including rules and regulations governing procedures for the filing of applications and the issuance of licenses or registrations thereunder. The rules and regulations adopted by the Secretary of State under this Act shall be effective in the manner provided for in "The Illinois Administrative Procedure Act", approved September 22, 1975, as amended.[2]

P.A. 76–1586, § 2–104, eff. July 1, 1970. Amended by P.A. 83–333, § 50, eff. Sept. 14, 1983.

Formerly Ill.Rev.Stat.1991, ch. 95 ½, ¶ 2–104.

[1] 625 ILCS 5/2–101 et seq. to 5/9–110 et seq.

[2] 5 ILCS 100/1–1 et seq.

5/2–105. Offices of Secretary of State

§ 2–105. Offices of Secretary of State. The Secretary of State shall maintain offices in the State capital and in such other places in the State as he may deem necessary to properly carry out the powers and duties vested in him.

The Secretary of State may construct and equip one or more buildings in the State of Illinois outside of the County of Sangamon as he deems necessary to properly carry out the powers and duties vested in him. The Secretary of State may, on behalf of the State of Illinois, acquire public or private property needed therefor by lease, purchase or eminent domain. The care, custody and control of such sites and buildings constructed thereon shall be vested in the Secretary of State. Expenditures for the construction and equipping of any of such buildings upon premises owned by another public entity shall not be subject to the provisions of any State law requiring that the State be vested with absolute fee title to the premises. The exercise of the authority vested in the Secretary of State by this Section is subject to the appropriation of the necessary funds.

Pursuant to Sections 4–6.2, 5–16.2, and 6–50.2 of The Election Code,[1] the Secretary of State shall make driver services facilities available for use as temporary places of registration. Registration within the offices shall be in the most public, orderly and convenient portions thereof, and Section 4–3, 5–3, and 11–4 of The Election Code [2] relative to the attendance of police officers during the conduct of registration shall apply. Registration under this Section shall be made in the manner provided by Sections 4–8, 4–10, 5–7, 5–9, 6–34, 6–35, and 6–37 of The Election Code.[3]

Within 30 days after the effective date of this amendatory Act of 1990, and no later than November 1 of each even-numbered year thereafter, the Secretary of State, to the extent practicable, shall designate to each election authority in the State a reasonable number of employees at each driver services facility registered to vote within the jurisdiction of such election authority and within adjacent election jurisdictions for appointment as deputy registrars by the election authority located within the election jurisdiction where the employees maintain their residences. Such designation shall be in writing and certified by the Secretary of State.

Each person applying at a driver services facility for a driver's license or permit, a corrected driver's license or permit, an Illinois identification card or a corrected Illinois identification card shall be notified that the person may register at such station to vote in the election jurisdiction in which the station is located or in an election jurisdiction adjacent to the location of the station and may also transfer his voter registration at such station to an address in the election jurisdiction within which the station is located or to an address in an adjacent election jurisdiction. Such notification may be made in writing or verbally issued by an employee or the Secretary of State.

The Secretary of State shall promulgate such rules as may be necessary for the efficient execution of his duties and the duties of his employees under this amendatory Act of 1990.

P.A. 76-1586, § 2-105, eff. July 1, 1970. Amended by P.A. 77-2302, § 1, eff. Aug. 13, 1972; P.A. 83-1059, § 4, eff. July 1, 1984; P.A. 86-1435, § 3, eff. Sept. 21, 1990; P.A. 90-89, § 15, eff. Jan. 1, 1998.

Formerly Ill.Rev.Stat.1991, ch. 95 ½, ¶ 2-105.

1 10 ILCS 5/4-6.2, 5/5-16.2, and 5/6-50.2.

2 10 ILCS 5/4-3, 5/5-3, and 5/11-4.

3 10 ILCS 5/4-8, 5/4-10, 5/5-7, 5/5-9, 5/6-34, 5/6-35, and 5/6-37.

Validity

Voter-registration notice provisions pursuant to this section were found inadequate in Orr v. Edgar, App. 1 Dist.1996, 219 Ill.Dec. 355, 283 Ill.App.3d 1088, 670 N.E.2d 1243.

5/2-106. Secretary of State to prescribe forms

§ 2-106. Secretary of State to prescribe forms. The Secretary of State shall prescribe or provide suitable forms of applications, certificates of title, registration cards, driver's licenses and such other forms requisite or deemed necessary to carry out the provisions of this Act and any other laws pertaining to vehicles the enforcement and administration of which are vested in the Secretary of State.

P.A. 76-1586, § 2-106, eff. July 1, 1970.

Formerly Ill.Rev.Stat.1991, ch. 95 ½, ¶ 2-106.

5/2-107. Authority to administer oaths

§ 2-107. Authority to administer oaths. Officers and employees of the Secretary of State designated by him are, for the purpose of administering the motor vehicle laws and any other laws relating to the use and operation of motor vehicles, authorized to administer oaths and acknowledge signatures, and shall do so without fee.

P.A. 76-1586, § 2-107, eff. July 1, 1970.

Formerly Ill.Rev.Stat.1991, ch. 95 ½, ¶ 2-107.

5/2-108. Authority to certify copies of records

§ 2-108. Authority to certify copies of records. The Secretary of State is hereby authorized to prepare under the seal of the Secretary of State certified copies of any records of his office and every such certified copy shall be admissible in any proceeding in any court in like manner as the original thereof.

P.A. 76-1586, § 2-108, eff. July 1, 1970.

Formerly Ill.Rev.Stat.1991, ch. 95 ½, ¶ 2-108.

5/2-109. Records of Secretary of State

§ 2-109. Records of Secretary of State. The Secretary of State may destroy any records of his office relating to the administration of any laws relating to the use and operation of motor vehicles the enforcement and administration of which are vested in him, if such records have been maintained on file for 4 years. Such records may be destroyed prior thereto with the approval of the State Records Commission.

P.A. 76-1586, § 2-109, eff. July 1, 1970.

Formerly Ill.Rev.Stat.1991, ch. 95 ½, ¶ 2-109.

5/2-109.1. Exchange of information

§ 2-109.1. Exchange of information.

(a) The Secretary of State shall exchange information with the Illinois Department of Public Aid which may be necessary for the establishment of paternity and the establishment, modification, and enforcement of child support orders pursuant to the Illinois Public Aid Code, [1] the Illinois Marriage and Dissolution of Marriage Act, [2] the Non-Support of Spouse and Children Act, [3] the Non-Support Punishment Act, [4] the Revised Uniform Reciprocal Enforcement of Support Act, [5] the Uniform Interstate Family Support Act, [6] or the Illinois Parentage Act of 1984.[7]

(b) Notwithstanding any provisions in this Code to the contrary, the Secretary of State shall not be liable to any person for any disclosure of information to the Illinois Department of Public Aid under subsection (a) or for any other action taken in good faith to comply with the requirements of subsection (a).

P.A. 76-1586, § 2-109.1, added by P.A. 90-18, § 80, eff. July 1, 1997. Amended by P.A. 91-613, § 945, eff. July 1, 2000.

1 305 ILCS 5/1-1 et seq.

2 750 ILCS 5/101 et seq.

3 750 ILCS 15/1 et seq.

4 750 ILCS 16/1 et seq.

5 750 ILCS 20/1 et seq.

6 750 ILCS 22/100 et seq.

7 750 ILCS 45/1 et seq.

For emergency rules to implement the amendatory changes of P.A. 90-18, see note following 5 ILCS 100/10-65.

5/2-110. Authority to grant or refuse applications

§ 2-110. Authority to grant or refuse applications. The Secretary of State shall examine and determine the genuineness, regularity and legality of every application for registration of a vehicle, for a certificate of title therefor, and for a driver's license and of any other application lawfully made to the Secretary of State, and may in all cases make investigation as may be deemed necessary or require additional information, and shall reject any such application if not satisfied of the genuineness, regularity or legality thereof or the truth of any statement contained therein, or for any other reason, when authorized by law.

P.A. 76-1586, § 2-110, eff. July 1, 1970.

Formerly Ill.Rev.Stat.1991, ch. 95 ½, ¶ 2-110.

5/2-111. Seizure of documents and plates

§ 2-111. Seizure of documents and plates. The Secretary of State is authorized to take possession of any certificate of title, registration card, permit, license, registration plate, plates, person with disabilities license plate or parking decal or device, or registration sticker issued by him upon expiration, revocation, cancellation or suspension thereof, or which is fictitious, or which has been unlawfully or erroneously issued. Police officers who have reasonable grounds to believe that any item or items listed in this section should be seized shall request the Secretary of State to take possession of such item or items.

P.A. 76–1586, § 2–111, eff. July 1, 1970. Amended by P.A. 80–230, § 1, eff. Oct. 1, 1977; P.A. 82–433, § 1, eff. Sept. 8, 1981; P.A. 90–106, § 5, eff. Jan. 1, 1998.

Formerly Ill.Rev.Stat.1991, ch. 95 ½, ¶ 2–111.

Section 3 of P.A. 82–433 approved Sept. 8, 1981, provided:

"This Act takes effect upon its becoming a law, except that the provisions relating to safety tests and proof of financial responsibility for medical transport vehicles apply only to applications for and the issuance of registration plates which are required to be displayed on January 1, 1982 or thereafter."

5/2–112. Distribution of synopsis laws

§ 2–112. Distribution of synopsis laws. The Secretary of State may publish a synopsis or summary of the laws of this State regulating the operation of vehicles and may deliver a copy thereof without charge with each original vehicle registration and with each original driver's license.

P.A. 76–1586, § 2–112, eff. July 1, 1970.

Formerly Ill.Rev.Stat.1991, ch. 95 ½, ¶ 2–112.

5/2–113. Secretary of State may subpoena witnesses and request the production of books and records

§ 2–113. Secretary of State may subpoena witnesses and request the production of books and records. (a) The Secretary of State, or employees designated by him, may request the production of pertinent books, records, letters, contracts or other pertinent documents of any person licensed or required to be licensed or registered under any chapter of this Act, for the purpose of investigations or audits, which in the opinion of the Secretary of State, are necessary and proper for the enforcement of this Act and the collection of any fees or taxes required to be paid under this Act.

(b) For the purpose of all hearings which in the opinion of the Secretary of State are necessary and proper for the enforcement of this Act, the Secretary of State, or a person designated by him is empowered to administer oaths and affirmations, subpoena witnesses, take evidence, and require the production of any books, papers or other documents which the Secretary of State, or a person designated by him, deems relevant or material to the inquiry. Any circuit court of this State, upon application by the Secretary of State and upon a proper showing may order the attendance of witnesses, the production of books, papers, accounts and documents and the giving of testimony before the Secretary of State, or a person designated by him; and any failure to obey such order may be punished by such circuit court as a contempt thereof. The fees of subpoenaed witnesses under this Act for attendance and travel shall be the same as fees of witnesses before the circuit courts of the State, such fees to be paid when the witness is excused from further attendance, provided, such witness is subpoenaed at the instance of the Secretary of State; and payment of such fees shall be made and audited in the same manner as other expenses of the Secretary of State. Whenever a subpoena is issued at the request of a complainant or respondent or defendant as the case may be, the Secretary of State may require that the cost of service and the fee of the witness shall be borne by the party at whose instance the witness is summoned. The Secretary of State shall have power in his discretion, to require a deposit to cover the cost of such service and witness fees and the payment of the legal witness fee and mileage to the witness served with subpoena. A subpoena issued under the provisions of this Act shall be served in the same manner as a subpoena issued out of a court.

P.A. 76–1586, § 2–113, eff. July 1, 1970. Amended by P.A. 76–2127, § 1, eff. July 1, 1970; P.A. 77–1541, § 1, eff. Sept. 17, 1971.

Formerly Ill.Rev.Stat.1991, ch. 95 ½, ¶ 2–113.

5/2–114. Giving of notice

§ 2–114. Giving of notice. Whenever the Secretary of State is authorized or required to give any notice under this Act or other law regulating the operation of vehicles, unless a different method of giving such notice is otherwise expressly prescribed, such notice shall be given either by personal delivery thereof to the person to be so notified or by deposit in the United States mail of such notice in an envelope with postage prepaid, addressed to such person at his address as shown by the records of the Office of the Secretary of State. The giving of notice by mail is complete upon the expiration of 4 days after such deposit of said notice. Proof of the giving of notice in either such manner may be made by the certificate of any officer or employee of the Secretary of State or affidavit of any person over 18 years of age, naming the person to whom such notice was given and specifying the time, place and manner of the giving thereof.

P.A. 76–1586, § 2–114, eff. July 1, 1970.

Formerly Ill.Rev.Stat.1991, ch. 95 ½, ¶ 2–114.

5/2–115. Investigators

§ 2–115. Investigators.

(a) The Secretary of State, for the purpose of more effectively carrying out the provisions of the laws in relation to motor vehicles, shall have power to appoint such number of investigators as he may deem necessary. It shall be the duty of such investigators to investigate and enforce violations of the provisions of this Act administered by the Secretary of State and provisions of Chapters 11, 12, 13, 14 and 15 [1] and to investigate and report any violation by any person who operates as a motor carrier of property as defined in Section 18–100 of this Act and does not hold a valid certificate or permit. Such investigators shall have and may exercise throughout the State all of the powers of peace officers.

No person may be retained in service as an investigator under this Section after he has reached 60 years of age.

The Secretary of State must authorize to each investigator employed under this Section and to any other employee of the Office of the Secretary of State exercising the powers of a peace officer a distinct badge that, on its face, (i) clearly states that the badge is authorized by the Office of the Secretary of State and (ii) contains a unique identifying number. No other badge shall be authorized by the Office of the Secretary of State.

(b) The Secretary may expend such sums as he deems necessary from Contractual Services appropriations for the Department of Police for the purchase of evidence, for the employment of persons to obtain evidence, and for the payment for any goods or services related to obtaining evidence. Such sums shall be advanced to investigators authorized by the Secretary to expend funds, on vouchers signed by the Secretary. In addition, the Secretary of State is authorized to maintain one or more commercial checking accounts with any State banking corporation or corporations organized under or subject to the Illinois Banking Act [2] for the deposit and withdrawal of moneys to be used solely for the purchase of evidence and for the employment of persons to obtain evidence, or for the payment for any goods or services related to obtaining evidence; provided that no check may be written on nor any withdrawal made from any such account except on the written signatures of 2 persons designated by the Secretary to write such checks and make such withdrawals, and provided further that the balance of moneys on deposit in any such account shall not exceed $5,000 at any time, nor shall any one check written on or single withdrawal made from any such account exceed $5,000.

All fines or moneys collected or received by the Department of Police under any State or federal forfeiture statute; including, but not limited to moneys forfeited under Section 12 of the Cannabis Control Act [3] and moneys distributed under Section 413 of the Illinois Controlled Substances Act, [4] shall be deposited into the Secretary of State Evidence Fund.

In all convictions for offenses in violation of this Act, the Court may order restitution to the Secretary of any or all sums expended for the purchase of evidence, for the employment of persons to obtain evidence, and for the payment for any goods or services related to obtaining evidence. All such restitution received by the Secretary shall be deposited into the Secretary of State Evidence Fund. Moneys deposited into the fund shall, subject to appropriation, be used by the Secretary of State for the purposes provided for under the provisions of this Section.

P.A. 76-1586, § 2-115, eff. July 1, 1970. Amended by P.A. 76-1797, eff. July 1, 1970; P.A. 78-298, § 1, eff. Jan. 1, 1974; P.A. 81-567, § 1, eff. Oct. 1, 1979; P.A. 82-977, § 1, eff. Jan. 1, 1983; P.A. 85-1204, § 1, eff. Aug. 26, 1988; P.A. 87-993, § 3, eff. Sept. 1, 1992; P.A. 88-517, § 10, eff. Nov. 16, 1993; P.A. 91-883, § 105, eff. Jan. 1, 2001.

Formerly Ill.Rev.Stat.1991, ch. 95 ½, ¶ 2-115.

1 625 ILCS 5/11-100 et seq. to 5/15-100 et seq.

2 205 ILCS 5/1 et seq.

3 720 ILCS 550/12.

4 720 ILCS 570/413.

5/2-116. Secretary of State Department of Police

§ 2-116. Secretary of State Department of Police.

(a) The Secretary of State and the officers, inspectors, and investigators appointed by him shall cooperate with the State Police and the sheriffs and police in enforcing the laws regulating the operation of vehicles and the use of the highways.

(b) The Secretary of State may provide training and education for members of his office in traffic regulation, the promotion of traffic safety and the enforcement of laws vested in the Secretary of State for administration and enforcement regulating the operation of vehicles and the use of the highways.

(c) The Secretary of State may provide distinctive uniforms and badges for officers, inspectors and investigators employed in the administration of laws relating to the operation of vehicles and the use of the highways and vesting the administration and enforcement of such laws in the Secretary of State.

(d) The Secretary of State Department of Police is authorized to:

(1) investigate the origins, activities, persons, and incidents of crime and the ways and means, if any, to redress the victims of crimes, and study the impact, if any, of legislation relative to the criminal laws of this State related thereto and conduct any other investigations as may be provided by law;

(2) employ skilled experts, technicians, investigators, special agents, or otherwise specially qualified persons to aid in preventing or detecting crime, apprehending criminals, or preparing and presenting evidence of violations of the criminal laws of the State;

(3) cooperate with the police of cities, villages, and incorporated towns, and with the police officers of any county, in enforcing the laws of the State and in making arrests;

(4) provide, as may be required by law, assistance to local law enforcement agencies through training, management, and consultant services for local law enforcement agencies, pertaining to law enforcement activities;

(5) exercise the rights, powers, and duties which have been vested in it by the Secretary of State Act [1] and this Code; [2] and

(6) enforce and administer any other laws in relation to law enforcement as may be vested in the Secretary of State Department of Police.

Persons within the Secretary of State Department of Police who exercise these powers are conservators of the peace and have all the powers possessed by policemen in municipalities and sheriffs, and may exercise these powers anywhere in the State in cooperation with local law enforcement officials. These persons may use false or fictitious names in the performance of their duties under this Section, upon approval of the Director of Police-Secretary of State, and shall not be subject to prosecution under the criminal laws for that use.

(e) The Secretary of State Department of Police may charge, collect, and receive fees or moneys equivalent to the cost of providing its personnel, equipment, and services to governmental agencies when explicitly requested by a governmental agency and according to an intergovernmental agreement or memorandums of understanding as provided by this Section, including but not limited to fees or moneys equivalent to the cost of providing training to other governmental agencies on terms and conditions that in the judgment of the Director of Police-Secretary of State are in the best interest of the Secretary of State. All fees received by the Secretary of State Police Department under this Act shall be deposited in a special fund in the State Treasury to be known as the Secretary of State Police Services Fund. The money deposited in the Secretary of State Police Services Fund shall be appropriated to the Secretary of State Department of Police as provided for in subsection (g).

(f) The Secretary of State Department of Police may apply for grants or contracts and receive, expend, allocate, or disburse moneys made available by public or private entities, including, but not limited to, contracts, bequests, grants, or receiving equipment from corporations, foundations, or public or private institutions of higher learning.

(g) The Secretary of State Police Services Fund is hereby created as a special fund in the State Treasury. All moneys received under this Section by the Secretary of State Department of Police shall be deposited into the Secretary of State Police Services Fund to be appropriated to the Secretary of State Department of Police for purposes as indicated by the grantor or contractor or, in the case of moneys bequeathed or granted for no specific purpose, for any purpose as deemed appropriate by the Director of Police-Secretary of State in administering the responsibilities of the Secretary of State Department of Police.

P.A. 76-1586, § 2-116, eff. July 1, 1970. Amended by P.A. 92-501, § 10, eff. Dec. 19, 2001.

Formerly Ill.Rev.Stat.1991, ch. 95 ½, ¶ 2-116.

1 15 ILCS 305/0.01 et seq.

2 625 ILCS 5/1-100 et seq.

5/2-117. Injunction

§ 2-117. Injunction. Whenever it shall appear to the Secretary of State that any person is engaged or about to engage in any acts or practices which constitute or will constitute a violation of the provisions of this Act, or of any rule or regulation prescribed under authority thereof, the Secretary of State may in his or her discretion, through the Attorney General, apply for an injunction without notice, and upon a proper showing, the circuit court shall have power to enter a permanent or preliminary injunction or a temporary restraining order without bond, to enforce the provisions of this Act, in addition to the penalties and other remedies in this Act provided; and either party may appeal as in other civil cases.

P.A. 76-1586, § 2-117, eff. July 1, 1970. Amended by P.A. 79-1358, § 43, eff. Oct. 1, 1976; P.A. 83-342, § 10, eff. Sept. 14, 1983.

Formerly Ill.Rev.Stat.1991, ch. 95 ½, ¶ 2-117.

5/2-118. Hearings

§ 2-118. Hearings.

(a) Upon the suspension, revocation or denial of the issuance of a license, permit, registration or certificate of title under this Code of any person the Secretary of State shall immediately notify such person in writing and upon his written request shall, within 20 days after receipt thereof, set a date for a hearing to commence within 90 calendar days from the date of the written request for all requests related to a suspension, revocation, or the denial of the issuance of a license, permit, registration, or certificate of title occurring after July 1, 2002, in the County of Sangamon, the County of Jefferson, or the County of Cook, as such person may specify, unless both parties agree that such hearing may be held in some other county. The Secretary may require the payment of a fee of not more than $50 for the filing of any petition, motion, or request for hearing conducted pursuant to this Section. These fees must be deposited into the Secretary of State DUI Administration Fund, a special fund created in the State treasury, and, subject to appropriation and as directed by the Secretary of State, shall be used for operation of the Department of Administrative Hearings of the Office of the Secretary of State and for no other purpose. The Secretary shall establish by rule the amount and the procedures, terms, and conditions relating to these fees.

(b) At any time after the suspension, revocation or denial of a license, permit, registration or certificate of title of any person as hereinbefore referred to, the Secretary of State, in his or her discretion and without the necessity of a request by such person, may hold such a hearing, upon not less than 10 days' notice in writing, in the Counties of Sangamon, Jefferson, or Cook or in any other county agreed to by the parties.

(c) Upon any such hearing, the Secretary of State, or his authorized agent may administer oaths and issue subpoenas for the attendance of witnesses and the production of relevant books and records and may require an examination of such person. Upon any such hearing, the Secretary of State shall either rescind or, good cause appearing therefor, continue, change or extend the Order of Revocation or Suspension, or upon petition therefore and subject to the provisions of this Code, issue a restricted driving permit or reinstate the license or permit of such person.

(d) All hearings and hearing procedures shall comply with requirements of the Constitution, so that no person is deprived of due process of law nor denied equal protection of the laws. All hearings shall be held before the Secretary of State or before such persons as may be designated by the Secretary of State and appropriate records of such hearings shall be kept. Where a transcript of the hearing is taken, the person requesting the hearing shall have the opportunity to order a copy thereof at his own expense. The Secretary of State shall enter an order upon any hearing conducted under this Section, related to a suspension, revocation, or the denial of the issuance of a license, permit, registration, or certificate of title occurring after July 1, 2002, within 90 days of its conclusion and shall immediately notify the person in writing of his or her action.

(e) The action of the Secretary of State in suspending, revoking or denying any license, permit, registration, or certificate of title shall be subject to judicial review in the Circuit Court of Sangamon County, in the Circuit Court of Jefferson County, or in the Circuit Court of Cook County, and the provisions of the Administrative Review Law,[1] and all amendments and modifications thereto, and the rules adopted pursuant thereto, are hereby adopted and shall apply to and govern every action for the judicial review of final acts or decisions of the Secretary of State hereunder.

P.A. 76-1586, § 2-118, eff. July 1, 1970. Amended by P.A. 78-244, § 1, eff. Aug. 13, 1973; P.A. 82-783, Art. XI, § 140, eff. July 13, 1982; P.A. 84-1394, § 5, eff. Sept. 18, 1986; P.A. 85-951, § 1, eff. July 1, 1988; P.A. 86-929, § 2, eff. Sept. 21, 1989; P.A. 89-145, § 10, eff. July 14, 1995; P.A. 91-823, § 5, eff. Jan. 1, 2001; P.A. 92-418, § 10, eff. Aug. 17, 2001.

Formerly Ill.Rev.Stat.1991, ch. 95 ½, ¶ 2-118.

[1] 735 ILCS 5/3-101 et seq.

5/2-118.1. Opportunity for hearing; statutory summary alcohol or other drug related suspension

§ 2-118.1. Opportunity for hearing; statutory summary alcohol or other drug related suspension.

(a) A statutory summary suspension of driving privileges under Section 11-501.1 shall not become effective until the person is notified in writing of the impending suspension and informed that he may request a hearing in the circuit court of venue under paragraph (b) of this Section and the statutory summary suspension shall become effective as provided in Section 11-501.1.

(b) Within 90 days after the notice of statutory summary suspension served under Section 11-501.1, the person may make a written request for a judicial hearing in the circuit court of venue. The request to the circuit court shall state the grounds upon which the person seeks to have the statutory summary suspension rescinded. Within 30 days after receipt of the written request or the first appearance date on the Uniform Traffic Ticket issued pursuant to a violation of Section 11-501, or a similar provision of a local ordinance, the hearing shall be conducted by the circuit court having jurisdiction. This judicial hearing, request, or process shall not stay or delay the statutory summary suspension. The hearings shall proceed in the court in the same manner as in other civil proceedings.

The hearing may be conducted upon a review of the law enforcement officer's own official reports; provided however, that the person may subpoena the officer. Failure of the officer to answer the subpoena shall be considered grounds for a continuance if in the court's discretion the continuance is appropriate.

The scope of the hearing shall be limited to the issues of:

1. Whether the person was placed under arrest for an offense as defined in Section 11-501, or a similar provision of a local ordinance, as evidenced by the issuance of a Uniform Traffic Ticket, or issued a Uniform Traffic Ticket out of state as provided in subsection (a) of Section 11-501.1; and

2. Whether the officer had reasonable grounds to believe that the person was driving or in actual physical control of a motor vehicle upon a highway while under the influence of alcohol, other drug, or combination of both; and

3. Whether the person, after being advised by the officer that the privilege to operate a motor vehicle would be suspended if the person refused to submit to and complete the test or tests, did refuse to submit to or complete the test or tests to determine the person's alcohol or drug concentration; or

4. Whether the person, after being advised by the officer that the privilege to operate a motor vehicle would be suspended if the person submits to a chemical test, or tests, and the test discloses an alcohol concentration of 0.08 or more, or any amount of a drug, substance, or compound in the person's blood or urine resulting from the unlawful use or consumption of cannabis listed in the Cannabis Control Act,[1] a controlled substance listed in the Illinois Controlled Substances Act, [2] or an intoxicating compound as listed in the use of Intoxicating Compounds Act,[3] and the person did submit to and complete the test or tests that determined an alcohol concentration of 0.08 or more.

Upon the conclusion of the judicial hearing, the circuit court shall sustain or rescind the statutory summary suspension and immediately notify the Secretary of State. Reports received by the Secretary of State under this Section shall be privileged information and for use only by the courts, police officers, and Secretary of State.

P.A. 76-1586, § 2-118.1, added by P.A. 84-272, § 7, eff. Jan. 1, 1986. Amended by P.A. 84-1394, § 5, eff. Sept. 18, 1986; P.A. 86-1019, § 7, eff. July 1, 1990; P.A. 87-1221, § 1, eff. July 1, 1993; P.A. 88-463, § 5, eff. Jan. 1, 1994; P.A. 89-156, § 5, eff. Jan. 1, 1996; P.A. 90-43, § 5, eff. July 2, 1997; P.A. 92-458, § 5, eff. Aug. 22, 2001.

Formerly Ill.Rev.Stat.1991, ch. 95 ½, ¶ 2-118.1.

1 720 ILCS 550/1 et seq.

2 720 ILCS 570/100 et seq.

3 720 ILCS 690/0.01 et seq.

5/2-119. Disposition of fees and taxes

§ 2-119. Disposition of fees and taxes.

(a) All moneys received from Salvage Certificates shall be deposited in the Common School Fund in the State Treasury.

(b) Beginning January 1, 1990 and concluding December 31, 1994, of the money collected for each certificate of title, duplicate certificate of title and corrected certificate of title, $0.50 shall be deposited into the Used Tire Management Fund. Beginning January 1, 1990 and concluding December 31, 1994, of the money collected for each certificate of title, duplicate certificate of title and corrected certificate of title, $1.50 shall be deposited in the Park and Conservation Fund.

Beginning January 1, 1995, of the money collected for each certificate of title, duplicate certificate of title and corrected certificate of title, $2 shall be deposited in the Park and Conservation Fund. The moneys deposited in the Park and Conservation Fund pursuant to this Section shall be used for the acquisition and development of bike paths as provided for in Section 805-420 of the Department of Natural Resources (Conservation) Law (20 ILCS 805/805-420).

Beginning January 1, 2000 and continuing through December 31, 2004, of the moneys collected for each certificate of title, duplicate certificate of title, and corrected certificate of title, $48 shall be deposited into the Road Fund and $4 shall be deposited into the Motor Vehicle License Plate Fund, except that if the balance in the Motor Vehicle License Plate Fund exceeds $40,000,000 on the last day of a calendar month, then during the next calendar month the $4 shall instead be deposited into the Road Fund.

Beginning January 1, 2005, of the moneys collected for each certificate of title, duplicate certificate of title, and corrected certificate of title, $52 shall be deposited into the Road Fund.

Except as otherwise provided in this Code, all remaining moneys collected for certificates of title, and all moneys collected for filing of security interests, shall be placed in the General Revenue Fund in the State Treasury.

(c) All moneys collected for that portion of a driver's license fee designated for driver education under Section 6-118 shall be placed in the Driver Education Fund in the State Treasury.

(d) Beginning January 1, 1999, of the monies collected as a registration fee for each motorcycle, motor driven cycle and motorized pedalcycle, 27% of each annual registration fee for such vehicle and 27% of each semiannual registration fee for such vehicle is deposited in the Cycle Rider Safety Training Fund.

(e) Of the monies received by the Secretary of State as registration fees or taxes or as payment of any other fee, as provided in this Act, except fees received by the Secretary under paragraph (7) of subsection (b) of Section 5-101 and Section 5-109 of this Code, 37% shall be deposited into the State Construction Fund.

(f) Of the total money collected for a CDL instruction permit or original or renewal issuance of a commercial driver's license (CDL) pursuant to the Uniform Commercial Driver's License Act (UCDLA) [1]: (i) $6 of the total fee for an original or renewal CDL, and $6 of the total CDL instruction permit fee when such permit is issued to any person holding a valid Illinois driver's license, shall be paid into the CDLIS/AAMVAnet Trust Fund (Commercial Driver's License Information System/American Association of Motor Vehicle Administrators network Trust Fund) and shall be used for the purposes provided in Section 6z-23 of the State Finance Act [2] and (ii) $20 of the total fee for an original or renewal CDL or commercial driver instruction permit shall be paid into the Motor Carrier Safety Inspection Fund, which is hereby created as a special fund in the State Treasury, to be used by the Department of State Police, subject to appropriation, to hire additional officers to conduct motor carrier safety inspections pursuant to Chapter 18b of this Code.[3]

(g) All remaining moneys received by the Secretary of State as registration fees or taxes or as payment of any other fee, as provided in this Act, except fees received by the Secretary under paragraph (7) of subsection (b) of Section 5-101 and Section 5-109 of this Code, shall be deposited in the Road Fund in the State Treasury. Moneys in the Road Fund shall be used for the purposes provided in Section 8.3 of the State Finance Act.[4]

(h) (Blank).

(i) (Blank).

(j) (Blank).

(k) There is created in the State Treasury a special fund to be known as the Secretary of State Special License Plate Fund. Money deposited into the Fund shall, subject to appropriation, be used by the Office of the Secretary of State (i) to help defray plate manufacturing and plate processing costs for the issuance and, when applicable, renewal of any new or existing special registration plates authorized under this Code and (ii) for grants made by the Secretary of State to benefit Illinois Veterans Home libraries.

On or before October 1, 1995, the Secretary of State shall direct the State Comptroller and State Treasurer to transfer any unexpended balance in the Special Environmental License Plate Fund, the Special Korean War Veteran License Plate Fund, and the Retired Congressional License Plate Fund to the Secretary of State Special License Plate Fund.

(*l*) The Motor Vehicle Review Board Fund is created as a special fund in the State Treasury. Moneys deposited into the Fund under paragraph (7) of subsection (b) of Section 5–101 and Section 5–109 shall, subject to appropriation, be used by the Office of the Secretary of State to administer the Motor Vehicle Review Board, including without limitation payment of compensation and all necessary expenses incurred in administering the Motor Vehicle Review Board under the Motor Vehicle Franchise Act.[5]

(m) Effective July 1, 1996, there is created in the State Treasury a special fund to be known as the Family Responsibility Fund. Moneys deposited into the Fund shall, subject to appropriation, be used by the Office of the Secretary of State for the purpose of enforcing the Family Financial Responsibility Law.

(n) The Illinois Fire Fighters' Memorial Fund is created as a special fund in the State Treasury. Moneys deposited into the Fund shall, subject to appropriation, be used by the Office of the State Fire Marshal for construction of the Illinois Fire Fighters' Memorial to be located at the State Capitol grounds in Springfield, Illinois. Upon the completion of the Memorial, moneys in the Fund shall be used in accordance with Section 3–634.

(*o*) Of the money collected for each certificate of title for all-terrain vehicles and off-highway motorcycles, $17 shall be deposited into the Off-Highway Vehicle Trails Fund.

P.A. 76–1586, § 2–119, eff. July 1, 1970. Amended by P.A. 78–860, § 2, eff. Jan. 1, 1974; P.A. 78–5, 3rd Sp.Sess., Part III, § 1, eff. Dec. 12, 1973; P.A. 78–1297, § 58, eff. March 4, 1975; P.A. 80–1185, § 1, eff. March 8, 1978; P.A. 81–3, 2nd Sp.Sess. § 15, eff. Sept. 19, 1979; P.A. 82–649, § 3, eff. Jan. 1, 1982; P.A. 83–12, § 1, eff. July 1, 1983; P.A. 84–470, § 1, eff. Sept. 17, 1985; P.A. 85–1144, § 1, eff. July 29, 1988; P.A. 86–452, § 12, eff. Aug. 31, 1989; P.A. 86–845, § 1, eff. April 1, 1990; P.A. 86–982, § 1, eff. July 1, 1990; P.A. 86–1005, § 3, eff. Dec. 28, 1989; P.A. 86–1019, § 2, eff. Jan. 1, 1990; P.A. 86–1475, Art. 2, § 2–25, eff. Jan. 10, 1990; P.A. 88–333, § 5, eff. Jan. 1, 1994; P.A. 88–485, § 10, eff. Jan. 1, 1994; P.A. 88–589, § 10, eff. Aug. 14, 1994; P.A. 88–670, Art. 2, § 2–59, eff. Dec. 2, 1994; P.A. 89–92, § 10, eff. July 1, 1996; P.A. 89–145, § 10, eff. July 14, 1995; P.A. 89–282, § 10, eff. Aug. 10, 1995; P.A. 89–612, § 10, eff. Aug. 9, 1996; P.A. 89–626, Art. 2, § 2–64, eff. Aug. 9, 1996; P.A. 89–639, § 5, eff. Jan. 1, 1997; P.A. 90–14, Art. 2, § 2–225, eff. July 1, 1997; P.A. 90–287, § 100, eff. Jan. 1, 1998; P.A. 90–622, § 5, eff. Jan. 1, 1999; P.A. 91–37, § 40, eff. July 1, 1999; P.A. 91–239, Art. 5, § 5–530, eff. Jan. 1, 2000; P.A. 91–537, § 10, eff. Aug. 13, 1999; P.A. 91–832, § 5, eff. June 16, 2000; P.A. 92–16, § 85, eff. June 28, 2001.

Formerly Ill.Rev.Stat.1991, ch. 95 ½, ¶ 2–119.

1 625 ILCS 5/6–500 et seq.

2 30 ILCS 105/6z–23.

3 625 ILCS 5/18b–100 et seq.

4 30 ILCS 105/8.3.

5 815 ILCS 710/1 et seq.

Section 4 of P.A. 83–12, approved July 1, 1983, provided:

"Effective date. This Act takes effect as provided in this Section.

"The amendments to those portions of Sections 3–815(a), 3–818 and 3–819(b) of 'The Illinois Vehicle Code' in Section 1 of this Act which create the 'X', 'Z', 'MX', 'MZ', 'MM' and 'TN' registration classifications and the fees and taxes imposed for those classifications, the amendments to Sections 2–119, 3–401 and 3–802 of 'The Illinois Vehicle Code' in Section 1 of this Act, and the amendments to Chapter 15 of 'The Illinois Vehicle Code' in Section 1 of this Act take effect July 1, 1983.

"The remaining amendments to 'The Illinois Vehicle Code' in Section 1 of this Act take effect July 1, 1983 and apply beginning with the 1985 registration year, except that the amendments to Sections 3–813 through 3–816 and Section 3–819 apply beginning with the 1984 registration year for those vehicles registered on a calendar year basis only.

"The amendments to Chapters 13 and 18 of 'The Illinois Vehicle Code' in Section 1 of this Act take effect January 1, 1984.

"Section 2 of this Act takes effect on the first day of the next succeeding month which commences at least 30 days after the date on which this Act becomes law.

"Section 3 of this Act takes effect July 1, 1983.

"Section 3.1 of this Act takes effect January 1, 1984.

"This Section 4 takes effect upon its becoming a law."

For purpose of revisory provisions of P.A. 91–239, see Historical and Statutory Notes under 20 ILCS 5/1–1.

5/2–120. Disposition of fines and forfeitures

§ 2–120. Disposition of fines and forfeitures.

(a) Except as provided in subsection (f) of Section 11–605 of this Code, fines and penalties recovered under the provisions of this Act administered by the Secretary of State, except those fines and penalties subject to disbursement by the circuit clerk under Section 27.5 of the Clerks of Courts Act,[1] shall be paid over and used as follows:

1. For violations of this Act committed within the limits of an incorporated city or village, to the treasurer of the particular city or village, if arrested by the authorities of the city or village and reasonably prosecuted for all fines and penalties under this Act by the police officers and officials of the city or village.

2. For violations of this Act committed outside the limits of an incorporated city or village to the county treasurer of the court where the offense was committed.

3. For the purposes of this Act an offense for violation of any provision of this Act not committed upon the highway shall be deemed to be committed where the violator resides or where he has a place of business requiring some registration, permit or license to operate such business under this Act.

(b) Failure, refusal or neglect on the part of any judicial or other officer or employee receiving or having custody of any such fine or forfeiture either before or after a deposit with the proper official as defined in paragraph (a) of this Section, shall constitute misconduct in office and shall be grounds for removal therefrom.

P.A. 76–1586, § 2–120, eff. July 1, 1970. Amended by P.A. 81–1509, Art. II, § 71, eff. Sept. 26, 1980; P.A. 87–671, § 3, eff. Jan. 1, 1992; P.A. 91–531, § 5, eff. Jan. 1, 2000.

Formerly Ill.Rev.Stat.1991, ch. 95 ½, ¶ 2–120.

1 705 ILCS 105/27.5.

5/2-121. Local Government Tax

§ 2-121. Local Government tax.

(a) No owner of a vehicle who shall have obtained a certificate from the Secretary of State and paid the registration fee and tax as provided in this Act, shall be required by any county, city, village, incorporated town, or other municipal corporation within the State other than a county, city, village, incorporated town, or other municipal corporation in which the owner resides or in which a vehicle has its situs or base, to pay any tax or license fee for the use of the vehicle. The county, city, village, or incorporated town in which the owner resides or in which a vehicle has its situs or base, except commercial motor vehicles as defined in paragraph (2) of Section 18b-101 that are registered under Section 3-402.1, may impose a tax or license fee as is provided in Section 8-11-4 of the Illinois Municipal Code[1] or a similar county ordinance that imposes a tax or license fee on an owner of a vehicle for the use of the vehicle.

Nor shall the owner be required to display upon his vehicle any plate or tax or license number other than that issued by the Secretary of State or by the county, city, village, incorporated town, or other municipal corporation within the State within which the owner resides or in which a vehicle has its situs or base. However, a resident owner shall not be required to display on his vehicle, the plate or tax or license number issued by the county, city, village, or incorporated town of his residence if his vehicle is displaying the plate or tax or license number issued by the place wherein the vehicle has its situs or base.

This subsection (a) applies to ordinances enacted by any county, city, village, incorporated town, or other municipal corporation. Any provision of an ordinance enacted by a county, city, village, incorporated town, or other municipal corporation that is inconsistent with this subsection (a) is null and void.

(b) No county, city, village, incorporated town, or other municipal corporation, including a home rule unit, may impose a tax or license fee under Section 8-11-4 of the Illinois Municipal Code, or impose a similar tax or license fee under home rule powers, upon any commercial vehicle as defined in paragraph (2) of Section 18b-101 that is registered under Section 3-402.1. This subsection (b) is a denial and limitation of home rule powers and functions under subsection (g) of Section 6 of Article VII of the Illinois Constitution.

P.A. 76-1586, § 2-121, eff. July 1, 1970. Amended by P.A. 78-231, § 1, eff. Jan. 1, 1974; P.A. 87-1063, § 1, eff. Jan. 1, 1993; P.A. 90-433, § 5, eff. Aug. 16, 1997.

Formerly Ill.Rev.Stat.1991, ch. 95 ½, ¶ 2-121.

[1] 65 ILCS 5/8-11-4.

5/2-122. Remittance agents

§ 2-122. Remittance agents. The Secretary of State shall administer the law relating to remittance agents pursuant to the law.

P.A. 76-1586, § 2-122, eff. July 1, 1970.

Formerly Ill.Rev.Stat.1991, ch. 95 ½, ¶ 2-122.

5/2-123. Sale and Distribution of Information

§ 2-123. Sale and Distribution of Information.

(a) Except as otherwise provided in this Section, the Secretary may make the driver's license, vehicle and title registration lists, in part or in whole, and any statistical information derived from these lists available to local governments, elected state officials, state educational institutions, and all other governmental units of the State and Federal Government requesting them for governmental purposes. The Secretary shall require any such applicant for services to pay for the costs of furnishing such services and the use of the equipment involved, and in addition is empowered to establish prices and charges for the services so furnished and for the use of the electronic equipment utilized.

(b) The Secretary is further empowered to and he may, in his discretion, furnish to any applicant, other than listed in subsection (a) of this Section, vehicle or driver data on a computer tape, disk, other electronic format or computer processable medium, or printout at a fixed fee of $250 in advance and require in addition a further sufficient deposit based upon the Secretary of State's estimate of the total cost of the information requested and a charge of $25 per 1,000 units or part thereof identified or the actual cost, whichever is greater. The Secretary is authorized to refund any difference between the additional deposit and the actual cost of the request. This service shall not be in lieu of an abstract of a driver's record nor of a title or registration search. This service may be limited to entities purchasing a minimum number of records as required by administrative rule. The information sold pursuant to this subsection shall be the entire vehicle or driver data list, or part thereof. The information sold pursuant to this subsection shall not contain personally identifying information unless the information is to be used for one of the purposes identified in subsection (f-5) of this Section. Commercial purchasers of driver and vehicle record databases shall enter into a written agreement with the Secretary of State that includes disclosure of the commercial use of the information to be purchased.

(c) Secretary of State may issue registration lists. The Secretary of State shall compile and publish, at least annually, a list of all registered vehicles. Each list of registered vehicles shall be arranged serially according to the registration numbers assigned to registered vehicles and shall contain in addition the names and addresses of registered owners and a brief description of each vehicle including the serial or other identifying number thereof. Such compilation may be in such form as in the discretion of the Secretary of State may seem best for the purposes intended.

(d) The Secretary of State shall furnish no more than 2 current available lists of such registrations to the sheriffs of all counties and to the chiefs of police of all cities and villages and towns of 2,000 population and over in this State at no cost. Additional copies may be purchased by the sheriffs or chiefs of police at the fee of $500 each or at the cost of producing the list as determined by the Secretary of State. Such lists are to be used for governmental purposes only.

(e) (Blank).

(e-1) (Blank).

(f) The Secretary of State shall make a title or registration search of the records of his office and a written report on the same for any person, upon written application of such person, accompanied by a fee of $5 for each registration or title search. The written application shall set forth the intended use of the requested information. No fee shall be charged for a title or registration search, or for the certification thereof requested by a government agency. The report of the title or registration search shall not contain personally identifying information unless the request for a search was made for one of the purposes identified in subsection (f-5) of this Section.

The Secretary of State shall certify a title or registration record upon written request. The fee for certification shall be $5 in addition to the fee required for a title or registration search. Certification shall be made under the signature of the Secretary of State and shall be authenticated by Seal of the Secretary of State.

The Secretary of State may notify the vehicle owner or registrant of the request for purchase of his title or registration information as the Secretary deems appropriate.

No information shall be released to the requestor until expiration of a 10 day period. This 10 day period shall not apply to requests for information made by law enforcement officials, government agencies, financial institutions, attorneys, insurers, employers, automobile associated businesses, persons licensed as a private detective or firms licensed as a private detective agency under the Private Detective, Private Alarm, and Private Security Act of 1983, [1] who are employed by or are acting on behalf of law enforcement officials, government agencies, financial institutions, attorneys, insurers, employers, automobile associated businesses, and other business entities for purposes consistent with the Illinois Vehicle Code, [2] the vehicle owner or registrant or other entities as the Secretary may exempt by rule and regulation.

Any misrepresentation made by a requestor of title or vehicle information shall be punishable as a petty offense, except in the case of persons licensed as a private detective or firms licensed as a private detective agency which shall be subject to disciplinary sanctions under Section 22 or 25 of the Private Detective, Private Alarm, and Private Security Act of 1983.

(f-5) The Secretary of State shall not disclose or otherwise make available to any person or entity any personally identifying information obtained by the Secretary of State in connection with a driver's license, vehicle, or title registration record unless the information is disclosed for one of the following purposes:

(1) For use by any government agency, including any court or law enforcement agency, in carrying out its functions, or any private person or entity acting on behalf of a federal, State, or local agency in carrying out its functions.

(2) For use in connection with matters of motor vehicle or driver safety and theft; motor vehicle emissions; motor vehicle product alterations, recalls, or advisories; performance monitoring of motor vehicles, motor vehicle parts, and dealers; and removal of non-owner records from the original owner records of motor vehicle manufacturers.

(3) For use in the normal course of business by a legitimate business or its agents, employees, or contractors, but only:

(A) to verify the accuracy of personal information submitted by an individual to the business or its agents, employees, or contractors; and

(B) if such information as so submitted is not correct or is no longer correct, to obtain the correct information, but only for the purposes of preventing fraud by, pursuing legal remedies against, or recovering on a debt or security interest against, the individual.

(4) For use in research activities and for use in producing statistical reports, if the personally identifying information is not published, redisclosed, or used to contact individuals.

(5) For use in connection with any civil, criminal, administrative, or arbitral proceeding in any federal, State, or local court or agency or before any self-regulatory body, including the service of process, investigation in anticipation of litigation, and the execution or enforcement of judgments and orders, or pursuant to an order of a federal, State, or local court.

(6) For use by any insurer or insurance support organization or by a self-insured entity or its agents, employees, or contractors in connection with claims investigation activities, antifraud activities, rating, or underwriting.

(7) For use in providing notice to the owners of towed or impounded vehicles.

(8) For use by any private investigative agency or security service licensed in Illinois for any purpose permitted under this subsection.

(9) For use by an employer or its agent or insurer to obtain or verify information relating to a holder of a commercial driver's license that is required under chapter 313 of title 49 of the United States Code.

(10) For use in connection with the operation of private toll transportation facilities.

(11) For use by any requester, if the requester demonstrates it has obtained the written consent of the individual to whom the information pertains.

(12) For use by members of the news media, as defined in Section 1-148.5, for the purpose of newsgathering when the request relates to the operation of a motor vehicle or public safety.

(13) For any other use specifically authorized by law, if that use is related to the operation of a motor vehicle or public safety.

(g) 1. The Secretary of State may, upon receipt of a written request and a fee of $6, furnish to the person or agency so requesting a driver's record. Such document may include a record of: current driver's license issuance information, except that the information on judicial driving permits shall be available only as otherwise provided by this Code; convictions; orders entered revoking, suspending or cancelling a driver's license or privilege; and notations of accident involvement. All other information, unless otherwise permitted by this Code, shall remain confidential. Information released pursuant to a request for a driver's record shall not contain personally identifying information, unless the request for the driver's record was made for one of the purposes set forth in subsection (f-5) of this Section.

2. The Secretary of State may certify an abstract of a driver's record upon written request therefor. Such certification shall be made under the signature of the Secretary of State and shall be authenticated by the Seal of his office.

3. All requests for driving record information shall be made in a manner prescribed by the Secretary and shall set forth the intended use of the requested information.

The Secretary of State may notify the affected driver of the request for purchase of his driver's record as the Secretary deems appropriate.

No information shall be released to the requester until expiration of a 10 day period. This 10 day period shall not apply to requests for information made by law enforcement officials, government agencies, financial institutions, attorneys, insurers, employers, automobile associated businesses, persons licensed as a private detective or firms licensed as a private detective agency under the Private Detective, Private Alarm, and Private Security Act of 1983, who are employed by or are acting on behalf of law enforcement officials, government agencies, financial institutions, attorneys, insurers, employers, automobile associated businesses, and other business entities for purposes consistent with the Illinois Vehicle Code, the affected driver or other entities as the Secretary may exempt by rule and regulation.

Any misrepresentation made by a requestor of driver information shall be punishable as a petty offense, except in the case of persons licensed as a private detective or firms licensed as a private detective agency which shall be subject to disciplinary sanctions under Section 22 or 25 of the Private Detective, Private Alarm, and Private Security Act of 1983.

4. The Secretary of State may furnish without fee, upon the written request of a law enforcement agency, any information from a driver's record on file with the Secretary of State when such information is required in the enforcement of this Code or any other law relating to the operation of motor vehicles, including records of dispositions; documented information involving the use of a motor vehicle; whether such individual has, or previously had, a driver's license; and the address and personal description as reflected on said driver's record.

5. Except as otherwise provided in this Section, the Secretary of State may furnish, without fee, information from an individual driver's record on file, if a written request therefor is submitted by any public transit system or authority, public defender, law enforcement agency, a state or federal agency, or an Illinois local intergovernmental association, if the request is for the purpose of a background check of applicants for employment with the requesting agency, or for the purpose of an official investigation conducted by the agency, or to determine a current address for the driver so public funds can be recovered or paid to the driver, or for any other purpose set forth in subsection (f–5) of this Section.

The Secretary may also furnish the courts a copy of an abstract of a driver's record, without fee, subsequent to an arrest for a violation of Section 11–501 or a similar provision of a local ordinance. Such abstract may include records of dispositions; documented information involving the use of a motor vehicle as contained in the current file; whether such individual has, or previously had, a driver's license; and the address and personal description as reflected on said driver's record.

6. Any certified abstract issued by the Secretary of State or transmitted electronically by the Secretary of State pursuant to this Section, to a court or on request of a law enforcement agency, for the record of a named person as to the status of the person's driver's license shall be prima facie evidence of the facts therein stated and if the name appearing in such abstract is the same as that of a person named in an information or warrant, such abstract shall be prima facie evidence that the person named in such information or warrant is the same person as the person named in such abstract and shall be admissible for any prosecution under this Code and be admitted as proof of any prior conviction or proof of records, notices, or orders recorded on individual driving records maintained by the Secretary of State.

7. Subject to any restrictions contained in the Juvenile Court Act of 1987, [3] and upon receipt of a proper request and a fee of $6, the Secretary of State shall provide a driver's record to the affected driver, or the affected driver's attorney, upon verification. Such record shall contain all the information referred to in paragraph 1 of this subsection (g) plus: any recorded accident involvement as a driver; information recorded pursuant to subsection (e) of Section 6–117 and paragraph (4) of subsection (a) of Section 6–204 of this Code. All other information, unless otherwise permitted by this Code, shall remain confidential.

(h) The Secretary shall not disclose social security numbers except pursuant to a written request by, or with the prior written consent of, the individual except: (1) to officers and employees of the Secretary who have a need to know the social security numbers in performance of their official duties, (2) to law enforcement officials for a lawful, civil or criminal law enforcement investigation, and if the head of the law enforcement agency has made a written request to the Secretary specifying the law enforcement investigation for which the social security numbers are being sought, (3) to the United States Department of Transportation, or any other State, pursuant to the administration and enforcement of the Commercial Motor Vehicle Safety Act of 1986, [4] (4) pursuant to the order of a court of competent jurisdiction, or (5) to the Department of Public Aid for utilization in the child support enforcement duties assigned to that Department under provisions of the Public Aid Code after the individual has received advanced meaningful notification of what redisclosure is sought by the Secretary in accordance with the federal Privacy Act.

(i) (Blank).

(j) Medical statements or medical reports received in the Secretary of State's Office shall be confidential. No confidential information may be open to public inspection or the contents disclosed to anyone, except officers and employees of the Secretary who have a need to know the information contained in the medical reports and the Driver License Medical Advisory Board, unless so directed by an order of a court of competent jurisdiction.

(k) All fees collected under this Section shall be paid into the Road Fund of the State Treasury, except that $3 of the $6 fee for a driver's record shall be paid into the Secretary of State Special Services Fund.

(*l*) (Blank).

(m) Notations of accident involvement that may be disclosed under this Section shall not include notations relating to damage to a vehicle or other property being transported by a tow truck. This information shall remain confidential, provided that nothing in this subsection (m) shall limit disclosure of any notification of accident involvement to any law enforcement agency or official.

(n) Requests made by the news media for driver's license, vehicle, or title registration information may be furnished without charge or at a reduced charge, as determined by the Secretary, when the specific purpose for requesting the documents is deemed to be in the public interest. Waiver or reduction of the fee is in the public interest if the principal purpose of the request is to access and disseminate information regarding the health, safety, and welfare or the legal rights of the general public and is not for the principal purpose of gaining a personal or commercial benefit. The information provided pursuant to this subsection shall not contain personally identifying information unless the information is to be used for one of the purposes identified in subsection (f–5) of this Section.

(*o*) The redisclosure of personally identifying information obtained pursuant to this Section is prohibited, except to the extent necessary to effectuate the purpose for which the original disclosure of the information was permitted.

(p) The Secretary of State is empowered to adopt rules to effectuate this Section.

P.A. 76–1586, § 2–123, added by P.A. 76–2128, § 1, eff. July 1, 1970. Amended by P.A. 81–982, § 1, eff. Jan. 1, 1980; P.A. 83–148, § 1, eff. Aug. 29, 1983; P.A. 83–1404, § 6, eff. Sept. 12, 1984; P.A. 84–411, § 1, eff. Jan. 1, 1986; P.A. 84–986, § 1, eff. Sept. 25, 1985; P.A. 84–1308, Art. II, § 96, eff. Aug. 25, 1986; P.A. 84–1394, § 5, eff. Sept. 18, 1986; P.A. 85–314, § 1, eff. Jan. 1, 1988; P.A. 85–1396, § 2, eff. Sept. 2, 1988; P.A. 86–549, § 1, eff. Jan. 1, 1990; P.A. 87–366, § 1, eff. Jan. 1, 1992; P.A. 87–623, § 1, eff. July 1, 1992; P.A. 87–895, Art. 2, § 2–45, eff. Aug. 14, 1992; P.A. 87–1074, § 2, eff. Jan. 1, 1993; P.A. 88–208, § 5, eff. Aug. 5, 1993; P.A. 88–363, § 293, eff. Jan. 1, 1994; P.A. 88–670, Art. 2, § 2–59, eff. Dec.

2, 1994; P.A. 89-503, § 10, eff. July 1, 1996; P.A. 90-144, § 15, eff. July 23, 1997; P.A. 90-330, § 5, eff. Aug. 8, 1997; P.A. 90-400, § 5, eff. Aug. 15, 1997; P.A. 90-655, § 153, eff. July 30, 1998; P.A. 91-37, § 40, eff. July 1, 1999; P.A. 91-357, § 231, eff. July 29, 1999; P.A. 91-716, § 5, eff. Oct. 1, 2000; P.A. 92-32, § 10, eff. July 1, 2001; P.A. 92-651, § 77, eff. July 11, 2002.

Formerly Ill.Rev.Stat.1991, ch. 95 ½, ¶ 2-123.

1 225 ILCS 445/1 (repealed).

2 635 ILCS 5/1-100 et seq.

3 705 ILCS 405/1-1 et seq.

4 49 App. U.S.C.A. § 2701 et seq. (repealed).

5/2-124. Audits, interest and penalties

§ 2-124. Audits, interest and penalties.

(a) Audits. The Secretary of State or employees and agents designated by him, may audit the books, records, tax returns, reports, and any and all other pertinent records or documents of any person licensed or registered, or required to be licensed or registered, under any provisions of this Act, for the purpose of determining whether such person has not paid any fees or taxes required to be paid to the Secretary of State and due to the State of Illinois. For purposes of this Section, "person" means an individual, corporation, or partnership, or an officer or an employee of any corporation, including a dissolved corporation, or a member or an employee of any partnership, who as an officer, employee, or member under a duty to perform the act in respect to which the violation occurs.

(b) Joint Audits. The Secretary of State may enter into reciprocal audit agreements with officers, agents or agencies of another State or States, for joint audits of any person subject to audit under this Act.

(c) Special Audits. If the Secretary of State is not satisfied with the books, records and documents made available for an audit, or if the Secretary of State is unable to determine therefrom whether any fees or taxes are due to the State of Illinois, or if there is cause to believe that the person audited has declined or refused to supply the books, records and documents necessary to determine whether a deficiency exists, the Secretary of State may either seek a court order for production of any and all books, records and documents he deems relevant and material, or, in his discretion, the Secretary of State may instead give written notice to such person requiring him to produce any and all books, records and documents necessary to properly audit and determine whether any fees or taxes are due to the State of Illinois. If such person fails, refuses or declines to comply with either the court order or written notice within the time specified, the Secretary of State shall then order a special audit at the expense of the person affected. Upon completion of the special audit, the Secretary of State shall determine if any fees or taxes required to be paid under this Act have not been paid, and make an assessment of any deficiency based upon the books, records and documents available to him, and in an assessment, he may rely upon records of other persons having an operation similar to that of the person audited specially. A person audited specially and subject to a court order and in default thereof, shall in addition, be subject to any penalty or punishment imposed by the court entering the order.

(d) Deficiency; Audit Costs. When a deficiency is found and any fees or taxes required to be paid under this Act have not been paid to the State of Illinois, the Secretary of State may impose an audit fee of $50 per day, or $25 per half-day, per auditor, plus in the case of out-of-state travel, transportation expenses incurred by the auditor or auditors. Where more than one person is audited on the same out-of-state trip, the additional transportation expenses may be apportioned. The actual costs of a special audit shall be imposed upon the person audited.

(e) Interest. When a deficiency is found and any fees or taxes required to be paid under this Act have not been paid to the State of Illinois, the amount of the deficiency, if greater than $100 for all registration years examined, shall also bear interest at the rate of ½ of 1% per month or fraction thereof, from the date when the fee or tax due should have been paid under the provisions of this Act, subject to a maximum of 6% per annum.

(f) Willful Negligence. When a deficiency is determined by the Secretary to be caused by the willful neglect or negligence of the person audited, an additional 10% penalty, that is 10% of the amount of the deficiency or assessment, shall be imposed, and the 10% penalty shall bear interest at the rate of ½ of 1% on and after the 30th day after the penalty is imposed until paid in full.

(g) Fraud or Evasion. When a deficiency is determined by the Secretary to be caused by fraud or willful evasion of the provisions of this Act, an additional penalty, that is 20% of the amount of the deficiency or assessment, shall be imposed, and the 20% penalty shall bear interest at the rate of ½ of 1% on and after the 30th day after the penalty is imposed until paid in full.

(h) Notice. The Secretary of State shall give written notice to any person audited, of the amount of any deficiency found or assessment made, of the costs of an audit or special audit, and of the penalty imposed, and payment shall be made within 30 days of the date of the notice unless such person petitions for a hearing.

However, except in the case of fraud or willful evasion, or the inaccessibility of books and records for audit or with the express consent of the person audited, no notice of a deficiency or assessment shall be issued by the Secretary for more than 3 registration years. This limitation shall commence on any January 1 as to calendar year registrations and on any July 1 as to fiscal year registrations. This limitation shall not apply for any period during which the person affected has declined or refuses to make his books and records available for audit, nor during any period of time in which an Order of any Court has the effect of enjoining or restraining the Secretary from making an audit or issuing a notice. Notwithstanding, each person licensed under the International Registration Plan and audited by this State or any member jurisdiction shall follow the assessment and refund procedures as adopted and amended by the International Registration Plan members. The Secretary of State shall have the final decision as to which registrants may be subject to the netting of audit fees as outlined in the International Registration Plan. Persons audited may be subject to a review process to determine the final outcome of the audit finding. This process shall follow the adopted procedure as outlined in the International Registration Plan. All decisions by the IRP designated tribunal shall be binding.

(i) Every person subject to licensing or registration and audit under the provisions of this Chapter shall retain all pertinent licensing and registration documents, books, records, tax returns, reports and all supporting records and documents for a period of 4 years.

(j) Hearings. Any person receiving written notice of a deficiency or assessment may, within 30 days after the date of the notice, petition for a hearing before the Secretary of State or his duly appointed hearing officer to contest the audit in whole or in part, and the petitioner shall simultaneously file a certified check or money order, or certificate of deposit, or a surety bond approved by the Secretary in the amount of the deficiency or assessment. Hearings shall be held pursuant to the provisions of Section 2–118 of this Act.

(k) Judgments. The Secretary of State may enforce any notice of deficiency or assessment pursuant to the provisions of Section 3–831 of this Act.

P.A. 76–1586, § 2–124, added by P.A. 77–1541, § 1, eff. Sept. 17, 1971. Amended by P.A. 79–1461, § 1, eff. Oct. 1, 1976; P.A. 85–512, § 1, eff. Jan. 1, 1988; P.A. 87–829, § 1, eff. Jan. 17, 1992; P.A. 87–832, § 3, eff. Jan. 17, 1992; P.A. 89–570, § 5, eff. July 26, 1996; P.A. 92–69, § 5, eff. July 12, 2001.

Formerly Ill.Rev.Stat.1991, ch. 95 ½, ¶ 2–124.

5/2–125. Maximum fees; rules and regulations

§ 2–125. The Secretary of State may in his discretion set maximum fees charged by any person, firm, corporation or private institution within the State of Illinois concerning the acceptance of applications for registration, certificate of title, or drivers license and for the distribution of motor vehicle license plates and other related functions of the Office. The Secretary of State may adopt and promulgate such rules and regulations as he shall deem necessary to effectuate and administer the provisions of this Section.

P.A. 76–1586, § 2–125, added by P.A. 80–469, § 1, eff. Sept. 3, 1977.

Formerly Ill.Rev.Stat.1991, ch. 95 ½, ¶ 2–125.

5/2–126. Drivers license exam stations; fees; temporary deposits

§ 2–126. Employees and agents of the Secretary of State, designated by him, who are employed at Drivers License Exam Stations throughout the State are authorized to deposit, on a temporary basis, fees and moneys collected at such stations in banks or savings and loan associations designated by the Secretary of State. Provided, however, that when such funds collected amount to $500 or more, or on the next succeeding 1st or 15th (disregarding Sundays and holidays) day of each month, whichever is earlier, such fees and moneys shall be forwarded to the Secretary of State by such designated banks or savings and loan associations for deposit with the State Treasurer.

No bank or savings and loan association shall receive public funds as permitted by this Section, unless it has complied with the requirements established pursuant to Section 6 of "An Act relating to certain investments of public funds by public agencies", approved July 23, 1943, as now or hereafter amended.[1]

P.A. 76–1586, § 2–126, added by P.A. 80–547, § 1, eff. Sept. 8, 1977. Amended by P.A. 80–1364, § 36, eff. Aug. 13, 1978; P.A. 83–541, § 52, eff. Sept. 17, 1983.

Formerly Ill.Rev.Stat.1991, ch. 95 ½, ¶ 2–126.

[1] 30 ILCS 235/6.

5/2–127. Transportation provided seniors

§ 2–127. The Secretary of State shall compile and maintain a listing of those services and agencies, both public and private, that provide transportation to senior citizens and shall make this information available to the public through the Drivers License Exam Stations.

P.A. 76–1586, § 2–127, added by P.A. 86–424, § 1, eff. Jan. 1, 1990.

Formerly Ill.Rev.Stat.1991, ch. 95 ½, ¶ 2–127.

5/2–128. § 2–128. Repealed by P.A. 87–564, § 1, eff. July 1, 1992

CHAPTER 3. CERTIFICATES OF TITLE AND REGISTRATION OF VEHICLES

Enactment

The Illinois Vehicle Code was enacted by P.A. 76–1586, effective July 1, 1970. The Code constitutes a consolidated recodification of various earlier laws and acts including the Illinois Motor Vehicle Law of 1957.

ARTICLE I. CERTIFICATES OF TITLE

Section

5/3–100. Definitions

§ 3–100. Definitions. For the purposes of this Chapter, the following words shall have the meanings ascribed to them:

"Electronic" includes electrical, digital, magnetic, optical, electromagnetic, or any other form of technology that entails capabilities similar to these technologies.

"Electronic record" means a record generated, communicated, received, or stored by electronic means for use in an information system or for transmission from one information system to another.

"Electronic signature" means a signature in electronic form attached to or logically associated with an electronic record.

"Owner" means a person who holds legal document of ownership of a vehicle, limited to a certificate of origin, certificate of title, salvage certificate, or junking certificate. However, in the event a vehicle is the subject of an agreement for the conditional sale or lease thereof with the right of purchase upon performance of the conditions stated in the agreement and with an immediate right of possession vested in the conditional vendee or lessee, or in the event a mortgagor of such vehicle is entitled to possession, then such conditional vendee or lessee or mortgagor shall be deemed the owner for the purpose of this Chapter, except as provided under paragraph (c) of Section 3-118.

"Record" means information that is inscribed, stored, or otherwise fixed on a tangible medium or that is stored in an electronic or other medium and is retrievable in perceivable form.

"Signature" or "signed" includes any symbol executed or adopted, or any security procedure employed or adopted, using electronic means or otherwise, by or on behalf of a person with intent to authenticate a record.

P.A. 76-1586, § 3-100, added by P.A. 78-858, § 1, eff. Jan. 1, 1974. Amended by P.A. 78-1205, § 1, eff. Sept. 5, 1974; P.A. 78-1297, § 58, eff. March 4, 1975; P.A. 83-831, § 1, eff. Jan. 1, 1984; P.A. 91-79, § 5, eff. July 9, 1999; P.A. 91-357, § 231, eff. July 29, 1999; P.A. 91-772, § 5, Jan. 1, 2001.

Formerly Ill.Rev.Stat.1991, ch. 95 ½, ¶ 3-100.

P.A. 91-772 incorporated the amendments by P.A. 91-79 and P.A. 91-357.

5/3-100.1. Use of electronic records

§ 3-100.1. Use of electronic records.

(a) To the extent authorized by the Secretary of State and in accordance with standards and procedures prescribed by the Secretary of State:

(1) Certificates, certifications, affidavits, applications, assignments, statements, notices, documents, and other records required under this Chapter may be created, distributed, and received in electronic form.

(2) Signatures required under this Chapter may be made as electronic signatures or may be waived.

(3) Delivery of records required under this Chapter may be made by any means, including electronic delivery.

(4) Fees and taxes required to be paid under this Chapter may be made by electronic means; provided that any forms, records, electronic records, and methods of electronic payment relating to the filing and payment of taxes shall be prescribed by the Department of Revenue.

(b) Electronic records accepted by the Secretary of State have the same force and effect as records created on paper by writing, typing, printing, or similar means. The procedures established by the Secretary of State concerning the acceptance of electronic filings and electronic records shall ensure that the electronic filings and electronic records are received and stored accurately and that they are readily available to satisfy any statutory requirements that call for a written record.

(c) Electronic signatures accepted by the Secretary of State shall have the same force and effect as manual signatures.

(d) Electronic delivery of records accepted by the Secretary of State shall have the same force and effect as physical delivery of records.

(e) Electronic records and electronic signatures accepted by the Secretary of State shall be admissible in all administrative, quasi-judicial, and judicial proceedings. In any such proceeding, nothing in the application of the rules of evidence shall apply so as to deny the admissibility of an electronic record or electronic signature into evidence on the sole ground that it is an electronic record or electronic signature, or on the grounds that it is not in its original form or is not an original. Information in the form of an electronic record shall be given due evidentiary weight by the trier of fact.

P.A. 76-1586, § 3-100.1, added by P.A. 91-772, § 5, eff. Jan. 1, 2001.

5/3-100.2. Electronic access; agreements with submitters

§ 3-100.2. Electronic access; agreements with submitters.

(a) The Secretary of State may allow, but not require, a person to submit any record required to be submitted to the Secretary of State by using electronic media deemed feasible by the Secretary of State, instead of requiring the actual submittal of the original paper record. The Secretary of State may also allow, but not require, a person to receive any record to be provided by the Secretary of State by using electronic media deemed feasible by the Secretary of State, instead of providing the original paper record.

(b) Electronic submittal, receipt, and delivery of records and electronic signatures may be authorized or accepted by the Secretary of State, when supported by a signed agreement between the Secretary of State and the submitter. The agreement shall require, at a minimum, each record to include all information necessary to complete a transaction, certification by the submitter upon its best knowledge as to the truthfulness of the data to be submitted to the Secretary of State, and retention by the submitter of supporting records.

(c) The Secretary of State may establish minimum transaction volume levels, audit and security standards, technological requirements, and other terms and conditions he or she deems necessary for approval of the electronic delivery process.

(d) When an agreement is made to accept electronic records, the Secretary of State shall not be required to produce a written record for the submitter with whom the Secretary of State has the agreement until requested to do so by the submitter.

(e) Upon the request of a lienholder submitter, the Secretary of State shall provide electronic notification to the lienholder submitter to verify the notation and perfection of the lienholder's security interest in a vehicle for which the certificate of title is an electronic record. Upon receipt of an electronic message from a lienholder submitter with a security interest in a vehicle for which the certificate of title is an electronic record that the lien should be released, the Secretary of State shall enter the appropriate electronic record of the release of lien and print and mail a paper certificate of title to the owner or lienholder at no expense. The Secretary of State may also mail the certificate to any other person that delivers to the Secretary of State an authorization from the owner to receive the certificate. If another lienholder holds a properly perfected security interest in the vehicle as reflected in the records of the Secretary of State, the certificate shall be delivered to that lienholder instead of the owner.

P.A. 76-1586, § 3-100.2, added by P.A. 91-772, § 5, eff. Jan. 1, 2001.

5/3-100.3. Rules

§ 3-100.3. Rules. The Secretary of State may adopt rules to implement this Article.

P.A. 76-1586, § 3-100.3, added by P.A. 91-772, § 5, eff. Jan. 1, 2001.

5/3-101. Certificate of title required

§ 3-101. Certificate of title required. (a) Except as provided in Section 3-102, every owner of a vehicle which is in this State and for which no certificate of title has been issued by the Secretary of State shall make application to the Secretary of State for a certificate of title of the vehicle.

(b) Every owner of a motorcycle or motor driven cycle purchased new on and after January 1, 1980 shall make application to the Secretary of State for a certificate of title. However, if such cycle is not properly manufactured or equipped for general highway use pursuant to the provisions of this Act, it shall not be eligible for license registration, but shall be issued a distinctive certificate of title except as provided in Sections 3-102 and 3-110 of this Act.

(c) The Secretary of State shall not register or renew the registration of a vehicle unless a certificate of title has been issued by the Secretary of State to the owner or an application therefor has been delivered by the owner to the Secretary of State.

(d) Every owner of an all-terrain vehicle or off-highway motorcycle purchased on or after January 1, 1998 shall make application to the Secretary of State for a certificate of title.

P.A. 76-1586, § 3-101, eff. July 1, 1970. Amended by P.A. 81-561, § 1, eff. Jan. 1, 1980; P.A. 90-287, § 100, eff. Jan. 1, 1998.

Formerly Ill.Rev.Stat.1991, ch. 95 ½, ¶ 3-101.

5/3-102. Exclusions

§ 3-102. Exclusions.

No certificate of title need be obtained for:

1. A vehicle owned by the State of Illinois; or a vehicle owned by the United States unless it is registered in this State;

2. A vehicle owned by a manufacturer or dealer and held for sale, even though incidentally moved on the highway or used for purposes of testing or demonstration, provided a dealer reassignment area is still available on the manufacturer's certificate of origin or the Illinois title; or a vehicle used by a manufacturer solely for testing;

3. A vehicle owned by a non-resident of this State and not required by law to be registered in this State;

4. A motor vehicle regularly engaged in the interstate transportation of persons or property for which a currently effective certificate of title has been issued in another State;

5. A vehicle moved solely by animal power;

6. An implement of husbandry;

7. Special mobile equipment;

8. An apportionable trailer or an apportionable semitrailer registered in the State prior to April 1, 1998.

P.A. 76-1586, § 3-102, eff. July 1, 1970. Amended by P.A. 89-710, § 15, eff. Feb. 14, 1997; P.A. 91-441, § 10, eff. Jan. 1, 2000.

Formerly Ill.Rev.Stat.1991, ch. 95 ½, ¶ 3-102.

5/3-103. Optional certificate of title

§ 3-103. Optional certificate of title. The owner of an implement of husbandry or special mobile equipment may apply for and obtain a certificate of title on it. All of the provisions of this Chapter, except part (e) of Section 3-104, are applicable to a certificate of title so issued, except that a person who receives a transfer of an interest in the vehicle without knowledge of the certificate of title is not prejudiced by reason of the existence of the certificate, and the perfection of a security interest under this Act is not effective until the lienholder has complied with the provisions of applicable law which otherwise relate to the perfection of security interests in personal property.

An application for an optional certificate of title must be accompanied by either an exemption determination from the Department of Revenue showing that no tax imposed under the "Use Tax Act" [1] or the "Retailers' Occupation Tax Act" [2] is owed by anyone with respect to that vehicle or by a receipt from the Department of Revenue showing that any tax so imposed has been paid. No optional certificate of title shall be issued in the absence of such a receipt or exemption determination.

If the proof of payment or of nonliability is, after the issuance of the optional certificate of title, found to be invalid, the Secretary of State shall revoke the optional certificate of title and require that it be returned to him.

P.A. 76-1586, § 3-103, eff. July 1, 1970. Amended by P.A. 78-1165, § 1, eff. Aug. 27, 1974.

Formerly Ill.Rev.Stat.1991, ch. 95 ½, ¶ 3-103.

[1] 35 ILCS 105/1 et seq.

[2] 35 ILCS 120/1 et seq.

5/3-104. Application for certificate of title

§ 3-104. Application for certificate of title.

(a) The application for a certificate of title for a vehicle in this State must be made by the owner to the Secretary of State on the form prescribed and must contain:

1. The name, Illinois residence and mail address of the owner;

2. A description of the vehicle including, so far as the following data exists: Its make, year-model, identifying number, type of body, whether new or used, as to house trailers as defined in Section 1-128 of this Code, the square footage of the house trailer based upon the outside dimensions of the house trailer excluding the length of the tongue and hitch, and, as to vehicles of the second division, whether for-hire, not-for-hire, or both for-hire and not-for-hire;

3. The date of purchase by applicant and, if applicable, the name and address of the person from whom the vehicle was acquired and the names and addresses of any lienholders in the order of their priority and signatures of owners;

4. The current odometer reading at the time of transfer and that the stated odometer reading is one of the following: actual mileage, not the actual mileage or mileage is in excess of its mechanical limits; and

5. Any further information the Secretary of State reasonably requires to identify the vehicle and to enable him to determine whether the owner is entitled to a certificate of title and the existence or nonexistence of security interests in the vehicle.

(b) If the application refers to a vehicle purchased from a dealer, it must also be signed by the dealer as well as the owner, and the dealer must promptly mail or deliver the application and required documents to the Secretary of State.

(c) If the application refers to a vehicle last previously registered in another State or country, the application must contain or be accompanied by:

1. Any certified document of ownership so recognized and issued by the other State or country and acceptable to the Secretary of State, and

2. Any other information and documents the Secretary of State reasonably requires to establish the ownership of the vehicle and the existence or nonexistence of security interests in it.

(d) If the application refers to a new vehicle it must be accompanied by the Manufacturer's Statement of Origin, or other documents as required and acceptable by the Secretary of State, with such assignments as may be necessary to show title in the applicant.

(e) If an application refers to a vehicle rebuilt from a vehicle previously salvaged, that application shall comply with the provisions set forth in Sections 3-302 through 3-304 of this Code.

(f) An application for a certificate of title for any vehicle, whether purchased in Illinois or outside Illinois, and even if previously registered in another State, must be accompanied by either an exemption determination from the Department of Revenue showing that no tax imposed pursuant to the Use Tax Act [1] or the vehicle use tax imposed by Section 3-1001 of the Illinois Vehicle Code is owed by anyone with respect to that vehicle, or a receipt from the Department of Revenue showing that any tax so imposed has been paid. An application for a certificate of title for any vehicle purchased outside Illinois, even if previously registered in another state, must be accompanied by either an exemption determination from the Department of Revenue showing that no tax imposed pursuant to the Municipal Use Tax Act[2] or the County Use Tax Act [3] is owed by anyone with respect to that vehicle, or a receipt from the Department of Revenue showing that any tax so imposed has been paid. In the absence of such a receipt for payment or determination of exemption from the Department, no certificate of title shall be issued to the applicant.

If the proof of payment of the tax or of nonliability therefor is, after the issuance of the certificate of title and display certificate of title, found to be invalid, the Secretary of State shall revoke the certificate and require that the certificate of title and, when applicable, the display certificate of title be returned to him.

(g) If the application refers to a vehicle not manufactured in accordance with federal safety and emission standards, the application must be accompanied by all documents required by federal governmental agencies to meet their standards before a vehicle is allowed to be issued title and registration.

(h) If the application refers to a vehicle sold at public sale by a sheriff, it must be accompanied by the required fee and a bill of sale issued and signed by a sheriff. The bill of sale must identify the new owner's name and address, the year model, make and vehicle identification number of the vehicle, court order document number authorizing such sale, if applicable, and the name and address of any lienholders in order of priority, if applicable.

(i) If the application refers to a vehicle for which a court of law determined the ownership, it must be accompanied with a certified copy of such court order and the required fee. The court order must indicate the new owner's name and address, the complete description of the vehicle, if known, the name and address of the lienholder, if any, and must be signed and dated by the judge issuing such order.

(j) If the application refers to a vehicle sold at public auction pursuant to the Labor and Storage Lien (Small Amount) Act,[4] it must be accompanied by an affidavit or affirmation furnished by the Secretary of State along with the documents described in the affidavit or affirmation and the required fee.

P.A. 76-1586, § 3-104, eff. July 1, 1970. Amended by P.A. 76-2129, § 1, eff. July 1, 1970; P.A. 78-858, § 1, eff. Jan. 1, 1974; P.A. 78-1142, § 3, eff. Aug. 26, 1974; P.A. 78-1205, § 1, eff. Sept. 5, 1974; P.A. 78-1297, § 30, eff. March 4, 1975; P.A. 81-3, 2nd Sp.Sess., § 19, eff. Jan. 1, 1980; P.A. 81-557, § 1, eff. Jan. 1, 1980; P.A. 81-1509, Art. I, § 57, eff. Sept. 26, 1980; P.A. 83-1473, § 1, eff. Jan. 1, 1985; P.A. 85-277, § 1, eff. Sept. 5, 1987; P.A. 85-1396, § 2, eff. Sept. 2, 1988; P.A. 86-444, § 1, eff. Jan. 1, 1990; P.A. 86-541, § 1, eff. Jan. 1, 1991; P.A. 86-1028, Art. II, § 2-44, eff. Feb. 5, 1990; P.A. 87-206, § 1, eff. Sept. 3, 1991; P.A. 88-45, Art. II, § 2-54, eff. July 6, 1993; P.A. 90-212, § 5, eff. Jan. 1, 1998; P.A. 90-422, § 5, eff. Aug. 15, 1997; P.A. 90-655, § 153, eff. July 30, 1998.

Formerly Ill.Rev.Stat.1991, ch. 95 ½, ¶ 3-104.

1 35 ILCS 105/1 et seq.

2 65 ILCS 5/8-11-6.

3 Former Ill.Rev.Stat. ch. 34, ¶ 409.10 (repealed).

4 770 ILCS 50/0.01 et seq.

P.A. 90-655, the First 1998 General Revisory Act, amended various Acts to delete obsolete text, to correct patent and technical errors, to revise cross references, to resolve multiple actions in the 89th and 90th General Assemblies and to make certain technical corrections in P.A. 89-708 through P.A. 90-566.

5/3-104.1. § 3-104.1. Repealed by P.A. 90-665, § 50, eff. Jan. 1, 1999

5/3-105. Examination of records

§ 3-105. Examination of records. The Secretary of State, upon receiving application for a first certificate of title, shall check the identifying number of the vehicle shown in the application against the records of vehicles required to be maintained by Section 3-107 and against the record of stolen and converted vehicles required to be maintained by Section 4-107.

P.A. 76-1586, § 3-105, eff. July 1, 1970.

Formerly Ill.Rev.Stat.1991, ch. 95 ½, ¶ 3-105.

5/3-106. Certificate of title—Issuance—Records

§ 3-106. Certificate of title—Issuance—Records. (a) The Secretary of State shall file each application received and, when satisfied as to its genuineness and regularity, and that no tax imposed by the "Use Tax Act" [1] or the vehicle use tax, as imposed by Section 3-1001 of "The Illinois Vehicle Code", or pursuant to the "Municipal Use Tax Act" [2] or pursuant to the "County Use Tax Act" [3] is owed as evidenced by the receipt for payment or determination of exemption from the Department of Revenue provided for in Section 3-104 of this Act, and that the applicant is entitled to the issuance of a certificate of title, shall issue a certificate of title of the vehicle.

(b) The Secretary of State shall maintain a record of all certificates of title issued by him under a distinctive title number assigned to the vehicle; and, in the discretion of the Secretary of State, in any other method determined.

P.A. 76-1586, § 3-106, eff. July 1, 1970. Amended by P.A. 76-2130, § 1, eff. July 1, 1970; P.A. 78-1142, § 3, eff. Aug. 26, 1974; P.A. 81-3, 2nd Sp.Sess. § 19, eff. Jan. 1, 1980; P.A. 86-444, § 1, eff. Jan. 1, 1990.

Formerly Ill.Rev.Stat.1991, ch. 95 ½, ¶ 3-106.

[1] 35 ILCS 105/1 et seq.

[2] 65 ILCS 5/8-11-6.

[3] Former Ill.Rev.Stat. ch. 34, ¶ 409.10 (repealed).

5/3-107. Contents and effect

§ 3-107. Contents and effect. (a) Each certificate of title issued by the Secretary of State shall contain:

1. the date issued;
2. the name and address of the owner;
3. the names and addresses of any lienholders, in the order of priority as shown on the application or, if the application is based on a certificate of title, as shown on the certificate;
4. the title number assigned to the vehicle;
5. a description of the vehicle including, so far as the following data exists: its make, year-model, identifying number, type of body, whether new or used, as to house trailers as defined in Section 1-128 of this Code, the square footage of the vehicle based upon the outside dimensions of the house trailer excluding the length of the tongue and hitch, and, if a new vehicle, the date of the first sale of the vehicle for use;
6. an odometer certification as provided for in this Code; and
7. any other data the Secretary of State prescribes.

(b) The certificate of title shall contain forms for assignment and warranty of title by the owner, and for assignment and warranty of title by a dealer, and may contain forms for applications for a certificate of title by a transferee, the naming of a lienholder and the assignment or release of the security interest of a lienholder.

(c) A certificate of title issued by the Secretary of State is prima facie evidence of the facts appearing on it.

(d) A certificate of title for a vehicle is not subject to garnishment, attachment, execution or other judicial process, but this subsection does not prevent a lawful levy upon the vehicle.

(e) Any certificate of title issued by the Secretary of State is subject to a lien in favor of the State of Illinois for any fees or taxes required to be paid under this Act and as have not been paid, as provided for in this Code.

P.A. 76-1586, § 3-107, eff. July 1, 1970. Amended by P.A. 77-641, § 1, eff. Aug. 4, 1971; P.A. 81-557, § 1, eff. Jan. 1, 1980; P.A. 81-1409, § 1, eff. Aug. 25, 1980; P.A. 85-1396, § 2, eff. Sept. 2, 1988; P.A. 86-541, § 1, eff. Jan. 1, 1991; P.A. 86-1028, Art. III, § 3-29, eff. Feb. 5, 1990; P.A. 87-206, § 1, eff. Sept. 3, 1991.

Formerly Ill.Rev.Stat.1991, ch. 95 ½, ¶ 3-107.

5/3-107.1. Presumption of tenancy

§ 3-107.1. Presumption of tenancy. When a certificate of title is made out to 2 or more persons, it shall be presumed that the title is held as joint tenants with right of survivorship.

P.A. 76-1586, § 3-107.1, added by P.A. 78-284, § 1, eff. Jan. 1, 1974. Amended by P.A. 79-482, § 2, eff. Oct. 1, 1975; P.A. 79-512, § 2, eff. Oct. 1, 1975; P.A. 79-1454, § 17[77], eff. Aug. 31, 1976.

Formerly Ill.Rev.Stat.1991, ch. 95 ½, ¶ 3-107.1.

5/3-108. Delivery

§ 3-108. Delivery.

The certificate of title shall be mailed or delivered to the first lienholder named in it or, if none, to the owner.

P.A. 76-1586, § 3-108, eff. July 1, 1970. Amended by P.A. 91-78, § 5, eff. July 9, 1999.

Formerly Ill.Rev.Stat.1991, ch. 95 ½, ¶ 3-108.

5/3-109. Registration without certificate of title; bond

§ 3-109. Registration without certificate of title; bond.

If the Secretary of State is not satisfied as to the ownership of the vehicle or that there are no undisclosed security interests in it, the Secretary of State may register the vehicle but shall either:

(a) Withhold issuance of a certificate of title until the applicant presents documents reasonably sufficient to satisfy the Secretary of State as to the applicant's ownership of the vehicle and that there are no undisclosed security interests in it; or

(b) As a condition of issuing a certificate of title, require the applicant to file with the Secretary of State a bond in the form prescribed by the Secretary of State and executed by the applicant, and either accompanied by the deposit of cash with the Secretary of State or also executed by a person authorized to conduct a surety business in this State. The bond shall be in an amount equal to one and one-half times the value of the vehicle as determined by the Secretary of State and conditioned to indemnify any prior owner and lienholder and any subsequent purchaser of the vehicle or person acquiring any security interest in it, and their respective successors in interest, against any expense, loss or damage, including reasonable attorney's fees, by reason of the issuance of the certificate of title of the vehicle or on account of any defect in or undisclosed security interest upon the right, title and interest of the applicant in and to the vehicle. Any such interested person has a right of action to recover on the bond for any breach of its conditions, but the aggregate liability of the surety to all persons shall not exceed the amount of the bond. The bond, and any deposit accompanying it, shall be returned at the end of three (3) years or prior thereto if the vehicle is no longer registered in this State and the currently valid certificate of title is surrendered to the Secretary of State, unless the Secretary of State has been notified of the pendency of an action to recover on the bond.

Security deposited as a bond hereunder shall be placed by the Secretary of State in the custody of the State Treasurer.

(c) During July, annually, the Secretary shall compile a list of all bonds on deposit, pursuant to this Section, for more than 3 years and concerning which he has received no notice as to the pendency of any judicial proceeding that could affect the disposition thereof. Thereupon, he shall promptly send a notice by certified mail to the last known address of each depositor advising him that his bond will be subject to escheat to the State of Illinois if not claimed within 30 days after the mailing date of such notice. At the expiration of such time, the Secretary of State shall file with the State Treasurer an order directing the transfer of such deposit to the Road Fund in the State Treasury. Upon receipt of such order, the State Treasurer shall make such transfer, after converting to cash any other type of security. Thereafter any person having a legal claim against such deposit may enforce it by appropriate proceedings in the Court of Claims subject to the limitations prescribed for such Court. At the expiration of such limitation period such deposit shall escheat to the State of Illinois.

P.A. 76-1586, § 3-109, eff. July 1, 1970. Amended by P.A. 81-1458, § 1, eff. Sept. 8, 1980.

Formerly Ill.Rev.Stat.1991, ch. 95 ½, ¶ 3-109.

5/3-110. Refusing certificate of title

§ 3-110. Refusing certificate of title. The Secretary of State shall refuse issuance of a certificate of title if any required fee is not paid or if he has reasonable grounds to believe that:

(a) The applicant is not the owner of the vehicle;

(b) The application contains a false or fraudulent statement; or

(c) The applicant fails to furnish required information or documents or any additional information the Secretary of State reasonably requires;

(d) The applicant has not paid to the Secretary of State any fees or taxes due under this Act and have not been paid upon reasonable notice and demand.

P.A. 76-1586, § 3-110, eff. July 1, 1970. Amended by P.A. 77-641, § 1, eff. Aug. 4, 1971.

Formerly Ill.Rev.Stat.1991, ch. 95 ½, ¶ 3-110.

5/3-111. Lost, stolen or mutilated certificates

§ 3-111. Lost, stolen or mutilated certificates. (a) If a certificate of title is lost, stolen, mutilated or destroyed or becomes illegible, the first lienholder or, if none, the owner or legal representative of the owner named in the certificate, as shown by the records of the Secretary of State, shall promptly make application for and may obtain a duplicate upon furnishing information satisfactory to the Secretary of State. The duplicate certificate of title shall contain the legend "This is a duplicate certificate and may be subject to the rights of a person under the original certificate." It shall be mailed to the first lienholder named in it or, if none, to the owner or the owner's designee.

(b) The Secretary of State shall not issue a duplicate certificate of title to any person within 15 days after the issuance of an original certificate of title to such person.

(c) A person recovering an original certificate of title for which a duplicate has been issued shall promptly surrender the original certificate to the Secretary of State.

(d) An application for a duplicate certificate of title must state the current vehicle odometer reading at the time of application and that the stated odometer reading is one of the following: actual mileage, not the actual mileage or mileage is in excess of its mechanical limits.

(e) If a Display certificate of title is lost, stolen, mutilated or destroyed or becomes illegible, the owner or legal representative of the owner named in the original Display certificate of title and in the certificate of title, as shown by the records of the Secretary of State, shall promptly make application for and may obtain a duplicate upon furnishing information satisfactory to the Secretary of State. The duplicate Display certificate of title shall contain the legend "Duplicate Display Certificate of Title." It shall be mailed to the owner or legal representative of the owner named in the original Display certificate of title and in the certificate of title. Such duplicate Display certificate of title shall be attached and displayed in the same manner and in the same place as the original Display certificate of title would have been attached and displayed had it not been lost, stolen, mutilated or destroyed or had it not become illegible.

P.A. 76-1586, § 3-111, eff. July 1, 1970. Amended by P.A. 85-457, § 1, eff. July 1, 1988; P.A. 85-1396, § 2, eff. Sept. 2, 1988; P.A. 86-444, § 1, eff. Jan. 1, 1990.

Formerly Ill.Rev.Stat.1991, ch. 95 ½, ¶ 3-111.

5/3-111.1. Corrected certificates

§ 3-111.1. Corrected certificates. An application for a corrected certificate of title must state the current vehicle odometer reading at the time of application and that the stated odometer reading is one of the following: actual mileage, not the actual mileage or mileage is in excess of its mechanical limits. The corrected certificate issued under this Section shall contain the notation "corrected".

P.A. 76-1586, § 3-111.1, added by P.A. 85-457, § 1, eff. July 1, 1988. Amended by P.A. 86-444, § 1, eff. Jan. 1, 1990; P.A. 90-212, § 5, eff. Jan. 1, 1998.

Formerly Ill.Rev.Stat.1991, ch. 95 ½, ¶ 3-111.1.

5/3-112. Transfer

§ 3-112. Transfer.

(a) If an owner transfers his interest in a vehicle, other than by the creation of a security interest, at the time of the delivery of the vehicle he shall execute to the transferee an assignment and warranty of title in the space provided on the certificate of title, or as the Secretary of State prescribes, and cause the certificate and assignment to be mailed or delivered to the transferee or to the Secretary of State.

If the vehicle is subject to a tax under the Mobile Home Local Services Tax Act [1] in a county with a population of less than 3,000,000, the owner shall also provide to the transferee a certification by the treasurer of the county in which the vehicle is situated that all taxes imposed upon the vehicle for the years the owner was the actual titleholder of the vehicle have been paid. The transferee shall be liable only for the taxes he or she incurred while he or she was the actual titleholder of the mobile home. The county treasurer shall refund any amount of taxes paid by the transferee that were imposed in years when the transferee was not the actual titleholder. The provisions of this amendatory Act of 1997 (P.A. 90-542) apply retroactively to January 1, 1996. In no event may the county treasurer refund amounts paid by the transferee during any year except the 10 years immediately preceding the year in which the refund is made. If the owner is a licensed dealer who has purchased the vehicle and is holding it for resale, in lieu of acquiring a certification from the county treasurer he shall forward the certification received from the previous owner to the next buyer of the vehicle. The owner shall cause the certification to be mailed or delivered to the Secretary of State with the certificate of title and assignment.

(b) Except as provided in Section 3-113, the transferee shall, promptly and within 20 days after delivery to him of the vehicle and the assigned title, execute the application for a new certificate of title in the space provided therefor on the certificate or as the Secretary of State prescribes, and cause the certificate and application to be mailed or delivered to the Secretary of State.

(c) Upon request of the owner or transferee, a lienholder in possession of the certificate of title shall, unless the transfer was a breach of his security agreement, either deliver the certificate to the transferee for delivery to the Secretary of State or, upon receipt from the transferee of the owner's assignment, the transferee's application for a new certificate and the required fee, mail or deliver them to the

Secretary of State. The delivery of the certificate does not affect the rights of the lienholder under his security agreement.

(d) If a security interest is reserved or created at the time of the transfer, the certificate of title shall be retained by or delivered to the person who becomes the lienholder, and the parties shall comply with the provisions of Section 3-203.

(e) Except as provided in Section 3-113 and as between the parties, a transfer by an owner is not effective until the provisions of this Section and Section 3-115 have been complied with; however, an owner who has delivered possession of the vehicle to the transferee and has complied with the provisions of this Section and Section 3-115 requiring action by him as not liable as owner for any damages thereafter resulting from operation of the vehicle.

(f) The Secretary of State shall not process any application for a transfer of an interest in a vehicle if any fees or taxes due under this Act from the transferor or the transferee have not been paid upon reasonable notice and demand.

(g) If the Secretary of State receives an application for transfer of a vehicle subject to a tax under the Mobile Home Local Services Tax Act in a county with a population of less than 3,000,000, such application must be accompanied by the required certification by the county treasurer or tax assessor authorizing the issuance of the title.

P.A. 76-1586, § 3-112, eff. July 1, 1970. Amended by P.A. 77-641, § 1, eff. Aug. 4, 1971; P.A. 83-871, § 1, eff. Sept. 26, 1983; P.A. 86-226, § 1, eff. Jan. 1, 1990; P.A. 86-460, § 2, eff. Jan. 1, 1990; P.A. 86-1028, Art. II, § 2-44, eff. Feb. 5, 1990; P.A. 90-212, § 5, eff. Jan. 1, 1998; P.A. 90-542, § 5, eff. Dec. 1, 1997; P.A. 90-655, § 153, eff. July 30, 1998; P.A. 92-651, § 77, eff. July 11, 2002.

Formerly Ill.Rev.Stat.1991, ch. 95 ½, ¶ 3-112.

[1] 35 ILCS 515/1 et seq.

P.A. 90-655, the First 1998 General Revisory Act, amended various Acts to delete obsolete text, to correct patent and technical errors, to revise cross references, to resolve multiple actions in the 89th and 90th General Assemblies and to make certain technical corrections in P.A. 89-708 through P.A. 90-566.

5/3-112.1. Odometer

§ 3-112.1. Odometer.

(a) All titles issued by the Secretary of State beginning January, 1990, shall provide for an odometer certification substantially as follows:

"I certify to the best of my knowledge that the odometer reading is and reflects the actual mileage of the vehicle unless one of the following statements is checked.

....

( ) 1. The mileage stated is in excess of its mechanical limits.

( ) 2. The odometer reading is not the actual mileage. Warning—Odometer Discrepancy."

(b) When executing any transfer of title which contains the odometer certification as described in paragraph (a) above, each transferor of a motor vehicle must supply on the title form the following information:

(1) The odometer reading at the time of transfer and an indication if the mileage is in excess of its mechanical limits or if it is not the actual mileage;

(2) The date of transfer;

(3) The transferor's printed name and signature; and

(4) The transferee's printed name and address.

(c) The transferee must sign on the title form indicating that he or she is aware of the odometer certification made by the transferor.

(d) The transferor will not be required to disclose the current odometer reading and the transferee will not have to acknowledge such disclosure under the following circumstances:

(1) A vehicle having a Gross Vehicle Weight Rating of more than 16,000 pounds;

(2) A vehicle that is not self-propelled;

(3) A vehicle that is 10 years old or older;

(4) A vehicle sold directly by the manufacturer to any agency of the United States; and

(5) A vehicle manufactured without an odometer.

(e) When the transferor signs the title transfer such transferor acknowledges that he or she is aware that Federal regulations and State law require him or her to state the odometer mileage upon transfer of ownership. An inaccurate or untruthful statement with intent to defraud subjects the transferor to liability for damages to the transferee pursuant to the federal Motor Vehicle Information and Cost Act of 1972, P.L. 92-513 as amended by P.L. 94-364.[1] No transferor shall be liable for damages as provided under this Section who transfers title to a motor vehicle which has an odometer reading that has been altered or tampered with by a previous owner, unless that transferor knew or had reason to know of such alteration or tampering and sold such vehicle with an intent to defraud. A cause of action is hereby created by which any person who, with intent to defraud, violates any requirement imposed under this Section shall be liable in an amount equal to the sum of:

(1) three times the amount of actual damages sustained or $1,500, whichever is the greater; and

(2) in the case of any successful action to enforce the foregoing liability, the costs of the action together with reasonable attorney fees as determined by the court.

Any recovery based on a cause of action under this Section shall be offset by any recovery made pursuant to the federal Motor Vehicle Information and Cost Savings Act of 1972.

(f) The provisions of this Section shall not apply to any motorcycle, motor driven cycle, moped or antique vehicle.

(g) The Secretary of State may adopt rules and regulations providing for a transition period for all non-conforming titles.

P.A. 76-1586, § 3-112.1, added by P.A. 81-1409, § 1, eff. Aug. 25, 1980. Amended by P.A. 85-1396, § 2, eff. Sept. 2, 1988; P.A. 86-444, § 1, eff. Jan. 1, 1990; P.A. 86-500, § 1, eff. Jan. 1, 1990; P.A. 86-1028, Art. II, § 2-44, eff. Feb. 5, 1990; P.A. 88-415, § 10, eff. Aug. 20, 1993; P.A. 91-357, § 231, eff. July 29, 1999; P.A. 92-651, § 77, eff. July 11, 2002.

Formerly Ill.Rev.Stat.1991, ch. 95 ½, ¶ 3-112.1.

[1] 15 U.S.C.A. § 1901 et seq.

5/3-113. Transfer to or from dealer; records

§ 3-113. Transfer to or from dealer; records.

(a) If a dealer buys a vehicle and holds it for resale and procures the certificate of title from the owner or the lienholder within 10 days after delivery to him of the vehicle, he need not send the certificate to the Secretary of State but, upon transferring the vehicle to another person other than by the creation of a security interest, shall promptly and within 20 days execute the assignment and warranty of title by a dealer, showing the names and addresses of the transferee and of any lienholder holding a security interest created or reserved at the time of the resale, in the spaces provided therefor on the certificate or as the Secretary of State prescribes, and mail or deliver the certificate to the Secretary of State with the transferee's application for a new certificate, except as provided in Section 3-117.2.

(b) The Secretary of State may decline to process any application for a transfer of an interest in a vehicle if any fees or taxes due under this Code from the transferor or the transferee have not been paid upon reasonable notice and demand.

(c) Any person who violates this Section shall be guilty of a petty offense.

P.A. 76-1586, § 3-113, eff. July 1, 1970. Amended by P.A. 77-641, § 1, eff. Aug. 4, 1971; P.A. 83-1473, § 1, eff. Jan. 1, 1985; P.A. 85-1204, § 1, eff. Aug. 26, 1988; P.A. 85-1396, § 2, eff. Sept. 2, 1988; P.A. 86-820, Art. II, § 2-8, eff. Sept. 7, 1989; P.A. 87-1225, § 2, eff. Dec. 22, 1992.

Formerly Ill.Rev.Stat.1991, ch. 95 ½, ¶ 3-113.

5/3-114. Transfer by operation of law

§ 3-114. Transfer by operation of law.

(a) If the interest of an owner in a vehicle passes to another other than by voluntary transfer, the transferee shall, except as provided in paragraph (b), promptly mail or deliver within 20 days to the Secretary of State the last certificate of title, if available, proof of the transfer, and his application for a new certificate in the form the Secretary of State prescribes. It shall be unlawful for any person having possession of a certificate of title for a motor vehicle, semitrailer, or house car by reason of his having a lien or encumbrance on such vehicle, to fail or refuse to deliver such certificate to the owner, upon the satisfaction or discharge of the lien or encumbrance, indicated upon such certificate of title.

(b) If the interest of an owner in a vehicle passes to another under the provisions of the Small Estates provisions of the Probate Act of 1975 [1]the transferee shall promptly mail or deliver to the Secretary of State, within 120 days, the last certificate of title, if available, the documentation required under the provisions of the Probate Act of 1975, and an application for certificate of title. The Small Estate Affidavit form shall be furnished by the Secretary of State. The transfer may be to the transferee or to the nominee of the transferee.

(c) If the interest of an owner in a vehicle passes to another under other provisions of the Probate Act of 1975, as amended, and the transfer is made by a representative or guardian, such transferee shall promptly mail or deliver to the Secretary of State, the last certificate of title, if available, and a certified copy of the letters of office or guardianship, and an application for certificate of title. Such application shall be made before the estate is closed. The transfer may be to the transferee or to the nominee of the transferee.

(d) If the interest of an owner in joint tenancy passes to the other joint tenant with survivorship rights as provided by law, the transferee shall promptly mail or deliver to the Secretary of State, the last certificate of title, if available, proof of death of the one joint tenant and survivorship of the surviving joint tenant, and an application for certificate of title. Such application shall be made within 120 days after the death of the joint tenant. The transfer may be to the transferee or to the nominee of the transferee.

(e) The Secretary of State shall transfer a decedent's vehicle title to any legatee, representative or heir of the decedent who submits to the Secretary a death certificate and an affidavit by an attorney at law on the letterhead stationery of the attorney at law stating the facts of the transfer.

(f) Repossession with assignment of title. In all cases wherein a lienholder has repossessed a vehicle by other than judicial process and holds it for resale under a security agreement, and the owner of record has executed an assignment of the existing certificate of title after default, the lienholder may proceed to sell or otherwise dispose of the vehicle as authorized under the Uniform Commercial Code.[2] Upon selling the vehicle to another person, the lienholder need not send the certificate of title to the Secretary of State, but shall promptly and within 20 days mail or deliver to the purchaser as transferee the existing certificate of title for the repossessed vehicle, reflecting the release of the lienholder's security interest in the vehicle. The application for a certificate of title made by the purchaser shall comply with subsection (a) of Section 3-104 and be accompanied by the existing certificate of title for the repossessed vehicle. The lienholder shall execute the assignment and warranty of title showing the name and address of the purchaser in the spaces provided therefor on the certificate of title or as the Secretary of State prescribes. The lienholder shall complete the assignment of title in the certificate of title to reflect the transfer of the vehicle to the lienholder and also a reassignment to reflect the transfer from the lienholder to the purchaser. For this purpose, the lienholder is specifically authorized to complete and execute the space reserved in the certificate of title for a dealer reassignment, notwithstanding that the lienholder is not a licensed dealer. Nothing herein shall be construed to mean that the lienholder is taking title to the repossessed vehicle for purposes of liability for retailer occupation, vehicle use, or other tax with respect to the proceeds from the repossession sale. Delivery of the existing certificate of title to the purchaser shall be deemed disclosure to the purchaser of the owner of the vehicle.

(f-5) Repossession without assignment of title. In all cases wherein a lienholder has repossessed a vehicle by other than judicial process and holds it for resale under a security agreement, and the owner of record has not executed an assignment of the existing certificate of title, the lienholder shall comply with the following provisions:

(1) Prior to sale, the lienholder shall deliver or mail to the owner at the owner's last known address and to any other lienholder of record, a notice of redemption setting forth the following information: (i) the name of the owner of record and in bold type at or near the top of the notice a statement that the owner's vehicle was repossessed on a specified date for failure to make payments on the loan (or other reason), (ii) a description of the vehicle subject to the lien sufficient to identify it, (iii) the right of the owner to redeem the vehicle, (iv) the lienholder's intent to sell or otherwise dispose of the vehicle after the expiration of 21 days from the date of mailing or delivery of the notice, and (v) the name, address, and telephone number of the lienholder from whom information may be obtained concerning the amount due to redeem the vehicle and from whom the vehicle may be redeemed under Section 9-623 of the Uniform Commercial Code.[3] At the lienholder's option, the information required to be set forth in this notice of redemption may be made a part of or accompany the notification of sale or other disposition required under Section 9-611 of the Uniform Commercial Code,[4] but none of the information required by this notice shall be construed to impose any requirement under Article 9 of the Uniform Commercial Code.[5]

(2) With respect to the repossession of a vehicle used primarily for personal, family, or household purposes, the lienholder shall also deliver or mail to the owner at the owner's last known address an affidavit of defense. The affidavit of defense shall accompany the notice of redemption required in subdivision (f–5)(1) of this Section. The affidavit of defense shall (i) identify the lienholder, owner, and the vehicle; (ii) provide space for the owner to state the defense claimed by the owner; and (iii) include an acknowledgment by the owner that the owner may be liable to the lienholder for fees, charges, and costs incurred by the lienholder in establishing the insufficiency or invalidity of the owner's defense. To stop the transfer of title, the affidavit of defense must be received by the lienholder no later than 21 days after the date of mailing or delivery of the notice required in subdivision (f–5)(1) of this Section. If the lienholder receives the affidavit from the owner in a timely manner, the lienholder must apply to a court of competent jurisdiction to determine if the lienholder is entitled to possession of the vehicle.

(3) Upon selling the vehicle to another person, the lienholder need not send the certificate of title to the Secretary of State, but shall promptly and within 20 days mail or deliver to the purchaser as transferee (i) the existing certificate of title for the repossessed vehicle, reflecting the release of the lienholder's security interest in the vehicle; and (ii) an affidavit of repossession made by or on behalf of the lienholder which provides the following information: that the vehicle was repossessed, a description of the vehicle sufficient to identify it, whether the vehicle has been damaged in excess of 33 ⅓% of its fair market value as required under subdivision (b)(3) of Section 3–117.1, that the owner and any other lienholder of record were given the notice required in subdivision (f–5)(1) of this Section, that the owner of record was given the affidavit of defense required in subdivision (f–5)(2) of this Section, that the interest of the owner was lawfully terminated or sold pursuant to the terms of the security agreement, and the purchaser's name and address. If the vehicle is damaged in excess of 33 ⅓% of its fair market value, the lienholder shall make application for a salvage certificate under Section 3–117.1 and transfer the vehicle to a person eligible to receive assignments of salvage certificates identified in Section 3–118.

(4) The application for a certificate of title made by the purchaser shall comply with subsection (a) of Section 3–104 and be accompanied by the affidavit of repossession furnished by the lienholder and the existing certificate of title for the repossessed vehicle. The lienholder shall execute the assignment and warranty of title showing the name and address of the purchaser in the spaces provided therefor on the certificate of title or as the Secretary of State prescribes. The lienholder shall complete the assignment of title in the certificate of title to reflect the transfer of the vehicle to the lienholder and also a reassignment to reflect the transfer from the lienholder to the purchaser. For this purpose, the lienholder is specifically authorized to execute the assignment on behalf of the owner as seller if the owner has not done so and to complete and execute the space reserved in the certificate of title for a dealer reassignment, notwithstanding that the lienholder is not a licensed dealer. Nothing herein shall be construed to mean that the lienholder is taking title to the repossessed vehicle for purposes of liability for retailer occupation, vehicle use, or other tax with respect to the proceeds from the repossession sale. Delivery of the existing certificate of title to the purchaser shall be deemed disclosure to the purchaser of the owner of the vehicle. In the event the lienholder does not hold the certificate of title for the repossessed vehicle, the lienholder shall make application for and may obtain a new certificate of title in the name of the lienholder upon furnishing information satisfactory to the Secretary of State. Upon receiving the new certificate of title, the lienholder may proceed with the sale described in subdivision (f–5)(3), except that upon selling the vehicle the lienholder shall promptly and within 20 days mail or deliver to the purchaser the new certificate of title reflecting the assignment and transfer of title to the purchaser.

(5) Neither the lienholder nor the owner shall file with the Office of the Secretary of State the notice of redemption or affidavit of defense described in subdivisions (f–5)(1) and (f–5)(2) of this Section. The Office of the Secretary of State shall not determine the merits of an owner's affidavit of defense, nor consider any allegations or assertions regarding the validity or invalidity of a lienholder's claim to the vehicle or an owner's asserted defenses to the repossession action.

(f–7) Notice of reinstatement in certain cases.

(1) If, at the time of repossession by a lienholder that is seeking to transfer title pursuant to subsection (f–5), the owner has paid an amount equal to 30% or more of the deferred payment price or total of payments due, the owner may, within 21 days of the date of repossession, reinstate the contract or loan agreement and recover the vehicle from the lienholder by tendering in a lump sum (i) the total of all unpaid amounts, including any unpaid delinquency or deferral charges due at the date of reinstatement, without acceleration; and (ii) performance necessary to cure any default other than nonpayment of the amounts due; and (iii) all reasonable costs and fees incurred by the lienholder in retaking, holding, and preparing the vehicle for disposition and in arranging for the sale of the vehicle. Reasonable costs and fees incurred by the lienholder include without limitation repossession and storage expenses and, if authorized by the contract or loan agreement, reasonable attorneys' fees and collection agency charges.

(2) Tender of payment and performance pursuant to this limited right of reinstatement restores to the owner his rights under the contract or loan agreement as though no default had occurred. The owner has the right to reinstate the contract or loan agreement and recover the vehicle from the lienholder only once under this subsection. The lienholder may, in the lienholder's sole discretion, extend the period during which the owner may reinstate the contract or loan agreement and recover the vehicle beyond the 21 days allowed under this subsection, and the extension shall not subject the lienholder to liability to the owner under the laws of this State.

(3) The lienholder shall deliver or mail written notice to the owner at the owner's last known address, within 3 business days of the date of repossession, of the owner's right to reinstate the contract or loan agreement and recover the vehicle pursuant to the limited right of reinstatement described in this subsection. At the lienholder's option, the information required to be set forth in this notice of reinstatement may be made part of or accompany the notice of redemption required in subdivision (f–5)(1) of this Section and the notification of sale or other disposition required under Section 9–611 of the Uniform Commercial Code, but none of the information required by this notice of reinstatement shall be construed to impose any requirement under Article 9 of the Uniform Commercial Code.

(4) The reinstatement period, if applicable, and the redemption period described in subdivision (f-5)(1) of this Section, shall run concurrently if the information required to be set forth in the notice of reinstatement is part of or accompanies the notice of redemption. In any event, the 21 day redemption period described in subdivision (f-5)(1) of this Section shall commence on the date of mailing or delivery to the owner of the information required to be set forth in the notice of redemption, and the 21 day reinstatement period described in this subdivision, if applicable, shall commence on the date of mailing or delivery to the owner of the information required to be set forth in the notice of reinstatement.

(5) The Office of the Secretary of State shall not determine the merits of an owner's claim of right to reinstatement, nor consider any allegations or assertions regarding the validity or invalidity of a lienholder's claim to the vehicle or an owner's asserted right to reinstatement. Where a lienholder is subject to licensing and regulatory supervision by the State of Illinois, the lienholder shall be subject to all of the powers and authority of the lienholder's primary State regulator to enforce compliance with the procedures set forth in this subsection (f-7).

(f-10) Repossession by judicial process. In all cases wherein a lienholder has repossessed a vehicle by judicial process and holds it for resale under a security agreement, order for replevin, or other court order establishing the lienholder's right to possession of the vehicle, the lienholder may proceed to sell or otherwise dispose of the vehicle as authorized under the Uniform Commercial Code or the court order. Upon selling the vehicle to another person, the lienholder need not send the certificate of title to the Secretary of State, but shall promptly and within 20 days mail or deliver to the purchaser as transferee (i) the existing certificate of title for the repossessed vehicle reflecting the release of the lienholder's security interest in the vehicle; (ii) a certified copy of the court order; and (iii) a bill of sale identifying the new owner's name and address and the year, make, model, and vehicle identification number of the vehicle. The application for a certificate of title made by the purchaser shall comply with subsection (a) of Section 3-104 and be accompanied by the certified copy of the court order furnished by the lienholder and the existing certificate of title for the repossessed vehicle. The lienholder shall execute the assignment and warranty of title showing the name and address of the purchaser in the spaces provided therefor on the certificate of title or as the Secretary of State prescribes. The lienholder shall complete the assignment of title in the certificate of title to reflect the transfer of the vehicle to the lienholder and also a reassignment to reflect the transfer from the lienholder to the purchaser. For this purpose, the lienholder is specifically authorized to execute the assignment on behalf of the owner as seller if the owner has not done so and to complete and execute the space reserved in the certificate of title for a dealer reassignment, notwithstanding that the lienholder is not a licensed dealer. Nothing herein shall be construed to mean that the lienholder is taking title to the repossessed vehicle for purposes of liability for retailer occupation, vehicle use, or other tax with respect to the proceeds from the repossession sale. Delivery of the existing certificate of title to the purchaser shall be deemed disclosure to the purchaser of the owner of the vehicle. In the event the lienholder does not hold the certificate of title for the repossessed vehicle, the lienholder shall make application for and may obtain a new certificate of title in the name of the lienholder upon furnishing information satisfactory to the Secretary of State. Upon receiving the new certificate of title, the lienholder may proceed with the sale described in this subsection, except that upon selling the vehicle the lienholder shall promptly and within 20 days mail or deliver to the purchaser the new certificate of title reflecting the assignment and transfer of title to the purchaser.

(f-15) The Secretary of State shall not issue a certificate of title to a purchaser under subsection (f), (f-5), or (f-10) of this Section, unless the person from whom the vehicle has been repossessed by the lienholder is shown to be the last registered owner of the motor vehicle. The Secretary of State may provide by rule for the standards to be followed by a lienholder in assigning and transferring certificates of title with respect to repossessed vehicles.

(f-20) If applying for a salvage certificate or a junking certificate, the lienholder shall within 20 days make an application to the Secretary of State for a salvage certificate or a junking certificate, as set forth in this Code. The Secretary of State shall not issue a salvage certificate or a junking certificate to such lienholder unless the person from whom such vehicle has been repossessed is shown to be the last registered owner of such motor vehicle and such lienholder establishes to the satisfaction of the Secretary of State that he is entitled to such salvage certificate or junking certificate. The Secretary of State may provide by rule for the standards to be followed by a lienholder in order to obtain a salvage certificate or junking certificate for a repossessed vehicle.

(f-25) If the interest of an owner in a mobile home, as defined in the Mobile Home Local Services Tax Act,[6] passes to another under the provisions of the Mobile Home Local Services Tax Enforcement Act, [7] the transferee shall promptly mail or deliver to the Secretary of State (i) the last certificate of title, if available, (ii) a certified copy of the court order ordering the transfer of title, and (iii) an application for certificate of title.

(g) A person holding a certificate of title whose interest in the vehicle has been extinguished or transferred other than by voluntary transfer shall mail or deliver the certificate, within 20 days upon request of the Secretary of State. The delivery of the certificate pursuant to the request of the Secretary of State does not affect the rights of the person surrendering the certificate, and the action of the Secretary of State in issuing a new certificate of title as provided herein is not conclusive upon the rights of an owner or lienholder named in the old certificate.

(h) The Secretary of State may decline to process any application for a transfer of an interest in a vehicle hereunder if any fees or taxes due under this Act from the transferor or the transferee have not been paid upon reasonable notice and demand.

(i) The Secretary of State shall not be held civilly or criminally liable to any person because any purported transferor may not have had the power or authority to make a transfer of any interest in any vehicle or because a certificate of title issued in error is subsequently used to commit a fraudulent act.

P.A. 76-1586, § 3-114, eff. July 1, 1970. Amended by P.A. 77-641, § 1, eff. Aug. 4, 1971; P.A. 78-286, § 1, eff. Aug. 13, 1973; P.A. 78-491, § 1, eff. Oct. 1, 1973; P.A. 78-1297, § 30, eff. March 4, 1975; P.A. 81-445, § 1, eff. Jan. 1, 1980; P.A. 83-388, § 53, eff. Sept. 16, 1983; P.A. 83-449, § 1, eff. Jan. 1, 1984; P.A. 83-706, § 41, eff. Sept. 23, 1983; P.A. 83-1362, Art. II, § 99, eff. Sept. 11, 1984; P.A. 83-1473, § 1, eff. Jan. 1, 1985; P.A. 84-1308, Art. III, § 38, eff. Aug. 25, 1986; P.A. 84-1390, § 3, eff. Sept. 18, 1986; P.A. 85-1396, § 2, eff. Sept. 2, 1988; P.A. 87-1225, § 2, eff. Dec. 22, 1992; P.A. 90-212,

§ 5, eff. Jan. 1, 1998; P.A. 90-665, § 45, eff. Jan. 1, 1999; P.A. 91-893, § 30, eff. July 1, 2001; P.A. 92-807, § 910, eff. Jan. 1, 2003.

Formerly Ill.Rev.Stat.1991, ch. 95 ½, ¶ 3-114.

[1] 755 ILCS 5/1-1 et seq.

[2] 810 ILCS 5/1-101 et seq.

[3] 810 ILCS 5/9-623.

[4] 810 ILCS 5/9-611.

[5] 810 ILCS 5/9-101 et seq.

[6] 35 ILCS 515/1 et seq.

[7] 35 ILCS 516/1 et seq.

5/3-114.1. Transfers to and from charitable organizations

§ 3-114.1. Transfers to and from charitable organizations. When a charitable not-for-profit organization that is exempt from federal income taxation under Section 501(c)(3) of the Internal Revenue Code [1] becomes the recipient of a motor vehicle by means of a donation from an individual, the organization need not send the certificate of title to the Secretary of State. Upon transferring the motor vehicle, the organization shall promptly and within 20 days execute the reassignment to reflect the transfer from the organization to the purchaser. The organization is specifically authorized to complete and execute the space reserved in the certificate of title for a dealer reassignment, not withstanding that the organization is not a licensed dealer. Nothing in this Section shall be construed to require the organization to become a licensed vehicle dealer.

P.A. 76-1586, § 3-114.1, added by P.A. 92-495, § 5, eff. Jan. 1, 2002.

[1] 25 U.S.C.A. § 501.

5/3-115. Fees—Registration cards—License plates

§ 3-115. Fees—Registration cards—License plates. (a) An application for a certificate of title shall be accompanied by an application for, or a transfer of, registration of the vehicle.

(b) An application for the naming of a lienholder or his assignee on a certificate of title shall be accompanied by the required fee when mailed or delivered to the Secretary of State.

(c) A transferor of a vehicle, other than a dealer transferring a new vehicle, shall deliver to the transferee at the time of the delivery of possession of the vehicle the properly assigned certificate of title of this vehicle.

(d) All applications shall be accompanied with the required fee or tax.

P.A. 76-1586, § 3-115, eff. July 1, 1970. Amended by P.A. 78-858, § 1, eff. Jan. 1, 1974; P.A. 81-557, § 1, eff. Jan. 1, 1980; P.A. 83-1473, § 1, eff. Jan. 1, 1985.

Formerly Ill.Rev.Stat.1991, ch. 95 ½, ¶ 3-115.

5/3-116. When Secretary of State to issue a certificate of title

§ 3-116. When Secretary of State to issue a certificate of title. (a) The Secretary of State, upon receipt of a properly assigned certificate of title, with an application for a certificate of title, the required fee and any other documents required by law, shall issue a new certificate of title in the name of the transferee as owner and mail it to the first lienholder named in it or, if none, to the owner or owner's designee.

(b) The Secretary of State, upon receipt of an application for a new certificate of title by a transferee other than by voluntary transfer, with proof of the transfer, the required fee and any other documents required by law, shall issue a new certificate of title in the name of the transferee as owner.

(c) Any person, firm or corporation, who shall knowingly possess, buy, sell, exchange or give away, or offer to buy, sell, exchange or give away the certificate of title to any motor vehicle which is a junk or salvage, or who shall fail to surrender the certificate of title to the Secretary of State as required under the provisions of this Section and Section 3-117.2, shall be guilty of Class 3 felony.

(d) The Secretary of State shall file and retain for four (4) years a record of every surrendered certificate of title or proof of ownership accepted by the Secretary of State, the file to be maintained so as to permit the tracing of title of the vehicle designated therein.

(e) The Secretary of State, upon receipt of an application for corrected certificate of title, with the original title, the required fee and any other required documents, shall issue a corrected certificate of title in the name of the owner and mail it to the first lienholder named in it or, if none, to the owner or owner's designee.

(f) The Secretary of State, upon receipt of a certified copy of a court order awarding ownership to an applicant along with an application for a certificate of title and the required fee, shall issue a certificate of title to the applicant.

P.A. 76-1586, § 3-116, eff. July 1, 1970. Amended by P.A. 78-491, § 1, eff. Oct. 1, 1973; P.A. 81-557, § 1, eff. Jan. 1, 1980; P.A. 85-1204, § 1, eff. Aug. 26, 1988; P.A. 85-1396, § 2, eff. Sept. 2, 1988; P.A. 86-820, Art. II, § 2-8, eff. Sept. 7, 1989; P.A. 90-212, § 5, eff. Jan. 1, 1998.

Formerly Ill.Rev.Stat.1991, ch. 95 ½, ¶ 3-116.

5/3-117. § 3-117. Repealed by P.A. 83-1473, § 2, eff. Jan. 1, 1985

5/3-117.1. When junking certificates or salvage certificates must be obtained

§ 3-117.1. When junking certificates or salvage certificates must be obtained.

(a) Except as provided in Chapter 4 of this Code,[1] a person who possesses a junk vehicle shall within 15 days cause the certificate of title, salvage certificate, certificate of purchase, or a similarly acceptable out of state document of ownership to be surrendered to the Secretary of State along with an application for a junking certificate, except as provided in Section 3-117.2, whereupon the Secretary of State shall issue to such a person a junking certificate, which shall authorize the holder thereof to possess, transport, or, by an endorsement, transfer ownership in such junked vehicle, and a certificate of title shall not again be issued for such vehicle.

A licensee who possesses a junk vehicle and a Certificate of Title, Salvage Certificate, Certificate of Purchase, or a similarly acceptable out-of-state document of ownership for such junk vehicle, may transport the junk vehicle to another licensee prior to applying for or obtaining a junking certificate, by executing a uniform invoice. The licensee transferor shall furnish a copy of the uniform invoice to the licensee transferee at the time of transfer. In any case, the licensee transferor shall apply for a junking certificate in conformance with Section 3-117.1 of this Chapter. The following information shall be contained on a uniform invoice:

(1) The business name, address and dealer license number of the person disposing of the vehicle, junk vehicle or vehicle cowl;

(2) The name and address of the person acquiring the vehicle, junk vehicle or vehicle cowl, and if that person is a dealer, the Illinois or out-of-state dealer license number of that dealer;

(3) The date of the disposition of the vehicle, junk vehicle or vehicle cowl;

(4) The year, make, model, color and description of each vehicle, junk vehicle or vehicle cowl disposed of by such person;

(5) The manufacturer's vehicle identification number, Secretary of State identification number or Illinois Department of State Police number, for each vehicle, junk vehicle or vehicle cowl part disposed of by such person;

(6) The printed name and legible signature of the person or agent disposing of the vehicle, junk vehicle or vehicle cowl; and

(7) The printed name and legible signature of the person accepting delivery of the vehicle, junk vehicle or vehicle cowl.

The Secretary of State may certify a junking manifest in a form prescribed by the Secretary of State that reflects those vehicles for which junking certificates have been applied or issued. A junking manifest may be issued to any person and it shall constitute evidence of ownership for the vehicle listed upon it. A junking manifest may be transferred only to a person licensed under Section 5–301 of this Code as a scrap processor. A junking manifest will allow the transportation of those vehicles to a scrap processor prior to receiving the junk certificate from the Secretary of State.

(b) An application for a salvage certificate shall be submitted to the Secretary of State in any of the following situations:

(1) When an insurance company makes a payment of damages on a total loss claim for a vehicle, the insurance company shall be deemed to be the owner of such vehicle and the vehicle shall be considered to be salvage except that ownership of (i) a vehicle that has incurred only hail damage that does not affect the operational safety of the vehicle or (ii) any vehicle 9 model years of age or older may, by agreement between the registered owner and the insurance company, be retained by the registered owner of such vehicle. The insurance company shall promptly deliver or mail within 20 days the certificate of title along with proper application and fee to the Secretary of State, and a salvage certificate shall be issued in the name of the insurance company. An insurer making payment of damages on a total loss claim for the theft of a vehicle may exchange the salvage certificate for a certificate of title if the vehicle is recovered without damage. In such a situation, the insurer shall fill out and sign a form prescribed by the Secretary of State which contains an affirmation under penalty of perjury that the vehicle was recovered without damage and the Secretary of State may, by rule or regulation, require photographs to be submitted.

(2) When a vehicle the ownership of which has been transferred to any person through a certificate of purchase from acquisition of the vehicle at an auction, other dispositions as set forth in Sections 4–208 and 4–209 of this Code, a lien arising under Section 18a–501 of this Code, or a public sale under the Abandoned Mobile Home Act[2] shall be deemed salvage or junk at the option of the purchaser. The person acquiring such vehicle in such manner shall promptly deliver or mail, within 20 days after the acquisition of the vehicle, the certificate of purchase, the proper application and fee, and, if the vehicle is an abandoned mobile home under the Abandoned Mobile Home Act, a certification from a local law enforcement agency that the vehicle was purchased or acquired at a public sale under the Abandoned Mobile Home Act to the Secretary of State and a salvage certificate or junking certificate shall be issued in the name of that person. The salvage certificate or junking certificate issued by the Secretary of State under this Section shall be free of any lien that existed against the vehicle prior to the time the vehicle was acquired by the applicant under this Code.

(3) A vehicle which has been repossessed by a lienholder shall be considered to be salvage only when the repossessed vehicle, on the date of repossession by the lienholder, has sustained damage by collision, fire, theft, rust corrosion, or other means so that the cost of repairing such damage, including labor, would be greater than 33 ⅓% of its fair market value without such damage. If the lienholder determines that such vehicle is damaged in excess of 33 ⅓% of such fair market value, the lienholder shall, before sale, transfer or assignment of the vehicle, make application for a salvage certificate, and shall submit with such application the proper fee and evidence of possession. If the facts required to be shown in subsection (f) of Section 3–114 are satisfied, the Secretary of State shall issue a salvage certificate in the name of the lienholder making the application. In any case wherein the vehicle repossessed is not damaged in excess of 33 ⅓% of its fair market value, the lienholder shall comply with the requirements of subsections (f), (f–5), and (f–10) of Section 3–114, except that the affidavit of repossession made by or on behalf of the lienholder shall also contain an affirmation under penalty of perjury that the vehicle on the date of sale is not damaged in excess of 33 ⅓% of its fair market value. If the facts required to be shown in subsection (f) of Section 3–114 are satisfied, the Secretary of State shall issue a certificate of title as set forth in Section 3–116 of this Code. The Secretary of State may by rule or regulation require photographs to be submitted.

(4) A vehicle which is a part of a fleet of more than 5 commercial vehicles registered in this State or any other state or registered proportionately among several states shall be considered to be salvage when such vehicle has sustained damage by collision, fire, theft, rust, corrosion or similar means so that the cost of repairing such damage, including labor, would be greater than 33 ⅓% of the fair market value of the vehicle without such damage. If the owner of a fleet vehicle desires to sell, transfer, or assign his interest in such vehicle to a person within this State other than an insurance company licensed to do business within this State, and the owner determines that such vehicle, at the time of the proposed sale, transfer or assignment is damaged in excess of 33 ⅓% of its fair market value, the owner shall, before such sale, transfer or assignment, make application for a salvage certificate. The application shall contain with it evidence of possession of the vehicle. If the fleet vehicle at the time of its sale, transfer, or assignment is not damaged in excess of 33 ⅓% of its fair market value, the owner shall so state in a written affirmation on a form prescribed by the Secretary of State by rule or regulation. The Secretary of State may by rule or regulation require photographs to be submitted. Upon sale, transfer or assignment of the fleet vehicle the owner shall mail the affirmation to the Secretary of State.

(5) A vehicle that has been submerged in water to the point that rising water has reached over the door sill and has entered the passenger or trunk compartment is a

"flood vehicle". A flood vehicle shall be considered to be salvage only if the vehicle has sustained damage so that the cost of repairing the damage, including labor, would be greater than 33 ⅓% of the fair market value of the vehicle without that damage. The salvage certificate issued under this Section shall indicate the word "flood", and the word "flood" shall be conspicuously entered on subsequent titles for the vehicle. A person who possesses or acquires a flood vehicle that is not damaged in excess of 33 ⅓% of its fair market value shall make application for title in accordance with Section 3-116 of this Code, designating the vehicle as "flood" in a manner prescribed by the Secretary of State. The certificate of title issued shall indicate the word "flood", and the word "flood" shall be conspicuously entered on subsequent titles for the vehicle.

(c) Any person who without authority acquires, sells, exchanges, gives away, transfers or destroys or offers to acquire, sell, exchange, give away, transfer or destroy the certificate of title to any vehicle which is a junk or salvage vehicle shall be guilty of a Class 3 felony.

(d) Any person who knowingly fails to surrender to the Secretary of State a certificate of title, salvage certificate, certificate of purchase or a similarly acceptable out-of-state document of ownership as required under the provisions of this Section is guilty of a Class A misdemeanor for a first offense and a Class 4 felony for a subsequent offense; except that a person licensed under this Code who violates paragraph (5) of subsection (b) of this Section is guilty of a business offense and shall be fined not less than $1,000 nor more than $5,000 for a first offense and is guilty of a Class 4 felony for a second or subsequent violation.

(e) Any vehicle which is salvage or junk may not be driven or operated on roads and highways within this State. A violation of this subsection is a Class A misdemeanor. A salvage vehicle displaying valid special plates issued under Section 3-601(b) of this Code, which is being driven to or from an inspection conducted under Section 3-308 of this Code, is exempt from the provisions of this subsection. A salvage vehicle for which a short term permit has been issued under Section 3-307 of this Code is exempt from the provisions of this subsection for the duration of the permit.

P.A. 76-1586, § 3-117.1, added by P.A. 83-1473, § 1, eff. Jan. 1, 1985. Amended by P.A. 84-1302, § 1, eff. Jan. 1, 1987; P.A. 84-1304, § 1, eff. Jan. 1, 1987; P.A. 85-311, § 1, eff. Sept. 10, 1987; P.A. 85-572, § 1, eff. Sept. 18, 1987; P.A. 85-1204, § 1, eff. Aug. 26, 1988; P.A. 85-1209, Art. II, § 2-51, eff. Aug. 30, 1988; P.A. 85-1440, Art. II, § 2-54, eff. Feb. 1, 1989; P.A. 86-566, § 1, eff. Jan. 1, 1990; P.A. 86-1209, § 1, eff. Jan. 1, 1991; P.A. 86-1214, § 1, eff. Jan. 1, 1991; P.A. 86-1475, Art. 2, § 2-25, eff. Jan. 10, 1991; P.A. 87-1225, § 2, eff. Dec. 22, 1992; P.A. 88-516, § 95, eff. July 1, 1994; P.A. 88-685, § 5, eff. Jan. 24, 1995; P.A. 89-669, § 10, eff. Jan. 1, 1997; P.A. 90-665, § 45, eff. Jan. 1, 1999; P.A. 92-751, § 5, eff. Aug. 2, 2002.

Formerly Ill.Rev.Stat.1991, ch. 95 ½, ¶ 3-117.1.

[1] 625 ILCS 5/4-100 et seq.

[2] 210 ILCS 117/1 et seq.

5/3-117.2. Junk Vehicle Notification

§ 3-117.2. Junk Vehicle Notification. Beginning July 1, 1989 a person licensed as a scrap processor pursuant to Section 5-301 of this Code who acquires a properly assigned Certificate of Title, a Salvage Certificate, a Certificate of Purchase, or a similarly acceptable out-of-state document of ownership pursuant to Section 5-401.3 of this Code, shall within 15 days of acquiring such document, submit it to the Secretary of State along with a Junk Vehicle Notification, the form and manner for which shall be as prescribed by Secretary of State rule or regulation. A scrap processor who acquires the above named documents of ownership pursuant to Section 5-401.3 shall not be required to apply for or obtain a junking certificate. The information contained on a Junk Vehicle Notification shall be duly recorded by the Secretary of State upon the receipt of such Notification. The Secretary of State shall not again issue a Certificate of Title or Salvage Certificate for any vehicle listed on a Junk Vehicle Notification.

P.A. 76-1586, § 3-117.2, added by P.A. 85-1204, § 1, eff. Aug. 26, 1988.

Formerly Ill.Rev.Stat.1991, ch. 95 ½, ¶ 3-117.2.

5/3-118. Application for salvage or junking certificate; contents

§ 3-118. Application for salvage or junking certificate; contents. (a) An application for a salvage certificate or junking certificate shall be made upon the forms prescribed by the Secretary of State and contain:

1. The name and address of the owner;
2. A description of the vehicle including, so far as the following data exists: its make, year-model, identifying number, type of body, whether new or used;
3. The date of purchase by applicant; and
4. Any further information reasonably required by the Secretary of State.

(b) The application for salvage certificate must also contain the current odometer reading and that the stated odometer reading is one of the following: actual mileage, not the actual mileage or mileage is in excess of its mechanical limits.

(c) A salvage certificate may be assigned to any person licensed under this Act as a rebuilder, automotive parts recycler, scrap processor or an out-of-state salvage vehicle buyer. A junking certificate may be assigned to anyone. The provisions for reassignment by dealers under paragraph (a) of Section 3-113 shall apply to salvage certificates, except as provided in Section 3-117.2. A salvage certificate may be reassigned to one other person licensed under this Act.

P.A. 76-1586, § 3-118, eff. July 1, 1970. Amended by P.A. 78-858, § 1, eff. Jan. 1, 1974; P.A. 78-1205, § 1, eff. Sept. 5, 1974; P.A. 78-1297, § 58, eff. March 4, 1975; P.A. 83-1473, § 1, eff. Jan. 1, 1985; P.A. 84-1302, § 1, eff. Jan. 1, 1987; P.A. 84-1304, § 1, eff. Jan. 1, 1987; P.A. 85-572, § 1, eff. Sept. 18, 1987; P.A. 85-951, § 1, eff. July 1, 1988; P.A. 85-1204, § 1, eff. Aug. 26, 1988; P.A. 85-1209, Art. II, § 2-51, eff. Aug. 30, 1988; P.A. 86-444, § 1, eff. Jan. 1, 1990; P.A. 87-206, § 1, eff. Sept. 3, 1991.

Formerly Ill.Rev.Stat.1991, ch. 95 ½, ¶ 3-118.

5/3-118.1. Title certificates for salvaged vehicles; total loss from theft

§ 3-118.1. Whenever a certificate of title is issued for a vehicle with respect to which a salvage certificate has been previously issued, the new certificate of title shall bear the notation "REBUILT". However, insurance companies or persons licensed under Section 5-301 who are also licensed as a used vehicle dealer under Section 5-102 of this Code may exchange a salvage certificate for a certificate of title which does not bear the notation "REBUILT" when there is submitted with the application satisfactory proof that the salvage certificate was obtained because of a claim of total loss from theft and the vehicle was recovered without structural damage caused by collision, fire, flood, theft, rust, or corrosion. The Secretary may adopt rules governing the issuance of titles authorized under this Section.

P.A. 76–1586, § 3–118.1, added by P.A. 81–988, § 1, eff. Jan. 1, 1980. Amended by P.A. 83–306, § 1, eff. Jan. 1, 1984; P.A. 86–1179, § 2, eff. Aug. 17, 1990; P.A. 89–189, § 5, eff. Jan. 1, 1996.

Formerly Ill.Rev.Stat.1991, ch. 95 ½, ¶ 3–118.1.

5/3–119 to 5/3–121. §§ 3–119 to 3–121. Repealed by P.A. 85–1374, § 2, eff. Jan. 1, 1989

ARTICLE II. SECURITY INTERESTS

Section

5/3–201. Excepted liens and security interests

§ 3–201. Excepted liens and security interests.

This Article does not apply to or affect:

(a) A lien given by statute or rule of law to a supplier of services or materials for the vehicle;

(b) A lien given by statute to the United States, this State or any political subdivision of this State, except liens on trailer coaches and mobile homes for public assistance, as provided in Section 3–12 (now repealed) of the Illinois Public Aid Code.[1]

(c) A security interest in a vehicle created by a manufacturer or dealer who holds the vehicle for sale, but a buyer in the ordinary course of trade from the manufacturer or dealer takes free of the security interest.

P.A. 76–1586, § 3–201, eff. July 1, 1970. Amended by P.A. 90–655, § 153, eff. July 30, 1998.

Formerly Ill.Rev.Stat.1991, ch. 95 ½, ¶ 3–201.

[1] 305 ILCS 5/3–12 (repealed).

5/3–201.1. Terminal rent adjustment clause leases

§ 3–201.1. Terminal rent adjustment clause leases. In the case of motor vehicles or trailers, a transaction does not create a sale or a security interest merely because it provides that the rental price is permitted or required to be adjusted under the agreement either upward or downward by reference to the amount realized upon sale or other disposition of the motor vehicle or trailer.

P.A. 76–1586, § 3–201.1, added by P.A. 87–493, § 5, eff. Jan. 1, 1992.

Formerly Ill.Rev.Stat.1991, ch. 95 ½, ¶ 3–201.1.

5/3–202. Perfection of security interest

§ 3–202. Perfection of security interest.

(a) Unless excepted by Section 3–201, a security interest in a vehicle of a type for which a certificate of title is required is not valid against subsequent transferees or lienholders of the vehicle unless perfected as provided in this Act.

(b) A security interest is perfected by the delivery to the Secretary of State of the existing certificate of title, if any, an application for a certificate of title containing the name and address of the lienholder and the required fee. The security interest is perfected as of the time of its creation if the delivery to the Secretary of State is completed within 21 days after the creation of the security interest or receipt by the new lienholder of the existing certificate of title from a prior lienholder or licensed dealer, otherwise as of the time of the delivery.

(c) If a vehicle is subject to a security interest when brought into this State, the validity of the security interest is determined by the law of the jurisdiction where the vehicle was when the security interest attached, subject to the following:

1. If the parties understood at the time the security interest attached that the vehicle would be kept in this State and it was brought into this State within 30 days thereafter for purposes other than transportation through this State, the validity of the security interest in this State is determined by the law of this State.

2. If the security interest was perfected under the law of the jurisdiction where the vehicle was when the security interest attached, the following rules apply:

(A) If the name of the lienholder is shown on an existing certificate of title issued by that jurisdiction, his security interest continues perfected in this State.

(B) If the name of the lienholder is not shown on an existing certificate of title issued by that jurisdiction, a security interest may be perfected by the lienholder delivering to the Secretary of State the prescribed notice and by payment of the required fee. Such security interest is perfected as of the time of delivery of the prescribed notice and payment of the required fee.

3. If the security interest was not perfected under the law of the jurisdiction where the vehicle was when the security interest attached, it may be perfected in this State; in that case perfection dates from the time of perfection in this State.

4. A security interest may be perfected under paragraph 3 of this subsection either as provided in subsection (b) or by the lienholder delivering to the Secretary of State a notice of security interest in the form the Secretary of State prescribes and the required fee.

P.A. 76–1586, § 3–202, eff. July 1, 1970. Amended by P.A. 81–557, § 1, eff. Jan. 1, 1980; P.A. 91–893, § 31, eff. July 6, 2000.

Formerly Ill.Rev.Stat.1991, ch. 95 ½, ¶ 3–202.

5/3–203. Security interest

§ 3–203. Security interest. If an owner creates a security interest in a vehicle:

(a) The owner shall immediately execute the application, in the space provided therefor on the certificate of title or on a separate form the Secretary of State prescribes, to name the lienholder on the certificate, showing the name and address of the lienholder and cause the certificate, application and the required fee to be delivered to the lienholder.

(b) The lienholder shall immediately cause the certificate, application and the required fee to be mailed or delivered to the Secretary of State.

(c) Upon request of the owner or subordinate lienholder, a lienholder in possession of the certificate of title shall either mail or deliver the certificate to the subordinate lienholder for delivery to the Secretary of State or, upon receipt from the subordinate lienholder of the owner's application and the required fee, mail or deliver them to the Secretary of State with the certificate. The delivery of the certificate does not affect the rights of the first lienholder under his security agreement.

(d) Upon receipt of the certificate of title, application and the required fee, the Secretary of State shall issue a new certificate containing the name and address of the new lienholder, and mail the certificate to the first lienholder named in it.

P.A. 76-1586, § 3-203, eff. July 1, 1970. Amended by P.A. 81-557, § 1, eff. Jan. 1, 1980; P.A. 85-511, § 1, eff. Jan. 1, 1988.

Formerly Ill.Rev.Stat.1991, ch. 95 ½, ¶ 3-203.

5/3-204. Assignment by lienholder

§ 3-204. Assignment by lienholder. (a) A lienholder may assign, absolutely or otherwise, his security interest in the vehicle to a person other than the owner without affecting the interest of the owner or the validity of the security interest, but any person without notice of the assignment is protected in dealing with the lienholder as the holder of the security interest and the lienholder remains liable for any obligations as lienholder until the assignee is named as lienholder on the certificate.

(b) The assignee may, but need not to perfect the assignment, have the certificate of title issued with the assignee named as lienholder, upon delivering to the Secretary of State the certificate and an assignment by the lienholder named in the certificate in the form the Secretary of State prescribes.

P.A. 76-1586, § 3-204, eff. July 1, 1970. Amended by P.A. 85-511, § 1, eff. Jan. 1, 1988.

Formerly Ill.Rev.Stat.1991, ch. 95 ½, ¶ 3-204.

5/3-205. Release of security interest

§ 3-205. Release of security interest. (a) Upon the satisfaction of a security interest in a vehicle for which the certificate of title is in the possession of the lienholder, he shall, within ten (10) days after demand and, in any event, within thirty (30) days, execute a release of his security interest, and mail or deliver the certificate and release to the next lienholder named therein, or, if none, to the owner or any person who delivers to the lienholder an authorization from the owner to receive the certificate. If the owner desires a new certificate reflecting no lien, the certificate and release from the lienholder may be submitted to the Secretary of State, along with the prescribed application and required fee, for issuance of that new certificate.

(b) Upon the satisfaction of a security interest in a vehicle for which the certificate of title is in the possession of a prior lienholder, the lienholder whose security interest is satisfied shall within ten (10) days after demand and, in any event, within thirty (30) days execute a release and deliver the release to the owner or any person who delivers to the lienholder an authorization from the owner to receive it. The lienholder in possession of the certificate of title may either deliver the certificate to the owner, or the person authorized by him, for delivery to the Secretary of State, or, upon receipt of the release, may mail or may deliver the certificate and release, along with prescribed application and require fee, to the Secretary of State, who shall issue a new certificate.

P.A. 76-1586, § 3-205, eff. July 1, 1970. Amended by P.A. 81-557, § 1, eff. Jan. 1, 1980.

Formerly Ill.Rev.Stat.1991, ch. 95 ½, ¶ 3-205.

5/3-206. Duty of lienholder

§ 3-206. Duty of lienholder. A lienholder named in a certificate of title shall, upon written request of the owner or of another lienholder named on the certificate, disclose any pertinent information as to his security agreement and the indebtedness secured by it.

P.A. 76-1586, § 3-206, eff. July 1, 1970.

Formerly Ill.Rev.Stat.1991, ch. 95 ½, ¶ 3-206.

5/3-207. Exclusiveness of procedure

§ 3-207. Exclusiveness of procedure. The method provided in this act of perfecting and giving notice of security interests subject to this act is exclusive. Security interests subject to this act are hereby exempted from the provisions of law which otherwise require or relate to the recording or filing of instruments creating or evidencing security interests in vehicles including chattel mortgages and conditional sale agreements.

P.A. 76-1586, § 3-207, eff. July 1, 1970.

Formerly Ill.Rev.Stat.1991, ch. 95 ½, ¶ 3-207.

5/3-208. Suspension or revocation of certificates

§ 3-208. Suspension or revocation of certificates. (a) The Secretary of State may suspend or revoke a certificate of title, upon notice and reasonable opportunity to be heard in accordance with Section 2-118, when authorized by any other provision of law or if he finds:

1. The certificate of title was fraudulently procured or erroneously issued, or

2. The vehicle has been scrapped, dismantled or destroyed.

(b) Suspension or revocation of a certificate of title does not, in itself, affect the validity of a security interest noted on it.

(c) When the Secretary of State suspends or revokes a certificate of title, the owner or person in possession of it shall, immediately upon receiving notice of the suspension or revocation, mail or deliver the certificate to the Secretary of State.

(d) The Secretary of State may seize and impound any certificate of title which has been suspended or revoked.

P.A. 76-1586, § 3-208, eff. July 1, 1970.

Formerly Ill.Rev.Stat.1991, ch. 95 ½, ¶ 3-208.

5/3-209. Powers of Secretary of State

§ 3-209. Powers of Secretary of State. (a) The Secretary of State shall prescribe and provide suitable forms of applications, certificates of title, notices of security interests, and all other notices and forms necessary to carry out the provisions of this chapter.

(b) The Secretary of State may:

1. Make necessary investigations to procure information required to carry out the provisions of this Act;

2. Assign a new identifying number to a vehicle if it has none, or its identifying number is destroyed or obliterated, or its motor is changed, and shall either issue a new certificate

of title showing the new identifying number or make an appropriate endorsement on the original certificate.

P.A. 76–1586, § 3–209, eff. July 1, 1970.

Formerly Ill.Rev.Stat.1991, ch. 95 ½, ¶ 3–209.

5/3–210. Court review

§ 3–210. Court review. A person aggrieved by an act or omission to act of the Secretary of State under this Article is also entitled to a review thereof by the Circuit Court of Sangamon County in accordance with the Administrative Review Law, as amended.[1]

P.A. 76–1586, § 3–210, eff. July 1, 1970. Amended by P.A. 82–783, Art. XI, § 140, eff. July 13, 1982.

Formerly Ill.Rev.Stat.1991, ch. 95 ½, ¶ 3–210.

1 735 ILCS 5/3–101 et seq.

ARTICLE III. CERTIFICATE OF TITLE—REBUILT VEHICLES

Date Effective

Article III was added by P.A. 83–1473, § 1, eff. Jan. 1, 1985.

5/3–301. New certificate of title for rebuilt vehicle

§ 3–301. New certificate of title for rebuilt vehicle. (a) For vehicles 8 model years of age or newer, the Secretary of State shall issue a new certificate of title to any rebuilt vehicle or any vehicle which previously had been titled as salvage in this State or any other jurisdiction upon the successful inspection of the vehicle in accordance with Section 3–308 of this Article.

(b) Vehicles more than 8 model years old shall not be required to complete a successful inspection required under Section 3–308 of this Code before being issued a new certificate of title as provided under this Section.

(c) Vehicles designated as flood vehicles that have sustained damage greater than 33⅓% of their fair market value with that damage shall be required to complete a successful inspection required under Section 3–308 of this Code before being issued a new certificate of title provided under paragraph (5), subsection (b) of Section 3–117.1.

P.A. 76–1586, § 3–301, added by P.A. 83–1473, § 1, eff. Jan. 1, 1985. Amended by P.A. 84–1302, § 1, eff. Jan. 1, 1987; P.A. 84–1304, § 1, eff. Jan. 1, 1987; P.A. 88–685, § 5, eff. Jan. 24, 1995; P.A. 89–669, § 10, eff. Jan. 1, 1997.

Formerly Ill.Rev.Stat.1991, ch. 95 ½, ¶ 3–301.

5/3–302. Application for title; contents

§ 3–302. Application for title; contents. Every application for a certificate of title for a rebuilt vehicle shall be made upon a form prescribed by the Secretary of State, and shall include the following:

1. The name, residence and mailing address of the owner;

2. A description of the vehicle including, so far as the following data exists: its make, year-model, identifying number, type of body, whether new or used, and as to vehicles of the second division, whether for-hire, not-for-hire, or both for-hire and not-for-hire;

3. The date of purchase by applicant, the name and address of the person from whom the vehicle was acquired and the names and addresses of any lienholders in the order of their priority;

4. The current odometer reading at the time of transfer and that the stated odometer reading is one of the following: actual mileage, not the actual mileage or mileage is in excess of its mechanical limits; and

5. Any further information the Secretary of State reasonably requires to identify the vehicle and to enable him to determine whether the owner is entitled to a certificate of title and the existence or nonexistence of security interests in the vehicle.

P.A. 76–1586, § 3–302, added by P.A. 83–1473, § 1, eff. Jan. 1, 1985. Amended by P.A. 85–951, § 1, eff. July 1, 1988; P.A. 86–444, § 1, eff. Jan. 1, 1990; P.A. 87–206, § 1, eff. Sept. 3, 1991; P.A. 92–651, § 77, eff. July 11, 2002.

Formerly Ill.Rev.Stat.1991, ch. 95 ½, ¶ 3–302.

5/3–303. Application for title—attachments

§ 3–303. Application for title—attachments. Every application for a certificate of title for a rebuilt vehicle shall be accompanied by the following:

1. The salvage certificate or out-of-state title certificate previously issued for the rebuilt vehicle;

2. Bills of sale and other documents evidencing the acquisition of all essential parts used to rebuild the vehicle;

3. Photographs of the rebuilt vehicle if required by rule of the Secretary of State;

4. A Certificate of Safety furnished by the Department of Transportation as set forth in Section 13–109; and

5. A listing of all replaced essential parts of the rebuilt vehicle, and the identification number of the vehicle or vehicles from which the essential parts originated.

P.A. 76–1586, § 3–303, added by P.A. 83–1473, § 1, eff. Jan. 1, 1985. Amended by P.A. 85–572, § 1, eff. Sept. 18, 1987; P.A. 85–951, § 1, eff. July 1, 1988; P.A. 85–1209, Art. II, § 2–51, eff. Aug. 30, 1988.

Formerly Ill.Rev.Stat.1991, ch. 95 ½, ¶ 3–303.

P.A. 85–1209, the First 1988 Revisory Act, provides in Art. II, for the nonsubstantive revision or renumbering or repeal of certain sections of Acts of the 85th General Assembly through P.A. 85–1014, and corrects errors, revises cross-references and deletes obsolete text in such sections.

5/3–304. Application for title—affirmation

§ 3–304. Application for title—affirmation. The applicant applying for a certificate of title for a rebuilt vehicle shall sign a written affirmation which states the following:

1. He personally rebuilt the vehicle, personally supervised its rebuilding or contracted for rebuilding with a licensed rebuilder;

2. He personally inspected the completed vehicle, and it complies with all safety requirements set forth in this Code and any regulations promulgated thereunder by the Secretary of State;

3. The identification numbers of the rebuilt vehicle and its parts have not, to the knowledge of the applicant, been removed, destroyed, falsified, altered or defaced;

4. The salvage certificate or out-of-state title certificate attached to the application has not, to the knowledge of the applicant, been forged, falsified, altered or counterfeited; and

5. All information contained on the application and its attachments is true and correct to the knowledge of the applicant.

P.A. 76–1586, § 3–304, added by P.A. 83–1473, § 1, eff. Jan. 1, 1985. Amended by P.A. 85–572, § 1, eff. Sept. 18, 1987.

Formerly Ill.Rev.Stat.1991, ch. 95 ½, ¶ 3–304.

5/3–305. Inspection fee

§ 3–305. Inspection fee. The fee for the inspection of a rebuilt vehicle shall be $94. All such fees received by the Secretary of State shall be deposited into the Road Fund.

P.A. 76–1586, § 3–305 added by P.A. 83–1473, § 1, eff. Jan. 1, 1985. Amended by P.A. 84–1302, § 1, eff. Jan. 1, 1987; P.A. 84–1304, § 1, eff. Jan. 1, 1987; P.A. 91–37, § 40, eff. July 1, 1999.

Formerly Ill.Rev.Stat.1991, ch. 95 ½, ¶ 3–305.

5/3–306. Retention of documents

§ 3–306. Retention of documents. The original documents required to be submitted to the Secretary of State pursuant to Sections 3–301 through 3–305 shall be retained by the Secretary of State for a period determined by Secretary of State by rule or regulation.

P.A. 76–1586, § 3–306, added by P.A. 83–1473, § 1, eff. Jan. 1, 1985. Amended by P.A. 83–1528, Art. II, § 24, eff. Jan. 17, 1985.

Formerly Ill.Rev.Stat.1991, ch. 95 ½, ¶ 3–306.

5/3–307. Short term permit

§ 3–307. Short term permit. The Secretary of State shall issue at no charge a short term permit for any vehicle for which an application for a certificate of title has been made under this Article and which must be driven on the roads and highways of this State to a place of inspection.

P.A. 76–1586, § 3–307, added by P.A. 83–1473, § 1, eff. Jan. 1, 1985. Amended by P.A. 84–1302, § 1, eff. Jan. 1, 1987; P.A. 84–1304, § 1, eff. Jan. 1, 1987.

Formerly Ill.Rev.Stat.1991, ch. 95 ½, ¶ 3–307.

The amendments by P.A. 84–1302 and P.A. 84–1304 were identical.

5/3–308. Inspection of rebuilt vehicles

§ 3–308. Inspection of rebuilt vehicles.

(a) The Secretary of State shall inspect any vehicle 8 model years of age or newer for which an application for a certificate of title for a rebuilt vehicle will be submitted, or any foreign vehicle which is or may have been salvage as defined under the provisions of this Code.

(b) The inspection of the vehicle shall include an examination of the vehicle and its parts and of the application and proof of notification, if applicable, to determine that:

(1) the identification numbers of the vehicle or its parts have not been removed, falsified, altered, defaced, destroyed, or tampered with;

(2) all information contained in the application for a certificate of title is true and correct; and

(3) there are no indications that the vehicle or any of its parts have been stolen.

(c) The Secretary of State shall, by rule or regulation, carry out and implement the provisions contained in this Section.

(d) All fees received by the Secretary of State from the inspection of vehicles under this Section shall be applied towards the maintenance of the vehicle inspection program and the personnel costs required for the operation of such program.

P.A. 76–1586, § 3–308, added by P.A. 83–1473, § 1, eff. Jan. 1, 1985. Amended by P.A. 84–1302, § 1, eff. Jan. 1, 1987; P.A. 84–1304, § 1, eff. Jan. 1, 1987; P.A. 89–433, § 5, eff. Dec. 15, 1995.

Formerly Ill.Rev.Stat.1991, ch. 95 ½, ¶ 3–308.

ARTICLE IV. ORIGINAL AND RENEWAL OF REGISTRATION

5/3-400. Definition

§ 3-400. Definition. Notwithstanding the definition set forth in Chapter 1 of this Act,[1] for the purposes of this Article, the following words shall have the meaning ascribed to them as follows:

"Apportionable Fee" means any periodic recurring fee required for licensing or registering vehicles, such as, but not limited to, registration fees, license or weight fees.

"Apportionable Vehicle" means any vehicle, except recreational vehicles, vehicles displaying restricted plates, city pickup and delivery vehicles, buses used in transportation of chartered parties, and government owned vehicles that are used or intended for use in 2 or more member jurisdictions that allocate or proportionally register vehicles, in a fleet which is used for the transportation of persons for hire or the transportation of property and which has a gross vehicle weight in excess of 26,000 pounds; or has three or more axles regardless of weight; or is used in combination when the weight of such combination exceeds 26,000 pounds gross vehicle weight. Vehicles, or combinations having a gross vehicle weight of 26,000 pounds or less and two-axle vehicles may be proportionally registered at the option of such owner.

"Base Jurisdiction" means, for purposes of fleet registration, the jurisdiction where the registrant has an established place of business, where operational records of the fleet are maintained and where mileage is accrued by the fleet. In case a registrant operates more than one fleet, and maintains records for each fleet in different places, the "base jurisdiction" for a fleet shall be the jurisdiction where an established place of business is maintained, where records of the operation of that fleet are maintained and where mileage is accrued by that fleet.

"Operational Records" means documents supporting miles traveled in each jurisdiction and total miles traveled, such as fuel reports, trip leases, and logs.

Owner. A person who holds legal title of a motor vehicle, or in the event a motor vehicle is the subject of an agreement for the conditional sale or lease thereof with the right of purchase upon performance of the conditions stated in the agreement and with an immediate right of possession vested in the conditional vendee or lessee with right of purchase, or in the event a mortgagor of such motor vehicle is entitled to possession, or in the event a lessee of such motor vehicle is entitled to possession or control, then such conditional vendee or lessee with right of purchase or mortgagor or lessee is considered to be the owner for the purpose of this Act.

"Rental Owner" means an owner principally engaged, with respect to one or more rental fleets, in renting to others or offering for rental the vehicles of such fleets, without drivers.

"Restricted Plates" shall include but are not limited to dealer, manufacturer, transporter, farm, repossessor, and permanently mounted type plates. Vehicles displaying any of these type plates from a foreign jurisdiction that is a member of the International Registration Plan shall be granted reciprocity but shall be subject to the same limitations as similar plated Illinois registered vehicles.

P.A. 76-1586, § 3-400, eff. July 1, 1970. Amended by P.A. 79-1041, § 1, eff. Jan. 1, 1976; P.A. 81-1509, Art. II, § 71, eff. Sept. 26, 1980; P.A. 84-300, § 1, eff. Sept. 13, 1985; P.A. 87-1041, § 1, eff. Sept. 11, 1993; P.A. 89-571, § 5, eff. July 26, 1996; P.A. 90-89, § 15, eff. Jan. 1, 1998.

Formerly Ill.Rev.Stat.1991, ch. 95 ½, ¶ 3-400.

[1] 625 ILCS 5/1-100 et seq.

5/3-401. Effect of provisions

§ 3-401. Effect of provisions.

(a) It shall be unlawful for any person to violate any provision of this Chapter or to drive or move or for an owner knowingly to permit to be driven or moved upon any highway any vehicle of a type required to be registered hereunder which is not registered or for which the appropriate fee has not been paid when and as required hereunder, except that when application accompanied by proper fee has been made for registration of a vehicle it may be operated temporarily pending complete registration upon displaying a duplicate application duly verified or other evidence of such application or otherwise under rules and regulations promulgated by the Secretary of State.

(b) The appropriate fees required to be paid under the various provisions of this Act for registration of vehicles shall mean the fee or fees which would have been paid initially, if proper and timely application had been made to the Secretary of State for the appropriate registration required, whether such registration be a flat weight registration, a single trip permit, a reciprocity permit or a supplemental application to an original prorate application together with payment of fees due under the supplemental application for prorate decals.

(c) Effective October 1, 1984, no vehicle required to pay a Federal Highway Users Tax shall be registered unless proof of payment, in a form prescribed and approved by the Secretary of State, is submitted with the appropriate registration. Notwithstanding any other provision of this Code, failure of the applicant to comply with this paragraph shall be deemed grounds for the Secretary to refuse registration.

(d) Second division vehicles.

(1) A vehicle of the second division moved or operated within this State shall have had paid for it the appropriate registration fees and flat weight tax, as evidenced by the Illinois registration issued for that vehicle, for the gross weight of the vehicle and load being operated or moved within this State. Second division vehicles of foreign jurisdictions operated within this State under a single trip permit, fleet reciprocity plan, prorate registration plan, or apportional registration plan, instead of second division vehicle registration under Article VIII of this Chapter,[1] must have had paid for it the appropriate registration fees and flat weight tax in the base jurisdiction of that vehicle, as evidenced by the maximum gross weight shown on the foreign registration cards, plus any appropriate fees required under this Code.

(2) If a vehicle and load are operated in this State and the appropriate fees and taxes have not been paid or the vehicle and load exceed the registered gross weight for which the required fees and taxes have been paid by 2001 pounds or more, the operator or owner shall be fined as provided in Section 15-113 of this Code. However, an owner or operator shall not be subject to arrest under this subsection for any weight in excess of 80,000 pounds. Further, for any unregistered vehicle or vehicle displaying expired registration, no fine shall exceed the actual cost of what the appropriate registration for that vehicle and load should have been as established in subsection (a) of Section 3-815 of this Chapter regardless of the route traveled.

(3) Any person operating a legal combination of vehicles displaying valid registration shall not be considered in violation of the registration provision of this subsection unless the total gross weight of the combination exceeds the total licensed weight of the vehicles in the combination. The gross weight of a vehicle exempt from the registration

requirements of this Chapter shall not be included when determining the total gross weight of vehicles in combination.

(4) If the defendant claims that he or she had previously paid the appropriate Illinois registration fees and taxes for this vehicle before the alleged violation, the defendant shall have the burden of proving the existence of the payment by competent evidence. Proof of proper Illinois registration issued by the Secretary of State, or the appropriate registration authority from the foreign state, shall be the only competent evidence of payment.

P.A. 76-1586, § 3-401, eff. July 1, 1970. Amended by P.A. 77-1315, § 1, eff. Jan. 1, 1972; P.A. 77-2830, Art. 73, § 1, eff. Jan. 1, 1973; P.A. 79-1041, § 1, eff. Jan. 1, 1976; P.A. 80-911, § 1, eff. Oct. 1, 1977; P.A. 81-886, § 1, eff. July 1, 1980; P.A. 83-12, § 1, eff. July 1, 1983; P.A. 88-476, § 2, eff. July 1, 1994; P.A. 89-245, § 5, eff. Jan. 1, 1996.

Formerly Ill.Rev.Stat.1991, ch. 95 ½, ¶ 3-401.

1 625 ILCS 5/3-801 et seq.

Section 4 of P.A. 83-12, approved July 1, 1983, provided:

"Effective date. This Act takes effect as provided in this Section.

"The amendments to those portions of Sections 3-815(a), 3-818 and 3-819(b) of 'The Illinois Vehicle Code' in Section 1 of this Act which create the 'X', 'Z', 'MX', 'MZ', 'MM' and 'TN' registration classifications and the fees and taxes imposed for those classifications, the amendments to Sections 2-119, 3-401 and 3-802 of 'The Illinois Vehicle Code' in Section 1 of this Act, and the amendments to Chapter 15 of 'The Illinois Vehicle Code' in Section 1 of this Act take effect July 1, 1983.

"The remaining amendments to 'The Illinois Vehicle Code' in Section 1 of this Act take effect July 1, 1983 and apply beginning with the 1985 registration year, except that the amendments to Sections 3-813 through 3-816 and Section 3-819 apply beginning with the 1984 registration year for those vehicles registered on a calendar year basis only.

"The amendments to Chapters 13 and 18 of 'The Illinois Vehicle Code' in Section 1 of this Act take effect January 1, 1984.

"Section 2 of this Act takes effect on the first day of the next succeeding month which commences at least 30 days after the date on which this Act becomes law.

"Section 3 of this Act takes effect July 1, 1983.

"Section 3.1 of this Act takes effect January 1, 1984.

"This Section 4 takes effect upon its becoming a law."

5/3-402. Vehicles subject to registration; exceptions

§ 3-402. Vehicles subject to registration; exceptions.

A. Exemptions and Policy. Every motor vehicle, trailer, semitrailer and pole trailer when driven or moved upon a highway shall be subject to the registration and certificate of title provisions of this Chapter except:

(1) Any such vehicle driven or moved upon a highway in conformance with the provisions of this Chapter relating to manufacturers, transporters, dealers, lienholders or nonresidents or under a temporary registration permit issued by the Secretary of State;

(2) Any implement of husbandry whether of a type otherwise subject to registration hereunder or not which is only incidentally operated or moved upon a highway, which shall include a not-for-hire movement for the purpose of delivering farm commodities to a place of first processing or sale, or to a place of storage;

(3) Any special mobile equipment as herein defined;

(4) Any vehicle which is propelled exclusively by electric power obtained from overhead trolley wires though not operated upon rails;

(5) Any vehicle which is equipped and used exclusively as a pumper, ladder truck, rescue vehicle, searchlight truck, or other fire apparatus, but not a vehicle of a type which would otherwise be subject to registration as a vehicle of the first division;

(6) Any vehicle which is owned and operated by the federal government and externally displays evidence of federal ownership. It is the policy of the State of Illinois to promote and encourage the fullest use of its highways and to enhance the flow of commerce thus contributing to the economic, agricultural, industrial and social growth and development of this State, by authorizing the Secretary of State to negotiate and enter into reciprocal or proportional agreements or arrangements with other States, or to issue declarations setting forth reciprocal exemptions, benefits and privileges with respect to vehicles operated interstate which are properly registered in this and other States, assuring nevertheless proper registration of vehicles in Illinois as may be required by this Code;

(7) Any converter dolly or tow dolly which merely serves as substitute wheels for another legally licensed vehicle. A title may be issued on a voluntary basis to a tow dolly upon receipt of the manufacturer's certificate of origin or the bill of sale;

(8) Any house trailer found to be an abandoned mobile home under the Abandoned Mobile Home Act; [1]

(9) Any vehicle that is not properly registered or does not have registration plates issued to the owner or operator affixed thereto, or that does have registration plates issued to the owner or operator affixed thereto but the plates are not appropriate for the weight of the vehicle, provided that this exemption shall apply only while the vehicle is being transported or operated by a towing service and has a third tow plate affixed to it.

B. Reciprocity. Any motor vehicle, trailer, semitrailer or pole trailer need not be registered under this Code provided the same is operated interstate and in accordance with the following provisions and any rules and regulations promulgated pursuant thereto:

(1) A nonresident owner, except as otherwise provided in this Section, owning any foreign registered vehicle of a type otherwise subject to registration hereunder, may operate or permit the operation of such vehicle within this State in interstate commerce without registering such vehicle in, or paying any fees to, this State subject to the condition that such vehicle at all times when operated in this State is operated pursuant to a reciprocity agreement, arrangement or declaration by this State, and further subject to the condition that such vehicle at all times when operated in this State is duly registered in, and displays upon it, a valid registration card and registration plate or plates issued for such vehicle in the place of residence of such owner and is issued and maintains in such vehicle a valid Illinois reciprocity permit as required by the Secretary of State, and provided like privileges are afforded to residents of this State by the State of residence of such owner.

Every nonresident including any foreign corporation carrying on business within this State and owning and regularly operating in such business any motor vehicle, trailer or semitrailer within this State in intrastate commerce, shall be required to register each such vehicle and pay the same fees therefor as is required with reference to like vehicles owned by residents of this State.

(2) Any motor vehicle, trailer, semitrailer and pole trailer operated interstate need not be registered in this State, provided:

(a) that the vehicle is properly registered in another State pursuant to law or to a reciprocity agreement, arrangement or declaration; or

(b) that such vehicle is part of a fleet of vehicles owned or operated by the same person who registers such fleet of vehicles pro rata among the various States in which such fleet operates; or

(c) that such vehicle is part of a fleet of vehicles, a portion of which are registered with the Secretary of State of Illinois in accordance with an agreement or arrangement concurred in by the Secretary of State of Illinois based on one or more of the following factors: ratio of miles in Illinois as against total miles in all jurisdictions; situs or base of a vehicle, or where it is principally garaged, or from whence it is principally dispatched or where the movements of such vehicle usually originate; situs of the residence of the owner or operator thereof, or of his principal office or offices, or of his places of business; the routes traversed and whether regular or irregular routes are traversed, and the jurisdictions traversed and served; and such other factors as may be deemed material by the Secretary and the motor vehicle administrators of the other jurisdictions involved in such apportionment.

Such vehicles shall maintain therein any reciprocity permit which may be required by the Secretary of State pursuant to rules and regulations which the Secretary of State may promulgate in the administration of this Code, in the public interest.

(3) (a) In order to effectuate the purposes of this Code, the Secretary of State of Illinois is empowered to negotiate and execute written reciprocal agreements or arrangements with the duly authorized representatives of other jurisdictions, including States, districts, territories and possessions of the United States, and foreign states, provinces, or countries, granting to owners or operators of vehicles duly registered or licensed in such other jurisdictions and for which evidence of compliance is supplied, benefits, privileges and exemption from the payment, wholly or partially, of any taxes, fees or other charges imposed with respect to the ownership or operation of such vehicles by the laws of this State except the tax imposed by the Motor Fuel Tax Law, approved March 25, 1929, as amended, [2] and the tax imposed by the Use Tax Act, approved July 14, 1955, as amended. [3]

The Secretary of State may negotiate agreements or arrangements as are in the best interests of this State and the residents of this State pursuant to the policies expressed in this Section taking into consideration the reciprocal exemptions, benefits and privileges available and accruing to residents of this State and vehicles registered in this State.

(b) Such reciprocal agreements or arrangements shall provide that vehicles duly registered or licensed in this State when operated upon the highways of such other jurisdictions, shall receive exemptions, benefits and privileges of a similar kind or to a similar degree as extended to vehicles from such jurisdictions in this State.

(c) Such agreements or arrangements may also authorize the apportionment of registration or licensing of fleets of vehicles operated interstate, based on any or all of the following factors: ratio of miles in Illinois as against total miles in all jurisdictions; situs or base of a vehicle, or where it is principally garaged or from whence it is principally dispatched or where the movements of such vehicle usually originate; situs of the residence of the owner or operator thereof, or of his principal office or offices, or of his places of business; the routes traversed and whether regular or irregular routes are traversed, and the jurisdictions traversed and served; and such other factors as may be deemed material by the Secretary and the motor vehicle administrators of the other jurisdictions involved in such apportionment, and such vehicles shall likewise be entitled to reciprocal exemptions, benefits and privileges.

(d) Such agreements or arrangements shall also provide that vehicles being operated in intrastate commerce in Illinois shall comply with the registration and licensing laws of this State, except that vehicles which are part of an apportioned fleet may conduct an intrastate operation incidental to their interstate operations. Any motor vehicle properly registered and qualified under any reciprocal agreement or arrangement under this Code and not having a situs or base within Illinois may complete the inbound movement of a trailer or semitrailer to an Illinois destination that was brought into Illinois by a motor vehicle also properly registered and qualified under this Code and not having a situs or base within Illinois, or may complete an outbound movement of a trailer or semitrailer to an out-of-state destination that was originated in Illinois by a motor vehicle also properly registered and qualified under this Code and not having a situs or base in Illinois, only if the operator thereof did not break bulk of the cargo laden in such inbound or outbound trailer or semitrailer. Adding or unloading intrastate cargo on such inbound or outbound trailer or semitrailer shall be deemed as breaking bulk.

(e) Such agreements or arrangements may also provide for the determination of the proper State in which leased vehicles shall be registered based on the factors set out in subsection (c) above and for apportionment of registration of fleets of leased vehicles by the lessee or by the lessor who leases such vehicles to persons who are not fleet operators.

(f) Such agreements or arrangements may also include reciprocal exemptions, benefits or privileges accruing under The Illinois Driver Licensing Law [4] or The Driver License Compact. [5]

(4) The Secretary of State is further authorized to examine the laws and requirements of other jurisdictions, and, in the absence of a written agreement or arrangement, to issue a written declaration of the extent and nature of the exemptions, benefits and privileges accorded to vehicles of this State by such other jurisdictions, and the extent and nature of reciprocal exemptions, benefits and privileges thereby accorded by this State to the vehicles of such other jurisdictions. A declaration by the Secretary of State may include any, part or all reciprocal exemptions, benefits and privileges or provisions as may be included within an agreement or arrangement.

(5) All agreements, arrangements, declarations and amendments thereto, shall be in writing and become effective when signed by the Secretary of State, and copies of all such documents shall be available to the public upon request.

(6) The Secretary of State is further authorized to require the display by foreign registered trucks, truck-tractors and buses, entitled to reciprocal benefits, exemptions or privileges hereunder, a reciprocity permit for external display before any such reciprocal benefits, exemptions or

privileges are granted. The Secretary of State shall provide suitable application forms for such permit and shall promulgate and publish reasonable rules and regulations for the administration and enforcement of the provisions of this Code including a provision for revocation of such permit as to any vehicle operated wilfully in violation of the terms of any reciprocal agreement, arrangement or declaration or in violation of the Illinois Motor Carrier of Property Law, as amended. [6]

(7) (a) Upon the suspension, revocation or denial of one or more of all reciprocal benefits, privileges and exemptions existing pursuant to the terms and provisions of this Code or by virtue of a reciprocal agreement or arrangement or declaration thereunder; or, upon the suspension, revocation or denial of a reciprocity permit; or, upon any action or inaction of the Secretary in the administration and enforcement of the provisions of this Code, any person, resident or nonresident, so aggrieved, may serve upon the Secretary, a petition in writing and under oath, setting forth the grievance of the petitioner, the grounds and basis for the relief sought, and all necessary facts and particulars, and request an administrative hearing thereon. Within 20 days, the Secretary shall set a hearing date as early as practical. The Secretary may, in his discretion, supply forms for such a petition. The Secretary may require the payment of a fee of not more than $50 for the filing of any petition, motion, or request for hearing conducted pursuant to this Section. These fees must be deposited into the Secretary of State DUI Administration Fund, a special fund that is hereby created in the State treasury, and, subject to appropriation and as directed by the Secretary of State, shall be used to fund the operation of the hearings department of the Office of the Secretary of State and for no other purpose. The Secretary shall establish by rule the amount and the procedures, terms, and conditions relating to these fees.

(b) The Secretary may likewise, in his discretion and upon his own petition, order a hearing, when in his best judgment, any person is not entitled to the reciprocal benefits, privileges and exemptions existing pursuant to the terms and provisions of this Code or under a reciprocal agreement or arrangement or declaration thereunder or that a vehicle owned or operated by such person is improperly registered or licensed, or that an Illinois resident has improperly registered or licensed a vehicle in another jurisdiction for the purposes of violating or avoiding the registration laws of this State.

(c) The Secretary shall notify a petitioner or any other person involved of such a hearing, by giving at least 10 days notice, in writing, by U.S. Mail, Registered or Certified, or by personal service, at the last known address of such petitioner or person, specifying the time and place of such hearing. Such hearing shall be held before the Secretary, or any person as he may designate, and unless the parties mutually agree to some other county in Illinois, the hearing shall be held in the County of Sangamon or the County of Cook. Appropriate records of the hearing shall be kept, and the Secretary shall issue or cause to be issued, his decision on the case, within 30 days after the close of such hearing or within 30 days after receipt of the transcript thereof, and a copy shall likewise be served or mailed to the petitioner or person involved.

(d) The actions or inactions or determinations, or findings and decisions upon an administrative hearing, of the Secretary, shall be subject to judicial review in the Circuit Court of the County of Sangamon or the County of Cook, and the provisions of the Administrative Review Law, [7] and all amendments and modifications thereof and rules adopted pursuant thereto, apply to and govern all such reviewable matters.

Any reciprocal agreements or arrangements entered into by the Secretary of State or any declarations issued by the Secretary of State pursuant to any law in effect prior to the effective date of this Code are not hereby abrogated, and such shall continue in force and effect until amended pursuant to the provisions of this Code or expire pursuant to the terms or provisions thereof.

P.A. 76-1586, § 3-402, eff. July 1, 1970. Amended by P.A. 77-43, § 1, eff. Jan. 1, 1972; P.A. 77-1508, § 1, eff. Jan. 1, 1972; P.A. 77-1545, § 1, eff. Jan. 1, 1972; P.A. 77-2636, § 1, eff. Jan. 1, 1973; P.A. 78-255, § 25, eff. Oct. 1, 1973; P.A. 79-1021, § 1, eff. Oct. 1, 1975; P.A. 81-886, § 1, eff. July 1, 1980; P.A. 82-783, Art. XI, § 140, eff. July 13, 1982; P.A. 83-848, § 1, eff. Jan. 1, 1984; P.A. 83-1539, Art. IV, § 4, eff. Feb. 4, 1985; P.A. 84-986, § 1, eff. Sept. 25, 1985; P.A. 87-1203, § 1, eff. Sept. 25, 1992; P.A. 88-516, § 95, eff. July 1, 1994; P.A. 89-433, § 5, eff. Dec. 15, 1995; P.A. 90-89, § 15, eff. Jan. 1, 1998; P.A. 92-418, § 10, eff. Aug. 17, 2001; P.A. 92-651, § 77, eff. July 11, 2002.

Formerly Ill.Rev.Stat.1991, ch. 95 ½, ¶ 3-402.

1 210 ILCS 117/1 et seq.

2 35 ILCS 505/1 et seq.

3 35 ILCS 105/1 et seq.

4 625 ILCS 5/6-100 et seq.

5 625 ILCS 5/6-700 et seq.

6 625 ILCS 5/18-101 et seq. (repealed; see, now, 625 ILCS 5/18c-1101 et seq.).

7 735 ILCS 5/3-101 et seq.

Section 2 of P.A. 79-1021, certified Sept. 17, 1975, provided:

"This amendatory Act of 1975 takes effect beginning with motor vehicle registrations for 1977."

P.A. 92-651, the First 2002 General Revisory Act, amended various Acts to delete obsolete text, to correct patent and technical errors, to revise cross references, to resolve multiple actions in the 91st and 92nd General Assemblies and to make certain technical corrections in P.A. 91-937 through P.A. 92-520.

5/3-402.1. Proportional Registration

§ 3-402.1. Proportional Registration. Any owner or rental owner engaged in operating a fleet of apportionable vehicles in this state and one or more other states may, in lieu of registration of such vehicles under the general provisions of sections 3-402, 3-815 and 3-819, register and license such fleet for operations in this state by filing an application statement, signed under penalties of perjury, with the Secretary of State which shall be in such form and contain such information as the Secretary of State shall require, declaring the total mileage operated in all states by such fleet, the total mileage operated in this state by such fleet during the preceding year, and describing and identifying each apportionable vehicle to be operated in this state during the ensuing year. If mileage data is not available for the preceding year, the Secretary of State may accept the latest 12-month period available. "Preceding year" means the period of 12 consecutive months immediately prior to July 1st of the year immediately preceding the registration or license year for which proportional registration is sought.

Such owner shall determine the proportion of in-state miles to total fleet miles. Such percentage figure shall be such owner's apportionment factor. In determining the total fee payment, such owner shall first compute the license fee for each vehicle within the fleet which would otherwise be required, and then multiply the said amount by the Illinois apportionment factor adding the fees for each vehicle to arrive at a total amount for the fleet. Apportionable trailers and semitrailers will be registered in accordance with the provisions of Section 3-813 of this Code.

Upon receipt of the appropriate fees from such owner as computed under the provisions of this section, the Secretary of State shall, when this state is the base jurisdiction, issue to such owner number plates or other distinctive tags or such evidence of registration as the Secretary of State shall deem appropriate to identify each vehicle in the fleet as a part of a proportionally registered interstate fleet.

Vehicles registered under the provision of this section shall be considered fully licensed and properly registered in Illinois for any type of movement or operation. The proportional registration and licensing provisions of this section shall apply to vehicles added to fleets and operated in this state during the registration year, applying the same apportionment factor to such fees as would be payable for the remainder of the registration year.

Apportionment factors for apportionable vehicles not operated in this state during the preceding year shall be determined by the Secretary of State on the basis of a full statement of the proposed methods of operation and in conformity with an estimated mileage chart as calculated by the Secretary of State. An established fleet adding states at the time of renewal shall estimate mileage for the added states in conformity with a mileage chart developed by the Secretary of State.

P.A. 76–1586, § 3–402.1, added by P.A. 79–1041, § 1, eff. Jan. 1, 1976. Amended by P.A. 87–206, § 1, eff. Sept. 3, 1991; P.A. 87–1041, § 1, eff. Sept. 11, 1992; P.A. 90–89, § 15, eff. Jan. 1, 1998.

Formerly Ill.Rev.Stat.1991, ch. 95 ½, ¶ 3–402.1.

5/3–402.2. Audits

§ 3–402.2. Audits. In addition to audit authority set forth in Section 2–124 of this Act, the Secretary of State, when this state is the base jurisdiction, may audit such owners displaying a base plate of this state as to authenticity of mileage figures and registrations and at such time and frequency as determined by the Secretary of State. Audits may be made by officials of other jurisdictions which are members of an International Registration Plan (IRP) of which this state is also a member.

Upon completion of any such audit, the Secretary of State shall notify all jurisdictions in which such owner was proportionally registered on the accuracy of the records of such owner. Should such owner have underpaid or overpaid any jurisdiction in which his vehicles were proportionally registered, such information shall be furnished to the jurisdiction for processing in accordance with the procedures as set forth under the International Registration Plan.

P.A. 76–1586, § 3–402.2, added by P.A. 79–1041, § 1, eff. Jan. 1, 1976. Amended by P.A. 87–206, § 1, eff. Sept. 3, 1991; P.A. 92–69, § 5, eff. July 12, 2001.

Formerly Ill.Rev.Stat.1991, ch. 95 ½, ¶ 3–402.2.

5/3–402.3. Relation to other state laws

§ 3–402.3. Relation to other state laws. The provisions of Section 3–402.1 shall constitute complete authority for the registration of vehicles upon a proportional registration basis without reference to or application of any other statutes of this state.

P.A. 76–1586, § 3–402.3, added by P.A. 79–1041, § 1, eff. Jan. 1, 1976.

Formerly Ill.Rev.Stat.1991, ch. 95 ½, ¶ 3–402.3.

5/3–402.4. Administrative Agreements and Rules

§ 3–402.4. Administrative Agreements and Rules. The Secretary of State may enter into agreements, compacts, or arrangements with other jurisdictions or agents for such jurisdictions, such as the American Association of Motor Vehicle Administrators, on behalf of this state for allocation or proportional registration of apportionable vehicles in a manner provided in Section 3–402.1 for the purpose of facilitating the administration thereof, and also for the purpose of conforming procedures for proportional registration, pursuant to Sections 3–402.1 and 3–402.2, with those agreed to by two or more additional jurisdictions, including but not limited to, acceptance of base jurisdiction responsibilities for apportional registration and licensing of fleet vehicles in other jurisdiction. In addition, the Secretary of State may adopt and promulgate such rules and regulations as he shall deem necessary to effectuate and administer the provisions of Sections 3–402.1 and 3–402.2. Any reciprocal arrangements or agreements in effect with jurisdictions that cannot grant proportional registration shall remain in force until specifically cancelled by either jurisdiction or until such time that jurisdiction becomes a member of an International Registration Plan (IRP) of which this state is also a member.

P.A. 76–1586, § 3–402.4, added by P.A. 79–1041, § 1, eff. Jan. 1, 1976. Amended by P.A. 85–1144, § 1, eff. July 29, 1988; P.A. 87–206, § 1, eff. Sept. 3, 1991.

Formerly Ill.Rev.Stat.1991, ch. 95 ½, ¶ 3–402.4.

5/3–403. Trip and Short-term permits.

§ 3–403. Trip and Short-term permits.

(a) The Secretary of State may issue a short-term permit to operate a nonregistered first or second division vehicle within the State of Illinois for a period of not more than 7 days. Any second division vehicle operating on such permit may operate only on empty weight. The fee for the short-term permit shall be $6.

This permit may also be issued to operate an unladen registered vehicle which is suspended under the Vehicle Emissions Inspection Law [1] and allow it to be driven on the roads and highways of the State in order to be repaired or when travelling to and from an emissions inspection station.

(b) The Secretary of State may, subject to reciprocal agreements, arrangements or declarations made or entered into pursuant to Section 3–402, 3–402.4 or by rule, provide for and issue registration permits for the use of Illinois highways by vehicles of the second division on an occasional basis or for a specific and special short-term use, in compliance with rules and regulations promulgated by the Secretary of State, and upon payment of the prescribed fee as follows:

One-trip permits. A registration permit for one trip, or one round-trip into and out of Illinois, for a period not to exceed 72 consecutive hours or 3 calendar days may be provided, for a fee as prescribed in Section 3–811.

One-Month permits. A registration permit for 30 days may be provided for a fee of $13 for registration plus 1/10 of the flat weight tax. The minimum fee for such permit shall be $31.

In-transit permits. A registration permit for one trip may be provided for vehicles in transit by the driveaway or towaway method and operated by a transporter in compliance with the Illinois Motor Carrier of Property Law, [2] for a fee as prescribed in Section 3–811.

Illinois Temporary Apportionment Authorization Permits. An apportionment authorization permit for forty-five days for the immediate operation of a vehicle upon application for and prior to receiving apportioned credentials or interstate credentials from the State of Illinois. The fee for such permit shall be $3.

Illinois Temporary Prorate Authorization Permit. A prorate authorization permit for forty-five days for the immediate operation of a vehicle upon application for and prior to receiving prorate credentials or interstate credentials from the State of Illinois. The fee for such permit shall be $3.

(c) The Secretary of State shall promulgate by such rule or regulation, schedules of fees and taxes for such permits and in computing the amount or amounts due, may round off such amount to the nearest full dollar amount.

(d) The Secretary of State shall further prescribe the form of application and permit and may require such information and data as necessary and proper, including confirming the status or identity of the applicant and the vehicle in question.

(e) Rules or regulations promulgated by the Secretary of State under this Section shall provide for reasonable and proper limitations and restrictions governing the application for and issuance and use of permits, and shall provide for the number of permits per vehicle or per applicant, so as to preclude evasion of annual registration requirements as may be required by this Act.

(f) Any permit under this Section is subject to suspension or revocation under this Act, and in addition, any such permit is subject to suspension or revocation should the Secretary of State determine that the vehicle identified in any permit should be properly registered in Illinois. In the event any such permit is suspended or revoked, the permit is then null and void, may not be re-instated, nor is a refund therefor available. The vehicle identified in such permit may not thereafter be operated in Illinois without being properly registered as provided in this Chapter.

P.A. 76-1586, § 3-403, eff. July 1, 1970. Amended by P.A. 76-2132, § 1, eff. July 1, 1970; P.A. 77-526, § 1, eff. July 31, 1971; P.A. 81-865, § 1, eff. Dec. 1, 1979; P.A. 83-449, § 1, eff. Jan. 1, 1984; P.A. 84-986, § 1, eff. Sept. 25, 1985; P.A. 86-395, § 1, eff. Aug. 30, 1989; P.A. 86-444, § 1, eff. Jan. 1, 1990; P.A. 86-1028, Art. II, § 2-44, eff. Feb. 5, 1990; P.A. 87-206, § 1, eff. Sept. 3, 1991; P.A. 88-415, § 10, eff. Aug. 20, 1993; P.A. 91-37, § 40, eff. July 1, 1999; P.A. 92-680, § 15, eff. July 16, 2002.

Formerly Ill.Rev.Stat.1991, ch. 95 ½, ¶ 3-403.

1 625 ILCS 5/13A-101 et seq.

2 Former Ill.Rev.Stat. ch. 95½, ¶ 18-100 et seq. (repealed); see now, 625 ILCS 5/18c-1101 et seq.

5/3-404. Vehicles of second division carrying persons or property—Required documents

§ 3-404. Vehicles of second division carrying persons or property—Required documents. The Secretary of State shall require an appropriate document, including but not limited to a bill of lading, trip manifest or dispatch record, to be carried, on all vehicles of the second division, carrying persons or property setting forth therein:

(a) the point of origin and destination of the vehicle and its cargo or the persons being carried;

(b) whether the movement is for-hire or not-for-hire; and

(c) whether the movement is intrastate or interstate as defined by this Act.

The Secretary of State shall promulgate and publish reasonable rules and regulations for the administration and enforcement of this requirement. Vehicles bearing valid current Illinois registration plate or plates and registration stickers where applicable shall be exempted from such requirement by the Secretary of State whether the movement is "intrastate" or "interstate" as defined in this Act.

P.A. 76-1586, § 3-404, eff. July 1, 1970. Amended by P.A. 80-230, § 1, eff. Oct. 1, 1977.

Formerly Ill.Rev.Stat.1991, ch. 95 ½, ¶ 3-404.

5/3-405. Application for registration

§ 3-405. Application for registration.

(a) Every owner of a vehicle subject to registration under this Code shall make application to the Secretary of State for the registration of such vehicle upon the appropriate form or forms furnished by the Secretary. Every such application shall bear the signature of the owner written with pen and ink and contain:

1. The name, bona fide residence (except as otherwise provided in this paragraph 1) and mail address of the owner or business address of the owner if a firm, association or corporation. If the mailing address is a post office box number, the address listed on the driver license record may be used to verify residence. A police officer, a deputy sheriff, an elected sheriff, a law enforcement officer for the Department of State Police, or a fire investigator may elect to furnish the address of the headquarters of the governmental entity or police district where he or she works instead of his or her residence address, in which case that address shall be deemed to be his or her residence address for all purposes under this Chapter 3. The spouse and children of a person who may elect under this paragraph 1 to furnish the address of the headquarters of the government entity or police district where the person works instead of the person's residence address may, if they reside with that person, also elect to furnish the address of the headquarters of the government entity or police district where the person works as their residence address, in which case that address shall be deemed to be their residence address for all purposes under this Chapter 3. In this paragraph 1: (A) "police officer" has the meaning ascribed to "policeman" in Section 10-3-1 of the Illinois Municipal Code;[1] (B) "deputy sheriff" means a deputy sheriff appointed under Section 3-6008 of the Counties Code;[2] (C) "elected sheriff" means a sheriff commissioned pursuant to Section 3-6001 of the Counties Code;[3] and (D) "fire investigator" means a person classified as a peace officer under the Peace Officer Fire Investigation Act.[4]

2. A description of the vehicle, including such information as is required in an application for a certificate of title, determined under such standard rating as may be prescribed by the Secretary.

3. Information, as may be required by the Secretary, relating to the insurance policy for a motor vehicle, including, but not limited to, the name of the insurer which issued the policy.

4. Such further information as may reasonably be required by the Secretary to enable him to determine whether the vehicle is lawfully entitled to registration and the owner entitled to a certificate of title.

5. An affirmation by the applicant that all information set forth is true and correct. If the application is for the registration of a motor vehicle, the applicant also shall affirm that the motor vehicle is insured as required by this Code, that such insurance will be maintained throughout the period for which the motor vehicle shall be registered, and that neither the owner, nor any person operating the motor vehicle with the owner's permission, shall operate

interchange capabilities. The Secretary shall in his or her discretion determine other qualifications for fleet owners to register under this paragraph. In making the determination, the Secretary shall consider the size of the fleet and the past history of the registrant.

P.A. 76-1586, § 3-405.3, added by P.A. 92-629, § 5, eff. July 1, 2003.

5/3-405.4. Audits

Text of section added effective July 1, 2003

§ 3-405.4. Audits. In addition to audit authority set forth in Section 2-124 of this Code, the Secretary of State may audit the registration plates and the inventory of credentials of any fleet owner participating in the fleet registration plan.

P.A. 76-1586, § 3-405.4, added by P.A. 92-629, § 5, eff. July 1, 2003.

5/3-406. Application for specially constructed, reconstructed or foreign vehicles

§ 3-406. Application for specially constructed, reconstructed or foreign vehicles. (a) In the event the vehicle to be registered is a specially constructed, reconstructed or foreign vehicle, such fact shall be stated in the application and with reference to every foreign vehicle which has been registered heretofore outside of this State the owner shall surrender to the Secretary of State all registration plates, registration cards or other evidence of such foreign registration as may be in his possession or under his control except as provided in subdivision (b) hereof.

(b) Where in the course of interstate operation of a vehicle registered in another State, it is desirable to retain registration of said vehicle in such other State, such applicant need not surrender but shall submit for inspection said evidences of such foreign registration and the Secretary of State upon a proper showing shall register said vehicle in this State but shall not issue a certificate of title for such vehicle.

P.A. 76-1586, § 3-406, eff. July 1, 1970.

Formerly Ill.Rev.Stat.1991, ch. 95 ½, ¶ 3-406.

5/3-407. Temporary permit or registration pending registration

§ 3-407. Temporary permit or registration pending registration. (a) **Temporary Permit.** The Secretary of State in his discretion may grant a temporary permit or placard to operate a vehicle for which application for registration and certificate of title has been made where such application is accompanied by the proper fee, pending action upon said application by the Secretary of State. In lieu of payment of the proper fee, the Secretary of State may accept a bond therefor or a certificate of deposit, in the proper amount, and in the same form and subject to the same requirements as the payment of such fees or taxes on an installment basis, except that the fees or taxes due shall be payable and paid to the Secretary of State. The design, color and format of the temporary permit or placard shall be wholly within the discretion of the Secretary of State.

(b) **Temporary Registration.** The Secretary of State in his discretion may issue registration plates to an owner for which application and certificate of title has been made where such application is accompanied by the proper fee and tax, pending completion of the said application by the applicant and the Secretary, subject however to rules and regulations promulgated by the Secretary.

(c) **Revocation.** A temporary permit or registration is subject to revocation to the same extent as any other registration.

P.A. 76-1586, § 3-407, eff. July 1, 1970. Amended by P.A. 77-1508, § 1, eff. Jan. 1, 1972; P.A. 77-2751, § 1, eff. Sept. 1, 1972; P.A. 78-255, § 61, eff. Oct. 1, 1973; P.A. 88-298, § 5, eff. July 1, 1994.

Formerly Ill.Rev.Stat.1991, ch. 95 ½, ¶ 3-407.

5/3-408. Grounds for refusing registration or certificate of title

§ 3-408. Grounds for refusing registration or certificate of title. The Secretary of State shall refuse registration or any transfer of registration upon any of the following grounds:

1. That the application contains any false or fraudulent statement or that the applicant has failed to furnish required information or reasonable additional information requested by the Secretary of State or that the applicant is not entitled to the issuance of a certificate of title or registration of the vehicle under Chapter 3;

2. That the Secretary of State has reasonable ground to believe that the vehicle is a stolen or embezzled vehicle or that the granting of registration would constitute a fraud against the rightful owner or other person having valid lien upon such vehicle;

3. That the registration of the vehicle stands suspended or revoked for any reason as provided in the motor-vehicle laws of this State;

4. That the required fee has not been paid;

5. (a) In the case of medical transport vehicles and vehicles designed to carry 15 or fewer passengers operated by a contract carrier transporting employees in the course of their employment on a highway of this State, that the application does not contain a copy of a completed Vehicle Inspection Report issued by the Department of Transportation which certifies that the vehicle has been determined to be in safe mechanical condition by a safety test administered within the preceding 6 months; and (b) in the case of medical transport vehicles, other than vehicles owned or operated by a unit of local government, proof of financial responsibility; or

6. That the applicant is 90 days or more delinquent in court ordered child support payments or has been adjudicated in arrears in an amount equal to 90 days' obligation or more and has been found in contempt of court for failure to pay the support, subject to the requirements and procedures of Article VII of Chapter 7 of the Illinois Vehicle Code.[1]

P.A. 76-1586, § 3-408, eff. July 1, 1970. Amended by P.A. 82-433, § 1, eff. Sept. 8, 1981; P.A. 82-949, § 1, eff. Jan. 1, 1983; P.A. 90-733, § 10, eff. Aug. 11, 1998; P.A. 92-108, § 5, eff. Jan. 1, 2002.

[1] 625 ILCS 5/7-701 et seq.

Section 3 of P.A. 82-433 approved Sept. 8, 1981, provided:

"This Act takes effect upon its becoming a law, except that the provisions relating to safety tests and proof of financial responsibility for medical transport vehicles apply only to applications for and the issuance of registration plates which are required to be displayed on January 1, 1982 or thereafter."

5/3-409. Registration indexes

§ 3-409. Registration indexes. The Secretary of State shall file each application received and when satisfied as to the genuineness and regularity thereof, and that the applicant is entitled to register such vehicle and to the issuance of the motor vehicle unless the required insurance is in effect. If the person signing the affirmation is not the sole owner of the vehicle, such person shall be deemed to have affirmed on behalf of all the owners of the vehicle. If the person signing the affirmation is not an owner of the vehicle, such person shall be deemed to have affirmed on behalf of the owner or owners of the vehicle. The lack of signature on the application shall not in any manner exempt the owner or owners from any provisions, requirements or penalties of this Code.

(b) When such application refers to a new vehicle purchased from a dealer the application shall be accompanied by a Manufacturer's Statement of Origin from the dealer, and a statement showing any lien retained by the dealer.

P.A. 76–1586, § 3–405, eff. July 1, 1970. Amended by P.A. 78–1140, § 1, eff. Aug. 26, 1974; P.A. 84–1311, § 1, eff. Aug. 27, 1986; P.A. 85–1201, § 1, eff. July 1, 1989; P.A. 86–149, § 2, eff. Aug. 11, 1989; P.A 87–206, § 1, eff. Sept. 3, 1991; P.A. 88–315, § 5, eff. Jan. 1, 1994; P.A. 91–575, § 5, eff. Aug. 14, 1999.

Formerly Ill.Rev.Stat.1991, ch. 95 ½, ¶ 3–405.

1 65 ILCS 5/10–3–1.

2 55 ILCS 3/6008.

3 55 ILCS 3/6001.

4 20 ILCS 2910/0.01 et seq.

5/3–405.1. Application for vanity and personalized license plates

§ 3–405.1. Application for vanity and personalized license plates.

(a) Vanity license plates mean any license plates, assigned to a passenger motor vehicle of the first division, to a motor vehicle of the second division registered at not more than 8,000 pounds or to a recreational vehicle, which display a registration number containing 4 to 7 letters as requested by the owner of the vehicle and license plates issued to retired members of Congress under Section 3–610.1 or to retired members of the General Assembly as provided in Section 3–606.1. A license plate consisting of 3 letters and no numbers or of 1, 2 or 3 numbers, upon its becoming available, is a vanity license plate. Personalized license plates mean any license plates, assigned to a passenger motor vehicle of the first division, to a motor vehicle of the second division, or to a recreational vehicle, which display a registration number containing a combination of letters and numbers as prescribed by rule, as requested by the owner of the vehicle.

(b) For any registration period commencing after 1979, any person who is the registered owner of a passenger motor vehicle of the first division, of a motor vehicle of the second division registered at not more than 8,000 pounds or of a recreational vehicle registered with the Secretary of State or who makes application for an original registration of such a motor vehicle or renewal registration of such a motor vehicle may, upon payment of a fee prescribed in Section 3–806.1, apply to the Secretary of State for personalized license plates.

(c) Except as otherwise provided in this Chapter 3 , vanity and personalized license plates as issued under this Section shall be the same color and design as other passenger vehicle license plates and shall not in any manner conflict with any other existing passenger, commercial, trailer, motorcycle, or special license plate series. However, special registration plates issued under Sections 3–611 and 3–616 for vehicles operated by or for persons with disabilities may also be vanity or personalized license plates.

(d) Vanity and personalized license plates shall be issued only to the registered owner of the vehicle on which they are to be displayed, except as provided in Sections 3–611 and 3–616 for special registration plates for vehicles operated by or for persons with disabilities.

(e) An applicant for the issuance of vanity or personalized license plates or subsequent renewal thereof shall file an application in such form and manner and by such date as the Secretary of State may, in his discretion, require.

No vanity nor personalized license plates shall be approved, manufactured, or distributed that contain any characters, symbols other than the international accessibility symbol for vehicles operated by or for persons with disabilities, foreign words, or letters of punctuation.

(f) Vanity and personalized license plates as issued pursuant to this Act may be subject to the Staggered Registration System as prescribed by the Secretary of State.

P.A. 76–1586, § 3–405.1 added by P.A. 81–987, § 1, eff. Sept. 22, 1979. Amended by P.A. 82–1011, § 2, eff. Sept. 17, 1982; P.A. 83–453, § 1, eff. Jan. 1, 1984; P.A. 83–828, § 1, eff. Jan. 1, 1984; P.A. 83–1362, Art. II, § 99, eff. Sept. 11, 1984; P.A. 86–480, § 1, eff. Jan. 1, 1990; P.A. 88–685, § 5, eff. Jan. 24, 1995; P.A. 89–282, § 10, eff. Aug. 10, 1995; P.A. 89–611, § 15, eff. Jan. 1, 1997; P.A. 92–651, § 77, eff. July 11, 2002.

Formerly Ill.Rev.Stat.1991, ch. 95 ½, ¶ 3–405.1.

Section 2 of P.A. 83–828 provided:

"This Act takes effect with the 1985 registration year."

P.A. 89–611 incorporated the amendment by P.A. 89–282.

5/3–405.2. Improper plates

§ 3–405.2. Improper plates. The Secretary of State shall refuse to issue any license plates bearing a combination of letters or numbers, or both, which creates a potential duplication or, in the opinion of the Secretary, (1) would substantially interfere with plate identification for law enforcement purposes, (2) is misleading, or (3) creates a connotation that is offensive to good taste and decency.

The Secretary may revoke any such plates issued previously. Any person who has his or her plates revoked under this Section may acquire at no charge new plates and any required stickers of the same category and for the same period of registration.

P.A. 76–1586, § 3–405.2, added by P.A. 83–449, § 1, eff. Jan. 1, 1984.

Formerly Ill.Rev.Stat.1991, ch. 95 ½, ¶ 3–405.2.

5/3–405.3. Application for fleet vehicles

Text of section added effective July 1, 2003

§ 3–405.3. Application for fleet vehicles.

(a) An owner engaged in operating a fleet of motor vehicles of the first division in this State or a fleet of second division vehicles operated intrastate may register and license the fleet for operations in this State by filing an application statement with the Secretary of State, signed under penalties of perjury, which shall be in the form and contain the information required by the Secretary of State. First division vehicles registered under this Section must be registered in accordance with the fees prescribed in Section 3–806 of this Code. Second division vehicles registered under this Section must be registered in accordance with the fees prescribed in Section 3–815 of this Code.

(b) Participation in the fleet registration plan may be accomplished only by entering into a contractual agreement with the Secretary. The applicant must have electronic data a certificate of title, shall register the vehicle therein described and keep a suitable record thereof as follows:

1. Under a distinctive registration number assigned to the vehicle;

2. Under the identifying number of the vehicle;

3. Alphabetically, under the name of the owner;

4. In the discretion of the Secretary of State, in any other manner it may deem desirable.

P.A. 76-1586, § 3-409, eff. July 1, 1970.

Formerly Ill.Rev.Stat.1991, ch. 95 ½, ¶ 3-409.

5/3-410. Secretary of State to issue registration card

§ 3-410. Secretary of State to issue registration card. (a) The Secretary of State upon registering a vehicle shall issue a registration card.

(b) The registration card shall be delivered to the owner and shall contain upon the face thereof the date issued, the name and address of the owner, the registration number assigned to the vehicle and as to vehicles of the second division, whether the vehicle is for-hire or not-for-hire and such description of the vehicle as determined by the Secretary of State.

P.A. 76-1586, § 3-410, eff. July 1, 1970.

Formerly Ill.Rev.Stat.1991, ch. 95 ½, ¶ 3-410.

5/3-411. Registration card to be carried and exhibited on demand

§ 3-411. Registration card to be carried and exhibited on demand.

(a) Every registration card for a vehicle of the second division weighing more than 8,000 pounds or any vehicle of the second division weighing 8,000 pounds or less towing a trailer, except pole trailer or semitrailer shall at all times be carried in the vehicle to which it refers or shall be carried by the person driving or in control of such vehicle who shall display the same upon demand of a police officer or any officer or employee of the Secretary of State.

(b) The provisions of this Section requiring that a registration card be carried in the vehicle to which it refers or by the person driving the same shall not apply when such card is used for the purpose of making application for renewal of registration or upon a transfer of registration of said vehicle.

(c) Every owner or operator of a vehicle of the second division subject to a reciprocity agreement under subsection (b) of Section 3-402 of this Chapter shall at all times carry in the vehicle a copy of the reciprocity permit and shall display the same upon demand of a police officer or any officer or employee of the Secretary of State.

P.A. 76-1586, § 3-411, eff. July 1, 1970. Amended by P.A. 78-738, § 1, eff. Jan. 1, 1974; P.A. 86-444, § 1, eff. Jan. 1, 1990; P.A. 89-245, § 5, eff. Jan. 1, 1996; P.A. 89-687, § 5, eff. June 1, 1997.

Formerly Ill.Rev.Stat.1991, ch. 95 ½, ¶ 3-411.

P.A. 89-687 incorporated the amendment by P.A. 89-245.

5/3-412. Registration plates and registration stickers to be furnished by the Secretary of State

Text of section as amended by P.A. 92-651, § 77, eff. July 11, 2002

§ 3-412. Registration plates and registration stickers to be furnished by the Secretary of State.

(a) The Secretary of State upon registering a vehicle subject to annual registration for the first time shall issue or shall cause to be issued to the owner one registration plate for a motorcycle, trailer, semitrailer, motorized pedalcycle or truck-tractor, 2 registration plates for other motor vehicles and, where applicable, current registration stickers for motor vehicles of the first division. The provisions of this Section may be made applicable to such vehicles of the second division, as the Secretary of State may, from time to time, in his discretion designate. On subsequent annual registrations during the term of the registration plate as provided in Section 3-414.1, the Secretary shall issue or cause to be issued registration stickers as evidence of current registration. However, the issuance of annual registration stickers to vehicles registered under the provisions of Section 3-402.1 of this Code may not be required if the Secretary deems the issuance unnecessary.

(b) Every registration plate shall have displayed upon it the registration number assigned to the vehicle for which it is issued, the name of this State, which may be abbreviated, the year number for which it was issued, which may be abbreviated, the phrase "Land of Lincoln" (except as otherwise provided in this Chapter 3), and such other letters or numbers as the Secretary may prescribe. However, for apportionment plates issued to vehicles registered under Section 3-402.1, the phrase "Land of Lincoln" may be omitted to allow for the word "apportioned" to be displayed. The Secretary may in his discretion prescribe that letters be used as prefixes only on registration plates issued to vehicles of the first division which are registered under this Code and only as suffixes on registration plates issued to other vehicles. Every registration sticker issued as evidence of current registration shall designate the year number for which it is issued and such other letters or numbers as the Secretary may prescribe and shall be of a contrasting color with the registration plates and registration stickers of the previous year.

(c) Each registration plate and the required letters and numerals thereon, except the year number for which issued, shall be of sufficient size to be plainly readable from a distance of 100 feet during daylight, and shall be coated with reflectorizing material. The dimensions of the plate issued to vehicles of the first division shall be 6 by 12 inches.

(d) The Secretary of State shall issue for every passenger motor vehicle rented without a driver the same type of registration plates as the type of plates issued for a private passenger vehicle.

(e) The Secretary of State shall issue for every passenger car used as a taxicab or livery, distinctive registration plates.

(f) The Secretary of State shall issue for every motorcycle distinctive registration plates distinguishing between motorcycles having 150 or more cubic centimeters piston displacement, or having less than 150 cubic centimeter piston displacement.

(g) Registration plates issued to vehicles for-hire may display a designation as determined by the Secretary that such vehicles are for-hire.

(h) The Secretary of State shall issue for each electric vehicle distinctive registration plates which shall distinguish between electric vehicles having a maximum operating speed of 45 miles per hour or more and those having a maximum operating speed of less than 45 miles per hour.

(i) The Secretary of State shall issue for every public and private ambulance registration plates identifying the vehicle as an ambulance. The Secretary shall forward to the Department of Public Aid registration information for the purpose of verification of claims filed with the Department by ambulance owners for payment for services to public assistance recipients.

(j) The Secretary of State shall issue for every public and private medical carrier or rescue vehicle livery registration plates displaying numbers within ranges of numbers reserved respectively for medical carriers and rescue vehicles. The Secretary shall forward to the Department of Public Aid registration information for the purpose of verification of claims filed with the Department by owners of medical carriers or rescue vehicles for payment for services to public assistance recipients.

P.A. 76-1586, § 3-412, eff. July 1, 1970. Amended by P.A. 76-1622, § 1, eff. July 1, 1970; P.A. 77-512, § 1, eff. Jan. 1, 1972; P.A. 79-700, § 1, eff. Oct. 1, 1975; P.A. 80-230, § 1, eff. Oct. 1, 1977; P.A. 80-262, § 1, eff. Aug. 20, 1977; P.A. 80-1185, § 1, eff. March 8, 1978; P.A. 82-433, § 1, eff. Sept. 8, 1981; P.A. 87-1040, § 1, eff. Sept. 11, 1992; P.A. 87-1041, § 1, eff. Sept. 11, 1992; P.A. 88-45, Art. II, § 2-54, eff. July 6, 1993; P.A. 88-485, § 10, eff. Jan. 1, 1994; P.A. 89-424, § 15, eff. June 1, 1996; P.A. 89-564, § 5, eff. July 1, 1997; P.A. 89-612, § 10, eff. Aug. 9, 1996; P.A. 89-621, § 10, eff. Jan. 1, 1997; P.A. 89-639, § 5, eff. Jan. 1, 1997; P.A. 90-14, Art. 2, § 2-225, eff. July 1, 1997; P.A. 90-533, § 5, eff. Nov. 14, 1997; P.A. 90-655, § 153, eff. July 30, 1998; P.A. 92-651, § 77, eff. July 11, 2002.

Formerly Ill.Rev.Stat.1991, ch. 95 ½, ¶ 3-412.

For text of section as amended by P.A. 92-629, effective July 1, 2003, see 625 ILCS 5/3-412, post

For final legislative action, see note following 625 ILCS 5/6-206

P.A. 92-651, the First 2002 General Revisory Act, amended various Acts to delete obsolete text, to correct patent and technical errors, to revise cross references, to resolve multiple actions in the 91st and 92nd General Assemblies and to make certain technical corrections in P.A. 91-937 through P.A. 92-520.

5/3-412. Registration plates and registration stickers to be furnished by the Secretary of State

Text of section as amended by P.A. 92-629, effective July 1, 2003

§ 3-412. Registration plates and registration stickers to be furnished by the Secretary of State.

(a) The Secretary of State upon registering a vehicle subject to annual registration for the first time shall issue or shall cause to be issued to the owner one registration plate for a motorcycle, trailer, semitrailer, motorized pedalcycle or truck-tractor, 2 registration plates for other motor vehicles and, where applicable, current registration stickers for motor vehicles of the first division. The provisions of this Section may be made applicable to such vehicles of the second division, as the Secretary of State may, from time to time, in his discretion designate. On subsequent annual registrations during the term of the registration plate as provided in Section 3-414.1, the Secretary shall issue or cause to be issued registration stickers as evidence of current registration. However, the issuance of annual registration stickers to vehicles registered under the provisions of Sections 3-402.1 and 3-405.3 of this Code may not be required if the Secretary deems the issuance unnecessary.

(b) Every registration plate shall have displayed upon it the registration number assigned to the vehicle for which it is issued, the name of this State, which may be abbreviated, the year number for which it was issued, which may be abbreviated, the phrase "Land of Lincoln" (except as otherwise provided in this Code), and such other letters or numbers as the Secretary may prescribe. However, for apportionment plates issued to vehicles registered under Section 3-402.1 and fleet plates issued to vehicles registered under Section 3-405.3, the phrase "Land of Lincoln" may be omitted to allow for the word "apportioned", the word "fleet", or other similar language to be displayed. Registration plates issued to a vehicle registered as a fleet vehicle may display a designation determined by the Secretary.

The Secretary may in his discretion prescribe that letters be used as prefixes only on registration plates issued to vehicles of the first division which are registered under this Code and only as suffixes on registration plates issued to other vehicles. Every registration sticker issued as evidence of current registration shall designate the year number for which it is issued and such other letters or numbers as the Secretary may prescribe and shall be of a contrasting color with the registration plates and registration stickers of the previous year.

(c) Each registration plate and the required letters and numerals thereon, except the year number for which issued, shall be of sufficient size to be plainly readable from a distance of 100 feet during daylight, and shall be coated with reflectorizing material. The dimensions of the plate issued to vehicles of the first division shall be 6 by 12 inches.

(d) The Secretary of State shall issue for every passenger motor vehicle rented without a driver the same type of registration plates as the type of plates issued for a private passenger vehicle.

(e) The Secretary of State shall issue for every passenger car used as a taxicab or livery, distinctive registration plates.

(f) The Secretary of State shall issue for every motorcycle distinctive registration plates distinguishing between motorcycles having 150 or more cubic centimeters piston displacement, or having less than 150 cubic centimeter piston displacement.

(g) Registration plates issued to vehicles for-hire may display a designation as determined by the Secretary that such vehicles are for-hire.

(h) The Secretary of State shall issue for each electric vehicle distinctive registration plates which shall distinguish between electric vehicles having a maximum operating speed of 45 miles per hour or more and those having a maximum operating speed of less than 45 miles per hour.

(i) The Secretary of State shall issue for every public and private ambulance registration plates identifying the vehicle as an ambulance. The Secretary shall forward to the Department of Public Aid registration information for the purpose of verification of claims filed with the Department by ambulance owners for payment for services to public assistance recipients.

(j) The Secretary of State shall issue for every public and private medical carrier or rescue vehicle livery registration plates displaying numbers within ranges of numbers reserved respectively for medical carriers and rescue vehicles. The Secretary shall forward to the Department of Public Aid registration information for the purpose of verification of claims filed with the Department by owners of medical carriers or rescue vehicles for payment for services to public assistance recipients.

P.A. 76-1586, § 3-412, eff. July 1, 1970. Amended by P.A. 76-1622, § 1, eff. July 1, 1970; P.A. 77-512, § 1, eff. Jan. 1, 1972; P.A. 79-700, § 1, eff. Oct. 1, 1975; P.A. 80-230, § 1, eff. Oct. 1, 1977; P.A. 80-262, § 1, eff. Aug. 20, 1977; P.A. 80-1185, § 1, eff. March 8, 1978; P.A. 82-433, § 1, eff. Sept. 8, 1981; P.A. 87-1040, § 1, eff. Sept. 11, 1992; P.A. 87-1041, § 1, eff. Sept. 11, 1992; P.A. 88-45, Art. II, § 2-54, eff. July 6, 1993; P.A. 88-485, § 10, eff. Jan. 1, 1994; P.A. 89-424, § 15, eff. June 1, 1996; P.A. 89-564, § 5, eff. July 1, 1997; P.A. 89-612, § 10, eff. Aug. 9, 1996; P.A. 89-621, § 10, eff. Jan. 1, 1997; P.A. 89-639, § 5, eff. Jan. 1, 1997; P.A. 90-14, Art. 2, § 2-225, eff. July 1, 1997; P.A. 90-533, § 5, eff. Nov. 14, 1997; P.A. 90-655, § 153, eff. July 30, 1998; P.A. 92-629, § 5, eff. July 1, 2003.

Formerly Ill.Rev.Stat.1991, ch. 95 ½, ¶ 3-412.

For text of section as amended by P.A. 92-651, effective July 11, 2002, see 612 ILCS 5/3-412, ante

Section 3 of P.A. 82-433 approved Sept. 8, 1981, provided:

"This Act takes effect upon its becoming a law, except that the provisions relating to safety tests and proof of financial responsibility for medical transport vehicles apply only to applications for and the issuance of registration plates which are required to be displayed on January 1, 1982 or thereafter."

P.A. 90-655, the First 1998 General Revisory Act, amended various Acts to delete obsolete text, to correct patent and technical errors, to revise cross references, to resolve multiple actions in the 89th and 90th General Assemblies and to make certain technical corrections in P.A. 89-708 through P.A. 90-566.

Final legislative action, 92nd General Assembly:

P.A. 92-629—April 24, 2002

P.A. 92-651—May 14, 2002

See 5 ILCS 70/6 as to the effect of (1) more than one amendment of a section at the same session of the General Assembly or (2) two or more acts relating to the same subject matter enacted by the same General Assembly.

5/3-413. Display of registration plates, registration stickers and drive-away permits

§ 3-413. Display of registration plates, registration stickers and drive-away permits.

(a) Registration plates issued for a motor vehicle other than a motorcycle, trailer, semitrailer, truck-tractor, apportioned bus, or apportioned truck shall be attached thereto, one in the front and one in the rear. The registration plate issued for a motorcycle, trailer or semitrailer required to be registered hereunder and any apportionment plate issued to a bus under the provisions of this Code shall be attached to the rear thereof. The registration plate issued for a truck-tractor or an apportioned truck required to be registered hereunder shall be attached to the front thereof.

(b) Every registration plate shall at all times be securely fastened in a horizontal position to the vehicle for which it is issued so as to prevent the plate from swinging and at a height of not less than 5 inches from the ground, measuring from the bottom of such plate, in a place and position to be clearly visible and shall be maintained in a condition to be clearly legible, free from any materials that would obstruct the visibility of the plate, including, but not limited to, glass covers and tinted plastic covers. Clear plastic covers are permissible as long as they remain clear and do not obstruct the visibility of the plates. Registration stickers issued as evidence of renewed annual registration shall be attached to registration plates as required by the Secretary of State, and be clearly visible at all times.

(c) Every drive-away permit issued pursuant to this Code shall be firmly attached to the motor vehicle in the manner prescribed by the Secretary of State. If a drive-away permit is affixed to a motor vehicle in any other manner the permit shall be void and of no effect.

(d) The Illinois prorate decal issued to a foreign registered vehicle part of a fleet prorated or apportioned with Illinois, shall be displayed on a registration plate and displayed on the front of such vehicle in the same manner as an Illinois registration plate.

(e) The registration plate issued for a camper body mounted on a truck displaying registration plates shall be attached to the rear of the camper body.

(f) No person shall operate a vehicle, nor permit the operation of a vehicle, upon which is displayed an Illinois registration plate, plates or registration stickers after the termination of the registration period for which issued or after the expiration date set pursuant to Sections 3-414 and 3-414.1 of this Code.

P.A. 76-1586, § 3-413, eff. July 1, 1970. Amended by P.A. 77-1315, § 1, eff. Jan. 1, 1972; P.A. 78-335, § 1, eff. Jan. 1, 1974; P.A. 80-230, § 1, eff. Oct. 1, 1977; P.A. 80-891, § 1, eff. Jan. 1, 1978; P.A. 80-1364, § 36, eff. Aug. 13, 1978; P.A. 81-886, § 1, eff. July 1, 1980; P.A. 82-133, § 1, eff. Jan. 1, 1982; P.A. 85-1396, § 2, eff. Sept. 2, 1988; P.A. 86-417, § 1, eff. Jan. 1, 1990; P.A. 87-353, § 3, eff. Sept. 9, 1991; P.A. 87-1041, § 1, eff. Jan. 1, 1993; P.A. 89-245, § 5, eff. Jan. 1, 1996; P.A. 89-375, § 3, eff. Aug. 18, 1995; P.A. 92-668, § 5, eff. Jan. 1, 2003; P.A. 92-680, § 15, eff. July 16, 2002.

Formerly Ill.Rev.Stat.1991, ch. 95 ½, ¶ 3-413.

P.A. 89-375 included the amendment by P.A. 89-245.

See 5 ILCS 70/6 as to the effect of (1) more than one amendment of a section at the same session of the General Assembly or (2) two or more acts relating to the same subject matter enacted by the same General Assembly.

5/3-414. Expiration of registration

Text of section effective until July 1, 2003

§ 3-414. Expiration of registration.

(a) Every vehicle registration under this Chapter and every registration card and registration plate or registration sticker issued hereunder to a vehicle shall be for the periods specified in this Chapter and shall expire at midnight on the day and date specified in this Section as follows:

1. When registered on a calendar year basis commencing January 1, expiration shall be on the 31st day of December or at such other date as may be selected in the discretion of the Secretary of State; however, registrations of apportionable vehicles, motorcycles, motor driven cycles and pedalcycles shall commence on the first day of April and shall expire March 31st of the following calendar year;

2. When registered on a 2 calendar year basis commencing January 1 of an even-numbered year, expiration shall be on the 31st day of December of the ensuing odd-numbered year, or at such other later date as may be selected in the discretion of the Secretary of State not beyond March 1 next;

3. When registered on a fiscal year basis commencing July 1, expiration shall be on the 30th day of June or at such other later date as may be selected in the discretion of the Secretary of State not beyond September 1 next;

4. When registered on a 2 fiscal year basis commencing July 1 of an even-numbered year, expiration shall be on the 30th day of June of the ensuing even-numbered year, or at such other later date as may be selected in the discretion of the Secretary of State not beyond September 1 next;

5. When registered on a 4 fiscal year basis commencing July 1 of an even-numbered year, expiration shall be on the 30th day of June of the second ensuing even-numbered year, or at such other later date as may be selected in the discretion of the Secretary of State not beyond September 1 next;

(b) Vehicle registrations of vehicles of the first division shall be for a calendar year or 2 calendar year basis as provided for in this Chapter.

Vehicle registrations of vehicles under Sections 3-807, 3-808 and 3-809 shall be on an indefinite term basis or a 2 calendar year basis as provided for in this Chapter.

Vehicle registrations for vehicles of the second division shall be for a fiscal year, 2 fiscal year or calendar year basis as provided for in this Chapter.

Motor vehicles registered under the provisions of Section 3-402.1 shall be issued multi-year registration plates with a new registration card issued annually upon payment of the appropriate fees. Apportionable trailers and apportionable semitrailers registered under the provisions of Section 3-402.1 shall be issued multi-year registration plates and cards that will be subject to revocation for failure to pay annual fees required by Section 3-814.1. The Secretary shall determine when these vehicles shall be issued new registration plates.

(c) Every vehicle registration specified in Section 3-810 and every registration card and registration plate or registration sticker issued thereunder shall expire on the 31st day of December of each year or at such other date as may be selected in the discretion of the Secretary of State.

(d) Every vehicle registration for a vehicle of the second division weighing over 8,000 pounds, except as provided in paragraph (g) of this Section, and every registration card and registration plate or registration sticker, where applicable, issued hereunder to such vehicles shall be issued for a fiscal year commencing on July 1st of each registration year. However, the Secretary of State may, pursuant to an agreement or arrangement or declaration providing for apportionment of a fleet of vehicles with other jurisdictions, provide for registration of such vehicles under apportionment or for all of the vehicles registered in Illinois by an applicant who registers some of his vehicles under apportionment on a calendar year basis instead, and the fees or taxes to be paid on a calendar year basis shall be identical to those specified in this Act for a fiscal year registration. Provision for installment payment may also be made.

(e) Semitrailer registrations under apportionment may be on a calendar year under a reciprocal agreement or arrangement and all other semitrailer registrations shall be on fiscal year or 2 fiscal year or 4 fiscal year basis as provided for in this Chapter.

(f) The Secretary of State may convert annual registration plates or 2-year registration plates, whether registered on a calendar year or fiscal year basis, to multi-year plates. The determination of which plate categories and when to convert to multi-year plates is solely within the discretion of the Secretary of State.

(g) After January 1, 1975, each registration, registration card and registration plate or registration sticker, where applicable, issued for a recreational vehicle or recreational or camping trailer, except a house trailer, used exclusively by the owner for recreational purposes, and not used commercially nor as a truck or bus, nor for hire, shall be on a calendar year basis; except that the Secretary of State shall provide for registration and the issuance of registration cards and plates or registration stickers, where applicable, for one 6-month period in order to accomplish an orderly transition from a fiscal year to a calendar year basis. Fees and taxes due under this Act for a registration year shall be appropriately reduced for such 6-month transitional registration period.

(h) The Secretary of State may, in order to accomplish an orderly transition for vehicles registered under Section 3-402.1 of this Code from a calendar year registration to a March 31st expiration, require applicants to pay fees and taxes due under this Code on a 15 month registration basis. However, if in the discretion of the Secretary of State this creates an undue hardship on any applicant the Secretary may allow the applicant to pay 3 month fees and taxes at the time of registration and the additional 12 month fees and taxes to be payable no later than March 31 of the year after this amendatory Act of 1991 takes effect.

(i) The Secretary of State may stagger registrations, of vehicles for which multi-year plates are issued pursuant to Section 3-414.1, as necessary for the convenience of the public and the efficiency of his Office. In order to appropriately and effectively accomplish any such staggering, the Secretary of State is authorized to prorate required registration fees, but in no event for a period longer than 15 months, at a monthly rate for a 12 month registration fee.

P.A. 76-1586, § 3-414, eff. July 1, 1970. Amended by P.A. 76-1865, § 1, eff. July 1, 1970; P.A. 77-44, § 1, eff. Jan. 1, 1972; P.A. 77-1315, § 1, eff. Jan. 1, 1972; P.A. 77-2829, § 40, eff. Dec. 22, 1972; P.A. 78-255, § 61, eff. Oct. 1, 1973; P.A. 78-1146, § 1, eff. Jan. 1, 1975; P.A. 78-1297, § 58, eff. March 4, 1975; P.A. 79-1021, § 1; P.A. 79-1367, § 1, eff. Aug. 6, 1976; P.A. 80-230, § 1, eff. Oct. 1, 1977; P.A. 80-1185, § 1, eff. March 8, 1978; P.A. 81-1491, § 1, eff. Sept. 19, 1980; P.A. 83-449, § 1, eff. Jan. 1, 1984; P.A. 83-817, § 1, eff. Jan. 1, 1984; P.A. 83-1362, Art. II, § 99, eff. Sept. 11, 1984; P.A. 87-206, § 1, eff. Sept. 3, 1991; P.A. 87-1040, § 1, eff. Sept. 11, 1992; P.A. 89-245, § 5, eff. Jan. 1, 1996.

Formerly Ill.Rev.Stat.1991, ch. 95 ½, ¶ 3-414.

For text of section effective July 1, 2003, see 625 ILCS 5/3-414, post

5/3-414. Expiration of registration

Text of section effective July 1, 2003

§ 3-414. Expiration of registration.

(a) Every vehicle registration under this Chapter and every registration card and registration plate or registration sticker issued hereunder to a vehicle shall be for the periods specified in this Chapter and shall expire at midnight on the day and date specified in this Section as follows:

1. When registered on a calendar year basis commencing January 1, expiration shall be on the 31st day of December or at such other date as may be selected in the discretion of the Secretary of State; however, registrations of apportionable vehicles, motorcycles, motor driven cycles and pedalcycles shall commence on the first day of April and shall expire March 31st of the following calendar year;

2. When registered on a 2 calendar year basis commencing January 1 of an even-numbered year, expiration shall be on the 31st day of December of the ensuing odd-numbered year, or at such other later date as may be selected in the discretion of the Secretary of State not beyond March 1 next;

3. When registered on a fiscal year basis commencing July 1, expiration shall be on the 30th day of June or at

such other later date as may be selected in the discretion of the Secretary of State not beyond September 1 next;

4. When registered on a 2 fiscal year basis commencing July 1 of an even-numbered year, expiration shall be on the 30th day of June of the ensuing even-numbered year, or at such other later date as may be selected in the discretion of the Secretary of State not beyond September 1 next;

5. When registered on a 4 fiscal year basis commencing July 1 of an even-numbered year, expiration shall be on the 30th day of June of the second ensuing even-numbered year, or at such other later date as may be selected in the discretion of the Secretary of State not beyond September 1 next;

(b) Vehicle registrations of vehicles of the first division shall be for a calendar year or 2 calendar year basis as provided for in this Chapter.

Vehicle registrations of vehicles under Sections 3-807, 3-808 and 3-809 shall be on an indefinite term basis or a 2 calendar year basis as provided for in this Chapter.

Vehicle registrations for vehicles of the second division shall be for a fiscal year, 2 fiscal year or calendar year basis as provided for in this Chapter.

Motor vehicles registered under the provisions of Sections 3-402.1 and 3-405.3 shall be issued multi-year registration plates with a new registration card issued annually upon payment of the appropriate fees. Apportionable trailers and apportionable semitrailers registered under the provisions of Section 3-402.1 shall be issued multi-year registration plates and cards that will be subject to revocation for failure to pay annual fees required by Section 3-814.1. The Secretary shall determine when these vehicles shall be issued new registration plates.

(c) Every vehicle registration specified in Section 3-810 and every registration card and registration plate or registration sticker issued thereunder shall expire on the 31st day of December of each year or at such other date as may be selected in the discretion of the Secretary of State.

(d) Every vehicle registration for a vehicle of the second division weighing over 8,000 pounds, except as provided in paragraph (g) of this Section, and every registration card and registration plate or registration sticker, where applicable, issued hereunder to such vehicles shall be issued for a fiscal year commencing on July 1st of each registration year. However, the Secretary of State may, pursuant to an agreement or arrangement or declaration providing for apportionment of a fleet of vehicles with other jurisdictions, provide for registration of such vehicles under apportionment or for all of the vehicles registered in Illinois by an applicant who registers some of his vehicles under apportionment on a calendar year basis instead, and the fees or taxes to be paid on a calendar year basis shall be identical to those specified in this Act for a fiscal year registration. Provision for installment payment may also be made.

(e) Semitrailer registrations under apportionment may be on a calendar year under a reciprocal agreement or arrangement and all other semitrailer registrations shall be on fiscal year or 2 fiscal year or 4 fiscal year basis as provided for in this Chapter.

(f) The Secretary of State may convert annual registration plates or 2-year registration plates, whether registered on a calendar year or fiscal year basis, to multi-year plates. The determination of which plate categories and when to convert to multi-year plates is solely within the discretion of the Secretary of State.

(g) After January 1, 1975, each registration, registration card and registration plate or registration sticker, where applicable, issued for a recreational vehicle or recreational or camping trailer, except a house trailer, used exclusively by the owner for recreational purposes, and not used commercially nor as a truck or bus, nor for hire, shall be on a calendar year basis; except that the Secretary of State shall provide for registration and the issuance of registration cards and plates or registration stickers, where applicable, for one 6-month period in order to accomplish an orderly transition from a fiscal year to a calendar year basis. Fees and taxes due under this Act for a registration year shall be appropriately reduced for such 6-month transitional registration period.

(h) The Secretary of State may, in order to accomplish an orderly transition for vehicles registered under Section 3-402.1 of this Code from a calendar year registration to a March 31st expiration, require applicants to pay fees and taxes due under this Code on a 15 month registration basis. However, if in the discretion of the Secretary of State this creates an undue hardship on any applicant the Secretary may allow the applicant to pay 3 month fees and taxes at the time of registration and the additional 12 month fees and taxes to be payable no later than March 31 of the year after this amendatory Act of 1991 takes effect.

(i) The Secretary of State may stagger registrations, of vehicles for which multi-year plates are issued pursuant to Section 3-414.1, as necessary for the convenience of the public and the efficiency of his Office. In order to appropriately and effectively accomplish any such staggering, the Secretary of State is authorized to prorate required registration fees, but in no event for a period longer than 15 months, at a monthly rate for a 12 month registration fee.

P.A. 76-1586, § 3-414, eff. July 1, 1970. Amended by P.A. 76-1865, § 1, eff. July 1, 1970; P.A. 77-44, § 1, eff. Jan. 1, 1972; P.A. 77-1315, § 1, eff. Jan. 1, 1972; P.A. 77-2829, § 40, eff. Dec. 22, 1972; P.A. 78-255, § 61, eff. Oct. 1, 1973; P.A. 78-1146, § 1, eff. Jan. 1, 1975; P.A. 78-1297, § 58, eff. March 4, 1975; P.A. 79-1021, § 1; P.A. 79-1367, § 1, eff. Aug. 6, 1976; P.A. 80-230, § 1, eff. Oct. 1, 1977; P.A. 80-1185, § 1, eff. March 8, 1978; P.A. 81-1491, § 1, eff. Sept. 19, 1980; P.A. 83-449, § 1, eff. Jan. 1, 1984; P.A. 83-817, § 1, eff. Jan. 1, 1984; P.A. 83-1362, Art. II, § 99, eff. Sept. 11, 1984; P.A. 87-206, § 1, eff. Sept. 3, 1991; P.A. 87-1040, § 1, eff. Sept. 11, 1992; P.A. 89-245, § 5, eff. Jan. 1, 1996; P.A. 92-629, § 5, eff. July 1, 2003.

Formerly Ill.Rev.Stat.1991, ch. 95 ½, ¶ 3-414.

For text of section effective until July 1, 2003, see 625 ILCS 5/3-414, ante

Section 2 of P.A. 83-817 approved Sept. 24, 1983, provided: "This Act takes effect with the 1985 registration year."

5/3-414.1. Term of multi-year registration plates

§ 3-414.1. Term of multi-year registration plates.

(a) Registration plates issued for motor vehicles shall be valid for an indefinite term of not less than one year. Registration plates issued as two-year plates may be issued as multi-year plates at the discretion of the Secretary of State. Current renewal registration stickers, when necessary, are to be attached as provided in Section 3-413. The Secretary may in his discretion prescribe a term greater than one year or may extend the term of current registration plates for an additional calendar year by appropriate public announcement made before August 1 of the current registration year.

(b) Registration plates issued to owners of vehicles subject to annual registration for the first time during the term of the plates shall be valid until the expiration of the term. Current annual registration stickers are to be attached as provided in Section 3-413.

P.A. 76-1586, § 3-414.1, eff. July 1, 1970, added by P.A. 80-230, § 1, eff. Oct. 1, 1977. Amended by P.A. 83-828, § 1, eff. Jan. 1, 1984; P.A. 84-986, § 1, eff. Sept. 25, 1985; P.A. 89-245, § 5, eff. Jan. 1, 1996.

Formerly Ill.Rev.Stat.1991, ch. 95 ½, ¶ 3-414.1.

Section 2 of P.A. 83-828 provided:

"This Act takes effect with the 1985 registration year."

See 5 ILCS 70/6 as to the effect of (1) more than one amendment of a section at the same session of the General Assembly or (2) two or more acts relating to the same subject matter enacted by the same General Assembly.

5/3-415. Application for and renewal of registration

§ 3-415. Application for and renewal of registration. **(a) Calendar year.** Application for renewal of a vehicle registration shall be made by the owner, as to those vehicles required to be registered on a calendar registration year, not later than December 1 of each year, upon proper application and by payment of the registration fee and tax for such vehicle, as provided by law except that application for renewal of a vehicle registration, as to those vehicles required to be registered on a staggered calendar year basis, shall be made by the owner in the form and manner prescribed by the Secretary of State.

(b) Fiscal year. Application for renewal of a vehicle registration shall be made by the owner, as to those vehicles required to be registered on a fiscal registration year, not later than June 1 of each year, upon proper application and by payment of the registration fee and tax for such vehicle as provided by law, except that application for renewal of a vehicle registration, as to those vehicles required to be registered on a staggered fiscal year basis, shall be made by the owner in the form and manner prescribed by the Secretary of State.

(c) Two calendar years. Application for renewal of a vehicle registration shall be made by the owner, as to those vehicles required to be registered for 2 calendar years, not later than December 1 of the year preceding commencement of the 2-year registration period, except that application for renewal of a vehicle registration, as to those vehicles required to be registered for 2 years on a staggered registration basis, shall be made by the owner in the form and manner prescribed by the Secretary of State.

(d) Two fiscal years. Application for renewal of a vehicle registration shall be made by the owner, as to those vehicles required to be registered for 2 fiscal years, not later than June 1 immediately preceding commencement of the 2-year registration period, except that application for renewal of a vehicle registration, as to those vehicles required to be registered for 2 fiscal years on a staggered registration basis, shall be made by the owner in the form and manner prescribed by the Secretary of State.

(e) Time of application. The Secretary of State may receive applications for renewal of registration and grant the same and issue new registration cards and plates or registration stickers at any time prior to expiration of registration. No person shall display upon a vehicle, the new registration plates or registration stickers prior to the dates the Secretary of State in his discretion may select.

(f) Verification. The Secretary of State may further require, as to vehicles for-hire, that applications be accompanied by verification that fees due under the Illinois Motor Carrier of Property Law, as amended,[1] have been paid.

P.A. 76-1586, § 3-415, eff. July 1, 1970. Amended by P.A. 76-1624, § 1, eff. July 1, 1970; P.A. 78-1120, § 1, eff. Oct. 1, 1974; P.A. 80-230, § 1, eff. Oct. 1, 1977; P.A. 80-1185, § 1, eff. March 8, 1978.

Formerly Ill.Rev.Stat.1991, ch. 95 ½, ¶ 3-415.

[1] Former Ill.Rev.Stat. ch. 95½, ¶ 18-100 et seq. (repealed; see, now, 625 ILCS 5/18c-1101 et seq.).

See 5 ILCS 70/6 as to the effect of (1) more than one amendment of a section at the same session of the General Assembly or (2) two or more acts relating to the same subject matter enacted by the same General Assembly.

5/3-416. Notice of change of address or name

§ 3-416. Notice of change of address or name.

(a) Whenever any person after making application for or obtaining the registration of a vehicle shall move from the address named in the application or shown upon a registration card or certificate of title such person shall within 10 days thereafter notify the Secretary of State in writing of his old and new address.

(a-5) A police officer, a deputy sheriff, an elected sheriff, a law enforcement officer for the Department of State Police, or a fire investigator who, in accordance with Section 3-405, has furnished the address of the office of the headquarters of the governmental entity or police district where he or she works instead of his or her residence address shall, within 10 days after he or she is no longer employed by that governmental entity or police district as a police officer, a deputy sheriff, an elected sheriff, a law enforcement officer for the Department of State Police or a fire investigator, notify the Secretary of State of the old address and his or her new address. If, in accordance with Section 3-405, the spouse and children of a police officer, deputy sheriff, elected sheriff, law enforcement officer for the Department of State Police, or fire investigator have furnished the address of the office of the headquarters of the governmental entity or police district where the police officer, deputy sheriff, elected sheriff, law enforcement officer for the Department of State Police, or fire investigator works instead of their residence address, the spouse and children shall notify the Secretary of State of their old address and new address within 10 days after the police officer, deputy sheriff, elected sheriff, law enforcement officer for the Department of State Police, or fire investigator is no longer employed by that governmental entity or police district as a police officer, deputy sheriff, elected sheriff, law enforcement officer for the Department of State Police, or fire investigator.

(b) Whenever the name of any person who has made application for or obtained the registration of a vehicle is thereafter changed by marriage or otherwise such person shall within 10 days notify the Secretary of State of such former and new name.

(c) In either event, any such person may obtain a corrected registration card or certificate of title upon application and payment of the statutory fee.

P.A. 76-1586, § 3-416, eff. July 1, 1970. Amended by P.A. 77-364, § 1, eff. July 23, 1971; P.A. 91-575, § 5, eff. Aug. 14, 1999.

Formerly Ill.Rev.Stat.1991, ch. 95 ½, ¶ 3-416.

5/3-417. Lost or damaged or stolen cards, plates and registration stickers

§ 3-417. Lost or damaged or stolen cards, plates and registration stickers. (a) In the event any registration card, plate, registration sticker or other Illinois evidence of proper registration is lost, mutilated or becomes illegible, the owner or legal representative or successor in interest of the owner of the vehicle for which the same was issued as shown by the records of the Secretary of State shall immediately make application for and may obtain a duplicate under a new registration card, plate, registration sticker or other Illinois evidence of proper registration.

(b) In the event any registration card, plate, registration sticker or other Illinois evidence of proper registration is stolen from the owner, the owner or legal representative or successor in interest of the owner of the vehicle shall promptly notify the Secretary of State, and in order to comply with Section 3-413 of this Act the owner shall make application for and obtain a duplicate registration card, plate, registration sticker or other Illinois evidence of proper registration.

(c) The Secretary of State may, if advisable, issue a substitute or new registration number in lieu of issuing a duplicate.

(d) An applicant for a duplicate shall furnish information satisfactory to and prescribed by the Secretary of State, and he shall forward with the application, the fees prescribed by law.

P.A. 76-1586, § 3-417, eff. July 1, 1970. Amended by P.A. 77-649, § 1, eff. Jan. 1, 1972; P.A. 80-230, § 1, eff. Oct. 1, 1977; P.A. 81-308, § 1, eff. Jan. 1, 1980.

Formerly Ill.Rev.Stat.1991, ch. 95 ½, ¶ 3-417.

5/3-418. Registration under new identifying number

§ 3-418. Registration under new identifying number. When the Secretary of State issues a new identifying number, such motor vehicle shall be registered under such identifying number in lieu of the former identifying number.

P.A. 76-1586, § 3-418, eff. July 1, 1970.

Formerly Ill.Rev.Stat.1991, ch. 95 ½, ¶ 3-418.

5/3-419. Regulations governing change of motors

§ 3-419. Regulations governing change of motors. The Secretary of State is authorized to adopt and enforce such registration rules and regulations as may be deemed necessary and compatible with the public interest with respect to the change or substitution of one engine in place of another in any motor vehicle.

Where a substitution or change changes the classification of a motor vehicle for registration purposes resulting in requiring the payment of a greater fee or tax, the owner shall be required to reclassify the registration and pay the higher or greater fee or tax due.

P.A. 76-1586, § 3-419, eff. July 1, 1970. Amended by P.A. 77-364, § 1, eff. July 23, 1971.

Formerly Ill.Rev.Stat.1991, ch. 95 ½, ¶ 3-419.

5/3-420. § 3-420. Deleted by P.A. 83-148, § 1, eff. Aug. 29, 1983

The provisions of this section were completely stricken out by P.A. 83-148, § 1, eff. Aug. 29, 1983. The section was derived from:

5/3-421. Right of reassignment

§ 3-421. Right of reassignment. (a) Every natural person shall have the right of reassignment of the license number issued to him during the current registration plate term, for the ensuing registration plate term, provided his application for reassignment is received in the Office of the Secretary of State on or before September 30 of the final year of the registration plate term as to a vehicle registered on a calendar year, and on or before March 31 as to a vehicle registered on a fiscal year. The right of reassignment shall apply to every natural person under the staggered registration system provided the application for reassignment is received in the Office of the Secretary of State by the 1st day of the month immediately preceding the applicant's month of expiration.

In addition, every natural person shall have the right of reassignment of the license number issued to him for a two-year registration, for the ensuing two-year period. Where the two-year period is for two calendar years, the application for reassignment must be received by the Secretary of State on or before September 30th of the year preceding commencement of the two-year period. Where the two-year period is for two fiscal years commencing on July 1, the application for reassignment must be received by the Secretary of State on or before April 30th immediately preceding commencement of the two-year period.

(b) Notwithstanding the above provision, the Secretary of State shall, subject to the existing right of reassignment, have the authority to designate new specific combinations of numerical, alpha-numerical, and numerical-alpha licenses for vehicles registered on a calendar year or on a fiscal year, whether the license be issued for one or more years. The new combinations so specified shall not be subject to the right of reassignment, and no right of reassignment thereto may at any future time be acquired.

P.A. 76-1586, § 3-421, added by P.A. 77-512, § 1, eff. Jan. 1, 1972. Amended by P.A. 79-717, § 1, eff. Oct. 1, 1975; P.A. 80-230, § 1, eff. Oct. 1, 1977; P.A. 80-1185, § 1, eff. March 8, 1978.

Formerly Ill.Rev.Stat.1991, ch. 95 ½, ¶ 3-421.

See 5 ILCS 70/6 as to the effect of (1) more than one amendment of a section at the same session of the General Assembly or (2) two or more acts relating to the same subject matter enacted by the same General Assembly.

ARTICLE V. TRANSFER OF REGISTRATION

Section

5/3-501. Registration expires on transfer by owner

§ 3-501. Registration expires on transfer by owner. Whenever the owner of a registered vehicle transfers or assigns his title, or interest thereto, the registration of such vehicle shall expire and the owner shall not be entitled to any refund of the registration fee. The owner shall remove the registration plates and registration stickers, if any, therefrom and forward the same to the Secretary of State or may have such plates and registration stickers, if any, and the registration number thereon assigned to another vehicle upon payment of the fees required by law and subject to the rules and regulations of the Secretary of State.

P.A. 76-1586, § 3-501, eff. July 1, 1970. Amended by P.A. 77-325, § 1, eff. July 22, 1971; P.A. 80-230, § 1, eff. Oct. 1, 1977; P.A. 80-1185, § 1, eff. March 8, 1978.

Formerly Ill.Rev.Stat.1991, ch. 95 ½, ¶ 3-501.

See 5 ILCS 70/6 as to the effect of (1) more than one amendment of a section at the same session of the General Assembly or (2) two or more acts relating to the same subject matter enacted by the same General Assembly.

5/3-501.1. Transfer or return of vanity or personalized license plates

§ 3-501.1. Transfer or return of vanity or personalized license plates. When any person who has been issued vanity or personalized license plates sells, trades or otherwise releases the ownership of the vehicle upon which the vanity or personalized license plates have been displayed, he shall immediately report the transfer of such plates to an acquired motor vehicle pursuant to Section 3-501 and pay the transfer fee or shall, upon the request of the Secretary, immediately return such plates to the Secretary of State. The right to reassignment of the registration plate number shall apply as provided in Section 3-421 of this Code.

P.A. 76-1586, § 3-501.1, added by P.A. 81-987, § 1, eff. Sept. 22, 1979. Amended by P.A. 86-480, § 1, eff. Jan. 1, 1990; P.A. 86-1005, § 3, eff. Dec. 28, 1989; P.A. 88-78, § 15, eff. Sept. 7, 1993.

Formerly Ill.Rev.Stat.1991, ch. 95 ½, ¶ 3-501.1.

5/3-502. New owner must secure new registration

§ 3-502. New owner must secure new registration. The transferee before operating or permitting the operation of such vehicle upon a highway shall apply for and obtain the registration thereof, as upon an original registration, except as otherwise permitted in Sections 3-401, 3-503 and 3-504.

P.A. 76-1586, § 3-502, eff. July 1, 1970.

Formerly Ill.Rev.Stat.1991, ch. 95 ½, ¶ 3-502.

5/3-503. Transfers to dealers

§ 3-503. Transfers to dealers. When the transferee of a vehicle is a dealer who holds the same for resale and lawfully operates the same under dealers' number plates or when the transferee does not drive such vehicle or permit it to be driven upon the highways, such transferee shall not be required to obtain a new registration of said vehicle.

P.A. 76-1586, § 3-503, eff. July 1, 1970.

Formerly Ill.Rev.Stat.1991, ch. 95 ½, ¶ 3-503.

5/3-504. Transfer by operation of law

§ 3-504. Transfer by operation of law. Except in case of joint tenancy with the right of survivorship or surviving spouse or transfer pursuant to an order of the Illinois Commerce Commission or Interstate Commerce Commission, whenever the title or interest of an owner in or to a registered vehicle shall pass to another otherwise than by voluntary transfer, except a transfer pursuant to an order of the Illinois Commerce Commission or Interstate Commerce Commission, the registration thereof shall expire and the vehicle shall not be operated upon the highways unless and until the person entitled to possession of such vehicle shall apply for and obtain the registration thereof.

P.A. 76-1586, § 3-504, eff. July 1, 1970.

Formerly Ill.Rev.Stat.1991, ch. 95 ½, ¶ 3-504.

5/3-505. Transfer of reciprocity permit or prorate decals

§ 3-505. Transfer of reciprocity permit or prorate decals. Whenever the owner of a vehicle properly registered in another State transfers his interest thereto, Illinois evidence of proper registration in such other State, that is an Illinois Reciprocity Permit or a Prorate Decal, shall expire and the owner shall remove the same from such vehicle and forward the same to the Secretary of State.

The owner may, however, instead have such Illinois evidence of proper registration in another State assigned to another vehicle also properly registered in another State, upon payment of the fees required by law and subject to the rules and regulations of the Secretary.

P.A. 76-1586, § 3-505, added by P.A. 77-649, § 1, eff. Jan. 1, 1972. Amended by P.A. 81-886, § 1, eff. July 1, 1980.

Formerly Ill.Rev.Stat.1991, ch. 95 ½, ¶ 3-505.

ARTICLE VI. SPECIAL PLATES

Section

5/3-600. Requirements for issuance of special plates

§ 3-600. Requirements for issuance of special plates.

(a) The Secretary of State shall not issue a series of special plates unless applications, as prescribed by the Secretary, have been received for 10,000 plates of that series; except that the Secretary of State may prescribe some other required number of applications if that number is sufficient to pay for the total cost of designing, manufacturing and issuing the special license plate.

(b) The Secretary of State, upon issuing a new series of special license plates, shall notify all law enforcement officials of the design, color and other special features of the special license plate series.

(c) This Section shall not apply to special license plate categories in existence on the effective date of this amendatory Act of 1990, or to the Secretary of State's discretion as established in Section 3-611.

P.A. 76-1586, § 3-600, added by P.A. 86-1207, § 1, eff. Aug. 29, 1990.

Formerly Ill.Rev.Stat.1991, ch. 95 ½, ¶ 3-600.

5/3-601. Operation of vehicles under special plates

§ 3-601. Operation of vehicles under special plates. (a) A manufacturer owning any unregistered vehicle of a type otherwise required to be registered under this Act may operate or move such upon the highways without registering each such vehicle upon condition that any such vehicle display thereon a special plate or plates issued to such owner as provided in this Article.

(b) A dealer owning any unregistered vehicle of a type otherwise required to be registered under this Act and held by him for sale or resale, may operate or move such upon the highways without registering each such vehicle upon condition that any such vehicle display thereon a special plate or plates issued to such owner as provided in this Article.

(c) A transporter may operate or move any vehicle not owned by him upon the highways by the driveaway or towaway methods solely for the purpose of delivery upon likewise displaying thereon like plates issued to him as provided in this Article.

(d) A boat dealer owning any boat trailer of a type otherwise required to be registered under this Act may operate or move such upon the highways and haul a boat customarily sold with such boat trailer, without registering each such boat trailer upon condition that any such boat trailer display thereon, in the manner prescribed in Section 3-413, a special plate or plates issued to such owner as provided in this Article.

(e) Any person owning unregistered vehicles of a type required to be registered and which are exclusively operated off the highways and upon private property, may move such vehicles from one plant location to another upon the highways without registering each such vehicle upon conditions that any such vehicle display thereon a special plate or plates issued to such persons as provided in this Article. Such vehicles must be unladen and may not be operated upon any highways with such special plates except for the interplant movement.

(f) Any person owning a vehicle of a type required to be registered which when purchased is not yet equipped for work or service, may move such vehicle from the point of original manufacture or sale to a body shop or other place where the vehicle is to be equipped for work or service and from such point to the owner's place of business without first registering each such vehicle upon condition that any such vehicle display thereon a special plate or plates issued to such person as provided in this Article. Upon completion of such movement, any such vehicle subject to registration must be properly registered.

(g) Special plates issued under this Article must be displayed in the manner provided for in Section 3-413.

(h) Any such vehicle bearing such special plate or plates may be operated without registration for any purpose, except that no such special plate or plates shall be used on any vehicle which is rented by the manufacturer or dealer to another person or which is used to transport passengers or property for hire, nor, except as provided in paragraph (i) of this Section, shall any such special plate or plates be used on a second division vehicle which is carrying cargo or merchandise except in demonstrating such second division vehicle for the purposes of sale, or for the purpose of testing engine and driveline components.

(i) The provisions of this Article authorizing special plates shall not apply to work or service vehicles owned by a manufacturer, transporter or dealer except a truck up to 8,000 pounds gross weight owned by a dealer and used for hauling parts incidental to the operation of the dealer's business.

(j) The Secretary of State may limit the number of special plates issued to any applicant.

P.A. 76-1586, § 3-601, eff. July 1, 1970. Amended by P.A. 76-2134, § 1, eff. July 1, 1970; P.A. 77-75, § 1, eff. July 1, 1971; P.A. 77-1316, § 1, eff. Jan. 1, 1972; P.A. 77-2829, § 40, eff. Dec. 22, 1972; P.A. 78-255, § 61, eff. Oct. 1, 1973; P.A. 78-753, § 1, eff. Sept. 11, 1973; P.A. 78-1297, § 58, eff. March 4, 1975.

Formerly Ill.Rev.Stat.1991, ch. 95 ½, ¶ 3-601.

5/3-602. Certificate and special plates for dealers, manufacturers, and transporters

§ 3-602. Certificate and special plates for dealers, manufacturers, and transporters.

(a) Any dealer, manufacturer, or transporter may make application to the Secretary of State upon the appropriate form for a certificate containing a general distinguishing number and for one or more sets of special plates as appropriate to various types of vehicles subject to registration hereunder. The applicant shall submit such proof of his or her status as a bona fide dealer, manufacturer, or transporter as may be reasonably required by the Secretary of State.

(b) The Secretary of State, upon granting any such application, shall issue to the applicant a certificate containing the applicant's name and address and special plates as applied for. Both the certificates and special plates shall display the general distinguishing number assigned to the applicant.

(c) The Secretary of State shall issue special plates to dealers and manufacturers in accordance with the following formula:

number vehicles sold in previous calendar year	maximum number sets of special plates issued at fee set by Sec. 3-810	maximum number additional sets issued at fee set by Sec. 3-806
0	0	0
1-10	1	1
11-25	2	2
26-100	8	8
101-250	12	12
251-500	20	20
501-750	30	30
751-1000	40	40
1001-1500	50	50
1501-2000	60	60
2001-2500	70	70
2501+	90	90

For those Dealers with annual sales over 2501, special plates will be allocated based on 10 sets of plates under each section for each additional 500 vehicles sold.

The limit on the maximum number of additional sets issued to manufacturers at the fee set by Section 3-806 may be lifted at the discretion of the Secretary of State.

The Secretary shall issue to a new dealer or manufacturer not more than 8 sets of special plates at each fee. If the new dealer or manufacturer has acquired his or her business from a previous dealer or manufacturer, he or she may be issued a number of sets based upon the number of vehicles sold in the previous calendar year by the previous dealer or manufacturer. If the new dealer or manufacturer was in business for only a part of the previous calendar year, the number of special plates to which he or she is entitled may be extrapolated from the number of vehicles he or she sold during that part of the year.

(d) Any manufacturer of engine and driveline components may apply to the Secretary of State for a license to operate vehicles in which such components are installed on the public highways of the State for the purpose of testing such components. The application shall describe the components and the vehicles in which they are installed, and shall contain such additional information as the Secretary shall prescribe. Upon receipt of an application and an accompanying fee of $1000, the Secretary shall issue to the applicant a license for the entire test period of the components described in the application.

Every licensee shall keep a record of each vehicle operated under such license which shall be open to inspection by the Secretary or his authorized representative for inspection at any reasonable time during the day or night.

The license of a manufacturer of engine and driveline components may be denied, revoked or suspended if the Secretary finds that the manufacturer has:

(1) violated this Code;

(2) made any material misrepresentation to the Secretary of State in connection with an application for a license; or

(3) failed to produce for the Secretary of State any record required to be produced by this Code.

This amendatory Act of 1983 shall be applicable to the 1984 registration year and thereafter.

P.A. 76-1586, § 3-602, eff. July 1, 1970. Amended by P.A. 76-2135, § 1, eff. July 1, 1970; P.A. 77-1316, § 1, eff. Jan. 1, 1972; P.A. 83-765, § 1, eff. Sept. 23, 1983; P.A. 84-986, § 1, eff. Sept. 25, 1985; P.A. 86-444, § 1, eff. Jan. 1, 1990; P.A. 91-357, § 231, eff. July 29, 1999.

Formerly Ill.Rev.Stat.1991, ch. 95 ½, ¶ 3-602.

5/3-603. Application for drive-away permits

§ 3-603. Application for drive-away permits.

(a) A dealer who has sold a vehicle of a type otherwise required to be registered under this Act to a nonresident of this State who does not have currently valid registration in his home state, may provide for the operation of such vehicle without registration from the place of sale to the place of destination outside of the State of Illinois, by issuing a drive-away permit in the manner prescribed by the Secretary of State and by affixing the permit to such vehicle in the manner prescribed by the Secretary of State. Any vehicle being operated pursuant to a drive-away permit may not be used for any other purpose and such permits shall be effective only for a period of 7 days from the date of sale.

(b) Any dealer may make application to the Secretary of State upon the appropriate form for drive-away permits for motor vehicles sold by such dealer. Along with such application each applicant shall submit proof of his status as a bona fide dealer and any other information as may be required by the Secretary of State. A non-resident who has purchased a motor vehicle from a person who is not a dealer, may likewise apply to the Secretary of State for a drive-away permit for display upon such vehicle while being driven from Illinois to the State of residence of the applicant. Along with such application, the applicant shall submit proof of his non-residence and eligibility for a reciprocal exemption from registration in Illinois.

All drive-away permits issued under such application shall bear a distinguishing number and such other features as may be required by the Secretary of State.

P.A. 76-1586, § 3-603, eff. July 1, 1970. Amended by P.A. 77-1316, § 1, eff. Jan. 1, 1972; P.A. 78-753, § 1, eff. Sept. 11, 1973; P.A. 81-822, § 1, eff. Jan. 1, 1980; P.A. 86-444, § 1, eff. Jan. 1, 1990; P.A. 92-680, § 15, eff. July 16, 2002.

Formerly Ill.Rev.Stat.1991, ch. 95 ½, ¶ 3-603.

5/3-604. Expiration of special plates

§ 3-604. Expiration of special plates. Every special plate issued, except those issued for dealers, manufacturers and transporters under Section 3-602 and persons with disabilities under Sections 3-609 or 3-616, or deaf or hard of hearing under Section 3-616 of this Code, may be issued for a 2 year period beginning January 1st of each odd-numbered year and ending December 31st of the subsequent even-numbered year. The special plates issued to a person with disabilities or a person who is deaf or hard of hearing shall expire according to the multi-year procedure as established by Section 3-414 of this Code.

Special plates issued to members of the General Assembly under Section 3-606 shall expire at midnight on the 31st day of January in odd-numbered years.

P.A. 76-1586, § 3-604, eff. July 1, 1970. Amended by P.A. 81-179, § 1, eff. Jan. 1, 1980; P.A. 83-449, § 1, eff. Jan. 1, 1984; P.A. 83-1058, § 1, eff. July 1, 1984; P.A. 83-1362, Art. II, § 99, eff. Sept. 11, 1984; P.A. 85-413, § 1, eff. Jan. 1, 1988; P.A. 85-821, § 1, eff. Jan. 1, 1988; P.A. 85-1209, Art. II, § 2-51, eff. Aug. 30, 1988; P.A. 88-685, § 5, eff. Jan. 24, 1995; P.A. 89-245, § 5, eff. Jan. 1, 1996.

Formerly Ill.Rev.Stat.1991, ch. 95 ½, ¶ 3-604.

5/3-605. Manufacturers, engine and driveline component manufacturers, transporters, repossessors and dealers to maintain records

§ 3-605. Manufacturers, engine and driveline component manufacturers, transporters, repossessors and dealers to maintain records.

Every manufacturer, engine and driveline component manufacturer, repossessor, transporter or dealer shall keep a written record of the persons to whom such drive-away permits or special plates are assigned, which record shall be open to inspection by any public officer or any employee of the Secretary of State.

P.A. 76-1586, § 3-605, eff. July 1, 1970. Amended by P.A. 76-2136, § 1, eff. July 1, 1970; P.A. 92-680, § 15, eff. July 16, 2002.

Formerly Ill.Rev.Stat.1991, ch. 95 ½, ¶ 3-605.

5/3-606. Members of General Assembly

§ 3-606. Members of General Assembly. Upon receipt of a request of a member of the General Assembly, accompanied by the appropriate application and fee, the Secretary of State shall issue to the member 2 plates as described in this Section. If the member so requests, the Secretary shall issue 2 identical sets of such registration plates for use on 2 different motor vehicles. A member may request that the Secretary of State issue registration plates in the name of a corporation when the corporation owns or leases the vehicle to be registered and the member is an officer or director of that corporation. Such registration plates shall be issued for a 2-year period beginning January 1 of each odd-numbered year and ending December 31 of the subsequent even-numbered year. If the application is from a member of the Senate, there shall appear on the rear plate, in addition to the designation of the State and the year for which the license was issued, the word "official" and appropriate wording or abbreviation indicating that the holder is a member of the Senate, followed by the number of the senatorial district of the member. On the front plate, there shall appear appropriate wording or abbreviation indicating that the holder is a member of the Senate. If the application is from a member of the House of Representatives, there shall appear on the rear plate, in addition to the designation of the State and the year for which the license was issued, the word "official" and appropriate wording or abbreviation indicating that the holder is a member of the House of Representatives, followed by the number assigned to the member. On the front plate, there shall appear appropriate wording or abbreviation indicating that the holder is a member of the House of Representatives. Numbers 1 through 118 shall be assigned and members with the longest length of service as members of the legislature shall be given the lower numbers.

When members have an equal length of service, the lower numbers shall be given in alphabetical order based on surnames.

P.A. 76-1586, § 3-606, eff. July 1, 1970. Amended by P.A. 77-2628, § 1, eff. Oct. 1, 1972; P.A. 78-328, § 1, eff. Oct. 1, 1973; P.A. 79-1036, § 1, eff. Oct. 1, 1975; P.A. 80-230, § 1, eff. Oct. 1, 1977; P.A. 82-1011, § 2, eff. Sept. 17, 1982; P.A. 88-661, § 27, eff. Sept. 16, 1994.

Formerly Ill.Rev.Stat.1991, ch. 95 ½, ¶ 3-606.

5/3-606.1. Retired members of the General Assembly

§ 3-606.1. Retired members of the General Assembly. Upon receipt of a request from a retired member of the General Assembly, accompanied by the appropriate application and fee, the Secretary of State shall issue to such retired member plates bearing appropriate wording or abbreviations indicating that the holder is a retired member of the General Assembly. Such plates may be issued for a 2 year period beginning January 1st of each odd-numbered year and ending December 31st of the subsequent even-numbered year.

"Retired member" means any individual who (a) has served as a member of the General Assembly for a minimum of 6 years, or (b) is 62 or older, has served as a member of the General Assembly for a minimum of 4 years, and retired prior to the convening of the 83rd General Assembly.

The fees and procedures relating to such plates for retired members of the General Assembly shall be the same as the fees and procedures applicable to personalized plates issued under this Code.

P.A. 76-1586, § 3-606.1, added by P.A. 82-1011, § 2, eff. Sept. 17, 1982. Amended by P.A. 84-684, § 1, eff. Sept. 20, 1985; P.A. 85-413, § 1, eff. Jan. 1, 1988.

Formerly Ill.Rev.Stat.1991, ch. 95 ½, ¶ 3-606.1.

5/3-607. Amateur Radio Operators

§ 3-607. Amateur Radio Operators. Amateur radio operators may obtain the issuance of registration plates for motor vehicles of the first division, and second division motor vehicles under 8,000 pounds, corresponding to their call letters, provided they make application therefor, which is subject to the staggered registration system, prior to October 1st of the final year of the current registration plate term and pay an additional fee of $4.

P.A. 76-1586, § 3-607, eff. July 1, 1970. Amended by P.A. 80-230, § 1, eff. Oct. 1, 1977; P.A. 84-288, § 1, eff. Jan. 1, 1986; P.A. 84-986, § 1, eff. Sept. 25, 1985; P.A. 84-1308, Art. II, § 96, eff. Aug. 25, 1986; P.A. 91-37, § 40, eff. July 1, 1999.

Formerly Ill.Rev.Stat.1991, ch. 95 ½, ¶ 3-607.

5/3-608. § 3-608. Repealed by P.A. 76-2137, § 1, eff. July 1, 1970

5/3-609. Disabled Veterans' Plates

§ 3-609. Disabled Veterans' Plates. Any disabled veteran who has been or declared eligible for funds for the purchase of a motor vehicle of the first division or for a motor vehicle of the second division weighing not more than 8,000 pounds by the United States Federal Government because of his disability, may make application for the registration of one such vehicle, to the Secretary of State without the payment of any registration fee. Registration shall be for a multi-year period effective in 1980 and may be issued staggered registration.

Any disabled veteran of World War I, of World War II, of the National Emergency between June 25, 1950 and January 31, 1955 or of the period beginning February 1, 1955 and ending on the day before the first day thereafter in which individuals (other than individuals liable for induction by reason of prior deferment) are no longer liable for induction for training and service into the armed forces under the Military Selective Service Act of 1967,[1] or of any armed conflict involving the armed forces of the United States, who has a service-connected disability of such a nature that it would, if it had been incurred in World War II, have entitled him to be awarded an automobile by the United States Federal Government, or who is receiving compensation from the Veterans Administration for total service-connected disability, may make application to the Secretary of State for the registration of one motor vehicle of the first division without accompanying such application with the payment of any fee.

Renewal of such registration must be accompanied with documentation for eligibility of registration without fee unless the applicant has a permanent qualifying disability, and such registration plates may not be issued to any person not eligible therefor.

The Illinois Veterans Commission may assist in providing the documentation of disability.

P.A. 76-1586, § 3-609, eff. July 1, 1970. Amended by P.A. 76-1625, § 1, eff. July 1, 1970; P.A. 79-1021, § 1; P.A. 81-557, § 1, eff. Jan. 1, 1980; P.A. 84-986, § 1, eff. Sept. 25, 1985; P.A. 86-444, § 1, eff. Jan. 1, 1990; P.A. 87-895, Art. 3, § 3-52, eff. Aug. 14, 1992.

Formerly Ill.Rev.Stat.1991, ch. 95 ½, ¶ 3-609.

[1] 50 U.S.C.A. App. § 451 et seq.

Section 2 of P.A. 79-1021, certified Sept. 17, 1975, provided:

"This amendatory Act of 1975 takes effect beginning with motor vehicle registrations for 1977."

5/3-609.1. Congressional Medal of Honor plates

§ 3-609.1. Congressional Medal of Honor plates. Any resident of the State of Illinois who has been awarded the Congressional Medal of Honor may make application for the registration of a motor vehicle owned solely or in part by such recipient, to the Secretary of State without the payment of any registration fee. Registration shall be for a multi-year period effective from issuance. The Secretary of State shall furnish at his office at no cost to such Congressional Medal of Honor recipients, plates bearing up to 3 letters designating the recipient's initials followed by the letters C M H signifying the Congressional Medal of Honor. The plate shall be suitable for attachment to a motor vehicle or motorcycle registered under this Code.

P.A. 76-1586, § 3-609.1, added by P.A. 82-117, § 1, eff. Jan. 1, 1982. Amended by P.A. 92-545, § 5, eff. June 12, 2002.

Formerly Ill.Rev.Stat.1991, ch. 95 ½, ¶ 3-609.1.

5/3-610. Members of Congress

§ 3-610. Members of Congress. Upon receiving an application for a certificate of registration for a motor vehicle from a member of the Congress of the United States from Illinois, accompanied with payments of the registration fees and taxes required under this Act, the Secretary of State instead of issuing to such member number plates as hereinabove provided, shall, if such member so requests, issue to him two number plates as described in this Section. Two duplicate sets of these number plates may be issued if requested and may be used on 2 different motor vehicles. There shall appear, in addition to the designation of the State and the year for which such license was issued, if he is a member of the House of Representatives, the number of the congressional district of such member in the center of the plate followed in the next line by the words "U. S. Congressman"; if he is the senior Senator from Illinois, the number 1 shall be in the center of the plate followed in the next line by the word "Senator"; and if he is the junior Senator, the number 2 shall be in the center of the plate followed in the next line by the word "Senator".

Such plates may be issued for a 2 year period beginning January 1st of each odd-numbered year and ending December 31st of the subsequent even-numbered years.

P.A. 76-1586, § 3-610, eff. July 1, 1970. Amended by P.A. 78-328, § 1, eff. Oct. 1, 1973; P.A. 79-866, § 1, eff. Sept. 10, 1975; P.A. 85-413, § 1, eff. Jan. 1, 1988.

Formerly Ill.Rev.Stat.1991, ch. 95 ½, ¶ 3-610.

5/3-610.1. Retired members of the Illinois congressional delegation

§ 3-610.1. Retired members of the Illinois congressional delegation. Upon receipt of a request from a retired member of the Illinois congressional delegation, accompanied by the appropriate application and fee, the Secretary of State shall issue to the retired member special registration plates bearing appropriate wording or abbreviations indicating that the holder is a retired member of the Illinois congressional delegation. The plates may be issued for a 2 year period beginning January 1st of each odd-numbered year and ending December 31st of the subsequent even-numbered year.

An applicant shall be charged a $15 fee for original issuance in addition to the applicable registration fee. This additional fee shall be deposited into the Secretary of State Special License Plate Fund. For each registration renewal period, a $2 fee, in addition to the appropriate registration fee, shall be charged and shall be deposited into the Retired Members of the Illinois Congressional Delegation Fund.

"Retired member of the Illinois congressional delegation" means any individual who has served as a member of the U.S. Senate or U.S. House of Representatives representing the State of Illinois. The term does not include an individual who is serving in the U.S. Senate or U.S. House of Representatives.

P.A. 76-1586, § 3-610.1, added by P.A. 88-685, § 5, eff. Jan. 24, 1995. Amended by P.A. 89-282, § 10, eff. Aug. 10, 1995.

5/3-611. Special designations

§ 3-611. Special designations. The Secretary of State, in his discretion, may make special designations of certain designs or combinations of designs, or alphabetical letters or combination of letters, or colors or combination of colors pertaining to registration plates issued to vehicles owned by governmental agencies, vehicles owned and registered by State and federal elected officials, retired Illinois Supreme Court justices, and appointed federal cabinet officials, vehicles operated by taxi or livery businesses, operated in connection with mileage weight registrations, or operated by a dealer, transporter, or manufacturer as the Secretary of State may deem necessary for the proper administration of this Act. In the case of registration plates issued for vehicles operated by or for persons with disabilities, as defined by Section 1-159.1, under Section 3-616 of this Act, the Secretary of State, upon request, shall make such special designations so that automobiles bearing such plates are easily recognizable thru use of the international accessibility symbol as automobiles driven by or for such persons. In the case of registration plates issued for vehicles operated by a disabled person with a type four hearing disability, as defined pursuant to Section 4A of The Illinois Identification Card Act,[1] the Secretary of State, upon request, shall make such special designations so that a motor vehicle bearing such plate is easily recognizable by a special symbol indicating that such vehicle is driven by a person with a hearing disability. Registration plates issued to a person who is deaf or hard of hearing under this Section shall not entitle a motor vehicle bearing such plates to those parking privileges established for persons with disabilities under this Code. In the case of registration plates issued for State owned vehicles, they shall be manufactured in compliance with Section 2 of "An Act relating to identification and use of motor vehicles of the State, approved August 9, 1951, as amended".[2] In the case of plates issued for State officials, such plates may be issued for a 2 year period beginning January 1st of each odd-numbered year and ending December 31st of the subsequent even-numbered year.

P.A. 76-1586, § 3-611, eff. July 1, 1970. Amended by P.A. 78-321, § 1, eff. Oct. 1, 1973; P.A. 79-716, § 1, eff. Oct. 1, 1975; P.A. 80-486, § 1, eff. Oct. 1, 1977; P.A. 81-449, § 1, eff. Sept. 7, 1979; P.A. 83-1058, § 1, eff. July 1, 1984; P.A. 85-413, § 1, eff. Jan. 1, 1988; P.A. 85-821, § 1, eff. Jan. 1, 1988; P.A. 85-1209, Art. II, § 2-51, eff. Aug. 30, 1988; P.A. 87-829, § 1, eff. Jan. 17, 1992; P.A. 87-832, § 3, eff. Jan. 17, 1992; P.A. 87-1249, § 1, eff. Dec. 24, 1992; P.A. 88-685, § 5, eff. Jan. 24, 1995.

Formerly Ill.Rev.Stat.1991, ch. 95 ½, ¶ 3-611.

[1] 15 ILCS 335/4A.

[2] 30 ILCS 610/2.

5/3-612. Repossessor plates

§ 3-612. Repossessor plates. The Secretary, upon receipt of an application, made on the form prescribed by the Secretary of State may issue to financial institutions, to lending institutions and to persons engaged in the business of repossessing motor vehicles for others in situations where the motor vehicle is the security for the funds, special plates which may be used by such financial institutions, lending institutions and repossessors solely for the purpose of operating the motor vehicles which are repossessed by such repossessors upon a default in the contract.

Said special plates shall, in addition to the legends provided in Section 3-412 of this Act, contain a phrase "repossessor" and such other letters or numbers as the Secretary of State may prescribe. If an applicant for such plates is engaged in repossessing vehicles for other persons and does not hold a certificate, registration or permit from the Illinois Commerce Commission to conduct such an operation, the application shall be denied.

P.A. 76-1586, § 3-612, eff. July 1, 1970.

Formerly Ill.Rev.Stat.1991, ch. 95 ½, ¶ 3-612.

5/3-613. Special inaugural license plate

§ 3-613. Special inaugural license plate. Any resident of Illinois, being a member of the Official Presidential Inaugural Committee, may, during the period from January through February 15th of any year in which the President of the United States is being inaugurated, display a special inaugural license plate furnished by such person in lieu of the current and valid Illinois license plate issued to a motor vehicle of the first division owned by such person, provided that the official inaugural credentials or a valid certificate thereof acceptable to the Secretary of State and the valid and current Illinois license plates and registration card issued to such motor vehicle are simultaneously carried within such vehicle and available for inspection.

P.A. 76-1586, § 3-613, eff. July 1, 1970.

Formerly Ill.Rev.Stat.1991, ch. 95 ½, ¶ 3 613.

5/3-614. Manufacturers of engine and driveline components

§ 3-614. Manufacturers of engine and driveline components. The Secretary, upon receipt of an application made on the form prescribed by the Secretary of State, may issue to manufacturers of engine and driveline components special plates which may be used by such manufacturers solely for the purpose of operating motor vehicles of the second division to test engine and driveline components installed in such vehicles.

P.A. 76-1586, § 3-614, eff. July 1, 1970, added by P.A. 76-2138, § 1, eff. July 1, 1970. Amended by P.A. 85-1396, § 2, eff. Sept. 2, 1988.

Formerly Ill.Rev.Stat.1991, ch. 95 ½, ¶ 3-614.

5/3-615. Honorary Consular License Plate

§ 3-615. Honorary Consular License Plate. The Secretary, upon receipt of an application made on the form prescribed by the Secretary of State, may issue Illinois Honorary Consular license plates to any person who is a non-resident and an official or employee of the Coordination Council for North American Affairs as recognized in the Taiwan Relation Act, Public Law 96-8[1], and serving that instrumentality and temporarily residing in this State. In addition, these plates may be issued to United States nationals or permanent residents who are appointed Honorary Consular officers and confirmed by the Federal Department of State.

Such registration plates may be issued for a 2 year period beginning January 1 of each odd-numbered year and ending December 31 of the subsequent even-numbered year. Applicants shall verify their status as Honorary Consular or Taiwanese representatives on forms provided by the Department of State.

In the event any holder of such registration plates or card leaves this State or no longer serves as an Honorary Consular or Taiwanese official or employee, the registration plates and card issued to such persons shall terminate and the owner shall remove such plates from the vehicle so registered and return them and the registration card to the Secretary of State. Such plates may not be transferred to any other person by the holder or owner.

P.A. 76-1586, § 3-615, added by P.A. 77-48, § 1, eff. July 1, 1971. Amended by P.A. 80-230, § 1, eff. Oct. 1, 1977; P.A. 80-1185, § 1, eff. March 8, 1978; P.A. 82-676, § 2, eff. Oct. 29, 1981; P.A. 83-449, § 1, eff. Jan. 1, 1984; P.A. 85-992, § 1, eff. Jan. 5, 1988.

Formerly Ill.Rev.Stat.1991, ch. 95 ½, ¶ 3-615.

[1] 22 U.S.C.A. § 3301 et seq.

5/3-616. Person with disabilities license plates

§ 3-616. Person with disabilities license plates.

(a) Upon receiving an application for a certificate of registration for a motor vehicle of the first division or for a motor vehicle of the second division weighing no more than 8,000 pounds, accompanied with payment of the registration fees required under this Code from a person with disabilities or a person who is deaf or hard of hearing, the Secretary of State, if so requested, shall issue to such person registration plates as provided for in Section 3–611, provided that the person with disabilities or person who is deaf or hard of hearing must not be disqualified from obtaining a driver's license under subsection 8 of Section 6–103 of this Code, and further provided that any person making such a request must submit a statement certified by a licensed physician to the effect that such person is a person with disabilities as defined by Section 1–159.1 of this Code, or alternatively provide adequate documentation that such person has a Class 1A, Class 2A or Type Four disability under the provisions of Section 4A of the Illinois Identification Card Act. [1] For purposes of this Section, an Illinois Disabled Person Identification Card issued pursuant to the Illinois Identification Card Act [2] indicating that the person thereon named has a disability shall be adequate documentation of such a disability.

(b) The Secretary shall issue plates under this Section to a parent or legal guardian of a person with disabilities if the person with disabilities has a Class 1A or Class 2A disability as defined in Section 4A of the Illinois Identification Card Act or is a person with disabilities as defined by Section 1–159.1 of this Code, and does not possess a vehicle registered in his or her name, provided that the person with disabilities relies frequently on the parent or legal guardian for transportation. Only one vehicle per family may be registered under this subsection, unless the applicant can justify in writing the need for one additional set of plates. Any person requesting special plates under this subsection shall submit such documentation or such physician's statement as is required in subsection (a) and a statement describing the circumstances qualifying for issuance of special plates under this subsection.

(c) The Secretary may issue a person with disabilities parking decal or device to a person with disabilities as defined by Section 1–159.1 without regard to qualification of such person with disabilities for a driver's license or registration of a vehicle by such person with disabilities or such person's immediate family, provided such person with disabilities making such a request has been issued a Disabled Person Identification Card indicating that the person named thereon has a Class 1A or Class 2A disability, or alternatively, submits a statement certified by a licensed physician to the effect that such person is a person with disabilities as defined by Section 1–159.1.

(d) The Secretary shall prescribe by rules and regulations procedures to certify or re-certify as necessary the eligibility of persons whose disabilities are other than permanent for special plates or person with disabilities parking decals or devices issued under subsections (a), (b) and (c). Except as provided under subsection (f) of this Section, no such special plates, decals or devices shall be issued by the Secretary of State to or on behalf of any person with disabilities unless such person is certified as meeting the definition of a person with disabilities pursuant to Section 1–159.1 or meeting the requirement of a Type Four disability as provided under Section 4A of the Illinois Identification Card Act for the period of time that the physician determines the applicant will have the disability, but not to exceed 6 months from the date of certification or recertification.

(e) Any person requesting special plates under this Section may also apply to have the special plates personalized, as provided under Section 3–405.1.

(f) The Secretary of State, upon application, shall issue person with disabilities registration plates or a person with disabilities parking decal to corporations, school districts, State or municipal agencies, limited liability companies, nursing homes, convalescent homes, or special education cooperatives which will transport persons with disabilities. The Secretary shall prescribe by rule a means to certify or recertify the eligibility of organizations to receive person with disabilities plates or decals and to designate which of the 2 person with disabilities emblems shall be placed on qualifying vehicles.

(g) The Secretary of State, or his designee, may enter into agreements with other jurisdictions, including foreign jurisdictions, on behalf of this State relating to the extension of parking privileges by such jurisdictions to permanently disabled residents of this State who display a special license plate or parking device that contains the International symbol of access on his or her motor vehicle, and to recognize such plates or devices issued by such other jurisdictions. This State shall grant the same parking privileges which are granted to disabled residents of this State to any nonresident whose motor vehicle is licensed in another state, district, territory or foreign country if such vehicle displays the international symbol of access or a distinguishing insignia on license plates or parking device issued in accordance with the laws of the non-resident's state, district, territory or foreign country.

P.A. 76–1586, § 3–616, added by P.A. 78–321, § 1, eff. Oct. 1, 1973. Amended by P.A. 80–486, § 1, eff. Oct. 1, 1977; P.A. 83–828, § 1, eff. Jan. 1, 1984; P.A. 83–1058, § 1, eff. July 1, 1984; P.A. 83–1362, Art. II, § 99, eff. Sept. 11, 1984; P.A. 83–1421, § 10, eff. July 1, 1985; P.A. 84–734, § 1, eff. Jan. 1, 1986; P.A. 84–868, § 1, eff. Sept. 23, 1985; P.A. 84–1308, Art. II, § 96, eff. Aug. 25, 1986; P.A. 85–821, § 1, eff. Jan. 1, 1988; P.A. 86–539, § 1, eff. Jan. 1, 1990; P.A. 88–685, § 5, eff. Jan. 24, 1995; P.A. 91–769, § 5, eff. June 9, 2000; P.A. 92–16, § 85, eff. June 28, 2001; P.A. 92–411, § 5, eff. Jan. 1, 2002; P.A. 92–651, § 77, eff. July 11, 2002.

Formerly Ill.Rev.Stat.1991, ch. 95 ½, ¶ 3–616.

[1] 15 ILCS 335/4A.

[2] 15 ILCS 335/1 et seq.

Section 2 of P.A. 83–828 provided:

"This Act takes effect with the 1985 registration year."

P.A. 92–16, the First 2001 General Revisory Act, amended various Acts to delete obsolete text, to correct patent and technical errors, to revise cross references, to resolve multiple actions in the 91st General Assembly and to make certain technical corrections in P.A. 91–1 through P.A. 91–937.

P.A. 92–651, the First 2002 General Revisory Act, amended various Acts to delete obsolete text, to correct patent and technical errors, to revise cross references, to resolve multiple actions in the 91st and 92nd General Assemblies and to make certain technical corrections in P.A. 91–937 through P.A. 92–520.

5/3–617. Driver education plates

§ 3–617. Driver education plates. A High School operating passenger cars for a high school driver training program, may operate or move the same upon the highway without registering each such passenger car upon the condition that each such passenger car display thereon, in the manner prescribed by Section 3–413, special plates issued to the high school under the provisions of Section 3–808.

Such special plates may be issued only to a public high school or a high school operated by a religious institution, and may be used only on passenger cars used exclusively in high school driver training program approved by the State Board of Education.

P.A. 76–1586, § 3–617, added by P.A. 78–502, § 1, eff. Jan. 1, 1974. Amended by P.A. 81–1508, § 8, eff. Sept. 25, 1980.

Formerly Ill.Rev.Stat.1991, ch. 95 ½, ¶ 3–617.

5/3–618. Charitable vehicle plates

§ 3–618. Charitable vehicle plates. Charitable vehicle plates shall be of such color and design as prescribed by the Secretary. The fee for such plates shall be as prescribed in Section 3–808 of this Code. Such plates may be obtained by owners of charitable vehicles.

P.A. 76–1586, § 3–618, added by P.A. 79–698, § 1, eff. Jan. 1, 1976. Amended by P.A. 82–1011, § 2, eff. Sept. 17, 1982; P.A. 90–89, § 15, eff. Jan. 1, 1998.

Formerly Ill.Rev.Stat.1991, ch. 95 ½, ¶ 3–618.

Another § 3–618 relating to Sample Registration plates and stickers, was renumbered § 3–619 by P.A. 79–1454, § 44.

5/3–619. Sample Registration plates and stickers

§ 3–619. Sample Registration plates and stickers. The Secretary of State, upon receipt of an application made on the form prescribed by the Secretary, may issue to any law enforcement agency in this State, or to any authorized agency of any foreign jurisdiction, or to any motion picture or television industry, one or more Sample Registration Plates and stickers. The design of such plates and stickers shall be wholly within the discretion of the Secretary, and shall be issued without charge. The Secretary of State, upon receipt of an application made on the form prescribed by the Secretary, may issue to any other individual one or more Sample Registration Plates and stickers for a fee of $4 for each Sample Registration Plate and sticker.

P.A. 76–1586, § 3–618, added by P.A. 79–715, § 1, eff. Jan. 1, 1976. Renumbered § 3–619 and amended by P.A. 79–1454, § 44, eff. Aug. 31, 1976. Amended by P.A. 80–1185, § 1, eff. March 8, 1978; P.A. 81–823, § 1, eff. Jan. 1, 1980; P.A. 85–951, § 1, eff. July 1, 1988; P.A. 91–37, § 40, eff. July 1, 1999.

Formerly Ill.Rev.Stat.1991, ch. 95 ½, ¶ 3–619.

5/3–620. Prisoner of war special registration plates

§ 3–620. The Secretary, upon receipt of an application made on the form prescribed by the Secretary of State, may issue special registration plates to United States citizens, who are present or former members of the United States armed forces or any of its allies, and who were prisoners of war of World War I, World War II, the Korean Conflict, and the Vietnamese conflict, or to the widowed spouse of a former member of the United States armed forces, providing that widowed spouse was married to the POW at the time of death, and is a single person at the time of application. The special plates issued pursuant to this Section shall be affixed only to passenger vehicles of the first division subject to the staggered registration system, motorcycles, and vehicles of the second division having a gross weight of 8,000 pounds or less and shall be issued without charge. Only one set of plates may be issued at no fee.

The design and color of the prisoner of war plates shall be wholly within the discretion of the Secretary of State.

P.A. 76–1586, § 3–620, added by P.A. 81–169, § 1, eff. Jan. 1, 1980. Amended by P.A. 82–118, § 1, eff. Jan. 1, 1982; P.A. 83–61, § 1, eff. Jan. 1, 1984; P.A. 83–117, § 1, eff. Aug. 19, 1983; P.A. 83–1362, Art. II, § 99, eff. Sept. 11, 1984; P.A. 84–132, § 1, eff. Aug. 12, 1985; P.A. 84–986, § 1, eff. Sept. 25, 1985; P.A. 84–1308, Art. II, § 96, eff. Aug. 25, 1986; P.A. 92–545, § 5, eff. June 12, 2002.

Formerly Ill.Rev.Stat.1991, ch. 95 ½, ¶ 3–620.

Section 2 of P.A. 84–132, approved Aug. 12, 1985, provided:

"This Act shall take effect upon becoming law, and shall apply to registrations beginning with the 1987 registration year and thereafter."

Article II of P.A. 84–1308, the First 84th General Assembly Combining Revisory Act, provides for the nonsubstantive revision or renumbering or repeal of Sections of Acts necessitated by the amendment, addition or repeal of Sections by two or more Public Acts of the 84th General Assembly, which multiple action was not resolved by one of the Acts of the 84th General Assembly affecting the particular Section and makes technical corrections in Acts amended by the 84th General Assembly.

5/3–621. National Guard plates

§ 3–621. The Secretary, upon receipt of an application, made in the form prescribed by the Secretary of State, may issue to members of the Illinois National Guard, and to Illinois residents who are either former members of the Illinois National Guard or the surviving spouses of Illinois National Guard members, special registration plates. The special plates issued pursuant to this Section shall be affixed only to passenger vehicles of the first division, motorcycles, or motor vehicles of the second division weighing not more than 8,000 pounds subject to the staggered registration system.

The design and color of such plates shall be wholly within the discretion of the Secretary of State.

P.A. 76–1586, § 3–621, added by P.A. 82–118, § 1, eff. Jan. 1, 1982. Amended by P.A. 84–986, § 1, eff. Sept. 25, 1985; P.A. 92–545, § 5, eff. June 12, 2002; P.A. 92–699, § 5, eff. Jan. 1, 2003.

Formerly Ill.Rev.Stat.1991, ch. 95 ½, ¶ 3–621.

See 5 ILCS 70/6 as to the effect of (1) more than one amendment of a section at the same session of the General Assembly or (2) two or more acts relating to the same subject matter enacted by the same General Assembly.

5/3–622. Armed Forces Reserves plates

§ 3–622. The Secretary, upon receipt of an application made in the form prescribed by the Secretary of State, may issue to members of the United States Armed Forces Reserves who reside in Illinois, and to Illinois residents who are either former members of the United States Armed Forces Reserves or the surviving spouses of United States Armed Forces Reserve members who resided in Illinois, special registration plates. The special plates issued pursuant to this Section shall be affixed only to passenger vehicles of the first division, motorcycles, or motor vehicles of the second division weighing not more than 8,000 pounds subject to the staggered registration system. The design and color of such plates shall be wholly within the discretion of the Secretary of State.

P.A. 76–1586, § 3–622, added by P.A. 83–1473, § 1, eff. Jan. 1, 1985. Amended by P.A. 84–986, § 1, eff. Sept. 25, 1985; P.A. 92–545, § 5, eff. June 12, 2002; P.A. 92–699, § 5, eff. Jan. 1, 2003.

Formerly Ill.Rev.Stat.1991, ch. 95 ½, ¶ 3–622.

See 5 ILCS 70/6 as to the effect of (1) more than one amendment of a section at the same session of the General Assembly or (2) two or more acts relating to the same subject matter enacted by the same General Assembly.

5/3–623. Purple Heart Plates

§ 3–623. Purple Heart Plates. The Secretary, upon receipt of an application made in the form prescribed by the Secretary of State, may issue to recipients awarded the Purple Heart by a branch of the armed forces of the United States who reside in Illinois, special registration plates. The special plates issued pursuant to this Section should be affixed only to passenger vehicles of the 1st division, including motorcycles, or motor vehicles of the 2nd division weighing not more than 8,000 pounds.

The design and color of such plates shall be wholly within the discretion of the Secretary of State. Appropriate documentation, as determined by the Secretary, and the appropriate registration fee shall accompany the application. However, for an individual who has been issued Purple Heart plates for a vehicle and who has claimed and received a grant under the Senior Citizens and Disabled Persons Property Tax Relief and Pharmaceutical Assistance Act,[1] the annual fee for the registration of the vehicle shall be as provided in Section 3–806.3 of this Code.

P.A. 76–1586, § 3–623, added by P.A. 85–172, § 1, eff. Jan. 1, 1988. Amended by P.A. 89–98, § 5, eff. Jan. 1, 1996; P.A. 91–25, § 25, eff. June 9, 1999; P.A. 92–82, § 5, eff. Jan. 1, 2002; P.A. 92–699, § 5, eff. Jan. 1, 2003.

Formerly Ill.Rev.Stat.1991, ch. 95 ½, ¶ 3–623.

[1] 320 ILCS 25/1 et seq.

P.A. 92–699 incorporated the amendment by P.A. 92–82.

5/3–624. Retired members of Armed Forces

§ 3–624. The Secretary, upon receipt of an application made in the form prescribed by the Secretary of State, may issue to retired members of the United States Armed Forces who reside in Illinois, special registration plates. The special plates issued pursuant to this Section shall be affixed only to passenger vehicles of the first division, motorcycles, or motor vehicles of the second division weighing not more than 8,000 pounds and subject to the staggered registration system. The design and color of such plates shall be wholly within the discretion of the Secretary of State.

P.A. 76–1586, § 3–624, added by P.A. 86–165, § 1, eff. Aug. 13, 1989. Amended by P.A. 92–545, § 5, eff. June 12, 2002.

Formerly Ill.Rev.Stat.1991, ch. 95 ½, ¶ 3–624.

5/3–625. Pearl Harbor Plates

§ 3–625. Pearl Harbor Plates. The Secretary, upon receipt of an application made in the form prescribed by the Secretary of State, may issue special registration plates to any Illinois resident who, while a member of the armed forces of the United States, participated in the battle of Pearl Harbor on December 7, 1941, or to the widowed spouse of any Illinois resident who, while a member of the armed forces of the United States, participated in the battle of Pearl Harbor on December 7, 1941, provided that the widowed spouse was married to the battle of Pearl Harbor participant at the time of the participant's death and is a single person at the time of application. The special plates issued pursuant to this Section should be affixed only to passenger vehicles of the 1st division, motorcycles or motor vehicles of the 2nd division weighing not more than 8,000 pounds.

The design and color of such plates shall be wholly within the discretion of the Secretary of State. Appropriate documentation, as determined by the Secretary, and the appropriate registration fee shall accompany the application.

P.A. 76–1586, § 3–625, added by P.A. 86–1481, Art. 9, § 1, eff. Jan. 14, 1991. Amended by P.A. 89–571, § 5, eff. July 26, 1996; P.A. 89–620, § 10, eff. Jan. 1, 1997; P.A. 92–545, § 5, eff. June 12, 2002; P.A. 92–699, § 5, eff. Jan. 1, 2003.

Formerly Ill.Rev.Stat.1991, ch. 95 ½, ¶ 3–625.

The amendments by P.A. 89–571 and P.A. 89–620 were identical.

See 5 ILCS 70/6 as to the effect of (1) more than one amendment of a section at the same session of the General Assembly or (2) two or more acts relating to the same subject matter enacted by the same General Assembly.

5/3–626. Korean War Veteran license plates

§ 3–626. Korean War Veteran license plates.

(a) In addition to any other special license plate, the Secretary, upon receipt of all applicable fees and applications made in the form prescribed by the Secretary of State, may issue special registration plates designated as Korean War Veteran license plates to residents of Illinois who participated in the United States Armed Forces during the Korean War. The special plate issued under this Section shall be affixed only to passenger vehicles of the first division, motorcycles, motor vehicles of the second division weighing not more than 8,000 pounds, and recreational vehicles as defined by Section 1–169 of this Code. Plates issued under this Section shall expire according to the staggered multi-year procedure established by Section 3–414.1 of this Code.

(b) The design, color, and format of the plates shall be wholly within the discretion of the Secretary of State. The Secretary may, in his or her discretion, allow the plates to be issued as vanity plates or personalized in accordance with Section 3–405.1 of this Code. The plates are not required to designate "Land Of Lincoln", as prescribed in subsection (b) of Section 3–412 of this Code. The Secretary shall prescribe the eligibility requirements and, in his or her discretion, shall approve and prescribe stickers or decals as provided under Section 3–412.

(c) An applicant shall be charged a $15 fee for original issuance in addition to the applicable registration fee. Of this additional fee, $13 shall be deposited into the Secretary of State Special License Plate Fund and $2 shall be deposited into the Korean War Memorial Construction Fund. For each registration renewal period, a $2 fee, in addition to the appropriate registration fee, shall be charged and shall be deposited into the Secretary of State Special License Plate Fund.

(d) The Korean War Memorial Construction Fund is created as a special fund in the State treasury. All moneys in the Korean War Memorial Construction Fund shall, subject to appropriation, be used by the Department of Veteran Affairs to provide grants for construction of the Korean War Memorial to be located at Oak Ridge Cemetery in Springfield, Illinois. Upon the completion of the Memorial, the Department of Veteran Affairs shall certify to the State Treasurer that the construction of the Memorial has been completed. Upon the certification by the Department of Veteran Affairs, the State Treasurer shall transfer all moneys in the Fund and any future deposits into the Fund into the Secretary of State Special License Plate Fund.

(e) An individual who has been issued Korean War Veteran license plates for a vehicle and who has claimed and received a grant under the Senior Citizens and Disabled Persons Property Tax Relief and Pharmaceutical Assistance Act shall pay the original issuance and the regular annual fee for the registration of the vehicle as provided in Section 3–

806.3 of this Code in addition to the fees specified in subsection (c) of this Section.

P.A. 76-1586, § 3-626, added by P.A. 88-485, § 10, eff. Jan. 1, 1994. Amended by P.A. 88-560, § 10, eff. Aug. 4, 1994; P.A. 88-670, Art. 2, § 2-59, eff. Dec. 2, 1994; P.A. 89-98, § 5, eff. Jan. 1, 1996; P.A. 89-282, § 10, eff. Aug. 10, 1995; P.A. 89-626, Art. 2, § 2-64, eff. Aug. 9, 1996; P.A. 91-679, § 5, eff. Jan. 26, 2000; P.A. 92-545, § 5, eff. June 12, 2002.

Another § 3-626, relating to environmental license plates, was renumbered § 3-627 by P.A. 88-670, Art. 2, § 2-59.

5/3-627. Environmental License Plate

§ 3-627. Environmental License Plate.

(a) The Secretary, upon receipt of an application made in the form prescribed by the Secretary of State, may issue special registration plates designated to be environmental license plates. The special plates issued under this Section shall be affixed only to passenger vehicles of the first division, motor vehicles of the second division weighing not more than 8,000 pounds, and, as of January 1, 1996, recreational vehicles as defined by Section 1-169 of this Code. Plates issued under this Section shall expire according to the multi-year procedure established by Section 3-414.1 of this Code.

(b) The design and color of the plates shall be wholly within the discretion of the Secretary of State. Appropriate documentation, as determined by the Secretary, shall accompany the application. As of January 1, 1996, the Secretary may, in his or her discretion, allow the plates to be issued as vanity or personalized plates in accordance with Section 3-405.1 of this Code.

(c) An applicant shall be charged a $40 fee for original issuance in addition to the appropriate registration fee, if applicable. Of this fee, $25 shall be deposited into the State Parks Fund and $15 shall be deposited into the Secretary of State Special License Plate Fund, to be used by the Secretary of State to help defray the administrative processing costs. For each registration renewal period, a $27 fee, in addition to the appropriate registration fee, shall be charged. Of this fee, $25 shall be deposited into the State Parks Fund and $2 shall be deposited into the Secretary of State Special License Plate Fund .

P.A. 76-1586, § 3-626, added by 88-333, § 5, eff. Jan. 1, 1994. Renumbered § 3-627 and amended by P.A. 88-670, Art. 2, § 2-59, eff. Dec. 2, 1994. Amended by P.A. 89-282, § 10, eff. Aug. 10, 1995.

5/3-628. Bronze Star plates

§ 3-628. Bronze Star plates.

(a) Beginning January 1, 1996, in addition to any other special license plate, the Secretary, upon receipt of all applicable fees and applications made in the form prescribed by the Secretary of State, may issue special registration plates to residents of Illinois who have been awarded the Bronze Star by the United States Armed Forces. The special plate issued under this Section shall be affixed only to passenger vehicles of the first division, motorcycles, or motor vehicles of the second division weighing not more than 8,000 pounds. Plates issued under this Section shall expire according to the staggered multi-year procedure established by Section 3-414.1 of this Code.

(b) The design, color, and format of the plates shall be wholly within the discretion of the Secretary of State. The Secretary may, in his or her discretion, allow the plates to be issued as vanity plates or personalized in accordance with Section 3-405.1 of this Code. The plates are not required to designate "Land Of Lincoln", as prescribed in subsection (b) of Section 3-412 of this Code. The Secretary shall prescribe the eligibility requirements and, in his or her discretion, shall approve and prescribe stickers or decals as provided under Section 3-412.

(c) An applicant shall be charged a $15 fee for original issuance in addition to the appropriate registration fee.

This additional fee shall be deposited into the Secretary of State Special License Plate Fund. For each registration renewal period, a $2 fee, in addition to the appropriate registration fee, shall be charged and deposited into the Secretary of State Special License Plate Fund.

P.A. 76-1586, § 3-628, added by P.A. 88-589, § 10, eff. Aug. 14, 1994. Amended by P.A. 89-282, § 10, eff. Aug. 10, 1995; P.A. 92-545, § 5, eff. June 12, 2002.

5/3-629. Collegiate license plates; scholarship fund

§ 3-629. Collegiate license plates; scholarship fund.

(a) In addition to any other special license plate, the Secretary, upon receipt of all applicable fees and applications made in the form prescribed by the Secretary of State, may issue collegiate license plates. The collegiate plates issued under this Section shall be affixed only to passenger vehicles of the first division and motor vehicles of the second division weighing nor more than 8,000 pounds and subject to the staggered registration system. Plates issued under this Section shall expire according to the staggered multi-year procedure established under Section 3-414.1 of this Code.

(b) The design, color, and format of the plates shall be wholly within the discretion of the Secretary of State. The Secretary of State may, at his or her discretion, issue the plates for any public or degree-granting, not-for-profit private college or university located in this State. The Secretary may, in his or her discretion, allow the plates to be issued as vanity plates or personalized in accordance with Section 3-405.1 of this Code. The plates are not required to designate "Land Of Lincoln", as prescribed in subsection (b) of Section 3-412 of this Code. The Secretary shall prescribe the eligibility requirements including a minimum level of specialized license plates requests and, in his or her discretion, shall approve and prescribe stickers or decals as provided under Section 3-412.

(c) An applicant shall be charged a $40 fee for original issuance in addition to the applicable registration fee. Of the original issuance fee in the case of a public university or college, $25 shall be deposited into the State College and University Trust Fund and $15 shall be deposited into the Secretary of State Special License Plate Fund to be used by the Secretary of State, subject to appropriation, to help defray the administrative costs of issuing the plate. Of the original issuance fee in the case of a degree-granting, not-for-profit private college or university, $25 shall be deposited into the University Grant Fund and $15 shall be deposited into the Secretary of State Special License Plate Fund to be used by the Secretary of State, subject to appropriation, to help defray the administrative cost of issuing the plate. In addition to the regular renewal fee, an applicant shall be charged $27 for the renewal of each set of license plates issued under this Section; $25 shall be deposited into the State College and University Trust Fund in the case of a public university or college or into the University Grant Fund in the case of a degree-granting, not-for-profit private college or university, and $2 shall be deposited into the Secretary of State Special License Plate Fund plates for all collegiate plates.

(d) The State College and University Trust Fund is created as a special fund in the State treasury. The State Treasurer shall create separate accounts within the State College and University Trust Fund for each public university or college for which collegiate license plates have been issued. Moneys in the State College and University Trust Fund shall be allocated to each account in proportion to the number of plates sold in regard to each public university or college. Moneys Receipts deposited into the State College and University Trust Fund during the preceding calendar year shall be distributed, subject to appropriation, to each participating public university or college This revenue shall be used for the sole purpose of scholarship grant awards.

(e) The University Grant Fund is created as a special fund in the State treasury. All moneys in the University Grant Fund shall be appropriated to the Illinois Student Assistance Commission to make reimbursements to participating private colleges and universities under the Higher Education License Plate Grant Program.

P.A. 76–1586, § 3–629, added by P.A. 89–424, § 15, eff. June 1, 1996. Amended by P.A. 89–626, Art. 2, § 2–65, eff. Aug. 9, 1996; P.A. 90–14, Art. 2, § 2–225, eff. July 1, 1997; P.A. 90–278, § 20, eff. July 31, 1997; P.A. 90–774, § 5, eff. Aug. 14, 1998; P.A. 91–83, § 5, eff. Jan. 1, 2000.

Other §§ 3–629, relating to violence prevention license plates and Illinois Fire Fighters' License Plates, were renumbered §§ 3–630 and 3–634 by P.A. 89–626, Art. 2, § 2–65 and P.A. 90–14, Art. 2, § 2–225, respectively.

P.A. 90–14, Article 2, of the First 1997 General Revisory Act, resolved multiple actions in the 89th General Assembly and made certain technical corrections in P.A. 89–443 through P.A. 89–707.

P.A. 90–774 incorporated the amendments by P.A. 90–14 and P.A. 90–278.

5/3–630. Violence prevention license plate

§ 3–630. Violence prevention license plate.

(a) The Secretary, upon receipt of an application made in the form prescribed by the Secretary of State, may issue special registration plates designated to be Violence Prevention plates. The special plates issued under this Section shall be affixed only to passenger vehicles of the first division or motor vehicles of the second division weighing not more than 8,000 pounds. Plates issued under this Section shall expire according to the multi-year procedure established by Section 3–414.1 of this Code.

(b) The design and color of the plates shall be wholly within the discretion of the Secretary of State. Appropriate documentation, as determined by the Secretary, shall accompany the application. Beginning January 1, 1999, the Secretary may, in his or her discretion, allow the plates to be issued as vanity plates or personalized in accordance with Section 3–405.1 of this Code.

(c) An applicant shall be charged a $40 dollar fee for original issuance in addition to the appropriate registration fee, if applicable. Of this fee, $25 shall be deposited into the Violence Prevention Fund as created by this Act and $15 shall be deposited into the Secretary of State Special License Plate Fund to be used by the Secretary of State to help defray the administrative processing costs. For each registration renewal period a $27 fee, in addition to the appropriate registration fee, shall be charged. Of this fee, $25 shall be deposited into the Violence Prevention Fund and $2 shall be deposited into the Secretary of State Special License Plate Fund.

P.A. 76–1586, § 3–629, added by P.A. 89–353, § 100, eff. Aug. 17, 1995. Renumbered § 3–630 and amended by P.A. 89–626, Art. 2, § 2–65, eff. Aug. 9, 1996. Amended by P.A. 90–619, § 5, eff. Jan. 1, 1999.

5/3–631. Sportsmen Series license plate

§ 3–631. Sportsmen Series license plate.

(a) The Secretary, upon receipt of an application made in the form prescribed by the Secretary of State, may issue special registration plates designated to be Sportsmen Series license plates. The special plates issued under this Section shall be affixed only to passenger vehicles of the first division, motor vehicles of the second division weighing not more than 8,000 pounds, and recreational vehicles as defined by Section 1–169 of this Code. Plates issued under this Section shall expire according to the multi-year procedure established by Section 3–414.1 of this Code.

(b) The design and color of the plates shall be wholly within the discretion of the Secretary of State. Appropriate documentation, as determined by the Secretary, shall accompany the application. The Secretary may, in his or her discretion, allow the plates to be issued as vanity or personalized plates in accordance with Section 3–405.1 of this Code.

(c) An applicant shall be charged a $40 fee for original issuance in addition to the appropriate registration fee, if applicable. Of this fee, $25 shall be deposited into the Illinois Habitat Fund and $15 shall be deposited into the Secretary of State Special License Plate Fund, to be used by the Secretary of State to help defray the administrative processing costs. For each registration renewal period, a $27 fee, in addition to the appropriate registration fee, shall be charged. Of this fee, $25 shall be deposited into the Illinois Habitat Fund and $2 shall be deposited into the Secretary of State Special License Plate Fund.

P.A. 76–1586, § 3–631, added by P.A. 89–611, § 15, eff. Jan. 1, 1997. Amended by P.A. 90–14, Art. 2, § 2–225, eff. July 1, 1997.

Other §§ 3–631, relating to Universal Charitable Organization license plates, Master Mason plates, D.A.R.E. license plates and U.S. Veteran license plates, were renumbered §§ 3–633, 3–635, 3–637 and 3–638, respectively, by P.A. 90–14, Art. 2, § 2–225.

P.A. 90–14, Article 2, of the First 1997 General Revisory Act, resolved multiple actions in the 89th General Assembly and made certain technical corrections in P.A. 89–443 through P.A. 89–707.

5/3–632. Wildlife Prairie Park license plate

§ 3–632. Wildlife Prairie Park license plate.

(a) The Secretary, upon receipt of an application made in the form prescribed by the Secretary of State, may issue special registration plates to be designated Wildlife Prairie Park license plates. The special plates issued under this Section shall be affixed only to passenger vehicles of the first division, motor vehicles of the second division weighing not more than 8,000 pounds, and recreational vehicles as defined by Section 1–169 of this Code. Plates issued under this Section shall expire according to the multi-year procedure established by Section 3–414.1 of this Code.

(b) The design and color of the plates shall be wholly within the discretion of the Secretary of State. Appropriate documentation, as determined by the Secretary, shall accompany the application. The Secretary may, in his or her discretion, allow the plates to be issued as vanity or personalized plates in accordance with Section 3–405.1 of this Code.

(c) An applicant shall be charged a $40 fee for original issuance in addition to the appropriate registration fee, if applicable. Of this fee, $25 shall be deposited into the Wildlife Prairie Park Fund and $15 shall be deposited into the Secretary of State Special License Plate Fund, to be used by the Secretary of State to help defray the administrative processing costs. For each registration renewal period, a $27 fee, in addition to the appropriate registration fee, shall be charged. Of this fee, $25 shall be deposited into the Wildlife Prairie Park Fund and $2 shall be deposited into the Secretary of State Special License Plate Fund.

P.A. 76–1586, § 3–632, added by P.A. 89–611, § 15, eff. Jan. 1, 1997. Amended by P.A. 90–14, Art. 2, § 2–225, eff. July 1, 1997.

Another § 3–632, relating to Knights of Columbus plates, was renumbered § 3–636 by P.A. 90–14, Art. 2, § 2–225.

P.A. 90–14, Article 2, of the First 1997 General Revisory Act, resolved multiple actions in the 89th General Assembly and made certain technical corrections in P.A. 89–443 through P.A. 89–707.

5/3–633. Universal Charitable Organization license plate

§ 3–633. Universal Charitable Organization license plate.

(a) In addition to any other special license plate, the Secretary, upon receipt of all applicable fees and applications made in the form prescribed by the Secretary of State, may issue Universal Charitable Organization license plates to residents of Illinois on behalf of organizations that meet the requirements of Title 26, Section 501(c)(3) of the United States Code formed for any bona fide charitable, benevolent, philanthropic, or patriotic purpose. The Secretary of State may prescribe rules establishing additional eligibility criteria for charitable organizations under this Section. The special Universal Charitable Organization plate issued under this Section shall be affixed only to passenger vehicles of the first division and motor vehicles of the second division weighing not more than 8,000 pounds. Plates issued under this Section shall expire according to the staggered multi-year procedure established by Section 3–414.1 of this Code.

(b) The design, color, and format of the plates shall be wholly within the discretion of the Secretary of State. The plates are not required to designate "Land of Lincoln", as prescribed in subsection (b) of Section 3–412 of this Code. Charitable organizations deemed eligible by the Secretary of State shall design charitable decals to be affixed on plates issued under this Section. The Secretary may prescribe rules governing the requirements and approval of charitable decals.

(c) An applicant shall be charged a $15 fee for original issuance in addition to the applicable registration fee. This additional fee shall be deposited into the Secretary of State Special License Plate Fund. For each registration renewal period, a $2 fee, in addition to the appropriate registration fee, shall be charged and shall be deposited into the Secretary of State Special License Plate Fund. Charitable organizations may establish a fee for the purchase of their charitable decal and shall report by July 31 of each year to the Secretary of State Vehicle Services Department the sticker fee, the number of charitable decals sold, the total revenue received from the sale of charitable decals during the previous fiscal year, and any other information deemed necessary by the Secretary of State.

P.A. 76–1586, § 3–631, added by P.A. 89–564, § 5, eff. July 1, 1997. Renumbered § 3–633 and amended by P.A. 90–14, Art. 2, § 2–225, eff. July 1, 1997.

P.A. 90–14, Article 2, of the First 1997 General Revisory Act, resolved multiple actions in the 89th General Assembly and made certain technical corrections in P.A. 89–443 through P.A. 89–707.

5/3–634. Illinois Fire Fighters' License Plate

§ 3–634. Illinois Fire Fighters' License Plate.

(a) The Secretary, upon receipt of an application made in the form prescribed by the Secretary of State, may issue special registration plates designated to be Illinois Fire Fighters' Memorial license plates. The special plates issued under this Section shall be affixed only to passenger vehicles of the first division, motor vehicles of the second division weighing not more than 8,000 pounds, recreational vehicles as defined in Section 1–169 of this Code, and subject to the staggered registration system. Plates issued under this Section shall expire according to the multi-year procedure established by Section 3–414.1 of this Code.

(b) The design and color of the plates shall be wholly within the discretion of the Secretary of State. The Secretary of State may, in his or her discretion, allow the plates to be issued as vanity plates or personalized in accordance with Section 3–405.1 of this Code. The plates are not required to designate "Land of Lincoln", as prescribed in subsection (b) of Section 3–412 of this Code. The Secretary of State shall prescribe stickers or decals as provided under Section 3–412.

(c) An applicant shall be charged a $27 fee for original issuance in addition to the applicable registration fee. Of this additional fee, $15 shall be deposited into the Secretary of State Special License Plate Fund and $12 shall be deposited into the Illinois Fire Fighters' Memorial Fund. For each registration renewal period, a $17 fee, in addition to the appropriate registration fee, shall be charged. Of this fee, $2 shall be deposited into the Secretary of State Special License Plate Fund and $15 shall be deposited into the Illinois Fire Fighters' Memorial Fund.

(d) In addition to the purpose specified in Section 2–119(n), moneys in the Illinois Fire Fighters' Memorial Fund shall, subject to appropriation by the General Assembly and approval by the Secretary, be used for maintaining the Illinois Fire Fighters' Memorial, for holding an annual memorial commemoration, and for providing scholarships to children of fire fighters killed in the line of duty.

P.A. 76–1586, § 3–629, added by P.A. 89–612, § 10, eff. Aug. 9, 1996. Renumbered § 3–634 and amended by P.A. 90–14, Art. 2, § 2–225, eff. July 1, 1997. Amended by P.A. 91–832, § 5, eff. June 16, 2000.

P.A. 90–14, Article 2, of the First 1997 General Revisory Act, resolved multiple actions in the 89th General Assembly and made certain technical corrections in P.A. 89–443 through P.A. 89–707.

5/3–635. Master Mason plates

§ 3–635. Master Mason plates.

(a) The Secretary, upon receipt of all applicable fees and applications made in the form prescribed by the Secretary, may issue special registration plates designated as Master Mason license plates.

The special plates issued under this Section shall be affixed only to passenger vehicles of the first division or motor vehicles of the second division weighing not more than 8,000 pounds.

Plates issued under this Section shall expire according to the multi-year procedure established by Section 3–414.1 of this Code.

(b) The design and color of the special plates shall be wholly within the discretion of the Secretary. Appropriate documentation, as determined by the Secretary, shall accompany each application.

(c) An applicant for the special plate shall be charged a $25 fee for original issuance in addition to the appropriate registration fee. Of this fee, $10 shall be deposited into the Master Mason Fund and $15 shall be deposited into the Secretary of State Special License Plate Fund, to be used by the Secretary to help defray the administrative processing costs.

For each registration renewal period, a $25 fee, in addition to the appropriate registration fee, shall be charged. Of this fee, $23 shall be deposited into the Master Mason Fund and $2 shall be deposited into the Secretary of State Special License Plate Fund.

(d) The Master Mason Fund is created as a special fund in the State treasury. All money in the Master Mason Fund shall be paid, subject to appropriation by the General Assembly and approval by the Secretary, as grants to The Illinois Masonic Foundation for the Prevention of Drug and Alcohol Abuse Among Children, Inc., a not-for-profit corporation, for the purpose of providing Model Student Assistance Programs in public and private schools in Illinois.

P.A. 76-1586, § 3-631, added by P.A. 89-620, § 10, eff. Jan. 1, 1997. Renumbered § 3-635 and amended by P.A. 90-14, Art. 2, § 2-225, eff. July 1, 1997.

P.A. 90-14, Article 2, of the First 1997 General Revisory Act, resolved multiple actions in the 89th General Assembly and made certain technical corrections in P.A. 89-443 through P.A. 89-707.

5/3-636. Knights of Columbus plates

§ 3-636. Knights of Columbus plates.

(a) The Secretary, upon receipt of all applicable fees and applications made in the form prescribed by the Secretary, may issue special registration plates designated as Knights of Columbus license plates.

The special plates issued under this Section shall be affixed only to passenger vehicles of the first division or motor vehicles of the second division weighing not more than 8,000 pounds.

Plates issued under this Section shall expire according to the multi-year procedure established by Section 3-414.1 of this Code.

(b) The design and color of the special plates shall be wholly within the discretion of the Secretary. Appropriate documentation, as determined by the Secretary, shall accompany each application.

(c) An applicant for the special plate shall be charged a $25 fee for original issuance in addition to the appropriate registration fee. Of this fee, $10 shall be deposited into the Knights of Columbus Fund and $15 shall be deposited into the Secretary of State Special License Plate Fund, to be used by the Secretary to help defray the administrative processing costs.

For each registration renewal period, a $25 fee, in addition to the appropriate registration fee, shall be charged. Of this fee, $23 shall be deposited into the Knights of Columbus Fund and $2 shall be deposited into the Secretary of State Special License Plate Fund.

(d) The Knights of Columbus Fund is created as a special fund in the State treasury. All money in the Knights of Columbus Fund shall be paid, subject to appropriation by the General Assembly and approval by the Secretary, as grants for charitable purposes sponsored by the Knights of Columbus.

P.A. 76-1586, § 3-632, added by P.A. 89-620, § 10, eff. Jan. 1, 1997. Renumbered § 3-636 and amended by P.A. 90-14, Art. 2, § 2-225, eff. July 1, 1997.

P.A. 90-14, Article 2, of the First 1997 General Revisory Act, resolved multiple actions in the 89th General Assembly and made certain technical corrections in P.A. 89-443 through P.A. 89-707.

5/3-637. D.A.R.E. license plate

§ 3-637. D.A.R.E. license plate.

(a) The Secretary, upon receipt of an application made in the form prescribed by the Secretary of State, may issue special registration plates designated to be D.A.R.E. (Drug Abuse Resistance Education) license plates. The special plates issued under this Section shall be affixed only to passenger vehicles of the first division, motor vehicles of the second division weighing not more than 8,000 pounds, and recreational vehicles as defined by Section 1-169 of this Code. Plates issued under this Section shall expire according to the multi-year procedure established by Section 3-414.1 of this Code.

(b) The design and color of the plates shall be wholly within the discretion of the Secretary of State. Appropriate documentation, as determined by the Secretary, shall accompany the application. The Secretary may, in his or her discretion, allow the plates to be issued as vanity or personalized plates in accordance with Section 3-405.1 of this Code.

(c) An applicant shall be charged a $45 fee for original issuance in addition to the appropriate registration fee, if applicable. Of this fee, $10 shall be deposited into the State D.A.R.E. Fund; $10 shall be deposited into the County D.A.R.E. Fund if the county, as indicated by the applicant's address, has a D.A.R.E. program, otherwise the $10 fee shall be deposited into the State D.A.R.E. Fund; $10 shall be deposited into the Municipal D.A.R.E. Fund if the municipality, as indicated by the applicant's address, has a D.A.R.E. program, otherwise the $10 fee shall be deposited into the County D.A.R.E. Fund if the county, as indicated by the applicant's address, has a D.A.R.E. program, otherwise the $10 fee shall be deposited into the State D.A.R.E. Fund; and $15 shall be deposited into the Secretary of State Special License Plate Fund.

For each registration renewal period, a $29 fee, in addition to the appropriate registration fee, shall be charged. Of this fee, $9 shall be deposited into the State D.A.R.E. Fund; $9 shall be deposited into the County D.A.R.E. Fund if the county, as indicated by the applicant's address, has a D.A.R.E. program, otherwise the $9 fee shall be deposited into the State D.A.R.E. Fund; $9 shall be deposited into the Municipal D.A.R.E. Fund if the municipality, as indicated by the applicant's address, has a D.A.R.E. program, otherwise the $9 fee shall be deposited into the County D.A.R.E. Fund if the county, as indicated by the applicant's address, has a D.A.R.E. program, otherwise the $9 fee shall be deposited into the State D.A.R.E. Fund; and $2 shall be deposited into the Secretary of State Special License Plate Fund.

(d) The State D.A.R.E. Fund is created as a special fund in the State Treasury. All money in the State D.A.R.E. Fund shall be distributed, subject to appropriation by the General Assembly, to the Illinois State Police for its D.A.R.E. program.

The County D.A.R.E. Fund is created as a special fund in the State Treasury. All money in the County D.A.R.E. Fund shall be distributed, subject to appropriation by the General Assembly, to the Illinois State Police. The Illinois State

Police shall make grants of this money to counties for their D.A.R.E. programs based on the proportion of money the County D.A.R.E. Fund has received from each county, as indicated by the applicant's address.

The Municipal D.A.R.E. Fund is created as a special fund in the State Treasury. All money in the Municipal D.A.R.E. Fund shall be distributed, subject to appropriation by the General Assembly, to the Illinois State Police. The Illinois State Police shall make grants of this money to municipalities for their D.A.R.E. programs based on the proportion of money the Municipal D.A.R.E. Fund has received from each municipality, as indicated by the applicant's address.

P.A. 76–1586, § 3–631, added by P.A. 89–621, § 5, eff. Jan. 1, 1997. Renumbered § 3–637 and amended by P.A. 90–14, Art. 2, § 2–225, eff. July 1, 1997.

P.A. 90–14, Article 2, of the First 1997 General Revisory Act, resolved multiple actions in the 89th General Assembly and made certain technical corrections in P.A. 89–443 through P.A. 89–707.

5/3–638. U.S. Veteran license plates

§ 3–638. U.S. Veteran License Plates.

(a) In addition to any other special license plate, the Secretary, upon receipt of all applicable fees and applications made in the form prescribed by the Secretary of State, may issue U.S. Veteran license plates to residents of Illinois who meet eligibility requirements prescribed by the Secretary of State. The special U.S. Veteran plate issued under this Section shall be affixed only to passenger vehicles of the first division, motorcycles, and motor vehicles of the second division weighing not more than 8,000 pounds. Plates issued under this Section shall expire according to the staggered multi-year procedure established by Section 3–414.1 of this Code.

(b) The design, color, and format of the plates shall be wholly within the discretion of the Secretary of State. The Secretary may, in his or her discretion, allow the plates to be issued as vanity plates or personalized in accordance with Section 3–405.1 of this Code. The plates are not required to designate "Land Of Lincoln", as prescribed in subsection (b) of Section 3–412 of this Code. The Secretary shall prescribe the eligibility requirements and, in his or her discretion, shall approve and prescribe stickers or decals as provided under Section 3–412.

(c) An applicant shall be charged a $15 fee for original issuance in addition to the applicable registration fee. This additional fee shall be deposited into the Secretary of State Special License Plate Fund. For each registration renewal period, a $2 fee, in addition to the appropriate registration fee, shall be charged and shall be deposited into the Secretary of State Special License Plate Fund.

P.A. 76–1586, § 3–631, added by P.A. 89–639, § 5, eff. Jan. 1, 1997. Renumbered § 3–638 and amended by P.A. 90–14, Art. 2, § 2–225, eff. July 1, 1997; P.A. 92–545, § 5, eff. June 12, 2002.

P.A. 90–14, Article 2, of the First 1997 General Revisory Act, resolved multiple actions in the 89th General Assembly and made certain technical corrections in P.A. 89–443 through P.A. 89–707.

5/3–639. Special registration plate for a president of a village or incorporated town or mayor

§ 3–639. Special registration plate for a president of a village or incorporated town or mayor.

(a) The Secretary, upon receipt of all applicable fees and applications made in the form prescribed by the Secretary, may issue special registration plates to presidents of villages and incorporated towns and mayors.

The special plates issued under this Section shall be affixed only to passenger vehicles of the first division or motor vehicles of the second division weighing not more than 8,000 pounds.

Plates issued under this Section shall expire according to the multi-year procedure established by Section 3–414.1 of this Code.

(b) The design and color of the special plates shall be wholly within the discretion of the Secretary. Appropriate documentation, as determined by the Secretary, shall accompany each application.

(c) An applicant for the special plate shall be charged a $15 fee for original issuance in addition to the appropriate registration fee. This additional fee shall be deposited into the Secretary of State Special License Plate Fund, to be used by the Secretary to help defray the administrative processing costs.

For each registration renewal period, a $2 fee, in addition to the appropriate registration fee, shall be charged. This additional fee shall be deposited into the Secretary of State Special License Plate Fund.

P.A. 76–1586, § 3–639, added by P.A. 90–527, § 5, eff. Nov. 13, 1997. Amended by P.A. 90–655, § 153, July 30, 1998.

Other §§ 3–639, relating to deceased police officer or firefighter plates and Silver Star plates, were renumbered § 3–641 and § 3–642, respectively, by P.A. 90–655, § 153.

P.A. 90–655, the First 1998 General Revisory Act, amended various Acts to delete obsolete text, to correct patent and technical errors, to revise cross references, to resolve multiple actions in the 89th and 90th General Assemblies and to make certain technical corrections in P.A. 89–708 through P.A. 90–566.

5/3–640. Illinois and Michigan Canal plates

§ 3–640. Illinois and Michigan Canal plates.

(a) The Secretary, upon receipt of all applicable fees and applications made in the form prescribed by the Secretary, may issue special registration plates designated as Illinois and Michigan Canal license plates.

The special plates issued under this Section shall be affixed only to passenger vehicles of the first division or motor vehicles of the second division weighing not more than 8,000 pounds.

Plates issued under this Section shall expire according to the multi-year procedure established by Section 3–414.1 of this Code.

(b) The design and color of the special plates shall be wholly within the discretion of the Secretary. Appropriate documentation, as determined by the Secretary, shall accompany each application.

(c) An applicant for the special plate shall be charged a $40 fee for original issuance in addition to the appropriate registration fee. Of this fee, $25 shall be deposited into the Illinois and Michigan Canal Fund and $15 shall be deposited into the Secretary of State Special License Plate Fund, to be used by the Secretary to help defray the administrative processing costs.

For each registration renewal period, a $27 fee, in addition to the appropriate registration fee, shall be charged. Of this fee, $25 shall be deposited into the Illinois and Michigan Canal Fund and $2 shall be deposited into the Secretary of State Special License Plate Fund.

(d) The Illinois and Michigan Canal Fund is created as a special fund in the State treasury. All money in the Illinois and Michigan Canal Fund shall be used, subject to appropriation by the General Assembly, by the Department of Natural Resources for restoration and improvements of the Illinois and Michigan Canal and its adjacent structures.

P.A. 76-1586, § 3-640, added by P.A. 90-527, § 5, eff. Nov. 13, 1997.

5/3-641. Deceased police officer or firefighter plates

§ 3-641. Deceased police officer or firefighter plates.

(a) The Secretary, upon receipt of all applicable fees and applications made in the form prescribed by the Secretary, may issue special registration plates to the surviving spouse or, if no spouse exists, the parents of a police officer or firefighter who has died in the line of duty in this State. The special plates issued pursuant to this Section shall be affixed only to passenger vehicles of the first division or motor vehicles of the second division weighing not more than 8,000 pounds.

Plates issued under this Section shall expire according

to the multi-year procedure established by Section 3-414.1 of this Code.

(b) The design and color of the special plates shall be wholly within the discretion of the Secretary. Appropriate documentation, as determined by the Secretary, shall accompany each application.

(c) An applicant for the special plate shall be charged a $15 fee for original issuance in addition to the appropriate registration fee. This additional fee shall be deposited into the Secretary of State Special License Plate Fund, to be used by the Secretary to help defray the administrative processing costs.

For each registration renewal period, a $2 fee, in addition to the appropriate registration fee, shall be charged. This additional fee shall be deposited into the Secretary of State Special License Plate Fund.

P.A. 76-1586, § 3-639, added by P.A. 90-530, § 5, eff. Jan. 1, 1998. Renumbered § 3-641 and amended by P.A. 90-655, § 153, eff. July 30, 1998.

P.A. 90-655, the First 1998 General Revisory Act, amended various Acts to delete obsolete text, to correct patent and technical errors, to revise cross references, to resolve multiple actions in the 89th and 90th General Assemblies and to make certain technical corrections in P.A. 89-708 through P.A. 90-566.

5/3-642. Silver Star plates

§ 3-642. Silver Star plates.

(a) The Secretary, upon receipt of all applicable fees and applications made in the form prescribed by the Secretary, may issue special registration plates to residents of Illinois who have been awarded the Silver Star by the United States Armed Forces. The special plate issued under this Section shall be affixed only to passenger vehicles of the first division, motorcycles, or motor vehicles of the second division weighing not more than 8,000 pounds. Plates issued under this Section shall expire according to the staggered multi-year procedure established by Section 3-414.1 of this Code.

(b) The design, color, and format of the plates shall be wholly within the discretion of the Secretary. The Secretary may, in his or her discretion, allow the plates to be issued as vanity plates or personalized in accordance with Section 3-405.1 of this Code. The plates are not required to designate "Land Of Lincoln", as prescribed in subsection (b) of Section 3-412 of this Code. The Secretary shall prescribe the eligibility requirements and, in his or her discretion, shall approve and prescribe stickers or decals as provided under Section 3-412.

(c) An applicant shall be charged a $15 fee for original issuance in addition to the appropriate registration fee.

This additional fee shall be deposited into the Secretary of State Special License Plate Fund. For each registration renewal period, a $2 fee, in addition to the appropriate registration fee, shall be charged and deposited into the Secretary of State Special License Plate Fund.

P.A. 76-1586, § 3-639, added by P.A. 90-533, § 5, eff. Nov. 14, 1997. Renumbered § 3-642 and amended by P.A. 90-655, § 153, eff. July 30, 1998; P.A. 92-545, § 5, eff. June 12, 2002.

P.A. 90-655, the First 1998 General Revisory Act, amended various Acts to delete obsolete text, to correct patent and technical errors, to revise cross references, to resolve multiple actions in the 89th and 90th General Assemblies and to make certain technical corrections in P.A. 89-708 through P.A. 90-566.

5/3-643. Mammogram license plates

§ 3-643. Mammogram license plates.

(a) The Secretary, upon receipt of an application made in the form prescribed by the Secretary, may issue special registration plates designated as Mammogram license plates. The special plates issued under this Section shall be affixed only to passenger vehicles of the first division and motor vehicles of the second division weighing not more than 8,000 pounds. Plates issued under this Section shall expire according to the multi-year procedure established by Section 3-414.1 of this Code.

(b) The design and color of the plates is wholly within the discretion of the Secretary, except that the following phrases shall be on the plates: (i) "Mammograms Save Lives" and (ii) "The Susan G. Komen Foundation". The Secretary may allow the plates to be issued as vanity plates or personalized under Section 3-405.1 of the Code. The Secretary shall prescribe stickers or decals as provided under Section 3-412 of this Code.

(c) An applicant for the special plate shall be charged a $25 fee for original issuance in addition to the appropriate registration fee. Of this fee, $10 shall be deposited into the Mammogram Fund and $15 shall be deposited into the Secretary of State Special License Plate Fund, to be used by the Secretary to help defray the administrative processing costs.

For each registration renewal period, a $25 fee, in addition to the appropriate registration fee, shall be charged. Of this fee, $23 shall be deposited into the Mammogram Fund and $2 shall be deposited into the Secretary of State Special License Plate Fund.

(d) The Mammogram Fund is created as a special fund in the State treasury. All money in the Mammogram Fund shall be paid, subject to appropriation by the General Assembly and approval by the Secretary, as grants to the Susan G. Komen Foundation for breast cancer research, education, screening, and treatment.

P.A. 76-1586, § 3-643, added by P.A. 90-675, § 10, eff. Jan. 1, 1999 Amended by P.A. 91-357, § 231, eff. July 29, 1999.

Another § 3-643, relating to Police Memorial Committee license plates, was renumbered § 3-644 by P.A. 91-357, § 231.

P.A. 91-357, the First 1999 General Revisory Act, amended various Acts to delete obsolete text, to correct patent and technical errors, to revise cross references, to resolve multiple actions in the 90th General Assembly and to make certain technical corrections in P.A. 90-567 through P.A. 90-810.

5/3-644. Police Memorial Committee license plates

§ 3-644. Police Memorial Committee license plates.

(a) The Secretary, upon receipt of an application made in the form prescribed by the Secretary, may issue special registration plates designated as Police Memorial Committee license plates. The special plates issued under this Section shall be affixed only to passenger vehicles of the first division and motor vehicles of the second division weighing not more than 8,000 pounds. Plates issued under this Section shall expire according to the multi-year procedure established by Section 3-414.1 of this Code.

(b) The design and color of the plates is wholly within the discretion of the Secretary. The Secretary may allow the plates to be issued as vanity plates or personalized under Section 3-405.1 of the Code. The Secretary shall prescribe stickers or decals as provided under Section 3-412 of this Code.

(c) An applicant for the special plate shall be charged a $25 fee for original issuance in addition to the appropriate registration fee. Of this fee, $10 shall be deposited into the Police Memorial Committee Fund and $15 shall be deposited into the Secretary of State Special License Plate Fund, to be used by the Secretary to help defray the administrative processing costs.

For each registration renewal period, a $25 fee, in addition to the appropriate registration fee, shall be charged. Of this fee, $23 shall be deposited into the Police Memorial Committee Fund and $2 shall be deposited into the Secretary of State Special License Plate Fund.

(d) The Police Memorial Committee Fund is created as a special fund in the State treasury. All money in the Police Memorial Committee Fund shall be paid, subject to appropriation by the General Assembly and approval by the Secretary, as grants to the Police Memorial Committee for maintaining a memorial statue, holding an annual memorial commemoration, and giving scholarships to children of police officers killed in the line of duty.

P.A. 76-1586, § 3-643, added by P.A. 90-729, § 10, eff. Jan. 1, 1999. Renumbered § 3-644 and amended by P.A. 91-357, § 231, eff. July 29, 1999.

P.A. 91-357, the First 1999 General Revisory Act, amended various Acts to delete obsolete text, to correct patent and technical errors, to revise cross references, to resolve multiple actions in the 90th General Assembly and to make certain technical corrections in P.A. 90-567 through P.A. 90-810.

5/3-645. Vietnam Veteran License Plates

§ 3-645. Vietnam Veteran License Plates.

(a) In addition to any other special license plate, the Secretary, upon receipt of all applicable fees and applications made in the form prescribed by the Secretary of State, may issue Vietnam Veteran license plates to residents of Illinois who meet eligibility requirements prescribed by the Secretary of State. The special Vietnam Veteran plate issued under this Section shall be affixed only to passenger vehicles of the first division, motorcycles, and motor vehicles of the second division weighing not more than 8,000 pounds. Plates issued under this Section shall expire according to the staggered multi-year procedure established by Section 3-414.1 of this Code.

(b) The design, color, and format of the plates shall be wholly within the discretion of the Secretary of State. The Secretary may, in his or her discretion, allow the plates to be issued as vanity plates or personalized in accordance with Section 3-405.1 of this Code. The plates are not required to designate "Land Of Lincoln", as prescribed in subsection (b) of Section 3-412 of this Code. The Secretary shall prescribe the eligibility requirements and, in his or her discretion, shall approve and prescribe stickers or decals as provided under Section 3-412.

(c) An applicant shall be charged a $15 fee for original issuance in addition to the applicable registration fee. This additional fee shall be deposited into the Secretary of State Special License Plate Fund. For each registration renewal period, a $2 fee, in addition to the appropriate registration fee, shall be charged and shall be deposited into the Secretary of State Special License Plate Fund.

P.A. 76-1586, § 3-645, added by P.A. 91-805, § 10, eff. Jan. 1, 2001. Amended by P.A. 92-545, § 5, eff. June 12, 2002.

5/3-646. Organ Donor Awareness license plates

§ 3-646. Organ Donor Awareness license plates.

(a) The Secretary, upon receipt of an application made in the form prescribed by the Secretary, may issue special registration plates designated as Organ Donor Awareness license plates. The special plates issued under this Section shall be affixed only to passenger vehicles of the first division and motor vehicles of the second division weighing not more than 8,000 pounds. Plates issued under this Section shall expire according to the multi-year procedure established by Section 3-414.1 of this Code.

(b) The design and color of the plates is wholly within the discretion of the Secretary, except that the phrase "Be An Organ Donor" shall be on the plates, and the design of the plates shall incorporate a reference to the Chicago Bears organization and Walter Payton. The Secretary may allow the plates to be issued as vanity plates or personalized under Section 3-405.1 of the Code. The Secretary shall prescribe stickers or decals as provided under Section 3-412 of this Code.

(c) An applicant for the special plate shall be charged a $25 fee for original issuance in addition to the appropriate registration fee. Of this additional fee, $10 shall be deposited into the Organ Donor Awareness Fund and $15 shall be deposited into the Secretary of State Special License Plate Fund, to be used by the Secretary to help defray the administrative processing costs.

For each registration renewal period, a $25 fee, in addition to the appropriate registration fee, shall be charged. Of this additional fee, $23 shall be deposited into the Organ Donor Awareness Fund and $2 shall be deposited into the Secretary of State Special License Plate Fund.

(d) The Organ Donor Awareness Fund is created as a special fund in the State treasury. Subject to appropriation by the General Assembly and approval by the Secretary, 50% of the moneys in the Organ Donor Awareness Fund shall be paid as grants to the Regional Organ Bank of Illinois, and the remaining 50% of the moneys in that fund shall be paid as grants to Mid-America Transplant Services.

P.A. 76-1586, § 3-646, added by P.A. 91-805, § 10, eff. Jan. 1, 2001.

5/3-647. World War II Veteran License Plates

§ 3-647. World War II Veteran License Plates.

(a) In addition to any other special license plate, the Secretary, upon receipt of all applicable fees and applications made in the form prescribed by the Secretary of State, may issue World War II Veteran license plates to residents of Illinois who meet eligibility requirements prescribed by the Secretary of State. The special World War II Veteran plate issued under this Section shall be affixed only to passenger vehicles of the first division, motorcycles, and motor vehicles of the second division weighing not more than 8,000 pounds. Plates issued under this Section shall expire according to the staggered multi-year procedure established by Section 3–414.1 of this Code.

(b) The design, color, and format of the plates shall be wholly within the discretion of the Secretary of State. The Secretary may, in his or her discretion, allow the plates to be issued as vanity plates or personalized in accordance with Section 3–405.1 of this Code. The plates are not required to designate "Land Of Lincoln", as prescribed in subsection (b) of Section 3–412 of this Code. The Secretary shall prescribe the eligibility requirements and, in his or her discretion, shall approve and prescribe stickers or decals as provided under Section 3–412.

(c) An applicant shall be charged a $15 fee for original issuance in addition to the applicable registration fee. This additional fee shall be deposited into the Secretary of State Special License Plate Fund. For each registration renewal period, a $2 fee, in addition to the appropriate registration fee, shall be charged and shall be deposited into the Secretary of State Special License Plate Fund.

P.A. 76–1586, § 3–647, added by P.A. 91–805, § 10, eff. Jan. 1, 2001. Amended by P.A. 92–545, § 5, eff. June 12, 2002.

5/3–648. Education license plates

Text of section as added by P.A. 92–445, § 15, and amended by P.A. 92–651, § 77, and P.A. 92–845, § 10, eff. January 1, 2003

§ 3–648. Education license plates.

(a) The Secretary, upon receipt of an application made in the form prescribed by the Secretary, may issue special registration plates designated as Education license plates. The special plates issued under this Section shall be affixed only to passenger vehicles of the first division and motor vehicles of the second division weighing not more than 8,000 pounds. Plates issued under this Section shall expire according to the multi-year procedure established by Section 3–414.1 of this Code.

(b) The design and color of the plates shall be determined by a contest that every elementary school pupil in the State of Illinois is eligible to enter. The designs submitted for the contest shall be judged on September 30, 2002, and the winning design shall be selected by a committee composed of the Secretary, the Director of State Police, 2 members of the Senate, one member chosen by the President of the Senate and one member chosen by the Senate Minority Leader, and 2 members of the House of Representatives, one member chosen by the Speaker of the House and one member chosen by the House Minority Leader. The Secretary may allow the plates to be issued as vanity or personalized plates under Section 3–405.1 of the Code. The Secretary shall prescribe stickers or decals as provided under Section 3–412 of this Code.

(c) An applicant for the special plate shall be charged a $40 fee for original issuance, in addition to the appropriate registration fee. Of this $40 additional original issuance fee, $15 shall be deposited into the Secretary of State Special License Plate Fund, to be used by the Secretary to help defray the administrative processing costs, and $25 shall be deposited into the Illinois Future Teacher Corps Scholarship Fund. For each registration renewal period, a $40 fee, in addition to the appropriate registration fee, shall be charged. Of this $40 additional renewal fee, $2 shall be deposited into the Secretary of State Special License Plate Fund and $38 shall be deposited into the Illinois Future Teacher Corps Scholarship Fund. Each fiscal year, once deposits from the additional original issuance and renewal fees into the Secretary of State Special License Plate Fund have reached $500,000, all the amounts received for the additional fees for the balance of the fiscal year shall be deposited into the Illinois Future Teacher Corps Scholarship Fund.

(d) The Illinois Future Teacher Corps Scholarship Fund is created as a special fund in the State treasury. Ninety-five percent of the moneys in the Illinois Future Teacher Corps Scholarship Fund shall be appropriated to the Illinois Student Assistance Commission for scholarships under Section 52 or 65.65 of the Higher Education Student Assistance Act,[1] and 5% of the moneys in the Illinois Future Teacher Corps Scholarship Fund shall be appropriated to the State Board of Education for grants to the Golden Apple Foundation for Excellence in Teaching, a recognized charitable organization that meets the requirements of Title 26, Section 501(c)(3) of the United States Code.

P.A. 76–1586, § 3–648, added by P.A. 92–445, § 15, eff. Aug. 17, 2001. Amended by P.A. 92–651, § 77, eff. July 11, 2002; P.A. 92–845, § 10, eff. Jan. 1, 2003.

[1] 110 ILCS 947/65.65.

For text of section as added by P.A. 92–693, § 10, relating to Hospice license plates, see 625 ILCS 5/3–648, post

P.A. 92–651, the First 2002 General Revisory Act, amended various Acts to delete obsolete text, to correct patent and technical errors, to revise cross references, to resolve multiple actions in the 91st and 92nd General Assemblies and to make certain technical corrections in P.A. 91–937 through P.A. 92–520.

P.A. 92–845 incorporated the amendment by P.A. 92–445.

See 5 ILCS 70/6 as to the effect of (1) more than one amendment of a section at the same session of the General Assembly or (2) two or more acts relating to the same subject matter enacted by the same General Assembly.

5/3–648. Hospice license plates

Text of section as added by P.A. 92–693, § 10, effective January 1, 2003

§ 3–648. Hospice license plates.

(a) The Secretary, upon receipt of an application made in the form prescribed by the Secretary, may issue special registration plates designated as Hospice license plates. The special plates issued under this Section shall be affixed only to passenger vehicles of the first division and motor vehicles of the second division weighing not more than 8,000 pounds. Plates issued under this Section shall expire according to the multi-year procedure established by Section 3–414.1 of this Code.

(b) The color of the plates is wholly within the discretion of the Secretary. The design of the plates shall include the word "Hospice" above drawings of two lilies and a butterfly. The Secretary may allow the plates to be issued as vanity plates or personalized under Section 3–405.1 of the Code. The Secretary shall prescribe stickers or decals as provided under Section 3–412 of this Code.

(c) An applicant for the special plate shall be charged a $25 fee for original issuance in addition to the appropriate registration fee. Of this fee, $10 shall be deposited into the Hospice Fund and $15 shall be deposited into the Secretary of State Special License Plate Fund, to be used by the Secretary to help defray the administrative processing costs.

For each registration renewal period, a $25 fee, in addition to the appropriate registration fee, shall be charged. Of this fee, $23 shall be deposited into the Hospice Fund and $2 shall be deposited into the Secretary of State Special License Plate Fund.

(d) The Hospice Fund is created as a special fund in the State treasury. All money in the Hospice Fund shall be paid, subject to appropriation by the General Assembly and approval by the Secretary, to the Department of Public Health for distribution as grants for hospice services as defined in the Hospice Program Licensing Act.[1] The Director of Public Health shall adopt rules for the distribution of these grants.

P.A. 76-1586, § 3-648, added by P.A. 92-693, § 10, eff. Jan. 1, 2003.

[1] 210 ILCS 60/1 et seq.

For text of section as added by P.A. 92-445 and amended by P.A. 92-651 and P.A. 92-845, effective January 1, 2003, see 625 ILCS 5/3-648, ante

Other § 3-648 were amended and redesignated as § 3-650 through § 3-653 by P.A. 92-545, 92-651, and 92-699.

See 5 ILCS 70/6 as to the effect of (1) more than one amendment of a section at the same session of the General Assembly or (2) two or more acts relating to the same subject matter enacted by the same General Assembly.

5/3-649. West Point Bicentennial license plates

§ 3-649. West Point Bicentennial license plates.

(a) In addition to any other special license plate, the Secretary, upon receipt of all applicable fees and applications made in the form prescribed by the Secretary of State, may issue West Point Bicentennial license plates to commemorate the 200th anniversary of the founding of the United States Military Academy at West Point, N.Y. The special West Point Bicentennial plate issued under this Section shall be affixed only to passenger vehicles of the first division and motor vehicles of the second division weighing not more than 8,000 pounds. Plates issued under this Section shall expire according to the staggered multi-year procedure established by Section 3-414. 1 of this Code.

(b) The design, color, and format of the plates shall be wholly within the discretion of the Secretary of State. The Secretary may, in his or her discretion, allow the plates to be issued as vanity plates or personalized in accordance with Section 3-405.1 of this Code. The plates are not required to designate "Land Of Lincoln", as prescribed in subsection (b) of Section 3-412 of this Code. The Secretary shall approve and prescribe stickers or decals as provided under Section 3-412.

(c) An applicant shall be charged a $15 fee for original issuance in addition to the applicable registration fee. This additional fee shall be deposited into the Secretary of State Special License Plate Fund. For each registration renewal period, a $2 fee, in addition to the appropriate registration fee, shall be charged and shall be deposited into the Secretary of State Special License Plate Fund.

P.A. 76-1586, § 3-649, added by P.A. 92-477, § 10, eff. Jan. 1, 2002.

5/3-650. Army Combat Veteran license plates.

§ 3-650. Army Combat Veteran license plates.

(a) In addition to any other special license plate, the Secretary, upon receipt of all applicable fees and applications made in the form prescribed by the Secretary of State, may issue Army Combat Veteran license plates to residents of Illinois who meet eligibility requirements prescribed by the Secretary of State. The special Army Combat Veteran plate issued under this Section shall be affixed only to passenger vehicles of the first division, motorcycles, and motor vehicles of the second division weighing not more than 8,000 pounds. Plates issued under this Section shall expire according to the staggered multi-year procedure established by Section 3-414.1 of this Code.

(b) The plates shall display the Army Combat Infantry Badge. In all other respects, the design, color, and format of the plates shall be within the discretion of the Secretary of State. The Secretary may, in his or her discretion, allow the plates to be issued as vanity plates or personalized in accordance with Section 3-405.1 of this Code. The plates are not required to designate "Land Of Lincoln", as prescribed in subsection (b) of Section 3-412 of this Code. The Secretary shall prescribe the eligibility requirements and, in his or her discretion, shall approve and prescribe stickers or decals as provided under Section 3-412.

(c) An applicant shall be charged a $15 fee for original issuance in addition to the applicable registration fee. This additional fee shall be deposited into the Secretary of State Special License Plate Fund. For each registration renewal period, a $2 fee, in addition to the appropriate registration fee, shall be charged and shall be deposited into the Secretary of State Special License Plate Fund.

P.A. 76-1586, § 3-648, added by P.A. 92-79, § 5, eff. Jan. 1, 2002. Renumbered § 3-650 and amended by P.A. 92-545, § 5, eff. June 12, 2002; P.A. 92-651, § 77, eff. July 11, 2002; P.A. 92-699, § 5, eff. Jan. 1, 2003.

P.A. 92-651, the First 2002 General Revisory Act, amended various Acts to delete obsolete text, to correct patent and technical errors, to revise cross references, to resolve multiple actions in the 91st and 92nd General Assemblies and to make certain technical corrections in P.A. 91-937 through P.A. 92-520.

See 5 ILCS 70/6 as to the effect of (1) more than one amendment of a section at the same session of the General Assembly or (2) two or more acts relating to the same subject matter enacted by the same General Assembly.

5/3-651. U.S. Marine Corps license plates.

§ 3-651. U.S. Marine Corps license plates.

(a) In addition to any other special license plate, the Secretary, upon receipt of all applicable fees and applications made in the form prescribed by the Secretary of State, may issue special registration plates designated as U.S. Marine Corps license plates to residents of Illinois who meet eligibility requirements prescribed by the Secretary of State. The special plate issued under this Section shall be affixed only to passenger vehicles of the first division, motorcycles, motor vehicles of the second division weighing not more than 8,000 pounds, and recreational vehicles as defined by Section 1-169 of this Code. Plates issued under this Section shall expire according to the staggered multi-year procedure established by Section 3-414.1 of this Code.

(b) The design, color, and format of the plates shall be wholly within the discretion of the Secretary of State, except that the U.S. Marine Corps emblem shall appear on the plates. The Secretary may, in his or her discretion, allow the plates to be issued as vanity or personalized plates in accordance with Section 3-405.1 of this Code. The plates are not required to designate "Land Of Lincoln", as prescribed in subsection (b) of Section 3-412 of this Code. The Secretary shall prescribe the eligibility requirements and, in his or her discretion, shall approve and prescribe stickers or decals as provided under Section 3-412.

(c) An applicant shall be charged a $20 fee for original issuance in addition to the applicable registration fee. Of this additional fee, $15 shall be deposited into the Secretary of State Special License Plate Fund and $5 shall be deposited into the Marine Corps Scholarship Fund. For each registration renewal period, a $20 fee, in addition to the appropriate registration fee, shall be charged. Of this additional fee, $2 shall be deposited into the Secretary of State Special License Plate Fund and $18 shall be deposited into the Marine Corps Scholarship Fund.

(d) The Marine Corps Scholarship Fund is created as a special fund in the State treasury. All moneys in the Marine Corps Scholarship Fund shall, subject to appropriation by the General Assembly and approval by the Secretary, be used by the Marine Corps Scholarship Foundation, Inc., a recognized charitable organization that meets the requirements of Title 26, Section 501(c)(3) of the United States Code, to provide grants for scholarships for higher education. The scholarship recipients must be the children of current or former members of the United States Marine Corps who meet the academic, financial, and other requirements established by the Marine Corps Scholarship Foundation. In addition, the recipients must be Illinois residents and must attend a college or university located within the State of Illinois.

The State Treasurer shall require the Marine Corps Scholarship Foundation to establish a separate account for receipt of the proceeds of the Marine Corps Scholarship Fund. That account shall be subject to audit either annually or at another interval, as determined by the State Treasurer. Proceeds from the Marine Corps Scholarship Fund shall be transferred on a quarterly basis by the State Treasurer's office to this separate account.

P.A. 76-1586, § 3-648, added by P.A. 92-467, § 10, eff. Jan. 1, 2002. Renumbered § 3-651 and amended by P.A. 92-545, § 5, eff. June 12, 2002; P.A. 92-651, § 77, eff. July 11, 2002; P.A. 92-699, § 5, eff. Jan. 1, 2003.

P.A. 92-651, the First 2002 General Revisory Act, amended various Acts to delete obsolete text, to correct patent and technical errors, to revise cross references, to resolve multiple actions in the 91st and 92nd General Assemblies and to make certain technical corrections in P.A. 91-937 through P.A. 92-520.

See 5 ILCS 70/6 as to the effect of (1) more than one amendment of a section at the same session of the General Assembly or (2) two or more acts relating to the same subject matter enacted by the same General Assembly.

5/3-652. Chicago and Northeast Illinois District Council of Carpenters license plates

§ 3-652. Chicago and Northeast Illinois District Council of Carpenters license plates.

(a) The Secretary, upon receipt of all applicable fees and applications made in the form prescribed by the Secretary, may issue special registration plates designated as Chicago and Northeast Illinois District Council of Carpenters license plates.

The special plates issued under this Section shall be affixed only to passenger vehicles of the first division or motor vehicles of the second division weighing not more than 8,000 pounds.

Plates issued under this Section shall expire according to the multi-year procedure established by Section 3-414.1 of this Code.

(b) The design and color of the special plates shall be wholly within the discretion of the Secretary. Appropriate documentation, as determined by the Secretary, shall accompany each application. The Secretary may allow the plates to be issued as vanity plates or personalized plates under Section 3-405.1 of this Code. The Secretary shall prescribe stickers or decals as provided under Section 3-412 of this Code.

(c) An applicant for the special plate shall be charged a $25 fee for original issuance in addition to the appropriate registration fee. Of this fee, $10 shall be deposited into the Chicago and Northeast Illinois District Council of Carpenters Fund and $15 shall be deposited into the Secretary of State Special License Plate Fund, to be used by the Secretary to help defray the administrative processing costs.

For each registration renewal period, a $25 fee, in addition to the appropriate registration fee, shall be charged. Of this fee, $23 shall be deposited into the Chicago and Northeast Illinois District Council of Carpenters Fund and $2 shall be deposited into the Secretary of State Special License Plate Fund.

(d) The Chicago and Northeast Illinois District Council of Carpenters Fund is created as a special fund in the State treasury. All moneys in the Chicago and Northeast Illinois District Council of Carpenters Fund shall be paid, subject to appropriation by the General Assembly and approval by the Secretary, as grants for charitable purposes sponsored by the Chicago and Northeast Illinois District Council of Carpenters.

P.A. 76-1586, § 3-648, added by P.A. 92-477, § 10, eff. Jan. 1, 2002. Renumbered § 3-652 and amended by P.A. 92-651, § 77, eff. July 11, 2002.

P.A. 92-651, the First 2002 General Revisory Act, amended various Acts to delete obsolete text, to correct patent and technical errors, to revise cross references, to resolve multiple actions in the 91st and 92nd General Assemblies and to make certain technical corrections in P.A. 91-937 through P.A. 92-520.

5/3-653. Pet Friendly license plates

Text of section as added by P.A. 92-520, § 10, effective January 1, 2003

§ 3-653. Pet Friendly license plates.

(a) The Secretary, upon receipt of an application made in the form prescribed by the Secretary, may issue special registration plates designated as Pet Friendly license plates. The special plates issued under this Section shall be affixed only to passenger vehicles of the first division, motor vehicles of the second division weighing not more than 8,000 pounds, and recreational vehicles as defined in Section 1-169 of this Code. Plates issued under this Section shall expire according to the multi-year procedure established by Section 3-414.1 of this Code.

(b) The design and color of the plates is wholly within the discretion of the Secretary, except that the phrase "I am pet friendly" shall be on the plates. The Secretary may allow the plates to be issued as vanity plates or personalized plates under Section 3-405.1 of the Code. The Secretary shall prescribe stickers or decals as provided under Section 3-412 of this Code.

(c) An applicant for the special plate shall be charged a $40 fee for original issuance in addition to the appropriate registration fee. Of this additional fee, $25 shall be deposited into the Pet Overpopulation Control Fund and $15 shall be deposited into the Secretary of State Special License Plate Fund, to be used by the Secretary to help defray the administrative processing costs.

For each registration renewal period, a $27 fee, in addition to the appropriate registration fee, shall be charged. Of this additional fee, $25 shall be deposited into the Pet Overpopulation Control Fund and $2 shall be deposited into the Secretary of State Special License Plate Fund.

(d) The Pet Overpopulation Control Fund is created as a special fund in the State treasury. All moneys in the Pet

Overpopulation Control Fund shall be paid, subject to appropriation by the General Assembly and approval by the Secretary, as grants to humane societies exempt from federal income taxation under Section 501(c)(3) of the Internal Revenue Code [1] to be used solely for the humane sterilization of dogs and cats in the State of Illinois. In approving grants under this subsection (d), the Secretary shall consider recommendations for grants made by a volunteer board appointed by the Secretary that shall consist of 5 Illinois residents who are officers or directors of humane societies operating in different regions in Illinois.

P.A. 76-1586, § 3-648, added by P.A. 92-520, § 10, eff. June 1, 2002. Renumbered § 3-653 and amended by P.A. 92-651, § 77, eff. July 11, 2002.

[1] 26 U.S.C.A. § 501.

For other §§ 3-653, see multiple added text of 625 ILCS 5/3-653, post

P.A. 92-651, the First 2002 General Revisory Act, amended various Acts to delete obsolete text, to correct patent and technical errors, to revise cross references, to resolve multiple actions in the 91st and 92nd General Assemblies and to make certain technical corrections in P.A. 91-937 through P.A. 92-520.

5/3-653. Lewis and Clark Bicentennial license plates

Text of section as added by P.A. 92-694, § 10, effective January 1, 2003

§ 3-653. Lewis and Clark Bicentennial license plates.

(a) In addition to any other special license plate, the Secretary, upon receipt of all applicable fees and applications made in the form prescribed by the Secretary of State, may issue special registration plates designated as Lewis and Clark Bicentennial license plates to residents of Illinois. The special plate issued under this Section shall be affixed only to passenger vehicles of the first division, motor vehicles of the second division weighing not more than 8,000 pounds, and recreational vehicles as defined by Section 1-169 of this Code. Plates issued under this Section shall expire according to the staggered multi-year procedure established by Section 3-414.1 of this Code.

(b) The Secretary of State shall confer with the Governor's Illinois Lewis and Clark Bicentennial Commission regarding the design, color, and format of the plates. The Secretary may, in his or her discretion, allow the plates to be issued as vanity or personalized plates in accordance with Section 3-405.1 of this Code. The plates are not required to designate "Land Of Lincoln", as prescribed in subsection (b) of Section 3-412 of this Code. The Secretary, in his or her discretion, shall approve and prescribe stickers or decals as provided under Section 3-412.

(c) An applicant shall be charged a $40 fee for original issuance in addition to the applicable registration fee. Of this additional fee, $15 shall be deposited into the Secretary of State Special License Plate Fund and $25 shall be deposited into the Lewis and Clark Bicentennial Fund. For each registration renewal period, a $27 fee, in addition to the appropriate registration fee, shall be charged. Of this additional fee, $2 shall be deposited into the Secretary of State Special License Plate Fund and $25 shall be deposited into the Lewis and Clark Bicentennial Fund.

(d) The Secretary of State shall issue special license plates under this Section on and before September 1, 2008. The Secretary may not issue special plates under this Section after September 1, 2008.

(e) The Lewis and Clark Bicentennial Fund is created as a special fund in the State treasury. All moneys in the Lewis and Clark Bicentennial Fund shall, subject to appropriation by the General Assembly and approval by the Secretary, be used by the Department of Commerce and Community Affairs to promote tourism and education related to the Lewis and Clark Expedition and for historic preservation purposes related to the Expedition.

The State Treasurer shall transfer any moneys remaining in the Lewis and Clark Bicentennial Fund on September 1, 2009 and any moneys received for deposit into that Fund on or after September 1, 2009 into the Secretary of State Special License Plate Fund.

P.A. 76-1586, § 3-653, added by P.A. 92-694, § 10, eff. Jan. 1, 2003.

For other §§ 3-653, see multiple added text of 625 ILCS 5/3-653, ante and post

5/3-653. September 11th license plates

Text of section as added by P.A. 92-704, § 20, eff. July 19, 2002

§ 3-653. September 11th license plates.

(a) Beginning on September 11, 2002, the Secretary, upon receipt of all applicable fees and applications made in the form prescribed by the Secretary, may issue special registration plates designated as September 11th license plates.

The special plates issued under this Section shall be affixed only to passenger vehicles of the first division or motor vehicles of the second division weighing not more than 8,000 pounds.

Plates issued under this Section shall expire according to the multi-year procedure established by Section 3-414.1 of this Code.

(b) The design and color of the special plates shall be wholly within the discretion of the Secretary. The Secretary may allow the plates to be issued as vanity or personalized plates under Section 3-405.1 of this Code. The Secretary shall prescribe stickers or decals as provided under Section 3-412 of this Code.

(c) An applicant for the special plate shall be charged a $40 fee for original issuance in addition to the appropriate registration fee. Of this fee, $25 shall be deposited into the September 11th Fund and $15 shall be deposited into the Secretary of State Special License Plate Fund, to be used by the Secretary to help defray the administrative processing costs.

For each registration renewal period, a $27 fee, in addition to the appropriate registration fee, shall be charged. Of this fee, $25 shall be deposited into the September 11th Fund and $2 shall be deposited into the Secretary of State Special License Plate Fund.

(d) The September 11th Fund is created as a special fund in the State treasury. Subject to appropriation by the General Assembly and approval by the Secretary, the Director of Commerce and Community Affairs shall pay all moneys in the September 11th Fund as grants to aid victims of terrorism and as grants to local governments to cover the costs of training, equipment, and other items related to public safety initiatives intended to prevent further acts of terrorism or to respond to further acts of terrorism or other disasters or emergency situations in Illinois.

P.A. 76-1586, § 3-653, added by P.A. 92-704, § 20, eff. July 19, 2002.

For other §§ 3-653, see multiple added text of 625 ILCS 5/3-653, ante and post

5/3-653. Illinois Route 66 license plates

Text of section as added by P.A. 92-706, § 10, eff. January 1, 2003

§ 3-653. Illinois Route 66 license plates.

(a) The Secretary, upon receipt of all applicable fees and applications made in the form prescribed by the Secretary, may issue special registration plates designated as Illinois Route 66 license plates. The special plates issued under this Section shall be affixed only to passenger vehicles of the first division or motor vehicles of the second division weighing not more than 8,000 pounds. Plates issued under this Section shall expire according to the multi-year procedure established by Section 3-414.1 of this Code.

(b) The design and color of the special plates shall be wholly within the discretion of the Secretary. The Secretary may, in his or her discretion, allow the plates to be issued as vanity or personalized plates in accordance with Section 3-405.1 of this Code. The plates are not required to designate "Land of Lincoln", as prescribed in subsection (b) of Section 3-412 of this Code. The Secretary, in his or her discretion, shall approve and prescribe stickers or decals as provided under Section 3-412.

(c) An applicant for the special plate shall be charged a $40 fee for original issuance in addition to the appropriate registration fee. Of this fee, $25 shall be deposited into the Illinois Route 66 Heritage Project Fund and $15 shall be deposited into the Secretary of State Special License Plate Fund, to be used by the Secretary to help defray the administrative processing costs.

For each registration renewal period, a $27 fee, in addition to the appropriate registration fee, shall be charged. Of this fee, $25 shall be deposited into the Illinois Route 66 Heritage Project Fund and $2 shall be deposited into the Secretary of State Special License Plate Fund.

(d) The Illinois Route 66 Heritage Project Fund is created as a special fund in the State treasury. Subject to appropriation by the General Assembly and approval by the Secretary, Illinois Route 66 Heritage Project, Inc. shall use all moneys in the Illinois Route 66 Heritage Project Fund for the development of tourism, through education and interpretation, preservation, and promotion of the former U.S. Route 66 in Illinois.

P.A. 76-1586, § 3-653, added by P.A. 92-706, § 10, eff. Jan. 1, 2003.

For other §§ 3-653, see multiple added texts of 625 ILCS 5/3-653, ante

See 5 ILCS 70/6 as to the effect of (1) more than one amendment of a section at the same session of the General Assembly or (2) two or more acts relating to the same subject matter enacted by the same General Assembly.

5/3-654. Illinois Public Broadcasting System Stations special license plates

Text of section as added by P.A. 92-695, § 10, effective January 1, 2003

§ 3-654. Illinois Public Broadcasting System Stations special license plates.

(a) The Secretary, upon receipt of all applicable fees and applications made in the form prescribed by the Secretary, may issue special registration plates designated as Illinois Public Broadcasting System Stations special license plates. The special plates issued under this Section shall be affixed only to passenger vehicles of the first division or motor vehicles of the second division weighing not more than 8,000 pounds. Plates issued under this Section shall expire according to the multi-year procedure established by Section 3-414.1 of this Code.

(b) The design and color of the special plates shall be wholly within the discretion of the Secretary. The Secretary may, in his or her discretion, allow the plates to be issued as vanity or personalized plates in accordance with Section 3-405.1 of this Code. The plates are not required to designate "Land of Lincoln", as prescribed in subsection (b) of Section 3-412 of this Code. The Secretary, in his or her discretion, shall approve and prescribe stickers or decals as provided under Section 3-412.

(c) An applicant for the special plate shall be charged a $40 fee for original issuance in addition to the appropriate registration fee. Of this fee, $25 shall be deposited into the Public Broadcasting Fund and $15 shall be deposited into the Secretary of State Special License Plate Fund, to be used by the Secretary to help defray the administrative processing costs.

For each registration renewal period, a $27 fee, in addition to the appropriate registration fee, shall be charged. Of this fee, $25 shall be deposited into the Public Broadcasting Fund and $2 shall be deposited into the Secretary of State Special License Plate Fund.

(d) The Public Broadcasting Fund is created as a special fund in the State treasury. Subject to appropriation by the General Assembly and approval by the Secretary, the Secretary shall pay all moneys in the Public Broadcasting Fund to the various Public Broadcasting System stations in Illinois for operating costs.

P.A. 76-1586, § 3-654, added by P.A. 92-695, § 10, eff. Jan. 1, 2003.

For other §§ 3-654, see multiple added texts of 625 ILCS 5/3-654, post

5/3-654. Park District Youth Program license plates

Text of section as added by P.A. 92-697, § 10, eff. July 19, 2002

§ 3-654. Park District Youth Program license plates.

(a) In addition to any other special license plate, the Secretary, upon receipt of all applicable fees and applications made in the form prescribed by the Secretary of State, may issue Park District Youth Program license plates. The special Park District Youth Program plate issued under this Section shall be affixed only to passenger vehicles of the first division and motor vehicles of the second division weighing not more than 8,000 pounds. Plates issued under this Section shall expire according to the staggered multi-year procedure established by Section 3-414.1 of this Code.

(b) The design, color, and format of the plates shall be wholly within the discretion of the Secretary of State. Appropriate documentation, as determined by the Secretary, must accompany each application. The Secretary, in his or her discretion, shall approve and prescribe stickers or decals as provided under Section 3-412.

(c) An applicant for the special plate shall be charged a $40 fee for original issuance in addition to the appropriate registration fee. Of this fee, $25 shall be deposited into the Park District Youth Program Fund and $15 shall be deposited into the Secretary of State Special License Plate Fund, to be used by the Secretary to help defray the administrative processing costs.

For each registration renewal period, a $27 fee, in addition to the appropriate registration fee, shall be charged. Of this fee, $25 shall be deposited into the Park District Youth Program Fund and $2 shall be deposited into the Secretary of State Special License Plate Fund.

(d) The Park District Youth Program Fund is created as a special fund in the State treasury. All money in the Park District Youth Program Fund shall be paid, subject to appropriation by the General Assembly and approval by the Secretary, as grants to the Illinois Association of Park Districts, a not-for-profit corporation, for grants to park districts and recreation agencies providing innovative after school programming for Illinois youth.

P.A. 92-697, § 10, eff. July 19, 2002.

For other § 3-654, see multiple added texts of 625 ILCS 5/3-654, ante and post

5/3-654. Professional Sports Teams license plates

Text of section as added by P.A. 92-699, § 5, effective January 1, 2003

§ 3-654. Professional Sports Teams license plates.

(a) The Secretary, upon receipt of an application made in the form prescribed by the Secretary, may issue special registration plates designated as Professional Sports Teams license plates. The special plates issued under this Section shall be affixed only to passenger vehicles of the first division and motor vehicles of the second division weighing not more than 8,000 pounds. Plates issued under this Section shall expire according to the multi-year procedure established by Section 3-414.1 of this Code.

(b) The design and color of the plates is wholly within the discretion of the Secretary, except that the plates shall, subject to the permission of the applicable team owner, display the logo of the Chicago Bears, the Chicago Bulls, the Chicago Black Hawks, the Chicago Cubs, the Chicago White Sox, the St. Louis Rams, or the St. Louis Cardinals, at the applicant's option. The Secretary may allow the plates to be issued as vanity or personalized plates under Section 3-405.1 of the Code. The Secretary shall prescribe stickers or decals as provided under Section 3-412 of this Code.

(c) An applicant for the special plate shall be charged a $40 fee for original issuance in addition to the appropriate registration fee. Of this fee, $25 shall be deposited into the Professional Sports Teams Education Fund and $15 shall be deposited into the Secretary of State Special License Plate Fund, to be used by the Secretary to help defray the administrative processing costs.

For each registration renewal period, a $27 fee, in addition to the appropriate registration fee, shall be charged. Of this fee, $25 shall be deposited into the Professional Sports Teams Education Fund and $2 shall be deposited into the Secretary of State Special License Plate Fund.

(d) The Professional Sports Teams Education Fund is created as a special fund in the State treasury. All moneys in the Professional Sports Teams Education Fund shall, subject to appropriation by the General Assembly and approval by the Secretary, be deposited every 6 months into the Common School Fund.

P.A. 76-1586, § 3-654, added by P.A. 92-699, § 5, eff. Jan. 1, 2003.

For other §§ 3-654, see multiple added texts of 625 ILCS 5/3-654, ante and post

5/3-654. Pan Hellenic license plates

Text of section as added by P.A. 92-702, § 10, eff. January 1, 2003

§ 3-654. Pan Hellenic license plates.

(a) The Secretary, upon receipt of all applicable fees and applications made in the form prescribed by the Secretary, may issue special registration plates designated as Pan Hellenic license plates. The special plates issued under this Section shall be affixed only to passenger vehicles of the first division or motor vehicles of the second division weighing not more than 8,000 pounds. Plates issued under this Section shall expire according to the multi-year procedure established by Section 3-414.1 of this Code.

(b) The design and color of the special plates shall be wholly within the discretion of the Secretary, except that an emblem of a Pan Hellenic eligible member shall be on the plate. Appropriate documentation, as determined by the Secretary, shall accompany each application. The Secretary may, in his or her discretion, allow the plates to be issued as vanity or personalized plates in accordance with Section 3-405.1 of this Code. The plates are not required to designate "Land of Lincoln" as prescribed in subsection (b) of Section 3-412 of this Code. The Secretary, in his or her discretion, may prescribe rules governing the requirements and approval of the special plates.

(c) An applicant for the special plate shall be charged a $40 fee for original issuance in addition to the appropriate registration fee. Of this fee, $25 shall be deposited into the Illinois Pan Hellenic Trust Fund and $15 shall be deposited into the Secretary of State Special License Plate Fund, to be used by the Secretary to help defray the administrative processing costs. For each registration renewal period, a $27 fee, in addition to the appropriate registration fee, shall be charged. Of this fee, $25 shall be deposited into the Illinois Pan Hellenic Trust Fund and $2 shall be deposited into the Secretary of State Special License Plate Fund.

(d) The Illinois Pan Hellenic Trust Fund is created as a special fund in the State Treasury. The State Treasurer shall create separate accounts within the Illinois Pan Hellenic Trust Fund for each eligible member for which Pan Hellenic license plates have been issued. Moneys in the Illinois Pan Hellenic Trust Fund shall be allocated to each account in proportion to the number of plates sold in regard to each fraternity or sorority. All moneys in the Illinois Pan Hellenic Trust Fund shall be distributed, subject to appropriation by the General Assembly and approval by the Secretary, as grants to the Illinois Alpha Kappa Alpha Charitable Foundation, Illinois Delta Sigma Theta Charitable Foundation, Illinois Zeta Phi Beta Charitable Foundation, Illinois Sigma Gamma Rho Charitable Foundation, Illinois Alpha Phi Alpha Charitable Foundation, Illinois Omega Psi Phi Charitable Foundation, Illinois Kappa Alpha Psi Charitable Foundation, Illinois Phi Beta Sigma Charitable Foundation, or Illinois Iota Phi Theta Charitable Foundation for charitable purposes sponsored by the African-American fraternity or sorority.

P.A. 76-1586, § 3-654, added by P.A. 92-702, § 10, eff. Jan. 1, 2003.

For other §§ 3-654, see multiple added texts of 625 ILCS 5/3-654, ante and post

5/3–654. Stop Neuroblastoma license plates

Text of section as added by P.A. 92–711, § 10, eff. July 19, 2002

§ 3–654. Stop Neuroblastoma license plates.

(a) The Secretary, upon receipt of an application made in the form prescribed by the Secretary, may issue special registration plates designated as Stop Neuroblastoma license plates. The special plates issued under this Section shall be affixed only to passenger vehicles of the first division and motor vehicles of the second division weighing not more than 8,000 pounds. Plates issued under this Section shall expire according to the multi-year procedure established by Section 3–414.1 of this Code.

(b) The design and color of the plates is wholly within the discretion of the Secretary, except that the following phrases shall be on the plates: (i) "Stop Neuroblastoma" and (ii) "Stop Cancer". The Secretary may allow the plates to be issued as vanity plates or personalized under Section 3–405.1 of this Code. The Secretary shall prescribe stickers or decals as provided under Section 3–412 of this Code.

(c) An applicant for the special plate shall be charged a $25 fee for original issuance in addition to the appropriate registration fee. Of this fee, $10 shall be deposited into the Stop Neuroblastoma Fund and $15 shall be deposited into the Secretary of State Special License Plate Fund, to be used by the Secretary to help defray the administrative processing costs.

For each registration renewal period, a $25 fee, in addition to the appropriate registration fee, shall be charged. Of this fee, $23 shall be deposited into the Stop Neuroblastoma Fund and $2 shall be deposited into the Secretary of State Special License Plate Fund.

(d) The Stop Neuroblastoma Fund is created as a special fund in the State treasury. All money in the Stop Neuroblastoma Fund shall be paid, subject to appropriation by the General Assembly and approval by the Secretary, as grants to the American Cancer Society for neuroblastoma and cancer research, education, screening, and treatment.

P.A. 76–1586, § 3–654, added by P.A. 92–711, § 10, eff. July 19, 2002.

For other §§ 3–654, see multiple added texts of 625 ILCS 5/3–654, ante

See 5 ILCS 70/6 as to the effect of (1) more than one amendment of a section at the same session of the General Assembly or (2) two or more acts relating to the same subject matter enacted by the same General Assembly.

ARTICLE VII. OFFENSES AGAINST REGISTRATION AND CERTIFICATE OF TITLE LAWS OR REVOCATION OF REGISTRATION OR CERTIFICATE OF TITLE

Section

Section

5/3–701. Operation of vehicles without evidence of registration—Operation under mileage plates when odometer broken or disconnected

§ 3–701. Operation of vehicles without evidence of registration—Operation under mileage plates when odometer broken or disconnected.

No person shall operate, nor shall an owner knowingly permit to be operated, upon any highway unless there shall be attached thereto and displayed thereon when and as required by law, proper evidence of registration in Illinois, as follows:

(1) A vehicle required to be registered in Illinois. A current and valid Illinois registration sticker or stickers and plate or plates, or an Illinois temporary registration permit, or a drive-away or in-transit permit, issued therefor by the Secretary of State; or

(2) A vehicle eligible for Reciprocity. A current and valid reciprocal foreign registration plate or plates properly issued to such vehicle or a temporary registration issued therefor, by the reciprocal State, and, in addition, when required by the Secretary, a current and valid Illinois Reciprocity Permit or Prorate Decal issued therefor by the Secretary of State; or except as otherwise expressly provided for in this Chapter.

No person shall operate, nor shall any owner knowingly permit to be operated, any vehicle of the second division for which the owner has made an election to pay the mileage tax in lieu of the annual flat weight tax, at any time when the odometer of such vehicle is broken or disconnected, or is inoperable or not operating.

P.A. 76–1586, § 3–701, eff. July 1, 1970. Amended by P.A. 77–1315, § 1, eff. Jan. 1, 1972; P.A. 77–2830, Art. 73, § 1, eff. Jan. 1, 1973; P.A. 80–230, § 1, eff. Oct. 1, 1977; P.A. 80–911, § 1, eff. Oct. 1, 1977; P.A. 80–1185, § 1, eff. March 8, 1978; P.A. 81–886, § 1, eff. July 1, 1980; P.A. 92–680, § 15, eff. July 16, 2002.

Formerly Ill.Rev.Stat.1991, ch. 95 ½, ¶ 3–701.

5/3–702. Operation of vehicle when registration cancelled, suspended or revoked

§ 3–702. Operation of vehicle when registration cancelled, suspended or revoked.

(a) No person shall operate, nor shall an owner knowingly permit to be operated, upon any highway:

(1) A vehicle the registration of which has been cancelled, suspended or revoked; or

(2) A vehicle properly registered in another Reciprocal State, the foreign registration of which, or the Illinois Reciprocity Permit or Decal of which, has been cancelled, suspended or revoked.

(b) No person shall use, nor shall any owner use or knowingly permit the use of any Illinois registration plate, plates or registration sticker, or any Illinois Reciprocity Permit or Prorate Decal which has been cancelled, suspended or revoked.

(c) Any violation of this Section is a Class A misdemeanor unless:

1. the registration of the motor vehicle has been suspended for noninsurance, then the provisions of Section 3-708 of this Code apply in lieu of this Section.

2. the registration of the motor vehicle has been suspended for failure to purchase a vehicle tax sticker pursuant to Section 3-704.1 of this Code, then the violation shall be considered a business offense and the person shall be required to pay a fine in excess of $500, but not more than $1,000.

P.A. 76-1586, § 3-702, eff. July 1, 1970. Amended by P.A. 77-1315, § 1, eff. Jan. 1, 1972; P.A. 77-2830, Art. 73, § 1, eff. Jan. 1, 1973; P.A. 80-230, § 1, eff. Oct. 1, 1977; P.A. 81-886, § 1, eff. July 1, 1980; P.A. 86-149, § 2, eff. Aug. 11, 1989; P.A. 87-1225, § 2, eff. Dec. 22, 1992.

Formerly Ill.Rev.Stat.1991, ch. 95 ½, ¶ 3-702.

5/3-703. Improper use of evidences of registration or certificate of title

§ 3-703. Improper use of evidences of registration or certificate of title. No person shall lend to another any certificate of title, registration card, registration plate, registration sticker, special plate or permit or other evidences of proper registration issued to him if the person desiring to borrow the same would not be entitled to the use thereof, nor shall any person knowingly permit the use of any of the same by one not entitled thereto, nor shall any person display upon a vehicle any registration card, registration sticker, registration plate or other evidences of proper registration not issued for such vehicle or not otherwise lawfully used thereon under this Code. No person shall duplicate, alter or attempt to reproduce in any manner a registration plate or registration sticker issued under this Code. No person shall make fraudulent use of evidences of registration or certificates of title issued erroneously by the Secretary of State. No person shall manufacture, advertise, distribute or sell any certificate of title, registration card, registration plate, registration sticker, special plate or permit or other evidences of proper registration which purports to have been issued under this Code. The Secretary of State may request the Attorney General to seek a restraining order in the circuit court against any person who violates this Section by advertising such fraudulent items. Any violation of this Section is a Class C misdemeanor.

P.A. 76-1586, § 3-703, eff. July 1, 1970. Amended by P.A. 77-1315, § 1, eff. Jan. 1, 1972; P.A. 77-2830, Art. 73, § 1, eff. Jan. 1, 1973; P.A. 80-230, § 1, eff. Oct. 1, 1977; P.A. 80-911, § 1, Oct. 1, 1977; P.A. 80-1364, § 36, eff. Aug. 13, 1978; P.A. 83-449, § 1, eff. Jan. 1, 1984; P.A. 86-551, § 1, eff. Jan. 1, 1990.

Formerly Ill.Rev.Stat.1991, ch. 95 ½, ¶ 3-703.

5/3-704. Authority of Secretary of State to suspend or revoke a registration or certificate of title; authority to suspend or revoke the registration of a vehicle

§ 3-704. Authority of Secretary of State to suspend or revoke a registration or certificate of title; authority to suspend or revoke the registration of a vehicle.

(a) The Secretary of State may suspend or revoke the registration of a vehicle or a certificate of title, registration card, registration sticker, registration plate, person with disabilities parking decal or device, or any nonresident or other permit in any of the following events:

1. When the Secretary of State is satisfied that such registration or that such certificate, card, plate, registration sticker or permit was fraudulently or erroneously issued;

2. When a registered vehicle has been dismantled or wrecked or is not properly equipped;

3. When the Secretary of State determines that any required fees have not been paid to either the Secretary of State or the Illinois Commerce Commission and the same are not paid upon reasonable notice and demand;

4. When a registration card, registration plate, registration sticker or permit is knowingly displayed upon a vehicle other than the one for which issued;

5. When the Secretary of State determines that the owner has committed any offense under this Chapter involving the registration or the certificate, card, plate, registration sticker or permit to be suspended or revoked;

6. When the Secretary of State determines that a vehicle registered not-for-hire is used or operated for-hire unlawfully, or used or operated for purposes other than those authorized;

7. When the Secretary of State determines that an owner of a for-hire motor vehicle has failed to give proof of financial responsibility as required by this Act;

8. When the Secretary determines that the vehicle is not subject to or eligible for a registration;

9. When the Secretary determines that the owner of a vehicle registered under the mileage weight tax option fails to maintain the records specified by law, or fails to file the reports required by law, or that such vehicle is not equipped with an operable and operating speedometer or odometer;

10. When the Secretary of State is so authorized under any other provision of law;

11. When the Secretary of State determines that the holder of a person with disabilities parking decal or device has committed any offense under Chapter 11 of this Code [1] involving the use of a person with disabilities parking decal or device.

(b) The Secretary of State may suspend or revoke the registration of a vehicle as follows:

1. When the Secretary of State determines that the owner of a vehicle has not paid a civil penalty or a settlement agreement arising from the violation of rules adopted under the Illinois Motor Carrier Safety Law [2] or the Illinois Hazardous Materials Transportation Act [3] or that a vehicle, regardless of ownership, was the subject of violations of these rules that resulted in a civil penalty or settlement agreement which remains unpaid.

2. When the Secretary of State determines that a vehicle registered for a gross weight of more than 16,000 pounds

within an affected area is not in compliance with the provisions of Section 13–109.1 of the Illinois Vehicle Code.[4]

P.A. 76–1586, § 3–704, eff. July 1, 1970. Amended by P.A. 77–1315, § 1, eff. Jan. 1, 1972; P.A. 80–230, § 1, eff. Oct. 1, 1977; P.A. 90–106, § 5, eff. Jan. 1, 1998; P.A. 92–437, § 5, eff. Aug. 17, 2001.

Formerly Ill.Rev.Stat.1991, ch. 95 ½, ¶ 3–704.

[1] 625 ILCS 5/11–100 et seq.

[2] 625 ILCS 5/18b–100 et seq.

[3] 430 ILCS 30/1 et seq.

[4] 625 ILCS 5/13–109.1.

5/3–704.1. Municipal vehicle tax liability; suspension of registration

§ 3–704.1. Municipal vehicle tax liability; suspension of registration.

(a) As used in this Section:

(1) "Municipality" means a city, village or incorporated town with a population over 1,000,000.

(2) "Vehicle tax" means a motor vehicle tax and any related late fees or charges imposed by a municipality under Section 8–11–4 or the Illinois Municipal Code [1] or under the municipality's home rule powers.

(3) "Vehicle owner" means the registered owner or owners of a vehicle who are residents of the municipality.

(b) A municipality that imposes a vehicle tax may, by ordinance adopted under this Section, establish a system whereby the municipality notifies the Secretary of State of vehicle tax liability and the Secretary of State suspends the registration of vehicles for which the tax has not been paid. An ordinance establishing a system must provide for the following:

(1) A first notice for failure to pay a vehicle tax shall be sent by first class mail to the vehicle owner at the owner's address recorded with the Secretary of State whenever the municipality has reasonable cause to believe that the vehicle owner has failed to pay a vehicle tax as required by ordinance. The notice shall include at least the following:

(A) The name and address of the vehicle owner.

(B) The registration plate number of the vehicle.

(C) The period for which the vehicle tax is due.

(D) The amount of vehicle tax that is due.

(E) A statement that the vehicle owner's registration for the vehicle will be subject to suspension proceedings unless the vehicle owner pays the vehicle tax or successfully contests the owner's alleged liability within 30 days of the date of the notice.

(F) An explanation of the vehicle owner's opportunity to be heard under subsection (c).

(2) If a vehicle owner fails to pay the vehicle tax or to contest successfully the owner's alleged liability within the period specified in the first notice, a second notice of impending registration suspension shall be sent by first class mail to the vehicle owner at the owner's address recorded with the Secretary of State. The notice shall contain the same information as the first notice, but shall also state that the failure to pay the amount owing, or to contest successfully the alleged liability within 45 days of the date of the second notice, will result in the municipality's notification of the Secretary of State that the vehicle owner is eligible for initiation of suspension proceedings under this Section.

(c) An ordinance adopted under this Section must also give the vehicle owner an opportunity to be heard upon the filing of a timely petition with the municipality. A vehicle owner may contest the alleged tax liability either through an adjudication by mail or at an administrative hearing, at the option of the vehicle owner. The grounds upon which the liability may be contested may be limited to the following:

(1) The alleged vehicle owner does not own the vehicle.

(2) The vehicle is not subject to the vehicle tax by law.

(3) The vehicle tax for the period in question has been paid.

At an administrative hearing, the formal or technical rules of evidence shall not apply. The hearing shall be recorded. The person conducting the hearing shall have the power to administer oaths and to secure by subpoena the attendance and testimony of witnesses and the production of relevant documents.

(d) If a vehicle owner who has been sent a first notice of failure to pay a vehicle tax and a second notice of impending registration suspension fails to pay the vehicle tax or to contest successfully the vehicle owner's liability within the periods specified in the notices, the appropriate official shall cause a certified report to be sent to the Secretary of State under subsection (e).

(e) A report of a municipality notifying the Secretary of State of a vehicle owner's failure to pay a vehicle tax or related fines or penalties under this Section shall be certified by the appropriate official and shall contain the following:

(1) The name, last known address and registration plate number of the vehicle of the person who failed to pay the vehicle tax.

(2) The name of the municipality making the report.

(3) A statement that the municipality sent notices as required by subsection (b); the date on which the notices were sent; the address to which the notices were sent; and the date of the hearing, if any.

(f) Following receipt of the certified report under this Section, the Secretary of State shall notify the vehicle owner that the vehicle's registration will be suspended at the end of a reasonable specified period of time unless the Secretary of State is presented with a notice from the municipality certifying that the person has paid the necessary vehicle tax, or that inclusion of that person's name or registration number on the certified report was in error. The Secretary's notice shall state in substance the information contained in the certified report from the municipality to the Secretary, and shall be effective as specified by subsection (c) of Section 6–211 of this Code. The notice shall also inform the person of the person's right to a hearing under subsection (g).

(g) An administrative hearing with the Office of the Secretary of State to contest an impending suspension or a suspension made under this Section may be had upon filing a written request with the Secretary of State. The filing fee for this hearing shall be $20 to be paid at the time the request is made.

(1) The scope of any administrative hearing with the Secretary of State to contest an impending suspension under this Section shall be limited to the following issues:

(A) Whether the report of the appropriate official of the municipality was certified and contained the information required by this Section.

(B) Whether the municipality making the certified report to the Secretary of State established procedures by ordinance for persons to challenge the accuracy of the certified report.

(C) Whether the Secretary of State notified the vehicle owner that the vehicle's registration would be suspended at the end of the specified time period unless the Secretary of State was presented with a notice from the municipality certifying that the person has purchased the necessary vehicle tax sticker or that inclusion of that person's name or registration number on the certified report was in error.

A municipality that files a certified report with the Secretary of State under this Section shall reimburse the Secretary for all reasonable costs incurred by the Secretary as a result of the filing of the report, including but not limited to the costs of providing the notice required under subsection (f) and the costs incurred by the Secretary in any hearing conducted with respect to the report under this subsection and any appeal from that hearing.

(h) After the expiration of the time specified under subsection (g), the Secretary of State shall, unless the suspension is successfully contested, suspend the registration of the vehicle until the Secretary receives notice under subsection (i).

(i) Any municipality making a certified report to the Secretary of State under this subsection shall notify the Secretary of State, in a form prescribed by the Secretary, whenever a person named in the certified report has subsequently paid a vehicle tax or whenever the municipality determines that the original report was in error. A certified copy of the notification shall also be given upon request and at no additional charge to the person named in the report. Upon receipt of the notification or presentation of a certified copy of the notification by the municipality, the Secretary of State shall terminate the suspension.

P.A. 76–1586, § 3–704.1, added by P.A. 87–1225, § 2, eff. Dec. 22, 1992.

Formerly Ill.Rev.Stat., ch. 95½, ¶ 3–704.1.

[1] 65 ILCS 5/8–11–4.

5/3–704.2. Failure to satisfy fines or penalties for toll violations or evasions; suspension of vehicle registration

§ 3–704.2. Failure to satisfy fines or penalties for toll violations or evasions; suspension of vehicle registration.

(a) Upon receipt of a certified report, as prescribed by subsection (c) of this Section, from the Authority stating that the owner of a registered vehicle has failed to satisfy any fine or penalty resulting from a final order issued by the Authority relating directly or indirectly to 5 or more toll violations, toll evasions, or both, the Secretary of State shall suspend the vehicle registration of the person in accordance with the procedures set forth in this Section.

(b) Following receipt of the certified report of the Authority as specified in the Section, the Secretary of State shall notify the person whose name appears on the certified report that the person's vehicle registration will be suspended at the end of a specified period unless the Secretary of State is presented with a notice from the Authority certifying that the fines or penalties owing the Authority have been satisfied or that inclusion of that person's name on the certified report was in error. The Secretary's notice shall state in substance the information contained in the Authority's certified report to the Secretary, and shall be effective as specified by subsection (c) of Section 6–211 of this Code.

(c) The report from the Authority notifying the Secretary of unsatisfied fines or penalties pursuant to this Section shall be certified and shall contain the following:

(1) The name, last known address, and driver's license number of the person who failed to satisfy the fines or penalties and the registration number of any vehicle known to be registered in this State to that person.

(2) A statement that the Authority sent a notice of impending suspension of the person's driver's license, vehicle registration, or both, as prescribed by rules enacted pursuant to subsection (a–5) of Section 10 of the Toll Highway Act,[1] to the person named in the report at the address recorded with the Secretary of State; the date on which the notice was sent; and the address to which the notice was sent.

(d) The Authority, after making a certified report to the Secretary pursuant to this Section, shall notify the Secretary, on a form prescribed by the Secretary, whenever a person named in the certified report has satisfied the previously reported fines or penalties or whenever the Authority determines that the original report was in error. A certified copy of the notification shall also be given upon request and at no additional charge to the person named therein. Upon receipt of the Authority's notification or presentation of a certified copy of the notification, the Secretary shall terminate the suspension.

(e) The Authority shall, by rule, establish procedures for persons to challenge the accuracy of the certified report made pursuant to this Section. The rule shall also provide the grounds for a challenge, which may be limited to:

(1) the person not having been the owner or lessee of the vehicle or vehicles receiving 5 or more toll violation or toll evasion notices on the date or dates the notices were issued; or

(2) the person having already satisfied the fines or penalties for the 5 or more toll violations or toll evasions indicated on the certified report.

(f) All notices sent by the Authority to persons involved in administrative adjudications, hearings, and final orders issued pursuant to rules implementing subsection (a–5) of Section 10 of the Toll Highway Act shall state that failure to satisfy any fine or penalty imposed by the Authority shall result in the Secretary of State suspending the driving privileges, vehicle registration, or both, of the person failing to satisfy the fines or penalties imposed by the Authority.

(g) A person may request an administrative hearing to contest an impending suspension or a suspension made pursuant to this Section upon filing a written request with the Secretary. The filing fee for this hearing is $20, to be paid at the time of the request. The Authority shall reimburse the Secretary for all reasonable costs incurred by the Secretary as a result of the filing of a certified report pursuant to this Section, including, but not limited to, the costs of providing notice required pursuant to subsection (b) and the costs incurred by the Secretary in any hearing conducted with respect to the report pursuant to this subsection and any appeal from that hearing.

(h) The Secretary and the Authority may promulgate rules to enable them to carry out their duties under this Section.

(i) The Authority shall cooperate with the Secretary in the administration of this Section and shall provide the Secretary with any information the Secretary may deem necessary for these purposes, including regular and timely access to toll violation enforcement records.

The Secretary shall cooperate with the Authority in the administration of this Section and shall provide the Authority with any information the Authority may deem necessary for the purposes of this Section, including regular and timely access to vehicle registration records. Section 2-123 of this Code shall not apply to the provision of this information, but the Secretary shall be reimbursed for the cost of providing this information.

(j) For purposes of this Section, the term "Authority" means the Illinois State Toll Highway Authority.

P.A. 76-1586, § 3-704.2, added by P.A. 91-277, § 5, eff. Jan. 1, 2000.

1 605 ILCS 10/10.

5/3-705. Suspending or revoking certificate or special plates of a manufacturer, engine and driveline component manufacturer, transporter, repossessor or dealer

§ 3-705. Suspending or revoking certificate or special plates of a manufacturer, engine and driveline component manufacturer, transporter, repossessor or dealer. The Secretary of State is also authorized to suspend or revoke a certificate or the special plates issued to a manufacturer, engine and driveline component manufacturer, transporter, repossessor or dealer upon determining that any such person is not lawfully entitled thereto or has made or knowingly permitted any illegal use of such plates or has committed fraud in the registration of vehicles or failed to give notices of transfers when and as required by this Chapter.

P.A. 76-1586, § 3-705, eff. July 1, 1970. Amended by P.A. 76-2139, § 1, eff. July 1, 1970.

Formerly Ill.Rev.Stat.1991, ch. 95 ½, ¶ 3-705.

5/3-706. Owner to return evidences of registration upon cancellation, revocation or suspension

§ 3-706. Owner to return evidences of registration upon cancellation, revocation or suspension. Whenever the Secretary of State cancels or revokes the registration of a vehicle or a certificate of title, registration card, registration sticker or stickers, registration plate or plates, or a nonresident or other permit or the license of any dealer or wrecker, the owner or person in possession of the same shall immediately return the evidences of registration, title or license so cancelled or revoked to the Secretary.

Whenever the Secretary suspends the registration of a vehicle or the license of any dealer or wrecker, the owner or person in possession of the same, upon request by the Secretary, shall immediately return all evidence of the registration or the license so suspended to the Secretary.

P.A. 76-1586, § 3-706, eff. July 1, 1970. Amended by P.A. 80-230, § 1, eff. Oct. 1, 1977; P.A. 80-1185, § 1, eff. March 8, 1978; P.A. 85-1201, § 1, eff. July 1, 1989.

Formerly Ill.Rev.Stat.1991, ch. 95 ½, ¶ 3-706.

5/3-707. Operation of uninsured motor vehicle—penalty

Text of section effective until July 1, 2003

§ 3-707. Operation of uninsured motor vehicle—penalty. No person shall operate a motor vehicle unless the motor vehicle is covered by a liability insurance policy in accordance with Section 7-601 of this Code.

Any person who fails to comply with a request by a law enforcement officer for display of evidence of insurance, as required under Section 7-602 of this Code, shall be deemed to be operating an uninsured motor vehicle.

Any operator of a motor vehicle subject to registration under this Code who is convicted of violating this Section is guilty of a business offense and shall be required to pay a fine in excess of $500, but not more than $1,000. However, no person charged with violating this Section shall be convicted if such person produces in court satisfactory evidence that at the time of the arrest the motor vehicle was covered by a liability insurance policy in accordance with Section 7-601 of this Code. The chief judge of each circuit may designate an officer of the court to review the documentation demonstrating that at the time of arrest the motor vehicle was covered by a liability insurance policy in accordance with Section 7-601 of this Code.

P.A. 76-1586, § 3-707, added by P.A. 85-1201, § 1, eff. July 1, 1989. Amended by P.A. 86-149, § 2, eff. Aug. 11, 1989; P.A. 86-1179, § 2, eff. Aug. 17, 1990; P.A. 88-315, § 5, eff. Jan. 1, 1994.

Formerly Ill.Rev.Stat.1991, ch. 95 ½, ¶ 3-707.

For text of section effective July 1, 2003, see 625 ILCS 5/3-707, post

5/3-707. Operation of uninsured motor vehicle—penalty

Text of section effective July 1, 2003

§ 3-707. Operation of uninsured motor vehicle—penalty.

(a) No person shall operate a motor vehicle unless the motor vehicle is covered by a liability insurance policy in accordance with Section 7-601 of this Code.

(b) Any person who fails to comply with a request by a law enforcement officer for display of evidence of insurance, as required under Section 7-602 of this Code, shall be deemed to be operating an uninsured motor vehicle.

(c) Any operator of a motor vehicle subject to registration under this Code who is convicted of violating this Section is guilty of a business offense and shall be required to pay a fine in excess of $500, but not more than $1,000. However, no person charged with violating this Section shall be convicted if such person produces in court satisfactory evidence that at the time of the arrest the motor vehicle was covered by a liability insurance policy in accordance with Section 7-601 of this Code. The chief judge of each circuit may designate an officer of the court to review the documentation demonstrating that at the time of arrest the motor vehicle was covered by a liability insurance policy in accordance with Section 7-601 of this Code.

(d) A person convicted a third or subsequent time of violating this Section or a similar provision of a local ordinance must give proof to the Secretary of State of the person's financial responsibility as defined in Section 7-315. The person must maintain the proof in a manner satisfactory to the Secretary for a minimum period of one year after the date the proof is first filed. The Secretary must suspend the driver's license of any person determined by the Secretary not to have provided adequate proof of financial responsibility as required by this subsection.

For text of section effective until July 1, 2003, see 625 ILCS 5/3-707, ante

P.A. 76-1586, § 3-707, added by P.A. 85-1201, § 1, eff. July 1, 1989. Amended by P.A. 86-149, § 2, eff. Aug. 11, 1989; P.A. 86-1179, § 2, eff. Aug. 17, 1990; P.A. 88-315, § 5, eff. Jan. 1, 1994; P.A. 92-775, § 5, eff. July 1, 2003.

Formerly Ill.Rev.Stat.1991, ch. 95 ½, ¶ 3-707.

5/3-708. Operation of motor vehicle when registration suspended for noninsurance

§ 3-708. Operation of motor vehicle when registration suspended for noninsurance. No person shall operate a vehicle the registration of which is suspended pursuant to Section 7-606 or 7-607 of this Code.

Any person convicted of violating this Section is guilty of a business offense and shall be required to pay a fine of not less than $1,000 and not more than $2,000. Any person convicted of a second or subsequent violation of this Section is guilty of a Class B misdemeanor and shall be required to pay a fine of not less than $1,000 and not more than $2,000.

P.A. 76-1586, § 3-708, added by P.A. 85-1201, § 1, eff. July 1, 1989. Amended by P.A. 86-149, § 2, eff. Aug. 11, 1989; P.A. 90-559, § 5, eff. June 1, 1998.

Formerly Ill.Rev.Stat.1991, ch. 95 ½, ¶ 3-708.

5/3-709. § 3-709. Repealed by P.A. 86-149, § 3, eff. Aug. 11, 1989

5/3-710. Display of false insurance card

§ 3-710. Display of false insurance card. No person shall display evidence of insurance to a law enforcement officer, court, or officer of the court, knowing there is no valid liability insurance in effect on the motor vehicle as required under Section 7-601 of this Code or knowing the evidence of insurance is illegally altered, counterfeit, or otherwise invalid as evidence of insurance required under Section 7-602 of this Code. If the law enforcement officer issues a citation to a motor vehicle operator for displaying invalid evidence of insurance, the officer shall confiscate the evidence for presentation in court.

Any person convicted of violating this Section is guilty of a Class A misdemeanor.

P.A. 76-1586, § 3-710, added by P.A. 85-1201, § 1, eff. July 1, 1989. Amended by P.A. 86-149, § 2, eff. Aug. 11, 1989; P.A. 89-565, § 5, eff. July 26, 1996.

Formerly Ill.Rev.Stat.1991, ch. 95 ½, ¶ 3-710.

5/3-711. Reports of orders of supervision

§ 3-711. Whenever a court convicts a person of a violation of Section 3-707, 3-708 or 3-710 of this Code, or enters an order placing on supervision the person charged with the violation, the clerk of the court within 10 days shall forward a report of the conviction or order of supervision to the Secretary of State in a form prescribed by the Secretary. In any case where the person charged with the violation fails to appear in court, the procedures provided in Section 6-306.3 or 6-306.4 of this Code, whichever is applicable shall apply.

The Secretary shall keep records of such reports. However, reports of orders of supervision shall not be released to any outside source, except the affected driver and law enforcement agencies, and shall be used only to inform the Secretary and the courts that such driver previously has been assigned court supervision.

P.A. 76-1586, § 3-711, added by P.A. 86-149, § 2, eff. Aug. 11, 1989.

Formerly Ill.Rev.Stat.1991, ch. 95 ½, ¶ 3-711.

ARTICLE VIII. REGISTRATION AND LICENSE FEES

5/3-801. Registration

§ 3-801. Registration. (a) Except as provided herein for new residents, every owner of any vehicle which shall be operated upon the public highways of this State shall, within 24 hours after becoming the owner or at such time as such vehicle becomes subject to registration under the provisions of this Act, file in an office of the Secretary of State, an application for registration properly completed and executed. New residents need not secure registration until 30 days after establishing residency in this State, provided the vehicle is properly registered in another jurisdiction. By the expiration of such 30 day statutory grace period, a new resident shall comply with the provisions of this Act and apply for Illinois vehicle registration. All applications for registration shall be accompanied by all documentation required under the provisions of this Act. The appropriate registration fees and taxes provided for in this Article of this Chapter shall be paid to the Secretary of State with the application for registration of vehicles subject to registration under this Act.

(b) Any resident of this State, who has been serving as a member of the United States Armed Services outside of the State of Illinois, need not secure registration until 45 days after returning to this State, provided the vehicle displays temporary military registration.

(c) When an application is submitted by mail, the applicant may not submit cash or postage stamps for payment of fees or taxes due. The Secretary in his discretion, may decline to accept a personal or company check in payment of fees or taxes. An application submitted to a dealer, or a remittance made to the Secretary of State shall be deemed in compliance with this Section.

P.A. 76–1586, § 3–801, eff. July 1, 1970. Amended by P.A. 77–364, § 1, eff. July 23, 1971; P.A. 79–516, § 1, eff. Oct. 1, 1975; P.A. 85–951, § 1, eff. July 1, 1988; P.A. 85–992, § 1, eff. Jan. 5, 1988; P.A. 85–1209, Art. II, § 2–51, eff. Aug. 30, 1988.

Formerly Ill.Rev.Stat.1991, ch. 95 ½, ¶ 3–801.

P.A. 85–1209, the First 1988 Revisory Act, provides in Art. II, for the nonsubstantive revision or renumbering or repeal of certain sections of Acts of the 85th General Assembly through P.A. 85–1014, and corrects errors, revises cross-references and deletes obsolete text in such sections.

5/3-802. Reclassifications and upgrades

§ 3–802. Reclassifications and upgrades.

(a) Definitions. For the purposes of this Section, the following words shall have the meanings ascribed to them as follows:

"Reclassification" means changing the registration of a vehicle from one plate category to another.

"Upgrade" means increasing the registered weight of a vehicle within the same plate category.

(b) When reclassing the registration of a vehicle from one plate category to another, the owner shall receive credit for the unused portion of the present plate and be charged the current portion fees for the new plate. In addition, the appropriate replacement plate and replacement sticker fees shall be assessed.

(c) When upgrading the weight of a registration within the same plate category, the owner shall pay the difference in current period fees between the two plates. In addition, the appropriate replacement plate and replacement sticker fees shall be assessed. In the event new plates are not required, the corrected registration card fee shall be assessed.

(d) In the event the owner of the vehicle desires to change the registered weight and change the plate category, the owner shall receive credit for the unused portion of the registration fee of the current plate and pay the current portion of the registration fee for the new plate, and in addition, pay the appropriate replacement plate and replacement sticker fees.

(e) Reclassing from one plate category to another plate category can be done only once within any registration period.

(f) No refunds shall be made in any of the circumstances found in subsection (b), subsection (c), or subsection (d).

(g) In the event the registration of a vehicle registered under the mileage tax option is revoked, the owner shall be required to pay the annual registration fee in the new plate category and shall not receive any credit for the mileage plate fees.

(h) Certain special interest plates may be displayed on first division vehicles, second division vehicles weighing 8,000 pounds or less, and recreational vehicles. Those plates can be transferred within those vehicle groups.

(i) Plates displayed on second division vehicles weighing 8,000 pounds or less and passenger vehicle plates may be reclassed from one division to the other.

(j) Other than in subsection (i), reclassing from one division to the other division is prohibited. In addition, a reclass from a motor vehicle to a trailer or a trailer to a motor vehicle is prohibited.

P.A. 76–1586, § 3–802, eff. July 1, 1970. Amended by P.A. 76–1626, § 1, eff. July 1, 1970; P.A. 77–364, § 1, eff. July 23, 1971; P.A. 78–328, eff. Oct. 1, 1973; P.A. 79–1367, § 1, eff. Aug. 6, 1976; P.A. 80–1185, § 1, eff. March 8, 1978; P.A. 80–1463, § 1, eff. Jan. 1, 1979; P.A. 83–12, § 1, eff. July 1, 1983; P.A. 86–444, § 1, eff. Jan. 1, 1990; P.A. 89–245, § 5, eff. Jan. 1, 1996; P.A. 90–774, § 5, eff. Aug. 14, 1998.

Formerly Ill.Rev.Stat.1991, ch. 95 ½, ¶ 3–802.

5/3-803. Reductions

§ 3–803. Reductions. (a) Reduction of fees and taxes prescribed in this Chapter shall be applicable only to vehicles newly-acquired by the owner after the beginning of a registration period or which become subject to registration after the beginning of a registration period as specified in this Act. The Secretary of State may deny a reduction as to any vehicle operated in this State without being properly and timely registered in Illinois under this Chapter, of a vehicle in violation of any provision of this Chapter, or upon detection of such violation by an audit, or upon determining that such vehicle was operated in Illinois before such violation. Bond or other security in the proper amount may be required by the Secretary of State while the matter is under investigation. Reductions shall be granted if a person becomes the owner after the dates specified or if a vehicle becomes subject to registration under this Act, as amended, after the dates specified.

(b) Vehicles of the First Division. The annual fees and taxes prescribed by Section 3–806 shall be reduced by 50% on and after June 15, except as provided in Sections 3–414 and 3–802 of this Act.

(c) Vehicles of the Second Division. The annual fees and taxes prescribed by Sections 3–402, 3–402.1, 3–815 and 3–819 and paid on a calendar year for such vehicles shall be reduced on a quarterly basis if the vehicle becomes subject to registration on and after March 31, June 30 or September 30. Where such fees and taxes are payable on a fiscal year basis, they shall be reduced on a quarterly basis on and after September 30, December 31 or March 31.

(d) Two-year Registrations. The fees and taxes prescribed by Section 3-808 for 2-year registrations shall not be reduced in any event. However, the fees and taxes prescribed for all other 2-year registrations by this Act, shall be reduced as follows:

By 25% on and after June 15;

By 50% on and after December 15;

By 75% on and after the next ensuing June 15.

(e) The registration fees and taxes imposed upon certain vehicles shall not be reduced by any amount in any event in the following instances:

Permits under Sections 3-403 and 3-811;

Municipal Buses under Section 3-807;

Governmental or charitable vehicles under Section 3-808;

Farm Machinery under Section 3-809;

Soil and conservation equipment under Section 3-809.1;

Special Plates under Section 3-810;

Permanently mounted equipment under Section 3-812;

Registration fee under Section 3-813;

Semitrailer fees under Section 3-814;

Farm trucks under Section 3-815;

Mileage weight tax option under Section 3-818;

Farm trailers under Section 3-819;

Duplicate plates under Section 3-820;

Fees under Section 3-821;

Security Fees under Section 3-822;

Search Fees under Section 3-823.

(f) The reductions provided for shall not apply to any vehicle of the first or second division registered by the same applicant in the prior registration year. This bill takes effect with the 1986 Calendar Registration Year.

(g) Reductions shall in no event result in payment of a fee or tax less than $6, and the Secretary of State shall promulgate schedules of fees reflecting applicable reductions. Where any reduced amount is not stated in full dollars, the Secretary of State may adjust the amount due to the nearest full dollar amount.

(h) The reductions provided for in subsections (a) through (g) of this Section shall not apply to those vehicles of the first or second division registered on a staggered registration basis.

(i) A vehicle which becomes subject to registration during the last month of the current registration year is exempt from any applicable reduced fourth quarter or second semi-annual registration fee, and may register for the subsequent registration year as its initial registration. This subsection does not include those apportioned and prorated fees under Sections 3-402 and 3-402.1 of this Code.

P.A. 76-1586, § 3-803, eff. July 1, 1970. Amended by P.A. 77-1541, § 1, eff. Sept. 17, 1971; P.A. 78-328, § 1, eff. Oct. 1, 1973; P.A. 79-627, § 1, eff. Aug. 28, 1975; P.A. 80-1185, § 1, eff. March 8, 1978; P.A. 81-323, § 1, eff. Aug. 30, 1979; P.A. 82-136, § 1, eff. Oct. 1, 1981; P.A. 83-455, § 1, eff. Oct. 1, 1983; P.A. 84-210, § 1, eff. Jan. 1, 1986; P.A. 84-1311, § 1, eff. Aug. 27, 1986.

Formerly Ill.Rev.Stat.1991, ch. 95 ½, ¶ 3-803.

P.A. 84-1311 incorporated the amendment by P.A. 84-210.

5/3-804. Antique vehicles

§ 3-804. Antique vehicles.

(a) The owner of an antique vehicle may register such vehicle for a fee not to exceed $13 for a 2-year antique plate. The application for registration must be accompanied by an affirmation of the owner that such vehicle will be driven on the highway only for the purpose of going to and returning from an antique auto show or an exhibition, or for servicing or demonstration and also affirming that the mechanical condition, physical condition, brakes, lights, glass and appearance of such vehicle is the same or as safe as originally equipped. The Secretary may, in his discretion prescribe that antique vehicle plates be issued for a definite or an indefinite term, such term to correspond to the term of registration plates issued generally, as provided in Section 3-414.1. In no event may the registration fee for antique vehicles exceed $6 per registration year. Any person requesting antique plates under this Section may also apply to have vanity or personalized plates as provided under Section 3-405.1.

(b) Any person who is the registered owner of an antique vehicle may display a historical license plate from or representing the model year of the vehicle, furnished by such person, in lieu of the current and valid Illinois antique vehicle plates issued thereto, provided that valid and current Illinois antique vehicle plates and registration card issued to such antique vehicle are simultaneously carried within such vehicle and are available for inspection.

P.A. 76-1586, § 3-804, eff. July 1, 1970. Amended by P.A. 76-1627, § 1, eff. Dec. 1, 1970; P.A. 77-217, § 1, eff. Jan. 1, 1972; P.A. 77-1910, § 1, eff. July 1, 1972; P.A. 78-255, § 61, eff. Oct. 1, 1973; P.A. 78-667, § 1, eff. July 1, 1974; P.A. 78-1297, § 58, eff. Mar. 4, 1975; P.A. 80-230, § 1, eff. Oct. 1, 1977; P.A. 83-145, § 1, eff. Jan. 1, 1984; P.A. 83-449, § 1, eff. Jan. 1, 1984; P.A. 83-1362, Art. II, § 99, eff. Sept. 11, 1984; P.A. 86-480, § 1, eff. Jan. 1, 1990; P.A. 91-37, § 40, eff. July 1, 1999.

Formerly Ill.Rev.Stat.1991, ch. 95 ½, ¶ 3-804.

5/3-804.02. Commuter Vans

§ 3-804.02. Commuter Vans. The owner of a commuter van may register such van for an annual fee not to exceed $63. The Secretary may prescribe that commuter van plates be issued for an indefinite term, such term to correspond to the term of registration plates issued generally. In no event may the registration fee for commuter vans exceed $63 per registration year.

P.A. 76-1586, § 3-804.02, added by P.A. 81-492, eff. Jan. 1, 1980. Amended by P.A. 90-89, § 15, eff. Jan. 1, 1998; P.A. 91-37, § 40, eff. July 1, 1999.

Formerly Ill.Rev.Stat.1991, ch. 95 ½, ¶ 3-804.02.

5/3-804.1. Custom vehicles

§ 3-804.1. Custom vehicles.

(a) The owner of a custom vehicle may register that vehicle for the standard registration fee for a vehicle of the first division, other than a motorcycle, motor driven cycle, or pedalcycle, and obtain a custom vehicle plate. An applicant for the special plate shall be charged, in addition to the standard registration fee, $15 for original issuance to be deposited into the Secretary of State Special License Plate Fund, to be used by the Secretary to help defray administrative costs. For each renewal period, in addition to the standard registration fee, the applicant shall be charged $2, which shall be deposited into the Secretary of State Special

License Plate Fund. The application for registration must be accompanied by an affirmation of the owner that the vehicle will be maintained for occasional transportation, exhibitions, club activities, parades, tours, and similar uses and will not be used for general daily transportation. The Secretary may, in his or her discretion, prescribe that custom vehicle plates be issued for a definite or an indefinite term, the term to correspond to the term of registration plates issued generally, as provided in Section 3–414.1. Any person requesting custom vehicle plates under this Section may also apply to have vanity or personalized plates as provided under Section 3–405.1.

(b) Upon initial registration of a custom vehicle, the owner of the custom vehicle must provide proof acceptable to the Secretary that, no more than 3 months before the date of the application for registration, the custom vehicle passed a safety inspection that (i) has been approved by the Secretary and (ii) is equivalent to the National Street Rod Association's prescribed vehicle safety inspection.

Except where otherwise provided, custom vehicles are considered to be in compliance with all vehicle equipment requirements if they have passed the approved vehicle safety inspection.

P.A. 76–1586, § 3–804.1, added by P.A. 92–668, § 5, eff. Jan. 1, 2003.

5/3–804.2. Street rods

§ 3–804.2. Street rods.

(a) The owner of a street rod may register the vehicle for the standard registration fee for a vehicle of the first division, other than a motorcycle, motor driven cycle, or pedalcycle, and obtain a street rod plate. An applicant for the special plate shall be charged, in addition to the standard registration fee, $15 for original issuance to be deposited into the Secretary of State Special License Plate Fund, to be used by the Secretary to help defray administrative costs. For each renewal period, in addition to the standard registration fee, the applicant shall be charged $2, which shall be deposited into the Secretary of State Special License Plate Fund. The application for registration must be accompanied by an affirmation of the owner that the vehicle will be maintained for occasional transportation, exhibitions, club activities, parades, tours, and similar uses and will not be used for general daily transportation. The Secretary may, in his or her discretion, prescribe that street rod plates be issued for a definite or an indefinite term, the term to correspond to the term of registration plates issued generally, as provided in Section 3–414.1. Any person requesting street rod plates under this Section may also apply to have vanity or personalized plates as provided under Section 3–405.1.

(b) Upon initial registration of a street rod, the owner of the street rod must provide proof acceptable to the Secretary that, no more than 3 months before the date of the application for registration, the street rod passed a safety inspection that (i) has been approved by the Secretary and (ii) is equivalent to the National Street Rod Association's prescribed vehicle safety inspection.

Except where otherwise provided, street rods are considered to be in compliance with all vehicle equipment requirements if they have passed the approved vehicle safety inspection.

P.A. 76–1586, § 3–804.2, added by P.A. 92–668, § 5, eff. Jan. 1, 2003.

5/3–805. Electric vehicles

§ 3–805. Electric vehicles. The owner of a motor vehicle of the first division propelled by an electric engine and not utilizing motor fuel, may register such vehicle for a fee not to exceed $35 for a 2–year registration period. The Secretary may, in his discretion, prescribe that electric vehicle registration plates be issued for an indefinite term, such term to correspond to the term of registration plates issued generally, as provided in Section 3–414.1. In no event may the registration fee for electric vehicles exceed $18 per registration year.

P.A. 76–1586, § 3–805, eff. July 1, 1970. Amended by P.A. 76–1628, § 1, eff. Dec. 1, 1970; P.A. 77–1315, § 1, eff. Jan. 1, 1972; P.A. 77–1910, § 1, eff. July 1, 1972; P.A. 78–255, § 61, eff. Oct. 1, 1973; P.A. 80–230, § 1, eff. Oct. 1, 1977; P.A. 89–245, § 5, eff. Jan. 1, 1996; P.A. 91–37, § 40, eff. July 1, 1999.

Formerly Ill.Rev.Stat.1991, ch. 95 ½, ¶ 3–805.

5/3–806. Registration Fees; Motor Vehicles of the First Division

§ 3–806. Registration Fees; Motor Vehicles of the First Division. Every owner of any other motor vehicle of the first division, except as provided in Sections 3–804, 3–805, 3–806.3, and 3–808, and every second division vehicle weighing 8,000 pounds or less, shall pay the Secretary of State an annual registration fee at the following rates:

SCHEDULE OF REGISTRATION FEES
REQUIRED BY LAW
Beginning with the 1986 registration year

	Annual Fee	Reduced Fee On and After June 15
Motor vehicles of the first division other than Motorcycles, Motor Driven Cycles and Pedalcycles	$48	$24
		Reduced Fee September 16 to March 31
Motorcycles, Motor Driven Cycles and Pedalcycles	30	15

SCHEDULE OF REGISTRATION FEES
REQUIRED BY LAW
Beginning with the 2001 registration year

	Annual Fee	Reduced Fee On and After June 15
Motor vehicles of the first division other than Motorcycles, Motor Driven Cycles and Pedalcycles	$78	$39
		Reduced Fee September 16 to March 31
Motorcycles, Motor Driven Cycles and Pedalcycles	38	19

P.A. 76–1586, § 3–806, eff. July 1, 1970. Amended by P.A. 76–2140, § 1, eff. July 1, 1970; P.A. 78–1146, § 1, eff. Jan. 1, 1975; P.A. 79–516, § 1, eff. Oct. 1, 1975; P.A. 80–262, § 1, eff. Aug. 30, 1977; P.A. 82–648, § 1, eff. July 1, 1982; P.A.

82–649, § 3, eff. Jan. 1, 1982; P.A. 82–783, Art. III, § 37, eff. July 13, 1982; P.A. 83–12, § 1, eff. July 1, 1983; P.A. 83–817, § 1, eff. Jan. 1, 1984; P.A. 83–1362, Art. II, § 99, eff. Sept. 11, 1984; P.A. 83–1457, § 2, eff. Jan. 1, 1985; P.A. 89–245, § 5, eff. Jan. 1, 1996; P.A. 91–37, § 40, eff. July 1, 1999.

Formerly Ill.Rev.Stat.1991, ch. 95 ½, ¶ 3–806.

Section 4 of P.A. 83–12, approved July 1, 1983, provided:

"Effective date. This Act takes effect as provided in this Section.

"The amendments to those portions of Sections 3–815(a), 3–818 and 3–819(b) of 'The Illinois Vehicle Code' in Section 1 of this Act which create the 'X', 'Z', 'MX', 'MZ', 'MM' and 'TN' registration classifications and the fees and taxes imposed for those classifications, the amendments to Sections 2–119, 3–401 and 3–802 of 'The Illinois Vehicle Code' in Section 1 of this Act, and the amendments to Chapter 15 of 'The Illinois Vehicle Code' in Section 1 of this Act take effect July 1, 1983.

"The remaining amendments to 'The Illinois Vehicle Code' in Section 1 of this Act take effect July 1, 1983 and apply beginning with the 1985 registration year, except that the amendments to Sections 3–813 through 3–816 and Section 3–819 apply beginning with the 1984 registration year for those vehicles registered on a calendar year basis only.

"The amendments to Chapters 13 and 18 of 'The Illinois Vehicle Code' in Section 1 of this Act take effect January 1, 1984.

"Section 2 of this Act takes effect on the first day of the next succeeding month which commences at least 30 days after the date on which this Act becomes law.

"Section 3 of this Act takes effect July 1, 1983.

"Section 3.1 of this Act takes effect January 1, 1984.

"This Section 4 takes effect upon its becoming a law."

For effective date of amendment by P.A. 83–817, see note under 625 ILCS 5/3–414.

Section 2 of P.A. 83–817 approved Sept. 24, 1983, provided:

"This Act takes effect with the 1985 registration year."

5/3–806.1. Additional fees for vanity license plates

§ 3–806.1. Additional fees for vanity license plates. In addition to the regular registration fee, an applicant shall be charged $94 for each set of vanity license plates issued to a motor vehicle of the first division or a motor vehicle of the second division registered at not more than 8,000 pounds or to a recreational vehicle and $50 for each set of vanity plates issued to a motorcycle. In addition to the regular renewal fee, an applicant shall be charged $13 for the renewal of each set of vanity license plates.

P.A. 76–1586, § 3–806.1, added by P.A. 81–987, § 1, eff. Sept. 17, 1982. Amended by P.A. 83–12, § 1, eff. July 1, 1983; P.A. 83–828, § 1, eff. Jan. 1, 1984; P.A. 83–1362, Art. II, § 99, eff. Sept. 11, 1984; P.A. 86–480, § 1, eff. Jan. 1, 1990; P.A. 91–37, § 40, eff. July 1, 1999.

Formerly Ill.Rev.Stat.1991, ch. 95 ½, ¶ 3–806.1.

Section 4 of P.A. 83–12, approved July 1, 1983, provided:

"Effective date. This Act takes effect as provided in this Section.

"The amendments to those portions of Sections 3–815(a), 3–818 and 3–819(b) of 'The Illinois Vehicle Code' in Section 1 of this Act which create the 'X', 'Z', 'MX', 'MZ', 'MM' and 'TN' registration classifications and the fees and taxes imposed for those classifications, the amendments to Sections 2–119, 3–401 and 3–802 of 'The Illinois Vehicle Code' in Section 1 of this Act, and the amendments to Chapter 15 of 'The Illinois Vehicle Code' in Section 1 of this Act take effect July 1, 1983.

"The remaining amendments to 'The Illinois Vehicle Code' in Section 1 of this Act take effect July 1, 1983 and apply beginning with the 1985 registration year, except that the amendments to Sections 3–813 through 3–816 and Section 3–819 apply beginning with the 1984 registration year for those vehicles registered on a calendar year basis only.

"The amendments to Chapters 13 and 18 of 'The Illinois Vehicle Code' in Section 1 of this Act take effect January 1, 1984.

"Section 2 of this Act takes effect on the first day of the next succeeding month which commences at least 30 days after the date on which this Act becomes law.

"Section 3 of this Act takes effect July 1, 1983.

"Section 3.1 of this Act takes effect January 1, 1984.

"This Section 4 takes effect upon its becoming a law."

Section 2 of P.A. 83–828 provided:

"This Act takes effect with the 1985 registration year."

5/3–806.2. Limitations on no-fee plates

§ 3–806.2. Limitations on no-fee plates. No individual shall be issued more than one pair of plates of any category for which no fee is required. The Secretary of State may issue additional pairs of plates of any such category upon receiving the required application and registration fees.

P.A. 76–1586, § 3–806.2, added by P.A. 82–1011, § 2, eff. Sept. 17, 1982. Amended by P.A. 88–517, § 10, eff. Nov. 16, 1993.

Formerly Ill.Rev.Stat.1991, ch. 95 ½, ¶ 3–806.2.

5/3–806.3. Senior Citizens

§ 3–806.3. Senior Citizens.

Commencing with the 2001 registration year and extending through the 2003 registration year, the registration fee paid by any vehicle owner who has claimed and received a grant under the Senior Citizens and Disabled Persons Property Tax Relief and Pharmaceutical Assistance Act or who is the spouse of such a person shall be $24 instead of the fee otherwise provided in this Code for passenger cars displaying standard multi-year registration plates issued under Section 3–414.1, motor vehicles displaying special registration plates issued under Section 3–616, motor vehicles registered at 8,000 pounds or less under Section 3–815(a) and recreational vehicles registered at 8,000 pounds or less under Section 3–815(b). Widows and widowers of claimants shall also be entitled to this reduced registration fee for the registration year in which the claimant was eligible.

Commencing with the 2004 registration year, the registration fee paid by any vehicle owner who has claimed and received a grant under the Senior Citizens and Disabled Persons Property Tax Relief and Pharmaceutical Assistance Act or who is the spouse of such a person shall be $24 instead of the fee otherwise provided in this Code for passenger cars displaying standard multi-year registration plates issued under Section 3–414.1, motor vehicles displaying special registration plates issued under Section 3–616, 3–621, 3–622, 3–623, 3–624, 3–625, 3–626, 3–628, 3–638, 3–642, 3–645, 3–647, 3–650, or 3–651, motor vehicles registered at 8,000 pounds or less under Section 3–815(a), and recreational vehicles registered at 8,000 pounds or less under Section 3–815(b). Widows and widowers of claimants shall also be entitled to this reduced registration fee for the registration year in which the claimant was eligible.

No more than one reduced registration fee under this Section shall be allowed during any 12 month period based on the primary eligibility of any individual, whether such reduced registration fee is allowed to the individual or to the spouse, widow or widower of such individual. This Section does not apply to the fee paid in addition to the registration fee for motor vehicles displaying vanity or special license plates.

P.A. 76–1586, § 3–806.3, added by P.A. 83–1457, § 2, eff. Jan. 1, 1985. Amended by P.A. 84–832, Art. III, § 11, eff. Sept. 23, 1985; P.A. 84–1390, § 4, eff. Sept. 18, 1986; P.A. 86–444,

§ 1, eff. Jan. 1, 1990; P.A. 91–37, § 40, eff. July 1, 1999; P.A. 92–651, § 77, eff. July 11, 2002; P.A. 92–699, § 5, eff. Jan. 1, 2003.

Formerly Ill.Rev.Stat.1991, ch. 95 ½, ¶ 3–806.3.

P.A. 92–651, the First 2002 General Revisory Act, amended various Acts to delete obsolete text, to correct patent and technical errors, to revise cross references, to resolve multiple actions in the 91st and 92nd General Assemblies and to make certain technical corrections in P.A. 91–937 through P.A. 92–520.

See 5 ILCS 70/6 as to the effect of (1) more than one amendment of a section at the same session of the General Assembly or (2) two or more acts relating to the same subject matter enacted by the same General Assembly.

5/3–806.4. Gold Star recipients

§ 3–806.4. Gold Star recipients. Commencing with the 1991 registration year, upon proper application, the Secretary of State shall issue one pair of registration plates to any Illinois resident, who as the surviving widow or widower, or in the absence thereof, as the surviving parent, is awarded the Gold Star by the United States in recognition of spouses or children who served in the Armed Forces of the United States and lost their lives while in service whether in peacetime or war. If the parent no longer survives, the Secretary of State shall issue the plates to a surviving sibling, of the person who served in the Armed Forces, who is an Illinois resident. No more than one set of plates shall be issued for each Gold Star awarded, and only one surviving parent, or in the absence of a surviving parent, only one surviving sibling shall be issued a set of registration plates, except for those surviving parents who, as recipients of the Gold Star, have legally separated or divorced, in which case each surviving parent shall be allowed one set of registration plates. Registration plates issued under this Section shall be for first division vehicles and second division vehicles of 8,000 pounds or less. An applicant shall be charged a $15 fee for the original issuance in addition to the appropriate registration fee which shall be deposited into the Road Fund to help defray the administrative processing costs. For each registration renewal period, a $2 fee, in addition to the appropriate registration fee, shall be charged and deposited into the Road Fund.

P.A. 76–1586, § 3–806.4, added by P.A. 86–390, § 1, eff. Jan. 1, 1990. Amended by P.A. 90–534, § 5, eff. Nov. 14, 1997.

Formerly Ill.Rev.Stat.1991, ch. 95 ½, ¶ 3–806.4.

5/3–807. Busses operating within Municipality; Registration Fee

§ 3–807. Busses operating within Municipality; Registration Fee. The registration fee of $13 per 2–year registration period shall be paid by the owners of 2 axle motor vehicles which are designed and used as busses in a public system for transporting more than 10 passengers, which vehicles are used as common carriers in the general transportation of passengers and not devoted to any specialized purpose, and which operate entirely within the territorial limits of a single municipality, or a single municipality and municipalities contiguous thereto, or in a close radius thereof, and whose operations are subject to the regulations of the Illinois Commerce Commission. Owners of such vehicles are exempt from paying either a flat weight tax or mileage weight tax. There shall be no reduction in such registration fee even though such registration is made after the beginning of the registration period.

P.A. 76–1586, § 3–807, eff. July 1, 1970. Amended by P.A. 76–2141, § 1, eff. July 1, 1970; P.A. 79–1021, § 1; P.A. 83–12, § 1, eff. July 1, 1983; P.A. 91–37, § 40, eff. July 1, 1999.

Formerly Ill.Rev.Stat.1991, ch. 95 ½, ¶ 3–807.

Section 2 of P.A. 79–1021, certified Sept. 17, 1975, provided:

"This amendatory Act of 1975 takes effect beginning with motor vehicle registrations for 1977."

Section 4 of P.A. 83–12, approved July 1, 1983, provided:

"Effective date. This Act takes effect as provided in this Section.

"The amendments to those portions of Sections 3–815(a), 3–818 and 3–819(b) of 'The Illinois Vehicle Code' in Section 1 of this Act which create the 'X', 'Z', 'MX', 'MZ', 'MM' and 'TN' registration classifications and the fees and taxes imposed for those classifications, the amendments to Sections 2–119, 3–401 and 3–802 of 'The Illinois Vehicle Code' in Section 1 of this Act, and the amendments to Chapter 15 of 'The Illinois Vehicle Code' in Section 1 of this Act take effect July 1, 1983.

"The remaining amendments to 'The Illinois Vehicle Code' in Section 1 of this Act take effect July 1, 1983 and apply beginning with the 1985 registration year, except that the amendments to Sections 3–813 through 3–816 and Section 3–819 apply beginning with the 1984 registration year for those vehicles registered on a calendar year basis only.

"The amendments to Chapters 13 and 18 of 'The Illinois Vehicle Code' in Section 1 of this Act take effect January 1, 1984.

"Section 2 of this Act takes effect on the first day of the next succeeding month which commences at least 30 days after the date on which this Act becomes law.

"Section 3 of this Act takes effect July 1, 1983.

"Section 3.1 of this Act takes effect January 1, 1984.

"This Section 4 takes effect upon its becoming a law."

5/3–808. Governmental and charitable vehicles; Registration fees

§ 3–808. Governmental and charitable vehicles; Registration fees.

(a) A registration fee of $10 per 2 year registration period shall be paid by the owner in the following cases:

1. Vehicles operated exclusively as a school bus for school purposes by any school district or any religious or denominational institution, except that such a school bus may be used by such a religious or denominational institution for the transportation of persons to or from any of its official activities.

2. Vehicles operated exclusively in a high school driver training program by any school district or school operated by a religious institution.

3. Rescue squad vehicles which are owned and operated by a corporation or association organized and operated not for profit for the purpose of conducting such rescue operations.

4. Vehicles, used exclusively as school buses for any school district, which are neither owned nor operated by such district.

5. Charitable vehicles.

(b) Annual vehicle registration plates shall be issued, at no charge, to the following:

1. Medical transport vehicles owned and operated by the State of Illinois or by any State agency financed by funds appropriated by the General Assembly.

2. Medical transport vehicles operated by or for any county, township or municipal corporation.

(c) Ceremonial plates. Upon payment of a registration fee of $78 per 2–year registration period, the Secretary of State shall issue registration plates to vehicles operated exclusively for ceremonial purposes by any not-for-profit veterans', fraternal, or civic organization. The Secretary of State may prescribe that ceremonial vehicle registration plates be issued for an indefinite term, that term to correspond to the term of registration plates issued generally, as provided in Section 3–414.1.

(d) In any event, any vehicle registered under this Section used or operated for purposes other than those herein prescribed shall be subject to revocation, and in that event, the owner may be required to properly register such vehicle under the provisions of this Code.

(e) As a prerequisite to registration under this Section, the Secretary of State may require the vehicle owners listed in subsection (a) of this Section who are exempt from federal income taxation under subsection (c) of Section 501 of the Internal Revenue Code of 1986, as now or hereafter amended,[1] to submit to him a determination letter, ruling or other written evidence of tax exempt status issued by the Internal Revenue Service. The Secretary may accept a certified copy of the document issued by the Internal Revenue Service as evidence of the exemption. The Secretary may require documentation of eligibility under this Section to accompany an application for registration.

(f) Special event plates. The Secretary of State may issue registration plates in recognition or commemoration of special events which promote the interests of Illinois citizens. These plates shall be valid for no more than 60 days prior to the date of expiration. The Secretary shall require the applicant for such plates to pay for the costs of furnishing the plates.

Beginning July 1, 1991, all special event plates shall be recorded in the Secretary of State's files for immediate identification.

The Secretary of State, upon issuing a new series of special event plates, shall notify all law enforcement officials of the design and other special features of the special plate series.

All special event plates shall indicate, in the lower right corner, the date of expiration in characters no less than ½ inch high.

P.A. 76–1586, § 3–808, eff. July 1, 1970. Amended by P.A. 76–2142, § 1, eff. July 1, 1970; P.A. 77–1713, § 1, eff. Jan. 1, 1972; P.A. 77–2751, § 1, eff. Sept. 1, 1972; P.A. 78–255, § 61, eff. Oct. 1, 1973; P.A. 78–1119, § 1, eff. Oct. 1, 1974; P.A. 78–1297, § 58, eff. March 4, 1975; P.A. 79–798, § 1, eff. July 1, 1976; P.A. 79–1021, § 1; P.A. 79–1454, § 44, eff. Aug. 31, 1976; P.A. 80–230, § 1, eff. Oct. 1, 1977; P.A. 81–1496, § 1, eff. Jan. 1, 1982; P.A. 82–433, § 1, eff. Sept. 8, 1981; P.A. 82–1011, § 2, eff. Sept. 17, 1982; P.A. 83–12, § 1, eff. July 1, 1983; P.A. 83–743, § 1, eff. Jan. 1, 1984; P.A. 83–1362, Art. II, § 99, eff. Sept. 11, 1984; P.A. 86–1207, § 1, eff. Aug. 29, 1990; P.A. 88–470, § 10, eff. Sept. 1, 1993; P.A. 89–245, § 5, eff. Jan. 1, 1996; P.A. 89–564, § 5, eff. July 26, 1996; P.A. 89–626, Art. 3, § 3–37, eff. Aug. 9, 1996; P.A. 90–89, § 15, eff. Jan. 1, 1998; P.A. 91–37, § 40, eff. July 1, 1999.

Formerly Ill.Rev.Stat.1991, ch. 95 ½, ¶ 3–808.

[1] 26 U.S.C.A. § 501.

Section 2 of P.A. 79–1021, certified Sept. 17, 1975, provided:

"This amendatory Act of 1975 takes effect beginning with motor vehicle registrations for 1977."

Section 3 of P.A. 82–433 approved Sept. 8, 1981, provided:

"This Act takes effect upon its becoming a law, except that the provisions relating to safety tests and proof of financial responsibility for medical transport vehicles apply only to applications for and the issuance of registration plates which are required to be displayed on January 1, 1982 or thereafter."

Section 4 of P.A. 83–12, approved July 1, 1983, provided:

"Effective date. This Act takes effect as provided in this Section.

"The amendments to those portions of Sections 3–815(a), 3–818 and 3–819(b) of 'The Illinois Vehicle Code' in Section 1 of this Act which create the 'X', 'Z', 'MX', 'MZ', 'MM' and 'TN' registration classifications and the fees and taxes imposed for those classifications, the amendments to Sections 2–119, 3–401 and 3–802 of 'The Illinois Vehicle Code' in Section 1 of this Act, and the amendments to Chapter 15 of 'The Illinois Vehicle Code' in Section 1 of this Act take effect July 1, 1983.

"The remaining amendments to 'The Illinois Vehicle Code' in Section 1 of this Act take effect July 1, 1983 and apply beginning with the 1985 registration year, except that the amendments to Sections 3–813 through 3–816 and Section 3–819 apply beginning with the 1984 registration year for those vehicles registered on a calendar year basis only.

"The amendments to Chapters 13 and 18 of 'The Illinois Vehicle Code' in Section 1 of this Act take effect January 1, 1984.

"Section 2 of this Act takes effect on the first day of the next succeeding month which commences at least 30 days after the date on which this Act becomes law.

"Section 3 of this Act takes effect July 1, 1983.

"Section 3.1 of this Act takes effect January 1, 1984.

"This Section 4 takes effect upon its becoming a law."

5/3–808.1. Vehicle registration plates; persons with disabilities; government owned vehicles

§ 3–808.1. (a) Permanent vehicle registration plates shall be issued, at no charge, to the following:

1. Vehicles, other than medical transport vehicles, owned and operated by the State of Illinois or by any State agency financed by funds appropriated by the General Assembly;

2. Special person with disabilities plates issued to vehicles owned and operated by the State of Illinois or by any State agency financed by funds appropriated by the General Assembly.

(b) Permanent vehicle registration plates shall be issued, for a one time fee of $8.00, to the following:

1. Vehicles, other than medical transport vehicles, operated by or for any county, township or municipal corporation;

2. Vehicles owned by counties, townships or municipal corporations for persons with disabilities.

3. Beginning with the 1991 registration year, county-owned vehicles operated by or for any county sheriff and designated deputy sheriffs. These registration plates shall contain the specific county code and unit number.

4. All-terrain vehicles owned by counties, townships, or municipal corporations and used for law enforcement purposes when the Manufacturer's Statement of Origin is accompanied with a letter from the original manufacturer or a manufacturer's franchised dealer stating that this all-terrain vehicle has been converted to a street worthy vehicle that meets the equipment requirements set forth in Chapter 12 of this Code.

5. Beginning with the 2001 registration year, municipally-owned vehicles operated by or for any police department. These registration plates shall contain the designation "municipal police" and shall be numbered and distributed as prescribed by the Secretary of State.

P.A. 76–1586, § 3–808.1, added by P.A. 81–1496, § 1, eff. Jan. 1, 1982. Amended by P.A. 82–433, § 1, eff. Sept. 8, 1981; P.A. 86–480, § 1, eff. Jan. 1, 1990; P.A. 88–685, § 5, eff. Jan. 24, 1995; P.A. 90–324, § 5, eff. Aug. 1, 1997; P.A. 91–383, § 5, eff. July 30, 1999.

Formerly Ill.Rev.Stat.1991, ch. 95 ½, ¶ 3–808.1.

Section 3 of P.A. 82–433 approved Sept. 8, 1981, provided:

"This Act takes effect upon its becoming a law, except that the provisions relating to safety tests and proof of financial responsibility for medical transport vehicles apply only to applications for and the

issuance of registration plates which are required to be displayed on January 1, 1982 or thereafter."

5/3-809. Farm machinery, exempt vehicles and fertilizer spreaders—registration fee

§ 3-809. Farm machinery, exempt vehicles and fertilizer spreaders—registration fee.

(a) Vehicles of the second division having a corn sheller, a well driller, hay press, clover huller, feed mixer and unloader, or other farm machinery permanently mounted thereon and used solely for transporting the same, farm wagon type trailers having a fertilizer spreader attachment permanently mounted thereon, having a gross weight of not to exceed 36,000 pounds and used only for the transportation of bulk fertilizer, and farm wagon type tank trailers of not to exceed 3,000 gallons capacity, used during the liquid fertilizer season as field-storage "nurse tanks" supplying the fertilizer to a field applicator and moved on highways only for bringing the fertilizer from a local source of supply to farm or field or from one farm or field to another, or used during the lime season and moved on the highways only for bringing from a local source of supply to farm or field or from one farm or field to another, shall be registered upon the filing of a proper application and the payment of a registration fee of $13 per 2-year registration period. This registration fee of $13 shall be paid in full and shall not be reduced even though such registration is made after the beginning of the registration period.

(b) Vehicles exempt from registration under the provisions of Section 3-402.A of this Act, as amended, except those vehicles required to be registered under paragraph (c) of this Section, may, at the option of the owner, be identified as exempt vehicles by displaying registration plates issued by the Secretary of State. The owner thereof may apply for such registration plates upon the filing of a proper application and the payment of a registration fee of $13, and this registration shall be valid for a 2 year registration period. This $13 fee shall be paid in full and shall not be reduced even though the application is made after the beginning of the registration period. The application for and display of such registration plates for identification purposes by vehicles exempt from registration shall not be deemed as a waiver or recision of its exempt status, nor make such vehicle subject to registration.

(c) Any single unit self-propelled agricultural fertilizer implement, designed for both on and off road use, equipped with flotation tires and otherwise specially adapted for the application of plant food materials or agricultural chemicals, desiring to be operated upon the highways ladened with load shall be registered upon the filing of a proper application and payment of a registration fee of $250. The registration fee shall be paid in full and shall not be reduced even though such registration is made during the second half of the registration year. These vehicles shall, whether loaded or unloaded, be limited to a maximum gross weight of 36,000 pounds, restricted to a highway speed of not more than 30 miles per hour and a legal width of not more than 12 feet. Such vehicles shall be limited to the furthering of agricultural or horticultural pursuits and in furtherance of these pursuits, such vehicles may be operated upon the highway, within a 50 mile radius of their point of loading as indicated on the written or printed statement required by the "Illinois Fertilizer Act of 1961",[1] as amended, for the purpose of moving plant food materials or agricultural chemicals to the field, or from field to field, for the sole purpose of application.

No single unit self-propelled agricultural fertilizer implement, designed for both on and off road use, equipped with flotation tires and otherwise specially adapted for the application of plant food materials or agricultural chemicals, having a width of more than 12 feet or a gross weight in excess of 36,000 pounds, shall be permitted to operate upon the highways ladened with load.

Whenever any vehicle is operated in violation of Section 3-809 (c) of this Act, the owner or the driver of such vehicle shall be deemed guilty of a petty offense and either may be prosecuted for such violation.

P.A. 76-1586, § 3-809, eff. July 1, 1970. Amended by P.A. 76-2143, § 1, eff. July 1, 1970; P.A. 79-1021, § 1; P.A. 81-327, § 1, eff. Jan. 1, 1980; P.A. 82-783, Art. IV, § 25, eff. July 13, 1982; P.A. 83-12, § 1, eff. July 1, 1983; P.A. 84-986, § 1, eff. Sept. 25, 1985; P.A. 86-1236, § 1, eff. Jan. 1, 1991; P.A. 91-37, § 40, eff. July 1, 1999; P.A. 92-15, § 5, eff. July 1, 2001.

Formerly Ill.Rev.Stat.1991, ch. 95 ½, ¶ 3-809.

1 505 ILCS 80/1 et seq.

Section 2 of P.A. 79-1021, certified Sept. 17, 1975, provided:

"This amendatory Act of 1975 takes effect beginning with motor vehicle registrations for 1977."

Section 4 of P.A. 83-12, approved July 1, 1983, provided:

"Effective date. This Act takes effect as provided in this Section.

"The amendments to those portions of Sections 3-815(a), 3-818 and 3-819(b) of 'The Illinois Vehicle Code' in Section 1 of this Act which create the 'X', 'Z', 'MX', 'MZ', 'MM' and 'TN' registration classifications and the fees and taxes imposed for those classifications, the amendments to Sections 2-119, 3-401 and 3-802 of 'The Illinois Vehicle Code' in Section 1 of this Act, and the amendments to Chapter 15 of 'The Illinois Vehicle Code' in Section 1 of this Act take effect July 1, 1983.

"The remaining amendments to 'The Illinois Vehicle Code' in Section 1 of this Act take effect July 1, 1983 and apply beginning with the 1985 registration year, except that the amendments to Sections 3-813 through 3-816 and Section 3-819 apply beginning with the 1984 registration year for those vehicles registered on a calendar year basis only.

"The amendments to Chapters 13 and 18 of 'The Illinois Vehicle Code' in Section 1 of this Act take effect January 1, 1984.

"Section 2 of this Act takes effect on the first day of the next succeeding month which commences at least 30 days after the date on which this Act becomes law.

"Section 3 of this Act takes effect July 1, 1983.

"Section 3.1 of this Act takes effect January 1, 1984.

"This Section 4 takes effect upon its becoming a law."

5/3-809.1. Vehicles of second division used for transporting soil and conservation machinery and equipment—Registration fee

§ 3-809.1. Vehicles of second division used for transporting soil and conservation machinery and equipment—Registration fee. Not for hire vehicles of the second division used, only in the territory within a 75 mile radius of the owner's headquarters, solely for transporting the owner's machinery, equipment, plastic tubing, tile and steel reinforcement materials used exclusively for soil and water conservation work on farms, other work on farms and in drainage districts organized for agricultural purposes, shall be registered upon the filing of a proper application and the payment of a registration fee of $488 per annum. The registration fee of $488 shall be paid in full and shall not be reduced even though such registration is made during the second half of the registration year.

P.A. 76-1586, § 3-809.1, added by P.A. 77-71, § 1, eff. July 1, 1971. Amended by P.A. 78-271, § 1, eff. Aug. 13, 1973;

P.A. 80–842, § 1, eff. Sept. 20, 1977; P.A. 83–12, § 1, eff. July 1, 1983; P.A. 85–1396, § 2, eff. Sept. 2, 1988; P.A. 91–37, § 40, eff. July 1, 1999.

Formerly Ill.Rev.Stat.1991, ch. 95 ½, ¶ 3–809.1.

Section 4 of P.A. 83–12, approved July 1, 1983, provided:

"Effective date. This Act takes effect as provided in this Section.

"The amendments to those portions of Sections 3–815(a), 3–818 and 3–819(b) of 'The Illinois Vehicle Code' in Section 1 of this Act which create the 'X', 'Z', 'MX', 'MZ', 'MM' and 'TN' registration classifications and the fees and taxes imposed for those classifications, the amendments to Sections 2–119, 3–401 and 3–802 of 'The Illinois Vehicle Code' in Section 1 of this Act, and the amendments to Chapter 15 of 'The Illinois Vehicle Code' in Section 1 of this Act take effect July 1, 1983.

"The remaining amendments to 'The Illinois Vehicle Code' in Section 1 of this Act take effect July 1, 1983 and apply beginning with the 1985 registration year, except that the amendments to Sections 3–813 through 3–816 and Section 3–819 apply beginning with the 1984 registration year for those vehicles registered on a calendar year basis only.

"The amendments to Chapters 13 and 18 of 'The Illinois Vehicle Code' in Section 1 of this Act take effect January 1, 1984.

"Section 2 of this Act takes effect on the first day of the next succeeding month which commences at least 30 days after the date on which this Act becomes law.

"Section 3 of this Act takes effect July 1, 1983.

"Section 3.1 of this Act takes effect January 1, 1984.

"This Section 4 takes effect upon its becoming a law."

5/3–810. Dealers, Manufacturers, Engine and Driveline Component Manufacturers, Transporters and Repossessors—Registration Plates.

§ 3–810. Dealers, Manufacturers, Engine and Driveline Component Manufacturers, Transporters and Repossessors—Registration Plates.

(a) Dealers, manufacturers and transporters registered under this Act may obtain registration plates for use as provided in this Act, at the following rates:

Initial set of dealer's, manufacturer's or transporter's "in-transit" plates: $45

Duplicate Plates: $13

Manufacturers of engine and driveline components registered under this Act may obtain registration plates at the following rates:

Initial set of "test vehicle" plates: $94

Duplicate plates: $25

Repossessors and other persons qualified and registered under Section 3–601 of this Act may obtain registration plates at the rate of $45 per set.

P.A. 76–1586, § 3–810, eff. July 1, 1970. Amended by P.A. 76–2144, § 1, eff. July 1, 1970; P.A. 77–1316, § 1, eff. Jan. 1, 1972; P.A. 78–753, § 1, eff. Sept. 11, 1973; P.A. 83–12, § 1, eff. July 1, 1983; P.A. 91–37, § 40, eff. July 1, 1999.

Formerly Ill.Rev.Stat.1991, ch. 95 ½, ¶ 3–810.

Effective date and application of P.A. 83–12, see note under 615 ILCS 5/2–119.

5/3–810.1. Tow-Truck—Registration Plates

§ 3–810.1. Tow-Truck—Registration Plates. Tow-Truck operators registered under this Act may obtain registration plates for use as provided in this Act at the rate per set provided in subsection (a) of Section 3–815 of this Code for each vehicle so registered.

P.A. 76–1586, § 3–810.1, added by P.A. 83–1473, § 1, eff. Jan. 1, 1985.

Formerly Ill.Rev.Stat.1991, ch. 95 ½, ¶ 3–810.1.

5/3–811. Drive-away and other permits—Fees

§ 3–811. Drive-away and other permits—Fees.

(a) Dealers may obtain drive-away permits for use as provided in this Code, for a fee of $6 per permit.

(b) Transporters may obtain one-trip permits for vehicles in transit for use as provided in this Code, for a fee of $6 per permit.

(c) Non-residents may likewise obtain a drive-away permit from the Secretary of State to export a motor vehicle purchased in Illinois, for a fee of $6 per permit.

(d) One-trip permits may be obtained for an occasional single trip by a vehicle as provided in this Code, upon payment of a fee of $19.

(e) One month permits may likewise be obtained for the fees and taxes prescribed in this Code and as promulgated by the Secretary of State.

P.A. 76–1586, § 3–811, eff. July 1, 1970. Amended by P.A. 76–2145, § 1, eff. July 1, 1970; P.A. 77–526, § 1, eff. July 31, 1971; P.A. 83–12, § 1, eff. July 1, 1983; P.A. 88–415, § 10, eff. Aug. 20, 1993; P.A. 91–37, § 40, eff. July 1, 1999; P.A. 92–680, § 15, eff. July 16, 2002.

Formerly Ill.Rev.Stat.1991, ch. 95 ½, ¶ 3–811.

Section 4 of P.A. 83–12, approved July 1, 1983, provided:

"Effective date. This Act takes effect as provided in this Section.

"The amendments to those portions of Sections 3–815(a), 3–818 and 3–819(b) of 'The Illinois Vehicle Code' in Section 1 of this Act which create the 'X', 'Z', 'MX', 'MZ', 'MM' and 'TN' registration classifications and the fees and taxes imposed for those classifications, the amendments to Sections 2–119, 3–401 and 3–802 of 'The Illinois Vehicle Code' in Section 1 of this Act, and the amendments to Chapter 15 of 'The Illinois Vehicle Code' in Section 1 of this Act take effect July 1, 1983.

"The remaining amendments to 'The Illinois Vehicle Code' in Section 1 of this Act take effect July 1, 1983 and apply beginning with the 1985 registration year, except that the amendments to Sections 3–813 through 3–816 and Section 3–819 apply beginning with the 1984 registration year for those vehicles registered on a calendar year basis only.

"The amendments to Chapters 13 and 18 of 'The Illinois Vehicle Code' in Section 1 of this Act take effect January 1, 1984.

"Section 2 of this Act takes effect on the first day of the next succeeding month which commences at least 30 days after the date on which this Act becomes law.

"Section 3 of this Act takes effect July 1, 1983.

"Section 3.1 of this Act takes effect January 1, 1984.

"This Section 4 takes effect upon its becoming a law."

5/3–812. Vehicles with Permanently Mounted Equipment—Registration Fees

§ 3–812. Vehicles with Permanently Mounted Equipment—Registration Fees. Vehicles having permanently mounted equipment thereon used exclusively by the owner for the transporting of such permanently mounted equipment and tools and equipment to be used incidentally in the work to be performed with the permanently mounted equipment and provided such vehicle is not used for hire shall be registered upon the filing of a proper application and the payment of a registration fee based upon a rate of $45 per year (or fraction of a year) for each 10,000 pounds (or portion thereof) of the gross weight of such motor vehicle and equipment, according to the following table of fees:

SCHEDULE OF FEES REQUIRED BY LAW

Gross Weight in Lbs. Including Vehicle and Equipment	Total Annual Fees
10,000 lbs. and less	$45
10,001 lbs. to 20,000 lbs.	90
20,001 lbs. to 30,000 lbs.	135
30,001 lbs. to 40,000 lbs.	180
40,001 lbs. to 50,000 lbs.	225
50,001 lbs. to 60,000 lbs.	270
60,001 lbs. to 70,000 lbs.	315
70,001 lbs. to 73,280 lbs.	340
73,281 lbs. to 80,000 lbs.	385

P.A. 76-1586, § 3-812, eff. July 1, 1970. Amended by P.A. 83-12, § 1, eff. July 1, 1983; P.A. 83-315, § 1, eff. Jan. 1, 1984; P.A. 83-1362, Art. II, § 99, eff. Sept. 11, 1984; P.A. 84-213, § 1, eff. Jan. 1, 1986; P.A. 91-37, § 40, eff. July 1, 1999.

Formerly Ill.Rev.Stat.1991, ch. 95 ½, ¶ 3-812.

Section 4 of P.A. 83-12, approved July 1, 1983, provided:

"Effective date. This Act takes effect as provided in this Section.

"The amendments to those portions of Sections 3-815(a), 3-818 and 3-819(b) of 'The Illinois Vehicle Code' in Section 1 of this Act which create the 'X', 'Z', 'MX', 'MZ', 'MM' and 'TN' registration classifications and the fees and taxes imposed for those classifications, the amendments to Sections 2-119, 3-401 and 3-802 of 'The Illinois Vehicle Code' in Section 1 of this Act, and the amendments to Chapter 15 of 'The Illinois Vehicle Code' in Section 1 of this Act take effect July 1, 1983.

"The remaining amendments to 'The Illinois Vehicle Code' in Section 1 of this Act take effect July 1, 1983 and apply beginning with the 1985 registration year, except that the amendments to Sections 3-813 through 3-816 and Section 3-819 apply beginning with the 1984 registration year for those vehicles registered on a calendar year basis only.

"The amendments to Chapters 13 and 18 of 'The Illinois Vehicle Code' in Section 1 of this Act take effect January 1, 1984.

"Section 2 of this Act takes effect on the first day of the next succeeding month which commences at least 30 days after the date on which this Act becomes law.

"Section 3 of this Act takes effect July 1, 1983.

"Section 3.1 of this Act takes effect January 1, 1984.

"This Section 4 takes effect upon its becoming a law."

Section 2 of P.A. 84-213, provided:

"This Act takes effect January 1, 1986 and applies to registrations beginning with the 1987 registration year."

5/3-813. Vehicles of second division—Registration fee

§ 3-813. Vehicles of second division—Registration fee. Except as otherwise provided in this Code, all owners of vehicles of the second division which are designed, equipped or used for carrying freight, goods, wares, merchandise, or for use as living quarters; and all owners of vehicles of the first division which have been remodelled and are being used for such purposes; and all owners of motor vehicles operated as truck tractors to the weights of which are added to the gross weights of semitrailers with their maximum loads when drawn by such truck tractors; and all owners of vehicles of the second division which are used for carrying more than 10 persons, shall pay to the Secretary of State for each registration year, for the use of the public highways of this State, a registration fee of $10 for each such vehicle. A self-propelled vehicle operated as a truck tractor and one semitrailer or a combination of a truck tractor and semitrailer drawing a trailer or a semitrailer converted to a trailer through use of an auxiliary axle or any combination of apportioned vehicles shall be considered as one vehicle in computing the flat weight taxes under Section 3-815.

P.A. 76-1586, § 3-813, eff. July 1, 1970. Amended by P.A. 76-2146, § 1, eff. July 1, 1970; P.A. 82-392, § 1, eff. Jan. 1, 1982; P.A. 83-12, § 1, eff. July 1, 1983; P.A. 87-206, § 1, eff. Sept. 3, 1991.

Formerly Ill.Rev.Stat.1991, ch. 95 ½, ¶ 3-813.

Section 2 of P.A. 82-392 approved Sept. 4, 1981, provided:

"This Act takes effect with the 1984 registration year."

Section 4 of P.A. 83-12, approved July 1, 1983, provided:

"Effective date. This Act takes effect as provided in this Section.

"The amendments to those portions of Sections 3-815(a), 3-818 and 3-819(b) of 'The Illinois Vehicle Code' in Section 1 of this Act which create the 'X', 'Z', 'MX', 'MZ', 'MM' and 'TN' registration classifications and the fees and taxes imposed for those classifications, the amendments to Sections 2-119, 3-401 and 3-802 of 'The Illinois Vehicle Code' in Section 1 of this Act, and the amendments to Chapter 15 of 'The Illinois Vehicle Code' in Section 1 of this Act take effect July 1, 1983.

"The remaining amendments to 'The Illinois Vehicle Code' in Section 1 of this Act take effect July 1, 1983 and apply beginning with the 1985 registration year, except that the amendments to Sections 3-813 through 3-816 and Section 3-819 apply beginning with the 1984 registration year for those vehicles registered on a calendar year basis only.

"The amendments to Chapters 13 and 18 of 'The Illinois Vehicle Code' in Section 1 of this Act take effect January 1, 1984.

"Section 2 of this Act takes effect on the first day of the next succeeding month which commences at least 30 days after the date on which this Act becomes law.

"Section 3 of this Act takes effect July 1, 1983.

"Section 3.1 of this Act takes effect January 1, 1984.

"This Section 4 takes effect upon its becoming a law."

5/3-814. Semitrailer registration fees

§ 3-814. Semitrailer registration fees. Effective with the 1984 registration year to the end of the 1998 registration year, an owner of a semitrailer shall pay to the Secretary of State, for the use of the public highways of this State, a flat weight tax of $60, which includes the registration fee, for a 5 year semitrailer plate.

Effective with the 1999 registration year an owner of a semitrailer shall pay to the Secretary of State, for the use of the public highways of this State, a one time flat tax of $15, which includes the registration fee, for a permanent non-transferrable semitrailer plate.

Effective with the 2001 registration year, an owner of a semitrailer shall pay to the Secretary of State, for the use of public highways of this State, a one-time flat tax of $19, which includes the registration fee, for a permanent non-transferrable semitrailer plate.

P.A. 76-1586, § 3-814, eff. July 1, 1970. Amended by P.A. 76-2147, § 1, eff. July 1, 1970; P.A. 82-392, § 1, eff. Jan. 1, 1982; P.A. 83-12, § 1, eff. July 1, 1983; P.A. 87-206, § 1, eff. Sept. 3, 1991; P.A. 87-1040, § 1, eff. Sept. 11, 1992; P.A. 89-710, § 15, eff. Feb. 14, 1997; P.A. 91-37, § 40, eff. July 1, 1999.

Formerly Ill.Rev.Stat.1991, ch. 95 ½, ¶ 3-814.

Section 4 of P.A. 83-12, approved July 1, 1983, provided:

"Effective date. This Act takes effect as provided in this Section.

"The amendments to those portions of Sections 3-815(a), 3-818 and 3-819(b) of 'The Illinois Vehicle Code' in Section 1 of this Act which create the 'X', 'Z', 'MX', 'MZ', 'MM' and 'TN' registration classifications and the fees and taxes imposed for those classifications, the amendments to Sections 2-119, 3-401 and 3-802 of 'The Illinois Vehicle Code' in Section 1 of this Act, and the amendments to Chapter 15 of 'The Illinois Vehicle Code' in Section 1 of this Act take effect July 1, 1983.

"The remaining amendments to 'The Illinois Vehicle Code' in Section 1 of this Act take effect July 1, 1983 and apply beginning with the 1985 registration year, except that the amendments to Sections 3-813 through 3-816 and Section 3-819 apply beginning with the 1984 registration year for those vehicles registered on a calendar year basis only.

"The amendments to Chapters 13 and 18 of 'The Illinois Vehicle Code' in Section 1 of this Act take effect January 1, 1984.

"Section 2 of this Act takes effect on the first day of the next succeeding month which commences at least 30 days after the date on which this Act becomes law.

"Section 3 of this Act takes effect July 1, 1983.

"Section 3.1 of this Act takes effect January 1, 1984.

"This Section 4 takes effect upon its becoming a law."

5/3-814.1. Apportionable trailer and semitrailer fees

§ 3-814.1. Apportionable trailer and semitrailer fees. Beginning April 1, 1994 through March 31, 1998, an owner of an apportionable trailer or apportionable semitrailer registered under Section 3-402.1 shall pay an annual registration fee of $12 to the Secretary of State.

Beginning April 1, 1998 through March 31, 2000, an owner of an apportionable trailer or apportionable semitrailer registered under Section 3-402.1 shall pay a one time registration fee of $15 to the Secretary of State for a permanent non-transferrable plate.

Beginning April 1, 2000, an owner of an apportionable trailer or apportionable semitrailer registered under Section 3-402.1 shall pay a one-time registration fee of $19 to the Secretary of State for a permanent non-transferrable plate.

P.A. 76-1586, § 3-814.1, added by P.A. 87-1040, § 1, eff. Sept. 11, 1992. Amended by P.A. 89-710, § 15, eff. Feb. 14, 1997; P.A. 91-37, § 40, eff. July 1, 1999.

Formerly Ill.Rev.Stat., ch. 95½, ¶ 3-814.1.

5/3-814.2. Optional registration of converter devices

§ 3-814.2. Optional registration of converter devices.

(a) The Secretary of State may provide for optional registration of devices that convert a semitrailer to a trailer and are exempt from vehicle registration requirements. The rules adopted for purposes of this Section may provide for the registration of this category of vehicle or type vehicle. Upon request of an owner, the Secretary of State may issue registration for a vehicle that meets the requirements of rules adopted under this Section. A registration fee for this vehicle may be imposed by rule.

(b) A vehicle that is registered under this Section is subject to the same provisions, conditions, fees, and other requirements under this Code.

P.A. 76-1586, § 3-814.2, added by P.A. 89-710, § 15, eff. Feb. 14, 1997.

5/3-814.3. Registration of fleets of semitrailers or apportionable semitrailers

§ 3-814.3. Registration of fleets of semitrailers or apportionable semitrailers. The Secretary of State may provide for the registration of large fleets of semitrailers or apportionable semitrailers by accepting the appropriate fees and issuing the registration plate prior to the plate being assigned to a specific vehicle. The registration indexes will be updated on a date predetermined by the Secretary of State. In determining this date, the Secretary of State shall take into consideration the number of vehicles in each fleet.

P.A. 76-1586, § 3-814.3, added by P.A. 89-710, § 15, eff. Feb. 14, 1997.

5/3-814.4. Registration of fleet vehicles

Text of section added effective July 1, 2003

§ 3-814.4 Registration of fleet vehicles. The Secretary may issue fleet vehicle registration plates to owners of vehicle fleets registered in accordance with Section 3-405.3 of this Code in bulk before plates are assigned to specific vehicles. A registration plate may not be displayed on a vehicle, however, until the plate has been activated on the Secretary's registration file and the proper fee has been forwarded to the Secretary.

P.A. 76-1586, § 3-814.4, added by P.A. 92-629, § 5, eff. July 1, 2003.

5/3-815. Flat weight tax; vehicles of the second division.

§ 3-815. Flat weight tax; vehicles of the second division.

(a) Except as provided in Section 3-806.3, every owner of a vehicle of the second division registered under Section 3-813, and not registered under the mileage weight tax under Section 3-818, shall pay to the Secretary of State, for each registration year, for the use of the public highways, a flat weight tax at the rates set forth in the following table, the rates including the $10 registration fee:

SCHEDULE OF FLAT WEIGHT
TAX REQUIRED BY LAW

Gross Weight in Lbs. Including Vehicle and Maximum Load	Class	Total Fees each Fiscal year
8,000 lbs. and less	B	$78
8,001 lbs. to 12,000 lbs.	D	138
12,001 lbs. to 16,000 lbs.	F	242
16,001 lbs. to 26,000 lbs.	H	490
26,001 lbs. to 28,000 lbs.	J	630
28,001 lbs. to 32,000 lbs.	K	842
32,001 lbs. to 36,000 lbs.	L	982
36,001 lbs. to 40,000 lbs.	N	1,202
40,001 lbs. to 45,000 lbs.	P	1,390
45,001 lbs. to 50,000 lbs.	Q	1,538
50,001 lbs. to 54,999 lbs.	R	1,698
55,000 lbs. to 59,500 lbs.	S	1,830
59,501 lbs. to 64,000 lbs.	T	1,970
64,001 lbs. to 73,280 lbs.	V	2,294
73,281 lbs. to 77,000 lbs.	X	2,622
77,001 lbs. to 80,000 lbs.	Z	2,790

(a-1) A Special Hauling Vehicle is a vehicle or combination of vehicles of the second division registered under Section 3-813 transporting asphalt or concrete in the plastic state or a vehicle or combination of vehicles that are subject to the gross weight limitations in subsection (b) of Section 15-111 for which the owner of the vehicle or combination of vehicles has elected to pay, in addition to the registration fee in subsection (a), $125 to the Secretary of State for each registration year. The Secretary shall designate this class of vehicle as a Special Hauling Vehicle.

(b) Except as provided in Section 3–806.3, every camping trailer, motor home, mini motor home, travel trailer, truck camper or van camper used primarily for recreational purposes, and not used commercially, nor for hire, nor owned by a commercial business, may be registered for each registration year upon the filing of a proper application and the payment of a registration fee and highway use tax, according to the following table of fees:

MOTOR HOME, MINI MOTOR HOME, TRUCK CAMPER OR VAN CAMPER

Gross Weight in Lbs. Including Vehicle and Maximum Load	Total Fees Each Calendar Year
8,000 lbs and less	$78
8,001 Lbs. to 10,000 Lbs.	90
10,001 Lbs. and Over	102

CAMPING TRAILER OR TRAVEL TRAILER

Gross Weight in Lbs. Including Vehicle and Maximum Load	Total Fees Each Calendar Year
3,000 Lbs. and Less	$18
3,001 Lbs. to 8,000 Lbs.	30
8,001 Lbs. to 10,000 Lbs.	38
10,001 Lbs. and Over	50

Every house trailer must be registered under Section 3–819.

(c) Farm Truck. Any truck used exclusively for the owner's own agricultural, horticultural or livestock raising operations and not-for-hire only, or any truck used only in the transportation for-hire of seasonal, fresh, perishable fruit or vegetables from farm to the point of first processing, may be registered by the owner under this paragraph in lieu of registration under paragraph (a), upon filing of a proper application and the payment of the $10 registration fee and the highway use tax herein specified as follows:

SCHEDULE OF FEES AND TAXES

Gross Weight in Lbs. Including Truck and Maximum Load	Class	Total Amount for each Fiscal Year
16,000 lbs. or less	VF	$150
16,001 to 20,000 lbs.	VG	226
20,001 to 24,000 lbs.	VH	290
24,001 to 28,000 lbs.	VJ	378
28,001 to 32,000 lbs.	VK	506
32,001 to 36,000 lbs.	VL	610
36,001 to 45,000 lbs.	VP	810
45,001 to 54,999 lbs.	VR	1,026
55,000 to 64,000 lbs.	VT	1,202
64,001 to 73,280 lbs.	VV	1,290
73,281 to 77,000 lbs.	VX	1,350
77,001 to 80,000 lbs.	VZ	1,490

In the event the Secretary of State revokes a farm truck registration as authorized by law, the owner shall pay the flat weight tax due hereunder before operating such truck.

Any combination of vehicles having 5 axles, with a distance of 42 feet or less between extreme axles, that are subject to the weight limitations in subsection (a) and (b) of Section 15–111 for which the owner of the combination of vehicles has elected to pay, in addition to the registration fee in subsection (c), $125 to the Secretary of State for each registration year shall be designated by the Secretary as a Special Hauling Vehicle.

(d) The number of axles necessary to carry the maximum load provided shall be determined from Chapter 15 of this Code.[1]

(e) An owner may only apply for and receive 5 farm truck registrations, and only 2 of those 5 vehicles shall exceed 59,500 gross weight in pounds per vehicle.

(f) Every person convicted of violating this Section by failure to pay the appropriate flat weight tax to the Secretary of State as set forth in the above tables shall be punished as provided for in Section 3–401.

P.A. 76–1586, § 3–815, eff. July 1, 1970. Amended by P.A. 76–2148, § 1, eff. July 1, 1970; P.A. 77–137, § 1, eff. July 1, 1972; P.A. 77–720, § 1, eff. July 1, 1972; P.A. 77–1633, § 1, eff. Sept. 23, 1971; P.A. 77–2829, § 40, eff. Dec. 22, 1972; P.A. 78–255, § 61, eff. Oct. 1, 1973; P.A. 78–335, § 1, eff. Jan. 1, 1974; P.A. 78–1146, § 1, eff. Jan. 1, 1975; P.A. 78–1297, § 58, eff. March 4, 1975; P.A. 80–758, § 1, eff. Oct. 1, 1977; P.A. 81–969, § 1, eff. Jan. 1, 1980; P.A. 82–392, § 1, eff. Jan. 1, 1982; P.A. 83–12, § 1, eff. July 1, 1983; P.A. 83–799, § 1, eff. Jan. 1, 1984; P.A. 83–1362, Art. II, § 99, eff. Sept. 11, 1984; P.A. 83–1457, § 2, eff. Jan. 1, 1985; P.A. 84–213, § 1, eff. Jan. 1, 1986; P.A. 84–986, § 1, eff. Sept. 25, 1985; P.A. 84–1308, Art. II, § 96, eff. Aug. 25, 1986; P.A. 85–678, § 1, eff. July 1, 1989; P.A. 86–845, § 2, eff. July 1, 1990; P.A. 86–1171, § 1, eff. Jan. 1, 1991; P.A. 88–403, § 5, eff. Jan. 1, 1994; P.A. 88–476, § 2, eff. July 1, 1994; P.A. 88–617, § 5, eff. Sept. 9, 1994; P.A. 88–670, Art. 2, § 2–59, eff. Dec. 2, 1994; P.A. 89–710, § 15, eff. Feb. 14, 1997; P.A. 91–37, § 40, eff. July 1, 1999.

Formerly Ill.Rev.Stat.1991, ch. 95 ½, ¶ 3–815.

[1] 625 ILCS 5/15–100 et seq.

Section 3 of P.A. 81–969, approved Sept. 22, 1979, provided:

"This amendatory Act takes effect at the start of the 1981 registration year."

Section 2 of P.A. 82–392 approved Sept. 4, 1981, provided:

"This Act takes effect with the 1984 registration year."

Section 4 of P.A. 83–12, approved July 1, 1983, provided:

"Effective date. This Act takes effect as provided in this Section.

"The amendments to those portions of Sections 3–815(a), 3–818 and 3–819(b) of 'The Illinois Vehicle Code' in Section 1 of this Act which create the 'X', 'Z', 'MX', 'MZ', 'MM' and 'TN' registration classifications and the fees and taxes imposed for those classifications, the amendments to Sections 2–119, 3–401 and 3–802 of 'The Illinois Vehicle Code' in Section 1 of this Act, and the amendments to Chapter 15 of 'The Illinois Vehicle Code' in Section 1 of this Act take effect July 1, 1983.

"The remaining amendments to 'The Illinois Vehicle Code' in Section 1 of this Act take effect July 1, 1983 and apply beginning with the 1985 registration year, except that the amendments to Sections 3–813 through 3–816 and Section 3–819 apply beginning with the 1984 registration year for those vehicles registered on a calendar year basis only.

"The amendments to Chapters 13 and 18 of 'The Illinois Vehicle Code' in Section 1 of this Act take effect January 1, 1984.

"Section 2 of this Act takes effect on the first day of the next succeeding month which commences at least 30 days after the date on which this Act becomes law.

"Section 3 of this Act takes effect July 1, 1983.

"Section 3.1 of this Act takes effect January 1, 1984.

"This Section 4 takes effect upon its becoming a law."

5/3–816. Installment Payments

§ 3–816. Installment Payments.

(a) The flat weight tax required to be paid by Section 3–815 for any vehicles on a calendar year basis may be paid if the owner so elects, in equal semi-annual installments due on January 1 and July 1 of each licensing year. Effective with the 1984 registration year the owners of semitrailers registered under Section 3-814 shall have the option of paying the designated fees to the Secretary in the following manner:

If registered in the first year the owner shall have the option of paying $30 the first year and the remaining $30 by the start of the second year;

If registered in the second year the owner shall have the option of paying $24 the first year and the remaining $24 by the start of the third year;

If registered in the third year the owner shall pay $36 for each semitrailer;

If registered in the fourth year the owner shall pay $24 for each semitrailer; and

If registered in the fifth year the owner shall pay $12 for each semitrailer.

Every such owner who elects to pay such tax in such installments shall file with the Secretary of State a surety bond or certificate of deposit, as hereinafter provided, in the amount of the sum of the second installment of taxes on his vehicle.

Such bond shall be in the form approved by the Secretary of State and with a surety company approved by the Department of Insurance to transact business in this State, as surety, and shall be conditioned upon such owner's paying to the State of Illinois all monies becoming due by reason of his operation of the second division motor vehicle in this State, together with all penalties and interest thereon.

The State Treasurer shall issue a certificate of deposit to any such owner who deposits with the State Treasurer securities of the Federal Government or the State of Illinois endorsed in blank by such owner, or a certificate of deposit issued by any bank or savings and loan association authorized to do business in Illinois, payable to the Secretary of State on or after July 1 of the year of registration. Such certificate of deposit and securities shall be approved by and deposited with the State Treasurer, and shall have a current market value in the total amount which would cover all monies becoming due and payable to the State of Illinois by reason of his operation of a second division motor vehicle in this State, together with all penalties and interest thereon.

The liability of the surety hereunder shall be absolute and upon notice from the Secretary of State that the second installment has not been paid on July 1 of any licensing year the surety shall immediately pay the second installment to the Secretary of State.

Upon notice by the Secretary of State that the second installment of such owner's taxes has not been paid on July 1 of any licensing year, the State Treasurer shall sell such securities and deliver the proceeds thereof to the Secretary of State to satisfy all monies becoming due by reason of such owner's operation of a second division motor vehicle in this State, together with all penalties and interest thereon.

If the owner's liability for the second installment is evidenced by a certificate of deposit payable to the Secretary of State, the Secretary of State shall, upon failure of the owner to pay the second installment by July 1, endorse the certificate of deposit which is in the custody of the State Treasurer, and thereafter the State Treasurer shall present the certificate of deposit for payment to the proper bank or savings and loan association. Upon receipt of payment, the State Treasurer shall forward to the Secretary of State all monies due by reason of such owner's operation of a second division motor vehicle in this State, and return the excess, if any, to the owner on whose behalf the certificate of deposit was previously deposited.

The State Treasurer shall return securities or proceeds in excess of that needed to satisfy the Secretary of State for all monies becoming due by reason of such owner's operation of a second division motor vehicle in this State, together with all penalties and interest thereon. Upon notice by the Secretary of State that the second installment has been paid, the State Treasurer shall return such certificate of deposit or securities deposited with him under this Section to the owner thereof.

(b) The flat weight tax required by Section 3-815 to be paid on a fiscal year basis may be paid, if the owner so elects, in equal semi-annual installments due on July 1st and January 1st of each registration year. From July 1, 1983 through November 30, 1983, the flat weight tax required by Section 3-814 for semitrailers previously registered on a fiscal year basis may be paid, if the owner so elects, by paying the Secretary of State $33 at the time of registration and the remaining $25 by January 1, 1985 for each 5 ½ year semitrailer plate. Every such owner who elects to pay such tax in such installments shall file with the Secretary of State a surety bond or certificate of deposit, as hereinafter provided, in the amount of the sum of the second installment of taxes on his vehicle.

Such bond shall be in the form approved by the Secretary of State and with a surety company approved by the Department of Insurance to transact business in this State, as surety, and shall be conditioned upon such owner's paying to the State of Illinois all monies becoming due by reason of his operation of the second division motor vehicle in this State, together with all penalties and interest thereon.

The liability of the surety hereunder shall be absolute and upon notice from the Secretary of State that the second installment has not been paid on January 1st of any registration year the surety shall immediately pay the second installment to the Secretary of State.

Upon notice by the Secretary of State that the second installment of such owner's taxes has not been paid on January 1st of any registration year, the State Treasurer shall sell such securities and deliver the proceeds thereof to the Secretary of State to satisfy all monies becoming due by reason of such owner's operation of a second division motor vehicle in this State, together with all penalties and interest thereon.

If the owner's liability for the second installment is evidenced by a certificate of deposit payable to the Secretary of State, the Secretary of State shall, upon failure of the owner to pay the second installment by January 1st, endorse the certificate of deposit which is in the custody of the State Treasurer, and thereafter the State Treasurer shall present the certificate of deposit for payment to the proper bank or savings and loan association. Upon receipt of payment, the State Treasurer shall forward to the Secretary of State all monies due by reason of such owner's operation of a second division motor vehicle in this State, and return the excess, if any, to the owner on whose behalf the certificate of deposit was previously deposited.

The State Treasurer shall return securities or proceeds in excess of that needed to satisfy the Secretary of State for all monies becoming due by reason of such owner's operation of a second division motor vehicle in this State, together with all penalties and interest thereon. Upon notice by the Secretary of State that the second installment has been paid, the State Treasurer shall return such certificate of deposit or securities deposited with him under this Section to the owner thereof.

(c) The flat weight tax required under Section 3-815 for vehicles registered in accordance with Section 3-402.1 may be paid, if the owner elects, in equal semi-annual installments due on April 1 and October 1 of each licensing year.

(d) In the event any surety pays for any second installment under this Section, the surety shall have recourse only against the principal and owner of the vehicles involved and shall have no right or privilege to demand revocation or suspension of the registration plates or registration stickers of the vehicles involved. Such surety may, however, impress a lien as provided in Section 3–828.

P.A. 76–1586, § 3–816, eff. July 1, 1970. Amended by P.A. 77–1464, § 1, eff. Sept. 7, 1971; P.A. 79–1038, § 1, eff. Oct. 1, 1975; P.A. 80–230, § 1, eff. Oct. 1, 1977; P.A. 80–674, § 1, eff. Oct. 1, 1977; P.A. 80–1364, § 36, eff. Aug. 13, 1978; P.A. 82–392, § 1, eff. Jan. 1, 1982; P.A. 83–12, § 1, eff. July 1, 1983; P.A. 83–541, § 52, eff. Sept. 17, 1983; P.A. 83–1362, Art. II, § 99, eff. Sept. 11, 1984; P.A. 87–1041, § 1, eff. Sept. 11, 1992; P.A. 91–357, § 231, eff. July 29, 1999.

Formerly Ill.Rev.Stat.1991, ch. 95 ½, ¶ 3–816.

Section 2 of P.A. 82–392 approved Sept. 4, 1981, provided:

"This Act takes effect with the 1984 registration year."

Section 4 of P.A. 83–12, approved July 1, 1983, provided:

"Effective date. This Act takes effect as provided in this Section.

"The amendments to those portions of Sections 3–815(a), 3–818 and 3–819(b) of 'The Illinois Vehicle Code' in Section 1 of this Act which create the 'X', 'Z', 'MX', 'MZ', 'MM' and 'TN' registration classifications and the fees and taxes imposed for those classifications, the amendments to Sections 2–119, 3–401 and 3–802 of 'The Illinois Vehicle Code' in Section 1 of this Act, and the amendments to Chapter 15 of 'The Illinois Vehicle Code' in Section 1 of this Act take effect July 1, 1983.

"The remaining amendments to 'The Illinois Vehicle Code' in Section 1 of this Act take effect July 1, 1983 and apply beginning with the 1985 registration year, except that the amendments to Sections 3–813 through 3–816 and Section 3–819 apply beginning with the 1984 registration year for those vehicles registered on a calendar year basis only.

"The amendments to Chapters 13 and 18 of 'The Illinois Vehicle Code' in Section 1 of this Act take effect January 1, 1984.

"Section 2 of this Act takes effect on the first day of the next succeeding month which commences at least 30 days after the date on which this Act becomes law.

"Section 3 of this Act takes effect July 1, 1983.

"Section 3.1 of this Act takes effect January 1, 1984.

"This Section 4 takes effect upon its becoming a law."

5/3–817. § 3–817. Repealed by P.A. 80–891, § 2, eff. Jan. 1, 1978

5/3–818. Mileage weight tax option

§ 3–818. (a) Mileage weight tax option. Any owner of a vehicle of the second division may elect to pay a mileage weight tax for such vehicle in lieu of the flat weight tax set out in Section 3–815. Such election shall be binding to the end of the registration year. Renewal of this election must be filed with the Secretary of State on or before July 1 of each registration period. In such event the owner shall, at the time of making such election, pay the $10 registration fee and the minimum guaranteed mileage weight tax, as hereinafter provided, which payment shall permit the owner to operate that vehicle the maximum mileage in this State hereinafter set forth. Any vehicle being operated on mileage plates cannot be operated outside of this State. In addition thereto, the owner of that vehicle shall pay a mileage weight tax at the following rates for each mile traveled in this State in excess of the maximum mileage provided under the minimum guaranteed basis:

BUS, TRUCK OR TRUCK TRACTOR

Gross Weight Vehicle and Load	Class	Minimum Guaranteed Mileage Weight Tax	Maximum Mileage Permitted Under Guaranteed Tax	Mileage Weight Tax for Mileage in excess of Guaranteed Mileage
12,000 lbs. or less	MD	$73	5,000	26 Mills
12,001 to 16,000 lbs.	MF	120	6,000	34 Mills
16,001 to 20,000 lbs.	MG	180	6,000	46 Mills
20,001 to 24,000 lbs.	MH	235	6,000	63 Mills
24,001 to 28,000 lbs.	MJ	315	7,000	63 Mills
28,001 to 32,000 lbs.	MK	385	7,000	83 Mills
32,001 to 36,000 lbs.	ML	485	7,000	99 Mills
36,001 to 40,000 lbs.	MN	615	7,000	128 Mills
40,001 to 45,000 lbs.	MP	695	7,000	139 Mills
45,001 to 54,999 lbs.	MR	853	7,000	156 Mills
55,000 to 59,500 lbs.	MS	920	7,000	178 Mills
59,501 to 64,000 lbs.	MT	985	7,000	195 Mills
64,001 to 73,280 lbs.	MV	1,173	7,000	225 Mills
73,281 to 77,000 lbs.	MX	1,328	7,000	258 Mills
77,001 to 80,000 lbs.	MZ	1,415	7,000	275 Mills

TRAILER

Gross Weight Vehicle and Load	Class	Minimum Guaranteed Mileage Weight Tax	Maximum Mileage Permitted Under Guaranteed Tax	Mileage Weight Tax for Mileage in excess of Guaranteed Mileage
14,000 lbs. or less	ME	$75	5,000	31 Mills
14,001 to 20,000 lbs.	MF	135	6,000	36 Mills
20,001 to 36,000 lbs.	ML	540	7,000	103 Mills
36,001 to 40,000 lbs.	MM	750	7,000	150 Mills

(a–1) A Special Hauling Vehicle is a vehicle or combination of vehicles of the second division registered under Section 3–813 transporting asphalt or concrete in the plastic state or a vehicle or combination of vehicles that are subject to the gross weight limitations in subsection (b) of Section 15–111 for which the owner of the vehicle or combination of vehicles has elected to pay, in addition to the registration fee in subsection (a), $125 to the Secretary of State for each registration year. The Secretary shall designate this class of vehicle as a Special Hauling Vehicle.

In preparing rate schedules on registration applications, the Secretary of State shall add to the above rates, the $10 registration fee. The Secretary may decline to accept any renewal filed after July 1st.

The number of axles necessary to carry the maximum load provided shall be determined from Chapter 15 of this Code.[1]

Every owner of a second division motor vehicle for which he has elected to pay a mileage weight tax shall keep a daily record upon forms prescribed by the Secretary of State, showing the mileage covered by that vehicle in this State. Such record shall contain the license number of the vehicle and the miles traveled by the vehicle in this State for each day of the calendar month. Such owner shall also maintain records of fuel consumed by each such motor vehicle and fuel purchases therefor. On or before the 10th day of January and July the owner shall certify to the Secretary of State upon forms prescribed therefor, summaries of his daily records which shall show the miles traveled by the vehicle in this State during the preceding 6 months and such other information as the Secretary of State may require. The daily record and fuel records shall be filed, preserved and available for audit for a period of 3 years. Any owner filing a return hereunder shall certify that such return is a true, correct and complete return. Any person who willfully makes a false return hereunder is guilty of perjury and shall be punished in the same manner and to the same extent as is provided therefor.

At the time of filing his return, each owner shall pay to the Secretary of State the proper amount of tax at the rate herein imposed.

Every owner of a vehicle of the second division who elects to pay on a mileage weight tax basis and who operates the vehicle within this State, shall file with the Secretary of State a bond in the amount of $500. The bond shall be in a form approved by the Secretary of State and with a surety company approved by the Illinois Department of Insurance to transact business in this State as surety, and shall be conditioned upon such applicant's paying to the State of Illinois all money becoming due by reason of the operation of the second division vehicle in this State, together with all penalties and interest thereon.

Upon notice from the Secretary that the registrant has failed to pay the excess mileage fees, the surety shall immediately pay the fees together with any penalties and interest thereon in an amount not to exceed the limits of the bond.

P.A. 76-1586, § 3-818, eff. July 1, 1970. Amended by P.A. 76-2150, § 1, eff. July 1, 1970; P.A. 77-1301, § 1, eff. Aug. 27, 1971; P.A. 77-2751, § 1, eff. Sept. 1, 1972; P.A. 78-255, § 61, eff. Oct. 1, 1973; P.A. 78-855, § 1, eff. Jan. 1, 1975; P.A. 78-1297, § 58, eff. March 4, 1975; P.A. 81-1440, § 1, eff. Sept. 4, 1980; P.A. 82-392, § 1, eff. Jan. 1, 1982; P.A. 83-12, § 1, eff. July 1, 1983; P.A. 83-449, § 1, eff. Jan. 1, 1984; P.A. 83-1362, Art. II, § 99, eff. Sept. 11, 1984; P.A. 84-986, § 1, eff. Sept. 25, 1985; P.A. 85-678, § 1, eff. July 1, 1989; P.A. 87-206, § 1, eff. Sept. 3, 1991; P.A. 88-403, § 5, eff. Jan. 1, 1994; P.A. 89-571, § 5, eff. July 26, 1996; P.A. 89-710, § 15, eff. Feb. 14, 1997; P.A. 91-37, § 40, eff. July 1, 1999; P.A. 91-499, § 5, eff. Aug. 13, 1999; P.A. 92-16, § 85, eff. June 28, 2001.

Formerly Ill.Rev.Stat.1991, ch. 95 ½, ¶ 3-818.

[1] 625 ILCS 5/15-100 et seq.

Section 2 of P.A. 82-392 approved Sept. 4, 1981, provided:

"This Act takes effect with the 1984 registration year."

Section 4 of P.A. 83-12, approved July 1, 1983, provided:

"Effective date. This Act takes effect as provided in this Section.

"The amendments to those portions of Sections 3-815(a), 3-818 and 3-819(b) of 'The Illinois Vehicle Code' in Section 1 of this Act which create the 'X', 'Z', 'MX', 'MZ', 'MM' and 'TN' registration classifications and the fees and taxes imposed for those classifications, the amendments to Sections 2-119, 3-401 and 3-802 of 'The Illinois Vehicle Code' in Section 1 of this Act, and the amendments to Chapter 15 of 'The Illinois Vehicle Code' in Section 1 of this Act take effect July 1, 1983.

"The remaining amendments to 'The Illinois Vehicle Code' in Section 1 of this Act take effect July 1, 1983 and apply beginning with the 1985 registration year, except that the amendments to Sections 3-813 through 3-816 and Section 3-819 apply beginning with the 1984 registration year for those vehicles registered on a calendar year basis only.

"The amendments to Chapters 13 and 18 of 'The Illinois Vehicle Code' in Section 1 of this Act take effect January 1, 1984.

"Section 2 of this Act takes effect on the first day of the next succeeding month which commences at least 30 days after the date on which this Act becomes law.

"Section 3 of this Act takes effect July 1, 1983.

"Section 3.1 of this Act takes effect January 1, 1984.

"This Section 4 takes effect upon its becoming a law."

5/3-819. Trailer; Flat weight tax.

§ 3-819. Trailer; Flat weight tax.

(a) Farm Trailer. Any farm trailer drawn by a motor vehicle of the second division registered under paragraph (a) or (c) of Section 3-815 and used exclusively by the owner for his own agricultural, horticultural or livestock raising operations and not used for hire, or any farm trailer utilized only in the transportation for-hire of seasonal, fresh, perishable fruit or vegetables from farm to the point of first processing, and any trailer used with a farm tractor that is not an implement of husbandry may be registered under this paragraph in lieu of registration under paragraph (b) of this Section upon the filing of a proper application and the payment of the $10 registration fee and the highway use tax herein for use of the public highways of this State, at the following rates which include the $10 registration fee:

SCHEDULE OF FEES AND TAXES

Gross Weight in Lbs. Including Vehicle and Maximum Load	Class	Total Amount each Fiscal Year
10,000 lbs. or less	VDD	$60
10,001 to 14,000 lbs.	VDE	106
14,001 to 20,000 lbs.	VDG	166
20,001 to 28,000 lbs.	VDJ	378
28,001 to 36,000 lbs.	VDL	650

An owner may only apply for and receive two farm trailer registrations.

(b) All other owners of trailers, other than apportionable trailers registered under Section 3-402.1 of this Code, used with a motor vehicle on the public highways, shall pay to the Secretary of State for each registration year a flat weight tax, for the use of the public highways of this State, at the following rates (which includes the registration fee of $10 required by Section 3-813):

SCHEDULE OF TRAILER FLAT WEIGHT TAX REQUIRED BY LAW

Gross Weight in Lbs. Including Vehicle and Maximum Load	Class	Total Fees each Fiscal Year
3,000 lbs. and less	TA	$18
5,000 lbs. and more than 3,000	TB	54
8,000 lbs. and more than 5,000	TC	58
10,000 lbs. and more than 8,000	TD	106
14,000 lbs. and more than 10,000	TE	170
20,000 lbs. and and more than 14,000	TG	258
32,000 lbs. and more than 20,000	TK	722
36,000 lbs. and more than 32,000	TL	1,082
40,000 lbs. and more than 36,000	TN	1,502

(c) The number of axles necessary to carry the maximum load provided shall be determined from Chapter 15 of this Code.[1]

P.A. 76-1586, § 3-819, eff. July 1, 1970. Amended by P.A. 76-2151, § 1, eff. July 1, 1970; P.A. 77-137, § 1, eff. July 1, 1972; P.A. 80-674, § 1, eff. Oct. 1, 1977; P.A. 82-392, § 1, eff. Jan. 1, 1982; P.A. 83-12, § 1, eff. July 1, 1983; P.A. 86-1340, § 1, eff. July 1, 1991; P.A. 87-206, § 1, eff. Sept. 3, 1991; P.A. 91-37, § 40, eff. July 1, 1999.

Formerly Ill.Rev.Stat.1991, ch. 95 ½, ¶ 3-819.

[1] 625 ILCS 5/15-100 et seq.

Section 2 of P.A. 82-392 approved Sept. 4, 1981, provided:

"This Act takes effect with the 1984 registration year."

Section 4 of P.A. 83-12, approved July 1, 1983, provided:

"Effective date. This Act takes effect as provided in this Section.

"The amendments to those portions of Sections 3–815(a), 3–818 and 3–819(b) of 'The Illinois Vehicle Code' in Section 1 of this Act which create the 'X', 'Z', 'MX', 'MZ', 'MM' and 'TN' registration classifications and the fees and taxes imposed for those classifications, the amendments to Sections 2–119, 3–401 and 3–802 of 'The Illinois Vehicle Code' in Section 1 of this Act, and the amendments to Chapter 15 of 'The Illinois Vehicle Code' in Section 1 of this Act take effect July 1, 1983.

"The remaining amendments to 'The Illinois Vehicle Code' in Section 1 of this Act take effect July 1, 1983 and apply beginning with the 1985 registration year, except that the amendments to Sections 3–813 through 3–816 and Section 3–819 apply beginning with the 1984 registration year for those vehicles registered on a calendar year basis only.

"The amendments to Chapters 13 and 18 of 'The Illinois Vehicle Code' in Section 1 of this Act take effect January 1, 1984.

"Section 2 of this Act takes effect on the first day of the next succeeding month which commences at least 30 days after the date on which this Act becomes law.

"Section 3 of this Act takes effect July 1, 1983.

"Section 3.1 of this Act takes effect January 1, 1984.

"This Section 4 takes effect upon its becoming a law."

5/3–820. Duplicate Number Plates

§ 3–820. Duplicate Number Plates. Upon filing in the Office of the Secretary of State an affidavit to the effect that an original number plate for a vehicle is lost, stolen or destroyed, a duplicate number plate shall be furnished upon payment of a fee of $6 for each duplicate plate and a fee of $9 for a pair of duplicate plates.

Upon filing in the Office of the Secretary of State an affidavit to the effect that an original registration sticker for a vehicle is lost, stolen or destroyed, a new registration sticker shall be furnished upon payment of a fee of $5.

The Secretary of State may, in his discretion, assign a new number plate or plates in lieu of a duplicate of the plate or plates so lost, stolen or destroyed, but such assignment of a new plate or plates shall not affect the right of the owner to secure a reassignment of his original registration number in the manner provided in this Act. The fee for one new number plate shall be $6, and for a pair of new number plates, $9.

For the administration of this Section, the Secretary shall consider the loss of a registration plate or plates with properly affixed registration stickers as requiring the payment of either $11 for each duplicate or $14 for a pair of duplicate plates or $19 for a pair of duplicate plates if stickers are required on both front and rear registration plates.

P.A. 76–1586, § 3–820, eff. July 1, 1970. Amended by P.A. 78–143, § 1, eff. Jan. 1, 1972; P.A. 80–230, § 1, eff. Oct. 1, 1977; P.A. 80–1185, § 1, eff. March 8, 1978; P.A. 83–12, § 1, eff. July 1, 1983; P.A. 91–37, § 40, eff. July 1, 1999.

Formerly Ill.Rev.Stat.1991, ch. 95 ½, ¶ 3–820.

Section 4 of P.A. 83–12, approved July 1, 1983, provided:

"Effective date. This Act takes effect as provided in this Section.

"The amendments to those portions of Sections 3–815(a), 3–818 and 3–819(b) of 'The Illinois Vehicle Code' in Section 1 of this Act which create the 'X', 'Z', 'MX', 'MZ', 'MM' and 'TN' registration classifications and the fees and taxes imposed for those classifications, the amendments to Sections 2–119, 3–401 and 3–802 of 'The Illinois Vehicle Code' in Section 1 of this Act, and the amendments to Chapter 15 of 'The Illinois Vehicle Code' in Section 1 of this Act take effect July 1, 1983.

"The remaining amendments to 'The Illinois Vehicle Code' in Section 1 of this Act take effect July 1, 1983 and apply beginning with the 1985 registration year, except that the amendments to Sections 3–813 through 3–816 and Section 3–819 apply beginning with the 1984 registration year for those vehicles registered on a calendar year basis only.

"The amendments to Chapters 13 and 18 of 'The Illinois Vehicle Code' in Section 1 of this Act take effect January 1, 1984.

"Section 2 of this Act takes effect on the first day of the next succeeding month which commences at least 30 days after the date on which this Act becomes law.

"Section 3 of this Act takes effect July 1, 1983.

"Section 3.1 of this Act takes effect January 1, 1984.

"This Section 4 takes effect upon its becoming a law."

5/3–821. Miscellaneous Registration and Title Fees

§ 3–821. Miscellaneous Registration and Title Fees.

(a) The fee to be paid to the Secretary of State for the following certificates, registrations or evidences of proper registration, or for corrected or duplicate documents shall be in accordance with the following schedule:

Certificate of Title, except for an all-terrain vehicle or off- highway motorcycle	$65
Certificate of Title for an all-terrain vehicle or off-highway motorcycle	$30
Certificate of Title for an all-terrain vehicle or off-highway motorcycle used for production agriculture, or accepted by a dealer in trade	13
Transfer of Registration or any evidence of proper registration	15
Duplicate Registration Card for plates or other evidence of proper registration	3
Duplicate Registration Sticker or Stickers, each	5
Duplicate Certificate of Title	65
Corrected Registration Card or Card for other evidence of proper registration	3
Corrected Certificate of Title	65
Salvage Certificate	4
Fleet Reciprocity Permit	15
Prorate Decal	1
Prorate Backing Plate	3

There shall be no fee paid for a Junking Certificate.

(b) The Secretary may prescribe the maximum service charge to be imposed upon an applicant for renewal of a registration by any person authorized by law to receive and remit or transmit to the Secretary such renewal application and fees therewith.

(c) If a check is delivered to the Office of the Secretary of State as payment of any fee or tax under this Code, and such check is not honored by the bank on which it is drawn for any reason, the registrant or other person tendering the check remains liable for the payment of such fee or tax. The Secretary of State may assess a service charge of $19 in addition to the fee or tax due and owing for all dishonored checks.

If the total amount then due and owing exceeds the sum of $50 and has not been paid in full within 60 days from the date such fee or tax became due to the Secretary of State, the Secretary of State shall assess a penalty of 25% of such amount remaining unpaid.

All amounts payable under this Section shall be computed to the nearest dollar.

(d) The minimum fee and tax to be paid by any applicant for apportionment of a fleet of vehicles under this Code shall be $15 if the application was filed on or before the date specified by the Secretary together with fees and taxes due. If an application and the fees or taxes due are filed after the date specified by the Secretary, the Secretary may prescribe the payment of interest at the rate of ½ of 1% per month or fraction thereof after such due date and a minimum of $8.

(e) Trucks, truck tractors, truck tractors with loads, and motor buses, any one of which having a combined total weight in excess of 12,000 lbs. shall file an application for a Fleet Reciprocity Permit issued by the Secretary of State. This permit shall be in the possession of any driver operating a vehicle on Illinois highways. Any foreign licensed vehicle of the second division operating at any time in Illinois without a Fleet Reciprocity Permit or other proper Illinois registration, shall subject the operator to the penalties provided in Section 3-834 of this Code. For the purposes of this Code, "Fleet Reciprocity Permit" means any second division motor vehicle with a foreign license and used only in interstate transportation of goods. The fee for such permit shall be $15 per fleet which shall include all vehicles of the fleet being registered.

(f) For purposes of this Section, "all-terrain vehicle or off-highway motorcycle used for production agriculture" means any all-terrain vehicle or off-highway motorcycle used in the raising of or the propagation of livestock, crops for sale for human consumption, crops for livestock consumption, and production seed stock grown for the propagation of feed grains and the husbandry of animals or for the purpose of providing a food product, including the husbandry of blood stock as a main source of providing a food product. "All-terrain vehicle or off-highway motorcycle used in production agriculture" also means any all-terrain vehicle or off-highway motorcycle used in animal husbandry, floriculture, aquaculture, horticulture, and viticulture.

P.A. 76-1586, § 1, eff. July 1, 1970. Amended by P.A. 76-2152, § 3-821, eff. July 1, 1970; P.A. 77-364, § 1, eff. July 23, 1971; P.A. 77-649, § 1, eff. Jan. 1, 1972; P.A. 77-2829, § 40, eff. Dec. 22, 1972; P.A. 78-255, § 61, eff. Oct. 1, 1973; P.A. 78-859, § 1, eff. Jan. 1, 1974; P.A. 78-1297, § 58, eff. March 4, 1975; P.A. 79-718, § 1, eff. Oct. 1, 1975; P.A. 79-1458, § 1, eff. Sept. 1, 1976; P.A. 80-230, § 1, eff. Oct. 1, 1977; P.A. 80-1185, § 1, eff. March 8, 1978; P.A. 81-886, § 1, eff. July 1, 1980; P.A. 83-12, § 1, eff. July 1, 1983; P.A. 83-953, § 1, eff. Dec. 2, 1983; P.A. 86-466, § 1, eff. Jan. 1, 1990; P.A. 86-1019, § 2, eff. Jan. 1, 1990; P.A. 87-1225, § 2, eff. Dec. 22, 1992; P.A. 88-78, § 15, eff. Sept. 7, 1993; P.A. 90-287, § 100, eff. Jan. 1, 1998; P.A. 90-774, § 5, eff. Aug. 14, 1998; P.A. 91-37, § 40, eff. July 1, 1999; P.A. 91-441, § 10, eff. Jan. 1, 2000; P.A. 92-16, § 85, eff. June 28, 2001.

Formerly Ill.Rev.Stat.1991, ch. 95 ½, ¶ 3-821.

Section 4 of P.A. 83-12, approved July 1, 1983, provided:

"Effective date. This Act takes effect as provided in this Section.

"The amendments to those portions of Sections 3-815(a), 3-818 and 3-819(b) of 'The Illinois Vehicle Code' in Section 1 of this Act which create the 'X', 'Z', 'MX', 'MZ', 'MM' and 'TN' registration classifications and the fees and taxes imposed for those classifications, the amendments to Sections 2-119, 3-401 and 3-802 of 'The Illinois Vehicle Code' in Section 1 of this Act, and the amendments to Chapter 15 of 'The Illinois Vehicle Code' in Section 1 of this Act take effect July 1, 1983.

"The remaining amendments to 'The Illinois Vehicle Code' in Section 1 of this Act take effect July 1, 1983 and apply beginning with the 1985 registration year, except that the amendments to Sections 3-813 through 3-816 and Section 3-819 apply beginning with the 1984 registration year for those vehicles registered on a calendar year basis only.

"The amendments to Chapters 13 and 18 of 'The Illinois Vehicle Code' in Section 1 of this Act take effect January 1, 1984.

"Section 2 of this Act takes effect on the first day of the next succeeding month which commences at least 30 days after the date on which this Act becomes law.

"Section 3 of this Act takes effect July 1, 1983.

"Section 3.1 of this Act takes effect January 1, 1984.

"This Section 4 takes effect upon its becoming a law."

5/3-821.1. Fees for record searches

§ 3-821.1. Fees for record searches. The fee to be paid to the Secretary of State by any towing service requesting a record search shall be in the amount the Secretary of State prescribes by rule.

P.A. 76-1586, § 3-821.1, added by P.A. 89-433, § 5, eff. Dec. 15, 1995.

5/3-822. Fees relating to security interests

§ 3-822. Fees relating to security interests. There shall be paid to the Secretary of State a filing fee of $2.00 for the filing of a notice of a security interest and for the filing of a release of a security interest for each motor vehicle subject to such security interest.

P.A. 76-1586, § 3-822, eff. July 1, 1970.

Formerly Ill.Rev.Stat.1991, ch. 95 ½, ¶ 3-822.

5/3-823. § 3-823. Deleted by P.A. 83-148, § 1, eff. Aug. 29, 1983

The provisions of this section, which related to title or registration search fees, were completely stricken out by P.A. 83-148, § 1. The section was derived from:

5/3-824. When fees returnable

§ 3-824. When fees returnable.

(a) Whenever any application to the Secretary of State is accompanied by any fee as required by law and such application is refused or rejected, said fee shall be returned to said applicant.

(b) Whenever the Secretary of State collects any fee not required to be paid under the provisions of this Act, the same shall be refunded to the person paying the same upon application therefor made within 6 months after the date of such payment, except as follows: (1) whenever a refund is determined to be due and owing as a result of an audit, by this State or any other state or province, in accordance with Section 2-124 of this Code, of a prorate or apportion license fee payment pursuant to any reciprocal compact or agreement between this State and any other state or province, and the Secretary for any reason fails to promptly make such refund, the licensee shall have one year from the date of the notification of the audit result to file, with the Secretary, an application for refund found to be due and owing as a result of such audit; and (2) whenever a person eligible for a reduced registration fee pursuant to Section 3-806.3 of this Code has paid in excess of the reduced registration fee owed, the refund applicant shall have 2 years from the date of overpayment to apply with the Secretary for a refund of that part of payment made in excess of the established reduced registration fee.

(c) Whenever a person dies after making application for registration, application for a refund of the registration fees and taxes may be made if the vehicle is then sold or disposed of so that the registration plates, registration sticker and card are never used. The Secretary of State shall refund the registration fees and taxes upon receipt within 6 months after the application for registration of an application for refund accompanied with the unused registration plates or registration sticker and card and proof of both the death of the applicant and the sale or disposition of the vehicle.

(d) Any application for refund received after the times specified in this Section shall be denied and the applicant in order to receive a refund must apply to the Court of Claims.

(e) The Secretary of State is authorized to maintain a two signature revolving checking account with a suitable commercial bank for the purpose of depositing and withdrawal-for-return those monies received and determined upon receipt to be in excess of the amount or amounts required by law.

(f) Refunds on audits performed by Illinois or another member of the International Registration Plan shall be made in accordance with the procedures as set forth in the agreement.

P.A. 76-1586, § 3-824, eff. July 1, 1970. Amended by P.A. 77-325, § 1, eff. July 22, 1971; P.A. 79-1107, § 1, eff. Sept. 26, 1975; P.A. 80-230, § 1, eff. Oct. 1, 1977; P.A. 83-1276, § 1, eff. Jan. 1, 1985; P.A. 86-131, § 1, eff. Jan. 1, 1990; P.A. 92-69, § 5, eff. July 12, 2001.

Formerly Ill.Rev.Stat.1991, ch. 95 ½, ¶ 3-824.

5/3-824.5. Applicability of fee and tax increases

§ 3-824.5. Applicability of fee and tax increases. The fee and tax increases in this Code made by this amendatory Act of the 91st General Assembly that apply to registrations apply to registration year 2001 and thereafter. The registration fees and taxes in existence on the day prior to the effective date of this amendatory Act of the 91st General Assembly apply throughout registration year 2000. All other fee and tax increases in this Code made by this amendatory Act of the 91st General Assembly shall apply beginning January 1, 2000 and thereafter.

P.A. 76-1586, § 3-824.5, added by P.A. 91-37, § 40, eff. July 1, 1999.

5/3-825. Certificate of Safety

§ 3-825. Certificate of Safety. Every application for registration of a motor vehicle which is subject to vehicle inspection may be accompanied by proof that a valid and unrevoked Certificate of Safety has been issued for each such vehicle. The Secretary of State may at his discretion decline to register any such vehicle unless the application is accompanied with such proof.

P.A. 76-1586, § 3-825, eff. July 1, 1970. Amended by P.A. 76-1997, § 1, eff. July 1, 1970.

Formerly Ill.Rev.Stat.1991, ch. 95 ½, ¶ 3-825.

5/3-826. § 3-826. Repealed by P.A. 78-433, § 1, eff. Oct. 1, 1973

5/3-827. § 3-827. Repealed by P.A. 88-415, § 15, eff. August 20, 1993

5/3-828. Lien for violations

§ 3-828. Lien for violations. Any vehicle used in violation of the provisions of this Act shall be subject to a lien for the full amount of all unpaid registration fees, flat weight taxes, and penalties. Such lien shall not release the offender from the full payment of all such fees, taxes, penalties and damages. The lien shall attach at the time of operation of any such vehicle within this State and shall remain effective until all unpaid registration fees, flat weight taxes, penalties and audit fees are paid, or until the vehicle is sold for the payment thereof. Such liens shall be superior to any other lien except that:

(a) no lien for any amounts due or assessed pursuant to this Section shall be enforceable against any vehicle which prior to such assessment had been transferred in good faith to a bona fide transferee for value;

(b) the lien of any amounts due or assessed shall be subject to a prior lien of any indebtedness existing against such vehicle which is noted on the certificate of title of such vehicle issued under this Act, or as to a vehicle from another jurisdiction, if written notice thereof is filed with the Secretary of State before such lien becomes operative and if

(1) Such prior indebtedness was incurred in good faith to secure all or a portion of the purchase price of such vehicle, and

(2) Such prior indebtedness is secured by a chattel mortgage or conditional sales agreement duly filed or perfected in this State pursuant to law and such chattel mortgage or conditional sales was not given directly or indirectly, to any officer, director or shareholder of a corporation, or to a partner of a partnership, or to a trustee or beneficiary of a trust, owning or having the lawful use or control of such vehicle, whether as a purchase money mortgage or otherwise.

The lien imposed under this Section shall be enforceable as to any equity after the encumbrance of any such chattel mortgage or conditional sales contract, and in the event any such vehicle subject to a lien hereunder is repossessed by a chattel mortgagee or a conditional vendor, such vehicle shall not be sold at any public or private sale unless at least 5 days written notice by registered mail is served upon the Secretary of State.

The Secretary of State, upon perfecting a prior lien hereunder for any flat weight taxes required to be paid under Section 3-815 may in his discretion waive the requirement for the surety bond specified in Section 3-816, providing that the said prior lien is so noted on the certificate of title for such vehicle or vehicles.

Any surety making payment of a second installment of taxes under Section 3-816 of this Act, may impress a lien similar to that of the Secretary of State, and such lien may be noted on title records and documents. The surety shall, however, pay any statutory fees therefor.

P.A. 76-1586, § 3-828, eff. July 1, 1970. Amended by P.A. 77-1464, § 1, eff. Sept. 7, 1971.

Formerly Ill.Rev.Stat.1991, ch. 95 ½, ¶ 3-828.

5/3-829. Foreclosure of lien—Service of processes—Notices

§ 3-829. Foreclosure of lien—Service of processes—Notices. In any action to foreclose the lien imposed by Section 3-828 service of process on all known owners and parties in interest shall be made in the manner now prescribed by law, and, as to all unknown owners and parties in interest, notice of the pendency of such action shall be given by publication in some newspaper of general circulation published in the county where the suit is pending, or if there is no such newspaper, then in a newspaper of general circulation published in an adjoining county in this State and having a general circulation in the county in which such suit is pending. Such notice shall contain the title of the court; the title of the case, showing the names of all known owners and parties in interest; a statement that publication is being made as to unknown owners and parties in interest; and the date on or after which default may be entered against the defendants.

P.A. 76-1586, § 3-829, eff. July 1, 1970.

Formerly Ill.Rev.Stat.1991, ch. 95 ½, ¶ 3-829.

5/3-830. Notice of pendency of action—Time and number of publications—Default

§ 3-830. Notice of pendency of action—Time and number of publications—Default. The notice required by Section 3-829 may be given at any time after commencement of the suit, and shall be published at least once each week for 3 successive weeks. No default or other proceeding shall be taken against any defendant as to whom publication was made and who does not appear, unless the first publication is at least 30 days prior to the time when the default or other proceeding is sought to be taken.

P.A. 76-1586, § 3-830, eff. July 1, 1970.

Formerly Ill.Rev.Stat.1991, ch. 95 ½, ¶ 3-830.

5/3-831. Secretary to institute suits

§ 3-831. Secretary to institute suits. The Secretary of State may institute, in the name of the People of the State of Illinois, a suit or suits in the circuit court to enforce the collection of any fees, taxes, interest, penalties or damages provided for in this Act, or to enjoin violations of this Act.

P.A. 76-1586, § 3-831, eff. July 1, 1970. Amended by P.A. 77-1541, § 1, eff. Sept. 17, 1971; P.A. 79-1358, § 43, eff. Oct. 1, 1976.

Formerly Ill.Rev.Stat.1991, ch. 95 ½, ¶ 3-831.

5/3-832. Service of process

§ 3-832. Service of process. The operation, with the consent of the owner, upon the highways of the State of any motor vehicle of the second division shall be deemed an appointment by the owner of the driver of the vehicle as the owner's agent upon whom may be served process in any civil or criminal proceeding against such owner based upon failure to register, improper registration or failure to pay the proper fees or taxes with respect to any motor vehicles of the second division of such owner.

P.A. 76-1586, § 3-832, eff. July 1, 1970.

Formerly Ill.Rev.Stat.1991, ch. 95 ½, ¶ 3-832.

5/3-833. Unlawful acts

§ 3-833. Unlawful acts. It shall be unlawful for any person to own or operate a vehicle on the public highways of this State without complying with this Act.

P.A. 76-1586, § 3-833, eff. July 1, 1970.

Formerly Ill.Rev.Stat.1991, ch. 95 ½, ¶ 3-833.

5/3-834. Violations of this Chapter 3

§ 3-834. Violations of this Chapter 3.

(a) It is unlawful for any person to violate any of the provisions of this Chapter 3, except as provided in paragraph (b) of this Section, unless such violation is by this Code or other law of this State declared to be a felony.

(b) Every person convicted of a misdemeanor for a violation of any of the provisions of this Chapter 3 for which another penalty is not provided shall for a first and second conviction be guilty of a petty offense; upon a third or subsequent conviction within one year after the first conviction such person shall be guilty of a Class C misdemeanor. Compliance with the registration provisions of this Code after apprehension or arrest shall not excuse imposition of the penalties herein provided nor be cause for dismissal of the arrest or of the summons nor be a basis for setting aside a conviction therefor.

P.A. 76-1586, § 3-834, eff. July 1, 1970. Amended by P.A. 77-76, § 1, eff. Jan. 1, 1972; P.A. 77-2720, § 1, eff. Jan. 1, 1973; P.A. 78-255, § 61, eff. Oct. 1, 1973; P.A. 80-911, § 1, eff. Oct. 1, 1977; P.A. 82-392, § 1, eff. Jan. 1, 1982; P.A. 84-980, § 1, eff. Sept. 25, 1985; P.A. 88-476, § 2, eff. July 1, 1994.

Formerly Ill.Rev.Stat.1991, ch. 95 ½, ¶ 3-834.

Section 2 of P.A. 82-392 approved Sept. 4, 1981, provided:
"This Act takes effect with the 1984 registration year."

ARTICLE IX. REMITTANCE AGENTS

Date Effective

Article IX was added by P.A. 76-1705, § 1, effective July 1, 1970.

5/3-900. § 3-900. Repealed by P.A. 90-89, § 20, eff. Jan. 1, 1998

5/3-901. Purpose of Article

§ 3-901. Purpose of Article. Many persons throughout the State hold themselves out to the public as being engaged in, and have engaged in, accepting money from members of the public for remittance to the State of Illinois, and its licensing and taxing agencies in payment of vehicle taxes or vehicle license or registration fees. Some of these persons have failed to make such remittance with the consequent loss to the remitters. It is the public policy of this State that its people be protected against such hazards.

P.A. 76-1586, § 3-901, added by P.A. 76-1705, § 1, eff. July 1, 1970.

Formerly Ill.Rev.Stat.1991, ch. 95 ½, ¶ 3-901.

5/3-902. Application of Article

§ 3-902. Application of Article. This Article shall not apply to (1) any person who accepts for remittance only such sums as he is authorized to collect by the remittee as its agent, and (2) to any person who, in connection with the issuance of a license to him to conduct a business in this State, shall have filed, pursuant to a statutory requirement, a surety bond covering the proper discharge of any liability incurred by him in connection with the acceptance for remittance of money for the purposes designated in the Article pursuant to which he is licensed; provided he does not accept any money for remittance, as a remittance agent, the proper transmittal of which is not covered by said bond.

P.A. 76–1586, § 3–902, added by P.A. 76–1705, § 1, eff. July 1, 1970.

Formerly Ill.Rev.Stat.1991, ch. 95 ½, ¶ 3–902.

5/3–903. License

§ 3–903. License. It shall be unlawful for any person, either as principal or agent, to act as a "remittance agent" in the State of Illinois without first having obtained or renewed, as the case may be, a license and posted a bond, as hereafter provided.

P.A. 76–1586, § 3–903, added by P.A. 76–1705, § 1, eff. July 1, 1970.

Formerly Ill.Rev.Stat.1991, ch. 95 ½, ¶ 3–903.

5/3–904. Application—Contents—Affidavits

§ 3–904. Application—Contents—Affidavits. Any person who desires to act as a "remittance agent" shall first file with the Secretary of State a written application for a license. The application shall be under oath and shall contain the following:

1. The name and address of the applicant.

2. The address of each location at which the applicant intends to act as a remittance agent.

3. The applicant's business, occupation or profession.

4. A statement disclosing whether he has been involved in any civil or criminal litigation and if so, the material facts pertaining thereto.

The application shall be accompanied by the affidavits of two persons residing in the city or town of such applicant's residence. Such affiants shall state that they have known the applicant for a period of at least two years; that the applicant is of good moral character and that his reputation for honesty and business integrity in the community in which he resides is good. If the applicant is not an individual, the requirements of this paragraph shall apply to each of its officers or members.

P.A. 76–1586, § 3–904, added by P.A. 76–1705, § 1, eff. July 1, 1970. Amended by P.A. 83–387, § 1, eff. Jan. 1, 1984.

Formerly Ill.Rev.Stat.1991, ch. 95 ½, ¶ 3–904.

5/3–905. Bond; Fee; Duration of license

§ 3–905. Bond; Fee; Duration of license. Such applicant shall, with his application, deposit with the Secretary of State a bond as hereinafter provided, for each location at which the applicant intends to act as a remittance agent. The application shall be accompanied by the payment of a license fee in the sum of $50.00 (or $25.00 if such application is filed after July 1) for each location at which he proposes to act as a remittance agent. If the applicant shall have complied with all of the requirements of this Section and the Secretary of State shall find after investigation that the applicant is financially sound and of good business integrity, he shall issue the required license. Such license shall terminate on December 31 of the year for which it is issued, but upon application prior to November 15 of any year for which a license is in effect may be renewed for the next succeeding calendar year. Such application shall be accompanied by the payment of an annual license fee of $50.00 for each location at which the applicant proposes to act as a remittance agent and the posting of the bond herein provided, for each such location.

The bond required by this Section shall be for the term of the license, or renewal thereof, for which application is made, and shall run to the People of the State of Illinois, with surety by a bonding or insurance company authorized to do business in this State, to be approved by the Secretary of State. It shall be conditioned upon the proper transmittal of all remittances by the applicant as a remittance agent and the performance of all undertakings in connection therewith. It shall be in the minimum sum of $10,000, or in an amount equal to the aggregate sum of money transmitted to the State by the applicant during the highest 15 day period in the fiscal year immediately preceding the one for which application is made (rounded to the nearest $1,000), whichever is the greater. However, for the purpose of determining the bond requirements hereunder, remittances made by applicants in the form of money orders or checks which are made payable directly to the Secretary of State or the Illinois Department of Revenue by the remitter, shall not be considered in the aggregate. The bond requirement of this Section shall not apply to banks, savings and loan associations, and credit unions chartered by the State of Illinois or the United States; provided that the banks, savings and loan associations, and credit unions provide to the Secretary of State an affidavit stating that the bank, savings and loan association, or credit union is sufficiently bonded to meet the requirements as required above. Such affidavit shall be signed by an officer of the bank, savings and loan association, or credit union and shall be notarized.

P.A. 76–1586, § 3–905, added by P.A. 76–1705, § 1, eff. July 1, 1970. Amended by P.A. 81–322, § 1, eff. Jan. 1, 1980; P.A. 83–449, § 1, eff. Jan. 1, 1984; P.A. 87–206, § 1, eff. Sept. 3, 1991; P.A. 88–470, § 10, eff. Sept. 1, 1993; P.A. 88–643, § 935, eff. Jan. 1, 1995.

Formerly Ill.Rev.Stat.1991, ch. 95 ½, ¶ 3–905.

P.A. 88–643 incorporated the amendment by P.A. 88–470.

5/3–906. Denial

§ 3–906. Denial. The Secretary of State shall deny any application under this Article upon any of the following grounds:

(1) That the application contains any false or fraudulent statement; or

(2) That the applicant has failed to furnish the information required by the Secretary or to file a bond as required; or

(3) That the required fee has not been paid; or

(4) That the applicant has failed to remit fees to the Secretary of State; or

(5) That the applicant has engaged in fraudulent practices; or

(6) That the applicant or a member of his immediate family is an employee of the Secretary of State; or

(7) That the Secretary of State is authorized under any other provision of law.

If the Secretary of State denies the application for a license, or renewal thereof, or revokes a license, he shall so order in writing and notify the applicant thereof by certified mail. Upon the denial of an application for a license, or renewal thereof, he shall return the license fee. No application shall be denied unless the applicant has had an opportunity for a fair hearing in connection therewith.

P.A. 76–1586, § 3–906, added by P.A. 76–1705, § 1, eff. July 1, 1970. Amended by P.A. 77–84, § 1, eff. Jan. 1, 1972.

Formerly Ill.Rev.Stat.1991, ch. 95 ½, ¶ 3–906.

5/3-907. Suspension or revocation

§ 3-907. Suspension or revocation. Such license may be suspended or revoked by the Secretary of State for the violation of any provision of this Act or any rule or regulation of the Secretary of State and for any reason which, had it existed or been known to the Secretary of State at the time of the filing of the application for such license, would have been good cause for the denial of such application. A licensee may, upon receipt of an order of suspension or revocation seek a hearing to review such order.

P.A. 76-1586, § 3-907, added by P.A. 76-1705, § 1, eff. July 1, 1970. Amended by P.A. 77-84, § 1, eff. Jan. 1, 1972.

Formerly Ill.Rev.Stat.1991, ch. 95 ½, ¶ 3-907.

5/3-908. Location

§ 3-908. Location. A licensee may not do business at a location not set forth in his license, but the Secretary of State may issue an amended license covering an additional location or locations, upon application therefor, the payment of an additional license fee and the posting of the required bond for each such location.

P.A. 76-1586, § 3-908, added by P.A. 76-1705, § 1, eff. July 1, 1970.

Formerly Ill.Rev.Stat.1991, ch. 95 ½, ¶ 3-908.

5/3-909. Money accepted for remittance—Obligations of licensee

§ 3-909. Money accepted for remittance—Obligations of licensee. Each licensee shall forward to the remittee all money accepted for remittance not later than the fifth calendar day after the date upon which such money was received by the licensee, and shall promptly fulfill any other obligation it has undertaken in connection therewith.

P.A. 76-1586, § 3-909, added by P.A. 76-1705, § 1, eff. July 1, 1970.

Formerly Ill.Rev.Stat.1991, ch. 95 ½, ¶ 3-909.

5/3-910. Records of transactions

§ 3-910. Records of transactions. Each licensee shall maintain for a period of three years the following records with reference to each transaction involving a remittance:

1. The address of the location at which the transaction occurred.
2. The name and address of the remitter.
3. The name and address of the remittee.
4. The purpose of the remittance.
5. The amount of money received for remittance.
6. The date of receipt of the money for remittance by the licensee.
7. The date such money was forwarded to the remittee.
8. If applicable, the date the license plate, vehicle tax sticker, license or other instrument issued by the remittee, was delivered to the remitter by the licensee.

P.A. 76-1586, § 3-910, added by P.A. 76-1705, § 1, eff. July 1, 1970.

Formerly Ill.Rev.Stat.1991, ch. 95 ½, ¶ 3-910.

5/3-911. Examination of business

§ 3-911. Examination of business. The Secretary of State or any of his representatives designated by him may examine the business of any person who acts, or may be acting, as a remittance agent, to determine whether such person is complying with the provisions of this Act and with such rules and regulations as may be promulgated by the Secretary of State pursuant to its provisions. For that purpose, the Secretary of State or his representatives shall have free access to the offices, places of business, and records of any such person.

P.A. 76-1586, § 3-911, added by P.A. 76-1705, § 1, eff. July 1, 1970.

Formerly Ill.Rev.Stat.1991, ch. 95 ½, ¶ 3-911.

5/3-912. Rules and regulations

§ 3-912. Rules and regulations. The Secretary of State may make such rules, regulations, direction, orders, decisions and findings as may be necessary for the enforcement of this Act and the purposes sought to be attained herein.

P.A. 76-1586, § 3-912, added by P.A. 76-1705, § 1, eff. July 1, 1970.

Formerly Ill.Rev.Stat.1991, ch. 95 ½, ¶ 3-912.

5/3-913. Hearing—Subpoenas

§ 3-913. Hearing—Subpoenas. Hearings under this Article shall be governed by Section 2-118 of this Act and the Administrative Review Law as amended,[1] shall apply to and govern all proceedings for judicial review of any final order issued by the Secretary of State. For the purposes of this Act, the Secretary of State, or the hearing officer as hereinafter provided, has power to require by subpoena the attendance and testimony of witnesses, and the production of all documentary evidence relating to any matter under hearing pursuant to this Act, and shall issue such subpoenas at the request of an interested party. The hearing officer may sign subpoenas in the name of the Secretary of State.

The Secretary of State may, in his discretion, direct that any hearing pursuant to this Act, shall be held before a competent and qualified agent of the Secretary of State, whom the Secretary of State shall designate as the hearing officer in such matter. The Secretary of State and the hearing officer are hereby empowered to, and shall, administer oaths and affirmations to all witnesses appearing before them. The hearing officer, upon the conclusion of the hearing before him, shall certify the evidence to the Secretary of State, and may make recommendations in connection therewith.

Any Circuit Court of this State, within the jurisdiction of which such hearing is carried on, may, in case of contumacy, or refusal of a witness to obey a subpoena, issue an order requiring such witness to appear before the Secretary of State, or the hearing officer, or to produce documentary evidence, or to give testimony touching the matter in question, and any failure to obey such order of the court may be punished by such court as a contempt thereof.

P.A. 76-1586, § 3-913, added by P.A. 76-1705, § 1, eff. July 1, 1970. Amended by P.A. 77-84, § 1, eff. Jan. 1, 1972; P.A. 82-783, Art. XI, § 140, eff. July 13, 1982.

Formerly Ill.Rev.Stat.1991, ch. 95 ½, ¶ 3-913.

[1] 735 ILCS 5/3-101 et seq.

5/3-914. Violations—Injunction

§ 3-914. Violations—Injunction. The violation of any provision of this Act by any remittance agent may be restrained by the issuance of an injunction by the circuit court, against him and any other person who shall aid or abet him in such violation, upon filing of a complaint by any person adversely affected thereby, the State's Attorney of such county, or by the Attorney General of the State of Illinois.

P.A. 76–1586, § 3–914, added by P.A. 76–1705, § 1, eff. July 1, 1970. Amended by P.A. 79–1358, § 43, eff. Oct. 1, 1976.

Formerly Ill.Rev.Stat.1991, ch. 95 ½, ¶ 3–914.

5/3–915. Violations

§ 3–915. Any person who violates, or who aids or abets another in the violation, of any provision of this Act or any rule or regulation promulgated thereunder, or does any act prohibited by this Act, or who fails, neglects, or refuses to perform any duty required by any provision of this Act or rule or regulation of the Secretary of State, within the time prescribed by the Secretary of State, or who fails, neglects, or refuses to obey any lawful order given or made by the Secretary of State, shall be guilty of a Class B misdemeanor, and each such act, failure, neglect, or refusal shall constitute a separate and distinct offense.

P.A. 76–1586, § 3–915, added by P.A. 76–1705, § 1, eff. July 1, 1970. Amended by P.A. 77–2720, § 1, eff. Jan. 1, 1973.

Formerly Ill.Rev.Stat.1991, ch. 95 ½, ¶ 3–915.

5/3–916. Issuance of license—Effect

§ 3–916. Issuance of license—Effect. The issuance of a license pursuant to the provisions of this Act shall not be construed to grant to any remittance agent the authority to act as agent for the State of Illinois or any of its instrumentalities or political subdivisions, or for any of their officials or for any other person.

P.A. 76–1586, § 3–916, added by P.A. 76–1705, § 1, eff. July 1, 1970.

Formerly Ill.Rev.Stat.1991, ch. 95 ½, ¶ 3–916.

5/3–917. Recovery of damages

§ 3–917. Recovery of damages. Any person who shall have been damaged by reason of the failure of any "remittance agent" to fulfill the conditions of any bond filed pursuant to the provisions of this Act may maintain a suit thereon to recover his damages and his reasonable attorney's fees, against such "remittance agent" or his surety, or both: provided, however, the aggregate liability of the surety to all such persons shall, in no event, exceed the sum of such bond.

P.A. 76–1586, § 3–917, added by P.A. 76–1705, § 1, eff. July 1, 1970.

Formerly Ill.Rev.Stat.1991, ch. 95 ½, ¶ 3–917.

ARTICLE X. VEHICLE USE TAX

Date Effective

Article X was added by P.A. 81–3, 2nd Sp.Sess., eff. Jan. 1, 1980.

5/3–1001. Imposition of tax; exceptions

§ 3–1001. A tax is hereby imposed on the privilege of using, in this State, any motor vehicle as defined in Section 1–146 of this Code acquired by gift, transfer, or purchase, and having a year model designation preceding the year of application for title by 5 or fewer years prior to October 1, 1985 and 10 or fewer years on and after October 1, 1985 and prior to January 1, 1988. On and after January 1, 1988, the tax shall apply to all motor vehicles without regard to model year. Except that the tax shall not apply

(i) if the use of the motor vehicle is otherwise taxed under the Use Tax Act; [1]

(ii) if the motor vehicle is bought and used by a governmental agency or a society, association, foundation or institution organized and operated exclusively for charitable, religious or educational purposes;

(iii) if the use of the motor vehicle is not subject to the Use Tax Act by reason of subsection (a), (b), (c), (d), (e) or (f) of Section 3–55 of that Act [2] dealing with the prevention of actual or likely multistate taxation;

(iv) to implements of husbandry;

(v) when a junking certificate is issued pursuant to Section 3–117(a) of this Code;

(vi) when a vehicle is subject to the replacement vehicle tax imposed by Section 3–2001 of this Act;

(vii) when the transfer is a gift to a beneficiary in the administration of an estate and the beneficiary is a surviving spouse.

Prior to January 1, 1988, the rate of tax shall be 5% of the selling price for each purchase of a motor vehicle covered by Section 3–1001 of this Code. Except as hereinafter provided, beginning January 1, 1988, the rate of tax shall be as follows for transactions in which the selling price of the motor vehicle is less than $15,000:

Number of Years Transpired After Model Year of Motor Vehicle	Applicable Tax
1 or less	$390
2	290
3	215
4	165
5	115
6	90
7	80
8	65
9	50
10	40
over 10	25

Except as hereinafter provided, beginning January 1, 1988, the rate of tax shall be as follows for transactions in which the selling price of the motor vehicle is $15,000 or more:

Selling Price	Applicable Tax
$15,000–$19,999	$ 750
$20,000–$24,999	$1,000
$25,000–$29,999	$1,250
$30,000 and over	$1,500

For the following transactions, the tax rate shall be $15 for each motor vehicle acquired in such transaction:

(i) when the transferee or purchaser is the spouse, mother, father, brother, sister or child of the transferor;

(ii) when the transfer is a gift to a beneficiary in the administration of an estate and the beneficiary is not a surviving spouse;

(iii) when a motor vehicle which has once been subjected to the Illinois retailers' occupation tax or use tax is transferred in connection with the organization, reorganization, dissolution or partial liquidation of an incorporated or unincorporated business wherein the beneficial ownership is not changed.

A claim that the transaction is taxable under subparagraph (i) shall be supported by such proof of family relationship as provided by rules of the Department.

For a transaction in which a motorcycle, motor driven cycle or motorized pedalcycle is acquired the tax rate shall be $25.

On and after October 1, 1985, 1/12 of $5,000,000 of the moneys received by the Department of Revenue pursuant to this Section shall be paid each month into the Build Illinois Fund and the remainder into the General Revenue Fund.

At the end of any fiscal year in which the moneys received by the Department of Revenue pursuant to this Section exceeds the Annual Specified Amount, as defined in Section 3 of the Retailers' Occupation Tax Act,[3] the State Comptroller shall direct the State Treasurer to transfer such excess amount from the General Revenue Fund to the Build Illinois Purposes Fund.

The tax imposed by this Section shall be abated and no longer imposed when the amount deposited to secure the bonds issued pursuant to the Build Illinois Bond Act[4] is sufficient to provide for the payment of the principal of, and interest and premium, if any, on the bonds, as certified to the State Comptroller and the Director of Revenue by the Director of the Bureau of the Budget.

P.A. 76-1586, § 3-1001, added by P.A. 81-3, 2nd Sp.Sess., § 18, eff. Jan. 1, 1980. Amended by P.A. 83-1353, § 1, eff. Sept. 8, 1984; P.A. 84-109, Art. 20, § 20-1, eff. July 25, 1985; P.A. 84-112, § 1, eff. July 25, 1985; P.A. 84-1308, Art. II, § 96, eff. Aug. 25, 1986; P.A. 84-1454, Art. I, § 1, eff. Jan. 6, 1987; P.A. 85-444, § 1, eff. Jan. 1, 1988; P.A. 86-152, § 1, eff. Jan. 1, 1990; P.A. 86-1475, Art. 5, § 5-8, eff. Jan. 10, 1991; P.A. 88-194, § 35, eff. Jan. 1, 1994; P.A. 90-89, § 15, eff. Jan. 1, 1998.

Formerly Ill.Rev.Stat.1991, ch. 95 ½, ¶ 3-1001.

1 35 ILCS 105/1 et seq.

2 35 ILCS 105/3-55.

3 35 ILCS 120/3.

4 30 ILCS 425/1 et seq.

For intent of P.A. 86-1475, Art. 5, see note following 35 ILCS 105/3.

5/3-1002. Returns; verification; payment to secure title; receipts

§ 3-1002. The purchaser shall file a return signed by the purchaser with the Department of Revenue on a form prescribed by the Department. Such return shall contain substantially the following and such other information as the Department may reasonably require:

VERIFICATION

I declare that I have examined this return and to the best of my knowledge it is true, correct and complete. I understand that the penalty for willfully filing a false return shall be a fine not to exceed $1,000 or imprisonment in a penal institution other than the penitentiary not to exceed one year, or both fine and imprisonment.

....
Date Signature of purchaser

Such return and payment from the purchaser shall be submitted to the Department after the sale and shall be a condition to securing in order to secure the title to the motor vehicle from the Secretary of State.

When a purchaser pays the tax imposed by Section 3-1001 of this Code, the Department (upon request therefor from such purchaser) shall issue an appropriate receipt to such purchaser showing that he has paid such tax to the Department. Such receipt shall be sufficient to relieve the purchaser from further liability for the tax to which such receipt may refer.

P.A. 76-1586, § 3-1002, added by P.A. 81-3, 2nd Sp.Sess., § 18, eff. Jan. 1, 1980. Amended by P.A. 81-1468, § 1, eff. Sept. 9, 1980; P.A. 84-109, Art. 20, § 20-1, eff. July 25, 1985.

Formerly Ill.Rev.Stat.1991, ch. 95 ½, ¶ 3-1002.

5/3-1002.1. False or incomplete returns

§ 3-1002.1. Any person required to file a return under this Article who willfully files a false or incomplete return is guilty of a Class A misdemeanor.

P.A. 76-1586, § 3-1002.1, added by P.A. 84-109, Art. 20, § 20-1, eff. July 25, 1985.

Formerly Ill.Rev.Stat.1991, ch. 95 ½, ¶ 3-1002.1.

Another § 3-1002.1, relating to selling price information, was renumbered as § 3-1002.2 by P.A. 84-1438, Art. II, § 30.

Article II of P.A. 84-1438, the Second 84th General Assembly Combining Revisory Act, provides for the nonsubstantive revision or renumbering or repeal of Sections of Acts necessitated by the amendment, addition or repeal of Sections by two or more 1986 Public Acts, which multiple action was not resolved by one of the 1986 Acts affecting the particular Section and makes technical corrections in Acts of the 84th General Assembly.

5/3-1002.2. Selling price information

§ 3-1002.2. For the purpose of assisting in determining the validity of the "selling price" reported on returns filed with the Department, the Department may furnish the following information to persons with whom the Department has contracted for service related to making such determination: the selling price stated on the return; vehicle identification number; year, make and model name or number of the vehicle; county code; purchase date; and mileage.

P.A. 76-1586, § 3-1002.1, added by P.A. 84-1307, § 1, eff. Aug. 22, 1986. Renumbered § 3-1002.2 and amended by P.A. 84-1438, Art. II, § 30, eff. Dec. 22, 1986.

Formerly Ill.Rev.Stat.1991, ch. 95 ½, ¶ 3-1002.2.

Article II of P.A. 84-1438, the Second 84th General Assembly Combining Revisory Act, provides for the nonsubstantive revision or renumbering or repeal of Sections of Acts necessitated by the amendment, addition or repeal of Sections by two or more 1986 Public Acts, which multiple action was not resolved by one of the 1986 Acts affecting the particular Section and makes technical corrections in Acts of the 84th General Assembly.

5/3-1003. Administration and enforcement; conformity with Use Tax Act

§ 3-1003. The Department shall have full power to administer and enforce this Article; to collect all taxes, penalties and interest due hereunder; to dispose of taxes, penalties and interest so collected in the manner hereinafter provided, and to determine all rights to credit memoranda or refunds arising on account of the erroneous payment of tax penalty or interest hereunder. In the administration of, and compliance with, this Article, the Department and persons who are subject to this Article shall have the same rights, remedies, privileges, immunities, powers and duties, and be subject to the same conditions, restrictions, limitations, penalties and definitions of terms, and employ the same modes of procedure, as are prescribed in the Use Tax Act, as now or hereafter amended,[1] which are not inconsistent with this Article, as fully as if provisions contained in those Sections of the Use Tax Act were set forth in this Article.

In addition to any other penalties imposed under law, any person convicted of violating the provisions of this Article, shall be assessed a fine of $1,000.

P.A. 76-1586, § 3-1003, added by P.A. 81-3, 2nd Sp.Sess., § 18, eff. Jan. 1, 1980. Amended by P.A. 85-444, § 1, eff. Jan. 1, 1988.

Formerly Ill.Rev.Stat.1991, ch. 95 ½, ¶ 3-1003.

[1] 35 ILCS 105/1 et seq.

5/3-1004. Disposition of funds

§ 3-1004. The State Department of Revenue shall, upon collecting any taxes as provided in this Article, pay such taxes over to the General Revenue Fund.

P.A. 76-1586, § 3-1004, added by P.A. 81-3, 2nd Sp.Sess., § 18, eff. Jan. 1, 1980. Amended by P.A. 82-783, Art. IV, § 25, eff. July 13, 1982; P.A. 84-471, § 1, eff. July 1, 1986.

Formerly Ill.Rev.Stat.1991, ch. 95 ½, ¶ 3-1004.

5/3-1005. Rules and regulations

§ 3-1005. The Department shall have the authority to adopt such rules and regulations as are reasonable and necessary to implement the provisions of this Article.

P.A. 76-1586, § 3-1005, added by P.A. 81-3, 2nd Sp.Sess., § 18, eff. Jan. 1, 1980.

Formerly Ill.Rev.Stat.1991, ch. 95 ½, ¶ 3-1005.

5/3-1006. Department

§ 3-1006. For the purposes of this Article, "Department" is the Department of Revenue of the State of Illinois.

P.A. 76-1586, § 3-1006, added by P.A. 81-3, 2nd Sp.Sess., § 18, eff. Jan. 1, 1980.

Formerly Ill.Rev.Stat.1991, ch. 95 ½, ¶ 3-1006.

ARTICLE XI. REPLACEMENT VEHICLE TAX

Date Effective

Article XI was added by P.A. 83-114, § 1, eff. Aug. 19, 1983.

Section

5/3-2001. Imposition of tax

§ 3-2001. A tax of $200 is hereby imposed on the purchase of any passenger car as defined in Section 1-157 of this Code, purchased in Illinois by or on behalf of an insurance company to replace a passenger car of an insured person in settlement of a total loss claim. The tax imposed by this Section shall apply only to that portion of the purchase price of the replacement vehicle paid by the insurance company in settlement of the total loss claim, but not including any portion of such insurance payment which exceeds the market value of the total loss vehicle.

P.A. 76-1586, § 3-2001, added by P.A. 83-114, § 1, eff. Aug. 19, 1983. Amended by P.A. 83-1353, § 1, eff. Sept. 8, 1984.

Formerly Ill.Rev.Stat.1991, ch. 95 ½, ¶ 3-2001.

5/3-2002. Returns from purchaser insurance company or broker; return and payment to secure title; receipts

§ 3-2002. The purchaser insurance company or broker for an insurance company shall file a return with the Department of Revenue on a form prescribed by the Department. Such return shall contain such information as the Department may reasonably require. Such return and payment from the purchaser shall be submitted to the Department after the sale in order to secure the title to the motor vehicle.

When a purchaser pays the tax imposed by Section 3-2001 of this Code, the Department (upon request therefor from such purchaser) shall issue an appropriate receipt to such purchaser showing that he has paid such tax to the Department. Such receipt shall be sufficient to relieve the purchaser from further liability for the tax to which such receipt may refer.

P.A. 76-1586, § 3-2002, added by P.A. 83-114, § 1, eff. Aug. 19, 1983.

Formerly Ill.Rev.Stat.1991, ch. 95 ½, ¶ 3-2002.

5/3-2003. Administration and enforcement; conformity with Use Tax Act

§ 3-2003. The Department shall have full power to administer and enforce this Article; to collect all taxes, penalties and interest due hereunder; to dispose of taxes, penalties and interest so collected in the manner hereinafter provided, and to determine all rights to credit memoranda or refunds arising on account of the erroneous payment of tax penalty or interest hereunder. In the administration of, and compliance with, this Article, the Department and persons who are subject to this Article shall have the same rights, remedies, privileges, immunities, powers and duties, and be subject to the same conditions, restrictions, limitations, penalties and definitions of terms, and employ the same modes of procedure, as are prescribed in the Use Tax Act, as now or hereafter amended,[1] which are not inconsistent with this Article, as fully as if provisions contained in those Sections of the Use Tax Act were set forth in this Article.

P.A. 76-1586, § 3-2003, added by P.A. 83-114, § 1, eff. Aug. 19, 1983.

Formerly Ill.Rev.Stat.1991, ch. 95 ½, ¶ 3-2003.

[1] 35 ILCS 105/1 et seq.

5/3-2004. Disposition of funds

§ 3-2004. The State Department of Revenue shall, upon collecting any taxes as provided in this Article, pay such taxes over to the General Revenue Fund.

P.A. 76-1586, § 3-2004, added by P.A. 83-114, § 1, eff. Aug. 19, 1983. Amended by P.A. 84-471, § 1, eff. July 1, 1986.

Formerly Ill.Rev.Stat.1991, ch. 95 ½, ¶ 3-2004.

5/3–2005. Rules and regulations

§ 3–2005. The Department shall have the authority to adopt such rules and regulations as are reasonable and necessary to implement the provisions of this Article.

P.A. 76–1586, § 3–2005, added by P.A. 83–114, § 1, eff. Aug. 19, 1983.

Formerly Ill.Rev.Stat.1991, ch. 95 ½, ¶ 3–2005.

5/3–2006. Department

§ 3–2006. For the purposes of this Article, "Department" is the Department of Revenue of the State of Illinois.

P.A. 76–1586, § 3–2006, added by P.A. 83–114, § 1, eff. Aug. 19, 1983.

Formerly Ill.Rev.Stat.1991, ch. 95 ½, ¶ 3–2006.

CHAPTER 4. ANTI–THEFT LAWS AND ABANDONED VEHICLES

Enactment

The Illinois Vehicle Code was enacted by P.A. 76–1586, effective July 1, 1970. The Code constitutes a consolidated recodification of various earlier laws and acts including the Illinois Motor Vehicle Law of 1957.

ARTICLE I. ANTI–THEFT LAWS

Section

5/4–100. § 4–100. Repealed by P.A. 90–89, § 20, eff. Jan. 1, 1998

5/4–101. Applicability of this Chapter

§ 4–101. Applicability of this Chapter. The provisions of this Chapter apply to all vehicles.

P.A. 76–1586, § 4–101, eff. July 1, 1970.

Formerly Ill.Rev.Stat.1991, ch. 95 ½, ¶ 4–101.

5/4–102. Offenses relating to motor vehicles and other vehicles—Misdemeanors

§ 4–102. Offenses relating to motor vehicles and other vehicles—Misdemeanors.

(a) It is a violation of this Chapter for:

(1) A person, without authority to do so, to damage a vehicle or to damage or remove any part of a vehicle;

(2) A person, without authority to do so, to tamper with a vehicle or go in it, on it, or work or attempt to work any of its parts, or set or attempt to set it in motion;

(3) A person to fail to report a vehicle as unclaimed in accordance with the provisions of Section 4–107.

(b) Sentence. A person convicted of a violation of this Section shall be guilty of a Class A misdemeanor. A person convicted of a violation of this Section a second or subsequent time, shall be guilty of a Class 4 felony.

P.A. 76–1586, § 4–102, eff. July 1, 1970. Amended by P.A. 78–858, § 1, eff. Jan. 1, 1974; P.A. 81–932, § 1, eff. Sept. 22, 1979; P.A. 83–1473, § 1, eff. Jan. 1, 1985; P.A. 84–1302, § 1, eff. Jan. 1, 1987; P.A. 84–1304, § 1, eff. Jan. 1, 1987; P.A. 86–1209, § 1, eff. Jan. 1, 1991.

Formerly Ill.Rev.Stat.1991, ch. 95 ½, ¶ 4–102.

Validity

The Supreme Court of Illinois has held that provisions of Vehicle Code under which it is a misdemeanor for person who lacks authority or permission to do so to damage or remove any part of, or tamper with, a vehicle, which do not require a culpable mental state, violate the due process clauses of Federal and State Constitutions in the case of In re K.C., 1999, 186 Ill.2d 542, 714 N.E.2d 491, 239 Ill.Dec. 572.

5/4–103. Offenses relating to motor vehicles and other vehicles—Felonies

§ 4–103. Offenses relating to motor vehicles and other vehicles—Felonies.

(a) It is a violation of this Chapter for:

(1) A person not entitled to the possession of a vehicle or essential part of a vehicle to receive, possess, conceal, sell, dispose, or transfer it, knowing it to have been stolen or converted; additionally the General Assembly finds that the acquisition and disposition of vehicles and their essential parts are strictly controlled by law and that such acquisitions and dispositions are reflected by documents of title, uniform invoices, rental contracts, leasing agreements and bills of sale. It may be inferred, therefore that a person exercising exclusive unexplained possession over a stolen or converted vehicle or an essential part of a stolen or converted vehicle has knowledge that such vehicle or essential part is stolen or converted, regardless of whether the date on which such vehicle or essential part was stolen is recent or remote;

(2) A person to knowingly remove, alter, deface, destroy, falsify, or forge a manufacturer's identification number of a vehicle or an engine number of a motor vehicle or any essential part thereof having an identification number;

(3) A person to knowingly conceal or misrepresent the identity of a vehicle or any essential part thereof;

(4) A person to buy, receive, possess, sell or dispose of a vehicle, or any essential part thereof, with knowledge that the identification number of the vehicle or any essential

part thereof having an identification number has been removed or falsified;

(5) A person to knowingly possess, buy, sell, exchange, give away, or offer to buy, sell, exchange or give away, any manufacturer's identification number plate, mylar sticker, federal certificate label, State police reassignment plate, Secretary of State assigned plate, rosette rivet, or facsimile of such which has not yet been attached to or has been removed from the original or assigned vehicle. It is an affirmative defense to subsection (a) of this Section that the person possessing, buying, selling or exchanging a plate mylar sticker or label described in this paragraph is a police officer doing so as part of his official duties, or is a manufacturer's authorized representative who is replacing any manufacturer's identification number plate, mylar sticker or Federal certificate label originally placed on the vehicle by the manufacturer of the vehicle or any essential part thereof;

(6) A person to knowingly make a false report of the theft or conversion of a vehicle to any police officer of this State or any employee of a law enforcement agency of this State designated by the law enforcement agency to take, receive, process, or record reports of vehicle theft or conversion.

(b) Sentence. A person convicted of a violation of this Section shall be guilty of a Class 2 felony.

(c) The offenses set forth in subsection (a) of this Section shall not include the offense set forth in Section 4–103.2 of this Code.

P.A. 76–1586, § 4–103, eff. July 1, 1970. Amended by P.A. 78–858, § 1, eff. Jan. 1, 1974; P.A. 81–932, § 1, eff. Sept. 22, 1979; P.A. 83–830, § 1, eff. Sept. 24, 1983; P.A. 83–1473, § 1, eff. Jan. 1, 1985; P.A. 85–572, § 1, eff. Sept. 18, 1987; P.A. 86–1209, § 1, eff. Jan. 1, 1991; P.A. 90–89, § 15, eff. Jan. 1, 1998; P.A. 91–450, § 5, eff. Jan. 1, 2000.

Formerly Ill.Rev.Stat.1991, ch. 95 ½, ¶ 4–103.

5/4–103.1. Vehicle theft conspiracy

§ 4–103.1 Vehicle theft conspiracy. (a) Elements of the offense. A person commits vehicle theft conspiracy when, with intent that a violation of Section 4–103 of this Code be committed, he agrees with another to the commission of such an offense. No person may be convicted of vehicle theft conspiracy unless an overt act in furtherance of such an agreement is alleged and proved to have been committed by him or by a co-conspirator, and the accused is part of a common plan or scheme to engage in the unlawful activity.

(b) Co-conspirators. It shall not be a defense to vehicle theft conspiracy that the person or persons with whom the accused is alleged to have conspired:

(1) has not been prosecuted or convicted;

(2) has been convicted of a different offense;

(3) is not amenable to justice;

(4) has been acquitted; or

(5) lacked the capacity to commit an offense.

(c) Sentence. Vehicle theft conspiracy to violate Section 4–103 of this Code is a Class 2 felony. Vehicle theft conspiracy to violate Section 4–103.2 of this Code is a Class 1 felony.

P.A. 76–1586, § 4–103.1, added by P.A. 83–830, § 1, eff. Sept. 24, 1983. Amended by P.A. 83–1473, § 1, eff. Jan. 1, 1985; P.A. 86–1209, § 1, eff. Jan. 1, 1991.

Formerly Ill.Rev.Stat.1991, ch. 95 ½, ¶ 4–103.1.

5/4–103.2. Aggravated offenses relating to motor vehicles and other vehicles—Felonies

§ 4–103.2. Aggravated offenses relating to motor vehicles and other vehicles—Felonies.

(a) It is a violation of this Chapter for:

(1) a person not entitled to the possession of 3 or more vehicles, 3 or more essential parts of different vehicles, or a combination thereof, to receive, possess, conceal, sell, dispose of or transfer, those vehicles or parts of vehicles at the same time or within a one year period knowing that these vehicles or parts of vehicles are stolen or converted;

(2) a person to buy, receive, possess, sell or dispose of 3 or more vehicles, 3 or more essential parts of different vehicles, or a combination thereof, at the same time or within a one year period, knowing that the identification numbers of the vehicles or the essential parts with an identification number have been removed or falsified;

(3) a person not entitled to the possession of a vehicle having a value of $25,000 or greater to receive, possess, conceal, sell, dispose or transfer the vehicle, knowing that the vehicle has been stolen or converted;

(4) a person to knowingly possess, buy, sell, exchange or give away, at the same time or within a one year period, 3 or more manufacturer's identification number plates, mylar stickers, federal certificate labels, State Police reassignment plates, Secretary of State assigned plates or a facsimile of those items, or a combination thereof, which have not yet been attached to or have been removed from an original or assigned vehicle or essential part of a vehicle. It is an affirmative defense that the person possessing, buying, selling or exchanging a plate, mylar sticker or label is a police officer doing so as part of his official duties or is a manufacturer's authorized representative who is replacing any manufacturer's identification number plate, mylar sticker or federal certificate label originally placed on a vehicle by the manufacturer of a vehicle or any essential part of a vehicle;

(5) a person not entitled to the possession of any second division vehicle, semitrailer, farm tractor, tow truck, rescue squad vehicle, medical transport vehicle, fire engine, special mobile equipment, dump truck, truck mounted transit mixer, crane or the engine, transmission, cab, cab clip or vehicle cowl of any of the above vehicles, to receive, possess, conceal, sell, dispose of or transfer the vehicle or vehicle part described in this paragraph knowing it is stolen or converted;

(6) a person not entitled to the possession of a vehicle which is owned or operated by a law enforcement agency to receive, possess, conceal, sell, or dispose of or transfer such vehicle knowing it is the property of a law enforcement agency and knowing it to be stolen or converted;

(7) a person:

(A) who is the driver or operator of a vehicle and is not entitled to the possession of that vehicle and who knows the vehicle is stolen or converted, or

(B) who is the driver or operator of a vehicle being used to transport or haul a vehicle or essential part of a vehicle and is not entitled to the possession of that vehicle or essential part being transported or hauled and who knows the transported or hauled vehicle or essential part is stolen or converted,

who has been given a signal by a peace officer directing him to bring the vehicle to a stop, to willfully fail or refuse to obey such direction, increase his speed, extinguish his lights or otherwise flee or attempt to elude the officer. The signal given by the peace officer may be by hand, voice, siren, or red or blue light. The officer giving the signal, if driving a vehicle, shall display the vehicle's illuminated, oscillating, rotating or flashing red or blue lights, which when used in conjunction with an audible horn or siren would indicate that the vehicle is an official police vehicle. Such requirement shall not preclude the use of amber or white oscillating, rotating or flashing lights in conjunction with red or blue oscillating, rotating or flashing lights as required in Section 12-215 of this Code; or

(8) a person, at the same time or within a one year period, to make a false report of the theft or conversion of 3 or more vehicles to any police officer or police officers of this State.

(b) The inference contained in paragraph (1) of subsection (a) of Section 4-103 of this Code shall apply to subsection (a) of this Section.

(c) A person convicted of violating this Section shall be guilty of a Class 1 felony.

(d) The offenses set forth in subsection (a) of this Section shall not include the offenses set forth in Section 4-103 of this Code.

P.A. 76-1586, § 4-103.2, added by P.A. 86-1209, § 1, eff. Jan. 1, 1991.

Formerly Ill.Rev.Stat.1991, ch. 95 ½, ¶ 4-103.2.

5/4-103.3. Organizer of an aggravated vehicle theft conspiracy

§ 4-103.3. Organizer of an aggravated vehicle theft conspiracy.

(a) A person commits the offense of organizer of a vehicle theft conspiracy if:

(1) the person intentionally violates Section 4-103.2 of this Code with the agreement of 3 or more persons; and

(2) the person is known by other co-conspirators as the organizer, supervisor, financier or otherwise leader of the conspiracy.

(b) No person may be convicted of organizer of a vehicle theft conspiracy unless an overt act in furtherance of the agreement is alleged and proved to have been committed by him or by a co-conspirator, and the accused is part of a common plan or scheme to engage in the unlawful activity.

(c) It shall not be a defense to organizer of a vehicle theft conspiracy that the person or persons with whom the accused is alleged to have conspired:

(1) has not been prosecuted or convicted;

(2) has been convicted of a different offense;

(3) is not amenable to justice;

(4) has been acquitted; or

(5) lacked the capacity to commit an offense.

(d) Notwithstanding Section 8-5 of the Criminal Code of 1961,[1] a person may be convicted and sentenced for both the offense of organizer of a vehicle theft conspiracy and any other offense in this Chapter which is the object of the conspiracy.

(e) Organizer of a vehicle theft conspiracy is a Class X felony.

P.A. 76-1586, § 4-103.3, added by P.A. 86-1209, § 1, eff. Jan. 1, 1991.

Formerly Ill.Rev.Stat.1991, ch. 95 ½, ¶ 4-103.3.

[1] 720 ILCS 5/8-5.

5/4-104. Offenses relating to possession of titles and registration

§ 4-104. Offenses relating to possession of titles and registration.

(a) It is a violation of this Chapter for:

1. A person to possess without authority any manufacturers statement of origin, certificate of title, salvage certificate, junking certificate, display certificate of title, registration card, license plate, registration sticker or temporary registration permit, whether blank or otherwise;

2. A person to possess any manufacturers certificate of origin, salvage certificate, junking certificate, certificate of title, display certificate without complete assignment;

3. A person to possess any manufacturers statement of origin, salvage certificate, junking certificate, display certificate or certificate of title, temporary registration permit, registration card, license plate or registration sticker knowing it to have been stolen, converted, altered, forged or counterfeited;

4. A person to display or affix to a vehicle any certificate of title, manufacturers statement of origin, salvage certificate, junking certificate, display certificate, temporary registration permit, registration card, license plate or registration sticker not authorized by law for use on such vehicle;

5. A person to permit another, not entitled thereto, to use or have possession of any manufacturers statement of origin, salvage certificate, junking certificate, display certificate or certificate of title, registration card, license plate, temporary registration permit, or registration sticker;

6. A person to fail to mail or deliver to the proper person within a reasonable period of time after receipt from the Secretary of State, any certificate of title, salvage certificate, junking certificate, display certificate, registration card, temporary registration permit, license plate or registration sticker. If a person mails or delivers reasonable notice to the proper person after receipt from the Secretary of State, a presumption of delivery within a reasonable period of time shall exist; provided, however, the delivery is made, either by mail or otherwise, within 20 days from the date of receipt from the Secretary of State.

(b) Sentence:

1. A person convicted of a violation of subsection 1 or 2 of paragraph (a) of this Section is guilty of a Class 4 felony.

2. A person convicted of a violation of subsection 3 of paragraph (a) of this Section is guilty of a Class 2 felony.

3. A person convicted of a violation of either subsection 4 or 5 of paragraph (a) of this Section is guilty of a Class A misdemeanor and upon a second or subsequent conviction of such a violation is guilty of a Class 4 felony.

4. A person convicted of a violation of subsection 6 of paragraph (a) of this Section is guilty of a petty offense.

P.A. 76-1586, § 4-104, eff. July 1, 1970. Amended by P.A. 78-858, § 1, eff. Jan. 1, 1974; P.A. 80-230, § 1, eff. Oct. 1, 1977; P.A. 81-932, § 1, eff. Sept. 22, 1979; P.A. 83-1473, § 1, eff. Jan. 1, 1985; P.A. 87-854, § 3, eff. May 8, 1992; P.A. 87-1225, § 2, eff. Dec. 22, 1992; P.A. 88-45, Art. II, § 2-54, eff. July 6, 1993.

Formerly Ill.Rev.Stat.1991, ch. 95 ½, ¶ 4-104.

Validity

Provision making it a Class 2 felony for a motor vehicle owner to alter his or her own temporary registration permit has been held unconstitutional by the Illinois Supreme Court in the case of People v. Morris, 136 Ill.2d 157, 554 N.E.2d 235, 143 Ill. Dec. 300 (1990). See Notes of Decisions, post.

P.A. 88-45, Article II, of the First 1993 General Revisory Act, resolved multiple actions in the 87th General Assembly and made certain technical corrections in P.A. 87-895 through P.A. 87-1280.

5/4-105. Offenses relating to disposition of titles and registration

§ 4-105. Offenses relating to disposition of titles and registration. (a) It is a violation of this Chapter for:

1. a person to alter, forge, or counterfeit any manufacturers statement of origin, certificate of title, salvage certificate, junking certificate, display certificate, registration sticker, registration card, or temporary registration permit;

2. a person to alter, forge, or counterfeit an assignment of any manufacturers statement of origin, certificate of title, salvage certificate or junking certificate;

3. a person to alter, forge, or counterfeit a release of a security interest on any manufacturers statement of origin, certificate of title, salvage certificate or junking certificate;

4. a person to alter, forge, or counterfeit an application for any certificate of title, salvage certificate, junking certificate, display certificate, registration sticker, registration card, temporary registration permit or license plate;

5. a person to use a false or fictitious name or address or altered, forged, counterfeited or stolen manufacturer's identification number, or make a material false statement, or fail to disclose a security interest, or conceal any other material fact on any application for any manufacturers statement of origin, certificate of title, junking certificate, salvage certificate, registration card, license plate, temporary registration permit, or registration sticker or commit a fraud in connection with any application under this Act;

6. an unauthorized person to have in his possession a blank Illinois certificate of title paper;

7. a person to surrender or cause to be surrendered any certificate of title, salvage or junking certificate in exchange for a certificate of title or other title document from any other state or foreign jurisdiction for the purpose of changing or deleting an "S.V." or "REBUILT" notation, odometer reading, or any other information contained on such Illinois certificate.

(b) Sentence:

A person convicted of a violation of this Section shall be guilty of a Class 2 felony.

P.A. 76-1586, § 4-105, eff. July 1, 1970. Amended by P.A. 78-858, § 1, eff. Jan. 1, 1974; P.A. 80-230, § 1, eff. Oct. 1, 1977; P.A. 81-932, § 1, eff. Sept. 22, 1979; P.A. 82-131, § 1, eff. Jan. 1, 1982; P.A. 83-1473, § 1, eff. Jan. 1, 1985; P.A. 84-986, § 1, eff. Sept. 25, 1985.

Formerly Ill.Rev.Stat.1991, ch. 95 ½, ¶ 4-105.

5/4-105.1. Offenses relating to deletion or falsification of information on title document

§ 4-105.1. Offenses relating to deletion or falsification of information on title document. (a) It is a violation of this Code for a person to knowingly, with the intent to defraud, surrender or cause to be surrendered any manufacturer's statement of origin, certificate of title, salvage certificate, junking certificate, or other title document, in exchange for a certificate of title or other title document of this State or of any other State or foreign jurisdiction which results in or attempts to result in:

1. The deletion of the words "S.V.", "REBUILT" or similar notation.

2. The falsification of an odometer reading; or

3. The alteration or deletion of any other information required to be contained on such certificate of title or any other title document of any State or foreign jurisdiction.

(b) Presumptions. A title surrendered to another jurisdiction that is subsequently submitted to any person, corporation, or other legal entity, residing or doing business within Illinois, the following presumption shall apply; if the title document fails to contain all of the previous information required by Illinois law, it shall be presumed to have been done so knowingly.

It shall be a rebuttable presumption that any title document surrendered or submitted with a false odometer reading shall be presumed to have been done so knowingly.

(c) Sentence. A person convicted of a violation of this Section shall be guilty of a Class A misdemeanor. A person convicted of violating this Section a second or subsequent time shall be guilty of a Class 3 felony.

P.A. 76-1586, § 4-105.1, added by P.A. 84-986, § 1, eff. Sept. 25, 1985. Amended by P.A. 91-571, § 5, eff. Jan. 1, 2000.

Formerly Ill.Rev.Stat.1991, ch. 95 ½, ¶ 4-105.1.

5/4-105.5. Attempt

§ 4-105.5. Attempt. As defined in Section 8-4 of the Criminal Code of 1961.[1]

P.A. 76-1586, § 4-105.5, added by P.A. 81-932, § 1, eff. Sept. 22, 1979.

Formerly Ill.Rev.Stat.1991, ch. 95 ½, ¶ 4-105.5.

[1] 720 ILCS 5/8-4.

5/4-106. Principals

§ 4-106. Principals. It shall be a violation of the provisions of this Chapter for a person, whether present or absent, to aid, abet, induce, procure or cause the commission of an act which, if done directly by him, would constitute a violation of the provisions of this Chapter.

P.A. 76-1586, § 4-106, eff. July 1, 1970.

Formerly Ill.Rev.Stat.1991, ch. 95 ½, ¶ 4-106.

5/4-107. Stolen, converted, recovered and unclaimed vehicles

§ 4-107. Stolen, converted, recovered and unclaimed vehicles.

(a) Every Sheriff, Superintendent of police, Chief of police or other police officer in command of any Police department in any City, Village or Town of the State, shall, by the fastest means of communications available to his law enforcement agency, immediately report to the State Police, in Springfield, Illinois, the theft or recovery of any stolen or converted vehicle within his district or jurisdiction. The report shall give the date of theft, description of the vehicle including color, year of manufacture, manufacturer's trade name, manufacturer's series name, body style, vehicle identification number and license registration number, including the state in which the license was issued and the year of issuance, together with the name, residence address, business address, and telephone number of the owner. The report shall be routed by the originating law enforcement agency through the State Police District in which such agency is located.

(b) A registered owner or a lienholder may report the theft by conversion of a vehicle, to the State Police, or any other police department or Sheriff's office. Such report will be accepted as a report of theft and processed only if a formal complaint is on file and a warrant issued.

(c) An operator of a place of business for garaging, repairing, parking or storing vehicles for the public, in which a vehicle remains unclaimed, after being left for the purpose of garaging, repairing, parking or storage, for a period of 15 days, shall, within 5 days after the expiration of that period, report the vehicle as unclaimed to the municipal police when the vehicle is within the corporate limits of any City, Village or incorporated Town, or the County Sheriff, or State Police when the vehicle is outside the corporate limits of a City, Village or incorporated Town. This Section does not apply to any vehicle:

(1) removed to a place of storage by a law enforcement agency having jurisdiction, in accordance with Sections 4–201 and 4–203 of this Act; or

(2) left under a garaging, repairing, parking, or storage order signed by the owner, lessor, or other legally entitled person.

Failure to comply with this Section will result in the forfeiture of storage fees for that vehicle involved.

(d) The State Police shall keep a complete record of all reports filed under this Section of the Act. Upon receipt of such report, a careful search shall be made of the records of the office of the State Police, and where it is found that a vehicle reported recovered was stolen in a County, City, Village or Town other than the County, City, Village or Town in which it is recovered, the State Police shall immediately notify the Sheriff, Superintendent of police, Chief of police, or other police officer in command of the Sheriff's office or Police department of the County, City, Village or Town in which the vehicle was originally reported stolen, giving complete data as to the time and place of recovery.

(e) Notification of the theft or conversion of a vehicle will be furnished to the Secretary of State by the State Police. The Secretary of State shall place the proper information in the license registration and title registration files to indicate the theft or conversion of a motor vehicle or other vehicle. Notification of the recovery of a vehicle previously reported as a theft or a conversion will be furnished to the Secretary of State by the State Police. The Secretary of State shall remove the proper information from the license registration and title registration files that has previously indicated the theft or conversion of a vehicle. The Secretary of State shall suspend the registration of a vehicle upon receipt of a report from the State Police that such vehicle was stolen or converted.

(f) When the Secretary of State receives an application for a certificate of title or an application for registration of a vehicle and it is determined from the records of the office of the Secretary of State that such vehicle has been reported stolen or converted, the Secretary of State shall immediately notify the State Police and shall give the State Police the name and address of the person or firm titling or registering the vehicle, together with all other information contained in the application submitted by such person or firm.

(g) During the usual course of business the manufacturer of any vehicle shall place an original manufacturer's vehicle identification number on all such vehicles manufactured and on any part of such vehicles requiring an identification number.

(h) If a manufacturer's vehicle identification number is missing or has been removed, changed or mutilated on any vehicle, or any part of such vehicle requiring an identification number, the State Police shall restore, restamp or reaffix the vehicle identification number plate, or affix a new plate bearing the original manufacturer's vehicle identification number on each such vehicle and on all necessary parts of the vehicles. A vehicle identification number so affixed, restored, restamped, reaffixed or replaced is not falsified, altered or forged within the meaning of this Act.

(i) If a vehicle or part of any vehicle is found to have the manufacturer' s identification number removed, altered, defaced or destroyed, the vehicle or part shall be seized by any law enforcement agency having jurisdiction and held for the purpose of identification. In the event that the manufacturer's identification number of a vehicle or part cannot be identified, the vehicle or part shall be considered contraband, and no right of property shall exist in any person owning, leasing or possessing such property, unless the person owning, leasing or possessing the vehicle or part acquired such without knowledge that the manufacturer's vehicle identification number has been removed, altered, defaced, falsified or destroyed.

Either the seizing law enforcement agency or the State's Attorney of the county where the seizure occurred may make an application for an order of forfeiture to the circuit court in the county of seizure. The application for forfeiture shall be independent from any prosecution arising out of the seizure and is not subject to any final determination of such prosecution. The circuit court shall issue an order forfeiting the property to the seizing law enforcement agency if the court finds that the property did not at the time of seizure possess a valid manufacturer's identification number and that the original manufacturer's identification number cannot be ascertained. The seizing law enforcement agency may:

(1) retain the forfeited property for official use; or

(2) sell the forfeited property and distribute the proceeds in accordance with Section 4–211 of this Code, or dispose of the forfeited property in such manner as the law enforcement agency deems appropriate.

(i–1) If a motorcycle is seized under subsection (i), the motorcycle must be returned within 45 days of the date of seizure to the person from whom it was seized, unless (i) criminal charges are pending against that person or (ii) an application for an order of forfeiture has been submitted to the circuit in the county of seizure or (iii) the circuit court in the county of seizure has received from the seizing law enforcement agency and has granted a petition to extend, for a single 30 day period, the 45 days allowed for return of the motorcycle. Except as provided in subsection (i–2), a motorcycle returned to the person from whom it was seized must be returned in essentially the same condition it was in at the time of seizure.

(i–2) If any part or parts of a motorcycle seized under subsection (i) are found to be stolen and are removed, the seizing law enforcement agency is not required to replace the part or parts before returning the motorcycle to the person from whom it was seized.

(j) The State Police shall notify the Secretary of State each time a manufacturer's vehicle identification number is affixed, reaffixed, restored or restamped on any vehicle. The Secretary of State shall make the necessary changes or corrections in his records, after the proper applications and fees have been submitted, if applicable.

(k) Any vessel, vehicle or aircraft used with knowledge and consent of the owner in the commission of, or in the attempt to commit as defined in Section 8-4 of the Criminal Code of 1961,[1] an offense prohibited by Section 4-103 of this Chapter, including transporting of a stolen vehicle or stolen vehicle parts, shall be seized by any law enforcement agency. The seizing law enforcement agency may:

(1) return the vehicle to its owner if such vehicle is stolen; or

(2) confiscate the vehicle and retain it for any purpose which the law enforcement agency deems appropriate; or

(3) sell the vehicle at a public sale or dispose of the vehicle in such other manner as the law enforcement agency deems appropriate.

If the vehicle is sold at public sale, the proceeds of the sale shall be paid to the law enforcement agency.

The law enforcement agency shall not retain, sell or dispose of a vehicle under paragraphs (2) or (3) of this subsection (k) except upon an order of forfeiture issued by the circuit court. The circuit court may issue such order of forfeiture upon application of the law enforcement agency or State's Attorney of the county where the law enforcement agency has jurisdiction, or in the case of the Department of State Police or the Secretary of State, upon application of the Attorney General.

The court shall issue the order if the owner of the vehicle has been convicted of transporting stolen vehicles or stolen vehicle parts and the evidence establishes that the owner's vehicle has been used in the commission of such offense.

The provisions of subsection (k) of this Section shall not apply to any vessel, vehicle or aircraft, which has been leased, rented or loaned by its owner, if the owner did not have knowledge of and consent to the use of the vessel, vehicle or aircraft in the commission of, or in an attempt to commit, an offense prohibited by Section 4-103 of this Chapter.

P.A. 76-1586, § 4-107, eff. July 1, 1970. Amended by P.A. 77-65, § 1, eff. July 1, 1971; P.A. 78-858, § 1, eff. Jan. 1, 1974; P.A. 79-866, § 1, eff. Sept. 10, 1975; P.A. 83-830, § 1, eff. Sept. 24, 1983; P.A. 83-1473, § 1, eff. Jan. 1, 1985; P.A. 84-25, Art. IV, § 27, eff. July 18, 1985; P.A. 86-1275, § 1, eff. Jan. 1, 1991; P.A. 89-433, § 5, eff. Dec. 15, 1995; P.A. 92-443, § 5, eff. Jan. 1, 2002.

Formerly Ill.Rev.Stat.1991, ch. 95 ½, ¶ 4-107.

1 720 ILCS 5/8-4.

5/4-108. Violations of this Chapter

§ 4-108. Violations of this Chapter. (a) Any person who violates or aids or abets in the violation of any of the provisions of Section 4-102, 4-103, 4-104 or 4-105 shall be guilty of such offense and be subject to the same sentence as if he had committed the offense himself.

(b) Any person who is convicted of any offense under Chapter 4 of this Act,[1] in addition to any other fines or penalties provided therein, may be required to compensate the victim, if known, involved in the related offense, for any loss that the victim sustains to his person or property.

(c) The amount and method of payment of the compensation award shall be determined at the time of the conviction.

(d) For purposes of this Section, "victim" shall mean the owner or other legally entitled person.

P.A. 76-1586, § 4-108, eff. July 1, 1970. Amended by P.A. 77-2720, § 1, eff. Jan. 1, 1973; P.A. 82-695, § 1, eff. Jan. 1, 1982; P.A. 83-1473, § 1, eff. Jan. 1, 1985.

Formerly Ill.Rev.Stat.1991, ch. 95 ½, ¶ 4-108.

1 625 ILCS 5/4-100 et seq.

5/4-109. Motor Vehicle Theft Prevention Program

§ 4-109. Motor Vehicle Theft Prevention Program. The Secretary of State, in conjunction with the Motor Vehicle Theft Prevention Council, is hereby authorized to establish and operate a Motor Vehicle Theft Prevention Program as follows:

(a) Voluntary program participation.

(b) The registered owner of a motor vehicle interested in participating in the program shall sign an informed consent agreement designed by the Secretary of State under subsection (e) of this Section indicating that the motor vehicle registered to him is not normally operated between the hours of 1:00 a.m. and 5:00 a.m. The form and fee, if any, shall be submitted to the Secretary of State for processing.

(c) Upon processing the form, the Secretary of State shall issue to the registered owner a decal. The registered owner shall affix the decal in a conspicuous place on his motor vehicle as prescribed by the Secretary of State.

(d) Whenever any law enforcement officer shall see a motor vehicle displaying a decal issued under the provisions of subsection (c) of this Section being operated upon the public highways of this State between the hours of 1:00 a.m. and 5:00 a.m., the officer is authorized to stop that motor vehicle and to request the driver to produce a valid driver's license and motor vehicle registration card if required to be carried in the vehicle. Whenever the operator of a motor vehicle displaying a decal is unable to produce the documentation set forth in this Section, the police officer shall investigate further to determine if the person operating the motor vehicle is the registered owner or has the authorization of the owner to operate the vehicle.

(e) The Secretary of State, in consultation with the Director of the Department of State Police and Motor Vehicle Theft Prevention Council, shall design the manner and form of the informed consent agreement required under subsection (b) of this Section and the decal required under subsection (c) of this Section.

(f) The Secretary of State shall provide for the recording of registered owners of motor vehicles who participate in the program. The records shall be available to all law enforcement departments, agencies, and forces. The Secretary of State shall cooperate with and assist all law enforcement officers and other agencies in tracing or examining any questionable motor vehicles in order to determine the ownership of the motor vehicles.

(g) A fee not to exceed $10 may be charged for the informed consent form and decal provided under this Section. The fee, if any, shall be set by the Motor Vehicle Theft Prevention Council and shall be collected by the Secretary of State and deposited into the Motor Vehicle Theft Prevention Trust Fund.

(h) The Secretary of State, in consultation with the Director of the Department of State Police and the Motor Vehicle Theft Prevention Council shall promulgate rules and regulations to effectuate the purposes of this Section.

P.A. 76-1586, § 4-109, added by P.A. 88-128, § 5, eff. Jan. 1, 1994. Amended by P.A. 88-684, § 5, eff. Jan. 24, 1995.

ARTICLE II. ABANDONED, LOST, STOLEN OR UNCLAIMED VEHICLES

Section

5/4-200. § 4-200. Renumbered § 4-201 and amended by P.A. 78-858, § 1, eff. Jan. 1, 1974

5/4-201. Abandonment of vehicles prohibited

§ 4-201. Abandonment of vehicles prohibited.

(a) The abandonment of a vehicle or any part thereof on any highway in this State is unlawful and subject to penalties as set forth under Penalty Section 4-214 of this Chapter.

(b) The abandonment of a vehicle or any part thereof on private or public property, other than a highway, in view of the general public, anywhere in this State is unlawful except on property of the owner or bailee of such abandoned vehicle. A vehicle or any part thereof so abandoned on private property shall be authorized for removal, by a law enforcement agency having jurisdiction, after a waiting period of 7 days or more, or may be removed immediately if determined to be a hazardous dilapidated motor vehicle under Section 11-40-3.1 of the Illinois Municipal Code.[1] A violation of subsections (a) or (b) of this Section is subject to penalties as set forth under Section 4-214 of this Chapter.

(c) A towing service may begin to process an unclaimed vehicle as abandoned by requesting a record search by the Secretary of State up to 10 days after the date of the tow, or any later date acceptable to the Secretary of State. This subsection (c) shall not apply to vehicles towed by order or authorization of a law enforcement agency.

P.A. 76-1586, § 4-200, added by P.A. 76-1437, § 1, eff. July 1, 1970. Renumbered § 4-201 and amended by P.A. 78-858, § 1, eff. Jan. 1, 1974. Amended by P.A. 81-653, § 2, eff. Sept. 14, 1979; P.A. 86-460, § 2, eff. Jan. 1, 1990; P.A. 90-330, § 5, eff. Aug. 8, 1997.

Formerly Ill.Rev.Stat.1991, ch. 95 ½, ¶ 4-201.

[1] 65 ILCS 5/11-40-3.1.

5/4-202. Abandoned, lost, stolen or unclaimed vehicle—Notification to law enforcement agencies

§ 4-202. Abandoned, lost, stolen or unclaimed vehicle—Notification to law enforcement agencies. When an abandoned, lost, stolen or unclaimed vehicle comes into the temporary possession or custody of a person in this State, not the owner of the vehicle, such person shall immediately notify the municipal police when the vehicle is within the corporate limits of any city, village or town having a duly authorized police department, or the State Police or the county sheriff when the vehicle is outside the corporate limits of a city, village or town. Upon receipt of such notification, the municipal police, State Police or county sheriff will authorize a towing service to remove and take possession of the abandoned, lost, stolen or unclaimed vehicle. The towing service will safely keep the towed vehicle and its contents, maintain a record of the tow as set forth in Section 4-204 for law enforcement agencies, until the vehicle is claimed by the owner or any other person legally entitled to possession thereof or until it is disposed of as provided in this Chapter.

P.A. 76-1586, § 4-201, eff. July 1, 1970. Amended by P.A. 76-1437, § 1, eff. July 1, 1970. Renumbered § 4-202 and amended by P.A. 78-858, § 1, eff. Jan. 1, 1974.

Formerly Ill.Rev.Stat.1991, ch. 95 ½, ¶ 4-202.

5/4-203. Removal of motor vehicles or other vehicles; Towing or hauling away

§ 4-203. Removal of motor vehicles or other vehicles; Towing or hauling away.

(a) When a vehicle is abandoned, or left unattended, on a toll highway, interstate highway, or expressway for 2 hours or more, its removal by a towing service may be authorized by a law enforcement agency having jurisdiction.

(b) When a vehicle is abandoned on a highway in an urban district 10 hours or more, its removal by a towing service may be authorized by a law enforcement agency having jurisdiction.

(c) When a vehicle is abandoned or left unattended on a highway other than a toll highway, interstate highway, or expressway, outside of an urban district for 24 hours or more, its removal by a towing service may be authorized by a law enforcement agency having jurisdiction.

(d) When an abandoned, unattended, wrecked, burned or partially dismantled vehicle is creating a traffic hazard because of its position in relation to the highway or its physical appearance is causing the impeding of traffic, its immediate removal from the highway or private property adjacent to the highway by a towing service may be authorized by a law enforcement agency having jurisdiction.

(e) Whenever a peace officer reasonably believes that a person under arrest for a violation of Section 11-501 of this Code or a similar provision of a local ordinance is likely, upon release, to commit a subsequent violation of Section 11-501, or a similar provision of a local ordinance, the arresting officer shall have the vehicle which the person was operating at the time of the arrest impounded for a period of not more than 12 hours after the time of arrest. However, such vehicle may be released by the arresting law enforcement agency prior to the end of the impoundment period if:

(1) the vehicle was not owned by the person under arrest, and the lawful owner requesting such release pos-

sesses a valid operator's license, proof of ownership, and would not, as determined by the arresting law enforcement agency, indicate a lack of ability to operate a motor vehicle in a safe manner, or who would otherwise, by operating such motor vehicle, be in violation of this Code; or

(2) the vehicle is owned by the person under arrest, and the person under arrest gives permission to another person to operate such vehicle, provided however, that the other person possesses a valid operator's license and would not, as determined by the arresting law enforcement agency, indicate a lack of ability to operate a motor vehicle in a safe manner or who would otherwise, by operating such motor vehicle, be in violation of this Code.

(e-5) Whenever a registered owner of a vehicle is taken into custody for operating the vehicle in violation of Section 11-501 of this Code or a similar provision of a local ordinance or Section 6-303 of this Code, a law enforcement officer may have the vehicle immediately impounded for a period not less than:

(1) 24 hours for a second violation of Section 11-501 of this Code or a similar provision of a local ordinance or Section 6-303 of this Code or a combination of these offenses; or

(2) 48 hours for a third violation of Section 11-501 of this Code or a similar provision of a local ordinance or Section 6-303 of this Code or a combination of these offenses.

The vehicle may be released sooner if the vehicle is owned by the person under arrest and the person under arrest gives permission to another person to operate the vehicle and that other person possesses a valid operator's license and would not, as determined by the arresting law enforcement agency, indicate a lack of ability to operate a motor vehicle in a safe manner or would otherwise, by operating the motor vehicle, be in violation of this Code.

(f) Except as provided in Chapter 18a of this Code,[1] the owner or lessor of privately owned real property within this State, or any person authorized by such owner or lessor, or any law enforcement agency in the case of publicly owned real property may cause any motor vehicle abandoned or left unattended upon such property without permission to be removed by a towing service without liability for the costs of removal, transportation or storage or damage caused by such removal, transportation or storage. The towing or removal of any vehicle from private property without the consent of the registered owner or other legally authorized person in control of the vehicle is subject to compliance with the following conditions and restrictions:

1. Any towed or removed vehicle must be stored at the site of the towing service's place of business. The site must be open during business hours, and for the purpose of redemption of vehicles, during the time that the person or firm towing such vehicle is open for towing purposes.

2. The towing service shall within 30 minutes of completion of such towing or removal, notify the law enforcement agency having jurisdiction of such towing or removal, and the make, model, color and license plate number of the vehicle, and shall obtain and record the name of the person at the law enforcement agency to whom such information was reported.

3. If the registered owner or legally authorized person entitled to possession of the vehicle shall arrive at the scene prior to actual removal or towing of the vehicle, the vehicle shall be disconnected from the tow truck and that person shall be allowed to remove the vehicle without interference, upon the payment of a reasonable service fee of not more than one half the posted rate of the towing service as provided in paragraph 6 of this subsection, for which a receipt shall be given.

4. The rebate or payment of money or any other valuable consideration from the towing service or its owners, managers or employees to the owners or operators of the premises from which the vehicles are towed or removed, for the privilege of removing or towing those vehicles, is prohibited. Any individual who violates this paragraph shall be guilty of a Class A misdemeanor.

5. Except for property appurtenant to and obviously a part of a single family residence, and except for instances where notice is personally given to the owner or other legally authorized person in control of the vehicle that the area in which that vehicle is parked is reserved or otherwise unavailable to unauthorized vehicles and they are subject to being removed at the owner or operator's expense, any property owner or lessor, prior to towing or removing any vehicle from private property without the consent of the owner or other legally authorized person in control of that vehicle, must post a notice meeting the following requirements:

a. The notice must be prominently placed at each driveway access or curb cut allowing vehicular access to the property within 5 feet from the public right-of-way line. If there are no curbs or access barriers, the sign must be posted not less than one sign each 100 feet of lot frontage.

b. The notice must indicate clearly, in not less than 2 inch high light-reflective letters on a contrasting background, that unauthorized vehicles will be towed away at the owner's expense.

c. The notice must also provide the name and current telephone number of the towing service towing or removing the vehicle.

d. The sign structure containing the required notices must be permanently installed with the bottom of the sign not less than 4 feet above ground level, and must be continuously maintained on the property for not less than 24 hours prior to the towing or removing of any vehicle.

6. Any towing service that tows or removes vehicles and proposes to require the owner, operator, or person in control of the vehicle to pay the costs of towing and storage prior to redemption of the vehicle must file and keep on record with the local law enforcement agency a complete copy of the current rates to be charged for such services, and post at the storage site an identical rate schedule and any written contracts with property owners, lessors, or persons in control of property which authorize them to remove vehicles as provided in this Section.

7. No person shall engage in the removal of vehicles from private property as described in this Section without filing a notice of intent in each community where he intends to do such removal, and such notice shall be filed at least 7 days before commencing such towing.

8. No removal of a vehicle from private property shall be done except upon express written instructions of the owners or persons in charge of the private property upon which the vehicle is said to be trespassing.

9. Vehicle entry for the purpose of removal shall be allowed with reasonable care on the part of the person or firm towing the vehicle. Such person or firm shall be liable for any damages occasioned to the vehicle if such entry is not in accordance with the standards of reasonable care.

10. When a vehicle has been towed or removed pursuant to this Section, it must be released to its owner or custodian within one half hour after requested, if such request is made during business hours. Any vehicle owner or custodian or agent shall have the right to inspect the vehicle before accepting its return, and no release or waiver of any kind which would release the towing service from liability for damages incurred during the towing and storage may be required from any vehicle owner or other legally authorized person as a condition of release of the vehicle. A detailed, signed receipt showing the legal name of the towing service must be given to the person paying towing or storage charges at the time of payment, whether requested or not.

This Section shall not apply to law enforcement, firefighting, rescue, ambulance, or other emergency vehicles which are marked as such or to property owned by any governmental entity.

When an authorized person improperly causes a motor vehicle to be removed, such person shall be liable to the owner or lessee of the vehicle for the cost or removal, transportation and storage, any damages resulting from the removal, transportation and storage, attorney's fee and court costs.

Any towing or storage charges accrued shall be payable by the use of any major credit card, in addition to being payable in cash.

11. Towing companies shall also provide insurance coverage for areas where vehicles towed under the provisions of this Chapter will be impounded or otherwise stored, and shall adequately cover loss by fire, theft or other risks.

Any person who fails to comply with the conditions and restrictions of this subsection shall be guilty of a Class C misdemeanor and shall be fined not less than $100 nor more than $500.

(g) When a vehicle is determined to be a hazardous dilapidated motor vehicle pursuant to Section 11-40-3.1 of the Illinois Municipal Code,[2] its removal and impoundment by a towing service may be authorized by a law enforcement agency with appropriate jurisdiction.

When a vehicle removal from either public or private property is authorized by a law enforcement agency, the owner of the vehicle shall be responsible for all towing and storage charges.

Vehicles removed from public or private property and stored by a commercial vehicle relocator or any other towing service in compliance with this Section and Sections 4-201 and 4-202 of this Code, shall be subject to a possessor lien for services pursuant to "An Act concerning liens for labor, services, skill or materials furnished upon or storage furnished for chattels", filed July 24, 1941, as amended, and the provisions of Section 1 of that Act relating to notice and implied consent shall be deemed satisfied by compliance with Section 18a-302 and subsection (6) of Section 18a-300. In no event shall such lien be greater than the rate or rates established in accordance with subsection (6) of Section 18a-200 of this Code. In no event shall such lien be increased or altered to reflect any charge for services or materials rendered in addition to those authorized by this Act. Every such lien shall be payable by use of any major credit card, in addition to being payable in cash.

P.A. 76-1586, § 4-202, eff. July 1, 1970. Amended by P.A. 76-1437, § 1, eff. July 1, 1970. Renumbered § 4-203 and amended by 78-858, § 1, eff. Jan. 1, 1974. Amended by P.A. 83-879, § 2, eff. July 1, 1984; P.A. 84-1311, § 1, eff. Aug. 27, 1986; P.A. 85-963, § 1, eff. July 1, 1988; P.A. 85-1237, § 1, eff. Jan. 1, 1989; P.A. 86-460, § 2, eff. Jan. 1, 1990; P.A. 86-820, Art. III, § 3-35, eff. Sept. 7, 1989; P.A. 86-1028, Art. II, § 2-44, eff. Feb. 5, 1990; P.A. 87-531, § 1, eff. Jan. 1, 1992; P.A. 90-738, § 5, eff. Jan. 1, 1999.

Formerly Ill.Rev.Stat.1991, ch. 95 ½, ¶ 4-203.

1 625 ILCS 5/18a-100 et seq.

2 65 ILCS 5/11-40-3.1.

5/4-204. Police tows; reports, release of vehicles, payment

§ 4-204. Police tows; reports, release of vehicles, payment.

When a vehicle is authorized to be towed away as provided in Section 4-202 or 4-203:

(a) The authorization, any hold order, and any release shall be in writing, or confirmed in writing, with a copy given to the towing service.

(b) The police headquarters or office of the law officer authorizing the towing shall keep and maintain a record of the vehicle towed, listing the color, year of manufacture, manufacturer's trade name, manufacturer's series name, body style. Vehicle Identification Number, license plate year and number and registration sticker year and number displayed on the vehicle. The record shall also include the date and hour of tow, location towed from, location towed to, reason for towing and the name of the officer authorizing the tow.

(c) The owner, operator, or other legally entitled person shall be responsible to the towing service for payment of applicable removal, towing, storage, and processing charges and collection costs associated with a vehicle towed or held under order or authorization of a law enforcement agency. If a vehicle towed or held under order or authorization of a law enforcement agency is seized by the ordering or authorizing agency or any other law enforcement or governmental agency and sold, any unpaid removal, towing, storage, and processing charges and collection costs shall be paid to the towing service from the proceeds of the sale. If applicable law provides that the proceeds are to be paid into the treasury of the appropriate civil jurisdiction, then any unpaid removal, towing, storage, and processing charges and collection costs shall be paid to the towing service from the treasury of the civil jurisdiction. That payment shall not, however, exceed the amount of proceeds from the sale, with the balance to be paid by the owner, operator, or other legally entitled person.

(d) Upon delivery of a written release order to the towing service, a vehicle subject to a hold order shall be released to the owner, operator, or other legally entitled person upon proof of ownership or other entitlement and upon payment of applicable removal, towing, storage, and processing charges and collection costs.

P.A. 76-1586, § 4-203, eff. July 1, 1970. Amended by P.A. 76-1437, § 1, eff. July 1, 1970. Renumbered § 4-204 and amended by P.A. 78-858, § 1, eff. Jan. 1, 1974. Amended by P.A. 80-230, § 1, eff. Oct. 1, 1977; P.A. 89-433, § 5, eff. Dec. 15, 1995.

Formerly Ill.Rev.Stat.1991, ch. 95 ½, ¶ 4-204.

5/4-205. Record searches

§ 4-205. Record searches.

(a) When a law enforcement agency authorizing the impounding of a vehicle does not know the identity of the registered owner, lienholder or other legally entitled person, that law enforcement agency will cause the vehicle registration records of the State of Illinois to be searched by the Secretary of State for the purpose of obtaining the required ownership information.

(b) The law enforcement agency authorizing the impounding of a vehicle will cause the stolen motor vehicle files of the State Police to be searched by a directed communication to the State Police for stolen or wanted information on the vehicle. When the State Police files are searched with negative results, the information contained in the National Crime Information Center (NCIC) files will be searched by the State Police. The information determined from these record searches will be returned to the requesting law enforcement agency for that agency's use in sending a notification by certified mail to the registered owner, lienholder and other legally entitled persons advising where the vehicle is held, requesting a disposition be made and setting forth public sale information. Notification shall be sent no later than 10 business days after the date the law enforcement agency impounds or authorizes the impounding of a vehicle, provided that if the law enforcement agency is unable to determine the identity of the registered owner, lienholder or other person legally entitled to ownership of the impounded vehicle within a 10 business day period after impoundment, then notification shall be sent no later than 2 days after the date the identity of the registered owner, lienholder or other person legally entitled to ownership of the impounded vehicle is determined. Exceptions to a notification by certified mail to the registered owner, lienholder and other legally entitled persons are set forth in Section 4-209 of this Code.

(c) When ownership information is needed for a towing service to give notification as required under this Code, the towing service may cause the vehicle registration records of the State of Illinois to be searched by the Secretary of State.

The written request of a towing service, in the form and containing the information prescribed by the Secretary of State by rule, may be transmitted to the Secretary of State in person, by U.S. mail or other delivery service, by facsimile transmission, or by other means the Secretary of State deems acceptable.

The Secretary of State shall provide the required information, or a statement that the information was not found in the vehicle registration records of the State, by U.S. mail or other delivery service, facsimile transmission, as requested by the towing service, or by other means acceptable to the Secretary of State.

(d) The Secretary of State may prescribe standards and procedures for submission of requests for record searches and replies via computer link.

(e) Fees for services provided under this Section shall be in amounts prescribed by the Secretary of State under Section 3-821.1 of this Code. Payment may be made by the towing service using cash, any commonly accepted credit card, or any other means of payment deemed acceptable by the Secretary of State.

P.A. 76-1586, § 4-204, eff. July 1, 1970. Amended by P.A. 76-1437, § 1, eff. July 1, 1970. Renumbered § 4-205 and amended by P.A. 78-858, § 1, eff. Jan. 1, 1974. Amended by P.A. 82-363, § 1, eff. Jan. 1, 1982; P.A. 84-402, § 1, eff. Jan. 1, 1986; P.A. 86-947, § 2, eff. Nov. 13, 1989; P.A. 89-179, § 5, eff. Jan. 1, 1996; P.A. 89-433, § 5, eff. Dec. 15, 1995.

Formerly Ill.Rev.Stat.1991, ch. 95 ½, ¶ 4-205.

P.A. 89-433 incorporated the amendment by P.A. 89-179.

5/4-206. Identifying and tracing of vehicle ownership by Illinois State Police

§ 4-206. Identifying and tracing of vehicle ownership by Illinois State Police. When the registered owner, lienholder or other person legally entitled to the possession of a vehicle cannot be identified from the registration files of this State or from the registration files of a foreign state, if applicable, the law enforcement agency having custody of the vehicle shall notify the State Police, for the purpose of identifying the vehicle owner or other person legally entitled to the possession of the vehicle. The information obtained by the State Police will be immediately forwarded to the law enforcement agency having custody of the vehicle for notification purposes as set forth in Section 4-205 of this Code.

P.A. 76-1586, § 4-205, eff. July 1, 1970. Amended by P.A. 76-1437, § 1, eff. July 1, 1970. Renumbered § 4-206 and amended by P.A. 78-858, § 1, eff. Jan. 1, 1974. Amended by P.A. 82-363, § 1, eff. Jan. 1, 1982.

Formerly Ill.Rev.Stat.1991, ch. 95 ½, ¶ 4-206.

5/4-207. Reclaimed vehicles; expenses

§ 4-207. Reclaimed vehicles; expenses.

(a) Any time before a vehicle is sold at public sale or disposed of as provided in Section 4-208, the owner, lienholder or other person legally entitled to its possession may reclaim the vehicle by presenting to the law enforcement agency having custody of the vehicle proof of ownership or proof of the right to possession of the vehicle.

(b) No vehicle shall be released to the owner, lienholder, or other person under this Section until all towing, storage, and processing charges have been paid.

P.A. 76-1586, § 4-206, eff. July 1, 1970. Amended by P.A. 76-1437, § 1, eff. July 1, 1970. Renumbered § 4-207 and amended by P.A. 78-858, § 1, eff. Jan. 1, 1974. Amended by P.A. 82-363, § 1, eff. Jan. 1, 1982; P.A. 89-433, § 5, eff. Dec. 15, 1995.

Formerly Ill.Rev.Stat.1991, ch. 95 ½, ¶ 4-207.

5/4-208. Disposal of unclaimed vehicles

§ 4-208. Disposal of unclaimed vehicles.

(a) In cities having a population of more than 500,000, whenever an abandoned, lost, stolen or unclaimed vehicle, or vehicle determined to be a hazardous dilapidated motor vehicle pursuant to Section 11-40-3.1 of the Illinois Municipal Code,[1] remains unclaimed by the registered owner, lienholder or other legally entitled person for a period of 15 days after notice has been given under Sections 4-205 and 4-206 of this Code, the vehicle shall be disposed, pursuant to the provisions of the "Municipal purchasing act for cities of 500,000 or more population", to a person licensed as an automotive parts recycler, rebuilder or scrap processor under Chapter 5 of this Code.[2]

(b) Except as provided in Section 4-208 for cities with more than 500,000 inhabitants, when an abandoned, lost, stolen or unclaimed vehicle 7 years of age or newer remains unclaimed by the registered owner, lienholder or other legally entitled persons for a period of 30 days after notice has been given as provided in Sections 4-205 and 4-206 of this Code, the law enforcement agency or towing service having possession of the vehicle shall cause it to be sold at public auction to a person licensed as an automotive parts recycler, rebuilder or scrap processor under Chapter 5 of this Code or the towing operator which towed the vehicle. Notice of the time and place of the sale shall be posted in a conspicuous place for at least 10 days prior to the sale on the premises where the vehicle has been impounded. At least 10 days prior to the sale, the law enforcement agency where the vehicle is impounded, or the towing service where the vehicle is impounded, shall cause a notice of the time and place of the sale to be sent by certified mail to the registered owner, lienholder, or other legally entitled persons. Notice as provided in Sections 4-205 and 4-206 of this Code and as provided in this subsection (b) shall state the time and place of sale and shall contain a complete description of the vehicle to be sold and what steps must be taken by any legally entitled person to reclaim the vehicle.

(c) If an abandoned, lost, stolen, or unclaimed vehicle displays dealer plates, notice under this Section and Section 4-209 of this Code shall be sent to both the dealer and the registered owner, lienholder, or other legally entitled persons.

(d) In those instances where the certified notification specified in Sections 4-205 and 4-206 of this Code has been returned by the postal authorities to the law enforcement agency or towing service, the sending of a second certified notice will not be required.

P.A. 76-1586, § 4-207, eff. July 1, 1970. Amended by P.A. 76-1437, § 1, eff. July 1, 1970. Renumbered § 4-208 and amended by P.A. 78-858, § 1, eff. Jan. 1, 1974. Amended by P.A. 82-363, § 1, eff. Jan. 1, 1982; P.A. 83-1473, § 1, eff. Jan. 1, 1985; P.A. 84-1302, § 1, eff. Jan. 1, 1987; P.A. 84-1304, § 1, eff. Jan. 1, 1987; P.A. 86-460, § 2, eff. Jan. 1, 1990; P.A. 86-1260, § 1, eff. Jan. 1, 1991; P.A. 89-433, § 5, eff. Dec. 15, 1995; P.A. 90-330, § 5, eff. Aug. 8, 1997.

Formerly Ill.Rev.Stat.1991, ch. 95 ½, ¶ 4-208.

1 65 ILCS 5/11-40-3.1.

2 625 ILCS 5/5-100 et seq.

5/4-209. Disposal of unclaimed vehicles more than 7 years of age; disposal of abandoned or unclaimed vehicles without notice

§ 4-209. Disposal of unclaimed vehicles more than 7 years of age; disposal of abandoned or unclaimed vehicles without notice.

(a) When the identity of the registered owner, lienholder, or other legally entitled persons of an abandoned, lost, or unclaimed vehicle of 7 years of age or newer cannot be determined by any means provided for in this Chapter, the vehicle may be sold as provided in Section 4-208 without notice to any person whose identity cannot be determined.

(b) When an abandoned vehicle of more than 7 years of age is impounded as specified by this Chapter, or when any such vehicle is towed at the request or with the consent of the owner or operator and is subsequently abandoned, it will be kept in custody or storage for a minimum of 10 days for the purpose of determining the identity of the registered owner, lienholder, or other legally entitled persons and contacting the registered owner, lienholder, or other legally entitled persons by the U. S. Mail, public service or in person for a determination of disposition; and, an examination of the State Police stolen vehicle files for theft and wanted information. At the expiration of the 10 day period, without the benefit of disposition information being received from the registered owner, lienholder, or other legally entitled persons, the vehicle may be disposed of in either of the following ways:

(1) The law enforcement agency having jurisdiction will authorize the disposal of the vehicle as junk or salvage.

(2) The towing service may sell the vehicle in the manner provided in Section 4-208 of this Code, provided that this paragraph (2) shall not apply to vehicles towed by order or authorization of a law enforcement agency.

(c) A vehicle classified as an antique vehicle, custom vehicle, or street rod may however be sold to a person desiring to restore it.

P.A. 76-1586, § 4-208, eff. July 1, 1970. Amended by P.A. 78-738, § 1, eff. Jan. 1, 1974. Renumbered § 4-209 and amended by P.A. 78-858, § 1, eff. Jan. 1, 1974. Amended by P.A. 78-1205, § 1, eff. Sept. 5, 1974; P.A. 78-1297, § 58, eff. March 4, 1975; P.A. 81-653, § 2, eff. Sept. 14, 1979; P.A. 82-363, § 1, eff. Jan. 1, 1982; P.A. 83-449, § 1, eff. Jan. 1, 1984; P.A. 85-951, § 1, eff. July 1, 1988; P.A. 86-1260, § 1, eff. Jan. 1, 1991; P.A. 89-433, § 5, eff. Dec. 15, 1995; P.A. 92-668, § 5, eff. Jan. 1, 2003.

Formerly Ill.Rev.Stat.1991, ch. 95 ½, ¶ 4-209.

Validity

Provision for post-tow notice by U.S. mail to owner of impounded vehicle more than 7 years old has been held unconstitutional by the U.S. District Court, Northern District of Illinois, in the case of Kohn v. Mucia, N.D. Ill.1991, 776 F.Supp. 348. See Notes of Decisions.

5/4-209.1. Disposal of hazardous dilapidated motor vehicles

§ 4-209.1. Disposal of hazardous dilapidated motor vehicles. Any hazardous dilapidated motor vehicle impounded pursuant to the provisions of this Article and Section 11-40-3.1 of the Illinois Municipal Code,[1] whether impounded at a public facility or on the property of private towing service, shall be kept in custody for a period of 10 days for the purpose of determining the identity of the registered owner or lienholder and contacting such owner or lienholder, if known, by regular U.S. Mail. At the expiration of the 10-day period, without benefit of disposition information being received from the registered owner or lienholder, the law enforcement agency having jurisdiction will authorize the disposal of the vehicle as junk.

P.A. 76-1586, § 4-209.1, added by P.A. 86-460, § 2, eff. Jan. 1, 1990.

Formerly Ill.Rev.Stat.1991, ch. 95 ½, ¶ 4-209.1.

1 65 ILCS 5/11-40-3.1.

5/4-209.2. Collection of unpaid charges

§ 4-209.2. Collection of unpaid charges. In an action to collect towing, storage, and processing charges that remain unpaid after disposition of a vehicle towed or relocated under this Code, the towing service may recover reasonable collection costs.

P.A. 76-1586, § 4-209.2, added by P.A. 89-433, § 5, eff. Dec. 15, 1995.

5/4-210. Police reports after vehicle is reclaimed or disposed of

§ 4-210. Police reports after vehicle is reclaimed or disposed of. When a vehicle in the custody of a law enforcement agency is reclaimed by the registered owner, lienholder or other legally entitled person, or when the vehicle is sold at public sale or otherwise disposed of as provided in this Chapter, a report of the transaction will be maintained by that law enforcement agency for a period of one year from the date of the sale or disposal.

P.A. 76-1586, § 4-210, eff. July 1, 1970. Amended by P.A. 76-1437, § 1, eff. July 1, 1970; P.A. 78-858, § 1, eff. Jan. 1, 1974; P.A. 82-363, § 1, eff. Jan. 1, 1982.

Formerly Ill.Rev.Stat.1991, ch. 95 ½, ¶ 4-210.

5/4-211. Disposition of proceeds of sale of unclaimed vehicles

§ 4-211. Disposition of proceeds of sale of unclaimed vehicles. (a) When a vehicle located within the corporate limits of a city, village or town is authorized to be towed away by a law enforcement agency having jurisdiction and disposed of as set forth in this Chapter, the proceeds of the public sale or disposition after the deduction of towing, storage and processing charges shall be deposited in the treasury of such city, village or town.

(b) When a vehicle located outside the corporate limits of a city, village, or town is authorized to be towed away by a law enforcement agency having jurisdiction and disposed of as set forth in this Chapter, the proceeds of the public sale or disposition, after deducting towing, storage and processing costs shall be deposited in the county treasury of the county where the vehicle was located at the time of the tow.

(c) The provisions of this Section shall not apply to vehicles disposed of or sold at public sale under subsection (k) of Section 4-107 of this Code.

P.A. 76-1586, § 4-211, eff. July 1, 1970. Amended by P.A. 76-1437, § 1, eff. July 1, 1970; P.A. 83-830, § 1, eff. Sept. 24, 1983.

Formerly Ill.Rev.Stat.1991, ch. 95 ½, ¶ 4-211.

5/4-212. Ownership documents for vehicles after public sale—removal of liens

§ 4-212. Ownership documents for vehicles after public sale—removal of liens.

When an applicant for a salvage certificate or junking certificate under this Chapter presents to the Secretary of State proof that he has purchased or acquired a vehicle at a public sale as authorized by this Chapter and such fact is certified to by the law enforcement agency having jurisdiction over the public sale of a vehicle, the Secretary of State shall issue a salvage certificate or junking certificate for the vehicle upon receipt of the statutory fee and a properly executed application for a salvage certificate or junking certificate. The salvage certificate or junking certificate issued by the Secretary of State under this Section shall be free of any lien that existed against the vehicle prior to the time the vehicle was acquired by the applicant under this Chapter.

P.A. 76-1586, § 4-212, eff. July 1, 1970. Amended by P.A. 76-1437, § 1, eff. July 1, 1970; P.A. 78-858, § 1, eff. Jan. 1, 1974; P.A. 85-951, § 1, eff. July 1, 1988.

Formerly Ill.Rev.Stat.1991, ch. 95 ½, ¶ 4-212.

5/4-212.1. Department to perform duties related to abandoned, lost, stolen or unclaimed vehicles

§ 4-212.1. In cities with more than 500,000 inhabitants, the corporate authorities may, by ordinance, designate any department of municipal government to do any of the following:

(1) To perform any of the duties and functions specified for law enforcement agencies in subsection (a) of Section 4-205 and in Sections 4-201, 4-203, 4-204, 4-206, 4-207, 4-208, 4-209, 4-210, 4-211 and 4-212; and

(2) To authorize a towing service to remove and take possession of abandoned, lost, stolen or unclaimed vehicles, in the manner that municipal police may make such authorization pursuant to Section 4-202; and

(3) To send notifications as required under subsection (b) of Section 4-205.

P.A. 76-1586, § 4-212.1, added by P.A. 86-947, § 2, eff. Nov. 13, 1989.

Formerly Ill.Rev.Stat.1991, ch. 95 ½, ¶ 4-212.1.

5/4-213. Liability of law enforcement officers, agencies, and towing services

§ 4-213. Liability of law enforcement officers, agencies, and towing services.

(a) A law enforcement officer or agency, a department of municipal government designated under Section 4-212.1 or its officers or employees, or a towing service owner, operator, or employee shall not be held to answer or be liable for damages in any action brought by the registered owner, former registered owner, or his legal representative, lienholder or any other person legally entitled to the possession of a vehicle when the vehicle was processed and sold or disposed of as provided by this Chapter.

(b) A towing service, and any of its officers or employees, that removes or tows a vehicle as a result of being directed to do so by a law enforcement officer or agency or a department of municipal government or its officers or employees shall not be held to answer or be liable for injury to, loss of, or damages to any real or personal property that occurs in the course of the removal or towing of a vehicle or its contents on a limited access highway in a designated Incident Management Program that uses fast lane clearance techniques as defined by the Department of Transportation.

P.A. 76-1586, § 4-213, eff. July 1, 1970. Amended by P.A. 76-1437, § 1, eff. July 1, 1970; P.A. 78-858, § 1, eff. Jan. 1, 1974; P.A. 82-363, § 1, eff. Jan. 1, 1982; P.A. 86-947, § 2, eff. Nov. 13, 1989; P.A. 89-433, § 5, eff. Dec. 15, 1995.

Formerly Ill.Rev.Stat.1991, ch. 95 ½, ¶ 4-213.

5/4-214. Violations of section 4-201

§ 4-214. Violations of Section 4-201.

(a) Any person who violates Section 4-201 of this Code or who aids and abets in that violation:

(1) shall be subject to a mandatory fine of $200; and

(2) shall be required by the court to make a disposition on the abandoned or unclaimed vehicle and pay all towing, storage, and processing charges and collection costs pursuant to Section 4-203, subsections (a) and (e).

(b) When a vehicle is abandoned, it shall be presumed that the last registered owner is responsible for the abandonment and shall be liable for all towing, storage, and processing charges and collection costs, less any amounts realized in the disposal of the vehicle. The last registered owner's liability for storage fees may not exceed a maximum of 30 days' storage fees.

The presumption established under this subsection may be rebutted by a showing that, prior to the time of the tow:

(1) a report of vehicle theft was filed with respect to the vehicle; or

(2) the vehicle was sold or transferred and the last registered owner provides the towing service with the

correct identity and address of the new owner at the time of the sale or transfer.

If the presumption established under this subsection is rebutted, the person responsible for theft of the vehicle or to whom the vehicle was sold or transferred is liable for all towing, storage, and processing charges and collection costs.

P.A. 76-1586, § 4-214, added by P.A. 76-1437, § 1, eff. July 1, 1970. Amended by P.A. 77-2720, § 1, eff. Jan. 1, 1973; P.A. 85-963, § 1, eff. July 1, 1988; P.A. 86-460, § 2, eff. Jan. 1, 1990; P.A. 89-433, § 5, eff. Dec. 15, 1995.

Formerly Ill.Rev.Stat.1991, ch. 95 ½, ¶ 4-214.

5/4-214.1. Failure to pay fines, charges, and costs on an abandoned vehicle

§ 4-214.1. Failure to pay fines, charges, and costs on an abandoned vehicle.

(a) Whenever any resident of this State fails to pay any fine, charge, or cost imposed for a violation of Section 4-201 of this Code, or a similar provision of a local ordinance, the clerk may notify the Secretary of State, on a report prescribed by the Secretary, and the Secretary shall prohibit the renewal, reissue, or reinstatement of the resident's driving privileges until the fine, charge, or cost has been paid in full. The clerk shall provide notice to the driver, at the driver's last known address as shown on the court's records, stating that the action will be effective on the 46th day following the date of the above notice if payment is not received in full by the court of venue.

(b) Following receipt of the report from the clerk, the Secretary of State shall make the proper notation to the driver's file to prohibit the renewal, reissue, or reinstatement of the driver's driving privileges. Except as provided in subsection (d) of this Section, the notation shall not be removed from the driver's record until the driver satisfies the outstanding fine, charge, or cost and an appropriate notice on a form prescribed by the Secretary is received by the Secretary from the court of venue, stating that the fine, charge, or cost has been paid in full. Upon payment in full of a fine, charge, or court cost which has previously been reported under this Section as unpaid, the clerk of the court shall present the driver with a signed receipt containing the seal of the court indicating that the fine, charge, or cost has been paid in full, and shall forward immediately to the Secretary of State a notice stating that the fine, charge, or cost has been paid in full.

(c) Notwithstanding the receipt of a report from the clerk as prescribed in subsection (a), nothing in this Section is intended to place any responsibility upon the Secretary of State to provide independent notice to the driver of any potential action to disallow the renewal, reissue, or reinstatement of the driver's driving privileges.

(d) The Secretary of State shall renew, reissue, or reinstate a driver's driving privileges which were previously refused under this Section upon presentation of an original receipt which is signed by the clerk of the court and contains the seal of the court indicating that the fine, charge, or cost has been paid in full. The Secretary of State shall retain the receipt for his or her records.

P.A. 76-1586, § 4-214.1, added by P.A. 92-654, § 5, eff. Jan. 1, 2003.

5/4-215. Rebuilt vehicles; clean titles

§ 4-215. Rebuilt vehicles; clean titles. Persons licensed under Section 5-301 of this Code may obtain a certificate of title that does not bear the notation "REBUILT" from a certificate of purchase when the damage to the vehicle is 25% or less of its market value, there has been no structural damage to the vehicle, there is no history of a salvage certificate, and the vehicle has undergone a salvage inspection by the Secretary of State and a safety inspection under Section 13-101 of this Code. The application for a certificate of title shall contain an affirmation under penalty for perjury that the vehicle on the date of the application is not damaged in excess of 25% of its market value, has no structural damage, and has no history of salvage.

P.A. 76-1586, § 4-215, added by P.A. 89-433, § 5, eff. Dec. 15, 1995.

ARTICLE III. VEHICLE RECYCLING BOARD

Date Effective

Article 3 was added by P.A. 78-857, effective September 14, 1973.

Section

5/4-300. Definitions

§ 4-300. Definitions. For the purposes of this Article, the following word shall have the meaning ascribed to it as follows:

Board. The Vehicle Recycling Board of the State of Illinois, acting directly or through its duly authorized officers and agents.

P.A. 76-1586, § 4-300, added by P.A. 78-857, § 1, eff. Sept. 14, 1973.

Formerly Ill.Rev.Stat.1991, ch. 95 ½, ¶ 4-300.

5/4-301. State policy

§ 4-301. State policy. The General Assembly finds that abandoned and derelict vehicles: constitute a safety hazard and a public nuisance; are detrimental to the health, safety and welfare of the general public by harboring disease, providing breeding places for vermin, inviting plundering, creating fire hazards, and presenting physical dangers to children and others; produce scenic blights which degrade the environment and adversely affect land values and the proper maintenance and continuing development of the State of Illinois and all of its subdivisions; represent a resource out of place and an energy loss to the Illinois economy, and require state and local governmental attention, in conjunction with any federal governmental attention, in order to assure the expeditious removal and recycling of these abandoned and derelict vehicles.

The General Assembly declares therefore, that it is the policy of the State of Illinois, to:

1. Prohibit the abandonment of vehicles and the retention of derelicts, and to enforce such prohibition by law while reminding vehicle owners of their own individual responsibility to dispose of such vehicles;

2. Encourage the development of procedures and techniques to facilitate the expeditious removal of abandoned and derelict vehicles from public or private premises;

3. Encourage the State of Illinois and all of its political subdivisions, in cooperation with the federal government and the private sector of our State, and in cooperation with other states of the United States, to recover and recycle the resource represented by abandoned and derelict vehicles to the fullest extent practicable.

P.A. 76-1586, § 4-301, added by P.A. 78-857, § 1, eff. Sept. 14, 1973. Amended by P.A. 81-653, § 2, eff. Sept. 14, 1979.

Formerly Ill.Rev.Stat.1991, ch. 95 ½, ¶ 4-301.

5/4-302. Vehicle Recycling Board

§ 4-302. Vehicle Recycling Board. There is hereby created the Vehicle Recycling Board of the State of Illinois composed of the Secretary of Transportation, the Director of State Police, the Director of Public Health, the Director of the Environmental Protection Agency, the Superintendent of State Troopers or their designated representatives. The Governor shall designate the Chairman and Secretary of the Board.

The Board shall appoint an advisory committee, of no less than 10 members, to include an official representative of the Office of the Secretary of State as designated by the Secretary; and other appropriate representatives from such sources as: statewide associations of city, county and township governing bodies; knowledgeable successful leaders from the auto recycling private sector; the State associations of chiefs of police, county sheriffs, police officers; and State agencies having a direct or indirect relationship with vehicle recycling.

P.A. 76-1586, § 4-302, added by P.A. 78-857, § 1, eff. Sept. 14, 1973. Amended by P.A. 81-653, § 2, eff. Sept. 14, 1979; P.A. 84-25, Art. IV, § 27, eff. July 18, 1985.

Formerly Ill.Rev.Stat.1991, ch. 95 ½, ¶ 4-302.

5/4-303. Tenure, vacancies and expenses

§ 4-303. Tenure, vacancies and expenses. State officers and their designated representatives on the Board and representatives of the State agencies serving on the advisory committee, shall serve without additional compensation and their necessary expenses shall be borne by the State office or agency represented. Members of the advisory committee shall be reimbursed for their necessary expenses in their attendance to meetings and functions as required by the Board.

The Board shall employ such personnel as deemed necessary by the Board to implement and administer this Act and any expenses incurred in its administration may be incurred and expended only within and pursuant to the appropriations made by the General Assembly.

The records of the Board shall be subject to audit by the Auditor General.

P.A. 76-1586, § 4-303, added by P.A. 78-857, § 1, eff. Sept. 14, 1973. Amended by P.A. 81-653, § 2, eff. Sept. 14, 1979.

Formerly Ill.Rev.Stat.1991, ch. 95 ½, ¶ 4-303.

5/4-304. Implementation and administration of policy

§ 4-304. Implementation and administration of policy. The Board shall consider and adopt such programs as are designed to implement and administer the policies hereinbefore expressed and within the appropriations provided for by the General Assembly.

In adopting such programs, the Board shall take into consideration the programs of the federal government in the same field, so as to assure full coordination therewith and that the State of Illinois does not duplicate federal actions and programs. The programs to be considered by the Board shall in addition be designed to:

1. Effect the efficient removal of abandoned vehicles from the highways, streets, roads, other public property, as well as from private property within Illinois.

2. Effect the efficient removal of abandoned and derelict vehicles from private property to be junked, salvaged, recycled, or reclaimed, to wrecking, recycling or salvaging facilities, or to a temporary impoundment or area collection center.

3. Effect efficient recycling or scrap processing of retired vehicles and the salvaging of usable parts.

4. Permit the restoration of antique and historic vehicles by private persons or agencies.

5. Work with other State agencies to effect the efficient and effective recycling of solid and liquid motor vehicle waste, including motor vehicle drain oil, derived in the recycling of a motor vehicle.

6. Recoup the costs of removal and disposal of abandoned and derelict vehicles from vehicle owners, land owners and persons who abandon or discard such vehicles and from other suitable sources.

7. Promote and publicize individual responsibility of vehicle owners for their personal disposal of unwanted and discarded vehicles and develop an effective promotional campaign to show owners how to properly dispose of such vehicles; and the legal consequences of not doing so.

8. Provide State coordination, expertise and assistance to all local units of government, as needed, seeking legislative remedy where appropriate regarding: vehicle detitling procedure; impoundment time periods; the legal restrictions unnecessarily delaying vehicle disposal; and, to promote and advance the technology, growth and development of the legitimate auto recycling industry to the end that this industry can effectively recycle all vehicles annually retired and accumulated in Illinois with a minimum of assistance from the State or its subdivisions.

The Board is empowered to negotiate and enter into reciprocal agreements with other states and State and federal agencies, in furtherance of the provisions of this Act, as amended; provided, however, that no such reciprocal agreement may be entered into without the approval and authorization of the State body legally required to approve such agreements.

The Board shall make rules, regulations and by-laws, not inconsistent with this Act or any other law of this State, as to its own organization and conduct and for the implementation and administration of this Act.

The Board is further empowered to enter into an agreement with any State agency represented on the Board, to carry out the administration of the abandoned and derelict vehicle abatement program of the Board, and to make such funds available as may be found necessary by the Board, as appropriated by the General Assembly.

P.A. 76-1586, § 4-304, added by P.A. 78-857, § 1, eff. Sept. 14, 1973. Amended by P.A. 81-653, § 2, eff. Sept. 14, 1979; P.A. 84-470, § 1, eff. Sept. 17, 1985; P.A. 90-655, § 153, eff. July 30, 1998; P.A. 91-357, § 231, eff. July 29, 1999.

Formerly Ill.Rev.Stat.1991, ch. 95 ½, ¶ 4-304.

5/4-305. Inventory, collection and disposal facilities

§ 4-305. Inventory, collection and disposal facilities. If not otherwise economically practicable, the Board may provide by contract with private persons or agencies, or with political subdivisions of the State of Illinois and all local governmental units of government, for the inventory, collection and disposal or any portion thereof, of abandoned and derelict vehicles to wrecking, salvage or recycling plants, or, provide facilities for the collection and proper disposal of any vehicle under the provisions of this Act, as amended.

The Board may further formulate a program, statewide or within prescribed areas, for the inventory and collection of abandoned and derelict vehicles and to provide for their junking, salvage or recycling. In all cases, the Board shall coordinate such program with each affected State agency, local governmental unit, and local law enforcement agencies.

The Board may further subsidize political subdivisions of this State, local governmental units and local law enforcement agencies for their costs, provable by audit and not otherwise recoverable from any proceeds derived from any sale of abandoned and derelict vehicles, in collecting, storing and disposing of such vehicles during a reimbursement period set by the Board.

Any expenditure of funds hereunder shall be subject to audit by the Auditor General, within the appropriations for this purpose by the General Assembly, and may be made only in the event that cost-analysis and program efficiency show that such reimbursement subsidy is justified. No owner of any abandoned or derelict vehicle shall in any way, receive any funds hereunder. This shall not, however, prohibit the Board from examining the strategy of paying owners of discarded vehicles a limited sum for delivering their vehicles to a collection point when scrap prices are depressed; and bringing emergency measures such as this to the attention of the General Assembly for its consideration at a later time.

P.A. 76-1586, § 4-305, added by P.A. 78-857, § 1, eff. Sept. 14, 1973. Amended by P.A. 81-653, § 2, eff. Sept. 14, 1979.

Formerly Ill.Rev.Stat.1991, ch. 95 ½, ¶ 4-305.

5/4-306. Federal aid

§ 4-306. Federal aid. The Board is authorized and empowered to do all things necessary and proper to fully cooperate with any agency of the United States in the administration of any federal act relating to abandoned and derelict vehicles or the recycling or scrapping of vehicles now in effect or hereafter enacted for the purpose of appropriation of funds for the payment to or toward the junking, salvaging, recycling or scrapping of retired and discarded vehicles.

Whenever federal funds are expended to provide for the payment to or toward the junking, salvaging, recycling or scrapping of such vehicles, the amount received as reimbursement therefor shall be paid into the fund or trust fund in the State Treasury from which such expenditure was made.

P.A. 76-1586, § 4-306, added by P.A. 78-857, § 1, eff. Sept. 14, 1973. Amended by P.A. 81-653, § 2, eff. Sept. 14, 1979.

Formerly Ill.Rev.Stat.1991, ch. 95 ½, ¶ 4-306.

5/4-307. Funding and fees

§ 4-307. Funding and fees. (a) The programs initiated by the Board shall be funded by appropriations by the General Assembly to the Board. In addition to any fees enacted by the General Assembly, the Board shall recommend additional and optional methods of financing such programs to the end that the programs shall become self-sufficient.

(b) In addition to any provisions made by the General Assembly, the Board shall recommend incentives to induce the junking of abandoned and derelict vehicles not suitable for rebuilding or restoring as antiques or historic vehicles. The Board may further recommend a subsidy to implement Section 4-305.

P.A. 76-1586, § 4-307, added by P.A. 78-857, § 1, eff. Sept. 14, 1973. Amended by P.A. 79-1107, § 2, eff. Sept. 26, 1975; P.A. 81-653, § 2, eff. Sept. 14, 1979; P.A. 84-470, § 1, eff. Sept. 17, 1985.

Formerly Ill.Rev.Stat.1991, ch. 95 ½, ¶ 4-307.

CHAPTER 5. DEALERS, TRANSPORTERS, WRECKERS AND REBUILDERS

Enactment

The Illinois Vehicle Code was enacted by P.A. 76-1586, effective July 1, 1970. The Code constitutes a consolidated recodification of various earlier laws and acts including the Illinois Motor Vehicle Law of 1957.

5/5-100. Definitions

§ 5-100. Definitions. For the purposes of this Chapter, the following words shall have the meanings ascribed to them as follows:

"Additional place of business" means a place owned or leased and occupied by the dealer in addition to its established place of business, at which the dealer conducts or intends to conduct business on a permanent or long term basis. The term does not include an area where an off site sale or exhibition is conducted. The Secretary of State shall adopt guidelines for the administration and enforcement of this definition by rule.

"Display exhibition" means a temporary display of vehicles by a dealer licensed under Section 5-101 or 5-102, at a location at which no vehicles are offered for sale, that is conducted at a place other than the dealer's established and additional places of business.

"Established place of business" means the place owned or leased and occupied by any person duly licensed or required to be licensed as a dealer for the purpose of engaging in selling, buying, bartering, displaying, exchanging or dealing in, on consignment or otherwise, vehicles and their essential parts and for such other ancillary purposes as may be permitted by the Secretary by rule. It shall include an office in which the dealer's records shall be separate and distinct from any other business or tenant which may occupy space in the same building except as provided in Section 5-101.1. This office shall not be located in a house trailer, residence, tent, temporary stand, temporary address, room or rooms in a hotel or rooming house, nor the premises occupied by a single or multiple unit residence. The established place of business of a scrap processor shall be the fixed location where the scrap processor maintains its principal place of business. The Secretary of State shall, by rule and regulation, adopt guidelines for the administration and enforcement of this definition, such as, but not limited to issues concerning the required hours of operation, describing where vehicles are displayed and offered for sale, where books and records are maintained and requirements for the fulfillment of warranties. A dealer may have an additional place of business as defined under this Section.

"Motor vehicle financing affiliate" means a business organization registered to do business in Illinois that, pursuant to a written contract with either (1) a single new or used motor vehicle dealer or (2) a single group of new or used motor vehicle dealers that share a common ownership within the group, purchases new or used motor vehicles on behalf of the dealer or group of dealers and then sells, transfers, or assigns those motor vehicles to the dealer or group of dealers. The motor vehicle financing affiliate must be incorporated or organized solely to purchase new or used vehicles on behalf of the new or used motor vehicle dealer or group of dealers with which it has contracted, shall not sell motor vehicles at retail, shall perform only those business functions related to the purchasing of motor vehicles and selling, transferring, or assigning those motor vehicles to the dealer or group of dealers. The motor vehicle financing affiliate must be licensed under the provisions of Section 5-101.1 and must not be licensed as a new or used motor vehicle dealer.

"Off site sale" means the temporary display and sale of vehicles, for a period of not more than 7 calendar days (excluding Sundays), by a dealer licensed under Section 5-101 or 5-102 at a place other than the dealer's established and additional places of business.

"Relevant market area", for a new vehicle dealer licensed under Section 5-101 and for a used vehicle dealer licensed under Section 5-102, means the area within 10 miles of the established or additional place of business of the dealer located in a county with a population of 300,000 or more, or within 15 miles if the established place of business is located in a county with a population of less than 300,000.

"Trade show exhibition" means a temporary display of vehicles, by dealers licensed under Section 5-101 or 5-102, or any other person as defined in subsection (c) of Section 5-102.1, at a location at which no vehicles are offered for sale that is conducted at a place other than the dealer's established and additional places of business. In order for a display exhibition to be considered a trade show exhibition, it must be participated in by at least 3 dealers, 2 of which must be licensed under Section 5-101 or 5-102; and a trade show exhibition of new vehicles shall only be participated in by licensed new vehicle dealers at least 2 of which must be licensed under Section 5-101.

P.A. 76-1586, § 5-100, eff. July 1, 1970. Amended by P.A. 77-1316, § 1, eff. Jan. 1, 1972; P.A. 77-2751, § 1, eff. Sept. 1, 1972; P.A. 78-255, § 61, eff. Oct. 1, 1973; P.A. 78-858, § 1, eff. Jan. 1, 1974; P.A. 78-1165, § 1, eff. Aug. 27, 1974; P.A. 78-1205, § 1, eff. Sept. 5, 1974; P.A. 78-1297, § 30, eff. March 4, 1975; P.A. 81-932, § 1, eff. Sept. 22, 1979; P.A. 83-1473, § 1, eff. Jan. 1, 1985; P.A. 84-1302, § 1, eff. Jan. 1 1987; P.A. 84-1304, § 1, eff. Jan. 1, 1987; P.A. 85-572, § 1, eff. Sept. 18, 1987; P.A. 85-1204, § 1, eff. Aug. 26, 1988; P.A. 86-444, § 1, eff. Jan. 1, 1990; P.A. 87-380, § 1, eff. July 1, 1992; P.A. 87-1249, § 1, eff. Dec. 24, 1992; P.A. 88-470, § 10, eff. Sept. 1, 1993; P.A. 88-588, § 5, eff. Jan. 1, 1995; P.A. 88-685, § 5, eff. Jan. 24, 1995; P.A. 89-235, Art. 2, § 2-120, eff. Aug. 4, 1995; P.A. 90-89, § 15, eff. Jan. 1, 1998; P.A. 91-415, § 5, eff. Jan. 1, 2000.

Formerly Ill.Rev.Stat.1991, ch. 95 ½, ¶ 5-100.

5/5-100-1. Findings and Purpose

§ 5-100-1. Findings and Purpose. The General Assembly finds that: (1) crimes involving the theft of vehicles and their parts have risen steadily over the past years, with a resulting loss of millions of dollars to the residents of this State; (2) essential to the criminal enterprise of vehicle theft operations is the ability of thieves to transfer or sell stolen vehicles or their parts through legitimate commercial channels, making them available for sale to the automotive industry; (3) vehicle dealers, scrap processors, automotive parts recyclers, repairers and rebuilders who comprise the vast majority of the persons engaged in the automotive business in this State are frequently exposed to pressures and influences from motor vehicle thieves; (4) elements of organized crime are constantly attempting to influence businessmen engaged in the sale and repair of motor vehicles so as to further their own criminal interests; and (5) close and strict government regulation of vehicle dealers, scrap processors, automotive parts recyclers, repairers and rebuilders will provide a system of tracking the flow of vehicles and their essential parts and therefore significantly reduce the numbers of vehicle-related thefts in this State. It is, therefore, the intent of the General Assembly to establish a system of mandatory licensing and record keeping which will prevent or reduce the transfer or sale of stolen vehicles or their parts within this State.

It further is the intent of the General Assembly that government agencies work in cooperation with vehicle dealers, scrap processors, automotive parts recyclers, repairers and rebuilders, utilizing their professional expertise in the development and execution of programs and strategies to reduce vehicle-related crime and maximize consumer protection while ensuring a healthy business climate for the legitimate automotive industry.

P.A. 76-1586, § 5-100-1, added by P.A. 82-984, § 1, eff. Jan. 1, 1983. Amended by P.A. 84-1302, § 1, eff. Jan. 1, 1987; P.A. 84-1304, § 1, eff. Jan. 1, 1987; P.A. 85-572, § 1, eff. Sept. 18, 1987.

Formerly Ill.Rev.Stat.1991, ch. 95 ½, ¶ 5-100-1.

ARTICLE I. DEALERS

5/5-101. New vehicle dealers must be licensed

Text of section effective until June 1, 2003

§ 5-101. New vehicle dealers must be licensed.

(a) No person shall engage in this State in the business of selling or dealing in, on consignment or otherwise, new vehicles of any make, or act as an intermediary or agent or broker for any licensed dealer or vehicle purchaser other than as a salesperson, or represent or advertise that he is so engaged or intends to so engage in such business unless licensed to do so in writing by the Secretary of State under the provisions of this Section.

(b) An application for a new vehicle dealer's license shall be filed with the Secretary of State, duly verified by oath, on such form as the Secretary of State may by rule or regulation prescribe and shall contain:

1. The name and type of business organization of the applicant and his established and additional places of business, if any, in this State.

2. If the applicant is a corporation, a list of its officers, directors, and shareholders having a ten percent or greater ownership interest in the corporation, setting forth the residence address of each; if the applicant is a sole proprietorship, a partnership, an unincorporated association, a trust, or any similar form of business organization, the name and residence address of the proprietor or of each partner, member, officer, director, trustee, or manager.

3. The make or makes of new vehicles which the applicant will offer for sale at retail in this State.

4. The name of each manufacturer or franchised distributor, if any, of new vehicles with whom the applicant has contracted for the sale of such new vehicles. As evidence of this fact, the application shall be accompanied by a signed statement from each such manufacturer or franchised distributor. If the applicant is in the business of offering for sale new conversion vehicles, trucks or vans, except for trucks modified to serve a special purpose which includes but is not limited to the following vehicles: street sweepers, fertilizer spreaders, emergency vehicles, implements of husbandry or maintenance type vehicles, he must furnish evidence of a sales and service agreement from both the chassis manufacturer and second stage manufacturer.

5. A statement that the applicant has been approved for registration under the Retailers' Occupation Tax Act [1] by the Department of Revenue: Provided that this requirement does not apply to a dealer who is already licensed hereunder with the Secretary of State, and who is merely applying for a renewal of his license. As evidence of this fact, the application shall be accompanied by a certification from the Department of Revenue showing that that Department has approved the applicant for registration under the Retailers' Occupation Tax Act.

6. A statement that the applicant has complied with the appropriate liability insurance requirement. A Certificate of Insurance in a solvent company authorized to do business in the State of Illinois shall be included with each application covering each location at which he proposes to act as a new vehicle dealer. The policy must provide liability coverage in the minimum amounts of $100,000 for bodily injury to, or death of, any person, $300,000 for bodily injury to, or death of, two or more persons in any one accident, and $50,000 for damage to property. Such policy shall expire not sooner than December 31 of the year for which the license was issued or renewed. The expiration of the insurance policy shall not terminate the liability under the policy arising during the period for which the policy was filed. Trailer and mobile home dealers are exempt from this requirement.

7. (A) An application for a new motor vehicle dealer's license shall be accompanied by the following license fees:

$100 for applicant's established place of business, and $50 for each additional place of business, if any, to which the application pertains; but if the application is made after June 15 of any year, the license fee shall be $50 for applicant's established place of business plus $25 for each additional place of business, if any, to which the application pertains. License fees shall be returnable only in the event that the application is denied by the Secretary of State. All moneys received by the Secretary of State as license fees under this Section shall be deposited into the Motor Vehicle Review Board Fund and shall be used to administer the Motor Vehicle Review Board under the Motor Vehicle Franchise Act.[2]

(B) An application for a new vehicle dealer's license, other than for a new motor vehicle dealer's license, shall be accompanied by the following license fees:

$50 for applicant's established place of business, and $25 for each additional place of business, if any, to which the application pertains; but if the application is made after June 15 of any year, the license fee shall be $25 for applicant's established place of business plus $12.50 for each additional place of business, if any, to which the application pertains. License fees shall be returnable only in the event that the application is denied by the Secretary of State.

8. A statement that the applicant's officers, directors, shareholders having a 10% or greater ownership interest therein, proprietor, a partner, member, officer, director, trustee, manager or other principals in the business have not committed in the past 3 years any one violation as determined in any civil, criminal or administrative proceedings of any one of the following Acts:

(A) The Anti Theft Laws of the Illinois Vehicle Code; [3]

(B) The Certificate of Title Laws of the Illinois Vehicle Code; [4]

(C) The Offenses against Registration and Certificates of Title Laws of the Illinois Vehicle Code; [5]

(D) The Dealers, Transporters, Wreckers and Rebuilders Laws of the Illinois Vehicle Code; [6]

(E) Section 21-2 of the Criminal Code of 1961,[7] Criminal Trespass to Vehicles; or

(F) The Retailers' Occupation Tax Act.

9. A statement that the applicant's officers, directors, shareholders having a 10% or greater ownership interest therein, proprietor, partner, member, officer, director, trustee, manager or other principals in the business have not committed in any calendar year 3 or more violations, as determined in any civil, criminal or administrative proceedings, of any one or more of the following Acts:

(A) The Consumer Finance Act; [8]

(B) The Consumer Installment Loan Act; [9]

(C) The Retail Installment Sales Act; [10]

(D) The Motor Vehicle Retail Installment Sales Act; [11]

(E) The Interest Act; [12]

(F) The Illinois Wage Assignment Act; [13]

(G) Part 8 of Article XII of the Code of Civil Procedure; [14] or

(H) The Consumer Fraud Act.[15]

10. A bond or certificate of deposit in the amount of $20,000 for each location at which the applicant intends to act as a new vehicle dealer. The bond shall be for the term of the license, or its renewal, for which application is

made, and shall expire not sooner than December 31 of the year for which the license was issued or renewed. The bond shall run to the People of the State of Illinois, with surety by a bonding or insurance company authorized to do business in this State. It shall be conditioned upon the proper transmittal of all title and registration fees and taxes (excluding taxes under the Retailers' Occupation Tax Act) accepted by the applicant as a new vehicle dealer.

11. Such other information concerning the business of the applicant as the Secretary of State may by rule or regulation prescribe.

12. A statement that the applicant understands Chapter One through Chapter Five of this Code.

(c) Any change which renders no longer accurate any information contained in any application for a new vehicle dealer's license shall be amended within 30 days after the occurrence of such change on such form as the Secretary of State may prescribe by rule or regulation, accompanied by an amendatory fee of $2.

(d) Anything in this Chapter 5 to the contrary notwithstanding no person shall be licensed as a new vehicle dealer unless:

1. He is authorized by contract in writing between himself and the manufacturer or franchised distributor of such make of vehicle to so sell the same in this State, and

2. Such person shall maintain an established place of business as defined in this Act.

(e) The Secretary of State shall, within a reasonable time after receipt, examine an application submitted to him under this Section and unless he makes a determination that the application submitted to him does not conform with the requirements of this Section or that grounds exist for a denial of the application, under Section 5-501 of this Chapter, grant the applicant an original new vehicle dealer's license in writing for his established place of business and a supplemental license in writing for each additional place of business in such form as he may prescribe by rule or regulation which shall include the following:

1. The name of the person licensed;

2. If a corporation, the name and address of its officers or if a sole proprietorship, a partnership, an unincorporated association or any similar form of business organization, the name and address of the proprietor or of each partner, member, officer, director, trustee or manager;

3. In the case of an original license, the established place of business of the licensee;

4. In the case of a supplemental license, the established place of business of the licensee and the additional place of business to which such supplemental license pertains;

5. The make or makes of new vehicles which the licensee is licensed to sell.

(f) The appropriate instrument evidencing the license or a certified copy thereof, provided by the Secretary of State, shall be kept posted conspicuously in the established place of business of the licensee and in each additional place of business, if any, maintained by such licensee.

(g) Except as provided in subsection (h) hereof, all new vehicle dealer's licenses granted under this Section shall expire by operation of law on December 31 of the calendar year for which they are granted unless sooner revoked or cancelled under the provisions of Section 5-501 of this Chapter.

(h) A new vehicle dealer's license may be renewed upon application and payment of the fee required herein, and submission of proof of coverage under an approved bond under the "Retailers' Occupation Tax Act" or proof that applicant is not subject to such bonding requirements, as in the case of an original license, but in case an application for the renewal of an effective license is made during the month of December, the effective license shall remain in force until the application is granted or denied by the Secretary of State.

(i) All persons licensed as a new vehicle dealer are required to furnish each purchaser of a motor vehicle:

1. In the case of a new vehicle a manufacturer's statement of origin and in the case of a used motor vehicle a certificate of title, in either case properly assigned to the purchaser;

2. A statement verified under oath that all identifying numbers on the vehicle agree with those on the certificate of title or manufacturer's statement of origin;

3. A bill of sale properly executed on behalf of such person;

4. A copy of the Uniform Invoice-transaction reporting return referred to in Section 5-402 hereof;

5. In the case of a rebuilt vehicle, a copy of the Disclosure of Rebuilt Vehicle Status; and

6. In the case of a vehicle for which the warranty has been reinstated, a copy of the warranty.

(j) Except at the time of sale or repossession of the vehicle, no person licensed as a new vehicle dealer may issue any other person a newly created key to a vehicle unless the new vehicle dealer makes a copy of the driver's license or State identification card of the person requesting or obtaining the newly created key. The new vehicle dealer must retain the copy for 30 days.

A new vehicle dealer who violates this subsection (j) is guilty of a petty offense. Violation of this subsection (j) is not cause to suspend, revoke, cancel, or deny renewal of the new vehicle dealer's license.

This amendatory Act of 1983 shall be applicable to the 1984 registration year and thereafter.

P.A. 76-1586, § 5-101, eff. July 1, 1970. Amended by P.A. 77-2751, § 1, eff. Sept. 1, 1972; P.A. 81-759, § 6, eff. Sept. 16, 1979; P.A. 81-932, § 1, eff. Sept. 22, 1979; P.A. 82-783, Art. XI, § 140, eff. July 13, 1982; P.A. 83-765, § 1, eff. Sept. 23, 1983; P.A. 83-1473, § 1, eff. Jan. 1, 1985; P.A. 84-986, § 1, eff. Sept. 25, 1985; P.A. 85-340, § 2, eff. Sept. 10, 1987; P.A. 85-1396, § 2, eff. Sept. 2, 1988; P.A. 86-444, § 1, eff. Jan. 1, 1990; P.A. 86-971, § 1, eff. Jan. 1, 1991; P.A. 86-1028, Art. II, § 2-44, eff. Feb. 5, 1990; P.A. 86-1179, § 2, eff. Aug. 17, 1990; P.A. 87-380, § 1, eff. July 1, 1992; P.A. 87-435, Art. 2, § 2-19, eff. Sept. 10, 1991; P.A. 87-895, Art. 2, § 2-45, eff. Aug. 14, 1992; P.A. 88-158, § 5, eff. Jan. 1, 1994; P.A. 89-145, § 10, eff. July 14, 1995; P.A. 89-189, § 5, eff. Jan. 1, 1996; P.A. 89-433, § 5, eff. Dec. 15, 1995; P.A. 92-391, § 5, eff. Aug. 16, 2001.

Formerly Ill.Rev.Stat.1991, ch. 95 ½, ¶ 5-101.

[1] 35 ILCS 120/1 et seq.

[2] 815 ILCS 710/1 et seq.

[3] 625 ILCS 5/4-100 et seq.

[4] 625 ILCS 5/3-100 et seq.

[5] 625 ILCS 5/3-701 et seq.

[6] 625 ILCS 5/5-100 et seq.

[7] 720 ILCS 5/21-2.

[8] Former Ill.Rev.Stat. ch. 17, ¶ 5601 et seq. (repealed).

[9] 205 ILCS 670/1 et seq.

[10] 815 ILCS 405/1 et seq.

11 815 ILCS 375/1 et seq.

12 815 ILCS 205/0.01 et seq.

13 740 ILCS 170/.01 et seq.

14 735 ILCS 5/12-101 et seq.

15 815 ILCS 505/1 et seq.

For text of section effective June 1, 2003, see 625 ILCS 5/5-101, post

5/5-101. New vehicle dealers must be licensed

Text of section effective June 1, 2003

§ 5-101. New vehicle dealers must be licensed.

(a) No person shall engage in this State in the business of selling or dealing in, on consignment or otherwise, new vehicles of any make, or act as an intermediary or agent or broker for any licensed dealer or vehicle purchaser other than as a salesperson, or represent or advertise that he is so engaged or intends to so engage in such business unless licensed to do so in writing by the Secretary of State under the provisions of this Section.

(b) An application for a new vehicle dealer's license shall be filed with the Secretary of State, duly verified by oath, on such form as the Secretary of State may by rule or regulation prescribe and shall contain:

1. The name and type of business organization of the applicant and his established and additional places of business, if any, in this State.

2. If the applicant is a corporation, a list of its officers, directors, and shareholders having a ten percent or greater ownership interest in the corporation, setting forth the residence address of each; if the applicant is a sole proprietorship, a partnership, an unincorporated association, a trust, or any similar form of business organization, the name and residence address of the proprietor or of each partner, member, officer, director, trustee, or manager.

3. The make or makes of new vehicles which the applicant will offer for sale at retail in this State.

4. The name of each manufacturer or franchised distributor, if any, of new vehicles with whom the applicant has contracted for the sale of such new vehicles. As evidence of this fact, the application shall be accompanied by a signed statement from each such manufacturer or franchised distributor. If the applicant is in the business of offering for sale new conversion vehicles, trucks or vans, except for trucks modified to serve a special purpose which includes but is not limited to the following vehicles: street sweepers, fertilizer spreaders, emergency vehicles, implements of husbandry or maintenance type vehicles, he must furnish evidence of a sales and service agreement from both the chassis manufacturer and second stage manufacturer.

5. A statement that the applicant has been approved for registration under the Retailers' Occupation Tax Act [1] by the Department of Revenue: Provided that this requirement does not apply to a dealer who is already licensed hereunder with the Secretary of State, and who is merely applying for a renewal of his license. As evidence of this fact, the application shall be accompanied by a certification from the Department of Revenue showing that that Department has approved the applicant for registration under the Retailers' Occupation Tax Act.

6. A statement that the applicant has complied with the appropriate liability insurance requirement. A Certificate of Insurance in a solvent company authorized to do business in the State of Illinois shall be included with each application covering each location at which he proposes to act as a new vehicle dealer. The policy must provide liability coverage in the minimum amounts of $100,000 for bodily injury to, or death of, any person, $300,000 for bodily injury to, or death of, two or more persons in any one accident, and $50,000 for damage to property. Such policy shall expire not sooner than December 31 of the year for which the license was issued or renewed. The expiration of the insurance policy shall not terminate the liability under the policy arising during the period for which the policy was filed. Trailer and mobile home dealers are exempt from this requirement.

If the permitted user has a liability insurance policy that provides automobile liability insurance coverage of at least $100,000 for bodily injury to or the death of any person, $300,000 for bodily injury to or the death of any 2 or more persons in any one accident, and $50,000 for damage to property, then the permitted user's insurer shall be the primary insurer and the dealer's insurer shall be the secondary insurer. If the permitted user does not have a liability insurance policy that provides automobile liability insurance coverage of at least $100,000 for bodily injury to or the death of any person, $300,000 for bodily injury to or the death of any 2 or more persons in any one accident, and $50,000 for damage to property, or does not have any insurance at all, then the dealer's insurer shall be the primary insurer and the permitted user's insurer shall be the secondary insurer.

When a permitted user is "test driving" a new vehicle dealer's automobile, the new vehicle dealer's insurance shall be primary and the permitted user's insurance shall be secondary.

As used in this paragraph 6, a "permitted user" is a person who, with the permission of the new vehicle dealer or an employee of the new vehicle dealer, drives a vehicle owned and held for sale or lease by the new vehicle dealer which the person is considering to purchase or lease, in order to evaluate the performance, reliability, or condition of the vehicle. The term "permitted user" also includes a person who, with the permission of the new vehicle dealer, drives a vehicle owned or held for sale or lease by the new vehicle dealer for loaner purposes while the user's vehicle is being repaired or evaluated.

As used in this paragraph 6, "test driving" occurs when a permitted user who, with the permission of the new vehicle dealer or an employee of the new vehicle dealer, drives a vehicle owned and held for sale or lease by a new vehicle dealer that the person is considering to purchase or lease, in order to evaluate the performance, reliability, or condition of the vehicle.

As used in this paragraph 6, "loaner purposes" means when a person who, with the permission of the new vehicle dealer, drives a vehicle owned or held for sale or lease by the new vehicle dealer while the user's vehicle is being repaired or evaluated.

7. (A) An application for a new motor vehicle dealer's license shall be accompanied by the following license fees:

$100 for applicant's established place of business, and $50 for each additional place of business, if any, to which the application pertains; but if the application is made after June 15 of any year, the license fee shall be $50 for applicant's established place of business plus $25 for each additional place of business, if any, to which the application pertains. License fees shall be returnable only in the event that the application is denied by the Secretary of State. All moneys received by the Secretary of State as license fees under this Section shall be deposited into the Motor Vehicle Review Board Fund and shall be used to administer the Motor Vehicle Review Board under the Motor Vehicle Franchise Act.[2]

(B) An application for a new vehicle dealer's license, other than for a new motor vehicle dealer's license, shall be accompanied by the following license fees:

$50 for applicant's established place of business, and $25 for each additional place of business, if any, to which the application pertains; but if the application is made after June 15 of any year, the license fee shall be $25 for applicant's established place of business plus $12.50 for each additional place of business, if any, to which the application pertains. License fees shall be returnable only in the event that the application is denied by the Secretary of State.

8. A statement that the applicant's officers, directors, shareholders having a 10% or greater ownership interest therein, proprietor, a partner, member, officer, director, trustee, manager or other principals in the business have not committed in the past 3 years any one violation as determined in any civil, criminal or administrative proceedings of any one of the following Acts:

(A) The Anti Theft Laws of the Illinois Vehicle Code; [3]

(B) The Certificate of Title Laws of the Illinois Vehicle Code; [4]

(C) The Offenses against Registration and Certificates of Title Laws of the Illinois Vehicle Code; [5]

(D) The Dealers, Transporters, Wreckers and Rebuilders Laws of the Illinois Vehicle Code; [6]

(E) Section 21-2 of the Criminal Code of 1961,[7] Criminal Trespass to Vehicles; [7] or

(F) The Retailers' Occupation Tax Act.

9. A statement that the applicant's officers, directors, shareholders having a 10% or greater ownership interest therein, proprietor, partner, member, officer, director, trustee, manager or other principals in the business have not committed in any calendar year 3 or more violations, as determined in any civil, criminal or administrative proceedings, of any one or more of the following Acts:

(A) The Consumer Finance Act; [8]

(B) The Consumer Installment Loan Act; [9]

(C) The Retail Installment Sales Act; [10]

(D) The Motor Vehicle Retail Installment Sales Act; [11]

(E) The Interest Act; [12]

(F) The Illinois Wage Assignment Act; [13]

(G) Part 8 of Article XII of the Code of Civil Procedure; [14] or

(H) The Consumer Fraud Act.[15]

10. A bond or certificate of deposit in the amount of $20,000 for each location at which the applicant intends to act as a new vehicle dealer. The bond shall be for the term of the license, or its renewal, for which application is made, and shall expire not sooner than December 31 of the year for which the license was issued or renewed. The bond shall run to the People of the State of Illinois, with surety by a bonding or insurance company authorized to do business in this State. It shall be conditioned upon the proper transmittal of all title and registration fees and taxes (excluding taxes under the Retailers' Occupation Tax Act) accepted by the applicant as a new vehicle dealer.

11. Such other information concerning the business of the applicant as the Secretary of State may by rule or regulation prescribe.

12. A statement that the applicant understands Chapter One through Chapter Five of this Code.

(c) Any change which renders no longer accurate any information contained in any application for a new vehicle dealer's license shall be amended within 30 days after the occurrence of such change on such form as the Secretary of State may prescribe by rule or regulation, accompanied by an amendatory fee of $2.

(d) Anything in this Chapter 5 to the contrary notwithstanding no person shall be licensed as a new vehicle dealer unless:

1. He is authorized by contract in writing between himself and the manufacturer or franchised distributor of such make of vehicle to so sell the same in this State, and

2. Such person shall maintain an established place of business as defined in this Act.

(e) The Secretary of State shall, within a reasonable time after receipt, examine an application submitted to him under this Section and unless he makes a determination that the application submitted to him does not conform with the requirements of this Section or that grounds exist for a denial of the application, under Section 5-501 of this Chapter, grant the applicant an original new vehicle dealer's license in writing for his established place of business and a supplemental license in writing for each additional place of business in such form as he may prescribe by rule or regulation which shall include the following:

1. The name of the person licensed;

2. If a corporation, the name and address of its officers or if a sole proprietorship, a partnership, an unincorporated association or any similar form of business organization, the name and address of the proprietor or of each partner, member, officer, director, trustee or manager;

3. In the case of an original license, the established place of business of the licensee;

4. In the case of a supplemental license, the established place of business of the licensee and the additional place of business to which such supplemental license pertains;

5. The make or makes of new vehicles which the licensee is licensed to sell.

(f) The appropriate instrument evidencing the license or a certified copy thereof, provided by the Secretary of State, shall be kept posted conspicuously in the established place of business of the licensee and in each additional place of business, if any, maintained by such licensee.

(g) Except as provided in subsection (h) hereof, all new vehicle dealer's licenses granted under this Section shall expire by operation of law on December 31 of the calendar year for which they are granted unless sooner revoked or cancelled under the provisions of Section 5-501 of this Chapter.

(h) A new vehicle dealer's license may be renewed upon application and payment of the fee required herein, and submission of proof of coverage under an approved bond under the "Retailers' Occupation Tax Act" or proof that applicant is not subject to such bonding requirements, as in the case of an original license, but in case an application for the renewal of an effective license is made during the month of December, the effective license shall remain in force until the application is granted or denied by the Secretary of State.

(i) All persons licensed as a new vehicle dealer are required to furnish each purchaser of a motor vehicle:

1. In the case of a new vehicle a manufacturer's statement of origin and in the case of a used motor vehicle a certificate of title, in either case properly assigned to the purchaser;

2. A statement verified under oath that all identifying numbers on the vehicle agree with those on the certificate of title or manufacturer's statement of origin;

3. A bill of sale properly executed on behalf of such person;

4. A copy of the Uniform Invoice-transaction reporting return referred to in Section 5-402 hereof;

5. In the case of a rebuilt vehicle, a copy of the Disclosure of Rebuilt Vehicle Status; and

6. In the case of a vehicle for which the warranty has been reinstated, a copy of the warranty.

(j) Except at the time of sale or repossession of the vehicle, no person licensed as a new vehicle dealer may issue any other person a newly created key to a vehicle unless the new vehicle dealer makes a copy of the driver's license or State identification card of the person requesting or obtaining the newly created key. The new vehicle dealer must retain the copy for 30 days.

A new vehicle dealer who violates this subsection (j) is guilty of a petty offense. Violation of this subsection (j) is not cause to suspend, revoke, cancel, or deny renewal of the new vehicle dealer's license.

This amendatory Act of 1983 shall be applicable to the 1984 registration year and thereafter.

P.A. 76-1586, § 5-101, eff. July 1, 1970. Amended by P.A. 77-2751, § 1, eff. Sept. 1, 1972; P.A. 81-759, § 6, eff. Sept. 16, 1979; P.A. 81-932, § 1, eff. Sept. 22, 1979; P.A. 82-783, Art. XI, § 140, eff. July 13, 1982; P.A. 83-765, § 1, eff. Sept. 23, 1983; P.A. 83-1473, § 1, eff. Jan. 1, 1985; P.A. 84-986, § 1, eff. Sept. 25, 1985; P.A. 85-340, § 2, eff. Sept. 10, 1987; P.A. 85-1396, § 2, eff. Sept. 2, 1988; P.A. 86-444, § 1, eff. Jan. 1, 1990; P.A. 86-971, § 1, eff. Jan. 1, 1991; P.A. 86-1028, Art. II, § 2-44, eff. Feb. 5, 1990; P.A. 86-1179, § 2, eff. Aug. 17, 1990; P.A. 87-380, § 1, eff. July 1, 1992; P.A. 87-435, Art. 2, § 2-19, eff. Sept. 10, 1991; P.A. 87-895, Art. 2, § 2-45, eff. Aug. 14, 1992; P.A. 88-158, § 5, eff. Jan. 1, 1994; P.A. 89-145, § 10, eff. July 14, 1995; P.A. 89-189, § 5, eff. Jan. 1, 1996; P.A. 89-433, § 5, eff. Dec. 15, 1995; P.A. 92-391, § 5, eff. Aug. 16, 2001; P.A. 92-835, § 5, eff. June 1, 2003.

Formerly Ill.Rev.Stat.1991, ch. 95 ½, ¶ 5-101.

[1] 35 ILCS 120/1 et seq.

[2] 815 ILCS 710/1 et seq.

[3] 625 ILCS 5/4-100 et seq.

[4] 625 ILCS 5/3-100 et seq.

[5] 625 ILCS 5/3-701 et seq.

[6] 625 ILCS 5/5-100 et seq.

[7] 720 ILCS 5/21-2.

[8] Former Ill.Rev.Stat. ch. 17, ¶5601 et seq. (repealed).

[9] 205 ILCS 670/1 et seq.

[10] 815 ILCS 405/1 et seq.

[11] 815 ILCS 375/1 et seq.

[12] 815 ILCS 205/0.01 et seq.

[13] 740 ILCS 170/.01 et seq.

[14] 735 ILCS 5/12-801 et seq.

[15] 815 ILCS 505/1 et seq.

For text of section effective until June 1, 2003, see 625 ILCS 5/5-101, ante

P.A. 92-835 incorporated the amendment by P.A. 92-391.

5/5-101.1. Motor vehicle financing affiliates; licensing

§ 5-101.1. Motor vehicle financing affiliates; licensing.

(a) In this State no business shall engage in the business of a motor vehicle financing affiliate without a license to do so in writing from the Secretary of State.

(b) An application for a motor vehicle financing affiliate's license must be filed with the Secretary of State, duly verified by oath, on a form prescribed by the Secretary of State and shall contain all of the following:

(1) The name and type of business organization of the applicant and the applicant's established place of business and any additional places of business in this State.

(2) The name and address of the licensed new or used vehicle dealer to which the applicant will be selling, transferring, or assigning new or used motor vehicles pursuant to a written contract. If more than one dealer is on the application, the applicant shall state in writing the basis of common ownership among the dealers.

(3) A list of the business organization's officers, directors, members, and shareholders having a 10% or greater ownership interest in the business, providing the residential address for each person listed.

(4) If selling, transferring, or assigning new motor vehicles, the make or makes of new vehicles that it will sell, assign, or otherwise transfer to the contracting new motor vehicle dealer listed on the application pursuant to paragraph (2).

(5) The name of each manufacturer or franchised distributor, if any, of new vehicles with whom the applicant has contracted for the sale of new vehicles and a signed statement from each manufacturer or franchised distributor acknowledging the contract.

(6) A statement that the applicant has been approved for registration under the Retailers' Occupation Tax Act [1] by the Department of Revenue. This requirement does not apply to a motor vehicle financing affiliate that is already licensed with the Secretary of State and is applying for a renewal of its license.

(7) A statement that the applicant has complied with the appropriate liability insurance requirement and a Certificate of Insurance that shall not expire before December 31 of the year for which the license was issued or renewed with a minimum liability coverage of $100,000 for the bodily injury or death of any person, $300,000 for the bodily injury or death of 2 or more persons in any one accident, and $50,000 for damage to property. The expiration of the insurance policy shall not terminate the liability under the policy arising during the period for which the policy was filed. Trailer and mobile home dealers are exempt from the requirements of this paragraph. A motor vehicle financing affiliate is exempt from the requirements of this paragraph if it is covered by the insurance policy of the new or used dealer listed on the application pursuant to paragraph (2).

(8) A license fee of $1,000 for the applicant's established place of business and $250 for each additional place of business, if any, to which the application pertains. Howev-

er, if the application is made after June 15 of any year, the license fee shall be $500 for the applicant's established place of business and $125 for each additional place of business, if any, to which the application pertains. These license fees shall be returnable only in the event that the application is denied by the Secretary of State.

(9) A statement incorporating the requirements of paragraphs 8 and 9 of subsection (b) of Section 5-101.

(10) Any other information concerning the business of the applicant as the Secretary of State may prescribe.

(11) A statement that the applicant understands Chapter 1 through Chapter 5 of this Code. [2]

(c) Any change which renders no longer accurate any information contained in any application for a motor vehicle financing affiliate's license shall be amended within 30 days after the occurrence of the change on a form prescribed by the Secretary of State, accompanied by an amendatory fee of $2.

(d) If a new vehicle dealer is not listed on the application, pursuant to paragraph (2) of subsection (b), the motor vehicle financing affiliate shall not receive, possess, or transfer any new vehicle. If a new motor vehicle dealer is listed on the application, pursuant to paragraph (2) of subsection (b), the new motor vehicle dealer can only receive those new cars it is permitted to receive under its franchise agreement. If both a new and used motor vehicle dealer are listed on the application, pursuant to paragraph (2) of subsection (b), only the new motor vehicle dealer may receive new motor vehicles. If a used motor vehicle is listed on the application, pursuant to paragraph (2) of subsection (b), the used motor vehicle dealer shall not receive any new motor vehicles.

(e) The applicant and dealer provided pursuant to paragraph (2) of subsection (b) must be business organizations registered to conduct business in Illinois. Three-fourths of the dealer's board of directors must be members of the motor vehicle financing affiliate's board of directors, if applicable.

(f) Unless otherwise provided in this Chapter 5, no business organization registered to do business in Illinois shall be licensed as a motor vehicle financing affiliate unless:

(1) The motor vehicle financing affiliate shall only sell, transfer, or assign motor vehicles to the licensed new or used dealer listed on the application pursuant to paragraph (2) of subsection (b).

(2) The motor vehicle financing affiliate sells, transfers, or assigns to the new motor vehicle dealer listed on the application, if any, only those new motor vehicles the motor vehicle financing affiliate has received under the contract set forth in paragraph (5) of subsection (b).

(3) Any new vehicle dealer listed pursuant to paragraph (2) of subsection (b) has a franchise agreement that permits the dealer to receive motor vehicles from the motor vehicle franchise affiliate.

(4) The new or used motor vehicle dealer listed on the application pursuant to paragraph (2) of subsection (b) has one established place of business or supplemental places of business as referenced in subsection (g).

(g) The Secretary of State shall, within a reasonable time after receipt, examine an application submitted pursuant to this Section and, unless it is determined that the application does not conform with the requirements of this Section or that grounds exist for a denial of the application under Section 5-501, grant the applicant a motor vehicle financing affiliate license in writing for the applicant's established place of business and a supplemental license in writing for each additional place of business in a form prescribed by the Secretary, which shall include all of the following:

(1) The name of the business licensed;

(2) The name and address of its officers, directors, or members, as applicable;

(3) In the case of an original license, the established place of business of the licensee; and

(4) If applicable, the make or makes of new vehicles which the licensee is licensed to sell to the new motor vehicle dealer listed on the application pursuant to paragraph (2) of subsection (b).

(h) The appropriate instrument evidencing the license or a certified copy, provided by the Secretary of State, shall be kept posted conspicuously in the established place of business of the licensee.

(i) Except as provided in subsection (h), all motor vehicle financing affiliate's licenses granted under this Section shall expired by operation of law on December 31 of the calendar year for which they are granted, unless revoked or canceled at an earlier date pursuant to Section 5-501.

(j) A motor vehicle financing affiliate's license may be renewed upon application and payment of the required fee. However, when an application for renewal of a motor vehicle financing affiliate's license is made during the month of December, the effective license shall remain in force until the application is granted or denied by the Secretary of State.

(k) The contract a motor vehicle financing affiliate has with a manufacturer or franchised distributor, as provided in paragraph (5) of subsection (b), shall only permit the applicant to sell, transfer, or assign new motor vehicles to the new motor vehicle dealer listed on the application pursuant to paragraph (2) of subsection (b). The contract shall specifically prohibit the motor vehicle financing affiliate from selling motor vehicles at retail. This contract shall not be considered the granting of a franchise as defined in Section 2 of the Motor Vehicle Franchise Act. [3]

(*l*) When purchasing of a motor vehicle by a new or used motor vehicle dealer, all persons licensed as a motor vehicle financing affiliate are required to furnish all of the following:

(1) For a new vehicle, a manufacturer's statement of origin properly assigned to the purchasing dealer. For a used vehicle, a certificate of title properly assigned to the purchasing dealer.

(2) A statement verified under oath that all identifying numbers on the vehicle agree with those on the certificate of title or manufacturer's statement of origin.

(3) A bill of sale properly executed on behalf of the purchasing dealer.

(4) A copy of the Uniform Invoice-transaction report pursuant to Section 5-402.

(5) In the case of a rebuilt vehicle, a copy of the Disclosure of Rebuilt Vehicle Status pursuant to Section 5-104.3.

(6) In the case of a vehicle for which a warranty has been reinstated, a copy of the warranty.

(m) The motor vehicle financing affiliate shall use the established and supplemental place or places of business the new or used vehicle dealer listed on the application pursuant to paragraph (2) of subsection (b) as its established and supplemental place or places of business.

(n) The motor vehicle financing affiliate shall keep all books and records required by this Code with the books and records of the new or used vehicle dealer listed on the application pursuant to paragraph (2) of subsection (b). The motor vehicle financing affiliate may use the books and records of the new or used motor vehicle dealer listed on the application pursuant to paragraph (2) of subsection (b).

(o) Under no circumstances shall a motor vehicle financing affiliate sell, transfer, or assign a new vehicle to any place of business of a new motor vehicle dealer, unless that place of business is licensed under this Chapter to sell, assign, or otherwise transfer the make of the new motor vehicle transferred.

(p) All moneys received by the Secretary of State as license fees under this Section shall be deposited into the Motor Vehicle Review Board Fund and shall be used to administer the Motor Vehicle Review Board under the Motor Vehicle Franchise Act. [4]

(q) Except as otherwise provided in this Section, a motor vehicle financing affiliate shall comply with all provisions of this Code.

P.A. 76-1586, § 5-101.1, added by P.A. 91-415, § 5, eff. Jan. 1, 2000.

[1] 35 ILCS 120/1 et seq.

[2] 625 ILCS 5/1-100 et seq. through 5/5-100 et seq.

[3] 815 ILCS 710/2.

[4] 815 ILCS 710/1 et seq.

5/5-102. Used vehicle dealers must be licensed

Text of section effective until June 1, 2003

§ 5-102. Used vehicle dealers must be licensed.

(a) No person, other than a licensed new vehicle dealer, shall engage in the business of selling or dealing in, on consignment or otherwise, 5 or more used vehicles of any make during the year (except house trailers as authorized by paragraph (j) of this Section and rebuilt salvage vehicles sold by their rebuilders to persons licensed under this Chapter), or act as an intermediary, agent or broker for any licensed dealer or vehicle purchaser (other than as a salesperson) or represent or advertise that he is so engaged or intends to so engage in such business unless licensed to do so by the Secretary of State under the provisions of this Section.

(b) An application for a used vehicle dealer's license shall be filed with the Secretary of State, duly verified by oath, in such form as the Secretary of State may by rule or regulation prescribe and shall contain:

1. The name and type of business organization established and additional places of business, if any, in this State.

2. If the applicant is a corporation, a list of its officers, directors, and shareholders having a ten percent or greater ownership interest in the corporation, setting forth the residence address of each; if the applicant is a sole proprietorship, a partnership, an unincorporated association, a trust, or any similar form of business organization, the names and residence address of the proprietor or of each partner, member, officer, director, trustee or manager.

3. A statement that the applicant has been approved for registration under the Retailers' Occupation Tax Act [1] by the Department of Revenue. However, this requirement does not apply to a dealer who is already licensed hereunder with the Secretary of State, and who is merely applying for a renewal of his license. As evidence of this fact, the application shall be accompanied by a certification from the Department of Revenue showing that the Department has approved the applicant for registration under the Retailers' Occupation Tax Act.

4. A statement that the applicant has complied with the appropriate liability insurance requirement. A Certificate of Insurance in a solvent company authorized to do business in the State of Illinois shall be included with each application covering each location at which he proposes to act as a used vehicle dealer. The policy must provide liability coverage in the minimum amounts of $100,000 for bodily injury to, or death of, any person, $300,000 for bodily injury to, or death of, two or more persons in any one accident, and $50,000 for damage to property. Such policy shall expire not sooner than December 31 of the year for which the license was issued or renewed. The expiration of the insurance policy shall not terminate the liability under the policy arising during the period for which the policy was filed. Trailer and mobile home dealers are exempt from this requirement.

5. An application for a used vehicle dealer's license shall be accompanied by the following license fees:

$50 for applicant's established place of business, and $25 for each additional place of business, if any, to which the application pertains; however, if the application is made after June 15 of any year, the license fee shall be $25 for applicant's established place of business plus $12.50 for each additional place of business, if any, to which the application pertains. License fees shall be returnable only in the event that the application is denied by the Secretary of State.

6. A statement that the applicant's officers, directors, shareholders having a 10% or greater ownership interest therein, proprietor, partner, member, officer, director, trustee, manager or other principals in the business have not committed in the past 3 years any one violation as determined in any civil, criminal or administrative proceedings of any one of the following Acts:

(A) The Anti Theft Laws of the Illinois Vehicle Code; [2]

(B) The Certificate of Title Laws of the Illinois Vehicle Code; [3]

(C) The Offenses against Registration and Certificates of Title Laws of the Illinois Vehicle Code; [4]

(D) The Dealers, Transporters, Wreckers and Rebuilders Laws of the Illinois Vehicle Code; [5]

(E) Section 21-2 of the Illinois Criminal Code of 1961,[6] Criminal Trespass to Vehicles; or

(F) The Retailers' Occupation Tax Act.

7. A statement that the applicant's officers, directors, shareholders having a 10% or greater ownership interest therein, proprietor, partner, member, officer, director, trustee, manager or other principals in the business have not committed in any calendar year 3 or more violations, as determined in any civil or criminal or administrative proceedings, of any one or more of the following Acts:

(A) The Consumer Finance Act; [7]

(B) The Consumer Installment Loan Act; [8]

(C) The Retail Installment Sales Act; [9]

(D) The Motor Vehicle Retail Installment Sales Act; [10]

(E) The Interest Act; [11]

(F) The Illinois Wage Assignment Act; [12]

(G) Part 8 of Article XII of the Code of Civil Procedure; [13] or

(H) The Consumer Fraud Act.[14]

8. A bond or Certificate of Deposit in the amount of $20,000 for each location at which the applicant intends to

act as a used vehicle dealer. The bond shall be for the term of the license, or its renewal, for which application is made, and shall expire not sooner than December 31 of the year for which the license was issued or renewed. The bond shall run to the People of the State of Illinois, with surety by a bonding or insurance company authorized to do business in this State. It shall be conditioned upon the proper transmittal of all title and registration fees and taxes (excluding taxes under the Retailers' Occupation Tax Act) accepted by the applicant as a used vehicle dealer.

9. Such other information concerning the business of the applicant as the Secretary of State may by rule or regulation prescribe.

10. A statement that the applicant understands Chapter 1 through Chapter 5 of this Code.

(c) Any change which renders no longer accurate any information contained in any application for a used vehicle dealer's license shall be amended within 30 days after the occurrence of each change on such form as the Secretary of State may prescribe by rule or regulation, accompanied by an amendatory fee of $2.

(d) Anything in this Chapter to the contrary notwithstanding, no person shall be licensed as a used vehicle dealer unless such person maintains an established place of business as defined in this Chapter.

(e) The Secretary of State shall, within a reasonable time after receipt, examine an application submitted to him under this Section. Unless the Secretary makes a determination that the application submitted to him does not conform to this Section or that grounds exist for a denial of the application under Section 5-501 of this Chapter, he must grant the applicant an original used vehicle dealer's license in writing for his established place of business and a supplemental license in writing for each additional place of business in such form as he may prescribe by rule or regulation which shall include the following:

1. The name of the person licensed;

2. If a corporation, the name and address of its officers or if a sole proprietorship, a partnership, an unincorporated association or any similar form of business organization, the name and address of the proprietor or of each partner, member, officer, director, trustee or manager;

3. In case of an original license, the established place of business of the licensee;

4. In the case of a supplemental license, the established place of business of the licensee and the additional place of business to which such supplemental license pertains.

(f) The appropriate instrument evidencing the license or a certified copy thereof, provided by the Secretary of State shall be kept posted, conspicuously, in the established place of business of the licensee and in each additional place of business, if any, maintained by such licensee.

(g) Except as provided in subsection (h) of this Section, all used vehicle dealer's licenses granted under this Section expire by operation of law on December 31 of the calendar year for which they are granted unless sooner revoked or cancelled under Section 5-501 of this Chapter.

(h) A used vehicle dealer's license may be renewed upon application and payment of the fee required herein, and submission of proof of coverage by an approved bond under the "Retailers' Occupation Tax Act" or proof that applicant is not subject to such bonding requirements, as in the case of an original license, but in case an application for the renewal of an effective license is made during the month of December, the effective license shall remain in force until the application for renewal is granted or denied by the Secretary of State.

(i) All persons licensed as a used vehicle dealer are required to furnish each purchaser of a motor vehicle:

1. A certificate of title properly assigned to the purchaser;

2. A statement verified under oath that all identifying numbers on the vehicle agree with those on the certificate of title;

3. A bill of sale properly executed on behalf of such person;

4. A copy of the Uniform Invoice-transaction reporting return referred to in Section 5-402 of this Chapter;

5. In the case of a rebuilt vehicle, a copy of the Disclosure of Rebuilt Vehicle Status; and

6. In the case of a vehicle for which the warranty has been reinstated, a copy of the warranty.

(j) A real estate broker holding a valid certificate of registration issued pursuant to "The Real Estate Brokers and Salesmen License Act" [15] may engage in the business of selling or dealing in house trailers not his own without being licensed as a used vehicle dealer under this Section; however such broker shall maintain a record of the transaction including the following:

(1) the name and address of the buyer and seller,

(2) the date of sale,

(3) a description of the mobile home, including the vehicle identification number, make, model, and year, and

(4) the Illinois certificate of title number.

The foregoing records shall be available for inspection by any officer of the Secretary of State's Office at any reasonable hour.

(k) Except at the time of sale or repossession of the vehicle, no person licensed as a used vehicle dealer may issue any other person a newly created key to a vehicle unless the used vehicle dealer makes a copy of the driver's license or State identification card of the person requesting or obtaining the newly created key. The used vehicle dealer must retain the copy for 30 days.

A used vehicle dealer who violates this subsection (k) is guilty of a petty offense. Violation of this subsection (k) is not cause to suspend, revoke, cancel, or deny renewal of the used vehicle dealer's license.

P.A. 76-1586, § 5-102, eff. July 1, 1970. Amended by P.A. 77-2751, § 1, eff. Sept. 1, 1973; P.A. 81-932, § 1, eff. Sept. 22, 1979; P.A. 81-1458, § 1, eff. Sept. 8, 1980; P.A. 82-783, Art. XI, § 140, eff. July 13, 1982; P.A. 83-765, § 1, eff. Sept. 23, 1983; P.A. 83-1473, § 1, eff. Jan. 1, 1985; P.A. 84-986, § 1, eff. Sept. 25, 1985; P.A. 84-1302, § 1, eff. Jan. 1, 1987; P.A. 84-1304, § 1, eff. Jan. 1, 1987; P.A. 85-340, § 2, eff. Sept. 10, 1987; P.A. 85-1396, § 2, eff. Sept. 2, 1988; P.A. 86-444, § 1, eff. Jan. 1, 1990; P.A. 87-380, § 1, eff. July 1, 1992; P.A. 88-158, § 5, eff. Jan. 1, 1994; P.A. 89-189, § 5, eff. Jan. 1, 1996; P.A. 92-391, § 5, eff. Aug. 16, 2001.

Formerly Ill.Rev.Stat.1991, ch. 95 ½, ¶ 5-102.

[1] 35 ILCS 120/1 et seq.

[2] 625 ILCS 5/1-100 et seq.

[3] 625 ILCS 5/3-100 et seq.

[4] 625 ILCS 5/3-701 et seq.

[5] 625 ILCS 5/5-100 et seq.

[6] 720 ILCS 5/21-2.

[7] Former Ill.Rev.Stat. ch. 17, ¶ 5601 et seq. (repealed).

[8] 205 ILCS 670/1 et seq.

9 815 ILCS 405/1 et seq.

10 815 ILCS 375/1 et seq.

11 815 ILCS 205/0.01 et seq.

12 740 ILCS 170/.01 et seq.

13 735 ILCS 5/12–101 et seq.

14 815 ILCS 505/1 et seq.

15 Former Ill.Rev.Stat. ch.111, ¶ 5701 et seq. (repealed; see, now, 225 ILCS 455/1 et seq.

For text of section effective June 1, 2003, see 625 ILCS 5/5–102, post

5/5–102. Used vehicle dealers must be licensed

Text of section effective June 1, 2003

§ 5–102. Used vehicle dealers must be licensed.

(a) No person, other than a licensed new vehicle dealer, shall engage in the business of selling or dealing in, on consignment or otherwise, 5 or more used vehicles of any make during the year (except house trailers as authorized by paragraph (j) of this Section and rebuilt salvage vehicles sold by their rebuilders to persons licensed under this Chapter), or act as an intermediary, agent or broker for any licensed dealer or vehicle purchaser (other than as a salesperson) or represent or advertise that he is so engaged or intends to so engage in such business unless licensed to do so by the Secretary of State under the provisions of this Section.

(b) An application for a used vehicle dealer's license shall be filed with the Secretary of State, duly verified by oath, in such form as the Secretary of State may by rule or regulation prescribe and shall contain:

1. The name and type of business organization established and additional places of business, if any, in this State.

2. If the applicant is a corporation, a list of its officers, directors, and shareholders having a ten percent or greater ownership interest in the corporation, setting forth the residence address of each; if the applicant is a sole proprietorship, a partnership, an unincorporated association, a trust, or any similar form of business organization, the names and residence address of the proprietor or of each partner, member, officer, director, trustee or manager.

3. A statement that the applicant has been approved for registration under the Retailers' Occupation Tax Act by the Department of Revenue. However, this requirement does not apply to a dealer who is already licensed hereunder with the Secretary of State, and who is merely applying for a renewal of his license. As evidence of this fact, the application shall be accompanied by a certification from the Department of Revenue showing that the Department has approved the applicant for registration under the Retailers' Occupation Tax Act.[1]

4. A statement that the applicant has complied with the appropriate liability insurance requirement. A Certificate of Insurance in a solvent company authorized to do business in the State of Illinois shall be included with each application covering each location at which he proposes to act as a used vehicle dealer. The policy must provide liability coverage in the minimum amounts of $100,000 for bodily injury to, or death of, any person, $300,000 for bodily injury to, or death of, two or more persons in any one accident, and $50,000 for damage to property. Such policy shall expire not sooner than December 31 of the year for which the license was issued or renewed. The expiration of the insurance policy shall not terminate the liability under the policy arising during the period for which the policy was filed. Trailer and mobile home dealers are exempt from this requirement.

If the permitted user has a liability insurance policy that provides automobile liability insurance coverage of at least $100,000 for bodily injury to or the death of any person, $300,000 for bodily injury to or the death of any 2 or more persons in any one accident, and $50,000 for damage to property, then the permitted user's insurer shall be the primary insurer and the dealer's insurer shall be the secondary insurer. If the permitted user does not have a liability insurance policy that provides automobile liability insurance coverage of at least $100,000 for bodily injury to or the death of any person, $300,000 for bodily injury to or the death of any 2 or more persons in any one accident, and $50,000 for damage to property, or does not have any insurance at all, then the dealer's insurer shall be the primary insurer and the permitted user's insurer shall be the secondary insurer.

When a permitted user is "test driving" a used vehicle dealer's automobile, the used vehicle dealer's insurance shall be primary and the permitted user's insurance shall be secondary.

As used in this paragraph 4, a "permitted user" is a person who, with the permission of the used vehicle dealer or an employee of the used vehicle dealer, drives a vehicle owned and held for sale or lease by the used vehicle dealer which the person is considering to purchase or lease, in order to evaluate the performance, reliability, or condition of the vehicle. The term "permitted user" also includes a person who, with the permission of the used vehicle dealer, drives a vehicle owned or held for sale or lease by the used vehicle dealer for loaner purposes while the user's vehicle is being repaired or evaluated.

As used in this paragraph 4, "test driving" occurs when a permitted user who, with the permission of the used vehicle dealer or an employee of the used vehicle dealer, drives a vehicle owned and held for sale or lease by a used vehicle dealer that the person is considering to purchase or lease, in order to evaluate the performance, reliability, or condition of the vehicle.

As used in this paragraph 4, "loaner purposes" means when a person who, with the permission of the used vehicle dealer, drives a vehicle owned or held for sale or lease by the used vehicle dealer while the user's vehicle is being repaired or evaluated.

5. An application for a used vehicle dealer's license shall be accompanied by the following license fees:

$50 for applicant's established place of business, and $25 for each additional place of business, if any, to which the application pertains; however, if the application is made after June 15 of any year, the license fee shall be $25 for applicant's established place of business plus $12.50 for each additional place of business, if any, to which the application pertains. License fees shall be returnable only in the event that the application is denied by the Secretary of State.

6. A statement that the applicant's officers, directors, shareholders having a 10% or greater ownership interest therein, proprietor, partner, member, officer, director, trustee, manager or other principals in the business have not committed in the past 3 years any one violation as determined in any civil, criminal or administrative proceedings of any one of the following Acts:

(A) The Anti Theft Laws of the Illinois Vehicle Code;[2]

(B) The Certificate of Title Laws of the Illinois Vehicle Code; [3]

(C) The Offenses against Registration and Certificates of Title Laws of the Illinois Vehicle Code; [4]

(D) The Dealers, Transporters, Wreckers and Rebuilders Laws of the Illinois Vehicle Code; [5]

(E) Section 21-2 of the Illinois Criminal Code of 1961, [6] Criminal Trespass to Vehicles; or

(F) The Retailers' Occupation Tax Act.

7. A statement that the applicant's officers, directors, shareholders having a 10% or greater ownership interest therein, proprietor, partner, member, officer, director, trustee, manager or other principals in the business have not committed in any calendar year 3 or more violations, as determined in any civil or criminal or administrative proceedings, of any one or more of the following Acts:

(A) The Consumer Finance Act; [7]

(B) The Consumer Installment Loan Act; [8]

(C) The Retail Installment Sales Act; [9]

(D) The Motor Vehicle Retail Installment Sales Act; [10]

(E) The Interest Act; [11]

(F) The Illinois Wage Assignment Act; [12]

(G) Part 8 of Article XII of the Code of Civil Procedure; [13] or

(H) The Consumer Fraud Act.[14]

8. A bond or Certificate of Deposit in the amount of $20,000 for each location at which the applicant intends to act as a used vehicle dealer. The bond shall be for the term of the license, or its renewal, for which application is made, and shall expire not sooner than December 31 of the year for which the license was issued or renewed. The bond shall run to the People of the State of Illinois, with surety by a bonding or insurance company authorized to do business in this State. It shall be conditioned upon the proper transmittal of all title and registration fees and taxes (excluding taxes under the Retailers' Occupation Tax Act) accepted by the applicant as a used vehicle dealer.

9. Such other information concerning the business of the applicant as the Secretary of State may by rule or regulation prescribe.

10. A statement that the applicant understands Chapter 1 through Chapter 5 of this Code.[15]

(c) Any change which renders no longer accurate any information contained in any application for a used vehicle dealer's license shall be amended within 30 days after the occurrence of each change on such form as the Secretary of State may prescribe by rule or regulation, accompanied by an amendatory fee of $2.

(d) Anything in this Chapter to the contrary notwithstanding, no person shall be licensed as a used vehicle dealer unless such person maintains an established place of business as defined in this Chapter.

(e) The Secretary of State shall, within a reasonable time after receipt, examine an application submitted to him under this Section. Unless the Secretary makes a determination that the application submitted to him does not conform to this Section or that grounds exist for a denial of the application under Section 5-501 of this Chapter, he must grant the applicant an original used vehicle dealer's license in writing for his established place of business and a supplemental license in writing for each additional place of business in such form as he may prescribe by rule or regulation which shall include the following:

1. The name of the person licensed;

2. If a corporation, the name and address of its officers or if a sole proprietorship, a partnership, an unincorporated association or any similar form of business organization, the name and address of the proprietor or of each partner, member, officer, director, trustee or manager;

3. In case of an original license, the established place of business of the licensee;

4. In the case of a supplemental license, the established place of business of the licensee and the additional place of business to which such supplemental license pertains.

(f) The appropriate instrument evidencing the license or a certified copy thereof, provided by the Secretary of State shall be kept posted, conspicuously, in the established place of business of the licensee and in each additional place of business, if any, maintained by such licensee.

(g) Except as provided in subsection (h) of this Section, all used vehicle dealer's licenses granted under this Section expire by operation of law on December 31 of the calendar year for which they are granted unless sooner revoked or cancelled under Section 5-501 of this Chapter.

(h) A used vehicle dealer's license may be renewed upon application and payment of the fee required herein, and submission of proof of coverage by an approved bond under the "Retailers' Occupation Tax Act" or proof that applicant is not subject to such bonding requirements, as in the case of an original license, but in case an application for the renewal of an effective license is made during the month of December, the effective license shall remain in force until the application for renewal is granted or denied by the Secretary of State.

(i) All persons licensed as a used vehicle dealer are required to furnish each purchaser of a motor vehicle:

1. A certificate of title properly assigned to the purchaser;

2. A statement verified under oath that all identifying numbers on the vehicle agree with those on the certificate of title;

3. A bill of sale properly executed on behalf of such person;

4. A copy of the Uniform Invoice-transaction reporting return referred to in Section 5-402 of this Chapter;

5. In the case of a rebuilt vehicle, a copy of the Disclosure of Rebuilt Vehicle Status; and

6. In the case of a vehicle for which the warranty has been reinstated, a copy of the warranty.

(j) A real estate broker holding a valid certificate of registration issued pursuant to "The Real Estate Brokers and Salesmen License Act" [16] may engage in the business of selling or dealing in house trailers not his own without being licensed as a used vehicle dealer under this Section; however such broker shall maintain a record of the transaction including the following:

(1) the name and address of the buyer and seller,

(2) the date of sale,

(3) a description of the mobile home, including the vehicle identification number, make, model, and year, and

(4) the Illinois certificate of title number. The foregoing records shall be available for inspection by any officer of the Secretary of State's Office at any reasonable hour.

(k) Except at the time of sale or repossession of the vehicle, no person licensed as a used vehicle dealer may issue any other person a newly created key to a vehicle unless the used vehicle dealer makes a copy of the driver's license or State identification card of the person requesting or obtaining the newly created key. The used vehicle dealer must retain the copy for 30 days.

A used vehicle dealer who violates this subsection (k) is guilty of a petty offense. Violation of this subsection (k) is not cause to suspend, revoke, cancel, or deny renewal of the used vehicle dealer's license.

P.A. 76–1586, § 5–102, eff. July 1, 1970. Amended by P.A. 77–2751, § 1, eff. Sept. 1, 1973; P.A. 81–932, § 1, eff. Sept. 22, 1979; P.A. 81–1458, § 1, eff. Sept. 8, 1980; P.A. 82–783, Art. XI, § 140, eff. July 13, 1982; P.A. 83–765, § 1, eff. Sept. 23, 1983; P.A. 83–1473, § 1, eff. Jan. 1, 1985; P.A. 84–986, § 1, eff. Sept. 25, 1985; P.A. 84–1302, § 1, eff. Jan. 1, 1987; P.A. 84–1304, § 1, eff. Jan. 1, 1987; P.A. 85–340, § 2, eff. Sept. 10, 1987; P.A. 85–1396, § 2, eff. Sept. 2, 1988; P.A. 86–444, § 1, eff. Jan. 1, 1990; P.A. 87–380, § 1, eff. July 1, 1992; P.A. 88–158, § 5, eff. Jan. 1, 1994; P.A. 89–189, § 5, eff. Jan. 1, 1996; P.A. 92–391, § 5, eff. Aug. 16, 2001; P.A. 92–835, § 5, eff. June 1, 2003.

Formerly Ill.Rev.Stat.1991, ch. 95 ½, ¶ 5–102.

1 35 ILCS 120/1 et seq.

2 625 ILCS 5/4–100 et seq.

3 625 ILCS 5/3–100 et seq.

4 625 ILCS 5/3–701 et seq.

5 625 ILCS 5/5–100 et seq.

6 720 ILCS 5/21–2.

7 Former Ill.Rev.Stat. ch. 17, ¶5601 et seq. (repealed).

8 205 ILCS 670/1 et seq.

9 815 ILCS 405/1 et seq.

10 815 ILCS 375/1 et seq.

11 815 ILCS 205/0.01 et seq.

12 740 ILCS 170/.01 et seq.

13 735 ILCS 5/12–801 et seq.

14 815 ILCS 505/1 et seq.

15 625 ILCS 5/1–100 et seq.

16 Former Ill.Rev.Stat. ch. 111, ¶5701 et seq. (repealed; see, now, 225 ILCS 455/1 et seq.).

For text of section effective until June 1, 2003, see 625 ILCS 5/5–102, ante

P.A. 92–835 incorporated the amendment by P.A. 92–391.

5/5–102.1. Permits for off site sales and exhibitions

§ 5–102.1. Permits for off site sales and exhibitions.

(a) A licensed new or used motor vehicle dealer licensed under Section 5–101 or 5–102 shall not engage in any off site sale without an off site sale permit issued by the Secretary under this Section.

The Secretary shall issue an off site sale permit to a dealer if:

(1) an application therefor is received by the Secretary prior to the beginning date of the proposed off site sale, accompanied by a fee of $25;

(2) the applicant is a licensed new vehicle dealer or used vehicle dealer in good standing; and

(3) the Secretary determines that the proposed off site sale will conform with the requirements imposed by law.

However, in no event shall an off site sale permit be issued to any licensed new or used vehicle dealer for any off site sale to be conducted outside that dealer's relevant market area, as that term is defined in this Chapter, except that this restriction shall not apply to off site sales of motor homes or recreational vehicles.

The provisions of this subsection shall not apply to self-contained motor homes, mini motor homes, van campers, and recreational trailers, including trailers designed and used to transport vessels or watercraft.

An off site sale permit does not authorize the sale of vehicles on a Sunday.

(b) Only a new or used vehicle dealer licensed under Section 5–101 or 5–102 may participate in a display exhibition and shall obtain a display exhibition permit issued by the Secretary under this Section.

The Secretary shall issue a display exhibition permit to a dealer if:

(1) an application therefor is received by the Secretary prior to the beginning date of the proposed exhibition, accompanied by a fee of $10;

(2) the applicant is a licensed new vehicle dealer or used vehicle dealer in good standing; and

(3) the Secretary determines that the proposed exhibition will conform with the requirements imposed by law.

A display exhibition permit shall be valid for a period of no longer than 30 days.

(c) A licensed new or used motor vehicle dealer under Section 5–101 or 5–102, or any other person as defined in this Section, may participate in a trade show exhibition and must obtain a trade show exhibition permit issued by the Secretary under this Section.

The Secretary shall issue a trade show exhibition permit if:

(1) an application is received by the Secretary before the beginning date of the proposed trade show exhibition, accompanied by a fee of $10;

(2) the applicant is a licensed new vehicle dealer or used vehicle dealer in good standing; and

(3) the Secretary determines that the proposed trade show exhibition shall conform with the requirements imposed by law.

A trade show exhibition permit shall be valid for a period of no longer than 30 days.

The provisions of this subsection shall not apply to self-contained motor homes, mini motor homes, van campers, and recreational trailers, including trailers designed and used to transport vessels or watercraft.

The term "any other person" shall mean new or used vehicle dealers licensed by other states; provided however, a trade show exhibition of new vehicles shall only be participated in by licensed new vehicle dealers, at least 2 of which must be licensed under Section 5–101.

(d) An Illinois or out-of-state licensed new or used trailer dealer, manufactured home dealer, motor home dealer, mini motor home dealer, or van camper dealer shall not engage in any off site sale or trade show exhibition without first acquiring a permit issued by the Secretary under this subsection. However, the provisions of this Section shall not apply to a licensed trailer dealer selling a mobile home or manufactured housing, as defined in the Illinois Manufactured Housing and Mobile Home Safety Act,[1] if the manufactured housing or mobile home has utilities permanently attached. The Secretary shall issue a permit to an Illinois dealer if:

(1) an application is received by the Secretary before the beginning date of the proposed off site sale or trade show exhibition, accompanied by a fee of $25;

(2) the applicant is a licensed new or used vehicle dealer in good standing; and

(3) the Secretary determines that the proposed off site sale or trade show exhibition will conform with the requirements imposed by law.

The Secretary shall issue a permit to an out-of-state dealer if the requirements of subdivisions (1), (2), and (3) of this subsection (d) are met and at least 2 licensed Illinois dealers will participate in the off site sale or trade show exhibition.

A permit issued pursuant to this subsection shall allow for the sale of vehicles at either an off site sale or at a trade show exhibition. The permit shall be valid for a period not to exceed 30 days.

(e) The Secretary of State may adopt rules regulating the conduct of off site sales and exhibitions, and governing the issuance and enforcement of the permits authorized under this Section.

P.A. 76–1586, § 5–102.1, added by P.A. 87–380, § 1, eff. July 1, 1992. Amended by P.A. 87–1249, § 1, eff. Dec. 24, 1992; P.A. 88–470, § 10, eff. Sept. 1, 1993; P.A. 88–588, § 5, eff. Jan. 1, 1995; P.A. 88–685, § 5, eff. Jan. 24, 1995; P.A. 89–235, Art. 2, § 2–120, eff. Aug. 4, 1995; P.A. 89–551, § 5, eff. Jan. 1, 1997; P.A. 90–718, § 5, eff. Jan. 1, 1999; P.A. 90–774, § 5, eff. Aug. 14, 1998; P.A. 91–357, § 231, eff. July 29, 1999.

Formerly Ill.Rev.Stat.1991, ch. 95 ½, ¶ 5–102.1.

[1] 430 ILCS 115/1 et seq.

5/5–103. Specifications of delivery and preparation obligations of vehicle dealers prior to delivery of new vehicles to retail buyers; inspection; applicability

§ 5–103. (a) Every new vehicle manufacturer shall specify the delivery and preparation obligations of its vehicle dealers prior to delivery of new vehicles to retail buyers. A copy of the delivery and preparation obligations of its dealers shall be filed with the Secretary of State by every vehicle manufacturer and shall constitute the vehicle dealer's only responsibility for product liability as between the dealer and the manufacturer. A manufacturer's product or warranty liability to the dealer shall extend to any mechanical, body or parts defect constituting a breach of any express or implied warranty of the manufacturer. The manufacturer shall reasonably compensate any authorized dealer who rectifies a defect which constitutes a breach of any express or implied warranty of the manufacturer and for preparation and delivery obligations. Every dealer shall perform the preparation and get ready services specified by the manufacturer to be performed prior to the delivery of the new vehicle to the buyer.

(b) The owner of the vehicle may cause the vehicle to be inspected according to this Section and have the original manufacturer's warranty reinstated if the vehicle is a theft recovery that has been salvaged and is recovered without structural damage or missing essential parts, excluding wheels, damage to the steering column, and radios provided the owner:

(1) Submits the vehicle to a franchised dealer for a complete inspection, including fluids, frame, essential parts, and other items deemed by the manufacturer as essential for verification of the condition of the vehicle at the time of recovery.

(2) Submits a copy of the police recovery report to the inspecting dealer.

(3) Paid the inspection fee charged by the franchised dealer.

The manufacturer shall reinstate the original manufacturer's warranty if a vehicle is certified by a franchised dealer as having complied with the provisions of this Section. The manufacturer shall, in addition to reinstating the warranty, provide the owner with a written statement indicating that the original manufacturer's warranty has been reinstated.

(c) Nothing in this Section shall affect a cause of action a buyer may have against a dealer or manufacturer under present applicable statutory or case law.

P.A. 76–1586, § 5–103, added by P.A. 77–1640, § 1, eff. Sept. 24, 1971. Amended by P.A. 77–2751, § 1, eff. Sept. 1, 1972; P.A. 78–255, § 61, eff. Oct. 1, 1973; P.A. 83–405, § 1, eff. Jan. 1, 1984; P.A. 89–189, § 5, eff. Jan. 1, 1996; P.A. 92–458, § 5, eff. Aug. 22, 2001.

Formerly Ill.Rev.Stat.1991, ch. 95 ½, ¶ 5–103.

5/5–104. Disclosure of miles per gallon in tests conducted by the U.S. Environmental Protection Agency

§ 5–104. (a) On and after January 1, 1976, each manufacturer of a 1976 or later model year vehicle of the first division manufactured for sale in this State, other than a motorcycle, shall clearly and conspicuously indicate, on the price listing affixed to the vehicle pursuant to the "Automobile Information Disclosure Act", (15 United States Code 1231 through 1233),[1] the following, with the appropriate gasoline mileage figure:

"In tests for fuel economy in city and highway driving conducted by the United States Environmental Protection Agency, this passenger vehicle obtained .... miles per gallon of gasoline."

P.A. 76–1586, § 5–104, added by P.A. 79–747, § 1, eff. Oct. 1, 1975.

Formerly Ill.Rev.Stat.1991, ch. 95 ½, ¶ 5–104.

[1] 15 U.S.C.A. § 1231 et seq.

5/5–104.1. Informational labels on pickup trucks; penalty

§ 5-104.1. Informational labels on pickup trucks; penalty. (1) Every manufacturer of second division vehicles having a gross vehicle weight rating of 8,500 pounds or less which are sold or offered for sale for use upon the public streets or highways within this State shall, prior to the delivery of the second division vehicle to an Illinois dealer, or on or prior to the introduction date of new models delivered to an Illinois dealer, securely affix to the windshield or side window of the second division vehicle a label upon which the manufacturer shall endorse clearly, distinctly and legibly true and correct entries disclosing information identical to and in the same manner as required on new first division vehicles. The label shall remain affixed to the second division vehicle until delivery of the second division vehicle to the ultimate purchaser. Any manufacturer who shall willfully fail to affix a proper label required by this Section or any person who shall willfully remove, alter or mutilate a label prior to delivery of the second division vehicle to the ultimate purchaser is guilty of a misdemeanor. This Section shall not apply to such second division vehicles for which the annual sales in Illinois of the previous model year were less than 200.

(2) This Section shall apply to second division vehicles having a gross vehicle weight rating of 8,500 pounds or less built after December 31, 1987.

P.A. 76-1586, § 5-104.1, added by P.A. 85-387, § 1, eff. Jan. 1, 1988.

Formerly Ill.Rev.Stat.1991, ch. 95 ½, ¶ 5-104.1.

5/5-104.2. Nonconforming vehicles; sale

§ 5-104.2. Nonconforming vehicles; sale.

(a) Every manufacturer shall be prohibited from reselling any motor vehicle that has been finally ordered, determined, or adjudicated as having a nonconformity under the New Vehicle Buyer Protection Act [1] or a similar law of any state, territory, or country, and that the manufacturer repurchased or replaced because of the nonconformity, unless the manufacturer has corrected the nonconformity and issues a disclosure statement prior to resale stating that the vehicle was repurchased or replaced under the New Vehicle Buyer Protection Act or similar law of any other state, territory, or country; identifying the nonconformity; and warranting that the nonconformity has been corrected. The disclosure statement must accompany the vehicle through the first retail purchase.

(b) "Nonconformity" refers to a new vehicle's failure to conform to all express warranties applicable to the vehicle, which failure substantially impairs the use, market value, or safety of the vehicle.

(c) The disclosure statement referred to in subsection (a) shall be in substantially the same form as below:

"IMPORTANT

Vehicle Identification Number (VIN): (Insert VIN Number); Year: (Insert Year); Make (Insert Make); Model: (Insert Model). This vehicle was previously sold as new. It was subsequently ordered as having a nonconformity by final decision of court proceeding or State run arbitration. It was subsequently repurchased by its manufacturer because it did not conform to the manufacturer's express warranty and the nonconformity was not cured within a reasonable time as provided by Illinois law. The following nonconformities have been corrected (a minimum of 5 numbered lines shall be provided to describe the nonconformity or nonconformities)."

The customer shall sign the disclosure statement. This disclosure language shall be in at least 8-point type.

P.A. 76-1586, § 5-104.2, added by P.A. 88-415, § 10, eff. Aug. 20, 1993.

1 815 ILCS 380/1 et seq.

5/5-104.3. Disclosure of rebuilt vehicle

§ 5-104.3. Disclosure of rebuilt vehicle.

(a) No person shall knowingly, with intent to defraud or deceive another, sell a vehicle for which a rebuilt title has been issued unless that vehicle is accompanied by a Disclosure of Rebuilt Vehicle Status form, properly signed and delivered to the buyer.

(b) The Secretary of State may by rule or regulation prescribe the format and information contained in the Disclosure of Rebuilt Vehicle Status form.

(c) A violation of subsection (a) of this Section is a Class A misdemeanor. A second or subsequent violation of subsection (a) of this Section is a Class 4 felony.

P.A. 76-1586, § 5-104.3, added by P.A. 89-189, § 5, eff. Jan. 1, 1996. Amended by P.A. 91-891, § 5, eff. July 6, 2000.

5/5-105. Investigation of licensee required

§ 5-105. Investigation of licensee required. Every person seeking a license under Chapter 5 of this Act, as part of the application process, authorizes an investigation to determine if the applicant has ever been convicted of a crime and if so, the disposition of those convictions. This authorization shall indicate the scope of the inquiry and the agencies which may be contacted. Upon this authorization the Secretary of State may request and receive information and assistance from any Federal, State or local governmental agency as part of the authorized investigation. The Department of State Police shall provide information concerning any criminal convictions and their disposition brought against the applicant upon request of the Secretary of State when the request is made in the form and manner required by the Department of State Police. The information derived from this investigation, including the source of this information, and any conclusions or recommendations derived from this information by the Secretary of State shall be provided to the applicant or his designee. Upon request to the Secretary of State prior to any final action by the Secretary of State on the application, no information obtained from such investigation may be placed in any automated information system. Any criminal convictions and their disposition information obtained by the Secretary of State shall be confidential and may not be transmitted outside the Office of the Secretary of State, except as required herein, and may not be transmitted to anyone within the Office of the Secretary of State except as needed for the purpose of evaluating the application. All criminal convictions and their disposition and information obtained by the Division of Investigation shall be destroyed no later than 60 days after the Division of Investigation has made a final ruling on the application, and all rights of appeal have expired and pending appeals have been completed. The only physical identity materials which the applicant can be required to provide the Secretary of State are photographs or fingerprints. Only information and standards which bear a reasonable and rational relation to the performance of a licensee shall be used by the Secretary of State. The Secretary of State shall adopt rules and regulations for the administration of this Section. Any employee of the Secretary of State who gives or causes to be given away any confidential information concerning any criminal convictions and their disposition of an applicant shall be guilty of a Class A misdemeanor.

P.A. 76-1586, § 5-105, added by P.A. 81-932, § 1, eff. Sept. 22, 1979. Amended by P.A. 84-25, Art. IV, § 27, eff. July 18, 1985.

Formerly Ill.Rev.Stat.1991, ch. 95 ½, ¶ 5-105.

5/5-106. Sales on Sunday

§ 5-106. No person may keep open, operate, or assist in keeping open or operating any established or additional place of business for the purpose of buying, selling, bartering, exchanging, or leasing for a period of 1 year or more, or offering for sale, barter, exchange, or lease for a period of 1 year or more, any motor vehicle, whether new or used, on the first day of the week, commonly called Sunday; provided, that this Section does not apply to the opening of an established or additional place of business on Sunday for the following purposes:

(1) to sell petroleum products, tires or repair parts and accessories;

(2) to operate and conduct a motor vehicle repair shop;

(3) to supply services for the washing, towing or wrecking of motor vehicles;

(4) to participate in a trade show exhibition or display exhibition by a dealer who has been granted a permit by the Secretary of State pursuant to Section 5-102.1 of this Article;

(5) to sell motorcycles, motor driven cycles, motorized pedalcycles when offered for sale by a dealer licensed under Sections 5-101 and 5-102 to sell only such motor vehicles;

(6) to offer for sale manufactured housing;

(7) to sell self-contained motor homes, mini motor homes, van campers and recreational trailers when offered for sale by a dealer at an established or additional place of business where only such vehicles are displayed or offered for sale. This exemption includes dealers with off site sales or trade show exhibition permits issued pursuant to subsection (d) of Section 5-102.1 of this Article.

P.A. 76-1586, § 5-106, added by P.A. 82-788, § 1, eff. Jan. 1, 1983. Amended by P.A. 84-818, § 1, eff. Sept. 22, 1985; P.A. 85-1374, § 1, eff. Jan. 1, 1989; P.A. 86-444, § 1, eff. Jan. 1, 1990; P.A. 89-551, § 5, eff. Jan. 1, 1997.

Formerly Ill.Rev.Stat.1991, ch. 95 ½, ¶ 5-106.

5/5-107. Bond exemption

§ 5-107. Bond exemption. The following persons shall be exempt from the bond required in Sections 5-101 and 5-102: (1) Any person who has been continuously licensed under Section 5-101 or 5-102 since calendar year 1983; (2) any licensee who as determined by the Secretary of State, has faithfully and continuously complied with conditions of the bond requirement for a period of 36 consecutive months.

This exemption shall continue for each licensee until such time as he may be determined by the Secretary of State to be delinquent or deficient in the transmittal of title and registration fees or taxes.

This amendatory Act of 1983 shall be applicable to the 1984 registration year and thereafter.

A person whose license is cancelled due to the voluntary surrender of such license, who applies for a new license for the same license year or one license year after the license year of the cancelled license, will remain exempt under paragraph (1) above if the only break in the continuous licensure is caused by the cancellation due to the voluntary surrender of the license.

P.A. 76-1586, § 5-107, added by P.A. 83-765, § 1, eff. Sept. 23, 1983. Amended by P.A. 85-572, § 1, eff. Sept. 18, 1987; P.A. 85-1209, Art. III, § 3-60, eff. Aug. 30, 1988; P.A. 88-158, § 5, eff. Jan. 1, 1994; P.A. 88-520, § 5, eff. Nov. 16, 1993.

Formerly Ill.Rev.Stat.1991, ch. 95 ½, ¶ 5-107.

P.A. 88-520 incorporated the amendment by P.A. 88-158.

5/5-108. Vehicle Referral and Marketing Services

§ 5-108. Vehicle Referral and Marketing Services. Nothing in this Code shall be construed to prohibit a credit union, as defined in the Illinois Credit Union Act,[1] a bank, as defined in the Illinois Banking Act,[2] or any firm, copartnership, association or corporation from advertising the sale of motor vehicles by licensed dealers or advertising motor vehicle purchase opportunities from licensed dealers, from referring potential purchasers of motor vehicles to licensed dealers, or from soliciting purchasers of motor vehicles for licensed dealers. However, any motor vehicle sale resulting from those activities may only be consummated by a dealer licensed under Section 5-101 or 5-102 of this Code.

P.A. 76-1586, § 5-108, added by P.A. 87-380, § 1, eff. July 1, 1992.

Formerly Ill.Rev.Stat.1991, ch. 95 ½, ¶ 5-108.

[1] 205 ILCS 305/1 et seq.

[2] 205 ILCS 5/1 et seq.

5/5-109. Manufacturers and Distributors; Fees

§ 5-109. Manufacturers and Distributors; Fees.

(a) "Manufacturer" means any person who manufactures or assembles new motor vehicles either within or without of this State.

(b) "Distributor" means any person who distributes or sells new motor vehicles to new vehicle dealers, or who maintains distributor representatives in this State, and who is not a manufacturer.

(c) Each manufacturer and distributor doing business in this State shall pay an annual fee of $1500 to the Secretary of State.

P.A. 76-1586, § 5-109, added by P.A. 89-145, § 10, eff. July 14, 1995. Amended by P.A. 89-433, § 5, eff. Dec. 15, 1995.

ARTICLE II. TRANSPORTERS

5/5-201. Transporters must apply for in-transit plates

§ 5-201. Transporters must apply for in-transit plates. (a) No person shall engage in this State in the business as a transporter until such person shall apply for and receive from the Secretary of State a generally distinctive set of two "in-transit license plates" for any vehicle so transported by him.

(b) An application for a generally distinctive number under this Article shall be filed with the Secretary of State, duly verified by oath and in such form as the Secretary of State may by rule or regulation prescribe and shall contain the name and business address of such person, the certificate, registration or permit number issued by the Illinois Commerce Commission and such other information concerning the business of the applicant as the Secretary of State may by rule or regulation prescribe. If the applicant does not hold a certificate, registration or permit from the Illinois Commerce Commission to so transport, such application shall be denied.

(c) An application for a generally distinctive set of two "in-transit license plates" shall be accompanied by the prescribed fee. Upon the payment of such license fee, such application shall be filed and recorded in the office of the Secretary of State. Thereupon the Secretary of State shall assign and issue to such person a generally distinctive number and without any further expense to him shall deliver to such person at his business address a certificate of registration in such form as the Secretary of State may prescribe and one set of two "in-transit license plates" with a number corresponding to the number of such certificate of registration. Such in-transit plates shall be used by such person only on vehicles transported, but not owned, by him.

(d) Except as provided in sub-section (3) hereof, all certificates of registration and "in-transit plates" granted under this Section shall expire by operation of law on December 31 of the calendar year for which they are granted unless sooner revoked under the provisions of Section 5–501 of this Chapter.

(e) A certificate of registration under this Article may be renewed upon application and payment of the fee required herein as in the case of an original application, provided, however, that in case an application for renewal of an effective registration is made during the month of December, such existing registration shall remain in force until such application for renewal is granted by the Secretary of State.

(f) Any person registered as a transporter under the Article may make application for additional duplicate sets of "in-transit plates" on such form as the Secretary of State may by rule or regulation prescribe, from time to time to obtain as many duplicate sets of "in-transit plates" as he may desire upon payment of the prescribed fee for each set. Such duplicate plates shall bear the number of that person's original certificate of registration.

(g) In case of loss or destruction of one license plate issued to a transporter under this Section, such transporter may obtain a duplicate of the same by filing an affidavit to that effect with the Secretary of State, accompanied by the prescribed fee.

(h) An original "in-transit plate" or a duplicate shall be attached to the front and rear of each vehicle so transported in this State; provided, that if one such vehicle is towing another such vehicle, one plate or duplicate plate shall be attached to the front of the towing vehicle and one such plate to the rear of the rearmost towed vehicle.

(i) Anything in this Chapter to the contrary notwithstanding, the provisions of this Section shall not apply to a nonresident engaged in such business and using the public highways of this State if he has an "in-transit plate" or license from the State, foreign country or province, territory or federal district of which he is a resident and such State, country, province, territory or district grants a like exemption to residents of this State.

P.A. 76–1586, § 5–201, eff. July 1, 1970.

Formerly Ill.Rev.Stat.1991, ch. 95 ½, ¶ 5–201.

5/5–202. Tow or Wrecker operators must register tow or wrecker vehicles

§ 5–202. Tow or Wrecker operators must register tow or wrecker vehicles. (a) No person in this State shall engage in the business of operating a tow truck or wrecker or operate a tow or wrecker vehicle until such person shall register any vehicle to be used for such purpose and apply for and receive from the Secretary of State a generally distinctive set of 3 "tow truck" plates for any towing or wrecker vehicle operated by him.

(b) An application for registration for a generally distinctive set of 3 "tow truck" plates under this Article shall be filed with the Secretary of State, duly verified by oath and in such form as the Secretary of State may by rule or regulation prescribe and shall contain the name and business address of such person, the vehicle identification number of the vehicle for which such application is made, proof of insurance as set forth in paragraph (d) of Section 12–606 of this Code, and such other information concerning the business of the applicant as the Secretary of State may by rule or regulation prescribe.

(c) The application for registration and a generally distinctive set of 3 "tow truck" plates shall be accompanied by the prescribed fee. Upon payment of such fee, such registration and application shall be filed and recorded in the office of the Secretary of State. Thereupon the Secretary of State shall assign and issue to such person a generally distinctive number for each vehicle and without further expense to him shall deliver to such person at his place of business address one set of 3 "tow truck" plates. Such "tow truck" plates shall be used by such person only on the vehicle for which application was made and the vehicle being towed, and are not transferable.

(d) All "tow truck" plates granted under this Section shall expire by operation of law on December 31 of the calendar year for which they are granted unless sooner revoked under the provisions of Section 5–501 of this Chapter.

(e) One "tow truck" plate shall be attached to the front and rear of each registered vehicle, and one "tow truck" plate shall be attached to the rear of the vehicle being towed unless the towed vehicle displays a valid registration plate visible from the rear while being towed, so that the numbers and letter on the plate are clearly visible to any person following the vehicle being towed. However, illumination of the rear plate required by subsection (c) of Section 12–201 of this Code shall not apply to the third plate displayed on the towed vehicle. In addition, the vehicle registration plates assigned to the vehicle being towed shall be displayed as provided in Section 3–413 of this Code.

P.A. 76–1586, § 5–202, added by P.A. 83–1473, § 1, eff. Jan. 1, 1985. Amended by P.A. 86–444, § 1, eff. Jan. 1, 1990; P.A. 86–565, § 1, eff. Jan. 1, 1990; P.A. 86–1028, Art. II, § 2–44, eff. Feb. 5, 1990.

Formerly Ill.Rev.Stat.1991, ch. 95 ½, ¶ 5–202.

P.A. 86–1028, the First 1990 Revisory Act, provides in Art. II, for the revision and renumbering of certain Sections of Acts which have been added or amended by more than one Act of the 86th General Assembly; repeals certain Sections that have been both amended and repealed in the 86th General Assembly and incorporates amendments into successor laws; corrects errors, revises cross-references and deletes obsolete text in such sections contained in P.A. 86–1 through P.A. 86–1009.

5/5–207. Licensing of towing services as dealers

§ 5–207. Licensing of towing services as dealers. Any towing service that sells or disposes of 5 or more vehicles in a calendar year to anyone other than a person licensed under Chapter 5 of this Code must also be licensed under Section 5–102 of this Chapter.

P.A. 76–1586, § 5–207, added by P.A. 89–433, § 5, eff. Dec. 15, 1995.

ARTICLE III. USED PARTS DEALERS, SCRAP PROCESSORS, AUTOMOTIVE PARTS RECYCLERS AND REBUILDERS

Article III heading which formerly read "Used Parts Dealers, Wreckers and Rebuilders" was amended by P.A. 78–1205, § 2, eff. Sept. 5, 1974.

Section

5/5-301. Automotive parts recyclers, scrap processors, repairers and rebuilders must be licensed

§ 5-301. Automotive parts recyclers, scrap processors, repairers and rebuilders must be licensed.

(a) No person in this State shall, except as an incident to the servicing of vehicles, carry on or conduct the business of a automotive parts recyclers, a scrap processor, a repairer, or a rebuilder, unless licensed to do so in writing by the Secretary of State under this Section. No person shall rebuild a salvage vehicle unless such person is licensed as a rebuilder by the Secretary of State under this Section. Each license shall be applied for and issued separately, except that a license issued to a new vehicle dealer under Section 5-101 of this Code shall also be deemed to be a repairer license.

(b) Any application filed with the Secretary of State, shall be duly verified by oath, in such form as the Secretary of State may by rule or regulation prescribe and shall contain:

1. The name and type of business organization of the applicant and his principal or additional places of business, if any, in this State.

2. The kind or kinds of business enumerated in subsection (a) of this Section to be conducted at each location.

3. If the applicant is a corporation, a list of its officers, directors, and shareholders having a ten percent or greater ownership interest in the corporation, setting forth the residence address of each; if the applicant is a sole proprietorship, a partnership, an unincorporated association, a trust, or any similar form of business organization, the names and residence address of the proprietor or of each partner, member, officer, director, trustee or manager.

4. A statement that the applicant's officers, directors, shareholders having a ten percent or greater ownership interest therein, proprietor, partner, member, officer, director, trustee, manager, or other principals in the business have not committed in the past three years any one violation as determined in any civil or criminal or administrative proceedings of any one of the following Acts:

(a) The Anti Theft Laws of the Illinois Vehicle Code;[1]

(b) The "Certificate of Title Laws" of the Illinois Vehicle Code;[2]

(c) The "Offenses against Registration and Certificates of Title Laws" of the Illinois Vehicle Code;[3]

(d) The "Dealers, Transporters, Wreckers and Rebuilders Laws" of the Illinois Vehicle Code;[4]

(e) Section 21-2 of the Criminal Code of 1961,[5] Criminal Trespass to Vehicles; or

(f) The Retailers Occupation Tax Act.[6]

5. A statement that the applicant's officers, directors, shareholders having a ten percent or greater ownership interest therein, proprietor, partner, member, officer, director, trustee, manager or other principals in the business have not committed in any calendar year 3 or more violations, as determined in any civil or criminal or administrative proceedings, of any one or more of the following Acts:

(a) The Consumer Finance Act;[7]

(b) The Consumer Installment Loan Act;[8]

(c) The Retail Installment Sales Act;[9]

(d) The Motor Vehicle Retail Installment Sales Act;[10]

(e) The Interest Act;[11]

(f) The Illinois Wage Assignment Act;[12]

(g) Part 8 of Article XII of the Code of Civil Procedure;[13] or

(h) The Consumer Fraud Act.[14]

6. An application for a license shall be accompanied by the following fees: $50 for applicant's established place of business; $25 for each additional place of business, if any, to which the application pertains; provided, however, that if such an application is made after June 15 of any year, the license fee shall be $25 for applicant's established place of business plus $12.50 for each additional place of business, if any, to which the application pertains. License fees shall be returnable only in the event that such application shall be denied by the Secretary of State.

7. A statement that the applicant understands Chapter 1 through Chapter 5 of this Code.[15]

8. A statement that the applicant shall comply with subsection (e) of this Section.

(c) Any change which renders no longer accurate any information contained in any application for a license filed with the Secretary of State shall be amended within 30 days after the occurrence of such change on such form as the Secretary of State may prescribe by rule or regulation, accompanied by an amendatory fee of $2.

(d) Anything in this chapter to the contrary, notwithstanding, no person shall be licensed under this Section unless such person shall maintain an established place of business as defined in this Chapter.

(e) The Secretary of State shall within a reasonable time after receipt thereof, examine an application submitted to him under this Section and unless he makes a determination that the application submitted to him does not conform with the requirements of this Section or that grounds exist for a denial of the application, as prescribed in Section 5-501 of this Chapter, grant the applicant an original license as applied for in writing for his established place of business and a supplemental license in writing for each additional place of business in such form as he may prescribe by rule or regulation which shall include the following:

1. The name of the person licensed;

2. If a corporation, the name and address of its officers or if a sole proprietorship, a partnership, an unincorporated association or any similar form of business organization, the name and address of the proprietor or of each partner, member, officer, director, trustee or manager;

3. A designation of the kind or kinds of business enumerated in subsection (a) of this Section to be conducted at each location;

4. In the case of an original license, the established place of business of the licensee;

5. In the case of a supplemental license, the established place of business of the licensee and the additional place of business to which such supplemental license pertains.

(f) The appropriate instrument evidencing the license or a certified copy thereof, provided by the Secretary of State shall be kept, posted, conspicuously in the established place of business of the licensee and in each additional place of business, if any, maintained by such licensee. The licensee also shall post conspicuously in the established place of business and in each additional place of business a notice which states that such business is required to be licensed by the Secretary of State under Section 5-301, and which provides the license number of the business and the license expiration date. This notice also shall advise the consumer that any complaints as to the quality of service may be brought to the attention of the Attorney General. The information required on this notice also shall be printed conspicuously on all estimates and receipts for work by the licensee subject to this Section. The Secretary of State shall prescribe the specific format of this notice.

(g) Except as provided in subsection (h) hereof, licenses granted under this Section shall expire by operation of law on December 31 of the calendar year for which they are granted unless sooner revoked or cancelled under the provisions of Section 5-501 of this Chapter.

(h) Any license granted under this Section may be renewed upon application and payment of the fee required herein as in the case of an original license, provided, however, that in case an application for the renewal of an effective license is made during the month of December, such effective license shall remain in force until such application is granted or denied by the Secretary of State.

(i) All automotive repairers and rebuilders shall, in addition to the requirements of subsections (a) through (h) of this Section, meet the following licensing requirements:

1. Provide proof that the property on which first time applicants plan to do business is in compliance with local zoning laws and regulations, and a listing of zoning classification;

2. Provide proof that the applicant for a repairer's license complies with the proper workers' compensation rate code or classification, and listing the code of classification for that industry;

3. Provide proof that the applicant for a rebuilder's license complies with the proper workers' compensation rate code or classification for the repair industry or the auto parts recycling industry and listing the code of classification;

4. Provide proof that the applicant has obtained or applied for a hazardous waste generator number, and listing the actual number if available or certificate of exemption;

5. Provide proof that applicant has proper liability insurance, and listing the name of the insurer and the policy number; and

6. Provide proof that the applicant has obtained or applied for the proper State sales tax classification and federal identification tax number, and listing the actual numbers if available.

(j) All automotive parts recyclers shall, in addition to the requirements of subsections (a) through (h) of this Section, meet the following licensing requirements:

1. A statement that the applicant purchases 5 vehicles per year or has 5 hulks or chassis in stock;

2. Provide proof that the property on which all first time applicants will do business does comply to the proper local zoning laws in existence, and a listing of zoning classifications;

3. Provide proof that applicant complies with the proper workers' compensation rate code or classification, and listing the code of classification; and

4. Provide proof that applicant has obtained or applied for the proper State sales tax classification and federal identification tax number, and listing the actual numbers if available.

P.A. 76-1586, § 5-301, eff. July 1, 1970. Amended by P.A. 77-643, § 1, eff. Aug. 4, 1971; P.A. 78-858, § 1, eff. Jan. 1, 1974; P.A. 78-1205, § 1, eff. Sept. 5, 1974; P.A. 78-1297, § 58, eff. March 4, 1975; P.A. 81-932, § 1, eff. Sept. 22, 1979; P.A. 82-783, Art. XI, § 140, eff. July 13, 1982; P.A. 83-1473, § 1, eff. Jan. 1, 1985; P.A. 84-680, § 2, eff. Jan. 1, 1986; P.A. 84-1302, § 1, eff. Jan. 1, 1987; P.A. 84-1304, § 1, eff. Jan. 1, 1987; P.A. 85-1396, § 2, eff. Sept. 2, 1988; P.A. 86-295, § 1, eff. Aug. 30, 1989; P.A. 86-444, § 1, eff. Jan. 1, 1990; P.A. 86-1028, Art. II, § 2-44, eff. Feb. 5, 1990; P.A. 87-682, § 1, eff. Jan. 1, 1992; P.A. 89-189, § 5, eff. Jan. 1, 1996.

Formerly Ill.Rev.Stat.1991, ch. 95 ½, ¶ 5-301.

1 625 ILCS 5/4-100 et seq.

2 625 ILCS 5/3-100 et seq.

3 625 ILCS 5/3-701 et seq.

4 625 ILCS 5/5-100 et seq.

5 720 ILCS 5/21-2.

6 35 ILCS 120/1 et seq.

7 Former Ill.Rev.Stat. ch. 17, ¶ 5601 et seq. (repealed).

8 205 ILCS 670/1 et seq.

9 815 ILCS 405/1 et seq.

10 815 ILCS 375/1 et seq.

11 815 ILCS 205/0.01 et seq.

12 740 ILCS 170/.01 et seq.

13 735 ILCS 5/12-801 et seq.

14 815 ILCS 505/1 et seq.

15 625 ILCS 5/1-100 et seq. to 5/5-100 et seq.

5/5-302. Out-of-state salvage vehicle buyer must be licensed

§ 5-302. Out-of-state salvage vehicle buyer must be licensed. (a) No person in this State shall sell or offer at auction salvage vehicles to a nonresident who has not been issued an out-of-state salvage vehicle buyer's ID card from the Secretary of State under this Section. To qualify for this ID card, the applicant shall submit with the application an out-of-state dealer license which is issued by the applicant's state and is substantially equivalent to that of a rebuilder, automotive parts recycler or scrap processor, as licensed under this Code.

(b) Any application filed with the Secretary of State, shall be duly verified by oath, in such form as the Secretary of State may by rule or regulation prescribe.

(c) An application for an out-of-state ID card shall be accompanied by a fee of $100; provided however, that if an application is made after June 15 of any year, the ID card fee shall be $50. Any fees shall be returnable only in the event that such application is denied by the Secretary of State.

(d) The Secretary of State shall within a reasonable time after receipt thereof, examine an application submitted to him under this Section and unless he makes a determination that the application submitted to him does not conform with the requirements of this Section or that grounds exist for a denial of the application, as prescribed in Section 5-501 of this Chapter, grant the applicant an out-of-state salvage vehicle buyer's ID card.

(e) Except as provided in subsection (f) of this Section, licenses granted under this Section shall expire by operation of law on December 31 of the calendar year for which they are granted unless revoked or cancelled under the provisions of Section 5-501 of this Chapter.

(f) Any license granted under this Section may be renewed upon application and payment of the fee required for an original license, provided however, that where an application for the renewal of a license is made during the month of December, the license in effect at the time of application for renewal shall remain in force until such application is granted or denied by the Secretary of State.

(g) An out-of-state salvage vehicle buyer shall be subject to the inspection of records pertaining to the acquisition of salvage vehicles in this State in accordance with this Code and such rules as the Secretary of State may promulgate.

(h) Beginning July 1, 1988, the application filed with the Secretary of State shall also contain:

1. The name and type of business organization of the applicant and his principal or other places of business;

2. If the applicant is a corporation, a list of its officers, directors, and shareholders having a 10% or greater ownership interest in the corporation, setting forth the residence address of each; if the applicant is a sole proprietorship, a partnership, an unincorporated association, a trust, or any similar form of business organization, the names and residence address of the proprietor, or of each partner, member, officer, director, trustee or manager;

3. A statement that the applicant's officers, directors, shareholders having a 10% or greater ownership interest therein, proprietor, partner, member, officer, director, trustee, manager, or other principals in the business have not committed in the past 3 years any one violation as determined in any civil or criminal or administrative proceedings of any one of the following Acts:

(A) The "Anti Theft Laws" of the Illinois Vehicle Code; [1]

(B) The "Certificate of Title Laws" of the Illinois Vehicle Code; [2]

(C) The "Offenses against Registration and Certificates of Title Laws" of the Illinois Vehicle Code; [3]

(D) The "Dealers, Transporters, Wreckers and Rebuilders Laws" of the Illinois Vehicle Code; [4]

(E) Section 21-2 of the Criminal Code of 1961,[5] Criminal Trespass to Vehicles; or

(F) The "Retailers Occupation Tax Act"; [6]

4. A statement that the applicant's officers, directors, shareholders having a 10% or greater ownership interest therein, proprietor, partner, member, officer, director, trustee, manager or other principals in the business have not committed in any calendar year 3 or more violations, as determined in any civil or criminal or administrative proceedings, of any one or more of the following Acts:

(A) The "Consumer Finance Act"; [7]

(B) The "Consumer Installment Loan Act"; [8]

(C) The "Retail Installment Sales Act"; [9]

(D) The "Motor Vehicle Retail Installment Sales Act"; [10]

(E) "An Act in relation to the rate of interest and other charges in connection with sales on credit and the lending of money", approved May 24, 1879, as amended; [11]

(F) "An Act to promote the welfare of wage earners by regulating the assignment of wages, and prescribing a penalty for the violation thereof", approved July 1, 1935, as amended; [12]

(G) Part 8 of Article XII of the Code of Civil Procedure; [13] or

(H) The "Consumer Fraud Act"; [14] and

5. A statement that the applicant understands Chapters 1 through 5 of this Code.[15]

(i) Any change which renders no longer accurate any information contained in any application for a license filed with the Secretary of State shall be amended within 30 days after the occurrence of such change on such form as the Secretary of State may prescribe by rule or regulation, accompanied by an amendatory fee of $2.

P.A. 76-1586, § 5-302, added by P.A. 85-572, § 1, eff. Sept. 18, 1987. Amended by P.A. 85-1396, § 2, eff. Sept. 2, 1988; P.A. 86-444, § 1, eff. Jan. 1, 1990.

Formerly Ill.Rev.Stat.1991, ch. 95 ½, ¶ 5-302.

1 625 ILCS 5/4-100 et seq.

2 625 ILCS 5/3-100 et seq.

3 625 ILCS 5/3-701 et seq.

4 625 ILCS 5/5-100 et seq.

5 720 ILCS 5/21-2.

6 35 ILCS 120/1 et seq.

7 Former Ill.Rev.Stat. ch. 17, ¶ 5601 et seq. (repealed).

8 205 ILCS 670/1 et seq.

9 815 ILCS 405/1 et seq.

10 815 ILCS 375/1 et seq.

11 815 ILCS 205/1 et seq.

12 740 ILCS 170/.01 et seq.

13 735 ILCS 5/12-801 et seq.

14 815 ILCS 505/1 et seq.

15 625 ILCS 5/1-100 et seq. to 5/5-100 et seq.

ARTICLE IV. RECORDS REQUIRED TO BE KEPT

Section

5/5-401 to 5/5-401.1. §§ 5-401 to 5-401.1. Repealed by P.A. 83-1473, § 2, eff. Jan. 1, 1985

5/5-401.2. Licensees required to keep records and make inspections

§ 5-401.2. Licensees required to keep records and make inspections.

(a) Every person licensed or required to be licensed under Section 5-101, 5-101.1, 5-102, 5-301 or 5-302 of this Code, shall, with the exception of scrap processors, maintain for 3 years, in a form as the Secretary of State may by rule or regulation prescribe, at his established place of business, additional place of business, or principal place of business if licensed under Section 5-302, the following records relating to the acquisition or disposition of vehicles and their essential parts possessed in this State, brought into this State from another state, territory or country, or sold or transferred to another person in this State or in another state, territory, or country.

(1) The following records pertaining to new or used vehicles shall be kept:

(A) the year, make, model, style and color of the vehicle;

(B) the vehicle's manufacturer's identification number or, if applicable, the Secretary of State or Illinois Department of State Police identification number;

(C) the date of acquisition of the vehicle;

(D) the name and address of the person from whom the vehicle was acquired and, if that person is a dealer, the Illinois or out-of-state dealer license number of such person;

(E) the signature of the person making the inspection of a used vehicle as required under subsection (d) of this Section, if applicable;

(F) the purchase price of the vehicle, if applicable;

(G) the date of the disposition of the vehicle;

(H) the name and address of the person to whom any vehicle was disposed, and if that person is a dealer, the Illinois or out-of-State dealer's license number of that dealer;

(I) the uniform invoice number reflecting the disposition of the vehicle, if applicable; and

(J) The sale price of the vehicle, if applicable.

(2) (A) The following records pertaining to used essential parts other than quarter panels and transmissions of vehicles of the first division shall be kept:

(i) the year, make, model, color and type of such part;

(ii) the vehicle's manufacturer's identification number, derivative number, or, if applicable, the Secretary of State or Illinois Department of State Police identification number of such part;

(iii) the date of the acquisition of each part;

(iv) the name and address of the person from whom the part was acquired and, if that person is a dealer, the Illinois or out-of-state dealer license number of such person; if the essential part being acquired is from a person other than a dealer, the licensee shall verify and record that person's identity by recording the identification numbers from at least two sources of identification, one of which shall be a drivers license or State identification card;

(v) the uniform invoice number or out-of-state bill of sale number reflecting the acquisition of such part;

(vi) the stock number assigned to the essential part by the licensee, if applicable;

(vii) the date of the disposition of such part;

(viii) the name and address of the person to whom such part was disposed of and, if that person is a dealer, the Illinois or out-of-state dealer license number of that person;

(ix) the uniform invoice number reflecting the disposition of such part.

(B) Inspections of all essential parts shall be conducted in accordance with Section 5-402.1.

(C) A separate entry containing all of the information required to be recorded in subparagraph (A) of paragraph (2) of subsection (a) of this Section shall be made for each separate essential part. Separate entries shall be made regardless of whether the part was a large purchase acquisition. In addition, a separate entry shall be made for each part acquired for immediate sale or transfer, or for placement into the overall inventory or stock to be disposed of at a later time, or for use on a vehicle to be materially altered by the licensee, or acquired for any other purpose or reason. Failure to make a separate entry for each essential part acquired or disposed of, or a failure to record any of the specific information required to be recorded concerning the acquisition or disposition of each essential part as set forth in subparagraph (A) of paragraph (2) of subsection (a) shall constitute a failure to keep records.

(D) The vehicle's manufacturer's identification number or Secretary of State or Illinois Department of State Police identification number for the essential part shall be ascertained and recorded even if such part is acquired from a person or dealer located in a State, territory, or country which does not require that such information be recorded. If the vehicle's manufacturer's identification number or Secretary of State or Illinois Department of State Police identification number for an essential part cannot be obtained, that part shall not be acquired by the licensee or any of his agents or employees. If such part or parts were physically acquired by the licensee or any of his agents or employees while the licensee or agent or employee was outside this State, that licensee or agent or employee was outside the State, that licensee, agent or employee shall not bring such essential part into this State or cause it to be brought into this State. The acquisition or disposition of an essential part by a licensee without the recording of the vehicle identification number or Secretary of State identification number for such part or the transportation into the State by the licensee or his agent or employee of such part or parts shall constitute a failure to keep records.

(E) The records of essential parts required to be kept by this Section shall apply to all hulks, chassis, frames or cowls, regardless of the age of those essential parts. The records required to be kept by this Section for essential parts other than hulks, chassis, frames or cowls, shall apply only to those essential parts which are 6 model years of age or newer. In determining the model year of such an essential part it may be presumed that the identification number of the vehicle from which the essential part came or the identification number affixed to the essential part itself acquired by the licensee denotes the model year of that essential part. This presumption, however, shall not apply if the gross appearance of the essential part does not correspond to the year, make or model of either the identification number of the vehicle from which the essential part is alleged to have come or the identification number which is affixed to the essential part itself. To determine whether an essential part is 6 years of age or newer within this paragraph, the model year of the essential part shall be subtracted from the calendar year in which the essential part is acquired or disposed of by the licensee. If the remainder is 6 or less, the record of the acquisition or disposition of that essential part shall be kept as required by this Section.

(F) The requirements of paragraph (2) of subsection (a) of this Section shall not apply to the disposition of an essential part other than a cowl which has been damaged or altered to a state in which it can no longer be returned to a usable condition and which is being sold or transferred to a scrap processor or for delivery to a scrap processor.

(3) the following records for vehicles on which junking certificates are obtained shall be kept:

(A) the year, make, model, style and color of the vehicle;

(B) the vehicle's manufacturer's identification number or, if applicable, the Secretary of State or Illinois Department of State Police identification number;

(C) the date the vehicle was acquired;

(D) the name and address of the person from whom the vehicle was acquired and, if that person is a dealer, the

Illinois or out-of-state dealer license number of that person;

(E) the certificate of title number or salvage certificate number for the vehicle, if applicable;

(F) the junking certificate number obtained by the licensee; this entry shall be recorded at the close of business of the fifth business day after receiving the junking certificate;

(G) the name and address of the person to whom the junking certificate has been assigned, if applicable, and if that person is a dealer, the Illinois or out-of-state dealer license number of that dealer;

(H) if the vehicle or any part of the vehicle is dismantled for its parts to be disposed of in any way, or if such parts are to be used by the licensee to materially alter a vehicle, those essential parts shall be recorded and the entries required by paragraph (2) of subsection (a) shall be made.

(4) The following records for rebuilt vehicles shall be kept:

(A) the year, make, model, style and color of the vehicle;

(B) the vehicle's manufacturer's identification number of the vehicle or, if applicable, the Secretary of State or Illinois Department of State Police identification number;

(C) the date the vehicle was acquired;

(D) the name and address of the person from whom the vehicle was acquired, and if that person is a dealer, the Illinois or out-of-state dealer license number of that person;

(E) the salvage certificate number for the vehicle;

(F) the newly issued certificate of title number for the vehicle;

(G) the date of disposition of the vehicle;

(H) the name and address of the person to whom the vehicle was disposed, and if a dealer, the Illinois or out-of-state dealer license number of that dealer;

(I) The sale price of the vehicle.

(a-1) A person licensed or required to be licensed under Section 5-101 or Section 5-102 of this Code who issues temporary registration permits as permitted by this Code and by rule must electronically file the registration with the Secretary and must maintain records of the registration in the manner prescribed by the Secretary.

(b) A failure to make separate entries for each vehicle acquired, disposed of, or assigned, or a failure to record any of the specific information required to be recorded concerning the acquisition or disposition of each vehicle as set forth in paragraphs (1), (3) and (4) of subsection (a) shall constitute a failure to keep records.

(c) All entries relating to the acquisition of a vehicle or essential part required by subsection (a) of this Section shall be recorded no later than the close of business on the seventh calendar day following such acquisition. All entries relating to the disposition of a vehicle or an essential part shall be made at the time of such disposition. If the vehicle or essential part was disposed of on the same day as its acquisition or the day thereafter, the entries relating to the acquisition of the vehicle or essential part shall be made at the time of the disposition of the vehicle or essential part. Failure to make the entries required in or at the times prescribed by this subsection following the acquisition or disposition of such vehicle or essential part shall constitute a failure to keep records.

(d) Every person licensed or required to be licensed shall, before accepting delivery of a used vehicle, inspect the vehicle to determine whether the manufacturer's public vehicle identification number has been defaced, destroyed, falsified, removed, altered, or tampered with in any way. If the person making the inspection determines that the manufacturer's public vehicle identification number has been altered, removed, defaced, destroyed, falsified or tampered with he shall not acquire that vehicle but instead shall promptly notify law enforcement authorities of his finding.

(e) The information required to be kept in subsection (a) of this Section shall be kept in a manner prescribed by rule or regulation of the Secretary of State.

(f) Every person licensed or required to be licensed shall have in his possession a separate certificate of title, salvage certificate, junking certificate, certificate of purchase, uniform invoice, out-of-state bill of sale or other acceptable documentary evidence of his right to the possession of every vehicle or essential part.

(g) Every person licensed or required to be licensed as a transporter under Section 5-201 shall maintain for 3 years, in such form as the Secretary of State may by rule or regulation prescribe, at his principal place of business a record of every vehicle transported by him, including numbers of or other marks of identification thereof, the names and addresses of persons from whom and to whom the vehicle was delivered and the dates of delivery.

(h) No later than 15 days prior to going out of business, selling the business, or transferring the ownership of the business, the licensee shall notify the Secretary of State that he is going out of business or that he is transferring the ownership of the business. Failure to notify under this paragraph shall constitute a failure to keep records.

(i) (Blank).

(j) A person who knowingly fails to comply with the provisions of this Section or knowingly fails to obey, observe, or comply with any order of the Secretary or any law enforcement agency issued in accordance with this Section is guilty of a Class B misdemeanor for the first violation and a Class A misdemeanor for the second and subsequent violations. Each violation constitutes a separate and distinct offense and a separate count may be brought in the same indictment or information for each vehicle or each essential part of a vehicle for which a record was not kept as required by this Section.

(k) Any person convicted of failing to keep the records required by this Section with intent to conceal the identity or origin of a vehicle or its essential parts or with intent to defraud the public in the transfer or sale of vehicles or their essential parts is guilty of a Class 2 felony. Each violation constitutes a separate and distinct offense and a separate count may be brought in the same indictment or information for each vehicle or essential part of a vehicle for which a record was not kept as required by this Section.

(*l*) A person may not be criminally charged with or convicted of both a knowing failure to comply with this Section and a knowing failure to comply with any order, if both offenses involve the same record keeping violation.

(m) The Secretary shall adopt rules necessary for implementation of this Section, which may include the imposition of administrative fines.

P.A. 76-1586, § 5-401.2, added by P.A. 83-1473, § 1, eff. Jan. 1, 1985. Amended by P.A. 83-1528, Art. II, § 24, eff. Jan. 17, 1985; P.A. 84-25, Art. IV, § 27, eff. July 18, 1985; P.A. 84-1105, § 1, eff. Dec. 10, 1985; P.A. 84-1302, § 1, eff. Jan. 1, 1987; P.A. 84-1304, § 1, eff. Jan. 1, 1987; P.A. 85-572, § 1, eff. Sept. 18, 1987; P.A. 85-1209, Art. III, § 3-60, eff. Aug. 30, 1988; P.A. 85-1396, § 2, eff. Sept. 2, 1988; P.A. 85-1440, Art. II, § 2-25, eff. Feb. 1, 1989; P.A. 86-444, § 1, eff.

Jan. 1, 1990; P.A. 86–1179, § 2, eff. Aug. 17, 1990; P.A. 86–1209, § 1, eff. Jan. 1, 1991; P.A. 89–189, § 5, eff. Jan. 1, 1996; P.A. 89–235, Art. 2, § 2–120, eff. Aug. 4, 1995; P.A. 91–415, § 5, eff. Jan. 1, 2000; P.A. 92–773, § 5, eff. Aug. 6, 2002.

Formerly Ill.Rev.Stat.1991, ch. 95 ½, ¶ 5–401.2.

Validity

The Supreme Court of Illinois has held that the provision making the known failure to maintain records of the acquisition and disposition of vehicles a Class 2 felony an unconstitutional violation of due process in the case of People v. Wright, 194 Ill.2d 1, 740 N.E.2d 755, 251 Ill.Dec. 469 (2000), rehearing denied (Nov. 27, 2000).

5/5–401.3. Scrap processors required to keep records

§ 5–401.3. Scrap processors required to keep records. (a) Every person licensed or required to be licensed as a scrap processor pursuant to Section 5–301 of this Chapter shall maintain for 3 years, at his established place of business, the following records relating to the acquisition of a vehicle, junk vehicle, or vehicle cowl which has been acquired for the purpose of processing into a form other than a vehicle, junk vehicle or vehicle cowl which is possessed in the State or brought into this State from another state, territory or country. No scrap metal processor shall sell a vehicle or essential part, as such, except for engines, transmissions, and powertrains, unless licensed to do so under another provision of this Code. A scrap processor who is additionally licensed as an automotive parts recycler shall not be subject to the record keeping requirements for a scrap processor when acting as an automotive parts recycler.

(1) For a vehicle, junk vehicle, or vehicle cowl acquired from a person who is licensed under this Chapter, the scrap processor shall record the name and address of the person, and the Illinois or out-of-state dealer license number of such person on the scrap processor's weight ticket at the time of the acquisition. The person disposing of the vehicle, junk vehicle, or vehicle cowl shall furnish the scrap processor with documentary proof of ownership of the vehicle, junk vehicle, or vehicle cowl in one of the following forms: a Certificate of Title, a Salvage Certificate, a Junking Certificate, a Secretary of State Junking Manifest, a Uniform Invoice, a Certificate of Purchase, or other similar documentary proof of ownership. The scrap processor shall not acquire a vehicle, junk vehicle or vehicle cowl without obtaining one of the aforementioned documentary proofs of ownership.

(2) For a vehicle, junk vehicle or vehicle cowl acquired from a person who is not licensed under this Chapter, the scrap processor shall verify and record that person's identity by recording the identification of such person from at least 2 sources of identification, one of which shall be a driver's license or State Identification Card, on the scrap processor's weight ticket at the time of the acquisition. The person disposing of the vehicle, junk vehicle, or vehicle cowl shall furnish the scrap processor with documentary proof of ownership of the vehicle, junk vehicle, or vehicle cowl in one of the following forms: a Certificate of Title, a Salvage Certificate, a Junking Certificate, a Secretary of State Junking Manifest, a Certificate of Purchase, or other similar documentary proof of ownership. The scrap processor shall not acquire a vehicle, junk vehicle or vehicle cowl without obtaining one of the aforementioned documentary proofs of ownership.

(3) In addition to the other information required on the scrap processor's weight ticket, a scrap processor who at the time of acquisition of a vehicle, junk vehicle, or vehicle cowl is furnished a Certificate of Title, Salvage Certificate or Certificate of Purchase shall record the vehicle Identification Number on the weight ticket or affix a copy of the Certificate of Title, Salvage Certificate or Certificate of Purchase to the weight ticket and the identification of the person acquiring the information on the behalf of the scrap processor.

(4) The scrap processor shall maintain a copy of a Junk Vehicle Notification relating to any Certificate of Title, Salvage Certificate, Certificate of Purchase or similarly acceptable out-of-state document surrendered to the Secretary of State pursuant to the provisions of Section 3–117.2 of this Code.

(b) Any licensee who knowingly fails to record any of the specific information required to be recorded on the weight ticket or who knowingly fails to acquire and maintain for 3 years documentary proof of ownership in one of the prescribed forms shall be guilty of a Class A misdemeanor and subject to a fine not to exceed $1,000. Each violation shall constitute a separate and distinct offense and a separate count may be brought in the same complaint for each violation. Any licensee who commits a second violation of this Section within two years of a previous conviction of a violation of this Section shall be guilty of a Class 4 felony.

(c) It shall be an affirmative defense to an offense brought under paragraph (b) of this Section that the licensee or person required to be licensed both reasonably and in good faith relied on information appearing on a Certificate of Title, a Salvage Certificate, a Junking Certificate, a Secretary of State Manifest, a Secretary of State's Uniform Invoice, a Certificate of Purchase, or other documentary proof of ownership prepared under Section 3–117.1(a) of this Code, relating to the transaction for which the required record was not kept which was supplied to the licensee by another licensee or out-of-state dealer.

(d) No later than 15 days prior to going out of business, selling the business, or transferring the ownership of the business, the scrap processor shall notify the Secretary of that fact. Failure to so notify the Secretary of State shall constitute a failure to keep records under this Section.

(e) Evidence derived directly or indirectly from the keeping of records required to be kept under this Section shall not be admissible in a prosecution of the licensee for an alleged violation of Section 4–102(a)(3) of this Code.

P.A. 76–1586, § 5–401.3, added by P.A. 83–1473, § 1, eff. Jan. 1, 1985. Amended by P.A. 84–1302, § 1, eff. Jan. 1, 1987; P.A. 84–1304, § 1, eff. Jan. 1, 1987; P.A. 85–1204, § 1, eff. Aug. 26, 1988; P.A. 86–444, § 1, eff. Jan. 1, 1990; P.A. 90–89, § 15, eff. Jan. 1, 1998.

Formerly Ill.Rev.Stat.1991, ch. 95 ½, ¶ 5–401.3.

5/5–402. Use of Department of Revenue Uniform Invoice for vehicle

§ 5–402. Use of Department of Revenue Uniform Invoice for vehicle. Every person licensed as a new vehicle dealer, or as a used vehicle dealer, or as a motor vehicle financing affiliate shall issue a Uniform Invoice with respect to each transaction wherein he disposes of a vehicle, except that where, in the same transaction, a vehicle dealer transfers more than one vehicle to another vehicle dealer for the purpose of resale, such seller for resale may issue one Uniform Invoice to the purchaser covering all the vehicles involved in that transaction and may report the transfer of all the vehicles involved in that transaction to the Department on the same Uniform Invoice-transaction reporting return form. Every person licensed as a rebuilder shall likewise issue a Uniform Invoice with respect to each transaction wherein he disposes of a rebuilt or restored vehicle. Such Uniform Invoice shall be the same document as the transaction reporting return referred to in Section 3 of the Retailers' Occupation Tax Act.[1] Such Uniform Invoice shall contain complete financial details of the transaction in such form as shall be prescribed by the Department of Revenue. Such Uniform Invoice shall include an affidavit by both the seller and the buyer that any trade-in title has been properly assigned from the buyer to the seller and that all information on the Uniform Invoice-transaction reporting return is true and accurate.

P.A. 76-1586, § 5-402, eff. July 1, 1970. Amended by P.A. 78-858, § 1, eff. Jan. 1, 1974; P.A. 83-1473, § 1, eff. Jan. 1, 1985; P.A. 85-1396, § 2, eff. Sept. 2, 1988; P.A. 91-415, § 5, eff. Jan. 1, 2000.

Formerly Ill.Rev.Stat.1991, ch. 95 ½, ¶ 5-402.

1 35 ILCS 120/3.

5/5-402.1. Use of Secretary of State Uniform Invoice for Essential Parts

§ 5-402.1. Use of Secretary of State Uniform Invoice for Essential Parts.

(a) Except for scrap processors, every person licensed or required to be licensed under Section 5-101, 5-101.1, 5-102 or 5-301 of this Code shall issue, in a form the Secretary of State may by rule or regulation prescribe, a Uniform Invoice, which may also act as a bill of sale, made out in triplicate with respect to each transaction in which he disposes of an essential part other than quarter panels and transmissions of vehicles of the first division. Such Invoice shall be made out at the time of the disposition of the essential part. If the licensee disposes of several essential parts in the same transaction, the licensee may issue one Uniform Invoice covering all essential parts disposed of in that transaction.

(b) The following information shall be contained on the Uniform Invoice:

(1) the business name, address and dealer license number of the person disposing of the essential part;

(2) the name and address of the person acquiring the essential part, and if that person is a dealer, the Illinois or out-of-state dealer license number of that dealer;

(3) the date of the disposition of the essential part;

(4) the year, make, model, color and description of each essential part disposed of by the person;

(5) the manufacturer's vehicle identification number, Secretary of State identification number or Illinois Department of State Police identification number, for each essential part disposed of by the person;

(6) the printed name and legible signature of the person or agent disposing of the essential part; and

(7) if the person is a dealer the printed name and legible signature of the dealer or his agent or employee accepting delivery of the essential part.

(c) Except for scrap processors, and except as set forth in subsection (d) of this Section, whenever a person licensed or required to be licensed by Section 5-101, 5-101.1, 5-102, or 5-301 accepts delivery of an essential part, other than quarter panels and transmissions of vehicles of the first division, that person shall, at the time of the acceptance or delivery, comply with the following procedures:

(1) Before acquiring or accepting delivery of any essential part, the licensee or his authorized agent or employee shall inspect the part to determine whether the vehicle identification number, Secretary of State identification number, Illinois Department of State Police identification number, or identification plate or sticker attached to or stamped on any part being acquired or delivered has been removed, falsified, altered, defaced, destroyed, or tampered with. If the licensee or his agent or employee determines that the vehicle identification number, Secretary of State identification number. Illinois Department of State Police identification number, identification plate or identification sticker containing an identification number, or Federal Certificate label of an essential part has been removed, falsified, altered, defaced, destroyed or tampered with, the licensee or agent shall not accept or receive that part.

If that part was physically acquired by or delivered to a licensee or his agent or employee while that licensee, agent or employee was outside this State, that licensee or agent or employee shall not bring that essential part into this State or cause it to be brought into this State.

(2) If the person disposing of or delivering the essential part to the licensee is a licensed in-state or out-of-state dealer, the licensee or his agent or employee, after inspecting the essential part as required by paragraph (1) of this subsection (c), shall examine the Uniform Invoice, or bill of sale, as the case may be, to ensure that it contains all the information required to be provided by persons disposing of essential parts as set forth in subsection (b) of this Section. If the Uniform Invoice or bill of sale does not contain all the information required to be listed by subsection (b) of this Section, the dealer disposing of or delivering such part or his agent or employee shall record such additional information or other needed modifications on the Uniform Invoice or bill of sale or, if needed, an attachment thereto. The dealer or his agent or employee delivering the essential part shall initial all additions or modifications to the Uniform Invoice or bill of sale and legibly print his name at the bottom of each document containing his initials. If the transaction involves a bill of sale rather than a Uniform Invoice, the licensee or his agent or employee accepting delivery of or acquiring the essential part shall affix his printed name and legible signature on the space on the bill of sale provided for his signature or, if no space is provided, on the back of the bill of sale. If the dealer or his agent or employee disposing of or delivering the essential part cannot or does not provide all the information required by subsection (b) of this Section, the licensee or his agent or employee shall not accept or receive any essential part for which that required information is not provided. If such essential part for which the information required is not fully provided was physically acquired while the licensee or his agent or employee was outside this State, the licensee or his agent or employee shall not bring that essential part into this State or cause it to be brought into this State.

(3) If the person disposing of the essential part is not a licensed dealer, the licensee or his agent or employee shall, after inspecting the essential part as required by paragraph (1) of subsection (c) of this Section verify the identity of the person disposing of the essential part by examining 2 sources of identification, one of which shall be either a driver's license or state identification card. The licensee or his agent or employee shall then prepare a Uniform Invoice listing all the information required to be provided by subsection (b) of this Section. In the space on the Uniform Invoice provided for the dealer license num-

ber of the person disposing of the part, the licensee or his agent or employee shall list the numbers taken from the documents of identification provided by the person disposing of the part. The person disposing of the part shall affix his printed name and legible signature on the space on the Uniform Invoice provided for the person disposing of the essential part and the licensee or his agent or employee acquiring the part shall affix his printed name and legible signature on the space provided on the Uniform Invoice for the person acquiring the essential part. If the person disposing of the essential part cannot or does not provide all the information required to be provided by this paragraph, or does not present 2 satisfactory forms of identification, the licensee or his agent or employee shall not acquire that essential part.

(d) If an essential part other than quarter panels and transmissions of vehicles of the first division was delivered by a licensed commercial delivery service delivering such part on behalf of a licensed dealer, the person required to comply with subsection (c) of this Section may conduct the inspection of that part required by paragraph (1) of subsection (c) and examination of the Uniform Invoice or bill of sale required by paragraph (2) of subsection (c) of this Section immediately after the acceptance of the part.

(1) If the inspection of the essential part pursuant to paragraph (1) of subsection (c) reveals that the vehicle identification number, Secretary of State identification number, Illinois Department of State Police identification number, identification plate or sticker containing an identification number, or Federal Certificate label of an essential part has been removed, falsified, altered, defaced, destroyed or tampered with, the licensee or his agent shall immediately record such fact on the Uniform Invoice or bill of sale, assign the part an inventory or stock number, place such inventory or stock number on both the essential part and the Uniform Invoice or bill of sale, and record the date of the inspection of the part on the Uniform Invoice or bill of sale. The licensee shall, within 7 days of such inspection, return such part to the dealer from whom it was acquired.

(2) If the examination of the Uniform Invoice or bill of sale pursuant to paragraph (2) of subsection (c) reveals that any of the information required to be listed by subsection (b) of this Section is missing, the licensee or person required to be licensed shall immediately assign a stock or inventory number to such part, place such stock or inventory number on both the essential part and the Uniform Invoice or bill of sale, and record the date of examination on the Uniform Invoice or bill of sale. The licensee or person required to be licensed shall acquire the information missing from the Uniform Invoice or bill of sale within 7 days of the examination of such Uniform Invoice or bill of sale. Such information may be received by telephone conversation with the dealer from whom the part was acquired. If the dealer provides the missing information the licensee shall record such information on the Uniform Invoice or bill of sale along with the name of the person providing the information. If the dealer does not provide the required information within the aforementioned 7 day period, the licensee shall return the part to that dealer.

(e) Except for scrap processors, all persons licensed or required to be licensed who acquire or dispose of essential parts other than quarter panels and transmissions of vehicles of the first division shall retain a copy of the Uniform Invoice required to be made by subsections (a), (b) and (c) of this Section for a period of 3 years.

(f) Except for scrap processors, any person licensed or required to be licensed under Sections 5-101, 5-102 or 5-301 who knowingly fails to record on a Uniform Invoice any of the information or entries required to be recorded by subsections (a), (b) and (c) of this Section, or who knowingly places false entries or other misleading information on such Uniform Invoice, or who knowingly fails to retain for 3 years a copy of a Uniform Invoice reflecting transactions required to be recorded by subsections (a), (b) and (c) of this Section, or who knowingly acquires or disposes of essential parts without receiving, issuing, or executing a Uniform Invoice reflecting that transaction as required by subsections (a), (b) and (c) of this Section, or who brings or causes to be brought into this State essential parts for which the information required to be recorded on a Uniform Invoice is not recorded as prohibited by subsection (c) of this Section, or who knowingly fails to comply with the provisions of this Section in any other manner shall be guilty of a Class 2 felony. Each violation shall constitute a separate and distinct offense and a separate count may be brought in the same indictment or information for each essential part for which a record was not kept as required by this Section or for which the person failed to comply with other provisions of this Section.

(g) The records required to be kept by this Section may be examined by a person or persons making a lawful inspection of the licensee's premises pursuant to Section 5-403.

(h) The records required to be kept by this Section shall be retained by the licensee at his principal place of business for a period of 7 years.

(i) The requirements of this Section shall not apply to the disposition of an essential part other than a cowl which has been damaged or altered to a state in which it can no longer be returned to a usable condition and which is being sold or transferred to a scrap processor or for delivery to a scrap processor.

P.A. 76-1586, § 5-402.1, added by P.A. 83-1473, § 1, eff. Jan. 1, 1985. Amended by P.A. 84-25, Art. IV, § 27, eff. July 18, 1985; P.A. 84-1302, § 1, eff. Jan. 1, 1987; P.A. 84-1304, § 1, eff. Jan. 1, 1987; P.A. 85-1204, § 1, eff. Aug. 26, 1988; P.A. 85-1396, § 2, eff. Sept. 2, 1988; P.A. 85-1440, Art. II, § 2-25, eff. Feb. 1, 1989; P.A. 86-1179, § 2, eff. Aug. 17, 1990; P.A. 86-1209, § 1, eff. Jan. 1, 1991; P.A. 86-1475, Art. 2, § 2-25, eff. Jan. 10, 1991; P.A. 91-415, § 5, eff. Jan. 1, 2000.

Formerly Ill.Rev.Stat.1991, ch. 95 ½, ¶ 5-402.1.

5/5-403. Inspection of records; notice; presence of licensee during inspection; duration; search warrants; public complaints

§ 5-403. (1) Authorized representatives of the Secretary of State including officers of the Secretary of State's Department of Police, other peace officers, and such other individuals as the Secretary may designate from time to time shall make inspections of individuals and facilities licensed or required to be licensed under Chapter 5 of the Illinois Vehicle Code for the purpose of reviewing records required to be maintained under Chapter 5 for accuracy and completeness and reviewing and examining the premises of the licensee's established or additional place of business for the purpose of determining the accuracy of the required records. Premises that may be inspected in order to determine the accuracy of the books and records required to be kept includes all premises used by the licensee to store vehicles and parts that are reflected by the required books and records.

(2) Persons having knowledge of or conducting inspections pursuant to this Chapter shall not in advance of such inspec-

tions knowingly notify a licensee or representative of a licensee of the contemplated inspection unless the Secretary or an individual designated by him for this purpose authorizes such notification. Any individual who, without authorization, knowingly violates this subparagraph shall be guilty of a Class A misdemeanor.

(3) The licensee or a representative of the licensee shall be entitled to be present during an inspection conducted pursuant to Chapter 5, however, the presence of the licensee or an authorized representative of the licensee is not a condition precedent to such an inspection.

(4) Inspection conducted pursuant to Chapter 5 may be initiated at any time that business is being conducted or work is being performed, whether or not open to the public or when the licensee or a representative of the licensee, other than a mere custodian or watchman, is present. The fact that a licensee or representative of the licensee leaves the licensed premises after an inspection has been initiated shall not require the termination of the inspection.

(5) Any inspection conducted pursuant to Chapter 5 shall not continue for more than 24 hours after initiation.

(6) In the event information comes to the attention of the individuals conducting an inspection that may give rise to the necessity of obtaining a search warrant, and in the event steps are initiated for the procurement of a search warrant, the individuals conducting such inspection may take all necessary steps to secure the premises under inspection until the warrant application is acted upon by a judicial officer.

(7) No more than 6 inspections of a premises may be conducted pursuant to Chapter 5 within any 6 month period except pursuant to a search warrant. Notwithstanding this limitation, nothing in this subparagraph shall be construed to limit the authority of law enforcement agents to respond to public complaints of violations of the Code. For the purpose of this subparagraph, a public complaint is one in which the complainant identifies himself or herself and sets forth, in writing, the specific basis for their complaint against the licensee.

(8) Nothing in this Section shall be construed to limit the authority of individuals by the Secretary pursuant to this Section to conduct searches of licensees pursuant to a duly issued and authorized search warrant.

(9) Any licensee who, having been informed by a person authorized to make inspections and examine records under this Section that he desires to inspect records and the licensee's premises as authorized by this Section, refuses either to produce for that person records required to be kept by this Chapter or to permit such authorized person to make an inspection of the premises in accordance with this Section shall subject the license to immediate suspension by the Secretary of State.

(10) Beginning July 1, 1988, any person licensed under 5–302 shall produce for inspection upon demand those records pertaining to the acquisition of salvage vehicles in this State. This inspection may be conducted at the principal offices of the Secretary of State.

P.A. 76–1586, § 5–403, added by P.A. 82–984, § 1, eff. Jan. 1, 1983. Amended by P.A. 83–1473, § 1, eff. Jan. 1, 1985; P.A. 85–572, § 1, eff. Sept. 18, 1987; P.A. 86–444, § 1, eff. Jan. 1, 1990.

Formerly Ill.Rev.Stat.1991, ch. 95 ½, ¶ 5–403.

5/5–403.1. Inventory System

§ 5–403.1. Inventory System.

(a) Every person licensed or required to be licensed under the provisions of Sections 5–101, 5–101.1, 5–102 and 5–301 of this Code shall, under rule and regulation prescribed by the Secretary of State, maintain an inventory system of all vehicles or essential parts in such a manner that a person making an inspection pursuant to the provisions of Section 5–403 of this Code can readily ascertain the identity of such vehicles or essential parts and readily locate such parts on the licensees premises.

(b) Failure to maintain an inventory system as required under this Section is a Class A misdemeanor.

(c) This Section does not apply to vehicles or essential parts which have been acquired by a scrap processor for processing into a form other than a vehicle or essential part.

P.A. 76–1586, § 5–403.1, added by P.A. 83–1473, § 1, eff. Jan. 1, 1985. Amended by P.A. 86–1209, § 1, eff. Jan. 1, 1991; P.A. 91–415, § 5, eff. Jan. 1, 2000.

Formerly Ill.Rev.Stat.1991, ch. 95 ½, ¶ 5–403.1.

5/5–404. § 5–404. Repealed by P.A. 86–1209, § 2, eff. Jan. 1, 1991

ARTICLE V. LICENSES—INJUNCTIONS

Article V heading which formerly read "Licenses" was amended by P.A. 78–1165, § 2, eff. Aug. 27, 1974.

5/5–501. Denial, suspension or revocation or cancellation of a license

§ 5–501. Denial, suspension or revocation or cancellation of a license. (a) The license of a person issued under this Chapter may be denied, revoked or suspended if the Secretary of State finds that the applicant, or the officer, director, shareholder having a ten percent or greater ownership interest in the corporation, owner, partner, trustee, manager, employee or the licensee has:

1. Violated this Act;

2. Made any material misrepresentation to the Secretary of State in connection with an application for a license, junking certificate, salvage certificate, title or registration;

3. Committed a fraudulent act in connection with selling, bartering, exchanging, offering for sale or otherwise dealing in vehicles, chassis, essential parts, or vehicle shells;

4. As a new vehicle dealer has no contract with a manufacturer or enfranchised distributor to sell that new vehicle in this State;

5. Not maintained an established place of business as defined in this Code;

6. Failed to file or produce for the Secretary of State any application, report, document or other pertinent books, records, documents, letters, contracts, required to be filed or produced under this Code or any rule or regulation made by the Secretary of State pursuant to this Code;

7. Previously had, within 3 years, such a license denied, suspended, revoked, or cancelled under the provisions of subsection (c)(2) of this Section;

8. Has committed in any calendar year 3 or more violations, as determined in any civil or criminal proceeding, of any one or more of the following Acts:

a. the "Consumer Finance Act";[1]

b. the "Consumer Installment Loan Act";[2]

c. the "Retail Installment Sales Act";[3]

d. the "Motor Vehicle Retail Installment Sales Act";[4]

e. "An Act in relation to the rate of interest and other charges in connection with sales on credit and the lending of money", approved May 24, 1879, as amended;[5]

f. "An Act to promote the welfare of wage-earners by regulating the assignment of wages, and prescribing a penalty for the violation thereof", approved July 1, 1935, as amended;[6]

g. Part 8 of Article XII of the Code of Civil Procedure;[7] or

h. the "Consumer Fraud Act";[8]

9. Failed to pay any fees or taxes due under this Act, or has failed to transmit any fees or taxes received by him for transmittal by him to the Secretary of State or the State of Illinois;

10. Converted an abandoned vehicle;

11. Used a vehicle identification plate or number assigned to a vehicle other than the one to which originally assigned;

12. Violated the provisions of Chapter 5 of this Act, as amended;

13. Violated the provisions of Chapter 4 of this Act, as amended;

14. Violated the provisions of Chapter 3 of this Act, as amended;

15. Violated Section 21-2 of the Criminal Code of 1961,[9] Criminal Trespass to Vehicles;

16. Made or concealed a material fact in connection with his application for a license;

17. Acted in the capacity of a person licensed or acted as a licensee under this Chapter without having a license therefor;

18. Failed to pay, within 90 days after a final judgment, any fines assessed against the licensee pursuant to an action brought under Section 5-404.

(b) In addition to other grounds specified in this Chapter, the Secretary of State, on complaint of the Department of Revenue, shall refuse the issuance of renewal of a license, or suspend or revoke such license, for any of the following violations of the "Retailers' Occupation Tax Act":[10]

1. Failure to make a tax return;

2. The filing of a fraudulent return;

3. Failure to pay all or part of any tax or penalty finally determined to be due;

4. Failure to comply with the bonding requirements of the "Retailers' Occupation Tax Act".

(c) Cancellation of a license.

1. The license of a person issued under this Chapter may be cancelled by the Secretary of State prior to its expiration in any of the following situations:

A. When a license is voluntarily surrendered, by the licensed person; or

B. If the business enterprise is a sole proprietorship, which is not a franchised dealership, when the sole proprietor dies or is imprisoned for any period of time exceeding 30 days; or

C. If the license was issued to the wrong person or corporation, or contains an error on its face. If any person above whose license has been cancelled wishes to apply for another license, whether during the same license year or any other year, that person shall be treated as any other new applicant and the cancellation of the person's prior license shall not, in and of itself, be a bar to the issuance of a new license.

2. The license of a person issued under this Chapter may be cancelled without a hearing when the Secretary of State is notified that the applicant, or any officer, director, shareholder having a 10 per cent or greater ownership interest in the corporation, owner, partner, trustee, manager, employee or member of the applicant or the licensee has been convicted of any felony involving the selling, bartering, exchanging, offering for sale, or otherwise dealing in vehicles, chassis, essential parts, vehicle shells, or ownership documents relating to any of the above items.

P.A. 76-1586, § 5-501, eff. July 1, 1970. Amended by P.A. 77-643, § 1, eff. Aug. 4, 1971; P.A. 78-858, § 1, eff. Jan. 1, 1974; P.A. 81-932, § 1, eff. Sept. 22, 1979; P.A. 82-783, Art. XI, § 140, eff. July 13, 1982; P.A. 83-1473, § 1, eff. Jan. 1, 1985; P.A. 85-572, § 1, eff. Sept. 18, 1987; P.A. 85-1204, § 1, eff. Aug. 26, 1988; P.A. 85-1396, § 2, eff. Sept. 2, 1988; P.A. 86-820, Art. II, § 2-8, eff. Sept. 7, 1989.

Formerly Ill.Rev.Stat.1991, ch. 95 ½, ¶ 5-501.

1 Former Ill.Rev.Stat. ch. 17, ¶ 5601 et seq. (repealed).

2 205 ILCS 670/1 et seq.

3 815 ILCS 405/1 et seq.

4 815 ILCS 375/1 et seq.

5 815 ILCS 205/0.01 et seq.

6 740 ILCS 170/.01 et seq.

7 735 ILCS 5/12-801 et seq.

8 815 ILCS 505/1 et seq.

9 720 ILCS 5/21-2.

10 35 ILCS 120/1 et seq.

P.A. 86-820, the Second 1989 Revisory Act, provides in Art. II, for the nonsubstantive revision, renumbering, repeal or rerepeal of certain Acts both amended and repealed by Acts of the 85th General Assembly and, where successor laws have been enacted, incorporates such amendments into successor laws, and corrects errors, revises cross-references and deletes obsolete text in such sections contained in P.A. 85-1 through P.A. 85-1451.

5/5-502. Injunctions

§ 5-502. Injunctions. If any person operates in violation of any provision of this Chapter, or any rule, regulation, order or decision of the Secretary of State, or of any term, condition or limitation of any license, the Secretary of State, or any person injured thereby, or any interested person, may apply to the Circuit Court of the county in which such violation or some part thereof occurred, or in which the person complained of has his established or additional place of business or resides, to prevent such violation. The Court has jurisdiction to enforce obedience by injunction or other process restraining such person from further violation and enjoining upon him obedience.

P.A. 76-1586, § 5-502, added by P.A. 78-1165, § 1, eff. Aug. 27, 1974. Amended by P.A. 86-444, § 1, eff. Jan. 1, 1990.

Formerly Ill.Rev.Stat.1991, ch. 95 ½, ¶ 5-502.

5/5–503. Failure to obtain dealer's license, operation of a business with a suspended or revoked license

§ 5–503. Failure to obtain dealer's license, operation of a business with a suspended or revoked license. (a) Any person operating a business for which he is required to be licensed under Section 5–101, 5–102, 5–201 or 5–301 who fails to apply for such a license or licenses within 15 days after being informed in writing by the Secretary of State that he must obtain such a license or licenses is subject to a civil action brought by the Secretary of State for operating a business without a license in the circuit court in the county in which the business is located. If the person is found to be in violation of Section 5–101, 5–102, 5–201 or 5–301 by carrying on a business without being properly licensed, that person shall be fined $300 for each business day he conducted his business without such a license after the expiration of the 15 day period specified in this subsection (a).

(b) Any person who, having had his license or licenses issued under Section 5–101, 5–102, 5–201 or 5–301 suspended, revoked, cancelled or denied by the Secretary of State under Section 5–501, continues to operate business after the effective date of such revocation, suspension, cancellation or denial may be sued in a civil action by the Secretary of State in the county in which the established or additional place of such business is located. If such person is found by the court to have operated such a business after the license or licenses required for conducting such business have been suspended, revoked, cancelled or denied, that person shall be fined $500 for each day he conducted business thereafter.

P.A. 76–1586, § 5–503, added by P.A. 83–1473, § 1, eff. Jan. 1, 1985. Amended by P.A. 86–444, § 1, eff. Jan. 1, 1990.

Formerly Ill.Rev.Stat.1991, ch. 95 ½, ¶ 5–503.

5/5–504. Effect of revoked or denied license—Notification to prospective buyers—Rescinding of contracts

§ 5–504. Effect of revoked or denied license—Notification to prospective buyers—Rescinding of contracts. (a) No license shall be issued to any person to conduct the business of a new vehicle dealer, used vehicle dealer, scrap processor, automotive parts recycler, repairer, or rebuilder at a location or at property at which that person or any other person had his license as a new vehicle dealer, used vehicle dealer, scrap processor, automotive parts recycler, repairer, or rebuilder revoked or denied after a revocation or pending revocation within 2 months after such revocation or denial.

(b) A licensee who has been notified by the Secretary of State that the Secretary of State may take action to revoke the dealer's license or licenses of that licensee shall inform in writing any prospective buyer of his business of such possible action by the Secretary of State.

(c) If any person purchases or contracts to purchase a business required to be licensed by Section 5–101, 5–102, 5–201 or 5–301 without being informed in writing by the prior owner or owners that, at the time of the sale or making of contract to purchase, the prior owner or owners had been informed by the Secretary of State that the Secretary of State may be taking action to revoke the license or licenses of the prior owner or owners, the person who has purchased or contracted to purchase such business may, within one year after being informed that his application for a dealer's license at that location had been denied due to the revocation of the license or licenses of any prior owner or owners, rescind the purchase or contract to purchase such business or the property, both real and otherwise, at which the business is located.

(d) Notwithstanding the provisions of subsection (a) of this Section, the Secretary of State may issue a license to a person applying for a license as a new vehicle dealer, used vehicle dealer, scrap processor, automotive parts recycler, repairer or rebuilder if the Secretary of State, solely in his discretion, determines that a denial of the license under the circumstances would place extreme undue hardship upon the applicant.

No license shall be issued under this subsection to a person who is a spouse, offspring, sibling, parent, grandparent, grandchild, uncle or aunt, nephew or niece, cousin or in-law of the person whose license to do business at that location had been revoked or denied nor to a person who was an officer or employee of the business firm in relation to which the license was revoked or denied.

Notwithstanding the provisions of subsection (e) of Section 2–118 of this Code, the venue for judicial review of final acts or decisions under this subsection shall be the Circuit Court of Sangamon County.

P.A. 76–1586, § 5–504, added by P.A. 83–1473, § 1, eff. Jan. 1, 1985. Amended by P.A. 84–1302, § 1, eff. Jan. 1, 1987; P.A. 84–1304, § 1, eff. Jan. 1, 1987.

Formerly Ill.Rev.Stat.1991, ch. 95 ½, ¶ 5–504.

The amendments by P.A. 84–1302 and P.A. 84–1304 were identical.

ARTICLE VI. CREDIT OR CONDITIONAL SALES—INSURANCE

Section

5/5–601. Credit or conditional sale of certain motor vehicles—Liability insurance status stamped on bill of sale

§ 5–601. Credit or conditional sale of certain motor vehicles—Liability insurance status stamped on bill of sale. Whenever, in connection with the credit sale of or conditional sale of a motor vehicle designed and used for the carrying of not more than 10 passengers, the agreement provides that all or any of the consideration to be paid by the buyer or conditional buyer may be paid more than 30 days after possession of such motor vehicle is transferred to such buyer or conditional buyer, and a policy of insurance which does not cover such buyer or conditional buyer for the risk of liability to the public arising out of the operation, use or maintenance of such motor vehicle, is issued in connection with such transaction, the seller or conditional seller shall stamp or have imprinted thereon a statement on the bill of sale at the time the transaction is consummated that no such coverage is included in such policy. Such statement shall be in the following form and shall be in bold type not less than one-half inch in height:

NO PUBLIC LIABILITY INSURANCE ISSUED WITH THIS TRANSACTION

P.A. 76–1586, § 5–601, eff. July 1, 1970.

Formerly Ill.Rev.Stat.1991, ch. 95 ½, ¶ 5–601.

5/5-602. Violations of this Article

§ 5-602. Whoever violates any of the provisions of this Article shall be guilty of a petty offense and shall be fined not more than $500.

P.A. 76-1586, § 5-602, eff. July 1, 1970. Amended by P.A. 77-2720, § 1, eff. Jan. 1, 1972.

Formerly Ill.Rev.Stat.1991, ch. 95 ½, ¶ 5-602.

ARTICLE VII. VEHICLE AUCTIONEERS

Date Effective

Article 7 was added by P.A. 81-908, eff. Sept. 22, 1979.

5/5-700. Definitions

§ 5-700. Definitions. For the purposes of this Article, the following phrases have the meanings ascribed to them in this Section:

Place of business for a vehicle auctioneer. This means the place owned and regularly occupied by a vehicle auctioneer licensee, within or without the State, for the primary and principal purpose of keeping and maintaining the books and records required for the conduct of business, with the personnel available during normal business hours or an automatic telephone answering service during normal business hours. The additional place of business means that place within the State where the auction is held, which place of business shall contain the books and records required for said auction with personnel available during normal business hours. The Secretary of State shall be notified of the additional place of business at least 10 days before the auction.

Auctioning vehicles. This means arranging for and handling the sale of vehicles, not the property of the auctioneer, by auction to the highest bidder.

P.A. 76-1586, § 5-700, added by P.A. 81-908, § 1, eff. Sept. 22, 1979. Amended by P.A. 89-663, § 5, eff. Aug. 14, 1996.

Formerly Ill.Rev.Stat.1991, ch. 95 ½, ¶ 5-700.

5/5-701. Vehicle auctioneers to be licensed

§ 5-701. Vehicle auctioneers to be licensed. (a) No person, other than a licensed new vehicle dealer, a licensed used vehicle dealer, or municipality, shall engage in this State in the business of auctioning vehicles, for more than one owner, at auction or shall offer to sell, solicit or advertise the sale of a vehicle at auction without first acquiring a commercial vehicle auctioneer license from the Secretary of State under the provisions of this Section. A vehicle auction licensee shall be entitled thereunder to sell, solicit, and advertise the sale of used vehicles belonging to others at auction.

(b) An application for a vehicle auctioneer license shall be filed with the Secretary of State, duly verified by oath, in such form as the Secretary of State may by rule or regulation prescribe and shall contain:

1. The name and type of business organization established and the address of the place of business;

2. If the applicant is a corporation, a list of its officers and directors, setting forth the residence address of each; if the applicant is a sole proprietorship, a partnership, an unincorporated association, trust or any similar form of business organization, the names and residence addresses of the proprietor or of each partner, member, officer, director, trustee, manager and shareholder having 10% or greater ownership interest in the corporation;

3. A statement that the applicant has been approved for registration under the Retailers' Occupation Tax Act, approved June 28, 1933, as amended,[1] by the Department of Revenue. However, this requirement does not apply to licensee who is already licensed hereunder with the Secretary of State, and who is merely applying for a renewal of his license. As evidence of this fact, the application shall be accompanied by a certification from the Department of Revenue showing that the Department has approved the applicant for registration under the Retailers' Occupation Tax Act;

4. A statement that the applicant has complied with the bonding requirements of the "Retailers' Occupation Tax Act", approved June 28, 1933, as amended. As evidence of this fact, the application shall be accompanied by a certification from the Department of Revenue showing that the applicant is in compliance with the bonding requirements of the "Retailers' Occupation Tax Act" or that the applicant is not required to be bonded with the Department of Revenue under the "Retailers' Occupation Tax Act";

5. Such other information concerning the business of the applicant as the Secretary of State may by rule or regulation prescribe;

6. An application for a vehicle auctioneer license shall be accompanied by the following license fees: $50 for applicant's place of business plus $25 for each additional place of business, if any, to which the application pertains, provided, however, that if such an application is made after July 1 of any year, the license fee shall be $25 for applicant's place of business plus $12.50 for each additional place of business, if any, to which the application pertains. License fees shall be returnable only in the event that such application shall be denied by the Secretary of State.

7. A statement that the licensee has irrevocably consented to the appointment of the Secretary of State as its agent for service of process with the State of Illinois. Said service of process shall be accomplished as provided in Section 10-301 of the Illinois Vehicle Code.

(c) Any change which renders no longer accurate any information contained in any application for a vehicle auctioneer shall be amended within thirty days after the occurrence of each change on such form as the Secretary of State may prescribe by rule or regulation, accompanied by an amendatory fee of $2.

(d) Anything in this Chapter to the contrary notwithstanding, no person shall be licensed as a vehicle auctioneer unless such person shall maintain a place of business as defined in this Chapter.

(e) The Secretary of State shall, within a reasonable time after receipt, examine an application submitted to him under this Section. Unless the Secretary makes a determination that the application submitted to him does not conform to this Section or that grounds exist for a denial of the application under Section 5-501 of this Chapter, he must grant the applicant an original vehicle auctioneer license in writing for his place of business and a supplemental license in writing for each additional place of business, in such form as he may prescribe by rule or regulation which shall include the following:

1. The name of the person licensed;

2. If a corporation, the name and address of its officers or if a sole proprietorship, a partnership, an unincorporated association or any similar form of business organization, the

name and address of the proprietor or of each partner, member, officer, director, trustee or manager;

3. Complete address of the place of business of the licensee;

4. In the case of supplemental license, the place of business of the licensee and the place of business to which such supplemental license pertains.

(f) The appropriate instruments evidencing the license or a certified copy thereof, provided by the Secretary of State shall be kept posted, conspicuously, in the place of business of the licensee within the State and in each additional place of business, if any, maintained by such licensee.

(g) Except as provided in subsection (h) of this Section, all vehicle auctioneer licenses granted under this Section expire on December 31 of the calendar year for which they are granted unless sooner revoked under Section 5-501 of this Chapter.

(h) A vehicle auctioneer license may be renewed upon application and payment of the fee required herein, and submission of proof of coverage by an approved bond under the "Retailers' Occupation Tax Act" or proof that applicant is not subject to such bonding requirements, as in the case of an original license, but in case an application for the renewal of an effective license is made during the month of December, the effective license shall remain in force until the application for renewal is granted or denied by the Secretary of State.

(i) Each person licensed as a vehicle auctioneer or a licensed new or used car dealer when auctioning vehicles is required to furnish each purchaser of a motor vehicle the following:

1. A certificate of title properly assigned to the purchaser;

2. A statement verified under oath that all identifying numbers on the vehicle agree with those on the certificate of title;

3. A bill of sale properly executed on behalf of such person.

P.A. 76-1586, § 5-701, added by P.A. 81-908, § 1, eff. Sept. 22, 1979. Amended by P.A. 85-1396, § 2, eff. Sept. 1, 1988.

Formerly Ill.Rev.Stat.1991, ch. 95 ½, ¶ 5-701.

1 35 ILCS 120/1 et seq.

5/5-702. Salvage certificate vehicles; auction prohibition

§ 5-702. No person shall engage in the business of auctioning any vehicles for which a salvage certificate is required by law except to a bidder who is properly licensed as a rebuilder, automotive parts recycler, scrap processor or out-of-state salvage buyer, as required by Sections 5-301 and 5-302 of this Chapter.

P.A. 76-1586, § 5-702, added by P.A. 81-908, § 1, eff. Sept. 22, 1979. Amended by P.A. 85-572, § 1, eff. Sept. 18, 1987; P.A. 85-951, § 1, eff. July 1, 1988; P.A. 85-1209, Art. II, § 2-51, eff. Aug. 30, 1988; P.A. 89-663, § 5, eff. Aug. 14, 1996.

Formerly Ill.Rev.Stat.1991, ch. 95 ½, ¶ 5-702.

ARTICLE VIII. PENALTIES

Section

5/5-801. Penalties

§ 5-801. Penalties. Any person who violates any of the provisions of this Chapter, except as otherwise indicated, shall be guilty of a Class A misdemeanor. Any person who violates any provisions of Section 5-701 shall be guilty of a Class 3 felony.

P.A. 76-1586, § 5-801, eff. July 1, 1970. Amended by P.A. 77-2720, § 1, eff. Jan. 1, 1972; P.A. 83-1473, § 1, eff. Jan. 1, 1985.

Formerly Ill.Rev.Stat.1991, ch. 95 ½, ¶ 5-801.

5/5-802. Criminal offense

§ 5-802. The violation of any rule or regulation promulgated by the Office of the Secretary of State under this Chapter shall not in and of itself constitute a criminal offense.

P.A. 76-1586, § 5-802, added by P.A. 85-1204, § 1, eff. Aug. 26, 1988.

Formerly Ill.Rev.Stat.1991, ch. 95 ½, ¶ 5-802.

CHAPTER 6. THE ILLINOIS DRIVER LICENSING LAW

ARTICLE I. ISSUANCE OF LICENSES, EXPIRATION AND RENEWAL

Section

5/6-100. Definitions

§ 6-100. Definitions. For the purposes of this Chapter, the following words shall have the meanings ascribed to them:

(a) Application Process. The process of obtaining a driver's license, identification card, or permit. The process begins when a person enters a Secretary of State Driver Services facility and requests a driver's license, identification card or permit.

(b) Conviction. A final adjudication of guilty by a court of competent jurisdiction either after a bench trial, trial by jury, plea of guilty, order of forfeiture, or default.

(c) Identification Card. A document made or issued by or under the authority of the United States Government, the State of Illinois or any other state or political subdivision thereof, or any governmental or quasi-governmental organization that, when completed with information concerning the individual, is of a type intended or commonly accepted for the purpose of identifying the individual.

P.A. 76-1586, § 6-100, added by P.A. 78-663, § 1, eff. Jan. 1, 1974. Amended by P.A. 85-813, § 1, eff. Jan. 1, 1988; P.A. 89-283, § 10, eff. Jan. 1, 1996.

Formerly Ill.Rev.Stat.1991, ch. 95 ½, ¶ 6-100.

5/6-101. Drivers must have licenses or Permits

§ 6-101. Drivers must have licenses or Permits. (a) No person, except those expressly exempted by Section 6-102, shall drive any motor vehicle upon a highway in this State unless such person has a valid license or permit, or a restricted driving permit, issued under the provisions of this Act.

(b) No person shall drive a motor vehicle unless he holds a valid license or permit, or a restricted driving permit issued under the provisions of Section 6-205, 6-206, or 6-113 of this Act. Any person to whom a license is issued under the provisions of this Act must surrender to the Secretary of State all valid licenses or permits. No drivers license shall be issued to any person who holds a valid Foreign State license unless such person first surrenders to the Secretary of State any such valid Foreign State license.

(c) Any person licensed as a driver hereunder shall not be required by any city, village, incorporated town or other municipal corporation to obtain any other license to exercise the privilege thereby granted.

(d) In addition to other penalties imposed under this Section, any person in violation of this Section who is also in violation of Section 7-601 of this Code relating to mandatory insurance requirements shall have his or her motor vehicle immediately impounded by the arresting law enforcement officer. The motor vehicle may be released to any licensed driver upon a showing of proof of insurance for the motor vehicle that was impounded and the notarized written consent for the release by the vehicle owner.

P.A. 76-1586, § 6-101, eff. July 1, 1970. Amended by P.A. 86-549, § 1, eff. Jan. 1, 1990; P.A. 90-559, § 5, eff. June 1, 1998.

Formerly Ill.Rev.Stat.1991, ch. 95 ½, ¶ 6-101.

5/6-102. What persons are exempt

§ 6-102. What persons are exempt. The following persons are exempt from the requirements of Section 6-101 and are not required to have an Illinois drivers license or permit if one or more of the following qualifying exemptions are met and apply:

1. Any employee of the United States Government or any member of the Armed Forces of the United States, while operating a motor vehicle owned by or leased to the United States Government and being operated on official business need not be licensed;

2. A nonresident who has in his immediate possession a valid license issued to him in his home state or country may operate a motor vehicle for which he is licensed for the period during which he is in this State;

3. A nonresident and his spouse and children living with him who is a student at a college or university in Illinois who have a valid license issued by their home State.

4. A person operating a road machine temporarily upon a highway or operating a farm tractor between the home farm buildings and any adjacent or nearby farm land for the exclusive purpose of conducting farm operations need not be licensed as a driver.

5. A resident of this State who has been serving as a member of the Armed Forces of the United States outside the Continental limits of the United States, for a period of 45 days following his return to the continental limits of the United States.

6. A nonresident on active duty in the Armed Forces of the United States who has a valid license issued by his home state and such nonresident's spouse, and dependent children and living with parents, who have a valid license issued by their home state.

7. A nonresident who becomes a resident of this State, may for a period of the first 90 days of residence in Illinois operate any motor vehicle which he was qualified or licensed to drive by his home state or country so long as he has in his possession, a valid and current license issued to him by his home state or country. Upon expiration of such 90 day period, such new resident must comply with the provisions of this Act and apply for an Illinois license or permit.

8. An engineer, conductor, brakeman, or any other member of the crew of a locomotive or train being operated upon rails, including operation on a railroad crossing over a public street, road or highway. Such person is not required to display a driver's license to any law enforcement officer in connection with the operation of a locomotive or train within this State.

The provisions of this Section granting exemption to any nonresident shall be operative to the same extent that the laws of the State or country of such nonresident grant like exemption to residents of this State.

The Secretary of State may implement the exemption provisions of this Section by inclusion thereof in a reciprocity agreement, arrangement or declaration issued pursuant to this Act.

P.A. 76-1586, § 6-102, eff. July 1, 1970. Amended by P.A. 76-1905, § 1; P.A. 77-21, § 1, eff. April 27, 1971; P.A. 79-1141, § 1, eff. Jan. 1, 1976; P.A. 86-1258, § 1, eff. Jan. 1, 1991.

Formerly Ill.Rev.Stat.1991, ch. 95 ½, ¶ 6-102.

5/6-103. What persons shall not be licensed as drivers or granted permits

§ 6-103. What persons shall not be licensed as drivers or granted permits. The Secretary of State shall not issue, renew, or allow the retention of any driver's license nor issue any permit under this Code:

1. To any person, as a driver, who is under the age of 18 years except as provided in Section 6-107, and except that an instruction permit may be issued under paragraphs (a) and (b) of Section 6-105 to a child who is not less than 15 years of age if the child is enrolled in an approved driver education course as defined in Section 1-103 of this Code and requires an instruction permit to participate therein, except that an instruction permit may be issued under the provisions of Section 6-107.1 to a child who is 17 years and 9 months of age without the child having enrolled in an approved driver education course and except that an instruction permit may be issued to a child who is at least 15 years and 6 months of age, is enrolled in school, meets the educational requirements of the Driver Education Act,[1] and has passed examinations the Secretary of State in his or her discretion may prescribe;

2. To any person who is under the age of 18 as an operator of a motorcycle other than a motor driven cycle unless the person has, in addition to meeting the provisions of Section 6-107 of this Code, completed a motorcycle training course approved by the Illinois Department of Transportation and successfully completes the required Secretary of State's motorcycle driver's examination;

3. To any person, as a driver, whose driver's license or permit has been suspended, during the suspension, nor to any person whose driver's license or permit has been revoked, except as provided in Sections 6-205, 6-206, and 6-208;

4. To any person, as a driver, who is a user of alcohol or any other drug to a degree that renders the person incapable of safely driving a motor vehicle;

5. To any person, as a driver, who has previously been adjudged to be afflicted with or suffering from any mental or physical disability or disease and who has not at the time of application been restored to competency by the methods provided by law;

6. To any person, as a driver, who is required by the Secretary of State to submit an alcohol and drug evaluation or take an examination provided for in this Code unless the person has successfully passed the examination and submitted any required evaluation;

7. To any person who is required under the provisions of the laws of this State to deposit security or proof of financial responsibility and who has not deposited the security or proof;

8. To any person when the Secretary of State has good cause to believe that the person by reason of physical or mental disability would not be able to safely operate a motor vehicle upon the highways, unless the person shall furnish to the Secretary of State a verified written statement, acceptable to the Secretary of State, from a competent medical specialist to the effect that the operation of a motor vehicle by the person would not be inimical to the public safety;

9. To any person, as a driver, who is 69 years of age or older, unless the person has successfully complied with the provisions of Section 6-109;

10. To any person convicted, within 12 months of application for a license, of any of the sexual offenses enumerated in paragraph 2 of subsection (b) of Section 6-205;

11. To any person who is under the age of 21 years with a classification prohibited in paragraph (b) of Section 6-104 and to any person who is under the age of 18 years with a classification prohibited in paragraph (c) of Section 6-104;

12. To any person who has been either convicted of or adjudicated under the Juvenile Court Act of 1987[2] based upon a violation of the Cannabis Control Act[3] or the Illinois Controlled Substances Act[4] while that person was in actual physical control of a motor vehicle. For purposes of this Section, any person placed on probation under Section 10 of the Cannabis Control Act[5] or Section 410 of the Illinois Controlled Substances Act[6] shall not be considered convicted. Any person found guilty of this offense, while in actual physical control of a motor vehicle, shall have an entry made in the court record by the judge that this offense did occur while the person was in actual physical control of a motor vehicle and order the clerk of the court to report the violation to the Secretary of State as such. The Secretary of State shall not issue a new license or permit for a period of one year;

13. To any person who is under the age of 18 years and who has committed the offense of operating a motor vehicle without a valid license or permit in violation of Section 6-101

14. To any person who is 90 days or more delinquent in court ordered child support payments or has been adjudicated in arrears in an amount equal to 90 days' obligation or more and who has been found in contempt of court for failure to pay the support, subject to the requirements and procedures of Article VII of Chapter 7 of the Illinois Vehicle Code;[7] or

15. To any person released from a term of imprisonment for violating Section 9-3 of the Criminal Code of 1961[8] relating to reckless homicide within 24 months of release from a term of imprisonment.

The Secretary of State shall retain all conviction information, if the information is required to be held confidential under the Juvenile Court Act of 1987.

P.A. 76-1586, § 6-103, eff. July 1, 1970. Amended by P.A. 77-51, § 1, eff. July 1, 1971; P.A. 77-670, § 1, eff. Jan. 1, 1972; P.A. 77-2829, § 40, eff. Dec. 22, 1972; P.A. 78-255, § 61, eff. Oct. 1, 1973; P.A. 79-1141, § 1, eff. Jan. 1, 1976; P.A. 83-820, § 1, eff. Jan. 1, 1984; P.A. 85-951, § 1, eff. July 1, 1988; P.A. 86-1450, § 2, eff. July 1, 1991; P.A. 87-1114, § 1, eff. Sept. 15, 1992; P.A. 88-212, § 5, eff. Jan. 1, 1994; P.A. 90-369, § 5, eff. Jan. 1, 1998; P.A. 90-733, § 10, eff. Aug. 11, 1998; P.A. 92-343, § 5, eff. Jan. 1, 2002.

Formerly Ill.Rev.Stat.1991, ch. 95 ½, ¶ 6-103.

[1] 105 ILCS 5/27-24 et seq.

[2] 705 ILCS 405/1-1 et seq.

[3] 720 ILCS 550/1 et seq.

[4] 720 ILCS 570/100 et seq.

[5] 720 ILCS 550/10.

[6] 720 ILCS 570/410 et seq.

[7] 625 ILCS 5/7-700 et seq.

[8] 720 ILCS 5/9-3.

5/6-104. Classification of Driver—Special Restrictions

§ 6-104. Classification of Driver—Special Restrictions.

(a) A driver's license issued under the authority of this Act shall indicate the classification for which the applicant therefor has qualified by examination or by such other means that the Secretary of State shall prescribe. Driver's license classifications shall be prescribed by rule or regulation promulgated by the Secretary of State and such may specify classifications as to operation of motor vehicles of the first division, or of those of the second division, whether operated singly or in lawful combination, and whether for-hire or not-for-hire, and may specify such other classifications as the Secretary deems necessary.

No person shall operate a motor vehicle unless such person has a valid license with a proper classification to permit the operation of such vehicle, except that any person may operate a motorized pedalcycle if such person has a valid current Illinois driver's license, regardless of classification.

(b) No person who is under the age of 21 years or has had less than 1 year of driving experience shall drive: (1) in connection with the operation of any school, day camp, summer camp, or nursery school, any public or private motor vehicle for transporting children to or from any school, day camp, summer camp, or nursery school, or (2) any motor vehicle of the second division when in use for the transportation of persons for compensation.

(c) No person who is under the age of 18 years shall be issued a license for the purpose of transporting property for hire, or for the purpose of transporting persons for compensation in a motor vehicle of the first division.

(d) No person shall drive: (1) a school bus when transporting school children unless such person possesses a valid school bus driver permit or is accompanied and supervised, for the specific purpose of training prior to routine operation of a school bus, by a person who has held a valid school bus driver permit for at least one year; or (2) any other vehicle owned or operated by or for a public or private school, or a school operated by a religious institution, where such vehicle is being used over a regularly scheduled route for the transportation of persons enrolled as a student in grade 12 or below, in connection with any activity of the entities unless such person possesses a valid school bus driver permit.

(d–5) No person may drive a bus that has been chartered for the sole purpose of transporting students regularly enrolled in grade 12 or below to or from interscholastic athletic or interscholastic or school sponsored activities unless the person has a valid school bus driver permit in addition to any other permit or license that is required to operate that bus. This subsection (d–5) does not apply to any bus driver employed by a public transportation provider authorized to conduct local or interurban transportation of passengers when the bus is not traveling a specific school bus route but is on a regularly scheduled route for the transporting of other fare paying passengers.

(e) No person shall drive a religious organization bus unless such person has a valid and properly classified drivers license or a valid school bus driver permit.

(f) No person shall drive a motor vehicle for the purpose of providing transportation for the elderly in connection with the activities of any public or private organization unless such person has a valid and properly classified driver's license issued by the Secretary of State.

(g) No person shall drive a bus which meets the special requirements for school buses provided in Section 12–801, 12–802, 12–803 and 12–805 of this Code for the purpose of transporting persons 18 years of age or less in connection with any youth camp licensed under the Youth Camp Act [1] or any child care facility licensed under the Child Care Act of 1969 [2] unless such person possesses a valid school bus driver permit or is accompanied and supervised, for the specific purpose of training prior to routine operation of a school bus, by a person who has held a valid school bus driver permit for at least one year; however, a person who has a valid and properly classified driver's license issued by the Secretary of State may operate a school bus for the purpose of transporting persons 18 years of age or less in connection with any such youth camp or child care facility if the "SCHOOL BUS" signs are covered or concealed and the stop signal arm and flashing signal systems are not operable through normal controls.

P.A. 76–1586, § 6–104, eff. July 1, 1970. Amended by P.A. 76–1751, § 1; P.A. 78–499, § 1, eff. Aug. 30, 1973; P.A. 78–1244, § 1, eff. Sept. 5, 1974; P.A. 78–1297, § 58, eff. March 4, 1975; P.A. 79–798, § 1, eff. July 1, 1976; P.A. 79–1141, § 1, eff. Jan. 1, 1976; P.A. 79–1454, § 44, eff. Aug. 31, 1976; P.A. 80–262, § 1, eff. Aug. 20, 1977; P.A. 81–509, § 1, eff. Jan. 1, 1980; P.A. 82–532, § 1, eff. Jan. 1, 1982; P.A. 84–1311, § 2, eff. Aug. 27, 1986; P.A. 88–612, § 15, eff. July 1, 1995; P.A. 92–849, § 5, eff. Jan. 1, 2003.

Formerly Ill.Rev.Stat.1991, ch. 95 ½, ¶ 6–104.

[1] 210 ILCS 100/1 et seq.

[2] 225 ILCS 10/1 et seq.

5/6–105. Instruction permits and temporary licenses for persons 18 years of age or older

§ 6–105. Instruction permits and temporary licenses for persons 18 years of age or older.

(a) Except as provided in this Section, the Secretary of State upon receiving proper application and payment of the required fee may issue an instruction permit to any person 18 years of age or older who is not ineligible for a license under paragraphs 1, 3, 4, 5, 7, or 8 of Section 6–103, after the applicant has successfully passed such examination as the Secretary of State in his discretion may prescribe.

1. An instruction permit entitles the holder while having the permit in his immediate possession to drive a motor vehicle, excluding a motor driven cycle or motorcycle, upon the highways for a period of 12 months after the date of its issuance when accompanied by a licensed driver who is 21 years of age or older, who has had a valid driver's license classification to operate such vehicle for at least one year and has had one year of driving experience with such classification and who is occupying a seat beside the driver.

2. A 12 month instruction permit for a motor driven cycle or motorcycle may be issued to a person 18 years of age or more, and entitles the holder to drive upon the highways during daylight under the direct supervision of a licensed motor driven cycle operator or motorcycle operator with the same or greater classification, who is 21 years of age or older and who has at least one year of driving experience.

3. (Blank).

(b) (Blank).

(c) The Secretary of State may issue a temporary driver's license to an applicant for a license permitting the operation of a motor vehicle while the Secretary is completing an investigation and determination of all facts relative to such applicant's eligibility to receive such license, or for any other reason prescribed by rule or regulation promulgated by the Secretary of State. Such permit must be in the applicant's immediate possession while operating a motor vehicle, and it shall be invalid when the applicant's driver's license has been issued or for good cause has been refused. In each case the Secretary of State may issue the temporary driver's license for such period as appropriate but in no event for longer than 90 days.

P.A. 76–1586, § 6–105, eff. July 1, 1970. Amended by P.A. 76–1906, § 1; P.A. 76–2153, § 1, eff. July 1, 1970; P.A. 77–670, § 1, eff. Jan. 1, 1972; P.A. 77–2805, § 1, eff. Oct. 1, 1972; P.A. 78–255, § 61, eff. Oct. 1, 1973; P.A. 79–1141, § 1, eff. Jan. 1, 1976; P.A. 83–820, § 1, eff. Jan. 1, 1984; P.A. 85–522, § 1, eff. Jan. 1, 1988; P.A. 90–369, § 5, eff. Jan. 1, 1998.

Formerly Ill.Rev.Stat.1991, ch. 95 ½, ¶ 6–105.

5/6–106. Application for license or instruction permit

§ 6–106. Application for license or instruction permit.

(a) Every application for any permit or license authorized to be issued under this Act shall be made upon a form furnished by the Secretary of State. Every application shall be accompanied by the proper fee and payment of such fee shall entitle the applicant to not more than 3 attempts to pass the examination within a period of 1 year after the date of application.

(b) Every application shall state the name, social security number, zip code, date of birth, sex, and residence address of the applicant; briefly describe the applicant; state whether the applicant has theretofore been licensed as a driver, and, if so, when and by what state or country, and whether any such license has ever been cancelled, suspended, revoked or refused, and, if so, the date and reason for such cancellation, suspension, revocation or refusal; shall include an affirmation by the applicant that all information set forth is true and correct; and shall bear the applicant's signature. The application form may also require the statement of such additional relevant information as the Secretary of State shall deem necessary to determine the applicant's competency and eligibility. The Secretary of State may in his discretion substitute a federal tax number in lieu of a social security number, or he may instead assign an additional distinctive number in lieu thereof, where an applicant is prohibited by bona fide religious convictions from applying or is exempt from applying for a social security number. The Secretary of State shall, however, determine which religious orders or sects have such bona fide religious convictions. The Secretary of State may, in his discretion, by rule or regulation, provide that an application for a drivers license or permit may include a suitable photograph of the applicant in the form prescribed by the Secretary, and he may further provide that each drivers license shall include a photograph of the driver. The Secretary of State may utilize a photograph process or system most suitable to deter alteration or improper reproduction of a drivers license and to prevent substitution of another photo thereon.

(c) The application form shall include a notice to the applicant of the registration obligations of sex offenders under the Sex Offender Registration Act.[1] The notice shall be provided in a form and manner prescribed by the Secretary of State. For purposes of this subsection (c), "sex offender" has the meaning ascribed to it in Section 2 of the Sex Offender Registration Act.[2]

(d) Any male United States citizen or immigrant who applies for any permit or license authorized to be issued under this Act or for a renewal of any permit or license, and who is at least 18 years of age but less than 26 years of age, must be registered in compliance with the requirements of the federal Military Selective Service Act.[3] The Secretary of State must forward in an electronic format the necessary personal information regarding the applicants identified in this subsection (d) to the Selective Service System. The applicant's signature on the application serves as an indication that the applicant either has already registered with the Selective Service System or that he is authorizing the Secretary to forward to the Selective Service System the necessary information for registration. The Secretary must notify the applicant at the time of application that his signature constitutes consent to registration with the Selective Service System, if he is not already registered.

P.A. 76–1586, § 6–106, eff. July 1, 1970. Amended by P.A. 77–105, § 1, eff. Jan. 1, 1972; P.A. 78–197, § 1, eff. Jan. 1, 1974; P.A. 78–663, § 1, eff. Jan. 1, 1974; P.A. 78–1297, § 30, eff. March 4, 1975; P.A. 86–503, § 1, eff. Sept. 1, 1989; P.A. 87–233, § 1, eff. Jan. 1, 1992; P.A. 89–8, Art. 20, § 20–15, eff. Jan. 1, 1996; P.A. 90–191, § 10, eff. Jan. 1, 1998; P.A. 92–117, § 5, eff. Jan. 1, 2002.

Formerly Ill.Rev.Stat.1991, ch. 95 ½, ¶ 6–106.

1 730 ILCS 150/1 et seq.

2 730 ILCS 150/2.

3 50 App. U.S.C.A. §451 et seq.

5/6–106.1. School bus driver permit

§ 6–106.1. School bus driver permit.

(a) The Secretary of State shall issue a school bus driver permit to those applicants who have met all the requirements of the application and screening process under this Section to insure the welfare and safety of children who are transported on school buses throughout the State of Illinois. Applicants shall obtain the proper application required by the Secretary of State from their prospective or current employer and submit the completed application to the prospective or current employer along with the necessary fingerprint submission as required by the Department of State Police to conduct fingerprint based criminal background checks on current and future information available in the state system and current information available through the Federal Bureau of Investigation's system. Applicants who have completed the fingerprinting requirements shall not be subjected to the fingerprinting process when applying for subsequent permits or submitting proof of successful completion of the annual refresher course. Individuals who on the effective date of this Act possess a valid school bus driver permit that has been previously issued by the appropriate Regional School Superintendent are not subject to the fingerprinting provisions of this Section as long as the permit remains valid and does not lapse. The applicant shall be required to pay all related application and fingerprinting fees as established by rule including, but not limited to, the amounts established by the Department of State Police and the Federal Bureau of Investigation to process fingerprint based criminal background investigations. All fees paid for fingerprint processing services under this Section shall be deposited into the State Police Services Fund for the cost incurred in processing the fingerprint based criminal background investigations. All other fees paid under this Section shall be deposited into the Road Fund for the purpose of defraying the costs of the Secretary of State in administering this Section. All applicants must:

1. be 21 years of age or older;

2. possess a valid and properly classified driver's license issued by the Secretary of State;

3. possess a valid driver's license, which has not been revoked, suspended, or canceled for 3 years immediately prior to the date of application, or have not had his or her commercial motor vehicle driving privileges disqualified within the 3 years immediately prior to the date of application;

4. successfully pass a written test, administered by the Secretary of State, on school bus operation, school bus safety, and special traffic laws relating to school buses and submit to a review of the applicant's driving habits by the Secretary of State at the time the written test is given;

5. demonstrate ability to exercise reasonable care in the operation of school buses in accordance with rules promulgated by the Secretary of State;

6. demonstrate physical fitness to operate school buses by submitting the results of a medical examination, including tests for drug use for each applicant not subject to such testing pursuant to federal law, conducted by a licensed physician, an advanced practice nurse who has a written collaborative agreement with a collaborating physician which authorizes him or her to perform medical examinations, or a physician assistant who has been delegated the performance of medical examinations by his or her supervising physician within 90 days of the date of application according to standards promulgated by the Secretary of State;

7. affirm under penalties of perjury that he or she has not made a false statement or knowingly concealed a material fact in any application for permit;

8. have completed an initial classroom course, including first aid procedures, in school bus driver safety as promulgated by the Secretary of State; and after satisfactory completion of said initial course an annual refresher course; such courses and the agency or organization conducting such courses shall be approved by the Secretary of State; failure to complete the annual refresher course, shall result in cancellation of the permit until such course is completed;

9. not have been convicted of 2 or more serious traffic offenses, as defined by rule, within one year prior to the date of application that may endanger the life or safety of any of the driver's passengers within the duration of the permit period;

10. not have been convicted of reckless driving, driving while intoxicated, or reckless homicide resulting from the operation of a motor vehicle within 3 years of the date of application;

11. not have been convicted of committing or attempting to commit any one or more of the following offenses: (i) those offenses defined in Sections 9-1, 9-1.2, 9-2, 9-2.1, 9-3, 9-3.2, 9-3.3, 10-1, 10-2, 10-3.1, 10-4, 10-5, 10-6, 10-7, 11-6, 11-9, 11-9.1, 11-14, 11-15, 11-15.1, 11-16, 11-17, 11-18, 11-19, 11-19.1, 11-19.2, 11-20, 11-20.1, 11-21, 11-22, 12-3.1, 12-4.1, 12-4.2, 12-4.3, 12-4.4, 12-4.5, 12-6, 12-6.2, 12-7.1, 12-7.3, 12-7.4, 12-11, 12-13, 12-14, 12-14.1, 12-15, 12-16, 12-16.2, 12-21.5, 12-21.6, 12-33, 18-1, 18-2, 18-3, 18-4, 18-5, 20-1, 20-1.1, 20-2, 24-1, 24-1.1, 24-1.2, 24-3.3, 31A-1, 31A-1.1, and 33A-2, and in subsection (a) and subsection (b), clause (1), of Section 12-4 of the Criminal Code of 1961; [1] (ii) those offenses defined in the Cannabis Control Act [2] except those offenses defined in subsections (a) and (b) of Section 4, and subsection (a) of Section 5 of the Cannabis Control Act; [3] (iii) those offenses defined in the Illinois Controlled Substances Act; [4] (iv) any offense committed or attempted in any other state or against the laws of the United States, which if committed or attempted in this State would be punishable as one or more of the foregoing offenses; (v) the offenses defined in Section 4.1 and 5.1 of the Wrongs to Children Act [5] and (vi) those offenses defined in Section 6-16 of the Liquor Control Act of 1934; [6]

12. not have been repeatedly involved as a driver in motor vehicle collisions or been repeatedly convicted of offenses against laws and ordinances regulating the movement of traffic, to a degree which indicates lack of ability to exercise ordinary and reasonable care in the safe operation of a motor vehicle or disrespect for the traffic laws and the safety of other persons upon the highway;

13. not have, through the unlawful operation of a motor vehicle, caused an accident resulting in the death of any person; and

14. not have, within the last 5 years, been adjudged to be afflicted with or suffering from any mental disability or disease.

(b) A school bus driver permit shall be valid for a period specified by the Secretary of State as set forth by rule. It shall be renewable upon compliance with subsection (a) of this Section.

(c) A school bus driver permit shall contain the holder's driver's license number, name, address, zip code, social security number and date of birth, a brief description of the holder and a space for signature. The Secretary of State may require a suitable photograph of the holder.

(d) The employer shall be responsible for conducting a pre-employment interview with prospective school bus driver candidates, distributing school bus driver applications and medical forms to be completed by the applicant, and submitting the applicant's fingerprint cards to the Department of State Police that are required for the criminal background investigations. The employer shall certify in writing to the Secretary of State that all pre-employment conditions have been successfully completed including the successful completion of an Illinois specific criminal background investigation through the Department of State Police and the submission of necessary fingerprints to the Federal Bureau of Investigation for criminal history information available through the Federal Bureau of Investigation system. The applicant shall present the certification to the Secretary of State at the time of submitting the school bus driver permit application.

(e) Permits shall initially be provisional upon receiving certification from the employer that all pre-employment conditions have been successfully completed, and upon successful completion of all training and examination requirements for the classification of the vehicle to be operated, the Secretary of State shall provisionally issue a School Bus Driver Permit. The permit shall remain in a provisional status pending the completion of the Federal Bureau of Investigation's criminal background investigation based upon fingerprinting specimens submitted to the Federal Bureau of Investigation by the Department of State Police. The Federal Bureau of Investigation shall report the findings directly to the Secretary of State. The Secretary of State shall remove the bus driver permit from provisional status upon the applicant's successful completion of the Federal Bureau of Investigation's criminal background investigation.

(f) A school bus driver permit holder shall notify the employer and the Secretary of State if he or she is convicted in another state of an offense that would make him or her ineligible for a permit under subsection (a) of this Section. The written notification shall be made within 5 days of the entry of the conviction. Failure of the permit holder to provide the notification is punishable as a petty offense for a first violation and a Class B misdemeanor for a second or subsequent violation.

(g) Cancellation; suspension; notice and procedure.

(1) The Secretary of State shall cancel a school bus driver permit of an applicant whose criminal background

investigation discloses that he or she is not in compliance with the provisions of subsection (a) of this Section.

(2) The Secretary of State shall cancel a school bus driver permit when he or she receives notice that the permit holder fails to comply with any provision of this Section or any rule promulgated for the administration of this Section.

(3) The Secretary of State shall cancel a school bus driver permit if the permit holder's restricted commercial or commercial driving privileges are withdrawn or otherwise invalidated.

(4) The Secretary of State may not issue a school bus driver permit for a period of 3 years to an applicant who fails to obtain a negative result on a drug test as required in item 6 of subsection (a) of this Section or under federal law.

(5) The Secretary of State shall forthwith suspend a school bus driver permit for a period of 3 years upon receiving notice that the holder has failed to obtain a negative result on a drug test as required in item 6 of subsection (a) of this Section or under federal law.

The Secretary of State shall notify the State Superintendent of Education and the permit holder's prospective or current employer that the applicant has (1) has failed a criminal background investigation or (2) is no longer eligible for a school bus driver permit; and of the related cancellation of the applicant's provisional school bus driver permit. The cancellation shall remain in effect pending the outcome of a hearing pursuant to Section 2–118 of this Code. The scope of the hearing shall be limited to the issuance criteria contained in subsection (a) of this Section. A petition requesting a hearing shall be submitted to the Secretary of State and shall contain the reason the individual feels he or she is entitled to a school bus driver permit. The permit holder's employer shall notify in writing to the Secretary of State that the employer has certified the removal of the offending school bus driver from service prior to the start of that school bus driver's next workshift. An employing school board that fails to remove the offending school bus driver from service is subject to the penalties defined in Section 3–14.23 of the School Code.[7] A school bus contractor who violates a provision of this Section is subject to the penalties defined in Section 6–106.11.

All valid school bus driver permits issued under this Section prior to January 1, 1995, shall remain effective until their expiration date unless otherwise invalidated.

P.A. 76–1586, § 6–106.1, added by P.A. 78–1244, § 1, eff. Sept. 5, 1974. Amended by P.A. 79–845, § 1, eff. Jan. 1, 1976; P.A. 79–1399, § 1, eff. Oct. 1, 1976; P.A. 80–506, § 1, eff. Oct. 1, 1977; P.A. 81–509, § 1, eff. Jan. 1, 1980; P.A. 81–1508, § 8, eff. Sept. 25, 1980; P.A. 83–831, § 1, eff. Jan. 1, 1984; P.A. 83–1067, § 19, eff. July 1, 1984; P.A. 83–1286, § 1, eff. Aug. 31, 1984; P.A. 83–1362, Art. II, § 99, eff. Sept. 11, 1984; P.A. 84–1450, § 7, eff. July 1, 1987; P.A. 86–508, § 1, eff. Jan. 1, 1990; P.A. 86–578, § 1, eff. Jan. 1, 1990; P.A. 86–1028, Art. II, § 2–44, eff. Feb. 5, 1990; P.A. 86–1465, § 1, eff. April 1, 1992; P.A. 87–526, § 2, eff. Sept. 16, 1991; P.A. 87–895, Art. 3, § 3–52, eff. Aug. 14, 1992; P.A. 88–612, § 15, eff. July 1, 1995; P.A. 89–71, § 5, eff. Jan. 1, 1996; P.A. 89–120, § 10, eff. July 7, 1995; P.A. 89–375, § 3, eff. Aug. 18, 1995; P.A. 89–428, Art. 2, § 250, eff. Dec. 13, 1995; P.A. 89–462, Art. 2, § 250, eff. May 29, 1996; P.A. 89–626, Art. 2, § 2–66, eff. Aug. 9, 1996; P.A. 90–191, § 10, eff. Jan. 1, 1998; P.A. 91–500, § 5, eff. Aug. 13, 1999; P.A. 92–703, § 10, eff. July 19, 2002.

Formerly Ill.Rev.Stat.1991, ch. 95 ½, ¶ 6–106.1.

[1] 720 ILCS 5/9–1 et seq.

[2] 720 ILCS 550/1 et seq.

[3] 720 ILCS 550/5.

[4] 720 ILCS 570/100 et seq.

[5] 720 ILCS 150/4.1 and 150/5.1.

[6] 235 ILCS 556161–16.

[7] 105 ILCS 5/3–14.23.

For saving clause, construction and application of P.A. 83–1067, see note following 720 ILCS 5/12–12.

P.A. 89–428 was held by the Illinois Supreme Court to be in violation of the single subject requirement of subsection (d) of Section 8 of Article IV of the Illinois Constitution in the case of Johnson v. Edgar, 1997, 176 Ill.2d 499, 680 N.E.2d 1372, 224 Ill.Dec. 1. Public Act 89–462 reenacted the amendment of this text by P.A. 89–428.

5/6–106.1a. Cancellation of school bus driver permit; trace of alcohol

§ 6–106.1a. Cancellation of school bus driver permit; trace of alcohol.

(a) A person who has been issued a school bus driver permit by the Secretary of State in accordance with Section 6–106.1 of this Code and who drives or is in actual physical control of a school bus or any other vehicle owned or operated by or for a public or private school, or a school operated by a religious institution, when the vehicle is being used over a regularly scheduled route for the transportation of persons enrolled as students in grade 12 or below, in connection with any activity of the entities listed, upon the public highways of this State shall be deemed to have given consent to a chemical test or tests of blood, breath, or urine for the purpose of determining the alcohol content of the person's blood if arrested, as evidenced by the issuance of a Uniform Traffic Ticket for any violation of this Code or a similar provision of a local ordinance, if a police officer has probable cause to believe that the driver has consumed any amount of an alcoholic beverage based upon evidence of the driver's physical condition or other first hand knowledge of the police officer. The test or tests shall be administered at the direction of the arresting officer. The law enforcement agency employing the officer shall designate which of the aforesaid tests shall be administered. A urine test may be administered even after a blood or breath test or both has been administered.

(b) A person who is dead, unconscious, or who is otherwise in a condition rendering that person incapable of refusal, shall be deemed not to have withdrawn the consent provided by paragraph (a) of this Section and the test or tests may be administered subject to the following provisions:

(1) Chemical analysis of the person's blood, urine, breath, or other substance, to be considered valid under the provisions of this Section, shall have been performed according to standards promulgated by the Department of State Police by an individual possessing a valid permit issued by the Department of State Police for this purpose. The Director of State Police is authorized to approve satisfactory techniques or methods, to ascertain the qualifications and competence of individuals to conduct analyses, to issue permits that shall be subject to termination or revocation at the direction of the Department of State Police, and to certify the accuracy of breath testing equipment. The Department of State Police shall prescribe rules as necessary.

(2) When a person submits to a blood test at the request of a law enforcement officer under the provisions of this Section, only a physician authorized to practice medicine, a registered nurse, or other qualified person trained in veni-

puncture and acting under the direction of a licensed physician may withdraw blood for the purpose of determining the alcohol content. This limitation does not apply to the taking of breath or urine specimens.

(3) The person tested may have a physician, qualified technician, chemist, registered nurse, or other qualified person of his or her own choosing administer a chemical test or tests in addition to any test or tests administered at the direction of a law enforcement officer. The test administered at the request of the person may be admissible into evidence at a hearing conducted in accordance with Section 2–118 of this Code. The failure or inability to obtain an additional test by a person shall not preclude the consideration of the previously performed chemical test.

(4) Upon a request of the person who submits to a chemical test or tests at the request of a law enforcement officer, full information concerning the test or tests shall be made available to the person or that person's attorney by the requesting law enforcement agency within 72 hours of receipt of the test result.

(5) Alcohol concentration means either grams of alcohol per 100 milliliters of blood or grams of alcohol per 210 liters of breath.

(6) If a driver is receiving medical treatment as a result of a motor vehicle accident, a physician licensed to practice medicine, registered nurse, or other qualified person trained in venipuncture and acting under the direction of a licensed physician shall withdraw blood for testing purposes to ascertain the presence of alcohol upon the specific request of a law enforcement officer. However, that testing shall not be performed until, in the opinion of the medical personnel on scene, the withdrawal can be made without interfering with or endangering the well-being of the patient.

(c) A person requested to submit to a test as provided in this Section shall be warned by the law enforcement officer requesting the test that a refusal to submit to the test, or submission to the test resulting in an alcohol concentration of more than 0.00, may result in the loss of that person's privilege to possess a school bus driver permit. The loss of the individual's privilege to possess a school bus driver permit shall be imposed in accordance with Section 6–106.1b of this Code.

(d) If the person refuses testing or submits to a test that discloses an alcohol concentration of more than 0.00, the law enforcement officer shall immediately submit a sworn report to the Secretary of State on a form prescribed by the Secretary of State certifying that the test or tests were requested under subsection (a) and the person refused to submit to a test or tests or submitted to testing which disclosed an alcohol concentration of more than 0.00. The law enforcement officer shall submit the same sworn report when a person who has been issued a school bus driver permit and who was operating a school bus or any other vehicle owned or operated by or for a public or private school, or a school operated by a religious institution, when the vehicle is being used over a regularly scheduled route for the transportation of persons enrolled as students in grade 12 or below, in connection with any activity of the entities listed, submits to testing under Section 11–501.1 of this Code and the testing discloses an alcohol concentration of more than 0.00 and less than the alcohol concentration at which driving or being in actual physical control of a motor vehicle is prohibited under paragraph (1) of subsection (a) of Section 11–501.

Upon receipt of the sworn report of a law enforcement officer, the Secretary of State shall enter the school bus driver permit sanction on the individual's driving record and the sanction shall be effective on the 46th day following the date notice of the sanction was given to the person.

The law enforcement officer submitting the sworn report shall serve immediate notice of this school bus driver permit sanction on the person and the sanction shall be effective on the 46th day following the date notice was given.

In cases where the blood alcohol concentration of more than 0.00 is established by a subsequent analysis of blood or urine, the police officer or arresting agency shall give notice as provided in this Section or by deposit in the United States mail of that notice in an envelope with postage prepaid and addressed to that person at his or her last known address and the loss of the school bus driver permit shall be effective on the 46th day following the date notice was given.

Upon receipt of the sworn report of a law enforcement officer, the Secretary of State shall also give notice of the school bus driver permit sanction to the driver and the driver's current employer by mailing a notice of the effective date of the sanction to the individual. However, shall the sworn report be defective by not containing sufficient information or be completed in error, the notice of the school bus driver permit sanction may not be mailed to the person or his current employer or entered to the driving record, but rather the sworn report shall be returned to the issuing law enforcement agency.

(e) A driver may contest this school bus driver permit sanction by requesting an administrative hearing with the Secretary of State in accordance with Section 2–118 of this Code. An individual whose blood alcohol concentration is shown to be more than 0.00 is not subject to this Section if he or she consumed alcohol in the performance of a religious service or ceremony. An individual whose blood alcohol concentration is shown to be more than 0.00 shall not be subject to this Section if the individual's blood alcohol concentration resulted only from ingestion of the prescribed or recommended dosage of medicine that contained alcohol. The petition for that hearing shall not stay or delay the effective date of the impending suspension. The scope of this hearing shall be limited to the issues of:

(1) whether the police officer had probable cause to believe that the person was driving or in actual physical control of a school bus or any other vehicle owned or operated by or for a public or private school, or a school operated by a religious institution, when the vehicle is being used over a regularly scheduled route for the transportation of persons enrolled as students in grade 12 or below, in connection with any activity of the entities listed, upon the public highways of the State and the police officer had reason to believe that the person was in violation of any provision of this Code or a similar provision of a local ordinance; and

(2) whether the person was issued a Uniform Traffic Ticket for any violation of this Code or a similar provision of a local ordinance; and

(3) whether the police officer had probable cause to believe that the driver had consumed any amount of an alcoholic beverage based upon the driver's physical actions or other first-hand knowledge of the police officer; and

(4) whether the person, after being advised by the officer that the privilege to possess a school bus driver permit would be canceled if the person refused to submit to and complete the test or tests, did refuse to submit to or complete the test or tests to determine the person's alcohol concentration; and

(5) whether the person, after being advised by the officer that the privileges to possess a school bus driver permit would be canceled if the person submits to a chemical test or tests and the test or tests disclose an alcohol concentration of more than 0.00 and the person did submit to and complete the test or tests that determined an alcohol concentration of more than 0.00; and

(6) whether the test result of an alcohol concentration of more than 0.00 was based upon the person's consumption of alcohol in the performance of a religious service or ceremony; and

(7) whether the test result of an alcohol concentration of more than 0.00 was based upon the person's consumption of alcohol through ingestion of the prescribed or recommended dosage of medicine.

The Secretary of State may adopt administrative rules setting forth circumstances under which the holder of a school bus driver permit is not required to appear in person at the hearing.

Provided that the petitioner may subpoena the officer, the hearing may be conducted upon a review of the law enforcement officer's own official reports. Failure of the officer to answer the subpoena shall be grounds for a continuance if, in the hearing officer's discretion, the continuance is appropriate. At the conclusion of the hearing held under Section 2-118 of this Code, the Secretary of State may rescind, continue, or modify the school bus driver permit sanction.

(f) The results of any chemical testing performed in accordance with subsection (a) of this Section are not admissible in any civil or criminal proceeding, except that the results of the testing may be considered at a hearing held under Section 2-118 of this Code. However, the results of the testing may not be used to impose driver's license sanctions under Section 11-501.1 of this Code. A law enforcement officer may, however, pursue a statutory summary suspension of driving privileges under Section 11-501.1 of this Code if other physical evidence or first hand knowledge forms the basis of that suspension.

(g) This Section applies only to drivers who have been issued a school bus driver permit in accordance with Section 6-106.1 of this Code at the time of the issuance of the Uniform Traffic Ticket for a violation of this Code or a similar provision of a local ordinance, and a chemical test request is made under this Section.

(h) The action of the Secretary of State in suspending, revoking, canceling, or denying any license, permit, registration, or certificate of title shall be subject to judicial review in the Circuit Court of Sangamon County or in the Circuit Court of Cook County, and the provisions of the Administrative Review Law [1] and its rules are hereby adopted and shall apply to and govern every action for the judicial review of final acts or decisions of the Secretary of State under this Section.

P.A. 76-1586, § 6-106.1a, added by P.A. 90-107, § 5, eff. Jan. 1, 1998. Amended by P.A. 91-124, § 5, eff. July 16, 1999; P.A. 91-828, § 5, eff. Jan. 1, 2001.

1 735 ILCS 5/3-101 et seq.

P.A. 91-828 incorporated the amendment by P.A. 91-124.

5/6-106.1b. Loss of school bus driver permit privileges; failure or refusal to submit to chemical testing

§ 6-106.1b. Loss of school bus driver permit privileges; failure or refusal to submit to chemical testing. Unless the loss of school bus driver permit privileges based upon consumption of alcohol by an individual who has been issued a school bus driver permit in accordance with Section 6-106.1 of this Code or refusal to submit to testing has been rescinded by the Secretary of State in accordance with subsection (c) of Section 6-206 of this Code, a person whose privilege to possess a school bus driver permit has been canceled under Section 6-106.1a is not eligible for restoration of the privilege until the expiration of 3 years from the effective date of the cancellation for a person who has refused or failed to complete a test or tests to determine blood alcohol concentration or has submitted to testing with a blood alcohol concentration of more than 0.00.

P.A. 76-1586, § 6-106.1b, added by P.A. 90-107, § 5, eff. Jan. 1, 1998. Amended by P.A. 91-124, § 5, eff. July 16, 1999.

5/6-106.2. Religious organization bus driver

§ 6-106.2. Religious organization bus driver. A religious organization bus driver shall meet the following requirements:

1. is 21 years of age or older;

2. has a valid and properly classified driver's license issued by the Secretary of State;

3. has held a valid driver's license, not necessarily of the same classification, for 3 years prior to the date of application;

4. has demonstrated an ability to exercise reasonable care in the safe operation of religious organization buses in accordance with such standards as the Secretary of State prescribes including a driving test in a religious organization bus; and

5. has not been convicted of any of the following offenses within 3 years of the date of application: Sections 11-401 (leaving the scene of a traffic accident involving death or personal injury), 11-501 (driving under the influence), 11-503 (reckless driving) and 11-504 (drag racing) of this Code, or Sections 9-3 (manslaughter or reckless homicide) and 12-5 (reckless conduct arising from the use of a motor vehicle) of the Criminal Code of 1961.[1]

P.A. 76-1586, § 6-106.2, added by P.A. 79-798, § 1, eff. July 1, 1976. Amended by P.A. 82-532, § 1, eff. Jan. 1, 1982; P.A. 83-831, § 1, eff. Jan. 1, 1984; P.A. 84-641, § 1, eff. Sept. 20, 1985.

Formerly Ill.Rev.Stat.1991, ch. 95 ½, ¶ 6-106.2.

1 720 ILCS 5/9-3 and 5/12-5.

5/6-106.3. Senior citizen transportation—driver

§ 6-106.3. Senior citizen transportation—driver. A driver of a vehicle operated solely for the purpose of providing transportation for the elderly in connection with the activities of any public or private organization shall meet the following requirements:

(1) is 21 years of age or older;

(2) has a valid and properly classified driver's license issued by the Secretary of State;

(3) has had a valid driver's license, not necessarily of the same classification, for 3 years prior to the date of application;

(4) has demonstrated his ability to exercise reasonable care in the safe operation of a motor vehicle which will be utilized to transport persons in accordance with such standards as the Secretary of State prescribes including a driving test in such motor vehicle; and

(5) has not been convicted of any of the following offenses within 3 years of the date of application: Sections 11-401

(leaving the scene of a traffic accident involving death or personal injury), 11-501 (driving under the influence), 11-503 (reckless driving) and 11-504 (drag racing) of this Code, or Sections 9-3 (manslaughter or reckless homicide) and 12-5 (reckless conduct arising from the use of a motor vehicle) of the Criminal Code of 1961.[1]

P.A. 76-1586, § 6-106.3, added by P.A. 82-532, § 1, eff. Jan. 1, 1982. Amended by P.A. 84-641, § 1, eff. Sept. 20, 1985.

Formerly Ill.Rev.Stat.1991, ch. 95 ½, ¶ 6-106.3.

1 720 ILCS 5/9-3 and 5/12-5.

5/6-106.4. For-profit ridesharing arrangement—driver

§ 6-106.4. For-profit ridesharing arrangement—driver. No person may drive a commuter van while it is being used for a for-profit ridesharing arrangement unless such person:

(1) is 21 years of age or older;

(2) has a valid and properly classified driver's license issued by the Secretary of State;

(3) has held a valid driver's license, not necessarily of the same classification, for 3 years prior to the date of application;

(4) has demonstrated his ability to exercise reasonable care in the safe operation of commuter vans used in for-profit ridesharing arrangements in accordance with such standards as the Secretary of State may prescribe, which standards may require a driving test in a commuter van; and

(5) has not been convicted of any of the following offenses within 3 years of the date of application: Sections 11-401 (leaving the scene of a traffic accident involving death or personal injury), 11-501 (driving under the influence), 11-503 (reckless driving) and 11-504 (drag racing) of this Code, or Sections 9-3 (manslaughter or reckless homicide) and 12-5 (reckless conduct arising from the use of a motor vehicle) of the Criminal Code of 1961.[1]

P.A. 76-1586, § 6-106.4, added by P.A. 83-1091, § 1, eff. July 1, 1984. Amended by P.A. 84-641, § 1, eff. Sept. 20, 1985.

Formerly Ill.Rev.Stat.1991, ch. 95 ½, ¶ 6-106.4.

1 720 ILCS 5/9-3 and 5/12-5.

5/6-106.11. Violations; penalties

§ 6-106.11. (a) Any individual, corporation, partnership or association, who through contractual arrangements with a school district transports students, teachers or other personnel of that district for compensation, shall not permit any person to operate a school bus pursuant to that contract if the driver has not complied with the provisions of Sections 6-106.1 of this Code or such other rules or regulations that the Secretary of State may prescribe for the classification, restriction or licensing of school bus drivers.

(b) A violation of this Section is a business offense and shall subject the offender to a fine of no less than $1,000 nor more than $10,000 for a first offense, no less than $1,500 nor more than $15,000 for a second offense, and no less than $2,000 nor more than $20,000 for a third or subsequent offense. In addition to any fines imposed under this subsection, any offender who has been convicted three times under the provisions of subsection (a) shall, upon a fourth or subsequent conviction be prohibited from transporting or contracting to transport students, teachers or other personnel of a school district for a period of five years beginning with the date of conviction of such fourth or subsequent conviction.

P.A. 76-1586, § 6-106.11, added by P.A. 83-1286, § 1, eff. Aug. 31, 1984.

Formerly Ill.Rev.Stat.1991, ch. 95 ½, ¶ 6-106.11.

5/6-107. Graduated license

§ 6-107. Graduated license.

(a) The purpose of the Graduated Licensing Program is to develop safe and mature driving habits in young, inexperienced drivers and reduce or prevent motor vehicle accidents, fatalities, and injuries by:

(1) providing for an increase in the time of practice period before granting permission to obtain a driver's license;

(2) strengthening driver licensing and testing standards for persons under the age of 21 years;

(3) sanctioning driving privileges of drivers under age 21 who have committed serious traffic violations or other specified offenses; and

(4) setting stricter standards to promote the public's health and safety.

(b) The application of any person under the age of 18 years, and not legally emancipated by marriage, for a drivers license or permit to operate a motor vehicle issued under the laws of this State, shall be accompanied by the written consent of either parent of the applicant; otherwise by the guardian having custody of the applicant, or in the event there is no parent or guardian, then by another responsible adult.

No graduated driver's license shall be issued to any applicant under 18 years of age, unless the applicant has:

(1) Held a valid instruction permit for a minimum of 3 months.

(2) Passed an approved driver education course and submits proof of having passed the course as may be required.

(3) Certification by the parent, legal guardian, or responsible adult that the applicant has had a minimum of 25 hours of behind-the-wheel practice time and is sufficiently prepared and able to safely operate a motor vehicle.

(c) No graduated driver's license or permit shall be issued to any applicant under 18 years of age who has committed the offense of operating a motor vehicle without a valid license or permit in violation of Section 6-101 of this Code and no graduated driver's license or permit shall be issued to any applicant under 18 years of age who has committed an offense that would otherwise result in a mandatory revocation of a license or permit as provided in Section 6-205 of this Code or who has been either convicted of or adjudicated a delinquent based upon a violation of the Cannabis Control Act [1] or the Illinois Controlled Substances Act,[2] while that individual was in actual physical control of a motor vehicle. For purposes of this Section, any person placed on probation under Section 10 of the Cannabis Control Act [3] or Section 410 of the Illinois Controlled Substances Act [4] shall not be considered convicted. Any person found guilty of this offense, while in actual physical control of a motor vehicle, shall have an entry made in the court record by the judge that this offense did occur while the person was in actual physical control of a motor vehicle and order the clerk of the court to report the violation to the Secretary of State as such.

(d) No graduated driver's license shall be issued for 6 months to any applicant under the age of 18 years who has been convicted of any offense defined as a serious traffic violation in this Code or a similar provision of a local ordinance.

(e) No graduated driver's license holder under the age of 18 years shall operate any motor vehicle, except a motor driven cycle or motorcycle, with more than one passenger in the front seat of the motor vehicle and no more passengers in the back seats than the number of available seat safety belts as set forth in Section 12–603 of this Code.

(f) No graduated driver's license holder under the age of 18 shall operate a motor vehicle unless each driver and front or back seat passenger under the age of 18 is wearing a properly adjusted and fastened seat safety belt.

P.A. 76–1586, § 6–107, eff. July 1, 1970. Amended by P.A. 77–51, § 1, eff. July 1, 1971; P.A. 77–2805, § 1, eff. Oct. 1, 1972; P.A. 78–255, § 61, eff. Oct. 1, 1973; P.A. 80–359, § 1, eff. Oct. 1, 1977; P.A. 86–1450, § 2, eff. July 1, 1991; P.A. 88–197, § 5, eff. Aug. 5, 1993; P.A. 90–369, § 5, eff. Jan. 1, 1998.

Formerly Ill.Rev.Stat.1991, ch. 95 ½, ¶ 6–107.

[1] 720 ILCS 550/1 et seq.

[2] 720 ILCS 570/100 et seq.

[3] 720 ILCS 550/10.

[4] 720 ILCS 570/410.

5/6–107.1. Instruction permit for a minor.

§ 6–107.1. Instruction permit for a minor.

(a) The Secretary of State, upon receiving proper application and payment of the required fee, may issue an instruction permit to any person under the age of 18 years who is not ineligible for a license under paragraphs 1, 3, 4, 5, 7, or 8 of Section 6–103, after the applicant has successfully passed such examination as the Secretary of State in his discretion may prescribe.

(1) An instruction permit issued under this Section shall be valid for a period of 24 months after the date of its issuance and shall be restricted, by the Secretary of State, to the operation of a motor vehicle by the minor only when accompanied by the adult instructor of a driver education program during enrollment in the program or when practicing with a parent, legal guardian, family member, or a person in loco parentis who is 21 years of age or more, has a license classification to operate such vehicle and at least one year of driving experience, and who is occupying a seat beside the driver.

(2) A 24 month instruction permit for a motor driven cycle may be issued to a person 16 or 17 years of age and entitles the holder to drive upon the highways during daylight under direct supervision of a licensed motor driven cycle operator or motorcycle operator 21 years of age or older who has a license classification to operate such motor driven cycle or motorcycle and at least one year of driving experience.

(3) A 24 month instruction permit for a motorcycle other than a motor driven cycle may be issued to a person 16 or 17 years of age in accordance with the provisions of paragraph 2 of Section 6–103 and entitles a holder to drive upon the highways during daylight under the direct supervision of a licensed motorcycle operator 21 years of age or older who has at least one year of driving experience.

(b) An instruction permit issued under this Section when issued to a person under the age of 17 years shall, as a matter of law, be invalid for the operation of any motor vehicle during the same time the child is prohibited from being on any street or highway under the provisions of the Child Curfew Act.[1]

(c) Any person under the age of 16 years who possesses an instruction permit and whose driving privileges have been suspended or revoked under the provisions of this Code shall not be granted a Family Financial Responsibility Driving Permit or a Restricted Driving Permit.

P.A. 76–1586, § 6–107.1, added by P.A. 90–369, § 5, eff. Jan. 1, 1998.

[1] 720 ILCS 555/0.01 et seq.

5/6–107.2. Rules for graduated licenses

§ 6–107.2. Rules for graduated licenses. The Secretary of State, using the authority to license motor vehicle operators, may adopt such rules as may be necessary to establish standards, policies, and procedures for graduated licenses.

P.A. 76–1586, § 6–107.2, added by P.A. 90–369, § 5, eff. Jan. 1, 1998.

5/6–107.3. Distinct nature of driver's license dependent on age

§ 6–107.3. Distinct nature of driver's license dependent on age. The Secretary of State shall provide that each graduated driver's license and each regular driver's license issued to individuals under 21 years of age shall be of a distinct nature from those driver's licenses issued to individuals 21 years of age and older. The colors designated for the graduated driver's license and regular driver's license shall be at the discretion of the Secretary of State.

P.A. 76–1586, § 6–107.3, added by P.A. 90–369, § 5, eff. Jan. 1, 1998.

5/6–108. Cancellation of license issued to minor

§ 6–108. Cancellation of license issued to minor.

(a) The Secretary of State shall cancel the license or permit of any minor under the age of 18 years in any of the following events:

1. Upon the verified written request of the person who consented to the application of the minor that the license or permit be cancelled;

2. Upon receipt of satisfactory evidence of the death of the person who consented to the application of the minor;

3. Upon receipt of satisfactory evidence that the person who consented to the application of a minor no longer has legal custody of the minor.

After cancellation, the Secretary of State shall not issue a new license or permit until the applicant meets the provisions of Section 6–107 of this Code.

(b) The Secretary of State shall cancel the license or permit of any person under the age of 18 years if he or she is convicted of violating the Cannabis Control Act[1] or the Illinois Controlled Substances Act[2] while that person was in actual physical control of a motor vehicle. For purposes of this Section, any person placed on probation under Section 10 of the Cannabis Control Act[3] or Section 410 of the Illinois Controlled Substances Act[4] shall not be considered convicted. Any person found guilty of this offense, while in actual physical control of a motor vehicle, shall have an entry made in the court record by the judge that this offense did occur while the person was in actual physical control of a motor vehicle and order the clerk of the court to report the violation to the Secretary of State as such. After the cancellation, the Secretary of State shall not issue a new license or permit for a period of one year after the date of cancellation or until the minor attains the age of 18 years, whichever is longer. However, upon application, the Secretary of State may, if satisfied that the person applying will not endanger the public safety, or welfare, issue a restricted driving permit granting the privilege of driving a motor vehicle between the person's residence and person's place of employment or within the scope of the person's employment related duties, or to allow transportation for the person or a household member of the person's family for the receipt of necessary medical care or, if the professional evaluation indicates, provide transportation for the petitioner for alcohol remedial or rehabilitative activity, or for the person to attend classes, as a student, in an accredited educational institution; if the person is able to demonstrate that no alternative means of transportation is reasonably available; provided that the Secretary's discretion shall be limited to cases where undue hardship would result from a failure to issue such restricted driving permit. In each case the Secretary of State may issue a restricted driving permit for a period as he deems appropriate, except that the permit shall expire within one year from the date of issuance. A restricted driving permit issued hereunder shall be subject to cancellation, revocation, and suspension by the Secretary of State in like manner and for like cause as a driver's license issued hereunder may be cancelled, revoked, or suspended; except that a conviction upon one or more offenses against laws or ordinances regulating the movement of traffic shall be deemed sufficient cause for the revocation, suspension, or cancellation of a restricted driving permit. The Secretary of State may, as a condition to the issuance of a restricted driving permit, require the applicant to participate in a driver remedial or rehabilitative program. Thereafter, upon reapplication for a license as provided in Section 6–106 of this Code or a permit as provided in Section 6–105 of this Code and upon payment of the appropriate application fee, the Secretary of State shall issue the applicant a license as provided in Section 6–106 of this Code or shall issue the applicant a permit as provided in Section 6–105.

P.A. 76–1586, § 6–108, eff. July 1, 1970. Amended by P.A. 77–2805, § 1, eff. Oct. 1, 1972; P.A. 86–1450, § 2, eff. July 1, 1991; P.A. 87–1114, § 1, eff. Sept. 15, 1992.

Formerly Ill.Rev.Stat.1991, ch. 95 ½, ¶ 6–108.

1 720 ILCS 550/1 et seq.

2 720 ILCS 570/100 et seq.

3 720 ILCS 550/10.

4 720 ILCS 570/410.

5/6–108.1. Notice to Secretary; denial of license; persons under 18

§ 6–108.1. Notice to Secretary; denial of license; persons under 18.

(a) The State's Attorney must notify the Secretary of the charges pending against any person younger than 18 years of age who has been charged with a violation of this Code or the Criminal Code of 1961 [1] arising out of an accident in which the person was involved as a driver and that caused the death of or a type A injury to another person. A "type A injury" includes severely bleeding wounds, distorted extremities, and injuries that require the injured party to be carried from the scene. The State's Attorney must notify the Secretary on a form prescribed by the Secretary.

(b) The Secretary, upon receiving notification from the State's Attorney, may deny any driver's license to any person younger than 18 years of age against whom the charges are pending.

(c) The State's Attorney must notify the Secretary of the final disposition of the case of any person who has been denied a driver's license under subsection (b).

(d) The Secretary must adopt rules for implementing this Section.

P.A. 76–1586, § 6–108.1, added by P.A. 92–137, § 5, eff. July 24, 2001.

1 720 ILCS 5/1–1 et seq.

5/6–109. Examination of Applicants

§ 6–109. Examination of Applicants.

(a) The Secretary of State shall examine every applicant for a driver's license or permit who has not been previously licensed as a driver under the laws of this State or any other state or country, or any applicant for renewal of such driver's license or permit when such license or permit has been expired for more than one year. The Secretary of State shall, subject to the provisions of paragraph (c), examine every licensed driver at least every 8 years, and may examine or re-examine any other applicant or licensed driver, provided that during the years 1984 through 1991 those drivers issued a license for 3 years may be re-examined not less than every 7 years or more than every 10 years.

The Secretary of State shall require the testing of the eyesight of any driver's license or permit applicant who has not been previously licensed as a driver under the laws of this State and shall promulgate rules and regulations to provide for the orderly administration of all the provisions of this Section.

(b) Except as provided for those applicants in paragraph (c), such examination shall include a test of the applicant's eyesight, his ability to read and understand official traffic control devices, his knowledge of safe driving practices and the traffic laws of this State, and may include an actual demonstration of the applicant's ability to exercise ordinary and reasonable control of the operation of a motor vehicle, and such further physical and mental examination as the Secretary of State finds necessary to determine the applicant's fitness to operate a motor vehicle safely on the highways, except the examination of an applicant 75 years of age or older shall include an actual demonstration of the applicant's ability to exercise ordinary and reasonable control of the operation of a motor vehicle. All portions of written and verbal examinations under this Section, excepting where the English language appears on facsimiles of road signs, may be given in the Spanish language and, at the discretion of the Secretary of State, in any other language as well as in English upon request of the examinee. Deaf persons who are otherwise qualified are not prohibited from being issued a license, other than a commercial driver's license, under this Code.

(c) Re-examination for those applicants who at the time of renewing their driver's license possess a driving record devoid of any convictions of traffic violations or evidence of committing an offense for which mandatory revocation would be required upon conviction pursuant to Section 6–205 at the time of renewal shall be in a manner prescribed by the Secretary in order to determine an applicant's ability to safely operate a motor vehicle, except that every applicant for the renewal of a driver's license who is 75 years of age or older must prove, by an actual demonstration, the applicant's ability to exercise reasonable care in the safe operation of a motor vehicle.

(d) In the event the applicant is not ineligible under the provisions of Section 6–103 to receive a driver's license, the Secretary of State shall make provision for giving an examination, either in the county where the applicant resides or at a place adjacent thereto reasonably convenient to the applicant, within not more than 30 days from the date said application is received.

P.A. 76-1586, § 6-109, eff. July 1, 1970. Amended by P.A. 76-1750, § 1; P.A. 77-1774, § 1, eff. July 1, 1972; P.A. 78-738, § 1, eff. Jan. 1, 1974; P.A. 79-1141, § 1, eff. Jan. 1, 1976; P.A. 82-628, § 1, eff. July 1, 1982; P.A. 83-56, § 1, eff. Jan. 1, 1984; P.A. 83-239, § 1, eff. Jan. 1, 1984; P.A. 83-1362, Art. II, § 99, eff. Sept. 11, 1984; P.A. 83-1458, § 1, eff. Sept. 17, 1984; P.A. 86-467, § 1, eff. Aug. 31, 1989; P.A. 89-569, § 10, eff. Jan. 1, 1997; P.A. 91-350, § 5, eff. July 29, 1999.

Formerly Ill.Rev.Stat.1991, ch. 95 ½, ¶ 6-109.

5/6-110. Licenses issued to drivers

§ 6-110. Licenses issued to drivers.

(a) The Secretary of State shall issue to every qualifying applicant a driver's license as applied for, which license shall bear a distinguishing number assigned to the licensee, the name, social security number, zip code, date of birth, address, and a brief description of the licensee, and a space where the licensee may write his usual signature.

If the licensee is less than 17 years of age, the license shall, as a matter of law, be invalid for the operation of any motor vehicle during any time the licensee is prohibited from being on any street or highway under the provisions of the Child Curfew Act. [1]

Licenses issued shall also indicate the classification and the restrictions under Section 6-104 of this Code.

In lieu of the social security number, the Secretary may in his discretion substitute a federal tax number or other distinctive number.

A driver's license issued may, in the discretion of the Secretary, include a suitable photograph of a type prescribed by the Secretary.

(b) The Secretary of State shall provide a format on the reverse of each driver's license issued which the licensee may use to execute a document of gift conforming to the provisions of the Uniform Anatomical Gift Act. [2] The format shall allow the licensee to indicate the gift intended, whether specific organs, any organ, or the entire body, and shall accommodate the signatures of the donor and 2 witnesses. The Secretary shall also inform each applicant or licensee of this format, describe the procedure for its execution, and may offer the necessary witnesses; provided that in so doing, the Secretary shall advise the applicant or licensee that he or she is under no compulsion to execute a document of gift. A brochure explaining this method of executing an anatomical gift document shall be given to each applicant or licensee. The brochure shall advise the applicant or licensee that he or she is under no compulsion to execute a document of gift, and that he or she may wish to consult with family, friends or clergy before doing so. The Secretary of State may undertake additional efforts, including education and awareness activities, to promote organ and tissue donation.

(c) The Secretary of State shall designate on each driver's license issued a space where the licensee may place a sticker or decal of the uniform size as the Secretary may specify, which sticker or decal may indicate in appropriate language that the owner of the license carries an Emergency Medical Information Card.

The sticker may be provided by any person, hospital, school, medical group, or association interested in assisting in implementing the Emergency Medical Information Card, but shall meet the specifications as the Secretary may by rule or regulation require.

(d) The Secretary of State shall designate on each driver's license issued a space where the licensee may indicate his blood type and RH factor.

(e) The Secretary of State shall provide that each original or renewal driver's license issued to a licensee under 21 years of age shall be of a distinct nature from those driver's licenses issued to individuals 21 years of age and older. The color designated for driver's licenses for licensees under 21 years of age shall be at the discretion of the Secretary of State.

(e-1) The Secretary shall provide that each driver's license issued to a person under the age of 21 displays the date upon which the person becomes 18 years of age and the date upon which the person becomes 21 years of age.

(f) The Secretary of State shall inform all Illinois licensed commercial motor vehicle operators of the requirements of the Uniform Commercial Driver License Act, Article V of this Chapter, and shall make provisions to insure that all drivers, seeking to obtain a commercial driver's license, be afforded an opportunity prior to April 1, 1992, to obtain the license. The Secretary is authorized to extend driver's license expiration dates, and assign specific times, dates and locations where these commercial driver's tests shall be conducted. Any applicant, regardless of the current expiration date of the applicant's driver's license, may be subject to any assignment by the Secretary. Failure to comply with the Secretary's assignment may result in the applicant's forfeiture of an opportunity to receive a commercial driver's license prior to April 1, 1992.

(g) The Secretary of State shall designate on a driver's license issued, a space where the licensee may indicate that he or she has drafted a living will in accordance with the Illinois Living Will Act [3] or a durable power of attorney for health care in accordance with the Illinois Power of Attorney Act. [4]

(g-1) The Secretary of State, in his or her discretion, may designate on each driver's license issued a space where the licensee may place a sticker or decal, issued by the Secretary of State, of uniform size as the Secretary may specify, that shall indicate in appropriate language that the owner of the license has renewed his or her driver's license.

(h) A person who acts in good faith in accordance with the terms of this Section is not liable for damages in any civil action or subject to prosecution in any criminal proceeding for his or her act.

P.A. 76-1586, § 6-110, eff. July 1, 1970. Amended by P.A. 77-105, § 1, eff. Jan. 1, 1972; P.A. 78-197, § 1, eff. Jan. 1, 1974; P.A. 79-158, § 1, eff. July 9, 1975; P.A. 79-416, § 1, eff. Aug. 14, 1975; P.A. 79-1454, § 44, eff. Aug. 31, 1976; P.A. 80-516, § 1, eff. Jan. 1, 1978; P.A. 80-534, § 1, eff. Jan. 1, 1978; P.A. 80-1364, § 36, eff. Aug. 13, 1978; P.A. 82-278, § 1, eff. July 1, 1982; P.A. 84-270, § 1, eff. Jan. 1, 1986; P.A. 84-1409, § 7, eff. Jan. 1, 1987; P.A. 85-192, § 1, eff. Aug. 21, 1987; P.A. 86-845, § 1, eff. April 1, 1990; P.A. 87-590, § 1, eff. Jan. 1, 1992; P.A. 88-78, § 20, eff. July 9, 1993; P.A. 88-393, § 5, eff. Jan. 1, 1994; P.A. 88-670, Art. 2, § 2-59, eff. Dec. 2, 1994; P.A. 89-569, § 10, eff. Jan. 1, 1997; P.A. 90-191, § 10, eff. Jan. 1, 1998; P.A. 91-357, § 231, eff. July 29, 1999; P.A. 92-689, § 5, eff. Jan. 1, 2003.

Formerly Ill.Rev.Stat.1991, ch. 95 ½, ¶ 6-110.

[1] 720 ILCS 555/0.01 et seq.

[2] 755 ILCS 50/1 et seq.

[3] 755 ILCS 35/1 et seq.

[4] 755 ILCS 45/1-1 et seq.

5/6-110.1. Confidentiality of captured photographs or images

§ 6-110.1. Confidentiality of captured photographs or images. The Secretary of State shall maintain a file on or contract to file all photographs and signatures obtained in the process of issuing a driver's license, permit, or identification card. The photographs and signatures shall be confidential and shall not be disclosed except to the following persons:

(1) the individual upon written request;

(2) officers and employees of the Secretary of State who have a need to have access to the stored images for purposes of issuing and controlling driver's licenses, permits, or identification cards;

(3) law enforcement officials for a lawful civil or criminal law enforcement investigation; or

(4) other entities that the Secretary may exempt by rule.

P.A. 76-1586, § 6-110.1, added by P.A. 90-191, § 10, eff. Jan. 1, 1998. Amended by P.A. 92-16, § 85, eff. June 28, 2001.

5/6-111. § 6-111. Repealed by P.A. 76-1906, § 2, eff. July 1, 1970

5/6-112. License and permits to be carried and exhibited on demand

§ 6-112. License and permits to be carried and exhibited on demand. Every licensee or permittee shall have his drivers license or permit in his immediate possession at all times when operating a motor vehicle and, for the purpose of indicating compliance with this requirement, shall display such license or permit if it is in his possession upon demand made, when in uniform or displaying a badge or other sign of authority, by a member of the State Police, a sheriff or other police officer or designated agent of the Secretary of State. However, no person charged with violating this Section shall be convicted if he produces in court satisfactory evidence that a drivers license was theretofor issued to him and was valid at the time of his arrest.

For the purposes of this section, "display" means the manual surrender of his license certificate into the hands of the demanding officer for his inspection thereof.

P.A. 76-1586, § 6-112, eff. July 1, 1970. Amended by P.A. 76-1749, § 1, eff. July 1, 1970.

Formerly Ill.Rev.Stat.1991, ch. 95 ½, ¶ 6-112.

5/6-113. Restricted licenses and permits

§ 6-113. Restricted licenses and permits.

(a) The Secretary of State upon issuing a drivers license or permit shall have the authority whenever good cause appears to impose restrictions suitable to the licensee's driving ability with respect to the type of, or special mechanical control devices required on, a motor vehicle which the licensee may operate or such other restrictions applicable to the licensee as the Secretary of State may determine to be appropriate to assure the safe operation of a motor vehicle by the licensee.

(b) The Secretary of State may either issue a special restricted license or permit or may set forth such restrictions upon the usual license or permit form.

(c) The Secretary of State may issue a probationary license to a person whose driving privileges have been suspended pursuant to subsection (d) of this Section or subsections (a)(2), (a)(19) and (a)(20) of Section 6-206 of this Code. The Secretary of State shall promulgate rules pursuant to The Illinois Administrative Procedure Act,[1] setting forth the conditions and criteria for the issuance and cancellation of probationary licenses.

(d) The Secretary of State may upon receiving satisfactory evidence of any violation of the restrictions of such license or permit suspend, revoke or cancel the same without preliminary hearing, but the licensee or permittee shall be entitled to a hearing as in the case of a suspension or revocation.

(e) It is unlawful for any person to operate a motor vehicle in any manner in violation of the restrictions imposed on a restricted license or permit issued to him.

(f) Whenever the holder of a restricted driving permit is issued a citation for any of the following offenses including similar local ordinances, the restricted driving permit is immediately invalidated:

1. Reckless homicide resulting from the operation of a motor vehicle;

2. Violation of Section 11-501 of this Act relating to the operation of a motor vehicle while under the influence of intoxicating liquor or narcotic drugs;

3. Violation of Section 11-401 of this Act relating to the offense of leaving the scene of a traffic accident involving death or injury; or

4. Violation of Section 11-504 of this Act relating to the offense of drag racing;

The police officer issuing the citation shall confiscate the restricted driving permit and forward it, along with the citation, to the Clerk of the Circuit Court of the county in which the citation was issued.

(g) The Secretary of State may issue a special restricted license for a period of 12 months to individuals using vision aid arrangements other than standard eyeglasses or contact lenses, allowing the operation of a motor vehicle during nighttime hours. The Secretary of State shall adopt rules defining the terms and conditions by which the individual may obtain and renew this special restricted license. At a minimum, all drivers must meet the following requirements:

1. Possess a valid driver's license and have operated a motor vehicle during daylight hours for a period of 12 months using vision aid arrangements other than standard eyeglasses or contact lenses.

2. Have a driving record that does not include any traffic accidents that occurred during nighttime hours, for which the driver has been found to be at fault, during the 12 months before he or she applied for the special restricted license.

3. Successfully complete a road test administered during nighttime hours.

At a minimum, all drivers renewing this license must meet the following requirements:

1. Successfully complete a road test administered during nighttime hours.

2. Have a driving record that does not include any traffic accidents that occurred during nighttime hours, for which the driver has been found to be at fault, during the 12 months before he or she applied for the special restricted license.

(h) Any driver issued a special restricted license as defined in subsection (g) whose privilege to drive during nighttime hours has been suspended due to an accident occurring during nighttime hours may request a hearing as provided in Section 2-118 of this Code to contest that suspension. If it is determined that the accident for which the driver was at fault was not influenced by the driver's use of vision aid arrangements other than standard eyeglasses or contact lenses, the Secretary may reinstate that driver's privilege to drive during nighttime hours.

P.A. 76-1586, § 6-113, eff. July 1, 1970. Amended by P.A. 77-2830, Art. 73, § 1, eff. Jan. 1, 1973; P.A. 80-911, § 1, eff. Oct. 1, 1977; P.A. 81-1400, § 1, eff. Aug. 25, 1980; P.A. 84-510, § 1, eff. Jan. 1, 1986; P.A. 84-793, § 2, eff. Jan. 1, 1986; P.A. 84-1308, Art. II, § 96, eff. Aug. 25, 1986; P.A. 84-1450, § 7, eff. July 1, 1987; P.A. 85-293, Art. II, § 13, eff. Sept. 8, 1987; P.A. 85-813, § 1, eff. Jan. 1, 1988; P.A. 86-549, § 1, eff. Jan. 1, 1990; P.A. 92-274, § 5, eff. Jan. 1, 2002.

Formerly Ill.Rev.Stat.1991, ch. 95 ½, ¶ 6-113.

1 5 ILCS 100/1-1 et seq.

5/6-114. Duplicate and corrected licenses and permits

§ 6-114. Duplicate and corrected licenses and permits. In the event that a drivers license or permit issued under the provisions of this Act is lost or destroyed, the person to whom the same was issued may upon application and payment of the required fee obtain a duplicate or substitute thereof, upon furnishing evidence satisfactory to the Secretary of State that such permit or license has been lost or destroyed and if such applicant is not then ineligible under Section 6-103 of this Act. Any person to whom has been issued a drivers license or permit under the provisions of this Act and who desires to obtain a corrected permit or license to indicate a change of name or address or to correct a statement appearing upon the original permit or license may upon application and payment of the required fee obtain a corrected permit or license. The original permit or license must accompany the application for correction or evidence must be furnished satisfactory to the Secretary of State that such permit or license has been lost or destroyed.

P.A. 76-1586, § 6-114, eff. July 1, 1970.

Formerly Ill.Rev.Stat.1991, ch. 95 ½, ¶ 6-114.

5/6-115. Expiration of driver's license

§ 6-115. Expiration of driver's license.

(a) Except as provided elsewhere in this Section, every driver's license issued under the provisions of this Code shall expire 4 years from the date of its issuance, or at such later date, as the Secretary of State may by proper rule and regulation designate, not to exceed 12 calendar months; in the event that an applicant for renewal of a driver's license fails to apply prior to the expiration date of the previous driver's license, the renewal driver's license shall expire 4 years from the expiration date of the previous driver's license, or at such later date as the Secretary of State may by proper rule and regulation designate, not to exceed 12 calendar months.

The Secretary of State may, however, issue to a person not previously licensed as a driver in Illinois a driver's license which will expire not less than 4 years nor more than 5 years from date of issuance, except as provided elsewhere in this Section.

The Secretary of State is authorized to issue driver's licenses during the years 1984 through 1987 which shall expire not less than 3 years nor more than 5 years from the date of issuance, except as provided elsewhere in this Section, for the purpose of converting all driver's licenses issued under this Code to a 4 year expiration. Provided that all original driver's licenses, except as provided elsewhere in this Section, shall expire not less than 4 years nor more than 5 years from the date of issuance.

(b) Before the expiration of a driver's license, except those licenses expiring on the individual's 21st birthday, or 3 months after the individual's 21st birthday, the holder thereof may apply for a renewal thereof, subject to all the provisions of Section 6-103, and the Secretary of State may require an examination of the applicant. A licensee whose driver's license expires on his 21st birthday, or 3 months after his 21st birthday, may not apply for a renewal of his driving privileges until he reaches the age of 21.

(c) The Secretary of State shall, 30 days prior to the expiration of a driver's license, forward to each person whose license is to expire a notification of the expiration of said license which may be presented at the time of renewal of said license.

There may be included with such notification information explaining the anatomical gift and Emergency Medical Information Card provisions of Section 6-110. The format and text of such information shall be prescribed by the Secretary.

There shall be included with such notification, for a period of 4 years beginning January 1, 2000 information regarding the Illinois Adoption Registry and Medical Information Exchange established in Section 18.1 of the Adoption Act.[1]

(d) The Secretary may defer the expiration of the driver's license of a licensee, spouse, and dependent children who are living with such licensee while on active duty, serving in the Armed Forces of the United States outside of the State of Illinois, and 45 days thereafter, upon such terms and conditions as the Secretary may prescribe.

(e) The Secretary of State may decline to process a renewal of a driver's license of any person who has not paid any fee or tax due under this Code and is not paid upon reasonable notice and demand.

(f) The Secretary shall provide that each original or renewal driver's license issued to a licensee under 21 years of age shall expire 3 months after the licensee's 21st birthday. Persons whose current driver's licenses expire on their 21st birthday on or after January 1, 1986 shall not renew their driver's license before their 21st birthday, and their current driver's license will be extended for an additional term of 3 months beyond their 21st birthday. Thereafter, the expiration and term of the driver's license shall be governed by subsection (a) hereof.

(g) The Secretary shall provide that each original or renewal driver's license issued to a licensee 81 years of age through age 86 shall expire 2 years from the date of issuance, or at such later date as the Secretary may by rule and regulation designate, not to exceed an additional 12 calendar months. The Secretary shall also provide that each original or renewal driver's license issued to a licensee 87 years of age or older shall expire 12 months from the date of issuance, or at such later date as the Secretary may by rule and regulation designate, not to exceed an additional 12 calendar months.

(h) The Secretary of State shall provide that each special restricted driver's license issued under subsection (g) of Section 6-113 of this Code shall expire 12 months from the date of issuance. The Secretary shall adopt rules defining renewal requirements.

P.A. 76-1586, § 6-115, eff. July 1, 1970. Amended by P.A. 76-1904, § 1; P.A. 77-642, § 1, eff. Aug. 4, 1971; P.A. 79-1141, § 1, eff. Jan. 1, 1976; P.A. 82-278, § 1, eff. July 1, 1982; P.A. 83-239, § 1, eff. Jan. 1, 1984; P.A. 84-270, § 1, eff. Jan. 1, 1986; P.A. 86-467, § 2, eff. Jan. 1, 1990; P.A. 91-417, § 7, eff. Jan. 1, 2000; P.A. 92-274, § 5, eff. Jan. 1, 2002.

Formerly Ill.Rev.Stat.1991, ch. 95 ½, ¶ 6-115.

1 750 ILCS 50/18.1.

5/6-116. Notice of change of address or name

§ 6-116. Notice of change of address or name. Whenever any person after applying for or receiving a drivers license or permit moves from the address named in such application or on the license or permit issued to him or when the name of a licensee or permittee is changed by marriage or otherwise such person shall within 10 days thereafter notify the Drivers Services Department of the Secretary of State's Office in writing of his old and new addresses or of such former and new names and of the number of any license or permit then held by him. Such person may obtain a corrected license or permit as provided in Section 6-114.

P.A. 76-1586, § 6-116, eff. July 1, 1970. Amended by P.A. 79-1141, § 1, eff. Jan. 1, 1976.

Formerly Ill.Rev.Stat.1991, ch. 95 ½, ¶ 6-116.

5/6-116.5. Driver's duty to report medical condition

§ 6-116.5. Driver's duty to report medical condition. Every driver shall report to the Secretary any medical condition, as defined by the Driver's License Medical Review Law of 1992,[1] that is likely to cause loss of consciousness or any loss of ability to safely operate a motor vehicle within 10 days of the driver becoming aware of the condition. The Secretary, in conjunction with the Driver's License Medical Advisory Board, shall determine by administrative rule the temporary conditions not required to be reported under the provisions of this Section. All information furnished to the Secretary under the provisions of this Section shall be deemed confidential and for the privileged use of the Secretary in accordance with the provisions of subsection (j) of Section 2-123 of this Code.

P.A. 76-1586, § 6-116.5, added by P.A. 89-584, § 5, eff. July 31, 1996.

1 625 ILCS 5/6-900 et seq.

5/6-117. Records to be kept by the Secretary of State

§ 6-117. Records to be kept by the Secretary of State.

(a) The Secretary of State shall file every application for a license or permit accepted under this Chapter, and shall maintain suitable indexes thereof. The records of the Secretary of State shall indicate the action taken with respect to such applications.

(b) The Secretary of State shall maintain appropriate records of all licenses and permits refused, cancelled, revoked or suspended and of the revocation and suspension of driving privileges of persons not licensed under this Chapter, and such records shall note the reasons for such action.

(c) The Secretary of State shall maintain appropriate records of convictions reported under this Chapter. Records of conviction may be maintained in a computer processible medium.

(d) The Secretary of State may also maintain appropriate records of any accident reports received.

(e) The Secretary of State shall also maintain appropriate records of any disposition of supervision or records relative to a driver's referral to a driver remedial or rehabilitative program, as required by the Secretary of State or the courts. Such records shall only be available for use by the Secretary, law enforcement agencies, the courts, and the affected driver or, upon proper verification, such affected driver's attorney.

(f) The Secretary of State shall also maintain or contract to maintain appropriate records of all photographs and signatures obtained in the process of issuing any driver's license, permit, or identification card. The record shall be confidential and shall not be disclosed except to those entities listed under Section 6-110.1 of this Code.

P.A. 76-1586, § 6-117, eff. July 1, 1970. Amended by P.A. 82-311, § 1, eff. Jan. 1, 1982; P.A. 84-596, § 1, eff. Jan. 1, 1986; P.A. 85-1396, § 2, eff. Sept. 2, 1988; P.A. 90-191, § 10, eff. Jan. 1, 1998; P.A. 92-458, § 5, eff. Aug. 22, 2001.

Formerly Ill.Rev.Stat.1991, ch. 95 ½, ¶ 6-117.

5/6-118. Fees

§ 6-118. Fees.

(a) The fee for licenses and permits under this Article is as follows:

Original driver's license $10
Original or renewal driver's license issued to 18, 19 and 20 year olds 5
All driver's licenses for persons age 69 through age 80 5
All driver's licenses for persons age 81 through age 86 2
All driver's licenses for persons age 87 or older 0
Renewal driver's license (except for applicants ages 18, 19 and 20 or age 69 and older) 10
Original instruction permit issued to persons (except those age 69 and older) who do not hold or have not previously held an Illinois instruction permit or driver's license 20
Instruction permit issued to any person holding an Illinois driver's license who wishes a change in classifications, other than at the time of renewal 5
Any instruction permit issued to a person age 69 and older 5
Instruction permit issued to any person, under age 69, not currently holding a valid Illinois driver's license or instruction permit but who has previously been issued either document in Illinois 10
Restricted driving permit 8
Duplicate or corrected driver's license or permit 5
Duplicate or corrected restricted driving permit 5
Original or renewal M or L endorsement 5

SPECIAL FEES FOR COMMERCIAL DRIVER'S LICENSE

The fees for commercial driver licenses and permits under Article V [1] shall be as follows:

Commercial driver's license: $6 for the CDLIS/AAMVAnet Fund (Commercial Driver's License Information System/American Association of Motor Vehicle Administrators network Trust Fund); $20 for the Motor Carrier Safety Inspection Fund; $10 for the driver's license; and $24 for the CDL: $60
Renewal commercial driver's license: $6 for the CDLIS/AAMVAnet Trust Fund; $20 for the Motor Carrier Safety Inspection Fund; $10 for the driver's license; and $24 for the CDL: $60
Commercial driver instruction permit issued to any person holding a valid Illinois driver's license for the purpose of changing to a CDL classification: $6 for the CDLIS/AAMVAnet Trust Fund; $20 for the Motor Carrier Safety Inspection Fund; and $24 for the CDL classification $50

Commercial driver instruction permit issued to any person holding a valid Illinois CDL for the purpose of making a change in a classification, endorsement or restriction $5
CDL duplicate or corrected license $5

In order to ensure the proper implementation of the Uniform Commercial Driver License Act,[2] Article V of this Chapter, the Secretary of State is empowered to pro-rate the $24 fee for the commercial driver's license proportionate to the expiration date of the applicant's Illinois driver's license.

The fee for any duplicate license or permit shall be waived for any person age 60 or older who presents the Secretary of State's office with a police report showing that his license or permit was stolen.

No additional fee shall be charged for a driver's license, or for a commercial driver's license, when issued to the holder of an instruction permit for the same classification or type of license who becomes eligible for such license.

(b) Any person whose license or privilege to operate a motor vehicle in this State has been suspended or revoked under any provision of Chapter 6, Chapter 11, or Section 7–702 of the Family Financial Responsibility Law of this Code,[3] shall in addition to any other fees required by this Code, pay a reinstatement fee as follows:

Summary suspension under Section 11–501.1 . . . . $60
Other suspension $30
Revocation $60

However, any person whose license or privilege to operate a motor vehicle in this State has been suspended or revoked for a second or subsequent time for a violation of Section 11–501 or 11–501.1 of this Code or a similar provision of a local ordinance or a similar out-of-state offense or Section 9–3 of the Criminal Code of 1961[4] and each suspension or revocation was for a violation of Section 11–501 or 11–501.1 of this Code or a similar provision of a local ordinance or a similar out of state offense or Section 9–3 of the Criminal Code of 1961 shall pay, in addition to any other fees required by this Code, a reinstatement fee as follows:

Summary suspension under Section 11–501.1 . . . . $250
Revocation $250

(c) All fees collected under the provisions of this Chapter 6 shall be paid into the Road Fund in the State Treasury except as follows:

1. The following amounts shall be paid into the Driver Education Fund:

(A) $16 of the $20 fee for an original driver's instruction permit;

(B) $5 of the $10 fee for an original driver's license;

(C) $5 of the $10 fee for a 4 year renewal driver's license; and

(D) $4 of the $8 fee for a restricted driving permit.

2. $30 of the $60 fee for reinstatement of a license summarily suspended under Section 11–501.1 shall be deposited into the Drunk and Drugged Driving Prevention Fund. However, for a person whose license or privilege to operate a motor vehicle in this State has been suspended or revoked for a second or subsequent time for a violation of Section 11–501 or 11–501.1 of this Code or Section 9–3 of the Criminal Code of 1961, $190 of the $250 fee for reinstatement of a license summarily suspended under Section 11–501.1, and $190 of the $250 fee for reinstatement of a revoked license shall be deposited into the Drunk and Drugged Driving Prevention Fund.

3. $6 of such original or renewal fee for a commercial driver's license and $6 of the commercial driver instruction permit fee when such permit is issued to any person holding a valid Illinois driver's license, shall be paid into the CDLIS/AAMVAnet Trust Fund.

4. The fee for reinstatement of a license suspended under the Family Financial Responsibility Law[5] shall be paid into the Family Responsibility Fund.

5. The $5 fee for each original or renewal M or L endorsement shall be deposited into the Cycle Rider Safety Training Fund.

6. $20 of any original or renewal fee for a commercial driver's license or commercial driver instruction permit shall be paid into the Motor Carrier Safety Inspection Fund.

P.A. 76–1586, § 6–118, eff. July 1, 1970. Amended by P.A. 78–820, § 1, eff. Jan. 1, 1974; P.A. 81–462, § 1, eff. Jan. 1, 1980; P.A. 81–844, § 1, eff. Jan. 1, 1980; P.A. 81–1509, Art. I, § 57, eff. Sept. 26, 1980; P.A. 82–617, § 1, eff. Jan. 1, 1982; P.A. 83–148, § 1, eff. Aug. 29, 1983; P.A. 83–239, § 1, eff. Jan. 1, 1984; P.A. 83–1362, Art. II, § 99, eff. Sept. 11, 1984; P.A. 84–270, § 1, eff. Jan. 1, 1986; P.A. 84–272, § 7, eff. Jan. 1, 1986; P.A. 84–1308, Art. II, § 96, eff. Aug. 25, 1986; P.A. 84–1394, § 5, eff. Sept. 18, 1986; P.A. 85–1304, § 1, eff. Jan. 1, 1989; P.A. 86–467, § 2, eff. Jan. 1, 1990; P.A. 86–525, § 1, eff. Jan. 1, 1990; P.A. 86–845, § 1, eff. April 1, 1990; P.A. 86–1028, Art. II, § 2–44, eff. Feb. 5, 1990; P.A. 89–92, § 10, eff. July 1, 1996; P.A. 90–622, § 5, eff. March 1, 1999; P.A. 90–738, § 5, eff. Jan. 1, 1999; P.A. 91–357, § 231, eff. July 29, 1999; P.A. 91–537, § 10, eff. Aug. 13, 1999; P.A. 92–458, § 5, eff. Aug. 22, 2001.

Formerly Ill.Rev.Stat.1991, ch. 95 ½, ¶ 6–118.

[1] 625 ILCS 5/5–100 et seq.

[2] 625 ILCS 5/6–500 et seq.

[3] 625 ILCS 5/6–100 et seq., 5/11–100 et seq., or 5/7–702.

[4] 720 ILCS 5/9–3.

[5] 625 ILCS 5/7–701 et seq.

5/6–119. When fees returnable—Drivers license

§ 6–119. When fees returnable—Drivers license. (a) Whenever any application to the Secretary of State is accompanied by any fee as required by law and such application is refused or rejected, said fee shall be returned to said applicant.

(b) Whenever the Secretary of State through error collects any fee not required to be paid hereunder, the same shall be refunded to the person paying the same upon application therefor made within 6 months after the date of such payment.

(c) Whenever a person dies after making application for a drivers license or permit under this Article, application for a refund of the drivers license or permit may be made if the person dies prior to the effective date for which application has been made, and if the drivers license or permit has never been used. The Secretary of State shall refund the drivers license or permit fees upon receipt within 3 months after the application for a drivers license or permit of an application for refund accompanied with the drivers license or permit and proof of death of the applicant.

(d) Any application for refund received after the times specified in this Section shall be denied and the applicant in order to receive a refund must apply to the Court of Claims.

P.A. 76–1586, § 6–119, eff. July 1, 1970. Amended by P.A. 78–756, § 1, eff. Oct. 1, 1973.

Formerly Ill.Rev.Stat.1991, ch. 95 ½, ¶ 6–119.

5/6–120. Inter-agency agreement for information

§ 6–120. Inter-agency agreement for information. Notwithstanding any other provision of this Code, the Secretary of State shall enter into an inter-agency agreement with the Department of Children and Family Services to establish a procedure by which employees of the Department of Children and Family Services may have immediate access to driver's license records maintained by the Secretary of State if the Department of Children and Family Services determines the information is necessary to perform its duties under the Abused and Neglected Child Reporting Act,[1] the Child Care Act of 1969,[2] and the Children and Family Services Act.[3]

P.A. 76–1586, § 6–120, added by P.A. 88–614, § 108, eff. Sept. 7, 1994.

1 325 ILCS 5/1 et seq.

2 225 ILCS 10/1 et seq.

3 20 ILCS 505/1 et seq.

ARTICLE II. CANCELLATION, SUSPENSION, OR REVOCATION OF LICENSES AND PERMITS

5/6–201. Authority to cancel licenses and permits

§ 6–201. Authority to cancel licenses and permits.

(a) The Secretary of State is authorized to cancel any license or permit upon determining that the holder thereof:

1. was not entitled to the issuance thereof hereunder; or

2. failed to give the required or correct information in his application; or

3. failed to pay any fees, civil penalties owed to the Illinois Commerce Commission, or taxes due under this Act and upon reasonable notice and demand; or

4. committed any fraud in the making of such application; or

5. is ineligible therefor under the provisions of Section 6–103 of this Act, as amended; or

6. has refused or neglected to submit an alcohol, drug, and intoxicating compound evaluation or to submit to examination or re-examination as required under this Act; or

7. has been convicted of violating the Cannabis Control Act,[1] the Illinois Controlled Substances Act,[2] or the Use of Intoxicating Compounds Act [3] while that individual was in actual physical control of a motor vehicle. For purposes of this Section, any person placed on probation under Section 10 of the Cannabis Control Act [4] or Section 410 of the Illinois Controlled Substances Act [5] shall not be considered convicted. Any person found guilty of this offense, while in actual physical control of a motor vehicle, shall have an entry made in the court record by the judge that this offense did occur while the person was in actual physical control of a motor vehicle and order the clerk of the court to report the violation to the Secretary of State as such. After the cancellation, the Secretary of State shall not issue a new license or permit for a period of one year after the date of cancellation. However, upon application, the Secretary of State may, if satisfied that the person applying will not endanger the public safety, or welfare, issue a restricted driving permit granting the privilege of driving a motor vehicle between the person's residence and person's place of employment or within the scope of the person's employment related duties, or to allow transportation for the person or a household member of the person's family for the receipt of necessary medical care or, if the professional evaluation indicates, provide transportation for the petitioner for alcohol remedial or rehabilitative activity, or for the person to attend classes, as a student, in an accredited educational institution; if the person is able to demonstrate that no alternative means of transportation is reasonably available; provided that the Secretary's discretion shall be limited to cases where undue hardship would result from a failure to issue such restricted driving permit. In each case the Secretary of State may issue such restricted driving permit for such period as he deems appropriate, except that such permit shall expire within one year from the date of issuance. A restricted driving permit issued hereunder shall be subject to cancellation, revocation and suspension by the Secretary of State in like manner and for like cause as a driver's license issued hereunder may be cancelled, revoked or suspended; except that a conviction upon one or more offenses against laws or ordinances regulating the movement of traffic shall be deemed sufficient cause for the revocation, suspension or cancellation of a restricted driving permit. The Secretary of State may, as a condition to the issuance of a restricted driving permit, require the applicant to participate in a driver remedial or rehabilitative program; or

8. failed to submit a report as required by Section 6–116.5 of this Code.

(b) Upon such cancellation the licensee or permittee must surrender the license or permit so cancelled to the Secretary of State.

(c) Except as provided in Sections 6–206.1 and 7–702.1, the Secretary of State shall have exclusive authority to grant, issue, deny, cancel, suspend and revoke driving privileges, drivers' licenses and restricted driving permits.

P.A. 76–1586, § 6–201, eff. July 1, 1970. Amended by P.A. 77–642, § 1, eff. Aug. 4, 1971; P.A. 79–1141, § 1, eff. Jan. 1, 1976; P.A. 84–272, § 7, eff. Jan. 1, 1986; P.A. 86–1450, § 2, eff. July 1, 1991; P.A. 88–212, § 5, eff. Jan. 1, 1994; P.A. 88–415, § 10, eff. Aug. 20, 1993; P.A. 88–670, Art. 2, § 2–59, eff. Dec. 2, 1994; P.A. 89–92, § 10, eff. July 1, 1996; P.A. 89–584, § 5, eff. July 31, 1996; P.A. 90–779, § 5, eff. Jan. 1, 1999.

Formerly Ill.Rev.Stat.1991, ch. 95 ½, ¶ 6–201.

1 720 ILCS 550/1 et seq.

2 720 ILCS 570/100 et seq.

3 720 ILCS 690/0.01 et seq.

4 720 ILCS 550/10.

5 720 ILCS 570/410.

5/6–202. Non-residents and unlicensed persons—Revocation and suspension—Reporting convictions

§ 6–202. Non-residents and unlicensed persons—Revocation and suspension—Reporting convictions. (a) The privilege of driving a motor vehicle on highways of this State given to a nonresident hereunder and the privilege which an unlicensed person might have to obtain a license under this Act shall be subject to suspension or revocation by the Secretary of State in like manner and for like cause as a drivers license issued hereunder may be suspended or revoked.

(b) The Secretary of State is authorized, upon receiving a report of the conviction in this State of a nonresident driver of a motor vehicle of any offense under the laws of this State relating to operation, custody or ownership of motor vehicles, to forward a copy or abstract of such report to the motor vehicle administrator of the State wherein the person so convicted is a resident.

(c) When a nonresident's operating privilege is suspended or revoked, the Secretary of State shall forward a certified copy of the record of such action to the motor vehicle administrator in the State where such person resides.

(d) This section is subject to the provisions of the Driver License Compact.[1]

P.A. 76–1586, § 6–202, eff. July 1, 1970. Amended by P.A. 76–1752, § 1, eff. July 1, 1970.

Formerly Ill.Rev.Stat.1991, ch. 95 ½, ¶ 6–202.

1 625 ILCS 5/6–700 et seq.

5/6–203. Suspending or revoking license or privilege upon conviction in another state

§ 6–203. Suspending or revoking license or privilege upon conviction in another state. The Secretary of State is authorized to suspend or revoke the license of any resident of this State or the privilege of a nonresident to drive a motor vehicle in this State upon receiving notice of the conviction of such person in another State of an offense therein which, if committed in this State would be grounds for the suspension or revocation of the license of a driver.

This Section is subject to the provisions of the Driver License Compact.[1]

P.A. 76–1586, § 6–203, eff. July 1, 1970.

Formerly Ill.Rev.Stat.1991, ch. 95 ½, ¶ 6–203.

1 625 ILCS 5/6–700 et seq.

5/6–203.1. Suspension of driving privileges; persons arrested in another state

§ 6–203.1. (a) The Secretary of State is authorized to suspend the driving privileges of persons arrested in another state for driving under the influence of alcohol, other drug or drugs, or intoxicating compound or compounds, or any combination thereof, or a similar provision, and who has refused to submit to a chemical test or tests under the provisions of implied consent.

(b) When a driving privilege has been suspended for a refusal as provided in paragraph (a) and the person is subsequently convicted of the underlying charge, for the same incident, any period served on suspension shall be credited toward the minimum period of revocation of driving privileges imposed pursuant to Section 6–206.

P.A. 76–1586, § 6–203.1, added by P.A. 84–272, § 7, eff. Jan. 1, 1986. Amended by P.A. 84–1394, § 5, eff. Sept. 18, 1986; P.A. 90–779, § 5, eff. Jan. 1, 1999.

Formerly Ill.Rev.Stat.1991, ch. 95 ½, ¶ 6–203.1.

5/6–204. When Court to forward License and Reports

§ 6–204. When Court to forward License and Reports.

(a) For the purpose of providing to the Secretary of State the records essential to the performance of the Secretary's duties under this Code to cancel, revoke or suspend the driver's license and privilege to drive motor vehicles of certain minors adjudicated truant minors in need of supervision, addicted, or delinquent and of persons found guilty of the criminal offenses or traffic violations which this Code recognizes as evidence relating to unfitness to safely operate motor vehicles, the following duties are imposed upon public officials:

(1) Whenever any person is convicted of any offense for which this Code makes mandatory the cancellation or revocation of the driver's license or permit of such person by the Secretary of State, the judge of the court in which such conviction is had shall require the surrender to the clerk of the court of all driver's licenses or permits then held by the person so convicted, and the clerk of the court shall, within 10 days thereafter, forward the same, together with a report of such conviction, to the Secretary.

(2) Whenever any person is convicted of any offense under this Code or similar offenses under a municipal ordinance, other than regulations governing standing, parking or weights of vehicles, and excepting the following enumerated Sections of this Code: Sections 11–1406 (obstruction to driver's view or control), 11–1407 (improper opening of door into traffic), 11–1410 (coasting on downgrade), 11–1411 (following fire apparatus), 11–1419.01 (Motor Fuel Tax I.D. Card), 12–101 (driving vehicle which is in unsafe condition or improperly equipped), 12–201(a) (daytime lights on motorcycles), 12–202 (clearance, identification and side marker lamps), 12–204 (lamp or flag on projecting load), 12–205 (failure to display the safety lights required), 12–401 (restrictions as to tire equipment), 12–502 (mirrors), 12–503 (windshields must be unobstructed and equipped with wipers), 12–601 (horns and warning devices), 12–602 (mufflers, prevention of noise or smoke), 12–603 (seat safety belts), 12–702 (certain vehicles to carry flares or other warning devices), 12–703 (vehicles for oiling roads operated on highways), 12–710 (splash guards and replacements), 13–101 (safety tests), 15–101 (size, weight and load), 15–102 (width), 15–103 (height), 15–104 (name and address on second division vehicles), 15–107 (length of vehicle), 15–109.1 (cover or tarpaulin), 15–111 (weights),

15-112 (weights), 15-301 (weights), 15-316 (weights), 15-318 (weights), and also excepting the following enumerated Sections of the Chicago Municipal Code: Sections 27-245 (following fire apparatus), 27-254 (obstruction of traffic), 27-258 (driving vehicle which is in unsafe condition), 27-259 (coasting on downgrade), 27-264 (use of horns and signal devices), 27-265 (obstruction to driver's view or driver mechanism), 27-267 (dimming of headlights), 27-268 (unattended motor vehicle), 27-272 (illegal funeral procession), 27-273 (funeral procession on boulevard), 27-275 (driving freight hauling vehicles on boulevard), 27-276 (stopping and standing of buses or taxicabs), 27-277 (cruising of public passenger vehicles), 27-305 (parallel parking), 27-306 (diagonal parking), 27-307 (parking not to obstruct traffic), 27-308 (stopping, standing or parking regulated), 27-311 (parking regulations), 27-312 (parking regulations), 27-313 (parking regulations), 27-314 (parking regulations), 27-315 (parking regulations), 27-316 (parking regulations), 27-317 (parking regulations), 27-318 (parking regulations), 27-319 (parking regulations), 27-320 (parking regulations), 27-321 (parking regulations), 27-322 (parking regulations), 27-324 (loading and unloading at an angle), 27-333 (wheel and axle loads), 27-334 (load restrictions in the downtown district), 27-335 (load restrictions in residential areas), 27-338 (width of vehicles), 27-339 (height of vehicles), 27-340 (length of vehicles), 27-352 (reflectors on trailers), 27-353 (mufflers), 27-354 (display of plates), 27-355 (display of city vehicle tax sticker), 27-357 (identification of vehicles), 27-358 (projecting of loads), and also excepting the following enumerated paragraphs of Section 2-201 of the Rules and Regulations of the Illinois State Toll Highway Authority: (*l*) (driving unsafe vehicle on tollway), (m) (vehicles transporting dangerous cargo not properly indicated), it shall be the duty of the clerk of the court in which such conviction is had within 10 days thereafter to forward to the Secretary of State a report of the conviction and the court may recommend the suspension of the driver's license or permit of the person so convicted.

The reporting requirements of this subsection shall apply to all violations stated in paragraphs (1) and (2) of this subsection when the individual has been adjudicated under the Juvenile Court Act [1] or the Juvenile Court Act of 1987.[2] Such reporting requirements shall also apply to individuals adjudicated under the Juvenile Court Act or the Juvenile Court Act of 1987 who have committed a violation of Section 11-501 of this Code, or similar provision of a local ordinance, or Section 9-3 of the Criminal Code of 1961, as amended,[3] relating to the offense of reckless homicide. The reporting requirements of this subsection shall also apply to a truant minor in need of supervision, an addicted minor, or a delinquent minor and whose driver's license and privilege to drive a motor vehicle has been ordered suspended for such times as determined by the Court, but only until he or she attains 18 years of age. It shall be the duty of the clerk of the court in which adjudication is had within 10 days thereafter to forward to the Secretary of State a report of the adjudication and the court order requiring the Secretary of State to suspend the minor's driver's license and driving privilege for such time as determined by the Court, but only until he or she attains the age of 18 years. All juvenile court dispositions reported to the Secretary of State under this provision shall be processed by the Secretary of State as if the cases had been adjudicated in traffic or criminal court. However, information reported relative to the offense of reckless homicide, or Section 11-501 of this Code, or a similar provision of a local ordinance, shall be privileged and available only to the Secretary of State, courts, and police officers.

(3) Whenever an order is entered vacating the forfeiture of any bail, security or bond given to secure appearance for any offense under this Code or similar offenses under municipal ordinance, it shall be the duty of the clerk of the court in which such vacation was had or the judge of such court if such court has no clerk, within 10 days thereafter to forward to the Secretary of State a report of the vacation.

(4) A report of any disposition of court supervision for a violation of Sections 6-303, 11-401, 11-501 or a similar provision of a local ordinance, 11-503 and 11-504 shall be forwarded to the Secretary of State. A report of any disposition of court supervision for a violation of an offense defined as a serious traffic violation in this Code or a similar provision of a local ordinance committed by a person under the age of 21 years shall be forwarded to the Secretary of State.

(5) Reports of conviction under this Code and sentencing hearings under the Juvenile Court Act of 1987 in an electronic format or a computer processible medium shall be forwarded to the Secretary of State via the Supreme Court in the form and format required by the Illinois Supreme Court and established by a written agreement between the Supreme Court and the Secretary of State. In counties with a population over 300,000, instead of forwarding reports to the Supreme Court, reports of conviction under this Code and sentencing hearings under the Juvenile Court Act of 1987 in an electronic format or a computer processible medium may be forwarded to the Secretary of State by the Circuit Court Clerk in a form and format required by the Secretary of State and established by written agreement between the Circuit Court Clerk and the Secretary of State. Failure to forward the reports of conviction or sentencing hearing under the Juvenile Court Act of 1987 as required by this Section shall be deemed an omission of duty and it shall be the duty of the several State's Attorneys to enforce the requirements of this Section.

(b) Whenever a restricted driving permit is forwarded to a court, as a result of confiscation by a police officer pursuant to the authority in Section 6-113(f), it shall be the duty of the clerk, or judge, if the court has no clerk, to forward such restricted driving permit and a facsimile of the officer's citation to the Secretary of State as expeditiously as practicable.

(c) For the purposes of this Code, a forfeiture of bail or collateral deposited to secure a defendant's appearance in court when forfeiture has not been vacated, or the failure of a defendant to appear for trial after depositing his driver's license in lieu of other bail, shall be equivalent to a conviction.

(d) For the purpose of providing the Secretary of State with records necessary to properly monitor and assess driver performance and assist the courts in the proper disposition of repeat traffic law offenders, the clerk of the court shall forward to the Secretary of State, on a form prescribed by the Secretary, records of a driver's participation in a driver remedial or rehabilitative program which was required, through a court order or court supervision, in relation to the driver's arrest for a violation of Section 11-501 of this Code or a similar provision of a local ordinance. The clerk of the court shall also forward to the Secretary, either on paper or in an electronic format or a computer processible medium as required under paragraph (5) of subsection (a) of this Section, any disposition of court supervision for any traffic violation, excluding those offenses listed in paragraph (2) of subsection (a) of this Section. These reports shall be sent within 10 days after disposition, or, if the driver is referred to a driver remedial or rehabilitative program, within 10 days of the driver's referral to that program. These reports received by the Secretary of State, including those required to be forwarded under paragraph (a)(4), shall be privileged information, available only (i) to the affected driver and (ii) for use by the courts, police officers, prosecuting authorities, and the Secretary of State.

P.A. 76-1586, § 6-204, eff. July 1, 1970. Amended by P.A. 76-2154, § 1, eff. July 1, 1970; P.A. 77-38, § 1, eff. Jan. 1, 1972; P.A. 81-348, § 1, eff. Jan. 1, 1980; P.A. 81-804, § 1, eff. Sept. 19, 1979; P.A. 81-840, § 41, eff. Sept. 19, 1979; P.A. 81-1400, § 1, eff. Aug. 25, 1980; P.A. 81-1509, Art. I, § 57, eff. Sept. 26, 1980; P.A. 82-311, § 1, eff. Jan. 1, 1982; P.A. 83-208, § 1, eff. Jan. 1, 1984; P.A. 84-272, § 7, eff. Jan. 1, 1986; P.A. 84-596, § 1, eff. Jan. 1, 1986; P.A. 84-1308, Art. II, § 96, eff. Aug. 25, 1986; P.A. 84-1394, § 5, eff. Sept. 18, 1986; P.A. 84-1395, § 11, eff. Jan. 1, 1987; P.A. 85-293, Art. II, § 13, eff. Sept. 8, 1987; P.A. 85-981, Art. III, § 2, eff. Dec. 16, 1987; P.A. 85-1209, Art. II, § 2-51, eff. Aug. 30, 1988; P.A. 85-1396, § 2, eff. Sept. 2, 1988; P.A. 85-1440, Art. II, § 2-54, eff. Feb. 1, 1989; P.A. 86-1450, § 2, eff. July 1, 1991; P.A. 88-415, § 10, eff. Aug. 20, 1993; P.A. 90-369, § 5, eff. Jan. 1, 1998; P.A. 90-590, Art. 3001, § 3001-5, eff. Jan. 1, 1999; P.A. 91-357, § 231, eff. July 29, 1999; P.A. 91-716, § 5, eff. Oct. 1, 2000; P.A. 92-458, § 5, eff. Aug. 22, 2001.

Formerly Ill.Rev.Stat.1991, ch. 95 ½, ¶ 6-204.

[1] Former Ill.Rev.Stat. ch. 37, ¶ 701-1 (repealed).

[2] 705 ILCS 405/1-1 et seq.

[3] 720 ILCS 5/9-3.

5/6-205. Mandatory revocation of license or permit; Hardship cases

§ 6-205. Mandatory revocation of license or permit; Hardship cases.

(a) Except as provided in this Section, the Secretary of State shall immediately revoke the license, permit, or driving privileges of any driver upon receiving a report of the driver's conviction of any of the following offenses:

1. Reckless homicide resulting from the operation of a motor vehicle;

2. Violation of Section 11-501 of this Code or a similar provision of a local ordinance relating to the offense of operating or being in physical control of a vehicle while under the influence of alcohol, other drug or drugs, intoxicating compound or compounds, or any combination thereof;

3. Any felony under the laws of any State or the federal government in the commission of which a motor vehicle was used;

4. Violation of Section 11-401 of this Code relating to the offense of leaving the scene of a traffic accident involving death or personal injury;

5. Perjury or the making of a false affidavit or statement under oath to the Secretary of State under this Code or under any other law relating to the ownership or operation of motor vehicles;

6. Conviction upon 3 charges of violation of Section 11-503 of this Code relating to the offense of reckless driving committed within a period of 12 months;

7. Conviction of any offense defined in Section 4-102 of this Code;

8. Violation of Section 11-504 of this Code relating to the offense of drag racing;

9. Violation of Chapters 8 and 9 of this Code; [1]

10. Violation of Section 12-5 of the Criminal Code of 1961 [2] arising from the use of a motor vehicle;

11. Violation of Section 11-204.1 of this Code relating to aggravated fleeing or attempting to elude a police officer;

12. Violation of paragraph (1) of subsection (b) of Section 6-507, or a similar law of any other state, relating to the unlawful operation of a commercial motor vehicle;

13. Violation of paragraph (a) of Section 11-502 of this Code or a similar provision of a local ordinance if the driver has been previously convicted of a violation of that Section or a similar provision of a local ordinance and the driver was less than 21 years of age at the time of the offense.

(b) The Secretary of State shall also immediately revoke the license or permit of any driver in the following situations:

1. Of any minor upon receiving the notice provided for in Section 5-901 of the Juvenile Court Act of 1987 [3] that the minor has been adjudicated under that Act [4] as having committed an offense relating to motor vehicles prescribed in Section 4-103 of this Code;

2. Of any person when any other law of this State requires either the revocation or suspension of a license or permit.

(c) Whenever a person is convicted of any of the offenses enumerated in this Section, the court may recommend and the Secretary of State in his discretion, without regard to whether the recommendation is made by the court may, upon application, issue to the person a restricted driving permit granting the privilege of driving a motor vehicle between the petitioner's residence and petitioner's place of employment or within the scope of the petitioner's employment related duties, or to allow transportation for the petitioner or a household member of the petitioner's family for the receipt of necessary medical care or, if the professional evaluation indicates, provide transportation for the petitioner for alcohol remedial or rehabilitative activity, or for the petitioner to attend classes, as a student, in an accredited educational institution; if the petitioner is able to demonstrate that no alternative means of transportation is reasonably available and the petitioner will not endanger the public safety or welfare; provided that the Secretary's discretion shall be limited to cases where undue hardship would result from a failure to issue the restricted driving permit.

If a person's license or permit has been revoked or suspended due to 2 or more convictions of violating Section 11-501 of this Code or a similar provision of a local ordinance or a similar out-of-state offense, arising out of separate occurrences, that person, if issued a restricted driving permit, may not operate a vehicle unless it has been equipped with an ignition interlock device as defined in Section 1-129.1.

If a person's license or permit has been revoked or suspended 2 or more times within a 10 year period due to a single conviction of violating Section 11-501 of this Code or a similar provision of a local ordinance or a similar out-of-state offense, and a statutory summary suspension under Section 11-501.1, or 2 or more statutory summary suspensions, or combination of 2 offenses, or of an offense and a statutory summary suspension, arising out of separate occurrences, that person, if issued a restricted driving permit, may not operate a vehicle unless it has been equipped with an ignition interlock device as defined in Section 1-129.1. The person must pay to the Secretary of State DUI Administration Fund an amount not to exceed $20 per month. The Secretary shall establish by rule the amount and the procedures, terms, and conditions relating to these fees. If the restricted driving permit was issued for employment purposes, then this provision does not apply to the operation of an occupational vehicle owned or leased by that person's employer. In each case the Secretary of State may issue a restricted driving permit for a period he deems appropriate, except that the permit shall expire within one year from the date of issuance. The Secretary may not, however, issue a restricted driving permit to any person whose current revocation is the result of a second or subsequent conviction for a violation of Section 11-501 of this Code or a similar provision of a local ordinance relating to the offense of operating or being in physical control of a motor vehicle while under the influence of alcohol, other drug or drugs, intoxicating compound or compounds, or any similar out-of-state offense, or any combination thereof, until the expiration of at least one year from the date of the revocation. A restricted driving permit issued under this Section shall be subject to cancellation, revocation, and suspension by the Secretary of State in like manner and for like cause as a driver's license issued under this Code may be cancelled, revoked, or suspended; except that a conviction upon one or more offenses against laws or ordinances regulating the movement of traffic shall be deemed sufficient cause for the revocation, suspension, or cancellation of a restricted driving permit. The Secretary of State may, as a condition to the issuance of a restricted driving permit, require the applicant to participate in a designated driver remedial or rehabilitative program. The Secretary of State is authorized to cancel a restricted driving permit if the permit holder does not successfully complete the program. However, if an individual's driving privileges have been revoked in accordance with paragraph 13 of subsection (a) of this Section, no restricted driving permit shall be issued until the individual has served 6 months of the revocation period.

(d) Whenever a person under the age of 21 is convicted under Section 11-501 of this Code or a similar provision of a local ordinance, the Secretary of State shall revoke the driving privileges of that person. One year after the date of revocation, and upon application, the Secretary of State may, if satisfied that the person applying will not endanger the public safety or welfare, issue a restricted driving permit granting the privilege of driving a motor vehicle only between the hours of 5 a.m. and 9 p.m. or as otherwise provided by this Section for a period of one year. After this one year period, and upon reapplication for a license as provided in Section 6-106, upon payment of the appropriate reinstatement fee provided under paragraph (b) of Section 6-118, the Secretary of State, in his discretion, may issue the applicant a license, or extend the restricted driving permit as many times as the Secretary of State deems appropriate, by additional periods of not more than 12 months each, until the applicant attains 21 years of age.

If a person's license or permit has been revoked or suspended due to 2 or more convictions of violating Section 11-501 of this Code or a similar provision of a local ordinance or a similar out-of-state offense, arising out of separate occurrences, that person, if issued a restricted driving permit, may not operate a vehicle unless it has been equipped with an ignition interlock device as defined in Section 1-129.1.

If a person's license or permit has been revoked or suspended 2 or more times within a 10 year period due to a single conviction of violating Section 11-501 of this Code or a similar provision of a local ordinance or a similar out-of-state offense, and a statutory summary suspension under Section 11-501.1, or 2 or more statutory summary suspensions, or combination of 2 offenses, or of an offense and a statutory summary suspension, arising out of separate occurrences, that person, if issued a restricted driving permit, may not operate a vehicle unless it has been equipped with an ignition interlock device as defined in Section 1-129.1. The person must pay to the Secretary of State DUI Administration Fund an amount not to exceed $20 per month. The Secretary shall establish by rule the amount and the procedures, terms, and conditions relating to these fees. If the restricted driving permit was issued for employment purposes, then this provision does not apply to the operation of an occupational vehicle owned or leased by that person's employer. A restricted driving permit issued under this Section shall be subject to cancellation, revocation, and suspension by the Secretary of State in like manner and for like cause as a driver's license issued under this Code may be cancelled, revoked, or suspended; except that a conviction upon one or more offenses against laws or ordinances regulating the movement of traffic shall be deemed sufficient cause for the revocation, suspension, or cancellation of a restricted driving permit. The revocation periods contained in this subparagraph shall apply to similar out-of-state convictions.

(e) This Section is subject to the provisions of the Driver License Compact.[5]

(f) Any revocation imposed upon any person under subsections 2 and 3 of paragraph (b) that is in effect on December 31, 1988 shall be converted to a suspension for a like period of time.

(g) The Secretary of State shall not issue a restricted driving permit to a person under the age of 16 years whose driving privileges have been revoked under any provisions of this Code.

(h) The Secretary of State shall require the use of ignition interlock devices on all vehicles owned by an individual who has been convicted of a second or subsequent offense under Section 11-501 of this Code or a similar provision of a local ordinance. The Secretary shall establish by rule and regulation the procedures for certification and use of the interlock system.

(i) The Secretary of State may not issue a restricted driving permit for a period of one year after a second or subsequent revocation of driving privileges under clause (a)(2) of this Section; however, one year after the date of a second or subsequent revocation of driving privileges under clause (a)(2) of this Section, the Secretary of State may, upon application, issue a restricted driving permit under the terms and conditions of subsection (c).

P.A. 76-1586, § 6-205, eff. July 1, 1970. Amended by P.A. 76-2155, § 1, eff. July 1, 1970; P.A. 78-663, § 1, eff. Jan. 1, 1974; P.A. 81-1400, § 1, eff. Aug. 25, 1980; P.A. 82-311, § 1, eff. Jan. 1, 1982; P.A. 83-1067, § 19, eff. July 1, 1984; P.A. 83-1326, § 1, eff. July 1, 1985; P.A. 84-1381, § 2, eff. Sept. 12, 1986; P.A. 84-1394, § 5, eff. Sept. 18, 1986; P.A. 84-1450, § 7, eff. July 1, 1987; P.A. 85-293, Art. II, § 13, eff. Sept. 8, 1987; P.A. 85-876, § 1, eff. Nov. 6, 1987; P.A. 85-951, § 1, eff. July 1, 1988; P.A. 85-1209, Art. II, § 2-51, eff. Aug. 30, 1988; P.A. 85-1259, § 3, eff. Jan. 1, 1989; P.A. 85-1440, Art. II, § 2-24, eff. Feb. 1, 1989; P.A. 86-845, § 1, eff. April 1, 1990; P.A. 86-929, § 2, eff. Sept. 21, 1989; P.A. 86-1028, Art. II, § 2-44, eff. Feb. 5, 1990; P.A. 87-1114, § 1, eff. Sept. 15, 1992; P.A. 88-209, § 5, eff. Jan. 1, 1994; P.A. 89-156, § 5, eff. Jan. 1, 1996; P.A. 89-245, § 5, eff. Jan. 1, 1996; P.A. 89-626, Art. 2, § 2-66, eff. Aug. 9, 1996; P.A. 90-369, § 5, eff. Jan. 1, 1998; P.A. 90-590, Art. 2001, § 2001-7, eff. Jan. 1, 1999; P.A. 90-611, § 5, eff. Jan. 1, 1999; P.A. 90-779, § 5, eff. Jan. 1, 1999; P.A. 91-357, § 231, eff. July 29, 1999; P.A. 92-248, § 5, eff. Aug. 3, 2001; P.A. 92-418, § 10, eff. Aug. 17, 2001; P.A. 92-651, § 77, eff. July 11, 2002; P.A. 92-834, § 5, eff. Aug. 22, 2002.

Formerly Ill.Rev.Stat.1991, ch. 95 ½, ¶ 6-205.

1 625 ILCS 5/8-101 et seq.

2 720 ILCS 5/12-5.

3 705 ILCS 405/5-901.

4 705 ILCS 405/1-1 et seq.

5 625 ILCS 5/6-700 et seq.

P.A. 92-651, the First 2002 General Revisory Act, amended various Acts to delete obsolete text, to correct patent and technical errors, to revise cross references, to resolve multiple actions in the 91st and 92nd General Assemblies and to make certain technical corrections in P.A. 91-937 through P.A. 92-520.

P.A. 92-834 incorporated the amendments by P.A. 92-248 and P.A. 92-418.

5/6-205.1. § 6-205.1. Repealed by P.A. 92-458, § 15, eff. Aug. 22, 2001

5/6-206. Discretionary authority to suspend or revoke license or permit; Right to a hearing.

Text of section as amended by P.A. 92-651 and P.A. 92-804, effective January 1, 2003

§ 6-206. Discretionary authority to suspend or revoke license or permit; Right to a hearing.

(a) The Secretary of State is authorized to suspend or revoke the driving privileges of any person without preliminary hearing upon a showing of the person's records or other sufficient evidence that the person:

1. Has committed an offense for which mandatory revocation of a driver's license or permit is required upon conviction;

2. Has been convicted of not less than 3 offenses against traffic regulations governing the movement of vehicles committed within any 12 month period. No revocation or suspension shall be entered more than 6 months after the date of last conviction;

3. Has been repeatedly involved as a driver in motor vehicle collisions or has been repeatedly convicted of offenses against laws and ordinances regulating the movement of traffic, to a degree that indicates lack of ability to exercise ordinary and reasonable care in the safe operation of a motor vehicle or disrespect for the traffic laws and the safety of other persons upon the highway;

4. Has by the unlawful operation of a motor vehicle caused or contributed to an accident resulting in death or injury requiring immediate professional treatment in a medical facility or doctor's office to any person, except that any suspension or revocation imposed by the Secretary of State under the provisions of this subsection shall start no later than 6 months after being convicted of violating a law or ordinance regulating the movement of traffic, which violation is related to the accident, or shall start not more than one year after the date of the accident, whichever date occurs later;

5. Has permitted an unlawful or fraudulent use of a driver's license, identification card, or permit;

6. Has been lawfully convicted of an offense or offenses in another state, including the authorization contained in Section 6-203.1, which if committed within this State would be grounds for suspension or revocation;

7. Has refused or failed to submit to an examination provided for by Section 6-207 or has failed to pass the examination;

8. Is ineligible for a driver's license or permit under the provisions of Section 6-103;

9. Has made a false statement or knowingly concealed a material fact or has used false information or identification in any application for a license, identification card, or permit;

10. Has possessed, displayed, or attempted to fraudulently use any license, identification card, or permit not issued to the person;

11. Has operated a motor vehicle upon a highway of this State when the person's driving privilege or privilege to obtain a driver's license or permit was revoked or suspended unless the operation was authorized by a judicial driving permit, probationary license to drive, or a restricted driving permit issued under this Code;

12. Has submitted to any portion of the application process for another person or has obtained the services of another person to submit to any portion of the application process for the purpose of obtaining a license, identification card, or permit for some other person;

13. Has operated a motor vehicle upon a highway of this State when the person's driver's license or permit was invalid under the provisions of Sections 6-107.1 and 6-110;

14. Has committed a violation of Section 6-301, 6-301.1, or 6-301.2 of this Act, or Section 14, 14A, or 14B of the Illinois Identification Card Act; [1]

15. Has been convicted of violating Section 21-2 of the Criminal Code of 1961 [2] relating to criminal trespass to vehicles in which case, the suspension shall be for one year;

16. Has been convicted of violating Section 11-204 of this Code relating to fleeing from a police officer;

17. Has refused to submit to a test, or tests, as required under Section 11-501.1 of this Code and the person has not sought a hearing as provided for in Section 11-501.1;

18. Has, since issuance of a driver's license or permit, been adjudged to be afflicted with or suffering from any mental disability or disease;

19. Has committed a violation of paragraph (a) or (b) of Section 6-101 relating to driving without a driver's license;

20. Has been convicted of violating Section 6-104 relating to classification of driver's license;

21. Has been convicted of violating Section 11-402 of this Code relating to leaving the scene of an accident resulting in damage to a vehicle in excess of $1,000, in which case the suspension shall be for one year;

22. Has used a motor vehicle in violating paragraph (3), (4), (7), or (9) of subsection (a) of Section 24-1 of the Criminal Code of 1961 [3] relating to unlawful use of weapons, in which case the suspension shall be for one year;

23. Has, as a driver, been convicted of committing a violation of paragraph (a) of Section 11-502 of this Code for a second or subsequent time within one year of a similar violation;

24. Has been convicted by a court-martial or punished by non-judicial punishment by military authorities of the

United States at a military installation in Illinois of or for a traffic related offense that is the same as or similar to an offense specified under Section 6–205 or 6–206 of this Code;

25. Has permitted any form of identification to be used by another in the application process in order to obtain or attempt to obtain a license, identification card, or permit;

26. Has altered or attempted to alter a license or has possessed an altered license, identification card, or permit;

27. Has violated Section 6–16 of the Liquor Control Act of 1934; [4]

28. Has been convicted of the illegal possession, while operating or in actual physical control, as a driver, of a motor vehicle, of any controlled substance prohibited under the Illinois Controlled Substances Act [5] or any cannabis prohibited under the provisions of the Cannabis Control Act, [6] in which case the person's driving privileges shall be suspended for one year, and any driver who is convicted of a second or subsequent offense, within 5 years of a previous conviction, for the illegal possession, while operating or in actual physical control, as a driver, of a motor vehicle, of any controlled substance prohibited under the provisions of the Illinois Controlled Substances Act or any cannabis prohibited under the Cannabis Control Act shall be suspended for 5 years. Any defendant found guilty of this offense while operating a motor vehicle, shall have an entry made in the court record by the presiding judge that this offense did occur while the defendant was operating a motor vehicle and order the clerk of the court to report the violation to the Secretary of State;

29. Has been convicted of the following offenses that were committed while the person was operating or in actual physical control, as a driver, of a motor vehicle: criminal sexual assault, predatory criminal sexual assault of a child, aggravated criminal sexual assault, criminal sexual abuse, aggravated criminal sexual abuse, juvenile pimping, soliciting for a juvenile prostitute and the manufacture, sale or delivery of controlled substances or instruments used for illegal drug use or abuse in which case the driver's driving privileges shall be suspended for one year;

30. Has been convicted a second or subsequent time for any combination of the offenses named in paragraph 29 of this subsection, in which case the person's driving privileges shall be suspended for 5 years;

31. Has refused to submit to a test as required by Section 11–501.6 or has submitted to a test resulting in an alcohol concentration of 0.08 or more or any amount of a drug, substance, or compound resulting from the unlawful use or consumption of cannabis as listed in the Cannabis Control Act, a controlled substance as listed in the Illinois Controlled Substances Act, or an intoxicating compound as listed in the Use of Intoxicating Compounds Act, [7] in which case the penalty shall be as prescribed in Section 6–208.1;

32. Has been convicted of Section 24–1.2 of the Criminal Code of 1961 [8] relating to the aggravated discharge of a firearm if the offender was located in a motor vehicle at the time the firearm was discharged, in which case the suspension shall be for 3 years;

33. Has as a driver, who was less than 21 years of age on the date of the offense, been convicted a first time of a violation of paragraph (a) of Section 11–502 of this Code or a similar provision of a local ordinance;

34. Has committed a violation of Section 11–1301.5 of this Code;

35. Has committed a violation of Section 11–1301.6 of this Code;

36. Is under the age of 21 years at the time of arrest and has been convicted of not less than 2 offenses against traffic regulations governing the movement of vehicles committed within any 24 month period. No revocation or suspension shall be entered more than 6 months after the date of last conviction;

37. Has committed a violation of subsection (c) of Section 11–907 of this Code; or

38. Has been convicted of a violation of Section 6–20 of the Liquor Control Act of 1934 or a similar provision of a local ordinance.

For purposes of paragraphs 5, 9, 10, 12, 14, 19, 25, 26, and 27 of this subsection, license means any driver's license, any traffic ticket issued when the person's driver's license is deposited in lieu of bail, a suspension notice issued by the Secretary of State, a duplicate or corrected driver's license, a probationary driver's license or a temporary driver's license.

(b) If any conviction forming the basis of a suspension or revocation authorized under this Section is appealed, the Secretary of State may rescind or withhold the entry of the order of suspension or revocation, as the case may be, provided that a certified copy of a stay order of a court is filed with the Secretary of State. If the conviction is affirmed on appeal, the date of the conviction shall relate back to the time the original judgment of conviction was entered and the 6 month limitation prescribed shall not apply.

(c) 1. Upon suspending or revoking the driver's license or permit of any person as authorized in this Section, the Secretary of State shall immediately notify the person in writing of the revocation or suspension. The notice to be deposited in the United States mail, postage prepaid, to the last known address of the person.

2. If the Secretary of State suspends the driver's license of a person under subsection 2 of paragraph (a) of this Section, a person's privilege to operate a vehicle as an occupation shall not be suspended, provided an affidavit is properly completed, the appropriate fee received, and a permit issued prior to the effective date of the suspension, unless 5 offenses were committed, at least 2 of which occurred while operating a commercial vehicle in connection with the driver's regular occupation. All other driving privileges shall be suspended by the Secretary of State. Any driver prior to operating a vehicle for occupational purposes only must submit the affidavit on forms to be provided by the Secretary of State setting forth the facts of the person's occupation. The affidavit shall also state the number of offenses committed while operating a vehicle in connection with the driver's regular occupation. The affidavit shall be accompanied by the driver's license. Upon receipt of a properly completed affidavit, the Secretary of State shall issue the driver a permit to operate a vehicle in connection with the driver's regular occupation only. Unless the permit is issued by the Secretary of State prior to the date of suspension, the privilege to drive any motor vehicle shall be suspended as set forth in the notice that was mailed under this Section. If an affidavit is received subsequent to the effective date of this suspension, a permit may be issued for the remainder of the suspension period.

The provisions of this subparagraph shall not apply to any driver required to obtain a commercial driver's license under Section 6–507 during the period of a disqualification of commercial driving privileges under Section 6–514.

Any person who falsely states any fact in the affidavit required herein shall be guilty of perjury under Section 6–

302 and upon conviction thereof shall have all driving privileges revoked without further rights.

3. At the conclusion of a hearing under Section 2-118 of this Code, the Secretary of State shall either rescind or continue an order of revocation or shall substitute an order of suspension; or, good cause appearing therefor, rescind, continue, change, or extend the order of suspension. If the Secretary of State does not rescind the order, the Secretary may upon application, to relieve undue hardship, issue a restricted driving permit granting the privilege of driving a motor vehicle between the petitioner's residence and petitioner's place of employment or within the scope of his employment related duties, or to allow transportation for the petitioner, or a household member of the petitioner's family, to receive necessary medical care and if the professional evaluation indicates, provide transportation for alcohol remedial or rehabilitative activity, or for the petitioner to attend classes, as a student, in an accredited educational institution; if the petitioner is able to demonstrate that no alternative means of transportation is reasonably available and the petitioner will not endanger the public safety or welfare.

If a person's license or permit has been revoked or suspended due to 2 or more convictions of violating Section 11-501 of this Code or a similar provision of a local ordinance or a similar out-of-state offense, arising out of separate occurrences, that person, if issued a restricted driving permit, may not operate a vehicle unless it has been equipped with an ignition interlock device as defined in Section 1-129.1.

If a person's license or permit has been revoked or suspended 2 or more times within a 10 year period due to a single conviction of violating Section 11-501 of this Code or a similar provision of a local ordinance or a similar out-of-state offense, and a statutory summary suspension under Section 11-501.1, or 2 or more statutory summary suspensions, or combination of 2 offenses, or of an offense and a statutory summary suspension, arising out of separate occurrences, that person, if issued a restricted driving permit, may not operate a vehicle unless it has been equipped with an ignition interlock device as defined in Section 1-129.1. The person must pay to the Secretary of State DUI Administration Fund an amount not to exceed $20 per month. The Secretary shall establish by rule the amount and the procedures, terms, and conditions relating to these fees. If the restricted driving permit was issued for employment purposes, then this provision does not apply to the operation of an occupational vehicle owned or leased by that person's employer. In each case the Secretary may issue a restricted driving permit for a period deemed appropriate, except that all permits shall expire within one year from the date of issuance. The Secretary may not, however, issue a restricted driving permit to any person whose current revocation is the result of a second or subsequent conviction for a violation of Section 11-501 of this Code or a similar provision of a local ordinance relating to the offense of operating or being in physical control of a motor vehicle while under the influence of alcohol, other drug or drugs, intoxicating compound or compounds, or any similar out-of-state offense, or any combination of those offenses, until the expiration of at least one year from the date of the revocation. A restricted driving permit issued under this Section shall be subject to cancellation, revocation, and suspension by the Secretary of State in like manner and for like cause as a driver's license issued under this Code may be cancelled, revoked, or suspended; except that a conviction upon one or more offenses against laws or ordinances regulating the movement of traffic shall be deemed sufficient cause for the revocation, suspension, or cancellation of a restricted driving permit. The Secretary of State may, as a condition to the issuance of a restricted driving permit, require the applicant to participate in a designated driver remedial or rehabilitative program. The Secretary of State is authorized to cancel a restricted driving permit if the permit holder does not successfully complete the program.

(c-5) The Secretary of State may, as a condition of the reissuance of a driver's license or permit to an applicant whose driver's license or permit has been suspended before he or she reached the age of 18 years pursuant to any of the provisions of this Section, require the applicant to participate in a driver remedial education course and be retested under Section 6-109 of this Code.

(d) This Section is subject to the provisions of the Drivers License Compact.

(e) The Secretary of State shall not issue a restricted driving permit to a person under the age of 16 years whose driving privileges have been suspended or revoked under any provisions of this Code.

P.A. 76-1586, § 6-206, eff. July 1, 1970. Amended by P.A. 76-2156, § 1, eff. July 1, 1970; P.A. 77-2739, § 1, eff. Oct. 1, 1972; P.A. 78-663, § 1, eff. Jan. 1, 1974; P.A. 79-1141, § 1, eff. Jan. 1, 1976; P.A. 81-1400, § 1, eff. Aug. 25, 1980; P.A. 82-141, § 1, eff. Jan. 1, 1982; P.A. 82-311, § 1, eff. Jan. 1, 1982; P.A. 82-783, Art. III, § 37, eff. July 13, 1982; P.A. 83-466, § 1, eff. Sept. 17, 1983; P.A. 83-905, § 1, eff. Jan. 1, 1984; P.A. 83-1362, Art. II, § 99, eff. Sept. 11, 1984; P.A. 84-112, § 1, eff. July 25, 1985; P.A. 84-272, § 7, eff. Jan. 1, 1986; P.A. 84-300, § 1, eff. Sept. 13, 1985; P.A. 84-551, § 50, eff. Sept. 18, 1985; P.A. 84-772, § 1, eff. Jan. 1, 1986; P.A. 84-1308, Art. II, § 96, eff. Aug. 25, 1986; P.A. 84-1394, § 5, eff. Sept. 18, 1986; P.A. 85-813, § 1, eff. Jan. 1, 1988; P.A. 85-1259, § 3, eff. Jan. 1, 1989; P.A. 86-879, § 1, eff. Jan. 1, 1990; P.A. 86-929, § 2, eff. Sept. 21, 1989; P.A. 86-947, § 2, eff. Jan. 1, 1991; P.A. 86-1019, § 7, eff. July 1, 1990; P.A. 86-1475, Art. 2, § 2-25, eff. Jan. 10, 1991; P.A. 87-233, § 1, eff. Jan. 1, 1992; P.A. 87-929, § 1, eff. Jan. 1, 1993; P.A. 87-1114, § 1, eff. Sept. 15, 1992; P.A. 88-45, Art. II, § 2-54, eff. July 6, 1993; P.A. 88-209, § 5, eff. Jan. 1, 1994; P.A. 88-211, § 5, eff. Jan. 1, 1994; P.A. 88-670, Art. 2, § 2-59, eff. Dec. 2, 1994; P.A. 89-283, § 10, eff. Jan. 1, 1996; P.A. 89-428, Art. 2, § 250, eff. Dec. 13, 1995; P.A. 89-462, Art. 2, § 250, eff. May 29, 1996; P.A. 90-43, § 5, eff. July 2, 1997; P.A. 90-106, § 5, eff. Jan. 1, 1998; P.A. 90-369, § 5, eff. Jan. 1, 1998; P.A. 90-655, § 153, eff. July 30, 1998; P.A. 92-283, § 5, eff. Jan. 1, 2002; P.A. 92-418, § 10, eff. Aug. 17, 2001; P.A. 92-458, § 5, eff. Aug. 22, 2001; P.A. 92-651, § 77, eff. July 11, 2002; P.A. 92-804, § 10, eff. Jan. 1, 2003.

Formerly Ill.Rev.Stat.1991, ch. 95 ½, ¶ 6-206.

1 15 ILSC 335/14, 335/14A, or 335/14B.

2 720 ILSC 5/21-2.

3 720 ILSC 5/24-1.

4 235 ILSC 5/6-16.

5 720 ILSC 570/100 et seq.

6 720 ILSC 550/1 et seq.

7 720 ILSC 690/0.01 et seq.

8 720 ILSC 5/24-1.2.

For text of section as amended by P.A. 92-651 and P.A. 92-814, effective January 1, 2003, see 625 ILCS 5/6-206, post

For final legislative action, see note following 625 ILCS 5/6-206, post

P.A. 89-428 was held by the Illinois Supreme Court to be in violation of the single subject requirement of subsection (d) of Section 8 of Article IV of the Illinois Constitution in the case of Johnson v. Edgar, 1997, 176 Ill.2d 499, 680 N.E.2d 1372, 224 Ill.Dec. 1. Public Act 89-462 reenacted the amendment of this text by P.A. 89-428.

P.A. 92-283, in subsec. (a), inserted par. 37 relating to violations of Section 11-907(c); and made nonsubstantive changes.

P.A. 92-418, in subsec. (c)3, inserted the second paragraph; and in the third paragraph, inserted the first four and the sixth sentences.

P.A. 92-458, in subsec. (a)31, inserted "or an intoxicating compound as listed in the use of Intoxicating Compounds Act," and made nonsubstantive changes; in subsec. (c-5), deleted "under the age of 18 years" preceding "whose driver's license" and inserted "before he or she reached the age of 18 years".

P.A. 92-651, the First 2002 General Revisory Act, amended various Acts to delete obsolete text, to correct patent and technical errors, to revise cross references, to resolve multiple actions in the 91st and 92nd General Assemblies and to make certain technical corrections in P.A. 91-937 through P.A. 92-520.

P.A. 92-804 incorporated the amendments by P.A. 92-283, 92-418, and 92-458.

See 5 ILCS 70/6 as to the effect of (1) more than one amendment of a section at the same session of the General Assembly or (2) two or more acts relating to the same subject matter enacted by the same General Assembly.

5/6-206. Discretionary authority to suspend or revoke license or permit; Right to a hearing.

Text of section as amended by P.A. 92-651 and P.A. 92-814, effective January 1, 2003

§ 6-206. Discretionary authority to suspend or revoke license or permit; Right to a hearing.

(a) The Secretary of State is authorized to suspend or revoke the driving privileges of any person without preliminary hearing upon a showing of the person's records or other sufficient evidence that the person:

1. Has committed an offense for which mandatory revocation of a driver's license or permit is required upon conviction;

2. Has been convicted of not less than 3 offenses against traffic regulations governing the movement of vehicles committed within any 12 month period. No revocation or suspension shall be entered more than 6 months after the date of last conviction;

3. Has been repeatedly involved as a driver in motor vehicle collisions or has been repeatedly convicted of offenses against laws and ordinances regulating the movement of traffic, to a degree that indicates lack of ability to exercise ordinary and reasonable care in the safe operation of a motor vehicle or disrespect for the traffic laws and the safety of other persons upon the highway;

4. Has by the unlawful operation of a motor vehicle caused or contributed to an accident resulting in death or injury requiring immediate professional treatment in a medical facility or doctor's office to any person, except that any suspension or revocation imposed by the Secretary of State under the provisions of this subsection shall start no later than 6 months after being convicted of violating a law or ordinance regulating the movement of traffic, which violation is related to the accident, or shall start not more than one year after the date of the accident, whichever date occurs later;

5. Has permitted an unlawful or fraudulent use of a driver's license, identification card, or permit;

6. Has been lawfully convicted of an offense or offenses in another state, including the authorization contained in Section 6-203.1, which if committed within this State would be grounds for suspension or revocation;

7. Has refused or failed to submit to an examination provided for by Section 6-207 or has failed to pass the examination;

8. Is ineligible for a driver's license or permit under the provisions of Section 6-103;

9. Has made a false statement or knowingly concealed a material fact or has used false information or identification in any application for a license, identification card, or permit;

10. Has possessed, displayed, or attempted to fraudulently use any license, identification card, or permit not issued to the person;

11. Has operated a motor vehicle upon a highway of this State when the person's driving privilege or privilege to obtain a driver's license or permit was revoked or suspended unless the operation was authorized by a judicial driving permit, probationary license to drive, or a restricted driving permit issued under this Code;

12. Has submitted to any portion of the application process for another person or has obtained the services of another person to submit to any portion of the application process for the purpose of obtaining a license, identification card, or permit for some other person;

13. Has operated a motor vehicle upon a highway of this State when the person's driver's license or permit was invalid under the provisions of Sections 6-107.1 and 6-110;

14. Has committed a violation of Section 6-301, 6-301.1, or 6-301.2 of this Act, or Section 14, 14A, or 14B of the Illinois Identification Card Act; [1]

15. Has been convicted of violating Section 21-2 of the Criminal Code of 1961 [2] relating to criminal trespass to vehicles in which case, the suspension shall be for one year;

16. Has been convicted of violating Section 11-204 of this Code relating to fleeing from a police officer;

17. Has refused to submit to a test, or tests, as required under Section 11-501.1 of this Code and the person has not sought a hearing as provided for in Section 11-501.1;

18. Has, since issuance of a driver's license or permit, been adjudged to be afflicted with or suffering from any mental disability or disease;

19. Has committed a violation of paragraph (a) or (b) of Section 6-101 relating to driving without a driver's license;

20. Has been convicted of violating Section 6-104 relating to classification of driver's license;

21. Has been convicted of violating Section 11-402 of this Code relating to leaving the scene of an accident resulting in damage to a vehicle in excess of $1,000, in which case the suspension shall be for one year;

22. Has used a motor vehicle in violating paragraph (3), (4), (7), or (9) of subsection (a) of Section 24-1 of the Criminal Code of 1961 [3] relating to unlawful use of weapons, in which case the suspension shall be for one year;

23. Has, as a driver, been convicted of committing a violation of paragraph (a) of Section 11-502 of this Code for a second or subsequent time within one year of a similar violation;

24. Has been convicted by a court-martial or punished by non-judicial punishment by military authorities of the

United States at a military installation in Illinois of or for a traffic related offense that is the same as or similar to an offense specified under Section 6–205 or 6–206 of this Code;

25. Has permitted any form of identification to be used by another in the application process in order to obtain or attempt to obtain a license, identification card, or permit;

26. Has altered or attempted to alter a license or has possessed an altered license, identification card, or permit;

27. Has violated Section 6–16 of the Liquor Control Act of 1934; [4]

28. Has been convicted of the illegal possession, while operating or in actual physical control, as a driver, of a motor vehicle, of any controlled substance prohibited under the Illinois Controlled Substances Act [5] or any cannabis prohibited under the provisions of the Cannabis Control Act, [6] in which case the person's driving privileges shall be suspended for one year, and any driver who is convicted of a second or subsequent offense, within 5 years of a previous conviction, for the illegal possession, while operating or in actual physical control, as a driver, of a motor vehicle, of any controlled substance prohibited under the provisions of the Illinois Controlled Substances Act or any cannabis prohibited under the Cannabis Control Act shall be suspended for 5 years. Any defendant found guilty of this offense while operating a motor vehicle, shall have an entry made in the court record by the presiding judge that this offense did occur while the defendant was operating a motor vehicle and order the clerk of the court to report the violation to the Secretary of State;

29. Has been convicted of the following offenses that were committed while the person was operating or in actual physical control, as a driver, of a motor vehicle: criminal sexual assault, predatory criminal sexual assault of a child, aggravated criminal sexual assault, criminal sexual abuse, aggravated criminal sexual abuse, juvenile pimping, soliciting for a juvenile prostitute and the manufacture, sale or delivery of controlled substances or instruments used for illegal drug use or abuse in which case the driver's driving privileges shall be suspended for one year;

30. Has been convicted a second or subsequent time for any combination of the offenses named in paragraph 29 of this subsection, in which case the person's driving privileges shall be suspended for 5 years;

31. Has refused to submit to a test as required by Section 11–501.6 or has submitted to a test resulting in an alcohol concentration of 0.08 or more or any amount of a drug, substance, or compound resulting from the unlawful use or consumption of cannabis as listed in the Cannabis Control Act, a controlled substance as listed in the Illinois Controlled Substances Act, or an intoxicating compound as listed in the Use of Intoxicating Compounds Act, [7] in which case the penalty shall be as prescribed in Section 6–208.1;

32. Has been convicted of Section 24–1.2 of the Criminal Code of 1961 [8] relating to the aggravated discharge of a firearm if the offender was located in a motor vehicle at the time the firearm was discharged, in which case the suspension shall be for 3 years;

33. Has as a driver, who was less than 21 years of age on the date of the offense, been convicted a first time of a violation of paragraph (a) of Section 11–502 of this Code or a similar provision of a local ordinance;

34. Has committed a violation of Section 11–1301.5 of this Code;

35. Has committed a violation of Section 11–1301.6 of this Code;

36. Is under the age of 21 years at the time of arrest and has been convicted of not less than 2 offenses against traffic regulations governing the movement of vehicles committed within any 24 month period. No revocation or suspension shall be entered more than 6 months after the date of last conviction;

37. Has committed a violation of subsection (c) of Section 11–907 of this Code; or

38. Has committed a second or subsequent violation of Section 11–1201 of this Code.

For purposes of paragraphs 5, 9, 10, 12, 14, 19, 25, 26, and 27 of this subsection, license means any driver's license, any traffic ticket issued when the person's driver's license is deposited in lieu of bail, a suspension notice issued by the Secretary of State, a duplicate or corrected driver's license, a probationary driver's license or a temporary driver's license.

(b) If any conviction forming the basis of a suspension or revocation authorized under this Section is appealed, the Secretary of State may rescind or withhold the entry of the order of suspension or revocation, as the case may be, provided that a certified copy of a stay order of a court is filed with the Secretary of State. If the conviction is affirmed on appeal, the date of the conviction shall relate back to the time the original judgment of conviction was entered and the 6 month limitation prescribed shall not apply.

(c) 1. Upon suspending or revoking the driver's license or permit of any person as authorized in this Section, the Secretary of State shall immediately notify the person in writing of the revocation or suspension. The notice to be deposited in the United States mail, postage prepaid, to the last known address of the person.

2. If the Secretary of State suspends the driver's license of a person under subsection 2 of paragraph (a) of this Section, a person's privilege to operate a vehicle as an occupation shall not be suspended, provided an affidavit is properly completed, the appropriate fee received, and a permit issued prior to the effective date of the suspension, unless 5 offenses were committed, at least 2 of which occurred while operating a commercial vehicle in connection with the driver's regular occupation. All other driving privileges shall be suspended by the Secretary of State. Any driver prior to operating a vehicle for occupational purposes only must submit the affidavit on forms to be provided by the Secretary of State setting forth the facts of the person's occupation. The affidavit shall also state the number of offenses committed while operating a vehicle in connection with the driver's regular occupation. The affidavit shall be accompanied by the driver's license. Upon receipt of a properly completed affidavit, the Secretary of State shall issue the driver a permit to operate a vehicle in connection with the driver's regular occupation only. Unless the permit is issued by the Secretary of State prior to the date of suspension, the privilege to drive any motor vehicle shall be suspended as set forth in the notice that was mailed under this Section. If an affidavit is received subsequent to the effective date of this suspension, a permit may be issued for the remainder of the suspension period.

The provisions of this subparagraph shall not apply to any driver required to obtain a commercial driver's license under Section 6–507 during the period of a disqualification of commercial driving privileges under Section 6–514.

Any person who falsely states any fact in the affidavit required herein shall be guilty of perjury under Section 6–302 and upon conviction thereof shall have all driving privileges revoked without further rights.

3. At the conclusion of a hearing under Section 2-118 of this Code, the Secretary of State shall either rescind or continue an order of revocation or shall substitute an order of suspension; or, good cause appearing therefor, rescind, continue, change, or extend the order of suspension. If the Secretary of State does not rescind the order, the Secretary may upon application, to relieve undue hardship, issue a restricted driving permit granting the privilege of driving a motor vehicle between the petitioner's residence and petitioner's place of employment or within the scope of his employment related duties, or to allow transportation for the petitioner, or a household member of the petitioner's family, to receive necessary medical care and if the professional evaluation indicates, provide transportation for alcohol remedial or rehabilitative activity, or for the petitioner to attend classes, as a student, in an accredited educational institution; if the petitioner is able to demonstrate that no alternative means of transportation is reasonably available and the petitioner will not endanger the public safety or welfare.

If a person's license or permit has been revoked or suspended due to 2 or more convictions of violating Section 11-501 of this Code or a similar provision of a local ordinance or a similar out-of-state offense, arising out of separate occurrences, that person, if issued a restricted driving permit, may not operate a vehicle unless it has been equipped with an ignition interlock device as defined in Section 1-129.1.

If a person's license or permit has been revoked or suspended 2 or more times within a 10 year period due to a single conviction of violating Section 11-501 of this Code or a similar provision of a local ordinance or a similar out-of-state offense, and a statutory summary suspension under Section 11-501.1, or 2 or more statutory summary suspensions, or combination of 2 offenses, or of an offense and a statutory summary suspension, arising out of separate occurrences, that person, if issued a restricted driving permit, may not operate a vehicle unless it has been equipped with an ignition interlock device as defined in Section 1-129.1. The person must pay to the Secretary of State DUI Administration Fund an amount not to exceed $20 per month. The Secretary shall establish by rule the amount and the procedures, terms, and conditions relating to these fees. If the restricted driving permit was issued for employment purposes, then this provision does not apply to the operation of an occupational vehicle owned or leased by that person's employer. In each case the Secretary may issue a restricted driving permit for a period deemed appropriate, except that all permits shall expire within one year from the date of issuance. The Secretary may not, however, issue a restricted driving permit to any person whose current revocation is the result of a second or subsequent conviction for a violation of Section 11-501 of this Code or a similar provision of a local ordinance relating to the offense of operating or being in physical control of a motor vehicle while under the influence of alcohol, other drug or drugs, intoxicating compound or compounds, or any similar out-of-state offense, or any combination of those offenses, until the expiration of at least one year from the date of the revocation. A restricted driving permit issued under this Section shall be subject to cancellation, revocation, and suspension by the Secretary of State in like manner and for like cause as a driver's license issued under this Code may be cancelled, revoked, or suspended; except that a conviction upon one or more offenses against laws or ordinances regulating the movement of traffic shall be deemed sufficient cause for the revocation, suspension, or cancellation of a restricted driving permit. The Secretary of State may, as a condition to the issuance of a restricted driving permit, require the applicant to participate in a designated driver remedial or rehabilitative program. The Secretary of State is authorized to cancel a restricted driving permit if the permit holder does not successfully complete the program.

(c-5) The Secretary of State may, as a condition of the reissuance of a driver's license or permit to an applicant whose driver's license or permit has been suspended before he or she reached the age of 18 years pursuant to any of the provisions of this Section, require the applicant to participate in a driver remedial education course and be retested under Section 6-109 of this Code.

(d) This Section is subject to the provisions of the Drivers License Compact.

(e) The Secretary of State shall not issue a restricted driving permit to a person under the age of 16 years whose driving privileges have been suspended or revoked under any provisions of this Code.

P.A. 76-1586, § 6-206, eff. July 1, 1970. Amended by P.A. 76-2156, § 1, eff. July 1, 1970; P.A. 77-2739, § 1, eff. Oct. 1, 1972; P.A. 78-663, § 1, eff. Jan. 1, 1974; P.A. 79-1141, § 1, eff. Jan. 1, 1976; P.A. 81-1400, § 1, eff. Aug. 25, 1980; P.A. 82-141, § 1, eff. Jan. 1, 1982; P.A. 82-311, § 1, eff. Jan. 1, 1982; P.A. 82-783, Art. III, § 37, eff. July 13, 1982; P.A. 83-466, § 1, eff. Sept. 17, 1983; P.A. 83-905, § 1, eff. Jan. 1, 1984; P.A. 83-1362, Art. II, § 99, eff. Sept. 11, 1984; P.A. 84-112, § 1, eff. July 25, 1985; P.A. 84-272, § 7, eff. Jan. 1, 1986; P.A. 84-300, § 1, eff. Sept. 13, 1985; P.A. 84-551, § 50, eff. Sept. 18, 1985; P.A. 84-772, § 1, eff. Jan. 1, 1986; P.A. 84-1308, Art. II, § 96, eff. Aug. 25, 1986; P.A. 84-1394, § 5, eff. Sept. 18, 1986; P.A. 85-813, § 1, eff. Jan. 1, 1988; P.A. 85-1259, § 3, eff. Jan. 1, 1989; P.A. 86-879, § 1, eff. Jan. 1, 1990; P.A. 86-929, § 2, eff. Sept. 21, 1989; P.A. 86-947, § 2, eff. Jan. 1, 1991; P.A. 86-1019, § 7, eff. July 1, 1990; P.A. 86-1475, Art. 2, § 2-25, eff. Jan. 10, 1991; P.A. 87-233, § 1, eff. Jan. 1, 1992; P.A. 87-929, § 1, eff. Jan. 1, 1993; P.A. 87-1114, § 1, eff. Sept. 15, 1992; P.A. 88-45, Art. II, § 2-54, eff. July 6, 1993; P.A. 88-209, § 5, eff. Jan. 1, 1994; P.A. 88-211, § 5, eff. Jan. 1, 1994; P.A. 88-670, Art. 2, § 2-59, eff. Dec. 2, 1994; P.A. 89-283, § 10, eff. Jan. 1, 1996; P.A. 89-428, Art. 2, § 250, eff. Dec. 13, 1995; P.A. 89-462, Art. 2, § 250, eff. May 29, 1996; P.A. 90-43, § 5, eff. July 2, 1997; P.A. 90-106, § 5, eff. Jan. 1, 1998; P.A. 90-369, § 5, eff. Jan. 1, 1998; P.A. 90-655, § 153, eff. July 30, 1998; P.A. 92-283, § 5, eff. Jan. 1, 2002; P.A. 92-418, § 10, eff. Aug. 17, 2001; P.A. 92-458, § 5, eff. Aug. 22, 2001; P.A. 92-651, § 77, eff. July 11, 2002; P.A. 92-814, § 5, eff. Jan. 1, 2003.

Formerly Ill.Rev.Stat.1991, ch. 95 ½, ¶ 6-206.

1 15 ILCS 335/14, 335/14A, or 335/14B.

2 720 ILCS 5/21-2.

3 720 ILCS 5/24.1.

4 235 ILCS 5/6-16.

5 720 ILCS 570/100 et seq.

6 720 ILCS 550/1 et seq.

7 720 ILSC 690/0.01 et seq.

8 720 ILSC 5/24-1.2.

For text of section as amended by P.A. 92-651 and P.A. 92-804, effective January 1, 2003, see 625 ILCS 5/6-206, ante

P.A. 89-428 was held by the Illinois Supreme Court to be in violation of the single subject requirement of subsection (d) of Section 8 of Article IV of the Illinois Constitution in the case of Johnson v. Edgar, 1997, 176 Ill.2d 499, 680 N.E.2d 1372, 224 Ill.Dec. 1. Public Act 89-462 reenacted the amendment of this text by P.A. 89-428.

P.A. 92-651, the First 2002 General Revisory Act, amended various Acts to delete obsolete text, to correct patent and technical errors, to revise cross references, to resolve multiple actions in the 91st and 92nd General Assemblies and to make certain technical corrections in P.A. 91-937 through P.A. 92-520.

P.A. 92-814 incorporated the amendments by P.A. 92-283, 92-418, and 92-458.

Final legislative action, 92nd General Assembly:

P.A. 92-651—May 14, 2002

P.A. 92-804—May 23, 2002

P.A. 92-814—May 31, 2002

See 5 ILCS 70/6 as to the effect of (1) more than one amendment of a section at the same session of the General Assembly or (2) two or more acts relating to the same subject matter enacted by the same General Assembly.

5/6-206.1. Judicial Driving Permit

§ 6-206.1. Judicial Driving Permit. Declaration of Policy. It is hereby declared a policy of the State of Illinois that the driver who is impaired by alcohol, other drug or drugs, or intoxicating compound or compounds is a threat to the public safety and welfare. Therefore, to provide a deterrent to such practice and to remove problem drivers from the highway, a statutory summary driver's license suspension is appropriate. It is also recognized that driving is a privilege and therefore, that in some cases the granting of limited driving privileges, where consistent with public safety, is warranted during the period of suspension in the form of a judicial driving permit to drive for the purpose of employment, receiving drug treatment or medical care, and educational pursuits, where no alternative means of transportation is available.

The following procedures shall apply whenever a first offender is arrested for any offense as defined in Section 11-501 or a similar provision of a local ordinance:

(a) Subsequent to a notification of a statutory summary suspension of driving privileges as provided in Section 11-501.1, the first offender as defined in Section 11-500 may petition the circuit court of venue for a Judicial Driving Permit, hereinafter referred as a JDP, to relieve undue hardship. The court may issue a court order, pursuant to the criteria contained in this Section, directing the Secretary of State to issue such a JDP to the petitioner. A JDP shall not become effective prior to the 31st day of the original statutory summary suspension and shall always be subject to the following criteria:

1. If ordered for the purposes of employment, the JDP shall be only for the purpose of providing the petitioner the privilege of driving a motor vehicle between the petitioner's residence and the petitioner's place of employment and return; or within the scope of the petitioner's employment related duties, shall be effective only during and limited to those specific times and routes actually required to commute or perform the petitioner's employment related duties.

2. The court, by a court order, may also direct the Secretary of State to issue a JDP to allow transportation for the petitioner, or a household member of the petitioner's family, to receive alcohol, drug, or intoxicating compound treatment or medical care, if the petitioner is able to demonstrate that no alternative means of transportation is reasonably available. Such JDP shall be effective only during the specific times actually required to commute.

3. The court, by a court order, may also direct the Secretary of State to issue a JDP to allow transportation by the petitioner for educational purposes upon demonstrating that there are no alternative means of transportation reasonably available to accomplish those educational purposes. Such JDP shall be only for the purpose of providing transportation to and from the petitioner's residence and the petitioner's place of educational activity, and only during the specific times and routes actually required to commute or perform the petitioner's educational requirement.

4. The Court shall not issue an order granting a JDP to:

(i) Any person unless and until the court, after considering the results of a current professional evaluation of the person's alcohol or other drug use by an agency pursuant to Section 15-10 of the Alcoholism and Other Drug Abuse and Dependency Act [1] and other appropriate investigation of the person, is satisfied that granting the privilege of driving a motor vehicle on the highways will not endanger the public safety or welfare.

(ii) Any person who has been convicted of reckless homicide within the previous 5 years.

(iii) Any person whose privilege to operate a motor vehicle was invalid at the time of arrest for the current violation of Section 11-501, or a similar provision of a local ordinance, except in cases where the cause for a driver's license suspension has been removed at the time a JDP is effective. In any case, should the Secretary of State enter a suspension or revocation of driving privileges pursuant to the provisions of this Code while the JDP is in effect or pending, the Secretary shall take the prescribed action and provide a notice to the person and the court ordering the issuance of the JDP that all driving privileges, including those provided by the issuance of the JDP, have been withdrawn.

(iv) Any person under the age of 18 years.

(b) Prior to ordering the issuance of a JDP the Court should consider at least, but not be limited to, the following issues:

1. Whether the person is employed and no other means of commuting to the place of employment is available or that the person must drive as a condition of employment. The employer shall certify the hours of employment and the need and parameters necessary for driving as a condition to employment.

2. Whether the person must drive to secure alcohol or other medical treatment for himself or a family member.

3. Whether the person must drive for educational purposes. The educational institution shall certify the person's enrollment in and academic schedule at the institution.

4. Whether the person has been repeatedly convicted of traffic violations or involved in motor vehicle accidents to a degree which indicates disrespect for public safety.

5. Whether the person has been convicted of a traffic violation in connection with a traffic accident resulting in the death of any person within the last 5 years.

6. Whether the person is likely to obey the limited provisions of the JDP.

7. Whether the person has any additional traffic violations pending in any court.

For purposes of this Section, programs conducting professional evaluations of a person's alcohol, other drug, or intoxicating compound use must report, to the court of venue, using a form prescribed by the Secretary of State. A copy of such evaluations shall be sent to the Secretary of State by the court. However, the evaluation information shall be privileged and only available to courts and to the Secretary of State, but shall not be admissible in the subsequent trial on the underlying charge.

(c) The scope of any court order issued for a JDP under this Section shall be limited to the operation of a motor vehicle as provided for in subsection (a) of this Section and shall specify the petitioner's residence, place of employment or location of educational institution, and the scope of job related duties, if relevant. The JDP shall also specify days of the week and specific hours of the day when the petitioner is able to exercise the limited privilege of operating a motor vehicle. If the Petitioner, who has been granted a JDP, is issued a citation for a traffic related offense, including operating a motor vehicle outside the limitations prescribed in the JDP or a violation of Section 6–303, or is convicted of any such an offense during the term of the JDP, the court shall consider cancellation of the limited driving permit. In any case, if the Petitioner commits an offense, as defined in Section 11–501, or a similar provision of a local ordinance, as evidenced by the issuance of a Uniform Traffic Ticket, the JDP shall be forwarded by the court of venue to the court ordering the issuance of the JDP, for cancellation. The court shall notify the Secretary of State of any such cancellation.

(d) The Secretary of State shall, upon receiving a court order from the court of venue, issue a JDP to a successful Petitioner under this Section. Such court order form shall also contain a notification, which shall be sent to the Secretary of State, providing the name, driver's license number and legal address of the successful petitioner, and the full and detailed description of the limitations of the JDP. This information shall be available only to the courts, police officers, and the Secretary of State, except during the actual period the JDP is valid, during which time it shall be a public record. The Secretary of State shall design and furnish to the courts an official court order form to be used by the courts when directing the Secretary of State to issue a JDP.

Any submitted court order that contains insufficient data or fails to comply with this Code shall not be utilized for JDP issuance or entered to the driver record but shall be returned to the issuing court indicating why the JDP cannot be so entered. A notice of this action shall also be sent to the JDP petitioner by the Secretary of State.

(e) The circuit court of venue may conduct the judicial hearing, as provided in Section 2–118.1, and the JDP hearing provided in this Section, concurrently. Such concurrent hearing shall proceed in the court in the same manner as in other civil proceedings.

(f) The circuit court of venue may, as a condition of the issuance of a JDP, prohibit the person from operating a motor vehicle not equipped with an ignition interlock device.

P.A. 76–1586, § 6–206.1, added by P.A. 84–272, § 7, eff. Jan. 1, 1986. Amended by P.A. 84–1394, § 5, eff. Sept. 18, 1986; P.A. 85–965, Art. XII, § 5, eff. July 1, 1988; P.A. 86–929, § 2, eff. Sept. 21, 1989; P.A. 88–670, Art. 3, § 3–80, eff. Dec. 2, 1994; P.A. 90–369, § 5, eff. Jan. 1, 1998; P.A. 90–779, § 5, eff. Jan. 1, 1999; P.A. 91–127, § 5, eff. Jan. 1, 2000.

Formerly Ill.Rev.Stat.1991, ch. 95 ½, ¶ 6–206.1.

1 20 ILCS 30/15–10.

5/6–206.2. Violations relating to an ignition interlock device

§ 6–206.2. Violations relating to an ignition interlock device.

(a) It is unlawful for any person whose driving privilege is restricted by being prohibited from operating a motor vehicle not equipped with an ignition interlock device to request or solicit any other person to blow into an ignition interlock device or to start a motor vehicle equipped with the device for the purpose of providing the person so restricted with an operable motor vehicle.

(b) It is unlawful to blow into an ignition interlock device or to start a motor vehicle equipped with the device for the purpose of providing an operable motor vehicle to a person whose driving privilege is restricted by being prohibited from operating a motor vehicle not equipped with an ignition interlock device.

(c) It is unlawful to tamper with, or circumvent the operation of, an ignition interlock device.

(d) Except as provided in subsection (c)(17) of Section 5–6–3.1 of the Unified Code of Corrections [1] or by rule, no person shall knowingly rent, lease, or lend a motor vehicle to a person known to have his or her driving privilege restricted by being prohibited from operating a vehicle not equipped with an ignition interlock device, unless the vehicle is equipped with a functioning ignition interlock device. Any person whose driving privilege is so restricted shall notify any person intending to rent, lease, or loan a motor vehicle to the restricted person of the driving restriction imposed upon him or her.

A person convicted of a violation of this subsection shall be punished by imprisonment for not more than 6 months or by a fine of not more than $5,000, or both.

(e) If a person prohibited under paragraph (2) or paragraph (3) of subsection (c–4) of Section 11–501 from driving any vehicle not equipped with an ignition interlock device nevertheless is convicted of driving a vehicle that is not equipped with the device, that person is prohibited from driving any vehicle not equipped with an ignition interlock device for an additional period of time equal to the initial time period that the person was required to use an ignition interlock device.

P.A. 76–1586, § 6–206.2, added by P.A. 91–127, § 5, eff. Jan. 1, 2000. Amended by P.A. 92–418, § 10, eff. Aug. 17, 2001.

1 730 ILCS 5/5–6–3.1.

5/6–207. Secretary of State may require reexamination or reissuance of a license

§ 6–207. Secretary of State may require reexamination or reissuance of a license.

(a) The Secretary of State, having good cause to believe that a licensed driver or person holding a permit or applying for a license or license renewal is incompetent or otherwise not qualified to hold a license or permit, may upon written notice of at least 5 days to the person require the person to submit to an examination as prescribed by the Secretary.

Refusal or neglect of the person to submit an alcohol, drug, or intoxicating compound evaluation or submit to or failure to successfully complete the examination is grounds for suspension of the person's license or permit under Section 6–206 of this Act or cancellation of his license or permit under Section 6–201 of this Act.

(b) The Secretary of State, having issued a driver's license or permit in error, may upon written notice of at least 5 days to the person, require the person to appear at a Driver Services facility to have the license or permit error corrected and a new license or permit issued.

Refusal or neglect of the person to appear is grounds for cancellation of the person's license or permit under Section 6–201 of this Act.

P.A. 76–1586, § 6–207, eff. July 1, 1970. Amended by P.A. 87–1114, § 1, eff. Sept. 15, 1992; P.A. 88–212, § 5, eff. Jan. 1, 1994; P.A. 90–779, § 5, eff. Jan. 1, 1999.

Formerly Ill.Rev.Stat.1991, ch. 95 ½, ¶ 6–207.

5/6–208. Period of Suspension—Application After Revocation

§ 6–208. Period of Suspension—Application After Revocation.

(a) Except as otherwise provided by this Code or any other law of this State, the Secretary of State shall not suspend a driver's license, permit or privilege to drive a motor vehicle on the highways for a period of more than one year.

(b) Any person whose license, permit or privilege to drive a motor vehicle on the highways has been revoked shall not be entitled to have such license, permit or privilege renewed or restored. However, such person may, except as provided under subsection (d) of Section 6–205, make application for a license pursuant to Section 6–106 (i) if the revocation was for a cause which has been removed or (ii) as provided in the following subparagraphs:

1. Except as provided in subparagraphs 2, 3, and 4, the person may make application for a license after the expiration of one year from the effective date of the revocation or, in the case of a violation of paragraph (b) of Section 11–401 of this Code or a similar provision of a local ordinance, after the expiration of 3 years from the effective date of the revocation or, in the case of a violation of Section 9–3 of the Criminal Code of 1961 [1] relating to the offense of reckless homicide, after the expiration of 2 years from the effective date of the revocation or after the expiration of 24 months from the date of release from a period of imprisonment as provided in Section 6–103 of this Code, whichever is later.

2. If such person is convicted of committing a second violation within a 20 year period of:

(A) Section 11–501 of this Code, or a similar provision of a local ordinance; or

(B) Paragraph (b) of Section 11–401 of this Code, or a similar provision of a local ordinance; or

(C) Section 9–3 of the Criminal Code of 1961, as amended, relating to the offense of reckless homicide; or

(D) any combination of the above offenses committed at different instances;

then such person may not make application for a license until after the expiration of 5 years from the effective date of the most recent revocation. The 20 year period shall be computed by using the dates the offenses were committed and shall also include similar out-of-state offenses.

3. However, except as provided in subparagraph 4, if such person is convicted of committing a third, or subsequent, violation or any combination of the above offenses, including similar out-of-state offenses, contained in subparagraph 2, then such person may not make application for a license until after the expiration of 10 years from the effective date of the most recent revocation.

4. The person may not make application for a license if the person is convicted of committing a fourth or subsequent violation of Section 11–501 of this Code or a similar provision of a local ordinance, Section 11–401 of this Code, Section 9–3 of the Criminal Code of 1961, or a combination of these offenses or similar provisions of local ordinances or similar out-of-state offenses.

Notwithstanding any other provision of this Code, all persons referred to in this paragraph (b) may not have their privileges restored until the Secretary receives payment of the required reinstatement fee pursuant to subsection (b) of Section 6–118.

In no event shall the Secretary issue such license unless and until such person has had a hearing pursuant to this Code and the appropriate administrative rules and the Secretary is satisfied, after a review or investigation of such person, that to grant the privilege of driving a motor vehicle on the highways will not endanger the public safety or welfare.

(c) If a person prohibited under paragraph (2) or paragraph (3) of subsection (c–4) of Section 11–501 from driving any vehicle not equipped with an ignition interlock device nevertheless is convicted of driving a vehicle that is not equipped with the device, that person is prohibited from driving any vehicle not equipped with an ignition interlock device for an additional period of time equal to the initial time period that the person was required to use an ignition interlock device.

P.A. 76–1586, § 6–208, eff. July 1, 1970. Amended by P.A. 81–462, § 1, eff. Jan. 1, 1980; P.A. 84–1381, § 2, eff. Sept. 12, 1986; P.A. 85–303, § 1, eff. Jan. 1, 1988; P.A. 85–951, § 1, eff. July 1, 1988; P.A. 85–1209, Art. II, § 2–51, eff. Aug. 30, 1988; P.A. 89–156, § 5, eff. Jan. 1, 1996; P.A. 90–543, § 5, eff. Dec. 1, 1997; P.A. 90–738, § 5, eff. Jan. 1, 1999; P.A. 91–357, § 231, eff. July 29, 1999; P.A. 92–343, § 5, eff. Jan. 1, 2002; P.A. 92–418, § 10, eff. Aug. 17, 2001; P.A. 92–458, § 5, eff. Aug. 22, 2001; P.A. 92–651, § 77, eff. July 11, 2002.

Formerly Ill.Rev.Stat.1991, ch. 95 ½, ¶ 6–208.

[1] 720 ILCS 5/9–3.

P.A. 92–651, the First 2002 General Revisory Act, amended various Acts to delete obsolete text, to correct patent and technical errors, to revise cross references, to resolve multiple actions in the 91st and 92nd General Assemblies and to make certain technical corrections in P.A. 91–937 through P.A. 92–520.

5/6–208.1. Period of statutory summary alcohol, other drug, or intoxicating compound related suspension

§ 6–208.1. Period of statutory summary alcohol, other drug, or intoxicating compound related suspension.

(a) Unless the statutory summary suspension has been rescinded, any person whose privilege to drive a motor vehicle on the public highways has been summarily suspended, pursuant to Section 11–501.1, shall not be eligible for restoration of the privilege until the expiration of:

1. Six months from the effective date of the statutory summary suspension for a refusal or failure to complete a test or tests to determine the alcohol, drug, or intoxicating compound concentration, pursuant to Section 11–501.1; or

2. Three months from the effective date of the statutory summary suspension imposed following the person's submission to a chemical test which disclosed an alcohol concentration of 0.08 or more, or any amount of a drug, substance, or intoxicating compound in such person's breath, blood, or urine resulting from the unlawful use or consumption of cannabis listed in the Cannabis Control Act,[1] a controlled substance listed in the Illinois Controlled Substances Act,[2] or an intoxicating compound listed in the Use of Intoxicating Compounds Act,[3] pursuant to Section 11–501.1; or

3. Three years from the effective date of the statutory summary suspension for any person other than a first offender who refuses or fails to complete a test or tests to determine the alcohol, drug, or intoxicating compound concentration pursuant to Section 11–501.1; or

4. One year from the effective date of the summary suspension imposed for any person other than a first offender following submission to a chemical test which disclosed an alcohol concentration of 0.08 or more pursuant to Section 11–501.1 or any amount of a drug, substance or compound in such person's blood or urine resulting from the unlawful use or consumption of cannabis listed in the Cannabis Control Act, a controlled substance listed in the Illinois Controlled Substances Act, or an intoxicating compound listed in the Use of Intoxicating Compounds Act.

(b) Following a statutory summary suspension of the privilege to drive a motor vehicle under Section 11–501.1, full driving privileges shall be restored unless the person is otherwise disqualified by this Code. If the court has reason to believe that the person's driving privilege should not be restored, the court shall notify the Secretary of State prior to the expiration of the statutory summary suspension so appropriate action may be taken pursuant to this Code.

(c) Full driving privileges may not be restored until all applicable reinstatement fees, as provided by this Code, have been paid to the Secretary of State and the appropriate entry made to the driver's record.

(d) Where a driving privilege has been summarily suspended under Section 11–501.1 and the person is subsequently convicted of violating Section 11–501, or a similar provision of a local ordinance, for the same incident, any period served on statutory summary suspension shall be credited toward the minimum period of revocation of driving privileges imposed pursuant to Section 6–205.

(e) Following a statutory summary suspension of driving privileges pursuant to Section 11–501.1, for a first offender, the circuit court may, after at least 30 days from the effective date of the statutory summary suspension, issue a judicial driving permit as provided in Section 6–206.1.

(f) Subsequent to an arrest of a first offender, for any offense as defined in Section 11–501 or a similar provision of a local ordinance, following a statutory summary suspension of driving privileges pursuant to Section 11–501.1, for a first offender, the circuit court may issue a court order directing the Secretary of State to issue a judicial driving permit as provided in Section 6–206.1. However, this JDP shall not be effective prior to the 31st day of the statutory summary suspension.

(g) Following a statutory summary suspension of driving privileges pursuant to Section 11–501.1 where the person was not a first offender, as defined in Section 11–500, the Secretary of State may not issue a restricted driving permit.

(h) (Blank).

P.A. 76–1586, § 6–208.1, added by P.A. 84–272, § 7, eff. Jan. 1, 1986. Amended by P.A. 84–1394, § 5, eff. Sept. 18, 1986; P.A. 86–929, § 2, eff. Sept. 21, 1989; P.A. 86–1019, § 7, eff. July 1, 1990; P.A. 87–461, § 1, eff. Jan. 1, 1992; P.A. 88–415, § 10, eff. Aug. 20, 1993; P.A. 89–203, § 20, eff. July 21, 1995; P.A. 90–43, § 5, eff. July 2, 1997; P.A. 90–738, § 5, eff. Jan. 1, 1999; P.A. 90–779, § 5, eff. Jan. 1, 1999; P.A. 91–357, § 231, eff. July 29, 1999; P.A. 92–248, § 5, eff. Aug. 3, 2001.

Formerly Ill.Rev.Stat.1991, ch. 95 ½, ¶ 6–208.1.

1 720 ILCS 550/1 et seq.

2 35 ILCS 570/1 et seq.

3 720 ILCS 690/0.01 et seq.

Validity

On November 18, 1999, the Supreme Court of Illinois held that P.A. 89–203 violated the single-subject rule of the Illinois Constitution in the case of People v. Wooters, 1999, 243 Ill.Dec. 33, 188 Ill.2d 500, 722 N.E.2d 1102.

5/6–208.2. Restoration of driving privileges; persons under age 21

§ 6–208.2. Restoration of driving privileges; persons under age 21.

(a) Unless the suspension based upon consumption of alcohol by a minor or refusal to submit to testing has been rescinded by the Secretary of State in accordance with item (c)(3) of Section 6–206 of this Code, a person whose privilege to drive a motor vehicle on the public highways has been suspended under Section 11–501.8 is not eligible for restoration of the privilege until the expiration of:

1. Six months from the effective date of the suspension for a refusal or failure to complete a test or tests to determine the alcohol concentration under Section 11–501.8;

2. Three months from the effective date of the suspension imposed following the person's submission to a chemical test which disclosed an alcohol concentration greater than 0.00 under Section 11–501.8;

3. Two years from the effective date of the suspension for a person who has been previously suspended under Section 11–501.8 and who refuses or fails to complete a test or tests to determine the alcohol concentration under Section 11–501.8; or

4. One year from the effective date of the suspension imposed for a person who has been previously suspended under Section 11–501.8 following submission to a chemical test that disclosed an alcohol concentration greater than 0.00 under Section 11–501.8.

(b) Following a suspension of the privilege to drive a motor vehicle under Section 11–501.8, full driving privileges shall be restored unless the person is otherwise disqualified by this Code.

(c) Full driving privileges may not be restored until all applicable reinstatement fees, as provided by this Code, have been paid to the Secretary of State and the appropriate entry made to the driver's record. The Secretary of State may also, as a condition of the reissuance of a driver's license or permit to an individual under the age of 18 years whose driving privileges have been suspended pursuant to Section 11–501.8, require the applicant to participate in a driver remedial education course and be retested under Section 6–109.

(d) Where a driving privilege has been suspended under Section 11–501.8 and the person is subsequently convicted of violating Section 11–501, or a similar provision of a local ordinance, for the same incident, any period served on that suspension shall be credited toward the minimum period of revocation of driving privileges imposed under Section 6–205.

(e) Following a suspension of driving privileges under Section 11–501.8 for a person who has not had his or her driving privileges previously suspended under that Section, the Secretary of State may issue a restricted driving permit after at least 30 days from the effective date of the suspension.

(f) Following a second or subsequent suspension of driving privileges under Section 11–501.8, the Secretary of State may issue a restricted driving permit after at least 12 months from the effective date of the suspension.

(g) (Blank).

(h) Any restricted driving permit considered under this Section is subject to the provisions of item (e) of Section 11–501.8.

P.A. 76–1586, § 6–208.2, added by P.A. 88–588, § 5, eff. Jan. 1, 1995. Amended by P.A. 90–774, § 5, eff. Aug. 14, 1998; P.A. 92–248, § 5, eff. Aug. 3, 2001.

5/6–209. Notice of cancellation, suspension or revocation—Surrender and return of license

§ 6–209. Notice of cancellation, suspension or revocation—Surrender and return of license. The Secretary of State upon cancelling, suspending or revoking a license or permit shall immediately notify the holder thereof in writing and shall require that such license or permit shall be surrendered to and retained by the Secretary of State. However, upon payment of the reinstatement fee set out in subsection (g) of Section 6–118 at the end of any period of suspension of a license the licensee, if not ineligible for some other reason, shall be entitled to reinstatement of driving privileges and the return of his license if it has not then expired; or, in case it has expired, to apply for a new license.

P.A. 76–1586, § 6–209, eff. July 1, 1970. Amended by P.A. 81–462, § 1, eff. Jan. 1, 1980.

Formerly Ill.Rev.Stat.1991, ch. 95 ½, ¶ 6–209.

5/6–210. No operation under foreign license during suspension or revocation in this State

§ 6–210. No operation under foreign license during suspension or revocation in this State.

Any resident or nonresident whose drivers license or permit or privilege to operate a motor vehicle in this State has been suspended or revoked as provided in this Act shall not operate a motor vehicle in this State:

(1) during the period of such suspension, except as permitted by a restricted driving permit issued under the provisions of Section 6–206 of this Act; or

(2) after such revocation until a license is obtained when and as permitted under this Act, except as permitted by a restricted driving permit issued under the provisions of Section 6–205 of this Act.

P.A. 76–1586, § 6–210, eff. July 1, 1970. Amended by P.A. 92–16, § 85, eff. June 28, 2001.

Formerly Ill.Rev.Stat.1991, ch. 95 ½, ¶ 6–210.

5/6–211. Secretary of State to administer act—Notices required

§ 6–211. Secretary of State to administer act—Notices required. (a) The Secretary of State shall administer the provisions of this Chapter and may make and enforce rules and regulations relating to its administration.

(b) The Secretary of State shall either provide or prescribe suitable forms requisite or deemed necessary by him for the purposes of this Chapter.

(c) Whenever under the provisions of this Chapter the Secretary of State is required to give notice to any person such notice shall be deemed to have been served either when personally delivered or when deposited in the United States mail, in a sealed envelope, with postage prepaid, addressed to the party affected thereby at his last known residence or place of business.

P.A. 76–1586, § 6–211, eff. July 1, 1970.

Formerly Ill.Rev.Stat.1991, ch. 95 ½, ¶ 6–211.

5/6–212. Court Review

§ 6–212. Court Review. The provisions of the Administrative Review Law, and all amendments and modifications thereof,[1] and the rules adopted pursuant thereto, shall apply to and govern all proceedings for the judicial review of final administrative decisions of the Secretary of State hereunder.

P.A. 76–1586, § 6–212, eff. July 1, 1970. Amended by P.A. 82–783, Art. XI, § 140, eff. July 13, 1982.

Formerly Ill.Rev.Stat.1991, ch. 95 ½, ¶ 6–212.

[1] 735 ILCS 5/3–101 et seq.

ARTICLE III. VIOLATION OF LICENSE PROVISIONS

Section

5/6-301. Unlawful use of license or permit

§ 6-301. Unlawful use of license or permit.

(a) It is a violation of this Section for any person:

1. To display or cause to be displayed or have in his possession any cancelled, revoked or suspended license or permit;

2. To lend his license or permit to any other person or knowingly allow the use thereof by another;

3. To display or represent as his own any license or permit issued to another;

4. To fail or refuse to surrender to the Secretary of State or his agent or any peace officer upon his lawful demand, any license or permit, which has been suspended, revoked or cancelled;

5. To allow any unlawful use of a license or permit issued to him;

6. To submit to an examination or to obtain the services of another person to submit to an examination for the purpose of obtaining a drivers license or permit for some other person.

(b) Sentence.

1. Any person convicted of a violation of this Section shall be guilty of a Class A misdemeanor and shall be sentenced to a minimum fine of $500 or 50 hours of community service, preferably at an alcohol abuse prevention program, if available.

2. Any person convicted of a second or subsequent violation of this Section shall be guilty of a Class 4 felony.

3. In addition to any other sentence imposed under paragraph 1 or 2 of this subsection (b), a person convicted of a violation of paragraph 6 of subsection (a) shall be imprisoned for not less than 7 days.

(c) This Section does not prohibit any lawfully authorized investigative, protective, law enforcement or other activity of any agency of the United States, State of Illinois or any other state or political subdivision thereof.

(d) This Section does not apply to licenses and permits invalidated under Section 6-301.3 of this Code.

P.A. 76-1586, § 6-301, eff. July 1, 1970. Amended by P.A. 77-2830, Art. 73, § 1, eff. Jan. 1, 1973; P.A. 80-911, § 1, eff. Oct. 1, 1977; P.A. 81-306, § 1, eff. Aug. 30, 1979; P.A. 86-503, § 1, eff. Sept. 1, 1989; P.A. 88-197, § 5, eff. Aug. 5, 1993; P.A. 88-210, § 10, eff. Jan. 1, 1994; P.A. 88-670, Art. 2, § 2-59, eff. Dec. 2, 1994; P.A. 92-647, § 5, eff. Jan. 1, 2003; P.A. 92-883, § 5, eff. Jan. 13, 2003.

Formerly Ill.Rev.Stat.1991, ch. 95 ½, ¶ 6-301.

P.A. 88-670, Article 2, of the First 1994 General Revisory Act, resolved multiple actions in the 88th General Assembly and made certain technical corrections in P.A. 88-1 through P.A. 88-538.

P.A. 92-883 incorporated the amendment by P.A. 92-647.

5/6-301.1. Fictitious or unlawfully altered driver's license or permit

§ 6-301.1. Fictitious or unlawfully altered driver's license or permit.

(a) As used in this Section:

1. "A fictitious driver's license or permit" means any issued license or permit for which a computerized number and file have been created by the Secretary of State or other official driver's license agency in another jurisdiction which contains false information concerning the identity of the individual issued the license or permit;

2. "False information" means any information concerning the name, sex, date of birth, social security number or any photograph that falsifies all or in part the actual identity of the individual issued the license or permit;

3. "An unlawfully altered driver's license or permit" means any issued license or permit for which a computerized number and file have been created by the Secretary of State or other official driver's license agency in another jurisdiction which has been physically altered or changed in such a manner that false information appears upon the license or permit;

4. "A document capable of defrauding another" includes, but is not limited to, any document by which any right, obligation or power with reference to any person or property may be created, transferred, altered or terminated;

5. "An identification document" means any document made or issued by or under the authority of the United States Government, the State of Illinois or any other state or political subdivision thereof, or any other governmental or quasi-governmental organization which, when completed with information concerning the individual, is of a type intended or commonly accepted for the purpose of identification of an individual;

6. "Common carrier" means any public or private provider of transportation, whether by land, air, or water.

(b) It is a violation of this Section for any person:

1. To knowingly possess any fictitious or unlawfully altered driver's license or permit;

2. To knowingly possess, display or cause to be displayed any fictitious or unlawfully altered driver's license or permit for the purpose of obtaining any account, credit, credit card or debit card from a bank, financial institution or retail mercantile establishment;

3. To knowingly possess any fictitious or unlawfully altered driver's license or permit with the intent to commit a theft, deception or credit or debit card fraud in violation of any law of this State or any law of any other jurisdiction;

4. To knowingly possess any fictitious or unlawfully altered driver's license or permit with the intent to commit any other violation of any law of this State or any law of any other jurisdiction for which a sentence to a term of imprisonment in a penitentiary for one year or more is provided;

5. To knowingly possess any fictitious or unlawfully altered driver's license or permit while in possession without authority of any document, instrument or device capable of defrauding another;

6. To knowingly possess any fictitious or unlawfully altered driver's license or permit with the intent to use the license or permit to acquire any other identification document;

7. To knowingly issue or assist in the issuance of any fictitious driver's license or permit;

8. To knowingly alter or attempt to alter any driver's license or permit;

9. To knowingly manufacture, possess, transfer or provide any identification document whether real or fictitious for the purpose of obtaining a fictitious driver's license or permit;

10. To knowingly use any fictitious or unlawfully altered driver's license or permit to purchase or attempt to purchase any ticket for a common carrier or to board or attempt to board any common carrier;

11. To knowingly possess any fictitious or unlawfully altered driver's license or permit if the person has at the time a different driver's license issued by the Illinois Secretary of State or other official driver's license agency in another jurisdiction that is suspended or revoked.

(c) Sentence.

1. Any person convicted of a violation of paragraph 1 of subsection (b) of this Section shall be guilty of a Class A misdemeanor and shall be sentenced to minimum fine of $500 or 50 hours of community service, preferably at an alcohol abuse prevention program, if available. A person convicted of a second or subsequent violation shall be guilty of a Class 4 felony.

2. Any person convicted of a violation of paragraph 3 of subsection (b) of this Section who at the time of arrest had in his possession two or more fictitious or unlawfully altered driver's licenses or permits shall be guilty of a Class 4 felony.

3. Any person convicted of a violation of any of paragraphs 2 through 11 of subsection (b) of this Section shall be guilty of a Class 4 felony. A person convicted of a second or subsequent violation shall be guilty of a Class 3 felony.

(d) This Section does not prohibit any lawfully authorized investigative, protective, law enforcement or other activity of any agency of the United States, State of Illinois or any other state or political subdivision thereof.

P.A. 76-1586, § 6-301.1, added by P.A. 81-306, § 1, eff. Aug. 30, 1979. Amended by P.A. 86-503, § 1, eff. Sept. 1, 1989; P.A. 86-551, § 1, eff. Jan. 1, 1990; P.A. 86-1028, Art. II, § 2-44, eff. Feb. 5, 1990; P.A. 88-210, § 10, eff. Jan. 1, 1994; P.A. 92-673, § 5, eff. Jan. 1, 2003.

Formerly Ill.Rev.Stat.1991, ch. 95 ½, ¶ 6-301.1.

5/6-301.2. Fraudulent driver's license or permit

§ 6-301.2. Fraudulent driver's license or permit.

(a) (Blank).

(b) It is a violation of this Section for any person:

1. To knowingly possess any fraudulent driver's license or permit;

2. To knowingly possess, display or cause to be displayed any fraudulent driver's license or permit for the purpose of obtaining any account, credit, credit card or debit card from a bank, financial institution or retail mercantile establishment;

3. To knowingly possess any fraudulent driver's license or permit with the intent to commit a theft, deception or credit or debit card fraud in violation of any law of this State or any law of any other jurisdiction;

4. To knowingly possess any fraudulent driver's license or permit with the intent to commit any other violation of any laws of this State or any law of any other jurisdiction for which a sentence to a term of imprisonment in a penitentiary for one year or more is provided;

5. To knowingly possess any fraudulent driver's license or permit while in unauthorized possession of any document, instrument or device capable of defrauding another;

6. To knowingly possess any fraudulent driver's license or permit with the intent to use the license or permit to acquire any other identification document;

7. To knowingly possess without authority any driver's license-making or permit-making implement;

8. To knowingly possess any stolen driver's license-making or permit- making implement;

9. To knowingly duplicate, manufacture, sell or transfer any fraudulent driver's license or permit;

10. To advertise or distribute any information or materials that promote the selling, giving, or furnishing of a fraudulent driver's license or permit;

11. To knowingly use any fraudulent driver's license or permit to purchase or attempt to purchase any ticket for a common carrier or to board or attempt to board any common carrier. As used in this Section, "common carrier" means any public or private provider of transportation, whether by land, air, or water;

12. To knowingly possess any fraudulent driver's license or permit if the person has at the time a different driver's license issued by the Secretary of State or another official driver's license agency in another jurisdiction that is suspended or revoked.

(c) Sentence.

1. Any person convicted of a violation of paragraph 1 of subsection (b) of this Section shall be guilty of a Class 4 felony and shall be sentenced to a minimum fine of $500 or 50 hours of community service, preferably at an alcohol abuse prevention program, if available.

2. Any person convicted of a violation of any of paragraphs 2 through 9 or paragraph 11 or 12 of subsection (b) of this Section shall be guilty of a Class 4 felony. A person convicted of a second or subsequent violation shall be guilty of a Class 3 felony.

3. Any person convicted of a violation of paragraph 10 of subsection (b) of this Section shall be guilty of a Class B misdemeanor.

(d) This Section does not prohibit any lawfully authorized investigative, protective, law enforcement or other activity of any agency of the United States, State of Illinois or any other state or political subdivision thereof.

(e) The Secretary may request the Attorney General to seek a restraining order in the circuit court against any person who violates this Section by advertising fraudulent driver's licenses or permits.

P.A. 76-1586, § 6-301.2, added by P.A. 86-503, § 1, eff. Sept. 1, 1989. Amended by P.A. 86-1028, Art. II, § 2-44, eff. Feb. 5, 1990; P.A. 88-210, § 10, eff. Jan. 1, 1994; P.A. 89-283, § 10, eff. Jan. 1, 1996; P.A. 90-89, § 15, eff. Jan. 1, 1998; P.A. 90-191, § 10, eff. Jan. 1, 1998; P.A. 90-655, § 153, eff. July 30, 1998; P.A. 92-673, § 5, eff. Jan. 1, 2003.

Formerly Ill.Rev.Stat.1991, ch. 95 ½, ¶ 6-301.2.

P.A. 90-655, the First 1998 General Revisory Act, amended various Acts to delete obsolete text, to correct patent and technical errors, to revise cross references, to resolve multiple actions in the 89th and 90th General Assemblies and to make certain technical corrections in P.A. 89-708 through P.A. 90-566.

5/6-301.3. Invalidation of a driver's license or permit

§ 6-301.3. Invalidation of a driver's license or permit.

(a) The Secretary of State may invalidate a driver's license or permit when:

(1) when the holder voluntarily surrenders the license or permit and declares his or her intention to do so in writing to the Secretary;

(2) when the Secretary receives a certified court order indicating the holder is to refrain from driving;

(3) upon the death of the holder; or

(4) as the Secretary deems appropriate by administrative rule.

(b) A driver's license or permit invalidated under this Section shall nullify the holder's driving privileges. If a license is invalidated under subdivision (a)(3) of this Section, the actual license or permit may be released to a relative of the decedent; provided, the actual license or permit bears a readily identifiable designation evidencing invalidation as prescribed by the Secretary.

P.A. 76-1586, § 6-301.3, added by P.A. 88-197, § 5, eff. Aug. 5, 1993 Amended by P.A. 91-357, § 231, eff. July 29, 1999.

5/6-302. Making false application or affidavit—Perjury

§ 6-302. Making false application or affidavit—Perjury.

(a) It is a violation of this Section for any person:

1. To display or present any document for the purpose of making application for a driver's license or permit knowing that such document contains false information concerning the identity of the applicant;

2. To accept or allow to be accepted any document displayed or presented for the purpose of making application for a driver's license or permit knowing that such document contains false information concerning the identity of the applicant;

3. To knowingly make any false affidavit or swear or affirm falsely to any matter or thing required by the terms of this Act to be sworn to or affirmed.

(b) Sentence.

1. Any person convicted of a violation of this Section shall be guilty of a Class 4 felony.

2. Any person convicted of a second or subsequent violation of this Section shall be guilty of a Class 3 felony.

(c) This Section does not prohibit any lawfully authorized investigative, protective, law enforcement or other activity of any agency of the United States, State of Illinois or any other state or political subdivision thereof.

P.A. 76-1586, § 6-302, eff. July 1, 1970. Amended by P.A. 86-503, § 1, eff. Sept. 1, 1989.

Formerly Ill.Rev.Stat.1991, ch. 95 ½, ¶ 6-302.

5/6-303. Driving while driver's license, permit or privilege to operate a motor vehicle is suspended or revoked

§ 6-303. Driving while driver's license, permit or privilege to operate a motor vehicle is suspended or revoked.

(a) Any person who drives or is in actual physical control of a motor vehicle on any highway of this State at a time when such person's driver's license, permit or privilege to do so or the privilege to obtain a driver's license or permit is revoked or suspended as provided by this Code or the law of another state, except as may be specifically allowed by a judicial driving permit, family financial responsibility driving permit, probationary license to drive, or a restricted driving permit issued pursuant to this Code or under the law of another state, shall be guilty of a Class A misdemeanor.

(b) The Secretary of State upon receiving a report of the conviction of any violation indicating a person was operating a motor vehicle during the time when said person's driver's license, permit or privilege was suspended by the Secretary, by the appropriate authority of another state, or pursuant to Section 11-501.1; except as may be specifically allowed by a probationary license to drive, judicial driving permit or restricted driving permit issued pursuant to this Code or the law of another state; shall extend the suspension for the same period of time as the originally imposed suspension; however, if the period of suspension has then expired, the Secretary shall be authorized to suspend said person's driving privileges for the same period of time as the originally imposed suspension; and if the conviction was upon a charge which indicated that a vehicle was operated during the time when the person's driver's license, permit or privilege was revoked; except as may be allowed by a restricted driving permit issued pursuant to this Code or the law of another state; the Secretary shall not issue a driver's license for an additional period of one year from the date of such conviction indicating such person was operating a vehicle during such period of revocation.

(c) Any person convicted of violating this Section shall serve a minimum term of imprisonment of 10 consecutive days or 30 days of community service when the person's driving privilege was revoked or suspended as a result of:

(1) a violation of Section 11-501 of this Code or a similar provision of a local ordinance relating to the offense of operating or being in physical control of a vehicle while under the influence of alcohol, any other drug or any combination thereof; or

(2) a violation of paragraph (b) of Section 11-401 of this Code or a similar provision of a local ordinance relating to the offense of leaving the scene of a motor vehicle accident involving personal injury or death; or

(3) a violation of Section 9-3 of the Criminal Code of 1961,[1] as amended, relating to the offense of reckless homicide; or

(4) a statutory summary suspension under Section 11-501.1 of this Code.

Such sentence of imprisonment or community service shall not be subject to suspension in order to reduce such sentence.

(c-1) Except as provided in subsection (d), any person convicted of a second violation of this Section shall be ordered by the court to serve a minimum of 100 hours of community service.

(c-2) In addition to other penalties imposed under this Section, the court may impose on any person convicted a fourth time of violating this Section any of the following:

(1) Seizure of the license plates of the person's vehicle.

(2) Immobilization of the person's vehicle for a period of time to be determined by the court.

(d) Any person convicted of a second violation of this Section shall be guilty of a Class 4 felony and shall serve a minimum term of imprisonment of 30 days or 300 hours of community service, as determined by the court, if the revocation or suspension was for a violation of Section 11-401 or 11-501 of this Code, or a similar out-of-state offense, or a similar provision of a local ordinance, a violation of Section 9-

3 of the Criminal Code of 1961, relating to the offense of reckless homicide, or a similar out-of-state offense, or a statutory summary suspension under Section 11–501.1 of this Code.

(d–1) Except as provided in subsection (d–2) and subsection (d–3), any person convicted of a third or subsequent violation of this Section shall serve a minimum term of imprisonment of 30 days or 300 hours of community service, as determined by the court.

(d–2) Any person convicted of a third violation of this Section is guilty of a Class 4 felony and must serve a minimum term of imprisonment of 30 days if the revocation or suspension was for a violation of Section 11–401 or 11–501 of this Code, or a similar out-of-state offense, or a similar provision of a local ordinance, a violation of Section 9–3 of the Criminal Code of 1961, relating to the offense of reckless homicide, or a similar out-of-state offense, or a statutory summary suspension under Section 11–501. 1 of this Code.

(d–3) Any person convicted of a fourth or subsequent violation of this Section is guilty of a Class 4 felony and must serve a minimum term of imprisonment of 180 days if the revocation or suspension was for a violation of Section 11–401 or 11–501 of this Code, or a similar out-of-state offense, or a similar provision of a local ordinance, a violation of Section 9–3 of the Criminal Code of 1961, relating to the offense of reckless homicide, or a similar out-of-state offense, or a statutory summary suspension under Section 11–501.1 of this Code.

(e) Any person in violation of this Section who is also in violation of Section 7–601 of this Code relating to mandatory insurance requirements, in addition to other penalties imposed under this Section, shall have his or her motor vehicle immediately impounded by the arresting law enforcement officer. The motor vehicle may be released to any licensed driver upon a showing of proof of insurance for the vehicle that was impounded and the notarized written consent for the release by the vehicle owner.

(f) For any prosecution under this Section, a certified copy of the driving abstract of the defendant shall be admitted as proof of any prior conviction.

(g) The motor vehicle used in a violation of this Section is subject to seizure and forfeiture as provided in Sections 36–1 and 36–2 of the Criminal Code of 1961 if the person's driving privilege was revoked or suspended as a result of a violation listed in paragraph (1), (2), or (3) of subsection (c) of this Section or as a result of a summary suspension as provided in paragraph (4) of subsection (c) of this Section.

P.A. 76–1586, § 6–303, eff. July 1, 1970. Amended by P.A. 77–2720, § 1, eff. Jan. 1, 1973; P.A. 80–1462, § 1, eff. Jan. 1, 1979; P.A. 83–206, § 2, eff. Jan. 1, 1984; P.A. 84–272, § 7, eff. Jan. 1, 1986; P.A. 84–1394, § 5, eff. Sept. 18, 1986; P.A. 88–383, § 5, eff. Jan. 1, 1994; P.A. 88–680, Art. 20, § 20–900, eff. Jan. 1, 1995; P.A. 89–8, Art. 1, § 1–5, eff. March 21, 1995; P.A. 89–92, § 10, eff. July 1, 1996; P.A. 89–156, § 5, eff. Jan. 1, 1996; P.A. 89–626, Art. 2, § 2–66, eff. Aug. 9, 1996; P.A. 90–400, § 5, eff. Aug. 15, 1997; P.A. 90–738, § 5, eff. Jan. 1, 1999; Re-enacted by P.A; 91–692, Art. 20, § 20–900, eff. April 13, 2000. Amended by P.A. 92–340, § 5, eff. Aug. 10, 2001; P.A. 92–688, § 5, eff. July 16, 2002.

Formerly Ill.Rev.Stat.1991, ch. 95 ½, ¶ 6–303.

1 720 ILCS 5/9–3.

Validity

The Supreme Court of Illinois held that P.A. 88–680 violated the single-subject rule of the Illinois Constitution in the case of People v. Cervantes, 1999, 243 Ill.Dec. 233, 189 Ill.2d 80, 723 N.E.2d 265; P.A. 91–692 re-enacted this section as contained in P.A. 88–680, including subsequent amendments in order "to remove any question as to the validity or content of those provisions."

Section 1 of P.A. 91–692, approved and eff. April 13, 2000, provides: "Purpose.

"(1) The General Assembly finds and declares that:

"(i) Public Act 88–680, effective January 1, 1995, contained provisions amending the Illinois Vehicle Code. Public Act 88–680 also contained other provisions.

"(ii) In addition, Public Act 88–680 was entitled "AN ACT to create a Safe Neighborhoods Law". (A) Article 5 was entitled JUVENILE JUSTICE and amended the Juvenile Court Act of 1987. (B) Article 15 was entitled GANGS and amended various provisions of the Criminal Code of 1961 and the Unified Code of Corrections. (C) Article 20 was entitled ALCOHOL ABUSE and amended various provisions of the Illinois Vehicle Code. (D) Article 25 was entitled DRUG ABUSE and amended the Cannabis Control Act and the Illinois Controlled Substances Act. (E) Article 30 was entitled FIREARMS and amended the Criminal Code of 1961 and the Code of Criminal Procedure of 1963. (F) Article 35 amended the Criminal Code of 1961, the Rights of Crime Victims and Witnesses Act, and the Unified Code of Corrections. (G) Article 40 amended the Criminal Code of 1961 to increase the penalty for compelling organization membership of persons. (H) Article 45 created the Secure Residential Youth Care Facility Licensing Act and amended the State Finance Act, the Juvenile Court Act of 1987, the Unified Code of Corrections, and the Private Correctional Facility Moratorium Act. (I) Article 50 amended the WIC Vendor Management Act, the Firearm Owners Identification Card Act, the Juvenile Court Act of 1987, the Criminal Code of 1961, the Wrongs to Children Act, and the Unified Code of Corrections.

"(iii) On December 2, 1999, the Illinois Supreme Court, in People v. Cervantes, Docket No. 87229, ruled that Public Act 88–680 violates the single subject clause of the Illinois Constitution (Article IV, Section 8 (d)) and was unconstitutional in its entirety.

"(iv) The provisions of Public Act 88–680 amending the Illinois Vehicle Code are of vital concern to the people of this State and legislative action concerning those provisions of Public Act 88–680 is necessary.

"(2) It is the purpose of this Act to re-enact the provisions of Public Act 88–680 amending the Illinois Vehicle Code, including subsequent amendments. This re-enactment is intended to remove any question as to the validity or content of those provisions.

"(3) This Act re-enacts various provisions of Public Act 88–680 amending the Illinois Vehicle Code, including subsequent amendments, to remove any question as to the validity or content of those provisions; it is not intended to supersede any other Public Act that amends the text of the Sections as set forth in this Act. The material is shown as existing text (i.e., without underscoring)."

P.A. 92–688 incorporated the amendment by P.A. 92–340.

5/6-304. Permitting unauthorized person to drive

§ 6–304. Permitting unauthorized person to drive. No person shall cause, authorize or knowingly permit a motor vehicle owned by him or under his control to be driven upon any highway by any person who is not authorized hereunder or in violation of any of the provisions of this Act.

P.A. 76–1586, § 6–304, eff. July 1, 1970.

Formerly Ill.Rev.Stat.1991, ch. 95 ½, ¶ 6–304.

5/6-304.1. Permitting a driver under the influence to operate a motor vehicle

§ 6–304.1. Permitting a driver under the influence to operate a motor vehicle. No person shall knowingly cause, authorize, or permit a motor vehicle owned by, or under the control of, such person to be driven or operated upon a highway by anyone who is under the influence of alcohol, other drugs, or combination thereof. This provision shall not apply to a spouse of the person who owns or has control of, or a co-owner of, a motor vehicle or to a bailee for hire.

Any person convicted of violating this Section shall be guilty of a Class A misdemeanor.

P.A. 76-1586, § 6-304.1, added by P.A. 84-272, § 7, eff. Jan. 1, 1986. Amended by P.A. 84-1394, § 5, eff. Sept. 18, 1986. **Formerly** Ill.Rev.Stat.1991, ch. 95 ½, ¶ 6-304.1.

5/6-305. Renting motor vehicle to another

§ 6-305. Renting motor vehicle to another.

(a) No person shall rent a motor vehicle to any other person unless the latter person, or a driver designated by a nondriver with disabilities and meeting any minimum age and driver's record requirements that are uniformly applied by the person renting a motor vehicle, is then duly licensed hereunder or, in the case of a nonresident, then duly licensed under the laws of the State or country of his residence unless the State or country of his residence does not require that a driver be licensed.

(b) No person shall rent a motor vehicle to another until he has inspected the drivers license of the person to whom the vehicle is to be rented, or by whom it is to be driven, and compared and verified the signature thereon with the signature of such person written in his presence unless, in the case of a nonresident, the State or country wherein the nonresident resides does not require that a driver be licensed.

(c) No person shall rent a motorcycle to another unless the latter person is then duly licensed hereunder as a motorcycle operator, and in the case of a nonresident, then duly licensed under the laws of the State or country of his residence, unless the State or country of his residence does not require that a driver be licensed.

(d) (Blank).

(e) (Blank).

(f) Any person who rents a motor vehicle to another shall only advertise, quote, and charge a rental rate that includes the entire amount except taxes and a mileage charge, if any, which a renter must pay to hire or lease the vehicle for the period of time to which the rental rate applies. Such person shall not charge in addition to the rental rate, taxes, and mileage charge, if any, any fee which must be paid by the renter as a condition of hiring or leasing the vehicle, such as, but not limited to, required fuel or airport surcharges, nor any fee for transporting the renter to the location where the rented vehicle will be delivered to the renter. In addition to the rental rate, taxes, and mileage charge, if any, such person may charge for an item or service provided in connection with a particular rental transaction if the renter can avoid incurring the charge by choosing not to obtain or utilize the optional item or service. Items and services for which such person may impose an additional charge include, but are not limited to, optional insurance and accessories requested by the renter, service charges incident to the renter's optional return of the vehicle to a location other than the location where the vehicle was hired or leased, and charges for refueling the vehicle at the conclusion of the rental transaction in the event the renter did not return the vehicle with as much fuel as was in the fuel tank at the beginning of the rental.

(g) Every person renting a motor vehicle to another shall keep a record of the registration number of the motor vehicle so rented, the name and address of the person to whom the vehicle is rented, the number of the license, if any, of said latter person, and the date and place when and where the license, if any, was issued. Such record shall be open to inspection by any police officer or designated agent of the Secretary of State.

(h) A person licensed as a new car dealer under Section 5-101 of this Code shall not be subject to the provisions of this Section regarding the rental of private passenger motor vehicles when providing, free of charge, temporary substitute vehicles for customers to operate during a period when a customer's vehicle, which is either leased or owned by that customer, is being repaired, serviced, replaced or otherwise made unavailable to the customer in accordance with an agreement with the licensed new car dealer or vehicle manufacturer, so long as the customer orally or in writing is made aware that the temporary substitute vehicle will be covered by his or her insurance policy and the customer shall only be liable to the extent of any amount deductible from such insurance coverage in accordance with the terms of the policy.

(i) This Section, except the requirements of subsection (g), also applies to rental agreements of 30 continuous days or less involving a motor vehicle that was delivered by an out of State person or business to a renter in this State.

(j) A public airport may, if approved by its local government corporate authorities or its airport authority, impose a customer facility charge upon customers of rental car companies for the purposes of financing, designing, constructing, operating, and maintaining consolidated car rental facilities and common use transportation equipment and facilities, which are used to transport the customer, connecting consolidated car rental facilities with other airport facilities.

Notwithstanding subsection (f) of this Section, the customer facility charge shall be collected by the rental car company as a separate charge, and clearly indicated as a separate charge on the rental agreement and invoice. Facility charges shall be immediately deposited into a trust account for the benefit of the airport and remitted at the direction of the airport, but not more often than once per month. The charge shall be uniformly calculated on a per-contract or per-day basis. Facility charges imposed by the airport may not exceed the reasonable costs of financing, designing, constructing, operating, and maintaining the consolidated car rental facilities and common use transportation equipment and facilities and may not be used for any other purpose.

Notwithstanding any other provision of law, the charges collected under this Section are not subject to retailer occupation, sales, use, or transaction taxes.

(k) When a rental car company states a rental rate in any of its rate advertisements, its proprietary computer reservation systems, or its in-person quotations intended to apply to an airport rental, a company that collects from its customers a customer facility charge for that rental under subsection (j) shall do all of the following:

(1) Clearly and conspicuously disclose in any radio, television, or other electronic media advertisements the existence and amount of the charge if the advertisement is intended for rentals at an airport imposing the charge or, if the advertisement covers an area with multiple airports with different charges, a range of amounts of customer facility charges if the advertisement is intended for rentals at an airport imposing the charge.

(2) Clearly and conspicuously disclose in any print rate advertising the existence and amount of the charge if the advertisement is intended for rentals at an airport imposing the charge or, if the print rate advertisement covers an area with multiple airports with different charges, a range of amounts of customer facility charges if the advertise-

ment is intended for rentals at an airport imposing the charge.

(3) Clearly and conspicuously disclose the existence and amount of the charge in any telephonic, in-person, or computer-transmitted quotation from the rental car company's proprietary computer reservation system at the time of making an initial quotation of a rental rate if the quotation is made by a rental car company location at an airport imposing the charge and at the time of making a reservation of a rental car if the reservation is made by a rental car company location at an airport imposing the charge.

(4) Clearly and conspicuously display the charge in any proprietary computer-assisted reservation or transaction directly between the rental car company and the customer, shown or referenced on the same page on the computer screen viewed by the customer as the displayed rental rate and in a print size not smaller than the print size of the rental rate.

(5) Clearly and conspicuously disclose and separately identify the existence and amount of the charge on its rental agreement.

(6) A rental car company that collects from its customers a customer facility charge under subsection (j) and engages in a practice which does not comply with subsections (f), (j), and (k) commits an unlawful practice within the meaning of the Consumer Fraud and Deceptive Business Practices Act.[1]

P.A. 76-1586, § 6-305, eff. July 1, 1970. Amended by P.A. 85-1374, § 1, eff. Jan. 1, 1989; P.A. 86-779, § 1, eff. July 1, 1990; P.A. 86-880, § 1, eff. Jan. 1, 1990; P.A. 87-1220, § 1, eff. July 1, 1993; P.A. 88-661, § 27, eff. Sept. 16, 1994; P.A. 89-248, § 5, eff. Aug. 4, 1995; P.A. 90-113, § 900, eff. July 14, 1997; P.A. 92-426, § 5, eff. Jan. 1, 2002.

Formerly Ill.Rev.Stat.1991, ch. 95 ½, ¶ 6-305.

[1] 815 ILCS 505/1 et seq.

5/6-305.1. Unlawful subleasing of a motor vehicle

§ 6-305.1. Unlawful subleasing of a motor vehicle. (a) It is unlawful for any person who is not a party to a lease contract, conditional sale contract, or security agreement which transfers any right or interest in a motor vehicle to:

(1) obtain or exercise control over a motor vehicle and then sell, transfer, assign, or lease the motor vehicle to another person without first obtaining written authorization from the secured creditor, lessor, or lienholder for the sale, transfer, assignment, or lease if he receives compensation or other consideration for the sale, transfer, assignment, or lease of the motor vehicle; or

(2) assist, cause, or arrange the actual or purported sale, transfer, assignment, or lease of a motor vehicle to another person without first obtaining written authorization from the secured creditor, lessor, or lienholder for the sale, transfer, assignment, or lease if he receives compensation or other consideration for assisting, causing, or arranging the sale, transfer, assignment, or lease of the motor vehicle.

(3) this subsection shall not apply to any employee acting upon request of his employer.

(b) Any person who violates the provisions of this Section is guilty of a Class A misdemeanor.

(c) Notwithstanding any other remedy or relief to which a person is entitled, anyone suffering damage as a result of a violation of this Section may bring an action to recover or obtain actual damages, equitable relief, including, but not limited to, an injunction or restitution of money and property, reasonable attorney's fees and costs, and any other relief the court deems proper.

P.A. 76-1586, § 6-305.1, added by P.A. 86-748, § 1, eff. July 1, 1990.

Formerly Ill.Rev.Stat.1991, ch. 95 ½, ¶ 6-305.1.

5/6-305.2. Limited liability for damage

§ 6-305.2. Limited liability for damage.

(a) Damage to private passenger vehicle. A person who rents a motor vehicle to another may hold the renter liable to the extent permitted under subsections (b) through (d) for physical or mechanical damage to the rented motor vehicle that occurs during the time the motor vehicle is under the rental agreement.

(b) Limits on liability. The total liability of a renter under subsection (a) for damage to a motor vehicle may not exceed all of the following:

(1) The lesser of:

(A) Actual and reasonable costs that the person who rents a motor vehicle to another incurred to repair the motor vehicle or that the rental company would have incurred if the motor vehicle had been repaired, which shall reflect any discounts, price reductions, or adjustments available to the rental company; or

(B) The fair market value of that motor vehicle immediately before the damage occurred, as determined in the customary market for the retail sale of that motor vehicle; and

(2) Actual and reasonable costs incurred by the loss due to theft of the rental motor vehicle up to $2,000; provided, however, that if it is established that the renter or an authorized driver failed to exercise ordinary care while in possession of the vehicle or that the renter or an authorized driver committed or aided and abetted the commission of the theft, then the damages shall be the actual and reasonable costs of the rental vehicle up to its fair market value, as determined by the customary market for the sale of that vehicle.

For purposes of this subsection (b), for the period prior to June 1, 1998, the maximum amount that may be recovered from an authorized driver shall not exceed $6,000; for the period beginning June 1, 1998 through May 31, 1999, the maximum recovery shall not exceed $7,500; and for the period beginning June 1, 1999 through May 31, 2000, the maximum recovery shall not exceed $9,000. Beginning June 1, 2000, and annually each June 1 thereafter, the maximum amount that may be recovered from an authorized driver shall be increased by $500 above the maximum recovery allowed immediately prior to June 1 of that year.

(c) Multiple recoveries prohibited. Any person who rents a motor vehicle to another may not hold the renter liable for any amounts that the rental company recovers from any other party.

(d) Repair estimates. A person who rents a motor vehicle to another may not collect or attempt to collect the amount described in subsection (b) unless the rental company obtains an estimate from a repair company or an appraiser in the business of providing such appraisals on the costs of repairing the motor vehicle, makes a copy of the estimate available upon request to the renter who may be liable under subsection (a), or the insurer of the renter, and submits a copy of the estimate with any claim to collect the amount described in subsection (b).

(e) Duty to mitigate. A claim against a renter resulting from damage or loss to a rental vehicle must be reasonably and rationally related to the actual loss incurred. A rental company shall mitigate damages where possible and shall not assert or collect any claim for physical damage which exceeds the actual costs of the repair, including all discounts or price reductions.

(f) No rental company shall require a deposit or an advance charge against the credit card of a renter, in any form, for damages to a vehicle which is in the renter's possession, custody, or control. No rental company shall require any payment for damage to the rental vehicle, upon the renter's return of the vehicle in a damaged condition, until after the cost of the damage to the vehicle and liability therefor is agreed to between the rental company and renter or is determined pursuant to law.

(g) If insurance coverage exists under the renter's personal insurance policy and the coverage is confirmed during regular business hours, the renter may require that the rental company must submit any claims to the renter's personal insurance carrier as the renter's agent. The rental company shall not make any written or oral representations that it will not present claims or negotiate with the renter's insurance carrier. For purposes of this Section, confirmation of coverage includes telephone confirmation from insurance company representatives during regular business hours. After confirmation of coverage, the amount of claim shall be resolved between the insurance carrier and the rental company.

P.A. 76–1586, § 6–305.2, added by P.A. 90–113, § 900, eff. July 14, 1997.

5/6–306. § 6–306. Repealed by P.A. 83–385, § 2, eff. Jan. 1, 1984

5/6–306.1. § 6–306.1. Repealed by P.A. 85–876, § 3, eff. Nov. 6, 1987

Section 4 of P.A. 85–876, veto overridden Nov. 6, 1987, provided:

"Sections 2 and 3 of this Act shall apply only to violations of a municipality's vehicular standing and parking regulations which occur on or after the effective date of this Act."

5/6–306.2. § 6–306.2. Repealed by P.A. 84–1231, § 2, eff. July 28, 1986

5/6–306.3. License as bail

§ 6–306.3. License as bail.

(a) Except as provided in Section 6–306.4 of this Code, any person arrested and charged with violation of Section 3–701, 3–707, or 3–710, or of any violation of Chapters 11 or 12 of this Code,[1] except the provisions of Sections 3–708, 11–401, 11–501, 11–503 or 11–504 of this Code shall have the option of depositing his valid driver's license issued under this Code with the officer demanding bail in lieu of any other security for his appearance in court in answer to any such charge.

(b) However, a uniform bail schedule and regulations adopted pursuant to Supreme Court Rule or Order may require that a driver's license issued under this Code must be deposited, in addition to appropriate cash deposit, where persons arrested and charged with violating Sections 3–708, 11–401, 11–501, 11–503 or 11–504 of this Code elect to take advantage of the uniform schedule establishing the amount of bail in such cases.

(c) When a license is deposited as security in lieu of or in addition to bail, the judge, court clerk, or other official accepting such deposit shall issue to the licensee a receipt for such license upon a form approved or provided by the Secretary of State.

(d) If the licensee whose license has been deposited as security for bail does not appear in court in compliance with the time and place for hearing as notified in such receipt, or the continued date thereof, if any has been ordered by the court, the court shall continue the case for a minimum of 30 days and require a notice of the continued court date be sent to the licensee at his last known address. The clerk of such court shall notify the licensee of the court's order. If the licensee does not appear in and surrender on the continued court date, or within such period, satisfy the court that his appearance in and surrender to the court is impossible and without any fault on his part, the court shall enter an order of failure to appear to answer such charge after depositing license in lieu of bail. The clerk of such court shall notify the Secretary of State of the court's order.

The Secretary of State, when notified by the clerk of such court that an order of failure to appear to answer such charge after depositing license in lieu of bail has been entered, shall immediately suspend the driver's license of such licensee without a hearing and shall not remove such suspension, nor issue any hardship license or privilege to such licensee thereafter until notified by such court that the licensee has appeared and answered the charges placed against him.

(e) 1. Any Illinois resident who has executed a written promise to comply with Section 6–306.2 of this Code, in effect until July 28, 1986, shall continue to be suspended until he or she complies with the terms and conditions of the written promise.

2. The Secretary of State, when notified by the clerk of such court that an order of failure to appear to answer a charge after promising to appear has been entered, shall immediately suspend the driver's license of such licensee without a hearing and shall not remove such suspension, nor issue a hardship license or privilege to such licensee thereafter until notified by such court that the licensee has appeared and answered the charges placed against him.

P.A. 76–1586, § 6–306.3, added by P.A. 84–1231, § 1, eff. July 28, 1986. Amended by P.A. 85–992, § 1, eff. Jan. 5, 1988; P.A. 86–149, § 2, eff. Aug. 11, 1989; P.A. 88–315, § 5, eff. Jan. 1, 1994; P.A. 88–415, § 10, eff. Aug. 20, 1993; P.A. 88–670, Art. 2, § 2–59, eff. Dec. 2, 1994.

Formerly Ill.Rev.Stat.1991, ch. 95 ½, ¶ 6–306.3.

1 625 ILCS 5/11–100 et seq. or 625 ILCS 5/12–100 et seq.

P.A. 88–670, Article 2, of the First 1994 General Revisory Act, resolved multiple actions in the 88th General Assembly and made certain technical corrections in P.A. 88–1 through P.A. 88–538.

5/6–306.4. Procedures for residents of other states

§ 6–306.4. Procedures for residents of other states. (a) Except as provided in paragraph (b) of this Section, any resident of another state which is a member of the Nonresident Violator Compact of 1977,[1] who is cited by a police officer for violating a traffic law or ordinance, shall have the option of (1) being taken without unnecessary delay before a court of jurisdiction or (2) executing a written promise to comply with the terms of the citation by signing at least one copy of a Uniform Traffic Ticket prepared by the police officer. The police officer may refuse to permit a nonresident violator to execute a written promise to comply with the terms of the citation if the nonresident violator cannot furnish satisfactory evidence of identity or if the officer has probable cause to believe the nonresident violator cited will disregard the written promise to comply with the citation.

If the person cited is a resident of another State which is not a member of the Nonresident Violator Compact of 1977, then the rules established by the Supreme Court for bail bond and appearance procedures apply.

(b) Any person cited for violating the following provisions of this Code or a similar provision of local ordinances shall be governed by the bail provisions of the Illinois Supreme Court Rules when it is not practical or feasible to take the person before a judge to have bail set or to avoid undue delay because of the hour or circumstances: Section 3-101, Section 3-702, Sections 3-707, 3-708 or 3-710, Chapter 4,[2] Chapter 5,[3] Section 6-101, Section 6-104, Section 6-113, Section 6-301, Section 6-303, Section 8-115, Section 11-204, Section 11-310, Section 11-311, Section 11-312, Section 11-401, Section 11-402, Section 11-403, Section 11-404, Section 11-409, Section 11-501, Section 11-503, Section 11-504, Section 11-601, when more than 30 m.p.h. over the posted limit, Section 11-1006, Section 11-1414, Section 15-102, Section 15-103, Section 15-107, Section 15-111, paragraph (f) of Section 15-112 or paragraph (j) of Section 15-301.

(c) If the person fails to comply with the executed written promise to comply with the original terms of the citation as indicated in paragraph (a) of this Section, the court shall continue the case for a minimum of 30 days and require that a notice of the continued court date be sent to the last known address of such person. If the person does not appear or otherwise satisfy the court on or before the continued court date, the court shall enter an order of failure to appear to answer such charge. The clerk of such court shall notify the Secretary of State of the court's order within 21 days.

(d) Upon receiving such notice, the Secretary of State shall comply with the provisions of Section 6-803 of this Code.

P.A. 76-1586, § 6-306.4, added by P.A. 84-1231, § 1, eff. July 28, 1986. Amended by P.A. 85-424, § 1, eff. Jan. 1, 1988; P.A. 86-149, § 2, eff. Aug. 11, 1989.

Formerly Ill.Rev.Stat.1991, ch. 95 ½, ¶ 6-306.4.

[1] 625 ILCS 5/6-800 et seq.

[2] 625 ILCS 5/4-100 et seq.

[3] 625 ILCS 5/5-100 et seq.

5/6-306.5. Failure to pay fine or penalty for standing, parking, or compliance violations; suspension of driving privileges

§ 6-306.5. Failure to pay fine or penalty for standing, parking, or compliance violations; suspension of driving privileges.

(a) Upon receipt of a certified report, as prescribed by subsection (c) of this Section, from any municipality stating that the owner of a registered vehicle has failed to pay any fine or penalty due and owing as a result of 10 or more violations of a municipality's vehicular standing, parking, or compliance regulations established by ordinance pursuant to Section 11-208.3 of this Code, the Secretary of State shall suspend the driving privileges of such person in accordance with the procedures set forth in this Section. The Secretary shall also suspend the driving privileges of an owner of a registered vehicle upon receipt of a certified report, as prescribed by subsection (f) of this Section, from any municipality stating that such person has failed to satisfy any fines or penalties imposed by final judgments for 10 or more violations of local standing, parking, or compliance regulations after exhaustion of judicial review procedures.

(b) Following receipt of the certified report of the municipality as specified in this Section, the Secretary of State shall notify the person whose name appears on the certified report that the person's drivers license will be suspended at the end of a specified period of time unless the Secretary of State is presented with a notice from the municipality certifying that the fine or penalty due and owing the municipality has been paid or that inclusion of that person's name on the certified report was in error. The Secretary's notice shall state in substance the information contained in the municipality's certified report to the Secretary, and shall be effective as specified by subsection (c) of Section 6-211 of this Code.

(c) The report of the appropriate municipal official notifying the Secretary of State of unpaid fines or penalties pursuant to this Section shall be certified and shall contain the following:

(1) The name, last known address and drivers license number of the person who failed to pay the fine or penalty and the registration number of any vehicle known to be registered to such person in this State.

(2) The name of the municipality making the report pursuant to this Section.

(3) A statement that the municipality sent a notice of impending drivers license suspension as prescribed by ordinance enacted pursuant to Section 11-208.3, to the person named in the report at the address recorded with the Secretary of State; the date on which such notice was sent; and the address to which such notice was sent. In a municipality with a population of 1,000,000 or more, the report shall also include a statement that the alleged violator's State vehicle registration number and vehicle make are correct as they appear on the citations.

(d) Any municipality making a certified report to the Secretary of State pursuant to this Section shall notify the Secretary of State, in a form prescribed by the Secretary, whenever a person named in the certified report has paid the previously reported fine or penalty or whenever the municipality determines that the original report was in error. A certified copy of such notification shall also be given upon request and at no additional charge to the person named therein. Upon receipt of the municipality's notification or presentation of a certified copy of such notification, the Secretary of State shall terminate the suspension.

(e) Any municipality making a certified report to the Secretary of State pursuant to this Section shall also by ordinance establish procedures for persons to challenge the accuracy of the certified report. The ordinance shall also state the grounds for such a challenge, which may be limited to (1) the person not having been the owner or lessee of the vehicle or vehicles receiving 10 or more standing, parking, or compliance violation notices on the date or dates such notices were issued; and (2) the person having already paid the fine or penalty for the 10 or more violations indicated on the certified report.

(f) Any municipality, other than a municipality establishing vehicular standing, parking, and compliance regulations pursuant to Section 11-208.3, may also cause a suspension of a person's drivers license pursuant to this Section. Such municipality may invoke this sanction by making a certified report to the Secretary of State upon a person's failure to satisfy any fine or penalty imposed by final judgment for 10 or more violations of local standing, parking, or compliance regulations after exhaustion of judicial review procedures, but only if:

(1) the municipality complies with the provisions of this Section in all respects except in regard to enacting an ordinance pursuant to Section 11-208.3;

(2) the municipality has sent a notice of impending drivers license suspension as prescribed by an ordinance enacted pursuant to subsection (g) of this Section; and

(3) in municipalities with a population of 1,000,000 or more, the municipality has verified that the alleged violator's State vehicle registration number and vehicle make are correct as they appear on the citations.

(g) Any municipality, other than a municipality establishing standing, parking, and compliance regulations pursuant to Section 11–208.3, may provide by ordinance for the sending of a notice of impending drivers license suspension to the person who has failed to satisfy any fine or penalty imposed by final judgment for 10 or more violations of local standing, parking, or compliance regulations after exhaustion of judicial review procedures. An ordinance so providing shall specify that the notice sent to the person liable for any fine or penalty shall state that failure to pay the fine or penalty owing within 45 days of the notice's date will result in the municipality notifying the Secretary of State that the person's drivers license is eligible for suspension pursuant to this Section. The notice of impending drivers license suspension shall be sent by first class United States mail, postage prepaid, to the address recorded with the Secretary of State.

(h) An administrative hearing to contest an impending suspension or a suspension made pursuant to this Section may be had upon filing a written request with the Secretary of State. The filing fee for this hearing shall be $20, to be paid at the time the request is made. A municipality which files a certified report with the Secretary of State pursuant to this Section shall reimburse the Secretary for all reasonable costs incurred by the Secretary as a result of the filing of the report, including but not limited to the costs of providing the notice required pursuant to subsection (b) and the costs incurred by the Secretary in any hearing conducted with respect to the report pursuant to this subsection and any appeal from such a hearing.

(i) The provisions of this Section shall apply on and after January 1, 1988.

(j) For purposes of this Section, the term "compliance violation" is defined as in Section 11–208.3.

P.A. 76–1586, § 6–306.5, added by P.A. 85–876, § 2, eff. Nov. 6, 1987. Amended by P.A. 89–190, § 5, eff. Jan. 1, 1996; P.A. 90–145, § 15, eff. Jan. 1, 1998; P.A. 90–481, § 30, eff. Aug. 17, 1997.

Formerly Ill.Rev.Stat.1991, ch. 95 ½, ¶ 6–306.5.

Section 4 of P.A. 85–876, veto overridden Nov. 6, 1987, provided:

"Sections 2 and 3 of this Act shall apply only to violations of a municipality's vehicular standing and parking regulations which occur on or after the effective date of this Act."

The amendments by P.A. 90–145 and P.A. 90–481 were identical.

5/6–306.6. Failure to pay traffic fines, penalties, and court costs

§ 6–306.6. Failure to pay traffic fines, penalties, and court costs.

(a) Whenever any resident of this State fails to pay any traffic fine, penalty, and cost imposed for a violation of this Code, or similar provision of local ordinance, the clerk may notify the Secretary of State, on a report prescribed by the Secretary, and the Secretary shall prohibit the renewal, reissue or reinstatement of such resident's driving privileges until such fine, penalty, and cost have been paid in full. The clerk shall provide notice to the driver, at the driver's last known address as shown on the court's records, stating that such action will be effective on the 46th day following the date of the above notice if payment is not received in full by the court of venue.

(b) Following receipt of the report from the clerk, the Secretary of State shall make the proper notation to the driver's file to prohibit the renewal, reissue or reinstatement of such driver's driving privileges. Except as provided in paragraph (2) of subsection (d) of this Section, such notation shall not be removed from the driver's record until the driver satisfies the outstanding fine, penalty, and cost and an appropriate notice on a form prescribed by the Secretary is received by the Secretary from the court of venue, stating that such fine, penalty, and cost has been paid in full. Upon payment in full of a traffic fine, penalty, and court cost which has previously been reported under this Section as unpaid, the clerk of the court shall present the driver with a signed receipt containing the seal of the court indicating that such fine, penalty, and cost have been paid in full, and shall forward forthwith to the Secretary of State a notice stating that the fine, penalty, and cost have been paid in full.

(c) The provisions of this Section shall be limited to a single action per arrest and as a post conviction measure only. Fines, penalty, and costs to be collected subsequent to orders of court supervision, or other available court diversions are not applicable to this Section. A driver making a partial payment of any outstanding fine, penalty, and cost is not a sufficient basis for the clerk to notify the Secretary for any subsequent action pursuant to this Section.

(d)(1) Notwithstanding the receipt of a report from the clerk as prescribed in subsection (a), nothing in this Section is intended to place any responsibility upon the Secretary of State to provide independent notice to the driver of any potential action to disallow the renewal, reissue or reinstatement of such driver's driving privileges. (2) The Secretary of State shall renew, reissue or reinstate a driver's driving privileges which were previously refused pursuant to this Section upon presentation of an original receipt which is signed by the clerk of the court and contains the seal of the court indicating that the fine, penalty, and cost have been paid in full. The Secretary of State shall retain such receipt for his records.

P.A. 76–1586, § 6–306.6, added by P.A. 86–609, § 1, eff. July 1, 1991. Amended by P.A. 89–71, § 5, eff. Jan. 1, 1996.

Formerly Ill.Rev.Stat.1991, ch. 95 ½, ¶ 6–306.6.

5/6–306.7. Failure to satisfy fines or penalties for toll violations or evasions; suspension of driving privileges

§ 6–306.7. Failure to satisfy fines or penalties for toll violations or evasions; suspension of driving privileges.

(a) Upon receipt of a certified report, as prescribed by subsection (c) of this Section, from the Authority stating that the owner of a registered vehicle has failed to satisfy any fine or penalty resulting from a final order issued by the Authority relating directly or indirectly to 5 or more toll violations, toll evasions, or both, the Secretary of State shall suspend the driving privileges of the person in accordance with the procedures set forth in this Section.

(b) Following receipt of the certified report of the Authority as specified in the Section, the Secretary of State shall notify the person whose name appears on the certified report that the person's driver's license will be suspended at the end of a specified period unless the Secretary of State is presented with a notice from the Authority certifying that the fines or penalties owing the Authority have been satisfied or that inclusion of that person's name on the certified report was in error. The Secretary's notice shall state in substance the information contained in the Authority's certified report to the Secretary, and shall be effective as specified by subsection (c) of Section 6-211 of this Code.

(c) The report from the Authority notifying the Secretary of unsatisfied fines or penalties pursuant to this Section shall be certified and shall contain the following:

(1) The name, last known address, and driver's license number of the person who failed to satisfy the fines or penalties and the registration number of any vehicle known to be registered in this State to that person.

(2) A statement that the Authority sent a notice of impending suspension of the person's driver's license, vehicle registration, or both, as prescribed by rules enacted pursuant to subsection (a-5) of Section 10 of the Toll Highway Act,[1] to the person named in the report at the address recorded with the Secretary of State; the date on which the notice was sent; and the address to which the notice was sent.

(d) The Authority, after making a certified report to the Secretary pursuant to this Section, shall notify the Secretary, on a form prescribed by the Secretary, whenever a person named in the certified report has satisfied the previously reported fines or penalties or whenever the Authority determines that the original report was in error. A certified copy of the notification shall also be given upon request and at no additional charge to the person named therein. Upon receipt of the Authority's notification or presentation of a certified copy of the notification, the Secretary shall terminate the suspension.

(e) The Authority shall, by rule, establish procedures for persons to challenge the accuracy of the certified report made pursuant to this Section. The rule shall also provide the grounds for a challenge, which may be limited to:

(1) the person not having been the owner or lessee of the vehicle or vehicles receiving 5 or more toll violations or toll evasion notices on the date or dates the notices were issued; or

(2) the person having already satisfied the fines or penalties for the 5 or more toll violations or toll evasions indicated on the certified report.

(f) All notices sent by the Authority to persons involved in administrative adjudications, hearings, and final orders issued pursuant to rules implementing subsection (a-5) of Section 10 of the Toll Highway Act shall state that failure to satisfy any fine or penalty imposed by the Authority shall result in the Secretary of State suspending the driving privileges, vehicle registration, or both, of the person failing to satisfy the fines or penalties imposed by the Authority.

(g) A person may request an administrative hearing to contest an impending suspension or a suspension made pursuant to this Section upon filing a written request with the Secretary. The filing fee for this hearing is $20, to be paid at the time of the request. The Authority shall reimburse the Secretary for all reasonable costs incurred by the Secretary as a result of the filing of a certified report pursuant to this Section, including, but not limited to, the costs of providing notice required pursuant to subsection (b) and the costs incurred by the Secretary in any hearing conducted with respect to the report pursuant to this subsection and any appeal from that hearing.

(h) The Secretary and the Authority may promulgate rules to enable them to carry out their duties under this Section.

(i) The Authority shall cooperate with the Secretary in the administration of this Section and shall provide the Secretary with any information the Secretary may deem necessary for these purposes, including regular and timely access to toll violation enforcement records.

The Secretary shall cooperate with the Authority in the administration of this Section and shall provide the Authority with any information the Authority may deem necessary for the purposes of this Section, including regular and timely access to vehicle registration records. Section 2-123 of this Code shall not apply to the provision of this information, but the Secretary shall be reimbursed for the cost of providing this information.

(j) For purposes of this Section, the term "Authority" means the Illinois State Toll Highway Authority.

P.A. 76-1586, § 6-306.7, added by P.A. 91-277, § 5, eff. Jan. 1, 2000.

[1] 605 ILCS 10/10.

5/6-307. Injunctions

§ 6-307. Injunctions. If any person operates in violation of any provision of this Chapter, or any rule, regulation, order or decision of the Secretary of State, or of any term, condition or limitation of any license, the Secretary of State, or any person injured thereby, or any interested person, may apply to the Circuit Court of the county in which such violation or some part thereof occurred, or in which the person complained of has his place of business or resides, to prevent such violation. The Court has jurisdiction to enforce obedience by injunction or other process restraining such person from further violation and enjoining upon him obedience.

P.A. 76-1586, § 6-307, added by P.A. 81-306, § 1, eff. Aug. 30, 1979.

Formerly Ill.Rev.Stat.1991, ch. 95 ½, ¶ 6-307.

ARTICLE IV. COMMERCIAL DRIVER TRAINING SCHOOLS

Section

5/6-401. Driver training schools—License required

§ 6-401. Driver training schools—License required. No person, firm, association, partnership or corporation shall operate a driver training school or engage in the business of giving instruction for hire or for a fee in the driving of motor vehicles or in the preparation of an applicant for examination given by the Secretary of State for a drivers license or permit, unless a license therefor has been issued by the Secretary.

This section shall not apply to public schools or to educational institutions in which driving instruction is part of the curriculum or to employers giving instruction to their employees.

P.A. 76-1586, § 6-401, eff. July 1, 1970.

Formerly Ill.Rev.Stat.1991, ch. 95 ½, ¶ 6-401.

5/6-402. Qualifications of driver training schools

§ 6-402. Qualifications of driver training schools. In order to qualify for a license to operate a driver training school, each applicant must:

(a) be of good moral character;

(b) be at least 21 years of age;

(c) maintain an established place of business open to the public which meets the requirements of Section 6-403 through 6-407;

(d) maintain bodily injury and property damage liability insurance on motor vehicles while used in driving instruction, insuring the liability of the driving school, the driving instructors and any person taking instruction in at least the following amounts: $50,000 for bodily injury to or death of one person in any one accident and, subject to said limit for one person, $100,000 for bodily injury to or death of 2 or more persons in any one accident and the amount of $10,000 for damage to property of others in any one accident. Evidence of such insurance coverage in the form of a certificate from the insurance carrier shall be filed with the Secretary of State, and such certificate shall stipulate that the insurance shall not be cancelled except upon 10 days prior written notice to the Secretary of State. The decal showing evidence of insurance shall be affixed to the windshield of the vehicle;

(e) provide a continuous surety company bond in the principal sum of $10,000 for the protection of the contractual rights of students in such form as will meet with the approval of the Secretary of State and written by a company authorized to do business in this State. However, the aggregate liability of the surety for all breaches of the condition of the bond in no event shall exceed the principal sum of $10,000. The surety on any such bond may cancel such bond on giving 30 days notice thereof in writing to the Secretary of State and shall be relieved of liability for any breach of any conditions of the bond which occurs after the effective date of cancellation;

(f) have the equipment necessary to the giving of proper instruction in the operation of motor vehicles;

(g) have and use a business telephone listing for all business purposes; and

(h) pay to the Secretary of State an application fee of $250.

No license shall be issued under this Section to a person who is a spouse, offspring, sibling, parent, grandparent, grandchild, uncle or aunt, nephew or niece, cousin, or in-law of the person whose license to do business at that location has been revoked or denied or to a person who was an officer or employee of a business firm that has had its license revoked or denied, unless the Secretary of State is satisfied the application was submitted in good faith and not for the purpose or effect of defeating the intent of this Code.

P.A. 76-1586, § 6-402, eff. July 1, 1970. Amended by P.A. 76-1838, § 1, eff. July 1, 1970; P.A. 87-829, § 1, eff. Jan. 17, 1992; P.A. 87-832, § 3, eff. Jan. 17, 1992; P.A. 87-895, Art. 2, § 2-45, eff. Aug. 14, 1992.

Formerly Ill.Rev.Stat.1991, ch. 95 ½, ¶ 6-402.

P.A. 87-895, the First 1992 General Revisory Act, provides in Article 2 for the revision and renumbering of certain Sections of Acts which have been added or amended by more than one Act of the 87th General Assembly; incorporates amendments to repealed Acts into successor laws passed by the same General Assembly; corrects errors, revises cross-references and deletes obsolete text in such Sections contained in Public Acts through P.A. 87-855.

5/6-403. Established place of business

§ 6-403. Established place of business. The established place of business of each driver training school must be owned or leased by the driver training school and regularly occupied and primarily used by that driver training school for the business of selling and giving driving instructions for hire or for a fee, and the business of preparing members of the public for examination given by the Secretary of State for a drivers license.

P.A. 76-1586, § 6-403, eff. July 1, 1970.

Formerly Ill.Rev.Stat.1991, ch. 95 ½, ¶ 6-403.

5/6-404. Location of schools

§ 6-404. Location of schools. The established place of business of each driver training school must be located in a district which is zoned for business or commercial purposes. The driver training school office must have a permanent sign clearly readable from the street, from a distance of no less than 100 feet, with the name of the driving school upon it.

P.A. 76-1586, § 6-404, eff. July 1, 1970. Amended by P.A. 76-1753, § 1, eff. July 1, 1970.

Formerly Ill.Rev.Stat.1991, ch. 95 ½, ¶ 6-404.

5/6-405. Restrictions of locations

§ 6-405. Restrictions of locations. The established place of business, or branch office, branch class room or advertised address of any driver training school shall not consist of or include a house trailer, residence, tent, temporary stand, temporary address, office space, a room or rooms in a hotel, rooming house or apartment house, or premises occupied by a single or multiple unit dwelling house or telephone answering service.

P.A. 76-1586, § 6-405, eff. July 1, 1970.

Formerly Ill.Rev.Stat.1991, ch. 95 ½, ¶ 6-405.

5/6-406. Required facilities

§ 6-406. Required facilities. (a) The established place of business of each driver training school must consist of at least the following permanent facilities:

(1) An office facility;

(2) A class room facility.

(b) The main class room facility of each driver training school must be reasonably accessible to the main office facility of the driver training school.

(c) All class room facilities must have adequate lighting, heating, ventilation, and must comply with all state, and local laws relating to public health, safety and sanitation.

(d) The main office facility and branch office facility of each driver training school must contain sufficient space, equipment, records and personnel to carry on the business of the driver training school. The main office facility must be specifically devoted to driver training school business.

(e) A driver training school which as an established place of business and a main office facility, may operate a branch office or a branch class room provided that all the requirements for the main office or main class room are met and that such branch office bears the same name and is operated as a part of the same business entity as the main office facility.

(f) No driver training school may share any main or branch facility or facilities with any other driver training school.

P.A. 76-1586, § 6-406, eff. July 1, 1970.

Formerly Ill.Rev.Stat.1991, ch. 95 ½, ¶ 6-406.

5/6-407. Locations and state facilities

§ 6-407. Locations and state facilities. No office or place of business of a driver training school shall be established within 1,500 feet of any building used as an office by any department of the Secretary of State having to do with the administration of any laws relating to motor vehicles, nor may any driving school solicit or advertise for business within 1,500 feet of any building used as an office by the Secretary of State having to do with the administration of any laws relating to motor vehicles.

P.A. 76-1586, § 6-407, eff. July 1, 1970.

Formerly Ill.Rev.Stat.1991, ch. 95 ½, ¶ 6-407.

5/6-408. Records

§ 6-408. Records. All driver training schools licensed by the Secretary of State must maintain a permanent record of instructions given to each student. The record must contain the name of the school and the name of the student, the number of all licenses or permits held by the student, the type and date of instruction given, whether class room or behind the wheel, and the signature of the instructor.

All permanent student instruction records must be kept on file in the main office of each driver training school for a period of 3 calendar years after the student has ceased taking instruction at or with the school.

The records should show the fees and charges of the school and also the record should show the course content and instructions given to each student.

P.A. 76-1586, § 6-408, eff. July 1, 1970. Amended by P.A. 76-1754, § 1, eff. July 1, 1970.

Formerly Ill.Rev.Stat.1991, ch. 95 ½, ¶ 6-408.

5/6-408.5 Courses for students or high school dropouts; limitation

§ 6-408.5. Courses for students or high school dropouts; limitation. (a) No driver training school or driving training instructor licensed under this Act may request a certificate of completion from the Secretary of State as provided in Section 6-411 for any person who is enrolled as a student in any public or non-public secondary school at the time such instruction is to be provided, or who was so enrolled during the semester last ended if that instruction is to be provided between semesters or during the summer after the regular school term ends, unless that student has received a passing grade in at least 8 courses during the 2 semesters last ending prior to requesting a certificate of completion from the Secretary of State for the student.

(b) No driver training school or driving training instructor licensed under this Act may request a certificate of completion from the Secretary of State as provided in Section 6-411 for any person who has dropped out of school and has not yet attained the age of 18 years unless the driver training school or driving training instructor has: 1) obtained written documentation verifying the dropout's enrollment in a GED or alternative education program or has obtained a copy of the dropout's GED certificate; 2) obtained verification that the student prior to dropping out had received a passing grade in at least 8 courses during the 2 previous semesters last ending prior to requesting a certificate of completion; or 3) obtained written consent from the dropout's parents or guardians and the regional superintendent.

(c) Students shall be informed of the eligibility requirements of this Act in writing at the time of registration.

(d) The superintendent of schools of the school district in which the student resides and attends school or in which the student resides at the time he or she drops out of school (with respect to a public high school student or a dropout from the public high school) or the chief school administrator (with respect to a student who attends a non-public high school or a dropout from a non-public high school) may waive the requirements of this Section if the superintendent or chief school administrator, as the case may be, deems it to be in the best interests of the student or dropout. Before requesting a certificate of completion from the Secretary of State for any person who is enrolled as a student in any public or non-public secondary school or who was so enrolled in the semester last ending prior to the request for a certificate of completion from the Secretary of State or who is of high school age, the driver training school shall determine from the school district in which that person resides or resided at the time of dropping out of school, or from the chief administrator of the non-public high school attended or last attended by such person, as the case may be, that such person is not ineligible to receive a certificate of completion under this Section.

(e) By January 1, 1997, the Secretary of State, in cooperation with the State Board of Education, shall complete, and submit to the General Assembly, a report that examines the impact of this Section and other changes made by Public Act 88-188.

P.A. 76-1586, § 6-408.5, added by P.A. 88-188, § 10, eff. Jan. 1, 1994. Amended by P.A. 88-628, § 10, eff. Sept. 9, 1994.

5/6-409. Display of license

§ 6-409. Display of license. Each driver training school must display at a prominent place in its main office all of the following:

(a) The State license issued to the school;

(b) The names and addresses and State instructors licenses of all instructors employed by the school;

(c) The address of all branch offices and branch class rooms.

P.A. 76-1586, § 6-409, eff. July 1, 1970.

Formerly Ill.Rev.Stat.1991, ch. 95 ½, ¶ 6-409.

5/6-410. Vehicle inspections

§ 6-410. Vehicle inspections. The Department of Transportation shall provide for the inspection of all motor vehicles used for driver training, and shall issue a safety inspection sticker provided:

(a) The motor vehicle has been inspected by the Department and found to be in safe mechanical condition;

(b) The motor vehicle is equipped with dual control brakes and a mirror on each side of the motor vehicle so located as to reflect to the driver a view of the highway for a distance of at least 200 feet to the rear of such motor vehicle; and

(c) The motor vehicle is equipped with a sign or signs visible from the front and the rear in letters no less than 2 inches tall, listing the full name of the driver training school which has registered and insured the motor vehicle.

P.A. 76–1586, § 6–410, eff. July 1, 1970. Amended by P.A. 77–170, § 1, eff. Jan. 1, 1972; P.A. 85–951, § 1, eff. July 1, 1988.

Formerly Ill.Rev.Stat.1991, ch. 95 ½, ¶ 6–410.

5/6–411. Qualifications of Driver Training Instructors

§ 6–411. Qualifications of Driver Training Instructors. In order to qualify for a license as an instructor for a driving school, an applicant must:

(a) Be of good moral character;

(b) Authorize an investigation to determine if the applicant has ever been convicted of a crime and if so, the disposition of those convictions; this authorization shall indicate the scope of the inquiry and the agencies which may be contacted. Upon this authorization the Secretary of State may request and receive information and assistance from any federal, state or local governmental agency as part of the authorized investigation. The Department of State Police shall provide information concerning any criminal convictions, and their disposition, brought against the applicant upon request of the Secretary of State when the request is made in the form and manner required by the Department of State Police. The information derived from this investigation including the source of this information, and any conclusions or recommendations derived from this information by the Secretary of State shall be provided to the applicant, or his designee, upon request to the Secretary of State, prior to any final action by the Secretary of State on the application. No information obtained from such investigation may be placed in any automated information system. Any criminal convictions and their disposition information obtained by the Secretary of State shall be confidential and may not be transmitted outside the Office of the Secretary of State, except as required herein, and may not be transmitted to anyone within the Office of the Secretary of State except as needed for the purpose of evaluating the applicant. The only physical identity materials which the applicant can be required to provide the Secretary of State are photographs or fingerprints; these shall be returned to the applicant upon request to the Secretary of State, after the investigation has been completed and no copy of these materials may be kept by the Secretary of State or any agency to which such identity materials were transmitted. Only information and standards which bear a reasonable and rational relation to the performance of a driver training instructor shall be used by the Secretary of State. Any employee of the Secretary of State who gives or causes to be given away any confidential information concerning any criminal charges and their disposition of an applicant shall be guilty of a Class A misdemeanor unless release of such information is authorized by this Section;

(c) Pass such examination as the Secretary of State shall require on (1) traffic laws, (2) safe driving practices, (3) operation of motor vehicles, and (4) qualifications of teacher;

(d) Be physically able to operate safely a motor vehicle and to train others in the operation of motor vehicles. An instructors license application must be accompanied by a medical examination report completed by a competent physician licensed to practice in the State of Illinois;

(e) Hold a valid Illinois drivers license;

(f) Have graduated from an accredited high school after at least 4 years of high school education or the equivalent; and

(g) Pay to the Secretary of State an application and license fee of $35.

If a driver training school class room instructor teaches an approved driver education course, as defined in Section 1–103 of this Code, to students under 18 years of age, he or she shall furnish to the Secretary of State a certificate issued by the State Board of Education that the said instructor is qualified and meets the minimum educational standards for teaching driver education courses in the local public or parochial school systems, except that no State Board of Education certification shall be required of any instructor who teaches exclusively in a commercial driving school. On and after July 1, 1986, the existing rules and regulations of the State Board of Education concerning commercial driving schools shall continue to remain in effect but shall be administered by the Secretary of State until such time as the Secretary of State shall amend or repeal the rules in accordance with The Illinois Administrative Procedure Act.[1] Upon request, the Secretary of State shall issue a certificate of completion to a student under 18 years of age who has completed an approved driver education course at a commercial driving school.

P.A. 76–1586, § 6–411, eff. July 1, 1970. Amended by P.A. 80–1447, § 1, eff. Sept. 15, 1978; P.A. 81–1508, § 8, eff. Sept. 25, 1980; P.A. 81–1509, Art. II, § 71, eff. Sept. 26, 1980; P.A. 81–1550, Art. I, § 22, eff. Jan. 8, 1981; P.A. 84–25, Art. IV, § 27, eff. July 18, 1985; P.A. 84–863, § 1, eff. July 1, 1986; P.A. 84–1308, Art. II, § 96, eff. Aug. 25, 1986; P.A. 87–829, § 1, eff. Jan. 17, 1992; P.A. 87–832, § 3, eff. Jan. 17, 1992.

Formerly Ill.Rev.Stat.1991, ch. 95 ½, ¶ 6–411.

[1] 5 ILCS 100/1–1 et seq.

The amendments by P.A. 87–829 and P.A. 87–832 were identical.

5/6–412. Issuance of licenses to driver training schools and driver training instructors

§ 6–412. Issuance of licenses to driver training schools and driver training instructors. The Secretary of State shall issue a license certificate to each applicant to conduct a driver training school or to each driver training instructor when the Secretary of State is satisfied that such person has met the qualifications required under this Act.

P.A. 76–1586, § 6–412, eff. July 1, 1970.

Formerly Ill.Rev.Stat.1991, ch. 95 ½, ¶ 6–412.

5/6–413. Expiration of Licenses

§ 6–413. Expiration of Licenses. All outstanding licenses issued to any driver training school or driver training instructor under this Act shall expire by operation of law 12 months from the date of issuance, unless sooner cancelled, suspended or revoked under the provisions of Section 6–420.

P.A. 76–1586, § 6–413, eff. July 1, 1970. Amended by P.A 87–829, § 1, eff. Jan. 17, 1992; P.A. 87–832, § 3, eff. Jan. 17, 1992.

Formerly Ill.Rev.Stat.1991, ch. 95 ½, ¶ 6–413.

The amendments by P.A. 87–829 and P.A. 87–832 were identical.

5/6–414. Renewal of Licenses

§ 6–414. Renewal of Licenses. The license of each driver training school may be renewed subject to the same conditions as the original license, and upon the payment of an annual renewal license fee of $250.

P.A. 76–1586, § 6–414, eff. July 1, 1970. Amended by P.A. 87–829, § 1, eff. Jan. 17, 1992; P.A. 87–832, § 3, eff. Jan. 17, 1992.

Formerly Ill.Rev.Stat.1991, ch. 95 ½, ¶ 6–414.

The amendments by P.A. 87–829 and P.A. 87–832 were identical.

5/6–415. Renewal Fee

§ 6–415. Renewal Fee. The license of each driver training instructor may be renewed subject to the same conditions of the original license, and upon the payment of annual renewal license fee of $35.

P.A. 76–1586, § 6–415, eff. July 1, 1970. Amended by P.A. 87–829, § 1, eff. Jan. 17, 1992; P.A. 87–832, § 3, eff. Jan. 17, 1992.

Formerly Ill.Rev.Stat.1991, ch. 95 ½, ¶ 6–415.

5/6–416. Licenses: Form and Filing

§ 6–416. Licenses: Form and Filing. All applications for renewal of a driver training school license or driver training instructor's license shall be on a form prescribed by the Secretary, and must be filed with the Secretary not less than 15 days preceding the expiration date of the license to be renewed.

P.A. 76–1586, § 6–416, eff. July 1, 1970. Amended by P.A. 87–829, § 1, eff. Jan. 17, 1992; P.A. 87–832, § 3, eff. Jan. 17, 1992.

Formerly Ill.Rev.Stat.1991, ch. 95 ½, ¶ 6–416.

The amendments by P.A. 87–829 and P.A. 87–832 were identical.

5/6–417. Instructor's license

§ 6–417. Instructor's license. Each driver training instructor's license shall authorize the licensee to instruct only at or for the driver training school indicated on the license. The Secretary shall not issue a driver training instructor's license to any individual who is licensed to instruct at or for another driver training school.

P.A. 76–1586, § 6–417, eff. July 1, 1970.

Formerly Ill.Rev.Stat.1991, ch. 95 ½, ¶ 6–417.

5/6–418. Instructor's records

§ 6–418. Instructor's records. Every licensee shall keep a record showing the name and address of each person given instruction and the instruction permit or driver's license number of every person given instruction in the driving of a motor vehicle, and shall show the particular type of instruction given and how much time was devoted to each such type of instruction. Such records shall be open to the inspection of the Secretary or his representatives at all reasonable times, but shall be for the confidential use of the Secretary.

P.A. 76–1586, § 6–418, eff. July 1, 1970.

Formerly Ill.Rev.Stat.1991, ch. 95 ½, ¶ 6–418.

5/6–419. Rules and regulations

§ 6–419. Rules and regulations. The Secretary is authorized to prescribe by rule standards for the eligibility, conduct and operation of driver training schools, and instructors and to adopt other reasonable rules and regulations necessary to carry out the provisions of this Act.

P.A. 76–1586, § 6–419, eff. July 1, 1970.

Formerly Ill.Rev.Stat.1991, ch. 95 ½, ¶ 6–419.

5/6–420. Denial, Cancellation, Suspension, Revocation and Failure to Renew License

§ 6–420. Denial, Cancellation, Suspension, Revocation and Failure to Renew License. The Secretary may deny, cancel, suspend or revoke, or refuse to renew any driver training school license or any driver training instructor license:

(1) When the Secretary is satisfied that the licensee fails to meet the requirements to receive or hold a license under this Code;

(2) Whenever the licensee fails to keep the records required by this Code;

(3) Whenever the licensee permits fraud or engages in fraudulent practices either with reference to a student or the Secretary, or induces or countenances fraud or fraudulent practices on the part of any applicant for a driver's license or permit;

(4) Whenever the licensee fails to comply with any provision of this Code or any rule of the Secretary made pursuant thereto;

(5) Whenever the licensee represents himself as an agent or employee of the Secretary or uses advertising designed to lead or which would reasonably have the effect of leading persons to believe that such licensee is in fact an employee or representative of the Secretary;

(6) Whenever the licensee or any employee or agent of the licensee solicits driver training or instruction in an office of any department of the Secretary of State having to do with the administration of any law relating to motor vehicles, or within 1,500 feet of any such office;

(7) Whenever the licensee is convicted of driving while under the influence of alcohol, other drugs, or a combination thereof; leaving the scene of an accident; reckless homicide or reckless driving; or

(8) Whenever a driver training school advertises that a driver's license is guaranteed upon completion of the course of instruction.

P.A. 76–1586, § 6–420, eff. July 1, 1970. Amended by P.A. 85–951, § 1, eff. July 1, 1988.

Formerly Ill.Rev.Stat.1991, ch. 95 ½, ¶ 6–420.

5/6–421. Judicial Review

§ 6–421. Judicial Review. The action of the Secretary in cancelling, suspending, revoking or denying any license under this Act shall be subject to judicial review in the Circuit Court of Sangamon County or the Circuit Court of Cook County, and the provisions of the Administrative Review Law, and all amendments and modifications thereto,[1] and the rules adopted pursuant thereto, are hereby adopted and shall apply to and govern every action for judicial review of the final acts or decisions of the Secretary under this Act.

P.A. 76–1586, § 6–421, eff. July 1, 1970. Amended by P.A. 82–783, Art. XI, § 140, eff. July 13, 1982.

Formerly Ill.Rev.Stat.1991, ch. 95 ½, ¶ 6–421.

[1] 735 ILCS 5/3–101 et seq.

5/6–422. Prior law and licenses thereunder

§ 6–422. Prior law and licenses thereunder. This Act shall not affect the validity of any outstanding license issued to any driver training school or driver training instructor by the Secretary of State under any prior law, nor shall this Act affect the validity or legality of any contract, agreement or undertaking entered into by any driver training school or driver training instructor, or any person, firm, corporation, partnership or association based on those provisions of any prior law.

P.A. 76-1586, § 6-422, eff. July 1, 1970.

Formerly Ill.Rev.Stat.1991, ch. 95 ½, ¶ 6-422.

5/6-423. Deposit of fees

§ 6-423. Deposit of fees. Fees collected under this Article shall be deposited in the Road Fund.

P.A. 76-1586, § 6-423, eff. July 1, 1970.

Formerly Ill.Rev.Stat.1991, ch. 95 ½, ¶ 6-423.

5/6-424. Injunctions

§ 6-424. Injunctions. If any person operates in violation of any provision of this Article, or any rule, regulation, order, or decision of the Secretary of State established under this Article, or in violation of any term, condition or limitation of any license issued under this Article, the Secretary of State, or any other person injured as a result, or any interested person, may apply to the circuit court of the county where the violation or some part occurred, or where the person complained of has an established or additional place of business or resides, to prevent the violation. The court may enforce compliance by injunction or other process restraining the person from further violation and compliance.

P.A. 76-1586, § 6-424, added by P.A. 87-829, § 1, eff. Jan. 17, 1992; P.A. 87-832, § 3, eff. Jan. 17, 1992.

Formerly Ill.Rev.Stat.1991, ch. 95 ½, ¶ 6-424.

P.A. 87-829 and P.A. 87-832 added identical versions of this section.

ARTICLE V. UNIFORM COMMERCIAL DRIVER'S LICENSE ACT

Date Effective

Article VI was added by P.A. 85-630, § 1, eff. Sept. 20, 1987, and editorially renumbered as Art. V.

P.A. 86-620, Art. III, § 3-36, eff. Sept. 7, 1989, renumbered the Article.

Section

Section

5/6-500. Definitions of words and phrases

§ 6-500. Definitions of words and phrases. Notwithstanding the definitions set forth elsewhere in this Code, for purposes of the Uniform Commercial Driver's License Act (UCDLA),[1] the words and phrases listed below have the meanings ascribed to them as follows:

(1) Alcohol. "Alcohol" means any substance containing any form of alcohol, including but not limited to ethanol, methanol, propanol, and isopropanol.

(2) Alcohol concentration. "Alcohol concentration" means:

(A) the number of grams of alcohol per 210 liters of breath; or

(B) the number of grams of alcohol per 100 milliliters of blood; or

(C) the number of grams of alcohol per 67 milliliters of urine.

Alcohol tests administered within 2 hours of the driver being "stopped or detained" shall be considered that driver's "alcohol concentration" for the purposes of enforcing this UCDLA.

(3) (Blank).

(4) (Blank).

(5) (Blank).

(6) Commercial Motor Vehicle.

(A) "Commercial motor vehicle" means a motor vehicle, except those referred to in subdivision (B), designed to transport passengers or property if:

(i) the vehicle has a GVWR of 26,001 pounds or more or such a lesser GVWR as subsequently determined by federal regulations or the Secretary of State; or any combination of vehicles with a GCWR of 26,001 pounds or more, provided the GVWR of any vehicle or vehicles being towed is 10,001 pounds or more; or

(ii) the vehicle is designed to transport 16 or more persons; or

(iii) the vehicle is transporting hazardous materials and is required to be placarded in accordance with 49 C.F.R. Part 172, subpart F.

(B) Pursuant to the interpretation of the Commercial Motor Vehicle Safety Act of 1986[2] by the Federal Highway Administration, the definition of "commercial motor vehicle" does not include:

(i) recreational vehicles, when operated primarily for personal use;

(ii) United States Department of Defense vehicles being operated by non-civilian personnel. This includes any operator on active military duty; members of the Reserves; National Guard; personnel on part-time training; and National Guard military technicians (civilians who are required to wear military uniforms and are subject to the Code of Military Justice); or

(iii) firefighting and other emergency equipment with audible and visual signals, owned or operated by or for a governmental entity, which is necessary to the preservation of life or property or the execution of emergency governmental functions which are normally not subject to general traffic rules and regulations.

(7) Controlled Substance. "Controlled substance" shall have the same meaning as defined in Section 102 of the Illinois Controlled Substances Act,[3] and shall also include cannabis as defined in Section 3 of the Cannabis Control Act.[4]

(8) Conviction. "Conviction" means an unvacated adjudication of guilt or a determination that a person has violated or failed to comply with the law in a court of original jurisdiction or an authorized administrative tribunal; an unvacated forfeiture of bail or collateral deposited to secure the person's appearance in court; the payment of a fine or court cost regardless of whether the imposition of sentence is deferred and ultimately a judgment dismissing the underlying charge is entered; or a violation of a condition of release without bail, regardless of whether or not the penalty is rebated, suspended or probated.

(9) (Blank).

(10) (Blank).

(11) (Blank).

(12) (Blank).

(13) Driver. "Driver" means any person who drives, operates, or is in physical control of a commercial motor vehicle, or who is required to hold a CDL.

(14) Employee. "Employee" means a person who is employed as a commercial motor vehicle driver. A person who is self-employed as a commercial motor vehicle driver must comply with the requirements of this UCDLA pertaining to employees. An owner-operator on a long-term lease shall be considered an employee.

(15) Employer. "Employer" means a person (including the United States, a State or a local authority) who owns or leases a commercial motor vehicle or assigns employees to operate such a vehicle. A person who is self-employed as a commercial motor vehicle driver must comply with the requirements of this UCDLA.

(16) (Blank).

(17) Foreign jurisdiction. "Foreign jurisdiction" means a sovereign jurisdiction that does not fall within the definition of "State".

(18) (Blank).

(19) (Blank).

(20) Hazardous Material. Upon a finding by the United States Secretary of Transportation, in his or her discretion, under 49 App. U.S.C. 5103(a), that the transportation of a particular quantity and form of material in commerce may pose an unreasonable risk to health and safety or property, he or she shall designate the quantity and form of material or group or class of the materials as a hazardous material. The materials so designated may include but are not limited to explosives, radioactive materials, etiologic agents, flammable liquids or solids, combustible liquids or solids, poisons, oxidizing or corrosive materials, and compressed gases.

(21) Long-term lease. "Long-term lease" means a lease of a commercial motor vehicle by the owner-lessor to a lessee, for a period of more than 29 days.

(22) Motor Vehicle. "Motor vehicle" means every vehicle which is self-propelled, and every vehicle which is propelled by electric power obtained from over head trolley wires but not operated upon rails, except vehicles moved solely by human power and motorized wheel chairs.

(23) Non-resident CDL. "Non-resident CDL" means a commercial driver's license issued by a state to an individual who is domiciled in a foreign jurisdiction.

(24) (Blank).

(25) (Blank).

(25.5) Railroad-Highway Grade Crossing Violation. "Railroad-highway grade crossing violation" means a violation, while operating a commercial motor vehicle, of any of the following:

(A) Section 11-1201, 11-1202, or 11-1425 of this Code.

(B) Any other similar law or local ordinance of any state relating to railroad-highway grade crossing.

(26) Serious Traffic Violation. "Serious traffic violation" means:

(A) a conviction when operating a commercial motor vehicle of:

(i) a violation relating to excessive speeding, involving a single speeding charge of 15 miles per hour or more above the legal speed limit; or

(ii) a violation relating to reckless driving; or

(iii) a violation of any State law or local ordinance relating to motor vehicle traffic control (other than parking violations) arising in connection with a fatal traffic accident; or

(iv) a violation of Section 6-501, relating to having multiple driver's licenses; or

(v) a violation of paragraph (a) of Section 6-507, relating to the requirement to have a valid CDL; or

(vi) a violation relating to improper or erratic traffic lane changes; or

(vii) a violation relating to following another vehicle too closely; or

(B) any other similar violation of a law or local ordinance of any state relating to motor vehicle traffic control, other than a parking violation, which the Secretary of State determines by administrative rule to be serious.

(27) State. "State" means a state of the United States, the District of Columbia and any province or territory of Canada.

(28) (Blank).

(29) (Blank).

(30) (Blank).

(31) (Blank).

P.A. 76-1586, § 6-500, added by P.A. 85-630, § 1, eff. Sept. 20, 1987. Amended by P.A. 85-1396, § 2, eff. Sept. 2, 1988; P.A. 86-845, § 1, eff. April 1, 1990; P.A. 87-829, § 1, eff. Jan. 17, 1992; P.A. 87-832, § 3, eff. Jan. 17, 1992; P.A. 89-179, § 5, eff. Jan. 1, 1996; P.A. 89-571, § 5, eff. July 26, 1996; P.A. 90-89, § 15, eff. Jan. 1, 1998; P.A. 92-249, § 5, eff. Jan. 1, 2002; P.A. 92-651, § 77, eff. July 11, 2002; P.A. 92-834, § 5, eff. Aug. 22, 2002.

Formerly Ill.Rev.Stat.1991, ch. 95 ½, ¶ 6-500.

[1] 625 ILCS 5/6-500 et seq.

[2] 49 App. U.S.C.A. § 2701 et seq. (repealed).

[3] 720 ILCS 570/102.

[4] 720 ILCS 550/3.

See 5 ILCS 70/6 as to the effect of (1) more than one amendment of a section at the same session of the General Assembly or (2) two or more acts relating to the same subject matter enacted by the same General Assembly.

P.A. 92-834 incorporated the amendment by P.A. 92-249.

5/6-500.1. Short title

§ 6-500.1. Short title. This Article may be cited as the Uniform Commercial Driver's License Act or "UCDLA".

P.A. 76-1586, § 6-500.1, added by P.A. 86-845, § 1, eff. April 1, 1990.

Formerly Ill.Rev.Stat.1991, ch. 95 ½, ¶ 6-500.1.

5/6-500.2. Statement of intent and purpose

§ 6-500.2. Statement of intent and purpose. The purpose of this UCDLA is to implement the federal Commercial Motor Vehicle Safety Act of 1986 (CMVSA) (Title XII of Pub. Law 99-570) and reduce or prevent commercial motor vehicle accidents, fatalities and injuries by:

(a) permitting commercial drivers to hold only one driver's license;

(b) disqualifying commercial drivers who have committed certain serious traffic violations, or other specified offenses; and

(c) strengthening commercial driver licensing and testing standards.

This UCDLA is remedial in nature and should be liberally construed to promote the public's health, safety and welfare. To the extent that this UCDLA conflicts with any other provisions of this Code, the UCDLA shall prevail. Where this UCDLA is silent, the other general provisions of this Code shall apply.

P.A. 76-1586, § 6-500.2, added by P.A. 86-845, § 1, eff. April 1, 1990.

Formerly Ill.Rev.Stat.1991, ch. 95 ½, ¶ 6-500.2.

5/6-501. Commercial drivers—permitted only one driver's license

§ 6-501. Commercial drivers—permitted only one driver's license. No person who drives a commercial motor vehicle, on the highways, shall have more than one driver's license, except during the 10-day period beginning on the date such person is issued a CDL.

Any person convicted of violating this Section shall be guilty of a Class A misdemeanor.

P.A. 76-1586, § 6-501, added by P.A. 85-630, § 1, eff. Sept. 20, 1987. Amended by P.A. 86-845, § 1, eff. April 1, 1990.

Formerly Ill.Rev.Stat.1991, ch. 95 ½, ¶ 6-501.

5/6-502. Commercial motor vehicle drivers—reporting of traffic violations to the Secretary of State

§ 6-502. Commercial motor vehicle drivers—reporting of traffic violations to the Secretary of State. When required by the Commercial Motor Vehicle Safety Act of 1986, [1] every person who has been issued an Illinois non-resident CDL or who is a domiciliary of this State and drives a commercial motor vehicle in violation of a law or local ordinance of any State relating to motor vehicle traffic control (other than parking violations) in any other state, shall notify the Secretary of State, on a form and in a manner prescribed by the Secretary, of such violation within 30 days after the date such person has been convicted of such offense.

P.A. 76-1586, § 6-502, added by P.A. 85-630, § 1, eff. Sept. 20, 1987. Amended by P.A. 86-845, § 1, eff. April 1, 1990.

Formerly Ill.Rev.Stat.1991, ch. 95 ½, ¶ 6-502.

[1] 49 App. U.S.C.A. § 2701.

5/6-503. Commercial motor vehicle drivers—reporting of traffic violations to employer

§ 6-503. Commercial motor vehicle drivers—reporting of traffic violations to employer. Every person who is a domiciliary of this State or who has been issued an Illinois non-resident CDL and drives a commercial motor vehicle in violation of a law or local ordinance of any State relating to motor vehicle traffic control (other than parking violations) in this or any other state, shall notify such person's employer of such violation within 30 days after the date such person is convicted of such offense.

In the event such person is a "common carrier of property by motor vehicle", as defined in Section 18c-1104 of this Code, such person shall notify the principal lessor of such within 30 days after the date such person is convicted of the violation. However, if such person is an independent contractor or owner operator, such report shall be kept at the principal place of business and available during normal office hours for inspection and auditing purposes by an authorized agency.

P.A. 76-1586, § 6-503, added by P.A. 85-630, § 1, eff. Sept. 20, 1987. Amended by P.A. 85-1396, § 2, eff. Sept. 2, 1988; P.A. 86-845, § 1, eff. April 1, 1990.

Formerly Ill.Rev.Stat.1991, ch. 95 ½, ¶ 6-503.

5/6-504. Commercial motor vehicle drivers—other reporting requirements

§ 6-504. Commercial motor vehicle drivers—other reporting requirements. All drivers of commercial motor vehicles licensed or domiciled in Illinois:

(1) who have their driving privileges suspended, revoked or cancelled by any state; or

(2) who lose their privilege to operate a commercial motor vehicle in any state for any period; or

(3) who are disqualified from driving a commercial motor vehicle for any period; or

(4) who are placed "out-of-service" pursuant to Section 6-515;

shall notify: (i) their employer of such suspension, revocation, cancellation, lost right, disqualification, or "out-of-service" action before the end of the business day following the day the driver received notice of such action; and within 30 days after the effective date of such action.

(ii) the Secretary of State of any such out-of-state suspension, revocation, cancellation, lost right, disqualification, or "out-of-service" action within 30 days after the effective date of such action.

P.A. 76-1586, § 6-504, added by P.A. 85-630, § 1, eff. Sept. 20, 1987. Amended by P.A. 85-1396, § 2, eff. Sept. 2, 1988; P.A. 86-845, § 1, eff. April 1, 1990.

Formerly Ill.Rev.Stat.1991, ch. 95 ½, ¶ 6-504.

5/6-505. Commercial motor vehicle driver—duty to report certain previous employment to potential employer

§ 6-505. Commercial motor vehicle driver—duty to report certain previous employment to potential employer. Each person who applies for employment as a driver of a commercial motor vehicle, with any employer, shall notify such potential employer at the time of such application of any and all previous employment for the last 10 years, as a driver of a commercial motor vehicle including, but not necessarily limited to, the dates between which the applicant drove for each employer, the reason for leaving each such employment and the information contained in the notification requirements of Section 6-504.

P.A. 76-1586, § 6-505, added by P.A. 85-630, § 1, eff. Sept. 20, 1987. Amended by P.A. 86-845, § 1, eff. April 1, 1990.

Formerly Ill.Rev.Stat.1991, ch. 95 ½, ¶ 6-505.

5/6-506. Commercial motor vehicle driver—employer/owner responsibilities

§ 6-506. Commercial motor vehicle driver—employer/owner responsibilities.

(a) No employer or commercial motor vehicle owner shall knowingly allow, permit, or authorize an employee to drive a commercial motor vehicle on the highways during any period in which such employee:

(1) has a driver's license suspended, revoked or cancelled by any state; or

(2) has lost the privilege to drive a commercial motor vehicle in any state; or

(3) has been disqualified from driving a commercial motor vehicle; or

(4) has more than one driver's license, except as provided by this UCDLA; or

(5) is subject to or in violation of an "out-of-service" order.

(b) No employer or commercial motor vehicle owner shall knowingly allow, permit, authorize, or require a driver to operate a commercial motor vehicle in violation of any law or regulation pertaining to railroad-highway grade crossings.

(c) Any employer convicted of violating subsection (a) of this Section, whether individually or in connection with one or more other persons, or as principal agent, or accessory, shall be guilty of a Class A misdemeanor.

P.A. 76-1586, § 6-506, added by P.A. 85-630, § 1, eff. Sept. 20, 1987. Amended by P.A. 86-845, § 1, eff. April 1, 1990; P.A. 92-249, § 5, eff. Jan. 1, 2002; P.A. 92-834, § 5, eff. Aug. 22, 2002.

Formerly Ill.Rev.Stat.1991, ch. 95 ½, ¶ 6-506.

P.A. 92-834 incorporated the amendment by P.A. 92-249.

5/6-507. Commercial Driver's License (CDL) Required

§ 6-507. Commercial Driver's License (CDL) Required.

(a) Except as expressly permitted by this UCDLA,[1] or when driving pursuant to the issuance of a commercial driver instruction permit and accompanied by the holder of a CDL valid for the vehicle being driven; no person shall drive a commercial motor vehicle on the highways unless the person has been issued, and is in the immediate possession of, a CDL bearing all applicable endorsements valid for type or classification of the commercial vehicle being driven.

(b) Except as otherwise provided by this Code, no person may drive a commercial motor vehicle on the highways while such person's driving privilege, license or permit is:

(1) Suspended, revoked, cancelled, or subject to disqualification. Any person convicted of violating this provision or a similar provision of this or any other state shall have their driving privileges revoked under paragraph 12 of subsection (a) of Section 6-205 of this Code.

(2) Subject to or in violation of an "out-of-service" order. Any person who has been issued a CDL and is convicted of violating this provision or a similar provision of any other state shall be disqualified from operating a commercial motor vehicle under subsection (i) of Section 6-514 of this Code.

(3) Subject to or in violation of an "out of service" order and while transporting passengers or hazardous materials. Any person who has been issued a CDL and is convicted of violating this provision or a similar provision of this or any other state shall be disqualified from operating a commercial motor vehicle under subsection (i) of Section 6-514 of this Code.

(c) Pursuant to the options provided to the States by FHWA Docket No. MC-88-8, the driver of any motor vehicle controlled or operated by or for a farmer is waived from the requirements of this Section, when such motor vehicle is being used to transport: agricultural products; implements of husbandry; or farm supplies; as long as such movement is not over 150 air miles from the originating farm. This waiver does not apply to the driver of any motor vehicle being used in a common or contract carrier type operation. However, for those drivers of any truck-tractor semitrailer combination or combinations registered under subsection (c) of Section 3-815 of this Code, this waiver shall apply only when the driver is a farmer or a member of the farmer's family and the driver is 21 years of age or more and has successfully completed any tests the Secretary of State deems necessary.

In addition, the farmer or a member of the farmer's family who operates a truck-tractor semitrailer combination or combinations pursuant to this waiver shall be granted all of the rights and shall be subject to all of the duties and restrictions with respect to Sections 6-514 and 6-515 of this Code applicable to the driver who possesses a commercial driver's license issued under this Code, except that the driver shall not be subject to any additional duties or restrictions contained in Part 382 of the Federal Motor Carrier Safety Regulations that are not otherwise imposed under Section 6-514 or 6-515 of this Code.

For purposes of this subsection (c), a member of the farmer's family is a natural or in-law spouse, child, parent, or sibling.

(c-5) An employee of a township or road district with a population of less than 3,000 operating a vehicle within the boundaries of the township or road district for the purpose of removing snow or ice from a roadway by plowing, sanding, or salting is waived from the requirements of this Section when the employee is needed to operate the vehicle because the employee of the township or road district who ordinarily operates the vehicle and who has a commercial driver's license is unable to operate the vehicle or is in need of additional assistance due to a snow emergency.

(d) Any person convicted of violating this Section, shall be guilty of a Class A misdemeanor.

(e) Any person convicted of violating paragraph (b) of this Section, shall have all driving privileges revoked by the Secretary of State.

(f) This Section shall not apply to:

(1) A person who currently holds a valid Illinois driver's license, for the type of vehicle being operated, until the expiration of such license or April 1, 1992, whichever is earlier; or

(2) A non-Illinois domiciliary who is properly licensed in another State, until April 1, 1992. A non-Illinois domiciliary, if such domiciliary is properly licensed in another State or foreign jurisdiction, until April 1, 1992.

P.A. 76–1586, § 6–507, added by P.A. 86–845, § 1, eff. April 1, 1990. Amended by P.A. 89–245, § 5, eff. Jan. 1, 1996; P.A. 89–658, § 5, eff. Oct. 1, 1996; P.A. 90–386, § 5, eff. Aug. 15, 1997; P.A. 90–655, § 153, eff. July 30, 1998.

Formerly Ill.Rev.Stat.1991, ch. 95 ½, ¶ 6–507.

1 625 ILCS 5/6–500 et seq.

P.A. 90–655, the First 1998 General Revisory Act, amended various Acts to delete obsolete text, to correct patent and technical errors, to revise cross references, to resolve multiple actions in the 89th and 90th General Assemblies and to make certain technical corrections in P.A. 89–708 through P.A. 90–566.

5/6–508. Commercial Driver's License (CDL)—qualification standards

§ 6–508. Commercial Driver's License (CDL)—qualification standards.

(a) Testing.

(1) General. No person shall be issued an original or renewal CDL unless that person is domiciled in this State. The Secretary shall cause to be administered such tests as the Secretary deems necessary to meet the requirements of 49 C.F.R. Part 383, subparts G and H.

(2) Third party testing. The Secretary of state may authorize a "third party tester", pursuant to 49 C.F.R. Part 383.75, to administer the skills test or tests specified by Federal Highway Administration pursuant to the Commercial Motor Vehicle Safety Act of 1986 [1] and any appropriate federal rule.

(b) Waiver of Skills Test. The Secretary of State may waive the skills test specified in this Section for a commercial driver license applicant who meets the requirements of 49 C.F.R. Part 383.77.

(c) Limitations on issuance of a CDL. A CDL, or a commercial driver instruction permit, shall not be issued to a person while the person is subject to a disqualification from driving a commercial motor vehicle, or unless otherwise permitted by this Code, while the person's driver's license is suspended, revoked or cancelled in any state, or any territory or province of Canada; nor may a CDL be issued to a person who has a CDL issued by any other state, or foreign jurisdiction, unless the person first surrenders all such licenses. No CDL shall be issued to or renewed for a person who does not meet the requirement of 49 CFR 391.41(b)(11). The requirement may be met with the aid of a hearing aid.

(d) Commercial driver instruction permit. A commercial driver instruction permit may be issued to any person holding a valid Illinois driver's license if such person successfully passes such tests as the Secretary determines to be necessary. A commercial driver instruction permit shall not be issued to a person who does not meet the requirements of 49 CFR 391.41 (b)(11), except for the renewal of a commercial driver instruction permit for a person who possesses a commercial instruction permit prior to the effective date of this amendatory Act of 1999.

P.A. 76–1586, § 6–508, added by P.A. 86–845, § 1, eff. April 1, 1990. Amended by P.A. 91–350, § 5, eff. July 29, 1999.

Formerly Ill.Rev.Stat.1991, ch. 95 ½, ¶ 6–508.

1 49 U.S.C.A. § 2701 et seq. (repealed).

5/6–509. Non-resident commercial driver's license

§ 6–509. Non-resident commercial driver's license. The Secretary of State may issue a non-resident CDL to a domiciliary of a foreign jurisdiction if the United States Secretary of Transportation has determined that the commercial motor vehicle testing and licensing standards, in that foreign jurisdiction, do not meet the testing standards established in 49 C.F.R. Part 383. The word "Non-resident" must appear on the face of the non-resident CDL. An applicant must surrender any non-resident CDL, license or permit issued by any other state.

P.A. 76–1586, § 6–509, added by P.A. 86–845, § 1, eff. April 1, 1990.

Formerly Ill.Rev.Stat.1991, ch. 95 ½, ¶ 6–509.

5/6–510. Application for Commercial Driver's License (CDL)

§ 6–510. Application for Commercial Driver's License (CDL). (a) The application for a CDL or commercial driver instruction permit, must include, but not necessarily be limited to, the following:

(1) the full name and current Illinois domiciliary address (unless the application is for a Non-resident CDL) of the applicant;

(2) a physical description of the applicant including sex, height, weight, color of eyes and hair color;

(3) date of birth;

(4) the applicant's social security number or other identifying number acceptable to the Secretary of State;

(5) the applicant's signature;

(6) certifications required by 49 C.F.R. Part 383.71; and

(7) any other information required by the Secretary of State.

P.A. 76–1586, § 6–510, added by P.A. 86–845, § 1, eff. April 1, 1990.

Formerly Ill.Rev.Stat.1991, ch. 95 ½, ¶ 6–510.

5/6–511. Change of name or domiciliary address

§ 6–511. Change of name or domiciliary address. All persons to whom a CDL has been issued, must notify the Driver Services Department of the Secretary of State's Office within 10 days of any name change or change in domiciliary address. In addition, such person shall make application for a corrected CDL within 30 days of any such change.

P.A. 76–1586, § 6–511, added by P.A. 86–845, § 1, eff. April 1, 1990.

Formerly Ill.Rev.Stat.1991, ch. 95 ½, ¶ 6–511.

5/6–512. Unlawful operation of a commercial motor vehicle pursuant to a non-Illinois issued CDL

§ 6–512. Unlawful operation of a commercial motor vehicle pursuant to a non-Illinois issued CDL. No person, after becoming a domiciliary of this State for 30 days or more, shall drive a commercial motor vehicle on the highways of this State pursuant to the authority of a CDL issued by any other State or foreign jurisdiction.

P.A. 76–1586, § 6–512, added by P.A. 86–845, § 1, eff. April 1, 1990.

Formerly Ill.Rev.Stat.1991, ch. 95 ½, ¶ 6–512.

5/6-513. Commercial Driver's License or CDL

§ 6-513. Commercial Driver's License or CDL. The content of the CDL shall include, but not necessarily be limited to the following:

(a) A CDL shall be distinctly marked "Commercial Driver's License" or "CDL". It must include, but not necessarily be limited to, the following information:

(1) the name and the Illinois domiciliary address (unless it is a Non-resident CDL) of the person to whom the CDL is issued;

(2) the person's color photograph;

(3) a physical description of the person including sex, height, and may include weight, color of eyes and hair color;

(4) date of birth;

(5) a CDL or file number assigned by the Secretary of State;

(6) it also may include the applicant's Social Security Number pursuant to Section 6-106;

(7) the person's signature;

(8) the class or type of commercial vehicle or vehicles which the person is authorized to drive together with any endorsements or restrictions;

(9) the name of the issuing state; and

(10) the issuance and expiration dates of the CDL.

(b) Applicant Record Check.

Prior to the issuance of a CDL, the Secretary of State shall obtain and review the applicant's driving record as required by the CMVSA and the United States Secretary of Transportation.

(c) Notification of Commercial Driver's License (CDL) Issuance.

Within 10 days after issuing a CDL, the Secretary of State must notify the Commercial Driver License Information System of that fact, and provide all information required to ensure identification of the person.

(d) Renewal.

Every person applying for a renewal of a CDL must complete the appropriate application form required by this Code and any other test deemed necessary by the Secretary.

P.A. 76-1586, § 6-513, added by P.A. 86-845, § 1, eff. April 1, 1990. Amended by P.A. 87-829, § 1, eff. Jan. 17, 1992; P.A. 87-832, § 3, eff. Jan. 17, 1992.

Formerly Ill.Rev.Stat.1991, ch. 95 ½, ¶ 6-513.

The amendments by P.A. 87-829 and P.A. 87-832 were identical.

5/6-514. Commercial Driver's License (CDL)—Disqualifications

§ 6-514. Commercial Driver's License (CDL)—Disqualifications.

(a) A person shall be disqualified from driving a commercial motor vehicle for a period of not less than 12 months for the first violation of:

(1) Refusing to submit to or failure to complete a test or tests to determine the driver's blood concentration of alcohol, other drug, or both, while driving a commercial motor vehicle; or

(2) Operating a commercial motor vehicle while the alcohol concentration of the person's blood, breath or urine is at least 0.04, or any amount of a drug, substance, or compound in the person's blood or urine resulting from the unlawful use or consumption of cannabis listed in the Cannabis Control Act [1] or a controlled substance listed in the Illinois Controlled Substances Act [2] as indicated by a police officer's sworn report or other verified evidence; or

(3) Conviction for a first violation of:

(i) Driving a commercial motor vehicle while under the influence of alcohol, or any other drug, or combination of drugs to a degree which renders such person incapable of safely driving; or

(ii) Knowingly and wilfully leaving the scene of an accident while operating a commercial motor vehicle; or

(iii) Driving a commercial motor vehicle while committing any felony.

If any of the above violations or refusals occurred while transporting hazardous material(s) required to be placarded, the person shall be disqualified for a period of not less than 3 years.

(b) A person is disqualified for life for a second conviction of any of the offenses specified in paragraph (a), or any combination of those offenses, arising from 2 or more separate incidents.

(c) A person is disqualified from driving a commercial motor vehicle for life who uses a commercial motor vehicle in the commission of any felony involving the manufacture, distribution, or dispensing of a controlled substance, or possession with intent to manufacture, distribute or dispense a controlled substance.

(d) The Secretary of State may, when the United States Secretary of Transportation so authorizes, issue regulations in which a disqualification for life under paragraph (b) may be reduced to a period of not less than 10 years. If a reinstated driver is subsequently convicted of another disqualifying offense, as specified in subsection (a) of this Section, he or she shall be permanently disqualified for life and shall be ineligible to again apply for a reduction of the lifetime disqualification.

(e) A person is disqualified from driving a commercial motor vehicle for a period of not less than 2 months if convicted of 2 serious traffic violations, committed in a commercial motor vehicle, arising from separate incidents, occurring within a 3 year period. However, a person will be disqualified from driving a commercial motor vehicle for a period of not less than 4 months if convicted of 3 serious traffic violations, committed in a commercial motor vehicle, arising from separate incidents, occurring within a 3 year period.

(f) Notwithstanding any other provision of this Code, any driver disqualified from operating a commercial motor vehicle, pursuant to this UCDLA, shall not be eligible for restoration of commercial driving privileges during any such period of disqualification.

(g) After suspending, revoking, or cancelling a commercial driver's license, the Secretary of State must update the driver's records to reflect such action within 10 days. After suspending or revoking the driving privilege of any person who has been issued a CDL or commercial driver instruction permit from another jurisdiction, the Secretary shall originate notification to such issuing jurisdiction within 10 days.

(h) The "disqualifications" referred to in this Section shall not be imposed upon any commercial motor vehicle driver, by the Secretary of State, unless the prohibited action(s) occurred after March 31, 1992.

(i) A person is disqualified from driving a commercial motor vehicle in accordance with the following:

(1) For 6 months upon a first conviction of paragraph (2) of subsection (b) of Section 6-507 of this Code.

(2) For one year upon a second conviction of paragraph (2) of subsection (b) of Section 6-507 of this Code within a 10-year period.

(3) For 3 years upon a third or subsequent conviction of paragraph (2) of subsection (b) of Section 6-507 of this Code within a 10-year period.

(4) For one year upon a first conviction of paragraph (3) of subsection (b) of Section 6-507 of this Code.

(5) For 3 years upon a second conviction of paragraph (3) of subsection (b) of Section 6-507 of this Code within a 10-year period.

(6) For 5 years upon a third or subsequent conviction of paragraph (3) of subsection (b) of Section 6-507 of this Code within a 10-year period.

(j) Disqualification for railroad-highway grade crossing violation.

(1) General rule. A driver who is convicted of a violation of a federal, State, or local law or regulation pertaining to one of the following 6 offenses at a railroad-highway grade crossing must be disqualified from operating a commercial motor vehicle for the period of time specified in paragraph (2) of this subsection (j) if the offense was committed while operating a commercial motor vehicle:

(i) For drivers who are not required to always stop, failing to slow down and check that the tracks are clear of an approaching train, as described in subsection (a-5) of Section 11-1201 of this Code;

(ii) For drivers who are not required to always stop, failing to stop before reaching the crossing, if the tracks are not clear, as described in subsection (a) of Section 11-1201 of this Code;

(iii) For drivers who are always required to stop, failing to stop before driving onto the crossing, as described in Section 11-1202 of this Code;

(iv) For all drivers, failing to have sufficient space to drive completely through the crossing without stopping, as described in subsection (b) of Section 11-1425 of this Code;

(v) For all drivers, failing to obey a traffic control device or the directions of an enforcement official at the crossing, as described in subdivision (a)2 of Section 11-1201 of this Code;

(vi) For all drivers, failing to negotiate a crossing because of insufficient undercarriage clearance, as described in subsection (d-1) of Section 11-1201 of this Code.

(2) Duration of disqualification for railroad-highway grade crossing violation.

(i) First violation. A driver must be disqualified from operating a commercial motor vehicle for not less than 60 days if the driver is convicted of a violation described in paragraph (1) of this subsection (j) and, in the three-year period preceding the conviction, the driver had no convictions for a violation described in paragraph (1) of this subsection (j).

(ii) Second violation. A driver must be disqualified from operating a commercial motor vehicle for not less than 120 days if the driver is convicted of a violation described in paragraph (1) of this subsection (j) and, in the three-year period preceding the conviction, the driver had one other conviction for a violation described in paragraph (1) of this subsection (j) that was committed in a separate incident.

(iii) Third or subsequent violation. A driver must be disqualified from operating a commercial motor vehicle for not less than one year if the driver is convicted of a violation described in paragraph (1) of this subsection (j) and, in the three-year period preceding the conviction, the driver had 2 or more other convictions for violations described in paragraph (1) of this subsection (j) that were committed in separate incidents.

P.A. 76-1586, § 6-514, added by P.A. 86-845, § 1, eff. April 1, 1990. Amended by P.A. 88-212, § 5, eff. Jan. 1, 1994; P.A. 89-245, § 5, eff. Jan. 1, 1996; P.A. 90-422, § 5, eff. Jan. 1, 1998; P.A. 92-249, § 5, eff. Jan. 1, 2002; P.A. 92-834, § 5, eff. Aug. 22, 2002.

Formerly Ill.Rev.Stat.1991, ch. 95 ½, ¶ 6-514.

1 720 ILCS 550/1 et seq.

2 720 ILCS 570/100 et seq.

P.A. 92-834 incorporated the amendment by P.A. 92-249.

5/6-515. Prohibitions against a person driving a commercial motor vehicle while having any alcohol, other drug, or both in such person's system

§ 6-515. Prohibitions against a person driving a commercial motor vehicle while having any alcohol, other drug, or both in such person's system.

(a) Notwithstanding any other provisions of this Code, a person shall not drive a commercial motor vehicle while having any alcohol, other drug, or both in such person's system.

(b) A person who drives a commercial motor vehicle while having any alcohol, other drug, or both, in such person's system or who refuses to submit to or fails to complete an alcohol or other drug test or tests pursuant to Section 6-517, as evidenced by the issuance of a Sworn Report by a police officer, must be placed "out-of-service" for at least 24 hours.

(c) The police officer shall provide the Secretary of State with a copy of all Sworn Reports issued pursuant to this UCDLA.

(d) The "out-of-service" referred to in this Section shall not be entered to the record of any Illinois commercial motor vehicle driver, by the Secretary of State, unless the prohibited action or actions occurred after March 31, 1992.

P.A. 76-1586, § 6-515, added by P.A. 86-845, § 1, eff. April 1, 1990. Amended by P.A. 88-212, § 5, eff. Jan. 1, 1994.

Formerly Ill.Rev.Stat.1991, ch. 95 ½, ¶ 6-515.

5/6-516. Implied consent requirements for commercial motor vehicle drivers

§ 6-516. Implied consent requirements for commercial motor vehicle drivers.

(a) Effective April 1, 1992, any person who drives a commercial motor vehicle upon the highways is hereby deemed to have given consent to submit to a test or tests, subject to the provisions of Section 11-501.2 of this Code, of such person's breath, blood or urine for the purpose of determining the presence of alcohol, or other drugs, in such person's system.

(b) A test or tests may be administered at the direction of a law enforcement officer, who after stopping or detaining the commercial motor vehicle driver, has probable cause to believe that driver was driving a commercial motor vehicle while having alcohol or any amount of a drug, substance, or compound resulting from the unlawful use or consumption of cannabis listed in the Cannabis Control Act [1] or a controlled substance listed in the Illinois Controlled Substances Act [2] in such driver's system.

(c) Effective April 1, 1992, any person who operates a school bus at the time of an accident involving the school bus is hereby deemed to have given consent to submit to a test or tests to be administered at the direction of a law enforcement officer, subject to the provisions of Section 11–501.2 of this Code, of the driver's breath, blood or urine for the purpose of determining the presence of alcohol, or other drugs, in the person's system.

P.A. 76–1586, § 6–516, added by P.A. 86–845, § 1, eff. April 1, 1990. Amended by P.A. 86–1465, § 1, eff. April 1, 1992; P.A. 88–212, § 5, eff. Jan. 1, 1994.

Formerly Ill.Rev.Stat.1991, ch. 95 ½, ¶ 6–516.

1 720 ILCS 550/1 et seq.

2 720 ILCS 570/100 et seq.

5/6–517. Commercial driver; implied consent warnings

§ 6–517. Commercial driver; implied consent warnings.

(a) Any person driving a commercial motor vehicle who is requested by a police officer, pursuant to Section 6–516, to submit to a chemical test or tests to determine the alcohol concentration or any amount of a drug, substance, or compound resulting from the unlawful use or consumption of cannabis listed in the Cannabis Control Act [1] or a controlled substance listed in the Illinois Controlled Substances Act [2] in such person's system, must be warned by the police officer requesting the test or tests that a refusal to submit to the test or tests will result in that person being immediately placed out-of-service for a period of 24 hours and being disqualified from operating a commercial motor vehicle for a period of not less than 12 months; the person shall also be warned that if such person submits to testing which discloses an alcohol concentration of greater than 0.00 but less than 0.04 or any amount of a drug, substance, or compound in such person's blood or urine resulting from the unlawful use or consumption of cannabis listed in the Cannabis Control Act or a controlled substance listed in the Illinois Controlled Substances Act, such person shall be placed immediately out-of-service for a period of 24 hours; if the person submits to testing which discloses an alcohol concentration of 0.04 or more or any amount of a drug, substance, or compound in such person's blood or urine resulting from the unlawful use or consumption of cannabis listed in the Cannabis Control Act or a controlled substance listed in the Illinois Controlled Substances Act, such person shall be placed immediately out-of-service and disqualified from driving a commercial motor vehicle for a period of at least 12 months; also the person shall be warned that if such testing discloses an alcohol concentration of 0.08, or more or any amount of a drug, substance, or compound in such person's blood or urine resulting from the unlawful use or consumption of cannabis listed in the Cannabis Control Act or a controlled substance listed in the Illinois Controlled Substances Act, in addition to the person being immediately placed out-of-service and disqualified for 12 months as provided in this UCDLA, the results of such testing shall also be admissible in prosecutions for violations of Section 11–501 of this Code, or similar violations of local ordinances, however, such results shall not be used to impose any driving sanctions pursuant to Section 11–501.1 of this Code.

The person shall also be warned that any disqualification imposed pursuant to this Section, shall be for life for any such offense or refusal, or combination thereof; including a conviction for violating Section 11–501 while driving a commercial motor vehicle, or similar provisions of local ordinances, committed a second time involving separate incidents.

(b) If the person refuses or fails to complete testing, or submits to a test which discloses an alcohol concentration of at least 0.04, or any amount of a drug, substance, or compound in such person's blood or urine resulting from the unlawful use or consumption of cannabis listed in the Cannabis Control Act or a controlled substance listed in the Illinois Controlled Substances Act, the law enforcement officer must submit a Sworn Report to the Secretary of State, in a form prescribed by the Secretary, certifying that the test or tests was requested pursuant to paragraph (a); that the person was warned, as provided in paragraph (a) and that such person refused to submit to or failed to complete testing, or submitted to a test which disclosed an alcohol concentration of 0.04 or more, or any amount of a drug, substance, or compound in such person's blood or urine resulting from the unlawful use or consumption of cannabis listed in the Cannabis Control Act or a controlled substance listed in the Illinois Controlled Substances Act.

(c) The police officer submitting the Sworn Report under this Section shall serve notice of the CDL disqualification on the person and such CDL disqualification shall be effective as provided in paragraph (d). In cases where the blood alcohol concentration of 0.04 or more, or any amount of a drug, substance, or compound in such person's blood or urine resulting from the unlawful use or consumption of cannabis listed in the Cannabis Control Act or a controlled substance listed in the Illinois Controlled Substances Act, is established by subsequent analysis of blood or urine collected at the time of the request, the police officer shall give notice as provided in this Section or by deposit in the United States mail of such notice as provided in this Section or by deposit in the United States mail of such notice in an envelope with postage prepaid and addressed to such person's domiciliary address as shown on the Sworn Report and the CDL disqualification shall begin as provided in paragraph (d).

(d) The CDL disqualification referred to in this Section shall take effect on the 46th day following the date the Sworn Report was given to the affected person.

(e) Upon receipt of the Sworn Report from the police officer, the Secretary of State shall disqualify the person from driving any commercial motor vehicle and shall confirm the CDL disqualification by mailing the notice of the effective date to the person. However, should the Sworn Report be defective by not containing sufficient information or be completed in error, the confirmation of the CDL disqualification shall not be mailed to the affected person or entered into the record, instead the Sworn Report shall be forwarded to the issuing agency identifying any such defect.

P.A. 76–1586, § 6–517, added by P.A. 86–845, § 1, eff. April 1, 1990. Amended by P.A. 88–212, § 5, eff. Jan. 1, 1994; P.A. 90–43, § 5, eff. July 2, 1997; P.A. 91–357, § 231, eff. July 29, 1999.

Formerly Ill.Rev.Stat.1991, ch. 95 ½, ¶ 6–517.

1 720 ILCS 550/1 et seq.

2 570 ILCS 570/100 et seq.

5/6–518. Notification of Traffic Convictions

§ 6–518. Notification of Traffic Convictions. Within 10 days after receiving a report of an Illinois conviction, or other verified evidence, of any driver who has been issued a CDL by another State, for a violation of any law or local ordinance of this State, relating to motor vehicle traffic control, other than parking violations, committed in a commercial motor vehicle, the Secretary of State must notify the driver licensing authority which issued such CDL of said conviction.

P.A. 76–1586, § 6–518, added by P.A. 86–845, § 1, eff. April 1, 1990.

Formerly Ill.Rev.Stat.1991, ch. 95 ½, ¶ 6–518.

5/6–519. Driving Record Information To Be Furnished

§ 6–519. Driving Record Information To Be Furnished. Notwithstanding any other provision of law to the contrary, the Secretary of State shall furnish full information regarding a commercial driver's driving record to the driver licensing administrator of any other State requesting such information; and any other entity or person authorized to receive such information pursuant to Section 2–123 of this Code.

P.A. 76–1586, § 6–519, added by P.A. 86–845, § 1, eff. April 1, 1990.

Formerly Ill.Rev.Stat.1991, ch. 95 ½, ¶ 6–519.

5/6–520. CDL disqualification or out-of-service order; hearing

§ 6–520. CDL disqualification or out-of-service order; hearing.

(a) A disqualification of commercial driving privileges by the Secretary of State, pursuant to this UCDLA, shall not become effective until the person is notified in writing, by the Secretary, of the impending disqualification and advised that a CDL hearing may be requested.

(b) Upon receipt of the notice of a CDL disqualification not based upon a conviction, an out-of-service order, or notification that a CDL disqualification is forthcoming, the person may make a written petition in a form, approved by the Secretary of State, for a CDL hearing. Such petition must state the grounds upon which the person seeks to have the CDL disqualification rescinded or the out-of-service order removed from the person's driving record. Within 10 days after the receipt of such petition, it shall be reviewed by the Director of the Department of Administrative Hearings, Office of the Secretary of State, or by an appointed designee. If it is determined that the petition on its face does not state grounds upon which the relief may be based, the petition for a CDL hearing shall be denied and the disqualification shall become effective as if no petition had been filed and the out-of-service order shall be sustained. If such petition is so denied, the person may submit another petition.

(c) The scope of a CDL hearing, for any disqualification imposed pursuant to paragraphs (1) and (2) of subsection (a) of Section 6–514 shall be limited to the following issues:

1. Whether the person was operating a commercial motor vehicle;

2. Whether, after making the initial stop, the police officer had probable cause to issue a Sworn Report;

3. Whether the person was verbally warned of the ensuing consequences prior to submitting to any type of chemical test or tests to determine such person's blood concentration of alcohol, other drug, or both; and

4. Whether the person did refuse to submit to or failed to complete the chemical testing or did submit to such test or tests and such test or tests disclosed an alcohol concentration of at least 0.04 or any amount of a drug, substance, or compound resulting from the unlawful use or consumption of cannabis listed in the Cannabis Control Act [1] or a controlled substance listed in the Illinois Controlled Substances Act [2] in the person's system;

5. Whether the person was warned that if the test or tests disclosed an alcohol concentration of 0.08 or more or any amount of a drug, substance, or compound resulting from the unlawful use or consumption of cannabis listed in the Cannabis Control Act or a controlled substance listed in the Illinois Controlled Substances Act, such results could be admissible in a subsequent prosecution under Section 11–501 of this Code or similar provision of local ordinances; and

6. Whether such results could not be used to impose any driver's license sanctions pursuant to Section 11–501.1.

Upon the conclusion of the above CDL hearing, the CDL disqualification imposed shall either be sustained or rescinded.

(d) The scope of a CDL hearing for any out-of-service sanction, imposed pursuant to Section 6–515, shall be limited to the following issues:

1. Whether the person was driving a commercial motor vehicle;

2. Whether, while driving such commercial motor vehicle, the person had alcohol or any amount of a drug, substance, or compound resulting from the unlawful use or consumption of cannabis listed in the Cannabis Control Act or a controlled substance listed in the Illinois Controlled Substances Act in such person's system; or

3. Whether the person was verbally warned of the ensuing consequences prior to being asked to submit to any type of chemical test or tests to determine such person's alcohol, other drug, or both, concentration; and

4. Whether, after being so warned, the person did refuse to submit to or failed to complete such chemical test or tests or did submit to such test or tests and such test or tests disclosed an alcohol concentration greater than 0.00 or any amount of a drug, substance, or compound resulting from the unlawful use or consumption of cannabis listed in the Cannabis Control Act or a controlled substance listed in the Illinois Controlled Substances Act.

Upon the conclusion of the above CDL hearing, the out-of-service sanction shall either be sustained or removed from the person's driving record.

(e) If any person petitions for a hearing relating to any CDL disqualification based upon a conviction, as defined in this UCDLA, said hearing shall not be conducted as a CDL hearing, but shall be conducted as any other driver's license hearing, whether formal or informal, as promulgated in the rules and regulations of the Secretary.

(f) Any evidence of alcohol or other drug consumption, for the purposes of this UCDLA, shall be sufficient probable cause for requesting the driver to submit to a chemical test or tests to determine the presence of alcohol, other drug, or both in the person's system and the subsequent issuance of an out-of-service order or a Sworn Report by a police officer.

(g) For the purposes of this UCDLA, a CDL "hearing" shall mean a hearing before the Office of the Secretary of State in accordance with Section 2–118 of this Code, for the purpose of resolving differences or disputes specifically related to the scope of the issues identified in this Section. These proceedings will be a matter of record and a final appealable order issued. The petition for a CDL hearing shall not stay or delay the effective date of the impending disqualification.

(h) The CDL hearing may be conducted upon a review of the police officer's own official reports; provided however, that the petitioner may subpoena the officer. Failure of the officer to answer the subpoena shall be grounds for a continuance.

P.A. 76-1586, § 6-520, added by P.A. 86-845, § 1, eff. April 1, 1990. Amended by P.A. 87-829, § 1, eff. Jan. 17, 1992; P.A. 87-832, § 3, eff. Jan. 17, 1992; P.A. 87-895, Art. 2, § 2-45, eff. Aug. 14, 1992; P.A. 88-212, § 5, eff. Jan. 1, 1994; P.A. 88-670, Art. 3, § 3-80, eff. Dec. 2, 1994; P.A. 90-43, § 5, eff. July 2, 1997; P.A. 91-357, § 231, eff. July 29, 1999.

Formerly Ill.Rev.Stat.1991, ch. 95 ½, ¶ 6-520.

1 720 ILCS 550/100 et seq.

2 720 ILCS 570/100 et seq.

5/6-521. Rulemaking Authority

§ 6-521. Rulemaking Authority.

(a) The Secretary of State, using the authority to license motor vehicle operators under this Code, may adopt such rules and regulations as may be necessary to establish standards, policies and procedures for the licensing of commercial motor vehicle drivers in order to meet the requirements of the Commercial Motor Vehicle Act of 1986 (CMVSA);[1] subsequent federal rulemaking under 49 C.F.R. Part 383; and administrative and policy decisions of the U.S. Secretary of Transportation and the Federal Highway Administration. The Secretary may, as provided in the CMVSA, establish stricter requirements for the licensing of commercial motor vehicle drivers than those established by the federal government.

(b) By January 1, 1994, the Secretary of State shall establish rules and regulations for the issuance of a restricted commercial driver's license for farm-related service industries consistent with federal guidelines. The restricted license shall be available for a seasonal period or periods not to exceed a total of 180 days in any 12 month period.

(c) By July 1, 1995, the Secretary of State shall establish rules and regulations, to be consistent with federal guidelines, for the issuance and cancellation or withdrawal of a restricted commercial driver's license that is limited to the operation of a school bus. A driver whose restricted commercial driver's license has been cancelled or withdrawn may contest the sanction by requesting a hearing pursuant to Section 2-118 of this Code. The cancellation or withdrawal of the restricted commercial driver's license shall remain in effect pending the outcome of that hearing.

(d) By July 1, 1995, the Secretary of State shall establish rules and regulations for the issuance and cancellation of a School Bus Driver's Permit. The permit shall be required for the operation of a school bus as provided in subsection (c), a non-restricted CDL with passenger endorsement, or a properly classified driver's license. The permit will establish that the school bus driver has met all the requirements of the application and screening process established by Section 6-106.1 of this Code.

P.A. 76-1586, § 6-521, added by P.A. 86-845, § 1, eff. April 1, 1990. Amended by P.A. 88-450, § 5, eff. Aug. 20, 1993; P.A. 88-612, § 15, eff. July 1, 1995.

Formerly Ill.Rev.Stat.1991, ch. 95 ½, ¶ 6-521.

1 49 App. U.S.C.A. § 2701.

P.A. 88-612 incorporated the amendment by P.A. 88-450.

5/6-522. Authority to Enter Agreements

§ 6-522. Authority to Enter Agreements. The Secretary of State may enter into or make agreements, arrangements, or declarations to carry out the provisions of this UCDLA.

P.A. 76-1586, § 6-522, added by P.A. 86-845, § 1, eff. April 1, 1990.

Formerly Ill.Rev.Stat.1991, ch. 95 ½, ¶ 6-522.

5/6-523. Reciprocity

§ 6-523. Reciprocity. (a) Notwithstanding any law to the contrary, a person may drive a commercial motor vehicle in this State if such person has a valid commercial driver's license or CDL instruction permit issued by another State or foreign jurisdiction as long as such person has not been an established domiciliary of this State for 30 days or more.

(b) The Secretary of State shall give out of state convictions full faith and credit and treat them for sanctioning purposes, under this UCDLA, just as if they occurred in this State.

P.A. 76-1586, § 6-523, added by P.A. 86-845, § 1, eff. April 1, 1990.

Formerly Ill.Rev.Stat.1991, ch. 95 ½, ¶ 6-523.

5/6-524. Penalties

§ 6-524. Penalties.

(a) Every person convicted of violating any provision of this UCDLA for which another penalty is not provided shall for a first offense be guilty of a petty offense; and for a second conviction for any offense committed within 3 years of any previous offense, shall be guilty of a Class B misdemeanor.

(b) Any person convicted of violating subsection (b) of Section 6-506 of this Code shall be subject to a civil penalty of not more than $10,000.

P.A. 76-1586, § 6-524, added by P.A. 86-845, § 1, eff. April 1, 1990. Amended by P.A. 92-249, § 5, eff. Jan. 1, 2002.

Formerly Ill.Rev.Stat.1991, ch. 95 ½, ¶ 6-524.

5/6-525. Severability

§ 6-525. Severability. The provisions of this UCLDA shall be severable and if any phrase, clause, sentence or provision of this UCLDA is declared to be contrary to the Constitutions of this State, or of the United States, such unconstitutionality shall not affect the validity of the remainder of this UCDLA.

P.A. 76-1586, § 6-525, added by P.A. 86-845, § 1, eff. April 1, 1990.

Formerly Ill.Rev.Stat.1991, ch. 95 ½, ¶ 6-525.

ARTICLE VI. PENALTIES

Section

5/6-601. Penalties

Text of section as amended by P.A. 92-622 and P.A. 92-883

§ 6-601. Penalties.

(a) It is a petty offense for any person to violate any of the provisions of this Chapter unless such violation is by this Code or other law of this State declared to be a misdemeanor or a felony.

(b) General penalties. Unless another penalty is in this Code or other laws of this State, every person convicted of a petty offense for the violation of any provision of this Chapter shall be punished by a fine of not more than $500.

(c) Unlicensed driving. Except as hereinafter provided a violation of Section 6-101 shall be:

1. A Class A misdemeanor if the person failed to obtain a driver's license or permit after expiration of a period of revocation.

2. A Class B misdemeanor if the person has been issued a driver's license or permit, which has expired, and if the period of expiration is greater than one year; or if the person has never been issued a driver's license or permit, or is not qualified to obtain a driver's license or permit because of his age.

If a licensee under this Code is convicted of violating Section 6-101 for operating a motor vehicle during a time when such licensee's driver's license was invalid under the provisions of Section 6-110, then conviction under such circumstances shall be punishable by a fine of not more than $25.

If a licensee under this Code is convicted of violating Section 6-303 for operating a motor vehicle during a time when such licensee's driver's license was suspended under the provisions of Section 6-306.3, then such act shall be a petty offense (provided the licensee has answered the charge which was the basis of the suspension under Section 6-306.3), and there shall be imposed no additional like period of suspension as provided in paragraph (b) of Section 6-303.

P.A. 76-1586, § 6-601, eff. July 1, 1970. Amended by P.A. 76-2157, § 1, eff. July 1, 1970; P.A. 77-2720, § 1, eff. Jan. 1, 1973; P.A. 80-911, § 1, eff. Oct. 1, 1977; P.A. 80-1462, § 1, eff. Jan. 1, 1979; P.A. 83-385, § 1, eff. Jan. 1, 1984; P.A. 84-1231, § 1, eff. July 28, 1986; P.A. 85-992, § 1, eff. Jan. 5, 1988; P.A. 92-622, § 5, eff. Jan. 1, 2003; P.A. 92-883, § 5, eff. Jan. 13, 2003.

Formerly Ill.Rev.Stat.1991, ch. 95 ½, ¶ 6-601.

For text of section as amended by P.A. 92-647 and P.A. 92-883, see 625 ILCS 5/6-601, post

P.A. 92-883 incorporated the amendment by P.A. 92-622.

5/6-601. Penalties

Text of Section as amended by P.A. 92-647 and P.A. 92-883

§ 6-601. Penalties.

(a) It is a petty offense for any person to violate any of the provisions of this Chapter unless such violation is by this Code or other law of this State declared to be a misdemeanor or a felony.

(b) General penalties. Unless another penalty is in this Code or other laws of this State, every person convicted of a petty offense for the violation of any provision of this Chapter shall be punished by a fine of not more than $500.

(c) Unlicensed driving. Except as hereinafter provided a violation of Section 6-101 shall be:

1. A Class A misdemeanor if the person failed to obtain a driver's license or permit after expiration of a period of revocation.

2. A Class B misdemeanor if the person has been issued a driver's license or permit, which has expired, and if the period of expiration is greater than one year; or if the person has never been issued a driver's license or permit, or is not qualified to obtain a driver's license or permit because of his age.

If a licensee under this Code is convicted of violating Section 6-101 for operating a motor vehicle during a time when such licensee's driver's license was invalid under the provisions of Section 6-110, then conviction under such circumstances shall be punishable by a fine of not more than $25.

If a licensee under this Code is convicted of violating Section 6-303 for operating a motor vehicle during a time when such licensee's driver's license was suspended under the provisions of Section 6-306.3, then such act shall be a petty offense (provided the licensee has answered the charge which was the basis of the suspension under Section 6-306.3), and there shall be imposed no additional like period of suspension as provided in paragraph (b) of Section 6-303.

P.A. 76-1586, § 6-601, eff. July 1, 1970. Amended by P.A. 76-2157, § 1, eff. July 1, 1970; P.A. 77-2720, § 1, eff. Jan. 1, 1973; P.A. 80-911, § 1, eff. Oct. 1, 1977; P.A. 80-1462, § 1, eff. Jan. 1, 1979; P.A. 83-385, § 1, eff. Jan. 1, 1984; P.A. 84-1231, § 1, eff. July 28, 1986; P.A. 85-992, § 1, eff. Jan. 5, 1988; P.A. 92-622, § 5, eff. Jan. 1, 2003; P.A. 92-647, § 5, eff. Jan. 1, 2003; P.A. 92-883, § 5, eff. Jan. 13, 2003.

Formerly Ill.Rev.Stat.1991, ch. 95 ½, ¶ 6-601.

For text of section as amended by P.A. 92-622 and P.A. 92-883, see 625 ILCS 5/6-601, ante

P.A. 92-883 incorporated the amendment by P.A. 92-647.

See 5 ILCS 70/6 as to the effect of (1) more than one amendment of a section at the same session of the General Assembly or (2) two or more acts relating to the same subject matter enacted by the same General Assembly.

ARTICLE VII. DRIVER LICENSE COMPACT

Date Effective

Article VII was added by P.A. 76-1615, § 1, effective July 1, 1970.

Section

5/6-700. Definitions

§ 6-700. Definitions. As used in this compact:

(a) "State" means a state, territory or possession of the United States, the District of Columbia, or the Commonwealth of Puerto Rico.

(b) "Home state" means the state which has issued and has the power to suspend or revoke the use of the license or permit to operate a motor vehicle.

(c) "Conviction" means a conviction of any offense related to the use or operation of a motor vehicle which is prohibited by state law, municipal ordinance or administrative rule or regulation, or a forfeiture of bail, bond or other security deposited to secure appearance by a person charged with having committed any such offense, and which conviction or forfeiture is required to be reported to the licensing authority.

P.A. 76-1586, § 6-700, added by P.A. 76-1615, § 1, eff. July 1, 1970.

Formerly Ill.Rev.Stat.1991, ch. 95 ½, ¶ 6-700.

5/6–701. Findings and declaration of policy

§ 6–701. Findings and declaration of policy.

(a) The party states find that:

1. The safety of their streets and highways is materially affected by the degree of compliance with state laws and local ordinances relating to the operation of motor vehicles.

2. Violation of such a law or ordinance is evidence that the violator engages in conduct which is likely to endanger the safety of persons and property.

3. The continuance in force of a license to drive is predicated upon compliance with laws and ordinances relating to the operation of motor vehicles, in whichever jurisdiction the vehicle is operated.

(b) It is the policy of each of the party states to:

1. Promote compliance with the laws, ordinances and administrative rules and regulations relating to the operation of motor vehicles by their operators in each of the jurisdictions where such operators drive motor vehicles.

2. Make the reciprocal recognition of licenses to drive and eligibility therefor more just and equitable by considering the over-all compliance with motor vehicle laws, ordinances and administrative rules and regulations as a condition precedent to the continuance or issuance of any license by reason of which the licensee is authorized or permitted to operate a motor vehicle in any of the party states.

P.A. 76–1586, § 6–701, added by P.A. 76–1615, § 1, eff. July 1, 1970.

Formerly Ill.Rev.Stat.1991, ch. 95 ½, ¶ 6–701.

5/6–702. Reports of conviction

§ 6–702. Reports of conviction. The licensing authority of a party state shall report each conviction of a person from another party state occurring within its jurisdiction to the licensing authority of the home state of the licensee. Such report shall clearly identify the person convicted; describe the violation specifying the section of the statute, code or ordinance violated; identify the court in which action was taken; indicate whether a plea of guilty or not guilty was entered, or the conviction was a result of the forfeiture of bail, bond or other security; and shall include any special findings made in connection therewith.

P.A. 76–1586, § 6–702, added by P.A. 76–1615, § 1, eff. July 1, 1970.

Formerly Ill.Rev.Stat.1991, ch. 95 ½, ¶ 6–702.

5/6–703. Effect of conviction

§ 6–703. Effect of conviction. (a) The licensing authority in the home state, for the purposes of suspension, revocation or limitation of the license to operate a motor vehicle, shall give the same effect to the conduct reported, pursuant to Section 6–702, as it would if such conduct had occurred in the home state, in the case of convictions for:

1. Manslaughter or negligent homicide resulting from the operation of a motor vehicle;

2. Driving a motor vehicle while under the influence of intoxicating liquor or a narcotic drug, or under the influence of any other drug to a degree which renders the driver incapable of safely driving a motor vehicle;

3. Any felony in the commission of which a motor vehicle is used;

4. Failure to stop and render aid in the event of a motor vehicle accident resulting in the death or personal injury of another.

(b) As to other convictions, reported pursuant to Section 6–702, the licensing authority in the home state shall give such effect to the conduct as is provided by the laws of the home state.

(c) If the laws of a party state do not provide for offenses or violations denominated or described in precisely the words employed in paragraph (a) of this Section, such party state shall construe the denominations and descriptions appearing in paragraph (a) hereof as being applicable to and identifying those offenses or violations of a substantially similar nature, and the laws of such party state shall contain such provision as may be necessary to ensure that full force and effect is given to this Section.

P.A. 76–1586, § 6–703, added by P.A. 76–1615, § 1, eff. July 1, 1970.

Formerly Ill.Rev.Stat.1991, ch. 95 ½, ¶ 6–703.

5/6–704. Applications for new licenses

§ 6–704. Applications for new licenses. Upon application for a license to drive, the licensing authority in a party state shall ascertain whether the applicant has ever held, or is the holder of a license to drive issued by any other party state. The licensing authority in the state where application is made shall not issue a license to drive to the applicant if:

1. The applicant has held such a license, but the same has been suspended by reason, in whole or in part, of a violation and if such suspension period has not terminated.

2. The applicant has held such a license, but the same has been revoked by reason, in whole or in part, of a violation and if such revocation has not terminated, except that after the expiration of one year from the date the license was revoked, such person may make application for a new license if permitted by law. The licensing authority may refuse to issue a license to any such applicant if, after investigation, the licensing authority determines that it will not be safe to grant to such person the privilege of driving a motor vehicle on the public highways.

3. The applicant is the holder of a license to drive issued by another party state and currently in force unless the applicant surrenders such license.

P.A. 76–1586, § 6–704, added by P.A. 76–1615, § 1, eff. July 1, 1970.

Formerly Ill.Rev.Stat.1991, ch. 95 ½, ¶ 6–704.

5/6–705. Applicability of other laws

§ 6–705. Applicability of other laws. Except as expressly required by provisions of this compact, nothing contained herein shall be construed to affect the right of any party state to apply any of its other laws relating to the licenses to drive to any person or circumstance, nor to invalidate or prevent any driver license agreement or other cooperative arrangement between a party state and a nonparty state.

P.A. 76–1586, § 6–705, added by P.A. 76–1615, § 1, eff. July 1, 1970.

Formerly Ill.Rev.Stat.1991, ch. 95 ½, ¶ 6–705.

5/6–706. Compact administrator and interchange of information

§ 6–706. Compact administrator and interchange of information. (a) The head of the licensing authority of each party state shall be administrator of this compact for his state. The administrators, acting jointly, shall have the power to formulate all necessary and proper procedures for the exchange of information under this compact.

(b) The administrator of each party state shall furnish to the administrator of each other party state any information or documents reasonably necessary to facilitate the administration of this compact.

P.A. 76-1586, § 6-706, added by P.A. 76-1615, § 1, eff. July 1, 1970.

Formerly Ill.Rev.Stat.1991, ch. 95 ½, ¶ 6-706.

5/6-707. Entry into force and withdrawal

§ 6-707. Entry into force and withdrawal. (a) This compact shall enter into force and become effective as to any state when it has enacted the same into law.

(b) Any party state may withdraw from this compact by enacting a statute repealing the same, but no such withdrawal shall take effect until 6 months after the executive head of the withdrawing state has given notice of the withdrawal to the executive heads of all other party states. No withdrawal shall affect the validity or applicability by the licensing authorities of states remaining party to the compact of any report of conviction occurring prior to the withdrawal.

P.A. 76-1586, § 6-707, added by P.A. 76-1615, § 1, eff. July 1, 1970.

Formerly Ill.Rev.Stat.1991, ch. 95 ½, ¶ 6-707.

5/6-708. Construction and Severability

§ 6-708. Construction and Severability. (a) This compact shall be liberally construed so as to effectuate the purposes thereof. The provisions of this compact shall be severable and if any phrase, clause, sentence or provision of this compact is declared to be contrary to the constitution of any party state or of the United States or the applicability thereof to any government, agency, person or circumstance is held invalid, the validity of the remainder of this compact and the applicability thereof to any government, agency, person or circumstance shall not be affected thereby. If this compact shall be held contrary to the constitution of any state party thereto, the compact shall remain in full force and effect as to the remaining states and in full force and effect as to the state affected as to all severable matters.

(b) As used in the compact, the term "licensing authority" with reference to this state, means the Secretary of State. The Secretary of State shall furnish to the appropriate authorities of any other party state any information or documents reasonably necessary to facilitate the administration of Sections 6-702, 6-703 and 6-704 of the compact.

(c) The compact administrator provided for in Section 6-706 of the compact shall not be entitled to any additional compensation on account of his service as such administrator, but shall be entitled to expenses incurred in connection with his duties and responsibilities as such administrator, in the same manner as for expenses incurred in connection with any other duties or responsibilities of his office or employment.

(d) As used in the compact, with reference to this state, the term "executive head" shall mean the Governor.

(e) The phrase "manslaughter or negligent homicide," as used in subparagraph (1) of paragraph (a) of Section 6-703 of the compact includes the offense of reckless homicide as defined in Section 9-3 of the "Criminal Code of 1961," as heretofore or hereafter amended,[1] or in any predecessor statute, as well as the offenses of second degree murder and involuntary manslaughter.

The offense described in subparagraph (2) of paragraph (a) of Section 6-703 of the compact includes any violation of Section 11-501 of this Code or any similar provision of a local ordinance.

The offense described in subparagraph (4) of paragraph (a) of Section 6-703 of the compact includes any violation of paragraph (a) of Section 11-401 of this Code.

P.A. 76-1586, § 6-708, added by P.A. 76-1615, § 1, eff. July 1, 1970. Amended by P.A. 84-1450, § 7, eff. July 1, 1987; P.A. 85-951, § 1, eff. July 1, 1988.

Formerly Ill.Rev.Stat.1991, ch. 95 ½, ¶ 6-708.

[1] 720 ILCS 5/9-3.

ARTICLE VIII. NONRESIDENT VIOLATOR COMPACT

Date Effective

Article VIII was added by P.A. 83-385, § 1, eff. Jan. 1, 1984.

Section

5/6-800. Enactment

§ 6-800. The Nonresident Violator Compact, hereinafter referred to as the Compact, is hereby enacted into law and entered into with all other jurisdictions legally joining therein.

P.A. 76-1586, § 6-800, added by P.A. 83-385, § 1, eff. Jan. 1, 1984.

Formerly Ill.Rev.Stat.1991, ch. 95 ½, ¶ 6-800.

5/6-801. Findings, Declaration of Policy and Purpose

§ 6-801. Findings, Declaration of Policy and Purpose. (a) The party jurisdictions find that:

1. In most instances, a motorist who is cited for a traffic violation in a jurisdiction other than the motorist's home jurisdiction:

(i) Must post collateral or bond to secure appearance for trial at a later date; or

(ii) If unable to post collateral or bond, is taken into custody until the collateral or bond is posted; or

(iii) Is taken directly to court for immediate disposition.

2. A motorist receiving a traffic citation in the motorist's home jurisdiction is permitted, except for certain violations, to accept the citation from the officer at the scene of the violation, voluntarily deposit a valid driver's license and immediately continue after promising or being instructed to comply with the terms of the citation.

3. The purpose of the practices described in subsections 1 and 2 of paragraph (a) is to ensure compliance with the terms of a traffic citation by the motorist who, if permitted to continue after receiving the traffic citation, could return to the motorist's home jurisdiction and disregard any duty under the terms of the traffic citation.

4. The practice described in subsection 1 of paragraph (a) causes unnecessary inconvenience and, at times, a hardship for the motorist who is unable at the time to post collateral, furnish a bond, stand trial, or pay the fine, and thus is compelled to remain in custody until some arrangement can be made.

5. The deposit of a driver's license as a bail bond, as described in subsection 2 of paragraph (a), is viewed with disfavor.

6. The practices described herein consume an undue amount of law enforcement time.

(b) It is the policy of the party jurisdictions to:

1. Seek compliance with the laws, ordinances, and administrative rules and regulations relating to the operation of motor vehicles in each of the jurisdictions.

2. Allow a motorist to accept a traffic citation for certain violations and proceed without delay whether or not the motorist is a resident of the jurisdiction in which the citation was issued.

3. Extend cooperation to its fullest extent among the jurisdictions for obtaining compliance with the terms of a traffic citation issued in one jurisdiction to a resident of another jurisdiction.

4. Maximize effective utilization of law enforcement personnel and assist court systems in the efficient disposition of traffic violations.

(c) The purpose of the Compact is to:

1. Provide a means through which the party jurisdictions may participate in a reciprocal program to effectuate the policies enumerated in paragraph (b) above in a uniform and orderly manner.

2. Provide for the fair and impartial treatment of traffic violators operating within party jurisdictions in recognition of the motorist's right of due process and the sovereign status of a party jurisdiction.

P.A. 76-1586, § 6-801, added by P.A. 83-385, § 1, eff. Jan. 1, 1984.

Formerly Ill.Rev.Stat.1991, ch. 95 ½, ¶ 6-801.

5/6-802. Definitions

§ 6-802. Definitions. In the Nonresident Violator Compact, the following words have the meanings indicated, unless the context requires otherwise.

1. "Citation" means any summons, ticket, or other official document issued by a police officer for a traffic violation containing an order which requires the motorist to respond.

2. "Collateral" means any cash or other security deposited to secure an appearance for trial, following the issuance by a police officer of a citation for a traffic violation.

3. "Court" means a court of law or traffic tribunal.

4. "Driver's license" means any license or privilege to operate a motor vehicle issued under the laws of this State.

5. "Home Jurisdiction" means the jurisdiction that issued the driver's license of the traffic violator.

6. "Issuing jurisdiction" means the jurisdiction in which the traffic citation was issued to the motorist.

7. "Jurisdiction" means a state, territory, or possession of the United States, the District of Columbia, or the Commonwealth of Puerto Rico.

8. "Motorist" means a driver of a motor vehicle operating in a party jurisdiction.

9. "Personal recognizance" means an agreement by a motorist made at the time of issuance of the traffic citation that such motorist will comply with the terms of that traffic citation.

10. "Police officer" means every officer authorized to make arrests and issue citations for traffic violations.

11. "Secretary" means the Illinois Secretary of State.

12. "Terms of the citation" means those options expressly stated upon the citation.

P.A. 76-1586, § 6-802, added by P.A. 83-385, § 1, eff. Jan. 1, 1984.

Formerly Ill.Rev.Stat.1991, ch. 95 ½, ¶ 6-802.

5/6-803. Procedure for Issuing Jurisdiction

§ 6-803. Procedure for Issuing Jurisdiction. (a) When issuing a citation for a traffic violation, a police officer shall issue the citation to a motorist who possesses a valid driver's license issued by a party jurisdiction and shall not, subject to the exceptions noted in Section 6-306.4 of this Code and paragraph (b) of this Section, require the motorist to post collateral to secure appearance, if the officer receives the motorist's personal recognizance to comply with the terms of the citation.

(b) Personal recognizance is acceptable only if not prohibited by law. If mandatory appearance is required, it must take place according to law, following issuance of the citation.

(c) Upon failure of a motorist to comply with the terms of a traffic citation, the appropriate official shall report the failure to comply, in a manner prescribed by the Secretary, to the licensing authority of the jurisdiction in which the traffic citation was issued. The report shall be made in accordance with procedures specified by the Secretary and shall contain information as specified by the Secretary as minimum requirements for effective processing by the home jurisdiction.

(d) Upon receipt of the report, the Secretary shall transmit to the licensing authority in the home jurisdiction of the motorist the information in a form and content as contained in the Compact Manual.

(e) The Secretary may not, except as provided under Section 6-306.4 of this Code, suspend the privileges of a motorist for whom a report has been transmitted, under the terms of this Compact, to another member jurisdiction.

(f) The Secretary shall not transmit a report on any violation if the date of transmission is more than 6 months after the date on which the traffic citation was issued.

(g) The Secretary shall not transmit a report on any violation where the date of issuance of the citation predates the most recent of the effective dates of entry for the two jurisdictions affected.

P.A. 76-1586, § 6-803, added by P.A. 83-385, § 1, eff. Jan. 1, 1984. Amended by P.A. 84-1231, § 1, eff. July 28, 1986.

Formerly Ill.Rev.Stat.1991, ch. 95 ½, ¶ 6-803.

5/6-804. Procedure for Home Jurisdiction

§ 6-804. Procedure for Home Jurisdiction. (a) Upon receipt of a report of a failure to comply from the Secretary, the licensing authority of the home jurisdiction shall notify the motorist and initiate a suspension action in accordance with the home jurisdiction's procedures to suspend the motorist's driver's license until satisfactory evidence of compliance with the terms of the traffic citation has been furnished to the Secretary. Due process safeguards will be accorded.

(b) The Secretary shall maintain a record of actions taken and make reports to issuing jurisdictions as provided in the Compact Manual.

P.A. 76-1586, § 6-804, added by P.A. 83-385, § 1, eff. Jan. 1, 1984.

Formerly Ill.Rev.Stat.1991, ch. 95 ½, ¶ 6-804.

5/6-805. Applicability of Other Laws

§ 6-805. Applicability of Other Laws. Except as expressly required by provisions of this Compact, nothing contained herein shall be construed to affect the right of any party jurisdiction to apply any of its other laws relating to licenses to drive to any person or circumstance, or to invalidate or prevent any driver license agreement or other cooperative agreement between a party jurisdiction and a nonparty jurisdiction.

P.A. 76-1586, § 6-805, added by P.A. 83-385, § 1, eff. Jan. 1, 1984.

Formerly Ill.Rev.Stat.1991, ch. 95 ½, ¶ 6-805.

5/6-806. Compact Administrator Procedures

§ 6-806. Compact Administrator Procedures. (a) For the purpose of administering the provisions of this Compact and to serve as a governing body for the resolution of all matters relating to the operation of this Compact, a Board of Compact Administrators is established. The Board shall be composed of one representative from each party jurisdiction to be known as the Compact Administrator. The Compact Administrator shall be appointed by the Secretary and will serve and be subject to removal in accordance with the laws of the jurisdiction represented. A Compact Administrator may provide for the discharge of duties and the performance of the functions as a Board Member to an alternate. An alternate may not be entitled to serve unless written identification notice has been given to the Board.

(b) Each member of the Board of Compact Administrators shall be entitled to one vote. No action of the Board shall be binding unless taken at a meeting at which a majority of the total number of votes on the Board are cast in favor. Action by the Board shall be only at a meeting at which a majority of the party jurisdictions are represented.

(c) The Board shall elect annually, from its membership, a Chairman and Vice Chairman.

(d) The Board shall adopt bylaws, not inconsistent with the provisions of this Compact or the laws of a party jurisdiction, for the conduct of its business and shall have the power to amend and rescind its bylaws.

(e) The Board may accept, for any of its purposes and functions under this Compact, any and all donations, grants of money, equipment, supplies, materials and services, conditional or otherwise, from any jurisdiction, the United States, or any other governmental agency, and may receive, utilize and dispose of the same.

(f) The Board may contract with, or accept services or personnel from, any governmental or intergovernmental agency, person, firm, or corporation, or any private nonprofit organization or institution.

(g) The Board shall formulate all necessary procedures and develop uniform forms and documents for administering the provisions of this Compact. All procedures and forms adopted pursuant to Board action shall be contained in the Compact Manual.

P.A. 76-1586, § 6-806, added by P.A. 83-385, § 1, eff. Jan. 1, 1984.

Formerly Ill.Rev.Stat.1991, ch. 95 ½, ¶ 6-806.

5/6-807. Entry into Compact and Withdrawal

§ 6-807. Entry into Compact and Withdrawal. (a) This Compact shall become effective when it has been adopted by at least 2 jurisdictions.

(b) Entry into the Compact shall be made by a Resolution of Ratification executed by the Secretary and submitted to the Chairman of the Board.

1. The resolution shall be in a form and content as provided in the Compact Manual and shall include statements that in substance are as follows:

(i) A citation of the authority by which the jurisdiction is empowered to become a party to this Compact.

(ii) Agreement to comply with the terms and provisions of the Compact.

(iii) That Compact entry is with all jurisdictions then party to the Compact and with any jurisdiction that legally becomes a party to the Compact.

2. The effective date of entry shall be specified by the Secretary, but it shall not be before July 1, 1984 nor fewer than 60 days after notice has been given by the Chairman of the Board of Compact Administrators or by the American Association of Motor Vehicle Administrators that each party jurisdiction has received the Secretary's resolution.

A withdrawal shall not take effect until 90 days after notice of withdrawal is given. The notice shall be directed to the Compact Administrator of each member jurisdiction. No withdrawal shall affect the validity of this Compact as to the remaining party jurisdictions.

P.A. 76-1586, § 6-807, added by P.A. 83-385, § 1, eff. Jan. 1, 1984.

Formerly Ill.Rev.Stat.1991, ch. 95 ½, ¶ 6-807.

5/6-808. Exceptions

§ 6-808. Exceptions. The provisions of this Compact shall not apply to parking or standing violations, highway weight limit violations, or to violations of law governing the transportation of hazardous materials.

P.A. 76-1586, § 6-808, added by P.A. 83-385, § 1, eff. Jan. 1, 1984.

Formerly Ill.Rev.Stat.1991, ch. 95 ½, ¶ 6-808.

5/6-809. Amendments to the Compact

§ 6-809. Amendments to the Compact. (a) This Compact may be amended from time to time. Amendments shall be presented in resolution form to the Chairman of the Board of Compact Administrators and may be initiated by one or more party jurisdictions.

(b) Adoption of an amendment shall require endorsement of all party jurisdictions and shall become effective 30 days after the date of the last endorsement.

(c) Failure of a party jurisdiction to respond to the Compact Chairman within 12 days after receipt of the proposed amendment shall constitute endorsement.

P.A. 76-1586, § 6-809, added by P.A. 83-385, § 1, eff. Jan. 1, 1984.

Formerly Ill.Rev.Stat.1991, ch. 95 ½, ¶ 6-809.

5/6-810. Construction

§ 6-810. Construction. This Compact shall be liberally construed so as to effectuate the purposes stated herein.

If this Compact shall be held contrary to the Constitution of any jurisdiction party thereto, the Compact shall remain in full force and effect as to the remaining jurisdictions.

P.A. 76–1586, § 6–810, added by P.A. 83–385, § 1, eff. Jan. 1, 1984.

Formerly Ill.Rev.Stat.1991, ch. 95 ½, ¶ 6–810.

ARTICLE IX. DRIVER'S LICENSE MEDICAL REVIEW LAW OF 1992

Date Effective

Article IX was added by P.A. 87–1249, § 1, eff. Dec. 24, 1992.

5/6–900. Short title

§ 6–900. Short title. This Article may be cited as the Driver's License Medical Review Law of 1992.

P.A. 76–1586, § 6–900, added by P.A. 87–1249, § 1, eff. Dec. 24, 1992.

Formerly Ill.Rev.Stat., ch. 95½, ¶ 6–900.

5/6–901. Definitions

§ 6–901. Definitions. For the purposes of this Article:

"Board" means the Driver's License Medical Advisory Board.

"Medical examiner" or "medical practitioner" means any person licensed to practice medicine in all its branches in the State of Illinois.

P.A. 76–1586, § 6–901, added by P.A. 87–1249, § 1, eff. Dec. 24, 1992. Amended by P.A. 90–89, § 15, eff. Jan. 1, 1998; P.A. 92–703, § 10, eff. July 19, 2002.

Formerly Ill.Rev.Stat., ch. 95½, ¶ 6–901.

5/6–902. Driver's License Medical Advisory Board; membership; terms; compensation; meetings

§ 6–902. Driver's License Medical Advisory Board; membership; terms; compensation; meetings.

(a) There is established within the Office of the Secretary of State a Driver's License Medical Advisory Board consisting of at least 9 members appointed by the Secretary. Members' terms of service shall be set by the Secretary at his or her discretion. The members of the Board shall receive compensation from the Secretary at a rate per day designated by the Secretary for each day required for transacting business of the Board and shall be reimbursed for expenses reasonably incurred in the performance of their duties. The Secretary may also call in allied medical personnel to advise and consult with the Board. The Secretary shall select one of the members to act as Chairperson.

(b) The Board, or any of its subdivisions, may meet at any place within the State and shall meet at the call of the Secretary as frequently as he or she deems necessary in order to properly discharge the functions prescribed by this Act.

P.A. 76–1586, § 6–902, added by P.A. 87–1249, § 1, eff. Dec. 24, 1992.

Formerly Ill.Rev.Stat., ch. 95½, ¶ 6–902.

5/6–903. Standard for determining medical limitation; records

§ 6–903. Standard for determining medical limitation; records.

(a) The Secretary in cooperation with the Board shall establish standards for determining the degree to which a person's medical condition constitutes a limitation to the person's ability to operate a motor vehicle or causes the person to be a driving hazard.

(b) The standards may include, but need not be limited to, the following:

(1) Physical disorders characterized by momentary or prolonged lapses of consciousness or control.

(2) Disorders and impairments affecting the cardiovascular functions.

(3) Musculoskeletal disabilities and disorders affecting musculoskeletal functions.

(4) Vision and disorders affecting vision.

(5) The use of or dependence upon alcohol or drugs.

(6) The extent to which compensatory aids and devices may be utilized.

(7) Conditions or disorders that medically impair a person's mental health.

P.A. 76–1586, § 6–903, added by P.A. 87–1249, § 1, eff. Dec. 24, 1992.

Formerly Ill.Rev.Stat., ch. 95½, ¶ 6–903.

5/6–904. Referral of cases by the Secretary

§ 6–904. Referral of cases by the Secretary. The Secretary shall, when he or she has good cause to believe an individual by reason of a medical limitation would not be able to operate a motor vehicle safely, refer a case to the Board for consideration.

P.A. 76–1586, § 6–904, added by P.A. 87–1249, § 1, eff. Dec. 24, 1992.

Formerly Ill.Rev.Stat., ch. 95½, ¶ 6–904.

5/6–905. Medical evaluations of individuals under review; scope of driving privileges; report to the Secretary

§ 6–905. Medical evaluations of individuals under review; scope of driving privileges; report to the Secretary.

(a) Within the scope of the case request, as sent by the Secretary, a function of the Board shall be to make medical evaluations of the individual under review and determine what medical conditions exist that may impair the individual's ability to operate a motor vehicle safely.

(b) Based on the medical evaluations and determination under subsection (a) and in accordance with established standards, the Board shall, among other things, indicate the scope of driving privileges that would enable the individual under review to operate a motor vehicle safely, including the extent to which compensatory aids and devices must be used and the need for ongoing review or evaluation.

(c) The findings, determination, and recommendations of the Board or its subdivisions shall be forwarded to the Secretary who shall then take the action in accordance with the Board's recommendation.

P.A. 76-1586, § 6-905, added by P.A. 87-1249, § 1, eff. Dec. 24, 1992.

Formerly Ill.Rev.Stat., ch. 95½, ¶ 6-905.

5/6-906. Request for a hearing

§ 6-906. Request for a hearing.

(a) After utilizing all possible review by the Board under this Act or any regulation promulgated by the Secretary, any person who has their driver's license restricted or canceled or is otherwise denied a license has a right to request a hearing under Section 2-118 of this Code. The request for a hearing shall be in writing.

(b) The Secretary shall prescribe by rule and regulation the procedures to be followed at the hearing.

P.A. 76-1586, § 6-906, added by P.A. 87-1249, § 1, eff. Dec. 24, 1992.

Formerly Ill.Rev.Stat., ch. 95½, ¶ 6-906.

5/6-907. Cooperation required of person under review

§ 6-907. Cooperation required of person under review.

(a) In making an inquiry or conducting a hearing the Secretary or Board may require the person under review to:

(1) Submit to a medical examination by a medical examiner of the person's choice who is acceptable to the Secretary or Board.

(2) Submit to a medical examination by an impartial medical examiner after the person has submitted information from that person's own medical examiner.

(3) Consent to make available to the Secretary or Board all medical records pertaining to the reported conditions that may be necessary to aid the Board in formulating its findings and recommendations.

(b) Any person under review who refuses to submit to an examination or to consent to provide information, or both, shall as a matter of law be considered unqualified to operate a motor vehicle until the individual complies with the Secretary's or Board's request and the Board is able to make its findings and recommendations, at which time the findings and recommendations shall control.

(c) The results of any examination ordered or conducted by the Secretary or the Board shall be made available to the individual under review.

P.A. 76-1586, § 6-907, added by P.A. 87-1249, § 1, eff. Dec. 24, 1992.

Formerly Ill.Rev.Stat., ch. 95½, ¶ 6-907.

5/6-908. Confidential information

§ 6-908. Confidential information. As provided in subsection (j) of Section 2-123 of this Code, all information furnished to the Secretary or Board, the results of all examinations made at their direction, and all medical findings of the Board shall be confidential and for the sole use of the Board and the Secretary which may have access to the same for the purposes as set forth in this Act. No confidential information may be open to public inspection or the contents disclosed to anyone, except the person under review and then only to the extent necessary to comply with a request for discovery during the hearing process, unless so directed by a court of competent jurisdiction.

P.A. 76-1586, § 6-908, added by P.A. 87-1249, § 1, eff. Dec. 24, 1992.

Formerly Ill.Rev.Stat., ch. 95½, ¶ 6-908.

5/6-909. Rules and regulations; review under Administrative Review Law

§ 6-909. Rules and regulations; review under Administrative Review Law. The Secretary, in cooperation with the Board, shall administer and enforce this Act and shall have the power to make and institute reasonable rules and regulations as necessary to carry out the provisions of this Act.

P.A. 76-1586, § 6-909, added by P.A. 87-1249, § 1, eff. Dec. 24, 1992.

Formerly Ill.Rev.Stat., ch. 95½, ¶ 6-909.

5/6-910. Liability of persons for information supplied to Board or Secretary

§ 6-910. Liability of persons for information supplied to Board or Secretary. No member of the Board, medical practitioner, clinic, hospital, or mental institution, whether public or private, shall be liable or subject to criminal or civil action for any opinions, findings, or recommendations, or for any information supplied to the Secretary or the Board regarding persons under review, or for reports required by this Act, except for willful and wanton misconduct.

P.A. 76-1586, § 6-910, added by P.A. 87-1249, § 1, eff. Dec. 24, 1992.

Formerly Ill.Rev.Stat., ch. 95½, ¶ 6-910.

5/6-911. Information submitted by medical practitioners; police officers; State's attorneys; or members of the judiciary

§ 6-911. Information submitted by medical practitioners; police officers; State's attorneys; or members of the judiciary. Any qualified medical practitioner, commissioned police officer, State's attorney, or member of the judiciary acting in his or her official capacity may submit information to the Secretary relative to the medical condition of a person, including suspected chronic alcoholism or habitual use of narcotics or dangerous drugs, if the condition interferes with the person's ability to operate a motor vehicle safely. Persons reporting under this Section shall enjoy the same immunities granted members of the Board under Section 6-910.

P.A. 76-1586, § 6-911, added by P.A. 87-1249, § 1, eff. Dec. 24, 1992.

Formerly Ill.Rev.Stat., ch. 95½, ¶ 6-911.

5/6–912. Severability

§ 6–912. Severability. The provisions of this Article are severable under Section 1.31 of the Statute on Statutes.[1]

P.A. 76–1586, § 6–912, added by P.A. 87–1249, § 1, eff. Dec. 24, 1992.

Formerly Ill.Rev.Stat., ch. 95½, ¶ 6–912.

[1] 5 ILCS 70/1.31.

CHAPTER 7. ILLINOIS SAFETY AND FAMILY FINANCIAL RESPONSIBILITY LAW

Enactment

The Illinois Vehicle Code was enacted by P.A. 76–1586, effective July 1, 1970. The Code constitutes a consolidated recodification of various earlier laws and acts including the Illinois Motor Vehicle Law of 1957.

ARTICLE I. ADMINISTRATION

5/7–100. Definition of words and phrases

§ 7–100. Definition of words and phrases. Notwithstanding the definitions set forth in Chapter 1,[1] for the purposes of this Chapter, the following words shall have the following meanings ascribed to them:

Administrator. The Department of Transportation.

Arrearage. The total amount of unpaid support obligations.

Authenticated document. A document from a court which contains a court stamp, showing it is filed with the court, or notarized, or is certified by the custodian of the original.

Compliance with a court order of support. The support obligor is no more than an amount equal to 90 days obligation in arrears in making payments in full for current support, or in making periodic payments on a support arrearage as determined by a court.

Court order of support. A judgment order for the support of dependent children issued by a court of this State, including a judgment of dissolution of marriage.

Driver's license. A license or permit to operate a motor vehicle in the State, including the privilege of a person to drive a motor vehicle whether or not the person holds a valid license or permit.

Family financial responsibility driving permit. A permit granting limited driving privileges for employment or medical purposes following a suspension of driving privileges under the Family Financial Responsibility Law.[2] This permit is valid only after the entry of a court order granting the permit and issuance of the permit by the Secretary of State's Office. An individual's driving privileges must be valid except for the family financial responsibility suspension in order for this permit to be issued. In order to be valid, the permit must be in the immediate possession of the driver to whom it is issued.

Judgment. A final judgment of any court of competent jurisdiction of any State, against a person as defendant for damages on account of bodily injury to or death of any person or damages to property resulting from the operation of any motor vehicle.

Obligor. The individual who owes a duty to make payments under a court order of support.

Obligee. The individual or other legal entity to whom a duty of support is owed through a court order of support or the individual's legal representatives.

P.A. 76–1586, § 7–100, eff. July 1, 1970, added by P.A. 76–2473, § 1, eff. July 1, 1971. Amended by P.A. 77–42, § 1, eff. July 1, 1971; P.A. 77–1910, § 1, eff. July 1, 1972; P.A. 78–255, § 61, eff. Oct. 1, 1973; P.A. 83–831, § 1, eff. Jan. 1, 1984; P.A. 84–797, § 1, eff. Jan. 1, 1986; P.A. 86–500, § 1, eff. Jan. 1, 1990; P.A. 89–92, § 10, eff. July 1, 1996; P.A. 90–89, § 15, eff. Jan. 1, 1998.

Formerly Ill.Rev.Stat.1991, ch. 95 ½, ¶ 7–100.

[1] 625 ILCS 5/1–100 et seq.

[2] 625 ILCS 5/7–701 et seq.

5/7–101. Administration of Illinois Safety and Family Financial Responsibility Law

§ 7–101. Administration of Illinois Safety and Family Financial Responsibility Law.[1] The Secretary of State and the Department, within the scope of their respective duties and powers under this Code, shall administer and enforce this Chapter and may make rules and regulations necessary for its administration and shall provide for hearings upon request of persons aggrieved by orders or acts of the Secretary of State, and the Department under this Section. However, the Secretary of State and the clerks of the circuit courts, within the scope of their respective duties and powers under this Code, shall administer and enforce Article VII of this Chapter.

P.A. 76–1586, § 7–101, eff. July 1, 1970. Amended by P.A. 76–2473, § 1, eff. July 1, 1971; P.A. 77–42, § 1, eff. July 1, 1971; P.A. 77–1910, § 1, eff. July 1, 1972; P.A. 78–255, § 61, eff. Oct. 1, 1973; P.A. 83–831, § 1, eff. Jan. 1, 1984; P.A. 89–92, § 10, eff. July 1, 1996.

Formerly Ill.Rev.Stat.1991, ch. 95 ½, ¶ 7–101.

[1] 625 ILCS 5/7–100 et seq.

5/7–102. Court Review

§ 7–102. Court Review. The provisions of the Administrative Review Law,[1] and all amendments and modifications thereof, and the rules adopted pursuant thereto, shall apply to and govern all proceedings for the judicial review of final administrative decisions of the Administrator or the Secretary of State hereunder.

P.A. 76–1586, § 7–102, eff. July 1, 1970. Amended by P.A. 76–2473, § 1, eff. July 1, 1971; P.A. 77–42, § 1, eff. July 1, 1971; P.A. 82–783, Art. XI, § 140, eff. July 13, 1982; P.A. 90–89, § 15, eff. Jan. 1, 1998.

Formerly Ill.Rev.Stat.1991, ch. 95 ½, ¶ 7–102.

[1] 735 ILCS 5/3–101 et seq.

ARTICLE II. SECURITY FOLLOWING ACCIDENT

5/7-201. Application of Article II

§ 7-201. Application of Article II. The Administrator as soon as practicable after the receipt of the report, required to be filed under Sections 11-406 and 11-410, of a motor vehicle accident occurring within this State and that has resulted in bodily injury or death of any person or that damage to the property of any one person in excess of $500 was sustained, shall determine:

1. Whether Section 7-202 of this Code requires the deposit of security by or on behalf of any person who was the operator or owner of any motor vehicle in any manner involved in the accident and;

2. What amount of security shall be sufficient to satisfy any potential judgment or judgments for money damages resulting from the accident as may be recovered against the operator or owner, which amount shall in no event be less than $500.

P.A. 76-1586, § 7-201, eff. July 1, 1970. Amended by P.A. 76-1616, § 1, eff. July 1, 1970; P.A. 76-2473, § 1, eff. July 1, 1971; P.A. 77-42, § 1, eff. July 1, 1971; P.A. 77-327, § 1, eff. July 22, 1971; P.A. 77-1910, § 1, eff. July 1, 1972; P.A. 78-255, § 61, eff. Oct. 1, 1973; P.A. 84-797, § 1, eff. Jan. 1, 1986; P.A. 87-829, § 1, eff. Jan. 17, 1992.

Formerly Ill.Rev.Stat.1991, ch. 95 ½, ¶ 7-201.

5/7-201.1. Request for missing report or missing information

§ 7-201.1. If the Administrator has not received a report required to be filed under Sections 11-406 and 11-410, or if the information contained in a report is insufficient, the Administrator shall send to the person required to file the report a written request for the missing report or the missing information. The Administrator shall send such request no later than 45 days after the accident or 7 days after receiving information that such accident has occurred, whichever is later.

If the request is sent to a driver involved in an accident, the request or an attachment thereto shall contain in bold print a warning that failure to comply with the request within 15 days may result in the suspension of the driver's license.

P.A. 76-1586, § 7-201.1, eff. July 1, 1970. Amended by P.A. 76-2473, § 1, eff. July 1, 1971; P.A. 77-42, § 1, eff. July 1, 1971; P.A. 77-1910, § 1, eff. July 1, 1972; P.A. 78-255, § 61, eff. Oct. 1, 1973; P.A. 84-797, § 1, eff. Jan. 1, 1986.

Formerly Ill.Rev.Stat.1991, ch. 95 ½, ¶ 7-201.1.

5/7-201.2. Accident information; certification to Secretary of State; notice to persons whose names are certified

§ 7-201.2. The Administrator, within 30 days after compiling sufficient information on a motor vehicle accident, shall certify to the Secretary of State the name of each owner and the name of each operator of any vehicle involved in the accident, his determination that security is required under this Code, and the amount of the security. The Administrator also shall supply to the Secretary of State a copy of any accident report requested by the Secretary.

The Administrator shall send a copy of the certification to each person whose name is certified. The copy, or an attachment thereto, shall contain in bold print an explanation that, because the person did not furnish the Department of Transportation with evidence that he or she is insured or otherwise able to pay for damages resulting from the accident, the person's name has been forwarded to the Secretary of State for possible suspension of his or her driver's license.

P.A. 76-1586, § 7-201.2, added by P.A. 84-797, § 1, eff. Jan. 1, 1986.

Formerly Ill.Rev.Stat.1991, ch. 95 ½, ¶ 7-201.2.

5/7-201.3. Administrator to itemize potential claims

§ 7-201.3. Administrator to itemize potential claims. The Administrator shall send by mail to the person required to deposit security an itemization of each potential claim of personal injury or property damage and the name and address of each potential claimant within the knowledge of the Administrator and upon which the determination of the amount of security is based.

P.A. 76-1586, § 7-201.3, added by P.A. 84-797, § 1, eff. Jan. 1, 1986.

Formerly Ill.Rev.Stat.1991, ch. 95 ½, ¶ 7-201.3.

5/7-202. Exceptions to requirements of security

§ 7-202. Exceptions to requirements of security. (a) The requirements as to security and suspension as provided by Sections 7-201 and 7-205 shall not apply:

1. To the driver or owner if such owner had in effect at the time of such motor vehicle accident a liability policy covering such driver and owner with respect to the vehicle involved in such motor vehicle accident;

2. To the driver, if not the owner of such vehicle, if there was in effect at the time of such motor vehicle accident a liability policy or bond with respect to the operation of motor vehicles not owned by the driver;

3. To the driver or owner if the liability of such driver or owner for damages resulting from such motor vehicle accident is covered by any other form of liability insurance policy or bond;

4. To the driver or owner, if such owner is qualified as a self-insurer as provided in Section 7-502;

5. To the owner if such owner at the time of such motor vehicle accident was in compliance with Section 8-101 or Section 9-101;

6. To the driver or owner if such owner at the time of such motor vehicle accident was in compliance with the Federal Revised Interstate Commerce Act (P.L. 95-473), as now or hereafter amended;[1]

7. To the owner if the vehicle involved in such motor vehicle accident was owned by the United States, this State or any political sub-division of this State, any municipality therein, or any local Mass Transit District;

8. To the driver or the owner of a vehicle involved in a motor vehicle accident wherein no injury or damage was caused to the person or property of any one other than such driver or owner;

9. To the driver or the owner of a vehicle which at the time of the motor vehicle accident was parked, unless such vehicle was parked at a place where parking was at the time of the accident prohibited under any applicable law or ordinance;

10. To the owner of a vehicle if at the time of the motor vehicle accident the vehicle was being operated without his permission, express or implied, or was parked by a person who had been operating such motor vehicle without such permission;

11. To the driver, if not the owner, of a commercial motor vehicle on which there was no liability policy or bond with respect to the operation of such vehicle in effect at the time of the motor vehicle accident when the driver was operating the vehicle in the course of the driver's employment and had no actual knowledge of such lack of a liability policy or bond prior to the motor vehicle accident.

(b) If at the time of the motor vehicle accident, an owner or driver is covered by a motor vehicle liability policy or bond meeting the requirements of this Code, such owner or driver shall be exempt from suspension under Section 7–205 as to that motor vehicle accident, if the company issuing the policy or bond has failed, and such policy or bond was not effective at the time of the motor vehicle accident or any time thereafter, provided, that the owner or driver had no knowledge of the company's failure prior to the motor vehicle accident, and such owner or driver has secured within 30 days after learning of such failure another liability policy or bond meeting the requirements of the Code relating to future occurrences or motor vehicle accidents.

As used in this paragraph, the words "failed" or "failure" mean that the company has suspended operations by order of a court.

P.A. 76–1586, § 7–202, eff. July 1, 1970. Amended by P.A. 76–1616, § 1, eff. July 1, 1970; P.A. 76–2473, § 1, eff. July 1, 1971; P.A. 77–42, § 1, eff. July 1, 1971; P.A. 80–593, § 1, eff. Oct. 1, 1977; P.A. 81–1269, § .01, eff. June 30, 1980; P.A. 83–333, § 50, eff. Sept. 14, 1983; P.A. 83–831, § 1, eff. Jan. 1, 1984; P.A. 83–1362, Art. II, § 99, eff. Sept. 11, 1984; P.A. 85–293, Art. III, § 21, eff. Sept. 8, 1987.

Formerly Ill.Rev.Stat.1991, ch. 95 ½, ¶ 7–202.

[1] 49 U.S.C.A. § 10101 et seq.

5/7–203. Requirements as to policy or bond

§ 7–203. Requirements as to policy or bond. No such policy or bond referred to in Section 7–202 shall be effective under this Section unless issued by an insurance company or surety company authorized to do business in this State, except that if such motor vehicle was not registered in this State, or was a motor vehicle which was registered elsewhere than in this State at the effective date of the policy or bond, or the most recent renewal thereof, such policy or bond shall not be effective under this Section unless the insurance company or surety company, if not authorized to do business in this State, shall execute a power of attorney authorizing the Secretary of State to accept service on its behalf of notice or process in any action upon such policy or bond arising out of such motor vehicle accident. However, every such policy or bond is subject, if the motor vehicle accident has resulted in bodily injury or death, to a limit, exclusive of interest and costs, of not less than $20,000 because of bodily injury to or death of any one person in any one motor vehicle accident and, subject to said limit for one person, to a limit of not less than $40,000 because of bodily injury to or death of 2 or more persons in any one motor vehicle accident, and, if the motor vehicle accident has resulted in injury to or destruction of property, to a limit of not less than $15,000 because of injury to or destruction of property of others in any one motor vehicle accident.

Upon receipt of a written motor vehicle accident report from the Administrator the insurance company or surety company named in such notice shall notify the Administrator within such time and in such manner as the Administrator may require, in case such policy or bond was not in effect at the time of such motor vehicle accident.

P.A. 76–1586, § 7–203, eff. July 1, 1970. Amended by P.A. 76–2473, § 1, eff. July 1, 1971; P.A. 77–42, § 1, eff. July 1, 1971; P.A. 81–1202, § 2, eff. March 1, 1980; P.A. 83–831, § 1, eff. Jan. 1, 1984; P.A. 85–730, § 1, eff. Jan. 1, 1988.

Formerly Ill.Rev.Stat.1991, ch. 95 ½, ¶ 7–203.

5/7–204. Form and amount of security—Definition

§ 7–204. Form and amount of security—Definition. (A) Any security required to be deposited under this Act shall be in the form as the Secretary of State may require by administrative rule, and in the amounts as the Administrator may determine to be sufficient to satisfy any judgment or judgments for damages against an operator or owner but in no case in excess of the limits specified in Section 7–203 of this Act in reference to the acceptable limits of a policy or bond nor for an amount less than $500.

(B) The person depositing security shall specify in writing the person or persons on whose behalf the deposit is made and, while at any time the deposit is in the custody of the Secretary of State or State Treasurer, the person depositing it may, in writing, amend the specification of the person or persons on whose behalf the deposit is made to include an additional person or persons; provided, however, that a single deposit of security shall be applicable only on behalf of persons, required to furnish security because of the same accident.

(C) Within 10 days after any security required under the provisions of this Article is deposited with the Secretary of State, the Secretary shall send notice of the security deposit to the following, if known:

1. To each owner and operator of any vehicle involved in the accident that sustained damage in excess of $500;

2. To any person who sustained damage to personal or real property in excess of $500;

3. To any person who was injured as a result of the accident; and

4. To the estate of any person killed as a result of the accident.

P.A. 76–1586, § 7–204, eff. July 1, 1970. Amended by P.A. 76–1617, § 1, eff. July 1, 1970; P.A. 76–2473, § 1, eff. July 1, 1971; P.A. 77–42, § 1, eff. July 1, 1971; P.A. 77–327, § 1, eff. July 22, 1971; P.A. 77–1910, § 1, eff. July 1, 1972; P.A. 78–255, § 61, eff. Oct. 1, 1973; P.A. 84–300, § 1, eff. Sept. 13, 1985; P.A. 84–570, § 1, eff. Jan. 1, 1986; P.A. 84–1308, Art. II, § 96, eff. Aug. 25, 1986; P.A. 87–829, § 1, eff. Jan. 17, 1992.

Formerly Ill.Rev.Stat.1991, ch. 95 ½, ¶ 7–204.

5/7-205. Failure to deposit security—Hearings and suspensions

§ 7-205. Failure to deposit security—Hearings and suspensions. The Secretary of State, within 15 days after receipt of the determination of the Administrator that a deposit of security is required under this Code, shall review all reports, documents and other pertinent evidence in his possession, and make a preliminary finding as to whether or not there is reasonable possibility of a civil judgment being entered in a court of proper jurisdiction against the person so certified by the Administrator under this Code.

(a) Upon a preliminary finding that there is such a reasonable possibility, the Secretary of State shall notify such person by mail that his driving privileges, driver's license or registration will be suspended 45 days after the date of the mailing of the notice unless the person can prove to the satisfaction of the Secretary of State that he has deposited or has had deposited and filed on his behalf the security required under this Code or, within 15 days of the mailing of such notice, requests a formal hearing to determine whether his driving privileges, driver's license or registration should be suspended or whether the Secretary should enter an order of exoneration, and that such hearing shall be scheduled within 45 days after the mailing of such notice in accordance with the rules and regulations of the Secretary of State.

(b) Upon a preliminary finding that there is not such a reasonable possibility, the Secretary of State may elect to take no further action.

(c) In the event an order of suspension so entered applies to a nonresident owner or driver, then the privilege of driving or using a motor vehicle within the territorial limits of this State shall be so suspended.

P.A. 76-1586, § 7-205, eff. July 1, 1970. Amended by P.A. 76-1864, § 1, eff. July 1, 1970; P.A. 76-2473, § 1, eff. July 1, 1970; P.A. 77-42, § 1, eff. July 1, 1971; P.A. 77-327, § 1, eff. July 22, 1971; P.A. 77-1910, § 1, eff. July 1, 1972; P.A. 78-255, § 61, eff. Oct. 1, 1973; P.A. 83-831, § 1, eff. Jan. 1, 1984; P.A. 83-1081, § 1, eff. July 1, 1984; P.A. 83-1362, Art. II, § 99, eff. Sept. 11, 1984; P.A. 84-797, § 1, eff. Jan. 1, 1986.

Formerly Ill.Rev.Stat.1991, ch. 95 ½, ¶ 7-205.

5/7-206. Release from liability

§ 7-206. Release from liability. (a) A person shall be relieved from the requirement for deposit of security required by Section 7-201 in the event there shall be filed with the Secretary of State satisfactory evidence that the person who would otherwise be required to deposit security has been released from liability.

(b) A covenant not to sue shall relieve the parties thereto as to each other from the security requirements of this Article.

P.A. 76-1586, § 7-206, eff. July 1, 1970. Amended by P.A. 83-831, § 1, eff. Jan. 1, 1984.

Formerly Ill.Rev.Stat.1991, ch. 95 ½, ¶ 7-206.

5/7-207. Adjudication of non-liability

§ 7-207. Adjudication of non-liability. A person shall be relieved from the requirement for deposit of security, required by Section 7-201 of this Act, in the event there shall be filed with the Secretary of State evidence satisfactory of a final adjudication of non-liability.

P.A. 76-1586, § 7-207, eff. July 1, 1970. Amended by P.A. 77-327, § 1, eff. July 22, 1971.

Formerly Ill.Rev.Stat.1991, ch. 95 ½, ¶ 7-207.

5/7-208. Agreements for payment of damages

§ 7-208. Agreements for payment of damages. (a) Any 2 or more of the persons involved in a motor vehicle accident subject to the provisions of Section 7-201 or their authorized representatives, may at any time enter into a written agreement for the payment of an agreed amount in installments, with respect to all claims for injuries or damages resulting from the motor vehicle accident.

(b) The Secretary of State, to the extent provided by any such written agreement properly filed with him, shall not require the deposit of security and shall terminate any prior order of suspension, or, if security has previously been deposited, the Secretary of State shall immediately return such security to the depositor or an appropriate personal representative.

(c) In the event of a default in any payment under such agreement and upon notice of such default the Secretary of State shall forthwith suspend the driver's license and registration, or nonresident's operating privileges, of such person in default which shall not be restored unless and until:

1. Such person deposits and thereafter maintains security as required under Section 7-201 in such amount as the Secretary of State may then determine,

2. Two years have elapsed since the acceptance of the notice of default by the Secretary of State and during such period no action upon such agreement has been instituted in any court having jurisdiction, or

3. The person enters into a second written agreement for the payment of an agreed amount in installments with respect to all claims for injuries or damages resulting from the motor vehicle accident.

P.A. 76-1586, § 7-208, eff. July 1, 1970. Amended by P.A. 77-327, § 1, eff. July 22, 1971; P.A. 83-831, § 1, eff. Jan. 1, 1984; P.A. 84-300, § 1, eff. Sept. 13, 1985; P.A. 85-321, § 1, eff. Jan. 1, 1988; P.A. 90-774, § 5, eff. Aug. 14, 1998.

Formerly Ill.Rev.Stat.1991, ch. 95 ½, ¶ 7-208.

5/7-209. Payment upon judgment

§ 7-209. Payment upon judgment. The payment of a judgment arising out of a motor vehicle accident or the payment upon such judgment of an amount equal to the maximum amount which could be required for deposit under this Article shall for the purposes of this Code be deemed satisfied.

P.A. 76-1586, § 7-209, eff. July 1, 1970. Amended by P.A. 83-831, § 1, eff. Jan. 1, 1984.

Formerly Ill.Rev.Stat.1991, ch. 95 ½, ¶ 7-209.

5/7-210. Termination of security requirement

§ 7-210. Termination of security requirement. The Secretary of State, if satisfied as to the existence of any fact which under Sections 7-206, 7-207, 7-208, or 7-209 would entitle a person to be relieved from the security requirements of this Article, shall not require the deposit of security by the person so relieved from such requirement and shall terminate any prior order of suspension in respect to such person, or if security has previously been deposited by such person, the Secretary of State shall immediately return such deposit to such person.

P.A. 76-1586, § 7-210, eff. July 1, 1970.

Formerly Ill.Rev.Stat.1991, ch. 95 ½, ¶ 7-210.

5/7-211. Duration of suspension

§ 7-211. Duration of suspension.

(a) Unless a suspension is terminated under other provisions of this Code, the driver's license or registration and nonresident's operating privilege suspended as provided in Section 7-205 shall remain suspended and shall not be renewed nor shall any license or registration be issued to the person until:

1. The person deposits or there shall be deposited and filed on the person's behalf the security required under Section 7-201;

2. Two years have elapsed following the date the driver's license and registrations were suspended and evidence satisfactory to the Secretary of State that during the period no action for damages arising out of a motor vehicle accident has been properly filed;

3. Receipt of proper notice that the person has filed bankruptcy which would include all claims for personal injury and property damage resulting from the accident; or

4. After the expiration of 5 years from the date of the accident, the Secretary of State has not received documentation that any action at law for damages arising out of the motor vehicle accident has been filed against the person.

An affidavit that no action at law for damages arising out of the motor vehicle accident has been filed against the applicant, or if filed that it is not still pending shall be prima facie evidence of that fact. The Secretary of State may take whatever steps are necessary to verify the statement set forth in the applicant's affidavit.

(b) The driver's license or registration and nonresident's operating privileges suspended as provided in Section 7-205 shall also remain suspended and shall not be renewed nor shall any license or registration be issued to the person until the person gives proof of his or her financial responsibility in the future as provided in Section 1-164.5. The proof is to be maintained by the person in a manner satisfactory to the Secretary of State for a period of 3 years after the date the proof is first filed.

P.A. 76-1586, § 7-211, eff. July 1, 1970. Amended by P.A. 77-327, § 1, eff. July 22, 1971; P.A. 83-831, § 1, eff. Jan. 1, 1984; P.A. 84-832, Art. III, § 11, eff. Sept. 23, 1985; P.A. 85-321, § 1, eff. Jan. 1, 1988; P.A. 86-549, § 1, eff. Jan. 1, 1990; P.A. 87-1114, § 1, eff. Sept. 15, 1992; P.A. 90-264, § 5, eff. Jan. 1, 1998; P.A. 91-80, § 5, eff. July 9, 1999.

Formerly Ill.Rev.Stat.1991, ch. 95 ½, ¶ 7-211.

5/7-212. Authority of Administrator and Secretary of State to decrease amount of security

§ 7-212. Authority of Administrator and Secretary of State to decrease amount of security. The Administrator may reduce the amount of security ordered in any case within one year after the date of the accident, but in no event for an amount less than $500, if, in the judgment of the Administrator the amount ordered is excessive, or may revoke or rescind its order requiring the deposit of security in any case within one year after the date of the accident if, in the judgment of the Administrator, the provisions of Sections 7-202 and 7-203 excuse or exempt the operator or owner from the requirement of the deposit. In case the security originally ordered has been deposited the excess of the reduced amount ordered shall be returned to the depositor or his personal representative forthwith, notwithstanding the provisions of Section 7-214. The Secretary of State likewise shall have authority granted to the Administrator to reduce the amount of security ordered by the Administrator.

P.A. 76-1586, § 7-212, eff. July 1, 1970. Amended by P.A. 76-2473, § 1, eff. July 1, 1971; P.A. 77-42, § 1, eff. July 1, 1971; P.A. 77-1910, § 1, eff. July 1, 1972; P.A. 78-255, § 61, eff. Oct. 1, 1973; P.A. 87-829, § 1, eff. Jan. 17, 1992.

Formerly Ill.Rev.Stat.1991, ch. 95 ½, ¶ 7-212.

5/7-213. Custody of security

§ 7-213. Custody of security. Security deposited in compliance with the requirements of this Article shall be placed by the Secretary of State in the custody of the State Treasurer.

P.A. 76-1586, § 7-213, eff. July 1, 1970. Amended by P.A. 83-831, § 1, eff. Jan. 1, 1984.

Formerly Ill.Rev.Stat.1991, ch. 95 ½, ¶ 7-213.

5/7-214. Disposition of Security

§ 7-214. Disposition of Security.

Such security shall be applicable only to the payment of a judgment or judgments, rendered against the person or persons on whose behalf the deposit was made, for damages arising out of the accident in question, in an action at law, begun not later than two years after the later of (i) the date the driver's license and registration were suspended following the accident or (ii) the date of any default in any payment under an installment agreement for payment of damages, and such deposit or any balance thereof shall be returned to the depositor or his personal representative when evidence satisfactory to the Secretary of State has been filed with him:

1. that there has been a release from liability, or a final adjudication of non-liability; or

2. a duly acknowledged written agreement in accordance with Section 7-208 of this Act; or

3. whenever after the expiration of two years after the later of (i) the date the driver's license and registration were suspended following the accident or (ii) the date of any default in any payment under an installment agreement for payment of damages, the Secretary of State shall be given reasonable evidence that there is no such action pending and no judgment rendered in such action left unpaid.

P.A. 76-1586, § 7-214, eff. July 1, 1970. Amended by P.A. 90-774, § 5, eff. Aug. 14, 1998.

Formerly Ill.Rev.Stat.1991, ch. 95 ½, ¶ 7-214.

5/7-215. Matters not to be evidence in civil suits

§ 7-215. Matters not to be evidence in civil suits. Any action taken pursuant to this Chapter, or the Rules and Regulations adopted hereunder, or findings of the Administrator or the Secretary of State upon which such action is based, or the security filed as provided in this Article shall not be referred to in any way, nor shall it be any evidence of the negligence or due care of either party, at the trial of any civil action to recover damages.

P.A. 76-1586, § 7-215, eff. July 1, 1970. Amended by P.A. 76-2473, § 1, eff. July 1, 1971; P.A. 77-42, § 1, eff. July 1, 1971; P.A. 77-979, § 1, eff. Jan. 1, 1972; P.A. 77-1910, § 1, eff. July 1, 1972; P.A. 78-255, § 61, eff. Oct. 1, 1973; P.A. 83-831, § 1, eff. Jan. 1, 1984.

Formerly Ill.Rev.Stat.1991, ch. 95 ½, ¶ 7-215.

5/7-216. Reciprocity—Residents and nonresidents—Licensing of nonresidents

§ 7-216. Reciprocity—Residents and nonresidents—Licensing of nonresidents. (a) When a nonresident's operating privilege is suspended pursuant to Section 7-205 the Secretary of State shall transmit a certified copy of the record of such action to the official in charge of the issuance of driver's license and registration certificates in the state in which such nonresident resides, if the law of such other state provides for action in relation thereto similar to that provided for in paragraph (b).

(b) Upon receipt of such certification that the operating privilege of a resident of this State has been suspended or revoked in any such other state pursuant to a law providing for its suspension or revocation for failure to deposit security for the payment of judgments arising out of a motor vehicle accident, or for failure to deposit security under circumstances which would require the Secretary of State to suspend a nonresident's operating privilege had the motor vehicle accident occurred in this State, the Secretary of State shall suspend the driver's license of such resident and all other registrations. Such suspension shall continue until such resident furnishes evidence of compliance with the law of such other state relating to the deposit of such security.

(c) In case the operator or the owner of a motor vehicle involved in a motor vehicle accident within this State has no driver's license or registration, such operator shall not be allowed a driver's license or registration until the operator has complied with the requirements of Sections 7-201 thru 7-216 to the same extent that would be necessary if, at the time of the motor vehicle accident, such operator had held a license and registration.

P.A. 76-1586, § 7-216, eff. July 1, 1970. Amended by P.A. 83-831, § 1, eff. Jan. 1, 1984.

Formerly Ill.Rev.Stat.1991, ch. 95 ½, ¶ 7-216.

ARTICLE III. PROOF OF FINANCIAL RESPONSIBILITY FOR THE FUTURE

Section

Section

5/7-301. Application of Article III

§ 7-301. Application of Article III. The provisions of this Article requiring the deposit of proof of financial responsibility for the future, subject to certain exemptions, shall apply with respect to persons whose driver's license or driving privileges have been revoked as provided by this Code, or who have failed to pay judgments amounting to $500 or more as defined in Section 7-303.

P.A. 76-1586, § 7-301, eff. July 1, 1970. Amended by P.A. 83-831, § 1, eff. Jan. 1, 1984; P.A. 86-549, § 1, eff. Jan. 1, 1990; P.A. 87-829, § 1, eff. Jan. 17, 1992.

Formerly Ill.Rev.Stat.1991, ch. 95 ½, ¶ 7-301.

5/7-302. § 7-302. Repealed by P.A. 90-89, § 20, eff. Jan. 1, 1998

5/7-303. Suspension of driver's licenses, registration certificates, license plates and registration stickers for failure to satisfy judgment

§ 7-303. Suspension of driver's licenses, registration certificates, license plates and registration stickers for failure to satisfy judgment. (a) The Secretary of State shall, except as provided in paragraph (d), suspend the driver's license issued to any person upon receiving an authenticated report as hereinafter provided for in Section 7-307 that such person has failed for a period of 30 days to satisfy any final judgment in amounts as hereinafter stated, and shall also suspend all registration certificates, license plates and registration stickers issued to the person named as the judgment debtor in any such authenticated report.

(b) The term "judgment" shall mean: A final judgment of any court of competent jurisdiction of any State, against a person as defendant for damages on account of bodily injury to or death of any person or damages to property resulting from the operation, on and after July 12, 1938, of any motor vehicle.

(c) The term "State" shall mean: Any State, Territory, or possession of the United States, the District of Columbia, or any province of the Dominion of Canada.

(d) The Secretary of State shall not suspend the driver's license, registration certificates, registration stickers or license plates of the judgment debtor, nor shall such judgment debtor be subject to the suspension provisions of Sections 7-308 and 7-309 if all the following conditions are met:

1. At the time of the motor vehicle accident which gave rise to the unsatisfied judgment the judgment debtor was covered by a motor vehicle liability policy or bond meeting the requirements of this Chapter;

2. The insurance company which issued the policy or bond has failed and has suspended operations by order of a court;

3. The judgment debtor had no knowledge of the insurance company's failure prior to the motor vehicle accident;

4. Within 30 days after learning of the insurance company's failure the judgment debtor secured another liability policy or bond meeting the requirements of this Article relating to future occurrences or accidents;

5. The insurance company which issued the motor vehicle liability policy or bond that covered the judgment debtor at the time of the motor vehicle accident is unable to satisfy the judgment in the amounts specified in Section 7-311;

6. The judgment debtor presents to the Secretary of State such certified documents or other proofs as the Secretary of State may require that all of the conditions set forth in this Section have been met.

P.A. 76-1586, § 7-303, eff. July 1, 1970. Amended by P.A. 79-1358, § 43, eff. Oct. 1, 1976; P.A. 80-230, § 1, eff. Oct. 1, 1977; P.A. 83-831, § 1, eff. Jan. 1, 1984; P.A. 85-321, § 1, eff. Jan. 1, 1988.

Formerly Ill.Rev.Stat.1991, ch. 95 ½, ¶ 7-303.

5/7-304. Proof required

§ 7-304. Proof required. Upon the revocation of a driver's license of any person as provided in Section 6-113, 6-205 or 6-206, the Secretary of State shall suspend any and all of the registration certificates, license plates and registration stickers issued for any motor vehicle registered in the name of such person as owner except that the Secretary shall not suspend such evidences of registration in the event such owner has previously given or shall immediately give the Secretary and thereafter maintain for a period of 3 years, proof of financial responsibility in the manner hereinafter specified in this Article with respect to each and every motor vehicle owned and registered by such person.

P.A. 76-1586, § 7-304, eff. July 1, 1970. Amended by P.A. 80-230, § 1, eff. Oct. 1, 1977; P.A. 83-831, § 1, eff. Jan. 1, 1984.

Formerly Ill.Rev.Stat.1991, ch. 95 ½, ¶ 7-304.

5/7-305. Suspension until proof furnished

§ 7-305. Suspension until proof furnished. The suspension of such certificates of registration, license plates and registration stickers of such person as provided for in Section 7-304 shall remain in effect and the Secretary of State shall not issue to any such person any new or renewal of driver's license and shall not register or re-register in the name of such person any motor vehicle until permitted under this Article and not then unless and until said person gives proof of his financial responsibility in the future, as defined in this Code, such proof to be maintained by said person in a manner satisfactory to the Secretary of State for a period of 3 years after the date such proof is first filed.

P.A. 76-1586, § 7-305, eff. July 1, 1970. Amended by P.A. 80-230, § 1, eff. Oct. 1, 1977; P.A. 83-831, § 1, eff. Jan. 1, 1984; P.A. 84-112, § 1, eff. July 25, 1985; P.A. 90-89, § 15, eff. Jan. 1, 1998.

Formerly Ill.Rev.Stat.1991, ch. 95 ½, ¶ 7-305.

5/7-306. Action in respect to an unlicensed driver

§ 7-306. Action in respect to an unlicensed driver. Whenever any person who is not a resident of this State has been convicted of an offense which would require the revocation of the driver's license of a resident, such nonresident shall not operate any motor vehicle in this State nor shall any motor vehicle owned by such nonresident be operated within this State by any person, and the Secretary of State shall not issue to such nonresident any driver's license and shall not register any motor vehicle owned by such nonresident unless and until such nonresident shall give proof of financial responsibility.

P.A. 76-1586, § 7-306, eff. July 1, 1970. Amended by P.A. 83-831, § 1, eff. Jan. 1, 1984.

Formerly Ill.Rev.Stat.1991, ch. 95 ½, ¶ 7-306.

5/7-307. Courts to report nonpayments of judgment

§ 7-307. Courts to report nonpayments of judgment. The clerk of a court, or the judge of a court which has no clerk shall forward to the Secretary of State, on a form prescribed by the Secretary, a certified record of any judgment for damages, the rendering and nonpayment of which judgment required the suspension of the driver's license and registrations in the name of the judgment debtor hereunder, such record to be forwarded to the Secretary of State upon request by the plaintiff after the expiration of 30 days after such judgment has become final and when such judgment has not been stayed or satisfied within the amounts specified in this Article as shown by the records of the Court.

P.A. 76-1586, § 7-307, eff. July 1, 1970. Amended by P.A. 80-849, § 1, eff. Oct. 1, 1977; P.A. 83-831, § 1, eff. Jan. 1, 1984; P.A. 86-549, § 1, eff. Jan. 1, 1990.

Formerly Ill.Rev.Stat.1991, ch. 95 ½, ¶ 7-307.

5/7-308. Action in respect to nonresident for nonpayment of judgment

§ 7-308. Action in respect to nonresident for nonpayment of judgment. (a) If a person, whose failure to satisfy a judgment within 30 days after the same became final would require a suspension or revocation hereunder in respect to a resident, shall not be a resident of this State, such nonresident shall not operate any motor vehicle in this State, nor shall any motor vehicle owned by such nonresident be operated in this State by any person and the Secretary of State shall not issue to such nonresident a driver's license and shall not register any motor vehicle owned by such nonresident unless and until such nonresident shall give proof of financial responsibility and shall satisfy any such judgment as required with respect to a resident of this State.

(b) The Secretary of State shall forward to the Motor Vehicle Commissioner or state officer performing the functions of a Commissioner in the state, foreign country, or province of the Dominion of Canada in which a judgment debtor resides, a certified record of any unsatisfied judgment rendered against such nonresident which requires suspension of such nonresident's driving privileges in this State.

P.A. 76-1586, § 7-308, eff. July 1, 1970. Amended by P.A. 83-831, § 1, eff. Jan. 1, 1984.

Formerly Ill.Rev.Stat.1991, ch. 95 ½, ¶ 7-308.

5/7-309. Suspension to continue until judgments paid and proof given

§ 7-309. Suspension to continue until judgments paid and proof given.

(a) The suspension of such driver's license, license plates and registration stickers shall remain in effect and no other vehicle shall be registered in the name of such judgment debtor, nor any new license issued to such person (including any such person not previously licensed), unless and until the

Secretary of State receives authenticated documentation that such judgment is satisfied, or dormant as provided for in Section 12-108 of the Code of Civil Procedure, as now or hereafter amended,[1] or stayed by court order, and the judgment debtor gives proof of financial responsibility, as hereinafter provided. The Secretary of State may terminate the suspension of such person's driver's license, license plates and registration stickers and no proof of financial responsibility shall be required on any existing suspensions under this Article which are more than 20 years old.

(b) Whenever, after one judgment is satisfied and proof of financial responsibility is given as herein required, another such judgment is rendered against the judgment debtor for any motor vehicle accident occurring prior to the date of the giving of said proof and such person fails to satisfy the latter judgment within the amounts specified herein within 30 days after the same becomes final, then the Secretary of State shall again suspend the driver's license of such judgment debtor and shall again suspend the registration of any vehicle registered in the name of such judgment debtor as owner. Such driver's license and registration shall not be renewed nor shall a driver's license and registration of any vehicle be issued to such judgment debtor while such latter judgment remains in effect and unsatisfied within the amount specified herein.

P.A. 76-1586, § 7-309, eff. July 1, 1970. Amended by P.A. 80-230, § 1, eff. Oct. 1, 1977; P.A. 83-831, § 1, eff. Jan. 1, 1984; P.A. 84-112, § 1, eff. July 25, 1985; P.A. 86-500, § 1, eff. Jan. 1, 1990; P.A. 90-655, § 153, eff. July 30, 1998.

Formerly Ill.Rev.Stat.1991, ch. 95 ½, ¶ 7-309.

1 735 ILCS 5/12-108.

5/7-310. Petition for discharge filed in bankruptcy

§ 7-310. Petition for discharge filed in bankruptcy. A petition for discharge filed in bankruptcy following the rendering of any judgment shall relieve the judgment debtor from any of the requirements of this Chapter 7.

A petition for discharge filed in bankruptcy of the owner or lessee of a commercial vehicle by whom the judgment debtor is employed at the time of the motor vehicle accident that gives rise to the judgment also shall relieve the judgment debtor so employed from any of the requirements of this Chapter 7 if the discharge of the owner or lessee follows the rendering of the judgment and if the judgment debtor so employed was operating the commercial vehicle in connection with his regular employment or occupation at the time of the accident. This amendatory act of 1985 applies to all cases irrespective of whether the accident giving rise to the suspension of license or registration occurred before, on, or after its effective date.

P.A. 76-1586, § 7-310, eff. July 1, 1970. Amended by P.A. 78-233, § 1, eff. Aug. 6, 1973; P.A. 83-368, § 1, eff. Jan. 1, 1984; P.A. 84-406, § 1, eff. Jan. 1, 1986; P.A. 86-549, § 1, eff. Jan. 1, 1990; P.A. 87-1114, § 1, eff. Sept. 15, 1992.

Formerly Ill.Rev.Stat.1991, ch. 95 ½, ¶ 7-310.

5/7-311. Payments sufficient to satisfy requirements

§ 7-311. Payments sufficient to satisfy requirements. (a) Judgments herein referred to arising out of motor vehicle accidents occurring on or after January 1, 1956, shall for the purpose of this Chapter be deemed satisfied:

1. When $20,000 has been credited upon any judgment or judgments rendered in excess of that amount for bodily injury to or the death of one person as the result of any one motor vehicle accident; or

2. When, subject to said limit of $20,000 as to any one person, the sum of $40,000 has been credited upon any judgment or judgments rendered in excess of that amount for bodily injury to or the death of more than one person as the result of any one motor vehicle accident; or

3. When $15,000 has been credited upon any judgment or judgments, rendered in excess of that amount for damages to property of others as a result of any one motor vehicle accident.

(b) Credit for such amounts shall be deemed a satisfaction of any such judgment or judgments in excess of said amounts only for the purposes of this Chapter.

(c) Whenever payment has been made in settlement of any claim for bodily injury, death or property damage arising from a motor vehicle accident resulting in injury, death or property damage to two or more persons in such accident, any such payment shall be credited in reduction of the amounts provided for in this Section.

P.A. 76-1586, § 7-311, eff. July 1, 1970. Amended by P.A. 81-1202, § 2, eff. March 1, 1980; P.A. 83-831, § 1, eff. Jan. 1, 1984; P.A. 85-730, § 1, eff. Jan. 1, 1988.

Formerly Ill.Rev.Stat.1991, ch. 95 ½, ¶ 7-311.

5/7-312. Installment payment

§ 7-312. Installment payment. (a) A judgment debtor upon 5 days notice to the judgment creditor may apply to the trial court in which the judgment was entered for the privilege of paying such judgment in installments and the court in its discretion and without prejudice to any other judicial remedies which the judgment creditor may have may so[1] order, fixing the amounts and times of payment of the installments.

(b) The Secretary of State shall not suspend the driver's license, registration or nonresident's operating privilege, and any suspended driver's license or registration following nonpayment of a final judgment shall be restored when the judgment debtor gives proof of financial responsibility and when the judgment debtor obtains an order from the trial court permitting the payment of such judgment in installments and while the payment of any such installment is not in default.

P.A. 76-1586, § 7-312, eff. July 1, 1970. Amended by P.A. 83-345, § 52, eff. Sept. 14, 1983; P.A. 83-831, § 1, eff. Jan. 1, 1984; P.A. 83-1362, Art. II, § 99, eff. Sept. 11, 1984.

Formerly Ill.Rev.Stat.1991, ch. 95 ½, ¶ 7-312.

1 So in enrolled bill.

P.A. 83-1362, Art. II, the 1984 Revisory Act provided in § 0.1:

"This Article provides for the nonsubstantive revision or renumbering or repeal of Sections of Acts necessitated by the amendment, addition or repeal of Sections by two or more Public Acts of the 83rd General Assembly, which multiple action was not resolved by one of the Acts of the 83rd General Assembly affecting the particular Section."

5/7-313. Suspension required upon breach of agreement

§ 7-313. Suspension required upon breach of agreement. In the event the judgment debtor fails to pay any installments as permitted by the order of the court upon notice of such default, the Secretary of State, upon receipt of a court order, shall forthwith suspend the driver's license, registration certificate, license plates, registration stickers or nonresident's operating privilege of the judgment debtor until said judgment is satisfied as provided in Section 7-311 or a second installment payment plan is accepted as provided in Section 7-312.

P.A. 76-1586, § 7-313, eff. July 1, 1970. Amended by P.A. 80-230, § 1, eff. Oct. 1, 1977; P.A. 80-1185, § 1, eff. March 8, 1978; P.A. 83-831, § 1, eff. Jan. 1, 1984; P.A. 85-321, § 1, eff. Jan. 1, 1988; P.A. 90-774, § 5, eff. Aug. 14, 1998.

Formerly Ill.Rev.Stat.1991, ch. 95 ½, ¶ 7-313.

5/7-314. Alternate methods of giving proof

§ 7-314. Alternate methods of giving proof. Proof of financial responsibility when required under this Article may be given by filing with the Secretary of State:

1. A certificate of insurance as provided in Section 7-315 or Section 7-316;

2. A bond as provided in Section 7-320; or

3. A deposit of securities as provided in Section 7-323.

P.A. 76-1586, § 7-314, eff. July 1, 1970. Amended by P.A. 83-831, § 1, eff. Jan. 1, 1984.

Formerly Ill.Rev.Stat.1991, ch. 95 ½, ¶ 7-314.

5/7-315. A certificate of insurance proof

§ 7-315. A certificate of insurance proof. (a) Proof of financial responsibility may be made by filing with the Secretary of State the written certificate of any insurance carrier duly authorized to do business in this State, certifying that it has issued to or for the benefit of the person furnishing such proof and named as the insured in a motor vehicle liability policy, a motor vehicle liability policy or policies or in certain events an operator's policy meeting the requirements of this Code and that said policy or policies are then in full force and effect.

(b) Such certificate or certificates shall give the dates of issuance and expiration of such policy or policies and certify that the same shall not be canceled unless 15 days' prior written notice thereof be given to the Secretary of State and shall explicitly describe all motor vehicles covered thereby unless the policy or policies are issued to a person who is not the owner of a motor vehicle.

(c) The Secretary of State shall not accept any certificate or certificates unless the same shall cover all motor vehicles then registered in this State in the name of the person furnishing such proof as owner and an additional certificate or certificates shall be required as a condition precedent to the subsequent registration of any motor vehicle or motor vehicles in the name of the person giving such proof as owner.

P.A. 76-1586, § 7-315, eff. July 1, 1970. Amended by P.A. 83-831, § 1, eff. Jan. 1, 1984; P.A. 90-774, § 5, eff. Aug. 14, 1998.

Formerly Ill.Rev.Stat.1991, ch. 95 ½, ¶ 7-315.

5/7-316. Certificate furnished by nonresident as proof

§ 7-316. Certificate furnished by nonresident as proof. Any nonresident owner of a motor vehicle not registered in this State may give proof of financial responsibility by filing with the Secretary of State a certificate or certificates of an insurance carrier authorized to transact business in the state or province of the Dominion of Canada in which the motor vehicle or motor vehicles described in such certificate are registered, or if such nonresident does not own a motor vehicle then in the state or province of the Dominion of Canada in which the insured resides, and otherwise conforming to the provisions of this Code, and the Secretary of State shall accept the same if such carrier shall:

1. Execute a power of attorney authorizing the Secretary of State to accept service on its behalf of notice of process in any action arising out of a motor vehicle accident in this State;

2. Duly adopt a resolution which shall be binding upon it declaring that its policies shall be deemed to be varied to comply with the laws of this State relating to the terms of motor vehicle liability policies as required by Section 7-317; and

3. Agree to accept as final and binding any final judgment duly rendered in any action arising out of a motor vehicle accident in any court of competent jurisdiction in this State.

P.A. 76-1586, § 7-316, eff. July 1, 1970. Amended by P.A. 83-831, § 1, eff. Jan. 1, 1984.

Formerly Ill.Rev.Stat.1991, ch. 95 ½, ¶ 7-316.

5/7-317. "Motor vehicle liability policy" defined

§ 7-317. "Motor vehicle liability policy" defined. (a) **Certification.**—A "motor vehicle liability policy", as that term is used in this Act, means an "owner's policy" or an "operator's policy" of liability insurance, certified as provided in Section 7-315 or Section 7-316 as proof of financial responsibility for the future, and issued, except as otherwise provided in Section 7-316, by an insurance carrier duly authorized to transact business in this State, to or for the benefit of the person named therein as insured.

(b) **Owner's Policy.**—Such owner's policy of liability insurance:

1. Shall designate by explicit description or by appropriate reference, all motor vehicles with respect to which coverage is thereby intended to be granted;

2. Shall insure the person named therein and any other person using or responsible for the use of such motor vehicle or vehicles with the express or implied permission of the insured;

3. Shall insure every named insured and any other person using or responsible for the use of any motor vehicle owned by the named insured and used by such other person with the express or implied permission of the named insured on account of the maintenance, use or operation of any motor vehicle owned by the named insured, within the continental limits of the United States or the Dominion of Canada against loss from liability imposed by law arising from such maintenance, use or operation, to the extent and aggregate amount, exclusive of interest and cost, with respect to each motor vehicle, of $20,000 for bodily injury to or death of one person as a result of any one accident and, subject to such limit as to one person, the amount of $40,000 for bodily injury to or death of all persons as a result of any one accident and the amount of $15,000 for damage to property of others as a result of any one accident.

(c) **Operator's Policy.**—When an operator's policy is required, it shall insure the person named therein as insured against the liability imposed by law upon the insured for bodily injury to or death of any person or damage to property to the amounts and limits above set forth and growing out of the use or operation by the insured within the continental limits of the United States or the Dominion of Canada of any motor vehicle not owned by him.

(d) **Required Statements in Policies.**—Every motor vehicle liability policy must specify the name and address of the insured, the coverage afforded by the policy, the premium charged therefor, the policy period, and the limits of liability, and shall contain an agreement that the insurance thereunder is provided in accordance with the coverage defined in this Act, as respects bodily injury and death or property damage or both, and is subject to all the provisions of this Act.

(e) **Policy Need Not Insure Workers' Compensation.**—Any liability policy or policies issued hereunder need not cover any liability of the insured assumed by or imposed upon the insured under any workers' compensation law nor any liability for damage to property in charge of the insured or the insured's employees.

(f) **Provisions Incorporated in Policy.**—Every motor vehicle liability policy is subject to the following provisions which need not be contained therein:

1. The liability of the insurance carrier under any such policy shall become absolute whenever loss or damage covered by the policy occurs and the satisfaction by the insured of a final judgment for such loss or damage shall not be a condition precedent to the right or obligation of the carrier to make payment on account of such loss or damage.

2. No such policy may be cancelled or annulled as respects any loss or damage, by any agreement between the carrier and the insured after the insured has become responsible for such loss or damage, and any such cancellation or annulment shall be void.

3. The insurance carrier shall, however, have the right to settle any claim covered by the policy, and if such settlement is made in good faith, the amount thereof shall be deductible from the limits of liability specified in the policy.

4. The policy, the written application therefor, if any, and any rider or endorsement which shall not conflict with the provisions of this Act shall constitute the entire contract between the parties.

(g) **Excess or Additional Coverage.**—Any motor vehicle liability policy may, however, grant any lawful coverage in excess of or in addition to the coverage herein specified or contain any agreements, provisions, or stipulations not in conflict with the provisions of this Act and not otherwise contrary to law.

(h) **Reimbursement Provision Permitted.**—The policy may provide that the insured, or any other person covered by the policy shall reimburse the insurance carrier for payment made on account of any loss or damage claim or suit involving a breach of the terms, provisions or conditions of the policy; and further, if the policy shall provide for limits in excess of the limits specified in this Act, the insurance carrier may plead against any plaintiff, with respect to the amount of such excess limits of liability, any defense which it may be entitled to plead against the insured.

(i) **Proration of Insurance Permitted.**—The policy may provide for the pro-rating of the insurance thereunder with other applicable valid and collectible insurance.

(j) **Binders.**—Any binder pending the issuance of any policy, which binder contains or by reference includes the provisions hereunder shall be sufficient proof of ability to respond in damages.

(k) **Copy of Policy to Be Filed with Department of Insurance—Approval.**—A copy of the form of every motor vehicle liability policy which is to be used to meet the requirements of this Act must be filed, by the company offering such policy, with the Department of Insurance, which shall approve or disapprove the policy within 30 days of its filing. If the Department approves the policy in writing within such 30 day period or fails to take action for 30 days, the form of policy shall be deemed approved as filed. If within the 30 days the Department disapproves the form of policy filed upon the ground that it does not comply with the requirements of this Act, the Department shall give written notice of its decision and its reasons therefor to the carrier and the policy shall not be accepted as proof of financial responsibility under this Act.

(*l*) **Insurance Carrier Required to File Certificate.**—An insurance carrier who has issued a motor vehicle liability policy or policies or an operator's policy meeting the requirements of this Act shall, upon the request of the insured therein, deliver to the insured for filing, or at the request of the insured, shall file direct, with the Secretary of State a certificate, as required by this Act, which shows that such policy or policies have been issued. No insurance carrier may require the payment of any extra fee or surcharge, in addition to the insurance premium, for the execution, delivery or filing of such certificate.

(m) **Proof When Made By Endorsement.**—Any motor vehicle liability policy which by endorsement contains the provisions required hereunder shall be sufficient proof of ability to respond in damages.

P.A. 76–1586, § 7–317, eff. July 1, 1970. Amended by P.A. 77–1337, § 1, eff. Aug. 27, 1971; P.A. 80–1495, § 36, eff. Jan. 8, 1979; P.A. 81–992, § 1, eff. Jan. 1, 1980; P.A. 81–1202, § 2, eff. March 1, 1980; P.A. 81–1509, Art. I, § 57, eff. Sept. 26, 1980; P.A. 85–730, § 1, eff. Jan. 1, 1988.

Formerly Ill.Rev.Stat.1991, ch. 95 ½, ¶ 7–317.

5/7–318. Notice of Cancellation or Termination of Certified Policy

§ 7–318. Notice of Cancellation or Termination of Certified Policy. When an insurance carrier has certified a motor vehicle liability policy or policies under this Act, it shall notify the Secretary of State of any cancellation by mailing a written notice at least 15 days prior to cancellation of such policy and the policy shall continue in full force and effect until the date of cancellation specified in such notice or until its expiration, except that such a policy subsequently procured and certified shall, on the effective date of its certification, terminate the insurance previously certified with respect to any vehicle designated in both certificates.

P.A. 76–1586, § 7–318, eff. July 1, 1970. Amended by P.A. 86–549, § 1, eff. Jan. 1, 1990.

Formerly Ill.Rev.Stat.1991, ch. 95 ½, ¶ 7–318.

5/7–319. This Act not to affect other policies

§ 7–319. This Act not to affect other policies. Sections 7–301 through 7–329, each inclusive, of this Act shall not be held to apply to or affect bonds or policies of automobile insurance against liability which may now or hereafter be required by any other provision of this Act and such bonds or policies, if endorsed to conform to the requirements of this Act, shall be accepted as proof of financial responsibility when required under this Act. This Act shall not be held to apply to or affect policies insuring solely the insured named in the policy against liability resulting from the maintenance, operation or use by persons in the insured's employ or in his behalf of motor vehicles not owned by the insured.

P.A. 76–1586, § 7–319, eff. July 1, 1970.

Formerly Ill.Rev.Stat.1991, ch. 95 ½, ¶ 7–319.

5/7–320. Bond as Proof

§ 7–320. Bond as Proof. A person required to give proof of financial responsibility may file with the Secretary of State a bond, executed by the person giving such proof and by a surety company, duly authorized to transact business within the State; or by the person, giving such proof and by 2 individual sureties, each owning real estate within this State and having an equity therein in the amount of such bond, which real estate shall be scheduled therein.

1. The Secretary of State shall not accept any such real estate bond unless it is first approved by a judge of a court.

2. The Secretary of State shall not accept any such bond unless it is conditioned for payment in amounts and under the same circumstances as would be required in a motor vehicle liability policy furnished by the person giving such proof under this Act.

3. No such bond shall be cancelled unless 10 days' prior written notice is given to the Secretary of State, but cancellation of such bond shall not prevent recovery thereon with respect to any right or cause of action arising prior to the date of cancellation.

4. The principal and sureties of every such real estate bond shall execute and deliver an original and one copy of the bond and schedule and in addition, when the real property or any part thereof, listed or described in the schedule, shall lie in more than one county, then as many extra copies as there are counties in which the real property, or any part thereof, shall lie, to the judge to whom such bond is presented for approval, who shall, if he approved the bond, endorse upon the original and each copy of the bond the date of the approval thereof; and the clerk of the court shall immediately file one of the copies with the recorder in each county in which is situated any of the non-registered real property so scheduled.

5. If any of the lands so scheduled shall have been registered under "An Act concerning land titles", approved May 1, 1897,[1] as amended, the clerk of the court in which the bond is approved shall immediately file with the registrar of titles in and for each county in which any of the registered land so scheduled is situated, a notice stating that such land has been so scheduled, and the registrar shall thereupon enter a memorial of such fact upon the record.

6. The clerk of the court in which the bond is approved shall endorse upon the original of each such real estate bond approved the date upon which he or she filed a copy of such bond with the recorder in each county in which is situated any of the non-registered real property so scheduled or the notice with the registrar of titles in and for each county in which any of the registered land scheduled is situated and shall deliver such original bond to the principal thereon.

P.A. 76-1586, § 7-320, eff. July 1, 1970. Amended by P.A. 83-345, § 52, eff. Sept. 14, 1983; P.A. 83-358, § 67, eff. Sept. 14, 1983; P.A. 83-1362, Art. II, § 99, eff. Sept. 11, 1984.

Formerly Ill.Rev.Stat.1991, ch. 95 ½, ¶ 7-320.

1 765 ILCS 35/1 et seq.

P.A. 83-1362, Art. II, the 1984 Revisory Act provided in § 0.1:

"This Article provides for the nonsubstantive revision or renumbering or repeal of Sections of Acts necessitated by the amendment, addition or repeal of Sections by two or more Public Acts of the 83rd General Assembly, which multiple action was not resolved by one of the Acts of the 83rd General Assembly affecting the particular Section."

5/7-321. When Bond Shall Constitute a Lien

§ 7-321. When Bond Shall Constitute a Lien. Such bond shall constitute a lien upon the unregistered real estate so scheduled of any surety from the time when a copy of such bond is filed in the office of the recorder in and for the county in which such non-registered real property so scheduled is situated, and such bond shall be a lien upon all registered real property listed or described in the accompanying schedule from the time when notice, as aforesaid, is filed in the office of the registrar of titles in and for the county in which such registered real estate so scheduled is situated. Such lien shall exist in favor of the People of the State of Illinois for the use of any holder of a final judgment against the principal on such bond upon a liability covered by the conditions of such bond.

P.A. 76-1586, § 7-321, eff. July 1, 1970. Amended by P.A. 80-1495, § 36, eff. Jan. 8, 1979; P.A. 83-358, § 67, eff. Sept. 14, 1983.

Formerly Ill.Rev.Stat.1991, ch. 95 ½, ¶ 7-321.

5/7-322. Action on bond

§ 7-322. Action on bond. If a judgment is rendered against the principal of any such surety or real estate bond upon a liability covered by the conditions of such bond and such judgment is not satisfied within thirty (30) days after it becomes final, then the judgment creditor may, for his own use and benefit, and at his sole expense, bring an action or actions in the name of the State against the company or persons who executed such bond including an action or proceeding to foreclose any lien that may exist upon the real estate of a person who has executed such bond, which action shall be brought in like manner and subject to all the provisions of law applicable to an action to foreclose a mortgage upon real estate.

P.A. 76-1586, § 7-322, eff. July 1, 1970.

Formerly Ill.Rev.Stat.1991, ch. 95 ½, ¶ 7-322.

5/7-323. Money or securities as proof

§ 7-323. Money or securities as proof. A person may give proof of financial responsibility by delivering to the Secretary of State a receipt of the State Treasurer showing the deposit with said State Treasurer of money in amount or securities endorsed in blank by the owner thereof and approved by said State Treasurer and of a market value in a total amount as would be required for coverage in a motor vehicle liability policy furnished by the person giving such proof under this Act. Such securities shall be of the type which may legally be purchased as investments of trust funds by trustees.

P.A. 76-1586, § 7-323, eff. July 1, 1970.

Formerly Ill.Rev.Stat.1991, ch. 95 ½, ¶ 7-323.

5/7-324. Application of deposit

§ 7-324. Application of deposit. All money or securities so deposited shall be subject to execution to satisfy any judgment mentioned in this Act but shall not otherwise be subject to attachment or execution. The State Treasurer shall not accept any such deposit or issue a certificate therefor, and the Secretary of State shall not accept such certificate unless accompanied by evidence that there are no unsatisfied judgments against the depositor registered in the county where the depositor resides.

P.A. 76-1586, § 7-324, eff. July 1, 1970.

Formerly Ill.Rev.Stat.1991, ch. 95 ½, ¶ 7-324.

5/7-325. Owner may give proof for others

§ 7-325. Owner may give proof for others. Whenever the Secretary of State determines that any person required to give proof under this Article by reason of a revocation is not the owner of a motor vehicle but was, at the time of such conviction a driver in the employ of an owner of a motor vehicle, or a member of the immediate family or household of the owner of a motor vehicle, the Secretary of State shall accept proof of financial responsibility given by such owner in lieu of proof given by such other person so long as such other person is operating a motor vehicle for which the owner has given proof as herein provided.

P.A. 76-1586, § 7-325, eff. July 1, 1970. Amended by P.A. 83-831, § 1, eff. Jan. 1, 1984.

Formerly Ill.Rev.Stat.1991, ch. 95 ½, ¶ 7-325.

5/7-326. Substitution of proof

§ 7-326. Substitution of proof. The Secretary of State shall cancel any bond or return any certificate of insurance, or the Secretary of State shall direct and the State Treasurer shall return any money or securities to the person entitled thereto, upon the substitution and acceptance of other adequate proof of financial responsibility pursuant to this Article.

P.A. 76-1586, § 7-326, eff. July 1, 1970. Amended by P.A. 83-831, § 1, eff. Jan. 1, 1984.

Formerly Ill.Rev.Stat.1991, ch. 95 ½, ¶ 7-326.

5/7-327. Other proof may be required

§ 7-327. Other proof may be required. Whenever any evidence of proof of ability to respond in damages filed under the provisions of this Article no longer fulfills the purpose for which required, the Secretary of State shall, for the purposes of this Chapter, require other evidence of ability to respond in damages as required by this Article, and the driver's license, registration certificates, license plates and registration stickers involved shall be suspended by the Secretary of State pending such proof.

P.A. 76-1586, § 7-327, eff. July 1, 1970. Amended by P.A. 80-230, § 1, eff. Oct. 1, 1977; P.A. 83-831, § 1, eff. Jan. 1, 1984.

Formerly Ill.Rev.Stat.1991, ch. 95 ½, ¶ 7-327.

5/7-328. Duration of proof—When proof may be canceled or returned

§ 7-328. Duration of proof—When proof may be canceled or returned. The Secretary of State shall upon request cancel any bond or return any certificate of insurance, or the Secretary of State shall direct and the State Treasurer shall return to the person entitled thereto any money or securities, deposited pursuant to this Chapter as proof of financial responsibility or waive the requirements of filing proof of financial responsibility in any of the following events:

1. In the event of the death of the person on whose behalf such proof was filed, or the permanent incapacity of such person to operate a motor vehicle;

2. In the event the person who has given proof of financial responsibility surrenders such person's driver's license, registration certificates, license plates and registration stickers, but the Secretary of State shall not release such proof in the event any action for damages upon a liability referred to in this Article is then pending or any judgment upon any such liability is then outstanding and unsatisfied or in the event the Secretary of State has received notice that such person has, within the period of 3 months immediately preceding, been involved as a driver in any motor vehicle accident. An affidavit of the applicant of the nonexistence of such facts shall be sufficient evidence thereof in the absence of evidence to the contrary in the records of the Secretary of State. Any person who has not completed the required 3 year period of proof of financial responsibility pursuant to Section 7-304, and to whom proof has been surrendered as provided in this paragraph applies for a driver's license or the registration of a motor vehicle shall have the application denied unless the applicant re-establishes such proof for the remainder of such period.

3. In the event that proof of financial responsibility has been deposited voluntarily, at any time upon request of the person entitled thereto, provided that the person on whose behalf such proof was given has not, during the period between the date of the original deposit thereof and the date of such request, been convicted of any offense for which revocation is mandatory as provided in Section 6-205; provided, further, that no action for damages is pending against such person on whose behalf such proof of financial responsibility was furnished and no judgment against such person is outstanding and unsatisfied in respect to bodily injury, or in respect to damage to property resulting from the ownership, maintenance, use or operation hereafter of a motor vehicle. An affidavit of the applicant under this Section shall be sufficient evidence of the facts in the absence of evidence to the contrary in the records of the Secretary of State.

P.A. 76-1586, § 7-328, eff. July 1, 1970. Amended by P.A. 80-230, § 1, eff. Oct. 1, 1977; P.A. 83-831, § 1, eff. Jan. 1, 1984; P.A. 85-321, § 1, eff. Jan. 1, 1988.

Formerly Ill.Rev.Stat.1991, ch. 95 ½, ¶ 7-328.

5/7-329. Proof of financial responsibility made voluntarily

§ 7-329. Proof of financial responsibility made voluntarily. 1. Proof of financial responsibility may be voluntarily by or on behalf of any person. The privilege of operation of any motor vehicle within this State by such person shall not be suspended or withdrawn under the provisions of this Article if such proof of financial responsibility has been voluntarily filed or deposited prior to the offense or accident out of which any conviction, judgment, or order arises and if such proof, at the date of such conviction, judgment, or order, is valid and sufficient for the requirements of this Code.

2. If the Secretary of State receives record of any conviction or judgment against such person which, in the absence of such proof of financial responsibility would have caused the suspension of the driver's license of such person, the Secretary of State shall forthwith notify the insurer or surety of such person of the conviction or judgment so reported.

P.A. 76-1586, § 7-329, eff. July 1, 1970. Amended by P.A. 83-831, § 1, eff. Jan. 1, 1984.

Formerly Ill.Rev.Stat.1991, ch. 95 ½, ¶ 7-329.

ARTICLE IV. VIOLATIONS OF PROVISIONS OF FINANCIAL RESPONSIBILITY ACT

Section

5/7-401. Transfer of registration to defeat purposes of act prohibited

§ 7-401. Transfer of registration to defeat purposes of act prohibited. (a) If an owner's registration has been suspended hereunder, such registration shall not be transferred nor the vehicle in respect to which such registration was issued be registered in any other name until the Secretary of State is satisfied that such transfer of registration is proposed in good faith and not for the purpose or with the effect of defeating the purposes of this act.

(b) Nothing in this section shall in any wise affect the rights of any conditional vendor, chattel mortgagee or lessor of such a vehicle registered in the name of another as owner who becomes subject to the provisions of this act.

(c) The Secretary of State shall suspend the registration of any vehicle transferred in violation of the provisions of this section.

P.A. 76–1586, § 7–401, eff. July 1, 1970.

Formerly Ill.Rev.Stat.1991, ch. 95 ½, ¶ 7–401.

5/7–402. Surrender of license to drive and registration

§ 7–402. Surrender of license to drive and registration. Except as otherwise provided in this Code or Article V of the Supreme Court Rules, any person whose license to drive has been suspended shall immediately return to the Secretary of State any driver's license, instruction permit, restricted driving permit or other evidence of driving privileges held by such person. Any driving authorization document issued under Section 6–206.1 or 11–501.1 of this Code shall be returned to the issuing court for proper processing. Any person whose vehicle registration has been suspended shall, upon the request of the Secretary, immediately return to the Secretary any license plates or other evidences of registration held by such person.

The Secretary is authorized to take possession of any license to drive, registration certificate, registration sticker or license plates upon the suspension thereof under the provisions of this Code or to direct any law enforcement officer to take possession thereof and to return the same to the Secretary.

Any person willfully failing to comply with this Section is guilty of a Class A misdemeanor and shall be punished as provided in Section 9–110 of this Code.

P.A. 76–1586, § 7–402, eff. July 1, 1970. Amended by P.A. 77–2830, Art. 73, § 1, eff. Jan. 1, 1973; P.A. 80–230, § 1, eff. Oct. 1, 1977; P.A. 80–1185, § 1, eff. March 8, 1978; P.A. 85–1201, § 1, eff. July 1, 1989; P.A. 91–357, § 231, eff. July 29, 1999.

Formerly Ill.Rev.Stat.1991, ch. 95 ½, ¶ 7–402.

5/7–403. Forged proof

§ 7–403. Forged proof. Any person who shall forge, or, without authority, sign any evidence of proof of financial responsibility for the future, or who files or offers for filing any such evidence of proof knowing or having reason to believe that it is forged or signed without authority, shall be guilty of a Class A misdemeanor.

P.A. 76–1586, § 7–403, eff. July 1, 1970. Amended by P.A. 77–2720, § 1, eff. Jan. 1, 1973.

Formerly Ill.Rev.Stat.1991, ch. 95 ½, ¶ 7–403.

ARTICLE V. MISCELLANEOUS PROVISIONS RELATING TO FINANCIAL RESPONSIBILITY

Section

5/7–501. Assigned Risk Plans

§ 7–501. Assigned Risk Plans. If, on or before January 1, 1946, every insurance carrier authorized to write automobile bodily injury liability insurance in this State shall not subscribe to an assigned risk plan approved by the Director of Insurance, providing that no carrier may withdraw therefrom after approval of the Director, the Director of Insurance shall, when he finds that an application for bodily injury or property damage insurance by a risk, which may become subject to this Act or is a local public entity subject to the Local Governmental and Governmental Employees Tort Immunity Act, [1] and in good faith is entitled to such insurance, has been rejected by 3 insurance carriers, designate an insurance carrier which shall be obligated to issue forthwith its usual form of policy providing such insurance for such risk. The Director shall make equitable distribution of such assignments among insurance carriers proportionate, so far as practicable, by premiums to the respective net direct automobile bodily injury premium writings of the carriers authorized to do business in this State. The Director of Insurance shall establish rules and regulations for the administration of the provisions of this Section.

If any carrier refuses or neglects to comply with the provisions of this Section or with any lawful order or ruling made by the Director of Insurance pursuant to this Section, the Director may, after notice and hearing, suspend the license of such carrier to transact any insurance business in this State until such carrier shall have complied with such order. The provisions of the Administrative Review Law, [2] and all amendments and modifications thereof, and the rules adopted pursuant thereto, shall apply to and govern all proceedings for the judicial review of final administrative decisions of the Director of Insurance hereunder.

P.A. 76–1586, § 7–501, eff. July 1, 1970. Amended by P.A. 80–824, § 1, eff. Oct. 1, 1977; P.A. 82–783, Art. XI, § 140, eff. July 13, 1982; P.A. 90–89, § 15, eff. Jan. 1, 1998; P.A. 92–651, § 77, eff. July 11, 2002.

Formerly Ill.Rev.Stat.1991, ch. 95 ½, ¶ 7–501.

[1] 745 ILCS 10/1–101 et seq.

[2] 735 ILCS 5/3–101 et seq.

5/7–502. Self-insurers

§ 7–502. Self-insurers. Any person in whose name more than 25 motor vehicles are registered may qualify as a self-insurer by obtaining a certificate of self-insurance issued by the Director of the Department of Insurance as provided in this Section.

The Director may, in his discretion, upon the application of such a person, issue a certificate of self-insurance when he is satisfied that such person is possessed and will continue to be possessed of ability to pay judgment obtained against such person.

Upon not less than 5 days' notice, and a hearing pursuant to such notice, the Director may upon reasonable grounds cancel a certificate of self-insurance. Failure to pay any judgment against any person covered by such certificate of self-insurance and arising out of any accident in which a motor vehicle covered by such certificate of self-insurance has been involved within 30 days after such judgment shall have become final shall constitute a reasonable ground for the cancellation of a certificate of self-insurance.

P.A. 76-1586, § 7-502, eff. July 1, 1970. Amended by P.A. 77-2743, § 1, eff. July 1, 1972; P.A. 82-138, § 1, eff. Jan. 1, 1982.

Formerly Ill.Rev.Stat.1991, ch. 95 ½, ¶ 7-502.

5/7-503. Unclaimed security deposits

§ 7-503. Unclaimed security deposits. During July, annually, the Secretary shall compile a list of all securities on deposit, pursuant to this Article, for more than 3 years and concerning which he has received no notice as to the pendency of any judicial proceeding that could affect the disposition thereof. Thereupon, he shall promptly send a notice by certified mail to the last known address of each depositor advising him that his deposit will be subject to escheat to the State of Illinois if not claimed within 30 days after the mailing date of such notice. At the expiration of such time, the Secretary of State shall file with the State Treasurer an order directing the transfer of such deposit to the general revenue fund in the State Treasury. Upon receipt of such order, the State Treasurer shall make such transfer, after converting to cash any other type of security. Thereafter any person having a legal claim against such deposit may enforce it by appropriate proceedings in the Court of Claims subject to the limitations prescribed for such Court. At the expiration of such limitation period such deposit shall escheat to the State of Illinois.

P.A. 76-1586, § 7-503, eff. July 1, 1970.

Formerly Ill.Rev.Stat.1991, ch. 95 ½, ¶ 7-503.

5/7-504. Emergency telephone system outages; reimbursement

§ 7-504. Emergency telephone system outages; reimbursement. Any person who negligently causes a motor vehicle accident that causes an emergency telephone system outage must reimburse the public safety agency that provides personnel to answer calls or to maintain or operate an emergency telephone system during the outage for the agency's costs associated with answering calls or maintaining or operating the system during the outage. For the purposes of this Section, "public safety agency" means the same as in Section 2.02 of the Emergency Telephone System Act.

P.A. 76-1586, § 7-504, added by P.A. 92-149, § 10, eff. Jan. 1, 2002.

ARTICLE VI. MANDATORY INSURANCE

Date Effective

Article VI was added by P.A. 85-1201, § 1, eff. July 1, 1989.

Section

5/7-601. Required liability insurance policy

§ 7-601. Required liability insurance policy.

(a) No person shall operate, register or maintain registration of, and no owner shall permit another person to operate, register or maintain registration of, a motor vehicle designed to be used on a public highway unless the motor vehicle is covered by a liability insurance policy.

The insurance policy shall be issued in amounts no less than the minimum amounts set for bodily injury or death and for destruction of property under Section 7-203 of this Code, and shall be issued in accordance with the requirements of Sections 143a and 143a-2 of the Illinois Insurance Code, as amended.[1] No insurer other than an insurer authorized to do business in this State shall issue a policy pursuant to this Section for any vehicle subject to registration under this Code. Nothing herein shall deprive an insurer of any policy defense available at common law.

(b) The following vehicles are exempt from the requirements of this Section:

(1) vehicles subject to the provisions of Chapters 8 or 18a,[2] Article III[3] or Section 7-609 of Chapter 7, or Sections 12-606 or 12-707.01 of Chapter 12 of this Code;

(2) vehicles required to file proof of liability insurance with the Illinois Commerce Commission;

(3) vehicles covered by a certificate of self-insurance under Section 7-502 of this Code;

(4) vehicles owned by the United States, the State of Illinois, or any political subdivision, municipality or local mass transit district;

(5) implements of husbandry;

(6) other vehicles complying with laws which require them to be insured in amounts meeting or exceeding the minimum amounts required under this Section; and

(7) inoperable or stored vehicles that are not operated, as defined by rules and regulations of the Secretary.

(c) Every employee of a State agency, as that term is defined in the Illinois State Auditing Act,[4] who is assigned a specific vehicle owned or leased by the State on an ongoing basis shall provide the certification described in this Section annually to the director or chief executive officer of his or her agency.

The certification shall affirm that the employee is duly licensed to drive the assigned vehicle and that (i) the employee has liability insurance coverage extending to the employee when the assigned vehicle is used for other than official State business, or (ii) the employee has filed a bond with the Secretary of State as proof of financial responsibility, in an amount equal to, or in excess of the requirements stated within this Section. Upon request of the agency director or chief executive officer, the employee shall present evidence to support the certification.

The certification shall be provided during the period July 1 through July 31 of each calendar year, or within 30 days of any new assignment of a vehicle on an ongoing basis, whichever is later.

The employee's authorization to use the assigned vehicle shall automatically be rescinded upon:

(1) the revocation or suspension of the license required to drive the assigned vehicle;

(2) the cancellation or termination for any reason of the automobile liability insurance coverage as required in item (c) (i); or

(3) the termination of the bond filed with the Secretary of State.

All State employees providing the required certification shall immediately notify the agency director or chief executive officer in the event any of these actions occur.

All peace officers employed by a State agency who are primarily responsible for prevention and detection of crime and the enforcement of the criminal, traffic, or highway laws of this State, and prohibited by agency rule or policy to use an assigned vehicle owned or leased by the State for regular personal or off-duty use, are exempt from the requirements of this Section.

P.A. 76-1586, § 7-601, added by P.A. 85-1201, § 1, eff. July 1, 1989. Amended by P.A. 86-149, § 2, eff. Aug. 11, 1989; P.A. 86-880, § 1, eff. Jan. 1, 1990; P.A. 86-1028, Art. II, § 2-44, eff. Feb. 5, 1990; P.A. 88-315, § 5, eff. Jan. 1, 1994; P.A. 89-669, § 10, eff. Jan. 1, 1997; P.A. 91-661, § 5, eff. Dec. 22, 1999.

Formerly Ill.Rev.Stat.1991, ch. 95 ½, ¶ 7-601.

1 215 ILCS 5/143a and 143a-2.

2 625 ILCS 5/8-101 et seq. or 5/18a-100 et seq.

3 625 ILCS 5/7-301 et seq.

4 30 ILCS 5/1-1 et seq.

5/7-602. Insurance card

§ 7-602. Insurance card. Every operator of a motor vehicle subject to Section 7-601 of this Code shall carry within the vehicle evidence of insurance. The evidence shall be legible and sufficient to demonstrate that the motor vehicle currently is covered by a liability insurance policy as required under Section 7-601 of this Code and may include, but is not limited to, the following:

(a) an insurance card provided by the insurer under this Section;

(b) the combination of proof of purchase of the motor vehicle within the previous 60 days and a current insurance card issued for the motor vehicle replaced by such purchase;

(c) the current declarations page of a liability insurance policy;

(d) a liability insurance binder, certificate of liability insurance or receipt for payment to an insurer or its authorized representative for a liability insurance premium, provided such document contains all information the Secretary of State by rule and regulation may require;

(e) a current rental agreement;

(f) registration plates, registration sticker or other evidence of registration issued by the Secretary only upon submission of proof of liability insurance pursuant to this Code;

(g) a certificate, decal, or other document or device issued by a governmental agency for a motor vehicle indicating the vehicle is insured for liability pursuant to law.

An insurance card shall be provided for each motor vehicle insured by the insurer issuing the liability insurance policy.

The form, contents and manner of issuance of the insurance card shall be prescribed by rules and regulations of the Secretary of State. The insurance card shall display an effective date and an expiration date covering a period of time not to exceed 12 months. The insurance card shall contain the following disclaimer: "Examine policy exclusions carefully. This form does not constitute any part of your insurance policy." If the insurance policy represented by the insurance card does not cover any driver operating the motor vehicle with the owner's permission, or the owner when operating a motor vehicle other than the vehicle for which the policy is issued, the insurance card shall contain a warning of such limitations in the coverage provided by the policy.

No insurer shall issue a card, similar in appearance, form and content to the insurance card required under this Section, in connection with an insurance policy that does not provide the liability insurance coverage required under Section 7-601 of this Code.

The evidence of insurance shall be displayed upon request made by any law enforcement officer wearing a uniform or displaying a badge or other sign of authority. Any person who fails or refuses to comply with such request is in violation of Section 3-707 of this Code. Any person who displays evidence of insurance, knowing there is no valid liability insurance in effect on the motor vehicle as required under Section 7-601 of this Code or knowing the evidence of insurance is illegally altered, counterfeit or otherwise invalid, is in violation of Section 3-710 of this Code.

"Display" means the manual surrender of the evidence of insurance into the hands of the law enforcement officer, court, or officer of the court making the request for the officer's, court's, or officer of the court's inspection thereof.

P.A. 76-1586, § 7-602, added by P.A. 85-1201, § 1, eff. July 1, 1989. Amended by P.A. 86-149, § 2, eff. Aug. 11, 1989; P.A. 88-315, § 5, eff. Jan. 1, 1994; P.A. 89-565, § 5, eff. July 26, 1996.

Formerly Ill.Rev.Stat.1991, ch. 95 ½, ¶ 7-602.

5/7-603. Illegal insurance cards—penalty

§ 7-603. Illegal insurance cards—penalty. No person shall alter an invalid insurance card to make it appear valid. No person knowingly shall make, sell or otherwise make available an invalid or counterfeit insurance card.

Any person convicted of a violation of this Section is guilty of a Class 4 felony.

P.A. 76-1586, § 7-603, added by P.A. 85-1201, § 1, eff. July 1, 1989.

Formerly Ill.Rev.Stat.1991, ch. 95 ½, ¶ 7-603.

5/7-604. Verification of liability insurance policy

§ 7-604. Verification of liability insurance policy.

(a) The Secretary of State may select random samples of registrations of motor vehicles subject to Section 7-601 of this Code, or owners thereof, for the purpose of verifying whether or not the motor vehicles are insured.

In addition to such general random samples of motor vehicle registrations, the Secretary may select for verification other random samples, including, but not limited to registrations of motor vehicles owned by persons:

(1) whose motor vehicle registrations during the preceding 4 years have been suspended pursuant to Section 7-606 or 7-607 of this Code;

(2) who during the preceding 4 years have been convicted of violating Section 3-707, 3-708 or 3-710 of this Code while operating vehicles owned by other persons;

(3) whose driving privileges have been suspended during the preceding 4 years;

(4) who during the preceding 4 years acquired ownership of motor vehicles while the registrations of such vehicles under the previous owners were suspended pursuant to Section 7-606 or 7-607 of this Code; or

(5) who during the preceding 4 years have received a disposition of supervision under subsection (c) of Section

5-6-1 of the Unified Code of Corrections [1] for a violation of Section 3-707, 3-708, or 3-710 of this Code.

(b) Upon receiving certification from the Department of Transportation under Section 7-201.2 of this Code of the name of an owner or operator of any motor vehicle involved in an accident, the Secretary may verify whether or not at the time of the accident such motor vehicle was covered by a liability insurance policy in accordance with Section 7-601 of this Code.

(c) In preparation for selection of random samples and their verification, the Secretary may send to owners of randomly selected motor vehicles, or to randomly selected motor vehicle owners, requests for information about their motor vehicles and liability insurance coverage. The request shall require the owner to state whether or not the motor vehicle was insured on the verification date stated in the Secretary's request and the request may require, but is not limited to, a statement by the owner of the names and addresses of insurers, policy numbers, and expiration dates of insurance coverage.

(d) Within 30 days after the Secretary mails a request, the owner to whom it is sent shall furnish the requested information to the Secretary above the owner's signed affirmation that such information is true and correct. Proof of insurance in effect on the verification date, as prescribed by the Secretary, may be considered by the Secretary to be a satisfactory response to the request for information.

Any owner whose response indicates that his or her vehicle was not covered by a liability insurance policy in accordance with Section 7-601 of this Code shall be deemed to have registered or maintained registration of a motor vehicle in violation of that Section. Any owner who fails to respond to such a request shall be deemed to have registered or maintained registration of a motor vehicle in violation of Section 7-601 of this Code.

(e) If the owner responds to the request for information by asserting that his or her vehicle was covered by a liability insurance policy on the verification date stated in the Secretary's request, the Secretary may conduct a verification of the response by furnishing necessary information to the insurer named in the response. The insurer shall within 45 days inform the Secretary whether or not on the verification date stated the motor vehicle was insured by the insurer in accordance with Section 7-601 of this Code. The Secretary may by rule and regulation prescribe the procedures for verification.

(f) No random sample selected under this Section shall be categorized on the basis of race, color, religion, sex, national origin, ancestry, age, marital status, physical or mental disability, economic status or geography.

P.A. 76-1586, § 7-604, added by P.A. 85-1201, § 1, eff. July 1, 1989. Amended by P.A. 86-149, § 2, eff. Aug. 11, 1989; P.A. 88-315, § 5, eff. Jan. 1, 1994; P.A. 88-685, § 5, eff. Jan. 24, 1995; P.A. 92-458, § 5, eff. Aug. 22, 2001.

Formerly Ill.Rev.Stat.1991, ch. 95 ½, ¶ 7-604.

[1] 730 ILCS 5/5-6-1.

5/7-605. Uninsured motor vehicles—notice

§ 7-605. Uninsured motor vehicles—notice. If the Secretary determines that an owner has registered or maintained the registration of a motor vehicle without a liability insurance policy in accordance with Section 7-601 of this Code, the Secretary shall notify the owner that such owner's vehicle registration shall be suspended 45 days after the date of the mailing of the notice unless the owner within 30 days furnishes proof of insurance in effect on the verification date, as prescribed by the Secretary.

P.A. 76-1586, § 7-605, added by P.A. 85-1201, § 1, eff. July 1, 1989. Amended by P.A. 86-149, § 2, eff. Aug. 11, 1989.

Formerly Ill.Rev.Stat.1991, ch. 95 ½, ¶ 7-605.

5/7-606. Uninsured motor vehicles—suspension and reinstatement

§ 7-606. Uninsured motor vehicles—suspension and reinstatement. The Secretary shall suspend the vehicle registration of any motor vehicle determined by the Secretary to be in violation of Section 7-601 of this Code, including any motor vehicle operated in violation of Section 3-707, 3-708 or 3-710 of this Code by an operator other than the owner of the vehicle. Neither the fact that, subsequent to the date of verification or conviction, the owner acquired the required liability insurance policy nor the fact that the owner terminated ownership of the motor vehicle shall have any bearing upon the Secretary's decision to suspend.

The Secretary is authorized to suspend the registration of any motor vehicle registered in this State upon receiving notice of the conviction of the operator of the motor vehicle in another State of an offense which, if committed in this State, would constitute a violation of Section 7-601 of this Code.

Until it is terminated, the suspension shall remain in force after the registration is renewed or a new registration is acquired for the motor vehicle. The suspension also shall apply to any motor vehicle to which the owner transfers the registration.

In the case of a first violation, the Secretary shall terminate the suspension upon payment by the owner of a reinstatement fee of $100 and submission of proof of insurance as prescribed by the Secretary.

In the case of a second or subsequent violation by a person having ownership interest in a motor vehicle or vehicles within the preceding 4 years, or a violation of Section 3-708 of this Code, the Secretary shall terminate the suspension 4 months after its effective date upon payment by the owner of a reinstatement fee of $100 and submission of proof of insurance as prescribed by the Secretary.

All fees collected under this Section shall be deposited into the Road Fund of the State treasury.

P.A. 76-1586, § 7-606, added by P.A. 85-1201, § 1, eff. July 1, 1989. Amended by P.A. 86-149, § 2, eff. Aug. 11, 1989; P.A. 88-315, § 5, eff. Jan. 1, 1994.

Formerly Ill.Rev.Stat.1991, ch. 95 ½, ¶ 7-606.

5/7-607. Submission of false proof—penalty

§ 7-607. Submission of false proof—penalty. If the Secretary determines that the proof of insurance submitted by a motor vehicle owner under Section 7-604, 7-605 or 7-606 of this Code is false, the Secretary shall suspend the owner's vehicle registration. The Secretary shall terminate the suspension 6 months after its effective date upon payment by the owner of a reinstatement fee of $200 and submission of proof of insurance as prescribed by the Secretary.

All fees collected under this Section shall be deposited into the Road Fund of the State treasury.

P.A. 76-1586, § 7-607, added by P.A. 85-1201, § 1, eff. July 1, 1989.

Formerly Ill.Rev.Stat.1991, ch. 95 ½, ¶ 7-607.

5/7-608. Verification—limitation

§ 7-608. Verification—limitation. No verification procedure established under this Code shall include individual inspections of vehicles on a highway solely for the purpose of verifying the existence of an insurance policy. No law enforcement officer shall stop a vehicle solely for the purpose of verifying the existence of a valid insurance policy.

P.A. 76-1586, § 7-608, added by P.A. 85-1201, § 1, eff. July 1, 1989. Amended by P.A. 86-149, § 2, eff. Aug. 11, 1989.

Formerly Ill.Rev.Stat.1991, ch. 95 ½, ¶ 7-608.

5/7-609. Exemption for certain religious organizations

§ 7-609. Exemption for certain religious organizations. (a) Pursuant to the following minimum criteria, the Secretary may exempt from the provisions of Section 7-601 of this Code motor vehicles owned by a religious organization or its members:

(1) The religious organization and its members hold a bona fide conviction that the acquisition of insurance is contrary to their religious beliefs.

(2) The religious organization and its members submit to the Secretary evidence that historically, over a period of time not less than two years, they have paid or, by agreement with the other party or parties involved, are paying in a timely manner for all damages for which they were or are liable.

(3) The religious organization has filed with the Secretary a current, irrevocable letter of credit, valid for a period of 12 months and issued in accordance with this Section and Article 5 of the Uniform Commercial Code, approved July 31, 1961, as amended,[1] by a financial institution chartered by an agency of State or federal government. The Secretary of State by rule and regulation shall establish the minimum amount of credit required.

(4) The religious organization and its members meet other requirements which the Secretary by rule and regulation may prescribe.

(b) Upon accepting a letter of credit from a religious organization, the Secretary shall issue a certificate of exemption for each motor vehicle covered. The certificate of exemption shall serve as evidence of insurance in accordance with Section 7-602 of this Code.

Not less than 30 days before a current letter of credit expires, or by agreement between the issuer and customer is revoked, the religious organization shall file with the Secretary a new letter of credit. If a new letter of credit is not on file with the Secretary at the time the current letter of credit expires or is revoked, the exemption of the religious organization and its members shall expire and their certificates of exemption shall become invalid.

(c) If credit is used to the extent that the remaining amount of credit does not meet the minimum requirements of this Section, and the issuer declines to reinstate the used portion of the credit or issue a new letter of credit, the issuer immediately shall send written notice to the customer and the Secretary that the current letter of credit on file with the Secretary no longer meets the minimum requirements of the law.

If, within 30 days of receiving the notice, the Secretary has not received and accepted a new letter of credit from the customer, the exemption of that religious organization and its members shall expire and their certificates of exemption shall become invalid.

(d) Upon the request of the plaintiff, if a person, known by the court to be covered by a current letter of credit issued pursuant to this Section, fails to pay a judgment for damages within 30 days after the judgment has become final, the clerk of the court within 10 days shall forward to the Secretary a report of the person's failure to pay. The report shall indicate that the person is covered by a letter of credit and, if known by the court, the names of the issuer and the customer.

Upon receiving the report from the court, the Secretary shall notify the religious organization that, unless the payment is made, 30 days after the date of the mailing of the notice the exemption of the religious organization and its members shall be terminated and their certificates of exemption shall become invalid. If within the 30 days the religious organization does not submit evidence that the payment has been made, or furnish valid reasons why the payment has been delayed or not made, the Secretary shall terminate the exemptions.

(e) The Secretary is authorized to promulgate rules and regulations necessary for the administration of the provisions of this Section.

P.A. 76-1586, § 7-609, added by P.A. 86-149, § 2, eff. Aug. 11, 1989.

Formerly Ill.Rev.Stat.1991, ch. 95 ½, ¶ 7-609.

[1] 810 ILCS 5/5-101 et seq.

5/7-610. Immunity

§ 7-610. Immunity. No state or local governmental unit and no government official or employee acting in the course of his or her official duties in the administration or enforcement of Section 7-601 and related provisions of this Code shall be liable for any damages, brought directly or indirectly by the injured party or a third party, except for damages resulting from willful and wanton misconduct or gross negligence on the part of the governmental unit, official or employee.

P.A. 76-1586, § 7-610, added by P.A. 86-149, § 2, eff. Aug. 11, 1989.

Formerly Ill.Rev.Stat.1991, ch. 95 ½, ¶ 7-610.

5/7-611. § 7-611. Repealed by P.A. 88-315, § 10, eff. Jan. 1, 1994

ARTICLE VII. FAMILY FINANCIAL RESPONSIBILITY LAW

Date Effective

Article VII was added by P.A. 89-92, § 10, eff. July 1, 1996.

Section

5/7–701. Findings and purpose

§ 7–701. Findings and purpose. The General Assembly finds that the timely receipt of adequate financial support has the effect of reducing poverty and State expenditures for welfare dependency among children, and that the timely payment of adequate child support demonstrates financial responsibility. Further, the General Assembly finds that the State has a compelling interest in ensuring that drivers within the State demonstrate financial responsibility, including family financial responsibility, in order to safely own and operate a motor vehicle. To this end, the Secretary of State is authorized to establish systems to suspend driver's licenses for failure to comply with court orders of support.

P.A. 76–1586, § 7–701, added by P.A. 89–92, § 10, eff. July 1, 1996. Amended by P.A. 91–613, § 945, eff. July 1, 2000.

5/7–702. Suspension of driver's license for failure to pay child support

§ 7–702. Suspension of driver's license for failure to pay child support.

(a) The Secretary of State shall suspend the driver's license issued to an obligor upon receiving an authenticated report provided for in subsection (a) of Section 7–703, that the person is 90 days or more delinquent in court ordered child support payments or has been adjudicated in arrears in an amount equal to 90 days obligation or more, and has been found in contempt by the court for failure to pay the support.

(b) The Secretary of State shall suspend the driver's license issued to an obligor upon receiving an authenticated document provided for in subsection (b) of Section 7–703, that the person has been adjudicated in arrears in court ordered child support payments in an amount equal to 90 days obligation or more, but has not been held in contempt of court, and that the court has ordered that the person's driving privileges be suspended. The obligor's driver's license shall be suspended until such time as the Secretary of State receives authenticated documentation that the obligor is in compliance with the court order of support. When the obligor complies with the court ordered child support payments, the circuit court shall report the obligor's compliance with the court order of support to the Secretary of State, on a form prescribed by the Secretary of State, and shall order that the obligor's driver's license be reinstated.

P.A. 76–1586, § 7–702, added by P.A. 89–92, § 10, eff. July 1, 1996. Amended by P.A. 91–613, § 945, eff. July 1, 2000.

5/7–702.1. Family financial responsibility driving permits

§ 7–702.1. Family financial responsibility driving permits. Following the entry of an order that an obligor has been found in contempt by the court for failure to pay court ordered child support payments or upon a motion by the obligor who is subject to having his or her driver's license suspended pursuant to subsection (b) of Section 7–703, the court may enter an order directing the Secretary of State to issue a family financial responsibility driving permit for the purpose of providing the obligor the privilege of operating a motor vehicle between the obligor's residence and place of employment, or within the scope of employment related duties; or for the purpose of providing transportation for the obligor or a household member to receive alcohol treatment, other drug treatment, or medical care. The court may enter an order directing the issuance of a permit only if the obligor has proven to the satisfaction of the court that no alternative means of transportation are reasonably available for the above stated purposes. No permit shall be issued to a person under the age of 16 years who possesses an instruction permit.

Upon entry of an order granting the issuance of a permit to an obligor, the court shall report this finding to the Secretary of State on a form prescribed by the Secretary. This form shall state whether the permit has been granted for employment or medical purposes and the specific days and hours for which limited driving privileges have been granted.

The family financial responsibility driving permit shall be subject to cancellation, invalidation, suspension, and revocation by the Secretary of State in the same manner and for the same reasons as a driver's license may be cancelled, invalidated, suspended, or revoked.

The Secretary of State shall, upon receipt of a certified court order from the court of jurisdiction, issue a family financial responsibility driving permit. In order for this permit to be issued, an individual's driving privileges must be valid except for the family financial responsibility suspension. This permit shall be valid only for employment and medical purposes as set forth above. The permit shall state the days and hours for which limited driving privileges have been granted.

Any submitted court order that contains insufficient data or fails to comply with any provision of this Code shall not be used for issuance of the permit or entered to the individual's driving record but shall be returned to the court of jurisdiction indicating why the permit cannot be issued at that time. The Secretary of State shall also send notice of the return of the court order to the individual requesting the permit.

P.A. 76–1586, § 7–702.1, added by P.A. 89–92, § 10, eff. July 1, 1996. Amended by P.A. 90–369, § 5, eff. Jan. 1, 1998; P.A. 91–613, § 945, eff. July 1, 2000.

5/7–702.2. Written agreement to pay past-due support

§ 7–702.2. Written agreement to pay past-due support.

(a) An obligor who is presently unable to pay all past-due support and is subject to having his or her license suspended pursuant to subsection (b) of Section 7–703 may come into compliance with the court order for support by executing a written payment agreement that is approved by the court and by complying with that agreement. A condition of a written payment agreement must be that the obligor pay the current child support when due. Before a written payment agreement is executed, the obligor shall:

(1) Disclose fully to the court in writing, on a form prescribed by the court, the obligor's financial circumstances, including income from all sources, assets, liabilities, and work history for the past year; and

(2) Provide documentation to the court concerning the obligor's financial circumstances, including copies of the most recent State and federal income tax returns, both personal and business; a copy of a recent pay stub representative of current income; and copies of other records that show the obligor's income and the present level of assets held by the obligor.

(b) After full disclosure, the court may determine the obligor's ability to pay past-due support and may approve a written payment agreement consistent with the obligor's ability to pay, not to exceed the court-ordered support.

P.A. 76-1586, § 7-702.2, added by P.A. 91-613, § 945, eff. July 1, 2000.

5/7-703. Courts to report non-payment of court ordered support

§ 7-703. Courts to report non-payment of court ordered support.

(a) The clerk of the circuit court, as provided in subsection (b) of Section 505 of the Illinois Marriage and Dissolution of Marriage Act [1] or as provided in Section 15 of the Illinois Parentage Act of 1984, [2] shall forward to the Secretary of State, on a form prescribed by the Secretary, an authenticated document certifying the court's order suspending the driving privileges of the obligor. For any such certification, the clerk of the court shall charge the obligor a fee of $5 as provided in the Clerks of Courts Act.[3]

(b) If an obligor has been adjudicated in arrears in court ordered child support payments in an amount equal to 90 days obligation or more but has not been held in contempt of court, the circuit court may order that the obligor's driving privileges be suspended. If the circuit court orders that the obligor's driving privileges be suspended, it shall forward to the Secretary of State, on a form prescribed by the Secretary, an authenticated document certifying the court's order suspending the driving privileges of the obligor. The authenticated document shall be forwarded to the Secretary of State by the court no later than 45 days after entry of the order suspending the obligor's driving privileges.

P.A. 76-1586, § 7-703, added by P.A. 89-92, § 10, eff. July 1, 1996. Amended by P.A. 89-626, Art. 3, § 3-37, eff. Aug. 9, 1996; P.A. 91-613, § 945, eff. July 1, 2000.

[1] 750 ILCS 5/1505.

[2] 750 ILCS 45/15.

[3] 705 ILCS 105/0.01 et seq.

5/7-704. Suspension to continue until compliance with court order of support

§ 7-704. Suspension to continue until compliance with court order of support.

(a) The suspension of a driver's license shall remain in effect unless and until the Secretary of State receives authenticated documentation that the obligor is in compliance with a court order of support or that the order has been stayed by a subsequent order of the court. Full driving privileges shall not be issued by the Secretary of State until notification of compliance has been received from the court. The circuit clerks shall report the obligor's compliance with a court order of support to the Secretary of State, on a form prescribed by the Secretary.

(b) Whenever, after one suspension of an individual's driver's license for failure to pay child support, another order of non-payment is entered against the obligor and the person fails to come into compliance with the court order of support, then the Secretary shall again suspend the driver's license of the individual and that suspension shall not be removed unless the obligor is in full compliance with the court order of support and has made full payment on all arrearages.

P.A. 76-1586, § 7-704, added by P.A. 89-92, § 10, eff. July 1, 1996.

5/7-705. Notice

§ 7-705. Notice. The Secretary of State, prior to suspending a driver's license under this Chapter, shall serve written notice upon an obligor that the individual's driver's license will be suspended in 60 days from the date on the notice unless the obligor satisfies the court order of support and the circuit clerk notifies the Secretary of State of this compliance.

P.A. 76-1586, § 7-705, added by P.A. 89-92, § 10, eff. July 1, 1996.

5/7-705.1. Notice of noncompliance with support order

§ 7-705.1. Notice of noncompliance with support order. Before forwarding to the Secretary of State the authenticated document under subsection (b) of Section 7-703, the circuit court must serve notice upon the obligor of its intention to suspend the obligor's driver's license for being adjudicated in arrears in court ordered child support payments in an amount equal to 90 days obligation. The notice must inform the obligor that:

(a) If the obligor is presently unable to pay all past-due support, the obligor may come into compliance with the support order by executing a written payment agreement with the court, as provided in Section 7-702.2, and by complying with that agreement;

(b) The obligor may contest the issue of compliance at a hearing;

(c) A request for a hearing must be made in writing and must be received by the clerk of the circuit court;

(d) If the obligor does not request a hearing to contest the issue of compliance within 45 days after the notice of noncompliance is mailed, the court may order that the obligor's driver's license be suspended as provided for in subsection (b) of Section 7-703;

(e) If the circuit court certifies the obligor to the Secretary of State for noncompliance with an order of support, the Secretary of State must suspend any driver's license or instruction permit the obligor holds and the obligor's right to apply for or obtain a driver's license or instruction permit until the obligor comes into compliance with the order of support;

(f) If the obligor files a motion to modify support with the court or requests the court to modify a support obligation, the circuit court shall stay action to certify the obligor to the Secretary of State for noncompliance with an order of support; and

(g) The obligor may comply with an order of support by doing all of the following:

(1) Paying the current support;

(2) Paying all past-due support or, if unable to pay all past-due support and a periodic payment for past-due support has not been ordered by the court, by making periodic payments in accordance with a written payment agreement approved by the court; and

(3) Meeting the obligor's health insurance obligation.

The notice must include the address and telephone number of the clerk of the circuit court. The clerk of the circuit court shall attach a copy of the obligor's order of support to the notice. The notice must be served by certified mail, return receipt requested, by service in hand, or as specified in the Code of Civil Procedure. [1]

P.A. 76-1586, § 7-705.1, added by P.A. 91-613, § 945, eff. July 1, 2000.

[1] 735 ILCS 5/1-101 et seq.

5/7-706. Administrative hearing

§ 7-706. Administrative hearing. A driver may contest this driver's license sanction by requesting an administrative hearing in accordance with Section 2-118 of this Code. If a written request for this hearing is received prior to the effective date of the suspension, the suspension shall be stayed. If a stay of the suspension is granted, it shall remain in effect until a hearing decision is entered. At the conclusion of this hearing, the Secretary of State may rescind or impose the driver's license suspension. If the suspension is upheld, it shall become effective 10 days from the date the hearing decision is entered. If the decision is to rescind the suspension, no suspension of driving privileges shall be entered. The scope of this hearing shall be limited to the following issues:

(a) Whether the driver is the obligor covered by the court order of support.

(b) Whether the authenticated document of a court order of support indicates that the obligor is 90 days or more delinquent or has been adjudicated in arrears in an amount equal to 90 days obligation or more and has been found in contempt of court for failure to pay child support.

(c) Whether a superseding authenticated document of any court order of support has been entered.

P.A. 76-1586, § 7-706, added by P.A. 89-92, § 10, eff. July 1, 1996.

5/7-706.1. Hearing for compliance with support order

§ 7-706.1. Hearing for compliance with support order.

(a) An obligor may request in writing to the clerk of the circuit court a hearing to contest the claim of noncompliance with an order of support and his or her subsequent driver's license suspension under subsection (b) of Section 7-702.

(b) If a written request for a hearing is received by the clerk of the circuit court, the clerk of the circuit court shall set the hearing before the circuit court.

(c) Upon the obligor's written request, the court must set a date for a hearing and afford the obligor an opportunity for a hearing as early as practical.

(d) The scope of this hearing is limited to the following issues:

(1) Whether the obligor is required to pay child support under an order of support.

(2) Whether the obligor has been adjudicated in arrears in court ordered child support payments in an amount equal to 90 days obligation or more.

(3) Any additional issues raised by the obligor, including the reasonableness of a payment agreement in light of the obligor's current financial circumstances, to be preserved for appeal.

(e) All hearings and hearing procedures shall comply with requirements of the Illinois Constitution and the United States Constitution, so that no person is deprived of due process of law nor denied equal protection of the laws. All hearings shall be held before a judge of the circuit court in the county in which the support order has been entered. Appropriate records of the hearings shall be kept. Where a transcript of the hearing is taken, the person requesting the hearing shall have the opportunity to order a copy of the transcript at his or her own expense.

(f) The action of the circuit court resulting in the suspension of any driver's license shall be a final judgment for purposes of appellate review.

P.A. 76-1586, § 7-706.1, added by P.A. 91-613, § 945, eff. July 1, 2000.

5/7-707. Payment of reinstatement fee

§ 7-707. Payment of reinstatement fee. When an obligor receives notice from the Secretary of State that the suspension of driving privileges has been terminated based upon receipt of notification from the circuit clerk of the obligor's compliance with a court order of support, the obligor shall pay a $30 reinstatement fee to the Secretary of State as set forth in Section 6-118 of this Code. The fee shall be deposited into the Family Responsibility Fund. In accordance with subsection (e) of Section 6-115 of this Code, the Secretary of State may decline to process a renewal of a driver's license of a person who has not paid this fee.

P.A. 76-1586, § 7-707, added by P.A. 89-92, § 10, eff. July 1, 1996. Amended by P.A. 92-16, § 85, eff. June 28, 2001.

5/7-708. Rules

§ 7-708. Rules. The Secretary of State, using the authority to license motor vehicle operators, may adopt such rules as may be necessary to establish standards, policies, and procedures for the suspension of driver's licenses for non-compliance with a court order of support.

P.A. 76-1586, § 7-708, added by P.A. 89-92, § 10, eff. July 1, 1996.

CHAPTER 8. MOTOR VEHICLES USED FOR TRANSPORTATION OF PASSENGERS

Section

Enactment

The Illinois Vehicle Code was enacted by P.A. 76-1586, effective July 1, 1970. The Code constitutes a consolidated recodification of various earlier laws and acts including the Illinois Motor Vehicle Law of 1957.

5/8–101. Proof of financial responsibility—Persons who operate motor vehicles in transportation of passengers for hire

§ 8–101. Proof of financial responsibility—Persons who operate motor vehicles in transportation of passengers for hire. It is unlawful for any person, firm or corporation to operate any motor vehicle along or upon any public street or highway in any incorporated city, town or village in this State for the carriage of passengers for hire, accepting and discharging all such persons as may offer themselves for transportation unless such person, firm or corporation has given, and there is in full force and effect and on file with the Secretary of State of Illinois, proof of financial responsibility provided in this Act. In addition this Section shall also apply to persons, firms or corporations who are in the business of providing transportation services for minors to or from educational or recreational facilities, except that this Section shall not apply to public utilities subject to regulation under "An Act concerning public utilities," approved June 29, 1921, as amended,[1] or to school buses which are operated by public or parochial schools and are engaged solely in the transportation of the pupils who attend such schools. This Section also applies to a contract carrier transporting employees in the course of their employment on a highway of this State in a vehicle designed to carry 15 or fewer passengers. This Section shall not apply to any person participating in a ridesharing arrangement or operating a commuter van, but only during the performance of activities authorized by the Ridesharing Arrangements Act.[2]

If the person operating such motor vehicle is not the owner, then proof of financial responsibility filed hereunder must provide that the owner is primarily liable.

P.A. 76–1586, § 8–101, eff. July 1, 1970. Amended by P.A. 77–2743, § 1, eff. July 1, 1972; P.A. 82–656, § 7, eff. Jan. 1, 1982; P.A. 92–108, § 5, eff. Jan. 1, 2002.

1 220 ILCS 5/1–101 et seq.

2 625 ILCS 30/1 et seq.

5/8–101.1. Proof of financial responsibility—Persons who operate medical transport vehicles

§ 8–101.1. Proof of financial responsibility—Persons who operate medical transport vehicles. It is unlawful for any person, firm or corporation, other than a unit of local government, to operate any medical transport vehicle along or upon any public street or highway in any incorporated city, town or village in this State unless such person, firm or corporation has given, and there is in full force and effect and on file with the Secretary of State, proof of financial responsibility provided in this Code.

If the person operating such motor vehicle is not the owner, then proof of financial responsibility filed hereunder must provide that the owner is primarily liable.

P.A. 76–1586, § 8–101.1, added by P.A. 82–433, § 1, eff. Sept. 8, 1981. Amended by P.A. 82–949, § 1, eff. Jan. 1, 1983.

Formerly Ill.Rev.Stat.1991, ch. 95 ½, ¶ 8–101.1.

Section 3 of P.A. 82–433 approved Sept. 8, 1981, provided:

"This Act takes effect upon its becoming a law, except that the provisions relating to safety tests and proof of financial responsibility for medical transport vehicles apply only to applications for and the issuance of registration plates which are required to be displayed on January 1, 1982 or thereafter."

5/8–102. Alternate methods of giving proof

§ 8–102. Alternate methods of giving proof. Proof of financial responsibility, when required under Section 8–101 or 8–101.1, may be given by filing with the Secretary of State one of the following:

1. A bond as provided in Section 8–103;

2. An insurance policy or other proof of insurance in a form to be prescribed by the Secretary as provided in Section 8–108;

3. A certificate of self-insurance issued by the Director;

4. A certificate of self-insurance issued to the Regional Transportation Authority by the Director naming municipal or non-municipal public carriers included therein;

5. A certificate of coverage issued by an intergovernmental risk management association evidencing coverages which meet or exceed the amounts required under this Code.

P.A. 76–1586, § 8–102, eff. July 1, 1970. Amended by P.A. 77–2743, § 1; P.A. 81–1269, § .01, eff. June 30, 1980; P.A. 82–138, § 1, eff. Jan. 1, 1982; P.A. 82–433, § 1, eff. Sept. 8, 1981; P.A. 82–783, Art. III, § 37, eff. July 13, 1982; P.A. 86–444, § 1, eff. Jan. 1, 1990.

Formerly Ill.Rev.Stat.1991, ch. 95 ½, ¶ 8–102.

Section 2 of P.A. 77–2743 provided:

"This amendatory Act shall take effect on July 1, 1972, as to motor vehicles registered on a fiscal year basis and January 1, 1973 as to motor vehicles registered on a calendar year basis."

Section 3 of P.A. 82–433 approved Sept. 8, 1981, provided:

"This Act takes effect upon its becoming a law, except that the provisions relating to safety tests and proof of financial responsibility for medical transport vehicles apply only to applications for and the issuance of registration plates which are required to be displayed on January 1, 1982 or thereafter."

5/8–103. Bond as proof of financial responsibility

§ 8–103. Bond as proof of financial responsibility. 1. A bond of the owner of motor vehicles, subject to the provisions of Section 8–101 or 8–101.1, with a solvent and responsible surety company authorized to do business under the laws of this State as surety thereon; or

2. A bond of such owner, with one or more personal sureties, owning real estate in the State of Illinois, of the value in the aggregate of $250,000 over and above all encumbrances, when approved by the Secretary of State shall be proof of financial responsibility as required by Section 8–101 or 8–101.1.

3. The bond shall not be approved unless accompanied by affidavits of the personal sureties, attached, stating the location, legal description, market value, nature and amount of encumbrances (if any), and the value above all encumbrances of such real estate scheduled to qualify on such bond, and not then unless all requirements for such bond as provided for by this Code have been met.

P.A. 76–1586, § 8–103, eff. July 1, 1970. Amended by P.A. 77–2743, § 1, eff. July 1, 1972; P.A. 82–433, § 1, eff. Sept. 8, 1981; P.A. 82–949, § 1, eff. Jan. 1, 1983.

Formerly Ill.Rev.Stat.1991, ch. 95 ½, ¶ 8–103.

Section 2 of P.A. 77–2743 provided:

"This amendatory Act shall take effect on July 1, 1972, as to motor vehicles registered on a fiscal year basis and January 1, 1973 as to motor vehicles registered on a calendar year basis."

Section 3 of P.A. 82–433 approved Sept. 8, 1981, provided:

"This Act takes effect upon its becoming a law, except that the provisions relating to safety tests and proof of financial responsibility for medical transport vehicles apply only to applications for and the

issuance of registration plates which are required to be displayed on January 1, 1982 or thereafter."

P.A. 82-949 incorporated the amendment by P.A. 82-433.

5/8-104. Requirements of bond

§ 8-104. Requirements of bond. 1. A surety bond or real estate bond filed as proof as provided in Section 8-103 shall be in the sum of $250,000 for each motor vehicle operated by the owner providing the motor vehicle is subject to Section 8-101 or 8-101.1.

2. The surety of real estate bond shall provide for the payment of each judgment by the owner of the motor vehicle (giving its manufacturer's name and number and state license number) within 30 days after it becomes final, provided each judgment shall have been rendered against such owner or any person operating the motor vehicle with the owner's express or implied consent, for any injury to or death of any person or for damage to property other than such motor vehicle, resulting from the negligence of such owner, his agent, or any person operating the motor vehicle with his express or implied consent, provided that the maximum payment required of the surety or sureties, on all judgments recovered against an owner hereunder, shall not exceed the sum of $250,000 for each motor vehicle operated, under Section 8-101 or 8-101.1.

P.A. 76-1586, § 8-104, eff. July 1, 1970. Amended by P.A. 77-2743, § 1, eff. July 1, 1972; P.A. 82-433, § 1, eff. Sept. 8, 1981; P.A. 82-949, § 1, eff. Jan. 1, 1983.

Formerly Ill.Rev.Stat.1991, ch. 95 ½, ¶ 8-104.

Section 2 of P.A. 77-2743 provided:

"This amendatory Act shall take effect on July 1, 1972, as to motor vehicles registered on a fiscal year basis and January 1, 1973 as to motor vehicles registered on a calendar year basis."

Section 3 of P.A. 82-433 approved Sept. 8, 1981, provided:

"This Act takes effect upon its becoming a law, except that the provisions relating to safety tests and proof of financial responsibility for medical transport vehicles apply only to applications for and the issuance of registration plates which are required to be displayed on January 1, 1982 or thereafter."

P.A. 82-949 incorporated the amendment by P.A. 82-433.

5/8-105. Action on bond

§ 8-105. Action on bond. The surety bond shall, by its terms, inure to the benefit of the person recovering any such judgment, and shall provide that an action may be brought in any court of competent jurisdiction upon such bond by the owner of any such judgment; and such bond, for the full amount thereof shall, by its terms, be a lien for the benefit of the beneficiaries of said bond on such real estate so scheduled, and shall be recorded in the office of the recorder in each county in which such real estate is located.

P.A. 76-1586, § 8-105, eff. July 1, 1970. Amended by P.A. 83-358, § 67, eff. Sept. 14, 1983.

Formerly Ill.Rev.Stat.1991, ch. 95 ½, ¶ 8-105.

Validity

Provision of 1923 motor vehicle law that surety bond of owner of motor vehicle used for transportation of passengers becomes a lien on real estate scheduled in the bond, without providing for discharge of the lien, which is continued in this Section, has been held unconstitutional by the Illinois Supreme Court in the case of Weksler v. Collins, 317 Ill. 132, 147 N.E. 797 (1925).

5/8-106. Withdrawal by sureties from bond—Notice

§ 8-106. Withdrawal by sureties from bond—Notice. Any surety or sureties may withdraw from any such bond by serving ten days previous notice in writing upon such owner and the Secretary of State, either personally or by registered mail, whereupon it shall be the duty of such owner to file another bond or insurance policy in accordance with the provisions of this Act. Upon the expiration of said ten days, the Secretary of State shall mark said bond "withdrawn", with the date such withdrawal became effective, and thereupon the liability of the sureties on such bond shall cease as to any injury or damages sustained after the date such withdrawal became effective.

P.A. 76-1586, § 8-106, eff. July 1, 1970. Amended by P.A. 80-1495, § 36, eff. Jan. 8, 1979.

Formerly Ill.Rev.Stat.1991, ch. 95 ½, ¶ 8-106.

5/8-107. Authority to require replacement of bond

§ 8-107. Authority to require replacement of bond. If, at any time, in the judgment of the Secretary of State, said bond is not sufficient for any good cause, he may require the owner of such motor vehicle who filed the same to replace said bond with another good and sufficient bond or insurance policy, in accordance with the provisions of this Act, and upon such replacement, the liability of the surety or sureties on such prior bond shall cease as to any injury or damage sustained after such replacement.

P.A. 76-1586, § 8-107, eff. July 1, 1970. Amended by P.A. 80-1495, § 36, eff. Jan. 8, 1979.

Formerly Ill.Rev.Stat.1991, ch. 95 ½, ¶ 8-107.

5/8-108. Insurance policy as bond

§ 8-108. Insurance policy as bond. A policy of insurance in a solvent and responsible company authorized to do business in the State of Illinois, and having admitted net assets of not less than $300,000 insuring the owner, his agent or any person operating the motor vehicle with the owner's express or implied consent against liability for any injury to or death of any person or for damage to property other than the motor vehicle resulting from the negligence of such owner, his agent or any person operating the vehicle with his express or implied consent, when accepted by the Secretary of State, shall be proof of financial responsibility as required by Section 8-101 or 8-101.1.

P.A. 76-1586, § 8-108, eff. July 1, 1970. Amended by P.A. 82-433, § 1, eff. Sept. 8, 1981.

Formerly Ill.Rev.Stat.1991, ch. 95 ½, ¶ 8-108.

Section 3 of P.A. 82-433 approved Sept. 8, 1981, provided:

"This Act takes effect upon its becoming a law, except that the provisions relating to safety tests and proof of financial responsibility for medical transport vehicles apply only to applications for and the issuance of registration plates which are required to be displayed on January 1, 1982 or thereafter."

5/8-109. Requirements of policy

§ 8-109. Requirements of policy. 1. The policy of insurance may cover one or more motor vehicles and for each such vehicle shall insure such owner against liability upon the owner to a minimum amount of $250,000 for bodily injury to, or death of, any person, and $50,000 for damage to property, provided that the maximum payment required of such company on all judgments recovered against an owner hereunder shall not exceed the sum of $300,000 for each motor vehicle operated under the provisions of this Section.

2. The policy of insurance shall provide for payment and satisfaction of any judgment within 30 days after it becomes final rendered against the owner or any person operating the motor vehicle with the owner's express or implied consent for such injury, death or damage to property other than the motor vehicle, and shall provide that suit may be brought in any court of competent jurisdiction upon such insurance policy by the owner of any such judgment.

3. The insurance policy shall contain a description of each motor vehicle, giving the manufacturer's name and number and state license number.

P.A. 76-1586, § 8-109, eff. July 1, 1970. Amended by P.A. 79-1141, § 1, eff. Jan. 1, 1976; P.A. 82-433, § 1, eff. Sept. 8, 1981; P.A. 82-949, § 1, eff. Jan. 1, 1983.

Formerly Ill.Rev.Stat.1991, ch. 95 ½, ¶ 8-109.

Section 3 of P.A. 82-433 approved Sept. 8, 1981, provided:

"This Act takes effect upon its becoming a law, except that the provisions relating to safety tests and proof of financial responsibility for medical transport vehicles apply only to applications for and the issuance of registration plates which are required to be displayed on January 1, 1982 or thereafter."

P.A. 82-949 recognized the amendment by P.A. 82-433.

5/8-110. Cancellation of insurance policy—Notice

§ 8-110. Cancellation of insurance policy—Notice. 1. In the event said policy of insurance be cancelled by the issuing company, or the authority of said issuing company to do business in the State of Illinois be revoked, the Secretary of State shall require the owner who filed the same either to furnish a bond or to replace said policy with another policy according to the provisions of this Act.

2. Said policy of insurance shall also contain a provision that the same cannot be cancelled by the company issuing it without giving ten days notice in writing of such cancellation to the owner and the Secretary of State, either personally or by registered mail.

3. Whenever the issuing company gives such notice of cancellation, the Secretary of State shall, at the expiration of said ten days, mark said insurance policy "Withdrawn" with the date such withdrawal became effective, and thereupon the liability of such company on said policy shall cease as to any injury or damage sustained after the date such withdrawal becomes effective.

P.A. 76-1586, § 8-110, eff. July 1, 1970.

Formerly Ill.Rev.Stat.1991, ch. 95 ½, ¶ 8-110.

5/8-111. Proof required after cancellation

§ 8-111. Proof required after cancellation. If, at any time, in the judgment of the Secretary of State, said policy of insurance is not sufficient for any good cause, he may require the owner of such motor vehicle who filed the same, to replace said policy of insurance with another good and sufficient bond or insurance policy, in accordance with the provisions of this Act, and upon such replacement, the liability of the company on said insurance policy shall cease as to any injury or damage sustained after such replacement.

P.A. 76-1586, § 8-111, eff. July 1, 1970.

Formerly Ill.Rev.Stat.1991, ch. 95 ½, ¶ 8-111.

5/8-112. When bond on policy to expire

§ 8-112. When bond on policy to expire. All bonds and policies of insurance filed with the Secretary of State, under this Act, shall expire not sooner than the 31st day of December as to a vehicle registered on a calendar year basis and not sooner than the 30th day of June as to a vehicle registered on a fiscal year basis in each year, provided, that the expiration of same shall not terminate liabilities upon such bonds and policies of insurance arising during the period for which the bonds and policies of insurance were filed.

P.A. 76-1586, § 8-112, eff. July 1, 1970. Amended by P.A. 77-99, § 1, eff. Jan. 1, 1972.

Formerly Ill.Rev.Stat.1991, ch. 95 ½, ¶ 8-112.

5/8-113. Secretary of State to suspend registration certificates, registration plates and registration sticker when bond or policy cancelled or withdrawn

§ 8-113. Secretary of State to suspend registration certificates, registration plates and registration sticker when bond or policy cancelled or withdrawn. In the event that a bond or policy of insurance is cancelled or withdrawn with respect to a vehicle or vehicles, subject to the provisions of Section 8-101 or 8-101.1, for which the bond or policy of insurance was issued, then the Secretary of State immediately shall suspend the registration certificates, registration plates and registration sticker or stickers of the owner, with respect to such motor vehicle or vehicles, and said registration certificates, registration plates and registration sticker or stickers shall remain suspended and no registration shall be permitted or renewed unless and until the owner of the motor vehicle shall have filed proof of financial responsibility as provided by Section 8-101 or 8-101.1.

P.A. 76-1586, § 8-113, eff. July 1, 1970. Amended by P.A. 80-230, § 1, eff. Oct. 1, 1977; P.A. 80-1185, § 1, eff. March 8, 1978; P.A. 82-433, § 1, eff. Sept. 8, 1981.

Formerly Ill.Rev.Stat.1991, ch. 95 ½, ¶ 8-113.

Section 3 of P.A. 82-433 approved Sept. 8, 1981, provided:

"This Act takes effect upon its becoming a law, except that the provisions relating to safety tests and proof of financial responsibility for medical transport vehicles apply only to applications for and the issuance of registration plates which are required to be displayed on January 1, 1982 or thereafter."

5/8-114. Issuance of license upon proof of financial responsibility

§ 8-114. Issuance of license upon proof of financial responsibility. The Secretary of State shall issue to each person who has in effect proof of financial responsibility as required by Section 8-101 or 8-101.1, a certificate for each motor vehicle operated by such person and included within the proof of financial responsibility. Each certificate shall specify the Illinois registration plate and registration sticker number of the vehicle, a statement that proof of financial responsibility has been filed, and the period for which the certificate was issued.

P.A. 76-1586, § 8-114, eff. July 1, 1970. Amended by P.A. 80-230, § 1, eff. Oct. 1, 1977; P.A. 82-433, § 1, eff. Sept. 8, 1981.

Formerly Ill.Rev.Stat.1991, ch. 95 ½, ¶ 8-114.

Section 3 of P.A. 82-433 approved Sept. 8, 1981, provided:

"This Act takes effect upon its becoming a law, except that the provisions relating to safety tests and proof of financial responsibility for medical transport vehicles apply only to applications for and the issuance of registration plates which are required to be displayed on January 1, 1982 or thereafter."

5/8-115. Display of certificate—Enforcement

§ 8-115. Display of certificate—Enforcement. The certificate issued pursuant to Section 8-114 shall be displayed upon a window of the motor vehicle for which it was issued, in such manner as to be visible to the passengers carried therein. This Section and Section 8-114 shall be enforced by the State Police, the Secretary of State, and other police officers.

P.A. 76-1586, § 8-115, eff. July 1, 1970. Amended by P.A. 82-433, § 1, eff. Sept. 8, 1981.

Formerly Ill.Rev.Stat.1991, ch. 95 ½, ¶ 8-115.

Section 3 of P.A. 82-433 approved Sept. 8, 1981, provided:

"This Act takes effect upon its becoming a law, except that the provisions relating to safety tests and proof of financial responsibility for medical transport vehicles apply only to applications for and the issuance of registration plates which are required to be displayed on January 1, 1982 or thereafter."

5/8-116. Failure to comply with provisions; punishment

§ 8-116. Any person who fails to comply with the provisions of this Chapter, or who fails to obey, observe or comply with any order of the Secretary of State or any law enforcement agency issued in accordance with the provisions of this Chapter is guilty of a Class A misdemeanor.

P.A. 76-1586, § 8-116, added by P.A. 77-2838, § 1, eff. Jan. 3, 1973.

Formerly Ill.Rev.Stat.1991, ch. 95 ½, ¶ 8-116.

CHAPTER 9. OWNERS OF FOR-RENT VEHICLES FOR-HIRE

Enactment

The Illinois Vehicle Code was enacted by P.A. 76-1586, effective July 1, 1970. The Code constitutes a consolidated recodification of various earlier laws and acts including the Illinois Motor Vehicle Law of 1957.

5/9-101. Owner of for-rent motor vehicle to give proof of financial responsibility

§ 9-101. Owner of for-rent motor vehicle to give proof of financial responsibility. For purposes of this Chapter, "for rent" means any transfer of the possession of or right to possession of a motor vehicle to a user for a valuable consideration for a period of less than one year, and "to lease" means any transfer of the possession of or right to possession of a motor vehicle to a user for a period of one year or more. It is unlawful for the owner of any motor vehicle to engage in the business, or to hold himself out to the public generally as being engaged in the business of renting out such motor vehicle to be operated by the customer, unless the owner has given, and there is in full force and effect and on file with the Secretary of State proof of financial responsibility as hereinafter provided. The delivery of a vehicle owned by an out of State person or business to a renter in this State shall constitute engaging in the rental business in this State for purposes of this Section.

All owners of motor vehicles which are leased for a period of one year or more are not required to provide proof of insurance as required under this chapter, but instead must comply with Section 7-601 of this Code and obtain vehicle insurance in amounts no less than the minimum amount set for bodily injury or death and for destruction of property pursuant to Section 7-203 of this Code.

P.A. 76-1586, § 9-101, eff. July 1, 1970. Amended by P.A. 86-880, § 1, eff. Jan. 1, 1990; P.A. 87-1220, § 1, eff. July 1, 1993.

Formerly Ill.Rev.Stat.1991, ch. 95 ½, ¶ 9-101.

5/9-102. Alternate methods of giving proof of financial responsibility

§ 9-102. Alternate methods of giving proof of financial responsibility. Proof of financial responsibility when required under Section 9-101 may be given by the following methods. By filing with the Secretary of State:

1. A bond as provided in Section 9-103.
2. An insurance policy or other proof of insurance in a form to be prescribed by the Secretary as provided in Section 9-105.
3. A certificate of self insurance issued by the Director.

P.A. 76-1586, § 9-102, eff. July 1, 1970. Amended by P.A. 77-736, § 1, eff. Aug. 12, 1971; P.A. 77-2743, § 1; P.A. 78-255, § 61, eff. Oct. 1, 1973; P.A. 82-138, § 1, eff. Jan. 1, 1982; P.A. 86-444, § 1, eff. Jan. 1, 1990.

Formerly Ill.Rev.Stat.1991, ch. 95 ½, ¶ 9-102.

5/9-103. Bond as proof—requirements

§ 9-103. Bond as proof—requirements. A motor vehicle liability bond, conditioned that the owner of the motor vehicle will pay any judgment within 30 days after it becomes final, recovered against the customer and the owner of the motor vehicle or against any person operating the motor vehicle with the customer's and the owner's express or implied consent for damage to property other than to the rented motor vehicle, or for an injury to, or for the death of any person including an occupant of the rented motor vehicle, resulting from the operation of the motor vehicle, provided, however, every such bond is in the penal sum of $100,000.

The bond shall be executed by a solvent and responsible surety company authorized to do business in the State of Illinois, or by one or more personal sureties to be approved by the Secretary of State.

The personal sureties shall own real estate in the State of Illinois of the aggregate value of $100,000, over and above all encumbrances, and each of the personal sureties shall make an affidavit concerning the property which he schedules for the purpose of qualifying as surety, stating the location, legal description, market value, and the amount and nature of any encumbrances.

P.A. 76-1586, § 9-103, eff. July 1, 1970. Amended by P.A. 76-1718, § 1; P.A. 77-2743, § 1, eff. July 1, 1972; P.A. 83-566, § 1, eff. Jan. 1, 1984; P.A. 86-444, § 1, eff. Jan. 1, 1990.

Formerly Ill.Rev.Stat.1991, ch. 95 ½, ¶ 9-103.

Section 2 of P.A. 77-2743 provided:

"This amendatory Act shall take effect on July 1, 1972, as to motor vehicles registered on a fiscal year basis and January 1, 1973 as to motor vehicles registered on a calendar year basis."

5/9-104. Withdrawal of sureties—Notice

§ 9-104. Withdrawal of sureties—Notice. Any surety may withdraw from the bond by serving ten days previous notice in writing, either personally or by registered mail, upon the owner of the motor vehicle, and upon the Secretary of State, whereupon it shall be the duty of such owner to file another bond or insurance policy, in accordance with the provisions of this Act. Upon the expiration of the ten days, the Secretary of State shall mark the bond "Cancelled".

P.A. 76-1586, § 9-104, eff. July 1, 1970.

Formerly Ill.Rev.Stat.1991, ch. 95 ½, ¶ 9-104.

5/9-105. Insurance policy as proof—requirements

§ 9-105. Insurance policy as proof—requirements. A motor vehicle liability policy in a solvent and responsible company, authorized to do business in the State of Illinois, providing that the insurance carrier will pay any judgment within 30 days after it becomes final, recovered against the customer or against any person operating the motor vehicle with the customer's express or implied consent, for damage to property other than to the rented motor vehicles, or for an injury to or for the death of any person, including an occupant of the rented motor vehicle, resulting from the operation of the motor vehicle shall serve as proof of financial responsibility; provided however, every such policy provides insurance insuring the operator of the rented motor vehicle against liability upon such insured to a minimum amount of $50,000 because of bodily injury to, or death of any one person or damage to property and $100,000 because of bodily injury to or death of 2 or more persons in any one motor vehicle accident.

P.A. 76-1586, § 9-105, eff. July 1, 1970. Amended by P.A. 76-1718, § 1; P.A. 77-2743, § 1; P.A. 85-1374, § 1, eff. Jan. 1, 1989; P.A. 86-880, § 1, eff. Jan. 1, 1990.

Formerly Ill.Rev.Stat.1991, ch. 95 ½, ¶ 9-105.

Section 2 of P.A. 77-2743 provided:

"This amendatory Act shall take effect on July 1, 1972, as to motor vehicles registered on a fiscal year basis and January 1, 1973 as to motor vehicles registered on a calendar year basis."

5/9-106. Cancellation of policy—Notices

§ 9-106. Cancellation of policy—Notices. The policy shall provide that the insurance carrier may cancel it by serving 10 days' previous notice in writing, either personally or by registered mail, upon the owner of the motor vehicle and upon the Secretary of State. Whenever any such policy shall be so cancelled, the Secretary of State shall mark same "Cancelled" and shall require such owner either to furnish a bond or a new policy of insurance, in accordance with this Act.

All policies filed with the Secretary of State shall expire not sooner than the 31st day of December as to vehicles registered on a calendar year nor sooner than the 30th day of June as to vehicles registered on a fiscal year.

P.A. 76-1586, § 9-106, eff. July 1, 1970. Amended by P.A. 77-99, § 1, eff. Jan. 1, 1972.

Formerly Ill.Rev.Stat.1991, ch. 95 ½, ¶ 9-106.

5/9-107. Authority to require replacement of bond

§ 9-107. Authority to require replacement of bond. If, at any time, in the judgment of the Secretary of State, the liability policy filed hereunder, is not sufficient for any good cause, he may require the owner of such motor vehicle who filed the same to replace, within fifteen (15) days from the date of notice given, said policy with another good and sufficient liability policy or bond, in accordance with the provisions of this Act. At the time of replacement or at the expiration of the fifteen (15) day period, as the case may be, the Secretary of State shall mark the policy "Cancelled."

Upon the cancellation of any liability policy hereunder the liabilities on said policy shall thereupon cease as to any future damage or injury.

P.A. 76-1586, § 9-107, eff. July 1, 1970.

Formerly Ill.Rev.Stat.1991, ch. 95 ½, ¶ 9-107.

5/9-108. Application for approval of insurance policy or bond required

§ 9-108. Application for approval of insurance policy or bond required. Every person desiring to engage in the business of renting out a motor vehicle, to be operated by the customer, shall file with the Secretary of State, an application for the approval of the Secretary of State of the insurance policy or bond tendered under the provisions of this Act, by such person, and if the Secretary of State shall determine that such insurance policy or bond complies with the provisions of this Act, he shall accept such insurance policy or bond, and shall thereupon issue to such applicant a certificate setting forth the fact that the applicant has, in respect to the vehicle described therein, complied with the provisions of this Act.

P.A. 76-1586, § 9-108, eff. July 1, 1970.

Formerly Ill.Rev.Stat.1991, ch. 95 ½, ¶ 9-108.

5/9-109. Secretary of State to cancel certificate and to suspend license plates and registration stickers when bond or policy cancelled or withdrawn

§ 9-109. Secretary of State to cancel certificate and to suspend license plates and registration stickers when bond or policy cancelled or withdrawn. (a) If any insurance policy or bond filed hereunder shall for any reason become inoperative, the Secretary of State shall forthwith cancel the certificate of compliance with the owner and it shall be unlawful for the owner to rent out the motor vehicle, covered by said certificate, until a policy or bond meeting the requirements of this Act is filed with the Secretary of State and a certificate has been issued by him as provided by Section 9-108.

(b) The Secretary of State shall also suspend the registration certificate, license plates and registration sticker or stickers of the owner, with respect to the motor vehicle for which the insurance policy or bond had been issued, and said registration certificates, license plates and registration sticker or stickers shall remain suspended and no registration shall be permitted or renewed unless and until the owner of said motor vehicle shall have complied with the provisions of this Act.

P.A. 76-1586, § 9-109, eff. July 1, 1970. Amended by P.A. 80-230, § 1, eff. Oct. 1, 1977; P.A. 80-1185, § 1, eff. March 8, 1978.

Formerly Ill.Rev.Stat.1991, ch. 95 ½, ¶ 9-109.

5/9-110. Penalties for violations of this Act

§ 9-110. Penalties for violations of this Act. Any person who fails to comply with the provisions of this Chapter, or who fails to obey, observe or comply with any order of the

Secretary of State, in accordance with the provisions of this Chapter, is guilty of a Class A misdemeanor.

P.A. 76-1586, § 9-110, eff. July 1, 1970. Amended by P.A. 77-2720, § 1, eff. Jan. 1, 1972.

Formerly Ill.Rev.Stat.1991, ch. 95 ½, ¶ 9-110.

CHAPTER 10. CIVIL LIABILITY

Enactment

The Illinois Vehicle Code was enacted by P.A. 76-1586, effective July 1, 1970. The Code constitutes a consolidated recodification of various earlier laws and acts including the Illinois Motor Vehicle Law of 1957.

ARTICLE I. LIABILITY OF COUNTIES, MUNICIPALITIES AND OTHER PUBLIC CORPORATIONS

5/10-101. Insurance

§ 10-101. Insurance. (a) Any public entity or corporation may insure against the liability imposed by law and may insure persons who are legally entitled to recover damages from owners and operators of uninsured motor vehicles and hit-and-run motor vehicles because of bodily injury, sickness or disease including death incurred while using a motor vehicle of such public entity or corporation with any insurance carrier duly authorized to transact business in this State and the premium for such insurance shall be a proper charge against the general fund or any applicable special fund of such entity or corporation.

(b) Every employee of the State, who operates for purposes of State business a vehicle not owned, leased or controlled by the State shall procure insurance in the limit of the amounts of liability not less than the amounts required in Section 7-203 of this Act. The State may provide such insurance for the benefit of, and without cost to, such employees and may include such coverage in a plan of self-insurance under Section 405-105 of the Department of Central Management Services Law (20 ILCS 405/405-105). The State may also obtain uninsured or hit-and-run vehicle coverage, as defined in Section 143a of the "Illinois Insurance Code".[1] Any public liability insurance furnished by the State under this Section shall be under the policy or policies contracted for or under a self-insurance plan implemented by the Department of Central Management Services pursuant to Section 405-105 of the Department of Central Management Services Law (20 ILCS 405/405-105), the costs for procuring such insurance to be charged, collected and received as provided in that Section 25-105.

P.A. 76-1586, § 10-101, eff. July 1, 1970. Amended by P.A. 77-472, § 1, eff. July 27, 1971; P.A. 77-473, § 1, eff. July 27, 1971; P.A. 77-2829, § 40, eff. Dec. 22, 1972; P.A. 78-255, § 61, eff. Oct. 1, 1973; P.A. 79-352, § 1, eff. Aug. 7, 1975; P.A. 79-1331, § 4, eff. July 28, 1976; P.A. 80-57, § 16, eff. July 1, 1977; P.A. 82-413, § 2, eff. Sept. 4, 1981; P.A. 82-789, Art. I, § 24, eff. July 13, 1982; P.A. 91-239, Art. 5, § 5-530, eff. Jan. 1, 2000.

Formerly Ill.Rev.Stat.1991, ch. 95 ½, ¶ 10-101.

1 215 ILCS 5/143a.

ARTICLE II. LIABILITY TO GUESTS

Caption to article II amended by P.A. 76-2158, eff. July 1, 1970. The caption formerly read, "Imputing Negligence to Guests."

5/10-201. Liability for bodily injury to or death of guest

§ 10-201. Liability for bodily injury to or death of guest. No person riding in or upon a motor vehicle or motorcycle as a guest without payment for such ride and who has solicited such ride in violation of Subsection (a) of Section 11-1006 of this Act, nor his personal representative in the event of the death of such guest, shall have a cause of action for damages against the driver or operator of such motor vehicle or motorcycle, or its owner or his employee or agent for injury, death or loss, in case of accident, unless such accident has been caused by the willful and wanton misconduct of the driver or operator of such motor vehicle or motorcycle or its owner or his employee or agent and unless such willful and wanton misconduct contributed to the injury, death or loss for which the action is brought.

Nothing contained in this section relieves a motor vehicle or motorcycle carrier of passengers for hire of responsibility for injury or death sustained by any passenger for hire.

This amendatory Act of 1971 shall apply only to causes of action arising from accidents occurring after its effective date.

P.A. 76-1586, § 10-201, eff. July 1, 1970. Amended by P.A. 77-1482, § 1, eff. Jan. 1, 1972.

Formerly Ill.Rev.Stat.1991, ch. 95 ½, ¶ 10-201.

5/10-202. Liability of employer in regard to ridesharing

§ 10-202. Liability of employer in regard to ridesharing. (a) An employer shall not be liable for injuries to passengers and other persons resulting from the operation or use of a passenger car or commuter van in a ridesharing arrangement which is not owned, leased, contracted for or driven by the employer, and for which the employer has not paid wages to an employee for services rendered in driving the vehicle, provided, that wages shall not include a portion of the fares collected by the driver and shall not include expenses for gasoline or passenger car or commuter van repairs.

(b) An employer shall not be liable for injuries to passengers and other persons because he provides information, incentives or otherwise encourages his employees to participate in ridesharing arrangements.

P.A. 76-1586, § 10-202, added by P.A. 81-1452, § 1, eff. Jan. 1, 1981. Amended by P.A. 83-1091, § 1, eff. July 1, 1984.

Formerly Ill.Rev.Stat.1991, ch. 95 ½, ¶ 10-202.

ARTICLE III. PROCESS ON NON-RESIDENT

5/10–301. Service of process on non-resident

§ 10–301. Service of process on non-resident.

(a) The use and operation by any person or his duly authorized agent or employee of a vehicle over or upon the highways of the State of Illinois, shall be deemed an appointment by such person of the Secretary of State to be his true and lawful attorney upon whom may be served all legal process in any action or proceeding against him, growing out of such use or resulting in damage or loss to person or property, and the use or operation shall be signification of his agreement that such process against him which is so served, shall be of the same legal force and validity as though served upon him personally if such person is a non-resident of this State or at the time a cause of action arises is a resident of this State but subsequently becomes a non-resident of this State, or in the event the vehicle is owned by a non-resident and is being operated over and upon the highways of this State with the owner's express or implied permission.

(b) Service of such process shall be made by serving a copy upon the Secretary of State or any employee in his office designated by him to accept such service for him, or by filing such copy in his office, together with an affidavit of compliance from the plaintiff instituting the action, suit, or proceeding, which states that this Section is applicable to the proceeding and that the plaintiff has complied with the requirements of this Section, and a fee of $5 and such service shall be sufficient service upon the person, if notice of such service and a copy of the process are, within 10 days thereafter, sent by registered mail by the plaintiff to the defendant, at the last known address of the defendant, and the plaintiff's affidavit of compliance herewith is appended to the summons.

(c) The court in which the action is pending may order such continuances as may be necessary to afford the defendant reasonable opportunity to defend the action. The fee of $5 paid by the plaintiff to the Secretary of State at the time of the service shall be taxed as his cost, if he prevails in the action.

(d) The Secretary of State shall keep a record of all such processes, which shall show the day and hour of such service.

(e) When a final judgment is entered against any non-resident defendant who has not received notice and a copy of the process by registered mail, required to be sent to him as above provided, and such person, his heirs, legatees, executor, administrator or other legal representatives, as the case may require, shall within one year after the written notice given to him of such judgment, or within 5 years after such judgment, if no such notice has been given, as stated above, appear and petition the court to be heard regarding such judgment, and shall pay such costs as the court may deem reasonable in that behalf, the person so petitioning the court may appear and answer the plaintiff's allegations, and thereupon such proceeding shall be had as if the defendant had appeared in due time and no judgment had been entered. If it appears upon the hearing that such judgment ought not to have been entered against the defendant, the judgment may be set aside, altered or amended as shall appear just; otherwise, it shall be ordered that the judgment stands confirmed against the defendant. The judgment shall, after 5 years from the entry thereof, if not set aside in the manner stated above, be deemed and adjudged confirmed against such defendant, and all persons claiming under him by virtue of any act done subsequent to the commencement of such action, and at the end of the 5 years, the court may enter such further orders as shall be required for the enforcement of the judgment.

(f) Any person instituting any action, suit, or proceeding who uses this Section to effect service of process shall be liable for the attorney's fees and costs of the defendant if the court finds that the person instituting the action knew or should have known that this Section is not applicable for effecting service in such action.

P.A. 76–1586, § 10–301, eff. July 1, 1970. Amended by P.A. 77–100, § 1, eff. Jan. 1, 1972; P.A. 84–549, § 20, eff. Sept. 18, 1985; P.A. 85–412, § 1, eff. Jan. 1, 1988; P.A. 91–357, § 231, eff. July 29, 1999.

Formerly Ill.Rev.Stat.1991, ch. 95 ½, ¶ 10–301.

CHAPTER 11. RULES OF THE ROAD

Enactment

The Illinois Vehicle Code was enacted by P.A. 76–1586, effective July 1, 1970. The Code constitutes a consolidated recodification of various earlier laws and acts including the Uniform Act Regulating Traffic on Highways, 1935.

ARTICLE I. SPECIAL DEFINITIONS

Section

5/11–100. Definition of Administrator

§ 11–100. Definition of Administrator. For the purposes of this Chapter, "Administrator" means the Administrator of the Illinois Safety and Family Financial Responsibility Law in Chapter 7 of this Code.[1]

P.A. 76–1586, § 11–100, eff. July 1, 1970. Amended by P.A. 76–1618, § 1, eff. July 1, 1970; P.A. 77–42, § 1, eff. July 1, 1971; P.A. 77–170, § 1, eff. Jan. 1, 1972; P.A. 77–1910, § 1, eff. July 1, 1972; P.A. 78–255, § 61, eff. Oct. 1, 1973; P.A. 83–1473, § 3, eff. Jan. 1, 1985; P.A. 89–92, § 10, eff. July 1, 1996; P.A. 90–89, § 15, eff. Jan. 1, 1998.

Formerly Ill.Rev.Stat.1991, ch. 95 ½, ¶ 11–100.

[1] 625 ILCS 5/7–100 et seq.

ARTICLE II. OBEDIENCE TO AND EFFECT OF TRAFFIC LAWS

Section

5/11–208.2. Limitation on home rule units.

5/11-201. Provisions of act refer to vehicles upon the highways—Exceptions

§ 11-201. Provisions of act refer to vehicles upon the highways—Exceptions. The provisions of this Chapter relating to the operation of vehicles refer exclusively to the operation of vehicles upon highways except:

1. Where a different place is specifically referred to in a given section.

2. The provisions of Articles IV and V of this Chapter shall apply upon highways and elsewhere throughout the State.

P.A. 76-1586, § 11-201, eff. July 1, 1970.

Formerly Ill.Rev.Stat.1991, ch. 95 ½, ¶ 11-201.

5/11-202. Required obedience to traffic laws

§ 11-202. Required obedience to traffic laws. It is unlawful and, unless otherwise declared in this Chapter with respect to particular offenses, it is a petty offense for any person to do any act forbidden or fail to perform any Act required in this Chapter.

P.A. 76-1586, § 11-202, eff. July 1, 1970. Amended by P.A. 77-2830, Art. 73, § 1, eff. Jan. 1, 1973; P.A. 80-911, § 1, eff. Oct. 1, 1977.

Formerly Ill.Rev.Stat.1991, ch. 95 ½, ¶ 11-202.

5/11-203. Obedience to police officers

§ 11-203. Obedience to police officers. No person shall wilfully fail or refuse to comply with any lawful order or direction of any police officer, fireman, or school crossing guard invested by law with authority to direct, control, or regulate traffic. Any person convicted of violating this Section is guilty of a petty offense and shall be subject to a mandatory fine of $150.

P.A. 76-1586, § 11-203, eff. July 1, 1970. Amended by P.A. 84-873, § 1, eff. Jan. 1, 1986; P.A. 90-749, § 5, eff. Jan. 1, 1999.

Formerly Ill.Rev.Stat.1991, ch. 95 ½, ¶ 11-203.

5/11-204. Fleeing or attempting to elude police officer

§ 11-204. Fleeing or attempting to elude police officer. (a) Any driver or operator of a motor vehicle who, having been given a visual or audible signal by a peace officer directing such driver or operator to bring his vehicle to a stop, wilfully fails or refuses to obey such direction, increases his speed, extinguishes his lights, or otherwise flees or attempts to elude the officer, is guilty of a Class A misdemeanor. The signal given by the peace officer may be by hand, voice, siren, red or blue light. Provided, the officer giving such signal shall be in police uniform, and, if driving a vehicle, such vehicle shall display illuminated oscillating, rotating or flashing red or blue lights which when used in conjunction with an audible horn or siren would indicate the vehicle to be an official police vehicle. Such requirement shall not preclude the use of amber or white oscillating, rotating or flashing lights in conjunction with red or blue oscillating, rotating or flashing lights as required in Section 12-215 of Chapter 12.

(b) Upon receiving notice of such conviction the Secretary of State shall suspend the drivers license of the person so convicted for a period of not more than 6 months for a first conviction and not more than 12 months for a second conviction.

(c) A third or subsequent violation of this Section is a Class 4 felony.

P.A. 76-1586, § 11-204, eff. July 1, 1970. Amended by P.A. 77-2720, § 1, eff. Jan. 1, 1972; P.A. 85-830, § 1, eff. Sept. 24, 1987; P.A. 90-134, § 5, eff. July 22, 1997.

Formerly Ill.Rev.Stat.1991, ch. 95 ½, ¶ 11-204.

5/11-204.1. Aggravated fleeing or attempt to elude a police officer

§ 11-204.1. Aggravated fleeing or attempt to elude a police officer.

(a) The offense of aggravated fleeing or attempting to elude a police officer is committed by any driver or operator of a motor vehicle who flees or attempts to elude a police officer, after being given a visual or audible signal by a police officer in the manner prescribed in subsection (a) of Section 11-204 of this Code, and such flight or attempt to elude:

(1) is at a rate of speed at least 21 miles per hour over the legal speed limit;

(2) causes bodily injury to any individual; or

(3) causes damage in excess of $300 to property.

(b) Any person convicted of a first violation of this Section shall be guilty of a Class 4 felony. Upon notice of such a conviction the Secretary of State shall forthwith revoke the driver's license of the person so convicted, as provided in Section 6-205 of this Code. Any person convicted of a second or subsequent violation of this Section shall be guilty of a Class 3 felony, and upon notice of such a conviction the Secretary of State shall forthwith revoke the driver's license of the person convicted, as provided in Section 6-205 of the Code.

(c) The motor vehicle used in a violation of this Section is subject to seizure and forfeiture as provided in Sections 36-1 and 36-2 of the Criminal Code of 1961.[1]

P.A. 76-1586, § 11-204.1, added by P.A. 83-1326, § 1, eff. July 1, 1985. Amended by P.A. 88-679, § 15, eff. July 1, 1995; P.A. 90-134, § 5, eff. July 22, 1997.

Formerly Ill.Rev.Stat.1991, ch. 95 ½, ¶ 11-204.1.

[1] 720 ILCS 5/36-1 and 5/36-2.

5/11-205. Public officers and employees to obey Act—Exceptions

§ 11-205. Public officers and employees to obey Act—Exceptions.

(a) The provisions of this Chapter applicable to the drivers of vehicles upon the highways shall apply to the drivers of all vehicles owned or operated by the United States, this State or any county, city, town, district or any other political subdivision of the State, except as provided in this Section and subject to such specific exceptions as set forth in this Chapter with reference to authorized emergency vehicles.

(b) The driver of an authorized emergency vehicle, when responding to an emergency call or when in the pursuit of an actual or suspected violator of the law or when responding to but not upon returning from a fire alarm, may exercise the privileges set forth in this Section, but subject to the conditions herein stated.

(c) The driver of an authorized emergency vehicle may:

1. Park or stand, irrespective of the provisions of this Chapter;

2. Proceed past a red or stop signal or stop sign, but only after slowing down as may be required and necessary for safe operation;

3. Exceed the maximum speed limits so long as he does not endanger life or property;

4. Disregard regulations governing direction of movement or turning in specified directions.

(d) The exceptions herein granted to an authorized emergency vehicle, other than a police vehicle, shall apply only when the vehicle is making use of either an audible signal when in motion or visual signals meeting the requirements of Section 12-215 of this Act.

(e) The foregoing provisions do not relieve the driver of an authorized emergency vehicle from the duty of driving with due regard for the safety of all persons, nor do such provisions protect the driver from the consequences of his reckless disregard for the safety of others.

(f) Unless specifically made applicable, the provisions of this Chapter, except those contained in Section 11-204 and Articles IV and V of this Chapter,[1] shall not apply to persons, motor vehicles and equipment while actually engaged in work upon a highway but shall apply to such persons and vehicles when traveling to or from such work.

P.A. 76-1586, § 11-205, eff. July 1, 1970. Amended by P.A. 76-1737, § 1; P.A. 76-1997, § 1, eff. July 1, 1970; P.A. 78-510, § 1, eff. Oct. 1, 1973; P.A. 79-1069, § 1, eff. Jan. 1, 1976; P.A. 89-710, § 15, eff. Feb. 14, 1997; P.A. 90-257, § 5, eff. July 30, 1997.

Formerly Ill.Rev.Stat.1991, ch. 95 ½, ¶ 11-205.

[1] 625 ILCS 5/11-401 et seq. and 5/11-500 et seq.

5/11-206. Traffic laws apply to persons riding animals or driving animal-drawn vehicles

§ 11-206. Traffic laws apply to persons riding animals or driving animal-drawn vehicles. Every person riding an animal or driving any animal-drawn vehicle upon a roadway shall be granted all of the rights and shall be subject to all of the duties applicable to the driver of a vehicle by this chapter, except those provisions of this chapter which by their very nature can have no application.

P.A. 76-1586, § 11-206, eff. July 1, 1970. Amended by P.A. 78-850, Art. II, § 1, eff. July 1, 1974; P.A. 79-858, § 1, eff. Jan. 1, 1976.

Formerly Ill.Rev.Stat.1991, ch. 95 ½, ¶ 11-206.

5/11-207. Provisions of this Chapter uniform throughout State

§ 11-207. Provisions of this Chapter uniform throughout State. The provisions of this Chapter shall be applicable and uniform throughout this State and in all political subdivisions and municipalities therein, and no local authority shall enact or enforce any ordinance rule or regulation in conflict with the provisions of this Chapter unless expressly authorized herein. Local authorities may, however, adopt additional traffic regulations which are not in conflict with the provisions of this Chapter, but such regulations shall not be effective until signs giving reasonable notice thereof are posted.

P.A. 76-1586, § 11-207, eff. July 1, 1970. Amended by P.A. 85-532, § 1, eff. Jan. 1, 1988; P.A. 92-651, § 77, eff. July 11, 2002.

Formerly Ill.Rev.Stat.1991, ch. 95 ½, ¶ 11-207.

5/11-208. Powers of local authorities

§ 11-208. Powers of local authorities.

(a) The provisions of this Code shall not be deemed to prevent local authorities with respect to streets and highways under their jurisdiction and within the reasonable exercise of the police power from:

1. Regulating the standing or parking of vehicles, except as limited by Section 11-1306 of this Act;

2. Regulating traffic by means of police officers or traffic control signals;

3. Regulating or prohibiting processions or assemblages on the highways;

4. Designating particular highways as one-way highways and requiring that all vehicles thereon be moved in one specific direction;

5. Regulating the speed of vehicles in public parks subject to the limitations set forth in Section 11-604;

6. Designating any highway as a through highway, as authorized in Section 11-302, and requiring that all vehicles stop before entering or crossing the same or designating any intersection as a stop intersection or a yield right-of-way intersection and requiring all vehicles to stop or yield the right-of-way at one or more entrances to such intersections;

7. Restricting the use of highways as authorized in Chapter 15;

8. Regulating the operation of bicycles and requiring the registration and licensing of same, including the requirement of a registration fee;

9. Regulating or prohibiting the turning of vehicles or specified types of vehicles at intersections;

10. Altering the speed limits as authorized in Section 11-604;

11. Prohibiting U-turns;

12. Prohibiting pedestrian crossings at other than designated and marked crosswalks or at intersections;

13. Prohibiting parking during snow removal operation;

14. Imposing fines in accordance with Section 11-1301.3 as penalties for use of any parking place reserved for persons with disabilities, as defined by Section 1-159.1, or disabled veterans by any person using a motor vehicle not bearing registration plates specified in Section 11-1301.1 or a special decal or device as defined in Section 11-1301.2 as evidence that the vehicle is operated by or for a person with disabilities or disabled veteran;

15. Adopting such other traffic regulations as are specifically authorized by this Code; or

16. Enforcing the provisions of subsection (f) of Section 3-413 of this Code or a similar local ordinance.

(b) No ordinance or regulation enacted under subsections 1, 4, 5, 6, 7, 9, 10, 11 or 13 of paragraph (a) shall be effective until signs giving reasonable notice of such local traffic regulations are posted.

(c) The provisions of this Code shall not prevent any municipality having a population of 500,000 or more inhabitants from prohibiting any person from driving or operating any motor vehicle upon the roadways of such municipality with headlamps on high beam or bright.

(d) The provisions of this Code shall not be deemed to prevent local authorities within the reasonable exercise of their police power from prohibiting, on private property, the unauthorized use of parking spaces reserved for persons with disabilities.

(e) No unit of local government, including a home rule unit, may enact or enforce an ordinance that applies only to motorcycles if the principal purpose for that ordinance is to restrict the access of motorcycles to any highway or portion of a highway for which federal or State funds have been used for the planning, design, construction, or maintenance of that highway. No unit of local government, including a home rule unit, may enact an ordinance requiring motorcycle users to wear protective headgear. Nothing in this subsection (e) shall affect the authority of a unit of local government to regulate motorcycles for traffic control purposes or in accordance with Section 12-602 of this Code. No unit of local government, including a home rule unit, may regulate motorcycles in a manner inconsistent with this Code. This subsection (e) is a limitation under subsection (i) of Section 6 of Article VII of the Illinois Constitution on the concurrent exercise by home rule units of powers and functions exercised by the State.

P.A. 76-1586, § 11-208, eff. July 1, 1970. Amended by P.A. 81-176, § 1, eff. Jan. 1, 1980; P.A. 83-831, § 1, eff. Jan. 1, 1984; P.A. 83-1058, § 1, eff. July 1, 1984; P.A. 83-1110, § 2, eff. May 25, 1984; P.A. 83-1316, § 1, eff. Jan. 1, 1985; P.A. 83-1362, Art. II, § 99, eff. Sept. 11, 1984; P.A. 83-1528, Art. II, § 24, eff. Jan. 17, 1985; P.A. 85-532, § 1, eff. Jan. 1, 1988; P.A. 88-685, § 5, eff. Jan. 24, 1995; P.A. 90-106, § 5, eff. Jan. 1, 1998; P.A. 90-513, § 5, eff. Aug. 22, 1997; P.A. 90-655, § 153, eff. July 30, 1998; P.A. 91-519, § 5, eff. Jan. 1, 2000.

Formerly Ill.Rev.Stat.1991, ch. 95 ½, ¶ 11-208.

5/11-208.1. Uniformity

§ 11-208.1. Uniformity. The provisions of this Chapter of this Act, as amended, and the rules and regulations promulgated thereunder by any State Officer, Office, Agency, Department or Commission, shall be applicable and uniformly applied and enforced throughout this State, in all other political subdivisions and in all units of local government.

P.A. 76-1586, § 11-208.1, added by P.A. 77-706, § 1, eff. Aug. 12, 1971.

Formerly Ill.Rev.Stat.1991, ch. 95 ½, ¶ 11-208.1.

5/11-208.2. Limitation on home rule units

Text of section effective until June 1, 2003

§ 11-208.2. Limitation on home rule units. The provisions of this Chapter of this Act limit the authority of home rule units to adopt local police regulations inconsistent herewith except pursuant to Sections 11-208 and 11-209 of this Chapter of this Act.

P.A. 76-1586, § 11-208.2, added by P.A. 77-706, § 1, eff. Aug. 12, 1971.

Formerly Ill.Rev.Stat.1991, ch. 95 ½, ¶ 11-208.2.

For text of section effective June 1, 2003, see 625 ILCS 5/11-208.2, post

5/11-208.2. Limitation on home rule units

Text of section effective June 1, 2003

§ 11-208.2. Limitation on home rule units.

The provisions of this Chapter of this Act limit the authority of home rule units to adopt local police regulations inconsistent herewith except pursuant to Sections 11-208, 11-209, 11-1005.1, 11-1412.1, and 11-1412.2 of this Chapter of this Act.

P.A. 76-1586, § 11-208.2, added by P.A. 77-706, § 1, eff. Aug. 12, 1971. Amended by P.A. 92-868, § 5, eff. June 1, 2003.

Formerly Ill.Rev.Stat.1991, ch. 95 ½, ¶ 11-208.2.

For text of section effective until June 1, 2003, see 625 ILCS 5/11-208.2, ante

5/11-208.3. Administrative adjudication of violations of traffic regulations concerning the standing, parking, or condition of vehicles

§ 11-208.3. Administrative adjudication of violations of traffic regulations concerning the standing, parking, or condition of vehicles.

(a) Any municipality may provide by ordinance for a system of administrative adjudication of vehicular standing and parking violations and vehicle compliance violations as defined in this subsection. The administrative system shall have as its purpose the fair and efficient enforcement of municipal regulations through the administrative adjudication of violations of municipal ordinances regulating the standing and parking of vehicles, the condition and use of vehicle equipment, and the display of municipal wheel tax licenses within the municipality's borders. The administrative system shall only have authority to adjudicate civil offenses carrying fines not in excess of $250 that occur after the effective date of the ordinance adopting such a system under this Section. For purposes of this Section, "compliance violation" means a violation of a municipal regulation governing the condition or use of equipment on a vehicle or governing the display of a municipal wheel tax license.

(b) Any ordinance establishing a system of administrative adjudication under this Section shall provide for:

(1) A traffic compliance administrator authorized to adopt, distribute and process parking and compliance violation notices and other notices required by this Section, collect money paid as fines and penalties for violation of parking and compliance ordinances, and operate an administrative adjudication system. The traffic compliance administrator also may make a certified report to the Secretary of State under Section 6-306.5.

(2) A parking, standing, or compliance violation notice that shall specify the date, time, and place of violation of a parking, standing, or compliance regulation; the particular regulation violated; the fine and any penalty that may be assessed for late payment, when so provided by ordinance; the vehicle make and state registration number; and the

identification number of the person issuing the notice. With regard to municipalities with a population of 1 million or more, it shall be grounds for dismissal of a parking violation if the State registration number or vehicle make specified is incorrect. The violation notice shall state that the payment of the indicated fine, and of any applicable penalty for late payment, shall operate as a final disposition of the violation. The notice also shall contain information as to the availability of a hearing in which the violation may be contested on its merits. The violation notice shall specify the time and manner in which a hearing may be had.

(3) Service of the parking, standing, or compliance violation notice by affixing the original or a facsimile of the notice to an unlawfully parked vehicle or by handing the notice to the operator of a vehicle if he or she is present. A person authorized by ordinance to issue and serve parking, standing, and compliance violation notices shall certify as to the correctness of the facts entered on the violation notice by signing his or her name to the notice at the time of service or in the case of a notice produced by a computerized device, by signing a single certificate to be kept by the traffic compliance administrator attesting to the correctness of all notices produced by the device while it was under his or her control. The original or a facsimile of the violation notice or, in the case of a notice produced by a computerized device, a printed record generated by the device showing the facts entered on the notice, shall be retained by the traffic compliance administrator, and shall be a record kept in the ordinary course of business. A parking, standing, or compliance violation notice issued, signed and served in accordance with this Section, a copy of the notice, or the computer generated record shall be prima facie correct and shall be prima facie evidence of the correctness of the facts shown on the notice. The notice, copy, or computer generated record shall be admissible in any subsequent administrative or legal proceedings.

(4) An opportunity for a hearing for the registered owner of the vehicle cited in the parking, standing, or compliance violation notice in which the owner may contest the merits of the alleged violation, and during which formal or technical rules of evidence shall not apply; provided, however, that under Section 11-1306 of this Code the lessee of a vehicle cited in the violation notice likewise shall be provided an opportunity for a hearing of the same kind afforded the registered owner. The hearings shall be recorded, and the person conducting the hearing on behalf of the traffic compliance administrator shall be empowered to administer oaths and to secure by subpoena both the attendance and testimony of witnesses and the production of relevant books and papers. Persons appearing at a hearing under this Section may be represented by counsel at their expense. The ordinance may also provide for internal administrative review following the decision of the hearing officer.

(5) Service of additional notices, sent by first class United States mail, postage prepaid, to the address of the registered owner of the cited vehicle as recorded with the Secretary of State or, under Section 11-1306 of this Code, to the lessee of the cited vehicle at the last address known to the lessor of the cited vehicle at the time of lease. The service shall be deemed complete as of the date of deposit in the United States mail. The notices shall be in the following sequence and shall include but not be limited to the information specified herein:

(i) A second notice of violation. This notice shall specify the date and location of the violation cited in the parking, standing, or compliance violation notice, the particular regulation violated, the vehicle make and state registration number, the fine and any penalty that may be assessed for late payment when so provided by ordinance, the availability of a hearing in which the violation may be contested on its merits, and the time and manner in which the hearing may be had. The notice of violation shall also state that failure either to pay the indicated fine and any applicable penalty, or to appear at a hearing on the merits in the time and manner specified, will result in a final determination of violation liability for the cited violation in the amount of the fine or penalty indicated, and that, upon the occurrence of a final determination of violation liability for the failure, and the exhaustion of, or failure to exhaust, available administrative or judicial procedures for review, any unpaid fine or penalty will constitute a debt due and owing the municipality.

(ii) A notice of final determination of parking, standing, or compliance violation liability. This notice shall be sent following a final determination of parking, standing, or compliance violation liability and the conclusion of judicial review procedures taken under this Section. The notice shall state that the unpaid fine or penalty is a debt due and owing the municipality. The notice shall contain warnings that failure to pay any fine or penalty due and owing the municipality within the time specified may result in the municipality's filing of a petition in the Circuit Court to have the unpaid fine or penalty rendered a judgment as provided by this Section, or may result in suspension of the person's drivers license for failure to pay fines or penalties for 10 or more parking violations under Section 6-306.5.

(6) A Notice of impending drivers license suspension. This notice shall be sent to the person liable for any fine or penalty that remains due and owing on 10 or more parking violations. The notice shall state that failure to pay the fine or penalty owing within 45 days of the notice's date will result in the municipality notifying the Secretary of State that the person is eligible for initiation of suspension proceedings under Section 6-306.5 of this Code. The notice shall also state that the person may obtain a photostatic copy of an original ticket imposing a fine or penalty by sending a self addressed, stamped envelope to the municipality along with a request for the photostatic copy. The notice of impending drivers license suspension shall be sent by first class United States mail, postage prepaid, to the address recorded with the Secretary of State.

(7) Final determinations of violation liability. A final determination of violation liability shall occur following failure to pay the fine or penalty after a hearing officer's determination of violation liability and the exhaustion of or failure to exhaust any administrative review procedures provided by ordinance. Where a person fails to appear at a hearing to contest the alleged violation in the time and manner specified in a prior mailed notice, the hearing officer's determination of violation liability shall become final: (A) upon denial of a timely petition to set aside that determination, or (B) upon expiration of the period for filing the petition without a filing having been made.

(8) A petition to set aside a determination of parking, standing, or compliance violation liability that may be filed by a person owing an unpaid fine or penalty. The petition shall be filed with and ruled upon by the traffic compliance administrator in the manner and within the time specified by ordinance. The grounds for the petition may be limited to: (A) the person not having been the owner or lessee of

the cited vehicle on the date the violation notice was issued, (B) the person having already paid the fine or penalty for the violation in question, and (C) excusable failure to appear at or request a new date for a hearing. With regard to municipalities with a population of 1 million or more, it shall be grounds for dismissal of a parking violation if the State registration number or vehicle make specified is incorrect. After the determination of parking, standing, or compliance violation liability has been set aside upon a showing of just cause, the registered owner shall be provided with a hearing on the merits for that violation.

(9) Procedures for non-residents. Procedures by which persons who are not residents of the municipality may contest the merits of the alleged violation without attending a hearing.

(10) A schedule of civil fines for violations of vehicular standing, parking, and compliance regulations enacted by ordinance pursuant to this Section, and a schedule of penalties for late payment of the fines, provided, however, that the total amount of the fine and penalty for any one violation shall not exceed $250.

(11) Other provisions as are necessary and proper to carry into effect the powers granted and purposes stated in this Section.

(c) Any municipality establishing vehicular standing, parking, and compliance regulations under this Section may also provide by ordinance for a program of vehicle immobilization for the purpose of facilitating enforcement of those regulations. The program of vehicle immobilization shall provide for immobilizing any eligible vehicle upon the public way by presence of a restraint in a manner to prevent operation of the vehicle. Any ordinance establishing a program of vehicle immobilization under this Section shall provide:

(1) Criteria for the designation of vehicles eligible for immobilization. A vehicle shall be eligible for immobilization when the registered owner of the vehicle has accumulated the number of unpaid final determinations of parking, standing, or compliance violation liability as determined by ordinance.

(2) A notice of impending vehicle immobilization and a right to a hearing to challenge the validity of the notice by disproving liability for the unpaid final determinations of parking, standing, or compliance violation liability listed on the notice.

(3) The right to a prompt hearing after a vehicle has been immobilized or subsequently towed without payment of the outstanding fines and penalties on parking, standing, or compliance violations for which final determinations have been issued. An order issued after the hearing is a final administrative decision within the meaning of Section 3-101 of the Code of Civil Procedure.[1]

(4) A post immobilization and post-towing notice advising the registered owner of the vehicle of the right to a hearing to challenge the validity of the impoundment.

(d) Judicial review of final determinations of parking, standing, and compliance violations and final administrative decisions issued after hearings regarding vehicle immobilization and impoundment made under this Section shall be subject to the provisions of the Administrative Review Law.[2]

(e) Any fine, penalty, or part of any fine or any penalty remaining unpaid after the exhaustion of, or the failure to exhaust, administrative remedies created under this Section and the conclusion of any judicial review procedures shall be a debt due and owing the municipality and, as such, may be collected in accordance with applicable law. Payment in full of any fine or penalty resulting from a standing, parking, or compliance violation shall constitute a final disposition of that violation.

(f) After the expiration of the period within which judicial review may be sought for a final determination of parking, standing, or compliance violation, the municipality may commence a proceeding in the Circuit Court for purposes of obtaining a judgment on the final determination of violation. Nothing in this Section shall prevent a municipality from consolidating multiple final determinations of parking, standing, or compliance violation against a person in a proceeding. Upon commencement of the action, the municipality shall file a certified copy of the final determination of parking, standing, or compliance violation, which shall be accompanied by a certification that recites facts sufficient to show that the final determination of violation was issued in accordance with this Section and the applicable municipal ordinance. Service of the summons and a copy of the petition may be by any method provided by Section 2-203 of the Code of Civil Procedure[3] or by certified mail, return receipt requested, provided that the total amount of fines and penalties for final determinations of parking, standing, or compliance violations does not exceed $2500. If the court is satisfied that the final determination of parking, standing, or compliance violation was entered in accordance with the requirements of this Section and the applicable municipal ordinance, and that the registered owner or the lessee, as the case may be, had an opportunity for an administrative hearing and for judicial review as provided in this Section, the court shall render judgment in favor of the municipality and against the registered owner or the lessee for the amount indicated in the final determination of parking, standing, or compliance violation, plus costs. The judgment shall have the same effect and may be enforced in the same manner as other judgments for the recovery of money.

P.A. 76-1586, § 11-208.3, added by P.A. 85-876, § 2, eff. Nov. 6, 1987. Amended by P.A. 86-947, § 2, eff. Nov. 13, 1989; P.A. 87-181, § 1, eff. Sept. 3, 1991; P.A. 88-415, § 10, eff. Aug. 20, 1993; P.A. 88-437, § 5, eff. Jan. 1, 1994; P.A. 88-670, Art. 2, § 2-59, eff. Dec. 2, 1994; P.A. 89-190, § 5, eff. Jan. 1, 1996; P.A. 92-695, § 10, eff. Jan. 1, 2003.

[1] 735 ILCS 5/3-101.

[2] 735 ILCS 5/3-101 et seq.

[3] 735 ILCS 5/2-203.

5/11-208.4. § 11-208.4. Repealed effective Dec. 31, 1994

5/11-209. Powers of municipalities and counties—Contract with school boards, hospitals, churches, condominium complex unit owners' associations, and commercial and industrial facility, shopping center, and apartment complex owners for regulation of traffic

§ 11-209. Powers of municipalities and counties—Contract with school boards, hospitals, churches, condominium complex unit owners' associations, and commercial and industrial facility, shopping center, and apartment complex owners for regulation of traffic.

(a) The corporate authorities of any municipality or the county board of any county, and a school board, hospital, church, condominium complex unit owners' association, or owner of any commercial and industrial facility, shopping center, or apartment complex which controls a parking area located within the limits of the municipality, or outside the limits of the municipality and within the boundaries of the county, may, by contract, empower the municipality or county to regulate the parking of automobiles and the traffic at such parking area. Such contract shall empower the municipality or county to accomplish all or any part of the following:

1. The erection of stop signs, flashing signals, person with disabilities parking area signs or yield signs at specified locations in a parking area and the adoption of appropriate regulations thereto pertaining, or the designation of any intersection in the parking area as a stop intersection or as a yield intersection and the ordering of like signs or signals at one or more entrances to such intersection, subject to the provisions of this Chapter.

2. The prohibition or regulation of the turning of vehicles or specified types of vehicles at intersections or other designated locations in the parking area.

3. The regulation of a crossing of any roadway in the parking area by pedestrians.

4. The designation of any separate roadway in the parking area for one-way traffic.

5. The establishment and regulation of loading zones.

6. The prohibition, regulation, restriction or limitation of the stopping, standing or parking of vehicles in specified areas of the parking area.

7. The designation of safety zones in the parking area and fire lanes.

8. Providing for the removal and storage of vehicles parked or abandoned in the parking area during snowstorms, floods, fires, or other public emergencies, or found unattended in the parking area, (a) where they constitute an obstruction to traffic, or (b) where stopping, standing or parking is prohibited, and for the payment of reasonable charges for such removal and storage by the owner or operator of any such vehicle.

9. Providing that the cost of planning, installation, maintenance and enforcement of parking and traffic regulations pursuant to any contract entered into under the authority of this paragraph (a) of this Section be borne by the municipality or county, or by the school board, hospital, church, property owner, apartment complex owner, or condominium complex unit owners' association, or that a percentage of the cost be shared by the parties to the contract.

10. Causing the installation of parking meters on the parking area and establishing whether the expense of installing said parking meters and maintenance thereof shall be that of the municipality or county, or that of the school board, hospital, church, condominium complex unit owners' association, shopping center or apartment complex owner. All moneys obtained from such parking meters as may be installed on any parking area shall belong to the municipality or county.

11. Causing the installation of parking signs in accordance with Section 11–301 in areas of the parking lots covered by this Section and where desired by the person contracting with the appropriate authority listed in paragraph (a) of this Section, indicating that such parking spaces are reserved for persons with disabilities.

12. Contracting for such additional reasonable rules and regulations with respect to traffic and parking in a parking area as local conditions may require for the safety and convenience of the public or of the users of the parking area.

(b) No contract entered into pursuant to this Section shall exceed a period of 20 years. No lessee of a shopping center or apartment complex shall enter into such a contract for a longer period of time than the length of his lease.

(c) Any contract entered into pursuant to this Section shall be recorded in the office of the recorder in the county in which the parking area is located, and no regulation made pursuant to the contract shall be effective or enforceable until 3 days after the contract is so recorded.

(d) At such time as parking and traffic regulations have been established at any parking area pursuant to the contract as provided for in this Section, then it shall be a petty offense for any person to do any act forbidden or to fail to perform any act required by such parking or traffic regulation. If the violation is the parking in a parking space reserved for persons with disabilities under paragraph (11) of this Section, by a person without special registration plates issued to a person with disabilities, as defined by Section 1–159.1, pursuant to Section 3–616 of this Code, or to a disabled veteran pursuant to Section 3–609 of this Code, the local police of the contracting corporate municipal authorities shall issue a parking ticket to such parking violator and issue a fine in accordance with Section 11–1301.3.

(e) The term "shopping center", as used in this Section, means premises having one or more stores or business establishments in connection with which there is provided on privately-owned property near or contiguous thereto an area, or areas, of land used by the public as the means of access to and egress from the stores and business establishments on such premises and for the parking of motor vehicles of customers and patrons of such stores and business establishments on such premises.

(f) The term "parking area", as used in this Section, means an area, or areas, of land near or contiguous to a school, church, or hospital building, shopping center, apartment complex, or condominium complex, but not the public highways or alleys, and used by the public as the means of access to and egress from such buildings and the stores and business establishments at a shopping center and for the parking of motor vehicles.

(g) The terms "owner", "property owner", "shopping center owner", and "apartment complex owner", as used in this Section, mean the actual legal owner of the shopping center parking area or apartment complex, the trust officer of a banking institution having the right to manage and control such property, or a person having the legal right, through lease or otherwise, to manage or control the property.

(g–5) The term "condominium complex unit owners' association", as used in this Section, means a "unit owners' association" as defined in Section 2 of the Condominium Property Act.[1]

(h) The term "fire lane", as used in this Section, means travel lanes for the fire fighting equipment upon which there shall be no standing or parking of any motor vehicle at any time so that fire fighting equipment can move freely thereon.

(i) The term "apartment complex", as used in this Section, means premises having one or more apartments in connection with which there is provided on privately-owned property near or contiguous thereto an area, or areas, of land used by occupants of such apartments or their guests as a means of access to and egress from such apartments or for the parking of motor vehicles of such occupants or their guests.

(j) The term "condominium complex", as used in this Section, means the units, common elements, and limited common elements that are located on the parcels, as those terms are defined in Section 2 of the Condominium Property Act.

(k) The term "commercial and industrial facility", as used in this Section, means a premises containing one or more commercial and industrial facility establishments in connection with which there is provided on privately-owned property near or contiguous to the premises an area or areas of land used by the public as the means of access to and egress from the commercial and industrial facility establishment on the premises and for the parking of motor vehicles of customers, patrons, and employees of the commercial and industrial facility establishment on the premises.

(*l*) The provisions of this Section shall not be deemed to prevent local authorities from enforcing, on private property, local ordinances imposing fines, in accordance with Section 11-1301.3, as penalties for use of any parking place reserved for persons with disabilities, as defined by Section 1-159.1, or disabled veterans by any person using a motor vehicle not bearing registration plates specified in Section 11-1301.1 or a special decal or device as defined in Section 11-1301.2 as evidence that the vehicle is operated by or for a person with disabilities or disabled veteran.

This amendatory Act of 1972 is not a prohibition upon the contractual and associational powers granted by Article VII, Section 10 of the Illinois Constitution.

P.A. 76-1586, § 11-209, eff. July 1, 1970. Amended by P.A. 77-1191, § 1, eff. Aug. 9, 1971; P.A. 77-2298, § 1, eff. Oct. 1, 1972; P.A. 77-2720, § 1, eff. Jan. 1, 1973; P.A. 78-255, § 26, eff. Oct. 1, 1973; P.A. 81-171, § 1, eff. Jan. 1, 1980; P.A. 83-358, § 67, eff. Sept. 14, 1983; P.A. 83-1058, § 1, eff. July 1, 1984; P.A. 83-1316, § 1, eff. Jan. 1, 1985; P.A. 83-1362, Art. II, § 99, eff. Sept. 11, 1984; P.A. 86-1179, § 2, eff. Aug. 17, 1990; P.A. 88-685, § 5, eff. Jan. 24, 1995; P.A. 89-551, § 5, eff. Jan. 1, 1997; P.A. 90-106, § 5, eff. Jan. 1, 1998; P.A. 90-145, § 15, eff. Jan. 1, 1998; P.A. 90-481, § 30, eff. Aug. 17, 1997; P.A. 90-655, § 153, eff. July 30, 1998.

Formerly Ill.Rev.Stat.1991, ch. 95 ½, ¶ 11-209.

1 765 ILCS 605/2.

P.A. 90-655, the First 1998 General Revisory Act, amended various Acts to delete obsolete text, to correct patent and technical errors, to revise cross references, to resolve multiple actions in the 89th and 90th General Assemblies and to make certain technical corrections in P.A. 89-708 through P.A. 90-566.

5/11-209.1. Powers of local authorities—enforcing the provisions of this Code on private streets and roads

§ 11-209.1. Powers of local authorities—enforcing the provisions of this Code on private streets and roads. (a) Any person or board of directors owning, operating or representing a residential subdivision, development, apartment house or apartment project, containing a minimum of 10 apartments or single family residences may file a written request, with the appropriate local authority wherein such property is situated, requesting their law enforcement agency enforce the provisions of this Code on all private streets or roads open to or used by the tenants, owners, employees or the public for the purposes of vehicular traffic by permission of such person or board of directors and not as a matter of public right. Notwithstanding Section 1-126 and Section 1-201 of this Code, if the local authority grants such request by the adoption of an enabling ordinance then all such private streets or roads shall be considered "highways" only for the enforcement purposes of this Code.

(b) All regulations adopted and traffic control devices employed by a local authority in the enforcement of this Code on such streets or roads within any private area, pursuant to this Section, shall be consistent with the provisions of this Code and shall conform to the Illinois Manual on Uniform Traffic Control Devices.

A local authority may require that any person who files a request for the installation of traffic signs pay for the cost of such traffic signs. Such traffic signs shall be in conformity with Section 11-604 of this Code.

(c) Any person or board of directors which has filed such a request under this Section, may rescind that request by filing with the appropriate local authority a written request for such rescission. Upon receipt of the written request, the local authority shall subsequently repeal the original enabling ordinance. Such repeal shall not take effect until the first day of January following any such action by the local authorities. However, no such rescission request may be filed within 12 months of the date of the original written request.

(d) The filing of a written request or the adoption of the enabling ordinance under this Section in no way constitutes a dedication to public use of any street, road, driveway, trail, terrace, bridle path, parkway, parking area, or other roadway open to or used by vehicular traffic, nor does it prevent such person or board of directors, as owners of such property, from requiring additional regulations than those specified by the local authorities or otherwise regulating such use as may seem best to such person or board of directors as long as they do not conflict with the powers granted to local authorities under Section 11-208 of this Code.

(e) This amendatory act of 1972 is not a prohibition upon the contractual and associational powers granted by Article VII, Section 10 of the Illinois Constitution.

P.A. 76-1586, § 11-209.1, added by P.A. 77-2296, § 1, eff. Oct. 1, 1972. Amended by P.A. 83-1473, § 3, eff. Jan. 1, 1985; P.A. 84-986, § 1, eff. Sept. 25, 1985; P.A. 86-521, § 1, eff. Sept. 1, 1989.

Formerly Ill.Rev.Stat.1991, ch. 95 ½, ¶ 11-209.1.

5/11-210. This Chapter not to interfere with rights of owners of real property with reference thereto

§ 11-210. This Chapter not to interfere with rights of owners of real property with reference thereto. Nothing in this Chapter shall be construed to prevent the owner of real property used by the public for purposes of vehicular travel by permission of the owner and not as matter of right from prohibiting such use, or from requiring other or different or additional conditions than those specified in this Chapter, or otherwise regulating such use as may seem best to such owner.

P.A. 76-1586, § 11-210, eff. July 1, 1970.

Formerly Ill.Rev.Stat.1991, ch. 95 ½, ¶ 11-210.

5/11-211. Local laws

§ 11-211. Local laws. No owner of a motor vehicle shall be limited as to speed upon any public place, at any time when the same is or may hereafter be opened to the use of persons having or using other vehicles, nor be required to comply with other provisions or conditions as to the use of such motor vehicles except as in this Chapter provided, and except as is provided in this Act.

P.A. 76-1586, § 11-211, eff. July 1, 1970. Amended by P.A. 77-1344, § 1, eff. Aug. 27, 1971.

Formerly Ill.Rev.Stat.1991, ch. 95 ½, ¶ 11-211.

ARTICLE III. TRAFFIC SIGNS, SIGNALS AND MARKINGS

5/11-301. Department to adopt sign manual

§ 11-301. Department to adopt sign manual.

(a) The Department shall adopt a State manual and specifications for a uniform system of traffic-control devices consistent with this Chapter for use upon highways within this State. Such manual shall include the adoption of the R 7-8 sign adopted by the United States Department of Transportation to designate the reservation of parking facilities for a person with disabilities. Non-conforming signs in use prior to January 1, 1985 shall not constitute a violation during their useful lives, which shall not be extended by other means than normal maintenance. The manual shall also specify insofar as practicable the minimum warrants justifying the use of the various traffic control devices. Such uniform system shall correlate with and, where not inconsistent with Illinois highway conditions, conform to the system set forth in the most recent edition of the national manual on Uniform Traffic Control Devices for Streets and Highways.

(b) Signs adopted by the Department to designate the reservation of parking facilities for a person with disabilities shall also exhibit, in a manner determined by the Department, the words "$100 Fine".

(c) If the amount of a fine is changed, the Department shall change the design of the signs to indicate the current amount of the fine.

P.A. 76-1586, § 11-301, eff. July 1, 1970. Amended by P.A. 76-2159, § 1, eff. July 1, 1970; P.A. 83-1316, § 1, eff. Jan. 1, 1985; P.A. 85-484, § 1, eff. Jan. 1, 1988; P.A. 88-685, § 5, eff. Jan. 24, 1995; P.A. 89-533, § 5, eff. Jan. 1, 1997.

Formerly Ill.Rev.Stat.1991, ch. 95 ½, ¶ 11-301.

5/11-301.1. Person with disabilities sign

§ 11-301.1. Beginning July 1, 1988, all signs erected and used to designate the reservation of parking facilities for a person with disabilities shall be in a form and manner prescribed under Section 11-301 of this Code, and all parking spaces reserved for a person with disabilities, except those reserving on-street parking areas, shall be at least 16 feet wide. Non-conforming signs in use prior to July 1, 1988 shall not constitute a violation during their useful lives, which shall not be extended by means other than normal maintenance. Beginning October 1, 1992, all parking spaces reserved for a person with disabilities, except those reserving on-street parking areas, shall be at least 16 feet wide.

P.A. 76-1586, § 11-301.1, added by P.A. 85-484, § 1, eff. Jan. 1, 1988. Amended by P.A. 87-562, § 1, eff. Jan. 1, 1992; P.A. 88-685, § 5, eff. Jan. 24, 1995.

Formerly Ill.Rev.Stat.1991, ch. 95 ½, ¶ 11-301.1.

5/11-302. Authority to designate through highway and stop and yield intersections

§ 11-302. Authority to designate through highway and stop and yield intersections. (a) The Department with reference to State highways under its jurisdiction, local authorities and road district highway commissioners with reference to other highways under their jurisdiction may designate through highways and erect stop signs or yield signs at specified entrances thereto, or may designate any intersection as a stop intersection or as a yield intersection and erect stop signs or yield signs at one or more entrances to such intersection. Designation of through highways and stop or yield intersections and the erection of stop signs or yield signs on township or road district roads are subject to the written approval of the county engineer or superintendent of highways.

(b) Every stop sign and yield sign shall conform to the State Manual and Specifications and shall be located as near as practicable to the nearest line of the crosswalk on the near side of the intersection or, if there is no crosswalk, then as close as practicable to the nearest line of the intersecting roadway.

(c) The Department may in its discretion and when traffic conditions warrant such action give preference to traffic upon any of the State highways under its jurisdiction over traffic crossing or entering such highway by erecting appropriate traffic control devices.

P.A. 76-1586, § 11-302, eff. July 1, 1970. Amended by P.A. 87-217, § 4, eff. Jan. 1, 1992.

Formerly Ill.Rev.Stat.1991, ch. 95 ½, ¶ 11-302.

5/11-303. The Department to place signs on all State highways

§ 11-303. The Department to place signs on all State highways.

(a) The Department shall place and maintain such traffic-control devices, conforming to its manual and specifications on all highways under its jurisdiction as it shall deem necessary to indicate and to carry out the provisions of this Chapter or to regulate, warn or guide traffic.

(b) No local authority shall place or maintain any traffic-control device upon any highway under the jurisdiction of the Department except by the latter's permission.

(c) The Department shall erect and maintain guide, warning and direction signs upon highways in cities, towns and villages of which portions or lanes of such highways are under the control and jurisdiction of the Department or for which the Department has maintenance responsibility.

(d) Nothing in this Chapter shall divest the corporate authorities of park districts of power to prohibit or restrict the use of highways under their jurisdiction by certain types or weights of motor vehicles or the power of cities, villages, incorporated towns and park districts to designate highways for one-way traffic or the power of such municipal corporations to erect and maintain appropriate signs respecting such uses.

(e) Nothing in this Section shall prohibit a municipality, township, or county from erecting signs as required under the Illinois Adopt-A-Highway Act.[1]

P.A. 76-1586, § 11-303, eff. July 1, 1970. Amended by P.A. 80-1495, § 36, eff. Jan. 8, 1979; P.A. 87-1118, § 90, eff. Sept. 16, 1992.

Formerly Ill.Rev.Stat.1991, ch. 95 ½, ¶ 11-303.

[1] 605 ILCS 120/1 et seq.

5/11-304. Local traffic-control devices; tourist oriented businesses signs

§ 11-304. Local traffic-control devices; tourist oriented businesses signs.

Local authorities and road district highway commissioners in their respective maintenance jurisdiction shall place and maintain such traffic-control devices upon highways under their maintenance jurisdiction as are required to indicate and carry out the provisions of this Chapter, and local traffic ordinances or to regulate, warn, or guide traffic. All such traffic control devices shall conform to the State Manual and Specifications and shall be justified by traffic warrants stated in the Manual. Placement of traffic-control devices on township or road district roads also shall be subject to the written approval of the county engineer or superintendent of highways.

Local authorities and road district highway commissioners in their respective maintenance jurisdictions shall have the authority to install signs, in conformance with the State Manual and specifications, alerting motorists of the tourist oriented businesses available on roads under local jurisdiction in rural areas as may be required to guide motorists to the businesses. The local authorities and road district highway commissioners shall also have the authority to sell or lease space on these signs to the owners or operators of the businesses.

P.A. 76-1586, § 11-304, eff. July 1, 1970. Amended by P.A. 87-217, § 4, eff. Jan. 1, 1992; P.A. 90-519, § 5, eff. June 1, 1998.

Formerly Ill.Rev.Stat.1991, ch. 95 ½, ¶ 11-304.

5/11-305. Obedience to and required traffic-control devices

§ 11-305. Obedience to and required traffic-control devices. (a) The driver of any vehicle shall obey the instructions of any official traffic-control device applicable thereto placed or held in accordance with the provisions of this Act, unless otherwise directed by a police officer, subject to the exceptions granted the driver of an authorized emergency vehicle in this Act.

(b) It is unlawful for any person to leave the roadway and travel across private property to avoid an official traffic control device.

(c) No provision of this Act for which official traffic-control devices are required shall be enforced against an alleged violator if at the time and place of the alleged violation an official device is not in proper position and sufficiently legible to be seen by an ordinarily observant person. Whenever a particular section does not state that official traffic-control devices are required, such section shall be effective even though no devices are erected or in place.

(d) Whenever any official traffic-control device is placed or held in position approximately conforming to the requirements of this Act and purports to conform to the lawful requirements pertaining to such device, such device shall be presumed to have been so placed or held by the official act or direction of lawful authority, and comply with the requirements of this Act, unless the contrary shall be established by competent evidence.

(e) The driver of a vehicle approaching a traffic control signal on which no signal light facing such vehicle is illuminated shall stop before entering the intersection in accordance with rules applicable in making a stop at a stop sign.

P.A. 76-1586, § 11-305, eff. July 1, 1970. Amended by P.A. 76-2160, § 1, eff. July 1, 1970; P.A. 79-1069, § 1, eff. Jan. 1, 1976; P.A. 80-267, § 1, eff. Oct. 1, 1977; P.A. 84-873, § 1, eff. Jan. 1, 1986.

Formerly Ill.Rev.Stat.1991, ch. 95 ½, ¶ 11-305.

5/11-306. Traffic-control signal legend

§ 11-306. Traffic-control signal legend. Whenever traffic is controlled by traffic-control signals exhibiting different colored lights or color lighted arrows, successively one at a time or in combination, only the colors green, red and yellow shall be used, except for special pedestrian signals carrying a word legend, and the lights shall indicate and apply to drivers of vehicles and pedestrians as follows:

(a) Green indication.

1. Vehicular traffic facing a circular green signal may proceed straight through or turn right or left unless a sign at such place prohibits either such turn. Vehicular traffic, including vehicles turning right or left, shall yield the right of way to other vehicles and to pedestrians lawfully within the intersection or an adjacent crosswalk at the time such signal is exhibited.

2. Vehicular traffic facing a green arrow signal, shown alone or in combination with another indication, may cautiously enter the intersection only to make the movement indicated by such arrow, or such other movement as is permitted by other indications shown at the same time. Such vehicular traffic shall yield the right of way to pedestrians lawfully within an adjacent crosswalk and to other traffic lawfully using the intersection.

3. Unless otherwise directed by a pedestrian-control signal, as provided in Section 11-307, pedestrians facing any green signal, except when the sole green signal is a turn arrow, may proceed across the roadway within any marked or unmarked crosswalk.

(b) Steady yellow indication.

1. Vehicular traffic facing a steady circular yellow or yellow arrow signal is thereby warned that the related green movement is being terminated or that a red indication will be exhibited immediately thereafter.

2. Pedestrians facing a steady circular yellow or yellow arrow signal, unless otherwise directed by a pedestrian-control signal as provided in Section 11-307, are thereby advised that there is insufficient time to cross the roadway before a red indication is shown and no pedestrian shall then start to cross the roadway.

(c) Steady red indication.

1. Except as provided in paragraph 3 of this subsection (c), vehicular traffic facing a steady circular red signal alone shall stop at a clearly marked stop line, but if there is no such stop line, before entering the crosswalk on the near side of the intersection, or if there is no such crosswalk, then before entering the intersection, and shall remain standing until an indication to proceed is shown.

2. Except as provided in paragraph 3 of this subsection (c), vehicular traffic facing a steady red arrow signal shall not enter the intersection to make the movement indicated by the arrow and, unless entering the intersection to make a movement permitted by another signal, shall stop at a clearly marked stop line, but if there is no such stop line, before entering the crosswalk on the near side of the intersection, or if there is no such crosswalk, then before entering the intersection, and shall remain standing until an indication permitting the movement indicated by such red arrow is shown.

3. Except when a sign is in place prohibiting a turn and local authorities by ordinance or State authorities by rule or regulation prohibit any such turn, vehicular traffic facing any steady red signal may cautiously enter the intersection to turn right, or to turn left from a one-way street into a one-way street, after stopping as required by paragraph 1 or paragraph 2 of this subsection. After stopping, the driver shall yield the right of way to any vehicle in the intersection or approaching on another roadway so closely as to constitute an immediate hazard during the time such driver is moving across or within the intersection or junction or roadways. Such driver shall yield the right of way to pedestrians within the intersection or an adjacent crosswalk.

4. Unless otherwise directed by a pedestrian-control signal as provided in Section 11-307, pedestrians facing a steady circular red or red arrow signal alone shall not enter the roadway.

5. A municipality with a population of 1,000,000 or more may enact an ordinance that provides for the use of an automated red light enforcement system to enforce violations of this subsection (c) that result in or involve a motor vehicle accident, leaving the scene of a motor vehicle accident, or reckless driving that results in bodily injury.

This paragraph 5 is subject to prosecutorial discretion that is consistent with applicable law.

(d) In the event an official traffic control signal is erected and maintained at a place other than an intersection, the provisions of this Section shall be applicable except as to provisions which by their nature can have no application. Any stop required shall be at a traffic sign or a marking on the pavement indicating where the stop shall be made or, in the absence of such sign or marking, the stop shall be made at the signal.

(e) The motorman of any streetcar shall obey the above signals as applicable to vehicles.

P.A. 76-1586, § 11-306, eff. July 1, 1970. Amended by P.A. 76-1737, § 1; P.A. 78-24, § 1, eff. Jan. 1, 1974; P.A. 79-1069, § 1, eff. Jan. 1, 1976; P.A. 81-861, § 1, eff. Jan. 1, 1980; P.A. 81-1509, Art. II, § 71, eff. Sept. 26, 1980; P.A. 84-873, § 1, eff. Jan. 1, 1986; P.A. 90-86, § 5, eff. July 10, 1997; P.A. 91-357, § 231, eff. July 29, 1999.

Formerly Ill.Rev.Stat.1991, ch. 95 ½, ¶ 11-306.

5/11-307. Pedestrian-control signals

§ 11-307. Pedestrian-control signals. Whenever special pedestrian-control signals exhibiting the words "Walk" or "Don't Walk" or the illuminated symbols of a walking person or an upraised palm are in place such signals shall indicate as follows:

(a) Walk or walking person symbol. Pedestrians facing such signal may proceed across the roadway in the direction of the signal, and shall be given the right of way by the drivers of all vehicles.

(b) Don't Walk or upraised palm symbol. No pedestrian shall start to cross the roadway in the direction of such signal, but any pedestrian who has partly completed his crossing on the Walk signal or walking person symbol shall proceed to a sidewalk or safety island while the "Don't Walk" signal or upraised palm symbol is illuminated, steady, or flashing.

P.A. 76-1586, § 11-307, eff. July 1, 1970. Amended by P.A. 79-1069, § 1, eff. Jan. 1, 1976; P.A. 81-553, § 1, eff. Jan. 1, 1980.

Formerly Ill.Rev.Stat.1991, ch. 95 ½, ¶ 11-307.

5/11-308. Lane-control signals

§ 11-308. Lane-control signals. Whenever lane-control signals are used in conjunction with official signs, they shall have the following meanings:

(a) Downward-pointing green arrow. A driver facing this indication is permitted to drive in the lane over which the arrow signal is located. Otherwise he shall obey all other traffic controls present and follow normal safe driving practices.

(b) Red X symbol. A driver facing this indication shall not drive in the lane over which the signal is located, and this indication shall modify accordingly the meaning of all other traffic controls present. Otherwise he shall obey all other traffic controls and follow normal safe driving practices.

(c) Yellow X (steady). A driver facing this indication should prepare to vacate the lane over which the signal is located, in a safe manner to avoid, if possible, occupying that lane when a steady red X is displayed.

(d) Flashing yellow arrow. A driver facing this indication may use the lane only for the purpose of approaching and making a left turn.

P.A. 76-1586, § 11-308, eff. July 1, 1970. Amended by P.A. 76-2161, § 1, eff. July 1, 1970; P.A. 81-552, § 1, eff. Jan. 1, 1980.

Formerly Ill.Rev.Stat.1991, ch. 95 ½, ¶ 11-308.

5/11-309. Flashing signals

§ 11-309. Flashing signals. Whenever an illuminated flashing red or yellow signal is used in conjunction with a traffic control device it shall require obedience by vehicular traffic as follows:

1. Flashing red (stop signal). When a red lens is illuminated with rapid intermittent flashes, drivers of vehicles shall stop at a clearly marked stop line, but if none, before entering the crosswalk on the near side of the intersection, or if none, then at a point nearest the intersecting roadway where the driver has a view of approaching traffic on the intersecting roadway before entering the intersection and the right to proceed shall be subject to the rules applicable after making a stop at a stop sign.

2. Flashing yellow (caution signal). When a yellow lens is illuminated with rapid intermittent flashes, drivers of vehicles may proceed through the intersection or past such signal only with caution.

3. This section does not apply at railroad grade crossings. Conduct of drivers of vehicles approaching railroad grade crossings shall be governed by Section 11-1201 of this Act.

P.A. 76-1586, § 11-309, eff. July 1, 1970. Amended by P.A. 76-1737, § 1; P.A. 76-2162, § 1, eff. July 1, 1970.

Formerly Ill.Rev.Stat.1991, ch. 95 ½, ¶ 11-309.

5/11-310. Display of Unauthorized Signs, Signals or Markings

§ 11-310. Display of Unauthorized Signs, Signals or Markings.

(a) No person shall place, maintain or display upon or in view of any highway any unauthorized sign, signal, marking, or device which purports to be or is an imitation of or resembles an official traffic-control device or railroad sign or signal, or which attempts to direct the movement of traffic, or which hides from view or interferes with the movement of traffic or the effectiveness of an official traffic-control device or any railroad sign or signal.

(b) No person shall place or maintain nor shall any public authority permit upon any highway any traffic sign or signal bearing thereon any commercial advertising.

(c) Every such prohibited sign, signal or marking is hereby declared to be a public nuisance and the authority having jurisdiction over the highway is hereby empowered to remove the same or cause it to be removed without notice.

(d) No person shall sell or offer for sale any traffic control device to be used on any street or highway in this State which does not conform to the requirements of this Chapter.

(e) This Section shall not be deemed to prohibit the erection upon private property adjacent to highways of signs giving useful directional information and of a type that cannot be mistaken for official signs.

(f) This Section shall not be deemed to prohibit the erection of Illinois Adopt-A-Highway signs by municipalities, townships, or counties as provided in the Illinois Adopt-A-Highway Act.[1]

(g) Any person failing to comply with this Section shall be guilty of a Class A misdemeanor.

P.A. 76-1586, § 11-310, eff. July 1, 1970. Amended by P.A. 77-49, § 1, eff. Jan. 1, 1972; P.A. 77-732, § 1, eff. Aug. 12, 1971; P.A. 77-2829, § 40, eff. Dec. 22, 1972; P.A. 78-255, § 61, eff. Oct. 1, 1973; P.A. 79-1069, § 1, eff. Jan. 1, 1976; P.A. 80-911, § 1, eff. Oct. 1, 1977; P.A. 81-1509, Art. II, § 71, eff. Sept. 26, 1980; P.A. 87-1118, § 90, eff. Sept. 16, 1992.

Formerly Ill.Rev.Stat.1991, ch. 95 ½, ¶ 11-310.

1 605 ILCS 120/1 et seq.

5/11-311. Interference with official traffic-control devices or railroad signs or signals

§ 11-311. Interference with official traffic-control devices or railroad signs or signals. No person shall without lawful authority attempt to or in fact alter, deface, injure, knock down, or remove any official traffic-control device, or any railroad sign or signal or any inscription, shield, or insignia thereon, or any other part thereof.

Every person who is convicted of a violation of this Section shall be guilty of a Class A misdemeanor, punishable by a fine of at least $250 in addition to any other penalties which may be imposed.

P.A. 76-1586, § 11-311, eff. July 1, 1970. Amended by P.A. 80-911, § 1, eff. Oct. 1, 1977; P.A. 83-672, § 1, eff. Jan. 1, 1984.

Formerly Ill.Rev.Stat.1991, ch. 95 ½, ¶ 11-311.

5/11-312. Unlawful Use or Damage to Highways, Appurtenances and Structures

§ 11-312. Unlawful Use or Damage to Highways, Appurtenances and Structures. It shall be unlawful for any person to wilfully injure or damage any public highway or street or any bridge or culvert, or to wilfully damage, injure or remove any sign, signpost, or structure upon or used or constructed in connection with any public highway or street for the protection thereof or for protection or regulation of traffic thereon by any wilfully unusual, improper or unreasonable use thereof, or by wilfully careless driving or use of any vehicle thereon, or by the wilful mutilation, defacing, destruction or removal thereof.

Every person who is convicted of a violation of this Section shall be guilty of a Class A misdemeanor, punishable by a fine of at least $250 in addition to any other penalty which may be imposed.

P.A. 76-1586, § 11-312, eff. July 1, 1970. Amended by P.A. 80-911, § 1, eff. Oct. 1, 1977; P.A. 81-1509, Art. II, § 71, eff. Sept. 26, 1980; P.A. 83-672, § 1, eff. Jan. 1, 1984.

Formerly Ill.Rev.Stat.1991, ch. 95 ½, ¶ 11-312.

5/11-313. Unlawful possession of highway sign or marker

§ 11-313. Unlawful possession of highway sign or marker. The Department and local authorities, with reference to traffic control signs, signals, or markers owned by the Department or local authority, are authorized to indicate the ownership of the signs, signals, or markers in letters not less than ⅜ inch or more than ¾ inch in height, by use of a metal stamp, etching, or other permanent means and, except for employees of the Department or local authorities, police officers, contractors and their employees engaged in a highway construction contract or work on the highway approved by the Department or local authority, it is unlawful for any person to possess such sign, signal, or marker so identified.

P.A. 76-1586, § 11-313, added by P.A. 77-1230, § 1, eff. Aug. 24, 1971. Amended by P.A. 77-2830, Art. 73, § 1, eff. Jan. 1, 1973; P.A. 80-526, § 1, eff. Oct. 1, 1977; P.A. 80-911, § 1, eff. Oct. 1, 1977; P.A. 80-1364, § 36, eff. Aug. 13, 1978; P.A. 91-512, § 5, eff. Aug. 13, 1999.

Formerly Ill.Rev.Stat.1991, ch. 95 ½, ¶ 11-313.

ARTICLE IV. ACCIDENTS

Section

5/11-401. Motor vehicle accidents involving death or personal injuries

§ 11-401. Motor vehicle accidents involving death or personal injuries.

(a) The driver of any vehicle involved in a motor vehicle accident resulting in personal injury to or death of any person shall immediately stop such vehicle at the scene of such accident, or as close thereto as possible and shall then forthwith return to, and in every event shall remain at the scene of the accident until the requirements of Section 11-403 have been fulfilled. Every such stop shall be made without obstructing traffic more than is necessary.

(b) Any person who has failed to stop or to comply with the requirements of paragraph (a) shall, as soon as possible but in no case later than one hour after such motor vehicle accident, or, if hospitalized and incapacitated from reporting at any time during such period, as soon as possible but in no case later than one hour after being discharged from the hospital, report the place of the accident, the date, the approximate time, the driver's name and address, the registration number of the vehicle driven, and the names of all other occupants of such vehicle, at a police station or sheriff's office near the place where such accident occurred. No report made as required under this paragraph shall be used, directly or indirectly, as a basis for the prosecution of any violation of paragraph (a).

For purposes of this Section, personal injury shall mean any injury requiring immediate professional treatment in a medical facility or doctor's office.

(c) Any person failing to comply with paragraph (a) shall be guilty of a Class A misdemeanor.

(d) Any person failing to comply with paragraph (b) is guilty of a Class 4 felony if the motor vehicle accident does not result in the death of any person. Any person failing to comply with paragraph (b) when the accident results in the death of any person is guilty of a Class 2 felony, for which the person, if sentenced to a term of imprisonment, shall be sentenced to a term of not less than 3 years and not more than 14 years.

(e) The Secretary of State shall revoke the driving privilege of any person convicted of a violation of this Section.

P.A. 76-1586, § 11-401, eff. July 1, 1970. Amended by P.A. 77-2720, § 1, eff. Jan. 1, 1973; P.A. 82-141, § 1, eff. Jan. 1, 1982; P.A. 83-831, § 1, eff. Jan. 1, 1984; P.A. 84-272, § 7, eff. Jan. 1, 1986; P.A. 90-543, § 5, eff. Dec. 1, 1997.

Formerly Ill.Rev.Stat.1991, ch. 95 ½, ¶ 11-401.

5/11-402. Motor vehicle accident involving damage to vehicle

§ 11-402. Motor vehicle accident involving damage to vehicle. (a) The driver of any vehicle involved in a motor vehicle accident resulting only in damage to a vehicle which is driven or attended by any person shall immediately stop such vehicle at the scene of such motor vehicle accident or as close thereto as possible, but shall forthwith return to and in every event shall remain at the scene of such motor vehicle accident until the requirements of Section 11-403 have been fulfilled. Every such stop shall be made without obstructing traffic more than is necessary.

Any person failing to comply with this Section shall be guilty of a Class A misdemeanor.

(b) Upon conviction of a violation of this Section, the court shall make a finding as to whether the damage to a vehicle is in excess of $1,000, and in such case a statement of this finding shall be reported to the Secretary of State with the report of conviction as required by Section 6-204 of this Code. Upon receipt of such report of conviction and statement of finding that the damage to a vehicle is in excess of $1,000, the Secretary of State shall suspend the driver's license or any nonresident's driving privilege.

P.A. 76-1586, § 11-402, eff. July 1, 1970. Amended by P.A. 80-911, § 1, eff. Oct. 1, 1977; P.A. 82-141, § 1, eff. Jan. 1, 1982; P.A. 83-831, § 1, eff. Jan. 1, 1984.

Formerly Ill.Rev.Stat.1991, ch. 95 ½, ¶ 11-402.

5/11-403. Duty to give information and render aid

§ 11-403. Duty to give information and render aid. The driver of any vehicle involved in a motor vehicle accident resulting in injury to or death of any person or damage to any vehicle which is driven or attended by any person shall give the driver's name, address, registration number and owner of the vehicle the driver is operating and shall upon request and if available exhibit such driver's license to the person struck or the driver or occupant of or person attending any vehicle collided with and shall render to any person injured in such accident reasonable assistance, including the carrying or the making of arrangements for the carrying of such person to a physician, surgeon or hospital for medical or surgical treatment, if it is apparent that such treatment is necessary or if such carrying is requested by the injured person.

If none of the persons entitled to information pursuant to this Section is in condition to receive and understand such information and no police officer is present, such driver after rendering reasonable assistance shall forthwith report such motor vehicle accident at the nearest office of a duly authorized police authority, disclosing the information required by this Section.

Any person failing to comply with this Section shall be guilty of a Class A misdemeanor.

P.A. 76-1586, § 11-403, eff. July 1, 1970. Amended by P.A. 80-911, § 1, eff. Oct. 1, 1977; P.A. 83-831, § 1, eff. Jan. 1, 1984.

Formerly Ill.Rev.Stat.1991, ch. 95 ½, ¶ 11-403.

5/11-404. Duty upon damaging unattended vehicle or other property

§ 11-404. Duty upon damaging unattended vehicle or other property. The driver of any vehicle which collides with or is involved in a motor vehicle accident with any vehicle which is unattended, or other property, resulting in any damage to such other vehicle or property shall immediately stop and shall then and there either locate and notify the operator or owner of such vehicle or other property of the driver's name, address, registration number and owner of the vehicle the driver was operating or shall attach securely in a conspicuous place on or in the vehicle or other property struck a written notice giving the driver's name, address, registration number and owner of the vehicle the driver was driving and shall without unnecessary delay notify the nearest office of a duly authorized police authority and shall make a written report of such accident when and as required in Section 11-406. Every such stop shall be made without obstructing traffic more than is necessary.

Any person failing to comply with this Section shall be guilty of a Class A misdemeanor.

P.A. 76-1586, § 11-404, eff. July 1, 1970. Amended by P.A. 76-1737, § 1; P.A. 80-911, § 1, eff. Oct. 1, 1977; P.A. 83-831, § 1, eff. Jan. 1, 1984.

Formerly Ill.Rev.Stat.1991, ch. 95 ½, ¶ 11-404.

5/11–405. § 11–405. Repealed by P.A. 76–1738, § 2

5/11–406. Duty to report accident

§ 11–406. Duty to report accident. (a) The driver of a vehicle that is in any manner involved in an accident within this State, resulting in injury to or death of any person, or in which damage to the property of any one person, including himself, in excess of $500 is sustained, shall, as soon as possible but not later than 10 days after the accident, forward a written report of the accident to the Administrator.

(b) Whenever a school bus is involved in an accident in this State, caused by a collision, a sudden stop or otherwise, resulting in any property damage, personal injury or death and whenever an accident occurs within 50 feet of a school bus in this State resulting in personal injury to or the death of any person while awaiting or preparing to board the bus or immediately after exiting the bus, the driver shall as soon as possible but not later than 10 days after the accident, forward a written report to the Department of Transportation. If a report is also required under Subsection (a) of this Section, that report and the report required by this Subsection shall be submitted on a single form.

(c) The Administrator may require any driver, occupant or owner of a vehicle involved in an accident of which report must be made as provided in this Section or Section 11–410 of this Chapter to file supplemental reports whenever the original report is insufficient in the opinion of the Secretary of State or the Administrator, and may require witnesses of the accident to submit written reports to the Administrator. The report may include photographs, charts, sketches, and graphs.

(d) Should the Administrator learn through other reports of accidents required by law of the occurrence of an accident reportable under this Article and the driver, owner, or witness has not reported as required under Subsections (a), (b) or (c) of this Section or Section 11–410, within the time specified, the person is not relieved of the responsibility and the Administrator shall notify the person by first class mail directed to his last known address of his legal obligation. However, the notification is not a condition precedent to impose the penalty for failure to report as provided in Subsection (e).

(e) The Secretary of State shall suspend the driver's license or any non-resident's driving privilege of any person who fails or neglects to make report of a traffic accident as required or as required by any other law of this State.

P.A. 76–1586, § 11–406, eff. July 1, 1970. Amended by P.A. 76–2473, § 1, eff. July 1, 1971; P.A. 77–42, § 1, eff. July 1, 1971; P.A. 77–1910, § 1, eff. July 1, 1972; P.A. 78–255, § 61, eff. Oct. 1, 1973; P.A. 78–1244, § 1, eff. Sept. 5, 1974; P.A. 78–1297, § 58, eff. March 4, 1975; P.A. 80–746, § 1, eff. Oct. 1, 1977; P.A. 87–829, § 1, eff. Jan. 17, 1992.

Formerly Ill.Rev.Stat.1991, ch. 95 ½, ¶ 11–406.

5/11–407. Immediate notice of accident

§ 11–407. Immediate notice of accident. (a) The driver of a vehicle which is in any manner involved in an accident described in Section 11–406 of this Chapter shall, if no police officer is present, give notice of the accident by the fastest available means of communication to the local police department if such accident occurs within a municipality or otherwise to the nearest office of the county sheriff or nearest headquarters of the Illinois State Police.

(b) Whenever the driver of a vehicle is physically incapable of giving immediate notice of an accident as required in Subsection (a) and there was another occupant in the vehicle at the time of the accident capable of doing so, that occupant must give notice as required in Subsection (a).

P.A. 76–1586, § 11–407, eff. July 1, 1970. Amended by P.A. 76–2163, § 1, eff. July 1, 1970.

Formerly Ill.Rev.Stat.1991, ch. 95 ½, ¶ 11–407.

5/11–408. Police to report motor vehicle accident investigations

§ 11–408. Police to report motor vehicle accident investigations.

(a) Every law enforcement officer who investigates a motor vehicle accident for which a report is required by this Article or who prepares a written report as a result of an investigation either at the time and scene of such motor vehicle accident or thereafter by interviewing participants or witnesses shall forward a written report of such motor vehicle accident to the Administrator on forms provided by the Administrator under Section 11–411 within 10 days after investigation of the motor vehicle accident, or within such other time as is prescribed by the Administrator. Such written reports required to be forwarded by law enforcement officers and the information contained therein are privileged as to the Secretary of State and the Department and, in the case of second division vehicles operated under certificate of convenience and necessity issued by the Illinois Commerce Commission, to the Commission, but shall not be held confidential by the reporting law enforcement officer or agency. The Secretary of State may also disclose notations of accident involvement maintained on individual driving records. However, the Administrator or the Secretary of State may require a supplemental written report from the reporting law enforcement officer and such supplemental report shall be for the privileged use of the Secretary of State and the Department and shall be held confidential.

(b) The Department at its discretion may require a supplemental written report from the reporting law enforcement officer on a form supplied by the Department to be submitted directly to the Department. Such supplemental report may be used only for accident studies and statistical or analytical purposes, and shall be for the privileged use of the Department and shall be held confidential.

(c) The Department at its discretion may also provide for in-depth investigations of a motor vehicle accident by individuals or special investigation groups, including but not limited to police officers, photographers, engineers, doctors, mechanics, and as a result of the investigation may require the submission of written reports, photographs, charts, sketches, graphs, or a combination of all. Such individual written reports, photographs, charts, sketches, or graphs may be used only for accident studies and statistical or analytical purposes, shall be for the privileged use of the Department and held confidential, and shall not be used in any trial, civil or criminal.

(d) On and after July 1, 1997, law enforcement officers who have reason to suspect that the motor vehicle accident was the result of a driver's loss of consciousness due to a medical condition, as defined by the Driver's License Medical Review Law of 1992,[1] or the result of any medical condition that impaired the driver's ability to safely operate a motor vehicle shall notify the Secretary of this determination. The Secretary, in conjunction with the Driver's License Medical Advisory Board, shall determine by administrative rule the temporary conditions not required to be reported under the provisions of this Section. The Secretary shall, in conjunction with the Illinois State Police and representatives of local and county law enforcement agencies, promulgate any rules necessary and develop the procedures and documents that may be required to obtain written, electronic, or other agreed upon methods of notification to implement the provisions of this Section.

(e) Law enforcement officers reporting under the provisions of subsection (d) of this Section shall enjoy the same immunities granted members of the Driver's License Medical Advisory Board under Section 6-910 of this Code.

(f) All information furnished to the Secretary under subsection (d) of this Section shall be deemed confidential and for the privileged use of the Secretary in accordance with the provisions of subsection (j) of Section 2-123 of this Code.

P.A. 76-1586, § 11-408, eff. July 1, 1970. Amended by P.A. 76-2473, § 1, eff. July 1, 1971; P.A. 77-42, § 1, eff. July 1, 1971; P.A. 77-1910, § 1, eff. July 1, 1972; P.A. 78-255, § 61, eff. Oct. 1, 1973; P.A. 79-865, § 1, eff. Jan. 1, 1976; P.A. 83-831, § 1, eff. Jan. 1, 1984; P.A. 89-503, § 10, eff. July 1, 1996; P.A. 89-584, § 5, eff. July 31, 1996; P.A. 90-14, Art. 2, § 2-225, eff. July 1, 1997.

Formerly Ill.Rev.Stat.1991, ch. 95 ½, ¶ 11-408.

[1] 625 ILCS 5/6-900 et seq.

P.A. 90-14, Article 2, of the First 1997 General Revisory Act, resolved multiple actions in the 89th General Assembly and made certain technical corrections in P.A. 89-443 through P.A. 89-707.

5/11-409. False motor vehicle accident reports or notices

§ 11-409. False motor vehicle accident reports or notices. Any person who provides information in an oral or written report required by this Code with knowledge or reason to believe that such information is false shall be guilty of a Class C misdemeanor.

P.A. 76-1586, § 11-409, eff. July 1, 1970. Amended by P.A. 77-2720, § 1, eff. Jan. 2, 1972; P.A. 80-911, § 1, eff. Oct. 1, 1977; P.A. 81-1509, Art. II, § 71, eff. Sept. 26, 1980; P.A. 83-831, § 1, eff. Jan. 1, 1984.

Formerly Ill.Rev.Stat.1991, ch. 95 ½, ¶ 11-409.

5/11-410. When driver fails to report a motor vehicle accident

§ 11-410. When driver fails to report a motor vehicle accident. Whenever the driver of a vehicle is physically incapable of making a required written accident report and if there was another occupant in the vehicle at the time of the motor vehicle accident capable of making a written report, such occupant shall make or cause to be made such written report. If said driver fails for any reason to make such report, the owner of the vehicle involved in such motor vehicle accident, shall, as soon as practicable, make said report to the Administrator.

P.A. 76-1586, § 11-410, eff. July 1, 1970. Amended by P.A. 76-2473, § 1, eff. July 1, 1971; P.A. 77-42, § 1, eff. July 1, 1971; P.A. 83-831, § 1, eff. Jan. 1, 1984.

Formerly Ill.Rev.Stat.1991, ch. 95 ½, ¶ 11-410.

5/11-411. Accident report forms

§ 11-411. Accident report forms. (a) The Administrator must prepare and upon request supply to police departments, sheriffs and other appropriate agencies or individuals, forms for written accident reports as required hereunder, suitable with respect to the persons required to make such reports and the purposes to be served. The written reports must call for sufficiently detailed information to disclose with reference to a vehicle accident the cause, conditions then existing, and the persons and vehicles involved or any other data concerning such accident that may be required for a complete analysis of all related circumstances and events leading to the accident or subsequent to the occurrence.

(b) Every accident report required to be made in writing must be made on an appropriate form approved or provided by the Administrator and must contain all the information required therein unless that information is not available.

(c) Should special accident studies be required by the Administrator, the Administrator may provide the supplemental forms for the special studies.

P.A. 76-1586, § 11-411, eff. July 1, 1970. Amended by P.A. 76-2473, § 1, eff. July 1, 1971; P.A. 77-42, § 1, eff. July 1, 1971; P.A. 77-1910, § 1, eff. July 1, 1972; P.A. 78-255, § 61, eff. Oct. 1, 1973.

Formerly Ill.Rev.Stat.1991, ch. 95 ½, ¶ 11-411.

5/11-412. Motor vehicle accident reports confidential

§ 11-412. Motor vehicle accident reports confidential. All required written motor vehicle accident reports and supplemental reports shall be without prejudice to the individual so reporting and shall be for the confidential use of the Department and the Secretary of State and, in the case of second division vehicles operated under certificate of convenience and necessity issued by the Illinois Commerce Commission, of the Commission, except that the Administrator or the Secretary of State or the Commission may disclose the identity of a person involved in a motor vehicle accident when such identity is not otherwise known or when such person denies his presence at such motor vehicle accident and the Department shall disclose the identity of the insurance carrier, if any, upon demand. The Secretary of State may also disclose notations of accident involvement maintained on individual driving records. The Department may furnish copies of its written accident reports to federal and State agencies that are engaged in highway safety research and studies. Reports furnished to any agency other than the Secretary of State or the Illinois Commerce Commission may be used only for statistical or analytical purposes and shall be held confidential by that agency. No such written report shall be used as evidence in any trial, civil or criminal, arising out of a motor vehicle accident, except that the Administrator shall furnish upon demand of any person who has, or claims to have, made such a written report, or upon demand of any court, a certificate showing that a specified written accident report has or has not been made to the Administrator solely to prove a compliance or a failure to comply with the requirement that such a written report be made to the Administrator.

The Department of Transportation at its discretion may provide for in-depth investigations of accidents involving Department employees. A written report describing the preventability of such an accident may be prepared to enhance the safety of Department employees. Such reports and any opinions expressed in the review of the accident as to the preventability of the accident shall be for the privileged use of the Department and held confidential and shall not be obtainable or used in any civil or criminal proceeding.

P.A. 76-1586, § 11-412, eff. July 1, 1970. Amended by P.A. 76-2473, § 1, eff. July 1, 1971; P.A. 77-42, § 1, eff. July 1, 1971; P.A. 77-330, § 1, eff. July 22, 1971; P.A. 77-1910, § 1, eff. July 1, 1972; P.A. 78-255, § 61, eff. Oct. 1, 1973; P.A. 79-865, § 1, eff. Jan. 1, 1976; P.A. 82-523, § 1, eff. Jan. 1, 1982; P.A. 83-831, § 1, eff. Jan. 1, 1984; P.A. 86-564, § 1, eff. Jan. 1, 1990; P.A. 89-503, § 10, eff. July 1, 1996.

Formerly Ill.Rev.Stat.1991, ch. 95 ½, ¶ 11-412.

5/11-413. Coroners to report

§ 11-413. Coroners to report. All coroners shall on or before the 10th day of each month report in writing to the Administrator the death of any person within their respective jurisdiction, during the preceding calendar month, as the result of a traffic accident giving the time and place of the accident and the circumstances relating thereto.

P.A. 76-1586, § 11-413, eff. July 1, 1970. Amended by P.A. 76-2473, § 1, eff. July 1, 1971; P.A. 77-42, § 1, eff. July 1, 1971; P.A. 83-831, § 1, eff. Jan. 1, 1984.

Formerly Ill.Rev.Stat.1991, ch. 95 ½, ¶ 11-413.

5/11-414. Department to tabulate and analyze motor vehicle accident reports

§ 11-414. Department to tabulate and analyze motor vehicle accident reports. The Department shall tabulate and may analyze all written motor vehicle accident reports received in compliance with this Code and shall publish annually or at more frequent intervals statistical information based thereon as to the number and circumstances of traffic accidents. The Department:

1. shall submit a report of school bus accidents and accidents resulting in personal injury to or the death of any person within 50 feet of a school bus while awaiting or preparing to board the bus or immediately after exiting the bus to the National Highway Safety Advisory Committee annually or as requested by the Committee;

2. shall compile, maintain, and make available to the public statistical information relating to traffic accidents involving medical transport vehicles;

3. may conduct special investigations of motor vehicle accidents and may solicit supplementary reports from drivers, owners, police departments, sheriffs, coroners, or any other individual. Failure of any individual to submit a supplementary report subjects such individual to the same penalties for failure to report as designated under Section 11-406.

P.A. 76-1586, § 11-414, eff. July 1, 1970. Amended by P.A. 76-2473, § 1, eff. July 1, 1971; P.A. 78-1244, § 1, eff. Sept. 5, 1974; P.A. 82-433, § 1, eff. Sept. 8, 1981; P.A. 83-831, § 1, eff. Jan. 1, 1984.

Formerly Ill.Rev.Stat.1991, ch. 95 ½, ¶ 11-414.

Section 3 of P.A. 82-433 approved Sept. 8, 1981, provided:

"This Act takes effect upon its becoming a law, except that the provisions relating to safety tests and proof of financial responsibility for medical transport vehicles apply only to applications for and the issuance of registration plates which are required to be displayed on January 1, 1982 or thereafter."

5/11-415. Municipalities may require traffic accident reports

§ 11-415. Municipalities may require traffic accident reports. Municipalities may by ordinance require that the driver or owner of a vehicle involved in a traffic accident file with the designated municipal office a written report of such accident. All such reports shall be for the confidential use of the municipal office and subject to the provisions of Section 11-412.

P.A. 76-1586, § 11-415, eff. July 1, 1970. Amended by P.A. 76-2164, § 1, eff. July 1, 1970; P.A. 83-831, § 1, eff. Jan. 1, 1984.

Formerly Ill.Rev.Stat.1991, ch. 95 ½, ¶ 11-415.

5/11-416. Furnishing copies—Fees

§ 11-416. Furnishing copies—Fees. The Department of State Police may furnish copies of an Illinois State Police Traffic Accident Report that has been investigated by the State Police and shall be paid a fee of $5 for each such copy, or in the case of an accident which was investigated by an accident reconstruction officer or accident reconstruction team, a fee of $20 shall be paid.

Other State law enforcement agencies or law enforcement agencies of local authorities may furnish copies of traffic accident reports prepared by such agencies and may receive a fee not to exceed $5 for each copy or in the case of an accident which was investigated by an accident reconstruction officer or accident reconstruction team, the State or local law enforcement agency may receive a fee not to exceed $20.

Any written accident report required or requested to be furnished the Administrator shall be provided without cost or fee charges authorized under this Section or any other provision of law.

P.A. 76-1586, § 11-416, eff. July 1, 1970. Amended by P.A. 76-2743, § 1, eff. July 1, 1971; P.A. 77-534, § 1, eff. July 31, 1971; P.A. 83-310, § 1, eff. Sept. 14, 1983; P.A. 84-25, Art. IV, § 27, eff. July 18, 1985; P.A. 84-1044, § 1, eff. July 1, 1986; P.A. 84-1308, Art. II, § 96, eff. Aug. 25, 1986; P.A. 90-89, § 15, eff. Jan. 1, 1998.

Formerly Ill.Rev.Stat.1991, ch. 95 ½, ¶ 11-416.

ARTICLE V. DRIVING WHILE INTOXICATED, TRANSPORTING ALCOHOLIC LIQUOR, AND RECKLESS DRIVING

Section

5/11-500. Definitions

§ 11-500. Definitions. For the purposes of interpreting Sections 6-206.1 and 6-208.1 of this Code, "first offender" shall mean any person who has not had a previous conviction or court assigned supervision for violating Section 11-501, or a similar provision of a local ordinance, or a conviction in any other state for a violation of driving while under the influence or a similar offense where the cause of action is the same or substantially similar to this Code or any person who has not had a driver's license suspension for violating Section 11-501.1 within 5 years prior to the date of the current offense, except in cases where the driver submitted to chemical testing resulting in an alcohol concentration of 0.08 or more, or any amount of a drug, substance, or compound in such person's blood or urine resulting from the unlawful use or consumption of cannabis listed in the Cannabis Control Act,[1] a controlled substance listed in the Illinois Controlled Substances Act,[2] or an intoxicating compound listed in the Use of Intoxicating Compounds Act[3] and was subsequently found not guilty of violating Section 11-501, or a similar provision of a local ordinance.

P.A. 76-1586, § 11-500, added by P.A. 84-272, § 7, eff. Jan. 1, 1986. Amended by P.A. 86-929, § 2, eff. Sept. 21, 1989; P.A. 86-1019, § 7, eff. July 1, 1990; P.A. 86-1475, Art. 2, § 2-25, eff. Jan. 10, 1991; P.A. 90-43, § 5, eff. July 2, 1997; P.A. 90-779, § 5, eff. Jan. 1, 1999.

Formerly Ill.Rev.Stat.1991, ch. 95 ½, ¶ 11-500.

1 720 ILCS 550/1 et seq.

2 720 ILCS 570/100 et seq.

3 720 ILCS 690/0.01 et seq.

P.A. 90-779 incorporated the amendment by P.A. 90-43.

5/11-500.1. Immunity

§ 11-500.1. Immunity.

(a) A person authorized under this Article to withdraw blood or collect urine shall not be civilly liable for damages when the person, in good faith, withdraws blood or collects urine for evidentiary purposes under this Code, upon the request of a law enforcement officer, unless the act is performed in a willful and wanton manner.

(b) As used in this Section, "willful and wanton manner" means a course of action that shows an actual or deliberate intention to cause harm or which, if not intentional, shows an utter indifference to or conscious disregard for the health or safety of another.

P.A. 76-1586, § 11-500.1, added by P.A. 89-689, § 70, eff. Dec. 31, 1996.

5/11-501. Driving while under the influence of alcohol, other drug or drugs, intoxicating compound or compounds or any combination thereof

§ 11-501. Driving while under the influence of alcohol, other drug or drugs, intoxicating compound or compounds or any combination thereof.

(a) A person shall not drive or be in actual physical control of any vehicle within this State while:

(1) the alcohol concentration in the person's blood or breath is 0.08 or more based on the definition of blood and breath units in Section 11-501.2;

(2) under the influence of alcohol;

(3) under the influence of any intoxicating compound or combination of intoxicating compounds to a degree that renders the person incapable of driving safely;

(4) under the influence of any other drug or combination of drugs to a degree that renders the person incapable of safely driving;

(5) under the combined influence of alcohol, other drug or drugs, or intoxicating compound or compounds to a degree that renders the person incapable of safely driving; or

(6) there is any amount of a drug, substance, or compound in the person's breath, blood, or urine resulting from the unlawful use or consumption of cannabis listed in the Cannabis Control Act,[1] a controlled substance listed in the Illinois Controlled Substances Act,[2] or an intoxicating compound listed in the Use of Intoxicating Compounds Act.[3]

(b) The fact that any person charged with violating this Section is or has been legally entitled to use alcohol, other drug or drugs, or intoxicating compound or compounds, or any combination thereof, shall not constitute a defense against any charge of violating this Section.

(c) Except as provided under paragraphs (c-3), (c-4), and (d) of this Section, every person convicted of violating this Section or a similar provision of a local ordinance, shall be guilty of a Class A misdemeanor and, in addition to any other criminal or administrative action, for any second conviction of violating this Section or a similar provision of a law of another state or local ordinance committed within 5 years of a previous violation of this Section or a similar provision of a local ordinance shall be mandatorily sentenced to a minimum of 5 days of imprisonment or assigned to a minimum of 30 days of community service as may be determined by the court. Every person convicted of violating this Section or a similar provision of a local ordinance shall be subject to an additional mandatory minimum fine of $500 and an additional mandatory 5 days of community service in a program benefiting children if the person committed a violation of paragraph (a) or a similar provision of a local ordinance while transporting a person under age 16. Every person convicted a second time for violating this Section or a similar provision of a local ordinance within 5 years of a previous violation of this Section or a similar provision of a law of another state or local ordinance shall be subject to an additional mandatory minimum fine of $500 and an additional 10 days of mandatory community service in a program benefiting children if the current offense was committed while transporting a person under age 16. The imprisonment or assignment under this subsection shall not be subject to suspension nor shall the person be eligible for probation in order to reduce the sentence or assignment.

(c-1) (1) A person who violates this Section during a period in which his or her driving privileges are revoked or suspended, where the revocation or suspension was for a violation of this Section, Section 11-501.1, paragraph (b) of Section 11-401, or Section 9-3 of the Criminal Code of 1961[4] is guilty of a Class 4 felony.

(2) A person who violates this Section a third time during a period in which his or her driving privileges are revoked or suspended where the revocation or suspension was for a violation of this Section, Section 11-501. 1, paragraph (b) of Section 11-401, or Section 9-3 of the Criminal Code of 1961 is guilty of a Class 3 felony.

(3) A person who violates this Section a fourth or subsequent time during a period in which his or her driving privileges are revoked or suspended where the revocation or suspension was for a violation of this Section, Section 11-501.1, paragraph (b) of Section 11-401, or Section 9-3 of the Criminal Code of 1961 is guilty of a Class 2 felony.

(c-2) (Blank).

(c-3) Every person convicted of violating this Section or a similar provision of a local ordinance who had a child under age 16 in the vehicle at the time of the offense shall have his or her punishment under this Act enhanced by 2 days of imprisonment for a first offense, 10 days of imprisonment for a second offense, 30 days of imprisonment for a third offense, and 90 days of imprisonment for a fourth or subsequent offense, in addition to the fine and community service required under subsection (c) and the possible imprisonment required under subsection (d). The imprisonment or assignment under this subsection shall not be subject to suspension nor shall the person be eligible for probation in order to reduce the sentence or assignment.

(c-4) When a person is convicted of violating Section 11-501 of this Code or a similar provision of a local ordinance, the following penalties apply when his or her blood, breath, or urine was .16 or more based on the definition of blood, breath, or urine units in Section 11-501.2 or when that person is convicted of violating this Section while transporting a child under the age of 16:

(1) A person who is convicted of violating subsection (a) of Section 11-501 of this Code a first time, in addition to any other penalty that may be imposed under subsection (c), is subject to a mandatory minimum of 100 hours of community service and a minimum fine of $500.

(2) A person who is convicted of violating subsection (a) of Section 11-501 of this Code a second time within 10 years, in addition to any other penalty that may be imposed under subsection (c), is subject to a mandatory minimum of 2 days of imprisonment and a minimum fine of $1,250.

(3) A person who is convicted of violating subsection (a) of Section 11-501 of this Code a third time within 20 years is guilty of a Class 4 felony and, in addition to any other penalty that may be imposed under subsection (c), is subject to a mandatory minimum of 90 days of imprisonment and a minimum fine of $2,500.

(4) A person who is convicted of violating this subsection (c-4) a fourth or subsequent time is guilty of a Class 2 felony and, in addition to any other penalty that may be imposed under subsection (c), is not eligible for a sentence of probation or conditional discharge and is subject to a minimum fine of $2,500.

(d) (1) Every person convicted of committing a violation of this Section shall be guilty of aggravated driving under the influence of alcohol, other drug or drugs, or intoxicating compound or compounds, or any combination thereof if:

(A) the person committed a violation of this Section, or a similar provision of a law of another state or a local ordinance when the cause of action is the same as or substantially similar to this Section, for the third or subsequent time;

(B) the person committed a violation of paragraph (a) while driving a school bus with children on board;

(C) the person in committing a violation of paragraph (a) was involved in a motor vehicle accident that resulted in great bodily harm or permanent disability or disfigurement to another, when the violation was a proximate cause of the injuries;

(D) the person committed a violation of paragraph (a) for a second time and has been previously convicted of violating Section 9-3 of the Criminal Code of 1961 relating to reckless homicide in which the person was determined to have been under the influence of alcohol, other drug or drugs, or intoxicating compound or compounds as an element of the offense or the person has previously been convicted under subparagraph (C) of this paragraph (1); or

(E) the person, in committing a violation of paragraph (a) while driving at any speed in a school speed zone at a time when a speed limit of 20 miles per hour was in effect under subsection (a) of Section 11-605 of this Code, was involved in a motor vehicle accident that resulted in bodily harm, other than great bodily harm or permanent disability or disfigurement, to another person, when the violation of paragraph (a) was a proximate cause of the bodily harm.

(2) Aggravated driving under the influence of alcohol, other drug or drugs, or intoxicating compound or compounds, or any combination thereof is a Class 4 felony. For a violation of subparagraph (C) of paragraph (1) of this subsection (d), the defendant, if sentenced to a term of imprisonment, shall be sentenced to not less than one year nor more than 12 years. For any prosecution under this subsection (d), a certified copy of the driving abstract of the defendant shall be admitted as proof of any prior conviction.

(e) After a finding of guilt and prior to any final sentencing, or an order for supervision, for an offense based upon an arrest for a violation of this Section or a similar provision of a local ordinance, individuals shall be required to undergo a professional evaluation to determine if an alcohol, drug, or intoxicating compound abuse problem exists and the extent of the problem, and undergo the imposition of treatment as appropriate. Programs conducting these evaluations shall be licensed by the Department of Human Services. The cost of any professional evaluation shall be paid for by the individual required to undergo the professional evaluation.

(f) Every person found guilty of violating this Section, whose operation of a motor vehicle while in violation of this Section proximately caused any incident resulting in an appropriate emergency response, shall be liable for the expense of an emergency response as provided under Section 5-5-3 of the Unified Code of Corrections. [5]

(g) The Secretary of State shall revoke the driving privileges of any person convicted under this Section or a similar provision of a local ordinance.

(h) Every person sentenced under paragraph (2) or (3) of subsection (c-1) of this Section or subsection (d) of this Section and who receives a term of probation or conditional discharge shall be required to serve a minimum term of either 60 days community service or 10 days of imprisonment as a condition of the probation or conditional discharge. This mandatory minimum term of imprisonment or assignment of community service shall not be suspended and shall not be subject to reduction by the court.

(i) The Secretary of State shall require the use of ignition interlock devices on all vehicles owned by an individual who has been convicted of a second or subsequent offense of this Section or a similar provision of a local ordinance. The Secretary shall establish by rule and regulation the procedures for certification and use of the interlock system.

(j) In addition to any other penalties and liabilities, a person who is found guilty of or pleads guilty to violating this Section, including any person placed on court supervision for violating this Section, shall be fined $100, payable to the circuit clerk, who shall distribute the money to the law enforcement agency that made the arrest. If the person has been previously convicted of violating this Section or a similar provision of a local ordinance, the fine shall be $200. In the event that more than one agency is responsible for the arrest, the $100 or $200 shall be shared equally. Any moneys received by a law enforcement agency under this subsection (j) shall be used to purchase law enforcement equipment that will assist in the prevention of alcohol related criminal violence throughout the State. This shall include, but is not limited to, in-car video cameras, radar and laser speed detection devices, and alcohol breath testers. Any moneys received by the Department of State Police under this subsection (j) shall be deposited into the State Police DUI Fund and shall be used to purchase law enforcement equipment that will assist in the prevention of alcohol related criminal violence throughout the State.

P.A. 76–1586, § 11–501, eff. July 1, 1970. Amended by P.A. 76–1738, § 1; P.A. 77–575, § 1, eff. July 31, 1971; P.A. 77–2720, § 1, eff. Jan. 1, 1973; P.A. 78–255, § 61, eff. Oct. 1, 1973; P.A. 80–1495, § 36, eff. Jan. 8, 1979; P.A. 82–221, § 3, eff. Jan. 1, 1982; P.A. 82–311, § 1, eff. Jan. 1, 1982; P.A. 82–783, Art. III, § 37, eff. July 13, 1982; P.A. 83–204, § 2, eff. Jan. 1, 1984; P.A. 83–1281, § 1, eff. July 1, 1985; P.A. 84–272, § 7, eff. Jan. 1, 1986; P.A. 84–899, § 1, eff. Jan. 1, 1986; P.A. 84–916, § 2, eff. Jan. 1, 1986; P.A. 84–1308, Art. II, § 96, eff. Aug. 25, 1986; P.A. 84–1394, § 5, eff. Sept. 18, 1986; P.A. 85–303, § 1, eff. Jan. 1, 1988; P.A. 86–581, § 2, eff. Jan. 1, 1990; P.A. 86–1019, § 7, eff. July 1, 1990; P.A. 86–1475, Art. 2, § 2–25, eff. Jan. 10, 1991; P.A. 87–274, § 2, eff. Jan. 1, 1992; P.A. 87–1073, § 2, eff. Jan. 1, 1993; P.A. 87–1074, § 2, eff. Jan. 1, 1993; P.A. 87–1075, § 2, eff. Jan. 1, 1993; P.A. 87–1198, § 6, eff. Sept. 25, 1992; P.A. 87–1222, § 1, eff. July 1, 1993; P.A. 88–45, Art. II, § 2–54, eff. July 6, 1993; P.A. 88–238, § 5, eff. Jan. 1, 1994; P.A. 88–433, § 1, eff. Jan. 1, 1994; P.A. 88–670, Art. 2, § 2–59, eff. Dec. 2, 1994; P.A. 88–680, Art. 20, § 20–900, eff. Jan. 1, 1995; P.A. 89–8, Art. 1, § 1–5, eff. March 21, 1995; P.A. 89–156, § 5, eff. Jan. 1, 1996; P.A. 89–203, § 25, eff. July 21, 1995; P.A. 89–507, Art. 90, § 90C–31, eff. July 1, 1997; P.A. 89–626, Art. 2, § 2–66, eff. Aug. 9, 1996; P.A. 90–43, § 5, eff. July 2, 1997; P.A. 90–400, § 5, eff. Aug. 15, 1997; P.A. 90–611, § 5, eff. Jan. 1, 1999; P.A. 90–655, § 153, eff. July 30, 1998; P.A. 90–738, § 5, eff. Jan. 1, 1999; P.A. 90–779, § 5, eff. Jan. 1, 1999; P.A. 91–126, § 5, eff. July 16, 1999; P.A. 91–357, § 231, eff. July 29, 1999. Re-enacted by P.A. 91–692, Art. 20, § 20–900, eff. April 13, 2000. Amended by P.A. 91–822, § 10, eff. June 13, 2000; P.A. 92–248, § 5, eff. Aug. 3, 2001; P.A. 92–418, § 10, eff. Aug. 17, 2001; P.A. 92–420, § 5, eff. Aug. 17, 2001; P.A. 92–429, § 5, eff. Jan. 1, 2002; P.A. 92–431, § 10, eff. Jan. 1, 2002; P.A. 92–651, § 77, eff. July 11, 2002.

Formerly Ill.Rev.Stat.1991, ch. 95 ½, ¶ 11–501.

[1] 720 ILCS 550/1 et seq.

[2] 35 ILCS 570/1 et seq.

[3] 720 ILCS 690/0.01 et seq.

[4] 720 ILCS 5/11–501, 5/1–401, 5/9–3.

[5] 730 ILCS 5/5–5–3.

Validity

The Supreme Court of Illinois held that P.A. 88–680 violated the single-subject rule of the Illinois Constitution in the case of People v. Cervantes, 1999, 243 Ill.Dec. 233, 189 Ill.2d 80, 723 N.E.2d 265; P.A. 91–692 re-enacted this section as contained in P.A. 88–680, including subsequent amendments in order "to remove any question as to the validity or content of those provisions."

On November 18, 1999, the Supreme Court of Illinois held that P.A. 89–203 violated the single-subject rule of the Illinois Constitution in the case of People v. Wooters, 1999, 243 Ill.Dec. 33, 188 Ill.2d 500, 722 N.E.2d 1102.

For purpose of P.A. 91–692, see Historical and Statutory Notes following 625 ILCS 5/6–303.

P.A. 92–651, the First 2002 General Revisory Act, amended various Acts to delete obsolete text, to correct patent and technical errors, to revise cross references, to resolve multiple actions in the 91st and 92nd General Assemblies and to make certain technical corrections in P.A. 91–937 through P.A. 92–520.

See 5 ILCS 70/6 as to the effect of (1) more than one amendment of a section at the same session of the General Assembly or (2) two or more acts relating to the same subject matter enacted by the same General Assembly.

5/11–501.1. Suspension of drivers license; statutory summary alcohol, other drug or drugs, or intoxicating compound or compounds related suspension; implied consent

§ 11–501.1. Suspension of drivers license; statutory summary alcohol, other drug or drugs, or intoxicating compound or compounds related suspension; implied consent.

(a) Any person who drives or is in actual physical control of a motor vehicle upon the public highways of this State shall be deemed to have given consent, subject to the provisions of Section 11–501.2, to a chemical test or tests of blood, breath, or urine for the purpose of determining the content of alcohol, other drug or drugs, or intoxicating compound or compounds or any combination thereof in the person's blood if arrested, as evidenced by the issuance of a Uniform Traffic Ticket, for any offense as defined in Section 11–501 or a similar provision of a local ordinance. The test or tests shall be administered at the direction of the arresting officer. The law enforcement agency employing the officer shall designate which of the aforesaid tests shall be administered. A urine test may be administered even after a blood or breath test or both has been administered. For purposes of this Section, an Illinois law enforcement officer of this State who is investigating the person for any offense defined in Section 11-501 may travel into an adjoining state, where the person has been transported for medical care, to complete an investigation and to request that the person submit to the test or tests set forth in this Section. The requirements of this Section that the person be arrested are inapplicable, but the officer shall issue the person a Uniform Traffic Ticket for an offense as defined in Section 11-501 or a similar provision of a local ordinance prior to requesting that the person submit to the test or tests. The issuance of the Uniform Traffic Ticket shall not constitute an arrest, but shall be for the purpose of notifying the person that he or she is subject to the provisions of this Section and of the officer's belief of the existence of probable cause to arrest. Upon returning to this State, the officer shall file the Uniform Traffic Ticket with the Circuit Clerk of the county where the offense was committed, and shall seek the issuance of an arrest warrant or a summons for the person.

(b) Any person who is dead, unconscious, or who is otherwise in a condition rendering the person incapable of refusal, shall be deemed not to have withdrawn the consent provided by paragraph (a) of this Section and the test or tests may be administered, subject to the provisions of Section 11-501.2.

(c) A person requested to submit to a test as provided above shall be warned by the law enforcement officer requesting the test that a refusal to submit to the test will result in the statutory summary suspension of the person's privilege to operate a motor vehicle as provided in Section 6-208.1 of this Code. The person shall also be warned by the law enforcement officer that if the person submits to the test or tests provided in paragraph (a) of this Section and the alcohol concentration in the person's blood or breath is 0.08 or greater, or any amount of a drug, substance, or compound resulting from the unlawful use or consumption of cannabis as covered by the Cannabis Control Act,[1] a controlled substance listed in the Illinois Controlled Substances Act,[2] or an intoxicating compound listed in the Use of Intoxicating Compounds Act[3] is detected in the person's blood or urine, a statutory summary suspension of the person's privilege to operate a motor vehicle, as provided in Sections 6-208.1 and 11-501.1 of this Code, will be imposed.

A person who is under the age of 21 at the time the person is requested to submit to a test as provided above shall, in addition to the warnings provided for in this Section, be further warned by the law enforcement officer requesting the test that if the person submits to the test or tests provided in paragraph (a) of this Section and the alcohol concentration in the person's blood or breath is greater than 0.00 and less than 0.08, a suspension of the person's privilege to operate a motor vehicle, as provided under Sections 6-208.2 and 11-501.8 of this Code, will be imposed. The results of this test shall be admissible in a civil or criminal action or proceeding arising from an arrest for an offense as defined in Section 11-501 of this Code or a similar provision of a local ordinance or pursuant to Section 11-501.4 in prosecutions for reckless homicide brought under the Criminal Code of 1961.[4] These test results, however, shall be admissible only in actions or proceedings directly related to the incident upon which the test request was made.

(d) If the person refuses testing or submits to a test that discloses an alcohol concentration of 0.08 or more, or any amount of a drug, substance, or intoxicating compound in the person's breath, blood, or urine resulting from the unlawful use or consumption of cannabis listed in the Cannabis Control Act, a controlled substance listed in the Illinois Controlled Substances Act, or an intoxicating compound listed in the Use of Intoxicating Compounds Act, the law enforcement officer shall immediately submit a sworn report to the circuit court of venue and the Secretary of State, certifying that the test or tests was or were requested under paragraph (a) and the person refused to submit to a test, or tests, or submitted to testing that disclosed an alcohol concentration of 0.08 or more.

(e) Upon receipt of the sworn report of a law enforcement officer submitted under paragraph (d), the Secretary of State shall enter the statutory summary suspension for the periods specified in Section 6-208.1, and effective as provided in paragraph (g).

If the person is a first offender as defined in Section 11-500 of this Code, and is not convicted of a violation of Section 11-501 of this Code or a similar provision of a local ordinance, then reports received by the Secretary of State under this Section shall, except during the actual time the Statutory Summary Suspension is in effect, be privileged information and for use only by the courts, police officers, prosecuting authorities or the Secretary of State.

(f) The law enforcement officer submitting the sworn report under paragraph (d) shall serve immediate notice of the statutory summary suspension on the person and the suspension shall be effective as provided in paragraph (g). In cases where the blood alcohol concentration of 0.08 or greater or any amount of a drug, substance, or compound resulting from the unlawful use or consumption of cannabis as covered by the Cannabis Control Act, a controlled substance listed in the Illinois Controlled Substances Act, or an intoxicating compound listed in the Use of Intoxicating Compounds Act is established by a subsequent analysis of blood or urine collected at the time of arrest, the arresting officer or arresting agency shall give notice as provided in this Section or by deposit in the United States mail of the notice in an envelope with postage prepaid and addressed to the person at his address as shown on the Uniform Traffic Ticket and the statutory summary suspension shall begin as provided in paragraph (g). The officer shall confiscate any Illinois driver's license or permit on the person at the time of arrest. If the person has a valid driver's license or permit, the officer shall issue the person a receipt, in a form prescribed by the Secretary of State, that will allow that person to drive during the periods provided for in paragraph (g). The officer shall immediately forward the driver's license or permit to the circuit court of venue along with the sworn report provided for in paragraph (d).

(g) The statutory summary suspension referred to in this Section shall take effect on the 46th day following the date the notice of the statutory summary suspension was given to the person.

(h) The following procedure shall apply whenever a person is arrested for any offense as defined in Section 11-501 or a similar provision of a local ordinance:

Upon receipt of the sworn report from the law enforcement officer, the Secretary of State shall confirm the statutory summary suspension by mailing a notice of the effective date of the suspension to the person and the court of venue. However, should the sworn report be defective by not containing sufficient information or be completed in error, the confirmation of the statutory summary suspension shall not be mailed to the person or entered to the record; instead, the sworn report shall be forwarded to the court of venue with a copy returned to the issuing agency identifying any defect.

P.A. 76-1586, § 11-501.1, added by P.A. 77-1800, § 1, eff. July 1, 1971. Amended by P.A. 77-1881, § 1, eff. July 1, 1972; P.A. 77-1884, § 1, eff. June 30, 1972; P.A. 78-255, § 27, eff. Oct. 1, 1973; P.A. 79-1363, § 12, eff. Oct. 1, 1976;

P.A. 82-221, § 3, eff. Jan. 1, 1982; P.A. 82-311, § 1, eff. Jan. 1, 1982; P.A. 82-783, Art. III, § 37, eff. July 13, 1982; P.A. 84-272, § 7, eff. Jan. 1, 1986; P.A. 84-1394, § 5, eff. Sept. 18, 1986; P.A. 86-929, § 2, eff. Sept. 21, 1989; P.A. 86-1019, § 7, eff. July 1, 1990; P.A. 86-1475, Art. 2, § 2-25, eff. Jan. 10, 1991; P.A. 87-1221, § 1, eff. July 1, 1993; P.A. 88-169, § 1, eff. Jan. 1, 1994; P.A. 88-588, § 5, eff. Jan. 1, 1995; P.A. 90-43, § 5, eff. July 2, 1997; P.A. 90-779, § 5, eff. Jan. 1, 1999; P.A. 91-357, § 231, eff. July 29, 1999.

Formerly Ill.Rev.Stat.1991, ch. 95 ½, ¶ 11-501.1.

1 720 ILCS 550/1 et seq.

2 720 ILCS 570/100 et seq.

3 720 ILCS 690/0.01 et seq.

4 720 ILCS 5/1-1 et seq.

5/11-501.2. Chemical and other tests

§ 11-501.2. Chemical and other tests.

(a) Upon the trial of any civil or criminal action or proceeding arising out of an arrest for an offense as defined in Section 11-501 or a similar local ordinance or proceedings pursuant to Section 2-118.1, evidence of the concentration of alcohol, other drug or drugs, or intoxicating compound or compounds, or any combination thereof in a person's blood or breath at the time alleged, as determined by analysis of the person's blood, urine, breath or other bodily substance, shall be admissible. Where such test is made the following provisions shall apply:

1. Chemical analyses of the person's blood, urine, breath or other bodily substance to be considered valid under the provisions of this Section shall have been performed according to standards promulgated by the Department of State Police by a licensed physician, registered nurse, trained phlebotomist acting under the direction of a licensed physician, certified paramedic, or other individual possessing a valid permit issued by that Department for this purpose. The Director of State Police is authorized to approve satisfactory techniques or methods, to ascertain the qualifications and competence of individuals to conduct such analyses, to issue permits which shall be subject to termination or revocation at the discretion of that Department and to certify the accuracy of breath testing equipment. The Department of State Police shall prescribe regulations as necessary to implement this Section.

2. When a person in this State shall submit to a blood test at the request of a law enforcement officer under the provisions of Section 11-501.1, only a physician authorized to practice medicine, a registered nurse, trained phlebotomist, or certified paramedic, or other qualified person approved by the Department of State Police may withdraw blood for the purpose of determining the alcohol, drug, or alcohol and drug content therein. This limitation shall not apply to the taking of breath or urine specimens.

When a blood test of a person who has been taken to an adjoining state for medical treatment is requested by an Illinois law enforcement officer, the blood may be withdrawn only by a physician authorized to practice medicine in the adjoining state, a registered nurse, a trained phlebotomist acting under the direction of the physician, or certified paramedic. The law enforcement officer requesting the test shall take custody of the blood sample, and the blood sample shall be analyzed by a laboratory certified by the Department of State Police for that purpose.

3. The person tested may have a physician, or a qualified technician, chemist, registered nurse, or other qualified person of their own choosing administer a chemical test or tests in addition to any administered at the direction of a law enforcement officer. The failure or inability to obtain an additional test by a person shall not preclude the admission of evidence relating to the test or tests taken at the direction of a law enforcement officer.

4. Upon the request of the person who shall submit to a chemical test or tests at the request of a law enforcement officer, full information concerning the test or tests shall be made available to the person or such person's attorney.

5. Alcohol concentration shall mean either grams of alcohol per 100 milliliters of blood or grams of alcohol per 210 liters of breath.

(b) Upon the trial of any civil or criminal action or proceeding arising out of acts alleged to have been committed by any person while driving or in actual physical control of a vehicle while under the influence of alcohol, the concentration of alcohol in the person's blood or breath at the time alleged as shown by analysis of the person's blood, urine, breath, or other bodily substance shall give rise to the following presumptions:

1. If there was at that time an alcohol concentration of 0.05 or less, it shall be presumed that the person was not under the influence of alcohol.

2. If there was at that time an alcohol concentration in excess of 0.05 but less than 0.08, such facts shall not give rise to any presumption that the person was or was not under the influence of alcohol, but such fact may be considered with other competent evidence in determining whether the person was under the influence of alcohol.

3. If there was at that time an alcohol concentration of 0.08 or more, it shall be presumed that the person was under the influence of alcohol.

4. The foregoing provisions of this Section shall not be construed as limiting the introduction of any other relevant evidence bearing upon the question whether the person was under the influence of alcohol.

(c) 1. If a person under arrest refuses to submit to a chemical test under the provisions of Section 11-501.1, evidence of refusal shall be admissible in any civil or criminal action or proceeding arising out of acts alleged to have been committed while the person under the influence of alcohol, other drug or drugs, or intoxicating compound or compounds, or any combination thereof was driving or in actual physical control of a motor vehicle.

2. Notwithstanding any ability to refuse under this Code to submit to these tests or any ability to revoke the implied consent to these tests, if a law enforcement officer has probable cause to believe that a motor vehicle driven by or in actual physical control of a person under the influence of alcohol, other drug or drugs, or intoxicating compound or compounds, or any combination thereof has caused the death or personal injury to another, that person shall submit, upon the request of a law enforcement officer, to a chemical test or tests of his or her blood, breath or urine for the purpose of determining the alcohol content thereof or the presence of any other drug or combination of both.

This provision does not affect the applicability of or imposition of driver's license sanctions under Section 11-501.1 of this Code.

3. For purposes of this Section, a personal injury includes any Type A injury as indicated on the traffic accident report completed by a law enforcement officer that requires immediate professional attention in either a doctor's office or a medical facility. A Type A injury

includes severe bleeding wounds, distorted extremities, and injuries that require the injured party to be carried from the scene.

P.A. 76-1586, § 11-501.2, added by P.A. 82-311, § 1, eff. Jan. 1, 1982. Amended by P.A. 84-25, Art. IV, § 27, July 18, 1985; P.A. 86-929, § 2, eff. Sept. 21, 1989; P.A. 87-1221, § 1, eff. July 1, 1993; P.A. 88-632, § 5, eff. Jan. 1, 1995; P.A. 90-43, § 5, eff. July 2, 1997; P.A. 90-779, § 5, eff. Jan. 1, 1999; P.A. 91-828, § 5, eff. Jan. 1, 2001.

Formerly Ill.Rev.Stat.1991, ch. 95 ½, ¶ 11-501.2.

5/11-501.3. § 11-501.3. Repealed by P.A. 84-1394, § 7, eff. Sept. 18, 1986

5/11-501.4. Admissibility of chemical tests of blood conducted in the regular course of providing emergency medical treatment

§ 11-501.4. Admissibility of chemical tests of blood conducted in the regular course of providing emergency medical treatment.

(a) Notwithstanding any other provision of law, the results of blood tests performed for the purpose of determining the content of alcohol, other drug or drugs, or intoxicating compound or compounds, or any combination thereof, of an individual's blood conducted upon persons receiving medical treatment in a hospital emergency room are admissible in evidence as a business record exception to the hearsay rule only in prosecutions for any violation of Section 11-501 of this Code or a similar provision of a local ordinance, or in prosecutions for reckless homicide brought under the Criminal Code of 1961,[1] when each of the following criteria are met:

(1) the chemical tests performed upon an individual's blood were ordered in the regular course of providing emergency medical treatment and not at the request of law enforcement authorities;

(2) the chemical tests performed upon an individual's blood were performed by the laboratory routinely used by the hospital; and

(3) results of chemical tests performed upon an individual's blood are admissible into evidence regardless of the time that the records were prepared.

(b) The confidentiality provisions of law pertaining to medical records and medical treatment shall not be applicable with regard to chemical tests performed upon an individual's blood under the provisions of this Section in prosecutions as specified in subsection (a) of this Section. No person shall be liable for civil damages as a result of the evidentiary use of chemical testing of an individual's blood test results under this Section, or as a result of that person's testimony made available under this Section.

P.A. 76-1586, § 11-501.4, added by P.A. 85-992, § 1, eff. Jan. 5, 1988. Amended by P.A. 88-212, § 5, eff. Jan. 1, 1994; P.A. 88-523, § 5, eff. July 1, 1994; P.A. 88-632, § 5, eff. Jan. 1, 1995; P.A. 88-670, Art. 2, § 2-59, eff. Dec. 2, 1994; P.A. 90-779, § 5, eff. Jan. 1, 1999.

Formerly Ill.Rev.Stat.1991, ch. 95 ½, ¶ 11-501.4.

[1] 720 ILCS 5/1-1 et seq.

Another § 11-501.4 was renumbered as § 11-501.5.

5/11-501.4-1. Reporting of test results of blood or urine conducted in the regular course of providing emergency medical treatment

§ 11-501.4-1. Reporting of test results of blood or urine conducted in the regular course of providing emergency medical treatment.

(a) Notwithstanding any other provision of law, the results of blood or urine tests performed for the purpose of determining the content of alcohol, other drug or drugs, or intoxicating compound or compounds, or any combination thereof, in an individual's blood or urine conducted upon persons receiving medical treatment in a hospital emergency room for injuries resulting from a motor vehicle accident shall be disclosed to the Department of State Police or local law enforcement agencies of jurisdiction, upon request. Such blood or urine tests are admissible in evidence as a business record exception to the hearsay rule only in prosecutions for any violation of Section 11-501 of this Code or a similar provision of a local ordinance, or in prosecutions for reckless homicide brought under the Criminal Code of 1961.[1]

(b) The confidentiality provisions of law pertaining to medical records and medical treatment shall not be applicable with regard to tests performed upon an individual's blood or urine under the provisions of subsection (a) of this Section. No person shall be liable for civil damages or professional discipline as a result of the disclosure or reporting of the tests or the evidentiary use of an individual's blood or urine test results under this Section or Section 11-501.4 or as a result of that person's testimony made available under this Section or Section 11-501.4, except for willful or wanton misconduct.

P.A. 76-1586, § 11-501.4-1, added by P.A. 89-517, § 10, eff. Jan. 1, 1997. Amended by P.A. 90-779, § 5, eff. Jan. 1, 1999; P.A. 91-125, § 5, eff. Jan. 1, 2000.

[1] 720 ILCS 5/1-1 et seq.

5/11-501.5. Preliminary Breath Screening Test

§ 11-501.5. Preliminary Breath Screening Test.

(a) If a law enforcement officer has reasonable suspicion to believe that a person is violating or has violated Section 11-501 or a similar provision of a local ordinance, the officer, prior to an arrest, may request the person to provide a sample of his or her breath for a preliminary breath screening test using a portable device approved by the Department of State Police. The person may refuse the test. The results of this preliminary breath screening test may be used by the law enforcement officer for the purpose of assisting with the determination of whether to require a chemical test as authorized under Sections 11-501.1 and 11-501.2, and the appropriate type of test to request. Any chemical test authorized under Sections 11-501.1 and 11-501.2 may be requested by the officer regardless of the result of the preliminary breath screening test, if probable cause for an arrest exists. The result of a preliminary breath screening test may be used by the defendant as evidence in any administrative or court proceeding involving a violation of Section 11-501 or 11-501.1.

(b) The Department of State Police shall create a pilot program to establish the effectiveness of pupillometer technology (the measurement of the pupil's reaction to light) as a noninvasive technique to detect and measure possible impairment of any person who drives or is in actual physical control of a motor vehicle resulting from the suspected usage of alcohol, other drug or drugs, intoxicating compound or compounds or any combination thereof. This technology shall also be used to detect fatigue levels of the operator of a Commercial Motor Vehicle as defined in Section 6-500(6), pursuant to Section 18b-105 (Part 395-Hours of Service of Drivers) of the Illinois Vehicle Code. A State Police officer may request that the operator of a commercial motor vehicle have his or her eyes examined or tested with a pupillometer device. The person may refuse the examination or test. The State Police officer shall have the device readily available to limit undue delays.

If a State Police officer has reasonable suspicion to believe that a person is violating or has violated Section 11-501, the officer may use the pupillometer technology, when available. The officer, prior to an arrest, may request the person to have his or her eyes examined or tested with a pupillometer device. The person may refuse the examination or test. The results of this examination or test may be used by the officer for the purpose of assisting with the determination of whether to require a chemical test as authorized under Sections 11-501.1 and 11-501.2 and the appropriate type of test to request. Any chemical test authorized under Sections 11-501. 1 and 11-501.2 may be requested by the officer regardless of the result of the pupillometer examination or test, if probable cause for an arrest exists. The result of the examination or test may be used by the defendant as evidence in any administrative or court proceeding involving a violation of 11-501 or 11-501.1.

The pilot program shall last for a period of 18 months and involve the testing of 15 pupillometer devices. Within 90 days of the completion of the pilot project, the Department of State Police shall file a report with the President of the Senate and Speaker of the House evaluating the project.

P.A. 76-1586, § 11-501.4, added by P.A. 85-485, § 1, eff. Jan. 1, 1988. Renumbered § 11-501.5 and amended by P.A. 85-1209, Art. II, § 2-51, eff. Aug. 30, 1988. Amended by P.A. 86-1019, § 7, eff. July 1, 1990; P.A. 88-169, § 1, eff. Jan. 1, 1994; P.A. 91-828, § 5, eff. Jan. 1, 2001; P.A. 91-881, § 5, eff. June 30, 2000; P.A. 92-16, § 85, eff. June 28, 2001.

Formerly Ill.Rev.Stat.1991, ch. 95 ½, ¶ 11-501.5.

5/11-501.6. Driver involvement in personal injury or fatal motor vehicle accident—chemical test

§ 11-501.6. Driver involvement in personal injury or fatal motor vehicle accident—chemical test.

(a) Any person who drives or is in actual control of a motor vehicle upon the public highways of this State and who has been involved in a personal injury or fatal motor vehicle accident, shall be deemed to have given consent to a breath test using a portable device as approved by the Department of State Police or to a chemical test or tests of blood, breath, or urine for the purpose of determining the content of alcohol, other drug or drugs, or intoxicating compound or compounds of such person's blood if arrested as evidenced by the issuance of a Uniform Traffic Ticket for any violation of the Illinois Vehicle Code [1] or a similar provision of a local ordinance, with the exception of equipment violations contained in Chapter 12 of this Code, or similar provisions of local ordinances. The test or tests shall be administered at the direction of the arresting officer. The law enforcement agency employing the officer shall designate which of the aforesaid tests shall be administered. A urine test may be administered even after a blood or breath test or both has been administered. Compliance with this Section does not relieve such person from the requirements of Section 11-501.1 of this Code.

(b) Any person who is dead, unconscious or who is otherwise in a condition rendering such person incapable of refusal shall be deemed not to have withdrawn the consent provided by subsection (a) of this Section. In addition, if a driver of a vehicle is receiving medical treatment as a result of a motor vehicle accident, any physician licensed to practice medicine, registered nurse or a phlebotomist acting under the direction of a licensed physician shall withdraw blood for testing purposes to ascertain the presence of alcohol, other drug or drugs, or intoxicating compound or compounds, upon the specific request of a law enforcement officer. However, no such testing shall be performed until, in the opinion of the medical personnel on scene, the withdrawal can be made without interfering with or endangering the well-being of the patient.

(c) A person requested to submit to a test as provided above shall be warned by the law enforcement officer requesting the test that a refusal to submit to the test, or submission to the test resulting in an alcohol concentration of 0.08 or more, or any amount of a drug, substance, or intoxicating compound resulting from the unlawful use or consumption of cannabis, as covered by the Cannabis Control Act, [2] a controlled substance listed in the Illinois Controlled Substances Act, [3] or an intoxicating compound listed in the Use of Intoxicating Compounds Act [4] as detected in such person's blood or urine, may result in the suspension of such person's privilege to operate a motor vehicle. The length of the suspension shall be the same as outlined in Section 6-208.1 of this Code regarding statutory summary suspensions.

(d) If the person refuses testing or submits to a test which discloses an alcohol concentration of 0.08 or more, or any amount of a drug, substance, or intoxicating compound in such person's blood or urine resulting from the unlawful use or consumption of cannabis listed in the Cannabis Control Act, a controlled substance listed in the Illinois Controlled Substances Act, or an intoxicating compound listed in the Use of Intoxicating Compounds Act, the law enforcement officer shall immediately submit a sworn report to the Secretary of State on a form prescribed by the Secretary, certifying that the test or tests were requested pursuant to subsection (a) and the person refused to submit to a test or tests or submitted to testing which disclosed an alcohol concentration of 0.08 or more, or any amount of a drug, substance, or intoxicating compound in such person's blood or urine, resulting from the unlawful use or consumption of cannabis listed in the Cannabis Control Act, a controlled substance listed in the Illinois Controlled Substances Act, or an intoxicating compound listed in the Use of Intoxicating Compounds Act.

Upon receipt of the sworn report of a law enforcement officer, the Secretary shall enter the suspension to the individual's driving record and the suspension shall be effective on the 46th day following the date notice of the suspension was given to the person.

The law enforcement officer submitting the sworn report shall serve immediate notice of this suspension on the person and such suspension shall be effective on the 46th day following the date notice was given.

In cases where the blood alcohol concentration of 0.08 or more, or any amount of a drug, substance, or intoxicating compound resulting from the unlawful use or consumption of cannabis as listed in the Cannabis Control Act, a controlled substance listed in the Illinois Controlled Substances Act, or an intoxicating compound listed in the Use of Intoxicating Compounds Act, is established by a subsequent analysis of blood or urine collected at the time of arrest, the arresting officer shall give notice as provided in this Section or by deposit in the United States mail of such notice in an envelope with postage prepaid and addressed to such person at his address as shown on the Uniform Traffic Ticket and the suspension shall be effective on the 46th day following the date notice was given.

Upon receipt of the sworn report of a law enforcement officer, the Secretary shall also give notice of the suspension to the driver by mailing a notice of the effective date of the suspension to the individual. However, should the sworn report be defective by not containing sufficient information or be completed in error, the notice of the suspension shall not be mailed to the person or entered to the driving record, but rather the sworn report shall be returned to the issuing law enforcement agency.

(e) A driver may contest this suspension of his driving privileges by requesting an administrative hearing with the Secretary in accordance with Section 2-118 of this Code. At the conclusion of a hearing held under Section 2-118 of this Code, the Secretary may rescind, continue, or modify the order of suspension. If the Secretary does not rescind the order, a restricted driving permit may be granted by the Secretary upon application being made and good cause shown. A restricted driving permit may be granted to relieve undue hardship to allow driving for employment, educational, and medical purposes as outlined in Section 6-206 of this Code. The provisions of Section 6-206 of this Code shall apply.

(f) (Blank).

(g) For the purposes of this Section, a personal injury shall include any type A injury as indicated on the traffic accident report completed by a law enforcement officer that requires immediate professional attention in either a doctor's office or a medical facility. A type A injury shall include severely bleeding wounds, distorted extremities, and injuries that require the injured party to be carried from the scene.

P.A. 76-1586, § 11-501.6, added by P.A. 86-947, § 2, eff. Jan. 1, 1991. Amended by P.A. 86-1275, § 1, eff. Jan. 1, 1991; P.A. 88-211, § 5, eff. Jan. 1, 1994; P.A. 90-43, § 5, eff. July 2, 1997; P.A. 90-779, § 5, eff. Jan. 1, 1999; P.A. 91-357, § 231, eff. July 29, 1999; P.A. 91-828, § 5, eff. Jan. 1, 2001.

Formerly Ill.Rev.Stat.1991, ch. 95 ½, ¶ 11-501.6.

1 625 ILCS 5/1-100 et seq.

2 720 ILCS 550/1 et seq.

3 720 ILCS 570/100 et seq.

4 720 ILCS 690/0.01 et seq.

Validity

The Illinois Supreme Court has held in the case of King v. Ryan, 153 Ill.2d 449, 607 N.E.2d 154, 180 Ill.Dec. 260 (1992) that implied consent for drug and alcohol testing of driver who is believed to have caused an accident involving death or personal injury pursuant to this Section is an unconstitutional violation of the 4th Amendment to the U.S. Constitution and Article I, § 6 of the Illinois Constitution.

P.A. 91-828 incorporated the amendment by P.A. 91-357.

5/11-501.7. Youthful Intoxicated Drivers' Visitation Program

§ 11-501.7. (a) As a condition of probation or discharge of a person convicted of a violation of Section 11-501 of this Code, who was less than 21 years of age at the time of the offense, or a person adjudicated delinquent pursuant to the Juvenile Court Act,[1] for violation of Section 11-501 of this Code, the Court may order the offender to participate in the Youthful Intoxicated Drivers' Visitation Program. The Program shall consist of a supervised visitation as provided by this Section by the person to at least one of the following, to the extent that personnel and facilities are available:

(1) A State or private rehabilitation facility that cares for victims of motor vehicle accidents involving persons under the influence of alcohol.

(2) A facility which cares for advanced alcoholics to observe persons in the terminal stages of alcoholism, under the supervision of appropriately licensed medical personnel.

(3) If approved by the coroner of the county where the person resides, the county coroner's office or the county morgue to observe appropriate victims of motor vehicle accidents involving persons under the influence of alcohol, under the supervision of the coroner or deputy coroner.

(b) The Program shall be operated by the appropriate probation authorities of the courts of the various circuits. The youthful offender ordered to participate in the Program shall bear all costs associated with participation in the Program. A parent or guardian of the offender may assume the obligation of the offender to pay the costs of the Program. The court may waive the requirement that the offender pay the costs of participation in the Program upon a finding of indigency.

(c) As used in this Section, "appropriate victims" means victims whose condition is determined by the visit supervisor to demonstrate the results of motor vehicle accidents involving persons under the influence of alcohol without being excessively gruesome or traumatic to the observer.

(d) Any visitation shall include, before any observation of victims or disabled persons, a comprehensive counseling session with the visitation supervisor at which the supervisor shall explain and discuss the experiences which may be encountered during the visitation in order to ascertain whether the visitation is appropriate.

P.A. 76-1586, § 11-501.7, added by P.A. 86-1242, § 1, eff. Jan. 1, 1991.

Formerly Ill.Rev.Stat.1991, ch. 95 ½, ¶ 11-501.7.

1 705 ILCS 405/1-1 et seq.

5/11-501.8. Suspension of driver's license; persons under age 21

§ 11-501.8. Suspension of driver's license; persons under age 21.

(a) A person who is less than 21 years of age and who drives or is in actual physical control of a motor vehicle upon the public highways of this State shall be deemed to have given consent to a chemical test or tests of blood, breath, or urine for the purpose of determining the alcohol content of the person's blood if arrested, as evidenced by the issuance of a Uniform Traffic Ticket for any violation of the Illinois Vehicle Code [1] or a similar provision of a local ordinance, if a police officer has probable cause to believe that the driver has consumed any amount of an alcoholic beverage based upon evidence of the driver's physical condition or other first hand knowledge of the police officer. The test or tests shall be administered at the direction of the arresting officer. The law enforcement agency employing the officer shall designate which of the aforesaid tests shall be administered. A urine test may be administered even after a blood or breath test or both has been administered.

(b) A person who is dead, unconscious, or who is otherwise in a condition rendering that person incapable of refusal, shall be deemed not to have withdrawn the consent provided by paragraph (a) of this Section and the test or tests may be administered subject to the following provisions:

(i) Chemical analysis of the person's blood, urine, breath, or other bodily substance, to be considered valid under the provisions of this Section, shall have been performed according to standards promulgated by the Department of State Police by an individual possessing a valid permit issued by that Department for this purpose. The Director of State Police is authorized to approve satisfactory techniques or methods, to ascertain the qualifications and competence of individuals to conduct analyses, to issue permits that shall be subject to termination or revocation at the direction of that Department, and to certify the accuracy of breath testing equipment. The Department of State Police shall prescribe regulations as necessary.

(ii) When a person submits to a blood test at the request of a law enforcement officer under the provisions of this Section, only a physician authorized to practice medicine, a registered nurse, or other qualified person trained in venipuncture and acting under the direction of a licensed physician may withdraw blood for the purpose of determining the alcohol content therein. This limitation does not apply to the taking of breath or urine specimens.

(iii) The person tested may have a physician, qualified technician, chemist, registered nurse, or other qualified person of his or her own choosing administer a chemical test or tests in addition to any test or tests administered at the direction of a law enforcement officer. The failure or inability to obtain an additional test by a person shall not preclude the consideration of the previously performed chemical test.

(iv) Upon a request of the person who submits to a chemical test or tests at the request of a law enforcement officer, full information concerning the test or tests shall be made available to the person or that person's attorney.

(v) Alcohol concentration means either grams of alcohol per 100 milliliters of blood or grams of alcohol per 210 liters of breath.

(vi) If a driver is receiving medical treatment as a result of a motor vehicle accident, a physician licensed to practice medicine, registered nurse, or other qualified person trained in venipuncture and acting under the direction of a licensed physician shall withdraw blood for testing purposes to ascertain the presence of alcohol upon the specific request of a law enforcement officer. However, that testing shall not be performed until, in the opinion of the medical personnel on scene, the withdrawal can be made without interfering with or endangering the well-being of the patient.

(c) A person requested to submit to a test as provided above shall be warned by the law enforcement officer requesting the test that a refusal to submit to the test, or submission to the test resulting in an alcohol concentration of more than 0.00, may result in the loss of that person's privilege to operate a motor vehicle. The loss of driving privileges shall be imposed in accordance with Section 6–208.2 of this Code.

(d) If the person refuses testing or submits to a test that discloses an alcohol concentration of more than 0.00, the law enforcement officer shall immediately submit a sworn report to the Secretary of State on a form prescribed by the Secretary of State, certifying that the test or tests were requested under subsection (a) and the person refused to submit to a test or tests or submitted to testing which disclosed an alcohol concentration of more than 0.00. The law enforcement officer shall submit the same sworn report when a person under the age of 21 submits to testing under Section 11–501.1 of this Code and the testing discloses an alcohol concentration of more than 0.00 and less than 0.08.

Upon receipt of the sworn report of a law enforcement officer, the Secretary of State shall enter the driver's license sanction on the individual's driving record and the sanctions shall be effective on the 46th day following the date notice of the sanction was given to the person. If this sanction is the individual's first driver's license suspension under this Section, reports received by the Secretary of State under this Section shall, except during the time the suspension is in effect, be privileged information and for use only by the courts, police officers, prosecuting authorities, the Secretary of State, or the individual personally.

The law enforcement officer submitting the sworn report shall serve immediate notice of this driver's license sanction on the person and the sanction shall be effective on the 46th day following the date notice was given.

In cases where the blood alcohol concentration of more than 0.00 is established by a subsequent analysis of blood or urine, the police officer or arresting agency shall give notice as provided in this Section or by deposit in the United States mail of that notice in an envelope with postage prepaid and addressed to that person at his last known address and the loss of driving privileges shall be effective on the 46th day following the date notice was given.

Upon receipt of the sworn report of a law enforcement officer, the Secretary of State shall also give notice of the driver's license sanction to the driver by mailing a notice of the effective date of the sanction to the individual. However, should the sworn report be defective by not containing sufficient information or be completed in error, the notice of the driver's license sanction may not be mailed to the person or entered to the driving record, but rather the sworn report shall be returned to the issuing law enforcement agency.

(e) A driver may contest this driver's license sanction by requesting an administrative hearing with the Secretary of State in accordance with Section 2–118 of this Code. An individual whose blood alcohol concentration is shown to be more than 0.00 is not subject to this Section if he or she consumed alcohol in the performance of a religious service or ceremony. An individual whose blood alcohol concentration is shown to be more than 0.00 shall not be subject to this Section if the individual's blood alcohol concentration resulted only from ingestion of the prescribed or recommended dosage of medicine that contained alcohol. The petition for that hearing shall not stay or delay the effective date of the impending suspension. The scope of this hearing shall be limited to the issues of:

(1) whether the police officer had probable cause to believe that the person was driving or in actual physical control of a motor vehicle upon the public highways of the State and the police officer had reason to believe that the person was in violation of any provision of the Illinois Vehicle Code or a similar provision of a local ordinance; and

(2) whether the person was issued a Uniform Traffic Ticket for any violation of the Illinois Vehicle Code or a similar provision of a local ordinance; and

(3) whether the police officer had probable cause to believe that the driver had consumed any amount of an alcoholic beverage based upon the driver's physical actions or other first-hand knowledge of the police officer; and

(4) whether the person, after being advised by the officer that the privilege to operate a motor vehicle would be

suspended if the person refused to submit to and complete the test or tests, did refuse to submit to or complete the test or tests to determine the person's alcohol concentration; and

(5) whether the person, after being advised by the officer that the privileges to operate a motor vehicle would be suspended if the person submits to a chemical test or tests and the test or tests disclose an alcohol concentration of more than 0.00, did submit to and complete the test or tests that determined an alcohol concentration of more than 0.00; and

(6) whether the test result of an alcohol concentration of more than 0.00 was based upon the person's consumption of alcohol in the performance of a religious service or ceremony; and

(7) whether the test result of an alcohol concentration of more than 0.00 was based upon the person's consumption of alcohol through ingestion of the prescribed or recommended dosage of medicine.

Provided that the petitioner may subpoena the officer, the hearing may be conducted upon a review of the law enforcement officer's own official reports. Failure of the officer to answer the subpoena shall be grounds for a continuance if, in the hearing officer's discretion, the continuance is appropriate. At the conclusion of the hearing held under Section 2-118 of this Code, the Secretary of State may rescind, continue, or modify the driver's license sanction. If the Secretary of State does not rescind the sanction, a restricted driving permit may be granted by the Secretary of State upon application being made and good cause shown. A restricted driving permit may be granted to relieve undue hardship by allowing driving for employment, educational, and medical purposes as outlined in item (3) of part (c) of Section 6-206 of this Code. The provisions of item (3) of part (c) of Section 6-206 of this Code shall apply. The Secretary of State shall promulgate rules providing for participation in an alcohol education and awareness program or activity, a drug education and awareness program or activity, or both as a condition to the issuance of a restricted driving permit for suspensions imposed under this Section.

(f) The results of any chemical testing performed in accordance with subsection (a) of this Section are not admissible in any civil or criminal proceeding, except that the results of the testing may be considered at a hearing held under Section 2-118 of this Code. However, the results of the testing may not be used to impose driver's license sanctions under Section 11-501.1 of this Code. A law enforcement officer may, however, pursue a statutory summary suspension of driving privileges under Section 11-501.1 of this Code if other physical evidence or first hand knowledge forms the basis of that suspension.

(g) This Section applies only to drivers who are under age 21 at the time of the issuance of a Uniform Traffic Ticket for a violation of the Illinois Vehicle Code or a similar provision of a local ordinance, and a chemical test request is made under this Section.

(h) The action of the Secretary of State in suspending, revoking, or denying any license, permit, registration, or certificate of title shall be subject to judicial review in the Circuit Court of Sangamon County or in the Circuit Court of Cook County, and the provisions of the Administrative Review Law [2] and its rules are hereby adopted and shall apply to and govern every action for the judicial review of final acts or decisions of the Secretary of State under this Section.
P.A. 76-1586, § 11-501.8, added by P.A. 88-588, § 5, eff. Jan. 1, 1995. Amended by P.A. 90-43, § 5, eff. July 2, 1997; P.A. 91-357, § 231, eff. July 29, 1999; P.A. 91-828, § 5, eff. Jan. 1, 2001.

[1] 625 ILCS 5/1-100 et seq.

[2] 735 ILCS 5/3-101 et seq.

P.A. 91-828 incorporated the amendment by P.A. 91-357.

5/11-502. Transportation or possession of alcoholic liquor in a motor vehicle

§ 11-502. Transportation or possession of alcoholic liquor in a motor vehicle. (a) Except as provided in paragraph (c), no driver may transport, carry, possess or have any alcoholic liquor within the passenger area of any motor vehicle upon a highway in this State except in the original container and with the seal unbroken.

(b) Except as provided in paragraph (c), no passenger may carry, possess or have any alcoholic liquor within any passenger area of any motor vehicle upon a highway in this State except in the original container and with the seal unbroken.

(c) This Section shall not apply to the passengers in a limousine when it is being used for purposes for which a limousine is ordinarily used, the passengers on a chartered bus when it is being used for purposes for which chartered buses are ordinarily used or on a motor home or mini motor home as defined in Section 1-145.01 of this Code. However, the driver of any such vehicle is prohibited from consuming or having any alcoholic liquor in or about the driver's area. Any evidence of alcoholic consumption by the driver shall be prima facie evidence of such driver's failure to obey this Section. For the purposes of this Section, a limousine is a motor vehicle of the first division with the passenger compartment enclosed by a partition or dividing window used in the for-hire transportation of passengers and operated by an individual in possession of a valid Illinois driver's license of the appropriate classification pursuant to Section 6-104 of this Code.

(d) The exemption applicable to chartered buses under paragraph (c) does not apply to any chartered bus being used for school purposes.

(e) Any driver who is convicted of violating subsection (a) of this Section for a second or subsequent time within one year of a similar conviction shall be subject to suspension of driving privileges as provided, in paragraph 23 of subsection (a) of Section 6-206 of this Code.

(f) Any driver, who is less than 21 years of age at the date of the offense and who is convicted of violating subsection (a) of this Section or a similar provision of a local ordinance, shall be subject to the loss of driving privileges as provided in paragraph 13 of subsection (a) of Section 6-205 of this Code and paragraph 33 of subsection (a) of Section 6-206 of this Code.

P.A. 76-1586, § 11-502, eff. July 1, 1970. Amended by P.A. 77-680, § 1, eff. Aug. 9, 1971; P.A. 77-2720, § 1, eff. Jan. 1, 1973; P.A. 78-255, § 28, eff. Oct. 1, 1973; P.A. 80-911, § 1, eff. Oct. 1, 1977; P.A. 80-1463, § 1, eff. Jan. 1, 1979; P.A. 83-205, § 1, eff. Jan. 1, 1984; P.A. 84-272, § 7, eff. Jan. 1, 1986; P.A. 85-951, § 1, eff. July 1, 1988; P.A. 86-747, § 1, eff. Jan. 1, 1990; P.A. 88-209, § 5, eff. Jan. 1, 1994.

Formerly Ill.Rev.Stat.1991, ch. 95 ½, ¶ 11-502.

5/11-503. Reckless driving; aggravated reckless driving

§ 11-503. Reckless driving; aggravated reckless driving. (a) Any person who drives any vehicle with a willful or wanton disregard for the safety of persons or property is guilty of reckless driving.

(b) Every person convicted of reckless driving shall be guilty of a Class A misdemeanor, except as provided under subsection (c) of this Section.

(c) Every person convicted of committing a violation of subsection (a) shall be guilty of aggravated reckless driving if the violation results in great bodily harm or permanent disability or disfigurement to another. Aggravated reckless driving is a Class 4 felony.

P.A. 76–1586, § 11–503, eff. July 1, 1970. Amended by P.A. 77–2720, § 1, eff. Jan. 1, 1973; P.A. 80–911, § 1, eff. Oct. 1, 1977; P.A. 86–581, § 2, eff. Jan. 1, 1990; P.A. 88–679, § 15, eff. July 1, 1995.

Formerly Ill.Rev.Stat.1991, ch. 95 ½, ¶ 11–503.

5/11–504. Drag racing

§ 11–504. Drag racing. Any person who, as an operator of a motor vehicle, is convicted of being a participant in drag racing shall be guilty of a Class C misdemeanor, and the driver's license of such person shall be revoked in the manner provided by Section 6–205.

"Drag racing" means the act of 2 or more individuals competing or racing on any street or highway in this State in a situation in which one of the motor vehicles is beside or to the rear of a motor vehicle operated by a competing driver and the one driver attempts to prevent the competing driver from passing or overtaking, either by acceleration or maneuver, or one or more individuals competing in a race against time on any street or highway in this State.

P.A. 76–1586, § 11–504, eff. July 1, 1970. Amended by P.A. 77–2720, § 1, eff. Jan. 1, 1973; P.A. 80–911, § 1, eff. Oct. 1, 1977; P.A. 83–831, § 1, eff. Jan. 1, 1984.

Formerly Ill.Rev.Stat.1991, ch. 95 ½, ¶ 11–504.

5/11–505. Squealing or screeching

§ 11–505. No person shall operate any motor vehicle in such a manner as to cause or allow to be emitted squealing, screeching or other such noise from the vehicle's tires due to rapid acceleration or excessive speed around corners or other such reason.

This Section shall not apply to the following conditions:

(a) an authorized emergency vehicle, when responding to an emergency call or when in the pursuit of an actual or suspected violator; nor

(b) the emergency operation of a motor vehicle when avoiding imminent danger; nor

(c) any raceway, racing facility or other public event, not part of a highway, sanctioned by the appropriate governmental authority.

P.A. 76–1586, § 11–505, added by P.A. 86–664, § 1, eff. Sept. 1, 1989.

Formerly Ill.Rev.Stat.1991, ch. 95 ½, ¶ 11–505.

ARTICLE VI. SPEED RESTRICTIONS

5/11–601. General speed restrictions

§ 11–601. General speed restrictions.

(a) No vehicle may be driven upon any highway of this State at a speed which is greater than is reasonable and proper with regard to traffic conditions and the use of the highway, or endangers the safety of any person or property. The fact that the speed of a vehicle does not exceed the applicable maximum speed limit does not relieve the driver from the duty to decrease speed when approaching and crossing an intersection, approaching and going around a curve, when approaching a hill crest, when traveling upon any narrow or winding roadway, or when special hazard exists with respect to pedestrians or other traffic or by reason of weather or highway conditions. Speed must be decreased as may be necessary to avoid colliding with any person or vehicle on or entering the highway in compliance with legal requirements and the duty of all persons to use due care.

(b) No person may drive a vehicle upon any highway of this State at a speed which is greater than the applicable statutory maximum speed limit established by paragraphs (c), (d), (e), (f) or (g) of this Section, by Section 11–605 or by a regulation or ordinance made under this Chapter.

(c) Unless some other speed restriction is established under this Chapter, the maximum speed limit in an urban district for all vehicles is:

1. 30 miles per hour; and
2. 15 miles per hour in an alley.

(d) Unless some other speed restriction is established under this Chapter, the maximum speed limit outside an urban district for any vehicle of the first division or a second division vehicle designed or used for the carrying of a gross weight of 8,000 pounds or less (including the weight of the vehicle and maximum load) is (1) 65 miles per hour (i) for all highways under the jurisdiction of the Illinois State Toll Highway Authority and (ii) for all or part of highways that are designated by the Department, have at least 4 lanes of traffic, and have a separation between the roadways moving in opposite directions and (2) 55 miles per hour for all other highways, roads, and streets.

(e) Unless some lesser speed restriction is established under this Chapter, the maximum speed limit outside an urban district for a second division vehicle designed or used for the carrying of a gross weight of 8,001 pounds or more (including the weight of the vehicle and maximum load) is 55 miles per hour.

(f) Unless some other speed restriction is established under this Chapter, the maximum speed limit outside an urban district for a bus is:

1. 65 miles per hour upon any highway which has at least 4 lanes of traffic and of which the roadways for traffic moving in opposite directions are separated by a strip of ground which is not surfaced or suitable for vehicular traffic, except that the maximum speed limit for a bus on

all highways, roads, or streets not under the jurisdiction of the Department or the Illinois State Toll Highway Authority is 55 miles per hour; and

2. 60 miles per hour on any other highway, except that the maximum speed limit for a bus on all highways, roads, or streets not under the jurisdiction of the Department or the Illinois State Toll Highway Authority is 55 miles per hour.

(g) Unless some other speed restriction is established under this Chapter, the maximum speed limit outside an urban district for a house car, camper, private living coach, vehicles licensed as recreational vehicles, and any vehicle towing any other vehicle is 55 miles per hour or the posted speed limit, whichever is less.

P.A. 76–1586, § 11–601, eff. July 1, 1970. Amended by P.A. 77–66, § 1, eff. July 1, 1971; P.A. 78–954, § 1, eff. Feb. 25, 1974; P.A. 79–267, § 1, eff. July 14, 1975; P.A. 84–730, § 1, eff. July 1, 1986; P.A. 89–444, § 5, eff. Jan. 25, 1996; P.A. 89–551, § 5, eff. Jan. 1, 1997.

Formerly Ill.Rev.Stat.1991, ch. 95 ½, ¶ 11–601.

P.A. 89–551 incorporated the amendment by P.A. 89–444.

5/11–601.5. Driving 40 miles per hour or more in excess of applicable limit

§ 11–601.5. Driving 40 miles per hour or more in excess of applicable limit. A person who drives a vehicle upon any highway of this State at a speed that is 40 miles per hour or more in excess of the applicable maximum speed limit established under this Chapter or a local ordinance commits a Class A misdemeanor.

P.A. 76–1586, § 11–601.5, added by P.A. 91–469, § 5, eff. Jan. 1, 2000.

5/11–602. Alteration of limits by Department

§ 11–602. Alteration of limits by Department. Whenever the Department determines, upon the basis of an engineering and traffic investigation concerning any highway for which the Department has maintenance responsibility, that a maximum speed limit prescribed in Section 11–601 of this Chapter is greater or less than is reasonable or safe with respect to the conditions found to exist at any intersection or other place on such highway or along any part or zone thereof, the Department shall determine and declare a reasonable and safe absolute maximum speed limit applicable to such intersection or place, or along such part or zone. However, such limit shall not exceed 65 miles per hour, or 55 miles per hour for a second division vehicle designed or used for the carrying of a gross weight of 8,001 pounds or more (including the weight of the vehicle and maximum load), on a highway or street which is especially designed for through traffic and to, from, or over which owners of or persons having an interest in abutting property or other persons have no right or easement, or only a limited right or easement, of access, crossing, light, air, or view, and shall not exceed 55 miles per hour on any other highway. A limit so determined and declared becomes effective, and suspends the applicability of the limit prescribed in Section 11–601 of this Chapter, when appropriate signs giving notice of the limit are erected at such intersection or other place, or along such part or zone of the highway. Electronic speed-detecting devices shall not be used within 500 feet beyond any such sign in the direction of travel; if so used in violation hereof, evidence obtained thereby shall be inadmissible in any prosecution for speeding. However, nothing in this Section prohibits the use of such electronic speed-detecting devices within 500 feet of a sign within a special school speed zone indicating such zone, conforming to the requirements of Section 11–605 of this Act, nor shall evidence obtained thereby be inadmissible in any prosecution for speeding provided the use of such device shall apply only to the enforcement of the speed limit in such special school speed zone.

P.A. 76–1586, § 11–602, eff. July 1, 1970. Amended by P.A. 77–101, § 1, eff. Jan. 1, 1972; P.A. 78–954, § 1, eff. Feb. 5, 1974; P.A. 79–267, § 1, eff. July 14, 1975; P.A. 89–444, § 5, eff. Jan. 25, 1996; P.A. 89–551, § 5, eff. Jan. 1, 1997.

Formerly Ill.Rev.Stat.1991, ch. 95 ½, ¶ 11–602.

P.A. 89–551 incorporated the amendment by P.A. 89–444.

5/11–603. Alteration of limits by Toll Highway Authority

§ 11–603. Alteration of limits by Toll Highway Authority. Whenever the Illinois State Toll Highway Authority determines, upon the basis of an engineering and traffic investigation concerning a toll highway under its jurisdiction, that a maximum speed limit prescribed in Section 11–601 of this Chapter is greater or less than is reasonable or safe with respect to conditions found to exist at any place or along any part or zone of such highway, the Authority shall determine and declare by regulation a reasonable and safe absolute maximum speed limit at such place or along such part or zone, not exceeding 65 miles per hour. A limit so determined and declared becomes effective, and suspends the application of the limit prescribed in Section 11–601 of this Chapter, when (a) the Department concurs in writing with the Authority's regulation, and (b) appropriate signs giving notice of the limit are erected at such place or along such part or zone of the highway. Electronic speed-detecting devices shall not be used within 500 feet beyond any such sign in the direction of travel; if so used in violation hereof, evidence obtained thereby shall be inadmissible in any prosecution for speeding.

P.A. 76–1586, § 11–603, eff. July 1, 1970. Amended by P.A. 77–643, § 1, eff. Aug. 4, 1971; P.A. 78–954, § 1, eff. Feb. 25, 1974; P.A. 79–267, § 1, eff. July 14, 1975; P.A. 89–444, § 5, eff. Jan. 25, 1996.

Formerly Ill.Rev.Stat.1991, ch. 95 ½, ¶ 11–603.

5/11–604. Alteration of limits by local authorities

§ 11–604. Alteration of limits by local authorities. Subject to the limitations set forth in this Section, the county board of a county may establish absolute maximum speed limits on all county highways, township roads and district roads as defined in the Illinois Highway Code,[1] except those under the jurisdiction of the Department or of the Illinois State Toll Highway Authority, as described in Sections 11–602 and 11–603 of this Chapter; and any park district, city, village, or incorporated town may establish absolute maximum speed limits on all streets which are within its corporate limits and which are not under the jurisdiction of the Department or of such Authority, and for which the county or a highway commissioner of such county does not have maintenance responsibility.

Whenever any such park district, city, village, or incorporated town determines, upon the basis of an engineering or traffic investigation concerning a highway or street on which it is authorized by this Section to establish speed limits, that a maximum speed limit prescribed in Section 11–601 of this Chapter is greater or less than is reasonable or safe with respect to the conditions found to exist at any place or along any part or zone of such highway or street, the local authority or park district shall determine and declare by ordinance a reasonable and safe absolute maximum speed limit at such place or along such part or zone, which:

(1) Decreases the limit within an urban district, but not to less than 20 miles per hour; or

(2) Increases the limit within an urban district, but not to more than 55 miles per hour; or

(3) Decreases the limit outside of an urban district, but not to less than 35 miles per hour, except as otherwise provided in subparagraph 4 of this paragraph; or

(4) Decreases the limit within a residence district, but not to less than 25 miles per hour, except as otherwise provided in subparagraph 1 of this paragraph.

The park district, city, village, or incorporated town may make such limit applicable at all times or only during certain specified times. Not more than 6 such alterations shall be made per mile along a highway or street; and the difference in limit between adjacent altered speed zones shall not be more than 10 miles per hour.

A limit so determined and declared by a park district, city, village, or incorporated town becomes effective, and suspends the application of the limit prescribed in Section 11-601 of this Chapter, when appropriate signs giving notice of the limit are erected at the proper place or along the proper part or zone of the highway or street. Electronic speed-detecting devices shall not be used within 500 feet beyond any such sign in the direction of travel; if so used in violation of this Section evidence obtained thereby shall be inadmissible in any prosecution for speeding. However, nothing in this Section prohibits the use of such electronic speed-detecting devices within 500 feet of a sign within a special school speed zone indicating such zone, conforming to the requirements of Section 11-605 of this Act, nor shall evidence obtained thereby be inadmissible in any prosecution for speeding provided the use of such device shall apply only to the enforcement of the speed limit in such special school speed zone. A county engineer or superintendent of highways may submit to the Department for approval, a county policy for establishing altered speed zones on township and county highways based upon engineering and traffic investigations.

Whenever the county board of a county determines that a maximum speed limit is greater or less than is reasonable or safe with respect to the conditions found to exist at any place or along any part or zone of the highway or road, the county board shall determine and declare by ordinance a reasonable and safe absolute maximum speed limit at that place or along that part or zone. However, the maximum speed limit shall not exceed 55 miles per hour. The limit becomes effective, and suspends the application of the limit prescribed in Section 11-601 of this Chapter, when appropriate signs giving notice of the limit are erected at the proper place or along the proper part of the zone of the highway. Electronic speed-detecting devices shall not be used within 500 feet beyond any such sign in the direction of travel; if so used in violation of this Section, evidence obtained thereby shall be inadmissible in any prosecution for speeding. However, nothing in this Section prohibits the use of such electronic speed-detecting devices within 500 feet of a sign within a special school speed zone indicating such zone, conforming to the requirements of Section 11-605 of this Act, nor shall evidence obtained thereby be inadmissible in any prosecution for speeding provided the use of such device shall apply only to the enforcement of the speed limit in such special school speed zone.

P.A. 76-1586, § 11-604, eff. July 1, 1970. Amended by P.A. 77-50, § 1, eff. Jan. 1, 1972; P.A. 77-101, § 1, eff. Jan. 1, 1972; P.A. 77-643, § 1, eff. Aug. 4, 1971; P.A. 77-2829, § 40, eff. Dec. 22, 1972; P.A. 78-255, § 61, eff. Oct. 1, 1973; P.A. 78-954, § 1, eff. Feb. 25, 1974; P.A. 78-1297, § 58, eff. March 4, 1975; P.A. 79-267, § 1, eff. July 14, 1975; P.A. 80-693, § 1, eff. Oct. 1, 1977; P.A. 81-875, § 1, eff. Jan. 1, 1980; P.A. 85-547, § 1, eff. Jan. 1, 1988; P.A. 87-217, § 4, eff. Jan. 1, 1992; P.A. 89-444, § 5, eff. Jan. 25, 1996.

Formerly Ill.Rev.Stat.1991, ch. 95 ½, ¶ 11-604.

[1] 605 ILCS 5/1-101 et seq.

5/11-605. Special speed limit while passing schools or while traveling through highway construction or maintenance zones

§ 11-605. Special speed limit while passing schools or while traveling through highway construction or maintenance zones.

(a) For the purpose of this Section, "school" means the following entities:

(1) A public or private primary or secondary school.

(2) A primary or secondary school operated by a religious institution.

(3) A public, private, or religious nursery school.

On a school day when school children are present and so close thereto that a potential hazard exists because of the close proximity of the motorized traffic, no person shall drive a motor vehicle at a speed in excess of 20 miles per hour while passing a school zone or while traveling on a roadway on public school property or upon any public thoroughfare where children pass going to and from school.

For the purpose of this Section a school day shall begin at seven ante meridian and shall conclude at four post meridian.

This Section shall not be applicable unless appropriate signs are posted upon streets and highways under their respective jurisdiction and maintained by the Department, township, county, park district, city, village or incorporated town wherein the school zone is located. With regard to the special speed limit while passing schools, such signs shall give proper due warning that a school zone is being approached and shall indicate the school zone and the maximum speed limit in effect during school days when school children are present.

(b) No person shall operate a motor vehicle in a construction or maintenance zone at a speed in excess of the posted speed limit when workers are present and so close to the moving traffic that a potential hazard exists because of the motorized traffic.

(c) Nothing in this Chapter shall prohibit the use of electronic speed-detecting devices within 500 feet of signs within a special school speed zone or a construction or maintenance zone indicating such zone, as defined in this Section, nor shall evidence obtained thereby be inadmissible in any prosecution for speeding provided the use of such device shall apply only to the enforcement of the speed limit in such special school speed zone or a construction or maintenance zone.

(d) For the purpose of this Section, a construction or maintenance zone is an area in which the Department, Toll Highway Authority, or local agency has determined that the preexisting established speed limit through a highway construction or maintenance project is greater than is reasonable or safe with respect to the conditions expected to exist in the construction or maintenance zone and has posted a lower speed limit with a highway construction or maintenance zone special speed limit sign.

Highway construction or maintenance zone special speed limit signs shall be of a design approved by the Department. The signs shall give proper due warning that a construction or maintenance zone is being approached and shall indicate the maximum speed limit in effect. The signs shall also state the amount of the minimum fine for a violation when workers are present.

(e) A first violation of this Section is a petty offense with a minimum fine of $150. A second or subsequent violation of this Section is a petty offense with a minimum fine of $300.

(f) When a fine for a violation of subsection (a) is $150 or greater, the person who violates subsection (a) shall be charged an additional $50 to be paid to the unit school district where the violation occurred for school safety purposes. If the violation occurred in a dual school district, $25 of the surcharge shall be paid to the elementary school district for school safety purposes and $25 of the surcharge shall be paid to the high school district for school safety purposes. Notwithstanding any other provision of law, the entire $50 surcharge shall be paid to the appropriate school district or districts.

For purposes of this subsection (f), "school safety purposes" includes the costs associated with school zone safety education and the purchase, installation, and maintenance of caution lights which are mounted on school speed zone signs.

(g) When a fine for a violation of subsection (b) is $150 or greater, the person who violates subsection (b) shall be charged an additional $50. The $50 surcharge shall be deposited into the Transportation Safety Highway Hire-back Fund.

(h) The Transportation Safety Highway Hire-back Fund is created as a special fund in the State treasury. Subject to appropriation by the General Assembly and approval by the Secretary, the Secretary of Transportation shall use all moneys in the Transportation Safety Highway Hire-back Fund to hire off-duty Department of State Police officers to monitor construction or maintenance zones.

P.A. 76-1586, § 11-605, eff. July 1, 1970. Amended by P.A. 77-101, § 1, eff. Jan. 1, 1972; P.A. 82-124, § 1, eff. Jan. 1, 1982; P.A. 89-251, § 5, eff. Jan. 1, 1996; P.A. 89-559, § 5, eff. Jan. 1, 1997; P.A. 91-531, § 5, eff. Jan. 1, 2000; P.A. 92-242, § 5, eff. Jan. 1, 2002; P.A. 92-619, § 10, eff. Jan. 1, 2003; P.A. 92-780, § 5, eff. Aug. 6, 2002.

Formerly Ill.Rev.Stat.1991, ch. 95 ½, ¶ 11-605.

P.A. 92-619 incorporated the amendment by P.A. 92-242.

P.A. 92-780 incorporated the amendment by P.A. 92-242.

See 5 ILCS 70/6 as to the effect of (1) more than one amendment of a section at the same session of the General Assembly or (2) two or more acts relating to the same subject matter enacted by the same General Assembly.

5/11-606. Minimum speed regulation

§ 11-606. Minimum speed regulation. (a) No person shall drive a motor vehicle at such a slow speed as to impede or block the normal and reasonable movement of traffic except when reduced speed is necessary for safe operation of his vehicle or in compliance with law.

(b) Whenever the Department, The Illinois State Toll Highway Authority, or a local authority described in Section 11-604 of this Chapter determines, upon the basis of an engineering and traffic investigation concerning a highway or street under its jurisdiction that slow vehicle speeds along any part or zone of such highway or street consistently impede the normal and reasonable movement of traffic, the Department, the Toll Highway Authority, or local authority (as appropriate) may determine and declare by proper regulation or ordinance a minimum speed limit below which no person shall drive except when necessary for safe operation of his vehicle or in compliance with law. A limit so determined and declared becomes effective when appropriate signs giving notice of the limit are erected along such part or zone of the highway or street.

P.A. 76-1586, § 11-606, eff. July 1, 1970. Amended by P.A. 81-840, § 41, eff. Sept. 19, 1979.

Formerly Ill.Rev.Stat.1991, ch. 95 ½, ¶ 11-606.

5/11-607. § 11-607. Repealed by P.A. 78-253, § 2, eff. Oct. 1, 1973

5/11-608. Special speed limitation on elevated structures

§ 11-608. Special speed limitation on elevated structures. (a) No person shall drive a vehicle over any bridge or other elevated structure constituting a part of a highway at a speed which is greater than the maximum speed which can be maintained with safety to such bridge or structure, when such structure is sign posted as provided in this Section.

(b) The Department upon request from any local authority shall, or upon its own initiative may, conduct an investigation of any bridge or other elevated structure constituting a part of a highway, and if it shall thereupon find that such structure cannot with safety to itself withstand vehicles traveling at the speed otherwise permissible under this Chapter, the Department shall determine and declare the maximum speed of vehicles which such structure can safely withstand, and shall cause or permit suitable signs stating such maximum speed to be erected and maintained before each end of such structure.

(c) Upon the trial of any person charged with a violation of this Section, proof of the determination of the maximum speed by the Department and the existence of such signs is conclusive evidence of the maximum speed which can be maintained with safety to such bridge or structure.

P.A. 76-1586, § 11-608, eff. July 1, 1970.

Formerly Ill.Rev.Stat.1991, ch. 95 ½, ¶ 11-608.

5/11-609. § 11-609. Repealed by P.A. 76-2165, § 1, eff. July 1, 1970

5/11-610. Charging violations and rule in civil actions

§ 11-610. Charging violations and rule in civil actions. (a) In every charge of violation of any speed regulation in this article the complaint, and also the summons or notice to appear, shall specify the speed at which the defendant is alleged to have driven and the maximum speed applicable within the district or at the location.

(b) The provision of this article declaring maximum speed limitations shall not be construed to relieve the plaintiff in any action from the burden of proving negligence on the part of the defendant as the proximate cause of an accident.

P.A. 76-1586, § 11-610, eff. July 1, 1970. Amended by P.A. 79-1069, § 1, eff. Jan. 1, 1976.

Formerly Ill.Rev.Stat.1991, ch. 95 ½, ¶ 11-610.

5/11-611. Maximum attainable operating speed

§ 11-611. No person shall drive or operate any motor vehicle on any street or highway in this State where the minimum allowable speed on that street or highway, as posted, is greater than the maximum attainable operating speed of the vehicle. Maximum attainable operating speed shall be determined by the manufacturer of the vehicle and clearly published in the manual of specifications and operation, or it shall be determined by applicable rule and regulation promulgated by the Secretary of State.

P.A. 76-1586, § 11-611, added by P.A. 79-700, § 1, eff. Oct. 1, 1975.

Formerly Ill.Rev.Stat.1991, ch. 95 ½, ¶ 11-611.

ARTICLE VII. DRIVING ON RIGHT SIDE OF ROADWAY—OVERTAKING AND PASSING, ETC.

5/11-701. Drive on right side of roadway—Exceptions

§ 11-701. Drive on right side of roadway—Exceptions. (a) Upon all roadways of sufficient width a vehicle shall be driven upon the right half of the roadway, except as follows:

1. When overtaking and passing another vehicle proceeding in the same direction under the rules governing such movements;

2. When an obstruction exists making it necessary to drive to the left of the center of the roadway; provided, any person so doing shall yield the right-of-way to all vehicles traveling in the proper direction upon the unobstructed portion of the roadway within such distance as to constitute an immediate hazard;

3. Upon a roadway divided into three marked lanes for traffic under the rules applicable thereon;

4. Upon a roadway restricted to one way traffic;

5. Whenever there is a single track paved road on one side of the public highway and 2 vehicles meet thereon, the driver on whose right is the wider shoulder shall give the right-of-way on such pavement to the other vehicle.

(b) Upon all roadways any vehicle proceeding at less than the normal speed of traffic at the time and place and under the conditions then existing shall be driven in the right-hand lane available for traffic, or as close as practicable to the right hand curb or edge of the roadway, except when overtaking and passing another vehicle proceeding in the same direction or when preparing for a left turn at an intersection or into a private road or driveway.

(c) Upon any roadway having 4 or more lanes for moving traffic and providing for 2-way movement of traffic, no vehicle shall be driven to the left of the center line of the roadway, except when authorized by official traffic-control devices designating certain lanes to the left side of the center of the roadway for use by traffic not otherwise permitted to use such lanes, or except as permitted under Subsection (a)2. However, this Subsection shall not be construed as prohibiting the crossing of the center line in making a left turn into or from an alley, private road or driveway.

P.A. 76-1586, § 11-701, eff. July 1, 1970. Amended by P.A. 76-1739, § 1; P.A. 76-2166, § 1, eff. July 1, 1970; P.A. 77-1344, § 1, eff. Aug. 27, 1971.

Formerly Ill.Rev.Stat.1991, ch. 95 ½, ¶ 11-701.

5/11-702. Passing vehicles proceeding in opposite directions

§ 11-702. Passing vehicles proceeding in opposite directions. Drivers of vehicles proceeding in opposite directions shall pass each other to the right, and upon roadways having width for not more than one line of traffic in each direction each driver shall give to the other at least one-half of the main-traveled portion of the roadway as nearly as possible.

P.A. 76-1586, § 11-702, eff. July 1, 1970. Amended by P.A. 79-1069, § 1, eff. Jan. 1, 1976.

Formerly Ill.Rev.Stat.1991, ch. 95 ½, ¶ 11-702.

5/11-703. Overtaking a vehicle on the left

§ 11-703. Overtaking a vehicle on the left. The following rules govern the overtaking and passing of vehicles proceeding in the same direction, subject to those limitations, exceptions, and special rules otherwise stated in this Chapter:

(a) The driver of a vehicle overtaking another vehicle proceeding in the same direction shall pass to the left thereof at a safe distance and shall not again drive to the right side of the roadway until safely clear of the overtaken vehicle. In no event shall such movement be made by driving off the pavement or the main traveled portion of the roadway.

(b) Except when overtaking and passing on the right is permitted, the driver of an overtaken vehicle shall give way to the right in favor of the overtaking vehicle on audible signal and shall not increase the speed of his vehicle until completely passed by the overtaking vehicle.

(c) The driver of a 2 wheeled vehicle may not, in passing upon the left of any vehicle proceeding in the same direction, pass upon the right of any vehicle proceeding in the same direction unless there is an unobstructed lane of traffic available to permit such passing maneuver safely.

P.A. 76-1586, § 11-703, eff. July 1, 1970.

Formerly Ill.Rev.Stat.1991, ch. 95 ½, ¶ 11-703.

5/11-704. When overtaking on the right is permitted

§ 11-704. When overtaking on the right is permitted. (a) The driver of a vehicle with 3 or more wheels may overtake and pass upon the right of another vehicle only under the following conditions:

1. When the vehicle overtaken is making or about to make a left turn;

2. Upon a roadway with unobstructed pavement of sufficient width for two or more lines of vehicles moving lawfully in the direction being traveled by the overtaking vehicle.

3. Upon a one-way street, or upon any roadway on which traffic is restricted to one direction of movement, where the roadway is free from obstructions and of sufficient width for 2 or more lines of moving vehicles.

(b) The driver of a 2 wheeled vehicle may not pass upon the right of any other vehicle proceeding in the same direction unless the unobstructed pavement to the right of the vehicle being passed is of a width of not less than 8 feet.

(c) The driver of a vehicle may overtake and pass another vehicle upon the right only under conditions permitting such movement in safety. Such movement shall not be made by driving off the roadway.

P.A. 76-1586, § 11-704, eff. July 1, 1970. Amended by P.A. 84-873, § 1, eff. Jan. 1, 1986.

Formerly Ill.Rev.Stat.1991, ch. 95 ½, ¶ 11-704.

5/11-705. Limitations on overtaking on the left

§ 11-705. Limitations on overtaking on the left. No vehicle shall be driven to the left side of the center of the roadway in overtaking and passing another vehicle proceeding in the same direction unless authorized by the provisions of this Chapter and unless such left side is clearly visible and is free of oncoming traffic for a sufficient distance ahead to permit such overtaking and passing to be completely made without interfering with the safe operation of any vehicle approaching from the opposite direction or any vehicle overtaken. In every event the overtaking vehicle must return to an authorized lane of travel as soon as practicable and in the event the passing movement involves the use of a lane authorized for vehicles approaching from the opposite direction, before coming within 200 feet of any vehicle approaching from the opposite direction.

P.A. 76-1586, § 11-705, eff. July 1, 1970.

Formerly Ill.Rev.Stat.1991, ch. 95 ½, ¶ 11-705.

5/11-706. Further limitations on driving to the left of center of roadway

§ 11-706. Further limitations on driving to the left of center of roadway. (a) No vehicle shall be driven on the left side of the roadway under the following conditions:

1. When approaching or upon the crest of a grade or a curve in the highway where the driver's view is obstructed within such distance as to create a hazard in the event another vehicle might approach from the opposite direction.

2. When approaching within 100 feet of or traversing any intersection or railroad grade crossing.

3. When the view is obstructed upon approaching within 100 feet of any bridge, viaduct or tunnel.

(b) The limitations in sub-paragraphs 1, 2 and 3 do not apply upon a one-way roadway nor upon a roadway with unobstructed pavement of sufficient width for 2 or more lanes of moving traffic in each direction nor to the driver of a vehicle turning left into or from an alley, private road or driveway when such movements can be made with safety.

P.A. 76-1586, § 11-706, eff. July 1, 1970. Amended by P.A. 76-1739, § 1; P.A. 79-1069, § 1, eff. Jan. 1, 1976.

Formerly Ill.Rev.Stat.1991, ch. 95 ½, ¶ 11-706.

5/11-707. No-passing zones

§ 11-707. No-passing zones. (a) The Department and local authorities are authorized to determine those portions of any highway under their respective jurisdictions where overtaking and passing or driving on the left of the roadway would be especially hazardous and may by appropriate signs or markings on the roadway indicate the beginning and end of such zones. Upon request of a local school board, the Department or local authority which has jurisdiction over the roadway in question, shall determine whether a hazardous situation exists at a particular location and warrants a no-passing zone. If the Department or local authority determines that a no-passing zone is warranted, the school board and the Department or local authority shall share equally the cost of designating the no-passing zone by signs and markings. When such signs or markings are in place and clearly visible to an ordinarily observant person every driver of a vehicle shall obey the directions thereof.

(b) Where signs or markings are in place to define a no-passing zone as set forth in paragraph (a) no driver may at any time drive on the left side of the roadway within the no-passing zone or on the left side of any pavement striping designed to mark such no-passing zone throughout its length.

(c) This Section does not apply under the conditions described in Section 11-701(a)2, nor to the driver of a vehicle turning left into or from an alley, private road or driveway. The pavement striping designed to mark the no-passing zone may be crossed from the left hand lane for the purpose of completing a pass that was begun prior to the beginning of the zone in the driver's direction of travel.

(d) Special speed limit areas required under Section 11-605 of this Code in unincorporated areas only shall also be no-passing zones.

P.A. 76-1586, § 11-707, eff. July 1, 1970. Amended by P.A. 76-1739, § 1; P.A. 79-918, § 1, eff. Oct. 1, 1975; P.A. 79-1068, § 1, eff. Jan. 1, 1976; P.A. 79-1454, § 44, eff. Aug. 31, 1976; P.A. 86-471, § 1, eff. July 1, 1990.

Formerly Ill.Rev.Stat.1991, ch. 95 ½, ¶ 11-707.

5/11-708. One-way roadways and rotary traffic islands

§ 11-708. One-way roadways and rotary traffic islands. (a) The Department and local authorities, with respect to highways under their respective jurisdictions, may designate any highway, roadway, part of a roadway or specific lanes upon which vehicular traffic shall proceed in one direction at all or such times as shall be indicated by official traffic control devices.

(b) Upon a roadway so designated for one-way traffic, a vehicle shall be driven only in the direction designated at all or such times as shall be indicated by official traffic control devices.

(c) A vehicle passing around a rotary traffic island must be driven only to the right of such island.

(d) Whenever any highway has been divided into 2 or more roadways by leaving an intervening space or by a physical barrier or a clearly indicated dividing section so constructed as to impede vehicular traffic, every vehicle must be driven only upon the right-hand roadway unless directed or permitted to use another roadway by official traffic-control devices or police officers. No vehicle may be driven over, across, or within any such dividing space, barrier, or section, except through an opening in the physical barrier, or dividing section, or space, or at a cross-over or intersection as established by public authority.

(e) The driver of a vehicle may turn left across a paved noncurbed dividing space unless prohibited by an official traffic-control device.

P.A. 76-1586, § 11-708, eff. July 1, 1970. Amended by P.A. 76-1739, § 1; P.A. 84-873, § 1, eff. Jan. 1, 1986.

Formerly Ill.Rev.Stat.1991, ch. 95 ½, ¶ 11-708.

5/11-709. Driving on roadways laned for traffic

§ 11-709. Driving on roadways laned for traffic. Whenever any roadway has been divided into 2 or more clearly marked lanes for traffic the following rules in addition to all others consistent herewith shall apply.

(a) A vehicle shall be driven as nearly as practicable entirely within a single lane and shall not be moved from such lane until the driver has first ascertained that such movement can be made with safety.

(b) Upon a roadway which is divided into 3 lanes and provides for two-way movement of traffic, a vehicle shall not be driven in the center lane except when overtaking and passing another vehicle traveling in the same direction when such center lane is clear of traffic within a safe distance, or in preparation for making a left turn or where such center lane is at the time allocated exclusively to traffic moving in the same direction that the vehicle is proceeding and such allocation is designated by official traffic control devices.

(c) Official traffic control devices may be erected directing specific traffic to use a designated lane or designating those lanes to be used by traffic moving in a particular direction regardless of the center of the roadway and drivers of vehicles shall obey the directions of every such device. On multi-lane controlled access highways with 3 or more lanes in one direction or on any multi-laned highway with 2 or more lanes in one direction, the Department may designate lanes of traffic to be used by different types of motor vehicles. Drivers must obey lane designation signing except when it is necessary to use a different lane to make a turning maneuver.

(d) Official traffic control devices may be installed prohibiting the changing of lanes on sections of roadway and drivers of vehicles shall obey the directions of every such device.

P.A. 76-1586, § 11-709, eff. July 1, 1970. Amended by P.A. 77-67, § 1, eff. July 1, 1971; P.A. 84-1311, § 1, eff. Aug. 27, 1986.

Formerly Ill.Rev.Stat.1991, ch. 95 ½, ¶ 11-709.

5/11-709.1. Driving on shoulder

§ 11-709.1. (a) Vehicles shall be driven on a roadway, and shall only be driven on the shoulder for the purpose of stopping or accelerating from a stop while merging into traffic. It shall be a violation of this Section if while merging into traffic and while on the shoulder, the vehicle passes any other vehicle on the roadway adjacent to it.

(b) This Section shall not apply to any authorized emergency vehicle, or to any service vehicle while engaged in maintenance of the highway or related work.

P.A. 76-1586, § 11-709.1, added by P.A. 86-664, § 1, eff. Sept. 1, 1989.

Formerly Ill.Rev.Stat.1991, ch. 95 ½, ¶ 11-709.1.

5/11-710. Following too closely

§ 11-710. Following too closely. (a) The driver of a motor vehicle shall not follow another vehicle more closely than is reasonable and prudent, having due regard for the speed of such vehicles and the traffic upon and the condition of the highway.

(b) The driver of any truck or motor vehicle drawing another vehicle when traveling upon a roadway outside of a business or residence district and which is following another truck or motor vehicle drawing another vehicle shall, whenever conditions permit, leave sufficient space so that an overtaking vehicle may enter and occupy such space without danger, except that this shall not prevent a truck or motor vehicle drawing another vehicle from overtaking and passing any vehicle or combination of vehicles.

(c) Motor vehicles being driven upon any roadway outside of a business or residence district in a caravan or motorcade whether or not towing other vehicles shall be so operated as to allow sufficient space between each such vehicle or combination of vehicles so as to enable any other vehicle to enter and occupy such space without danger. This provision shall not apply to funeral processions.

P.A. 76-1586, § 11-710, eff. July 1, 1970. Amended by P.A. 79-1069, § 1, eff. Jan. 1, 1976.

Formerly Ill.Rev.Stat.1991, ch. 95 ½, ¶ 11-710.

5/11-711. Restrictions on use of controlled access highway

§ 11-711. Restrictions on use of controlled access highway. (a) No person may drive a vehicle onto or from any controlled access highway except at entrances and exits established by public authority.

(b) The Department with respect to any controlled access highway under its jurisdiction may prohibit the use of any such highways by pedestrians (except in authorized areas or facilities), bicycles, farm tractors, implements of husbandry, funeral processions, and any vehicle unable to maintain the minimum speed for which the highway is posted, or other non-motorized traffic or by any person operating a motor driven cycle. The Department may also prohibit the use of such highway to school buses picking up and discharging children and mail delivery vehicles picking up or delivering mail. The Department shall erect and maintain official signs on the controlled access highway on which such prohibitions are applicable and when so erected no person may disobey the restrictions stated on such sign.

P.A. 76-1586, § 11-711, eff. July 1, 1970.

Formerly Ill.Rev.Stat.1991, ch. 95 ½, ¶ 11-711.

ARTICLE VIII. TURNING AND STARTING AND SIGNALS ON STOPPING AND TURNING

Section

5/11-801. Required position and method of turning

§ 11-801. Required position and method of turning. (a) The driver of a vehicle intending to turn at an intersection shall do so as follows:

(1) Both the approach for a right turn and a right turn shall be made as close as practical to the right-hand curb or edge of the roadway.

(2) The driver of a vehicle intending to turn left at any intersection shall approach the intersection in the extreme left-hand lane lawfully available to traffic moving in the direction of travel of such vehicle, and after entering the intersection, the left turn shall be made so as to leave the intersection in a lane lawfully available to traffic moving in such direction upon the roadway being entered. Whenever practicable the left turn shall be made in that portion of the intersection to the left of the center of the intersection.

(3) The Department and local authorities in their respective jurisdictions may cause official traffic control devices to be placed within or adjacent to intersections and thereby require and direct that a different course from that specified in this Section be traveled by vehicles turning at an intersection, and when such devices are so placed no driver of a vehicle shall turn a vehicle at an intersection other than as directed and required by such devices.

(b) Two-way left turn lanes. Where a special lane for making left turns by drivers proceeding in opposite directions has been indicated by official traffic-control devices:

(1) A left turn shall not be made from any other lane.

(2) A vehicle shall not be driven in the lane except when preparing for or making a left turn from or into the roadway or when preparing for or making a U turn when otherwise permitted by law.

(c) When a motor vehicle and a mass transit bus are traveling in the same direction on the same multi-laned highway, street or road, the operator of the motor vehicle overtaking such bus, which is stopped at an intersection on the right side of the roadway to receive or discharge passengers, shall pass to the left of the bus at a safe distance and shall not turn to the right in front of the bus at that intersection.

P.A. 76-1586, § 11-801, eff. July 1, 1970. Amended by P.A. 76-1739, § 1; P.A. 81-860, § 1, eff. Jan. 1, 1980; P.A. 84-873, § 1, eff. Jan. 1, 1986; P.A. 85-786, § 1, eff. Jan. 1, 1988.

Formerly Ill.Rev.Stat.1991, ch. 95 ½, ¶ 11-801.

5/11-802. Limitations on U turns

§ 11-802. Limitations on U turns. (a) The driver of any vehicle shall not turn such vehicle so as to proceed in the opposite direction unless such movement can be made in safety and without interfering with other traffic.

(b) No vehicle shall be turned so as to proceed in the opposite direction upon any curve, or upon the approach to or near the crest of a grade, where such vehicle cannot be seen by the driver of any other vehicle approaching from either direction within 500 feet.

P.A. 76-1586, § 11-802, eff. July 1, 1970. Amended by P.A. 79-1068, § 1, eff. Jan. 1, 1976; P.A. 82-783, Art. IV, § 25, eff. July 13, 1982.

Formerly Ill.Rev.Stat.1991, ch. 95 ½, ¶ 11-802.

5/11-803. Starting parked vehicle

§ 11-803. Starting parked vehicle. No person shall start a vehicle which is stopped, standing, or parked unless and until such movement can be made with reasonable safety.

P.A. 76-1586, § 11-803, eff. July 1, 1970.

Formerly Ill.Rev.Stat.1991, ch. 95 ½, ¶ 11-803.

5/11-804. When signal required

§ 11-804. When signal required. (a) No person may turn a vehicle at an intersection unless the vehicle is in proper position upon the roadway as required in Section 11-801 or turn a vehicle to enter a private road or driveway, or otherwise turn a vehicle from a direct course or move right or left upon a roadway unless and until such movement can be made with reasonable safety. No person may so turn any vehicle without giving an appropriate signal in the manner hereinafter provided.

(b) A signal of intention to turn right or left when required must be given continuously during not less than the last 100 feet traveled by the vehicle before turning within a business or residence district, and such signal must be given continuously during not less than the last 200 feet traveled by the vehicle before turning outside a business or residence district.

(c) No person may stop or suddenly decrease the speed of a vehicle without first giving an appropriate signal in the manner provided in this Chapter to the driver of any vehicle immediately to the rear when there is opportunity to give such a signal.

(d) The electric turn signal device required in Section 12-208 of this Act must be used to indicate an intention to turn, change lanes or start from a parallel parked position but must not be flashed on one side only on a parked or disabled vehicle or flashed as a courtesy or "do pass" signal to operators of other vehicles approaching from the rear. However, such signal devices may be flashed simultaneously on both sides of a motor vehicle to indicate the presence of a vehicular traffic hazard requiring unusual care in approaching, overtaking and passing.

P.A. 76-1586, § 11-804, eff. July 1, 1970. Amended by P.A. 76-2167, § 1, eff. July 1, 1970; P.A. 78-510, § 1, eff. Oct. 1, 1973; P.A. 78-738, § 1, eff. Jan. 1, 1974; P.A. 78-1297, § 58, eff. March 4, 1975.

Formerly Ill.Rev.Stat.1991, ch. 95 ½, ¶ 11-804.

5/11-805. Signal by hand or arm or signal device

§ 11-805. Signal by hand or arm or signal device. Any stop or turn signal when required herein shall be given either by means of the hand and arm or by an electric turn signal device conforming to the requirements provided in Section 12-208 of this act.

P.A. 76-1586, § 11-805, eff. July 1, 1970. Amended by P.A. 79-1069, § 1, eff. Jan. 1, 1976.

Formerly Ill.Rev.Stat.1991, ch. 95 ½, ¶ 11-805.

5/11-806. Method of giving hand and arm signals

§ 11-806. Method of giving hand and arm signals. All signals herein required given by hand and arm shall be given from the left side of the vehicle in the following manner and such signals shall indicate as follows:

1. Left turn—Hand and arm extended horizontally.
2. Right turn—Hand and arm extended upward.
3. Stop or decrease of speed—Hand and arm extended downward.

P.A. 76-1586, § 11-806, eff. July 1, 1970.

Formerly Ill.Rev.Stat.1991, ch. 95 ½, ¶ 11-806.

ARTICLE IX. RIGHT-OF-WAY

Section

5/11-901. Vehicles approaching or entering intersection

§ 11-901. Vehicles approaching or entering intersection. (a) When 2 vehicles approach or enter an intersection from different roadways at approximately the same time, the driver of the vehicle on the left must yield the right-of-way to the vehicle on the right.

(b) The right-of-way rule declared in paragraph (a) of this Section is modified at through highways and otherwise as stated in this Chapter.

P.A. 76-1586, § 11-901, eff. July 1, 1970. Amended by P.A. 76-1739, § 1, eff. Oct. 6, 1969.

Formerly Ill.Rev.Stat.1991, ch. 95 ½, ¶ 11-901.

5/11-901.01. Vehicles approaching or entering a "T" intersection

§ 11-901.01. Vehicles approaching or entering a "T" intersection. The driver of a vehicle approaching the intersection of a highway from a highway which terminates at the intersection, not otherwise regulated by this Act or controlled by traffic control signs or signals, shall stop, yield, and grant the privilege of immediate use of the intersection to another vehicle which has entered the intersection from the non-terminating highway or is approaching the intersection on the non-terminating highway in such proximity as to constitute a hazard and after stopping may proceed when the driver may safely enter the intersection without interference or collision with the traffic using the non-terminating highway.

P.A. 76-1586, § 11-901.01, added by P.A. 81-860, § 1, eff. Jan. 1, 1980.

Formerly Ill.Rev.Stat.1991, ch. 95 ½, ¶ 11-901.01.

5/11-902. Vehicle turning left

§ 11-902. Vehicle turning left. The driver of a vehicle intending to turn to the left within an intersection or into an alley, private road, or driveway shall yield the right-of-way to any vehicle approaching from the opposite direction which is so close as to constitute an immediate hazard, but said driver, having so yielded may proceed at such time as a safe interval occurs.

P.A. 76-1586, § 11-902, eff. July 1, 1970.

Formerly Ill.Rev.Stat.1991, ch. 95 ½, ¶ 11-902.

5/11-903. Vehicles entering stop crosswalk

§ 11-903. Vehicles entering stop crosswalk. Where stop signs or flashing red signals are in place at an intersection or flashing red signals are in place at a plainly marked crosswalk between intersections, drivers of vehicles shall stop before entering the nearest crosswalk and pedestrians within or entering the crosswalk at either edge of the roadway shall have the right-of-way over vehicles so stopped. Drivers of vehicles having so yielded the right-of-way to pedestrians entering or within the nearest crosswalk at an intersection shall also yield the right-of-way to pedestrians within any other crosswalk at the intersection.

P.A. 76-1586, § 11-903, eff. July 1, 1970.

Formerly Ill.Rev.Stat.1991, ch. 95 ½, ¶ 11-903.

5/11-904. Vehicle entering stop or yield intersection

§ 11-904. Vehicle entering stop or yield intersection. (a) Preferential right-of-way at an intersection may be indicated by stop or yield signs as authorized in Section 11-302 of this Chapter.

(b) Except when directed to proceed by a police officer or traffic-control signal, every driver of a vehicle approaching a stop intersection indicated by a stop sign shall stop at a clearly marked stop line, but if none, before entering the crosswalk on the near side of the intersection, or if none, then at the point nearest the intersecting roadway where the driver has a view of approaching traffic on the intersecting roadway before entering the intersection. After having stopped, the driver shall yield the right-of-way to any vehicle which has entered the intersection from another roadway or which is approaching so closely on the roadway as to constitute an immediate hazard during the time when the driver is moving across or within the intersection, but said driver having so yielded may proceed at such time as a safe interval occurs.

(c) The driver of a vehicle approaching a yield sign shall in obedience to such sign slow down to a speed reasonable for the existing conditions and, if required for safety to stop, shall stop at a clearly marked stop line, but if none, before entering the crosswalk on the near side of the intersection, or if none, then at the point nearest the intersecting roadway where the driver has a view of approaching traffic on the intersecting roadway. After slowing or stopping, the driver shall yield the right-of-way to any vehicle in the intersection or approaching on another roadway so closely as to constitute an immediate hazard during the time such driver is moving across or within the intersection.

(d) If a driver is involved in a collision at an intersection or interferes with the movement of other vehicles after driving past a yield right-of-way sign, such collision or interference shall be deemed prima facie evidence of the driver's failure to yield right-of-way.

P.A. 76-1586, § 11-904, eff. July 1, 1970. Amended by P.A. 76-1739, § 1, eff. Oct. 6, 1969.

Formerly Ill.Rev.Stat.1991, ch. 95 ½, ¶ 11-904.

5/11-905. Merging traffic

§ 11-905. Merging traffic. Notwithstanding the right of way provision in Sec. 11-901 of this Act, at an intersection where traffic lanes are provided for merging traffic the driver of each vehicle on the converging roadways is required to adjust his vehicular speed and lateral position so as to avoid a collision with another vehicle.

P.A. 76-1586, § 11-905, eff. July 1, 1970. Amended by P.A. 81-860, § 1, eff. Jan. 1, 1980.

Formerly Ill.Rev.Stat.1991, ch. 95 ½, ¶ 11-905.

5/11-906. Vehicle entering highway from private road or driveway

§ 11-906. Vehicle entering highway from private road or driveway. The driver of a vehicle about to enter or cross a highway from an alley, building, private road or driveway shall yield the right-of-way to all vehicles approaching on the highway to be entered.

P.A. 76-1586, § 11-906, eff. July 1, 1970. Amended by P.A. 76-1739, § 1, eff. Oct. 6, 1969.

Formerly Ill.Rev.Stat.1991, ch. 95 ½, ¶ 11-906.

5/11–907. Operation of vehicles and streetcars on approach of authorized emergency vehicles.

Text of section effective until June 1, 2003

(a) Upon the immediate approach of an authorized emergency vehicle making use of audible and visual signals meeting the requirements of this Code or a police vehicle properly and lawfully making use of an audible or visual signal,

(1) the driver of every other vehicle shall yield the right-of-way and shall immediately drive to a position parallel to, and as close as possible to, the right-hand edge or curb of the highway clear of any intersection and shall, if necessary to permit the safe passage of the emergency vehicle, stop and remain in such position until the authorized emergency vehicle has passed, unless otherwise directed by a police officer and

(2) the operator of every streetcar shall immediately stop such car clear of any intersection and keep it in such position until the authorized emergency vehicle has passed, unless otherwise directed by a police officer.

(b) This Section shall not operate to relieve the driver of an authorized emergency vehicle from the duty to drive with due regard for the safety of all persons using the highway.

(c) Upon approaching a stationary authorized emergency vehicle, when the authorized emergency vehicle is giving a signal by displaying alternately flashing red, red and white, blue, or red and blue lights or amber or yellow warning lights, a person who drives an approaching vehicle shall:

(1) proceeding with due caution, yield the right-of-way by making a lane change into a lane not adjacent to that of the authorized emergency vehicle, if possible with due regard to safety and traffic conditions, if on a highway having at least 4 lanes with not less than 2 lanes proceeding in the same direction as the approaching vehicle; or

(2) proceeding with due caution, reduce the speed of the vehicle, maintaining a safe speed for road conditions, if changing lanes would be impossible or unsafe.

As used in this subsection (c), "authorized emergency vehicle" includes any vehicle authorized by law to be equipped with oscillating, rotating, or flashing lights under Section 12–215 of this Code, while the owner or operator of the vehicle is engaged in his or her official duties.

(d) A person who violates subsection (c) of this Section commits a business offense punishable by a fine of not more than $10,000. It is a factor in aggravation if the person committed the offense while in violation of Section 11–501 of this Code.

(e) If a violation of subsection (c) of this Section results in damage to the property of another person, in addition to any other penalty imposed, the person's driving privileges shall be suspended for a fixed period of not less than 90 days and not more than one year.

(f) If a violation of subsection (c) of this Section results in injury to another person, in addition to any other penalty imposed, the person's driving privileges shall be suspended for a fixed period of not less than 180 days and not more than 2 years.

(g) If a violation of subsection (c) of this Section results in the death of another person, in addition to any other penalty imposed, the person's driving privileges shall be suspended for 2 years.

(h) The Secretary of State shall, upon receiving a record of a judgment entered against a person under subsection (c) of this Section:

(1) suspend the person's driving privileges for the mandatory period; or

(2) extend the period of an existing suspension by the appropriate mandatory period.

P.A. 76–1586, § 11–907, eff. July 1, 1970. Amended by P.A. 83–781, § 1, eff. Jan. 1, 1984; P.A. 92–283, § 5, eff. Jan. 1, 2002.

Formerly Ill.Rev.Stat.1991, ch. 95 ½, ¶ 11–907.

For text of section effective June 1, 2003, see 625 ILCS 5/11–907, post

5/11–907. Operation of vehicles and streetcars on approach of authorized emergency vehicles.

Text of section effective June 1, 2003

§ 11–907. Operation of vehicles and streetcars on approach of authorized emergency vehicles.

(a) Upon the immediate approach of an authorized emergency vehicle making use of audible and visual signals meeting the requirements of this Code or a police vehicle properly and lawfully making use of an audible or visual signal,

(1) the driver of every other vehicle shall yield the right-of-way and shall immediately drive to a position parallel to, and as close as possible to, the right-hand edge or curb of the highway clear of any intersection and shall, if necessary to permit the safe passage of the emergency vehicle, stop and remain in such position until the authorized emergency vehicle has passed, unless otherwise directed by a police officer and

(2) the operator of every streetcar shall immediately stop such car clear of any intersection and keep it in such position until the authorized emergency vehicle has passed, unless otherwise directed by a police officer.

(b) This Section shall not operate to relieve the driver of an authorized emergency vehicle from the duty to drive with due regard for the safety of all persons using the highway.

(c) Upon approaching a stationary authorized emergency vehicle, when the authorized emergency vehicle is giving a signal by displaying alternately flashing red, red and white, blue, or red and blue lights or amber or yellow warning lights, a person who drives an approaching vehicle shall:

(1) proceeding with due caution, yield the right-of-way by making a lane change into a lane not adjacent to that of the authorized emergency vehicle, if possible with due regard to safety and traffic conditions, if on a highway having at least 4 lanes with not less than 2 lanes proceeding in the same direction as the approaching vehicle; or

(2) proceeding with due caution, reduce the speed of the vehicle, maintaining a safe speed for road conditions, if changing lanes would be impossible or unsafe.

As used in this subsection (c), "authorized emergency vehicle" includes any vehicle authorized by law to be equipped with oscillating, rotating, or flashing lights under Section 12–215 of this Code, while the owner or operator of the vehicle is engaged in his or her official duties.

(d) A person who violates subsection (c) of this Section commits a business offense punishable by a fine of not more than $10,000. A person charged with the offense must appear in court to answer the charges. It is a factor in aggravation if the person committed the offense while in violation of Section 11–501 of this Code.

(e) If a violation of subsection (c) of this Section results in damage to the property of another person, in addition to any other penalty imposed, the person's driving privileges shall be suspended for a fixed period of not less than 90 days and not more than one year.

(f) If a violation of subsection (c) of this Section results in injury to another person, in addition to any other penalty imposed, the person's driving privileges shall be suspended for a fixed period of not less than 180 days and not more than 2 years.

(g) If a violation of subsection (c) of this Section results in the death of another person, in addition to any other penalty imposed, the person's driving privileges shall be suspended for 2 years.

(h) The Secretary of State shall, upon receiving a record of a judgment entered against a person under subsection (c) of this Section:

(1) suspend the person's driving privileges for the mandatory period; or

(2) extend the period of an existing suspension by the appropriate mandatory period.

P.A. 76-1586, § 11-907, eff. July 1, 1970. Amended by P.A. 83-781, § 1, eff. Jan. 1, 1984; P.A. 92-283, § 5, eff. Jan. 1, 2002; P.A. 92-872, § 5, eff. June 1, 2003.

Formerly Ill.Rev.Stat.1991, ch. 95 ½, ¶ 11-907.

For text of section effective until June 1, 2003, see 625 ILCS 5/11-907, ante

5/11-908. Vehicle approaching highway construction or maintenance area

Text of section effective until June 1, 2003

§ 11-908. Vehicle approaching highway construction or maintenance area. (a) The driver of a vehicle shall yield the right of way to any authorized vehicle or pedestrian actually engaged in work upon a highway within any highway construction or maintenance area indicated by official traffic-control devices.

(b) The driver of a vehicle shall yield the right of way to any authorized vehicle obviously and actually engaged in work upon a highway whenever the vehicle engaged in construction or maintenance work displays flashing lights as provided in Section 12-215 of this Act.

(c) The driver of a vehicle shall stop if signaled to do so by a flagger or a traffic control signal and remain in such position until signaled to proceed. If a driver of a vehicle fails to stop when signaled to do so by a flagger, the flagger is authorized to report such offense to the State's Attorney or authorized prosecutor.

P.A. 76-1586, § 11-908, added by P.A. 81-312, § 1, eff. Jan. 1, 1980. Amended by P.A. 84-873, § 1, eff. Jan. 1, 1986; P.A. 86-611, § 1, eff. Sept. 1, 1989.

Formerly Ill.Rev.Stat.1991, ch. 95 ½, ¶ 11-908.

For text of section effective June 1, 2003, see 625 ILCS 5/11-908, post

5/11-908. Vehicle approaching or entering a highway construction or maintenance area or zone

Text of section effective June 1, 2003

§ 11-908. Vehicle approaching or entering a highway construction or maintenance area or zone.

(a) The driver of a vehicle shall yield the right of way to any authorized vehicle or pedestrian actually engaged in work upon a highway within any highway construction or maintenance area indicated by official traffic-control devices.

(a-1) Upon entering a construction or maintenance zone when workers are present, a person who drives a vehicle shall:

(1) proceeding with due caution, make a lane change into a lane not adjacent to that of the workers present, if possible with due regard to safety and traffic conditions, if on a highway having at least 4 lanes with not less than 2 lanes proceeding in the same direction as the approaching vehicle; or

(2) proceeding with due caution, reduce the speed of the vehicle, maintaining a safe speed for road conditions, if changing lanes would be impossible or unsafe.

(a-2) A person who violates subsection (a-1) of this Section commits a business offense punishable by a fine of not more than $10,000. A person charged with the offense must appear in court to answer the charges. It is a factor in aggravation if the person committed the offense while in violation of Section 11-501 of this Code.

(a-3) If a violation of subsection (a-1) of this Section results in damage to the property of another person, in addition to any other penalty imposed, the person's driving privileges shall be suspended for a fixed period of not less than 90 days and not more than one year.

(a-4) If a violation of subsection (a-1) of this Section results in injury to another person, in addition to any other penalty imposed, the person's driving privileges shall be suspended for a fixed period of not less than 180 days and not more than 2 years.

(a-5) If a violation of subsection (a-1) of this Section results in the death of another person, in addition to any other penalty imposed, the person's driving privileges shall be suspended for 2 years.

(a-6) The Secretary of State shall, upon receiving a record of a judgment entered against a person under subsection (a-1) of this Section:

(1) suspend the person's driving privileges for the mandatory period; or

(2) extend the period of an existing suspension by the appropriate mandatory period.

(b) The driver of a vehicle shall yield the right of way to any authorized vehicle obviously and actually engaged in work upon a highway whenever the vehicle engaged in construction or maintenance work displays flashing lights as provided in Section 12-215 of this Act.

(c) The driver of a vehicle shall stop if signaled to do so by a flagger or a traffic control signal and remain in such position until signaled to proceed. If a driver of a vehicle fails to stop when signaled to do so by a flagger, the flagger is authorized to report such offense to the State's Attorney or authorized prosecutor. The penalties imposed for a violation of this subsection (c) shall be in addition to any penalties imposed for a violation of subsection (a-1).

P.A. 76-1586, § 11-908, added by P.A. 81-312, § 1, eff. Jan. 1, 1980. Amended by P.A. 84-873, § 1, eff. Jan. 1, 1986; P.A. 86-611, § 1, eff. Sept. 1, 1989; P.A. 92-872, § 5, eff. June 1, 2003.

Formerly Ill.Rev.Stat.1991, ch. 95 ½, ¶ 11-908.

For text of section effective until June 1, 2003, see 625 ILCS 5/11-908, ante

ARTICLE X. PEDESTRIANS' RIGHTS AND DUTIES

5/11-1001. Pedestrian obedience to traffic control devices and traffic regulations

§ 11-1001. Pedestrian obedience to traffic control devices and traffic regulations.

(a) A pedestrian shall obey the instructions of any official traffic control device specifically applicable to him, unless otherwise directed by a police officer.

(b) Pedestrians shall be subject to traffic and pedestrian control signals provided in Sections 11-306 and 11-307 of this Chapter, but at all other places pedestrians shall be accorded the privileges and shall be subject to the restrictions stated in this Article.

P.A. 76-1586, § 11-1001, eff. July 1, 1970. Amended by P.A. 76-1734, § 1, eff. Oct. 6, 1969.

Formerly Ill.Rev.Stat.1991, ch. 95 ½, ¶ 11-1001.

5/11-1002. Pedestrians' right-of-way at crosswalks

§ 11-1002. Pedestrians' right-of-way at crosswalks. (a) When traffic control signals are not in place or not in operation the driver of a vehicle shall yield the right-of-way, slowing down or stopping if need be to so yield, to a pedestrian crossing the roadway within a crosswalk when the pedestrian is upon the half of the roadway upon which the vehicle is traveling, or when the pedestrian is approaching so closely from the opposite half of the roadway as to be in danger.

(b) No pedestrian shall suddenly leave a curb or other place of safety and walk or run into the path of a moving vehicle which is so close as to constitute an immediate hazard.

(c) Paragraph (a) shall not apply under the condition stated in Section 11-1003(b).

(d) Whenever any vehicle is stopped at a marked crosswalk or at any unmarked crosswalk at an intersection to permit a pedestrian to cross the roadway, the driver of any other vehicle approaching from the rear shall not overtake and pass such stopped vehicle.

(e) Whenever stop signs or flashing red signals are in place at an intersection or at a plainly marked crosswalk between intersections, drivers shall yield right-of-way to pedestrians as set forth in Section 11-904 of this Chapter.

P.A. 76-1586, § 11-1002, eff. July 1, 1970. Amended by P.A. 76-2168, § 1, eff. July 1, 1970; P.A. 77-329, § 1, eff. Jan. 1, 1972; P.A. 79-857, § 1, eff. Jan. 1, 1976.

Formerly Ill.Rev.Stat.1991, ch. 95 ½, ¶ 11-1002.

5/11-1003. Crossing at other than crosswalks

§ 11-1003. Crossing at other than crosswalks.

(a) Every pedestrian crossing a roadway at any point other than within a marked crosswalk or within an unmarked crosswalk at an intersection shall yield the right-of-way to all vehicles upon the roadway.

(b) Any pedestrian crossing a roadway at a point where a pedestrian tunnel or overhead pedestrian crossing has been provided shall yield the right-of-way to all vehicles upon the roadway.

(c) Between adjacent intersections at which traffic-control signals are in operation pedestrians shall not cross at any place except in a marked crosswalk.

(d) No pedestrian shall cross a roadway intersection diagonally unless authorized by official traffic-control devices; and, when authorized to cross diagonally, pedestrians shall cross only in accordance with the official traffic-control devices pertaining to such crossing movements.

(e) Pedestrians with disabilities may cross a roadway at any point other than within a marked crosswalk or within an unmarked crosswalk where the intersection is physically inaccessible to them but they shall yield the right-of-way to all vehicles upon the roadway.

P.A. 76-1586, § 11-1003, eff. July 1, 1970. Amended by P.A. 76-2169, § 1, eff. July 1, 1970; P.A. 79-857, § 1, eff. Jan. 1, 1976; P.A. 80-1495, § 36, eff. Jan. 8, 1979; P.A. 88-685, § 5, eff. Jan. 24, 1995.

Formerly Ill.Rev.Stat.1991, ch. 95 ½, ¶ 11-1003.

5/11-1003.1. Drivers to exercise due care

§ 11-1003.1. Drivers to exercise due care. Notwithstanding other provisions of this Code or the provisions of any local ordinance, every driver of a vehicle shall exercise due care to avoid colliding with any pedestrian, or any person operating a bicycle or other device propelled by human power and shall give warning by sounding the horn when necessary and shall exercise proper precaution upon observing any child or any obviously confused, incapacitated or intoxicated person.

P.A. 76-1586, § 11-1003.1, added by P.A. 79-857, § 2, eff. Jan. 1, 1976. Amended by P.A. 82-132, § 1, eff. Jan. 1, 1982.

Formerly Ill.Rev.Stat.1991, ch. 95 ½, ¶ 11-1003.1.

5/11-1004. Pedestrian with disabilities; right-of-way

§ 11-1004. Pedestrian with disabilities; right-of-way. The driver of a vehicle shall yield the right-of-way to any pedestrian with clearly visible disabilities.

P.A. 76-1586, § 11-1004, eff. July 1, 1970. Amended by P.A. 79-857, § 1, eff. Jan. 1, 1976; P.A. 82-222, § 5, eff. Jan. 1, 1982; P.A. 83-93, § 5, eff. Jan. 1, 1984; P.A. 88-685, § 5, eff. Jan. 24, 1995.

Formerly Ill.Rev.Stat.1991, ch. 95 ½, ¶ 11-1004.

5/11–1004.1. Motorized wheelchairs

§ 11–1004.1. Motorized wheelchairs. Every person operating a motorized wheelchair upon a sidewalk or roadway shall be granted all the rights and shall be subject to all the duties applicable to a pedestrian.

P.A. 76–1586, § 11–1004.1, added by P.A. 84–672, § 1, eff. Sept. 20, 1985.

Formerly Ill.Rev.Stat.1991, ch. 95 ½, ¶ 11–1004.1.

5/11–1005. Pedestrians to use right half of crosswalks

§ 11–1005. Pedestrians to use right half of crosswalks. Pedestrians shall move, whenever practicable, upon the right half of crosswalks.

P.A. 76–1586, § 11–1005, eff. July 1, 1970.

Formerly Ill.Rev.Stat.1991, ch. 95 ½, ¶ 11–1005.

5/11–1005.1. Electric personal assistive mobility devices

Text of section added effective June 1, 2003

§ 11–1005.1. Electric personal assistive mobility devices. Every person operating an electric personal assistive mobility device upon a sidewalk or roadway has all the rights and is subject to all the duties applicable to a pedestrian. Nothing in this Section shall be deemed to limit or preempt the authority of any home rule or non-home rule unit of local government from regulating or prohibiting the use of electric personal assistive mobility devices.

P.A. 76–1586, § 11–1005.1, added by P.A. 92–868, § 5, eff. June 1, 2003.

5/11–1006. Pedestrians soliciting rides or business

§ 11–1006. Pedestrians soliciting rides or business. (a) No person shall stand in a roadway for the purpose of soliciting a ride from the driver of any vehicle.

(b) No person shall stand on a highway for the purpose of soliciting employment or business from the occupant of any vehicle.

(c) No person shall stand on a highway for the purpose of soliciting contributions from the occupant of any vehicle except within a municipality when expressly permitted by municipal ordinance. The local municipality, city, village, or other local governmental entity in which the solicitation takes place shall determine by ordinance where and when solicitations may take place based on the safety of the solicitors and the safety of motorists. The decision shall also take into account the orderly flow of traffic and may not allow interference with the operation of official traffic control devices. The soliciting agency shall be:

1. registered with the Attorney General as a charitable organization as provided by "An Act to regulate solicitation and collection of funds for charitable purposes, providing for violations thereof, and making an appropriation therefor", approved July 26, 1963, as amended;[1]

2. engaged in a Statewide fund raising activity; and

3. liable for any injuries to any person or property during the solicitation which is causally related to an act of ordinary negligence of the soliciting agent.

Any person engaged in the act of solicitation shall be 16 years of age or more and shall be wearing a high visibility vest.

(d) No person shall stand on or in the proximity of a highway for the purpose of soliciting the watching or guarding of any vehicle while parked or about to be parked on a highway.

(e) Every person who is convicted of a violation of this Section shall be guilty of a Class A misdemeanor.

P.A. 76–1586, § 11–1006, eff. July 1, 1970. Amended by P.A. 76–1734, § 1; P.A. 79–857, § 1, eff. Jan. 1, 1976; P.A. 80–911, § 1, eff. Oct. 1, 1977; P.A. 81–29, § 1, eff. Jan. 1, 1980; P.A. 88–589, § 10, eff. Aug. 14, 1994.

Formerly Ill.Rev.Stat.1991, ch. 95 ½, ¶ 11–1006.

[1] 225 ILCS 460/1 et seq.

5/11–1007. Pedestrians walking on highways

§ 11–1007. Pedestrians walking on highways. (a) Where a sidewalk is provided and its use is practicable, it shall be unlawful for any pedestrian to walk along and upon an adjacent roadway.

(b) Where a sidewalk is not available, any pedestrian walking along and upon a highway shall walk only on a shoulder, as far as practicable from the edge of the roadway.

(c) Where neither a sidewalk nor a shoulder is available, any pedestrian walking along and upon a highway shall walk as near as practicable to an outside edge of a roadway, and, if on a two-way roadway, shall walk only on the left side of the roadway.

(d) Except as otherwise provided in this Chapter, any pedestrian upon a roadway shall yield the right-of-way to all vehicles upon the roadway.

P.A. 76–1586, § 11–1007, eff. July 1, 1970. Amended by P.A. 79–857, § 1, eff. Jan. 1, 1976.

Formerly Ill.Rev.Stat.1991, ch. 95 ½, ¶ 11–1007.

5/11–1007.1. § 11–1007.1. Repealed by P.A. 77–329, § 2, eff. Jan. 1, 1972

5/11–1008. Right-of-way on sidewalks

§ 11–1008. Right-of-way on sidewalks. The driver of a vehicle shall yield the right-of-way to any pedestrian on a sidewalk.

P.A. 76–1586, § 11–1008, added by P.A. 79–857, § 2, eff. Jan. 1, 1976.

Formerly Ill.Rev.Stat.1991, ch. 95 ½, ¶ 11–1008.

5/11–1009. Pedestrians yield to authorized emergency vehicles

§ 11–1009. Pedestrians yield to authorized emergency vehicles. Upon the immediate approach of an authorized emergency vehicle making use of an audible signal and visual signals meeting the requirements of Section 12–217 of this Chapter, or of a police vehicle properly and lawfully making use of an audible signal only, every pedestrian shall yield the right-of-way to the authorized emergency vehicle.

P.A. 76–1586, § 11–1009, added by P.A. 79–857, § 2, eff. Jan. 1, 1976.

Formerly Ill.Rev.Stat.1991, ch. 95 ½, ¶ 11–1009.

5/11–1010. Pedestrians under influence of alcohol or drugs

§ 11–1010. Pedestrians under influence of alcohol or drugs. A pedestrian who is under the influence of alcohol or any drug to a degree which renders himself a hazard shall not walk or be upon a highway except on a sidewalk.

P.A. 76–1586, § 11–1010, added by P.A. 79–857, § 2, eff. Jan. 1, 1976.

Formerly Ill.Rev.Stat.1991, ch. 95 ½, ¶ 11–1010.

5/11-1011. Bridge and railroad signals

§ 11-1011. Bridge and railroad signals.

(a) No pedestrian shall enter or remain upon any bridge or approach thereto beyond the bridge signal, gate, or barrier after a bridge operation signal indication has been given.

(b) No pedestrian shall pass through, around, over, or under any crossing gate or barrier at a railroad grade crossing or bridge while such gate or barrier is closed or is being opened or closed.

(c) No pedestrian shall enter, remain upon or traverse over a railroad grade crossing or pedestrian walkway crossing a railroad track when an audible bell or clearly visible electric or mechanical signal device is operational giving warning of the presence, approach, passage, or departure of a railroad train.

(d) A violation of any part of this Section is a petty offense for which a $250 fine shall be imposed for a first violation, and a $500 fine shall be imposed for a second or subsequent violation. The court may impose 25 hours of community service in place of the $250 fine for a first violation.

(e) Local authorities shall impose fines as established in subsection (d) for pedestrians who fail to obey signals indicating the presence, approach, passage, or departure of a train.

P.A. 76-1586, § 11-1011, added by P.A. 79-857, § 2, eff. Jan. 1, 1976. Amended by P.A. 86-429, § 1, eff. Jan. 1, 1990; P.A. 86-1028, Art. III, § 3-29, eff. Feb. 5, 1990; P.A. 89-186, § 5, eff. Jan. 1, 1996; P.A. 89-658, § 5, eff. Jan. 1, 1997; P.A. 92-814, § 5, eff. Jan. 1, 2003.

Formerly Ill.Rev.Stat.1991, ch. 95 ½, ¶ 11-1011.

P.A. 89-658 incorporated the amendment by P.A. 89-186.

ARTICLE XI. STREET CARS AND SAFETY ZONES

Section

5/11-1101. Passing street car on left

§ 11-1101. Passing street car on left. (a) The driver of a vehicle shall not overtake and pass upon the left nor drive upon the left side of any street car proceeding in the same direction, whether such street car is actually in motion or temporarily at rest, except:

1. When so directed by a police officer;
2. When upon a one-way street; or
3. When upon a street where the tracks are so located as to prevent compliance with the section.

(b) The driver of any vehicle when permitted to overtake and pass upon the left of a street car which has stopped for the purpose of receiving or discharging any passenger shall reduce speed and may proceed only upon exercising due caution for pedestrians and shall accord pedestrians the right-of-way when required by other Sections of this Chapter.

P.A. 76-1586, § 11-1101, eff. July 1, 1970.

Formerly Ill.Rev.Stat.1991, ch. 95 ½, ¶ 11-1101.

5/11-1102. Passing street car on right

§ 11-1102. Passing street car on right. The driver of a vehicle overtaking upon the right any street car stopped or about to stop for the purpose of receiving or discharging any passenger shall stop such vehicle at least ten feet to the rear of the nearest running board or door of such street car and thereupon remain standing until all passengers have boarded such car or upon alighting have reached a place of safety, except that where a safety zone has been established a vehicle need not be brought to a stop before passing any such street car but may proceed past such car at a speed not greater than is reasonable and proper and with due caution for the safety of pedestrians.

P.A. 76-1586, § 11-1102, eff. July 1, 1970.

Formerly Ill.Rev.Stat.1991, ch. 95 ½, ¶ 11-1102.

5/11-1103. Driving on street car tracks

§ 11-1103. Driving on street car tracks. (a) The driver of any vehicle proceeding upon any street car track in front of a street car upon a street shall remove such vehicle from the track as soon as practical after signal from the operator of said street car.

(b) The driver of a vehicle upon overtaking and passing a street car shall not turn in front of such street car so as to interfere with or impede its movement.

P.A. 76-1586, § 11-1103, eff. July 1, 1970.

Formerly Ill.Rev.Stat.1991, ch. 95 ½, ¶ 11-1103.

5/11-1104. Driving through safety zone prohibited

§ 11-1104. Driving through safety zone prohibited. No vehicle shall at any time be driven through or within a safety zone.

P.A. 76-1586, § 11-1104, eff. July 1, 1970.

Formerly Ill.Rev.Stat.1991, ch. 95 ½, ¶ 11-1104.

ARTICLE XII. SPECIAL STOPS REQUIRED

Section

5/11-1201. Obedience to signal indicating approach of train

§ 11-1201. Obedience to signal indicating approach of train.

(a) Whenever any person driving a vehicle approaches a railroad grade crossing where the driver is not always required to stop, the person must exercise due care and caution as the existence of a railroad track across a highway is a warning of danger, and under any of the circumstances stated in this Section, the driver shall stop within 50 feet but not less than 15 feet from the nearest rail of the railroad and shall not proceed until the tracks are clear and he or she can do so safely. The foregoing requirements shall apply when:

1. A clearly visible electric or mechanical signal device gives warning of the immediate approach of a railroad train;

2. A crossing gate is lowered or a human flagman gives or continues to give a signal of the approach or passage of a railroad train;

3. A railroad train approaching a highway crossing emits a warning signal and such railroad train, by reason of its speed or nearness to such crossing, is an immediate hazard;

4. An approaching railroad train is plainly visible and is in hazardous proximity to such crossing;

5. A railroad train is approaching so closely that an immediate hazard is created.

(a-5) Whenever a person driving a vehicle approaches a railroad grade crossing where the driver is not always required to stop but must slow down, the person must exercise due care and caution as the existence of a railroad track across a highway is a warning of danger, and under any of the circumstances stated in this Section, the driver shall slow down within 50 feet but not less than 15 feet from the nearest rail of the railroad and shall not proceed until he or she checks that the tracks are clear of an approaching train.

(b) No person shall drive any vehicle through, around or under any crossing gate or barrier at a railroad crossing while such gate or barrier is closed or is being opened or closed.

(c) The Department, and local authorities with the approval of the Department, are hereby authorized to designate particularly dangerous highway grade crossings of railroads and to erect stop signs thereat. When such stop signs are erected the driver of any vehicle shall stop within 50 feet but not less than 15 feet from the nearest rail of such railroad and shall proceed only upon exercising due care.

(d) At any railroad grade crossing provided with railroad crossbuck signs, without automatic, electric, or mechanical signal devices, crossing gates, or a human flagman giving a signal of the approach or passage of a train, the driver of a vehicle shall in obedience to the railroad crossbuck sign, yield the right-of-way and slow down to a speed reasonable for the existing conditions and shall stop, if required for safety, at a clearly marked stopped line, or if no stop line, within 50 feet but not less than 15 feet from the nearest rail of the railroad and shall not proceed until he or she can do so safely. If a driver is involved in a collision at a railroad crossing or interferes with the movement of a train after driving past the railroad crossbuck sign, the collision or interference is prima facie evidence of the driver's failure to yield right-of-way.

(d-1) No person shall, while driving a commercial motor vehicle, fail to negotiate a railroad-highway grade railroad crossing because of insufficient undercarriage clearance.

(d-5) (Blank.)

(e) It is unlawful to violate any part of this Section.

(1) A violation of this Section is a petty offense for which a fine of $250 shall be imposed for a first violation, and a fine of $500 shall be imposed for a second or subsequent violation. The court may impose 25 hours of community service in place of the $250 fine for the first violation.

(2) For a second or subsequent violation, the Secretary of State may suspend the driving privileges of the offender for a minimum of 6 months.

(f) Corporate authorities of municipal corporations regulating operators of vehicles that fail to obey signals indicating the presence, approach, passage, or departure of a train shall impose fines as established in subsection (e) of this Section.

P.A. 76-1586, § 11-1201, eff. July 1, 1970. Amended by P.A. 76-2170, § 1, eff. July 1, 1970; P.A. 79-1069, § 1, eff. Jan. 1, 1976; P.A. 89-186, § 5, eff. Jan. 1, 1996; P.A. 89-658, § 5, eff. Jan. 1, 1997; P.A. 92-245, § 5, eff. Aug. 3, 2001; P.A. 92-249, § 5, eff. Jan. 1, 2002; P.A. 92-651, § 77, eff. July 11, 2002; P.A. 92-814, § 5, eff. Jan. 1, 2003; P.A. 92-834, § 5, eff. Aug. 22, 2002.

Formerly Ill.Rev.Stat.1991, ch. 95 ½, ¶ 11-1201.

P.A. 92-814 incorporated the amendments by P.A. 92-245 and 92-249.

P.A. 92-834 incorporated the amendments by P.A. 92-245 and P.A. 92-249.

See 5 ILCS 70/6 as to the effect of (1) more than one amendment of a section at the same session of the General Assembly of (2) two or more acts relating to the same subject matter enacted by the same General Assembly

5/11-1201.1. Automated Railroad Crossing Enforcement System

§ 11-1201.1. Automated Railroad Crossing Enforcement System.

(a) For the purposes of this Section, an automated railroad grade crossing enforcement system is a system operated by a law enforcement agency that records a driver's response to automatic, electrical or mechanical signal devices and crossing gates. The system shall be designed to obtain a clear photograph or other recorded image of the vehicle, vehicle operator and the vehicle registration plate of a vehicle in violation of Section 11-1201. The photograph or other recorded image shall also display the time, date and location of the violation.

(b) Commencing on January 1, 1996, the Illinois Commerce Commission and the Commuter Rail Board of the Regional Transportation Authority shall, in cooperation with local law enforcement agencies, establish a 5 year pilot program within a county with a population of between 750,000 and 1,000,000 using an automated railroad grade crossing enforcement system. The Commission shall determine the 3 railroad grade crossings within that county that pose the greatest threat to human life based upon the number of accidents and fatalities at the crossings during the past 5 years and with approval of the local law enforcement agency equip the crossings with an automated railroad grade crossing enforcement system.

(b-1) Commencing on July 20, 2001 (the effective date of Public Act 92-98) , the Illinois Commerce Commission and the Commuter Rail Board may, in cooperation with the local law enforcement agency, establish in a county with a population of between 750,000 and 1,000,000 a 2 year pilot program using an automated railroad grade crossing enforcement system. This pilot program may be established at a railroad grade crossing designated by local authorities. No State moneys may be expended on the automated railroad grade crossing enforcement system established under this pilot program.

(c) For each violation of Section 11-1201 recorded by an automatic railroad grade crossing system, the local law enforcement agency having jurisdiction shall issue a written Uniform Traffic Citation of the violation to the registered owner of the vehicle as the alleged violator. The Uniform Traffic Citation shall be delivered to the registered owner of the vehicle, by mail, within 30 days of the violation. The Uniform Traffic Citation shall include the name and address of vehicle owner, the vehicle registration number, the offense charged, the time, date, and location of the violation, the first available court date and that the basis of the citation is the photograph or other recorded image from the automated railroad grade crossing enforcement system.

(d) The Uniform Traffic Citation issued to the registered owner of the vehicle shall be accompanied by a written notice, the contents of which is set forth in subsection (d-1) of this Section, explaining how the registered owner of the vehicle can elect to proceed by either paying the fine or challenging the issuance of the Uniform Traffic Citation.

(d-1) The written notice explaining the alleged violator's rights and obligations must include the following text:

"You have been served with the accompanying Uniform Traffic Citation and cited with having violated Section 11-1201 of the Illinois Vehicle Code. You can elect to proceed by:

1. Paying the fine; or

2. Challenging the issuance of the Uniform Traffic Citation in court; or

3. If you were not the operator of the vehicle at the time of the alleged offense, notifying in writing the local law enforcement agency that issued the Uniform Traffic Citation of the number of the Uniform Traffic Citation received and the name and address of the person operating the vehicle at the time of the alleged offense. If you fail to so notify in writing the local law enforcement agency of the name and address of the operator of the vehicle at the time of the alleged offense, you may be presumed to have been the operator of the vehicle at the time of the alleged offense."

(d-2) If the registered owner of the vehicle was not the operator of the vehicle at the time of the alleged offense, and if the registered owner notifies the local law enforcement agency having jurisdiction of the name and address of the operator of the vehicle at the time of the alleged offense, the local law enforcement agency having jurisdiction shall then issue a written Uniform Traffic Citation to the person alleged by the registered owner to have been the operator of the vehicle at the time of the alleged offense. If the registered owner fails to notify in writing the local law enforcement agency having jurisdiction of the name and address of the operator of the vehicle at the time of the alleged offense, the registered owner may be presumed to have been the operator of the vehicle at the time of the alleged offense.

(e) Evidence.

(i) A certificate alleging that a violation of Section 11-1201 occurred, sworn to or affirmed by a duly authorized agency, based on inspection of recorded images produced by an automated railroad crossing enforcement system are evidence of the facts contained in the certificate and are admissible in any proceeding alleging a violation under this Section.

(ii) Photographs or recorded images made by an automatic railroad grade crossing enforcement system are confidential and shall be made available only to the alleged violator and governmental and law enforcement agencies for purposes of adjudicating a violation of Section 11-1201 of the Illinois Vehicle Code. However, any photograph or other recorded image evidencing a violation of Section 11-1201 shall be admissible in any proceeding resulting from the issuance of the Uniform Traffic Citation when there is reasonable and sufficient proof of the accuracy of the camera or electronic instrument recording the image. There is a rebuttable presumption that the photograph or recorded image is accurate if the camera or electronic recording instrument was in good working order at the beginning and the end of the day of the alleged offense.

(f) Rail crossings equipped with an automatic railroad grade crossing enforcement system shall be posted with a sign visible to approaching traffic stating that the railroad grade crossing is being monitored, that citations will be issued, and the amount of the fine for violation.

(g) Except as provided in subsection (b-1), the cost of the installation and maintenance of each automatic railroad grade crossing enforcement system shall be paid from the Grade Crossing Protection Fund if the rail line is not owned by Commuter Rail Board of the Regional Transportation Authority. Except as provided in subsection (b-1), if the rail line is owned by the Commuter Rail Board of the Regional Transportation Authority, the costs of the installation and maintenance shall be paid from the Regional Transportation Authority's portion of the Public Transportation Fund.

(h) The Illinois Commerce Commission shall issue a report to the General Assembly at the conclusion of the 5 year pilot program established under subsection (b) on the effectiveness of the automatic railroad grade crossing enforcement system.

(i) If any part or parts of this Section are held by a court of competent jurisdiction to be unconstitutional, the unconstitutionality shall not affect the validity of the remaining parts of this Section. The General Assembly hereby declares that it would have passed the remaining parts of this Section if it had known that the other part or parts of this Section would be declared unconstitutional.

(j) Penalty.

(i) A violation of this Section is a petty offense for which a fine of $250 shall be imposed for a first violation, and a fine of $500 shall be imposed for a second or subsequent violation. The court may impose 25 hours of community service in place of the $250 fine for the first violation.

(ii) For a second or subsequent violation, the Secretary of State may suspend the registration of the motor vehicle for a period of at least 6 months.

P.A. 76-1586, § 1201.1, added by P.A. 89-454, § 10, eff. May 17, 1996. Renumbered § 11-1201.1 and amended by P.A. 90-14, Art. 2, § 2-225, eff. July 1, 1997. Amended by P.A. 92-98, § 5, eff. July 18, 2001; P.A. 92-245, § 5, eff. Aug. 3, 2001; P.A. 92-651, § 77, eff. July 11, 2002; P.A. 92-814, § 5, eff. Jan. 1, 2003.

P.A. 92-651, the First 2002 General Revisory Act, amended various Acts to delete obsolete text, to correct patent and technical errors, to revise cross references, to resolve multiple actions in the 91st and 92nd General Assemblies and to make certain technical corrections in P.A. 91-937 through P.A. 92-520.

P.A. 92-814 incorporated the amendments by P.A. 92-98 and 92-245.

See 5 ILCS 70/6 as to the effect of (1) more than one amendment of a section at the same session of the General Assembly or (2) two or more acts relating to the same subject matter enacted by the same General Assembly.

5/11-1202. Certain vehicles must stop at all railroad grade crossings

§ 11-1202. Certain vehicles must stop at all railroad grade crossings. (a) The driver of any of the following vehicles shall, before crossing a railroad track or tracks at grade, stop such vehicle within 50 feet but not less than 15 feet from the nearest rail and, while so stopped, shall listen and look for the approach of a train and shall not proceed until such movement can be made with safety:

1. Any second division vehicle carrying passengers for hire;

2. Any bus that meets all of the special requirements for school buses in Sections 12-801, 12-803, and 12-805 of this Code ;

3. Any other vehicle which is required by Federal or State law to be placarded when carrying as a cargo or part of a cargo hazardous material as defined in the "Illinois Hazardous Materials Transportation Act".[1] After stopping as required in this Section, the driver shall proceed only in a gear not requiring a change of gears during the crossing, and the driver shall not shift gears while crossing the track or tracks.

(b) This Section shall not apply:

1. At any railroad grade crossing where traffic is controlled by a police officer or flagperson;

2. At any railroad grade crossing controlled by a functioning traffic-control signal transmitting a green indication which, under law, permits the vehicle to proceed across the railroad tracks without slowing or stopping, except that subsection (a) shall apply to any school bus;

3. At any streetcar grade crossing within a business or residence district; or

4. At any abandoned, industrial or spur track railroad grade crossing designated as exempt by the Illinois Commerce Commission and marked with an official sign as authorized in the State Manual on Uniform Traffic Control Devices for Streets and Highways.

P.A. 76-1586, § 11-1202, eff. July 1, 1970. Amended by P.A. 76-2171, § 1, eff. July 1, 1970; P.A. 79-1069, § 1, eff. Jan. 1, 1976; P.A. 80-506, § 1, eff. Oct. 1, 1977; P.A. 81-805, § 1, eff. Jan. 1, 1980; P.A. 83-905, § 1, eff. Jan. 1, 1984; P.A. 84-1246, § 1, eff. July 29, 1986; P.A. 86-499, § 1, eff. Jan. 1, 1990; P.A. 89-658, § 5, eff. Jan. 1, 1997.

Formerly Ill.Rev.Stat.1991, ch. 95 ½, ¶ 11-1202.

[1] 430 ILCS 30/1 et seq.

5/11-1203. Moving heavy equipment at railroad grade crossing

§ 11-1203. Moving heavy equipment at railroad grade crossing. (a) No person shall operate or move any crawler-type tractor, power shovel, derrick, roller, or any equipment or structure having a normal operating speed of 10 or less miles per hour, or, for such equipment with 18 feet or less distance between two adjacent axles, having a vertical body or load clearance of less than 9 inches above a level surface, or, for such equipment with more than 18 feet between two adjacent axles, having a vertical body or load clearance of less than ½ inch per foot of distance between such adjacent axles above a level surface upon or across any tracks at a railroad grade crossing without first complying with this Section.

(b) Notice of any such intended crossing shall be given to a superintendent of such railroad and a reasonable time be given to such railroad to provide proper protection at such crossing.

(c) Before making any such crossing the person operating or moving any such vehicle or equipment shall first stop the same not less than 15 feet nor more than 50 feet from the nearest rail of such railway and while so stopped shall listen and look in both directions along such track for any approaching train and for signals indicating the approach of a train, and shall not proceed until the crossing can be made safely.

(d) No such crossing shall be made when warning is given by automatic signal or crossing gates or a flagman or otherwise of the immediate approach of a railroad train or car.

P.A. 76-1586, § 11-1203, eff. July 1, 1970. Amended by P.A. 76-2172, § 1, eff. July 1, 1970.

Formerly Ill.Rev.Stat.1991, ch. 95 ½, ¶ 11-1203.

5/11-1204. Stop and yield signs

§ 11-1204. Stop and yield signs. (a) Preferential right-of-way at an intersection may be indicated by stop signs or yield signs as authorized in Section 11-302 of this Act.

(b) Except when directed to proceed by a police officer or traffic control signal, every driver of a vehicle and every motorman of a streetcar approaching a stop intersection indicated by a stop sign shall stop before entering the crosswalk on the near side of the intersection or, in the event there is no crosswalk, shall stop at a clearly marked stop line, but if none, then at the point nearest the intersection roadway where the driver has a view of approaching traffic on the intersecting roadway before entering the intersection.

(c) The driver of a vehicle approaching a yield sign if required for safety to stop shall stop before entering the crosswalk on the near side of the intersection or, in the event there is no crosswalk, at a clearly marked stop line, but if none, then at the point nearest the intersecting roadway where the driver has a view of approaching traffic on the intersecting roadway.

P.A. 76-1586, § 11-1204, eff. July 1, 1970.

Formerly Ill.Rev.Stat.1991, ch. 95 ½, ¶ 11-1204.

5/11-1205. Emerging from alley, building, private road or driveway

§ 11-1205. Emerging from alley, building, private road or driveway. The driver of a vehicle emerging from an alley, building, private road or driveway within an urban area shall stop such vehicle immediately prior to driving into the sidewalk area extending across such alley, building entrance, road or driveway, or in the event there is no sidewalk area, shall stop at the point nearest the street to be entered where the driver has a view of approaching traffic thereon, and shall yield the right-of-way to any pedestrian as may be necessary to avoid collision, and upon entering the roadway shall yield the right-of-way to all vehicles approaching on such roadway.

P.A. 76-1586, § 11-1205, eff. July 1, 1970. Amended by P.A. 76-1735, § 1; P.A. 77-1344, § 1, eff. Aug. 27, 1971.

Formerly Ill.Rev.Stat.1991, ch. 95 ½, ¶ 11-1205.

ARTICLE XIII. STOPPING, STANDING, AND PARKING

5/11-1301. Stopping, standing or parking outside of business or residence district

§ 11-1301. Stopping, standing or parking outside of business or residence district.

(a) Outside a business or residence district, no person shall stop, park or leave standing any vehicle, whether attended or unattended, upon the roadway when it is practicable to stop, park or so leave such vehicle off the roadway, but in every event an unobstructed width of the highway opposite a standing vehicle shall be left for the free passage of other vehicles and a clear view of such stopped vehicle shall be available from a distance of 200 feet in each direction upon such highway.

(b) The Department with respect to highways under its jurisdiction or for the maintenance of which it is responsible may place signs prohibiting or restricting the stopping, standing or parking of vehicles on any highway where in its opinion such stopping, standing or parking is dangerous to those using the highway or where the stopping, standing or parking of vehicles would unduly interfere with the free movement of traffic thereon. Any such regulations adopted by the Department regarding the stopping, standing or parking of vehicles upon any specific street, streets or highways become effective at the time of the erection of appropriate signs indicating such regulations. Any such signs may be erected either by the Department or by a local authority with the approval of the Department.

(c) This Section, Section 11-1303 and Section 11-1304 shall not apply to the driver of any vehicle which is disabled in such manner and to such extent that it is impossible to avoid stopping and temporarily leaving the vehicle in such position.

(d) Any second division vehicle used exclusively for the collection of garbage, refuse, or recyclable material may stop or stand on the road in a business, rural, or residential district for the sole purpose of collecting garbage, refuse, or recyclable material. The vehicle, in addition to having its hazard lights lighted at all times that it is engaged in stopping or standing, shall also use its amber oscillating, rotating, or flashing light or lights as authorized under paragraph 12 of subsection (b) of Section 12-215, if so equipped.

P.A. 76-1586, § 11-1301, eff. July 1, 1970. Amended by P.A. 76-2173, § 1, eff. July 1, 1970; P.A. 79-1069, § 1, eff. Jan. 1, 1976; P.A. 91-869, § 5, eff. Jan. 1, 2001.

Formerly Ill.Rev.Stat.1991, ch. 95 ½, ¶ 11-1301.

5/11-1301.1. Persons with disabilities—Parking privileges—Exemptions

§ 11-1301.1. Persons with disabilities—Parking privileges—Exemptions. A motor vehicle bearing registration plates issued to a person with disabilities, as defined by Section 1-159.1, pursuant to Section 3-616 or to a disabled veteran pursuant to Section 3-609 or a special decal or device issued pursuant to Section 3-616 or pursuant to Section 11-1301.2 of this Code or a motor vehicle registered in another jurisdiction, state, district, territory or foreign country upon which is displayed a registration plate, special decal or device issued by the other jurisdiction designating the vehicle is operated by or for a person with disabilities shall be exempt from the payment of parking meter fees and exempt from any statute or ordinance imposing time limitations on parking, except limitations of one-half hour or less, on any street or highway zone, or any parking lot or parking place which are owned, leased or owned and leased by a municipality or a municipal parking utility; and shall be recognized by state and local authorities as a valid license plate or parking device and shall receive the same parking privileges as residents of this State; but, such vehicle shall be subject to the laws which prohibit parking in "no stopping" and "no standing" zones in front of or near fire hydrants, driveways, public building entrances and exits, bus stops and loading areas, and is prohibited from parking where the motor vehicle constitutes a traffic hazard, whereby such motor vehicle shall be moved at the instruction and request of a law enforcement officer to a location designated by the officer. Any motor vehicle bearing registration plates or a special decal or device specified in this Section or in Section 3-616 of this Code or such parking device as specifically authorized in Section 11-1301.2 as evidence that the vehicle is operated by or for a person with disabilities or disabled veteran may park, in addition to any other lawful place, in any parking place specifically reserved for such vehicles by the posting of an official sign as provided under Section 11-301. Parking privileges granted by this Section are strictly limited to the person to whom the special registration plates, special decal or device were issued and to qualified operators acting under his express direction while the person with disabilities is present. A person to whom privileges were granted shall, at the request of a police officer or any other person invested by law with authority to direct, control, or regulate traffic, present an identification card with a picture as verification that the person is the person to whom the special registration plates, special decal or device was issued.

Such parking privileges granted by this Section are also extended to motor vehicles of not-for-profit organizations used for the transportation of persons with disabilities when such motor vehicles display the decal or device issued pursuant to Section 11-1301.2 of this Code.

No person shall use any area for the parking of any motor vehicle pursuant to Section 11-1303 of this Code or where an official sign controlling such area expressly prohibits parking at any time or during certain hours.

P.A. 76-1586, § 11-1301.1, added by P.A. 79-974, § 1, eff. Oct. 1, 1975. Amended by P.A. 81-171, § 1, eff. Jan. 1, 1980; P.A. 81-176, § 1, eff. Jan. 1, 1980; P.A. 81-1509, Art. 1, § 57, eff. Sept. 26, 1980; P.A. 83-1058, § 1, eff. July 1, 1984; P.A. 83-1316, § 1, eff. Jan. 1, 1985; P.A. 84-980, § 1, eff. Sept. 25, 1985; P.A. 86-539, § 1, eff. Jan. 1, 1990; P.A. 88-685, § 5, eff. Jan. 24, 1995; P.A. 90-106, § 5, eff. Jan. 1, 1998.

Formerly Ill.Rev.Stat.1991, ch. 95 ½, ¶ 11-1301.1.

5/11-1301.2. Special decals for a person with disabilities parking

§ 11-1301.2. Special decals for a person with disabilities parking.

(a) The Secretary of State shall provide for, by administrative rules, the design, size, color, and placement of a person with disabilities motorist decal or device and shall provide for, by administrative rules, the content and form of an application for a person with disabilities motorist decal or device, which shall be used by local authorities in the issuance thereof to a person with temporary disabilities, provided that the decal or device is valid for no more than 90 days, subject to renewal for like periods based upon continued disability, and further provided that the decal or device clearly sets forth the date that the decal or device expires. The application shall include the requirement of an Illinois Identification Card number or a State of Illinois driver's license number. This decal or device shall be the property of such person with disabilities and may be used by that person to designate and identify a vehicle not owned or displaying a registration plate as provided in Sections 3-609 and 3-616 of this Act to designate when the vehicle is being used to transport said person or persons with disabilities, and thus is entitled to enjoy all the privileges that would be afforded a person with disabilities licensed vehicle. Person with disabilities decals or devices issued and displayed pursuant to this Section shall be recognized and honored by all local authorities regardless of which local authority issued such decal or device.

The decal or device shall be issued only upon a showing by adequate documentation that the person for whose benefit the decal or device is to be used has a temporary disability as defined in Section 1-159.1 of this Code.

(b) The local governing authorities shall be responsible for the provision of such decal or device, its issuance and designated placement within the vehicle. The cost of such decal or device shall be at the discretion of such local governing authority.

(c) The Secretary of State may, pursuant to Section 3-616(c), issue a person with disabilities parking decal or device to a person with disabilities as defined by Section 1-159.1. Any person with disabilities parking decal or device issued by the Secretary of State shall be registered to that person with disabilities in the form to be prescribed by the Secretary of State. The person with disabilities parking decal or device shall not display that person's address. One additional decal or device may be issued to an applicant upon his or her written request and with the approval of the Secretary of State. The written request must include a justification of the need for the additional decal or device.

(d) Replacement decals or devices may be issued for lost, stolen, or destroyed decals upon application and payment of a $10 fee. The replacement fee may be waived for individuals that have claimed and received a grant under the Senior Citizens and Disabled Persons Property Tax Relief and Pharmaceutical Assistance Act.[1]

P.A. 76-1586, § 11-1301.2, added by P.A. 81-171, § 1, eff. Jan. 1, 1980. Amended by P.A. 82-1011, § 2, eff. Sept. 17, 1982; P.A. 83-1058, § 1, eff. July 1, 1984; P.A. 83-1421, § 10, eff. July 1, 1985; P.A. 85-484, § 1, eff. Jan. 1, 1988; P.A. 88-685, § 5, eff. Jan. 24, 1995; P.A. 90-106, § 5, eff. Jan. 1, 1998; P.A. 92-411, § 5, eff. Jan. 1, 2002.

Formerly Ill.Rev.Stat.1991, ch. 95 ½, ¶ 11-1301.2.

[1] 320 ILCS 25/1 et seq.

Another § 11-1301.2 was renumbered § 11-1301.3.

5/11-1301.3. Unauthorized use of parking places reserved for persons with disabilities

§ 11-1301.3. Unauthorized use of parking places reserved for persons with disabilities.

(a) It shall be prohibited to park any motor vehicle which is not properly displaying registration plates or decals issued to a person with disabilities, as defined by Section 1-159.1, pursuant to Sections 3-616, 11-1301.1 or 11-1301.2, or to a disabled veteran pursuant to Section 3-609 of this Act, as evidence that the vehicle is operated by or for a person with disabilities or disabled veteran, in any parking place, including any private or public offstreet parking facility, specifically reserved, by the posting of an official sign as designated under Section 11-301, for motor vehicles displaying such registration plates. It shall be prohibited to park any motor vehicle in a designated access aisle adjacent to any parking place specifically reserved for persons with disabilities, by the posting of an official sign as designated under Section 11-301, for motor vehicles displaying such registration plates. When using the parking privileges for persons with disabilities, the parking decal or device must be displayed properly in the vehicle where it is clearly visible to law enforcement personnel, either hanging from the rearview mirror or placed on the dashboard of the vehicle in clear view. An individual with a vehicle properly displaying a person with disabilities license plate or parking decal or device issued to a disabled person under Sections 3-616, 11-1301.1, or 11-1301.2 is in violation of this Section if the person is not the authorized holder of a person with disabilities license plate or parking decal or device and is not transporting the authorized holder of a person with disabilities license plate or parking decal or device to or from the parking location and the person uses the person with disabilities license plate or parking decal or device to exercise any privileges granted through the person with disabilities license plates or parking decals or devices under this Code. Any motor vehicle properly displaying a person with disabilities license plate or a person with disabilities parking decal or device containing the International symbol of access issued to persons with disabilities by any local authority, state, district, territory or foreign country shall be recognized by State and local authorities as a valid license plate or device and receive the same parking privileges as residents of this State.

(b) Any person or local authority owning or operating any public or private offstreet parking facility may, after notifying the police or sheriff's department, remove or cause to be removed to the nearest garage or other place of safety any vehicle parked within a stall or space reserved for use by a person with disabilities which does not display person with disabilities registration plates or a special decal or device as required under this Section.

(c) Any person found guilty of violating the provisions of this Section shall be fined $100 in addition to any costs or charges connected with the removal or storage of any motor vehicle authorized under this Section; but municipalities by ordinance may impose a fine up to $200 and shall display signs indicating the fine imposed. If the amount of the fine is subsequently changed, the municipality shall change the sign to indicate the current amount of the fine. It shall not be a defense to a charge under this Section that the sign posted pursuant to this Section does not comply with the technical requirements of Section 11-301, Department regulations, or local ordinance if a reasonable person would be made aware by the sign or notice on or near the parking place that the place is reserved for a person with disabilities.

(d) Local authorities shall impose fines as established in subsection (c) for violations of this Section.

(e) As used in this Section, "authorized holder" means an individual issued a person with disabilities license plate under Section 3-616 of this Code or an individual issued a person with disabilities parking decal or device under Section 11-1301.2 of this Code.

P.A. 76-1586, § 11-1301.2, added by P.A. 81-176, § 1, eff. Jan. 1, 1980. Renumbered § 11-1301.3 and amended by P.A. 81-1509, Art. I, § 57, eff. Sept. 26, 1980. Amended by P.A. 82-226, § 1, eff. Jan. 1, 1982; P.A. 83-1058, § 1, eff. July 1, 1984; P.A. 83-1316, § 1, eff. Jan. 1, 1985; P.A. 86-539, § 1, eff. Jan. 1, 1990; P.A. 88-685, § 5, eff. Jan. 24, 1995; P.A. 89-275, § 5, eff. Jan. 1, 1996; P.A. 89-533, § 5, eff. Jan. 1, 1997; P.A. 89-626, Art. 2, § 2-66, eff. Aug. 9, 1996; P.A. 90-106, § 5, eff. Jan. 1, 1998; P.A. 91-427, § 5, eff. Aug. 6, 1999; P.A. 92-411, § 5, eff. Jan. 1, 2002; P.A. 92-637, § 5, eff. Jan. 1, 2003.

Formerly Ill.Rev.Stat.1991, ch. 95 ½, ¶ 11-1301.3.

P.A. 92-637 incorporated the amendment by P.A. 92-411.

5/11-1301.4. Reciprocal agreements with other jurisdictions

§ 11-1301.4. Reciprocal agreements with other jurisdictions. The Secretary of State, or his designee, may enter into agreements with other jurisdictions, including foreign jurisdictions, on behalf of this State relating to the extension of parking privileges by such jurisdictions to permanently disabled residents of this State who display a special license plate or parking device that contains the International symbol of access on his or her motor vehicle, and to recognize such plates or devices issued by such other jurisdictions. This State shall grant the same parking privileges which are granted to disabled residents of this State to any non-resident whose motor vehicle is licensed in another state, district, territory or foreign country if such vehicle displays the International symbol of access or a distinguishing insignia on license plates or parking device issued in accordance with the laws of the non-resident's state, district, territory or foreign country.

P.A. 76-1586, § 11-1301.4, added by P.A. 84-868, § 1, eff. Sept. 23, 1985. Amended by P.A. 86-539, § 1, eff. Jan. 1, 1990.

Formerly Ill.Rev.Stat.1991, ch. 95 ½, ¶ 11-1301.4.

5/11-1301.5. Fictitious or unlawfully altered person with disabilities license plate or parking decal or device

§ 11-1301.5. Fictitious or unlawfully altered person with disabilities license plate or parking decal or device.

(a) As used in this Section:

"Fictitious person with disabilities license plate or parking decal or device" means any issued person with disabilities license plate or parking decal or device that has been issued by the Secretary of State or an authorized unit of local government that was issued based upon false information contained on the required application.

"False information" means any incorrect or inaccurate information concerning the name, date of birth, social security number, driver's license number, physician certification, or any other information required on the application for a person with disabilities license plate or parking permit or device that falsifies the content of the application.

"Unlawfully altered person with disabilities license plate or parking permit or device" means any person with disabilities license plate or parking permit or device issued by the Secretary of State or an authorized unit of local government that has been physically altered or changed in such manner that false information appears on the license plate or parking decal or device.

"Authorized holder" means an individual issued a person with disabilities license plate under Section 3-616 of this Code or an individual issued a person with disabilities parking decal or device under Section 11-1301.2 of this Code.

(b) It is a violation of this Section for any person:

(1) to knowingly possess any fictitious or unlawfully altered person with disabilities license plate or parking decal or device;

(2) to knowingly issue or assist in the issuance of, by the Secretary of State or unit of local government, any fictitious person with disabilities license plate or parking decal or device;

(3) to knowingly alter any person with disabilities license plate or parking decal or device;

(4) to knowingly manufacture, possess, transfer, or provide any documentation used in the application process whether real or fictitious, for the purpose of obtaining a fictitious person with disabilities license plate or parking decal or device;

(5) to knowingly provide any false information to the Secretary of State or a unit of local government in order to obtain a person with disabilities license plate or parking decal or device; or

(6) to knowingly transfer a person with disabilities license plate or parking decal or device for the purpose of exercising the privileges granted to an authorized holder of a person with disabilities license plate or parking decal or device under this Code in the absence of the authorized holder.

(c) Sentence.

(1) Any person convicted of a violation of this Section shall be guilty of a Class A misdemeanor.

(2) Any person who commits a violation of this Section may have his or her driving privileges suspended or revoked by the Secretary of State for a period of time determined by the Secretary of State.

(3) Any police officer may seize the parking decal or device from any person who commits a violation of this Section. Any police officer may seize the person with disabilities license plate upon authorization from the Secretary of State. Any police officer may request that the Secretary of State revoke the parking decal or device or the person with disabilities license plate of any person who commits a violation of this Section.

P.A. 76-1586, § 11-1301.5, added by P.A. 90-106, § 5, eff. Jan. 1, 1998. Amended by P.A. 90-655, § 153, eff. July 30, 1998; P.A. 92-411, § 5, eff. Jan. 1, 2002.

Another § 11–1301.5, relating to appointed volunteers and contracted entities for policing disabled person parking violations, was renumbered § 11–1301.7 by P.A. 90–655, § 153.

5/11–1301.6. Fraudulent person with disabilities license plate or parking decal or device

§ 11–1301.6. Fraudulent person with disabilities license plate or parking decal or device.

(a) As used in this Section:

"Fraudulent person with disabilities license plate or parking decal or device" means any person with disabilities license plate or parking decal or device that purports to be an official person with disabilities license plate or parking decal or device and that has not been issued by the Secretary of State or an authorized unit of local government.

"Person with disabilities license plate or parking decal or device-making implement" means any implement specially designed or primarily used in the manufacture, assembly, or authentication of a person with disabilities license plate or parking decal or device issued by the Secretary of State or a unit of local government.

(b) It is a violation of this Section for any person:

(1) to knowingly possess any fraudulent person with disabilities license plate or parking decal;

(2) to knowingly possess without authority any person with disabilities license plate or parking decal or device-making implement;

(3) to knowingly duplicate, manufacture, sell, or transfer any fraudulent or stolen person with disabilities license plate or parking decal or device;

(4) to knowingly assist in the duplication, manufacturing, selling, or transferring of any fraudulent or stolen person with disabilities license plate or parking decal or device; or

(5) to advertise or distribute a fraudulent person with disabilities license plate or parking decal or device.

(c) Sentence.

(1) Any person convicted of a violation of this Section shall be guilty of a Class 4 felony.

(2) Any person who commits a violation of this Section may have his or her driving privileges suspended or revoked by the Secretary of State for a period of time determined by the Secretary of State.

(3) Any police officer may seize the parking decal or device from any person who commits a violation of this Section. Any police officer may seize the person with disabilities license plate upon authorization from the Secretary of State. Any police officer may request that the Secretary of State revoke the parking decal or device or the person with disabilities license plate of any person who commits a violation of this Section.

P.A. 76–1586, § 11–1301.6, added by P.A. 90–106, § 5, eff. Jan. 1, 1998. Amended by P.A. 92–411, § 5, eff. Jan. 1, 2002.

5/11–1301.7. Appointed volunteers and contracted entities; disabled person parking violations

§ 11–1301.7. Appointed volunteers and contracted entities; disabled person parking violations.

(a) The chief of police of a municipality and the sheriff of a county authorized to enforce parking laws may appoint volunteers or contract with public or private entities to issue parking violation notices for violations of Section 11–1301.3 or ordinances dealing with parking privileges for persons with disabilities. Volunteers appointed under this Section and any employees of public or private entities that the chief of police or sheriff has contracted with under this Section who are issuing these parking violation notices must be at least 21 years of age. The chief of police or sheriff appointing the volunteers or contracting with public or private entities may establish any other qualifications that he or she deems desirable.

(b) The chief of police or sheriff appointing volunteers under this Section shall provide training to the volunteers before authorizing them to issue parking violation notices.

(c) A parking violation notice issued by a volunteer appointed under this Section or by a public or private entity that the chief of police or sheriff has contracted with under this Section shall have the same force and effect as a parking violation notice issued by a police officer for the same offense.

(d) All funds collected as a result of the payment of the parking violation notices issued under this Section shall go to the municipality or county where the notice is issued.

(e) An appointed volunteer or private or public entity under contract pursuant to this Section is not liable for his or her or its act or omission in the execution or enforcement of laws or ordinances if acting within the scope of the appointment or contract authorized by this Section, unless the act or omission constitutes willful and wanton conduct.

(f) Except as otherwise provided by statute, a local government, a chief of police, sheriff, or employee of a police department or sheriff, as such and acting within the scope of his or her employment, is not liable for an injury caused by the act or omission of an appointed volunteer or private or public entity under contract pursuant to this Section. No local government, chief of police, sheriff, or an employee of a local government, police department or sheriff shall be liable for any actions regarding the supervision or direction, or the failure to supervise and direct, an appointed volunteer or private or public entity under contract pursuant to this Section unless the act or omission constitutes willful and wanton conduct.

(g) An appointed volunteer or private or public entity under contract pursuant to this Section shall assume all liability for and hold the property owner and his agents and employees harmless from any and all claims of action resulting from the work of the appointed volunteer or public or private entity.

P.A. 76–1586, § 11–1301.5, added by P.A. 90–181, § 5, eff. July 23, 1997. Renumbered § 11–1301.7 and amended by P.A. 90–655, § 153, eff. July 30, 1998.

P.A. 90–655, the First 1998 General Revisory Act, amended various Acts to delete obsolete text, to correct patent and technical errors, to revise cross references, to resolve multiple actions in the 89th and 90th General Assemblies and to make certain technical corrections in P.A. 89–708 through P.A. 90–566.

5/11–1302. Officers authorized to remove vehicles

§ 11–1302. Officers authorized to remove vehicles. (a) Whenever any police officer finds a vehicle in violation of any of the provisions of Section 11–1301 such officer is hereby authorized to move such vehicle, or require the driver or other person in charge of the vehicle to move the same, to a position off the roadway.

(b) Any police officer is hereby authorized to remove or cause to be removed to a place of safety any unattended vehicle illegally left standing upon any highway, bridge, causeway, or in a tunnel, in such a position or under such circumstances as to obstruct the normal movement of traffic.

Whenever the Department finds an abandoned or disabled vehicle standing upon the paved or main-traveled part of a highway, which vehicle is or may be expected to interrupt the free flow of traffic on the highway or interfere with the maintenance of the highway, the Department is authorized to move the vehicle to a position off the paved or improved or main-traveled part of the highway.

(c) Any police officer is hereby authorized to remove or cause to be removed to the nearest garage or other place of safety any vehicle found upon a highway when:

1. Report has been made that such vehicle has been stolen or taken without the consent of its owner, or

2. The person or persons in charge of such vehicle are unable to provide for its custody or removal, or

3. When the person driving or in control of such vehicle is arrested for an alleged offense for which the officer is required by law to take the person arrested before a proper magistrate without unnecessary delay.

P.A. 76–1586, § 11–1302, eff. July 1, 1970. Amended by P.A. 76–1735, § 1; P.A. 79–1069, § 1, eff. Jan. 1, 1976.

Formerly Ill.Rev.Stat.1991, ch. 95 ½, ¶ 11–1302.

5/11–1303. Stopping, standing or parking prohibited in specified places

§ 11–1303. Stopping, standing or parking prohibited in specified places.

(a) Except when necessary to avoid conflict with other traffic, or in compliance with law or the directions of a police officer or official traffic-control device, no person shall:

1. Stop, stand or park a vehicle:

a. On the roadway side of any vehicle stopped or parked at the edge or curb of a street;

b. On a sidewalk;

c. Within an intersection;

d. On a crosswalk;

e. Between a safety zone and the adjacent curb or within 30 feet of points on the curb immediately opposite the ends of a safety zone, unless a different length is indicated by signs or markings;

f. Alongside or opposite any street excavation or obstruction when stopping, standing or parking would obstruct traffic;

g. Upon any bridge or other elevated structure upon a highway or within a highway tunnel;

h. On any railroad tracks. A violation of any part of this subparagraph h. shall result in a mandatory fine of $500 or 50 hours of community service.

i. At any place where official signs prohibit stopping;

j. On any controlled-access highway;

k. In the area between roadways of a divided highway, including crossovers;

l. In a public parking area if the vehicle does not display a current annual registration sticker or current temporary permit pending registration.

2. Stand or park a vehicle, whether occupied or not, except momentarily to pick up or discharge passengers:

a. In front of a public or private driveway;

b. Within 15 feet of a fire hydrant;

c. Within 20 feet of a crosswalk at an intersection;

d. Within 30 feet upon the approach to any flashing signal, stop sign, yield sign, or traffic control signal located at the side of a roadway;

e. Within 20 feet of the driveway entrance to any fire station and on the side of a street opposite the entrance to any fire station within 75 feet of such entrance (when properly sign-posted);

f. At any place where official signs prohibit standing.

3. Park a vehicle, whether occupied or not, except temporarily for the purpose of and while actually engaged in loading or unloading property or passengers:

a. Within 50 feet of the nearest rail of a railroad crossing;

b. At any place where official signs prohibit parking.

(b) No person shall move a vehicle not lawfully under his control into any such prohibited area or away from a curb such distance as is unlawful.

P.A. 76–1586, § 11–1303, eff. July 1, 1970. Amended by P.A. 77–1345, § 1, eff. Aug. 27, 1971; P.A. 79–1069, § 1, eff. Jan. 1, 1976; P.A. 89–245, § 5, eff. Jan. 1, 1996; P.A. 89–658, § 5, eff. Jan. 1, 1997.

Formerly Ill.Rev.Stat.1991, ch. 95 ½, ¶ 11–1303.

P.A. 89–658 incorporated the amendment by P.A. 89–245.

5/11–1304. Additional parking regulations

§ 11–1304. Additional parking regulations. (a) Except as otherwise provided in this section, every vehicle stopped or parked upon a two-way roadway shall be so stopped or parked with the right-hand wheels parallel to and within 12 inches of the right-hand curb or as close as practicable to the right edge of the right-hand shoulder.

(b) Except when otherwise provided by local ordinance, every vehicle stopped or parked upon a one-way roadway shall be so stopped or parked parallel to the curb or edge of the roadway, in the direction of authorized traffic movement, with its right-hand wheels within 12 inches of the right-hand curb or as close as practicable to the right edge of the right-hand shoulder, or with its left-hand wheels within 12 inches of the left-hand curb or as close as practicable to the left edge of the left-hand shoulder.

(c) Local authorities may permit angle parking on any roadway, except that angle parking shall not be permitted on any federal-aid or State highway unless the Department has determined that the roadway is of sufficient width to permit angle parking without interfering with the free movement of traffic.

(d) The Department with respect to highways under its jurisdiction may place signs prohibiting, limiting, or restricting the stopping, standing or parking of vehicles on any highway where in its opinion such stopping, standing or parking is dangerous to those using the highway or where the stopping, standing or parking of vehicles would unduly interfere with the free movement of traffic thereon. No person shall stop, stand or park any vehicle in violation of the restrictions indicated by such devices.

P.A. 76–1586, § 11–1304, eff. July 1, 1970. Amended by P.A. 79–801, § 1, eff. Oct. 1, 1975; P.A. 79–1069, § 1, eff. Jan. 1, 1976; P.A. 79–1454, § 44, eff. Aug. 31, 1976.

Formerly Ill.Rev.Stat.1991, ch. 95 ½, ¶ 11–1304.

5/11–1304.5. Parking of vehicle with expired registration

§ 11–1304.5. Parking of vehicle with expired registration. No person may stop, park, or leave standing upon a public street, highway, or roadway a vehicle upon which is displayed an Illinois registration plate or plates or registration sticker after the termination of the registration period for which the registration plate or plates or registration sticker was issued or after the expiration date set under Section 3–414 or 3–414.1 of this Code.

P.A. 76–1586, § 11–1304.5, added by P.A. 91–487, § 5, eff. Jan. 1, 2000.

5/11-1305. Lessors of visitor vehicles—Duty upon receiving notice of violation of this Article or local parking regulation

§ 11–1305. Lessors of visitor vehicles—Duty upon receiving notice of violation of this Article or local parking regulation. Every person in whose name a vehicle is registered pursuant to law and who leases such vehicle to others, after receiving written notice of a violation of this Article or a parking regulation of a local authority involving such vehicle, shall upon request provide such police officers as have authority of the offense, and the court having jurisdiction thereof, with a written statement of the name and address of the lessee at the time of such offense and the identifying number upon the registration plates and registration sticker or stickers of such vehicle.

P.A. 76–1586, § 11–1305, eff. July 1, 1970. Amended by P.A. 77–2720, § 1, eff. Jan. 1, 1973; P.A. 80–230, § 1, eff. Oct. 1, 1977; P.A. 80–911, § 1, eff. Oct. 1, 1977; P.A. 80–1185, § 1, eff. March 8, 1978.

Formerly Ill.Rev.Stat.1991, ch. 95 ½, ¶ 11–1305.

See 5 ILCS 70/6 as to the effect of (1) more than one amendment of a section at the same session of the General Assembly or (2) two or more acts relating to the same subject matter enacted by the same General Assembly.

5/11-1306. Parking liability of lessor

§ 11–1306. Parking liability of lessor. No person who is the lessor of a vehicle pursuant to a written lease agreement shall be liable for the violation of any parking or standing regulation of this Act, or of a local authority, involving such vehicle during the period of the lease; provided that upon the request of the appropriate authority received within 120 days after the violation occurred, the lessor provides within 60 days after such receipt the name and address of the lessee. The drivers license number of a lessee may be subsequently individually requested by the appropriate authority if needed for enforcement of the Act.

P.A. 76–1586, § 11–1306, added by P.A. 83–1110, § 2, eff. May 25, 1984. Amended by P.A. 84–354, § 1, eff. Sept. 14, 1985.

Formerly Ill.Rev.Stat.1991, ch. 95 ½, ¶ 11–1306.

ARTICLE XIV. MISCELLANEOUS LAWS

5/11-1401. Unattended motor vehicles

§ 11–1401. Unattended motor vehicles. No person driving or in charge of a motor vehicle shall permit it to stand unattended without first stopping the engine, locking the ignition, removing the key from the ignition, effectively setting the brake thereon and, when standing upon any perceptible grade, turning the front wheels to the curb or side of the highway.

P.A. 76–1586, § 11–1401, eff. July 1, 1970. Amended by P.A. 76–2174, § 1, eff. July 1, 1970; P.A. 79–1069, § 1, eff. Jan. 1, 1976.

Formerly Ill.Rev.Stat.1991, ch. 95 ½, ¶ 11–1401.

5/11-1402. Limitations on backing

§ 11-1402. Limitations on backing. (a) The driver of a vehicle shall not back the same unless such movement can be made with safety and without interfering with other traffic.

(b) The driver of a vehicle shall not back the same upon any shoulder or roadway of any controlled-access highway.

P.A. 76-1586, § 11-1402, eff. July 1, 1970. Amended by P.A. 79-1069, § 1, eff. Jan. 1, 1976.

Formerly Ill.Rev.Stat.1991, ch. 95 ½, ¶ 11-1402.

5/11-1403. Riding on motorcycles

§ 11-1403. Riding on motorcycles. (a) A person operating a motorcycle shall ride only upon the permanent and regular seat attached thereto, and such operator shall not carry any other person nor shall any other person ride on a motorcycle unless such motorcycle is designed to carry more than one person, in which event a passenger may ride upon the permanent and regular seat if designed for 2 persons, or upon another seat firmly attached to the motorcycle at the rear or side of the operator.

(b) A person shall ride upon a motorcycle only while sitting astride the seat, facing forward, with one leg on each side of the motorcycle.

(c) No person shall operate any motorcycle with handlebars higher than the height of the shoulders of the operator when the operator is seated in the normal driving position astride that portion of the seat or saddle occupied by the operator.

P.A. 76-1586, § 11-1403, eff. July 1, 1970. Amended by P.A. 84-602, § 1, eff. Jan. 1, 1986.

Formerly Ill.Rev.Stat.1991, ch. 95 ½, ¶ 11-1403.

5/11-1403.1. Riding on motorized pedalcycles

§ 11-1403.1. Riding on motorized pedalcycles. (a) The operator of a motorized pedalcycle shall ride only astride the permanent and regular seat attached thereto, and shall not permit 2 persons to ride thereon at the same time, unless the motorized pedalcycle is designed to carry 2 persons; any motorized pedalcycle designed for 2 persons must be equipped with a passenger seat and footrests for use of a passenger.

(b) The provisions of Article XV shall be applicable to the operation of motorized pedalcycles, except for those provisions which by their nature can have no application to motorized pedalcycles.

P.A. 76-1586, § 11-403.1, added by P.A. 80-262, § 1, eff. Aug. 20, 1977. Renumbered § 11-1403.1 and amended by P.A. 82-783, Art. IV, § 25, eff. July 13, 1982. Amended by P.A. 84-602, § 1, eff. Jan. 1, 1986; P.A. 85-830, § 1, eff. Sept. 24, 1987.

Formerly Ill.Rev.Stat.1991, ch. 95 ½, ¶ 11-1403.1.

5/11-1403.2. Operation on one wheel

§ 11-1403.2. No person shall operate a motorcycle, motor driven cycle, or motorized pedalcycle on one wheel.

P.A. 76-1586, § 11-1403.2, added by P.A. 81-844, § 1, eff. Jan. 1, 1980. Amended by P.A. 85-830, § 1, eff. Sept. 24, 1987.

Formerly Ill.Rev.Stat.1991, ch. 95 ½, ¶ 11-1403.2.

5/11-1403.3. Intercom helmets

§ 11-1403.3. Intercom helmets. Any driver of a vehicle defined in Section 1-145.001, 1-147, or 1-148.2 of this Code may use a helmet equipped with an electronic intercom system permitting 2-way vocal communication with drivers of any such vehicles or passengers on such vehicles.

P.A. 76-1586, § 11-1403.3, added by P.A. 85-273, § 1, eff. Jan. 1, 1988. Amended by P.A. 90-89, § 15, eff. Jan. 1, 1998.

Formerly Ill.Rev.Stat.1991, ch. 95 ½, ¶ 11-1403.3.

5/11-1404. Special equipment for persons riding motorcycles, motor driven cycles or motorized pedalcycles

§ 11-1404. Special equipment for persons riding motorcycles, motor driven cycles or motorized pedalcycles.

(a) The operator of a motorcycle, motor driven cycle or motorized pedalcycle and every passenger thereon shall be protected by glasses, goggles or a transparent shield.

(b) For the purposes of this Section, glasses, goggles, and transparent shields are defined as follows:

"Glasses" means ordinary eye pieces such as spectacles or sunglasses worn before the eye, made of shatter-resistant material. Shatter-resistant material, as used in this Section, means material so manufactured, fabricated, or created that it substantially prevents shattering or flying when struck or broken.

"Goggles" means a device worn before the eyes, the predominant function of which is protecting the eyes without obstructing peripheral vision. Goggles shall provide protection from the front and sides, and may or may not form a complete seal with the face.

"Transparent shield" means a windshield attached to the front of a motorcycle that extends above the eyes when an operator is seated in the normal, upright riding position, made of shatter-resistant material, or a shatter-resistant protective face shield that covers the wearer's eyes and face at least to a point approximately to the tip of the nose.

(c) Contact lenses are not acceptable eye protection devices.

P.A. 76-1586, § 11-1404, eff. July 1, 1970. Amended by P.A. 76-2175, § 1, eff. July 1, 1970; P.A. 78-748, § 1, eff. Jan. 1, 1974; P.A. 85-830, § 1, eff. Sept. 24, 1987; P.A. 89-271, § 5, eff. Jan. 1, 1996.

Formerly Ill.Rev.Stat.1991, ch. 95 ½, ¶ 11-1404.

5/11-1405. Required equipment on motorcycles

§ 11-1405. Required equipment on motorcycles. Any motorcycle carrying a passenger, other than in a sidecar or enclosed cab, shall be equipped with footrests for such passenger.

P.A. 76-1586, § 11-1405, eff. July 1, 1970. Amended by P.A. 76-1736, § 1; P.A. 81-804, § 1, eff. Sept. 19, 1979; P.A. 84-602, § 1, eff. Jan. 1, 1986.

Formerly Ill.Rev.Stat.1991, ch. 95 ½, ¶ 11-1405.

5/11-1406. Obstruction of driver's view or driving mechanism

§ 11-1406. Obstruction of driver's view or driving mechanism. (a) No person shall drive a vehicle when it is so loaded, or when there are in the front seat such a number of persons, exceeding three, as to obstruct the view of the driver to the front or sides of the vehicle or as to interfere with the driver's control over the driving mechanism of the vehicle.

(b) No passenger in a vehicle or streetcar shall ride in such position as to interfere with the driver's or motorman's view ahead or to the sides, or to interfere with his control over the driving mechanism of the vehicle or streetcar.

(c) No passenger on a school bus may ride or stand in a position as to interfere with the driver's view ahead or to the side or to the rear, or to interfere with his control of the driving mechanism of the bus.

P.A. 76-1586, § 11-1406, eff. July 1, 1970. Amended by P.A. 78-499, § 1, eff. Aug. 30, 1973; P.A. 79-1069, § 1, eff. Jan. 1, 1976.

Formerly Ill.Rev.Stat.1991, ch. 95 ½, ¶ 11-1406.

5/11-1407. Opening and closing vehicle doors

§ 11-1407. Opening and closing vehicle doors. No person shall open the door of a vehicle on the side available to moving traffic unless and until it is reasonably safe to do so, and can be done without interfering with the movement of other traffic, nor shall any person leave a door open on the side of a vehicle available to moving traffic for a period of time longer than necessary to load or unload passengers.

P.A. 76-1586, § 11-1407, eff. July 1, 1970. Amended by P.A. 79-1069, § 1, eff. Jan. 1, 1976.

Formerly Ill.Rev.Stat.1991, ch. 95 ½, ¶ 11-1407.

5/11-1408. Riding in house trailers

§ 11-1408. Riding in house trailers. No person or persons shall occupy a house trailer, travel trailer while it is being towed upon a public highway.

P.A. 76-1586, § 11-1408, eff. July 1, 1970. Amended by P.A. 81-969, § 1, eff. Jan. 1, 1980.

Formerly Ill.Rev.Stat.1991, ch. 95 ½, ¶ 11-1408.

Section 3 of P.A. 81-969, approved Sept. 22, 1979, provided:

"This amendatory Act takes effect at the start of the 1981 registration year."

5/11-1409. Driving on mountain highways

§ 11-1409. Driving on mountain highways. The driver of a motor vehicle traveling through defiles or canyons or on mountain highways shall hold such motor vehicle under control and as near the right-hand edge of the roadway as reasonably possible and, except when driving entirely to the right of the center of the roadway, shall give audible warning with the horn of such motor vehicle upon approaching any curve where the view is obstructed within a distance of 200 feet along the highway.

P.A. 76-1586, § 11-1409, eff. July 1, 1970. Amended by P.A. 79-1069, § 1, eff. Jan. 1, 1976.

Formerly Ill.Rev.Stat.1991, ch. 95 ½, ¶ 11-1409.

5/11-1410. Coasting prohibited

§ 11-1410. Coasting prohibited. (a) The driver of any motor vehicle when traveling upon a down grade shall not coast with the gears or transmission of such vehicle in neutral.

(b) The driver of a truck or bus when traveling upon a down grade shall not coast with the clutch disengaged.

P.A. 76-1586, § 11-1410, eff. July 1, 1970. Amended by P.A. 76-1736, § 1; P.A. 79-1069, § 1, eff. Jan. 1, 1976.

Formerly Ill.Rev.Stat.1991, ch. 95 ½, ¶ 11-1410.

5/11-1411. Following fire apparatus prohibited

§ 11-1411. Following fire apparatus prohibited. The driver of any vehicle other than one on official business shall not follow any fire apparatus traveling in response to a fire alarm closer than 500 feet or stop such vehicle within 500 feet of any fire apparatus stopped in answer to a fire alarm.

P.A. 76-1586, § 11-1411, eff. July 1, 1970. Amended by P.A. 79-1069, § 1, eff. Jan. 1, 1976.

Formerly Ill.Rev.Stat.1991, ch. 95 ½, ¶ 11-1411.

5/11-1412. Crossing fire hose

§ 11-1412. Crossing fire hose. No vehicle shall be driven over any unprotected hose of a fire department when laid down on any street, private road or driveway to be used at any fire or alarm of fire, without the consent of the fire department official in command.

P.A. 76-1586, § 11-1412, eff. July 1, 1970. Amended by P.A. 76-1736, § 1, eff. Oct. 6, 1969.

Formerly Ill.Rev.Stat.1991, ch. 95 ½, ¶ 11-1412.

5/11-1412.1. Driving upon sidewalk

Text of section effective until June 1, 2003

§ 11-1412.1. Driving upon sidewalk. No person shall drive any vehicle upon a sidewalk or sidewalk area except upon a permanent or duly authorized temporary driveway. This Section does not apply to any vehicle moved exclusively by human power nor to any motorized wheelchair.

P.A. 76-1586, § 11-1412.1, added by P.A. 76-1736, § 1. Amended by P.A. 79-1069, § 1, eff. Jan. 1, 1976; P.A. 84-672, § 1, eff. Sept. 20, 1985.

Formerly Ill.Rev.Stat.1991, ch. 95 ½, ¶ 11-1412.1.

For text of section effective June 1, 2003, see 625 ILCS 5/11-1412.1, post

5/11-1412.1. Driving upon sidewalk

Text of section effective June 1, 2003

§ 11-1412.1. Driving upon sidewalk. No person shall drive any vehicle upon a sidewalk or sidewalk area except upon a permanent or duly authorized temporary driveway. This Section does not apply to any vehicle moved exclusively by human power, to any electric personal assistive mobility device, nor to any motorized wheelchair. Nothing in this Section shall be deemed to limit or preempt the authority of any home rule or non-home rule unit of local government from regulating or prohibiting the use of electric personal assistive mobility devices.

P.A. 76-1586, § 11-1412.1, added by P.A. 76-1736, § 1. Amended by P.A. 79-1069, § 1, eff. Jan. 1, 1976; P.A. 84-672, § 1, eff. Sept. 20, 1985; P.A. 92-868, § 5, eff. June 1, 2003.

Formerly Ill.Rev.Stat.1991, ch. 95 ½, ¶ 11-1412.1.

For text of section effective until June 1, 2003, see 625 ILCS 5/11-1412.1, ante

5/11-1412.2. Operating an electric personal assistive mobility device on a public sidewalk

Text of section added effective June 1, 2003

§ 11-1412.2. Operating an electric personal assistive mobility device on a public sidewalk. A person may not operate an electric personal assistive mobility device upon a public sidewalk at a speed greater than 8 miles per hour. Nothing in this Section shall be deemed to limit or preempt the authority of any home rule or non-home rule unit of local government from regulating or prohibiting the use of electric personal assistive mobility devices.

P.A. 76-1586, § 11-1412.2, added by P.A. 92-868, § 5, eff. June 1, 2003.

5/11-1413. Depositing material on highway prohibited

§ 11-1413. Depositing material on highway prohibited.

(a) No person shall throw, spill or deposit upon any highway any bottle, glass, nails, tacks, wire, cans, or any litter (as defined in Section 3 of the Litter Control Act).[1]

(b) Any person who violates subsection (a) upon any highway shall immediately remove such material or cause it to be removed.

(c) Any person removing a wrecked or damaged vehicle from a highway shall remove any glass or other debris, except any hazardous substance as defined in Section 3.215 of the Environmental Protection Act,[2] hazardous waste as defined in Section 3.220 of the Environmental Protection Act,[3] and potentially infectious medical waste as defined in Section 3.360 of the Environmental Protection Act,[4] dropped upon the highway from such vehicle.

P.A. 76-1586, § 11-1413, eff. July 1, 1970. Amended by P.A. 79-1069, § 1, eff. Jan. 1, 1976; P.A. 86-664, § 1, eff. Sept. 1, 1989; P.A. 87-190, § 1, eff. Jan. 1, 1992; P.A. 88-415, § 10, eff. Aug. 20, 1993; P.A. 88-670, Art. 3, § 3-80, eff. Dec. 2, 1994; P.A. 92-574, § 70, eff. June 26, 2002.

Formerly Ill.Rev.Stat.1991, ch. 95½, ¶ 11-1413.

1 415 ILCS 105/3.

2 415 ILCS 5/3.215.

3 415 ILCS 5/3.220.

4 415 ILCS 5/3.360.

P.A. 88-670, Article 3, of the First 1994 General Revisory Act, amended various Acts to delete obsolete text, to correct patent and technical errors, and to revise cross references.

5/11-1414. Approaching, overtaking, and passing school bus

§ 11-1414. Approaching, overtaking, and passing school bus.

(a) The driver of a vehicle shall stop such vehicle before meeting or overtaking, from either direction, any school bus stopped for the purpose of receiving or discharging pupils on a highway, on a roadway on school property, or upon a private road within an area that is covered by a contract or agreement executed pursuant to Section 11-209.1 of this Code. Such stop is required before reaching the school bus when there is in operation on the school bus the visual signals as specified in Sections 12-803 and 12-805 of this Code. The driver of the vehicle shall not proceed until the school bus resumes motion or the driver of the vehicle is signaled by the school bus driver to proceed or the visual signals are no longer actuated.

(b) The stop signal arm required by Section 12-803 of this Code shall be extended after the school bus has come to a complete stop for the purpose of loading or discharging pupils and shall be closed before the school bus is placed in motion again. The stop signal arm shall not be extended at any other time.

(c) The alternately flashing red signal lamps of an 8-lamp flashing signal system required by Section 12-805 of this Code shall be actuated after the school bus has come to a complete stop for the purpose of loading or discharging pupils and shall be turned off before the school bus is placed in motion again. The red signal lamps shall not be actuated at any other time except as provided in paragraph (d) of this Section.

(d) The alternately flashing amber signal lamps of an 8-lamp flashing signal system required by Section 12-805 of this Code shall be actuated continuously during not less than the last 100 feet traveled by the school bus before stopping for the purpose of loading or discharging pupils within an urban area and during not less than the last 200 feet traveled by the school bus outside an urban area. The amber signal lamps shall remain actuated until the school bus is stopped. The amber signal lamps shall not be actuated at any other time.

(e) The driver of a vehicle upon a highway having 4 or more lanes which permits at least 2 lanes of traffic to travel in opposite directions need not stop such vehicle upon meeting a school bus which is stopped in the opposing roadway; and need not stop such vehicle when driving upon a controlled access highway when passing a school bus traveling in either direction that is stopped in a loading zone adjacent to the surfaced or improved part of the controlled access highway where pedestrians are not permitted to cross.

(f) Beginning with the effective date of this amendatory Act of 1985, the Secretary of State shall suspend for a period of 3 months the driving privileges of any person convicted of a violation of subsection (a) of this Section or a similar provision of a local ordinance; the Secretary shall suspend for a period of one year the driving privileges of any person convicted of a second or subsequent violation of subsection (a) of this Section or a similar provision of a local ordinance if the second or subsequent violation occurs within 5 years of a prior conviction for the same offense. In addition to the suspensions authorized by this Section, any person convicted of violating this Section or a similar provision of a local ordinance shall be subject to a mandatory fine of $150 or, upon a second or subsequent violation, $500. The Secretary may also grant, for the duration of any suspension issued under this subsection, a restricted driving permit granting the privilege of driving a motor vehicle between the driver's residence and place of employment or within other proper limits that the Secretary of State shall find necessary to avoid any undue hardship. A restricted driving permit issued hereunder shall be subject to cancellation, revocation and suspension by the Secretary of State in like manner and for like cause as a driver's license may be cancelled, revoked or suspended; except that a conviction upon one or more offenses against laws or ordinances regulating the movement of traffic shall be deemed sufficient cause for the revocation, suspension or cancellation of the restricted driving permit. The Secretary of State may, as a condition to the issuance of a restricted driving permit, require the applicant to participate in a designated driver remedial or rehabilitative program. Any conviction for a violation of this subsection shall be included as an offense for the purposes of determining suspension action under any other provision of this Code, provided however, that the penalties provided under this subsection shall be imposed unless those penalties imposed under other applicable provisions are greater.

The owner of any vehicle alleged to have violated paragraph (a) of this Section shall, upon appropriate demand by the State's Attorney or other authorized prosecutor acting in response to a signed complaint, provide a written statement or deposition identifying the operator of the vehicle if such operator was not the owner at the time of the alleged violation. Failure to supply such information shall be construed to be the same as a violation of paragraph (a) and shall be subject to the same penalties herein provided. In the event the owner has assigned control for the use of the vehicle to another, the person to whom control was assigned shall comply with the provisions of this paragraph and be subject to the same penalties as herein provided.

P.A. 76-1586, § 11-1414, eff. July 1, 1970. Amended by P.A. 76-1723, § 1; P.A. 78-510, § 1, eff. Oct. 1, 1973; P.A. 78-738, § 1, eff. Jan. 1, 1974; P.A. 78-1244, § 1, eff. Sept. 5, 1974; P.A. 78-1297, § 58, eff. March 4, 1975; P.A. 79-63, § 1, eff. June 26, 1975; P.A. 80-506, § 1, eff. Oct. 1, 1977; P.A. 82-648, § 1, eff. July 1, 1982; P.A. 83-905, § 1, eff. Jan. 1, 1984; P.A. 84-112, § 1, eff. July 25, 1985; P.A. 89-210, § 5, eff. Aug. 2, 1995; P.A. 91-260, § 5, eff. Jan. 1, 2000.

Formerly Ill.Rev.Stat.1991, ch. 95 ½, ¶ 11-1414.

5/11-1414.1. School transportation of students

§ 11-1414.1. School transportation of students.

(a) Every student enrolled in grade 12 or below in any entity listed in paragraph (a) of Section 1-182 of this Code who is transported in a second division motor vehicle owned or operated by or for that entity, in connection with any official activity of such entity, must be transported in a school bus or a bus described in subparagraph (1) of paragraph (b) of Section 1-182.

(b) This Section shall not apply to any second division vehicle being used by such entity in a parade, homecoming or similar school activity, nor to a motor vehicle designed for the transportation of not less than 7 nor more than 16 persons while that vehicle is being operated by or for a public or private primary or secondary school, including any primary or secondary school operated by a religious institution, for the purpose of transporting not more than 15 students to and from interscholastic athletic or other interscholastic or school sponsored activities.

P.A. 76-1586, § 11-1414.1, added by P.A. 83-299, § 1, eff. Jan. 1, 1984. Amended by P.A. 89-132, § 10, eff. July 14, 1995.

Formerly Ill.Rev.Stat.1991, ch. 95 ½, ¶ 11-1414.1.

5/11-1415. School buses stopping, loading and discharging passengers on one-way roadways on highways having 4 or more lanes

§ 11-1415. School buses stopping, loading and discharging passengers on one-way roadways on highways having 4 or more lanes. (a) A school bus traveling on a one-way roadway or a highway having 4 or more lanes for vehicular traffic shall stop for the loading or discharging of passengers only on the right side of the highway. If the highway has 4 or more lanes and permits traffic to operate in both directions, the school bus shall load or discharge only those passengers whose residences are located to the right of the highway. The routes of school buses shall be so arranged that no child shall be required to cross a highway of 4 or more lanes to board a school bus or to reach such child's residence after leaving the school bus. A school child in an urban area shall cross a highway only at a crossing for pedestrians, except as provided in paragraph (b) of this Section.

(b) With respect to school children crossing a highway at other than a pedestrian crossing, this Section shall not apply when children are escorted or controlled by competent persons designated by the school authorities or by police officers.

P.A. 76-1586, § 11-1415, eff. July 1, 1970. Amended by P.A. 83-905, § 1, eff. Jan. 1, 1984.

Formerly Ill.Rev.Stat.1991, ch. 95½, ¶ 11-1415.

5/11-1416. Obstructing person in highways

§ 11-1416. Obstructing person in highways. No person shall wilfully and unnecessarily hinder, obstruct or delay, or wilfully and unnecessarily attempt to delay, hinder or obstruct any other person in lawfully driving or traveling along or upon any highway within this State or offer for barter or sale merchandise on said highway so as to interfere with the effective movement of traffic.

P.A. 76-1586, § 11-1416, eff. July 1, 1970. Amended by P.A. 77-2830, Art. 73, § 1, eff. Jan. 1, 1973; P.A. 78-494, § 1, eff. Oct. 1, 1973; P.A. 80-911, § 1, eff. Oct. 1, 1977.

Formerly Ill.Rev.Stat.1991, ch. 95 ½, ¶ 11-1416.

5/11-1417. Travel regulated

§ 11-1417. Travel regulated. It shall be unlawful for any person to drive or cause to be driven a vehicle of any description in or upon any portion of the highway immediately after the same has been dragged and before such portion of the highway shall have partially dried out or frozen; provided, that nothing in this Section shall apply in those instances where it is impossible to drive with safety at one side of said dragged portion of the road, or where a vehicle does not make a rut on such dragged portion of the road, injurious to the work accomplished by use of the road drag or where a vehicle does not make a rut nearer than nine (9) feet from the center of the dragged portion of the road.

P.A. 76-1586, § 11-1417, eff. July 1, 1970.

Formerly Ill.Rev.Stat.1991, ch. 95 ½, ¶ 11-1417.

5/11-1418. Farm tractor operation regulated

§ 11-1418. Farm tractor operation regulated.

No person shall operate a farm tractor on a highway unless the tractor is being used as an implement of husbandry in connection with farming operations.

For the purpose of this Section, use of a farm tractor as an implement of husbandry in connection with farming operations shall be deemed to include use of the tractor in connection with the transportation of agricultural products and of farm machinery, equipment and supplies as well as transportation of the implement of husbandry from its place of purchase to its place of storage, in connection with the obtaining of repairs of the implement of husbandry, and the towing of a registered truck not more than 8,000 pounds for use as return transportation after the tractor is left at the place of work or repair.

P.A. 76-1586, § 11-1418, eff. July 1, 1970. Amended by P.A. 77-631, § 1, eff. Aug. 4, 1971; P.A. 87-1028, § 1, eff. Jan. 1, 1993.

Formerly Ill.Rev.Stat.1991, ch. 95 ½, ¶ 11-1418.

5/11-1419. Operation of motor vehicles—Duration—Exceptions

§ 11-1419. Operation of motor vehicles—Duration—Exceptions. It is unlawful for any owner to require, permit or allow any operator of any of his motor vehicles of the second division to operate any such motor vehicle for a longer period than 10 hours following 8 consecutive hours off-duty or drive for any period after having been on duty 15 hours following 8 consecutive hours off-duty, or to be or remain on duty more than 60 hours in any 7 consecutive days, and whenever any such operator has operated such motor vehicle for 10 hours following 8 consecutive hours off-duty or has been on duty 15 hours following 8 consecutive hours off-duty, he or she shall be relieved and not required, permitted or allowed again to operate any such motor vehicle until he or she has had at least 8 consecutive hours off-duty. The Department of State Police shall fix by general rule or temporary order the circumstances and regulations under which in case of emergency or unusual temporary demands for transportation any such operator may be permitted to operate any such motor vehicle or to stay on duty for longer periods of time than set by this Section.

The provisions of this Section shall not apply to any public utility in the operation of any motor vehicle not for hire in case of emergency or in case of unusual temporary necessity for transportation of persons or property or safeguarding of vehicles and their loads, nor shall such provisions apply to operation of any motor vehicle as a part of the agricultural operations of canning, packing or freezing establishments engaged in the growing and processing of perishable fruits and vegetables, including the hauling of such products between fields and such canning, packing or freezing establishments and between such establishments, nor shall such provisions apply to operation of any motor vehicle being used for transportation of construction materials or equipment to, on or from construction sites within a radius of 50 miles of such construction sites, nor to driver sales persons operating within a radius of 50 miles of their principal place of business.

P.A. 76–1586, § 11–1419, eff. July 1, 1970. Amended by P.A. 76–2176, § 1, eff. July 1, 1970; P.A. 84–25, Art. IV, § 27, eff. July 18, 1985; P.A. 84–551, § 50, eff. Sept. 18, 1985; P.A. 84–1308, Art. II, § 96, eff. Aug. 25, 1986.

Formerly Ill.Rev.Stat.1991, ch. 95 ½, ¶ 11–1419.

Article II of P.A. 84–1308, the First 84th General Assembly Combining Revisory Act, provides for the nonsubstantive revision or renumbering or repeal of Sections of Acts necessitated by the amendment, addition or repeal of Sections by two or more Public Acts of the 84th General Assembly, which multiple action was not resolved by one of the Acts of the 84th General Assembly affecting the particular Section and makes technical corrections in Acts amended by the 84th General Assembly.

5/11–1419.01. Operating without a valid single trip permit

§ 11–1419.01. Operating without a valid single trip permit. If a single trip permit is required by Section 13a.5 of the Motor Fuel Tax Law,[1] a motor carrier shall not operate in Illinois without a single trip permit issued by the Department of Revenue or its agents.

If a commercial motor vehicle is found operating in Illinois without displaying a required valid single trip permit, the operator is guilty of a petty offense as provided in Section 13a.6 of the Motor Fuel Tax Law.[2]

P.A. 76–1586, § 11–1419.01, added by P.A. 81–348, § 1, eff. Jan. 1, 1980. Amended by P.A. 88–669, Art. 90, § 90–9.5, eff. Nov. 29, 1994; P.A. 89–399, § 35, eff. Aug. 20, 1995.

Formerly Ill.Rev.Stat.1991, ch. 95 ½, ¶ 11–1419.01.

1 35 ILCS 505/13a.5.

2 35 ILCS 505/13a.6.

5/11–1419.02. Failure to display a valid motor fuel use tax license

§ 11–1419.02. Failure to display a valid motor fuel use tax license.

(a) If required by Section 13a.4 of the Motor Fuel Tax Law,[1] every valid motor fuel use tax license, or an authorized reproduction, shall at all times be carried in the cab of the vehicle. The operator shall display the license or reproduction upon demand of a police officer or agent of the Department of Revenue. An operator who fails to display a valid motor fuel use tax license is guilty of a petty offense as provided in Section 13a.6 of the Motor Fuel Tax Law.[2]

(b) As used in this Section:

"Display" means the manual surrender of the motor fuel use tax license into the hands of the demanding officer or agent for inspection.

"Motor fuel use tax license" means a motor fuel use tax license issued by the Department of Revenue or by any member jurisdiction under the International Fuel Tax Agreement, or a valid 30 day International Fuel Tax Agreement temporary permit.

P.A. 76–1586, § 11–1419.02, added by P.A. 83–1426, § 1, eff. Jan. 1, 1985. Amended by P.A. 84–1076, § 1, eff. July 1, 1986; P.A. 85–340, § 2, eff. Sept. 10, 1987; P.A. 88–669, Art. 90, § 90–9.5, eff. Nov. 29, 1994; P.A. 89–399, § 35, eff. Aug. 20, 1995.

Formerly Ill.Rev.Stat.1991, ch. 95 ½, ¶ 11–1419.02.

1 35 ILCS 505/13a.4.

2 35 ILCS 505/13a.6.

5/11–1419.03. Failure to Display Valid External Motor Fuel Use Tax Decals

§ 11–1419.03. Failure to Display Valid External Motor Fuel Use Tax Decals.

(a) Except as provided in the Motor Fuel Tax Law,[1] a motor carrier shall not operate or cause to be operated a commercial motor vehicle upon the highways of this State unless there is properly affixed to that commercial vehicle 2 valid external motor use tax decals required by Section 13a.4 of the Motor Fuel Tax Law.[2] An operator who operates a commercial motor vehicle without 2 properly displayed valid external motor fuel use tax decals is guilty of a petty offense as provided in Section 13a.6 of the Motor Fuel Tax Law.[3] A valid 30–day International Fuel Tax Agreement temporary permit may be displayed instead of decals during the temporary period specified on the permit.

(b) As used in this Section:

"Properly displayed" means 2 motor fuel use tax decals, one placed on each side of the exterior of the cab. In the case of transporters, manufacturers, dealers, or driveaway operations, the decals need not be permanently affixed but may be temporarily displayed in a visible manner on the exterior sides of the cab.

"Commercial motor vehicle" means a motor vehicle used, designed, or maintained for the transportation of people or property and either having 2 axles and a gross vehicle weight or registered gross vehicle weight exceeding 26,000 pounds or 11,793 kilograms, or having 3 or more axles regardless of weight, or that is used in combination, when the weight of the combination exceeds 26,000 pounds or 11,793 kilograms gross vehicle weight or registered gross vehicle weight except for motor vehicles operated by this State or the United States, recreational vehicles, school buses, and commercial motor vehicles operated solely within this State for which all motor fuel is purchased within this State.

"Motor carrier" means any person who operates or causes to be operated any commercial motor vehicle on any highway within this State.

P.A. 76-1586, § 11-1419.03, added by P.A. 88-669, Art. 90, § 90-9.5, eff. Nov. 29, 1994. Amended by P.A. 89-399, § 35, eff. Aug. 20, 1995.

1 35 ILCS 505/1 et seq.

2 35 ILCS 505/13a.4.

3 35 ILCS 505/13a.6.

5/11-1419.04. Failure to carry a manifest

§ 11-1419.04. Failure to carry a manifest. Any person who acts as a motor carrier and who fails to carry a manifest as provided in Section 5.5 of the Motor Fuel Tax Law[1] is guilty of a Class A misdemeanor. For each subsequent offense, the person is guilty of a Class 4 felony.

P.A. 76-1586, § 11-1419.04, added by P.A. 89-399, § 35, eff. Aug. 20, 1995.

1 35 ILCS 505/5.5.

5/11-1419.05. Operation of commercial motor vehicle with revoked motor fuel use tax license

§ 11-1419.05. A motor carrier shall not operate or cause to be operated a commercial motor vehicle upon the highways of this State with a revoked motor fuel use tax license. Any person who operates a commercial motor vehicle with a revoked motor fuel use tax license is guilty of a petty offense as provided in Section 13a.6 of the Motor Fuel Tax Law.[1] When a commercial motor vehicle is found to be operating in Illinois with a revoked motor fuel use tax license, the vehicle shall be placed out of service and not allowed to operate in Illinois until the motor fuel use tax license is reinstated.

P.A. 76-1586, § 11-1419.05, added by P.A. 91-173, § 15, eff. Jan. 1, 2000.

1 35 ILCS 505/13a.6.

5/11-1420. Funeral processions

§ 11-1420. Funeral processions.

(a) Funeral processions have the right-of-way at intersections when vehicles comprising such procession have their headlights lighted, subject to the following conditions and exceptions:

1. Operators of vehicles in a funeral procession shall yield the right-of-way upon the approach of an authorized emergency vehicle giving an audible or visible signal;

2. Operators of vehicles in a funeral procession shall yield the right-of-way when directed to do so by a traffic officer;

3. The operator of the leading vehicle in a funeral procession shall comply with stop signs and traffic control signals but when the leading vehicle has proceeded across an intersection in accordance with such signal or after stopping as required by the stop sign, all vehicles in such procession may proceed without stopping, regardless of the sign or signal and the leading vehicle and the vehicles in procession shall proceed with due caution.

(b) The operator of a vehicle not in the funeral procession shall not drive his vehicle in the funeral procession except when authorized to do so by a traffic officer or when such vehicle is an authorized emergency vehicle giving audible or visible signal.

(c) Operators of vehicles not a part of a funeral procession may not form a procession or convoy and have their headlights lighted for the purpose of securing the right-of-way granted by this Section to funeral processions.

(d) The operator of a vehicle not in a funeral procession may overtake and pass the vehicles in such procession if such overtaking and passing can be accomplished without causing a traffic hazard or interfering with such procession.

(e) The lead vehicle in the funeral procession may be equipped with a flashing amber light which may be used only when such vehicle is used as a lead vehicle in such procession. Vehicles comprising a funeral procession may utilize funeral pennants or flags or windshield stickers or flashing hazard warning signal flashers to identify the individual vehicles in such a procession.

P.A. 76-1586, § 11-1420, eff. July 1, 1970. Amended by P.A. 90-58, § 5, eff. Jan. 1, 1998.

Formerly Ill.Rev.Stat.1991, ch. 95 ½, ¶ 11-1420.

5/11-1421. Conditions for operating ambulances and rescue vehicles

§ 11-1421. Conditions for operating ambulances and rescue vehicles.

(a) No person shall operate an ambulance or rescue vehicle in a manner not conforming to the motor vehicle laws and regulations of this State or of any political subdivision of this State as such laws and regulations apply to motor vehicles in general, unless in compliance with the following conditions:

1. The person operating the ambulance shall be either responding to a bona fide emergency call or specifically directed by a licensed physician to disregard traffic laws in operating the ambulance during and for the purpose of the specific trip or journey that is involved;

2. The ambulance or rescue vehicle shall be equipped with a siren producing an audible signal of an intensity of 100 decibels at a distance of 50 feet from the siren, and with a lamp or lamps emitting an oscillating, rotating or flashing red beam directed in part toward the front of the vehicle, and these lamps shall have sufficient intensity to be visible at 500 feet in normal sunlight, and in addition to other lighting requirements, excluding those vehicles operated in counties with a population in excess of 2,000,000, may also operate with a lamp or lamps emitting an oscillating, rotating, or flashing green light;

3. The aforesaid siren and lamp or lamps shall be in operation at all times when it is reasonably necessary to warn pedestrians and other drivers of the approach thereof during such trip or journey;

4. Whenever the ambulance or rescue vehicle is operated at a speed in excess of 40 miles per hour, the ambulance or rescue vehicle shall be operated in complete conformance with every other motor vehicle law and regulation of this State and of the political subdivision in which the ambulance or rescue vehicle is operated, relating to the operation of motor vehicles, as such provision applies to motor vehicles in general, except laws and regulations pertaining to compliance with official traffic-control devices or to vehicular operation upon the right half of the roadway; and

5. The ambulance shall display registration plates identifying the vehicle as an ambulance.

(b) The foregoing provisions do not relieve the driver of an ambulance or rescue vehicle from the duty of driving with due regard for the safety of all persons, nor do such provisions protect the driver from the consequences resulting from the reckless disregard for the safety of others.

P.A. 76-1586, § 11-1421, eff. July 1, 1970. Amended by P.A. 82-433, § 1, eff. Sept. 8, 1981; P.A. 83-831, § 1, eff. Jan. 1, 1984; P.A. 88-517, § 10, eff. Nov. 16, 1993.

Formerly Ill.Rev.Stat.1991, ch. 95 ½, ¶ 11-1421.

Section 3 of P.A. 82-433 approved Sept. 8, 1981, provided:

"This Act takes effect upon its becoming a law, except that the provisions relating to safety tests and proof of financial responsibility for medical transport vehicles apply only to applications for and the issuance of registration plates which are required to be displayed on January 1, 1982 or thereafter."

5/11-1422. Illegal operation of an ambulance or rescue vehicle—Penalty

§ 11-1422. Illegal operation of an ambulance or rescue vehicle—Penalty. A person who operates an ambulance or rescue vehicle in violation of Section 11-1421 shall be subject to the penalty prescribed by the applicable law, or regulation or ordinance of this State or any political subdivision thereof.

P.A. 76-1586, § 11-1422, eff. July 1, 1970. Amended by P.A. 83-831, § 1, eff. Jan. 1, 1984.

Formerly Ill.Rev.Stat.1991, ch. 95 ½, ¶ 11-1422.

5/11-1423. Passengers boarding or exiting a school bus

§ 11-1423. Passengers boarding or exiting a school bus. (a) At all pick-up points where it is necessary for a school bus passenger to cross the roadway to board the bus, the school bus driver shall signal the awaiting passenger when it is safe to cross the roadway ahead of the bus.

(b) At all discharge points where it is necessary for a school bus passenger to cross the roadway, the school bus driver shall direct the passenger to a point approximately 10 feet in front of the bus on the shoulder and shall then signal the passenger when it is safe to cross the roadway.

P.A. 76-1586, § 11-1423, added by P.A. 78-1244, § 1, eff. Sept. 5, 1974.

Formerly Ill.Rev.Stat.1991, ch. 95 ½, ¶ 11-1423.

5/11-1424. Operation of religious organization bus

§ 11-1424. Operation of a religious organization bus. (a) No religious organization bus may be operated on any street or highway unless all passengers, except for supervisory personnel, are seated in seats permanently mounted to the vehicle, and the aisle of the bus is kept clean and open.

(b) No religious organization bus may be operated on any street or highway while carrying more than the manufacturer's rated passenger capacity for such bus, or at a gross weight in excess of the chassis manufacturer's gross vehicle weight rating (GVWR) or gross axle weight rating (GAWR), or in excess of the weight load ratings of the tires on such bus. For Buses or tires on which the manufacturer has not shown such ratings, by a label, embossment, molding or equivalent means, the Department shall provide, or assist in obtaining, the necessary ratings and may publish such ratings.

(c) In loading or unloading passengers, the religious organization bus driver shall stop the bus out of the lane of moving traffic at any bus stop, officially designated as such by government authorities or in a parking lane on the pavement of the highway or on the shoulder off of the highway, if wide enough to permit the safe loading or unloading of passengers. If, however, there is no such bus stop, parking lane or shoulder within 50 feet of the residence or temporary residence of the passenger transported or to be transported by the bus or within 50 feet of the religious facility, the driver may stop the bus on the pavement of the highway after activating unison amber warning lights for not less than 200 feet before the bus is brought to a stop and while passengers are being loaded or unloaded, or if the bus is equipped as a school bus and meets the requirements of Article VIII of this Act,[1] by complying with the subsections (b), (c) and (d) of Section 11-1414.

(d) At all pickup points where it is necessary for a religious organization bus passenger under the age of 12 years to cross the roadway to board the bus, a responsible supervisor on the bus shall personally escort the awaiting passenger when it is safe to cross the roadway ahead of the bus.

(e) At all discharge points where it is necessary for a religious organization bus passenger under the age of 12 to cross the roadway, a responsible supervisor on the bus shall personally escort the passenger to a point approximately 10 feet in front of the bus on the shoulder and then, when it is safe to cross the roadway, across the roadway to a place of safety.

(f) If a school bus is used by a religious organization bus for the purposes specified in subsection (a) of Section 1-111.1a and activates the visual signals as required by subsections (b), (c) and (d) of Section 11-1414 when picking up or discharging passengers, compliance with subsections (d) and (e) of this Section is optional.

P.A. 76-1586, § 11-1424, added by P.A. 79-798, § 1, eff. July 1, 1976. Amended by P.A. 80-506, § 1, eff. Oct. 1, 1977; P.A. 90-89, § 15, eff. Jan. 1, 1998.

Formerly Ill.Rev.Stat.1991, ch. 95 ½, ¶ 11-1424.

[1] 625 ILCS 5/6-800 et seq.

Another § 11-1424, relating to stop when traffic obstructed, was renumbered as § 11-1425 by P.A. 79-1454, § 44.

5/11-1425. Stop when traffic obstructed

§ 11-1425. Stop when traffic obstructed.

(a) No driver shall enter an intersection or a marked crosswalk or drive onto any railroad grade crossing unless there is sufficient space on the other side of the intersection, crosswalk or railroad grade crossing to accommodate the vehicle he is operating without obstructing the passage of other vehicles, pedestrians or railroad trains notwithstanding any traffic-control signal indication to proceed.

(b) No driver shall enter a highway rail grade crossing unless there is sufficient space on the other side of the highway rail grade crossing to accommodate the vehicle being operated without obstructing the passage of a train or other railroad equipment using the rails, notwithstanding any traffic-control signal indication to proceed. Any person found in violation of subsection (b) shall be subject to a mandatory fine of $500 or 50 hours of community service.

(c) Local authorities shall impose fines as established in subsection (b) for persons found in violation of this Section or any similar local ordinance.

P.A. 76-1586, § 11-1424, added by P.A. 79-1068, § 1, eff. Jan. 1, 1976. Renumbered § 11-1425 and amended by P.A. 79-1454, § 44, eff. Aug. 31, 1976. Amended by P.A. 91-532, § 5, eff. Jan. 1, 2000.

Formerly Ill.Rev.Stat.1991, ch. 95 ½, ¶ 11-1425.

5/11-1426. Operation of all-terrain vehicles and off-highway motorcycles on streets, roads and highways

§ 11-1426. Operation of all-terrain vehicles and off-highway motorcycles on streets, roads and highways.

(a) Except as provided under this Section, it shall be unlawful for any person to drive or operate any all-terrain vehicle or off-highway motorcycle upon any street, highway or roadway in this State.

(b) Except as provided under subsection (c) of this Section, all-terrain vehicles and off-highway motorcycles may make a direct crossing provided:

(1) The crossing is made at an angle of approximately 90 degrees to the direction of the street, road or highway and at a place where no obstruction prevents a quick and safe crossing; and

(2) The all-terrain vehicle or off-highway motorcycle is brought to a complete stop before attempting a crossing; and

(3) The operator of the all-terrain vehicle or off-highway motorcycle yields the right of way to all pedestrian and vehicular traffic which constitutes a hazard; and

(4) That when crossing a divided highway, the crossing is made only at an intersection of the highway with another public street, road, or highway; and

(5) That when accessing township roadways in counties which contain a tract of the Shawnee National Forest, the accessing complies with rules promulgated by the Department of Natural Resources to govern the accessing.

(c) No person operating an all-terrain vehicle or off-highway motorcycle shall make a direct crossing upon or across any tollroad, interstate highway, or controlled access highway in this State.

(d) The corporate authorities of a county, road district, township, city, village, or incorporated town may adopt ordinances or resolutions allowing all-terrain vehicles and off-highway motorcycles to be operated on roadways under their jurisdiction, designated by signs as may be prescribed by the Department, when it is necessary to cross a bridge or culvert or when it is impracticable to gain immediate access to an area adjacent to a highway where an all-terrain vehicle or off-highway motorcycle is to be operated. The crossing shall be made in the same direction as traffic.

(e) The corporate authorities of a county, road district, township, city, village, or incorporated town may adopt ordinances or resolutions designating one or more specific public highways or streets under their jurisdiction as egress and ingress routes for the use of all-terrain vehicles and off-highway motorcycles. Operation of all-terrain vehicles and off-highway motorcycles on the routes shall be in the same direction as traffic. Corporate authorities acting under the authority of this subsection (e) shall erect and maintain signs, as may be prescribed by the Department, giving proper notice of the designation.

P.A. 76-1586, § 11-1426, added by P.A. 85-830, § 1, eff. Sept. 24, 1987. Amended by P.A. 86-1091, § 1, eff. July 13, 1990; P.A. 89-445, § 9A-87, eff. Feb. 7, 1996; P.A. 90-287, § 100, eff. Jan. 1, 1998.

Formerly Ill.Rev.Stat.1991, ch. 95 ½, ¶ 11-1426.

5/11-1427. Illegal operation of an all-terrain vehicle or off-highway motorcycle

§ 11-1427. Illegal operation of an all-terrain vehicle or off-highway motorcycle. It is unlawful for any person to drive or operate any all-terrain vehicle or off-highway motorcycle in the following ways:

(a) Careless Operation. No person shall operate any all-terrain vehicle or off-highway motorcycle in a careless or heedless manner so as to be grossly indifferent to the person or property of other persons, or at a rate of speed greater than will permit him in the exercise of reasonable care to bring the all-terrain vehicle or off-highway motorcycle to a stop within the assured clear distance ahead.

(b) Reckless Operation. No person shall operate any all-terrain vehicle or off-highway motorcycle in such a manner as to endanger the life, limb or property of any person.

(c) Within any nature preserve as defined in Section 3.11 of the Illinois Natural Areas Preservation Act.[1]

(d) On the tracks or right of way of an operating railroad.

(e) In any tree nursery or planting in a manner which damages or destroys growing stock, or creates a substantial risk thereto.

(f) On private property, without the written or verbal consent of the owner or lessee thereof. Any person operating an all-terrain vehicle or off-highway motorcycle upon lands of another shall stop and identify himself upon the request of the landowner or his duly authorized representative, and, if requested to do so by the landowner shall promptly remove the all-terrain vehicle or off-highway motorcycle from the premises.

(g) Notwithstanding any other law to the contrary, an owner, lessee, or occupant of premises owes no duty of care to keep the premises safe for entry or use by others for use by an all-terrain vehicle or off-highway motorcycle, or to give warning of any condition, use, structure or activity on such premises. This subsection does not apply where permission to drive or operate an all-terrain vehicle or off-highway motorcycle is given for a valuable consideration other than to this State, any political subdivision or municipality of this State, or any landowner who is paid with funds from the Off-Highway Vehicle Trails Fund. In the case of land leased to the State or a subdivision of the State, any consideration received is not valuable consideration within the meaning of this Section.

Nothing in this subsection limits in any way liability which otherwise exists for willful or malicious failure to guard or warn against a dangerous condition, use, structure, or activity.

(h) On publicly owned lands unless such lands are designated for use by all-terrain vehicles or off-highway motorcycles. For publicly owned lands to be designated for use by all-terrain vehicles or off-highway motorcycles a public hearing shall be conducted by the governmental entity that has jurisdiction over the proposed land prior to the designation.

Nothing in this subsection limits in any way liability which otherwise exists for willful or malicious failure to guard or warn against a dangerous condition, use, structure, or activity.

(h-1) At a rate of speed too fast for conditions, and the fact that the speed of the all-terrain vehicle or off-highway motorcycle does not exceed the applicable maximum speed limit allowed does not relieve the driver from the duty to decrease speed as may be necessary to avoid colliding with any person, vehicle, or object within legal requirements and the duty of all persons to use due care.

(h-2) On the frozen surface of public waters of this State within 100 feet of a person, including a skater, not in or upon an all-terrain vehicle or off-highway motorcycle; within 100 feet of a person engaged in fishing, except at the minimum speed required to maintain forward movement of the all-terrain vehicle or off-highway motorcycle; on an area which has been cleared of snow for skating purposes unless the area is necessary for access to the frozen waters of this State.

(h-3) Within 100 feet of a dwelling between midnight and 6 a.m. at a speed greater than the minimum required to maintain forward movement of the all-terrain vehicle or off-highway motorcycle. This subdivision (h-5) does not apply on private property where verbal or written consent of the owner or lessee has been granted to drive or operate an all-terrain vehicle or off-highway motorcycle upon the private property or frozen waters of this State.

(i) Other Prohibitions.

(1) No person, except persons permitted by law, shall operate or ride any all-terrain vehicle or off-highway motorcycle with any firearm in his or her possession unless he or she is in compliance with Section 2.33 of the Wildlife Code.[2]

(2) No person shall operate any all-terrain vehicle or off-highway motorcycle emitting pollutants in violation of standards established pursuant to the Environmental Protection Act.[3]

(3) No person shall deposit from an all-terrain vehicle or off-highway motorcycle on the snow, ice or ground surface, trash, glass, garbage, insoluble material, or other offensive matter.

P.A. 76-1586, § 11.1427, added by P.A. 86-1091, § 1, eff. July 13, 1990. Renumbered § 11-1427 and amended by P.A. 90-14, Art. 2, § 2-225, eff. July 1, 1997. Amended by P.A. 90-287, § 100, eff. Jan. 1, 1998.

Formerly Ill.Rev.Stat.1991, ch. 95 ½, ¶ 11-1427.

[1] 525 ILCS 30/3.11.

[2] 520 ILCS 5/2.33.

[3] 415 ILCS 5/1 et seq.

P.A. 90-14, Article 2, of the First 1997 General Revisory Act, resolved multiple actions in the 89th General Assembly and made certain technical corrections in P.A. 89-443 through P.A. 89-707.

5/11-1427.1. Operation of an all-terrain vehicle or off-highway motorcycle on ice

§ 11-1427.1. Operation of an all-terrain vehicle or off-highway motorcycle on ice. All-terrain vehicles and off-highway motorcycles may be operated on the frozen waters of this State subject to the provisions of this Section and the rules of the Department of Natural Resources.

P.A. 76-1586, § 11-1427.1, added by P.A. 90-287, § 100, eff. Jan. 1, 1998.

5/11-1427.2. Special all-terrain vehicle or off-highway motorcycle event

§ 11-1427.2. Special all-terrain vehicle or off-highway motorcycle event. Nothing contained in Section 11-1426, 11-1427, or 11-1427.1 shall be construed to prohibit any local authority of this State from designating a special all-terrain vehicle or off-highway motorcycle event. In such case the provisions of Sections 11-1426, 11-1427, and 11-1427.1 shall not apply to areas or highways under the jurisdiction of that local authority.

P.A. 76-1586, § 11-1427.2, added by P.A. 90-287, § 100, eff. Jan. 1, 1998.

5/11-1427.3. Rules for all-terrain vehicles and off-highway motorcycles

§ 11-1427.3. Rules for all-terrain vehicles and off-highway motorcycles. The Department of Natural Resources shall adopt rules to implement and administer the provisions of Sections 11-1426, 11-1427, 11-1427.1, and 11-1427.2.

P.A. 76-1586, § 11-1427.3, added by P.A. 90-287, § 100, eff. Jan. 1, 1998.

5/11-1427.4. Signal from officer to stop

§ 11-1427.4. Signal from officer to stop. An all-terrain vehicle or off-highway motorcycle operator, after having received a visual or audible signal from a law enforcement officer to come to a stop, may not:

(1) operate an all-terrain vehicle or off-highway motorcycle in willful or wanton disregard of the signal to stop;

(2) interfere with or endanger the law enforcement officer or another person or vehicle; or

(3) increase speed or attempt to flee or elude the officer.

P.A. 76-1586, § 11-1427.4, added by P.A. 90-287, § 100, eff. Jan. 1, 1998.

5/11-1428. Operation of golf carts on streets, roads and highways

§ 11-1428. Operation of golf carts on streets, roads and highways.

(a) Except as otherwise provided in this Section, it shall be unlawful for any person to drive or operate any golf cart upon any street, highway or roadway in this State.

(b) Except as provided under subsection (c) of this Section, golf carts may make a direct crossing over a street, highway or roadway that runs through a golf course provided:

(1) The crossing is made at an interchange approved by the local unit of government and at a place where no obstruction prevents a quick and safe crossing; and

(2) The golf cart is brought to a complete stop before attempting a crossing; and

(3) The operator of the golf cart yields the right of way to all pedestrian and vehicular traffic which constitutes a hazard; and

(4) There is no tunnel or overpass ramp provided for the golf cart to cross through the golf course.

(c) No person operating a golf cart shall make a direct crossing upon or across any highway under the jurisdiction of the State, tollroad, interstate highway, or controlled access highway in this State.

(d) For purposes of this Section, "golf cart" means a vehicle specifically designed and intended for the purposes of transporting one or more persons and their golf clubs or maintenance equipment while engaged in the playing of golf, supervising the play of golf, or maintaining the condition of the grounds on a public or private golf course.

(e) Subject to subsection (b), a municipality, township, county, or other unit of local government may authorize, by ordinance or resolution, the operation of golf carts on roadways under their respective jurisdictions. The Department may authorize the operation of golf carts on the roadways under its jurisdiction.

Before permitting the operation of golf carts on its roadway, a municipality, township, county, other unit of local government, or the Department must consider the volume, speed, and character of traffic on the roadway and determine whether golf carts may safely travel on or cross the roadway. Upon determining that golf carts may safely operate on a roadway and the adoption of an ordinance or resolution by a municipality, township, county or other unit of local government, or authorization by the Department, appropriate signs shall be posted.

If a roadway is under the jurisdiction of more than one unit of government, golf carts may not be operated on the roadway unless each unit of government agrees and takes action as provided in this subsection.

No golf cart may be operated on a roadway unless, at a minimum, it has the following: brakes, a steering apparatus, tires, a rearview mirror, red reflectorized warning devices in the front and rear, a slow moving emblem (as required of other vehicles in Section 12-709) on the rear of the golf cart, a headlight that emits a white light visible from a distance of 500 feet to the front, a tail lamp that emits a red light visible from at least 100 feet from the rear, brake lights, and turn signals. When operated on a roadway, a golf cart shall have its headlight and tail lamps lighted as required by Section 12-201.

(f) A person who drives or is in actual physical control of a golf cart on a roadway while under the influence is subject to Section 11-500 through 11-502.

P.A. 76-1586, § 11-1428, added by P.A. 87-847, § 105, eff. July 1, 1992. Amended by P.A. 90-683, § 5, eff. Jan. 1, 1999.

Formerly Ill.Rev.Stat.1991, ch. 95 ½, ¶ 11-1428.

ARTICLE XV. BICYCLES

5/11-1501. Application of rules

§ 11-1501. Application of rules. (a) It is unlawful for any person to do any act forbidden or fail to perform any act required in Article XV of Chapter 11 of this Code.

(b) The parent of any child and the guardian of any ward shall not authorize or knowingly permit any such child or ward to violate any of the provisions of this Code.

P.A. 76-1586, § 11-1501, added by P.A. 79-858, § 1, eff. Jan. 1, 1976. Amended by P.A. 80-911, § 1, eff. Oct. 1, 1977; P.A. 82-132, § 1, eff. Jan. 1, 1982.

Formerly Ill.Rev.Stat.1991, ch. 95 ½, ¶ 11-1501.

5/11-1502. Traffic laws apply to persons riding bicycles

§ 11-1502. Traffic laws apply to persons riding bicycles. Every person riding a bicycle upon a highway shall be granted all of the rights and shall be subject to all of the duties applicable to the driver of a vehicle by this Code, except as to special regulations in this Article XV and except as to those provisions of this Code which by their nature can have no application.

P.A. 76-1586, § 11-1502, added by P.A. 79-858, § 1, eff. Jan. 1, 1976. Amended by P.A. 82-132, § 1, eff. Jan. 1, 1982.

Formerly Ill.Rev.Stat.1991, ch. 95 ½, ¶ 11-1502.

5/11-1503. Riding on bicycles

§ 11-1503. Riding on bicycles. (a) A person propelling a bicycle shall not ride other than upon or astride a permanent and regular seat attached thereto.

(b) No bicycle shall be used to carry more persons at one time than the number for which it is designed and equipped, except that an adult rider may carry a child securely attached to his person in a back pack or sling.

P.A. 76-1586, § 11-1503, added by P.A. 79-858, § 1, eff. Jan. 1, 1976. Amended by P.A. 82-132, § 1, eff. Jan. 1, 1982.

Formerly Ill.Rev.Stat.1991, ch. 95 ½, ¶ 11-1503.

5/11-1504. Clinging to vehicles

§ 11-1504. Clinging to vehicles. No person riding upon any bicycle, coaster, roller skates, sled or toy vehicle shall attach the same or himself to any vehicle upon a roadway.

P.A. 76-1586, § 11-1504, added by P.A. 79-858, § 1, eff. Jan. 1, 1976. Amended by P.A. 82-132, § 1, eff. Jan. 1, 1982.

Formerly Ill.Rev.Stat.1991, ch. 95 ½, ¶ 11-1504.

5/11-1505. Position of bicycles and motorized pedal cycles on roadways—Riding on roadways and bicycle paths

§ 11-1505. Position of bicycles and motorized pedal cycles on roadways—Riding on roadways and bicycle paths. (a) Any person operating a bicycle or motorized pedal cycle upon a roadway at less than the normal speed of traffic at the time and place and under the conditions then existing shall ride as close as practicable to the right-hand curb or edge of the roadway except under the following situations:

1. When overtaking and passing another bicycle, motorized pedal cycle or vehicle proceeding in the same direction; or

2. When preparing for a left turn at an intersection or into a private road or driveway; or

3. When reasonably necessary to avoid conditions including, but not limited to, fixed or moving objects, parked or moving vehicles, bicycles, motorized pedal cycles, pedestrians, animals, surface hazards, or substandard width lanes that make it unsafe to continue along the right-hand curb or edge. For purposes of this subsection, a "substandard width lane" means a lane that is too narrow for a bicycle or motorized pedal cycle and a vehicle to travel safely side by side within the lane.

(b) Any person operating a bicycle or motorized pedal cycle upon a one-way highway with two or more marked traffic lanes may ride as near the left-hand curb or edge of such roadway as practicable.

P.A. 76-1586, § 11-1505, added by P.A. 79-858, § 1, eff. Jan. 1, 1976. Amended by P.A. 82-132, § 1, eff. Jan. 1, 1982; P.A. 83-549, § 1, eff. Jan. 1, 1984.

Formerly Ill.Rev.Stat.1991, ch. 95 ½, ¶ 11-1505.

5/11-1505.1. Riding bicycles or motorized pedal cycles on roadways

§ 11-1505.1. Persons riding bicycles or motorized pedal cycles upon a roadway shall not ride more than 2 abreast, except on paths or parts of roadways set aside for their exclusive use. Persons riding 2 abreast shall not impede the normal and reasonable movement of traffic and, on a laned roadway, shall ride within a single lane subject to the provisions of Section 11-1505.

P.A. 76-1586, § 11-1505.1, added by P.A. 83-549, § 1, eff. Jan. 1, 1984.

Formerly Ill.Rev.Stat.1991, ch. 95 ½, ¶ 11-1505.1.

5/11-1506. Carrying articles

§ 11-1506. Carrying articles. No person operating a bicycle shall carry any package, bundle or article which prevents the use of both hands in the control and operation of the bicycle. A person operating a bicycle shall keep at least one hand on the handlebars at all times.

P.A. 76-1586, § 11-1506, added by P.A. 79-858, § 1, eff. Jan. 1, 1976. Amended by P.A. 82-132, § 1, eff. Jan. 1, 1982.

Formerly Ill.Rev.Stat.1991, ch. 95 ½, ¶ 11-1506.

5/11-1507. Lamps and other equipment on bicycles

§ 11-1507. Lamps and other equipment on bicycles. (a) Every bicycle when in use at nighttime shall be equipped with a lamp on the front which shall emit a white light visible from a distance of at least 500 feet to the front and with a red reflector on the rear of a type approved by the Department which shall be visible from all distances from 100 feet to 600 feet to the rear when directly in front of lawful lower beams of headlamps on a motor vehicle. A lamp emitting a red light visible from a distance of 500 feet to the rear may be used in addition to the red reflector.

(b) A bicycle shall not be equipped with nor shall any person use upon a bicycle any siren.

(c) Every bicycle shall be equipped with a brake which will adequately control movement of and stop and hold such bicycle.

(d) No person shall sell a new bicycle or pedal for use on a bicycle that is not equipped with a reflex reflector conforming to specifications prescribed by the Department, on each pedal, visible from the front and rear of the bicycle during darkness from a distance of 200 feet.

(e) No person shall sell or offer for sale a new bicycle that is not equipped with side reflectors. Such reflectors shall be visible from each side of the bicycle from a distance of 500 feet and shall be essentially colorless or red to the rear of the center of the bicycle and essentially colorless or amber to the front of the center of the bicycle provided. The requirements of this paragraph may be met by reflective materials which shall be at least $\frac{3}{16}$ of an inch wide on each side of each tire or rim to indicate as clearly as possible the continuous circular shape and size of the tires or rims of such bicycle and which reflective materials may be of the same color on both the front and rear tire or rim. Such reflectors shall conform to specifications prescribed by the Department.

(f) No person shall sell or offer for sale a new bicycle that is not equipped with an essentially colorless front-facing reflector.

P.A. 76-1586, § 11-1507, added by P.A. 79-858, § 1, eff. Jan. 1, 1976. Amended by P.A. 80-506, § 1, eff. Oct. 1, 1977; P.A. 82-132, § 1, eff. Jan. 1, 1982.

Formerly Ill.Rev.Stat.1991, ch. 95 ½, ¶ 11-1507.

5/11-1507.1. Lamps on motorized pedalcycles

§ 11-1507.1. Lamps on motorized pedalcycles. Every motorized pedalcycle, when in use at nighttime, shall be equipped with a lamp on the front which shall emit a white light visible from a distance of at least 500 feet to the front, and with a red reflector on the rear of a type approved by the Department which shall be visible from all distances from 100 feet to 600 feet to the rear when in front of lawful, low-powered beams of head lamps on a motor vehicle. A lamp emitting a red light visible from a distance of 500 feet to the rear may be used in addition to the red reflector.

P.A. 76-1586, § 11-1507.1, added by P.A. 80-262, § 1, eff. Aug. 20, 1977.

Formerly Ill.Rev.Stat.1991, ch. 95 ½, ¶ 11-1507.1.

5/11-1508. Bicycle identifying number

§ 11-1508. Bicycle identifying number. A person engaged in the business of selling bicycles at retail shall not sell any bicycle unless the bicycle has an identifying number permanently stamped or cast on its frame.

P.A. 76-1586, § 11-1508, added by 82-132, § 1, eff. Jan. 1, 1982.

Formerly Ill.Rev.Stat.1991, ch. 95 ½, ¶ 11-1508.

5/11-1509. Inspecting bicycles

§ 11-1509. Inspecting bicycles. A uniformed police officer may at any time upon reasonable cause to believe that a bicycle is unsafe or not equipped as required by law, or that its equipment is not in proper adjustment or repair, require the person riding the bicycle to stop and submit the bicycle to an inspection and such test with reference thereto as may be appropriate.

P.A. 76-1586, § 11-1509, added by P.A. 82-132, § 1, eff. Jan. 1, 1982.

Formerly Ill.Rev.Stat.1991, ch. 95 ½, ¶ 11-1509.

5/11-1510. Left Turns

§ 11-1510. Left Turns. (a) A person riding a bicycle or motorized pedalcycle intending to turn left shall follow a course described in Section 11-801 or in paragraph (b) of this Section.

(b) A person riding a bicycle or motorized pedalcycle intending to turn left shall approach the turn as close as practicable to the right curb or edge of the roadway. After proceeding across the intersecting roadway to the far corner of the curb or intersection of the roadway edges, the bicyclist or motorized pedalcycle driver shall stop, as much as practicable out of the way of traffic. After stopping the person shall yield to any traffic proceeding in either direction along the roadway such person had been using. After yielding, the bicycle or motorized pedalcycle driver shall comply with any official traffic control device or police officer regulating traffic on the highway along which he intends to proceed, and the bicyclist or motorized pedalcycle driver may proceed in the new direction.

(c) Notwithstanding the foregoing provisions, the Department and local authorities in their respective jurisdictions may cause official traffic-control devices to be placed and thereby require and direct that a specific course be traveled by turning bicycles and motorized pedalcycles, and when such devices are so placed, no person shall turn a bicycle or motorized pedalcycle other than as directed and required by such devices.

P.A. 76-1586, § 11-1510, added by P.A. 82-132, § 1, eff. Jan. 1, 1982. Amended by P.A. 85-951, § 1, eff. July 1, 1988.

Formerly Ill.Rev.Stat.1991, ch. 95 ½, ¶ 11-1510.

5/11-1511. Turn and stop signals

§ 11-1511. Turn and stop signals. (a) Except as provided in this Section, a person riding a bicycle shall comply with Section 11-804.

(b) A signal of intention to turn right or left when required shall be given during not less than the last 100 feet traveled by the bicycle before turning, and shall be given while the bicycle is stopped waiting to turn. A signal by hand and arm need not be given continuously if the hand is needed in the control or operation of the bicycle.

P.A. 76-1586, § 11-1511, added by P.A. 82-132, § 1, eff. Jan. 1, 1982.

Formerly Ill.Rev.Stat.1991, ch. 95 ½, ¶ 11-1511.

5/11-1512. Bicycles on sidewalks

§ 11-1512. Bicycles on sidewalks. (a) A person propelling a bicycle upon and along a sidewalk, or across a roadway upon and along a crosswalk, shall yield the right of way to any pedestrian and shall give audible signal before overtaking and passing such pedestrian.

(b) A person shall not ride a bicycle upon and along a sidewalk, or across a roadway upon and along a crosswalk, where such use of bicycles is prohibited by official traffic-control devices.

(c) A person propelling a bicycle upon and along a sidewalk, or across a roadway upon and along a crosswalk, shall have all the rights and duties applicable to a pedestrian under the same circumstances.

P.A. 76-1586, § 11-1512, added by P.A. 82-132, § 1, eff. Jan. 1, 1982.

Formerly Ill.Rev.Stat.1991, ch. 95 ½, ¶ 11-1512.

5/11-1513. Bicycle parking

§ 11-1513. Bicycle parking. (a) A person may park a bicycle on a sidewalk unless prohibited or restricted by an official traffic-control device.

(b) A bicycle parked on a sidewalk shall not impede the normal and reasonable movement of pedestrian or other traffic.

(c) A bicycle may be parked on the roadway at any angle to the curb or edge of the roadway at any location where parking is allowed.

(d) A bicycle may be parked on the roadway abreast of another bicycle or bicycles near the side of the roadway at any location where parking is allowed.

(e) A person shall not park a bicycle on a roadway in such a manner as to obstruct the movement of a legally parked motor vehicle.

(f) In all other respects, bicycles parked anywhere on a highway shall conform with the provisions of this Code regulating the parking of vehicles.

P.A. 76-1586, § 11-1513, added by P.A. 82-132, § 1, eff. Jan. 1, 1982.

Formerly Ill.Rev.Stat.1991, ch. 95 ½, ¶ 11-1513.

5/11-1514. Bicycle racing

§ 11-1514. Bicycle racing. (a) Bicycle racing on a highway shall not be unlawful when a racing event has been approved by State or local authorities on any highway under their respective jurisdictions. Approval of bicycle highway racing events shall be granted only under conditions which assure reasonable safety for all race participants, spectators and other highway users, and which prevent unreasonable interference with traffic flow which would seriously inconvenience other highway users.

(b) By agreement with the approving authority, participants, in an approved bicycle highway racing event may be exempted from compliance with any traffic laws otherwise applicable thereto, provided that traffic control is adequate to assure the safety of all highway users.

P.A. 76-1586, § 11-1514, added by P.A. 82-132, § 1, eff. Jan. 1, 1982.

Formerly Ill.Rev.Stat.1991, ch. 95 ½, ¶ 11-1514.

5/11-1515. Operation of a commercial bicycle messenger service; insurance coverage

§ 11-1515. No person, firm, or corporation shall operate a commercial bicycle messenger service in a city with a population of more than 2,000,000 unless the bicycles used are covered by a liability insurance policy at the expense of the person, firm, or corporation. The insurance policy shall be issued in amounts no less than the minimum amounts set for bodily injury or death and for destruction of property under Section 7-203 of this Code. No insurer other than an insurer authorized to do business in this State shall issue a policy under this Section.

P.A. 76-1586, § 11-1515, added by P.A. 87-1203, § 1, eff. Sept. 25, 1992.

Formerly Ill.Rev.Stat., ch. 95½, ¶ 11-1515.

CHAPTER 12. EQUIPMENT OF VEHICLES

Enactment

The Illinois Vehicle Code was enacted by P.A. 76-1586, effective July 1, 1970. The Code constitutes a consolidated recodification of various earlier laws and acts including the Uniform Act Regulating Traffic on Highways.

Chapter 12 was amended, divided into Articles 1 to 7 and resectioned by P.A. 77-37, effective January 1, 1972.

ARTICLE I. GENERAL PROVISIONS

5/12-100. § 12-100. Repealed by P.A. 90-89, § 20, eff. Jan. 1, 1998

5/12-101. Scope and effect of equipment requirements

§ 12-101. Scope and effect of equipment requirements. (a) It is unlawful for any person to drive or move or for the owner to cause or knowingly permit to be driven or moved on any highway any vehicle or combination of vehicles which is in such unsafe condition as to endanger any person or property, or which does not contain those parts or is not at all times equipped with such lamps and other equipment in proper condition and adjustment as required in this Chapter 12, or which is equipped in any manner in violation of this Code, or for any person to do any act forbidden or fail to perform any act required under this Chapter 12.

(b) The provisions of this Chapter 12 with respect to equipment on vehicles shall not apply to implements of husbandry, road machinery, road rollers, or farm tractors or to farm-wagon type trailers having a fertilizer spreader attachment permanently mounted thereon, having a gross weight of not to exceed 36,000 pounds and used only for the transportation of bulk fertilizer or to farm-wagon type tank trailers of not to exceed 2,000 gallons capacity, used during the liquid fertilizer season as field-storage "nurse tanks" supplying the fertilizer to a field applicator and moved on highways only for bringing the fertilizer from a local source of supply to farm or field or from one farm or field to another.

P.A. 76-1586, § 12-101, eff. July 1, 1970. Amended by P.A. 77-37, § 1, eff. Jan. 1, 1972; P.A. 81-327, § 1, eff. Jan. 1, 1980; P.A. 82-523, § 1, eff. Jan. 1, 1982.

Formerly Ill.Rev.Stat.1991, ch. 95 ½, ¶ 12-101.

ARTICLE II. LIGHTS AND LAMPS

Section

5/12-201. When lighted lamps are required

§ 12-201. When lighted lamps are required.

(a) When operated upon any highway in this State, every motorcycle shall at all times exhibit at least one lighted lamp, showing a white light visible for at least 500 feet in the direction the motorcycle is proceeding. However, in lieu of such lighted lamp, a motorcycle may be equipped with and use a means of modulating the upper beam of the head lamp between high and a lower brightness. No such head lamp shall be modulated, except to otherwise comply with this Code, during times when lighted lamps are required for other motor vehicles.

(b) All other motor vehicles shall exhibit at least 2 lighted head lamps, with at least one on each side of the front of the vehicle, which satisfy United States Department of Transportation requirements, showing white lights, including that emitted by high intensity discharge (HID) lamps, or lights of a yellow or amber tint, during the period from sunset to sunrise, at times when rain, snow, fog, or other atmospheric conditions require the use of windshield wipers, and at any other times when, due to insufficient light or unfavorable atmospheric conditions, persons and vehicles on the highway are not clearly discernible at a distance of 1000 feet. Parking lamps may be used in addition to but not in lieu of such head lamps. Every motor vehicle, trailer, or semi-trailer shall also exhibit at least 2 lighted lamps, commonly known as tail lamps, which shall be mounted on the left rear and right rear of the vehicle so as to throw a red light visible for at least 500 feet in the reverse direction, except that a truck tractor or road tractor manufactured before January 1, 1968 and all motorcycles need be equipped with only one such tail lamp.

(c) Either a tail lamp or a separate lamp shall be so constructed and placed as to illuminate with a white light a rear registration plate when required and render it clearly legible from a distance of 50 feet to the rear. Any tail lamp or tail lamps, together with any separate lamp or lamps for illuminating a rear registration plate, shall be so wired as to be lighted whenever the head lamps or auxiliary driving lamps are lighted.

(d) A person shall install only head lamps that satisfy United States Department of Transportation regulations and show white light, including that emitted by HID lamps, or light of a yellow or amber tint for use by a motor vehicle.

(e) For purposes of this Section, a custom vehicle or street rod is considered to be in compliance with all vehicle lamp requirements if it has passed the approved safety inspection provided for in Section 3-804.1 or 3-804.2.

P.A. 76-1586, § 12-102, eff. July 1, 1970. Amended by P.A. 76-2177, § 1, eff. July 1, 1970. Renumbered § 12-201 by P.A. 77-37, § 1, eff. Jan. 1, 1972. Amended by P.A. 81-804, § 1, eff. Sept. 19, 1979; P.A. 83-331, § 1, eff. Jan. 1, 1984; P.A. 88-147, § 5, eff. Jan. 1, 1994; P.A. 91-130, § 5, eff. Jan. 1, 2000; P.A. 91-135, § 5, eff. Jan. 1, 2000; P.A. 92-16, § 85, eff. June 28, 2001; P.A. 92-668, § 5, eff. Jan. 1, 2003.

Formerly Ill.Rev.Stat.1991, ch. 95 ½, ¶ 12-201.

P.A. 92-668 incorporated the amendment by P.A. 92-16.

5/12-202. Clearance, identification and side marker lamps

§ 12-202. Clearance, identification and side marker lamps. (a) Every motor vehicle of the second division, the length of which together with any trailer or trailers in tow thereof, is more than 25 feet or the width of which is more than 80 inches exclusive of mirrors, bumpers and other required safety devices, while being operated on the highways of this State during the period from sunset to sunrise, shall display on the front of the vehicle 2 yellow or amber lights, one on each upper front corner of the vehicle, which shall be plainly visible at a distance of at least 500 feet; also on the rear thereof in a horizontal line, 3 red lights plainly visible at a distance of not less than 500 feet; also on the front of the body of that vehicle near the lower left hand corner one yellow or amber tinted reflector, and near the lower right hand corner one yellow or amber tinted reflector; also red reflectors on the rear of the body of that vehicle, not more than 12 inches from the lower left and right hand corners. All motor vehicles of the second division more than 20 feet long, and all trailers and semitrailers, except trailers and semitrailers having a gross weight of 3,000 pounds or less including the weight of the trailer and maximum load, while being operated on the highways of this State during the period from sunset to sunrise, shall display on each side of the vehicle at approximately the one-third points of the length of the same, at a height not exceeding 5 feet above the surface of the road, and reflecting on a line approximately at right angles to the center line of the vehicle, 2 amber tinted reflectors. After January, 1974, all new motor vehicles of the second division more than 20 feet long, and all trailers and semitrailers except trailers and semitrailers having a gross weight of 3,000 pounds or less including the weight of the trailer and maximum load sold as new in this State, while being operated on the highways of this State during period from sunset to sunrise, shall display on each side of the vehicle, not more than 12 inches from the front, one amber tinted reflector, and not more than 12 inches from the rear one red reflector at a height not exceeding 5 feet above the surface of the road, and reflecting on a line approximately at right angles to the center line of the vehicle, approved by the Department.

(b) Every trailer and semitrailer having a gross weight of 3,000 pounds or less including the weight of the trailer and maximum load, towed either by a motor vehicle of the first division or a motor vehicle of the second division shall be equipped with 2 red reflectors, which will be visible when hit by headlight beams 300 feet away at night, on the rear of the body of such trailer, not more than 12 inches from the lower left hand and lower right hand corners.

(c) Every vehicle designated in paragraph (a) or (b) of this Section that is manufactured after December 31, 1973, shall, at the places and times specified in paragraph (a) or (b) of this Section, display reflectors and clearance, identification, and side marker lamps in conformance with the specifications prescribed by the Department.

P.A. 76–1586, § 12–103, eff. July 1, 1970. Amended by P.A. 76–1725, § 1, eff. July 1, 1970; P.A. 76–1997, § 1, eff. July 1, 1970. Renumbered § 12–202 by P.A. 77–37, § 1, eff. Jan. 1, 1972. Amended by P.A. 78–748, § 1, eff. Jan. 1, 1974; P.A. 78–501, § 1, eff. Oct. 1, 1973; P.A. 78–1297, § 30, eff. March 4, 1975.

Formerly Ill.Rev.Stat.1991, ch. 95 ½, ¶ 12–202.

5/12–203. Lamps on parked vehicles

§ 12–203. Lamps on parked vehicles. (a) During the period from sunset to sunrise every motorcycle or motor vehicle which is standing on any highway shall display a parking light on the front and at the rear of the same. However, any city, village or incorporated town may by ordinance, under rules and regulations it may prescribe, designate any part or parts of any street, or other highway under their jurisdiction, as parking places in which motorcycles and motor vehicles may be parked without having their lamps lighted, as otherwise required by this Section.

(b) Any lighted driving lamps upon a parked vehicle shall be depressed or dimmed.

P.A. 76–1586, § 12–104, eff. July 1, 1970. Renumbered § 12–203 by P.A. 77–37, § 1, eff. Jan. 1, 1972.

Formerly Ill.Rev.Stat.1991, ch. 95 ½, ¶ 12–203.

5/12–204. Lamp or flag on projecting load

§ 12–204. Lamp or flag on projecting load. Whenever the load upon any vehicle extends to the rear 4 feet, or more beyond the bed or body of such vehicle there shall be displayed at the extreme rear end of the load, at the times specified in Section 12–201 hereof, a red light or lantern plainly visible from a distance of at least 500 feet to the sides and rear. The red light or lantern required under this Section shall be in addition to the red rear light required upon every vehicle. At any other time there shall be displayed at the extreme rear end of such load a red flag or cloth not less than 12 inches square.

P.A. 76–1586, § 12–105, eff. July 1, 1970. Renumbered § 12–204 by P.A. 77–37, § 1, eff. Jan. 1, 1972.

Formerly Ill.Rev.Stat.1991, ch. 95 ½, ¶ 12–204.

5/12–205. Lamps on other vehicles and equipment

§ 12–205. Lamps on other vehicles and equipment. Every vehicle, including animal drawn vehicles, referred to in paragraph (b) of Section 12–101, not specifically required by the provisions of this Article to be equipped with lamps or other lighting devices, shall at all times specified in Section 12–201 of this Act be equipped with at least 2 lamps on the power or towing unit, displaying a white light visible from a distance of not less than 1,000 feet to the front of such vehicle and shall also be equipped with 2 lamps each displaying a red light visible from a distance of not less than 1,000 feet to the rear of such vehicle.

Where the towed unit or any load thereon partially or totally obscures the 2 lamps displaying red light to the rear of the towing unit, the rearmost towed unit shall be equipped with 2 lamps displaying red light visible from a distance of not less than 1,000 feet to the rear of such towed unit which are positioned in such a manner as to not obstruct the visibility of the red light to any vehicle operator approaching from the rear of such vehicle or combination of vehicles.

Where the 2 lamps displaying red light are not obscured by the towed unit or its load, then either towing unit or towed unit, or both, may be equipped with the 2 lamps displaying red light as required.

The preceding paragraph does not apply to antique vehicles, custom vehicles, or street rods. An antique vehicle shall be equipped with lamps of the same type originally installed by the manufacturer as original equipment and in working order.

P.A. 76–1586, § 12–106. Amended by P.A. 76–1627, § 1, eff. Dec. 1, 1970; P.A. 76–2178, § 1, eff. July 1, 1970. Renumbered § 12–205 by P.A. 77–37, § 1, eff. Jan. 1, 1972. Amended by P.A. 85–830, § 1, eff. Sept. 24, 1987; P.A. 92–668, § 5, eff. Jan. 1, 2003.

Formerly Ill.Rev.Stat.1991, ch. 95 ½, ¶ 12–205.

5/12–205.1. Implements of husbandry or slow-moving vehicles—Display of amber signal lamp

§ 12–205.1. Implements of husbandry or slow-moving vehicles—Display of amber signal lamp. Every animal drawn vehicle, farm tractor, implement of husbandry and special mobile equipment, except when used for road construction or maintenance within the limits of a construction or maintenance project where traffic control devices are used in compliance with the applicable provisions of the manual and specifications adopted under Section 11–301 of the Illinois Vehicle Code, when operated on a highway during a time when lighted lamps are required by Section 12–201 of this Chapter, shall display to the rear at least one flashing amber signal lamp mounted as high as practicable and of sufficient intensity to be visible for a distance of at least 500 feet in normal sunlight; provided, that only the rearmost vehicle of a combination of vehicles coupled together need display such lamp. The flashing amber signal lamp may be operated lighted during daylight hours when other lamps are not required to be lighted when vehicles authorized in this Section are operated on a highway. Implements of husbandry manufactured on or after January 1, 2003 and operated on public roads between sunset and sunrise shall display markings and lighting that meet or exceed the design, performance, and mounting specifications adopted by the American Society of Agricultural Engineers and published by that body as ASAE S279.11 APR01.

P.A. 76-1586, § 12-205.1, added by P.A. 78-253, § 1, eff. Oct. 1, 1973. Amended by P.A. 84-285, § 1, eff. Jan. 1, 1986; P.A. 91-505, § 5, eff. Jan. 1, 2000; P.A. 92-820, § 5, eff. Aug. 21, 2002.

Formerly Ill.Rev.Stat.1991, ch. 95 ½, ¶ 12-205.1.

5/12-206. § 12-206. Repealed by P.A. 79-858, § 2, eff. Jan. 1, 1976

5/12-207. Spot lamps and auxiliary driving lamps

§ 12-207. Spot lamps and auxiliary driving lamps.

(a) Any motor vehicle may be equipped with not to exceed one spot lamp and every lighted spot lamp shall be so aimed and used upon approaching another vehicle that no part of the high-intensity portion of the beam will be directed to the left of the prolongation of the extreme left side of the vehicle nor more than 100 feet ahead of the vehicle.

(b) Any motor vehicle may be equipped with not to exceed three auxiliary driving lamps mounted on the front at a height not less than 12 inches nor more than 42 inches above the level surface upon which the vehicle stands.

(c) The restrictions of subsections 12-207 (a) and 12-207 (b) of this Act shall not apply to authorized emergency vehicles or equipment used for snow and ice removal operations if owned or operated by or for any governmental body.

(d) The minimum and maximum height restrictions prescribed in subsection (b) of Section 12-207 shall not apply to privately owned motor vehicles on which a snow plow is mounted, while in transit between or during snow and ice removal operations. This exemption shall apply only during the period from November 15 through April 1, and only when the snow plow blade, commonly referred to as a "moldboard", is properly and securely affixed to the front of the motor vehicle.

P.A. 76-1586, § 12-108, eff. July 1, 1970. Renumbered § 12-207 by P.A. 77-37 § 1, eff. Jan. 1, 1972. Amended by P.A. 77-63, § 1, eff. July 1, 1971; P.A. 77-2829, § 40, eff. Dec. 22, 1972; P.A. 78-255, § 61, eff. Oct. 1, 1973; P.A. 78-510, § 1, eff. Oct. 1, 1973; P.A. 78-1297, § 58, eff. March 4, 1975; P.A. 84-677, § 1, eff. Jan. 1, 1986; P.A. 85-1010, § 1, eff. March 2, 1988.

Formerly Ill.Rev.Stat.1991, ch. 95 ½, ¶ 12-207.

5/12-208. Signal lamps and signal devices

§ 12-208. Signal lamps and signal devices.

(a) Every vehicle other than an antique vehicle displaying an antique plate operated in this State shall be equipped with a stop lamp or lamps on the rear of the vehicle which shall display a red or amber light visible from a distance of not less than 500 feet to the rear in normal sunlight and which shall be actuated upon application of the service (foot) brake, and which may but need not be incorporated with other rear lamps. During times when lighted lamps are not required, an antique vehicle may be equipped with a stop lamp or lamps on the rear of such vehicle of the same type originally installed by the manufacturer as original equipment and in working order. However, at all other times, such antique vehicle must be equipped with stop lamps meeting the requirements of Section 12-208 of this Act.

(b) Every motor vehicle other than an antique vehicle displaying an antique plate shall be equipped with an electric turn signal device which shall indicate the intention of the driver to turn to the right or to the left in the form of flashing lights located at and showing to the front and rear of the vehicle on the side of the vehicle toward which the turn is to be made. The lamps showing to the front shall be mounted on the same level and as widely spaced laterally as practicable and, when signaling, shall emit a white or amber light, or any shade of light between white and amber. The lamps showing to the rear shall be mounted on the same level and as widely spaced laterally as practicable and, when signaling, shall emit a red or amber light. An antique vehicle shall be equipped with a turn signal device of the same type originally installed by the manufacturer as original equipment and in working order.

(c) Every trailer and semitrailer shall be equipped with an electric turn signal device which indicates the intention of the driver in the power unit to turn to the right or to the left in the form of flashing red or amber lights located at the rear of the vehicle on the side toward which the turn is to be made and mounted on the same level and as widely spaced laterally as practicable.

(d) Turn signal lamps must be visible from a distance of not less than 300 feet in normal sunlight.

(e) Motorcycles and motor-driven cycles need not be equipped with electric turn signals. Antique vehicles need not be equipped with turn signals unless such were installed by the manufacturer as original equipment.

(f) For purposes of this Section, a custom vehicle or street rod is considered to be in compliance with all signal lamp and signal device requirements if it has passed the approved safety inspection provided for in Section 3-804.1 or 3-804.2.

P.A. 76-1586, § 12-109. Amended by P.A. 76-1627, § 1, eff. Dec. 1, 1970; P.A. 76-2179, § 1, eff. July 1, 1970. Renumbered § 12-208 by P.A. 77-37, § 1, eff. Jan. 1, 1972. Amended by P.A. 92-668, § 5, eff. Jan. 1, 2003.

Formerly Ill.Rev.Stat.1991, ch. 95 ½, ¶ 12-208.

5/12-209. Additional lighting equipment

§ 12-209. Additional lighting equipment. (a) Any motor vehicle may be equipped with not more than 2 side cowl or fender lamps which shall emit an amber or white light without glare.

(b) Any motor vehicle may be equipped with not more than one running board courtesy lamp on each side thereof which shall emit a white or amber light without glare.

(c) Any motor vehicle may be equipped with one or more back-up lamps either separately or in combination with other lamps; but any such back-up lamp or lamps shall not be lighted when the motor vehicle is in forward motion.

P.A. 76-1586, § 12-110, eff. July 1, 1970. Amended by P.A. 76-2180, § 1, eff. July 1, 1970. Renumbered § 12-209 by P.A. 77-37, § 1, eff. Jan. 1, 1972.

Formerly Ill.Rev.Stat.1991, ch. 95 ½, ¶ 12-209.

5/12-210. Use of head lamps and auxiliary driving lamps

§ 12-210. Use of head lamps and auxiliary driving lamps. (a) Whenever the driver of any vehicle equipped with an electric driving head lamp, driving head lamps, auxiliary driving lamp or auxiliary driving lamps is within 500 feet of another vehicle approaching from the opposite direction, the driver shall dim or drop such head lamp or head lamps and shall extinguish all auxiliary driving lamps.

(b) The driver of any vehicle equipped with an electric driving head lamp, head lamps, auxiliary driving lamp or auxiliary driving lamps shall dim or drop such head lamp or head lamps and shall extinguish all auxiliary driving lamps when there is another vehicle traveling in the same direction less than 300 feet to the front of him.

(c) No vehicle shall have the lighting system modified to allow more than 2 electric head lamps to be lighted while operating in the dimmed or dropped position.

(d) Nothing in this Section shall prohibit the use of auxiliary driving lamps, commonly referred to as "fog" lamps, when used in conjunction with head lamps, if such auxiliary driving lamps are adjusted and so aimed that the glaring rays are not projected into the eyes of drivers of oncoming vehicles.

P.A. 76-1586, § 12-111, eff. July 1, 1970. Renumbered § 12-210 by P.A. 77-37, § 1, eff. Jan. 1, 1972. Amended by P.A. 85-830, § 1, eff. Sept. 24, 1987; P.A. 85-1144, § 1, eff. July 29, 1988.

Formerly Ill.Rev.Stat.1991, ch. 95 ½, ¶ 12-210.

P.A. 85-1144 incorporated the amendment by P.A. 85-830.

5/12-211. Number of driving lamps required or permitted

§ 12-211. Number of driving lamps required or permitted. (a) At all times specified in Section 12-201, at least 2 lighted driving lamps shall be displayed, one on each side of the front of every motor vehicle other than a motorcycle, except when such vehicle is parked subject to the regulations governing lights on parked vehicles.

(b) Whenever a motor vehicle equipped with driving lamps as herein required is also equipped with any auxiliary driving lamps or a spot lamp or any other lamp on the front thereof, not more than a total of 4 of any such lamps on the front of a vehicle shall be lighted at any one time when upon a highway.

P.A. 76-1586, § 12-112, eff. July 1, 1970. Amended by P.A. 76-2181, § 1, eff. July 1, 1970. Renumbered § 12-211 by P.A. 77-37, § 1, eff. Jan. 1, 1972. Amended by P.A. 86-1236, § 1, eff. Jan. 1, 1991.

Formerly Ill.Rev.Stat.1991, ch. 95 ½, ¶ 12-211.

5/12-212. Special restrictions on lamps

§ 12-212. Special restrictions on lamps. (a) No person shall drive or move any vehicle or equipment upon any highway with any lamp or device on the vehicle or equipment displaying a red light visible from directly in front of the vehicle or equipment except as otherwise provided in this Act.

(b) Subject to the restrictions of this Act, flashing lights are prohibited on motor vehicles except as a means for indicating a right or left turn as provided in Section 12-208 or the presence of a vehicular traffic hazard requiring unusual care as expressly provided in Sections 11-804 or 12-215.

(c) Unless otherwise expressly authorized by this Code, all other lighting or combination of lighting on any vehicle shall be prohibited.

P.A. 76-1586, § 12-113, eff. July 1, 1970. Renumbered § 12-212 by P.A. 77-37, § 1, eff. Jan. 1, 1972. Amended by P.A. 81-879, § 1, eff. Sept. 21, 1979; P.A. 86-664, § 1, eff. Sept. 1, 1989.

Formerly Ill.Rev.Stat.1991, ch. 95 ½, ¶ 12-212.

5/12-213. § 12-213. Repealed by P.A. 78-1244, § 4, eff. Sept. 5, 1974

5/12-214. Special lighting equipment on rural mail delivery vehicles

§ 12-214. Special lighting equipment on rural mail delivery vehicles. If a rural mail delivery vehicle is equipped with special signal lamps, there shall be displayed to the front 2 such alternately flashing amber lamps located at the same level and mounted as high and as widely spaced laterally as practicable and to the rear 2 alternately flashing amber lamps located at the same level and mounted as high and as widely spaced laterally as practicable. Such lamps shall be of sufficient intensity to be visible at 500 feet in normal sunlight and shall be controlled so that they will only be used to indicate to other traffic that a stop is being made for the purpose of picking up or delivering U. S. mail.

P.A. 76-1586, § 12-115, eff. July 1, 1970. Renumbered § 12-214 by P.A. 77-37, § 1, eff. Jan. 1, 1972.

Formerly Ill.Rev.Stat.1991, ch. 95 ½, ¶ 12-214.

5/12-214.1. Tow trucks meeting federal motor carrier safety requirements; lighting and signalling equipment

§ 12-214.1. Tow trucks meeting federal motor carrier safety requirements; lighting and signalling equipment. Any tow truck that meets the requirements of the Federal Motor Carrier Safety Regulations of the United States Department of Transportation, regarding lighting and signalling equipment required on commercial motor vehicles, shall be deemed to comply with the provisions of this Chapter regarding required lighting and signalling equipment.

P.A. 76-1586, § 12-214.1, added by P.A. 89-433, § 5, eff. Dec. 15, 1995.

5/12-215. Oscillating, rotating or flashing lights on motor vehicles

Text of section effective until June 1, 2003

§ 12-215. Oscillating, rotating or flashing lights on motor vehicles. Except as otherwise provided in this Code:

(a) The use of red or white oscillating, rotating or flashing lights, whether lighted or unlighted, is prohibited except on:

1. Law enforcement vehicles of State, Federal or local authorities;

2. A vehicle operated by a police officer or county coroner and designated or authorized by local authorities, in writing, as a law enforcement vehicle; however, such designation or authorization must be carried in the vehicle;

3. Vehicles of local fire departments and State or federal firefighting vehicles;

4. Vehicles which are designed and used exclusively as ambulances or rescue vehicles; furthermore, such lights shall not be lighted except when responding to an emergency call for and while actually conveying the sick or injured;

5. Tow trucks licensed in a state that requires such lights; furthermore, such lights shall not be lighted on any such tow truck while the tow truck is operating in the State of Illinois;

6. Vehicles of the Illinois Emergency Management Agency, and vehicles of the Department of Nuclear Safety; and

7. Vehicles operated by a local or county emergency management services agency as defined in the Illinois Emergency Management Agency Act.

(b) The use of amber oscillating, rotating or flashing lights, whether lighted or unlighted, is prohibited except on:

1. Second division vehicles designed and used for towing or hoisting vehicles; furthermore, such lights shall not be lighted except as required in this paragraph 1; such lights shall be lighted when such vehicles are actually being used at the scene of an accident or disablement; if the towing vehicle is equipped with a flat bed that supports all wheels of the vehicle being transported, the lights shall not be lighted while the vehicle is engaged in towing on a highway; if the towing vehicle is not equipped with a flat bed that supports all wheels of a vehicle being transported, the lights shall be lighted while the towing vehicle is engaged in towing on a highway during all times when the use of headlights is required under Section 12-201 of this Code;

2. Motor vehicles or equipment of the State of Illinois, local authorities and contractors; furthermore, such lights shall not be lighted except while such vehicles are engaged in maintenance or construction operations within the limits of construction projects;

3. Vehicles or equipment used by engineering or survey crews; furthermore, such lights shall not be lighted except while such vehicles are actually engaged in work on a highway;

4. Vehicles of public utilities, municipalities, or other construction, maintenance or automotive service vehicles except that such lights shall be lighted only as a means for indicating the presence of a vehicular traffic hazard requiring unusual care in approaching, overtaking or passing while such vehicles are engaged in maintenance, service or construction on a highway;

5. Oversized vehicle or load; however, such lights shall only be lighted when moving under permit issued by the Department under Section 15-301 of this Code;

6. The front and rear of motorized equipment owned and operated by the State of Illinois or any political subdivision thereof, which is designed and used for removal of snow and ice from highways;

7. Fleet safety vehicles registered in another state, furthermore, such lights shall not be lighted except as provided for in Section 12-212 of this Code;

8. Such other vehicles as may be authorized by local authorities;

9. Law enforcement vehicles of State or local authorities when used in combination with red oscillating, rotating or flashing lights;

9.5. Propane delivery trucks;

10. Vehicles used for collecting or delivering mail for the United States Postal Service provided that such lights shall not be lighted except when such vehicles are actually being used for such purposes;

11. Any vehicle displaying a slow-moving vehicle emblem as provided in Section 12-205.1;

12. All trucks equipped with self-compactors or roll-off hoists and roll- on containers for garbage or refuse hauling. Such lights shall not be lighted except when such vehicles are actually being used for such purposes;

13. Vehicles used by a security company, alarm responder, or control agency; and

14. Security vehicles of the Department of Human Services; however, the lights shall not be lighted except when being used for security related purposes under the direction of the superintendent of the facility where the vehicle is located.

(c) The use of blue oscillating, rotating or flashing lights, whether lighted or unlighted, is prohibited except on:

1. Rescue squad vehicles not owned by a fire department and vehicles owned or fully operated by a:

voluntary firefighter;

paid firefighter;

part-paid firefighter;

call firefighter;

member of the board of trustees of a fire protection district;

paid or unpaid member of a rescue squad;

paid or unpaid member of a voluntary ambulance unit; or

paid or unpaid members of a local or county emergency management services agency as defined in the Illinois Emergency Management Agency Act,[1] designated or authorized by local authorities, in writing, and carrying that designation or authorization in the vehicle.

However, such lights are not to be lighted except when responding to a bona fide emergency.

2. Police department vehicles in cities having a population of 500,000 or more inhabitants.

3. Law enforcement vehicles of State or local authorities when used in combination with red oscillating, rotating or flashing lights.

4. Vehicles of local fire departments and State or federal firefighting vehicles when used in combination with red oscillating, rotating or flashing lights.

5. Vehicles which are designed and used exclusively as ambulances or rescue vehicles when used in combination with red oscillating, rotating or flashing lights; furthermore, such lights shall not be lighted except when responding to an emergency call.

6. Vehicles that are equipped and used exclusively as organ transport vehicles when used in combination with red oscillating, rotating, or flashing lights; furthermore, these lights shall only be lighted when the transportation is declared an emergency by a member of the transplant team or a representative of the organ procurement organization.

7. Vehicles of the Illinois Emergency Management Agency and vehicles of the Department of Nuclear Safety, when used in combination with red oscillating, rotating, or flashing lights.

8. Vehicles operated by a local or county emergency management services agency as defined in the Illinois Emergency Management Agency Act, when used in combination with red oscillating, rotating, or flashing lights.

(c-1) In addition to the blue oscillating, rotating, or flashing lights permitted under subsection (c), and notwithstanding subsection (a), a vehicle operated by a voluntary firefighter may be equipped with flashing white headlights and blue grill lights, which may be used only in responding to an emergency call.

(c-2) In addition to the blue oscillating, rotating, or flashing lights permitted under subsection (c), and notwithstanding subsection (a), a vehicle operated by a paid or unpaid member of a local or county emergency management services agency as defined in the Illinois Emergency Management

Agency Act, may be equipped with white oscillating, rotating, or flashing lights to be used in combination with blue oscillating, rotating, or flashing lights, if authorization by local authorities is in writing and carried in the vehicle.

(d) The use of a combination of amber and white oscillating, rotating or flashing lights, whether lighted or unlighted, is prohibited, except motor vehicles or equipment of the State of Illinois, local authorities and contractors may be so equipped; furthermore, such lights shall not be lighted except while such vehicles are engaged in highway maintenance or construction operations within the limits of highway construction projects.

(e) All oscillating, rotating or flashing lights referred to in this Section shall be of sufficient intensity, when illuminated, to be visible at 500 feet in normal sunlight.

(f) Nothing in this Section shall prohibit a manufacturer of oscillating, rotating or flashing lights or his representative from temporarily mounting such lights on a vehicle for demonstration purposes only.

(g) Any person violating the provisions of subsections (a), (b), (c) or (d) of this Section who without lawful authority stops or detains or attempts to stop or detain another person shall be guilty of a Class 4 felony.

(h) Except as provided in subsection (g) above, any person violating the provisions of subsections (a) or (c) of this Section shall be guilty of a Class A misdemeanor.

P.A. 76–1586, § 12–116, eff. July 1, 1970. Amended by P.A. 76–2182, § 1, eff. July 1, 1970. Renumbered § 12–215 by P.A. 77–37, § 1, eff. Jan. 1, 1972. Amended by P.A. 77–103, § 1, eff. Jan. 1, 1972; P.A. 77–2829, § 40, eff. Dec. 22, 1972; P.A. 78–255, § 61, eff. Oct. 1, 1973; P.A. 78–509, § 1, eff. Jan. 1, 1974; P.A. 78–1203, § 1, eff. Sept. 5, 1974; P.A. 78–1297, § 58, eff. March 4, 1975; P.A. 79–537, § 1, eff. Oct. 1, 1975; P.A. 79–870, § 1, eff. Oct. 1, 1975; P.A. 79–916, § 1, eff. Oct. 1, 1975; P.A. 79–1454, § 44, eff. Aug. 31, 1976; P.A. 80–1013, § 1, eff. Oct. 1, 1977; P.A. 81–1509, Art. II, § 71, eff. Sept. 26, 1980; P.A. 83–769, § 1, eff. Jan. 1, 1984; P.A. 84–256, § 1, eff. Jan. 1, 1986; P.A. 84–285, § 1, eff. Jan. 1, 1986; P.A. 84–1105, § 1, eff. Dec. 10, 1985; P.A. 84–1231, § 1, eff. July 28, 1986; P.A. 84–1308, Art. II, § 96, eff. Aug. 25, 1986; P.A. 84–1438, Art. II, § 30, eff. Dec. 22, 1986; P.A. 85–586, § 1, eff. Sept. 20, 1987; P.A. 85–1368, § 1, eff. Jan. 1, 1989; P.A. 86–611, § 1, eff. Sept. 1, 1989; P.A. 87–531, § 1, eff. Jan. 1, 1992; P.A. 88–58, § 5, eff. Jan. 1, 1994; P.A. 88–341, § 1, eff. Jan. 1, 1994; P.A. 88–670, Art. 2, § 2–59, eff. Dec. 2, 1994; P.A. 89–433, § 5, eff. Dec. 15, 1995; P.A. 89–507, Art. 90, § 90D–84, eff. July 1, 1997; P.A. 90–330, § 5, eff. Aug. 8, 1997; P.A. 90–347, § 5, eff. Jan. 1, 1998; P.A. 90–655, § 153, eff. July 30, 1998; P.A. 91–357, § 231, eff. July 29, 1999; P.A. 92–138, § 5, eff. July 24, 2001; P.A. 92–407, § 5, eff. Aug. 17, 2001; P.A. 92–651, § 77, eff. July 11, 2002; P.A. 92–782, § 5, eff. Aug. 6, 2002; P.A. 92–820, § 5, eff. Aug. 21, 2002.

Formerly Ill.Rev.Stat.1991, ch. 95 ½, ¶ 12–215.

[1] 20 ILCS 3305/1 et seq.

For text of section effective June 1, 2003, see 625 ILCS 5/12–215, post

P.A. 92–651, the First 2002 General Revisory Act, amended various Acts to delete obsolete text, to correct patent and technical errors, to revise cross references, to resolve multiple actions in the 91st and 92nd General Assemblies and to make certain technical corrections in P.A. 91–937 through P.A. 92–520.

P.A. 92–782 incorporated the amendments by P.A. 92–138 and P.A. 92–407.

P.A. 92–820 incorporated the amendments by P.A. 92–138 and P.A. 92–407.

5/12–215. Oscillating, rotating or flashing lights on motor vehicles

Text of section effective June 1, 2003

§ 12–215. Oscillating, rotating or flashing lights on motor vehicles. Except as otherwise provided in this Code:

(a) The use of red or white oscillating, rotating or flashing lights, whether lighted or unlighted, is prohibited except on:

1. Law enforcement vehicles of State, Federal or local authorities;

2. A vehicle operated by a police officer or county coroner and designated or authorized by local authorities, in writing, as a law enforcement vehicle; however, such designation or authorization must be carried in the vehicle;

3. Vehicles of local fire departments and State or federal firefighting vehicles;

4. Vehicles which are designed and used exclusively as ambulances or rescue vehicles; furthermore, such lights shall not be lighted except when responding to an emergency call for and while actually conveying the sick or injured;

5. Tow trucks licensed in a state that requires such lights; furthermore, such lights shall not be lighted on any such tow truck while the tow truck is operating in the State of Illinois;

6. Vehicles of the Illinois Emergency Management Agency, and vehicles of the Department of Nuclear Safety; and

7. Vehicles operated by a local or county emergency management services agency as defined in the Illinois Emergency Management Agency Act.

(b) The use of amber oscillating, rotating or flashing lights, whether lighted or unlighted, is prohibited except on:

1. Second division vehicles designed and used for towing or hoisting vehicles; furthermore, such lights shall not be lighted except as required in this paragraph 1; such lights shall be lighted when such vehicles are actually being used at the scene of an accident or disablement; if the towing vehicle is equipped with a flat bed that supports all wheels of the vehicle being transported, the lights shall not be lighted while the vehicle is engaged in towing on a highway; if the towing vehicle is not equipped with a flat bed that supports all wheels of a vehicle being transported, the lights shall be lighted while the towing vehicle is engaged in towing on a highway during all times when the use of headlights is required under Section 12–201 of this Code;

2. Motor vehicles or equipment of the State of Illinois, local authorities and contractors; furthermore, such lights shall not be lighted except while such vehicles are engaged in maintenance or construction operations within the limits of construction projects;

3. Vehicles or equipment used by engineering or survey crews; furthermore, such lights shall not be lighted except while such vehicles are actually engaged in work on a highway;

4. Vehicles of public utilities, municipalities, or other construction, maintenance or automotive service vehicles except that such lights shall be lighted only as a means for indicating the presence of a vehicular traffic hazard requiring unusual care in approaching, overtaking or passing

while such vehicles are engaged in maintenance, service or construction on a highway;

5. Oversized vehicle or load; however, such lights shall only be lighted when moving under permit issued by the Department under Section 15-301 of this Code;

6. The front and rear of motorized equipment owned and operated by the State of Illinois or any political subdivision thereof, which is designed and used for removal of snow and ice from highways;

7. Fleet safety vehicles registered in another state, furthermore, such lights shall not be lighted except as provided for in Section 12-212 of this Code;

8. Such other vehicles as may be authorized by local authorities;

9. Law enforcement vehicles of State or local authorities when used in combination with red oscillating, rotating or flashing lights;

9.5. Propane delivery trucks;

10. Vehicles used for collecting or delivering mail for the United States Postal Service provided that such lights shall not be lighted except when such vehicles are actually being used for such purposes;

11. Any vehicle displaying a slow-moving vehicle emblem as provided in Section 12-205.1;

12. All trucks equipped with self-compactors or roll-off hoists and roll- on containers for garbage or refuse hauling. Such lights shall not be lighted except when such vehicles are actually being used for such purposes;

13. Vehicles used by a security company, alarm responder, or control agency;

14. Security vehicles of the Department of Human Services; however, the lights shall not be lighted except when being used for security related purposes under the direction of the superintendent of the facility where the vehicle is located; and

15. Vehicles of union representatives, except that the lights shall be lighted only while the vehicle is within the limits of a construction project or while the vehicle is parked alongside any roadway.

(c) The use of blue oscillating, rotating or flashing lights, whether lighted or unlighted, is prohibited except on:

1. Rescue squad vehicles not owned by a fire department and vehicles owned or fully operated by a:

voluntary firefighter;

paid firefighter;

part-paid firefighter;

call firefighter;

member of the board of trustees of a fire protection district;

paid or unpaid member of a rescue squad;

paid or unpaid member of a voluntary ambulance unit; or

paid or unpaid members of a local or county emergency management services agency as defined in the Illinois Emergency Management Agency Act,[1] designated or authorized by local authorities, in writing, and carrying that designation or authorization in the vehicle.

However, such lights are not to be lighted except when responding to a bona fide emergency.

2. Police department vehicles in cities having a population of 500,000 or more inhabitants.

3. Law enforcement vehicles of State or local authorities when used in combination with red oscillating, rotating or flashing lights.

4. Vehicles of local fire departments and State or federal firefighting vehicles when used in combination with red oscillating, rotating or flashing lights.

5. Vehicles which are designed and used exclusively as ambulances or rescue vehicles when used in combination with red oscillating, rotating or flashing lights; furthermore, such lights shall not be lighted except when responding to an emergency call.

6. Vehicles that are equipped and used exclusively as organ transport vehicles when used in combination with red oscillating, rotating, or flashing lights; furthermore, these lights shall only be lighted when the transportation is declared an emergency by a member of the transplant team or a representative of the organ procurement organization.

7. Vehicles of the Illinois Emergency Management Agency and vehicles of the Department of Nuclear Safety, when used in combination with red oscillating, rotating, or flashing lights.

8. Vehicles operated by a local or county emergency management services agency as defined in the Illinois Emergency Management Agency Act, when used in combination with red oscillating, rotating, or flashing lights.

(c-1) In addition to the blue oscillating, rotating, or flashing lights permitted under subsection (c), and notwithstanding subsection (a), a vehicle operated by a voluntary firefighter, a voluntary member of a rescue squad, or a member of a voluntary ambulance unit may be equipped with flashing white headlights and blue grill lights, which may be used only in responding to an emergency call.

(c-2) In addition to the blue oscillating, rotating, or flashing lights permitted under subsection (c), and notwithstanding subsection (a), a vehicle operated by a paid or unpaid member of a local or county emergency management services agency as defined in the Illinois Emergency Management Agency Act, may be equipped with white oscillating, rotating, or flashing lights to be used in combination with blue oscillating, rotating, or flashing lights, if authorization by local authorities is in writing and carried in the vehicle.

(d) The use of a combination of amber and white oscillating, rotating or flashing lights, whether lighted or unlighted, is prohibited, except motor vehicles or equipment of the State of Illinois, local authorities, contractors, and union representatives may be so equipped; furthermore, such lights shall not be lighted on vehicles of the State of Illinois, local authorities, and contractors except while such vehicles are engaged in highway maintenance or construction operations within the limits of highway construction projects, and shall not be lighted on the vehicles of union representatives except when those vehicles are within the limits of a construction project.

(e) All oscillating, rotating or flashing lights referred to in this Section shall be of sufficient intensity, when illuminated, to be visible at 500 feet in normal sunlight.

(f) Nothing in this Section shall prohibit a manufacturer of oscillating, rotating or flashing lights or his representative from temporarily mounting such lights on a vehicle for demonstration purposes only.

(g) Any person violating the provisions of subsections (a), (b), (c) or (d) of this Section who without lawful authority stops or detains or attempts to stop or detain another person shall be guilty of a Class 4 felony.

(h) Except as provided in subsection (g) above, any person violating the provisions of subsections (a) or (c) of this Section shall be guilty of a Class A misdemeanor.

P.A. 76-1586, § 12-116, eff. July 1, 1970. Amended by P.A. 76-2182, § 1, eff. July 1, 1970. Renumbered § 12-215 by P.A. 77-37, § 1, eff. Jan. 1, 1972. Amended by P.A. 77-103, § 1, eff. Jan. 1, 1972; P.A. 77-2829, § 40, eff. Dec. 22, 1972; P.A. 78-255, § 61, eff. Oct. 1, 1973; P.A. 78-509, § 1, eff. Jan. 1, 1974; P.A. 78-1203, § 1, eff. Sept. 5, 1974; P.A. 78-1297, § 58, eff. March 4, 1975; P.A. 79-537, § 1, eff. Oct. 1, 1975; P.A. 79-870, § 1, eff. Oct. 1, 1975; P.A. 79-916, § 1, eff. Oct. 1, 1975; P.A. 79-1454, § 44, eff. Aug. 31, 1976; P.A. 80-1013, § 1, eff. Oct. 1, 1977; P.A. 81-1509, Art. II, § 71, eff. Sept. 26, 1980; P.A. 83-769, § 1, eff. Jan. 1, 1984; P.A. 84-256, § 1, eff. Jan. 1, 1986; P.A. 84-285, § 1, eff. Jan. 1, 1986; P.A. 84-1105, § 1, eff. Dec. 10, 1985; P.A. 84-1231, § 1, eff. July 28, 1986; P.A. 84-1308, Art. II, § 96, eff. Aug. 25, 1986; P.A. 84-1438, Art. II, § 30, eff. Dec. 22, 1986; P.A. 85-586, § 1, eff. Sept. 20, 1987; P.A. 85-1368, § 1, eff. Jan. 1, 1989; P.A. 86-611, § 1, eff. Sept. 1, 1989; P.A. 87-531, § 1, eff. Jan. 1, 1992; P.A. 88-58, § 5, eff. Jan. 1, 1994; P.A. 88-341, § 1, eff. Jan. 1, 1994; P.A. 88-670, Art. 2, § 2-59, eff. Dec. 2, 1994; P.A. 89-433, § 5, eff. Dec. 15, 1995; P.A. 89-507, Art. 90, § 90D-84, eff. July 1, 1997; P.A. 90-330, § 5, eff. Aug. 8, 1997; P.A. 90-347, § 5, eff. Jan. 1, 1998; P.A. 90-655, § 153, eff. July 30, 1998; P.A. 91-357, § 231, eff. July 29, 1999; P.A. 92-138, § 5, eff. July 24, 2001; P.A. 92-407, § 5, eff. Aug. 17, 2001; P.A. 92-651, § 77, eff. July 11, 2002; P.A. 92-782, § 5, eff. Aug. 6, 2002; P.A. 92-820, § 5, eff. Aug. 21, 2002; P.A. 92-872, § 5, eff. June 1, 2003.

Formerly Ill.Rev.Stat.1991, ch. 95 ½, ¶ 12-215.

1 20 ILCS 3305/1 et seq.

For text of section effective until June 1, 2003, see 625 ILCS 5/12-215, ante

P.A. 92-407 inserted subpar. (c-1).

P.A. 92-651, the First 2002 General Revisory Act, amended various Acts to delete obsolete text, to correct patent and technical errors, to revise cross references, to resolve multiple actions in the 91st and 92nd General Assemblies and to make certain technical corrections in P.A. 91-937 through P.A. 92-520.

P.A. 92-782 incorporated the amendments by P.A. 92-138 and P.A. 92-407.

P.A. 92-820 incorporated the amendments by P.A. 92-138 and P.A. 92-407.

See 5 ILCS 70/6 as to the effect of (1) more than one amendment of a section at the same session of the General Assembly or (2) two or more acts relating to the same subject matter enacted by the same General Assembly.

5/12-216. Operation of oscillating, rotating or flashing lights

§ 12-216. Operation of oscillating, rotating or flashing lights. Oscillating, rotating or flashing lights located on or within police vehicles in this State shall be lighted whenever a police officer is in pursuit of a violator of a traffic law or regulation.

P.A. 76-1586, § 12-117, eff. July 1, 1970. Renumbered § 12-216 by P.A. 77-37, § 1, eff. Jan. 1, 1972. Amended by P.A. 85-830, § 1, eff. Sept. 24, 1987.

Formerly Ill.Rev.Stat.1991, ch. 95 ½, ¶ 12-216.

5/12-217. Special lighting equipment for interstate transportation authority

§ 12-217. Special lighting equipment for interstate transportation authority. (a) Notwithstanding any other provisions of this Chapter, an interstate transportation authority, as defined in this Section, in addition to headlights and other required or authorized lighting, may affix to the top front of its buses, 2 sets of lights, each containing up to 5 stationary lights, of different colors, including the colors white, yellow, blue, green and purple, and excepting, however, the color red. Such lights shall be located symmetrically above the windshield with one set of lights on each side of the headsign and may reflect an intensity of up to 64 candlepower each. Provided further however, that normally no more than 3 of such colored lights on each set of lights may be on or displayed at any one time. Such lights shall be stationary only, and shall not be oscillating, rotating, or flashing. The lights shall be displayed only on the top front of such buses, lighted in various combinations to indicate the route, the destination, and the express or local nature of the service.

(b) As used herein, the term "interstate transportation authority" shall mean any body, agency, entity, or political subdivision created by compact between Illinois and another state, which is a body corporate and politic, and which operates a public mass transportation or transit system.

P.A. 76-1586, § 12-217, added by P.A. 85-1144, § 1, eff. July 29, 1988.

Formerly Ill.Rev.Stat.1991, ch. 95 ½, ¶ 12-217.

ARTICLE III. BRAKES

5/12-301. Brakes

§ 12-301. Brakes.

(a) Brake equipment required.

1. Every motor vehicle, other than a motor-driven cycle and an antique vehicle displaying an antique plate, when operated upon a highway shall be equipped with brakes adequate to control the movement of and to stop and hold such vehicle, including 2 separate means of applying the brakes, each of which means shall be effective to apply the brakes to at least one wheel on a motorcycle and at least 2 wheels on all other first division and second division vehicles. If these 2 separate means of applying the brakes are connected in any way, they shall be so constructed that failure of any one part of the operating mechanism shall not leave the motor vehicle without brakes.

2. Every motor-driven cycle when operated upon a highway shall be equipped with at least one brake which may be operated by hand or foot.

3. Every antique vehicle shall be equipped with the brakes of the same type originally installed by the manufacturer as original equipment and in working order.

4. Every trailer or semitrailer of a gross weight of over 3,000 pounds, when operated upon a highway must be equipped with brakes adequate to control the movement of, to stop and to hold such vehicle, and designed so as to be operable by the driver of the towing vehicle from its cab. Such brakes must be so designed and connected that

in case of an accidental breakaway of a towed vehicle over 5,000 pounds, the brakes are automatically applied.

5. Every motor vehicle, trailer, pole trailer or semitrailer, sold in this State or operated upon the highways shall be equipped with service brakes upon all wheels of every such vehicle, except any motor-driven cycle, and except that any trailer, pole trailer or semitrailer 3,000 pounds gross weight or less need not be equipped with brakes, and except that any trailer or semitrailer with gross weight over 3,000 pounds but under 5,001 pounds need be equipped with brakes on only one wheel on each side of the vehicle. Any motor vehicle and truck tractor having 3 or more axles and manufactured prior to July 25, 1980 need not have brakes on the front wheels, except when such vehicles are equipped with at least 2 steerable axles, the wheels of one such axle need not be equipped with brakes. However, a vehicle that is more than 30 years of age and which is driven on the highways only in going to and returning from an antique auto show or for servicing or for a demonstration need be equipped with 2 wheel brakes only.

(b) Performance ability of brakes.

1. The service brakes upon any motor vehicle or combination of vehicles operating on a level surface shall be adequate to stop such vehicle or vehicles when traveling 20 miles per hour within a distance of 30 feet when upon dry asphalt or concrete pavement surface free from loose material.

2. Under the above conditions the hand brake shall be adequate to stop such vehicle or vehicles, except any motorcycle, within a distance of 55 feet and the hand brake shall be adequate to hold such vehicle or vehicles stationary on any grade upon which operated.

3. Under the above conditions the service brakes upon an antique vehicle shall be adequate to stop the vehicle within a distance of 40 feet and the hand brake adequate to stop the vehicle within a distance of 55 feet.

4. All braking distances specified in this Section apply to all vehicles mentioned, whether such vehicles are unloaded or are loaded to the maximum capacity permitted under this Act.

5. All brakes shall be maintained in good working order and shall be so adjusted as to operate as equally as practicable with respect to the wheels on opposite sides of the vehicle.

6. Brake assembly requirements for mobile homes shall be the standards required by the United States Department of Housing and Urban Development adopted under Title VI of the Housing and Community Development Act of 1974.[1]

(c) For purposes of this Section, a custom vehicle or street rod is considered to be in compliance with all brake equipment requirements if it has passed the approved vehicle safety inspection provided for in Section 3-804.1 or 3-804.2.

P.A. 76-1586, § 12-118, eff. July 1, 1970. Amended by P.A. 76-1627, § 1, eff. July 1, 1970; P.A. 76-1997, § 1, eff. July 1, 1970. Renumbered § 12-301 by P.A. 77-37, § 1, eff. Jan. 1, 1972. Amended by P.A. 77-217, § 1, eff. Jan. 1, 1972; P.A. 77-2829, § 40, eff. Dec. 22, 1972; P.A. 78-255, § 61, eff. Oct. 1, 1973; P.A. 80-1038, § 1, eff. Sept. 27, 1977; P.A. 86-447, § 2, eff. Aug. 30, 1989; P.A. 86-1340, § 1, eff. July 1, 1990; P.A. 92-668, § 5, eff. Jan. 1, 2003.

Formerly Ill.Rev.Stat.1991, ch. 95 ½, ¶ 12-301.

[1] 42 U.S.C.A. § 5401 et seq.

P.A. 86-1340 incorporated the amendment by P.A. 86-447.

5/12-302. Brake fluid

§ 12-302. Brake fluid. No person shall sell, offer for sale or distribute brake fluid for use on motor vehicles for repair purposes unless such fluid conforms to specifications prescribed by the Department.

P.A. 76-1586, § 12-119, eff. July 1, 1970. Renumbered § 12-302 by P.A. 77-37, § 1, eff. Jan. 1, 1972. Amended by P.A. 77-2830, Art. 73, § 1, eff. Jan. 1, 1973; P.A. 78-748, § 1, eff. Jan. 1, 1974.

Formerly Ill.Rev.Stat.1991, ch. 95 ½, ¶ 12-302.

ARTICLE IV. TIRES

Section

5/12-401. Restriction as to tire equipment

§ 12-401. Restriction as to tire equipment. No metal tired vehicle, including tractors, motor vehicles of the second division, traction engines and other similar vehicles, shall be operated over any improved highway of this State, if such vehicle has on the periphery of any of the road wheels any block, stud, flange, cleat, ridge, lug or any projection of metal or wood which projects radially beyond the tread or traffic surface of the tire. This prohibition does not apply to pneumatic tires with metal studs used on vehicles operated by rural letter carriers who are employed or enjoy a contract with the United States Postal Service for the purpose of delivering mail if such vehicle is actually used for such purpose during operations between November 15 of any year and April 1 of the following year, or to motor vehicles displaying a person with disabilities or disabled veteran license plate whose owner resides in an unincorporated area located upon a county or township highway or road and possesses a valid driver's license and operates the vehicle with such tires only during the period heretofore described, or to tracked type motor vehicles when that part of the vehicle coming in contact with the road surface does not contain any projections of any kind likely to injure the surface of the road; however, tractors, traction engines, and similar vehicles may be operated which have upon their road wheels V-shaped, diagonal or other cleats arranged in such a manner as to be continuously in contact with the road surface, provided that the gross weight upon such wheels per inch of width of such cleats in contact with the road surface, when measured in the direction of the axle of the vehicle, does not exceed 800 pounds.

All motor vehicles and all other vehicles in tow thereof, or thereunto attached, operating upon any roadway, shall have tires of rubber or some material of equal resiliency. Solid tires shall be considered defective and shall not be permitted to be used if the rubber or other material has been worn or otherwise reduced to a thickness of less than three-fourths of an undue vibration when the vehicle is in motion or to cause undue concentration of the wheel load on the surface of the road. The requirements of this Section do not apply to agricultural tractors or traction engines or to agricultural machinery, including wagons being used for agricultural purposes in tow thereof, or to road rollers or road building machinery operated at a speed not in excess of 10 miles per hour. All motor vehicles of the second division, operating upon any roadway shall have pneumatic tires, unless exempted herein.

Nothing in this Section shall be deemed to prohibit the use of tire chains of reasonable proportion upon any vehicle when required for safety because of snow, ice or other conditions tending to cause a vehicle to skid.

P.A. 76-1586, § 12-124, eff. July 1, 1970. Amended by P.A. 76-2184, § 1, eff. July 1, 1970. Renumbered § 12-401 by P.A. 77-37, § 1, eff. Jan. 1, 1972. Amended by P.A. 78-381, § 1, eff. Oct. 1, 1973; P.A. 79-466, § 1, eff. Aug. 21, 1975; P.A. 83-213, § 1, eff. Jan. 1, 1984; P.A. 83-888, § 1, eff. Nov. 2, 1983; P.A. 83-1362, Art. II, § 99, eff. Sept. 11, 1984; P.A. 88-685, § 5, eff. Jan. 24, 1995.

Formerly Ill.Rev.Stat.1991, ch. 95 ½, ¶ 12-401.

5/12-402. Sale or lease of siped or regrooved pneumatic tire

§ 12-402. Sale or lease of siped or regrooved pneumatic tire. No person or organization shall sell or lease or offer for sale or lease, for use on a highway, any pneumatic tire, either original tread or retread, on which the tread is siped or regrooved to a depth equal to or deeper than the molded groove depth, unless the tire was constructed or retreaded with sufficient tread material and type of labels to permit such siping or regrooving. Such labels and siping or regrooving shall be in compliance with Part 569 of Title 49 of the Code of Federal Regulations, and after siping or regrooving the tire shall conform to that Part.

For the purpose of this Article, siped shall mean cut without removing material, and regrooved shall mean the tread groove pattern is renewed, or a new pattern generated, or both, without additional tread material being added.

P.A. 76-1586, § 12-134, eff. July 1, 1970. Renumbered § 12-402 by P.A. 77-37, § 1, eff. Jan. 1, 1972. Amended by P.A. 83-213, § 1, eff. Jan. 1, 1984.

Formerly Ill.Rev.Stat.1991, ch. 95 ½, ¶ 12-402.

5/12-403. Sale or lease of retreaded or "recapped" pneumatic tire

§ 12-403. Sale or lease of retreaded or "recapped" pneumatic tire. No person or organization shall sell or lease or offer for sale or lease, for use on a highway, any pneumatic tire produced or rebuilt by a process in which tread material is attached to a used tire, unless the tire, tread material, labelling and certification, before and after processing, conform to Part 571.117 of Title 49 of the Code of Federal Regulations.

P.A. 76-1586, § 12-135, eff. July 1, 1970. Renumbered § 12-403 by P.A. 77-37, § 1, eff. Jan. 1, 1972. Amended by P.A. 83-213, § 1, eff. Jan. 1, 1984.

Formerly Ill.Rev.Stat.1991, ch. 95 ½, ¶ 12-403.

5/12-404. Sale or lease of pneumatic tire without marking

§ 12-404. Sale or lease of pneumatic tire without marking. No person or organization shall sell or lease or offer for sale or lease, for use on a highway, any pneumatic tire that does not bear the special marking required by this Section.

(a) Regrooved or siped tire. In addition to the identification, labelling and certification required under Section 12-402, either the word "regrooved" or the word "siped" shall be branded on each side of a pneumatic tire on which the tread is either regrooved or siped, as the case may be. In the case of a tire that is both regrooved and siped, the word "regrooved" alone on each side shall suffice, although both words may appear on each side. Each branding shall be conspicuous but shall be sized, located and applied so as not to weaken or damage the tire or otherwise degrade the performance of the tire or shorten its useful life.

(b) Retreaded tire. In addition to the labelling, identification, certification and other marking required under Section 12-403, the word "retreaded" shall be branded or molded into or onto each side of a pneumatic tire that has been retreaded or "recapped". Each molding or branding shall be conspicuous but shall be sized, located and applied so as not to weaken or damage the tire or otherwise degrade the performance of the tire or shorten its useful life.

(c) New tire. The labelling, identification, certification and other marking required by Part 571.109 of Title 49 of the Code of Federal Regulations shall appear on each new pneumatic tire intended for use on a passenger car other than a multipurpose passenger vehicle. The labelling, identification, certification and other marking required by Part 571.119 of Title 49 of the Code of Federal Regulations shall appear on each new pneumatic tire intended for use on either a multipurpose passenger vehicle or other type of vehicle that is not a passenger car.

P.A. 76-1586, § 12-136, eff. July 1, 1970. Renumbered § 12-404 by P.A. 77-37, § 1, eff. Jan. 1, 1972. Amended by P.A. 83-213, § 1, eff. Jan. 1, 1984.

Formerly Ill.Rev.Stat.1991, ch. 95 ½, ¶ 12-404.

5/12-405. Operating condition of pneumatic tires

§ 12-405. Operating condition of pneumatic tires. **(a) Definition.** The term "spare tire" as used in this Section 12-405 means any new, used or specially constructed tire that is either carried or installed for short term emergency use.

(b) Promulgated Rules. The Department shall promulgate rules concerning unsafe operating conditions of pneumatic tires. The rules shall be enforced by police officers by visual inspection of tires, including visual comparison with simple measuring scales or gauges. The rules shall include precepts and standards for determining unsafe conditions, including the determination of an effective depth of tread groove, and shall be based upon, to the extent that it is reasonable and practical, all provisions set forth in paragraph (d) of this Section.

(c) Use of Unsafe Tire. 1. No person or organization shall place, drive or move, or cause or allow to be placed, driven or moved, on a highway of this State, any vehicle equipped with one or more pneumatic tires deemed to be unsafe under a provision of paragraph (d) of this Section or a rule promulgated under paragraph (b) of this Section.

2. Exemptions. Any restriction stated in this paragraph (c) shall not apply:

(i) To a tire on a damaged, disabled, abandoned, or other unsafe or unwanted vehicle being legally towed, pushed or otherwise transferred to a repair, relocation, storage, salvage, junking, or other collection site;

(ii) To a tire on a racing or other competitive vehicle being legally moved or transported, not under its own power, to a lawful competition site or to a bona fide testing site; or

(iii) To a spare tire either carried or in short term emergency use for only such distance or time as is reasonably necessary to accomplish the repair or replacement of the damaged or unsafe tire for which the spare was substituted.

(d) Criteria for Unsafe Pneumatic Tires. A pneumatic tire shall be deemed to be unsafe if it has:

1. Any part of a ply or cord exposed;

2. A tread or sidewall crack, cut, snag, or other surface interruption deep enough to expose a ply or cord;

3. Any bulge, knot, or separation;

4. Tread wear indicators flush with the tread outer surface in any 2 or more adjacent tread grooves at 3 locations approximately equally spaced around the circumference of the tire;

5. A depth of tread groove less than $\frac{2}{32}$ of an inch or less than $\frac{1}{32}$ of an inch if on a motorcycle or truckster, measured in any 2 or more adjacent tread grooves at 3 locations approximately equally spaced around the circumference of the tire, at least one of which, in the judgment of the inspecting officer, is a location at which the tread is thinnest, providing that any measurement over a tie bar, tread wear indicator, hump or fillet is excluded;

6. A depth of tread groove less than $\frac{4}{32}$ of an inch at any one location and the tire is mounted on the front wheel of a motor vehicle subject to the provisions of Chapter 18B of this Code, provided that any measurement over a tie bar, tread wear indicator, hump or fillet is excluded;

7. A marking which indicates that the tire is not intended for use on a public highway;

8. Been regrooved or recut below the bottom of an original tread groove, except in the case of a special "regroovable" tire that was manufactured or retreaded with thick undertread, identified and regrooved in compliance with the applicable federal standard in Title 49 of the Code of Federal Regulations, and in compliance with each applicable Section of this Code; or

9. Other condition, marking or lack of marking that may be reasonably demonstrated to identify the tire as unsuitable for highway use, including inflation, load, speed or installation condition seriously incompatible with the tire size, construction, or other pertinent marking or feature.

(e) Sale, Lease or Installation of Pneumatic Tires. 1. No person or organization shall sell, lease, or offer for sale or lease, or mount, install, or cause or allow to be mounted or installed, for use on a highway, any pneumatic tire deemed to be unsafe under paragraph (d) of this Section or under a rule promulgated under paragraph (b) of this Section. Except as provided in paragraph (c) of this Section, any person or organization offering a vehicle for sale or lease shall, prior to its being placed, driven or moved on a highway, correct any unsafe tire condition.

2. No person or organization shall sell, lease, or offer for sale or lease, for highway use, any pneumatic tire, or any vehicle equipped with a pneumatic tire, which has a depth of tread groove less than $\frac{2}{32}$ of an inch; except a pneumatic tire on a motorcycle or truckster may have a depth of tire groove of not less than $\frac{1}{32}$ of an inch. Groove depth shall not be measured where a tie bar, tread wear indicator, hump or fillet is located.

(f) Compliance and Enforcement. Any police officer, upon reasonable cause to believe that a person or organization has acted or is acting in violation of any provision of this Section, shall require the driver, owner, or other appropriate custodian to submit the tire or tires to an inspection. When so required, the owner or other appropriate custodian shall allow the tire inspection and the driver of a vehicle or combination of vehicles shall stop at a designated location and allow the tire or tires to be inspected or shall move the vehicle or combination to a location that is reasonably convenient and is suitable for such inspection.

P.A. 76-1586, § 12-405, added by P.A. 77-2770, § 1, eff. Jan. 1, 1973. Amended by P.A. 83-213, § 1, eff. Jan. 1, 1984.

Formerly Ill.Rev.Stat.1991, ch. 95 ½, ¶ 12-405.

5/12-406. § 12-406. Repealed by P.A. 80-911, § 2, eff. Oct. 1, 1977

5/12-407. Rules and regulations

§ 12-407. Rules and regulations. The Department may promulgate rules and regulations to clarify or specify the requirements of this Article IV.

P.A. 76-1586, § 12-407, added by P.A. 83-213, § 1, eff. Jan. 1, 1984.

Formerly Ill.Rev.Stat.1991, ch. 95 ½, ¶ 12-407.

ARTICLE V. GLASS, WINDSHIELDS AND MIRRORS

Section

5/12-500. § 12-500. Repealed by P.A. 90-89, § 20, eff. Jan. 1, 1998

5/12-501. Windshields and safety glazing material in motor vehicles

§ 12-501. Windshields and safety glazing material in motor vehicles.

(a) Every motor vehicle operated upon the highways of this State shall be equipped with a front windshield which complies with those standards as established pursuant to this Section and Section 12-503 of this Code. This subsection shall not apply to motor vehicles designed and used exclusively for off-highway use, motorcycles, motor-driven cycles, motorized pedalcycles, nor to motor vehicles registered as antique vehicles, custom vehicles, or street rods when the original design of such vehicles did not include front windshields.

(b) No person shall knowingly sell any 1936 or later model motor vehicle unless such vehicle is equipped with safety glazing material conforming to specifications prescribed by the Department wherever glazing material is used in doors, windows and windshields. Regulations promulgated by the Department specifying standards for safety glazing material on windshields shall, as a minimum, conform with those applicable Federal Motor Vehicles Safety Standards (49 CFR 571.205). These provisions apply to all motor vehicles of the first and second division but with respect to trucks, including truck tractors, the requirements as to safety glazing material apply to all glazing material used in doors, windows and windshields in the drivers' compartments of such vehicles.

(c) It is unlawful for the owner or any other person knowingly to install or cause to be installed in any motor vehicle any glazing material other than safety glazing material conforming to the specifications prescribed by the Department.

P.A. 76-1586, § 12-126, eff. July 1, 1970. Resectioned in part § 12-501 by P.A. 77-37, § 1, eff. Jan. 1, 1972. Amended by P.A. 78-748, § 1, eff. Jan. 1, 1974; P.A. 85-1144, § 1, eff. July 29, 1988; P.A. 92-668, § 5, eff. Jan. 1, 2003.

Formerly Ill.Rev.Stat.1991, ch. 95 ½, ¶ 12-501.

5/12-502. Mirrors

§ 12-502. Mirrors. Every motor vehicle, operated singly or when towing another vehicle, shall be equipped with a mirror so located as to reflect to the driver a view of the highway for a distance of at least 200 feet to the rear of such motor vehicle.

P.A. 76-1586, § 12-122, eff. July 1, 1970. Renumbered § 12-502 by P.A. 77-37, § 1, eff. Jan. 1, 1972. Amended by P.A. 82-122, § 1, eff. Jan. 1, 1982.

Formerly Ill.Rev.Stat.1991, ch. 95 ½, ¶ 12-502.

5/12-503. Windshields must be unobstructed and equipped with wipers

§ 12-503. Windshields must be unobstructed and equipped with wipers.

(a) No person shall drive a motor vehicle with any sign, poster, window application, reflective material, nonreflective material or tinted film upon the front windshield, sidewings or side windows immediately adjacent to each side of the driver. A nonreflective tinted film may be used along the uppermost portion of the windshield if such material does not extend more than 6 inches down from the top of the windshield. Nothing in this Section shall create a cause of action on behalf of a buyer against a dealer or manufacturer who sells a motor vehicle with a window which is in violation of this Section.

(b) Nothing contained in this Section shall prohibit the use of nonreflective, smoked or tinted glass, nonreflective film, perforated window screen or other decorative window application on windows to the rear of the driver's seat, except that any motor vehicle with a window to the rear of the driver's seat treated in this manner shall be equipped with a side mirror on each side of the motor vehicle which are in conformance with Section 12-502.

(c) No person shall drive a motor vehicle with any objects placed or suspended between the driver and the front windshield, rear window, side wings or side windows immediately adjacent to each side of the driver which materially obstructs the driver's view.

(d) Every motor vehicle, except motorcycles, shall be equipped with a device, controlled by the driver, for cleaning rain, snow, moisture or other obstructions from the windshield; and no person shall drive a motor vehicle with snow, ice, moisture or other material on any of the windows or mirrors, which materially obstructs the driver's clear view of the highway.

(e) No person shall drive a motor vehicle when the windshield, side or rear windows are in such defective condition or repair as to materially impair the driver's view to the front, side or rear. A vehicle equipped with a side mirror on each side of the vehicle which are in conformance with Section 12-502 will be deemed to be in compliance in the event the rear window of the vehicle is materially obscured.

(f) Paragraphs (a) and (b) of this Section shall not apply to:

(1) motor vehicles manufactured prior to January 1, 1982; or

(2) to those motor vehicles properly registered in another jurisdiction.

(g) Paragraph (a) of this Section shall not apply to any motor vehicle with a window treatment, including but not limited to a window application, reflective material, nonreflective material, or tinted film, applied or affixed to the motor vehicle for the purposes set forth in item (1) or (2) before the effective date of this amendatory Act of 1997 and:

(1) that is owned and operated by a person afflicted with or suffering from a medical illness, ailment, or disease which would require that person to be shielded from the direct rays of the sun; or

(2) that is used in transporting a person when the person resides at the same address as the registered owner of the vehicle and the person is afflicted with or suffering from a medical illness, ailment or disease which would require the person to be shielded from the direct rays of the sun;

It must be certified by a physician licensed to practice medicine in Illinois that such person owning and operating or being transported in a motor vehicle is afflicted with or suffers from such illness, ailment, or disease and such certification must be carried in the motor vehicle at all times. The certification shall be legible and shall contain the date of issuance, the name, address and signature of the attending physician, and the name, address, and medical condition of the person requiring exemption. The information on the certificate for a window treatment applied or affixed before the effective date of this amendatory Act of 1997 must remain current and shall be renewed annually by the attending physician, but in no event shall a certificate issued for purposes of this subsection be valid on or after January 1, 2008. The person shall also submit a copy of the certification to the Secretary of State. The Secretary of State may forward notice of certification to law enforcement agencies.

This subsection shall not be construed to authorize window treatments applied or affixed on or after the effective date of this amendatory Act of 1997.

The exemption provided by this subsection (g) shall not apply to any motor vehicle on and after January 1, 2008.

(h) Paragraph (a) of this Section shall not apply to motor vehicle stickers or other certificates issued by State or local authorities which are required to be displayed upon motor vehicle windows to evidence compliance with requirements concerning motor vehicles.

(i) Those motor vehicles exempted under paragraph (f)(1) of this Section shall not cause their windows to be treated as described in paragraph (a) after January 1, 1993.

(j) A person found guilty of violating paragraphs (a), (b), or (i) of this Section shall be guilty of a petty offense and fined no less than $50 nor more than $500. A second or subsequent violation of paragraphs (a), (b), or (i) of this Section shall be treated as a Class C misdemeanor and the violator fined no less than $100 nor more than $500. Any person convicted under paragraphs (a), (b), or (i) of this Section shall be ordered to alter any nonconforming windows into compliance with this Section.

P.A. 76-1586, § 12-123, eff. July 1, 1970. Amended by P.A. 76-1997, § 1, eff. July 1, 1970. Renumbered § 12-503 and amended by P.A. 77-37, § 1, eff. Jan. 1, 1972. Amended by P.A. 78-462, § 1, eff. Jan. 1, 1974; P.A. 82-122, § 1, eff. Jan. 1, 1982; P.A. 85-1144, § 1, eff. July 29, 1988; P.A. 86-488, § 1, eff. Jan. 1, 1990; P.A. 87-1203, § 1, eff. Sept. 25, 1992; P.A. 88-52, § 5, eff. July 7, 1993; P.A. 90-389, § 5, eff. Jan. 1, 1998.

Formerly Ill.Rev.Stat.1991, ch. 95 ½, ¶ 12-503.

ARTICLE VI. MISCELLANEOUS REQUIREMENTS

5/12-600. § 12-600. Repealed by P.A. 90-89, § 20, eff. Jan. 1, 1998

5/12-601. Horns and warning devices

§ 12-601. Horns and warning devices.

(a) Every motor vehicle when operated upon a highway shall be equipped with a horn in good working order and capable of emitting sound audible under normal conditions from a distance of not less than 200 feet, but no horn or other warning device shall emit an unreasonable loud or harsh sound or a whistle. The driver of a motor vehicle shall when reasonably necessary to insure safe operation give audible warning with his horn but shall not otherwise use such horn when upon a highway.

(b) No vehicle shall be equipped with nor shall any person use upon a vehicle any siren, whistle, or bell, except as otherwise permitted in this section. Any authorized emergency vehicle or organ transport vehicle as defined in Chapter 1 of this Act [1] may be equipped with a siren, whistle, or bell, capable of emitting sound audible under normal conditions from a distance of not less than 500 feet, but such siren, whistle or bell, shall not be used except when such vehicle is operated in response to an emergency call or in the immediate pursuit of an actual or suspected violator of the law in either of which events the driver of such vehicle shall sound such siren, whistle or bell, when necessary to warn pedestrians and other drivers of the approach thereof.

(c) Trackless trolley coaches, as defined by Section 1-206 of this Code, and replica trolleys, as defined by Section 1-171.04 of this Code, may be equipped with a bell or bells in lieu of a horn, and may, in addition to the requirements of paragraph (a) of this Section, use a bell or bells for the purpose of indicating arrival or departure at designated stops during the hours of scheduled operation.

P.A. 76-1586, § 12-120. Renumbered § 12-601 by P.A. 77-37, § 1, eff. Jan. 1, 1972. Amended by P.A. 79-858, § 1, eff. Jan. 1, 1976; P.A. 89-345, § 10, eff. Jan. 1, 1996; P.A. 89-687, § 5, eff. June 1, 1997; P.A. 90-347, § 5, eff. Jan. 1, 1998; P.A. 90-655, § 153, eff. July 30, 1998.

Formerly Ill.Rev.Stat.1991, ch. 95 ½, ¶ 12-601.

[1] 625 ILCS 5/1-100 et seq.

P.A. 90-655, the First 1998 General Revisory Act, amended various Acts to delete obsolete text, to correct patent and technical errors, to revise cross references, to resolve multiple actions in the 89th and 90th General Assemblies and to make certain technical corrections in P.A. 89-708 through P.A. 90-566.

5/12-602. Mufflers, prevention of noise

§ 12-602. Mufflers, prevention of noise. Every motor vehicle driven or operated upon the highways of this State shall at all times be equipped with an adequate muffler or exhaust system in constant operation and properly maintained to prevent any excessive or unusual noise. No such muffler or exhaust system shall be equipped with a cutout, bypass or similar device. No person shall modify the exhaust system of a motor vehicle in a manner which will amplify or increase the noise of such vehicle above that emitted by the muffler originally installed on the vehicle, and such original muffler shall comply with all the requirements of this Section.

P.A. 76-1586, § 12-121, eff. July 1, 1970. Amended by P.A. 76-2183, § 1, eff. July 1, 1970. Resectioned in part § 12-602 by P.A. 77-37, § 1, eff. Jan. 1, 1972.

Formerly Ill.Rev.Stat.1991, ch. 95 ½, ¶ 12-602.

5/12-603. Seat safety belts

§ 12-603. Seat safety belts.

(a) No person shall sell any 1965 or later model motor vehicle of the first division unless the front seat of such motor vehicle is equipped with 2 sets of seat safety belts. Motorcycles are exempted from the provisions of this Section.

(b) No person shall operate any 1965 or later model motor vehicle of the first division that is titled or licensed by the Secretary of State unless the front seat of such motor vehicle is equipped with 2 sets of seat safety belts.

(b-5) No person under the age of 18 years shall operate any motor vehicle, except a motor driven cycle or motorcycle, with more than one passenger in the front seat of the motor vehicle and no more passengers in the back seats than the number of available seat safety belts, except that each driver under the age of 18 years operating a second division vehicle having a gross vehicle weight rating of 8,000 pounds or less that contains only a front seat may operate the vehicle with more than one passenger in the front seat, provided that each passenger is wearing a properly adjusted and fastened seat safety belt.

(c) (Blank).

(d) The Department shall establish performance specifications for seat safety belts and for the attachment and installation thereof.

P.A. 76-1586, § 12-127, eff. July 1, 1970. Amended by P.A. 76-2185, § 1, eff. July 1, 1970. Renumbered § 12-603 by P.A. 77-37, § 1, eff. Jan. 1, 1972. Amended by P.A. 78-748, § 1, eff. Jan. 1, 1974; P.A. 89-120, § 10, eff. July 7, 1995; P.A. 90-89, § 15, eff. Jan. 1, 1998; P.A. 90-369, § 5, eff. Jan. 1, 1998; P.A. 90-655, § 153, eff. July 30, 1998.

Formerly Ill.Rev.Stat.1991, ch. 95 ½, ¶ 12-603.

P.A. 90-655, the First 1998 General Revisory Act, amended various Acts to delete obsolete text, to correct patent and technical errors, to revise cross references, to resolve multiple actions in the 89th and 90th General Assemblies and to make certain technical corrections in P.A. 89-708 through P.A. 90-566.

5/12-603.1. Driver and passenger required to use safety belts, exceptions and penalty

§ 12-603.1. Driver and passenger required to use safety belts, exceptions and penalty.

(a) Each driver and front seat passenger of a motor vehicle operated on a street or highway in this State shall wear a properly adjusted and fastened seat safety belt; except that, a child less than 6 years of age shall be protected as required pursuant to the Child Passenger Protection Act.[1] Each driver under the age of 18 years and each of the driver's passengers under the age of 18 years of a motor vehicle operated on a street or highway in this State shall wear a properly adjusted and fastened seat safety belt. Each driver of a motor vehicle transporting a child 6 years of age or more, but less than 16 years of age, in the front seat of the motor vehicle shall secure the child in a properly adjusted and fastened seat safety belt.

(b) Paragraph (a) shall not apply to any of the following:

1. A driver or passenger frequently stopping and leaving the vehicle or delivering property from the vehicle, if the speed of the vehicle between stops does not exceed 15 miles per hour.

2. A driver or passenger possessing a written statement from a physician that such person is unable, for medical or physical reasons, to wear a seat safety belt.

3. A driver or passenger possessing an official certificate or license endorsement issued by the appropriate agency in another state or country indicating that the driver is unable for medical, physical, or other valid reasons to wear a seat safety belt.

4. A driver operating a motor vehicle in reverse.

5. A motor vehicle with a model year prior to 1965.

6. A motorcycle or motor driven cycle.

7. A motorized pedalcycle.

8. A motor vehicle which is not required to be equipped with seat safety belts under federal law.

9. A motor vehicle operated by a rural letter carrier of the United States postal service while performing duties as a rural letter carrier.

(c) Failure to wear a seat safety belt in violation of this Section shall not be considered evidence of negligence, shall not limit the liability of an insurer, and shall not diminish any recovery for damages arising out of the ownership, maintenance, or operation of a motor vehicle.

(d) A violation of this Section shall be a petty offense and subject to a fine not to exceed $25.

(e) No motor vehicle, or driver or passenger of such vehicle, shall be stopped or searched by any law enforcement officer solely on the basis of a violation or suspected violation of this Section.

P.A. 76-1586, § 12-603.1, added by P.A. 83-1507, § 1, eff. July 1, 1985. Amended by P.A. 85-291, § 2, eff. Jan. 1, 1988; P.A. 90-369, § 5, eff. Jan. 1, 1998.

Formerly Ill.Rev.Stat.1991, ch. 95 ½, ¶ 12-603.1.

1 625 ILCS 25/1 et seq.

5/12-604. Television receivers

§ 12-604. Television receivers.

(a) No motor vehicle operated on the highways of this State shall be equipped with television broadcast receiver equipment so located that the viewer or screen is visible from the driver's seat.

(b) A visual display device permitted under this Section shall be attached to the vehicle in a manner that meets all applicable federal motor vehicle dash safety standards.

(c) This section does not prohibit the use of television-type receiving equipment used exclusively for safety or traffic engineering studies.

P.A. 76-1586, § 12-138, eff. July 1, 1970. Renumbered § 12-604 by P.A. 77-37, § 1, eff. Jan. 1, 1972. Amended by P.A. 77-1344, § 1, eff. Aug. 27, 1971; P.A. 77-2829, § 40, eff. Dec. 22, 1972; P.A. 78-255, § 61, eff. Oct. 1, 1973; P.A. 88-415, § 10, eff. Aug. 20, 1993.

Formerly Ill.Rev.Stat.1991, ch. 95 ½, ¶ 12-604.

5/12-605. Taxicabs—Bullet proof shields

§ 12-605. Taxicabs—Bullet proof shields. In municipalities with 1,000,000 or more population, any taxicab manufactured, owned or operated after September 1, 1970, and regularly operated in such a municipality must have a bullet proof shield completely separating the driver's seat from the back seat.

P.A. 76-1586, § 12-605, added by P.A. 77-37, § 1, eff. Jan. 1, 1972. Amended by P.A. 77-2720, § 1, eff. Jan. 1, 1973; P.A. 78-255, § 61, eff. Oct. 1, 1973; P.A. 80-911, § 1, eff. Oct. 1, 1977.

Formerly Ill.Rev.Stat.1991, ch. 95 ½, ¶ 12-605.

5/12-605.1. Buses; two-way radios

§ 12-605.1. (a) On or after two years from the effective date of this Act, no bus which was first placed in service after July 1, 1969, or which has undergone complete renovation and restoration since July 1, 1969 shall be operated as a part of any local mass transit system in this State unless the vehicle is equipped with radio facilities permitting two-way vocal communications between the bus and a local transit control office. This Section does not apply to buses used for charter service, school buses, intrastate carriers while not providing transportation services pursuant to contracts with any local mass transit system, private non-profit carriers receiving assistance under Section 16(b)2 of the Urban Mass Transportation Act of 1964 as amended,[1] carriers receiving assistance pursuant to Article III of the Downstate Public Transportation Act,[2] or interstate carriers and buses owned by a private local mass transit system;

(b) A local mass transit system operating a bus not in compliance with the requirements of subsection (a) shall not be in violation of that subsection, provided that the bus is brought into compliance within a reasonable time (in no event to exceed 1 week) following written notification to the mass transit system of the fact that the bus is not in compliance.

P.A. 76-1586, § 12-605.1, added by P.A. 81-1184, § 1, eff. July 1, 1980. Amended by P.A. 90-89, § 15, eff. Jan. 1, 1998.

Formerly Ill.Rev.Stat.1991, ch. 95 ½, ¶ 12-605.1.

1 49 U.S.C.A. § 1601 et seq. (repealed; see, now, 49 U.S.C.A. § 5301 et seq.)

2 30 ILCS 740/3-1 et seq.

5/12-605.2. Consumption of food or drink on bus

§ 12-605.2. Beginning 30 days after the effective date of this amendatory Act of 1988, no person shall consume any food or drink, excluding any medicine, upon any bus operated as a part of any local mass transit system in this State. This Section does not apply to buses used for charter service, school buses, intrastate carriers while not providing transportation services pursuant to contracts with any local mass transit system, and private non-profit carriers.

Persons found guilty of violating this Section shall be fined $100.

P.A. 76-1586, § 12-605.2, added by P.A. 85-1364, § 1, eff. Jan. 1, 1989. Amended by P.A. 90-89, § 15, eff. Jan. 1, 1998.

Formerly Ill.Rev.Stat.1991, ch. 95 ½, ¶ 12-605.2.

5/12-606. Tow-trucks; identification; equipment; insurance

§ 12-606. Tow-trucks; identification; equipment; insurance.

(a) Every tow-truck, except those owned by governmental agencies, shall have displayed on each side thereof, a sign with letters not less than 2 inches in height, contrasting in color to that of the background, stating the full legal name, complete address (including street address and city), and telephone number of the owner or operator thereof. This information shall be permanently affixed to the sides of the tow truck.

(b) Every tow-truck shall be equipped with:

(1) One or more brooms and shovels;

(2) One or more trash cans of at least 5 gallon capacity; and

(3) One fire extinguisher. This extinguisher shall be either:

(i) of the dry chemical or carbon dioxide type with an aggregate rating of at least 4-B, C units, and bearing the approval of a laboratory qualified by the Division of Fire Prevention for this purpose; or

(ii) One that meets the requirements of the Federal Motor Carrier Safety Regulations of the United States Department of Transportation for fire extinguishers on commercial motor vehicles.

(c) Every owner or operator and driver of a tow-truck shall comply with Section 11-1413 of this Act and shall remove or cause to be removed all glass and debris, except any (i) hazardous substance as defined in Section 3.215 of the Environmental Protection Act,[1] (ii) hazardous waste as defined in Section 3.220 of the Environmental Protection Act,[2] and (iii) medical samples or waste, including but not limited to any blood samples, used syringes, other used medical supplies, or any other potentially infectious medical waste as defined in Section 3.360 of the Environmental Protection Act,[3] deposited upon any street or highway by the disabled vehicle being serviced, and shall in addition, spread dirt or sand or oil absorbent upon that portion of any street or highway where oil or grease has been deposited by the disabled vehicle being serviced.

(d) Every tow-truck operator shall in addition file an indemnity bond, insurance policy, or other proof of insurance in a form to be prescribed by the Secretary for: garagekeepers liability insurance, in an amount no less than a combined single limit of $500,000, and truck (auto) liability insurance in an amount no less than a combined single limit of $500,000, on hook coverage or garagekeepers coverage in an amount of no less than $25,000 which shall indemnify or insure the tow-truck operator for the following:

(1) Bodily injury or damage to the property of others.

(2) Damage to any vehicle towed by the tower.

(3) In case of theft, loss of, or damage to any vehicle stored, garagekeepers legal liability coverage in an amount of no less than $25,000.

(4) In case of injury to or occupational illness of the tow truck driver or helper, workers compensation insurance meeting the minimum requirements of the Workers' Compensation Act.[4]

Any such bond or policy shall be issued only by a bonding or insuring firm authorized to do business as such in the State of Illinois, and a certificate of such bond or policy shall be carried in the cab of each tow-truck.

(e) The bond or policy required in subsection (d) shall provide that the insurance carrier may cancel it by serving previous notice, as required by Sections 143.14 and 143.16 of the Illinois Insurance Code,[5] in writing, either personally or by registered mail, upon the owner or operator of the motor vehicle and upon the Secretary of State. Whenever any such bond or policy shall be so cancelled, the Secretary of State shall mark the policy "Cancelled" and shall require such owner or operator either to furnish a new bond or policy, in accordance with this Act.

P.A. 76-1586, § 12-606, added by P.A. 78-324, § 1, eff. Jan. 1, 1974. Amended by P.A. 83-1473, § 1, eff. Jan. 1, 1985; P.A. 85-1396, § 2, eff. Sept. 2, 1988; P.A. 86-444, § 1, eff. Jan. 1, 1990; P.A. 86-563, § 1, eff. Jan. 1, 1990; P.A. 86-1028, Art. II, § 2-44, eff. Feb. 5, 1990; P.A. 87-190, § 1, eff. Jan. 1, 1992; P.A. 87-757, § 3, eff. Oct. 3, 1991; P.A. 87-895, Art. 2, § 2-45, eff. Aug. 14, 1992; P.A. 88-415, § 10, eff. Aug. 20, 1993; P.A. 88-670, Art. 3, § 3-80, eff. Dec. 2, 1994; P.A. 89-433, § 5, eff. Dec. 15, 1995; P.A. 92-574, § 70, eff. June 26, 2002.

Formerly Ill.Rev.Stat.1991, ch. 95 ½, ¶ 12-606.

[1] 415 ILCS 5/3.215.

[2] 415 ILCS 5/3.220.

[3] 415 ILCS 5/3.360.

[4] 820 ILCS 305/1 et seq.

[5] 215 ILCS 5561143.14 and 5/143.16.

Another § 12-606 was added by P.A. 78-436; see § 12-608, post.

5/12-607. Suspension System

§ 12-607. Suspension System.

(a) It shall be unlawful to operate a motor vehicle on any highway of this State when the suspension system has been modified from the original manufactured design by lifting the body from the chassis in excess of 3 inches or to cause the horizontal line from the front to the rear bumper to vary over 3 inches in height when measured from a level surface of the highway to the lower edge of the bumper, except that it is unlawful to operate a street rod or custom vehicle when the suspension system has been modified from the original manufactured design so that the horizontal line from the front to the rear bumper varies over 7 inches in height when measured from a level surface of the highway to the lower edge of the bumper.

(b) Nothing in this Section shall prevent the installation of manufactured heavy duty equipment to include shock absorbers and overload springs, nor shall anything contained in this Section prevent a person to operate a motor vehicle on any highway of this State with normal wear of the suspension system if normal wear does not affect the control or safe operation of the vehicle. This Section shall not apply to motor vehicles designed or modified primarily for off-highway racing purposes while such vehicles are in tow or to motorcycles or motor driven cycles.

P.A. 76-1586, § 12-607, added by P.A. 78-436, § 1, eff. Jan. 1, 1974. Amended by P.A. 92-668, § 5, eff. Jan. 1, 2003.

Formerly Ill.Rev.Stat.1991, ch. 95 ½, ¶ 12-607.

5/12-607.1. Frame and floor height

§ 12-607.1. Frame and floor height. (a) No person shall operate upon a highway a first division vehicle which has a clearance between the frame and ground in excess of 22 inches. The lowest portion of the body floor shall not be more than 4 inches above the top of the frame. No such vehicle shall be modified to cause the vehicle body or chassis to come in contact with the ground, expose the fuel tank to damage from collision or cause the wheels to come in contact with the body under normal operation.

(b) No person shall operate upon a highway a second division vehicle which has a clearance between the frame and ground which is in excess of the limits specified within this subsection for its gross vehicle weight rating (GVWR) category. For the purpose of this section, GVWR means the manufacturer's gross vehicle weight rating whether or not the vehicle is modified by the use of parts not originally installed by the manufacturer. The stacking or attaching of vehicle frames (one frame on top of or beneath another frame) is prohibited. No portion of the body floor shall be raised above the frame.

(1) The frame height of second division vehicles, whose GVWR is under 4,500 pounds, shall be no more than 24 inches.

(2) The frame height of second division vehicles, whose GVWR is more than 4,500 pounds and less than 7,500 pounds, shall be no more than 26 inches.

(3) The frame height of second division vehicles, whose GVWR is more than 7,500 pounds and less than 10,000 pounds, shall be no more than 28 inches.

(c) Under subsections (a) or (b) of this Section, measurements shall be made when a vehicle is unladen on a level surface at the lowest point from the bottom of the original vehicle manufacturer's longitudinal frame rail between the front axle and second axle on the vehicle.

(d) This Section does not apply to specially designed or modified motor vehicles when operated off the highways. Such motor vehicles may be transported upon the highway only by use of a trailer or semitrailer. The specially designed or modified motor vehicle may also be transported upon another vehicle, providing that the entire weight of the specifically designed or modified vehicle is resting upon the transporting vehicle.

(e) Any violation of this Section is a Class C misdemeanor. A second conviction under this Section shall be punished with a fine of not less than $500. An officer making an arrest under this Section shall order the vehicle driver to remove the vehicle from the highway. A person convicted under this Section shall be ordered to bring his vehicle into compliance with this Section.

P.A. 76-1586, § 12-607.1, added by P.A. 86-498, § 1, eff. Jan. 1, 1990. Amended by P.A. 90-89, § 15, eff. Jan. 1, 1998.

Formerly Ill.Rev.Stat.1991, ch. 95 ½, ¶ 12-607.1.

5/12-608. Bumpers

§ 12-608. Bumpers.

(a) It shall be unlawful to operate any motor vehicle with a gross vehicle weight rating of 9,000 pounds or less or any motor vehicle registered as a recreational vehicle under this Code on any highway of this State unless such motor vehicle is equipped with both a front and rear bumper.

Except as indicated below, maximum bumper heights of such motor vehicles shall be determined by weight category of gross vehicle weight rating (GVWR) measured from a level surface to the highest point of the bottom of the bumper when the vehicle is unloaded and the tires are inflated to the manufacturer's recommended pressure.

Maximum bumper heights are as follows:

	Maximum Front Bumper height	Maximum Rear Bumper Height
All motor vehicles of the first division except multipurpose passenger vehicles:	22 inches	22 inches
Multipurpose passenger vehicles and all other motor vehicles:		
4,500 lbs. and under GVWR	24 inches	26 inches
4,501 lbs. through 7,500 lbs. GVWR	27 inches	29 inches
7,501 lbs. through 9,000 lbs. GVWR	28 inches	30 inches

For any vehicle with bumpers or attaching components which have been modified or altered from the original manufacturer's design in order to conform with the maximum bumper requirements of this section, the bumper height shall be measured from a level surface to the bottom of the vehicle frame rail at the most forward and rearward points of the frame rail. The bumper on any vehicle so modified or altered shall be at least 4.5 inches in vertical height and extend no less than the width of the respective wheel tracks outermost distance.

However, nothing in this Section shall prevent the installation of bumper guards.

(b) This Section shall not apply to street rods, custom vehicles, motor vehicles designed or modified primarily for off-highway purposes while such vehicles are in tow or to motorcycles or motor driven cycles, nor to motor vehicles registered as antique vehicles when the original design of such antique vehicles did not include bumpers. The provisions of this Section shall not apply to any motor vehicle driven during the first 1000 recorded miles of that vehicle, when such vehicle is owned or operated by a manufacturer, dealer or transporter displaying a special plate or plates as described in Chapter 3 of this Code while such vehicle is (1) being delivered from the manufacturing or assembly plant directly to the purchasing dealer or distributor, or from one dealership or distributor to another; (2) being moved by the most direct route from one location to another for the purpose of installing special bodies or equipment; or (3) being driven for purposes of demonstration by a prospective buyer with the dealer or his agent present in the cab of the vehicle during the demonstration.

The dealer shall, prior to the receipt of any deposit made or any contract signed by the buyer to secure the purchase of a vehicle, inform such buyer, by written statement signed by the purchaser to indicate acknowledgement of the contents thereof, of the legal requirements of this Section regarding front and rear bumpers if such vehicle is not to be equipped with bumpers at the time of delivery.

(c) Any violation of this Section is a Class C misdemeanor. A second conviction under this Section shall be punishable with a fine of not less than $500. An officer making an arrest under this Section shall order the vehicle driver to remove the vehicle from the highway. A person convicted under this Section shall be ordered to bring his vehicle into compliance with this Section.

P.A. 76-1586, § 12-606, added by P.A. 78-436, § 1, eff. Jan. 1, 1974. Renumbered § 12-608 and amended by P.A. 78-1297, § 30, eff. March 4, 1975. Amended by P.A. 83-838, § 1, eff. Jan. 1, 1984; P.A. 83-1386, § 1, eff. Jan. 1, 1985; P.A. 86-498, § 1, eff. Jan. 1, 1990; P.A. 92-668, § 5, eff. Jan. 1, 2003.

Formerly Ill.Rev.Stat.1991, ch. 95 ½, ¶ 12-608.

5/12-609. Disposal of motor vehicles bearing police markings

§ 12-609. No official or employee of the State or any political subdivision thereof shall sell, trade or otherwise dispose of any motor vehicle bearing equipment, markings, or other indicia of police authority unless, prior to delivery of the vehicle, the equipment and markings have been sufficiently altered or obliterated to remove the appearance of such authority.

P.A. 76-1586, § 12-609, added by P.A. 79-544, § 1, eff. Oct. 1, 1975. Amended by P.A. 79-1454, § 44, eff. Aug. 31, 1976.

Formerly Ill.Rev.Stat.1991, ch. 95 ½, ¶ 12-609.

Another § 12-609 was renumbered as § 12-610 by P.A. 85-273, § 1, eff. Jan. 1, 1988.

5/12-610. Headset receivers

§ 12-610. Headset receivers.

(a) Except as provided under Section 11-1403.3, no driver of a motor vehicle on the highways of this State shall wear headset receivers while driving.

(b) This Section does not prohibit the use of a headset type receiving equipment used exclusively for safety or traffic engineering studies, by law enforcement personnel on duty, or emergency medical services and fire service personnel.

(c) This Section does not prohibit the use of any single sided headset type receiving and transmitting equipment designed to be used in or on one ear which is used exclusively for providing two-way radio vocal communications by an individual in possession of a current and valid novice class or higher amateur radio license issued by the Federal Communications Commission and an amateur radio operator special registration plate issued under Section 3-607 of this Code.

(d) This Section does not prohibit the use of a single-sided headset or earpiece with a cellular or other mobile telephone.

P.A. 76-1586, § 12-609, added by P.A. 80-361, § 1, eff. Aug. 26, 1977. Renumbered § 12-610 and amended by P.A. 85-273, § 1, eff. Jan. 1, 1988; P.A. 85-293, Art. III, § 21, eff. Sept. 8, 1987. Amended by P.A. 86-1193, § 1, eff. Aug. 29, 1990; P.A. 89-551, § 5, eff. Jan. 1, 1997; P.A. 92-152, § 5, eff. July 25, 2001.

Formerly Ill.Rev.Stat.1991, ch. 95 ½, ¶ 12-610.

5/12-610.5. Tinted registration plate covers

§ 12-610.5. Tinted registration plate covers.

(a) It shall be unlawful to operate any motor vehicle that is equipped with tinted plastic or tinted glass registration plate covers.

(b) A violation of this Section or a similar provision of a local ordinance shall be an offense against laws and ordinances regulating the movement of traffic.

P.A. 76-1586, § 12-610.5, added by P.A. 89-245, § 5, eff. Jan. 1, 1996.

5/12-611. Sound amplification systems

§ 12-611. No driver of any motor vehicle within this State shall operate or permit operation of any sound amplification system which can be heard outside the vehicle from 75 or more feet when the vehicle is being operated upon a highway, unless such system is being operated to request assistance or warn of a hazardous situation.

This Section does not apply to authorized emergency vehicles.

Any violation of the provisions of this Section shall be a petty offense punishable by a fine not to exceed $50.

P.A. 76-1586, § 12-611, added by P.A. 86-1240, § 1, eff. Jan. 1, 1991. Amended by P.A. 91-919, § 5, eff. Jan. 1, 2001.

Formerly Ill.Rev.Stat.1991, ch. 95 ½, ¶ 12-611.

Validity

The Supreme Court of Illinois has held that this section violates the First Amendment's free speech guarantee in the case of People v. Jones, 1999, 188 Ill.2d 352, 242 Ill.Dec. 267, 721 N.E.2d 546. P.A. 91-919 amended this section to delete the exception for vehicles engaged in advertising.

5/12-612. False or secret compartment in a motor vehicle

§ 12-612. False or secret compartment in a motor vehicle.

(a) Offenses. It is unlawful for any person to own or operate any motor vehicle he or she knows to contain a false or secret compartment. It is unlawful for any person to knowingly install, create, build, or fabricate in any motor vehicle a false or secret compartment.

(b) Definitions. For purposes of this Section, a "false or secret compartment" means any enclosure that is intended and designed to be used to conceal, hide, and prevent discovery by law enforcement officers of the false or secret compartment, or its contents, and which is integrated into a vehicle. For purpose of this Section, a person's intention to use a false or secret compartment to conceal the contents of the compartment from a law enforcement officer may be inferred from factors including, but not limited to, the discovery of a person, firearm, controlled substance, or other contraband within the false or secret compartment, or from the discovery of evidence of the previous placement of a person, firearm, controlled substance, or other contraband within the false or secret compartment.

(c) Forfeiture. Any motor vehicle containing a false or secret compartment, as well as any items within that compartment, shall be subject to seizure by the Department of State Police or by any municipal or other local law enforcement agency within whose jurisdiction that property is found as provided in Sections 36-1 and 36-2 of the Criminal Code of 1961 (720 ILCS 5/36-1 and 5/36-2).

(d) Sentence. A violation of this Section is a Class C misdemeanor.

P.A. 76-1586, § 12-612, added by P.A. 91-359, § 5, eff. Jan. 1, 2000.

ARTICLE VII. SPECIAL REQUIREMENTS FOR VEHICLES OF THE SECOND DIVISION

Section

5/12–701. Tractors, traction engines and motor trucks—Operation on highways—Turning on highways during farming operations—Violations

§ 12–701. Tractors, traction engines and motor trucks—Operation on highways—Turning on highways during farming operations—Violations. No tractor, traction engine, motor truck or other similar vehicle shall be operated across, over or along any public highway of this State which has been oil-treated, if any such vehicle has on the periphery of any of the road wheels any block, stud, flange, cleat, ridge, lug, or any projection of metal or wood which projects radially beyond the tread or traffic surface of the tire; except that this prohibition shall not apply to tractors or traction engines equipped with what is known as crawler type tractors, when the same does not contain any projections of any kind likely to injure the surface of the road, nor to tractors, traction engines and similar vehicles which have upon their road wheels V-shaped, diagonal or other cleats arranged in such a manner as to be continuously in contact with the road surface. In no event shall the oil mat surface of any oil-treated public road be used as an area or space for turning any tractor or other farm machinery in carrying on or performing any farming operations upon the adjacent land. Provided, that nothing in this Section contained shall prohibit the operation of tractors, traction engines or motor trucks across any oil-treated road in order to reach adjacent lands or the operation of any such vehicles upon the treated portion of such oil-treated roads if there is no untreated portion thereof over which they may be operated or the operation of any such vehicles on oil-treated roads if in passing along said road they travel over the portion of said road which does not constitute the oil mat surface created by said oil treatment or the use of flexible tire chains on any tractor, traction engine, motor truck or other similar vehicle being operated upon any such oil-treated road.

It is unlawful for any person to operate any tractor, traction engine, motor truck or other similar vehicle over and along any public highway of this State, which has been oil-treated, in violation of the provisions of this Section.

P.A. 76–1586, § 12–125, eff. July 1, 1970. Renumbered § 12–701 by P.A. 77–37, § 1, eff. Jan. 1, 1972. Amended by P.A. 77–2720, § 1, eff. Jan. 1, 1973; P.A. 78–255, § 61, eff. Oct. 1, 1973; P.A. 80–911, § 1, eff. Oct. 1, 1977.

Formerly Ill.Rev.Stat.1991, ch. 95 ½, ¶ 12–701.

5/12–702. Certain vehicles to carry flares or other warning devices

§ 12–702. Certain vehicles to carry flares or other warning devices.

(a) No person shall operate any motor vehicle of the second division weighing more than 8,000 pounds or any vehicle of the second division weighing 8,000 pounds or less towing a trailer or any motor vehicle towing a house trailer upon any highway outside an urban district at any time unless there is carried in such vehicle the following equipment, except as provided in paragraph (b) of this Section:

1. At least 3 liquid-burning flares, or 3 red electric lanterns or 3 portable red emergency reflectors, each of which is capable of being seen and distinguished at a distance of not less than 500 feet when lighted lamps are required, provided that emergency reflectors meeting the requirements of Federal Motor Vehicle Safety Standard No. 125 shall be deemed acceptable as regards visibility and color; and

2. At least 3 red-burning 15–minute fusees unless red electric lanterns or portable red emergency reflectors are carried; and

3. At least 2 red-cloth flags, not less than 12 inches square, with standards to support flags or in lieu thereof, 2 portable emergency reflectors meeting the requirements of Federal Motor Vehicle Safety Standard No. 125.

(b) No person shall operate at the time and under the conditions stated in paragraph (a) of this Section any motor vehicle used for the transportation of explosives, any cargo tank truck used for the transportation of flammable liquids or compressed gases or any motor vehicle using compressed gas as a fuel unless there is carried in such vehicle 3 red electric lanterns or 3 portable red emergency reflectors meeting the requirements of paragraph (a) of this Section, and such vehicle shall not carry any flares, fusees or signals produced by flame.

(c) Whenever any motor vehicle of the second division weighing more than 8,000 pounds or any vehicle of the second division weighing 8,000 pounds or less towing a trailer or any motor vehicle towing a house trailer is disabled upon the roadway of any highway or the shoulder thereof outside an urban district or on any controlled access highway within an urban district at any time when lighted lamps are required, the driver of such vehicle shall display the following warning devices upon the highway during the time the vehicle is so disabled, except as provided in paragraph (d) of this Section:

1. A lighted fusee, a lighted red electric lantern or a portable red emergency reflector shall be immediately placed at the traffic side of the vehicle in the direction of the nearest approaching traffic. However, the driver of such vehicle upon learning of the disability may simultaneously flash the 2 front and 2 rear turn signals as a vehicular traffic warning and continue such flashing until the portable signals have been placed as required by this Section and during the time such portable emergency signals are being picked up for storage prior to the movement of the vehicle.

2. As soon thereafter as possible, but in any event within the burning period of the fusee (15 minutes), the driver shall place 3 liquid-burning flares, or 3 lighted red electric lanterns or 3 portable red emergency reflectors on

the roadway or shoulder of the highway in the following order:

One approximately 100 feet from the disabled vehicle in the center of the lane or shoulder occupied by such vehicle and toward traffic approaching in that lane; and

One approximately 100 feet in the opposite direction from the disabled vehicle and in the center of the traffic lane or shoulder occupied by such vehicle; and

One at the traffic side of the disabled vehicle not less than 10 feet to the rear or forward thereof in the direction of the nearest approaching traffic. If a lighted red electric lantern or a portable red emergency reflector has been placed at the traffic side of the vehicle in accordance with paragraph (c)(1) of this Section, it may be used for this purpose.

(d) Whenever any vehicle referred to in this Section is disabled within 500 feet of a curve, hill crest or other obstruction to view, the warning signal in that direction shall be so placed as to afford ample warning to other users of the highway, but in no case less than 100 feet nor more than 500 feet from the disabled vehicle.

(e) Whenever any vehicle of a type referred to in this Section is disabled upon any roadway or shoulder of a divided highway during the time that lighted lamps are required, the appropriate warning devices prescribed in paragraph (a)(1) and (2) of this Section shall be placed as follows:

One at a distance of approximately 200 feet from the vehicle in the center of the lane or shoulder occupied by the stopped vehicle and in the direction of traffic approaching in that lane; and

One at a distance of approximately 100 feet from the vehicle in the center of the lane or shoulder occupied by the vehicle and in the direction of traffic approaching in that lane; and

One at the traffic side of the vehicle and approximately 10 feet from the vehicle in the direction of the nearest approaching traffic.

(f) Whenever any vehicle of a type referred to in this Section is disabled upon the roadway of any highway or the shoulder thereof outside an urban district or on any controlled access highway within an urban district at any time when the display of fusees, flares, red electric lanterns or portable red emergency reflectors are not required, the driver of the vehicle shall display 2 red-cloth flags or 2 portable emergency reflectors meeting the requirements of Federal Motor Vehicle Safety Standard No. 125 upon the roadway or shoulder in the lane of traffic occupied by the disabled vehicle in the following order:

One at a distance of approximately 100 feet in advance of the vehicle; and

One at a distance of approximately 100 feet in the rear of the vehicle.

(g) Whenever any vehicle of a type referred to in this Section is disabled upon any roadway or shoulder of a divided highway during the time that lighted lamps are not required, the driver of such vehicle shall display 2 red-cloth flags or 2 portable emergency reflectors meeting the requirements of Federal Motor Vehicle Safety Standard No. 125 upon the roadway or shoulder in the center of the lane of traffic occupied by the disabled vehicle in the following order:

One at a distance of approximately 200 feet to the rear of the vehicle; and

One at a distance of approximately 100 feet to the rear of the vehicle.

(h) Whenever any motor vehicle used for the transportation of explosives, or any cargo tank truck used for the transportation of any flammable liquid or compressed flammable gas or any motor vehicle using compressed gas as a fuel is disabled upon a highway of this State at any time or place mentioned in paragraph (c) of this Section, the driver of such vehicle shall immediately display 3 red electric lanterns or portable red emergency reflectors placed in the following order:

One at the traffic side of the vehicle and approximately 10 feet from the vehicle in the direction of the nearest approaching traffic; and

One at a distance of approximately 100 feet to the front of the disabled vehicle in the center of the lane of traffic or shoulder occupied by such vehicle; and

One at a distance of approximately 100 feet to the rear of the disabled vehicle in the center of the lane of traffic or shoulder occupied by such vehicle. Flares, fusees or signals produced by flame shall not be used as warning devices for disabled vehicles of the type mentioned in this paragraph.

(i) The flares, fusees, red electric lanterns, portable red emergency reflectors and flags to be displayed as required in this Section shall conform with the requirements of paragraphs (a) and (b) of this Section applicable thereto.

P.A. 76-1586, § 12-128, eff. July 1, 1970. Amended by P.A. 76-1725, § 1, eff. July 1, 1970; P.A. 76-2187, § 1, eff. July 1, 1970. Renumbered § 12-702 by P.A. 77-37, § 1, eff. Jan. 1, 1972. Amended by P.A. 78-280, § 1, eff. Jan. 1, 1974; P.A. 78-693, § 1, eff. Jan. 1, 1974; P.A. 78-1297, § 30, eff. March 4, 1975; P.A. 89-687, § 5, eff. June 1, 1997.

Formerly Ill.Rev.Stat.1991, ch. 95 ½, ¶ 12-702.

5/12-703. Road oil vehicles—Dripping on certain highways forbidden

§ 12-703. Road oil vehicles—Dripping on certain highways forbidden. No person shall operate, on a durable all-weather highway of a type other than gravel or crushed stone, any vehicle used for the purpose of applying road oil, liquid asphalt or similar material to road surfaces unless such vehicle is so equipped as to absolutely prevent such material from dripping on such highway, nor shall such material be allowed to drip on any such highway.

P.A. 76-1586, § 12-129, eff. July 1, 1970. Renumbered § 12-703 by P.A. 77-37, § 1, eff. Jan. 1, 1972.

Formerly Ill.Rev.Stat.1991, ch. 95 ½, ¶ 12-703.

5/12-704, 5/12-704.1. §§ 12-704, 12-704.1. Repealed by P.A. 88-415, § 15, eff. Aug. 20, 1993

5/12-704.3. Motor vehicles using alternate fuels; markings

§ 12-704.3. Motor vehicles using alternate fuels; markings. Notwithstanding any other regulation or requirement, every motor vehicle using liquefied petroleum gas or compressed natural gas must be marked in accordance with guidelines established by the National Fire Protection Association's (NFPA) standards for the Storage and Handling of Liquefied Petroleum Gases and for Compressed Natural Gas Vehicular Fuel Systems and published by that body as NFPA 58 and NFPA 52 dated February 10, 1992 and August 14, 1992, respectively.

The sign or decal shall be maintained in good legible condition. A sign or decal that is deteriorated or defaced so as to impair its legibility, quick recognition, or meaning shall be replaced by a new sign or decal.

P.A. 76–1586, § 12–704.3, added by P.A. 83–1027, § 2, eff. July 1, 1984. Amended by P.A. 88–415, § 10, eff. Aug. 20, 1993.

Formerly Ill.Rev.Stat.1991, ch. 95 ½, ¶ 12–704.3.

5/12–705. § 12–705. Repealed by P.A. 88–415, § 15, eff. Aug. 20, 1993

5/12–706. Fire apparatus—Safety belts

§ 12–706. Fire apparatus—Safety belts. No fire apparatus equipped to carry firemen on the outside of such vehicle on the sides, or rear, or both, shall be operated without first installing on the fire apparatus on the sides and rear thereof a sufficient number of safety belts and safety belt connections to protect the maximum number of firemen who can occupy the sides and rear of such apparatus while responding to alarms of fire. The municipality shall cause inspection of such safety equipment at least semi-annually.

P.A. 76–1586, § 12–139, added by P.A. 76–2190, § 1, eff. July 1, 1970. Renumbered § 12–706 by P.A. 77–37, § 1, eff. Jan. 1, 1972.

Formerly Ill.Rev.Stat.1991, ch. 95 ½, ¶ 12–706.

5/12–707. Vehicle passenger capacity

§ 12–707. Vehicle passenger capacity. No school bus, commuter van or motor vehicle owned by or used for hire by and in connection with the operation of private or public schools, day camps, summer camps or nursery schools or in charter operations, and no commuter van or passenger car used for a for-profit ridesharing arrangement, shall be operated if it is occupied by more passengers than recommended by the manufacturer thereof if the vehicle is manufactured as a passenger vehicle; if the vehicle is manufactured for use other than passenger, then it shall not accommodate more passengers than provided for by the manufacturer in passenger vehicles of like style or rating.

P.A. 76–1586, § 12–133, eff. July 1, 1970. Renumbered § 12–707 by P.A. 77–37, § 1, eff. Jan. 1, 1972. Amended by P.A. 78–499, § 1, eff. Aug. 30, 1973; P.A. 80–529, § 1, eff. Jan. 1, 1979; P.A. 81–509, § 1, eff. Jan. 1, 1980; P.A. 83–1091, § 1, eff. July 1, 1984.

Formerly Ill.Rev.Stat.1991, ch. 95 ½, ¶ 12–707.

5/12–707.01. Liability insurance

§ 12–707.01. Liability insurance. No school bus, commuter van or motor vehicle owned by or used for hire by and in connection with the operation of private or public schools, day camps, summer camps or nursery schools, and no commuter van or passenger car used for a for-profit ridesharing arrangement, shall be operated for such purposes unless the owner thereof shall carry a minimum of personal injury liability insurance in the amount of $25,000 for any one person in any one accident, and subject to the limit for one person, $100,000 for two or more persons injured by reason of the operation of the vehicle in any one accident.

P.A. 76–1586, § 12–707.01, added by P.A. 81–509, § 1, eff. Jan. 1, 1980. Amended by P.A. 83–1091, § 1, eff. July 1, 1984.

Formerly Ill.Rev.Stat.1991, ch. 95 ½, ¶ 12–707.01.

5/12–708. Operator protective frames on tractor-mower combinations

§ 12–708. Operator protective frames on tractor-mower combinations. No tractor unit over 16 engine horsepower designed for mowing or tractor-mower combination unit over 16 engine horsepower owned or leased by the Department, a municipal corporation or political subdivision shall be operated for the purpose of mowing vegetation on highway right-of-way unless the tractor of such unit is equipped with an operator protective frame conforming to the specifications prescribed by regulations under the United States Occupational Safety and Health Act of 1970, as amended,[1] and with a seat safety belt.

The operator protective frame may be incorporated into a cab which design shall conform to the specifications established by the United States Occupational Safety and Health Act of 1970, as amended.[1]

The seat safety belt must meet the requirements provided in Section 12–603 of this Act.

P.A. 76–1586, § 12–140, added by P.A. 76–2191, § 1, eff. July 1, 1970. Renumbered § 12–708 and amended by P.A. 77–37, § 1, eff. Jan. 1, 1972. Amended by P.A. 77–157, § 1, eff. Jan. 1, 1972; P.A. 77–202, § 1, eff. Jan. 1, 1972; P.A. 77–2829, § 40, eff. Dec. 22, 1972; P.A. 78–255, § 61, eff. Oct. 1, 1973; P.A. 78–748, § 1, eff. Jan. 1, 1974; P.A. 78–1297, § 58, eff. March 4, 1975; P.A. 81–435, § 1, eff. Jan. 1, 1980.

Formerly Ill.Rev.Stat.1991, ch. 95 ½, ¶ 12–708.

[1] 29 U.S.C.A. § 651 et seq.

5/12–709. Slow-moving vehicle emblem

§ 12–709. Slow-moving vehicle emblem.

(a) Every animal drawn vehicle, farm tractor, implement of husbandry and special mobile equipment, when operated on a highway must display a slow-moving vehicle emblem mounted on the rear except as provided in paragraph (b) of this Section. Special mobile equipment is exempt when operated within the limits of a construction or maintenance project where traffic control devices are used in compliance with the applicable provisions of the manual and specifications adopted under Section 11–301 of the "Illinois Vehicle Code".

(b) Every vehicle or unit described in paragraph (a) of this Section when operated in combination on a highway must display a slow-moving vehicle emblem as follows:

1. Where the towed unit or any load thereon partially or totally obscures the slow-moving vehicle emblem on the towing unit, the towed unit shall be equipped with a slow-moving vehicle emblem. In such cases the towing unit need not display the emblem.

2. Where the slow-moving vehicle emblem on the towing unit is not obscured by the towed unit or its load, then either or both may be equipped with the required emblem but it shall be sufficient if either displays it.

3. A registered truck towed behind a farm tractor in conformity with the provisions of Section 11–1418 of the "Illinois Vehicle Code" must display a slow-moving vehicle emblem in the manner provided in paragraph (c) while being towed on a highway if the emblem on the towing vehicle is partially or totally obscured.

(c) The slow-moving vehicle emblem required by paragraphs (a) and (b) of this Section must meet or exceed the specifications and mounting requirements established by the Department. Such specifications and mounting requirements shall, on and before August 31, 2004, be based on the specifications adopted by the American Society of Agricultural Engineers and published by that body as ASAE S 276.2 dated March, 1968 or as ASAE S 276.5. On and after September 1, 2004, the specifications and mounting requirements shall be based on the specifications adopted by the American Society of Agricultural Engineers and published by that body as ASAE S 276.5 NOV 97. No advertising or other marking shall appear upon the emblem except that specified by the American Society of Agricultural Engineers to identify the standard to which the material complies. Each original package containing a slow-moving vehicle emblem shall display a notice on the outside of the package stating that such emblem shall only be used for the purposes stated in subsections (a) and (b).

(d) A slow-moving vehicle emblem is intended as a safety identification device and shall not be displayed on any vehicle nor displayed in any manner other than as described in paragraphs (a), (b) and (c) of this Section. A violation of this subsection (d) is a petty offense punishable by a fine of $25 for the first offense and $75 for a second or subsequent offense within one year of the first offense.

P.A. 76–1586, § 12–141 added by P.A. 76–2192, § 1, eff. July 1, 1970. Renumbered § 12–709 by P.A. 77–37, § 1, eff. Jan. 1, 1972. Amended by P.A. 78–253, § 1, eff. Oct. 1, 1973; P.A. 78–748, § 1, eff. Jan. 1, 1974; P.A. 78–1297, § 58, eff. March 4, 1975; P.A. 86–1259, § 1, eff. Jan. 1, 1991; P.A. 91–505, § 5, eff. Jan. 1, 2000; P.A. 92–72, § 5, eff. Jan. 1, 2002.

Formerly Ill.Rev.Stat.1991, ch. 95 ½, ¶ 12–709.

5/12–710. Rear fender splash guards

§ 12–710. Rear fender splash guards. It is unlawful for any person to operate any vehicle of the second division, except a truck tractor, to which this Section is applicable upon any highway of this State unless such vehicle is equipped with rear fender splash guards of either the contour type or the flap type which comply with the specifications provided in this Section for the type of splash guards used on the vehicle, and which are so attached as to prevent the splashing of mud or water upon the windshield of other motor vehicles.

(a) Specifications for contour type splash guards. When contour type rear fender splash guards are used, they shall contour the wheel in such a manner that the relationship of the inside surface of any such splash guard to the tread surface of the tire or wheel shall be relatively parallel, both laterally and across the wheel, at least throughout the top 90 degrees of the rear 180 degrees of the wheel surface; provided however, on vehicles which have a clearance of less than 5 inches between the top of the tire or wheel and that part of the body of the vehicle directly above the tire or wheel when the vehicle is loaded to maximum legal capacity, the curved portion of the splash guard need only extend from a point directly behind the center of the rear axle and to the rear of the wheel surface upwards to within at least 2 inches of the bottom line of the body when the vehicle is loaded to maximum legal capacity. There shall be a downward extension of the curved surface which shall end not more than 12 inches from the ground when the vehicle is loaded to maximum legal capacity. This downward extension shall be part of the curved surface or attached directly to such curved surface, but it need not contour the wheel. Such contour type splash guards shall be wide enough to cover the full tread width of the tire or tires being protected and shall be installed not more than 6 inches from the tread surface of the tire or wheel when the vehicle is loaded to maximum legal capacity. The splash guard shall have a lip or flange on its outside edge to minimize side throw and splash. The lip or flange shall extend toward the center of the wheel, and shall be perpendicular to and extend not less than 2 inches below the inside or bottom surface line or plane of the guard. Such contour type splash guards may be constructed of either a rigid or flexible material, but shall be attached in such a manner that, regardless of movement either by the splash guards or the vehicle, the splash guards will retain their general parallel relationship to the tread surface of the tire or wheel under all ordinary operating conditions.

(b) Specifications for flap type splash guards. When flap type splash guards are used, they shall be wide enough to cover the full tread width of the tire or tires being protected; shall be so installed that they extend from the underside of the vehicle in a vertical plane behind the rear wheels to within 12 inches of the ground, when the vehicle is loaded to maximum legal capacity; shall be so constructed and attached so that when the vehicle is in forward motion such splash guard will not deviate or move backward from the vertical plane by an angle of more than 30 degrees measured from the vertical plane and so that when the forward motion of the vehicle causes such splash guard to deviate from the vertical plane, the bottom of such flap type splash guard will not be more than 15 inches from the ground, when the vehicle is loaded to maximum legal capacity. Such flap type splash guard may be constructed of either a rigid or flexible material.

(c) Exemptions. This Section shall not apply to vehicles the construction or design of which does not require such splash guards, nor to vehicles in-transit and capable only of using temporary splash guards prescribed by the Department, nor to pole trailers.

P.A. 76–1586, § 12–130. Renumbered § 12–710 by P.A. 77–37, § 1, eff. Jan. 1, 1972. Amended by P.A. 77–36, § 1, eff. July 1, 1971; P.A. 77–2829, § 40, eff. Dec. 22, 1972; P.A. 78–255, § 61, eff. Oct. 1, 1973; P.A. 78–748, § 1, eff. Jan. 1, 1974; P.A. 78–1297, § 58, eff. March 4, 1975; P.A. 85–830, § 1, eff. Sept. 24, 1987; P.A. 85–1010, § 1, eff. March 2, 1988; P.A. 89–117, § 10, eff. July 7, 1995.

Formerly Ill.Rev.Stat.1991, ch. 95 ½, ¶ 12–710.

P.A. 85–1010 recognized the amendment by P.A. 85–830.

5/12–711. Trucks equipped with self-compactors or roll-off hoists and roll-on containers for garbage or refuse hauls; audible warning signal

§ 12–711. Commencing January 1, 1987, all trucks equipped with self-compactors or roll-off hoists and roll-on containers for garbage or refuse hauls shall, before operating on any public or private highway, alley or parking area of this State, be equipped with an operably working external audible warning signal device that meets the standard of American National Standards Institute, SAE J994b, Type A, B or C, which is activated when the vehicle is operated in reverse or when top-hinged tailgates are open.

P.A. 76–1586, § 12–711, added by P.A. 84–813, § 1, eff. Sept. 22, 1985.

Formerly Ill.Rev.Stat.1991, ch. 95 ½, ¶ 12–711.

5/12–712. Construction equipment to display company name

§ 12–712. Construction equipment to display company name.

(a) Construction equipment that is capable of being self propelled or any construction equipment capable of being towed shall display on the side of the equipment the name of the company for which it is employed. The name shall be in letters at least 2 inches tall and one-half inch wide. This Section shall not apply to any motor vehicle upon which is affixed the insignia required under Section 18c-4701 of the Illinois Commercial Transportation Law.[1]

(b) Any person convicted of violating this Section shall be guilty of a petty offense and subject to a fine not to exceed $100.

P.A. 76-1586, § 12-712, added by P.A. 87-1160, § 1, eff. Jan. 1, 1993. Amended by P.A. 88-45, Art. II, § 2-54, eff. July 6, 1993.

Formerly Ill.Rev.Stat., ch. 95½, ¶ 12-712.

[1] 625 ILCS 5/18c-4701.

Former § 12-712, prohibiting the possession and use of radar detection devices, was renumbered § 12-714 by P.A. 88-45, Art. II, § 2-54.

P.A. 88-45, Article II, of the First 1993 General Revisory Act, resolved multiple actions in the 87th General Assembly and made certain technical corrections in P.A. 87-895 through P.A. 87-1280.

5/12-713. Commercial trucks used by construction contractors or subcontractors to display company name

§ 12-713. Commercial trucks used by construction contractors or subcontractors to display company name.

(a) Every second division vehicle operating commercially in this State that is used by a construction contractor or subcontractor shall display on the side of the vehicle or its trailer the name of the company for which it is employed. The name shall be in letters at least 2 inches tall and one-half inch wide. This Section shall not apply to any motor vehicle upon which is affixed the insignia required under Section 18c-4701 of the Illinois Commercial Transportation Law.[1]

(b) Any person convicted of violating this Section shall be guilty of a petty offense and subject to a fine not to exceed $100.

P.A. 76-1586, § 12-713, added by P.A. 87-1160, § 1, eff. Jan. 1, 1993. Amended by P.A. 88-45, Art. II, § 2-54, eff. July 6, 1993.

Formerly Ill.Rev.Stat., ch. 95½, ¶ 12-713.

[1] 625 ILCS 5/18c-4701.

Former § 12-713, prohibiting the possession and use of radar jamming devices, was renumbered § 12-715 by P.A. 88-45, Art. II, § 2-54.

P.A. 88-45, Article II, of the First 1993 General Revisory Act, resolved multiple actions in the 87th General Assembly and made certain technical corrections in P.A. 87-895 through P.A. 87-1280.

5/12-714. Possession and use of radar detection devices prohibited

§ 12-714. Possession and use of radar detection devices prohibited.

(a) No person shall operate or be in actual physical control of a commercial motor vehicle as defined in Section 6-500(6) of this Code while the motor vehicle is equipped with any instrument designed to detect the presence of police radar for the purpose of monitoring vehicular speed.

(b) Notwithstanding subsection (a) of this Section, a person operating a commercial motor vehicle as defined in Section 6-500(6) of this Code, who possesses within the vehicle a radar detecting device that is contained in a locked opaque box or similar container, or that is not in the passenger compartment of the vehicle, and that is not in operation, shall not be in violation of subsection (a) of this Section.

Any person found guilty of violating this Section shall be guilty of a petty offense. A minimum fine of $50 shall be imposed for a first offense and a minimum fine of $100 for a second or subsequent offense.

(c) The radar detection device or mechanism shall be seized by the law enforcement officer at the time of the violation if the offender has previously been convicted of violating this Section. This Section shall not be construed to authorize the permanent forfeiture to the State of any radar detection device or mechanism. Any such device or mechanism shall be taken and held for the period when needed as evidence. When no longer needed for evidence, the defendant may petition the court for the return of the device or mechanism; provided the defendant shall prove to the court by a preponderance of the evidence that the device or mechanism will be used only for a legitimate and lawful purpose.

(d) No commercial motor vehicle, or driver of such vehicle, shall be stopped or searched by any law enforcement officer solely on the basis of a violation or suspected violation of this Section.

P.A. 76-1586, § 12-712, added by P.A. 87-1202, § 1, eff. Jan. 1, 1993. Renumbered § 12-714 and amended by P.A. 88-45, Art. II, § 2-54, eff. July 6, 1993. Amended by P.A. 90-89, § 15, eff. Jan. 1, 1998.

Formerly Ill.Rev.Stat., ch. 95½, ¶ 12-712.

5/12-715. Possession and use of radar jamming devices prohibited

§ 12-715. Possession and use of radar jamming devices prohibited.

(a) No person shall operate or be in actual physical control of a commercial motor vehicle as defined in Section 6-500(6) of this Code while the motor vehicle is equipped with any instrument designed to interfere with microwaves or lasers at frequencies used by police radar for the purpose of monitoring vehicular speed.

(b) Notwithstanding subsection (a) of this Section, a person operating a commercial motor vehicle as defined in Section 6-500(6) of this Code, who possesses within the vehicle a radar or laser jamming device that is contained in a locked opaque box or similar container, or that is not in the passenger compartment of the vehicle, and that is not in operation, shall not be in violation of subsection (a) of this Section.

Any person found guilty of violating this Section shall be guilty of a petty offense. A minimum fine of $50 shall be imposed for a first offense and a minimum fine of $100 for a second or subsequent offense.

(c) The radar or laser jamming device or mechanism shall be seized by the law enforcement officer at the time of the violation. This Section shall not be construed to authorize the permanent forfeiture to the State of any radar or laser jamming device or mechanism. Any such device or mechanism shall be taken and held for the period when needed as evidence. When no longer needed for evidence, the defendant may petition the court for the return of the device or mechanism; provided the defendant shall prove to the court by a preponderance of the evidence that the device or mechanism will be used only for a legitimate and lawful purpose.

(d) No commercial motor vehicle, or driver of such vehicle, shall be stopped or searched by any law enforcement officer solely on the basis of a violation or suspected violation of this Section.

P.A. 76-1586, § 12-713, added by P.A. 87-1202, § 1, eff. Jan. 1, 1993. Renumbered § 12-715 and amended by P.A. 88-45, Art. II, § 2-54, eff. July 6, 1993. Amended by P.A. 90-89, § 15, eff. Jan. 1, 1998; P.A. 91-243, § 5, eff. Jan. 1, 2000.

Formerly Ill.Rev.Stat., ch. 95½, ¶ 12-713.

ARTICLE VIII. SPECIAL REQUIREMENTS FOR SCHOOL BUSES

Date Effective

Article VIII, consisting of Sections 12–800 to 12–812, was added by P.A. 78–1244, eff. Sept. 5, 1974.

5/12–800. § 12–800. Repealed by P.A. 90–89, § 20, eff. Jan. 1, 1998

5/12–801. Color

§ 12–801. Color. The exterior of each school bus shall be national school bus glossy yellow except as follows:

The rooftop may be white.

The fenders of school buses manufactured before January 1, 1976, may be black.

Body trim, rub rails, lettering other than on a stop signal arm and bumpers on a Type I school bus shall be glossy black.

Lettering on a stop signal arm shall be white on a red background.

Bumpers on a Type II school bus may be glossy black or a bright, light or colorless finish.

The hood and upper cowl may be lusterless black or lusterless school bus yellow.

Grilles on the front, lamp trim and hubcaps may be a bright finish.

The name or emblem of a manufacturer may be colorless or any color.

The exterior paint of any school bus shall match the central value, hue and chroma set forth in rules promulgated by the Department.

P.A. 76–1586, § 12–801, added by P.A. 78–1244, § 1, eff. Sept. 5, 1974. Amended by P.A. 79–845, § 1, eff. Jan. 1, 1976; P.A. 80–1495, § 36, eff. Jan. 8, 1979; P.A. 81–740, § 1, eff. Jan. 1, 1980; P.A. 88–415, § 10, eff. Aug. 20, 1993; P.A. 89–433, § 5, eff. Dec. 15, 1995.

Formerly Ill.Rev.Stat.1991, ch. 95 ½, ¶ 12–801.

5/12–802. Identification

§ 12–802. Identification. Each school bus shall have the sign "SCHOOL BUS" painted on both the front and rear of the bus as high as practicable in letters at least 8 inches high. The vehicle weight and the vehicle maximum passenger capacity recommended by the manufacturer of the bus, which shall be based upon provision for 13 inches of seating space for each passenger exclusive of the driver, shall be painted on the body to the left of the service door in letters at least 2 inches high. The name of the owner or the entity for which the school bus is operated or both shall be painted in a contrasting color on both sides, centered as high as practicable below the window line, in letters at least 4 inches high. A school bus identification number shall be painted as high as practicable on both the front and rear of the bus in letters at least 4 inches high. Decals may be used instead of painting.

P.A. 76–1586, § 12–802, added by P.A. 78–1244, § 1, eff. Sept. 5, 1974. Amended by P.A. 79–63, § 1, eff. June 26, 1975; P.A. 79–845, § 1, eff. Jan. 1, 1976; P.A. 79–1454, § 44, eff. Aug. 31, 1976; P.A. 82–111, § 1, eff. Aug. 6, 1981.

Formerly Ill.Rev.Stat.1991, ch. 95 ½, ¶ 12–802.

5/12–803. Stop signal arm

§ 12–803. (a) Each school bus shall be equipped with a stop signal arm on the driver's side of the school bus that may be operated either manually or mechanically. For each school bus manufactured on and after September 1, 1992, the stop signal arm shall be an octagon shaped semaphore that conforms to 49 C.F.R. 571.131, "SCHOOL BUS PEDESTRIAN SAFETY DEVICES", S5.1 through S5.5.

(b) Each school bus manufactured prior to September 1, 1992 shall be equipped with a stop signal arm that conforms to standards promulgated by the Department.

P.A. 76–1586, § 12–803, added by P.A. 78–1244, § 1, eff. Sept. 5, 1974. Amended by P.A. 79–63, § 1, eff. June 26, 1975; P.A. 79–845, § 1, eff. Jan. 1, 1976; P.A. 79–1454, § 44, eff. Aug. 31, 1976; P.A. 83–299, § 1, eff. Jan. 1, 1984; P.A. 88–415, § 10, eff. Aug. 20, 1993.

Formerly Ill.Rev.Stat.1991, ch. 95 ½, ¶ 12–803.

5/12–804. Other vehicles—Color, stop signal arm and identification

§ 12–804. Other vehicles—Color, stop signal arm and identification. No vehicle other than a school bus shall be identified with the sign "SCHOOL BUS", shall be equipped with a stop signal arm, shall be equipped with a strobe lamp or shall be equipped with a warning lamp system as described in Section 12–805 of this Act. No commuter van or bus other than a school bus shall be painted national school bus glossy yellow or a color that closely resembles national school bus glossy yellow.

P.A. 76–1586, § 12–804, added by P.A. 78–1244, § 1, eff. Sept. 5, 1974. Amended by P.A. 79–63, § 1, eff. June 26,

1975; P.A. 81-509, § 1, eff. Jan. 1, 1980; P.A. 81-740, § 1, eff. Jan. 1, 1980; P.A. 81-1509, Art. I, § 57, eff. Sept. 26, 1980.

Formerly Ill.Rev.Stat.1991, ch. 95 ½, ¶ 12-804.

Art. I, § 1 of P.A. 81-1509 provided in part:

"This Article provides for the nonsubstantive revision or renumbering or repeal of Sections of Acts necessitated by the amendment, addition or repeal of Sections by two or more Public Acts of the 81st General Assembly, through Public Act 81-1224, which multiple action was not resolved by one of the Acts affecting the particular Section."

5/12-805. Special lighting equipment

§ 12-805. Special lighting equipment. Each school bus purchased as a new vehicle after December 31, 1975 shall be equipped with an 8-lamp flashing signal system. Until December 31, 1978, all other school buses shall be equipped with either a 4-lamp or an 8-lamp flashing signal system. After December 31, 1978, all school buses shall be equipped with an 8-lamp flashing signal system.

A 4-lamp flashing signal system shall have 2 alternately flashing red lamps mounted as high and as widely spaced laterally on the same level as practicable at the front of the school bus and 2 such lamps mounted in the same manner at the rear.

An 8-lamp flashing signal system shall have, in addition to a 4-lamp system, 4 alternately flashing amber lamps. Each amber lamp shall be mounted next to a red lamp and at the same level but closer to the centerline of the school bus.

Each signal lamp shall be a sealed beam at least 5½ inches in diameter and shall have sufficient intensity to be visible at 500 feet in normal sunlight. Both the 4-lamp and 8-lamp system shall be actuated only by means of a manual switch. There shall be a device for indicating to the driver that the system is operating properly or is inoperative.

P.A. 76-1586, § 12-805, added by P.A. 78-1244, § 1, eff. Sept. 5, 1974. Amended by P.A. 79-1400, § 1, eff. Oct. 1, 1976.

Formerly Ill.Rev.Stat.1991, ch. 95 ½, ¶ 12-805.

5/12-806. Identification, stop signal arms and special lighting when not used as a school bus

§ 12-806. Identification, stop signal arms and special lighting when not used as a school bus. Except as provided in Section 12-806a, whenever a school bus is operated for the purpose of transporting passengers other than persons in connection with an activity of the school or religious organization which owns the school bus or for which the school bus is operated, the "SCHOOL BUS" signs shall be covered or concealed and the stop signal arm and flashing signal system shall not be operable through normal controls.

P.A. 76-1586, § 12-806, added by P.A. 78-1244, § 1, eff. Sept. 5, 1974. Amended by P.A. 79-798, § 1, eff. July 1, 1976; P.A. 84-1311, § 2, eff. Aug. 27, 1986.

Formerly Ill.Rev.Stat.1991, ch. 95 ½, ¶ 12-806.

5/12-806a. Identification, stop signal arms and special lighting on school buses used in connection with a youth camp, child care facility, or community based rehabilitation facility

§ 12-806a. Identification, stop signal arms and special lighting on school buses used in connection with a youth camp, child care facility, or community based rehabilitation facility.

(a) Subject to the conditions in Subsection (c), a bus which meets any of the special requirements for school buses in Section 12-801, 12-802, 12-803 and 12-805 of this Code may be used for the purpose of transporting persons 18 years of age or less in connection with any of the following facilities:

(i) any youth camp licensed under the Youth Camp Act; [1] and

(ii) any child care facility licensed under the Child Care Act of 1969.[2]

(b) Subject to the conditions in subsection (c), a bus which meets any of the special requirements for school buses in Sections 12-801, 12-802, 12-803 and 12-805 of this Code may be used for the purpose of transporting persons recognized as clients of a community based rehabilitation facility which is accredited by the Commission on Accreditation of Rehabilitation Facilities of Tucson, Arizona, and which is under a contractual agreement with the Department of Human Services.

(c) A bus used for transportation as provided in subsection (a) or (b) shall either (i) meet all of the special requirements for school buses in Section 12-801, 12-802, 12-803 and 12-805 or (ii) shall have the "SCHOOL BUS" signs covered or concealed and the stop signal arm and flashing signal system rendered inoperable through normal means. A bus which meets all of the special requirements for school buses in Section 12-801, 12-802, 12-803 and 12-805 shall be operated by a person who has a valid and properly classified driver's license issued by the Secretary of State and who possesses a valid school bus driver permit or is accompanied and supervised, for the specific purpose of training prior to routine operation of a school bus, by a person who has held a valid school bus driver permit for at least one year. A bus which has had the "SCHOOL BUS" signs covered or concealed and the stop signal arm and flashing signal system rendered inoperable through normal means may be operated by a person who has a valid and properly classified driver's license issued by the Secretary of State.

P.A. 76-1586, § 12-806a, added by P.A. 84-1311, § 2, eff. Aug. 27, 1986. Amended by P.A. 85-815, § 1, eff. Jan. 1, 1988; P.A. 89-507, Art. 90, § 90D-84, eff. July 1, 1997.

Formerly Ill.Rev.Stat.1991, ch. 95 ½, ¶ 12-806a.

[1] 210 ILCS 100/1 et seq.

[2] 225 ILCS 10/1 et seq.

5/12-807. Seat belt for driver

§ 12-807. Seat belt for driver. Each school bus shall be equipped with a retractable lap belt assembly for the driver's seat. No school bus shall be operated unless the driver has properly restrained himself with the lap belt assembly.

P.A. 76-1586, § 12-807, added by P.A. 78-1244, § 1, eff. Sept. 5, 1974.

Formerly Ill.Rev.Stat.1991, ch. 95 ½, ¶ 12-807.

5/12-807.1. Seat back height

§ 12-807.1. Seat back height. No Type I school bus manufactured after June 30, 1987 shall be sold for use as, or purchased for use as, or used as a school bus within this State unless such bus is equipped with passenger seat backs having a seat back height of 28 inches installed by the original bus body manufacturer.

P.A. 76-1586, § 12-807.1, added by P.A. 84-1334, § 2, eff. Sept. 9, 1986. Amended by P.A. 85-1010, § 1, eff. March 2, 1988.

Formerly Ill.Rev.Stat.1991, ch. 95 ½, ¶ 12-807.1.

5/12–807.2. Crossing control arms

§ 12–807.2. Crossing control arms.

(a) No Type I or Type II school bus may be operated or used as a school bus within this State after December 31, 1999 unless that bus is equipped with a crossing control arm on the front of the bus that conforms to equipment and installation standards that the Department of Transportation shall promulgate for purposes of this subsection.

(b) If a Type I or Type II school bus is manufactured after December 31, 1997, that bus shall not be sold for use as, or purchased for the use as, or used as a school bus within this State unless that bus is equipped with a crossing control arm that is installed on the front of the bus by the original bus body manufacturer and that conforms to equipment and installation standards that the Department shall promulgate for purposes of this subsection.

(c) A crossing control arm meeting standards promulgated by the Department under this Section shall be designed to swing out from the front of a school bus when the bus stops and opens its doors while school children enter or exit the bus, as prescribed in rules promulgated by the State Board of Education.

(d) This Section does not apply to the temporary operation in this State of a school bus that is legally registered in another state and is displaying valid registration plates of that state if (i) the bus is not operated in Illinois on a regular basis, and (ii) the bus is being operated in Illinois in connection with a cultural, tourist, athletic, or similar activity that is sponsored by one or more schools located outside of Illinois for the benefit of their enrolled students who are being transported to or from that activity.

P.A. 76–1586, § 12–807.2, added by P.A. 90–108, § 15, eff. July 14, 1997.

5/12–808. Fire extinguisher

§ 12–808. Fire extinguisher. Each school bus shall be equipped with at least one dry chemical gauge type fire extinguisher mounted in the extinguisher manufacturer's automobile type bracket in a position readily accessible to the driver.

P.A. 76–1586, § 12–808, added by P.A. 78–1244, § 1, eff. Sept. 5, 1974.

Formerly Ill.Rev.Stat.1991, ch. 95 ½, ¶ 12–808.

5/12–809. First aid kit

§ 12–809. First aid kit. Each school bus shall be equipped with a first aid kit mounted in full view of and readily accessible to the driver.

P.A. 76–1586, § 12–809, added by P.A. 78–1244, § 1, eff. Sept. 5, 1974.

Formerly Ill.Rev.Stat.1991, ch. 95 ½, ¶ 12–809.

5/12–810. Restraining devices for passengers who are persons with disabilities

§ 12–810. Restraining devices for passengers who are persons with disabilities.

Each school bus which is operated for transporting passengers who are persons with disabilities shall be equipped with an appropriate restraining or safety device for each such passenger.

P.A. 76–1586, § 12–810, added by P.A. 78–1244, § 1, eff. Sept. 5, 1974. Amended by P.A. 88–685, § 5, eff. Jan. 24, 1995.

Formerly Ill.Rev.Stat.1991, ch. 95 ½, ¶ 12–810.

5/12–811. Amber 3 bar clearance light

§ 12–811. Amber 3 bar clearance light. Each Type I school bus shall be equipped with an amber 3 bar clearance light on the front of the bus. The light shall be illuminated at all times when the bus is being operated between sunset and sunrise and in conditions of reduced visibility.

P.A. 76–1586, § 12–811, added by P.A. 78–1244, § 1, eff. Sept. 5, 1974. Amended by P.A. 79–63, § 1, eff. June 26, 1975.

Formerly Ill.Rev.Stat.1991, ch. 95 ½, ¶ 12–811.

5/12–812. Rules and regulations

§ 12–812. Rules and regulations.

(a) The Department may promulgate rules and regulations to more completely specify the equipment requirements of this Article.

(b) All rules, regulations and standards promulgated from time to time by the State Board of Education and the Department for the safety and construction of school buses shall be applicable to every motor vehicle in this State defined as a school bus under Section 1–182.

P.A. 76–1586, § 12–812, added by P.A. 78–1244, § 1, eff. Sept. 5, 1974. Amended by P.A. 81–1508, § 8, eff. Sept. 25, 1980.

Formerly Ill.Rev.Stat.1991, ch. 95 ½, ¶ 12–812.

5/12–812.1. Alternate fuels; use; rules and regulations

§ 12–812.1. (a) The Department shall adopt and promulgate rules and regulations governing the use of liquefied petroleum gases, compressed natural gases and liquefied natural gases as a propellant fuel in school buses. Such rules and regulations shall include the installation, maintenance and operation of such equipment installed on school buses and shall be based on the generally accepted standards of safety as recommended by the National Fire Protection Association.

(b) All school buses using liquefied petroleum gases, compressed natural gases or liquefied natural gases as a propellant fuel must conform to and obey any rule or regulation lawfully adopted by the Department.

P.A. 76–1586, § 12–812.1, added by P.A. 83–1027, § 2, eff. July 1, 1984.

Formerly Ill.Rev.Stat.1991, ch. 95 ½, ¶ 12–812.1.

5/12–813. § 12–813. Repealed by P.A. 80–506, § 2, eff. Oct. 1, 1977

5/12–813.1. Operation of a school bus while using a cellular radio telecommunication device

§ 12–813.1. Operation of a school bus while using a cellular radio telecommunication device.

(a) In this Section:

"School bus driver" means a person operating a school bus who has a valid school bus driver permit as required under Sections 6–104 and 6–106.1 of this Code.

"Cellular radio telecommunication device" means a device capable of sending or receiving telephone communications without an access line for service and which requires the operator to dial numbers manually. It does not, however, include citizens band radios or citizens band radio hybrids.

"Using a cellular radio telecommunication device" means talking or listening to or dialing a cellular radio telecommunication device.

To "operate" means to have the vehicle in motion while it contains one or more passengers.

(b) A school bus driver may not operate a school bus while using a cellular radio telecommunication device.

(c) This Section does not apply:

(1) To the use of a cellular radio telecommunication device for the purpose of communicating with any of the following regarding an emergency situation:

(A) an emergency response operator;

(B) a hospital;

(C) a physician's office or health clinic;

(D) an ambulance service;

(E) a fire department, fire district, or fire company; or

(F) a police department.

(2) To the use of a cellular radio telecommunication device to call for assistance in the event that there is a mechanical breakdown or other mechanical problem that impairs the safe operation of the bus.

(3) To the use of a cellular radio telecommunication device that has a digital two-way radio service capability owned and operated by the school district, when that device is being used as a digital two-way radio.

(4) When the school bus is parked.

(d) A school bus driver who violates this Section is guilty of a petty offense punishable by a fine of not less than $100 and not more than $250.

P.A. 76–1586, § 12–813.1, added by P.A. 92–730, § 5, eff. Jan. 1, 2003.

5/12–814. § 12–814. Repealed by P.A. 81–509, § 2, eff. Jan. 1, 1980

5/12–815. Strobe lamp on school bus

§ 12–815. Strobe lamp on school bus.

(a) A school bus manufactured prior to January 1, 2000 may be equipped with one strobe lamp that will emit 60 to 120 flashes per minute of white or bluish-white light visible to a motorist approaching the bus from any direction. A school bus manufactured on or after January 1, 2000 shall be equipped with one strobe lamp that will emit 60 to 120 flashes per minute of white or bluish-white light visible to a motorist approaching the bus from any direction. The lamp shall be of sufficient brightness to be visible in normal sunlight when viewed directly from a distance of at least one mile.

(b) The strobe lamp shall be mounted on the rooftop of the bus with the light generating element in the lamp located equidistant from each side and either at or behind the center of the rooftop. The maximum height of the element above the rooftop shall not exceed 1/30 of its distance from the rear of the rooftop. If the structure of the strobe lamp obscures the light generating element, the element shall be deemed to be in the center of the lamp with a maximum height 1/4 inch less than the maximum height of the strobe lamp unless otherwise indicated in rules and regulations promulgated by the Department. The Department may promulgate rules and regulations to govern measurements, glare, effectiveness and protection of strobe lamps on school buses, including higher strobe lamps than authorized in this paragraph.

(c) The strobe lamp may be lighted only when the school bus is actually being used as a school bus and:

1. is stopping or stopped for loading or discharging pupils on a highway outside an urban area; or

2. is bearing one or more pupils and is either stopped or, in the interest of safety, is moving very slowly at a speed:

(i) less than the posted minimum speed limit, or

(ii) less than 30 miles per hour on a highway outside an urban area.

P.A. 76–1586, § 12–815, added by P.A. 81–879, § 1, eff. Sept. 21, 1979. Amended by P.A. 87–768, § 2, eff. Oct. 10, 1991; P.A. 91–168, § 5, eff. Jan. 1, 2000; P.A. 91–679, § 5, eff. Jan. 26, 2000.

Formerly Ill.Rev.Stat.1991, ch. 95 ½, ¶ 12–815.

P.A. 91–679 incorporated the amendment by P.A. 91–168.

5/12–815.1. Emergency exits identification

§ 12–815.1. Emergency exits identification. On and after August 1, 2000, all emergency exits of a school bus shall be outlined around the perimeter of the exit with a minimum one inch wide yellow reflective tape or decal. This yellow reflective tape or decal shall be placed on the exterior surface of the school bus.

P.A. 76–1586, § 12–815.1, added by P.A. 91–168, § 5, eff. Jan. 1, 2000. Amended by P.A. 91–785, § 5, eff. June 9, 2000.

5/12–820. Nursery school buses

§ 12-820. Nursery school buses. The Department of Transportation, after conducting a Public Hearing, may, by regulation, modify and supplement the requirements pertaining to seat dimensions, spacing and height from the floor and to other safety features in the interior of a school bus used to transport preschool children, when such modification or supplementing will enhance the safety of the bus when transporting such children.

P.A. 76–1586, § 12–820, added by P.A. 79–845, § 1, eff. Jan. 1, 1976. Amended by P.A. 82–523, § 1, eff. Jan. 1, 1982; P.A. 85–828, § 7, eff. Jan. 1, 1988.

Formerly Ill.Rev.Stat.1991, ch. 95 ½, ¶ 12–820.

ARTICLE IX. SPECIAL REQUIREMENTS FOR RELIGIOUS ORGANIZATION BUSES

Section

5/12–900. Color and markings

§ 12–900. Color and markings. Each religious organization bus may be of any color and have any markings designating its purpose other than those required for school buses under Article VIII of this Act.

P.A. 76–1586, § 12–900, added by P.A. 79–798, § 1, eff. July 1, 1976.

Formerly Ill.Rev.Stat.1991, ch. 95 ½, ¶ 12–900.

5/12–901. Special lighting equipment

§ 12–901. Special lighting equipment. Any religious organization bus may be equipped with a 4-lamp flashing signal system having unison flashing amber lamps, 2 at the front and 2 at the rear of the bus, mounted as high and as widely spaced laterally on the same level as is practicable. If such equipment is installed, (a) each lamp must be a sealed beam at least 5½ inches in diameter and have sufficient intensity to be visible at 500 feet in normal sunlight, (b) the system shall be actuated only by means of a manual switch, and (c) there shall be a device for indicating to the driver that the system is operating properly or is inoperative.

P.A. 76-1586, § 12-901, added by P.A. 79-798, § 1, eff. July 1, 1976.

Formerly Ill.Rev.Stat.1991, ch. 95 ½, ¶ 12-901.

5/12-902. Rules and regulations

§ 12-902. Rules and regulations. The Department of Transportation may promulgate rules and regulations to more completely specify the equipment requirements for every motor vehicle defined as a religious organization bus under Section 1-111.1a.

P.A. 76-1586, § 12-902, added by P.A. 79-798, § 1, eff. July 1, 1976. Amended by P.A. 90-89, § 15, eff. Jan. 1, 1998.

Formerly Ill.Rev.Stat.1991, ch. 95 ½, ¶ 12-902.

CHAPTER 13. INSPECTION OF VEHICLES

Section

Enactment

The Illinois Vehicle Code was enacted by P.A. 76-1586, effective July 1, 1970. The Code constitutes a consolidated recodification of various earlier laws and acts including the Uniform Act Regulating Traffic on Highways.

5/13-100. § 13-100. Repealed by P.A. 90-89, § 20, eff. Jan. 1, 1998

5/13-100.1. Definitions

§ 13-100.1. Definitions. As used in this Chapter, "affected areas" means the counties of Cook, DuPage, Lake, Kane, McHenry, Will, Madison, St. Clair, and Monroe and the townships of Aux Sable and Goose Lake in Grundy County and the township of Oswego in Kendall County.

P.A. 76-1586, § 13-100.1, added by P.A. 91-254, § 10, eff. July 1, 2000.

5/13-101. Submission to safety test; Certificate of safety

§ 13-101. Submission to safety test; Certificate of safety. To promote the safety of the general public, every owner of a second division vehicle, medical transport vehicle, tow truck, or contract carrier transporting employees in the course of their employment on a highway of this State in a vehicle designed to carry 15 or fewer passengers shall, before operating the vehicle upon the highways of Illinois, submit it to a "safety test" and secure a certificate of safety furnished by the Department as set forth in Section 13-109. Each second division motor vehicle that pulls or draws a trailer, semitrailer or pole trailer, with a gross weight of more than 8,000 lbs or is registered for a gross weight of more than 8,000 lbs, motor bus, religious organization bus, school bus, senior citizen transportation vehicle, and limousine shall be subject to inspection by the Department and the Department is authorized to establish rules and regulations for the implementation of such inspections.

The owners of each salvage vehicle shall submit it to a "safety test" and secure a certificate of safety furnished by the Department prior to its salvage vehicle inspection pursuant to Section 3-308 of this Code.

However, none of the provisions of Chapter 13 requiring safety tests or a certificate of safety shall apply to:

(a) farm tractors, machinery and implements, wagons, wagon-trailers or like farm vehicles used primarily in agricultural pursuits;

(b) vehicles other than school buses, tow trucks and medical transport vehicles owned or operated by a municipal corporation or political subdivision having a population of 1,000,000 or more inhabitants and which are subject to safety tests imposed by local ordinance or resolution;

(c) a semitrailer or trailer having a gross weight of 5,000 pounds or less including vehicle weight and maximum load;

(d) recreational vehicles;

(e) vehicles registered as and displaying Illinois antique vehicle plates;

(f) house trailers equipped and used for living quarters;

(g) vehicles registered as and displaying Illinois permanently mounted equipment plates or similar vehicles eligible therefor but registered as governmental vehicles provided that if said vehicle is reclassified from a permanently mounted equipment plate so as to lose the exemption of not requiring a certificate of safety, such vehicle must be safety tested within 30 days of the reclassification;

(h) vehicles owned or operated by a manufacturer, dealer or transporter displaying a special plate or plates as described in Chapter 3 of this Code while such vehicle is being delivered from the manufacturing or assembly plant directly to the purchasing dealership or distributor, or being temporarily road driven for quality control testing, or from one dealer or distributor to another, or are being moved by the most direct route from one location to another for the purpose of installing special bodies or equipment, or driven for purposes of demonstration by a prospective buyer with the dealer or his agent present in the cab of the vehicle during the demonstration;

(i) pole trailers and auxiliary axles;

(j) special mobile equipment;

(k) vehicles properly registered in another State pursuant to law and displaying a valid registration plate;

(*l*) water-well boring apparatuses or rigs;

(m) any vehicle which is owned and operated by the federal government and externally displays evidence of such ownership; and

(n) second division vehicles registered for a gross weight of 8,000 pounds or less, except when such second division motor vehicles pull or draw a trailer, semi-trailer or pole trailer having a gross weight of or registered for a gross weight of more than 8,000 pounds; motor buses; religious organization buses; school buses; senior citizen transportation vehicles; medical transport vehicles and tow trucks.

The safety test shall include the testing and inspection of brakes, lights, horns, reflectors, rear vision mirrors, mufflers, safety chains, windshields and windshield wipers, warning flags and flares, frame, axle, cab and body, or cab or body, wheels, steering apparatus, and other safety devices and appliances required by this Code and such other safety tests as the Department may by rule or regulation require, for second division vehicles, school buses, medical transport vehicles, tow trucks, vehicles designed to carry 15 or fewer passengers operated by a contract carrier transporting employees in the course of their employment on a highway of this State, trailers, and semitrailers subject to inspection.

For tow trucks, the safety test and inspection shall also include the inspection of winch mountings, body panels, body mounts, wheel lift swivel points, and sling straps, and other tests and inspections the Department by rule requires for tow trucks.

For trucks, truck tractors, trailers, semi-trailers, and buses, the safety test shall be conducted in accordance with the Minimum Periodic Inspection Standards promulgated by the Federal Highway Administration of the U.S. Department of Transportation and contained in Appendix G to Subchapter B of Chapter III of Title 49 of the Code of Federal Regulations. Those standards, as now in effect, are made a part of this Code, in the same manner as though they were set out in full in this Code.

The passing of the safety test shall not be a bar at any time to prosecution for operating a second division vehicle, medical transport vehicle, or vehicle designed to carry 15 or fewer passengers operated by a contract carrier as provided in this Section which is unsafe as determined by the standards prescribed in this Code.

P.A. 76-1586, § 13-101, eff. July 1, 1970. Amended by P.A. 77-157, § 1, eff. Jan. 1, 1972; P.A. 77-170, § 1, eff. Jan. 1, 1972; P.A. 77-1633, § 1, eff. Sept. 23, 1972; P.A. 77-1688, § 1, eff. July 1, 1972; P.A. 77-2170, § 1, eff. Aug. 2, 1972; P.A. 78-255, § 61, eff. Oct. 1, 1973; P.A. 78-1244, § 1, eff. Sept. 5, 1974; P.A. 78-1297, § 58, eff. March 4, 1975; P.A. 79-798, § 1, eff. July 1, 1976; P.A. 79-865, § 1, eff. Jan. 1, 1976; P.A. 79-1454, § 44, eff. Aug. 31, 1976; P.A. 80-606, § 1, eff. Oct. 1, 1977; P.A. 80-1018, § 1, eff. Oct. 1, 1977; P.A. 80-1364, § 36, eff. Aug. 13, 1978; P.A. 81-1554, § 1, eff. Jan. 13, 1981; P.A. 82-433, § 1, eff. Sept. 8, 1981; P.A. 82-573, § 1, eff. Sept. 24, 1981; P.A. 82-783, Art. III, § 37, eff. July 13, 1982; P.A. 82-957, § 1, eff. Jan. 1, 1983; P.A. 83-315, § 1, eff. Jan. 1, 1984; P.A. 83-497, § 1, eff. Jan. 1, 1984; P.A. 83-831, § 1, eff. Jan. 1, 1984; P.A. 83-1260, § 1, eff. Aug. 16, 1984; P.A. 83-1362, Art. II, § 99, eff. Sept. 11, 1984; P.A. 84-832, Art. II, § 10, eff. Sept. 23, 1985; P.A. 84-1060, § 1, eff. July 1, 1986; P.A. 85-572, § 1, eff. Sept. 18, 1987; P.A. 86-408, § 1, eff. Jan. 1, 1990; P.A. 86-447, § 2, eff. Aug. 30, 1989; P.A. 86-1028, Art. II, § 2-44, eff. Feb. 5, 1990; P.A. 87-1111, § 1, eff. Sept. 15, 1992; P.A. 89-433, § 5, eff. Dec. 15, 1995; P.A. 92-108, § 5, eff. Jan. 1, 2002.

Formerly Ill.Rev.Stat.1991, ch. 95 ½, ¶ 13-101.

Section 3 of P.A. 82-433 approved Sept. 8, 1981, provided:

"This Act takes effect upon its becoming a law, except that the provisions relating to safety tests and proof of financial responsibility for medical transport vehicles apply only to applications for and the issuance of registration plates which are required to be displayed on January 1, 1982 or thereafter."

5/13-101.1. Senior citizen transportation vehicle

§ 13-101.1. Senior citizen transportation vehicle. Any vehicle of 12 or more passengers used in the transportation of senior citizens shall bear placards on both sides indicating it is being used for such purposes. The placards may be permanently or temporarily affixed to the vehicle. The size of the letters must be at least 2 inches high and the stroke of the brush must be at least ½ inch wide. Any such vehicle used for such purposes shall be subject to the inspections provided for vehicles of the second division and its operation shall be governed according to the requirements of this Code.

P.A. 76-1586, § 13-101.1, added by P.A. 82-957, § 1, eff. Jan. 1, 1983.

Formerly Ill.Rev.Stat.1991, ch. 95 ½, ¶ 13-101.1.

5/13-102. Tests and investigations

§ 13-102. Tests and investigations. The Department shall conduct tests and make investigations to determine the kind and type of equipment necessary to test the brakes, lights, frame, wheels, steering apparatus, including camber and caster of the axle, and toe-in and tracking of the wheels, and all other devices and appliances referred to in this Act; and shall make public its findings and furnish upon request a list of the various testing devices approved by it.

P.A. 76-1586, § 13-102, eff. July 1, 1970. Amended by P.A. 77-157, § 1, eff. Jan. 1, 1972; P.A. 77-170, § 1, eff. Jan. 1, 1972; P.A. 77-2829, § 40, eff. Dec. 22, 1972; P.A. 78-255, § 61, eff. Oct. 1, 1973; P.A. 78-1244, § 1, eff. Sept. 5, 1974; P.A. 78-1297, § 58, eff. March 4, 1975.

Formerly Ill.Rev.Stat.1991, ch. 95 ½, ¶ 13-102.

5/13-102.1. Diesel powered vehicle emission inspection report

§ 13-102.1. Diesel powered vehicle emission inspection report. Beginning July 1, 2000, the Department of Transportation and the Department of State Police shall each conduct an annual study concerned with the results of emission inspections for diesel powered vehicles registered for a gross weight of more than 16,000 pounds or having a gross vehicle weight rating of more than 16,000 pounds. The studies shall be reported to the General Assembly by June 30, 2001, and every June 30 thereafter. The studies shall also be sent to the Illinois Environmental Protection Agency for its use in environmental matters.

The studies shall include, but not be limited to, the following information:

(a) the number of diesel powered vehicles that were inspected for emission compliance by the respective departments pursuant to this Chapter 13 during the previous year;

(b) the number of diesel powered vehicles that failed and passed the emission inspections conducted by the respective departments required pursuant to this Chapter 13 during the previous year; and

(c) the number of diesel powered vehicles that failed the emission inspections conducted by the respective departments pursuant to this Chapter 13 more than once in the previous year.

P.A. 76-1586, § 13-102.1, added by P.A. 91-254, § 10, eff. July 1, 2000. Amended by P.A. 91-865, § 5, eff. July 1, 2000.

5/13-103. Official testing stations—Fee—Permit—Bond

§ 13-103. Official testing stations—Fee—Permit—Bond. Upon the payment of a fee of $10 and the filing of an application by the proprietor of any vehicle service station or public or private garage upon forms furnished by the Department, accompanied by proof of experience, training and ability of the operator of the testing equipment, together with proof of installation of approved testing equipment as defined in Section 13-102 and the giving of a bond conditioned upon faithful observance of this Section and of rules and regulations issued by the Department in the amount of $1,000 with security approved by the Department, the Department shall issue a permit to the proprietor of such vehicle service station or garage to operate an Official Testing Station. Such permit shall expire 12 months following its issuance, but may be renewed annually by complying with the requirements set forth in this Section and upon the payment of a renewal fee of $10. Proprietors of official testing stations for which permits have been issued prior to the effective date of this Act may renew such permits for the renewal fee of $10 on the expiration of each 12 months following issuance of such permits, by complying with the requirements set forth in this Section. However, any city, village or incorporated town shall upon application to the Department and without payment of any fee or filing of any bond, but upon proof of experience, training and ability of the operator of the testing equipment, and proof of the installation of approved testing equipment as defined in Section 13-102, be issued a permit to operate such testing station as an Official Testing Station under this Act. The permit so issued shall at all times be displayed in a prominent place in the vehicle service station, garage or municipal testing station which is licensed as an Official Testing Station under this Act. No person or vehicle service station, garage or municipal testing station shall in any manner claim or represent himself or itself to be an official testing station unless a permit has been issued to him or it as provided in this Section.

Any person or municipality who or which has received a permit under this Section may test his or its own second division vehicles and issue certificates of safety and conduct emission inspections of his or its own second division vehicles in accordance with the requirements of Section 13-109.1 with respect to any such second division vehicles owned, operated or controlled by him or it.

Each such permit issued by the Department shall state on its face the location of the official testing station to be operated under the permit and safety tests shall be made only at such location. However, the Department may, upon application, authorize a change in the location of the official testing station and the removal of the testing equipment to the new location. Upon approval of such application, the Department shall issue an endorsement which the applicant shall affix to his permit. Such endorsement constitutes authority for the applicant to make such change in location and to remove his testing equipment at the times and to the places stated in the endorsement.

P.A. 76-1586, § 13-103, eff. July 1, 1970. Amended by P.A. 76-1620, § 1, eff. July 1, 1970; P.A. 77-157, § 1, eff. Jan. 1, 1972; P.A. 77-170, § 1, eff. Jan. 1, 1972; P.A. 77-2829, § 40, eff. Dec. 22, 1972; P.A. 78-255, § 61, eff. Oct. 1, 1973; P.A. 80-606, § 1, eff. Oct. 1, 1977; P.A. 91-254, § 10, eff. July 1, 2000.

Formerly Ill.Rev.Stat.1991, ch. 95 ½, ¶ 13-103.

5/13-103.1. Annual certification of safety testers—Fee—Renewal

§ 13-103.1. Annual certification of safety testers—Fee—Renewal. Only certified safety testers are authorized to perform safety tests and affix Certificates of Safety to vehicles. The Department shall annually certify those safety testers who have met its requirements. Safety testers' certificates shall expire 12 months following the date of issue, but may be renewed annually by complying with the requirements as established by the Department.

P.A. 76-1586, § 13-103.1, added by P.A. 80-606, § 1, eff. Oct. 1, 1977.

Formerly Ill.Rev.Stat.1991, ch. 95 ½, ¶ 13-103.1.

5/13-103.2. Reclassification of nonconforming station

§ 13-103.2. Reclassification of nonconforming station. The Department may not change the administrative classification of a nonconforming official testing station from its present classification to a less favorable classification upon a change in ownership of the station, if (1) the nonconforming official testing station has held its present administrative classification since July 1, 1972, and (2) the station meets all requirements for its present classification, other than the requirement of having an exit door in direct line with the safety test equipment and (3) the station is located in a county with no other class "A" or class "C" official testing station.

P.A. 76-1586, § 13-103.2, added by P.A. 84-1422, § 1, eff. Sept. 24, 1986.

Formerly Ill.Rev.Stat.1991, ch. 95 ½, ¶ 13-103.2.

5/13-104. Obtaining or issuing a certificate of safety without proper test—Suspension or revocation of license

§ 13-104. Obtaining or issuing a certificate of safety without proper test—Suspension or revocation of license. Any motor vehicle owner, driver or operator who accepts, obtains or attempts to obtain a certificate of safety without securing a test, or by a test which is known by him to have been improperly made, shall be guilty of a petty offense and shall be fined not less than $5.00 nor more than $100.00 for the first such certificate so accepted or obtained, or attempted to be obtained; and for the second such certificate obtained or attempted to be obtained, not less than $25.00 nor more than $200.00; and for each certificate after the second certificate, obtained or attempted to be obtained, not less than $100.00 nor more than $300.00. The same penalties shall apply to official testing station operators who issue certificates of safety in violation of this Chapter.

When a license is suspended, the suspension shall be for not less than 30 nor more than 180 days. When a license is revoked, the owner of the station cannot make an application for a new license within the period of twelve months after the date of the revocation and then, upon his making an application, the Department of Transportation shall consider this record in deciding whether or not to grant the license.

P.A. 76–1586, § 13–104, eff. July 1, 1970. Amended by P.A. 77–157, § 1, eff. Jan. 1, 1972; P.A. 77–170, § 1, eff. Jan. 1, 1972; P.A. 77–2720, § 1, eff. Jan. 1, 1973; P.A. 78–255, § 61, eff. Oct. 1, 1973.

Formerly Ill.Rev.Stat.1991, ch. 95 ½, ¶ 13–104.

5/13–105. Inspection of official testing stations

§ 13–105. Inspection of official testing stations. Employees specifically authorized by the Department so to do shall inspect all "Official Testing Stations" at frequent intervals. Such employees shall have access to all records relating to tests and work done or parts sold as a result of such tests, to ascertain whether or not tests are properly, fairly and honestly made, and may examine the owner of the official testing station or any officer or employee thereof under oath. The Department shall conduct periodic nonscheduled inspection on owners premises of vehicles owned and operated by licensed "Independent Official Testing Stations."

P.A. 76–1586, § 13–105, eff. July 1, 1970. Amended by P.A. 77–157, § 1, eff. Jan. 1, 1972; P.A. 77–170, § 1, eff. Jan. 1, 1972; P.A. 77–2829, § 40, eff. Dec. 22, 1972; P.A. 78–255, § 61, eff. Oct. 1, 1973; P.A. 86–447, § 2, eff. Aug. 30, 1989.

Formerly Ill.Rev.Stat.1991, ch. 95 ½, ¶ 13–105.

5/13–106. Rates and charges by official testing stations—Schedule to be filed

§ 13–106. Rates and charges by official testing stations-Schedule to be filed. Every operator of an official testing station shall file with the Department, in the manner prescribed by the Department, a schedule of all rates and charges made by him for performing the tests provided for in Section 13–101 and Section 13–109.1. Such rate or charge shall include an amount to reimburse the operator of the official testing station for the purchase from the Department of the certificate of safety required by this chapter, not to exceed that fee paid to the Department by the operator authorized by this chapter. Such rates and charges shall be just and reasonable and the Department upon its own initiative or upon complaint of any person or corporation may require the testing station operator to appear for a hearing and prove that the rates so filed are just and reasonable. A "just and reasonable" rate or charge, for the purposes of this Section, means a rate or charge which is the same, or nearly the same, as the prevailing rate or charge for the same or similar tests made in the community where the station is located. No operator may change this schedule of rates and charges until the proposed changes are filed with and approved by the Department. No license may be issued to any official testing station unless the applicant has filed with the Department a proposed schedule of rates and charges and unless such rates and charges have been approved by the Department. No operator of an official testing station shall charge more or less than the rates so filed with and approved by the Department.

P.A. 76–1586, § 13–106, eff. July 1, 1970. Amended by P.A. 77–157, § 1, eff. Jan. 1, 1972; P.A. 77–170, § 1, eff. Jan. 1, 1972; P.A. 77–2829, § 40, eff. Dec. 22, 1972; P.A. 78–255, § 61, eff. Oct. 1, 1973; P.A. 80–606, § 1, eff. Oct. 1, 1977; P.A. 91–254, § 10, eff. July 1, 2000.

Formerly Ill.Rev.Stat.1991, ch. 95 ½, ¶ 13–106.

5/13–107. Investigation of complaints against official testing stations

§ 13–107. Investigation of complaints against official testing stations. The Department shall, upon its own motion, or upon charges made in writing verified under oath, investigate complaints that an official testing station is willfully falsifying records or tests, either for the purpose of selling parts or services not actually required, or for the purpose of issuing a certificate of safety for a vehicle designed to carry 15 or fewer passengers operated by a contract carrier transporting employees in the course of their employment on a highway of this State, second division vehicle, or medical transport vehicle that is not in safe mechanical condition as determined by the standards of this Chapter in violation of the provisions of this Chapter or of the rules and regulations issued by the Department.

The Secretary of Transportation, for the purpose of more effectively carrying out the provisions of Chapter 13, may appoint such a number of inspectors as he may deem necessary. Such inspectors shall inspect and investigate applicants for official testing station permits and investigate and report violations. With respect to enforcement of the provisions of this Chapter 13, such inspectors shall have and may exercise throughout the State all the powers of police officers.

The Secretary must authorize to each inspector and to any other employee of the Department exercising the powers of a peace officer a distinct badge that, on its face, (i) clearly states that the badge is authorized by the Department and (ii) contains a unique identifying number. No other badge shall be authorized by the Department.

P.A. 76–1586, § 13–107, eff. July 1, 1970. Amended by P.A. 76–2193, § 1, eff. July 1, 1970; P.A. 77–157, § 1, eff. Jan. 1, 1972; P.A. 77–170, § 1, eff. Jan. 1, 1972; P.A. 77–2829, § 40, eff. Dec. 22, 1972; P.A. 78–255, § 61, eff. Oct. 1, 1973; P.A. 82–433, § 1, eff. Sept. 8, 1981; P.A. 91–883, § 105, eff. Jan. 1, 2001; P.A. 92–108, § 5, eff. Jan. 1, 2002.

Formerly Ill.Rev.Stat.1991, ch. 95 ½, ¶ 13–107.

Section 3 of P.A. 82–433 approved Sept. 8, 1981, provided:

"This Act takes effect upon its becoming a law, except that the provisions relating to safety tests and proof of financial responsibility for medical transport vehicles apply only to applications for and the issuance of registration plates which are required to be displayed on January 1, 1982 or thereafter."

5/13–108. Hearing on complaint against official testing station—Suspension or revocation of permit

§ 13–108. Hearing on complaint against official testing station—Suspension or revocation of permit. If it appears to the Department, either through its own investigation or upon charges verified under oath, that any of the provisions of this Chapter or the rules and regulations of the Department, are being violated, the Department, shall after notice to the person, firm or corporation charged with such violation, conduct a hearing. At least 10 days prior to the date of such hearing the Department shall cause to be served upon the person, firm or corporation charged with such violation, a copy of such charge or charges by registered mail or by the personal service thereof, together with a notice specifying the time and place of such hearing. At the time and place specified in such notice the person, firm or corporation charged with such violation shall be given an opportunity to appear in person or by counsel and to be heard by the Secretary of Transportation or an officer or employee of the Department designated in writing by him to conduct such hearing. If it appears from the hearing that such person, firm or corporation is guilty of the charge preferred against him or it, the Secretary of Transportation may order the permit suspended or revoked, and the bond forfeited. Any such revocation or suspension shall not be a bar to subsequent arrest and prosecution for violation of this Chapter.

P.A. 76-1586, § 13-108, eff. July 1, 1970. Amended by P.A. 77-157, § 1, eff. Jan. 1, 1972; P.A. 77-170, § 1, eff. Jan. 1, 1972; P.A. 77-2829, § 40, eff. Dec. 22, 1972; P.A. 78-255, § 61, eff. Oct. 1, 1973.

Formerly Ill.Rev.Stat.1991, ch. 95 ½, ¶ 13-108.

5/13-109. Safety test prior to application for license—Subsequent tests—Repairs—Retest

§ 13-109. Safety test prior to application for license—Subsequent tests—Repairs—Retest.

(a) Except as otherwise provided in Chapter 13, each second division vehicle and medical transport vehicle, except those vehicles other than school buses or medical transport vehicles owned or operated by a municipal corporation or political subdivision having a population of 1,000,000 or more inhabitants which are subjected to safety tests imposed by local ordinance or resolution, operated in whole or in part over the highways of this State, and each vehicle designed to carry 15 or fewer passengers operated by a contract carrier transporting employees in the course of their employment on a highway of this State, shall be subjected to the safety test provided for in Chapter 13 of this Code. Tests shall be conducted at an official testing station within 6 months prior to the application for registration as provided for in this Code. Subsequently each vehicle shall be subject to tests at least every 6 months, and in the case of school buses at least every 6 months or 10,000 miles whichever occurs first, and according to schedules established by rules and regulations promulgated by the Department. Any component subject to regular inspection which is damaged in a reportable accident must be reinspected before the bus is returned to service.

(b) The Department shall also conduct periodic nonscheduled inspections of school buses, of buses registered as charitable vehicles and of religious organization buses. If such inspection reveals that a vehicle is not in substantial compliance with the rules promulgated by the Department, the Department shall remove the Certificate of Safety from the vehicle, and shall place the vehicle out-of-service. A bright orange, triangular decal shall be placed on an out-of-service vehicle where the Certificate of Safety has been removed. The vehicle must pass a safety test at an official testing station before it is again placed in service.

(c) If the violation is not substantial a bright yellow, triangular sticker shall be placed next to the Certificate of Safety at the time the nonscheduled inspection is made. The Department shall reinspect the vehicle after 3 working days to determine that the violation has been corrected and remove the yellow, triangular decal. If the violation is not corrected within 3 working days, the Department shall place the vehicle out-of-service in accordance with procedures in subsection (b).

(d) If a violation is not substantial and does not directly affect the safe operation of the vehicle, the Department shall issue a warning notice requiring correction of the violation. Such correction shall be accomplished as soon as practicable and a report of the correction shall be made to the Department within 30 days in a manner established by the Department. If the Department has not been advised that the corrections have been made, and the violations still exist, the Department shall place the vehicle out-of-service in accordance with procedures in subsection (b).

(e) The Department is authorized to promulgate regulations to implement its program of nonscheduled inspections. Causing or allowing the operation of an out-of-service vehicle with passengers or unauthorized removal of an out-of-service sticker is a Class 3 felony. Causing or allowing the operation of a vehicle with a 3-day sticker for longer than 3 days with the sticker attached or the unauthorized removal of a 3-day sticker is a Class C misdemeanor.

(f) If a second division vehicle, medical transport vehicle, or vehicle operated by a contract carrier as provided in subsection (a) of this Section is in safe mechanical condition, as determined pursuant to Chapter 13, the operator of the official testing station must at once issue to the second division vehicle or medical transport vehicle a certificate of safety, in the form and manner prescribed by the Department, which shall be affixed to the vehicle by the certified safety tester who performed the safety tests. The owner of the second division vehicle or medical transport vehicle or the contract carrier shall at all times display the Certificate of Safety on the second division vehicle, medical transport vehicle, or vehicle operated by a contract carrier in the manner prescribed by the Department.

(g) If a test shows that a second division vehicle, medical transport vehicle, or vehicle operated by a contract carrier is not in safe mechanical condition as provided in this Section, it shall not be operated on the highways until it has been repaired and submitted to a retest at an official testing station. If the owner or contract carrier submits the vehicle to a retest at a different official testing station from that where it failed to pass the first test, he shall present to the operator of the second station the report of the original test, and shall notify the Department in writing, giving the name and address of the original testing station and the defects which prevented the issuance of a Certificate of Safety, and the name and address of the second official testing station making the retest.

P.A. 76-1586, § 13-109, eff. July 1, 1970. Amended by P.A. 77-157, § 1, eff. Jan. 1, 1972; P.A. 77-170, § 1, eff. Jan. 1, 1972; P.A. 77-2170, § 1, eff. Aug. 2, 1972; P.A. 78-255, § 61, eff. Oct. 1, 1973; P.A. 78-1244, § 1, eff. Sept. 5, 1974; P.A. 78-1297, § 58, eff. March 4, 1975; P.A. 79-63, § 1, eff. June 26, 1975; P.A. 79-798, § 1, eff. July 1, 1976; P.A. 79-1454, § 44, eff. Aug. 31, 1976; P.A. 80-606, § 1, eff. Oct. 1, 1977; P.A. 82-433, § 1, eff. Sept. 8, 1981; P.A. 86-447, § 2, eff. Aug. 30, 1989; P.A. 86-1223, § 1, eff. Jan. 1, 1991; P.A. 92-108, § 5, eff. Jan. 1, 2002.

Formerly Ill.Rev.Stat.1991, ch. 95 ½, ¶ 13-109.

Section 3 of P.A. 82-433 approved Sept. 8, 1981, provided:

"This Act takes effect upon its becoming a law, except that the provisions relating to safety tests and proof of financial responsibility for medical transport vehicles apply only to applications for and the issuance of registration plates which are required to be displayed on January 1, 1982 or thereafter."

5/13-109.1. Annual and nonscheduled emission inspection tests; standards; penalties; funds

§ 13-109.1. Annual and nonscheduled emission inspection tests; standards; penalties; funds.

(a) For each diesel powered vehicle that (i) is registered for a gross weight of more than 16,000 pounds, (ii) is registered within an affected area, and (iii) is a 2 year or older model year, an annual emission inspection test shall be conducted at an official testing station certified by the Illinois Department of Transportation to perform diesel emission inspections pursuant to the standards set forth in subsection (b) of this Section. This annual emission inspection test may be conducted in conjunction with a semi-annual safety test.

(a-5) Beginning October 1, 2000, the Department of State Police is authorized to perform nonscheduled emission inspections for cause, at any place within an affected area, of any diesel powered vehicles that are operated on the roadways of this State, and are registered for a gross weight of more than 16,000 pounds or have a gross vehicle weight rating of more than 16,000 pounds. The inspections shall adhere to the procedures and standards set forth in subsection (b). These nonscheduled emission inspections shall be conducted by the Department of State Police at weigh stations, roadside, or other safe and reasonable locations within an affected area. Before any person may inspect a diesel vehicle under this Section, he or she must receive adequate training and certification for diesel emission inspections by the Department of State Police. The Department of State Police shall adopt rules for the training and certification of persons who conduct emission inspections under this Section.

(b) Diesel emission inspections conducted under this Chapter 13 shall be conducted in accordance with the Society of Automotive Engineers Recommended Practice J1667 "Snap-Acceleration Smoke Test Procedure for Heavy-Duty Diesel Powered Vehicles" and the cutpoint standards set forth in the United States Environmental Protection Agency guidance document "Guidance to States on Smoke Opacity Cutpoints to be used with the SAE J1667 In-Use Smoke Test Procedure". Those procedures and standards, as now in effect, are made a part of this Code, in the same manner as though they were set out in full in this Code.

Notwithstanding the above cutpoint standards, for motor vehicles that are model years 1973 and older, until December 31, 2002, the level of peak smoke opacity shall not exceed 70 percent. Beginning January 1, 2003, for motor vehicles that are model years 1973 and older, the level of peak smoke opacity shall not exceed 55 percent.

(c) If the annual emission inspection under subsection (a) reveals that the vehicle is not in compliance with the diesel emission standards set forth in subsection (b) of this Section, the operator of the official testing station shall issue a warning notice requiring correction of the violation. The correction shall be made and the vehicle submitted to an emissions retest at an official testing station certified by the Department to perform diesel emission inspections within 30 days from the issuance of the warning notice requiring correction of the violation.

If, within 30 days from the issuance of the warning notice, the vehicle is not in compliance with the diesel emission standards set forth in subsection (b) as determined by an emissions retest at an official testing station, the operator of the official testing station or the Department shall place the vehicle out-of-service in accordance with the rules promulgated by the Department. Operating a vehicle that has been placed out-of-service under this subsection (c) is a petty offense punishable by a $1,000 fine. The vehicle must pass a diesel emission inspection at an official testing station before it is again placed in service. The Secretary of State, Department of State Police, and other law enforcement officers shall enforce this Section. No emergency vehicle, as defined in Section 1-105, may be placed out-of-service pursuant to this Section.

The Department or an official testing station may issue a certificate of waiver subsequent to a reinspection of a vehicle that failed the emissions inspection. Certificate of waiver shall be issued upon determination that documented proof demonstrates that emissions repair costs for the noncompliant vehicle of at least $3,000 have been spent in an effort to achieve compliance with the emission standards set forth in subsection (b). The Department of Transportation shall adopt rules for the implementation of this subsection including standards of documented proof as well as the criteria by which a waiver shall be granted.

(c-5) If a nonscheduled inspection reveals that the vehicle is not in compliance with the diesel emission standards set forth in subsection (b), the operator of the vehicle is guilty of a petty offense punishable by a $400 fine, and a State Police officer shall issue a citation for a violation of the standards. A third or subsequent violation within one year of the first violation is a petty offense punishable by a $1,000 fine. An operator who receives a citation under this subsection shall not, within 30 days of the initial citation, receive a second or subsequent citation for operating the same vehicle in violation of the emission standards set forth in subsection (b).

(d) There is hereby created within the State Treasury a special fund to be known as the Diesel Emissions Testing Fund, constituted from the fines collected pursuant to subsections (c) and (c-5) of this Section. Subject to appropriation, moneys from the Diesel Emissions Testing Fund shall be available, as a supplement to moneys appropriated from the General Revenue Fund, to the Department of Transportation and the Department of State Police for their implementation of the diesel emission inspection requirements under this Chapter 13. All moneys received from fines imposed under this Section shall be paid into the Diesel Emissions Testing Fund. All citations issued pursuant to this Section shall be considered non-moving violations. The Department of Transportation and the Department of State Police are authorized to promulgate rules to implement their responsibilities under this Section.

P.A. 76-1586, § 13-109.1, added by P.A. 91-254, § 10, eff. July 1, 2000. Amended by P.A. 91-865, § 5, eff. July 1, 2000.

5/13-109.2. Pollution Control Board diesel emission standards and tests

§ 13-109.2. Pollution Control Board diesel emission standards and tests. Within 8 months of the effective date of this amendatory Act of the 91st General Assembly, the Pollution Control Board shall amend its heavy-duty diesel smoke opacity standards and test procedures to be consistent with the procedures and standards set forth in Section 13-109.1.

P.A. 76-1586, § 13-109.2, added by P.A. 91-254, § 10, eff. July 1, 2000.

5/13-109.3. Exemption from diesel emissions inspections

§ 13-109.3. Exemption from diesel emissions inspections. Second division vehicles being operated on plates issued pursuant to subsection (c) of Section 3-815 are exempt from the diesel emissions inspection requirements set forth in this Chapter.

P.A. 76–1586, § 13–109.3, added by P.A. 91–254, § 10, eff. July 1, 2000.

5/13–110. Certificate of safety

§ 13–110. Certificate of safety. (a) Certificates of Safety shall be in contrasting colors, with a number on the face of the Certificate indicating the month of the next inspection period the vehicle is subject to inspection. Certificates for school buses shall also indicate the mileage at which the school bus shall be subject to inspection if it occurs before the next regular inspection period. The colors of Certificates of Safety shall be prescribed by the Department.

(b) Certificates of Safety, which remain the property of the State of Illinois, will be provided to Official Testing Stations by the Department at the fee of $1 each. Certificates of Safety which remain unused at the end of each inspection period will be redeemed for the same amount in a manner prescribed by the Department.

(c) Nothing in this Chapter shall be construed as a suggestion or direction to any owner to require him to have any repairs made or any work done by any official testing station, but all tests must be made at an official testing station to secure the issuance of a certificate of safety, and no certificate of safety issued by any other than an official testing station shall be deemed a compliance with this Chapter.

P.A. 76–1586, § 13–110, eff. July 1, 1970. Amended by P.A. 80–606, § 1, eff. Oct. 1, 1977; P.A. 83–311, § 1, eff. Jan. 1, 1984.

Formerly Ill.Rev.Stat.1991, ch. 95 ½, ¶ 13–110.

5/13–111. Operation without certificate of safety attached; Effective date of certificate

§ 13–111. Operation without certificate of safety attached; Effective date of certificate.

(a) Except as provided for in Chapter 13, no person shall operate any vehicle required to be inspected by this Chapter upon the highways of this State unless there is affixed to that vehicle a certificate of safety then in effect. The Secretary of State, State Police, and other police officers shall enforce this Section. The Department shall determine the expiration date of the certificate of safety.

The certificates, all forms and records, reports of tests and retests, and the full procedure and methods of making the tests and retests, shall be in the form prescribed by the Department.

(b) Every person convicted of violating this Section is guilty of a Class C misdemeanor.

P.A. 76–1586, § 13–111, eff. July 1, 1970. Amended by P.A. 77–157, § 1, eff. Jan. 1, 1972; P.A. 77–170, § 1, eff. Jan. 1, 1972; P.A. 77–2170, § 1, eff. Aug. 2, 1972; P.A. 78–255, § 61, eff. Oct. 1, 1973; P.A. 81–1554, § 1, eff. Jan. 13, 1981; P.A. 82–433, § 1, eff. Sept. 8, 1981; P.A. 83–12, § 1, eff. Jan. 1, 1984; P.A. 88–415, § 10, eff. Aug. 20, 1993.

Formerly Ill.Rev.Stat.1991, ch. 95 ½, ¶ 13–111.

Section 3 of P.A. 82–433 approved Sept. 8, 1981, provided:

"This Act takes effect upon its becoming a law, except that the provisions relating to safety tests and proof of financial responsibility for medical transport vehicles apply only to applications for and the issuance of registration plates which are required to be displayed on January 1, 1982 or thereafter."

Section 4 of P.A. 83–12, approved July 1, 1983, provided:

"Effective date. This Act takes effect as provided in this Section.

"The amendments to those portions of Sections 3–815(a), 3–818 and 3–819(b) of 'The Illinois Vehicle Code' in Section 1 of this Act which create the 'X', 'Z', 'MX', 'MZ', 'MM' and 'TN' registration classifications and the fees and taxes imposed for those classifications, the amendments to Sections 2–119, 3–401 and 3–802 of 'The Illinois Vehicle Code' in Section 1 of this Act, and the amendments to Chapter 15 of 'The Illinois Vehicle Code' in Section 1 of this Act take effect July 1, 1983.

"The remaining amendments to 'The Illinois Vehicle Code' in Section 1 of this Act take effect July 1, 1983 and apply beginning with the 1985 registration year, except that the amendments to Sections 3–813 through 3–816 and Section 3–819 apply beginning with the 1984 registration year for those vehicles registered on a calendar year basis only.

"The amendments to Chapters 13 and 18 of 'The Illinois Vehicle Code' in Section 1 of this Act take effect January 1, 1984.

"Section 2 of this Act takes effect on the first day of the next succeeding month which commences at least 30 days after the date on which this Act becomes law.

"Section 3 of this Act takes effect July 1, 1983.

"Section 3.1 of this Act takes effect January 1, 1984.

"This Section 4 takes effect upon its becoming a law."

5/13–112. Exemption from local tests

§ 13–112. Exemption from local tests. Any second division vehicle or limousine displaying a certificate of safety issued under this Chapter is exempt from any test required by ordinance or otherwise in any city, village or incorporated town in this State.

P.A. 76–1586, § 13–101, eff. July 1, 1970. Amended by P.A. 77–157, § 1, eff. Jan. 1, 1972; P.A. 77–170, § 1, eff. Jan. 1, 1972; P.A. 77–1633, § 1, eff. Sept. 23, 1972; P.A. 77–1688, § 1, eff. July 1, 1972; P.A. 77–2170, § 1, eff. Aug. 2, 1972; P.A. 78–255, § 61, eff. Oct. 1, 1973; P.A. 78–1244, § 1, eff. Sept. 5, 1974; P.A. 78–1297, § 58, eff. March 4, 1975; P.A. 79–798, § 1, eff. July 1, 1976; P.A. 79–865, § 1, eff. Jan. 1, 1976; P.A. 79–1454, § 44, eff. Aug. 31, 1976; P.A. 80–606, § 1, eff. Oct. 1, 1977; P.A. 80–1018, § 1, eff. Oct. 1, 1977; P.A. 80–1364, § 36, eff. Aug. 13, 1978; P.A. 81–1554, § 1, eff. Jan. 13, 1981; P.A. 82–433, § 1, eff. Sept. 8, 1981; P.A. 82–573, § 1, eff. Sept. 24, 1981; P.A. 82–783, Art. III, § 37, eff. July 13, 1982; P.A. 82–957, § 1, eff. Jan. 1, 1983; P.A. 83–315, § 1, eff. Jan. 1, 1984; P.A. 83–497, § 1, eff. Jan. 1, 1984; P.A. 83–831, § 1, eff. Jan. 1, 1984; P.A. 83–1260, § 1, eff. Aug. 16, 1984; P.A. 83–1362, Art. II, § 99, eff. Sept. 11, 1984; P.A. 84–832, Art. II, § 10, eff. Sept. 23, 1985; P.A. 84–1060, § 1, eff. July 1, 1986; P.A. 85–572, § 1, eff. Sept. 18, 1987; P.A. 86–408, § 1, eff. Jan. 1, 1990; P.A. 86–447, § 2, eff. Aug. 30, 1989; P.A. 86–1028, Art. II, § 2–44, eff. Feb. 5, 1990; P.A. 87–1111, § 1, eff. Sept. 15, 1992.

Formerly Ill.Rev.Stat.1991, ch. 95 ½, ¶ 13–112.

5/13–113. Sale or exchange of used vehicle without certificate of safety

§ 13–113. Sale or exchange of used vehicle without certificate of safety. No person engaged in the business of buying, selling or exchanging motor vehicles shall sell, transfer or exchange any used second division vehicle or medical transport vehicle unless it has been tested and a currently valid certificate of safety has been issued therefor: Provided, that such person engaged in the business of buying, selling or exchanging motor vehicles may sell, transfer or exchange any used second division vehicle or medical transport vehicle without a valid certificate of safety if the sale, transfer or exchange is for the purpose of restoring or repairing such vehicle to a condition in which it can pass the test for a certificate of safety, or for the purpose of junking. Provided, however, that the used second division vehicle or medical transport vehicle is not moved under its own power to the location in which it will be restored, repaired or junked.

P.A. 76-1586, § 13-113, eff. July 1, 1970. Amended by P.A. 81-694, § 1, eff. Sept. 16, 1979; P.A. 82-433, § 1, eff. Sept. 8, 1981.

Formerly Ill.Rev.Stat.1991, ch. 95 ½, ¶ 13-113.

Section 3 of P.A. 82-433 approved Sept. 8, 1981, provided:

"This Act takes effect upon its becoming a law, except that the provisions relating to safety tests and proof of financial responsibility for medical transport vehicles apply only to applications for and the issuance of registration plates which are required to be displayed on January 1, 1982 or thereafter."

5/13-114. Interstate carriers of property

§ 13-114. Interstate carriers of property. Any vehicle registered in Illinois and operated by an interstate carrier of property shall be exempt from the provisions of this Chapter provided such carrier has registered with the Bureau of Motor Carrier Safety of the Federal Highway Administration as an interstate motor carrier of property and has been assigned a federal census number by such Bureau. An interstate carrier of property, however, is not exempt from the provisions of Section 13-111(b) of this Chapter.

Any vehicle registered in Illinois and operated by a private interstate carrier of property shall be exempt from the provisions of this Chapter, except the provisions of Section 13-111(b), provided it:

1. is registered with the Bureau of Motor Carrier Safety of the Federal Highway Administration, and
2. carries in the motor vehicle documentation issued by the Bureau of Motor Carrier Safety of the Federal Highway Administration displaying the federal census number assigned, and
3. displays on the sides of the motor vehicle the census number, which must be no less than 2 inches high, with a brush stroke no less than ¼ inch wide in a contrasting color.

Notwithstanding any other provision of this Section, each diesel powered vehicle that is registered for a gross weight of more than 16,000 pounds or has a gross vehicle weight rating of more than 16,000 pounds and that is operated by an interstate carrier of property or a private interstate carrier of property within the affected area is subject only to the provisions of this Chapter that pertain to nonscheduled diesel emission inspections.

P.A. 76-1586, § 13-114, eff. July 1, 1970. Amended by P.A. 76-1725, § 1, eff. July 1, 1970; P.A. 77-43, § 1, eff. Jan. 1, 1972; P.A. 78-498, § 1, eff. Oct. 1, 1973; P.A. 81-1554, § 1, eff. Jan. 13, 1981; P.A. 83-12, § 1, eff. Jan. 1, 1984; P.A. 85-560, § 1, eff. Sept. 18, 1987; P.A. 85-1407, § 2, eff. Sept. 22, 1988; P.A. 91-254, § 10, eff. July 1, 2000; P.A. 91-865, § 5, eff. July 1, 2000.

Formerly Ill.Rev.Stat.1991, ch. 95 ½, ¶ 13-114.

Section 4 of P.A. 83-12, approved July 1, 1983, provided:

"Effective date. This Act takes effect as provided in this Section.

"The amendments to those portions of Sections 3-815(a), 3-818 and 3-819(b) of 'The Illinois Vehicle Code' in Section 1 of this Act which create the 'X', 'Z', 'MX', 'MZ', 'MM' and 'TN' registration classifications and the fees and taxes imposed for those classifications, the amendments to Sections 2-119, 3-401 and 3-802 of 'The Illinois Vehicle Code' in Section 1 of this Act, and the amendments to Chapter 15 of 'The Illinois Vehicle Code' in Section 1 of this Act take effect July 1, 1983.

"The remaining amendments to 'The Illinois Vehicle Code' in Section 1 of this Act take effect July 1, 1983 and apply beginning with the 1985 registration year, except that the amendments to Sections 3-813 through 3-816 and Section 3-819 apply beginning with the 1984 registration year for those vehicles registered on a calendar year basis only.

"The amendments to Chapters 13 and 18 of 'The Illinois Vehicle Code' in Section 1 of this Act take effect January 1, 1984.

"Section 2 of this Act takes effect on the first day of the next succeeding month which commences at least 30 days after the date on which this Act becomes law.

"Section 3 of this Act takes effect July 1, 1983.

"Section 3.1 of this Act takes effect January 1, 1984.

"This Section 4 takes effect upon its becoming a law."

P.A. 91-865 incorporated the amendment by P.A. 91-254.

5/13-115. School buses—pretrip inspections

§ 13-115. School buses—pretrip inspections.

Each day that a school bus is operated the driver shall conduct a pretrip inspection of the mechanical and safety equipment on the bus as prescribed by rule or regulation of the Department. A person other than the driver may perform portions of the pretrip inspection as prescribed by rule of the Department.

P.A. 76-1586, § 13-115, added by P.A. 78-1244, § 1, eff. Sept. 5, 1974. Amended by P.A. 89-658, § 5, eff. Jan. 1, 1997.

Formerly Ill.Rev.Stat.1991, ch. 95 ½, ¶ 13-115.

5/13-116. Deposit of funds

§ 13-116. All funds collected by the Department under this Chapter shall be deposited in the road fund in the State Treasury.

P.A. 76-1586, § 13-116, added by P.A. 80-606, § 1, eff. Oct. 1, 1977.

Formerly Ill.Rev.Stat.1991, ch. 95 ½, ¶ 13-116.

5/13-116.1. Emission inspection funding

§ 13-116.1. Emission inspection funding. The Department of Transportation shall be reimbursed for all expenses related to the training, equipment, recordkeeping, and conducting of diesel powered emission inspections pursuant to this Chapter 13 when that testing is conducted within the affected areas, subject to appropriation, from the General Revenue Fund and the Diesel Emissions Testing Fund. No moneys from any funds other than the General Revenue Fund and the Diesel Emissions Testing Fund shall be appropriated for diesel emission inspections under this Chapter 13.

P.A. 76-1586, § 13-116.1, added by P.A. 91-254, § 10, eff. July 1, 2000.

5/13-117. Home rule

§ 13-117. Home rule. A unit of local government within the affected areas, including home rule units, shall not require or conduct a diesel emission inspection program that does not meet or exceed the standards of the diesel emission inspections provided for in this Chapter 13. A unit of local government within the affected areas, including home rule units, must affirmatively comply with the diesel emission inspection requirements of this Chapter 13. This Section is a limitation under subsection (i) of Section 6 of Article VII of the Illinois Constitution on the concurrent exercise by home rule units of powers and functions exercised by the State.

P.A. 76-1586, § 13-117, added by P.A. 91-254, § 10, eff. July 1, 2000.

CHAPTER 13A. EMISSION INSPECTION

Section

Enactment and Repeal

Chapter 13A was added by P.A. 83-1477, § 1, eff. Sept. 24, 1984, and was repealed eff. Jan. 1, 2003, pursuant to 625 ILCS 5/13A-115, as amended by P.A. 92-682.

5/13A-101 to 5/13A-115. §§ 13A-101 to 13A-115. Repealed eff. Jan. 1, 2003

CHAPTER 13B. EMISSION INSPECTION

Section

Enactment

Chapter 13B was added by P.A. 88-533, § 15, eff. Jan. 1, 1994

5/13B-1. Short title

§ 13B-1. Short title. This Chapter may be cited as the Vehicle Emissions Inspection Law of 1995.

P.A. 76-1586, § 13B-1, added by P.A. 88-533, § 15, eff. Jan. 18, 1994.

5/13B-5. Definitions

§ 13B-5. Definitions. For the purposes of this Chapter:

"Affected counties" means Cook County; DuPage County; Lake County; those parts of Kane County that are not included within any of the following ZIP code areas, as designated by the U.S. Postal Service on the effective date of this amendatory Act of 1994: 60109, 60119, 60135, 60140, 60142, 60144, 60147, 60151, 60152, 60178, 60182, 60511, 60520, 60545, and 60554; those parts of Kendall County that are not included within any of the following ZIP code areas, as designated by the U.S. Postal Service on the effective date of this amendatory Act of 1994: 60447, 60512, 60536, 60537, 60541, those parts of 60543 that are not within the census defined urbanized area, 60545, and 60560; those parts of McHenry County that are not included within any of the following ZIP code areas, as designated by the U.S. Postal Service on the effective date of this amendatory Act of 1994: 60001, 60033, 60034, 60071, 60072, 60097, 60098, 60142, 60152, and 60180; those parts of Will County that are not included within any of the following ZIP code areas, as designated by the U.S. Postal Service on the effective date of this amendatory Act of 1994: 60401, 60407, 60408, 60410, 60416, 60418, 60421, 60442, 60447, 60468, 60481, 60935 and 60950; those parts of Madison County that are not included within any of the following ZIP code areas, as designated by the U.S. Postal Service on the effective date of this amendatory Act of 1994: 62001, 62012, 62021, 62026, 62046, 62058, 62061, 62067, 62074, 62088, 62097, 62249, 62275, and 62281; those parts of Monroe County that are not included within any of the following ZIP code areas, as designated by the U.S. Postal Service on the effective date of this amendatory Act of 1994: 62244, 62248, 62256, 62261, 62276, 62278, 62279, 62295, and 62298; and those parts of St. Clair County that are not included within any of the following ZIP code areas, as designated by the U.S. Postal Service on the effective date of this amendatory Act of 1994: 62224, 62243, 62248, 62254, 62255, 62257, 62258, 62260, 62264, 62265, 62269, 62278, 62282, 62285, 62289, and 62298.

"Board" means the Illinois Pollution Control Board.

"Claim evaluation center" means an automotive diagnostic facility that meets the standards prescribed by the Agency for performing examinations of vehicle emissions inspection damage claims.

"Contractor" means the vehicle emissions test contractor for Official Inspection Stations described in Section 13B-45.

"Inspection area" means Cook County, DuPage County, Lake County and those portions of Kane, Kendall, Madison, McHenry, Monroe, Will, and St. Clair Counties included in the definition of "affected counties".

"Owner" means the registered owner of the vehicle, as indicated on the vehicle's registration. In the case of an unregistered vehicle, "owner" has the meaning set forth in Section 1-155 of this Code.

"Program" means the vehicle emission inspection program established under this Chapter.

"Resident" includes natural persons, foreign and domestic corporations, partnerships, associations, and all other commercial and governmental entities. For the purpose of determining residence, the owner of a vehicle shall be presumed to reside at the address indicated on the vehicle's registration. A governmental entity, including the federal government and its agencies, and any unit of local government or school district, any part of which is located within an affected county, shall be deemed a resident of an affected county for the purpose of any vehicle that is owned by the governmental entity and regularly operated in an affected county.

"Registration" of a vehicle means its registration under Article IV of Chapter 3 of this Code.[1]

P.A. 76-1586, § 13B-5, added by P.A. 88-533, § 15, eff. Jan. 18, 1994. Amended by P.A. 90-89, § 15, eff. Jan. 1, 1998; P.A. 92-821, § 5, eff. Aug. 21, 2002.

[1] 625 ILCS 5/3-400 et seq.

5/13B-10. Program

§ 13B-10. Program.

(a) The Agency shall establish a program to begin January 1, 1995, to reduce the emission of pollutants by motor vehicles. At a minimum, this program shall provide for all of the following:

(1) The inspection of certain motor vehicles every 2 years, as required under Section 13B-15.

(2) The establishment and operation of official inspection stations.

(3) The designation of official test equipment and testing procedures.

(4) The training and supervision of inspectors and other personnel.

(5) Procedures to assure the correct operation, maintenance and calibration of test equipment.

(6) Procedures for certifying test results and for reporting and maintaining relevant data and records.

(b) The Agency shall provide for the operation of a sufficient number of official inspection stations to prevent undue difficulty in obtaining the inspections required under this Chapter. In the event that the Agency operates inspection stations or contracts with one or more parties to operate inspection stations on its behalf, the Agency shall endeavor to: (i) locate the stations so that the owners of vehicles subject to inspection reside within 12 miles of an official inspection station; and (ii) have sufficient inspection capacity at the stations so that the usual wait before the start of an inspection does not exceed 20 minutes.

P.A. 76-1586, § 13B-10, added by P.A. 88-533, § 15, eff. Jan. 18, 1994.

5/13B-15. Inspections

§ 13B-15. Inspections.

(a) Beginning with the implementation of the program required by this Chapter, every motor vehicle that is owned by a resident of an affected county, other than a vehicle that is exempt under subsection (f) or (g), is subject to inspection under the program.

The Agency shall send notice of the assigned inspection month, at least 15 days before the beginning of the assigned month, to the owner of each vehicle subject to the program. For a vehicle that was subject to inspection before the effective date of this amendatory Act of 1994 and for which an initial inspection sticker or initial inspection certificate has already been issued, the month to be assigned by the Agency for that vehicle shall not be earlier than the current assigned month, unless so requested by the owner. If the assigned month is later than the current assigned month, the Agency shall issue either a corrected inspection sticker or corrected certificate for that vehicle.

Initial emission inspection stickers or initial inspection certificates, as the case may be, expire on the last day of the third month following the month assigned by the Agency for the first inspection of the vehicle. Renewal inspection stickers or certificates expire on the last day of the third month following the month assigned for inspection in the year in which the vehicle's next inspection is required.

The Agency or its agent may issue an interim emission inspection sticker or certificate for any vehicle subject to inspection that does not have a currently valid emission inspection sticker or certificate at the time the Agency is notified by the Secretary of State of its registration by a new owner, and for which an initial emission inspection sticker or certificate has already been issued. Interim emission inspection stickers or certificates expire no later than the last day of the sixth complete calendar month after the date the Agency issued the interim emission inspection sticker or certificate.

The owner of each vehicle subject to inspection shall obtain an emission inspection sticker or certificate for the vehicle in accordance with this subsection. Before the expiration of the emission inspection sticker or certificate, the owner shall have the vehicle inspected and, upon demonstration of compliance, obtain a renewal emission inspection sticker or certificate. A renewal emission inspection sticker or certificate shall not be issued more than 5 months before the expiration date of the previous inspection sticker or certificate.

(b) Except as provided in subsection (c), vehicles shall be inspected every 2 years on a schedule that begins either in the second, fourth, or later calendar year after the vehicle model year. The beginning test schedule shall be set by the Agency and shall be consistent with the State's requirements for emission reductions as determined by the applicable United States Environmental Protection Agency vehicle emissions estimation model and applicable guidance and rules.

(c) A vehicle may be inspected out of its 2-year inspection schedule when a new owner acquires the vehicle and it should have been, but was not, in compliance with this Act when the vehicle was acquired by the new owner.

(d) The owner of a vehicle subject to inspection shall have the vehicle inspected and obtain and display on the vehicle or carry within the vehicle, in a manner specified by the Agency, a valid unexpired emission inspection sticker or certificate in the manner specified by the Agency.

Any person who violates this subsection (d) is guilty of a petty offense, except that a third or subsequent violation within one year of the first violation is a Class C misdemeanor. The fine imposed for a violation of this subsection shall be not less than $50 if the violation occurred within 60 days following the date by which a new or renewal emission inspection sticker or certificate was required to be obtained for the vehicle, and not less than $300 if the violation occurred more than 60 days after that date.

(e) (1) For a $20 fee, to be paid into the Vehicle Inspection Fund, the Agency shall inspect:

(A) Vehicles operated on federal installations within an affected county, pursuant to Title 40, Section 51.356 of the Code of Federal Regulations.

(B) Federally owned vehicles operated in affected counties.

(2) For a fee of $20, to be paid into the Vehicle Inspection Fund, the Agency may inspect:

(A) Vehicles registered in and subject to emission inspections requirements of another state.

(B) Vehicles presented for inspection on a voluntary basis.

Any fees collected under this subsection shall not offset normally appropriated Motor Fuel Tax Funds.

(f) The following vehicles are not subject to inspection:

(1) Vehicles not subject to registration under Article IV of Chapter 3 of this Code,[1] other than vehicles owned by the federal government.

(2) Motorcycles, motor driven cycles, and motorized pedalcycles.

(3) Farm vehicles and implements of husbandry.

(4) Implements of warfare owned by the State or federal government.

(5) Antique vehicles, custom vehicles, street rods, and vehicles of model year 1967 or before.

(6) Vehicles operated exclusively for parade or ceremonial purposes by any veterans, fraternal, or civic organization, organized on a not-for-profit basis.

(7) Vehicles for which a Junking Certificate has been issued by the Secretary of State under Section 3-117 of this Code.

(8) Diesel powered vehicles, and vehicles that are powered exclusively by electricity.

(9) Vehicles operated exclusively in organized amateur or professional sporting activities, as defined in the Environmental Protection Act.[2]

(10) Vehicles registered in, subject to, and in compliance with the emission inspection requirements of another state.

The Agency may issue temporary or permanent exemption stickers or certificates for vehicles temporarily or permanently exempt from inspection under this subsection (f). An exemption sticker or certificate does not need to be displayed.

(g) According to criteria the Agency may adopt, a motor vehicle may be exempted from the inspection requirements of this Section by the Agency on the basis of an Agency determination that the vehicle is located and primarily used outside of the affected counties or in other jurisdictions where vehicle emission inspections are not required. The Agency may issue an annual exemption sticker or certificate without inspection for any vehicle exempted from inspection under this subsection.

(h) Any owner or lessee of a fleet of 15 or more motor vehicles which are subject to inspection under this Section may apply to the Agency for a permit to establish and operate a Private Official Inspection Station.

(i) Pursuant to Title 40, Section 51.371 of the Code of Federal Regulations, the Agency shall establish a program of on-road testing of in-use vehicles through the use of remote sensing devices. The Agency shall evaluate the emission performance of 0.5% of the subject fleet or 20,000 vehicles, whichever is less. Under no circumstances shall on-road testing include any sort of roadblock or roadside pullover or cause any type of traffic delay.

If, during the course of on-road inspections, a vehicle is found to exceed the on-road emissions standards established for the model year and type of vehicle, the Agency shall send a notice to the vehicle owner. The notice shall document the occurrence and results of on-road exceedances. The notice of a second on-road exceedance shall indicate that the vehicle has been reassigned and is subject to an out-of-cycle follow-up inspection at an official inspection station. In no case shall the Agency send a notice of an on-road exceedance to the owner of a vehicle that was found to exceed the on-road emission standards established for the model year and type of vehicle if the vehicle is registered outside of the affected counties.

P.A. 76–1586, § 13B–15, added by P.A. 88–533, § 15, eff. Jan. 18, 1994. Amended by P.A. 90–475, § 10, eff. Aug. 17, 1997; P.A. 92–668, § 5, eff. Jan. 1, 2003.

1 625 ILCS 5/3–400 et seq.

2 415 ILCS 5/1 et seq.

5/13B–20. Rules and standards

§ 13B–20. Rules and standards.

(a) The Agency shall propose standards necessary to achieve reductions in the emission of hydrocarbons, carbon monoxide, and oxides of nitrogen from motor vehicles subject to inspection under this Chapter. Within 120 days after the Agency proposes these standards, the Board shall adopt rules establishing standards for the emission of hydrocarbons, carbon monoxide, and oxides of nitrogen from motor vehicles subject to inspection under this Chapter. These rules may be amended from time to time pursuant to Agency proposals. The Board shall set standards necessary to achieve the reductions in vehicle hydrocarbons, carbon monoxide, and oxides of nitrogen emissions, as determined by the applicable vehicle emission estimation model and rules developed by the United States Environmental Protection Agency, required by the federal Clean Air Act.[1] A predetermined rate of failure shall not be used in determining standards necessary to achieve the reductions in vehicle hydrocarbons, carbon monoxide and oxides of nitrogen emissions. The emission standards established by the Board for vehicles of model year 1981 or later shall be identical in substance, as defined in Section 7.2(a) of the Environmental Protection Act,[2] to the emission standards promulgated by the United States Environmental Protection Agency.

If the Administrator of the United States Environmental Protection Agency finds that oxides of nitrogen emission reductions are not beneficial under Title 40, Section 51.351(d) of the Code of Federal Regulations, the Board shall not adopt rules establishing such standards for the emission of oxides of nitrogen under this Chapter. Any rules establishing these standards that have already been adopted before the findings by the United States Environmental Protection Agency shall be repealed by the Board by preemptory rulemaking under the Illinois Administrative Procedure Act [3] upon petition by the Agency.

Except as otherwise provided in this subsection, subsection (b) of Section 27 of the Environmental Protection Act [4] and the rulemaking provisions of the Illinois Administrative Procedure Act shall not apply to rules adopted by the Board under this subsection. Challenges to the validity of rules adopted by the Board under this subsection (a) may only be brought by filing a petition for review in the Appellate Court under Section 29 of the Environmental Protection Act within 35 days after the rule is filed with the Secretary of State.

(b) The Agency shall establish, and may from time to time amend, procedures designed to implement this Chapter.

P.A. 76–1586, § 13B–20, added by P.A. 88–533, § 15, eff. Jan. 18, 1994.

1 42 U.S.C.A. § 7401 et seq.

2 415 ILCS 5/7.2.

3 5 ILCS 100/1–1 et seq.

4 415 ILCS 5/27.

5/13B–25. Performance of inspections

§ 13B–25. Performance of inspections.

(a) The inspection of vehicles required under this Chapter shall be performed only: (i) by inspectors who have been certified by the Agency after successfully completing a course of training and successfully passing a written test; (ii) at official inspection stations or official on-road inspection sites established under this Chapter; and (iii) with equipment that has been approved by the Agency for these inspections.

(b) Except as provided in subsections (c) and (d), the inspection shall consist of (i) a loaded mode exhaust gas analysis; (ii) an evaporative system integrity test; (iii) an on-board computer diagnostic system check; and (iv) a verification that all required emission-related recall repairs have been made under Title 40, Section 51.370 of the Code of Federal Regulations; and may also include an evaporative system purge test. The owner of the vehicle or the owner's agent shall be entitled to an emission inspection certificate issued by an inspector only if all required tests are passed at the time of the inspection.

(c) A steady-state idle exhaust gas analysis may be substituted for the loaded mode exhaust gas analysis and the evaporative purge system test in the following cases:

(1) On any vehicle of model year 1980 or older.

(2) On any heavy duty vehicle with a manufacturer gross vehicle weight rating in excess of 8,500 pounds.

(3) On any vehicle for which loaded mode testing is not possible due to vehicle design or configuration.

(d) The procedures contained in subsections (d)(1) and (d)(2) of this Section shall be followed on model year 1996 and newer vehicles equipped with OBD on-board computer diagnostic equipment, as required.

(1) Beginning on July 1, 2002, and continuing through December 31, 2003, such vehicles shall be given a complete on-board diagnostic test consistent with the requirements of paragraphs (d)(1)(A) through (d)(1)(D) of this Section.

(A) If the vehicle meets the standards set for the complete on-board computer diagnostic test, neither the loaded mode exhaust gas analysis nor the idle exhaust gas analysis shall be performed; however, all other elements of the test contained in subsection (b) of this Section shall be performed.

(B) If, however, the vehicle fails to meet the standard for the complete on-board computer diagnostic test, it shall be given the loaded mode exhaust gas analysis or the idle exhaust gas analysis, as required, and all other elements of the test contained in subsection (b) of this Section, unless the owner of the vehicle chooses to avoid the loaded mode exhaust gas analysis or idle exhaust gas analysis and proceed directly under paragraph (d)(1)(C) of this Section. For those vehicles that fail to meet the standard for the complete on-board computer diagnostic test, the owner of the vehicle must be informed that he or she has the option to have the vehicle tested using the less stringent loaded mode exhaust gas analysis or the idle exhaust gas analysis, as appropriate, for one test cycle.

(C) If the vehicle fails to meet the standard for the complete on-board computer diagnostic test and the standard for the loaded mode exhaust gas analysis or the idle exhaust gas analysis, as required, or the owner of the vehicle has chosen to avoid the loaded mode exhaust gas analysis or idle exhaust gas analysis and proceed directly under this paragraph, the vehicle must be repaired to pass either the complete on-board computer diagnostic test or the loaded mode exhaust gas analysis or idle exhaust gas analysis, as required, and all other elements of the test contained in subsection (b) of this Section.

(D) The on-board computer diagnostic test shall not be a required element of the inspection mandated by this Section for such vehicles for which on-board computer diagnostic testing is not possible due to the vehicle's originally certified design or its design as modified in accordance with federal law and regulations, or for vehicles with known on-board diagnostic communications or software problems, as determined by the Agency. In such cases, all other elements of the inspection required under this Section shall be performed on such vehicles, including the exhaust gas analysis as specified in subsection (b) of this Section.

By April 15, 2003, the Agency shall submit to the General Assembly a report detailing the effectiveness of the use of the on-board computer diagnostic test. The report shall include the number of failures, the reason for each failure, the number of vehicle damage complaints, and the average wait time at the test stations.

(2) Beginning on January 1, 2004, such vehicles shall be given a complete on-board diagnostic test consistent with the requirements of paragraphs (d)(2)(A) and (d)(2)(B) of this Section.

(A) The loaded mode exhaust gas analysis specified in subsection (b) of this Section shall not be performed on such vehicles for which the on-board computer diagnostic test specified in subsection (h) of this Section can be performed. All other elements of the inspection required for such vehicles shall be performed in accordance with the provisions of this Section.

(B) The on-board computer diagnostic test shall not be a required element of the inspection mandated by this Section for such vehicles for which on-board computer diagnostic testing is not possible due to the vehicle's originally certified design or its design as modified in accordance with federal law and regulations, or for vehicles with known on-board diagnostic communications or software problems, as determined by the Agency. In such cases, all other elements of the inspection required under this Section shall be performed on such vehicles, including the exhaust gas analysis as specified in subsection (b) of this Section.

(e) The exhaust gas analysis shall consist of a test of an exhaust gas sample to determine whether the quantities of exhaust gas pollutants emitted by the vehicle meet the standards set for vehicles of that type under Section 13B-20. A vehicle shall be deemed to have passed this portion of the inspection if the evaluation of the exhaust gas sample indicates that the quantities of exhaust gas pollutants emitted by the vehicle do not exceed the standards set for vehicles of that type under Section 13B-20 or an inspector certifies that the vehicle qualifies for a waiver of the exhaust gas pollutant standards under Section 13B-30.

(f) The evaporative system integrity test shall consist of a procedure to determine if leaks exist in all or a portion of the vehicle fuel evaporation emission control system. A vehicle shall be deemed to have passed this test if it meets the criteria that the Board may adopt for an evaporative system integrity test.

(g) The evaporative system purge test shall consist of a procedure to verify the purging of vapors stored in the evaporative canister. A vehicle shall be deemed to have passed this test if it meets the criteria that the Board may adopt for an evaporative system purge test.

(h) The on-board computer diagnostic test shall consist of accessing the vehicle's on-board computer system, if so equipped, and reading any stored diagnostic codes that may be present. The vehicle shall be deemed to have passed this test if the codes observed did not exceed standards set for vehicles of that type under Section 13B-20.

P.A. 76-1586, § 13B-25, added by P.A. 88-533, § 15, eff. Jan. 18, 1994. Amended by P.A. 90-475, § 10, eff. Aug. 17, 1997; P.A. 92-682, § 5, eff. July 16, 2002.

5/13B-30. Waivers

§ 13B-30. Waivers.

(a) The Agency shall certify that a vehicle that has failed a vehicle emission retest qualifies for a waiver of the emission inspection standards if the following criteria are met:

(1) The vehicle has received all repairs and adjustments for which it is eligible under any emission performance warranty provided under Section 207 of the federal Clean Air Act.[1]

(2) The Agency determines by normal inspection procedures that the vehicle's emission control devices are present and appear to be properly connected and operating.

(3) Consistent with Title 40, Section 51.360 of the Code of Federal Regulations, for vehicles required to be tested

under this Chapter, a minimum expenditure of at least $450 in emission-related repairs exclusive of tampering-related repairs have been made.

(4) Repairs for vehicles of model year 1981 and later are conducted by a recognized repair technician.

(5) Evidence of repair is presented consisting of either signed and dated receipts identifying the vehicle and describing the work performed and amount charged for eligible emission-related repairs, or an affidavit executed by the person performing the eligible emission related repairs.

(6) The repairs have resulted in an improvement in vehicle emissions as determined by comparison of initial and final retest results.

(b) The Agency may issue an emission inspection certificate to vehicles failing a transient loaded mode emission retest if a complete documented physical and functional diagnosis and inspection shows that no additional emission-related repairs are needed. This diagnostic inspection must be performed by the Agency or its designated agent and shall be available only to motorists whose vehicle was repaired by a recognized repair technician.

(c) The Agency may extend the emission inspection certificate expiration date by one year upon receipt of a petition by the vehicle owner that needed repairs cannot be made due to economic hardship. Consistent with Title 40, Section 51.360 of the Code of Federal Regulations, this extension may be granted more than once during the life of the vehicle.

(d) The Agency shall propose procedures, practices, and performance requirements for operation of vehicle scrappage programs by any person that wants to receive credits for certain emissions reductions from these vehicles. The proposal shall include the method of vehicle selection, testing of vehicle emissions, documentation of annual vehicle miles traveled, determination of emissions, and determination of emissions reductions credits. Any applicable guidance available from the United States Environmental Protection Agency regarding these programs shall also be considered by the Agency. Within 180 days after the Agency files this proposal, the Board shall adopt rules for vehicle scrappage programs. Subsection (b) of Section 27 of the Environmental Protection Act [2] and the rulemaking provisions of the Illinois Administrative Procedure Act [3] shall not apply to rules adopted by the Board under this subsection (d).

(e) The Agency may adopt procedures to purchase vehicles for scrap that are unable to meet emission inspection standards and for which motorists provide a signed estimate from a recognized repair technician that the cost of emission-related repairs is expected to exceed an amount equal to one-half of the current minimum expenditure required in item (3) of subsection (a) of this Section. If the Agency adopts such procedures, they must be included in the vehicle scrappage programs in subsection (d). Such procedures shall require the Agency to arrange for private sector funding for the purchase of at least 90% of the vehicles which will be purchased for scrap.

(f) The Agency may issue an emission inspection certificate for vehicles subject to inspection under this Chapter that are located and primarily used in an area subject to the vehicle emission inspection requirements of another state. Emission inspection certificates shall be issued under this subsection only upon receipt by the Agency of evidence that the vehicle has been inspected and is in compliance with the emission inspection requirements and standards applicable in the state or local jurisdiction where the vehicle is being used.

P.A. 76–1586, § 13B–30, added by P.A. 88–533, § 15, eff. Jan. 18, 1994. Amended by P.A. 90–475, § 10, eff. Aug. 17, 1997.

1 42 U.S.C.A. § 7541.

2 415 ILCS 5/27.

3 5 ILCS 100/1–1 et seq.

5/13B–35. Inquiries

§ 13B–35. Inquiries. The Agency shall develop a means of responding to inquiries from inspectors and members of the public concerning the program, including (i) when inspections are required, (ii) what kind of inspections are required, (iii) whether emission inspection stickers or certificates previously required for a vehicle have been obtained, and (iv) the procedures for resolving disputes concerning inspections.

P.A. 76–1586, § 13B–35, added by P.A. 88–533, § 15, eff. Jan. 18, 1994.

5/13B–40. Grievance and damage claim requirements and procedures

§ 13B–40. Grievance and damage claim requirements and procedures.

(a) Emissions inspection and waiver denial grievance procedures. Any person aggrieved by a decision regarding the failure of an emissions test or the denial of a waiver may file a petition with the Agency within 30 days after the decision was made, and the Agency shall thereupon investigate the matter. Within 45 days after its receipt of the petition, the Agency shall submit to the petitioner and any affected inspector or station its written determination of the correctness or incorrectness of the decision complained of. The written determination shall include a statement of the facts relied upon and the legal and technical issues decided by the Agency in making its determination, and may also include an order directing the inspector (i) to issue an emission inspection certificate for the vehicle effective on such date as the Agency may specify, (ii) to reinspect the vehicle, (iii) to apply the standards that the Agency has determined to be applicable, or (iv) to take any other action that the Agency deems to be appropriate. In conducting the investigation, the Agency may require the petitioner to present the vehicle for inspection by the Agency or its designated agent. The written determination of the Agency shall be subject to review in circuit court in accordance with the provisions of the Administrative Review Law,[1] except that no challenge to the validity of a rule adopted by the Board under subsection (a) of Section 13B–20 shall be heard by the circuit court if the challenge could have been raised in a timely petition for review under Section 13B–20.

(b) Vehicle damage claim requirements and procedures.

(1) The contractor shall make vehicle damage claim forms authorized by the Agency available for vehicle owners in sufficient quantities at all official inspection stations.

(2) Notice of the vehicle damage claim procedures and the vehicle owner's rights in relation to a vehicle damage claim shall be conspicuously posted at all official inspection stations.

(3) If a vehicle owner believes that his or her vehicle was damaged by an act or omission of the contractor during or as a result of an emissions inspection performed on or after August 1, 2002, the owner may initiate resolution of the damage claim under this subsection by complying with the following:

(A) Within 30 days of the date of the vehicle emissions inspection that allegedly caused the vehicle damage, the vehicle owner shall submit a vehicle damage claim to the contractor at the Official Inspection Station at which the vehicle damage allegedly occurred.

(B) Within 30 days of filing the claim, the owner shall submit to the contractor any relevant information relating to the owner's claim for vehicle damage, including but not limited to evaluations conducted by a claims evaluation center or automotive repair shop meeting standards prescribed by the Agency.

(4) The contractor shall promptly notify the Agency of each vehicle damage claim received by the contractor under subdivision (b)(3) and shall forward to the Agency any additional information provided by the owner.

(5) Within 60 days after the filing of a vehicle damage claim, the contractor shall notify the vehicle owner of its proposed resolution of the damage claim.

(6) Within 30 days after receiving the contractor's proposed resolution of the damage claim, the owner may petition the Agency for a review of the adequacy and completeness of the contractor's proposed resolution. The petition shall be in a form specified by the Agency.

(7) Upon receiving a petition for review, the Agency shall request the contractor to deliver to the Agency a copy of the contractor's proposed resolution of the damage claim, together with all documents, videotapes, and information relevant to the damage claim and the proposed resolution. The contractor shall provide the requested materials to the Agency within 15 days of receiving the Agency's request.

(8) Within 30 days after receiving the relevant materials from the contractor, the Agency shall review the materials and determine whether the contractor's proposed resolution of the damage claim is adequate and complete. The Agency may deem the proposed resolution of the damage claim to be adequate and complete. If the Agency does not deem the proposed resolution of the damage claim to be adequate and complete, it may request the contractor to further investigate and evaluate the damage claim and resubmit its proposed resolution of the claim. The contractor shall then have 30 days to respond in writing to the Agency with the results of its further evaluation of the damage claim and its proposed resolution.

(9) The Agency shall notify the vehicle owner in writing of the result of its review of the adequacy and completeness of the contractor's proposed resolution of the damage claim. Copies of all correspondence between the Agency and the contractor relating to the damage claim shall also be sent to the vehicle owner.

(10) If, after the Agency's review, the vehicle owner still does not agree with all or a portion of the proposed resolution of the damage claim by the contractor, the vehicle owner may further pursue the damage claim through the binding arbitration process established by the contractor and accepted by the Agency, or in circuit court.

(11) The Agency's review of the adequacy and completeness of the contractor's proposed resolution of a damage claim is not binding upon the vehicle owner or the contractor and does not affect the rights of the vehicle owner or the contractor under law. The Agency's review of the adequacy and completeness of the contractor's proposed resolution of a damage claim is not a final action subject to administrative review and is not subject to review by the Pollution Control Board or otherwise appealable.

P.A. 76-1586, § 13B-40, added by P.A. 88-533, § 15, eff. Jan. 18, 1994. Amended by P.A. 92-821, § 5, eff. Aug. 21, 2002.

[1] 735 ILCS 5/13-101 et seq.

5/13B-45. Contracts

§ 13B-45. Contracts.

(a) The Agency may enter into contracts with one or more responsible parties to construct and operate official inspection stations, provide and maintain approved test equipment, administer tests, certify results, issue emission inspection stickers or certificates, maintain records, train personnel, or provide information to the public concerning the program.

These contracts (i) shall be subject to the Illinois Purchasing Act,[1] (ii) may be for a term of up to 9 years, (iii) shall be in writing, and (iv) shall not take effect until a copy of the contract is filed with the State Comptroller.

(b) In preparing its proposals for bidding by potential contractors, the Agency shall endeavor to include provisions relating to the following factors:

(1) The demonstrated financial responsibility of the potential contractor.

(2) The specialized experience and technical competence of the potential contractor in connection with the type of services required and the complexity of the project.

(3) The potential contractor's past record of performance on contracts with the Agency, with other government agencies or public bodies, and with private industry, including such items as cost, quality of work, and ability to meet schedules.

(4) The capacity of the potential contractor to perform the work within the time limitations.

(5) The familiarity of the potential contractor with the types of problems applicable to the project.

(6) The potential contractor's proposed method to accomplish the work required including, where appropriate, any demonstrated capability of exploring and developing innovative or advanced techniques and methods.

(7) Avoidance of personal and organizational conflicts of interest prohibited under federal, State, or local law.

(8) The potential contractor's present and prior involvement in the community and in the State of Illinois.

(c) Any contract for the operation of one or more official inspection stations shall include a provision that the contractor shall not perform emission-related repairs or adjustments to vehicles, other than to the contractor's own vehicles, necessary to enable vehicles to pass Illinois emission inspections.

P.A. 76-1586, § 13B-45, added by P.A. 88-533, § 15, eff. Jan. 18, 1994.

[1] 30 ILCS 505/1 et seq.

5/13B-50. Costs

§ 13B-50. Costs.

(a) Except as otherwise provided in subsection (e) of Section 13B-15, no fee shall be charged to motor vehicle owners for obtaining inspections required under this Chapter. The Vehicle Inspection Fund, which is a fund created in the State treasury for the purpose of receiving moneys from the Motor Fuel Tax Fund and other sources, shall be used, subject to appropriation, for the payment of the costs of the program, including reimbursement of those agencies of the State that incur expenses in the administration or enforcement of the program. The Vehicle Inspection Fund shall continue in existence notwithstanding the repeal of Chapter 13A.[1] Any money in the Vehicle Inspection Fund on January 1, 1995, shall be used for the purposes set forth in this Chapter.

(b) The Agency may acquire, own, maintain, operate, sell, lease and otherwise transfer real and personal property and interests in real and personal property for the purpose of creating or operating inspection stations and for any other purpose relating to the administration of this Chapter, and may use money from the Vehicle Inspection Fund for these purposes.

P.A. 76-1586, § 13B-50, added by P.A. 88-533, § 15, eff. Jan. 18, 1994.

1 625 ILCS 5/13A-101 et seq.

5/13B-55. Enforcement

§ 13B-55. Enforcement.

(a) The Agency shall cooperate in the enforcement of this Chapter by (i) identifying probable violations through computer matching of vehicle registration records and inspection records; (ii) sending one notice to each suspected violator identified through such matching, stating that registration and inspection records indicate that the vehicle owner has not complied with this Chapter; (iii) directing the vehicle owner to notify the Agency or the Secretary of State if he or she has ceased to own the vehicle or has changed residence; and (iv) advising the vehicle owner of the consequences of violating this Chapter.

The Agency shall cooperate with the Secretary of State in the administration of this Chapter and the related provisions of Chapter 3,[1] and shall provide the Secretary of State with such information as the Secretary of State may deem necessary for these purposes, including regular and timely access to vehicle inspection records. The Agency shall be reimbursed for the cost of providing this information.

The Secretary of State shall cooperate with the Agency in the administration of this Chapter and shall provide the Agency with such information as the Agency may deem necessary for the purposes of this Chapter, including regular and timely access to vehicle registration records. Section 2-123 of this Code shall not apply to the provision of this information, but the Secretary of State shall be reimbursed for the cost of providing the information.

(b) The Secretary of State shall suspend either the driving privileges or the vehicle registration, or both, of any vehicle owner who has not complied with this Chapter, if (i) the vehicle owner failed to satisfactorily respond to the one notice sent by the Agency under subsection (a), and (ii) the Secretary of State has mailed the vehicle owner a notice that the suspension will be imposed if the owner does not comply within a stated period, and the Secretary of State has not received satisfactory evidence of compliance within that period. The Secretary of State shall send this notice only after receiving a statement from the Agency that the vehicle owner has failed to comply with this Section. Notice shall be effective as specified in subsection (c) of Section 6-211 of this Code.

A suspension under this subsection shall not be terminated until satisfactory proof of compliance has been submitted to the Secretary of State. No driver's license or permit, or renewal of a license or permit, may be issued to a person whose driving privileges have been suspended under this Section until the suspension has been terminated. No vehicle registration or registration plate that has been suspended under this Section may be reinstated or renewed, or transferred by the owner to any other vehicle, until the suspension has been terminated.

The filing fee for an administrative hearing to contest a suspension made under this Section shall be $20, to be paid by the vehicle owner at the time written request for the hearing is made to the Secretary of State.

The Secretary of State may promulgate rules to enable him or her to carry out his or her duties under this Chapter.

P.A. 76-1586, § 13B-55, added by P.A. 88-533, § 15, eff. Jan. 18, 1994.

1 625 ILCS 5/3-100 et seq.

5/13B-60. Other offenses

§ 13B-60. Other offenses.

(a) Any person who knowingly displays an emission inspection sticker or exemption sticker on any vehicle other than the one for which the sticker was lawfully issued in accordance with the provisions of this Chapter, or duplicates, alters, uses, possesses, issues, or distributes any emission inspection sticker, exemption sticker, inspection certificate, or facsimile thereof, except in accordance with the provisions of this Chapter and the rules and regulations adopted hereunder, is guilty of a Class C misdemeanor.

(b) A vehicle owner shall pay a monetary fine equivalent to the test fee plus the applicable waiver repair expenditure for the continued operation of a noncomplying vehicle beyond 4 months past the expiration of the vehicle emission inspection certificate. Any fines collected under this Section shall be divided equally between the local jurisdiction issuing the citation and the Vehicle Inspection Fund.

P.A. 76-1586, § 13B-60, added by P.A. 88-533, § 15, eff. Jan. 18, 1994.

5/13B-70. Legislative intent

§ 13B-70. Legislative intent. It is the intent of the General Assembly that, to the greatest extent possible, there be continuity in the operation of the Vehicle Emissions Inspection Programs under this Chapter and Chapter 13A[1] during the transition phase when certain affected counties become subject to the program under this Chapter instead of the program under Chapter 13A.

P.A. 76-1586, § 13B-70, added by P.A. 88-533, § 15, eff. Jan. 18, 1994.

1 625 ILCS 5/13A-101 et seq.

5/13B-75. Home rule

§ 13B-75. Home rule. Pursuant to subsections (h) and (i) of Section 6 of Article VII of the Illinois Constitution, the exercise by a home rule unit of any power which is inconsistent with this Chapter is hereby specifically denied and preempted, and the vehicle emission inspection program created by this Chapter is hereby declared to be the subject of exclusive State jurisdiction.

P.A. 76-1586, § 13B-75, added by P.A. 88-533, § 15, eff. Jan. 18, 1994.

CHAPTER 14. VEHICLE EQUIPMENT SAFETY COMPACT

5/14-101 to 5/14-110. §§ 14-101 to 14-110. Repealed by P.A. 83-821, § 2, eff. Sept. 24, 1983

CHAPTER 15. SIZE, WEIGHT, AND LOAD PERMITS

Enactment

The Illinois Vehicle Code was enacted by P.A. 76–1586, effective July 1, 1970. The Code constitutes a consolidated recodification of various earlier laws and acts including the Uniform Act Regulating Traffic on Highways.

5/15–100. § 15–100. Repealed by P.A. 90–89, § 20, eff. Jan. 1, 1998

ARTICLE I. SIZE, WEIGHT AND LOAD

5/15–101. Scope and effect of Chapter 15

§ 15–101. Scope and effect of Chapter 15. (a) It is unlawful for any person to drive or move on, upon or across or for the owner to cause or knowingly permit to be driven or moved on, upon or across any highway any vehicle or vehicles of a size and weight exceeding the limitations stated in this Chapter or otherwise in violation of this Chapter, and the maximum size and weight of vehicles herein specified shall be lawful throughout this State, and local authorities shall have no power or authority to alter such limitations except as express authority may be granted in this Chapter.

(b) The provisions of this Chapter governing size, weight and load do not apply to fire apparatus or equipment for snow and ice removal operations owned or operated by any governmental body, or to implements of husbandry, as defined in Chapter 1 of this Code,[1] temporarily operated or towed in a combination upon a highway provided such combination does not consist of more than 3 vehicles or, in the case of hauling fresh, perishable fruits or vegetables from farm to the point of first processing, not more than 3 wagons being towed by an implement of husbandry, or to a vehicle operated under the terms of a special permit issued hereunder.

P.A. 76–1586, § 15–101, eff. July 1, 1970. Amended by P.A. 76–1694, § 1; P.A. 76–2194, § 1, eff. July 1, 1970; P.A. 83–831, § 1, eff. Jan. 1, 1984; P.A. 92–417, § 5, eff. Jan. 1, 2002.

Formerly Ill.Rev.Stat.1991, ch. 95 ½, ¶ 15–101.

[1] 625 ILCS 5/1–101 et seq.

5/15–102. Width of Vehicles

§ 15–102. Width of Vehicles.

(a) On Class III and non-designated State and local highways, the total outside width of any vehicle or load thereon shall not exceed 8 feet.

(b) Except during those times when, due to insufficient light or unfavorable atmospheric conditions, persons and vehicles on the highway are not clearly discernible at a distance of 1000 feet, the following vehicles may exceed the 8 feet limitation during the period from a half hour before sunrise to a half hour after sunset:

(1) Loads of hay, straw or other similar farm products provided that the load is not more than 12 feet wide.

(2) Implements of husbandry being transported on another vehicle and the transporting vehicle while loaded.

The following requirements apply to the transportation on another vehicle of an implement of husbandry wider than 8 feet 6 inches on the National System of Interstate and Defense Highways or other highways in the system of State highways:

(A) The driver of a vehicle transporting an implement of husbandry that exceeds 8 feet 6 inches in width shall obey all traffic laws and shall check the roadways prior to making a movement in order to ensure that adequate clearance is available for the movement. It is prima facie evidence that the driver of a vehicle transporting an implement of husbandry has failed to check the roadway prior to making a movement if the vehicle is involved in a collision with a bridge, overpass, fixed structure, or properly placed traffic control device or if the vehicle blocks traffic due to its inability to proceed because of a bridge, overpass, fixed structure, or properly placed traffic control device.

(B) Flags shall be displayed so as to wave freely at the extremities of overwidth objects and at the extreme ends of all protrusions, projections, and overhangs. All flags shall be clean, bright red flags with no advertising, wording, emblem, or insignia inscribed upon them and at least 18 inches square.

(C) "OVERSIZE LOAD" signs are mandatory on the front and rear of all vehicles with loads over 10 feet wide. These signs must have 12–inch high black letters with a 2–inch stroke on a yellow sign that is 7 feet wide by 18 inches high.

(D) One civilian escort vehicle is required for a load that exceeds 14 feet 6 inches in width and 2 civilian escort vehicles are required for a load that exceeds 16 feet in width on the National System of Interstate and Defense Highways or other highways in the system of State highways.

(E) The requirements for a civilian escort vehicle and driver are as follows:

(1) The civilian escort vehicle shall be a passenger car or a second division vehicle not exceeding a gross vehicle weight of 8,000 pounds that is designed to afford clear and unobstructed vision to both front and rear.

(2) The escort vehicle driver must be properly licensed to operate the vehicle.

(3) While in use, the escort vehicle must be equipped with illuminated rotating, oscillating, or flashing amber lights or flashing amber strobe lights mounted on top that are of sufficient intensity to be visible at 500 feet in normal sunlight.

(4) "OVERSIZE LOAD" signs are mandatory on all escort vehicles. The sign on an escort vehicle shall

have 8-inch high black letters on a yellow sign that is 5 feet wide by 12 inches high.

(5) When only one escort vehicle is required and it is operating on a two-lane highway, the escort vehicle shall travel approximately 300 feet ahead of the load. The rotating, oscillating, or flashing lights or flashing amber strobe lights and an "OVERSIZE LOAD" sign shall be displayed on the escort vehicle and shall be visible from the front. When only one escort vehicle is required and it is operating on a multilane divided highway, the escort vehicle shall travel approximately 300 feet behind the load and the sign and lights shall be visible from the rear.

(6) When 2 escort vehicles are required, one escort shall travel approximately 300 feet ahead of the load and the second escort shall travel approximately 300 feet behind the load. The rotating, oscillating, or flashing lights or flashing amber strobe lights and an "OVERSIZE LOAD" sign shall be displayed on the escort vehicles and shall be visible from the front on the lead escort and from the rear on the trailing escort.

(7) When traveling within the corporate limits of a municipality, the escort vehicle shall maintain a reasonable and proper distance from the oversize load, consistent with existing traffic conditions.

(8) A separate escort shall be provided for each load hauled.

(9) The driver of an escort vehicle shall obey all traffic laws.

(10) The escort vehicle must be in safe operational condition.

(11) The driver of the escort vehicle must be in radio contact with the driver of the vehicle carrying the oversize load.

(F) A transport vehicle while under load of more than 8 feet 6 inches in width must be equipped with an illuminated rotating, oscillating, or flashing amber light or lights or a flashing amber strobe light or lights mounted on the top of the cab that are of sufficient intensity to be visible at 500 feet in normal sunlight. If the load on the transport vehicle blocks the visibility of the amber lighting from the rear of the vehicle, the vehicle must also be equipped with an illuminated rotating, oscillating, or flashing amber light or lights or a flashing amber strobe light or lights mounted on the rear of the load that are of sufficient intensity to be visible at 500 feet in normal sunlight.

(G) When a flashing amber light is required on the transport vehicle under load and it is operating on a two-lane highway, the transport vehicle shall display to the rear at least one rotating, oscillating, or flashing light or a flashing amber strobe light and an "OVERSIZE LOAD" sign. When a flashing amber light is required on the transport vehicle under load and it is operating on a multilane divided highway, the sign and light shall be visible from the rear.

(H) Maximum speed shall be 45 miles per hour on all such moves or 5 miles per hour above the posted minimum speed limit, whichever is greater, but the vehicle shall not at any time exceed the posted maximum speed limit.

(3) Portable buildings designed and used for agricultural and livestock raising operations that are not more than 14 feet wide and with not more than a 1 foot overhang along the left side of the hauling vehicle. However, the buildings shall not be transported more than 10 miles and not on any route that is part of the National System of Interstate and Defense Highways.

All buildings when being transported shall display at least 2 red cloth flags, not less than 12 inches square, mounted as high as practicable on the left and right side of the building.

A State Police escort shall be required if it is necessary for this load to use part of the left lane when crossing any 2 laned State highway bridge.

(c) Vehicles propelled by electric power obtained from overhead trolley wires operated wholly within the corporate limits of a municipality are also exempt from the width limitation.

(d) Exemptions are also granted to vehicles designed for the carrying of more than 10 persons under the following conditions:

(1) (Blank);

(2) When operated within any public transportation service with the approval of local authorities or an appropriate public body authorized by law to provide public transportation. Any vehicle so operated may be 8 feet 6 inches in width; or

(3) When a county engineer or superintendent of highways, after giving due consideration to the mass transportation needs of the area and to the width and condition of the road, has determined that the operation of buses wider than 8 feet will not pose an undue safety hazard on a particular county or township road segment, he or she may authorize buses not to exceed 8 feet 6 inches in width on any highway under that engineer's or superintendent's jurisdiction.

(e) A vehicle and load traveling upon the National System of Interstate and Defense Highways or any other highway in the system of State highways that has been designated as a Class I or Class II highway by the Department, or any street or highway designated by local authorities or road district commissioners, may have a total outside width of 8 feet 6 inches, provided that certain safety devices that the Department determines as necessary for the safe and efficient operation of motor vehicles shall not be included in the calculation of width.

(e-1) A vehicle and load more than 8 feet wide but not exceeding 8 feet 6 inches in width is allowed access according to the following:

(1) A vehicle and load not exceeding 73,280 pounds in weight is allowed access from any State designated highway onto any county, township, or municipal highway for a distance of 5 highway miles for the purpose of loading and unloading, provided:

(A) The vehicle and load does not exceed 65 feet overall length.

(B) There is no sign prohibiting that access.

(C) The route is not being used as a thoroughfare between State designated highways.

(2) A vehicle and load not exceeding 73,280 pounds in weight is allowed access from any State designated highway onto any county or township highway for a distance of 5 highway miles or onto any municipal highway for a distance of one highway mile for the purpose of food, fuel, repairs, and rest, provided:

(A) The vehicle and load does not exceed 65 feet overall length.

(B) There is no sign prohibiting that access.

(C) The route is not being used as a thoroughfare between State designated highways.

(3) A vehicle and load not exceeding 80,000 pounds in weight is allowed access from a Class I highway onto any street or highway for a distance of one highway mile for the purpose of loading, unloading, food, fuel, repairs, and rest, provided there is no sign prohibiting that access.

(4) A vehicle and load not exceeding 80,000 pounds in weight is allowed access from a Class I or Class II highway onto any State highway or any locally designated highway for a distance of 5 highway miles for the purpose of loading, unloading, food, fuel, repairs, and rest.

(5) A trailer or semi-trailer not exceeding 28 feet 6 inches in length, that was originally in combination with a truck tractor, shall have unlimited access to points of loading and unloading.

(6) All household goods carriers shall have unlimited access to points of loading and unloading.

Section 5–35 of the Illinois Administrative Procedure Act [1] relating to procedures for rulemaking shall not apply to the designation of highways under this paragraph (e).

(f) Mirrors required by Section 12–502 of this Code and other safety devices identified by the Department may project up to 14 inches beyond each side of a bus and up to 6 inches beyond each side of any other vehicle, and that projection shall not be deemed a violation of the width restrictions of this Section.

(g) Any person who is convicted of violating this Section is subject to the penalty as provided in paragraph (b) of Section 15–113.

P.A. 76–1586, § 15–102, eff. July 1, 1970. Amended by P.A. 76–2195, § 1, eff. July 1, 1970; P.A. 77–123, § 1, eff. Jan. 1, 1972; P.A. 78–510, § 1, eff. Oct. 1, 1973; P.A. 80–574, § 1, eff. Oct. 1, 1977; P.A. 80–1173, § 1, eff. July 1, 1978; P.A. 80–1364, § 36, eff. Aug. 13, 1978; P.A. 83–12, § 1, eff. July 1, 1983; P.A. 83–848, § 1, eff. Jan. 1, 1984; P.A. 83–1362, Art. II, § 99, eff. Sept. 11, 1984; P.A. 84–691, § 1, eff. Jan. 1, 1986; P.A. 86–1236, § 1, eff. Jan. 1, 1991; P.A. 87–217, § 4, eff. Jan. 1, 1992; P.A. 87–1160, § 1, eff. Jan. 1, 1993; P.A. 87–1203, § 1, eff. Sept. 25, 1992; P.A. 88–45, Art. II, § 2–54, eff. July 6, 1993; P.A. 88–476, § 2, eff. July 1, 1994; P.A. 88–517, § 10, eff. Nov. 16, 1993; P.A. 88–589, § 10, eff. Aug. 14, 1994; P.A. 88–670, Art. 2, § 2–59, eff. Dec. 2, 1994; P.A. 88–675, § 5, eff. Dec. 14, 1994; P.A. 88–684, § 5, eff. Jan. 24, 1995; P.A. 89–551, § 5, eff. Jan. 1, 1997; P.A. 89–658, § 5, eff. Jan. 1, 1997; P.A. 90–14, Art. 2, § 2–225, eff. July 1, 1997; P.A. 91–780, § 5, eff. June 9, 2000; P.A. 92–417, § 5, eff. Jan. 1, 2002.

Formerly Ill.Rev.Stat.1991, ch. 95 ½, ¶ 15–102.

[1] 5 ILCS 100/5–35.

Section 4 of P.A. 83–12, approved July 1, 1983, provided:

"Effective date. This Act takes effect as provided in this Section.

"The amendments to those portions of Sections 3–815(a), 3–818 and 3–819(b) of 'The Illinois Vehicle Code' in Section 1 of this Act which create the 'X', 'Z', 'MX', 'MZ', 'MM' and 'TN' registration classifications and the fees and taxes imposed for those classifications, the amendments to Sections 2–119, 3–401 and 3–802 of 'The Illinois Vehicle Code' in Section 1 of this Act, and the amendments to Chapter 15 of 'The Illinois Vehicle Code' in Section 1 of this Act take effect July 1, 1983.

"The remaining amendments to 'The Illinois Vehicle Code' in Section 1 of this Act take effect July 1, 1983 and apply beginning with the 1985 registration year, except that the amendments to Sections 3–813 through 3–816 and Section 3–819 apply beginning with the 1984 registration year for those vehicles registered on a calendar year basis only.

"The amendments to Chapters 13 and 18 of 'The Illinois Vehicle Code' in Section 1 of this Act take effect January 1, 1984.

"Section 2 of this Act takes effect on the first day of the next succeeding month which commences at least 30 days after the date on which this Act becomes law.

"Section 3 of this Act takes effect July 1, 1983.

"Section 3.1 of this Act takes effect January 1, 1984.

"This Section 4 takes effect upon its becoming a law."

5/15–103. Height of vehicles

§ 15–103. Height of vehicles. The height of a vehicle from the under side of the tire to the top of the vehicle, inclusive of load, shall not exceed 13 feet, 6 inches on any highway in the State.

A person convicted of violating this Section is subject to the penalty provided in paragraph (b) of Section 15–113.

P.A. 76–1586, § 15–103, eff. July 1, 1970. Amended by P.A. 83–831, § 1, eff. Jan. 1, 1984; P.A. 92–417, § 5, eff. Jan. 1, 2002.

Formerly Ill.Rev.Stat.1991, ch. 95 ½, ¶ 15–103.

5/15–104. § 15–104. Repealed by P.A. 83–527, § 1, eff. Sept. 17, 1983

5/15–105. Projecting loads on passenger vehicles

§ 15–105. Projecting loads on passenger vehicles. No passenger-type vehicle shall be operated on any highway with any load carried thereon extending beyond the line of the fenders on the left side of such vehicle nor extending more than 6 inches beyond the line of the fenders on the right side thereof.

P.A. 76–1586, § 15–105, eff. July 1, 1970.

Formerly Ill.Rev.Stat.1991, ch. 95 ½, ¶ 15–105.

5/15–106. Protruding members of vehicles

§ 15–106. Protruding members of vehicles.

No vehicle with boom, arm, drill rig or other protruding component shall be operated upon any highway in this State unless such protruding component is fastened so as to prevent shifting, bouncing or moving in any manner.

P.A. 76–1586, § 15–106, eff. July 1, 1970. Amended by P.A. 92–417, § 5, eff. Jan. 1, 2002.

Formerly Ill.Rev.Stat.1991, ch. 95 ½, ¶ 15–106.

5/15–107. Length of vehicles

§ 15–107. Length of vehicles.

(a) The maximum length of a single vehicle on any highway of this State may not exceed 42 feet except the following:

(1) Semitrailers.

(2) Charter or regulated route buses may be up to 45 feet in length, not including energy absorbing bumpers.

(a–1) A motor home as defined in Section 1–145.01 may be up to 45 feet in length, not including energy absorbing bumpers. The length limitations described in this subsection (a–1) shall be exclusive of energy-absorbing bumpers and rear view mirrors.

(b) On all non-State highways, the maximum length of vehicles in combinations is as follows:

(1) A truck tractor in combination with a semitrailer may not exceed 55 feet overall dimension.

(2) A truck tractor-semitrailer-trailer may not exceed 60 feet overall dimension.

(3) Combinations specially designed to transport motor vehicles or boats may not exceed 60 feet overall dimension.

Vehicles operating during daylight hours when transporting poles, pipes, machinery, or other objects of a structural nature that cannot readily be dismembered are exempt from length limitations, provided that no object may exceed 80 feet in length and the overall dimension of the vehicle including the load may not exceed 100 feet. This exemption does not apply to operation on a Saturday, Sunday, or legal holiday. Legal holidays referred to in this Section are the days on which the following traditional holidays are celebrated: New Year's Day; Memorial Day; Independence Day; Labor Day; Thanksgiving Day; and Christmas Day.

Vehicles and loads operated by a public utility while en route to make emergency repairs to public service facilities or properties are exempt from length limitations, provided that during night operations every vehicle and its load must be equipped with a sufficient number of clearance lamps on both sides and marker lamps on the extreme ends of any projecting load to clearly mark the dimensions of the load.

A tow truck in combination with a disabled vehicle or combination of disabled vehicles, as provided in paragraph (6) of subsection (c) of this Section, is exempt from length limitations.

All other combinations not listed in this subsection (b) may not exceed 60 feet overall dimension.

(c) Combinations of vehicles may not exceed a total of 2 vehicles except the following:

(1) A truck tractor semitrailer may draw one trailer.

(2) A truck tractor semitrailer may draw one converter dolly.

(3) A truck tractor semitrailer may draw one vehicle that is defined in Chapter 1 [1] as special mobile equipment, provided the overall dimension does not exceed 60 feet.

(4) A truck in transit may draw 3 trucks in transit coupled together by the triple saddlemount method.

(5) Recreational vehicles consisting of 3 vehicles, provided the following:

(A) The total overall dimension does not exceed 60 feet.

(B) The towing vehicle is a properly registered vehicle capable of towing another vehicle using a fifth-wheel type assembly.

(C) The second vehicle in the combination of vehicles is a recreational vehicle that is towed by a fifth-wheel assembly. This vehicle must be properly registered and must be equipped with brakes, regardless of weight.

(D) The third vehicle must be the lightest of the 3 vehicles and be a trailer or semitrailer designed or used for transporting a boat, all-terrain vehicle, personal watercraft, or motorcycle.

(E) The towed vehicles may be only for the use of the operator of the towing vehicle.

(F) All vehicles must be properly equipped with operating brakes and safety equipment required by this Code, except the additional brake requirement in subdivision (C) of this subparagraph (5).

(6) A tow truck in combination with a disabled vehicle or combination of disabled vehicles, provided the towing vehicle:

(A) Is specifically designed as a tow truck having a gross vehicle weight rating of at least 18,000 pounds and equipped with air brakes, provided that air brakes are required only if the towing vehicle is towing a vehicle, semitrailer, or tractor-trailer combination that is equipped with air brakes. For the purpose of this subsection, gross vehicle weight rating, or GVWR, means the value specified by the manufacturer as the loaded weight of the tow truck.

(B) Is equipped with flashing, rotating, or oscillating amber lights, visible for at least 500 feet in all directions.

(C) Is capable of utilizing the lighting and braking systems of the disabled vehicle or combination of vehicles.

(D) Does not engage a tow exceeding 50 highway miles from the initial point of wreck or disablement to a place of repair. Any additional movement of the vehicles may occur only upon issuance of authorization for that movement under the provisions of Sections 15-301 through 15-319 of this Code.

The Department may by rule or regulation prescribe additional requirements regarding length limitations for a tow truck towing another vehicle.

For purposes of this Section, a tow-dolly that merely serves as substitute wheels for another legally licensed vehicle is considered part of the licensed vehicle and not a separate vehicle.

(d) On Class I highways there are no overall length limitations on motor vehicles operating in combinations provided:

(1) The length of a semitrailer, unladen or with load, in combination with a truck tractor may not exceed 53 feet.

(2) The distance between the kingpin and the center of the rear axle of a semitrailer longer than 48 feet, in combination with a truck tractor, may not exceed 45 feet 6 inches.

(3) The length of a semitrailer or trailer, unladen or with load, operated in a truck tractor-semitrailer-trailer combination, may not exceed 28 feet 6 inches.

(4) Maxi-cube combinations, as defined in Chapter 1, may not exceed 65 feet overall dimension.

(5) Combinations of vehicles specifically designed to transport motor vehicles or boats may not exceed 65 feet overall dimension. The length limitation is inclusive of front and rear bumpers but exclusive of the overhang of the transported vehicles, as provided in paragraph (i) of this Section.

(6) Stinger steered semitrailer vehicles as defined in Chapter 1, specifically designed to transport motor vehicles or boats, may not exceed 75 feet overall dimension. The length limitation is inclusive of front and rear bumpers but exclusive of the overhang of the transported vehicles, as provided in paragraph (i) of this Section.

(7) A truck in transit transporting 3 trucks coupled together by the triple saddlemount method may not exceed 75 feet overall dimension.

Vehicles operating during daylight hours when transporting poles, pipes, machinery, or other objects of a structural nature that cannot readily be dismembered are exempt from length limitations, provided that no object may exceed 80 feet in length and the overall dimension of the vehicle including the load may not exceed 100 feet. This exemption does not apply to operation on a Saturday, Sunday, or legal holiday. Legal holidays referred to in this Section are the days on which the following traditional holidays are celebrated: New Year's Day; Memorial Day; Independence Day; Labor Day; Thanksgiving Day; and Christmas Day.

Vehicles and loads operated by a public utility while en route to make emergency repairs to public service facilities or properties are exempt from length limitations, provided that during night operations every vehicle and its load must be equipped with a sufficient number of clearance lamps on both sides and marker lamps on the extreme ends of any projecting load to clearly mark the dimensions of the load.

A tow truck in combination with a disabled vehicle or combination of disabled vehicles, as provided in paragraph (6) of subsection (c) of this Section, is exempt from length limitations.

The length limitations described in this paragraph (d) shall be exclusive of safety and energy conservation devices, such as bumpers, refrigeration units or air compressors and other devices, that the Department may interpret as necessary for safe and efficient operation; except that no device excluded under this paragraph shall have by its design or use the capability to carry cargo.

Section 5-35 of the Illinois Administrative Procedure Act [2] relating to procedures for rulemaking shall not apply to the designation of highways under this paragraph (d).

(e) On Class II highways there are no overall length limitations on motor vehicles operating in combinations, provided:

(1) The length of a semitrailer, unladen or with load, in combination with a truck tractor, may not exceed 53 feet overall dimension.

(2) The distance between the kingpin and the center of the rear axle of a semitrailer longer than 48 feet, in combination with a truck tractor, may not exceed 45 feet 6 inches.

(3) A truck tractor-semitrailer-trailer combination may not exceed 65 feet in dimension from front axle to rear axle.

(4) The length of a semitrailer or trailer, unladen or with load, operated in a truck tractor-semitrailer-trailer combination, may not exceed 28 feet 6 inches.

(5) Maxi-cube combinations, as defined in Chapter 1, may not exceed 65 feet overall dimension.

(6) A combination of vehicles, specifically designed to transport motor vehicles or boats, may not exceed 65 feet overall dimension. The length limitation is inclusive of front and rear bumpers but exclusive of the overhang of the transported vehicles, as provided in paragraph (i) of this Section.

(7) Stinger steered semitrailer vehicles, as defined in Chapter 1, specifically designed to transport motor vehicles or boats, may not exceed 75 feet overall dimension. The length limitation is inclusive of front and rear bumpers but exclusive of the overhang of the transported vehicles, as provided in paragraph (i) of this Section.

(8) A truck in transit transporting 3 trucks coupled together by the triple saddlemount method may not exceed 75 feet overall dimension.

Vehicles operating during daylight hours when transporting poles, pipes, machinery, or other objects of a structural nature that cannot readily be dismembered are exempt from length limitations, provided that no object may exceed 80 feet in length and the overall dimension of the vehicle including the load may not exceed 100 feet. This exemption does not apply to operation on a Saturday, Sunday, or legal holiday. Legal holidays referred to in this Section are the days on which the following traditional holidays are celebrated: New Year's Day; Memorial Day; Independence Day; Labor Day; Thanksgiving Day; and Christmas Day.

Vehicles and loads operated by a public utility while en route to make emergency repairs to public service facilities or properties are exempt from length limitations, provided that during night operations every vehicle and its load must be equipped with a sufficient number of clearance lamps on both sides and marker lamps on the extreme ends of any projecting load to clearly mark the dimensions of the load.

A tow truck in combination with a disabled vehicle or combination of disabled vehicles, as provided in paragraph (6) of subsection (c) of this Section, is exempt from length limitations.

Local authorities and road district commissioners, with respect to streets and highways under their jurisdiction, may also by ordinance or resolution allow length limitations of this subsection (e).

The length limitations described in this paragraph (e) shall be exclusive of safety and energy conservation devices, such as bumpers, refrigeration units or air compressors and other devices, that the Department may interpret as necessary for safe and efficient operation; except that no device excluded under this paragraph shall have by its design or use the capability to carry cargo.

(e-1) Combinations of vehicles not exceeding 65 feet overall length are allowed access as follows:

(1) From any State designated highway onto any county, township, or municipal highway for a distance of 5 highway miles for the purpose of loading and unloading, provided:

(A) The vehicle does not exceed 73,280 pounds in gross weight and 8 feet 6 inches in width.

(B) There is no sign prohibiting that access.

(C) The route is not being used as a thoroughfare between State designated highways.

(2) From any State designated highway onto any county or township highway for a distance of 5 highway miles or onto any municipal highway for a distance of one highway mile for the purpose of food, fuel, repairs, and rest, provided:

(A) The vehicle does not exceed 73,280 pounds in gross weight and 8 feet 6 inches in width.

(B) There is no sign prohibiting that access.

(C) The route is not being used as a thoroughfare between State designated highways.

(e-2) Except as provided in subsection (e-3), combinations of vehicles over 65 feet in length, with no overall length limitation except as provided in subsections (d) and (e) of this Section, are allowed access as follows:

(1) From a Class I highway onto any street or highway for a distance of one highway mile for the purpose of loading, unloading, food, fuel, repairs, and rest, provided there is no sign prohibiting that access.

(2) From a Class I or Class II highway onto any State highway or any locally designated highway for a distance of 5 highway miles for the purpose of loading, unloading, food, fuel, repairs, and rest.

(e-3) Combinations of vehicles over 65 feet in length operated by household goods carriers, with no overall length limitations except as provided in subsections (d) and (e) of this Section, have unlimited access to points of loading and unloading.

Section 5-35 of the Illinois Administrative Procedure Act relating to procedures for rulemaking shall not apply to the designation of highways under this paragraph (e).

(f) On Class III and other non-designated State highways, the length limitations for vehicles in combination are as follows:

(1) Truck tractor-semitrailer combinations, must comply with either a maximum 55 feet overall wheel base or a maximum 65 feet extreme overall dimension.

(2) Semitrailers, unladen or with load, may not exceed 53 feet overall dimension.

(3) No truck tractor-semitrailer-trailer combination may exceed 60 feet extreme overall dimension.

(4) The distance between the kingpin and the center axle of a semitrailer longer than 48 feet, in combination with a truck tractor, may not exceed 42 feet 6 inches.

(g) Length limitations in the preceding subsections of this Section 15–107 do not apply to the following:

(1) Vehicles operated in the daytime, except on Saturdays, Sundays, or legal holidays, when transporting poles, pipe, machinery, or other objects of a structural nature that cannot readily be dismembered, provided the overall length of vehicle and load may not exceed 100 feet and no object exceeding 80 feet in length may be transported unless a permit has been obtained as authorized in Section 15–301.

(2) Vehicles and loads operated by a public utility while en route to make emergency repairs to public service facilities or properties, but during night operation every vehicle and its load must be equipped with a sufficient number of clearance lamps on both sides and marker lamps upon the extreme ends of any projecting load to clearly mark the dimensions of the load.

(3) A tow truck in combination with a disabled vehicle or combination of disabled vehicles, provided the towing vehicle meets the following conditions:

(A) It is specifically designed as a tow truck having a gross vehicle weight rating of at least 18,000 pounds and equipped with air brakes, provided that air brakes are required only if the towing vehicle is towing a vehicle, semitrailer, or tractor-trailer combination that is equipped with air brakes.

(B) It is equipped with flashing, rotating, or oscillating amber lights, visible for at least 500 feet in all directions.

(C) It is capable of utilizing the lighting and braking systems of the disabled vehicle or combination of vehicles.

(D) It does not engage in a tow exceeding 50 miles from the initial point of wreck or disablement.

The Department may by rule or regulation prescribe additional requirements regarding length limitations for a tow truck towing another vehicle.

For the purpose of this subsection, gross vehicle weight rating, or GVWR, shall mean the value specified by the manufacturer as the loaded weight of the tow truck. Legal holidays referred to in this Section shall be specified as the day on which the following traditional holidays are celebrated:

New Year's Day;

Memorial Day;

Independence Day;

Labor Day;

Thanksgiving Day; and

Christmas Day.

(h) The load upon any vehicle operated alone, or the load upon the front vehicle of a combination of vehicles, shall not extend more than 3 feet beyond the front wheels of the vehicle or the front bumper of the vehicle if it is equipped with a front bumper. The provisions of this subsection (h) shall not apply to any vehicle or combination of vehicles specifically designed for the collection and transportation of waste, garbage, or recyclable materials during the vehicle's operation in the course of collecting garbage, waste, or recyclable materials if the vehicle is traveling at a speed not in excess of 15 miles per hour during the vehicle's operation and in the course of collecting garbage, waste, or recyclable materials. However, in no instance shall the load extend more than 7 feet beyond the front wheels of the vehicle or the front bumper of the vehicle if it is equipped with a front bumper.

(i) The load upon the front vehicle of a combination of vehicles specifically designed to transport motor vehicles shall not extend more than 3 feet beyond the foremost part of the transporting vehicle and the load upon the rear transporting vehicle shall not extend more than 4 feet beyond the rear of the bed or body of the vehicle. This paragraph shall only be applicable upon highways designated in paragraphs (d) and (e) of this Section.

(j) Articulated vehicles comprised of 2 sections, neither of which exceeds a length of 42 feet, designed for the carrying of more than 10 persons, may be up to 60 feet in length, not including energy absorbing bumpers, provided that the vehicles are:

1. operated by or for any public body or motor carrier authorized by law to provide public transportation services; or

2. operated in local public transportation service by any other person and the municipality in which the service is to be provided approved the operation of the vehicle.

(j–1) (Blank).

(k) Any person who is convicted of violating this Section is subject to the penalty as provided in paragraph (b) of Section 15–113.

(*l*) (Blank).

P.A. 76–1586, § 15–107, eff. July 1, 1970. Amended by P.A. 76–2196, § 1, eff. July 1, 1970; P.A. 77–58, § 1, eff. July 1, 1971; P.A. 77–1344, § 1, eff. Aug. 27, 1971; P.A. 77–2637, § 1, eff. Oct. 1, 1972; P.A. 77–2829, §§ 40, 67, eff. Dec. 22, 1972; P.A. 78–255, § 29, eff. Oct. 1, 1973; P.A. 78–486, § 1, eff. Jan. 1, 1974; P.A. 78–1297, § 58, eff. March 4, 1975; P.A. 81–967, § 1, eff. Jan. 1, 1980; P.A. 82–198, § 1, eff. Jan. 1, 1982; P.A. 82–573, § 1, eff. Sept. 24, 1981; P.A. 82–649, § 1, eff. July 1, 1982; P.A. 82–783, Art. III, § 37, eff. July 13, 1982; P.A. 83–12, § 1, eff. July 1, 1983; P.A. 83–475, § 1, eff. Jan. 1, 1984; P.A. 83–781, § 1, eff. Jan. 1, 1984; P.A. 83–953, § 1, eff. Dec. 2, 1983; P.A. 83–1362, Art. II, § 99, eff. Sept. 11, 1984; P.A. 84–1061, § 1, eff. July 1, 1986; P.A. 85–505, § 1, eff. Sept. 18, 1987; P.A. 85–562, § 1, eff. Sept. 18, 1987; P.A. 85–830, § 1, eff. Sept. 24, 1987; P.A. 85–1209, Art. II, § 2–51, eff. Aug. 30, 1988; P.A. 85–1345, § 1, eff. Aug. 31, 1988; P.A. 85–1440, Art. II, § 2–54, eff. Feb. 1, 1989; P.A. 86–419, § 1, eff. Aug. 30, 1989; P.A. 86–447, § 2, eff. Aug. 30, 1989; P.A. 86–589, § 1, eff. Jan. 1, 1990; P.A. 86–1028, Art. II, § 2–44, eff. Feb. 5, 1990; P.A. 87–1203, § 1, eff. Sept. 25, 1992; P.A. 88–45, Art. III, § 3–128, eff. July 6, 1993; P.A. 88–384, § 5, eff. Jan. 1, 1994; P.A. 88–670, Art. 2, § 2–59, eff. Dec. 2, 1994; P.A. 89–219, § 5, eff. Jan. 1, 1996; P.A. 89–434, § 5, eff. June 1, 1996; P.A. 89–626, Art. 2, § 2–66, eff. Aug. 9, 1996; P.A. 90–89, § 15, eff. Jan. 1, 1998; P.A. 90–147, § 5, eff. July 23, 1997; P.A. 90–407, § 5, eff. Aug. 15, 1997; P.A.

90-655, § 153, eff. July 30, 1998; P.A. 92-417, § 5, eff. Jan. 1, 2002; P.A. 92-766, § 5, eff. Jan. 1, 2003; P.A. 92-883, § 5, eff. Jan. 13, 2003.

Formerly Ill.Rev.Stat.1991, ch. 95 ½, ¶ 15-107.

1 625 ILCS 5/1-101 et seq.

2 5 ILCS 100/5-35.

Section 4 of P.A. 83-12, approved July 1, 1983, provided:

"Effective date. This Act takes effect as provided in this Section.

"The amendments to those portions of Sections 3-815(a), 3-818 and 3-819(b) of 'The Illinois Vehicle Code' in Section 1 of this Act which create the 'X', 'Z', 'MX', 'MZ', 'MM' and 'TN' registration classifications and the fees and taxes imposed for those classifications, the amendments to Sections 2-119, 3-401 and 3-802 of 'The Illinois Vehicle Code' in Section 1 of this Act, and the amendments to Chapter 15 of 'The Illinois Vehicle Code' in Section 1 of this Act take effect July 1, 1983.

"The remaining amendments to 'The Illinois Vehicle Code' in Section 1 of this Act take effect July 1, 1983 and apply beginning with the 1985 registration year, except that the amendments to Sections 3-813 through 3-816 and Section 3-819 apply beginning with the 1984 registration year for those vehicles registered on a calendar year basis only.

"The amendments to Chapters 13 and 18 of 'The Illinois Vehicle Code' in Section 1 of this Act take effect January 1, 1984.

"Section 2 of this Act takes effect on the first day of the next succeeding month which commences at least 30 days after the date on which this Act becomes law.

"Section 3 of this Act takes effect July 1, 1983.

"Section 3.1 of this Act takes effect January 1, 1984.

"This Section 4 takes effect upon its becoming a law."

P.A. 92-766 incorporated the amendment by P.A. 92-417.

P.A. 92-883 incorporated the amendments by P.A. 92-417 and P.A. 92-766.

5/15-108. Planking edge of a pavement

§ 15-108. Planking edge of a pavement. No tractor, traction engine or other metal tired vehicle, weighing more than 4 tons, including the weight of the vehicle and its load, shall drive up onto, off or over the edge of any paved public highway in this State, without protecting such edge by putting down solid planks or other suitable device to prevent such vehicle from breaking off the edges or corners of such pavement.

P.A. 76-1586, § 15-108, eff. July 1, 1970. Amended by P.A. 90-655, § 153, eff. July 30, 1998.

Formerly Ill.Rev.Stat.1991, ch. 95 ½, ¶ 15-108.

5/15-109. Spilling loads on highways prohibited

§ 15-109. Spilling loads on highways prohibited. (a) No vehicle shall be driven or moved on any highway unless such vehicle is so constructed or loaded as to prevent any of its load from dropping, shifting, leaking or otherwise escaping therefrom, except that sand may be dropped for the purpose of securing traction, or water or other substance may be sprinkled on a roadway in cleaning or maintaining such roadway.

(b) No person shall operate on any highway any vehicle with any load unless said load and any covering thereon is securely fastened so as to prevent said covering or load from becoming loose, detached, or in any manner a hazard to other users of the highway.

(c) The Department shall adopt such rules and regulations it deems appropriate which require the securing of steel rolls and other objects on flatbed trucks so as to prevent injury to users of highways and damage to property. Any person who operates a flatbed truck on any highway in violation of the rules and regulations promulgated by the Department under this subsection shall be guilty of a Class A misdemeanor.

P.A. 76-1586, § 15-109, eff. July 1, 1970. Amended by P.A. 82-231, § 1, eff. Jan. 1, 1982.

Formerly Ill.Rev.Stat.1991, ch. 95 ½, ¶ 15-109.

5/15-109.1. Covers or tarpaulins required for certain loads

§ 15-109.1. Covers or tarpaulins required for certain loads.

(a) No person shall operate or cause to be operated, on a highway, any second division vehicle loaded with dirt, aggregate, garbage, refuse, or other similar material, when any portion of the load is falling, sifting, blowing, dropping or in any way escaping from the vehicle.

(b) No person shall operate or cause to be operated, on a highway, any second division vehicle having a gross vehicle weight rating of 8,000 pounds or more loaded with dirt, aggregate, garbage, refuse, or other similar material in or on any part of the vehicle other than in the cargo area. In addition, no person shall operate on any highway, such vehicle unless the tailgate on the vehicle is in good repair and operating condition and closes securely so as to prevent any load, residue, or other material from escaping.

(c) This Section shall not apply to the operation of highway maintenance vehicles engaged in removing snow and ice from the roadway, nor to implements of husbandry or other farm vehicles while transporting agricultural products to or from the original place of production.

(d) For the purpose of this Section "aggregate" shall include all ores, minerals, sand, gravel, shale, coal, clay, limestone or any other ore or mineral which may be mined.

(e) Notwithstanding any other penalty, whenever a police officer determines that the operator of a vehicle is in violation of this Section, as evidenced by the issuance of a citation for a violation of Section 15-109.1 of this Code, or where a police officer determines that a dangerous condition exists whereby any portion of the load may fall, sift, blow, drop, or in any way escape or fall from the vehicle, the police officer shall require the operator to stop the vehicle in a suitable place and keep such vehicle stationary until the load has either been reduced, secured, or covered with a cover or tarpaulin of sufficient size to prevent any further violation of this Section.

(f) Any violation of the provisions of this Section shall be a petty offense punishable by a fine not to exceed $250.

P.A. 76-1586, § 15-109.1, added by P.A. 84-226, § 1, eff. Jan. 1, 1986. Amended by P.A. 91-858, § 5, eff. Jan. 1, 2001.

Formerly Ill.Rev.Stat.1991, ch. 95 ½, ¶ 15-109.1.

5/15-110. Towed vehicles

§ 15-110. Towed vehicles. (a) When one vehicle is towing another, the drawbar or other connection shall be of sufficient strength to pull all the weight towed thereby and the drawbar or other connection shall not exceed 15 feet from one vehicle to the other, except for the connection between any 2 vehicles transporting poles, pipes, machinery or other objects of structural nature which cannot readily be dismembered.

(b) Outside a business, residential or suburban district or on any controlled access highway, no vehicle other than a pole trailer or a semitrailer which is being towed by a truck tractor and is connected by the means of a fifth wheel shall be towed on a roadway except by a drawbar and each such vehicle so towed shall, in addition, be coupled with 2 safety chains or cables to the towing vehicle. Such chains or cables shall be of sufficient size and strength to prevent the towed vehicle parting from the drawing vehicle in case the drawbar should break or become disengaged.

(c) The provisions of this section shall not apply to any second division vehicle owned, operated or controlled by any person who is registered with the Bureau of Motor Carrier Safety of the Federal Highway Administration and has complied with the federal safety provisions of the Bureau of Motor Carrier Safety of the Federal Highway Administration and the rules and regulations of the Bureau.

P.A. 76–1586, § 15–110, eff. July 1, 1970. Amended by P.A. 77–22, § 1, eff. July 1, 1971.

Formerly Ill.Rev.Stat.1991, ch. 95 ½, ¶ 15–110.

5/15–111. Wheel and axle loads and gross weights

§ 15–111. Wheel and axle loads and gross weights.

(a) On non-designated highways, no vehicle or combination of vehicles equipped with pneumatic tires may be operated, unladen or with load, when the total weight transmitted to the road surface exceeds 18,000 pounds on a single axle or 32,000 pounds on a tandem axle with no axle within the tandem exceeding 18,000 pounds except:

(1) when a different limit is established and posted in accordance with Section 15–316 of this Code;

(2) vehicles for which the Department of Transportation and local authorities issue overweight permits under authority of Section 15–301 of this Code;

(3) tow trucks subject to the conditions provided in subsection (d) may not exceed 24,000 pounds on a single rear axle or 44,000 pounds on a tandem rear axle;

(4) any single axle of a 2–axle truck weighing 36,000 pounds or less and not a part of a combination of vehicles, shall not exceed 20,000 pounds;

(5) any single axle of a 2–axle truck equipped with a personnel lift or digger derrick, weighing 36,000 pounds or less, owned and operated by a public utility, shall not exceed 20,000 pounds;

(6) any single axle of a 2–axle truck specially equipped with a front loading compactor used exclusively for garbage, refuse, or recycling may not exceed 20,000 pounds per axle, provided that the gross weight of the vehicle does not exceed 40,000 pounds;

(7) a truck, not in combination and specially equipped with a selfcompactor or an industrial roll-off hoist and roll-off container, used exclusively for garbage or refuse operations may, when laden, transmit upon the road surface the following maximum weights: 22,000 pounds on a single axle; 40,000 pounds on a tandem axle;

(8) a truck, not in combination and used exclusively for the collection of rendering materials, may, when laden, transmit upon the road surface the following maximum weights: 22,000 pounds on a single axle; 40,000 pounds on a tandem axle;

(9) tandem axles on a 3–axle truck registered as a Special Hauling Vehicle, manufactured prior to or in the model year of 2004 and first registered in Illinois prior to January 1, 2005, with a distance greater than 72 inches but not more than 96 inches between any series of 2 axles, is allowed a combined weight on the series not to exceed 36,000 pounds and neither axle of the series may exceed 18,000 pounds. Any vehicle of this type manufactured after the model year of 2004 or first registered in Illinois after December 31, 2004 may not exceed a combined weight of 32,000 pounds through the series of 2 axles and neither axle of the series may exceed 18,000 pounds;

(10) tandem axles on a 4–axle truck mixer, whose fourth axle is a road surface engaging mixer trailing axle, registered as a Special Hauling Vehicle, used exclusively for the mixing and transportation of concrete and manufactured prior to or in the model year of 2004 and first registered in Illinois prior to January 1, 2005, with a distance greater than 72 inches but not more than 96 inches between any series of 2 axles, is allowed a combined weight on the series not to exceed 36,000 pounds and neither axle of the series may exceed 18,000 pounds. Any vehicle of this type manufactured after the model year of 2004 or first registered in Illinois after December 31, 2004 may not exceed a combined weight of 32,000 pounds through the series of 2 axles and neither axle of the series may exceed 18,000 pounds;

(11) 4–axle vehicles or a 5 or more axle combination of vehicles: The weight transmitted upon the road surface through any series of 3 axles whose centers are more than 96 inches apart, measured between extreme axles in the series, may not exceed those allowed in the table contained in subsection (f) of this Section. No axle or tandem axle of the series may exceed the maximum weight permitted under this Section for a single or tandem axle.

No vehicle or combination of vehicles equipped with other than pneumatic tires may be operated, unladen or with load, upon the highways of this State when the gross weight on the road surface through any wheel exceeds 800 pounds per inch width of tire tread or when the gross weight on the road surface through any axle exceeds 16,000 pounds.

(b) On non-designated highways, the gross weight of vehicles and combination of vehicles including the weight of the vehicle or combination and its maximum load shall be subject to the foregoing limitations and further shall not exceed the following gross weights dependent upon the number of axles and distance between extreme axles of the vehicle or combination measured longitudinally to the nearest foot.

VEHICLES HAVING 2 AXLES .... 36,000 pounds

VEHICLES OR COMBINATIONS
HAVING 3 AXLES

With Tandem Axles Minimum distance to nearest foot between extreme axles	Maximum Gross Weight (pounds)	With or Without Tandem Axles Minimum distance to nearest foot between extreme axles	Maximum Gross Weight (pounds)
10 feet	41,000	16 feet	46,000
11	42,000	17	47,000
12	43,000	18	47,500
13	44,000	19	48,000
14	44,500	20	49,000
15	45,000	21 feet or more	50,000

VEHICLES OR COMBINATIONS
HAVING 4 AXLES

Minimum distance to nearest foot between extreme axles	Maximum Gross Weight (pounds)	Minimum distance to nearest foot between extreme axles	Maximum Gross Weight (pounds)
15 feet	50,000	26 feet	57,500

Minimum distance to nearest foot between extreme axles	Maximum Gross Weight (pounds)	Minimum distance to nearest foot between extreme axles	Maximum Gross Weight (pounds)
16	50,500	27	58,000
17	51,500	28	58,500
18	52,000	29	59,500
19	52,500	30	60,000
20	53,500	31	60,500
21	54,000	32	61,500
22	54,500	33	62,000
23	55,500	34	62,500
24	56,000	35	63,500
25	56,500	36 feet or more	64,000

A vehicle not in a combination having more than 4 axles may not exceed the weight in the table in this subsection (b) for 4 axles measured between the extreme axles of the vehicle.

COMBINATIONS HAVING 5 OR MORE AXLES

Minimum distance to nearest foot between extreme axles	Maximum Gross Weight (pounds)
42 feet or less	72,000
43	73,000
44 feet or more	73,280

VEHICLES OPERATING ON CRAWLER TYPE TRACKS .... 40,000 pounds

TRUCKS EQUIPPED WITH SELFCOMPACTORS OR ROLL-OFF HOISTS AND ROLL-OFF CONTAINERS FOR GARBAGE OR REFUSE HAULS ONLY AND TRUCKS USED FOR THE COLLECTION OF RENDERING MATERIALS

On Highway Not Part of National System of Interstate and Defense Highways

with 2 axles	36,000 pounds
with 3 axles	54,000 pounds

TWO AXLE TRUCKS EQUIPPED WITH A FRONT LOADING COMPACTOR USED EXCLUSIVELY FOR THE COLLECTION OF GARBAGE, REFUSE, OR RECYCLING

with 2 axles	40,000 pounds

(c) Cities having a population of more than 50,000 may permit by ordinance axle loads on 2 axle motor vehicles 33 ½ % above those provided for herein, but the increase shall not become effective until the city has officially notified the Department of the passage of the ordinance and shall not apply to those vehicles when outside of the limits of the city, nor shall the gross weight of any 2 axle motor vehicle operating over any street of the city exceed 40,000 pounds.

(d) Weight limitations shall not apply to vehicles (including loads) operated by a public utility when transporting equipment required for emergency repair of public utility facilities or properties or water wells.

A combination of vehicles, including a tow truck and a disabled vehicle or disabled combination of vehicles, that exceeds the weight restriction imposed by this Code, may be operated on a public highway in this State provided that neither the disabled vehicle nor any vehicle being towed nor the tow truck itself shall exceed the weight limitations permitted under this Chapter. During the towing operation, neither the tow truck nor the vehicle combination shall exceed 24,000 pounds on a single rear axle and 44,000 pounds on a tandem rear axle, provided the towing vehicle:

(1) is specifically designed as a tow truck having a gross vehicle weight rating of at least 18,000 pounds and is equipped with air brakes, provided that air brakes are required only if the towing vehicle is towing a vehicle, semitrailer, or tractor-trailer combination that is equipped with air brakes;

(2) is equipped with flashing, rotating, or oscillating amber lights, visible for at least 500 feet in all directions;

(3) is capable of utilizing the lighting and braking systems of the disabled vehicle or combination of vehicles; and

(4) does not engage in a tow exceeding 20 miles from the initial point of wreck or disablement. Any additional movement of the vehicles may occur only upon issuance of authorization for that movement under the provisions of Sections 15-301 through 15-319 of this Code.

Gross weight limits shall not apply to the combination of the tow truck and vehicles being towed. The tow truck license plate must cover the operating empty weight of the tow truck only. The weight of each vehicle being towed shall be covered by a valid license plate issued to the owner or operator of the vehicle being towed and displayed on that vehicle. If no valid plate issued to the owner or operator of that vehicle is displayed on that vehicle, or the plate displayed on that vehicle does not cover the weight of the vehicle, the weight of the vehicle shall be covered by the third tow truck plate issued to the owner or operator of the tow truck and temporarily affixed to the vehicle being towed.

The Department may by rule or regulation prescribe additional requirements. However, nothing in this Code shall prohibit a tow truck under instructions of a police officer from legally clearing a disabled vehicle, that may be in violation of weight limitations of this Chapter, from the roadway to the berm or shoulder of the highway. If in the opinion of the police officer that location is unsafe, the officer is authorized to have the disabled vehicle towed to the nearest place of safety.

For the purpose of this subsection, gross vehicle weight rating, or GVWR, shall mean the value specified by the manufacturer as the loaded weight of the tow truck.

(e) No vehicle or combination of vehicles equipped with pneumatic tires shall be operated, unladen or with load, upon the highways of this State in violation of the provisions of any permit issued under the provisions of Sections 15-301 through 15-319 of this Chapter.

(f) On designated Class I, II, or III highways and the National System of Interstate and Defense Highways, no vehicle or combination of vehicles with pneumatic tires may be operated, unladen or with load, when the total weight on the road surface exceeds the following: 20,000 pounds on a single axle; 34,000 pounds on a tandem axle with no axle within the tandem exceeding 20,000 pounds; 80,000 pounds gross weight for vehicle combinations of 5 or more axles; or a total weight on a group of 2 or more consecutive axles in excess of that weight produced by the application of the following formula: W = 500 times the sum of (LN divided by N-1) + 12N + 36, where "W" equals overall total weight on any group of 2 or more consecutive axles to the nearest 500 pounds, "L" equals the distance measured to the nearest foot between extremes of any group of 2 or more consecutive axles, and "N" equals the number of axles in the group under consideration.

The above formula when expressed in tabular form results in allowable loads as follows:

Distance measured to the nearest foot between the extremes of any group of 2 or more consecutive axles	Maximum weight in pounds of any group of 2 or more consecutive axles				
feet	2 axles	3 axles	4 axles	5 axles	6 axles
4	34,000				
5	34,000				
6	34,000				
7	34,000				
8	38,000*	42,000			
9	39,000	42,500			
10	40,000	43,500			
11		44,000			
12		45,000	50,000		
13		45,500	50,500		
14		46,500	51,500		
15		47,000	52,000		
16		48,000	52,500	58,000	
17		48,500	53,500	58,500	
18		49,500	54,000	59,000	
19		50,000	54,500	60,000	
20		51,000	55,500	60,500	66,000
21		51,500	56,000	61,000	66,500
22		52,500	56,500	61,500	67,000
23		53,000	57,500	62,500	68,000
24		54,000	58,000	63,000	68,500
25		54,500	58,500	63,500	69,000
26		55,500	59,500	64,000	69,500
27		56,000	60,000	65,000	70,000
28		57,000	60,500	65,500	71,000
29		57,500	61,500	66,000	71,500
30		58,500	62,000	66,500	72,000
31		59,000	62,500	67,500	72,500
32		60,000	63,500	68,000	73,000
33			64,000	68,500	74,000
34			64,500	69,000	74,500
35			65,500	70,000	75,000
36			66,000	70,500	75,500
37			66,500	71,000	76,000
38			67,500	72,000	77,000
39			68,000	72,500	77,500
40			68,500	73,000	78,000
41			69,500	73,500	78,500
42			70,000	74,000	79,000
43			70,500	75,000	80,000
44			71,500	75,500	
45			72,000	76,000	
46			72,500	76,500	
47			73,500	77,500	
48			74,000	78,000	
49			74,500	78,500	
50			75,500	79,000	
51			76,000	80,000	
52			76,500		
53			77,500		
54			78,000		
55			78,500		
56			79,500		
57			80,000		

* If the distance between 2 axles is 96 inches or less, the 2 axles are tandem axles and the maximum total weight may not exceed 34,000 pounds, notwithstanding the higher limit resulting from the application of the formula.

Vehicles not in a combination having more than 4 axles may not exceed the weight in the table in this subsection (f) for 4 axles measured between the extreme axles of the vehicle.

Vehicles in a combination having more than 6 axles may not exceed the weight in the table in this subsection (f) for 6 axles measured between the extreme axles of the combination.

Local authorities and road district highway commissioners, with respect to streets and highways under their jurisdiction, without additional fees, may also by ordinance or resolution allow the weight limitations of this subsection, provided the maximum gross weight on any one axle shall not exceed 20,000 pounds and the maximum total weight on any tandem axle shall not exceed 34,000 pounds, on designated highways when appropriate regulatory signs giving notice are erected upon the street or highway or portion of any street or highway affected by the ordinance or resolution.

The following are exceptions to the above formula:

(1) Two consecutive sets of tandem axles may carry a total weight of 34,000 pounds each if the overall distance between the first and last axles of the consecutive sets of tandem axles is 36 feet or more.

(2) Vehicles for which a different limit is established and posted in accordance with Section 15–316 of this Code.

(3) Vehicles for which the Department of Transportation and local authorities issue overweight permits under authority of Section 15–301 of this Code. These vehicles are not subject to the bridge formula.

(4) Tow trucks subject to the conditions provided in subsection (d) may not exceed 24,000 pounds on a single rear axle or 44,000 pounds on a tandem rear axle.

(5) A tandem axle on a 3–axle truck registered as a Special Hauling Vehicle, manufactured prior to or in the model year of 2004, and registered in Illinois prior to January 1, 2005, with a distance between 2 axles in a series greater than 72 inches but not more than 96 inches may not exceed a total weight of 36,000 pounds and neither axle of the series may exceed 18,000 pounds.

(6) A truck not in combination, equipped with a self compactor or an industrial roll-off hoist and roll-off container, used exclusively for garbage or refuse operations, may, when laden, transmit upon the road surface, except when on part of the National System of Interstate and Defense Highways, the following maximum weights: 22,000 pounds on a single axle; 40,000 pounds on a tandem axle; 36,000 pounds gross weight on a 2–axle vehicle; 54,000 pounds gross weight on a 3–axle vehicle. This vehicle is not subject to the bridge formula.

(7) Combinations of vehicles, registered as Special Hauling Vehicles that include a semitrailer manufactured prior to or in the model year of 2004, and registered in Illinois prior to January 1, 2005, having 5 axles with a distance of 42 feet or less between extreme axles, may not exceed the following maximum weights: 18,000 pounds on a single axle; 32,000 pounds on a tandem axle; and 72,000 pounds gross weight. This combination of vehicles is not subject to the bridge formula. For all those combinations of vehicles that include a semitrailer manufactured after the effective date of this amendatory Act of the 92nd General Assembly, the overall distance between the first and last axles of the 2 sets of tandems must be 18 feet 6 inches or more. Any combination of vehicles that has had its cargo container replaced in its entirety after December 31, 2004 may not exceed the weights allowed by the bridge formula.

No vehicle or combination of vehicles equipped with other than pneumatic tires may be operated, unladen or with load, upon the highways of this State when the gross weight on the road surface through any wheel exceeds 800 pounds per inch width of tire tread or when the gross weight on the road surface through any axle exceeds 16,000 pounds.

(f-1) A vehicle and load not exceeding 73,280 pounds is allowed access as follows:

(1) From any State designated highway onto any county, township, or municipal highway for a distance of 5 highway miles for the purpose of loading and unloading, provided:

(A) The vehicle and load does not exceed 8 feet 6 inches in width and 65 feet overall length.

(B) There is no sign prohibiting that access.

(C) The route is not being used as a thoroughfare between State designated highways.

(2) From any State designated highway onto any county or township highway for a distance of 5 highway miles, or any municipal highway for a distance of one highway mile for the purpose of food, fuel, repairs, and rest, provided:

(A) The vehicle and load does not exceed 8 feet 6 inches in width and 65 feet overall length.

(B) There is no sign prohibiting that access.

(C) The route is not being used as a thoroughfare between State designated highways.

(f-2) A vehicle and load greater than 73,280 pounds in weight but not exceeding 80,000 pounds is allowed access as follows:

(1) From a Class I highway onto any street or highway for a distance of one highway mile for the purpose of loading, unloading, food, fuel, repairs, and rest, provided there is no sign prohibiting that access.

(2) From a Class I, II, or III highway onto any State highway or any local designated highway for a distance of 5 highway miles for the purpose of loading, unloading, food, fuel, repairs, and rest.

Section 5-35 of the Illinois Administrative Procedure Act [1] relating to procedures for rulemaking shall not apply to the designation of highways under this subsection.

(g) No person shall operate a vehicle or combination of vehicles over a bridge or other elevated structure constituting part of a highway with a gross weight that is greater than the maximum weight permitted by the Department, when the structure is sign posted as provided in this Section.

(h) The Department upon request from any local authority shall, or upon its own initiative may, conduct an investigation of any bridge or other elevated structure constituting a part of a highway, and if it finds that the structure cannot with safety to itself withstand the weight of vehicles otherwise permissible under this Code the Department shall determine and declare the maximum weight of vehicles that the structures can withstand, and shall cause or permit suitable signs stating maximum weight to be erected and maintained before each end of the structure. No person shall operate a vehicle or combination of vehicles over any structure with a gross weight that is greater than the posted maximum weight.

(i) Upon the trial of any person charged with a violation of subsections (g) or (h) of this Section, proof of the determination of the maximum allowable weight by the Department and the existence of the signs, constitutes conclusive evidence of the maximum weight that can be maintained with safety to the bridge or structure.

P.A. 76-1586, § 15-111, eff. July 1, 1970. Amended by P.A. 76-2197, § 1, eff. July 1, 1970; P.A. 77-643, § 1, eff. Aug. 4, 1971; P.A. 77-1226, § 1, eff. Aug. 24, 1971; P.A. 77-1418, § 1, eff. Jan. 1, 1972; P.A. 77-2829, § 40, eff. Dec. 22, 1972; P.A. 78-255, § 61, eff. Oct. 1, 1973; P.A. 78-324, § 1, eff. Jan. 1, 1974; P.A. 78-1297, § 58, eff. March 4, 1975; P.A. 79-628, § 1, eff. Aug. 28, 1975; P.A. 83-12, § 1, eff. July 1, 1983; P.A. 83-953, § 1, eff. Dec. 2, 1983; P.A. 83-1478, § 1, eff. Jan. 1, 1985; P.A. 84-598, § 1, eff. Jan. 1, 1986; P.A. 84-1007, § 1, eff. Oct. 31, 1985; P.A. 84-1061, § 1, eff. July 1, 1986; P.A. 84-1308, Art. II, § 96, eff. Aug. 25, 1986; P.A. 84-1311, § 1, eff. Aug. 27, 1986; P.A. 84-1330, § 1, eff. Sept. 9, 1986; P.A. 84-1438, Art. II, § 30, eff. Dec. 22, 1986; P.A. 85-561, § 1, eff. Sept. 18, 1987; P.A. 85-563, § 1, eff. Sept. 18, 1987; P.A. 85-678, § 1, eff. July 1, 1989; P.A. 85-757, § 1, eff. Sept. 23, 1987; P.A. 85-1209, Art. II, § 2-51, eff. Aug. 30, 1988; P.A. 85-1345, § 1, eff. Aug. 31, 1988; P.A. 85-1440, Art. II, § 2-25, eff. Feb. 1, 1989; P.A. 86-409, § 1, eff. Aug. 30, 1989; P.A. 86-519, § 1, eff. Sept. 1, 1989; P.A. 86-1005, § 3, eff. Dec. 28, 1989; P.A. 86-1028, Art. II, § 2-44, eff. Feb. 5, 1990; P.A. 86-1236, § 1, eff. Jan. 1, 1991; P.A. 87-1203, § 1, eff. Sept. 25, 1992; P.A. 87-1249, § 1, eff. Dec. 24, 1992; P.A. 88-45, Art. III, § 3-128, eff. July 6, 1993; P.A. 88-385, § 5, eff. Jan. 1, 1994; P.A. 88-403, § 5, eff. Jan. 1, 1994; P.A. 88-476, § 2, eff. July 1, 1994; P.A. 88-670, Art. 2, § 2-59, eff. Dec. 2, 1994; P.A. 89-117, § 10, eff. July 7, 1995; P.A. 89-433, § 5, eff. Dec. 15, 1995; P.A. 90-89, § 15, eff. Jan. 1, 1998; P.A. 90-330, § 5, eff. Aug. 8, 1997; P.A. 90-655, § 153, eff. July 30, 1998; P.A. 92-417, § 5, eff. Jan. 1, 2002.

Formerly Ill.Rev.Stat.1991, ch. 95 ½, ¶ 15-111.

[1] 5 ILCS 100/5-35.

Effective date and application of P.A. 83-12, see note under 625 ILCS 5/2-119.

5/15-112. Officers to weigh vehicles and require removal of excess loads

§ 15-112. Officers to weigh vehicles and require removal of excess loads.

(a) Any police officer having reason to believe that the weight of a vehicle and load is unlawful shall require the driver to stop and submit to a weighing of the same either by means of a portable or stationary scales that have been tested and approved at a frequency prescribed by the Illinois Department of Agriculture, or for those scales operated by the State, when such tests are requested by the Department of State Police, whichever is more frequent. If such scales are not available at the place where such vehicle is stopped, the police officer shall require that such vehicle be driven to the nearest available scale that has been tested and approved pursuant to this Section by the Illinois Department of Agriculture. Notwithstanding any provisions of the Weights and Measures Act [1] or the United States Department of Commerce NIST handbook 44, multi or single draft weighing is an acceptable method of weighing by law enforcement for determining a violation of Chapter 3 or 15 of this Code.[2] Law enforcement is exempt from the requirements of commercial weighing established in NIST handbook 44.

Within 18 months after the effective date of this amendatory Act of the 91st General Assembly, all municipal and county officers, technicians, and employees who set up and operate portable scales for wheel load or axle load or both and issue citations based on the use of portable scales for wheel load or axle load or both and who have not successfully completed initial classroom and field training regarding the set up and operation of portable scales, shall attend and successfully complete initial classroom and field training administered by the Illinois Law Enforcement Training Standards Board.

(b) Whenever an officer, upon weighing a vehicle and the load, determines that the weight is unlawful, such officer shall require the driver to stop the vehicle in a suitable place and remain standing until such portion of the load is removed as may be necessary to reduce the weight of the vehicle to the limit permitted under this Chapter, or to the limit permitted under the terms of a permit issued pursuant to Sections 15–301 through 15–318 and shall forthwith arrest the driver or owner. All material so unloaded shall be cared for by the owner or operator of the vehicle at the risk of such owner or operator; however, whenever a 3 or 4 axle vehicle with a tandem axle dimension greater than 72 inches, but less than 96 inches and registered as a Special Hauling Vehicle is transporting asphalt or concrete in the plastic state that exceeds axle weight or gross weight limits by less than 4,000 pounds, the owner or operator of the vehicle shall accept the arrest ticket or tickets for the alleged violations under this Section and proceed without shifting or reducing the load being transported or may shift or reduce the load under the provisions of subsection (d) or (e) of this Section, when applicable. Any fine imposed following an overweight violation by a vehicle registered as a Special Hauling Vehicle transporting asphalt or concrete in the plastic state shall be paid as provided in subsection 4 of paragraph (a) of Section 16–105 of this Code.

(c) The Department of Transportation may, at the request of the Department of State Police, erect appropriate regulatory signs on any State highway directing second division vehicles to a scale. The Department of Transportation may also, at the direction of any State Police officer, erect portable regulating signs on any highway directing second division vehicles to a portable scale. Every such vehicle, pursuant to such sign, shall stop and be weighed.

(d) Whenever any axle load of a vehicle exceeds the axle or tandem axle weight limits permitted by paragraph (a) or (f) of Section 15–111 by 2000 pounds or less, the owner or operator of the vehicle must shift or remove the excess so as to comply with paragraph (a) or (f) of Section 15–111. No overweight arrest ticket shall be issued to the owner or operator of the vehicle by any officer if the excess weight is shifted or removed as required by this paragraph.

(e) Whenever the gross weight of a vehicle with a registered gross weight of 73,280 pounds or less exceeds the weight limits of paragraph (b) or (f) of Section 15–111 of this Chapter by 2000 pounds or less, the owner or operator of the vehicle must remove the excess. Whenever the gross weight of a vehicle with a registered gross weight of 73,281 pounds or more exceeds the weight limits of paragraph (b) or (f) of Section 15–111 by 1,000 pounds or less or 2,000 pounds or less if weighed on wheel load weighers, the owner or operator of the vehicle must remove the excess. In either case no arrest ticket for any overweight violation of this Code shall be issued to the owner or operator of the vehicle by any officer if the excess weight is removed as required by this paragraph. A person who has been granted a special permit under Section 15–301 of this Code shall not be granted a tolerance on wheel load weighers.

(f) Whenever an axle load of a vehicle exceeds axle weight limits allowed by the provisions of a permit an arrest ticket shall be issued, but the owner or operator of the vehicle may shift the load so as to comply with the provisions of the permit. Where such shifting of a load to comply with the permit is accomplished, the owner or operator of the vehicle may then proceed.

(g) Any driver of a vehicle who refuses to stop and submit his vehicle and load to weighing after being directed to do so by an officer or removes or causes the removal of the load or part of it prior to weighing is guilty of a business offense and shall be fined not less than $500 nor more than $2,000.

P.A. 76–1586, § 15–112, eff. July 1, 1970. Amended by P.A. 76–2198, § 1, eff. July 1, 1970; P.A. 77–77, § 1, eff. July 1, 1971; P.A. 77–170, § 1, eff. Jan. 1, 1972; P.A. 77–1225, § 1, eff. Aug. 24, 1971; P.A. 77–2720, § 1, eff. Jan. 1, 1973; P.A. 77–2830, Art. 73, § 1, eff. Jan. 1, 1973; P.A. 78–255, § 61, eff. Oct. 1, 1973; P.A. 81–942, § 1, eff. Jan. 1, 1980; P.A. 83–12, § 1, eff. July 1, 1983; P.A. 83–953, § 1, eff. Dec. 2, 1983; P.A. 84–25, Art. IV, § 27, eff. July 18, 1985; P.A. 85–830, § 1, eff. Sept. 24, 1987; P.A. 86–849, § 1, eff. Sept. 7, 1989; P.A. 88–403, § 5, eff. Jan. 1, 1994; P.A. 88–476, § 2, eff. July 1, 1994; P.A. 88–535, § 25, eff. Jan. 26, 1994; P.A. 91–129, § 10, eff. July 16, 1999; P.A. 92–417, § 5, eff. Jan. 1, 2002.

Formerly Ill.Rev.Stat.1991, ch. 95 ½, ¶ 15–112.

1 225 ILCS 470/1 et seq.

2 625 ILCS 5/1–100 or 5/15–100 et seq.

Section 4 of P.A. 83–12, approved July 1, 1983, provided:

"Effective date. This Act takes effect as provided in this Section.

"The amendments to those portions of Sections 3–815(a), 3–818 and 3–819(b) of 'The Illinois Vehicle Code' in Section 1 of this Act which create the 'X', 'Z', 'MX', 'MZ', 'MM' and 'TN' registration classifications and the fees and taxes imposed for those classifications, the amendments to Sections 2–119, 3–401 and 3–802 of 'The Illinois Vehicle Code' in Section 1 of this Act, and the amendments to Chapter 15 of 'The Illinois Vehicle Code' in Section 1 of this Act take effect July 1, 1983.

"The remaining amendments to 'The Illinois Vehicle Code' in Section 1 of this Act take effect July 1, 1983 and apply beginning with the 1985 registration year, except that the amendments to Sections 3–813 through 3–816 and Section 3–819 apply beginning with the 1984 registration year for those vehicles registered on a calendar year basis only.

"The amendments to Chapters 13 and 18 of 'The Illinois Vehicle Code' in Section 1 of this Act take effect January 1, 1984.

"Section 2 of this Act takes effect on the first day of the next succeeding month which commences at least 30 days after the date on which this Act becomes law.

"Section 3 of this Act takes effect July 1, 1983.

"Section 3.1 of this Act takes effect January 1, 1984.

"This Section 4 takes effect upon its becoming a law."

5/15–113. Violations; Penalties

§ 15–113. Violations; Penalties.

(a) Whenever any vehicle is operated in violation of the provisions of Section 15–111 or subsection (d) of Section 3–401, the owner or driver of such vehicle shall be deemed guilty of such violation and either the owner or the driver of such vehicle may be prosecuted for such violation. Any person charged with a violation of any of these provisions who pleads not guilty shall be present in court for the trial on the charge. Any person, firm or corporation convicted of any violation of Section 15–111 including, but not limited to, a maximum axle or gross limit specified on a regulatory sign posted in accordance with paragraph (g) or (h) of Section 15–111, shall be fined according to the following schedule:

Up to and including	2000 pounds overweight	=	$50
from 2001 through	2500 pounds overweight	=	the fine is $135
from 2501 through	3000 pounds overweight	=	the fine is $165
from 3001 through	3500 pounds overweight	=	the fine is $260
from 3501 through	4000 pounds overweight	=	the fine is $300
from 4001 through	4500 pounds overweight	=	the fine is $425
from 4501 through	5000 pounds overweight	=	the fine is $475
from 5001 or more pounds	overweight	=	the fine shall be computed by assessing $750 for the first 5000 pounds overweight and $75 for each additional increment of 500 pounds overweight or fraction thereof.

In addition any person, firm or corporation convicted of 4 or more violations of Section 15–111 within any 12 month period shall be fined an additional amount of $2500 for the fourth and each subsequent conviction within the 12 month period. Provided, however, that with regard to a firm or corporation, a fourth or subsequent conviction shall mean a fourth or subsequent conviction attributable to any one employee-driver.

(b) Whenever any vehicle is operated in violation of the provisions of Sections 15–102, 15–103 or 15–107, the owner or driver of such vehicle shall be deemed guilty of such violation and either may be prosecuted for such violation. Any person, firm or corporation convicted of any violation of Sections 15–102, 15–103 or 15–107 shall be fined for the first or second conviction an amount equal to not less than $50 nor more than $500, and for the third and subsequent convictions by the same person, firm or corporation within a period of one year after the date of the first offense, not less than $500 nor more than $1,000.

P.A. 76–1586, § 15–113, eff. July 1, 1970. Amended by P.A. 81–199, § 1, eff. Jan. 1, 1980; P.A. 81–942, § 1, eff. Jan. 1, 1980; P.A. 81–1509, Art. I, § 57, eff. Sept. 26, 1980; P.A. 83–12, § 1, eff. July 1, 1983; P.A. 83–838, § 1, eff. Jan. 1, 1984; P.A. 83–953, § 1, eff. Dec. 2, 1983; P.A. 86–664, § 1, eff. Sept. 1, 1989; P.A. 88–476, § 2, eff. July 1, 1994; P.A. 89–117, § 10, eff. July 7, 1995; P.A. 89–245, § 5, eff. Jan. 1, 1996.

Formerly Ill.Rev.Stat.1991, ch. 95 ½, ¶ 15–113.

Section 4 of P.A. 83–12, approved July 1, 1983, provided:

"Effective date. This Act takes effect as provided in this Section.

"The amendments to those portions of Sections 3–815(a), 3–818 and 3–819(b) of 'The Illinois Vehicle Code' in Section 1 of this Act which create the 'X', 'Z', 'MX', 'MZ', 'MM' and 'TN' registration classifications and the fees and taxes imposed for those classifications, the amendments to Sections 2–119, 3–401 and 3–802 of 'The Illinois Vehicle Code' in Section 1 of this Act, and the amendments to Chapter 15 of 'The Illinois Vehicle Code' in Section 1 of this Act take effect July 1, 1983.

"The remaining amendments to 'The Illinois Vehicle Code' in Section 1 of this Act take effect July 1, 1983 and apply beginning with the 1985 registration year, except that the amendments to Sections 3–813 through 3–816 and Section 3–819 apply beginning with the 1984 registration year for those vehicles registered on a calendar year basis only.

"The amendments to Chapters 13 and 18 of 'The Illinois Vehicle Code' in Section 1 of this Act take effect January 1, 1984.

"Section 2 of this Act takes effect on the first day of the next succeeding month which commences at least 30 days after the date on which this Act becomes law.

"Section 3 of this Act takes effect July 1, 1983.

"Section 3.1 of this Act takes effect January 1, 1984.

"This Section 4 takes effect upon its becoming a law."

The amendments by P.A. 89–117 and P.A. 89–245 were identical.

5/15–113.1. Violations—Sentence of permit moves

§ 15–113.1. Violations—Sentence of permit moves. Whenever any vehicle is operated in violation of the provisions of a permit issued under the provisions of Sections 15–301 through 15–319 of this Chapter by operating under a fraudulent permit or under a permit not specifically covering the move, the owner or driver of such vehicle shall be deemed guilty of a business offense and either the owner or the driver of such vehicle may be prosecuted for such violation. When any person, firm or corporation is convicted of such violation, the permit shall be null and void and such person, firm or corporation shall be fined in an amount not less than 10 cents per pound for each pound the gross weight of the vehicle exceeds the gross weight of such vehicles allowable under Section 15–111 of this Chapter.

Penalties for violations of this section shall be in addition to any penalties imposed for violation of Section 15–301(j) of this Chapter.

P.A. 76–1586, § 15–113.1, added by P.A. 77–1224, § 1, eff. Aug. 24, 1971. Amended by P.A. 77–2830, Art. 73, § 1, eff. Jan. 1, 1973.

Formerly Ill.Rev.Stat.1991, ch. 95 ½, ¶ 15–113.1.

5/15–113.2. Violations—Sentence of permit moves exceeding axle weights

§ 15–113.2. Violations—Sentence of permit moves exceeding axle weights. Whenever any vehicle is operated in violation of the provisions of a permit issued under the provisions of Sections 15–301 through 15–319 of this Chapter by operating with axle weights in excess of those authorized in such permit, the owner or driver of such vehicle shall be deemed guilty of a business offense and either the owner or the driver of such vehicle may be prosecuted for such violation. Any person, firm or corporation convicted of such violation shall be fined in an amount not less than 2 cents nor more than 5 cents per pound for each pound of excess weight on such axle or tandem axle in excess of the weight authorized in the permit when the excess is 1,000 pounds or less; not less than 5 cents nor more than 10 cents per pound for each pound of excess weight when the excess exceeds 1,000 pounds and is 2,000 pounds or less; not less than 10 cents nor more than 15 cents per pound for each pound of excess weight when the excess exceeds 2,000 pounds and is 3,000 pounds or less; and not less than 15 cents nor more than 20 cents per pound for each pound of excess weight when the excess exceeds 3,000 pounds.

Penalties for violations of this section shall be in addition to any penalties imposed for violation of Section 15–301(j) of this Chapter.

P.A. 76–1586, § 15–113.2, added by P.A. 77–1224, § 1, eff. Aug. 24, 1971. Amended by P.A. 77–2830, Art. 73, § 1, eff. Jan. 1, 1973; P.A. 81–199, § 1, eff. Jan. 1, 1980.

Formerly Ill.Rev.Stat.1991, ch. 95 ½, ¶ 15–113.2.

5/15–113.3. Violations—Sentence of permit moves exceeding gross weight

§ 15–113.3. Violations—Sentence of permit moves exceeding gross weight. Whenever any vehicle is operated in violation of the provisions of a permit issued under the provisions of Sections 15–301 through 15–319 of this Chapter by operating with the gross weight in excess of that authorized in such permit, the owner or driver of such vehicle shall be deemed guilty of a business offense and either the owner or the driver of such vehicle may be prosecuted for such violation. Any person, firm or corporation convicted of such violation shall be fined in an amount not less than 2 cents nor more than 5 cents per pound for each pound of excess weight in excess of the gross weight authorized in the permit when the excess is 1,000 pounds or less; not less than 4 cents nor more than 7 cents per pound for each pound of excess weight when the excess exceeds 1,000 pounds and is 2,000 pounds or less; not less than 7 cents nor more than 10 cents per pound for each pound of excess weight when the excess exceeds 2,000 pounds and is 3,000 pounds or less; not less than 10 cents nor more than 15 cents per pound for each pound of excess weight when the excess exceeds 3,000 pounds and is 4,000 pounds or less; not less than 15 cents nor more than 20 cents per pound for each pound of excess weight when the excess exceeds 4,000 pounds and is 5,000 pounds or less; and not less than 17 cents nor more than 25 cents per pound for each pound of excess weight when the excess exceeds 5,000 pounds.

Penalties for violations of this section shall be in addition to any penalties imposed for violation of Section 15-301(j) of this Chapter.

P.A. 76-1586, § 15-113.3, added by P.A. 77-1224, § 1, eff. Aug. 24, 1971. Amended by P.A. 77-2830, Art. 73, § 1, eff. Jan. 1, 1973.

Formerly Ill.Rev.Stat.1991, ch. 95 ½, ¶ 15-113.3.

5/15-114. Pushing of disabled vehicles

§ 15-114. Pushing of disabled vehicles. It is unlawful under any circumstances for any vehicle to push any other vehicle on or along any highway outside an urban area in this State, except in an extreme emergency and then the vehicle shall not be pushed farther than is reasonably necessary to remove it from the roadway or from the immediate hazard that exists.

P.A. 76-1586, § 15-114, added by P.A. 78-486, § 1, eff. Jan. 1, 1974.

Formerly Ill.Rev.Stat.1991, ch. 95 ½, ¶ 15-114.

5/15-115. Report; operation of larger vehicles; consumption of diesel fuel by first and second division vehicles

§ 15-115. By July 1, 1985, and every 3 years thereafter, the Department of Transportation shall publish and deliver to the Governor and the General Assembly a report which assesses the damage done to public highways in the State of Illinois by virtue of the increased lengths, widths and weight loads allowed under this amendatory Act of 1983 and which determines whether the proceeds of the taxes imposed by the addition of Section 2(c) to "The Motor Fuel Tax Law" [1] in Section 2 of this amendatory Act of 1983 and the proceeds of the fees and taxes paid by the owners of vehicles classified in the "X", "Z", "MX" and "MZ" classifications under the amendments to Sections 3-815(a) and 3-818 in Section 1 of this amendatory Act of 1983 are sufficient to cover the costs of permitting the operation of such larger vehicles. The report shall also assess the consumption of diesel fuel by first and second division motor vehicles.

P.A. 76-1586, § 15-115, added by P.A. 83-12, § 1, eff. July 1, 1983.

Formerly Ill.Rev.Stat.1991, ch. 95 ½, ¶ 15-115.

[1] 35 ILCS 505/2.

ARTICLE II. VEHICLES EXCEEDING WEIGHT LIMITS

5/15-201. Vehicles exceeding prescribed weight limits—Preventing use of highway by

§ 15-201. Vehicles exceeding prescribed weight limits—Preventing use of highway by. The Department of State Police is directed to institute and maintain a program designed to prevent the use of public highways by vehicles which exceed the maximum weights allowed by Section 15-111 of this Act or which exceeds the maximum weights allowed as evidenced by the license plates attached to such vehicle and which license is required by this Act.

P.A. 76-1586, § 15-201, eff. July 1, 1970. Amended by P.A. 77-1057, § 1, eff. Aug. 17, 1971; P.A. 84-25, Art. IV, § 27, eff. July 18, 1985.

Formerly Ill.Rev.Stat.1991, ch. 95 ½, ¶ 15-201.

5/15-202. Enforcement

§ 15-202. Enforcement. Such program shall make provision for an intensive campaign by the State Police to apprehend any violators of the acts above mentioned, and at all times to maintain a vigilant watch for possible violators of such acts.

P.A. 76-1586, § 15-202, eff. July 1, 1970. Amended by P.A. 77-506, § 1, eff. Jan. 1, 1972.

Formerly Ill.Rev.Stat.1991, ch. 95 ½, ¶ 15-202.

5/15-203. Records of violations

§ 15-203. Records of violations. The Department of State Police shall maintain records of the number of violators of such acts apprehended and the number of convictions obtained. A resume of such records shall be included in the Department's annual report to the Governor; and the Department shall also present such resume to each regular session of the General Assembly.

The requirement for reporting to the General Assembly shall be satisfied by filing copies of the report with the Speaker, the Minority Leader and the Clerk of the House of Representatives and the President, the Minority Leader and the Secretary of the Senate and the Legislative Research Unit, as required by Section 3.1 of "An Act to revise the law in relation to the General Assembly", approved February 25, 1874, as amended,[1] and filing such additional copies with the State Government Report Distribution Center for the General Assembly as is required under paragraph (t) of Section 7 of the State Library Act.[2]

P.A. 76-1586, § 15-203, eff. July 1, 1970. Amended by P.A. 77-1058, § 1, eff. Aug. 17, 1971; P.A. 83-784, § 51, eff. Jan. 1, 1984; P.A. 84-25, Art. IV, § 27, eff. July 18, 1985; P.A. 84-1438, Art. III, § 46, eff. Dec. 22, 1986.

Formerly Ill.Rev.Stat.1991, ch. 95 ½, ¶ 15-203.

[1] 25 ILCS 5/3.1.

[2] 15 ILCS 320/7.

5/15-204 to 5/15-211. §§ 15-204 to 15-211. Repealed by P.A. 77-506, § 2, eff. Jan. 1, 1972

ARTICLE III. PERMITS

5/15–301. Permits for excess size and weight

§ 15–301. Permits for excess size and weight.

(a) The Department with respect to highways under its jurisdiction and local authorities with respect to highways under their jurisdiction may, in their discretion, upon application and good cause being shown therefor, issue a special permit authorizing the applicant to operate or move a vehicle or combination of vehicles of a size or weight of vehicle or load exceeding the maximum specified in this Act or otherwise not in conformity with this Act upon any highway under the jurisdiction of the party granting such permit and for the maintenance of which the party is responsible. Applications and permits other than those in written or printed form may only be accepted from and issued to the company or individual making the movement. Except for an application to move directly across a highway, it shall be the duty of the applicant to establish in the application that the load to be moved by such vehicle or combination is composed of a single nondivisible object that cannot reasonably be dismantled or disassembled. For the purpose of over length movements, more than one object may be carried side by side as long as the height, width, and weight laws are not exceeded and the cause for the over length is not due to multiple objects. For the purpose of over height movements, more than one object may be carried as long as the cause for the over height is not due to multiple objects and the length, width, and weight laws are not exceeded. For the purpose of an over width movement, more than one object may be carried as long as the cause for the over width is not due to multiple objects and length, height, and weight laws are not exceeded. No state or local agency shall authorize the issuance of excess size or weight permits for vehicles and loads that are divisible and that can be carried, when divided, within the existing size or weight maximums specified in this Chapter. Any excess size or weight permit issued in violation of the provisions of this Section shall be void at issue and any movement made thereunder shall not be authorized under the terms of the void permit. In any prosecution for a violation of this Chapter when the authorization of an excess size or weight permit is at issue, it is the burden of the defendant to establish that the permit was valid because the load to be moved could not reasonably be dismantled or disassembled, or was otherwise nondivisible.

(b) The application for any such permit shall: (1) state whether such permit is requested for a single trip or for limited continuous operation; (2) state if the applicant is an authorized carrier under the Illinois Motor Carrier of Property Law, if so, his certificate, registration or permit number issued by the Illinois Commerce Commission; (3) specifically describe and identify the vehicle or vehicles and load to be operated or moved except that for vehicles or vehicle combinations registered by the Department as provided in Section 15–319 of this Chapter, only the Illinois Department of Transportation's (IDT) registration number or classification need be given; (4) state the routing requested including the points of origin and destination, and may identify and include a request for routing to the nearest certified scale in accordance with the Department's rules and regulations, provided the applicant has approval to travel on local roads; and (5) state if the vehicles or loads are being transported for hire. No permits for the movement of a vehicle or load for hire shall be issued to any applicant who is required under the Illinois Motor Carrier of Property Law to have a certificate, registration or permit and does not have such certificate, registration or permit.

(c) The Department or local authority when not inconsistent with traffic safety is authorized to issue or withhold such permit at its discretion; or, if such permit is issued at its discretion to prescribe the route or routes to be traveled, to limit the number of trips, to establish seasonal or other time limitations within which the vehicles described may be operated on the highways indicated, or otherwise to limit or prescribe conditions of operations of such vehicle or vehicles, when necessary to assure against undue damage to the road foundations, surfaces or structures, and may require such undertaking or other security as may be deemed necessary to compensate for any injury to any roadway or road structure. The Department shall maintain a daily record of each permit issued along with the fee and the stipulated dimensions, weights, conditions and restrictions authorized and this record shall be presumed correct in any case of questions or dispute. The Department shall install an automatic device for recording applications received and permits issued by telephone. In making application by telephone, the Department and applicant waive all objections to the recording of the conversation.

(d) The Department shall, upon application in writing from any local authority, issue an annual permit authorizing the local authority to move oversize highway construction, transportation, utility and maintenance equipment over roads under the jurisdiction of the Department. The permit shall be applicable only to equipment and vehicles owned by or registered in the name of the local authority, and no fee shall be charged for the issuance of such permits.

(e) As an exception to paragraph (a) of this Section, the Department and local authorities, with respect to highways under their respective jurisdictions, in their discretion and upon application in writing may issue a special permit for limited continuous operation, authorizing the applicant to move loads of sweet corn, soybeans, corn, wheat, milo, other small grains and ensilage during the harvest season only on a 2 axle single vehicle registered by the Secretary of State with axle loads not to exceed 35% above those provided in Section 15–111. Permits may be issued for a period not to exceed 40 days and moves may be made of a distance not to exceed 25 miles from a field to a specified processing plant over any highway except the National System of Interstate and Defense Highways. All such vehicles shall be operated in the daytime except when weather or crop conditions require emergency operation at night, but with respect to such night operation, every such vehicle with load shall be equipped with flashing amber lights as specified under Section 12-215. Upon a declaration by the Governor that an emergency harvest situation exists, a special permit issued by the Department under this Section shall not be required from September 1 through December 31 during harvest season emergencies, provided that the weight does not exceed 20% above the limits provided in Section 15-111. All other restrictions that apply to permits issued under this Section shall apply during the declared time period. With respect to highways under the jurisdiction of local authorities, the local authorities may, at their discretion, waive special permit requirements during harvest season emergencies. This permit exemption shall apply to all vehicles eligible to obtain permits under this Section, including commercial vehicles in use during the declared time period.

(f) The form and content of the permit shall be determined by the Department with respect to highways under its jurisdiction and by local authorities with respect to highways under their jurisdiction. Every permit shall be in written form and carried in the vehicle or combination of vehicles to which it refers and shall be open to inspection by any police officer or authorized agent of any authority granting the permit and no person shall violate any of the terms or conditions of such special permit. Violation of the terms and conditions of the permit shall not be deemed a revocation of the permit; however, any vehicle and load found to be off the route prescribed in the permit shall be held to be operating without a permit. Any off route vehicle and load shall be required to obtain a new permit or permits, as necessary, to authorize the movement back onto the original permit routing. No rule or regulation, nor anything herein shall be construed to authorize any police officer, court, or authorized agent of any authority granting the permit to remove the permit from the possession of the permittee unless the permittee is charged with a fraudulent permit violation as provided in paragraph (i). However, upon arrest for an offense of violation of permit, operating without a permit when the vehicle is off route, or any size or weight offense under this Chapter when the permittee plans to raise the issuance of the permit as a defense, the permittee, or his agent, must produce the permit at any court hearing concerning the alleged offense.

If the permit designates and includes a routing to a certified scale, the permitee, while enroute to the designated scale, shall be deemed in compliance with the weight provisions of the permit provided the axle or gross weights do not exceed any of the permitted limits by more than the following amounts:

Single axle	2000 pounds
Tandem axle	3000 pounds
Gross	5000 pounds

(g) The Department is authorized to adopt, amend, and to make available to interested persons a policy concerning reasonable rules, limitations and conditions or provisions of operation upon highways under its jurisdiction in addition to those contained in this Section for the movement by special permit of vehicles, combinations, or loads which cannot reasonably be dismantled or disassembled, including manufactured and modular home sections and portions thereof. All rules, limitations and conditions or provisions adopted in the policy shall have due regard for the safety of the traveling public and the protection of the highway system and shall have been promulgated in conformity with the provisions of the Illinois Administrative Procedure Act.[1] The requirements of the policy for flagmen and escort vehicles shall be the same for all moves of comparable size and weight. When escort vehicles are required, they shall meet the following requirements:

(1) All operators shall be 18 years of age or over and properly licensed to operate the vehicle.

(2) Vehicles escorting oversized loads more than 12-feet wide must be equipped with a rotating or flashing amber light mounted on top as specified under Section 12-215.

The Department shall establish reasonable rules and regulations regarding liability insurance or self insurance for vehicles with oversized loads promulgated under The Illinois Administrative Procedure Act. Police vehicles may be required for escort under circumstances as required by rules and regulations of the Department.

(h) Violation of any rule, limitation or condition or provision of any permit issued in accordance with the provisions of this Section shall not render the entire permit null and void but the violator shall be deemed guilty of violation of permit and guilty of exceeding any size, weight or load limitations in excess of those authorized by the permit. The prescribed route or routes on the permit are not mere rules, limitations, conditions, or provisions of the permit, but are also the sole extent of the authorization granted by the permit. If a vehicle and load are found to be off the route or routes prescribed by any permit authorizing movement, the vehicle and load are operating without a permit. Any off route movement shall be subject to the size and weight maximums, under the applicable provisions of this Chapter, as determined by the type or class highway upon which the vehicle and load are being operated.

(i) Whenever any vehicle is operated or movement made under a fraudulent permit the permit shall be void, and the person, firm, or corporation to whom such permit was granted, the driver of such vehicle in addition to the person who issued such permit and any accessory, shall be guilty of fraud and either one or all persons may be prosecuted for such violation. Any person, firm, or corporation committing such violation shall be guilty of a Class 4 felony and the Department shall not issue permits to the person, firm or corporation convicted of such violation for a period of one year after the date of conviction. Penalties for violations of this Section shall be in addition to any penalties imposed for violation of other Sections of this Act.

(j) Whenever any vehicle is operated or movement made in violation of a permit issued in accordance with this Section, the person to whom such permit was granted, or the driver of such vehicle, is guilty of such violation and either, but not both, persons may be prosecuted for such violation as stated in this subsection (j). Any person, firm or corporation convicted of such violation shall be guilty of a petty offense and shall be fined for the first offense, not less than $50 nor more than $200 and, for the second offense by the same person, firm or corporation within a period of one year, not less than $200 nor more than $300 and, for the third offense by the same person, firm or corporation within a period of one year after the date of the first offense, not less than $300 nor more than $500 and the Department shall not issue permits to the person, firm or corporation convicted of a third offense during a period of one year after the date of conviction for such third offense.

(k) Whenever any vehicle is operated on local roads under permits for excess width or length issued by local authorities, such vehicle may be moved upon a State highway for a distance not to exceed one-half mile without a permit for the purpose of crossing the State highway.

(*l*) Notwithstanding any other provision of this Section, the Department, with respect to highways under its jurisdiction, and local authorities, with respect to highways under their jurisdiction, may at their discretion authorize the movement of a vehicle in violation of any size or weight requirement, or both, that would not ordinarily be eligible for a permit, when there is a showing of extreme necessity that the vehicle and load should be moved without unnecessary delay.

For the purpose of this subsection, showing of extreme necessity shall be limited to the following: shipments of livestock, hazardous materials, liquid concrete being hauled in a mobile cement mixer, or hot asphalt.

(m) Penalties for violations of this Section shall be in addition to any penalties imposed for violating any other Section of this Code.

(n) The Department with respect to highways under its jurisdiction and local authorities with respect to highways under their jurisdiction, in their discretion and upon application in writing, may issue a special permit for continuous limited operation, authorizing the applicant to operate a tow-truck that exceeds the weight limits provided for in subsection (d) of Section 15-111, provided:

(1) no rear single axle of the tow-truck exceeds 26,000 pounds;

(2) no rear tandem axle of the tow-truck exceeds 50,000 pounds;

(3) neither the disabled vehicle nor the disabled combination of vehicles exceed the weight restrictions imposed by this Chapter 15, or the weight limits imposed under a permit issued by the Department prior to hookup;

(4) the tow-truck prior to hookup does not exceed the weight restrictions imposed by this Chapter 15;

(5) during the tow operation the tow-truck does not violate any weight restriction sign;

(6) the tow-truck is equipped with flashing, rotating, or oscillating amber lights, visible for at least 500 feet in all directions;

(7) the tow-truck is specifically designed and licensed as a tow-truck;

(8) the tow-truck has a gross vehicle weight rating of sufficient capacity to safely handle the load;

(9) the tow-truck is equipped with air brakes;

(10) the tow-truck is capable of utilizing the lighting and braking systems of the disabled vehicle or combination of vehicles;

(11) the tow distance of the tow does not exceed 50 miles from the point of disablement to a place of repair or safekeeping;

(12) the permit issued to the tow-truck is carried in the tow-truck and exhibited on demand by a police officer; and

(13) the movement shall be valid only on state routes approved by the Department.

P.A. 76-1586, § 15-301, eff. July 1, 1970. Amended by P.A. 76-2202, § 1, eff. July 1, 1970; P.A. 77-1223, § 1, eff. Aug. 24, 1971; P.A. 77-2720, § 1, eff. Jan. 1, 1973; P.A. 78-255, § 61, eff. Oct. 1, 1973; P.A. 78-692, § 1, eff. Oct. 1, 1973; P.A. 78-802, § 1, eff. Oct. 1, 1973; P.A. 78-1297, § 30, eff. March 4, 1975; P.A. 81-199, § 1, eff. Jan. 1, 1980; P.A. 82-783, Art. XI, § 140, eff. July 13, 1982; P.A. 84-986, § 1, eff. Sept. 25, 1985; P.A. 86-1232, § 1, eff. Jan. 1, 1991; P.A. 88-291, § 5, eff. Aug. 11, 1993; P.A. 88-476, § 2, eff. July 1, 1994; P.A. 88-670, Art. 2, § 2-59, eff. Dec. 2, 1994; P.A. 90-89, § 15, eff. Jan. 1, 1998; P.A. 90-228, § 5, eff. July 25, 1997; P.A. 90-655, § 153, eff. July 30, 1998; P.A. 90-676, § 5, eff. July 31, 1998; P.A. 91-569, § 5, eff. Jan. 1, 2000.

Formerly Ill.Rev.Stat.1991, ch. 95 ½, ¶ 15-301.

[1] 5 ILCS 100/1-1 et seq.

5/15-302. Fees for special permits

§ 15-302. Fees for special permits. The Department with respect to highways under its jurisdiction shall collect a fee from the applicant for the issuance of a permit to operate or move a vehicle or combination of vehicles or load as authorized in Section 15-301. The charge for each permit shall consist of:

1. a service charge for special handling of a permit when requested by an applicant;

2. fees for any dimension, axle weight or gross weight in excess of the maximum size or weight specified in this Chapter; and

3. additional fees for special investigations as in Section 15-311 and special police escort as in Section 15-312 when required.

With respect to overweight fees, the charge shall be sufficient to compensate in part for the cost of the extra wear and tear on the mileage of highways over which the load is to be moved. With respect to over-dimension permits, the fee shall be sufficient to compensate in part for the special privilege of transporting oversize vehicle or vehicle combination and load and to compensate in part for the economic loss of operators of vehicles in regular operation due to inconvenience occasioned by the oversize movements.

Fees to be paid by the applicant are to be at the rates specified in this Chapter. In determining the fees in Section 15-306 and paragraph (f) of Section 15-307, all weights shall be to the next highest 1,000 pounds and all distances shall be determined from the Illinois Official Highway Map.

For repeated moves of like objects which cannot be dismantled or disassembled and which are monolithically structured for permanent use in the transported form, the fees specified in Sections 15-305, 15-306 and 15-307 for other than the first move shall be reduced by $4 provided the objects are to be moved from the same origin to the same destination, the number of trips will not be less than 5, the trips will be completed within 30 days, and all applications are submitted at one time. Round trip permits shall be the same as a single trip permit except the fee shall be computed based upon the total distance traveled, and shall be for the same vehicle, vehicle combination or like load traveling both directions over the same route, provided a description including make and model of the equipment being transported is furnished to the Department, except that a vehicle combination registered by the Department as provided in Section 15-319 may be one of the same class. Limited continuous operation permits are to be valid for a period of 90 days or one year, and shall be for the same vehicle, vehicle combination or like load.

P.A. 76-1586, § 15-302, eff. July 1, 1970. Amended by P.A. 76-2203, § 1, eff. July 1, 1970; P.A. 81-199, § 1, eff. Jan. 1, 1980; P.A. 83-831, § 1, eff. Jan. 1, 1984; P.A. 84-566, § 1, eff. Jan. 1, 1986; P.A. 89-219, § 5, eff. Jan. 1, 1996; P.A. 91-357, § 231, eff. July 29, 1999.

Formerly Ill.Rev.Stat.1991, ch. 95 ½, ¶ 15-302.

5/15–303. Transmission fees

§ 15–303. Transmission Fees. When special transmission of permits is requested by an applicant, a service charge in an amount sufficient to defray the cost shall be charged.

P.A. 76–1586, § 15–303, eff. July 1, 1970. Amended by P.A. 76–2204, § 1, eff. July 1, 1970; P.A. 81–199, § 1, eff. Jan. 1, 1980.

Formerly Ill.Rev.Stat.1991, ch. 95 ½, ¶ 15–303.

5/15–303.1. § 15–303.1. Repealed by P.A. 81–199, § 2, eff. Jan. 1, 1980

5/15–304. Fees for house trailer combinations, or a unit carrying roof or floor trusses

§ 15–304. Fees for house trailer combinations, or a unit carrying roof or floor trusses. Fees for special permits to move a house trailer, oversize storage building, modular home section, or a unit carrying roof or floor trusses in combination with a towing vehicle shall be paid by the applicant to the Department at the following rates:

	Single Trip	90 Day Limited Continuous Operation	Annual Limited Continuous Operation
(a) Maximum overall width of 10 feet or less; maximum overall height of 14 feet 6 inches or less; or maximum overall length, including the towing vehicle, of 70 feet or less:		$100.00	$400.00
For the first 90 miles	$12.00		
From 90 miles to 180 miles	$15.00		
From 180 miles to 270 miles	$18.00		
For more than 270 miles	$21.00		
(b) Maximum overall width of 12 feet or less, plus an additional 2 inch overhang on each side to allow for eaves, drip edges or guttering that is at least 9 feet above the surface of the pavement; maximum overall height of 14 feet 6 inches or less; or maximum overall length, including the towing vehicle, of 115 feet or less:		$150.00	$600.00
For the first 90 miles	$15.00		
From 90 miles to 180 miles	$20.00		
From 180 miles to 270 miles	$25.00		
For more than 270 miles	$30.00		

(c) Maximum overall width of 14 feet or less; maximum overall height of 15 feet or less; maximum overall length, including the towing vehicle, of 115 feet or less;

	Single Trip	90 Day Limited Continuous Operation	Annual Limited Continuous Operation
		$250.00	$1000.00
For the first 90 miles	$25.00		
From 90 miles to 180 miles	$30.00		
From 180 miles to 270 miles	$35.00		
For more than 270 miles	$40.00		

(d) Maximum overall width of 14 feet 4 inches or less, maximum overall height of 15 feet or less; or maximum overall length, including the towing vehicle, of 115 feet or less:

	Single Trip	90 Day Limited Continuous Operation	Annual Limited Continuous Operation
		$250.00	$1000.00
For the first 90 miles	$30.00		
From 90 miles to 180 miles	$40.00		
From 180 miles to 270 miles	$50.00		
From 270 miles or more	$60.00		

(e) Maximum overall width of 16 feet or less provided that a tolerance in width of up to 3 inches will be allowed for house trailer combinations; or maximum overall height of 15 feet or less; or maximum overall length, including the towing vehicle of 115 feet or less:

	Single Trip Only	90 Day Limited Continuous Operation	Annual Limited Continuous Operation
For the first 90 miles	$30.00	$250.00	$1000.00
From 90 miles to 180 miles	$40.00		
From 180 miles to 270 miles	$50.00		
From 270 miles or more	$60.00		

P.A. 76–1586, § 15–304, eff. July 1, 1970. Amended by P.A. 76–2206, § 1, eff. July 1, 1970; P.A. 78–802, § 1, eff. Oct. 1, 1973; P.A. 81–199, § 1, eff. Jan. 1, 1980; P.A. 83–821, § 1, eff. Sept. 24, 1983; P.A. 86–1223, § 1, eff. Jan. 1, 1991; P.A. 87–140, § 1, eff. Aug. 16, 1991; P.A. 88–517, § 10, eff. Nov. 16, 1993; P.A. 89–219, § 5, eff. Jan. 1, 1996; P.A. 90–148, § 5, eff. July 23, 1997.

Formerly Ill.Rev.Stat.1991, ch. 95 ½, ¶ 15–304.

5/15–305. Fees for legal weight but overdimension vehicles, combinations, and loads, other than house trailer combinations

§ 15–305. Fees for legal weight but overdimension Vehicles, Combinations, and Loads, other than House Trailer Combinations. Fees for special permits to move overdimension vehicles, combinations, and loads, other than house trailer combinations, shall be paid by the applicant to the Department at the following rates:

	Single Trip	90 Day Limited Continuous Operation	Annual Limited Continuous Operation
(a) Overall width of 10 feet or less, overall height of 14 feet 6 inches or less, and overall length of 70 feet or less		$100.00	$ 400.00
For the first 90 miles	$ 12.00		
From 90 miles to 180 miles	15.00		
From 180 miles to 270 miles	18.00		
For more than 270 miles	$ 21.00		
(b) Overall width of 12 feet or less, overall height of 14 feet 6 inches or less, and overall length of 85 feet or less		$150.00	$ 600.00
For the first 90 miles	$ 15.00		
From 90 miles to 180 miles	$ 20.00		
From 180 miles to 270 miles	$ 25.00		
For more than 270 miles	$ 30.00		
(c) Overall width of 14 feet or less, overall height of 15 feet or less, and overall length of 100 feet or less		Single Trip Only	
For the first 90 miles	$ 25.00		
From 90 miles to 180 miles	$ 30.00		
From 180 miles to 270 miles	$ 35.00		
For more than 270 miles	$ 40.00		
(d) Overall width of 18 feet or less (authorized only under special conditions and for limited distances), overall height of 16 feet or less, and overall length of 120 feet or less		Single Trip Only	
For the first 90 miles	$ 30.00		
From 90 miles to 180 miles	$ 40.00		
From 180 miles to 270 miles	$ 50.00		
For more than 270 miles	$ 60.00		
(e) Overall width of more than 18 feet (authorized only under special conditions and for limited distances), overall height more than 16 feet, and overall length more than 120 feet		Single Trip Only	
For the first 90 miles	$ 50.00		
From 90 miles to 180 miles	$ 75.00		
From 180 miles to 270 miles	$100.00		
For more than 270 miles	$125.00		

Permits issued under this Section shall be for a vehicle, or vehicle combination and load not exceeding legal weights; and, in the case of the limited continuous operation, shall be for the same vehicle, vehicle combination or like load.

Escort requirements shall be as prescribed in the Department's Rules and Regulations. Fees for the State Police vehicle escort, when required, shall be in addition to the permit fees.

P.A. 76-1586, § 15-305, eff. July 1, 1970. Amended by P.A. 78-270, § 1, eff. Aug. 13, 1973; P.A. 81-199, § 1, eff. Jan. 1, 1980; P.A. 89-219, § 5, eff. Jan. 1, 1996.

Formerly Ill.Rev.Stat.1991, ch. 95 ½, ¶ 15-305.

5/15-306. Fees for Overweight-Axle Loads

§ 15-306. Fees for Overweight-Axle Loads. Fees for special permits to move legal gross weight vehicles, combinations of vehicles and loads with overweight-axle loads shall be paid by the applicant to the Department as follows:

For each overweight single axle or tandem axle group, the flat rate fees herein scheduled for increments of 45 miles or fraction thereof including issuance fee predicated upon an 18,000 pound single axle equivalency.

18,000 Pound Single Axle Equivalency Fees

Axle weight in excess	2-Axle Single Axle	3-Axle Tandem	Tandem Tandem
1-6000 lbs.	$ 5	$ 5	$ 5
6001-11,000 lbs.	8	7	6
11,001-17,000 lbs.	not permitted	8	7
17,001-22,000 lbs.	not permitted	not permitted	9
22,001-29,000 lbs.	not permitted	not permitted	11

P.A. 76-1586, § 15-306, eff. July 1, 1970. Amended by P.A. 81-199, § 1, eff. Jan. 1, 1980; P.A. 90-676, § 5, eff. July 31, 1998.

Formerly Ill.Rev.Stat.1991, ch. 95 ½, ¶ 15-306.

5/15-307. Fees for Overweight-Gross Loads

§ 15-307. Fees for Overweight-Gross Loads. Fees for special permits to move vehicles, combinations of vehicles and loads with overweight-gross loads shall be paid at the flat rate fees established in this Section for weights in excess of legal gross weights, by the applicant to the Department.

(a) With respect to fees for overweight-gross loads listed in this Section and for overweight-axle loads listed in Section 15-306, one fee only shall be charged, whichever is the greater, but not for both.

(b) In lieu of the fees stated in this Section and Section 15-306, with respect to combinations of vehicles consisting of a 3-axle truck tractor with a tandem axle composed of 2 consecutive axles drawing a semitrailer, or other vehicle approved by the Department, equipped with a tandem axle composed of 3 consecutive axles, weighing over 73,280 pounds but not more than 88,000 pounds gross weight, the fees shall be at the following rates:

Distance	Rate
For the first 45 miles	$10
From 45 miles to 90 miles	12.50
From 90 miles to 135 miles	15.00
From 135 miles to 180 miles	17.50
From 180 miles to 225 miles	20.00
For each additional 45 miles or part thereof in excess of the rate for 225 miles, an additional	2.50

For such combinations weighing over 88,000 pounds but not more than 100,000 pounds gross weight, the fees shall be at the following rates:

Distance	Rate
For the first 45 miles	15
From 45 miles to 90 miles	25
From 90 miles to 135 miles	35
From 135 miles to 180 miles	45
From 180 miles to 225 miles	55
For each additional 45 miles or part thereof in excess of the rate for 225 miles, an additional	10

For such combination weighing over 100,000 pounds but not more than 110,000 pounds gross weight, the fees shall be at the following rates:

Distance	Rate
For the first 45 miles	$20
From 45 miles to 90 miles	32.50
From 90 miles to 135 miles	45
From 135 miles to 180 miles	57.50
From 180 miles to 225 miles	70

Distance	Rate
For each additional 45 miles or part thereof in excess of the rate for 225 miles an additional	12.50

For such combinations weighing over 110,000 pounds but not more than 120,000 pounds gross weight, the fees shall be at the following rates:

Distance	Rate
For the first 45 miles	$30
From 46 miles to 90 miles	55
From 90 miles to 135 miles	80
From 135 miles to 180 miles	105
From 180 miles to 225 miles	130
For each additional 45 miles or part thereof in excess of the rate for 225 miles an additional	25

Payment of overweight fees for the above combinations also shall include fees for overwidth dimensions of 4 feet or less, overheight and overlength. Any overwidth in excess of 4 feet shall be charged an additional fee of $15.

(c) In lieu of the fees stated in this Section and Section 15–306 of this Chapter, with respect to combinations of vehicles consisting of a 3–axle truck tractor with a tandem axle composed of 2 consecutive axles drawing a semitrailer, or other vehicle approved by the Department, equipped with a tandem axle composed of 2 consecutive axles, weighing over 73,280 pounds but not more than 88,000 pounds gross weight, the fees shall be at the following rates:

Distance	Rate
For the first 45 miles	$20
From 45 miles to 90 miles	32.50
From 90 miles to 135 miles	45
From 135 miles to 180 miles	57.50
From 180 miles to 225 miles	70
For each additional 60 miles or part thereof in excess of the rate for 225 miles an additional	12.50

For such combination weighing over 88,000 pounds but not more than 100,000 pounds gross weight, the fees shall be at the following rates:

Distance	Rate
For the first 45 miles	$30
From 46 miles to 90 miles	55
From 90 miles to 135 miles	80
From 135 miles to 180 miles	105
From 180 miles to 225 miles	130
For each additional 45 miles or part thereof in excess of the rate for 225 miles an additional	25

Payment of overweight fees for the above combinations also shall include fees for overwidth dimension of 4 feet or less, overheight and overlength. Any overwidth in excess of 4 feet shall be charged an additional overwidth fee of $15.

(d) In lieu of the fees stated in this Section and in Section 15–306 of this Chapter, with respect to a 3 (or more) axle mobile crane or water well-drilling vehicle consisting of a single axle and a tandem axle or 2 tandem axle groups composed of 2 consecutive axles each, with a distance of extreme axles not less than 18 feet, weighing not more than 60,000 pounds gross with no single axle weighing more than 21,000 pounds, or any tandem axle group to exceed 40,000 pounds, the fees shall be at the following rates:

Distance	Rate
For the first 45 miles	$12.50
For each additional 45 miles or portion thereof	9.00

For such vehicles weighing over 60,000 pounds but not more than 68,000 pounds with no single axle weighing more than 21,000 pounds and no tandem axle group exceeding 48,000 pounds, the fees shall be at the following rates:

Distance	Rate
For the first 45 miles	$20
For each additional 45 miles or portion thereof	12.50

Payment of overweight fees for the above vehicle shall include overwidth dimension of 4 feet or less, overheight and overlength. Any overwidth in excess of 4 feet shall be charged an additional overwidth fee of $15.

(e) In lieu of the fees stated in this Section and in Section 15–306 of this Chapter, with respect to a 4 (or more) axle mobile crane or water well drilling vehicle consisting of 2 sets of tandem axles composed of 2 or more consecutive axles each with a distance between extreme axles of not less than 23 feet weighing not more than 72,000 pounds with axle weights on one set of tandem axles not more than 34,000 pounds, and weight in the other set of tandem axles not to exceed 40,000 pounds, the fees shall be at the following rates:

Distance	Rate
For the first 45 miles	$15
For each additional 45 miles or portion thereof	10

For such vehicles weighing over 72,000 pounds but not more than 76,000 pounds with axle weights on either set of tandem axles not more than 44,000 pounds, the fees shall be at the following rates:

Distance	Rate
For the first 45 miles	$20
For each additional 45 miles or portion thereof	12.50

Payment of overweight fees for the above vehicle shall include overwidth dimension of 4 feet or less, overheight and overlength. Any overwidth in excess of 4 feet shall be charged an additional fee of $15.

(f) In lieu of fees stated in this Section and in Section 15–306 of this Chapter, with respect to a two axle mobile crane or water well-drilling vehicle consisting of 2 single axles weighing not more than 48,000 pounds with no single axle weighing more than 25,000 pounds, the fees shall be at the following rates:

Distance	Rate
For the first 45 miles	$15
For each additional 45 miles or portion thereof	10

For such vehicles weighing over 48,000 pounds but not more than 54,000 pounds with no single axle weighing more than 28,000 pounds, the fees shall be at the following rates:

Distance	Rate
For the first 45 miles	$20
For each additional 45 miles or portion thereof	12.50

Payment of overweight fees for the above vehicle shall include overwidth dimension of 4 feet or less, overheight and overlength. Any overwidth in excess of 4 feet shall be charged an additional overwidth fee of $15.

(g) Fees for special permits to move vehicles, combinations of vehicles, and loads with overweight gross loads not included in the fee categories shall be paid by the applicant to the Department at the rate of $50 plus 3.5 cents per ton-mile in excess of legal weight.

With respect to fees for overweight gross loads not included in the schedules specified in paragraphs (a) through (e) of Section 15-307 and for overweight axle loads listed in Section 15-306, one fee only shall be charged, whichever is the greater, but not both. An additional fee in accordance with the schedule set forth in Section 15-305 shall be charged for each overdimension.

P.A. 76-1586, § 15-307, eff. July 1, 1970. Amended by P.A. 76-2207, § 1, eff. July 1, 1970; P.A. 77-1221, § 1, eff. Aug. 24, 1971; P.A. 78-1165, § 1, eff. Aug. 27, 1974; P.A. 81-199, § 1, eff. Jan. 1, 1980; P.A. 82-783, Art. IV, § 25, eff. July 13, 1982; P.A. 84-566, § 1, eff. Jan. 1, 1986; P.A. 90-228, § 5, eff. July 25, 1997; P.A. 90-676, § 5, eff. July 31, 1998.

Formerly Ill.Rev.Stat.1991, ch. 95 ½, ¶ 15-307.

P.A. 90-676 incorporated the amendment by P.A. 90-228.

5/15-308. Fees for overweight trucks hauling sweet corn

§ 15-308. Fees for overweight trucks hauling sweet corn. Fees for special permits for two axle truck with gross axle load not to exceed 35 percent in excess of the legal axle load to be used for hauling sweet corn and ensilage, for a period of 40 days only during harvest season; limited continuous operation permit only, $10.

P.A. 76-1586, § 15-308, eff. July 1, 1970.

Formerly Ill.Rev.Stat.1991, ch. 95 ½, ¶ 15-308.

5/15-308.1. Fees for moving oversize or overweight equipment to the site of rail derailments

§ 15-308.1. Fees for moving oversize or overweight equipment to the site of rail derailments. Fees for permits to move oversize or overweight equipment to the sites of train derailments shall include all equipment otherwise eligible to obtain single trip permits under normal situations. The permit shall be valid for a period of one year and can be used at any time for movement to the site of a train derailment during an emergency. The amount of the fee shall be $500.

P.A. 76-1586, § 15-308.1, added by P.A. 90-273, § 65, eff. July 30, 1997.

5/15-308.2. Fees for special permits for tow-trucks

§ 15-308.2. Fees for special permits for tow-trucks. The fee for a special permit to operate a tow-truck pursuant to subsection (n) of Section 15-301 is $500 quarterly and $2,000 annually.

P.A. 76-1586, § 15-308.2, added by P.A. 91-569, § 5, eff. Jan. 1, 2000.

5/15-309. Fees for moves directly across highway

§ 15-309. Fees for moves directly across highway. Fees for special permits for vehicles or vehicle combinations exceeding the legal sizes and weights specified in this Chapter either empty or hauling material directly across a highway making repeated moves in the course of industrial operations, for a period of 6 months; limited continuous operation permit only, $15.

P.A. 76-1586, § 15-309, eff. July 1, 1970. Amended by P.A. 81-199, § 1, eff. Jan. 1, 1980.

Formerly Ill.Rev.Stat.1991, ch. 95 ½, ¶ 15-309.

5/15-310. Fees for buildings and special moves

§ 15-310. Fees for buildings and special moves. Fees for special permits for moving buildings or large machines.

(a) When moved on house moving equipment or on own trucks or tracks fees will be based on maximum overall dimensions, plus engineering investigation and police escort fees when required; single trip only.

(b) When moved on a vehicle or vehicle combination applicable overdimension and overweight fees shall apply; single trip only.

P.A. 76-1586, § 15-310, eff. July 1, 1970.

Formerly Ill.Rev.Stat.1991, ch. 95 ½, ¶ 15-310.

5/15-311. Fees for Engineering Inspections or Field Investigations

§ 15-311. Fees for Engineering Inspections or Field Investigations. Engineering inspections or field investigations will be made by the Department and the following fees shall be paid by the applicant: for normal field investigations, or for special engineering investigations requiring assessment of work to be done on the highway and final inspection, $40 per hour.

P.A. 76-1586, § 15-311, eff. July 1, 1970. Amended by P.A. 81-199, § 1, eff. Jan. 1, 1980; P.A. 84-566, § 1, eff. Jan. 1, 1986.

Formerly Ill.Rev.Stat.1991, ch. 95 ½, ¶ 15-311.

5/15-312. Fees for Police Escort

§ 15-312. Fees for Police Escort. When State Police escorts are required by the Department for the safety of the motoring public, the following fees shall be paid by the applicant to the Department: $40 per hour per vehicle based upon pre-estimated time of movement to be agreed upon between Department and applicant. Minimum fee $80 per vehicle.

P.A. 76-1586, § 15-312, eff. July 1, 1970. Amended by P.A. 81-199, § 1, eff. Jan. 1, 1980; P.A. 84-566, § 1, eff. Jan. 1, 1986.

Formerly Ill.Rev.Stat.1991, ch. 95 ½, ¶ 15-312.

5/15-313. Supplemental permit fee

§ 15-313. Supplemental permit fee. The Department shall collect a fee of $5 and other applicable fees to cover the cost of processing an application for supplemental special permit. This fee shall be charged for each supplemental special permit issued. In addition, if the supplemental permit provides for an increase in size or weight or both over that specified in the original special permit, additional fees shall be charged as provided in Sections 15-303 through 15-312 as applicable, to correct for the increase.

P.A. 76-1586, § 15-313, eff. July 1, 1970. Amended by P.A. 81-199, § 1, eff. Jan. 1, 1980.

Formerly Ill.Rev.Stat.1991, ch. 95 ½, ¶ 15-313.

5/15-314. Payment of Fees

§ 15-314. Payment of Fees. The Department shall prescribe the time and method of payment of all appropriate fees authorized by Section 15-302 through 15-313.

The Department may, at its discretion, establish credit accounts with billing to be made at intervals not exceeding one month.

Failure to pay invoices in full within a period of 30 days after the billing date shall be sufficient cause for the Department to withhold issuance of any further permits or credit to the individual, company, or subsidiary firm.

The Department is authorized to charge a service fee of $3 for a check returned for any reason. All money received by the Department under the provisions of this Section shall be deposited in the Road Fund. No refund shall be made to applicant following issuance of a permit if move is not completed.

P.A. 76-1586, § 15-314, eff. July 1, 1970. Amended by P.A. 81-199, § 1, eff. Jan. 1, 1980.

Formerly Ill.Rev.Stat.1991, ch. 95 ½, ¶ 15-314.

5/15-315. Exemptions to requirement of fees

§ 15-315. Exemptions to requirement of fees. (a) The requirements as to fees authorized by Sections 15-302 through 15-314 shall not apply to the owner of the vehicle or vehicle combination if owned by the United States, this State, or any political subdivision of this State, or any municipality therein.

(b) The provisions of Sections 15-302 through 15-314 requiring fees for a permit shall not modify, alter or in any manner affect either the provisions of Section 15-301, or the policy of the Department adopted for the administration of this Chapter.

P.A. 76-1586, § 15-315, eff. July 1, 1970. Amended by P.A. 83-831, § 1, eff. Jan. 1, 1984.

Formerly Ill.Rev.Stat.1991, ch. 95 ½, ¶ 15-315.

5/15-316. When the Department, local authority or road district highway commissioner may restrict right to use highways

§ 15-316. When the Department, local authority or road district highway commissioner may restrict right to use highways.

(a) Local authorities and road district highway commissioners with respect to highways under their jurisdiction may by ordinance or resolution prohibit the operation of vehicles upon any such highway or impose restrictions as to the weight of vehicles to be operated upon any such highway, for a total period of not to exceed 90 days in any one calendar year, whenever any said highway by reason of deterioration, rain, snow, or other climate conditions will be seriously damaged or destroyed unless the use of vehicles thereon is prohibited or the permissible weights thereof reduced.

(b) The local authority or road district highway commissioner enacting any such ordinance or resolution shall erect or cause to be erected and maintained signs designating the provision of the ordinance or resolution at each end of that portion of any highway affected thereby, and the ordinance or resolution shall not be effective unless and until such signs are erected and maintained.

(c) Local authorities and road district highway commissioners with respect to highways under their jurisdiction may also, by ordinance or resolution, prohibit the operation of trucks or other commercial vehicles, or may impose limitations as the weight thereof, on designated highways, which prohibitions and limitations shall be designated by appropriate signs placed on such highways.

(c-1) (Blank).

(d) The Department shall likewise have authority as hereinbefore granted to local authorities and road district highway commissioners to determine by resolution and to impose restrictions as to the weight of vehicles operated upon any highway under the jurisdiction of said department, and such restrictions shall be effective when signs giving notice thereof are erected upon the highway or portion of any highway affected by such resolution.

(d-1) (Blank).

(d-2) (Blank).

(e) When any vehicle is operated in violation of this Section, the owner or driver of the vehicle shall be deemed guilty of a violation and either the owner or the driver of the vehicle may be prosecuted for the violation. Any person, firm, or corporation convicted of violating this Section shall be fined $50 for any weight exceeding the posted limit up to the axle or gross weight limit allowed a vehicle as provided for in subsections (a) or (b) of Section 15-111 and $75 per every 500 pounds or fraction thereof for any weight exceeding that which is provided for in subsections (a) or (b) of Section 15-111.

(f) A municipality is authorized to enforce a county weight limit ordinance applying to county highways within its corporate limits and is entitled to the proceeds of any fines collected from the enforcement.

P.A. 76-1586, § 15-316, eff. July 1, 1970. Amended by P.A. 81-540, § 1, eff. Jan. 1, 1980; P.A. 86-447, § 2, eff. Aug. 30, 1989; P.A. 87-1203, § 1, eff. Sept. 25, 1992; P.A. 88-384, § 5, eff. Jan. 1, 1994; P.A. 89-117, § 10, eff. July 7, 1995; P.A. 89-687, § 5, eff. June 1, 1997; P.A. 90-211, § 5, eff. Jan. 1, 1998; P.A. 92-417, § 5, eff. Jan. 1, 2002.

Formerly Ill.Rev.Stat.1991, ch. 95 ½, ¶ 15-316.

5/15-317. Special weight limitation on elevated structures

§ 15-317. Special weight limitation on elevated structures. (a) No person shall operate a vehicle or combination of vehicles over a bridge or other elevated structure constituting a part of a highway with a gross weight which is greater than the maximum weight permitted by the Department, when such structure is sign posted as provided in this Section.

(b) The Department upon request from any local authority shall, or upon its own initiative may, conduct an investigation of any bridge or other elevated structure constituting a part of a highway, and if it finds that such structure cannot with safety to itself withstand the weight of vehicles otherwise permissible under this Chapter the Department shall determine and declare the maximum weight of vehicles which such structure can withstand, and shall cause or permit suitable signs stating maximum weight to be erected and maintained before each end of such structure.

(c) Upon the trial of any person charged with a violation of this Section, proof of the determination of the maximum allowable weight by the Department and the existence of the signs, constitutes conclusive evidence of the maximum weight which can be maintained with safety to such bridge or structure.

P.A. 76-1586, § 15-317, eff. July 1, 1970.

Formerly Ill.Rev.Stat.1991, ch. 95 ½, ¶ 15-317.

5/15-318. Liability if highway or structure damaged

§ 15-318. Liability if highway or structure damaged. (a) Any person driving any vehicle, object or contrivance upon any highway or highway structure is liable for all damage which the highway or structure may sustain as a result of any illegal operation, driving or moving of such vehicle, object or contrivance, or as a result of operating, driving, or moving any vehicle, object, or contrivance exceeding the maximum dimensions or weighing in excess of the maximum weight specified in this Chapter but authorized by a special permit issued as provided in this Chapter. The measure of liability is the cost of repairing a facility partially damaged or the depreciated replacement cost of a facility damaged beyond repair together with all other expenses incurred by the authorities in control of the highway or highway structure in providing a temporary detour, including a temporary structure, to serve the needs of traffic during the period of repair or replacement of the damaged highway or highway structure.

(b) Whenever such driver is not the owner of such vehicle, object, or contrivance, but is so operating, driving, or moving the same with the express or implied permission of such owner, then the owner and driver are jointly and severally liable to the extent provided in paragraph (a) of this Section.

(c) Recovery may be had in a civil action brought by the authorities in control of such highway or highway structure.

P.A. 76-1586, § 15-318, eff. July 1, 1970. Amended by P.A. 81-199, § 1, eff. Jan. 1, 1980.

Formerly Ill.Rev.Stat.1991, ch. 95 ½, ¶ 15-318.

5/15-319. Special registration of vehicles by department

§ 15-319. Special registration of vehicles by department. (a) Applicants for special permits authorized in Section 15-301 may apply to the Department for an Illinois Department of Transportation (IDT) registration number and classification identification label issued for the purpose of identifying and classifying vehicles or combinations of vehicles that may be operated or moved by special permit. Applications shall be made on a form provided by the Department and certified to be true.

(b) For a fee of $5 and following an analysis of data submitted by the applicant, the Department may, at its discretion, issue an Illinois Department of Transportation (IDT) registration number and classification identification label. The label shall be issued for a period of not to exceed 2 years or for a lesser period of time in conformance with rules to be established by the Department and to be valid must be displayed in a conspicuous place on the outside of a vehicle as designated by the Department. The label, all forms, records, rules, procedures, methods of analysis, and classification shall be in the form or as prescribed in rules promulgated by the Department.

(c) All monies received by the Department under the provisions of this Section shall be deposited in the Road Fund. Vehicle classification shall be for identification purposes and shall not alter or in any manner affect either the provisions of Section 15-301 or the policy adopted by the Department for the administration thereof.

P.A. 76-1586, § 15-319, eff. July 1, 1970, added by P.A. 76-2208, § 1, eff. July 1, 1970. Amended by P.A. 81-199, § 1, eff. Jan. 1, 1980; P.A. 83-831, § 1, eff. Jan. 1, 1984.

Formerly Ill.Rev.Stat.1991, ch. 95 ½, ¶ 15-319.

CHAPTER 16. ENFORCEMENT, PENALTIES AND DISPOSITION OF FINES AND FORFEITURES, AND CRIMINAL CASES

Enactment

The Illinois Vehicle Code was enacted by P.A. 76-1586, effective July 1, 1970. The Code constitutes a consolidated recodification of various earlier laws and acts including the Uniform Act Regulating Traffic on Highways.

ARTICLE I. ENFORCEMENT, PENALTIES AND DISPOSITION OF FINES AND FORFEITURES

Section

5/16-101. Applicability

§ 16-101. Applicability. The provisions of this Chapter shall be applicable to the enforcement of this entire Code, except where another penalty is set forth in a specific Chapter which is applicable to that Chapter or a designated part or Section thereof.

P.A. 76-1586, § 16-101, eff. July 1, 1970. Amended by P.A. 82-695, § 2, eff. July 1, 1982; P.A. 82-1011, § 2, eff. Sept. 17, 1982.

Formerly Ill.Rev.Stat.1991, ch. 95 ½, ¶ 16-101.

P.A. 82-1011 recognized the amendment by P.A. 82-695.

5/16-102. Arrests—Investigations—Prosecutions

§ 16-102. Arrests—Investigations—Prosecutions. The State Police shall patrol the public highways and make arrests for violation of the provisions of this Act.

The Secretary of State, through the investigators provided for in this Act shall investigate and report violations of the provisions of this Act in relation to the equipment and operation of vehicles as provided for in Section 2-115 and for such purposes these investigators have and may exercise throughout the State all of the powers of police officers.

The State's Attorney of the county in which the violation occurs shall prosecute all violations except when the violation occurs within the corporate limits of a municipality, the municipal attorney may prosecute if written permission to do so is obtained from the State's Attorney.

P.A. 76–1586, § 16–102, eff. July 1, 1970. Amended by P.A. 76–1863, § 1, eff. July 1, 1970; P.A. 78–885, § 1, eff. Jan. 1, 1974; P.A. 83–341, § 5, eff. Sept. 14, 1983.

Formerly Ill.Rev.Stat.1991, ch. 95 ½, ¶ 16–102.

5/16–102.5. Enforcement by municipality

§ 16–102.5. Enforcement by municipality.

(a) If a municipality adopts an ordinance similar to subsection (f) of Section 3–413 or Section 11–1304.5 of this Code, any person that a municipality designates to enforce ordinances regulating the standing or parking of vehicles shall have the authority to enforce the provisions of subsection (f) of Section 3–413 or Section 11–1304.5 of this Code or the similar local ordinance. However, the authority to enforce subsection (f) of Section 3–413 or Section 11–1304.5 of this Code or a similar local ordinance shall not be given to an appointed volunteer or private or public entity under contract to enforce person with disabilities parking laws.

(b) To enforce the provisions of subsection (f) of Section 3–413 or Section 11–1304.5 of this Code or a similar local ordinance, a municipality shall impose a fine not exceeding $25.

P.A. 76–1586, § 16–102.5, added by P.A. 90–513, § 5, eff. Aug. 22, 1997. Amended by P.A. 90–655, § 153, eff. July 30, 1998; P.A. 91–487, § 5, eff. Jan. 1, 2000.

5/16–103. Arrest outside county where violation committed

§ 16–103. Arrest outside county where violation committed. Whenever a defendant is arrested upon a warrant charging a violation of this Act in a county other than that in which such warrant was issued, the arresting officer, immediately upon the request of the defendant, shall take such defendant before a circuit judge or associate circuit judge in the county in which the arrest was made who shall admit the defendant to bail for his appearance before the court named in the warrant. On taking such bail the circuit judge or associate circuit judge shall certify such fact on the warrant and deliver the warrant and undertaking of bail or other security, or the drivers license of such defendant if deposited, under the law relating to such licenses, in lieu of such security, to the officer having charge of the defendant. Such officer shall then immediately discharge the defendant from arrest and without delay deliver such warrant and such undertaking of bail, or other security or drivers license to the court before which the defendant is required to appear.

P.A. 76–1586, § 16–103, eff. July 1, 1970. Amended by P.A. 77–1280, § 1, eff. Aug. 24, 1971.

Formerly Ill.Rev.Stat.1991, ch. 95 ½, ¶ 16–103.

5/16–104. Penalties

§ 16–104. Penalties. Every person convicted of a violation of any provision of this Code for which another penalty is not provided shall, for a first or second conviction thereof, be guilty of a petty offense and, for a third or subsequent conviction within one year after the first conviction, be guilty of a Class C misdemeanor.

P.A. 76–1586, § 16–104, eff. July 1, 1970. Amended by P.A. 77–493, § 1, eff. July 28, 1971; P.A. 77–2720, § 1, eff. Jan. 1, 1973; P.A. 78–255, § 61, eff. Oct. 1, 1973; P.A. 80–911, § 1, eff. Oct. 1, 1977; P.A. 91–357, § 231, eff. July 29, 1999.

Formerly Ill.Rev.Stat.1991, ch. 95 ½, ¶ 16–104.

5/16–104a. Additional penalty for certain violations

§ 16–104a. Additional penalty for certain violations. There is added to every fine imposed upon conviction of an offense reportable to the Secretary of State under the provisions of subdivision (a) (2) of Section 6–204 of this Act an additional penalty of $4 for each $40, or fraction thereof, of fine imposed. Each such additional penalty received shall be remitted within one month to the State Treasurer to be deposited into the Drivers Education Fund, unless the additional penalty is subject to disbursement by the circuit clerk under Section 27.5 of the Clerks of Courts Act.[1] Such additional amounts shall be assessed by the court and shall be collected by the Clerk of the Circuit Court in addition to the fine and costs in the case. Such additional penalty shall not be considered a part of the fine for purposes of any reduction made in the fine for time served either before or after sentencing. Not later than March 1 of each year the Clerk of the Circuit Court shall submit to the State Comptroller a report of the amount of funds remitted by him to the State Treasurer under this Section during the preceding calendar year. Except as otherwise provided by Supreme Court Rules, if a court in sentencing an offender levies a gross amount for fine, costs, fees and penalties, the amount of the additional penalty provided for herein shall be computed on the amount remaining after deducting from the gross amount levied all fees of the Circuit Clerk, the State's Attorney and the Sheriff. After deducting from the gross amount levied the fees and additional penalty provided for herein, less any other additional penalties provided by law, the clerk shall remit the net balance remaining to the entity authorized by law to receive the fine imposed in the case. For purposes of this Section "fees of the Circuit Clerk" shall include, if applicable, the fee provided for under Section 27.3a of the Clerks of Courts Act[2] and the fee, if applicable, payable to the county in which the violation occurred pursuant to Section 5–1101 of the Counties Code.[3]

When bail is forfeited for failure to appear in connection with an offense reportable to the Secretary of State under subdivision (a) (2) of Section 6–204 of this Act, and no fine is imposed ex parte, $4 of every $40 cash deposit, or fraction thereof, given to secure appearance shall be remitted within one month to the State Treasurer to be deposited into the Drivers Education Fund, unless the bail is subject to disbursement by the circuit clerk under Section 27.5 of the Clerks of Courts Act.

P.A. 76–1586, § 16–104a, added by P.A. 82–695, § 2, eff. July 1, 1982. Amended by P.A. 84–1313, § 7, eff. Aug. 28, 1986; P.A. 85–757, § 1, eff. Sept. 23, 1987; P.A. 86–1475, Art. 3, § 3–42, eff. Jan. 10, 1991; P.A. 87–670, § 6, eff. Jan. 1, 1992; P.A. 91–716, § 5, eff. Oct. 1, 2000.

Formerly Ill.Rev.Stat.1991, ch. 95 ½, ¶ 16–104a.

[1] 705 ILCS 105/27.5.

[2] 705 ILCS 105/27.3a.

[3] 55 ILCS 5/5–1101.

5/16–104b. Amounts for Trauma Center Fund

§ 16–104b. Amounts for Trauma Center Fund. In counties that have elected not to distribute moneys under the disbursement formulas in Sections 27.5 and 27.6 of the Clerks of Courts Act,[1] the Circuit Clerk of the County, when collecting fees, fines, costs, additional penalties, bail balances assessed or forfeited, and any other amount imposed upon a conviction of or an order of supervision for a violation of laws or ordinances regulating the movement of traffic that amounts to $55 or more, shall remit $5 of the total amount collected, less 2 ½% of the $5 to help defray the administrative costs incurred by the Clerk, except that upon a conviction or order of supervision for driving under the influence of alcohol or drugs the Clerk shall remit $105 of the total amount collected ($5 for a traffic violation that amounts to $55 or more and an additional fee of $100 to be collected by the Circuit Clerk for a conviction or order of supervision for driving under the influence of alcohol or drugs), less the 2 ½ %, within 60 days to the State Treasurer to be deposited into the Trauma Center Fund. Of the amounts deposited into the Trauma Center Fund under this Section, 50% shall be disbursed to the Department of Public Health and 50% shall be disbursed to the Department of Public Aid. Not later than March 1 of each year the Circuit Clerk shall submit a report of the amount of funds remitted to the State Treasurer under this Section during the preceding calendar year.

P.A. 76–1586, § 16–104b, added by P.A. 87–1229, § 3, eff. Jan. 1, 1993. Amended by P.A. 88–667, § 15, eff. Sept. 16, 1994; P.A. 89–105, § 10, eff. Jan. 1, 1996; P.A. 92–431, § 10, eff. Jan. 1, 2002.

Formerly Ill.Rev.Stat., ch. 95½, ¶ 16–104b.

[1] 705 ILCS 105/27.5 and 105/27.6.

5/16–105. Disposition of fines and forfeitures

§ 16–105. Disposition of fines and forfeitures.

(a) Except as provided in Section 16–104a of this Act and except for those amounts required to be paid into the Traffic and Criminal Conviction Surcharge Fund in the State Treasury pursuant to Section 9.1 of the Illinois Police Training Act [1] and Section 5–9–1 of the Unified Code of Corrections [2] and except those amounts subject to disbursement by the circuit clerk under Section 27.5 of the Clerks of Courts Act,[3] fines and penalties recovered under the provisions of Chapters 11 through 16 [4] inclusive of this Code shall be paid and used as follows:

1. For offenses committed upon a highway within the limits of a city, village, or incorporated town or under the jurisdiction of any park district, to the treasurer of the particular city, village, incorporated town or park district, if the violator was arrested by the authorities of the city, village, incorporated town or park district, provided the police officers and officials of cities, villages, incorporated towns and park districts shall seasonably prosecute for all fines and penalties under this Code. If the violation is prosecuted by the authorities of the county, any fines or penalties recovered shall be paid to the county treasurer. Provided further that if the violator was arrested by the State Police, fines and penalties recovered under the provisions of paragraph (a) of Section 15–113 of this Code or paragraph (e) of Section 15–316 of this Code shall be paid over to the Department of State Police which shall thereupon remit the amount of the fines and penalties so received to the State Treasurer who shall deposit the amount so remitted in the special fund in the State treasury known as the Road Fund except that if the violation is prosecuted by the State's Attorney, 10% of the fine or penalty recovered shall be paid to the State's Attorney as a fee of his office and the balance shall be paid over to the Department of State Police for remittance to and deposit by the State Treasurer as hereinabove provided.

2. Except as provided in paragraph 4, for offenses committed upon any highway outside the limits of a city, village, incorporated town or park district, to the county treasurer of the county where the offense was committed except if such offense was committed on a highway maintained by or under the supervision of a township, township district, or a road district to the Treasurer thereof for deposit in the road and bridge fund of such township or other district; Provided, that fines and penalties recovered under the provisions of paragraph (a) of Section 15–113, paragraph (d) of Section 3–401, or paragraph (e) of Section 15–316 of this Code shall be paid over to the Department of State Police which shall thereupon remit the amount of the fines and penalties so received to the State Treasurer who shall deposit the amount so remitted in the special fund in the State treasury known as the Road Fund except that if the violation is prosecuted by the State's Attorney, 10% of the fine or penalty recovered shall be paid to the State's Attorney as a fee of his office and the balance shall be paid over to the Department of State Police for remittance to and deposit by the State Treasurer as hereinabove provided.

3. Notwithstanding subsections 1 and 2 of this paragraph, for violations of overweight and overload limits found in Sections 15–101 through 15–203 of this Code, which are committed upon the highways belonging to the Illinois State Toll Highway Authority, fines and penalties shall be paid over to the Illinois State Toll Highway Authority for deposit with the State Treasurer into that special fund known as the Illinois State Toll Highway Authority Fund, except that if the violation is prosecuted by the State's Attorney, 10% of the fine or penalty recovered shall be paid to the State's Attorney as a fee of his office and the balance shall be paid over to the Illinois State Toll Highway Authority for remittance to and deposit by the State Treasurer as hereinabove provided.

4. With regard to violations of overweight and overload limits found in Sections 15–101 through 15–203 of this Code committed by operators of vehicles registered as Special Hauling Vehicles, for offenses committed upon a highway within the limits of a city, village, or incorporated town or under the jurisdiction of any park district, all fines and penalties shall be paid over or retained as required in paragraph 1. However, with regard to the above offenses committed by operators of vehicles registered as Special Hauling Vehicles upon any highway outside the limits of a city, village, incorporated town or park district, fines and penalties shall be paid over or retained by the entity having jurisdiction over the road or highway upon which the offense occurred, except that if the violation is prosecuted by the State's Attorney, 10% of the fine or penalty recovered shall be paid to the State's Attorney as a fee of his office.

(b) Failure, refusal or neglect on the part of any judicial or other officer or employee receiving or having custody of any such fine or forfeiture either before or after a deposit with the proper official as defined in paragraph (a) of this Section, shall constitute misconduct in office and shall be grounds for removal therefrom.

P.A. 76–1586, § 16–105, eff. July 1, 1970. Amended by P.A. 76–2209, § 1, eff. July 1, 1970; P.A. 81–1468, § 1, eff. Sept. 9, 1980; P.A. 82–604, § 1, eff. Jan. 1, 1982; P.A. 82–695, § 2, eff. July 1, 1982; P.A. 82–739, § 4, eff. Jan. 1, 1982; P.A. 82–783, Art. III, § 37, eff. July 13, 1982; P.A. 84–25, Art. IV, § 27, eff. July 18, 1985; P.A. 87–670, § 6, eff. Jan. 1, 1992; P.A. 88–403, § 5, eff. Jan. 1, 1994; P.A. 88–476, § 2, eff. July 1, 1994; P.A. 88–535, § 25, eff. Jan. 26, 1994; P.A. 89–117, § 10, eff. July 7, 1995.

Formerly Ill.Rev.Stat.1991, ch. 95 ½, ¶ 16–105.

[1] 50 ILCS 705/9.1.

[2] 730 ILCS 5/5–9–1.

[3] 705 ILCS 105/27.5.

[4] 625 ILCS 5/11–101 et seq. to 5/16–101 et seq.

5/16–105.5. Payment to municipality

§ 16–105.5. Payment to municipality. All revenues derived from the issuance of citations for violations of subsection (f) of Section 3–413 of this Code or a similar local ordinance that are required to be paid to a municipality under this Code shall be deposited into the general fund of the municipality.

P.A. 76–1586, § 16–105.5, added by P.A. 90–513, § 5, eff. Aug. 22, 1997.

5/16–106. Notice to accused concerning multiple court appearances

§ 16–106. For offenses committed under the provisions of this Act or the ordinances of any municipality, park district or county which involve the regulation of the ownership, use or operation of vehicles, the police officers and officials of such municipalities and park districts, and sheriffs shall, when issuing a traffic ticket, other citation, or Notice to Appear in lieu of either, in counties other than Cook, also issue written notice to the accused in substantially the following form:

AVOID MULTIPLE COURT APPEARANCES

If you intend to plead "not guilty" to this charge, or if, in addition, you intend to demand a trial by jury, so notify the clerk of the court at least 5 days (excluding Saturdays, Sundays or holidays) before the day set for your appearance. A new appearance date will be set, and arrangements will be made to have the arresting officer present on that new date. Failure to notify the clerk of either your intention to plead "not guilty" or your intention to demand a jury trial, may result in your having to return to court, if you plead "not guilty" on the date originally set for your court appearance. Upon timely receipt of notice that the accused intends to plead "not guilty", the clerk shall set a new appearance date not less than 7 days nor more than 49 days after the original appearance date set by the arresting officer, and notify all parties of the new date and the time for appearance. If the accused fails to notify the clerk as provided above, the arresting officer's failure to appear on the date originally set for appearance may, in counties other than Cook, be considered good cause for a continuance.

P.A. 76–1586, § 16–106, added by P.A. 78–273, § 1, eff. Oct. 1, 1973. Amended by P.A. 81–781, § 1, eff. Jan. 1, 1980.

Formerly Ill.Rev.Stat.1991, ch. 95 ½, ¶ 16–106.

5/16–106.5. Pilot project; notice of violation to owner

§ 16–106.5. Pilot project; notice of violation to owner.

(a) A pilot project is created that shall be in operation from January 1, 2002 through December 31, 2003 in the counties of DuPage, Kendall, and Sangamon. Under the pilot project, when a traffic citation is issued for a violation of this Code to a person who is under the age of 18 years, who is a resident of the county in which the traffic citation was issued, and who is not the registered owner of the vehicle named in the traffic citation, the circuit clerk of the county in which the traffic citation was issued shall, within 10 days after the traffic citation is filed with the circuit clerk, send notice of the issuance of the traffic citation to the registered owner of the vehicle. The notice must include:

(1) the date and time the violation was alleged to have been committed;

(2) the location where the violation was alleged to have been committed;

(3) the name of the person cited for committing the alleged violation;

(4) the violation alleged to have been committed; and

(5) the date and time of any required court appearance by the person cited for committing the alleged violation.

(b) On or before March 31, 2004, the Department of State Police shall report to the General Assembly on the effectiveness of the pilot project.

P.A. 76–1586, § 16–106.5, added by P.A. 92–344, § 5, eff. Aug. 10, 2001.

5/16–107. Appearance of parent or guardian of minor in certain court proceedings—Judicial discretion

§ 16–107. Appearance of parent or guardian of minor in certain court proceedings—Judicial discretion. (a) Whenever an unemancipated minor is required to appear in court pursuant to a citation for violation of any Section or any subsection of any Section of this Act specified in subsection (b) of this Section, the court may require that a parent or guardian of the minor accompany the minor and appear before the court with the minor, unless, in the discretion of the court, such appearance would be unreasonably burdensome under the circumstances.

(b) This Section shall apply whenever an unemancipated minor is charged with violation of any of the following Sections and subsections of this Act:

1) Sections 3–701, 3–702 and 3–703;

2) Sections 4–102, 4–103, 4–104 and 4–105;

3) Section 6–101, subsections (a), (b) and (c) of Section 6–104, and Sections 6–113, 6–301, 6–302, 6–303 and 6–304;

4) Sections 11–203 and 11–204, subsection (b) of Section 11–305, Sections 11–311, 11–312, 11–401, 11–402, 11–403, 11–404, 11–407, 11–409, 11–501, 11–502, 11–503 and 11–504, subsection (b) of Section 11–601, Sections 11–704, 11–707, 11–1007, 11–1403, 11–1404 and subsection (a) of Section 11–1414.

P.A. 76–1586, § 16–107, added by P.A. 80–646, § 1, eff. Oct. 1, 1977.

Formerly Ill.Rev.Stat.1991, ch. 95 ½, ¶ 16–107.

5/16–108. Claims of diplomatic immunity

§ 16–108. Claims of diplomatic immunity.

(a) This Section applies only to an individual that displays to a police officer a driver's license issued by the U.S. Department of State or that otherwise claims immunities or privileges under Title 22, Chapter 6 of the United States Code with respect to the individual's violation of Section 9–3 or Section 9–3.2 of the Criminal Code of 1961 [1] or his or her violation of a traffic regulation governing the movement of vehicles under this Code or a similar provision of a local ordinance.

(b) If a driver subject to this Section is stopped by a police officer that has probable cause to believe that the driver has committed a violation described in subsection (a) of this Section, the police officer shall:

(1) As soon as practicable contact the U.S. Department of State office in order to verify the driver's status and immunity, if any;

(2) Record all relevant information from any driver's license or identification card, including a driver's license or identification card issued by the U.S. Department of State; and

(3) Within 5 workdays after the date of the stop, forward the following to the Secretary of State of Illinois:

(A) A vehicle accident report, if the driver was involved in a vehicle accident;

(B) If a citation or charge was issued to the driver, a copy of the citation or charge; and

(C) If a citation or charge was not issued to the driver, a written report of the incident.

(c) Upon receiving material submitted under paragraph (3) of subsection (b) of this Section, the Secretary of State shall:

(1) File each vehicle accident report, citation or charge, and incident report received;

(2) Keep convenient records or make suitable notations showing each:

(A) Conviction;

(B) Disposition of court supervision for any violation of Section 11-501 of this Code; and

(C) Vehicle accident; and

(3) Send a copy of each document and record described in paragraph (2) of this subsection (c) to the Bureau of Diplomatic Security, Office of Foreign Missions, of the U.S. Department of State.

(d) This Section does not prohibit or limit the application of any law to a criminal or motor vehicle violation by an individual who has or claims immunities or privileges under Title 22, Chapter 6 of the United States Code.

P.A. 76-1586, § 16-108, added by P.A. 92-160, § 5, eff. July 25, 2001.

[1] 720 ILCS 5/9-3 or 5/9-3.2.

ARTICLE II. PARTIES IN CRIMINAL CASES

5/16-201. Parties to a crime

§ 16-201. Parties to a crime. Every person who commits, attempts to commit, conspires to commit, or aids, or abets in the commission of any act declared to be a crime, whether individually or in connection with one or more other persons or as principal, agent or accessory, shall be guilty of such offense, and every person who falsely, fraudulently, forcibly, or wilfully induces, causes, coerces, requires, permits, or directs another to violate any provision of this Act is likewise guilty of such offense.

P.A. 76-1586, § 16-201, eff. July 1, 1970.

Formerly Ill.Rev.Stat.1991, ch. 95 ½, ¶ 16-201.

5/16-202. Offenses by persons owning or controlling vehicles

§ 16-202. Offenses by persons owning or controlling vehicles. It is unlawful for the owner, or any other person, employing or otherwise directing the driver of any vehicle to require or knowingly to permit the operation of such vehicle upon a highway in any manner contrary to law.

P.A. 76-1586, § 16-202, eff. July 1, 1970.

Formerly Ill.Rev.Stat.1991, ch. 95 ½, ¶ 16-202.

CHAPTER 17. ILLINOIS HIGHWAY SAFETY LAW

Enactment

The Illinois Vehicle Code was enacted by P.A. 76-1586, effective July 1, 1970. The Code constitutes a consolidated recodification of various earlier laws and acts including the Illinois Motor Vehicle Law of 1957.

5/17-101. Powers and duties of Governor

§ 17-101. Powers and duties of Governor.

The Governor, in addition to other duties and responsibilities conferred upon him by the constitution and laws of this State is empowered to contract and to do all other things necessary in behalf of this State to secure the full benefits available to this State under the Federal Highway Safety Act of 1966, as amended,[1] and in so doing, to cooperate with Federal and State agencies, agencies private and public, interested organizations, and with individuals, to effectuate the purposes of that enactment, and any and all subsequent amendments thereto. The Governor is the official of this State having the ultimate responsibility for dealing with the Federal Government with respect to programs and activities pursuant to the National Highway Safety Act of 1966 and any amendments thereto. To that end he shall coordinate the activities of the Secretary of State and the State Board of Education and of any and all departments and agencies of this State and its subdivisions, relating thereto.

P.A. 76-1586, § 17-101, eff. July 1, 1970. Amended by P.A. 81-1508, § 8, eff. Sept. 25, 1980.

Formerly Ill.Rev.Stat.1991, ch. 95 ½, ¶ 17-101.

[1] 23 U.S.C.A. § 401 et seq.

5/17-102 to 5/17-105. §§ 17-102 to 17-105. Repealed by P.A. 82-523, § 2, eff. Jan. 1, 1982

CHAPTER 18. ILLINOIS MOTOR CARRIER OF PROPERTY LAW

5/18-100 to 5/18-903. §§ 18-100 to 18-903. Repealed by P.A. 81-501, § 2, eff. Jan. 1, 1980; P.A. 84-796, § 21, eff. Jan. 1, 1986; P.A. 84-1308, Art. II, § 97, eff. Aug. 25, 1986

Article II of P.A. 84-1308, the First 84th General Assembly Combining Revisory Act, provides for the nonsubstantive revision or renumbering or repeal of Sections of Acts necessitated by the amendment, addition or repeal of Sections by two or more Public Acts of the 84th General Assembly, which multiple action was not resolved by one of the Acts of the 84th General Assembly affecting the particular Section and makes technical corrections in Acts amended by the 84th General Assembly.

CHAPTER 18a. ILLINOIS COMMERCIAL RELOCATION OF TRESPASSING VEHICLES LAW

Enactment

Chapter 18a was added by P.A. 80-1459, § 2, effective January 1, 1979

ARTICLE I. DEFINITIONS, POLICY AND JURISDICTION

5/18a-100. Definitions

§ 18a-100. Definitions. As used in this Chapter: (1) "Commercial vehicle relocator" or "relocator" means any person or entity engaged in the business of removing trespassing vehicles from private property by means of towing or otherwise, and thereafter relocating and storing such vehicles;

(2) "Commission" means the Illinois Commerce Commission;

(3) "Operator" means any person who, as an employee of a commercial vehicle relocator, removes trespassing vehicles from private property by means of towing or otherwise. This term includes the driver of any vehicle used in removing a trespassing vehicle from private property, as well as any person other than the driver who assists in the removal of a trespassing vehicle from private property;

(4) "Operator's employment permit" means a license issued to an operator in accordance with Sections 18a-403 or 18a-405 of this Chapter;

(5) "Relocator's license" means a license issued to a commercial vehicle relocator in accordance with Sections 18a-400 or 18a-401 of this Chapter;

(6) "Dispatcher" means any person who, as an employee or agent of a commercial vehicle relocator, dispatches vehicles to or from locations from which operators perform removal activities; and

(7) "Dispatcher's employment permit" means a license issued to a dispatcher in accordance with Sections 18a-407 or 18a-408 of this Chapter.

P.A. 76-1586, § 18a-100, added by P.A. 80-1459, § 2, eff. Jan. 1, 1979. Amended by P.A. 82-616, § 1, eff. Jan. 1, 1982; P.A. 85-923, § 1, eff. Dec. 1, 1987.

Formerly Ill.Rev.Stat.1991, ch. 95 ½, ¶ 18a-100.

5/18a-101. Declaration of policy and delegation of jurisdiction

§ 18a-101. Declaration of policy and delegation of jurisdiction. It is hereby declared to be the policy of the State of Illinois to supervise and regulate the commercial removal of trespassing vehicles from private property, and the subsequent relocation and storage of such vehicles in such manner as to fairly distribute rights and responsibilities among vehicle owners, private property owners and commercial vehicle relocators, and for this purpose the power and authority to administer and to enforce the provisions of this Chapter shall be vested in the Illinois Commerce Commission.

P.A. 76-1586, § 18a-101, added by P.A. 80-1459, § 2, eff. Jan. 1, 1979.

Formerly Ill.Rev.Stat.1991, ch. 95 ½, ¶ 18a-101.

5/18a-102. Local regulation

§ 18a-102. Local regulation. Nothing contained in this Chapter shall be construed to infringe upon the right of non-home rule units of local government to regulate the commercial relocation of vehicles in a manner consistent with, or in addition to, State or federal laws or regulations. Nothing in this Chapter shall constitute a limitation on the authority of any home rule unit; however, the provisions of this Chapter shall remain in full force and effect in home rule units notwithstanding any applicable ordinances of home rule units.

P.A. 76-1586, § 18a-102, added by P.A. 80-1459, § 2, eff. Jan. 1, 1979.

Formerly Ill.Rev.Stat.1991, ch. 95 ½, ¶ 18a-102.

5/18a-103. Review

§ 18a-103. Review. A person aggrieved by an order of the Commission under this Chapter is entitled, in addition to any other remedy, to a review thereof by the Circuit Court in accordance with the Administrative Review Law, as amended.[1]

P.A. 76-1586, § 18a-103, added by P.A. 80-1459, § 2, eff. Jan. 1, 1979. Amended by P.A. 82-783, Art. XI, § 140, eff. July 13, 1982.

Formerly Ill.Rev.Stat.1991, ch. 95 ½, ¶ 18a-103.

[1] 735 ILCS 5/3-101 et seq.

5/18a-104. Towing performed pursuant to police order

§ 18a-104. Towing performed pursuant to police order. Nothing contained in this Chapter shall be construed to regulate or otherwise affect towing performed by any relocator pursuant to the order of a law enforcement official or agency in accordance with Sections 4-201 through 4-214 of the Illinois Vehicle Code.

P.A. 76-1586, § 18a-104, added by P.A. 80-1459, § 2, eff. Jan. 1, 1979.

Formerly Ill.Rev.Stat.1991, ch. 95 ½, ¶ 18a-104.

5/18a-105. Exemptions

§ 18a-105. Exemptions. This Chapter shall not apply to the relocation of:

(1) Vehicles registered for a gross weight in excess of 10,000 pounds, or if the vehicle is not registered, with a gross weight in excess of 10,000 pounds including vehicle weight and maximum load; or

(2) Motorcycles.

Such relocation shall be governed by the provisions of Section 4-203 of this Code.

P.A. 76-1586, § 18a-105, added by P.A. 85-923, § 1, eff. Dec. 1, 1987.

Formerly Ill.Rev.Stat.1991, ch. 95 ½, ¶ 18a-105.

ARTICLE II. DUTIES AND POWERS

5/18a–200. General powers and duties of Commission

§ 18a–200. General powers and duties of Commission. The Commission shall:

(1) Regulate commercial vehicle relocators and their employees or agents in accordance with this Chapter and to that end may establish reasonable requirements with respect to proper service and practices relating thereto;

(2) Require the maintenance of uniform systems of accounts, records and the preservation thereof;

(3) Require that all drivers and other personnel used in relocation be employees of a licensed relocator;

(4) Regulate equipment leasing to and by relocators;

(5) Adopt reasonable and proper rules covering the exercise of powers conferred upon it by this Chapter, and reasonable rules governing investigations, hearings and proceedings under this Chapter;

(6) Set reasonable rates for the commercial towing or removal of trespassing vehicles from private property. The rates shall not exceed the mean average of the 5 highest rates for police tows within the territory to which this Chapter applies that are performed under Sections 4–201 and 4–214 of this Code and that are of record at hearing; provided that the Commission shall not re-calculate the maximum specified herein if the order containing the previous calculation was entered within one calendar year of the date on which the new order is entered. Set reasonable rates for the storage, for periods in excess of 24 hours, of the vehicles in connection with the towing or removal; however, no relocator shall impose charges for storage for the first 24 hours after towing or removal. Set reasonable rates for other services provided by relocators, provided that the rates shall not be charged to the owner or operator of a relocated vehicle. Any fee charged by a relocator for the use of a credit card that is used to pay for any service rendered by the relocator shall be included in the total amount that shall not exceed the maximum reasonable rate established by the Commission. The Commission shall require a relocator to refund any amount charged in excess of the reasonable rate established by the Commission, including any fee for the use of a credit card;

(7) Investigate and maintain current files of the criminal records, if any, of all relocators and their employees and of all applicants for relocator's license, operator's licenses and dispatcher's licenses;

(8) Issue relocator's licenses, dispatcher's employment permits, and operator's employment permits in accordance with Article IV of this Chapter; [1]

(9) Establish fitness standards for applicants seeking relocator licensees and holders of relocator licenses;

(10) Upon verified complaint in writing by any person, organization or body politic, or upon its own initiative may, investigate whether any commercial vehicle relocator, operator, dispatcher, or person otherwise required to comply with any provision of this Chapter or any rule promulgated hereunder, has failed to comply with any provision or rule;

(11) Whenever the Commission receives notice from the Secretary of State that any domestic or foreign corporation regulated under this Chapter has not paid a franchise tax, license fee or penalty required under the Business Corporation Act of 1983,[2] institute proceedings for the revocation of the license or right to engage in any business required under this Chapter or the suspension thereof until such time as the delinquent franchise tax, license fee or penalty is paid.

P.A. 76–1586, § 18a–200, added by P.A. 80–1459, § 2, eff. Jan. 1, 1979. Amended by P.A. 81–332, § 2, eff. Jan. 1, 1980; P.A. 81–333, § 1, eff. Jan. 1, 1980; P.A. 82–616, § 1, eff. Jan. 1, 1982; P.A. 83–1295, § 1, eff. July 1, 1985; P.A. 83–1362, Art. IV, § 15, eff. Sept. 11, 1984; P.A. 83–1528, Art. II, § 24, eff. Jan. 17, 1985; P.A. 84–796, § 1, eff. Jan. 1, 1986; P.A. 85–923, § 1, eff. Dec. 1, 1987; P.A. 86–492, § 1, eff. Sept. 1, 1989; P.A. 88–448, § 1, eff. Aug. 20, 1993.

Formerly Ill.Rev.Stat.1991, ch. 95 ½, ¶ 18a–200.

1 625 ILCS 5/18a–400 et seq.

2 805 ILCS 5/1.01 et seq.

5/18a–201. Additional officers and employees

§ 18a–201. Additional officers and employees. The Commission, for the purpose of more effectively carrying out the provisions of this Chapter, shall obtain pursuant to the provisions of the "Personnel Code" [1] such officers and employees as it may deem necessary to carry out the provisions of this Chapter or to perform the duties and exercise the powers conferred by law upon the Commission.

P.A. 76–1586, § 18a–201, added by P.A. 80–1459, § 2, eff. Jan. 1, 1979.

Formerly Ill.Rev.Stat.1991, ch. 95 ½, ¶ 18a–201.

1 20 ILCS 415/1 et seq.

ARTICLE III. REQUIREMENTS AND PROHIBITIONS

Section

5/18a–300. Commercial vehicle relocators—Unlawful practices

§ 18a–300. Commercial vehicle relocators—Unlawful practices. It shall be unlawful for any commercial vehicle relocator:

(1) To operate in any county in which this Chapter is applicable without a valid, current relocator's license as provided in Article IV of this Chapter; [1]

(2) To employ as an operator, or otherwise so use the services of, any person who does not have at the commencement of employment or service, or at any time during the course of employment or service, a valid, current operator's employment permit, or temporary operator's employment permit issued in accordance with Sections 18a–403 or 18a–405 of this Chapter; or to fail to notify the Commission, in writing, of any known criminal conviction of any employee occurring at any time before or during the course of employment or service;

(3) To employ as a dispatcher, or otherwise so use the services of, any person who does not have at the commencement of employment or service, or at any time during the course of employment or service, a valid, current dispatcher's or operator's employment permit or temporary dispatcher's or operator's employment permit issued in accordance with Sections 18a–403 or 18a–407 of this Chapter; or to fail to notify the Commission, in writing, of any known criminal conviction of any employee occurring at any time before or during the course of employment or service;

(4) To operate upon the highways of this State any vehicle used in connection with any commercial vehicle relocation service unless:

(A) There is painted or firmly affixed to the vehicle on both sides of the vehicle in a color or colors vividly contrasting to the color of the vehicle the name, address and telephone number of the relocator. The Commission shall prescribe reasonable rules and regulations pertaining to insignia to be painted or firmly affixed to vehicles and shall waive the requirements of the address on any vehicle in cases where the operator of a vehicle has painted or otherwise firmly affixed to the vehicle a seal or trade mark that clearly identifies the operator of the vehicle; and

(B) There is carried in the power unit of the vehicle a certified copy of the currently effective relocator's license and operator's employment permit. Copies may be photographed, photocopied, or reproduced or printed by any other legible and durable process. Any person guilty of not causing to be displayed a copy of his relocator's license and operator's employment permit may in any hearing concerning the violation be excused from the payment of the penalty hereinafter provided upon a showing that the license was issued by the Commission, but was subsequently lost or destroyed;

(5) To operate upon the highways of this State any vehicle used in connection with any commercial vehicle relocation service that bears the name or address and telephone number of any person or entity other than the relocator by which it is owned or to which it is leased;

(6) To advertise in any newspaper, book, list, classified directory or other publication unless there is contained in the advertisement the license number of the relocator;

(7) To remove any vehicle from private property without having first obtained the written authorization of the property owner or other person in lawful possession or control of the property, his authorized agent, or an authorized law enforcement officer. The authorization may be on a contractual basis covering a period of time or limited to a specific removal;

(8) To charge the private property owner, who requested that an unauthorized vehicle be removed from his property, with the costs of removing the vehicle contrary to any terms that may be a part of the contract between the property owner and the commercial relocator. Nothing in this paragraph shall prevent a relocator from assessing, collecting, or receiving from the property owner, lessee, or their agents any fee prescribed by the Commission;

(9) To remove a vehicle when the owner or operator of the vehicle is present or arrives at the vehicle location at any time prior to the completion of removal, and is willing and able to remove the vehicle immediately;

(10) To remove any vehicle from property on which signs are required and on which there are not posted appropriate signs under Section 18a–302;

(11) To fail to notify law enforcement authorities in the jurisdiction in which the trespassing vehicle was removed within one hour of the removal. Notification shall include a complete description of the vehicle, registration numbers if possible, the locations from which and to which the vehicle was removed, the time of removal, and any other information required by regulation, statute or ordinance;

(12) To impose any charge other than in accordance with the rates set by the Commission as provided in paragraph (6) of Section 18a–200 of this Chapter;

(13) To fail, in the office or location at which relocated vehicles are routinely returned to their owners, to prominently post the name, address and telephone number of the nearest office of the Commission to which inquiries or complaints may be sent;

(13.1) To fail to distribute to each owner or operator of a relocated vehicle, in written form as prescribed by Commission rule or regulation, the relevant statutes, regulations and ordinances governing commercial vehicle relocators, including, in at least 12 point boldface type, the name, address and telephone number of the nearest office of the Commission to which inquiries or complaints may be sent;

(14) To remove any vehicle, otherwise in accordance with this Chapter, more than 15 air miles from its location when towed from a location in an unincorporated area of a county or more than 10 air miles from its location when towed from any other location;

(15) To fail to make a telephone number available to the police department of any municipality in which a relocator operates at which the relocator or an employee of the relocator may be contacted at any time during the hours in which the relocator is engaged in the towing of vehicles, or advertised as engaged in the towing of vehicles, for the purpose of effectuating the release of a towed vehicle; or to fail to include the telephone number in any advertisement of the relocator's services published or otherwise appearing on or after the effective date of this amendatory Act; or to fail to have an employee available at any time on the premises owned or controlled by the relocator for the purposes of arranging for the immediate release of the vehicle.

Apart from any other penalty or liability authorized under this Act, if after a reasonable effort, the owner of the vehicle is unable to make telephone contact with the relocator for a period of one hour from his initial attempt during any time period in which the relocator is required to respond at the number, all fees for towing, storage, or otherwise are to be waived. Proof of 3 attempted phone calls to the number provided to the police department by an officer or employee of the department on behalf of the vehicle owner within the space of one hour, at least 2 of which are separated by 45 minutes, shall be deemed sufficient proof of the owner's reasonable effort to make contact with the vehicle relocator. Failure of the relocator to respond to the phone calls is not a criminal violation of this Chapter;

(16) To use equipment which the relocator does not own, except in compliance with Section 18a–306 of this Chapter and Commission regulations. No equipment can be leased to more than one relocator at any time. Equipment leases shall be filed with the Commission. If equipment is leased to one relocator, it cannot thereafter be leased to another relocator until a written cancellation of lease is properly filed with the Commission;

(17) To use drivers or other personnel who are not employees or contractors of the relocator;

(18) To fail to refund any amount charged in excess of the reasonable rate established by the Commission;

(19) To violate any other provision of this Chapter, or of Commission regulations or orders adopted under this Chapter.

P.A. 76–1586, § 18a–300, added by P.A. 80–1459, § 2, eff. Jan. 1, 1979. Amended by P.A. 80–1495, § 36, eff. Jan. 8, 1979; P.A. 81–332, § 2, eff. Jan. 1, 1980; P.A. 81–333, § 1, eff. Jan. 1, 1980; P.A. 81–990, § 1, eff. Jan. 1, 1980; P.A. 81–1509, Art. I, § 57, eff. Sept. 26, 1980; P.A. 82–616, § 1, eff. Jan. 1, 1982; P.A. 83–879, § 2, eff. July 1, 1984; P.A. 85–923, § 1, eff. Dec. 1, 1987; P.A. 86–1272, § 1, eff. Jan. 1, 1991; P.A. 88–448, § 1, eff. Aug. 20, 1993.

Formerly Ill.Rev.Stat.1991, ch. 95 ½, ¶ 18a–300.

[1] 625 ILCS 5/18a–400 et seq.

5/18a–301. Commercial vehicle relocators—Security requirements

§ 18a–301. Commercial vehicle relocators—Security requirements. Every commercial vehicle relocator shall file with the Commission and have in effect an indemnity bond or insurance policy or certificates of bonds or insurance in lieu thereof which shall indemnify or insure the relocator for its liability: (1) for injury to person, in an amount not less than $100,000 to any one person and $300,000 for any one accident; (2) in case of damage to property other than a vehicle being removed, in an amount not less than $50,000 for any one accident; and (3) in case of damage to any vehicle relocated or stored by the relocator, in an amount not less than $15,000 per vehicle. Any such bond or policy shall be issued by a bonding or insurance firm authorized to do business as such in the State of Illinois. All certificates or indemnity bonds or insurance filed with the Commission must show the coverage effective continuously until cancelled, and the Commission may require such evidence of continued validity as it deems necessary.

P.A. 76–1586, § 18a–301, added by P.A. 80–1459, § 2, eff. Jan. 1, 1979. Amended by P.A. 85–1396, § 2, eff. Sept. 2, 1988.

Formerly Ill.Rev.Stat.1991, ch. 95 ½, ¶ 18a–301.

5/18a–302. Owner or other person in lawful possession or control of private property—Right to employ relocation service

§ 18a–302. Owner or other person in lawful possession or control of private property—Right to employ relocation service. It shall be unlawful for an owner or other person in lawful possession or control of private property to remove or employ a commercial relocator to remove an unauthorized vehicle from such property unless written notice is provided to the effect that such vehicles will be removed, including the name, address and telephone number of the appropriate commercial vehicle relocator, if any. Such notice shall consist of a sign, posted in a conspicuous place in the affected area, of a size at least 24 inches in height by 36 inches in width. Such sign shall be at least 4 feet from the ground but less than 8 feet from the ground and shall be either illuminated or painted with reflective paint, or both. Such sign shall state the amount of towing charges to which the person parking may be subject. This provision shall not be construed as prohibiting any unit of local government from imposing additional or greater notice requirements.

No express notice shall be required under this Section upon residential property which, paying due regard to the circumstances and the surrounding area, is clearly reserved or intended exclusively for the use or occupation of residents or their vehicles.

P.A. 76–1586, § 18a–302, added by P.A. 80–1459, § 2, eff. Jan. 1, 1979. Amended by P.A. 81–332, § 2, eff. Jan. 1, 1980.

Formerly Ill.Rev.Stat.1991, ch. 95 ½, ¶ 18a–302.

5/18a–303. Civil and Criminal liability

§ 18a–303. Civil and Criminal liability. Nothing in this Chapter shall be construed to limit or alter the vehicle owner's civil or criminal liability for trespass. Nothing in this Chapter shall be construed to limit or alter the civil or criminal liability of any person or entity for any act or omission. All penalties accruing under this Law shall be cumulative of each other and a suit for recovery of one penalty shall not bar or affect the recovery of another penalty.

P.A. 76–1586, § 18a–303, added by P.A. 80–1459, § 2, eff. Jan. 1, 1979. Amended by P.A. 82–616, § 1, eff. Jan. 1, 1982; P.A. 85–923, § 1, eff. Dec. 1, 1987.

Formerly Ill.Rev.Stat.1991, ch. 95 ½, ¶ 18a–303.

5/18a–304. Operators—Unlawful Practices

§ 18a–304. Operators—Unlawful Practices. It shall be unlawful for any operator:

(1) To act as an operator without a valid, current operator's employment permit.

(2) To violate any other provision of this Chapter, or of Commission regulations or orders adopted under this Chapter.

P.A. 76–1586, § 18a–304, added by P.A. 85–923, § 1, eff. Dec. 1, 1987.

Formerly Ill.Rev.Stat.1991, ch. 95 ½, ¶ 18a–304.

5/18a–305. Aiding and abetting

§ 18a–305. Aiding and abetting. It shall be unlawful for any person to aid or abet in any violation of this Chapter, or of Commission regulations or orders adopted under this Chapter.

P.A. 76–1586, § 18a–305, added by P.A. 85–923, § 1, eff. Dec. 1, 1987.

Formerly Ill.Rev.Stat.1991, ch. 95 ½, ¶ 18a–305.

5/18a–306. Equipment Leasing

§ 18a–306. Equipment Leasing. Provisions in Section 18c-4103 of the Illinois Commercial Transportation Law, as amended,[1] shall likewise govern equipment leasing by relocators except to the extent as otherwise provided in this Law.

P.A. 76–1586, § 18a–306, added by P.A. 85–923, § 1, eff. Dec. 1, 1987.

Formerly Ill.Rev.Stat.1991, ch. 95 ½, ¶ 18a–306.

[1] 625 ILCS 5/18c–4103.

5/18a–307. Enforcement

§ 18a–307. Enforcement. Provisions in Article VII of subchapter 1 of the Illinois Commercial Transportation Law,[1] governing enforcement of the Illinois Commercial Transportation Law, shall likewise govern the enforcement of this Chapter.

P.A. 76–1586, § 18a–307, added by P.A. 85–923, § 1, eff. Dec. 1, 1987.

Formerly Ill.Rev.Stat.1991, ch. 95 ½, ¶ 18a–307.

[1] 625 ILCS 5/18c–1701 et seq.

ARTICLE IV. LICENSES

5/18a–400. Relocator's licenses—Applications, original determinations

§ 18a–400. Relocator's licenses—Applications, original determinations. (a) Each application for a license to operate as a commercial vehicle relocator shall be made in writing to the Commission, shall be verified under oath, shall be in such form and contain such information as the Commission may by regulation require, and shall be accompanied by the required application fee and proof of security.

(b) Upon the filing of such application, the Commission shall, within a reasonable time, fix a time and place for public hearing thereon. At least 10 days before the hearing, the Commission shall notify the applicant and all parties of record to such proceeding of the time and place of such hearing, by mailing a notice thereof to each such party to the address of such party shown in the records of such proceeding. Any person having an interest in the subject matter may appear at the hearing in support of or in objection to the application.

(c) The applicant shall publish a notice on a form prescribed by the Commission covering the filing of such application at least 10 days prior to the time of the initial hearing in (i) the official newspaper selected by the Department of Finance of the State of Illinois pursuant to Section 4 of the Illinois Purchasing Act,[1] and (ii) a secular newspaper of general circulation and published in the county in the State of Illinois, wherein the applicant or applicants propose to maintain their principal office and place of business within the State of Illinois. The Commission may by regulation or otherwise order applicants to give such further notice as it deems required. The Commission may give additional notice of the filing of such application as it may deem reasonable and proper as prescribed in its rules. The Director of the Department of Finance of the State of Illinois for the purposes hereof shall over his or her signature as such Director annually and immediately upon selecting the official newspaper certify to the Illinois Commerce Commission the name and address of said newspaper, together with the date of expiration of the period of one year for which said newspaper was so selected and the Commission shall filemark each such certification as of the date it receives the same and shall keep an official file of said certifications of said Director conveniently available at its office in Springfield, Illinois; provided, however, that in any and all events and for all purposes of this Section and this Chapter, should the aforesaid Director for any reason fail to make said certification annually, the newspaper set forth in the certification aforesaid of said Director filemarked by the Commission as of the most recent date shall be the official newspaper in which publication is required hereby. In case publication is required hereby in a newspaper published in a particular county and no newspaper is so published, then and in that case publication shall be made in a newspaper published in the closest county thereto which meets the circulation requirements of this Section.

(d) The Commission shall issue a relocator's license to any qualified applicant therefor after hearing, pursuant to an application filed, if it is found that the applicant is fit, willing and able properly to perform the service proposed and to conform to provisions of this Chapter and the requirements, rules and regulations of the Commission thereunder; otherwise such application shall be denied. The order of the Commission granting or denying a relocator's license shall set forth the specific findings of fact on which such order is based. Notwithstanding any other provision of this Chapter no such license shall be issued to any person who has failed to pay any registration fee or any tax due from such person to the State of Illinois for the privilege of operating any motor vehicle on the public highways in the State of Illinois.

(e) Operation over the public highways of this State conducted pursuant to a relocator's license shall be in conformity with all of the laws of this State pertaining to motor vehicle operation over such public highways.

(f) No relocator's license shall confer any proprietary or property rights in the use of the public highways.

P.A. 76–1586, § 18a–400, added by P.A. 80–1459, § 2, eff. Jan. 1, 1979.

Formerly Ill.Rev.Stat.1991, ch. 95 ½, ¶ 18a–400.

[1] 30 ILCS 505/4.

5/18a–401. Relocator's licenses—Expiration and renewal

§ 18a–401. Relocator's licenses—Expiration and renewal. All relocator's licenses shall expire 2 years from the date of issuance by the Commission. The Commission may temporarily extend the duration of a license for the pendency of a renewal application until formally approved or denied. Upon filing, no earlier than 90 days nor later than 45 days prior to such expiration, of written application for renewal, verified under oath, in such form and containing such information as the Commission shall by regulation require, and accompanied by the required application fee and proof of security, the Commission shall, unless it has received information of cause not to do so, renew the license. If the Commission has information of cause not to renew such license, it shall so notify the applicant, and shall hold a hearing as provided for in Section 18a–400. The Commission may at any time during the term of the license make inquiry into the management, conduct of business, or otherwise to determine that the provisions of this Chapter 18A and the regulations of the Commission promulgated thereunder are being observed.

P.A. 76–1586, § 18a–401, added by P.A. 80–1459, § 2, eff. Jan. 1, 1979. Amended by P.A. 82–616, § 1, eff. Jan. 1, 1982.

Formerly Ill.Rev.Stat.1991, ch. 95 ½, ¶ 18a–401.

5/18a–402. Relocator's license—Transfer

§ 18a–402. Relocator's license—Transfer. A relocator's license is not transferable.

P.A. 76–1586, § 18a–402, added by P.A. 80–1459, § 2, eff. Jan. 1, 1979.

Formerly Ill.Rev.Stat.1991, ch. 95 ½, ¶ 18a–402.

5/18a-403. Operator's or dispatcher's employment permits—Applications, original determinations

§ 18a-403. Operator's or dispatcher's employment permits—Applications, original determinations. (1) Each application for an operator's or dispatcher's employment permit shall be made in writing to the Commission, shall be acknowledged before a notary public, shall be in such form and shall contain such information as the Commission may by regulation require, and shall be accompanied by the required application fee and proof, in a form prescribed by the Commission, that the operator applicant has a valid driver's license issued by the Secretary of State.

(2) Upon the filing of such application, the Commission shall conduct an investigation of the criminal record, if any, of the applicant. The Commission shall, within 3 working days, issue to any new applicant for an employment permit a provisional operator's or dispatcher's employment permit unless the Commission finds that the applicant has committed an offense for which the permit could be revoked under Section 18a-404 of this Chapter. This provisional employment permit shall be valid for a period of 1 year unless suspended or revoked by order of the Commission. At the end of 1 year, the provisional permit shall automatically become permanent unless the permit was revoked by order of the Commission during the preceding year. The permanent permit shall remain valid unless suspended or revoked by order of the Commission under this law.

(3) The permit shall identify the operator or dispatcher by name and address, and shall identify the relocator by which the operator or dispatcher will be employed by name, address and relocator's permit number. The permit shall be valid only when the operator or dispatcher is employed by the relocator identified thereon.

Operation over the public highways of this State conducted pursuant to an operator's license issued under the provisions of this Section shall be in conformity with all the laws of this State pertaining to motor vehicle operation over such public highways.

P.A. 76-1586, § 18a-403, added by P.A. 80-1459, § 2, eff. Jan. 1, 1979. Amended by P.A. 82-616, § 1, eff. Jan. 1, 1982; P.A. 85-923, § 1, eff. Dec. 1, 1987.

Formerly Ill.Rev.Stat.1991, ch. 95 ½, ¶ 18a-403.

5/18a-404. Operator's and dispatcher's employment permits—Revocation

§ 18a-404. Operator's and dispatcher's employment permits—Revocation. (1) The Commission shall suspend or revoke the permit of an operator if it finds that:

(a) The operator or dispatcher made a false statement on the application for an operator's or dispatcher's employment permit;

(b) The operator's or dispatcher's driver's license issued by the Secretary of State has been suspended or revoked; or

(c) The operator or dispatcher has been convicted, during the preceding 5 years, of any criminal offense of the State of Illinois or any other jurisdiction involving any of the following, and the holder does not make a compelling showing that he is nevertheless fit to hold an operator's license:

(i) Bodily injury or attempt to inflict bodily injury to another;

(ii) Theft of property or attempted theft of property; or

(iii) Sexual assault or attempted sexual assault of any kind.

(2) The Commission, upon notification and verification of any conviction described in this Section, of any person to whom license has been issued, occurring within the 5 years prior to such issuance or any time thereafter, shall immediately suspend the employment permit of such person, and issue an order setting forth the grounds for revocation. The person and his employer shall be notified of such suspension. Such person shall not thereafter be employed by a relocator until a final order is issued by the Commission either reinstating the employment permit, upon a finding that the reinstatement of an employment permit to the person constitutes no threat to the public safety, or revoking the employment permit.

(3) If the employment permit is revoked, the person shall not thereafter be employed by a relocator until he obtains an employment permit license under Article IV of this Chapter.

P.A. 76-1586, § 18a-404, added by P.A. 80-1459, § 2, eff. Jan. 1, 1979. Amended by P.A. 82-616, § 1, eff. Jan. 1, 1982; P.A. 85-923, § 1, eff. Dec. 1, 1987.

Formerly Ill.Rev.Stat.1991, ch. 95 ½, ¶ 18a-404.

5/18a-405. Operator's employment permits—Expiration and renewal

§ 18a-405. Operator's employment permits—Expiration and renewal. All operator's employment permits shall expire 2 years from the date of issuance by the Commission. The Commission may temporarily extend the duration of an employment permit for the pendency of a renewal application until formally approved or denied. Upon filing, no earlier than 90 nor later than 45 days prior to such expiration, of written application for renewal, acknowledged before a notary public, in such form and containing such information as the Commission shall by regulation require, and accompanied by the required fee and proof of possession of a valid driver's license issued by the Secretary of State, the Commission shall, unless it has received information of cause not to do so, renew the applicant's operator's employment permit. If the Commission does not renew such employment permit, it shall issue an order setting forth the grounds for denial. The Commission may at any time during the term of the employment permit make inquiry into the conduct of the permittee to determine that the provisions of this Chapter 18A and the regulations of the Commission promulgated thereunder are being adhered to.

P.A. 76-1586, § 18a-405, added by P.A. 80-1459, § 2, eff. Jan. 1, 1979. Amended by P.A. 82-616, § 1, eff. Jan. 1, 1982; P.A. 85-923, § 1, eff. Dec. 1, 1987.

Formerly Ill.Rev.Stat.1991, ch. 95 ½, ¶ 18a-405.

5/18a-406. Operator's employment permits—Transfer

§ 18a-406. Operator's employment permits—Transfer. An operator's employment permit is not transferrable to another operator or to another relocator.

P.A. 76-1586, § 18a-406, added by P.A. 80-1459, § 2, eff. Jan. 1, 1979. Amended by P.A. 85-923, § 1, eff. Dec. 1, 1987.

Formerly Ill.Rev.Stat.1991, ch. 95 ½, ¶ 18a-406.

5/18a-407. Dispatcher's employment permits, expiration and renewal

§ 18a-407. Dispatcher's employment permits, expiration and renewal. All dispatcher's employment permits shall expire 2 years from the date of issuance by the Commission. The Commission may temporarily extend the duration of an employment permit for the pendency of a renewal application until formally approved or denied. Upon filing, no earlier than 90 nor later than 45 days prior to such expiration, of written application for renewal, acknowledged before a notary public, in such form and containing such information as the Commission shall by regulation require, and accompanied by the required fee, the Commission shall, unless it has received information of cause not to do so, renew the applicant's dispatcher's employment permit. If the Commission does not renew such employment permit, it shall issue an order setting forth the grounds for denial. The Commission may at any time during the term of the employment permit make inquiry into the conduct of the permittee to determine that the provisions of this Chapter 18A and the regulations of the Commission promulgated thereunder are being observed.

P.A. 76–1586, § 18a–407, added by P.A. 82–616, § 1, eff. Jan. 1, 1982. Amended by P.A. 85–923, § 1, eff. Dec. 1, 1987.

Formerly Ill.Rev.Stat.1991, ch. 95 ½, ¶ 18a–407.

5/18a–408. Dispatcher's employment permit—Transfer

§ 18a–408. Dispatcher's employment permit—Transfer. A dispatcher's employment permit is not transferable to another dispatcher or to another relocator.

P.A. 76–1586, § 18a–408, added by P.A. 82–616, § 1, eff. Jan. 1, 1982. Amended by P.A. 85–923, § 1, eff. Dec. 1, 1987.

Formerly Ill.Rev.Stat.1991, ch. 95 ½, ¶ 18a–408.

ARTICLE V. RATES AND CHARGES—LIENS

Section

5/18a–500. Posting of rates

§ 18a–500. Posting of rates. Every commercial vehicle relocator shall print and keep open to the public, all authorized rates and charges for towing, otherwise moving, and storing vehicles in connection with removal of unauthorized vehicles from private property. Such rates and charges shall be clearly stated in terms of lawful money of the United States, and shall be posted in such form and manner, and shall contain such information as the Commission shall by regulation prescribe.

P.A. 76–1586, § 18a–500, added by P.A. 80–1459, § 2, eff. Jan. 1, 1979.

Formerly Ill.Rev.Stat.1991, ch. 95 ½, ¶ 18a–500.

5/18a–501. Liens against relocated vehicles

§ 18a–501. Liens against relocated vehicles. Unauthorized vehicles removed and stored by a commercial vehicle relocator in compliance with this Chapter shall be subject to a possessory lien for services pursuant to the Labor and Storage Lien (Small Amount) Act [1], and the provisions of Section 1 of that Act [2] relating to notice and implied consent shall be deemed satisfied by compliance with Section 18a–302 and item (10) of Section 18a–300. In no event shall such lien be greater than the rate or rates established in accordance with item (6) of Section 18a–200. In no event shall such lien be increased or altered to reflect any charge for services or materials rendered in addition to those authorized by this Act. Every such lien shall be payable by use of any major credit card, in addition to being payable in cash. Upon receipt of a properly signed credit card receipt, a relocator shall become a holder in due course, and neither the holder of the credit card nor the company which issued the credit card may thereafter refuse to remit payment in the amount shown on the credit card receipt minus the ordinary charge assessed by the credit card company for processing the charge. The Commission may adopt regulations governing acceptance of credit cards by a relocator.

P.A. 76–1586, § 18a–501, added by P.A. 80–1459, § 2, eff. Jan. 1, 1979. Amended by P.A. 85–923, § 1, eff. Dec. 1, 1987; P.A. 91–357, § 231, eff. July 29, 1999.

Formerly Ill.Rev.Stat.1991, ch. 95 ½, ¶ 18a–501.

1 770 ILCS 50/0.01 et seq.

2 770 ILCS 50/1.

ARTICLE VI. FEES

Section

5/18a–600. Relocator's license

§ 18a–600. Relocator's license. Each application for a license to operate as a commercial vehicle relocator, or for a renewal of such license, shall be accompanied by a filing fee in the amount provided or prescribed by the Commission.

P.A. 76–1586, § 18a–600, added by P.A. 80–1459, § 2, eff. Jan. 1, 1979. Amended by P.A. 82–616, § 1, eff. Jan. 1, 1982; P.A. 85–923, § 1, eff. Dec. 1, 1987.

Formerly Ill.Rev.Stat.1991, ch. 95 ½, ¶ 18a–600.

5/18a–601. Operator's or dispatcher's employment permit

§ 18a–601. Operator's or dispatcher's employment permit. Each application for dispatcher's or an operator's employment permit shall be accompanied by a filing fee in the amount provided or prescribed by the Commission. Each application for renewal of an operator's or dispatcher's employment permit shall be accompanied by a filing fee in the amount provided herein or prescribed by the Commission.

P.A. 76–1586, § 18a–601, added by P.A. 80–1459, § 2, eff. Jan. 1, 1979. Amended by P.A. 82–616, § 1, eff. Jan. 1, 1982; P.A. 85–923, § 1, eff. Dec. 1, 1987; P.A. 85–1209, Art. III, § 3–60, eff. Aug. 30, 1988.

Formerly Ill.Rev.Stat.1991, ch. 95 ½, ¶ 18a–601.

5/18a–602. Establishment and Adjustment of Fees

§ 18a–602. Establishment and Adjustment of Fees.

(1) General Provisions. The Commission may exercise any and all powers with respect to establishment and adjustment of fees with respect to commercial vehicle relocators which it may exercise with respect to motor carriers under subsections (2), (3) and (4) of Section 18c–1501 of the Illinois Commercial Transportation Law.

(2) Initial fees. The Commission shall set initial fees by rulemaking in accordance with Section 5–50 of the Illinois Administrative Procedure Act.[1] Initial fees shall be set and take effect within 60 days after December 1, 1987. Such fees

shall remain in effect until adjusted by the Commission in accordance with subsection (1) of this Section.

P.A. 76–1586, § 18a–602, added by P.A. 80–1459, § 2, eff. Jan. 1, 1979. Amended by P.A. 84–796, § 1, eff. Jan. 1, 1986; P.A. 85–923, § 1, eff. Dec. 1, 1987; P.A. 88–45, Art. III, § 3–128, eff. July 6, 1993.

Formerly Ill.Rev.Stat.1991, ch. 95 ½, ¶ 18a–602.

[1] 5 ILCS 100/5–50.

5/18a–603. Disposition of funds

§ 18a–603. Disposition of funds. All fees and fines collected by the Commission under this Chapter shall be paid into the Transportation Regulatory Fund in the State Treasury. The money in that fund shall be used to defray the expenses of the administration of this Chapter and for the purposes specified in Section 18c–1601 of this Code.

P.A. 76–1586, § 18a–603, added by P.A. 85–923, § 1, eff. Dec. 1, 1987.

Formerly Ill.Rev.Stat.1991, ch. 95 ½, ¶ 18a–603.

ARTICLE VII. COUNTIES COVERED

Section

5/18a–700. Counties covered

§ 18a–700. Counties covered. (a) The provisions of this Chapter apply to all the activities of relocators and operators in any counties of 1,000,000 or more and in any county of less than 1,000,000 which adopts regulation under this Chapter as provided in this Section.

(b) Any operation of a relocator or operator involving the removal or storage of a given vehicle which takes place in any part in a regulated county shall subject all the activities of the relocator and operator involving that vehicle to regulation under this Chapter, except operations which take place entirely within the territory of a city, village or incorporated town excluded from this Chapter under paragraph (d).

(c) Any county of under 1,000,000 may elect to be covered under this Chapter by the adoption of a resolution by the County Board, approved by a majority of its members, providing that the county shall be subject to this Chapter. The county clerk shall certify to the Commission that the County Board has adopted the resolution. The Commission shall certify to such County Board an effective date for the applicability of this Chapter in such county. Such effective date shall be no earlier than 30 days from certification to the County Board nor later than 6 months from such certification or the beginning of the next fiscal year, whichever is last.

(d) Cities, villages and incorporated towns in counties to which the provisions of this Chapter apply may, by resolution adopted by a majority of the members of the corporate authorities and filed with the County Clerk of such county and with the Illinois Commerce Commission, choose to be excluded from the provisions of this Chapter. Upon the filing of such resolution, the provisions of this Chapter shall not be applicable to operations of relocators or operators which take place entirely within the territory of such city, village or incorporated town.

P.A. 76–1586, § 18a–700, added by P.A. 80–1459, § 2, eff. Jan. 1, 1979. Amended by P.A. 80–1495, § 36, eff. Jan. 8, 1979; P.A. 86–492, § 1, eff. Sept. 1, 1989.

Formerly Ill.Rev.Stat.1991, ch. 95 ½, ¶ 18a–700.

CHAPTER 18b. MOTOR CARRIER SAFETY REGULATIONS

Enactment

Chapter 18b was added by P.A. 82–657, § 1, effective January 1, 1982

ARTICLE I. FEDERAL MOTOR CARRIER SAFETY REGULATIONS

Section

5/18b–100. Short Title

§ 18b–100. Short Title. This Chapter shall be known and may be cited as "The Illinois Motor Carrier Safety Law".

P.A. 76–1586, § 18b–100, added by P.A. 82–657, § 1, eff. Jan. 1, 1982. Amended by P.A. 82–887, § 1, eff. Aug. 2, 1982; P.A. 83–12, § 1, eff. Jan. 1, 1984; P.A. 83–542, § 1, eff. Jan. 1, 1984; P.A. 83–1362, Art. II, § 99, eff. Sept. 11, 1984; P.A. 84–1246, § 1, eff. July 29, 1986; P.A. 85–1144, § 1, eff. July 29, 1988; P.A. 86–611, § 1, eff. Sept. 1, 1989.

Formerly Ill.Rev.Stat.1991, ch. 95 ½, ¶ 18b–100.

Section 4 of P.A. 83–12, approved July 1, 1983, provided:

"Effective date. This Act takes effect as provided in this Section.

"The amendments to those portions of Sections 3–815(a), 3–818 and 3–819(b) of 'The Illinois Vehicle Code' in Section 1 of this Act which create the 'X', 'Z', 'MX', 'MZ', 'MM' and 'TN' registration classifications and the fees and taxes imposed for those classifications, the amendments to Sections 2–119, 3–401 and 3–802 of 'The Illinois Vehicle Code' in Section 1 of this Act, and the amendments to Chapter 15 of 'The Illinois Vehicle Code' in Section 1 of this Act take effect July 1, 1983.

"The remaining amendments to 'The Illinois Vehicle Code' in Section 1 of this Act take effect July 1, 1983 and apply beginning with the 1985 registration year, except that the amendments to Sections 3–813 through 3–816 and Section 3–819 apply beginning with the 1984 registration year for those vehicles registered on a calendar year basis only.

"The amendments to Chapters 13 and 18 of 'The Illinois Vehicle Code' in Section 1 of this Act take effect January 1, 1984.

"Section 2 of this Act takes effect on the first day of the next succeeding month which commences at least 30 days after the date on which this Act becomes law.

"Section 3 of this Act takes effect July 1, 1983.

"Section 3.1 of this Act takes effect January 1, 1984.

"This Section 4 takes effect upon its becoming a law."

5/18b–101. Definitions

§ 18b–101. Definitions. Unless the context otherwise clearly requires, as used in this Chapter:

"Commercial motor vehicle" means any self propelled or towed vehicle used on public highways in interstate and intrastate commerce to transport passengers or property when the vehicle has a gross vehicle weight, a gross vehicle weight rating, a gross combination weight, or a gross combination weight rating of 10,001 or more pounds; or the vehicle is designed to transport more than 15 passengers, including the driver; or the vehicle is designed to carry 15 or fewer passengers and is operated by a contract carrier transporting employees in the course of their employment on a highway of this State; or the vehicle is used in the transportation of hazardous materials in a quantity requiring placarding under the Illinois Hazardous Materials Transportation Act.[1] This definition shall not include farm machinery, fertilizer spreaders, and other special agricultural movement equipment described in Section 3–809 nor implements of husbandry as defined in Section 1–130;

"Officer" means Illinois State Police Officer;

"Person" means any natural person or individual, governmental body, firm, association, partnership, copartnership, joint venture, company, corporation, joint stock company, trust, estate or any other legal entity or their legal representative, agent or assigns.

P.A. 76–1586, § 18b–101, added by P.A. 86–611, § 1, eff. Sept. 1, 1989. Amended by P.A. 87–829, § 1, eff. Jan. 17, 1992; P.A. 90–89, § 15, eff. Jan. 1, 1998; P.A. 91–179, § 5, eff. Jan. 1, 2000; P.A. 92–108, § 5, eff. Jan. 1, 2002.

Formerly Ill.Rev.Stat.1991, ch. 95 ½, ¶ 18b–101.

1 430 ILCS 30/1 et seq.

5/18b–102. Authority of Department

§ 18b–102. Authority of Department. To the extent necessary to administer this Chapter, the Department is authorized to:

(a) Adopt by reference all or any portion of the Federal Motor Carrier Safety Regulations of the United States Department of Transportation, as they are now or hereafter amended.

(b) Conduct investigations; make reports; issue subpoenas; conduct hearings; require the production of relevant documents, records and property; take depositions; and, in conjunction with the Illinois State Police, conduct directly or indirectly research, development, demonstrations and training activities.

(c) Authorize any officer or Department employee to enter upon, inspect and examine at reasonable times and in a reasonable manner, the records and properties of persons to the extent such records and properties relate to the transportation by motor vehicle of persons or property.

(d) Conduct a continuing review of all aspects of the transportation of persons and property by motor vehicle in order to determine and recommend appropriate steps to assure safe transportation by motor vehicle in Illinois.

(e) Administer and enforce the provisions of this Chapter and any rules and regulations issued under this Chapter. Only the Illinois State Police shall be authorized to stop and inspect any commercial motor vehicle or driver at any time for the purpose of determining compliance with the provisions of this Chapter or rules and regulations issued under this Chapter.

P.A.76–1586, § 18b–102, added by P.A. 86–611, § 1, eff. Sept. 1, 1989. Amended by P.A. 87–829, § 1, eff. Jan. 17, 1992; P.A. 90–89, § 15, eff. Jan. 1, 1998.

Formerly Ill.Rev.Stat.1991, ch. 95 ½, ¶ 18b–102.

5/18b–103. Compliance with this Chapter

§ 18b–103. Compliance with this Chapter. Transportation by motor vehicle of persons or property in commerce that is not in compliance with this Chapter or any rules and regulations issued under this Act is prohibited.

P.A. 76–1586, § 18b–103, added by P.A. 86–611, § 1, eff. Sept. 1, 1989.

Formerly Ill.Rev.Stat.1991, ch. 95 ½, ¶ 18b–103.

5/18b–103.1. Obedience to Police Officer

§ 18b–103.1. Obedience to Police Officer.

(a) No person shall willfully fail or refuse to comply with any lawful order or direction of any officer authorized by law to enforce this Chapter and to perform vehicle and driver motor carrier safety inspections under this Chapter. Lawful orders or directions shall include providing documentation and answering questions necessary to determine compliance with the provisions of this Chapter. The driver or owner shall assist the officer, as needed, during the course of any such inspection.

(b) Any person who violates this Section shall be guilty of a Class C misdemeanor offense.

P.A. 76–1586, § 18b–103.1, added by P.A. 87–768, § 2, eff. Oct. 10, 1991. Amended by P.A. 88–476, § 2, eff. July 1, 1994.

Formerly Ill.Rev.Stat.1991, ch. 95 ½, ¶ 18b–103.1.

5/18b–104. Cooperation with State Agencies—Records and Data—Availability

§ 18b–104. Cooperation with State Agencies—Records and Data—Availability. The Department shall cooperate with other State agencies regulating transportation by motor vehicles and may enter into interagency agreements for the purpose of sharing data. The Department shall enter into an interagency agreement with the Illinois State Police for the purpose of enforcing any provisions of this Chapter and the rules and regulations issued under this Chapter.

P.A. 76–1586, § 18b–104, added by P.A. 86–611, § 1, eff. Sept. 1, 1989.

Formerly Ill.Rev.Stat.1991, ch. 95 ½, ¶ 18b–104.

5/18b–105. Rules and Regulations

§ 18b–105. Rules and Regulations.

(a) The Department is authorized to make and adopt reasonable rules and regulations and orders consistent with law necessary to carry out the provisions of this Chapter.

(b) The following parts of Title 49 of the Code of Federal Regulations, as now in effect, are hereby adopted by reference as though they were set out in full:

Part 383—Commercial Driver's License Standards, Requirements, and Penalties;

Part 385—Safety Fitness Procedures;

Part 390—Federal Motor Carrier Safety Regulations: General;

Part 391—Qualifications of Drivers;

Part 392—Driving of Motor Vehicles;

Part 393—Parts and Accessories Necessary for Safe Operation;

Part 395—Hours of Service of Drivers, except as provided in Section 18b–106.1; and

Part 396—Inspection, Repair and Maintenance.

(b–5) Individuals who meet the requirements set forth in the definition of "medical examiner" in Section 390.5 of Part 390 of Title 49 of the Code of Federal Regulations may act as medical examiners in accordance with Part 391 of Title 49 of the Code of Federal Regulations.

(c) The following parts and Sections of the Federal Motor Carrier Safety Regulations shall not apply to those intrastate carriers, drivers or vehicles subject to subsection (b).

(1) Section 393.93 of Part 393 for those vehicles manufactured before June 30, 1972.

(2) Section 393.86 of Part 393 for those vehicles which are registered as farm trucks under subsection (c) of Section 3–815 of this Code.

(3) (Blank).

(4) (Blank).

(5) Paragraph (b)(1) of Section 391.11 of Part 391.

(6) All of Part 395 for all agricultural movements as defined in Chapter 1, between the period of February 1 through November 30 each year, and all farm to market agricultural transportation as defined in Chapter 1 and for grain hauling operations within a radius of 200 air miles of the normal work reporting location.

(7) Paragraphs (b)(3) (insulin dependent diabetic) and (b)(10) (minimum visual acuity) of Section 391.41 of part 391, but only for any driver who immediately prior to July 29, 1986 was eligible and licensed to operate a motor vehicle subject to this Section and was engaged in operating such vehicles, and who was disqualified on July 29, 1986 by the adoption of Part 391 by reason of the application of paragraphs (b)(3) and (b)(10) of Section 391.41 with respect to a physical condition existing at that time unless such driver has a record of accidents which would indicate a lack of ability to operate a motor vehicle in a safe manner.

(d) Intrastate carriers subject to the recording provisions of Section 395.8 of Part 395 of the Federal Motor Carrier Safety Regulations shall be exempt as established under paragraph (1) of Section 395.8; provided, however, for the purpose of this Code, drivers shall operate within a 150 air-mile radius of the normal work reporting location to qualify for exempt status.

(e) Regulations adopted by the Department subsequent to those adopted under subsection (b) hereof shall be identical in substance to the Federal Motor Carrier Safety Regulations of the United States Department of Transportation and adopted in accordance with the procedures for rulemaking in Section 5–35 of the Illinois Administrative Procedure Act. [1]

P.A. 76–1586, § 18b–105, added by P.A. 86–611, § 1, eff. Sept. 1, 1989. Amended by P.A. 87–829, § 1, eff. Jan. 17, 1992; P.A. 88–45, Art. III, § 3–128, eff. July 6, 1993; P.A. 88–476, § 2, eff. July 1, 1994; P.A. 90–89, § 15, eff. Jan. 1, 1998; P.A. 90–228, § 5, eff. July 25, 1997; P.A. 90–655, § 153, eff. July 30, 1998; P.A. 91–179, § 5, eff. Jan. 1, 2000; P.A. 92–108, § 5, eff. Jan. 1, 2002; P.A. 92–249, § 5, eff. Jan. 1, 2002; P.A. 92–651, § 77, eff. July 11, 2002; P.A. 92–703, § 10, eff. July 19, 2002.

Formerly Ill.Rev.Stat.1991, ch. 95 ½, ¶ 18b–105.

[1] 5 ILCS 100/5–35.

P.A. 92–651, the First 2002 General Revisory Act, amended various Acts to delete obsolete text, to correct patent and technical errors, to revise cross references, to resolve multiple actions in the 91st and 92nd General Assemblies and to make certain technical corrections in P.A. 91–937 through P.A. 92–520.

See 5 ILCS 70/6 as to the effect of (1) more than one amendment of a section at the same session of the General Assembly or (2) two or more acts relating to the same subject matter enacted by the same General Assembly.

5/18b–106. Application of Chapter and Regulations

§ 18b–106. Application of Chapter and Regulations. Except as expressly specified within this Chapter, this Chapter and the rules and regulations issued under this Chapter shall be applicable to all persons employing drivers, drivers and commercial motor vehicles which transport property or passengers in interstate or intrastate commerce.

P.A. 76–1586, § 18b–106, added by P.A. 86–611, § 1, eff. Sept. 1, 1989. Amended by P.A. 87–829, § 1, eff. Jan. 17, 1992.

Formerly Ill.Rev.Stat.1991, ch. 95½, ¶ 18b–106.

5/18b–106.1. Hours of service of drivers employed by contract carriers transporting employees in the course of their employment

§ 18b–106.1. Hours of service of drivers employed by contract carriers transporting employees in the course of their employment. A contract carrier shall limit the hours of service by a driver transporting employees in the course of their employment on a road or highway of this State in a vehicle designed to carry 15 or fewer passengers to 12 hours of vehicle operation per day, 15 hours of on-duty service per day, and 70 hours of on-duty service in 7 consecutive days. The contract carrier shall require a driver who has 12 hours of vehicle operation per day or 15 hours of on-duty service per day to have at least 8 consecutive hours off duty before operating a vehicle again.

P.A. 76–1586, § 18b–106.1, added by P.A. 92–108, § 5, eff. Jan. 1, 2002.

5/18b–107. Violations—Civil penalties

§ 18b–107. Violations—Civil penalties.

Except as provided in Section 18b–108, any person who is determined by the Department after reasonable notice and opportunity for a fair and impartial hearing to have committed an act in violation of this Chapter or any rule or regulation issued under this Chapter is liable to the State for a civil penalty. Such person is subject to a civil penalty of not more than $5,000 for such violation, except that a person committing a railroad-highway grade crossing violation is subject to a civil penalty of not more than $10,000, and, if any such violation is a continuing one, each day of violation constitutes a separate offense. The amount of any such penalty shall be assessed by the Department by a written notice. In determining the amount of such penalty, the Department shall take into account the nature, circumstances, extent and gravity of the violation and, with respect to a person found to have committed such violation, the degree of culpability, history or prior offenses, ability to pay, effect on ability to continue to do business and such other matters as justice may require.

Such civil penalty is recoverable in an action brought by the State's Attorney or the Attorney General on behalf of the State in the circuit court or, prior to referral to the State's Attorney or the Attorney General, such civil penalty may be compromised by the Department. The amount of such penalty when finally determined (or agreed upon in compromise), may be deducted from any sums owed by the State to the person charged. All civil penalties collected under this subsection shall be deposited in the Road Fund.

P.A. 76–1586, § 18b–107, added by P.A. 86–611, § 1, eff. Sept. 1, 1989. Amended by P.A. 86–1236, § 1, eff. Jan. 1, 1991; P.A. 92–249, § 5, eff. Jan. 1, 2002.

Formerly Ill.Rev.Stat.1991, ch. 95 ½, ¶ 18b–107.

5/18b–108. Violations; Criminal penalties

§ 18b–108. Violations; Criminal penalties.

(a) The provisions of Chapter 16 [1] shall be applicable to acts committed by a driver of a motor vehicle that violate this Chapter or any rule or regulation issued under this Chapter.

(b) Any driver who willfully violates any provision of this Chapter or any rule or regulation issued under this Chapter is guilty of a Class 4 felony. In addition to any other penalties prescribed by law, the maximum fine for each offense is $10,000. Such violation shall be prosecuted by the State's Attorney or the Attorney General.

(c) Any person, other than a driver, who willfully violates or causes another to violate any provision of this Chapter or any rule or regulation issued under this Chapter is guilty of a Class 3 felony. In addition to any other penalties prescribed by law, the maximum fine for each offense is $25,000. Such violation shall be prosecuted at the request of the Department by the State's Attorney or the Attorney General.

P.A. 76–1586, § 18b–108, added by P.A. 86–611, § 1, eff. Sept. 1, 1989. Amended by P.A. 86–1236, § 1, eff. Jan. 1, 1991; P.A. 88–476, § 2, eff. July 1, 1994; P.A. 89–179, § 5, eff. Jan. 1, 1996.

Formerly Ill.Rev.Stat.1991, ch. 95 ½, ¶ 18b–108.

[1] 625 ILCS 5/16–101 et seq.

5/18b–109. Enforcement of Rules and Regulations

§ 18b–109. Enforcement of Rules and Regulations. Only the Illinois State Police shall enforce the rules and regulations issued under this Chapter against drivers. The Department and the Illinois State Police shall enforce the rules and regulations issued under this Chapter against persons other than drivers.

P.A. 76–1586, § 18b–109, added by P.A. 86–611, § 1, eff. Sept. 1, 1989.

Formerly Ill.Rev.Stat.1991, ch. 95 ½, ¶ 18b–109.

5/18b–110. Conflict With Other Laws

§ 18b–110. Conflict With Other Laws. This Chapter is not intended to affect any State law or ordinance of a local authority now in effect or intrude upon the duties and responsibilities of any State or local officer with respect to matters related to the subject to this Chapter, but in the case of any conflict with other State laws or ordinance of local authorities relating to the transportation of persons or property by highway, the provisions of this Chapter shall control.

P.A. 76–1586, § 18b–110, added by P.A. 86–611, § 1, eff. Sept. 1, 1989.

Formerly Ill.Rev.Stat.1991, ch. 95 ½, ¶ 18b–110.

5/18b–111. Review Under Administrative Review Law

§ 18b–111. Review Under Administrative Review Law. All administrative decisions of the Department under this Chapter shall be subject to judicial review under the Administrative Review Law, as now or hereafter amended.[1]

P.A. 76–1586, § 18b–111, added by P.A. 86–611, § 1, eff. Sept. 1, 1989. Amended by P.A. 90–89, § 15, eff. Jan. 1, 1998.

Formerly Ill.Rev.Stat.1991, ch. 95 ½, ¶ 18b–111.

[1] 735 ILCS 5/3–101 et seq.

5/18b–112. Intermodal trailer, chassis, and safety

§ 18b–112. Intermodal trailer, chassis, and safety.

(a) Definitions. For purposes of this Section:

"Department" means the Department of State Police.

"Equipment interchange agreement" means a written document executed by the intermodal equipment provider and operator at the time the equipment is interchanged by the provider to the operator.

"Equipment provider" is the owner of an intermodal trailer, chassis, or container. This includes any forwarding company, water carrier, steamship line, railroad, vehicle equipment leasing company, and their subsidiary or affiliated companies owning the equipment.

"Federal motor carrier safety regulations" means regulations promulgated by the United States Department of Transportation governing the condition and maintenance of commercial motor vehicles contained in Title 49 of the United States Code of Federal Regulations on the day of enactment of this Act or as amended or revised by the United States Department of Transportation thereafter.

"Interchange" means the act of providing a vehicle to a motor carrier by an equipment provider for the purpose of transporting the vehicle for loading or unloading by another party or the repositioning of the vehicle for the benefit of the equipment provider. "Interchange" does not include the leasing of the vehicle by a motor carrier from an owner-operator pursuant to subpart B of Part 376 of Title 49 of the Code of Federal Regulations or the leasing of a vehicle to a motor carrier for use in the motor carrier's over-the-road freight hauling operations.

"Operator" means a motor carrier or driver of a commercial motor vehicle.

"Vehicle" means an intermodal trailer, chassis, or container.

(b) Responsibility of equipment provider. An equipment provider shall not interchange or offer for interchange a vehicle with an operator for use on a highway which vehicle is in violation of the requirements contained in the federal motor carrier safety regulations. It is the responsibility of the equipment provider to inspect and, if a vehicle at the time of inspection does not comply with all federal motor carrier safety regulation requirements, perform the necessary repairs on, all vehicles prior to interchange or offering for interchange.

(c) Duty of inspection by the operator. Before interchanging a vehicle with an operator, an equipment provider must provide the operator the opportunity and facilities to perform a visual inspection of the equipment. The operator must determine if it complies with the provisions of the federal motor carrier safety regulation capable of being determined from an inspection. If the operator determines that the vehicle does not comply with the provisions of the federal motor carrier safety regulations, the equipment provider shall immediately perform the necessary repairs to the vehicle so that it complies with the federal motor carrier safety regulations or shall immediately provide the operator with another vehicle.

(d) Presumption of defect prior to interchange.

(1) If as a result of a roadside inspection by the Department, any of the defects listed in paragraph (2) are discovered, a rebuttable presumption existed at the time of the interchange. If a summons or complaint is issued to the operator, the operator may seek relief pursuant to paragraph (3).

(2) A rebuttable presumption exists that the following defects were present at the time of the interchange:

(A) There is a defect with the brake drum when:

(I) the drum cracks;

(II) the lining is loose or missing; or

(III) the lining is saturated with oil.

(B) There is a defect of inoperative brakes when:

(I) there is no movement of any components;

(II) there are missing, broken, or loose components; or

(III) there are mismatched components.

(C) There is a defect with the air lines and tubing when:

(I) there is a bulge and swelling;

(II) there is an audible air leak; or

(III) there are air lines broken,cracked, or crimped.

(D) There is a defect with the reservoir tank when there is any separation of original attachment points.

(E) There is a defect with the frames when:

(I) there is any cracked, loose, sagging, or broken frame members which measure one and one-half inch in web or one inch or longer in bottom flange or any crack extending from web radius into bottom flange; or

(II) there is any condition which causes moving parts to come in contact with the frame.

(F) There is an electrical defect when wires are chaffed.

(G) There is a defect with the wheel assembly when:

(I) there is low or no oil;

(II) there is oil leakage on brake components;

(III) there are lug nuts that are loose or missing; or

(IV) the wheel bearings are not properly maintained.

(H) There is a defect with the tires when:

(I) there is improper inflation;

(II) there is tire separation from the casing; or

(III) there are exposed plys or belting material.

(I) There is defect with rim cracks when:

(I) there is any circumferential crack, except a manufactured crack; or

(II) there is a lock or side ring cracked, bent, broken, sprung, improperly seated, or mismatched.

(J) There is a defect with the suspension when:

(I) there are spring assembly leaves broken, missing, or separated; or

(II) there are spring hanger, u-bolts, or axle positioning components cracked, broken loose, or missing.

(K) There is a defect with the chassis locking pins when there is any twist lock or fitting for securement that is sprung, broken, or improperly latched.

(3) If an operator receives a citation for a violation due to a defect in any equipment specified in subsection (d)(2), the equipment provider shall reimburse the operator for any:

(A) fines and costs, including court costs and reasonable attorneys fees, incurred as a result of the citation; and

(B) costs incurred by the operator to repair the defects specified in the citation, including any towing costs incurred.

The equipment provider shall reimburse the operator within 30 days of the final court action. If the equipment provider fails to reimburse the operator within 30 days, the operator has a civil cause of action against the equipment provider.

(e) Fines and penalties. Any person violating the provisions of this Section shall be fined no less than $50 and no more than $500 for each violation.

(f) Obligation of motor carrier. Nothing in Section is intended to eliminate the responsibility and obligation of a motor carrier and operator to maintain and operate vehicles in accordance with the federal motor carrier safety regulations and applicable State and local laws and regulations.

(g) This Section shall not be applied, construed, or implemented in any manner inconsistent with, or in conflict with, any provision of the federal motor carrier safety regulations.

P.A. 76–1586, § 18b–112, added by P.A. 91–662, § 5, eff. July 1, 2000.

CHAPTER 18c. ILLINOIS COMMERCIAL TRANSPORTATION LAW

Enactment

Chapter 18c was added by P.A. 84–796, § 1, eff. Jan. 1, 1986.

SUB–CHAPTER 1. GENERAL PROVISIONS

ARTICLE I. SHORT TITLE, LEGISLATIVE INTENT, STATE TRANSPORTATION POLICY, AND DEFINITIONS

Section

ARTICLE II. JURISDICTION AND POWER OF THE COMMISSION

ARTICLE I. SHORT TITLE, LEGISLATIVE INTENT, STATE TRANSPORTATION POLICY, AND DEFINITIONS

5/18c-1101. Short Title

§ 18c-1101. Short Title. This Chapter shall be known and may be cited as the "Illinois Commercial Transportation Law".

P.A. 76-1586, § 18c-1101, added by P.A. 84-796, § 1, eff. Jan. 1, 1986.

Formerly Ill.Rev.Stat.1991, ch. 95 ½, ¶ 18c-1101.

5/18c-1102. Legislative Intent

§ 18c-1102. Legislative Intent. The General Assembly finds that:

(a) a comprehensive recodification of existing transportation regulatory statutes is needed to delete obsolete provisions and facilitate a coordinated approach to regulation of motor carriers, rail carriers, and brokers;

(b) the accelerating pace of change in the transportation industry, as an outgrowth of changing economic conditions and federal legislation, necessitates the streamlining of regulatory procedures to allow for prompt action to protect the interests of the people of the State of Illinois; and

(c) an increasing incidence of unlawful activity by unlicensed carriers and others has rendered existing enforcement mechanisms inadequate.

Where the language of any provision in this Chapter is substantially similar to the language in the predecessor statute, the legislative intent expressed in this Chapter shall be the same as the legislative intent embodied in the predecessor statute as construed by the courts of this State and, where appropriate, reports of the Illinois Motor Vehicle Laws Commission.

P.A. 76-1586, § 18c-1102, added by P.A. 84-796, § 1, eff. Jan. 1, 1986. Amended by P.A. 89-42, § 10, eff. Jan. 1, 1996; P.A. 91-357, § 231, eff. July 29, 1999.

Formerly Ill.Rev.Stat.1991, ch. 95 ½, ¶ 18c-1102.

5/18c-1103. State Transportation Policy

§ 18c-1103. State Transportation Policy. It is hereby declared to be the policy of the State of Illinois to actively supervise and regulate commercial transportation of persons and property within this state. This policy shall be carried out in such manner as to: (a) promote adequate, economical, efficient and responsive commercial transportation service, with adequate revenues to carriers and reasonable rates to the public, and without discrimination; (b) recognize and preserve the inherent advantages of, and foster sound economic conditions in, the several modes of commercial transportation in the public interest; (c) develop and preserve a commercial transportation system properly supportive of the broad economic development goals of the State of Illinois; (d) create economic and employment opportunities in commercial transportation and affected industries through economic growth and development; (e) encourage fair wages and safe and suitable working conditions in the transportation industry; (f) protect the public safety through administration of a program of safety standards and insurance; (g) insure a stable and well-coordinated transportation system for shippers, carriers and the public; and (h) cooperate with the federal government, the several states, and with the organizations representing states and commercial transportation service providers and consumers.

P.A. 76-1586, § 18c-1103, added by P.A. 84-796, § 1, eff. Jan. 1, 1986.

Formerly Ill.Rev.Stat.1991, ch. 95 ½, ¶ 18c-1103.

5/18c-1104. Definitions

§ 18c-1104. Definitions. The following terms, when used in this Chapter, have the hereinafter designated meanings unless their context clearly indicates otherwise:

(1) "Broker" means any person other than a motor carrier of property, that arranges, offers to arrange, or holds itself out, by solicitation, advertisement, or otherwise, as arranging or offering to arrange for-hire transportation of property or other service in connection therewith by a motor carrier of

property which holds or is required to hold a license issued by the Commission.

(2) "Carrier" means any motor carrier or rail carrier other than a private carrier.

(3) "Certificate" means a certificate of public convenience and necessity issued under this Chapter to common carriers of household goods.

(4) "Commission" means the Illinois Commerce Commission.

(5) "Commission regulations and orders" means rules and regulations adopted and orders or decisions issued by the Commission pursuant to this Chapter; any certificate, permit, broker's license or other license or registration issued pursuant to such rules, regulations, orders and decisions; and all terms, conditions, or limitations thereof.

(6) (Blank).

(7) (Blank).

(8) (Blank).

(9) "Discrimination" means undue discrimination in the context of the particular mode of transportation involved.

(10) "Farm crossing" means a crossing used for agricultural and livestock purposes only.

(11) "For-hire" means for compensation or hire, regardless of the form of compensation and whether compensation is direct or indirect.

(12) "Freight forwarder" means any person other than a motor carrier, rail carrier, or common carrier by pipeline which holds itself out as a common carrier to provide transportation of property, for compensation or hire, which, in the rendition of its services:

(a) Undertakes responsibility for the consolidation (where applicable), transportation, break-bulk (where applicable), and distribution of such property from the point of receipt to the point of delivery; and

(b) Utilizes, for the transportation of such property, the services of one or more motor carriers or rail carriers.

(13) "Hazardous material" means any substance or material in a quantity and form determined by the federal Office of Hazardous Materials and the Federal Railroad Administration to be capable of posing an unreasonable risk to health, safety, or property when transported in commerce.

(13.1) "Household goods" means:

(A) Personal effects and property used or to be used in a dwelling when a part of the equipment or supply of such dwelling; except that this subdivision (13.1) shall not be construed to include property moving from a factory or store, except such property as the householder has purchased with intent to use in his or her dwelling and that is transported at the request of, and the transportation charges paid to the carrier by, the householder;

(B) Furniture, fixtures, equipment, and the property of stores, offices, museums, institutions, hospitals, or other establishments, when a part of the stock, equipment, or supply of such stores, offices, museums, institutions, hospitals, or other establishments; except that this subdivision (13.1) shall not be construed to include the stock-in-trade of any establishment, whether consignor or consignee, other than used furniture and used fixtures, except when transported as an incident to the moving of the establishment, or a portion thereof, from one location to another; and

(C) Articles, including, but not limited to, objects of art, displays, and exhibits, which, because of their unusual nature or value, require the specialized handling and equipment usually employed in moving household goods; except that this subdivision (13.1) shall not be construed to include any article, whether crated or uncrated, that does not, because of its unusual nature or value, require the specialized handling and equipment usually employed in moving household goods.

(13.2) "Household goods carrier" means a motor carrier of property authorized to transport household goods.

(13.3) "Household goods common carrier" means any household goods carrier engaged in transportation for the general public over regular or irregular routes. Household goods common carriers may also be referred to as "common carriers of household goods".

(13.4) "Household goods contract carrier" means any household goods carrier engaged in transportation under contract with a limited number of shippers (that shall not be freight forwarders, shippers' agents or brokers) that either (a) assigns motor vehicles for a continuing period of time to the exclusive use of the shipper or shippers served, or (b) furnishes transportation service designed to meet the distinct need of the shipper or shippers served. Household goods contract carriers may also be referred to as "contract carriers of household goods".

(14) "Interstate carrier" means any person engaged in the for-hire transportation of persons or property in interstate or foreign commerce in this State, whether or not such transportation is pursuant to authority issued to it by the Interstate Commerce Commission.

(15) "Intrastate carrier" means any person engaged in the for-hire transportation of persons or property in intrastate commerce in this State.

(16) "Interstate commerce" means commerce between a point in the State of Illinois and a point outside the State of Illinois, or between points outside the State of Illinois when such commerce moves through Illinois, or between points in Illinois moving through another state in a bona fide operation that is either exempt from federal regulation or moves under a certificate or permit issued by the Interstate Commerce Commission authorizing interstate transportation, whether such commerce moves wholly by motor vehicle or partly by motor vehicle and partly by any other regulated means of transportation where the commodity does not come to rest or change its identity during the movement, and includes commerce originating or terminating in a foreign country moving through the State of Illinois.

(17) "Intrastate commerce" means commerce moving wholly between points within the State of Illinois, whether such commerce moves wholly by one transportation mode or partly by one mode and partly by any other mode of transportation.

(18) "License" means any certificate, permit, broker's license, or other license issued under this Chapter. For purposes of Article III of Sub-chapter 4 of this Chapter,[1] "license" does not include a "public carrier certificate".

(19) "Motor carrier" means any person engaged in the transportation of property or passengers, or both, for hire, over the public roads of this State, by motor vehicle. Motor carriers engaged in the transportation of property are referred to as "motor carriers of property"; motor carriers engaged in the transportation of passengers are referred to as "motor carriers of passengers" or "bus companies".

(20) "Motor vehicle" means any vehicle, truck, trucktractor, trailer or semitrailer propelled or drawn by mechanical power and used upon the highways of the State in the transportation of property or passengers.

(21) "Non-relocation towing" means the:

(a) For-hire transportation of vehicles by use of wrecker or towing equipment, other than the removal of trespassing vehicles from private property subject to the provisions of Chapter 18a of this Code,[2] and other than transportation exempted by Section 18c–4102; and

(b) For-hire towing of wheeled property other than vehicles.

(22) "Notice" means with regard to all proceedings except enforcement proceedings instituted on the motion of the Commission, and except for interstate motor carrier registrations, public notice by publication in the official state newspaper, unless otherwise provided in this Chapter.

(23) "Official state newspaper" means the newspaper designated and certified to the Commission annually by the Director of Central Management Services of the State of Illinois, or, if said Director fails to certify to the Commission the name and address of the official newspaper selected by the Director prior to expiration of the previous certification, the newspaper designated in the most recent certification.

(24) "Party" means any person admitted as a party to a Commission proceeding or seeking and entitled as a matter of right to admission as a party to a Commission proceeding.

(25) "Permit" means a permit issued under this Chapter to contract carriers of property by motor vehicle.

(26) "Person" means any natural person or legal entity, whether such entity is a proprietorship, partnership, corporation, association, or other entity, and, where a provision concerns the acts or omissions of a person, includes the partners, officers, employees, and agents of the person, as well as any trustees, assignees, receivers, or personal representatives of the person.

(27) "Private carrier by motor vehicle" means any person engaged in the transportation of property or passengers by motor vehicle other than for hire, whether the person is the owner, lessee or bailee of the lading or otherwise, when the transportation is for the purpose of sale, lease, or bailment and in furtherance of the person's primary business, other than transportation. "Private carriers by motor vehicle" may be referred to as "private carriers". Ownership, lease or bailment of the lading is not sufficient proof of a private carrier operation if the carrier is, in fact, engaged in the transportation of property for-hire.

(27.1) "Public carrier" means a motor carrier of property, other than a household goods carrier.

(27.2) "Public carrier certificate" means a certificate issued to a motor carrier to transport property, other than household goods, in intrastate commerce. The issuance of a public carrier certificate shall not be subject to the provisions of Article I of Sub-chapter 2 of this Chapter.[3]

(28) "Public convenience and necessity" shall be construed to have the same meaning under this Chapter as it was construed by the courts to have under the Illinois Motor Carrier of Property Law,[4] with respect to motor carriers of property, and the Public Utilities Act [5] with respect to motor carriers of passengers and rail carriers.

(29) "Public interest" shall be construed to have the same meaning under this Chapter as it was construed by the courts to have under the Illinois Motor Carrier of Property Law.

(30) "Rail carrier" means any person engaged in the transportation of property or passengers for hire by railroad, together with all employees or agents of such person or entity, and all property used, controlled, or owned by such person or entity.

(31) "Railroad" means track and associated structures, including bridges, tunnels, switches, spurs, terminals and other facilities, and equipment, including engines, freight cars, passenger cars, cabooses, and other equipment, used in the transportation of property or passengers by rail.

(32) "Rail yard" means a system of parallel tracks, crossovers and switches where cars are switched and made up into trains, and where cars, locomotives, and other rolling stock are kept when not in use or awaiting repairs. A "rail yard" may also be referred to as a "yard".

(33) "Rate" means every individual or joint rate, fare, toll, or charge of any carrier or carriers, any provisions relating to application thereof, and any tariff or schedule containing rates and provisions. The term "tariff" refers to a publication or document containing motor common carrier rates and provisions or rates and provisions applicable via rail carrier under contracts established pursuant to 49 U.S. Code 10713. The term "schedule" refers to a publication or document containing motor contract carrier rates and provisions.

(34) "Registration" means a registration issued to an interstate carrier.

(35) "Shipper" means the consignor or consignee.

(36) "Terminal area" means, in addition to the area within the corporate boundary of an incorporated city, village, municipality, or community center, the area (whether incorporated or unincorporated) within 10 air miles of the corporate limits of the base city, village, municipality, or community center, including all of any city, village or municipality which lies within such area.

(37) "Transfer" means the sale, lease, consolidation, merger, acquisition or change of control, or other transfer of a license, in whole or in part.

(38) "Transportation" means the actual movement of property or passengers by motor vehicle (without regard to ownership of vehicles or equipment used in providing transportation service) or rail together with loading, unloading, and any other accessorial or ancillary service provided by the carrier in connection with movement by motor vehicle or rail, which is performed by or on behalf of the carriers, its employees or agents, or under the authority or direction of the carrier or under the apparent authority or direction and with the knowledge of the carrier. Transportation of property by motor vehicle includes driveaway or towaway delivery service.

(39) "Towing" means the pushing, towing, or drawing of wheeled property by means of a crane, hoist, towbar, towline, or auxiliary axle.

(40) "Wrecker or towing equipment" means tow trucks or auxiliary axles, when used in relation to towing accidentally wrecked or disabled vehicles; and roll-back carriers or trailers, when used in relation to transporting accidentally wrecked or disabled vehicles. Wrecker or towing equipment does not include car carriers or trailers other than roll-back car carriers or trailers.

P.A. 76–1586, § 18c–1104, added by P.A. 84–796, § 1, eff. Jan. 1, 1986. Amended by P.A. 84–1025, § 2, eff. Jan. 1, 1986; P.A. 84–1311, § 1, eff. Aug. 27, 1986; P.A. 85–553, § 2, eff. Sept. 18, 1987; P.A. 85–963, § 1, eff. July 1, 1988; P.A. 85–1209, Art. II, § 2–51, eff. Aug. 30, 1988; P.A. 89–42, § 10, eff. Jan. 1, 1996; P.A. 89–444, § 5, eff. Jan. 25, 1996; P.A. 90–14, Art. 2, § 2–225, eff. July 1, 1997.

Formerly Ill.Rev.Stat.1991, ch. 95 ½, ¶ 18c–1104.

1 625 ILCS 5/18c–4301 et seq.

2 625 ILCS 5/18a–100 et seq.

3 625 ILCS 5/18c–2101 et seq.

4 625 ILCS 5/18–101 et seq. (repealed).

5 220 ILCS 5/1–101 et seq.

P.A. 90–14, Article 2, of the First 1997 General Revisory Act, resolved multiple actions in the 89th General Assembly and made certain technical corrections in P.A. 89–443 through P.A. 89–707.

ARTICLE II. JURISDICTION AND POWER OF THE COMMISSION

5/18c–1201. Jurisdiction

§ 18c–1201. Jurisdiction. The jurisdiction of the Commission under this Chapter shall extend to for-hire transportation by motor carrier and rail carrier, the activities of brokers, and to other activities specifically enumerated herein, within the State of Illinois, and except as otherwise provided elsewhere in this Chapter shall extend only to intrastate commerce.

P.A. 76–1586, § 18c–1201, added by P.A. 84–796, § 1, eff. Jan. 1, 1986. Amended by P.A. 89–42, § 10, eff. Jan. 1, 1996.

Formerly Ill.Rev.Stat.1991, ch. 95 ½, ¶ 18c–1201.

5/18c–1202. Enumeration of Powers

§ 18c–1202. Enumeration of Powers. The Commission shall have the power to:

(1) Administer and enforce provisions of this Chapter;

(2) Regulate the entry, exit, and services of carriers; as to public carriers, this power is limited to matters relating to insurance and safety standards;

(3) Regulate rates and practices of household goods carriers, rail carriers, passenger carriers, and common carriers by pipeline;

(4) Establish and maintain systems of accounting as well as reporting and record-keeping requirements for household goods carriers, rail carriers, passenger carriers, and common carriers by pipeline;

(5) Establish and maintain systems for the classification of carriers, commodities and services;

(6) Regulate practices, terms and conditions relating to the leasing of equipment and to the interchange of equipment among carriers; as to public carriers, this power is limited to matters relating to insurance and safety standards;

(7) Protect the public safety through insurance and safety standards;

(8) Regulate brokers in accordance with provisions of this Chapter;

(9) Adopt appropriate regulations setting forth the standards and procedures by which it will administer and enforce this Chapter, with such regulations being uniform for all modes of transportation or different for the different modes as will, in the opinion of the Commission, best effectuate the purposes of this Chapter;

(10) Conduct hearings and investigations, on its own motion or the motion of a person;

(11) Adjudicate disputes, hear complaints or other petitions for relief, and settle such matters by stipulation or agreement;

(12) Create special procedures for the receipt and handling of consumer complaints;

(13) Issue certificates describing the extent to which a person is exempt under the provisions of this Chapter;

(14) Construe this Chapter, Commission regulations and orders, except that the rule of ejusdem generis shall not be applicable in the construction or interpretation of any license, certificate or permit originally issued under the Illinois Motor Carrier of Property Law and now governed by subchapter 4 of this Chapter [1] or issued under subchapter 4 of this Chapter prior to July 1, 1989;

(15) Employ such persons as are needed to administer and enforce this Chapter, in such capacities as they are needed, whether as hearings examiners, special examiners, enforcement officers, investigators, or otherwise;

(16) Create advisory committees made up of representatives of the various transportation modes, shippers, receivers, or other members of the public;

(17) Initiate and participate in proceedings in the federal or State courts, and in proceedings before federal or other State agencies, to the extent necessary to effectuate the purposes of this Chapter, provided that participation in specific proceedings is directed, in writing, by the Commission;

(18) Direct any telecommunications carrier to disconnect the telephone number published in any commercial listing of any household goods carrier that does not have a valid license issued by the Commission.

P.A. 76–1586, § 18c–1202, added by P.A. 84–796, § 1, eff. Jan. 1, 1986. Amended by P.A. 85–553, § 2, eff. Sept. 18, 1987; P.A. 86–1005, § 3, eff. Dec. 28, 1989; P.A. 89–444, § 5, eff. Jan. 25, 1996.

Formerly Ill.Rev.Stat.1991, ch. 95 ½, ¶ 18c–1202.

1 Former Ill.Rev.Stat. ch. 95½, ¶ 18–100 et seq. (repealed; see, now, 625 ILCS 5/18c–4101 et seq.).

5/18c–1203. Initial Decisions

§ 18c–1203. Initial Decisions. (1) Delegation of Authority. (a) General Delegation. The power to make an initial decision in all matters under this Chapter and Chapter 18a [1] which are interlocutory or which are not the subject of an active controversy between parties, except in motor carrier of property licensing cases and cases assigned for hearing, is delegated to one or more staff members who shall be designated by the Commission. (b) Delegation to Examiners. The power to make initial decisions shall be vested in the examiner, in all cases assigned for hearing, except in household goods carrier licensing cases.

(2) Form of Decisions. Decisions under this Section shall be by letter notice or directive, signed by the person authorized to make the initial decision. Such notice or directive shall be effective and enforceable in the same manner as an order of the Commission.

(3) Appeal of Initial Decisions. All initial decisions rendered under this Section may be appealed to the Commission. Appeal of interlocutory decisions by an examiner in a case assigned for hearing shall be in accordance with the Commission's Rules of Practice. Appeal of other initial decisions shall be by motion for reconsideration in accordance with Section 18c–2110 of this Chapter.

(4) Enforcement. An initial decision which has not been administratively appealed or the administrative appeal of which has been denied shall be effective and enforceable in the same manner as an order of the Commission.

P.A. 76–1586, § 18c–1203, added by P.A. 85–553, § 2, eff. Sept. 18, 1987. Amended by P.A. 89–444, § 5, eff. Jan. 25, 1996.

Formerly Ill.Rev.Stat.1991, ch. 95 ½, ¶ 18c–1203.

1 625 ILCS 5/18a–100 et seq.

5/18c–1204. Transportation Division

§ 18c–1204. Transportation Division.

(1) Establishment. There shall be established within the staff of the Commission a Transportation Division in which

primary staff responsibility for the administration and enforcement of this Chapter and Chapter 18a shall be vested. The Transportation Division shall be headed by a division manager responsible to the executive director.

(2) Structure. The Transportation Division shall consist of 4 programs and 2 offices. The 4 programs shall be Compliance, Review and Examination, Docketing and Processing, and Rail Safety. Each program shall be headed by a program director and responsible to the division manager, except that in the Compliance Program the 3 staff supervisors shall each be responsible to the division manager. The 2 offices shall be the Office of Transportation Counsel and the Office of the Division Manager. The Office of Transportation Counsel shall be headed by a Chief Counsel responsible to the Division Manager. The Division Manager shall coordinate the activities and responsibilities of the Office of Transportation Counsel with the executive director and the personal assistant serving as staff counsel to the executive director in the office of the executive director, and with the Commission.

(a) The Compliance Program.

(i) The Compliance Program shall consist of a police staff, a rate auditing staff, and a civil penalties staff. These staffs shall be headed by a Chief of Police, a Supervisor of Tariffs and Audits, and a Supervisor of Civil Penalties, respectively.

(ii) The police staff shall be divided into districts with a field office in each district. Each district shall be headed by a working supervisor responsible to the Chief of Police. All staff responsibility for enforcement of this Chapter, except with regard to rail safety, shall be vested in the Compliance Program.

(b) The Review and Examination Program.

(i) Staff responsibility for review of all nonhearing matters under this Chapter and Chapter 18a and examination of all matters assigned for hearing under this Chapter and Chapter 18a shall be vested in the Review and Examination Program, except as otherwise provided in Section 18c–1204b.

(ii) Hearing examiners in the program shall have responsibility for developing a full, complete and impartial record on all issues to be decided in a proceeding; recommending disposition of the issues or making an initial decision on them, as provided in this Chapter; and setting forth in writing the basis for their recommendations or initial decisions. The program director shall be the chief hearing examiner for matters under this Chapter and Chapter 18a with responsibility to insure consistency of recommendations and initial decisions.

(c) The Processing and Docketing Program. All staff responsibility for docketing and processing filings, accounting of receipts and expenditures, issuing, file maintenance and other processing functions under this Chapter and Chapter 18a shall be vested in the Processing Program.

(d) The Rail Safety Program. Staff responsibility for administration and enforcement of the rail safety provisions of this Chapter shall be vested in the Rail Safety Program.

(e) The Office of Transportation Counsel.

(i) All Commission staff responsibility for provision of legal services in connection with any matter under this Chapter, excepting any matter under subchapters 7 and 8 of this Chapter, or in connection with any matter under Chapter 18a shall, except with regard to functions vested in the review and examination program under paragraph (b) of this subsection, be vested exclusively in the Office of Transportation Counsel.

(ii) The Office of Transportation Counsel shall, when directed through the division manager to do so, represent the Commission or Commission staff in administrative or judicial proceedings and render staff advisory opinions to the executive director and the Commission.

(f) Levels of Administration. No additional levels of administration, supervision or authority shall be superimposed, or remain superimposed, between levels prescribed under this Section, and no organizational units may be created within the Transportation Division except as prescribed under this Section.

(3) Additional functions. Staff functions relating to rulemaking, policy recommendations and advisory committees under this Chapter and Chapter 18a shall be vested in the Transportation Division.

The staff shall prepare and distribute to the General Assembly, in April of each year, a report on railway accidents in Illinois which involve hazardous materials. The report shall include the location, substance involved, amounts involved, and the suspected reason for each accident. The report shall also reveal the rail line and point of origin of the hazardous material involved in each accident.

P.A. 76–1586, § 18c–1204, added by P.A. 85–553, § 2, eff. Sept. 18, 1987. Amended by P.A. 86–1005, § 3, eff. Dec. 28, 1989; P.A. 86–1166, § 1, eff. Aug. 10, 1990; P.A. 88–415, § 10, eff. Aug. 20, 1993.

Formerly Ill.Rev.Stat.1991, ch. 95 ½, ¶ 18c–1204.

5/18c–1204a. Docketing Procedures

§ 18c–1204a. Docketing Procedures. (1) Mandatory Docketing Requirement. All pleadings filed with the Commission under this Chapter and Chapter 18a shall be docketed in a timely manner.

(2) Staff Objections. If staff believes a pleading filed with the Commission under this Chapter and Chapter 18a to be defective in any respect, it may file its objection with the Commission in writing, provided a copy of the objection is simultaneously served on the person who filed the pleading and 15 days are allowed for the filing of a reply. The Commission may, if it finds that the pleading is defective, either dismiss the proceeding or permit amendment of the pleading, provided that intervenors are permitted adequate time after amendment to prepare for continuation of the proceeding.

P.A. 76–1586, § 18c–1204a, added by P.A. 85–553, § 2, eff. Sept. 18, 1987.

Formerly Ill.Rev.Stat.1991, ch. 95 ½, ¶ 18c–1204a.

5/18c–1204b. Certification of Records

§ 18c–1204b. Certification of Records. Copies of all official documents and orders filed or deposited according to the law in the office of the Commission under this Chapter or Chapter 18a, certified by the director of the processing and docketing program to be true copies of the originals, under the official seal of the Commission, shall be evidence in like manner as the originals.

P.A. 76–1586, § 18c–1204b, added by P.A. 85–553, § 2, eff. Sept. 18, 1987.

Formerly Ill.Rev.Stat.1991, ch. 95 ½, ¶ 18c–1204b.

5/18c–1204c. Independent Review of Decisions on Administrative Appeal

§ 18c–1204c. Independent Review of Decisions on Administrative Appeal. (1) Requirement of Independent Review. Except as otherwise provided in subsection (3) of this Section:

(a) Review of Staff Decisions. No decision made by other than the Commission shall be reviewed on administrative appeal by the person or board which made the decision, unless the appeal requests review by the person or board which made the decision.

(b) Review of Commission or Employee Board Decisions. No decision made by the Commission or an employee board shall be reviewed on administrative appeal by the person or board which made the formal recommendation pursuant to which the decision was made, unless the appeal requests review by the person or board which made the formal recommendation.

(2) Independent Review Board. (a) Establishment of an Independent Review Board. The Commission shall establish an Independent Review Board which shall review motions for rehearing and reconsideration which do not request review by the person or board which made the decision or the formal recommendation pursuant to which the decision was made.

(b) Composition of the Independent Review Board. The Board shall consist of 3 members appointed by the Commission, one of whom shall be designated as the chairman. The Commission shall appoint the members from Commission staff whose expenses may be allocated to the Transportation Regulatory Fund under Section 18c–1603. If the Transportation Division is not represented on the Board by a voting member, the Commission shall appoint a nonvoting member from the Transportation Division.

(c) Functions of the Independent Review Board. The Board shall review all motions presented to it under this Section. The Board may, in its discretion, review the record of the proceeding and hear oral argument by the parties. The Board shall recommend a decision by the Commission. If a Board member dissents from the recommendation, any dissenting opinion supplied by the member shall be attached.

(3) Applicability of Section. The provisions of this Section shall not apply to any matter arising under Subchapter 7 of this Chapter.

P.A. 76–1586, § 18c–1204c, added by P.A. 85–553, § 2, eff. Sept. 18, 1987. Amended by P.A. 86–1005, § 3, eff. Dec. 28, 1989.

Formerly Ill.Rev.Stat.1991, ch. 95 ½, ¶ 18c–1204c.

5/18c–1204d. Staff participation

§ 18c–1204d. Staff participation. (1) General Provisions. Except as otherwise provided in this Section, Commission staff participation in the administration or enforcement of this Law in a supervisory, advisory, or other capacity shall be limited to personnel whose expenses are, in whole or in part, allocable to the Transportation Regulatory Fund.

(2) Exceptions. The provisions of subsection (1) of this Section shall not apply to:

(a) Staff of the office of chairman and commissioners serving as personal assistants or clerical support to the members;

(b) Members of the Independent Review Board serving on the effective date of this amendatory Act of 1989, while serving in their current capacities; or

(c) Commission staff other than the staff of the office of chairman and commissioners participating in proceedings involving subchapters 5, 6, 7 or 8 of this Chapter.

P.A. 76–1586, § 18c–1204d, added by P.A. 86–1005, § 3, eff. Dec. 28, 1989.

Formerly Ill.Rev.Stat.1991, ch. 95 ½, ¶ 18c–1204d.

5/18c–1204e. Communications with the Office of Chairman and Commissioners

§ 18c–1204e. Communications with the Office of Chairman and Commissioners. (1) The chairman, members and executive director shall jointly adopt and adhere to written procedures concerning communication with staff of the Transportation Division to insure that:

(a) Communications from the members or staff of the office of chairman and commissioners which do not require substantial work from staff shall be transmitted to the manager of the Transportation Division; and

(b) Communications from the members or staff of the office of chairman and commissioners which do require substantial work from staff shall be transmitted to the executive director.

(2) The executive director shall establish written procedures, which staff other than staff of the office of chairman and commissioners shall adhere to, in regard to communications of such staff to the chairman, members or staff of the office of chairman and commissioners.

P.A. 76–1586, § 18c–1204e, added by P.A. 86–1005, § 3, eff. Dec. 28, 1989.

Formerly Ill.Rev.Stat.1991, ch. 95 ½, ¶ 18c–1204e.

5/18c–1205. Qualifications of Transportation Compliance Program Staff

§ 18c–1205. Qualifications of Transportation Compliance Program Staff.

(1) General provisions. The manager of the Transportation Division shall establish and adhere to written professional standards and procedures for the employment, education and training, performance and dismissal of all nonclerical compliance program personnel. Such standards and procedures shall include:

(a) Merit standards and procedures, and education requirements, applicable to State troopers, and training requirements at least equivalent to that received from a police training school approved by the Illinois Law Enforcement Training Standards Board, together with such additional qualifications as are needed under this Chapter, for all nonclerical field operations personnel;

(b) Successful completion of an accredited accounting or transportation-related education program, or at least 4 years experience in motor carrier rate analysis or auditing, plus such additional qualifications as are needed under this Chapter, for all nonclerical rate auditing personnel; and

(c) Successful completion of an accredited legal or paralegal education program, or equivalent administrative law experience, plus such additional qualifications as are needed under this Chapter, for all nonclerical civil penalties program personnel.

(2) Merit Selection Committee. Standards and procedures under this Section for police shall include the establishment of one or more merit selection committees, each composed of one Commission employee and no fewer than 3, nor more than 5, persons who are not employed by the Commission, each of whom shall from time to time be designated by

the division manager, subject to the approval of the Commission. The division manager shall submit a list of candidates to the committee or subcommittee thereof for its consideration. The committee or subcommittee thereof shall interview each candidate on the list and rate those interviewed as "most qualified", "qualified", or "not qualified". The committee shall recommend candidates rated "most qualified" and "qualified" to the division manager. In filling positions to which this Section applies, the division manager shall first offer the position to persons rated "most qualified". If all persons rated "most qualified" have been offered the position and each failed to accept the offer within the time specified by the division manager in the offer, the position may be offered to a person rated "qualified". Only persons rated "most qualified" or "qualified" shall be offered positions within the Compliance Program.

(3) The Commission shall authorize to each employee of the Commission exercising the powers of a peace officer a distinct badge that, on its face, (i) clearly states the badge is authorized by the Commission and (ii) contains a unique identifying number. No other badge shall be authorized by the Commission.

P.A. 76–1586, § 18c–1205, added by P.A. 85–553, § 2, eff. Sept. 18, 1987. Amended by P.A. 86–1005, § 3, eff. Dec. 28, 1989; P.A. 88–415, § 10, eff. Aug. 20, 1993; P.A. 89–444, § 5, eff. Jan. 25, 1996; P.A. 91–357, § 231, eff. July 29, 1999; P.A. 91–883, § 105, eff. Jan. 1, 2001.

Formerly Ill.Rev.Stat.1991, ch. 95 ½, ¶ 18c–1205.

P.A. 91–883 incorporated the amendment by P.A. 91–357.

ARTICLE III. EMPLOYEE BOARDS

5/18c–1301. Employee Boards Generally

§ 18c–1301. Employee Boards Generally. The Commission may, except as expressly provided in this Section, delegate one or more of its functions under this Chapter to Transportation Employee Boards. The Commission shall reserve to itself the function of making transportation policy. The Board shall be subject, in its deliberations, to all restraints which would govern the Commission if such functions had not been delegated to a Board, and to such other restraints as the Commission may by regulation prescribe. All decisions delegated to an Employee Board shall be appealable to the Commission.

P.A. 76–1586, § 18c–1301, added by P.A. 84–796, § 1, eff. Jan. 1, 1986.

Formerly Ill.Rev.Stat.1991, ch. 95 ½, ¶ 18c–1301.

5/18c–1302. Members of Employee Boards

§ 18c–1302. Members of Employee Boards. (1) Appointment of Members. Each board shall have 3 members. Members of employee boards established under provisions of this Article shall be appointed by the Commission. When any member is unable to act upon any matter before a Board because of absence, conflict, or other cause, and a qualified alternate appointed by the Commission is available, such alternate shall be called upon to serve on the Board. If no qualified alternate is available, the Chairman of the Commission may designate another qualified employee to serve temporarily until a member appointed by the Commission is available to serve.

(2) Qualification of Members. The Commission or its Chairman may, subject to limitations set forth in this Section, appoint any manager, section chief, examiner, attorney, or other qualified professional employee to serve on an Employee Board, either as a regular member or as an alternate member. No Employee Board member shall participate in any decision in which such person has a pecuniary or other direct interest. No 3 sitting members of an Employee Board shall be employed in the same division of the Commission.

P.A. 76–1586, § 18c–1302, added by P.A. 84–796, § 1, eff. Jan. 1, 1986. Amended by P.A. 86–1166, § 1, eff. Aug. 10, 1990.

Formerly Ill.Rev.Stat.1991, ch. 95 ½, ¶ 18c–1302.

5/18c–1303. Conduct of Employee Board Proceedings

§ 18c–1303. Conduct of Employee Board Proceedings. A majority of an Employee Board shall constitute a quorum for the transaction of business. Decisions on matters before an Employee Board shall be by majority vote of members present. Any party may appear before an Employee Board and be heard, in person or by representative, to the extent such party would be permitted to appear and be heard before the Commission itself. Each meeting of an Employee Board shall be a public meeting. Every vote and official act of an Employee Board shall be entered of record, and such records shall be made public on request.

P.A. 76–1586, § 18c–1303, added by P.A. 84–796, § 1, eff. Jan. 1, 1986.

Formerly Ill.Rev.Stat.1991, ch. 95 ½, ¶ 18c–1303.

5/18c–1304. Orders of Employee Boards

§ 18c–1304. Orders of Employee Boards. Employee Board orders shall be served, in writing, on all parties to the proceeding in which the order is entered. Such orders shall contain, in addition to the decision of the Board, a statement of findings, conclusions, or other reasons therefore. Employee Board decisions and orders shall have the same force and effect, and may be made, issued, and evidenced in the same manner, as if the decision had been made and the order issued by the Commission itself. The filing of a timely motion for reconsideration shall, unless otherwise provided by the Commission, stay the effect of an Employee Board order pending reconsideration.

P.A. 76–1586, § 18c–1304, added by P.A. 84–796, § 1, eff. Jan. 1, 1986.

Formerly Ill.Rev.Stat.1991, ch. 95 ½, ¶ 18c–1304.

ARTICLE IV. MODIFICATION OF STANDARDS AND PROCEDURES

5/18c–1401. Modification of Standards and Procedures in Response to Preemptive Federal Legislation

§ 18c–1401. Modification of Standards and Procedures in Response to Preemptive Federal Legislation. The Commission may, except with regard to licensing and ratemaking standards for motor carriers of property or passengers, conform its standards and procedures to the standards and procedures in a valid, preemptive federal statute where the provisions of this Chapter are in conflict with and would otherwise be preempted by such statute, any other provision of this Chapter notwithstanding.

P.A. 76–1586, § 18c–1401, added by P.A. 84–796, § 1, eff. Jan. 1, 1986.

Formerly Ill.Rev.Stat.1991, ch. 95 ½, ¶ 18c–1401.

5/18c-1402. Interim Rulemaking

§ 18c-1402. Interim Rulemaking. The Commission may, by publishing interim rules in the official state newspaper and simultaneously initiating rulemaking proceedings in accordance with the Administrative Procedure Act: [1]

(1) Modify its standards and procedures in accordance with Section 18c-1401 of this Chapter; or

(2) Modify its procedures in accordance with this Chapter in response to other circumstances impacting on the jurisdiction of the Commission in the field of transportation which are not of the Commission's own making but which necessitate adoption or amendment of regulations prior to the completion of normal rulemaking proceedings pursuant to the Illinois Administrative Procedure Act. Nothing in this subsection shall be construed to permit modification of licensing or ratemaking standards for motor carriers of property or passengers.

Such interim rules shall remain in effect only until regulations are adopted in accordance with the Administrative Procedure Act.

P.A. 76-1586, § 18c-1402, added by P.A. 84-796, § 1, eff. Jan. 1, 1986.

Formerly Ill.Rev.Stat.1991, ch. 95 ½, ¶ 18c-1402.

[1] 5 ILCS 100/1-1 et seq.

ARTICLE V. FEES AND TAXES

5/18c-1501. Franchise, Franchise Renewal, Filing and Other Fees for Motor Carriers of Property

§ 18c-1501. Franchise, Franchise Renewal, Filing and Other Fees for Motor Carriers of Property. (1) Franchise, Franchise Renewal, Filing, and Other Fee Levels in Effect Absent Commission Regulations Prescribing Different Fee Levels. The levels of franchise, franchise renewal, filing, and other fees for motor carriers of property in effect, absent Commission regulations prescribing different fee levels, shall be:

(a) Franchise and franchise renewal fees: $19 for each motor vehicle operated by a motor carrier of property in intrastate commerce, and $2 for each motor vehicle operated by a motor carrier of property in interstate commerce.

(b) Filing fees: $100 for each application seeking a Commission license or other authority, the reinstatement of a cancelled license or authority, or authority to establish a rate, other than by special permission, excluding both released rate applications and rate filings which may be investigated or suspended but which require no prior authorization for filing; $25 for each released rate application and each application to register as an interstate carrier; $15 for each application seeking special permission in regard to rates; and $15 for each equipment lease.

(2) Adjustment of Fee Levels. The Commission may, by rulemaking in accordance with provisions of The Illinois Administrative Procedure Act,[1] adjust franchise, franchise renewal, filing, and other fees for motor carriers of property by increasing or decreasing them from levels in effect absent Commission regulations prescribing different fee levels. Franchise and franchise renewal fees prescribed by the Commission for motor carriers of property shall not exceed:

(a) $50 for each motor vehicle operated by a household goods carrier in intrastate commerce;

(a-5) $5 for each motor vehicle operated by a public carrier in intrastate commerce; and

(b) $7 for each motor vehicle operated by a motor carrier of property in interstate commerce.

(3) Late-Filing Fees.

(a) Commission to Prescribe Late-Filing Fees. The Commission may prescribe fees for the late filing of proof of insurance, operating reports, franchise or franchise renewal fee applications, or other documents required to be filed on a periodic basis with the Commission.

(b) Late-filing Fees to Accrue Automatically. Late-filing fees shall accrue automatically from the filing deadline set forth in Commission regulations, and all persons or entities required to make such filings shall be on notice of such deadlines.

(c) Maximum Fees. Late-filing fees prescribed by the Commission shall not exceed $100 for an initial period, plus $10 for each day after the expiration of the initial period. The Commission may provide for waiver of all or part of late-filing fees accrued under this subsection on a showing of good cause.

(d) Effect of Failure to Make Timely Filings and Pay Late-Filing Fees. Failure of a person to file proof of continuous insurance coverage or to make other periodic filings required under Commission regulations shall make licenses and registrations held by the person subject to revocation or suspension. The licenses or registrations cannot thereafter be returned to good standing until after payment of all late-filing fees accrued and not waived under this subsection.

(4) Payment of Fees.

(a) Franchise and Franchise Renewal Fees. Franchise and franchise renewal fees for motor carriers of property shall be due and payable on or before the 31st day of December of the calendar year preceding the calendar year for which the fees are owing, unless otherwise provided in Commission regulations.

(b) Filing and Other Fees. Filing and other fees (including late-filing fees) shall be due and payable on the date of filing, or on such other date as is set forth in Commission regulations.

(5) When Fees Returnable.

(a) Whenever an application to the Illinois Commerce Commission is accompanied by any fee as required by law and such application is refused or rejected, said fee shall be returned to said applicant.

(b) The Illinois Commerce Commission may reduce by interlineation the amount of any personal check or corporate check or company check drawn on the account of and delivered by any person for payment of a fee required by the Illinois Commerce Commission.

(c) Any check altered pursuant to above shall be endorsed by the Illinois Commerce Commission as follows: "This check is warranted to subsequent holders and to the drawee to be in the amount $____."

(d) All applications to the Illinois Commerce Commission requiring fee payment upon reprinting shall contain the following authorization statement: "My signature authorizes the Illinois Commerce Commission to lower the amount of check if fee submitted exceeds correct amount."

P.A. 76-1586, § 18c-1501, added by P.A. 84-796, § 1, eff. Jan. 1, 1986. Amended by P.A. 85-553, § 2, eff. Sept. 18, 1987; P.A. 86-1005, § 3, eff. Dec. 28, 1989; P.A. 89-444, § 5, eff. Jan. 25, 1996.

Formerly Ill.Rev.Stat.1991, ch. 95 ½, ¶ 18c-1501.

[1] 5 ILCS 100/1-1 et seq.

5/18c-1502. Gross Receipts Taxes For Motor Carriers of Passengers and Rail Carriers

§ 18c-1502. Gross Receipts Taxes For Motor Carriers of Passengers and Rail Carriers. Each motor carrier of passengers and rail carrier shall pay to the Commission, in accordance with Sections 2-202, 3-120 and 3-121 of "The Public Utilities Act", as amended,[1] a gross receipts tax in the amount provided herein.

The amount of the tax for motor carriers of passengers shall be prescribed by the Commission by rulemaking in accordance with provisions of The Illinois Administrative Procedure Act,[2] and shall not exceed 0.1% of the carrier's gross Illinois intrastate revenues for each calendar year.

The amount of the tax for rail carriers shall be 0.15% of the carrier's gross Illinois intrastate revenues for each calendar year.

P.A. 76-1586, § 18c-1502, added by P.A. 84-796, § 1, eff. Jan. 1, 1986. Amended by P.A. 84-1025, § 2, eff. Jan. 1, 1986; P.A. 85-6, § 1, eff. June 30, 1987; P.A. 85-553, § 2, eff. Sept. 18, 1987; P.A. 85-1209, Art. II, § 2-51, eff. Aug. 30, 1988; P.A. 89-42, § 10, eff. Jan. 1, 1996; P.A. 89-699, § 15, eff. Jan. 16, 1997.

Formerly Ill.Rev.Stat.1991, ch. 95 ½, ¶ 18c-1502.

[1] 220 ILCS 5/2-202, 5/3-120, and 5/3-121.

[2] 5 ILCS 100/1-1 et seq.

P.A. 89-699 incorporated the amendment by P.A. 89-42.

5/18c-1502.05. Route Mileage Fee for Rail Carriers

§ 18c-1502.05. Route Mileage Fee for Rail Carriers. Beginning with calendar year 1997, every rail carrier shall pay to the Commission for each calendar year a route mileage fee of $37 for each route mile of railroad right of way owned by the rail carrier in Illinois. The fee shall be based on the number of route miles as of January 1 of the year for which the fee is due, and the payment of the route mileage fee shall be due by February 1 of each calendar year.

P.A. 76-1586, § 18c-1502.05, added by P.A. 89-699, § 15, eff. Jan. 16, 1997.

5/18c-1502.10. Railroad-Highway Grade Crossing and Grade Separation Fee

§ 18c-1502.10. Railroad-Highway Grade Crossing and Grade Separation Fee. Beginning with calendar year 1997, every rail carrier shall pay to the Commission for each calendar year a fee of $23 for each location at which the rail carrier's track crosses a public road, highway, or street, whether the crossing be at grade, by overhead structure, or by subway. The fee shall be based on the number of the crossings as of January 1 of each calendar year, and the fee shall be due by February 1 of each calendar year.

P.A. 76-1586, § 18c-1502.10, added by P.A. 89-699, § 15, eff. Jan. 16, 1997.

5/18c-1503. Legislative Intent

§ 18c-1503. Legislative Intent. It is the intent of the Legislature that the exercise of powers under Sections 18c-1501 and 18c-1502 of this Chapter shall not diminish revenues to the Commission, and that any surplus or deficit of revenues in the Transportation Regulatory Fund, together with any projected changes in the cost of administering and enforcing this Chapter, should be considered in establishing or adjusting fees and taxes in succeeding years. The Commission shall administer fees and taxes under this Chapter in such a manner as to insure that any surplus generated or accumulated in the Transportation Regulatory Fund does not exceed the surplus accumulated in the Motor Vehicle Fund during fiscal year 1984, and shall adjust the level of such fees and taxes to insure compliance with this provision.

P.A. 76-1586, § 18c-1503, added by P.A. 84-796, § 1, eff. Jan. 1, 1986.

Formerly Ill.Rev.Stat.1991, ch. 95 ½, ¶ 18c-1503.

5/18c-1504. Reciprocity

§ 18c-1504. Reciprocity. The Commission may enter into agreements with agencies in other jurisdictions for the reciprocal waiver of motor carrier fees or taxes administered by the Commission, and may revoke such agreements where another jurisdiction does not extend reciprocal treatment to carriers based in the State of Illinois. The Commission may, in addition, and notwithstanding any other provision of this Chapter, prescribe fees for carriers based in jurisdictions other than the State of Illinois equal to fees charged to Illinois carriers by such other jurisdictions.

P.A. 76-1586, § 18c-1504, added by P.A. 84-796, § 1, eff. Jan. 1, 1986.

Formerly Ill.Rev.Stat.1991, ch. 95 ½, ¶ 18c-1504.

5/18c-1505. Proration of Fees

§ 18c-1505. Proration of Fees. The Commission may prorate fees and levies provided in this Chapter throughout the calendar year.

P.A. 76-1586, § 18c-1505, added by P.A. 84-796, § 1, eff. Jan. 1, 1986.

Formerly Ill.Rev.Stat.1991, ch. 95 ½, ¶ 18c-1505.

ARTICLE VI. TRANSPORTATION REGULATORY FUND

5/18c-1601. Deposit of Monies into the Transportation Regulatory Fund

§ 18c-1601. Deposit of Monies into the Transportation Regulatory Fund.

(1) Deposit of Fees, Taxes, and Monies Other Than Criminal Fines. All fees, penalties (other than criminal penalties) or monies collected in settlement of enforcement proceedings, taxes, and other monies collected under this Chapter or which are transferred, appropriated or reimbursed to the Commission for the purpose of administering and enforcing this Chapter, shall be promptly paid into a special fund in the State treasury known as the Transportation Regulatory Fund.

(2) Accounting for Monies Received. The Commission shall account separately for the receipt of monies from the following classes:

(a) motor carriers of property (other than carriers engaged in nonrelocation towing);

(b) rail carriers; and

(c) other monies.

The Commission may account separately with regard to groups of persons within the foregoing classes.

(3) Deposit of criminal fines. Criminal fines collected under this Chapter from motor carriers of property or persons or entities found to have aided or abetted motor carriers of property or passengers in violation of this Chapter shall be disposed of in accordance with Section 16-105 of this Code. Other criminal fines collected under this Chapter

shall be deposited into the Transportation Regulatory Fund in accordance with subsection (1) of this Section.

(4) (Blank).

P.A. 76-1586, § 18c-1601, added by P.A. 84-796, § 1, eff. Jan. 1, 1986. Amended by P.A. 85-7, § 1, eff. June 30, 1987; P.A. 85-553, § 2, eff. Sept. 18, 1987; P.A. 85-1209, Art. II, § 2-51, eff. Aug. 30, 1988; P.A. 87-838, § 155, eff. Jan. 24, 1992; P.A. 90-372, Art. 10, § 10-125, eff. July 1, 1998.

Formerly Ill.Rev.Stat.1991, ch. 95 ½, ¶ 18c-1601.

5/18c-1602. Appropriations from the Transportation Regulatory Fund

§ 18c-1602. Appropriations from the Transportation Regulatory Fund. (1) Appropriation of Monies. Appropriations from the Transportation Regulatory Fund shall be separately identified both in the Commission's appropriations request and the Act by which appropriations from the Fund are made.

(2) Authorization of Staff Positions. Authorized staff positions to be funded with monies appropriated from the Transportation Regulatory Fund shall be separately identified in the Commission's appropriations request.

(3) Appropriations and Authorizations Not Transferable. Appropriations from the Transportation Regulatory Fund shall be used only for the administration and enforcement of this Chapter and Chapter 18a. Such appropriations and authorized headcount may be transferred within the Transportation Regulatory Fund, but may not be transferred to any other fund.

P.A. 76-1586, § 18c-1602, added by P.A. 85-553, § 2, eff. Sept. 18, 1987.

Formerly Ill.Rev.Stat.1991, ch. 95 ½, ¶ 18c-1602.

5/18c-1603. Expenditures from the Transportation Regulatory Fund

§ 18c-1603. Expenditures from the Transportation Regulatory Fund. (1) Authorization of Expenditures from the Fund. Monies deposited in the Transportation Regulatory Fund shall be expended only for the administration and enforcement of this Chapter and Chapter 18a.

(2) Allocation of Expenses to the Fund. (a) Expenses Allocated Entirely to the Transportation Regulatory Fund. All expenses of the Transportation Division shall be allocated to the Transportation Regulatory Fund, provided that they were:

(i) Incurred by and for staff employed within the Transportation Division and accountable, directly or through a program director or staff supervisor, to the Transportation Division manager;

(ii) Incurred exclusively in the administration and enforcement of this Chapter and Chapter 18a; and

(iii) Authorized by the Transportation Division manager.

(b) Expenses Partially Allocated to the Transportation Regulatory Fund. A portion of expenses for the following persons and activities may be allocated to the Transportation Regulatory Fund:

(i) The Executive Director, his deputies and personal assistants, and their clerical support;

(ii) The legislative liaison activities of the Office of Legislative Affairs, its constituent elements and successors;

(iii) The activities of the Administrative Services Division on the effective date of this amendatory Act of 1987, exclusive of the Chief Clerk's office;

(iv) The payroll expenses of Commissioners' assistants;

(v) The internal auditor; and

(vi) The in-state travel expenses of the Commissioners to and from the offices of the Commission.

(c) Allocation Methodology for Expenses Other Than Administrative Services Division and Commissioners' Assistants. The portion of total expenses (other than Administrative Services Division and commissioners' assistants' expenses) allocated to the Transportation Regulatory Fund under paragraph (b) of this subsection shall be the lessor of:

(i) The portion of staff time spent exclusively on administration and enforcement of this Chapter and Chapter 18a, as shown by a time study updated at least once each 6 months; and

(ii) The percentage of total authorized Commission staff for the fiscal year which is employed in Transportation Division (based on the average for the fiscal year).

(d) Allocation Methodology for Expenses of Administration Services Division. The portion of expenses for Administrative Services Division allocated to the Transportation Regulatory Fund under paragraph (b) of this subsection shall not exceed:

(i) The portion allocable under paragraph (c) of this subsection, for staff payroll expenses; and

(ii) The portion used exclusively in the administration and enforcement of this Chapter and Chapter 18a, for other than staff payroll expenses.

(e) Allocation methodology for Commissioners' Assistants Expenses. Five percent of the payroll expenses of commissioners' assistants may be allocated to the Transportation Regulatory Fund.

(f) Expenses not allocable to the Transportation Regulatory Fund. No expenses shall be allocated to or paid from the Transportation Regulatory Fund except as expressly authorized in paragraphs (a) through (e) of this subsection. In particular, no expenses shall be allocated to the Fund which were incurred by or in relation to the following persons and activities:

(i) Commissioners' travel, except as otherwise provided in paragraphs (b) and (c) of this subsection;

(ii) Commissioners' assistants except as otherwise provided in paragraphs (b) and (e) of this subsection;

(iii) The Policy Analysis and Research Division, its constituent elements and successors;

(iv) The Chief Clerk's office, its constituent elements and successors;

(v) The Hearing Examiners Division, its constituent elements and successors, and any hearing examiners or hearings conducted, in whole or in part, outside the Transportation Division;

(vi) The Public Affairs Group, its constituent elements and successors;

(vii) The Office of General Counsel, its constituent elements and successors, including but not limited to the Office of Public Utility Counsel and any legal staff in the office of the executive director, but not including the personal assistant serving as staff counsel to the executive director as provided in Section 18c-1204(2) and the Office of Transportation Counsel; and

(viii) Any other expenses or portion thereof not expressly authorized in this subsection to be allocated to the Fund.

The constituent elements of the foregoing shall, for purposes of this Section, be their constituent elements on the effective date of this amendatory Act of 1987.

(3) Allocation of Expenses Within the Fund. (a) Monies deposited in the Transportation Regulatory Fund shall be expended only in the regulation of that class of persons as defined in subsection (2) of Section 18c–1601 of this Chapter from or in relation to which the monies were received.

(b) Expenses incurred exclusively in relation to one class shall be allocated to that class and no other.

(c) A portion of each expense incurred in relation to more than one class may be allocated to each of the involved classes based on time study or actual use, provided that the portion allocated to any class shall not exceed the maximum specified in paragraph (d) of this subsection.

(d) Total expenses allocated to any one class under paragraph (c) of this subsection shall not exceed the amount which bears the same percentage relationship to expenses allocated to that class under paragraph (b) of this subsection ((c) divided by (b)) as total expenses allocated to all classes under paragraph (b) bear to total expenses allocated to all classes under paragraph (c) ((c) divided by (b)).

(4) Effective Date of Section. The Commission shall have 180 calendar days from the effective date of this amendatory Act of 1987 to comply fully with this Section.

P.A. 76–1586, § 18c–1603, added by P.A. 85–553, § 2, eff. Sept. 18, 1987. Amended by P.A. 86–1005, § 3, eff. Dec. 28, 1989.

Formerly Ill.Rev.Stat.1991, ch. 95 ½, ¶ 18c–1603.

5/18c–1604. Annual Report of Expenditures

§ 18c–1604. Annual Report of Expenditures. The Commission shall, within 60 calendar days after the end of each fiscal year, submit to the Governor and the General Assembly a report of the following for such fiscal year:

(1) All monies deposited in the Transportation Regulatory Fund, showing the total and subtotals by class as defined in subsection (2) of Section 18c-1601 of this Chapter;

(2) All expenditures from the Transportation Regulatory Fund, showing the total and the sub-totals by class as defined in subsection (2) of Section 18c-1601 of this Chapter;

(3) A listing and description by function of all staff positions actually funded, in whole or in part, at any time during the fiscal year, from the Transportation Regulatory Fund; and

(4) The methods used to allocate expenses between the Transportation Regulatory Fund and other funds, and between classes within the Transportation Regulatory Fund.

P.A. 76–1586, § 18c–1604, added by P.A. 85–553, § 2, eff. Sept. 18, 1987.

Formerly Ill.Rev.Stat.1991, ch. 95 ½, ¶ 18c–1604.

ARTICLE VII. VIOLATIONS OF THE LAW

5/18c–1701. Violations Defined

§ 18c–1701. Violations Defined. Each person who fails to comply, in whole or in part, with any provision of this Chapter, Commission regulations or orders shall have committed a violation of this Chapter. Likewise, any person who aids or abets another in such failure to comply shall have committed a violation of this Chapter. The agent of a carrier shall not be found to have aided or abetted in violation of this Chapter where the act of the agent was required by this Chapter, Commission regulations or orders. The act or omission of any officer, employee, or agent within the scope of such person's office, employment or agency shall be deemed the act or omission of the business entity; such entity shall be named as the party defendant or respondent and the officer, employee, or agent shall not be held liable. Failure to comply with more than one provision of this Chapter or regulations or orders hereunder shall constitute multiple violations. Each day's continuance of a violation shall constitute a separate violation.

P.A. 76–1586, § 18c–1701, added by P.A. 84–796, § 1, eff. Jan. 1, 1986.

Formerly Ill.Rev.Stat.1991, ch. 95 ½, ¶ 18c–1701.

5/18c–1702. Responsibility for Enforcement

§ 18c–1702. Responsibility for Enforcement. It shall be the duty of the Commission and of the State Police and the Secretary of State to conduct investigations, make arrests, and take any other action necessary for the enforcement of this Chapter.

P.A. 76–1586, § 18c–1702, added by P.A. 84–796, § 1, eff. Jan. 1, 1986.

Formerly Ill.Rev.Stat.1991, ch. 95 ½, ¶ 18c–1702.

5/18c–1703. Investigations and Arrests

§ 18c-1703. Investigations and Arrests. (1) Enforcement Officers and Investigators. Enforcement officers and investigators appointed by the Commission shall have, and may exercise throughout the state, all the powers of police officers when enforcing provisions of this Chapter, subject to the regulations and orders of the Commission.

(2) Investigations.

(a) General Provisions. The Commission, through its employees, shall conduct such investigations as are necessary for the enforcement of this Chapter.

(b) Examination, Audit and Production of Records. Authorized employees of the Commission shall have the power at any and all times to examine, audit, or demand production of all accounts, books, records, memoranda, and other papers in the possession or control of a license or registration holder, its employees or agents. In addition, every person other than a license or registration holder and every officer, employee or agent of such person shall permit every authorized employee of the Commission, upon administrative subpoena issued by the Chairman or his designee or the Attorney General, to inspect and copy any accounts, books, records, memoranda, letters, checks, vouchers, telegrams, documents, or other papers in its possession or control which the Commission deems necessary to the proper conduct of an investigation to determine whether provisions of this Chapter, Commission regulations or orders, have been violated.

(c) Inspection of Equipment and Facilities. Authorized employees of the Commission shall have the power at all times to inspect the equipment, facilities, and other property of the licensee in the possession or control of a carrier or broker, its employees or agents.

(d) Special Investigations. The Commission may also conduct special investigations as necessary for the enforcement of this Chapter. Where such person is found by the Commission to have violated this Chapter, and where the Commission imposes a sanction for such violation under Section 18c-1704 of this Chapter, the Commission may impose on such person an assessment of reasonable expenses incurred by the Commission in the investigation and subsequent proceeding. Such assessment shall not exceed a fee of $100 per work day or $50 per half work day, per employee, for the payroll costs of the Commission staff, plus actual transportation (in accordance with applicable state employee travel expense reimbursement regulations) and all other actual expenses incurred in the special investigation and subsequent proceeding.

(3) Arrests and Citations. The Commission shall make arrests and issue notices of civil violations where necessary for the enforcement of this Chapter. No rail carrier employee shall be arrested for violation of this Chapter. No person operating a motor vehicle in violation of the licensing or safety provisions of this Chapter shall be permitted to transport property or passengers beyond the point of arrest unless, in the opinion of the officer making the arrest, it is necessary to transport the property or passengers to another location to insure their safety or to preserve or tend cargo carried in the vehicle.

P.A. 76–1586, § 18c–1703, added by P.A. 84–796, § 1, eff. Jan. 1, 1986. Amended by P.A. 85–553, § 2, eff. Sept. 18, 1987.

Formerly Ill.Rev.Stat.1991, ch. 95 ½, ¶ 18c–1703.

5/18c–1704. Sanctions

§ 18c–1704. Sanctions. Each violation of this Chapter shall subject the violator to the following sanctions, except as otherwise provided elsewhere in this Chapter. Sanctions provided for in this Section may be imposed by the Commission only in compliance with the notice and hearing requirements of Section 18c–2102 of this Chapter.

(1) Criminal Misdemeanor Penalties. Each violation of this Chapter shall constitute a Class C misdemeanor.

(2) Civil Penalties. The Commission may assess, against any person found by it to have violated this Chapter, a civil penalty not greater than $1,000 nor less than $100 per violation. The penalty assessed by the Commission shall reflect the number and severity of violations found to have been committed. Penalties assessed by the Commission shall be enforced by any court having venue in enforcement cases under this Chapter.

(3) Cease and Desist Orders. The Commission may, where a person is found after hearing to have violated this Chapter, Commission regulations or orders, and justice requires, order the person to cease and desist from further or from any future violations. A cease and desist order may be entered on the Commission's own motion or by agreement between the parties. Orders and agreements under this Section shall be valid and enforceable for the period stated therein, not to exceed 2 years from the date the order or agreement is approved by the Commission, unless the parties stipulate otherwise. Such orders and agreements shall be enforceable in any court of this State having venue and jurisdiction in enforcement actions under this Chapter. Failure to comply with a Commission cease and desist order shall constitute a violation of this Chapter separate and apart from any underlying violations.

(4) Stipulated Settlements.

(a) General Provisions. The Commission may accept a reasonable monetary settlement, suspension or revocation of a license or registration, or any other reasonable terms stipulated between the respondent and staff, with or without a finding of violations.

(b) Presumption of Reasonableness. Such stipulations shall be presumed reasonable. Unless the terms of a stipulation exceed such parameters as the Commission may establish, this presumption is rebuttable only by evidence of record at hearing.

(c) Parameters. Parameters for settlement shall be based on type of violation; severity, as measured by revenues from unlawful activities; and number of violations. Minimum settlement amounts may be established.

(d) Orders. Orders suspending proposed settlements shall cite reasons for suspension which are specific to the case. Orders rejecting proposed settlements shall recite the grounds on which the settlements are found to be unreasonable and describe the evidence which supports such findings.

(5) Injunctive Relief. Any court with jurisdiction and venue for purposes of enforcing this Chapter shall have the power to enjoin any person from committing violations of this Chapter. Suit for penalties shall not be a prerequisite to injunctive relief. No bond shall be required when injunctive relief is granted at the request of the Commission.

(6) Suspension or Revocation of Licenses and Registrations.

(a) Availability of Suspension and Revocation as Sanctions. Violation of this Chapter by a motor carrier of property or passengers shall, in addition to other sanctions provided herein, subject the violator to suspension or revocation of any or all Commission licenses and registrations. The Commission may impose the sanctions of suspension and revocation. Where the violation is failure of a motor carrier of property or passengers to have in effect and file proof of continuous insurance coverage in accordance with this Chapter, Commission regulations and orders, the license or registration or both may be suspended by telephonic or telegraphic directive, confirmed by certified or registered mail or personal service, pending final disposition of revocation proceedings.

(b) Suspension Pending Adjudication. Where the violation is failure of a motor carrier of property to pay a franchise or franchise renewal fee, the license or registration or both may be suspended by certified or registered mail or personally served directive, pending final disposition of revocation proceedings.

(c) Special Revocation Procedures.

(i) Notice. The Commission shall serve notice upon all persons who have failed to pay a franchise tax, license fee, or penalty required under the Business Corporation Act of 1983,[1] or who have failed to comply with this Chapter, Commission regulations and orders, regarding the filing of proof of continuous insurance or bond coverage, the payment of periodic fees, the filing of periodic reports, the payment of civil penalties, or the filing of rates to the full extent of a carrier's authority. The notice shall advise such person of the apparent violations and state that, unless the Commission receives a written request for hearing or extension of time within 30 days from the date the notice is served, the person's license or registration will be revoked by operation of law without further action by the Commission.

(ii) Extensions of Time. The Commission may grant one extension of time not exceeding 60 days where the extension will not endanger the public.

(iii) Request for Hearing. If a timely written request for hearing is received, no further action shall be taken until the requirements of Section 18c–2102 of this Chapter have been satisfied.

(iv) Revocation by Operation of Law. If, at the expiration of the applicable time period, the person has not complied with the pertinent requirements, and a written request for hearing has not been received, the person will be deemed to have waived hearing and the license or registration shall be revoked by operation of law without further action by the Commission as if the Commission has served an order on the date following expiration revoking the license or registration.

(7) Probation. The Commission may probate the imposition of any of the sanctions set forth in this Section.

P.A. 76–1586, § 18c–1704, added by P.A. 84–796, § 1, eff. Jan. 1, 1986. Amended by P.A. 85–553, § 2, eff. Sept. 18, 1987; P.A. 86–1286, § 1, eff. Sept. 6, 1990; P.A. 88–415, § 10, eff. Aug. 20, 1993.

Formerly Ill.Rev.Stat.1991, ch. 95 ½, ¶ 18c–1704.

1 805 ILCS 5/1.01 et seq.

5/18c–1705. Expedited Enforcement Procedures

§ 18c–1705. Expedited Enforcement Procedures. The Commission shall, within 60 days from the effective date of this amendatory Act of 1987, implement expedited administrative enforcement procedures.

(a) Initiation of Administrative Enforcement Proceedings. The Transportation Division Manager or his designee shall have the power to issue, or refuse to issue, a notice or citation instituting an administrative enforcement proceeding.

(b) Settlement of Enforcement Proceedings by Stipulation.

(i) Power to Negotiate Settlements. The Transportation Division Manager or his designee shall have the power to negotiate and sign proposed settlements of enforcement proceedings by written stipulation.

(ii) Review and Acceptance of Stipulations. The Commission shall provide for any appropriate and necessary review of proposed settlements within 30 days after a stipulation is signed by the parties. Unless a stipulation is suspended for review by order of the Commission served within 30 calendar days after it was signed by the parties, it shall be deemed accepted by operation of law. A stipulation which has been suspended for review shall likewise be deemed accepted by operation of law unless it is rejected by order of the Commission served within 45 days after it was suspended. A stipulation which is deemed accepted under this sub-paragraph shall become effective and shall be enforceable in the same manner as an order of the Commission.

(iii) Administrative Appeal of Settlements. Administrative appeal of a stipulation which has been approved by order of the Commission or by operation of law shall be by motion for rehearing or reconsideration in accordance with Section 18c–2110 of this Chapter. The right to administratively appeal a settlement may be waived by written stipulation.

P.A. 76–1586, § 18c–1705, added by P.A. 85–553, § 2, eff. Sept. 18, 1987. Amended by P.A. 86–1005, § 3, eff. Dec. 28, 1989; P.A. 86–1166, § 1, eff. Aug. 10, 1990; P.A. 91–357, § 231, eff. July 29, 1999.

Formerly Ill.Rev.Stat.1991, ch. 95 ½, ¶ 18c–1705.

ARTICLE VIII. SERVICE OF NOTICES, ORDERS AND PROCESS

5/18c–1801. Persons Who May Be Served

§ 18c–1801. Persons Who May be Served. It shall be the responsibility of each person subject to the licensing or ratemaking provisions of this Chapter to keep on file with the Commission the name of a person upon whom notices, orders, or process in administrative or judicial proceedings under this Chapter may be served, together with a current address within the State of Illinois at which such person may be served. The Commission shall maintain a file of such "agents for service of process." Service of any Commission notice, order, or process on the agent for service of process at the address shown in the file shall be conclusively presumed to be service on the carrier, broker, or other person. If a person fails to make the filing required herein, the person may be served at the most current address in other records of the Commission, or at the address on file with the Secretary of State for service of process, and the same conclusive presumption shall apply.

P.A. 76–1586, § 18c–1801, added by P.A. 84–796, § 1, eff. Jan. 1, 1986.

Formerly Ill.Rev.Stat.1991, ch. 95 ½, ¶ 18c–1801.

5/18c–1802. Time of Service

§ 18c–1802. Time of Service. Notices, orders, process and other correspondence of the Commission shall be deemed served at the time they are deposited in the United States mail or delivered to a commercial delivery service or delivered in person by an employee or agent of the Commission. Notices, orders, process and other correspondence shall be deemed served on the Commission at the time of receipt.

P.A. 76–1586, § 18c–1802, added by P.A. 84–796, § 1, eff. Jan. 1, 1986.

Formerly Ill.Rev.Stat.1991, ch. 95 ½, ¶ 18c–1802.

SUB–CHAPTER 2. PROCEEDINGS BEFORE THE COMMISSION AND THE COURTS

ARTICLE I. ADMINISTRATIVE PROCEEDINGS BEFORE THE COMMISSION

ARTICLE II. JUDICIAL REVIEW PROCEEDINGS

ARTICLE III. ADMINISTRATIVE AND JUDICIAL ENFORCEMENT PROCEEDINGS

ARTICLE I. ADMINISTRATIVE PROCEEDINGS BEFORE THE COMMISSION

5/18c–2101. Hearings in household goods carrier licensing cases

§ 18c–2101. Hearings in household goods carrier licensing cases. (1) Hearing required. The Commission shall issue orders in household goods carrier licensing cases only after notice and hearing in accordance with the rules of practice applicable to proceedings under this Chapter.

(2) Hearing not required. Hearing shall be required in household goods carrier licensing cases, except as provided in Sections 18c–2107 and 18c–4306 of this Chapter.

P.A. 76–1586, § 18c–2101, added by P.A. 84–796, § 1, eff. Jan. 1, 1986. Amended by P.A. 85–553, § 2, eff. Sept. 18, 1987; P.A. 89–444, § 5, eff. Jan. 25, 1996.

Formerly Ill.Rev.Stat.1991, ch. 95 ½, ¶ 18c–2101.

5/18c–2102. Hearings in other than household goods carrier authority cases

§ 18c–2102. Hearings in other than household goods carrier authority cases. (1) Hearing required. Except as otherwise provided in subsection (2) of this Section, and in Section 18c–2108 of this Chapter the Commission shall, in other than household goods carrier authority cases, issue orders granting authority or other relief, prescribing rates, imposing sanctions, or directing that a person take, continue to take, refrain from taking or cease and desist from continuing to take any action, only after notice and hearing in accordance with the rules of practice applicable to proceedings under this Chapter.

(2) Hearing not required. Except as otherwise provided in Section 18c–2108 of this Chapter, the Commission may, in other than household goods carrier authority cases, conduct its review and issue orders without hearing, the taking of evidence, or the making of a record where action taken in the order:

(a) Was not opposed in a timely pleading addressed to the Commission;

(b) Was opposed in a timely pleading, but such opposition was later withdrawn or the parties in opposition waived further hearing and taking of evidence;

(c) Was taken on an emergency temporary or interim basis in accordance with Section 18c–2108 of this Chapter; or

(d) Is interlocutory in nature.

(3) Section not applicable to household goods carrier authority cases. Nothing in this Section shall have application to any household goods carrier authority case.

P.A. 76–1586, § 18c–2102, added by P.A. 84–796, § 1, eff. Jan. 1, 1986. Amended by P.A. 89–444, § 5, eff. Jan. 25, 1996.

Formerly Ill.Rev.Stat.1991, ch. 95 ½, ¶ 18c–2102.

5/18c–2103. Rules of Practice

§ 18c–2103. Rules of Practice. (1) General Provisions. The Commission shall adopt General and Special rules of practice to govern administrative proceedings under this Chapter. Such rules shall be designed to effectuate the purposes of this Chapter. Rules of practice heretofore issued by the Commission shall be the rules of practice applicable under this Chapter unless changed, repealed, or supplemented by the Commission.

(2) Verification of Pleadings. Unless otherwise expressly provided therein, the signature on any pleading, document, or other paper filed with the Commission on which a verification or oath is required under applicable statutes or regulations shall constitute the verification or oath of the signatory and no further verification or oath shall be required. False verification or oath shall be a violation of this Chapter.

P.A. 76–1586, § 18c–2103, added by P.A. 84–796, § 1, eff. Jan. 1, 1986.

Formerly Ill.Rev.Stat.1991, ch. 95 ½, ¶ 18c–2103.

5/18c–2104. Rules of Evidence

§ 18c–2104. Rules of Evidence. The rules of evidence which apply in civil cases before the circuit courts of this State shall, except as otherwise provided herein, apply to proceedings before the Commission under this Chapter. Evidence not admissible under the rules of evidence applicable in civil courts may be admitted if it is of a type commonly relied upon by prudent persons in the conduct of their affairs. Objections must be made at hearing to preserve them on appeal. Evidence may be received orally or in writing.

P.A. 76–1586, § 18c–2104, added by P.A. 84–796, § 1, eff. Jan. 1, 1986.

Formerly Ill.Rev.Stat.1991, ch. 95 ½, ¶ 18c–2104.

5/18c–2105. Discovery

§ 18c–2105. Discovery. (1) Discovery Generally. Any party may utilize written interrogatories, depositions, requests for discovery or inspection of documents or property and other discovery tools commonly utilized in civil actions in the circuit courts in the State of Illinois in the manner contemplated by the Code of Civil Procedure[1] and the Rules of the Supreme Court of Illinois; except that discovery must be completed by the 30th day after the party filed its petition for leave to intervene, unless the period of discovery is extended by agreement of the parties or by the Commission. The Chairman or a hearing examiner may, at any time, on his own motion or at the request of a party, issue such rulings denying, limiting, conditioning, or regulating discovery as justice requires, and may supervise all or part of any discovery procedure. Parties to proceedings before the Commission are encouraged to clarify and resolve issues where possible through the use of pre-hearing discovery. However, discovery order should be calculated to lessen the time and expense required to reach an informed resolution of the issues.

(2) Subpoenas. The Chairman or a hearing examiner may, for good cause, issue a subpoena directing a person to appear and testify, and to produce records, documents, or other papers, at a time and place set forth in the subpoena, in connection with a proceeding before the Commission. Service of the subpoena shall be in the same manner as a subpoena issued by a court. The Commission may, on its own motion or the motion of a person served with a subpoena, quash the subpoena, in whole or in part.

(3) Appeal from Discovery and Subpoenas. A person served with a discovery request or subpoena may appeal such interlocutory matter to the Commission. Such appeals shall set forth grounds for seeking to quash or limit the scope of the discovery or subpoena, as well as the specific relief sought, and must be filed within 10 days after service of the discovery or subpoena. If discovery is stayed by the Commission, the person served shall be excused from compliance with the discovery order or subpoena until a decision on its appeal is made by the Commission.

(4) Assessment and Payment of Discovery Costs. The Commission may assess the costs of discovery, including fees for witness attendance and travel, against the party by which discovery was requested. Where a subpoena is issued on the Commission's own motion, fees for witness attendance and travel shall be paid by the Commission on request. Witness fees shall be the same as for a circuit court proceeding. Deposits to insure payment of costs and fees may be required.

(5) Enforcement of Discovery Procedures. The Commission may, where a person has failed to comply with or permit discovery authorized hereunder, determine any or all issues within the scope of the discovery or subpoena adverse to such person without further evidence. The Commission may, in addition, assess civil penalties under Article VII of Subchapter 1 of this Chapter for such violator for contempt and may assess the costs of enforcement, both before the Commission and before the court, against the violator.

P.A. 76–1586, § 18c–2105, added by P.A. 84–796, § 1, eff. Jan. 1, 1986.

Formerly Ill.Rev.Stat.1991, ch. 95 ½, ¶ 18c–2105.

1 735 ILCS 5/1–101 et seq.

5/18c–2106. Standing

§ 18c–2106. Standing. (1) General Provisions. Each person with an administratively cognizable interest in a proceeding before the Commission shall, upon compliance with procedural rules adopted by the Commission for such proceedings, be entitled to appear and participate as a party to the proceeding. The Commission may, in addition, grant leave to appear and participate on such terms as it may prescribe, where to do so would assist the Commission in reaching an informed and just decision in the proceeding.

(2) Definition of Administratively Cognizable Interest. The following persons or entities shall be deemed to have an administratively cognizable interest in proceedings under this Chapter:

(a) Licensing Proceedings. A person shall be deemed to have an administratively cognizable interest in a proceeding in which an application for a new, amended, or extended intrastate license is under consideration only if:

(i) The person possesses a license authorizing all or part of the service for which authority is sought, such license is in good standing, and the person has transported or actively solicited traffic or both within the scope of the application during the 12 month period immediately preceding initiation of the proceeding; or

(ii) The proceeding involves an application for a household goods carrier license and the person is an organization representing employees of a household goods carrier .

(b) Rate Proceedings. A person shall be deemed to have an administratively cognizable interest in a proceeding in which new or amended rates are under consideration only if the person is:

(i) A carrier authorized to transport traffic such as would be subject to or affected by the rates;

(ii) A shipper or receiver of traffic such as would be subject to or affected by the rates;

(iii) An association of two or more carriers, acting at the request of and on behalf of one or more carriers authorized to transport traffic such as would be subject to or affected by the rates; or an association of two or more shippers or receivers acting at the request of and on behalf of one or more shippers or receivers of such traffic; or

(iv) An organization representing employees of a household goods carrier.

(c) Proceedings to Transfer a License. A person shall be deemed to have an administratively cognizable interest in a proceeding to transfer an intrastate license only if the person:

(i) Has an ownership interest in or control of the license which is the subject of the proceeding;

(ii) Would, if the proposed transfer is approved, acquire ownership or control of the license which is the subject of the proceeding;

(iii) Possesses a license authorizing all or part of the service authorized by the license sought to be transferred, such license is in good standing, and the person or entity has transported or actively solicited traffic within the scope of the license sought to be transported during the 12 months period immediately preceding initiation of the proceeding;

(iv) Would be directly affected by the transfer; or

(v) Is an organization representing employees of a household goods carrier.

(d) Complaint and Enforcement Proceedings. A person shall be deemed to have an administratively cognizable interest in a complaint proceeding if the person:

(i) Has an ownership interest in or control of the license which is the subject of the proceeding;

(ii) Would be directly and adversely affected by failure to grant relief sought in the complaint or enforcement action and such adverse effect is contrary to the purposes of this Chapter; or

(iii) Is an organization representing employees of a household goods carrier of property.

(e) All Proceedings. Notwithstanding the provisions of subsections (2)(a) through (2)(d) of this Section, a person shall be deemed to have an administratively cognizable interest in a proceeding other than a complaint proceeding if the person:

(i) Filed the pleading pursuant to which the proceeding was initiated; or

(ii) Is an organization representing employees of a household goods carrier.

P.A. 76–1586, § 18c–2106, added by P.A. 84–796, § 1, eff. Jan. 1, 1986. Amended by P.A. 85–553, § 2, eff. Sept. 18, 1987; P.A. 89–444, § 5, eff. Jan. 25, 1996.

Formerly Ill.Rev.Stat.1991, ch. 95 ½, ¶ 18c–2106.

5/18c–2107. Orders in household goods carrier authority proceedings

§ 18c–2107. Orders in household goods carrier authority proceedings. (1) Emergency Proceedings Orders. The Commission may, on request, and upon a finding that urgent and immediate public need requires emergency temporary action, issue orders granting emergency temporary relief in household goods carrier authority proceedings. The Commission shall promptly post notice of any such request at a prominent location at the Commission offices in Springfield and Chicago, and where action affecting a specific named person is requested shall promptly notify the person by telephone or telegram. Such orders may be issued without hearing and shall remain in effect pending notice and hearing in accordance with subsection (1) of Section 18c-2101 of this Chapter, but shall not remain in effect for a period exceeding 45 days from issuance, and shall not be renewed or extended. Any person in opposition to such relief shall be entitled, on request, to an oral hearing on the request for emergency temporary relief. The filing or granting of a request for an oral hearing shall not, unless the Commission so provides, stay the issuance or effect of any emergency temporary order under this subsection.

(2) Interim orders. The Commission may, on request, issue interim orders for temporary authority in household goods carrier authority proceedings making temporary disposition of issues in a proceeding after notice and review of verified supporting statements. Such orders shall remain in effect pending final disposition in accordance with Section 18c-2101 of this Chapter unless otherwise provided in the interim order or the interim order is modified or rescinded by the Commission. Any person in opposition to such relief shall be entitled, on request, to an oral hearing on the request for temporary relief. The filing or granting of such a request for an oral hearing shall not, unless the Commission so provides, stay the issuance or effect of any interim order under this subsection. A request for oral hearing on a request for interim relief shall, unless otherwise specified by the party making the request for oral hearing, be construed as a request for oral hearing on the application for permanent relief as well.

(3) Final Orders. Final orders shall be issued in household goods carrier of property authority proceedings only after an oral hearing.

P.A. 76-1586, § 18c-2107, added by P.A. 84-796, § 1, eff. Jan. 1, 1986. Amended by P.A. 89-444, § 5, eff. Jan. 25, 1996.

Formerly Ill.Rev.Stat.1991, ch. 95 ½, ¶ 18c-2107.

5/18c-2108. Orders in other than household goods carrier authority and enforcement proceedings

§ 18c-2108. Orders in other than household goods carriers authority and enforcement proceedings.

(1) Emergency Orders. The Commission may, on request, and upon a finding that urgent and immediate public need requires emergency temporary action, issue orders granting emergency temporary relief in other than household goods carrier authority or enforcement cases. The Commission shall promptly post notice of any such request at a prominent location at the Commission offices in Springfield and Chicago, and where action affecting a specific named person is requested shall promptly notify the person by telephone or telegram. Such orders may be issued without hearing and shall remain in effect pending notice and hearing in accordance with subsection (1) of Section 18c-2101 of this Chapter, but shall not remain in effect for a period exceeding 45 days from issuance, and shall not be renewed or extended. Any person in opposition to such relief shall be entitled, on request, to an oral hearing on the request for emergency temporary relief. The filing or granting of such request for oral hearing shall not, unless the Commission so provides, stay the issuance or effect of any emergency temporary order under this subsection.

(2) Interim Orders. The Commission may, on request, issue interim orders making temporary disposition of issues in a proceeding, other than a household goods carrier authority or enforcement proceeding, after notice and hearing on written submissions. Such orders shall remain in effect pending final disposition in accordance with Section 18c-2102 of this Chapter unless otherwise provided in the interim order or the interim order is modified or rescinded by the Commission. Any person in opposition to such relief shall be entitled, on request, to an oral hearing on the request for temporary relief. The filing or granting of such a request for oral hearing shall not, unless the Commission so provides, stay the issuance or effect of any interim order under this subsection. A request for oral hearing on a request for temporary relief shall, unless otherwise specified by the party making the request for oral hearing, be construed as a request for oral hearing on the application for permanent relief as well.

(3) Final orders. Any party to a proceeding before the Commission shall be entitled, on timely written request, to an oral hearing prior to issuance of a final order in the proceeding. Where the Commission has issued an interim order and no timely request for oral hearing has been filed or is pending, the Commission may issue a final order without oral hearing, except in household goods carrier authority proceedings.

(4) Section not applicable to household goods carrier authority proceedings. Nothing in this Section shall have application to any household goods carrier authority proceeding.

P.A. 76-1586, § 18c-2108, added by P.A. 84-796, § 1, eff. Jan. 1, 1986. Amended by P.A. 89-444, § 5, eff. Jan. 25, 1996; P.A. 92-651, § 77, eff. July 11, 2002.

Formerly Ill.Rev.Stat.1991, ch. 95 ½, ¶ 18c-2108.

5/18c-2109. Prompt Final Disposition of Proceedings

§ 18c-2109. Prompt Final Disposition of Proceedings. The Commission shall consider matters properly before it in the most expeditious manner possible, and in no case shall the final order resolving matters in a proceeding be entered later than the 90th day following the close of oral hearing. Proceedings may be reassigned in order to expedite consideration and disposition.

P.A. 76-1586, § 18c-2109, added by P.A. 84-796, § 1, eff. Jan. 1, 1986. Amended by P.A. 85-553, § 2, eff. Sept. 18, 1987.

Formerly Ill.Rev.Stat.1991, ch. 95 ½, ¶ 18c-2109.

5/18c-2110. Reconsideration, Rehearing and Reopening of Proceedings

§ 18c-2110. Reconsideration, Rehearing and Reopening of Proceedings. (1) Motions for Rehearing or Reconsideration.

(a) Who May File Motions. Any party of record to an administrative proceeding before the Commission may file a motion administratively appealing the action or inaction of the Commission, Employee Board, or Commission staff.

(b) Relief Which May Be Sought. A motion may request modification or rescission of a Commission or Employee Board order, or of the action or inaction of the Commission, Employee Board, or Commission staff; the Commission or Employee Board may likewise request such relief.

(c) To Whom Motions May Be Addressed. If the order appealed is a nonfinal order of an Employee Board, the motion may be addressed to the Board or to the Commission; otherwise, the motion must be addressed to the Commission.

(d) Deadline For Filing Motions. The motion must be filed within 30 days after service of the order, or of the action or inaction appealed, unless the time for filing a motion is extended by the Commission in writing.

(e) Style and Contents of Motions. The motion must set forth specific grounds for modification or rescission of the order. Appeals from orders issued by the Commission, or from the action or inaction of the Commission shall be styled "motions for rehearing;" appeals from orders of an Employee Board, or from the action or inaction of Employee Board or staff, shall be styled "motions for reconsideration."

(f) Grant or Denial of Motions. The Commission may grant or deny such motions, in whole or in part. If the Commission grants such a motion a new order shall be issued within 180 days after service of the order granting the motion unless the order granting the motion also disposed of the issues in the proceeding and is therefore a final, appealable order. If the Commission fails to act on any such motion within 45 days after it is filed, or up to 90 days if the period for acting on the motion has been extended by the Commission in writing, the motion shall be deemed to have been denied by operation of law.

(g) Appeals of Rulings by Hearing Examiners. Notwithstanding any other provision of this Section, interlocutory appeals of rulings by hearing examiners shall be as provided by the Commission's Rules of Practice; no other appeals of action or inaction by a hearing examiner may be taken.

(2) Motions to Reopen. The Commission may, at any time after notice to the parties and the public, reopen a proceeding to consider clarification, modification, or rescission of its order. Reopening may be on the Commission's own motion or on the motion of any interested person. Upon a finding of clerical or technical error the Commission may modify or rescind its order in the proceeding. The Commission may not, on reopening, impair the vested rights of any person.

P.A. 76–1586, § 18c–2110, added by P.A. 84–796, § 1, eff. Jan. 1, 1986. Amended by P.A. 84–1025, § 2, eff. Jan. 1, 1986; P.A. 85–553, § 2, eff. Sept. 18, 1987.

Formerly Ill.Rev.Stat.1991, ch. 95 ½, ¶ 18c–2110.

ARTICLE II. JUDICIAL REVIEW PROCEEDINGS

5/18c–2201. Availability of Judicial Review

§ 18c–2201. Availability of Judicial Review. (1) Standing to Seek Judicial Review. No person shall have standing to seek judicial review of a Commission action unless such person shall have an administratively cognizable interest in the order, be aggrieved by it, and have exhausted its administrative remedies. A person admitted as a party to an administrative proceeding shall be presumed to have an administratively cognizable interest in orders issued in the proceeding for purposes of standing to seek judicial review.

(2) Exhaustion of Administrative Remedies. A person shall be deemed to have exhausted its administrative remedies only if:

(a) The person participated as a party to the proceeding before the Commission, or filed a timely pleading seeking to participate as a party and was entitled as matter of right to participate as a party;

(b) The person filed a timely motion for reconsideration or rehearing which was denied by the Commission or by operation of law, unless the Commission expressly waived the filing of such a motion; and

(c) The action of which judicial review is sought is, in all respects, a final order of the Commission.

(3) Deadline for Filing Petitions for Judicial Review. A petition for judicial review must be filed within 35 days after the order of the Commission becomes final.

(4) Remedy Exclusive. Judicial review as provided for under this Article shall be exclusive of all other remedies at law or equity in regard to review of Commission actions, regulations or orders.

P.A. 76–1586, § 18c–2201, added by P.A. 84–796, § 1, eff. Jan. 1, 1986. Amended by P.A. 84–1025, § 2, eff. Jan. 1, 1986.

Formerly Ill.Rev.Stat.1991, ch. 95 ½, ¶ 18c–2201.

5/18c–2202. Scope of Judicial Review

§ 18c–2202. Scope of Judicial Review. (1) Issues on Review. The reviewing court shall be limited in its review to whether:

(a) The Commission's order is against the manifest weight of evidence in the record before the Commission;

(b) The order is contrary to provisions of this Chapter or Commission regulations;

(c) The order is an abuse of discretion;

(d) The order is beyond the jurisdiction of the Commission; or

(e) The order denies constitutional rights of the person seeking judicial review.

(2) Record on Review. In reviewing an order of the Commission, the court shall be limited to issues of fact or law presented to the Commission in either a motion for reconsideration or a motion for rehearing, and to:

(a) Evidence in the record before the Commission;

(b) Evidence offered but erroneously excluded by the Commission from the record; and

(c) Evidence of procedural irregularities which could not, with reasonable diligence, have been offered, either at the administrative hearing or in the motion for reconsideration or rehearing.

P.A. 76–1586, § 18c–2202, added by P.A. 84–796, § 1, eff. Jan. 1, 1986.

Formerly Ill.Rev.Stat.1991, ch. 95 ½, ¶ 18c–2202.

5/18c–2203. Submission of the Administrative Record

§ 18c–2203. Submission of the Administrative Record. It shall be the responsibility of the Commission to submit to the court certified copies of the record before the Commission. The record submitted must be complete in all respects unless all parties have, by written stipulation, agreed to deletion of materials not relevant to the issues raised in the petition for judicial review. The cost of preparing certified copies of the record may be assessed, in whole or in part, to the party seeking judicial review, and failure to pay such costs shall be grounds for dismissal in accordance with the Illinois Administrative Review Law.[1]

P.A. 76–1586, § 18c–2203, added by P.A. 84–796, § 1, eff. Jan. 1, 1986.

Formerly Ill.Rev.Stat.1991, ch. 95 ½, ¶ 18c–2203.

[1] 735 ILCS 5/3–101 et seq.

5/18c–2204. Relief

§ 18c–2204. Relief. The reviewing court may grant relief in accordance with provisions of the Illinois Administrative Review Law.[1]

P.A. 76–1586, § 18c–2204, added by P.A. 84–796, § 1, eff. Jan. 1, 1986.

Formerly Ill.Rev.Stat.1991, ch. 95 ½, ¶ 18c–2204.

[1] 735 ILCS 5/3–101 et seq.

5/18c–2205. Stay of Action Pending Judicial Review

§ 18c–2205. Stay of Action Pending Judicial Review. (1) Commission Orders Not Stayed by Filing of Appeal. The filing or pendency of a petition for judicial review shall not of itself stay, suspend, restrain or enjoin the operation of a rule, regulation, order or decision of the Commission.

(2) Power of Court to Stay Commission Orders. During the pendency of a petition for judicial review the reviewing court in its discretion may, except as provided in this subsection, stay, suspend, restrain or enjoin, in whole or in part, the operation of a Commission regulation or order. No order staying, suspending, restraining or enjoining a Commission regulation or order shall be made by the court except upon 3 days' actual notice to the Commission and the Attorney General and after hearing. Where the Commission action relates to enforcement of this Chapter, the reviewing court shall not stay, suspend, restrain or enjoin the action of the Commission for a period longer than 180 days from the filing of the appeal; unless at the expiration of the initial 180 day period, the court finds that continuation is necessary for the informed and just resolution of the issues; and unless the court does continue the stay, suspension, restraint, or injunction in effect for one or more definite periods of time not to exceed 180 days each.

(3) Bond Required. In case an action, regulation or order of the Commission is stayed, suspended, restrained, or enjoined, the order of the court shall not become effective until a bond shall first have been executed and filed with and approved by the court, except as otherwise provided in this paragraph. Where the order under review does not relate to enforcement of this law, the court may, for good cause, waive the requirement of a bond.

P.A. 76–1586, § 18c–2205, added by P.A. 84–796, § 1, eff. Jan. 1, 1986.

Formerly Ill.Rev.Stat.1991, ch. 95 ½, ¶ 18c–2205.

5/18c–2206. Application of Illinois Administrative Review Law

§ 18c–2206. Application of the Illinois Administrative Review Law.[1] Where this Article is silent, proceedings for judicial review of a Commission action, regulation or order shall be governed by provisions of the Administrative Review Law.

P.A. 76–1586, § 18c–2206, added by P.A. 84–796, § 1, eff. Jan. 1, 1986.

Formerly Ill.Rev.Stat.1991, ch. 95 ½, ¶ 18c–2206.

[1] 735 ILCS 5/3–101 et seq.

ARTICLE III. ADMINISTRATIVE AND JUDICIAL ENFORCEMENT PROCEEDINGS

5/18c–2301. Initiation of Proceedings

§ 18c–2301. Initiation of Proceedings. The Commission may initiate either administrative or judicial proceedings, or both, to enforce provisions of this Chapter, and Commission regulations and orders. In addition, any interested person may apply to a circuit court, which has jurisdiction and venue as set out in this Chapter, for injunctive relief to enforce provisions of Sub-Chapter 4 of this Chapter, and Commission regulations and orders issued pursuant to Sub-Chapter 4.

P.A. 76–1586, § 18c–2301, added by P.A. 84–796, § 1, eff. Jan. 1, 1986.

Formerly Ill.Rev.Stat.1991, ch. 95 ½, ¶ 18c–2301.

5/18c–2302. Governing Procedures

§ 18c–2302. Governing Procedures. Administrative enforcement proceedings initiated hereunder shall be governed by the Commission's rules of practice. Judicial enforcement proceedings initiated hereunder shall be governed by the rules of procedure applicable in the courts of this State.

P.A. 76–1586, § 18c–2302, added by P.A. 84–796, § 1, eff. Jan. 1, 1986.

Formerly Ill.Rev.Stat.1991, ch. 95 ½, ¶ 18c–2302.

ARTICLE IV. VENUE AND JURISDICTION

5/18c–2401. Venue and Jurisdiction in Actions for Judicial Review

§ 18c–2401. Venue and Jurisdiction in Actions for Judicial Review. (1) Venue. Actions for judicial review under this Chapter may be filed in the circuit courts of Sangamon or Cook Counties.

(2) Jurisdiction. Jurisdiction in actions for judicial review under this Chapter shall be vested in the circuit courts of Sangamon and Cook Counties.

P.A. 76–1586, § 18c–2401, added by P.A. 84–796, § 1, eff. Jan. 1, 1986.

Formerly Ill.Rev.Stat.1991, ch. 95 ½, ¶ 18c–2401.

5/18c–2402. Venue and Jurisdiction in Actions to Enforce this Chapter

§ 18c–2402. Venue and Jurisdiction in Actions to Enforce this Chapter.

(a) Venue in Suits for Criminal Misdemeanor Penalties. Actions in which criminal misdemeanor penalties are sought may be brought in the county where any part of the subject matter is located, or part of the violation(s) occurred, or the arrest was made, and venue shall lie in that county; the case may be transferred to another county only with the approval of the court and the agreement of the parties.

(b) Venue in Actions Other Than Suits for Criminal Penalties. Actions to enforce this Chapter, Commission regulations and orders, other than suits for criminal misdemeanor penalties, may be brought in the circuit courts of any county in which any part of the subject matter is located, or any part of the violation(s) occurred; the case may be transferred to another county only with the approval of the court and the agreement of the parties.

P.A. 76–1586, § 18c–2402, added by P.A. 84–796, § 1, eff. Jan. 1, 1986. Amended by P.A. 85–553, § 2, eff. Sept. 18, 1987; P.A. 91–357, § 231, eff. July 29, 1999.

Formerly Ill.Rev.Stat.1991, ch. 95 ½, ¶ 18c–2402.

SUB–CHAPTER 3. SUBSTANTIVE PROVISIONS APPLICABLE TO MORE THAN ONE TRANSPORTATION MODE

ARTICLE I. LICENSING

Section

ARTICLE II. RATEMAKING

Section

ARTICLE III. OTHER PROVISIONS COMMON TO ALL TRANSPORTATION MODES

ARTICLE I. LICENSING

5/18c–3101. Terms, Conditions, and Limitations

§ 18c–3101. Terms, Conditions, and Limitations. The Commission may attach to the exercise of rights under any license or other authorization issued or granted by it such terms, conditions, and limitations as will protect the public interest and effectuate the purposes of this Chapter.

P.A. 76–1586, § 18c–3101, added by P.A. 84–796, § 1, eff. Jan. 1, 1986.

Formerly Ill.Rev.Stat.1991, ch. 95 ½, ¶ 18c–3101.

5/18c–3102. Geographical Restrictions

§ 18c–3102. Geographical Restrictions. A prima facie determination whether transportation is within the geographical scope of a license may be made by reference to a copy of the official state highway map and the distance scale shown thereon. Such a determination may be rebutted by a showing, based on a municipal ordinance; other official document; or commercially published map, chart or other competent evidence; that the geographical scope of the license is other than as represented on the official state highway map.

P.A. 76–1586, § 18c–3102, added by P.A. 84–796, § 1, eff. Jan. 1, 1986.

Formerly Ill.Rev.Stat.1991, ch. 95 ½, ¶ 18c–3102.

ARTICLE II. RATEMAKING

5/18c–3201. Prohibition of transportation services in the absence of effective rates

§ 18c–3201. Prohibition of transportation services in the absence of effective rates. No common carrier by pipeline, household goods carrier, rail carrier, or passenger carrier shall render service until such carrier has in effect a tariff or schedule of rates applicable to such service in compliance with this Chapter. Likewise, no such carrier shall render service under a license issued by the Commission if the Commission has suspended or cancelled the tariff or schedule of rates previously in effect and applicable to such service, or if the tariff or schedule is, by action of a party thereto or by its own terms, no longer effective.

P.A. 76–1586, § 18c–3201, added by P.A. 84–796, § 1, eff. Jan. 1, 1986. Amended by P.A. 89–444, § 5, eff. Jan. 25, 1996.

Formerly Ill.Rev.Stat.1991, ch. 95 ½, ¶ 18c–3201.

5/18c–3202. Effective Dates of New or Amended Rates

§ 18c–3202. Effective Dates of New or Amended Rates. The Commission shall prescribe the periods of notice which must elapse between the filing of a proposed rate and its proposed effective date. In no case shall the Commission prescribe a notice period greater than 30 days or the period established by a valid, preemptive federal statute.

P.A. 76–1586, § 18c–3202, added by P.A. 84–796, § 1, eff. Jan. 1, 1986. Amended by P.A. 85–553, § 2, eff. Sept. 18, 1987.

Formerly Ill.Rev.Stat.1991, ch. 95 ½, ¶ 18c–3202.

5/18c–3203. Filing, publishing and posting of tariffs and schedules

§ 18c–3203. Filing, publishing and posting of tariffs and schedules.

(1) General requirement of filing, publication and posting. Each common carrier of household goods or passengers shall file, publish, and make available for public inspection its current tariffs (other than rail contract rate tariffs). Copies of such tariffs shall be provided by the carrier to any member of the public on request and at a reasonable cost. Each contract carrier of household goods shall file its current schedule of rates and provisions.

(2) Tariff and schedule specifications. Tariffs and schedules filed in accordance with this subsection shall be in such form and contain such information as the Commission may specify. The Commission may, by special permission for good cause shown, grant permission to deviate from its tariff and schedule regulations.

(3) Rejection of tariffs and schedules. The Commission may, at any time prior to the effective date of a tariff or schedule, reject or suspend a tariff or schedule which does not conform to its specifications or which on its face is in violation of this Chapter, Commission regulations or orders.

(4) Right of independent action. Each carrier subject to this Chapter shall have the individual right to publish, file, and post any rate for transportation provided by such carrier or in connection with any other carrier. No carrier shall be a member of any bureau, tariff publishing agency, or other organization which, directly or indirectly, prohibits such carrier from publishing and filing any rate or which requires

that such rate be published or filed by the bureau, publishing agency, or other organization.

P.A. 76–1586, § 18c–3203, added by P.A. 84–796, § 1, eff. Jan. 1, 1986. Amended by P.A. 85–553, § 2, eff. Sept. 18, 1987; P.A. 89–444, § 5, eff. Jan. 25, 1996; P.A. 90–655, § 153, eff. July 30, 1998.

Formerly Ill.Rev.Stat.1991, ch. 95 ½, ¶ 18c–3203.

5/18c–3204. Rate Proceedings

§ 18c–3204. Rate Proceedings.

(1) Initiation of proceedings. The Commission may initiate a proceeding to investigate or prescribe tariffs or schedules on its own motion or on complaint.

(2) Suspension of tariffs and schedules.

(a) Suspension of tariffs. The Commission may suspend a tariff, in whole or in part, during the pendency of a proceeding to consider the reasonableness of the tariff, or to consider whether the tariff is discriminatory, or to consider whether the tariff otherwise violates provisions of this Chapter, Commission regulations or orders, provided the order of suspension is issued prior to the effective date of the tariff. The suspension shall remain in effect for the period allowed under this Chapter unless the Commission order provides for a shorter period of suspension. At the end of the statutory suspension period the suspension may be extended by agreement of the parties; otherwise, the tariff shall go into effect. The statutory suspension period is:

(i) Seven months for public carriers and household goods common carriers;

(ii) One hundred and twenty days for motor carriers of passengers; and

(iii) Five months for rail carriers, unless the period is extended for an additional 3 months in accordance with provisions of the Interstate Commerce Act.[1]

(b) Suspension of schedules. The Commission may suspend a household goods contract carrier schedule, in whole or in part, during the pendency of a proceeding to consider whether the schedule violates provisions of this Chapter, Commission regulations or orders, provided the order of suspension is issued prior to the effective date of the schedule. The suspension shall remain in effect for 7 months unless the Commission order provides for a shorter period of suspension. At the end of this period, the suspension may be extended by agreement of the parties; otherwise, the schedule shall go into effect.

(c) Burden of proof in investigation proceedings. The burden of proof in an investigation proceeding shall be on the proponent of the rate unless otherwise provided in a valid preemptive federal statute which governs the rate.

(3) Prescription of tariffs and schedules. The Commission may prescribe tariffs where it has determined, in accordance with Section 18c–2102 of this Chapter, that a tariff published by a carrier is unreasonable, discriminatory, or otherwise in violation of this Chapter, Commission regulations or orders. The Commission may prescribe schedules where it has determined, after hearing, that a schedule filed by a carrier is in violation of this Chapter, Commission regulations or orders.

(4) Relief. The Commission may, where it finds a tariff or schedule to be in violation of this Chapter, its regulations or orders, or finds rates or provisions in a tariff unjust, unreasonable, or discriminatory, and in accordance with Section 18c–2102 of this Chapter, direct the carrier to:

(a) Publish and file a supplement cancelling the tariff or file notice of cancellation of the schedule, in whole or in part;

(b) Publish and file a new tariff or file a new schedule containing rates and provisions prescribed by the Commission; and

(c) Repay any overcharges or collect any undercharges, and, except with regard to household goods carriers, pay reparations.

P.A. 76–1586, § 18c–3204, added by P.A. 84–796, § 1, eff. Jan. 1, 1986. Amended by P.A. 85–553, § 2, eff. Sept. 18, 1987; P.A. 89–42, § 10, eff. Jan. 1, 1996; P.A. 89–444, § 5, eff. Jan. 25, 1996; P.A. 90–14, Art. 2, § 2–225, eff. July 1, 1997.

Formerly Ill.Rev.Stat.1991, ch. 95 ½, ¶ 18c–3204.

[1] 49 U.S.C.A. § 10101 et seq.

P.A. 90–14, Article 2, of the First 1997 General Revisory Act, resolved multiple actions in the 89th General Assembly and made certain technical corrections in P.A. 89–443 through P.A. 89–707.

5/18c–3205. Ratemaking Standards

§ 18c–3205. Ratemaking Standards. (1) Reasonableness. Rates for household goods common carrier service must be just, reasonable, and not discriminatory.

(2) Factors to be Considered. The Commission shall, in exercising its ratemaking powers consider, among other factors, the inherent advantages of transportation by a particular class of carriers, the public need for and interest in adequate and efficient transportation service, at rates consistent with provision of such service, and the revenue needs of carriers under honest, economical and efficient management.

(3) Factors Not Considered. The Commission shall not, in exercising its ratemaking powers, consider the value of any operating authority held by a carrier, or the value of any goodwill or earning power connected with operations of the carrier.

P.A. 76–1586, § 18c–3205, added by P.A. 84–796, § 1, eff. Jan. 1, 1986. Amended by P.A. 89–444, § 5, eff. Jan. 25, 1996.

Formerly Ill.Rev.Stat.1991, ch. 95 ½, ¶ 18c–3205.

5/18c–3206. Charges to conform to tariffs or schedules and orders of the commission

§ 18c–3206. Charges to conform to tariffs or schedules and orders of the Commission. (1) Overcharges and undercharges prohibited. No common or contract household goods or passenger carrier shall offer, advertise, charge, demand, collect, or receive, in any manner, a greater, lesser, or different compensation for transportation or for any service in connection therewith than the rates and charges specified in tariffs or schedules on file with the Commission and in effect at the time the transportation or any other service is rendered; nor shall any such carrier offer, advertise, charge, demand, collect, or receive any compensation for transportation or for any other service rendered in connection therewith where there is not in effect at the time a lawfully applicable tariff or schedule. Likewise, no such carrier shall refund or remit, in any manner or by any device, whether directly or indirectly, or through any agent or otherwise, or pursuant to Commission order, any portion of the rates or charges specified in tariffs or schedules on file with the Commission and in effect at the time; nor shall any such carrier extend to any person any discount, value, privilege, or facilities for transportation or any service rendered in connection therewith, except as are specified in tariffs or schedules on file with the Commission and in effect at the time.

(2) Repayment of overcharges, collection of undercharges and reparations.

(a) Repayment of overcharges and payment of reparations. The Commission may, in accordance with Section 18c–2101 of this Chapter, order any carrier to pay to one or more shippers the amount by which the carrier received compensation greater than the rates and charges specified in tariffs or schedules in effect at the time the carrier rendered the transportation or other service in connection therewith. The Commission may likewise, in accordance with Section 18c–2101 of this Chapter, order any carrier other than a household goods carrier to pay to one or more shippers the amount by which the carrier received compensation greater than reasonable rates and charges as determined by the Commission.

(b) Collection of undercharges. The Commission may, in accordance to Section 18c–2101 of this Chapter, order any carrier to make all reasonable efforts to collect from one or more shippers the difference between amounts collected and the amount of compensation specified in tariffs or schedules in effect at the time the transportation or other service in connection therewith was rendered.

P.A. 76–1586, § 18c–3206, added by P.A. 84–796, § 1, eff. Jan. 1, 1986. Amended by P.A. 89–444, § 5, eff. Jan. 25, 1996.

Formerly Ill.Rev.Stat.1991, ch. 95 ½, ¶ 18c–3206.

5/18c–3207. Zones of Rate Flexibility

§ 18c–3207. Zones of Rate Flexibility. (1) Zone for Motor Carriers of Passengers. Notwithstanding any other provisions of this Sub-chapter, the Commission may not investigate, suspend, revise, or revoke any single-line rate proposed by a motor carrier of passengers, or joint rate proposed by one or more such companies, applicable to any transportation on the grounds that such rate is unreasonably high or low if:

(a) The rate was published in accordance with provisions of this Chapter, Commission regulations and orders;

(b) The Commission was properly notified that the carrier or carriers wish to have the rate considered pursuant to this subsection; and

(c) The net of all increases and decreases, during the calendar year in which the rate is to become effective, is not more than 25%.

(2) Zone for Rail Carriers. Notwithstanding any other provision of this Sub-chapter the Commission may not investigate, suspend, revise, or revoke any rate proposed by a rail carrier on the grounds that such rate is unreasonably high or low if:

(a) The rate was published in accordance with provisions of this Chapter and Commission regulations;

(b) Commission was properly notified that the carrier wished to have the rate to be considered pursuant to this subsection; and

(c) The net of all increases and decreases, during the calendar year in which the rate is to become effective, is not more than the amount specified under 49 U.S. Code 10707a and 10708.

(3) Commission to Adopt Regulations. The Commission may adopt regulations specifying procedures for determining whether a rate published by a carrier falls within the zone of rate flexibility.

P.A. 76–1586, § 18c–3207, added by P.A. 84–796, § 1, eff. Jan. 1, 1986.

Formerly Ill.Rev.Stat.1991, ch. 95 ½, ¶ 18c–3207.

5/18c–3208. Joint rates and routes

§ 18c–3208. Joint rates and routes. (1) Establishment by carriers. Two or more common carriers of household goods or passengers may establish through routes and joint rates, provided that the rates, and divisions and practices relating thereto, are just, reasonable, and not discriminatory.

(2) Establishment by the Commission. The Commission may, on its own motion or on petition or complaint, where 2 or more carriers have failed to establish through routes, joint rates, or divisions and practices relating thereto, establish such routes, rates, divisions and practices. The Commission shall take such action only after notice and hearing to consider whether any proposed routes, rates, divisions and practices are just, reasonable and not discriminatory, whether any carrier has a reasonable objection to establishment of such routes, rates, divisions and practices, and whether such objections can be satisfied by imposing reasonable terms and conditions on the application of such routes, rates, divisions and practices. The provisions of this subsection shall have no application to household goods carriers.

P.A. 76–1586, § 18c–3208, added by P.A. 84–796, § 1, eff. Jan. 1, 1986. Amended by P.A. 89–444, § 5, eff. Jan. 25, 1996.

Formerly Ill.Rev.Stat.1991, ch. 95 ½, ¶ 18c–3208.

5/18c–3209. Charges Not Part of Direct Transportation Cost

§ 18c–3209. Charges Not Part of Direct Transportation Cost. Any agreement, arrangement, or device, or part thereof, which, as a condition to the provision of transportation service, requires or permits any carrier, shipper, or receiver to pay a charge to any person, where such charge is not part of the direct cost of transportation service, shall be void.

P.A. 76–1586, § 18c–3209, added by P.A. 84–796, § 1, eff. Jan. 1, 1986. Amended by P.A. 85–553, § 2, eff. Sept. 18, 1987.

Formerly Ill.Rev.Stat.1991, ch. 95 ½, ¶ 18c–3209.

5/18c–3210. Presentation of freight bills, payment of freight charges, and extension of credit

§ 18c–3210. Presentation of freight bills, payment of freight charges, and extension of credit. Except as otherwise provided in this Chapter, this Section is applicable only to household goods carriers. (1) Presentation of freight bills. Freight bills shall be presented to the person responsible for payment of freight charges not later than the 7th day following delivery of the freight.

(2) Payment required before delivery or relinquishment of possession. Except as provided in subsection (3) of this Section, no common carrier shall deliver or relinquish possession of a shipment transported by it until all freight charges for such shipment under lawfully applicable rates have been paid to the carrier. Where credit has been extended in accordance with this Section, and all freight charges on the shipment under lawfully applicable rates have not been paid before expiration of the period for which credit has been extended, the carrier shall cease delivering or relinquishing

possession of the shipment and may decline to transport future shipments until all such charges have been paid.

(3) Exception: Delivery or relinquishment of possession before payment. A carrier may deliver or relinquish possession of a shipment transported by it in advance of payment of all freight charges on the shipment under lawfully applicable rates if the carrier has, in accordance with this Section, extended credit to the person responsible for payment of freight charges.

(4) Extension of credit. Credit, if extended by a carrier, must be extended without discrimination. Credit for payment of freight charges shown on the initial freight bill shall be for a period not to exceed 30 days, beginning on the later of the date of delivery or the date on which the freight bill is presented. If freight charges shown on the initial freight bill are paid and the carrier subsequently presents a supplemental freight bill, the carrier may extend credit in the amount of freight charges shown on the supplemental freight bill for an additional period not to exceed 15 days, beginning on the date on which the supplemental freight bill is presented.

(5) Commission regulation of credit terms. The Commission may regulate the extension and terms of credit extended by carriers under this Section, and no credit shall be extended except in accordance with such regulations.

(6) Use of U.S. Postal Service for presentation of bills or payment of charges. Where the United States Postal Service is used for the presentation of freight bills or payment of freight charges, the date of mailing, as indicated by the postmark, shall be the date of presentation or payment.

(7) Calculation of times for extension of credit. Time periods of extension of credit under this Section shall commence at midnight on the date of the event (delivery or presentation of freight bill). The initial 7 day period shall not include Saturdays, Sundays, or legal holidays.

P.A. 76–1586, § 18c–3210, added by P.A. 84–796, § 1, eff. Jan. 1, 1986. Amended by P.A. 85–553, § 2, eff. Sept. 18, 1987; P.A. 89–444, § 5, eff. Jan. 25, 1996.

Formerly Ill.Rev.Stat.1991, ch. 95 ½, ¶ 18c–3210.

5/18c–3211. Free or Reduced Rate Carriage

§ 18c–3211. Free or Reduced Rate Carriage. Nothing in this Chapter shall prevent a carrier from establishing reduced rate or free carriage rates applicable to transportation provided for the United States, the State of Illinois, or any municipality or subdivision of this State, where it is required by law that the carrier providing such transportation be selected by competitive bid. Such rates shall be filed in the form and manner required by the Commission.

P.A. 76–1586, § 18c–3211, added by P.A. 84–796, § 1, eff. Jan. 1, 1986.

Formerly Ill.Rev.Stat.1991, ch. 95 ½, ¶ 18c–3211.

5/18c–3212. Statute of Limitations for Freight Charges

§ 18c–3212. Statute of Limitations for Freight Charges. (1) Collection Actions. Actions to collect freight charges under lawfully applicable rates must be instituted within 3 years after rendition of the service.

(2) Reparations or Overcharge Proceedings. Petitions seeking reparations or repayment of overcharges must be filed with the Commission within 3 years after rendition of the service, and any action seeking judicial enforcement of a Commission order awarding reparations must be instituted within 1 year after issuance of such order. Where an action seeking judicial review of a Commission order awarding reparations is filed, the time preceding final adjudication of the action shall be excluded in computing the time for instituting the action seeking judicial enforcement of the Commission order.

P.A. 76–1586, § 18c–3212, added by P.A. 84–796, § 1, eff. Jan. 1, 1986.

Formerly Ill.Rev.Stat.1991, ch. 95 ½, ¶ 18c–3212.

5/18c–3213. Application of Rate Regulations to Exempt Traffic

§ 18c–3213. Application of Rate Regulations to Exempt Traffic. Notwithstanding any other provision of this Chapter to the contrary, the provisions of this Article shall not apply to traffic which is altogether exempt from Commission jurisdiction under this Chapter or a valid, preemptive federal statute.

P.A. 76–1586, § 18c–3213, added by P.A. 84–796, § 1, eff. Jan. 1, 1986.

Formerly Ill.Rev.Stat.1991, ch. 95 ½, ¶ 18c–3213.

ARTICLE III. OTHER PROVISIONS COMMON TO ALL TRANSPORTATION MODES

5/18c–3301. Certain Third Party Payments Prohibited

§ 18c–3301. Certain Third Party Payments Prohibited. Whenever a shipper or receiver of property requires that any person who owns or operates a motor vehicle transporting property in intrastate commerce under the provisions of this Chapter be assisted in the loading or unloading of such vehicle, the shipper or receiver shall be responsible for providing such assistance or shall compensate the owner or operator for all costs associated with securing and compensating the person or persons providing such assistance. It shall be unlawful to coerce or attempt to coerce any person providing transportation of property by motor vehicle for-hire in intrastate commerce to employ or pay one or more persons to load or unload any part of such property onto or from such vehicle, except that this subsection shall not be construed as making unlawful any activity which is not unlawful under the National Labor Relations Act[1] or any other acts governing labor practices.

P.A. 76–1586, § 18c–3301, added by P.A. 84–796, § 1, eff. Jan. 1, 1986.

Formerly Ill.Rev.Stat.1991, ch. 95 ½, ¶ 18c–3301.

[1] 29 U.S.C.A. § 151 et seq.

5/18c–3302. Prohibition against discrimination

§ 18c–3302. Prohibition against discrimination. It shall be unlawful for any household goods carrier, rail carrier, common carrier by pipeline, or passenger carrier to discriminate by giving or causing to be given any unreasonable preference or advantage to any person or traffic, or to subject any such person or traffic to unreasonable prejudice or disadvantage.

P.A. 76–1586, § 18c–3302, added by P.A. 84–796, § 1, eff. Jan. 1, 1986. Amended by P.A. 89–444, § 5, eff. Jan. 25, 1996.

Formerly Ill.Rev.Stat.1991, ch. 95 ½, ¶ 18c–3302.

5/18c–3303. Failure to Reject or Suspend, or to Invoke Sanctions, Not to be Construed as Acceptance

§ 18c–3303. Failure to Reject or Suspend, or to Invoke Sanctions, Not to be Construed as Acceptance. Failure of the Commission to reject or suspend any rate, contract, application, or other document filed with it, or to initiate enforcement proceedings or invoke sanctions against any person for action or violation of this Chapter, Commission regulations or orders, shall not be construed in any proceeding of either any administrative or judicial nature as authorization or acceptance of such document or action, or any portion thereof. Nothing in this Section shall be construed to affect the date on which a rate or tariff is lawfully in effect.

P.A. 76-1586, § 18c-3303, added by P.A. 84-796, § 1, eff. Jan. 1, 1986.

Formerly Ill.Rev.Stat.1991, ch. 95 ½, ¶ 18c-3303.

5/18c-3304. Records and accounts

§ 18c-3304. Records and accounts. Each household goods carrier, rail carrier, common carrier by pipeline, and passenger carrier shall:

(1) Keep written accounts and records of its revenues, expenses, contracts, and other activities subject to regulation under this Chapter in accordance with regulations prescribed by the Commission;

(2) Maintain, for a period of 3 years, copies of all accounts and records required by Commission regulations; and

(3) Make such accounts and records available for inspection, on request, by any authorized employee of the Commission.

Accounts and records kept pursuant to this Section shall be kept at an office in the State of Illinois unless the Commission shall have authorized maintenance at a location outside of the State.

P.A. 76-1586, § 18c-3304, added by P.A. 84-796, § 1, eff. Jan. 1, 1986. Amended by P.A. 89-444, § 5, eff. Jan. 25, 1996.

Formerly Ill.Rev.Stat.1991, ch. 95 ½, ¶ 18c-3304.

SUB-CHAPTER 4. MOTOR CARRIERS OF PROPERTY

ARTICLE I. GENERAL PROVISIONS GOVERNING MOTOR CARRIERS OF PROPERTY

ARTICLE I. GENERAL PROVISIONS GOVERNING MOTOR CARRIERS OF PROPERTY

5/18c-4101. Scope of Commission Jurisdiction

§ 18c-4101. Scope of Commission Jurisdiction. Except as provided in Section 18c-4102 of this Chapter, the jurisdiction of the Commission shall extend to all motor carriers of property operating within the State of Illinois.

P.A. 76-1586, § 18c-4101, added by P.A. 84-796, § 1, eff. Jan. 1, 1986.

Formerly Ill.Rev.Stat.1991, ch. 95 ½, ¶ 18c-4101.

5/18c-4102. Exemptions from Commission Jurisdiction

§ 18c-4102. Exemptions from Commission Jurisdiction. The provisions of this chapter shall not apply to transportation, by motor vehicle:

(a) of mail exclusively for the United States Postal Service;

(b) of agricultural commodities, farm supplies, and other commodities for sale by farm supply retail outlets, by an agricultural cooperative association as defined in the Illinois "Agricultural Co-Operative Act" as amended; [1]

(c) of farm or dairy products, livestock, poultry, fruits and agricultural products, by the producer thereof or by a producer on behalf of other producers from farm to a farm, market, warehouse, dairy or shipping terminal, for which no monetary compensation is paid or received;

(d) of livestock from farm to a farm market, farm to farm, or farm market to a farm as long as the vehicle is not registered for a gross vehicle weight that exceeds 28,000 pounds or a truck and trailer with a registered combined gross vehicle weight that does not exceed 28,000 pounds;

(e) by farm tractors and any other motorized, self-propelled machinery used in the production of agricultural commodities on a farm, where the transportation is provided by the owner of the machinery or another farmer as an incident to the business of farming;

(f) consisting of towing performed by any towing service pursuant to the written order of a law enforcement official or agency in accordance with Sections 4-201 through 4-214 of The Illinois Vehicle Code;

(g) of trespassing motor vehicles by a licensed commercial vehicle relocator;

(h) of newspapers being delivered to residential subscribers or to persons who will deliver the newspapers to residential subscribers;

(i) of waste having no commercial value to a disposal site for disposal;

(j) where the transportation is incidental to and within the scope of the person's primary business purpose, and the primary business is other than transportation;

(k) consisting of emergency transportation of a wrecked or disabled vehicle. Further movements to an additional place of repair or storage are not exempt under this subsection. Emergency transportation of wrecked or disabled vehicles shall include the transportation, pursuant to written authorization of law enforcement official if the owner is unavailable or unable to make the request, of wrecked or disabled vehicles which might otherwise constitute a public safety hazard along a street or highway, and transportation of wrecked or disabled vehicles in other bona fide emergency situations;

(*l*) consisting of transportation by a tow truck or rollback car carrier equipped as a tow truck of a motor vehicle when requested by the owner;

(m) of waste from the facilities of the generator of the waste to a recognized recycling or waste processing facility when the generator receives no direct or indirect compensation from anyone for the waste and when the transportation is by garbage trucks with self contained compacting devices, roll off trucks with containers, or vehicles or containers specially designed and used to receive separated recyclables, and when the transportation is an interim step toward recycling, reclamation, reuse, or disposal; and

(n) of potable water for human and livestock consumption transported in containers of 1,600 gallons or less. This subsection does not apply to vehicles transporting more than one container.

P.A. 76-1586, § 18c-4102, added by P.A. 84-796, § 1, eff. Jan. 1, 1986. Amended by P.A. 84-1308, Art. II, § 98, eff. Aug. 25, 1986; P.A. 85-553, § 2, eff. Sept. 18, 1987; P.A. 85-963, § 1, eff. July 1, 1988; P.A. 85-1209, Art. II, § 2-51, eff. Aug. 30, 1988; P.A. 86-564, § 1, eff. Jan. 1, 1990; P.A. 87-465, § 1, eff. Sept. 13, 1991; P.A. 87-531, § 1, eff. Jan. 1, 1992; P.A. 87-727, § 110, eff. Sept. 23, 1991; P.A. 87-768, § 2, eff. Oct. 10, 1991; P.A. 87-895, Art. 2, § 2-45, eff. Aug. 14, 1992; P.A. 87-1203, § 1, eff. Sept. 25, 1992; P.A. 87-1249, § 1, eff. Dec. 24, 1992.

Formerly Ill.Rev.Stat.1991, ch. 95 ½, ¶ 18c-4102.

[1] 805 ILCS 315/1 et seq.

P.A. 87-895, the First 1992 General Revisory Act, provides in Article 2 for the revision and renumbering of certain Sections of Acts which have been added or amended by more than one Act of the 87th General Assembly; incorporates amendments to repealed Acts into successor laws passed by the same General Assembly; corrects errors, revises cross-references and deletes obsolete text in such Sections contained in Public Acts through P.A. 87-855.

P.A. 87-1249 incorporated the amendments by P.A. 87-465, P.A. 87-531, P.A. 87-727, P.A. 87-768 and P.A. 87-1203 and included the amendment by P.A. 87-895.

5/18c-4103. Leasing

§ 18c-4103. Leasing. (1) Prohibition Against Single-Source Leasing. No private carrier shall lease any motor vehicle with driver, nor shall any person lease a motor vehicle with driver to any private carrier. Likewise, no person shall lease any motor vehicle to any private carrier and either:

(a) Procure or exercise control over drivers of such vehicles, directly or indirectly; or

(b) Be responsible for or hold itself out to be responsible for driver's wages, payroll, unemployment compensation, social security tax, income withholding tax or any other taxes or payments normally due by reason of the employer-employee relationship, or any other compensation to drivers.

The provision of motor vehicles with drivers shall constitute motor carrier operations subject to the licensing, ratemaking, and other jurisdiction of the Commission under this Chapter.

(2) Exclusive Use of Household Goods Contract Carrier Vehicles. The prohibition against single source leasing in subsection (1) of this Section shall not prohibit a household goods contract carrier from providing motor vehicles, with drivers, for exclusive use by a private carrier where:

(a) The private carrier is a contracting shipper;

(b) Operations conducted with such motor vehicles are within the scope of the household goods contract carrier's authority;

(c) The household goods contract carrier exercises direct supervision and control of such motor vehicles and drivers; and

(d) The lease does not have the effect of circumventing rate or other provisions of this Chapter, Commission regulations and orders.

This subsection shall apply regardless of whether the household goods contract carrier's permit expressly provides for the lease of vehicles, with drivers, to contracting shippers.

(3) Equipment Leasing.

(a) Requirements for Content, Filing, and Carrying of Leases. The Commission may prescribe requirements for the leasing of equipment, with driver, and of equipment without driver, to or by a motor carrier of property; provided that such regulations shall not encompass the leasing of equipment, without drivers, from a bona fide equipment leasing company to a motor carrier of property. Such leases shall be in writing, constitute the complete and exclusive statement of terms between the parties, specify the compensation for the lease and the duration of the lease, be signed by the parties thereto, be filed with the Commission, and be carried in each motor vehicle covered thereby, provided, however, that the Commission may exempt from the foregoing requirements leases between parties, all of whom hold public carrier certificates issued by the Commission. The provisions of this paragraph shall not apply to the interchange of equipment or drivers between carriers for use wholly within a county having a population of more than 1,000,000 inhabitants.

(b) Direction and Control of Leased Equipment. It shall be the responsibility of the license holder to exercise full direction and control of all equipment and personnel used in its operations. Equipment used in its operations must be owned by or under lease to the carrier.

P.A. 76–1586, § 18c–4103, added by P.A. 84–796, § 1, eff. Jan. 1, 1986. Amended by P.A. 85–553, § 2, eff. Sept. 18, 1987; P.A. 89–444, § 5, eff. Jan. 25, 1996.

Formerly Ill.Rev.Stat.1991, ch. 95 ½, ¶ 18c–4103.

5/18c–4104. Unlawful Operations

§ 18c–4104. Unlawful Operations. (1) Prohibition. Except as provided in Article I of this Sub-chapter, and subject to the provisions stated herein, it shall be unlawful for any person to:

(a) Operate as an intrastate motor carrier of property without a license from the Commission; or as an interstate motor carrier of property without a registration from the Commission.

(b) Operate as an intrastate household goods carrier in excess of the scope of a license issued to it by the Commission in regard to any of the following:

1. hauling unauthorized commodities;
2. operating outside authorized territory; or
3. violating other restrictions.

(c) Operate, as an intrastate motor carrier of property, any motor vehicle which does not carry a copy of a valid, current license issued by the Commission to such carrier; or operate, as an interstate motor carrier of property, any motor vehicle which does not carry a copy of a valid, current registration issued by the Commission to such carrier; or fail to produce such copy on request; provided that an authorized interstate motor carrier of property shall be exempted from the requirement that a copy of its registration be carried in each motor vehicle.

(d) Operate, as an intrastate household goods carrier, any motor vehicle not owned by the carrier, or operate as an intrastate public carrier, any motor vehicle not owned by the carrier or another intrastate public carrier, for which a valid lease is not on file in compliance with Section 18c–4103 of this Chapter, Commission regulations and orders.

(e) Operate, as an intrastate household goods carrier, any motor vehicle not owned by the carrier, or operate as an intrastate public carrier, any motor vehicle not owned by the carrier or another intrastate public carrier, which does not carry an executed copy of the lease required in paragraph (d) of this subsection; or fail to produce such copy on request.

(f) Operate, as an intrastate motor carrier of property, any motor vehicle for which the carrier has not executed a prescribed intrastate cab card, with current Illinois intrastate identifier printed thereon; or, as an interstate motor carrier of property, any motor vehicle for which the carrier has not executed a prescribed interstate cab card, with current Illinois interstate identifier affixed or printed thereon.

(g) Operate, as an intrastate motor carrier of property, any motor vehicle which does not carry the properly executed intrastate cab card, with current Illinois intrastate identifier printed thereon; or, as an interstate motor carrier of property, any motor vehicle which does not carry the properly executed interstate cab card, with current Illinois interstate identifier affixed or printed thereon.

(h) Operate, as an intrastate or interstate motor carrier of property, any motor vehicle which is not identified or is not properly identified in compliance with Section 18c–4701 of this Chapter, Commission regulations and orders.

(i) Operate, as an intrastate motor carrier of property, in violation of transfer requirements in Section 18c–4307 of this Chapter.

(j) Provide, as an intrastate household goods carrier, service at rates other than those contained in lawfully applicable tariffs or schedules for such service.

(k) Otherwise operate as a motor carrier of property in violation of any provision of this Chapter, Commission regulations and orders, or any other law of this State.

(*l*) Aid or abet any other person in a violation of this Chapter, Commission regulations or orders, by soliciting, receiving, or compensating service from a person not authorized to provide such service, or at other than lawful rates for such service, or otherwise.

(2) Provisos.

(a) Presentation of Documents at Hearing as Defense. Presentation, at hearing, of a copy of a current license or registration issued by the Commission to the carrier which was valid on the date the violation occurred shall, if no concurrent violations of this Chapter, Commission regulations or orders are found, excuse the carrier from any penalties under paragraph (c) of subsection (1) of this Section. Presentation, at hearing, of an executed copy of the current lease in the form prescribed by and on file with the Commission shall, if no concurrent violations of this Chapter, Commission regulations or orders are found, excuse the carrier from penalties under paragraph (d) of subsection (1) of this Section. Presentation, at hearing, of the required intrastate or interstate cab card, with the required Illinois intrastate or interstate identifier affixed or printed thereon, if valid on the date the violation occurred, and if no concurrent violations are found, shall excuse the carrier from penalties under paragraph (g) of subsection (1) of this Section.

(b) Lease Form Prescribed by the Commission. A lease shall, for purposes of paragraph (d) of subsection (1) of this Section, be deemed to be in the form prescribed by the Commission if it contains all provisions called for in the

Commission-prescribed lease and does not contain any provisions inconsistent therewith.

P.A. 76–1586, § 18c–4104, added by P.A. 84–796, § 1, eff. Jan. 1, 1986. Amended by P.A. 85–553, § 2, eff. Sept. 18, 1987; P.A. 89–444, § 5, eff. Jan. 25, 1996.

Formerly Ill.Rev.Stat.1991, ch. 95 ½, ¶ 18c–4104.

ARTICLE II. LICENSING

5/18c–4201. Licensing cases

§ 18c–4201. Licensing cases. (1) Scope of Section. The provisions of this Chapter relating to household goods carrier licensing apply to applications:

(a) For a license authorizing a carrier to operate as an intrastate household goods carrier;

(b) To transfer a certificate, permit, or license or to change the name on a certificate, permit, or license; and

(c) To convert household goods contract carrier authority to household goods common carrier authority.

(2) Form and content of household goods carrier licensing applications. Household goods carrier licensing applications shall be on such forms and contain such information as may be prescribed by the Commission, be verified under oath, and shall be accompanied by the required filing fee.

(3) Public notice of applications.

(a) Review of applications prior to publication. The Commission may provide for preliminary review of each application to determine if it is complete, if it gives adequate notice, and if the authority requested is unenforceably vague or otherwise contrary to the provisions of this Chapter.

(b) Authorization to submit application for publication. If the Commission determines after review that the application is defective in any respect, it shall promptly notify the applicant. No application shall be submitted to the official newspaper for publication until after it has been approved for publication, if the Commission has provided for preliminary review. If the Commission does not find that the application is defective, or if it finds that any defects have been removed by amendment, the applicant shall be permitted to submit the application to the official newspaper for publication. The Commission shall complete its review and notify the applicant within 15 days after filing of the application.

(c) Additional notice prescribed by the Commission. The Commission may direct applicant to give such further notice in connection with its application as the Commission deems necessary. The Commission may, itself, give such additional notice as it deems necessary.

(4) Hearing on licensing applications.

(a) Participation at hearing. Any person having standing to participate under this Chapter may appear and participate in a hearing before the Commission to the extent of its standing, provided that the person has complied with Commission regulations concerning the filing of petitions for leave to intervene and like pleadings. Petitions for leave to intervene must be filed within 15 days after publication, unless the Commission provides for filing at a later date. The Commission may permit additional persons to appear and participate, on such terms as the Commission shall prescribe, where such participation is deemed necessary to an informed and just resolution of the issues in the proceeding. No shipper representative shall be permitted to testify in support of an application for a motor common carrier certificate or a motor contract carrier permit on the issue of need for service unless:

(i) A supporting statement was filed on behalf of the shipper at least 10 days prior to the date of testimony; and

(ii) If the supporting statement was not filed with the application, the statement was served on all parties of record at least 10 days prior to the date of testimony.

(b) Setting, notice, and hearing. Notwithstanding any contrary provisions in Section 18c–2101 of this Chapter, a hearing shall be held on each licensing application to determine that the requirements of this Chapter have been satisfied, except as otherwise provided in Section 18c–4306 of this Chapter. The Commission shall set the hearing at a time not less than 15 days after publication in the official newspaper. The Commission shall serve notice of hearing on each party of record.

(c) Issuance of orders after hearing. The Commission may issue summary orders in cases where the licensing application was not opposed in a timely pleading addressed to the Commission, or was opposed in a timely pleading but such opposition was later withdrawn or the parties in opposition waived all right to other than a summary order. Summary orders shall be issued within 10 days after the close of oral hearing or such other period as the Commission may prescribe. Where a party requests, in a properly filed motion for reconsideration or rehearing, a detailed statement of findings and conclusions, the Commission shall vacate the summary order and issue a new order in accordance with Sub-chapters 1 and 2 of this Chapter.[1] Otherwise, orders shall be issued in accordance with provisions of Sub-chapters 1 and 2 of this Chapter.

P.A. 76–1586, § 18c–4201, added by P.A. 84–796, § 1, eff. Jan. 1, 1986. Amended by P.A. 85–553, § 2, eff. Sept. 18, 1987; P.A. 89–444, § 5, eff. Jan. 25, 1996.

Formerly Ill.Rev.Stat.1991, ch. 95 ½, ¶ 18c–4201.

1 625 ILCS 5/18–1101 et seq. and 5/18c–2101 et seq.

5/18c–4202. Household goods common carrier certificates

§ 18c–4202. Household goods common carrier certificates. (1) Prerequisite to operation as a household goods common carrier. No person shall operate as a household goods common carrier unless such person possesses a common carrier of household goods certificate issued by the Commission and in good standing.

(2) Requirements for issuance. The Commission shall grant an application for a common carrier of household goods certificate, in whole or in part, to the extent that it finds that the application was properly filed; a public need for the service exists; the applicant is fit, willing and able to provide the service in compliance with this Chapter, Commission regulations or orders; and the public convenience and necessity requires issuance of the certificate. Otherwise, the application shall be denied. The burden of proving that the requirements for issuance of a common carrier of household goods certificate have been met shall be borne by the applicant.

(3) Duties and practices of household goods common carriers. Household goods common carriers shall provide safe and adequate transportation service to the general public within the scope of their authorities and in compliance with this Chapter, Commission regulations and orders. Such service shall be at reasonable rates and without discrimination.

P.A. 76–1586, § 18c–4202, added by P.A. 84–796, § 1, eff. Jan. 1, 1986. Amended by P.A. 89–444, § 5, eff. Jan. 25, 1996.

Formerly Ill.Rev.Stat.1991, ch. 95 ½, ¶ 18c–4202.

5/18c–4203. Household goods contract carrier permits

§ 18c–4203. Household goods contract carrier permits. (1) Prerequisite to operation as a household goods contract carrier. No person shall operate as a household goods contract carrier of property unless such person possesses a household goods contract carrier permit issued by the Commission and in good standing.

(2) Requirements for issuance.

(a) General requirements. The Commission shall grant an application for a household goods contract carrier permit, in whole or in part, to the extent that it finds that the application was properly filed; supporting shippers need the proposed service; the applicant is fit, willing and able to provide the service in compliance with this Chapter, Commission regulations and orders; and issuance of the permit will be consistent with the public interest. Otherwise, the application shall be denied. The burden of proving that the requirements for issuance of a household goods contract carrier permit have been met shall be borne by the applicant.

(b) Conversion to household goods common carrier authority. The Commission may, at the request of the holder, authorize the conversion of household goods contract carrier authority to household goods common carrier authority, subject to the same terms, conditions, limitations, and regulations as other household goods common carriers.

(c) Cancellation and non-renewal of contracts. Cancellation or non-renewal of a contract, or failure to keep on file with the Commission a copy of a valid contract, shall render a permit void with regard to the involved shipper.

(3) Duties and practices of household goods contract carriers.

(a) Services. Household goods contract carriers shall provide safe and adequate transportation service to their contracting shippers within the scope of their authorities and contracts and in compliance with this Chapter, Commission regulations and orders.

(b) Contracts. Each household goods contract carrier shall file with the Commission a copy of each contract executed under authority of its permit, and shall provide no service except in accordance with contracts on file with the Commission. The Commission may, at any time, reject contracts filed with it which do not comply with the provisions of this Chapter, Commission regulations and orders.

P.A. 76–1586, § 18c–4203, added by P.A. 84–796, § 1, eff. Jan. 1, 1986. Amended by P.A. 89–444, § 5, eff. Jan. 25, 1996.

Formerly Ill.Rev.Stat.1991, ch. 95 ½, ¶ 18c–4203.

5/18c–4204. Standards to be considered in issuing common and contract household goods carrier licenses

§ 18c–4204. Standards to be considered in issuing common and contract household goods carrier licenses. The Commission shall exercise its discretion in regard to issuance of common carrier of household goods or contract carrier of household goods licenses in accordance with standards enumerated in this Section. (1) Standards relevant to both common and contract household goods carrier licenses. In determining whether to issue a common carrier of household goods certificate or a contract carrier of household goods permit under Sections 18c–4202 and 18c–4203 of this Chapter, the Commission shall consider, in addition to other standards enumerated in this Chapter:

(a) The characteristics of the supporting shipper or shippers transportation needs, including the total volume of shipments, the amounts handled by existing authorized carriers and others, the amounts which would be tendered to the applicant, the nature and location of points where traffic would be picked up and delivered, and any special transportation needs of the supporting shipper or shippers or their receiver or receivers;

(b) The existing authorized carriers' services, including the adequacy of such services and the effect which issuance of a new certificate or permit would have on such services;

(c) The proposed service, and whether it would meet the needs of the supporting shipper or shippers;

(d) Any evidence bearing on the fitness, willingness, or ability of the applicant, including but not limited to any past history of violations of this Chapter, Commission regulations or orders, whether or not such violations were the subject of an enforcement proceeding; and

(e) The effect which issuing the certificate or permit would have on the development, maintenance and preservation of the highways of this State for commercial and other public use.

(2) Additional standards relevant to household goods contract carrier licenses. In determining whether to issue a household goods contract carrier permit under Section 18c–4203 of this Chapter, the Commission shall consider, in addition to standards enumerated in subsection (1) of this Section or elsewhere in this Sub-chapter:

(a) Whether the proposed service is contract carrier service; and

(b) The effect which failure to issue the permit would have on the supporting shipper or shippers.

(3) Standards not relevant to either household goods common or household goods contract carrier licenses. In determining whether to issue a household goods common carrier certificate or a household goods contract carrier permit under Sections 18c–4202 and 18c–4203 of this Chapter, the Commission shall not consider:

(a) The mere preference of the supporting shipper or shippers or their receiver or receivers for the applicant's service; or

(b) Any illegal operations of the applicant as evidence of shipper need or the inadequacy of existing carriers' services.

P.A. 76–1586, § 18c–4204, added by P.A. 84–796, § 1, eff. Jan. 1, 1986. Amended by P.A. 85–553, § 2, eff. Sept. 18, 1987; P.A. 86–1005, § 3, eff. Dec. 28, 1989; P.A. 89–444, § 5, eff. Jan. 25, 1996.

Formerly Ill.Rev.Stat.1991, ch. 95 ½, ¶ 18c–4204.

5/18c–4204a. Fitness standards

§ 18c–4204a. Fitness standards. (1) Establishment of administrative standards. The Commission shall, within 180 days from the effective date of this amendatory Act of 1987, adopt and implement standards for determining fitness to hold or continue to hold a household goods carrier license.

(2) Statutory standards. A person shall not be considered fit for purposes of this Section unless the record shows that, at the time of hearing, the person:

(a) Is aware of its obligations under this Chapter, Commission regulations and orders, and other provisions of The Illinois Vehicle Code; [1]

(b) Has substantially complied with applicable statutes and regulations; and

(c) Possesses the equipment, facilities, financial resources, knowledge and experience to provide the proposed service and meet the needs of supporting shippers, in compliance with applicable statutes and regulations, on a long-term basis.

(3) Burden of proof in application proceedings. (a) Temporary authority. Each applicant for temporary household goods carrier authority shall have the burden of making a prima facie showing of fitness. The Commission may, in its discretion, deny an application for temporary household goods authority where the applicant's fitness is controverted by specific allegations, under oath, by an intervenor.

(b) Permanent authority. Each applicant for permanent household goods authority shall have the burden of proving its fitness by clear and convincing evidence.

(c) Findings. The order granting permanent household goods authority shall contain specific findings, with citation to the record, on each aspect of fitness.

(4) Revocation proceedings. If the record in a revocation proceeding shows that a licensee is no longer fit to hold a household goods carrier license, the Commission shall suspend or revoke the license. When a license is suspended under this Section, the holder shall have 6 months in which to demonstrate, by clear and convincing evidence, that its fitness has been restored. Unless the Commission finds that such a demonstration has been made, the license shall be revoked. A license revoked under this Section shall not be reinstated.

P.A. 76-1586, § 18c-4204a, added by P.A. 85-553, § 2, eff. Sept. 18, 1987. Amended by P.A. 89-444, § 5, eff. Jan. 25, 1996.

Formerly Ill.Rev.Stat.1991, ch. 95 ½, ¶ 18c-4204a.

[1] 625 ILCS 5/1-100 et seq.

5/18c-4205. § 18c-4205. Repealed by P.A. 85-553, § 3, eff. Sept. 18, 1987

5/18c-4206. Dual operations

§ 18c-4206. Dual operations. (1) Dual common/contract operations. No person shall hold both a household goods common carrier certificate and a household goods contract carrier permit unless the Commission determines, or has determined, that both licenses may be held consistent with the public interest and authorizes such dual licensing. Issuance of household goods contract carrier authority after the effective date of this amendatory Act of 1995 to a person that already holds household goods common carrier authority, or vice versa, shall be rebuttably presumed inconsistent with the public interest if the two authorities would be duplicative, in whole or in part.

(2) Merger of duplicative operating rights. The Commission may, except as otherwise provided in this subsection, order that duplicative operating rights, whether household goods common carrier or household goods contract carrier or both, be merged into a single license and may impose such requirements upon operations under such license as will promote the public interest and effectuate the purposes of this Chapter. The power of the Commission to order merger shall not extend to duplicative operating rights in existence on the effective date of this Chapter.

P.A. 76-1586, § 18c-4206, added by P.A. 84-796, § 1, eff. Jan. 1, 1986. Amended by P.A. 89-444, § 5, eff. Jan. 25, 1996.

Formerly Ill.Rev.Stat.1991, ch. 95 ½, ¶ 18c-4206.

5/18c-4207. Cessation of service under a license

§ 18c-4207. Cessation of service under a license. No household goods carrier shall abandon, discontinue, or suspend any service that it is authorized to provide pursuant to a license issued by the Commission without authorization by the Commission. If the Commission finds good cause for the abandonment, discontinuance, or suspension, it may approve same. If the Commission finds that a household goods carrier has abandoned, discontinued, or suspended service without authorization, it may revoke the carrier's license.

P.A. 76-1586, § 18c-4207, added by P.A. 84-796, § 1, eff. Jan. 1, 1986. Amended by P.A. 89-444, § 5, eff. Jan. 25, 1996.

Formerly Ill.Rev.Stat.1991, ch. 95 ½, ¶ 18c-4207.

ARTICLE III. TRANSFER OF LICENSES

5/18c-4301. Power of Commission to Approve Transfers

§ 18c-4301. Power of Commission to Approve Transfers. A license issued under this Sub-chapter may be transferred, with Commission approval, under the conditions specified in this Article and in accordance with such rules and regulations as the Commission may prescribe.

P.A. 76-1586, § 18c-4301, added by P.A. 84-796, § 1, eff. Jan. 1, 1986.

Formerly Ill.Rev.Stat.1991, ch. 95 ½, ¶ 18c-4301.

5/18c-4302. Types of Transfers Which May be Approved

§ 18c-4302. Types of Transfers Which May be Approved. It is lawful, with prior authorization from the Commission, for:

(1) Two or more motor carriers of property to consolidate or merge their properties into one business entity for the ownership, management, or operation of the properties theretofore in separate ownership;

(2) A motor carrier of property, or two or more such carriers jointly, to purchase, lease or contract to operate the properties of another such carrier;

(3) A motor carrier of property, or two or more such carriers jointly, to acquire control of another such carrier through ownership of its stock or otherwise;

(4) A person not a motor carrier of property, to acquire control of one or more such motor carriers through ownership of its or their stock or otherwise;

(5) A person not a motor carrier of property and which has control of one or more such carriers to acquire control of another carrier through ownership of its stock or otherwise; or

(6) A person to acquire possession, ownership, or control, by means of the sale or other conveyance of a license issued by the Commission to another person.

P.A. 76-1586, § 18c-4302, added by P.A. 84-796, § 1, eff. Jan. 1, 1986.

Formerly Ill.Rev.Stat.1991, ch. 95 ½, ¶ 18c-4302.

5/18c-4303. Applications for Approval

§ 18c-4303. Applications for Approval. Applications for approval of the transfer of a license shall be on forms prescribed by the Commission and shall, where possible, be accompanied by a copy of the written contract executed by parties to the proposed transfer. The contract must state that it:

(1) Is expressly conditioned on approval of the transfer by the Commission;

(2) Is a complete and exclusive statement of the rights of the parties in regard to the proposed transfer; and

(3) Cannot be amended without notice to and approval by the Commission. The application shall also be accompanied by an abstract of shipments performed by the transferor within the last year prior to the date of the contract showing the date of each shipment, the identification number of the shipment, the origin and destination of the shipment, and a description of the commodity shipped.

The application shall not be docketed until a contract and abstract have been filed. Where the contract cannot be signed because of some operation of law, the Commission may waive the signature of the transferor, but not the filing of the written contract.

P.A. 76-1586, § 18c-4303, added by P.A. 84-796, § 1, eff. Jan. 1, 1986.

Formerly Ill.Rev.Stat.1991, ch. 95 ½, ¶ 18c-4303.

5/18c-4304. Standard for Review of Applications

§ 18c-4304. Standard for Review of Applications. The Commission may approve a proposed transfer if it finds that:

(1) The license to be transferred is in good standing and has not been abandoned, discontinued, or suspended, in whole or in part;

(2) The proposed transferee is fit, willing, and able to provide service for which the license was issued, and to do so in compliance with provisions of this Chapter, Commission regulations and orders; and

(3) The transfer would be consistent with the public interest and the state transportation policy.

The Commission may approve or disapprove a transfer, in whole or in part, and may subject the transfer to such terms and conditions as will protect the public interest and effectuate the purposes of this Chapter.

P.A. 76-1586, § 18c-4304, added by P.A. 84-796, § 1, eff. Jan. 1, 1986.

Formerly Ill.Rev.Stat.1991, ch. 95 ½, ¶ 18c-4304.

5/18c-4305. Abandonment, Discontinuance, or Suspension of Service Under a License to be Transferred

§ 18c-4305. Abandonment, Discontinuance, or Suspension of Service Under a License to be Transferred. In determining whether the proposed transferor has abandoned, discontinued or suspended service without authorization, the Commission shall only consider the operations of the transferring party performed within the last 2 years prior to the date on which the contract between transferor and transferee was executed, or the date the application was filed.

P.A. 76-1586, § 18c-4305, added by P.A. 84-796, § 1, eff. Jan. 1, 1986.

Formerly Ill.Rev.Stat.1991, ch. 95 ½, ¶ 18c-4305.

5/18c-4306. Expedited Transfer Procedures

§ 18c-4306. Expedited Transfer Procedures.

(1) The Commission may provide for the transfer of a license, without notice and hearing, and without the necessity of making the findings specified above, when such transfer or control is to:

(a) A member or members of the transferor's immediate family;

(b) A corporation, the stock of which is wholly owned by the transferor or members of his immediate family or a member or members of the transferor partnership;

(c) A member or members of a partnership of which the transferor is a partner;

(d) A stockholder or stockholders of the transferor corporation or of a corporation wholly owned by the transferor or the transferor's immediate family;

(e) The heirs of a person who dies intestate or the legatees of a testator, upon order of the probate court having jurisdiction;

(f) The heirs or legatees of the transferor pursuant to the Probate Act of 1975, as amended;[1]

(g) A corporation, more than 50% of the stock of which is controlled by the stockholders of the transferor corporation; or

(h) A corporation, all of the stock of which is controlled by a member or members of the immediate family of the stockholder or stockholders of the transferor corporation.

(2) When a transfer of a license may be accomplished on an expedited basis without notice and hearing through 2 or more transactions of the type described in subsection (a), and they do, in fact, represent a single, contemporaneous transaction, then the Commission shall allow the transfer to be made as a single transaction in a single application. However, it shall be the applicants' burden to demonstrate that they are entitled to this treatment of their application by setting forth each of the individual qualifying transactions under subsection (1) with the same detail and specificity as if each individual application were filed.

P.A. 76-1586, § 18c-4306, added by P.A. 84-796, § 1, eff. Jan. 1, 1986. Amended by P.A. 85-553, § 2, eff. Sept. 18, 1987; P.A. 88-415, § 10, eff. Aug. 20, 1993.

Formerly Ill.Rev.Stat.1991, ch. 95 ½, ¶ 18c-4306.

[1] 755 ILCS 5/1-1 et seq.

5/18c-4307. Unapproved Transfers

§ 18c-4307. Unapproved Transfers. (1) Unapproved Transfers Prohibited. Except as provided in this Article, no person may enter into a transaction to accomplish or effectuate, or participate in accomplishing or effectuating, the ownership, control or management of any one or more motor carriers, however such result is attained, whether directly or indirectly by use of common directors, officers, or stockholders, a holding or investment company, a voting trust, or in any other manner, and regardless of whether or not the carrier received compensation or value from the transaction. Nor shall any person continue to maintain control or management accomplished or effectuated in violation of this Article. The words "control or management," when used in this Article, shall be construed to include the power to exercise control or management.

(2) Direct Supervision and Control by License Holder Required. The holder of a motor carrier license shall exercise direct supervision and control over all operations conducted with vehicles registered under its license or utilized in conducting operations under its license. The holder may be called upon to demonstrate that it is exercising direct supervision and control. Failure to exercise active supervision and control shall constitute the unauthorized transfer of operating rights in violation of this Chapter. Where an unauthorized transfer occurs, both the transferor and transferee shall have committed violations of this Chapter. Nothing contained herein shall prevent the holder from exercising such supervision and control through a manager or other

bona fide employee of the holder. Elements to be considered in evaluating whether supervision and control is being exercised include solicitation; public identification; billing; collecting; dispatching drivers and equipment; hiring; evaluation and firing of drivers and other personnel; liability for cargo loss or damage; and responsibility for payment of carrier expenses.

P.A. 76–1586, § 18c–4307, added by P.A. 84–796, § 1, eff. Jan. 1, 1986. Amended by P.A. 85–553, § 2, eff. Sept. 18, 1987.

Formerly Ill.Rev.Stat.1991, ch. 95 ½, ¶ 18c–4307.

5/18c–4308. Enforcement of Transfer Requirements

§ 18c–4308. Enforcement of Transfer Requirements. The Commission may, on its own motion or on complaint, investigate and determine whether violations of this Article have occurred. When the Commission determines that a carrier or other person is violating the provisions of this Article it shall by order require the carrier or other person to take whatever action is necessary to prevent continuance of the violation, and may, in addition, impose sanctions as provided in this Chapter.

P.A. 76–1586, § 18c–4308, added by P.A. 84–796, § 1, eff. Jan. 1, 1986.

Formerly Ill.Rev.Stat.1991, ch. 95 ½, ¶ 18c–4308.

5/18c–4309. Temporary Suspension and Transfer

§ 18c–4309. Temporary Suspension and Transfer. Periods during which a license is temporarily suspended by order of the Commission shall not be considered as part of the 1-year period for which an abstract of shipments must be provided for application to transfer a license pursuant to Section 18c–4303 of this Chapter, or for the 2-year period used to determine whether a proposed transferor has abandoned, discontinued or suspended service without Commission authorization pursuant to Section 18c–4305 of this Chapter. This Section shall apply to all temporary suspension applications filed, and all temporary suspensions granted, on or after January 1, 1986.

P.A. 76–1586, § 18c–4309, added by P.A. 85–553, § 2, eff. Sept. 18, 1987.

Formerly Ill.Rev.Stat.1991, ch. 95 ½, ¶ 18c–4309.

ARTICLE IV. RATE FILINGS AND REGISTRATION OF INTRASTATE PUBLIC CARRIERS AND EQUIPMENT AND REGISTRATION OF INTERSTATE CARRIERS AND EQUIPMENT

5/18c–4401. Registration required

§ 18c–4401. Registration required. (1) General provisions. No intrastate public carrier and no interstate motor carrier of property shall operate over the public roads of this State without a registration issued pursuant to this Article and in effect at the time operations are conducted.

(2) Interstate intercorporate hauling and single-source leasing. Persons or entities engaged in interstate compensated intercorporate hauling, and interstate private carriers which lease equipment, with drivers, are interstate carriers for purposes of this Article notwithstanding any other provision of this Chapter. However, the Commission may:

(a) Exempt such carriers from the requirements of this Article;

(b) Subject any such exemption to such reasonable terms and conditions as the Commission deems necessary to effectuate the purposes of this Chapter; and

(c) Revoke any exemption granted hereunder if it deems revocation necessary to effectuate the purposes of this Chapter.

P.A. 76–1586, § 18c–4401, added by P.A. 84–796, § 1, eff. Jan. 1, 1986. Amended by P.A. 85–553, § 2, eff. Sept. 18, 1987; P.A. 89–444, § 5, eff. Jan. 25, 1996.

Formerly Ill.Rev.Stat.1991, ch. 95 ½, ¶ 18c–4401.

5/18c–4402. Registration Standards

§ 18c–4402. Registration Standards. The Commission shall not issue a registration until after the carrier has:

(1) Properly filed an application for registration; and

(2) Complied with Commission regulations and orders regarding:

(a) Application, franchise, franchise renewal, and other fees and levies; and

(b) Proof of insurance.

P.A. 76–1586, § 18c–4402, added by P.A. 84–796, § 1, eff. Jan. 1, 1986. Amended by P.A. 85–553, § 2, eff. Sept. 18, 1987.

Formerly Ill.Rev.Stat.1991, ch. 95 ½, ¶ 18c–4402.

5/18c–4403. Issuance of registrations

§ 18c–4403. Issuance of registrations. The Commission may issue registrations to any qualified applicant authorizing bona fide intrastate public carrier or interstate operations, if it is found that the applicant is fit, willing, and able to provide service in conformity with the requirements of this Chapter, Commission regulations and orders.

P.A. 76–1586, § 18c–4403, added by P.A. 84–796, § 1, eff. Jan. 1, 1986. Amended by P.A. 89–444, § 5, eff. Jan. 25, 1996.

Formerly Ill.Rev.Stat.1991, ch. 95 ½, ¶ 18c–4403.

5/18c–4404. Revocation of Registrations

§ 18c–4404. Revocation of Registrations. The Commission may revoke any registration if it determines that the carrier has failed to comply with this Chapter, Commission regulations or orders, or with any other statute or regulation of this State relating to the privilege of operating motor vehicles over the public roads of the State.

P.A. 76–1586, § 18c–4404, added by P.A. 84–796, § 1, eff. Jan. 1, 1986.

Formerly Ill.Rev.Stat.1991, ch. 95 ½, ¶ 18c–4404.

5/18c–4405. Intrastate public carrier rate filings

§ 18c–4405. Intrastate public carrier rate filings. Public carriers that voluntarily file rates under an agreement approved by the Commission under Section 18c–4502 of this Chapter are subject to all provisions of Sub-chapter 3, Article II,[1] and Section 18c–4501 of this Chapter 18c.

[1] 625 ILCS 5/18c–3201 et seq.

P.A. 76–1586, § 18c–4405, added by P.A. 89–444, § 5, eff. Jan. 25, 1996.

ARTICLE V. RATEMAKING

5/18c–4501. Jurisdiction and power of the Commission

§ 18c–4501. Jurisdiction and power of the Commission. (1) Power to set rates. The Commission shall have jurisdiction and power to set the maximum or minimum, or maximum and minimum, lawful rates for intrastate service by common carriers of household goods, to set the minimum lawful rates for contract carriers of household goods, and to prescribe the form and content of tariffs and schedules containing such rates.

(2) Power to Establish Ratemaking Procedures. The Commission may establish procedures for the filing, publication, investigation, suspension and prescription of rates. The Commission may provide that rates for particular services will go into effect unless suspended by the Commission, or may require that rates for such services be approved by the Commission before going into effect.

P.A. 76–1586, § 18c–4501, added by P.A. 84–796, § 1, eff. Jan. 1, 1986. Amended by P.A. 89–444, § 5, eff. Jan. 25, 1996.

Formerly Ill.Rev.Stat.1991, ch. 95 ½, ¶ 18c–4501.

5/18c–4502. Collective Ratemaking

§ 18c–4502. Collective Ratemaking. (1) Application for Approval. Any carrier party to an agreement between or among 2 or more carriers relating to rates, fares, classifications, divisions, allowances, or charges (including charges between carriers and compensation paid or received for the use of facilities and equipment), or rules and regulations pertaining thereto, or procedures for the joint consideration, initiation or establishment thereof, whether such conference, bureau, committee, or other organization be a "for-profit" or "not-for-profit" corporate entity or whether or not such conference, bureau, committee or other organization is or will be controlled by other businesses may, under such rules and regulations as the Commission may prescribe, apply to the Commission for approval of the agreement, and the Commission shall by order approve any such agreement, if approval thereof is not prohibited by subsection (3), (4), or (5) of this Section, if it finds that, by reason of furtherance of the State transportation policy declared in Section 18c–1103 of this Chapter, the relief provided in subsection (8) should apply with respect to the making and carrying out of such agreement; otherwise the application shall be denied. The approval of the Commission shall be granted only upon such terms and conditions as the Commission may prescribe as necessary to enable it to grant its approval in accordance with the standard above set forth in this paragraph.

(2) Accounts, Reporting, and Internal Procedures. Each conference, bureau, committee, or other organization established or continued pursuant to any agreement approved by the Commission under the provisions of this Section shall maintain such accounts, records, files and memoranda and shall submit to the Commission such reports, as may be prescribed by the Commission, and all such accounts, records, files, and memoranda shall be subject to inspection by the Commission or its duly authorized representatives. Any conference, bureau committee, or other organization described in subsection (1) of this Section shall cause to be published notice of the final disposition of any action taken by such entity together with a concise statement of the reasons therefore. The Commission shall withhold approval of any agreement under this Section unless the agreement specifies a reasonable period of time within which proposals by parties to the agreement will be finally acted upon by the conference, bureau, committee, or other organization.

(3) Matters Which May Be the Subject of Agreements Approved By the Commission. The Commission shall not approve under this Section any agreement between or among carriers of different classes unless it finds that such agreement is of the character described in subsection (1) of this Section and is limited to matters relating to transportation under joint rates or over through routes. For purposes of this paragraph carriers by railroad and express companies are carriers of one class; carriers by motor vehicle are carriers of one class and carriers by water are carriers of one class.

(4) Non-Applicability of Section to Transfers. The Commission shall not approve under this Section any agreement which it finds is an agreement with respect to a pooling, division, or other matter or transaction, to which Section 18c–4302 of this Chapter is applicable.

(5) Independent Action. The Commission shall not approve under this Section any agreement which establishes a procedure for the determination of any matter through joint consideration unless it finds that under the agreement there is accorded to each party the free and unrestrained right to take independent action either before or after any determination arrived at through such procedures. The Commission shall not find that each party has a free and unrestrained right to take independent action if the conference, bureau, committee, or other organization is granted by the agreement any right to engage in proceedings before the Commission or before any court regarding any action taken by a party to an agreement authorized by this Section, or by any other party providing or seeking authority to provide transportation services.

(6) Investigation of Activities. The Commission is authorized, upon complaint or upon its own initiative without complaint, to investigate and determine whether any agreement previously approved by it under this Section, or terms and conditions upon which such approval was granted, is not or are not in conformity with the standard, set forth in subsection (1), or whether any such terms and conditions are not necessary for purposes of conformity with such standard, and, after such investigation, the Commission shall by order terminate or modify its approval of such agreement if it finds such action necessary to insure conformity with such standard, and shall modify the terms and conditions upon which such approval was granted to the extent it finds necessary to insure conformity with such standard or to the extent to which it finds such terms and conditions not necessary to insure such conformity. The effective date of any order terminating or modifying approval, or modifying terms and conditions, shall be postponed for such period as the Commission determines to be reasonably necessary to avoid undue hardship.

(7) Hearings and Orders. No order shall be entered under this Section except after interested parties have been afforded reasonable opportunity for hearing.

(8) Exemption From State Antitrust Laws. Parties to any agreement approved by the Commission under this Section and other persons are, if the approval of such agreement is not prohibited by subsection (3), (4), or (5), hereby relieved from the operation of the antitrust laws with respect to the making of such agreement, and with respect to the carrying out of such agreement in conformity with its provisions and in conformity with the terms and conditions prescribed by the Commission.

(9) Other Laws Not Affected. Any action of the Commission under this Section in approving an agreement, or in denying an application for such approval, or in terminating or modifying its approval of an agreement, or in prescribing the terms and conditions upon which its approval is to be granted, or in modifying such terms and conditions, shall be construed as having effect solely with reference to the appli-

cability of the relief provisions of paragraph subsection (8) of this Section.

P.A. 76-1586, § 18c-4502, added by P.A. 84-796, § 1, eff. Jan. 1, 1986.

Formerly Ill.Rev.Stat.1991, ch. 95 ½, ¶ 18c-4502.

5/18c-4503. Terminal Area Operations

§ 18c-4503. Terminal Area Operations.

(1) Exemption From Rate Regulation. Except as provided in subsection (2) of this Section, nothing contained in this Chapter shall be construed to require any carrier engaged in the transportation of property by motor vehicle between points wholly within a terminal area to comply with the provisions of this Chapter with respect to the filing, publishing, observance or enforcement of tariffs or schedules of rates with respect to transportation wholly within any such area.

(2) Application of Section. Notwithstanding any contrary provisions therein, the ratemaking provisions of subsection (1) of this Section shall have no application to transportation of household goods, as defined in Commission regulations, wholly within a county having a population of more than 1,000,000.

P.A. 76-1586, § 18c-4503, added by P.A. 85-553, § 2, eff. Sept. 18, 1987.

Formerly Ill.Rev.Stat.1991, ch. 95 ½, ¶ 18c-4503.

ARTICLE VI. CAB CARDS AND IDENTIFIERS

5/18c-4601. Cab Card and Identifier to be Carried and Displayed in Each Vehicle

§ 18c-4601. Cab Card and Identifier to be Carried and Displayed in Each Vehicle.

(1) General Provisions.

(a) Carrying Requirement. Each motor vehicle used in for-hire transportation upon the public roads of this State shall carry a current cab card together with an identifier issued by or under authority of the Commission. If the carrier is an intrastate motor carrier of property, the prescribed intrastate cab card and identifier shall be required; if the carrier is an interstate motor carrier of property, the prescribed interstate cab card and identifier shall be required.

(b) Execution and Presentation Requirement. Such cab card shall be properly executed by the carrier. The cab card, with an identifier affixed or printed thereon, shall be carried in the vehicle for which it was executed. The cab card and identifier shall be presented upon request to any authorized employee of the Commission or the State Police or Secretary of State.

(c) Deadlines for Execution, Carrying, and Presentation. Cab cards and identifiers shall be executed, carried, and presented no earlier than December 1 of the calendar year preceding the calendar year for which fees are owing, and no later than February 1 of the calendar year for which fees are owing, unless otherwise provided in Commission regulations and orders.

(2) Interstate Compensated Intercorporate Hauling and Single-Source Leasing. The provisions of subsection (1) of this Section apply to motor vehicles used in interstate compensated intercorporate hauling or which are leased, with drivers, to private carriers for use in interstate commerce, as well as to other motor vehicles used in for-hire transportation upon the public roads of this State. However, the Commission may:

(a) Exempt such carriers from the requirements of this Article;

(b) Subject any exemption to such reasonable terms and conditions as the Commission deems necessary to effectuate the purposes of this Chapter; and

(c) Revoke any exemption granted hereunder if it deems revocation necessary to effectuate the purposes of this Chapter.

P.A. 76-1586, § 18c-4601, added by P.A. 84-796, § 1, eff. Jan. 1, 1986. Amended by P.A. 85-553, § 2, eff. Sept. 18, 1987.

Formerly Ill.Rev.Stat.1991, ch. 95 ½, ¶ 18c-4601.

5/18c-4602. Commission to Prescribe Cab Cards and Identifiers

§ 18c-4602. Commission to Prescribe Cab Cards and Identifiers. The Commission shall prescribe the cab cards and identifiers required under Section 18c-4601 of this Chapter.

P.A. 76-1586, § 18c-4602, added by P.A. 84-796, § 1, eff. Jan. 1, 1986. Amended by P.A. 85-553, § 2, eff. Sept. 18, 1987.

Formerly Ill.Rev.Stat.1991, ch. 95 ½, ¶ 18c-4602.

5/18c-4603. Issuance of Cab Cards and Identifiers

§ 18c-4603. Issuance of Cab Cards and Identifiers. (1) Applications for Cards and Identifiers. Applications for cab cards and identifiers shall be on forms prescribed by the Commission and shall be accompanied by the per vehicle franchise or franchise renewal fee prescribed by the Commission.

(2) Expiration and Renewal of Cab Cards and Identifiers. Identifiers issued by or under authority of the Commission shall expire automatically on January 31 of each year, or on such other date as the Commission may prescribe. It shall be the responsibility of each carrier to insure that the cab cards and identifiers in its vehicles are current.

(3) Issuance of Cards and Identifiers. Applications and fees for cab cards and identifiers may be filed with, and cards or identifiers may be issued by, the Commission or its agent. The Commission shall issue intrastate cab cards and identifiers and interstate identifiers as proof of payment of franchise and franchise renewal fees by licensed intrastate and registered interstate carriers. Upon payment of the intrastate fee by a licensed intrastate motor carrier of property, the Commission shall issue a current Illinois cab card with identifier printed thereon. Upon payment of the interstate fee by a registered interstate motor carrier of property, the Commission shall issue a current Illinois interstate identifier which the carrier shall affix to the interstate cab card.

P.A. 76-1586, § 18c-4603, added by P.A. 84-796, § 1, eff. Jan. 1, 1986. Amended by P.A. 85-553, § 2, eff. Sept. 18, 1987.

Formerly Ill.Rev.Stat.1991, ch. 95 ½, ¶ 18c-4603.

5/18c-4604. Enforcement

§ 18c-4604. Enforcement. It shall be a violation of this Chapter, separate and apart from any other violation, for a person to:

(1) Operate a vehicle without a current, executed cab card and identifier as required by this Article;

(2) Transfer a cab card and identifier to a vehicle other than the vehicle for which it was originally executed, except in accordance with Commission regulations;

(3) Use a cab card and identifier issued to another carrier or permit the use of a cab card by another carrier except in accordance with Commission regulations; or

(4) Fail to present a cab card and identifier as required by this Article.

P.A. 76–1586, § 18c–4604, added by P.A. 84–796, § 1, eff. Jan. 1, 1986. Amended by P.A. 85–553, § 2, eff. Sept. 18, 1987.

Formerly Ill.Rev.Stat.1991, ch. 95 ½, ¶ 18c–4604.

ARTICLE VII. IDENTIFICATION OF CARRIERS

5/18c–4701. Insignia on Vehicles

§ 18c–4701. Insignia on Vehicles.

(1) General Requirements to be Prescribed by Commission. Except as otherwise provided in this Section, no intrastate carrier shall operate any motor vehicle upon the public roads of this State unless there is painted or affixed to both sides of the cab or power unit, in accordance with such specifications as the Commission may prescribe, the trade name of the carrier as it appears on the carrier's license or the carrier's recognized logo, together with the license and registration number of the carrier. Likewise, no interstate carrier shall operate any motor vehicle upon the public roads of this State unless there is painted or affixed to both sides of the cab or power unit, in accordance with such specifications as the Commission may prescribe, the registration or authority number of the carrier.

(2) Use of ICC–Prescribed Identification. Identifying information prescribed by the Interstate Commerce Commission may be used in satisfaction of requirements established under this Section, including special orders granting a petition for waiver of Sections 1057.22(a) and 1057.22(c)(2) and (4), as they relate to equipment receipts, of the Lease and Interchange of Vehicle Regulations (49 CFR 1057), in lieu of numbers or symbols prescribed by the Commission.

(3) Identification of Trip Lessees. Notwithstanding any other provision of this Section to the contrary, a motor vehicle trip leased in accordance with this Chapter, Commission regulations and orders shall not be required to bear the name and license number of the lessee if:

(a) the motor vehicle bears the name and license or registration number of the lessor in accordance with subsection (1) of this Section, Commission regulations and orders;

(b) the lessor and lessee are commonly-owned; and

(c) the vehicle carries a photocopy of a letter signed by the lessor, on file with the Commission, stating that the lessor and lessee are commonly-owned.

(4) Rules not superseded. The authority of the Illinois Commerce Commission to regulate the identification of motor vehicles of intrastate and interstate carriers, engaged in the transportation of hazardous materials, shall not supersede or replace the rules and regulations of the Illinois Department of Transportation and Federal Motor Carrier Safety regulations Part 390.21, as relates now or hereafter to the markings and identification of such vehicles.

(5) Identification on vehicles under 9,000 pounds gross vehicle weight (GVW). Vehicles with a gross vehicle weight (GVW) less than 9,000 pounds may, in lieu of identification required under subsection (1) of this Section display the trade name of the carrier as it appears on the carrier's license or the carrier's recognized logo, together with the license and registration number of the carrier in such manner as to be clearly legible and visible from both sides of the vehicle at a distance of 25 feet, when the vehicle is not in motion, and in accordance with such specifications as the Commission may prescribe.

P.A. 76–1586, § 18c–4701, added by P.A. 84–796, § 1, eff. Jan. 1, 1986. Amended by P.A. 85–553, § 2, eff. Sept. 18, 1987; P.A. 85–786, § 1, eff. Jan. 1, 1988; P.A. 85–809, § 1, eff. Sept. 24, 1987; P.A. 85–1209, Art. II, § 2–51, eff. Aug. 30, 1988; P.A. 85–1407, § 2, eff. Sept. 22, 1988; P.A. 85–1440, Art. II, § 2–54, eff. Feb. 1, 1989; P.A. 88–415, § 10, eff. Aug. 20, 1993; P.A. 91–357, § 231, eff. July 29, 1999.

Formerly Ill.Rev.Stat.1991, ch. 95 ½, ¶ 18c–4701.

5/18c–4702. Identification of Carrier in Advertising, Solicitation, and Other Documents

§ 18c–4702. Identification of Carrier in Advertising, Solicitation, and other Documents. No carrier shall use in any advertising, solicitation, correspondence, publication, or other document connected with its transportation service any name other than its name or trade name as it appears on the carrier's license or registration. Each advertisement, solicitation, correspondence, publication, or other document shall contain the carrier's license or registration number unless otherwise provided in Commission regulations or orders.

P.A. 76–1586, § 18c–4702, added by P.A. 84–796, § 1, eff. Jan. 1, 1986. Amended by P.A. 85–553, § 2, eff. Sept. 18, 1987.

Formerly Ill.Rev.Stat.1991, ch. 95 ½, ¶ 18c–4702.

ARTICLE VIII. BILLS OF LADING

5/18c–4801. Rights, Obligations and Liabilities

§ 18c–4801. Rights, Obligations, and Liabilities. The provisions of Sections 7–101, 7–102, 7–103, 7–104, 7–105, 7–301, 7–302, 7–303, 7–304, 7–305, 7–306, 7–307, 7–308, 7–309, 7–401, 7–402, 7–403, 7–404, 7–501, 7–502, 7–503, 7–504, 7–505, 7–506, 7–507, 7–508, 7–509, 7–601, 7–602, 7–603 of the "Uniform Commercial Code", as amended,[1] are adopted by reference to the extent that they relate to bills of lading and the intrastate transportation of property by a motor common carrier.

P.A. 76–1586, § 18c–4801, added by P.A. 84–796, § 1, eff. Jan. 1, 1986.

Formerly Ill.Rev.Stat.1991, ch. 95 ½, ¶ 18c–4801.

[1] 810 ILCS 5/7–101, 5/7–102, 5/7–103, 5/7–104, 5/7–105, 5/7–301, 5/7–302, 5/7–303, 5/7–304, 5/7–305, 5/7–306, 5/7–307, 5/7–308, 5/7–309, 5/7–401, 5/7–402, 5/7–403, 5/7–404, 5/7–501, 5/7–502, 5/7–503, 5/7–504, 5/7–505, 5/7–506, 5/7–507, 5/7–508, 5/7–509, 5/7–601, 5/7–602, 5/7–603.

5/18c–4802. Straight Bill of Lading

§ 18c–4802. Straight Bill of Lading. A bill in which it is stated that the goods are consigned or destined to a specific person is a straight bill.

P.A. 76–1586, § 18c–4802, added by P.A. 84–796, § 1, eff. Jan. 1, 1986.

Formerly Ill.Rev.Stat.1991, ch. 95 ½, ¶ 18c–4802.

5/18c–4803. Order Bill of Lading

§ 18c–4803. Order Bill of Lading. A bill of lading in which it is stated that the goods are consigned or destined to the order of any person named in such bill is an order bill of lading. Any provision in such a bill or in any notice, contract, regulation, or tariff that it is nonnegotiable shall be null and void unless upon its face and in writing such provision is agreed to by the shipper.

P.A. 76–1586, § 18c–4803, added by P.A. 84–796, § 1, eff. Jan. 1, 1986.

Formerly Ill.Rev.Stat.1991, ch. 95 ½, ¶ 18c–4803.

5/18c–4804. Limitation of Liability

§ 18c–4804. Limitation of Liability. The provisions of this Section respecting liability for full actual loss, damage or injury, notwithstanding subsection 2 of Section 7–309 of the "Uniform Commercial Code", as amended,[1] do not apply to property received for transportation concerning which the carrier is expressly authorized or required by order of the Commission to establish rates based on value declared in writing by the shipper or agreed upon by the shipper, in writing, as the released value of the property. Such declarations or agreements have no other effect than to limit liability to an amount not exceeding the value declared or released, and are not in violation of this Chapter. A tariff containing such rates shall contain specific reference to the Commission order authorizing them.

P.A. 76–1586, § 18c–4804, added by P.A. 84–796, § 1, eff. Jan. 1, 1986.

Formerly Ill.Rev.Stat.1991, ch. 95 ½, ¶ 18c–4804.

[1] 810 ILCS 5/7–309.

5/18c–4805. Other Remedies Available to Holder of Bill of Lading Not Preempted

§ 18c–4805. Other Remedies Available to Holder of Bill of Lading Not Preempted. This Article does not deprive any holder of a receipt or bill of lading of any remedy or right of action had under existing law.

P.A. 76–1586, § 18c–4805, added by P.A. 84–796, § 1, eff. Jan. 1, 1986.

Formerly Ill.Rev.Stat.1991, ch. 95 ½, ¶ 18c–4805.

5/18c–4806. Delivering Carrier Defined

§ 18c–4806. Delivering Carrier Defined. For the purposes of this Section the delivering carrier is the carrier performing transportation service to or nearest to the point of destination.

P.A. 76–1586, § 18c–4806, added by P.A. 84–796, § 1, eff. Jan. 1, 1986.

Formerly Ill.Rev.Stat.1991, ch. 95 ½, ¶ 18c–4806.

5/18c–4807. Bill of Lading or Similar Documentation Required

§ 18c–4807. Bill of Lading or Similar Documentation Required. (1) General Requirements. Except as provided in subsection (2) of this Section, every motor common carrier of property shall be required to issue a bill of lading and freight bill indicating the commodities transported, weight thereof (where freight charges are assessed by weight), the points of origin and destination of such commodities, the consignor and consignee, and the charge therefor. If the commodities are not delivered by the originating carrier, the bill of lading or freight bill shall indicate the point of interchange and the connecting carrier. This Section shall not apply to motor contract carriers of property.

(2) Exceptions.

(a) Simplified Documentation. The Commission may prescribe simplified documentation to be issued by classes of carriers where such requirements would be less burdensome and would effectuate the purposes of this Chapter. Simplified documentation shall be prescribed for the following classes of carriers:

(i) Motor common carriers of shipments composed of parcels weighing 100 pounds or less and not exceeding 200 pounds from one consignor to one consignee on one day;

(ii) Carriers of agricultural or dairy products, poultry, eggs, or fruits;

(iii) Aggregate carriers; and

(iv) Messenger carriers; and

(v) Such other classes as the Commission may, from time to time, determine.

(b) Supplementary Requirements. The Commission may adopt supplementary requirements for the issuance or carrying of documentation for household goods carriers or other carriers where large numbers of non-commercial shippers may be affected and such documentation is necessary to effectuate the purposes of this Chapter.

(c) Commodity descriptions for shipments weighing 10 pounds or less. Where a shipment weighs ten pounds or less, except when it contains dangerous articles or hazardous materials, the following may be used in lieu of a commodity description: "Parcel 10 Pounds or Under".

P.A. 76–1586, § 18c–4807, added by P.A. 84–796, § 1, eff. Jan. 1, 1986. Amended by P.A. 85–1407, § 2, eff. Sept. 22, 1988.

Formerly Ill.Rev.Stat.1991, ch. 95 ½, ¶ 18c–4807.

ARTICLE IX. SAFETY REGULATIONS FOR MOTOR CARRIERS OF PROPERTY: INSURANCE

5/18c–4901. Insurance Coverage as a Prerequisite to Operations

§ 18c–4901. Insurance Coverage as a Prerequisite to Operations. No motor carrier of property shall operate within this State unless it has on file with the Commission or its agent proof of continuous insurance or surety coverage in accordance with Commission regulations.

P.A. 76–1586, § 18c–4901, added by P.A. 84–796, § 1, eff. Jan. 1, 1986. Amended by P.A. 85–553, § 2, eff. Sept. 18, 1987.

Formerly Ill.Rev.Stat.1991, ch. 95 ½, ¶ 18c–4901.

5/18c–4902. Commission to Set Insurance Coverage Limits and Establish Procedures

§ 18c–4902. Commission to Set Insurance Coverage Limits and Establish Procedures. The Commission shall prescribe the amounts of insurance or surety coverage required as a minimum, the maximum allowable deductible limits, procedures for the filing and rejection or return of filings, and such other reasonable regulations regarding insurance or surety coverage as are necessary to protect the travelling and shipping or receiving public.

P.A. 76–1586, § 18c–4902, added by P.A. 84–796, § 1, eff. Jan. 1, 1986. Amended by P.A. 84–1025, § 2, eff. Jan. 1, 1986; P.A. 85–553, § 2, eff. Sept. 18, 1987.

Formerly Ill.Rev.Stat.1991, ch. 95 ½, ¶ 18c–4902.

5/18c–4903. Implied Terms of Insurance Coverage

§ 18c–4903. Implied Terms of Insurance Coverage. Each certificate or other proof of insurance or surety coverage shall have, as an implied term, that the insurance or surety coverage will remain in effect continuously until notice of cancellation is filed in accordance with Commission regulations, and that all motor vehicles operated by or under authority of the carrier will be covered, whether or not such vehicles have been reported to the insurance, surety, or other company. Filing proof of insurance with the Commission shall constitute acceptance of this implied term, and such acceptance may not thereafter be withdrawn except on withdrawal of all proof of insurance or surety coverage.

P.A. 76–1586, § 18c–4903, added by P.A. 84–796, § 1, eff. Jan. 1, 1986. Amended by P.A. 85–553, § 2, eff. Sept. 18, 1987.

Formerly Ill.Rev.Stat.1991, ch. 95 ½, ¶ 18c–4903.

5/18c–4904. Liability to Be Covered by Insurance

§ 18c–4904. Liability to Be Covered by Insurance. Insurance or surety under this Article shall cover the carrier's liability for injury to persons and damage to property other than cargo. Coverage shall, in the case of motor common carriers, also extend to cargo damage.

P.A. 76–1586, § 18c–4904, added by P.A. 84–796, § 1, eff. Jan. 1, 1986. Amended by P.A. 85–553, § 2, eff. Sept. 18, 1987.

Formerly Ill.Rev.Stat.1991, ch. 95 ½, ¶ 18c–4904.

5/18c–4905. Self-insurance

§ 18c–4905. Self-insurance. The Commission may exempt a carrier from the requirement of Sections 18c–4901, 18c–4902, 18c–4903, and 18c–4904 of this Chapter if it determines that the carrier has the financial ability to pay for any and all damages the liability for which would otherwise be assumed by an insurance or surety company under the referenced sections. Each carrier so exempted shall file periodic reports, at such intervals as the Commission shall specify, showing its continuing ability to act as a self-insurer. The Commission may rescind an exemption on 10 days' notice if rescission appears necessary to protect the public. Upon the granting or rescission of a self-insured status of a carrier by the Commission, the Commission shall immediately notify, in writing, the Illinois Department of Transportation of the name, address, and other pertinent information required by the Department of Transportation concerning the status of the carrier.

P.A. 76–1586, § 18c–4905, added by P.A. 84–796, § 1, eff. Jan. 1, 1986. Amended by P.A. 84–1246, § 1, eff. July 29, 1986.

Formerly Ill.Rev.Stat.1991, ch. 95 ½, ¶ 18c–4905.

SUB–CHAPTER 5. SPECIAL PROVISIONS APPLICABLE TO TRANSPORTATION OF PROPERTY OVER PUBLIC ROADS

ARTICLE I. BROKERS

Section

ARTICLE II. RESOLUTION OF HOUSEHOLD GOODS DISPUTES

Section

ARTICLE III. NON–RELOCATION TOWING

ARTICLE I. BROKERS

5/18c–5101. Unlawful Activities

§ 18c–5101. Unlawful Activities. It shall be unlawful for any person:

(1) To act as a broker without a license in good standing issued to it by the Commission;

(2) To act as a broker in violation of any provision of this Chapter, Commission regulations and orders, or any other law of this state;

(3) To act as a broker of any shipment which the person owns or in which the person has a beneficial interest;

(4) To act as a broker of any shipment over which the person is able to exercise control because the person acting as a broker owns or controls the shipper, the shipper owns or controls the person acting as a broker, or there is a common ownership or control of the two;

(5) Which is also a broker to act or represent itself as a shipper in dealing with a common or contract carrier of property by motor vehicle;

(6) To act as a broker in connection with transportation by a person other than an authorized common or contract carrier of property by motor vehicle, unless the carrier does not require authorization to transport the shipment;

(7) To act as a broker in connection with transportation at other than lawfully applicable rates for the motor carrier service;

(8) To act as a broker in any name other than that which appears on its Commission license;

(9) To act as a broker without fully disclosing its brokering status;

(10) To provide transportation service with regard to freight for which it was the broker;

(11) To receive any compensation for brokering services other than a fee assessed to the shipper or, alternatively, to the carrier, in addition to freight charges at lawfully applicable rates for the motor carrier service;

(12) To advertise, offer, or give anything of value to a shipper, consignor, or consignee, other than inexpensive promotional items; or

(13) Act as a broker of household goods.

P.A. 76-1586, § 18c-5101, added by P.A. 84-796, § 1, eff. Jan. 1, 1986.

Formerly Ill.Rev.Stat.1991, ch. 95 ½, ¶ 18c-5101.

5/18c-5102. Licensing of Brokers

§ 18c-5102. Licensing of Brokers. (1) Procedures for Issuing Brokers' Licenses. The Provisions of Article II of Sub-chapter 4 of this Chapter which govern the form and manner of filing of applications for authority, notice to be given to the public, and hearing, shall likewise govern the issuance of a brokers' license.

(2) Standards for Review of Brokers' License Applications. The Commission shall issue a license authorizing a person to act as a statewide broker of general commodities where:

(a) The person has properly filed an application on forms prescribed by the Commission;

(b) The person has remitted the filing fee prescribed by the Commission;

(c) The person has filed proof of bond or insurance as required by Commission regulations; and

(d) The Commission has determined that the person is fit, willing, and able to;

(i) Act as a statewide broker of general commodities as authorized by the license; and

(ii) Comply with provisions of this Chapter, Commission regulations and orders. Otherwise, the application shall be denied.

(3) Suspension or Revocation of Brokers' Licenses. If at any time the Commission determines after notice and hearing that the holder of a broker's license is not fit, willing, or able to continue to act as a broker, the Commission may suspend or revoke the license.

P.A. 76-1586, § 18c-5102, added by P.A. 84-796, § 1, eff. Jan. 1, 1986.

Formerly Ill.Rev.Stat.1991, ch. 95 ½, ¶ 18c-5102.

5/18c-5103. The Fitness Standard

§ 18c-5103. The Fitness Standard. A person shall be rebuttably presumed unfit to act or to continue to act as a broker if:

(1) The person has violated any provision of this Chapter, Commission regulations or orders, or any other law governing its activities as a broker;

(2) The person has violated any fiduciary or other obligation with regard to transmittal of monies, bills, or other matters entrusted to it as broker; or

(3) The person is applying for a broker's license and any other person the ownership, management, or control of which is or was in substantial identity with the applicant has committed an act of the type described in (1) or (2), above. The Commission may consider any relevant facts in determining whether a person is fit to act or to continue to act as a broker, or whether any presumption which arises under this Section has been rebutted.

P.A. 76-1586, § 18c-5103, added by P.A. 84-796, § 1, eff. Jan. 1, 1986.

Formerly Ill.Rev.Stat.1991, ch. 95 ½, ¶ 18c-5103.

5/18c-5104. Transfer of Brokers' Licenses

§ 18c-5104. Transfer of Brokers' Licenses. (1) Transfer of Brokers' Licenses Permitted. A broker's license may be transferred, with Commission approval, under the conditions specified in this Section and in accordance with such regulations as the Commission may prescribe.

(2) Procedures for Transferring Brokers' Licenses. The provisions of Article III of the Sub-chapter 4 of this Chapter that define a transfer and which govern the form and manner of filing of applications for approval of the transfer of a motor carrier of property license, notice to be given to the public, and hearing, shall likewise govern the transfer of a broker's license.

(3) Standards for Review of Transfer Applications. The Commission shall grant an application for authority to transfer a broker's license where:

(a) The application was properly filed on forms prescribed by the Commission;

(b) The person has remitted the filing fee prescribed by the Commission; and

(c) The transferee is fit, willing, and able under the terms of Section 18c-5103 of this Chapter.

Otherwise, the application shall be denied.

P.A. 76-1586, § 18c-5104, added by P.A. 84-796, § 1, eff. Jan. 1, 1986.

Formerly Ill.Rev.Stat.1991, ch. 95 ½, ¶ 18c-5104.

5/18c-5105. Bonds and Insurance

§ 18c-5105. Bonds and Insurance. The Commission may prescribe for brokers such requirements regarding bonds, insurance, and the terms of coverage thereof, as the Commission determines are needed to protect carriers, shippers, consignors, and consignees of freight with respect to which brokering service is provided. Unless otherwise provided by the Commission, such requirements shall be the same as are applicable to property brokers under the Interstate Commerce Act [1] and regulations adopted thereunder.

P.A. 76-1586, § 18c-5105, added by P.A. 84-796, § 1, eff. Jan. 1, 1986.

Formerly Ill.Rev.Stat.1991, ch. 95 ½, ¶ 18c-5105.

[1] 49 U.S.C.A. § 10101 et seq.

5/18c-5106. Records of Brokers

§ 18c-5106. Records of Brokers. (1) Records to be Kept by Brokers. A broker shall keep a record of each transaction which shows:

(a) The name, address, and license number of the motor carrier or carriers;

(b) The name and address of the shipper, consignor, and consignee;

(c) The Bill of Lading or freight bill number;

(d) The amount of compensation received by the broker for brokering service, and the identity of the payor;

(e) A description of any non-brokering service provided in connection with each shipment or other activity, the amount of compensation received for such non-brokering service, and the identity of the payor;

(f) The amount of any freight charges collected by the broker, the date on which such charges were paid over to the carrier, and the amount of payment to the carrier; and

(g) Any other information which the Commission may prescribe.

(2) Maintenance of Records. Records required to be kept under this Section shall be maintained at an office within the State of Illinois, unless maintenance of an office outside the State of Illinois is expressly authorized by the Commission,

and shall be maintained for a period of 3 years after the date on which the shipment was delivered.

(3) Accounting. Each broker which engages in other business shall maintain accounts so that the brokering portion of its business or businesses is segregated from its other activities.

P.A. 76–1586, § 18c–5106, added by P.A. 84–796, § 1, eff. Jan. 1, 1986.

Formerly Ill.Rev.Stat.1991, ch. 95 ½, ¶ 18c–5106.

5/18c–5107. Brokers and Motor Carrier Applications

§ 18c–5107. Brokers and Motor Carrier Applications. A Broker shall not have standing to support any application for motor carrier of property authority.

P.A. 76–1586, § 18c–5107, added by P.A. 84–796, § 1, eff. Jan. 1, 1986.

Formerly Ill.Rev.Stat.1991, ch. 95 ½, ¶ 18c–5107.

ARTICLE II. RESOLUTION OF HOUSEHOLD GOODS DISPUTES

5/18c–5201. Application of Article

§ 18c–5201. Application of Article. The provisions of this Article apply to the collect-on-delivery transportation of household goods for non-commercial use where:

(1) The dispute relates to the propriety of charges for services rendered or loss of or damage to lading from the loading, unloading, or transportation thereof;

(2) The movement to which the dispute relates was between points in the State of Illinois; or

(3) Either the movement was made under authority issued by the Commission or the movement was such that it could have been lawfully made only under authority issued by the Commission.

P.A. 76–1586, § 18c–5201, added by P.A. 84–796, § 1, eff. Jan. 1, 1986.

Formerly Ill.Rev.Stat.1991, ch. 95 ½, ¶ 18c–5201.

5/18c–5202. Commission to prescribe dispute resolution procedure

§ 18c–5202. Commission to prescribe dispute resolution procedures. (1) Within 180 days after the effective date of this amendatory Act of 1995, the Commission shall propose rules specifying the procedures by which disputes between carriers and shippers to which this Sub-chapter is applicable will be resolved. Upon adoption, the rules will be applicable to all household goods carriers.

(2) Standards for dispute resolution procedures. The rules adopted by the Commission shall be calculated to provide for the objective, expeditious, and inexpensive resolution of household goods disputes, and shall include, without limitation, provisions dealing with: the location of any required hearings; required notifications; whether participation in a dispute resolution procedure is mandatory; and how the fees and costs of the procedures shall be distributed. To the extent authorized by Commission rules, procedures adopted under this Article may specify that dispute resolution services will be provided by the Commission, and in accordance with procedural rules adopted by the Commission.

(3) Grounds for Resolution of Household Goods Disputes. A dispute under this Article shall be resolved adverse to the carrier if:

(a) The carrier assessed a rate not contained in a lawfully applicable tariff or tariffs for such services;

(b) The carrier failed to fully apprise the shipper, prior to execution of any contract or contract amendment covering the services, of the lawful rates and charges for such services;

(c) Damages to lading occurred during the loading, transportation, or unloading of the shipments, or rendition of any accessorial service by the carrier, its employees or agents, without regard to negligence or fault, and the shipper did not elect in writing to assume liability for all or part of such damages.

P.A. 76–1586, § 18c–5202, added by P.A. 84–796, § 1, eff. Jan. 1, 1986. Amended by P.A. 89–444, § 5, eff. Jan. 25, 1996.

Formerly Ill.Rev.Stat.1991, ch. 95 ½, ¶ 18c–5202.

5/18c–5203. Award of Attorney Fees

§ 18c–5203. Award of Attorneys Fees. (1) Award to Complaining Shipper. In any court action to resolve a dispute within the scope of this Article, the court shall award reasonable attorney's fees to the complaining shipper if:

(a) The shipper submitted a claim to the carrier within 120 days after delivery of the shipment is completed;

(b) The shipper prevailed in the court action; and

(c) Either:

(i) No certified private dispute resolution procedure was available for use by the shipper at the time the court action was initiated; or

(ii) (Blank).

(iii) The court action was to enforce a timely decision rendered under the dispute resolution procedures specified by the Commission under this amendatory Act of 1995.

(2) Award to carrier. In any court action to resolve a dispute within the scope of this Article, the court may award reasonable attorney's fees to the carrier if the shipper brought the action in bad faith after submitting the dispute for resolution under the dispute resolution procedures specified by the Commission.

P.A. 76–1586, § 18c–5203, added by P.A. 84–796, § 1, eff. Jan. 1, 1986. Amended by P.A. 89–444, § 5, eff. Jan. 25, 1996.

Formerly Ill.Rev.Stat.1991, ch. 95 ½, ¶ 18c–5203.

5/18c–5204. Investigation of Practices of Household Goods Carriers

§ 18c–5204. Investigation of Practices of Household Goods Carriers. The Commission may, on its own motion or on complaint, conduct an investigation to determine whether a household goods carrier has, with or without the license required under Sub-chapter 4 of this Chapter,[1] engaged in a pattern or practice of underestimating freight charges for household goods shipments, or has otherwise violated provisions of this Chapter, Commission regulations or orders, and may invoke any or all sanctions provided for in Article VII of Sub-chapter 1 of this Chapter [2] against the carrier if such a pattern or practice, or any other violation, is found to have occurred.

P.A. 76–1586, § 18c–5204, added by P.A. 84–796, § 1, eff. Jan. 1, 1986. Amended by P.A. 90–89, § 15, eff. Jan. 1, 1998.

Formerly Ill.Rev.Stat.1991, ch. 95 ½, ¶ 18c–5204.

1 625 ILCS 5/18c–4101 et seq.

2 625 ILCS 5/18c–1701 et seq.

5/18c–5205. Applicability of Article

§ 18c–5205. Applicability of Article. This Article applies to disputes arising from transactions which occur at least 180 days after the effective date of this amendatory Act of 1985.

P.A. 76–1586, § 18c–5205, added by P.A. 84–796, § 1, eff. Jan. 1, 1986.

Formerly Ill.Rev.Stat.1991, ch. 95 ½, ¶ 18c–5205.

ARTICLE III. NON-RELOCATION TOWING

Enactment

Article III was added by P.A. 84–1311, § 1, eff. Aug. 27, 1986.

5/18c–5301. Application of Article

§ 18c–5301. Application of Article. The provisions of this Article shall apply to non-relocation towing. Where the provisions of this Article conflict with any other provisions in this Chapter, the provisions of this Article shall govern.

P.A. 76–1586, § 18c–5301, added by P.A. 84–1311, § 1, eff. Aug. 27, 1986.

Formerly Ill.Rev.Stat.1991, ch. 95 ½, ¶ 18c–5301.

5/18c–5302. Commission to Adopt Special Rules

§ 18c–5302. Commission to Adopt Special Rules.

(1) General Provisions. The Commission shall, within 180 days after the effective date of this Article, have finally adopted special forms and regulations applicable to non-relocation towing. Such regulations shall encompass definitions of terms, licensing, ratemaking, record-keeping, insurance or surety coverage, fees, and such other provisions as are necessary to effectuate the purposes of this Article. Such regulations shall be consistent with the provisions of this Article and shall implement such provisions with regard to non-relocation towing in a manner which recognizes the special circumstances and conditions which pertain to non-relocation towing as distinguished from other forms of motor carriage of property.

(2) Towing at Owner's Request. The Commission shall, within 60 days from July 1, 1988, adopt rules in accordance with Section 5–50 of the Illinois Administrative Procedure Act [1] which implement the provisions of this Chapter dealing with the exemption of non-relocation towing at the request of the vehicle owner.

P.A. 76–1586, § 18c–5302, added by P.A. 84–1311, § 1, eff. Aug. 27, 1986. Amended by P.A. 85–963, § 1, eff. July 1, 1988; P.A. 88–45, Art. III, § 3–128, eff. July 6, 1993.

Formerly Ill.Rev.Stat.1991, ch. 95 ½, ¶ 18c–5302.

[1] 5 ILCS 100/5–50.

5/18c–5303. Fitness Test

§ 18c–5303. The Fitness Test.

(1) Prima Facie Evidence of Applicant Fitness in Licensing Cases. Applicants for non-relocation towing licenses may establish a prima facie showing of fitness by the following evidence:

(a) A summary statement of net worth;

(b) A listing of applicant's drivers and any persons who assist or supervise drivers;

(c) A description of equipment to be used in providing service under the license;

(d) A statement that the applicant has not:

(i) Been convicted, during the 2 years immediately preceding the filing of the application, of a felony involving theft of property, violence to persons, or criminal damage to property; or

(ii) Been convicted, during the year immediately preceding the filing of the application, of safety violations on 3 or more occasions in which its vehicle or vehicles were taken out of service, or which otherwise show the applicant to be unfit;

(e) A statement that the applicant does not and will not employ or lease any driver, or any person who will assist or supervise drivers, who has been convicted, during the applicable time frames, of the foregoing violations;

(f) A statement that the applicant does not and will not employ or lease any driver who does not hold a valid classified driver's license to operate a tow truck;

(g) A statement that the applicant is familiar with and will comply with the provisions of this Chapter, Commission regulations and orders; and

(h) Proof of insurance in compliance with Commission regulations and orders.

(2) Prima Facie Evidence of Licensee Fitness in Enforcement Cases. The respondent in a proceeding to consider whether to suspend or revoke a license authorizing non-relocation towing or to impose other sanctions on grounds of unfitness may establish a prima facie showing of fitness in the manner provided in subsection (1) of this Section.

(3) Rebuttal of Prima Facie Showing of Fitness. A prima facie showing of applicant or licensee fitness may be rebutted by other evidence of record, either from the applicant or otherwise.

P.A. 76–1586, § 18c–5303, added by P.A. 84–1311, § 1, eff. Aug. 27, 1986.

Formerly Ill.Rev.Stat.1991, ch. 95 ½, ¶ 18c–5303.

5/18c–5304. Public Need/Public Convenience and Necessity Test

§ 18c–5304. The Public Need/Public Convenience and Necessity Test. Applicants for non-relocation towing licenses may establish, and other parties may rebut, a prima facie showing of public need/public convenience and necessity by the following evidence:

(1) Existing Towing Companies.

(a) Evidentiary Standard. Any person engaged in non-relocation towing between July 1, 1985 and January 1, 1986 may establish a prima facie showing of public convenience and necessity to the extent of such operations by submitting a statement:

(i) Affirming that the person was engaged in non-relocation during the foregoing time period; and

(ii) Describing its operations during such period.

(b) Extent of Existing Operations. The extent of the applicant's operations shall be presumed to encompass non-relocation towing within the following territory, unless otherwise shown on the record:

(i) Movements within a 50 mile radius of the applicant's principal place of business in Illinois; and

(ii) Movements from points within the foregoing radius to points in Illinois, and vice versa.

(c) Deadline for Filing Applications. Applications under this subsection must be filed within 9 months after the effective date of this amendatory Act of 1986, or by July 1, 1987, whichever is later.

(2) New Towing Companies and Extension of Existing Company Operations. Applications for non-relocation towing

licenses need not be supported by shippers intending to use the carrier's service if other evidence of public need/public convenience and necessity is offered by carrier witnesses, non-carrier witnesses from other than shippers intending to use the carrier's service, or others.

(3) Rebuttal of Prima Facie Showing of Public Need/Public Convenience and Necessity. A prima facie showing of public need/public convenience and necessity may be rebutted by other evidence of record, either from the applicant or otherwise.

P.A. 76–1586, § 18c–5304, added by P.A. 84–1311, § 1, eff. Aug. 27, 1986.

Formerly Ill.Rev.Stat.1991, ch. 95 ½, ¶ 18c–5304.

5/18c–5305. Hearings in Non-Relocation Towing Authority Cases

§ 18c–5305. Hearings in Non-Relocation Towing Authority Cases.

(1) Hearings on Fitness Required. Hearings on applications for non-relocation towing licenses shall be governed by the provisions of Section 18c–2101 of this Code, with regard to the issue of fitness; and by the provisions of subsection (2) of Section 18c–2102 of this Code, with regard to the issue of public need/public convenience and necessity. Hearings in other non-relocation towing cases shall be governed by the provisions of Section 18c–2102 of this Code.

(2) Setting and Conduct of Licensing Hearings.

(a) Regional Hearings. Hearings on applications for non-relocation towing licenses shall be consolidated and conducted regionally for the convenience of the parties. Where practicable:

(i) Hearings shall be conducted at a location not more than 50 miles from the principal place of the applicant's business;

(ii) The Commission shall schedule joint hearings at each regional location.

(b) Scheduling of Hearings. Hearings on applications for non-relocation towing licenses shall be scheduled and concluded so as to minimize inconvenience to the parties. Where practicable, hearings on an application shall be concluded in a single day, unless:

(i) Continuance is required for the applicant to produce evidence of its fitness; or

(ii) A petition for leave to intervene in opposition is properly filed and granted.

P.A. 76–1586, § 18c–5305, added by P.A. 84–1311, § 1, eff. Aug. 27, 1986.

Formerly Ill.Rev.Stat.1991, ch. 95 ½, ¶ 18c–5305.

5/18c–5306. Denial, Suspension or Revocation of Licenses

§ 18c–5306. Denial, Suspension, or Revocation of Licenses. If, at any time during or after adjudication of a non-relocation towing license application, there exists an issue with regard to the fitness of the applicant, the Commission may suspend any temporary license granted to the applicant. If the applicant is not shown to be fit, the Commission shall revoke the temporary license and deny the application for a permanent license. If, at any time subsequent to the grant of a permanent license, the holder is determined to be unfit, the Commission shall suspend or revoke the license. Suspension or revocation shall be after notice and hearing, absent waiver of same by respondent, as provided for other than motor carrier of property authority cases under Section 18c–2102 of this Code.

P.A. 76–1586, § 18c–5306, added by P.A. 84–1311, § 1, eff. Aug. 27, 1986.

Formerly Ill.Rev.Stat.1991, ch. 95 ½, ¶ 18c–5306.

5/18c–5307. False Statements by Applicant

§ 18c–5307. False Statements by Applicant. Any false statement of a material fact by an applicant shall be grounds for denial or revocation of a license.

P.A. 76–1586, § 18c–5307, added by P.A. 84–1311, § 1, eff. Aug. 27, 1986.

Formerly Ill.Rev.Stat.1991, ch. 95 ½, ¶ 18c–5307.

5/18c–5308. Intervention in Opposition to Non-Relocation Towing Applications

§ 18c–5308. Intervention in Opposition to Non-Relocation Towing Applications.

(1) Filing Fee for Petitions for Leave to Intervene in Opposition. The Commission shall prescribe a filing fee of not less than $100 for each petition for leave to intervene in opposition in a non-relocation towing authority case.

(2) Standing to Participate and Intervene. Any person with evidence relating to the fitness of an applicant for a non-relocation towing license may be permitted, at the discretion of the examiner, to present such evidence at hearing. The provisions of paragraph (a) of subsection (2) of Section 18c–2106 of this Code shall not apply to persons filing petitions for leave to intervene in opposition to non-relocation towing license applications, unless the issue of public need/public convenience and necessity is controverted by such persons at hearing.

P.A. 76–1586, § 18c–5308, added by P.A. 84–1311, § 1, eff. Aug. 27, 1986.

Formerly Ill.Rev.Stat.1991, ch. 95 ½, ¶ 18c–5308.

5/18c–5309. Ratemaking

§ 18c–5309. Ratemaking. Unless otherwise specified in the tariff, rates applicable to non-relocation towing shall be the maximum rates which may be charged by carriers participating in the tariff for such service.

P.A. 76–1586, § 18c–5309, added by P.A. 84–1311, § 1, eff. Aug. 27, 1986.

Formerly Ill.Rev.Stat.1991, ch. 95 ½, ¶ 18c–5309.

5/18c–5310. Insurance

§ 18c–5310. Insurance.

(1) Implied Garagekeeper's Liability. The filing of a form E certificate of insurance shall constitute a representation by the insurance company that the underlying insurance policy includes, with regard to non-relocation towing, liability for damage to vehicles in the custody of the non-relocation towing company, whether in transit or otherwise, in an amount not less than the amount of cargo insurance required under Commission regulations and orders, unless otherwise specified by the insurance company on the form E certificate of liability insurance.

(2) Filing Proof of Cargo Insurance. Except where the form E certificate of liability insurance indicates, in accordance with subsection (1) of this Section, that garagekeeper's liability is not covered by the underlying policy of insurance,

a non-relocation towing company shall not be required to file proof of cargo insurance for the transportation of vehicles.

P.A. 76–1586, § 18c–5310, added by P.A. 84–1311, § 1, eff. Aug. 27, 1986.

Formerly Ill.Rev.Stat.1991, ch. 95 ½, ¶ 18c–5310.

SUB–CHAPTER 6. MOTOR CARRIERS OF PASSENGERS

ARTICLE I. GENERAL PROVISIONS GOVERNING MOTOR CARRIERS OF PASSENGERS

ARTICLE I. GENERAL PROVISIONS GOVERNING MOTOR CARRIERS OF PASSENGERS

5/18c–6101. Scope of Commission Jurisdiction

§ 18c–6101. Scope of Commission Jurisdiction. Except as provided in Section 18c–6102 of this Chapter, the jurisdiction of the Commission shall extend to all motor carriers of passengers operating within the State of Illinois.

P.A. 76–1586, § 18c–6101, added by P.A. 84–796, § 1, eff. Jan. 1, 1986.

Formerly Ill.Rev.Stat.1991, ch. 95 ½, ¶ 18c–6101.

5/18c–6102. Exemptions From Commission Jurisdiction

§ 18c–6102. Exemptions From Commission Jurisdiction. The provisions of this Sub-chapter shall not, except as provided in Section 18c–6501 of this Chapter, apply to:

(1) carriers owned by any political subdivision, school district, institution of higher education, or municipality, and operated either by such political subdivision, institution of higher education, or municipality or its lessee or agent;

(2) commuter vans as defined in this Code;

(3) carriers transporting passengers without fixed routes or schedules and charging on a time or distance basis, including taxicabs, charter operations, and contract bus operations;

(4) carriers transporting passengers with fixed routes and schedules and charging on a per passenger fixed charge basis and which do not include an airport as a point to be served on the route, in whole or in part;

(5) transportation in vehicles with a manufacturer's rated seating capacity of less than 8 persons, including the driver;

(6) transportation subject to the Ridesharing Arrangements Act; [1]

(7) commuter buses offering short-haul for-hire regularly scheduled passenger transportation service within metropolitan and suburban areas, over regular routes with fixed schedules, and utilized primarily by passengers using reduced-fare, multiple-ride, or commutation tickets during morning and evening peak periods in travelling to and from their places of employment; and

(8) those persons owning and operating school buses, as defined in this Code, and regulated by other provisions of this Code.

P.A. 76–1586, § 18c–6102, added by P.A. 84–796, § 1, eff. Jan. 1, 1986. Amended by P.A. 84–1025, § 2, eff. Jan. 1, 1986; P.A. 84–1246, § 1, eff. July 29, 1986; P.A. 85–809, § 1, eff. Sept. 24, 1987; P.A. 90–407, § 5, eff. Aug. 15, 1997; P.A. 91–357, § 231, eff. July 29, 1999.

Formerly Ill.Rev.Stat.1991, ch. 95 ½, ¶ 18c–6102.

[1] 625 ILCS 30/1 et seq.

5/18c–6103. Unlawful Operations

§ 18c–6103. Unlawful Operations. Except as provided in Article I of this Sub-chapter, and subject to the provisions stated herein, no person shall:

(1) Operate as a motor carrier of passengers unless the person possesses a valid license authorizing such operations.

(2) Provide service at rates other than those contained in lawfully applicable tariffs for such service;

(3) Otherwise operate as a motor carrier of passengers in violation of any provision of this Chapter, Commission regulations and orders, or any other law of this state; or

(4) Aid or abet any other person in a violation of this Chapter, Commission regulations or orders, by soliciting or receiving, or by compensating service from a person not authorized to provide such service, or at other than lawful rates for such service, or otherwise.

P.A. 76–1586, § 18c–6103, added by P.A. 84–796, § 1, eff. Jan. 1, 1986.

Formerly Ill.Rev.Stat.1991, ch. 95 ½, ¶ 18c–6103.

ARTICLE II. LICENSING

5/18c–6201. Requirements for Issuance of Licenses

§ 18c–6201. Requirements for Issuance of Licenses. (1) General Requirements. Except as provided in subsection (2) of this Section, the Commission shall grant an application for a motor carrier of passengers license, in whole or in part, to the extent that it finds that the application was properly filed, a need for the proposed service exists, the applicant if fit, willing, and able to provide the service in compliance with this Chapter, Commission regulations and orders, absent a showing that issuance of the license would be inconsistent with the public interest. Otherwise, the application shall be denied. In determining whether issuance of a motor carrier of passengers license would be inconsistent with the public interest, the Commission shall consider:

(a) The value of competition which would result from issuance to the travelling public;

(b) The effect of issuance on motor carrier of passengers service to small communities;

(c) The effect of issuance on the ability of any other carrier to provide a substantial portion of the passenger service such carrier provides over its entire system, except that diversion of revenue or traffic from a carrier in and of itself shall not be sufficient to support a finding that issuance of the license would impair the ability of the other carrier to provide a substantial portion of the passenger service such carrier provides over its entire system; and

(d) Any other factor relevant to the public interest.

(2) Motor Carriers of Passengers Providing Service to or from Airports. The Commission shall grant an application for a motor carrier of passengers license authorizing service along any route where an airport is a point to be served on the route, in whole or in part, to the extent that it finds that the application was properly filed, a need for the proposed service exists, the applicant is fit, willing, and able to provide the service in compliance with this Chapter, Commission regulations and orders, and the public convenience and necessity requires issuance of the license. Otherwise, the application shall be denied. The provisions of this subsection shall be construed to impose the same entry requirements as were previously applicable under Section 55 of "An Act concerning public utilities", approved June 29, 1921, as amended.[1]

P.A. 76–1586, § 18c–6201, added by P.A. 84–796, § 1, eff. Jan. 1, 1986. Amended by P.A. 85–553, § 2, eff. Sept. 18, 1987.

Formerly Ill.Rev.Stat.1991, ch. 95 ½, ¶ 18c–6201.

[1] Former Ill.Rev.Stat. ch. 111⅔, ¶ 55 (repealed; see, now 220 ILCS 5/8–302).

5/18c–6202. Other Provisions Relating to Licensing and Registration

§ 18c–6202. Other Provisions Relating to Licensing and Registration. Provisions in Articles II, III, and IV of Subchapter 4 of this Chapter, governing the suspension, revocation, and transfer of motor carrier of property licenses, the registration of interstate motor carriers of property shall likewise govern motor carriers of passengers as if all references therein were to motor carriers of passengers.

P.A. 76–1586, § 18c–6202, added by P.A. 84–796, § 1, eff. Jan. 1, 1986. Amended by P.A. 85–553, § 2, eff. Sept. 18, 1987.

Formerly Ill.Rev.Stat.1991, ch. 95 ½, ¶ 18c–6202.

ARTICLE III. ADDITION, CHANGE, REDUCTION, OR DISCONTINUANCE OF SCHEDULED MOTOR BUS SERVICE

5/18c–6301. General Provisions

§ 18c–6301. General Provisions. No motor common carrier of passengers shall add to, change, reduce, or discontinue service to any point along a route over which the carrier is authorized to provide intrastate service, except in accordance with the provisions of this Article.

P.A. 76–1586, § 18c–6301, added by P.A. 84–796, § 1, eff. Jan. 1, 1986. Amended by P.A. 85–553, § 2, eff. Sept. 18, 1987.

Formerly Ill.Rev.Stat.1991, ch. 95 ½, ¶ 18c–6301.

5/18c–6302. Definitions

§ 18c–6302. Definitions. The following terms, when used in this Article, shall have the hereinafter designated meanings.

(1) "Addition" to service means the institution of new scheduled service.

(2) "Change" in service means a change in the time or times of scheduled service which does not constitute a reduction or discontinuance of service.

(3) "Reduction" of service means any reduction in the level of scheduled service which does not constitute discontinuance of the carrier's service.

(4) "Discontinuance" of service means total discontinuance of service to any point along a route over which the carrier is authorized to provide service or reduction in the level of service to any such point to less than one round trip per weekday (Monday through Friday).

P.A. 76–1586, § 18c–6302, added by P.A. 84–796, § 1, eff. Jan. 1, 1986. Amended by P.A. 90–655, § 153, eff. July 30, 1998.

Formerly Ill.Rev.Stat.1991, ch. 95 ½, ¶ 18c–6302.

5/18c–6303. Schedule Changes and Reductions in Service

§ 18c–6303. Schedule Changes and Reductions in Service. Any motor common carrier of passengers may add to, change, or reduce the level of its service to any point along a route over which the carrier is authorized to provide service, provided that the addition, change or reduction does not constitute discontinuance of service to any point along a route over which the carrier is authorized to serve, after the carrier has served notice in accordance with Commission regulations adopted pursuant to this Article, and without prior authorization.

P.A. 76–1586, § 18c–6303, added by P.A. 84–796, § 1, eff. Jan. 1, 1986.

Formerly Ill.Rev.Stat.1991, ch. 95 ½, ¶ 18c–6303.

5/18c–6304. Discontinuances

§ 18c–6304. Discontinuances. No motor common carrier of passengers shall discontinue service to any point along a route over which the carrier is authorized to provide service except in accordance with provisions of Section 18c–6305 of this Chapter.

P.A. 76–1586, § 18c–6304, added by P.A. 84–796, § 1, eff. Jan. 1, 1986.

Formerly Ill.Rev.Stat.1991, ch. 95 ½, ¶ 18c–6304.

5/18c–6305. Prior Notice and Petition for Authorization

§ 18c–6305. Prior Notice and Petition for Authorization. (1) Annual and Amended Lists of Points Under Consideration for Discontinuance. By March of each calendar year, each motor carrier of passengers shall submit to the Commission a list of routes and points which it is authorized to serve which the carrier has under consideration for discontinuance within the following 12 months. A carrier may amend its list on the 1st day of each subsequent month.

(2) Notice of Intent to Discontinue. Not less than 30 days after a point appears on a list of points under consideration for discontinuance, the carrier may serve on the Commission the carrier's Notice of Intent to discontinue service. Such notice shall be for the purpose of alerting the Commission

and allowing a period of time during which alternatives to discontinuance, or alternative service, may be explored.

(3) Petitions to Discontinue. Not less than 60 nor more than 90 days after the filing of a Notice of Intent to discontinue, the carrier may formally propose discontinuance by filing in accordance with such requirements as to form and content as the Commission may prescribe. The Commission may investigate the proposal, and may suspend the discontinuance pending the outcome of the investigation for a period not to exceed 90 days from the date the proposal is filed. The Commission shall determine, after considering the public need for service, revenues (both those which have been received and those which might be received, by subsidy or otherwise) and variable costs associated with the service, and the availability of reasonable alternative transportation service whether the public convenience and necessity requires continuation of the service proposed to be discontinued. If the Commission determines that the public convenience and necessity requires continuation, it shall so order; otherwise, the proceeding shall be dismissed.

(4) Waiver or Notice. Prior notice requirements under this Section may be waived for good cause or where the carrier has made substantial compliance with such prior notice requirements or compliance is not necessary to effectuate the purposes of this Chapter.

P.A. 76–1586, § 18c–6305, added by P.A. 84–796, § 1, eff. Jan. 1, 1986.

Formerly Ill.Rev.Stat.1991, ch. 95 ½, ¶ 18c–6305.

ARTICLE IV. RATEMAKING

5/18c–6401. Ratemaking

§ 18c–6401. Ratemaking. The Commission may exercise, with respect to rate regulation of motor carriers of passengers, any and all power which it may exercise with respect to rate regulation of motor carriers of property. Motor carriers of passengers shall be in all respects subject to provisions of this Chapter governing ratemaking for motor carriers of property, except as provided in 49 U.S. Code 11501(e).

P.A. 76–1586, § 18c–6401, added by P.A. 84–796, § 1, eff. Jan. 1, 1986.

Formerly Ill.Rev.Stat.1991, ch. 95 ½, ¶ 18c–6401.

ARTICLE V. SAFETY REQUIREMENTS FOR MOTOR CARRIERS OF PASSENGERS

5/18c–6501. Hours of Service for Drivers

§ 18c–6501. Hours of Service for Drivers. No motor carrier of passengers shall operate any vehicle with a manufacturer's rated seating capacity of more than 8 persons, including the driver, except in compliance with federal hours of service regulations codified at 49 Code of Federal Regulations Part 395, Hours of Service of Drivers, as amended.

P.A. 76–1586, § 18c–6501, added by P.A. 84–796, § 1, eff. Jan. 1, 1986.

Formerly Ill.Rev.Stat.1991, ch. 95 ½, ¶ 18c–6501.

5/18c–6502. Report and Investigations of Accidents

§ 18c–6502. Report and Investigation of Accidents. (1) Reports. Every motor carrier of passengers shall report to the Commission, by the speediest means possible, whether telephone, telegraph, or otherwise, every accident involving its equipment which resulted in loss of life to any person. In addition to reports required to be filed with the Department of Transportation, under Article IV of Chapter 11 and Chapter 7 of this Code,[1] such carrier shall file a written report with the Commission, in accordance with regulations adopted hereunder, of any accident which results in injury or loss of life to any employee, or damage to the person or property of any member of the public. The Commission and the Department of Transportation may adopt, by reference, such state or federal reporting requirements as will effectuate the purposes of this Section and promote uniformity in bus accident reporting.

(2) Investigations. The Commission and the Department of Transportation may investigate any bus accident reported to it or of which it acquires knowledge independent of reports made by motor carriers of passengers, and shall have the power to enter such orders and adopt such regulations as will minimize the risk of future accidents.

P.A. 76–1586, § 18c–6502, added by P.A. 84–796, § 1, eff. Jan. 1, 1986. Amended by P.A. 84–1246, § 1, eff. July 29, 1986.

Formerly Ill.Rev.Stat.1991, ch. 95 ½, ¶ 18c–6502.

[1] 625 ILCS 5/11–401 et seq. and 5/7–100 et seq.

5/18c–6503. Insurance

§ 18c–6503. Insurance. The provisions of Article IX of Subchapter 4 of this Chapter regarding insurance for motor carriers of property shall apply to motor carriers of passengers subject to the jurisdiction of the Commission under this Subchapter as if all references in Article IX were to motor carriers of passengers.

P.A. 76–1586, § 18c–6503, added by P.A. 84–1025, § 2, eff. Jan. 1, 1986.

Formerly Ill.Rev.Stat.1991, ch. 95 ½, ¶ 18c–6503.

SUB–CHAPTER 7. RAIL CARRIERS

ARTICLE I. JURISDICTION OVER RAIL CARRIERS

Section

ARTICLE II. REGISTRATION AND SERVICES OF RAIL CARRIERS

ARTICLE III. RATEMAKING

ARTICLE IV. SAFETY REQUIREMENTS FOR RAIL CARRIERS

ARTICLE V. MISCELLANEOUS PROVISIONS

ARTICLE I. JURISDICTION OVER RAIL CARRIERS

5/18c-7101. Jurisdiction Over Rail Carriers

§ 18c-7101. Jurisdiction Over Rail Carriers. The jurisdiction of the Commission under this Sub-chapter shall be exclusive and shall extend to all intrastate and interstate rail carrier operations within this State, except to the extent that its jurisdiction is preempted by valid provisions of the Staggers Rail Act of 1980 [1] or other valid federal statute, regulation, or order.

P.A. 76-1586, § 18c-7101, added by P.A. 84-796, § 1, eff. Jan. 1, 1986. Amended by P.A. 85-406, § 1, eff. Sept. 15, 1987.

Formerly Ill.Rev.Stat.1991, ch. 95 ½, ¶ 18c-7101.

[1] 49 U.S.C.A. § 10101 et seq.

ARTICLE II. REGISTRATION AND SERVICES OF RAIL CARRIERS

5/18c-7201. Registration as a Rail Carrier

§ 18c-7201. Registration as a Rail Carrier. (1) General Provisions. Except as provided in subsection (2) of this Section, no person shall operate as a rail carrier, and no person shall begin or continue construction of any track or other facilities, other than the repair or replacement of existing plant, for use in operations as a rail carrier unless such person has registered with the Commission as a rail carrier.

(2) Exceptions. Each rail carrier operating within the State of Illinois on the effective date of this Chapter shall automatically be deemed, as of that date, to have registered as a rail carrier for purposes of this Section. Such constructive registration shall expire on the 180th day after the effective date of this amendatory Act of 1985.

P.A. 76-1586, § 18c-7201, added by P.A. 84-796, § 1, eff. Jan. 1, 1986.

Formerly Ill.Rev.Stat.1991, ch. 95 ½, ¶ 18c-7201.

5/18c-7202. Duties and Obligations of Rail Carriers

§ 18c-7202. Duties and Obligations of Rail Carriers. Each rail carrier shall provide adequate service to the public at reasonable rates and without discrimination.

P.A. 76-1586, § 18c-7202, added by P.A. 84-796, § 1, eff. Jan. 1, 1986.

Formerly Ill.Rev.Stat.1991, ch. 95 ½, ¶ 18c-7202.

5/18c-7203. § 18c-7203. Repealed by P.A. 90-257, § 10, eff. July 30, 1997

ARTICLE III. RATEMAKING

5/18c-7301, 5/18c-7302. §§ 18c-7301, 18c-7302. Repealed by P.A. 90-257, § 10, eff. July 30, 1997

ARTICLE IV. SAFETY REQUIREMENTS FOR RAIL CARRIERS

5/18c-7401. Safety Requirements for Track, Facilities, and Equipment

§ 18c-7401. Safety Requirements for Track, Facilities, and Equipment.

(1) General Requirements. Each rail carrier shall, consistent with rules, orders, and regulations of the Federal Railroad Administration, construct, maintain, and operate all of its equipment, track, and other property in this State in such a manner as to pose no undue risk to its employees or the person or property of any member of the public.

(2) Adoption of Federal Standards. The track safety standards and accident/incident standards promulgated by the Federal Railroad Administration shall be safety standards of the Commission. The Commission may, in addition, adopt by reference in its regulations other federal railroad safety standards, whether contained in federal statutes or in regulations adopted pursuant to such statutes.

(3) Railroad Crossings. No public road, highway, or street shall hereafter be constructed across the track of any rail carrier at grade, nor shall the track of any rail carrier be constructed across a public road, highway or street at grade, without having first secured the permission of the Commission; provided, that this Section shall not apply to the replacement of lawfully existing roads, highways and tracks. No public pedestrian bridge or subway shall be constructed across the track of any rail carrier without having first secured the permission of the Commission. The Commission shall have the right to refuse its permission or to grant it upon such terms and conditions as it may prescribe. The Commission shall have power to determine and prescribe the manner, including the particular point of crossing, and the terms of installation, operation, maintenance, use and protection of each such crossing.

The Commission shall also have power, after a hearing, to require major alteration of or to abolish any crossing, heretofore or hereafter established, when in its opinion, the public safety requires such alteration or abolition, and, except in cities, villages and incorporated towns of 1,000,000 or more inhabitants, to vacate and close that part of the highway on such crossing altered or abolished and cause barricades to be erected across such highway in such manner as to prevent the use of such crossing as a highway, when, in the opinion of the Commission, the public convenience served by the crossing in question is not such as to justify the further retention thereof; or to require a separation of grades, at railroad-highway grade crossings; or to require a separation of grades at any proposed crossing where a proposed public highway may cross the tracks of any rail carrier or carriers; and to prescribe, after a hearing of the parties, the terms upon which such separations shall be made and the proportion in which the expense of the alteration or abolition of such crossings or the separation of such grades, having regard to the benefits, if any, accruing to the rail carrier or any party in interest, shall be divided between the rail carrier or carriers affected, or between such carrier or carriers and the State, county, municipality or other public authority in interest. However, a public hearing by the Commission to abolish a crossing shall not be required when the public highway authority in interest vacates the highway. In such instance the rail carrier, following notification to the Commission and the highway authority, shall remove any grade crossing warning devices and the grade crossing surface.

The Commission shall also have power by its order to require the reconstruction, minor alteration, minor relocation or improvement of any crossing (including the necessary highway approaches thereto) of any railroad across any highway or public road, pedestrian bridge, or pedestrian subway, whether such crossing be at grade or by overhead structure or by subway, whenever the Commission finds after a hearing or without a hearing as otherwise provided in this paragraph that such reconstruction, alteration, relocation or improvement is necessary to preserve or promote the safety or convenience of the public or of the employees or passengers of such rail carrier or carriers. By its original order or supplemental orders in such case, the Commission may direct such reconstruction, alteration, relocation, or improvement to be made in such manner and upon such terms and conditions as may be reasonable and necessary and may apportion the cost of such reconstruction, alteration, relocation or improvement and the subsequent maintenance thereof, having regard to the benefits, if any, accruing to the railroad or any party in interest, between the rail carrier or carriers and public utilities affected, or between such carrier or carriers and public utilities and the State, county, municipality or other public authority in interest. The cost to be so apportioned shall include the cost of changes or alterations in the equipment of public utilities affected as well as the cost of the relocation, diversion or establishment of any public highway, made necessary by such reconstruction, alteration, relocation or improvement of said crossing. A hearing shall not be required in those instances when the Commission enters an order confirming a written stipulation in which the Commission, the public highway authority or other public authority in interest, the rail carrier or carriers affected, and in instances involving the use of the Grade Crossing Protection Fund, the Illinois Department of Transportation, agree on the reconstruction, alteration, relocation, or improvement and the subsequent maintenance thereof and the division of costs of such changes of any grade crossing (including the necessary highway approaches thereto) of any railroad across any highway, pedestrian bridge, or pedestrian subway.

Every rail carrier operating in the State of Illinois shall construct and maintain every highway crossing over its tracks within the State so that the roadway at the intersection shall be as flush with the rails as superelevated curves will allow, and, unless otherwise ordered by the Commission, shall construct and maintain the approaches thereto at a grade of not more than 5% within the right of way for a distance of not less the 6 feet on each side of the centerline of such tracks; provided, that the grades at the approaches may be maintained in excess of 5% only when authorized by the Commission.

Every rail carrier operating within this State shall remove from its right of way at all railroad-highway grade crossings within the State, such brush, shrubbery, and trees as is reasonably practical for a distance of not less than 500 feet in either direction from each grade crossing. The Commission shall have power, upon its own motion, or upon complaint, and after having made proper investigation, to require the installation of adequate and appropriate luminous reflective warning signs, luminous flashing signals, crossing gates illuminated at night, or other protective devices in order to promote and safeguard the health and safety of the public. Luminous flashing signal or crossing gate devices installed at grade crossings, which have been approved by the Commission, shall be deemed adequate and appropriate. The Commission shall have authority to determine the number, type, and location of such signs, signals, gates, or other protective devices which, however, shall conform as near as may be with generally recognized national standards, and the Commission shall have authority to prescribe the division of the cost of the installation and subsequent maintenance of such signs, signals, gates, or other protective devices between the rail carrier or carriers, the public highway authority or other public authority in interest, and in instances involving the use of the Grade Crossing Protection Fund, the Illinois Department of Transportation.

No railroad may change or modify the warning device system at a railroad-highway grade crossing, including warning systems interconnected with highway traffic control signals, without having first received the approval of the Commission. The Commission shall have the further power, upon application, upon its own motion, or upon complaint and after having made proper investigation, to require the interconnection of grade crossing warning devices with traffic control signals at highway intersections located at or near railroad crossings within the distances described by the State Manual on Uniform Traffic Control Devices adopted pursuant to Section 11–301 of this Code. In addition, State and local authorities may not install, remove, modernize, or otherwise modify traffic control signals at a highway intersection that is interconnected or proposed to be interconnected with grade crossing warning devices when the change affects the number, type, or location of traffic control devices on the track approach leg or legs of the intersection or the timing of the railroad preemption sequence of operation until the Commission has approved the installation, removal, modernization, or modification. Commission approval shall be limited to consideration of issues directly affecting the public safety at the railroad-highway grade crossing. The electrical circuit devices, alternate warning devices, and preemption sequences shall conform as nearly as possible, considering the particular characteristics of the crossing and intersection area, to the State manual adopted by the Illinois Department of Transportation pursuant to Section 11–301 of this Code and such federal standards as are made applicable by subsection (2) of this Section. In order to carry out this authority, the Commission shall have the authority to determine the number, type, and location of traffic control devices on the track approach leg or legs of the intersection and the timing of the railroad preemption sequence of operation. The Commission shall prescribe the division of costs for installation and maintenance of all devices required by this paragraph between the railroad or railroads and the highway authority in interest and in instances involving the use of the Grade Crossing Protection Fund or a State highway, the Illinois Department of Transportation.

Any person who unlawfully or maliciously removes, throws down, damages or defaces any sign, signal, gate or other protective device, located at or near any public grade crossing, shall be guilty of a petty offense and fined not less than $50 nor more than $200 for each offense. In addition to fines levied under the provisions of this Section a person adjudged guilty hereunder may also be directed to make restitution for the costs of repair or replacement, or both, necessitated by his misconduct.

It is the public policy of the State of Illinois to enhance public safety by establishing safe grade crossings. In order to implement this policy, the Illinois Commerce Commission is directed to conduct public hearings and to adopt specific criteria by July 1, 1994, that shall be adhered to by the Illinois Commerce Commission in determining if a grade crossing should be opened or abolished. The following factors shall be considered by the Illinois Commerce Commission in developing the specific criteria for opening and abolishing grade crossings:

(a) timetable speed of passenger trains;

(b) distance to an alternate crossing;

(c) accident history for the last 5 years;

(d) number of vehicular traffic and posted speed limits;

(e) number of freight trains and their timetable speeds;

(f) the type of warning device present at the grade crossing;

(g) alignments of the roadway and railroad, and the angle of intersection of those alignments;

(h) use of the grade crossing by trucks carrying hazardous materials, vehicles carrying passengers for hire, and school buses; and

(i) use of the grade crossing by emergency vehicles.

The Illinois Commerce Commission, upon petition to open or abolish a grade crossing, shall enter an order opening or abolishing the crossing if it meets the specific criteria adopted by the Commission.

Except as otherwise provided in this subsection (3), in no instance shall a grade crossing be permanently closed without public hearing first being held and notice of such hearing being published in an area newspaper of local general circulation.

(4) Freight Trains—Radio Communications. The Commission shall after hearing and order require that every main line railroad freight train operating on main tracks outside of yard limits within this State shall be equipped with a radio communication system. The Commission after notice and hearing may grant exemptions from the requirements of this Section as to secondary and branch lines.

(5) Railroad Bridges and Trestles—Walkway and Handrail. In cases in which the Commission finds the same to be practical and necessary for safety of railroad employees, bridges and trestles, over and upon which railroad trains are operated, shall include as a part thereof, a safe and suitable walkway and handrail on one side only of such bridge or trestle, and such handrail shall be located at the outer edge of the walkway and shall provide a clearance of not less than 8 feet, 6 inches, from the center line of the nearest track, measured at right angles thereto.

(6) Packages Containing Articles for First Aid to Injured on Trains. All rail carriers shall provide a package containing the articles prescribed by the Commission, on each train or engine, for first aid to persons who may be injured in the course of the operation of such trains.

(7) Abandoned Bridges, Crossings, and Other Rail Plant. The Commission shall have authority, after notice and hearing, to order:

(a) The removal of any abandoned railroad tracks from roads, streets or other thoroughfares in this State; and

(b) The removal of abandoned overhead railroad structures crossing highways, waterways, or railroads.

The Commission may equitably apportion the cost of such actions between the rail carrier or carriers, public utilities, and the State, county, municipality, township, road district, or other public authority in interest.

(8) Railroad–Highway Bridge Clearance. A vertical clearance of not less than 23 feet above the top of rail shall be provided for all new or reconstructed highway bridges constructed over a railroad track. The Commission may permit a lesser clearance if it determines that the 23 foot clearance standard cannot be justified based on engineering, operational, and economic conditions.

P.A. 76–1586, § 18c–7401, added by P.A. 84–796, § 1, eff. Jan. 1, 1986. Amended by P.A. 88–296, § 5, eff. Jan. 1, 1994; P.A. 89–699, § 15, eff. Jan. 16, 1997; P.A. 90–691, § 10, eff. Jan. 1, 1999; P.A. 91–725, § 10, eff. June 2, 2000.

Formerly Ill.Rev.Stat.1991, ch. 95 ½, ¶ 18c–7401.

5/18c–7402. Safety Requirements for Railroad Operations

§ 18c–7402. Safety Requirements for Railroad Operations.

(1) Obstruction of Crossings.

(a) Obstruction of Emergency Vehicles. Every railroad shall be operated in such a manner as to minimize obstruction of emergency vehicles at crossings. Where such obstruction occurs and the train crew is aware of the obstruction, the train crew shall immediately take any action, consistent with safe operating procedure, necessary to remove the obstruction. In the Chicago and St. Louis switching districts, every railroad dispatcher or other person responsible for the movement of railroad equipment in a specific area who receives notification that railroad equipment is obstructing the movement of an emergency vehicle at any crossing within such area shall immediately notify the train crew through use of existing communication facilities. Upon notification, the train crew shall take immediate action in accordance with this paragraph.

(b) Obstruction of Highway at Grade Crossing Prohibited. It is unlawful for a rail carrier to permit any train, railroad car or engine to obstruct public travel at a railroad-highway grade crossing for a period in excess of 10 minutes, except where such train or railroad car is continuously moving or cannot be moved by reason of circumstances over which the rail carrier has no reasonable control.

In a county with a population of greater than 1,000,000, as determined by the most recent federal census, during the hours of 7:00 a.m. through 9:00 a. m. and 4:00 p.m. through 6:00 p.m. it is unlawful for a rail carrier to permit any single train or railroad car to obstruct public travel at a railroad-highway grade crossing in excess of a total of 10 minutes during a 30 minute period, except where the train or railroad car cannot be moved by reason or circumstances over which the rail carrier has no reasonable control. Under no circumstances will a moving train be stopped for the purposes of issuing a citation related to this Section.

However, no employee acting under the rules or orders of the rail carrier or its supervisory personnel may be prosecuted for a violation of this subsection (b).

(c) Punishment for Obstruction of Grade Crossing. Any rail carrier violating paragraph (b) of this subsection shall be guilty of a petty offense and fined not less than $200 nor more than $500 if the duration of the obstruction is in excess of 10 minutes but no longer than 15 minutes. If the duration of the obstruction exceeds 15 minutes the violation shall be a business offense and the following fines shall be imposed: if the duration of the obstruction is in excess of 15 minutes but no longer than 20 minutes, the fine shall be $500; if the duration of the obstruction is in excess of 20 minutes but no longer than 25 minutes, the fine shall be $700; if the duration of the obstruction is in excess of 25 minutes, but no longer than 30 minutes, the fine shall be $900; if the duration of the obstruction is in excess of 30 minutes but no longer than 35 minutes, the fine shall be $1,000; if the duration of the obstruction is in excess of 35 minutes, the fine shall be $1,000 plus an additional $500 for each 5 minutes of obstruction in excess of 25 minutes of obstruction.

(2) Other Operational Requirements.

(a) Bell and Whistle-Crossings. Every rail carrier shall cause a bell, and a whistle or horn to be placed and kept on each locomotive, and shall cause the same to be rung or sounded by the engineer or fireman, at the distance of a least 1,320 feet, from the place where the railroad crosses or intersects any public highway, and shall be kept ringing or sounding until the highway is reached; provided that at crossings where the Commission shall by order direct, only after a hearing has been held to determine the public is reasonably and sufficiently protected, the rail carrier may be excused from giving warning provided by this paragraph.

(a–5) The requirements of paragraph (a) of this subsection (2) regarding ringing a bell and sounding a whistle or horn do not apply at a railroad crossing that has a permanently installed automated audible warning device authorized by the Commission under Section 18c–7402.1 that sounds automatically when an approaching train is at least 1,320 feet from the crossing and that keeps sounding until the lead locomotive has crossed the highway. The engineer or fireman may ring the bell or sound the whistle or horn at a railroad crossing that has a permanently installed audible warning device.

(b) Speed Limits. Each rail carrier shall operate its trains in compliance with speed limits set by the Commission. The Commission may set train speed limits only where such limits are necessitated by extraordinary circumstances effecting the public safety, and shall maintain such train speed limits in effect only for such time as the extraordinary circumstances prevail.

The Commission and the Department of Transportation shall conduct a study of the relation between train speeds and railroad-highway grade crossing safety. The Commission shall report the findings of the study to the General Assembly no later than January 5, 1997.

(c) Special Speed Limit; Pilot Project. The Commission and the Board of the Commuter Rail Division of the Regional Transportation Authority shall conduct a pilot project in the Village of Fox River Grove, the site of the fatal school bus accident at a railroad crossing on October 25, 1995, in order to improve railroad crossing safety. For this project, the Commission is directed to set the maximum train speed limit for Regional Transportation Authority trains at 50 miles per hour at intersections on that portion of the intrastate rail line located in the Village of Fox River Grove. If the Regional Transportation Authority deliberately fails to comply with this maximum speed limit, then any entity, governmental or otherwise, that provides capital or operational funds to the Regional Transportation Authority shall appropriately reduce or eliminate that funding. The Commission shall report to the Governor and the General Assembly on the results of this pilot project in January 1999, January 2000, and January 2001. The Commission shall also submit a final report on the pilot project to the Governor and the General Assembly in January 2001. The provisions of this subsection (c), other than this sentence, are inoperative after February 1, 2001.

(3) Report and Investigation of Rail Accidents.

(a) Reports. Every rail carrier shall report to the Commission, by the speediest means possible, whether telephone, telegraph, or otherwise, every accident involving its equipment, track, or other property which resulted in loss of life to any person. In addition, such carriers shall file a written report with the Commission. Reports submitted under this paragraph shall be strictly confidential, shall be specifically prohibited from disclosure, and shall not be admissible in any administrative or judicial proceeding relating to the accidents reported.

(b) Investigations. The Commission may investigate all railroad accidents reported to it or of which it acquires knowledge independent of reports made by rail carriers, and shall have the power, consistent with standards and procedures established under the Federal Railroad Safety Act, as amended,[1] to enter such temporary orders as will minimize the risk of future accidents pending notice, hearing, and final action by the Commission.

P.A. 76–1586, § 18c–7402, added by P.A. 84–796, § 1, eff. Jan. 1, 1986. Amended by P.A. 85–1144, § 1, eff. July 29, 1988; P.A. 89–699, § 15, eff. Jan. 16, 1997; P.A. 90–187, § 5, eff. Jan. 1, 1998; P.A. 91–675, § 5, eff. June 1, 2000; P.A. 92–284, § 5, eff. Aug. 9, 2001.

Formerly Ill.Rev.Stat.1991, ch. 95 ½, ¶ 18c–7402.

1 45 U.S.C.A. § 421 et seq.

5/18c–7402.1. Pilot projects; automated audible warning devices

§ 18c–7402.1. Pilot projects; automated audible warning devices.

(a) The General Assembly finds and declares that, for the communities of the State that are traversed by railroads, there is a growing need to mitigate train horn noise without compromising the safety of the public. Therefore, after applications are filed and approved by the Commission, the Commission shall authorize pilot projects in the counties of Cook, DuPage, Lake, and Will to test the utility and safety of stationary automated audible warning devices as an alternative to trains having to sound their horns as they approach highway-rail crossings.

(b) In light of the pending proposed ruling by the Federal Railroad Administration on the use of locomotive horns at all highway-rail crossings across the nation, it is in the best interest of the State for the Commission to expedite the pilot projects in order to contribute data to the federal rulemaking process regarding the possible inclusion of stationary automated warning devices in the counties of Cook, DuPage, Lake, and Will as a safety measure option to the proposed federal rule.

(c) The Commission shall adopt rules for implementing the pilot projects in the counties of Cook, DuPage, Lake, and Will.

P.A. 76–1586, § 18c–7402.1, added by P.A. 92–284, § 5, eff. Aug. 9, 2001.

5/18c–7402.5. § 18c–7402.5. Repealed effective Feb. 1, 2001

5/18c–7403. Enforcement and Waiver of Safety Requirements

§ 18c–7403. Enforcement and Waiver of Safety Requirements. (1) Enforcement. Except with regard to grade crossing obstructions under Section 18c–7402 of this Chapter and trespass on railroad rights of way and yards under

Section 18c-7503 of this Chapter, jurisdiction to initiate actions to enforce provisions of this Chapter is vested exclusively in the Commission. Where a valid federal statute, regulation, or order sets forth procedures or sanctions for violation of safety standards, and such procedures or sanctions are preemptive of state law, the Commission shall exercise its enforcement jurisdiction under this Article in accordance therewith. Otherwise, the provisions of this Chapter regarding enforcement procedures and sanctions shall apply.

(2) Waiver. The Commission may waive any of the safety requirements under this Article if continued adherence to the requirement or requirements is not required for the safety of railroad employees or the public.

P.A. 76-1586, § 18c-7403, added by P.A. 84-796, § 1, eff. Jan. 1, 1986. Amended by P.A. 90-257, § 5, eff. July 30, 1997.

Formerly Ill.Rev.Stat.1991, ch. 95 ½, ¶ 18c-7403.

5/18c-7404. Transportation of Hazardous Materials by Rail Carriers

§ 18c-7404. Transportation of Hazardous Materials by Rail Carriers. (1) Commission to Regulate Hazardous Materials Transportation by Rail Carrier.

(a) Powers of the Commission. The Commission is authorized to regulate the transportation of hazardous materials by rail carrier by:

(i) Adopting by reference the hazardous materials regulations of the Office of Hazardous Materials Transportation and the Federal Railroad Administration of the United States Department of Transportation, as amended;

(ii) Conducting investigations, issuing subpoenas, taking depositions, requiring the production of relevant documents, records and property, and conducting hearings in aid of such investigations;

(iii) Conducting a continuing review of all aspects of hazardous materials transportation by rail carrier to determine and recommend actions necessary to insure safe transportation of such materials;

(iv) Undertaking, directly or indirectly, research, development, demonstration and training activities;

(v) Cooperating with other State agencies and enter into interagency agreements; and

(vi) Entering upon, inspecting and examining the records and properties relating to the transportation of hazardous materials by rail, including all portions of any facility used in the loading, unloading, and actual movement of such materials, or in the storage of such materials incidental to actual movement by rail;

(vii) Stopping and inspecting trains, at reasonable times and locations and in a reasonable manner, or taking any other action necessary to administer or enforce the provisions of this Section.

(b) Scope of Section. The provisions of this Section apply generally to the transportation of hazardous materials by rail carrier within the State of Illinois, but do not apply to:

(i) Natural gas pipelines;

(ii) Transportation of firearms or ammunition for personal use or in commerce; or

(iii) Transportation exempted by the Commission where the exemption granted by the Commission is:

(A) Coextensive with an exemption granted by the Office of Hazardous Materials and the Federal Railroad Administration; or

(B) Otherwise exempt under statutes or regulations governing similar transportation in interstate commerce.

(c) Rail Carriers to Comply with Commission Regulations. No person shall transport hazardous materials by rail carrier except in compliance with this Section, Commission regulations and orders.

(2) Enforcement.

(a) Criminal Penalties. Any person who willfully violates the provisions of this Section, Commission regulations or orders shall have committed a class 3 felony and be subject to criminal penalties in an amount not to exceed $25,000.

(b) Civil Penalties. Any person who knowingly violates the provisions of this Section, Commission regulations or orders shall also be subject to civil penalties in an amount not to exceed $10,000.

(c) Injunctive Relief. The Commission may petition any circuit court with venue and jurisdiction to enforce this Chapter to enjoin actions which it has reason to believe may pose an imminent hazard, and to issue such other orders as will eliminate or ameliorate the imminent hazard. As used in this Section, "imminent hazard" means a substantial likelihood that death, serious illness, or severe personal injury will occur prior to the time during which an administrative proceeding to abate the danger could normally be completed.

(3) Commission to Adopt Regulations. The Commission may adopt regulations governing the transportation of hazardous materials by rail carrier where:

(a) The risk created by such transportation is susceptible to control by regulation;

(b) State regulation would be more effective in controlling the risk than federal regulation; and

(c) The regulations adopted by the Commission are not inconsistent with federal regulations.

P.A. 76-1586, § 18c-7404, added by P.A. 84-796, § 1, eff. Jan. 1, 1986. Amended by P.A. 85-815, § 1, eff. Jan. 1, 1988.

Formerly Ill.Rev.Stat.1991, ch. 95 ½, ¶ 18c-7404.

5/18c-7405. Accident counseling

§ 18c-7405. Accident counseling.

(a) Every Class I rail carrier, according to federal regulations, operating in this State must establish a counseling or trauma program and provide or make available counseling or other critical incident stress debriefing services to each member of an operating crew directly involved in an accident that results in loss of life or serious bodily injury on its railway or right-of-way.

(b) Each Class I rail carrier, according to federal regulations, operating in this State must file its counseling or trauma program with the processing section of the Transportation Division of the Illinois Commerce Commission, whose sole responsibility under this Section shall be to receive the program and make it available for public inspection.

P.A. 76-1586, § 18c-7405, added by P.A. 91-729, § 5, eff. Jan. 1, 2001.

ARTICLE V. MISCELLANEOUS PROVISIONS

5/18c-7501. Eminent Domain

§ 18c-7501. Eminent Domain. If any rail carrier shall be unable to agree with the owner for the purchase of any real estate required for the purposes of its incorporation, or the transaction of its business, or for its depots, station buildings, machine and repair shops, or for right of way or any other lawful purpose connected with or necessary to the building, operating or running of such rail carrier, such may acquire such title in the manner that may be now or hereafter provided for by the law of eminent domain.

A rail carrier may exercise quick take powers of eminent domain as provided in Article VII of the Code of Civil Procedure, as now or hereafter amended,[1] when all of the following conditions are met: (1) the complaint for condemnation is filed within one year of the effective date of this amendatory Act of 1988; (2) the purpose of the condemnation proceeding is to acquire land for the construction of an industrial harbor railroad port; and (3) the total amount of land to be acquired for that purpose is less than 75 acres and is adjacent to the Illinois River.

P.A. 76-1586, § 18c-7501, added by P.A. 84-796, § 1, eff. Jan. 1, 1986. Amended by P.A. 85-1159, § 2-3, eff. Aug. 4, 1988.

Formerly Ill.Rev.Stat.1991, ch. 95 ½, ¶ 18c-7501.

[1] 735 ILCS 5/7-101 et seq.

5/18c-7502. Malicious removal of or damage to railroad property or freight

§ 18c-7502. Malicious removal of or damage to railroad property or freight.

(a) Malicious removal of or damage to railroad property or freight.

A person is guilty of an offense if he or she is found to have:

(i) removed, taken, stolen, changed, added to, taken from, or in any manner changed, defaced, or interfered with any of the parts or attachments of any locomotive or car, or any plant or property used in or in connection with the operation of any railroad carrier, locomotive, car, or train, or shoots, throws, or drops any object onto or at any train, locomotive, or car;

(ii) willfully and with intent to permanently deprive the owner thereof, taken or removed railroad freight from any freight car, including a boxcar, container, or flatbed; or

(iii) bought or received any of the railroad freight described in item (ii), having reason to know that such freight was stolen.

(b) Penalties.

(1) If the railroad property damage does not exceed $500 and no bodily injury occurs to another as a result of a violation of this Section, the person shall be guilty of a Class A misdemeanor. Upon being found in violation of item (i) of subsection (a), the person shall, in addition to such other sanctions as may be deemed appropriate by the court, be subject to pay the railroad carrier involved the cost to repair any railroad property damaged, and to perform community service for not less than 30 hours or more than 120 hours. If community service is not available in the jurisdiction where the offense was committed, that person shall be subject to pay a fine of not less than $150 or more than $1,000, or imprisonment for not less than 5 days or more than 1 year, or both. If railroad property damage exceeds $500 or bodily injury occurs to another as a result of a violation of this Section, the person shall be guilty of a Class 4 felony. Upon being found in violation of item (i) of subsection (a), the person shall, in addition to such other sanctions as may be deemed appropriate by the court, be subject to pay the railroad carrier involved for the cost to repair any railroad property damaged, and shall be fined not less than $1,000, nor more than $25,000, or imprisonment for not less than 1 year, or more than 3 years, or both. If serious bodily injury or death occurs to another as a result of a violation of item (i) of subsection (a), the person shall be guilty of a Class 2 felony and shall, in addition to such sanctions as may be deemed appropriate by the court, be subject to pay the railroad carrier involved the cost to repair any railroad property damaged, and shall be fined not less than $5,000 nor more than $25,000, or imprisonment for not less than 3 years nor more than 7 years, or both. If any such action is malicious and is the cause of wrecking any train, locomotive, or car in this State whereby the life of any person is lost, the person found guilty thereof shall be liable for first degree murder and the person shall be subject to pay the railroad carrier involved the cost to repair any railroad property damaged.

(2) Upon being found in violation of item (ii) or (iii), the person shall be guilty of a Class 4 felony. In addition to such other sanctions as may be deemed appropriate by the court, the person shall be subject to pay the railroad carrier involved for the cost to repair any railroad property damaged, and shall be fined not less than $1,000, nor more than $25,000, or imprisoned for not less than 1 year nor more than 3 years.

(3) Local authorities shall impose fines as established in this subsection (b) for persons found in violation of this Section or any similar local ordinance.

(c) Definitions. As used in this Section:

"Bodily injury" means:

(i) a cut, abrasion, bruise, bump, or disfigurement;

(ii) physical pain;

(iii) illness;

(iv) impairment of the function of a bodily member, organ, or mental faculty; or

(v) any other injury to the body, no matter how temporary.

"Railroad" means any form of nonhighway ground transportation that runs on rails or electromagnetic guideways, including:

(i) commuter or other short-haul railroad passenger service in a metropolitan or urban area; and

(ii) high-speed ground transportation systems that connect metropolitan areas, but does not include rapid transit operations in an urban area that are not connected to the general railroad system of transportation.

"Railroad carrier" means a person providing railroad transportation.

"Railroad property" means all tangible property owned, leased, or operated by a railroad carrier including a right of way, track, bridge, yard, shop, station, tunnel, viaduct, trestle, depot, warehouse, terminal, or any other structure, appurtenance, or equipment owned, leased, or used in the operation of any railroad carrier including trains, locomotives, engines, railroad cars, work equipment, rolling stock, or safety devices. "Railroad property" does not include a railroad carrier's administrative buildings or offices, office equipment, or intangible property such as software or other information.

"Right of way" means the track or roadbed owned, leased, or operated by a rail carrier that is located on either side of its tracks and that is readily recognizable to a reasonable person as being railroad property or is reasonably identified as such by fencing or appropriate signs.

"Yard" means a system of parallel tracks, crossovers, and switches where railroad cars are switched and made up into

trains, and where railroad cars, locomotives, and other rolling stock is kept when not in use or when awaiting repair.

"Serious bodily injury" means bodily injury that involves:

(i) a substantial risk of death;

(ii) extreme physical pain;

(iii) protracted and obvious disfigurement; or

(iv) protracted loss or impairment of the function of a bodily member, organ, or mental faculty.

P.A. 76–1586, § 18c–7502, added by P.A. 84–796, § 1, eff. Jan. 1, 1986. Amended by P.A. 85–293, Art. III, § 21, eff. Sept. 8, 1987; P.A. 90–691, § 10, eff. Jan. 1, 1999; P.A. 91–532, § 5, eff. Jan. 1, 2000.

Formerly Ill.Rev.Stat.1991, ch. 95 ½, ¶ 18c–7502.

5/18c–7503. Trespassing on railroad property

§ 18c–7503. Trespassing on railroad property.

(1) Trespassing on railroad property prohibited.

(a) General prohibition. Except as otherwise provided in paragraph (b) of this subsection, no person may:

(i) walk, ride, drive or be upon or along the right of way or rail yard of a rail carrier within the State, at a place other than a public crossing;

(ii) enter or be upon any railroad property;

(iii) without lawful authority or the railroad carrier's consent, ride on the outside of a train or inside a passenger car, locomotive, or freight car, including a box car, flatbed, or container;

(iv) willfully lead or contrive any animal to go upon the railroad's rights of way for any reason other than to pass over such rights of way at a marked public crossing; or

(v) throw or cause to be thrown on to the railroad's rights of way any waste paper, ashes, household waste, glass, metal, tires, refuse, or rubbish.

(b) Exceptions. This subsection shall not apply to:

(i) fare paying passengers on trains or employees of a rail carrier;

(ii) railroad employees and an authorized representative of rail carrier employees, while performing required duties in accordance with reasonable rail carrier company guidelines;

(iii) a person going upon the right of way or into the rail yard to save human life or to remove an object that a reasonable person would believe poses an imminent threat to human life or limb;

(iv) a person being on the station grounds or in the depot of the rail carrier for the purpose of transacting business;

(v) a person, his family, or his employees or agents going across a farm crossing, as defined in this Chapter, for the purpose of crossing from one part to another part of a farm he owns or leases, where the farm lies on both sides of the right of way;

(vi) a person having written permission from the rail carrier to go upon the right of way or into the rail yard;

(vii) representatives of local, State, and federal governmental agencies in performance of their official duties; and

(viii) a person having written permission from the rail carrier to go in or be upon railroad property.

(2) Penalties.

(a) Any person found in violation of item (i), (ii), (iii) or (iv) of paragraph (a) of subsection (1) shall be guilty of a Class C misdemeanor for a first offense. In addition to such other sanctions as may be deemed appropriate by the court, the person shall be subject to a mandatory fine of not less than $150 or more than $500, or to imprisonment for not less than 5 days nor more than 30 days, or both. For each subsequent offense, the person shall be guilty of a Class A misdemeanor. In addition to such sanctions as may be deemed appropriate by the court, the person shall be subject to a mandatory fine of not less than $500 nor more than $1,000, or to imprisonment for not less than 10 days or more than one year, or both.

(b) Any person found in violation of item (v) of paragraph (a) of subsection (1) shall be guilty of an offense and in addition to such sanctions as may be deemed appropriate by the court shall be subject to a fine of not less than $100 nor more than $500, or community service of not less than 8 hours nor more than 50 hours, or both. If damage to any railroad property or bodily injury occurs to another as a result of a violation of item (v) of paragraph (a) of subsection (1), that person shall be charged with the offense of Malicious Removal of or Damage to Railroad Property or Freight pursuant to Section 18c–7502.

(c) Local authorities shall impose fines as established in paragraphs (a) and (b) of this subsection (2) for persons found in violation of this Section or any similar local ordinance.

(3) Definitions. For purposes of this Section:

"Passenger" means a person who is traveling by train with lawful authority and who does not participate in the train's operation. The term "passenger" does not include stowaways.

"Railroad" means any form of nonhighway ground transportation that runs on rails or electromagnetic guideways, including:

(i) commuter or other short-haul railroad passenger service in a metropolitan or urban area; and

(ii) high-speed ground transportation systems that connect metropolitan areas; but does not include rapid transit operations in an urban area that are not connected to the general railroad system of transportation.

"Railroad carrier" means a person providing railroad transportation.

"Railroad property" means all tangible property owned, leased, or operated by a railroad carrier including a right of way, track, bridge, yard, shop, station, tunnel, viaduct, trestle, depot, warehouse, terminal, or any other structure, appurtenance, or equipment owned, leased, or used in the operation of any railroad carrier including trains, locomotives, engines, railroad cars, work equipment, rolling stock, or safety devices. "Railroad property" does not include a railroad carrier's administrative buildings or offices, office equipment, or intangible property such as software or other information.

"Right of way" means the track or roadbed owned, leased, or operated by a rail carrier which is located on either side of its tracks and which is readily recognizable to a reasonable person as being railroad property or is reasonably identified as such by fencing or appropriate signs.

"Yard" means a system of parallel tracks, crossovers, and switches where railroad cars are switched and made up into

trains, and where railroad cars, locomotives, and other rolling stock is kept when not in use or when awaiting repair.

P.A. 76–1586, § 18c–7503, added by P.A. 84–796, § 1, eff. Jan. 1, 1986. Amended by P.A. 90–655, § 153, eff. July 30, 1998; P.A. 90–691, § 10, eff. Jan. 1, 1999; P.A. 91–532, § 5, eff. Jan. 1, 2000.

Formerly Ill.Rev.Stat.1991, ch. 95 ½, ¶ 18c–7503.

5/18c–7504. Construction of Fences, Farm Crossings, and Damages

§ 18c–7504. Construction of Fences, Farm Crossings, and Damages. (1) Fencing. Every rail carrier shall, within 6 months after any part of its line is open for use, erect and thereafter maintain fences on both sides of its road or so much thereof as is open for use, suitable and sufficient to prevent cattle, horses, sheep, hogs or other livestock from getting on such railroad, provided that the other 3 sides of the property are enclosed, except at the crossings of public roads and highways, and within such portion of cities and incorporated towns and villages as are or may be hereafter laid out and platted into lots and blocks, with gates at the farm crossings of such railroad, which farm crossings shall be constructed by such rail carrier when and where the same may become necessary, for the use of the proprietors of the lands adjoining such railroad; and when such fences are not made as aforesaid, or when such fences are not kept in good repair, such rail carrier shall be liable for all damages which may be done by the agents, engines or cars of such rail carrier, to such cattle, horses, sheep, hogs or other livestock thereof, and reasonable attorney's fees in any court wherein suit is brought for such damages, or to which the same may be appealed; but where such fences have been duly made and kept in good repair, such rail carrier shall not be liable for any such damages, unless negligently or willfully done.

(2) Enforcement. If the rail carrier, after being notified, shall refuse to build or repair such fence, gates, or farm crossings, in accordance with the provisions of this Section, the owner or occupant of the land required to be fenced shall be entitled to an order from any court of competent jurisdiction requiring the rail carrier to build or repair such fence, gates, or farm crossing and may recover interest at one percent per month of the cost of such building or repair, from the time the crossing or repair was requested, as damage in the circuit court, together with costs to be taxed by the court.

P.A. 76–1586, § 18c–7504, added by P.A. 84–796, § 1, eff. Jan. 1, 1986.

Formerly Ill.Rev.Stat.1991, ch. 95 ½, ¶ 18c–7504.

SUB–CHAPTER 8. COMMON CARRIERS BY PIPELINE

ARTICLE I. JURISDICTION AND POWER OVER COMMON CARRIERS BY PIPELINE

ARTICLE II. LICENSING AND RATEMAKING

ARTICLE III. SAFETY REGULATION

ARTICLE IV. MISCELLANEOUS PROVISIONS

ARTICLE I. JURISDICTION AND POWER OVER COMMON CARRIERS BY PIPELINE

5/18c–8101. § 18c–8101. Repealed by P.A. 89–42, § 15, eff. Jan. 1, 1996

ARTICLE II. LICENSING AND RATEMAKING

5/18c–8201. § 18c–8201. Repealed by P.A. 89–42, § 15, eff. Jan. 1, 1996

ARTICLE III. SAFETY REGULATION

5/18c–8301. § 18c–8301. Repealed by P.A. 89–42, § 15, eff. Jan. 1, 1996

ARTICLE IV. MISCELLANEOUS PROVISIONS

5/18c–8401. § 18c–8401. Repealed by P.A. 89–42, § 15, eff. Jan. 1, 1996

SUB–CHAPTER 9. MISCELLANEOUS PROVISIONS OF LAW

ARTICLE I. REMEDIES CUMULATIVE

ARTICLE II. GRANDFATHER PROVISIONS

ARTICLE I. REMEDIES CUMULATIVE

5/18c–9101. Remedies Cumulative

§ 18c–9101. Remedies Cumulative. Rights and remedies under this Chapter shall be cumulative of each other and of rights and remedies under other provisions of law, except as otherwise expressly provided herein. Exercise of one right or remedy under this Chapter shall not waive or bar exercise of any other, and imposition of one sanction under this Chapter shall not be a bar to imposition of any other sanction provided for in this Chapter.

P.A. 76–1586, § 18c–9101, added by P.A. 84–796, § 1, eff. Jan. 1, 1986.

Formerly Ill.Rev.Stat.1991, ch. 95 ½, ¶ 18c–9101.

ARTICLE II. GRANDFATHER PROVISIONS

5/18c–9201. Grandfather Clause

§ 18c-9201. Grandfather Clause. Except as otherwise expressly provided in this Chapter, valid regulations adopted, licenses, registrations, certifications and other authorizations issued or recognized, rates established or recognized, and forms promulgated or utilized under Acts or parts of Acts repealed by this Act shall have the same force and effect as if adopted, issued, established, or recognized under this Chapter.

P.A. 76–1586, § 18c–9201, added by P.A. 84–796, § 1, eff. Jan. 1, 1986. Amended by P.A. 85–553, § 2, eff. Sept. 18, 1987.

Formerly Ill.Rev.Stat.1991, ch. 95 ½, ¶ 18c–9201.

CHAPTER 19. ILLINOIS VEHICLE LAWS COMMISSION

5/19-101 to 5/19-104. §§ 19-101 to 19-104. Repealed by P.A. 83-1257, Art. 12, § 12-18, eff. Sept. 30, 1984

CHAPTER 20. MISCELLANEOUS PROVISIONS, EFFECT OF ACT AND REPEAL OF NAMED ACTS

Enactment

The Illinois Vehicle Code was enacted by P.A. 76-1586, effective July 1, 1970. The Code constitutes a consolidated recodification of various earlier laws and acts including the Illinois Motor Vehicle Law of 1957.

ARTICLE I. DISTRIBUTION OF FEES AND TAXES

5/20-101. Moneys derived from registration, operation and use of automobiles and from fuel taxes—Use

§ 20-101. Moneys derived from registration, operation and use of automobiles and from fuel taxes—Use. From and after the effective date of this Act, no public moneys derived from fees, excises or license taxes relating to registration, operation and use of vehicles on public highways or to fuels used for the propulsion of such vehicles, shall be appropriated or expended other than for costs of administering the laws imposing such fees, excises and license taxes, statutory refunds and adjustments allowed thereunder, administrative costs of the Department of Transportation, payment of debts and liabilities incurred in construction and reconstruction of public highways and bridges, acquisition of rights-of-way for, and the cost of construction, reconstruction, maintenance, repair and operation of public highways and bridges under the direction and supervision of the State, political subdivision or municipality collecting such moneys, and the costs for patrolling and policing the public highways (by the State, political subdivision or municipality collecting such money) for enforcement of traffic laws; provided, that such moneys may be used for the retirement of and interest on bonds heretofore issued for purposes other than the construction of public highways or bridges but not to a greater extent, nor a greater length of time, than is provided in acts theretofore adopted and now in force. Further the separation of grades of such highways with railroads and costs associated with protection of at-grade highway and railroad crossings shall also be permissible.

P.A. 76-1586, § 20-101, eff. July 1, 1970. Amended by P.A. 81-3, 2nd Sp.Sess., § 4, eff. Sept. 19, 1979.

Formerly Ill.Rev.Stat.1991, ch. 95 ½, ¶ 20-101.

ARTICLE II. EFFECT OF ACT

5/20-201. Effect of headings

§ 20-201. Effect of headings. Chapter, Article and Section headings contained herein shall not be deemed to govern, limit, modify or in any manner affect the scope, meaning or intent of the provisions of any Chapter, Article or Section hereof.

P.A. 76-1586, § 20-201, eff. July 1, 1970.

Formerly Ill.Rev.Stat.1991, ch. 95 ½, ¶ 20-201.

5/20-201.1. Gender

§ 20-201.1. Gender. When used in this Code, words importing the masculine may be applied to females and vice versa.

P.A. 76-1586, § 20-201.1, added by P.A. 82-123, § 1, eff. Jan. 1, 1982.

Formerly Ill.Rev.Stat.1991, ch. 95 ½, ¶ 20-201.1.

5/20-201.2. Number

§ 20-201.2. Number. When used in this Code, words importing the singular may extend and be applied to several persons or things, and words importing the plural number may include singular.

P.A. 76-1586, § 20-201.2, added by P.A. 82-123, § 1, eff. Jan. 1, 1982.

Formerly Ill.Rev.Stat.1991, ch. 95 ½, ¶ 20-201.2.

5/20-201.3. Tense

§ 20-201.3. Tense. When used in this Code, words importing the present tense may include the future and vice versa.

P.A. 76-1586, § 20-201.3, added by P.A. 82-123, § 1, eff. Jan. 1, 1982.

Formerly Ill.Rev.Stat.1991, ch. 95 ½, ¶ 20-201.3.

5/20-202. Act not retroactive

§ 20-202. Act not retroactive. This Act shall not have a retroactive effect and shall not apply to any traffic accident, to a cause of action arising out of a traffic accident or judgment arising therefrom, or to any violation of the laws of this State, occurring prior to the effective date of this Act.

P.A. 76-1586, § 20-202, eff. July 1, 1970.

Formerly Ill.Rev.Stat.1991, ch. 95 ½, ¶ 20-202.

5/20-203. Constitutionality

§ 20-203. Constitutionality. If any part or parts of this Act shall be held to be unconstitutional, such unconstitutionality shall not affect the validity of the remaining parts of this Act. The legislature hereby declares that it would have passed the remaining parts of this Act if it had known that such part or parts thereof would be declared unconstitutional.

P.A. 76-1586, § 20-203, eff. July 1, 1970.

Formerly Ill.Rev.Stat.1991, ch. 95 ½, ¶ 20-203.

5/20–204. Adoption by municipality by reference of all or part of Code

§ 20–204. The corporate authorities of a municipality may adopt all or any portion of this Illinois Vehicle Code by reference.

P.A. 76–1586, § 20–204, added by P.A. 78–738, § 1, eff. Jan. 1, 1974.

Formerly Ill.Rev.Stat.1991, ch. 95 ½, ¶ 20–204.

ARTICLE III. REPEAL OF NAMED ACTS

5/20–301. Repeal

§ 20–301. Repeal. The following acts are repealed:

(a) The "Illinois Vehicle Law", approved July 11, 1957, as amended.[1]

(b) "AN ACT in relation to motor vehicles and to repeal a certain act therein named", approved June 30, 1919, as amended.[2]

(c) "AN ACT in relation to the issuance of insurance policies in connection with certain transactions involving motor vehicles, and providing a penalty for the violation thereof", approved July 7, 1955, as amended.[3]

(d) "AN ACT providing for the use of public money derived from fees, excises, and license taxes relating to registration, operation and use of vehicles on public highways, and fuels used for the propulsion of such vehicles", approved July 21, 1947, as amended.[4]

(e) The "Uniform Act Regulating Traffic on Highways", approved July 9, 1935, as amended.[5]

(f) "AN ACT in relation to the prevention of the use of public highways by vehicles exceeding prescribed weight limits", approved August 6, 1949, as amended.[6]

(g) "AN ACT relating to the operation of ambulances", approved July 25, 1963.[7]

(h) "AN ACT to prevent the overloading of motor vehicles used in transporting children", approved July 22, 1959, as amended.[8]

(i) "AN ACT in relation to the sale of certain tires for use on motor vehicles", approved July 9, 1955, as amended.[9]

(j) The "Illinois Motor Carrier of Property Act", approved July 7, 1953, as amended.[10]

(k) "AN ACT to create a Motor Vehicle Laws Commission, to define its powers and duties, and to make an appropriation therefor", approved June 21, 1951, as amended.[11]

(*l*) "AN ACT to authorize the Department of Public Safety to furnish copies of traffic accident reports and be paid a fee therefor", approved April 17, 1967.[12]

(m) "AN ACT relating to the powers and duties of the Governor in connection with the Federal Highway Safety Act of 1966", approved August 18, 1967.[13]

(n) "AN ACT enacting and entering into the Driver Licenses Compact", approved August 19, 1963, as amended.[14]

(*o*) "AN ACT to adopt the Vehicle Equipment Safety Compact and to provide for the administration thereof", approved August 19, 1963.[15]

P.A. 76–1586, § 20–301, eff. July 1, 1970. Amended by P.A. 85–293, Art. III, § 21, eff. Sept. 8, 1987.

Formerly Ill.Rev.Stat.1991, ch. 95 ½, ¶ 20–301.

1 Former Ill.Rev.Stat. ch. 95½, ¶ 1 et seq. (repealed; see, now, 625 ILCS 5/1–101 et seq.).

2 Former Ill.Rev.Stat. ch. 95½, ¶ 1 et seq. (repealed; see, now, 625 ILCS 5/1–101 et seq.).

3 Former Ill.Rev.Stat. ch. 95½, ¶¶ 58p and 58q (repealed; see, now, 625 ILCS 5/5–601, 5/5–602).

4 Former Ill.Rev.Stat. ch. 95½, ¶ 73a (repealed; see, now, 625 ILCS 5/20–101).

5 Former Ill.Rev.Stat. ch. 95½, ¶ 98 et seq. (repealed).

6 Former Ill.Rev.Stat. ch. 95½, ¶ 239.1 et seq. (repealed; see, now, 625 ILCS 5/15–201 et seq.).

7 Former Ill.Rev.Stat. ch. 95½, ¶¶ 239.4 and 239.5 (repealed; see, now, 625 ILCS 5/11–1421, 5/11–1422).

8 Former Ill.Rev.Stat. ch. 95½, ¶ 239.21 et seq. (repealed).

9 Former Ill.Rev.Stat. ch. 95½, ¶ 239.21 et seq. (repealed; see, now, 625 ILCS 5/12–402).

10 Former Ill.Rev.Stat. ch. 95½, ¶ 282.1 et seq. (repealed).

11 Former Ill.Rev.Stat. ch. 95½, ¶ 401 et seq. (repealed).

12 Former Ill.Rev.Stat. ch. 95½, ¶ 411 (repealed; see, now, 625 ILCS 5/11–416).

13 Former Ill.Rev.Stat. ch. 95½, ¶ 421 (repealed; see, now, 625 ILCS 5/17–101).

14 Former Ill.Rev.Stat. ch. 95½, ¶ 501 et seq. (repealed; see, now, 625 ILCS 5/6-700 et seq.).

15 Former Ill.Rev.Stat. ch. 95½, ¶ 551 et seq. (repealed; see, now 625 ILCS 5/1-218).

ARTICLE IV. SAVINGS CLAUSE AND EFFECTIVE DATE

5/20–401. Saving provisions

§ 20–401. Saving provisions. The repeal of any Act by this Chapter shall not affect any right accrued or liability incurred under said repealed Act to the effective date hereof.

The provisions of this Act, insofar as they are the same or substantially the same as those of any prior Act, shall be construed as a continuation of said prior Act. Any license, permit, certificate, registration, registration plate, registration sticker, bond, policy of insurance or other instrument or document issued or filed or any deposit made under any such prior Act and still in effect on the effective date of this Act shall, except as otherwise specifically provided in this Act, be deemed the equivalent of a license, permit, certificate, registration, registration plate, registration sticker, bond, policy of insurance, or other instrument or document issued or filed or any deposit made under this Act, and shall continue in effect until its expiration or until suspended, revoked, cancelled or forfeited under this Act.

Furthermore, when any section of any of the various laws or acts repealed by this Act is amended by an Amendatory Act of the 76th General Assembly, and such amended section becomes law prior to the effective date of this Act, then it is the intent of the General Assembly that the corresponding section of this Code and Act be construed so as to give effect to such amendment as if it were made a part of this Code. Should, however, any such Amendatory Act amend a definition of a word or phrase in an act repealed by this Act, and such becomes law prior to the effective date of this Act, it is the further intent of the General Assembly that the corresponding section of this Code specifically defining such word or phrase be construed so as to give effect to such amendment, and if not specifically defined, that the corresponding section of Chapter 1 of this Code be construed so as to give effect to such amendment. In the event that a new section is added to an act repealed by this Act by an Act of the 76th General Assembly, it is the further intent of the General Assembly that this Code be construed as if such were made a part of this Code.

P.A. 76-1586, § 20-401, eff. July 1, 1970. Amended by P.A. 80-230, § 1, eff. Oct. 1, 1977.

Formerly Ill.Rev.Stat.1991, ch. 95 ½, ¶ 20-401.

5/20-402. Effective Date

§ 20-402. Effective Date. This Act is effective July 1, 1970.

P.A. 76-1586, § 20-402, eff. July 1, 1970.

Formerly Ill.Rev.Stat.1991, ch. 95 ½, ¶ 20-402.

ACT 10. MOTOR VEHICLE THEFT REPORTING ACT

CHAPTER 20. MISCELLANEOUS PROVISIONS, EFFECT OF ACT AND REPEAL OF NAMED ACTS

Section

10/1. Short title

§ 1. Short title. This Act may be cited as the Motor Vehicle Theft Reporting Act.

P.A. 88-566, § 1, eff. Jan. 1, 1995.

Title of Act:

An Act concerning motor vehicle theft. P.A. 88-566, approved Aug. 5, 1994, eff. Jan. 1, 1995.

10/5. Definitions

§ 5. Definitions.

"Motor vehicle repair station" means a place where the business of performing repair work on motor vehicles is conducted.

"Repair work" includes without limitation diagnosis, maintenance, alteration, adjustment, installation, or replacement of a part, component, or accessory for a motor vehicle.

P.A. 88-566, § 5, eff. Jan. 1, 1995.

10/10. Theft of motor vehicle; report to police

§ 10. Theft of motor vehicle; report to police. If a motor vehicle in the possession of a motor vehicle repair station is stolen, the operator of the motor vehicle repair station shall, immediately upon discovering the theft, report the theft to the police department or sheriff's department of the jurisdiction in which the motor vehicle repair station is located. As soon as possible after reporting the theft to the police department or sheriff's department, the operator of the motor vehicle repair station shall notify the customer whose motor vehicle was stolen of the theft.

P.A. 88-566, § 10, eff. Jan. 1, 1995.

10/15. Penalty

§ 15. Penalty. A person who violates Section 10 of this Act is guilty of a business offense and shall be fined not less than $501 and not more than $1,000.

P.A. 88-566, § 15, eff. Jan. 1, 1995.

ACT 15. CHINA AFFAIRS COUNCIL ACT

Section

15/0.01. Short title

§ 0.01. Short title. This Act may be cited as the China Affairs Council Act.

P.A. 82-676, § 0.01, added by P.A. 86-1324, § 57, eff. Sept. 6, 1990.

Formerly Ill.Rev.Stat.1991, ch. 1, ¶ 6000.

Title of Act:

An Act relating to the Coordination Council for North American Affairs of the Republic of China. P.A. 82-676, veto overridden and eff. Oct. 29, 1981.

15/1. Coordination Council for North American affairs; rights, privileges and immunities

§ 1. Every official or employee of an office of the Coordination Council for North American Affairs located in Illinois shall have the same rights, privileges and immunities enjoyed by officials and employees of any office of the Republic of China on Taiwan located in Illinois prior to January 1, 1979, including applying for and displaying special Illinois registration plates, registration stickers and cards as provided in Section 3-615 of the Illinois Vehicle Code.[1]

P.A. 82-676, § 1, eff. Oct. 29, 1981.

Formerly Ill.Rev.Stat.1991, ch. 1, ¶ 6001.

1 625 ILCS 5/3-615.

ACT 20. CHAUFFEUR PROTECTION ACT

Section

20/0.01. Short title

§ 0.01. Short title. This Act may be cited as the Chauffeur Protection Act.

Laws 1913, p. 334, § 0.01, added by P.A. 86-1324, § 461, eff. Sept. 6, 1990.

Formerly Ill.Rev.Stat.1991, ch. 48, ¶ 88.9.

Title of Act:

An Act to protect chauffeurs in their employment from dust, wind, and inclement weather. Laws 1913, p. 334, approved June 27, 1913, eff. July 1, 1913.

20/1. Shield and hood on delivery trucks and automobiles

§ 1. Every person or corporation owning, operating or controlling automobiles or auto trucks used for the delivery of merchandise, produce or freight, shall keep upon the front of the said automobiles or auto trucks a shield and hood as an inclosure to protect chauffeurs from wind, dust and inclement weather.

Laws 1913, p. 334, § 1, eff. July 1, 1913.

Formerly Ill.Rev.Stat.1991, ch. 48, ¶ 89.

20/2. Penalty for violation

§ 2. Every person or corporation owning, operating or controlling an automobile or auto truck who shall neglect or refuse to comply with the provisions of section 1 of this act upon conviction shall be guilty of a petty offense and fined not less than $10 nor more than $50 for each and every day and for each and every automobile or auto truck used and operated in violation of section 1 of this act.

Laws 1913, p. 334, § 2, eff. July 1, 1913. Amended by P.A. 77–2427, § 1, eff. Jan. 1, 1973.

Formerly Ill.Rev.Stat.1991, ch. 48, ¶ 90.

ACT 25. CHILD PASSENGER PROTECTION ACT

Section

25/1. Title and citation

§ 1. Title and citation. This Act shall be known and may be cited as the "Child Passenger Protection Act".

P.A. 83–8, § 1, eff. July 1, 1983.

Formerly Ill.Rev.Stat.1991, ch. 95 ½, ¶ 1101.

Title of Act:

An Act to protect children who are passengers in motor vehicles, as well as the motoring public in general. P.A. 83–8, approved June 27, 1983, eff. July 1, 1983.

25/2. Legislative Finding—Purpose

§ 2. Legislative Finding—Purpose. The General Assembly finds that a substantial number of passengers under the age of 6 years riding in motor vehicles, which are most frequently operated by a parent, annually die or sustain serious physical injury as a direct result of not being placed in a child passenger restraint system. The General Assembly further finds that the safety of the motoring public is seriously threatened as indicated by the significant number of traffic accidents annually caused, directly or indirectly, by driver distraction or other impairment of driving ability induced by the movement or actions of unrestrained passengers under the age of 6 years.

It is the purpose of this Act to further protect the health, safety and welfare of motor vehicle passengers under the age of 6 years and the motoring public through the proper utilization of approved child restraint systems.

P.A. 83–8, § 2, eff. July 1, 1983.

Formerly Ill.Rev.Stat.1991, ch. 95 ½, ¶ 1102.

25/3. Definitions

§ 3. Definitions. The terms "highway", "motor vehicle", "owner", "police officer", "recreational vehicle", "roadway", and "street" as used in this Act, unless the context otherwise requires, have the meaning ascribed to them in The Illinois Vehicle Code, as now or hereafter amended.[1] For the purpose of this Act, "motor vehicle" does not include motorcycles.

P.A. 83–8, § 3, eff. July 1, 1983.

Formerly Ill.Rev.Stat.1991, ch. 95 ½, ¶ 1103.

[1] 625 ILCS 5/1–100 et seq.

25/4. Transporting child under age of 4; restraint system

§ 4. When any person is transporting a child in this State under the age of 4 years in a non-commercial motor vehicle of the first division, a motor vehicle of the second division with a gross vehicle weight rating of 9,000 pounds or less, or a recreational vehicle on the roadways, streets or highways of this State, such person shall be responsible for providing for the protection of such child by properly securing him or her in a child restraint system. The parent or legal guardian of a child under the age of 4 years shall provide a child restraint system to any person who transports his or her child. Any person who transports the child of another shall not be in violation of this Section unless a child restraint system was provided by the parent or legal guardian but not used to transport the child.

For purposes of this Section and Section 4a, "child restraint system" means any device which meets the standards of the United States Department of Transportation designed to restrain, seat or position children.

P.A. 83–8, § 4, eff. July 1, 1983. Amended by P.A. 85–1209, Art. III, § 3–62, eff. Aug. 30, 1988; P.A. 86–1241, § 1, eff. Jan. 1, 1991; P.A. 88–17, § 5, eff. Jan. 1, 1994.

Formerly Ill.Rev.Stat.1991, ch. 95 ½, ¶ 1104.

25/4a. Children 4 years of age or older but under age of 16; restraint system or seat belts

§ 4a. Every person, when transporting a child 4 years of age or older but under the age of 16, as provided in Section 4 of this Act, shall be responsible for securing that child in either a child restraint system or seat belts.

P.A. 83–8, § 4a, eff. July 1, 1983. Amended by P.A. 86–1241, § 1, eff. Jan. 1, 1991; P.A. 88–17, § 5, eff. Jan. 1, 1994; P.A. 92–171, § 5, eff. Jan. 1, 2002.

Formerly Ill.Rev.Stat.1991, ch. 95 ½, ¶ 1104a.

25/4b. Children 6 years of age or older but under the age of 18; seat belts

§ 4b. Children 6 years of age or older but under the age of 18; seat belts. Every person under the age of 18 years, when transporting a child 6 years of age or older but under the age of 18 years, as provided in Section 4 of this Act, shall be responsible for securing that child in a properly adjusted and fastened seat safety belt.

P.A. 83–8, § 4b, added by P.A. 90–369, § 10, eff. Jan. 1, 1998.

25/5. Failure to secure or properly secure child; negligence; admissibility in trial

§ 5. In no event shall a person's failure to secure a child under 6 years of age in an approved child restraint system or properly secure such child, if age 4 or 5, in a seat belt constitute contributory negligence or be admissible as evidence in the trial of any civil action.

P.A. 83–8, § 5, eff. July 1, 1983. Amended by P.A. 86–1241, § 1, eff. Jan. 1, 1991.

Formerly Ill.Rev.Stat.1991, ch. 95 ½, ¶ 1105.

25/6. Violations; fines

§ 6. A violation of this Act is a petty offense punishable by a fine of not more than $50 waived upon proof of possession of an approved child restraint system as defined under this Act. A subsequent violation of this Act is a petty offense punishable by a fine of not more than $100.

P.A. 83–8, § 6, eff. July 1, 1983. Amended by P.A. 92–173, § 5, eff. Jan. 1, 2002.

Formerly Ill.Rev.Stat.1991, ch. 95 ½, ¶ 1106.

25/7. Arrests—Prosecutions

§ 7. Arrests—Prosecutions. The State Police shall patrol the public highways and make arrests for a violation of this Act. Police officers shall make arrests for violations of this Act occurring upon the highway within the limits of a county, city, village, or unincorporated town or park district.

The State's Attorney of the county in which the violation of this Act occurs shall prosecute all violations except when the violation occurs within the corporate limits of a municipality, the municipal attorney may prosecute if written permission to do so is obtained from the State's Attorney.

The provisions of this Act shall not apply to a child passenger with a physical disability of such a nature as to prevent appropriate restraint in a seat, provided that the disability is duly certified by a physician who shall state the nature of the disability, as well as the reason the restraint is inappropriate. No physician shall be liable, and no cause of action may be brought for personal injuries resulting from the exercise of good faith judgment in making certifications under this provision.

P.A. 83–8, § 7, eff. July 1, 1983. Amended by P.A. 85–1277, § 1, eff. Aug. 30, 1988; P.A. 88–685, § 10, eff. Jan. 24, 1995.

Formerly Ill.Rev.Stat.1991, ch. 95 ½, ¶ 1107.

25/8. Repealer

§ 8. The "Child Passenger Restraint Act", enacted by the 82nd General Assembly, is repealed.

P.A. 83–8, § 8, eff. July 1, 1983.

Formerly Ill.Rev.Stat.1991, ch. 95 ½, ¶ 1108.

25/9. Effective date

§ 9. This Act takes effect July 1, 1983.

P.A. 83–8, § 9, eff. July 1, 1983.

Formerly Ill.Rev.Stat.1991, ch. 95 ½, ¶ 1109.

ACT 27. RENTER'S FINANCIAL RESPONSIBILITY AND PROTECTION ACT

Section

Section

27/1. Short title

§ 1. Short title. This Act may be cited as the Renter's Financial Responsibility and Protection Act.

P.A. 90–113, § 1, eff. July 14, 1997.

Title of Act:

An Act concerning rental vehicles. P.A. 90–113, approved and eff. July 14, 1997.

27/5. Legislative findings

§ 5. Legislative findings. The General Assembly finds and declares the following:

(a) Amendments enacted in 1988 which limit negligent drivers' liability for damage to vehicles rented from motor vehicle rental companies to $200 have had the unintended, anti-consumer effect of unfairly transferring most of the costs of liability for renters' negligence to car rental companies.

(b) This transfer of liability from negligent renters has forced Illinois rental companies and dealers to experience significant financial losses in the form of actual costs to repair, service, and replace vehicles and loss of economic opportunity by being deprived of the rental use of damaged or destroyed rental cars; as a result, many Illinois vehicle rental companies in Illinois have been forced to close because of the current amendments, and high risk to capital threatens to close existing companies; economic losses have also resulted in Illinois renters paying daily and weekly vehicle rental rates almost two-fold higher than renters in other states, including those states surrounding Illinois.

(c) As the vast majority of renters in Illinois are non-Illinois residents, the increased damage costs of rental car companies and dealers are absorbed and paid by all Illinois consumers and business.

(d) The current law also threatens the public safety of all Illinois citizens as it has contributed to an almost three-fold increase in driver accident and fatality rates in Illinois.

P.A. 90–113, § 5, eff. July 14, 1997.

27/10. Definitions

§ 10. Definitions. As used in this Act:

"Rental Company" means a person or entity that rents private passenger vehicles to the public for 30 days or less.

"Renter" means a person or entity that obtains the use of a private passenger vehicle from a rental company under terms of a rental agreement.

"Rental Agreement" means an agreement for 30 days or less setting forth the terms and conditions governing the use of a private passenger vehicle provided by a rental company.

"Authorized Driver" means: the renter; the renter's spouse if the spouse is a licensed driver and satisfies the rental company's minimum age requirement; the renter's employer, employee, or co-worker if that person is a licensed driver, satisfies the rental company's minimum age requirement, and at the time of the rental is engaged in a business activity with the renter; any person who is expressly listed by the rental company on the rental agreement as an authorized driver; and any person driving directly to a medical or police facility under circumstances reasonably believed to constitute an emergency and who is a licensed driver.

"Damage Waiver" means a rental company's agreement not to hold an authorized driver liable for all or a part of any damage to or loss of a rented vehicle for which the renter may be liable pursuant to Section 6–305.2. "Damage Waiver" shall encompass within its meaning other similar terms used by rental companies, such as "Collision Damage Waiver", "Loss Damage Waiver", "Physical Damage Waiver", and the like.

P.A. 90–113, § 10, eff. July 14, 1997.

27/15. Prohibited practices

§ 15. Prohibited practices.

(a) A rental company may not sell a damage waiver unless the renter agrees to the damage waiver in writing at or prior to the time the rental agreement is executed.

(b) A rental company may not void a damage waiver except for one or more of the following reasons:

(1) Damage or loss while the rental vehicle is used to carry persons or property for a charge or fee.

(2) Damage or loss during an organized or agreed upon racing or speed contest or demonstration or pushing or pulling activity in which the rental vehicle is actively involved.

(3) Damage or loss that could reasonably be expected from an intentional or criminal act of the driver other than a traffic infraction.

(4) Damage or loss to any rental vehicle resulting from any auto business operation, including but not limited to repairing, servicing, testing, washing, parking, storing, or selling of automobiles.

(5) Damage or loss occurring to a rental vehicle if the rental contract is based on fraudulent or material misrepresentation by the renter.

(6) Damage or loss arising out of the use of the rental vehicle outside the continental United States when such use is specifically prohibited in the rental agreement.

(7) Damage or loss occurring while the rental vehicle is operated by a driver not permitted under the rental agreement.

(c) A rental company shall not charge more than $9 per full or partial 24 hour rental day for a collision damage waiver if the manufacturer's suggested retail price of the rental vehicle type is not greater than $30,000. A rental company shall not charge more than $12 per full or partial 24 hour rental day for a collision damage waiver if the manufacturer's suggested retail price of the rental vehicle type is greater than $30,000. On January 1, 2000, the maximum charges in this subsection (c) shall be increased to $9.50 and $12.50, respectively, and shall be subsequently increased to $10 and $13 on January 1, 2001 and $10.50 and $13.50 on January 1, 2002.

P.A. 90–113, § 15, eff. July 14, 1997.

27/20. Disclosure notice and advertising requirements

§ 20. Disclosure notice and advertising requirements.

(a) Each renter who purchases a damage waiver that is not included in the base rental shall be provided the following disclosure notice:

NOTICE: This contract offers, for an additional charge, a collision damage waiver to cover your financial responsibility for damage to the rental vehicle. The purchase of a collision damage waiver is optional and may be declined. You are advised to carefully consider whether to sign this waiver if you have rental vehicle collision coverage provided by your credit card or collision insurance on your own vehicle. Before deciding whether to purchase the collision damage waiver, you may wish to determine whether your own vehicle insurance affords you coverage for damage to the rental vehicle and the amount of deductible under your own insurance coverage.

(b) The disclosure notice required in subsection (a) shall be made on the face of the rental agreement either by stamp, label, or as part of the written contract, shall be set apart in boldface type and in no smaller print than 10 point type, and shall include a space for the renter to acknowledge his or her receipt of the notice. The contract shall also include in boldface type and in no smaller print than 10 point type, in simple and readable language, any other conditions and exclusions applicable to the collision damage waiver.

(c) Any rental company who states or permits to be stated the rental cost of a rental motor vehicle in any advertisement shall state conspicuously, in plain language and in conjunction with the advertised rental cost of the vehicle, the daily rate of the applicable collision damage waiver, that the rate constitutes an additional daily charge to the renter, that the collision damage waiver is optional, and that prospective renters should examine their automobile insurance policies for rental vehicle coverage.

(1) When a written advertisement, including all print media, contains the statement of the rental cost of a vehicle, the disclosure required by this subsection shall be printed in type no less than 10 point type.

(2) When the video presentation of a television advertisement contains the written statement of the rental cost of a vehicle, the depiction of the disclosure required by this subsection shall be no less than one-third the size of the depiction of the rental cost.

(3) When a radio advertisement or the audio presentation of a television advertisement contains the statement of the rental cost of the vehicle, the oral statement of the rental cost shall be immediately accompanied by an oral statement of the disclosure required by this subsection.

(d) Any rental company that makes any oral statement, excluding telephonic communications, or written statement of the rental cost of a vehicle shall disclose, in plain language and in conjunction with that statement, the daily rate of the applicable collision damage waiver and that the rate constitutes an additional daily charge to the renter.

(e) Any rental company that offers the collision damage waiver option to a renter shall inform the renter in posted signs or in pamphlets, written in plain language, of all of the information described in Sections 15 through 20. The requirements of this subsection shall be deemed to be satisfied if the rental company places the pamphlets or posted signs prominently and conspicuously where the posted signs and pamphlets may be easily seen or reached by renters.

P.A. 90–113, § 20, eff. July 14, 1997.

27/25. Mandatory charges

§ 25. Mandatory charges.

(a) As used in this Section, "mandatory charge" means any charge, surcharge, or fee in addition to the base rental rate for an item or service provided in connection with the rental transaction that the renter does not have the option of avoiding or declining and that is not otherwise imposed by law.

(b) A rental agreement containing any mandatory charge shall prominently display and fully disclose the charge separately on the face of the agreement.

(c) A mandatory charge shall also be prominently displayed and fully disclosed in all price advertising, price displays, price quotes, and price offers, including displays in computerized reservation systems.

(d) Notwithstanding the foregoing, a rental company may not impose or require the purchase of a damage waiver as a mandatory charge.

P.A. 90–113, § 25, eff. July 14, 1997.

27/999. Effective date

§ 999. Effective date. This Act takes effect upon becoming law.

P.A. 90–113, § 999, eff. July 14, 1997.

ACT 30. RIDESHARING ARRANGEMENTS ACT

30/1. Short title

§ 1. This Act shall be known and may be cited as the Ridesharing Arrangements Act.

P.A. 82–656, § 1, eff. Jan. 1, 1982.

Formerly Ill.Rev.Stat.1991, ch. 95 ½, ¶ 901.

Title of Act:

An Act in relation to ridesharing and amending a certain Act in connection therewith. P.A. 82–656, approved Sept. 25, 1981, eff. Jan. 1, 1982.

30/2. Definitions

§ 2. (a) "Ridesharing arrangement" means the transportation by motor vehicle of not more than 16 persons (including the driver):

(1) for purposes incidental to another purpose of the driver, for which no fee is charged or paid except to reimburse the driver or owner of the vehicle for his operating expenses on a nonprofit basis; or

(2) when such persons are travelling between their homes and their places of employment, or places reasonably convenient thereto, for which (i) no fee is charged or paid except to reimburse the driver or owner of the vehicle for his operating expenses on a nonprofit basis, or (ii) a fee is charged in accordance with the provisions of Section 6 of this Act.

(b) "For-profit ridesharing arrangement" means a ridesharing arrangement for which a fee is charged in accordance with Section 6 of this Act.

P.A. 82–656, § 2, eff. Jan. 1, 1982. Amended by P.A. 83–1091, § 2, eff. July 1, 1984.

Formerly Ill.Rev.Stat.1991, ch. 95 ½, ¶ 902.

30/3. Commerce commission; regulation; exemption

§ 3. No ridesharing arrangement, whether or not a fee is charged, shall be subject to regulation by the Illinois Commerce Commission.

P.A. 82–656, § 3, eff. Jan. 1, 1982. Amended by P.A. 83–1091, § 2, eff. July 1, 1984.

Formerly Ill.Rev.Stat.1991, ch. 95 ½, ¶ 903.

30/4. Vehicle code; compliance

§ 4. Persons participating in a ridesharing arrangement are not thereby relieved of compliance with The Illinois Safety Responsibility Law contained in Chapter 7 of The Illinois Vehicle Code.[1]

P.A. 82–656, § 4, eff. Jan. 1, 1982. Amended by P.A. 83–1091, § 2, eff. July 1, 1984.

Formerly Ill.Rev.Stat.1991, ch. 95 ½, ¶ 904.

1 625 ILCS 5/7–100 et seq.

30/5. Local government regulation; licenses; fares

§ 5. No unit of local government, whether or not it is a home rule unit, may:

(1) license or regulate ridesharing arrangements;

(2) impose any tax or fee upon the owner or operator of a motor vehicle because of its use in a ridesharing arrangement;

(3) prohibit or regulate the charging of fees for ridesharing arrangements in accordance with Section 6 of this Act.

This Act is declared to be a denial and limitation of the powers of home rule units pursuant to paragraph (g) of Section 6 of Article VII of the Illinois Constitution.

P.A. 82–656, § 5, eff. Jan. 1, 1982. Amended by P.A. 83–1091, § 2, eff. July 1, 1984.

Formerly Ill.Rev.Stat.1991, ch. 95 ½, ¶ 905.

30/6. Commercial vehicles; application of law

§ 6. (a) The operator of a ridesharing arrangement may charge his or her passengers a fee in excess of the amount required to reimburse the operator for his or her expenses, if:

(1) the operator makes no more than 2 round trips per day in the course of operating any ridesharing arrangement;

(2) any passenger so charged is a person whom the operator has agreed to transport in advance of such person presenting himself or herself at the pickup point; and

(3) the operator complies with Sections 6–106.4, 12–707 and 12–707.01 of the Illinois Vehicle Code.[1]

(b) A for-profit ridesharing arrangement may, but need not, be organized as a sole proprietorship, or as any other appropriate form of business entity.

P.A. 82–656, § 6, eff. Jan. 1, 1982. Amended by P.A. 83–1091, § 2, eff. July 1, 1984; P.A. 91–357, § 232, eff. July 29, 1999.

Formerly Ill.Rev.Stat.1991, ch. 95 ½, ¶ 906.

1 625 ILCS 5/6–106.4, 5/12–707 and 5/12–707.01.

ACT 32. EMPLOYEE COMMUTE OPTIONS ACT

32/1 to 32/99. §§ 1 to 99. Repealed by P.A. 89–493, § 45, eff. Jan. 1, 1997

Section 75 provided:

"Repealer. If Section 182(d)(1)(B) of the Clean Air Act is repealed or the United States Environmental Protection Agency determines that Section 182(d)(1)(B) no longer applies to any area in Illinois, this Act is repealed."

ACT 33. VOLUNTARY EMPLOYEE COMMUTE OPTIONS EMISSION REDUCTION CREDIT ACT

Section

33/1. Short title

§ 1. Short title. This Act may be cited as the Voluntary Employee Commute Options Emission Reduction Credit Act.

P.A. 89–493, § 1, eff. Jan. 1, 1997.

Title of Act:

An Act to create the Voluntary Employee Commute Options Emission Reduction Credit Act and to repeal the Employee Commute Options Act, amending named Acts. P.A. 89–493, approved June 21, 1996, eff. Jan. 1, 1997.

33/5. Purpose

§ 5. Purpose. It is the purpose of this Act to provide owners with the opportunity to implement voluntary employee commute options programs. These programs would enable the owners to obtain emission reductions that are creditable toward the level of emission reductions required under the federal Clean Air Act Amendments of 1990 [1] for the post–1996 period, including emission reductions required under Section 9.8 of the Environmental Protection Act.[2]

P.A. 89–493, § 5, eff. Jan. 1, 1997.

[1] 42 U.S.C.A. § 7401 et seq.

[2] 415 ILCS 5/9.8.

33/10. Definitions

§ 10. Definitions. For purposes of this Act:

"Agency" means the Environmental Protection Agency.

"Department" means the Illinois Department of Transportation.

"Owners" means employers in the Chicago, Illinois ozone nonattainment area who operate stationary sources that are subject to emission reduction requirements for the post–1996 period under the Clean Air Act Amendments of 1990.[1]

P.A. 89–493, § 10, eff. Jan. 1, 1997.

[1] 42 U.S.C.A. § 7401 et seq.

33/15. Voluntary Employee Commute Options Program

§ 15. Voluntary Employee Commute Options Program. Owners may implement voluntary programs to encourage the use of carpooling, mass transit, vanpooling, telecommuting, compressed work weeks, clean fuel vehicles, and other measures that either reduce the number of commuting trips by their employees or reduce the emissions associated with those commuting trips for the purpose of creating emission reduction credits that may be used by the owners of stationary sources to satisfy the post–1996 emission reduction requirements under the Clean Air Act Amendments of 1990.[1]

P.A. 89–493, § 15, eff. Jan. 1, 1997.

[1] 42 U.S.C.A. § 7401 et seq.

33/20. Submission of programs and awarding of credits

§ 20. Submission of programs and awarding of credits. Owners may submit voluntary programs as described in Section 15 to the Department for approval. The Department, after consultation with the Agency, shall determine the appropriate emission reduction credit to be awarded to owners who carry out their programs and to be used by the owners of stationary sources to satisfy the post–1996 emission reduction requirements under the Clean Air Act Amendments of 1990.[1] Emission reduction credits shall not be awarded to owners for programs that are required under the Clean Air Act or the Environmental Protection Act [2] or that are substantially the same as an owner's employees' existing level of use of employee commute options programs. The Department shall adjust credits to avoid duplicating the credits the State takes for similar transportation demand management practices under the applicable State Implementation Plan. Credits may be revoked for failure to achieve the reductions called for in the owner's voluntary program.

P.A. 89–493, § 20, eff. Jan. 1, 1997.

[1] 42 U.S.C.A. § 7401 et seq.

[2] 415 ILCS 5/1 et seq.

33/25. Voluntary compliance

§ 25. Voluntary compliance. Within 30 days after the effective date of this amendatory Act of 1996, the State of Illinois shall notify the United States Environmental Protection Agency to remove the mandated Employee Commute Options requirement from the State Implementation Plan for ozone. The State of Illinois shall also notify the United States Environmental Protection Agency that emissions reductions achieved from voluntary implementation of the Voluntary Employee Commute Options Emission Reduction Credit Act by an owner are creditable toward the level of emission reductions required under other post–1996 stationary source emission reduction programs.

P.A. 89–493, § 25, eff. Jan. 1, 1997.

33/30. Rules

§ 30. Rules. The Department is authorized to adopt rules that may be necessary to accomplish the purposes of this Act.

P.A. 89–493, § 30, eff. Jan. 1, 1997.

33/35. Review under Administrative Review Law; venue

§ 35. Review under Administrative Review Law; [1] venue. An owner who does not agree with the credit awarded for his or her program, whose program is disapproved, or whose credit is revoked may seek relief under the Administrative Review Law, as amended now or hereafter, and the rules adopted pursuant to that Law.

Those proceedings for judicial review of final administrative decisions of the Department under this Act shall be commenced in the Appellate Court in the District in which the party applying for review resides, but if the party is not a resident of this State, the venue shall be the Fourth Appellate District.

P.A. 89–493, § 35, eff. Jan. 1, 1997.

[1] 735 ILCS 5/3–101 et seq.

33/40. Repealer

§ 40. The State Finance Act is amended by repealing Section 5.354.[1]

P.A. 89–493, § 40, eff. Jan. 1, 1997.

[1] 30 ILCS 105/5.354 (repealed).

33/45. Repealer

§ 45. The Employee Commute Options Act [1] is repealed.

P.A. 89–493, § 45, eff. Jan. 1, 1997.

[1] 625 ILCS 32/1 et seq. (repealed).

ACT 35. CYCLE RIDER SAFETY TRAINING ACT

Section

35/1. Short title

§ 1. This Act shall be known and may be cited as the "Cycle Rider Safety Training Act". It is the policy of this State to promote safety for persons and property connected with the use and operation of motorcycles, motor driven cycles and motorized pedalcycles.

P.A. 82–649, § 1, eff. Jan. 1, 1982. Amended by P.A. 85–183, Art. X, § 10–1, eff. Aug. 30, 1989; P.A. 86–1005, § 4, eff. Dec. 28, 1989.

Formerly Ill.Rev.Stat.1991, ch. 95 ½, ¶ 801.

Title of Act:

An Act to create the "Cycle Rider Safety Training Act" and to amend Sections 2–119 and 3–806 of "The Illinois Vehicle Code", approved September 29, 1969, as amended, and to add Section 5.92 to "An Act in relation to State finance", approved June 10, 1911, as amended. P.A. 82–649, approved Sept. 25, 1981, eff. Jan. 1, 1982.

35/2. Definitions

§ 2. As used in this Act, the terms specified in Sections 2.01 through 2.06 have the meanings ascribed to them in those Sections unless the context clearly requires a different meaning.

P.A. 82–649, § 1, eff. Jan. 1, 1982.

Formerly Ill.Rev.Stat.1991, ch. 95 ½, ¶ 802.

35/2.01. "Cycle"

§ 2.01. "Cycle" means a motorcycle, motor driven cycle or motorized pedalcycle, as defined in The Illinois Vehicle Code [1].

P.A. 82–649, § 1, eff. Jan. 1, 1982. Amended by P.A. 85–183, Art. X, § 10–1, eff. Aug. 30, 1989; P.A. 86–1005, § 4, eff. Dec. 28, 1989.

Formerly Ill.Rev.Stat.1991, ch. 95 ½, ¶ 802.01.

[1] 625 ILCS 5/1–100 et seq.

35/2.02. "Cycle Rider"

§ 2.02. "Cycle Rider" means every person who rides and is in actual physical control of a cycle.

P.A. 82–649, § 1, eff. Jan. 1, 1982.

Formerly Ill.Rev.Stat.1991, ch. 95 ½, ¶ 802.02.

35/2.03. "Cycle Rider Safety Training Courses"

§ 2.03. "Cycle Rider Safety Training Courses" and "Courses" mean courses of instruction in the use and operation of cycles, including instruction in the safe on-road operation of cycles, the rules of the road and the laws of this State relating to motor vehicles, which courses meet the minimum requirements of this Act and the rules and regulations issued hereunder by the Department and which have been approved by the Department as meeting such requirements.

P.A. 82–649, § 1, eff. Jan. 1, 1982.

Formerly Ill.Rev.Stat.1991, ch. 95 ½, ¶ 802.03.

35/2.04. "Department"

§ 2.04. "Department" means the Illinois Department of Transportation.

P.A. 82–649, § 1, eff. Jan. 1, 1982.

Formerly Ill.Rev.Stat.1991, ch. 95 ½, ¶ 802.04.

35/2.05. "Driver's License"

§ 2.05. "Driver's License" means any license or permit to operate a motor vehicle under the laws of this State.

P.A. 82–649, § 1, eff. Jan. 1, 1982.

Formerly Ill.Rev.Stat.1991, ch. 95 ½, ¶ 802.05.

35/2.06. "Person"

§ 2.06. "Person" means every person, firm, partnership or corporation.

P.A. 82–649, § 1, eff. Jan. 1, 1982.

Formerly Ill.Rev.Stat.1991, ch. 95 ½, ¶ 802.06.

35/3. Powers and duties; department

§ 3. The Department shall have the power, duty and authority to administer this Act.

P.A. 82–649, § 1, eff. Jan. 1, 1982.

Formerly Ill.Rev.Stat.1991, ch. 95 ½, ¶ 803.

35/4. Regional centers; organization; curriculum

§ 4. Any State or community college, State university or community agency designated by the Department may organize a Regional Cycle Rider Safety Training Center and may offer cycle rider safety training courses through such Training Centers which it operates. The curriculum and accreditation for the courses, and the geographic areas in which each Training Center may offer the courses, shall be provided for by rules and regulations of the Department. Instructors of such courses shall meet the qualification and certification requirements of the regulations of the Department and the college, university or community agency offering the program and may be employed on a calendar year rather than a school year basis. Such courses shall be open to all residents of the State who hold a currently valid driver's license and who have reached their 16th birthday without regard to whether such person is enrolled in any other course offered by said State or community college, State university or community agency. Such courses may be offered throughout the calendar year. The courses may be offered as credit or noncredit courses, but no fee shall be charged except for a nominal registration fee which shall be refunded upon completion of the course.

P.A. 82–649, § 1, eff. Jan. 1, 1982. Amended by P.A. 85–183, Art. X, § 10–1, eff. Aug. 30, 1989; P.A. 86–1005, § 4, eff. Dec. 28, 1989.

Formerly Ill.Rev.Stat.1991, ch. 95 ½, ¶ 804.

35/5. Rules and regulations

§ 5. The Department may promulgate rules and regulations not inconsistent with the provisions of the Cycle Rider Safety Training Act for the administration of the Cycle Rider Safety Training Act.

P.A. 82–649, § 1, eff. Jan. 1, 1982.

Formerly Ill.Rev.Stat.1991, ch. 95 ½, ¶ 805.

35/6. Cycle Rider Safety Training Fund; deposits

§ 6. To finance the Cycle Rider Safety Training program and to pay the costs thereof, the Secretary of State will hereafter deposit with the State Treasurer an amount equal to each annual fee and each reduced fee, for the registration of each motorcycle, motor driven cycle and motorized pedalcycle processed by the Office of the Secretary of State during the preceding quarter as required in subsection (d) of Section 2–119 of the Illinois Vehicle Code,[1] which amount the State Comptroller shall transfer quarterly to a trust fund outside of the State treasury to be known as the Cycle Rider Safety Training Fund, which is hereby created. In addition, the Department may accept any federal, State, or private moneys for deposit into the Fund and shall be used by the Department only for the expenses of the Department in administering the provisions of this Act, for funding of contracts with approved Regional Cycle Rider Safety Training Centers for the conduct of courses, or for any purpose related or incident thereto and connected therewith.

P.A. 82–649, § 1, eff. Jan. 1, 1982. Amended by P.A. 85–183, Art. X, § 10–1, eff. Aug. 30, 1989; P.A. 86–1005, § 4, eff. Dec. 28, 1989; P.A. 87–838, § 165, eff. Jan. 24, 1992; P.A. 87–1217, § 1, eff. Jan. 1, 1993.

Formerly Ill.Rev.Stat.1991, ch. 95 ½, ¶ 806.

[1] 625 ILCS 5/2–119.

P.A. 87–1217 incorporated the amendment by P.A. 87–838.

35/7. Contracts; safety training courses

§ 7. The Department is authorized to and shall award contracts out of appropriations to the Department from "The Cycle Rider Safety Training Fund" to qualifying Regional Cycle Rider Safety Training Centers for the conduct of approved Cycle Rider Safety Training courses.

P.A. 82–649, § 1, eff. Jan. 1, 1982.

Formerly Ill.Rev.Stat.1991, ch. 95 ½, ¶ 807.

ACT 40. SNOWMOBILE REGISTRATION AND SAFETY ACT

Article

ARTICLE I. DEFINITIONS—APPLICATION—JURISDICTION

Section

40/1–1. Title and declaration of intent

§ 1–1. Title and declaration of intent. This Act shall be known and may be cited as the "Snowmobile Registration and Safety Act". It is the policy of this State to promote safety for persons and property in and connected with the use, operation and equipment of snowmobiles and to promote uniformity of laws relating thereto.

P.A. 77–1312, § 1–1, eff. Aug. 27, 1971.

Formerly Ill.Rev.Stat.1991, ch. 95 ½, ¶ 601–1.

Title of Act:

An Act for the registration of snowmobiles, providing for regulations pertaining to the operation thereof, and providing penalties for the violations thereof. P.A. 77–1312, approved and eff. Aug. 27, 1971.

40/1–2. Definitions

§ 1–2. Definitions. As used in this Act, the terms specified in Sections 1–2.01 through 1–2.20 [1] have the meanings ascribed to them in those Sections unless the context clearly requires a different meaning.

P.A. 77–1312, § 1–2, eff. Aug. 27, 1971. Resectioned §§ 1–2, 1–2.01 to 1–2.15 and amended by P.A. 78–856, § 1, eff. Sept. 14, 1973.

Formerly Ill.Rev.Stat.1991, ch. 95 ½, ¶ 601–2.

[1] 625 ILCS 40/1–2.01 to 40/1–2.15; no §§ 1–2.16 to 1–2.20 in enrolled bill.

40/1–2.01. Cowling

§ 1–2.01. "Cowling" means the forward portions of a snowmobile surrounding the motor and clutch assembly.

P.A. 77–1312, § 1–2, eff. Aug. 27, 1971. Resectioned in part § 1–2.01 by P.A. 78–856, § 1, eff. July 1, 1974.

Formerly Ill.Rev.Stat.1991, ch. 95 ½, ¶ 601–2.01.

40/1–2.02. Dealer

§ 1–2.02. "Dealer" means a person, partnership, or corporation engaged in the business of manufacturing, selling, or leasing snowmobiles at wholesale or retail.

P.A. 77–1312, § 1–2, eff. Aug. 27, 1971. Resectioned in part § 1–2.02 by P.A. 78–856, § 1, eff. July 1, 1974.

Formerly Ill.Rev.Stat.1991, ch. 95 ½, ¶ 601–2.02.

40/1–2.03. Dangerous drug

§ 1–2.03. "Dangerous drug" means any drug defined as a depressant or stimulant substance in the "Illinois Controlled Substances Act" [1] and cannabis as defined in the "Cannabis Control Act" [2].

P.A. 77–1312, § 1–2, eff. Aug. 27, 1971. Resectioned in part § 1–2.03 and amended by P.A. 78–856, § 1, eff. July 1, 1974.

Formerly Ill.Rev.Stat.1991, ch. 95 ½, ¶ 601–2.03.

[1] 720 ILCS 570/100 et seq.

[2] 720 ILCS 550/1 et seq.

40/1–2.04. Department

§ 1–2.04. "Department" means the Department of Natural Resources.

P.A. 77–1312, § 1–2, eff. Aug. 27, 1971. Resectioned in part § 1–2.04 by P.A. 78–856, § 1, eff. July 1, 1974. Amended by P.A. 89–445, § 9A–88, eff. Feb. 7, 1996.

Formerly Ill.Rev.Stat.1991, ch. 95 ½, ¶ 601–2.04.

40/1–2.05. Highway; state highway; Interstate highway; controlled access highway; tollroad

§ 1–2.05. (a) "Highway" means the entire width between the boundary lines of every way publicly maintained when any part thereof is open to the use of the public for purposes of vehicular travel.

(b) "State highway" means State highways as defined in the Illinois Highway Code.[1]

(c) "Interstate highway" means any highway which now is, or shall hereafter be a part of the national system of interstate and defense highways within this State.

(d) "Controlled access highway" means every highway, street or roadway in respect to which owners or occupants of abutting lands and other persons have no legal right of access to or from the same except at such points only and in such manner as may be determined by the public authority having jurisdiction over such highway, street or roadway.

(e) "Tollroad" means all highways under the jurisdiction of the Illinois State Toll Highway Authority.

P.A. 77–1312, § 1–2, eff. Aug. 27, 1971. Resectioned in part § 1–2.05 by P.A. 78–856, § 1, eff. Sept. 14, 1973. Amended by P.A. 83–789, § 1, eff. Jan. 1, 1984.

Formerly Ill.Rev.Stat.1991, ch. 95 ½, ¶ 601–2.05.

[1] 605 ILCS 5/1–101 et seq.

40/1–2.06. Intoxicating Beverage

§ 1–2.06. "Intoxicating Beverage" means any beverage enumerated in the "Liquor Control Act".[1]

P.A. 77–1312, § 1–2, eff. Aug. 27, 1971. Resectioned in part § 1–2.06 by P.A. 78–856, § 1, eff. Sept. 14, 1973.

Formerly Ill.Rev.Stat.1991, ch. 95 ½, ¶ 601–2.06.

[1] 235 ILCS 5/1–1 et seq.

40/1–2.07. Local Authority

§ 1–2.07. "Local Authority" means every county, municipal, and other local board or body having authority to adopt local police regulations under the Constitution and laws of this State.

P.A. 77–1312, § 1–2, eff. Aug. 27, 1971. Resectioned in part § 1–2.07 by P.A. 78–856, § 1, eff. Sept. 14, 1973.

Formerly Ill.Rev.Stat.1991, ch. 95 ½, ¶ 601–2.07.

40/1–2.08. Narcotic drug

§ 1–2.08. "Narcotic drug" means any substance defined as a narcotic drug in the "Illinois Controlled Substances Act.[1] "

P.A. 77–1312, § 1–2, eff. Aug. 27, 1971. Resectioned in part § 1–2.08 and amended by P.A. 78–856, § 1, eff. Sept. 14, 1973.

Formerly Ill.Rev.Stat.1991, ch. 95 ½, ¶ 601–2.08.

[1] 720 ILCS 570/100 et seq.

40/1–2.09. Operate

§ 1–2.09. "Operate" means to ride in or on, other than as a passenger, use or control the operation of a snowmobile in any manner, whether or not the snowmobile is under way.

P.A. 77–1312, § 1–2, eff. Aug. 27, 1971. Resectioned in part § 1–2.09 by P.A. 78–856, § 1, eff. Sept. 14, 1973.

Formerly Ill.Rev.Stat.1991, ch. 95 ½, ¶ 601–2.09.

40/1–2.10. Operator

§ 1–2.10. "Operator" means every person who operates or is in actual physical control of a snowmobile.

P.A. 77–1312, § 1–2, eff. Aug. 27, 1971. Resectioned in part § 1–2.10 by P.A. 78–856, § 1, eff. Sept. 14, 1973.

Formerly Ill.Rev.Stat.1991, ch. 95 ½, ¶ 601–2.10.

40/1–2.11. Owner

§ 1–2.11. "Owner" means a person, other than a lien holder, having title to a snowmobile. The term includes a person entitled to the use or possession of a snowmobile subject to an interest in another person, reserved or created by agreement and securing payment or performance of an obligation, but the term excludes a lessee under a lease not intended as security.

P.A. 77–1312, § 1–2, eff. Aug. 27, 1971. Resectioned in part § 1–2.11 by P.A. 78–856, § 1, eff. Sept. 14, 1973.

Formerly Ill.Rev.Stat.1991, ch. 95 ½, ¶ 601–2.11.

40/1–2.12. Person

§ 1–2.12. "Person" means an individual, partnership, firm, corporation, association, or other entity.

P.A. 77–1312, § 1–2, eff. Aug. 27, 1971. Resectioned in part § 1–2.12 by P.A. 78–856, § 1, eff. Sept. 14, 1973.

Formerly Ill.Rev.Stat.1991, ch. 95 ½, ¶ 601–2.12.

40/1-2.13. Register

§ 1-2.13. "Register" means the act of assigning a registration number to a snowmobile.

P.A. 77-1312, § 1-2, eff. Aug. 27, 1971. Resectioned in part § 1-2.13 by P.A. 78-856, § 1, eff. Sept. 14, 1973.

Formerly Ill.Rev.Stat.1991, ch. 95 ½, ¶ 601-2.13.

40/1-2.14. Roadway

§ 1-2.14. "Roadway" means that portion of a highway improved, designed or ordinarily used for vehicular travel, exclusive of the berm or shoulder. In the event a highway includes 2 or more separate roadways the term "roadway" as used in this Act refers to any such roadway separately but not to all such roadways collectively.

P.A. 77-1312, § 1-2, eff. Aug. 27, 1971. Resectioned in part § 1.14 by P.A. 78-856, § 1, eff. Sept. 14, 1973. Renumbered § 1-2.14 and amended by P.A. 79-885, § 1, eff. Oct. 1, 1975.

Formerly Ill.Rev.Stat.1991, ch. 95 ½, ¶ 601-2.14.

40/1-2.15. Snowmobile

§ 1-2.15. "Snowmobile" means a self-propelled device designed for travel on snow or ice or natural terrain steered by skis or runners, and supported in part by skis, belts, or cleats.

P.A. 77-1312, § 1-2, eff. Aug. 27, 1971. Resectioned in part § 1-2.15 by P.A. 78-856, § 1, eff. Sept. 14, 1973.

Formerly Ill.Rev.Stat.1991, ch. 95 ½, ¶ 601-2.15.

40/1-3. Application and jurisdiction

§ 1-3. Application and jurisdiction. The Department shall, for purposes of this Act, have the power, duty, and authority to administer and enforce all statutes, rules and regulations, except as otherwise provided by statute, relating to the operation and use of snowmobiles within the state.

P.A. 77-1312, § 1-3, eff. Aug. 27, 1971.

Formerly Ill.Rev.Stat.1991, ch. 95 ½, ¶ 601-3.

ARTICLE II. ENFORCEMENT—INSPECTION—PROSECUTIONS

40/2-1. Enforcement

§ 2-1. Enforcement. It is the duty of all Conservation Police Officers and all sheriffs, deputy sheriffs, and other police officers to arrest any person detected in violation of any of the provisions of this Act. It is further the duty of all such officers to make prompt investigation of any violation of the provisions of this Act reported by any other person, and to cause a complaint to be filed before the circuit court if there seems just ground for such complaint and evidence procurable to support the same.

P.A. 77-1312, § 2-1, eff. Aug. 27, 1971. Amended by P.A. 79-885, § 1, eff. Oct. 1, 1975.

Formerly Ill.Rev.Stat.1991, ch. 95 ½, ¶ 602-1.

40/2-2. Inspection

§ 2-2. Inspection. Agents of the Department or other duly authorized police officers may stop and inspect any snowmobile at any time for the purpose of determining if the provisions of this Act are being complied with. If the inspecting officer or agent discovers any violation of the provisions of this Act, he must issue a summons to the operator of such snowmobile requiring that the operator appear before the circuit court for the county within which the offense was committed.

Every snowmobile subject to this Act, if under way and upon being hailed by a designated law enforcement officer, must stop immediately.

P.A. 77-1312, § 2-2, eff. Aug. 27, 1971.

Formerly Ill.Rev.Stat.1991, ch. 95 ½, ¶ 602-2.

40/2-3. Prosecutions

§ 2-3. Prosecutions. All prosecutions under this Act shall be brought in the name and by the authority of the People of the State of Illinois before the circuit court having jurisdiction under the law relative to the enforcement of the provisions hereof. It is the duty of all State's Attorneys to enforce this Act in their respective counties and to prosecute all persons charged with violating the provisions hereof.

P.A. 77-1312, § 2-3, eff. Aug. 27, 1971.

Formerly Ill.Rev.Stat.1991, ch. 95 ½, ¶ 602-3.

40/2-4. Resistance to officers

§ 2-4. Resistance to officers. It is unlawful for any person to resist or obstruct any officer or employee of the Department in the discharge of his duties under this Act.

P.A. 77-1312, § 2-4, eff. Aug. 27, 1971.

Formerly Ill.Rev.Stat.1991, ch. 95 ½, ¶ 602-4.

40/2-5. False representation

§ 2-5. False representation. It is unlawful for any person to represent himself falsely to be an officer or employee of the Department or to assume to act as such without having been duly appointed and employed as such.

P.A. 77-1312, § 2-5, eff. Aug. 27, 1971.

Formerly Ill.Rev.Stat.1991, ch. 95 ½, ¶ 602-5.

ARTICLE III. REGISTRATION OF SNOWMOBILES

40/3-1. Operation of Unnumbered Snowmobiles

§ 3-1. Operation of Unnumbered Snowmobiles. Except as hereinafter provided, no person shall, after the effective date of this Act, operate any snowmobile within this State unless such snowmobile has been registered and numbered in accordance with the provisions of this Article, and unless

(1) the certificate of number awarded to such snowmobile is in full force and effect.

P.A. 77-1312, § 3-1, eff. Aug. 27, 1971. Amended by P.A. 81-702, § 1, eff. Jan. 1, 1981.

Formerly Ill.Rev.Stat.1991, ch. 95 ½, ¶ 603-1.

40/3-2. Identification Number Application

§ 3-2. Identification Number Application. The owner of each snowmobile requiring numbering by this State shall file an application for number with the Department on forms approved by it. The application shall be signed by the owner of the snowmobile and shall be accompanied by a fee of $18. When a snowmobile dealer sells a snowmobile the dealer shall, at the time of sale, require the buyer to complete an application for the registration certificate, collect the required fee and mail the application and fee to the Department no later than 14 days after the date of sale. Combination application-receipt forms shall be provided by the Department and the dealer shall furnish the buyer with the completed receipt showing that application for registration has been made. This completed receipt shall be in the possession of the user of the snowmobile until the registration certificate is received. No snowmobile dealer may charge an additional fee to the buyer for performing this service required under this subsection. However, no purchaser exempted under Section 3-11 of this Act shall be charged any fee or be subject to the other requirements of this Section. The application form shall so state in clear language the requirements of this Section and the penalty for violation near the place on the application form provided for indicating the intention to register in another jurisdiction. Each dealer shall maintain, for one year, a record in a form prescribed by the Department for each snowmobile sold. These records shall be open to inspection by the Department. Upon receipt of the application in approved form the Department shall enter the same upon the records of its office and issue to the applicant a certificate of number stating the number awarded to the snowmobile and the name and address of the owner.

P.A. 77-1312, § 3-2, eff. Aug. 27, 1971. Amended by P.A. 81-702, § 1, eff. Jan. 1, 1981; P.A. 82-195, § 1, eff. April 1, 1982; P.A. 84-151, § 2, eff. Jan. 1, 1986; P.A. 84-973, § 2, eff. Jan. 1, 1986; P.A. 92-174, § 5, eff. July 26, 2001.

Formerly Ill.Rev.Stat.1991, ch. 95 ½, ¶ 603-2.

40/3-3. Identification Number Display

§ 3-3. Identification Number Display. The Department shall issue to the snowmobile owner two registration expiration decals with the number awarded to that snowmobile imprinted upon the decals. The owner shall apply these decals on each side of the cowling of such snowmobile. The certificate of number shall be pocket size and shall be available at all times for inspection on the snowmobile for which issued, whenever such snowmobile is in operation.

P.A. 77-1312, § 3-3, eff. Aug. 27, 1971. Amended by P.A. 81-702, § 1, eff. Jan. 1, 1981; P.A. 81-1509, Art. II, § 73, eff. Sept. 26, 1980.

Formerly Ill.Rev.Stat.1991, ch. 95 ½, ¶ 603-3.

40/3-4. Destruction, sale, transfer or abandonment

§ 3-4. Destruction, sale, transfer or abandonment. The owner of any snowmobile shall within 15 days notify the Department if such snowmobile is destroyed or abandoned, or is sold or transferred either wholly or in part to another person or persons. In all such cases, the notice shall be accompanied by a surrender of the certificate of number. When the surrender of the certificate is by reason of the snowmobile being destroyed or abandoned, the Department shall cancel the certificate and enter such fact in its records. The Department shall be notified in writing of any change of address. Should the owner desire a new certificate of number, showing the new address, he shall surrender his old certificate and notify the Department of the new address, remitting one dollar to cover the issuance of a new certificate of number. If the surrender is by reason of a sale or transfer either wholly or in part to another person or persons, the owner surrendering the certificate shall state to the Department, under oath, the name of the purchaser or transferee.

P.A. 77-1312, § 3-4, eff. Aug. 27, 1971.

Formerly Ill.Rev.Stat.1991, ch. 95 ½, ¶ 603-4.

40/3-5. Transfer of Identification Number

§ 3-5. Transfer of Identification Number. The purchaser of a snowmobile shall, within 15 days after acquiring same, make application to the Department for the transfer to him of the certificate of number issued to the snowmobile, giving his name, his address and the number of the snowmobile. The purchaser shall apply for a transfer-renewal for a fee of $18 for approximately 3 years. All transfers will bear September 30 expiration dates in the calendar year of expiration. Upon receipt of the application and fee, the Department shall transfer the certificate of number issued to the snowmobile to the new owner. Unless the application is made and fee paid within 30 days, the snowmobile shall be deemed to be without certificate of number and it shall be unlawful for any person to operate the snowmobile until the certificate is issued.

P.A. 77-1312, § 3-5, eff. Aug. 27, 1971. Amended by P.A. 82-195, § 1, eff. April 1, 1982; P.A. 84-151, § 2, eff. Jan. 1, 1986; P.A. 84-973, § 2, eff. Jan. 1, 1986; P.A. 87-1109, § 2, eff. April 1, 1993; P.A. 92-174, § 5, eff. July 26, 2001.

Formerly Ill.Rev.Stat.1991, ch. 95 ½, ¶ 603-5.

40/3-6. Loss of certificate

§ 3-6. Loss of certificate. Should a certificate of number or registration expiration decal become lost, destroyed, or mutilated beyond legibility, the owner of the snowmobile shall make application to the Department for the replacement of the certificate or decal, giving his name, address, and the number of his snowmobile and shall at the same time pay to the Department a fee of $1.

P.A. 77-1312, § 3-6, eff. Aug. 27, 1971.

Formerly Ill.Rev.Stat.1991, ch. 95 ½, ¶ 603-6.

40/3-7. Department Records

§ 3-7. Department Records. All records of the Department made or kept under this Article shall be public records.

P.A. 77-1312, § 3-7, eff. Aug. 27, 1971. Amended by P.A. 79-885, § 1, eff. Oct. 1, 1975.

Formerly Ill.Rev.Stat.1991, ch. 95 ½, ¶ 603-7.

40/3-8. Certificate of Number

§ 3-8. Certificate of Number. Every certificate of number awarded under this Act shall continue in full force and effect for approximately 3 years unless sooner terminated or discontinued in accordance with this Act. All new certificates issued will bear September 30 expiration dates in the calendar year 3 years after the issuing date. Provided however, that the Department may, for purposes of implementing this Section, adopt rules for phasing in the issuance of new certificates and provide for 1, 2 or 3 year expiration dates and pro-rated payments or charges for each registration.

All certificates shall be renewed for 3 years from the nearest September 30 for a fee of $18. All certificates will be considered invalid after October 15 of the year of expiration. All certificates expiring in a given year shall be renewed between April 1 and September 30 of that year, in order to allow sufficient time for processing.

The Department shall issue "registration expiration decals" with all new certificates of number, all certificates of number transferred and renewed, and all certificates of number renewed. The decals issued for each year shall be of a different and distinct color from the decals of each year currently displayed. The decals shall be affixed to each side of the cowling of the snowmobile in the manner prescribed by the rules and regulations of the Department. The Department shall fix a day and month of the year on which certificates of number due to expire shall lapse and no longer be of any force and effect unless renewed pursuant to this Act.

No number or registration expiration decal, except a sticker or number which may be required by a political subdivision, municipality, or state, other than the registration expiration decal issued to a snowmobile or granted reciprocity pursuant to this Act, shall be painted, attached, or otherwise displayed on either side of the cowling of such snowmobile.

A dealer engaged in the manufacture, sale, or leasing of snowmobiles required to be numbered hereunder, upon application to the Department upon forms prescribed by it, may obtain certificates of number for use in the testing or demonstrating of such snowmobiles upon payment of $18 for each registration. Certificates of number so issued may be used by the applicant in the testing or demonstrating of snowmobiles by temporary placement of the registration expiration decals assigned by such certificates on the snowmobile so tested or demonstrated.

P.A. 77-1312, § 3-8, eff. Aug. 27, 1971. Amended by P.A. 78-856, § 1, eff. July 1, 1974; P.A. 82-195, § 1, eff. April 1, 1982; P.A. 84-151, § 2, eff. Jan. 1, 1986; P.A. 84-973, § 2, eff. Jan. 1, 1986; P.A. 92-174, § 5, eff. July 26, 2001.

Formerly Ill.Rev.Stat.1991, ch. 95 ½, ¶ 603-8.

40/3-9. Registration List

§ 3-9. Registration List.

A snowmobile registration list may be furnished for official use at no charge only to such federal, state, county and municipal enforcement agencies as may require such data. A snowmobile registration list may be furnished, at the cost of reproduction, to statewide not-for-profit Illinois snowmobile organizations for use only with educational programs.

P.A. 77-1312, § 3-9, eff. Aug. 27, 1971. Amended by P.A. 92-174, § 5, eff. July 26, 2001.

Formerly Ill.Rev.Stat.1991, ch. 95 ½, ¶ 603-9.

40/3-10. Penalty

§ 3-10. Penalty. No person shall at any time falsely alter or change in any manner the certificate of number issued under the provisions hereof, or falsify any record required by this Act, or counterfeit any form of license provided for by this Act.

P.A. 77-1312, § 3-10, eff. Aug. 27, 1971.

Formerly Ill.Rev.Stat.1991, ch. 95 ½, ¶ 603-10.

40/3-11. Exception from numbering provisions of this Act

§ 3-11. Exception from numbering provisions of this Act. A snowmobile shall not be required to be numbered under this Act if it is:

A. Owned and used by the United States, another state, or a political subdivision thereof, but such snowmobiles shall display the name of the owner on the cowling thereof.

B. Covered by a valid registration or license of another state, province or country which is the domicile of the owner of the snowmobile and is not operated within this State on more than 30 consecutive days in any calendar year.

C. Owned and operated on lands owned by the owner or operator or on lands to which he has a contractual right other than as a member of a club or association, provided the snowmobile is not operated elsewhere within the state.

D. Used only on international or national competition circuits in events for which written permission has been obtained by the sponsoring or sanctioning body from the governmental unit having jurisdiction over the location of any event held in this State.

E. Owned by persons domiciled in Illinois but used entirely in another jurisdiction when such owner has complied with the provisions of Section 3-2 of this Act.

F. Designed for use by small children primarily as a toy and used only on private property and not on any public use trail.

P.A. 77-1312, § 3-11, eff. Aug. 27, 1971. Amended by P.A. 78-856, § 1, eff. July 1, 1974; P.A. 81-702, § 1, eff. Jan. 1, 1981; P.A. 92-174, § 5, eff. July 26, 2001.

Formerly Ill.Rev.Stat.1991, ch. 95 ½, ¶ 603-11.

ARTICLE IV. SNOWMOBILE EQUIPMENT

40/4-1. Equipment

§ 4-1. Equipment. All snowmobiles operating within the State of Illinois shall be equipped with:

A. At least one white head-lamp having a minimum candlepower of sufficient intensity to exhibit a white light plainly visible from a distance of at least 500 feet ahead during hours of darkness under normal atmospheric conditions. If a snowmobile is equipped with a single beam lamp, such lamp shall be so aimed that when the vehicle is loaded none of the high intensity portion of the light, at a distance of 25 feet in front of the vehicle, projects higher than the level of the center of the lamp from which it originates.

B. At least one red tail lamp having a minimum candlepower of sufficient intensity to exhibit a red light plainly visible from a distance of five hundred feet to the rear during hours of darkness under normal atmospheric conditions.

C. A brake system in good mechanical condition.

D. Reflective material of a minimum area of 16 square inches mounted on each side of the cowling. Identifying numbers may be included in computing the required 16 square inch area.

E. Adequate sound suppression equipment. No snowmobile manufactured after June 1, 1972, shall be sold or offered for sale, unless it is equipped with sound suppression devices that limit total machine noise in accordance with noise pollution standards established pursuant to the Environmental Protection Act.[1]

P.A. 77-1312, § 4-1, eff. Aug. 27, 1971. Amended by P.A. 82-417, § 1, eff. Sept. 4, 1981.

Formerly Ill.Rev.Stat.1991, ch. 95 ½, ¶ 604-1.

[1] 415 ILCS 5/1 et seq.

40/4-2. Inspection and testing

§ 4-2. Inspection and testing. The Department may adopt rules and regulations with respect to the inspection of snowmobiles and the testing of machine noise.

P.A. 77-1312, § 4-2, eff. Aug. 27, 1971.

Formerly Ill.Rev.Stat.1991, ch. 95 ½, ¶ 604-2.

40/4-3. Sale prohibited

§ 4-3. Sale prohibited. No person shall have for sale, sell, or offer for sale in this State any snowmobile which fails to comply with Section 4-1, or which does not comply with the specifications for such equipment required by the rules and regulations of the Department after the effective date of such rules and regulations.

P.A. 77-1312, § 4-3, eff. Aug. 27, 1971.

Formerly Ill.Rev.Stat.1991, ch. 95 ½, ¶ 604-3.

40/4-4. Racing machines

§ 4-4. Racing machines. Snowmobiles used only on international or national competition circuits in events for which written permission has been obtained by the sponsoring or sanctioning body from the governmental unit having jurisdiction over the location of any event held in this State are exempt from the provisions of this Article.

P.A. 77-1312, § 4-4, eff. Aug. 27, 1971. Amended by P.A. 78-856, § 1, eff. Sept. 14, 1973.

Formerly Ill.Rev.Stat.1991, ch. 95 ½, ¶ 604-4.

ARTICLE V. CONTROL PROVISIONS

40/5-1. Operation Generally

§ 5-1. Operation Generally. It is unlawful for any person to drive or operate any snowmobile in the following ways:

A. At a rate of speed too fast for conditions and the fact that the speed of the snowmobile does not exceed the applicable maximum speed limit allowed does not relieve the driver from the duty to decrease speed as may be necessary to avoid colliding with any person or vehicle or object within legal requirements and the duty of all persons to use due care.

B. In a careless, reckless, or negligent manner.

C. (Blank)

D. At any time without at least one lighted headlamp and one lighted tail lamp on the snowmobile.

E. Within any nature preserve.

F. On the tracks or right of way of an operating railroad.

G. In any tree nursery or planting in a manner which damages or destroys growing stock, or creates a substantial risk thereto.

H. On private property, without the written or verbal consent of the owner or lessee thereof. Any person operating a snowmobile upon lands of another shall stop and identify himself upon the request of the landowner or his duly authorized representative, and, if requested to do so by the landowner shall promptly remove the snowmobile from the premises.

I. Notwithstanding any other law to the contrary, an owner, lessee, or occupant of premises owes no duty of care to keep the premises safe for entry or use by others for snowmobiling, or to give warning of any condition, use, structure or activity on such premises. This subsection does not apply where permission to snowmobile is given for a valuable consideration other than to this State, any political subdivision or municipality thereof, or any landowner who is paid with funds from the Snowmobile Trail Establishment Fund. In the case of land leased to the State or a subdivision thereof, any consideration received is not valuable consideration within the meaning of this section. Nothing in this section limits in any way liability which otherwise exists for willful or malicious failure to guard or warn against a dangerous condition, use, structure, or activity.

J. Notwithstanding any other law to the contrary, an owner, lessee or occupant of premises who gives permission to another to snowmobile upon such premises does not thereby extend any assurance that the premises are safe for such purpose, or assume responsibility for or incur liability for any injury to person or property caused by any act or omission of persons to whom the permission to snowmobile is granted. This subsection shall not apply where permission to snowmobile is given for a valuable consideration other than to this State, any political subdivision or municipality thereof, or any landowner who is paid with funds from the Snowmobile Trail Establishment Fund. In the case of land leased to the State or a subdivision thereof, any consideration received is not valuable consideration within the meaning of this section. Nothing in this section limits in any way liability which otherwise exists for willful or malicious failure to guard or warn against a dangerous condition, use, structure, or activity.

K. On the frozen surface of public waters of this State within 100 feet of a person, including a skater not in or upon a snowmobile; within 100 feet of a person engaged in fishing, except at the minimum speed required to maintain forward movement of the snowmobile; on an area which has been cleared of snow for skating purposes unless the area is necessary for access to the frozen waters of this State.

L. Within 100 feet of a dwelling between midnight and 6 a.m. at a speed greater than the minimum required to maintain forward movement of the snowmobile. This provision would not apply on private property where verbal or written consent of the owner or lessee has been granted to snowmobile upon such private property or frozen waters of this State.

M. Notwithstanding any other law to the contrary, any owner, lessee or occupant of premises or any person or association who, with the permission of the owner of the premises, places, maintains or displays a sign, signal, marking or device to give warning of any unsafe condition on the premises for snowmobiling shall not be liable for any personal injuries allegedly caused by his or her acts or omissions in providing such warning unless the alleged misconduct was willful or malicious. This subsection shall not apply where the owner, occupant or lessee of the premises grants express permission for snowmobiling in exchange for valuable consideration. However, this subsection will apply where such consideration is given to such owner, occupant or lessee by the State or one of its political subdivisions.

N. Notwithstanding any other law or Section of this Act to the contrary, the State and any political subdivision or municipality thereof owes no duty of care to keep the premises safe for entry or use by others for snowmobiling or to guard against or give warnings of any condition, use, structure or activity on property in which the State and any political subdivision or municipality thereof has any interest.

P.A. 77-1312, § 5-1, eff. Aug. 27, 1971. Amended by P.A. 78-856, § 1, eff. July 1, 1974; P.A. 81-701, § 1, eff. Jan. 1, 1980; P.A. 81-915, § 1, eff. Jan. 1, 1980; P.A. 81-1509, Art. I, § 58, eff. Sept. 26, 1980; P.A. 82-195, § 1, eff. April 1, 1982; P.A. 82-993, § 1, eff. Sept. 10, 1982; P.A. 83-1044, § 1, eff. Jan. 5, 1984; P.A. 84-151, § 2, eff. Jan. 1, 1986; P.A. 84-973, § 2, eff. Jan. 1, 1986; P.A. 89-55, § 5, eff. Jan. 1, 1996.

Formerly Ill.Rev.Stat.1991, ch. 95 ½, ¶ 605-1.

40/5-2. Operation on Highways

§ 5-2. Operation on Highways. It is unlawful for any person to drive or operate any snowmobile on a highway in this State except as follows:

A. On highways other than tollways, interstate highways and fully or limited access-controlled highways snowmobiles may make a direct crossing provided:

(1) the crossing is made at an angle of approximately 90 degrees to the direction of the highway and at a place where no obstruction prevents a quick and safe crossing; and

(2) the snowmobile is brought to a complete stop before crossing a roadway; and

(3) the operator yields the right of way to all oncoming traffic which constitutes a hazard.

B. On highways other than tollways, interstate highways and fully or limited access-controlled highways snowmobiles may be operated not less than 10 feet from the roadway and in the same direction as traffic. On such highways, other than State highways, the corporate authorities of a city, village or incorporated town may adopt ordinances providing for variance from the 10-foot separation requirement of this subsection, including ordinances permitting the operation of snowmobiles upon the roadways of such highways, other than State highways, within city, village or town limits. In addition, the corporate authorities of any unit of local government with jurisdiction over such highways may adopt ordinances authorizing the operation of snowmobiles within 10 feet of the roadway to avoid obstructions or hazardous terrain. Other than for State highways, corporate authorities of a city, village or incorporated town may adopt ordinances providing for trails, including the designation of the roadways of highways referred to in this paragraph as snowmobile trails, and regulating snowmobile operation within city, village or town limits.

C. On highways other than tollways, interstate highways and fully or limited access-controlled highways snowmobiles may be operated on roadways when it is necessary to cross a bridge or culvert or when it is impracticable to gain immediate access to an area adjacent to a highway where a snowmobile is to be operated.

D. Corporate authorities of a city, village or incorporated town may by ordinance designate 1 or more specific public highways or streets within their jurisdiction as egress and ingress routes for the use of snowmobiles. In the event that such public highways or streets are under the jurisdiction of the State of Illinois, express written consent of the Illinois Department of Transportation shall be required. Corporate authorities acting under the authority of this paragraph D shall erect and maintain signs giving proper notice thereof.

E. Snowmobiles may be lawfully driven or operated upon those highways where posted with signs giving proper notice and erected and maintained by the township road commissioner. A township or township road commissioner shall not be liable for any personal injuries caused as a result of the operation of a snowmobile on such highways. For purposes of this paragraph E, "highways" are defined as township roads pursuant to Section 2-205 of the Illinois Highway Code.[1]

P.A. 77-1312, § 5-2, eff. Aug. 27, 1971. Amended by P.A. 79-885, § 1, eff. Oct. 1, 1975; P.A. 81-828, § 1, eff. Jan. 1, 1980; P.A. 82-195, § 1, eff. April 1, 1982; P.A. 82-347, § 1, eff. Jan. 1, 1982; P.A. 82-377, § 1, eff. Sept. 2, 1981; P.A. 82-464, § 1, eff. Sept. 15, 1981; P.A. 82-783, Art. III, § 38, eff. July 13, 1982; P.A. 83-789, § 1, eff. Jan. 1, 1983; P.A. 84-151, § 2, eff. Jan. 1, 1986; P.A. 84-973, § 2, eff. Jan. 1, 1986; P.A. 91-357, § 233, eff. July 29, 1999.

Formerly Ill.Rev.Stat.1991, ch. 95 ½, ¶ 605-2.

1 605 ILCS 5/2-205.

40/5-3. Youthful Operators

§ 5-3. Youthful Operators.

A. No person under 10 years of age may operate a snowmobile, other than machines designed for use by small children primarily as a toy and used only on private property and not on any public use trail.

B. Persons at least 10 and less than 12 years of age may operate a snowmobile only if they are either accompanied on the snowmobile by a parent or guardian or a person at least 18 years of age designated by a parent or guardian.

C. Persons at least 12 and less than 16 years of age may operate a snowmobile only if they are either accompanied on the snowmobile by a parent or guardian or a person at least 16 years of age designated by a parent or guardian, or such operator is in possession of a certificate issued by the Department authorizing the holder to operate snowmobiles.

D. Any person who operates a snowmobile on a highway as provided in Section 5-2 shall (1) possess a valid motor vehicle driver's license; or (2) possess a safety certificate as provided for in this Section. Any such person less than 16 years of age shall also be under the immediate supervision of a parent or guardian or a person at least 18 years of age designated by the parent or guardian.

E. Violations of this Section done with the knowledge of a parent or guardian shall be deemed a violation by the parent or guardian and punishable under Article X of this Act.

F. The department shall establish a program of instruction on snowmobile laws, regulations, safety and related subjects. It is unlawful for any person under 16 years of age to operate a snowmobile on a public highway in this State.

The program shall be conducted by instructors certified by the department. The department may procure liability insurance coverage for certified instructors for work within the scope of their duties under this section. Persons satisfactorily completing this program shall receive certification from the department. The department may charge each person who enrolls in the course an instruction fee of $2.50. If a fee is authorized by the department, the department shall authorize instructors conducting such courses meeting standards established by it to retain $1 of the fee to defray expenses incurred locally to operate the program. The remaining $1.50 of the fee shall be retained by the department to defray a part of its expenses incurred to operate the safety and accident reporting program. A person over the age of 12 years but under the age of 16 years who holds a valid certificate issued by another state or province of the Dominion of Canada need not obtain a certificate from the department if the course content of the program in such other state or province substantially meets that established by the department under this section. A certificate issued by the Department, or by another State or a province of the Dominion of Canada, shall not constitute a valid motor vehicle operator's license for the purpose of this Section.

P.A. 77-1312, § 5-3, eff. Aug. 27, 1971. Amended by P.A. 79-1058, § 1, eff. Oct. 1, 1975; P.A. 84-151, § 2, eff. Jan. 1, 1986; P.A. 84-973, § 2, eff. Jan. 1, 1986; P.A. 85-293, Art. III, § 22, eff. Sept. 8, 1987; P.A. 92-174, § 5, eff. July 26, 2001.

Formerly Ill.Rev.Stat.1991, ch. 95 ½, ¶ 605-3.

40/5-4. Operation on Ice

§ 5-4. Operation on Ice.

Snowmobiles may be operated on the frozen waters of this State subject to the provisions of Section 5-1 and the rules and regulations of the Department.

P.A. 77-1312, § 5-4, eff. Aug. 27, 1971. Amended by P.A. 89-55, § 5, eff. Jan. 1, 1996.

Formerly Ill.Rev.Stat.1991, ch. 95 ½, ¶ 605-4.

40/5-5. Special events

§ 5-5. Special events. Nothing contained in this Article shall be construed to prohibit any local authority of this State from designating a special snowmobile event. In such case the provisions of this article shall not apply to areas or highways under the jurisdiction of that local authority.

P.A. 77-1312, § 5-5, eff. Aug. 27, 1971.

Formerly Ill.Rev.Stat.1991, ch. 95 ½, ¶ 605-5.

40/5-6. Other Prohibition

§ 5-6. Other Prohibition. A. No person, except persons permitted by law, shall operate or ride any snowmobile with any firearm in his possession unless it is unloaded and enclosed in a carrying case, or any bow unless it is unstrung in a carrying case.

B. No person shall operate any snowmobile emitting pollutants in accordance with standards established pursuant to the Environmental Protection Act.[1]

C. No person shall deposit from a snowmobile on the snow, ice, or ground surface, trash, glass, garbage, insoluble material, or other offensive matter.

D. No person shall use a snowmobile to take, pursue or intentionally harass or disturb wildlife as defined in Section 1.2t of the Wildlife Code, except such restriction shall not apply to any person acting to protect livestock from predatory animals.

P.A. 77-1312, § 5-6, eff. Aug. 12, 1971. Amended by P.A. 82-629, § 2, eff. Sept. 24, 1981.

Formerly Ill.Rev.Stat.1991, ch. 95 ½, ¶ 605-6.

[1] 415 ILCS 5/1 et seq.

40/5-7. Operating a snowmobile while under the influence of alcohol or other drug; criminal penalties; suspension of operating privileges

§ 5-7. Operating a snowmobile while under the influence of alcohol or other drug; criminal penalties; suspension of operating privileges.

(a) A person may not operate a snowmobile within this State while:

1. The alcohol concentration in that person's blood or breath is a concentration at which driving a motor vehicle is prohibited under subdivision (1) of subsection (a) of Section 11-501 of the Illinois Vehicle Code; [1]

2. The person is under the influence of alcohol;

3. The person is under the influence of any other drug or combination of drugs to a degree that renders that person incapable of safely operating a snowmobile;

4. The person is under the combined influence of alcohol and any other drug or drugs to a degree that renders that person incapable of safely operating a snowmobile; or

5. There is any amount of a drug, substance, or compound in that person's blood or urine resulting from the unlawful use or consumption of cannabis listed in the Cannabis Control Act,[2] or controlled substance listed in the Illinois Controlled Substances Act.[3]

(b) The fact that a person charged with violating this Section is or has been legally entitled to use alcohol or other drugs does not constitute a defense against a charge of violating this Section.

(c) Every person convicted of violating this Section or a similar provision of a local ordinance is guilty of a Class A misdemeanor, except as otherwise provided in this Section.

(d) Every person convicted of violating this Section is guilty of a Class 4 felony if:

1. The person has a previous conviction under this Section; or

2. The offense results in personal injury where a person other than the operator suffers great bodily harm or permanent disability or disfigurement, when the violation was a proximate cause of the injuries. A person guilty of a Class 4 felony under this paragraph 2, if sentenced to a term of imprisonment, shall be sentenced to not less than one year nor more than 12 years.

(e) Every person convicted of violating this Section is guilty of a Class 2 felony if the offense results in the death of a person. A person guilty of a Class 2 felony under this subsection (e), if sentenced to a term of imprisonment, shall be sentenced to a term of not less than 3 years and not more than 14 years.

(f) In addition to any criminal penalties imposed, the Department of Conservation shall suspend the snowmobile operation privileges of a person convicted of a misdemeanor under this Section for a period of one year or for a period of

5 years if the person is convicted of a felony under this Section.

P.A. 77-1312, § 5-7, added by P.A. 89-55, § 5, eff. Jan. 1, 1996. Amended by P.A. 90-215, § 5, eff. Jan. 1, 1998; P.A. 92-615, § 5, eff. Jan. 1, 2003.

1 625 ILCS 5/11-501.

2 720 ILCS 550/1 et seq.

3 720 ILCS 570/100 et seq.

40/5-7.1. Implied consent

§ 5-7.1. Implied consent.

(a) A person who operates a snowmobile in this State is deemed to have given consent to a chemical test or tests of blood, breath, or urine for the purpose of determining the alcohol or other drug content of that person's blood if arrested for a violation of Section 5-7. The test or tests shall be administered at the direction of the arresting officer. The law enforcement agency employing the officer shall designate which tests shall be administered. A urine test may be administered even after a blood or breath test or both has been administered.

(b) A person who is dead, unconscious, or who is otherwise in a condition rendering that person incapable of refusal, is deemed not to have withdrawn the consent provided in subsection (a).

(c) A person requested to submit to a test as provided in this Section shall be verbally advised by the law enforcement officer requesting the test that a refusal to submit to the test will result in suspension of that person's privilege to operate a snowmobile for a minimum of 2 years.

(d) Following this warning, if a person under arrest refuses upon the request of a law enforcement officer to submit to a test designated by the officer, no test may be given, but the law enforcement officer shall file with the clerk of the circuit court for the county in which the arrest was made, a sworn statement naming the person refusing to take and complete the test or tests requested under the provisions of this Section. The sworn statement shall identify the arrested person, the person's current residence address and shall specify that a refusal by that person to take the test or tests was made. The sworn statement shall include a statement that the officer had reasonable cause to believe the person was operating the snowmobile within this State while under the influence of alcohol or other drug and that test or tests were requested as an incident to and following the lawful arrest for an offense as defined in Section 5-7 or a similar provision of a local ordinance, and that the person, after being arrested for an offense arising out of acts alleged to have been committed while operating a snowmobile, refused to submit to and complete a test or tests as requested by the law enforcement officer.

(e) The clerk shall notify the person in writing that the person's privilege to operate a snowmobile will be suspended for a minimum of 2 years unless, within 28 days from the date of mailing of the notice, that person requests a hearing in writing.

If the person desires a hearing, the person shall file a complaint in the circuit court in the county where that person was arrested within 28 days from the date of mailing of the notice. The hearing shall proceed in the court in the same manner as other civil proceedings. The hearing shall cover only the following issues: (1) whether the person was placed under arrest for an offense as defined in Section 5-7 or a similar provision of a local ordinance as evidenced by the issuance of a uniform citation; (2) whether the arresting officer had reasonable grounds to believe that the person was operating a snowmobile while under the influence of alcohol or other drug; and (3) whether that person refused to submit and complete the test or tests upon the request of the law enforcement officer. Whether the person was informed that the person's privilege to operate a snowmobile would be suspended if that person refused to submit to the test or tests may not be an issue in the hearing.

If the court finds against the person on the issues before the court, the clerk shall immediately notify the Department of Conservation of the court's decision, and the Department shall suspend the snowmobile operation privileges of that person for at least 2 years.

(f) If the person fails to request a hearing in writing within 28 days of the date of mailing of the notice, the clerk shall immediately notify the Department of Conservation that no request for a hearing was received within the statutory time period, and the Department shall suspend the snowmobile operation privileges of that person for at least 2 years.

(g) A person must submit to each test offered by the law enforcement officer in order to comply with implied consent provisions of this Section.

(h) The provision of Section 11-501.2 of the Illinois Vehicle Code [1] concerning the certification and use of chemical tests applies to the use of those tests under this Section.

P.A. 77-1312, § 5-7.1, added by P.A. 89-55, § 5, eff. Jan. 1, 1996.

1 625 ILCS 5/11-501.2.

40/5-7.2. Chemical and other tests

§ 5-7.2. Chemical and other tests.

(a) Upon the trial of a civil or criminal action or proceeding arising out of acts alleged to have been committed while under the influence of alcohol, the concentration of alcohol in the person's blood or breath at the time alleged as shown by analysis of the person's blood, urine, breath, or other bodily substance gives rise to the presumptions specified in subdivisions 1, 2, and 3 of subsection (b) of Section 11-501.2 of the Illinois Vehicle Code.[1]

(b) The provisions of subsection (a) shall not be construed as limiting the introduction of any other relevant evidence bearing upon the question whether the person was under the influence of alcohol.

(c) If a person under arrest refuses to submit to a chemical test under the provisions of Section 5-7.1, evidence of refusal is admissible in a civil or criminal action or proceeding arising out of acts alleged to have been committed while the person under the influence of alcohol or other drugs was operating a snowmobile.

P.A. 77-1312, § 5-7.2, added by P.A. 89-55, § 5, eff. Jan. 1, 1996. Amended by P.A. 90-215, § 5, eff. Jan. 1, 1998.

1 625 ILCS 5/11-501.2.

40/5-7.3. Supervision of operator; notification; 6 hour operating limitation

§ 5-7.3. Supervision of operator; notification; 6 hour operating limitation.

(a) The owner of a snowmobile or person given supervisory authority over a snowmobile, may not knowingly permit a snowmobile to be operated by a person under the influence of alcohol or other drug.

(b) Whenever a person is convicted of a violation of Section 5-7, the court shall notify the Office of Law Enforcement of the Department with the records essential for the performance of the Department's duties to monitor and enforce an order of suspension or revocation concerning the person's privilege to operate a snowmobile.

(c) A person who has been arrested and charged with violating Section 5-7 may not operate a snowmobile within this State for a period of 6 hours after that person's arrest.

P.A. 77-1312, § 5-7.3, added by P.A. 89-55, § 5, eff. Jan. 1, 1996.

40/5-7.4. Admissibility of blood alcohol tests

§ 5-7.4. Admissibility of blood alcohol tests.

(a) Notwithstanding any other provision of law, the written results of blood alcohol tests conducted upon persons receiving medical treatment in a hospital emergency room are admissible in evidence as a business record exception to the hearsay rule only in prosecutions for a violation of Section 5-7 of this Act or a similar provision of a local ordinance or in prosecutions for reckless homicide brought under the Criminal Code of 1961. [1] The results of the tests are admissible only when each of the following criteria are met:

1. The blood alcohol tests were ordered by a physician on duty at the hospital emergency room and were performed in the regular course of providing emergency medical treatment in order to assist the physician in diagnosis or treatment;

2. The blood alcohol tests were performed by the hospital's own laboratory; and

3. The written results of the blood alcohol tests were received and considered by the physician on duty at the hospital emergency room to assist that physician in diagnosis or treatment.

(b) The confidentiality provisions of law pertaining to medical records and medical treatment are not applicable with regard to blood alcohol tests performed under the provisions of this Section in prosecutions as specified in subsection (a) of this Section. No person shall be liable for civil damages as a result of the evidentiary use of blood alcohol tests results under this Section or as a result of that person's testimony made available under this Section.

P.A. 77-1312, § 40/5-7.4, added by P.A. 89-55, § 5, eff. Jan. 1, 1996. Renumbered § 5-7.4 and amended by P.A. 89-626, Art. 3, § 3-38, eff. Aug. 9, 1996.

[1] 720 ILCS 5/1-1 et seq.

40/5-7.5. Preliminary breath screening test

§ 5-7.5. Preliminary breath screening test. If a law enforcement officer has probable cause to believe that a person is violating or has violated Section 5-7 or a similar provision of a local ordinance, the officer, before an arrest, may request the person to provide a sample of his or her breath for a preliminary breath screening test using a portable device approved by the Department of State Police. The results of this preliminary breath screening test may be used by the law enforcement officer for the purpose of assisting with the determination of whether to require a chemical test, as authorized under Sections 5-7.1 and 5-7.2 and the appropriate type of test to request. Any chemical test authorized under Sections 5-7.1 and 5-7.2 may be requested by the officer regardless of the result of the preliminary breath screening test if probable cause for an arrest exists. The result of a preliminary breath screening test may be used by the defendant as evidence in an administrative or court proceeding involving a violation of Section 5-7 or 5-7.1.

P.A. 77-1312, § 40/5-7.5, added by P.A. 89-55, § 5, eff. Jan. 1, 1996. Renumbered § 5-7.5 and amended by P.A. 89-626, Art. 3, § 3-38, eff. Aug. 9, 1996. Amended by P.A. 91-828, § 10, eff. Jan. 1, 2001.

ARTICLE VI. ACCIDENT REPORTS—OPERATOR'S RESPONSIBILITY—TRANSMITTAL OF INFORMATION

Section

40/6-1. Collisions, accidents, and casualties; reports

§ 6-1. Collisions, accidents, and casualties; reports.

A. The operator of a snowmobile involved in a collision, accident, or other casualty, shall render to other persons affected by this collision, accident, or other casualty such assistance as may be practicable and as may be necessary in order to save them from or minimize any danger caused by the collision, accident, or other casualty, and also shall give his name, address, and identification of his snowmobile to any person injured and to the owner of any property damaged in the collision, accident, or other casualty.

B. In the case of collision, accident, or other casualty involving the operation of a snowmobile, the operator thereof, if the collision, accident, or other casualty results in death or injury to a person or damage to property in excess of $750, shall file with the Department a full description of the collision, accident, or other casualty, including such information as the Department may, by regulation, require. Reports of such accidents must be filed with the Department on a Department Accident Report form within 5 days.

C. Reports of accidents resulting in personal injury, wherein a person is incapacitated for a period exceeding 72 hours, must be filed with the Department on a Department Accident Report form within 5 days. Accidents which result in loss of life shall be reported to the Department on a Department form within 48 hours.

D. All required accident reports and supplemental reports are without prejudice to the individual so reporting, and are for the confidential use of the Department, except that the Department may disclose the identity of a person involved in an accident when such identity is not otherwise known or when such person denies his presence at such accident. No such report may be used as evidence in any trial, civil or criminal, arising out of an accident, except that the Department must furnish upon demand of any person who has or claims to have made such a report, or upon demand of any court, a certificate showing that a specified accident report has or has not been made to the Department, solely to prove a compliance or a failure to comply with the requirements that such a report be made to the Department.

P.A. 77-1312, § 6-1, eff. Aug. 27, 1971. Amended by P.A. 92-174, § 5, eff. July 26, 2001.

Formerly Ill.Rev.Stat.1991, ch. 95 ½, ¶ 606-1.

40/6-2. Owner's and operator's responsibility

§ 6-2. Owner's and operator's responsibility. The owner and any operator of a snowmobile are jointly and severally liable for any injury or damage occasioned by the operation of such snowmobile.

P.A. 77–1312, § 6–2, eff. Aug. 27, 1971.

Formerly Ill.Rev.Stat.1991, ch. 95 ½, ¶ 606–2.

ARTICLE VII. LOCAL REGULATION

40/7–1. Local ordinances

§ 7–1. Local ordinances. This Act and other applicable laws of this State govern the operation, equipment, numbering and all other matters relating thereto whenever any snowmobile is operated within this State; but this Act does not prevent the adoption of any ordinance or local law by any political subdivision of the State relating to the operation and equipment of snowmobiles which is not inconsistent with this Act, amendments hereto or regulations issued hereunder. Such ordinances or local laws shall be operative only so long as they continue to be not inconsistent with this Act, amendments hereto or regulations issued hereunder. However, this Act is not a limit upon any home rule unit.

P.A. 77–1312, § 7–1, eff. Aug. 27, 1971. Amended by P.A. 78–856, § 1, eff. Sept. 14, 1973.

Formerly Ill.Rev.Stat.1991, ch. 95 ½, ¶ 607–1.

ARTICLE VIII. FILING OF REGULATIONS

40/8–1. Rules and regulations, filing

§ 8–1. Rules and regulations, filing. The implementation and administration of the provisions of this Act shall be by rules and regulations adopted by the Department of Natural Resources. A copy of the rules and regulations adopted pursuant to this Act, and of any amendments thereto, shall be filed in the office of the Department and in the office of the Secretary of State. Rules and regulations shall be published by the Department in a convenient form.

P.A. 77–1312, § 8–1, eff. Aug. 27, 1971. Amended by P.A. 84–151, § 2, eff. Jan. 1, 1986; P.A. 84–973, § 2, eff. Jan. 1, 1986; P.A. 89–445, § 9A–88, eff. Feb. 7, 1996.

Formerly Ill.Rev.Stat.1991, ch. 95 ½, ¶ 608–1.

ARTICLE IX. SNOWMOBILE REGISTRATION AND SAFETY ACT REVENUES

40/9–1. Special fund

§ 9–1. Special fund. Except as provided in Section 9–2, all revenues received under this Act, including registration fees, fines, bond forfeitures or other income of whatever kind or nature shall be deposited in the State Treasury in "The State Boating Act Fund". Appropriations of revenue received as a result of this Act from "The State Boating Act Fund" shall be made only to the Department for administering the registration of snowmobiles, snowmobile safety, snowmobile safety education and enforcement provisions of this Act or for any purpose related or connected thereto, including the construction, maintenance, and rehabilitation of snowmobile recreation areas or any other facilities for the use of snowmobiles, including plans and specifications, engineering surveys and supervision and land acquisition where necessary, and including the disbursement of funds to political subdivisions upon written application to and subsequent approval by the Department for construction, maintenance, and rehabilitation of snowmobile recreation areas or any other facilities for the use of snowmobiles, including plans and specifications, engineering surveys and supervision and land acquisition where necessary.

P.A. 77–1312, § 9–1, eff. Aug. 27, 1971. Amended by P.A. 78–856, § 1, eff. July 1, 1974; P.A. 82–195, § 1, eff. April 1, 1982.

Formerly Ill.Rev.Stat.1991, ch. 95 ½, ¶ 609–1.

40/9–2. Special fund

§ 9–2. Special fund. There is created a special fund in the State Treasury to be known as the Snowmobile Trail Establishment Fund. Thirty–three percent of each new, transfer-renewal and renewal registration fee collected under Sections 3–2, 3–5 and 3–8 of this Act shall be deposited in the fund. The fund shall be administered by the Department and shall be used for disbursement, upon written application to and subsequent approval by the Department, to nonprofit snowmobile clubs and organizations for construction, maintenance, and rehabilitation of snowmobile trails and areas for the use of snowmobiles, including plans and specifications, engineering surveys and supervision where necessary. The Department shall promulgate such rules or regulations as it deems necessary for the administration of the fund.

P.A. 77–1312, § 9–2, added by P.A. 82–195, § 1, eff. April 1, 1982. Amended by P.A. 82–993, § 1, eff. Sept. 10, 1982; P.A. 85–153, § 1, eff. Aug. 14, 1987; P.A. 92–174, § 5, eff. July 26, 2001.

Formerly Ill.Rev.Stat.1991, ch. 95 ½, ¶ 609–2.

ARTICLE X. PENALTIES

40/10–1. Violations

§ 10–1. Violations.

(a) Except as otherwise provided in this Act, a person who violates any of the provisions of this Act is guilty of a Class C misdemeanor.

(b) A person who violates subsection (B) of Section 5–1 of this Act is guilty of a Class B misdemeanor.

(c) A person who violates Section 2–4 or Section 5–7.3 of this Act is guilty of a Class A misdemeanor.

P.A. 77–1312, § 10–1, eff. Aug. 27, 1971. Amended by P.A. 77–2779, § 1, eff. Jan. 1, 1973; P.A. 78–255, § 61, eff. Oct. 1, 1973; P.A. 82–629, § 2, eff. Sept. 24, 1981; P.A. 84–151, § 2, eff. Jan. 1, 1986; P.A. 84–973, § 2, eff. Jan. 1, 1986; P.A. 89–55, § 5, eff. Jan. 1, 1996.

Formerly Ill.Rev.Stat.1991, ch. 95 ½, ¶ 610–1.

40/10–2. Denial of operating privilege

§ 10–2. Denial of operating privilege. A person who is convicted of a violation of subsection (B) of Section 5–1 or Section 5–7 of this Act, in addition to other penalties authorized in this Act, may in the discretion of the court be refused the privilege to operate a snowmobile in this State for a period of one year or more.

P.A. 77-1312, § 10-2, added by P.A. 89-55, § 5, eff. Jan. 1, 1996.

40/10-3. Unlawful operation of a snowmobile

§ 10-3. Unlawful operation of a snowmobile. A person who operates a snowmobile during the period when he or she is denied the privilege to operate a snowmobile is guilty of a Class A misdemeanor.

P.A. 77-1312, § 10-3, added by P.A. 89-55, § 5, eff. Jan. 1, 1996.

ARTICLE XI. PARTIAL INVALIDITY

Section

40/11-1. Invalid provisions and applications; effect

§ 11-1. If any provision of this Act, or the application of such provision to any persons, body or circumstances shall be held invalid, the remainder of this Act, or the application of such provision to persons, bodies or circumstances other than those as to which it shall have been held invalid, shall not be affected thereby.

P.A. 77-1312, § 11-1, eff. Aug. 27, 1971.

Formerly Ill.Rev.Stat.1991, ch. 95 ½, ¶ 611-1.

ARTICLE XII. APPROPRIATION

40/12.1. § 12.1. Repealed by P.A. 81-371, eff. Jan. 1, 1980

ACT 45. BOAT REGISTRATION AND SAFETY ACT

Article

ARTICLE I. DEFINITIONS—APPLICATION—JURISDICTION

Section

45/1-1. Title and declaration of intent

§ 1-1. Title and declaration of intent. This Act shall be known and may be cited as the "Boat Registration and Safety Act." It is the policy of this State to promote safety for persons and property in and connected with the use, operation and equipment of vessels and to promote uniformity of laws relating thereto.

Laws 1959, p. 1473, Art. I, § 1. Amended by Laws 1967, p. 2217, § 1. Renumbered § 1-1 and amended by P.A. 82-783, Art. VII, § 2, eff. July 13, 1982.

Formerly Ill.Rev.Stat.1991, ch. 95 ½, ¶ 311-1.

Title of Act:

An Act for the registration of boats, providing for regulations pertaining to the operation thereof, providing penalties for the violation thereof, and repealing certain Acts herein named. Laws 1959, p. 1473, approved July 17, 1959, eff. March 1, 1960.

45/1-2. Definitions

§ 1-2. Definitions. As used in this Act, unless the context clearly requires a different meaning:

"Vessel" or "Watercraft" means every description of watercraft used or capable of being used as a means of transportation on water, except a seaplane on the water, innertube, air mattress or similar device, and boats used for concession rides in artificial bodies of water designed and used exclusively for such concessions.

"Motorboat" means any vessel propelled by machinery, whether or not such machinery is the principal source of propulsion, but does not include a vessel which has a valid marine document issued by the Bureau of Customs of the United States Government or any Federal agency successor thereto.

"Sailboat" means any watercraft propelled by sail or canvas, including sailboards. For the purposes of this Act, any watercraft propelled by both sail or canvas and machinery of any sort shall be deemed a motorboat when being so propelled.

"Airboat" means any boat (but not including airplanes or hydroplanes) propelled by machinery applying force against the air rather than the water as a means of propulsion.

"Lifeboat" means a small boat kept on board a larger boat for use in emergency.

"Owner" means a person, other than lien holder, having title to a motorboat. The term includes a person entitled to the use or possession of a motorboat subject to an interest in another person, reserved or created by agreement and securing payment of performance of an obligation, but the term excludes a lessee under a lease not intended as security.

"Waters of this State" means any water within the jurisdiction of this State.

"Person" means an individual, partnership, firm, corporation, association, or other entity.

"Operate" means to navigate or otherwise use a motorboat or vessel.

"Department" means the Department of Natural Resources.

"Competent" means capable of assisting a skier in case of injury or accident.

"Personal flotation device" or "PFD" means a device that is approved by the Commandant, U.S. Coast Guard, under Part 160 of Title 46 of the Code of Federal Regulations.

"Recreational boat" means any vessel manufactured or used primarily for noncommercial use; or leased, rented or chartered to another for noncommercial use.

"Personal watercraft" means a vessel that uses an inboard motor powering a water jet pump as its primary source of motor power and that is designed to be operated by a person sitting, standing, or kneeling on the vessel, rather than the conventional manner of sitting or standing inside the vessel, and includes vessels that are similar in appearance and operation but are powered by an outboard or propeller drive motor.

"Specialty prop-craft" means a vessel that is similar in appearance and operation to a personal watercraft but that is powered by an outboard or propeller driven motor.

"Underway" applies to a vessel or watercraft at all times except when it is moored at a dock or anchorage area.

"Use" applies to all vessels on the waters of this State, whether moored or underway.

Laws 1959, p. 1473, Art. I, § 2. Amended by Laws 1967, p. 2217, § 1; P.A. 79–470, § 1, eff. Oct. 1, 1975. Renumbered § 1–2 and amended by P.A. 82–783, Art. VII, § 2, eff. July 13, 1982. Amended by P.A. 84–973, § 1, eff. Jan. 1, 1986; P.A. 85–149, § 1, eff. Jan. 1, 1988; P.A. 87–798, § 4, eff. Dec. 16, 1991; P.A. 89–445, § 9A–89, eff. Feb. 7, 1996.

Formerly Ill.Rev.Stat.1991, ch. 95 ½, ¶ 311–2.

45/1–3. Application and jurisdiction

§ 1–3. Application and jurisdiction. The Department shall, for the purposes of this Act, have full and complete jurisdiction of all waters within the boundaries of the State of Illinois, subject only to the paramount authority of the Federal Government with reference to the navigation of such stream or streams and further subject to such powers as may be granted to political subdivisions of the State. Wherever the provisions of this Act conflict with the laws and regulations of the Federal Government, the laws and regulations of the Federal Government shall take precedence.

Laws 1959, p. 1473, Art. I, § 3. Amended by Laws 1961, p. 3349, § 1. Renumbered § 1–3 and amended by P.A. 82–783, Art. VII, § 2, eff. July 13, 1982.

Formerly Ill.Rev.Stat.1991, ch. 95 ½, ¶ 311–3.

45/1–4. Rules

§ 1–4. The Department is authorized to issue administrative rules for carrying out, administering and enforcing the provisions of this Act. The administrative rules shall be promulgated in accordance with The Illinois Administrative Procedure Act.[1]

Such rules, after becoming effective, shall be enforced in the same manner as are any other provisions of this Act and violators thereof are subject to the penalties set out in this Act.

Laws 1959, p. 1473, Art. I, § 1–4, added by P.A. 85–149, § 1, eff. Jan. 1, 1988.

Formerly Ill.Rev.Stat.1991, ch. 95 ½, ¶ 311–4.

[1] 5 ILCS 100/1–1 et seq.

45/1–5. Reciprocal agreements

§ 1–5. The Department is authorized to cooperate with and to enter into reciprocal agreements with the appropriate departments of the federal government and other departments or agencies of other states for carrying out, administering, and enforcing the provisions of this Act.

Laws 1959, p. 1473, Art. I, § 1–5, added by P.A. 85–149, § 1, eff. Jan. 1, 1988.

Formerly Ill.Rev.Stat.1991, ch. 95 ½, ¶ 311–5.

ARTICLE II. ENFORCEMENT—INSPECTION—PROSECUTIONS

Section

45/2–1. Enforcement

§ 2–1. Enforcement. It is the duty of all Conservation Police Officers and other employees of the Department designated by the Director to enforce this Act, and all sheriffs, deputy sheriffs and other police officers to arrest any person detected in violation of any of the provisions of this Act. It is further the duty of all such officers to make prompt investigation of any violation of the provisions of this Act reported by any other person, and to cause a complaint to be filed before the circuit court if there seems just ground for such complaint and evidence procurable to support the same.

Laws 1959, p. 1473, Art. II, § 1. Amended by Laws 1965, p. 332, § 1; Laws 1965, p. 338, § 1; Laws 1967, p. 3943, § 1; P.A. 79–470, § 1, eff. Oct. 1, 1975. Renumbered § 2–1 and amended by P.A. 82–783, Art. VII, § 2, eff. July 13, 1982.

Formerly Ill.Rev.Stat.1991, ch. 95 ½, ¶ 312–1.

45/2–2. Inspection

§ 2–2. Inspection.

(a) Agents of the Department or other duly authorized police officers may board and inspect any boat at any time for the purpose of determining if this Act is being complied with. If the boarding officer or agent discovers any violation of this Act, he may issue a summons to the operator of the boat requiring that the operator appear before the circuit court for the county within which the offense was committed.

(b) Every vessel subject to this Act, if under way and upon being hailed by a designated law enforcement officer, must stop immediately and lay to.

(c) Agents of the Department and other duly authorized police officers may enforce all federal laws and regulations which have been mutually agreed upon by the federal and state governments and are applicable to the operation of watercraft on navigable waters and federal impoundments where concurrent jurisdiction exists between the federal and state governments.

(d) Agents of the Department and other duly authorized police officers may seize and impound, at the owner's or operator's expense, any watercraft involved in a boating accident or a violation of Section 3A–21, 5–1, 5–2, or 5–16 of this Act.

Laws 1959, p. 1473, Art. II, § 2. Amended by Laws 1963, p. 66, § 1; Laws 1965, p. 332, § 1; Laws 1967, p. 1054, § 1; Laws 1967, p. 2217, § 1; Laws 1968, p. 311, § 1, eff. July 1, 1969; P.A. 79–470, § 1, eff. Oct. 1, 1975. Renumbered § 2–2 and amended by P.A. 82–783, Art. VII, § 2, eff. July 13, 1982. Amended by P.A. 87–798, § 4, eff. Dec. 16, 1991; P.A. 88–670, Art. 3, § 3–81, eff. Dec. 2, 1994.

Formerly Ill.Rev.Stat.1991, ch. 95 ½, ¶ 312–2.

45/2–3. Prosecutions

§ 2–3. Prosecutions. All prosecutions under the provisions of this Act shall be brought in the name and by the authority of the People of the State of Illinois before the circuit court having jurisdiction under the law relative to the enforcement of the provisions hereof. It is the duty of all State's Attorneys to enforce the provisions of this Act in their respective counties, and to prosecute all persons charged with violating the provisions hereof.

Laws 1959, p. 1473, Art. II, § 3. Amended by Laws 1965, p. 332, § 1; Laws 1965, p. 627, § 1; Laws 1967, p. 3944, § 1. Renumbered § 2–3 and amended by P.A. 82–783, Art. VII, § 2, eff. July 13, 1982.

Formerly Ill.Rev.Stat.1991, ch. 95 ½, ¶ 312–3.

45/2–4. Resistance to officers

§ 2–4. Resistance to officers.

(a) It is unlawful for any person to resist or obstruct any officer or employee of the Department in the discharge of his duties under the provisions hereof.

(b) It is unlawful for the operator of a watercraft, having been given a signal by a conservation police officer, sheriff, deputy sheriff, or other police officer directing the operator of the watercraft to bring the watercraft to a stop, to willfully fail or refuse to obey the direction, to increase speed, to extinguish lights, or otherwise flee or attempt to elude the officer. The signal given by the officer may be by hand, voice, sign, siren, or blue or red light.

Laws 1959, p. 1473, Art. II, § 4, added by Laws 1963, p. 2012, § 1. Renumbered § 2–4 and amended by P.A. 82–783, Art. VII, § 2, eff. July 13, 1982. Amended by P.A. 88–524, § 1, eff. July 1, 1994.

Formerly Ill.Rev.Stat.1991, ch. 95 ½, ¶ 312–4.

45/2–5. False representation

§ 2–5. False representation. It is unlawful for any person to represent himself falsely to be an officer or employee of the Department or to assume to act as such without having been duly appointed and employed as such.

Laws 1959, p. 1473, Art. II, § 5, added by Laws 1963, p. 2012, § 1. Renumbered § 2–5 and amended by P.A. 82–783, Art. VII, § 2, eff. July 13, 1982.

Formerly Ill.Rev.Stat.1991, ch. 95 ½, ¶ 312–5.

ARTICLE III. REGISTRATION OF MOTORBOATS AND SAILBOATS OVER 12 FEET IN LENGTH

Section

Article III heading was amended by Laws 1967, p. 2217 and P.A. 76–1495, § 1.

45/3–1. Unlawful operation of unnumbered watercraft

§ 3-1. Unlawful operation of unnumbered watercraft. Every watercraft other than sailboards, on waters within the jurisdiction of this State shall be numbered. No person may operate or give permission for the operation of any such watercraft on such waters unless the watercraft is numbered in accordance with this Act, or in accordance with applicable Federal law, or in accordance with a Federally-approved numbering system of another State, and unless (1) the certificate of number awarded to such watercraft is in full force and effect, and (2) the identifying number set forth in the certificate of number is displayed on each side of the bow of such watercraft.

Laws 1959, p. 1473, Art. III, § 1. Amended by Laws 1967, p. 2217, § 1. Renumbered § 3–1 and amended by P.A. 82–783, Art. VII, § 2, eff. July 13, 1982. Amended by P.A. 84–973, § 1, eff. Jan. 1, 1986; P.A. 85–149, § 1, eff. Jan. 1, 1988.

Formerly Ill.Rev.Stat.1991, ch. 95 ½, ¶ 313–1.

45/3–2. Identification number application

§ 3–2. Identification number application. The owner of each watercraft requiring numbering by this State shall file an application for number with the Department on forms approved by it. The application shall be signed by the owner of the watercraft and shall be accompanied by a fee as follows:

A. Class A (all canoes and kayaks) $6
B. Class 1 (all watercraft less than 16 feet in length, except canoes and kayaks) $15
C. Class 2 (all watercraft 16 feet or more but less than 26 feet in length except canoes and kayaks) $20
D. Class 3 (all watercraft 26 feet or more but less than 40 feet in length) $25
E. Class 4 (all watercraft 40 feet in length or more) $30

Upon receipt of the application in approved form, and when satisfied that no tax imposed pursuant to the "Municipal Use Tax Act" [1] or the "County Use Tax Act" [2] is owed, or that such tax has been paid, the Department shall enter the same upon the records of its office and issue to the applicant a certificate of number stating the number awarded to the watercraft and the name and address of the owner.

Laws 1959, p. 1473, Art. III, § 2. Amended by Laws 1961, p. 3349, § 1; Laws 1963, p. 66, § 1; Laws 1963, p. 2012, § 1; Laws 1965, p. 332, § 1; Laws 1965, p. 1818, § 1; Laws 1967, p. 1054, § 1; Laws 1967, p. 2217, § 1; Laws 1968, p. 312, § 1, eff. July 1, 1969; P.A. 78–1142, § 5, eff. Aug. 26, 1974. Renumbered § 3–2 and amended by P.A. 82–783, Art. VII, § 2, eff. July 13, 1982. Amended by P.A. 84–973, § 1, eff. Jan. 1, 1986; P.A. 85–149, § 1, eff. Jan. 1, 1988; P.A. 88–91, § 125, eff. July 14, 1993.

Formerly Ill.Rev.Stat.1991, ch. 95 ½, ¶ 313–2.

1 65 ILCS 5/8–11–6 et seq.

2 35 ILCS 105/1 et seq.

45/3-3. Identification number display

§ 3-3. Identification number display. A. The owner shall paint on or attach to both sides of the bow (front) of a watercraft the identification number, which shall be of block characters at least 3 inches in height. The figures shall read from left to right, be of contrasting color to their background, and be maintained in a legible condition. No other number shall be displayed on the bow of the boat. In affixing the number to the boat, a space or a hyphen shall be provided between the IL and the number and another space or hyphen between the number and the letters which follow. On vessels of unconventional design or constructed so that it is impractical or impossible to display identification numbers in a prominent position on the forward half of their hulls or permanent substructures, numbers may be displayed in brackets or fixtures firmly attached to the vessel. Exact positioning of the numbers in brackets or protruding fixtures shall be discretionary with vessel owners, providing the numbers are placed on the forward half of the vessel and meet the standard requirements for legibility, size, style and contrast with the background.

B. A watercraft already covered by a number in full force and effect which has been awarded to it pursuant to Federal law is exempt from number display as prescribed by this Section.

C. All non-powered canoes and kayaks are exempt from number display as prescribed by this Section.

Laws 1959, p. 1473, Art. III, § 2. Amended by Laws 1961, p. 3349, § 1; Laws 1963, p. 66, § 1; Laws 1963, p. 2012, § 1; Laws 1965, p. 332, § 1; Laws 1965, p. 1818, § 1. Resectioned § 3 and amended by Laws 1967, p. 2217, § 1. Amended by Laws 1968, p. 312, § 1, eff. July 1, 1969. Renumbered § 3-3 and amended by P.A. 82-783, Art. VII, § 2, eff. July 13, 1982. Amended by P.A. 85-149, § 1, eff. Jan. 1, 1988; P.A. 85-1328, § 1, eff. Aug. 31, 1988; P.A. 87-391, § 1, eff. Jan. 1, 1992.

Formerly Ill.Rev.Stat.1991, ch. 95 ½, ¶ 313-3.

45/3-4. Destruction, sale, transfer or abandonment

§ 3-4. Destruction, sale, transfer or abandonment. The owner of any watercraft shall within 15 days notify the Department if the watercraft is destroyed or abandoned, or is sold or transferred either wholly or in part to another person or persons. In sale or transfer cases, the notice shall be accompanied by a surrender of the certificate of number. In destruction or abandonment cases, the notice shall be accompanied by a surrender of the certificate of title. When the surrender of the certificate is by reason of the watercraft being destroyed or abandoned, the Department shall cancel the certificate and enter such fact in its records. The Department shall be notified in writing of any change of address. Should the owner desire a new certificate of number, showing the new address, he shall surrender his old certificate and notify the Department of the new address, remitting $1 to cover the issuance of a new certificate of number. If the surrender is by reason of a sale or transfer either wholly or in part to another person or persons, the owner surrendering the certificate shall state to the Department, under oath, the name of the purchaser or transferee.

Laws 1959, p. 1473, Art. III, § 2. Amended by Laws 1961, p. 3349, § 1; Laws 1963, p. 66, § 1; Laws 1963, p. 2012, § 1; Laws 1965, p. 332, § 1; Laws 1965, p. 1818, § 1. Resectioned § 4 and amended by Laws 1967, p. 2217, § 1. Amended by Laws 1968, p. 312, § 1, eff. July 1, 1969. Renumbered § 3-4 and amended by P.A. 82-783, Art. VII, § 2, eff. July 13, 1982. Amended by P.A. 84-973, § 1, eff. Jan. 1, 1986; P.A. 85-149, § 1, eff. Jan. 1, 1988.

Formerly Ill.Rev.Stat.1991, ch. 95 ½, ¶ 313-4.

45/3-5. Transfer of Identification Number

§ 3-5. Transfer of Identification Number. The purchaser of a watercraft shall, within 15 days after acquiring same, make application to the Department for transfer to him of the certificate of number issued to the watercraft giving his name, address and the number of the boat. The purchaser shall apply for a transfer-renewal for a fee as prescribed under Section 3-2 of this Act for approximately 3 years. All transfers will bear June 30 expiration dates in the calendar year of expiration. Upon receipt of the application and fee, together with proof that any tax imposed under the Municipal Use Tax Act [1] or County Use Tax Act [2] has been paid or that no such tax is owed, the Department shall transfer the certificate of number issued to the watercraft to the new owner.

Unless the application is made and fee paid, and proof of payment of municipal use tax or county use tax or nonliability therefor is made, within 30 days, the watercraft shall be deemed to be without certificate of number and it shall be unlawful for any person to operate the watercraft until the certificate is issued.

Laws 1959, p. 1473, Art. III, § 2. Amended by Laws 1961, p. 3349, § 1; Laws 1963, p. 66, § 1; Laws 1963, p. 2012, § 1; Laws 1965, p. 332, § 1; Laws 1965, p. 1818, § 1. Resectioned § 5 and amended by Laws 1967, p. 2217, § 1. Amended by Laws 1968, p. 312, § 1, eff. July 1, 1969; P.A. 76-1495, § 1, eff. Sept. 22, 1969; P.A. 78-1142, § 5, eff. Aug. 26, 1974. Renumbered § 3-5 and amended by P.A. 82-783, Art. VII, § 2, eff. July 13, 1982. Amended by P.A. 84-973, § 1, eff. Jan. 1, 1986; P.A. 85-149, § 1, eff. Jan. 1, 1988; P.A. 87-1109, § 1, eff. Jan. 1, 1993.

Formerly Ill.Rev.Stat.1991, ch. 95 ½, ¶ 313-5.

[1] 65 ILCS 5/8-11-6.

[2] Former Ill.Rev.Stat. ch. 34, ¶ 409.10 (repealed).

45/3-6. Conformity with United States Government

§ 3-6. Conformity with United States Government. In the event that an agency of the United States Government has in force an over-all system of identification numbering for watercraft within the United States, the numbering system employed pursuant to this Act by the Department shall be in conformity therewith.

Laws 1959, p. 1473, Art. III, § 2. Amended by Laws 1961, p. 3349, § 1; Laws 1963, p. 66, § 1; Laws 1963, p. 2012, § 1; Laws 1965, p. 332, § 1; Laws 1965, p. 1818, § 1. Resectioned § 6 and amended by Laws 1967, p. 2217, § 1. Amended by Laws 1968, p. 312, § 1, eff. July 1, 1969. Renumbered § 3-6 and amended by P.A. 82-783, Art. VII, § 2, eff. July 13, 1982. Amended by P.A. 85-149, § 1, eff. Jan. 1, 1988.

Formerly Ill.Rev.Stat.1991, ch. 95 ½, ¶ 313-6.

45/3-7. Loss of certificate

§ 3-7. Loss of certificate. Should a certificate of number or registration expiration decal become lost, destroyed, or mutilated beyond legibility, the owner of the watercraft shall make application to the Department for the replacement of the certificate or decal, giving his name, address, and the number of his boat and shall at the same time pay to the Department a fee of $1.

Laws 1959, p. 1473, Art. III, § 2. Amended by Laws 1961, p. 3349, § 1; Laws 1963, p. 66, § 1; Laws 1963, p. 2012, § 1; Laws 1965, p. 332, § 1; Laws 1965, p. 1818, § 1. Resectioned § 7 and amended by Laws 1967, p. 2217, § 1. Amended by Laws 1968, p. 312, § 1, eff. July 1, 1969. Renumbered § 3-7 and amended by P.A. 82-783, Art. VII, § 2, eff. July 13, 1982. Amended by P.A. 85-149, § 1, eff. Jan. 1, 1988.

Formerly Ill.Rev.Stat.1991, ch. 95 ½, ¶ 313-7.

45/3-8. Department records

§ 3-8. Department records. All records of the Department made or kept pursuant to this Article shall be public records.

Laws 1959, p. 1473, Art. III, § 2. Amended by Laws 1961, p. 3349, § 1; Laws 1963, p. 66, § 1; Laws 1963, p. 2012, § 1; Laws 1965, p. 332, § 1; Laws 1965, p. 1818, § 1. Resectioned § 8 and amended by Laws 1967, p. 2217, § 1. Amended by Laws 1968, p. 312, § 1, eff. July 1, 1969; P.A. 79-470, § 1, eff. Oct. 1, 1975. Renumbered § 3-8 and amended by P.A. 82-783, Art. VII, § 2, eff. July 13, 1982. Amended by P.A. 86-1088, § 1, eff. July 13, 1990.

Formerly Ill.Rev.Stat.1991, ch. 95 ½, ¶ 313-8.

45/3-9. Certificate of Number

§ 3-9. Certificate of Number. Every certificate of number awarded pursuant to this Act shall continue in full force and effect for approximately 3 years unless sooner terminated or discontinued in accordance with this Act. All new certificates issued will bear June 30 expiration dates in the calendar year 3 years after the issuing date. Provided however, that the Department may, for purposes of implementing this Section, adopt rules for phasing in the issuance of new certificates and provide for 1, 2 or 3 year expiration dates and pro-rated payments or charges for each registration.

All certificates shall be renewed for 3 years from the nearest June 30 for a fee as prescribed in Section 3-2 of this Act. All certificates will be invalid after July 15 of the year of expiration. All certificates expiring in a given year shall be renewed between January 1 and June 30 of that year, in order to allow sufficient time for processing.

The Department shall issue "registration expiration decals" with all new certificates of number, all certificates of number transferred and renewed and all certificates of number renewed. The decals issued for each year shall be of a different and distinct color from the decals of each other year currently displayed. The decals shall be affixed to each side of the bow of the watercraft, except for federally documented vessels, in the manner prescribed by the rules and regulations of the Department. Federally documented vessels shall have decals affixed to the watercraft on each side of the federally documented name of the vessel in the manner prescribed by the rules and regulations of the Department.

The Department shall fix a day and month of the year on which certificates of number due to expire shall lapse and no longer be of any force and effect unless renewed pursuant to this Act.

No number or registration expiration decal other than the number awarded or the registration expiration decal issued to a watercraft or granted reciprocity pursuant to this Act shall be painted, attached, or otherwise displayed on either side of the bow of such watercraft. A person engaged in the operation of a licensed boat livery shall pay a fee as prescribed under Section 3-2 of this Act for each watercraft used in the livery operation.

A person engaged in the manufacture or sale of watercraft of a type otherwise required to be numbered hereunder, upon application to the Department upon forms prescribed by it, may obtain certificates of number for use in the testing or demonstrating of such watercraft upon payment of $10 for each registration. Certificates of number so issued may be used by the applicant in the testing or demonstrating of watercraft by temporary placement of the numbers assigned by such certificates on the watercraft so tested or demonstrated.

Laws 1959, p. 1473, Art. III, § 2. Amended by Laws 1961, p. 3349, § 1; Laws 1963, p. 66, § 1; Laws 1963, p. 2012, § 1; Laws 1965, p. 332, § 1; Laws 1965, p. 1818, § 1. Resectioned § 9 and amended by Laws 1967, p. 2217, § 1. Amended by Laws 1968, p. 312, § 1, eff. July 1, 1969; P.A. 76-1495, § 1, eff. Sept. 22, 1969. Renumbered § 3-9 and amended by P.A. 82-783, Art. VII, § 2, eff. July 13, 1982. Amended by P.A. 84-973, § 1, eff. Jan. 1, 1986; P.A. 85-149, § 1, eff. Jan. 1, 1988; P.A. 87-798, § 4, eff. Dec. 16, 1991.

Formerly Ill.Rev.Stat.1991, ch. 95 ½, ¶ 313-9.

45/3-10. Registration list

§ 3-10. Registration list. A boat registration list may be furnished for official use at no charge only to such federal, state, county and municipal enforcement agencies as may require such data.

Laws 1959, p. 1473, Art. III, § 2. Amended by Laws 1961, p. 3349, § 1; Laws 1963, p. 66, § 1; Laws 1963, p. 2012, § 1; Laws 1965, p. 332, § 1; Laws 1965, p. 1818, § 1. Resectioned § 10 and amended by Laws 1967, p. 2217, § 1. Amended by Laws 1968, p. 312, § 1, eff. July 1, 1969. Renumbered § 3-10 and amended by P.A. 82-783, Art. VII, § 2, eff. July 13, 1982.

Formerly Ill.Rev.Stat.1991, ch. 95 ½, ¶ 313-10.

45/3-11. Penalty

§ 3-11. Penalty. No person shall at any time falsely alter or change in any manner a certificate of number issued under the provisions hereof, or falsify any record required by this Act, or counterfeit any form of license provided for by this Act.

Laws 1959, p. 1473, Art. III, § 2. Amended by Laws 1961, p. 3349, § 1; Laws 1963, p. 66, § 1; Laws 1963, p. 2012, § 1; Laws 1965, p. 332, § 1; Laws 1965, p. 1818, § 1. Resectioned § 11 and amended by Laws 1967, p. 2217, § 1. Amended by Laws 1968, p. 312, § 1, eff. July 1, 1969. Renumbered § 3-11 and amended by P.A. 82-783, Art. VII, § 2, eff. July 13, 1982.

Formerly Ill.Rev.Stat.1991, ch. 95 ½, ¶ 313-11.

45/3-12. Exemption from numbering provisions of this Act

§ 3-12. Exemption from numbering provisions of this Act. A watercraft shall not be required to be numbered under this Act if it is:

A. A watercraft which has a valid marine document issued by the United States Coast Guard, provided the owner of any such vessel used upon the waters of this State for more than 60 days in any calendar year shall be required to comply with the registration requirements of Section 3-9 of this Act.

B. Already covered by a number in full force and effect which has been awarded to it pursuant to Federal law or a

Federally-approved numbering system of another State, if such boat will not be within this State for a period in excess of 60 consecutive days.

C. A watercraft from a country other than the United States temporarily using the waters of this State.

D. A watercraft whose owner is the United States, a State or a subdivision thereof, and used solely for official purposes and clearly identifiable.

E. A vessel used exclusively as a ship's lifeboat.

F. A watercraft belonging to a class of boats which has been exempted from numbering by the Department after such agency has found that an agency of the Federal Government has a numbering system applicable to the class of watercraft to which the watercraft in question belongs and would be exempt from numbering if it were subject to the Federal law.

G. Watercraft while competing in any race approved by the Department under the provisions of Section 5-15 of this Act or if the watercraft is designed and intended solely for racing while engaged in navigation that is incidental to preparation of the watercraft for the race. Preparation of the watercraft for the race may be accomplished only after obtaining the written authorization of the Department.

H. Non-powered, owned and operated on water completely impounded on land belonging to the owner of the watercraft. This Section does not apply to water controlled by a club or association.

I. A canoe or kayak which is owned by an organization which is organized and conducted on a not-for-profit basis with no personal profit inuring to anyone as a result of the operation.

Laws 1959, p. 1473, Art. III, § 3. Amended by Laws 1961, p. 3349, § 1; Laws 1963, p. 66, § 1; Laws 1963, p. 2012, § 1; Laws 1965, p. 332, § 1; Laws 1965, p. 1818, § 1. Renumbered § 12 and amended by Laws 1967, p. 2217, § 1. Amended by P.A. 79-470, § 1, eff. Oct. 1, 1975. Renumbered § 3-12 and amended by P.A. 82-783, Art. VII, § 2, eff. July 13, 1982. Amended by P.A. 85-149, § 1, eff. Jan. 1, 1988; P.A. 85-1323, § 1, eff. Aug. 31, 1988; P.A. 88-524, § 1, eff. July 1, 1994.

Formerly Ill.Rev.Stat.1991, ch. 95 ½, ¶ 313-12.

45/3-13. Hull identification numbers

§ 3-13. Hull identification numbers. Any watercraft manufactured after the effective date of this amendatory Act shall have a hull identification number carved, burned, stamped, embossed, or otherwise permanently affixed to the outboard side of the transom or, if there is no transom, to the outermost starboard side at the end of the hull that bears the rudder or other steering mechanism, above the water line in such a way that alteration, removal, or replacement would be obvious and evident. Any individual who manufactures any watercraft, either for private or public use, shall apply to the Department of Natural Resources for issuance of a Hull Identification Number and shall affix such number to watercraft as required by the rules and regulations of the Department.

Laws 1959, p. 1473, Art. III, § 13, added by P.A. 79-470, § 1, eff. Oct. 1, 1975. Renumbered § 3-13 and amended by P.A. 82-783, Art. VII, § 2, eff. July 13, 1982. Amended by P.A. 89-445, § 9A-89, eff. Feb. 7, 1996.

Formerly Ill.Rev.Stat.1991, ch. 95 ½, ¶ 313-13.

45/3-14. Historical watercraft identification plaque

§ 3-14. A. The Department may issue a historical watercraft identification plaque for a boat that is (1) at least 25 years of age and (2) powered by the boat's original type of power plant. Such a boat shall be known as a "heritage watercraft".

B. An application for such a plaque shall be on a form prescribed by the Department and shall be accompanied by a $25.00 fee. The heritage watercraft identification plaque shall be designed by the Department and shall be non-expiring.

C. When prominently displayed on the boat, a heritage watercraft identification plaque shall entitle the boat owner to apply to participate in parades, shows, and special events. The heritage watercraft plaque does not in itself qualify a boat for recreational use.

Laws 1959, p. 1473, Art. III, § 14, added by P.A. 82-109, § 1, eff. Jan. 1, 1982. Renumbered § 3-14 and amended by P.A. 82-783, Art. VII, § 2, eff. July 13, 1982.

Formerly Ill.Rev.Stat.1991, ch. 95 ½, ¶ 313-14.

ARTICLE IIIA. CERTIFICATE OF TITLE—MOTORBOATS AND SAILBOATS OVER 12 FEET IN LENGTH

Section

Enactment

Article IIIA was added by P.A. 81-1199, eff. Jan. 1, 1981.

45/3A-1. Certificate of title required

§ 3A-1. Certificate of title required.

(a) Every owner of a watercraft required to be numbered by this State and for which no certificate of title has been issued by the Department of Natural Resources shall make application to the Department of Natural Resources for a certificate of title either before or at the same time he next applies for issuance, transfer or renewal of a certificate of number. All watercraft already covered by a number in full force and effect which has been awarded to it pursuant to Federal law is exempt from titling requirements in this Act.

(b) The Department shall not issue, transfer or renew a certificate of number unless a certificate of title has been issued by the Department of Natural Resources or an application for a certificate of title has been delivered to the Department.

Laws 1959, p. 1473, Art. III, § 3A-1, added by P.A. 81-1199, § 1, eff. Jan. 1, 1981. Amended by P.A. 85-149, § 1, eff. Jan. 1, 1988; P.A. 89-445, § 9A-89, eff. Feb. 7, 1996.

Formerly Ill.Rev.Stat.1991, ch. 95 ½, ¶ 313A-1.

45/3A-2. Voluntary titling

§ 3A-2. Voluntary titling. The owner of any watercraft exempt from Section 3A-1(a) of this Act may apply to the Department of Natural Resources for a certificate of title by filing an application accompanied by the prescribed fee. Any owner exempt from this Act who obtains a certificate of title must also obtain a certificate of number as prescribed in Section 3-9 of this Act.

Laws 1959, p. 1473, Art. III, § 3A-2, added by P.A. 81-1199, § 1, eff. Jan. 1, 1981. Amended by P.A. 89-445, § 9A-89, eff. Feb. 7, 1996; P.A. 91-357, § 234, eff. July 29, 1999.

Formerly Ill.Rev.Stat.1991, ch. 95 ½, ¶ 313A-2.

45/3A-3. Application for first certificate of title

§ 3A-3. Application for first certificate of title.

(a) The application for the first certificate of title in this State must be made by the owner to the Department of Natural Resources on the form prescribed and must contain:

1. The name, residence and mail address of the owner;

2. A description of the watercraft so far as the following data exists: Its make, model, year of manufacture, manufacturer's serial number or builder's hull number, length and principal material used in construction;

3. The date of purchase by applicant, the name and address of the person from whom the watercraft was acquired and the names and addresses of any lienholders in the order of their priority and the dates of their security agreements; and

4. Any further information the Department of Natural Resources reasonably requires to identify the watercraft and to enable the Department to determine whether the owner is entitled to a certificate of title and the existence or nonexistence of security interests in the watercraft.

(b) If the application refers to a watercraft purchased from a dealer, it must contain the name and address of any lienholder holding a security interest created or reserved at the time of the sale and the date of his security agreement and be signed by the dealer as well as the owner, and the dealer must within 15 days mail or deliver the application to the Department of Natural Resources.

(c) If the application refers to a watercraft last previously registered in another State or country, the application must contain or be accompanied by:

1. Any certificate of title issued by the other State or country; and

2. Any other information and documents the Department of Natural Resources reasonably requires to establish ownership and the existence or nonexistence of security interests.

Laws 1959, p. 1473, Art. III, § 3A-3, added by P.A. 81-1199, § 1, eff. Jan. 1, 1981. Amended by P.A. 85-149, § 1, eff. Jan. 1, 1988; P.A. 89-445, § 9A-89, eff. Feb. 7, 1996; P.A. 91-357, § 234, eff. July 29, 1999.

Formerly Ill.Rev.Stat.1991, ch. 95 ½, ¶ 313A-3.

45/3A-4. Examination of records

§ 3A-4. Examination of records. The Department of Natural Resources, upon receiving application for a first certificate of title, shall check the identifying description of the watercraft shown in the application against the records required to be maintained by Section 3A-5 of this Article and against the record of stolen and converted watercraft required to be maintained by Section 3A-6 of this Article.

Laws 1959, p. 1473, Art. III, § 3A-4, added by P.A. 81-1199, § 1, eff. Jan. 1, 1981. Amended by P.A. 85-149, § 1, eff. Jan. 1, 1988; P.A. 89-445, § 9A-89, eff. Feb. 7, 1996.

Formerly Ill.Rev.Stat.1991, ch. 95 ½, ¶ 313A-4.

45/3A-5. Certificate of title—Issuance—Records

§ 3A-5. Certificate of title—Issuance—Records.

(a) The Department of Natural Resources shall file each application received and, when satisfied as to its genuineness and regularity, and that no tax imposed by the "Use Tax Act" [1] is owed as evidenced by the receipt for payment or determination of exemption from the Department of Revenue provided for in Section 3A-3 of this Article, and that the applicant is entitled to the issuance of a certificate of title, shall issue a certificate of title.

(b) The Department of Natural Resources shall maintain a record of all certificates of title issued under a distinctive title number assigned to the watercraft and, in the discretion of the Department, in any other method determined.

Laws 1959, p. 1473, Art. III, § 3A-5, added by P.A. 81-1199, § 1, eff. Jan. 1, 1981. Amended by P.A. 85-149, § 1, eff. Jan. 1, 1988; P.A. 89-445, § 9A-89, eff. Feb. 7, 1996.

Formerly Ill.Rev.Stat.1991, ch. 95 ½, ¶ 313A-5.

1 35 ILCS 105/1 et seq.

45/3A-6. Stolen and recovered watercraft

§ 3A-6. Stolen and recovered watercraft.

(a) Every sheriff, superintendent of police, chief of police or other police officer in command of any police department in any city, village or town of the State shall, by the fastest means of communications available to his or her law enforcement agency, immediately report to the Department of State Police the theft or recovery of any stolen or converted watercraft within his or her district or jurisdiction. The report shall give the date of theft, description of the watercraft including color, manufacturer's trade name, manufacturer's series name, identification number and registration number, including the state in which the registration number was issued, together with the name, residence address, business address, and telephone number of the owner. The report shall be routed by the originating law enforcement agency through the State Police in a form and manner prescribed by the Department of State Police.

(b) A registered owner or a lienholder may report the theft by conversion of a watercraft to the Department of State Police or any other police department or sheriff's office. The report will be accepted as a report of theft and processed only if a formal complaint is on file and a warrant issued.

(c) The Department of State Police shall keep a complete record of all reports filed under this Section. Upon receipt of the report, a careful search shall be made of the records of the Department of State Police, and where it is found that a watercraft reported recovered was stolen in a county, city, village or town other than the county, city, village or town in which it is recovered, the recovering agency shall notify the reporting agency of the recovery in a form and manner prescribed by the Department of State Police.

(d) Notification of the theft of a watercraft will be furnished to the Department of Natural Resources by the Department of State Police. The Department of Natural Resources shall place the proper information in the title registration files and in the certificate of number files to indicate the theft of a watercraft. Notification of the recovery of a watercraft previously reported as a theft or a conversion will be furnished to the Department of Natural Resources by the Department of State Police. The Department of Natural Resources shall remove the proper information from the certificate of number and title registration files that has previously indicated the theft of a watercraft. The Department of Natural Resources shall suspend the certificate of number of a watercraft upon receipt of a report that the watercraft was stolen.

(e) When the Department of Natural Resources receives an application for a certificate of title or an application for a certificate of number of a watercraft and it is determined from the records that the watercraft has been reported stolen, the Department of Natural Resources, Division of Law Enforcement, shall immediately notify the State Police and shall give the State Police the name and address of the person or firm titling or registering the watercraft, together with all other information contained in the application submitted by the person or firm.

Laws 1959, p. 1473, Art. III, § 3A-6, added by P.A. 81-1199, § 1, eff. Jan. 1, 1981. Amended by P.A. 84-25, Art. IV, § 28, eff. July 18, 1985; P.A. 85-149, § 1, eff. Jan. 1, 1988; P.A. 85-1042, § 3, eff. July 13, 1988; P.A. 87-803, § 1, eff. July 1, 1992; P.A. 89-445, § 9A-89, eff. Feb. 7, 1996.

Formerly Ill.Rev.Stat.1991, ch. 95 ½, ¶ 313A-6.

45/3A-7. Contents and effect

§ 3A-7. Contents and effect.

(a) Each certificate of title issued by the Department of Natural Resources shall contain:

1. The date issued;
2. The name and address of the owner;
3. The names and addresses of any lienholders, in the order of priority as shown on the application or, if the application is based on a certificate of title, as shown on the certificate;
4. The title number assigned to the watercraft;
5. A description of the watercraft including, so far as the following data exists: its make, model, year of manufacture, registration number, and manufacturer's serial number or, if none, the builder's hull number, length, purchase date, and the principal material used in construction;
6. Any other data the Department of Natural Resources prescribes.

(b) The certificate of title shall contain forms for assignment and warranty of title by the owner, and for assignment and warranty of title by a dealer, and may contain forms for applications for a certificate of title by a transferee, the naming of a lienholder and the assignment or release of the security interest of a lienholder.

(c) A certificate of title issued by the Department of Natural Resources is prima facie evidence of the facts appearing on it.

(d) A certificate of title is not subject to garnishment, attachment, execution or other judicial process, but this subsection does not prevent a lawful levy upon the watercraft.

(e) Any certificate of title issued by the Department of Natural Resources is subject to a lien in favor of the State of Illinois for any fees or taxes required to be paid under this Act and as have not been paid, as provided for in this Act.

Laws 1959, p. 1473, Art. III, § 3A-7, added by P.A. 81-1199, § 1, eff. Jan. 1, 1981. Amended by P.A. 89-445, § 9A-89, eff. Feb. 7, 1996.

Formerly Ill.Rev.Stat.1991, ch. 95 ½, ¶ 313A-7.

45/3A-8. Presumption of tenancy

§ 3A-8. Presumption of tenancy. When a certificate of title is made out to a husband and wife with the marital relationship shown on the certificate, it shall be presumed that the title is held as joint tenants with right of survivorship.

Laws 1959, p. 1473, Art. III, § 3A-8, added by P.A. 81-1199, § 1, eff. Jan. 1, 1981.

Formerly Ill.Rev.Stat.1991, ch. 95 ½, ¶ 313A-8.

45/3A-9. Delivery

§ 3A-9. Delivery. The certificate of title shall be mailed to the first lienholder named in it or, if none, to the owner.

Laws 1959, p. 1473, Art. III, § 3A-9, added by P.A. 81-1199, § 1, eff. Jan. 1, 1981.

Formerly Ill.Rev.Stat.1991, ch. 95 ½, ¶ 313A-9.

45/3A-10. Refusing certificate of title

§ 3A-10. Refusing certificate of title. The Department of Natural Resources shall refuse issuance of a certificate of title if any required fee is not paid or if he has reasonable grounds to believe that:

(a) The applicant is not the owner of the watercraft;

(b) The application contains a false or fraudulent statement; or

(c) The applicant fails to furnish required information or documents or any additional information the Department of Natural Resources reasonably requires;

(d) The applicant has not paid any fees or taxes due under this Act and have not been paid upon reasonable notice and demand.

Laws 1959, p. 1473, Art. III, § 3A-10, added by P.A. 81-1199, § 1, eff. Jan. 1, 1981. Amended by P.A. 89-445, § 9A-89, eff. Feb. 7, 1996.

Formerly Ill.Rev.Stat.1991, ch. 95 ½, ¶ 313A-10.

45/3A-11. Lost, stolen or mutilated certificates

§ 3A-11. Lost, stolen or mutilated certificates.

(a) If a certificate of title is lost, stolen, mutilated or destroyed or becomes illegible, the first lienholder or, if none, the owner or legal representative of the owner named in the certificate, as shown by the records of the Department of Natural Resources, shall promptly make application for and may obtain a duplicate upon furnishing information satisfactory to the Department of Natural Resources. The duplicate certificate of title shall contain the legend "This is a duplicate certificate and may be subject to the rights of a person under the original certificate." It shall be mailed to the first lienholder named in it or, if none, to the owner.

(b) The Department of Natural Resources shall not issue a duplicate certificate of title to any person within 15 days after the issuance of an original certificate of title to such person.

(c) A person recovering an original certificate of title for which a duplicate has been issued shall promptly surrender the original certificate to the Department of Natural Resources.

Laws 1959, p. 1473, Art. III, § 3A-11, added by P.A. 81-1199, § 1, eff. Jan. 1, 1981. Amended by P.A. 89-445, § 9A-89, eff. Feb. 7, 1996.

Formerly Ill.Rev.Stat.1991, ch. 95 ½, ¶ 313A-11.

45/3A-12. Transfer

§ 3A-12. Transfer.

(a) If an owner transfers his interest in a watercraft other than by the creation of a security interest, he shall, at the time of the delivery, execute an assignment and warranty of title to the transferee in the space provided therefor on the certificate or as the Department of Natural Resources prescribes and cause the certificate and assignment to be mailed or delivered to the transferee or to the Department of Natural Resources.

(b) Except as provided in Section 3A-14 of this Article, the transferee shall, promptly and within 15 days after delivery to him of the watercraft and the assigned title, execute the application for a new certificate of title in the space provided therefor on the certificate or as the Department of Natural Resources prescribes, and cause the certificate and application to be mailed or delivered to the Department of Natural Resources.

(c) Upon request of the owner or transferee, a lienholder in possession of the certificate of title shall, unless the transfer was a breach of his security agreement, either deliver the certificate to the transferee for delivery to the Department of Natural Resources or, upon receipt from the transferee of the owner's assignment, the transferee's application for a new certificate and the required fee, mail or deliver them to the Department of Natural Resources . The delivery of the certificate does not affect the rights of the lienholder under his security agreement.

(d) If a security interest is reserved or created at the time of the transfer, the certificate of title shall be retained by or delivered to the person who becomes the lienholder, and the parties shall comply with the provisions of Section 3B-3 of Article IIIB.[1]

(e) Except as provided in Section 3A-14 of this Article and as between the parties, a transfer by an owner is not effective until the provisions of this Section and Section 3A-16 of this Article have been complied with; however, an owner who has delivered possession of the watercraft to the transferee and has complied with the provisions of this Section and Section 3A-16 of this Article requiring action by him as not liable as owner for any damages thereafter resulting from operation of the watercraft.

(f) The Department of Natural Resources may decline to process any application for a transfer of an interest in a watercraft if any fees or taxes due under this Act from the transferor or the transferee have not been paid upon reasonable notice and demand.

Laws 1959, p. 1473, Art. III, § 3A-12, added by P.A. 81-1199, § 1, eff. Jan. 1, 1981. Amended by P.A. 85-149, § 1, eff. Jan. 1, 1988; P.A. 89-445, § 9A-89, eff. Feb. 7, 1996.

Formerly Ill.Rev.Stat.1991, ch. 95 ½, ¶ 313A-12.

[1] 625 ILCS 45/3B-1 et seq.

45/3A-13. Transfer to or from dealer—Manufacturer's or Importer's Certificate

§ 3A-13. Transfer to or from dealer—Manufacturer's or Importer's Certificate. (a) No dealer shall purchase or acquire a new watercraft without obtaining from the seller thereof a manufacturer's or importer's certificate.

(b) No manufacturer, importer, dealer or other person shall sell or otherwise dispose of a new watercraft to a dealer for purposes of display and resale, without delivering to such dealer a manufacturer's or importer's certificate.

Laws 1959, p. 1473, Art. III, § 3A-13, added by P.A. 81-1199, § 1, eff. Jan. 1, 1981.

Formerly Ill.Rev.Stat.1991, ch. 95 ½, ¶ 313A-13.

45/3A-14. Transfer to or from dealer—Records

§ 3A-14. Transfer to or from dealer—Records.

(a) If a dealer buys a watercraft and holds it for resale and procures the certificate of title from the owner or the lienholder within 10 days after delivery to him of the watercraft he need not send the certificate to the Department of Natural Resources but, upon transferring the watercraft to another person other than by the creation of a security interest, shall promptly and within 15 days execute the assignment and warranty of title by a dealer, showing the names and addresses of the transferee and of any lienholder holding a security interest created or reserved at the time of the resale and the date of his security agreement, in the spaces provided therefor on the certificate or as the Department of Natural Resources prescribes, and mail or deliver the certificate to the Department with the transferee's application for a new certificate.

(b) Every dealer shall maintain for 3 years a record in the form the Department of Natural Resources prescribes of every watercraft bought, sold or exchanged by him, or received by him for sale or exchange, which shall be open to inspection by a representative of the Department of Natural Resources or peace officer during reasonable business hours.

(c) The Department of Natural Resources may decline to process any application for a transfer of an interest in a watercraft if any fees or taxes due under this Act from the transferor or the transferee have not been paid upon reasonable notice and demand.

Laws 1959, p. 1473, Art. III, § 3A-14, added by P.A. 81-1199, § 1, eff. Jan. 1, 1981. Amended by P.A. 85-149, § 1, eff. Jan. 1, 1988; P.A. 89-445, § 9A-89, eff. Feb. 7, 1996.

Formerly Ill.Rev.Stat.1991, ch. 95 ½, ¶ 313A-14.

45/3A-15. Transfer by operation of law

§ 3A-15. Transfer by operation of law.

(a) If the interest of an owner in a watercraft passes to another other than by voluntary transfer, the transferee shall, except as provided in subsection (b), promptly mail or deliver within 15 days to the Department of Natural Resources the last certificate of title, if available, proof of the transfer, and his or her application for a new certificate in the form the Department prescribes. It shall be unlawful for any person having possession of a certificate of title for a watercraft by reason of his or her having a lien or encumbrance on such watercraft, to fail or refuse to deliver such certificate to the owner, upon the satisfaction or discharge of the lien or encumbrance, indicated upon such certificate of title.

(b) If the interest of an owner in a watercraft passes to another under the provisions of the Small Estates provisions of the Probate Act of 1975, as amended,[1] the transferee shall promptly mail or deliver to the Department of Natural Resources, within 120 days, the last certificate of title, if available, the documentation required under the provisions of the Probate Act of 1975, as amended, and an application for certificate of title. The transfer may be to the transferee or to the nominee of the transferee.

(c) If the interest of an owner in a watercraft passes to another under other provisions of the Probate Act of 1975, as amended, and the transfer is made by an executor, administrator, or guardian for a disabled person, such transferee shall promptly mail or deliver to the Department of Natural Resources, the last certificate of title, if available, and a certified copy of the letters testamentary, letters of administration or letters of guardianship, as the case may be, and an application for certificate of title. Such application shall be made before the estate is closed. The transfer may be to the transferee or to the nominee of the transferee.

(d) If the interest of an owner in joint tenancy passes to the other joint tenant with survivorship rights as provided by law, the transferee shall promptly mail or deliver to the Department of Natural Resources, the last certificate of title, if available, proof of death of the one joint tenant and survivorship of the surviving joint tenant, and an application for certificate of title. Such application shall be made within 120 days after the death of the joint tenant. The transfer may be to the transferee or to the nominee of the transferee.

(e) If the interest of the owner is terminated or the watercraft is sold under a security agreement by a lienholder named in the certificate of title, the transferee shall promptly mail or deliver within 15 days to the Department of Natural Resources the last certificate of title, his or her application for a new certificate in the form the Department prescribes, and an affidavit made by or on behalf of the lienholder that the watercraft was repossessed and that the interest of the owner was lawfully terminated or sold pursuant to the terms of the security agreement. In all cases wherein a lienholder has found it necessary to repossess a watercraft and desires to obtain certificate of title for such watercraft in the name of such lienholder, the Department of Natural Resources shall not issue a certificate of title to such lienholder unless the person from whom such watercraft has been repossessed, is shown to be the last registered owner of such watercraft and such lienholder establishes to the satisfaction of the Department that he or she is entitled to such certificate of title.

(f) A person holding a certificate of title whose interest in the watercraft has been extinguished or transferred other than by voluntary transfer shall mail or deliver the certificate within 15 days upon request of the Department of Natural Resources. The delivery of the certificate pursuant to the request of the Department of Natural Resources does not affect the rights of the person surrendering the certificate, and the action of the Department in issuing a new certificate of title as provided herein is not conclusive upon the rights of an owner or lienholder named in the old certificate.

(g) The Department of Natural Resources may decline to process any application for a transfer of an interest hereunder if any fees or taxes due under this Act from the transferor or the transferee have not been paid upon reasonable notice and demand.

(h) The Department of Natural Resources shall not be held civilly or criminally liable to any person because any purported transferor may not have had the power or authority to make a transfer of any interest in any watercraft.

Laws 1959, p. 1473, Art. III, § 3A-15, added by P.A. 81-1199, § 1, eff. Jan. 1, 1981. Amended by P.A. 83-706, § 42, eff. Sept. 23, 1983; P.A. 85-149, § 1, eff. Jan. 1, 1988; P.A. 89-445, § 9A-89, eff. Feb. 7, 1996.

Formerly Ill.Rev.Stat.1991, ch. 95 ½, ¶ 313A-15.

[1] 755 ILCS 5/1-1 et seq.

45/3A-16. Fees

§ 3A-16. Fees. Fees shall be paid according to the following schedule:

Certificate of title	$7
Duplicate certificate of title	5
Corrected certificate of title	5
Search	5

Laws 1959, p. 1473, Art. III, § 3A-16, added by P.A. 81-1199, § 1, eff. Jan. 1, 1981. Amended by P.A. 85-149, § 1, eff. Jan. 1, 1988.

Formerly Ill.Rev.Stat.1991, ch. 95 ½, ¶ 313A-16.

45/3A-17. Transfer of watercraft

§ 3A-17. Transfer of watercraft. A transferor of a watercraft other than a dealer transferring a new watercraft, shall deliver to the transferee at the time of delivery of possession of the watercraft the properly assigned certificate of title.

Laws 1959, p. 1473, Art. III, § 3A-17, added by P.A. 81-1199, § 1, eff. Jan. 1, 1981. Amended by P.A. 85-149, § 1, eff. Jan. 1, 1988.

Formerly Ill.Rev.Stat.1991, ch. 95 ½, ¶ 313A-17.

45/3A-18. Transfer or surrender of certificate of title

§ 3A-18. Transfer or surrender of certificate of title.

(a) The Department of Natural Resources, upon receipt of a properly assigned certificate of title, with an application for a new certificate of title, the required fee and any other documents required by law, shall issue a new certificate of title in the name of the transferee as owner and mail it to the first lienholder named in it or, if none, to the owner.

(b) The Department of Natural Resources, upon receipt of an application for a new certificate of title by a transferee other than by voluntary transfer, with proof of the transfer, the required fee and any other documents required by law, shall issue a new certificate of title in the name of the transferee as owner. If the outstanding certificate of title is not delivered to him, the Department shall make demand therefor from the holder thereof.

(c) The Department of Natural Resources shall file and retain for 4 years every surrendered Illinois certificate of title, the file to be maintained so as to permit the tracing of title of the watercraft designated therein.

Laws 1959, p. 1473, Art. III, § 3A-18, added by P.A. 81-1199, § 1, eff. Jan. 1, 1981. Amended by P.A. 89-445, § 9A-89, eff. Feb. 7, 1996.

Formerly Ill.Rev.Stat.1991, ch. 95 ½, ¶ 313A-18.

45/3A-19. Scrapping, junking or destroying a watercraft

§ 3A-19. Scrapping, junking or destroying a watercraft. An owner who scraps, junks or destroys a watercraft, or a person who purchases a watercraft as scrap or as a watercraft to be junked or destroyed shall immediately cause the certificate of title to be mailed or delivered to the Department of Natural Resources, and a certificate of title shall not again be issued for such watercraft. Upon receipt of the certificate of title, the Department shall cancel the certificate.

Laws 1959, p. 1473, Art. III, § 3A-19, added by P.A. 81-1199, § 1, eff. Jan. 1, 1981. Amended by P.A. 85-149, § 1, eff. Jan. 1, 1988; P.A. 89-445, § 9A-89, eff. Feb. 7, 1996.

Formerly Ill.Rev.Stat.1991, ch. 95 ½, ¶ 313A-19.

45/3A-20. Offenses relating to titling; misdemeanors

§ 3A-20. Offenses relating to titling; misdemeanors. Violation of any of the following provisions shall constitute a Class A misdemeanor:

(a) No person shall operate in this State a watercraft for which a certificate of title is required without having such certificate of title.

(b) No person shall sell, transfer or otherwise dispose of a watercraft without delivering to the purchaser or transferee a certificate of title, or a manufacturer's or importer's certificate, assigned to such purchaser or transferee as required by this Act.

(c) No person shall fail to surrender to the Department of Natural Resources any certificate of title upon cancellation of the same by the Department for any valid reason set forth in this Act or regulations adopted pursuant thereto.

Laws 1959, p. 1473, Art. III, § 3A-20, added by P.A. 81-1199, § 1, eff. Jan. 1, 1981. Amended by P.A. 85-149, § 1, eff. Jan. 1, 1988; P.A. 88-524, § 1, eff. July 1, 1994; P.A. 89-445, § 9A-89, eff. Feb. 7, 1996.

Formerly Ill.Rev.Stat.1991, ch. 95 ½, ¶ 313A-20.

45/3A-21. Offenses relating to titling; felonies

§ 3A-21. Offenses relating to titling; felonies. Violation of any of the following provisions shall constitute a Class 2 felony:

(a) No person shall alter, forge or counterfeit any certificate of title or a manufacturer's or importer's certificate to a watercraft.

(b) No person shall alter or falsify any assignment of a certificate of title, or an assignment or cancellation of a security interest on a certificate of title to a watercraft.

(c) No person shall hold or use a certificate of title to a watercraft nor hold or use any assignment or cancellation of a security interest on a certificate of title to a watercraft, knowing it to have been altered, forged, counterfeited or falsified.

(d) No person shall use a false or fictitious name or address, or make any material false statement, or conceal any material fact, in an application for a certificate of title, or in a bill of sale or sworn statement of ownership.

(e) No person shall procure or attempt to procure a certificate of title to a watercraft, or pass or attempt to pass a certificate of title or any assignment thereof to a watercraft, knowing or having reason to believe that such watercraft has been stolen.

(f) No person shall have possession of, buy, receive, sell or offer to sell, or otherwise dispose of a watercraft on which the manufacturer's or assigned serial number of the watercraft has been destroyed, removed, covered, altered, or defaced, knowing of such destruction, removal, covering, alteration or defacement of such manufacturer's or assigned serial number.

(g) No person shall destroy, remove, cover, alter or deface the manufacturer's or assigned serial number on any watercraft.

(h) No person shall possess, buy, sell, exchange or give away, or offer to buy, sell, exchange, or give away the certificate of title to any watercraft which is a junk or salvage.

Laws 1959, p. 1473, Art. III, § 3A-21, added by P.A. 81-1199, § 1, eff. Jan. 1, 1981. Amended by P.A. 81-1509, Art. II, § 72, eff. Sept. 26, 1980; P.A. 85-149, § 1, eff. Jan. 1, 1988; P.A. 88-524, § 1, eff. July 1, 1994.

Formerly Ill.Rev.Stat.1991, ch. 95 ½, ¶ 313A-21.

45/3A-22. § 3A-22. Repealed by P.A. 85-149, § 2, eff. Jan. 1, 1988

ARTICLE IIIB. SECURITY INTERESTS

Section

Enactment

Article IIIB was added by P.A. 81-1199, § 1, eff. Jan. 1, 1981.

45/3B-1. Excepted liens and security interests

§ 3B-1. Excepted liens and security interests. This Article does not apply to or affect:

(a) A lien given by statute or rule of law to a supplier of services or materials for the watercraft;

(b) A lien given by the statute to the United States, this State or any political subdivision of this State.

(c) A security interest in a watercraft created by a manufacturer or dealer who holds the watercraft for sale, but a buyer in the ordinary course of trade from the manufacturer or dealer takes free of the security interest.

Laws 1959, p. 1473, Art. III, § 3B-1, added by P.A. 81-1199, § 1, eff. Jan. 1, 1981.

Formerly Ill.Rev.Stat.1991, ch. 95 ½, ¶ 313B-1.

45/3B-2. Perfection of security interest

§ 3B-2. Perfection of security interest.

(a) Unless excepted by Section 3B-1, a security interest in a watercraft of a type for which a certificate of title is required is not valid against subsequent transferees or lienholders of the watercraft unless perfected as provided in this Act.

(b) A security interest is perfected by the delivery to the Department of Natural Resources of the existing certificate of title, if any, an application for a certificate of title containing the name and address of the lienholder and the date of his security agreement and the required fee. It is perfected as of the time of its creation if the delivery is completed within 21 days thereafter, otherwise as of the time of the delivery.

(c) If a watercraft is subject to a security interest when brought into this State, the validity of the security interest is determined by the law of the jurisdiction where the watercraft was when the security interest attached, subject to the following:

1. If the parties understood at the time the security interest attached that the watercraft would be kept in this State and it was brought into this State within 30 days thereafter for purposes other than transportation through this State, the validity of the security interest in this State is determined by the law of this State.

2. If the security interest was perfected under the law of the jurisdiction where the watercraft was when the security interest attached, the following rules apply:

(A) If the name of the lienholder is shown on an existing certificate of title issued by that jurisdiction, his security interest continues perfected in this State.

(B) If the name of the lienholder is not shown on an existing certificate of title issued by that jurisdiction, a security interest may be perfected by the lienholder delivering to the Department of Natural Resources the prescribed notice and by payment of the required fee. Such security interest is perfected as of the time of delivery of the prescribed notice and payment of the required fee.

3. If the security interest was not perfected under the law of the jurisdiction where the watercraft was when the security interest attached, it may be perfected in this State; in that case perfection dates from the time of perfection in this State.

4. A security interest may be perfected under paragraph 3 of this subsection either as provided in subsection (b) or by the lienholder delivering to the Department of Natural Resources a notice of security interest in the form the Department prescribes and the required fee.

Laws 1959, p. 1473, Art. III, § 3B–2, added by P.A. 81–1199, § 1, eff. Jan. 1, 1981. Amended by P.A. 85–149, § 1, eff. Jan. 1, 1988; P.A. 89–445, § 9A–89, eff. Feb. 7, 1996.

Formerly Ill.Rev.Stat.1991, ch. 95 ½, ¶ 313B–2.

45/3B-3. Security interest

§ 3B–3. Security interest. If an owner creates a security interest in a watercraft:

(a) The owner shall immediately execute the application, in the space provided therefor on the certificate of title or on a separate form the Department of Natural Resources prescribes, to name the lienholder on the certificate, showing the name and address of the lienholder and the date of his security agreement, and cause the certificate, application and the required fee to be delivered to the lienholder.

(b) The lienholder shall immediately cause the certificate, application and the required fee to be mailed or delivered to the Department of Natural Resources.

(c) Upon request of the owner or subordinate lienholder, a lienholder in possession of the certificate of title shall either mail or deliver the certificate to the subordinate lienholder for delivery to the Department of Natural Resources or, upon receipt from the subordinate lienholder of the owner's application and the required fee, mail or deliver them to the Department of Natural Resources with the certificate. The delivery of the certificate does not affect the rights of the first lienholder under his security agreement.

(d) Upon receipt of the certificate of title, application and the required fee, the Department of Natural Resources shall either endorse on the certificate or issue a new certificate containing the name and address of the new lienholder, and mail the certificate to the first lienholder named in it.

Laws 1959, p. 1473, Art. III, § 3B–3, added by P.A. 81–1199, § 1, eff. Jan. 1, 1981. Amended by P.A. 89–445, § 9A–89, eff. Feb. 7, 1996.

Formerly Ill.Rev.Stat.1991, ch. 95 ½, ¶ 313B–3.

45/3B-4. Assignment by lienholder

§ 3B–4. Assignment by lienholder. (a) A lienholder may assign, absolutely or otherwise, his security interest in the watercraft to a person other than the owner without affecting the interest of the owner or the validity of the security interest, but any person without notice of the assignment is protected in dealing with the lienholder as the holder of the security interest and the lienholder remains liable for any obligations as lienholder until the assignee is named as lienholder on the certificate.

(b) The assignee may, but need not to perfect the assignment, have the certificate of title endorsed or issued with the assignee named as lienholder, upon delivering to the Department of Natural Resources the certificate and an assignment by the lienholder named in the certificate in the form the Department prescribes.

Laws 1959, p. 1473, Art. III, § 3B–4, added by P.A. 81–1199, § 1, eff. Jan. 1, 1981. Amended by P.A. 89–445, § 9A–89, eff. Feb. 7, 1996.

Formerly Ill.Rev.Stat.1991, ch. 95 ½, ¶ 313B–4.

45/3B-5. Release of security interest

§ 3B–5. Release of security interest.

(a) Upon the satisfaction of a security interest in a watercraft for which the certificate of title is in the possession of the lienholder, he shall, within 10 days after demand and, in any event, within 30 days, execute a release of his security interest, and mail or deliver the certificate and release to the next lienholder named therein, or, if none, to the owner or any person who delivers to the lienholder an authorization from the owner to receive the certificate. The owner, other than a dealer holding the watercraft for resale, shall promptly cause the certificate and release to be mailed or delivered to the Department of Natural Resources, which shall release the lienholder's rights on the certificate or issue a new certificate.

(b) Upon the satisfaction of a security interest in a watercraft for which the certificate of title is in the possession of a prior lienholder, the lienholder whose security interest is satisfied shall within 10 days after demand and, in any event, within 30 days execute a release and deliver the release to the owner or any person who delivers to the lienholder an authorization from the owner to receive it. The lienholder in possession of the certificate of title shall either deliver the certificate to the owner, or the person authorized by him, for delivery to the Department of Natural Resources, or, upon receipt of the release, mail or deliver the certificate and release to the Department, which shall release the subordinate lienholder's rights on the certificate or issue a new certificate.

Laws 1959, p. 1473, Art. III, § 3B–5, added by P.A. 81–1199, § 1, eff. Jan. 1, 1981. Amended by P.A. 89–445, § 9A–89, eff. Feb. 7, 1996.

Formerly Ill.Rev.Stat.1991, ch. 95 ½, ¶ 313B–5.

45/3B-6. Duty of lienholder

§ 3B–6. Duty of lienholder. A lienholder named in a certificate of title shall, upon written request of the owner or of another lienholder named on the certificate, disclose any pertinent information as to his security agreement and the indebtedness secured by it.

Laws 1959, p. 1473, Art. III, § 3B–6, added by P.A. 81–1199, § 1, eff. Jan. 1, 1981.

Formerly Ill.Rev.Stat.1991, ch. 95 ½, ¶ 313B–6.

45/3B–7. Exclusiveness of procedure

§ 3B–7. Exclusiveness of procedure. The method provided in this Act of perfecting and giving notice of security interests subject to this Act is exclusive. Security interests subject to this Act are hereby exempted from the provisions of law which otherwise require or relate to the recording or filing of instruments creating or evidencing security interests in watercraft including chattel mortgages and conditional sale agreements.

Laws 1959, p. 1473, Art. III, § 3B–7, added by P.A. 81–1199, § 1, eff. Jan. 1, 1981. Amended by P.A. 85–149, § 1, eff. Jan. 1, 1988.

Formerly Ill.Rev.Stat.1991, ch. 95 ½, ¶ 313B–7.

45/3B–8. Suspension or revocation of certificates

§ 3B–8. Suspension or revocation of certificates.

(a) The Department of Natural Resources may suspend or revoke a certificate of title, upon notice and reasonable opportunity to be heard, when authorized by any other provision of law or if he finds:

1. The certificate of title was fraudulently procured or erroneously issued, or

2. The watercraft has been scrapped, dismantled or destroyed.

(b) Suspension or revocation of a certificate of title does not, in itself, affect the validity of a security interest noted on it.

(c) When the Department of Natural Resources suspends or revokes a certificate of title, the owner or person in possession of it shall, immediately upon receiving notice of the suspension or revocation, mail or deliver the certificate to the Department.

(d) The Department of Natural Resources may seize and impound any certificate of title which has been suspended or revoked.

Laws 1959, p. 1473, Art. III, § 3B–8, added by P.A. 81–1199, § 1, eff. Jan. 1, 1981. Amended by P.A. 89–445, § 9A–89, eff. Feb. 7, 1996.

Formerly Ill.Rev.Stat.1991, ch. 95 ½, ¶ 313B–8.

45/3B–9. Powers of Department of Natural Resources

§ 3B–9. Powers of Department of Natural Resources.

(a) The Department of Natural Resources shall prescribe and provide suitable forms of applications, certificates of title, notices of security interests, and all other notices and forms necessary to carry out the provisions of this Article and Article IIIA.[1]

(b) The Department of Natural Resources may:

1. Make necessary investigations to procure information required to carry out the provisions of this Article and Article IIIA;

2. Assign a new identifying number to a watercraft if it has none, or its identifying number is destroyed or obliterated, and shall either issue a new certificate of title showing the new identifying number or make an appropriate endorsement on the original certificate.

Laws 1959, p. 1473, Art. III, § 3B–9, added by P.A. 81–1199, § 1, eff. Jan. 1, 1981. Amended by P.A. 89–445, § 9A–89, eff. Feb. 7, 1996.

Formerly Ill.Rev.Stat.1991, ch. 95 ½, ¶ 313B–9.

[1] 625 ILCS 45/3A–1 et seq.

45/3B–10. Court Review

§ 3B–10. Court review. A person aggrieved by an act or omission to act of the Department of Natural Resources under this Article or Article IIIA [1] is also entitled to a review thereof by the Circuit Court of Sangamon County in accordance with the Administrative Review Law, as amended.[2]

Laws 1959, p. 1473, Art. III, § 3B–10, added by P.A. 81–1199, § 1, eff. Jan. 1, 1981. Amended by P.A. 82–783, Art. XI, § 141, eff. July 13, 1982; P.A. 89–445, § 9A–89, eff. Feb. 7, 1996.

Formerly Ill.Rev.Stat.1991, ch. 95 ½, ¶ 313B–10.

[1] 625 ILCS 45/3A–1 et seq.

[2] 735 ILCS 5/3–101 et seq.

ARTICLE IIIC. LOST AND ABANDONED WATERCRAFT

Section

Enactment

Article IIIC was added by P.A. 84–646, § 1, eff. Jan. 1, 1986.

45/3C–1. Abandonment of watercraft prohibited

§ 3C–1. Abandonment of watercraft prohibited. (a) The abandonment of a watercraft or any part thereof on any waters in this State is unlawful and subject to penalties as set forth under Section 3C–14.

(b) The abandonment of a watercraft or any part thereof on private or public property, other than a waterway, in view of the general public, anywhere in this State is unlawful except on property of the owner or bailee of such abandoned watercraft.

Laws 1959, p. 1473, Art. IIIC, § 3C–1, added by P.A. 84–646, § 1, eff. Jan. 1, 1986.

Formerly Ill.Rev.Stat.1991, ch. 95 ½, ¶ 313C–1.

45/3C–2. Notification to law enforcement agencies

§ 3C–2. Notification to law enforcement agencies. When an abandoned, lost, stolen or unclaimed watercraft comes into the temporary possession or custody of a person in this

State, not the owner of the watercraft, such person shall immediately notify the municipal police when the watercraft is within the corporate limits of any city, village or town having a duly authorized police department, or the State Police, Conservation Police or the county sheriff when the watercraft is outside the corporate limits of a city, village or town. Upon receipt of such notification, the municipal police, State Police, Conservation Police, or county sheriff will authorize a towing service to remove and take possession of the abandoned, lost, stolen or unclaimed watercraft. The towing service will safely keep the towed watercraft and its contents, and maintain a record of the tow as set forth in Section 3C–4 for law enforcement agencies, until the watercraft is claimed by the owner or any other person legally entitled to possession thereof or until it is disposed of as provided in this Article.

Laws 1959, p. 1473, Art. IIIC, § 3C–2, added by P.A. 84–646, § 1, eff. Jan. 1, 1986.

Formerly Ill.Rev.Stat.1991, ch. 95 ½, ¶ 313C–2.

45/3C–3. Removal of watercraft

§ 3C–3. Removal of watercraft. (a) When a watercraft is abandoned on any waters of this State for 24 hours or more, its removal by a towing service may be authorized by a law enforcement agency having jurisdiction.

(b) When an abandoned, unattended, wrecked, burned or partially dismantled watercraft is creating a traffic or navigational hazard because of its position in relation to the waterway or because its physical appearance is impeding traffic or navigation, its immediate removal from the waterway by a towing service may be authorized by a law enforcement agency having jurisdiction.

(c) When a watercraft removal from either public or private property is authorized by a law enforcement agency, the owner of the watercraft will be responsible for all towing costs. Watercraft removed from public or private property and stored by a commercial relocator or any other towing service shall be subject to a possessory lien for services pursuant to "An Act concerning liens for labor, services, skills or materials furnished upon or storage furnished for chattels", filed July 24, 1941, as amended,[1] and the provisions of Section 1 of that Act[2] relating to notice and implied consent shall be deemed satisfied. In no event shall such lien be greater than the rates established by that Act. In no event shall such lien be increased or altered to reflect any charge for services or materials rendered in addition to those authorized by this Article. Every such lien shall be payable in cash.

Laws 1959, p. 1473, Art. IIIC, § 3C–3, added by P.A. 84–646, § 1, eff. Jan. 1, 1986.

Formerly Ill.Rev.Stat.1991, ch. 95 ½, ¶ 313C–3.

1 770 ILCS 50/0.01 et seq.

2 770 ILCS 50/1.

45/3C–4. Reports on towed watercraft

§ 3C–4. Reports on towed watercraft. When a watercraft is authorized to be towed away as provided in Section 3C–2, the police headquarters or office of the law enforcement officer authorizing the towing shall keep and maintain a record of the watercraft towed, listing the color, manufacturer's trade name, manufacturer's series name, hull type, hull material, hull identification number, and registration number displayed on the watercraft. The record shall also include the date and hour of tow, location towed from, location towed to, and reason for towing and the name of the officer authorizing the tow.

Laws 1959, p. 1473, Art. IIIC, § 3C–4, added by P.A. 84–646, § 1, eff. Jan. 1, 1986.

Formerly Ill.Rev.Stat.1991, ch. 95 ½, ¶ 313C–4.

45/3C–5. Record searches

§ 3C–5. Record searches. When a law enforcement agency authorizing the impounding of a watercraft does not know the identity of the registered owner, lienholder or other legally entitled person, that law enforcement agency will cause the watercraft registration records of the State of Illinois to be searched by the Department of Natural Resources for the purpose of obtaining the required ownership information. The law enforcement agency authorizing the impounding of a watercraft will cause the stolen watercraft files of the State Police to be searched by a directed communication to the State Police for stolen or wanted information on the watercraft. When the State Police files are searched with negative results, the information contained in the National Crime Information Center (NCIC) files will be searched by the State Police. The information determined from these record searches will be returned to the requesting law enforcement agency for that agency's use in sending a notification by certified mail to the registered owner, lienholder and other legally entitled persons advising where the watercraft is held, requesting that a disposition be made and setting forth public sale information. Notification shall be sent no later than 10 days after the date the law enforcement agency impounds or authorizes the impounding of a watercraft, provided that if the law enforcement agency is unable to determine the identity of the registered owner, lienholder or other person legally entitled to ownership of the impounded watercraft within a 10 day period after impoundment, then notification shall be sent no later than 2 days after the date the identity of the registered owner, lienholder or other person legally entitled to ownership of the impounded watercraft is determined. Exceptions to a notification by certified mail to the registered owner, lienholder and other legally entitled persons are set forth in Section 3C–9.

Laws 1959, p. 1473, Art. IIIC, § 3C–5, added by P.A. 84–646, § 1, eff. Jan. 1, 1986. Amended by P.A. 85–149, § 1, eff. Jan. 1, 1988; P.A. 89–445, § 9A–89, eff. Feb. 7, 1996.

Formerly Ill.Rev.Stat.1991, ch. 95 ½, ¶ 313C–5.

45/3C–6. Identifying and tracing of watercraft ownership by the Department of Natural Resources

§ 3C–6. Identifying and tracing of watercraft ownership by the Department of Natural Resources. When the registered owner, lienholder or other person legally entitled to the possession of a watercraft cannot be identified from the registration files of this State or from the registration files of a foreign state, if applicable, the law enforcement agency having custody of the watercraft shall notify the Department of Natural Resources, for the purpose of identifying the watercraft owner or other person legally entitled to the possession of the watercraft. The information obtained by the Department of Natural Resources will be immediately forwarded to the law enforcement agency having custody of the watercraft for notification purposes as set forth in Section 3C–5.

Laws 1959, p. 1473, Art. IIIC, § 3C–6, added by P.A. 84–646, § 1, eff. Jan. 1, 1986. Amended by P.A. 89–445, § 9A–89, eff. Feb. 7, 1996.

Formerly Ill.Rev.Stat.1991, ch. 95 ½, ¶ 313C–6.

45/3C-7. Reclaimed watercraft

§ 3C-7. Reclaimed watercraft. Any time before a watercraft is sold at public sale or disposed of as provided in Section 3C-8, the owner, lienholder or other person legally entitled to its possession may reclaim the watercraft by presenting to the law enforcement agency having custody of the watercraft proof of ownership or proof of the right to possession of the watercraft. No watercraft shall be released to the owner, lienholder or other person under this Section until all towing and storage charges have been paid.

Laws 1959, p. 1473, Art. IIIC, § 3C-7, added by P.A. 84-646, § 1, eff. Jan. 1, 1986.

Formerly Ill.Rev.Stat.1991, ch. 95 ½, ¶ 313C-7.

45/3C-8. Disposal of unclaimed watercraft

§ 3C-8. Disposal of unclaimed watercraft. (a) In cities having a population of more than 500,000 inhabitants, whenever an abandoned, lost, stolen or unclaimed watercraft or other watercraft remains unclaimed by the registered owner, lienholder or other legally entitled person for a period of 15 days after notice has been given as provided in Sections 3C-5 and 3C-6, the watercraft may be disposed of as provided in the "Municipal purchasing act for cities of 500,000 or more population".[1]

(b) Except as provided in subsection (a), when an abandoned, lost, stolen or unclaimed watercraft 7 years of age or newer remains unclaimed by the registered owner, lienholder or other person legally entitled to its possession for a period of 30 days after notice has been given as provided in Sections 3C-5 and 3C-6, the law enforcement agency or towing service having possession of the watercraft shall cause it to be sold at public sale to the highest bidder. Notice of the time and place of the sale shall be posted in a conspicuous place for at least 10 days prior to the sale, on the premises where the watercraft has been impounded. At least 10 days prior to the sale, the law enforcement agency where the watercraft is impounded, or the towing service where the watercraft is impounded, shall cause a notice of the time and place of the sale to be sent by certified mail to the registered owner, lienholder and other persons known by the law enforcement agency or towing service to be legally entitled to the possession of the watercraft. Such notice shall contain a complete description of the watercraft to be sold and what steps must be taken by any legally entitled person to reclaim the watercraft. In those instances where the certified notification specified in Sections 3C-5 and 3C-6 has been returned by the postal authorities to the law enforcement agency or towing service due to the addressee having moved, or being unknown at the address obtained from the registration records of this State, the sending of a second certified notice will not be required.

Laws 1959, p. 1473, Art. IIIC, § 3C-8, added by P.A. 84-646, § 1, eff. Jan. 1, 1986.

Formerly Ill.Rev.Stat.1991, ch. 95 ½, ¶ 313C-8.

[1] 65 ILCS 5/8-10-1 et seq.

45/3C-9. Disposal of unclaimed watercraft without notice

§ 3C-9. Disposal of unclaimed watercraft without notice.

(a) When the identity of the registered owner, lienholder and other person legally entitled to the possession of an abandoned, lost or unclaimed watercraft of 7 years of age or newer cannot be determined by any means provided for in this Article, the watercraft may be sold as provided in Section 3C-8 without notice to any person whose identity cannot be determined.

(b) When an abandoned watercraft of more than 7 years of age is impounded as specified by this Article, it will be kept in custody for a minimum of 10 days for the purpose of determining the identity of the registered owner and lienholder, contacting the registered owner and lienholder for a determination of disposition, and an examination of the State Police stolen watercraft files for the theft and wanted information. At the expiration of the 10 day period, if disposition information has not been received from the registered owner or the lienholder, the law enforcement agency having jurisdiction will authorize the disposal of the watercraft as junk.

However if, in the opinion of the police officer processing the watercraft, it has a value of $200 or more and can be restored to safe operating condition, the law enforcement agency may authorize its purchase for salvage and the Department of Natural Resources may issue a certificate of title. A watercraft classified as a historical watercraft may be sold to a person desiring to restore it.

Laws 1959, p. 1473, Art. IIIC, § 3C-9, added by P.A. 84-646, § 1, eff. Jan. 1, 1986. Amended by P.A. 89-445, § 9A-89, eff. Feb. 7, 1996.

Formerly Ill.Rev.Stat.1991, ch. 95 ½, ¶ 313C-9.

45/3C-10. Police reports

§ 3C-10. Police reports. When a watercraft in the custody of a law enforcement agency is reclaimed by the registered owner, lienholder or other legally entitled person, or when the watercraft is sold at public sale or otherwise disposed of as provided in this Article, a report of the transaction will be maintained by the law enforcement agency for a period of one year from the date of the sale or disposal.

Laws 1959, p. 1473, Art. IIIC, § 3C-10, added by P.A. 84-646, § 1, eff. Jan. 1, 1986.

Formerly Ill.Rev.Stat.1991, ch. 95 ½, ¶ 313C-10.

45/3C-11. Disposition of proceeds

§ 3C-11. Disposition of proceeds. (a) When a watercraft located within the corporate limits of a city, village or town is towed away by a law enforcement agency having jurisdiction and disposed of as set forth in this Article, the proceeds of the public sale or disposition, after the deduction of towing, storage and processing charges, shall be deposited in the treasury of such city, village or town.

(b) When a watercraft located outside the corporate limits of any city, village or town is towed away by a law enforcement agency having jurisdiction and disposed of as set forth in this Article, the proceeds of the public sale or disposition, after deducting towing, storage and processing costs, shall be deposited in the county treasury of the county where the watercraft was located at the time of the tow.

Laws 1959, p. 1473, Art. IIIC, § 3C-11, added by P.A. 84-646, § 1, eff. Jan. 1, 1986.

Formerly Ill.Rev.Stat.1991, ch. 95 ½, ¶ 313C-11.

45/3C-12. Titling watercraft

§ 3C-12. Titling watercraft. When an applicant for a certificate of title presents to the Department of Natural Resources proof that he has purchased or acquired a watercraft at a public sale as authorized by this Article and such fact is certified by the law enforcement agency having jurisdiction over the public sale of the watercraft, the Department shall issue a certificate of title for the watercraft upon receipt of the statutory fee and a properly executed application for a certificate of title. The title issued by the Department under this Section shall be free of any lien that existed against the watercraft prior to the time the watercraft was acquired by the applicant under this Article.

Laws 1959, p. 1473, Art. IIIC, § 3C–12, added by P.A. 84–646, § 1, eff. Jan. 1, 1986. Amended by P.A. 89–445, § 9A–89, eff. Feb. 7, 1996.

Formerly Ill.Rev.Stat.1991, ch. 95 ½, ¶ 313C–12.

45/3C–13. Liability

§ 3C–13. Liability. A law enforcement officer or agency, towing service owner, operator or employee shall not be held liable for damages in any action brought by the registered owner, former registered owner or his legal representative, lienholder or any other person legally entitled to the possession of a watercraft when the watercraft was processed and sold or disposed of as provided by this Article.

Laws 1959, p. 1473, Art. IIIC, § 3C–13, added by P.A. 84–646, § 1, eff. Jan. 1, 1986.

Formerly Ill.Rev.Stat.1991, ch. 95 ½, ¶ 313C–13.

45/3C–14. Violations

§ 3C–14. Violations. Any person who violates or aids and abets in the violation of Section 3C–1 of this Act is guilty of a petty offense, and may be required by the court to make a disposition on the abandoned or unclaimed watercraft.

Laws 1959, p. 1473, Art. IIIC, § 3C 14, added by P.A. 84–646, § 1, eff. Jan. 1, 1986.

Formerly Ill.Rev.Stat.1991, ch. 95 ½, ¶ 313C–14.

ARTICLE IV. MOTORBOAT EQUIPMENT

45/4–1. Personal flotation devices

§ 4–1. Personal flotation devices.

A. No person may operate a watercraft unless at least one U.S. Coast Guard approved PFD of the following types or their equivalent is on board for each person: Type I, Type II or Type III.

B. No person may operate a personal watercraft or specialty prop-craft unless each person aboard is wearing a Type I, Type II, Type III or Type V PFD approved by the United States Coast Guard.

C. No person may operate a watercraft 16 feet or more in length, except a canoe or kayak, unless at least one Type IV U.S. Coast Guard approved PFD or its equivalent is on board in addition to the PFD's required in paragraph A of this Section.

D. A U.S. Coast Guard approved Type V personal flotation device may be carried in lieu of the Type I, II, III or IV personal flotation device required in this Section, if the Type V personal flotation device is approved for the activity in which it is being used.

E. When assisting a person on waterskis, aquaplane or similar device, there must be one U.S. Coast Guard approved PFD on board the watercraft for each person being assisted or towed or worn by the person being assisted or towed.

F. No person may operate a watercraft unless each device required by this Section is:

1. Readily accessible;
2. In serviceable condition;
3. Of the appropriate size for the person for whom it is intended; and
4. Legibly marked with the U.S. Coast Guard approval number.

G. Approved personal flotation devices are defined as follows:

Type I—A Type I personal flotation device is an approved device designed to turn an unconscious person in the water from a face downward position to a vertical or slightly backward position and to have more than 20 pounds of buoyancy.

Type II—A Type II personal flotation device is an approved device designed to turn an unconscious person in the water from a face downward position to a vertical or slightly backward position and to have at least 15½ pounds of buoyancy.

Type III—A Type III personal flotation device is an approved device designed to keep a conscious person in a vertical or slightly backward position and to have at least 15½ pounds of buoyancy.

Type IV—A Type IV personal flotation device is an approved device designed to be thrown to a person in the water and not worn. It is designed to have at least 16½ pounds of buoyancy.

Type V—A Type V personal flotation device is an approved device for restricted use and is acceptable only when used in the activity for which it is approved.

H. The provisions of subsections A through G of this Section shall not apply to sailboats.

I. No person may operate a watercraft under 26 feet in length unless a Type I, Type II, Type III, or Type V personal flotation device is being properly worn by each person under the age of 13 on board the watercraft at all times in which the watercraft is underway; however, this requirement shall not apply to persons who are below decks or in totally enclosed cabin spaces. The provisions of this subsection I shall not apply to a person operating a watercraft on private property.

Laws 1959, p. 1473, Art. IV, § 1. Amended by Laws 1965, p. 332, § 1; Laws 1967, p. 2217, § 1; P.A. 79–470, § 1, eff. Oct. 1, 1975; P.A. 80–560, § 1, eff. Oct. 1, 1977; P.A. 80–1495, § 37, eff. Jan. 8, 1979. Renumbered § 4–1 and amended by P.A. 82–783, Art. VII, § 2, eff. July 13, 1982. Amended by P.A. 85–149, § 1, eff. Jan. 1, 1988; P.A. 87–798, § 4, eff. Dec. 16, 1991; P.A. 87–391, § 1, eff. Jan. 1, 1992; P.A. 87–895, Art. 2, § 2–46, eff. Aug. 14, 1992; P.A. 90–411, § 5, eff. Jan. 1, 1998.

Formerly Ill.Rev.Stat.1991, ch. 95 ½, ¶ 314–1.

45/4–2. Lights

§ 4–2. Lights.

A. It is unlawful to operate any vessel less than 39 feet in length unless the following lights are carried and displayed when underway from sunset to sunrise:

1. A bright, white light after to show all around the horizon, visible for a distance of 2 miles. The word "visible" as used herein means visible on a dark night with clear atmosphere.

2. A combination light in the forepart of the boat lower than the white light after, showing green to starboard and red to port, so fixed as to throw a light from dead ahead to 2 points abaft the beam on their respective sides and visible for a distance of not less than 1 mile.

3. Lights under International Rules may be shown as an alternative to the above requirements.

B. Watercraft propelled by muscular power when underway shall carry on board from sunset to sunrise, but not fixed to any part of the boat, a lantern or flashlight capable of showing a white light visible all around the horizon at a distance of 2 miles or more, and shall display such lantern in sufficient time to avoid collision with another watercraft.

C. Every vessel 39 feet or more in length shall carry and display when underway such additional or alternate lights as shall be required by the U.S. Coast Guard for watercraft of equivalent length and type.

D. Sailboats equipped with motors and being propelled partly or solely by such motors shall carry and display the same lights required for motorboats of the same class. Sailboats being propelled entirely by sail between sunset and sunrise shall have lighted the combination running light, and a white light visible aft only. Sailboats 26 feet or more in length, equipped with motors but being propelled entirely by sail between sunset and sunrise, shall have lighted the colored side lights suitably screened, but not the white lights prescribed for motorboats.

E. Dinghies, tenders and other watercraft, whose principal function is as an auxiliary to other larger watercraft, when so operating need carry only a flashlight visible to other craft in the area, anything in this section to the contrary notwithstanding.

F. Vessels at anchor between the hours of sunset and sunrise, except those in a "Special Anchorage Area", shall display such anchor lights as shall be required by the U.S. Coast Guard for watercraft of equivalent length and type.

G. Watercraft operated manually or by motor which are located on bodies of water where motors of over 7½ horsepower are prohibited must be equipped during the hours between sunset and sunrise with a lantern or flashlight which is capable of showing a beam for 2 miles, anything in this Section to the contrary notwithstanding.

Laws 1959, p. 1473, Art. IV, § 2. Amended by Laws 1961, p. 3349, § 1; Laws 1963, p. 2012, § 1; Laws 1965, p. 332, § 1; Laws 1967, p. 2217, § 1. Renumbered § 4-2 and amended by P.A. 82-783, Art. VII, § 2, eff. July 13, 1982. Amended by P.A. 88-524, § 1, eff. July 1, 1994.

Formerly Ill.Rev.Stat.1991, ch. 95 ½, ¶ 314-2.

45/4-3. Mufflers

§ 4-3. Mufflers. A. All motorboats shall be equipped and maintained with an effective muffler or underwater exhaust system. For the purpose of this Section, an effective muffler or underwater exhaust system is one that does not produce sound levels that create excessive or unusual noise, or sound levels that are in excess of 90 decibels when subjected to a stationary sound level test as prescribed by the Society of Automotive Engineers in its procedure J2005.

B. No person may operate a motorboat on the waters of this State in a manner to exceed a noise level of 75 decibels measured as specified in the Society of Automotive Engineers in its procedure J1970 from any point on the shoreline, or from any point on the water within 20 feet of of the shoreline, of the body of water on which the motorboat is being operated.

C. No person may manufacture or offer for sale any motorboat for use on the waters of this State if that motorboat cannot be operated in compliance with the sound levels in subsections A and B above.

D. The provisions of this Section shall apply to all public waters over which the State has jurisdiction.

E. This Section does not apply to:

(1) a motorboat tuning up for or participating in official trials for a sanctioned race or regatta conducted as authorized by the appropriate unit of government, or

(2) a motorboat being operated by a boat or marine engine manufacturer for the purpose of testing or development as authorized by the appropriate unit of government.

F. Any person violating subsection A or B of this Section shall be required to:

(1) install an effective muffler system on the motorboat in violation;

(2) pass the sound level test prescribed by the Society of Automotive Engineers in its procedure J2005 before putting the motorboat back into use; and

(3) be subject to a Class B misdemeanor for the first offense and a Class A misdemeanor for any subsequent offense occurring within 3 years of the date of the most recent offense.

G. Any person violating subsection C of this Section shall be required to:

(1) install an effective muffler system on the motorboat in violation;

(2) pass the sound level test prescribed by the Society of Automotive Engineers in its procedure J2005 before putting the motorboat back into use; and

(3) be subject to a Class A misdemeanor for the first offense and a Class 4 felony for any subsequent offense.

H. Any person who operates any motorboat upon the waters of this State shall be deemed to have given consent to the test or tests as may be prescribed in this Section or by the Department to determine if the motorboat is in compliance with the provisions of this Section.

Laws 1959, p. 1473, Art. IV, § 3. Renumbered § 4-3 and amended by 82-783, Art. VII, § 2, eff. July 13, 1982. Amended by P.A. 87-391, § 1, eff. Jan. 1, 1992; P.A. 87-422, § 1, eff. Jan. 1, 1992; P.A. 87-895, Art. 2, § 2-46, eff. Aug. 14, 1992.

Formerly Ill.Rev.Stat.1991, ch. 95 ½, ¶ 314-3.

P.A. 87-895, the First 1992 General Revisory Act, provides in Article 2 for the revision and renumbering of certain Sections of Acts which have been added or amended by more than one Act of the 87th General Assembly; incorporates amendments to repealed Acts into successor laws passed by the same General Assembly; corrects errors, revises cross-references and deletes obsolete text in such Sections contained in Public Acts through P.A. 87-855.

45/4-4. Whistles

§ 4-4. Whistles. It is unlawful to operate a motorboat without a mouth, hand or power operated whistle, horn or other appliance, capable of producing a blast of 2 seconds or more duration and audible for at least one-half mile.

Laws 1959, p. 1473, Art. IV, § 4. Amended by Laws 1967, p. 2217, § 1; P.A. 79-470, § 1, eff. Oct. 1, 1975. Renumbered § 4-4 and amended by P.A. 82-783, Art. VII, § 2, eff. July 13, 1982.

Formerly Ill.Rev.Stat.1991, ch. 95 ½, ¶ 314-4.

45/4-5. Fire extinguisher

§ 4-5. Fire extinguisher. It is unlawful to operate a motorboat equipped with an internal combustion engine anywhere in this State without at least one U. S. Coast Guard approved fire extinguisher, so placed as to be readily accessible and in such condition as to be ready for immediate and effective use.

Laws 1959, p. 1473, Art. IV, § 5. Amended by Laws 1967, p. 2217, § 1; P.A. 79-470, § 1, eff. Oct. 1, 1975. Renumbered § 4-5 and amended by P.A. 82-783, Art. VII, § 2, eff. July 13, 1982. Amended by P.A. 85-149, § 1, eff. Jan. 1, 1988.

Formerly Ill.Rev.Stat.1991, ch. 95 ½, ¶ 314-5.

45/4-6. Carburetor arrestors

§ 4-6. Carburetor arrestors. Carburetors on all engines of motorboats other than those propelled by a detachable outboard motor shall be fitted with or protected by a U. S. Coast Guard approved device for arresting backfire.

Laws 1959, p. 1473, Art. IV, § 6. Renumbered § 4-6 and amended by P.A. 82-783, Art. VII, § 2, eff. July 13, 1982.

Formerly Ill.Rev.Stat.1991, ch. 95 ½, ¶ 314-6.

45/4-7. Ventilators

§ 4-7. Ventilators. Except for open boats, all motorboats which use fuel having a flashpoint of 110 degrees Fahrenheit or less shall have at least 2 ventilator ducts, fitted with cowls or their equivalent, for the efficient removal of explosive or flammable gases from the bilges of every engine and fuel tank compartment. There shall be at least one exhaust duct installed so as to extend from the open atmosphere to the lower portion of the bilge and at least one intake duct installed so as to extend to a point at least midway to the bilge or at least below the level of the carburetor air intake. The cowls shall be located and trimmed for maximum effectiveness and in such a manner so as to prevent displaced fumes from being recirculated.

Laws 1959, p. 1473, Art. IV, § 7. Amended by Laws 1967, p. 2217, § 1. Renumbered § 4-7 and amended by P.A. 82-783, Art. VII, § 2, eff. July 13, 1982.

Formerly Ill.Rev.Stat.1991, ch. 95 ½, ¶ 314-7.

45/4-8. Sirens and flashing lights

§ 4-8. Sirens and flashing lights.

(a) Except as provided in this Section, it shall be unlawful for any person to use a watercraft equipped with a siren or any red or blue oscillating, rotating, or flashing light. The use of a siren or light in violation of this Section shall constitute a public nuisance subject to confiscation and disposal as determined by a court of competent jurisdiction.

(b) Any authorized emergency watercraft described in subsection (c) or (d) may be equipped with a siren, but the siren shall not be used except when the watercraft is operating in response to an emergency call or in the immediate pursuit of an actual or suspected violator of the law.

(c) The use of blue oscillating, rotating, or flashing lights, whether lighted or unlighted, is prohibited except on law enforcement watercraft of State, federal, or local authorities.

(d) The use of red oscillating, rotating, or flashing lights, whether lighted or unlighted, is prohibited except on fire, rescue, or other emergency watercraft as authorized by State, federal, or local authorities having jurisdiction, provided the watercraft are clearly identifiable as such; the lights shall not be lighted except when responding to an emergency call or while actually engaged in a hazardous situation.

(e) The use of any other color of oscillating, rotating, or flashing lights, whether lighted or unlighted, is prohibited except as authorized by the Department.

Laws 1959, p. 1473, Art. IV, § 8. Renumbered § 4-8 and amended by P.A. 82-783, Art. VII, § 2, eff. July 13, 1982. Amended by P.A. 88-524, § 1, eff. July 1, 1994.

Formerly Ill.Rev.Stat.1991, ch. 95 ½, ¶ 314-8.

45/4-9. Sealing of marine heads

§ 4-9. Sealing of marine heads. No marine head (toilet) on any watercraft used upon waters of this State may be so constructed and operated as to permit the discharge of any sewage into the waters directly or indirectly.

Laws 1959, p. 1473, Art. IV, § 9, added by Laws 1967, p. 2217, § 1. Renumbered § 4-9 and amended by P.A. 82-783, Art. VII, § 2, eff. July 13, 1982. Amended by P.A. 88-524, § 1, eff. July 1, 1994.

Formerly Ill.Rev.Stat.1991, ch. 95 ½, ¶ 314-9.

45/4-10. Battery Covers

§ 4-10. Battery Covers. Every motorboat equipped with storage batteries shall be provided with suitable supports and secured against shifting with the motion of the boat. Such storage batteries shall be equipped with non-conductive shielding means to prevent accidental shorting of battery terminals.

Laws 1959, p. 1473, Art. IV, § 10, added by P.A. 76-1495, § 1, eff. Sept. 22, 1969. Renumbered § 4-10 and amended by P.A. 82-783, Art. VII, § 2, eff. July 13, 1982.

Formerly Ill.Rev.Stat.1991, ch. 95 ½, ¶ 314-10.

45/4-11. Lanyard cut-off switch

§ 4-11. Lanyard cut-off switch. No person may operate any motor boat, including personal watercraft or specialty prop-craft, which is equipped with a lanyard type engine cut-off switch unless such lanyard is properly attached to his or her person, clothing or worn PFD, as appropriate for the specific vessel.

Laws 1959, p. 1473, Art. IV, § 4-11, added by P.A. 87-798, § 4, eff. Dec. 16, 1991.

Formerly Ill.Rev.Stat.1991, ch. 95 ½, ¶ 314-11.

45/4-12. Visual distress signals

§ 4-12. Visual distress signals. It is unlawful to operate any watercraft on the waters of Lake Michigan without having onboard visual distress signals as required and approved by the U.S. Coast Guard, so placed as to be readily accessible and in such condition as to be ready for immediate and effective use.

Laws 1959, p. 1473, Art. IV, § 4-12, added by P.A. 88-524, § 1, eff. July 1, 1994.

ARTICLE V. OPERATION OF MOTORBOATS

45/5-1. Careless operation

§ 5-1. Careless operation. No person shall operate any watercraft in a careless or heedless manner so as to endanger any person or property or at a rate of speed greater than will permit him in the exercise of reasonable care to bring the watercraft to a stop within the assured clear distance ahead.

Laws 1959, p. 1473, Art. V, § 1. Renumbered § 5-1 and amended by P.A. 82-783, Art. VII, § 2, eff. July 13, 1982. Amended by P.A. 85-149, § 1, eff. Jan. 1, 1988.

Formerly Ill.Rev.Stat.1991, ch. 95 ½, ¶ 315-1.

45/5-2. Reckless operation

§ 5-2. Reckless operation. No person shall operate any watercraft, specialty prop-craft, personal watercraft or manipulate any water skis, aquaplane, or similar device in such a manner as to willfully or wantonly endanger the life, limb or property of any person, to weave through congested traffic, to jump the wake of another vessel unreasonably or unnecessarily close to the other vessel or when visibility around the other vessel is obstructed, to wait until the last possible moment to swerve to avoid collision, or operate any watercraft so as to approach or pass another watercraft in such a manner or at such a rate of speed as to create a hazardous wake or wash.

Laws 1959, p. 1473, Art. V, § 2. Amended by P.A. 79-875, § 1, eff. Oct. 1, 1975. Renumbered § 5-2 and amended by P.A. 82-783, Art. VII, § 2, eff. July 13, 1982. Amended by P.A. 85-149, § 1, eff. Jan. 1, 1988; P.A. 87-798, § 4, eff. Dec. 16, 1991.

Formerly Ill.Rev.Stat.1991, ch. 95 ½, ¶ 315-2.

45/5-2.1. § 5-2.1. Repealed by P.A. 80-268, § 1, eff. Jan. 1, 1978

45/5-3. Interference with navigation

§ 5-3. Interference with navigation. No person shall operate any watercraft in a manner which unreasonably or unnecessarily interferes with other watercraft or with the free and proper navigation of the waterways of the State. Anchoring under bridges or in heavily traveled channels constitutes such interference if unreasonable under the prevailing circumstances.

Laws 1959, p. 1473, Art. V, § 3. Amended by Laws 1961, p. 3349, § 1. Renumbered § 5-3 and amended by P.A. 82-783, Art. VII, § 2, eff. July 13, 1982.

Formerly Ill.Rev.Stat.1991, ch. 95 ½, ¶ 315-3.

45/5-4. Overloading

§ 5-4. Overloading. A. No motorboat may be loaded with passengers or cargo beyond its safe carrying capacity taking into consideration weather and other existing operating conditions.

B. Capacity plates. (1) Every vessel less than 26 feet in length, designed to carry 2 or more persons and to be propelled by machinery as its principal source of power or designed to be propelled by oars shall, if manufactured or offered for sale in this State, have affixed permanently thereto by the manufacturer a capacity plate as required by this Section. As used in this Section, "manufacture" means to construct or assemble a vessel or alter a vessel in such manner as to change its weight capacity.

(2) A capacity plate shall bear the following information permanently marked thereon in such manner as to be clearly visible and legible from the position designed or normally intended to be occupied by the operator of the vessel when under way:

a. For all vessels designed for or represented by the manufacturer as being suitable for use with outboard motor:

1. The total weight of persons, motor, gear and other articles placed aboard which the vessel is capable of carrying with safety under normal conditions.

2. The recommended number of persons commensurate with the weight capacity of the vessel and the presumed weight in pounds of each such person. In no instance may such presumed weight per person be less than 150 pounds.

3. Clear notice that the information appearing on the capacity plate is applicable under normal conditions and that the weight of the outboard motor and associated equipment is considered to be part of total weight capacity.

4. The maximum horsepower of the motor the vessel is designed or intended to accommodate.

b. For all other vessels to which this Section applies:

1. The total weight of persons, gear and other articles placed aboard which the vessel is capable of carrying with safety under normal conditions.

2. The recommended number of persons commensurate with the weight capacity of the vessel and the presumed weight in pounds of each such person. In no instance shall such presumed weight per person be less than 150 pounds.

3. Clear notice that the information appearing on the capacity plate is applicable under normal conditions.

(3) The information relating to maximum capacity required to appear on capacity plates by Subsection B(2) of this Section shall be determined in accordance with such methods and formulas as shall be prescribed by rule or regulation adopted by the Department. In prescribing such methods and formulas, the Department shall be guided by and give due regard to the necessity for uniformity in methods and formulas lawful for use in determining small vessel capacity in the several states and to any methods and formulas which may be recognized or recommended by the United States Coast Guard or any agency successor thereto.

(4) Any vessel to which this Section applies, not having a capacity plate meeting the requirements of law affixed thereto by the manufacturer thereof, may have such affixed by any other person in accordance with such rules and regulations as the Department may prescribe and may thereafter be offered for sale in this State, but no action taken pursuant to this Section, or in the manner described herein, shall relieve any manufacturer from liability for failure to comply with the requirements of this Section.

(5) The information appearing on a capacity plate shall be deemed to warrant that the manufacturer, or the person affixing the capacity plate is permitted by Subsection B(4) of this Section, as the case may be, has correctly and faithfully employed a method and formula for the calculation of maximum weight capacity prescribed by the Department and that the information appearing on the capacity plate with respect to maximum weight capacity and recommended number of persons is the result of the application of such method and formula, and with respect to information concerning horsepower limitations, that such information is not a deliberate or negligent misrepresentation.

(6) If any vessel required by this Section to have a capacity plate affixed thereto is of such design or construction as to make it impracticable or undesirable to affix such plate, the manufacturer, or other person having the responsibility for affixing the plate, may represent such impracticability or undesirability to the Department in writing. Upon determination by the Department that such representation has merit and that a proper and effective substitute for the capacity plate which will serve the same purpose is feasible, the Department may authorize such alternative compliance and such alternative compliance shall thereafter be deemed compliance with the capacity plate requirements of this Section.

(7) The Department may by rules or regulations exempt from the requirements of this Section vessels which it finds to be of such unconventional design or construction that the information required on capacity plates would not assist in promoting safety or is not reasonably obtainable.

(8) The Department is authorized to issue and amend rules and regulations to carry out the purposes of this Section.

Failure to affix a proper capacity plate shall constitute a separate violation of this subsection B for each vessel with respect to which such failure occurs.

Laws 1959, p. 1473, Art. V, § 4. Amended by Laws 1967, p. 707, § 1, eff. Jan. 1, 1968. Renumbered § 5-4 and amended by P.A. 82-783, Art. VII, § 2, eff. July 13, 1982.

Formerly Ill.Rev.Stat.1991, ch. 95 ½, ¶ 315-4.

45/5-5. Incapacity of operator

§ 5-5. Incapacity of operator. The owner of any motorboat or any person having such in charge or in control shall not authorize or knowingly permit the same to be operated by any person who by reason of physical or mental disability is incapable of operating such motorboat under the prevailing circumstances.

Laws 1959, p. 1473, Art. V, § 5. Renumbered § 5-5 and amended by P.A. 82-783, Art. VII, § 2, eff. July 13, 1982.

Formerly Ill.Rev.Stat.1991, ch. 95 ½, ¶ 315-5.

45/5-6. Overpowering

§ 5-6. Overpowering. No motorboat shall be equipped with any motor or other propulsion machinery beyond its safe power capacity taking into consideration the type and construction of such motorboat and other existing operating conditions.

Laws 1959, p. 1473, Art. V, § 6. Renumbered § 5-6 and amended by P.A. 82-783, Art. VII, § 2, eff. July 13, 1982.

Formerly Ill.Rev.Stat.1991, ch. 95 ½, ¶ 315-6.

45/5-7. Restricted areas

§ 5-7. Restricted areas. No person shall operate a watercraft within a water area that has been clearly marked by buoys or some other distinguishing device as a bathing, fishing, swimming or otherwise restricted area by the Department or a political subdivision of the State or by an owner or lessee of property in accordance with his or her rights to the use of the property, except in the manner prescribed by the buoys or other distinguishing devices. This Section shall not apply in the case of an emergency, or to patrol or rescue craft.

No person shall operate a watercraft within 150 feet of a public launching ramp owned, operated or maintained by the Department or a political subdivision of the State at greater than a "No Wake" speed as defined in Section 5-12 of this Act. Posting of the areas by the Department or a political subdivision of the State is not required.

The Department and other political subdivisions of the State may, within their discretion and after issuing an administrative rule in accordance with the Illinois Administrative Procedure Act, [1] designate certain areas by proper signs to be bathing, fishing, swimming or otherwise restricted areas, or eliminate, alter or otherwise modify existing areas. The Department or a political subdivision of the State shall further have the authority in order to fully carry out the provisions of this Act to place signs, beacons and buoys in designated areas controlling the flow of traffic.

It shall be unlawful for any person to deface, move, obliterate, tear down, or destroy, in whole or in part, or attempt to deface, move, obliterate, tear down or destroy any buoys or signs posted pursuant to the provisions of this Act, except as authorized by the Department.

Laws 1959, p. 1473, Art. V, § 7. Amended by Laws 1961, p. 3349, § 1; Laws 1963, p. 2012, § 1. Renumbered § 5-7 and amended by P.A. 82-783, Art. VII, § 2, eff. July 13, 1982. Amended by P.A. 85-149, § 1, eff. Jan. 1, 1988; P.A. 87-803, § 1, eff. July 1, 1992; P.A. 92-651, § 78, eff. July 11, 2002.

Formerly Ill.Rev.Stat.1991, ch. 95 ½, ¶ 315-7.

[1] 5 ILCS 100/1-1 et seq.

45/5-8 to 45/5-11. §§ 5-8 to 5-11. Repealed by P.A. 85-149, § 2, eff. Jan. 1, 1988

45/5-11a. § 5-11a. Renumbered as § 5-16a by P.A. 88-670, Art. 3, § 3-81, eff. Dec. 2, 1994

45/5-11b. § 5-11b. Renumbered as § 5-16b by P.A. 88-670, Art. 3, § 3-81, eff. Dec. 2, 1994

45/5-12. Wake; posted areas

§ 5-12. A wake is defined as a movement of the water created by a boat underway great enough to disturb a boat at rest, but under no circumstances shall a boat underway exceed 5 miles per hour while in a posted "No Wake" area. "No Wake" areas shall be clearly posted with buoys or appropriate signs except as provided in Section 5-7 of this

Act. All buoys or signs posting "No Wake" areas shall meet the specifications as prescribed by the United States Coast Guard or the Illinois Department of Natural Resources.

Laws 1959, p. 1473, Art. V, § 7.5, added by P.A. 79–470, § 1, eff. Oct. 1, 1975. Renumbered § 5–12 and amended by P.A. 82–783, Art. VII, § 2, eff. July 13, 1982. Amended by P.A. 87–803, § 1, eff. July 1, 1992; P.A. 89–445, § 9A–89, eff. Feb. 7, 1996.

Formerly Ill.Rev.Stat.1991, ch. 95 ½, ¶ 315–7.5.

45/5-13. Traffic rules

§ 5–13. Traffic rules. **A. Passing.** When 2 boats are approaching each other "head on" or nearly so (so as to involve risk of collision), each boat must bear to the right and pass the other boat on its left side.

B. Crossing. When boats approach each other obliquely or at right angles, the boat approaching on the right side has the right of way.

C. Overtaking. One boat may overtake another on either side but must grant right of way to the overtaken boat.

D. Sailboats and Rowboats. When a motorboat is approaching a boat propelled solely by sails or oars, the motorboat must yield the right of way to the sailboat or rowboat except, when a large craft is navigating in a confined channel, the large craft has the right of way over a boat propelled solely by oars or sails.

Laws 1959, p. 1473, Art. V, § 8. Amended by Laws 1967, p. 2217, § 1. Renumbered § 5–13 and amended by P.A. 82–783, Art. VII, § 2, eff. July 13, 1982.

Formerly Ill.Rev.Stat.1991, ch. 95 ½, ¶ 315–8.

45/5-14. Water Skiing

§ 5–14. Water Skiing. A. No person may operate a motorboat that has in tow or is otherwise assisting a person on water skis, an aquaplane, or a similar contrivance in or upon any waterway, unless the motorboat has a capacity of at least 3 persons and is occupied by at least 2 competent persons.

B. No person may operate a motorboat having in tow or otherwise be assisting a person on water skis, aquaplane or similar contrivance from the period of one-half hour after sunset to one-half hour before sunrise. This paragraph B does not apply to motorboats used in duly authorized water ski tournaments, competitions, exhibitions or trials therefor where adequate lighting is provided.

C. All persons operating a motorboat having in tow or otherwise assisting a person on water skis, aquaplane or similar contrivance, must be careful and prudent in their operation and keep at a reasonable distance from persons and property so as not to endanger the life or property of any person.

D. No person may operate or manipulate any vessel, tow rope or other device by which the direction or location of water skis, aquaplane, or similar device may be affected or controlled in such a way as to cause the water skis, aquaplane, or similar device, or any persons thereon to collide with or strike against any person or object, except ski jumps, buoys and like objects normally used in competitive or recreational skiing.

Laws 1959, p. 1473, Art. V, § 9. Amended by Laws 1961, p. 3349, § 1; Laws 1967, p. 2217, § 1; P.A. 76–1495, § 1, eff. Sept. 22, 1969. Renumbered § 5–14 and amended by P.A. 82–783, Art. VII, § 2, eff. July 13, 1982. Amended by P.A. 90–412, § 5, eff. Jan. 1, 1998.

Formerly Ill.Rev.Stat.1991, ch. 95 ½, ¶ 315–9.

45/5-15. Regattas and races

§ 5–15. Regattas and races. A. The Department may authorize the holding of regattas, motorboat or other boat races on any waters of this State. It shall adopt and may, from time to time, amend regulations concerning the safety of motorboats and other vessels and persons thereon, either observers or participants. Whenever a regatta, motorboat or other boat race is proposed to be held, the person in charge thereof, shall, at least 30 days prior thereto, file an application with the Department for permission to hold such regatta, motorboat or other boat race. The application shall set forth the date, time and location where it is proposed to hold such regatta, motorboat or other boat race and it shall not be conducted without authorization of the Department in writing.

B. When a regatta, motorboat or other boat race authorized or proposed to be authorized under subsection A of this Section is to be held on a body of water owned and operated by a unit of local government, the unit of local government may schedule those events, but only after adopting an ordinance providing for such scheduling and filing it with the Department.

C. The provisions of this Section do not exempt any person from compliance with applicable Federal law or regulation, but nothing contained herein may be construed to require the securing of a State permit pursuant to this Section if a permit therefor has been obtained from an authorized agency of the United States.

Laws 1959, p. 1473, Art. V, § 10. Amended by Laws 1967, p. 2217, § 1. Renumbered § 5–15 and amended by P.A. 82–783, Art. VII, § 2, eff. July 13, 1982. Amended by P.A. 84–559, § 1, eff. Jan. 1, 1986.

Formerly Ill.Rev.Stat.1991, ch. 95 ½, ¶ 315–10.

45/5-16. Operating a watercraft under the influence of alcohol, other drug, or combination thereof

§ 5–16. Operating a watercraft under the influence of alcohol, other drug, or combination thereof.

(A) 1. A person shall not operate any watercraft within this State while:

(a) The alcohol concentration in such person's blood or breath is a concentration at which driving a motor vehicle is prohibited under subdivision (1) of subsection (a) of Section 11–501 of the Illinois Vehicle Code; [1]

(b) Under the influence of alcohol;

(c) Under the influence of any other drug or combination of drugs to a degree which renders such person incapable of safely operating any watercraft;

(d) Under the combined influence of alcohol and any other drug or drugs to a degree which renders such person incapable of safely operating a watercraft; or

(e) There is any amount of a drug, substance, or compound in the person's blood or urine resulting from the unlawful use or consumption of cannabis as defined in the Cannabis Control Act [2] or a controlled substance listed in the Illinois Controlled Substances Act.[3]

2. The fact that any person charged with violating this Section is or has been legally entitled to use alcohol, or other drugs, or any combination of both, shall not constitute a defense against any charge of violating this Section.

3. Every person convicted of violating this Section shall be guilty of a Class A misdemeanor, except as otherwise provided in this Section.

4. Every person convicted of violating this Section shall be guilty of a Class 4 felony if:

(a) He has a previous conviction under this Section; or

(b) The offense results in personal injury where a person other than the operator suffers great bodily harm or permanent disability or disfigurement, when the violation was a proximate cause of the injuries. A person guilty of a Class 4 felony under this subparagraph (b), if sentenced to a term of imprisonment, shall be sentenced to a term of not less than one year nor more than 12 years.

5. Every person convicted of violating this Section shall be guilty of a Class 2 felony if the offense results in the death of a person. A person guilty of a Class 2 felony under this paragraph 5, if sentenced to a term of imprisonment, shall be sentenced to a term of not less than 3 years and not more than 14 years.

6. (a) In addition to any criminal penalties imposed, the Department of Natural Resources shall suspend the watercraft operation privileges of any person convicted of a misdemeanor under this Section for a period of one year.

(b) In addition to any criminal penalties imposed, the Department of Natural Resources shall suspend the watercraft operation privileges of any person convicted of a felony under this Section for a period of 3 years.

(B) 1. Any person who operates any watercraft upon the waters of this State shall be deemed to have given consent to a chemical test or tests of blood, breath or urine for the purpose of determining the alcohol, other drug, or combination thereof content of such person's blood if arrested for any offense of subsection (A) above. The test or tests shall be administered at the direction of the arresting officer.

2. Any person who is dead, unconscious or who is otherwise in a condition rendering such person incapable of refusal, shall be deemed not to have withdrawn the consent provided above.

3. A person requested to submit to a test as provided above shall be verbally advised by the law enforcement officer requesting the test that a refusal to submit to the test will result in suspension of such person's privilege to operate a watercraft. Following this warning, if a person under arrest refuses upon the request of a law enforcement officer to submit to a test designated by the officer, none shall be given, but the law enforcement officer shall file with the clerk of the circuit court for the county in which the arrest was made, a sworn statement naming the person refusing to take and complete the test or tests requested under the provisions of this Section. Such sworn statement shall identify the arrested person, such person's current residence address and shall specify that a refusal by such person to take the test or tests was made. Such sworn statement shall include a statement that the arresting officer had reasonable cause to believe the person was operating the watercraft within this State while under the influence of alcohol, other drug, or combination thereof and that such test or tests were made as an incident to and following the lawful arrest for an offense as defined in this Section or a similar provision of a local ordinance, and that the person after being arrested for an offense arising out of acts alleged to have been committed while so operating a watercraft refused to submit to and complete a test or tests as requested by the law enforcement officer.

The clerk shall thereupon notify such person in writing that the person's privilege to operate a watercraft will be suspended unless, within 28 days from the date of mailing of the notice, such person shall request in writing a hearing thereon; if the person desires a hearing, such person shall file a complaint in the circuit court for and in the county in which such person was arrested for such hearing. Such hearing shall proceed in the court in the same manner as other civil proceedings, shall cover only the issues of whether the person was placed under arrest for an offense as defined in this Section or a similar provision of a local ordinance as evidenced by the issuance of a uniform citation; whether the arresting officer had reasonable grounds to believe that such person was operating a watercraft while under the influence of alcohol, other drug, or combination thereof; and whether such person refused to submit and complete the test or tests upon the request of the law enforcement officer. Whether the person was informed that such person's privilege to operate a watercraft would be suspended if such person refused to submit to the test or tests shall not be an issue.

If the court finds against the person on the issues before the court, the clerk shall immediately notify the Department of Natural Resources of the court's decision, and the Department shall suspend the watercraft operation privileges of the person for at least 2 years.

4. A person must submit to each test offered by the law enforcement officer in order to comply with the implied consent provisions of this Section.

5. The provisions of Section 11-501.2 of the Illinois Vehicle Code, [4] as amended, concerning the certification and use of chemical tests apply to the use of such tests under this Section.

(C) Upon the trial of any civil or criminal action or proceeding arising out of acts alleged to have been committed by any person while operating a watercraft while under the influence of alcohol, the concentration of alcohol in the person's blood or breath at the time alleged as shown by analysis of a person's blood, urine, breath, or other bodily substance shall give rise to the presumptions specified in subdivisions 1, 2, and 3 of subsection (b) of Section 11–501.2 of the Illinois Vehicle Code. The foregoing provisions of this subsection (C) shall not be construed as limiting the introduction of any other relevant evidence bearing upon the question whether the person was under the influence of alcohol.

(D) If a person under arrest refuses to submit to a chemical test under the provisions of this Section, evidence of refusal shall be admissible in any civil or criminal action or proceeding arising out of acts alleged to have been committed while the person under the influence of alcohol, or other drugs, or combination of both was operating a watercraft.

(E) The owner of any watercraft or any person given supervisory authority over a watercraft, may not knowingly permit a watercraft to be operated by any person under the influence of alcohol, other drug, or combination thereof.

(F) Whenever any person is convicted of a violation of this Section, the court shall notify the Division of Law Enforcement of the Department of Natural Resources, to provide the Department with the records essential for the performance of the Department's duties to monitor and enforce any order of suspension or revocation concerning the privilege to operate a watercraft.

(G) No person who has been arrested and charged for violating paragraph 1 of subsection (A) of this Section shall operate any watercraft within this State for a period of 6 hours after such arrest.

Laws 1959, p. 1473, Art. V, § 11. Amended by Laws 1967, p. 2217, § 1. Renumbered § 5–16 and amended by P.A. 82–

783, Art. VII, § 2, eff. July 13, 1982. Amended by P.A. 84–515, § 1, eff. Jan. 1, 1986; P.A. 85–147, § 1, eff. Jan. 1, 1988; P.A. 85–1328, § 1, eff. Aug. 31, 1988; P.A. 86–535, § 1, eff. Jan. 1, 1990; P.A. 88–175, § 1, eff. Jan. 1, 1994; P.A. 88–670, Art. 2, § 2–60, eff. Dec. 2, 1994; P.A. 89–445, § 9A–89, eff. Feb. 7, 1996; P.A. 90–215, § 10, eff. Jan. 1, 1998; P.A. 90–655, § 154, eff. July 30, 1998; P.A. 92–615, § 10, eff. Jan. 1, 2003.

Formerly Ill.Rev.Stat.1991, ch. 95 ½, ¶ 315–11.

[1] 625 ILCS 5/11–501.

[2] 720 ILCS 550/1 et seq.

[3] 720 ILCS 570/100 et seq.

[4] 625 ILCS 5/11–501.2.

Another § 5–16, relating to unlawful operation of a personal watercraft or a specialty prop craft at night, was renumbered § 5–20 by P.A. 88–670, Art. 2, § 2–60.

P.A. 90–655, the First 1998 General Revisory Act, amended various Acts to delete obsolete text, to correct patent and technical errors, to revise cross references, to resolve multiple actions in the 89th and 90th General Assemblies and to make certain technical corrections in P.A. 89–708 through P.A. 90–566.

45/5–16a. Admissibility of written blood alcohol test results conducted in the regular course of providing emergency medical treatment

§ 5–16a. Admissibility of written blood alcohol test results conducted in the regular course of providing emergency medical treatment.

(a) Notwithstanding any other provision of law, the written results of blood alcohol tests conducted upon persons receiving medical treatment in a hospital emergency room are admissible in evidence as a business record exception to the hearsay rule only in prosecutions for any violation of Section 5–16 of this Act or a similar provision of a local ordinance or in prosecutions for reckless homicide brought under the Criminal Code of 1961,[1] when each of the following criteria are met:

(1) the blood alcohol tests were ordered by a physician on duty at the hospital emergency room and were performed in the regular course of providing emergency medical treatment in order to assist the physician in diagnosis or treatment;

(2) the blood alcohol tests were performed by the hospital's own laboratory; and

(3) the written results of the blood alcohol tests were received and considered by the physician on duty at the hospital emergency room to assist that physician in diagnosis or treatment.

(b) The confidentiality provisions of law pertaining to medical records and medical treatment shall not be applicable with regard to blood alcohol tests performed under the provisions of this Section in prosecutions as specified in subsection (a) of this Section. No person shall be liable for civil damages as a result of the evidentiary use of blood alcohol test results under this Section or as a result of that person's testimony made available under this Section.

Laws 1959, p. 1473, Art. V, § 5–11a, added by P.A. 87–803, § 1, eff. July 1, 1992. Renumbered § 5–16a and amended by P.A. 88–670, Art. 3, § 3–81, eff. Dec. 2, 1994.

Formerly Ill.Rev.Stat.1991, ch. 95 ½, ¶ 315–11a.

[1] 720 ILCS 5/1–1 et seq.

45/5–16b. Preliminary breath screening test

§ 5–16b. Preliminary breath screening test. If a law enforcement officer has reasonable suspicion to believe that a person is violating or has violated Section 5–16 or a similar provision of a local ordinance, the officer, prior to an arrest, may request the person to provide a sample of his or her breath for a preliminary breath screening test using a portable device approved by the Department of State Police. The results of this preliminary breath screening test may be used by the law enforcement officer for the purpose of assisting with the determination of whether to require a chemical test as authorized under Section 5–16 and the appropriate type of test to request. Any chemical test authorized under Section 5–16 may be requested by the officer regardless of the result of the preliminary breath screening test if probable cause for an arrest exists. The result of a preliminary breath screening test may be used by the defendant as evidence in any administrative or court proceeding involving a violation of Section 5–16.

Laws 1959, p. 1473, Art. V, § 5–11b, added by P.A. 87–803, § 1, eff. July 1, 1992. Renumbered § 5–16b and amended by P.A. 88–670, Art. 3, § 3–81, eff. Dec. 2, 1994. Amended by P.A. 90–215, § 10, eff. Jan. 1, 1998; P.A. 91–828, § 15, eff. Jan. 1, 2001.

Formerly Ill.Rev.Stat.1991, ch. 95 ½, ¶ 315–11b.

45/5–17. Uniform waterway marking system

§ 5–17. The Department is authorized and empowered to establish a system of regulatory aids on the waters of the State in accordance with United States Coast Guard specifications and as recommended by the Coast Guard as a uniform waterway marking system.

Laws 1959, p. 1473, Art. V, § 12, added by Laws 1965, p. 332, § 1. Renumbered § 5–17 and amended by P.A. 82–783, Art. VII, § 2, eff. July 13, 1982.

Formerly Ill.Rev.Stat.1991, ch. 95 ½, ¶ 315–12.

45/5–18. Age of operators; limitations; certificates

§ 5–18. No person under 10 years of age may operate a motorboat. Persons at least 10 years of age and less than 12 years of age may operate a motorboat only if they are accompanied on the motorboat and under the direct control of a parent or guardian or a person at least 18 years of age designated by a parent or guardian. Persons at least 12 years of age and less than 18 years of age may operate a motorboat only if they are accompanied on the motorboat and under the direct control of a parent or guardian or a person at least 18 years of age designated by a parent or guardian, or such motorboat operator is in possession of a Boating Safety Certificate issued by the Department of Natural Resources, Division of Law Enforcement, authorizing the holder to operate motorboats.

Violations of this Section done with the knowledge of a parent or guardian shall be deemed a violation by the parent or guardian and punishable under Section 11A–1–6.

The Department of Natural Resources, Division of Law Enforcement, shall establish a program of instruction on boating safety, laws, regulations and administrative laws, and any other subject matter which might be related to the subject of general boat safety. The program shall be conducted by instructors certified by the Department of Natural Resources, Division of Law Enforcement. The course of instruction for persons certified to teach boating safety shall be not less than 8 hours in length, and the Department shall have the authority to revoke the certification of any instructor who has demonstrated his inability to conduct courses on the subject matter. Students satisfactorily completing a program of not less than 8 hours in length shall receive a certificate of safety from the Department of Natural Resources, Division of Law Enforcement. The Department may cooperate with schools, private clubs and other organizations in offering boating safety courses throughout the State of Illinois.

The Department shall issue certificates of boating safety to persons 10 years of age or older successfully completing the prescribed course of instruction and passing such tests as may be prescribed by the Department. The Department may charge each person who enrolls in a course of instruction a fee not to exceed $5. If a fee is authorized by the Department, the Department shall authorize instructors conducting such courses meeting standards established by it to charge for the rental of facilities or for the cost of materials utilized in the course. Fees retained by the Department shall be utilized to defray a part of its expenses to operate the safety and accident reporting programs of the Department.

A person over the age of 12 years who holds a valid certificate issued by another state, a province of the Dominion of Canada, the United States Coast Guard Auxiliary or the United States Power Squadron need not obtain a certificate from the Department if the course content of the program in such other state, province or organization substantially meets that established by the Department under this Section. A certificate issued by the Department or by another state, province of the Dominion of Canada or approved organization shall not constitute an operator's license, but shall certify only that the student has successfully passed a course in boating safety instruction.

The Department of Natural Resources, Division of Law Enforcement, shall implement and enforce the provisions of this Section.

Laws 1959, p. 1473, Art. V, § 13, added by P.A. 80-268, § 2, eff. Jan. 1, 1978. Renumbered § 5-18 and amended by P.A. 82-783, Art. VII, § 2, eff. July 13, 1982. Amended by P.A. 87-798, § 4, eff. Dec. 16, 1991; P.A. 89-445, § 9A-89, eff. Feb. 7, 1996; P.A. 91-357, § 234, eff. July 29, 1999.

Formerly Ill.Rev.Stat.1991, ch. 95 ½, ¶ 315-13.

45/5-19. Skin diving

§ 5-19. Skin diving.

(A) 1. No person may engage in underwater diving or swimming with the use of swimming fins or skin diving in waters other than marked swimming areas or within 150 feet of shoreline.

2. No person may engage in underwater diving or swimming with the use of self-contained underwater breathing apparatus in waters other than marked swimming areas, unless the location of such diving or swimming is distinctly marked by a diver's flag, not less than 12 inches high and 15 inches long, displaying one diagonal white stripe 3 inches wide on a red background, and of a height above the water so as to be clearly apparent at a distance of 100 yards under normal conditions, and so designed and displayed as to be visible from any point on the horizon.

3. Except in case of emergency, anyone engaging in such diving or swimming shall not rise to the surface outside of a radius of 50 feet from such flag.

4. No person engaged in such diving or swimming shall interfere with the operation of anyone fishing, nor engage in such diving or swimming in established traffic lanes; nor shall any person acting alone, or with another, intentionally or unintentionally block or obstruct any boat in any manner from proceeding to its destination where a reasonable alternative is unavailable. A reasonable alternative route is available when the otherwise unobstructed boat can proceed to its destination without reducing its lawful speed, by passing to the right or to the left of a marked diving operation.

(B) An alternate flag recognized and approved by the United States Coast Guard may be substituted for the flag required in subsection (A)2 of this Section.

(C) No watercraft shall be operated within 150 feet of a diving flag except for watercraft directly associated with that diving activity.

Laws 1959, p. 1473, Art. V, § 5-14, added by P.A. 85-149, § 1, eff. Jan. 1, 1988. Amended by P.A. 85-1209, Art. III, § 3-61, eff. Aug. 30, 1988. Renumbered § 5-19 and amended by P.A. 87-895, Art. 3, § 3-53, eff. Aug. 14, 1992. Amended by P.A. 90-655, § 154, eff. July 30, 1998.

Formerly Ill.Rev.Stat.1991, ch. 95½, ¶ 315-14.

45/5-20. Unlawful operation at night

§ 5-20. Unlawful operation at night. Beginning July 1, 1994, no person shall operate a personal watercraft or a specialty prop craft between the hours of sunset and sunrise.

Laws 1959, p. 1473, Art. V, § 5-16, added by P.A. 88-524, § 1, eff. July 1, 1994. Renumbered § 5-20 and amended by P.A. 88-670, Art. 2, § 2-60, eff. Dec. 2, 1994.

P.A. 88-670, Article 2, of the First 1994 General Revisory Act, resolved multiple actions in the 88th General Assembly and made certain technical corrections in P.A. 88-1 through P.A. 88-538.

45/5-21. Passenger location

§ 5-21. Passenger location. No person operating a motorboat shall allow a person in the motorboat to ride or sit on the gunwales, tops of seat backs, or on the decking over the bow or stern of the motorboat while the motorboat is underway, unless the person is inboard of guards or rails provided on the motorboat to prevent passengers from being lost overboard.

Nothing in this Section shall be construed to prohibit entry upon the decking over the bow or stern of the motorboat for the purpose of anchoring, mooring, or casting off or some other necessary purpose nor to prohibit customary practices while lawfully engaged in commercial fishing under the provisions of the Fish and Aquatic Life Code [1] or hunting and trapping under the provisions of the Wildlife Code.[2]

The provisions of this Section shall not apply to the driver of the boat, a person while fishing or to a person on private property.

Laws 1959, p. 1473, Art. V, § 5-21, added by P.A. 90-412, § 5, eff. Jan. 1, 1998.

1 515 ILCS 5/1 et seq.

2 520 ILCS 5/1 et seq.

ARTICLE VI. ACCIDENT REPORTS—OPERATOR'S RESPONSIBILITY—TRANSMITTAL OF INFORMATION

Section

45/6-1. Collisions, accidents, and casualties; reports

§ 6-1. Collisions, accidents, and casualties; reports.

A. The operator of a vessel involved in a collision, accident, or other casualty, so far as he can without serious danger to his own vessel, crew, passengers and guests, if any, shall render to other persons affected by the collision, accident, or other casualty assistance as may be practicable and as may be necessary in order to save them from or minimize any danger caused by the collision, accident, or other casualty, and also shall give his name, address, and identification of his vessel to any person injured and to the owner of any property damaged in the collision, accident, or other casualty.

B. In the case of collision, accident, or other casualty involving a vessel, the operator, if the collision, accident, or other casualty results in death or injury to a person or damage to property in excess of $500, shall file with the Department a full description of the collision, accident, or other casualty, including information as the Department may by regulation require. Reports of the accidents must be filed with the Department on a Department Accident Report form within 5 days.

C. Reports of accidents resulting in personal injury, where a person is incapacitated for a period exceeding 72 hours, must be filed with the Department on a Department Accident Report form within 5 days. Accidents that result in loss of life shall be reported to the Department on a Department form within 48 hours.

D. All required accident reports and supplemental reports are without prejudice to the individual reporting, and are for the confidential use of the Department, except that the Department may disclose the identity of a person involved in an accident when the identity is not otherwise known or when the person denies his presence at the accident. No report may be used as evidence in any trial, civil or criminal, arising out of an accident, except that the Department must furnish upon demand of any person who has or claims to have made a report or upon demand of any court a certificate showing that a specified accident report has or has not been made to the Department solely to prove a compliance or a failure to comply with the requirements that a report be made to the Department.

E. (1) Every coroner or medical examiner shall on or before the 10th day of each month report in writing to the Department the circumstances surrounding the death of any person that has occurred as the result of a boating accident within the examiner's jurisdiction during the preceding calendar month.

(2) Within 6 hours after a death resulting from a boating accident, but in any case not more than 12 hours after the occurrence of the boating accident, a blood specimen of at least 10 cc shall be withdrawn from the body of the decedent by the coroner or medical examiner or by a qualified person at the direction of the physician. All morticians shall obtain a release from the coroner or medical examiner prior to proceeding with embalming any body coming under the scope of this Section. The blood so drawn shall be forwarded to a laboratory approved by the Department of State Police for analysis of the alcoholic content of the blood specimen. The coroner or medical examiner causing the blood to be withdrawn shall be notified of the results of each analysis made and shall forward the results of each analysis to the Department. The Department shall keep a record of all examinations to be used for statistical purposes only. The cumulative results of the examinations, without identifying the individuals involved, shall be disseminated and made public by the Department.

Laws 1959, p. 1473, Art. VI, § 1. Amended by Laws 1967, p. 2217, § 1. Renumbered § 6-1 and amended by P.A. 82-783, Art. VII, § 2, eff. July 13, 1982. Amended by P.A. 84-515, § 1, eff. Jan. 1, 1986; P.A. 85-149, § 1, eff. Jan. 1, 1988; P.A. 87-803, § 1, eff. July 1, 1992; P.A. 91-828, § 15, eff. Jan. 1, 2001.

Formerly Ill.Rev.Stat.1991, ch. 95 ½, ¶ 316-1.

45/6-2. Operator's responsibility

§ 6-2. Operator's responsibility. The operator of a watercraft is liable for any injury or damage occasioned by the negligent operation of such watercraft, whether such negligence consists of a violation of the provisions of the Statutes of this State, or in the failure to observe such ordinary care in such operation as the rules of the common law require.

Laws 1959, p. 1473, Art. VI, § 2. Renumbered § 6-2 and amended by P.A. 82-783, Art. VII, § 2, eff. July 13, 1982.

Formerly Ill.Rev.Stat.1991, ch. 95 ½, ¶ 316-2.

45/6-3. Transmittal of information

§ 6-3. Transmittal of information. In accordance with any request duly made by an authorized official or agency of the United States, any information compiled or otherwise available to the Department pursuant to subsection (B) of Section 6-1 [1] shall be transmitted to such official or agency of the United States.

Laws 1959, p. 1473, Art. VI, § 3. Renumbered § 6-3 and amended by P.A. 82-783, Art. VII, § 2, eff. July 13, 1982.

Formerly Ill.Rev.Stat.1991, ch. 95 ½, ¶ 316-3.

1 625 ILCS 45/6-1.

ARTICLE VII. BUSINESS OF BOAT RENTAL SERVICE

Section

45/7-1. License

§ 7-1. On and after March 1, 1960 it shall be unlawful for any person to engage in the business of operating a boat or boats carrying passengers for hire, or renting a boat or boats for hire without first having obtained a license so to do from the Department. Such license shall be renewable each year on March 1st, shall be good only for one year or portion of a year to March 1st, and it shall be unlawful for such person to so engage in such business without having a valid license currently then in force.

Laws 1959, p. 1473, Art. VII, § 1. Renumbered § 7-1 and amended by P.A. 82-783, Art. VII, § 2, eff. July 13, 1982. Amended by P.A. 85-149, § 1, eff. Jan. 1, 1988.

Formerly Ill.Rev.Stat.1991, ch. 95 ½, ¶ 317-1.

45/7-2. License fee

§ 7-2. License fee. The fee for a license to operate a boat for carrying passengers for hire shall be $50 for each boat. The fee for a license for engaging in the business of renting boats for hire shall be $30, plus an annual fee for each boat rented or offered for rent of $1 for each boat less than 16 feet in length; $2 for each boat 16 feet or over and less than 26 feet in length; and $8 for each boat 26 feet or over in length. No boat shall, after March 1, 1960, be rented or offered for rent until such license has been granted and the boat marked as hereinafter provided.

Laws 1959, p. 1473, Art. VII, § 2. Renumbered § 7-2 and amended by P.A. 82-783, Art. VII, § 2, eff. July 13, 1982. Amended by P.A. 85-149, § 1, eff. Jan. 1, 1988.

Formerly Ill.Rev.Stat.1991, ch. 95 ½, ¶ 317-2.

45/7-3. Rules and regulations

§ 7-3. Rules and regulations. The Department is hereby empowered, and it shall be their duty, to prescribe methods of inspection to determine the weight capacity for each boat carrying passengers for hire, or for rent, and to satisfy the Department that such boat is of a suitable structure for the service in which it is to be employed, and is in a condition to warrant the belief that it may be used in navigation with safety to life and property.

Laws 1959, p. 1473, Art. VII, § 3. Renumbered § 7-3 and amended by P.A. 82-783, Art. VII, § 2, eff. July 13, 1982. Amended by P.A. 85-149, § 1, eff. Jan. 1, 1988.

Formerly Ill.Rev.Stat.1991, ch. 95 ½, ¶ 317-3.

45/7-4. Weight capacity of boats; determination

§ 7-4. In order to authorize the maximum number of pounds of weight for boats less than 16 feet in length, the Department shall have their cubic foot capacity accurately determined, divide this number by twelve, and multiply the quotient by 150 pounds. The Department shall determine the basis for computing the weight capacity of boats 16 feet or over and less than 45 feet in length.

Laws 1959, p. 1473, Art. VII, § 4. Renumbered § 7-4 and amended by P.A. 82-783, Art. VII, § 2, eff. July 13, 1982.

Formerly Ill.Rev.Stat.1991, ch. 95 ½, ¶ 317-4.

45/7-5. Compliance with standards, rules and regulations

§ 7-5. It shall be the duty of the Department to see that all of such boats comply with the standards prescribed in this Act and the rules and regulations of the Department.

Laws 1959, p. 1473, Art. VII, § 5. Renumbered § 7-5 and amended by P.A. 82-783, Art. VII, § 2, eff. July 13, 1982. Amended by P.A. 85-149, § 1, eff. Jan. 1, 1988.

Formerly Ill.Rev.Stat.1991, ch. 95 ½, ¶ 317-5.

45/7-6. Non-compliance; notice to owner; rectification of defective conditions

§ 7-6. Whenever, it shall be found that any boat does not comply with the standards of this Act and the rules and regulations of the Department, it shall thereupon be the duty of the Department to notify the owner, proprietor or agent in charge of any such boat, the respect in which the boat fails to comply, and to demand that such defective conditions be rectified prior to further use of such boat.

Laws 1959, p. 1473, Art. VII, § 6. Renumbered § 7-6 and amended by P.A. 82-783, Art. VII, § 2, eff. July 13, 1982. Amended by P.A. 85-149, § 1, eff. Jan. 1, 1988.

Formerly Ill.Rev.Stat.1991, ch. 95 ½, ¶ 317-6.

45/7-7. Display of license or tags

§ 7-7. The Department shall furnish to the licensee an appropriate license which shall be prominently displayed in his place of business, or upon the boat if only one boat is involved. In addition to said license the Department shall also furnish to such licensee a durable tag or disc for each boat so licensed with such markings as the Department shall deem necessary, which tag or disc must be affixed to some prominent place at the bow of said boat plainly visible to the public. The licensee shall also cause to be painted on the after quarter of the boat the number of pounds of weight authorized to be carried therein, and no licensee or his agent shall knowingly permit more than that number of pounds of weight or number of persons to occupy said boat at any one given time.

Laws 1959, p. 1473, Art. VII, § 7. Renumbered § 7-7 and amended by P.A. 82-783, Art. VII, § 2, eff. July 13, 1982.

Formerly Ill.Rev.Stat.1991, ch. 95 ½, ¶ 317-7.

45/7-8. Equipment

§ 7-8. Equipment. Neither the owner of a boat livery, nor his agent or employee shall permit any watercraft to depart from his premises unless it has been provided, either by owner or renter, with the equipment required pursuant to Article IV of this Act and any rules and regulations made pursuant thereto.

Laws 1959, p. 1473, Art. VII, § 8. Renumbered § 7-8 and amended by P.A. 82-783, Art. VII, § 2, eff. July 13, 1982. Amended by P.A. 87-198, § 1, eff. Jan. 1, 1992.

Formerly Ill.Rev.Stat.1991, ch. 95 ½, ¶ 317-8.

45/7-9. Registration

§ 7-9. It shall be the responsibility of the owner of a boat livery, or his agent or employee, to determine that all watercraft are properly registered as required pursuant to Article III of this Act.

Laws 1959, p. 1473, Art. VII, § 9, added by Laws 1961, p. 3349, § 1. Renumbered § 7-9 and amended by P.A. 82-783, Art. VII, § 2, eff. July 13, 1982. Amended by P.A. 86-1340, § 2, eff. Sept. 7, 1990; P.A. 87-198, § 1, eff. Jan. 1, 1992.

Formerly Ill.Rev.Stat.1991, ch. 95 ½, ¶ 317-9.

45/7-10. Unlawful rental of personal watercraft or specialty prop-craft

§ 7-10. Unlawful rental of personal watercraft or specialty prop-craft.

(a) A livery shall not lease, hire or rent a personal watercraft or a specialty prop-craft to, or for operation by, any person who is under 16 years of age.

(b) Any person convicted of violating this Section is guilty of a Class A misdemeanor.

Laws 1959, p. 1473, Art. VII, § 7-10, added by P.A. 87-798, § 4, eff. Dec. 16, 1991. Amended by P.A. 90-412, § 5, eff. Jan. 1, 1998.

Formerly Ill.Rev.Stat.1991, ch. 95 ½, ¶ 317-10.

ARTICLE VIII. LOCAL REGULATION

Section

45/8-1. Local ordinances

§ 8-1. Local ordinances. The provisions of this Act, and of other applicable laws of this State shall govern the operation, equipment, numbering and all other matters relating thereto whenever any vessel shall be operated on the waters of this State, or when any activity regulated by this Act shall take place thereon; but nothing in this Act shall be construed to prevent the adoption of any ordinance or local law by any political subdivision of the State relating to operation and equipment of vessels the provisions of which are not inconsistent with the provisions of this Act, amendments thereto or regulations issued thereunder: Provided, that such ordinances or local laws shall be operative only so long as and to the extent that they continue to be not inconsistent with the provisions of this Act, amendments thereto or regulations issued thereunder.

Laws 1959, p. 1473, Art. VIII, § 1. Renumbered § 8-1 and amended by P.A. 82-783, Art. VII, § 2, eff. July 13, 1982.

Formerly Ill.Rev.Stat.1991, ch. 95 ½, ¶ 318-1.

45/8-2. Special rules—Application

§ 8-2. Special rules—Application. Any subdivision of this State may, at any time, but only after public notice, make formal application to the Department for special rules and regulations with reference to the operation of vessels on any waters within its territorial limits and shall set forth therein the reasons which make such special rules or regulations necessary or appropriate.

Laws 1959, p. 1473, Art. VIII, § 2. Renumbered § 8-2 and amended by P.A. 82-783, Art. VII, § 2, eff. July 13, 1982.

Formerly Ill.Rev.Stat.1991, ch. 95 ½, ¶ 318-2.

45/8-3. Special rules—Power

§ 8-3. Special rules—Power. The Department is hereby authorized to make special rules and regulations with reference to the operation of vessels on any waters within the territorial limits of any subdivision of this State.

Laws 1959, p. 1473, Art. VIII, § 3. Renumbered § 8-3 and amended by P.A. 82-783, Art. VII, § 2, eff. July 13, 1982.

Formerly Ill.Rev.Stat.1991, ch. 95 ½, ¶ 318-3.

ARTICLE IX. FILING OF REGULATIONS

Section

45/9-1. Rules and regulations, filing

§ 9-1. Rules and regulations, filing. The implementation and administration of the provisions of this Act shall be by rules and regulations adopted by the Department of Natural Resources. A copy of the rules and regulations adopted pursuant to this Act, and of any amendments thereto, shall be filed in the office of the Department and in the office of the Secretary of State. Rules and regulations shall be published by the Department in a convenient form.

Laws 1959, p. 1473, Art. IX, § 1. Renumbered § 9-1 and amended by P.A. 82-783, Art. VII, § 2, eff. July 13, 1982. Amended by P.A. 84-973, § 1, eff. Jan. 1, 1986; P.A. 89-445, § 9A-89, eff. Feb. 7, 1996.

Formerly Ill.Rev.Stat.1991, ch. 95 ½, ¶ 319-1.

ARTICLE X. THE STATE BOATING ACT FUND

Section

45/10-1. Special fund

§ 10-1. Special fund. All revenue received under the provisions of this Act, including registration fees, fines, or other income of any kind or nature, shall be deposited in the State Treasury and shall be set apart in a special fund to be known as the State Boating Act Fund, except that revenue from fines resulting from citations written by a county sheriff or his deputy shall be deposited in a county fund in the county where the citation was written. Appropriations from the State Boating Act Fund, excepting those revenues received as a result of the Snowmobile Registration and Safety Act,[1] shall be made to the Department, and shall be used for the expenses of the Department in administering the registration, boat safety, boat safety education, and enforcement provisions of this Act or for any purpose related or incident thereto and connected therewith, including the construction and improvement of boating facilities, such as access areas, launching sites, harbor facilities, lakes, and marinas, including plans and specifications, engineering surveys, and supervision and land acquisition where necessary. In addition to the foregoing, appropriations from the State Boating Act Fund, other than revenues received as a result of the Snowmobile Registration and Safety Act, may be made to the Department of Natural Resources to pay operational expenses for recreational boating facilities at McHenry Lock and Dam in McHenry County and Sinnissippi Dam in Whiteside County.

Laws 1959, p. 1473, Art. X, § 1. Amended by Laws 1963, p. 2598, § 1; P.A. 77-1314, § 1, eff. Aug. 27, 1971. Renumbered § 10-1 and amended by P.A. 82-783, Art. VII, § 2, eff. July 13, 1982. Amended by P.A. 83-971, § 1, eff. Dec. 2, 1983; P.A. 87-1109, § 1, eff. Jan. 1, 1993; P.A. 89-445, § 9E-46, eff. Feb. 7, 1996.

Formerly Ill.Rev.Stat.1991, ch. 95 ½, ¶ 320-1.

[1] 325 ILCS 40/1-1 et seq.

45/10-2. Snowmobile Registration and Safety Act Revenues

§ 10-2. Snowmobile Registration and Safety Act Revenues. All revenue received under the provisions of the "Snowmobile Registration and Safety Act",[1] including registration fees, fines, or other income of whatsoever kind or nature, shall be deposited in the State Treasury in "The State Boating Act Fund". Appropriations of such revenue shall be made only to the Department for administering the registration of snowmobiles, snowmobile safety, snowmobile safety education and enforcement provisions of the "Snowmobile Registration and Safety Act" or for any purpose related or connected thereto, including the construction, maintenance, and rehabilitation of snowmobile recreation areas or any other facilities for the use of snowmobiles, including plans and specifications, engineering surveys and supervision and land acquisition where necessary.

Laws 1959, p. 1473, Art. X, § 2, added by P.A. 77-1314, § 1, eff. Aug. 27, 1971. Renumbered § 10-2 and amended by P.A. 82-783, Art. VII, § 2, eff. July 13, 1982.

Formerly Ill.Rev.Stat.1991, ch. 95 ½, ¶ 320-2.

[1] 625 ILCS 40/1-1 et seq.

ARTICLE XI. PENALTIES

45/11-1 to 45/11-9. §§ 11-1 to 11-9. Repealed by P.A. 85-149, § 2, eff. Jan. 1, 1988

ARTICLE XIA. PENALTIES

Section

Enactment

Article XIA was added by P.A. 85-149, § 1, eff. Jan. 1, 1988.

45/11A-1. Violations; punishment

§ 11A-1. Except as otherwise provided in this Act, any person who violates any of the provisions of this Act shall be guilty of a petty offense.

Laws 1959, p. 1473, Art. XIA, § 11A-1, added by P.A. 85-149, § 1, eff. Jan. 1, 1988.

Formerly Ill.Rev.Stat.1991, ch. 95 ½, ¶ 321A-1.

45/11A-2. Violations of sections 3A-3, 3A-13, 3A-14, 3A-20 or 3A-21

§ 11A-2. A. Any person who violates Section 3A-3, 3A-13, 3A-14, or 3A-20 is guilty of a Class A misdemeanor.

B. Any person who violates Section 3A-21 is guilty of a Class 2 felony.

Laws 1959, p. 1473, Art. XIA, § 11A-2, added by P.A. 85-149, § 1, eff. Jan. 1, 1988. Amended by P.A. 88-524, § 1, eff. July 1, 1994.

Formerly Ill.Rev.Stat.1991, ch. 95 ½, ¶ 321A-2.

45/11A-3. Violations of sections 5-1 or 5-2

§ 11A-3. Any person who violates any of the provisions of Section 5-1 or 5-2 of this Act is guilty of a Class B misdemeanor.

Laws 1959, p. 1473, Art. XIA, § 11A-3, added by P.A. 85-149, § 1, eff. Jan. 1, 1988.

Formerly Ill.Rev.Stat.1991, ch. 95 ½, ¶ 321A-3.

45/11A-4. Additional penalties

§ 11A-4. Any person who is convicted of a violation of Sections 5-1, 5-2 or 11A-5 of this Act, in addition to any other penalties authorized in this Act, may in the discretion of the court be refused the privilege of operating any watercraft on any of the waterways of this State for a period of not less than one year.

Laws 1959, p. 1473, Art. XIA, § 11A-4, added by P.A. 85-149, § 1, eff. Jan. 1, 1988.

Formerly Ill.Rev.Stat.1991, ch. 95 ½, ¶ 321A-4.

45/11A-5. Operation of watercraft during period when privilege is denied

§ 11A-5. Any person who operates any watercraft during the period when he is denied the privilege to so operate is guilty of a Class A misdemeanor.

Laws 1959, p. 1473, Art. XIA, § 11A-5, added by P.A. 85-149, § 1, eff. Jan. 1, 1988.

Formerly Ill.Rev.Stat.1991, ch. 95 ½, ¶ 321A-5.

45/11A-6. Violations of section 2-4

§ 11A-6. Any person who violates any provision of Section 2-4 is guilty of a Class A misdemeanor.

Laws 1959, p. 1473, Art. XIA, § 11A-6, added by P.A. 85-149, § 1, eff. Jan. 1, 1988.

Formerly Ill.Rev.Stat.1991, ch. 95 ½, ¶ 321A-6.

ARTICLE XII. PARTIAL INVALIDITY

Section

45/12-1. Effect

§ 12-1. If any provision of this Act, or the application of such provision to any persons, body or circumstances shall be held invalid, the remainder of this Act, or the application of such provision to persons, bodies or circumstances other than those as to which it shall have been held invalid, shall not be affected thereby.

Laws 1959, p. 1473, Art. XII, § 1. Renumbered § 12-1 and amended by P.A. 82-783, Art. VII, § 2, eff. July 13, 1982.

Formerly Ill.Rev.Stat.1991, ch. 95 ½, ¶ 322-1.

ARTICLE XIII. EFFECTIVE DATE

Section

45/13-1. Effective date

§ 13-1. This Act takes effect on March 1, 1960.

Laws 1959, p. 1473, Art. XIII, § 1. Renumbered § 13-1 and amended by P.A. 82-783, Art. VII, § 2, eff. July 13, 1982.

Formerly Ill.Rev.Stat.1991, ch. 95 ½, ¶ 323-1.

ARTICLE XIV. REPEAL

Section

45/1. Repeal

§ 1. "An Act regulating Motorboats" approved July 15, 1941, as amended, and "An Act regulating the Operation of Motorboats", approved July 18, 1947,[1] are repealed.

Laws 1959, p. 1473, Art. XIV, § 1.

Formerly Ill.Rev.Stat.1991, ch. 95 ½, ¶ 324-1.

[1] Former Ill.Rev.Stat. ch. 95½, ¶¶ 283 to 303 (repealed).

ACT 50. PUBLIC CONVEYANCE NOTICE ACT

Section

50/0.01. Short title

§ 0.01. Short title. This Act may be cited as the Public Conveyance Notice Act.

Laws 1967, p. 2850, § 0.01, added by P.A. 86–1324, § 674, eff. Sept. 6, 1990.

Formerly Ill.Rev.Stat.1991, ch. 100, ¶ 30.

Title of Act:

An Act to require displaying of notices in conveyances used for the transportation of the public for hire in relation to aggravated assault and aggravated battery against a driver, operator, employee or passenger. Laws 1967, p. 2850, approved and eff. Aug. 11, 1967.

50/1. Form and contents of notice

§ 1. A notice shall be prominently displayed in each vehicle or conveyance used for the transportation of the public for hire which must state substantially the following: Any person who assaults or harms an individual whom he knows to be a driver, operator, employee or passenger of a transportation facility or system engaged in the business of transportation for hire and who is then performing in such capacity or using such public transportation as a passenger, if such individual is assaulted, commits a Class A misdemeanor, or if such individual is harmed, commits a Class 3 felony.

Laws 1967, p. 2850, § 1, eff. Aug. 11, 1967. Amended by P.A. 77–2830, Art. 74, § 1, eff. Jan. 1, 1973.

Formerly Ill.Rev.Stat.1991, ch. 100, ¶ 31.

INDEX

References are to Chapter, Act and Section

5/1-102.02. § 1-102.02. Renumbered as § 1-101.8 by P.A. 90-89, § 15, eff. Jan. 1, 1998

5/1-102.1. Antique vehicle

§ 1-102.1. Antique vehicle. A motor vehicle that is more than 25 years of age or a bona fide replica thereof and which is driven on the highways only going to and returning from an antique auto show or an exhibition, or for servicing or demonstration, or a fire-fighting vehicle more than 20 years old which is not used as fire-fighting equipment but is used only for the purpose of exhibition of demonstration.

P.A. 76-1586, § 1-102.1, added by P.A. 77-217, § 1, eff. Jan. 1, 1972. Amended by P.A. 78-667, § 1, eff. July 1, 1974.

Formerly Ill.Rev.Stat.1991, ch. 95 ½, ¶ 1-102.1.

5/1-102.2. Apportionable semitrailer

§ 1-102.2. Apportionable semitrailer. Through March 31, 1996, an apportionable semitrailer is a semitrailer that is paying annual fees to a foreign jurisdiction under the provisions of the International Registration Plan. Beginning April 1, 1996, an apportionable semitrailer is a semitrailer used in interstate commerce and registered with an apportioned power fleet.

P.A. 76-1586, § 1-102.2, added by P.A. 87-1040, § 1, eff. Sept. 11, 1992. Amended by P.A. 89-245, § 5, eff. Jan. 1, 1996.

Formerly Ill.Rev.Stat., ch. 95½, ¶ 1-102.2.

5/1-102.3. Apportionable trailer

§ 1-102.3. Apportionable trailer. A trailer involved in interstate commerce.

P.A. 76-1586, § 1-102.3, added by P.A. 87-1040, § 1, eff. Sept. 11, 1992.

Formerly Ill.Rev.Stat., ch. 95½, ¶ 1-102.3.

5/1-103. Approved driver education course

§ 1-103. Approved driver education course. (a) Any course of driver education approved by the State Board of Education, offered by public or private schools maintaining grades 9 through 12, and meeting at least the minimum requirements of the "Driver Education Act", as now or hereafter amended,[1] or (b) any course of driver education offered by a school licensed to give driver education instructions under this Act which meets at least the minimum educational requirements of the "Driver Education Act", as now or hereafter amended, and is approved by the State Board of Education or (c) any course of driver education given in another State to an Illinois resident attending school in such State and approved by the State administrator of the Driver Education Program of such other State.

P.A. 76-1586, § 1-103, eff. July 1, 1970. Amended by P.A. 76-2120, § 1, eff. July 1, 1970; P.A. 81-1508, § 8, eff. Sept. 25, 1980.

Formerly Ill.Rev.Stat.1991, ch. 95 ½, ¶ 1-103.

1 105 ILCS 5/27-24 et seq.

5/1-104. § 1-104. Repealed by P.A. 90-89, § 20, eff. Jan. 1, 1998

5/1-104.1. Article

§ 1-104.1. Article. The word "Article" as used in this Code shall, unless the context otherwise clearly indicates, mean an Article of a Chapter of "The Illinois Vehicle Code".[1]

P.A. 76-1586, § 1-104.1, added by P.A. 82-123, § 1, eff. Jan. 1, 1982.

Formerly Ill.Rev.Stat.1991, ch. 95 ½, ¶ 1-104.1.

1 625 ILCS 5/1-100 et seq.

5/1-105. Authorized emergency vehicle

§ 1-105. Authorized emergency vehicle.

Emergency vehicles of municipal departments or public service corporations as are designated or authorized by proper local authorities; police vehicles; vehicles of the fire department; ambulances; vehicles of the Illinois Emergency Management Agency; and vehicles of the Department of Nuclear Safety.

P.A. 76-1586, § 1-105, eff. July 1, 1970. Amended by P.A. 92-138, § 5, eff. July 24, 2001.

Formerly Ill.Rev.Stat.1991, ch. 95 ½, ¶ 1-105.

5/1-105.3. Automotive parts recycler

§ 1-105.3. Automotive parts recycler. A person who is in the business of acquiring previously owned vehicles and vehicle parts for the primary purpose of disposing of parts of vehicles in a manner other than that described in the definition of a "scrap processor" in this Code.

P.A. 76-1586, § 1-105.3, added by P.A. 90-89, § 15, eff. Jan. 1, 1998.

5/1-105.5. Automated red light enforcement system

§ 1-105.5. Automated red light enforcement system. A system in a municipality with a population of 1,000,000 or more operated by a governmental agency, in cooperation with a law enforcement agency, that photographically records a motor vehicle's response to a traffic control signal with a red light indication and is designed to obtain a clear photograph of the vehicle and the vehicle's license plate when the motor vehicle is involved in a motor vehicle accident, leaving the scene of a motor vehicle accident, or reckless driving that results in bodily injury.

P.A. 76-1586, § 1-105.5, added by P.A. 90-86, § 5, eff. July 10, 1997.

5/1-105.6. Axle load

§ 1-105.6. Axle load. The total load transmitted to the road by all wheels whose centers may be included between 2 parallel transverse vertical planes 40 inches apart extending across the full width of the vehicle.

P.A. 76-1586, § 1-105.6, added by P.A. 90-89, § 15, eff. Jan. 1, 1998.

5/1-106. Bicycle

§ 1-106. Bicycle. Every device propelled by human power upon which any person may ride, having two tandem wheels except scooters and similar devices.

P.A. 76-1586, § 1-106, eff. July 1, 1970. Amended by P.A. 85-951, § 1, eff. July 1, 1988.

Formerly Ill.Rev.Stat.1991, ch. 95 ½, ¶ 1-106.

5/1-106.5. Bumper

§ 1-106.5. Bumper. Any device or system of devices protruding from and attached to the front and rear of a motor vehicle that has been designed to be used to absorb the impact of a collision. For the purposes of this Code, a bumper also includes a device or system of devices similar in design to those with which new motor vehicles are equipped.

P.A. 76–1586, § 1–106.5, added by P.A. 90–89, § 15, eff. Jan. 1, 1998. Amended by P.A. 92–61, § 5, eff. Jan. 1, 2002.

5/1–107. Bus

§ 1–107. Bus. Every motor vehicle, other than a commuter van, designed for carrying more than 10 persons.

P.A. 76–1586, § 1–107, eff. July 1, 1970. Amended by P.A. 80–529, § 1, eff. Jan. 1, 1979; P.A. 82–1011, § 2, eff. Sept. 17, 1982.

Formerly Ill.Rev.Stat.1991, ch. 95 ½, ¶ 1–107.

5/1–108. Business district

§ 1–108. Business district. The territory contiguous to and including a highway when within any 600 feet along such highway there are buildings in use for business or industrial purposes, including but not limited to hotels, banks, or office buildings, railroad stations and public buildings which occupy at least 300 feet of frontage on one side or 300 feet collectively on both sides of the highway.

P.A. 76–1586, § 1–108, eff. July 1, 1970.

Formerly Ill.Rev.Stat.1991, ch. 95 ½, ¶ 1–108.

5/1–109. § 1–109. Repealed by P.A. 81–969, § 2

The repeal was effective at the "start of the 1981 registration year."

5/1–109.01. Camping trailer

§ 1–109.01. Camping trailer. A trailer, not used commercially, constructed with partial side walls which fold for towing and unfold to provide temporary living quarters for recreational camping or travel use and of a size or weight not requiring an overdimension permit when towed on a highway.

P.A. 76–1586, § 1–109.01, added by P.A. 81–969, § 1, eff. Jan. 1, 1980.

Formerly Ill.Rev.Stat.1991, ch. 95 ½, ¶ 1–109.01.

Section 3 of P.A. 81–969, approved Sept. 22, 1979, provided:

"This amendatory Act takes effect at the start of the 1981 registration year."

Effective date of P.A. 81–969: Section 3 of P.A. 81–969, approved Sept. 22, 1979, provided the Act would take effect at the start of the 1981 registration year.

5/1–110. Cancellation of driver's license

§ 1–110. Cancellation of driver's license. The annulment or termination by formal action of the Secretary of a person's driver's license because of some error or defect in the license or because the licensee is no longer entitled to such license, but, with the exception of Sections 6–107, 6–108 and 6–201, the cancellation of a license is without prejudice and application for a new license may be made at any time after such cancellation.

P.A. 76–1586, § 1–110, eff. July 1, 1970. Amended by P.A. 86–1450, § 2, eff. July 1, 1991.

Formerly Ill.Rev.Stat.1991, ch. 95 ½, ¶ 1–110.

5/1–110.1. § 1–110.1. Renumbered as § 1–111.1b by P.A. 90–89, § 15, eff. Jan. 1, 1998

Another § 1–110.1 was renumbered § 1–110.2 by P.A. 83–1528, Art. II, § 24, eff. Jan. 17, 1985.

5/1–110.2. Certificate of purchase

§ 1–110.2. Certificate of purchase. A bill of sale given to a licensee making an acquisition of a vehicle under Sections 4–208 and 4–209 of this Code.

P.A. 76–1586, § 1–110.1, added by P.A. 83–1473, § 1, eff. Jan. 1, 1985. Renumbered § 1–110.2 and amended by P.A. 83–1528, Art. II, § 24, eff. Jan. 17, 1985.

Formerly Ill.Rev.Stat.1991, ch. 95 ½, ¶ 1–110.2.

P.A. 83–1528, the Second 1984 Revisory Act, provides in Art. II, for the nonsubstantive revision or renumbering or repeal of sections of certain Acts of the 83rd General Assembly and for the correction of misspelled words and technical errors in Acts of the 83rd General Assembly.

5/1–110a. § 1–110a. Renumbered as § 1–111.1c by P.A. 90–89, § 15, eff. Jan. 1, 1998

5/1–111. § 1–111. Repealed by P.A. 90–89, § 20, eff. Jan. 1, 1998

5/1–111.1. Chapter

§ 1–111.1. Chapter. The word "Chapter" as used in this Code shall, unless the context otherwise clearly indicates, mean a Chapter of "The Illinois Vehicle Code".[1]

P.A. 76–1586, § 1–111.1, added by P.A. 82–123, § 1, eff. Jan. 1, 1982.

Formerly Ill.Rev.Stat.1991, ch. 95 ½, ¶ 1–111.1.

[1] 625 ILCS 5/1–100 et seq.

5/1–111.1a. Charitable vehicle

§ 1–111.1a. Charitable vehicle.

(a) Any vehicle that is exclusively owned and operated by a religious or charitable not-for-profit organization and is used primarily in conducting the official activities of such organization.

(b) This definition does not include:

(1) a bus operated by a public utility, municipal corporation or common carrier authorized to conduct local or interurban transportation of passengers when such bus is on a regularly scheduled route for the transportation of other fare paying passengers or furnishing charter service for the transportation of groups on special trips or in connection with special events and not over a regular or customary religious organization bus route;

(2) a school bus as defined in Section 1–182 of this Code; or

(3) a First Division vehicle, other than one designed for transporting not less than 7 nor more than 10 passengers, as defined in Section 1–217 of this Code; except that for purposes of determining the number of persons a vehicle is designed to carry, in any vehicle equipped with one or more wheelchair tiedowns, each wheelchair tiedown shall be counted as 4 persons.

P.A. 76–1586, § 1–171.01, added by P.A. 79–798, § 1, eff. July 1, 1976. Amended by P.A. 81–509, § 1, eff. Jan. 1, 1980; P.A. 82–1011, § 2, eff. Sept. 17, 1982; P.A. 83–743, § 1, eff. Jan. 1, 1984; P.A. 87–1025, § 1, eff. Jan. 1, 1993. Renumbered § 1–111.1a and amended by P.A. 90–89, § 15, eff. Jan. 1, 1998. Amended by P.A. 91–64, § 5, eff. Jan. 1, 2000.

Formerly Ill.Rev.Stat.1991, ch. 95 ½, ¶ 1–171.01.

5/1-111.1b. Chassis

§ 1-111.1b. Chassis. Every frame or supportive element of a vehicle whether or not a manufacturer's identification number, serial number, or other identifying numbers are present on said part.

P.A. 76-1586, § 1-110.1, added by P.A. 83-831, § 1, eff. Jan. 1, 1984. Renumbered § 1-111.1b and amended by P.A. 90-89, § 15, eff. Jan. 1, 1998.

Formerly Ill.Rev.Stat.1991, ch. 95 ½, ¶ 1-110.1.

5/1-111.1c. Chassis manufacturer

§ 1-111.1c. Chassis manufacturer. A person who manufactures and produces the frame upon which is mounted the body of a motor vehicle.

P.A. 76-1586, § 1-110a, added by P.A. 86-971, § 1, eff. Jan. 1, 1991. Renumbered § 1-111.1c and amended by P.A. 90-89, § 15, eff. Jan. 1, 1998.

Formerly Ill.Rev.Stat.1991, ch. 95 ½, ¶ 1-110a.

5/1-111.2. Code

§ 1-111.2. Code. The word "Code" as used in this Act shall, unless the context otherwise clearly indicates, mean "The Illinois Vehicle Code".[1]

P.A. 76-1586, § 1-111.2, added by P.A. 82-123, § 1, eff. Jan. 1, 1982.

Formerly Ill.Rev.Stat.1991, ch. 95 ½, ¶ 1-111.2.

[1] 625 ILCS 5/1-100 et seq.

5/1-111.3. Collection costs

§ 1-111.3. Collection costs. Collection costs consist of reasonable costs incurred in locating the owner, lienholder, or other legally entitled persons, and demanding payment, together with court costs and reasonable attorney's fees as determined by the court.

P.A. 76-1586, § 1-111.3, added by P.A. 89-433, § 5, eff. Dec. 15, 1995.

Another § 1-111.3, defining "component part", was enacted by P.A. 83-831, and was repealed by P.A. 83-1473, § 2, eff. Jan. 1, 1985.

5/1-111.4. Commerce

§ 1-111.4. Commerce. Trade, commerce, or transportation.

P.A. 76-1586, § 1-111.4, added by P.A. 90-89, § 15, eff. Jan. 1, 1998.

5/1-111.5. Commercial driver instruction permit

§ 1-111.5. Commercial driver instruction permit. A permit issued pursuant to Section 6-508 of this Code.

P.A. 76-1586, § 1-111.5, added by P.A. 90-89, § 15, eff. Jan. 1, 1998.

5/1-111.6. Commercial driver's license (CDL)

§ 1-111.6. Commercial driver's license (CDL). A driver's license issued by a state to a person that authorizes that person to drive a certain class of commercial motor vehicle or vehicles.

P.A. 76-1586, § 1-111.6, added by P.A. 90-89, § 15, eff. Jan. 1, 1998.

5/1-111.7. Commercial driver license information system (CDLIS)

§ 1-111.7. Commercial driver license information system (CDLIS). The information system established, pursuant to the Commercial Motor Vehicle Safety Act of 1986 (CMVSA) (49 U.S.C. 2701 et seq.), to serve as a clearinghouse for locating information related to the licensing and identification of commercial motor vehicle drivers.

P.A. 76-1586, § 1-111.7, added by P.A. 90-89, § 15, eff. Jan. 1, 1998.

5/1-111.8. Commercial vehicle

§ 1-111.8. Commercial vehicle. Any vehicle operated for the transportation of persons or property in the furtherance of any commercial or industrial enterprise, For-Hire or Not-For-Hire, but not including a commuter van, a vehicle used in a ridesharing arrangement when being used for that purpose, or a recreational vehicle not being used commercially.

P.A. 76-1586, § 1-114, eff. July 1, 1970. Amended by P.A. 76-1909, § 1; P.A. 80-529, § 1, eff. Jan. 1, 1979; P.A. 81-1452, § 1, eff. Jan. 1, 1981; P.A. 83-1091, § 1, eff. July 1, 1984. Renumbered § 1-111.8 and amended by P.A. 90-89, § 15, eff. Jan. 1, 1998.

Formerly Ill.Rev.Stat.1991, ch. 95 ½, ¶ 1-114.

5/1-111.9. Commuter van

§ 1-111.9. Commuter van. A motor vehicle designed for the transportation of not less than 7 nor more than 16 passengers, which is: (1) used in a ridesharing arrangement; or (2) owned or leased by or on behalf of a company or an employee organization and operated on a non-profit basis with the primary purpose of transporting employees of the company between the employees' homes and the company's place of business or a public transportation station and in which the operating, administrative, maintenance and reasonable depreciation costs are paid principally by the persons utilizing the commuter van.

P.A. 76-1586, § 1-114.1, added by P.A. 80-529, § 1, eff. Jan. 1, 1979. Amended by P.A. 81-492, § 1, eff. Jan. 1, 1980; P.A. 83-1091, § 1, eff. July 1, 1984; P.A. 84-603, § 1, eff. Jan. 1, 1986. Renumbered § 1-111.9 and amended by P.A. 90-89, § 15, eff. Jan. 1, 1998.

Formerly Ill.Rev.Stat.1991, ch. 95 ½, ¶ 1-114.1.

5/1-112. Controlled access highway

§ 1-112. Controlled access highway. Every highway, street or roadway in respect to which owners or occupants of abutting lands and other persons have no legal right of access to or from the same except at such points only and in such manner as may be determined by the public authority having jurisdiction over such highway, street or roadway.

P.A. 76-1586, § 1-112, eff. July 1, 1970.

Formerly Ill.Rev.Stat.1991, ch. 95 ½, ¶ 1-112.

5/1-112.1. Conversion

§ 1-112.1. Conversion. A motor vehicle, other than a motor home, which has been modified by a person other than the manufacturer of the chassis of the motor vehicle and which has not been the subject of a retail sale.

P.A. 76-1586, § 1-112.1, added by P.A. 86-971, § 1, eff. Jan. 1, 1991.

Formerly Ill.Rev.Stat.1991, ch. 95 ½, ¶ 1-112.1.

5/1-112.2. Converter or second stage manufacturer

§ 1-112.2. Converter or second stage manufacturer. A person who prior to the retail sale of a motor vehicle, assembles, installs or affixes a body, cab, or special equipment to a chassis, or who adds, subtracts from, or modifies a previously assembled or manufactured motor vehicle.

P.A. 76-1586, § 1-112.2, added by P.A. 86-971, § 1, eff. Jan. 1, 1991. Amended by P.A. 90-89, § 15, eff. Jan. 1, 1998.

Formerly Ill.Rev.Stat.1991, ch. 95 ½, ¶ 1-112.2.

5/1-112.3. Converter Dolly

§ 1-112.3. Converter Dolly. A vehicle consisting of a chassis equipped with one or more axles, a fifth wheel or an equivalent mechanism, and draw bar, the attachment of which converts a semitrailer to a full trailer.

P.A. 76-1586, § 1-112.3, added by P.A. 87-1203, § 1, eff. Sept. 25, 1992.

Formerly Ill.Rev.Stat., ch. 95½, ¶ 1-112.3.

5/1-112.5. Counterfeit

§ 1-112.5. Counterfeit. To copy or imitate, without legal authority, with the intent of deceiving or defrauding.

P.A. 76-1586, § 1-114.2, added by P.A. 83-1473, § 1, eff. Jan. 1, 1985. Renumbered § 1-112.5 and amended by P.A. 90-89, § 15, eff. Jan. 1, 1998.

Formerly Ill.Rev.Stat.1991, ch. 95 ½, ¶ 1-114.2.

5/1-112.7. Court

§ 1-112.7. Court. A court of law, traffic tribunal, or circuit court of Illinois, including a judge of a court of law, traffic tribunal, or circuit court of Illinois.

P.A. 76-1586, § 1-112.7, added by P.A. 90-89, § 15, eff. Jan. 1, 1998.

5/1-113. Crosswalk

§ 1-113. Crosswalk. (a) That part of a roadway at an intersection included within the connections of the lateral lines of the sidewalks on opposite sides of the highway measured from the curbs or, in the absence of curbs, from the edges of the traversable roadway, and in the absence of a sidewalk on one side of the highway, that part of the highway included within the extension of the lateral line of the existing sidewalk to the side of the highway without the sidewalk, with such extension forming a right angle to the centerline of the highway;

(b) Any portion of a roadway at an intersection or elsewhere distinctly indicated for pedestrian crossing by lines or other markings on the surface placed in accordance with the provisions in the Manual adopted by the Department of Transportation as authorized in Section 11-301.

P.A. 76-1586, § 1-113, eff. July 1, 1970. Amended by P.A. 76-2121, § 1, eff. July 1, 1970; P.A. 83-831, § 1, eff. Jan. 1, 1984.

Formerly Ill.Rev.Stat.1991, ch. 95 ½, ¶ 1-113.

5/1-113.1. Custom vehicle

§ 1-113.1. Custom vehicle. A motor vehicle that is at least 25 years of age and of a model year after 1948 or a vehicle that has been certified by an inspector of the National Street Rod Association, on a form prescribed by the Secretary of State, to be a custom vehicle manufactured to resemble a vehicle at least 25 years of age and of a model year after 1948 and has been altered from the manufacturer's original design or has a body constructed from non-original materials and which is maintained for occasional transportation, exhibitions, club activities, parades, tours, and similar uses and which is not used for general daily transportation.

P.A. 76-1586, § 1-113.1, added by P.A. 92-668, § 5, eff. Jan. 1, 2003.

5/1-114. § 1-114. Renumbered § 1-111.8 and amended by P.A. 90-89, § 15, eff. Jan. 1, 1998

5/1-114.1. § 1-114.1. Renumbered § 1-111.9 and amended by P.A. 90-89, § 15, eff. Jan. 1, 1998

5/1-114.2. § 1-114.2. Renumbered § 1-112.5 and amended by P.A. 90-89, § 15, eff. Jan. 1, 1998

5/1-115. Dealer

§ 1-115. Dealer. Every person engaged in the business of acquiring or disposing of vehicles or their essential parts and who has an established place of business for such purpose.

P.A. 76-1586, § 1-115, eff. July 1, 1970. Amended by P.A. 83-1473, § 1, eff. Jan. 1, 1985.

Formerly Ill.Rev.Stat.1991, ch. 95 ½, ¶ 1-115.

5/1-115.05. Department

§ 1-115.05. Department. The Department of Transportation of the State of Illinois, acting directly or through its duly authorized officers and agents, except that in Chapter 5 [1] and Articles X and XI of Chapter 3 of this Code,[2] "Department" means the Department of Revenue of the State of Illinois.

P.A. 76-1586, § 1-115.05, added by P.A. 90-89, § 15, eff. Jan. 1, 1998.

1 625 ILCS 5/1-100 et seq.

2 625 ILCS 5/3-1001 et seq. and 5/3-2001 et seq.

5/1-115.07. Derelict vehicle

§ 1-115.07. Derelict vehicle. Any inoperable, unregistered, discarded motor vehicle, regardless of title, having lost its character as a substantial property and left unattended without justification on the owner's land contrary to the public policy expressed in Section 4-301 of this Code.

P.A. 76-1586, § 1-115.07, added by P.A. 90-89, § 15, eff. Jan. 1, 1998.

5/1-115.1. Disposition of vehicle or vehicle part

§ 1-115.1. Disposition of vehicle or vehicle part. The purchase, exchange, transfer, sale, assignment or other change of ownership or possession or the junking or wrecking of a vehicle or vehicle part.

P.A. 76-1586, § 1-115.1, added by P.A. 83-1473, § 1, eff. Jan. 1, 1985.

Formerly Ill.Rev.Stat.1991, ch. 95 ½, ¶ 1-115.1.

5/1-115.3. Disqualification

§ 1-115.3. Disqualification. A withdrawal of the privilege to drive a commercial motor vehicle.

P.A. 76-1586, § 1-115.3, added by P.A. 90-89, § 15, eff. Jan. 1, 1998.

5/1-115.5. Domicile

§ 1-115.5. Domicile. A true, fixed, and permanent legal home of a person or the place to which the person intends to return even though the person may reside elsewhere. As a further explanation, "A person may have more than one residence but only one domicile".

P.A. 76-1586, § 1-115.5, added by P.A. 90-89, § 15, eff. Jan. 1, 1998.

5/1-115.6. Domiciliary

§ 1-115.6. Domiciliary. A person who is domiciled.

P.A. 76-1586, § 1-115.6, added by P.A. 90-89, § 15, eff. Jan. 1, 1998.

5/1-115.8. Drive

§ 1-115.8. Drive. To drive, operate, or be in physical control of a motor vehicle.

P.A. 76-1586, § 1-115.8, added by P.A. 90-89, § 15, eff. Jan. 1, 1998.

5/1-116. Driver

§ 1-116. Driver. Every person who drives or is in actual physical control of a vehicle.

P.A. 76-1586, § 1-116, eff. July 1, 1970.

Formerly Ill.Rev.Stat.1991, ch. 95 ½, ¶ 1-116.

5/1-116.1. Driver's license

§ 1-116.1. Driver's license. Any license to operate a motor vehicle issued under the laws of this State.

P.A. 76-1586, § 1-116.1, added by P.A. 84-1394, § 5, eff. Sept. 18, 1986.

Formerly Ill.Rev.Stat.1991, ch. 95 ½, ¶ 1-116.1.

5/1-117. Driver License Compact

§ 1-117. Driver License Compact. The Driver License Compact set forth in Chapter 6 of this Act.[1]

P.A. 76-1586, § 1-117, eff. July 1, 1970.

Formerly Ill.Rev.Stat.1991, ch. 95 ½, ¶ 1-117.

[1] 625 ILCS 5/6-700 et seq.

5/1-117.5. Driver's license or permit making implement

§ 1-117.5. Driver's license or permit making implement. Any implement specially designed or primarily used in the manufacture, assembly, or authentication of an official driver's license or permit issued by the Secretary of State or other official driver's license agency in another jurisdiction. These implements include, but are not limited to, cameras used for creating driver's license captured images, camera cards, or driver's license or permit laminates.

P.A. 76-1586, § 1-117.5, added by P.A. 90-89, § 15, eff. Jan. 1, 1998.

5/1-117.7. Electric personal assistive mobility device

Text of section added effective June 1, 2003

§ 1-117.7. Electric personal assistive mobility device. A self-balancing 2 non-tandem wheeled device designed to transport only one person with an electric propulsion system that limits the maximum speed of the device to 15 miles per hour or less.

P.A. 76-1586, § 1-117.7, added by P.A. 92-868, § 5, eff. June 1, 2003.

5/1-118. Essential Parts

§ 1-118. Essential Parts. All integral and body parts of a vehicle of a type required to be registered hereunder, the removal, alteration or substitution of which would tend to conceal the identity of the vehicle or substantially alter its appearance, model, type or mode of operation. "Essential parts" includes the following: vehicle hulks, shells, chassis, frames, front end assemblies (which may consist of headlight, grill, fenders and hood), front clip (front end assembly with cowl attached), rear clip (which may consist of quarter panels, fenders, floor and top), doors, hatchbacks, fenders, cabs, cab clips, cowls, hoods, trunk lids, deck lids, T-tops, sunroofs, moon roofs, astro roofs, transmissions of vehicles of the second division, seats, aluminum wheels, engines and similar parts. Essential parts shall also include stereo radios, cassette radios, compact disc radios, cassette/compact disc radios and compact disc players and compact disc changers which are either installed in dash or trunk-mounted.

An essential part which does not have affixed to it an identification number as defined in Section 1-129 adopts the identification number of the vehicle to which such part is affixed, installed or mounted.

P.A. 76-1586, § 1-118, eff. July 1, 1970. Amended by P.A. 83-1473, § 1, eff. Jan. 1, 1985; P.A. 86-1179, § 2, eff. Aug. 17, 1990; P.A. 86-1209, § 1, eff. Jan. 1, 1991; P.A. 87-435, Art. 2, § 2-19, eff. Sept. 10, 1991.

Formerly Ill.Rev.Stat.1991, ch. 95 ½, ¶ 1-118.

P.A. 87-435, the First 1991 Revisory Act, provides in Article 2 for the revision and renumbering of certain Sections of Acts which have been added or amended by more than one Act of the 86th General Assembly; incorporates amendments to repealed Acts into successor laws passed by the same General Assembly; corrects errors, revises cross-references and deletes obsolete text in such Sections contained in Public Acts through P.A. 86-1490.

5/1-119. Explosives

§ 1-119. Explosives. Any chemical compound or mechanical mixture that is commonly used or intended for the purpose of producing an explosion and which contains any oxidizing and combustive units or other ingredients in such proportions, quantities or packing that an ignition by fire, by friction, by concussion, by percussion or by detonator of any part of the compound or mixture may cause such a sudden generation of highly heated gases that the resultant gaseous pressures are capable of producing destructive effects on contiguous objects or of destroying life or limb.

P.A. 76-1586, § 1-119, eff. July 1, 1970.

Formerly Ill.Rev.Stat.1991, ch. 95 ½, ¶ 1-119.

5/1-119.3. Expressway

§ 1-119.3. Expressway. A freeway with full control access and with grade separations at intersections.

P.A. 76-1586, § 1-119.3, added by P.A. 90-89, § 15, eff. Jan. 1, 1998.

5/1-119.6. Farm to market agricultural transportation

§ 1-119.6. Farm to market agricultural transportation. The operation of a motor vehicle controlled and operated by a farmer who is a private motor carrier of property, who is using the vehicle to transport agricultural products to or from a farm operated by the farmer or to transport farm machinery or farm supplies to or from a farm operated by the farmer, and who is not using the commercial vehicle to transport hazardous materials of a type or quantity that requires the vehicle to be placarded in accordance with the Illinois Hazardous Materials Transportation Act.[1]

P.A. 76–1586, § 1–119.6, added by P.A. 90–89, § 15, eff. Jan. 1, 1998.

[1] 430 ILCS 30/1 et seq.

5/1–120. Farm tractor

§ 1–120. Farm tractor. Every motor vehicle designed and used primarily as a farm implement for drawing wagons, plows, mowing machines and other implements of husbandry, and every implement of husbandry which is self propelled, excluding all-terrain vehicles and off-highway motorcycles as defined in this Code.

P.A. 76–1586, § 1–120, eff. July 1, 1970. Amended by P.A. 85–830, § 1, eff. Sept. 24, 1987; P.A. 85–1010, § 1, eff. March 2, 1988.

Formerly Ill.Rev.Stat.1991, ch. 95 ½, ¶ 1–120.

P.A. 85–1010 incorporated the amendment by P.A. 85–830.

5/1–120.5. Fifth wheel assembly

§ 1–120.5. Fifth wheel assembly. A coupling device connecting 2 or more vehicles operating in combination. The lower half of a fifth wheel assembly mounted on a truck tractor or converter dolly must be secured to the frame of that vehicle with properly designed brackets, mounting plates, or angles and properly tightened bolts of adequate size and grade or devices that provide equivalent security. The installation shall not cause cracking, warping, or deformation of the frame. The installation shall include a device for positively preventing the lower half of the fifth wheel assembly from shifting on the frame to which it is attached.

The upper half of a fifth wheel assembly must be fastened to the motor vehicle with at least the same security required for the installation of the lower half on a truck tractor or converter dolly.

Every fifth wheel assembly shall have a locking mechanism. The locking mechanism and any adapter used in conjunction with it must prevent separation of the upper and lower halves of the fifth wheel assembly unless a positive manual release is activated. The release may be located so that the driver can operate it from the cab. If a motor vehicle has a fifth wheel assembly designed and constructed to be readily separable, the fifth wheel assembly locking devices shall apply automatically on coupling.

The lower half of a fifth wheel assembly shall be located so that, regardless of the condition of loading, the relationship between the kingpin and the rear axle or axles of the towing motor vehicle will properly distribute the gross weight of both the towed and towing vehicles on the axles of those vehicles, will not unduly interfere with the steering, braking, and other maneuvering of the towing vehicle, and will not otherwise contribute to unsafe operation of the vehicles comprising the combination. The upper half of a fifth wheel assembly shall be located so that the weight of the vehicles is properly distributed on their axles and the combination of vehicles will operate safely during normal operation.

P.A. 76–1586, § 1–120.5, added by P.A. 90–89, § 15, eff. Jan. 1, 1998.

5/1–121. Flammable liquid

§ 1–121. Flammable liquid. Any liquid which has a flash point of 70 degrees Fahrenheit, or less, as determined by a tagliabue or equivalent closed-cup test device.

P.A. 76–1586, § 1–121, eff. July 1, 1970. Amended by P.A. 91–357, § 231, eff. July 29, 1999.

Formerly Ill.Rev.Stat.1991, ch. 95 ½, ¶ 1–121.

5/1–122. Fleet

§ 1–122. Fleet. 1 or more commercial motor vehicles.

P.A. 76–1586, § 1–122, eff. July 1, 1970. Amended by P.A. 79–1041, § 1, eff. Jan. 1, 1976.

Formerly Ill.Rev.Stat.1991, ch. 95 ½, ¶ 1–122.

5/1–122.1. Fleet safety vehicle

§ 1–122.1. Fleet safety vehicle. Any motor vehicle which is used to supervise operations of vehicles of the second division on the highway so as to promote safety and legal operations of such second division vehicle.

P.A. 76–1586, § 1–122.1, added by P.A. 79–870, § 1, eff. Oct. 1, 1975.

Formerly Ill.Rev.Stat.1991, ch. 95 ½, ¶ 1–122.1.

5/1–122.5. For-hire

§ 1–122.5. For-hire. The operation of a vehicle for compensation and subject to federal regulation by the Interstate Commerce Commission or to state regulation by the Illinois Commerce Commission and those vehicles governed by Chapters 8 and 9 under this Code [1] and regulated by the Secretary of State.

P.A. 76–1586, § 1–124, eff. July 1, 1970. Amended by P.A. 86–880, § 1, eff. Jan. 1, 1990. Renumbered § 1–122.5 and amended by P.A. 90–89, § 15, eff. Jan. 1, 1998.

Formerly Ill.Rev.Stat.1991, ch. 95 ½, ¶ 1–124.

[1] 625 ILCS 5/8–100 et seq. and 5/9–100 et seq.

5/1–122.7. For-profit ridesharing arrangement

§ 1–122.7. For-profit ridesharing arrangement. The transportation by motor vehicle of not more than 16 persons, including the driver, for which a fee is charged in accordance with Section 6 of the Ridesharing Arrangements Act.[1]

P.A. 76–1586, § 1–122.7, added by P.A. 90–89, § 15, eff. Jan. 1, 1998.

[1] 625 ILCS 30/6 et seq.

5/1–123. Foreign vehicle

§ 1–123. Foreign vehicle. Every vehicle of a type required to be registered hereunder brought into this State from another State, territory or country other than in the ordinary course of business by or through a manufacturer or dealer and not registered in this State.

P.A. 76–1586, § 1–123, eff. July 1, 1970.

Formerly Ill.Rev.Stat.1991, ch. 95 ½, ¶ 1–123.

5/1–123.1. § 1–123.1. Repealed by P.A. 90–89, § 20, eff. Jan. 1, 1998

5/1–123.3. Frame

§ 1–123.3. Frame. The main longitudinal structural members of the chassis of the vehicle or, for vehicles with unitized body construction, the lowest main longitudinal structural members of the body of the vehicle.

P.A. 76-1586, § 1-123.3, added by P.A. 90-89, § 15, eff. Jan. 1, 1998.

5/1-123.4. Fraudulent driver's license or permit

§ 1-123.4. Fraudulent driver's license or permit. Any license or permit that purports to be an official driver's license or permit for which a computerized number and file have not been created by the Secretary of State or other official driver's license agency in another jurisdiction.

P.A. 76-1586, § 1-123.4, added by P.A. 90-89, § 15, eff. Jan. 1, 1998.

5/1-123.5. Freeway

§ 1-123.5. Freeway. A highway or street especially designed for through traffic and to, from, or over which owners of or persons having an interest in abutting land or other persons have no right or easement or only a limited right or easement of access, crossing, light, air, or view by reason of the fact that the property abuts upon the highway or street or for any other reason.

P.A. 76-1586, § 1-123.5, added by P.A. 90-89, § 15, eff. Jan. 1, 1998.

5/1-123.7. Garbage

§ 1-123.7. Garbage. Any material or load consisting of waste from the facilities of the generator of the waste when transported for disposal or to a permitted recycling or waste processing facility when the generator receives no direct or indirect compensation from anyone for the material or load and when transported by a truck specially equipped with a selfcompactor or an industrial roll-off hoist and roll-off container.

P.A. 76-1586, § 1-123.7, added by P.A. 90-89, § 15, eff. Jan. 1, 1998.

5/1-124. § 1-124. Renumbered as § 1-122.5 by P.A. 90-89, § 15, eff. Jan. 1, 1998

5/1-124.1. Grey Market Vehicle

§ 1-124.1. Grey Market Vehicle. A vehicle not originally manufactured in compliance with U.S. emission or safety standards.

P.A. 76-1586, § 1-124.1, added by P.A. 85-951, § 1, eff. July 1, 1988. Amended by P.A. 86-444, § 1, eff. Jan. 1, 1990.

Formerly Ill.Rev.Stat.1991, ch. 95 ½, ¶ 1-124.1.

5/1-124.5. Gross Vehicle Weight Rating (GVWR)

§ 1-124.5. Gross Vehicle Weight Rating (GVWR). The value specified by the manufacturer or manufacturers as the maximum loaded weight of a single vehicle. The GVWR of a combination of vehicles (commonly referred to as the "Gross Combination Weight Rating" or GCWR) is the GVWR of the power unit plus the GVWR of the towed unit or units. In the absence of a value specified by the manufacturer, GCWR is determined by adding the GVWR of the power unit and the total weight of the towed unit and any load on the unit.

P.A. 76-1586, § 1-124.5, added by P.A. 90-89, § 15, eff. Jan. 1, 1998.

5/1-125. Gross weight

§ 1-125. Gross weight. The weight of a vehicle whether operated singly or in combination without load plus the weight of the load thereon.

P.A. 76-1586, § 1-125, eff. July 1, 1970.

Formerly Ill.Rev.Stat.1991, ch. 95 ½, ¶ 1-125.

5/1-125.7. Headset receiver

§ 1-125.7. Headset receiver. Any device, other than a hearing aid, designed to be worn on a person's head that enables the wearer to hear or receive electronic communications.

P.A. 76-1586, § 1-125.7, added by P.A. 90-89, § 15, eff. Jan. 1, 1998.

5/1-126. Highway

§ 1-126. Highway.

The entire width between the boundary lines of every way publicly maintained when any part thereof is open to the use of the public for purposes of vehicular travel or located on public school property.

P.A. 76-1586, § 1-126, eff. July 1, 1970. Amended by P.A. 92-780, § 5, eff. Aug. 6, 2002.

Formerly Ill.Rev.Stat.1991, ch. 95 ½, ¶ 1-126.

5/1-126.1. Highway Designations

§ 1-126.1. Highway Designations. The Department of Transportation may designate streets or highways in the system of State highways as follows:

(a) Class I highways include interstate highways, expressways, tollways, and other highways deemed appropriate by the department.

(b) Class II highways include major arterials not built to interstate highway standards that have at least 11 feet lane widths.

(c) Class III highways include those State highways that have lane widths of less than 11 feet.

(d) Non-designated highways are highways in the system of State highways not designated as Class I, II, or III, or local highways which are part of any county, township, municipal, or district road system. Local authorities also may designate Class II or Class III highways within their systems of highways.

P.A. 76-1586, § 1-126.1, added by P.A. 92-417, § 5, eff. Jan. 1, 2002.

5/1-127. § 1-127. Repealed by P.A. 81-969, § 2

5/1-128. House trailer

§ 1-128. House trailer. (a) A trailer or semitrailer equipped and used for living quarters or for human habitation (temporarily or permanently) rather than for the transportation of freight, goods, wares and merchandise; or

(b) A house trailer or a semitrailer which is used commercially (temporarily or permanently), that is, for the advertising, sales, display or promotion of merchandise or services, or for any other commercial purpose except the transportation of property for hire or the transportation of property for distribution by a private carrier.

P.A. 76-1586, § 1-128, eff. July 1, 1970. Amended by P.A. 81-969, § 1, eff. Jan. 1, 1980.

Formerly Ill.Rev.Stat.1991, ch. 95 ½, ¶ 1-128.

Section 3 of P.A. 81-969, approved Sept. 22, 1979, provided:

"This amendatory Act takes effect at the start of the 1981 registration year."

5/1-129. Identification Number

§ 1-129. Identification Number. The numbers and letters, if any, on a vehicle or essential part, affixed by its manufacturer, the Illinois Secretary of State or the Illinois Department of State Police for the purpose of identifying the vehicle or essential part, or which is required to be affixed to the vehicle or part by federal or state law.

P.A. 76-1586, § 1-129, eff. July 1, 1970. Amended by P.A. 84-1302, § 1, eff. Jan. 1, 1987; P.A. 84-1304, § 1, eff. Jan. 1, 1987.

Formerly Ill.Rev.Stat.1991, ch. 95 ½, ¶ 1-129.

The amendments by P.A. 84-1302 and P.A. 84-1304 were identical.

5/1-129.1. Ignition interlock device

§ 1-129.1. Ignition interlock device. A device installed in a motor vehicle that prevents the vehicle from starting until the device has determined by an analysis of the driver's breath that the driver's blood alcohol is below a certain preset level.

P.A. 76-1586, § 1-129.1, added by P.A. 91-127, § 5, eff. Jan. 1, 2000.

5/1-130. Implement of husbandry

§ 1-130. Implement of husbandry. Every vehicle designed and adapted exclusively for agricultural, horticultural, or livestock raising operations, including farm wagons, wagon trailers or like vehicles used in connection therewith, or for lifting or carrying an implement of husbandry provided that no farm wagon, wagon trailer or like vehicle having a gross weight of more than 36,000 pounds, shall be included hereunder.

P.A. 76-1586, § 1-130, eff. July 1, 1970. Amended by P.A. 81-327, § 1, eff. Jan. 1, 1980.

Formerly Ill.Rev.Stat.1991, ch. 95 ½, ¶ 1-130.

5/1-131. Improved highway

§ 1-131. Improved highway. Any roadway of concrete, brick, asphalt, macadam and crushed stone or gravel.

P.A. 76-1586, § 1-131, eff. July 1, 1970.

Formerly Ill.Rev.Stat.1991, ch. 95 ½, ¶ 1-131.

5/1-132. Intersection

§ 1-132. Intersection. The area embraced within the prolongation or connection of the lateral curb lines, or, if none, then the lateral boundary lines of the roadways of two highways which join one another at, or approximately at, right angles or the area within which vehicles traveling upon different roadways joining at any other angle may come in conflict.

(b)[1] Where a highway includes two roadways 40 feet or more apart, then every crossing of each roadway of such divided highway by an intersecting highway shall be regarded as a separate intersection.

(c) The junction of an alley with a street or highway does not constitute an intersection.

P.A. 76-1586, § 1-132, eff. July 1, 1970. Amended by P.A. 77-321, § 1, eff. Jan. 1, 1972.

Formerly Ill.Rev.Stat.1991, ch. 95 ½, ¶ 1-132.

[1] No "(a)" in enrolled bill.

5/1-133. Interstate or interstate commerce

§ 1-133. Interstate or interstate commerce. Transportation between 2 or more States or transportation originating in one State and passing into or through other States for delivery in another State, and which is not intrastate.

P.A. 76-1586, § 1-133, eff. July 1, 1970.

Formerly Ill.Rev.Stat.1991, ch. 95 ½, ¶ 1-133.

5/1-133.05. Interstate carrier of property

§ 1-133.05. Interstate carrier of property. Any person who is engaged in the transportation of property only by motor vehicle in whole or in part in interstate or foreign commerce in this State either with or without authority issued from the Interstate Commerce Commission.

P.A. 76-1586, § 1-133.05, added by P.A. 90-89, § 15, eff. Jan. 1, 1998.

5/1-133.1. Interstate highway

§ 1-133.1. Interstate highway. Any highway which is now, or shall hereafter be, a part of the national system of interstate and defense highways within this State.

P.A. 76-1586, § 1-133.1, added by P.A. 85-830, § 1, eff. Sept. 24, 1987.

Formerly Ill.Rev.Stat.1991, ch. 95 ½, ¶ 1-133.1.

5/1-134. Intrastate or intrastate commerce

§ 1-134. Intrastate or intrastate commerce. Transportation originating at any point or place within this State and destined to any other point or place within this State, irrespective of the route, highway or highways traversed, and including transportation which passes into or through another State before delivery is made within this State, and including any act of transportation which includes or completes a pickup within Illinois for delivery within Illinois.

P.A. 76-1586, § 1-134, eff. July 1, 1970.

Formerly Ill.Rev.Stat.1991, ch. 95 ½, ¶ 1-134.

5/1-134.1. Junk vehicle

§ 1-134.1. Junk vehicle. A junk vehicle is a vehicle which has been or is being disassembled, crushed, compressed, flattened, destroyed or otherwise reduced to a state in which it no longer can be returned to an operable state.

P.A. 76-1586, § 1-134.1, added by P.A. 83-1473, § 1, eff. Jan. 1, 1985.

Formerly Ill.Rev.Stat.1991, ch. 95 ½, ¶ 1-134.1.

5/1-135. Lane-control signal

§ 1-135. Lane-control signal. An official traffic control device consisting of an electrically controlled and illuminated signal of a square or rectangular design and employing distinctive colors or symbols used to control the direction of vehicular flow on the particular lane to which the indication applies.

P.A. 76-1586, § 1-135, eff. July 1, 1970. Amended by P.A. 76-2122, § 1, eff. July 1, 1970.

Formerly Ill.Rev.Stat.1991, ch. 95 ½, ¶ 1-135.

5/1-136. Laned roadway

§ 1-136. Laned roadway. A roadway which is divided into two or more clearly marked lanes for vehicular traffic.

P.A. 76-1586, § 1-136, eff. July 1, 1970.

Formerly Ill.Rev.Stat.1991, ch. 95 ½, ¶ 1-136.

5/1-136.5. Law enforcement agency

§ 1-136.5. Law enforcement agency. Every governmental enforcement agency or officer having authority to enforce the provisions of this Act or applicable local vehicle ordinances.

P.A. 76-1586, § 1-136.5, added by P.A. 90-89, § 15, eff. Jan. 1, 1998.

5/1-137. Lease

§ 1-137. Lease. A written document vesting exclusive possession, use, control and responsibility of the lessee during the periods the vehicle is operated by or for the lessee for a specific period of time.

P.A. 76-1586, § 1-137, eff. July 1, 1970. Amended by P.A. 81-501, § 1, eff. Jan. 1, 1980.

Formerly Ill.Rev.Stat.1991, ch. 95 ½, ¶ 1-137.

5/1-138. License to drive

§ 1-138. License to drive. Any driver's license or any other license or permit to operate a motor vehicle issued under the laws of this State including:

1. Any temporary license or instruction permit;

2. The privilege of any person to drive a motor vehicle whether or not such person holds a valid license or permit.

3. Any nonresident's driving privilege as defined herein.

P.A. 76-1586, § 1-138, eff. July 1, 1970.

Formerly Ill.Rev.Stat.1991, ch. 95 ½, ¶ 1-138.

5/1-138.1. Licensee

§ 1-138.1. Licensee. A person licensed or required to be licensed under Sections 5-101, 5-102, 5-201 and 5-301 of this Code.

P.A. 76-1586, § 1-138.1, added by P.A. 83-1473, § 1, eff. Jan. 1, 1985.

Formerly Ill.Rev.Stat.1991, ch. 95 ½, ¶ 1-138.1.

5/1-139. Lienholder

§ 1-139. Lienholder. A person holding a security interest in a vehicle.

P.A. 76-1586, § 1-139, eff. July 1, 1970.

Formerly Ill.Rev.Stat.1991, ch. 95 ½, ¶ 1-139.

5/1-139.1. Limousine

§ 1-139.1. Limousine. Any privately owned first division vehicle intended to be used for the transportation of persons for-hire when the payment is not based on a meter charge, but is prearranged for a designated destination.

P.A. 76-1586, § 1-139.1, added by P.A. 88-415, § 10, eff. Aug. 20, 1993.

5/1-140. Local authorities

§ 1-140. Local authorities. Every county, municipal and other local board or body having authority to enact laws relating to traffic under the constitution and laws of this State.

P.A. 76-1586, § 1-140, eff. July 1, 1970.

Formerly Ill.Rev.Stat.1991, ch. 95 ½, ¶ 1-140.

5/1-140.5. Local mass transit system

§ 1-140.5. Local mass transit system. An organized system providing passenger transportation over regular routes within a designated municipality or area.

P.A. 76-1586, § 1-140.5, added by P.A. 90-89, § 15, eff. Jan. 1, 1998.

5/1-141. Mail

§ 1-141. Mail. To deposit in the United States mail properly addressed and with postage prepaid.

P.A. 76-1586, § 1-141, eff. July 1, 1970.

Formerly Ill.Rev.Stat.1991, ch. 95 ½, ¶ 1-141.

5/1-142. Manufacturer

§ 1-142. Manufacturer. Every person engaged in the business of manufacturing and assembling vehicles or reconstructed vehicles, or engine and driveline components for vehicles.

P.A. 76-1586, § 1-142, eff. July 1, 1970. Amended by P.A. 76-1798, § 1, eff. July 1, 1970.

Formerly Ill.Rev.Stat.1991, ch. 95 ½, ¶ 1-142.

5/1-142.01. Materially altered vehicle

§ 1-142.01. Materially altered vehicle. Any vehicle which has been modified, rebuilt, repaired, reconstructed, restored or specially constructed.

P.A. 76-1586, § 1-142.01, added by P.A. 83-1473, § 1, eff. Jan. 1, 1985.

Formerly Ill.Rev.Stat.1991, ch. 95 ½, ¶ 1-142.01.

5/1-142.05. Maxi-cube vehicle

§ 1-142.05. Maxi-cube vehicle. A combination of vehicles consisting of a truck-tractor, upon which is mounted a separable cargo carrying semi-trailer, and a trailing unit that is attached by a pintle hook or similar connection, with the separable cargo carrying semi-trailer designed so as to be loaded and unloaded through the trailing unit, except that the entire combination shall not exceed 65 feet in length and that neither the semi-trailer nor the trailing unit in the combination shall by itself exceed 34 feet in length.

P.A. 76-1586, § 1-142.05, added by P.A. 90-89, § 15, eff. Jan. 1, 1998.

5/1-142.1. Medical Carrier

§ 1-142.1. Medical Carrier. Any publicly or privately owned vehicle which is specifically designed, constructed or modified and equipped, and is intended to be used for, and is maintained or operated for the nonemergency transportation of persons for compensation for the purpose of obtaining medical services.

P.A. 76-1586, § 1-142.1, added by P.A. 82-433, § 1, eff. Sept. 8, 1981.

Formerly Ill.Rev.Stat.1991, ch. 95 ½, ¶ 1-142.1.

Section 3 of P.A. 82-433 approved Sept. 8, 1981, provided:

"This Act takes effect upon its becoming a law, except that the provisions relating to safety tests and proof of financial responsibility for medical transport vehicles apply only to applications for and the issuance of registration plates which are required to be displayed on January 1, 1982 or thereafter."

5/1-142.1a. § 1-142.1a. Repealed by P.A. 92-703, § 15, eff. July 19, 2002

5/1-142.1b. Medical limitation or condition

§ 1-142.1b. Medical limitation or condition. A scientifically recognized condition that may medically impair a person's physical or mental health to the extent the person is unable to safely operate a motor vehicle.

P.A. 76-1586, § 1-142.1b, added by P.A. 90-89, § 15, eff. Jan. 1, 1998.

5/1-142.2. Medical transport vehicle

§ 1-142.2. Medical transport vehicle. Includes ambulances, medical carriers, and rescue vehicles.

P.A. 76-1586, § 1-142.2, added by P.A. 82-433, § 1, eff. Sept. 8, 1981.

Formerly Ill.Rev.Stat.1991, ch. 95 ½, ¶ 1-142.2.

Effective date of P.A. 82-433, see Historical and Statutory Notes following 625 ILCS 5/1-102.01.

5/1-143, 5/1-144. §§ 1-143, 1-144. Repealed by P.A. 90-89, § 20, eff. Jan. 1, 1998

5/1-144.05. Model year

§ 1-144.05. Model year. The year of manufacture of a vehicle based upon the annual production period of the vehicle as designated by the manufacturer and indicated on the title and registration of the vehicle. If the manufacturer does not designate a production period for the vehicle, then "model year" means the calendar year of manufacture.

P.A. 76-1586, § 1-144.05, added by P.A. 90-89, § 15, eff. Jan. 1, 1998.

5/1-144.1. Modified vehicle

§ 1-144.1. Modified vehicle. Every vehicle of a type required to be registered under this Code altered by the addition, deletion, or modification of the body, chassis, component or essential parts, new or used.

P.A. 76-1586, § 1-144.1, added by P.A. 83-831, § 1, eff. Jan. 1, 1984.

Formerly Ill.Rev.Stat.1991, ch. 95 ½, ¶ 1-144.1.

5/1-145. Motor carrier

§ 1-145. Motor carrier. An operator of For-Hire vehicles pursuant to the Illinois Motor Carrier of Property Law.[1]

P.A. 76-1586, § 1-145, eff. July 1, 1970.

Formerly Ill.Rev.Stat.1991, ch. 95 ½, ¶ 1-145.

[1] Former Ill.Rev.Stat. ch. 95½, ¶ 18-100 et seq. (repealed).

5/1-145.001. Motor driven cycle

§ 1-145.001. Motor driven cycle. Every motorcycle and every motor scooter with less than 150 cubic centimeter piston displacement including motorized pedalcycles.

P.A. 76-1586, § 1-148, eff. July 1, 1970. Amended by P.A. 80-262, § 1, eff. Aug. 20, 1977. Renumbered § 1-145.001 and amended by P.A. 90-89, § 15, eff. Jan. 1, 1998.

Formerly Ill.Rev.Stat.1991, ch. 95 ½, ¶ 1-148.

5/1-145.01. Motor home, mini motor home or van camper

§ 1-145.01. Motor home, mini motor home or van camper. A self-contained motor vehicle, not used commercially, designed or permanently converted to provide living quarters for recreational, camping or travel use, with direct walk through access to the living quarters from the driver's seat. Such vehicles must include at least four of the following:

a) A cooking facility with an on-board fuel source;

b) A gas or electric refrigerator;

c) A toilet with exterior evacuation;

d) A heating or air conditioning system with an on-board power or fuel source separate from the vehicle engine;

e) A potable water supply system that includes at least a sink, a faucet, and a water tank with an exterior service supply connection;

f) A 110-125 volt electric power supply.

P.A. 76-1586, § 1-145.01, added by P.A. 81-969, § 1, eff. Jan. 1, 1980. Amended by P.A. 86-971, § 1, eff. Jan. 1, 1991.

Formerly Ill.Rev.Stat.1991, ch. 95 ½, ¶ 1-145.01.

Section 3 of P.A. 81-969, approved Sept. 22, 1979, provided:

"This amendatory Act takes effect at the start of the 1981 registration year."

5/1-146. Motor vehicle

§ 1-146. Motor vehicle. Every vehicle which is self-propelled and every vehicle which is propelled by electric power obtained from overhead trolley wires, but not operated upon rails, except for vehicles moved solely by human power and motorized wheelchairs. For this Act, motor vehicles are divided into two divisions:

First Division: Those motor vehicles which are designed for the carrying of not more than 10 persons.

Second Division: Those motor vehicles which are designed for carrying more than 10 persons, those motor vehicles designed or used for living quarters, those motor vehicles which are designed for pulling or carrying freight, cargo or implements of husbandry, and those motor vehicles of the First Division remodelled for use and used as motor vehicles of the Second Division.

P.A. 76-1586, § 1-146, eff. July 1, 1970. Amended by P.A. 84-672, § 1, eff. Sept. 20, 1985; P.A. 85-1010, § 1, eff. March 2, 1988.

Formerly Ill.Rev.Stat.1991, ch. 95 ½, ¶ 1-146.

5/1-147. Motorcycle

§ 1-147. Motorcycle. Every motor vehicle having a seat or saddle for the use of the rider and designed to travel on not more than 3 wheels in contact with the ground, but excluding a tractor.

P.A. 76-1586, § 1-147, eff. July 1, 1970. Amended by P.A. 80-262, § 1, eff. Aug. 20, 1977.

Formerly Ill.Rev.Stat.1991, ch. 95 ½, ¶ 1-147.

5/1-148. § 1-148. Renumbered as § 1-145.001 by P.A. 90-89, § 15, eff. Jan. 1, 1998

5/1-148.1. § 1-148.1. Renumbered as § 1-148.3b by P.A. 90-89, § 15, eff. Jan. 1, 1998

5/1-148.2. Motorized Pedalcycle

§ 1-148.2. Motorized Pedalcycle. A motorized pedalcycle is a motor-driven cycle whose speed attainable in one mile is 30 mph or less, which is equipped with a motor that produces 2 brake horsepower or less. If an internal combustion engine is used, the displacement shall not exceed 50 cubic centimeter displacement and the power drive system shall not require the operator to shift gears.

P.A. 76-1586, § 1-148.2, added by P.A. 80-262, § 1, eff. Aug. 20, 1977. Amended by P.A. 83-820, § 1, eff. Jan. 1, 1984.

Formerly Ill.Rev.Stat.1991, ch. 95 ½, ¶ 1-148.2.

5/1-148.3. Motorized wheelchair

§ 1-148.3. Motorized wheelchair. Any self-propelled vehicle, including a three-wheeled vehicle, designed for and used by a person with disabilities, that is incapable of a speed in excess of 8 miles per hour on level ground.

P.A. 76-1586, § 1-148.3, added by P.A. 84-672, § 1, eff. Sept. 20, 1985. Amended by P.A. 88-685, § 5, eff. Jan. 24, 1995.

Formerly Ill.Rev.Stat.1991, ch. 95 ½, ¶ 1-148.3.

5/1-148.3a. Muffler

§ 1-148.3a. Muffler. A device consisting of a series of chambers or baffle plates or other mechanical design for the purpose of receiving exhaust gas from an internal combustion engine or turbine wheels for the purpose of receiving exhaust gas from a diesel engine, all of which are effective in reducing noise.

P.A. 76-1586, § 1-148.3a, added by P.A. 90-89, § 15, eff. Jan. 1, 1998.

5/1-148.3b. Multipurpose passenger vehicle

§ 1-148.3b. Multipurpose passenger vehicle. A motor vehicle with motive power, except a trailer, designed to carry 10 persons or less that is constructed either on a truck chassis or with special features for occasional off-road operation.

P.A. 76-1586, § 1-148.1, added by P.A. 78-343, § 1, eff. Jan. 1, 1974. Renumbered § 1-148.3b and amended by P.A. 90-89, § 15, eff. Jan. 1, 1998.

Formerly Ill.Rev.Stat.1991, ch. 95 ½, ¶ 1-148.1.

5/1-148.4. New Vehicle

§ 1-148.4. New Vehicle. A new vehicle which has not been previously sold to any person except a franchised distributor or franchised new vehicle dealer.

P.A. 76-1586, § 1-148.4, added by P.A. 86-444, § 1, eff. Jan. 1, 1990.

Formerly Ill.Rev.Stat.1991, ch. 95 ½, ¶ 1-148.4.

5/1-148.5. News media

§ 1-148.5. News media. A newspaper or other periodical issued at regular intervals whether in print or electronic format, a news service whether in print or electronic format, a radio station, a television station, a television network, a community antenna television service, or a person or corporation engaged in making news reels or other motion picture news for public showing.

P.A. 76-1586, § 1-148.5, added by P.A. 90-144, § 15, eff. July 23, 1997. Amended by P.A. 92-335, § 30, eff. Aug. 10, 2001.

5/1-148.6. Noncommercial vehicle

§ 1-148.6. Noncommercial vehicle. Any vehicle that is not a commercial vehicle.

P.A. 76-1586, § 1-151, eff. July 1, 1970. Renumbered § 1-148.6 and amended by P.A. 90-89, § 15, eff. Jan. 1, 1998.

Formerly Ill.Rev.Stat.1991, ch. 95 ½, ¶ 1-151.

5/1-148.8. Nondivisible load or vehicle

§ 1-148.8. Nondivisible load or vehicle. A load or vehicle that when separated into smaller loads or vehicles further dismantling would:

(1) Compromise the intended use of the load or vehicle or make it unable to perform the function for which it was intended.

(2) Destroy the value of the load or vehicle or make it unusable for its intended purpose.

(3) Require more than 8 work hours to dismantle using appropriate equipment. The applicant for a nondivisible load has the burden of proof as to the number of work hours required to dismantle the load.

P.A. 76-1586, § 1-148.8, added by P.A. 90-89, § 15, eff. Jan. 1, 1998.

5/1-149. Nonresident

§ 1-149. Nonresident. Every person who is not a resident of this State.

P.A. 76-1586, § 1-149, eff. July 1, 1970.

Formerly Ill.Rev.Stat.1991, ch. 95 ½, ¶ 1-149.

5/1-150. Nonresident's driving privilege

§ 1-150. Nonresident's driving privilege. The privilege conferred upon a nonresident by the laws of this State pertaining to the operation by such person of a motor vehicle, or the use of a vehicle owned by such person, in this State.

P.A. 76-1586, § 1-150, eff. July 1, 1970.

Formerly Ill.Rev.Stat.1991, ch. 95 ½, ¶ 1-150.

5/1-151. § 1-151. Renumbered as § 1-148.6 by P.A. 90-89, § 15, eff. Jan. 1, 1998

5/1-152. § 1-152. Repealed by P.A. 79-1041, § 2, eff. Jan. 1, 1976

5/1-153. Not-for-hire

§ 1-153. Not-for-hire. Operation of a commercial vehicle in furtherance of any commercial or industrial enterprise but not For-Hire.

P.A. 76-1586, § 1-153, eff. July 1, 1970.

Formerly Ill.Rev.Stat.1991, ch. 95 ½, ¶ 1-153.

5/1-153.1. Off-highway motorcycle

§ 1-153.1. Off-highway motorcycle. Any motorized device designed to travel primarily off-highway on 2 wheels, having a seat or saddle for the use of the operator, upon or by which any person, persons or property may be transported or drawn.

P.A. 76-1586, § 1-153.1, added by P.A. 85-830, § 1, eff. Sept. 24, 1987.

Formerly Ill.Rev.Stat.1991, ch. 95 ½, ¶ 1-153.1.

5/1-154. Official traffic-control devices

§ 1-154. Official traffic-control devices. All signs, signals, markings, and devices which conform with the State Manual and not inconsistent with this Act placed or erected by authority of a public body or official having jurisdiction, for the purpose of regulating, warning, or guiding traffic.

P.A. 76-1586, § 1-154, eff. July 1, 1970.

Formerly Ill.Rev.Stat.1991, ch. 95 ½, ¶ 1-154.

5/1-154.1. Operate

§ 1-154.1. Operate. To ride in or on, other than as a passenger, use or control in any manner the operation of any device or vehicle whether motorized or propelled by human power.

P.A. 76-1586, § 1-154.1, added by P.A. 85-830, § 1, eff. Sept. 24, 1987.

Formerly Ill.Rev.Stat.1991, ch. 95 ½, ¶ 1-154.1.

5/1-154.2. Operator

§ 1-154.2. Operator. Every person who operates or is in actual physical control of any device or vehicle whether motorized or propelled by human power.

P.A. 76-1586, § 1-154.2, added by P.A. 85-830, § 1, eff. Sept. 24, 1987.

Formerly Ill.Rev.Stat.1991, ch. 95 ½, ¶ 1-154.2.

5/1-154.4. Organ transport vehicle

§ 1-154.4. Organ transport vehicle. A motor vehicle of the second division equipped and used exclusively for the transportation of organs for human transplant or the transportation of members of the surgical team performing the organ harvesting or transplant operations. Vehicles defined in this Section shall be owned or operated by a company that has a contractual agreement with a federally designated organ procurement organization for the purposes stated in this Section.

P.A. 76-1586, § 1-154.4, added by P.A. 90-347, § 5, eff. Jan. 1, 1998.

5/1-154.5. Out-of-service order

§ 1-154.5. Out-of-service order. A temporary prohibition against driving a commercial motor vehicle.

P.A. 76-1586, § 1-154.5, added by P.A. 90-89, § 15, eff. Jan. 1, 1998.

5/1-154.7. Out-of-state salvage vehicle buyer

§ 1-154.7. Out-of-state salvage vehicle buyer. A person who is licensed in another state for the primary purpose of acquiring salvage vehicles and who is issued an out-of-state salvage vehicle buyer's identification card in this State for the sole purpose of acquiring salvage vehicles and taking them out of state.

P.A. 76-1586, § 1-154.7, added by P.A. 90-89, § 15, eff. Jan. 1, 1998.

5/1-155. Owner

§ 1-155. Owner. A person who holds legal title of a vehicle, or in the event a vehicle is the subject of an agreement for the conditional sale or lease thereof with the right of purchase upon performance of the conditions stated in the agreement and with an immediate right of possession vested in the conditional vendee or lessee, or in the event a mortgagor of such vehicle is entitled to possession, then such conditional vendee or lessee or mortgagor shall be deemed the owner for the purpose of this Code.

P.A. 76-1586, § 1-155, eff. July 1, 1970. Amended by P.A. 85-1201, § 1, eff. July 1, 1989.

Formerly Ill.Rev.Stat.1991, ch. 95 ½, ¶ 1-155.

5/1-155.5. Owner-operator

§ 1-155.5. Owner-operator. A commercial motor vehicle lessor who leases the commercial motor vehicle, with driver, to a lessee.

P.A. 76-1586, § 1-155.5, added by P.A. 90-89, § 15, eff. Jan. 1, 1998.

5/1-156. Park or parking

§ 1-156. Park or parking. Means the standing of a vehicle, whether occupied or not, otherwise than when temporarily and actually engaged in loading or unloading merchandise or passengers.

P.A. 76-1586, § 1-156, eff. July 1, 1970.

Formerly Ill.Rev.Stat.1991, ch. 95 ½, ¶ 1-156.

5/1-156.5. Park district

§ 1-156.5. Park district. Any park district formed under the Park District Code [1] or any Submerged Land Park District as that term is defined in subsection (c) of Section 1-3 of the Park District Code.[2]

P.A. 76-1586, § 1-156.5, added by P.A. 90-89, § 15, eff. Jan. 1, 1998.

1 70 ILCS 1205/1-1 et seq.

2 70 ILCS 1205/1-3.

5/1-157. Passenger car

§ 1-157. Passenger car. A motor vehicle of the First Division including a multipurpose passenger vehicle, that is designed for carrying not more than 10 persons.

P.A. 76-1586, § 1-157, eff. July 1, 1970. Amended by P.A. 78-343, § 1, eff. Jan. 1, 1974.

Formerly Ill.Rev.Stat.1991, ch. 95 ½, ¶ 1-157.

5/1-158. Pedestrian

§ 1-158. Pedestrian.

Any person afoot, including a person with a physical, hearing, or visual disability.

P.A. 76-1586, § 1-158, eff. July 1, 1970. Amended by P.A. 88-685, § 5, eff. Jan. 24, 1995.

Formerly Ill.Rev.Stat.1991, ch. 95 ½, ¶ 1-158.

5/1-158.5. Penalties and offenses—definitions

§ 1-158.5. Penalties and offenses-definitions. The following words and phrases when used in this Act, shall for the purposes of this Act, have the meanings ascribed to them in Article V of the "Unified Code of Corrections", as now or hereafter amended: [1]

Business Offense;

Conviction;

Court;

Felony;

Class 1 Felony;

Class 2 Felony;

Class 3 Felony;

Class 4 Felony;

Imprisonment;

Judgment;

Misdemeanor;

Class A Misdemeanor;

Class B Misdemeanor;

Class C Misdemeanor;

Offense;

Petty Offense;

Sentence.

P.A. 76-1586, § 1-300, added by P.A. 78-142, § 1, eff. Oct. 1, 1973. Renumbered § 1-158.5 and amended by P.A. 90-89, § 15, eff. Jan. 1, 1998.

Formerly Ill.Rev.Stat.1991, ch. 95 ½, ¶ 1-300.

1 730 ILCS 5/5-1-1 et seq.

5/1-159. Person

§ 1-159. Person. Every natural person, firm, copartnership, association or corporation.

P.A. 76-1586, § 1-159, eff. July 1, 1970.

Formerly Ill.Rev.Stat.1991, ch. 95 ½, ¶ 1-159.

5/1-159.1. Person with disabilities

§ 1-159.1. Person with disabilities. A natural person who, as determined by a licensed physician: (1) cannot walk without the use of, or assistance from, a brace, cane, crutch, another person, prosthetic device, wheelchair, or other assistive device; (2) is restricted by lung disease to such an extent that his or her forced (respiratory) expiratory volume for one second, when measured by spirometry, is less than one liter, or the arterial oxygen tension is less than 60 mm/hg on room air at rest; (3) uses portable oxygen; (4) has a cardiac condition to the extent that the person's functional limitations are classified in severity as Class III or Class IV, according to standards set by the American Heart Association; (5) is severely limited in the person's ability to walk due to an arthritic, neurological, or orthopedic condition; or (6) cannot walk 200 feet without stopping to rest because of one of the above 5 conditions.

P.A. 76-1586, § 1-159.1, added by P.A. 78-321, § 1, eff. Oct. 1, 1973. Amended by P.A. 83-1058, § 1, eff. July 1, 1984; P.A. 88-685, § 5, eff. Jan. 24, 1995; P.A. 92-411, § 5, eff. Jan. 1, 2002.

Formerly Ill.Rev.Stat.1991, ch. 95 ½, ¶ 1-159.1.

5/1-159.2. Personally identifying information

§ 1-159.2. Personally identifying information. Information that identifies an individual, including his or her photograph, social security number, driver identification number, name, address (but not the 5 digit zip code), telephone number, and medical or disability information, but "personally identifying information" does not include information on vehicular accidents, driving violations, and driver's status.

P.A. 76-1586, § 1-159.2, added by P.A. 92-32, § 10, eff. July 1, 2001.

5/1-159.3. Photograph

§ 1-159.3. Photograph. Any color photograph or digitally produced and captured image of an applicant for a driver's license or permit.

P.A. 76-1586, § 1-159.3, added by P.A. 90-191, § 10, eff. Jan. 1, 1998.

5/1-160. Pneumatic tire

§ 1-160. Pneumatic tire. Every tire in which compressed air is designed to support the load.

P.A. 76-1586, § 1-160, eff. July 1, 1970.

Formerly Ill.Rev.Stat.1991, ch. 95 ½, ¶ 1-160.

5/1-161. Pole trailer

§ 1-161. Pole trailer. Every vehicle without motive power designed to be drawn by another vehicle and attached to the towing vehicle by means of a reach or pole, or by being boomed or otherwise secured to the towing vehicle, and ordinarily used for transporting long or irregularly shaped loads such as poles, pipes or structural members capable, generally, of sustaining themselves as beams between the supporting connections.

P.A. 76-1586, § 1-161, eff. July 1, 1970.

Formerly Ill.Rev.Stat.1991, ch. 95 ½, ¶ 1-161.

5/1-162. Police officer

§ 1-162. Police officer. Every officer authorized to direct or regulate traffic or to make arrests and issue citations for violations of traffic regulations.

P.A. 76-1586, § 1-162, eff. July 1, 1970. Amended by P.A. 90-89, § 15, eff. Jan. 1, 1998.

Formerly Ill.Rev.Stat.1991, ch. 95 ½, ¶ 1-162.

5/1-162.5. Principal place of business

§ 1-162.5. Principal place of business. The place where any person transacts his principal business, or where he makes up and approves his payroll, maintains a central file of records and maintains his principal executive offices. In the event that not all of these functions are performed in one place, then that place where a majority of such functions are performed or the place where such person does in fact principally transact and control his business affairs.

P.A. 76-1586, § 1-164, eff. July 1, 1970. Renumbered § 1-162.5 and amended by P.A. 90-89, § 15, eff. Jan. 1, 1998.

Formerly Ill.Rev.Stat.1991, ch. 95 ½, ¶ 1-164.

5/1-163. Private road or driveway

§ 1-163. Private road or driveway. Every way or place in private ownership and used for vehicular travel by the owner and those having express or implied permission from the owner, but not by other persons.

P.A. 76-1586, § 1-163, eff. July 1, 1970.

Formerly Ill.Rev.Stat.1991, ch. 95 ½, ¶ 1-163.

5/1-164. § 1-164. Renumbered as § 1-162.5 by P.A. 90-89, § 15, eff. Jan. 1, 1998

5/1-164.1. Probationary license to drive

§ 1-164.1. Probationary license to drive. A conditional license granting full driving privileges during a period of suspension.

P.A. 76-1586, § 1-164.1, added by P.A. 84-1394, § 5, eff. Sept. 18, 1986. Amended by P.A. 86-549, § 1, eff. Jan. 1, 1990.

Formerly Ill.Rev.Stat.1991, ch. 95 ½, ¶ 1-164.1.

5/1-164.2. Processing costs

§ 1-164.2. Processing costs. Processing costs consist of fees paid to the Secretary of State for a record search to determine the name and address of the last registered owner, lienholder, and other legally entitled persons, plus the cost of sending certified mail notice to those persons.

P.A. 76-1586, § 1-164.2, added by P.A. 89-433, § 5, eff. Dec. 15, 1995.

5/1-164.5. Proof of financial responsibility

§ 1-164.5. Proof of financial responsibility. Proof of ability to respond in damages for any liability thereafter incurred resulting from the ownership, maintenance, use or operation of a motor vehicle for bodily injury to or death of any person in the amount of $20,000, and subject to this limit for any one person injured or killed, in the amount of $40,000 for bodily injury to or death of 2 or more persons in any one accident, and for damage to property in the amount of $15,000 resulting from any one accident. This proof in these amounts shall be furnished for each motor vehicle registered by every person required to furnish this proof.

P.A. 76-1586, § 1-164.5, added by P.A. 90-89, § 15, eff. Jan. 1, 1998.

5/1-164.7. Public utility

§ 1-164.7. Public utility. Each firm lawfully licensed and engaged in any of the following: the transmission of telegraphic or telephonic messages; the production, storage, transmission, distribution, sale, delivery, or furnishing of heat, cold, light, power, electricity, gas, or water; the disposal of sewage; the conveyance of oil or gas by pipeline; the drilling of water wells; or the installation or repair of facilities for any of these foregoing activities.

P.A. 76-1586, § 1-164.7, added by P.A. 90-89, § 15, eff. Jan. 1, 1998.

5/1-165. § 1-165. Repealed by P.A. 81-969, § 2

The repeal was effective at the "start of the 1981 registration year."

5/1-166. Railroad

§ 1-166. Railroad. A carrier of persons or property upon cars, other than streetcars, operated upon stationary rails.

P.A. 76-1586, § 1-166, eff. July 1, 1970.

Formerly Ill.Rev.Stat.1991, ch. 95 ½, ¶ 1-166.

5/1-166.1. Railroad-highway grade crossing

§ 1-166.1. Railroad-highway grade crossing. The intersection of stationary rails owned or used in the operation of a railroad corporation across a highway.

P.A. 76-1586, § 1-166.1, added by P.A. 78-314, § 1, eff. Oct. 1, 1973.

Formerly Ill.Rev.Stat.1991, ch. 95 ½, ¶ 1-166.1.

5/1-167. Railroad sign or signal

§ 1-167. Railroad sign or signal. Any sign, signal or device, other than an official traffic control signal or device, erected in accordance with the laws governing same and intended to give notice of the presence of railroad tracks or the approach of a railroad train.

P.A. 76-1586, § 1-167, eff. July 1, 1970. Amended by P.A. 76-2124, § 1, eff. July 1, 1970; P.A. 83-831, § 1, eff. Jan. 1, 1984.

Formerly Ill.Rev.Stat.1991, ch. 95 ½, ¶ 1-167.

5/1-168. Railroad train

§ 1-168. Railroad train. A steam engine, electric or other motor, with or without cars coupled thereto, operated upon rails, except streetcars.

P.A. 76-1586, § 1-168, eff. July 1, 1970.

Formerly Ill.Rev.Stat.1991, ch. 95 ½, ¶ 1-168.

5/1-168.05. Rebuilder

§ 1-168.05. Rebuilder. A person who is in the business of returning a vehicle for which a salvage certificate has been previously issued back to its original or operating condition.

P.A. 76-1586, § 1-168.05, added by P.A. 90-89, § 15, eff. Jan. 1, 1998.

5/1-168.1. Rebuilt vehicle

§ 1-168.1. Rebuilt vehicle. A vehicle for which a salvage certificate has been issued and which subsequently has been put back into its original or operating condition by a licensed rebuilder and which has met all the requirements of a salvage vehicle inspection.

P.A. 76-1586, § 1-168.1, added by P.A. 83-1473, § 1, eff. Jan. 1, 1985. Amended by P.A. 85-951, § 1, eff. July 1, 1988.

Formerly Ill.Rev.Stat.1991, ch. 95 ½, ¶ 1-168.1.

5/1-168.5. Recognized repair technician

§ 1-168.5. Recognized repair technician. A person professionally engaged in vehicle repair, employed by a going concern whose purpose is vehicle repair, or possessing nationally recognized certification for emission-related diagnosis and repair.

P.A. 76-1586, § 1-168.5, added by P.A. 90-89, § 15, eff. Jan. 1, 1998.

5/1-169. Recreational vehicle

§ 1-169. Recreational vehicle. Every camping trailer, motor home, mini motor home, travel trailer, truck camper or van camper used primarily for recreational purposes and not used commercially nor owned by a commercial business.

P.A. 76-1586, § 1-169, eff. July 1, 1970. Amended by P.A. 78-343, § 1, eff. Jan. 1, 1974; P.A. 81-969, § 1, eff. Jan. 4, 1980; P.A. 84-986, § 1, eff. Sept. 25, 1985.

Formerly Ill.Rev.Stat.1991, ch. 95 ½, ¶ 1-169.

Section 3 of P.A. 81-969, approved Sept. 22, 1979, provided:

"This amendatory Act takes effect at the start of the 1981 registration year."

5/1-169.5. Refuse

§ 1-169.5. Refuse. Any material or load consisting of waste from the facilities of the generator of the waste when transported for disposal or to a permitted recycling or waste processing facility when the generator receives no direct or indirect compensation from anyone for the material or load and when transported by a truck specially equipped with a selfcompactor or an industrial roll-off hoist and roll-off container.

P.A. 76-1586, § 1-169.5, added by P.A. 90-89, § 15, eff. Jan. 1, 1998.

5/1-170. § 1-170. Repealed by P.A. 85-951, § 2, eff. July 1, 1988

5/1-171. Registration—Registration Sticker

§ 1-171. Registration—Registration Sticker. Registration. The registration certificate or certificates, registration plates and registration stickers issued under the laws of this State pertaining to the registration of vehicles.

Registration Sticker or Stickers. A device or devices to be attached to a rear registration plate that will renew the registration and registration plate or plates for a pre-determined period not to exceed one registration year except as provided in subsection (1) of Section 3-414 of this Code. Should the Secretary of State determine it is advisable to require a registration sticker to be attached to a front registration plate, he may require such action and provide the necessary additional sticker. Such determination shall be publicly announced at least 30 days in advance of a new annual registration year.

P.A. 76-1586, § 1-171, eff. July 1, 1970. Amended by P.A. 80-230, § 1, eff. Oct. 1, 1977; P.A. 80-1185, § 1, eff. March 8, 1978.

Formerly Ill.Rev.Stat.1991, ch. 95 ½, ¶ 1-171.

5/1-171.01. § 1-171.01. Renumbered as § 1-111.1a by P.A. 90-89, § 15, eff. Jan. 1, 1998

5/1-171.01a. Remittance agent

§ 1-171.01a. Remittance agent. For the purposes of Article IX of Chapter 3,[1] the term "remittance agent" means any person who holds himself or herself out to the public as being engaged in or who engages in accepting money for remittance to the State of Illinois or any of its instrumentalities or political subdivisions, or to any of their officials, for the payment of vehicle taxes or vehicle license or registration fees regardless of when the money is accepted from the public or remitted to the State, whether or not the person renders any other service in connection with the making of any such remittance or is engaged in any other endeavor. The term "remittance agent" does not include any licensed dealer in motor vehicles who accepts money for remittance to the State of Illinois for the payment of vehicle taxes or vehicle licenses or registration fees as an incident to his or her business as a motor vehicle dealer.

P.A. 76-1586, § 1-171.01a, added by P.A. 90-89, § 15, eff. Jan. 1, 1998.

1 625 ILCS 5/3-900 et seq.

5/1-171.01b. Remittee

§ 1-171.01b. Remittee. The State of Illinois location where the remittance agent brings the money and application he or she receives from the general public (remitter) to be processed by the State of Illinois.

P.A. 76-1586, § 1-171.01b, added by P.A. 90-89, § 15, eff. Jan. 1, 1998.

5/1-171.01c. Remitter

§ 1-171.01c. Remitter. Any person who gives money to a remittance agent to submit to the State of Illinois and its licensing and taxing agencies for the payment of vehicle taxes or vehicle license and registration fees.

P.A. 76-1586, § 1-171.01c, added by P.A. 90-89, § 15, eff. Jan. 1, 1998.

5/1-171.02. Repaired vehicle

§ 1-171.02. Repaired vehicle. A vehicle other than a rebuilt vehicle which has been put back into its original or operating condition by restoring, mending, straightening, replacing, altering or painting its essential parts by a licensed repairer.

P.A. 76-1586, § 1-171.02, added by P.A. 83-1473, § 1, eff. Jan. 1, 1985.

Formerly Ill.Rev.Stat.1991, ch. 95 ½, ¶ 1-171.02.

5/1-171.04. Replica trolley

§ 1-171.04. Replica trolley. A motor vehicle that is a replica of or is specifically designed to resemble a cable car or an antique trolley car, except that the vehicle is not operated on rails.

P.A. 76-1586, § 1-171.04, added by P.A. 89-687, § 5, eff. June 1, 1997.

5/1-171.3. Repairer

§ 1-171.3. Repairer. A person who is in the business of returning a vehicle other than a vehicle for which a salvage certificate has been issued back to its original or operating condition by restoring, mending, straightening, replacing, altering, or painting its essential parts.

P.A. 76-1586, § 1-171.3, added by P.A. 90-89, § 15, eff. Jan. 1, 1998.

5/1-171.6. Rescue squad

§ 1-171.6. Rescue squad. A voluntary association of individuals or a fire department dedicated to saving lives through the rescue of persons entrapped in wrecked vehicles or other hazardous circumstances and associated with some unit of government.

P.A. 76-1586, § 1-222, added by P.A. 79-537, § 1, eff. Oct. 1, 1975. Renumbered § 1-171.6 and amended by P.A. 90-89, § 15, eff. Jan. 1, 1998.

Formerly Ill.Rev.Stat.1991, ch. 95 ½, ¶ 1-222.

5/1-171.8. Rescue vehicle

§ 1-171.8. Rescue vehicle. Any publicly or privately owned vehicle which is specifically designed, configured, and equipped for the performance of access and extrication of persons from hazardous or life-endangering situations, as well as for the emergency transportation of persons who are sick, injured, wounded or otherwise incapacitated or helpless.

P.A. 76-1586, § 1-224, added by P.A. 82-433, § 1, eff. Sept. 8, 1981. Renumbered § 1-171.8 and amended by P.A. 90-89, § 15, eff. Jan. 1, 1998.

Formerly Ill.Rev.Stat.1991, ch. 95 ½, ¶ 1-224.

Section 3 of P.A. 82-433 approved Sept. 8, 1981, provided:

"This Act takes effect upon its becoming a law, except that the provisions relating to safety tests and proof of financial responsibility for medical transport vehicles apply only to applications for and the issuance of registration plates which are required to be displayed on January 1, 1982 or thereafter."

5/1-172. Residence district

§ 1-172. Residence district. The territory contiguous to and including a highway not comprising a business district when the property on such highway for a distance of 300 feet or more is in the main improved with residences or residences and buildings in use for business.

For purposes of establishing maximum speed limits, a residence district shall be at least a quarter of a mile long with residences or residences and buildings in use for businesses spaced no more than 300 feet apart.

P.A. 76-1586, § 1-172, eff. July 1, 1970. Amended by P.A. 81-875, § 1, eff. Jan. 1, 1980.

Formerly Ill.Rev.Stat.1991, ch. 95 ½, ¶ 1-172.

5/1-173. Resident

§ 1-173. Resident. (a) Every natural person who resides in this state shall be deemed a resident of this State.

(b) In the case of a firm, copartnership or association, if the principal place of business of such firm, copartnership or association is located in the State of Illinois, then such firm, copartnership or association shall be deemed a resident of the State of Illinois.

(c) In the case of a corporation, if the corporation was incorporated under the laws of the State of Illinois or if the principal place of business of such corporation is in the State of Illinois, then such corporation shall be deemed a resident of the State of Illinois.

P.A. 76-1586, § 1-173, eff. July 1, 1970.

Formerly Ill.Rev.Stat.1991, ch. 95 ½, ¶ 1-173.

5/1-173.1. Restricted Driving Permit

§ 1-173.1. Restricted Driving Permit. A restricted driving permit is that document which grants and specifies limited privileges to drivers of motor vehicles who have had their full driving privileges suspended, revoked or cancelled. The restricted driving permit is valid only when in the immediate possession of the driver to whom it is issued.

P.A. 76-1586, § 1-173.1, added by P.A. 81-1400, § 1, eff. Aug. 25, 1980.

Formerly Ill.Rev.Stat.1991, ch. 95 ½, ¶ 1-173.1.

5/1-174. Retail sale

§ 1-174. Retail sale. The act or attempted act of selling vehicles or otherwise disposing of a vehicle to a person for use as a consumer.

P.A. 76-1586, § 1-174, eff. July 1, 1970.

Formerly Ill.Rev.Stat.1991, ch. 95 ½, ¶ 1-174.

5/1-175. § 1-175. Repealed by P.A. 90-89, § 20, eff. Jan. 1, 1998

5/1-176. Revocation of driver's license

§ 1-176. Revocation of driver's license. The termination by formal action of the Secretary of a person's license or privilege to operate a motor vehicle on the public highways, which termination shall not be subject to renewal or restoration except that an application for a new license may be presented and acted upon by the Secretary after the expiration of at least one year after the date of revocation.

P.A. 76-1586, § 1-176, eff. July 1, 1970.

Formerly Ill.Rev.Stat.1991, ch. 95 ½, ¶ 1-176.

5/1-176.1. Ridesharing arrangement

§ 1-176.1. Ridesharing arrangement. The transportation by motor vehicle of not more than 16 persons, including the driver, (1) for purposes incidental to another purpose of the driver, for which no fee is charged or paid except to reimburse the driver or owner of the vehicle for his or her operating expenses on a nonprofit basis or (2) when these persons are traveling between their homes and their places of employment, or places reasonably convenient thereto, for which (i) no fee is charged or paid except to reimburse the driver or owner of the vehicle for his or her operating expenses on a nonprofit basis or (ii) a fee is charged in accordance with the provisions of Section 6 of the Ridesharing Arrangements Act.[1]

P.A. 76-1586, § 1-176.1, added by P.A. 81-1452, § 1, eff. Jan. 1, 1981. Amended by P.A. 83-1091, § 1, eff. July 1, 1984; P.A. 90-89, § 15, eff. Jan. 1, 1998.

Formerly Ill.Rev.Stat.1991, ch. 95 ½, ¶ 1-176.1.

[1] 625 ILCS 30/1 et seq.

5/1-177. Right-of-way

§ 1-177. Right-of-way. The right of one vehicle or pedestrian to proceed in a lawful manner in preference to another vehicle or pedestrian approaching under such circumstances of direction, speed and proximity as to give rise to danger of collision unless one grants precedence to the other.

P.A. 76-1586, § 1-177, eff. July 1, 1970.

Formerly Ill.Rev.Stat.1991, ch. 95 ½, ¶ 1-177.

5/1-178. Road tractor

§ 1-178. Road tractor. Every motor vehicle designed and used for drawing other vehicles and not so constructed as to carry any load thereon either independently or any part of the weight of a vehicle or load so drawn.

P.A. 76-1586, § 1-178, eff. July 1, 1970.

Formerly Ill.Rev.Stat.1991, ch. 95 ½, ¶ 1-178.

5/1-179. Roadway

§ 1-179. Roadway. That portion of a highway improved, designed or ordinarily used for vehicular travel, exclusive of the berm or shoulder. In the event a highway includes two or more separate roadways the term "roadway" as used herein shall refer to any such roadway separately but not to all such roadways collectively.

P.A. 76-1586, § 1-179, eff. July 1, 1970.

Formerly Ill.Rev.Stat.1991, ch. 95 ½, ¶ 1-179.

5/1-179.5. Rooftop

§ 1-179.5. Rooftop. The major uppermost portion of a bus body that is flat in a fore and aft direction.

P.A. 76-1586, § 1-179.5, added by P.A. 90-89, § 15, eff. Jan. 1, 1998.

5/1-180. Rural mail delivery vehicle

§ 1-180. Rural mail delivery vehicle. Every vehicle used to deliver U. S. mail on a rural mail delivery route.

P.A. 76-1586, § 1-180, eff. July 1, 1970.

Formerly Ill.Rev.Stat.1991, ch. 95 ½, ¶ 1-180.

5/1-180.5. Safety glazing material

§ 1-180.5. Safety glazing material. Any glazing material so constructed, treated, or combined with other materials as to reduce substantially, in comparison with ordinary sheet glass or plate glass, the likelihood of injury to persons by objects from exterior sources or by these safety glazing materials when they may be cracked or broken.

P.A. 76-1586, § 1-180.5, added by P.A. 90-89, § 15, eff. Jan. 1, 1998.

5/1-181. Safety zone

§ 1-181. Safety zone. The area or space officially set apart within a roadway for the exclusive use of pedestrians and which is protected or is so marked or indicated by adequate signs as to be plainly visible at all times while set apart as a safety zone.

P.A. 76-1586, § 1-181, eff. July 1, 1970.

Formerly Ill.Rev.Stat.1991, ch. 95 ½, ¶ 1-181.

5/1-182. School bus

§ 1-182. School bus.

(a) "School bus" means every motor vehicle, except as provided in paragraph (b) of this Section, owned or operated by or for any of the following entities for the transportation of persons regularly enrolled as students in grade 12 or below in connection with any activity of such entity:

Any public or private primary or secondary school;

Any primary or secondary school operated by a religious institution; or

Any public, private or religious nursery school.

(b) This definition shall not include the following:

1. A bus operated by a public utility, municipal corporation or common carrier authorized to conduct local or interurban transportation of passengers when such bus is not traveling a specific school bus route but is:

On a regularly scheduled route for the transportation of other fare paying passengers;

Furnishing charter service for the transportation of groups on field trips or other special trips or in connection with other special events; or

Being used for shuttle service between attendance centers or other educational facilities.

2. A motor vehicle of the First Division.

3. A motor vehicle designed for the transportation of not less than 7 nor more than 16 persons that is operated by or for a public or private primary or secondary school, including any primary or secondary school operated by a religious institution, for the purpose of transporting not more than 15 students to and from interscholastic athletic or other interscholastic or school sponsored activities.

P.A. 76-1586, § 1-182, eff. July 1, 1970. Amended by P.A. 78-1244, § 1, eff. Sept. 5, 1974; P.A. 79-63, § 1, eff. June 26, 1975; P.A. 79-798, § 1, eff. July 1, 1976; P.A. 79-1454, § 44, eff. Aug. 31, 1976; P.A. 80-1034, § 1, eff. Oct. 1, 1977; P.A. 81-509, § 1, eff. Jan. 1, 1980; P.A. 82-1011, § 2, eff. Sept. 17, 1982; P.A. 83-299, § 1, eff. Jan. 1, 1984; P.A. 89-132, § 10, eff. July 14, 1995.

Formerly Ill.Rev.Stat.1991, ch. 95 ½, ¶ 1-182.

5/1-182.3. Scrap processor

§ 1-182.3. Scrap processor. A person who purchases a vehicle, junk vehicle, or vehicle cowl for processing into a form other than a vehicle, junk vehicle, or vehicle cowl for remelting purposes only, who from a fixed location utilizes machinery and equipment for processing or manufacturing ferrous or nonferrous metallic scrap into prepared grades, and whose principal product is metallic scrap and who records the purchases on a weight ticket.

P.A. 76-1586, § 1-182.3, added by P.A. 90-89, § 15, eff. Jan. 1, 1998.

5/1-182.6. Seat safety belts

§ 1-182.6. Seat safety belts. A set of belts or a harness meeting the specifications established by the Department of Transportation and installed in such manner as to prevent or materially reduce the movement of the person using the belts or harness in the event of collision or upset of the vehicle.

P.A. 76-1586, § 1-182.6, added by P.A. 90-89, § 15, eff. Jan. 1, 1998.

5/1-182.8. Second stage manufacturer or converter

§ 1-182.8. Second stage manufacturer or converter. A person who prior to the retail sale of a motor vehicle, assembles, installs or affixes a body, cab, or special equipment to a chassis, or who adds, subtracts from, or modifies a previously assembled or manufactured motor vehicle.

P.A. 76-1586, § 1-182.8, added by P.A. 90-89, § 15, eff. Jan. 1, 1998.

5/1-183. Secretary

§ 1-183. Secretary. The Illinois Secretary of State or his or her designee.

P.A. 76-1586, § 1-183, eff. July 1, 1970. Amended by P.A. 90-89, § 15, eff. Jan. 1, 1998.

Formerly Ill.Rev.Stat.1991, ch. 95 ½, ¶ 1-183.

5/1-184. Secretary of State

§ 1-184. Secretary of State. The Secretary of State of Illinois.

P.A. 76-1586, § 1-184, eff. July 1, 1970.

Formerly Ill.Rev.Stat.1991, ch. 95 ½, ¶ 1-184.

5/1-185. Security agreement

§ 1-185. Security agreement. A written agreement which reserves or creates a security interest.

P.A. 76-1586, § 1-185, eff. July 1, 1970.

Formerly Ill.Rev.Stat.1991, ch. 95 ½, ¶ 1-185.

5/1-186. Security interest

§ 1-186. Security interest. An interest in a vehicle reserved or created by agreement and which secures payment or performance of an obligation. The term includes the interest of a lessor under a lease intended as security. A security interest is "perfected" when it is valid against third parties generally, subject only to specific statutory exceptions.

P.A. 76-1586, § 1-186, eff. July 1, 1970.

Formerly Ill.Rev.Stat.1991, ch. 95 ½, ¶ 1-186.

5/1-186.5. Selling price

§ 1-186.5. Selling price. The consideration received for a motor vehicle subject to the tax imposed by Section 3-1001 valued in money, whether received in money or otherwise, including cash, credits, service, or property. In the case of gifts or transfers without reasonable consideration, "selling price" shall be deemed to be the fair market value as determined by the Department of Revenue.

P.A. 76-1586, § 1-186.5, added by P.A. 90-89, § 15, eff. Jan. 1, 1998.

5/1-187. Semitrailer

§ 1-187. Semitrailer. Every vehicle without motive power, other than a pole trailer, designed for carrying persons or property and for being drawn by a motor vehicle and so constructed that some part of its weight and that of its load rests upon or is carried by another vehicle.

P.A. 76-1586, § 1-187, eff. July 1, 1970.

Formerly Ill.Rev.Stat.1991, ch. 95 ½, ¶ 1-187.

5/1-187.001. Serious traffic violation

§ 1-187.001. Serious traffic violation.

(a) A conviction when operating a motor vehicle for:

(1) a violation of subsection (a) of Section 11–402, relating to a motor vehicle accident involving damage to a vehicle;

(2) a violation of Section 11–403, relating to failure to stop and exchange information after a motor vehicle collision, property damage only;

(3) a violation of subsection (a) of Section 11–502, relating to illegal transportation, possession, or carrying of alcoholic liquor within the passenger area of any vehicle;

(4) a violation of Section 6–101 relating to operating a motor vehicle without a valid license or permit;

(5) a violation of Section 11–403, relating to failure to stop and exchange information or give aid after a motor vehicle collision involving personal injury or death;

(6) a violation relating to excessive speeding, involving a single speeding charge of 30 miles per hour or more above the legal speed limit;

(7) a violation relating to reckless driving;

(8) a violation of subsection (d) of Section 11–707, relating to passing in a no-passing zone;

(9) a violation of subsection (b) of Section 11–1402, relating to limitations on backing upon a controlled access highway;

(10) a violation of subsection (b) of Section 11–707, relating to driving on the left side of a roadway in a no-passing zone;

(11) a violation of subsection (e) of Section 11–1002, relating to failure to yield the right-of-way to a pedestrian at an intersection;

(12) a violation of Section 11–1008, relating to failure to yield to a pedestrian on a sidewalk; or

(13) a violation of Section 11–1201, relating to failure to stop for an approaching railroad train or signals; or

(b) Any other similar violation of a law or local ordinance of any state relating to motor vehicle traffic control, other than a parking violation.

(c) A violation of any of these defined serious traffic offenses shall not preclude the defendant from being eligible to receive an order of court supervision under Section 5–6–1 of the Unified Code of Corrections.[1]

P.A. 76–1586, § 1–187.001, added by P.A. 90–369, § 5, eff. Jan. 1, 1998.

1 730 ILCS 5/5–6–1.

5/1–187.01. Servicing of vehicles

§ 1–187.01. Servicing of vehicles. The altering or maintaining of the parts of a vehicle other than its essential parts. Regarding engines and transmissions, however, repair or replacement of parts, which does not result in the removal of all or any part of the identification number shall be deemed servicing of the vehicle.

P.A. 76–1586, § 1–187.01, added by P.A. 84–1302, § 1, eff. Jan. 1, 1987; P.A. 84–1304, § 1, eff. Jan. 1, 1987.

Formerly Ill.Rev.Stat.1991, ch. 95 ½, ¶ 1–187.01.

P.A. 84–1302 and P.A. 84–1304 enacted identical text.

5/1–187.1. Shoulder

§ 1–187.1. Shoulder. That portion of the highway adjacent to the roadway for accommodating stopped vehicles or for emergency use.

P.A. 76–1586, § 1–187.1, added by P.A. 84–873, § 1, eff. Jan. 1, 1986.

Formerly Ill.Rev.Stat.1991, ch. 95 ½, ¶ 1–187.1.

5/1–188. Sidewalk

§ 1–188. Sidewalk. That portion of a street between the curb lines, or the lateral lines of a roadway, and the adjacent property lines, intended for use of pedestrians.

P.A. 76–1586, § 1–188, eff. July 1, 1970.

Formerly Ill.Rev.Stat.1991, ch. 95 ½, ¶ 1–188.

5/1–188.2. Signature

§ 1–188.2. Signature. The name of a person as written by that person and captured in a manner acceptable to the Secretary of State.

P.A. 76–1586, § 1–188.2, added by P.A. 90–191, § 10, eff. Jan. 1, 1998.

5/1–189. Situs or base of vehicle

§ 1–189. Situs or base of vehicle. The place where a vehicle is principally garaged, or from whence it is principally dispatched, or where the movements of such vehicle usually originate.

P.A. 76–1586, § 1–189, eff. July 1, 1970.

Formerly Ill.Rev.Stat.1991, ch. 95 ½, ¶ 1–189.

5/1–190. Solid tire

§ 1–190. Solid tire. Every tire of rubber or other resilient material which does not depend upon compressed air for the support of the load.

P.A. 76–1586, § 1–190, eff. July 1, 1970.

Formerly Ill.Rev.Stat.1991, ch. 95 ½, ¶ 1–190.

5/1–190.05. Special hauling vehicle

§ 1–190.05. Special hauling vehicle. A vehicle or combination of vehicles transporting asphalt or concrete in the plastic state or a vehicle or combination of vehicles that is subject to the weight limitations in subsections (a) and (b) of Section 15–111 for which the owner of the vehicle or combination of vehicles has elected to pay, in addition to the registration fees stated in subsection (a) or (c) of Section 3–815 or Section 3–818, $100 to the Secretary of State for each registration year.

P.A. 76–1586, § 1–190.05, added by P.A. 90–89, § 15, eff. Jan. 1, 1998.

5/1–190.1. Special license plate

§ 1–190.1. Special license plate. Registration plates issued by the Secretary of State that by statute require, in addition to the applicable registration fee, an additional fee that is to be deposited into the Secretary of State Special License Plate Fund.

P.A. 76–1586, § 1–190.1, added by P.A. 89–282, § 10, eff. Aug. 10, 1995.

5/1–191. Special mobile equipment

§ 1–191. Special mobile equipment. Every vehicle not designed or used primarily for the transportation of persons or property and only incidentally operated or moved over a highway, including but not limited to: street sweepers, ditch digging apparatus, well boring apparatus and road construction and maintenance machinery such as asphalt spreaders, bituminous mixers, bucket loaders, tractors other than truck tractors, ditchers, levelling graders, finishing machines, motor graders, road rollers, scarifiers, earth moving carryalls and scrapers, power shovels and drag lines, and self-propelled cranes and earth moving equipment. The term does not include house trailers, dump trucks, truck mounted transit mixers, cranes or shovels, or other vehicles designed for the transportation of persons or property to which machinery has been attached.

P.A. 76-1586, § 1-191, eff. July 1, 1970. Amended by P.A. 85-951, § 1, eff. July 1, 1988.

Formerly Ill.Rev.Stat.1991, ch. 95 ½, ¶ 1-191.

5/1-192. Specially constructed vehicle

§ 1-192. Specially constructed vehicle. Every vehicle of a type required to be registered hereunder that: (a) has been materially altered from its original construction by the removal, addition or substitution of essential parts; or (b) was not originally constructed under a distinctive name by a generally recognized manufacturer of vehicles.

P.A. 76-1586, § 1-192, eff. July 1, 1970. Amended by P.A. 83-1473, § 1, eff. Jan. 1, 1985; P.A. 85-951, § 1, eff. July 1, 1988.

Formerly Ill.Rev.Stat.1991, ch. 95 ½, ¶ 1-192.

5/1-193. Speed-change lane

§ 1-193. Speed-change lane. An auxiliary lane, including tapered areas, primarily for the acceleration or deceleration of vehicles entering or leaving the through traffic lanes.

P.A. 76-1586, § 1-193, eff. July 1, 1970.

Formerly Ill.Rev.Stat.1991, ch. 95 ½, ¶ 1-193.

5/1-194. Stand or standing

§ 1-194. Stand or standing. Means the halting of a vehicle, whether occupied or not, otherwise than when temporarily and actually engaged in receiving or discharging passengers.

P.A. 76-1586, § 1-194, eff. July 1, 1970.

Formerly Ill.Rev.Stat.1991, ch. 95 ½, ¶ 1-194.

5/1-195. State

§ 1-195. State. A state, territory or possession of the United States, the District of Columbia, the Commonwealth of Puerto Rico or a province of the Dominion of Canada.

P.A. 76-1586, § 1-195, eff. July 1, 1970.

Formerly Ill.Rev.Stat.1991, ch. 95 ½, ¶ 1-195.

5/1-196. State highways

§ 1-196. State highways. Defined in the "Illinois Highway Code" as the same may from time to time be amended.[1]

P.A. 76-1586, § 1-196, eff. July 1, 1970.

Formerly Ill.Rev.Stat.1991, ch. 95 ½, ¶ 1-196.

[1] 605 ILCS 5/1-101 et seq.

5/1-197. State Police

§ 1-197. State Police. The Illinois State Police.

P.A. 76-1586, § 1-197, eff. July 1, 1970.

Formerly Ill.Rev.Stat.1991, ch. 95 ½, ¶ 1-197.

5/1-197.5. Statutory summary alcohol or other drug related suspension of driver's privileges

§ 1-197.5. Statutory summary alcohol or other drug related suspension of driver's privileges. The withdrawal by the circuit court of a person's license or privilege to operate a motor vehicle on the public highways for the periods provided in Section 6-208.1. Reinstatement after the suspension period shall occur after all appropriate fees have been paid, unless the court notifies the Secretary of State that the person should be disqualified. The bases for this withdrawal of driving privileges shall be the individual's refusal to submit to or failure to complete a chemical test or tests following an arrest for the offense of driving under the influence of alcohol, other drugs, or intoxicating compounds, or any combination thereof, or submission to such a test or tests indicating an alcohol concentration of 0.08 or more as provided in Section 11-501.1 of this Code.

P.A. 76-1586, § 1-203.1, added by P.A. 84-272, § 7, eff. Jan. 1, 1986. Amended by P.A. 84-1394, § 5, eff. Sept. 18, 1986; P.A. 90-43, § 5, eff. July 2, 1997. Renumbered § 1-197.5 and amended by P.A. 90-89, § 15, eff. Jan. 1, 1998. Amended by P.A. 90-655, § 153, eff. July 30, 1998; P.A. 92-834, § 5, eff. Aug. 22, 2002.

Formerly Ill.Rev.Stat.1991, ch. 95 ½, ¶ 1-203.1.

P.A. 90-655, the First 1998 General Revisory Act, amended various Acts to delete obsolete text, to correct patent and technical errors, to revise cross references, to resolve multiple actions in the 89th and 90th General Assemblies and to make certain technical corrections in P.A. 89-708 through P.A. 90-566.

5/1-198. Stinger-steered semitrailer

§ 1-198. Stinger-steered semitrailer. Every semitrailer which has its kingpin on a projection to the front of the structure of such semitrailer and is combined with the 5th wheel of the truck tractor at a point not less than two feet to the rear of the center of the rearmost axle of such tractor.

P.A. 76-1586, § 1-198, eff. July 1, 1970.

Formerly Ill.Rev.Stat.1991, ch. 95 ½, ¶ 1-198.

5/1-199. Stop

§ 1-199. Stop. When required means complete cessation from movement.

P.A. 76-1586, § 1-199, eff. July 1, 1970.

Formerly Ill.Rev.Stat.1991, ch. 95 ½, ¶ 1-199.

5/1-200. Stop or stopping

§ 1-200. Stop or stopping. Means any halting even momentarily of a vehicle, whether occupied or not, except when necessary to avoid conflict with other traffic or in compliance with the directions of a police officer or traffic-control sign or signal.

P.A. 76-1586, § 1-200, eff. July 1, 1970. Amended by P.A. 76-2125, § 1, eff. July 1, 1970.

Formerly Ill.Rev.Stat.1991, ch. 95 ½, ¶ 1-200.

5/1-201. Street

§ 1-201. Street. The entire width between boundary lines of every way publicly maintained, when any part thereof is open to the use of the public for purposes of vehicular travel.

P.A. 76-1586, § 1-201, eff. July 1, 1970. Amended by P.A. 90-655, § 153, eff. July 30, 1998.

Formerly Ill.Rev.Stat.1991, ch. 95 ½, ¶ 1-201.

5/1-202. Streetcar

§ 1-202. Streetcar. A car other than a railroad train for transporting persons or property and operated upon rails principally within a municipality.

P.A. 76-1586, § 1-202, eff. July 1, 1970.

Formerly Ill.Rev.Stat.1991, ch. 95 ½, ¶ 1-202.

5/1-202.1. Street rod

§ 1-202.1. Street rod. A motor vehicle that is a 1948 or older vehicle or a vehicle that has been certified by an inspector of the National Street Rod Association, on a form prescribed by the Secretary of State, to be a street rod that was manufactured after 1948 to resemble a vehicle that was manufactured before 1949 and has been altered from the manufacturer's original design or has a body constructed from non-original materials and which is maintained for occasional transportation, exhibitions, club activities, parades, tours, and similar uses and which is not used for general daily transportation.

P.A. 76-1586, § 1-202.1, added by P.A. 92-668, § 5, eff. Jan. 1, 2003.

5/1-202.5. Strobe lamp

§ 1-202.5. Strobe lamp. A vehicular signaling device that generates flashes of light by inducing intermittent flows of electricity through a gas.

P.A. 76-1586, § 1-202.5, added by P.A. 90-89, § 15, eff. Jan. 1, 1998.

5/1-203. Suburban district

§ 1-203. Suburban district. That portion of any city, village or incorporated town other than the business and residence districts.

P.A. 76-1586, § 1-203, eff. July 1, 1970.

Formerly Ill.Rev.Stat.1991, ch. 95 ½, ¶ 1-203.

5/1-203.1. § 1-203.1. Renumbered as § 1-197.5 by P.A. 90-89, § 15, eff. Jan. 1, 1998

5/1-204. Suspension of driver's license

§ 1-204. Suspension of driver's license. The temporary withdrawal by formal action of the Secretary of a person's license or privilege to operate a motor vehicle on the public highways, for a period specifically designated by the Secretary.

P.A. 76-1586, § 1-204, eff. July 1, 1970.

Formerly Ill.Rev.Stat.1991, ch. 95 ½, ¶ 1-204.

5/1-204.05. Suspension system

§ 1-204.05. Suspension system. The system of devices consisting of but not limited to springs, spring shackles, shock absorbers, torsion bars, a frame, or any other supporting members used to attach the body of a motor vehicle to its axles.

P.A. 76-1586, § 1-204.05, added by P.A. 90-89, § 15, eff. Jan. 1, 1998.

5/1-204.1. Sworn report

§ 1-204.1. Sworn report. A confirmation of correctness and truth by an affidavit, oath, deposition or a verification by certification executed pursuant to Section 1-109 of the Code of Civil Procedure.[1]

P.A. 76-1586, § 1-204.1, added by P.A. 85-992, § 1, eff. Jan. 5, 1988.

Formerly Ill.Rev.Stat.1991, ch. 95 ½, ¶ 1-204.1.

[1] 735 ILCS 5/1-109.

5/1-204.3. Tandem axles

§ 1-204.3. Tandem axles. Any 2 or more single axles whose centers are more than 40 inches and not more than 96 inches apart, measured to the nearest inch between extreme axles in the series, except as provided in Section 15-111 for special hauling vehicles.

P.A. 76-1586, § 1-204.3, added by P.A. 90-89, § 15, eff. Jan. 1, 1998.

5/1-204.4. Tank vehicle

§ 1-204.4. Tank vehicle. Any commercial motor vehicle that is designed to transport any liquid or gaseous material within a tank that is either permanently or temporarily attached to the vehicle or the chassis. Those vehicles include, but are not limited to, cargo tanks and portable tanks, as defined in 49 C.F.R. Part 171. However, for the purposes of Article V of Chapter 6 of this Code,[1] this definition does not include portable tanks having a rated capacity of less than 1,000 gallons.

P.A. 76-1586, § 1-204.4, added by P.A. 90-89, § 15, eff. Jan. 1, 1998.

[1] 625 ILCS 5/6-500 et seq.

5/1-205. Through highway

§ 1-205. Through highway. Every highway or portion thereof on which vehicular traffic is given preferential right of way, and at the entrances to which vehicular traffic from intersecting highways is required by law to yield right of way to vehicles on such through highway in obedience to either a stop sign or a yield sign, when such signs are erected as provided in this Act.

P.A. 76-1586, § 1-205, eff. July 1, 1970.

Formerly Ill.Rev.Stat.1991, ch. 95 ½, ¶ 1-205.

5/1-205.01. Tollroad or toll highway

§ 1-205.01. Tollroad or toll highway. All highways under the jurisdiction of the Illinois State Toll Highway Authority.

P.A. 76-1586, § 1-205.01, added by P.A. 85-830, § 1, eff. Sept. 24, 1987. Amended by P.A. 90-89, § 15, eff. Jan. 1, 1998.

Formerly Ill.Rev.Stat.1991, ch. 95 ½, ¶ 1-205.01.

5/1-205.1. Tow-Truck

§ 1-205.1. Tow-Truck. Every truck designed or altered and equipped for and used to push, tow, carry upon, or draw vehicles by means of a crane, hoist, towbar, towline or auxiliary axle, or carried upon to render assistance to disabled vehicles, except for any truck tractor temporarily converted to a tow truck by means of a portable wrecker unit attached to the fifth wheel of the truck tractor and used only by the owner to tow a disabled vehicle also owned by him or her and never used for hire.

P.A. 76-1586, § 1-205.1, added by P.A. 78-324, § 1, eff. Jan. 1, 1974. Amended by P.A. 83-1473, § 1, eff. Jan. 1, 1985; P.A. 89-245, § 5, eff. Jan. 1, 1996; P.A. 90-89, § 15, eff. Jan. 1, 1998.

Formerly Ill.Rev.Stat.1991, ch. 95 ½, ¶ 1-205.1.

5/1-205.2. Tower

§ 1-205.2. Tower. A person who owns or operates a tow-truck or a wrecker.

P.A. 76-1586, § 1-205.2, added by P.A. 83-1473, § 1, eff. Jan. 1, 1985.

Formerly Ill.Rev.Stat.1991, ch. 95 ½, ¶ 1-205.2.

5/1-206. Trackless trolley coach

§ 1-206. Trackless trolley coach. Every motor vehicle which is propelled by electric power obtained from overhead trolley wires but not operated upon rails.

P.A. 76-1586, § 1-206, eff. July 1, 1970.

Formerly Ill.Rev.Stat.1991, ch. 95 ½, ¶ 1-206.

5/1-207. Traffic

§ 1-207. Traffic. Pedestrians, ridden or herded animals, vehicles, streetcars and other conveyances either singly or together while using any highway for purposes of travel.

P.A. 76-1586, § 1-207, eff. July 1, 1970.

Formerly Ill.Rev.Stat.1991, ch. 95 ½, ¶ 1-207.

5/1-208. Traffic control signal

§ 1-208. Traffic control signal. Any official traffic control device other than a railroad sign or signal, whether manually, electrically or mechanically operated, by which traffic is alternately directed to stop and permitted to proceed.

P.A. 76-1586, § 1-208, eff. July 1, 1970. Amended by P.A. 76-2126, § 1, eff. July 1, 1970; P.A. 83-831, § 1, eff. Jan. 1, 1984.

Formerly Ill.Rev.Stat.1991, ch. 95 ½, ¶ 1-208.

5/1-209. Trailer

§ 1-209. Trailer. Every vehicle without motive power in operation, other than a pole trailer, designed for carrying persons or property and for being drawn by a motor vehicle and so constructed that no part of its weight rests upon the towing vehicle.

P.A. 76-1586, § 1-209, eff. July 1, 1970. Amended by P.A. 76-1798, § 1, eff. July 1, 1970.

Formerly Ill.Rev.Stat.1991, ch. 95 ½, ¶ 1-209.

5/1-209.5. Transportation

§ 1-209.5. Transportation. The actual movement of property or passengers by motor vehicle, together with loading, unloading, and any other accessorial or ancillary service provided by the carrier in connection with movement by motor vehicle.

P.A. 76-1586, § 1-209.5, added by P.A. 90-89, § 15, eff. Jan. 1, 1998.

5/1-210. Transporter

§ 1-210. Transporter. Every person engaged in the driveaway or towaway business of transporting vehicles, not his own, by driving, either singly or by the towbar, saddle mount or full mount methods or any combinations thereof or by drawing or towing house trailers, semitrailers or trailers, including their coupling devices, and using the public highways of this State therefor.

P.A. 76-1586, § 1-210, eff. July 1, 1970. Amended by P.A. 78-858, § 1, eff. Jan. 1, 1974.

Formerly Ill.Rev.Stat.1991, ch. 95 ½, ¶ 1-210.

5/1-210.01. Travel trailer

§ 1-210.01. Travel trailer. A trailer, not used commercially, designed to provide living quarters for recreational, camping or travel use, and of a size or weight not requiring an overdimension permit when towed on a highway.

P.A. 76-1586, § 1-210.01, added by P.A. 81-969, § 1, eff. Jan. 1, 1980.

Formerly Ill.Rev.Stat.1991, ch. 95 ½, ¶ 1-210.01.

5/1-211. Truck

§ 1-211. Truck. Every motor vehicle designed, used, or maintained primarily for the transportation of property.

P.A. 76-1586, § 1-211, eff. July 1, 1970. Amended by P.A. 86-1005, § 3, eff. Dec. 28, 1989; P.A. 88-476, § 2, eff. July 1, 1994.

Formerly Ill.Rev.Stat.1991, ch. 95 ½, ¶ 1-211.

5/1-211.01. Truck camper

§ 1-211.01. Truck camper. A truck, not used commercially, when equipped with a portable unit designed to be loaded onto the bed which is constructed to provide temporary living quarters for recreational, travel, or camping use.

P.A. 76-1586, § 1-211.01, added by P.A. 81-969, eff. Jan. 1, 1980. Amended by P.A. 91-357, § 231, eff. July 29, 1999.

Formerly Ill.Rev.Stat.1991, ch. 95 ½, ¶ 1-211.01.

5/1-211.1. § 1-211.1. Renumbered as § 1-212.5 by P.A. 90-89, § 15, eff. Jan. 1, 1998

5/1-212. Truck tractor

§ 1-212. Truck tractor. Every motor vehicle designed and used primarily for drawing other vehicles and not so constructed as to carry a load other than a part of the weight of the vehicle and load so drawn.

P.A. 76-1586, § 1-212, eff. July 1, 1970.

Formerly Ill.Rev.Stat.1991, ch. 95 ½, ¶ 1-212.

5/1-212.5. Truckster

§ 1-212.5. Truckster. Every motor vehicle or motorcycle with 3 wheels designed, used or maintained primarily for the transportation of property.

P.A. 76-1586, § 1-211.1, added by P.A. 77-1633, § 1, eff. Sept. 23, 1971. Renumbered § 1-212.5 and amended by P.A. 90-89, § 15, eff. Jan. 1, 1998.

Formerly Ill.Rev.Stat.1991, ch. 95 ½, ¶ 1-211.1.

5/1-213. § 1-213. Repealed by P.A. 90-89, § 20, eff. Jan. 1, 1998

5/1-213.4. Type I school bus

§ 1-213.4. Type I school bus. A school bus with a Gross Vehicle Weight Rating more than 10,000 pounds.

P.A. 76-1586, § 1-213.4, added by P.A. 90-89, § 15, eff. Jan. 1, 1998.

5/1-213.5. Type II school bus

§ 1-213.5. Type II school bus. A school bus with a Gross Vehicle Weight Rating of 10,000 pounds or less.

P.A. 76-1586, § 1-213.5, added by P.A. 90-89, § 15, eff. Jan. 1, 1998.

5/1-214. Urban district

§ 1-214. Urban district. The territory contiguous to and including any street which is built up with structures devoted to business, industry or dwelling houses situated at intervals of less than 100 feet for a distance of a quarter of a mile or more.

P.A. 76–1586, § 1–214, eff. July 1, 1970.

Formerly Ill.Rev.Stat.1991, ch. 95 ½, ¶ 1–214.

5/1–214.1. § 1–214.1. Renumbered as § 1–214.8 by P.A. 90–89, § 15, eff. Jan. 1, 1998

5/1–214.8. Urban area

§ 1–214.8. Urban area. An urban area is any incorporated or unincorporated area developed primarily for residential and/or business purposes.

P.A. 76–1586, § 1–214.1, added by P.A. 77–58, § 1, eff. July 1, 1971. Renumbered § 1–214.8 and amended by P.A. 90–89, § 15, eff. Jan. 1, 1998.

Formerly Ill.Rev.Stat.1991, ch. 95 ½, ¶ 1–214.1.

5/1–215. Used car dealer

§ 1–215. Used car dealer. Every person engaged in the business of buying, selling or exchanging used motor vehicles and who has an established place of business for such purpose in this State.

P.A. 76–1586, § 1–215, eff. July 1, 1970.

Formerly Ill.Rev.Stat.1991, ch. 95 ½, ¶ 1–215.

5/1–216. Used motor vehicle

§ 1–216. Used motor vehicle. Every motor vehicle which has been sold, bargained, exchanged, given away, or title transferred from the person who first acquired it from the manufacturer or importer, dealer, or agent of the manufacturer or importer and so used as to have become what is commonly known as "second hand" within the ordinary meaning thereof: Provided, that a new motor vehicle shall not be considered as a "used motor vehicle" until it has been placed in a bona fide consumer use, notwithstanding the number of transfers of such motor vehicle. The term "bona fide consumer use" means actual operation by an owner who acquired the vehicle for use in business or for pleasure purposes and who has been granted a Certificate of Title on such motor vehicle and has registered such motor vehicle, all in accordance with the laws of the residence of the owner.

P.A. 76–1586, § 1–216, eff. July 1, 1970.

Formerly Ill.Rev.Stat.1991, ch. 95 ½, ¶ 1–216.

5/1–217. Vehicle

§ 1–217. Vehicle. Every device, in, upon or by which any person or property is or may be transported or drawn upon a highway or requiring a certificate of title under Section 3–101(d) of this Code, except devices moved by human power, devices used exclusively upon stationary rails or tracks and snowmobiles as defined in the Snowmobile Registration and Safety Act.[1]

For the purposes of this Code, unless otherwise prescribed, a device shall be considered to be a vehicle until such time it either comes within the definition of a junk vehicle, as defined under this Code, or a junking certificate is issued for it.

For this Code, vehicles are divided into 2 divisions:

First Division: Those motor vehicles which are designed for the carrying of not more than 10 persons.

Second Division: Those vehicles which are designed for carrying more than 10 persons, those designed or used for living quarters and those vehicles which are designed for pulling or carrying property, freight or cargo, those motor vehicles of the First Division remodelled for use and used as motor vehicles of the Second Division, and those motor vehicles of the First Division used and registered as school buses.

P.A. 76–1586, § 1–217, eff. July 1, 1970. Amended by P.A. 76–1798, § 1, eff. July 1, 1970; P.A. 77–68, § 1, eff. Jan. 1, 1972; P.A. 77–1313, § 1, eff. Aug. 27, 1971; P.A. 77–2829, § 40, eff. Dec. 22, 1972; P.A. 78–255, § 61, eff. Oct. 1, 1973; P.A. 78–343, § 1, eff. Jan. 1, 1974; P.A. 78–1297, § 58, eff. March 4, 1975; P.A. 83–1473, § 1, eff. Jan. 1, 1985; P.A. 92–812, § 5, eff. Aug. 21, 2002.

Formerly Ill.Rev.Stat.1991, ch. 95 ½, ¶ 1–217.

1 625 ILCS 40/1–1 et seq.

5/1–217.1. Vehicle cowl

§ 1–217.1. Vehicle cowl. The portion of the vehicle that separates the front compartment from the rear compartment, commonly referred to as the firewall, to which a vehicle identification number is normally attached.

P.A. 76–1586, § 1–217.1, added by P.A. 85–1204, § 1, eff. Aug. 26, 1988.

Formerly Ill.Rev.Stat.1991, ch. 95 ½, ¶ 1–217.1.

5/1–218. § 1–218. Repealed by P.A. 90–89, § 20, eff. Jan. 1, 1998

5/1–218.1. Vehicle shell

§ 1–218.1. Vehicle shell. Every sheet metal part of a vehicle whether or not attached to a chassis or part of a chassis. For the purposes of this definition the term vehicle shell shall include the terms, shell, vehicle hulk, body, vehicle body.

P.A. 76–1586, § 1–218.1, added by P.A. 83–831, § 1, eff. Jan. 1, 1984.

Formerly Ill.Rev.Stat.1991, ch. 95 ½, ¶ 1–218.1.

5/1–218.5. Verified evidence

§ 1–218.5. Verified evidence. A document that is confirmed or substantiated by a sworn report or any public record received from a court of competent jurisdiction.

P.A. 76–1586, § 1–218.5, added by P.A. 90–89, § 15, eff. Jan. 1, 1998.

5/1–219. § 1–219. Repealed by P.A. 90–89, § 20, eff. Jan. 1, 1998

5/1–221. § 1–221. Repealed by P.A. 90–89, § 20, eff. Jan. 1, 1998

5/1–222. § 1–222. Renumbered as § 1–171.6 by P.A. 90–89, § 15, eff. Jan. 1, 1998

5/1–223. § 1–223. Repealed by P.A. 90–89, § 20, eff. Jan. 1, 1998

5/1–224. § 1–224. Renumbered as § 1–171.8 by P.A. 90–89, § 15, eff. Jan. 1, 1998

5/1–226 to 5/1–229. §§ 1–226 to 1–229. Repealed by P.A. 83–831, § 2, eff. Jan. 1, 1984

5/1–300. § 1–300. Renumbered as § 1–158.5 by P.A. 90–89, § 15, eff. Jan. 1, 1998

CHAPTER 2. THE SECRETARY OF STATE

Section

5/2–101. Administration vested in Secretary of State

§ 2–101. Administration vested in Secretary of State. The Secretary of State is hereby vested with powers and duties and jurisdiction of administering Chapters 2, 3, 4, 5, 6, 7, 8 and 9 of The Illinois Vehicle Code.[1]

P.A. 76–1586, § 2–101, eff. July 1, 1970.

Formerly Ill.Rev.Stat.1991, ch. 95 ½, ¶ 2–101.

[1] 625 ILCS 5/2–101 et seq. to 5/9–110 et seq.

5/2–102. Organization of administration

§ 2–102. Organization of administration. The Secretary of State shall organize the work of the administration of the portion of this Act delegated to him in such manner as he may deem necessary to carry out those provisions of this Act.

P.A. 76–1586, § 2–102, eff. July 1, 1970.

Formerly Ill.Rev.Stat.1991, ch. 95 ½, ¶ 2–102.

5/2–103. Secretary of State to appoint subordinates

§ 2–103. Secretary of State to appoint subordinates. The Secretary of State shall appoint such subordinate officers, clerks, investigators, and other employees as may be necessary to carry out the provisions of this Act.

P.A. 76–1586, § 2–103, eff. July 1, 1970. Amended by P.A. 82–783, Art. IV, § 25, eff. July 13, 1982.

Formerly Ill.Rev.Stat.1991, ch. 95 ½, ¶ 2–103.

5/2–104. Powers and duties of the Secretary of State

§ 2–104. Powers and duties of the Secretary of State. (a) The administration of Chapters 2, 3, 4, 5, 6, 7, 8 and 9 of this Act [1] is vested in the Secretary of State, who is charged with the duty of observing, administering and enforcing the provisions of this Act.

(b) The Secretary may from time to time make, amend, and rescind such rules and regulations as may be necessary in the public interest to carry out the provisions of this Act, including rules and regulations governing procedures for the filing of applications and the issuance of licenses or registrations thereunder. The rules and regulations adopted by the Secretary of State under this Act shall be effective in the manner provided for in "The Illinois Administrative Procedure Act", approved September 22, 1975, as amended.[2]

P.A. 76–1586, § 2–104, eff. July 1, 1970. Amended by P.A. 83–333, § 50, eff. Sept. 14, 1983.

Formerly Ill.Rev.Stat.1991, ch. 95 ½, ¶ 2–104.

[1] 625 ILCS 5/2–101 et seq. to 5/9–110 et seq.

[2] 5 ILCS 100/1–1 et seq.

5/2–105. Offices of Secretary of State

§ 2–105. Offices of Secretary of State. The Secretary of State shall maintain offices in the State capital and in such other places in the State as he may deem necessary to properly carry out the powers and duties vested in him.

The Secretary of State may construct and equip one or more buildings in the State of Illinois outside of the County of Sangamon as he deems necessary to properly carry out the powers and duties vested in him. The Secretary of State may, on behalf of the State of Illinois, acquire public or private property needed therefor by lease, purchase or eminent domain. The care, custody and control of such sites and buildings constructed thereon shall be vested in the Secretary of State. Expenditures for the construction and equipping of any of such buildings upon premises owned by another public entity shall not be subject to the provisions of any State law requiring that the State be vested with absolute fee title to the premises. The exercise of the authority vested in the Secretary of State by this Section is subject to the appropriation of the necessary funds.

Pursuant to Sections 4–6.2, 5–16.2, and 6–50.2 of The Election Code,[1] the Secretary of State shall make driver services facilities available for use as temporary places of registration. Registration within the offices shall be in the most public, orderly and convenient portions thereof, and Section 4–3, 5–3, and 11–4 of The Election Code [2] relative to the attendance of police officers during the conduct of registration shall apply. Registration under this Section shall be made in the manner provided by Sections 4–8, 4–10, 5–7, 5–9, 6–34, 6–35, and 6–37 of The Election Code.[3]

Within 30 days after the effective date of this amendatory Act of 1990, and no later than November 1 of each even-numbered year thereafter, the Secretary of State, to the extent practicable, shall designate to each election authority in the State a reasonable number of employees at each driver services facility registered to vote within the jurisdiction of such election authority and within adjacent election jurisdictions for appointment as deputy registrars by the election authority located within the election jurisdiction where the employees maintain their residences. Such designation shall be in writing and certified by the Secretary of State.

Each person applying at a driver services facility for a driver's license or permit, a corrected driver's license or permit, an Illinois identification card or a corrected Illinois identification card shall be notified that the person may register at such station to vote in the election jurisdiction in which the station is located or in an election jurisdiction adjacent to the location of the station and may also transfer his voter registration at such station to an address in the election jurisdiction within which the station is located or to an address in an adjacent election jurisdiction. Such notification may be made in writing or verbally issued by an employee or the Secretary of State.

The Secretary of State shall promulgate such rules as may be necessary for the efficient execution of his duties and the duties of his employees under this amendatory Act of 1990.

P.A. 76-1586, § 2-105, eff. July 1, 1970. Amended by P.A. 77-2302, § 1, eff. Aug. 13, 1972; P.A. 83-1059, § 4, eff. July 1, 1984; P.A. 86-1435, § 3, eff. Sept. 21, 1990; P.A. 90-89, § 15, eff. Jan. 1, 1998.

Formerly Ill.Rev.Stat.1991, ch. 95 ½, ¶ 2-105.

[1] 10 ILCS 5/4-6.2, 5/5-16.2, and 5/6-50.2.

[2] 10 ILCS 5/4-3, 5/5-3, and 5/11-4.

[3] 10 ILCS 5/4-8, 5/4-10, 5/5-7, 5/5-9, 5/6-34, 5/6-35, and 5/6-37.

Validity

Voter-registration notice provisions pursuant to this section were found inadequate in Orr v. Edgar, App. 1 Dist.1996, 219 Ill.Dec. 355, 283 Ill.App.3d 1088, 670 N.E.2d 1243.

5/2-106. Secretary of State to prescribe forms

§ 2-106. Secretary of State to prescribe forms. The Secretary of State shall prescribe or provide suitable forms of applications, certificates of title, registration cards, driver's licenses and such other forms requisite or deemed necessary to carry out the provisions of this Act and any other laws pertaining to vehicles the enforcement and administration of which are vested in the Secretary of State.

P.A. 76-1586, § 2-106, eff. July 1, 1970.

Formerly Ill.Rev.Stat.1991, ch. 95 ½, ¶ 2-106.

5/2-107. Authority to administer oaths

§ 2-107. Authority to administer oaths. Officers and employees of the Secretary of State designated by him are, for the purpose of administering the motor vehicle laws and any other laws relating to the use and operation of motor vehicles, authorized to administer oaths and acknowledge signatures, and shall do so without fee.

P.A. 76-1586, § 2-107, eff. July 1, 1970.

Formerly Ill.Rev.Stat.1991, ch. 95 ½, ¶ 2-107.

5/2-108. Authority to certify copies of records

§ 2-108. Authority to certify copies of records. The Secretary of State is hereby authorized to prepare under the seal of the Secretary of State certified copies of any records of his office and every such certified copy shall be admissible in any proceeding in any court in like manner as the original thereof.

P.A. 76-1586, § 2-108, eff. July 1, 1970.

Formerly Ill.Rev.Stat.1991, ch. 95 ½, ¶ 2-108.

5/2-109. Records of Secretary of State

§ 2-109. Records of Secretary of State. The Secretary of State may destroy any records of his office relating to the administration of any laws relating to the use and operation of motor vehicles the enforcement and administration of which are vested in him, if such records have been maintained on file for 4 years. Such records may be destroyed prior thereto with the approval of the State Records Commission.

P.A. 76-1586, § 2-109, eff. July 1, 1970.

Formerly Ill.Rev.Stat.1991, ch. 95 ½, ¶ 2-109.

5/2-109.1. Exchange of information

§ 2-109.1. Exchange of information.

(a) The Secretary of State shall exchange information with the Illinois Department of Public Aid which may be necessary for the establishment of paternity and the establishment, modification, and enforcement of child support orders pursuant to the Illinois Public Aid Code, [1] the Illinois Marriage and Dissolution of Marriage Act, [2] the Non-Support of Spouse and Children Act, [3] the Non-Support Punishment Act, [4] the Revised Uniform Reciprocal Enforcement of Support Act, [5] the Uniform Interstate Family Support Act, [6] or the Illinois Parentage Act of 1984.[7]

(b) Notwithstanding any provisions in this Code to the contrary, the Secretary of State shall not be liable to any person for any disclosure of information to the Illinois Department of Public Aid under subsection (a) or for any other action taken in good faith to comply with the requirements of subsection (a).

P.A. 76-1586, § 2-109.1, added by P.A. 90-18, § 80, eff. July 1, 1997. Amended by P.A. 91-613, § 945, eff. July 1, 2000.

[1] 305 ILCS 5/1-1 et seq.

[2] 750 ILCS 5/101 et seq.

[3] 750 ILCS 15/1 et seq.

[4] 750 ILCS 16/1 et seq.

[5] 750 ILCS 20/1 et seq.

[6] 750 ILCS 22/100 et seq.

[7] 750 ILCS 45/1 et seq.

For emergency rules to implement the amendatory changes of P.A. 90-18, see note following 5 ILCS 100/10-65.

5/2-110. Authority to grant or refuse applications

§ 2-110. Authority to grant or refuse applications. The Secretary of State shall examine and determine the genuineness, regularity and legality of every application for registration of a vehicle, for a certificate of title therefor, and for a driver's license and of any other application lawfully made to the Secretary of State, and may in all cases make investigation as may be deemed necessary or require additional information, and shall reject any such application if not satisfied of the genuineness, regularity or legality thereof or the truth of any statement contained therein, or for any other reason, when authorized by law.

P.A. 76-1586, § 2-110, eff. July 1, 1970.

Formerly Ill.Rev.Stat.1991, ch. 95 ½, ¶ 2-110.

5/2-111. Seizure of documents and plates

§ 2-111. Seizure of documents and plates. The Secretary of State is authorized to take possession of any certificate of title, registration card, permit, license, registration plate, plates, person with disabilities license plate or parking decal or device, or registration sticker issued by him upon expiration, revocation, cancellation or suspension thereof, or which is fictitious, or which has been unlawfully or erroneously issued. Police officers who have reasonable grounds to believe that any item or items listed in this section should be seized shall request the Secretary of State to take possession of such item or items.

P.A. 76-1586, § 2-111, eff. July 1, 1970. Amended by P.A. 80-230, § 1, eff. Oct. 1, 1977; P.A. 82-433, § 1, eff. Sept. 8, 1981; P.A. 90-106, § 5, eff. Jan. 1, 1998.

Formerly Ill.Rev.Stat.1991, ch. 95 ½, ¶ 2-111.

Section 3 of P.A. 82-433 approved Sept. 8, 1981, provided:

"This Act takes effect upon its becoming a law, except that the provisions relating to safety tests and proof of financial responsibility for medical transport vehicles apply only to applications for and the issuance of registration plates which are required to be displayed on January 1, 1982 or thereafter."

5/2-112. Distribution of synopsis laws

§ 2-112. Distribution of synopsis laws. The Secretary of State may publish a synopsis or summary of the laws of this State regulating the operation of vehicles and may deliver a copy thereof without charge with each original vehicle registration and with each original driver's license.

P.A. 76-1586, § 2-112, eff. July 1, 1970.

Formerly Ill.Rev.Stat.1991, ch. 95 ½, ¶ 2-112.

5/2-113. Secretary of State may subpoena witnesses and request the production of books and records

§ 2-113. Secretary of State may subpoena witnesses and request the production of books and records. (a) The Secretary of State, or employees designated by him, may request the production of pertinent books, records, letters, contracts or other pertinent documents of any person licensed or required to be licensed or registered under any chapter of this Act, for the purpose of investigations or audits, which in the opinion of the Secretary of State, are necessary and proper for the enforcement of this Act and the collection of any fees or taxes required to be paid under this Act.

(b) For the purpose of all hearings which in the opinion of the Secretary of State are necessary and proper for the enforcement of this Act, the Secretary of State, or a person designated by him is empowered to administer oaths and affirmations, subpoena witnesses, take evidence, and require the production of any books, papers or other documents which the Secretary of State, or a person designated by him, deems relevant or material to the inquiry. Any circuit court of this State, upon application by the Secretary of State and upon a proper showing may order the attendance of witnesses, the production of books, papers, accounts and documents and the giving of testimony before the Secretary of State, or a person designated by him; and any failure to obey such order may be punished by such circuit court as a contempt thereof. The fees of subpoenaed witnesses under this Act for attendance and travel shall be the same as fees of witnesses before the circuit courts of the State, such fees to be paid when the witness is excused from further attendance, provided, such witness is subpoenaed at the instance of the Secretary of State; and payment of such fees shall be made and audited in the same manner as other expenses of the Secretary of State. Whenever a subpoena is issued at the request of a complainant or respondent or defendant as the case may be, the Secretary of State may require that the cost of service and the fee of the witness shall be borne by the party at whose instance the witness is summoned. The Secretary of State shall have power in his discretion, to require a deposit to cover the cost of such service and witness fees and the payment of the legal witness fee and mileage to the witness served with subpoena. A subpoena issued under the provisions of this Act shall be served in the same manner as a subpoena issued out of a court.

P.A. 76-1586, § 2-113, eff. July 1, 1970. Amended by P.A. 76-2127, § 1, eff. July 1, 1970; P.A. 77-1541, § 1, eff. Sept. 17, 1971.

Formerly Ill.Rev.Stat.1991, ch. 95 ½, ¶ 2-113.

5/2-114. Giving of notice

§ 2-114. Giving of notice. Whenever the Secretary of State is authorized or required to give any notice under this Act or other law regulating the operation of vehicles, unless a different method of giving such notice is otherwise expressly prescribed, such notice shall be given either by personal delivery thereof to the person to be so notified or by deposit in the United States mail of such notice in an envelope with postage prepaid, addressed to such person at his address as shown by the records of the Office of the Secretary of State. The giving of notice by mail is complete upon the expiration of 4 days after such deposit of said notice. Proof of the giving of notice in either such manner may be made by the certificate of any officer or employee of the Secretary of State or affidavit of any person over 18 years of age, naming the person to whom such notice was given and specifying the time, place and manner of the giving thereof.

P.A. 76-1586, § 2-114, eff. July 1, 1970.

Formerly Ill.Rev.Stat.1991, ch. 95 ½, ¶ 2-114.

5/2-115. Investigators

§ 2-115. Investigators.

(a) The Secretary of State, for the purpose of more effectively carrying out the provisions of the laws in relation to motor vehicles, shall have power to appoint such number of investigators as he may deem necessary. It shall be the duty of such investigators to investigate and enforce violations of the provisions of this Act administered by the Secretary of State and provisions of Chapters 11, 12, 13, 14 and 15 [1] and to investigate and report any violation by any person who operates as a motor carrier of property as defined in Section 18-100 of this Act and does not hold a valid certificate or permit. Such investigators shall have and may exercise throughout the State all of the powers of peace officers.

No person may be retained in service as an investigator under this Section after he has reached 60 years of age.

The Secretary of State must authorize to each investigator employed under this Section and to any other employee of the Office of the Secretary of State exercising the powers of a peace officer a distinct badge that, on its face, (i) clearly states that the badge is authorized by the Office of the Secretary of State and (ii) contains a unique identifying number. No other badge shall be authorized by the Office of the Secretary of State.

(b) The Secretary may expend such sums as he deems necessary from Contractual Services appropriations for the Department of Police for the purchase of evidence, for the employment of persons to obtain evidence, and for the payment for any goods or services related to obtaining evidence. Such sums shall be advanced to investigators authorized by the Secretary to expend funds, on vouchers signed by the Secretary. In addition, the Secretary of State is authorized to maintain one or more commercial checking accounts with any State banking corporation or corporations organized under or subject to the Illinois Banking Act [2] for the deposit and withdrawal of moneys to be used solely for the purchase of evidence and for the employment of persons to obtain evidence, or for the payment for any goods or services related to obtaining evidence; provided that no check may be written on nor any withdrawal made from any such account except on the written signatures of 2 persons designated by the Secretary to write such checks and make such withdrawals, and provided further that the balance of moneys on deposit in any such account shall not exceed $5,000 at any time, nor shall any one check written on or single withdrawal made from any such account exceed $5,000.

All fines or moneys collected or received by the Department of Police under any State or federal forfeiture statute; including, but not limited to moneys forfeited under Section 12 of the Cannabis Control Act [3] and moneys distributed under Section 413 of the Illinois Controlled Substances Act, [4] shall be deposited into the Secretary of State Evidence Fund.

In all convictions for offenses in violation of this Act, the Court may order restitution to the Secretary of any or all sums expended for the purchase of evidence, for the employment of persons to obtain evidence, and for the payment for any goods or services related to obtaining evidence. All such restitution received by the Secretary shall be deposited into the Secretary of State Evidence Fund. Moneys deposited into the fund shall, subject to appropriation, be used by the Secretary of State for the purposes provided for under the provisions of this Section.

P.A. 76-1586, § 2-115, eff. July 1, 1970. Amended by P.A. 76-1797, eff. July 1, 1970; P.A. 78-298, § 1, eff. Jan. 1, 1974; P.A. 81-567, § 1, eff. Oct. 1, 1979; P.A. 82-977, § 1, eff. Jan. 1, 1983; P.A. 85-1204, § 1, eff. Aug. 26, 1988; P.A. 87-993, § 3, eff. Sept. 1, 1992; P.A. 88-517, § 10, eff. Nov. 16, 1993; P.A. 91-883, § 105, eff. Jan. 1, 2001.

Formerly Ill.Rev.Stat.1991, ch. 95 ½, ¶ 2-115.

[1] 625 ILCS 5/11-100 et seq. to 5/15-100 et seq.

[2] 205 ILCS 5/1 et seq.

[3] 720 ILCS 550/12.

[4] 720 ILCS 570/413.

5/2-116. Secretary of State Department of Police

§ 2-116. Secretary of State Department of Police.

(a) The Secretary of State and the officers, inspectors, and investigators appointed by him shall cooperate with the State Police and the sheriffs and police in enforcing the laws regulating the operation of vehicles and the use of the highways.

(b) The Secretary of State may provide training and education for members of his office in traffic regulation, the promotion of traffic safety and the enforcement of laws vested in the Secretary of State for administration and enforcement regulating the operation of vehicles and the use of the highways.

(c) The Secretary of State may provide distinctive uniforms and badges for officers, inspectors and investigators employed in the administration of laws relating to the operation of vehicles and the use of the highways and vesting the administration and enforcement of such laws in the Secretary of State.

(d) The Secretary of State Department of Police is authorized to:

(1) investigate the origins, activities, persons, and incidents of crime and the ways and means, if any, to redress the victims of crimes, and study the impact, if any, of legislation relative to the criminal laws of this State related thereto and conduct any other investigations as may be provided by law;

(2) employ skilled experts, technicians, investigators, special agents, or otherwise specially qualified persons to aid in preventing or detecting crime, apprehending criminals, or preparing and presenting evidence of violations of the criminal laws of the State;

(3) cooperate with the police of cities, villages, and incorporated towns, and with the police officers of any county, in enforcing the laws of the State and in making arrests;

(4) provide, as may be required by law, assistance to local law enforcement agencies through training, management, and consultant services for local law enforcement agencies, pertaining to law enforcement activities;

(5) exercise the rights, powers, and duties which have been vested in it by the Secretary of State Act [1] and this Code; [2] and

(6) enforce and administer any other laws in relation to law enforcement as may be vested in the Secretary of State Department of Police.

Persons within the Secretary of State Department of Police who exercise these powers are conservators of the peace and have all the powers possessed by policemen in municipalities and sheriffs, and may exercise these powers anywhere in the State in cooperation with local law enforcement officials. These persons may use false or fictitious names in the performance of their duties under this Section, upon approval of the Director of Police-Secretary of State, and shall not be subject to prosecution under the criminal laws for that use.

(e) The Secretary of State Department of Police may charge, collect, and receive fees or moneys equivalent to the cost of providing its personnel, equipment, and services to governmental agencies when explicitly requested by a governmental agency and according to an intergovernmental agreement or memorandums of understanding as provided by this Section, including but not limited to fees or moneys equivalent to the cost of providing training to other governmental agencies on terms and conditions that in the judgment of the Director of Police-Secretary of State are in the best interest of the Secretary of State. All fees received by the Secretary of State Police Department under this Act shall be deposited in a special fund in the State Treasury to be known as the Secretary of State Police Services Fund. The money deposited in the Secretary of State Police Services Fund shall be appropriated to the Secretary of State Department of Police as provided for in subsection (g).

(f) The Secretary of State Department of Police may apply for grants or contracts and receive, expend, allocate, or disburse moneys made available by public or private entities, including, but not limited to, contracts, bequests, grants, or receiving equipment from corporations, foundations, or public or private institutions of higher learning.

(g) The Secretary of State Police Services Fund is hereby created as a special fund in the State Treasury. All moneys received under this Section by the Secretary of State Department of Police shall be deposited into the Secretary of State Police Services Fund to be appropriated to the Secretary of State Department of Police for purposes as indicated by the grantor or contractor or, in the case of moneys bequeathed or granted for no specific purpose, for any purpose as deemed appropriate by the Director of Police-Secretary of State in administering the responsibilities of the Secretary of State Department of Police.

P.A. 76-1586, § 2-116, eff. July 1, 1970. Amended by P.A. 92-501, § 10, eff. Dec. 19, 2001.

Formerly Ill.Rev.Stat.1991, ch. 95 ½, ¶ 2-116.

[1] 15 ILCS 305/0.01 et seq.

[2] 625 ILCS 5/1-100 et seq.

5/2–117. Injunction

§ 2–117. Injunction. Whenever it shall appear to the Secretary of State that any person is engaged or about to engage in any acts or practices which constitute or will constitute a violation of the provisions of this Act, or of any rule or regulation prescribed under authority thereof, the Secretary of State may in his or her discretion, through the Attorney General, apply for an injunction without notice, and upon a proper showing, the circuit court shall have power to enter a permanent or preliminary injunction or a temporary restraining order without bond, to enforce the provisions of this Act, in addition to the penalties and other remedies in this Act provided; and either party may appeal as in other civil cases.

P.A. 76–1586, § 2–117, eff. July 1, 1970. Amended by P.A. 79–1358, § 43, eff. Oct. 1, 1976; P.A. 83–342, § 10, eff. Sept. 14, 1983.

Formerly Ill.Rev.Stat.1991, ch. 95 ½, ¶ 2–117.

5/2–118. Hearings

§ 2–118. Hearings.

(a) Upon the suspension, revocation or denial of the issuance of a license, permit, registration or certificate of title under this Code of any person the Secretary of State shall immediately notify such person in writing and upon his written request shall, within 20 days after receipt thereof, set a date for a hearing to commence within 90 calendar days from the date of the written request for all requests related to a suspension, revocation, or the denial of the issuance of a license, permit, registration, or certificate of title occurring after July 1, 2002, in the County of Sangamon, the County of Jefferson, or the County of Cook, as such person may specify, unless both parties agree that such hearing may be held in some other county. The Secretary may require the payment of a fee of not more than $50 for the filing of any petition, motion, or request for hearing conducted pursuant to this Section. These fees must be deposited into the Secretary of State DUI Administration Fund, a special fund created in the State treasury, and, subject to appropriation and as directed by the Secretary of State, shall be used for operation of the Department of Administrative Hearings of the Office of the Secretary of State and for no other purpose. The Secretary shall establish by rule the amount and the procedures, terms, and conditions relating to these fees.

(b) At any time after the suspension, revocation or denial of a license, permit, registration or certificate of title of any person as hereinbefore referred to, the Secretary of State, in his or her discretion and without the necessity of a request by such person, may hold such a hearing, upon not less than 10 days' notice in writing, in the Counties of Sangamon, Jefferson, or Cook or in any other county agreed to by the parties.

(c) Upon any such hearing, the Secretary of State, or his authorized agent may administer oaths and issue subpoenas for the attendance of witnesses and the production of relevant books and records and may require an examination of such person. Upon any such hearing, the Secretary of State shall either rescind or, good cause appearing therefor, continue, change or extend the Order of Revocation or Suspension, or upon petition therefore and subject to the provisions of this Code, issue a restricted driving permit or reinstate the license or permit of such person.

(d) All hearings and hearing procedures shall comply with requirements of the Constitution, so that no person is deprived of due process of law nor denied equal protection of the laws. All hearings shall be held before the Secretary of State or before such persons as may be designated by the Secretary of State and appropriate records of such hearings shall be kept. Where a transcript of the hearing is taken, the person requesting the hearing shall have the opportunity to order a copy thereof at his own expense. The Secretary of State shall enter an order upon any hearing conducted under this Section, related to a suspension, revocation, or the denial of the issuance of a license, permit, registration, or certificate of title occurring after July 1, 2002, within 90 days of its conclusion and shall immediately notify the person in writing of his or her action.

(e) The action of the Secretary of State in suspending, revoking or denying any license, permit, registration, or certificate of title shall be subject to judicial review in the Circuit Court of Sangamon County, in the Circuit Court of Jefferson County, or in the Circuit Court of Cook County, and the provisions of the Administrative Review Law,[1] and all amendments and modifications thereto, and the rules adopted pursuant thereto, are hereby adopted and shall apply to and govern every action for the judicial review of final acts or decisions of the Secretary of State hereunder.

P.A. 76–1586, § 2–118, eff. July 1, 1970. Amended by P.A. 78–244, § 1, eff. Aug. 13, 1973; P.A. 82–783, Art. XI, § 140, eff. July 13, 1982; P.A. 84–1394, § 5, eff. Sept. 18, 1986; P.A. 85–951, § 1, eff. July 1, 1988; P.A. 86–929, § 2, eff. Sept. 21, 1989; P.A. 89–145, § 10, eff. July 14, 1995; P.A. 91–823, § 5, eff. Jan. 1, 2001; P.A. 92–418, § 10, eff. Aug. 17, 2001.

Formerly Ill.Rev.Stat.1991, ch. 95 ½, ¶ 2–118.

[1] 735 ILCS 5/3–101 et seq.

5/2–118.1. Opportunity for hearing; statutory summary alcohol or other drug related suspension

§ 2–118.1. Opportunity for hearing; statutory summary alcohol or other drug related suspension.

(a) A statutory summary suspension of driving privileges under Section 11–501.1 shall not become effective until the person is notified in writing of the impending suspension and informed that he may request a hearing in the circuit court of venue under paragraph (b) of this Section and the statutory summary suspension shall become effective as provided in Section 11–501.1.

(b) Within 90 days after the notice of statutory summary suspension served under Section 11–501.1, the person may make a written request for a judicial hearing in the circuit court of venue. The request to the circuit court shall state the grounds upon which the person seeks to have the statutory summary suspension rescinded. Within 30 days after receipt of the written request or the first appearance date on the Uniform Traffic Ticket issued pursuant to a violation of Section 11–501, or a similar provision of a local ordinance, the hearing shall be conducted by the circuit court having jurisdiction. This judicial hearing, request, or process shall not stay or delay the statutory summary suspension. The hearings shall proceed in the court in the same manner as in other civil proceedings.

The hearing may be conducted upon a review of the law enforcement officer's own official reports; provided however, that the person may subpoena the officer. Failure of the officer to answer the subpoena shall be considered grounds for a continuance if in the court's discretion the continuance is appropriate.

The scope of the hearing shall be limited to the issues of:

1. Whether the person was placed under arrest for an offense as defined in Section 11-501, or a similar provision of a local ordinance, as evidenced by the issuance of a Uniform Traffic Ticket, or issued a Uniform Traffic Ticket out of state as provided in subsection (a) of Section 11-501.1; and

2. Whether the officer had reasonable grounds to believe that the person was driving or in actual physical control of a motor vehicle upon a highway while under the influence of alcohol, other drug, or combination of both; and

3. Whether the person, after being advised by the officer that the privilege to operate a motor vehicle would be suspended if the person refused to submit to and complete the test or tests, did refuse to submit to or complete the test or tests to determine the person's alcohol or drug concentration; or

4. Whether the person, after being advised by the officer that the privilege to operate a motor vehicle would be suspended if the person submits to a chemical test, or tests, and the test discloses an alcohol concentration of 0.08 or more, or any amount of a drug, substance, or compound in the person's blood or urine resulting from the unlawful use or consumption of cannabis listed in the Cannabis Control Act,[1] a controlled substance listed in the Illinois Controlled Substances Act, [2] or an intoxicating compound as listed in the use of Intoxicating Compounds Act,[3] and the person did submit to and complete the test or tests that determined an alcohol concentration of 0.08 or more.

Upon the conclusion of the judicial hearing, the circuit court shall sustain or rescind the statutory summary suspension and immediately notify the Secretary of State. Reports received by the Secretary of State under this Section shall be privileged information and for use only by the courts, police officers, and Secretary of State.

P.A. 76-1586, § 2-118.1, added by P.A. 84-272, § 7, eff. Jan. 1, 1986. Amended by P.A. 84-1394, § 5, eff. Sept. 18, 1986; P.A. 86-1019, § 7, eff. July 1, 1990; P.A. 87-1221, § 1, eff. July 1, 1993; P.A. 88-463, § 5, eff. Jan. 1, 1994; P.A. 89-156, § 5, eff. Jan. 1, 1996; P.A. 90-43, § 5, eff. July 2, 1997; P.A. 92-458, § 5, eff. Aug. 22, 2001.

Formerly Ill.Rev.Stat.1991, ch. 95 ½, ¶ 2-118.1.

[1] 720 ILCS 550/1 et seq.

[2] 720 ILCS 570/100 et seq.

[3] 720 ILCS 690/0.01 et seq.

5/2-119. Disposition of fees and taxes

§ 2-119. Disposition of fees and taxes.

(a) All moneys received from Salvage Certificates shall be deposited in the Common School Fund in the State Treasury.

(b) Beginning January 1, 1990 and concluding December 31, 1994, of the money collected for each certificate of title, duplicate certificate of title and corrected certificate of title, $0.50 shall be deposited into the Used Tire Management Fund. Beginning January 1, 1990 and concluding December 31, 1994, of the money collected for each certificate of title, duplicate certificate of title and corrected certificate of title, $1.50 shall be deposited in the Park and Conservation Fund.

Beginning January 1, 1995, of the money collected for each certificate of title, duplicate certificate of title and corrected certificate of title, $2 shall be deposited in the Park and Conservation Fund. The moneys deposited in the Park and Conservation Fund pursuant to this Section shall be used for the acquisition and development of bike paths as provided for in Section 805-420 of the Department of Natural Resources (Conservation) Law (20 ILCS 805/805-420).

Beginning January 1, 2000 and continuing through December 31, 2004, of the moneys collected for each certificate of title, duplicate certificate of title, and corrected certificate of title, $48 shall be deposited into the Road Fund and $4 shall be deposited into the Motor Vehicle License Plate Fund, except that if the balance in the Motor Vehicle License Plate Fund exceeds $40,000,000 on the last day of a calendar month, then during the next calendar month the $4 shall instead be deposited into the Road Fund.

Beginning January 1, 2005, of the moneys collected for each certificate of title, duplicate certificate of title, and corrected certificate of title, $52 shall be deposited into the Road Fund.

Except as otherwise provided in this Code, all remaining moneys collected for certificates of title, and all moneys collected for filing of security interests, shall be placed in the General Revenue Fund in the State Treasury.

(c) All moneys collected for that portion of a driver's license fee designated for driver education under Section 6-118 shall be placed in the Driver Education Fund in the State Treasury.

(d) Beginning January 1, 1999, of the monies collected as a registration fee for each motorcycle, motor driven cycle and motorized pedalcycle, 27% of each annual registration fee for such vehicle and 27% of each semiannual registration fee for such vehicle is deposited in the Cycle Rider Safety Training Fund.

(e) Of the monies received by the Secretary of State as registration fees or taxes or as payment of any other fee, as provided in this Act, except fees received by the Secretary under paragraph (7) of subsection (b) of Section 5-101 and Section 5-109 of this Code, 37% shall be deposited into the State Construction Fund.

(f) Of the total money collected for a CDL instruction permit or original or renewal issuance of a commercial driver's license (CDL) pursuant to the Uniform Commercial Driver's License Act (UCDLA) [1]: (i) $6 of the total fee for an original or renewal CDL, and $6 of the total CDL instruction permit fee when such permit is issued to any person holding a valid Illinois driver's license, shall be paid into the CDLIS/AAMVAnet Trust Fund (Commercial Driver's License Information System/American Association of Motor Vehicle Administrators network Trust Fund) and shall be used for the purposes provided in Section 6z-23 of the State Finance Act [2] and (ii) $20 of the total fee for an original or renewal CDL or commercial driver instruction permit shall be paid into the Motor Carrier Safety Inspection Fund, which is hereby created as a special fund in the State Treasury, to be used by the Department of State Police, subject to appropriation, to hire additional officers to conduct motor carrier safety inspections pursuant to Chapter 18b of this Code.[3]

(g) All remaining moneys received by the Secretary of State as registration fees or taxes or as payment of any other fee, as provided in this Act, except fees received by the Secretary under paragraph (7) of subsection (b) of Section 5-101 and Section 5-109 of this Code, shall be deposited in the Road Fund in the State Treasury. Moneys in the Road Fund shall be used for the purposes provided in Section 8.3 of the State Finance Act.[4]

(h) (Blank).

(i) (Blank).

(j) (Blank).

(k) There is created in the State Treasury a special fund to be known as the Secretary of State Special License Plate Fund. Money deposited into the Fund shall, subject to appropriation, be used by the Office of the Secretary of State (i) to help defray plate manufacturing and plate processing costs for the issuance and, when applicable, renewal of any new or existing special registration plates authorized under this Code and (ii) for grants made by the Secretary of State to benefit Illinois Veterans Home libraries.

On or before October 1, 1995, the Secretary of State shall direct the State Comptroller and State Treasurer to transfer any unexpended balance in the Special Environmental License Plate Fund, the Special Korean War Veteran License Plate Fund, and the Retired Congressional License Plate Fund to the Secretary of State Special License Plate Fund.

(*l*) The Motor Vehicle Review Board Fund is created as a special fund in the State Treasury. Moneys deposited into the Fund under paragraph (7) of subsection (b) of Section 5-101 and Section 5-109 shall, subject to appropriation, be used by the Office of the Secretary of State to administer the Motor Vehicle Review Board, including without limitation payment of compensation and all necessary expenses incurred in administering the Motor Vehicle Review Board under the Motor Vehicle Franchise Act.[5]

(m) Effective July 1, 1996, there is created in the State Treasury a special fund to be known as the Family Responsibility Fund. Moneys deposited into the Fund shall, subject to appropriation, be used by the Office of the Secretary of State for the purpose of enforcing the Family Financial Responsibility Law.

(n) The Illinois Fire Fighters' Memorial Fund is created as a special fund in the State Treasury. Moneys deposited into the Fund shall, subject to appropriation, be used by the Office of the State Fire Marshal for construction of the Illinois Fire Fighters' Memorial to be located at the State Capitol grounds in Springfield, Illinois. Upon the completion of the Memorial, moneys in the Fund shall be used in accordance with Section 3-634.

(*o*) Of the money collected for each certificate of title for all-terrain vehicles and off-highway motorcycles, $17 shall be deposited into the Off-Highway Vehicle Trails Fund.

P.A. 76-1586, § 2-119, eff. July 1, 1970. Amended by P.A. 78-860, § 2, eff. Jan. 1, 1974; P.A. 78-5, 3rd Sp.Sess., Part III, § 1, eff. Dec. 12, 1973; P.A. 78-1297, § 58, eff. March 4, 1975; P.A. 80-1185, § 1, eff. March 8, 1978; P.A. 81-3, 2nd Sp.Sess. § 15, eff. Sept. 19, 1979; P.A. 82-649, § 3, eff. Jan. 1, 1982; P.A. 83-12, § 1, eff. July 1, 1983; P.A. 84-470, § 1, eff. Sept. 17, 1985; P.A. 85-1144, § 1, eff. July 29, 1988; P.A. 86-452, § 12, eff. Aug. 31, 1989; P.A. 86-845, § 1, eff. April 1, 1990; P.A. 86-982, § 1, eff. July 1, 1990; P.A. 86-1005, § 3, eff. Dec. 28, 1989; P.A. 86-1019, § 2, eff. Jan. 1, 1990; P.A. 86-1475, Art. 2, § 2-25, eff. Jan. 10, 1990; P.A. 88-333, § 5, eff. Jan. 1, 1994; P.A. 88-485, § 10, eff. Jan. 1, 1994; P.A. 88-589, § 10, eff. Aug. 14, 1994; P.A. 88-670, Art. 2, § 2-59, eff. Dec. 2, 1994; P.A. 89-92, § 10, eff. July 1, 1996; P.A. 89-145, § 10, eff. July 14, 1995; P.A. 89-282, § 10, eff. Aug. 10, 1995; P.A. 89-612, § 10, eff. Aug. 9, 1996; P.A. 89-626, Art. 2, § 2-64, eff. Aug. 9, 1996; P.A. 89-639, § 5, eff. Jan. 1, 1997; P.A. 90-14, Art. 2, § 2-225, eff. July 1, 1997; P.A. 90-287, § 100, eff. Jan. 1, 1998; P.A. 90-622, § 5, eff. Jan. 1, 1999; P.A. 91-37, § 40, eff. July 1, 1999; P.A. 91-239, Art. 5, § 5-530, eff. Jan. 1, 2000; P.A. 91-537, § 10, eff. Aug. 13, 1999; P.A. 91-832, § 5, eff. June 16, 2000; P.A. 92-16, § 85, eff. June 28, 2001.

Formerly Ill.Rev.Stat.1991, ch. 95 ½, ¶ 2-119.

1 625 ILCS 5/6-500 et seq.

2 30 ILCS 105/6z-23.

3 625 ILCS 5/18b-100 et seq.

4 30 ILCS 105/8.3.

5 815 ILCS 710/1 et seq.

Section 4 of P.A. 83-12, approved July 1, 1983, provided:

"Effective date. This Act takes effect as provided in this Section.

"The amendments to those portions of Sections 3-815(a), 3-818 and 3-819(b) of 'The Illinois Vehicle Code' in Section 1 of this Act which create the 'X', 'Z', 'MX', 'MZ', 'MM' and 'TN' registration classifications and the fees and taxes imposed for those classifications, the amendments to Sections 2-119, 3-401 and 3-802 of 'The Illinois Vehicle Code' in Section 1 of this Act, and the amendments to Chapter 15 of 'The Illinois Vehicle Code' in Section 1 of this Act take effect July 1, 1983.

"The remaining amendments to 'The Illinois Vehicle Code' in Section 1 of this Act take effect July 1, 1983 and apply beginning with the 1985 registration year, except that the amendments to Sections 3-813 through 3-816 and Section 3-819 apply beginning with the 1984 registration year for those vehicles registered on a calendar year basis only.

"The amendments to Chapters 13 and 18 of 'The Illinois Vehicle Code' in Section 1 of this Act take effect January 1, 1984.

"Section 2 of this Act takes effect on the first day of the next succeeding month which commences at least 30 days after the date on which this Act becomes law.

"Section 3 of this Act takes effect July 1, 1983.

"Section 3.1 of this Act takes effect January 1, 1984.

"This Section 4 takes effect upon its becoming a law."

For purpose of revisory provisions of P.A. 91-239, see Historical and Statutory Notes under 20 ILCS 5/1-1.

5/2-120. Disposition of fines and forfeitures

§ 2-120. Disposition of fines and forfeitures.

(a) Except as provided in subsection (f) of Section 11-605 of this Code, fines and penalties recovered under the provisions of this Act administered by the Secretary of State, except those fines and penalties subject to disbursement by the circuit clerk under Section 27.5 of the Clerks of Courts Act,[1] shall be paid over and used as follows:

1. For violations of this Act committed within the limits of an incorporated city or village, to the treasurer of the particular city or village, if arrested by the authorities of the city or village and reasonably prosecuted for all fines and penalties under this Act by the police officers and officials of the city or village.

2. For violations of this Act committed outside the limits of an incorporated city or village to the county treasurer of the court where the offense was committed.

3. For the purposes of this Act an offense for violation of any provision of this Act not committed upon the highway shall be deemed to be committed where the violator resides or where he has a place of business requiring some registration, permit or license to operate such business under this Act.

(b) Failure, refusal or neglect on the part of any judicial or other officer or employee receiving or having custody of any such fine or forfeiture either before or after a deposit with the proper official as defined in paragraph (a) of this Section, shall constitute misconduct in office and shall be grounds for removal therefrom.

P.A. 76-1586, § 2-120, eff. July 1, 1970. Amended by P.A. 81-1509, Art. II, § 71, eff. Sept. 26, 1980; P.A. 87-671, § 3, eff. Jan. 1, 1992; P.A. 91-531, § 5, eff. Jan. 1, 2000.

Formerly Ill.Rev.Stat.1991, ch. 95 ½, ¶ 2-120.

1 705 ILCS 105/27.5.

5/2-121. Local Government Tax

§ 2-121. Local Government tax.

(a) No owner of a vehicle who shall have obtained a certificate from the Secretary of State and paid the registration fee and tax as provided in this Act, shall be required by any county, city, village, incorporated town, or other municipal corporation within the State other than a county, city, village, incorporated town, or other municipal corporation in which the owner resides or in which a vehicle has its situs or base, to pay any tax or license fee for the use of the vehicle. The county, city, village, or incorporated town in which the owner resides or in which a vehicle has its situs or base, except commercial motor vehicles as defined in paragraph (2) of Section 18b-101 that are registered under Section 3-402.1, may impose a tax or license fee as is provided in Section 8-11-4 of the Illinois Municipal Code [1] or a similar county ordinance that imposes a tax or license fee on an owner of a vehicle for the use of the vehicle.

Nor shall the owner be required to display upon his vehicle any plate or tax or license number other than that issued by the Secretary of State or by the county, city, village, incorporated town, or other municipal corporation within the State within which the owner resides or in which a vehicle has its situs or base. However, a resident owner shall not be required to display on his vehicle, the plate or tax or license number issued by the county, city, village, or incorporated town of his residence if his vehicle is displaying the plate or tax or license number issued by the place wherein the vehicle has its situs or base.

This subsection (a) applies to ordinances enacted by any county, city, village, incorporated town, or other municipal corporation. Any provision of an ordinance enacted by a county, city, village, incorporated town, or other municipal corporation that is inconsistent with this subsection (a) is null and void.

(b) No county, city, village, incorporated town, or other municipal corporation, including a home rule unit, may impose a tax or license fee under Section 8-11-4 of the Illinois Municipal Code, or impose a similar tax or license fee under home rule powers, upon any commercial vehicle as defined in paragraph (2) of Section 18b-101 that is registered under Section 3-402.1. This subsection (b) is a denial and limitation of home rule powers and functions under subsection (g) of Section 6 of Article VII of the Illinois Constitution.

P.A. 76-1586, § 2-121, eff. July 1, 1970. Amended by P.A. 78-231, § 1, eff. Jan. 1, 1974; P.A. 87-1063, § 1, eff. Jan. 1, 1993; P.A. 90-433, § 5, eff. Aug. 16, 1997.

Formerly Ill.Rev.Stat.1991, ch. 95 ½, ¶ 2-121.

[1] 65 ILCS 5/8-11-4.

5/2-122. Remittance agents

§ 2-122. Remittance agents. The Secretary of State shall administer the law relating to remittance agents pursuant to the law.

P.A. 76-1586, § 2-122, eff. July 1, 1970.

Formerly Ill.Rev.Stat.1991, ch. 95 ½, ¶ 2-122.

5/2-123. Sale and Distribution of Information

§ 2-123. Sale and Distribution of Information.

(a) Except as otherwise provided in this Section, the Secretary may make the driver's license, vehicle and title registration lists, in part or in whole, and any statistical information derived from these lists available to local governments, elected state officials, state educational institutions, and all other governmental units of the State and Federal Government requesting them for governmental purposes. The Secretary shall require any such applicant for services to pay for the costs of furnishing such services and the use of the equipment involved, and in addition is empowered to establish prices and charges for the services so furnished and for the use of the electronic equipment utilized.

(b) The Secretary is further empowered to and he may, in his discretion, furnish to any applicant, other than listed in subsection (a) of this Section, vehicle or driver data on a computer tape, disk, other electronic format or computer processable medium, or printout at a fixed fee of $250 in advance and require in addition a further sufficient deposit based upon the Secretary of State's estimate of the total cost of the information requested and a charge of $25 per 1,000 units or part thereof identified or the actual cost, whichever is greater. The Secretary is authorized to refund any difference between the additional deposit and the actual cost of the request. This service shall not be in lieu of an abstract of a driver's record nor of a title or registration search. This service may be limited to entities purchasing a minimum number of records as required by administrative rule. The information sold pursuant to this subsection shall be the entire vehicle or driver data list, or part thereof. The information sold pursuant to this subsection shall not contain personally identifying information unless the information is to be used for one of the purposes identified in subsection (f-5) of this Section. Commercial purchasers of driver and vehicle record databases shall enter into a written agreement with the Secretary of State that includes disclosure of the commercial use of the information to be purchased.

(c) Secretary of State may issue registration lists. The Secretary of State shall compile and publish, at least annually, a list of all registered vehicles. Each list of registered vehicles shall be arranged serially according to the registration numbers assigned to registered vehicles and shall contain in addition the names and addresses of registered owners and a brief description of each vehicle including the serial or other identifying number thereof. Such compilation may be in such form as in the discretion of the Secretary of State may seem best for the purposes intended.

(d) The Secretary of State shall furnish no more than 2 current available lists of such registrations to the sheriffs of all counties and to the chiefs of police of all cities and villages and towns of 2,000 population and over in this State at no cost. Additional copies may be purchased by the sheriffs or chiefs of police at the fee of $500 each or at the cost of producing the list as determined by the Secretary of State. Such lists are to be used for governmental purposes only.

(e) (Blank).

(e-1) (Blank).

(f) The Secretary of State shall make a title or registration search of the records of his office and a written report on the same for any person, upon written application of such person, accompanied by a fee of $5 for each registration or title search. The written application shall set forth the intended use of the requested information. No fee shall be charged for a title or registration search, or for the certification thereof requested by a government agency. The report of the title or registration search shall not contain personally identifying information unless the request for a search was made for one of the purposes identified in subsection (f-5) of this Section.

The Secretary of State shall certify a title or registration record upon written request. The fee for certification shall be $5 in addition to the fee required for a title or registration search. Certification shall be made under the signature of the Secretary of State and shall be authenticated by Seal of the Secretary of State.

The Secretary of State may notify the vehicle owner or registrant of the request for purchase of his title or registration information as the Secretary deems appropriate.

No information shall be released to the requestor until expiration of a 10 day period. This 10 day period shall not apply to requests for information made by law enforcement officials, government agencies, financial institutions, attorneys, insurers, employers, automobile associated businesses, persons licensed as a private detective or firms licensed as a private detective agency under the Private Detective, Private Alarm, and Private Security Act of 1983, [1] who are employed by or are acting on behalf of law enforcement officials, government agencies, financial institutions, attorneys, insurers, employers, automobile associated businesses, and other business entities for purposes consistent with the Illinois Vehicle Code, [2] the vehicle owner or registrant or other entities as the Secretary may exempt by rule and regulation.

Any misrepresentation made by a requestor of title or vehicle information shall be punishable as a petty offense, except in the case of persons licensed as a private detective or firms licensed as a private detective agency which shall be subject to disciplinary sanctions under Section 22 or 25 of the Private Detective, Private Alarm, and Private Security Act of 1983.

(f-5) The Secretary of State shall not disclose or otherwise make available to any person or entity any personally identifying information obtained by the Secretary of State in connection with a driver's license, vehicle, or title registration record unless the information is disclosed for one of the following purposes:

(1) For use by any government agency, including any court or law enforcement agency, in carrying out its functions, or any private person or entity acting on behalf of a federal, State, or local agency in carrying out its functions.

(2) For use in connection with matters of motor vehicle or driver safety and theft; motor vehicle emissions; motor vehicle product alterations, recalls, or advisories; performance monitoring of motor vehicles, motor vehicle parts, and dealers; and removal of non-owner records from the original owner records of motor vehicle manufacturers.

(3) For use in the normal course of business by a legitimate business or its agents, employees, or contractors, but only:

(A) to verify the accuracy of personal information submitted by an individual to the business or its agents, employees, or contractors; and

(B) if such information as so submitted is not correct or is no longer correct, to obtain the correct information, but only for the purposes of preventing fraud by, pursuing legal remedies against, or recovering on a debt or security interest against, the individual.

(4) For use in research activities and for use in producing statistical reports, if the personally identifying information is not published, redisclosed, or used to contact individuals.

(5) For use in connection with any civil, criminal, administrative, or arbitral proceeding in any federal, State, or local court or agency or before any self-regulatory body, including the service of process, investigation in anticipation of litigation, and the execution or enforcement of judgments and orders, or pursuant to an order of a federal, State, or local court.

(6) For use by any insurer or insurance support organization or by a self-insured entity or its agents, employees, or contractors in connection with claims investigation activities, antifraud activities, rating, or underwriting.

(7) For use in providing notice to the owners of towed or impounded vehicles.

(8) For use by any private investigative agency or security service licensed in Illinois for any purpose permitted under this subsection.

(9) For use by an employer or its agent or insurer to obtain or verify information relating to a holder of a commercial driver's license that is required under chapter 313 of title 49 of the United States Code.

(10) For use in connection with the operation of private toll transportation facilities.

(11) For use by any requester, if the requester demonstrates it has obtained the written consent of the individual to whom the information pertains.

(12) For use by members of the news media, as defined in Section 1-148.5, for the purpose of newsgathering when the request relates to the operation of a motor vehicle or public safety.

(13) For any other use specifically authorized by law, if that use is related to the operation of a motor vehicle or public safety.

(g) 1. The Secretary of State may, upon receipt of a written request and a fee of $6, furnish to the person or agency so requesting a driver's record. Such document may include a record of: current driver's license issuance information, except that the information on judicial driving permits shall be available only as otherwise provided by this Code; convictions; orders entered revoking, suspending or cancelling a driver's license or privilege; and notations of accident involvement. All other information, unless otherwise permitted by this Code, shall remain confidential. Information released pursuant to a request for a driver's record shall not contain personally identifying information, unless the request for the driver's record was made for one of the purposes set forth in subsection (f-5) of this Section.

2. The Secretary of State may certify an abstract of a driver's record upon written request therefor. Such certification shall be made under the signature of the Secretary of State and shall be authenticated by the Seal of his office.

3. All requests for driving record information shall be made in a manner prescribed by the Secretary and shall set forth the intended use of the requested information.

The Secretary of State may notify the affected driver of the request for purchase of his driver's record as the Secretary deems appropriate.

No information shall be released to the requester until expiration of a 10 day period. This 10 day period shall not apply to requests for information made by law enforcement officials, government agencies, financial institutions, attorneys, insurers, employers, automobile associated businesses, persons licensed as a private detective or firms licensed as a private detective agency under the Private Detective, Private Alarm, and Private Security Act of 1983, who are employed by or are acting on behalf of law enforcement officials, government agencies, financial institutions, attorneys, insurers, employers, automobile associated businesses, and other business entities for purposes consistent with the Illinois Vehicle Code, the affected driver or other entities as the Secretary may exempt by rule and regulation.

Any misrepresentation made by a requestor of driver information shall be punishable as a petty offense, except in the case of persons licensed as a private detective or firms licensed as a private detective agency which shall be subject to disciplinary sanctions under Section 22 or 25 of the Private Detective, Private Alarm, and Private Security Act of 1983.

4. The Secretary of State may furnish without fee, upon the written request of a law enforcement agency, any information from a driver's record on file with the Secretary of State when such information is required in the enforcement of this Code or any other law relating to the operation of motor vehicles, including records of dispositions; documented information involving the use of a motor vehicle; whether such individual has, or previously had, a driver's license; and the address and personal description as reflected on said driver's record.

5. Except as otherwise provided in this Section, the Secretary of State may furnish, without fee, information from an individual driver's record on file, if a written request therefor is submitted by any public transit system or authority, public defender, law enforcement agency, a state or federal agency, or an Illinois local intergovernmental association, if the request is for the purpose of a background check of applicants for employment with the requesting agency, or for the purpose of an official investigation conducted by the agency, or to determine a current address for the driver so public funds can be recovered or paid to the driver, or for any other purpose set forth in subsection (f–5) of this Section.

The Secretary may also furnish the courts a copy of an abstract of a driver's record, without fee, subsequent to an arrest for a violation of Section 11–501 or a similar provision of a local ordinance. Such abstract may include records of dispositions; documented information involving the use of a motor vehicle as contained in the current file; whether such individual has, or previously had, a driver's license; and the address and personal description as reflected on said driver's record.

6. Any certified abstract issued by the Secretary of State or transmitted electronically by the Secretary of State pursuant to this Section, to a court or on request of a law enforcement agency, for the record of a named person as to the status of the person's driver's license shall be prima facie evidence of the facts therein stated and if the name appearing in such abstract is the same as that of a person named in an information or warrant, such abstract shall be prima facie evidence that the person named in such information or warrant is the same person as the person named in such abstract and shall be admissible for any prosecution under this Code and be admitted as proof of any prior conviction or proof of records, notices, or orders recorded on individual driving records maintained by the Secretary of State.

7. Subject to any restrictions contained in the Juvenile Court Act of 1987, [3] and upon receipt of a proper request and a fee of $6, the Secretary of State shall provide a driver's record to the affected driver, or the affected driver's attorney, upon verification. Such record shall contain all the information referred to in paragraph 1 of this subsection (g) plus: any recorded accident involvement as a driver; information recorded pursuant to subsection (e) of Section 6–117 and paragraph (4) of subsection (a) of Section 6–204 of this Code. All other information, unless otherwise permitted by this Code, shall remain confidential.

(h) The Secretary shall not disclose social security numbers except pursuant to a written request by, or with the prior written consent of, the individual except: (1) to officers and employees of the Secretary who have a need to know the social security numbers in performance of their official duties, (2) to law enforcement officials for a lawful, civil or criminal law enforcement investigation, and if the head of the law enforcement agency has made a written request to the Secretary specifying the law enforcement investigation for which the social security numbers are being sought, (3) to the United States Department of Transportation, or any other State, pursuant to the administration and enforcement of the Commercial Motor Vehicle Safety Act of 1986, [4] (4) pursuant to the order of a court of competent jurisdiction, or (5) to the Department of Public Aid for utilization in the child support enforcement duties assigned to that Department under provisions of the Public Aid Code after the individual has received advanced meaningful notification of what redisclosure is sought by the Secretary in accordance with the federal Privacy Act.

(i) (Blank).

(j) Medical statements or medical reports received in the Secretary of State's Office shall be confidential. No confidential information may be open to public inspection or the contents disclosed to anyone, except officers and employees of the Secretary who have a need to know the information contained in the medical reports and the Driver License Medical Advisory Board, unless so directed by an order of a court of competent jurisdiction.

(k) All fees collected under this Section shall be paid into the Road Fund of the State Treasury, except that $3 of the $6 fee for a driver's record shall be paid into the Secretary of State Special Services Fund.

(*l*) (Blank).

(m) Notations of accident involvement that may be disclosed under this Section shall not include notations relating to damage to a vehicle or other property being transported by a tow truck. This information shall remain confidential, provided that nothing in this subsection (m) shall limit disclosure of any notification of accident involvement to any law enforcement agency or official.

(n) Requests made by the news media for driver's license, vehicle, or title registration information may be furnished without charge or at a reduced charge, as determined by the Secretary, when the specific purpose for requesting the documents is deemed to be in the public interest. Waiver or reduction of the fee is in the public interest if the principal purpose of the request is to access and disseminate information regarding the health, safety, and welfare or the legal rights of the general public and is not for the principal purpose of gaining a personal or commercial benefit. The information provided pursuant to this subsection shall not contain personally identifying information unless the information is to be used for one of the purposes identified in subsection (f–5) of this Section.

(*o*) The redisclosure of personally identifying information obtained pursuant to this Section is prohibited, except to the extent necessary to effectuate the purpose for which the original disclosure of the information was permitted.

(p) The Secretary of State is empowered to adopt rules to effectuate this Section.

P.A. 76–1586, § 2–123, added by P.A. 76–2128, § 1, eff. July 1, 1970. Amended by P.A. 81–982, § 1, eff. Jan. 1, 1980; P.A. 83–148, § 1, eff. Aug. 29, 1983; P.A. 83–1404, § 6, eff. Sept. 12, 1984; P.A. 84–411, § 1, eff. Jan. 1, 1986; P.A. 84–986, § 1, eff. Sept. 25, 1985; P.A. 84–1308, Art. II, § 96, eff. Aug. 25, 1986; P.A. 84–1394, § 5, eff. Sept. 18, 1986; P.A. 85–314, § 1, eff. Jan. 1, 1988; P.A. 85–1396, § 2, eff. Sept. 2, 1988; P.A. 86–549, § 1, eff. Jan. 1, 1990; P.A. 87–366, § 1, eff. Jan. 1, 1992; P.A. 87–623, § 1, eff. July 1, 1992; P.A. 87–895, Art. 2, § 2–45, eff. Aug. 14, 1992; P.A. 87–1074, § 2, eff. Jan. 1, 1993; P.A. 88–208, § 5, eff. Aug. 5, 1993; P.A. 88–363, § 293, eff. Jan. 1, 1994; P.A. 88–670, Art. 2, § 2–59, eff. Dec.

2, 1994; P.A. 89-503, § 10, eff. July 1, 1996; P.A. 90-144, § 15, eff. July 23, 1997; P.A. 90-330, § 5, eff. Aug. 8, 1997; P.A. 90-400, § 5, eff. Aug. 15, 1997; P.A. 90-655, § 153, eff. July 30, 1998; P.A. 91-37, § 40, eff. July 1, 1999; P.A. 91-357, § 231, eff. July 29, 1999; P.A. 91-716, § 5, eff. Oct. 1, 2000; P.A. 92-32, § 10, eff. July 1, 2001; P.A. 92-651, § 77, eff. July 11, 2002.

Formerly Ill.Rev.Stat.1991, ch. 95 ½, ¶ 2-123.

1 225 ILCS 445/1 (repealed).

2 635 ILCS 5/1-100 et seq.

3 705 ILCS 405/1-1 et seq.

4 49 App. U.S.C.A. § 2701 et seq. (repealed).

5/2-124. Audits, interest and penalties

§ 2-124. Audits, interest and penalties.

(a) Audits. The Secretary of State or employees and agents designated by him, may audit the books, records, tax returns, reports, and any and all other pertinent records or documents of any person licensed or registered, or required to be licensed or registered, under any provisions of this Act, for the purpose of determining whether such person has not paid any fees or taxes required to be paid to the Secretary of State and due to the State of Illinois. For purposes of this Section, "person" means an individual, corporation, or partnership, or an officer or an employee of any corporation, including a dissolved corporation, or a member or an employee of any partnership, who as an officer, employee, or member under a duty to perform the act in respect to which the violation occurs.

(b) Joint Audits. The Secretary of State may enter into reciprocal audit agreements with officers, agents or agencies of another State or States, for joint audits of any person subject to audit under this Act.

(c) Special Audits. If the Secretary of State is not satisfied with the books, records and documents made available for an audit, or if the Secretary of State is unable to determine therefrom whether any fees or taxes are due to the State of Illinois, or if there is cause to believe that the person audited has declined or refused to supply the books, records and documents necessary to determine whether a deficiency exists, the Secretary of State may either seek a court order for production of any and all books, records and documents he deems relevant and material, or, in his discretion, the Secretary of State may instead give written notice to such person requiring him to produce any and all books, records and documents necessary to properly audit and determine whether any fees or taxes are due to the State of Illinois. If such person fails, refuses or declines to comply with either the court order or written notice within the time specified, the Secretary of State shall then order a special audit at the expense of the person affected. Upon completion of the special audit, the Secretary of State shall determine if any fees or taxes required to be paid under this Act have not been paid, and make an assessment of any deficiency based upon the books, records and documents available to him, and in an assessment, he may rely upon records of other persons having an operation similar to that of the person audited specially. A person audited specially and subject to a court order and in default thereof, shall in addition, be subject to any penalty or punishment imposed by the court entering the order.

(d) Deficiency; Audit Costs. When a deficiency is found and any fees or taxes required to be paid under this Act have not been paid to the State of Illinois, the Secretary of State may impose an audit fee of $50 per day, or $25 per half-day, per auditor, plus in the case of out-of-state travel, transportation expenses incurred by the auditor or auditors. Where more than one person is audited on the same out-of-state trip, the additional transportation expenses may be apportioned. The actual costs of a special audit shall be imposed upon the person audited.

(e) Interest. When a deficiency is found and any fees or taxes required to be paid under this Act have not been paid to the State of Illinois, the amount of the deficiency, if greater than $100 for all registration years examined, shall also bear interest at the rate of ½ of 1% per month or fraction thereof, from the date when the fee or tax due should have been paid under the provisions of this Act, subject to a maximum of 6% per annum.

(f) Willful Negligence. When a deficiency is determined by the Secretary to be caused by the willful neglect or negligence of the person audited, an additional 10% penalty, that is 10% of the amount of the deficiency or assessment, shall be imposed, and the 10% penalty shall bear interest at the rate of ½ of 1% on and after the 30th day after the penalty is imposed until paid in full.

(g) Fraud or Evasion. When a deficiency is determined by the Secretary to be caused by fraud or willful evasion of the provisions of this Act, an additional penalty, that is 20% of the amount of the deficiency or assessment, shall be imposed, and the 20% penalty shall bear interest at the rate of ½ of 1% on and after the 30th day after the penalty is imposed until paid in full.

(h) Notice. The Secretary of State shall give written notice to any person audited, of the amount of any deficiency found or assessment made, of the costs of an audit or special audit, and of the penalty imposed, and payment shall be made within 30 days of the date of the notice unless such person petitions for a hearing.

However, except in the case of fraud or willful evasion, or the inaccessibility of books and records for audit or with the express consent of the person audited, no notice of a deficiency or assessment shall be issued by the Secretary for more than 3 registration years. This limitation shall commence on any January 1 as to calendar year registrations and on any July 1 as to fiscal year registrations. This limitation shall not apply for any period during which the person affected has declined or refuses to make his books and records available for audit, nor during any period of time in which an Order of any Court has the effect of enjoining or restraining the Secretary from making an audit or issuing a notice. Notwithstanding, each person licensed under the International Registration Plan and audited by this State or any member jurisdiction shall follow the assessment and refund procedures as adopted and amended by the International Registration Plan members. The Secretary of State shall have the final decision as to which registrants may be subject to the netting of audit fees as outlined in the International Registration Plan. Persons audited may be subject to a review process to determine the final outcome of the audit finding. This process shall follow the adopted procedure as outlined in the International Registration Plan. All decisions by the IRP designated tribunal shall be binding.

(i) Every person subject to licensing or registration and audit under the provisions of this Chapter shall retain all pertinent licensing and registration documents, books, records, tax returns, reports and all supporting records and documents for a period of 4 years.

(j) Hearings. Any person receiving written notice of a deficiency or assessment may, within 30 days after the date of the notice, petition for a hearing before the Secretary of State or his duly appointed hearing officer to contest the audit in whole or in part, and the petitioner shall simultaneously file a certified check or money order, or certificate of deposit, or a surety bond approved by the Secretary in the amount of the deficiency or assessment. Hearings shall be held pursuant to the provisions of Section 2-118 of this Act.

(k) Judgments. The Secretary of State may enforce any notice of deficiency or assessment pursuant to the provisions of Section 3-831 of this Act.

P.A. 76-1586, § 2-124, added by P.A. 77-1541, § 1, eff. Sept. 17, 1971. Amended by P.A. 79-1461, § 1, eff. Oct. 1, 1976; P.A. 85-512, § 1, eff. Jan. 1, 1988; P.A. 87-829, § 1, eff. Jan. 17, 1992; P.A. 87-832, § 3, eff. Jan. 17, 1992; P.A. 89-570, § 5, eff. July 26, 1996; P.A. 92-69, § 5, eff. July 12, 2001.

Formerly Ill.Rev.Stat.1991, ch. 95 ½, ¶ 2-124.

5/2-125. Maximum fees; rules and regulations

§ 2-125. The Secretary of State may in his discretion set maximum fees charged by any person, firm, corporation or private institution within the State of Illinois concerning the acceptance of applications for registration, certificate of title, or drivers license and for the distribution of motor vehicle license plates and other related functions of the Office. The Secretary of State may adopt and promulgate such rules and regulations as he shall deem necessary to effectuate and administer the provisions of this Section.

P.A. 76-1586, § 2-125, added by P.A. 80-469, § 1, eff. Sept. 3, 1977.

Formerly Ill.Rev.Stat.1991, ch. 95 ½, ¶ 2-125.

5/2-126. Drivers license exam stations; fees; temporary deposits

§ 2-126. Employees and agents of the Secretary of State, designated by him, who are employed at Drivers License Exam Stations throughout the State are authorized to deposit, on a temporary basis, fees and moneys collected at such stations in banks or savings and loan associations designated by the Secretary of State. Provided, however, that when such funds collected amount to $500 or more, or on the next succeeding 1st or 15th (disregarding Sundays and holidays) day of each month, whichever is earlier, such fees and moneys shall be forwarded to the Secretary of State by such designated banks or savings and loan associations for deposit with the State Treasurer.

No bank or savings and loan association shall receive public funds as permitted by this Section, unless it has complied with the requirements established pursuant to Section 6 of "An Act relating to certain investments of public funds by public agencies", approved July 23, 1943, as now or hereafter amended.[1]

P.A. 76-1586, § 2-126, added by P.A. 80-547, § 1, eff. Sept. 8, 1977. Amended by P.A. 80-1364, § 36, eff. Aug. 13, 1978; P.A. 83-541, § 52, eff. Sept. 17, 1983.

Formerly Ill.Rev.Stat.1991, ch. 95 ½, ¶ 2-126.

[1] 30 ILCS 235/6.

5/2-127. Transportation provided seniors

§ 2-127. The Secretary of State shall compile and maintain a listing of those services and agencies, both public and private, that provide transportation to senior citizens and shall make this information available to the public through the Drivers License Exam Stations.

P.A. 76-1586, § 2-127, added by P.A. 86-424, § 1, eff. Jan. 1, 1990.

Formerly Ill.Rev.Stat.1991, ch. 95 ½, ¶ 2-127.

5/2-128. § 2-128. Repealed by P.A. 87-564, § 1, eff. July 1, 1992

CHAPTER 3. CERTIFICATES OF TITLE AND REGISTRATION OF VEHICLES

Enactment

The Illinois Vehicle Code was enacted by P.A. 76-1586, effective July 1, 1970. The Code constitutes a consolidated recodification of various earlier laws and acts including the Illinois Motor Vehicle Law of 1957.

ARTICLE I. CERTIFICATES OF TITLE

Section

5/3-100. Definitions

§ 3-100. Definitions. For the purposes of this Chapter, the following words shall have the meanings ascribed to them:

"Electronic" includes electrical, digital, magnetic, optical, electromagnetic, or any other form of technology that entails capabilities similar to these technologies.

"Electronic record" means a record generated, communicated, received, or stored by electronic means for use in an information system or for transmission from one information system to another.

"Electronic signature" means a signature in electronic form attached to or logically associated with an electronic record.

"Owner" means a person who holds legal document of ownership of a vehicle, limited to a certificate of origin, certificate of title, salvage certificate, or junking certificate. However, in the event a vehicle is the subject of an agreement for the conditional sale or lease thereof with the right of purchase upon performance of the conditions stated in the agreement and with an immediate right of possession vested in the conditional vendee or lessee, or in the event a mortgagor of such vehicle is entitled to possession, then such conditional vendee or lessee or mortgagor shall be deemed the owner for the purpose of this Chapter, except as provided under paragraph (c) of Section 3-118.

"Record" means information that is inscribed, stored, or otherwise fixed on a tangible medium or that is stored in an electronic or other medium and is retrievable in perceivable form.

"Signature" or "signed" includes any symbol executed or adopted, or any security procedure employed or adopted, using electronic means or otherwise, by or on behalf of a person with intent to authenticate a record.

P.A. 76–1586, § 3–100, added by P.A. 78–858, § 1, eff. Jan. 1, 1974. Amended by P.A. 78–1205, § 1, eff. Sept. 5, 1974; P.A. 78–1297, § 58, eff. March 4, 1975; P.A. 83–831, § 1, eff. Jan. 1, 1984; P.A. 91–79, § 5, eff. July 9, 1999; P.A. 91–357, § 231, eff. July 29, 1999; P.A. 91–772, § 5, Jan. 1, 2001.

Formerly Ill.Rev.Stat.1991, ch. 95 ½, ¶ 3–100.

P.A. 91–772 incorporated the amendments by P.A. 91–79 and P.A. 91–357.

5/3–100.1. Use of electronic records

§ 3–100.1. Use of electronic records.

(a) To the extent authorized by the Secretary of State and in accordance with standards and procedures prescribed by the Secretary of State:

(1) Certificates, certifications, affidavits, applications, assignments, statements, notices, documents, and other records required under this Chapter may be created, distributed, and received in electronic form.

(2) Signatures required under this Chapter may be made as electronic signatures or may be waived.

(3) Delivery of records required under this Chapter may be made by any means, including electronic delivery.

(4) Fees and taxes required to be paid under this Chapter may be made by electronic means; provided that any forms, records, electronic records, and methods of electronic payment relating to the filing and payment of taxes shall be prescribed by the Department of Revenue.

(b) Electronic records accepted by the Secretary of State have the same force and effect as records created on paper by writing, typing, printing, or similar means. The procedures established by the Secretary of State concerning the acceptance of electronic filings and electronic records shall ensure that the electronic filings and electronic records are received and stored accurately and that they are readily available to satisfy any statutory requirements that call for a written record.

(c) Electronic signatures accepted by the Secretary of State shall have the same force and effect as manual signatures.

(d) Electronic delivery of records accepted by the Secretary of State shall have the same force and effect as physical delivery of records.

(e) Electronic records and electronic signatures accepted by the Secretary of State shall be admissible in all administrative, quasi-judicial, and judicial proceedings. In any such proceeding, nothing in the application of the rules of evidence shall apply so as to deny the admissibility of an electronic record or electronic signature into evidence on the sole ground that it is an electronic record or electronic signature, or on the grounds that it is not in its original form or is not an original. Information in the form of an electronic record shall be given due evidentiary weight by the trier of fact.

P.A. 76–1586, § 3–100.1, added by P.A. 91–772, § 5, eff. Jan. 1, 2001.

5/3–100.2. Electronic access; agreements with submitters

§ 3–100.2. Electronic access; agreements with submitters.

(a) The Secretary of State may allow, but not require, a person to submit any record required to be submitted to the Secretary of State by using electronic media deemed feasible by the Secretary of State, instead of requiring the actual submittal of the original paper record. The Secretary of State may also allow, but not require, a person to receive any record to be provided by the Secretary of State by using electronic media deemed feasible by the Secretary of State, instead of providing the original paper record.

(b) Electronic submittal, receipt, and delivery of records and electronic signatures may be authorized or accepted by the Secretary of State, when supported by a signed agreement between the Secretary of State and the submitter. The agreement shall require, at a minimum, each record to include all information necessary to complete a transaction, certification by the submitter upon its best knowledge as to the truthfulness of the data to be submitted to the Secretary of State, and retention by the submitter of supporting records.

(c) The Secretary of State may establish minimum transaction volume levels, audit and security standards, technological requirements, and other terms and conditions he or she deems necessary for approval of the electronic delivery process.

(d) When an agreement is made to accept electronic records, the Secretary of State shall not be required to produce a written record for the submitter with whom the Secretary of State has the agreement until requested to do so by the submitter.

(e) Upon the request of a lienholder submitter, the Secretary of State shall provide electronic notification to the lienholder submitter to verify the notation and perfection of the lienholder's security interest in a vehicle for which the certificate of title is an electronic record. Upon receipt of an electronic message from a lienholder submitter with a security interest in a vehicle for which the certificate of title is an electronic record that the lien should be released, the Secretary of State shall enter the appropriate electronic record of the release of lien and print and mail a paper certificate of title to the owner or lienholder at no expense. The Secretary of State may also mail the certificate to any other person that delivers to the Secretary of State an authorization from the owner to receive the certificate. If another lienholder holds a properly perfected security interest in the vehicle as reflected in the records of the Secretary of State, the certificate shall be delivered to that lienholder instead of the owner.

P.A. 76–1586, § 3–100.2, added by P.A. 91–772, § 5, eff. Jan. 1, 2001.

5/3-100.3. Rules

§ 3-100.3. Rules. The Secretary of State may adopt rules to implement this Article.

P.A. 76-1586, § 3-100.3, added by P.A. 91-772, § 5, eff. Jan. 1, 2001.

5/3-101. Certificate of title required

§ 3-101. Certificate of title required. (a) Except as provided in Section 3-102, every owner of a vehicle which is in this State and for which no certificate of title has been issued by the Secretary of State shall make application to the Secretary of State for a certificate of title of the vehicle.

(b) Every owner of a motorcycle or motor driven cycle purchased new on and after January 1, 1980 shall make application to the Secretary of State for a certificate of title. However, if such cycle is not properly manufactured or equipped for general highway use pursuant to the provisions of this Act, it shall not be eligible for license registration, but shall be issued a distinctive certificate of title except as provided in Sections 3-102 and 3-110 of this Act.

(c) The Secretary of State shall not register or renew the registration of a vehicle unless a certificate of title has been issued by the Secretary of State to the owner or an application therefor has been delivered by the owner to the Secretary of State.

(d) Every owner of an all-terrain vehicle or off-highway motorcycle purchased on or after January 1, 1998 shall make application to the Secretary of State for a certificate of title.

P.A. 76-1586, § 3-101, eff. July 1, 1970. Amended by P.A. 81-561, § 1, eff. Jan. 1, 1980; P.A. 90-287, § 100, eff. Jan. 1, 1998.

Formerly Ill.Rev.Stat.1991, ch. 95 ½, ¶ 3-101.

5/3-102. Exclusions

§ 3-102. Exclusions.

No certificate of title need be obtained for:

1. A vehicle owned by the State of Illinois; or a vehicle owned by the United States unless it is registered in this State;

2. A vehicle owned by a manufacturer or dealer and held for sale, even though incidentally moved on the highway or used for purposes of testing or demonstration, provided a dealer reassignment area is still available on the manufacturer's certificate of origin or the Illinois title; or a vehicle used by a manufacturer solely for testing;

3. A vehicle owned by a non-resident of this State and not required by law to be registered in this State;

4. A motor vehicle regularly engaged in the interstate transportation of persons or property for which a currently effective certificate of title has been issued in another State;

5. A vehicle moved solely by animal power;

6. An implement of husbandry;

7. Special mobile equipment;

8. An apportionable trailer or an apportionable semitrailer registered in the State prior to April 1, 1998.

P.A. 76-1586, § 3-102, eff. July 1, 1970. Amended by P.A. 89-710, § 15, eff. Feb. 14, 1997; P.A. 91-441, § 10, eff. Jan. 1, 2000.

Formerly Ill.Rev.Stat.1991, ch. 95 ½, ¶ 3-102.

5/3-103. Optional certificate of title

§ 3-103. Optional certificate of title. The owner of an implement of husbandry or special mobile equipment may apply for and obtain a certificate of title on it. All of the provisions of this Chapter, except part (e) of Section 3-104, are applicable to a certificate of title so issued, except that a person who receives a transfer of an interest in the vehicle without knowledge of the certificate of title is not prejudiced by reason of the existence of the certificate, and the perfection of a security interest under this Act is not effective until the lienholder has complied with the provisions of applicable law which otherwise relate to the perfection of security interests in personal property.

An application for an optional certificate of title must be accompanied by either an exemption determination from the Department of Revenue showing that no tax imposed under the "Use Tax Act" [1] or the "Retailers' Occupation Tax Act" [2] is owed by anyone with respect to that vehicle or by a receipt from the Department of Revenue showing that any tax so imposed has been paid. No optional certificate of title shall be issued in the absence of such a receipt or exemption determination.

If the proof of payment or of nonliability is, after the issuance of the optional certificate of title, found to be invalid, the Secretary of State shall revoke the optional certificate of title and require that it be returned to him.

P.A. 76-1586, § 3-103, eff. July 1, 1970. Amended by P.A. 78-1165, § 1, eff. Aug. 27, 1974.

Formerly Ill.Rev.Stat.1991, ch. 95 ½, ¶ 3-103.

[1] 35 ILCS 105/1 et seq.

[2] 35 ILCS 120/1 et seq.

5/3-104. Application for certificate of title

§ 3-104. Application for certificate of title.

(a) The application for a certificate of title for a vehicle in this State must be made by the owner to the Secretary of State on the form prescribed and must contain:

1. The name, Illinois residence and mail address of the owner;

2. A description of the vehicle including, so far as the following data exists: Its make, year-model, identifying number, type of body, whether new or used, as to house trailers as defined in Section 1-128 of this Code, the square footage of the house trailer based upon the outside dimensions of the house trailer excluding the length of the tongue and hitch, and, as to vehicles of the second division, whether for-hire, not-for-hire, or both for-hire and not-for-hire;

3. The date of purchase by applicant and, if applicable, the name and address of the person from whom the vehicle was acquired and the names and addresses of any lienholders in the order of their priority and signatures of owners;

4. The current odometer reading at the time of transfer and that the stated odometer reading is one of the following: actual mileage, not the actual mileage or mileage is in excess of its mechanical limits; and

5. Any further information the Secretary of State reasonably requires to identify the vehicle and to enable him to determine whether the owner is entitled to a certificate of title and the existence or nonexistence of security interests in the vehicle.

(b) If the application refers to a vehicle purchased from a dealer, it must also be signed by the dealer as well as the owner, and the dealer must promptly mail or deliver the application and required documents to the Secretary of State.

(c) If the application refers to a vehicle last previously registered in another State or country, the application must contain or be accompanied by:

1. Any certified document of ownership so recognized and issued by the other State or country and acceptable to the Secretary of State, and

2. Any other information and documents the Secretary of State reasonably requires to establish the ownership of the vehicle and the existence or nonexistence of security interests in it.

(d) If the application refers to a new vehicle it must be accompanied by the Manufacturer's Statement of Origin, or other documents as required and acceptable by the Secretary of State, with such assignments as may be necessary to show title in the applicant.

(e) If an application refers to a vehicle rebuilt from a vehicle previously salvaged, that application shall comply with the provisions set forth in Sections 3–302 through 3–304 of this Code.

(f) An application for a certificate of title for any vehicle, whether purchased in Illinois or outside Illinois, and even if previously registered in another State, must be accompanied by either an exemption determination from the Department of Revenue showing that no tax imposed pursuant to the Use Tax Act [1] or the vehicle use tax imposed by Section 3–1001 of the Illinois Vehicle Code is owed by anyone with respect to that vehicle, or a receipt from the Department of Revenue showing that any tax so imposed has been paid. An application for a certificate of title for any vehicle purchased outside Illinois, even if previously registered in another state, must be accompanied by either an exemption determination from the Department of Revenue showing that no tax imposed pursuant to the Municipal Use Tax Act[2] or the County Use Tax Act [3] is owed by anyone with respect to that vehicle, or a receipt from the Department of Revenue showing that any tax so imposed has been paid. In the absence of such a receipt for payment or determination of exemption from the Department, no certificate of title shall be issued to the applicant.

If the proof of payment of the tax or of nonliability therefor is, after the issuance of the certificate of title and display certificate of title, found to be invalid, the Secretary of State shall revoke the certificate and require that the certificate of title and, when applicable, the display certificate of title be returned to him.

(g) If the application refers to a vehicle not manufactured in accordance with federal safety and emission standards, the application must be accompanied by all documents required by federal governmental agencies to meet their standards before a vehicle is allowed to be issued title and registration.

(h) If the application refers to a vehicle sold at public sale by a sheriff, it must be accompanied by the required fee and a bill of sale issued and signed by a sheriff. The bill of sale must identify the new owner's name and address, the year model, make and vehicle identification number of the vehicle, court order document number authorizing such sale, if applicable, and the name and address of any lienholders in order of priority, if applicable.

(i) If the application refers to a vehicle for which a court of law determined the ownership, it must be accompanied with a certified copy of such court order and the required fee. The court order must indicate the new owner's name and address, the complete description of the vehicle, if known, the name and address of the lienholder, if any, and must be signed and dated by the judge issuing such order.

(j) If the application refers to a vehicle sold at public auction pursuant to the Labor and Storage Lien (Small Amount) Act,[4] it must be accompanied by an affidavit or affirmation furnished by the Secretary of State along with the documents described in the affidavit or affirmation and the required fee.

P.A. 76–1586, § 3–104, eff. July 1, 1970. Amended by P.A. 76–2129, § 1, eff. July 1, 1970; P.A. 78–858, § 1, eff. Jan. 1, 1974; P.A. 78–1142, § 3, eff. Aug. 26, 1974; P.A. 78–1205, § 1, eff. Sept. 5, 1974; P.A. 78–1297, § 30, eff. March 4, 1975; P.A. 81–3, 2nd Sp.Sess., § 19, eff. Jan. 1, 1980; P.A. 81–557, § 1, eff. Jan. 1, 1980; P.A. 81–1509, Art. I, § 57, eff. Sept. 26, 1980; P.A. 83–1473, § 1, eff. Jan. 1, 1985; P.A. 85–277, § 1, eff. Sept. 5, 1987; P.A. 85–1396, § 2, eff. Sept. 2, 1988; P.A. 86–444, § 1, eff. Jan. 1, 1990; P.A. 86–541, § 1, eff. Jan. 1, 1991; P.A. 86–1028, Art. II, § 2–44, eff. Feb. 5, 1990; P.A. 87–206, § 1, eff. Sept. 3, 1991; P.A. 88–45, Art. II, § 2–54, eff. July 6, 1993; P.A. 90–212, § 5, eff. Jan. 1, 1998; P.A. 90–422, § 5, eff. Aug. 15, 1997; P.A. 90–655, § 153, eff. July 30, 1998.

Formerly Ill.Rev.Stat.1991, ch. 95 ½, ¶ 3–104.

1 35 ILCS 105/1 et seq.

2 65 ILCS 5/8–11–6.

3 Former Ill.Rev.Stat. ch. 34, ¶ 409.10 (repealed).

4 770 ILCS 50/0.01 et seq.

P.A. 90–655, the First 1998 General Revisory Act, amended various Acts to delete obsolete text, to correct patent and technical errors, to revise cross references, to resolve multiple actions in the 89th and 90th General Assemblies and to make certain technical corrections in P.A. 89–708 through P.A. 90–566.

5/3–104.1. § 3–104.1. Repealed by P.A. 90–665, § 50, eff. Jan. 1, 1999

5/3–105. Examination of records

§ 3–105. Examination of records. The Secretary of State, upon receiving application for a first certificate of title, shall check the identifying number of the vehicle shown in the application against the records of vehicles required to be maintained by Section 3–107 and against the record of stolen and converted vehicles required to be maintained by Section 4–107.

P.A. 76–1586, § 3–105, eff. July 1, 1970.

Formerly Ill.Rev.Stat.1991, ch. 95 ½, ¶ 3–105.

5/3–106. Certificate of title—Issuance—Records

§ 3–106. Certificate of title—Issuance—Records. (a) The Secretary of State shall file each application received and, when satisfied as to its genuineness and regularity, and that no tax imposed by the "Use Tax Act" [1] or the vehicle use tax, as imposed by Section 3–1001 of "The Illinois Vehicle Code", or pursuant to the "Municipal Use Tax Act" [2] or pursuant to the "County Use Tax Act" [3] is owed as evidenced by the receipt for payment or determination of exemption from the Department of Revenue provided for in Section 3–104 of this Act, and that the applicant is entitled to the issuance of a certificate of title, shall issue a certificate of title of the vehicle.

(b) The Secretary of State shall maintain a record of all certificates of title issued by him under a distinctive title number assigned to the vehicle; and, in the discretion of the Secretary of State, in any other method determined.

P.A. 76–1586, § 3–106, eff. July 1, 1970. Amended by P.A. 76–2130, § 1, eff. July 1, 1970; P.A. 78–1142, § 3, eff. Aug. 26, 1974; P.A. 81–3, 2nd Sp.Sess. § 19, eff. Jan. 1, 1980; P.A. 86–444, § 1, eff. Jan. 1, 1990.

Formerly Ill.Rev.Stat.1991, ch. 95 ½, ¶ 3-106.

[1] 35 ILCS 105/1 et seq.

[2] 65 ILCS 5/8-11-6.

[3] Former Ill.Rev.Stat. ch. 34, ¶ 409.10 (repealed).

5/3-107. Contents and effect

§ 3-107. Contents and effect. (a) Each certificate of title issued by the Secretary of State shall contain:

1. the date issued;
2. the name and address of the owner;
3. the names and addresses of any lienholders, in the order of priority as shown on the application or, if the application is based on a certificate of title, as shown on the certificate;
4. the title number assigned to the vehicle;
5. a description of the vehicle including, so far as the following data exists: its make, year-model, identifying number, type of body, whether new or used, as to house trailers as defined in Section 1-128 of this Code, the square footage of the vehicle based upon the outside dimensions of the house trailer excluding the length of the tongue and hitch, and, if a new vehicle, the date of the first sale of the vehicle for use;
6. an odometer certification as provided for in this Code; and
7. any other data the Secretary of State prescribes.

(b) The certificate of title shall contain forms for assignment and warranty of title by the owner, and for assignment and warranty of title by a dealer, and may contain forms for applications for a certificate of title by a transferee, the naming of a lienholder and the assignment or release of the security interest of a lienholder.

(c) A certificate of title issued by the Secretary of State is prima facie evidence of the facts appearing on it.

(d) A certificate of title for a vehicle is not subject to garnishment, attachment, execution or other judicial process, but this subsection does not prevent a lawful levy upon the vehicle.

(e) Any certificate of title issued by the Secretary of State is subject to a lien in favor of the State of Illinois for any fees or taxes required to be paid under this Act and as have not been paid, as provided for in this Code.

P.A. 76-1586, § 3-107, eff. July 1, 1970. Amended by P.A. 77-641, § 1, eff. Aug. 4, 1971; P.A. 81-557, § 1, eff. Jan. 1, 1980; P.A. 81-1409, § 1, eff. Aug. 25, 1980; P.A. 85-1396, § 2, eff. Sept. 2, 1988; P.A. 86-541, § 1, eff. Jan. 1, 1991; P.A. 86-1028, Art. III, § 3-29, eff. Feb. 5, 1990; P.A. 87-206, § 1, eff. Sept. 3, 1991.

Formerly Ill.Rev.Stat.1991, ch. 95 ½, ¶ 3-107.

5/3-107.1. Presumption of tenancy

§ 3-107.1. Presumption of tenancy. When a certificate of title is made out to 2 or more persons, it shall be presumed that the title is held as joint tenants with right of survivorship.

P.A. 76-1586, § 3-107.1, added by P.A. 78-284, § 1, eff. Jan. 1, 1974. Amended by P.A. 79-482, § 2, eff. Oct. 1, 1975; P.A. 79-512, § 2, eff. Oct. 1, 1975; P.A. 79-1454, § 17[77], eff. Aug. 31, 1976.

Formerly Ill.Rev.Stat.1991, ch. 95 ½, ¶ 3-107.1.

5/3-108. Delivery

§ 3-108. Delivery.

The certificate of title shall be mailed or delivered to the first lienholder named in it or, if none, to the owner.

P.A. 76-1586, § 3-108, eff. July 1, 1970. Amended by P.A. 91-78, § 5, eff. July 9, 1999.

Formerly Ill.Rev.Stat.1991, ch. 95 ½, ¶ 3-108.

5/3-109. Registration without certificate of title; bond

§ 3-109. Registration without certificate of title; bond.

If the Secretary of State is not satisfied as to the ownership of the vehicle or that there are no undisclosed security interests in it, the Secretary of State may register the vehicle but shall either:

(a) Withhold issuance of a certificate of title until the applicant presents documents reasonably sufficient to satisfy the Secretary of State as to the applicant's ownership of the vehicle and that there are no undisclosed security interests in it; or

(b) As a condition of issuing a certificate of title, require the applicant to file with the Secretary of State a bond in the form prescribed by the Secretary of State and executed by the applicant, and either accompanied by the deposit of cash with the Secretary of State or also executed by a person authorized to conduct a surety business in this State. The bond shall be in an amount equal to one and one-half times the value of the vehicle as determined by the Secretary of State and conditioned to indemnify any prior owner and lienholder and any subsequent purchaser of the vehicle or person acquiring any security interest in it, and their respective successors in interest, against any expense, loss or damage, including reasonable attorney's fees, by reason of the issuance of the certificate of title of the vehicle or on account of any defect in or undisclosed security interest upon the right, title and interest of the applicant in and to the vehicle. Any such interested person has a right of action to recover on the bond for any breach of its conditions, but the aggregate liability of the surety to all persons shall not exceed the amount of the bond. The bond, and any deposit accompanying it, shall be returned at the end of three (3) years or prior thereto if the vehicle is no longer registered in this State and the currently valid certificate of title is surrendered to the Secretary of State, unless the Secretary of State has been notified of the pendency of an action to recover on the bond.

Security deposited as a bond hereunder shall be placed by the Secretary of State in the custody of the State Treasurer.

(c) During July, annually, the Secretary shall compile a list of all bonds on deposit, pursuant to this Section, for more than 3 years and concerning which he has received no notice as to the pendency of any judicial proceeding that could affect the disposition thereof. Thereupon, he shall promptly send a notice by certified mail to the last known address of each depositor advising him that his bond will be subject to escheat to the State of Illinois if not claimed within 30 days after the mailing date of such notice. At the expiration of such time, the Secretary of State shall file with the State Treasurer an order directing the transfer of such deposit to the Road Fund in the State Treasury. Upon receipt of such order, the State Treasurer shall make such transfer, after converting to cash any other type of security. Thereafter any person having a legal claim against such deposit may enforce it by appropriate proceedings in the Court of Claims subject to the limitations prescribed for such Court. At the expiration of such limitation period such deposit shall escheat to the State of Illinois.

P.A. 76–1586, § 3–109, eff. July 1, 1970. Amended by P.A. 81–1458, § 1, eff. Sept. 8, 1980.

Formerly Ill.Rev.Stat.1991, ch. 95 ½, ¶ 3–109.

5/3–110. Refusing certificate of title

§ 3–110. Refusing certificate of title. The Secretary of State shall refuse issuance of a certificate of title if any required fee is not paid or if he has reasonable grounds to believe that:

(a) The applicant is not the owner of the vehicle;

(b) The application contains a false or fraudulent statement; or

(c) The applicant fails to furnish required information or documents or any additional information the Secretary of State reasonably requires;

(d) The applicant has not paid to the Secretary of State any fees or taxes due under this Act and have not been paid upon reasonable notice and demand.

P.A. 76–1586, § 3–110, eff. July 1, 1970. Amended by P.A. 77–641, § 1, eff. Aug. 4, 1971.

Formerly Ill.Rev.Stat.1991, ch. 95 ½, ¶ 3–110.

5/3–111. Lost, stolen or mutilated certificates

§ 3–111. Lost, stolen or mutilated certificates. (a) If a certificate of title is lost, stolen, mutilated or destroyed or becomes illegible, the first lienholder or, if none, the owner or legal representative of the owner named in the certificate, as shown by the records of the Secretary of State, shall promptly make application for and may obtain a duplicate upon furnishing information satisfactory to the Secretary of State. The duplicate certificate of title shall contain the legend "This is a duplicate certificate and may be subject to the rights of a person under the original certificate." It shall be mailed to the first lienholder named in it or, if none, to the owner or the owner's designee.

(b) The Secretary of State shall not issue a duplicate certificate of title to any person within 15 days after the issuance of an original certificate of title to such person.

(c) A person recovering an original certificate of title for which a duplicate has been issued shall promptly surrender the original certificate to the Secretary of State.

(d) An application for a duplicate certificate of title must state the current vehicle odometer reading at the time of application and that the stated odometer reading is one of the following: actual mileage, not the actual mileage or mileage is in excess of its mechanical limits.

(e) If a Display certificate of title is lost, stolen, mutilated or destroyed or becomes illegible, the owner or legal representative of the owner named in the original Display certificate of title and in the certificate of title, as shown by the records of the Secretary of State, shall promptly make application for and may obtain a duplicate upon furnishing information satisfactory to the Secretary of State. The duplicate Display certificate of title shall contain the legend "Duplicate Display Certificate of Title." It shall be mailed to the owner or legal representative of the owner named in the original Display certificate of title and in the certificate of title. Such duplicate Display certificate of title shall be attached and displayed in the same manner and in the same place as the original Display certificate of title would have been attached and displayed had it not been lost, stolen, mutilated or destroyed or had it not become illegible.

P.A. 76–1586, § 3–111, eff. July 1, 1970. Amended by P.A. 85–457, § 1, eff. July 1, 1988; P.A. 85–1396, § 2, eff. Sept. 2, 1988; P.A. 86–444, § 1, eff. Jan. 1, 1990.

Formerly Ill.Rev.Stat.1991, ch. 95 ½, ¶ 3–111.

5/3–111.1. Corrected certificates

§ 3–111.1. Corrected certificates. An application for a corrected certificate of title must state the current vehicle odometer reading at the time of application and that the stated odometer reading is one of the following: actual mileage, not the actual mileage or mileage is in excess of its mechanical limits. The corrected certificate issued under this Section shall contain the notation "corrected".

P.A. 76–1586, § 3–111.1, added by P.A. 85–457, § 1, eff. July 1, 1988. Amended by P.A. 86–444, § 1, eff. Jan. 1, 1990; P.A. 90–212, § 5, eff. Jan. 1, 1998.

Formerly Ill.Rev.Stat.1991, ch. 95 ½, ¶ 3–111.1.

5/3–112. Transfer

§ 3–112. Transfer.

(a) If an owner transfers his interest in a vehicle, other than by the creation of a security interest, at the time of the delivery of the vehicle he shall execute to the transferee an assignment and warranty of title in the space provided on the certificate of title, or as the Secretary of State prescribes, and cause the certificate and assignment to be mailed or delivered to the transferee or to the Secretary of State.

If the vehicle is subject to a tax under the Mobile Home Local Services Tax Act [1] in a county with a population of less than 3,000,000, the owner shall also provide to the transferee a certification by the treasurer of the county in which the vehicle is situated that all taxes imposed upon the vehicle for the years the owner was the actual titleholder of the vehicle have been paid. The transferee shall be liable only for the taxes he or she incurred while he or she was the actual titleholder of the mobile home. The county treasurer shall refund any amount of taxes paid by the transferee that were imposed in years when the transferee was not the actual titleholder. The provisions of this amendatory Act of 1997 (P.A. 90–542) apply retroactively to January 1, 1996. In no event may the county treasurer refund amounts paid by the transferee during any year except the 10 years immediately preceding the year in which the refund is made. If the owner is a licensed dealer who has purchased the vehicle and is holding it for resale, in lieu of acquiring a certification from the county treasurer he shall forward the certification received from the previous owner to the next buyer of the vehicle. The owner shall cause the certification to be mailed or delivered to the Secretary of State with the certificate of title and assignment.

(b) Except as provided in Section 3–113, the transferee shall, promptly and within 20 days after delivery to him of the vehicle and the assigned title, execute the application for a new certificate of title in the space provided therefor on the certificate or as the Secretary of State prescribes, and cause the certificate and application to be mailed or delivered to the Secretary of State.

(c) Upon request of the owner or transferee, a lienholder in possession of the certificate of title shall, unless the transfer was a breach of his security agreement, either deliver the certificate to the transferee for delivery to the Secretary of State or, upon receipt from the transferee of the owner's assignment, the transferee's application for a new certificate and the required fee, mail or deliver them to the

Secretary of State. The delivery of the certificate does not affect the rights of the lienholder under his security agreement.

(d) If a security interest is reserved or created at the time of the transfer, the certificate of title shall be retained by or delivered to the person who becomes the lienholder, and the parties shall comply with the provisions of Section 3-203.

(e) Except as provided in Section 3-113 and as between the parties, a transfer by an owner is not effective until the provisions of this Section and Section 3-115 have been complied with; however, an owner who has delivered possession of the vehicle to the transferee and has complied with the provisions of this Section and Section 3-115 requiring action by him as not liable as owner for any damages thereafter resulting from operation of the vehicle.

(f) The Secretary of State shall not process any application for a transfer of an interest in a vehicle if any fees or taxes due under this Act from the transferor or the transferee have not been paid upon reasonable notice and demand.

(g) If the Secretary of State receives an application for transfer of a vehicle subject to a tax under the Mobile Home Local Services Tax Act in a county with a population of less than 3,000,000, such application must be accompanied by the required certification by the county treasurer or tax assessor authorizing the issuance of the title.

P.A. 76-1586, § 3-112, eff. July 1, 1970. Amended by P.A. 77-641, § 1, eff. Aug. 4, 1971; P.A. 83-871, § 1, eff. Sept. 26, 1983; P.A. 86-226, § 1, eff. Jan. 1, 1990; P.A. 86-460, § 2, eff. Jan. 1, 1990; P.A. 86-1028, Art. II, § 2-44, eff. Feb. 5, 1990; P.A. 90-212, § 5, eff. Jan. 1, 1998; P.A. 90-542, § 5, eff. Dec. 1, 1997; P.A. 90-655, § 153, eff. July 30, 1998; P.A. 92-651, § 77, eff. July 11, 2002.

Formerly Ill.Rev.Stat.1991, ch. 95 ½, ¶ 3-112.

[1] 35 ILCS 515/1 et seq.

P.A. 90-655, the First 1998 General Revisory Act, amended various Acts to delete obsolete text, to correct patent and technical errors, to revise cross references, to resolve multiple actions in the 89th and 90th General Assemblies and to make certain technical corrections in P.A. 89-708 through P.A. 90-566.

5/3-112.1. Odometer

§ 3-112.1. Odometer.

(a) All titles issued by the Secretary of State beginning January, 1990, shall provide for an odometer certification substantially as follows:

"I certify to the best of my knowledge that the odometer reading is and reflects the actual mileage of the vehicle unless one of the following statements is checked.

....

( ) 1. The mileage stated is in excess of its mechanical limits.

( ) 2. The odometer reading is not the actual mileage. Warning—Odometer Discrepancy."

(b) When executing any transfer of title which contains the odometer certification as described in paragraph (a) above, each transferor of a motor vehicle must supply on the title form the following information:

(1) The odometer reading at the time of transfer and an indication if the mileage is in excess of its mechanical limits or if it is not the actual mileage;

(2) The date of transfer;

(3) The transferor's printed name and signature; and

(4) The transferee's printed name and address.

(c) The transferee must sign on the title form indicating that he or she is aware of the odometer certification made by the transferor.

(d) The transferor will not be required to disclose the current odometer reading and the transferee will not have to acknowledge such disclosure under the following circumstances:

(1) A vehicle having a Gross Vehicle Weight Rating of more than 16,000 pounds;

(2) A vehicle that is not self-propelled;

(3) A vehicle that is 10 years old or older;

(4) A vehicle sold directly by the manufacturer to any agency of the United States; and

(5) A vehicle manufactured without an odometer.

(e) When the transferor signs the title transfer such transferor acknowledges that he or she is aware that Federal regulations and State law require him or her to state the odometer mileage upon transfer of ownership. An inaccurate or untruthful statement with intent to defraud subjects the transferor to liability for damages to the transferee pursuant to the federal Motor Vehicle Information and Cost Act of 1972, P.L. 92-513 as amended by P.L. 94-364.[1] No transferor shall be liable for damages as provided under this Section who transfers title to a motor vehicle which has an odometer reading that has been altered or tampered with by a previous owner, unless that transferor knew or had reason to know of such alteration or tampering and sold such vehicle with an intent to defraud. A cause of action is hereby created by which any person who, with intent to defraud, violates any requirement imposed under this Section shall be liable in an amount equal to the sum of:

(1) three times the amount of actual damages sustained or $1,500, whichever is the greater; and

(2) in the case of any successful action to enforce the foregoing liability, the costs of the action together with reasonable attorney fees as determined by the court.

Any recovery based on a cause of action under this Section shall be offset by any recovery made pursuant to the federal Motor Vehicle Information and Cost Savings Act of 1972.

(f) The provisions of this Section shall not apply to any motorcycle, motor driven cycle, moped or antique vehicle.

(g) The Secretary of State may adopt rules and regulations providing for a transition period for all non-conforming titles.

P.A. 76-1586, § 3-112.1, added by P.A. 81-1409, § 1, eff. Aug. 25, 1980. Amended by P.A. 85-1396, § 2, eff. Sept. 2, 1988; P.A. 86-444, § 1, eff. Jan. 1, 1990; P.A. 86-500, § 1, eff. Jan. 1, 1990; P.A. 86-1028, Art. II, § 2-44, eff. Feb. 5, 1990; P.A. 88-415, § 10, eff. Aug. 20, 1993; P.A. 91-357, § 231, eff. July 29, 1999; P.A. 92-651, § 77, eff. July 11, 2002.

Formerly Ill.Rev.Stat.1991, ch. 95 ½, ¶ 3-112.1.

[1] 15 U.S.C.A. § 1901 et seq.

5/3-113. Transfer to or from dealer; records

§ 3-113. Transfer to or from dealer; records.

(a) If a dealer buys a vehicle and holds it for resale and procures the certificate of title from the owner or the lienholder within 10 days after delivery to him of the vehicle, he need not send the certificate to the Secretary of State but, upon transferring the vehicle to another person other than by the creation of a security interest, shall promptly and within 20 days execute the assignment and warranty of title by a dealer, showing the names and addresses of the transferee and of any lienholder holding a security interest created or reserved at the time of the resale, in the spaces provided therefor on the certificate or as the Secretary of State prescribes, and mail or deliver the certificate to the Secretary of State with the transferee's application for a new certificate, except as provided in Section 3-117.2.

(b) The Secretary of State may decline to process any application for a transfer of an interest in a vehicle if any fees or taxes due under this Code from the transferor or the transferee have not been paid upon reasonable notice and demand.

(c) Any person who violates this Section shall be guilty of a petty offense.

P.A. 76-1586, § 3-113, eff. July 1, 1970. Amended by P.A. 77-641, § 1, eff. Aug. 4, 1971; P.A. 83-1473, § 1, eff. Jan. 1, 1985; P.A. 85-1204, § 1, eff. Aug. 26, 1988; P.A. 85-1396, § 2, eff. Sept. 2, 1988; P.A. 86-820, Art. II, § 2-8, eff. Sept. 7, 1989; P.A. 87-1225, § 2, eff. Dec. 22, 1992.

Formerly Ill.Rev.Stat.1991, ch. 95 ½, ¶ 3-113.

5/3-114. Transfer by operation of law

§ 3-114. Transfer by operation of law.

(a) If the interest of an owner in a vehicle passes to another other than by voluntary transfer, the transferee shall, except as provided in paragraph (b), promptly mail or deliver within 20 days to the Secretary of State the last certificate of title, if available, proof of the transfer, and his application for a new certificate in the form the Secretary of State prescribes. It shall be unlawful for any person having possession of a certificate of title for a motor vehicle, semi-trailer, or house car by reason of his having a lien or encumbrance on such vehicle, to fail or refuse to deliver such certificate to the owner, upon the satisfaction or discharge of the lien or encumbrance, indicated upon such certificate of title.

(b) If the interest of an owner in a vehicle passes to another under the provisions of the Small Estates provisions of the Probate Act of 1975 [1]the transferee shall promptly mail or deliver to the Secretary of State, within 120 days, the last certificate of title, if available, the documentation required under the provisions of the Probate Act of 1975, and an application for certificate of title. The Small Estate Affidavit form shall be furnished by the Secretary of State. The transfer may be to the transferee or to the nominee of the transferee.

(c) If the interest of an owner in a vehicle passes to another under other provisions of the Probate Act of 1975, as amended, and the transfer is made by a representative or guardian, such transferee shall promptly mail or deliver to the Secretary of State, the last certificate of title, if available, and a certified copy of the letters of office or guardianship, and an application for certificate of title. Such application shall be made before the estate is closed. The transfer may be to the transferee or to the nominee of the transferee.

(d) If the interest of an owner in joint tenancy passes to the other joint tenant with survivorship rights as provided by law, the transferee shall promptly mail or deliver to the Secretary of State, the last certificate of title, if available, proof of death of the one joint tenant and survivorship of the surviving joint tenant, and an application for certificate of title. Such application shall be made within 120 days after the death of the joint tenant. The transfer may be to the transferee or to the nominee of the transferee.

(e) The Secretary of State shall transfer a decedent's vehicle title to any legatee, representative or heir of the decedent who submits to the Secretary a death certificate and an affidavit by an attorney at law on the letterhead stationery of the attorney at law stating the facts of the transfer.

(f) Repossession with assignment of title. In all cases wherein a lienholder has repossessed a vehicle by other than judicial process and holds it for resale under a security agreement, and the owner of record has executed an assignment of the existing certificate of title after default, the lienholder may proceed to sell or otherwise dispose of the vehicle as authorized under the Uniform Commercial Code.[2] Upon selling the vehicle to another person, the lienholder need not send the certificate of title to the Secretary of State, but shall promptly and within 20 days mail or deliver to the purchaser as transferee the existing certificate of title for the repossessed vehicle, reflecting the release of the lienholder's security interest in the vehicle. The application for a certificate of title made by the purchaser shall comply with subsection (a) of Section 3-104 and be accompanied by the existing certificate of title for the repossessed vehicle. The lienholder shall execute the assignment and warranty of title showing the name and address of the purchaser in the spaces provided therefor on the certificate of title or as the Secretary of State prescribes. The lienholder shall complete the assignment of title in the certificate of title to reflect the transfer of the vehicle to the lienholder and also a reassignment to reflect the transfer from the lienholder to the purchaser. For this purpose, the lienholder is specifically authorized to complete and execute the space reserved in the certificate of title for a dealer reassignment, notwithstanding that the lienholder is not a licensed dealer. Nothing herein shall be construed to mean that the lienholder is taking title to the repossessed vehicle for purposes of liability for retailer occupation, vehicle use, or other tax with respect to the proceeds from the repossession sale. Delivery of the existing certificate of title to the purchaser shall be deemed disclosure to the purchaser of the owner of the vehicle.

(f-5) Repossession without assignment of title. In all cases wherein a lienholder has repossessed a vehicle by other than judicial process and holds it for resale under a security agreement, and the owner of record has not executed an assignment of the existing certificate of title, the lienholder shall comply with the following provisions:

(1) Prior to sale, the lienholder shall deliver or mail to the owner at the owner's last known address and to any other lienholder of record, a notice of redemption setting forth the following information: (i) the name of the owner of record and in bold type at or near the top of the notice a statement that the owner's vehicle was repossessed on a specified date for failure to make payments on the loan (or other reason), (ii) a description of the vehicle subject to the lien sufficient to identify it, (iii) the right of the owner to redeem the vehicle, (iv) the lienholder's intent to sell or otherwise dispose of the vehicle after the expiration of 21 days from the date of mailing or delivery of the notice, and (v) the name, address, and telephone number of the lienholder from whom information may be obtained concerning the amount due to redeem the vehicle and from whom the vehicle may be redeemed under Section 9-623 of the Uniform Commercial Code.[3] At the lienholder's option, the information required to be set forth in this notice of redemption may be made a part of or accompany the notification of sale or other disposition required under Section 9-611 of the Uniform Commercial Code,[4] but none of the information required by this notice shall be construed to impose any requirement under Article 9 of the Uniform Commercial Code.[5]

(2) With respect to the repossession of a vehicle used primarily for personal, family, or household purposes, the lienholder shall also deliver or mail to the owner at the owner's last known address an affidavit of defense. The affidavit of defense shall accompany the notice of redemption required in subdivision (f-5)(1) of this Section. The affidavit of defense shall (i) identify the lienholder, owner, and the vehicle; (ii) provide space for the owner to state the defense claimed by the owner; and (iii) include an acknowledgment by the owner that the owner may be liable to the lienholder for fees, charges, and costs incurred by the lienholder in establishing the insufficiency or invalidity of the owner's defense. To stop the transfer of title, the affidavit of defense must be received by the lienholder no later than 21 days after the date of mailing or delivery of the notice required in subdivision (f-5)(1) of this Section. If the lienholder receives the affidavit from the owner in a timely manner, the lienholder must apply to a court of competent jurisdiction to determine if the lienholder is entitled to possession of the vehicle.

(3) Upon selling the vehicle to another person, the lienholder need not send the certificate of title to the Secretary of State, but shall promptly and within 20 days mail or deliver to the purchaser as transferee (i) the existing certificate of title for the repossessed vehicle, reflecting the release of the lienholder's security interest in the vehicle; and (ii) an affidavit of repossession made by or on behalf of the lienholder which provides the following information: that the vehicle was repossessed, a description of the vehicle sufficient to identify it, whether the vehicle has been damaged in excess of 33 ⅓% of its fair market value as required under subdivision (b)(3) of Section 3-117.1, that the owner and any other lienholder of record were given the notice required in subdivision (f-5)(1) of this Section, that the owner of record was given the affidavit of defense required in subdivision (f-5)(2) of this Section, that the interest of the owner was lawfully terminated or sold pursuant to the terms of the security agreement, and the purchaser's name and address. If the vehicle is damaged in excess of 33 ⅓% of its fair market value, the lienholder shall make application for a salvage certificate under Section 3-117.1 and transfer the vehicle to a person eligible to receive assignments of salvage certificates identified in Section 3-118.

(4) The application for a certificate of title made by the purchaser shall comply with subsection (a) of Section 3-104 and be accompanied by the affidavit of repossession furnished by the lienholder and the existing certificate of title for the repossessed vehicle. The lienholder shall execute the assignment and warranty of title showing the name and address of the purchaser in the spaces provided therefor on the certificate of title or as the Secretary of State prescribes. The lienholder shall complete the assignment of title in the certificate of title to reflect the transfer of the vehicle to the lienholder and also a reassignment to reflect the transfer from the lienholder to the purchaser. For this purpose, the lienholder is specifically authorized to execute the assignment on behalf of the owner as seller if the owner has not done so and to complete and execute the space reserved in the certificate of title for a dealer reassignment, notwithstanding that the lienholder is not a licensed dealer. Nothing herein shall be construed to mean that the lienholder is taking title to the repossessed vehicle for purposes of liability for retailer occupation, vehicle use, or other tax with respect to the proceeds from the repossession sale. Delivery of the existing certificate of title to the purchaser shall be deemed disclosure to the purchaser of the owner of the vehicle. In the event the lienholder does not hold the certificate of title for the repossessed vehicle, the lienholder shall make application for and may obtain a new certificate of title in the name of the lienholder upon furnishing information satisfactory to the Secretary of State. Upon receiving the new certificate of title, the lienholder may proceed with the sale described in subdivision (f-5)(3), except that upon selling the vehicle the lienholder shall promptly and within 20 days mail or deliver to the purchaser the new certificate of title reflecting the assignment and transfer of title to the purchaser.

(5) Neither the lienholder nor the owner shall file with the Office of the Secretary of State the notice of redemption or affidavit of defense described in subdivisions (f-5)(1) and (f-5)(2) of this Section. The Office of the Secretary of State shall not determine the merits of an owner's affidavit of defense, nor consider any allegations or assertions regarding the validity or invalidity of a lienholder's claim to the vehicle or an owner's asserted defenses to the repossession action.

(f-7) Notice of reinstatement in certain cases.

(1) If, at the time of repossession by a lienholder that is seeking to transfer title pursuant to subsection (f-5), the owner has paid an amount equal to 30% or more of the deferred payment price or total of payments due, the owner may, within 21 days of the date of repossession, reinstate the contract or loan agreement and recover the vehicle from the lienholder by tendering in a lump sum (i) the total of all unpaid amounts, including any unpaid delinquency or deferral charges due at the date of reinstatement, without acceleration; and (ii) performance necessary to cure any default other than nonpayment of the amounts due; and (iii) all reasonable costs and fees incurred by the lienholder in retaking, holding, and preparing the vehicle for disposition and in arranging for the sale of the vehicle. Reasonable costs and fees incurred by the lienholder include without limitation repossession and storage expenses and, if authorized by the contract or loan agreement, reasonable attorneys' fees and collection agency charges.

(2) Tender of payment and performance pursuant to this limited right of reinstatement restores to the owner his rights under the contract or loan agreement as though no default had occurred. The owner has the right to reinstate the contract or loan agreement and recover the vehicle from the lienholder only once under this subsection. The lienholder may, in the lienholder's sole discretion, extend the period during which the owner may reinstate the contract or loan agreement and recover the vehicle beyond the 21 days allowed under this subsection, and the extension shall not subject the lienholder to liability to the owner under the laws of this State.

(3) The lienholder shall deliver or mail written notice to the owner at the owner's last known address, within 3 business days of the date of repossession, of the owner's right to reinstate the contract or loan agreement and recover the vehicle pursuant to the limited right of reinstatement described in this subsection. At the lienholder's option, the information required to be set forth in this notice of reinstatement may be made part of or accompany the notice of redemption required in subdivision (f-5)(1) of this Section and the notification of sale or other disposition required under Section 9-611 of the Uniform Commercial Code, but none of the information required by this notice of reinstatement shall be construed to impose any requirement under Article 9 of the Uniform Commercial Code.

(4) The reinstatement period, if applicable, and the redemption period described in subdivision (f–5)(1) of this Section, shall run concurrently if the information required to be set forth in the notice of reinstatement is part of or accompanies the notice of redemption. In any event, the 21 day redemption period described in subdivision (f–5)(1) of this Section shall commence on the date of mailing or delivery to the owner of the information required to be set forth in the notice of redemption, and the 21 day reinstatement period described in this subdivision, if applicable, shall commence on the date of mailing or delivery to the owner of the information required to be set forth in the notice of reinstatement.

(5) The Office of the Secretary of State shall not determine the merits of an owner's claim of right to reinstatement, nor consider any allegations or assertions regarding the validity or invalidity of a lienholder's claim to the vehicle or an owner's asserted right to reinstatement. Where a lienholder is subject to licensing and regulatory supervision by the State of Illinois, the lienholder shall be subject to all of the powers and authority of the lienholder's primary State regulator to enforce compliance with the procedures set forth in this subsection (f–7).

(f–10) Repossession by judicial process. In all cases wherein a lienholder has repossessed a vehicle by judicial process and holds it for resale under a security agreement, order for replevin, or other court order establishing the lienholder's right to possession of the vehicle, the lienholder may proceed to sell or otherwise dispose of the vehicle as authorized under the Uniform Commercial Code or the court order. Upon selling the vehicle to another person, the lienholder need not send the certificate of title to the Secretary of State, but shall promptly and within 20 days mail or deliver to the purchaser as transferee (i) the existing certificate of title for the repossessed vehicle reflecting the release of the lienholder's security interest in the vehicle; (ii) a certified copy of the court order; and (iii) a bill of sale identifying the new owner's name and address and the year, make, model, and vehicle identification number of the vehicle. The application for a certificate of title made by the purchaser shall comply with subsection (a) of Section 3–104 and be accompanied by the certified copy of the court order furnished by the lienholder and the existing certificate of title for the repossessed vehicle. The lienholder shall execute the assignment and warranty of title showing the name and address of the purchaser in the spaces provided therefor on the certificate of title or as the Secretary of State prescribes. The lienholder shall complete the assignment of title in the certificate of title to reflect the transfer of the vehicle to the lienholder and also a reassignment to reflect the transfer from the lienholder to the purchaser. For this purpose, the lienholder is specifically authorized to execute the assignment on behalf of the owner as seller if the owner has not done so and to complete and execute the space reserved in the certificate of title for a dealer reassignment, notwithstanding that the lienholder is not a licensed dealer. Nothing herein shall be construed to mean that the lienholder is taking title to the repossessed vehicle for purposes of liability for retailer occupation, vehicle use, or other tax with respect to the proceeds from the repossession sale. Delivery of the existing certificate of title to the purchaser shall be deemed disclosure to the purchaser of the owner of the vehicle. In the event the lienholder does not hold the certificate of title for the repossessed vehicle, the lienholder shall make application for and may obtain a new certificate of title in the name of the lienholder upon furnishing information satisfactory to the Secretary of State. Upon receiving the new certificate of title, the lienholder may proceed with the sale described in this subsection, except that upon selling the vehicle the lienholder shall promptly and within 20 days mail or deliver to the purchaser the new certificate of title reflecting the assignment and transfer of title to the purchaser.

(f–15) The Secretary of State shall not issue a certificate of title to a purchaser under subsection (f), (f–5), or (f–10) of this Section, unless the person from whom the vehicle has been repossessed by the lienholder is shown to be the last registered owner of the motor vehicle. The Secretary of State may provide by rule for the standards to be followed by a lienholder in assigning and transferring certificates of title with respect to repossessed vehicles.

(f–20) If applying for a salvage certificate or a junking certificate, the lienholder shall within 20 days make an application to the Secretary of State for a salvage certificate or a junking certificate, as set forth in this Code. The Secretary of State shall not issue a salvage certificate or a junking certificate to such lienholder unless the person from whom such vehicle has been repossessed is shown to be the last registered owner of such motor vehicle and such lienholder establishes to the satisfaction of the Secretary of State that he is entitled to such salvage certificate or junking certificate. The Secretary of State may provide by rule for the standards to be followed by a lienholder in order to obtain a salvage certificate or junking certificate for a repossessed vehicle.

(f–25) If the interest of an owner in a mobile home, as defined in the Mobile Home Local Services Tax Act,[6] passes to another under the provisions of the Mobile Home Local Services Tax Enforcement Act, [7] the transferee shall promptly mail or deliver to the Secretary of State (i) the last certificate of title, if available, (ii) a certified copy of the court order ordering the transfer of title, and (iii) an application for certificate of title.

(g) A person holding a certificate of title whose interest in the vehicle has been extinguished or transferred other than by voluntary transfer shall mail or deliver the certificate, within 20 days upon request of the Secretary of State. The delivery of the certificate pursuant to the request of the Secretary of State does not affect the rights of the person surrendering the certificate, and the action of the Secretary of State in issuing a new certificate of title as provided herein is not conclusive upon the rights of an owner or lienholder named in the old certificate.

(h) The Secretary of State may decline to process any application for a transfer of an interest in a vehicle hereunder if any fees or taxes due under this Act from the transferor or the transferee have not been paid upon reasonable notice and demand.

(i) The Secretary of State shall not be held civilly or criminally liable to any person because any purported transferor may not have had the power or authority to make a transfer of any interest in any vehicle or because a certificate of title issued in error is subsequently used to commit a fraudulent act.

P.A. 76–1586, § 3–114, eff. July 1, 1970. Amended by P.A. 77–641, § 1, eff. Aug. 4, 1971; P.A. 78–286, § 1, eff. Aug. 13, 1973; P.A. 78–491, § 1, eff. Oct. 1, 1973; P.A. 78–1297, § 30, eff. March 4, 1975; P.A. 81–445, § 1, eff. Jan. 1, 1980; P.A. 83–388, § 53, eff. Sept. 16, 1983; P.A. 83–449, § 1, eff. Jan. 1, 1984; P.A. 83–706, § 41, eff. Sept. 23, 1983; P.A. 83–1362, Art. II, § 99, eff. Sept. 11, 1984; P.A. 83–1473, § 1, eff. Jan. 1, 1985; P.A. 84–1308, Art. III, § 38, eff. Aug. 25, 1986; P.A. 84–1390, § 3, eff. Sept. 18, 1986; P.A. 85–1396, § 2, eff. Sept. 2, 1988; P.A. 87–1225, § 2, eff. Dec. 22, 1992; P.A. 90–212,

§ 5, eff. Jan. 1, 1998; P.A. 90-665, § 45, eff. Jan. 1, 1999; P.A. 91-893, § 30, eff. July 1, 2001; P.A. 92-807, § 910, eff. Jan. 1, 2003.

Formerly Ill.Rev.Stat.1991, ch. 95 ½, ¶ 3-114.

1 755 ILCS 5/1-1 et seq.

2 810 ILCS 5/1-101 et seq.

3 810 ILCS 5/9-623.

4 810 ILCS 5/9-611.

5 810 ILCS 5/9-101 et seq.

6 35 ILCS 515/1 et seq.

7 35 ILCS 516/1 et seq.

5/3-114.1. Transfers to and from charitable organizations

§ 3-114.1. Transfers to and from charitable organizations. When a charitable not-for-profit organization that is exempt from federal income taxation under Section 501(c)(3) of the Internal Revenue Code [1] becomes the recipient of a motor vehicle by means of a donation from an individual, the organization need not send the certificate of title to the Secretary of State. Upon transferring the motor vehicle, the organization shall promptly and within 20 days execute the reassignment to reflect the transfer from the organization to the purchaser. The organization is specifically authorized to complete and execute the space reserved in the certificate of title for a dealer reassignment, not withstanding that the organization is not a licensed dealer. Nothing in this Section shall be construed to require the organization to become a licensed vehicle dealer.

P.A. 76-1586, § 3-114.1, added by P.A. 92-495, § 5, eff. Jan. 1, 2002.

1 25 U.S.C.A. § 501.

5/3-115. Fees—Registration cards—License plates

§ 3-115. Fees—Registration cards—License plates. (a) An application for a certificate of title shall be accompanied by an application for, or a transfer of, registration of the vehicle.

(b) An application for the naming of a lienholder or his assignee on a certificate of title shall be accompanied by the required fee when mailed or delivered to the Secretary of State.

(c) A transferor of a vehicle, other than a dealer transferring a new vehicle, shall deliver to the transferee at the time of the delivery of possession of the vehicle the properly assigned certificate of title of this vehicle.

(d) All applications shall be accompanied with the required fee or tax.

P.A. 76-1586, § 3-115, eff. July 1, 1970. Amended by P.A. 78-858, § 1, eff. Jan. 1, 1974; P.A. 81-557, § 1, eff. Jan. 1, 1980; P.A. 83-1473, § 1, eff. Jan. 1, 1985.

Formerly Ill.Rev.Stat.1991, ch. 95 ½, ¶ 3-115.

5/3-116. When Secretary of State to issue a certificate of title

§ 3-116. When Secretary of State to issue a certificate of title. (a) The Secretary of State, upon receipt of a properly assigned certificate of title, with an application for a certificate of title, the required fee and any other documents required by law, shall issue a new certificate of title in the name of the transferee as owner and mail it to the first lienholder named in it or, if none, to the owner or owner's designee.

(b) The Secretary of State, upon receipt of an application for a new certificate of title by a transferee other than by voluntary transfer, with proof of the transfer, the required fee and any other documents required by law, shall issue a new certificate of title in the name of the transferee as owner.

(c) Any person, firm or corporation, who shall knowingly possess, buy, sell, exchange or give away, or offer to buy, sell, exchange or give away the certificate of title to any motor vehicle which is a junk or salvage, or who shall fail to surrender the certificate of title to the Secretary of State as required under the provisions of this Section and Section 3-117.2, shall be guilty of Class 3 felony.

(d) The Secretary of State shall file and retain for four (4) years a record of every surrendered certificate of title or proof of ownership accepted by the Secretary of State, the file to be maintained so as to permit the tracing of title of the vehicle designated therein.

(e) The Secretary of State, upon receipt of an application for corrected certificate of title, with the original title, the required fee and any other required documents, shall issue a corrected certificate of title in the name of the owner and mail it to the first lienholder named in it or, if none, to the owner or owner's designee.

(f) The Secretary of State, upon receipt of a certified copy of a court order awarding ownership to an applicant along with an application for a certificate of title and the required fee, shall issue a certificate of title to the applicant.

P.A. 76-1586, § 3-116, eff. July 1, 1970. Amended by P.A. 78-491, § 1, eff. Oct. 1, 1973; P.A. 81-557, § 1, eff. Jan. 1, 1980; P.A. 85-1204, § 1, eff. Aug. 26, 1988; P.A. 85-1396, § 2, eff. Sept. 2, 1988; P.A. 86-820, Art. II, § 2-8, eff. Sept. 7, 1989; P.A. 90-212, § 5, eff. Jan. 1, 1998.

Formerly Ill.Rev.Stat.1991, ch. 95 ½, ¶ 3-116.

5/3-117. § 3-117. Repealed by P.A. 83-1473, § 2, eff. Jan. 1, 1985

5/3-117.1. When junking certificates or salvage certificates must be obtained

§ 3-117.1. When junking certificates or salvage certificates must be obtained.

(a) Except as provided in Chapter 4 of this Code,[1] a person who possesses a junk vehicle shall within 15 days cause the certificate of title, salvage certificate, certificate of purchase, or a similarly acceptable out of state document of ownership to be surrendered to the Secretary of State along with an application for a junking certificate, except as provided in Section 3-117.2, whereupon the Secretary of State shall issue to such a person a junking certificate, which shall authorize the holder thereof to possess, transport, or, by an endorsement, transfer ownership in such junked vehicle, and a certificate of title shall not again be issued for such vehicle.

A licensee who possesses a junk vehicle and a Certificate of Title, Salvage Certificate, Certificate of Purchase, or a similarly acceptable out-of-state document of ownership for such junk vehicle, may transport the junk vehicle to another licensee prior to applying for or obtaining a junking certificate, by executing a uniform invoice. The licensee transferor shall furnish a copy of the uniform invoice to the licensee transferee at the time of transfer. In any case, the licensee transferor shall apply for a junking certificate in conformance with Section 3-117.1 of this Chapter. The following information shall be contained on a uniform invoice:

(1) The business name, address and dealer license number of the person disposing of the vehicle, junk vehicle or vehicle cowl;

(2) The name and address of the person acquiring the vehicle, junk vehicle or vehicle cowl, and if that person is a dealer, the Illinois or out-of-state dealer license number of that dealer;

(3) The date of the disposition of the vehicle, junk vehicle or vehicle cowl;

(4) The year, make, model, color and description of each vehicle, junk vehicle or vehicle cowl disposed of by such person;

(5) The manufacturer's vehicle identification number, Secretary of State identification number or Illinois Department of State Police number, for each vehicle, junk vehicle or vehicle cowl part disposed of by such person;

(6) The printed name and legible signature of the person or agent disposing of the vehicle, junk vehicle or vehicle cowl; and

(7) The printed name and legible signature of the person accepting delivery of the vehicle, junk vehicle or vehicle cowl.

The Secretary of State may certify a junking manifest in a form prescribed by the Secretary of State that reflects those vehicles for which junking certificates have been applied or issued. A junking manifest may be issued to any person and it shall constitute evidence of ownership for the vehicle listed upon it. A junking manifest may be transferred only to a person licensed under Section 5–301 of this Code as a scrap processor. A junking manifest will allow the transportation of those vehicles to a scrap processor prior to receiving the junk certificate from the Secretary of State.

(b) An application for a salvage certificate shall be submitted to the Secretary of State in any of the following situations:

(1) When an insurance company makes a payment of damages on a total loss claim for a vehicle, the insurance company shall be deemed to be the owner of such vehicle and the vehicle shall be considered to be salvage except that ownership of (i) a vehicle that has incurred only hail damage that does not affect the operational safety of the vehicle or (ii) any vehicle 9 model years of age or older may, by agreement between the registered owner and the insurance company, be retained by the registered owner of such vehicle. The insurance company shall promptly deliver or mail within 20 days the certificate of title along with proper application and fee to the Secretary of State, and a salvage certificate shall be issued in the name of the insurance company. An insurer making payment of damages on a total loss claim for the theft of a vehicle may exchange the salvage certificate for a certificate of title if the vehicle is recovered without damage. In such a situation, the insurer shall fill out and sign a form prescribed by the Secretary of State which contains an affirmation under penalty of perjury that the vehicle was recovered without damage and the Secretary of State may, by rule or regulation, require photographs to be submitted.

(2) When a vehicle the ownership of which has been transferred to any person through a certificate of purchase from acquisition of the vehicle at an auction, other dispositions as set forth in Sections 4–208 and 4–209 of this Code, a lien arising under Section 18a–501 of this Code, or a public sale under the Abandoned Mobile Home Act[2] shall be deemed salvage or junk at the option of the purchaser. The person acquiring such vehicle in such manner shall promptly deliver or mail, within 20 days after the acquisition of the vehicle, the certificate of purchase, the proper application and fee, and, if the vehicle is an abandoned mobile home under the Abandoned Mobile Home Act, a certification from a local law enforcement agency that the vehicle was purchased or acquired at a public sale under the Abandoned Mobile Home Act to the Secretary of State and a salvage certificate or junking certificate shall be issued in the name of that person. The salvage certificate or junking certificate issued by the Secretary of State under this Section shall be free of any lien that existed against the vehicle prior to the time the vehicle was acquired by the applicant under this Code.

(3) A vehicle which has been repossessed by a lienholder shall be considered to be salvage only when the repossessed vehicle, on the date of repossession by the lienholder, has sustained damage by collision, fire, theft, rust corrosion, or other means so that the cost of repairing such damage, including labor, would be greater than 33 ⅓% of its fair market value without such damage. If the lienholder determines that such vehicle is damaged in excess of 33 ⅓% of such fair market value, the lienholder shall, before sale, transfer or assignment of the vehicle, make application for a salvage certificate, and shall submit with such application the proper fee and evidence of possession. If the facts required to be shown in subsection (f) of Section 3–114 are satisfied, the Secretary of State shall issue a salvage certificate in the name of the lienholder making the application. In any case wherein the vehicle repossessed is not damaged in excess of 33 ⅓% of its fair market value, the lienholder shall comply with the requirements of subsections (f), (f–5), and (f–10) of Section 3–114, except that the affidavit of repossession made by or on behalf of the lienholder shall also contain an affirmation under penalty of perjury that the vehicle on the date of sale is not damaged in excess of 33 ⅓% of its fair market value. If the facts required to be shown in subsection (f) of Section 3–114 are satisfied, the Secretary of State shall issue a certificate of title as set forth in Section 3–116 of this Code. The Secretary of State may by rule or regulation require photographs to be submitted.

(4) A vehicle which is a part of a fleet of more than 5 commercial vehicles registered in this State or any other state or registered proportionately among several states shall be considered to be salvage when such vehicle has sustained damage by collision, fire, theft, rust, corrosion or similar means so that the cost of repairing such damage, including labor, would be greater than 33 ⅓% of the fair market value of the vehicle without such damage. If the owner of a fleet vehicle desires to sell, transfer, or assign his interest in such vehicle to a person within this State other than an insurance company licensed to do business within this State, and the owner determines that such vehicle, at the time of the proposed sale, transfer or assignment is damaged in excess of 33 ⅓% of its fair market value, the owner shall, before such sale, transfer or assignment, make application for a salvage certificate. The application shall contain with it evidence of possession of the vehicle. If the fleet vehicle at the time of its sale, transfer, or assignment is not damaged in excess of 33 ⅓% of its fair market value, the owner shall so state in a written affirmation on a form prescribed by the Secretary of State by rule or regulation. The Secretary of State may by rule or regulation require photographs to be submitted. Upon sale, transfer or assignment of the fleet vehicle the owner shall mail the affirmation to the Secretary of State.

(5) A vehicle that has been submerged in water to the point that rising water has reached over the door sill and has entered the passenger or trunk compartment is a

"flood vehicle". A flood vehicle shall be considered to be salvage only if the vehicle has sustained damage so that the cost of repairing the damage, including labor, would be greater than 33 ⅓% of the fair market value of the vehicle without that damage. The salvage certificate issued under this Section shall indicate the word "flood", and the word "flood" shall be conspicuously entered on subsequent titles for the vehicle. A person who possesses or acquires a flood vehicle that is not damaged in excess of 33 ⅓% of its fair market value shall make application for title in accordance with Section 3-116 of this Code, designating the vehicle as "flood" in a manner prescribed by the Secretary of State. The certificate of title issued shall indicate the word "flood", and the word "flood" shall be conspicuously entered on subsequent titles for the vehicle.

(c) Any person who without authority acquires, sells, exchanges, gives away, transfers or destroys or offers to acquire, sell, exchange, give away, transfer or destroy the certificate of title to any vehicle which is a junk or salvage vehicle shall be guilty of a Class 3 felony.

(d) Any person who knowingly fails to surrender to the Secretary of State a certificate of title, salvage certificate, certificate of purchase or a similarly acceptable out-of-state document of ownership as required under the provisions of this Section is guilty of a Class A misdemeanor for a first offense and a Class 4 felony for a subsequent offense; except that a person licensed under this Code who violates paragraph (5) of subsection (b) of this Section is guilty of a business offense and shall be fined not less than $1,000 nor more than $5,000 for a first offense and is guilty of a Class 4 felony for a second or subsequent violation.

(e) Any vehicle which is salvage or junk may not be driven or operated on roads and highways within this State. A violation of this subsection is a Class A misdemeanor. A salvage vehicle displaying valid special plates issued under Section 3-601(b) of this Code, which is being driven to or from an inspection conducted under Section 3-308 of this Code, is exempt from the provisions of this subsection. A salvage vehicle for which a short term permit has been issued under Section 3-307 of this Code is exempt from the provisions of this subsection for the duration of the permit.

P.A. 76-1586, § 3-117.1, added by P.A. 83-1473, § 1, eff. Jan. 1, 1985. Amended by P.A. 84-1302, § 1, eff. Jan. 1, 1987; P.A. 84-1304, § 1, eff. Jan. 1, 1987; P.A. 85-311, § 1, eff. Sept. 10, 1987; P.A. 85-572, § 1, eff. Sept. 18, 1987; P.A. 85-1204, § 1, eff. Aug. 26, 1988; P.A. 85-1209, Art. II, § 2-51, eff. Aug. 30, 1988; P.A. 85-1440, Art. II, § 2-54, eff. Feb. 1, 1989; P.A. 86-566, § 1, eff. Jan. 1, 1990; P.A. 86-1209, § 1, eff. Jan. 1, 1991; P.A. 86-1214, § 1, eff. Jan. 1, 1991; P.A. 86-1475, Art. 2, § 2-25, eff. Jan. 10, 1991; P.A. 87-1225, § 2, eff. Dec. 22, 1992; P.A. 88-516, § 95, eff. July 1, 1994; P.A. 88-685, § 5, eff. Jan. 24, 1995; P.A. 89-669, § 10, eff. Jan. 1, 1997; P.A. 90-665, § 45, eff. Jan. 1, 1999; P.A. 92-751, § 5, eff. Aug. 2, 2002.

Formerly Ill.Rev.Stat.1991, ch. 95 ½, ¶ 3-117.1.

1 625 ILCS 5/4-100 et seq.

2 210 ILCS 117/1 et seq.

5/3-117.2. Junk Vehicle Notification

§ 3-117.2. Junk Vehicle Notification. Beginning July 1, 1989 a person licensed as a scrap processor pursuant to Section 5-301 of this Code who acquires a properly assigned Certificate of Title, a Salvage Certificate, a Certificate of Purchase, or a similarly acceptable out-of-state document of ownership pursuant to Section 5-401.3 of this Code, shall within 15 days of acquiring such document, submit it to the Secretary of State along with a Junk Vehicle Notification, the form and manner for which shall be as prescribed by Secretary of State rule or regulation. A scrap processor who acquires the above named documents of ownership pursuant to Section 5-401.3 shall not be required to apply for or obtain a junking certificate. The information contained on a Junk Vehicle Notification shall be duly recorded by the Secretary of State upon the receipt of such Notification. The Secretary of State shall not again issue a Certificate of Title or Salvage Certificate for any vehicle listed on a Junk Vehicle Notification.

P.A. 76-1586, § 3-117.2, added by P.A. 85-1204, § 1, eff. Aug. 26, 1988.

Formerly Ill.Rev.Stat.1991, ch. 95 ½, ¶ 3-117.2.

5/3-118. Application for salvage or junking certificate; contents

§ 3-118. Application for salvage or junking certificate; contents. (a) An application for a salvage certificate or junking certificate shall be made upon the forms prescribed by the Secretary of State and contain:

1. The name and address of the owner;
2. A description of the vehicle including, so far as the following data exists: its make, year-model, identifying number, type of body, whether new or used;
3. The date of purchase by applicant; and
4. Any further information reasonably required by the Secretary of State.

(b) The application for salvage certificate must also contain the current odometer reading and that the stated odometer reading is one of the following: actual mileage, not the actual mileage or mileage is in excess of its mechanical limits.

(c) A salvage certificate may be assigned to any person licensed under this Act as a rebuilder, automotive parts recycler, scrap processor or an out-of-state salvage vehicle buyer. A junking certificate may be assigned to anyone. The provisions for reassignment by dealers under paragraph (a) of Section 3-113 shall apply to salvage certificates, except as provided in Section 3-117.2. A salvage certificate may be reassigned to one other person licensed under this Act.

P.A. 76-1586, § 3-118, eff. July 1, 1970. Amended by P.A. 78-858, § 1, eff. Jan. 1, 1974; P.A. 78-1205, § 1, eff. Sept. 5, 1974; P.A. 78-1297, § 58, eff. March 4, 1975; P.A. 83-1473, § 1, eff. Jan. 1, 1985; P.A. 84-1302, § 1, eff. Jan. 1, 1987; P.A. 84-1304, § 1, eff. Jan. 1, 1987; P.A. 85-572, § 1, eff. Sept. 18, 1987; P.A. 85-951, § 1, eff. July 1, 1988; P.A. 85-1204, § 1, eff. Aug. 26, 1988; P.A. 85-1209, Art. II, § 2-51, eff. Aug. 30, 1988; P.A. 86-444, § 1, eff. Jan. 1, 1990; P.A. 87-206, § 1, eff. Sept. 3, 1991.

Formerly Ill.Rev.Stat.1991, ch. 95 ½, ¶ 3-118.

5/3-118.1. Title certificates for salvaged vehicles; total loss from theft

§ 3-118.1. Whenever a certificate of title is issued for a vehicle with respect to which a salvage certificate has been previously issued, the new certificate of title shall bear the notation "REBUILT". However, insurance companies or persons licensed under Section 5-301 who are also licensed as a used vehicle dealer under Section 5-102 of this Code may exchange a salvage certificate for a certificate of title which does not bear the notation "REBUILT" when there is submitted with the application satisfactory proof that the salvage certificate was obtained because of a claim of total loss from theft and the vehicle was recovered without structural damage caused by collision, fire, flood, theft, rust, or corrosion. The Secretary may adopt rules governing the issuance of titles authorized under this Section.

P.A. 76-1586, § 3-118.1, added by P.A. 81-988, § 1, eff. Jan. 1, 1980. Amended by P.A. 83-306, § 1, eff. Jan. 1, 1984; P.A. 86-1179, § 2, eff. Aug. 17, 1990; P.A. 89-189, § 5, eff. Jan. 1, 1996.

Formerly Ill.Rev.Stat.1991, ch. 95 ½, ¶ 3-118.1.

5/3-119 to 5/3-121. §§ 3-119 to 3-121. Repealed by P.A. 85-1374, § 2, eff. Jan. 1, 1989

ARTICLE II. SECURITY INTERESTS

5/3-201. Excepted liens and security interests

§ 3-201. Excepted liens and security interests.

This Article does not apply to or affect:

(a) A lien given by statute or rule of law to a supplier of services or materials for the vehicle;

(b) A lien given by statute to the United States, this State or any political subdivision of this State, except liens on trailer coaches and mobile homes for public assistance, as provided in Section 3-12 (now repealed) of the Illinois Public Aid Code.[1]

(c) A security interest in a vehicle created by a manufacturer or dealer who holds the vehicle for sale, but a buyer in the ordinary course of trade from the manufacturer or dealer takes free of the security interest.

P.A. 76-1586, § 3-201, eff. July 1, 1970. Amended by P.A. 90-655, § 153, eff. July 30, 1998.

Formerly Ill.Rev.Stat.1991, ch. 95 ½, ¶ 3-201.

[1] 305 ILCS 5/3-12 (repealed).

5/3-201.1. Terminal rent adjustment clause leases

§ 3-201.1. Terminal rent adjustment clause leases. In the case of motor vehicles or trailers, a transaction does not create a sale or a security interest merely because it provides that the rental price is permitted or required to be adjusted under the agreement either upward or downward by reference to the amount realized upon sale or other disposition of the motor vehicle or trailer.

P.A. 76-1586, § 3-201.1, added by P.A. 87-493, § 5, eff. Jan. 1, 1992.

Formerly Ill.Rev.Stat.1991, ch. 95 ½, ¶ 3-201.1.

5/3-202. Perfection of security interest

§ 3-202. Perfection of security interest.

(a) Unless excepted by Section 3-201, a security interest in a vehicle of a type for which a certificate of title is required is not valid against subsequent transferees or lienholders of the vehicle unless perfected as provided in this Act.

(b) A security interest is perfected by the delivery to the Secretary of State of the existing certificate of title, if any, an application for a certificate of title containing the name and address of the lienholder and the required fee. The security interest is perfected as of the time of its creation if the delivery to the Secretary of State is completed within 21 days after the creation of the security interest or receipt by the new lienholder of the existing certificate of title from a prior lienholder or licensed dealer, otherwise as of the time of the delivery.

(c) If a vehicle is subject to a security interest when brought into this State, the validity of the security interest is determined by the law of the jurisdiction where the vehicle was when the security interest attached, subject to the following:

1. If the parties understood at the time the security interest attached that the vehicle would be kept in this State and it was brought into this State within 30 days thereafter for purposes other than transportation through this State, the validity of the security interest in this State is determined by the law of this State.

2. If the security interest was perfected under the law of the jurisdiction where the vehicle was when the security interest attached, the following rules apply:

(A) If the name of the lienholder is shown on an existing certificate of title issued by that jurisdiction, his security interest continues perfected in this State.

(B) If the name of the lienholder is not shown on an existing certificate of title issued by that jurisdiction, a security interest may be perfected by the lienholder delivering to the Secretary of State the prescribed notice and by payment of the required fee. Such security interest is perfected as of the time of delivery of the prescribed notice and payment of the required fee.

3. If the security interest was not perfected under the law of the jurisdiction where the vehicle was when the security interest attached, it may be perfected in this State; in that case perfection dates from the time of perfection in this State.

4. A security interest may be perfected under paragraph 3 of this subsection either as provided in subsection (b) or by the lienholder delivering to the Secretary of State a notice of security interest in the form the Secretary of State prescribes and the required fee.

P.A. 76-1586, § 3-202, eff. July 1, 1970. Amended by P.A. 81-557, § 1, eff. Jan. 1, 1980; P.A. 91-893, § 31, eff. July 6, 2000.

Formerly Ill.Rev.Stat.1991, ch. 95 ½, ¶ 3-202.

5/3-203. Security interest

§ 3-203. Security interest. If an owner creates a security interest in a vehicle:

(a) The owner shall immediately execute the application, in the space provided therefor on the certificate of title or on a separate form the Secretary of State prescribes, to name the lienholder on the certificate, showing the name and address of the lienholder and cause the certificate, application and the required fee to be delivered to the lienholder.

(b) The lienholder shall immediately cause the certificate, application and the required fee to be mailed or delivered to the Secretary of State.

(c) Upon request of the owner or subordinate lienholder, a lienholder in possession of the certificate of title shall either mail or deliver the certificate to the subordinate lienholder for delivery to the Secretary of State or, upon receipt from the subordinate lienholder of the owner's application and the required fee, mail or deliver them to the Secretary of State with the certificate. The delivery of the certificate does not affect the rights of the first lienholder under his security agreement.

(d) Upon receipt of the certificate of title, application and the required fee, the Secretary of State shall issue a new certificate containing the name and address of the new lienholder, and mail the certificate to the first lienholder named in it.

P.A. 76-1586, § 3-203, eff. July 1, 1970. Amended by P.A. 81-557, § 1, eff. Jan. 1, 1980; P.A. 85-511, § 1, eff. Jan. 1, 1988.

Formerly Ill.Rev.Stat.1991, ch. 95 ½, ¶ 3-203.

5/3-204. Assignment by lienholder

§ 3-204. Assignment by lienholder. (a) A lienholder may assign, absolutely or otherwise, his security interest in the vehicle to a person other than the owner without affecting the interest of the owner or the validity of the security interest, but any person without notice of the assignment is protected in dealing with the lienholder as the holder of the security interest and the lienholder remains liable for any obligations as lienholder until the assignee is named as lienholder on the certificate.

(b) The assignee may, but need not to perfect the assignment, have the certificate of title issued with the assignee named as lienholder, upon delivering to the Secretary of State the certificate and an assignment by the lienholder named in the certificate in the form the Secretary of State prescribes.

P.A. 76-1586, § 3-204, eff. July 1, 1970. Amended by P.A. 85-511, § 1, eff. Jan. 1, 1988.

Formerly Ill.Rev.Stat.1991, ch. 95 ½, ¶ 3-204.

5/3-205. Release of security interest

§ 3-205. Release of security interest. (a) Upon the satisfaction of a security interest in a vehicle for which the certificate of title is in the possession of the lienholder, he shall, within ten (10) days after demand and, in any event, within thirty (30) days, execute a release of his security interest, and mail or deliver the certificate and release to the next lienholder named therein, or, if none, to the owner or any person who delivers to the lienholder an authorization from the owner to receive the certificate. If the owner desires a new certificate reflecting no lien, the certificate and release from the lienholder may be submitted to the Secretary of State, along with the prescribed application and required fee, for issuance of that new certificate.

(b) Upon the satisfaction of a security interest in a vehicle for which the certificate of title is in the possession of a prior lienholder, the lienholder whose security interest is satisfied shall within ten (10) days after demand and, in any event, within thirty (30) days execute a release and deliver the release to the owner or any person who delivers to the lienholder an authorization from the owner to receive it. The lienholder in possession of the certificate of title may either deliver the certificate to the owner, or the person authorized by him, for delivery to the Secretary of State, or, upon receipt of the release, may mail or may deliver the certificate and release, along with prescribed application and require fee, to the Secretary of State, who shall issue a new certificate.

P.A. 76-1586, § 3-205, eff. July 1, 1970. Amended by P.A. 81-557, § 1, eff. Jan. 1, 1980.

Formerly Ill.Rev.Stat.1991, ch. 95 ½, ¶ 3-205.

5/3-206. Duty of lienholder

§ 3-206. Duty of lienholder. A lienholder named in a certificate of title shall, upon written request of the owner or of another lienholder named on the certificate, disclose any pertinent information as to his security agreement and the indebtedness secured by it.

P.A. 76-1586, § 3-206, eff. July 1, 1970.

Formerly Ill.Rev.Stat.1991, ch. 95 ½, ¶ 3-206.

5/3-207. Exclusiveness of procedure

§ 3-207. Exclusiveness of procedure. The method provided in this act of perfecting and giving notice of security interests subject to this act is exclusive. Security interests subject to this act are hereby exempted from the provisions of law which otherwise require or relate to the recording or filing of instruments creating or evidencing security interests in vehicles including chattel mortgages and conditional sale agreements.

P.A. 76-1586, § 3-207, eff. July 1, 1970.

Formerly Ill.Rev.Stat.1991, ch. 95 ½, ¶ 3-207.

5/3-208. Suspension or revocation of certificates

§ 3-208. Suspension or revocation of certificates. (a) The Secretary of State may suspend or revoke a certificate of title, upon notice and reasonable opportunity to be heard in accordance with Section 2-118, when authorized by any other provision of law or if he finds:

1. The certificate of title was fraudulently procured or erroneously issued, or

2. The vehicle has been scrapped, dismantled or destroyed.

(b) Suspension or revocation of a certificate of title does not, in itself, affect the validity of a security interest noted on it.

(c) When the Secretary of State suspends or revokes a certificate of title, the owner or person in possession of it shall, immediately upon receiving notice of the suspension or revocation, mail or deliver the certificate to the Secretary of State.

(d) The Secretary of State may seize and impound any certificate of title which has been suspended or revoked.

P.A. 76-1586, § 3-208, eff. July 1, 1970.

Formerly Ill.Rev.Stat.1991, ch. 95 ½, ¶ 3-208.

5/3-209. Powers of Secretary of State

§ 3-209. Powers of Secretary of State. (a) The Secretary of State shall prescribe and provide suitable forms of applications, certificates of title, notices of security interests, and all other notices and forms necessary to carry out the provisions of this chapter.

(b) The Secretary of State may:

1. Make necessary investigations to procure information required to carry out the provisions of this Act;

2. Assign a new identifying number to a vehicle if it has none, or its identifying number is destroyed or obliterated, or its motor is changed, and shall either issue a new certificate

of title showing the new identifying number or make an appropriate endorsement on the original certificate.

P.A. 76–1586, § 3–209, eff. July 1, 1970.

Formerly Ill.Rev.Stat.1991, ch. 95 ½, ¶ 3–209.

5/3–210. Court review

§ 3–210. Court review. A person aggrieved by an act or omission to act of the Secretary of State under this Article is also entitled to a review thereof by the Circuit Court of Sangamon County in accordance with the Administrative Review Law, as amended.[1]

P.A. 76–1586, § 3–210, eff. July 1, 1970. Amended by P.A. 82–783, Art. XI, § 140, eff. July 13, 1982.

Formerly Ill.Rev.Stat.1991, ch. 95 ½, ¶ 3–210.

[1] 735 ILCS 5/3–101 et seq.

ARTICLE III. CERTIFICATE OF TITLE—REBUILT VEHICLES

Date Effective

Article III was added by P.A. 83–1473, § 1, eff. Jan. 1, 1985.

Section

5/3–301. New certificate of title for rebuilt vehicle

§ 3–301. New certificate of title for rebuilt vehicle. (a) For vehicles 8 model years of age or newer, the Secretary of State shall issue a new certificate of title to any rebuilt vehicle or any vehicle which previously had been titled as salvage in this State or any other jurisdiction upon the successful inspection of the vehicle in accordance with Section 3–308 of this Article.

(b) Vehicles more than 8 model years old shall not be required to complete a successful inspection required under Section 3–308 of this Code before being issued a new certificate of title as provided under this Section.

(c) Vehicles designated as flood vehicles that have sustained damage greater than 33⅓% of their fair market value with that damage shall be required to complete a successful inspection required under Section 3–308 of this Code before being issued a new certificate of title provided under paragraph (5), subsection (b) of Section 3–117.1.

P.A. 76–1586, § 3–301, added by P.A. 83–1473, § 1, eff. Jan. 1, 1985. Amended by P.A. 84–1302, § 1, eff. Jan. 1, 1987; P.A. 84–1304, § 1, eff. Jan. 1, 1987; P.A. 88–685, § 5, eff. Jan. 24, 1995; P.A. 89–669, § 10, eff. Jan. 1, 1997.

Formerly Ill.Rev.Stat.1991, ch. 95 ½, ¶ 3–301.

5/3–302. Application for title; contents

§ 3–302. Application for title; contents. Every application for a certificate of title for a rebuilt vehicle shall be made upon a form prescribed by the Secretary of State, and shall include the following:

1. The name, residence and mailing address of the owner;

2. A description of the vehicle including, so far as the following data exists: its make, year-model, identifying number, type of body, whether new or used, and as to vehicles of the second division, whether for-hire, not-for-hire, or both for-hire and not-for-hire;

3. The date of purchase by applicant, the name and address of the person from whom the vehicle was acquired and the names and addresses of any lienholders in the order of their priority;

4. The current odometer reading at the time of transfer and that the stated odometer reading is one of the following: actual mileage, not the actual mileage or mileage is in excess of its mechanical limits; and

5. Any further information the Secretary of State reasonably requires to identify the vehicle and to enable him to determine whether the owner is entitled to a certificate of title and the existence or nonexistence of security interests in the vehicle.

P.A. 76–1586, § 3–302, added by P.A. 83–1473, § 1, eff. Jan. 1, 1985. Amended by P.A. 85–951, § 1, eff. July 1, 1988; P.A. 86–444, § 1, eff. Jan. 1, 1990; P.A. 87–206, § 1, eff. Sept. 3, 1991; P.A. 92–651, § 77, eff. July 11, 2002.

Formerly Ill.Rev.Stat.1991, ch. 95 ½, ¶ 3–302.

5/3–303. Application for title—attachments

§ 3–303. Application for title—attachments. Every application for a certificate of title for a rebuilt vehicle shall be accompanied by the following:

1. The salvage certificate or out-of-state title certificate previously issued for the rebuilt vehicle;

2. Bills of sale and other documents evidencing the acquisition of all essential parts used to rebuild the vehicle;

3. Photographs of the rebuilt vehicle if required by rule of the Secretary of State;

4. A Certificate of Safety furnished by the Department of Transportation as set forth in Section 13–109; and

5. A listing of all replaced essential parts of the rebuilt vehicle, and the identification number of the vehicle or vehicles from which the essential parts originated.

P.A. 76–1586, § 3–303, added by P.A. 83–1473, § 1, eff. Jan. 1, 1985. Amended by P.A. 85–572, § 1, eff. Sept. 18, 1987; P.A. 85–951, § 1, eff. July 1, 1988; P.A. 85–1209, Art. II, § 2–51, eff. Aug. 30, 1988.

Formerly Ill.Rev.Stat.1991, ch. 95 ½, ¶ 3–303.

P.A. 85–1209, the First 1988 Revisory Act, provides in Art. II, for the nonsubstantive revision or renumbering or repeal of certain sections of Acts of the 85th General Assembly through P.A. 85–1014, and corrects errors, revises cross-references and deletes obsolete text in such sections.

5/3–304. Application for title—affirmation

§ 3–304. Application for title—affirmation. The applicant applying for a certificate of title for a rebuilt vehicle shall sign a written affirmation which states the following:

1. He personally rebuilt the vehicle, personally supervised its rebuilding or contracted for rebuilding with a licensed rebuilder;

2. He personally inspected the completed vehicle, and it complies with all safety requirements set forth in this Code and any regulations promulgated thereunder by the Secretary of State;

3. The identification numbers of the rebuilt vehicle and its parts have not, to the knowledge of the applicant, been removed, destroyed, falsified, altered or defaced;

4. The salvage certificate or out-of-state title certificate attached to the application has not, to the knowledge of the applicant, been forged, falsified, altered or counterfeited; and

5. All information contained on the application and its attachments is true and correct to the knowledge of the applicant.

P.A. 76-1586, § 3-304, added by P.A. 83-1473, § 1, eff. Jan. 1, 1985. Amended by P.A. 85-572, § 1, eff. Sept. 18, 1987.

Formerly Ill.Rev.Stat.1991, ch. 95 ½, ¶ 3-304.

5/3-305. Inspection fee

§ 3-305. Inspection fee. The fee for the inspection of a rebuilt vehicle shall be $94. All such fees received by the Secretary of State shall be deposited into the Road Fund.

P.A. 76-1586, § 3-305 added by P.A. 83-1473, § 1, eff. Jan. 1, 1985. Amended by P.A. 84-1302, § 1, eff. Jan. 1, 1987; P.A. 84-1304, § 1, eff. Jan. 1, 1987; P.A. 91-37, § 40, eff. July 1, 1999.

Formerly Ill.Rev.Stat.1991, ch. 95 ½, ¶ 3-305.

5/3-306. Retention of documents

§ 3-306. Retention of documents. The original documents required to be submitted to the Secretary of State pursuant to Sections 3-301 through 3-305 shall be retained by the Secretary of State for a period determined by Secretary of State by rule or regulation.

P.A. 76-1586, § 3-306, added by P.A. 83-1473, § 1, eff. Jan. 1, 1985. Amended by P.A. 83-1528, Art. II, § 24, eff. Jan. 17, 1985.

Formerly Ill.Rev.Stat.1991, ch. 95 ½, ¶ 3-306.

5/3-307. Short term permit

§ 3-307. Short term permit. The Secretary of State shall issue at no charge a short term permit for any vehicle for which an application for a certificate of title has been made under this Article and which must be driven on the roads and highways of this State to a place of inspection.

P.A. 76-1586, § 3-307, added by P.A. 83-1473, § 1, eff. Jan. 1, 1985. Amended by P.A. 84-1302, § 1, eff. Jan. 1, 1987; P.A. 84-1304, § 1, eff. Jan. 1, 1987.

Formerly Ill.Rev.Stat.1991, ch. 95 ½, ¶ 3-307.

The amendments by P.A. 84-1302 and P.A. 84-1304 were identical.

5/3-308. Inspection of rebuilt vehicles

§ 3-308. Inspection of rebuilt vehicles.

(a) The Secretary of State shall inspect any vehicle 8 model years of age or newer for which an application for a certificate of title for a rebuilt vehicle will be submitted, or any foreign vehicle which is or may have been salvage as defined under the provisions of this Code.

(b) The inspection of the vehicle shall include an examination of the vehicle and its parts and of the application and proof of notification, if applicable, to determine that:

(1) the identification numbers of the vehicle or its parts have not been removed, falsified, altered, defaced, destroyed, or tampered with;

(2) all information contained in the application for a certificate of title is true and correct; and

(3) there are no indications that the vehicle or any of its parts have been stolen.

(c) The Secretary of State shall, by rule or regulation, carry out and implement the provisions contained in this Section.

(d) All fees received by the Secretary of State from the inspection of vehicles under this Section shall be applied towards the maintenance of the vehicle inspection program and the personnel costs required for the operation of such program.

P.A. 76-1586, § 3-308, added by P.A. 83-1473, § 1, eff. Jan. 1, 1985. Amended by P.A. 84-1302, § 1, eff. Jan. 1, 1987; P.A. 84-1304, § 1, eff. Jan. 1, 1987; P.A. 89-433, § 5, eff. Dec. 15, 1995.

Formerly Ill.Rev.Stat.1991, ch. 95 ½, ¶ 3-308.

ARTICLE IV. ORIGINAL AND RENEWAL OF REGISTRATION

Section

5/3-400. Definition

§ 3-400. Definition. Notwithstanding the definition set forth in Chapter 1 of this Act,[1] for the purposes of this Article, the following words shall have the meaning ascribed to them as follows:

"Apportionable Fee" means any periodic recurring fee required for licensing or registering vehicles, such as, but not limited to, registration fees, license or weight fees.

"Apportionable Vehicle" means any vehicle, except recreational vehicles, vehicles displaying restricted plates, city pickup and delivery vehicles, buses used in transportation of chartered parties, and government owned vehicles that are used or intended for use in 2 or more member jurisdictions that allocate or proportionally register vehicles, in a fleet which is used for the transportation of persons for hire or the transportation of property and which has a gross vehicle weight in excess of 26,000 pounds; or has three or more axles regardless of weight; or is used in combination when the weight of such combination exceeds 26,000 pounds gross vehicle weight. Vehicles, or combinations having a gross vehicle weight of 26,000 pounds or less and two-axle vehicles may be proportionally registered at the option of such owner.

"Base Jurisdiction" means, for purposes of fleet registration, the jurisdiction where the registrant has an established place of business, where operational records of the fleet are maintained and where mileage is accrued by the fleet. In case a registrant operates more than one fleet, and maintains records for each fleet in different places, the "base jurisdiction" for a fleet shall be the jurisdiction where an established place of business is maintained, where records of the operation of that fleet are maintained and where mileage is accrued by that fleet.

"Operational Records" means documents supporting miles traveled in each jurisdiction and total miles traveled, such as fuel reports, trip leases, and logs.

Owner. A person who holds legal title of a motor vehicle, or in the event a motor vehicle is the subject of an agreement for the conditional sale or lease thereof with the right of purchase upon performance of the conditions stated in the agreement and with an immediate right of possession vested in the conditional vendee or lessee with right of purchase, or in the event a mortgagor of such motor vehicle is entitled to possession, or in the event a lessee of such motor vehicle is entitled to possession or control, then such conditional vendee or lessee with right of purchase or mortgagor or lessee is considered to be the owner for the purpose of this Act.

"Rental Owner" means an owner principally engaged, with respect to one or more rental fleets, in renting to others or offering for rental the vehicles of such fleets, without drivers.

"Restricted Plates" shall include but are not limited to dealer, manufacturer, transporter, farm, repossessor, and permanently mounted type plates. Vehicles displaying any of these type plates from a foreign jurisdiction that is a member of the International Registration Plan shall be granted reciprocity but shall be subject to the same limitations as similar plated Illinois registered vehicles.

P.A. 76-1586, § 3-400, eff. July 1, 1970. Amended by P.A. 79-1041, § 1, eff. Jan. 1, 1976; P.A. 81-1509, Art. II, § 71, eff. Sept. 26, 1980; P.A. 84-300, § 1, eff. Sept. 13, 1985; P.A. 87-1041, § 1, eff. Sept. 11, 1993; P.A. 89-571, § 5, eff. July 26, 1996; P.A. 90-89, § 15, eff. Jan. 1, 1998.

Formerly Ill.Rev.Stat.1991, ch. 95 ½, ¶ 3-400.

[1] 625 ILCS 5/1-100 et seq.

5/3-401. Effect of provisions

§ 3-401. Effect of provisions.

(a) It shall be unlawful for any person to violate any provision of this Chapter or to drive or move or for an owner knowingly to permit to be driven or moved upon any highway any vehicle of a type required to be registered hereunder which is not registered or for which the appropriate fee has not been paid when and as required hereunder, except that when application accompanied by proper fee has been made for registration of a vehicle it may be operated temporarily pending complete registration upon displaying a duplicate application duly verified or other evidence of such application or otherwise under rules and regulations promulgated by the Secretary of State.

(b) The appropriate fees required to be paid under the various provisions of this Act for registration of vehicles shall mean the fee or fees which would have been paid initially, if proper and timely application had been made to the Secretary of State for the appropriate registration required, whether such registration be a flat weight registration, a single trip permit, a reciprocity permit or a supplemental application to an original prorate application together with payment of fees due under the supplemental application for prorate decals.

(c) Effective October 1, 1984, no vehicle required to pay a Federal Highway Users Tax shall be registered unless proof of payment, in a form prescribed and approved by the Secretary of State, is submitted with the appropriate registration. Notwithstanding any other provision of this Code, failure of the applicant to comply with this paragraph shall be deemed grounds for the Secretary to refuse registration.

(d) Second division vehicles.

(1) A vehicle of the second division moved or operated within this State shall have had paid for it the appropriate registration fees and flat weight tax, as evidenced by the Illinois registration issued for that vehicle, for the gross weight of the vehicle and load being operated or moved within this State. Second division vehicles of foreign jurisdictions operated within this State under a single trip permit, fleet reciprocity plan, prorate registration plan, or apportional registration plan, instead of second division vehicle registration under Article VIII of this Chapter,[1] must have had paid for it the appropriate registration fees and flat weight tax in the base jurisdiction of that vehicle, as evidenced by the maximum gross weight shown on the foreign registration cards, plus any appropriate fees required under this Code.

(2) If a vehicle and load are operated in this State and the appropriate fees and taxes have not been paid or the vehicle and load exceed the registered gross weight for which the required fees and taxes have been paid by 2001 pounds or more, the operator or owner shall be fined as provided in Section 15-113 of this Code. However, an owner or operator shall not be subject to arrest under this subsection for any weight in excess of 80,000 pounds. Further, for any unregistered vehicle or vehicle displaying expired registration, no fine shall exceed the actual cost of what the appropriate registration for that vehicle and load should have been as established in subsection (a) of Section 3-815 of this Chapter regardless of the route traveled.

(3) Any person operating a legal combination of vehicles displaying valid registration shall not be considered in violation of the registration provision of this subsection unless the total gross weight of the combination exceeds the total licensed weight of the vehicles in the combination. The gross weight of a vehicle exempt from the registration

requirements of this Chapter shall not be included when determining the total gross weight of vehicles in combination.

(4) If the defendant claims that he or she had previously paid the appropriate Illinois registration fees and taxes for this vehicle before the alleged violation, the defendant shall have the burden of proving the existence of the payment by competent evidence. Proof of proper Illinois registration issued by the Secretary of State, or the appropriate registration authority from the foreign state, shall be the only competent evidence of payment.

P.A. 76-1586, § 3-401, eff. July 1, 1970. Amended by P.A. 77-1315, § 1, eff. Jan. 1, 1972; P.A. 77-2830, Art. 73, § 1, eff. Jan. 1, 1973; P.A. 79-1041, § 1, eff. Jan. 1, 1976; P.A. 80-911, § 1, eff. Oct. 1, 1977; P.A. 81-886, § 1, eff. July 1, 1980; P.A. 83-12, § 1, eff. July 1, 1983; P.A. 88-476, § 2, eff. July 1, 1994; P.A. 89-245, § 5, eff. Jan. 1, 1996.

Formerly Ill.Rev.Stat.1991, ch. 95 ½, ¶ 3-401.

1 625 ILCS 5/3-801 et seq.

Section 4 of P.A. 83-12, approved July 1, 1983, provided:

"Effective date. This Act takes effect as provided in this Section.

"The amendments to those portions of Sections 3-815(a), 3-818 and 3-819(b) of 'The Illinois Vehicle Code' in Section 1 of this Act which create the 'X', 'Z', 'MX', 'MZ', 'MM' and 'TN' registration classifications and the fees and taxes imposed for those classifications, the amendments to Sections 2-119, 3-401 and 3-802 of 'The Illinois Vehicle Code' in Section 1 of this Act, and the amendments to Chapter 15 of 'The Illinois Vehicle Code' in Section 1 of this Act take effect July 1, 1983.

"The remaining amendments to 'The Illinois Vehicle Code' in Section 1 of this Act take effect July 1, 1983 and apply beginning with the 1985 registration year, except that the amendments to Sections 3-813 through 3-816 and Section 3-819 apply beginning with the 1984 registration year for those vehicles registered on a calendar year basis only.

"The amendments to Chapters 13 and 18 of 'The Illinois Vehicle Code' in Section 1 of this Act take effect January 1, 1984.

"Section 2 of this Act takes effect on the first day of the next succeeding month which commences at least 30 days after the date on which this Act becomes law.

"Section 3 of this Act takes effect July 1, 1983.

"Section 3.1 of this Act takes effect January 1, 1984.

"This Section 4 takes effect upon its becoming a law."

5/3-402. Vehicles subject to registration; exceptions

§ 3-402. Vehicles subject to registration; exceptions.

A. Exemptions and Policy. Every motor vehicle, trailer, semitrailer and pole trailer when driven or moved upon a highway shall be subject to the registration and certificate of title provisions of this Chapter except:

(1) Any such vehicle driven or moved upon a highway in conformance with the provisions of this Chapter relating to manufacturers, transporters, dealers, lienholders or nonresidents or under a temporary registration permit issued by the Secretary of State;

(2) Any implement of husbandry whether of a type otherwise subject to registration hereunder or not which is only incidentally operated or moved upon a highway, which shall include a not-for-hire movement for the purpose of delivering farm commodities to a place of first processing or sale, or to a place of storage;

(3) Any special mobile equipment as herein defined;

(4) Any vehicle which is propelled exclusively by electric power obtained from overhead trolley wires though not operated upon rails;

(5) Any vehicle which is equipped and used exclusively as a pumper, ladder truck, rescue vehicle, searchlight truck, or other fire apparatus, but not a vehicle of a type which would otherwise be subject to registration as a vehicle of the first division;

(6) Any vehicle which is owned and operated by the federal government and externally displays evidence of federal ownership. It is the policy of the State of Illinois to promote and encourage the fullest use of its highways and to enhance the flow of commerce thus contributing to the economic, agricultural, industrial and social growth and development of this State, by authorizing the Secretary of State to negotiate and enter into reciprocal or proportional agreements or arrangements with other States, or to issue declarations setting forth reciprocal exemptions, benefits and privileges with respect to vehicles operated interstate which are properly registered in this and other States, assuring nevertheless proper registration of vehicles in Illinois as may be required by this Code;

(7) Any converter dolly or tow dolly which merely serves as substitute wheels for another legally licensed vehicle. A title may be issued on a voluntary basis to a tow dolly upon receipt of the manufacturer's certificate of origin or the bill of sale;

(8) Any house trailer found to be an abandoned mobile home under the Abandoned Mobile Home Act; 1

(9) Any vehicle that is not properly registered or does not have registration plates issued to the owner or operator affixed thereto, or that does have registration plates issued to the owner or operator affixed thereto but the plates are not appropriate for the weight of the vehicle, provided that this exemption shall apply only while the vehicle is being transported or operated by a towing service and has a third tow plate affixed to it.

B. Reciprocity. Any motor vehicle, trailer, semitrailer or pole trailer need not be registered under this Code provided the same is operated interstate and in accordance with the following provisions and any rules and regulations promulgated pursuant thereto:

(1) A nonresident owner, except as otherwise provided in this Section, owning any foreign registered vehicle of a type otherwise subject to registration hereunder, may operate or permit the operation of such vehicle within this State in interstate commerce without registering such vehicle in, or paying any fees to, this State subject to the condition that such vehicle at all times when operated in this State is operated pursuant to a reciprocity agreement, arrangement or declaration by this State, and further subject to the condition that such vehicle at all times when operated in this State is duly registered in, and displays upon it, a valid registration card and registration plate or plates issued for such vehicle in the place of residence of such owner and is issued and maintains in such vehicle a valid Illinois reciprocity permit as required by the Secretary of State, and provided like privileges are afforded to residents of this State by the State of residence of such owner.

Every nonresident including any foreign corporation carrying on business within this State and owning and regularly operating in such business any motor vehicle, trailer or semitrailer within this State in intrastate commerce, shall be required to register each such vehicle and pay the same fees therefor as is required with reference to like vehicles owned by residents of this State.

(2) Any motor vehicle, trailer, semitrailer and pole trailer operated interstate need not be registered in this State, provided:

(a) that the vehicle is properly registered in another State pursuant to law or to a reciprocity agreement, arrangement or declaration; or

(b) that such vehicle is part of a fleet of vehicles owned or operated by the same person who registers such fleet of vehicles pro rata among the various States in which such fleet operates; or

(c) that such vehicle is part of a fleet of vehicles, a portion of which are registered with the Secretary of State of Illinois in accordance with an agreement or arrangement concurred in by the Secretary of State of Illinois based on one or more of the following factors: ratio of miles in Illinois as against total miles in all jurisdictions; situs or base of a vehicle, or where it is principally garaged, or from whence it is principally dispatched or where the movements of such vehicle usually originate; situs of the residence of the owner or operator thereof, or of his principal office or offices, or of his places of business; the routes traversed and whether regular or irregular routes are traversed, and the jurisdictions traversed and served; and such other factors as may be deemed material by the Secretary and the motor vehicle administrators of the other jurisdictions involved in such apportionment.

Such vehicles shall maintain therein any reciprocity permit which may be required by the Secretary of State pursuant to rules and regulations which the Secretary of State may promulgate in the administration of this Code, in the public interest.

(3) (a) In order to effectuate the purposes of this Code, the Secretary of State of Illinois is empowered to negotiate and execute written reciprocal agreements or arrangements with the duly authorized representatives of other jurisdictions, including States, districts, territories and possessions of the United States, and foreign states, provinces, or countries, granting to owners or operators of vehicles duly registered or licensed in such other jurisdictions and for which evidence of compliance is supplied, benefits, privileges and exemption from the payment, wholly or partially, of any taxes, fees or other charges imposed with respect to the ownership or operation of such vehicles by the laws of this State except the tax imposed by the Motor Fuel Tax Law, approved March 25, 1929, as amended,[2] and the tax imposed by the Use Tax Act, approved July 14, 1955, as amended.[3]

The Secretary of State may negotiate agreements or arrangements as are in the best interests of this State and the residents of this State pursuant to the policies expressed in this Section taking into consideration the reciprocal exemptions, benefits and privileges available and accruing to residents of this State and vehicles registered in this State.

(b) Such reciprocal agreements or arrangements shall provide that vehicles duly registered or licensed in this State when operated upon the highways of such other jurisdictions, shall receive exemptions, benefits and privileges of a similar kind or to a similar degree as extended to vehicles from such jurisdictions in this State.

(c) Such agreements or arrangements may also authorize the apportionment of registration or licensing of fleets of vehicles operated interstate, based on any or all of the following factors: ratio of miles in Illinois as against total miles in all jurisdictions; situs or base of a vehicle, or where it is principally garaged or from whence it is principally dispatched or where the movements of such vehicle usually originate; situs of the residence of the owner or operator thereof, or of his principal office or offices, or of his places of business; the routes traversed and whether regular or irregular routes are traversed, and the jurisdictions traversed and served; and such other factors as may be deemed material by the Secretary and the motor vehicle administrators of the other jurisdictions involved in such apportionment, and such vehicles shall likewise be entitled to reciprocal exemptions, benefits and privileges.

(d) Such agreements or arrangements shall also provide that vehicles being operated in intrastate commerce in Illinois shall comply with the registration and licensing laws of this State, except that vehicles which are part of an apportioned fleet may conduct an intrastate operation incidental to their interstate operations. Any motor vehicle properly registered and qualified under any reciprocal agreement or arrangement under this Code and not having a situs or base within Illinois may complete the inbound movement of a trailer or semitrailer to an Illinois destination that was brought into Illinois by a motor vehicle also properly registered and qualified under this Code and not having a situs or base within Illinois, or may complete an outbound movement of a trailer or semitrailer to an out-of-state destination that was originated in Illinois by a motor vehicle also properly registered and qualified under this Code and not having a situs or base in Illinois, only if the operator thereof did not break bulk of the cargo laden in such inbound or outbound trailer or semitrailer. Adding or unloading intrastate cargo on such inbound or outbound trailer or semitrailer shall be deemed as breaking bulk.

(e) Such agreements or arrangements may also provide for the determination of the proper State in which leased vehicles shall be registered based on the factors set out in subsection (c) above and for apportionment of registration of fleets of leased vehicles by the lessee or by the lessor who leases such vehicles to persons who are not fleet operators.

(f) Such agreements or arrangements may also include reciprocal exemptions, benefits or privileges accruing under The Illinois Driver Licensing Law[4] or The Driver License Compact.[5]

(4) The Secretary of State is further authorized to examine the laws and requirements of other jurisdictions, and, in the absence of a written agreement or arrangement, to issue a written declaration of the extent and nature of the exemptions, benefits and privileges accorded to vehicles of this State by such other jurisdictions, and the extent and nature of reciprocal exemptions, benefits and privileges thereby accorded by this State to the vehicles of such other jurisdictions. A declaration by the Secretary of State may include any, part or all reciprocal exemptions, benefits and privileges or provisions as may be included within an agreement or arrangement.

(5) All agreements, arrangements, declarations and amendments thereto, shall be in writing and become effective when signed by the Secretary of State, and copies of all such documents shall be available to the public upon request.

(6) The Secretary of State is further authorized to require the display by foreign registered trucks, truck-tractors and buses, entitled to reciprocal benefits, exemptions or privileges hereunder, a reciprocity permit for external display before any such reciprocal benefits, exemptions or

privileges are granted. The Secretary of State shall provide suitable application forms for such permit and shall promulgate and publish reasonable rules and regulations for the administration and enforcement of the provisions of this Code including a provision for revocation of such permit as to any vehicle operated wilfully in violation of the terms of any reciprocal agreement, arrangement or declaration or in violation of the Illinois Motor Carrier of Property Law, as amended. [6]

(7) (a) Upon the suspension, revocation or denial of one or more of all reciprocal benefits, privileges and exemptions existing pursuant to the terms and provisions of this Code or by virtue of a reciprocal agreement or arrangement or declaration thereunder; or, upon the suspension, revocation or denial of a reciprocity permit; or, upon any action or inaction of the Secretary in the administration and enforcement of the provisions of this Code, any person, resident or nonresident, so aggrieved, may serve upon the Secretary, a petition in writing and under oath, setting forth the grievance of the petitioner, the grounds and basis for the relief sought, and all necessary facts and particulars, and request an administrative hearing thereon. Within 20 days, the Secretary shall set a hearing date as early as practical. The Secretary may, in his discretion, supply forms for such a petition. The Secretary may require the payment of a fee of not more than $50 for the filing of any petition, motion, or request for hearing conducted pursuant to this Section. These fees must be deposited into the Secretary of State DUI Administration Fund, a special fund that is hereby created in the State treasury, and, subject to appropriation and as directed by the Secretary of State, shall be used to fund the operation of the hearings department of the Office of the Secretary of State and for no other purpose. The Secretary shall establish by rule the amount and the procedures, terms, and conditions relating to these fees.

(b) The Secretary may likewise, in his discretion and upon his own petition, order a hearing, when in his best judgment, any person is not entitled to the reciprocal benefits, privileges and exemptions existing pursuant to the terms and provisions of this Code or under a reciprocal agreement or arrangement or declaration thereunder or that a vehicle owned or operated by such person is improperly registered or licensed, or that an Illinois resident has improperly registered or licensed a vehicle in another jurisdiction for the purposes of violating or avoiding the registration laws of this State.

(c) The Secretary shall notify a petitioner or any other person involved of such a hearing, by giving at least 10 days notice, in writing, by U.S. Mail, Registered or Certified, or by personal service, at the last known address of such petitioner or person, specifying the time and place of such hearing. Such hearing shall be held before the Secretary, or any person as he may designate, and unless the parties mutually agree to some other county in Illinois, the hearing shall be held in the County of Sangamon or the County of Cook. Appropriate records of the hearing shall be kept, and the Secretary shall issue or cause to be issued, his decision on the case, within 30 days after the close of such hearing or within 30 days after receipt of the transcript thereof, and a copy shall likewise be served or mailed to the petitioner or person involved.

(d) The actions or inactions or determinations, or findings and decisions upon an administrative hearing, of the Secretary, shall be subject to judicial review in the Circuit Court of the County of Sangamon or the County of Cook, and the provisions of the Administrative Review Law, [7] and all amendments and modifications thereof and rules adopted pursuant thereto, apply to and govern all such reviewable matters.

Any reciprocal agreements or arrangements entered into by the Secretary of State or any declarations issued by the Secretary of State pursuant to any law in effect prior to the effective date of this Code are not hereby abrogated, and such shall continue in force and effect until amended pursuant to the provisions of this Code or expire pursuant to the terms or provisions thereof.

P.A. 76-1586, § 3-402, eff. July 1, 1970. Amended by P.A. 77-43, § 1, eff. Jan. 1, 1972; P.A. 77-1508, § 1, eff. Jan. 1, 1972; P.A. 77-1545, § 1, eff. Jan. 1, 1972; P.A. 77-2636, § 1, eff. Jan. 1, 1973; P.A. 78-255, § 25, eff. Oct. 1, 1973; P.A. 79-1021, § 1, eff. Oct. 1, 1975; P.A. 81-886, § 1, eff. July 1, 1980; P.A. 82-783, Art. XI, § 140, eff. July 13, 1982; P.A. 83-848, § 1, eff. Jan. 1, 1984; P.A. 83-1539, Art. IV, § 4, eff. Feb. 4, 1985; P.A. 84-986, § 1, eff. Sept. 25, 1985; P.A. 87-1203, § 1, eff. Sept. 25, 1992; P.A. 88-516, § 95, eff. July 1, 1994; P.A. 89-433, § 5, eff. Dec. 15, 1995; P.A. 90-89, § 15, eff. Jan. 1, 1998; P.A. 92-418, § 10, eff. Aug. 17, 2001; P.A. 92-651, § 77, eff. July 11, 2002.

Formerly Ill.Rev.Stat.1991, ch. 95 ½, ¶ 3-402.

[1] 210 ILCS 117/1 et seq.

[2] 35 ILCS 505/1 et seq.

[3] 35 ILCS 105/1 et seq.

[4] 625 ILCS 5/6-100 et seq.

[5] 625 ILCS 5/6-700 et seq.

[6] 625 ILCS 5/18-101 et seq. (repealed; see, now, 625 ILCS 5/18c-1101 et seq.).

[7] 735 ILCS 5/3-101 et seq.

Section 2 of P.A. 79-1021, certified Sept. 17, 1975, provided:

"This amendatory Act of 1975 takes effect beginning with motor vehicle registrations for 1977."

P.A. 92-651, the First 2002 General Revisory Act, amended various Acts to delete obsolete text, to correct patent and technical errors, to revise cross references, to resolve multiple actions in the 91st and 92nd General Assemblies and to make certain technical corrections in P.A. 91-937 through P.A. 92-520.

5/3-402.1. Proportional Registration

§ 3-402.1. Proportional Registration. Any owner or rental owner engaged in operating a fleet of apportionable vehicles in this state and one or more other states may, in lieu of registration of such vehicles under the general provisions of sections 3-402, 3-815 and 3-819, register and license such fleet for operations in this state by filing an application statement, signed under penalties of perjury, with the Secretary of State which shall be in such form and contain such information as the Secretary of State shall require, declaring the total mileage operated in all states by such fleet, the total mileage operated in this state by such fleet during the preceding year, and describing and identifying each apportionable vehicle to be operated in this state during the ensuing year. If mileage data is not available for the preceding year, the Secretary of State may accept the latest 12-month period available. "Preceding year" means the period of 12 consecutive months immediately prior to July 1st of the year immediately preceding the registration or license year for which proportional registration is sought.

Such owner shall determine the proportion of in-state miles to total fleet miles. Such percentage figure shall be such owner's apportionment factor. In determining the total fee payment, such owner shall first compute the license fee for each vehicle within the fleet which would otherwise be required, and then multiply the said amount by the Illinois apportionment factor adding the fees for each vehicle to arrive at a total amount for the fleet. Apportionable trailers and semitrailers will be registered in accordance with the provisions of Section 3-813 of this Code.

Upon receipt of the appropriate fees from such owner as computed under the provisions of this section, the Secretary of State shall, when this state is the base jurisdiction, issue to such owner number plates or other distinctive tags or such evidence of registration as the Secretary of State shall deem appropriate to identify each vehicle in the fleet as a part of a proportionally registered interstate fleet.

Vehicles registered under the provision of this section shall be considered fully licensed and properly registered in Illinois for any type of movement or operation. The proportional registration and licensing provisions of this section shall apply to vehicles added to fleets and operated in this state during the registration year, applying the same apportionment factor to such fees as would be payable for the remainder of the registration year.

Apportionment factors for apportionable vehicles not operated in this state during the preceding year shall be determined by the Secretary of State on the basis of a full statement of the proposed methods of operation and in conformity with an estimated mileage chart as calculated by the Secretary of State. An established fleet adding states at the time of renewal shall estimate mileage for the added states in conformity with a mileage chart developed by the Secretary of State.

P.A. 76-1586, § 3-402.1, added by P.A. 79-1041, § 1, eff. Jan. 1, 1976. Amended by P.A. 87-206, § 1, eff. Sept. 3, 1991; P.A. 87-1041, § 1, eff. Sept. 11, 1992; P.A. 90-89, § 15, eff. Jan. 1, 1998.

Formerly Ill.Rev.Stat.1991, ch. 95 ½, ¶ 3-402.1.

5/3-402.2. Audits

§ 3-402.2. Audits. In addition to audit authority set forth in Section 2-124 of this Act, the Secretary of State, when this state is the base jurisdiction, may audit such owners displaying a base plate of this state as to authenticity of mileage figures and registrations and at such time and frequency as determined by the Secretary of State. Audits may be made by officials of other jurisdictions which are members of an International Registration Plan (IRP) of which this state is also a member.

Upon completion of any such audit, the Secretary of State shall notify all jurisdictions in which such owner was proportionally registered on the accuracy of the records of such owner. Should such owner have underpaid or overpaid any jurisdiction in which his vehicles were proportionally registered, such information shall be furnished to the jurisdiction for processing in accordance with the procedures as set forth under the International Registration Plan.

P.A. 76-1586, § 3-402.2, added by P.A. 79-1041, § 1, eff. Jan. 1, 1976. Amended by P.A. 87-206, § 1, eff. Sept. 3, 1991; P.A. 92-69, § 5, eff. July 12, 2001.

Formerly Ill.Rev.Stat.1991, ch. 95 ½, ¶ 3-402.2.

5/3-402.3. Relation to other state laws

§ 3-402.3. Relation to other state laws. The provisions of Section 3-402.1 shall constitute complete authority for the registration of vehicles upon a proportional registration basis without reference to or application of any other statutes of this state.

P.A. 76-1586, § 3-402.3, added by P.A. 79-1041, § 1, eff. Jan. 1, 1976.

Formerly Ill.Rev.Stat.1991, ch. 95 ½, ¶ 3-402.3.

5/3-402.4. Administrative Agreements and Rules

§ 3-402.4. Administrative Agreements and Rules. The Secretary of State may enter into agreements, compacts, or arrangements with other jurisdictions or agents for such jurisdictions, such as the American Association of Motor Vehicle Administrators, on behalf of this state for allocation or proportional registration of apportionable vehicles in a manner provided in Section 3-402.1 for the purpose of facilitating the administration thereof, and also for the purpose of conforming procedures for proportional registration, pursuant to Sections 3-402.1 and 3-402.2, with those agreed to by two or more additional jurisdictions, including but not limited to, acceptance of base jurisdiction responsibilities for apportional registration and licensing of fleet vehicles in other jurisdiction. In addition, the Secretary of State may adopt and promulgate such rules and regulations as he shall deem necessary to effectuate and administer the provisions of Sections 3-402.1 and 3-402.2. Any reciprocal arrangements or agreements in effect with jurisdictions that cannot grant proportional registration shall remain in force until specifically cancelled by either jurisdiction or until such time that jurisdiction becomes a member of an International Registration Plan (IRP) of which this state is also a member.

P.A. 76-1586, § 3-402.4, added by P.A. 79-1041, § 1, eff. Jan. 1, 1976. Amended by P.A. 85-1144, § 1, eff. July 29, 1988; P.A. 87-206, § 1, eff. Sept. 3, 1991.

Formerly Ill.Rev.Stat.1991, ch. 95 ½, ¶ 3-402.4.

5/3-403. Trip and Short-term permits.

§ 3-403. Trip and Short-term permits.

(a) The Secretary of State may issue a short-term permit to operate a nonregistered first or second division vehicle within the State of Illinois for a period of not more than 7 days. Any second division vehicle operating on such permit may operate only on empty weight. The fee for the short-term permit shall be $6.

This permit may also be issued to operate an unladen registered vehicle which is suspended under the Vehicle Emissions Inspection Law [1] and allow it to be driven on the roads and highways of the State in order to be repaired or when travelling to and from an emissions inspection station.

(b) The Secretary of State may, subject to reciprocal agreements, arrangements or declarations made or entered into pursuant to Section 3-402, 3-402.4 or by rule, provide for and issue registration permits for the use of Illinois highways by vehicles of the second division on an occasional basis or for a specific and special short-term use, in compliance with rules and regulations promulgated by the Secretary of State, and upon payment of the prescribed fee as follows:

One-trip permits. A registration permit for one trip, or one round-trip into and out of Illinois, for a period not to exceed 72 consecutive hours or 3 calendar days may be provided, for a fee as prescribed in Section 3-811.

One-Month permits. A registration permit for 30 days may be provided for a fee of $13 for registration plus 1/10 of the flat weight tax. The minimum fee for such permit shall be $31.

In-transit permits. A registration permit for one trip may be provided for vehicles in transit by the driveaway or towaway method and operated by a transporter in compliance with the Illinois Motor Carrier of Property Law, [2] for a fee as prescribed in Section 3-811.

Illinois Temporary Apportionment Authorization Permits. An apportionment authorization permit for forty-five days for the immediate operation of a vehicle upon application for and prior to receiving apportioned credentials or interstate credentials from the State of Illinois. The fee for such permit shall be $3.

Illinois Temporary Prorate Authorization Permit. A prorate authorization permit for forty-five days for the immediate operation of a vehicle upon application for and prior to receiving prorate credentials or interstate credentials from the State of Illinois. The fee for such permit shall be $3.

(c) The Secretary of State shall promulgate by such rule or regulation, schedules of fees and taxes for such permits and in computing the amount or amounts due, may round off such amount to the nearest full dollar amount.

(d) The Secretary of State shall further prescribe the form of application and permit and may require such information and data as necessary and proper, including confirming the status or identity of the applicant and the vehicle in question.

(e) Rules or regulations promulgated by the Secretary of State under this Section shall provide for reasonable and proper limitations and restrictions governing the application for and issuance and use of permits, and shall provide for the number of permits per vehicle or per applicant, so as to preclude evasion of annual registration requirements as may be required by this Act.

(f) Any permit under this Section is subject to suspension or revocation under this Act, and in addition, any such permit is subject to suspension or revocation should the Secretary of State determine that the vehicle identified in any permit should be properly registered in Illinois. In the event any such permit is suspended or revoked, the permit is then null and void, may not be re-instated, nor is a refund therefor available. The vehicle identified in such permit may not thereafter be operated in Illinois without being properly registered as provided in this Chapter.

P.A. 76-1586, § 3-403, eff. July 1, 1970. Amended by P.A. 76-2132, § 1, eff. July 1, 1970; P.A. 77-526, § 1, eff. July 31, 1971; P.A. 81-865, § 1, eff. Dec. 1, 1979; P.A. 83-449, § 1, eff. Jan. 1, 1984; P.A. 84-986, § 1, eff. Sept. 25, 1985; P.A. 86-395, § 1, eff. Aug. 30, 1989; P.A. 86-444, § 1, eff. Jan. 1, 1990; P.A. 86-1028, Art. II, § 2-44, eff. Feb. 5, 1990; P.A. 87-206, § 1, eff. Sept. 3, 1991; P.A. 88-415, § 10, eff. Aug. 20, 1993; P.A. 91-37, § 40, eff. July 1, 1999; P.A. 92-680, § 15, eff. July 16, 2002.

Formerly Ill.Rev.Stat.1991, ch. 95 ½, ¶ 3-403.

1 625 ILCS 5/13A-101 et seq.

2 Former Ill.Rev.Stat. ch. 95½, ¶ 18-100 et seq. (repealed); see now, 625 ILCS 5/18c-1101 et seq.

5/3-404. Vehicles of second division carrying persons or property—Required documents

§ 3-404. Vehicles of second division carrying persons or property—Required documents. The Secretary of State shall require an appropriate document, including but not limited to a bill of lading, trip manifest or dispatch record, to be carried, on all vehicles of the second division, carrying persons or property setting forth therein:

(a) the point of origin and destination of the vehicle and its cargo or the persons being carried;

(b) whether the movement is for-hire or not-for-hire; and

(c) whether the movement is intrastate or interstate as defined by this Act.

The Secretary of State shall promulgate and publish reasonable rules and regulations for the administration and enforcement of this requirement. Vehicles bearing valid current Illinois registration plate or plates and registration stickers where applicable shall be exempted from such requirement by the Secretary of State whether the movement is "intrastate" or "interstate" as defined in this Act.

P.A. 76-1586, § 3-404, eff. July 1, 1970. Amended by P.A. 80-230, § 1, eff. Oct. 1, 1977.

Formerly Ill.Rev.Stat.1991, ch. 95 ½, ¶ 3-404.

5/3-405. Application for registration

§ 3-405. Application for registration.

(a) Every owner of a vehicle subject to registration under this Code shall make application to the Secretary of State for the registration of such vehicle upon the appropriate form or forms furnished by the Secretary. Every such application shall bear the signature of the owner written with pen and ink and contain:

1. The name, bona fide residence (except as otherwise provided in this paragraph 1) and mail address of the owner or business address of the owner if a firm, association or corporation. If the mailing address is a post office box number, the address listed on the driver license record may be used to verify residence. A police officer, a deputy sheriff, an elected sheriff, a law enforcement officer for the Department of State Police, or a fire investigator may elect to furnish the address of the headquarters of the governmental entity or police district where he or she works instead of his or her residence address, in which case that address shall be deemed to be his or her residence address for all purposes under this Chapter 3. The spouse and children of a person who may elect under this paragraph 1 to furnish the address of the headquarters of the government entity or police district where the person works instead of the person's residence address may, if they reside with that person, also elect to furnish the address of the headquarters of the government entity or police district where the person works as their residence address, in which case that address shall be deemed to be their residence address for all purposes under this Chapter 3. In this paragraph 1: (A) "police officer" has the meaning ascribed to "policeman" in Section 10-3-1 of the Illinois Municipal Code;[1] (B) "deputy sheriff" means a deputy sheriff appointed under Section 3-6008 of the Counties Code;[2] (C) "elected sheriff" means a sheriff commissioned pursuant to Section 3-6001 of the Counties Code;[3] and (D) "fire investigator" means a person classified as a peace officer under the Peace Officer Fire Investigation Act.[4]

2. A description of the vehicle, including such information as is required in an application for a certificate of title, determined under such standard rating as may be prescribed by the Secretary.

3. Information, as may be required by the Secretary, relating to the insurance policy for a motor vehicle, including, but not limited to, the name of the insurer which issued the policy.

4. Such further information as may reasonably be required by the Secretary to enable him to determine whether the vehicle is lawfully entitled to registration and the owner entitled to a certificate of title.

5. An affirmation by the applicant that all information set forth is true and correct. If the application is for the registration of a motor vehicle, the applicant also shall affirm that the motor vehicle is insured as required by this Code, that such insurance will be maintained throughout the period for which the motor vehicle shall be registered, and that neither the owner, nor any person operating the motor vehicle with the owner's permission, shall operate

interchange capabilities. The Secretary shall in his or her discretion determine other qualifications for fleet owners to register under this paragraph. In making the determination, the Secretary shall consider the size of the fleet and the past history of the registrant.

P.A. 76-1586, § 3-405.3, added by P.A. 92-629, § 5, eff. July 1, 2003.

5/3-405.4. Audits

Text of section added effective July 1, 2003

§ 3-405.4. Audits. In addition to audit authority set forth in Section 2-124 of this Code, the Secretary of State may audit the registration plates and the inventory of credentials of any fleet owner participating in the fleet registration plan.

P.A. 76-1586, § 3-405.4, added by P.A. 92-629, § 5, eff. July 1, 2003.

5/3-406. Application for specially constructed, reconstructed or foreign vehicles

§ 3-406. Application for specially constructed, reconstructed or foreign vehicles. (a) In the event the vehicle to be registered is a specially constructed, reconstructed or foreign vehicle, such fact shall be stated in the application and with reference to every foreign vehicle which has been registered heretofore outside of this State the owner shall surrender to the Secretary of State all registration plates, registration cards or other evidence of such foreign registration as may be in his possession or under his control except as provided in subdivision (b) hereof.

(b) Where in the course of interstate operation of a vehicle registered in another State, it is desirable to retain registration of said vehicle in such other State, such applicant need not surrender but shall submit for inspection said evidences of such foreign registration and the Secretary of State upon a proper showing shall register said vehicle in this State but shall not issue a certificate of title for such vehicle.

P.A. 76-1586, § 3-406, eff. July 1, 1970.

Formerly Ill.Rev.Stat.1991, ch. 95 ½, ¶ 3-406.

5/3-407. Temporary permit or registration pending registration

§ 3-407. Temporary permit or registration pending registration. (a) **Temporary Permit.** The Secretary of State in his discretion may grant a temporary permit or placard to operate a vehicle for which application for registration and certificate of title has been made where such application is accompanied by the proper fee, pending action upon said application by the Secretary of State. In lieu of payment of the proper fee, the Secretary of State may accept a bond therefor or a certificate of deposit, in the proper amount, and in the same form and subject to the same requirements as the payment of such fees or taxes on an installment basis, except that the fees or taxes due shall be payable and paid to the Secretary of State. The design, color and format of the temporary permit or placard shall be wholly within the discretion of the Secretary of State.

(b) **Temporary Registration.** The Secretary of State in his discretion may issue registration plates to an owner for which application and certificate of title has been made where such application is accompanied by the proper fee and tax, pending completion of the said application by the applicant and the Secretary, subject however to rules and regulations promulgated by the Secretary.

(c) **Revocation.** A temporary permit or registration is subject to revocation to the same extent as any other registration.

P.A. 76-1586, § 3-407, eff. July 1, 1970. Amended by P.A. 77-1508, § 1, eff. Jan. 1, 1972; P.A. 77-2751, § 1, eff. Sept. 1, 1972; P.A. 78-255, § 61, eff. Oct. 1, 1973; P.A. 88-298, § 5, eff. July 1, 1994.

Formerly Ill.Rev.Stat.1991, ch. 95 ½, ¶ 3-407.

5/3-408. Grounds for refusing registration or certificate of title

§ 3-408. Grounds for refusing registration or certificate of title. The Secretary of State shall refuse registration or any transfer of registration upon any of the following grounds:

1. That the application contains any false or fraudulent statement or that the applicant has failed to furnish required information or reasonable additional information requested by the Secretary of State or that the applicant is not entitled to the issuance of a certificate of title or registration of the vehicle under Chapter 3;

2. That the Secretary of State has reasonable ground to believe that the vehicle is a stolen or embezzled vehicle or that the granting of registration would constitute a fraud against the rightful owner or other person having valid lien upon such vehicle;

3. That the registration of the vehicle stands suspended or revoked for any reason as provided in the motor-vehicle laws of this State;

4. That the required fee has not been paid;

5. (a) In the case of medical transport vehicles and vehicles designed to carry 15 or fewer passengers operated by a contract carrier transporting employees in the course of their employment on a highway of this State, that the application does not contain a copy of a completed Vehicle Inspection Report issued by the Department of Transportation which certifies that the vehicle has been determined to be in safe mechanical condition by a safety test administered within the preceding 6 months; and (b) in the case of medical transport vehicles, other than vehicles owned or operated by a unit of local government, proof of financial responsibility; or

6. That the applicant is 90 days or more delinquent in court ordered child support payments or has been adjudicated in arrears in an amount equal to 90 days' obligation or more and has been found in contempt of court for failure to pay the support, subject to the requirements and procedures of Article VII of Chapter 7 of the Illinois Vehicle Code.[1]

P.A. 76-1586, § 3-408, eff. July 1, 1970. Amended by P.A. 82-433, § 1, eff. Sept. 8, 1981; P.A. 82-949, § 1, eff. Jan. 1, 1983; P.A. 90-733, § 10, eff. Aug. 11, 1998; P.A. 92-108, § 5, eff. Jan. 1, 2002.

[1] 625 ILCS 5/7-701 et seq.

Section 3 of P.A. 82-433 approved Sept. 8, 1981, provided:

"This Act takes effect upon its becoming a law, except that the provisions relating to safety tests and proof of financial responsibility for medical transport vehicles apply only to applications for and the issuance of registration plates which are required to be displayed on January 1, 1982 or thereafter."

5/3-409. Registration indexes

§ 3-409. Registration indexes. The Secretary of State shall file each application received and when satisfied as to the genuineness and regularity thereof, and that the applicant is entitled to register such vehicle and to the issuance of the motor vehicle unless the required insurance is in effect. If the person signing the affirmation is not the sole owner of the vehicle, such person shall be deemed to have affirmed on behalf of all the owners of the vehicle. If the person signing the affirmation is not an owner of the vehicle, such person shall be deemed to have affirmed on behalf of the owner or owners of the vehicle. The lack of signature on the application shall not in any manner exempt the owner or owners from any provisions, requirements or penalties of this Code.

(b) When such application refers to a new vehicle purchased from a dealer the application shall be accompanied by a Manufacturer's Statement of Origin from the dealer, and a statement showing any lien retained by the dealer.

P.A. 76–1586, § 3–405, eff. July 1, 1970. Amended by P.A. 78–1140, § 1, eff. Aug. 26, 1974; P.A. 84–1311, § 1, eff. Aug. 27, 1986; P.A. 85–1201, § 1, eff. July 1, 1989; P.A. 86–149, § 2, eff. Aug. 11, 1989; P.A 87–206, § 1, eff. Sept. 3, 1991; P.A. 88–315, § 5, eff. Jan. 1, 1994; P.A. 91–575, § 5, eff. Aug. 14, 1999.

Formerly Ill.Rev.Stat.1991, ch. 95 ½, ¶ 3–405.

1 65 ILCS 5/10–3–1.

2 55 ILCS 3/6008.

3 55 ILCS 3/6001.

4 20 ILCS 2910/0.01 et seq.

5/3–405.1. Application for vanity and personalized license plates

§ 3–405.1. Application for vanity and personalized license plates.

(a) Vanity license plates mean any license plates, assigned to a passenger motor vehicle of the first division, to a motor vehicle of the second division registered at not more than 8,000 pounds or to a recreational vehicle, which display a registration number containing 4 to 7 letters as requested by the owner of the vehicle and license plates issued to retired members of Congress under Section 3–610.1 or to retired members of the General Assembly as provided in Section 3–606.1. A license plate consisting of 3 letters and no numbers or of 1, 2 or 3 numbers, upon its becoming available, is a vanity license plate. Personalized license plates mean any license plates, assigned to a passenger motor vehicle of the first division, to a motor vehicle of the second division, or to a recreational vehicle, which display a registration number containing a combination of letters and numbers as prescribed by rule, as requested by the owner of the vehicle.

(b) For any registration period commencing after 1979, any person who is the registered owner of a passenger motor vehicle of the first division, of a motor vehicle of the second division registered at not more than 8,000 pounds or of a recreational vehicle registered with the Secretary of State or who makes application for an original registration of such a motor vehicle or renewal registration of such a motor vehicle may, upon payment of a fee prescribed in Section 3–806.1, apply to the Secretary of State for personalized license plates.

(c) Except as otherwise provided in this Chapter 3 , vanity and personalized license plates as issued under this Section shall be the same color and design as other passenger vehicle license plates and shall not in any manner conflict with any other existing passenger, commercial, trailer, motorcycle, or special license plate series. However, special registration plates issued under Sections 3–611 and 3–616 for vehicles operated by or for persons with disabilities may also be vanity or personalized license plates.

(d) Vanity and personalized license plates shall be issued only to the registered owner of the vehicle on which they are to be displayed, except as provided in Sections 3–611 and 3–616 for special registration plates for vehicles operated by or for persons with disabilities.

(e) An applicant for the issuance of vanity or personalized license plates or subsequent renewal thereof shall file an application in such form and manner and by such date as the Secretary of State may, in his discretion, require.

No vanity nor personalized license plates shall be approved, manufactured, or distributed that contain any characters, symbols other than the international accessibility symbol for vehicles operated by or for persons with disabilities, foreign words, or letters of punctuation.

(f) Vanity and personalized license plates as issued pursuant to this Act may be subject to the Staggered Registration System as prescribed by the Secretary of State.

P.A. 76–1586, § 3–405.1 added by P.A. 81–987, § 1, eff. Sept. 22, 1979. Amended by P.A. 82–1011, § 2, eff. Sept. 17, 1982; P.A. 83–453, § 1, eff. Jan. 1, 1984; P.A. 83–828, § 1, eff. Jan. 1, 1984; P.A. 83–1362, Art. II, § 99, eff. Sept. 11, 1984; P.A. 86–480, § 1, eff. Jan. 1, 1990; P.A. 88–685, § 5, eff. Jan. 24, 1995; P.A. 89–282, § 10, eff. Aug. 10, 1995; P.A. 89–611, § 15, eff. Jan. 1, 1997; P.A. 92–651, § 77, eff. July 11, 2002.

Formerly Ill.Rev.Stat.1991, ch. 95 ½, ¶ 3–405.1.

Section 2 of P.A. 83–828 provided:

"This Act takes effect with the 1985 registration year."

P.A. 89–611 incorporated the amendment by P.A. 89–282.

5/3–405.2. Improper plates

§ 3–405.2. Improper plates. The Secretary of State shall refuse to issue any license plates bearing a combination of letters or numbers, or both, which creates a potential duplication or, in the opinion of the Secretary, (1) would substantially interfere with plate identification for law enforcement purposes, (2) is misleading, or (3) creates a connotation that is offensive to good taste and decency.

The Secretary may revoke any such plates issued previously. Any person who has his or her plates revoked under this Section may acquire at no charge new plates and any required stickers of the same category and for the same period of registration.

P.A. 76–1586, § 3–405.2, added by P.A. 83–449, § 1, eff. Jan. 1, 1984.

Formerly Ill.Rev.Stat.1991, ch. 95 ½, ¶ 3–405.2.

5/3–405.3. Application for fleet vehicles

Text of section added effective July 1, 2003

§ 3–405.3. Application for fleet vehicles.

(a) An owner engaged in operating a fleet of motor vehicles of the first division in this State or a fleet of second division vehicles operated intrastate may register and license the fleet for operations in this State by filing an application statement with the Secretary of State, signed under penalties of perjury, which shall be in the form and contain the information required by the Secretary of State. First division vehicles registered under this Section must be registered in accordance with the fees prescribed in Section 3–806 of this Code. Second division vehicles registered under this Section must be registered in accordance with the fees prescribed in Section 3–815 of this Code.

(b) Participation in the fleet registration plan may be accomplished only by entering into a contractual agreement with the Secretary. The applicant must have electronic data a certificate of title, shall register the vehicle therein described and keep a suitable record thereof as follows:

1. Under a distinctive registration number assigned to the vehicle;

2. Under the identifying number of the vehicle;

3. Alphabetically, under the name of the owner;

4. In the discretion of the Secretary of State, in any other manner it may deem desirable.

P.A. 76–1586, § 3–409, eff. July 1, 1970.

Formerly Ill.Rev.Stat.1991, ch. 95 ½, ¶ 3–409.

5/3–410. Secretary of State to issue registration card

§ 3–410. Secretary of State to issue registration card. (a) The Secretary of State upon registering a vehicle shall issue a registration card.

(b) The registration card shall be delivered to the owner and shall contain upon the face thereof the date issued, the name and address of the owner, the registration number assigned to the vehicle and as to vehicles of the second division, whether the vehicle is for-hire or not-for-hire and such description of the vehicle as determined by the Secretary of State.

P.A. 76–1586, § 3–410, eff. July 1, 1970.

Formerly Ill.Rev.Stat.1991, ch. 95 ½, ¶ 3–410.

5/3–411. Registration card to be carried and exhibited on demand

§ 3–411. Registration card to be carried and exhibited on demand.

(a) Every registration card for a vehicle of the second division weighing more than 8,000 pounds or any vehicle of the second division weighing 8,000 pounds or less towing a trailer, except pole trailer or semitrailer shall at all times be carried in the vehicle to which it refers or shall be carried by the person driving or in control of such vehicle who shall display the same upon demand of a police officer or any officer or employee of the Secretary of State.

(b) The provisions of this Section requiring that a registration card be carried in the vehicle to which it refers or by the person driving the same shall not apply when such card is used for the purpose of making application for renewal of registration or upon a transfer of registration of said vehicle.

(c) Every owner or operator of a vehicle of the second division subject to a reciprocity agreement under subsection (b) of Section 3–402 of this Chapter shall at all times carry in the vehicle a copy of the reciprocity permit and shall display the same upon demand of a police officer or any officer or employee of the Secretary of State.

P.A. 76–1586, § 3–411, eff. July 1, 1970. Amended by P.A. 78–738, § 1, eff. Jan. 1, 1974; P.A. 86–444, § 1, eff. Jan. 1, 1990; P.A. 89–245, § 5, eff. Jan. 1, 1996; P.A. 89–687, § 5, eff. June 1, 1997.

Formerly Ill.Rev.Stat.1991, ch. 95 ½, ¶ 3–411.

P.A. 89–687 incorporated the amendment by P.A. 89–245.

5/3–412. Registration plates and registration stickers to be furnished by the Secretary of State

Text of section as amended by P.A. 92–651, § 77, eff. July 11, 2002

§ 3–412. Registration plates and registration stickers to be furnished by the Secretary of State.

(a) The Secretary of State upon registering a vehicle subject to annual registration for the first time shall issue or shall cause to be issued to the owner one registration plate for a motorcycle, trailer, semitrailer, motorized pedalcycle or truck-tractor, 2 registration plates for other motor vehicles and, where applicable, current registration stickers for motor vehicles of the first division. The provisions of this Section may be made applicable to such vehicles of the second division, as the Secretary of State may, from time to time, in his discretion designate. On subsequent annual registrations during the term of the registration plate as provided in Section 3–414.1, the Secretary shall issue or cause to be issued registration stickers as evidence of current registration. However, the issuance of annual registration stickers to vehicles registered under the provisions of Section 3–402.1 of this Code may not be required if the Secretary deems the issuance unnecessary.

(b) Every registration plate shall have displayed upon it the registration number assigned to the vehicle for which it is issued, the name of this State, which may be abbreviated, the year number for which it was issued, which may be abbreviated, the phrase "Land of Lincoln" (except as otherwise provided in this Chapter 3), and such other letters or numbers as the Secretary may prescribe. However, for apportionment plates issued to vehicles registered under Section 3–402.1, the phrase "Land of Lincoln" may be omitted to allow for the word "apportioned" to be displayed. The Secretary may in his discretion prescribe that letters be used as prefixes only on registration plates issued to vehicles of the first division which are registered under this Code and only as suffixes on registration plates issued to other vehicles. Every registration sticker issued as evidence of current registration shall designate the year number for which it is issued and such other letters or numbers as the Secretary may prescribe and shall be of a contrasting color with the registration plates and registration stickers of the previous year.

(c) Each registration plate and the required letters and numerals thereon, except the year number for which issued, shall be of sufficient size to be plainly readable from a distance of 100 feet during daylight, and shall be coated with reflectorizing material. The dimensions of the plate issued to vehicles of the first division shall be 6 by 12 inches.

(d) The Secretary of State shall issue for every passenger motor vehicle rented without a driver the same type of registration plates as the type of plates issued for a private passenger vehicle.

(e) The Secretary of State shall issue for every passenger car used as a taxicab or livery, distinctive registration plates.

(f) The Secretary of State shall issue for every motorcycle distinctive registration plates distinguishing between motorcycles having 150 or more cubic centimeters piston displacement, or having less than 150 cubic centimeter piston displacement.

(g) Registration plates issued to vehicles for-hire may display a designation as determined by the Secretary that such vehicles are for-hire.

(h) The Secretary of State shall issue for each electric vehicle distinctive registration plates which shall distinguish between electric vehicles having a maximum operating speed of 45 miles per hour or more and those having a maximum operating speed of less than 45 miles per hour.

(i) The Secretary of State shall issue for every public and private ambulance registration plates identifying the vehicle as an ambulance. The Secretary shall forward to the Department of Public Aid registration information for the purpose of verification of claims filed with the Department by ambulance owners for payment for services to public assistance recipients.

(j) The Secretary of State shall issue for every public and private medical carrier or rescue vehicle livery registration plates displaying numbers within ranges of numbers reserved respectively for medical carriers and rescue vehicles. The Secretary shall forward to the Department of Public Aid registration information for the purpose of verification of claims filed with the Department by owners of medical carriers or rescue vehicles for payment for services to public assistance recipients.

P.A. 76-1586, § 3-412, eff. July 1, 1970. Amended by P.A. 76-1622, § 1, eff. July 1, 1970; P.A. 77-512, § 1, eff. Jan. 1, 1972; P.A. 79-700, § 1, eff. Oct. 1, 1975; P.A. 80-230, § 1, eff. Oct. 1, 1977; P.A. 80-262, § 1, eff. Aug. 20, 1977; P.A. 80-1185, § 1, eff. March 8, 1978; P.A. 82-433, § 1, eff. Sept. 8, 1981; P.A. 87-1040, § 1, eff. Sept. 11, 1992; P.A. 87-1041, § 1, eff. Sept. 11, 1992; P.A. 88-45, Art. II, § 2-54, eff. July 6, 1993; P.A. 88-485, § 10, eff. Jan. 1, 1994; P.A. 89-424, § 15, eff. June 1, 1996; P.A. 89-564, § 5, eff. July 1, 1997; P.A. 89-612, § 10, eff. Aug. 9, 1996; P.A. 89-621, § 10, eff. Jan. 1, 1997; P.A. 89-639, § 5, eff. Jan. 1, 1997; P.A. 90-14, Art. 2, § 2-225, eff. July 1, 1997; P.A. 90-533, § 5, eff. Nov. 14, 1997; P.A. 90-655, § 153, eff. July 30, 1998; P.A. 92-651, § 77, eff. July 11, 2002.

Formerly Ill.Rev.Stat.1991, ch. 95 ½, ¶ 3-412.

For text of section as amended by P.A. 92-629, effective July 1, 2003, see 625 ILCS 5/3-412, post

For final legislative action, see note following 625 ILCS 5/6-206

P.A. 92-651, the First 2002 General Revisory Act, amended various Acts to delete obsolete text, to correct patent and technical errors, to revise cross references, to resolve multiple actions in the 91st and 92nd General Assemblies and to make certain technical corrections in P.A. 91-937 through P.A. 92-520.

5/3-412. Registration plates and registration stickers to be furnished by the Secretary of State

Text of section as amended by P.A. 92-629, effective July 1, 2003

§ 3-412. Registration plates and registration stickers to be furnished by the Secretary of State.

(a) The Secretary of State upon registering a vehicle subject to annual registration for the first time shall issue or shall cause to be issued to the owner one registration plate for a motorcycle, trailer, semitrailer, motorized pedalcycle or truck-tractor, 2 registration plates for other motor vehicles and, where applicable, current registration stickers for motor vehicles of the first division. The provisions of this Section may be made applicable to such vehicles of the second division, as the Secretary of State may, from time to time, in his discretion designate. On subsequent annual registrations during the term of the registration plate as provided in Section 3-414.1, the Secretary shall issue or cause to be issued registration stickers as evidence of current registration. However, the issuance of annual registration stickers to vehicles registered under the provisions of Sections 3-402.1 and 3-405.3 of this Code may not be required if the Secretary deems the issuance unnecessary.

(b) Every registration plate shall have displayed upon it the registration number assigned to the vehicle for which it is issued, the name of this State, which may be abbreviated, the year number for which it was issued, which may be abbreviated, the phrase "Land of Lincoln" (except as otherwise provided in this Code), and such other letters or numbers as the Secretary may prescribe. However, for apportionment plates issued to vehicles registered under Section 3-402.1 and fleet plates issued to vehicles registered under Section 3-405.3, the phrase "Land of Lincoln" may be omitted to allow for the word "apportioned", the word "fleet", or other similar language to be displayed. Registration plates issued to a vehicle registered as a fleet vehicle may display a designation determined by the Secretary.

The Secretary may in his discretion prescribe that letters be used as prefixes only on registration plates issued to vehicles of the first division which are registered under this Code and only as suffixes on registration plates issued to other vehicles. Every registration sticker issued as evidence of current registration shall designate the year number for which it is issued and such other letters or numbers as the Secretary may prescribe and shall be of a contrasting color with the registration plates and registration stickers of the previous year.

(c) Each registration plate and the required letters and numerals thereon, except the year number for which issued, shall be of sufficient size to be plainly readable from a distance of 100 feet during daylight, and shall be coated with reflectorizing material. The dimensions of the plate issued to vehicles of the first division shall be 6 by 12 inches.

(d) The Secretary of State shall issue for every passenger motor vehicle rented without a driver the same type of registration plates as the type of plates issued for a private passenger vehicle.

(e) The Secretary of State shall issue for every passenger car used as a taxicab or livery, distinctive registration plates.

(f) The Secretary of State shall issue for every motorcycle distinctive registration plates distinguishing between motorcycles having 150 or more cubic centimeters piston displacement, or having less than 150 cubic centimeter piston displacement.

(g) Registration plates issued to vehicles for-hire may display a designation as determined by the Secretary that such vehicles are for-hire.

(h) The Secretary of State shall issue for each electric vehicle distinctive registration plates which shall distinguish between electric vehicles having a maximum operating speed of 45 miles per hour or more and those having a maximum operating speed of less than 45 miles per hour.

(i) The Secretary of State shall issue for every public and private ambulance registration plates identifying the vehicle as an ambulance. The Secretary shall forward to the Department of Public Aid registration information for the purpose of verification of claims filed with the Department by ambulance owners for payment for services to public assistance recipients.

(j) The Secretary of State shall issue for every public and private medical carrier or rescue vehicle livery registration plates displaying numbers within ranges of numbers reserved respectively for medical carriers and rescue vehicles. The Secretary shall forward to the Department of Public Aid registration information for the purpose of verification of claims filed with the Department by owners of medical carriers or rescue vehicles for payment for services to public assistance recipients.

P.A. 76-1586, § 3-412, eff. July 1, 1970. Amended by P.A. 76-1622, § 1, eff. July 1, 1970; P.A. 77-512, § 1, eff. Jan. 1, 1972; P.A. 79-700, § 1, eff. Oct. 1, 1975; P.A. 80-230, § 1, eff. Oct. 1, 1977; P.A. 80-262, § 1, eff. Aug. 20, 1977; P.A. 80-1185, § 1, eff. March 8, 1978; P.A. 82-433, § 1, eff. Sept. 8, 1981; P.A. 87-1040, § 1, eff. Sept. 11, 1992; P.A. 87-1041, § 1, eff. Sept. 11, 1992; P.A. 88-45, Art. II, § 2-54, eff. July 6, 1993; P.A. 88-485, § 10, eff. Jan. 1, 1994; P.A. 89-424, § 15, eff. June 1, 1996; P.A. 89-564, § 5, eff. July 1, 1997; P.A. 89-612, § 10, eff. Aug. 9, 1996; P.A. 89-621, § 10, eff. Jan. 1, 1997; P.A. 89-639, § 5, eff. Jan. 1, 1997; P.A. 90-14, Art. 2, § 2-225, eff. July 1, 1997; P.A. 90-533, § 5, eff. Nov. 14, 1997; P.A. 90-655, § 153, eff. July 30, 1998; P.A. 92-629, § 5, eff. July 1, 2003.

Formerly Ill.Rev.Stat.1991, ch. 95 ½, ¶ 3-412.

For text of section as amended by P.A. 92-651, effective July 11, 2002, see 612 ILCS 5/3-412, ante

Section 3 of P.A. 82-433 approved Sept. 8, 1981, provided:

"This Act takes effect upon its becoming a law, except that the provisions relating to safety tests and proof of financial responsibility for medical transport vehicles apply only to applications for and the issuance of registration plates which are required to be displayed on January 1, 1982 or thereafter."

P.A. 90-655, the First 1998 General Revisory Act, amended various Acts to delete obsolete text, to correct patent and technical errors, to revise cross references, to resolve multiple actions in the 89th and 90th General Assemblies and to make certain technical corrections in P.A. 89-708 through P.A. 90-566.

Final legislative action, 92nd General Assembly:

P.A. 92-629—April 24, 2002

P.A. 92-651—May 14, 2002

See 5 ILCS 70/6 as to the effect of (1) more than one amendment of a section at the same session of the General Assembly or (2) two or more acts relating to the same subject matter enacted by the same General Assembly.

5/3-413. Display of registration plates, registration stickers and drive-away permits

§ 3-413. Display of registration plates, registration stickers and drive-away permits.

(a) Registration plates issued for a motor vehicle other than a motorcycle, trailer, semitrailer, truck-tractor, apportioned bus, or apportioned truck shall be attached thereto, one in the front and one in the rear. The registration plate issued for a motorcycle, trailer or semitrailer required to be registered hereunder and any apportionment plate issued to a bus under the provisions of this Code shall be attached to the rear thereof. The registration plate issued for a truck-tractor or an apportioned truck required to be registered hereunder shall be attached to the front thereof.

(b) Every registration plate shall at all times be securely fastened in a horizontal position to the vehicle for which it is issued so as to prevent the plate from swinging and at a height of not less than 5 inches from the ground, measuring from the bottom of such plate, in a place and position to be clearly visible and shall be maintained in a condition to be clearly legible, free from any materials that would obstruct the visibility of the plate, including, but not limited to, glass covers and tinted plastic covers. Clear plastic covers are permissible as long as they remain clear and do not obstruct the visibility of the plates. Registration stickers issued as evidence of renewed annual registration shall be attached to registration plates as required by the Secretary of State, and be clearly visible at all times.

(c) Every drive-away permit issued pursuant to this Code shall be firmly attached to the motor vehicle in the manner prescribed by the Secretary of State. If a drive-away permit is affixed to a motor vehicle in any other manner the permit shall be void and of no effect.

(d) The Illinois prorate decal issued to a foreign registered vehicle part of a fleet prorated or apportioned with Illinois, shall be displayed on a registration plate and displayed on the front of such vehicle in the same manner as an Illinois registration plate.

(e) The registration plate issued for a camper body mounted on a truck displaying registration plates shall be attached to the rear of the camper body.

(f) No person shall operate a vehicle, nor permit the operation of a vehicle, upon which is displayed an Illinois registration plate, plates or registration stickers after the termination of the registration period for which issued or after the expiration date set pursuant to Sections 3-414 and 3-414.1 of this Code.

P.A. 76-1586, § 3-413, eff. July 1, 1970. Amended by P.A. 77-1315, § 1, eff. Jan. 1, 1972; P.A. 78-335, § 1, eff. Jan. 1, 1974; P.A. 80-230, § 1, eff. Oct. 1, 1977; P.A. 80-891, § 1, eff. Jan. 1, 1978; P.A. 80-1364, § 36, eff. Aug. 13, 1978; P.A. 81-886, § 1, eff. July 1, 1980; P.A. 82-133, § 1, eff. Jan. 1, 1982; P.A. 85-1396, § 2, eff. Sept. 2, 1988; P.A. 86-417, § 1, eff. Jan. 1, 1990; P.A. 87-353, § 3, eff. Sept. 9, 1991; P.A. 87-1041, § 1, eff. Jan. 1, 1993; P.A. 89-245, § 5, eff. Jan. 1, 1996; P.A. 89-375, § 3, eff. Aug. 18, 1995; P.A. 92-668, § 5, eff. Jan. 1, 2003; P.A. 92-680, § 15, eff. July 16, 2002.

Formerly Ill.Rev.Stat.1991, ch. 95 ½, ¶ 3-413.

P.A. 89-375 included the amendment by P.A. 89-245.

See 5 ILCS 70/6 as to the effect of (1) more than one amendment of a section at the same session of the General Assembly or (2) two or more acts relating to the same subject matter enacted by the same General Assembly.

5/3-414. Expiration of registration

Text of section effective until July 1, 2003

§ 3-414. Expiration of registration.

(a) Every vehicle registration under this Chapter and every registration card and registration plate or registration sticker issued hereunder to a vehicle shall be for the periods specified in this Chapter and shall expire at midnight on the day and date specified in this Section as follows:

1. When registered on a calendar year basis commencing January 1, expiration shall be on the 31st day of December or at such other date as may be selected in the discretion of the Secretary of State; however, registrations of apportionable vehicles, motorcycles, motor driven cycles and pedalcycles shall commence on the first day of April and shall expire March 31st of the following calendar year;

2. When registered on a 2 calendar year basis commencing January 1 of an even-numbered year, expiration shall be on the 31st day of December of the ensuing odd-numbered year, or at such other later date as may be selected in the discretion of the Secretary of State not beyond March 1 next;

3. When registered on a fiscal year basis commencing July 1, expiration shall be on the 30th day of June or at such other later date as may be selected in the discretion of the Secretary of State not beyond September 1 next;

4. When registered on a 2 fiscal year basis commencing July 1 of an even-numbered year, expiration shall be on the 30th day of June of the ensuing even-numbered year, or at such other later date as may be selected in the discretion of the Secretary of State not beyond September 1 next;

5. When registered on a 4 fiscal year basis commencing July 1 of an even-numbered year, expiration shall be on the 30th day of June of the second ensuing even-numbered year, or at such other later date as may be selected in the discretion of the Secretary of State not beyond September 1 next;

(b) Vehicle registrations of vehicles of the first division shall be for a calendar year or 2 calendar year basis as provided for in this Chapter.

Vehicle registrations of vehicles under Sections 3–807, 3–808 and 3–809 shall be on an indefinite term basis or a 2 calendar year basis as provided for in this Chapter.

Vehicle registrations for vehicles of the second division shall be for a fiscal year, 2 fiscal year or calendar year basis as provided for in this Chapter.

Motor vehicles registered under the provisions of Section 3–402.1 shall be issued multi-year registration plates with a new registration card issued annually upon payment of the appropriate fees. Apportionable trailers and apportionable semitrailers registered under the provisions of Section 3–402.1 shall be issued multi-year registration plates and cards that will be subject to revocation for failure to pay annual fees required by Section 3–814.1. The Secretary shall determine when these vehicles shall be issued new registration plates.

(c) Every vehicle registration specified in Section 3–810 and every registration card and registration plate or registration sticker issued thereunder shall expire on the 31st day of December of each year or at such other date as may be selected in the discretion of the Secretary of State.

(d) Every vehicle registration for a vehicle of the second division weighing over 8,000 pounds, except as provided in paragraph (g) of this Section, and every registration card and registration plate or registration sticker, where applicable, issued hereunder to such vehicles shall be issued for a fiscal year commencing on July 1st of each registration year. However, the Secretary of State may, pursuant to an agreement or arrangement or declaration providing for apportionment of a fleet of vehicles with other jurisdictions, provide for registration of such vehicles under apportionment or for all of the vehicles registered in Illinois by an applicant who registers some of his vehicles under apportionment on a calendar year basis instead, and the fees or taxes to be paid on a calendar year basis shall be identical to those specified in this Act for a fiscal year registration. Provision for installment payment may also be made.

(e) Semitrailer registrations under apportionment may be on a calendar year under a reciprocal agreement or arrangement and all other semitrailer registrations shall be on fiscal year or 2 fiscal year or 4 fiscal year basis as provided for in this Chapter.

(f) The Secretary of State may convert annual registration plates or 2–year registration plates, whether registered on a calendar year or fiscal year basis, to multi-year plates. The determination of which plate categories and when to convert to multi-year plates is solely within the discretion of the Secretary of State.

(g) After January 1, 1975, each registration, registration card and registration plate or registration sticker, where applicable, issued for a recreational vehicle or recreational or camping trailer, except a house trailer, used exclusively by the owner for recreational purposes, and not used commercially nor as a truck or bus, nor for hire, shall be on a calendar year basis; except that the Secretary of State shall provide for registration and the issuance of registration cards and plates or registration stickers, where applicable, for one 6–month period in order to accomplish an orderly transition from a fiscal year to a calendar year basis. Fees and taxes due under this Act for a registration year shall be appropriately reduced for such 6–month transitional registration period.

(h) The Secretary of State may, in order to accomplish an orderly transition for vehicles registered under Section 3–402.1 of this Code from a calendar year registration to a March 31st expiration, require applicants to pay fees and taxes due under this Code on a 15 month registration basis. However, if in the discretion of the Secretary of State this creates an undue hardship on any applicant the Secretary may allow the applicant to pay 3 month fees and taxes at the time of registration and the additional 12 month fees and taxes to be payable no later than March 31 of the year after this amendatory Act of 1991 takes effect.

(i) The Secretary of State may stagger registrations, of vehicles for which multi-year plates are issued pursuant to Section 3–414.1, as necessary for the convenience of the public and the efficiency of his Office. In order to appropriately and effectively accomplish any such staggering, the Secretary of State is authorized to prorate required registration fees, but in no event for a period longer than 15 months, at a monthly rate for a 12 month registration fee.

P.A. 76–1586, § 3–414, eff. July 1, 1970. Amended by P.A. 76–1865, § 1, eff. July 1, 1970; P.A. 77–44, § 1, eff. Jan. 1, 1972; P.A. 77–1315, § 1, eff. Jan. 1, 1972; P.A. 77–2829, § 40, eff. Dec. 22, 1972; P.A. 78–255, § 61, eff. Oct. 1, 1973; P.A. 78–1146, § 1, eff. Jan. 1, 1975; P.A. 78–1297, § 58, eff. March 4, 1975; P.A. 79–1021, § 1; P.A. 79–1367, § 1, eff. Aug. 6, 1976; P.A. 80–230, § 1, eff. Oct. 1, 1977; P.A. 80–1185, § 1, eff. March 8, 1978; P.A. 81–1491, § 1, eff. Sept. 19, 1980; P.A. 83–449, § 1, eff. Jan. 1, 1984; P.A. 83–817, § 1, eff. Jan. 1, 1984; P.A. 83–1362, Art. II, § 99, eff. Sept. 11, 1984; P.A. 87–206, § 1, eff. Sept. 3, 1991; P.A. 87–1040, § 1, eff. Sept. 11, 1992; P.A. 89–245, § 5, eff. Jan. 1, 1996.

Formerly Ill.Rev.Stat.1991, ch. 95 ½, ¶ 3–414.

For text of section effective July 1, 2003, see 625 ILCS 5/3–414, post

5/3–414. Expiration of registration

Text of section effective July 1, 2003

§ 3–414. Expiration of registration.

(a) Every vehicle registration under this Chapter and every registration card and registration plate or registration sticker issued hereunder to a vehicle shall be for the periods specified in this Chapter and shall expire at midnight on the day and date specified in this Section as follows:

1. When registered on a calendar year basis commencing January 1, expiration shall be on the 31st day of December or at such other date as may be selected in the discretion of the Secretary of State; however, registrations of apportionable vehicles, motorcycles, motor driven cycles and pedalcycles shall commence on the first day of April and shall expire March 31st of the following calendar year;

2. When registered on a 2 calendar year basis commencing January 1 of an even-numbered year, expiration shall be on the 31st day of December of the ensuing odd-numbered year, or at such other later date as may be selected in the discretion of the Secretary of State not beyond March 1 next;

3. When registered on a fiscal year basis commencing July 1, expiration shall be on the 30th day of June or at

such other later date as may be selected in the discretion of the Secretary of State not beyond September 1 next;

4. When registered on a 2 fiscal year basis commencing July 1 of an even-numbered year, expiration shall be on the 30th day of June of the ensuing even-numbered year, or at such other later date as may be selected in the discretion of the Secretary of State not beyond September 1 next;

5. When registered on a 4 fiscal year basis commencing July 1 of an even-numbered year, expiration shall be on the 30th day of June of the second ensuing even-numbered year, or at such other later date as may be selected in the discretion of the Secretary of State not beyond September 1 next;

(b) Vehicle registrations of vehicles of the first division shall be for a calendar year or 2 calendar year basis as provided for in this Chapter.

Vehicle registrations of vehicles under Sections 3-807, 3-808 and 3-809 shall be on an indefinite term basis or a 2 calendar year basis as provided for in this Chapter.

Vehicle registrations for vehicles of the second division shall be for a fiscal year, 2 fiscal year or calendar year basis as provided for in this Chapter.

Motor vehicles registered under the provisions of Sections 3-402.1 and 3-405.3 shall be issued multi-year registration plates with a new registration card issued annually upon payment of the appropriate fees. Apportionable trailers and apportionable semitrailers registered under the provisions of Section 3-402.1 shall be issued multi-year registration plates and cards that will be subject to revocation for failure to pay annual fees required by Section 3-814.1. The Secretary shall determine when these vehicles shall be issued new registration plates.

(c) Every vehicle registration specified in Section 3-810 and every registration card and registration plate or registration sticker issued thereunder shall expire on the 31st day of December of each year or at such other date as may be selected in the discretion of the Secretary of State.

(d) Every vehicle registration for a vehicle of the second division weighing over 8,000 pounds, except as provided in paragraph (g) of this Section, and every registration card and registration plate or registration sticker, where applicable, issued hereunder to such vehicles shall be issued for a fiscal year commencing on July 1st of each registration year. However, the Secretary of State may, pursuant to an agreement or arrangement or declaration providing for apportionment of a fleet of vehicles with other jurisdictions, provide for registration of such vehicles under apportionment or for all of the vehicles registered in Illinois by an applicant who registers some of his vehicles under apportionment on a calendar year basis instead, and the fees or taxes to be paid on a calendar year basis shall be identical to those specified in this Act for a fiscal year registration. Provision for installment payment may also be made.

(e) Semitrailer registrations under apportionment may be on a calendar year under a reciprocal agreement or arrangement and all other semitrailer registrations shall be on fiscal year or 2 fiscal year or 4 fiscal year basis as provided for in this Chapter.

(f) The Secretary of State may convert annual registration plates or 2-year registration plates, whether registered on a calendar year or fiscal year basis, to multi-year plates. The determination of which plate categories and when to convert to multi-year plates is solely within the discretion of the Secretary of State.

(g) After January 1, 1975, each registration, registration card and registration plate or registration sticker, where applicable, issued for a recreational vehicle or recreational or camping trailer, except a house trailer, used exclusively by the owner for recreational purposes, and not used commercially nor as a truck or bus, nor for hire, shall be on a calendar year basis; except that the Secretary of State shall provide for registration and the issuance of registration cards and plates or registration stickers, where applicable, for one 6-month period in order to accomplish an orderly transition from a fiscal year to a calendar year basis. Fees and taxes due under this Act for a registration year shall be appropriately reduced for such 6-month transitional registration period.

(h) The Secretary of State may, in order to accomplish an orderly transition for vehicles registered under Section 3-402.1 of this Code from a calendar year registration to a March 31st expiration, require applicants to pay fees and taxes due under this Code on a 15 month registration basis. However, if in the discretion of the Secretary of State this creates an undue hardship on any applicant the Secretary may allow the applicant to pay 3 month fees and taxes at the time of registration and the additional 12 month fees and taxes to be payable no later than March 31 of the year after this amendatory Act of 1991 takes effect.

(i) The Secretary of State may stagger registrations, of vehicles for which multi-year plates are issued pursuant to Section 3-414.1, as necessary for the convenience of the public and the efficiency of his Office. In order to appropriately and effectively accomplish any such staggering, the Secretary of State is authorized to prorate required registration fees, but in no event for a period longer than 15 months, at a monthly rate for a 12 month registration fee.

P.A. 76-1586, § 3-414, eff. July 1, 1970. Amended by P.A. 76-1865, § 1, eff. July 1, 1970; P.A. 77-44, § 1, eff. Jan. 1, 1972; P.A. 77-1315, § 1, eff. Jan. 1, 1972; P.A. 77-2829, § 40, eff. Dec. 22, 1972; P.A. 78-255, § 61, eff. Oct. 1, 1973; P.A. 78-1146, § 1, eff. Jan. 1, 1975; P.A. 78-1297, § 58, eff. March 4, 1975; P.A. 79-1021, § 1; P.A. 79-1367, § 1, eff. Aug. 6, 1976; P.A. 80-230, § 1, eff. Oct. 1, 1977; P.A. 80-1185, § 1, eff. March 8, 1978; P.A. 81-1491, § 1, eff. Sept. 19, 1980; P.A. 83-449, § 1, eff. Jan. 1, 1984; P.A. 83-817, § 1, eff. Jan. 1, 1984; P.A. 83-1362, Art. II, § 99, eff. Sept. 11, 1984; P.A. 87-206, § 1, eff. Sept. 3, 1991; P.A. 87-1040, § 1, eff. Sept. 11, 1992; P.A. 89-245, § 5, eff. Jan. 1, 1996; P.A. 92-629, § 5, eff. July 1, 2003.

Formerly Ill.Rev.Stat.1991, ch. 95 ½, ¶ 3-414.

For text of section effective until July 1, 2003, see 625 ILCS 5/3-414, ante

Section 2 of P.A. 83-817 approved Sept. 24, 1983, provided: "This Act takes effect with the 1985 registration year."

5/3-414.1. Term of multi-year registration plates

§ 3-414.1. Term of multi-year registration plates.

(a) Registration plates issued for motor vehicles shall be valid for an indefinite term of not less than one year. Registration plates issued as two-year plates may be issued as multi-year plates at the discretion of the Secretary of State. Current renewal registration stickers, when necessary, are to be attached as provided in Section 3-413. The Secretary may in his discretion prescribe a term greater than one year or may extend the term of current registration plates for an additional calendar year by appropriate public announcement made before August 1 of the current registration year.

(b) Registration plates issued to owners of vehicles subject to annual registration for the first time during the term of the plates shall be valid until the expiration of the term. Current annual registration stickers are to be attached as provided in Section 3-413.

P.A. 76-1586, § 3-414.1, eff. July 1, 1970, added by P.A. 80-230, § 1, eff. Oct. 1, 1977. Amended by P.A. 83-828, § 1, eff. Jan. 1, 1984; P.A. 84-986, § 1, eff. Sept. 25, 1985; P.A. 89-245, § 5, eff. Jan. 1, 1996.

Formerly Ill.Rev.Stat.1991, ch. 95 ½, ¶ 3-414.1.

Section 2 of P.A. 83-828 provided:

"This Act takes effect with the 1985 registration year."

See 5 ILCS 70/6 as to the effect of (1) more than one amendment of a section at the same session of the General Assembly or (2) two or more acts relating to the same subject matter enacted by the same General Assembly.

5/3-415. Application for and renewal of registration

§ 3-415. Application for and renewal of registration. **(a) Calendar year.** Application for renewal of a vehicle registration shall be made by the owner, as to those vehicles required to be registered on a calendar registration year, not later than December 1 of each year, upon proper application and by payment of the registration fee and tax for such vehicle, as provided by law except that application for renewal of a vehicle registration, as to those vehicles required to be registered on a staggered calendar year basis, shall be made by the owner in the form and manner prescribed by the Secretary of State.

(b) Fiscal year. Application for renewal of a vehicle registration shall be made by the owner, as to those vehicles required to be registered on a fiscal registration year, not later than June 1 of each year, upon proper application and by payment of the registration fee and tax for such vehicle as provided by law, except that application for renewal of a vehicle registration, as to those vehicles required to be registered on a staggered fiscal year basis, shall be made by the owner in the form and manner prescribed by the Secretary of State.

(c) Two calendar years. Application for renewal of a vehicle registration shall be made by the owner, as to those vehicles required to be registered for 2 calendar years, not later than December 1 of the year preceding commencement of the 2-year registration period, except that application for renewal of a vehicle registration, as to those vehicles required to be registered for 2 years on a staggered registration basis, shall be made by the owner in the form and manner prescribed by the Secretary of State.

(d) Two fiscal years. Application for renewal of a vehicle registration shall be made by the owner, as to those vehicles required to be registered for 2 fiscal years, not later than June 1 immediately preceding commencement of the 2-year registration period, except that application for renewal of a vehicle registration, as to those vehicles required to be registered for 2 fiscal years on a staggered registration basis, shall be made by the owner in the form and manner prescribed by the Secretary of State.

(e) Time of application. The Secretary of State may receive applications for renewal of registration and grant the same and issue new registration cards and plates or registration stickers at any time prior to expiration of registration. No person shall display upon a vehicle, the new registration plates or registration stickers prior to the dates the Secretary of State in his discretion may select.

(f) Verification. The Secretary of State may further require, as to vehicles for-hire, that applications be accompanied by verification that fees due under the Illinois Motor Carrier of Property Law, as amended,[1] have been paid.

P.A. 76-1586, § 3-415, eff. July 1, 1970. Amended by P.A. 76-1624, § 1, eff. July 1, 1970; P.A. 78-1120, § 1, eff. Oct. 1, 1974; P.A. 80-230, § 1, eff. Oct. 1, 1977; P.A. 80-1185, § 1, eff. March 8, 1978.

Formerly Ill.Rev.Stat.1991, ch. 95 ½, ¶ 3-415.

[1] Former Ill.Rev.Stat. ch. 95½, ¶ 18-100 et seq. (repealed; see, now, 625 ILCS 5/18c-1101 et seq.).

See 5 ILCS 70/6 as to the effect of (1) more than one amendment of a section at the same session of the General Assembly or (2) two or more acts relating to the same subject matter enacted by the same General Assembly.

5/3-416. Notice of change of address or name

§ 3-416. Notice of change of address or name.

(a) Whenever any person after making application for or obtaining the registration of a vehicle shall move from the address named in the application or shown upon a registration card or certificate of title such person shall within 10 days thereafter notify the Secretary of State in writing of his old and new address.

(a-5) A police officer, a deputy sheriff, an elected sheriff, a law enforcement officer for the Department of State Police, or a fire investigator who, in accordance with Section 3-405, has furnished the address of the office of the headquarters of the governmental entity or police district where he or she works instead of his or her residence address shall, within 10 days after he or she is no longer employed by that governmental entity or police district as a police officer, a deputy sheriff, an elected sheriff, a law enforcement officer for the Department of State Police or a fire investigator, notify the Secretary of State of the old address and his or her new address. If, in accordance with Section 3-405, the spouse and children of a police officer, deputy sheriff, elected sheriff, law enforcement officer for the Department of State Police, or fire investigator have furnished the address of the office of the headquarters of the governmental entity or police district where the police officer, deputy sheriff, elected sheriff, law enforcement officer for the Department of State Police, or fire investigator works instead of their residence address, the spouse and children shall notify the Secretary of State of their old address and new address within 10 days after the police officer, deputy sheriff, elected sheriff, law enforcement officer for the Department of State Police, or fire investigator is no longer employed by that governmental entity or police district as a police officer, deputy sheriff, elected sheriff, law enforcement officer for the Department of State Police, or fire investigator.

(b) Whenever the name of any person who has made application for or obtained the registration of a vehicle is thereafter changed by marriage or otherwise such person shall within 10 days notify the Secretary of State of such former and new name.

(c) In either event, any such person may obtain a corrected registration card or certificate of title upon application and payment of the statutory fee.

P.A. 76-1586, § 3-416, eff. July 1, 1970. Amended by P.A. 77-364, § 1, eff. July 23, 1971; P.A. 91-575, § 5, eff. Aug. 14, 1999.

Formerly Ill.Rev.Stat.1991, ch. 95 ½, ¶ 3-416.

5/3-417. Lost or damaged or stolen cards, plates and registration stickers

§ 3-417. Lost or damaged or stolen cards, plates and registration stickers. (a) In the event any registration card, plate, registration sticker or other Illinois evidence of proper registration is lost, mutilated or becomes illegible, the owner or legal representative or successor in interest of the owner of the vehicle for which the same was issued as shown by the records of the Secretary of State shall immediately make application for and may obtain a duplicate under a new registration card, plate, registration sticker or other Illinois evidence of proper registration.

(b) In the event any registration card, plate, registration sticker or other Illinois evidence of proper registration is stolen from the owner, the owner or legal representative or successor in interest of the owner of the vehicle shall promptly notify the Secretary of State, and in order to comply with Section 3-413 of this Act the owner shall make application for and obtain a duplicate registration card, plate, registration sticker or other Illinois evidence of proper registration.

(c) The Secretary of State may, if advisable, issue a substitute or new registration number in lieu of issuing a duplicate.

(d) An applicant for a duplicate shall furnish information satisfactory to and prescribed by the Secretary of State, and he shall forward with the application, the fees prescribed by law.

P.A. 76-1586, § 3-417, eff. July 1, 1970. Amended by P.A. 77-649, § 1, eff. Jan. 1, 1972; P.A. 80-230, § 1, eff. Oct. 1, 1977; P.A. 81-308, § 1, eff. Jan. 1, 1980.

Formerly Ill.Rev.Stat.1991, ch. 95 ½, ¶ 3-417.

5/3-418. Registration under new identifying number

§ 3-418. Registration under new identifying number. When the Secretary of State issues a new identifying number, such motor vehicle shall be registered under such identifying number in lieu of the former identifying number.

P.A. 76-1586, § 3-418, eff. July 1, 1970.

Formerly Ill.Rev.Stat.1991, ch. 95 ½, ¶ 3-418.

5/3-419. Regulations governing change of motors

§ 3-419. Regulations governing change of motors. The Secretary of State is authorized to adopt and enforce such registration rules and regulations as may be deemed necessary and compatible with the public interest with respect to the change or substitution of one engine in place of another in any motor vehicle.

Where a substitution or change changes the classification of a motor vehicle for registration purposes resulting in requiring the payment of a greater fee or tax, the owner shall be required to reclassify the registration and pay the higher or greater fee or tax due.

P.A. 76-1586, § 3-419, eff. July 1, 1970. Amended by P.A. 77-364, § 1, eff. July 23, 1971.

Formerly Ill.Rev.Stat.1991, ch. 95 ½, ¶ 3-419.

5/3-420. § 3-420. Deleted by P.A. 83-148, § 1, eff. Aug. 29, 1983

The provisions of this section were completely stricken out by P.A. 83-148, § 1, eff. Aug. 29, 1983. The section was derived from:

5/3-421. Right of reassignment

§ 3-421. Right of reassignment. (a) Every natural person shall have the right of reassignment of the license number issued to him during the current registration plate term, for the ensuing registration plate term, provided his application for reassignment is received in the Office of the Secretary of State on or before September 30 of the final year of the registration plate term as to a vehicle registered on a calendar year, and on or before March 31 as to a vehicle registered on a fiscal year. The right of reassignment shall apply to every natural person under the staggered registration system provided the application for reassignment is received in the Office of the Secretary of State by the 1st day of the month immediately preceding the applicant's month of expiration.

In addition, every natural person shall have the right of reassignment of the license number issued to him for a two-year registration, for the ensuing two-year period. Where the two-year period is for two calendar years, the application for reassignment must be received by the Secretary of State on or before September 30th of the year preceding commencement of the two-year period. Where the two-year period is for two fiscal years commencing on July 1, the application for reassignment must be received by the Secretary of State on or before April 30th immediately preceding commencement of the two-year period.

(b) Notwithstanding the above provision, the Secretary of State shall, subject to the existing right of reassignment, have the authority to designate new specific combinations of numerical, alpha-numerical, and numerical-alpha licenses for vehicles registered on a calendar year or on a fiscal year, whether the license be issued for one or more years. The new combinations so specified shall not be subject to the right of reassignment, and no right of reassignment thereto may at any future time be acquired.

P.A. 76-1586, § 3-421, added by P.A. 77-512, § 1, eff. Jan. 1, 1972. Amended by P.A. 79-717, § 1, eff. Oct. 1, 1975; P.A. 80-230, § 1, eff. Oct. 1, 1977; P.A. 80-1185, § 1, eff. March 8, 1978.

Formerly Ill.Rev.Stat.1991, ch. 95 ½, ¶ 3-421.

See 5 ILCS 70/6 as to the effect of (1) more than one amendment of a section at the same session of the General Assembly or (2) two or more acts relating to the same subject matter enacted by the same General Assembly.

ARTICLE V. TRANSFER OF REGISTRATION

5/3-501. Registration expires on transfer by owner

§ 3-501. Registration expires on transfer by owner. Whenever the owner of a registered vehicle transfers or assigns his title, or interest thereto, the registration of such vehicle shall expire and the owner shall not be entitled to any refund of the registration fee. The owner shall remove the registration plates and registration stickers, if any, therefrom and forward the same to the Secretary of State or may have such plates and registration stickers, if any, and the registration number thereon assigned to another vehicle upon payment of the fees required by law and subject to the rules and regulations of the Secretary of State.

P.A. 76-1586, § 3-501, eff. July 1, 1970. Amended by P.A. 77-325, § 1, eff. July 22, 1971; P.A. 80-230, § 1, eff. Oct. 1, 1977; P.A. 80-1185, § 1, eff. March 8, 1978.

Formerly Ill.Rev.Stat.1991, ch. 95 ½, ¶ 3-501.

See 5 ILCS 70/6 as to the effect of (1) more than one amendment of a section at the same session of the General Assembly or (2) two or more acts relating to the same subject matter enacted by the same General Assembly.

5/3-501.1. Transfer or return of vanity or personalized license plates

§ 3-501.1. Transfer or return of vanity or personalized license plates. When any person who has been issued vanity or personalized license plates sells, trades or otherwise releases the ownership of the vehicle upon which the vanity or personalized license plates have been displayed, he shall immediately report the transfer of such plates to an acquired motor vehicle pursuant to Section 3-501 and pay the transfer fee or shall, upon the request of the Secretary, immediately return such plates to the Secretary of State. The right to reassignment of the registration plate number shall apply as provided in Section 3-421 of this Code.

P.A. 76-1586, § 3-501.1, added by P.A. 81-987, § 1, eff. Sept. 22, 1979. Amended by P.A. 86-480, § 1, eff. Jan. 1, 1990; P.A. 86-1005, § 3, eff. Dec. 28, 1989; P.A. 88-78, § 15, eff. Sept. 7, 1993.

Formerly Ill.Rev.Stat.1991, ch. 95 ½, ¶ 3-501.1.

5/3-502. New owner must secure new registration

§ 3-502. New owner must secure new registration. The transferee before operating or permitting the operation of such vehicle upon a highway shall apply for and obtain the registration thereof, as upon an original registration, except as otherwise permitted in Sections 3-401, 3-503 and 3-504.

P.A. 76-1586, § 3-502, eff. July 1, 1970.

Formerly Ill.Rev.Stat.1991, ch. 95 ½, ¶ 3-502.

5/3-503. Transfers to dealers

§ 3-503. Transfers to dealers. When the transferee of a vehicle is a dealer who holds the same for resale and lawfully operates the same under dealers' number plates or when the transferee does not drive such vehicle or permit it to be driven upon the highways, such transferee shall not be required to obtain a new registration of said vehicle.

P.A. 76-1586, § 3-503, eff. July 1, 1970.

Formerly Ill.Rev.Stat.1991, ch. 95 ½, ¶ 3-503.

5/3-504. Transfer by operation of law

§ 3-504. Transfer by operation of law. Except in case of joint tenancy with the right of survivorship or surviving spouse or transfer pursuant to an order of the Illinois Commerce Commission or Interstate Commerce Commission, whenever the title or interest of an owner in or to a registered vehicle shall pass to another otherwise than by voluntary transfer, except a transfer pursuant to an order of the Illinois Commerce Commission or Interstate Commerce Commission, the registration thereof shall expire and the vehicle shall not be operated upon the highways unless and until the person entitled to possession of such vehicle shall apply for and obtain the registration thereof.

P.A. 76-1586, § 3-504, eff. July 1, 1970.

Formerly Ill.Rev.Stat.1991, ch. 95 ½, ¶ 3-504.

5/3-505. Transfer of reciprocity permit or prorate decals

§ 3-505. Transfer of reciprocity permit or prorate decals. Whenever the owner of a vehicle properly registered in another State transfers his interest thereto, Illinois evidence of proper registration in such other State, that is an Illinois Reciprocity Permit or a Prorate Decal, shall expire and the owner shall remove the same from such vehicle and forward the same to the Secretary of State.

The owner may, however, instead have such Illinois evidence of proper registration in another State assigned to another vehicle also properly registered in another State, upon payment of the fees required by law and subject to the rules and regulations of the Secretary.

P.A. 76-1586, § 3-505, added by P.A. 77-649, § 1, eff. Jan. 1, 1972. Amended by P.A. 81-886, § 1, eff. July 1, 1980.

Formerly Ill.Rev.Stat.1991, ch. 95 ½, ¶ 3-505.

ARTICLE VI. SPECIAL PLATES

Section

5/3-600. Requirements for issuance of special plates

§ 3-600. Requirements for issuance of special plates.

(a) The Secretary of State shall not issue a series of special plates unless applications, as prescribed by the Secretary, have been received for 10,000 plates of that series; except that the Secretary of State may prescribe some other required number of applications if that number is sufficient to pay for the total cost of designing, manufacturing and issuing the special license plate.

(b) The Secretary of State, upon issuing a new series of special license plates, shall notify all law enforcement officials of the design, color and other special features of the special license plate series.

(c) This Section shall not apply to special license plate categories in existence on the effective date of this amendatory Act of 1990, or to the Secretary of State's discretion as established in Section 3-611.

P.A. 76-1586, § 3-600, added by P.A. 86-1207, § 1, eff. Aug. 29, 1990.

Formerly Ill.Rev.Stat.1991, ch. 95 ½, ¶ 3-600.

5/3-601. Operation of vehicles under special plates

§ 3-601. Operation of vehicles under special plates. (a) A manufacturer owning any unregistered vehicle of a type otherwise required to be registered under this Act may operate or move such upon the highways without registering each such vehicle upon condition that any such vehicle display thereon a special plate or plates issued to such owner as provided in this Article.

(b) A dealer owning any unregistered vehicle of a type otherwise required to be registered under this Act and held by him for sale or resale, may operate or move such upon the highways without registering each such vehicle upon condition that any such vehicle display thereon a special plate or plates issued to such owner as provided in this Article.

(c) A transporter may operate or move any vehicle not owned by him upon the highways by the driveaway or towaway methods solely for the purpose of delivery upon likewise displaying thereon like plates issued to him as provided in this Article.

(d) A boat dealer owning any boat trailer of a type otherwise required to be registered under this Act may operate or move such upon the highways and haul a boat customarily sold with such boat trailer, without registering each such boat trailer upon condition that any such boat trailer display thereon, in the manner prescribed in Section 3-413, a special plate or plates issued to such owner as provided in this Article.

(e) Any person owning unregistered vehicles of a type required to be registered and which are exclusively operated off the highways and upon private property, may move such vehicles from one plant location to another upon the highways without registering each such vehicle upon conditions that any such vehicle display thereon a special plate or plates issued to such persons as provided in this Article. Such vehicles must be unladen and may not be operated upon any highways with such special plates except for the interplant movement.

(f) Any person owning a vehicle of a type required to be registered which when purchased is not yet equipped for work or service, may move such vehicle from the point of original manufacture or sale to a body shop or other place where the vehicle is to be equipped for work or service and from such point to the owner's place of business without first registering each such vehicle upon condition that any such vehicle display thereon a special plate or plates issued to such person as provided in this Article. Upon completion of such movement, any such vehicle subject to registration must be properly registered.

(g) Special plates issued under this Article must be displayed in the manner provided for in Section 3-413.

(h) Any such vehicle bearing such special plate or plates may be operated without registration for any purpose, except that no such special plate or plates shall be used on any vehicle which is rented by the manufacturer or dealer to another person or which is used to transport passengers or property for hire, nor, except as provided in paragraph (i) of this Section, shall any such special plate or plates be used on a second division vehicle which is carrying cargo or merchandise except in demonstrating such second division vehicle for the purposes of sale, or for the purpose of testing engine and driveline components.

(i) The provisions of this Article authorizing special plates shall not apply to work or service vehicles owned by a manufacturer, transporter or dealer except a truck up to 8,000 pounds gross weight owned by a dealer and used for hauling parts incidental to the operation of the dealer's business.

(j) The Secretary of State may limit the number of special plates issued to any applicant.

P.A. 76-1586, § 3-601, eff. July 1, 1970. Amended by P.A. 76-2134, § 1, eff. July 1, 1970; P.A. 77-75, § 1, eff. July 1, 1971; P.A. 77-1316, § 1, eff. Jan. 1, 1972; P.A. 77-2829, § 40, eff. Dec. 22, 1972; P.A. 78-255, § 61, eff. Oct. 1, 1973; P.A. 78-753, § 1, eff. Sept. 11, 1973; P.A. 78-1297, § 58, eff. March 4, 1975.

Formerly Ill.Rev.Stat.1991, ch. 95 ½, ¶ 3-601.

5/3-602. Certificate and special plates for dealers, manufacturers, and transporters

§ 3-602. Certificate and special plates for dealers, manufacturers, and transporters.

(a) Any dealer, manufacturer, or transporter may make application to the Secretary of State upon the appropriate form for a certificate containing a general distinguishing number and for one or more sets of special plates as appropriate to various types of vehicles subject to registration hereunder. The applicant shall submit such proof of his or her status as a bona fide dealer, manufacturer, or transporter as may be reasonably required by the Secretary of State.

(b) The Secretary of State, upon granting any such application, shall issue to the applicant a certificate containing the applicant's name and address and special plates as applied for. Both the certificates and special plates shall display the general distinguishing number assigned to the applicant.

(c) The Secretary of State shall issue special plates to dealers and manufacturers in accordance with the following formula:

number vehicles sold in previous calendar year	maximum number sets of special plates issued at fee set by Sec. 3-810	maximum number additional sets issued at fee set by Sec. 3-806
0	0	0
1-10	1	1
11-25	2	2
26-100	8	8
101-250	12	12
251-500	20	20
501-750	30	30
751-1000	40	40
1001-1500	50	50
1501-2000	60	60
2001-2500	70	70
2501+	90	90

For those Dealers with annual sales over 2501, special plates will be allocated based on 10 sets of plates under each section for each additional 500 vehicles sold.

The limit on the maximum number of additional sets issued to manufacturers at the fee set by Section 3-806 may be lifted at the discretion of the Secretary of State.

The Secretary shall issue to a new dealer or manufacturer not more than 8 sets of special plates at each fee. If the new dealer or manufacturer has acquired his or her business from a previous dealer or manufacturer, he or she may be issued a number of sets based upon the number of vehicles sold in the previous calendar year by the previous dealer or manufacturer. If the new dealer or manufacturer was in business for only a part of the previous calendar year, the number of special plates to which he or she is entitled may be extrapolated from the number of vehicles he or she sold during that part of the year.

(d) Any manufacturer of engine and driveline components may apply to the Secretary of State for a license to operate vehicles in which such components are installed on the public highways of the State for the purpose of testing such components. The application shall describe the components and the vehicles in which they are installed, and shall contain such additional information as the Secretary shall prescribe. Upon receipt of an application and an accompanying fee of $1000, the Secretary shall issue to the applicant a license for the entire test period of the components described in the application.

Every licensee shall keep a record of each vehicle operated under such license which shall be open to inspection by the Secretary or his authorized representative for inspection at any reasonable time during the day or night.

The license of a manufacturer of engine and driveline components may be denied, revoked or suspended if the Secretary finds that the manufacturer has:

(1) violated this Code;

(2) made any material misrepresentation to the Secretary of State in connection with an application for a license; or

(3) failed to produce for the Secretary of State any record required to be produced by this Code.

This amendatory Act of 1983 shall be applicable to the 1984 registration year and thereafter.

P.A. 76-1586, § 3-602, eff. July 1, 1970. Amended by P.A. 76-2135, § 1, eff. July 1, 1970; P.A. 77-1316, § 1, eff. Jan. 1, 1972; P.A. 83-765, § 1, eff. Sept. 23, 1983; P.A. 84-986, § 1, eff. Sept. 25, 1985; P.A. 86-444, § 1, eff. Jan. 1, 1990; P.A. 91-357, § 231, eff. July 29, 1999.

Formerly Ill.Rev.Stat.1991, ch. 95 ½, ¶ 3-602.

5/3-603. Application for drive-away permits

§ 3-603. Application for drive-away permits.

(a) A dealer who has sold a vehicle of a type otherwise required to be registered under this Act to a nonresident of this State who does not have currently valid registration in his home state, may provide for the operation of such vehicle without registration from the place of sale to the place of destination outside of the State of Illinois, by issuing a drive-away permit in the manner prescribed by the Secretary of State and by affixing the permit to such vehicle in the manner prescribed by the Secretary of State. Any vehicle being operated pursuant to a drive-away permit may not be used for any other purpose and such permits shall be effective only for a period of 7 days from the date of sale.

(b) Any dealer may make application to the Secretary of State upon the appropriate form for drive-away permits for motor vehicles sold by such dealer. Along with such application each applicant shall submit proof of his status as a bona fide dealer and any other information as may be required by the Secretary of State. A non-resident who has purchased a motor vehicle from a person who is not a dealer, may likewise apply to the Secretary of State for a drive-away permit for display upon such vehicle while being driven from Illinois to the State of residence of the applicant. Along with such application, the applicant shall submit proof of his non-residence and eligibility for a reciprocal exemption from registration in Illinois.

All drive-away permits issued under such application shall bear a distinguishing number and such other features as may be required by the Secretary of State.

P.A. 76-1586, § 3-603, eff. July 1, 1970. Amended by P.A. 77-1316, § 1, eff. Jan. 1, 1972; P.A. 78-753, § 1, eff. Sept. 11, 1973; P.A. 81-822, § 1, eff. Jan. 1, 1980; P.A. 86-444, § 1, eff. Jan. 1, 1990; P.A. 92-680, § 15, eff. July 16, 2002.

Formerly Ill.Rev.Stat.1991, ch. 95 ½, ¶ 3-603.

5/3-604. Expiration of special plates

§ 3-604. Expiration of special plates. Every special plate issued, except those issued for dealers, manufacturers and transporters under Section 3-602 and persons with disabilities under Sections 3-609 or 3-616, or deaf or hard of hearing under Section 3-616 of this Code, may be issued for a 2 year period beginning January 1st of each odd-numbered year and ending December 31st of the subsequent even-numbered year. The special plates issued to a person with disabilities or a person who is deaf or hard of hearing shall expire according to the multi-year procedure as established by Section 3–414 of this Code.

Special plates issued to members of the General Assembly under Section 3–606 shall expire at midnight on the 31st day of January in odd-numbered years.

P.A. 76–1586, § 3–604, eff. July 1, 1970. Amended by P.A. 81–179, § 1, eff. Jan. 1, 1980; P.A. 83–449, § 1, eff. Jan. 1, 1984; P.A. 83–1058, § 1, eff. July 1, 1984; P.A. 83–1362, Art. II, § 99, eff. Sept. 11, 1984; P.A. 85–413, § 1, eff. Jan. 1, 1988; P.A. 85–821, § 1, eff. Jan. 1, 1988; P.A. 85–1209, Art. II, § 2–51, eff. Aug. 30, 1988; P.A. 88–685, § 5, eff. Jan. 24, 1995; P.A. 89–245, § 5, eff. Jan. 1, 1996.

Formerly Ill.Rev.Stat.1991, ch. 95 ½, ¶ 3–604.

5/3–605. Manufacturers, engine and driveline component manufacturers, transporters, repossessors and dealers to maintain records

§ 3–605. Manufacturers, engine and driveline component manufacturers, transporters, repossessors and dealers to maintain records.

Every manufacturer, engine and driveline component manufacturer, repossessor, transporter or dealer shall keep a written record of the persons to whom such drive-away permits or special plates are assigned, which record shall be open to inspection by any public officer or any employee of the Secretary of State.

P.A. 76–1586, § 3–605, eff. July 1, 1970. Amended by P.A. 76–2136, § 1, eff. July 1, 1970; P.A. 92–680, § 15, eff. July 16, 2002.

Formerly Ill.Rev.Stat.1991, ch. 95 ½, ¶ 3–605.

5/3–606. Members of General Assembly

§ 3–606. Members of General Assembly. Upon receipt of a request of a member of the General Assembly, accompanied by the appropriate application and fee, the Secretary of State shall issue to the member 2 plates as described in this Section. If the member so requests, the Secretary shall issue 2 identical sets of such registration plates for use on 2 different motor vehicles. A member may request that the Secretary of State issue registration plates in the name of a corporation when the corporation owns or leases the vehicle to be registered and the member is an officer or director of that corporation. Such registration plates shall be issued for a 2–year period beginning January 1 of each odd-numbered year and ending December 31 of the subsequent even-numbered year. If the application is from a member of the Senate, there shall appear on the rear plate, in addition to the designation of the State and the year for which the license was issued, the word "official" and appropriate wording or abbreviation indicating that the holder is a member of the Senate, followed by the number of the senatorial district of the member. On the front plate, there shall appear appropriate wording or abbreviation indicating that the holder is a member of the Senate. If the application is from a member of the House of Representatives, there shall appear on the rear plate, in addition to the designation of the State and the year for which the license was issued, the word "official" and appropriate wording or abbreviation indicating that the holder is a member of the House of Representatives, followed by the number assigned to the member. On the front plate, there shall appear appropriate wording or abbreviation indicating that the holder is a member of the House of Representatives. Numbers 1 through 118 shall be assigned and members with the longest length of service as members of the legislature shall be given the lower numbers.

When members have an equal length of service, the lower numbers shall be given in alphabetical order based on surnames.

P.A. 76–1586, § 3–606, eff. July 1, 1970. Amended by P.A. 77–2628, § 1, eff. Oct. 1, 1972; P.A. 78–328, § 1, eff. Oct. 1, 1973; P.A. 79–1036, § 1, eff. Oct. 1, 1975; P.A. 80–230, § 1, eff. Oct. 1, 1977; P.A. 82–1011, § 2, eff. Sept. 17, 1982; P.A. 88–661, § 27, eff. Sept. 16, 1994.

Formerly Ill.Rev.Stat.1991, ch. 95 ½, ¶ 3–606.

5/3–606.1. Retired members of the General Assembly

§ 3–606.1. Retired members of the General Assembly. Upon receipt of a request from a retired member of the General Assembly, accompanied by the appropriate application and fee, the Secretary of State shall issue to such retired member plates bearing appropriate wording or abbreviations indicating that the holder is a retired member of the General Assembly. Such plates may be issued for a 2 year period beginning January 1st of each odd-numbered year and ending December 31st of the subsequent even-numbered year.

"Retired member" means any individual who (a) has served as a member of the General Assembly for a minimum of 6 years, or (b) is 62 or older, has served as a member of the General Assembly for a minimum of 4 years, and retired prior to the convening of the 83rd General Assembly.

The fees and procedures relating to such plates for retired members of the General Assembly shall be the same as the fees and procedures applicable to personalized plates issued under this Code.

P.A. 76–1586, § 3–606.1, added by P.A. 82–1011, § 2, eff. Sept. 17, 1982. Amended by P.A. 84–684, § 1, eff. Sept. 20, 1985; P.A. 85–413, § 1, eff. Jan. 1, 1988.

Formerly Ill.Rev.Stat.1991, ch. 95 ½, ¶ 3–606.1.

5/3–607. Amateur Radio Operators

§ 3–607. Amateur Radio Operators. Amateur radio operators may obtain the issuance of registration plates for motor vehicles of the first division, and second division motor vehicles under 8,000 pounds, corresponding to their call letters, provided they make application therefor, which is subject to the staggered registration system, prior to October 1st of the final year of the current registration plate term and pay an additional fee of $4.

P.A. 76–1586, § 3–607, eff. July 1, 1970. Amended by P.A. 80–230, § 1, eff. Oct. 1, 1977; P.A. 84–288, § 1, eff. Jan. 1, 1986; P.A. 84–986, § 1, eff. Sept. 25, 1985; P.A. 84–1308, Art. II, § 96, eff. Aug. 25, 1986; P.A. 91–37, § 40, eff. July 1, 1999.

Formerly Ill.Rev.Stat.1991, ch. 95 ½, ¶ 3–607.

5/3–608. § 3–608. Repealed by P.A. 76–2137, § 1, eff. July 1, 1970

5/3–609. Disabled Veterans' Plates

§ 3–609. Disabled Veterans' Plates. Any disabled veteran who has been or declared eligible for funds for the purchase of a motor vehicle of the first division or for a motor vehicle of the second division weighing not more than 8,000 pounds by the United States Federal Government because of his disability, may make application for the registration of one such vehicle, to the Secretary of State without the payment of any registration fee. Registration shall be for a multi-year period effective in 1980 and may be issued staggered registration.

Any disabled veteran of World War I, of World War II, of the National Emergency between June 25, 1950 and January 31, 1955 or of the period beginning February 1, 1955 and ending on the day before the first day thereafter in which individuals (other than individuals liable for induction by reason of prior deferment) are no longer liable for induction for training and service into the armed forces under the Military Selective Service Act of 1967,[1] or of any armed conflict involving the armed forces of the United States, who has a service-connected disability of such a nature that it would, if it had been incurred in World War II, have entitled him to be awarded an automobile by the United States Federal Government, or who is receiving compensation from the Veterans Administration for total service-connected disability, may make application to the Secretary of State for the registration of one motor vehicle of the first division without accompanying such application with the payment of any fee.

Renewal of such registration must be accompanied with documentation for eligibility of registration without fee unless the applicant has a permanent qualifying disability, and such registration plates may not be issued to any person not eligible therefor.

The Illinois Veterans Commission may assist in providing the documentation of disability.

P.A. 76-1586, § 3-609, eff. July 1, 1970. Amended by P.A. 76-1625, § 1, eff. July 1, 1970; P.A. 79-1021, § 1; P.A. 81-557, § 1, eff. Jan. 1, 1980; P.A. 84-986, § 1, eff. Sept. 25, 1985; P.A. 86-444, § 1, eff. Jan. 1, 1990; P.A. 87-895, Art. 3, § 3-52, eff. Aug. 14, 1992.

Formerly Ill.Rev.Stat.1991, ch. 95 ½, ¶ 3-609.

[1] 50 U.S.C.A. App. § 451 et seq.

Section 2 of P.A. 79-1021, certified Sept. 17, 1975, provided:

"This amendatory Act of 1975 takes effect beginning with motor vehicle registrations for 1977."

5/3-609.1. Congressional Medal of Honor plates

§ 3-609.1. Congressional Medal of Honor plates. Any resident of the State of Illinois who has been awarded the Congressional Medal of Honor may make application for the registration of a motor vehicle owned solely or in part by such recipient, to the Secretary of State without the payment of any registration fee. Registration shall be for a multi-year period effective from issuance. The Secretary of State shall furnish at his office at no cost to such Congressional Medal of Honor recipients, plates bearing up to 3 letters designating the recipient's initials followed by the letters C M H signifying the Congressional Medal of Honor. The plate shall be suitable for attachment to a motor vehicle or motorcycle registered under this Code.

P.A. 76-1586, § 3-609.1, added by P.A. 82-117, § 1, eff. Jan. 1, 1982. Amended by P.A. 92-545, § 5, eff. June 12, 2002.

Formerly Ill.Rev.Stat.1991, ch. 95 ½, ¶ 3-609.1.

5/3-610. Members of Congress

§ 3-610. Members of Congress. Upon receiving an application for a certificate of registration for a motor vehicle from a member of the Congress of the United States from Illinois, accompanied with payments of the registration fees and taxes required under this Act, the Secretary of State instead of issuing to such member number plates as hereinabove provided, shall, if such member so requests, issue to him two number plates as described in this Section. Two duplicate sets of these number plates may be issued if requested and may be used on 2 different motor vehicles. There shall appear, in addition to the designation of the State and the year for which such license was issued, if he is a member of the House of Representatives, the number of the congressional district of such member in the center of the plate followed in the next line by the words "U. S. Congressman"; if he is the senior Senator from Illinois, the number 1 shall be in the center of the plate followed in the next line by the word "Senator"; and if he is the junior Senator, the number 2 shall be in the center of the plate followed in the next line by the word "Senator".

Such plates may be issued for a 2 year period beginning January 1st of each odd-numbered year and ending December 31st of the subsequent even-numbered years.

P.A. 76-1586, § 3-610, eff. July 1, 1970. Amended by P.A. 78-328, § 1, eff. Oct. 1, 1973; P.A. 79-866, § 1, eff. Sept. 10, 1975; P.A. 85-413, § 1, eff. Jan. 1, 1988.

Formerly Ill.Rev.Stat.1991, ch. 95 ½, ¶ 3-610.

5/3-610.1. Retired members of the Illinois congressional delegation

§ 3-610.1. Retired members of the Illinois congressional delegation. Upon receipt of a request from a retired member of the Illinois congressional delegation, accompanied by the appropriate application and fee, the Secretary of State shall issue to the retired member special registration plates bearing appropriate wording or abbreviations indicating that the holder is a retired member of the Illinois congressional delegation. The plates may be issued for a 2 year period beginning January 1st of each odd-numbered year and ending December 31st of the subsequent even-numbered year.

An applicant shall be charged a $15 fee for original issuance in addition to the applicable registration fee. This additional fee shall be deposited into the Secretary of State Special License Plate Fund. For each registration renewal period, a $2 fee, in addition to the appropriate registration fee, shall be charged and shall be deposited into the Retired Members of the Illinois Congressional Delegation Fund.

"Retired member of the Illinois congressional delegation" means any individual who has served as a member of the U.S. Senate or U.S. House of Representatives representing the State of Illinois. The term does not include an individual who is serving in the U.S. Senate or U.S. House of Representatives.

P.A. 76-1586, § 3-610.1, added by P.A. 88-685, § 5, eff. Jan. 24, 1995. Amended by P.A. 89-282, § 10, eff. Aug. 10, 1995.

5/3-611. Special designations

§ 3-611. Special designations. The Secretary of State, in his discretion, may make special designations of certain designs or combinations of designs, or alphabetical letters or combination of letters, or colors or combination of colors pertaining to registration plates issued to vehicles owned by governmental agencies, vehicles owned and registered by State and federal elected officials, retired Illinois Supreme Court justices, and appointed federal cabinet officials, vehicles operated by taxi or livery businesses, operated in connection with mileage weight registrations, or operated by a dealer, transporter, or manufacturer as the Secretary of State may deem necessary for the proper administration of this Act. In the case of registration plates issued for vehicles operated by or for persons with disabilities, as defined by Section 1-159.1, under Section 3-616 of this Act, the Secretary of State, upon request, shall make such special designations so that automobiles bearing such plates are easily recognizable thru use of the international accessibility symbol as automobiles driven by or for such persons. In the case of registration plates issued for vehicles operated by a disabled person with a type four hearing disability, as defined pursuant to Section 4A of The Illinois Identification Card Act,[1] the Secretary of State, upon request, shall make such special designations so that a motor vehicle bearing such plate is easily recognizable by a special symbol indicating that such vehicle is driven by a person with a hearing disability. Registration plates issued to a person who is deaf or hard of hearing under this Section shall not entitle a motor vehicle bearing such plates to those parking privileges established for persons with disabilities under this Code. In the case of registration plates issued for State owned vehicles, they shall be manufactured in compliance with Section 2 of "An Act relating to identification and use of motor vehicles of the State, approved August 9, 1951, as amended".[2] In the case of plates issued for State officials, such plates may be issued for a 2 year period beginning January 1st of each odd-numbered year and ending December 31st of the subsequent even-numbered year.

P.A. 76-1586, § 3-611, eff. July 1, 1970. Amended by P.A. 78-321, § 1, eff. Oct. 1, 1973; P.A. 79-716, § 1, eff. Oct. 1, 1975; P.A. 80-486, § 1, eff. Oct. 1, 1977; P.A. 81-449, § 1, eff. Sept. 7, 1979; P.A. 83-1058, § 1, eff. July 1, 1984; P.A. 85-413, § 1, eff. Jan. 1, 1988; P.A. 85-821, § 1, eff. Jan. 1, 1988; P.A. 85-1209, Art. II, § 2-51, eff. Aug. 30, 1988; P.A. 87-829, § 1, eff. Jan. 17, 1992; P.A. 87-832, § 3, eff. Jan. 17, 1992; P.A. 87-1249, § 1, eff. Dec. 24, 1992; P.A. 88-685, § 5, eff. Jan. 24, 1995.

Formerly Ill.Rev.Stat.1991, ch. 95 ½, ¶ 3-611.

[1] 15 ILCS 335/4A.

[2] 30 ILCS 610/2.

5/3-612. Repossessor plates

§ 3-612. Repossessor plates. The Secretary, upon receipt of an application, made on the form prescribed by the Secretary of State may issue to financial institutions, to lending institutions and to persons engaged in the business of repossessing motor vehicles for others in situations where the motor vehicle is the security for the funds, special plates which may be used by such financial institutions, lending institutions and repossessors solely for the purpose of operating the motor vehicles which are repossessed by such repossessors upon a default in the contract.

Said special plates shall, in addition to the legends provided in Section 3-412 of this Act, contain a phrase "repossessor" and such other letters or numbers as the Secretary of State may prescribe. If an applicant for such plates is engaged in repossessing vehicles for other persons and does not hold a certificate, registration or permit from the Illinois Commerce Commission to conduct such an operation, the application shall be denied.

P.A. 76-1586, § 3-612, eff. July 1, 1970.

Formerly Ill.Rev.Stat.1991, ch. 95 ½, ¶ 3-612.

5/3-613. Special inaugural license plate

§ 3-613. Special inaugural license plate. Any resident of Illinois, being a member of the Official Presidential Inaugural Committee, may, during the period from January through February 15th of any year in which the President of the United States is being inaugurated, display a special inaugural license plate furnished by such person in lieu of the current and valid Illinois license plate issued to a motor vehicle of the first division owned by such person, provided that the official inaugural credentials or a valid certificate thereof acceptable to the Secretary of State and the valid and current Illinois license plates and registration card issued to such motor vehicle are simultaneously carried within such vehicle and available for inspection.

P.A. 76-1586, § 3-613, eff. July 1, 1970.

Formerly Ill.Rev.Stat.1991, ch. 95 ½, ¶ 3 613.

5/3-614. Manufacturers of engine and driveline components

§ 3-614. Manufacturers of engine and driveline components. The Secretary, upon receipt of an application made on the form prescribed by the Secretary of State, may issue to manufacturers of engine and driveline components special plates which may be used by such manufacturers solely for the purpose of operating motor vehicles of the second division to test engine and driveline components installed in such vehicles.

P.A. 76-1586, § 3-614, eff. July 1, 1970, added by P.A. 76-2138, § 1, eff. July 1, 1970. Amended by P.A. 85-1396, § 2, eff. Sept. 2, 1988.

Formerly Ill.Rev.Stat.1991, ch. 95 ½, ¶ 3-614.

5/3-615. Honorary Consular License Plate

§ 3-615. Honorary Consular License Plate. The Secretary, upon receipt of an application made on the form prescribed by the Secretary of State, may issue Illinois Honorary Consular license plates to any person who is a non-resident and an official or employee of the Coordination Council for North American Affairs as recognized in the Taiwan Relation Act, Public Law 96-8[1], and serving that instrumentality and temporarily residing in this State. In addition, these plates may be issued to United States nationals or permanent residents who are appointed Honorary Consular officers and confirmed by the Federal Department of State.

Such registration plates may be issued for a 2 year period beginning January 1 of each odd-numbered year and ending December 31 of the subsequent even-numbered year. Applicants shall verify their status as Honorary Consular or Taiwanese representatives on forms provided by the Department of State.

In the event any holder of such registration plates or card leaves this State or no longer serves as an Honorary Consular or Taiwanese official or employee, the registration plates and card issued to such persons shall terminate and the owner shall remove such plates from the vehicle so registered and return them and the registration card to the Secretary of State. Such plates may not be transferred to any other person by the holder or owner.

P.A. 76-1586, § 3-615, added by P.A. 77-48, § 1, eff. July 1, 1971. Amended by P.A. 80-230, § 1, eff. Oct. 1, 1977; P.A. 80-1185, § 1, eff. March 8, 1978; P.A. 82-676, § 2, eff. Oct. 29, 1981; P.A. 83-449, § 1, eff. Jan. 1, 1984; P.A. 85-992, § 1, eff. Jan. 5, 1988.

Formerly Ill.Rev.Stat.1991, ch. 95 ½, ¶ 3-615.

[1] 22 U.S.C.A. § 3301 et seq.

5/3-616. Person with disabilities license plates

§ 3-616. Person with disabilities license plates.

(a) Upon receiving an application for a certificate of registration for a motor vehicle of the first division or for a motor vehicle of the second division weighing no more than 8,000 pounds, accompanied with payment of the registration fees required under this Code from a person with disabilities or a person who is deaf or hard of hearing, the Secretary of State, if so requested, shall issue to such person registration plates as provided for in Section 3–611, provided that the person with disabilities or person who is deaf or hard of hearing must not be disqualified from obtaining a driver's license under subsection 8 of Section 6–103 of this Code, and further provided that any person making such a request must submit a statement certified by a licensed physician to the effect that such person is a person with disabilities as defined by Section 1–159.1 of this Code, or alternatively provide adequate documentation that such person has a Class 1A, Class 2A or Type Four disability under the provisions of Section 4A of the Illinois Identification Card Act.[1] For purposes of this Section, an Illinois Disabled Person Identification Card issued pursuant to the Illinois Identification Card Act[2] indicating that the person thereon named has a disability shall be adequate documentation of such a disability.

(b) The Secretary shall issue plates under this Section to a parent or legal guardian of a person with disabilities if the person with disabilities has a Class 1A or Class 2A disability as defined in Section 4A of the Illinois Identification Card Act or is a person with disabilities as defined by Section 1–159.1 of this Code, and does not possess a vehicle registered in his or her name, provided that the person with disabilities relies frequently on the parent or legal guardian for transportation. Only one vehicle per family may be registered under this subsection, unless the applicant can justify in writing the need for one additional set of plates. Any person requesting special plates under this subsection shall submit such documentation or such physician's statement as is required in subsection (a) and a statement describing the circumstances qualifying for issuance of special plates under this subsection.

(c) The Secretary may issue a person with disabilities parking decal or device to a person with disabilities as defined by Section 1–159.1 without regard to qualification of such person with disabilities for a driver's license or registration of a vehicle by such person with disabilities or such person's immediate family, provided such person with disabilities making such a request has been issued a Disabled Person Identification Card indicating that the person named thereon has a Class 1A or Class 2A disability, or alternatively, submits a statement certified by a licensed physician to the effect that such person is a person with disabilities as defined by Section 1–159.1.

(d) The Secretary shall prescribe by rules and regulations procedures to certify or re-certify as necessary the eligibility of persons whose disabilities are other than permanent for special plates or person with disabilities parking decals or devices issued under subsections (a), (b) and (c). Except as provided under subsection (f) of this Section, no such special plates, decals or devices shall be issued by the Secretary of State to or on behalf of any person with disabilities unless such person is certified as meeting the definition of a person with disabilities pursuant to Section 1–159.1 or meeting the requirement of a Type Four disability as provided under Section 4A of the Illinois Identification Card Act for the period of time that the physician determines the applicant will have the disability, but not to exceed 6 months from the date of certification or recertification.

(e) Any person requesting special plates under this Section may also apply to have the special plates personalized, as provided under Section 3–405.1.

(f) The Secretary of State, upon application, shall issue person with disabilities registration plates or a person with disabilities parking decal to corporations, school districts, State or municipal agencies, limited liability companies, nursing homes, convalescent homes, or special education cooperatives which will transport persons with disabilities. The Secretary shall prescribe by rule a means to certify or recertify the eligibility of organizations to receive person with disabilities plates or decals and to designate which of the 2 person with disabilities emblems shall be placed on qualifying vehicles.

(g) The Secretary of State, or his designee, may enter into agreements with other jurisdictions, including foreign jurisdictions, on behalf of this State relating to the extension of parking privileges by such jurisdictions to permanently disabled residents of this State who display a special license plate or parking device that contains the International symbol of access on his or her motor vehicle, and to recognize such plates or devices issued by such other jurisdictions. This State shall grant the same parking privileges which are granted to disabled residents of this State to any non-resident whose motor vehicle is licensed in another state, district, territory or foreign country if such vehicle displays the international symbol of access or a distinguishing insignia on license plates or parking device issued in accordance with the laws of the non-resident's state, district, territory or foreign country.

P.A. 76–1586, § 3–616, added by P.A. 78–321, § 1, eff. Oct. 1, 1973. Amended by P.A. 80–486, § 1, eff. Oct. 1, 1977; P.A. 83–828, § 1, eff. Jan. 1, 1984; P.A. 83–1058, § 1, eff. July 1, 1984; P.A. 83–1362, Art. II, § 99, eff. Sept. 11, 1984; P.A. 83–1421, § 10, eff. July 1, 1985; P.A. 84–734, § 1, eff. Jan. 1, 1986; P.A. 84–868, § 1, eff. Sept. 23, 1985; P.A. 84–1308, Art. II, § 96, eff. Aug. 25, 1986; P.A. 85–821, § 1, eff. Jan. 1, 1988; P.A. 86–539, § 1, eff. Jan. 1, 1990; P.A. 88–685, § 5, eff. Jan. 24, 1995; P.A. 91–769, § 5, eff. June 9, 2000; P.A. 92–16, § 85, eff. June 28, 2001; P.A. 92–411, § 5, eff. Jan. 1, 2002; P.A. 92–651, § 77, eff. July 11, 2002.

Formerly Ill.Rev.Stat.1991, ch. 95 ½, ¶ 3–616.

[1] 15 ILCS 335/4A.

[2] 15 ILCS 335/1 et seq.

Section 2 of P.A. 83–828 provided:

"This Act takes effect with the 1985 registration year."

P.A. 92–16, the First 2001 General Revisory Act, amended various Acts to delete obsolete text, to correct patent and technical errors, to revise cross references, to resolve multiple actions in the 91st General Assembly and to make certain technical corrections in P.A. 91–1 through P.A. 91–937.

P.A. 92–651, the First 2002 General Revisory Act, amended various Acts to delete obsolete text, to correct patent and technical errors, to revise cross references, to resolve multiple actions in the 91st and 92nd General Assemblies and to make certain technical corrections in P.A. 91–937 through P.A. 92–520.

5/3–617. Driver education plates

§ 3–617. Driver education plates. A High School operating passenger cars for a high school driver training program, may operate or move the same upon the highway without registering each such passenger car upon the condition that each such passenger car display thereon, in the manner prescribed by Section 3–413, special plates issued to the high school under the provisions of Section 3–808.

Such special plates may be issued only to a public high school or a high school operated by a religious institution, and may be used only on passenger cars used exclusively in high school driver training program approved by the State Board of Education.

P.A. 76–1586, § 3–617, added by P.A. 78–502, § 1, eff. Jan. 1, 1974. Amended by P.A. 81–1508, § 8, eff. Sept. 25, 1980.

Formerly Ill.Rev.Stat.1991, ch. 95 ½, ¶ 3–617.

5/3–618. Charitable vehicle plates

§ 3–618. Charitable vehicle plates. Charitable vehicle plates shall be of such color and design as prescribed by the Secretary. The fee for such plates shall be as prescribed in Section 3–808 of this Code. Such plates may be obtained by owners of charitable vehicles.

P.A. 76–1586, § 3–618, added by P.A. 79–698, § 1, eff. Jan. 1, 1976. Amended by P.A. 82–1011, § 2, eff. Sept. 17, 1982; P.A. 90–89, § 15, eff. Jan. 1, 1998.

Formerly Ill.Rev.Stat.1991, ch. 95 ½, ¶ 3–618.

Another § 3–618 relating to Sample Registration plates and stickers, was renumbered § 3–619 by P.A. 79–1454, § 44.

5/3–619. Sample Registration plates and stickers

§ 3–619. Sample Registration plates and stickers. The Secretary of State, upon receipt of an application made on the form prescribed by the Secretary, may issue to any law enforcement agency in this State, or to any authorized agency of any foreign jurisdiction, or to any motion picture or television industry, one or more Sample Registration Plates and stickers. The design of such plates and stickers shall be wholly within the discretion of the Secretary, and shall be issued without charge. The Secretary of State, upon receipt of an application made on the form prescribed by the Secretary, may issue to any other individual one or more Sample Registration Plates and stickers for a fee of $4 for each Sample Registration Plate and sticker.

P.A. 76–1586, § 3–618, added by P.A. 79–715, § 1, eff. Jan. 1, 1976. Renumbered § 3–619 and amended by P.A. 79–1454, § 44, eff. Aug. 31, 1976. Amended by P.A. 80–1185, § 1, eff. March 8, 1978; P.A. 81–823, § 1, eff. Jan. 1, 1980; P.A. 85–951, § 1, eff. July 1, 1988; P.A. 91–37, § 40, eff. July 1, 1999.

Formerly Ill.Rev.Stat.1991, ch. 95 ½, ¶ 3–619.

5/3–620. Prisoner of war special registration plates

§ 3–620. The Secretary, upon receipt of an application made on the form prescribed by the Secretary of State, may issue special registration plates to United States citizens, who are present or former members of the United States armed forces or any of its allies, and who were prisoners of war of World War I, World War II, the Korean Conflict, and the Vietnamese conflict, or to the widowed spouse of a former member of the United States armed forces, providing that widowed spouse was married to the POW at the time of death, and is a single person at the time of application. The special plates issued pursuant to this Section shall be affixed only to passenger vehicles of the first division subject to the staggered registration system, motorcycles, and vehicles of the second division having a gross weight of 8,000 pounds or less and shall be issued without charge. Only one set of plates may be issued at no fee.

The design and color of the prisoner of war plates shall be wholly within the discretion of the Secretary of State.

P.A. 76–1586, § 3–620, added by P.A. 81–169, § 1, eff. Jan. 1, 1980. Amended by P.A. 82–118, § 1, eff. Jan. 1, 1982; P.A. 83–61, § 1, eff. Jan. 1, 1984; P.A. 83–117, § 1, eff. Aug. 19, 1983; P.A. 83–1362, Art. II, § 99, eff. Sept. 11, 1984; P.A. 84–132, § 1, eff. Aug. 12, 1985; P.A. 84–986, § 1, eff. Sept. 25, 1985; P.A. 84–1308, Art. II, § 96, eff. Aug. 25, 1986; P.A. 92–545, § 5, eff. June 12, 2002.

Formerly Ill.Rev.Stat.1991, ch. 95 ½, ¶ 3–620.

Section 2 of P.A. 84–132, approved Aug. 12, 1985, provided:

"This Act shall take effect upon becoming law, and shall apply to registrations beginning with the 1987 registration year and thereafter."

Article II of P.A. 84–1308, the First 84th General Assembly Combining Revisory Act, provides for the nonsubstantive revision or renumbering or repeal of Sections of Acts necessitated by the amendment, addition or repeal of Sections by two or more Public Acts of the 84th General Assembly, which multiple action was not resolved by one of the Acts of the 84th General Assembly affecting the particular Section and makes technical corrections in Acts amended by the 84th General Assembly.

5/3–621. National Guard plates

§ 3–621. The Secretary, upon receipt of an application, made in the form prescribed by the Secretary of State, may issue to members of the Illinois National Guard, and to Illinois residents who are either former members of the Illinois National Guard or the surviving spouses of Illinois National Guard members, special registration plates. The special plates issued pursuant to this Section shall be affixed only to passenger vehicles of the first division, motorcycles, or motor vehicles of the second division weighing not more than 8,000 pounds subject to the staggered registration system.

The design and color of such plates shall be wholly within the discretion of the Secretary of State.

P.A. 76–1586, § 3–621, added by P.A. 82–118, § 1, eff. Jan. 1, 1982. Amended by P.A. 84–986, § 1, eff. Sept. 25, 1985; P.A. 92–545, § 5, eff. June 12, 2002; P.A. 92–699, § 5, eff. Jan. 1, 2003.

Formerly Ill.Rev.Stat.1991, ch. 95 ½, ¶ 3–621.

See 5 ILCS 70/6 as to the effect of (1) more than one amendment of a section at the same session of the General Assembly or (2) two or more acts relating to the same subject matter enacted by the same General Assembly.

5/3–622. Armed Forces Reserves plates

§ 3–622. The Secretary, upon receipt of an application made in the form prescribed by the Secretary of State, may issue to members of the United States Armed Forces Reserves who reside in Illinois, and to Illinois residents who are either former members of the United States Armed Forces Reserves or the surviving spouses of United States Armed Forces Reserve members who resided in Illinois, special registration plates. The special plates issued pursuant to this Section shall be affixed only to passenger vehicles of the first division, motorcycles, or motor vehicles of the second division weighing not more than 8,000 pounds subject to the staggered registration system. The design and color of such plates shall be wholly within the discretion of the Secretary of State.

P.A. 76–1586, § 3–622, added by P.A. 83–1473, § 1, eff. Jan. 1, 1985. Amended by P.A. 84–986, § 1, eff. Sept. 25, 1985; P.A. 92–545, § 5, eff. June 12, 2002; P.A. 92–699, § 5, eff. Jan. 1, 2003.

Formerly Ill.Rev.Stat.1991, ch. 95 ½, ¶ 3–622.

See 5 ILCS 70/6 as to the effect of (1) more than one amendment of a section at the same session of the General Assembly or (2) two or more acts relating to the same subject matter enacted by the same General Assembly.

5/3-623. Purple Heart Plates

§ 3-623. Purple Heart Plates. The Secretary, upon receipt of an application made in the form prescribed by the Secretary of State, may issue to recipients awarded the Purple Heart by a branch of the armed forces of the United States who reside in Illinois, special registration plates. The special plates issued pursuant to this Section should be affixed only to passenger vehicles of the 1st division, including motorcycles, or motor vehicles of the 2nd division weighing not more than 8,000 pounds.

The design and color of such plates shall be wholly within the discretion of the Secretary of State. Appropriate documentation, as determined by the Secretary, and the appropriate registration fee shall accompany the application. However, for an individual who has been issued Purple Heart plates for a vehicle and who has claimed and received a grant under the Senior Citizens and Disabled Persons Property Tax Relief and Pharmaceutical Assistance Act,[1] the annual fee for the registration of the vehicle shall be as provided in Section 3-806.3 of this Code.

P.A. 76-1586, § 3-623, added by P.A. 85-172, § 1, eff. Jan. 1, 1988. Amended by P.A. 89-98, § 5, eff. Jan. 1, 1996; P.A. 91-25, § 25, eff. June 9, 1999; P.A. 92-82, § 5, eff. Jan. 1, 2002; P.A. 92-699, § 5, eff. Jan. 1, 2003.

Formerly Ill.Rev.Stat.1991, ch. 95 ½, ¶ 3-623.

[1] 320 ILCS 25/1 et seq.

P.A. 92-699 incorporated the amendment by P.A. 92-82.

5/3-624. Retired members of Armed Forces

§ 3-624. The Secretary, upon receipt of an application made in the form prescribed by the Secretary of State, may issue to retired members of the United States Armed Forces who reside in Illinois, special registration plates. The special plates issued pursuant to this Section shall be affixed only to passenger vehicles of the first division, motorcycles, or motor vehicles of the second division weighing not more than 8,000 pounds and subject to the staggered registration system. The design and color of such plates shall be wholly within the discretion of the Secretary of State.

P.A. 76-1586, § 3-624, added by P.A. 86-165, § 1, eff. Aug. 13, 1989. Amended by P.A. 92-545, § 5, eff. June 12, 2002.

Formerly Ill.Rev.Stat.1991, ch. 95 ½, ¶ 3-624.

5/3-625. Pearl Harbor Plates

§ 3-625. Pearl Harbor Plates. The Secretary, upon receipt of an application made in the form prescribed by the Secretary of State, may issue special registration plates to any Illinois resident who, while a member of the armed forces of the United States, participated in the battle of Pearl Harbor on December 7, 1941, or to the widowed spouse of any Illinois resident who, while a member of the armed forces of the United States, participated in the battle of Pearl Harbor on December 7, 1941, provided that the widowed spouse was married to the battle of Pearl Harbor participant at the time of the participant's death and is a single person at the time of application. The special plates issued pursuant to this Section should be affixed only to passenger vehicles of the 1st division, motorcycles or motor vehicles of the 2nd division weighing not more than 8,000 pounds.

The design and color of such plates shall be wholly within the discretion of the Secretary of State. Appropriate documentation, as determined by the Secretary, and the appropriate registration fee shall accompany the application.

P.A. 76-1586, § 3-625, added by P.A. 86-1481, Art. 9, § 1, eff. Jan. 14, 1991. Amended by P.A. 89-571, § 5, eff. July 26, 1996; P.A. 89-620, § 10, eff. Jan. 1, 1997; P.A. 92-545, § 5, eff. June 12, 2002; P.A. 92-699, § 5, eff. Jan. 1, 2003.

Formerly Ill.Rev.Stat.1991, ch. 95 ½, ¶ 3-625.

The amendments by P.A. 89-571 and P.A. 89-620 were identical.

See 5 ILCS 70/6 as to the effect of (1) more than one amendment of a section at the same session of the General Assembly or (2) two or more acts relating to the same subject matter enacted by the same General Assembly.

5/3-626. Korean War Veteran license plates

§ 3-626. Korean War Veteran license plates.

(a) In addition to any other special license plate, the Secretary, upon receipt of all applicable fees and applications made in the form prescribed by the Secretary of State, may issue special registration plates designated as Korean War Veteran license plates to residents of Illinois who participated in the United States Armed Forces during the Korean War. The special plate issued under this Section shall be affixed only to passenger vehicles of the first division, motorcycles, motor vehicles of the second division weighing not more than 8,000 pounds, and recreational vehicles as defined by Section 1-169 of this Code. Plates issued under this Section shall expire according to the staggered multi-year procedure established by Section 3-414.1 of this Code.

(b) The design, color, and format of the plates shall be wholly within the discretion of the Secretary of State. The Secretary may, in his or her discretion, allow the plates to be issued as vanity plates or personalized in accordance with Section 3-405.1 of this Code. The plates are not required to designate "Land Of Lincoln", as prescribed in subsection (b) of Section 3-412 of this Code. The Secretary shall prescribe the eligibility requirements and, in his or her discretion, shall approve and prescribe stickers or decals as provided under Section 3-412.

(c) An applicant shall be charged a $15 fee for original issuance in addition to the applicable registration fee. Of this additional fee, $13 shall be deposited into the Secretary of State Special License Plate Fund and $2 shall be deposited into the Korean War Memorial Construction Fund. For each registration renewal period, a $2 fee, in addition to the appropriate registration fee, shall be charged and shall be deposited into the Secretary of State Special License Plate Fund.

(d) The Korean War Memorial Construction Fund is created as a special fund in the State treasury. All moneys in the Korean War Memorial Construction Fund shall, subject to appropriation, be used by the Department of Veteran Affairs to provide grants for construction of the Korean War Memorial to be located at Oak Ridge Cemetery in Springfield, Illinois. Upon the completion of the Memorial, the Department of Veteran Affairs shall certify to the State Treasurer that the construction of the Memorial has been completed. Upon the certification by the Department of Veteran Affairs, the State Treasurer shall transfer all moneys in the Fund and any future deposits into the Fund into the Secretary of State Special License Plate Fund.

(e) An individual who has been issued Korean War Veteran license plates for a vehicle and who has claimed and received a grant under the Senior Citizens and Disabled Persons Property Tax Relief and Pharmaceutical Assistance Act shall pay the original issuance and the regular annual fee for the registration of the vehicle as provided in Section 3-

806.3 of this Code in addition to the fees specified in subsection (c) of this Section.

P.A. 76–1586, § 3–626, added by P.A. 88–485, § 10, eff. Jan. 1, 1994. Amended by P.A. 88–560, § 10, eff. Aug. 4, 1994; P.A. 88–670, Art. 2, § 2–59, eff. Dec. 2, 1994; P.A. 89–98, § 5, eff. Jan. 1, 1996; P.A. 89–282, § 10, eff. Aug. 10, 1995; P.A. 89–626, Art. 2, § 2–64, eff. Aug. 9, 1996; P.A. 91–679, § 5, eff. Jan. 26, 2000; P.A. 92–545, § 5, eff. June 12, 2002.

Another § 3–626, relating to environmental license plates, was renumbered § 3–627 by P.A. 88–670, Art. 2, § 2–59.

5/3–627. Environmental License Plate

§ 3–627. Environmental License Plate.

(a) The Secretary, upon receipt of an application made in the form prescribed by the Secretary of State, may issue special registration plates designated to be environmental license plates. The special plates issued under this Section shall be affixed only to passenger vehicles of the first division, motor vehicles of the second division weighing not more than 8,000 pounds, and, as of January 1, 1996, recreational vehicles as defined by Section 1–169 of this Code. Plates issued under this Section shall expire according to the multi-year procedure established by Section 3–414.1 of this Code.

(b) The design and color of the plates shall be wholly within the discretion of the Secretary of State. Appropriate documentation, as determined by the Secretary, shall accompany the application. As of January 1, 1996, the Secretary may, in his or her discretion, allow the plates to be issued as vanity or personalized plates in accordance with Section 3–405.1 of this Code.

(c) An applicant shall be charged a $40 fee for original issuance in addition to the appropriate registration fee, if applicable. Of this fee, $25 shall be deposited into the State Parks Fund and $15 shall be deposited into the Secretary of State Special License Plate Fund, to be used by the Secretary of State to help defray the administrative processing costs. For each registration renewal period, a $27 fee, in addition to the appropriate registration fee, shall be charged. Of this fee, $25 shall be deposited into the State Parks Fund and $2 shall be deposited into the Secretary of State Special License Plate Fund .

P.A. 76–1586, § 3–626, added by 88–333, § 5, eff. Jan. 1, 1994. Renumbered § 3–627 and amended by P.A. 88–670, Art. 2, § 2–59, eff. Dec. 2, 1994. Amended by P.A. 89–282, § 10, eff. Aug. 10, 1995.

5/3–628. Bronze Star plates

§ 3–628. Bronze Star plates.

(a) Beginning January 1, 1996, in addition to any other special license plate, the Secretary, upon receipt of all applicable fees and applications made in the form prescribed by the Secretary of State, may issue special registration plates to residents of Illinois who have been awarded the Bronze Star by the United States Armed Forces. The special plate issued under this Section shall be affixed only to passenger vehicles of the first division, motorcycles, or motor vehicles of the second division weighing not more than 8,000 pounds. Plates issued under this Section shall expire according to the staggered multi-year procedure established by Section 3–414.1 of this Code.

(b) The design, color, and format of the plates shall be wholly within the discretion of the Secretary of State. The Secretary may, in his or her discretion, allow the plates to be issued as vanity plates or personalized in accordance with Section 3–405.1 of this Code. The plates are not required to designate "Land Of Lincoln", as prescribed in subsection (b) of Section 3–412 of this Code. The Secretary shall prescribe the eligibility requirements and, in his or her discretion, shall approve and prescribe stickers or decals as provided under Section 3–412.

(c) An applicant shall be charged a $15 fee for original issuance in addition to the appropriate registration fee.

This additional fee shall be deposited into the Secretary of State Special License Plate Fund. For each registration renewal period, a $2 fee, in addition to the appropriate registration fee, shall be charged and deposited into the Secretary of State Special License Plate Fund.

P.A. 76–1586, § 3–628, added by P.A. 88–589, § 10, eff. Aug. 14, 1994. Amended by P.A. 89–282, § 10, eff. Aug. 10, 1995; P.A. 92–545, § 5, eff. June 12, 2002.

5/3–629. Collegiate license plates; scholarship fund

§ 3–629. Collegiate license plates; scholarship fund.

(a) In addition to any other special license plate, the Secretary, upon receipt of all applicable fees and applications made in the form prescribed by the Secretary of State, may issue collegiate license plates. The collegiate plates issued under this Section shall be affixed only to passenger vehicles of the first division and motor vehicles of the second division weighing nor more than 8,000 pounds and subject to the staggered registration system. Plates issued under this Section shall expire according to the staggered multi-year procedure established under Section 3–414.1 of this Code.

(b) The design, color, and format of the plates shall be wholly within the discretion of the Secretary of State. The Secretary of State may, at his or her discretion, issue the plates for any public or degree-granting, not-for-profit private college or university located in this State. The Secretary may, in his or her discretion, allow the plates to be issued as vanity plates or personalized in accordance with Section 3–405.1 of this Code. The plates are not required to designate "Land Of Lincoln", as prescribed in subsection (b) of Section 3–412 of this Code. The Secretary shall prescribe the eligibility requirements including a minimum level of specialized license plates requests and, in his or her discretion, shall approve and prescribe stickers or decals as provided under Section 3–412.

(c) An applicant shall be charged a $40 fee for original issuance in addition to the applicable registration fee. Of the original issuance fee in the case of a public university or college, $25 shall be deposited into the State College and University Trust Fund and $15 shall be deposited into the Secretary of State Special License Plate Fund to be used by the Secretary of State, subject to appropriation, to help defray the administrative costs of issuing the plate. Of the original issuance fee in the case of a degree-granting, not-for-profit private college or university, $25 shall be deposited into the University Grant Fund and $15 shall be deposited into the Secretary of State Special License Plate Fund to be used by the Secretary of State, subject to appropriation, to help defray the administrative cost of issuing the plate. In addition to the regular renewal fee, an applicant shall be charged $27 for the renewal of each set of license plates issued under this Section; $25 shall be deposited into the State College and University Trust Fund in the case of a public university or college or into the University Grant Fund in the case of a degree-granting, not-for-profit private college or university, and $2 shall be deposited into the Secretary of State Special License Plate Fund plates for all collegiate plates.

(d) The State College and University Trust Fund is created as a special fund in the State treasury. The State Treasurer shall create separate accounts within the State College and University Trust Fund for each public university or college for which collegiate license plates have been issued. Moneys in the State College and University Trust Fund shall be allocated to each account in proportion to the number of plates sold in regard to each public university or college. Moneys Receipts deposited into the State College and University Trust Fund during the preceding calendar year shall be distributed, subject to appropriation, to each participating public university or college This revenue shall be used for the sole purpose of scholarship grant awards.

(e) The University Grant Fund is created as a special fund in the State treasury. All moneys in the University Grant Fund shall be appropriated to the Illinois Student Assistance Commission to make reimbursements to participating private colleges and universities under the Higher Education License Plate Grant Program.

P.A. 76-1586, § 3-629, added by P.A. 89-424, § 15, eff. June 1, 1996. Amended by P.A. 89-626, Art. 2, § 2-65, eff. Aug. 9, 1996; P.A. 90-14, Art. 2, § 2-225, eff. July 1, 1997; P.A. 90-278, § 20, eff. July 31, 1997; P.A. 90-774, § 5, eff. Aug. 14, 1998; P.A. 91-83, § 5, eff. Jan. 1, 2000.

Other §§ 3-629, relating to violence prevention license plates and Illinois Fire Fighters' License Plates, were renumbered §§ 3-630 and 3-634 by P.A. 89-626, Art. 2, § 2-65 and P.A. 90-14, Art. 2, § 2-225, respectively.

P.A. 90-14, Article 2, of the First 1997 General Revisory Act, resolved multiple actions in the 89th General Assembly and made certain technical corrections in P.A. 89-443 through P.A. 89-707.

P.A. 90-774 incorporated the amendments by P.A. 90-14 and P.A. 90-278.

5/3-630. Violence prevention license plate

§ 3-630. Violence prevention license plate.

(a) The Secretary, upon receipt of an application made in the form prescribed by the Secretary of State, may issue special registration plates designated to be Violence Prevention plates. The special plates issued under this Section shall be affixed only to passenger vehicles of the first division or motor vehicles of the second division weighing not more than 8,000 pounds. Plates issued under this Section shall expire according to the multi-year procedure established by Section 3-414.1 of this Code.

(b) The design and color of the plates shall be wholly within the discretion of the Secretary of State. Appropriate documentation, as determined by the Secretary, shall accompany the application. Beginning January 1, 1999, the Secretary may, in his or her discretion, allow the plates to be issued as vanity plates or personalized in accordance with Section 3-405.1 of this Code.

(c) An applicant shall be charged a $40 dollar fee for original issuance in addition to the appropriate registration fee, if applicable. Of this fee, $25 shall be deposited into the Violence Prevention Fund as created by this Act and $15 shall be deposited into the Secretary of State Special License Plate Fund to be used by the Secretary of State to help defray the administrative processing costs. For each registration renewal period a $27 fee, in addition to the appropriate registration fee, shall be charged. Of this fee, $25 shall be deposited into the Violence Prevention Fund and $2 shall be deposited into the Secretary of State Special License Plate Fund.

P.A. 76-1586, § 3-629, added by P.A. 89-353, § 100, eff. Aug. 17, 1995. Renumbered § 3-630 and amended by P.A. 89-626, Art. 2, § 2-65, eff. Aug. 9, 1996. Amended by P.A. 90-619, § 5, eff. Jan. 1, 1999.

5/3-631. Sportsmen Series license plate

§ 3-631. Sportsmen Series license plate.

(a) The Secretary, upon receipt of an application made in the form prescribed by the Secretary of State, may issue special registration plates designated to be Sportsmen Series license plates. The special plates issued under this Section shall be affixed only to passenger vehicles of the first division, motor vehicles of the second division weighing not more than 8,000 pounds, and recreational vehicles as defined by Section 1-169 of this Code. Plates issued under this Section shall expire according to the multi-year procedure established by Section 3-414.1 of this Code.

(b) The design and color of the plates shall be wholly within the discretion of the Secretary of State. Appropriate documentation, as determined by the Secretary, shall accompany the application. The Secretary may, in his or her discretion, allow the plates to be issued as vanity or personalized plates in accordance with Section 3-405.1 of this Code.

(c) An applicant shall be charged a $40 fee for original issuance in addition to the appropriate registration fee, if applicable. Of this fee, $25 shall be deposited into the Illinois Habitat Fund and $15 shall be deposited into the Secretary of State Special License Plate Fund, to be used by the Secretary of State to help defray the administrative processing costs. For each registration renewal period, a $27 fee, in addition to the appropriate registration fee, shall be charged. Of this fee, $25 shall be deposited into the Illinois Habitat Fund and $2 shall be deposited into the Secretary of State Special License Plate Fund.

P.A. 76-1586, § 3-631, added by P.A. 89-611, § 15, eff. Jan. 1, 1997. Amended by P.A. 90-14, Art. 2, § 2-225, eff. July 1, 1997.

Other §§ 3-631, relating to Universal Charitable Organization license plates, Master Mason plates, D.A.R.E. license plates and U.S. Veteran license plates, were renumbered §§ 3-633, 3-635, 3-637 and 3-638, respectively, by P.A. 90-14, Art. 2, § 2-225.

P.A. 90-14, Article 2, of the First 1997 General Revisory Act, resolved multiple actions in the 89th General Assembly and made certain technical corrections in P.A. 89-443 through P.A. 89-707.

5/3-632. Wildlife Prairie Park license plate

§ 3-632. Wildlife Prairie Park license plate.

(a) The Secretary, upon receipt of an application made in the form prescribed by the Secretary of State, may issue special registration plates to be designated Wildlife Prairie Park license plates. The special plates issued under this Section shall be affixed only to passenger vehicles of the first division, motor vehicles of the second division weighing not more than 8,000 pounds, and recreational vehicles as defined by Section 1-169 of this Code. Plates issued under this Section shall expire according to the multi-year procedure established by Section 3-414.1 of this Code.

(b) The design and color of the plates shall be wholly within the discretion of the Secretary of State. Appropriate documentation, as determined by the Secretary, shall accompany the application. The Secretary may, in his or her discretion, allow the plates to be issued as vanity or personalized plates in accordance with Section 3-405.1 of this Code.

(c) An applicant shall be charged a $40 fee for original issuance in addition to the appropriate registration fee, if applicable. Of this fee, $25 shall be deposited into the Wildlife Prairie Park Fund and $15 shall be deposited into the Secretary of State Special License Plate Fund, to be used by the Secretary of State to help defray the administrative processing costs. For each registration renewal period, a $27 fee, in addition to the appropriate registration fee, shall be charged. Of this fee, $25 shall be deposited into the Wildlife Prairie Park Fund and $2 shall be deposited into the Secretary of State Special License Plate Fund.

P.A. 76-1586, § 3-632, added by P.A. 89-611, § 15, eff. Jan. 1, 1997. Amended by P.A. 90-14, Art. 2, § 2-225, eff. July 1, 1997.

Another § 3-632, relating to Knights of Columbus plates, was renumbered § 3-636 by P.A. 90-14, Art. 2, § 2-225.

P.A. 90-14, Article 2, of the First 1997 General Revisory Act, resolved multiple actions in the 89th General Assembly and made certain technical corrections in P.A. 89-443 through P.A. 89-707.

5/3-633. Universal Charitable Organization license plate

§ 3-633. Universal Charitable Organization license plate.

(a) In addition to any other special license plate, the Secretary, upon receipt of all applicable fees and applications made in the form prescribed by the Secretary of State, may issue Universal Charitable Organization license plates to residents of Illinois on behalf of organizations that meet the requirements of Title 26, Section 501(c)(3) of the United States Code formed for any bona fide charitable, benevolent, philanthropic, or patriotic purpose. The Secretary of State may prescribe rules establishing additional eligibility criteria for charitable organizations under this Section. The special Universal Charitable Organization plate issued under this Section shall be affixed only to passenger vehicles of the first division and motor vehicles of the second division weighing not more than 8,000 pounds. Plates issued under this Section shall expire according to the staggered multi-year procedure established by Section 3-414.1 of this Code.

(b) The design, color, and format of the plates shall be wholly within the discretion of the Secretary of State. The plates are not required to designate "Land of Lincoln", as prescribed in subsection (b) of Section 3-412 of this Code. Charitable organizations deemed eligible by the Secretary of State shall design charitable decals to be affixed on plates issued under this Section. The Secretary may prescribe rules governing the requirements and approval of charitable decals.

(c) An applicant shall be charged a $15 fee for original issuance in addition to the applicable registration fee. This additional fee shall be deposited into the Secretary of State Special License Plate Fund. For each registration renewal period, a $2 fee, in addition to the appropriate registration fee, shall be charged and shall be deposited into the Secretary of State Special License Plate Fund. Charitable organizations may establish a fee for the purchase of their charitable decal and shall report by July 31 of each year to the Secretary of State Vehicle Services Department the sticker fee, the number of charitable decals sold, the total revenue received from the sale of charitable decals during the previous fiscal year, and any other information deemed necessary by the Secretary of State.

P.A. 76-1586, § 3-631, added by P.A. 89-564, § 5, eff. July 1, 1997. Renumbered § 3-633 and amended by P.A. 90-14, Art. 2, § 2-225, eff. July 1, 1997.

P.A. 90-14, Article 2, of the First 1997 General Revisory Act, resolved multiple actions in the 89th General Assembly and made certain technical corrections in P.A. 89-443 through P.A. 89-707.

5/3-634. Illinois Fire Fighters' License Plate

§ 3-634. Illinois Fire Fighters' License Plate.

(a) The Secretary, upon receipt of an application made in the form prescribed by the Secretary of State, may issue special registration plates designated to be Illinois Fire Fighters' Memorial license plates. The special plates issued under this Section shall be affixed only to passenger vehicles of the first division, motor vehicles of the second division weighing not more than 8,000 pounds, recreational vehicles as defined in Section 1-169 of this Code, and subject to the staggered registration system. Plates issued under this Section shall expire according to the multi-year procedure established by Section 3-414.1 of this Code.

(b) The design and color of the plates shall be wholly within the discretion of the Secretary of State. The Secretary of State may, in his or her discretion, allow the plates to be issued as vanity plates or personalized in accordance with Section 3-405.1 of this Code. The plates are not required to designate "Land of Lincoln", as prescribed in subsection (b) of Section 3-412 of this Code. The Secretary of State shall prescribe stickers or decals as provided under Section 3-412.

(c) An applicant shall be charged a $27 fee for original issuance in addition to the applicable registration fee. Of this additional fee, $15 shall be deposited into the Secretary of State Special License Plate Fund and $12 shall be deposited into the Illinois Fire Fighters' Memorial Fund. For each registration renewal period, a $17 fee, in addition to the appropriate registration fee, shall be charged. Of this fee, $2 shall be deposited into the Secretary of State Special License Plate Fund and $15 shall be deposited into the Illinois Fire Fighters' Memorial Fund.

(d) In addition to the purpose specified in Section 2-119(n), moneys in the Illinois Fire Fighters' Memorial Fund shall, subject to appropriation by the General Assembly and approval by the Secretary, be used for maintaining the Illinois Fire Fighters' Memorial, for holding an annual memorial commemoration, and for providing scholarships to children of fire fighters killed in the line of duty.

P.A. 76-1586, § 3-629, added by P.A. 89-612, § 10, eff. Aug. 9, 1996. Renumbered § 3-634 and amended by P.A. 90-14, Art. 2, § 2-225, eff. July 1, 1997. Amended by P.A. 91-832, § 5, eff. June 16, 2000.

P.A. 90-14, Article 2, of the First 1997 General Revisory Act, resolved multiple actions in the 89th General Assembly and made certain technical corrections in P.A. 89-443 through P.A. 89-707.

5/3-635. Master Mason plates

§ 3-635. Master Mason plates.

(a) The Secretary, upon receipt of all applicable fees and applications made in the form prescribed by the Secretary, may issue special registration plates designated as Master Mason license plates.

The special plates issued under this Section shall be affixed only to passenger vehicles of the first division or motor vehicles of the second division weighing not more than 8,000 pounds.

Plates issued under this Section shall expire according to the multi-year procedure established by Section 3-414.1 of this Code.

(b) The design and color of the special plates shall be wholly within the discretion of the Secretary. Appropriate documentation, as determined by the Secretary, shall accompany each application.

(c) An applicant for the special plate shall be charged a $25 fee for original issuance in addition to the appropriate registration fee. Of this fee, $10 shall be deposited into the Master Mason Fund and $15 shall be deposited into the Secretary of State Special License Plate Fund, to be used by the Secretary to help defray the administrative processing costs.

For each registration renewal period, a $25 fee, in addition to the appropriate registration fee, shall be charged. Of this fee, $23 shall be deposited into the Master Mason Fund and $2 shall be deposited into the Secretary of State Special License Plate Fund.

(d) The Master Mason Fund is created as a special fund in the State treasury. All money in the Master Mason Fund shall be paid, subject to appropriation by the General Assembly and approval by the Secretary, as grants to The Illinois Masonic Foundation for the Prevention of Drug and Alcohol Abuse Among Children, Inc., a not-for-profit corporation, for the purpose of providing Model Student Assistance Programs in public and private schools in Illinois.

P.A. 76-1586, § 3-631, added by P.A. 89-620, § 10, eff. Jan. 1, 1997. Renumbered § 3-635 and amended by P.A. 90-14, Art. 2, § 2-225, eff. July 1, 1997.

P.A. 90-14, Article 2, of the First 1997 General Revisory Act, resolved multiple actions in the 89th General Assembly and made certain technical corrections in P.A. 89-443 through P.A. 89-707.

5/3-636. Knights of Columbus plates

§ 3-636. Knights of Columbus plates.

(a) The Secretary, upon receipt of all applicable fees and applications made in the form prescribed by the Secretary, may issue special registration plates designated as Knights of Columbus license plates.

The special plates issued under this Section shall be affixed only to passenger vehicles of the first division or motor vehicles of the second division weighing not more than 8,000 pounds.

Plates issued under this Section shall expire according to the multi-year procedure established by Section 3-414.1 of this Code.

(b) The design and color of the special plates shall be wholly within the discretion of the Secretary. Appropriate documentation, as determined by the Secretary, shall accompany each application.

(c) An applicant for the special plate shall be charged a $25 fee for original issuance in addition to the appropriate registration fee. Of this fee, $10 shall be deposited into the Knights of Columbus Fund and $15 shall be deposited into the Secretary of State Special License Plate Fund, to be used by the Secretary to help defray the administrative processing costs.

For each registration renewal period, a $25 fee, in addition to the appropriate registration fee, shall be charged. Of this fee, $23 shall be deposited into the Knights of Columbus Fund and $2 shall be deposited into the Secretary of State Special License Plate Fund.

(d) The Knights of Columbus Fund is created as a special fund in the State treasury. All money in the Knights of Columbus Fund shall be paid, subject to appropriation by the General Assembly and approval by the Secretary, as grants for charitable purposes sponsored by the Knights of Columbus.

P.A. 76-1586, § 3-632, added by P.A. 89-620, § 10, eff. Jan. 1, 1997. Renumbered § 3-636 and amended by P.A. 90-14, Art. 2, § 2-225, eff. July 1, 1997.

P.A. 90-14, Article 2, of the First 1997 General Revisory Act, resolved multiple actions in the 89th General Assembly and made certain technical corrections in P.A. 89-443 through P.A. 89-707.

5/3-637. D.A.R.E. license plate

§ 3-637. D.A.R.E. license plate.

(a) The Secretary, upon receipt of an application made in the form prescribed by the Secretary of State, may issue special registration plates designated to be D.A.R.E. (Drug Abuse Resistance Education) license plates. The special plates issued under this Section shall be affixed only to passenger vehicles of the first division, motor vehicles of the second division weighing not more than 8,000 pounds, and recreational vehicles as defined by Section 1-169 of this Code. Plates issued under this Section shall expire according to the multi-year procedure established by Section 3-414.1 of this Code.

(b) The design and color of the plates shall be wholly within the discretion of the Secretary of State. Appropriate documentation, as determined by the Secretary, shall accompany the application. The Secretary may, in his or her discretion, allow the plates to be issued as vanity or personalized plates in accordance with Section 3-405.1 of this Code.

(c) An applicant shall be charged a $45 fee for original issuance in addition to the appropriate registration fee, if applicable. Of this fee, $10 shall be deposited into the State D.A.R.E. Fund; $10 shall be deposited into the County D.A.R.E. Fund if the county, as indicated by the applicant's address, has a D.A.R.E. program, otherwise the $10 fee shall be deposited into the State D.A.R.E. Fund; $10 shall be deposited into the Municipal D.A.R.E. Fund if the municipality, as indicated by the applicant's address, has a D.A.R.E. program, otherwise the $10 fee shall be deposited into the County D.A.R.E. Fund if the county, as indicated by the applicant's address, has a D.A.R.E. program, otherwise the $10 fee shall be deposited into the State D.A.R.E. Fund; and $15 shall be deposited into the Secretary of State Special License Plate Fund.

For each registration renewal period, a $29 fee, in addition to the appropriate registration fee, shall be charged. Of this fee, $9 shall be deposited into the State D.A.R.E. Fund; $9 shall be deposited into the County D.A.R.E. Fund if the county, as indicated by the applicant's address, has a D.A.R.E. program, otherwise the $9 fee shall be deposited into the State D.A.R.E. Fund; $9 shall be deposited into the Municipal D.A.R.E. Fund if the municipality, as indicated by the applicant's address, has a D.A.R.E. program, otherwise the $9 fee shall be deposited into the County D.A.R.E. Fund if the county, as indicated by the applicant's address, has a D.A.R.E. program, otherwise the $9 fee shall be deposited into the State D.A.R.E. Fund; and $2 shall be deposited into the Secretary of State Special License Plate Fund.

(d) The State D.A.R.E. Fund is created as a special fund in the State Treasury. All money in the State D.A.R.E. Fund shall be distributed, subject to appropriation by the General Assembly, to the Illinois State Police for its D.A.R.E. program.

The County D.A.R.E. Fund is created as a special fund in the State Treasury. All money in the County D.A.R.E. Fund shall be distributed, subject to appropriation by the General Assembly, to the Illinois State Police. The Illinois State

Police shall make grants of this money to counties for their D.A.R.E. programs based on the proportion of money the County D.A.R.E. Fund has received from each county, as indicated by the applicant's address.

The Municipal D.A.R.E. Fund is created as a special fund in the State Treasury. All money in the Municipal D.A.R.E. Fund shall be distributed, subject to appropriation by the General Assembly, to the Illinois State Police. The Illinois State Police shall make grants of this money to municipalities for their D.A.R.E. programs based on the proportion of money the Municipal D.A.R.E. Fund has received from each municipality, as indicated by the applicant's address.

P.A. 76-1586, § 3-631, added by P.A. 89-621, § 5, eff. Jan. 1, 1997. Renumbered § 3-637 and amended by P.A. 90-14, Art. 2, § 2-225, eff. July 1, 1997.

P.A. 90-14, Article 2, of the First 1997 General Revisory Act, resolved multiple actions in the 89th General Assembly and made certain technical corrections in P.A. 89-443 through P.A. 89-707.

5/3-638. U.S. Veteran license plates

§ 3-638. U.S. Veteran License Plates.

(a) In addition to any other special license plate, the Secretary, upon receipt of all applicable fees and applications made in the form prescribed by the Secretary of State, may issue U.S. Veteran license plates to residents of Illinois who meet eligibility requirements prescribed by the Secretary of State. The special U.S. Veteran plate issued under this Section shall be affixed only to passenger vehicles of the first division, motorcycles, and motor vehicles of the second division weighing not more than 8,000 pounds. Plates issued under this Section shall expire according to the staggered multi-year procedure established by Section 3-414.1 of this Code.

(b) The design, color, and format of the plates shall be wholly within the discretion of the Secretary of State. The Secretary may, in his or her discretion, allow the plates to be issued as vanity plates or personalized in accordance with Section 3-405.1 of this Code. The plates are not required to designate "Land Of Lincoln", as prescribed in subsection (b) of Section 3-412 of this Code. The Secretary shall prescribe the eligibility requirements and, in his or her discretion, shall approve and prescribe stickers or decals as provided under Section 3-412.

(c) An applicant shall be charged a $15 fee for original issuance in addition to the applicable registration fee. This additional fee shall be deposited into the Secretary of State Special License Plate Fund. For each registration renewal period, a $2 fee, in addition to the appropriate registration fee, shall be charged and shall be deposited into the Secretary of State Special License Plate Fund.

P.A. 76-1586, § 3-631, added by P.A. 89-639, § 5, eff. Jan. 1, 1997. Renumbered § 3-638 and amended by P.A. 90-14, Art. 2, § 2-225, eff. July 1, 1997; P.A. 92-545, § 5, eff. June 12, 2002.

P.A. 90-14, Article 2, of the First 1997 General Revisory Act, resolved multiple actions in the 89th General Assembly and made certain technical corrections in P.A. 89-443 through P.A. 89-707.

5/3-639. Special registration plate for a president of a village or incorporated town or mayor

§ 3-639. Special registration plate for a president of a village or incorporated town or mayor.

(a) The Secretary, upon receipt of all applicable fees and applications made in the form prescribed by the Secretary, may issue special registration plates to presidents of villages and incorporated towns and mayors.

The special plates issued under this Section shall be affixed only to passenger vehicles of the first division or motor vehicles of the second division weighing not more than 8,000 pounds.

Plates issued under this Section shall expire according to the multi-year procedure established by Section 3-414.1 of this Code.

(b) The design and color of the special plates shall be wholly within the discretion of the Secretary. Appropriate documentation, as determined by the Secretary, shall accompany each application.

(c) An applicant for the special plate shall be charged a $15 fee for original issuance in addition to the appropriate registration fee. This additional fee shall be deposited into the Secretary of State Special License Plate Fund, to be used by the Secretary to help defray the administrative processing costs.

For each registration renewal period, a $2 fee, in addition to the appropriate registration fee, shall be charged. This additional fee shall be deposited into the Secretary of State Special License Plate Fund.

P.A. 76-1586, § 3-639, added by P.A. 90-527, § 5, eff. Nov. 13, 1997. Amended by P.A. 90-655, § 153, July 30, 1998.

Other §§ 3-639, relating to deceased police officer or firefighter plates and Silver Star plates, were renumbered § 3-641 and § 3-642, respectively, by P.A. 90-655, § 153.

P.A. 90-655, the First 1998 General Revisory Act, amended various Acts to delete obsolete text, to correct patent and technical errors, to revise cross references, to resolve multiple actions in the 89th and 90th General Assemblies and to make certain technical corrections in P.A. 89-708 through P.A. 90-566.

5/3-640. Illinois and Michigan Canal plates

§ 3-640. Illinois and Michigan Canal plates.

(a) The Secretary, upon receipt of all applicable fees and applications made in the form prescribed by the Secretary, may issue special registration plates designated as Illinois and Michigan Canal license plates.

The special plates issued under this Section shall be affixed only to passenger vehicles of the first division or motor vehicles of the second division weighing not more than 8,000 pounds.

Plates issued under this Section shall expire according to the multi-year procedure established by Section 3-414.1 of this Code.

(b) The design and color of the special plates shall be wholly within the discretion of the Secretary. Appropriate documentation, as determined by the Secretary, shall accompany each application.

(c) An applicant for the special plate shall be charged a $40 fee for original issuance in addition to the appropriate registration fee. Of this fee, $25 shall be deposited into the Illinois and Michigan Canal Fund and $15 shall be deposited into the Secretary of State Special License Plate Fund, to be used by the Secretary to help defray the administrative processing costs.

For each registration renewal period, a $27 fee, in addition to the appropriate registration fee, shall be charged. Of this fee, $25 shall be deposited into the Illinois and Michigan Canal Fund and $2 shall be deposited into the Secretary of State Special License Plate Fund.

(d) The Illinois and Michigan Canal Fund is created as a special fund in the State treasury. All money in the Illinois and Michigan Canal Fund shall be used, subject to appropriation by the General Assembly, by the Department of Natural Resources for restoration and improvements of the Illinois and Michigan Canal and its adjacent structures.

P.A. 76-1586, § 3-640, added by P.A. 90-527, § 5, eff. Nov. 13, 1997.

5/3-641. Deceased police officer or firefighter plates

§ 3-641. Deceased police officer or firefighter plates.

(a) The Secretary, upon receipt of all applicable fees and applications made in the form prescribed by the Secretary, may issue special registration plates to the surviving spouse or, if no spouse exists, the parents of a police officer or firefighter who has died in the line of duty in this State. The special plates issued pursuant to this Section shall be affixed only to passenger vehicles of the first division or motor vehicles of the second division weighing not more than 8,000 pounds.

Plates issued under this Section shall expire according

to the multi-year procedure established by Section 3-414.1 of this Code.

(b) The design and color of the special plates shall be wholly within the discretion of the Secretary. Appropriate documentation, as determined by the Secretary, shall accompany each application.

(c) An applicant for the special plate shall be charged a $15 fee for original issuance in addition to the appropriate registration fee. This additional fee shall be deposited into the Secretary of State Special License Plate Fund, to be used by the Secretary to help defray the administrative processing costs.

For each registration renewal period, a $2 fee, in addition to the appropriate registration fee, shall be charged. This additional fee shall be deposited into the Secretary of State Special License Plate Fund.

P.A. 76-1586, § 3-639, added by P.A. 90-530, § 5, eff. Jan. 1, 1998. Renumbered § 3-641 and amended by P.A. 90-655, § 153, eff. July 30, 1998.

P.A. 90-655, the First 1998 General Revisory Act, amended various Acts to delete obsolete text, to correct patent and technical errors, to revise cross references, to resolve multiple actions in the 89th and 90th General Assemblies and to make certain technical corrections in P.A. 89-708 through P.A. 90-566.

5/3-642. Silver Star plates

§ 3-642. Silver Star plates.

(a) The Secretary, upon receipt of all applicable fees and applications made in the form prescribed by the Secretary, may issue special registration plates to residents of Illinois who have been awarded the Silver Star by the United States Armed Forces. The special plate issued under this Section shall be affixed only to passenger vehicles of the first division, motorcycles, or motor vehicles of the second division weighing not more than 8,000 pounds. Plates issued under this Section shall expire according to the staggered multi-year procedure established by Section 3-414.1 of this Code.

(b) The design, color, and format of the plates shall be wholly within the discretion of the Secretary. The Secretary may, in his or her discretion, allow the plates to be issued as vanity plates or personalized in accordance with Section 3-405.1 of this Code. The plates are not required to designate "Land Of Lincoln", as prescribed in subsection (b) of Section 3-412 of this Code. The Secretary shall prescribe the eligibility requirements and, in his or her discretion, shall approve and prescribe stickers or decals as provided under Section 3-412.

(c) An applicant shall be charged a $15 fee for original issuance in addition to the appropriate registration fee.

This additional fee shall be deposited into the Secretary of State Special License Plate Fund. For each registration renewal period, a $2 fee, in addition to the appropriate registration fee, shall be charged and deposited into the Secretary of State Special License Plate Fund.

P.A. 76-1586, § 3-639, added by P.A. 90-533, § 5, eff. Nov. 14, 1997. Renumbered § 3-642 and amended by P.A. 90-655, § 153, eff. July 30, 1998; P.A. 92-545, § 5, eff. June 12, 2002.

P.A. 90-655, the First 1998 General Revisory Act, amended various Acts to delete obsolete text, to correct patent and technical errors, to revise cross references, to resolve multiple actions in the 89th and 90th General Assemblies and to make certain technical corrections in P.A. 89-708 through P.A. 90-566.

5/3-643. Mammogram license plates

§ 3-643. Mammogram license plates.

(a) The Secretary, upon receipt of an application made in the form prescribed by the Secretary, may issue special registration plates designated as Mammogram license plates. The special plates issued under this Section shall be affixed only to passenger vehicles of the first division and motor vehicles of the second division weighing not more than 8,000 pounds. Plates issued under this Section shall expire according to the multi-year procedure established by Section 3-414.1 of this Code.

(b) The design and color of the plates is wholly within the discretion of the Secretary, except that the following phrases shall be on the plates: (i) "Mammograms Save Lives" and (ii) "The Susan G. Komen Foundation". The Secretary may allow the plates to be issued as vanity plates or personalized under Section 3-405.1 of the Code. The Secretary shall prescribe stickers or decals as provided under Section 3-412 of this Code.

(c) An applicant for the special plate shall be charged a $25 fee for original issuance in addition to the appropriate registration fee. Of this fee, $10 shall be deposited into the Mammogram Fund and $15 shall be deposited into the Secretary of State Special License Plate Fund, to be used by the Secretary to help defray the administrative processing costs.

For each registration renewal period, a $25 fee, in addition to the appropriate registration fee, shall be charged. Of this fee, $23 shall be deposited into the Mammogram Fund and $2 shall be deposited into the Secretary of State Special License Plate Fund.

(d) The Mammogram Fund is created as a special fund in the State treasury. All money in the Mammogram Fund shall be paid, subject to appropriation by the General Assembly and approval by the Secretary, as grants to the Susan G. Komen Foundation for breast cancer research, education, screening, and treatment.

P.A. 76-1586, § 3-643, added by P.A. 90-675, § 10, eff. Jan. 1, 1999 Amended by P.A. 91-357, § 231, eff. July 29, 1999.

Another § 3-643, relating to Police Memorial Committee license plates, was renumbered § 3-644 by P.A. 91-357, § 231.

P.A. 91-357, the First 1999 General Revisory Act, amended various Acts to delete obsolete text, to correct patent and technical errors, to revise cross references, to resolve multiple actions in the 90th General Assembly and to make certain technical corrections in P.A. 90-567 through P.A. 90-810.

5/3-644. Police Memorial Committee license plates

§ 3-644. Police Memorial Committee license plates.

(a) The Secretary, upon receipt of an application made in the form prescribed by the Secretary, may issue special registration plates designated as Police Memorial Committee license plates. The special plates issued under this Section shall be affixed only to passenger vehicles of the first division and motor vehicles of the second division weighing not more than 8,000 pounds. Plates issued under this Section shall expire according to the multi-year procedure established by Section 3-414.1 of this Code.

(b) The design and color of the plates is wholly within the discretion of the Secretary. The Secretary may allow the plates to be issued as vanity plates or personalized under Section 3-405.1 of the Code. The Secretary shall prescribe stickers or decals as provided under Section 3-412 of this Code.

(c) An applicant for the special plate shall be charged a $25 fee for original issuance in addition to the appropriate registration fee. Of this fee, $10 shall be deposited into the Police Memorial Committee Fund and $15 shall be deposited into the Secretary of State Special License Plate Fund, to be used by the Secretary to help defray the administrative processing costs.

For each registration renewal period, a $25 fee, in addition to the appropriate registration fee, shall be charged. Of this fee, $23 shall be deposited into the Police Memorial Committee Fund and $2 shall be deposited into the Secretary of State Special License Plate Fund.

(d) The Police Memorial Committee Fund is created as a special fund in the State treasury. All money in the Police Memorial Committee Fund shall be paid, subject to appropriation by the General Assembly and approval by the Secretary, as grants to the Police Memorial Committee for maintaining a memorial statue, holding an annual memorial commemoration, and giving scholarships to children of police officers killed in the line of duty.

P.A. 76-1586, § 3-643, added by P.A. 90-729, § 10, eff. Jan. 1, 1999. Renumbered § 3-644 and amended by P.A. 91-357, § 231, eff. July 29, 1999.

P.A. 91-357, the First 1999 General Revisory Act, amended various Acts to delete obsolete text, to correct patent and technical errors, to revise cross references, to resolve multiple actions in the 90th General Assembly and to make certain technical corrections in P.A. 90-567 through P.A. 90-810.

5/3-645. Vietnam Veteran License Plates

§ 3-645. Vietnam Veteran License Plates.

(a) In addition to any other special license plate, the Secretary, upon receipt of all applicable fees and applications made in the form prescribed by the Secretary of State, may issue Vietnam Veteran license plates to residents of Illinois who meet eligibility requirements prescribed by the Secretary of State. The special Vietnam Veteran plate issued under this Section shall be affixed only to passenger vehicles of the first division, motorcycles, and motor vehicles of the second division weighing not more than 8,000 pounds. Plates issued under this Section shall expire according to the staggered multi-year procedure established by Section 3-414.1 of this Code.

(b) The design, color, and format of the plates shall be wholly within the discretion of the Secretary of State. The Secretary may, in his or her discretion, allow the plates to be issued as vanity plates or personalized in accordance with Section 3-405.1 of this Code. The plates are not required to designate "Land Of Lincoln", as prescribed in subsection (b) of Section 3-412 of this Code. The Secretary shall prescribe the eligibility requirements and, in his or her discretion, shall approve and prescribe stickers or decals as provided under Section 3-412.

(c) An applicant shall be charged a $15 fee for original issuance in addition to the applicable registration fee. This additional fee shall be deposited into the Secretary of State Special License Plate Fund. For each registration renewal period, a $2 fee, in addition to the appropriate registration fee, shall be charged and shall be deposited into the Secretary of State Special License Plate Fund.

P.A. 76-1586, § 3-645, added by P.A. 91-805, § 10, eff. Jan. 1, 2001. Amended by P.A. 92-545, § 5, eff. June 12, 2002.

5/3-646. Organ Donor Awareness license plates

§ 3-646. Organ Donor Awareness license plates.

(a) The Secretary, upon receipt of an application made in the form prescribed by the Secretary, may issue special registration plates designated as Organ Donor Awareness license plates. The special plates issued under this Section shall be affixed only to passenger vehicles of the first division and motor vehicles of the second division weighing not more than 8,000 pounds. Plates issued under this Section shall expire according to the multi-year procedure established by Section 3-414.1 of this Code.

(b) The design and color of the plates is wholly within the discretion of the Secretary, except that the phrase "Be An Organ Donor" shall be on the plates, and the design of the plates shall incorporate a reference to the Chicago Bears organization and Walter Payton. The Secretary may allow the plates to be issued as vanity plates or personalized under Section 3-405.1 of the Code. The Secretary shall prescribe stickers or decals as provided under Section 3-412 of this Code.

(c) An applicant for the special plate shall be charged a $25 fee for original issuance in addition to the appropriate registration fee. Of this additional fee, $10 shall be deposited into the Organ Donor Awareness Fund and $15 shall be deposited into the Secretary of State Special License Plate Fund, to be used by the Secretary to help defray the administrative processing costs.

For each registration renewal period, a $25 fee, in addition to the appropriate registration fee, shall be charged. Of this additional fee, $23 shall be deposited into the Organ Donor Awareness Fund and $2 shall be deposited into the Secretary of State Special License Plate Fund.

(d) The Organ Donor Awareness Fund is created as a special fund in the State treasury. Subject to appropriation by the General Assembly and approval by the Secretary, 50% of the moneys in the Organ Donor Awareness Fund shall be paid as grants to the Regional Organ Bank of Illinois, and the remaining 50% of the moneys in that fund shall be paid as grants to Mid-America Transplant Services.

P.A. 76-1586, § 3-646, added by P.A. 91-805, § 10, eff. Jan. 1, 2001.

5/3-647. World War II Veteran License Plates

§ 3-647. World War II Veteran License Plates.

(a) In addition to any other special license plate, the Secretary, upon receipt of all applicable fees and applications made in the form prescribed by the Secretary of State, may issue World War II Veteran license plates to residents of Illinois who meet eligibility requirements prescribed by the Secretary of State. The special World War II Veteran plate issued under this Section shall be affixed only to passenger vehicles of the first division, motorcycles, and motor vehicles of the second division weighing not more than 8,000 pounds. Plates issued under this Section shall expire according to the staggered multi-year procedure established by Section 3-414.1 of this Code.

(b) The design, color, and format of the plates shall be wholly within the discretion of the Secretary of State. The Secretary may, in his or her discretion, allow the plates to be issued as vanity plates or personalized in accordance with Section 3-405.1 of this Code. The plates are not required to designate "Land Of Lincoln", as prescribed in subsection (b) of Section 3-412 of this Code. The Secretary shall prescribe the eligibility requirements and, in his or her discretion, shall approve and prescribe stickers or decals as provided under Section 3-412.

(c) An applicant shall be charged a $15 fee for original issuance in addition to the applicable registration fee. This additional fee shall be deposited into the Secretary of State Special License Plate Fund. For each registration renewal period, a $2 fee, in addition to the appropriate registration fee, shall be charged and shall be deposited into the Secretary of State Special License Plate Fund.

P.A. 76-1586, § 3-647, added by P.A. 91-805, § 10, eff. Jan. 1, 2001. Amended by P.A. 92-545, § 5, eff. June 12, 2002.

5/3-648. Education license plates

Text of section as added by P.A. 92-445, § 15, and amended by P.A. 92-651, § 77, and P.A. 92-845, § 10, eff. January 1, 2003

§ 3-648. Education license plates.

(a) The Secretary, upon receipt of an application made in the form prescribed by the Secretary, may issue special registration plates designated as Education license plates. The special plates issued under this Section shall be affixed only to passenger vehicles of the first division and motor vehicles of the second division weighing not more than 8,000 pounds. Plates issued under this Section shall expire according to the multi-year procedure established by Section 3-414.1 of this Code.

(b) The design and color of the plates shall be determined by a contest that every elementary school pupil in the State of Illinois is eligible to enter. The designs submitted for the contest shall be judged on September 30, 2002, and the winning design shall be selected by a committee composed of the Secretary, the Director of State Police, 2 members of the Senate, one member chosen by the President of the Senate and one member chosen by the Senate Minority Leader, and 2 members of the House of Representatives, one member chosen by the Speaker of the House and one member chosen by the House Minority Leader. The Secretary may allow the plates to be issued as vanity or personalized plates under Section 3-405.1 of the Code. The Secretary shall prescribe stickers or decals as provided under Section 3-412 of this Code.

(c) An applicant for the special plate shall be charged a $40 fee for original issuance, in addition to the appropriate registration fee. Of this $40 additional original issuance fee, $15 shall be deposited into the Secretary of State Special License Plate Fund, to be used by the Secretary to help defray the administrative processing costs, and $25 shall be deposited into the Illinois Future Teacher Corps Scholarship Fund. For each registration renewal period, a $40 fee, in addition to the appropriate registration fee, shall be charged. Of this $40 additional renewal fee, $2 shall be deposited into the Secretary of State Special License Plate Fund and $38 shall be deposited into the Illinois Future Teacher Corps Scholarship Fund. Each fiscal year, once deposits from the additional original issuance and renewal fees into the Secretary of State Special License Plate Fund have reached $500,000, all the amounts received for the additional fees for the balance of the fiscal year shall be deposited into the Illinois Future Teacher Corps Scholarship Fund.

(d) The Illinois Future Teacher Corps Scholarship Fund is created as a special fund in the State treasury. Ninety-five percent of the moneys in the Illinois Future Teacher Corps Scholarship Fund shall be appropriated to the Illinois Student Assistance Commission for scholarships under Section 52 or 65.65 of the Higher Education Student Assistance Act,[1] and 5% of the moneys in the Illinois Future Teacher Corps Scholarship Fund shall be appropriated to the State Board of Education for grants to the Golden Apple Foundation for Excellence in Teaching, a recognized charitable organization that meets the requirements of Title 26, Section 501(c)(3) of the United States Code.

P.A. 76-1586, § 3-648, added by P.A. 92-445, § 15, eff. Aug. 17, 2001. Amended by P.A. 92-651, § 77, eff. July 11, 2002; P.A. 92-845, § 10, eff. Jan. 1, 2003.

[1] 110 ILCS 947/65.65.

For text of section as added by P.A. 92-693, § 10, relating to Hospice license plates, see 625 ILCS 5/3-648, post

P.A. 92-651, the First 2002 General Revisory Act, amended various Acts to delete obsolete text, to correct patent and technical errors, to revise cross references, to resolve multiple actions in the 91st and 92nd General Assemblies and to make certain technical corrections in P.A. 91-937 through P.A. 92-520.

P.A. 92-845 incorporated the amendment by P.A. 92-445.

See 5 ILCS 70/6 as to the effect of (1) more than one amendment of a section at the same session of the General Assembly or (2) two or more acts relating to the same subject matter enacted by the same General Assembly.

5/3-648. Hospice license plates

Text of section as added by P.A. 92-693, § 10, effective January 1, 2003

§ 3-648. Hospice license plates.

(a) The Secretary, upon receipt of an application made in the form prescribed by the Secretary, may issue special registration plates designated as Hospice license plates. The special plates issued under this Section shall be affixed only to passenger vehicles of the first division and motor vehicles of the second division weighing not more than 8,000 pounds. Plates issued under this Section shall expire according to the multi-year procedure established by Section 3-414.1 of this Code.

(b) The color of the plates is wholly within the discretion of the Secretary. The design of the plates shall include the word "Hospice" above drawings of two lilies and a butterfly. The Secretary may allow the plates to be issued as vanity plates or personalized under Section 3-405.1 of the Code. The Secretary shall prescribe stickers or decals as provided under Section 3-412 of this Code.

(c) An applicant for the special plate shall be charged a $25 fee for original issuance in addition to the appropriate registration fee. Of this fee, $10 shall be deposited into the Hospice Fund and $15 shall be deposited into the Secretary of State Special License Plate Fund, to be used by the Secretary to help defray the administrative processing costs.

For each registration renewal period, a $25 fee, in addition to the appropriate registration fee, shall be charged. Of this fee, $23 shall be deposited into the Hospice Fund and $2 shall be deposited into the Secretary of State Special License Plate Fund.

(d) The Hospice Fund is created as a special fund in the State treasury. All money in the Hospice Fund shall be paid, subject to appropriation by the General Assembly and approval by the Secretary, to the Department of Public Health for distribution as grants for hospice services as defined in the Hospice Program Licensing Act.[1] The Director of Public Health shall adopt rules for the distribution of these grants.

P.A. 76-1586, § 3-648, added by P.A. 92-693, § 10, eff. Jan. 1, 2003.

[1] 210 ILCS 60/1 et seq.

For text of section as added by P.A. 92-445 and amended by P.A. 92-651 and P.A. 92-845, effective January 1, 2003, see 625 ILCS 5/3-648, ante

Other § 3-648 were amended and redesignated as § 3-650 through § 3-653 by P.A. 92-545, 92-651, and 92-699.

See 5 ILCS 70/6 as to the effect of (1) more than one amendment of a section at the same session of the General Assembly or (2) two or more acts relating to the same subject matter enacted by the same General Assembly.

5/3-649. West Point Bicentennial license plates

§ 3-649. West Point Bicentennial license plates.

(a) In addition to any other special license plate, the Secretary, upon receipt of all applicable fees and applications made in the form prescribed by the Secretary of State, may issue West Point Bicentennial license plates to commemorate the 200th anniversary of the founding of the United States Military Academy at West Point, N.Y. The special West Point Bicentennial plate issued under this Section shall be affixed only to passenger vehicles of the first division and motor vehicles of the second division weighing not more than 8,000 pounds. Plates issued under this Section shall expire according to the staggered multi-year procedure established by Section 3-414. 1 of this Code.

(b) The design, color, and format of the plates shall be wholly within the discretion of the Secretary of State. The Secretary may, in his or her discretion, allow the plates to be issued as vanity plates or personalized in accordance with Section 3-405.1 of this Code. The plates are not required to designate "Land Of Lincoln", as prescribed in subsection (b) of Section 3-412 of this Code. The Secretary shall approve and prescribe stickers or decals as provided under Section 3-412.

(c) An applicant shall be charged a $15 fee for original issuance in addition to the applicable registration fee. This additional fee shall be deposited into the Secretary of State Special License Plate Fund. For each registration renewal period, a $2 fee, in addition to the appropriate registration fee, shall be charged and shall be deposited into the Secretary of State Special License Plate Fund.

P.A. 76-1586, § 3-649, added by P.A. 92-477, § 10, eff. Jan. 1, 2002.

5/3-650. Army Combat Veteran license plates.

§ 3-650. Army Combat Veteran license plates.

(a) In addition to any other special license plate, the Secretary, upon receipt of all applicable fees and applications made in the form prescribed by the Secretary of State, may issue Army Combat Veteran license plates to residents of Illinois who meet eligibility requirements prescribed by the Secretary of State. The special Army Combat Veteran plate issued under this Section shall be affixed only to passenger vehicles of the first division, motorcycles, and motor vehicles of the second division weighing not more than 8,000 pounds. Plates issued under this Section shall expire according to the staggered multi-year procedure established by Section 3-414.1 of this Code.

(b) The plates shall display the Army Combat Infantry Badge. In all other respects, the design, color, and format of the plates shall be within the discretion of the Secretary of State. The Secretary may, in his or her discretion, allow the plates to be issued as vanity plates or personalized in accordance with Section 3-405.1 of this Code. The plates are not required to designate "Land Of Lincoln", as prescribed in subsection (b) of Section 3-412 of this Code. The Secretary shall prescribe the eligibility requirements and, in his or her discretion, shall approve and prescribe stickers or decals as provided under Section 3-412.

(c) An applicant shall be charged a $15 fee for original issuance in addition to the applicable registration fee. This additional fee shall be deposited into the Secretary of State Special License Plate Fund. For each registration renewal period, a $2 fee, in addition to the appropriate registration fee, shall be charged and shall be deposited into the Secretary of State Special License Plate Fund.

P.A. 76-1586, § 3-648, added by P.A. 92-79, § 5, eff. Jan. 1, 2002. Renumbered § 3-650 and amended by P.A. 92-545, § 5, eff. June 12, 2002; P.A. 92-651, § 77, eff. July 11, 2002; P.A. 92-699, § 5, eff. Jan. 1, 2003.

P.A. 92-651, the First 2002 General Revisory Act, amended various Acts to delete obsolete text, to correct patent and technical errors, to revise cross references, to resolve multiple actions in the 91st and 92nd General Assemblies and to make certain technical corrections in P.A. 91-937 through P.A. 92-520.

See 5 ILCS 70/6 as to the effect of (1) more than one amendment of a section at the same session of the General Assembly or (2) two or more acts relating to the same subject matter enacted by the same General Assembly.

5/3-651. U.S. Marine Corps license plates.

§ 3-651. U.S. Marine Corps license plates.

(a) In addition to any other special license plate, the Secretary, upon receipt of all applicable fees and applications made in the form prescribed by the Secretary of State, may issue special registration plates designated as U.S. Marine Corps license plates to residents of Illinois who meet eligibility requirements prescribed by the Secretary of State. The special plate issued under this Section shall be affixed only to passenger vehicles of the first division, motorcycles, motor vehicles of the second division weighing not more than 8,000 pounds, and recreational vehicles as defined by Section 1-169 of this Code. Plates issued under this Section shall expire according to the staggered multi-year procedure established by Section 3-414.1 of this Code.

(b) The design, color, and format of the plates shall be wholly within the discretion of the Secretary of State, except that the U.S. Marine Corps emblem shall appear on the plates. The Secretary may, in his or her discretion, allow the plates to be issued as vanity or personalized plates in accordance with Section 3-405.1 of this Code. The plates are not required to designate "Land Of Lincoln", as prescribed in subsection (b) of Section 3-412 of this Code. The Secretary shall prescribe the eligibility requirements and, in his or her discretion, shall approve and prescribe stickers or decals as provided under Section 3-412.

(c) An applicant shall be charged a $20 fee for original issuance in addition to the applicable registration fee. Of this additional fee, $15 shall be deposited into the Secretary of State Special License Plate Fund and $5 shall be deposited into the Marine Corps Scholarship Fund. For each registration renewal period, a $20 fee, in addition to the appropriate registration fee, shall be charged. Of this additional fee, $2 shall be deposited into the Secretary of State Special License Plate Fund and $18 shall be deposited into the Marine Corps Scholarship Fund.

(d) The Marine Corps Scholarship Fund is created as a special fund in the State treasury. All moneys in the Marine Corps Scholarship Fund shall, subject to appropriation by the General Assembly and approval by the Secretary, be used by the Marine Corps Scholarship Foundation, Inc., a recognized charitable organization that meets the requirements of Title 26, Section 501(c)(3) of the United States Code, to provide grants for scholarships for higher education. The scholarship recipients must be the children of current or former members of the United States Marine Corps who meet the academic, financial, and other requirements established by the Marine Corps Scholarship Foundation. In addition, the recipients must be Illinois residents and must attend a college or university located within the State of Illinois.

The State Treasurer shall require the Marine Corps Scholarship Foundation to establish a separate account for receipt of the proceeds of the Marine Corps Scholarship Fund. That account shall be subject to audit either annually or at another interval, as determined by the State Treasurer. Proceeds from the Marine Corps Scholarship Fund shall be transferred on a quarterly basis by the State Treasurer's office to this separate account.

P.A. 76–1586, § 3–648, added by P.A. 92–467, § 10, eff. Jan. 1, 2002. Renumbered § 3–651 and amended by P.A. 92–545, § 5, eff. June 12, 2002; P.A. 92–651, § 77, eff. July 11, 2002; P.A. 92–699, § 5, eff. Jan. 1, 2003.

P.A. 92–651, the First 2002 General Revisory Act, amended various Acts to delete obsolete text, to correct patent and technical errors, to revise cross references, to resolve multiple actions in the 91st and 92nd General Assemblies and to make certain technical corrections in P.A. 91–937 through P.A. 92–520.

See 5 ILCS 70/6 as to the effect of (1) more than one amendment of a section at the same session of the General Assembly or (2) two or more acts relating to the same subject matter enacted by the same General Assembly.

5/3–652. Chicago and Northeast Illinois District Council of Carpenters license plates

§ 3–652. Chicago and Northeast Illinois District Council of Carpenters license plates.

(a) The Secretary, upon receipt of all applicable fees and applications made in the form prescribed by the Secretary, may issue special registration plates designated as Chicago and Northeast Illinois District Council of Carpenters license plates.

The special plates issued under this Section shall be affixed only to passenger vehicles of the first division or motor vehicles of the second division weighing not more than 8,000 pounds.

Plates issued under this Section shall expire according to the multi-year procedure established by Section 3–414.1 of this Code.

(b) The design and color of the special plates shall be wholly within the discretion of the Secretary. Appropriate documentation, as determined by the Secretary, shall accompany each application. The Secretary may allow the plates to be issued as vanity plates or personalized plates under Section 3–405.1 of this Code. The Secretary shall prescribe stickers or decals as provided under Section 3–412 of this Code.

(c) An applicant for the special plate shall be charged a $25 fee for original issuance in addition to the appropriate registration fee. Of this fee, $10 shall be deposited into the Chicago and Northeast Illinois District Council of Carpenters Fund and $15 shall be deposited into the Secretary of State Special License Plate Fund, to be used by the Secretary to help defray the administrative processing costs.

For each registration renewal period, a $25 fee, in addition to the appropriate registration fee, shall be charged. Of this fee, $23 shall be deposited into the Chicago and Northeast Illinois District Council of Carpenters Fund and $2 shall be deposited into the Secretary of State Special License Plate Fund.

(d) The Chicago and Northeast Illinois District Council of Carpenters Fund is created as a special fund in the State treasury. All moneys in the Chicago and Northeast Illinois District Council of Carpenters Fund shall be paid, subject to appropriation by the General Assembly and approval by the Secretary, as grants for charitable purposes sponsored by the Chicago and Northeast Illinois District Council of Carpenters.

P.A. 76–1586, § 3–648, added by P.A. 92–477, § 10, eff. Jan. 1, 2002. Renumbered § 3–652 and amended by P.A. 92–651, § 77, eff. July 11, 2002.

P.A. 92–651, the First 2002 General Revisory Act, amended various Acts to delete obsolete text, to correct patent and technical errors, to revise cross references, to resolve multiple actions in the 91st and 92nd General Assemblies and to make certain technical corrections in P.A. 91–937 through P.A. 92–520.

5/3–653. Pet Friendly license plates

Text of section as added by P.A. 92–520, § 10, effective January 1, 2003

§ 3–653. Pet Friendly license plates.

(a) The Secretary, upon receipt of an application made in the form prescribed by the Secretary, may issue special registration plates designated as Pet Friendly license plates. The special plates issued under this Section shall be affixed only to passenger vehicles of the first division, motor vehicles of the second division weighing not more than 8,000 pounds, and recreational vehicles as defined in Section 1–169 of this Code. Plates issued under this Section shall expire according to the multi-year procedure established by Section 3–414.1 of this Code.

(b) The design and color of the plates is wholly within the discretion of the Secretary, except that the phrase "I am pet friendly" shall be on the plates. The Secretary may allow the plates to be issued as vanity plates or personalized plates under Section 3–405.1 of the Code. The Secretary shall prescribe stickers or decals as provided under Section 3–412 of this Code.

(c) An applicant for the special plate shall be charged a $40 fee for original issuance in addition to the appropriate registration fee. Of this additional fee, $25 shall be deposited into the Pet Overpopulation Control Fund and $15 shall be deposited into the Secretary of State Special License Plate Fund, to be used by the Secretary to help defray the administrative processing costs.

For each registration renewal period, a $27 fee, in addition to the appropriate registration fee, shall be charged. Of this additional fee, $25 shall be deposited into the Pet Overpopulation Control Fund and $2 shall be deposited into the Secretary of State Special License Plate Fund.

(d) The Pet Overpopulation Control Fund is created as a special fund in the State treasury. All moneys in the Pet

Overpopulation Control Fund shall be paid, subject to appropriation by the General Assembly and approval by the Secretary, as grants to humane societies exempt from federal income taxation under Section 501(c)(3) of the Internal Revenue Code [1] to be used solely for the humane sterilization of dogs and cats in the State of Illinois. In approving grants under this subsection (d), the Secretary shall consider recommendations for grants made by a volunteer board appointed by the Secretary that shall consist of 5 Illinois residents who are officers or directors of humane societies operating in different regions in Illinois.

P.A. 76-1586, § 3-648, added by P.A. 92-520, § 10, eff. June 1, 2002. Renumbered § 3-653 and amended by P.A. 92-651, § 77, eff. July 11, 2002.

[1] 26 U.S.C.A. § 501.

For other §§ 3-653, see multiple added text of 625 ILCS 5/3-653, post

P.A. 92-651, the First 2002 General Revisory Act, amended various Acts to delete obsolete text, to correct patent and technical errors, to revise cross references, to resolve multiple actions in the 91st and 92nd General Assemblies and to make certain technical corrections in P.A. 91-937 through P.A. 92-520.

5/3-653. Lewis and Clark Bicentennial license plates

Text of section as added by P.A. 92-694, § 10, effective January 1, 2003

§ 3-653. Lewis and Clark Bicentennial license plates.

(a) In addition to any other special license plate, the Secretary, upon receipt of all applicable fees and applications made in the form prescribed by the Secretary of State, may issue special registration plates designated as Lewis and Clark Bicentennial license plates to residents of Illinois. The special plate issued under this Section shall be affixed only to passenger vehicles of the first division, motor vehicles of the second division weighing not more than 8,000 pounds, and recreational vehicles as defined by Section 1-169 of this Code. Plates issued under this Section shall expire according to the staggered multi-year procedure established by Section 3-414.1 of this Code.

(b) The Secretary of State shall confer with the Governor's Illinois Lewis and Clark Bicentennial Commission regarding the design, color, and format of the plates. The Secretary may, in his or her discretion, allow the plates to be issued as vanity or personalized plates in accordance with Section 3-405.1 of this Code. The plates are not required to designate "Land Of Lincoln", as prescribed in subsection (b) of Section 3-412 of this Code. The Secretary, in his or her discretion, shall approve and prescribe stickers or decals as provided under Section 3-412.

(c) An applicant shall be charged a $40 fee for original issuance in addition to the applicable registration fee. Of this additional fee, $15 shall be deposited into the Secretary of State Special License Plate Fund and $25 shall be deposited into the Lewis and Clark Bicentennial Fund. For each registration renewal period, a $27 fee, in addition to the appropriate registration fee, shall be charged. Of this additional fee, $2 shall be deposited into the Secretary of State Special License Plate Fund and $25 shall be deposited into the Lewis and Clark Bicentennial Fund.

(d) The Secretary of State shall issue special license plates under this Section on and before September 1, 2008. The Secretary may not issue special plates under this Section after September 1, 2008.

(e) The Lewis and Clark Bicentennial Fund is created as a special fund in the State treasury. All moneys in the Lewis and Clark Bicentennial Fund shall, subject to appropriation by the General Assembly and approval by the Secretary, be used by the Department of Commerce and Community Affairs to promote tourism and education related to the Lewis and Clark Expedition and for historic preservation purposes related to the Expedition.

The State Treasurer shall transfer any moneys remaining in the Lewis and Clark Bicentennial Fund on September 1, 2009 and any moneys received for deposit into that Fund on or after September 1, 2009 into the Secretary of State Special License Plate Fund.

P.A. 76-1586, § 3-653, added by P.A. 92-694, § 10, eff. Jan. 1, 2003.

For other §§ 3-653, see multiple added text of 625 ILCS 5/3-653, ante and post

5/3-653. September 11th license plates

Text of section as added by P.A. 92-704, § 20, eff. July 19, 2002

§ 3-653. September 11th license plates.

(a) Beginning on September 11, 2002, the Secretary, upon receipt of all applicable fees and applications made in the form prescribed by the Secretary, may issue special registration plates designated as September 11th license plates.

The special plates issued under this Section shall be affixed only to passenger vehicles of the first division or motor vehicles of the second division weighing not more than 8,000 pounds.

Plates issued under this Section shall expire according to the multi-year procedure established by Section 3-414.1 of this Code.

(b) The design and color of the special plates shall be wholly within the discretion of the Secretary. The Secretary may allow the plates to be issued as vanity or personalized plates under Section 3-405.1 of this Code. The Secretary shall prescribe stickers or decals as provided under Section 3-412 of this Code.

(c) An applicant for the special plate shall be charged a $40 fee for original issuance in addition to the appropriate registration fee. Of this fee, $25 shall be deposited into the September 11th Fund and $15 shall be deposited into the Secretary of State Special License Plate Fund, to be used by the Secretary to help defray the administrative processing costs.

For each registration renewal period, a $27 fee, in addition to the appropriate registration fee, shall be charged. Of this fee, $25 shall be deposited into the September 11th Fund and $2 shall be deposited into the Secretary of State Special License Plate Fund.

(d) The September 11th Fund is created as a special fund in the State treasury. Subject to appropriation by the General Assembly and approval by the Secretary, the Director of Commerce and Community Affairs shall pay all moneys in the September 11th Fund as grants to aid victims of terrorism and as grants to local governments to cover the costs of training, equipment, and other items related to public safety initiatives intended to prevent further acts of terrorism or to respond to further acts of terrorism or other disasters or emergency situations in Illinois.

P.A. 76-1586, § 3-653, added by P.A. 92-704, § 20, eff. July 19, 2002.

For other §§ 3-653, see multiple added text of 625 ILCS 5/3-653, ante and post

5/3–653. Illinois Route 66 license plates

Text of section as added by P.A. 92–706, § 10, eff. January 1, 2003

§ 3–653. Illinois Route 66 license plates.

(a) The Secretary, upon receipt of all applicable fees and applications made in the form prescribed by the Secretary, may issue special registration plates designated as Illinois Route 66 license plates. The special plates issued under this Section shall be affixed only to passenger vehicles of the first division or motor vehicles of the second division weighing not more than 8,000 pounds. Plates issued under this Section shall expire according to the multi-year procedure established by Section 3–414.1 of this Code.

(b) The design and color of the special plates shall be wholly within the discretion of the Secretary. The Secretary may, in his or her discretion, allow the plates to be issued as vanity or personalized plates in accordance with Section 3–405.1 of this Code. The plates are not required to designate "Land of Lincoln", as prescribed in subsection (b) of Section 3–412 of this Code. The Secretary, in his or her discretion, shall approve and prescribe stickers or decals as provided under Section 3–412.

(c) An applicant for the special plate shall be charged a $40 fee for original issuance in addition to the appropriate registration fee. Of this fee, $25 shall be deposited into the Illinois Route 66 Heritage Project Fund and $15 shall be deposited into the Secretary of State Special License Plate Fund, to be used by the Secretary to help defray the administrative processing costs.

For each registration renewal period, a $27 fee, in addition to the appropriate registration fee, shall be charged. Of this fee, $25 shall be deposited into the Illinois Route 66 Heritage Project Fund and $2 shall be deposited into the Secretary of State Special License Plate Fund.

(d) The Illinois Route 66 Heritage Project Fund is created as a special fund in the State treasury. Subject to appropriation by the General Assembly and approval by the Secretary, Illinois Route 66 Heritage Project, Inc. shall use all moneys in the Illinois Route 66 Heritage Project Fund for the development of tourism, through education and interpretation, preservation, and promotion of the former U.S. Route 66 in Illinois.

P.A. 76–1586, § 3–653, added by P.A. 92–706, § 10, eff. Jan. 1, 2003.

For other §§ 3–653, see multiple added texts of 625 ILCS 5/3–653, ante

See 5 ILCS 70/6 as to the effect of (1) more than one amendment of a section at the same session of the General Assembly or (2) two or more acts relating to the same subject matter enacted by the same General Assembly.

5/3–654. Illinois Public Broadcasting System Stations special license plates

Text of section as added by P.A. 92–695, § 10, effective January 1, 2003

§ 3–654. Illinois Public Broadcasting System Stations special license plates.

(a) The Secretary, upon receipt of all applicable fees and applications made in the form prescribed by the Secretary, may issue special registration plates designated as Illinois Public Broadcasting System Stations special license plates. The special plates issued under this Section shall be affixed only to passenger vehicles of the first division or motor vehicles of the second division weighing not more than 8,000 pounds. Plates issued under this Section shall expire according to the multi-year procedure established by Section 3–414.1 of this Code.

(b) The design and color of the special plates shall be wholly within the discretion of the Secretary. The Secretary may, in his or her discretion, allow the plates to be issued as vanity or personalized plates in accordance with Section 3–405.1 of this Code. The plates are not required to designate "Land of Lincoln", as prescribed in subsection (b) of Section 3–412 of this Code. The Secretary, in his or her discretion, shall approve and prescribe stickers or decals as provided under Section 3–412.

(c) An applicant for the special plate shall be charged a $40 fee for original issuance in addition to the appropriate registration fee. Of this fee, $25 shall be deposited into the Public Broadcasting Fund and $15 shall be deposited into the Secretary of State Special License Plate Fund, to be used by the Secretary to help defray the administrative processing costs.

For each registration renewal period, a $27 fee, in addition to the appropriate registration fee, shall be charged. Of this fee, $25 shall be deposited into the Public Broadcasting Fund and $2 shall be deposited into the Secretary of State Special License Plate Fund.

(d) The Public Broadcasting Fund is created as a special fund in the State treasury. Subject to appropriation by the General Assembly and approval by the Secretary, the Secretary shall pay all moneys in the Public Broadcasting Fund to the various Public Broadcasting System stations in Illinois for operating costs.

P.A. 76–1586, § 3–654, added by P.A. 92–695, § 10, eff. Jan. 1, 2003.

For other §§ 3–654, see multiple added texts of 625 ILCS 5/3–654, post

5/3–654. Park District Youth Program license plates

Text of section as added by P.A. 92–697, § 10, eff. July 19, 2002

§ 3–654. Park District Youth Program license plates.

(a) In addition to any other special license plate, the Secretary, upon receipt of all applicable fees and applications made in the form prescribed by the Secretary of State, may issue Park District Youth Program license plates. The special Park District Youth Program plate issued under this Section shall be affixed only to passenger vehicles of the first division and motor vehicles of the second division weighing not more than 8,000 pounds. Plates issued under this Section shall expire according to the staggered multi-year procedure established by Section 3–414.1 of this Code.

(b) The design, color, and format of the plates shall be wholly within the discretion of the Secretary of State. Appropriate documentation, as determined by the Secretary, must accompany each application. The Secretary, in his or her discretion, shall approve and prescribe stickers or decals as provided under Section 3–412.

(c) An applicant for the special plate shall be charged a $40 fee for original issuance in addition to the appropriate registration fee. Of this fee, $25 shall be deposited into the Park District Youth Program Fund and $15 shall be deposited into the Secretary of State Special License Plate Fund, to be used by the Secretary to help defray the administrative processing costs.

For each registration renewal period, a $27 fee, in addition to the appropriate registration fee, shall be charged. Of this fee, $25 shall be deposited into the Park District Youth Program Fund and $2 shall be deposited into the Secretary of State Special License Plate Fund.

(d) The Park District Youth Program Fund is created as a special fund in the State treasury. All money in the Park District Youth Program Fund shall be paid, subject to appropriation by the General Assembly and approval by the Secretary, as grants to the Illinois Association of Park Districts, a not-for-profit corporation, for grants to park districts and recreation agencies providing innovative after school programming for Illinois youth.

P.A. 92-697, § 10, eff. July 19, 2002.

For other § 3-654, see multiple added texts of 625 ILCS 5/3-654, ante and post

5/3-654. Professional Sports Teams license plates

Text of section as added by P.A. 92-699, § 5, effective January 1, 2003

§ 3-654. Professional Sports Teams license plates.

(a) The Secretary, upon receipt of an application made in the form prescribed by the Secretary, may issue special registration plates designated as Professional Sports Teams license plates. The special plates issued under this Section shall be affixed only to passenger vehicles of the first division and motor vehicles of the second division weighing not more than 8,000 pounds. Plates issued under this Section shall expire according to the multi-year procedure established by Section 3-414.1 of this Code.

(b) The design and color of the plates is wholly within the discretion of the Secretary, except that the plates shall, subject to the permission of the applicable team owner, display the logo of the Chicago Bears, the Chicago Bulls, the Chicago Black Hawks, the Chicago Cubs, the Chicago White Sox, the St. Louis Rams, or the St. Louis Cardinals, at the applicant's option. The Secretary may allow the plates to be issued as vanity or personalized plates under Section 3-405.1 of the Code. The Secretary shall prescribe stickers or decals as provided under Section 3-412 of this Code.

(c) An applicant for the special plate shall be charged a $40 fee for original issuance in addition to the appropriate registration fee. Of this fee, $25 shall be deposited into the Professional Sports Teams Education Fund and $15 shall be deposited into the Secretary of State Special License Plate Fund, to be used by the Secretary to help defray the administrative processing costs.

For each registration renewal period, a $27 fee, in addition to the appropriate registration fee, shall be charged. Of this fee, $25 shall be deposited into the Professional Sports Teams Education Fund and $2 shall be deposited into the Secretary of State Special License Plate Fund.

(d) The Professional Sports Teams Education Fund is created as a special fund in the State treasury. All moneys in the Professional Sports Teams Education Fund shall, subject to appropriation by the General Assembly and approval by the Secretary, be deposited every 6 months into the Common School Fund.

P.A. 76-1586, § 3-654, added by P.A. 92-699, § 5, eff. Jan. 1, 2003.

For other §§ 3-654, see multiple added texts of 625 ILCS 5/3-654, ante and post

5/3-654. Pan Hellenic license plates

Text of section as added by P.A. 92-702, § 10, eff. January 1, 2003

§ 3-654. Pan Hellenic license plates.

(a) The Secretary, upon receipt of all applicable fees and applications made in the form prescribed by the Secretary, may issue special registration plates designated as Pan Hellenic license plates. The special plates issued under this Section shall be affixed only to passenger vehicles of the first division or motor vehicles of the second division weighing not more than 8,000 pounds. Plates issued under this Section shall expire according to the multi-year procedure established by Section 3-414.1 of this Code.

(b) The design and color of the special plates shall be wholly within the discretion of the Secretary, except that an emblem of a Pan Hellenic eligible member shall be on the plate. Appropriate documentation, as determined by the Secretary, shall accompany each application. The Secretary may, in his or her discretion, allow the plates to be issued as vanity or personalized plates in accordance with Section 3-405.1 of this Code. The plates are not required to designate "Land of Lincoln" as prescribed in subsection (b) of Section 3-412 of this Code. The Secretary, in his or her discretion, may prescribe rules governing the requirements and approval of the special plates.

(c) An applicant for the special plate shall be charged a $40 fee for original issuance in addition to the appropriate registration fee. Of this fee, $25 shall be deposited into the Illinois Pan Hellenic Trust Fund and $15 shall be deposited into the Secretary of State Special License Plate Fund, to be used by the Secretary to help defray the administrative processing costs. For each registration renewal period, a $27 fee, in addition to the appropriate registration fee, shall be charged. Of this fee, $25 shall be deposited into the Illinois Pan Hellenic Trust Fund and $2 shall be deposited into the Secretary of State Special License Plate Fund.

(d) The Illinois Pan Hellenic Trust Fund is created as a special fund in the State Treasury. The State Treasurer shall create separate accounts within the Illinois Pan Hellenic Trust Fund for each eligible member for which Pan Hellenic license plates have been issued. Moneys in the Illinois Pan Hellenic Trust Fund shall be allocated to each account in proportion to the number of plates sold in regard to each fraternity or sorority. All moneys in the Illinois Pan Hellenic Trust Fund shall be distributed, subject to appropriation by the General Assembly and approval by the Secretary, as grants to the Illinois Alpha Kappa Alpha Charitable Foundation, Illinois Delta Sigma Theta Charitable Foundation, Illinois Zeta Phi Beta Charitable Foundation, Illinois Sigma Gamma Rho Charitable Foundation, Illinois Alpha Phi Alpha Charitable Foundation, Illinois Omega Psi Phi Charitable Foundation, Illinois Kappa Alpha Psi Charitable Foundation, Illinois Phi Beta Sigma Charitable Foundation, or Illinois Iota Phi Theta Charitable Foundation for charitable purposes sponsored by the African-American fraternity or sorority.

P.A. 76-1586, § 3-654, added by P.A. 92-702, § 10, eff. Jan. 1, 2003.

For other §§ 3-654, see multiple added texts of 625 ILCS 5/3-654, ante and post

5/3-654. Stop Neuroblastoma license plates

Text of section as added by P.A. 92-711, § 10, eff. July 19, 2002

§ 3-654. Stop Neuroblastoma license plates.

(a) The Secretary, upon receipt of an application made in the form prescribed by the Secretary, may issue special registration plates designated as Stop Neuroblastoma license plates. The special plates issued under this Section shall be affixed only to passenger vehicles of the first division and motor vehicles of the second division weighing not more than 8,000 pounds. Plates issued under this Section shall expire according to the multi-year procedure established by Section 3-414.1 of this Code.

(b) The design and color of the plates is wholly within the discretion of the Secretary, except that the following phrases shall be on the plates: (i) "Stop Neuroblastoma" and (ii) "Stop Cancer". The Secretary may allow the plates to be issued as vanity plates or personalized under Section 3-405.1 of this Code. The Secretary shall prescribe stickers or decals as provided under Section 3-412 of this Code.

(c) An applicant for the special plate shall be charged a $25 fee for original issuance in addition to the appropriate registration fee. Of this fee, $10 shall be deposited into the Stop Neuroblastoma Fund and $15 shall be deposited into the Secretary of State Special License Plate Fund, to be used by the Secretary to help defray the administrative processing costs.

For each registration renewal period, a $25 fee, in addition to the appropriate registration fee, shall be charged. Of this fee, $23 shall be deposited into the Stop Neuroblastoma Fund and $2 shall be deposited into the Secretary of State Special License Plate Fund.

(d) The Stop Neuroblastoma Fund is created as a special fund in the State treasury. All money in the Stop Neuroblastoma Fund shall be paid, subject to appropriation by the General Assembly and approval by the Secretary, as grants to the American Cancer Society for neuroblastoma and cancer research, education, screening, and treatment.

P.A. 76-1586, § 3-654, added by P.A. 92-711, § 10, eff. July 19, 2002.

For other §§ 3-654, see multiple added texts of 625 ILCS 5/3-654, ante

See 5 ILCS 70/6 as to the effect of (1) more than one amendment of a section at the same session of the General Assembly or (2) two or more acts relating to the same subject matter enacted by the same General Assembly.

ARTICLE VII. OFFENSES AGAINST REGISTRATION AND CERTIFICATE OF TITLE LAWS OR REVOCATION OF REGISTRATION OR CERTIFICATE OF TITLE

Section

5/3-701. Operation of vehicles without evidence of registration—Operation under mileage plates when odometer broken or disconnected

§ 3-701. Operation of vehicles without evidence of registration—Operation under mileage plates when odometer broken or disconnected.

No person shall operate, nor shall an owner knowingly permit to be operated, upon any highway unless there shall be attached thereto and displayed thereon when and as required by law, proper evidence of registration in Illinois, as follows:

(1) A vehicle required to be registered in Illinois. A current and valid Illinois registration sticker or stickers and plate or plates, or an Illinois temporary registration permit, or a drive-away or in-transit permit, issued therefor by the Secretary of State; or

(2) A vehicle eligible for Reciprocity. A current and valid reciprocal foreign registration plate or plates properly issued to such vehicle or a temporary registration issued therefor, by the reciprocal State, and, in addition, when required by the Secretary, a current and valid Illinois Reciprocity Permit or Prorate Decal issued therefor by the Secretary of State; or except as otherwise expressly provided for in this Chapter.

No person shall operate, nor shall any owner knowingly permit to be operated, any vehicle of the second division for which the owner has made an election to pay the mileage tax in lieu of the annual flat weight tax, at any time when the odometer of such vehicle is broken or disconnected, or is inoperable or not operating.

P.A. 76-1586, § 3-701, eff. July 1, 1970. Amended by P.A. 77-1315, § 1, eff. Jan. 1, 1972; P.A. 77-2830, Art. 73, § 1, eff. Jan. 1, 1973; P.A. 80-230, § 1, eff. Oct. 1, 1977; P.A. 80-911, § 1, eff. Oct. 1, 1977; P.A. 80-1185, § 1, eff. March 8, 1978; P.A. 81-886, § 1, eff. July 1, 1980; P.A. 92-680, § 15, eff. July 16, 2002.

Formerly Ill.Rev.Stat.1991, ch. 95 ½, ¶ 3-701.

5/3-702. Operation of vehicle when registration cancelled, suspended or revoked

§ 3-702. Operation of vehicle when registration cancelled, suspended or revoked.

(a) No person shall operate, nor shall an owner knowingly permit to be operated, upon any highway:

(1) A vehicle the registration of which has been cancelled, suspended or revoked; or

(2) A vehicle properly registered in another Reciprocal State, the foreign registration of which, or the Illinois Reciprocity Permit or Decal of which, has been cancelled, suspended or revoked.

(b) No person shall use, nor shall any owner use or knowingly permit the use of any Illinois registration plate, plates or registration sticker, or any Illinois Reciprocity Permit or Prorate Decal which has been cancelled, suspended or revoked.

(c) Any violation of this Section is a Class A misdemeanor unless:

1. the registration of the motor vehicle has been suspended for noninsurance, then the provisions of Section 3-708 of this Code apply in lieu of this Section.

2. the registration of the motor vehicle has been suspended for failure to purchase a vehicle tax sticker pursuant to Section 3-704.1 of this Code, then the violation shall be considered a business offense and the person shall be required to pay a fine in excess of $500, but not more than $1,000.

P.A. 76-1586, § 3-702, eff. July 1, 1970. Amended by P.A. 77-1315, § 1, eff. Jan. 1, 1972; P.A. 77-2830, Art. 73, § 1, eff. Jan. 1, 1973; P.A. 80-230, § 1, eff. Oct. 1, 1977; P.A. 81-886, § 1, eff. July 1, 1980; P.A. 86-149, § 2, eff. Aug. 11, 1989; P.A. 87-1225, § 2, eff. Dec. 22, 1992.

Formerly Ill.Rev.Stat.1991, ch. 95 ½, ¶ 3-702.

5/3-703. Improper use of evidences of registration or certificate of title

§ 3-703. Improper use of evidences of registration or certificate of title. No person shall lend to another any certificate of title, registration card, registration plate, registration sticker, special plate or permit or other evidences of proper registration issued to him if the person desiring to borrow the same would not be entitled to the use thereof, nor shall any person knowingly permit the use of any of the same by one not entitled thereto, nor shall any person display upon a vehicle any registration card, registration sticker, registration plate or other evidences of proper registration not issued for such vehicle or not otherwise lawfully used thereon under this Code. No person shall duplicate, alter or attempt to reproduce in any manner a registration plate or registration sticker issued under this Code. No person shall make fraudulent use of evidences of registration or certificates of title issued erroneously by the Secretary of State. No person shall manufacture, advertise, distribute or sell any certificate of title, registration card, registration plate, registration sticker, special plate or permit or other evidences of proper registration which purports to have been issued under this Code. The Secretary of State may request the Attorney General to seek a restraining order in the circuit court against any person who violates this Section by advertising such fraudulent items. Any violation of this Section is a Class C misdemeanor.

P.A. 76-1586, § 3-703, eff. July 1, 1970. Amended by P.A. 77-1315, § 1, eff. Jan. 1, 1972; P.A. 77-2830, Art. 73, § 1, eff. Jan. 1, 1973; P.A. 80-230, § 1, eff. Oct. 1, 1977; P.A. 80-911, § 1, Oct. 1, 1977; P.A. 80-1364, § 36, eff. Aug. 13, 1978; P.A. 83-449, § 1, eff. Jan. 1, 1984; P.A. 86-551, § 1, eff. Jan. 1, 1990.

Formerly Ill.Rev.Stat.1991, ch. 95 ½, ¶ 3-703.

5/3-704. Authority of Secretary of State to suspend or revoke a registration or certificate of title; authority to suspend or revoke the registration of a vehicle

§ 3-704. Authority of Secretary of State to suspend or revoke a registration or certificate of title; authority to suspend or revoke the registration of a vehicle.

(a) The Secretary of State may suspend or revoke the registration of a vehicle or a certificate of title, registration card, registration sticker, registration plate, person with disabilities parking decal or device, or any nonresident or other permit in any of the following events:

1. When the Secretary of State is satisfied that such registration or that such certificate, card, plate, registration sticker or permit was fraudulently or erroneously issued;

2. When a registered vehicle has been dismantled or wrecked or is not properly equipped;

3. When the Secretary of State determines that any required fees have not been paid to either the Secretary of State or the Illinois Commerce Commission and the same are not paid upon reasonable notice and demand;

4. When a registration card, registration plate, registration sticker or permit is knowingly displayed upon a vehicle other than the one for which issued;

5. When the Secretary of State determines that the owner has committed any offense under this Chapter involving the registration or the certificate, card, plate, registration sticker or permit to be suspended or revoked;

6. When the Secretary of State determines that a vehicle registered not-for-hire is used or operated for-hire unlawfully, or used or operated for purposes other than those authorized;

7. When the Secretary of State determines that an owner of a for-hire motor vehicle has failed to give proof of financial responsibility as required by this Act;

8. When the Secretary determines that the vehicle is not subject to or eligible for a registration;

9. When the Secretary determines that the owner of a vehicle registered under the mileage weight tax option fails to maintain the records specified by law, or fails to file the reports required by law, or that such vehicle is not equipped with an operable and operating speedometer or odometer;

10. When the Secretary of State is so authorized under any other provision of law;

11. When the Secretary of State determines that the holder of a person with disabilities parking decal or device has committed any offense under Chapter 11 of this Code [1] involving the use of a person with disabilities parking decal or device.

(b) The Secretary of State may suspend or revoke the registration of a vehicle as follows:

1. When the Secretary of State determines that the owner of a vehicle has not paid a civil penalty or a settlement agreement arising from the violation of rules adopted under the Illinois Motor Carrier Safety Law [2] or the Illinois Hazardous Materials Transportation Act [3] or that a vehicle, regardless of ownership, was the subject of violations of these rules that resulted in a civil penalty or settlement agreement which remains unpaid.

2. When the Secretary of State determines that a vehicle registered for a gross weight of more than 16,000 pounds

within an affected area is not in compliance with the provisions of Section 13–109.1 of the Illinois Vehicle Code.[4]

P.A. 76–1586, § 3–704, eff. July 1, 1970. Amended by P.A. 77–1315, § 1, eff. Jan. 1, 1972; P.A. 80–230, § 1, eff. Oct. 1, 1977; P.A. 90–106, § 5, eff. Jan. 1, 1998; P.A. 92–437, § 5, eff. Aug. 17, 2001.

Formerly Ill.Rev.Stat.1991, ch. 95 ½, ¶ 3–704.

1 625 ILCS 5/11–100 et seq.

2 625 ILCS 5/18b–100 et seq.

3 430 ILCS 30/1 et seq.

4 625 ILCS 5/13–109.1.

5/3–704.1. Municipal vehicle tax liability; suspension of registration

§ 3–704.1. Municipal vehicle tax liability; suspension of registration.

(a) As used in this Section:

(1) "Municipality" means a city, village or incorporated town with a population over 1,000,000.

(2) "Vehicle tax" means a motor vehicle tax and any related late fees or charges imposed by a municipality under Section 8–11–4 or the Illinois Municipal Code[1] or under the municipality's home rule powers.

(3) "Vehicle owner" means the registered owner or owners of a vehicle who are residents of the municipality.

(b) A municipality that imposes a vehicle tax may, by ordinance adopted under this Section, establish a system whereby the municipality notifies the Secretary of State of vehicle tax liability and the Secretary of State suspends the registration of vehicles for which the tax has not been paid. An ordinance establishing a system must provide for the following:

(1) A first notice for failure to pay a vehicle tax shall be sent by first class mail to the vehicle owner at the owner's address recorded with the Secretary of State whenever the municipality has reasonable cause to believe that the vehicle owner has failed to pay a vehicle tax as required by ordinance. The notice shall include at least the following:

(A) The name and address of the vehicle owner.

(B) The registration plate number of the vehicle.

(C) The period for which the vehicle tax is due.

(D) The amount of vehicle tax that is due.

(E) A statement that the vehicle owner's registration for the vehicle will be subject to suspension proceedings unless the vehicle owner pays the vehicle tax or successfully contests the owner's alleged liability within 30 days of the date of the notice.

(F) An explanation of the vehicle owner's opportunity to be heard under subsection (c).

(2) If a vehicle owner fails to pay the vehicle tax or to contest successfully the owner's alleged liability within the period specified in the first notice, a second notice of impending registration suspension shall be sent by first class mail to the vehicle owner at the owner's address recorded with the Secretary of State. The notice shall contain the same information as the first notice, but shall also state that the failure to pay the amount owing, or to contest successfully the alleged liability within 45 days of the date of the second notice, will result in the municipality's notification of the Secretary of State that the vehicle owner is eligible for initiation of suspension proceedings under this Section.

(c) An ordinance adopted under this Section must also give the vehicle owner an opportunity to be heard upon the filing of a timely petition with the municipality. A vehicle owner may contest the alleged tax liability either through an adjudication by mail or at an administrative hearing, at the option of the vehicle owner. The grounds upon which the liability may be contested may be limited to the following:

(1) The alleged vehicle owner does not own the vehicle.

(2) The vehicle is not subject to the vehicle tax by law.

(3) The vehicle tax for the period in question has been paid.

At an administrative hearing, the formal or technical rules of evidence shall not apply. The hearing shall be recorded. The person conducting the hearing shall have the power to administer oaths and to secure by subpoena the attendance and testimony of witnesses and the production of relevant documents.

(d) If a vehicle owner who has been sent a first notice of failure to pay a vehicle tax and a second notice of impending registration suspension fails to pay the vehicle tax or to contest successfully the vehicle owner's liability within the periods specified in the notices, the appropriate official shall cause a certified report to be sent to the Secretary of State under subsection (e).

(e) A report of a municipality notifying the Secretary of State of a vehicle owner's failure to pay a vehicle tax or related fines or penalties under this Section shall be certified by the appropriate official and shall contain the following:

(1) The name, last known address and registration plate number of the vehicle of the person who failed to pay the vehicle tax.

(2) The name of the municipality making the report.

(3) A statement that the municipality sent notices as required by subsection (b); the date on which the notices were sent; the address to which the notices were sent; and the date of the hearing, if any.

(f) Following receipt of the certified report under this Section, the Secretary of State shall notify the vehicle owner that the vehicle's registration will be suspended at the end of a reasonable specified period of time unless the Secretary of State is presented with a notice from the municipality certifying that the person has paid the necessary vehicle tax, or that inclusion of that person's name or registration number on the certified report was in error. The Secretary's notice shall state in substance the information contained in the certified report from the municipality to the Secretary, and shall be effective as specified by subsection (c) of Section 6–211 of this Code. The notice shall also inform the person of the person's right to a hearing under subsection (g).

(g) An administrative hearing with the Office of the Secretary of State to contest an impending suspension or a suspension made under this Section may be had upon filing a written request with the Secretary of State. The filing fee for this hearing shall be $20 to be paid at the time the request is made.

(1) The scope of any administrative hearing with the Secretary of State to contest an impending suspension under this Section shall be limited to the following issues:

(A) Whether the report of the appropriate official of the municipality was certified and contained the information required by this Section.

(B) Whether the municipality making the certified report to the Secretary of State established procedures by ordinance for persons to challenge the accuracy of the certified report.

(C) Whether the Secretary of State notified the vehicle owner that the vehicle's registration would be suspended at the end of the specified time period unless the Secretary of State was presented with a notice from the municipality certifying that the person has purchased the necessary vehicle tax sticker or that inclusion of that person's name or registration number on the certified report was in error.

A municipality that files a certified report with the Secretary of State under this Section shall reimburse the Secretary for all reasonable costs incurred by the Secretary as a result of the filing of the report, including but not limited to the costs of providing the notice required under subsection (f) and the costs incurred by the Secretary in any hearing conducted with respect to the report under this subsection and any appeal from that hearing.

(h) After the expiration of the time specified under subsection (g), the Secretary of State shall, unless the suspension is successfully contested, suspend the registration of the vehicle until the Secretary receives notice under subsection (i).

(i) Any municipality making a certified report to the Secretary of State under this subsection shall notify the Secretary of State, in a form prescribed by the Secretary, whenever a person named in the certified report has subsequently paid a vehicle tax or whenever the municipality determines that the original report was in error. A certified copy of the notification shall also be given upon request and at no additional charge to the person named in the report. Upon receipt of the notification or presentation of a certified copy of the notification by the municipality, the Secretary of State shall terminate the suspension.

P.A. 76-1586, § 3-704.1, added by P.A. 87-1225, § 2, eff. Dec. 22, 1992.

Formerly Ill.Rev.Stat., ch. 95½, ¶ 3-704.1.

[1] 65 ILCS 5/8-11-4.

5/3-704.2. Failure to satisfy fines or penalties for toll violations or evasions; suspension of vehicle registration

§ 3-704.2. Failure to satisfy fines or penalties for toll violations or evasions; suspension of vehicle registration.

(a) Upon receipt of a certified report, as prescribed by subsection (c) of this Section, from the Authority stating that the owner of a registered vehicle has failed to satisfy any fine or penalty resulting from a final order issued by the Authority relating directly or indirectly to 5 or more toll violations, toll evasions, or both, the Secretary of State shall suspend the vehicle registration of the person in accordance with the procedures set forth in this Section.

(b) Following receipt of the certified report of the Authority as specified in the Section, the Secretary of State shall notify the person whose name appears on the certified report that the person's vehicle registration will be suspended at the end of a specified period unless the Secretary of State is presented with a notice from the Authority certifying that the fines or penalties owing the Authority have been satisfied or that inclusion of that person's name on the certified report was in error. The Secretary's notice shall state in substance the information contained in the Authority's certified report to the Secretary, and shall be effective as specified by subsection (c) of Section 6-211 of this Code.

(c) The report from the Authority notifying the Secretary of unsatisfied fines or penalties pursuant to this Section shall be certified and shall contain the following:

(1) The name, last known address, and driver's license number of the person who failed to satisfy the fines or penalties and the registration number of any vehicle known to be registered in this State to that person.

(2) A statement that the Authority sent a notice of impending suspension of the person's driver's license, vehicle registration, or both, as prescribed by rules enacted pursuant to subsection (a-5) of Section 10 of the Toll Highway Act, [1] to the person named in the report at the address recorded with the Secretary of State; the date on which the notice was sent; and the address to which the notice was sent.

(d) The Authority, after making a certified report to the Secretary pursuant to this Section, shall notify the Secretary, on a form prescribed by the Secretary, whenever a person named in the certified report has satisfied the previously reported fines or penalties or whenever the Authority determines that the original report was in error. A certified copy of the notification shall also be given upon request and at no additional charge to the person named therein. Upon receipt of the Authority's notification or presentation of a certified copy of the notification, the Secretary shall terminate the suspension.

(e) The Authority shall, by rule, establish procedures for persons to challenge the accuracy of the certified report made pursuant to this Section. The rule shall also provide the grounds for a challenge, which may be limited to:

(1) the person not having been the owner or lessee of the vehicle or vehicles receiving 5 or more toll violation or toll evasion notices on the date or dates the notices were issued; or

(2) the person having already satisfied the fines or penalties for the 5 or more toll violations or toll evasions indicated on the certified report.

(f) All notices sent by the Authority to persons involved in administrative adjudications, hearings, and final orders issued pursuant to rules implementing subsection (a-5) of Section 10 of the Toll Highway Act shall state that failure to satisfy any fine or penalty imposed by the Authority shall result in the Secretary of State suspending the driving privileges, vehicle registration, or both, of the person failing to satisfy the fines or penalties imposed by the Authority.

(g) A person may request an administrative hearing to contest an impending suspension or a suspension made pursuant to this Section upon filing a written request with the Secretary. The filing fee for this hearing is $20, to be paid at the time of the request. The Authority shall reimburse the Secretary for all reasonable costs incurred by the Secretary as a result of the filing of a certified report pursuant to this Section, including, but not limited to, the costs of providing notice required pursuant to subsection (b) and the costs incurred by the Secretary in any hearing conducted with respect to the report pursuant to this subsection and any appeal from that hearing.

(h) The Secretary and the Authority may promulgate rules to enable them to carry out their duties under this Section.

(i) The Authority shall cooperate with the Secretary in the administration of this Section and shall provide the Secretary with any information the Secretary may deem necessary for these purposes, including regular and timely access to toll violation enforcement records.

The Secretary shall cooperate with the Authority in the administration of this Section and shall provide the Authority with any information the Authority may deem necessary for the purposes of this Section, including regular and timely access to vehicle registration records. Section 2-123 of this Code shall not apply to the provision of this information, but the Secretary shall be reimbursed for the cost of providing this information.

(j) For purposes of this Section, the term "Authority" means the Illinois State Toll Highway Authority.

P.A. 76-1586, § 3-704.2, added by P.A. 91-277, § 5, eff. Jan. 1, 2000.

[1] 605 ILCS 10/10.

5/3-705. Suspending or revoking certificate or special plates of a manufacturer, engine and driveline component manufacturer, transporter, repossessor or dealer

§ 3-705. Suspending or revoking certificate or special plates of a manufacturer, engine and driveline component manufacturer, transporter, repossessor or dealer. The Secretary of State is also authorized to suspend or revoke a certificate or the special plates issued to a manufacturer, engine and driveline component manufacturer, transporter, repossessor or dealer upon determining that any such person is not lawfully entitled thereto or has made or knowingly permitted any illegal use of such plates or has committed fraud in the registration of vehicles or failed to give notices of transfers when and as required by this Chapter.

P.A. 76-1586, § 3-705, eff. July 1, 1970. Amended by P.A. 76-2139, § 1, eff. July 1, 1970.

Formerly Ill.Rev.Stat.1991, ch. 95 ½, ¶ 3-705.

5/3-706. Owner to return evidences of registration upon cancellation, revocation or suspension

§ 3-706. Owner to return evidences of registration upon cancellation, revocation or suspension. Whenever the Secretary of State cancels or revokes the registration of a vehicle or a certificate of title, registration card, registration sticker or stickers, registration plate or plates, or a nonresident or other permit or the license of any dealer or wrecker, the owner or person in possession of the same shall immediately return the evidences of registration, title or license so cancelled or revoked to the Secretary.

Whenever the Secretary suspends the registration of a vehicle or the license of any dealer or wrecker, the owner or person in possession of the same, upon request by the Secretary, shall immediately return all evidence of the registration or the license so suspended to the Secretary.

P.A. 76-1586, § 3-706, eff. July 1, 1970. Amended by P.A. 80-230, § 1, eff. Oct. 1, 1977; P.A. 80-1185, § 1, eff. March 8, 1978; P.A. 85-1201, § 1, eff. July 1, 1989.

Formerly Ill.Rev.Stat.1991, ch. 95 ½, ¶ 3-706.

5/3-707. Operation of uninsured motor vehicle—penalty

Text of section effective until July 1, 2003

§ 3-707. Operation of uninsured motor vehicle—penalty. No person shall operate a motor vehicle unless the motor vehicle is covered by a liability insurance policy in accordance with Section 7-601 of this Code.

Any person who fails to comply with a request by a law enforcement officer for display of evidence of insurance, as required under Section 7-602 of this Code, shall be deemed to be operating an uninsured motor vehicle.

Any operator of a motor vehicle subject to registration under this Code who is convicted of violating this Section is guilty of a business offense and shall be required to pay a fine in excess of $500, but not more than $1,000. However, no person charged with violating this Section shall be convicted if such person produces in court satisfactory evidence that at the time of the arrest the motor vehicle was covered by a liability insurance policy in accordance with Section 7-601 of this Code. The chief judge of each circuit may designate an officer of the court to review the documentation demonstrating that at the time of arrest the motor vehicle was covered by a liability insurance policy in accordance with Section 7-601 of this Code.

P.A. 76-1586, § 3-707, added by P.A. 85-1201, § 1, eff. July 1, 1989. Amended by P.A. 86-149, § 2, eff. Aug. 11, 1989; P.A. 86-1179, § 2, eff. Aug. 17, 1990; P.A. 88-315, § 5, eff. Jan. 1, 1994.

Formerly Ill.Rev.Stat.1991, ch. 95 ½, ¶ 3-707.

For text of section effective July 1, 2003, see 625 ILCS 5/3-707, post

5/3-707. Operation of uninsured motor vehicle—penalty

Text of section effective July 1, 2003

§ 3-707. Operation of uninsured motor vehicle—penalty.

(a) No person shall operate a motor vehicle unless the motor vehicle is covered by a liability insurance policy in accordance with Section 7-601 of this Code.

(b) Any person who fails to comply with a request by a law enforcement officer for display of evidence of insurance, as required under Section 7-602 of this Code, shall be deemed to be operating an uninsured motor vehicle.

(c) Any operator of a motor vehicle subject to registration under this Code who is convicted of violating this Section is guilty of a business offense and shall be required to pay a fine in excess of $500, but not more than $1,000. However, no person charged with violating this Section shall be convicted if such person produces in court satisfactory evidence that at the time of the arrest the motor vehicle was covered by a liability insurance policy in accordance with Section 7-601 of this Code. The chief judge of each circuit may designate an officer of the court to review the documentation demonstrating that at the time of arrest the motor vehicle was covered by a liability insurance policy in accordance with Section 7-601 of this Code.

(d) A person convicted a third or subsequent time of violating this Section or a similar provision of a local ordinance must give proof to the Secretary of State of the person's financial responsibility as defined in Section 7-315. The person must maintain the proof in a manner satisfactory to the Secretary for a minimum period of one year after the date the proof is first filed. The Secretary must suspend the driver's license of any person determined by the Secretary not to have provided adequate proof of financial responsibility as required by this subsection.

For text of section effective until July 1, 2003, see 625 ILCS 5/3-707, ante

P.A. 76-1586, § 3-707, added by P.A. 85-1201, § 1, eff. July 1, 1989. Amended by P.A. 86-149, § 2, eff. Aug. 11, 1989; P.A. 86-1179, § 2, eff. Aug. 17, 1990; P.A. 88-315, § 5, eff. Jan. 1, 1994; P.A. 92-775, § 5, eff. July 1, 2003.

Formerly Ill.Rev.Stat.1991, ch. 95 ½, ¶ 3-707.

5/3-708. Operation of motor vehicle when registration suspended for noninsurance

§ 3-708. Operation of motor vehicle when registration suspended for noninsurance. No person shall operate a vehicle the registration of which is suspended pursuant to Section 7-606 or 7-607 of this Code.

Any person convicted of violating this Section is guilty of a business offense and shall be required to pay a fine of not less than $1,000 and not more than $2,000. Any person convicted of a second or subsequent violation of this Section is guilty of a Class B misdemeanor and shall be required to pay a fine of not less than $1,000 and not more than $2,000.

P.A. 76-1586, § 3-708, added by P.A. 85-1201, § 1, eff. July 1, 1989. Amended by P.A. 86-149, § 2, eff. Aug. 11, 1989; P.A. 90-559, § 5, eff. June 1, 1998.

Formerly Ill.Rev.Stat.1991, ch. 95 ½, ¶ 3-708.

5/3-709. § 3-709. Repealed by P.A. 86-149, § 3, eff. Aug. 11, 1989

5/3-710. Display of false insurance card

§ 3-710. Display of false insurance card. No person shall display evidence of insurance to a law enforcement officer, court, or officer of the court, knowing there is no valid liability insurance in effect on the motor vehicle as required under Section 7-601 of this Code or knowing the evidence of insurance is illegally altered, counterfeit, or otherwise invalid as evidence of insurance required under Section 7-602 of this Code. If the law enforcement officer issues a citation to a motor vehicle operator for displaying invalid evidence of insurance, the officer shall confiscate the evidence for presentation in court.

Any person convicted of violating this Section is guilty of a Class A misdemeanor.

P.A. 76-1586, § 3-710, added by P.A. 85-1201, § 1, eff. July 1, 1989. Amended by P.A. 86-149, § 2, eff. Aug. 11, 1989; P.A. 89-565, § 5, eff. July 26, 1996.

Formerly Ill.Rev.Stat.1991, ch. 95 ½, ¶ 3-710.

5/3-711. Reports of orders of supervision

§ 3-711. Whenever a court convicts a person of a violation of Section 3-707, 3-708 or 3-710 of this Code, or enters an order placing on supervision the person charged with the violation, the clerk of the court within 10 days shall forward a report of the conviction or order of supervision to the Secretary of State in a form prescribed by the Secretary. In any case where the person charged with the violation fails to appear in court, the procedures provided in Section 6-306.3 or 6-306.4 of this Code, whichever is applicable shall apply.

The Secretary shall keep records of such reports. However, reports of orders of supervision shall not be released to any outside source, except the affected driver and law enforcement agencies, and shall be used only to inform the Secretary and the courts that such driver previously has been assigned court supervision.

P.A. 76-1586, § 3-711, added by P.A. 86-149, § 2, eff. Aug. 11, 1989.

Formerly Ill.Rev.Stat.1991, ch. 95 ½, ¶ 3-711.

ARTICLE VIII. REGISTRATION AND LICENSE FEES

5/3-801. Registration

§ 3-801. Registration. (a) Except as provided herein for new residents, every owner of any vehicle which shall be operated upon the public highways of this State shall, within 24 hours after becoming the owner or at such time as such vehicle becomes subject to registration under the provisions of this Act, file in an office of the Secretary of State, an application for registration properly completed and executed. New residents need not secure registration until 30 days after establishing residency in this State, provided the vehicle is properly registered in another jurisdiction. By the expiration of such 30 day statutory grace period, a new resident shall comply with the provisions of this Act and apply for Illinois vehicle registration. All applications for registration shall be accompanied by all documentation required under the provisions of this Act. The appropriate registration fees and taxes provided for in this Article of this Chapter shall be paid to the Secretary of State with the application for registration of vehicles subject to registration under this Act.

(b) Any resident of this State, who has been serving as a member of the United States Armed Services outside of the State of Illinois, need not secure registration until 45 days after returning to this State, provided the vehicle displays temporary military registration.

(c) When an application is submitted by mail, the applicant may not submit cash or postage stamps for payment of fees or taxes due. The Secretary in his discretion, may decline to accept a personal or company check in payment of fees or taxes. An application submitted to a dealer, or a remittance made to the Secretary of State shall be deemed in compliance with this Section.

P.A. 76-1586, § 3-801, eff. July 1, 1970. Amended by P.A. 77-364, § 1, eff. July 23, 1971; P.A. 79-516, § 1, eff. Oct. 1, 1975; P.A. 85-951, § 1, eff. July 1, 1988; P.A. 85-992, § 1, eff. Jan. 5, 1988; P.A. 85-1209, Art. II, § 2-51, eff. Aug. 30, 1988.

Formerly Ill.Rev.Stat.1991, ch. 95 ½, ¶ 3-801.

P.A. 85-1209, the First 1988 Revisory Act, provides in Art. II, for the nonsubstantive revision or renumbering or repeal of certain sections of Acts of the 85th General Assembly through P.A. 85-1014, and corrects errors, revises cross-references and deletes obsolete text in such sections.

5/3-802. Reclassifications and upgrades

§ 3-802. Reclassifications and upgrades.

(a) Definitions. For the purposes of this Section, the following words shall have the meanings ascribed to them as follows:

"Reclassification" means changing the registration of a vehicle from one plate category to another.

"Upgrade" means increasing the registered weight of a vehicle within the same plate category.

(b) When reclassing the registration of a vehicle from one plate category to another, the owner shall receive credit for the unused portion of the present plate and be charged the current portion fees for the new plate. In addition, the appropriate replacement plate and replacement sticker fees shall be assessed.

(c) When upgrading the weight of a registration within the same plate category, the owner shall pay the difference in current period fees between the two plates. In addition, the appropriate replacement plate and replacement sticker fees shall be assessed. In the event new plates are not required, the corrected registration card fee shall be assessed.

(d) In the event the owner of the vehicle desires to change the registered weight and change the plate category, the owner shall receive credit for the unused portion of the registration fee of the current plate and pay the current portion of the registration fee for the new plate, and in addition, pay the appropriate replacement plate and replacement sticker fees.

(e) Reclassing from one plate category to another plate category can be done only once within any registration period.

(f) No refunds shall be made in any of the circumstances found in subsection (b), subsection (c), or subsection (d).

(g) In the event the registration of a vehicle registered under the mileage tax option is revoked, the owner shall be required to pay the annual registration fee in the new plate category and shall not receive any credit for the mileage plate fees.

(h) Certain special interest plates may be displayed on first division vehicles, second division vehicles weighing 8,000 pounds or less, and recreational vehicles. Those plates can be transferred within those vehicle groups.

(i) Plates displayed on second division vehicles weighing 8,000 pounds or less and passenger vehicle plates may be reclassed from one division to the other.

(j) Other than in subsection (i), reclassing from one division to the other division is prohibited. In addition, a reclass from a motor vehicle to a trailer or a trailer to a motor vehicle is prohibited.

P.A. 76-1586, § 3-802, eff. July 1, 1970. Amended by P.A. 76-1626, § 1, eff. July 1, 1970; P.A. 77-364, § 1, eff. July 23, 1971; P.A. 78-328, eff. Oct. 1, 1973; P.A. 79-1367, § 1, eff. Aug. 6, 1976; P.A. 80-1185, § 1, eff. March 8, 1978; P.A. 80-1463, § 1, eff. Jan. 1, 1979; P.A. 83-12, § 1, eff. July 1, 1983; P.A. 86-444, § 1, eff. Jan. 1, 1990; P.A. 89-245, § 5, eff. Jan. 1, 1996; P.A. 90-774, § 5, eff. Aug. 14, 1998.

Formerly Ill.Rev.Stat.1991, ch. 95 ½, ¶ 3-802.

5/3-803. Reductions

§ 3-803. Reductions. (a) Reduction of fees and taxes prescribed in this Chapter shall be applicable only to vehicles newly-acquired by the owner after the beginning of a registration period or which become subject to registration after the beginning of a registration period as specified in this Act. The Secretary of State may deny a reduction as to any vehicle operated in this State without being properly and timely registered in Illinois under this Chapter, of a vehicle in violation of any provision of this Chapter, or upon detection of such violation by an audit, or upon determining that such vehicle was operated in Illinois before such violation. Bond or other security in the proper amount may be required by the Secretary of State while the matter is under investigation. Reductions shall be granted if a person becomes the owner after the dates specified or if a vehicle becomes subject to registration under this Act, as amended, after the dates specified.

(b) Vehicles of the First Division. The annual fees and taxes prescribed by Section 3-806 shall be reduced by 50% on and after June 15, except as provided in Sections 3-414 and 3-802 of this Act.

(c) Vehicles of the Second Division. The annual fees and taxes prescribed by Sections 3-402, 3-402.1, 3-815 and 3-819 and paid on a calendar year for such vehicles shall be reduced on a quarterly basis if the vehicle becomes subject to registration on and after March 31, June 30 or September 30. Where such fees and taxes are payable on a fiscal year basis, they shall be reduced on a quarterly basis on and after September 30, December 31 or March 31.

(d) Two-year Registrations. The fees and taxes prescribed by Section 3-808 for 2-year registrations shall not be reduced in any event. However, the fees and taxes prescribed for all other 2-year registrations by this Act, shall be reduced as follows:

By 25% on and after June 15;

By 50% on and after December 15;

By 75% on and after the next ensuing June 15.

(e) The registration fees and taxes imposed upon certain vehicles shall not be reduced by any amount in any event in the following instances:

Permits under Sections 3-403 and 3-811;

Municipal Buses under Section 3-807;

Governmental or charitable vehicles under Section 3-808;

Farm Machinery under Section 3-809;

Soil and conservation equipment under Section 3-809.1;

Special Plates under Section 3-810;

Permanently mounted equipment under Section 3-812;

Registration fee under Section 3-813;

Semitrailer fees under Section 3-814;

Farm trucks under Section 3-815;

Mileage weight tax option under Section 3-818;

Farm trailers under Section 3-819;

Duplicate plates under Section 3-820;

Fees under Section 3-821;

Security Fees under Section 3-822;

Search Fees under Section 3-823.

(f) The reductions provided for shall not apply to any vehicle of the first or second division registered by the same applicant in the prior registration year. This bill takes effect with the 1986 Calendar Registration Year.

(g) Reductions shall in no event result in payment of a fee or tax less than $6, and the Secretary of State shall promulgate schedules of fees reflecting applicable reductions. Where any reduced amount is not stated in full dollars, the Secretary of State may adjust the amount due to the nearest full dollar amount.

(h) The reductions provided for in subsections (a) through (g) of this Section shall not apply to those vehicles of the first or second division registered on a staggered registration basis.

(i) A vehicle which becomes subject to registration during the last month of the current registration year is exempt from any applicable reduced fourth quarter or second semiannual registration fee, and may register for the subsequent registration year as its initial registration. This subsection does not include those apportioned and prorated fees under Sections 3-402 and 3-402.1 of this Code.

P.A. 76-1586, § 3-803, eff. July 1, 1970. Amended by P.A. 77-1541, § 1, eff. Sept. 17, 1971; P.A. 78-328, § 1, eff. Oct. 1, 1973; P.A. 79-627, § 1, eff. Aug. 28, 1975; P.A. 80-1185, § 1, eff. March 8, 1978; P.A. 81-323, § 1, eff. Aug. 30, 1979; P.A. 82-136, § 1, eff. Oct. 1, 1981; P.A. 83-455, § 1, eff. Oct. 1, 1983; P.A. 84-210, § 1, eff. Jan. 1, 1986; P.A. 84-1311, § 1, eff. Aug. 27, 1986.

Formerly Ill.Rev.Stat.1991, ch. 95 ½, ¶ 3-803.

P.A. 84-1311 incorporated the amendment by P.A. 84-210.

5/3-804. Antique vehicles

§ 3-804. Antique vehicles.

(a) The owner of an antique vehicle may register such vehicle for a fee not to exceed $13 for a 2-year antique plate. The application for registration must be accompanied by an affirmation of the owner that such vehicle will be driven on the highway only for the purpose of going to and returning from an antique auto show or an exhibition, or for servicing or demonstration and also affirming that the mechanical condition, physical condition, brakes, lights, glass and appearance of such vehicle is the same or as safe as originally equipped. The Secretary may, in his discretion prescribe that antique vehicle plates be issued for a definite or an indefinite term, such term to correspond to the term of registration plates issued generally, as provided in Section 3-414.1. In no event may the registration fee for antique vehicles exceed $6 per registration year. Any person requesting antique plates under this Section may also apply to have vanity or personalized plates as provided under Section 3-405.1.

(b) Any person who is the registered owner of an antique vehicle may display a historical license plate from or representing the model year of the vehicle, furnished by such person, in lieu of the current and valid Illinois antique vehicle plates issued thereto, provided that valid and current Illinois antique vehicle plates and registration card issued to such antique vehicle are simultaneously carried within such vehicle and are available for inspection.

P.A. 76-1586, § 3-804, eff. July 1, 1970. Amended by P.A. 76-1627, § 1, eff. Dec. 1, 1970; P.A. 77-217, § 1, eff. Jan. 1, 1972; P.A. 77-1910, § 1, eff. July 1, 1972; P.A. 78-255, § 61, eff. Oct. 1, 1973; P.A. 78-667, § 1, eff. July 1, 1974; P.A. 78-1297, § 58, eff. Mar. 4, 1975; P.A. 80-230, § 1, eff. Oct. 1, 1977; P.A. 83-145, § 1, eff. Jan. 1, 1984; P.A. 83-449, § 1, eff. Jan. 1, 1984; P.A. 83-1362, Art. II, § 99, eff. Sept. 11, 1984; P.A. 86-480, § 1, eff. Jan. 1, 1990; P.A. 91-37, § 40, eff. July 1, 1999.

Formerly Ill.Rev.Stat.1991, ch. 95 ½, ¶ 3-804.

5/3-804.02. Commuter Vans

§ 3-804.02. Commuter Vans. The owner of a commuter van may register such van for an annual fee not to exceed $63. The Secretary may prescribe that commuter van plates be issued for an indefinite term, such term to correspond to the term of registration plates issued generally. In no event may the registration fee for commuter vans exceed $63 per registration year.

P.A. 76-1586, § 3-804.02, added by P.A. 81-492, eff. Jan. 1, 1980. Amended by P.A. 90-89, § 15, eff. Jan. 1, 1998; P.A. 91-37, § 40, eff. July 1, 1999.

Formerly Ill.Rev.Stat.1991, ch. 95 ½, ¶ 3-804.02.

5/3-804.1. Custom vehicles

§ 3-804.1. Custom vehicles.

(a) The owner of a custom vehicle may register that vehicle for the standard registration fee for a vehicle of the first division, other than a motorcycle, motor driven cycle, or pedalcycle, and obtain a custom vehicle plate. An applicant for the special plate shall be charged, in addition to the standard registration fee, $15 for original issuance to be deposited into the Secretary of State Special License Plate Fund, to be used by the Secretary to help defray administrative costs. For each renewal period, in addition to the standard registration fee, the applicant shall be charged $2, which shall be deposited into the Secretary of State Special

License Plate Fund. The application for registration must be accompanied by an affirmation of the owner that the vehicle will be maintained for occasional transportation, exhibitions, club activities, parades, tours, and similar uses and will not be used for general daily transportation. The Secretary may, in his or her discretion, prescribe that custom vehicle plates be issued for a definite or an indefinite term, the term to correspond to the term of registration plates issued generally, as provided in Section 3-414.1. Any person requesting custom vehicle plates under this Section may also apply to have vanity or personalized plates as provided under Section 3-405.1.

(b) Upon initial registration of a custom vehicle, the owner of the custom vehicle must provide proof acceptable to the Secretary that, no more than 3 months before the date of the application for registration, the custom vehicle passed a safety inspection that (i) has been approved by the Secretary and (ii) is equivalent to the National Street Rod Association's prescribed vehicle safety inspection.

Except where otherwise provided, custom vehicles are considered to be in compliance with all vehicle equipment requirements if they have passed the approved vehicle safety inspection.

P.A. 76-1586, § 3-804.1, added by P.A. 92-668, § 5, eff. Jan. 1, 2003.

5/3-804.2. Street rods

§ 3-804.2. Street rods.

(a) The owner of a street rod may register the vehicle for the standard registration fee for a vehicle of the first division, other than a motorcycle, motor driven cycle, or pedalcycle, and obtain a street rod plate. An applicant for the special plate shall be charged, in addition to the standard registration fee, $15 for original issuance to be deposited into the Secretary of State Special License Plate Fund, to be used by the Secretary to help defray administrative costs. For each renewal period, in addition to the standard registration fee, the applicant shall be charged $2, which shall be deposited into the Secretary of State Special License Plate Fund. The application for registration must be accompanied by an affirmation of the owner that the vehicle will be maintained for occasional transportation, exhibitions, club activities, parades, tours, and similar uses and will not be used for general daily transportation. The Secretary may, in his or her discretion, prescribe that street rod plates be issued for a definite or an indefinite term, the term to correspond to the term of registration plates issued generally, as provided in Section 3-414.1. Any person requesting street rod plates under this Section may also apply to have vanity or personalized plates as provided under Section 3-405.1.

(b) Upon initial registration of a street rod, the owner of the street rod must provide proof acceptable to the Secretary that, no more than 3 months before the date of the application for registration, the street rod passed a safety inspection that (i) has been approved by the Secretary and (ii) is equivalent to the National Street Rod Association's prescribed vehicle safety inspection.

Except where otherwise provided, street rods are considered to be in compliance with all vehicle equipment requirements if they have passed the approved vehicle safety inspection.

P.A. 76-1586, § 3-804.2, added by P.A. 92-668, § 5, eff. Jan. 1, 2003.

5/3-805. Electric vehicles

§ 3-805. Electric vehicles. The owner of a motor vehicle of the first division propelled by an electric engine and not utilizing motor fuel, may register such vehicle for a fee not to exceed $35 for a 2-year registration period. The Secretary may, in his discretion, prescribe that electric vehicle registration plates be issued for an indefinite term, such term to correspond to the term of registration plates issued generally, as provided in Section 3-414.1. In no event may the registration fee for electric vehicles exceed $18 per registration year.

P.A. 76-1586, § 3-805, eff. July 1, 1970. Amended by P.A. 76-1628, § 1, eff. Dec. 1, 1970; P.A. 77-1315, § 1, eff. Jan. 1, 1972; P.A. 77-1910, § 1, eff. July 1, 1972; P.A. 78-255, § 61, eff. Oct. 1, 1973; P.A. 80-230, § 1, eff. Oct. 1, 1977; P.A. 89-245, § 5, eff. Jan. 1, 1996; P.A. 91-37, § 40, eff. July 1, 1999.

Formerly Ill.Rev.Stat.1991, ch. 95 ½, ¶ 3-805.

5/3-806. Registration Fees; Motor Vehicles of the First Division

§ 3-806. Registration Fees; Motor Vehicles of the First Division. Every owner of any other motor vehicle of the first division, except as provided in Sections 3-804, 3-805, 3-806.3, and 3-808, and every second division vehicle weighing 8,000 pounds or less, shall pay the Secretary of State an annual registration fee at the following rates:

SCHEDULE OF REGISTRATION FEES
REQUIRED BY LAW
Beginning with the 1986 registration year

	Annual Fee	Reduced Fee On and After June 15
Motor vehicles of the first division other than Motorcycles, Motor Driven Cycles and Pedalcycles	$48	$24
		Reduced Fee September 16 to March 31
Motorcycles, Motor Driven Cycles and Pedalcycles	30	15

SCHEDULE OF REGISTRATION FEES
REQUIRED BY LAW
Beginning with the 2001 registration year

	Annual Fee	Reduced Fee On and After June 15
Motor vehicles of the first division other than Motorcycles, Motor Driven Cycles and Pedalcycles	$78	$39
		Reduced Fee September 16 to March 31
Motorcycles, Motor Driven Cycles and Pedalcycles	38	19

P.A. 76-1586, § 3-806, eff. July 1, 1970. Amended by P.A. 76-2140, § 1, eff. July 1, 1970; P.A. 78-1146, § 1, eff. Jan. 1, 1975; P.A. 79-516, § 1, eff. Oct. 1, 1975; P.A. 80-262, § 1, eff. Aug. 30, 1977; P.A. 82-648, § 1, eff. July 1, 1982; P.A.

82-649, § 3, eff. Jan. 1, 1982; P.A. 82-783, Art. III, § 37, eff. July 13, 1982; P.A. 83-12, § 1, eff. July 1, 1983; P.A. 83-817, § 1, eff. Jan. 1, 1984; P.A. 83-1362, Art. II, § 99, eff. Sept. 11, 1984; P.A. 83-1457, § 2, eff. Jan. 1, 1985; P.A. 89-245, § 5, eff. Jan. 1, 1996; P.A. 91-37, § 40, eff. July 1, 1999.

Formerly Ill.Rev.Stat.1991, ch. 95 ½, ¶ 3-806.

Section 4 of P.A. 83-12, approved July 1, 1983, provided:

"Effective date. This Act takes effect as provided in this Section.

"The amendments to those portions of Sections 3-815(a), 3-818 and 3-819(b) of 'The Illinois Vehicle Code' in Section 1 of this Act which create the 'X', 'Z', 'MX', 'MZ', 'MM' and 'TN' registration classifications and the fees and taxes imposed for those classifications, the amendments to Sections 2-119, 3-401 and 3-802 of 'The Illinois Vehicle Code' in Section 1 of this Act, and the amendments to Chapter 15 of 'The Illinois Vehicle Code' in Section 1 of this Act take effect July 1, 1983.

"The remaining amendments to 'The Illinois Vehicle Code' in Section 1 of this Act take effect July 1, 1983 and apply beginning with the 1985 registration year, except that the amendments to Sections 3-813 through 3-816 and Section 3-819 apply beginning with the 1984 registration year for those vehicles registered on a calendar year basis only.

"The amendments to Chapters 13 and 18 of 'The Illinois Vehicle Code' in Section 1 of this Act take effect January 1, 1984.

"Section 2 of this Act takes effect on the first day of the next succeeding month which commences at least 30 days after the date on which this Act becomes law.

"Section 3 of this Act takes effect July 1, 1983.

"Section 3.1 of this Act takes effect January 1, 1984.

"This Section 4 takes effect upon its becoming a law."

For effective date of amendment by P.A. 83-817, see note under 625 ILCS 5/3-414.

Section 2 of P.A. 83-817 approved Sept. 24, 1983, provided:

"This Act takes effect with the 1985 registration year."

5/3-806.1. Additional fees for vanity license plates

§ 3-806.1. Additional fees for vanity license plates. In addition to the regular registration fee, an applicant shall be charged $94 for each set of vanity license plates issued to a motor vehicle of the first division or a motor vehicle of the second division registered at not more than 8,000 pounds or to a recreational vehicle and $50 for each set of vanity plates issued to a motorcycle. In addition to the regular renewal fee, an applicant shall be charged $13 for the renewal of each set of vanity license plates.

P.A. 76-1586, § 3-806.1, added by P.A. 81-987, § 1, eff. Sept. 17, 1982. Amended by P.A. 83-12, § 1, eff. July 1, 1983; P.A. 83-828, § 1, eff. Jan. 1, 1984; P.A. 83-1362, Art. II, § 99, eff. Sept. 11, 1984; P.A. 86-480, § 1, eff. Jan. 1, 1990; P.A. 91-37, § 40, eff. July 1, 1999.

Formerly Ill.Rev.Stat.1991, ch. 95 ½, ¶ 3-806.1.

Section 4 of P.A. 83-12, approved July 1, 1983, provided:

"Effective date. This Act takes effect as provided in this Section.

"The amendments to those portions of Sections 3-815(a), 3-818 and 3-819(b) of 'The Illinois Vehicle Code' in Section 1 of this Act which create the 'X', 'Z', 'MX', 'MZ', 'MM' and 'TN' registration classifications and the fees and taxes imposed for those classifications, the amendments to Sections 2-119, 3-401 and 3-802 of 'The Illinois Vehicle Code' in Section 1 of this Act, and the amendments to Chapter 15 of 'The Illinois Vehicle Code' in Section 1 of this Act take effect July 1, 1983.

"The remaining amendments to 'The Illinois Vehicle Code' in Section 1 of this Act take effect July 1, 1983 and apply beginning with the 1985 registration year, except that the amendments to Sections 3-813 through 3-816 and Section 3-819 apply beginning with the 1984 registration year for those vehicles registered on a calendar year basis only.

"The amendments to Chapters 13 and 18 of 'The Illinois Vehicle Code' in Section 1 of this Act take effect January 1, 1984.

"Section 2 of this Act takes effect on the first day of the next succeeding month which commences at least 30 days after the date on which this Act becomes law.

"Section 3 of this Act takes effect July 1, 1983.

"Section 3.1 of this Act takes effect January 1, 1984.

"This Section 4 takes effect upon its becoming a law."

Section 2 of P.A. 83-828 provided:

"This Act takes effect with the 1985 registration year."

5/3-806.2. Limitations on no-fee plates

§ 3-806.2. Limitations on no-fee plates. No individual shall be issued more than one pair of plates of any category for which no fee is required. The Secretary of State may issue additional pairs of plates of any such category upon receiving the required application and registration fees.

P.A. 76-1586, § 3-806.2, added by P.A. 82-1011, § 2, eff. Sept. 17, 1982. Amended by P.A. 88-517, § 10, eff. Nov. 16, 1993.

Formerly Ill.Rev.Stat.1991, ch. 95 ½, ¶ 3-806.2.

5/3-806.3. Senior Citizens

§ 3-806.3. Senior Citizens.

Commencing with the 2001 registration year and extending through the 2003 registration year, the registration fee paid by any vehicle owner who has claimed and received a grant under the Senior Citizens and Disabled Persons Property Tax Relief and Pharmaceutical Assistance Act or who is the spouse of such a person shall be $24 instead of the fee otherwise provided in this Code for passenger cars displaying standard multi-year registration plates issued under Section 3-414.1, motor vehicles displaying special registration plates issued under Section 3-616, motor vehicles registered at 8,000 pounds or less under Section 3-815(a) and recreational vehicles registered at 8,000 pounds or less under Section 3-815(b). Widows and widowers of claimants shall also be entitled to this reduced registration fee for the registration year in which the claimant was eligible.

Commencing with the 2004 registration year, the registration fee paid by any vehicle owner who has claimed and received a grant under the Senior Citizens and Disabled Persons Property Tax Relief and Pharmaceutical Assistance Act or who is the spouse of such a person shall be $24 instead of the fee otherwise provided in this Code for passenger cars displaying standard multi-year registration plates issued under Section 3-414.1, motor vehicles displaying special registration plates issued under Section 3-616, 3-621, 3-622, 3-623, 3-624, 3-625, 3-626, 3-628, 3-638, 3-642, 3-645, 3-647, 3-650, or 3-651, motor vehicles registered at 8,000 pounds or less under Section 3-815(a), and recreational vehicles registered at 8,000 pounds or less under Section 3-815(b). Widows and widowers of claimants shall also be entitled to this reduced registration fee for the registration year in which the claimant was eligible.

No more than one reduced registration fee under this Section shall be allowed during any 12 month period based on the primary eligibility of any individual, whether such reduced registration fee is allowed to the individual or to the spouse, widow or widower of such individual. This Section does not apply to the fee paid in addition to the registration fee for motor vehicles displaying vanity or special license plates.

P.A. 76-1586, § 3-806.3, added by P.A. 83-1457, § 2, eff. Jan. 1, 1985. Amended by P.A. 84-832, Art. III, § 11, eff. Sept. 23, 1985; P.A. 84-1390, § 4, eff. Sept. 18, 1986; P.A. 86-444,

§ 1, eff. Jan. 1, 1990; P.A. 91-37, § 40, eff. July 1, 1999; P.A. 92-651, § 77, eff. July 11, 2002; P.A. 92-699, § 5, eff. Jan. 1, 2003.

Formerly Ill.Rev.Stat.1991, ch. 95 ½, ¶ 3-806.3.

P.A. 92-651, the First 2002 General Revisory Act, amended various Acts to delete obsolete text, to correct patent and technical errors, to revise cross references, to resolve multiple actions in the 91st and 92nd General Assemblies and to make certain technical corrections in P.A. 91-937 through P.A. 92-520.

See 5 ILCS 70/6 as to the effect of (1) more than one amendment of a section at the same session of the General Assembly or (2) two or more acts relating to the same subject matter enacted by the same General Assembly.

5/3-806.4. Gold Star recipients

§ 3-806.4. Gold Star recipients. Commencing with the 1991 registration year, upon proper application, the Secretary of State shall issue one pair of registration plates to any Illinois resident, who as the surviving widow or widower, or in the absence thereof, as the surviving parent, is awarded the Gold Star by the United States in recognition of spouses or children who served in the Armed Forces of the United States and lost their lives while in service whether in peacetime or war. If the parent no longer survives, the Secretary of State shall issue the plates to a surviving sibling, of the person who served in the Armed Forces, who is an Illinois resident. No more than one set of plates shall be issued for each Gold Star awarded, and only one surviving parent, or in the absence of a surviving parent, only one surviving sibling shall be issued a set of registration plates, except for those surviving parents who, as recipients of the Gold Star, have legally separated or divorced, in which case each surviving parent shall be allowed one set of registration plates. Registration plates issued under this Section shall be for first division vehicles and second division vehicles of 8,000 pounds or less. An applicant shall be charged a $15 fee for the original issuance in addition to the appropriate registration fee which shall be deposited into the Road Fund to help defray the administrative processing costs. For each registration renewal period, a $2 fee, in addition to the appropriate registration fee, shall be charged and deposited into the Road Fund.

P.A. 76-1586, § 3-806.4, added by P.A. 86-390, § 1, eff. Jan. 1, 1990. Amended by P.A. 90-534, § 5, eff. Nov. 14, 1997.

Formerly Ill.Rev.Stat.1991, ch. 95 ½, ¶ 3-806.4.

5/3-807. Busses operating within Municipality; Registration Fee

§ 3-807. Busses operating within Municipality; Registration Fee. The registration fee of $13 per 2-year registration period shall be paid by the owners of 2 axle motor vehicles which are designed and used as busses in a public system for transporting more than 10 passengers, which vehicles are used as common carriers in the general transportation of passengers and not devoted to any specialized purpose, and which operate entirely within the territorial limits of a single municipality, or a single municipality and municipalities contiguous thereto, or in a close radius thereof, and whose operations are subject to the regulations of the Illinois Commerce Commission. Owners of such vehicles are exempt from paying either a flat weight tax or mileage weight tax. There shall be no reduction in such registration fee even though such registration is made after the beginning of the registration period.

P.A. 76-1586, § 3-807, eff. July 1, 1970. Amended by P.A. 76-2141, § 1, eff. July 1, 1970; P.A. 79-1021, § 1; P.A. 83-12, § 1, eff. July 1, 1983; P.A. 91-37, § 40, eff. July 1, 1999.

Formerly Ill.Rev.Stat.1991, ch. 95 ½, ¶ 3-807.

Section 2 of P.A. 79-1021, certified Sept. 17, 1975, provided:

"This amendatory Act of 1975 takes effect beginning with motor vehicle registrations for 1977."

Section 4 of P.A. 83-12, approved July 1, 1983, provided:

"Effective date. This Act takes effect as provided in this Section.

"The amendments to those portions of Sections 3-815(a), 3-818 and 3-819(b) of 'The Illinois Vehicle Code' in Section 1 of this Act which create the 'X', 'Z', 'MX', 'MZ', 'MM' and 'TN' registration classifications and the fees and taxes imposed for those classifications, the amendments to Sections 2-119, 3-401 and 3-802 of 'The Illinois Vehicle Code' in Section 1 of this Act, and the amendments to Chapter 15 of 'The Illinois Vehicle Code' in Section 1 of this Act take effect July 1, 1983.

"The remaining amendments to 'The Illinois Vehicle Code' in Section 1 of this Act take effect July 1, 1983 and apply beginning with the 1985 registration year, except that the amendments to Sections 3-813 through 3-816 and Section 3-819 apply beginning with the 1984 registration year for those vehicles registered on a calendar year basis only.

"The amendments to Chapters 13 and 18 of 'The Illinois Vehicle Code' in Section 1 of this Act take effect January 1, 1984.

"Section 2 of this Act takes effect on the first day of the next succeeding month which commences at least 30 days after the date on which this Act becomes law.

"Section 3 of this Act takes effect July 1, 1983.

"Section 3.1 of this Act takes effect January 1, 1984.

"This Section 4 takes effect upon its becoming a law."

5/3-808. Governmental and charitable vehicles; Registration fees

§ 3-808. Governmental and charitable vehicles; Registration fees.

(a) A registration fee of $10 per 2 year registration period shall be paid by the owner in the following cases:

1. Vehicles operated exclusively as a school bus for school purposes by any school district or any religious or denominational institution, except that such a school bus may be used by such a religious or denominational institution for the transportation of persons to or from any of its official activities.

2. Vehicles operated exclusively in a high school driver training program by any school district or school operated by a religious institution.

3. Rescue squad vehicles which are owned and operated by a corporation or association organized and operated not for profit for the purpose of conducting such rescue operations.

4. Vehicles, used exclusively as school buses for any school district, which are neither owned nor operated by such district.

5. Charitable vehicles.

(b) Annual vehicle registration plates shall be issued, at no charge, to the following:

1. Medical transport vehicles owned and operated by the State of Illinois or by any State agency financed by funds appropriated by the General Assembly.

2. Medical transport vehicles operated by or for any county, township or municipal corporation.

(c) Ceremonial plates. Upon payment of a registration fee of $78 per 2-year registration period, the Secretary of State shall issue registration plates to vehicles operated exclusively for ceremonial purposes by any not-for-profit veterans', fraternal, or civic organization. The Secretary of State may prescribe that ceremonial vehicle registration plates be issued for an indefinite term, that term to correspond to the term of registration plates issued generally, as provided in Section 3-414.1.

(d) In any event, any vehicle registered under this Section used or operated for purposes other than those herein prescribed shall be subject to revocation, and in that event, the owner may be required to properly register such vehicle under the provisions of this Code.

(e) As a prerequisite to registration under this Section, the Secretary of State may require the vehicle owners listed in subsection (a) of this Section who are exempt from federal income taxation under subsection (c) of Section 501 of the Internal Revenue Code of 1986, as now or hereafter amended,[1] to submit to him a determination letter, ruling or other written evidence of tax exempt status issued by the Internal Revenue Service. The Secretary may accept a certified copy of the document issued by the Internal Revenue Service as evidence of the exemption. The Secretary may require documentation of eligibility under this Section to accompany an application for registration.

(f) Special event plates. The Secretary of State may issue registration plates in recognition or commemoration of special events which promote the interests of Illinois citizens. These plates shall be valid for no more than 60 days prior to the date of expiration. The Secretary shall require the applicant for such plates to pay for the costs of furnishing the plates.

Beginning July 1, 1991, all special event plates shall be recorded in the Secretary of State's files for immediate identification.

The Secretary of State, upon issuing a new series of special event plates, shall notify all law enforcement officials of the design and other special features of the special plate series.

All special event plates shall indicate, in the lower right corner, the date of expiration in characters no less than ½ inch high.

P.A. 76–1586, § 3–808, eff. July 1, 1970. Amended by P.A. 76–2142, § 1, eff. July 1, 1970; P.A. 77–1713, § 1, eff. Jan. 1, 1972; P.A. 77–2751, § 1, eff. Sept. 1, 1972; P.A. 78–255, § 61, eff. Oct. 1, 1973; P.A. 78–1119, § 1, eff. Oct. 1, 1974; P.A. 78–1297, § 58, eff. March 4, 1975; P.A. 79–798, § 1, eff. July 1, 1976; P.A. 79–1021, § 1; P.A. 79–1454, § 44, eff. Aug. 31, 1976; P.A. 80–230, § 1, eff. Oct. 1, 1977; P.A. 81–1496, § 1, eff. Jan. 1, 1982; P.A. 82–433, § 1, eff. Sept. 8, 1981; P.A. 82–1011, § 2, eff. Sept. 17, 1982; P.A. 83–12, § 1, eff. July 1, 1983; P.A. 83–743, § 1, eff. Jan. 1, 1984; P.A. 83–1362, Art. II, § 99, eff. Sept. 11, 1984; P.A. 86–1207, § 1, eff. Aug. 29, 1990; P.A. 88–470, § 10, eff. Sept. 1, 1993; P.A. 89–245, § 5, eff. Jan. 1, 1996; P.A. 89–564, § 5, eff. July 26, 1996; P.A. 89–626, Art. 3, § 3–37, eff. Aug. 9, 1996; P.A. 90–89, § 15, eff. Jan. 1, 1998; P.A. 91–37, § 40, eff. July 1, 1999.

Formerly Ill.Rev.Stat.1991, ch. 95 ½, ¶ 3–808.

[1] 26 U.S.C.A. § 501.

Section 2 of P.A. 79–1021, certified Sept. 17, 1975, provided:

"This amendatory Act of 1975 takes effect beginning with motor vehicle registrations for 1977."

Section 3 of P.A. 82–433 approved Sept. 8, 1981, provided:

"This Act takes effect upon its becoming a law, except that the provisions relating to safety tests and proof of financial responsibility for medical transport vehicles apply only to applications for and the issuance of registration plates which are required to be displayed on January 1, 1982 or thereafter."

Section 4 of P.A. 83–12, approved July 1, 1983, provided:

"Effective date. This Act takes effect as provided in this Section.

"The amendments to those portions of Sections 3–815(a), 3–818 and 3–819(b) of 'The Illinois Vehicle Code' in Section 1 of this Act which create the 'X', 'Z', 'MX', 'MZ', 'MM' and 'TN' registration classifications and the fees and taxes imposed for those classifications, the amendments to Sections 2–119, 3–401 and 3–802 of 'The Illinois Vehicle Code' in Section 1 of this Act, and the amendments to Chapter 15 of 'The Illinois Vehicle Code' in Section 1 of this Act take effect July 1, 1983.

"The remaining amendments to 'The Illinois Vehicle Code' in Section 1 of this Act take effect July 1, 1983 and apply beginning with the 1985 registration year, except that the amendments to Sections 3–813 through 3–816 and Section 3–819 apply beginning with the 1984 registration year for those vehicles registered on a calendar year basis only.

"The amendments to Chapters 13 and 18 of 'The Illinois Vehicle Code' in Section 1 of this Act take effect January 1, 1984.

"Section 2 of this Act takes effect on the first day of the next succeeding month which commences at least 30 days after the date on which this Act becomes law.

"Section 3 of this Act takes effect July 1, 1983.

"Section 3.1 of this Act takes effect January 1, 1984.

"This Section 4 takes effect upon its becoming a law."

5/3–808.1. Vehicle registration plates; persons with disabilities; government owned vehicles

§ 3–808.1. (a) Permanent vehicle registration plates shall be issued, at no charge, to the following:

1. Vehicles, other than medical transport vehicles, owned and operated by the State of Illinois or by any State agency financed by funds appropriated by the General Assembly;

2. Special person with disabilities plates issued to vehicles owned and operated by the State of Illinois or by any State agency financed by funds appropriated by the General Assembly.

(b) Permanent vehicle registration plates shall be issued, for a one time fee of $8.00, to the following:

1. Vehicles, other than medical transport vehicles, operated by or for any county, township or municipal corporation;

2. Vehicles owned by counties, townships or municipal corporations for persons with disabilities.

3. Beginning with the 1991 registration year, county-owned vehicles operated by or for any county sheriff and designated deputy sheriffs. These registration plates shall contain the specific county code and unit number.

4. All–terrain vehicles owned by counties, townships, or municipal corporations and used for law enforcement purposes when the Manufacturer's Statement of Origin is accompanied with a letter from the original manufacturer or a manufacturer's franchised dealer stating that this all-terrain vehicle has been converted to a street worthy vehicle that meets the equipment requirements set forth in Chapter 12 of this Code.

5. Beginning with the 2001 registration year, municipally-owned vehicles operated by or for any police department. These registration plates shall contain the designation "municipal police" and shall be numbered and distributed as prescribed by the Secretary of State.

P.A. 76–1586, § 3–808.1, added by P.A. 81–1496, § 1, eff. Jan. 1, 1982. Amended by P.A. 82–433, § 1, eff. Sept. 8, 1981; P.A. 86–480, § 1, eff. Jan. 1, 1990; P.A. 88–685, § 5, eff. Jan. 24, 1995; P.A. 90–324, § 5, eff. Aug. 1, 1997; P.A. 91–383, § 5, eff. July 30, 1999.

Formerly Ill.Rev.Stat.1991, ch. 95 ½, ¶ 3–808.1.

Section 3 of P.A. 82–433 approved Sept. 8, 1981, provided:

"This Act takes effect upon its becoming a law, except that the provisions relating to safety tests and proof of financial responsibility for medical transport vehicles apply only to applications for and the

issuance of registration plates which are required to be displayed on January 1, 1982 or thereafter."

5/3-809. Farm machinery, exempt vehicles and fertilizer spreaders—registration fee

§ 3-809. Farm machinery, exempt vehicles and fertilizer spreaders—registration fee.

(a) Vehicles of the second division having a corn sheller, a well driller, hay press, clover huller, feed mixer and unloader, or other farm machinery permanently mounted thereon and used solely for transporting the same, farm wagon type trailers having a fertilizer spreader attachment permanently mounted thereon, having a gross weight of not to exceed 36,000 pounds and used only for the transportation of bulk fertilizer, and farm wagon type tank trailers of not to exceed 3,000 gallons capacity, used during the liquid fertilizer season as field-storage "nurse tanks" supplying the fertilizer to a field applicator and moved on highways only for bringing the fertilizer from a local source of supply to farm or field or from one farm or field to another, or used during the lime season and moved on the highways only for bringing from a local source of supply to farm or field or from one farm or field to another, shall be registered upon the filing of a proper application and the payment of a registration fee of $13 per 2-year registration period. This registration fee of $13 shall be paid in full and shall not be reduced even though such registration is made after the beginning of the registration period.

(b) Vehicles exempt from registration under the provisions of Section 3-402.A of this Act, as amended, except those vehicles required to be registered under paragraph (c) of this Section, may, at the option of the owner, be identified as exempt vehicles by displaying registration plates issued by the Secretary of State. The owner thereof may apply for such registration plates upon the filing of a proper application and the payment of a registration fee of $13, and this registration shall be valid for a 2 year registration period. This $13 fee shall be paid in full and shall not be reduced even though the application is made after the beginning of the registration period. The application for and display of such registration plates for identification purposes by vehicles exempt from registration shall not be deemed as a waiver or recision of its exempt status, nor make such vehicle subject to registration.

(c) Any single unit self-propelled agricultural fertilizer implement, designed for both on and off road use, equipped with flotation tires and otherwise specially adapted for the application of plant food materials or agricultural chemicals, desiring to be operated upon the highways ladened with load shall be registered upon the filing of a proper application and payment of a registration fee of $250. The registration fee shall be paid in full and shall not be reduced even though such registration is made during the second half of the registration year. These vehicles shall, whether loaded or unloaded, be limited to a maximum gross weight of 36,000 pounds, restricted to a highway speed of not more than 30 miles per hour and a legal width of not more than 12 feet. Such vehicles shall be limited to the furthering of agricultural or horticultural pursuits and in furtherance of these pursuits, such vehicles may be operated upon the highway, within a 50 mile radius of their point of loading as indicated on the written or printed statement required by the "Illinois Fertilizer Act of 1961",[1] as amended, for the purpose of moving plant food materials or agricultural chemicals to the field, or from field to field, for the sole purpose of application.

No single unit self-propelled agricultural fertilizer implement, designed for both on and off road use, equipped with flotation tires and otherwise specially adapted for the application of plant food materials or agricultural chemicals, having a width of more than 12 feet or a gross weight in excess of 36,000 pounds, shall be permitted to operate upon the highways ladened with load.

Whenever any vehicle is operated in violation of Section 3-809 (c) of this Act, the owner or the driver of such vehicle shall be deemed guilty of a petty offense and either may be prosecuted for such violation.

P.A. 76-1586, § 3-809, eff. July 1, 1970. Amended by P.A. 76-2143, § 1, eff. July 1, 1970; P.A. 79-1021, § 1; P.A. 81-327, § 1, eff. Jan. 1, 1980; P.A. 82-783, Art. IV, § 25, eff. July 13, 1982; P.A. 83-12, § 1, eff. July 1, 1983; P.A. 84-986, § 1, eff. Sept. 25, 1985; P.A. 86-1236, § 1, eff. Jan. 1, 1991; P.A. 91-37, § 40, eff. July 1, 1999; P.A. 92-15, § 5, eff. July 1, 2001.

Formerly Ill.Rev.Stat.1991, ch. 95 ½, ¶ 3-809.

1 505 ILCS 80/1 et seq.

Section 2 of P.A. 79-1021, certified Sept. 17, 1975, provided:

"This amendatory Act of 1975 takes effect beginning with motor vehicle registrations for 1977."

Section 4 of P.A. 83-12, approved July 1, 1983, provided:

"Effective date. This Act takes effect as provided in this Section.

"The amendments to those portions of Sections 3-815(a), 3-818 and 3-819(b) of 'The Illinois Vehicle Code' in Section 1 of this Act which create the 'X', 'Z', 'MX', 'MZ', 'MM' and 'TN' registration classifications and the fees and taxes imposed for those classifications, the amendments to Sections 2-119, 3-401 and 3-802 of 'The Illinois Vehicle Code' in Section 1 of this Act, and the amendments to Chapter 15 of 'The Illinois Vehicle Code' in Section 1 of this Act take effect July 1, 1983.

"The remaining amendments to 'The Illinois Vehicle Code' in Section 1 of this Act take effect July 1, 1983 and apply beginning with the 1985 registration year, except that the amendments to Sections 3-813 through 3-816 and Section 3-819 apply beginning with the 1984 registration year for those vehicles registered on a calendar year basis only.

"The amendments to Chapters 13 and 18 of 'The Illinois Vehicle Code' in Section 1 of this Act take effect January 1, 1984.

"Section 2 of this Act takes effect on the first day of the next succeeding month which commences at least 30 days after the date on which this Act becomes law.

"Section 3 of this Act takes effect July 1, 1983.

"Section 3.1 of this Act takes effect January 1, 1984.

"This Section 4 takes effect upon its becoming a law."

5/3-809.1. Vehicles of second division used for transporting soil and conservation machinery and equipment—Registration fee

§ 3-809.1. Vehicles of second division used for transporting soil and conservation machinery and equipment—Registration fee. Not for hire vehicles of the second division used, only in the territory within a 75 mile radius of the owner's headquarters, solely for transporting the owner's machinery, equipment, plastic tubing, tile and steel reinforcement materials used exclusively for soil and water conservation work on farms, other work on farms and in drainage districts organized for agricultural purposes, shall be registered upon the filing of a proper application and the payment of a registration fee of $488 per annum. The registration fee of $488 shall be paid in full and shall not be reduced even though such registration is made during the second half of the registration year.

P.A. 76-1586, § 3-809.1, added by P.A. 77-71, § 1, eff. July 1, 1971. Amended by P.A. 78-271, § 1, eff. Aug. 13, 1973;

P.A. 80–842, § 1, eff. Sept. 20, 1977; P.A. 83–12, § 1, eff. July 1, 1983; P.A. 85–1396, § 2, eff. Sept. 2, 1988; P.A. 91–37, § 40, eff. July 1, 1999.

Formerly Ill.Rev.Stat.1991, ch. 95 ½, ¶ 3–809.1.

Section 4 of P.A. 83–12, approved July 1, 1983, provided:

"Effective date. This Act takes effect as provided in this Section.

"The amendments to those portions of Sections 3–815(a), 3–818 and 3–819(b) of 'The Illinois Vehicle Code' in Section 1 of this Act which create the 'X', 'Z', 'MX', 'MZ', 'MM' and 'TN' registration classifications and the fees and taxes imposed for those classifications, the amendments to Sections 2–119, 3–401 and 3–802 of 'The Illinois Vehicle Code' in Section 1 of this Act, and the amendments to Chapter 15 of 'The Illinois Vehicle Code' in Section 1 of this Act take effect July 1, 1983.

"The remaining amendments to 'The Illinois Vehicle Code' in Section 1 of this Act take effect July 1, 1983 and apply beginning with the 1985 registration year, except that the amendments to Sections 3–813 through 3–816 and Section 3–819 apply beginning with the 1984 registration year for those vehicles registered on a calendar year basis only.

"The amendments to Chapters 13 and 18 of 'The Illinois Vehicle Code' in Section 1 of this Act take effect January 1, 1984.

"Section 2 of this Act takes effect on the first day of the next succeeding month which commences at least 30 days after the date on which this Act becomes law.

"Section 3 of this Act takes effect July 1, 1983.

"Section 3.1 of this Act takes effect January 1, 1984.

"This Section 4 takes effect upon its becoming a law."

5/3–810. Dealers, Manufacturers, Engine and Driveline Component Manufacturers, Transporters and Repossessors—Registration Plates.

§ 3–810. Dealers, Manufacturers, Engine and Driveline Component Manufacturers, Transporters and Repossessors—Registration Plates.

(a) Dealers, manufacturers and transporters registered under this Act may obtain registration plates for use as provided in this Act, at the following rates:

Initial set of dealer's, manufacturer's or transporter's "in-transit" plates: $45

Duplicate Plates: $13

Manufacturers of engine and driveline components registered under this Act may obtain registration plates at the following rates:

Initial set of "test vehicle" plates: $94

Duplicate plates: $25

Repossessors and other persons qualified and registered under Section 3–601 of this Act may obtain registration plates at the rate of $45 per set.

P.A. 76–1586, § 3–810, eff. July 1, 1970. Amended by P.A. 76–2144, § 1, eff. July 1, 1970; P.A. 77–1316, § 1, eff. Jan. 1, 1972; P.A. 78–753, § 1, eff. Sept. 11, 1973; P.A. 83–12, § 1, eff. July 1, 1983; P.A. 91–37, § 40, eff. July 1, 1999.

Formerly Ill.Rev.Stat.1991, ch. 95 ½, ¶ 3–810.

Effective date and application of P.A. 83–12, see note under 615 ILCS 5/2–119.

5/3–810.1. Tow-Truck—Registration Plates

§ 3–810.1. Tow-Truck—Registration Plates. Tow-Truck operators registered under this Act may obtain registration plates for use as provided in this Act at the rate per set provided in subsection (a) of Section 3–815 of this Code for each vehicle so registered.

P.A. 76–1586, § 3–810.1, added by P.A. 83–1473, § 1, eff. Jan. 1, 1985.

Formerly Ill.Rev.Stat.1991, ch. 95 ½, ¶ 3–810.1.

5/3–811. Drive-away and other permits—Fees

§ 3–811. Drive-away and other permits—Fees.

(a) Dealers may obtain drive-away permits for use as provided in this Code, for a fee of $6 per permit.

(b) Transporters may obtain one-trip permits for vehicles in transit for use as provided in this Code, for a fee of $6 per permit.

(c) Non-residents may likewise obtain a drive-away permit from the Secretary of State to export a motor vehicle purchased in Illinois, for a fee of $6 per permit.

(d) One-trip permits may be obtained for an occasional single trip by a vehicle as provided in this Code, upon payment of a fee of $19.

(e) One month permits may likewise be obtained for the fees and taxes prescribed in this Code and as promulgated by the Secretary of State.

P.A. 76–1586, § 3–811, eff. July 1, 1970. Amended by P.A. 76–2145, § 1, eff. July 1, 1970; P.A. 77–526, § 1, eff. July 31, 1971; P.A. 83–12, § 1, eff. July 1, 1983; P.A. 88–415, § 10, eff. Aug. 20, 1993; P.A. 91–37, § 40, eff. July 1, 1999; P.A. 92–680, § 15, eff. July 16, 2002.

Formerly Ill.Rev.Stat.1991, ch. 95 ½, ¶ 3–811.

Section 4 of P.A. 83–12, approved July 1, 1983, provided:

"Effective date. This Act takes effect as provided in this Section.

"The amendments to those portions of Sections 3–815(a), 3–818 and 3–819(b) of 'The Illinois Vehicle Code' in Section 1 of this Act which create the 'X', 'Z', 'MX', 'MZ', 'MM' and 'TN' registration classifications and the fees and taxes imposed for those classifications, the amendments to Sections 2–119, 3–401 and 3–802 of 'The Illinois Vehicle Code' in Section 1 of this Act, and the amendments to Chapter 15 of 'The Illinois Vehicle Code' in Section 1 of this Act take effect July 1, 1983.

"The remaining amendments to 'The Illinois Vehicle Code' in Section 1 of this Act take effect July 1, 1983 and apply beginning with the 1985 registration year, except that the amendments to Sections 3–813 through 3–816 and Section 3–819 apply beginning with the 1984 registration year for those vehicles registered on a calendar year basis only.

"The amendments to Chapters 13 and 18 of 'The Illinois Vehicle Code' in Section 1 of this Act take effect January 1, 1984.

"Section 2 of this Act takes effect on the first day of the next succeeding month which commences at least 30 days after the date on which this Act becomes law.

"Section 3 of this Act takes effect July 1, 1983.

"Section 3.1 of this Act takes effect January 1, 1984.

"This Section 4 takes effect upon its becoming a law."

5/3–812. Vehicles with Permanently Mounted Equipment—Registration Fees

§ 3–812. Vehicles with Permanently Mounted Equipment—Registration Fees. Vehicles having permanently mounted equipment thereon used exclusively by the owner for the transporting of such permanently mounted equipment and tools and equipment to be used incidentally in the work to be performed with the permanently mounted equipment and provided such vehicle is not used for hire shall be registered upon the filing of a proper application and the payment of a registration fee based upon a rate of $45 per year (or fraction of a year) for each 10,000 pounds (or portion thereof) of the gross weight of such motor vehicle and equipment, according to the following table of fees:

SCHEDULE OF FEES REQUIRED BY LAW

Gross Weight in Lbs. Including Vehicle and Equipment	Total Annual Fees
10,000 lbs. and less	$45
10,001 lbs. to 20,000 lbs.	90
20,001 lbs. to 30,000 lbs.	135
30,001 lbs. to 40,000 lbs.	180
40,001 lbs. to 50,000 lbs.	225
50,001 lbs. to 60,000 lbs.	270
60,001 lbs. to 70,000 lbs.	315
70,001 lbs. to 73,280 lbs.	340
73,281 lbs. to 80,000 lbs.	385

P.A. 76–1586, § 3–812, eff. July 1, 1970. Amended by P.A. 83–12, § 1, eff. July 1, 1983; P.A. 83–315, § 1, eff. Jan. 1, 1984; P.A. 83–1362, Art. II, § 99, eff. Sept. 11, 1984; P.A. 84–213, § 1, eff. Jan. 1, 1986; P.A. 91–37, § 40, eff. July 1, 1999.

Formerly Ill.Rev.Stat.1991, ch. 95 ½, ¶ 3–812.

Section 4 of P.A. 83–12, approved July 1, 1983, provided:

"Effective date. This Act takes effect as provided in this Section.

"The amendments to those portions of Sections 3–815(a), 3–818 and 3–819(b) of 'The Illinois Vehicle Code' in Section 1 of this Act which create the 'X', 'Z', 'MX', 'MZ', 'MM' and 'TN' registration classifications and the fees and taxes imposed for those classifications, the amendments to Sections 2–119, 3–401 and 3–802 of 'The Illinois Vehicle Code' in Section 1 of this Act, and the amendments to Chapter 15 of 'The Illinois Vehicle Code' in Section 1 of this Act take effect July 1, 1983.

"The remaining amendments to 'The Illinois Vehicle Code' in Section 1 of this Act take effect July 1, 1983 and apply beginning with the 1985 registration year, except that the amendments to Sections 3–813 through 3–816 and Section 3–819 apply beginning with the 1984 registration year for those vehicles registered on a calendar year basis only.

"The amendments to Chapters 13 and 18 of 'The Illinois Vehicle Code' in Section 1 of this Act take effect January 1, 1984.

"Section 2 of this Act takes effect on the first day of the next succeeding month which commences at least 30 days after the date on which this Act becomes law.

"Section 3 of this Act takes effect July 1, 1983.

"Section 3.1 of this Act takes effect January 1, 1984.

"This Section 4 takes effect upon its becoming a law."

Section 2 of P.A. 84–213, provided:

"This Act takes effect January 1, 1986 and applies to registrations beginning with the 1987 registration year."

5/3–813. Vehicles of second division—Registration fee

§ 3–813. Vehicles of second division—Registration fee. Except as otherwise provided in this Code, all owners of vehicles of the second division which are designed, equipped or used for carrying freight, goods, wares, merchandise, or for use as living quarters; and all owners of vehicles of the first division which have been remodelled and are being used for such purposes; and all owners of motor vehicles operated as truck tractors to the weights of which are added to the gross weights of semitrailers with their maximum loads when drawn by such truck tractors; and all owners of vehicles of the second division which are used for carrying more than 10 persons, shall pay to the Secretary of State for each registration year, for the use of the public highways of this State, a registration fee of $10 for each such vehicle. A self-propelled vehicle operated as a truck tractor and one semitrailer or a combination of a truck tractor and semitrailer drawing a trailer or a semitrailer converted to a trailer through use of an auxiliary axle or any combination of apportioned vehicles shall be considered as one vehicle in computing the flat weight taxes under Section 3–815.

P.A. 76–1586, § 3–813, eff. July 1, 1970. Amended by P.A. 76–2146, § 1, eff. July 1, 1970; P.A. 82–392, § 1, eff. Jan. 1, 1982; P.A. 83–12, § 1, eff. July 1, 1983; P.A. 87–206, § 1, eff. Sept. 3, 1991.

Formerly Ill.Rev.Stat.1991, ch. 95 ½, ¶ 3–813.

Section 2 of P.A. 82–392 approved Sept. 4, 1981, provided:

"This Act takes effect with the 1984 registration year."

Section 4 of P.A. 83–12, approved July 1, 1983, provided:

"Effective date. This Act takes effect as provided in this Section.

"The amendments to those portions of Sections 3–815(a), 3–818 and 3–819(b) of 'The Illinois Vehicle Code' in Section 1 of this Act which create the 'X', 'Z', 'MX', 'MZ', 'MM' and 'TN' registration classifications and the fees and taxes imposed for those classifications, the amendments to Sections 2–119, 3–401 and 3–802 of 'The Illinois Vehicle Code' in Section 1 of this Act, and the amendments to Chapter 15 of 'The Illinois Vehicle Code' in Section 1 of this Act take effect July 1, 1983.

"The remaining amendments to 'The Illinois Vehicle Code' in Section 1 of this Act take effect July 1, 1983 and apply beginning with the 1985 registration year, except that the amendments to Sections 3–813 through 3–816 and Section 3–819 apply beginning with the 1984 registration year for those vehicles registered on a calendar year basis only.

"The amendments to Chapters 13 and 18 of 'The Illinois Vehicle Code' in Section 1 of this Act take effect January 1, 1984.

"Section 2 of this Act takes effect on the first day of the next succeeding month which commences at least 30 days after the date on which this Act becomes law.

"Section 3 of this Act takes effect July 1, 1983.

"Section 3.1 of this Act takes effect January 1, 1984.

"This Section 4 takes effect upon its becoming a law."

5/3–814. Semitrailer registration fees

§ 3–814. Semitrailer registration fees. Effective with the 1984 registration year to the end of the 1998 registration year, an owner of a semitrailer shall pay to the Secretary of State, for the use of the public highways of this State, a flat weight tax of $60, which includes the registration fee, for a 5 year semitrailer plate.

Effective with the 1999 registration year an owner of a semitrailer shall pay to the Secretary of State, for the use of the public highways of this State, a one time flat tax of $15, which includes the registration fee, for a permanent non-transferrable semitrailer plate.

Effective with the 2001 registration year, an owner of a semitrailer shall pay to the Secretary of State, for the use of public highways of this State, a one-time flat tax of $19, which includes the registration fee, for a permanent non-transferrable semitrailer plate.

P.A. 76–1586, § 3–814, eff. July 1, 1970. Amended by P.A. 76–2147, § 1, eff. July 1, 1970; P.A. 82–392, § 1, eff. Jan. 1, 1982; P.A. 83–12, § 1, eff. July 1, 1983; P.A. 87–206, § 1, eff. Sept. 3, 1991; P.A. 87–1040, § 1, eff. Sept. 11, 1992; P.A. 89–710, § 15, eff. Feb. 14, 1997; P.A. 91–37, § 40, eff. July 1, 1999.

Formerly Ill.Rev.Stat.1991, ch. 95 ½, ¶ 3–814.

Section 4 of P.A. 83–12, approved July 1, 1983, provided:

"Effective date. This Act takes effect as provided in this Section.

"The amendments to those portions of Sections 3–815(a), 3–818 and 3–819(b) of 'The Illinois Vehicle Code' in Section 1 of this Act which create the 'X', 'Z', 'MX', 'MZ', 'MM' and 'TN' registration classifications and the fees and taxes imposed for those classifications, the amendments to Sections 2-119, 3-401 and 3-802 of 'The Illinois Vehicle Code' in Section 1 of this Act, and the amendments to Chapter 15 of 'The Illinois Vehicle Code' in Section 1 of this Act take effect July 1, 1983.

"The remaining amendments to 'The Illinois Vehicle Code' in Section 1 of this Act take effect July 1, 1983 and apply beginning with the 1985 registration year, except that the amendments to Sections 3-813 through 3-816 and Section 3-819 apply beginning with the 1984 registration year for those vehicles registered on a calendar year basis only.

"The amendments to Chapters 13 and 18 of 'The Illinois Vehicle Code' in Section 1 of this Act take effect January 1, 1984.

"Section 2 of this Act takes effect on the first day of the next succeeding month which commences at least 30 days after the date on which this Act becomes law.

"Section 3 of this Act takes effect July 1, 1983.

"Section 3.1 of this Act takes effect January 1, 1984.

"This Section 4 takes effect upon its becoming a law."

5/3-814.1. Apportionable trailer and semitrailer fees

§ 3-814.1. Apportionable trailer and semitrailer fees. Beginning April 1, 1994 through March 31, 1998, an owner of an apportionable trailer or apportionable semitrailer registered under Section 3-402.1 shall pay an annual registration fee of $12 to the Secretary of State.

Beginning April 1, 1998 through March 31, 2000, an owner of an apportionable trailer or apportionable semitrailer registered under Section 3-402.1 shall pay a one time registration fee of $15 to the Secretary of State for a permanent non-transferrable plate.

Beginning April 1, 2000, an owner of an apportionable trailer or apportionable semitrailer registered under Section 3-402.1 shall pay a one-time registration fee of $19 to the Secretary of State for a permanent non-transferrable plate.

P.A. 76-1586, § 3-814.1, added by P.A. 87-1040, § 1, eff. Sept. 11, 1992. Amended by P.A. 89-710, § 15, eff. Feb. 14, 1997; P.A. 91-37, § 40, eff. July 1, 1999.

Formerly Ill.Rev.Stat., ch. 95½, ¶ 3-814.1.

5/3-814.2. Optional registration of converter devices

§ 3-814.2. Optional registration of converter devices.

(a) The Secretary of State may provide for optional registration of devices that convert a semitrailer to a trailer and are exempt from vehicle registration requirements. The rules adopted for purposes of this Section may provide for the registration of this category of vehicle or type vehicle. Upon request of an owner, the Secretary of State may issue registration for a vehicle that meets the requirements of rules adopted under this Section. A registration fee for this vehicle may be imposed by rule.

(b) A vehicle that is registered under this Section is subject to the same provisions, conditions, fees, and other requirements under this Code.

P.A. 76-1586, § 3-814.2, added by P.A. 89-710, § 15, eff. Feb. 14, 1997.

5/3-814.3. Registration of fleets of semitrailers or apportionable semitrailers

§ 3-814.3. Registration of fleets of semitrailers or apportionable semitrailers. The Secretary of State may provide for the registration of large fleets of semitrailers or apportionable semitrailers by accepting the appropriate fees and issuing the registration plate prior to the plate being assigned to a specific vehicle. The registration indexes will be updated on a date predetermined by the Secretary of State. In determining this date, the Secretary of State shall take into consideration the number of vehicles in each fleet.

P.A. 76-1586, § 3-814.3, added by P.A. 89-710, § 15, eff. Feb. 14, 1997.

5/3-814.4. Registration of fleet vehicles

Text of section added effective July 1, 2003

§ 3-814.4 Registration of fleet vehicles. The Secretary may issue fleet vehicle registration plates to owners of vehicle fleets registered in accordance with Section 3-405.3 of this Code in bulk before plates are assigned to specific vehicles. A registration plate may not be displayed on a vehicle, however, until the plate has been activated on the Secretary's registration file and the proper fee has been forwarded to the Secretary.

P.A. 76-1586, § 3-814.4, added by P.A. 92-629, § 5, eff. July 1, 2003.

5/3-815. Flat weight tax; vehicles of the second division.

§ 3-815. Flat weight tax; vehicles of the second division.

(a) Except as provided in Section 3-806.3, every owner of a vehicle of the second division registered under Section 3-813, and not registered under the mileage weight tax under Section 3-818, shall pay to the Secretary of State, for each registration year, for the use of the public highways, a flat weight tax at the rates set forth in the following table, the rates including the $10 registration fee:

SCHEDULE OF FLAT WEIGHT
TAX REQUIRED BY LAW

Gross Weight in Lbs. Including Vehicle and Maximum Load	Class	Total Fees each Fiscal year
8,000 lbs. and less	B	$78
8,001 lbs. to 12,000 lbs.	D	138
12,001 lbs. to 16,000 lbs.	F	242
16,001 lbs. to 26,000 lbs.	H	490
26,001 lbs. to 28,000 lbs.	J	630
28,001 lbs. to 32,000 lbs.	K	842
32,001 lbs. to 36,000 lbs.	L	982
36,001 lbs. to 40,000 lbs.	N	1,202
40,001 lbs. to 45,000 lbs.	P	1,390
45,001 lbs. to 50,000 lbs.	Q	1,538
50,001 lbs. to 54,999 lbs.	R	1,698
55,000 lbs. to 59,500 lbs.	S	1,830
59,501 lbs. to 64,000 lbs.	T	1,970
64,001 lbs. to 73,280 lbs.	V	2,294
73,281 lbs. to 77,000 lbs.	X	2,622
77,001 lbs. to 80,000 lbs.	Z	2,790

(a-1) A Special Hauling Vehicle is a vehicle or combination of vehicles of the second division registered under Section 3-813 transporting asphalt or concrete in the plastic state or a vehicle or combination of vehicles that are subject to the gross weight limitations in subsection (b) of Section 15-111 for which the owner of the vehicle or combination of vehicles has elected to pay, in addition to the registration fee in subsection (a), $125 to the Secretary of State for each registration year. The Secretary shall designate this class of vehicle as a Special Hauling Vehicle.

(b) Except as provided in Section 3-806.3, every camping trailer, motor home, mini motor home, travel trailer, truck camper or van camper used primarily for recreational purposes, and not used commercially, nor for hire, nor owned by a commercial business, may be registered for each registration year upon the filing of a proper application and the payment of a registration fee and highway use tax, according to the following table of fees:

MOTOR HOME, MINI MOTOR HOME, TRUCK CAMPER OR VAN CAMPER

Gross Weight in Lbs. Including Vehicle and Maximum Load	Total Fees Each Calendar Year
8,000 lbs and less	$78
8,001 Lbs. to 10,000 Lbs.	90
10,001 Lbs. and Over	102

CAMPING TRAILER OR TRAVEL TRAILER

Gross Weight in Lbs. Including Vehicle and Maximum Load	Total Fees Each Calendar Year
3,000 Lbs. and Less	$18
3,001 Lbs. to 8,000 Lbs.	30
8,001 Lbs. to 10,000 Lbs.	38
10,001 Lbs. and Over	50

Every house trailer must be registered under Section 3-819.

(c) Farm Truck. Any truck used exclusively for the owner's own agricultural, horticultural or livestock raising operations and not-for-hire only, or any truck used only in the transportation for-hire of seasonal, fresh, perishable fruit or vegetables from farm to the point of first processing, may be registered by the owner under this paragraph in lieu of registration under paragraph (a), upon filing of a proper application and the payment of the $10 registration fee and the highway use tax herein specified as follows:

SCHEDULE OF FEES AND TAXES

Gross Weight in Lbs. Including Truck and Maximum Load	Class	Total Amount for each Fiscal Year
16,000 lbs. or less	VF	$150
16,001 to 20,000 lbs.	VG	226
20,001 to 24,000 lbs.	VH	290
24,001 to 28,000 lbs.	VJ	378
28,001 to 32,000 lbs.	VK	506
32,001 to 36,000 lbs.	VL	610
36,001 to 45,000 lbs.	VP	810
45,001 to 54,999 lbs.	VR	1,026
55,000 to 64,000 lbs.	VT	1,202
64,001 to 73,280 lbs.	VV	1,290
73,281 to 77,000 lbs.	VX	1,350
77,001 to 80,000 lbs.	VZ	1,490

In the event the Secretary of State revokes a farm truck registration as authorized by law, the owner shall pay the flat weight tax due hereunder before operating such truck.

Any combination of vehicles having 5 axles, with a distance of 42 feet or less between extreme axles, that are subject to the weight limitations in subsection (a) and (b) of Section 15-111 for which the owner of the combination of vehicles has elected to pay, in addition to the registration fee in subsection (c), $125 to the Secretary of State for each registration year shall be designated by the Secretary as a Special Hauling Vehicle.

(d) The number of axles necessary to carry the maximum load provided shall be determined from Chapter 15 of this Code.[1]

(e) An owner may only apply for and receive 5 farm truck registrations, and only 2 of those 5 vehicles shall exceed 59,500 gross weight in pounds per vehicle.

(f) Every person convicted of violating this Section by failure to pay the appropriate flat weight tax to the Secretary of State as set forth in the above tables shall be punished as provided for in Section 3-401.

P.A. 76-1586, § 3-815, eff. July 1, 1970. Amended by P.A. 76-2148, § 1, eff. July 1, 1970; P.A. 77-137, § 1, eff. July 1, 1972; P.A. 77-720, § 1, eff. July 1, 1972; P.A. 77-1633, § 1, eff. Sept. 23, 1971; P.A. 77-2829, § 40, eff. Dec. 22, 1972; P.A. 78-255, § 61, eff. Oct. 1, 1973; P.A. 78-335, § 1, eff. Jan. 1, 1974; P.A. 78-1146, § 1, eff. Jan. 1, 1975; P.A. 78-1297, § 58, eff. March 4, 1975; P.A. 80-758, § 1, eff. Oct. 1, 1977; P.A. 81-969, § 1, eff. Jan. 1, 1980; P.A. 82-392, § 1, eff. Jan. 1, 1982; P.A. 83-12, § 1, eff. July 1, 1983; P.A. 83-799, § 1, eff. Jan. 1, 1984; P.A. 83-1362, Art. II, § 99, eff. Sept. 11, 1984; P.A. 83-1457, § 2, eff. Jan. 1, 1985; P.A. 84-213, § 1, eff. Jan. 1, 1986; P.A. 84-986, § 1, eff. Sept. 25, 1985; P.A. 84-1308, Art. II, § 96, eff. Aug. 25, 1986; P.A. 85-678, § 1, eff. July 1, 1989; P.A. 86-845, § 2, eff. July 1, 1990; P.A. 86-1171, § 1, eff. Jan. 1, 1991; P.A. 88-403, § 5, eff. Jan. 1, 1994; P.A. 88-476, § 2, eff. July 1, 1994; P.A. 88-617, § 5, eff. Sept. 9, 1994; P.A. 88-670, Art. 2, § 2-59, eff. Dec. 2, 1994; P.A. 89-710, § 15, eff. Feb. 14, 1997; P.A. 91-37, § 40, eff. July 1, 1999.

Formerly Ill.Rev.Stat.1991, ch. 95 ½, ¶ 3-815.

[1] 625 ILCS 5/15-100 et seq.

Section 3 of P.A. 81-969, approved Sept. 22, 1979, provided:

"This amendatory Act takes effect at the start of the 1981 registration year."

Section 2 of P.A. 82-392 approved Sept. 4, 1981, provided:

"This Act takes effect with the 1984 registration year."

Section 4 of P.A. 83-12, approved July 1, 1983, provided:

"Effective date. This Act takes effect as provided in this Section.

"The amendments to those portions of Sections 3-815(a), 3-818 and 3-819(b) of 'The Illinois Vehicle Code' in Section 1 of this Act which create the 'X', 'Z', 'MX', 'MZ', 'MM' and 'TN' registration classifications and the fees and taxes imposed for those classifications, the amendments to Sections 2-119, 3-401 and 3-802 of 'The Illinois Vehicle Code' in Section 1 of this Act, and the amendments to Chapter 15 of 'The Illinois Vehicle Code' in Section 1 of this Act take effect July 1, 1983.

"The remaining amendments to 'The Illinois Vehicle Code' in Section 1 of this Act take effect July 1, 1983 and apply beginning with the 1985 registration year, except that the amendments to Sections 3-813 through 3-816 and Section 3-819 apply beginning with the 1984 registration year for those vehicles registered on a calendar year basis only.

"The amendments to Chapters 13 and 18 of 'The Illinois Vehicle Code' in Section 1 of this Act take effect January 1, 1984.

"Section 2 of this Act takes effect on the first day of the next succeeding month which commences at least 30 days after the date on which this Act becomes law.

"Section 3 of this Act takes effect July 1, 1983.

"Section 3.1 of this Act takes effect January 1, 1984.

"This Section 4 takes effect upon its becoming a law."

5/3-816. Installment Payments

§ 3-816. Installment Payments.

(a) The flat weight tax required to be paid by Section 3-815 for any vehicles on a calendar year basis may be paid if the owner so elects, in equal semi-annual installments due on January 1 and July 1 of each licensing year. Effective with the 1984 registration year the owners of semitrailers registered under Section 3-814 shall have the option of paying the designated fees to the Secretary in the following manner:

If registered in the first year the owner shall have the option of paying $30 the first year and the remaining $30 by the start of the second year;

If registered in the second year the owner shall have the option of paying $24 the first year and the remaining $24 by the start of the third year;

If registered in the third year the owner shall pay $36 for each semitrailer;

If registered in the fourth year the owner shall pay $24 for each semitrailer; and

If registered in the fifth year the owner shall pay $12 for each semitrailer.

Every such owner who elects to pay such tax in such installments shall file with the Secretary of State a surety bond or certificate of deposit, as hereinafter provided, in the amount of the sum of the second installment of taxes on his vehicle.

Such bond shall be in the form approved by the Secretary of State and with a surety company approved by the Department of Insurance to transact business in this State, as surety, and shall be conditioned upon such owner's paying to the State of Illinois all monies becoming due by reason of his operation of the second division motor vehicle in this State, together with all penalties and interest thereon.

The State Treasurer shall issue a certificate of deposit to any such owner who deposits with the State Treasurer securities of the Federal Government or the State of Illinois endorsed in blank by such owner, or a certificate of deposit issued by any bank or savings and loan association authorized to do business in Illinois, payable to the Secretary of State on or after July 1 of the year of registration. Such certificate of deposit and securities shall be approved by and deposited with the State Treasurer, and shall have a current market value in the total amount which would cover all monies becoming due and payable to the State of Illinois by reason of his operation of a second division motor vehicle in this State, together with all penalties and interest thereon.

The liability of the surety hereunder shall be absolute and upon notice from the Secretary of State that the second installment has not been paid on July 1 of any licensing year the surety shall immediately pay the second installment to the Secretary of State.

Upon notice by the Secretary of State that the second installment of such owner's taxes has not been paid on July 1 of any licensing year, the State Treasurer shall sell such securities and deliver the proceeds thereof to the Secretary of State to satisfy all monies becoming due by reason of such owner's operation of a second division motor vehicle in this State, together with all penalties and interest thereon.

If the owner's liability for the second installment is evidenced by a certificate of deposit payable to the Secretary of State, the Secretary of State shall, upon failure of the owner to pay the second installment by July 1, endorse the certificate of deposit which is in the custody of the State Treasurer, and thereafter the State Treasurer shall present the certificate of deposit for payment to the proper bank or savings and loan association. Upon receipt of payment, the State Treasurer shall forward to the Secretary of State all monies due by reason of such owner's operation of a second division motor vehicle in this State, and return the excess, if any, to the owner on whose behalf the certificate of deposit was previously deposited.

The State Treasurer shall return securities or proceeds in excess of that needed to satisfy the Secretary of State for all monies becoming due by reason of such owner's operation of a second division motor vehicle in this State, together with all penalties and interest thereon. Upon notice by the Secretary of State that the second installment has been paid, the State Treasurer shall return such certificate of deposit or securities deposited with him under this Section to the owner thereof.

(b) The flat weight tax required by Section 3-815 to be paid on a fiscal year basis may be paid, if the owner so elects, in equal semi-annual installments due on July 1st and January 1st of each registration year. From July 1, 1983 through November 30, 1983, the flat weight tax required by Section 3-814 for semitrailers previously registered on a fiscal year basis may be paid, if the owner so elects, by paying the Secretary of State $33 at the time of registration and the remaining $25 by January 1, 1985 for each 5 ½ year semitrailer plate. Every such owner who elects to pay such tax in such installments shall file with the Secretary of State a surety bond or certificate of deposit, as hereinafter provided, in the amount of the sum of the second installment of taxes on his vehicle.

Such bond shall be in the form approved by the Secretary of State and with a surety company approved by the Department of Insurance to transact business in this State, as surety, and shall be conditioned upon such owner's paying to the State of Illinois all monies becoming due by reason of his operation of the second division motor vehicle in this State, together with all penalties and interest thereon.

The liability of the surety hereunder shall be absolute and upon notice from the Secretary of State that the second installment has not been paid on January 1st of any registration year the surety shall immediately pay the second installment to the Secretary of State.

Upon notice by the Secretary of State that the second installment of such owner's taxes has not been paid on January 1st of any registration year, the State Treasurer shall sell such securities and deliver the proceeds thereof to the Secretary of State to satisfy all monies becoming due by reason of such owner's operation of a second division motor vehicle in this State, together with all penalties and interest thereon.

If the owner's liability for the second installment is evidenced by a certificate of deposit payable to the Secretary of State, the Secretary of State shall, upon failure of the owner to pay the second installment by January 1st, endorse the certificate of deposit which is in the custody of the State Treasurer, and thereafter the State Treasurer shall present the certificate of deposit for payment to the proper bank or savings and loan association. Upon receipt of payment, the State Treasurer shall forward to the Secretary of State all monies due by reason of such owner's operation of a second division motor vehicle in this State, and return the excess, if any, to the owner on whose behalf the certificate of deposit was previously deposited.

The State Treasurer shall return securities or proceeds in excess of that needed to satisfy the Secretary of State for all monies becoming due by reason of such owner's operation of a second division motor vehicle in this State, together with all penalties and interest thereon. Upon notice by the Secretary of State that the second installment has been paid, the State Treasurer shall return such certificate of deposit or securities deposited with him under this Section to the owner thereof.

(c) The flat weight tax required under Section 3-815 for vehicles registered in accordance with Section 3-402.1 may be paid, if the owner elects, in equal semi-annual installments due on April 1 and October 1 of each licensing year.

(d) In the event any surety pays for any second installment under this Section, the surety shall have recourse only against the principal and owner of the vehicles involved and shall have no right or privilege to demand revocation or suspension of the registration plates or registration stickers of the vehicles involved. Such surety may, however, impress a lien as provided in Section 3-828.

P.A. 76-1586, § 3-816, eff. July 1, 1970. Amended by P.A. 77-1464, § 1, eff. Sept. 7, 1971; P.A. 79-1038, § 1, eff. Oct. 1, 1975; P.A. 80-230, § 1, eff. Oct. 1, 1977; P.A. 80-674, § 1, eff. Oct. 1, 1977; P.A. 80-1364, § 36, eff. Aug. 13, 1978; P.A. 82-392, § 1, eff. Jan. 1, 1982; P.A. 83-12, § 1, eff. July 1, 1983; P.A. 83-541, § 52, eff. Sept. 17, 1983; P.A. 83-1362, Art. II, § 99, eff. Sept. 11, 1984; P.A. 87-1041, § 1, eff. Sept. 11, 1992; P.A. 91-357, § 231, eff. July 29, 1999.

Formerly Ill.Rev.Stat.1991, ch. 95 ½, ¶ 3-816.

Section 2 of P.A. 82-392 approved Sept. 4, 1981, provided:

"This Act takes effect with the 1984 registration year."

Section 4 of P.A. 83-12, approved July 1, 1983, provided:

"Effective date. This Act takes effect as provided in this Section.

"The amendments to those portions of Sections 3-815(a), 3-818 and 3-819(b) of 'The Illinois Vehicle Code' in Section 1 of this Act which create the 'X', 'Z', 'MX', 'MZ', 'MM' and 'TN' registration classifications and the fees and taxes imposed for those classifications, the amendments to Sections 2-119, 3-401 and 3-802 of 'The Illinois Vehicle Code' in Section 1 of this Act, and the amendments to Chapter 15 of 'The Illinois Vehicle Code' in Section 1 of this Act take effect July 1, 1983.

"The remaining amendments to 'The Illinois Vehicle Code' in Section 1 of this Act take effect July 1, 1983 and apply beginning with the 1985 registration year, except that the amendments to Sections 3-813 through 3-816 and Section 3-819 apply beginning with the 1984 registration year for those vehicles registered on a calendar year basis only.

"The amendments to Chapters 13 and 18 of 'The Illinois Vehicle Code' in Section 1 of this Act take effect January 1, 1984.

"Section 2 of this Act takes effect on the first day of the next succeeding month which commences at least 30 days after the date on which this Act becomes law.

"Section 3 of this Act takes effect July 1, 1983.

"Section 3.1 of this Act takes effect January 1, 1984.

"This Section 4 takes effect upon its becoming a law."

5/3-817. § 3-817. Repealed by P.A. 80-891, § 2, eff. Jan. 1, 1978

5/3-818. Mileage weight tax option

§ 3-818. (a) Mileage weight tax option. Any owner of a vehicle of the second division may elect to pay a mileage weight tax for such vehicle in lieu of the flat weight tax set out in Section 3-815. Such election shall be binding to the end of the registration year. Renewal of this election must be filed with the Secretary of State on or before July 1 of each registration period. In such event the owner shall, at the time of making such election, pay the $10 registration fee and the minimum guaranteed mileage weight tax, as hereinafter provided, which payment shall permit the owner to operate that vehicle the maximum mileage in this State hereinafter set forth. Any vehicle being operated on mileage plates cannot be operated outside of this State. In addition thereto, the owner of that vehicle shall pay a mileage weight tax at the following rates for each mile traveled in this State in excess of the maximum mileage provided under the minimum guaranteed basis:

BUS, TRUCK OR TRUCK TRACTOR

Gross Weight Vehicle and Load	Class	Minimum Guaranteed Mileage Weight Tax	Maximum Mileage Permitted Under Guaranteed Tax	Mileage Weight Tax for Mileage in excess of Guaranteed Mileage
12,000 lbs. or less	MD	$73	5,000	26 Mills
12,001 to 16,000 lbs.	MF	120	6,000	34 Mills
16,001 to 20,000 lbs.	MG	180	6,000	46 Mills
20,001 to 24,000 lbs.	MH	235	6,000	63 Mills
24,001 to 28,000 lbs.	MJ	315	7,000	63 Mills
28,001 to 32,000 lbs.	MK	385	7,000	83 Mills
32,001 to 36,000 lbs.	ML	485	7,000	99 Mills
36,001 to 40,000 lbs.	MN	615	7,000	128 Mills
40,001 to 45,000 lbs.	MP	695	7,000	139 Mills
45,001 to 54,999 lbs.	MR	853	7,000	156 Mills
55,000 to 59,500 lbs.	MS	920	7,000	178 Mills
59,501 to 64,000 lbs.	MT	985	7,000	195 Mills
64,001 to 73,280 lbs.	MV	1,173	7,000	225 Mills
73,281 to 77,000 lbs.	MX	1,328	7,000	258 Mills
77,001 to 80,000 lbs.	MZ	1,415	7,000	275 Mills

TRAILER

Gross Weight Vehicle and Load	Class	Minimum Guaranteed Mileage Weight Tax	Maximum Mileage Permitted Under Guaranteed Tax	Mileage Weight Tax for Mileage in excess of Guaranteed Mileage
14,000 lbs. or less	ME	$75	5,000	31 Mills
14,001 to 20,000 lbs.	MF	135	6,000	36 Mills
20,001 to 36,000 lbs.	ML	540	7,000	103 Mills
36,001 to 40,000 lbs.	MM	750	7,000	150 Mills

(a-1) A Special Hauling Vehicle is a vehicle or combination of vehicles of the second division registered under Section 3-813 transporting asphalt or concrete in the plastic state or a vehicle or combination of vehicles that are subject to the gross weight limitations in subsection (b) of Section 15-111 for which the owner of the vehicle or combination of vehicles has elected to pay, in addition to the registration fee in subsection (a), $125 to the Secretary of State for each registration year. The Secretary shall designate this class of vehicle as a Special Hauling Vehicle.

In preparing rate schedules on registration applications, the Secretary of State shall add to the above rates, the $10 registration fee. The Secretary may decline to accept any renewal filed after July 1st.

The number of axles necessary to carry the maximum load provided shall be determined from Chapter 15 of this Code.[1]

Every owner of a second division motor vehicle for which he has elected to pay a mileage weight tax shall keep a daily record upon forms prescribed by the Secretary of State, showing the mileage covered by that vehicle in this State. Such record shall contain the license number of the vehicle and the miles traveled by the vehicle in this State for each day of the calendar month. Such owner shall also maintain records of fuel consumed by each such motor vehicle and fuel purchases therefor. On or before the 10th day of January and July the owner shall certify to the Secretary of State upon forms prescribed therefor, summaries of his daily records which shall show the miles traveled by the vehicle in this State during the preceding 6 months and such other information as the Secretary of State may require. The daily record and fuel records shall be filed, preserved and available for audit for a period of 3 years. Any owner filing a return hereunder shall certify that such return is a true, correct and complete return. Any person who willfully makes a false return hereunder is guilty of perjury and shall be punished in the same manner and to the same extent as is provided therefor.

At the time of filing his return, each owner shall pay to the Secretary of State the proper amount of tax at the rate herein imposed.

Every owner of a vehicle of the second division who elects to pay on a mileage weight tax basis and who operates the vehicle within this State, shall file with the Secretary of State a bond in the amount of $500. The bond shall be in a form approved by the Secretary of State and with a surety company approved by the Illinois Department of Insurance to transact business in this State as surety, and shall be conditioned upon such applicant's paying to the State of Illinois all money becoming due by reason of the operation of the second division vehicle in this State, together with all penalties and interest thereon.

Upon notice from the Secretary that the registrant has failed to pay the excess mileage fees, the surety shall immediately pay the fees together with any penalties and interest thereon in an amount not to exceed the limits of the bond.

P.A. 76–1586, § 3–818, eff. July 1, 1970. Amended by P.A. 76–2150, § 1, eff. July 1, 1970; P.A. 77–1301, § 1, eff. Aug. 27, 1971; P.A. 77–2751, § 1, eff. Sept. 1, 1972; P.A. 78–255, § 61, eff. Oct. 1, 1973; P.A. 78–855, § 1, eff. Jan. 1, 1975; P.A. 78–1297, § 58, eff. March 4, 1975; P.A. 81–1440, § 1, eff. Sept. 4, 1980; P.A. 82–392, § 1, eff. Jan. 1, 1982; P.A. 83–12, § 1, eff. July 1, 1983; P.A. 83–449, § 1, eff. Jan. 1, 1984; P.A. 83–1362, Art. II, § 99, eff. Sept. 11, 1984; P.A. 84–986, § 1, eff. Sept. 25, 1985; P.A. 85–678, § 1, eff. July 1, 1989; P.A. 87–206, § 1, eff. Sept. 3, 1991; P.A. 88–403, § 5, eff. Jan. 1, 1994; P.A. 89–571, § 5, eff. July 26, 1996; P.A. 89–710, § 15, eff. Feb. 14, 1997; P.A. 91–37, § 40, eff. July 1, 1999; P.A. 91–499, § 5, eff. Aug. 13, 1999; P.A. 92–16, § 85, eff. June 28, 2001.

Formerly Ill.Rev.Stat.1991, ch. 95 ½, ¶ 3–818.

1 625 ILCS 5/15–100 et seq.

Section 2 of P.A. 82–392 approved Sept. 4, 1981, provided:

"This Act takes effect with the 1984 registration year."

Section 4 of P.A. 83–12, approved July 1, 1983, provided:

"Effective date. This Act takes effect as provided in this Section.

"The amendments to those portions of Sections 3–815(a), 3–818 and 3–819(b) of 'The Illinois Vehicle Code' in Section 1 of this Act which create the 'X', 'Z', 'MX', 'MZ', 'MM' and 'TN' registration classifications and the fees and taxes imposed for those classifications, the amendments to Sections 2–119, 3–401 and 3–802 of 'The Illinois Vehicle Code' in Section 1 of this Act, and the amendments to Chapter 15 of 'The Illinois Vehicle Code' in Section 1 of this Act take effect July 1, 1983.

"The remaining amendments to 'The Illinois Vehicle Code' in Section 1 of this Act take effect July 1, 1983 and apply beginning with the 1985 registration year, except that the amendments to Sections 3–813 through 3–816 and Section 3–819 apply beginning with the 1984 registration year for those vehicles registered on a calendar year basis only.

"The amendments to Chapters 13 and 18 of 'The Illinois Vehicle Code' in Section 1 of this Act take effect January 1, 1984.

"Section 2 of this Act takes effect on the first day of the next succeeding month which commences at least 30 days after the date on which this Act becomes law.

"Section 3 of this Act takes effect July 1, 1983.

"Section 3.1 of this Act takes effect January 1, 1984.

"This Section 4 takes effect upon its becoming a law."

5/3–819. Trailer; Flat weight tax.

§ 3–819. Trailer; Flat weight tax.

(a) Farm Trailer. Any farm trailer drawn by a motor vehicle of the second division registered under paragraph (a) or (c) of Section 3–815 and used exclusively by the owner for his own agricultural, horticultural or livestock raising operations and not used for hire, or any farm trailer utilized only in the transportation for-hire of seasonal, fresh, perishable fruit or vegetables from farm to the point of first processing, and any trailer used with a farm tractor that is not an implement of husbandry may be registered under this paragraph in lieu of registration under paragraph (b) of this Section upon the filing of a proper application and the payment of the $10 registration fee and the highway use tax herein for use of the public highways of this State, at the following rates which include the $10 registration fee:

SCHEDULE OF FEES AND TAXES

Gross Weight in Lbs. Including Vehicle and Maximum Load	Class	Total Amount each Fiscal Year
10,000 lbs. or less	VDD	$60
10,001 to 14,000 lbs.	VDE	106
14,001 to 20,000 lbs.	VDG	166
20,001 to 28,000 lbs.	VDJ	378
28,001 to 36,000 lbs.	VDL	650

An owner may only apply for and receive two farm trailer registrations.

(b) All other owners of trailers, other than apportionable trailers registered under Section 3–402.1 of this Code, used with a motor vehicle on the public highways, shall pay to the Secretary of State for each registration year a flat weight tax, for the use of the public highways of this State, at the following rates (which includes the registration fee of $10 required by Section 3–813):

SCHEDULE OF TRAILER FLAT WEIGHT TAX REQUIRED BY LAW

Gross Weight in Lbs. Including Vehicle and Maximum Load	Class	Total Fees each Fiscal Year
3,000 lbs. and less	TA	$18
5,000 lbs. and more than 3,000	TB	54
8,000 lbs. and more than 5,000	TC	58
10,000 lbs. and more than 8,000	TD	106
14,000 lbs. and more than 10,000	TE	170
20,000 lbs. and and more than 14,000	TG	258
32,000 lbs. and more than 20,000	TK	722
36,000 lbs. and more than 32,000	TL	1,082
40,000 lbs. and more than 36,000	TN	1,502

(c) The number of axles necessary to carry the maximum load provided shall be determined from Chapter 15 of this Code.[1]

P.A. 76–1586, § 3–819, eff. July 1, 1970. Amended by P.A. 76–2151, § 1, eff. July 1, 1970; P.A. 77–137, § 1, eff. July 1, 1972; P.A. 80–674, § 1, eff. Oct. 1, 1977; P.A. 82–392, § 1, eff. Jan. 1, 1982; P.A. 83–12, § 1, eff. July 1, 1983; P.A. 86–1340, § 1, eff. July 1, 1991; P.A. 87–206, § 1, eff. Sept. 3, 1991; P.A. 91–37, § 40, eff. July 1, 1999.

Formerly Ill.Rev.Stat.1991, ch. 95 ½, ¶ 3–819.

1 625 ILCS 5/15–100 et seq.

Section 2 of P.A. 82–392 approved Sept. 4, 1981, provided:

"This Act takes effect with the 1984 registration year."

Section 4 of P.A. 83–12, approved July 1, 1983, provided:

"Effective date. This Act takes effect as provided in this Section.

"The amendments to those portions of Sections 3–815(a), 3–818 and 3–819(b) of 'The Illinois Vehicle Code' in Section 1 of this Act which create the 'X', 'Z', 'MX', 'MZ', 'MM' and 'TN' registration classifications and the fees and taxes imposed for those classifications, the amendments to Sections 2–119, 3–401 and 3–802 of 'The Illinois Vehicle Code' in Section 1 of this Act, and the amendments to Chapter 15 of 'The Illinois Vehicle Code' in Section 1 of this Act take effect July 1, 1983.

"The remaining amendments to 'The Illinois Vehicle Code' in Section 1 of this Act take effect July 1, 1983 and apply beginning with the 1985 registration year, except that the amendments to Sections 3–813 through 3–816 and Section 3–819 apply beginning with the 1984 registration year for those vehicles registered on a calendar year basis only.

"The amendments to Chapters 13 and 18 of 'The Illinois Vehicle Code' in Section 1 of this Act take effect January 1, 1984.

"Section 2 of this Act takes effect on the first day of the next succeeding month which commences at least 30 days after the date on which this Act becomes law.

"Section 3 of this Act takes effect July 1, 1983.

"Section 3.1 of this Act takes effect January 1, 1984.

"This Section 4 takes effect upon its becoming a law."

5/3–820. Duplicate Number Plates

§ 3–820. Duplicate Number Plates. Upon filing in the Office of the Secretary of State an affidavit to the effect that an original number plate for a vehicle is lost, stolen or destroyed, a duplicate number plate shall be furnished upon payment of a fee of $6 for each duplicate plate and a fee of $9 for a pair of duplicate plates.

Upon filing in the Office of the Secretary of State an affidavit to the effect that an original registration sticker for a vehicle is lost, stolen or destroyed, a new registration sticker shall be furnished upon payment of a fee of $5.

The Secretary of State may, in his discretion, assign a new number plate or plates in lieu of a duplicate of the plate or plates so lost, stolen or destroyed, but such assignment of a new plate or plates shall not affect the right of the owner to secure a reassignment of his original registration number in the manner provided in this Act. The fee for one new number plate shall be $6, and for a pair of new number plates, $9.

For the administration of this Section, the Secretary shall consider the loss of a registration plate or plates with properly affixed registration stickers as requiring the payment of either $11 for each duplicate or $14 for a pair of duplicate plates or $19 for a pair of duplicate plates if stickers are required on both front and rear registration plates.

P.A. 76–1586, § 3–820, eff. July 1, 1970. Amended by P.A. 78–143, § 1, eff. Jan. 1, 1972; P.A. 80–230, § 1, eff. Oct. 1, 1977; P.A. 80–1185, § 1, eff. March 8, 1978; P.A. 83–12, § 1, eff. July 1, 1983; P.A. 91–37, § 40, eff. July 1, 1999.

Formerly Ill.Rev.Stat.1991, ch. 95 ½, ¶ 3–820.

Section 4 of P.A. 83–12, approved July 1, 1983, provided:

"Effective date. This Act takes effect as provided in this Section.

"The amendments to those portions of Sections 3–815(a), 3–818 and 3–819(b) of 'The Illinois Vehicle Code' in Section 1 of this Act which create the 'X', 'Z', 'MX', 'MZ', 'MM' and 'TN' registration classifications and the fees and taxes imposed for those classifications, the amendments to Sections 2–119, 3–401 and 3–802 of 'The Illinois Vehicle Code' in Section 1 of this Act, and the amendments to Chapter 15 of 'The Illinois Vehicle Code' in Section 1 of this Act take effect July 1, 1983.

"The remaining amendments to 'The Illinois Vehicle Code' in Section 1 of this Act take effect July 1, 1983 and apply beginning with the 1985 registration year, except that the amendments to Sections 3–813 through 3–816 and Section 3–819 apply beginning with the 1984 registration year for those vehicles registered on a calendar year basis only.

"The amendments to Chapters 13 and 18 of 'The Illinois Vehicle Code' in Section 1 of this Act take effect January 1, 1984.

"Section 2 of this Act takes effect on the first day of the next succeeding month which commences at least 30 days after the date on which this Act becomes law.

"Section 3 of this Act takes effect July 1, 1983.

"Section 3.1 of this Act takes effect January 1, 1984.

"This Section 4 takes effect upon its becoming a law."

5/3–821. Miscellaneous Registration and Title Fees

§ 3–821. Miscellaneous Registration and Title Fees.

(a) The fee to be paid to the Secretary of State for the following certificates, registrations or evidences of proper registration, or for corrected or duplicate documents shall be in accordance with the following schedule:

Certificate of Title, except for an all-terrain vehicle or off- highway motorcycle	$65
Certificate of Title for an all-terrain vehicle or off-highway motorcycle	$30
Certificate of Title for an all-terrain vehicle or off-highway motorcycle used for production agriculture, or accepted by a dealer in trade	13
Transfer of Registration or any evidence of proper registration	15
Duplicate Registration Card for plates or other evidence of proper registration	3
Duplicate Registration Sticker or Stickers, each	5
Duplicate Certificate of Title	65
Corrected Registration Card or Card for other evidence of proper registration	3
Corrected Certificate of Title	65
Salvage Certificate	4
Fleet Reciprocity Permit	15
Prorate Decal	1
Prorate Backing Plate	3

There shall be no fee paid for a Junking Certificate.

(b) The Secretary may prescribe the maximum service charge to be imposed upon an applicant for renewal of a registration by any person authorized by law to receive and remit or transmit to the Secretary such renewal application and fees therewith.

(c) If a check is delivered to the Office of the Secretary of State as payment of any fee or tax under this Code, and such check is not honored by the bank on which it is drawn for any reason, the registrant or other person tendering the check remains liable for the payment of such fee or tax. The Secretary of State may assess a service charge of $19 in addition to the fee or tax due and owing for all dishonored checks.

If the total amount then due and owing exceeds the sum of $50 and has not been paid in full within 60 days from the date such fee or tax became due to the Secretary of State, the Secretary of State shall assess a penalty of 25% of such amount remaining unpaid.

All amounts payable under this Section shall be computed to the nearest dollar.

(d) The minimum fee and tax to be paid by any applicant for apportionment of a fleet of vehicles under this Code shall be $15 if the application was filed on or before the date specified by the Secretary together with fees and taxes due. If an application and the fees or taxes due are filed after the date specified by the Secretary, the Secretary may prescribe the payment of interest at the rate of ½ of 1% per month or fraction thereof after such due date and a minimum of $8.

(e) Trucks, truck tractors, truck tractors with loads, and motor buses, any one of which having a combined total weight in excess of 12,000 lbs. shall file an application for a Fleet Reciprocity Permit issued by the Secretary of State. This permit shall be in the possession of any driver operating a vehicle on Illinois highways. Any foreign licensed vehicle of the second division operating at any time in Illinois without a Fleet Reciprocity Permit or other proper Illinois registration, shall subject the operator to the penalties provided in Section 3-834 of this Code. For the purposes of this Code, "Fleet Reciprocity Permit" means any second division motor vehicle with a foreign license and used only in interstate transportation of goods. The fee for such permit shall be $15 per fleet which shall include all vehicles of the fleet being registered.

(f) For purposes of this Section, "all-terrain vehicle or off-highway motorcycle used for production agriculture" means any all-terrain vehicle or off-highway motorcycle used in the raising of or the propagation of livestock, crops for sale for human consumption, crops for livestock consumption, and production seed stock grown for the propagation of feed grains and the husbandry of animals or for the purpose of providing a food product, including the husbandry of blood stock as a main source of providing a food product. "All-terrain vehicle or off-highway motorcycle used in production agriculture" also means any all-terrain vehicle or off-highway motorcycle used in animal husbandry, floriculture, aquaculture, horticulture, and viticulture.

P.A. 76-1586, § 1, eff. July 1, 1970. Amended by P.A. 76-2152, § 3-821, eff. July 1, 1970; P.A. 77-364, § 1, eff. July 23, 1971; P.A. 77-649, § 1, eff. Jan. 1, 1972; P.A. 77-2829, § 40, eff. Dec. 22, 1972; P.A. 78-255, § 61, eff. Oct. 1, 1973; P.A. 78-859, § 1, eff. Jan. 1, 1974; P.A. 78-1297, § 58, eff. March 4, 1975; P.A. 79-718, § 1, eff. Oct. 1, 1975; P.A. 79-1458, § 1, eff. Sept. 1, 1976; P.A. 80-230, § 1, eff. Oct. 1, 1977; P.A. 80-1185, § 1, eff. March 8, 1978; P.A. 81-886, § 1, eff. July 1, 1980; P.A. 83-12, § 1, eff. July 1, 1983; P.A. 83-953, § 1, eff. Dec. 2, 1983; P.A. 86-466, § 1, eff. Jan. 1, 1990; P.A. 86-1019, § 2, eff. Jan. 1, 1990; P.A. 87-1225, § 2, eff. Dec. 22, 1992; P.A. 88-78, § 15, eff. Sept. 7, 1993; P.A. 90-287, § 100, eff. Jan. 1, 1998; P.A. 90-774, § 5, eff. Aug. 14, 1998; P.A. 91-37, § 40, eff. July 1, 1999; P.A. 91-441, § 10, eff. Jan. 1, 2000; P.A. 92-16, § 85, eff. June 28, 2001.

Formerly Ill.Rev.Stat.1991, ch. 95 ½, ¶ 3-821.

Section 4 of P.A. 83-12, approved July 1, 1983, provided:

"Effective date. This Act takes effect as provided in this Section.

"The amendments to those portions of Sections 3-815(a), 3-818 and 3-819(b) of 'The Illinois Vehicle Code' in Section 1 of this Act which create the 'X', 'Z', 'MX', 'MZ', 'MM' and 'TN' registration classifications and the fees and taxes imposed for those classifications, the amendments to Sections 2-119, 3-401 and 3-802 of 'The Illinois Vehicle Code' in Section 1 of this Act, and the amendments to Chapter 15 of 'The Illinois Vehicle Code' in Section 1 of this Act take effect July 1, 1983.

"The remaining amendments to 'The Illinois Vehicle Code' in Section 1 of this Act take effect July 1, 1983 and apply beginning with the 1985 registration year, except that the amendments to Sections 3-813 through 3-816 and Section 3-819 apply beginning with the 1984 registration year for those vehicles registered on a calendar year basis only.

"The amendments to Chapters 13 and 18 of 'The Illinois Vehicle Code' in Section 1 of this Act take effect January 1, 1984.

"Section 2 of this Act takes effect on the first day of the next succeeding month which commences at least 30 days after the date on which this Act becomes law.

"Section 3 of this Act takes effect July 1, 1983.

"Section 3.1 of this Act takes effect January 1, 1984.

"This Section 4 takes effect upon its becoming a law."

5/3-821.1. Fees for record searches

§ 3-821.1. Fees for record searches. The fee to be paid to the Secretary of State by any towing service requesting a record search shall be in the amount the Secretary of State prescribes by rule.

P.A. 76-1586, § 3-821.1, added by P.A. 89-433, § 5, eff. Dec. 15, 1995.

5/3-822. Fees relating to security interests

§ 3-822. Fees relating to security interests. There shall be paid to the Secretary of State a filing fee of $2.00 for the filing of a notice of a security interest and for the filing of a release of a security interest for each motor vehicle subject to such security interest.

P.A. 76-1586, § 3-822, eff. July 1, 1970.

Formerly Ill.Rev.Stat.1991, ch. 95 ½, ¶ 3-822.

5/3-823. § 3-823. Deleted by P.A. 83-148, § 1, eff. Aug. 29, 1983

The provisions of this section, which related to title or registration search fees, were completely stricken out by P.A. 83-148, § 1. The section was derived from:

5/3-824. When fees returnable

§ 3-824. When fees returnable.

(a) Whenever any application to the Secretary of State is accompanied by any fee as required by law and such application is refused or rejected, said fee shall be returned to said applicant.

(b) Whenever the Secretary of State collects any fee not required to be paid under the provisions of this Act, the same shall be refunded to the person paying the same upon application therefor made within 6 months after the date of such payment, except as follows: (1) whenever a refund is determined to be due and owing as a result of an audit, by this State or any other state or province, in accordance with Section 2-124 of this Code, of a prorate or apportion license fee payment pursuant to any reciprocal compact or agreement between this State and any other state or province, and the Secretary for any reason fails to promptly make such refund, the licensee shall have one year from the date of the notification of the audit result to file, with the Secretary, an application for refund found to be due and owing as a result of such audit; and (2) whenever a person eligible for a reduced registration fee pursuant to Section 3-806.3 of this Code has paid in excess of the reduced registration fee owed, the refund applicant shall have 2 years from the date of overpayment to apply with the Secretary for a refund of that part of payment made in excess of the established reduced registration fee.

(c) Whenever a person dies after making application for registration, application for a refund of the registration fees and taxes may be made if the vehicle is then sold or disposed of so that the registration plates, registration sticker and card are never used. The Secretary of State shall refund the registration fees and taxes upon receipt within 6 months after the application for registration of an application for refund accompanied with the unused registration plates or registration sticker and card and proof of both the death of the applicant and the sale or disposition of the vehicle.

(d) Any application for refund received after the times specified in this Section shall be denied and the applicant in order to receive a refund must apply to the Court of Claims.

(e) The Secretary of State is authorized to maintain a two signature revolving checking account with a suitable commercial bank for the purpose of depositing and withdrawal-for-return those monies received and determined upon receipt to be in excess of the amount or amounts required by law.

(f) Refunds on audits performed by Illinois or another member of the International Registration Plan shall be made in accordance with the procedures as set forth in the agreement.

P.A. 76-1586, § 3-824, eff. July 1, 1970. Amended by P.A. 77-325, § 1, eff. July 22, 1971; P.A. 79-1107, § 1, eff. Sept. 26, 1975; P.A. 80-230, § 1, eff. Oct. 1, 1977; P.A. 83-1276, § 1, eff. Jan. 1, 1985; P.A. 86-131, § 1, eff. Jan. 1, 1990; P.A. 92-69, § 5, eff. July 12, 2001.

Formerly Ill.Rev.Stat.1991, ch. 95 ½, ¶ 3-824.

5/3-824.5. Applicability of fee and tax increases

§ 3-824.5. Applicability of fee and tax increases. The fee and tax increases in this Code made by this amendatory Act of the 91st General Assembly that apply to registrations apply to registration year 2001 and thereafter. The registration fees and taxes in existence on the day prior to the effective date of this amendatory Act of the 91st General Assembly apply throughout registration year 2000. All other fee and tax increases in this Code made by this amendatory Act of the 91st General Assembly shall apply beginning January 1, 2000 and thereafter.

P.A. 76-1586, § 3-824.5, added by P.A. 91-37, § 40, eff. July 1, 1999.

5/3-825. Certificate of Safety

§ 3-825. Certificate of Safety. Every application for registration of a motor vehicle which is subject to vehicle inspection may be accompanied by proof that a valid and unrevoked Certificate of Safety has been issued for each such vehicle. The Secretary of State may at his discretion decline to register any such vehicle unless the application is accompanied with such proof.

P.A. 76-1586, § 3-825, eff. July 1, 1970. Amended by P.A. 76-1997, § 1, eff. July 1, 1970.

Formerly Ill.Rev.Stat.1991, ch. 95 ½, ¶ 3-825.

5/3-826. § 3-826. Repealed by P.A. 78-433, § 1, eff. Oct. 1, 1973

5/3-827. § 3-827. Repealed by P.A. 88-415, § 15, eff. August 20, 1993

5/3-828. Lien for violations

§ 3-828. Lien for violations. Any vehicle used in violation of the provisions of this Act shall be subject to a lien for the full amount of all unpaid registration fees, flat weight taxes, and penalties. Such lien shall not release the offender from the full payment of all such fees, taxes, penalties and damages. The lien shall attach at the time of operation of any such vehicle within this State and shall remain effective until all unpaid registration fees, flat weight taxes, penalties and audit fees are paid, or until the vehicle is sold for the payment thereof. Such liens shall be superior to any other lien except that:

(a) no lien for any amounts due or assessed pursuant to this Section shall be enforceable against any vehicle which prior to such assessment had been transferred in good faith to a bona fide transferee for value;

(b) the lien of any amounts due or assessed shall be subject to a prior lien of any indebtedness existing against such vehicle which is noted on the certificate of title of such vehicle issued under this Act, or as to a vehicle from another jurisdiction, if written notice thereof is filed with the Secretary of State before such lien becomes operative and if

(1) Such prior indebtedness was incurred in good faith to secure all or a portion of the purchase price of such vehicle, and

(2) Such prior indebtedness is secured by a chattel mortgage or conditional sales agreement duly filed or perfected in this State pursuant to law and such chattel mortgage or conditional sales was not given directly or indirectly, to any officer, director or shareholder of a corporation, or to a partner of a partnership, or to a trustee or beneficiary of a trust, owning or having the lawful use or control of such vehicle, whether as a purchase money mortgage or otherwise.

The lien imposed under this Section shall be enforceable as to any equity after the encumbrance of any such chattel mortgage or conditional sales contract, and in the event any such vehicle subject to a lien hereunder is repossessed by a chattel mortgagee or a conditional vendor, such vehicle shall not be sold at any public or private sale unless at least 5 days written notice by registered mail is served upon the Secretary of State.

The Secretary of State, upon perfecting a prior lien hereunder for any flat weight taxes required to be paid under Section 3-815 may in his discretion waive the requirement for the surety bond specified in Section 3-816, providing that the said prior lien is so noted on the certificate of title for such vehicle or vehicles.

Any surety making payment of a second installment of taxes under Section 3-816 of this Act, may impress a lien similar to that of the Secretary of State, and such lien may be noted on title records and documents. The surety shall, however, pay any statutory fees therefor.

P.A. 76-1586, § 3-828, eff. July 1, 1970. Amended by P.A. 77-1464, § 1, eff. Sept. 7, 1971.

Formerly Ill.Rev.Stat.1991, ch. 95 ½, ¶ 3-828.

5/3-829. Foreclosure of lien—Service of processes—Notices

§ 3-829. Foreclosure of lien—Service of processes—Notices. In any action to foreclose the lien imposed by Section 3-828 service of process on all known owners and parties in interest shall be made in the manner now prescribed by law, and, as to all unknown owners and parties in interest, notice of the pendency of such action shall be given by publication in some newspaper of general circulation published in the county where the suit is pending, or if there is no such newspaper, then in a newspaper of general circulation published in an adjoining county in this State and having a general circulation in the county in which such suit is pending. Such notice shall contain the title of the court; the title of the case, showing the names of all known owners and parties in interest; a statement that publication is being made as to unknown owners and parties in interest; and the date on or after which default may be entered against the defendants.

P.A. 76-1586, § 3-829, eff. July 1, 1970.

Formerly Ill.Rev.Stat.1991, ch. 95 ½, ¶ 3-829.

5/3-830. Notice of pendency of action—Time and number of publications—Default

§ 3-830. Notice of pendency of action—Time and number of publications—Default. The notice required by Section 3-829 may be given at any time after commencement of the suit, and shall be published at least once each week for 3 successive weeks. No default or other proceeding shall be taken against any defendant as to whom publication was made and who does not appear, unless the first publication is at least 30 days prior to the time when the default or other proceeding is sought to be taken.

P.A. 76-1586, § 3-830, eff. July 1, 1970.

Formerly Ill.Rev.Stat.1991, ch. 95 ½, ¶ 3-830.

5/3-831. Secretary to institute suits

§ 3-831. Secretary to institute suits. The Secretary of State may institute, in the name of the People of the State of Illinois, a suit or suits in the circuit court to enforce the collection of any fees, taxes, interest, penalties or damages provided for in this Act, or to enjoin violations of this Act.

P.A. 76-1586, § 3-831, eff. July 1, 1970. Amended by P.A. 77-1541, § 1, eff. Sept. 17, 1971; P.A. 79-1358, § 43, eff. Oct. 1, 1976.

Formerly Ill.Rev.Stat.1991, ch. 95 ½, ¶ 3-831.

5/3-832. Service of process

§ 3-832. Service of process. The operation, with the consent of the owner, upon the highways of the State of any motor vehicle of the second division shall be deemed an appointment by the owner of the driver of the vehicle as the owner's agent upon whom may be served process in any civil or criminal proceeding against such owner based upon failure to register, improper registration or failure to pay the proper fees or taxes with respect to any motor vehicles of the second division of such owner.

P.A. 76-1586, § 3-832, eff. July 1, 1970.

Formerly Ill.Rev.Stat.1991, ch. 95 ½, ¶ 3-832.

5/3-833. Unlawful acts

§ 3-833. Unlawful acts. It shall be unlawful for any person to own or operate a vehicle on the public highways of this State without complying with this Act.

P.A. 76-1586, § 3-833, eff. July 1, 1970.

Formerly Ill.Rev.Stat.1991, ch. 95 ½, ¶ 3-833.

5/3-834. Violations of this Chapter 3

§ 3-834. Violations of this Chapter 3.

(a) It is unlawful for any person to violate any of the provisions of this Chapter 3, except as provided in paragraph (b) of this Section, unless such violation is by this Code or other law of this State declared to be a felony.

(b) Every person convicted of a misdemeanor for a violation of any of the provisions of this Chapter 3 for which another penalty is not provided shall for a first and second conviction be guilty of a petty offense; upon a third or subsequent conviction within one year after the first conviction such person shall be guilty of a Class C misdemeanor. Compliance with the registration provisions of this Code after apprehension or arrest shall not excuse imposition of the penalties herein provided nor be cause for dismissal of the arrest or of the summons nor be a basis for setting aside a conviction therefor.

P.A. 76-1586, § 3-834, eff. July 1, 1970. Amended by P.A. 77-76, § 1, eff. Jan. 1, 1972; P.A. 77-2720, § 1, eff. Jan. 1, 1973; P.A. 78-255, § 61, eff. Oct. 1, 1973; P.A. 80-911, § 1, eff. Oct. 1, 1977; P.A. 82-392, § 1, eff. Jan. 1, 1982; P.A. 84-980, § 1, eff. Sept. 25, 1985; P.A. 88-476, § 2, eff. July 1, 1994.

Formerly Ill.Rev.Stat.1991, ch. 95 ½, ¶ 3-834.

Section 2 of P.A. 82-392 approved Sept. 4, 1981, provided:
"This Act takes effect with the 1984 registration year."

ARTICLE IX. REMITTANCE AGENTS

Date Effective

Article IX was added by P.A. 76-1705, § 1, effective July 1, 1970.

5/3-900. § 3-900. Repealed by P.A. 90-89, § 20, eff. Jan. 1, 1998

5/3-901. Purpose of Article

§ 3-901. Purpose of Article. Many persons throughout the State hold themselves out to the public as being engaged in, and have engaged in, accepting money from members of the public for remittance to the State of Illinois, and its licensing and taxing agencies in payment of vehicle taxes or vehicle license or registration fees. Some of these persons have failed to make such remittance with the consequent loss to the remitters. It is the public policy of this State that its people be protected against such hazards.

P.A. 76-1586, § 3-901, added by P.A. 76-1705, § 1, eff. July 1, 1970.

Formerly Ill.Rev.Stat.1991, ch. 95 ½, ¶ 3-901.

5/3-902. Application of Article

§ 3-902. Application of Article. This Article shall not apply to (1) any person who accepts for remittance only such sums as he is authorized to collect by the remittee as its agent, and (2) to any person who, in connection with the issuance of a license to him to conduct a business in this State, shall have filed, pursuant to a statutory requirement, a surety bond covering the proper discharge of any liability incurred by him in connection with the acceptance for remittance of money for the purposes designated in the Article pursuant to which he is licensed; provided he does not accept any money for remittance, as a remittance agent, the proper transmittal of which is not covered by said bond.

P.A. 76-1586, § 3-902, added by P.A. 76-1705, § 1, eff. July 1, 1970.

Formerly Ill.Rev.Stat.1991, ch. 95 ½, ¶ 3-902.

5/3-903. License

§ 3-903. License. It shall be unlawful for any person, either as principal or agent, to act as a "remittance agent" in the State of Illinois without first having obtained or renewed, as the case may be, a license and posted a bond, as hereafter provided.

P.A. 76-1586, § 3-903, added by P.A. 76-1705, § 1, eff. July 1, 1970.

Formerly Ill.Rev.Stat.1991, ch. 95 ½, ¶ 3-903.

5/3-904. Application—Contents—Affidavits

§ 3-904. Application—Contents—Affidavits. Any person who desires to act as a "remittance agent" shall first file with the Secretary of State a written application for a license. The application shall be under oath and shall contain the following:

1. The name and address of the applicant.

2. The address of each location at which the applicant intends to act as a remittance agent.

3. The applicant's business, occupation or profession.

4. A statement disclosing whether he has been involved in any civil or criminal litigation and if so, the material facts pertaining thereto.

The application shall be accompanied by the affidavits of two persons residing in the city or town of such applicant's residence. Such affiants shall state that they have known the applicant for a period of at least two years; that the applicant is of good moral character and that his reputation for honesty and business integrity in the community in which he resides is good. If the applicant is not an individual, the requirements of this paragraph shall apply to each of its officers or members.

P.A. 76-1586, § 3-904, added by P.A. 76-1705, § 1, eff. July 1, 1970. Amended by P.A. 83-387, § 1, eff. Jan. 1, 1984.

Formerly Ill.Rev.Stat.1991, ch. 95 ½, ¶ 3-904.

5/3-905. Bond; Fee; Duration of license

§ 3-905. Bond; Fee; Duration of license. Such applicant shall, with his application, deposit with the Secretary of State a bond as hereinafter provided, for each location at which the applicant intends to act as a remittance agent. The application shall be accompanied by the payment of a license fee in the sum of $50.00 (or $25.00 if such application is filed after July 1) for each location at which he proposes to act as a remittance agent. If the applicant shall have complied with all of the requirements of this Section and the Secretary of State shall find after investigation that the applicant is financially sound and of good business integrity, he shall issue the required license. Such license shall terminate on December 31 of the year for which it is issued, but upon application prior to November 15 of any year for which a license is in effect may be renewed for the next succeeding calendar year. Such application shall be accompanied by the payment of an annual license fee of $50.00 for each location at which the applicant proposes to act as a remittance agent and the posting of the bond herein provided, for each such location.

The bond required by this Section shall be for the term of the license, or renewal thereof, for which application is made, and shall run to the People of the State of Illinois, with surety by a bonding or insurance company authorized to do business in this State, to be approved by the Secretary of State. It shall be conditioned upon the proper transmittal of all remittances by the applicant as a remittance agent and the performance of all undertakings in connection therewith. It shall be in the minimum sum of $10,000, or in an amount equal to the aggregate sum of money transmitted to the State by the applicant during the highest 15 day period in the fiscal year immediately preceding the one for which application is made (rounded to the nearest $1,000), whichever is the greater. However, for the purpose of determining the bond requirements hereunder, remittances made by applicants in the form of money orders or checks which are made payable directly to the Secretary of State or the Illinois Department of Revenue by the remitter, shall not be considered in the aggregate. The bond requirement of this Section shall not apply to banks, savings and loan associations, and credit unions chartered by the State of Illinois or the United States; provided that the banks, savings and loan associations, and credit unions provide to the Secretary of State an affidavit stating that the bank, savings and loan association, or credit union is sufficiently bonded to meet the requirements as required above. Such affidavit shall be signed by an officer of the bank, savings and loan association, or credit union and shall be notarized.

P.A. 76-1586, § 3-905, added by P.A. 76-1705, § 1, eff. July 1, 1970. Amended by P.A. 81-322, § 1, eff. Jan. 1, 1980; P.A. 83-449, § 1, eff. Jan. 1, 1984; P.A. 87-206, § 1, eff. Sept. 3, 1991; P.A. 88-470, § 10, eff. Sept. 1, 1993; P.A. 88-643, § 935, eff. Jan. 1, 1995.

Formerly Ill.Rev.Stat.1991, ch. 95 ½, ¶ 3-905.

P.A. 88-643 incorporated the amendment by P.A. 88-470.

5/3-906. Denial

§ 3-906. Denial. The Secretary of State shall deny any application under this Article upon any of the following grounds:

(1) That the application contains any false or fraudulent statement; or

(2) That the applicant has failed to furnish the information required by the Secretary or to file a bond as required; or

(3) That the required fee has not been paid; or

(4) That the applicant has failed to remit fees to the Secretary of State; or

(5) That the applicant has engaged in fraudulent practices; or

(6) That the applicant or a member of his immediate family is an employee of the Secretary of State; or

(7) That the Secretary of State is authorized under any other provision of law.

If the Secretary of State denies the application for a license, or renewal thereof, or revokes a license, he shall so order in writing and notify the applicant thereof by certified mail. Upon the denial of an application for a license, or renewal thereof, he shall return the license fee. No application shall be denied unless the applicant has had an opportunity for a fair hearing in connection therewith.

P.A. 76-1586, § 3-906, added by P.A. 76-1705, § 1, eff. July 1, 1970. Amended by P.A. 77-84, § 1, eff. Jan. 1, 1972.

Formerly Ill.Rev.Stat.1991, ch. 95 ½, ¶ 3-906.

5/3-907. Suspension or revocation

§ 3-907. Suspension or revocation. Such license may be suspended or revoked by the Secretary of State for the violation of any provision of this Act or any rule or regulation of the Secretary of State and for any reason which, had it existed or been known to the Secretary of State at the time of the filing of the application for such license, would have been good cause for the denial of such application. A licensee may, upon receipt of an order of suspension or revocation seek a hearing to review such order.

P.A. 76-1586, § 3-907, added by P.A. 76-1705, § 1, eff. July 1, 1970. Amended by P.A. 77-84, § 1, eff. Jan. 1, 1972.

Formerly Ill.Rev.Stat.1991, ch. 95 ½, ¶ 3-907.

5/3-908. Location

§ 3-908. Location. A licensee may not do business at a location not set forth in his license, but the Secretary of State may issue an amended license covering an additional location or locations, upon application therefor, the payment of an additional license fee and the posting of the required bond for each such location.

P.A. 76-1586, § 3-908, added by P.A. 76-1705, § 1, eff. July 1, 1970.

Formerly Ill.Rev.Stat.1991, ch. 95 ½, ¶ 3-908.

5/3-909. Money accepted for remittance—Obligations of licensee

§ 3-909. Money accepted for remittance—Obligations of licensee. Each licensee shall forward to the remittee all money accepted for remittance not later than the fifth calendar day after the date upon which such money was received by the licensee, and shall promptly fulfill any other obligation it has undertaken in connection therewith.

P.A. 76-1586, § 3-909, added by P.A. 76-1705, § 1, eff. July 1, 1970.

Formerly Ill.Rev.Stat.1991, ch. 95 ½, ¶ 3-909.

5/3-910. Records of transactions

§ 3-910. Records of transactions. Each licensee shall maintain for a period of three years the following records with reference to each transaction involving a remittance:

1. The address of the location at which the transaction occurred.
2. The name and address of the remitter.
3. The name and address of the remittee.
4. The purpose of the remittance.
5. The amount of money received for remittance.
6. The date of receipt of the money for remittance by the licensee.
7. The date such money was forwarded to the remittee.
8. If applicable, the date the license plate, vehicle tax sticker, license or other instrument issued by the remittee, was delivered to the remitter by the licensee.

P.A. 76-1586, § 3-910, added by P.A. 76-1705, § 1, eff. July 1, 1970.

Formerly Ill.Rev.Stat.1991, ch. 95 ½, ¶ 3-910.

5/3-911. Examination of business

§ 3-911. Examination of business. The Secretary of State or any of his representatives designated by him may examine the business of any person who acts, or may be acting, as a remittance agent, to determine whether such person is complying with the provisions of this Act and with such rules and regulations as may be promulgated by the Secretary of State pursuant to its provisions. For that purpose, the Secretary of State or his representatives shall have free access to the offices, places of business, and records of any such person.

P.A. 76-1586, § 3-911, added by P.A. 76-1705, § 1, eff. July 1, 1970.

Formerly Ill.Rev.Stat.1991, ch. 95 ½, ¶ 3-911.

5/3-912. Rules and regulations

§ 3-912. Rules and regulations. The Secretary of State may make such rules, regulations, direction, orders, decisions and findings as may be necessary for the enforcement of this Act and the purposes sought to be attained herein.

P.A. 76-1586, § 3-912, added by P.A. 76-1705, § 1, eff. July 1, 1970.

Formerly Ill.Rev.Stat.1991, ch. 95 ½, ¶ 3-912.

5/3-913. Hearing—Subpoenas

§ 3-913. Hearing—Subpoenas. Hearings under this Article shall be governed by Section 2-118 of this Act and the Administrative Review Law as amended,[1] shall apply to and govern all proceedings for judicial review of any final order issued by the Secretary of State. For the purposes of this Act, the Secretary of State, or the hearing officer as hereinafter provided, has power to require by subpoena the attendance and testimony of witnesses, and the production of all documentary evidence relating to any matter under hearing pursuant to this Act, and shall issue such subpoenas at the request of an interested party. The hearing officer may sign subpoenas in the name of the Secretary of State.

The Secretary of State may, in his discretion, direct that any hearing pursuant to this Act, shall be held before a competent and qualified agent of the Secretary of State, whom the Secretary of State shall designate as the hearing officer in such matter. The Secretary of State and the hearing officer are hereby empowered to, and shall, administer oaths and affirmations to all witnesses appearing before them. The hearing officer, upon the conclusion of the hearing before him, shall certify the evidence to the Secretary of State, and may make recommendations in connection therewith.

Any Circuit Court of this State, within the jurisdiction of which such hearing is carried on, may, in case of contumacy, or refusal of a witness to obey a subpoena, issue an order requiring such witness to appear before the Secretary of State, or the hearing officer, or to produce documentary evidence, or to give testimony touching the matter in question, and any failure to obey such order of the court may be punished by such court as a contempt thereof.

P.A. 76-1586, § 3-913, added by P.A. 76-1705, § 1, eff. July 1, 1970. Amended by P.A. 77-84, § 1, eff. Jan. 1, 1972; P.A. 82-783, Art. XI, § 140, eff. July 13, 1982.

Formerly Ill.Rev.Stat.1991, ch. 95 ½, ¶ 3-913.

[1] 735 ILCS 5/3-101 et seq.

5/3-914. Violations—Injunction

§ 3-914. Violations—Injunction. The violation of any provision of this Act by any remittance agent may be restrained by the issuance of an injunction by the circuit court, against him and any other person who shall aid or abet him in such violation, upon filing of a complaint by any person adversely affected thereby, the State's Attorney of such county, or by the Attorney General of the State of Illinois.

P.A. 76–1586, § 3–914, added by P.A. 76–1705, § 1, eff. July 1, 1970. Amended by P.A. 79–1358, § 43, eff. Oct. 1, 1976.

Formerly Ill.Rev.Stat.1991, ch. 95 ½, ¶ 3–914.

5/3–915. Violations

§ 3–915. Any person who violates, or who aids or abets another in the violation, of any provision of this Act or any rule or regulation promulgated thereunder, or does any act prohibited by this Act, or who fails, neglects, or refuses to perform any duty required by any provision of this Act or rule or regulation of the Secretary of State, within the time prescribed by the Secretary of State, or who fails, neglects, or refuses to obey any lawful order given or made by the Secretary of State, shall be guilty of a Class B misdemeanor, and each such act, failure, neglect, or refusal shall constitute a separate and distinct offense.

P.A. 76–1586, § 3–915, added by P.A. 76–1705, § 1, eff. July 1, 1970. Amended by P.A. 77–2720, § 1, eff. Jan. 1, 1973.

Formerly Ill.Rev.Stat.1991, ch. 95 ½, ¶ 3–915.

5/3–916. Issuance of license—Effect

§ 3–916. Issuance of license—Effect. The issuance of a license pursuant to the provisions of this Act shall not be construed to grant to any remittance agent the authority to act as agent for the State of Illinois or any of its instrumentalities or political subdivisions, or for any of their officials or for any other person.

P.A. 76–1586, § 3–916, added by P.A. 76–1705, § 1, eff. July 1, 1970.

Formerly Ill.Rev.Stat.1991, ch. 95 ½, ¶ 3–916.

5/3–917. Recovery of damages

§ 3–917. Recovery of damages. Any person who shall have been damaged by reason of the failure of any "remittance agent" to fulfill the conditions of any bond filed pursuant to the provisions of this Act may maintain a suit thereon to recover his damages and his reasonable attorney's fees, against such "remittance agent" or his surety, or both: provided, however, the aggregate liability of the surety to all such persons shall, in no event, exceed the sum of such bond.

P.A. 76–1586, § 3–917, added by P.A. 76–1705, § 1, eff. July 1, 1970.

Formerly Ill.Rev.Stat.1991, ch. 95 ½, ¶ 3–917.

ARTICLE X. VEHICLE USE TAX

Date Effective

Article X was added by P.A. 81–3, 2nd Sp.Sess., eff. Jan. 1, 1980.

5/3–1001. Imposition of tax; exceptions

§ 3–1001. A tax is hereby imposed on the privilege of using, in this State, any motor vehicle as defined in Section 1–146 of this Code acquired by gift, transfer, or purchase, and having a year model designation preceding the year of application for title by 5 or fewer years prior to October 1, 1985 and 10 or fewer years on and after October 1, 1985 and prior to January 1, 1988. On and after January 1, 1988, the tax shall apply to all motor vehicles without regard to model year. Except that the tax shall not apply

(i) if the use of the motor vehicle is otherwise taxed under the Use Tax Act; [1]

(ii) if the motor vehicle is bought and used by a governmental agency or a society, association, foundation or institution organized and operated exclusively for charitable, religious or educational purposes;

(iii) if the use of the motor vehicle is not subject to the Use Tax Act by reason of subsection (a), (b), (c), (d), (e) or (f) of Section 3–55 of that Act [2] dealing with the prevention of actual or likely multistate taxation;

(iv) to implements of husbandry;

(v) when a junking certificate is issued pursuant to Section 3–117(a) of this Code;

(vi) when a vehicle is subject to the replacement vehicle tax imposed by Section 3–2001 of this Act;

(vii) when the transfer is a gift to a beneficiary in the administration of an estate and the beneficiary is a surviving spouse.

Prior to January 1, 1988, the rate of tax shall be 5% of the selling price for each purchase of a motor vehicle covered by Section 3–1001 of this Code. Except as hereinafter provided, beginning January 1, 1988, the rate of tax shall be as follows for transactions in which the selling price of the motor vehicle is less than $15,000:

Number of Years Transpired After Model Year of Motor Vehicle	Applicable Tax
1 or less	$390
2	290
3	215
4	165
5	115
6	90
7	80
8	65
9	50
10	40
over 10	25

Except as hereinafter provided, beginning January 1, 1988, the rate of tax shall be as follows for transactions in which the selling price of the motor vehicle is $15,000 or more:

Selling Price	Applicable Tax
$15,000–$19,999	$ 750
$20,000–$24,999	$1,000
$25,000–$29,999	$1,250
$30,000 and over	$1,500

For the following transactions, the tax rate shall be $15 for each motor vehicle acquired in such transaction:

(i) when the transferee or purchaser is the spouse, mother, father, brother, sister or child of the transferor;

(ii) when the transfer is a gift to a beneficiary in the administration of an estate and the beneficiary is not a surviving spouse;

(iii) when a motor vehicle which has once been subjected to the Illinois retailers' occupation tax or use tax is transferred in connection with the organization, reorganization, dissolution or partial liquidation of an incorporated or unincorporated business wherein the beneficial ownership is not changed.

A claim that the transaction is taxable under subparagraph (i) shall be supported by such proof of family relationship as provided by rules of the Department.

For a transaction in which a motorcycle, motor driven cycle or motorized pedalcycle is acquired the tax rate shall be $25.

On and after October 1, 1985, 1/12 of $5,000,000 of the moneys received by the Department of Revenue pursuant to this Section shall be paid each month into the Build Illinois Fund and the remainder into the General Revenue Fund.

At the end of any fiscal year in which the moneys received by the Department of Revenue pursuant to this Section exceeds the Annual Specified Amount, as defined in Section 3 of the Retailers' Occupation Tax Act,[3] the State Comptroller shall direct the State Treasurer to transfer such excess amount from the General Revenue Fund to the Build Illinois Purposes Fund.

The tax imposed by this Section shall be abated and no longer imposed when the amount deposited to secure the bonds issued pursuant to the Build Illinois Bond Act[4] is sufficient to provide for the payment of the principal of, and interest and premium, if any, on the bonds, as certified to the State Comptroller and the Director of Revenue by the Director of the Bureau of the Budget.

P.A. 76–1586, § 3–1001, added by P.A. 81–3, 2nd Sp.Sess., § 18, eff. Jan. 1, 1980. Amended by P.A. 83–1353, § 1, eff. Sept. 8, 1984; P.A. 84–109, Art. 20, § 20–1, eff. July 25, 1985; P.A. 84–112, § 1, eff. July 25, 1985; P.A. 84–1308, Art. II, § 96, eff. Aug. 25, 1986; P.A. 84–1454, Art. I, § 1, eff. Jan. 6, 1987; P.A. 85–444, § 1, eff. Jan. 1, 1988; P.A. 86–152, § 1, eff. Jan. 1, 1990; P.A. 86–1475, Art. 5, § 5–8, eff. Jan. 10, 1991; P.A. 88–194, § 35, eff. Jan. 1, 1994; P.A. 90–89, § 15, eff. Jan. 1, 1998.

Formerly Ill.Rev.Stat.1991, ch. 95 ½, ¶ 3–1001.

[1] 35 ILCS 105/1 et seq.

[2] 35 ILCS 105/3–55.

[3] 35 ILCS 120/3.

[4] 30 ILCS 425/1 et seq.

For intent of P.A. 86–1475, Art. 5, see note following 35 ILCS 105/3.

5/3–1002. Returns; verification; payment to secure title; receipts

§ 3–1002. The purchaser shall file a return signed by the purchaser with the Department of Revenue on a form prescribed by the Department. Such return shall contain substantially the following and such other information as the Department may reasonably require:

VERIFICATION

I declare that I have examined this return and to the best of my knowledge it is true, correct and complete. I understand that the penalty for willfully filing a false return shall be a fine not to exceed $1,000 or imprisonment in a penal institution other than the penitentiary not to exceed one year, or both fine and imprisonment.

....
Date Signature of purchaser

Such return and payment from the purchaser shall be submitted to the Department after the sale and shall be a condition to securing in order to secure the title to the motor vehicle from the Secretary of State.

When a purchaser pays the tax imposed by Section 3–1001 of this Code, the Department (upon request therefor from such purchaser) shall issue an appropriate receipt to such purchaser showing that he has paid such tax to the Department. Such receipt shall be sufficient to relieve the purchaser from further liability for the tax to which such receipt may refer.

P.A. 76–1586, § 3–1002, added by P.A. 81–3, 2nd Sp.Sess., § 18, eff. Jan. 1, 1980. Amended by P.A. 81–1468, § 1, eff. Sept. 9, 1980; P.A. 84–109, Art. 20, § 20–1, eff. July 25, 1985.

Formerly Ill.Rev.Stat.1991, ch. 95 ½, ¶ 3–1002.

5/3–1002.1. False or incomplete returns

§ 3–1002.1. Any person required to file a return under this Article who willfully files a false or incomplete return is guilty of a Class A misdemeanor.

P.A. 76–1586, § 3–1002.1, added by P.A. 84–109, Art. 20, § 20–1, eff. July 25, 1985.

Formerly Ill.Rev.Stat.1991, ch. 95 ½, ¶ 3–1002.1.

Another § 3–1002.1, relating to selling price information, was renumbered as § 3–1002.2 by P.A. 84–1438, Art. II, § 30.

Article II of P.A. 84–1438, the Second 84th General Assembly Combining Revisory Act, provides for the nonsubstantive revision or renumbering or repeal of Sections of Acts necessitated by the amendment, addition or repeal of Sections by two or more 1986 Public Acts, which multiple action was not resolved by one of the 1986 Acts affecting the particular Section and makes technical corrections in Acts of the 84th General Assembly.

5/3–1002.2. Selling price information

§ 3–1002.2. For the purpose of assisting in determining the validity of the "selling price" reported on returns filed with the Department, the Department may furnish the following information to persons with whom the Department has contracted for service related to making such determination: the selling price stated on the return; vehicle identification number; year, make and model name or number of the vehicle; county code; purchase date; and mileage.

P.A. 76–1586, § 3–1002.1, added by P.A. 84–1307, § 1, eff. Aug. 22, 1986. Renumbered § 3–1002.2 and amended by P.A. 84–1438, Art. II, § 30, eff. Dec. 22, 1986.

Formerly Ill.Rev.Stat.1991, ch. 95 ½, ¶ 3–1002.2.

Article II of P.A. 84–1438, the Second 84th General Assembly Combining Revisory Act, provides for the nonsubstantive revision or renumbering or repeal of Sections of Acts necessitated by the amendment, addition or repeal of Sections by two or more 1986 Public Acts, which multiple action was not resolved by one of the 1986 Acts affecting the particular Section and makes technical corrections in Acts of the 84th General Assembly.

5/3–1003. Administration and enforcement; conformity with Use Tax Act

§ 3–1003. The Department shall have full power to administer and enforce this Article; to collect all taxes, penalties and interest due hereunder; to dispose of taxes, penalties and interest so collected in the manner hereinafter provided, and to determine all rights to credit memoranda or refunds arising on account of the erroneous payment of tax penalty or interest hereunder. In the administration of, and compliance with, this Article, the Department and persons who are subject to this Article shall have the same rights, remedies, privileges, immunities, powers and duties, and be subject to the same conditions, restrictions, limitations, penalties and definitions of terms, and employ the same modes of procedure, as are prescribed in the Use Tax Act, as now or hereafter amended,[1] which are not inconsistent with this Article, as fully as if provisions contained in those Sections of the Use Tax Act were set forth in this Article.

In addition to any other penalties imposed under law, any person convicted of violating the provisions of this Article, shall be assessed a fine of $1,000.

P.A. 76-1586, § 3-1003, added by P.A. 81-3, 2nd Sp.Sess., § 18, eff. Jan. 1, 1980. Amended by P.A. 85-444, § 1, eff. Jan. 1, 1988.

Formerly Ill.Rev.Stat.1991, ch. 95 ½, ¶ 3-1003.

[1] 35 ILCS 105/1 et seq.

5/3-1004. Disposition of funds

§ 3-1004. The State Department of Revenue shall, upon collecting any taxes as provided in this Article, pay such taxes over to the General Revenue Fund.

P.A. 76-1586, § 3-1004, added by P.A. 81-3, 2nd Sp.Sess., § 18, eff. Jan. 1, 1980. Amended by P.A. 82-783, Art. IV, § 25, eff. July 13, 1982; P.A. 84-471, § 1, eff. July 1, 1986.

Formerly Ill.Rev.Stat.1991, ch. 95 ½, ¶ 3-1004.

5/3-1005. Rules and regulations

§ 3-1005. The Department shall have the authority to adopt such rules and regulations as are reasonable and necessary to implement the provisions of this Article.

P.A. 76-1586, § 3-1005, added by P.A. 81-3, 2nd Sp.Sess., § 18, eff. Jan. 1, 1980.

Formerly Ill.Rev.Stat.1991, ch. 95 ½, ¶ 3-1005.

5/3-1006. Department

§ 3-1006. For the purposes of this Article, "Department" is the Department of Revenue of the State of Illinois.

P.A. 76-1586, § 3-1006, added by P.A. 81-3, 2nd Sp.Sess., § 18, eff. Jan. 1, 1980.

Formerly Ill.Rev.Stat.1991, ch. 95 ½, ¶ 3-1006.

ARTICLE XI. REPLACEMENT VEHICLE TAX

Date Effective

Article XI was added by P.A. 83-114, § 1, eff. Aug. 19, 1983.

Section

5/3-2001. Imposition of tax

§ 3-2001. A tax of $200 is hereby imposed on the purchase of any passenger car as defined in Section 1-157 of this Code, purchased in Illinois by or on behalf of an insurance company to replace a passenger car of an insured person in settlement of a total loss claim. The tax imposed by this Section shall apply only to that portion of the purchase price of the replacement vehicle paid by the insurance company in settlement of the total loss claim, but not including any portion of such insurance payment which exceeds the market value of the total loss vehicle.

P.A. 76-1586, § 3-2001, added by P.A. 83-114, § 1, eff. Aug. 19, 1983. Amended by P.A. 83-1353, § 1, eff. Sept. 8, 1984.

Formerly Ill.Rev.Stat.1991, ch. 95 ½, ¶ 3-2001.

5/3-2002. Returns from purchaser insurance company or broker; return and payment to secure title; receipts

§ 3-2002. The purchaser insurance company or broker for an insurance company shall file a return with the Department of Revenue on a form prescribed by the Department. Such return shall contain such information as the Department may reasonably require. Such return and payment from the purchaser shall be submitted to the Department after the sale in order to secure the title to the motor vehicle.

When a purchaser pays the tax imposed by Section 3-2001 of this Code, the Department (upon request therefor from such purchaser) shall issue an appropriate receipt to such purchaser showing that he has paid such tax to the Department. Such receipt shall be sufficient to relieve the purchaser from further liability for the tax to which such receipt may refer.

P.A. 76-1586, § 3-2002, added by P.A. 83-114, § 1, eff. Aug. 19, 1983.

Formerly Ill.Rev.Stat.1991, ch. 95 ½, ¶ 3-2002.

5/3-2003. Administration and enforcement; conformity with Use Tax Act

§ 3-2003. The Department shall have full power to administer and enforce this Article; to collect all taxes, penalties and interest due hereunder; to dispose of taxes, penalties and interest so collected in the manner hereinafter provided, and to determine all rights to credit memoranda or refunds arising on account of the erroneous payment of tax penalty or interest hereunder. In the administration of, and compliance with, this Article, the Department and persons who are subject to this Article shall have the same rights, remedies, privileges, immunities, powers and duties, and be subject to the same conditions, restrictions, limitations, penalties and definitions of terms, and employ the same modes of procedure, as are prescribed in the Use Tax Act, as now or hereafter amended,[1] which are not inconsistent with this Article, as fully as if provisions contained in those Sections of the Use Tax Act were set forth in this Article.

P.A. 76-1586, § 3-2003, added by P.A. 83-114, § 1, eff. Aug. 19, 1983.

Formerly Ill.Rev.Stat.1991, ch. 95 ½, ¶ 3-2003.

[1] 35 ILCS 105/1 et seq.

5/3-2004. Disposition of funds

§ 3-2004. The State Department of Revenue shall, upon collecting any taxes as provided in this Article, pay such taxes over to the General Revenue Fund.

P.A. 76-1586, § 3-2004, added by P.A. 83-114, § 1, eff. Aug. 19, 1983. Amended by P.A. 84-471, § 1, eff. July 1, 1986.

Formerly Ill.Rev.Stat.1991, ch. 95 ½, ¶ 3-2004.

5/3–2005. Rules and regulations

§ 3–2005. The Department shall have the authority to adopt such rules and regulations as are reasonable and necessary to implement the provisions of this Article.

P.A. 76–1586, § 3–2005, added by P.A. 83–114, § 1, eff. Aug. 19, 1983.

Formerly Ill.Rev.Stat.1991, ch. 95 ½, ¶ 3–2005.

5/3–2006. Department

§ 3–2006. For the purposes of this Article, "Department" is the Department of Revenue of the State of Illinois.

P.A. 76–1586, § 3–2006, added by P.A. 83–114, § 1, eff. Aug. 19, 1983.

Formerly Ill.Rev.Stat.1991, ch. 95 ½, ¶ 3–2006.

CHAPTER 4. ANTI–THEFT LAWS AND ABANDONED VEHICLES

Enactment

The Illinois Vehicle Code was enacted by P.A. 76–1586, effective July 1, 1970. The Code constitutes a consolidated recodification of various earlier laws and acts including the Illinois Motor Vehicle Law of 1957.

ARTICLE I. ANTI–THEFT LAWS

Section

5/4–100. § 4–100. Repealed by P.A. 90–89, § 20, eff. Jan. 1, 1998

5/4–101. Applicability of this Chapter

§ 4–101. Applicability of this Chapter. The provisions of this Chapter apply to all vehicles.

P.A. 76–1586, § 4–101, eff. July 1, 1970.

Formerly Ill.Rev.Stat.1991, ch. 95 ½, ¶ 4–101.

5/4–102. Offenses relating to motor vehicles and other vehicles—Misdemeanors

§ 4–102. Offenses relating to motor vehicles and other vehicles—Misdemeanors.

(a) It is a violation of this Chapter for:

(1) A person, without authority to do so, to damage a vehicle or to damage or remove any part of a vehicle;

(2) A person, without authority to do so, to tamper with a vehicle or go in it, on it, or work or attempt to work any of its parts, or set or attempt to set it in motion;

(3) A person to fail to report a vehicle as unclaimed in accordance with the provisions of Section 4–107.

(b) Sentence. A person convicted of a violation of this Section shall be guilty of a Class A misdemeanor. A person convicted of a violation of this Section a second or subsequent time, shall be guilty of a Class 4 felony.

P.A. 76–1586, § 4–102, eff. July 1, 1970. Amended by P.A. 78–858, § 1, eff. Jan. 1, 1974; P.A. 81–932, § 1, eff. Sept. 22, 1979; P.A. 83–1473, § 1, eff. Jan. 1, 1985; P.A. 84–1302, § 1, eff. Jan. 1, 1987; P.A. 84–1304, § 1, eff. Jan. 1, 1987; P.A. 86–1209, § 1, eff. Jan. 1, 1991.

Formerly Ill.Rev.Stat.1991, ch. 95 ½, ¶ 4–102.

Validity

The Supreme Court of Illinois has held that provisions of Vehicle Code under which it is a misdemeanor for person who lacks authority or permission to do so to damage or remove any part of, or tamper with, a vehicle, which do not require a culpable mental state, violate the due process clauses of Federal and State Constitutions in the case of In re K.C., 1999, 186 Ill.2d 542, 714 N.E.2d 491, 239 Ill.Dec. 572.

5/4–103. Offenses relating to motor vehicles and other vehicles—Felonies

§ 4–103. Offenses relating to motor vehicles and other vehicles—Felonies.

(a) It is a violation of this Chapter for:

(1) A person not entitled to the possession of a vehicle or essential part of a vehicle to receive, possess, conceal, sell, dispose, or transfer it, knowing it to have been stolen or converted; additionally the General Assembly finds that the acquisition and disposition of vehicles and their essential parts are strictly controlled by law and that such acquisitions and dispositions are reflected by documents of title, uniform invoices, rental contracts, leasing agreements and bills of sale. It may be inferred, therefore that a person exercising exclusive unexplained possession over a stolen or converted vehicle or an essential part of a stolen or converted vehicle has knowledge that such vehicle or essential part is stolen or converted, regardless of whether the date on which such vehicle or essential part was stolen is recent or remote;

(2) A person to knowingly remove, alter, deface, destroy, falsify, or forge a manufacturer's identification number of a vehicle or an engine number of a motor vehicle or any essential part thereof having an identification number;

(3) A person to knowingly conceal or misrepresent the identity of a vehicle or any essential part thereof;

(4) A person to buy, receive, possess, sell or dispose of a vehicle, or any essential part thereof, with knowledge that the identification number of the vehicle or any essential

part thereof having an identification number has been removed or falsified;

(5) A person to knowingly possess, buy, sell, exchange, give away, or offer to buy, sell, exchange or give away, any manufacturer's identification number plate, mylar sticker, federal certificate label, State police reassignment plate, Secretary of State assigned plate, rosette rivet, or facsimile of such which has not yet been attached to or has been removed from the original or assigned vehicle. It is an affirmative defense to subsection (a) of this Section that the person possessing, buying, selling or exchanging a plate mylar sticker or label described in this paragraph is a police officer doing so as part of his official duties, or is a manufacturer's authorized representative who is replacing any manufacturer's identification number plate, mylar sticker or Federal certificate label originally placed on the vehicle by the manufacturer of the vehicle or any essential part thereof;

(6) A person to knowingly make a false report of the theft or conversion of a vehicle to any police officer of this State or any employee of a law enforcement agency of this State designated by the law enforcement agency to take, receive, process, or record reports of vehicle theft or conversion.

(b) Sentence. A person convicted of a violation of this Section shall be guilty of a Class 2 felony.

(c) The offenses set forth in subsection (a) of this Section shall not include the offense set forth in Section 4-103.2 of this Code.

P.A. 76-1586, § 4-103, eff. July 1, 1970. Amended by P.A. 78-858, § 1, eff. Jan. 1, 1974; P.A. 81-932, § 1, eff. Sept. 22, 1979; P.A. 83-830, § 1, eff. Sept. 24, 1983; P.A. 83-1473, § 1, eff. Jan. 1, 1985; P.A. 85-572, § 1, eff. Sept. 18, 1987; P.A. 86-1209, § 1, eff. Jan. 1, 1991; P.A. 90-89, § 15, eff. Jan. 1, 1998; P.A. 91-450, § 5, eff. Jan. 1, 2000.

Formerly Ill.Rev.Stat.1991, ch. 95 ½, ¶ 4-103.

5/4-103.1. Vehicle theft conspiracy

§ 4-103.1 Vehicle theft conspiracy. (a) Elements of the offense. A person commits vehicle theft conspiracy when, with intent that a violation of Section 4-103 of this Code be committed, he agrees with another to the commission of such an offense. No person may be convicted of vehicle theft conspiracy unless an overt act in furtherance of such an agreement is alleged and proved to have been committed by him or by a co-conspirator, and the accused is part of a common plan or scheme to engage in the unlawful activity.

(b) Co-conspirators. It shall not be a defense to vehicle theft conspiracy that the person or persons with whom the accused is alleged to have conspired:

(1) has not been prosecuted or convicted;

(2) has been convicted of a different offense;

(3) is not amenable to justice;

(4) has been acquitted; or

(5) lacked the capacity to commit an offense.

(c) Sentence. Vehicle theft conspiracy to violate Section 4-103 of this Code is a Class 2 felony. Vehicle theft conspiracy to violate Section 4-103.2 of this Code is a Class 1 felony.

P.A. 76-1586, § 4-103.1, added by P.A. 83-830, § 1, eff. Sept. 24, 1983. Amended by P.A. 83-1473, § 1, eff. Jan. 1, 1985; P.A. 86-1209, § 1, eff. Jan. 1, 1991.

Formerly Ill.Rev.Stat.1991, ch. 95 ½, ¶ 4-103.1.

5/4-103.2. Aggravated offenses relating to motor vehicles and other vehicles—Felonies

§ 4-103.2. Aggravated offenses relating to motor vehicles and other vehicles—Felonies.

(a) It is a violation of this Chapter for:

(1) a person not entitled to the possession of 3 or more vehicles, 3 or more essential parts of different vehicles, or a combination thereof, to receive, possess, conceal, sell, dispose of or transfer, those vehicles or parts of vehicles at the same time or within a one year period knowing that these vehicles or parts of vehicles are stolen or converted;

(2) a person to buy, receive, possess, sell or dispose of 3 or more vehicles, 3 or more essential parts of different vehicles, or a combination thereof, at the same time or within a one year period, knowing that the identification numbers of the vehicles or the essential parts with an identification number have been removed or falsified;

(3) a person not entitled to the possession of a vehicle having a value of $25,000 or greater to receive, possess, conceal, sell, dispose or transfer the vehicle, knowing that the vehicle has been stolen or converted;

(4) a person to knowingly possess, buy, sell, exchange or give away, at the same time or within a one year period, 3 or more manufacturer's identification number plates, mylar stickers, federal certificate labels, State Police reassignment plates, Secretary of State assigned plates or a facsimile of those items, or a combination thereof, which have not yet been attached to or have been removed from an original or assigned vehicle or essential part of a vehicle. It is an affirmative defense that the person possessing, buying, selling or exchanging a plate, mylar sticker or label is a police officer doing so as part of his official duties or is a manufacturer's authorized representative who is replacing any manufacturer's identification number plate, mylar sticker or federal certificate label originally placed on a vehicle by the manufacturer of a vehicle or any essential part of a vehicle;

(5) a person not entitled to the possession of any second division vehicle, semitrailer, farm tractor, tow truck, rescue squad vehicle, medical transport vehicle, fire engine, special mobile equipment, dump truck, truck mounted transit mixer, crane or the engine, transmission, cab, cab clip or vehicle cowl of any of the above vehicles, to receive, possess, conceal, sell, dispose of or transfer the vehicle or vehicle part described in this paragraph knowing it is stolen or converted;

(6) a person not entitled to the possession of a vehicle which is owned or operated by a law enforcement agency to receive, possess, conceal, sell, or dispose of or transfer such vehicle knowing it is the property of a law enforcement agency and knowing it to be stolen or converted;

(7) a person:

(A) who is the driver or operator of a vehicle and is not entitled to the possession of that vehicle and who knows the vehicle is stolen or converted, or

(B) who is the driver or operator of a vehicle being used to transport or haul a vehicle or essential part of a vehicle and is not entitled to the possession of that vehicle or essential part being transported or hauled and who knows the transported or hauled vehicle or essential part is stolen or converted,

who has been given a signal by a peace officer directing him to bring the vehicle to a stop, to willfully fail or refuse to obey such direction, increase his speed, extinguish his lights or otherwise flee or attempt to elude the officer. The signal given by the peace officer may be by hand, voice, siren, or red or blue light. The officer giving the signal, if driving a vehicle, shall display the vehicle's illuminated, oscillating, rotating or flashing red or blue lights, which when used in conjunction with an audible horn or siren would indicate that the vehicle is an official police vehicle. Such requirement shall not preclude the use of amber or white oscillating, rotating or flashing lights in conjunction with red or blue oscillating, rotating or flashing lights as required in Section 12-215 of this Code; or

(8) a person, at the same time or within a one year period, to make a false report of the theft or conversion of 3 or more vehicles to any police officer or police officers of this State.

(b) The inference contained in paragraph (1) of subsection (a) of Section 4-103 of this Code shall apply to subsection (a) of this Section.

(c) A person convicted of violating this Section shall be guilty of a Class 1 felony.

(d) The offenses set forth in subsection (a) of this Section shall not include the offenses set forth in Section 4-103 of this Code.

P.A. 76-1586, § 4-103.2, added by P.A. 86-1209, § 1, eff. Jan. 1, 1991.

Formerly Ill.Rev.Stat.1991, ch. 95 ½, ¶ 4-103.2.

5/4-103.3. Organizer of an aggravated vehicle theft conspiracy

§ 4-103.3. Organizer of an aggravated vehicle theft conspiracy.

(a) A person commits the offense of organizer of a vehicle theft conspiracy if:

(1) the person intentionally violates Section 4-103.2 of this Code with the agreement of 3 or more persons; and

(2) the person is known by other co-conspirators as the organizer, supervisor, financier or otherwise leader of the conspiracy.

(b) No person may be convicted of organizer of a vehicle theft conspiracy unless an overt act in furtherance of the agreement is alleged and proved to have been committed by him or by a co-conspirator, and the accused is part of a common plan or scheme to engage in the unlawful activity.

(c) It shall not be a defense to organizer of a vehicle theft conspiracy that the person or persons with whom the accused is alleged to have conspired:

(1) has not been prosecuted or convicted;

(2) has been convicted of a different offense;

(3) is not amenable to justice;

(4) has been acquitted; or

(5) lacked the capacity to commit an offense.

(d) Notwithstanding Section 8-5 of the Criminal Code of 1961,[1] a person may be convicted and sentenced for both the offense of organizer of a vehicle theft conspiracy and any other offense in this Chapter which is the object of the conspiracy.

(e) Organizer of a vehicle theft conspiracy is a Class X felony.

P.A. 76-1586, § 4-103.3, added by P.A. 86-1209, § 1, eff. Jan. 1, 1991.

Formerly Ill.Rev.Stat.1991, ch. 95 ½, ¶ 4-103.3.

[1] 720 ILCS 5/8-5.

5/4-104. Offenses relating to possession of titles and registration

§ 4-104. Offenses relating to possession of titles and registration.

(a) It is a violation of this Chapter for:

1. A person to possess without authority any manufacturers statement of origin, certificate of title, salvage certificate, junking certificate, display certificate of title, registration card, license plate, registration sticker or temporary registration permit, whether blank or otherwise;

2. A person to possess any manufacturers certificate of origin, salvage certificate, junking certificate, certificate of title, display certificate without complete assignment;

3. A person to possess any manufacturers statement of origin, salvage certificate, junking certificate, display certificate or certificate of title, temporary registration permit, registration card, license plate or registration sticker knowing it to have been stolen, converted, altered, forged or counterfeited;

4. A person to display or affix to a vehicle any certificate of title, manufacturers statement of origin, salvage certificate, junking certificate, display certificate, temporary registration permit, registration card, license plate or registration sticker not authorized by law for use on such vehicle;

5. A person to permit another, not entitled thereto, to use or have possession of any manufacturers statement of origin, salvage certificate, junking certificate, display certificate or certificate of title, registration card, license plate, temporary registration permit, or registration sticker;

6. A person to fail to mail or deliver to the proper person within a reasonable period of time after receipt from the Secretary of State, any certificate of title, salvage certificate, junking certificate, display certificate, registration card, temporary registration permit, license plate or registration sticker. If a person mails or delivers reasonable notice to the proper person after receipt from the Secretary of State, a presumption of delivery within a reasonable period of time shall exist; provided, however, the delivery is made, either by mail or otherwise, within 20 days from the date of receipt from the Secretary of State.

(b) Sentence:

1. A person convicted of a violation of subsection 1 or 2 of paragraph (a) of this Section is guilty of a Class 4 felony.

2. A person convicted of a violation of subsection 3 of paragraph (a) of this Section is guilty of a Class 2 felony.

3. A person convicted of a violation of either subsection 4 or 5 of paragraph (a) of this Section is guilty of a Class A misdemeanor and upon a second or subsequent conviction of such a violation is guilty of a Class 4 felony.

4. A person convicted of a violation of subsection 6 of paragraph (a) of this Section is guilty of a petty offense.

P.A. 76-1586, § 4-104, eff. July 1, 1970. Amended by P.A. 78-858, § 1, eff. Jan. 1, 1974; P.A. 80-230, § 1, eff. Oct. 1, 1977; P.A. 81-932, § 1, eff. Sept. 22, 1979; P.A. 83-1473, § 1, eff. Jan. 1, 1985; P.A. 87-854, § 3, eff. May 8, 1992; P.A. 87-1225, § 2, eff. Dec. 22, 1992; P.A. 88-45, Art. II, § 2-54, eff. July 6, 1993.

Formerly Ill.Rev.Stat.1991, ch. 95 ½, ¶ 4-104.

Validity

Provision making it a Class 2 felony for a motor vehicle owner to alter his or her own temporary registration permit has been held unconstitutional by the Illinois Supreme Court in the case of People v. Morris, 136 Ill.2d 157, 554 N.E.2d 235, 143 Ill. Dec. 300 (1990). See Notes of Decisions, post.

P.A. 88–45, Article II, of the First 1993 General Revisory Act, resolved multiple actions in the 87th General Assembly and made certain technical corrections in P.A. 87–895 through P.A. 87–1280.

5/4–105. Offenses relating to disposition of titles and registration

§ 4–105. Offenses relating to disposition of titles and registration. (a) It is a violation of this Chapter for:

1. a person to alter, forge, or counterfeit any manufacturers statement of origin, certificate of title, salvage certificate, junking certificate, display certificate, registration sticker, registration card, or temporary registration permit;

2. a person to alter, forge, or counterfeit an assignment of any manufacturers statement of origin, certificate of title, salvage certificate or junking certificate;

3. a person to alter, forge, or counterfeit a release of a security interest on any manufacturers statement of origin, certificate of title, salvage certificate or junking certificate;

4. a person to alter, forge, or counterfeit an application for any certificate of title, salvage certificate, junking certificate, display certificate, registration sticker, registration card, temporary registration permit or license plate;

5. a person to use a false or fictitious name or address or altered, forged, counterfeited or stolen manufacturer's identification number, or make a material false statement, or fail to disclose a security interest, or conceal any other material fact on any application for any manufacturers statement of origin, certificate of title, junking certificate, salvage certificate, registration card, license plate, temporary registration permit, or registration sticker or commit a fraud in connection with any application under this Act;

6. an unauthorized person to have in his possession a blank Illinois certificate of title paper;

7. a person to surrender or cause to be surrendered any certificate of title, salvage or junking certificate in exchange for a certificate of title or other title document from any other state or foreign jurisdiction for the purpose of changing or deleting an "S.V." or "REBUILT" notation, odometer reading, or any other information contained on such Illinois certificate.

(b) Sentence:

A person convicted of a violation of this Section shall be guilty of a Class 2 felony.

P.A. 76–1586, § 4–105, eff. July 1, 1970. Amended by P.A. 78–858, § 1, eff. Jan. 1, 1974; P.A. 80–230, § 1, eff. Oct. 1, 1977; P.A. 81–932, § 1, eff. Sept. 22, 1979; P.A. 82–131, § 1, eff. Jan. 1, 1982; P.A. 83–1473, § 1, eff. Jan. 1, 1985; P.A. 84–986, § 1, eff. Sept. 25, 1985.

Formerly Ill.Rev.Stat.1991, ch. 95 ½, ¶ 4–105.

5/4–105.1. Offenses relating to deletion or falsification of information on title document

§ 4–105.1. Offenses relating to deletion or falsification of information on title document. (a) It is a violation of this Code for a person to knowingly, with the intent to defraud, surrender or cause to be surrendered any manufacturer's statement of origin, certificate of title, salvage certificate, junking certificate, or other title document, in exchange for a certificate of title or other title document of this State or of any other State or foreign jurisdiction which results in or attempts to result in:

1. The deletion of the words "S.V.", "REBUILT" or similar notation.

2. The falsification of an odometer reading; or

3. The alteration or deletion of any other information required to be contained on such certificate of title or any other title document of any State or foreign jurisdiction.

(b) Presumptions. A title surrendered to another jurisdiction that is subsequently submitted to any person, corporation, or other legal entity, residing or doing business within Illinois, the following presumption shall apply; if the title document fails to contain all of the previous information required by Illinois law, it shall be presumed to have been done so knowingly.

It shall be a rebuttable presumption that any title document surrendered or submitted with a false odometer reading shall be presumed to have been done so knowingly.

(c) Sentence. A person convicted of a violation of this Section shall be guilty of a Class A misdemeanor. A person convicted of violating this Section a second or subsequent time shall be guilty of a Class 3 felony.

P.A. 76–1586, § 4–105.1, added by P.A. 84–986, § 1, eff. Sept. 25, 1985. Amended by P.A. 91–571, § 5, eff. Jan. 1, 2000.

Formerly Ill.Rev.Stat.1991, ch. 95 ½, ¶ 4–105.1.

5/4–105.5. Attempt

§ 4–105.5. Attempt. As defined in Section 8–4 of the Criminal Code of 1961.[1]

P.A. 76–1586, § 4–105.5, added by P.A. 81–932, § 1, eff. Sept. 22, 1979.

Formerly Ill.Rev.Stat.1991, ch. 95 ½, ¶ 4–105.5.

1 720 ILCS 5/8–4.

5/4–106. Principals

§ 4–106. Principals. It shall be a violation of the provisions of this Chapter for a person, whether present or absent, to aid, abet, induce, procure or cause the commission of an act which, if done directly by him, would constitute a violation of the provisions of this Chapter.

P.A. 76–1586, § 4–106, eff. July 1, 1970.

Formerly Ill.Rev.Stat.1991, ch. 95 ½, ¶ 4–106.

5/4–107. Stolen, converted, recovered and unclaimed vehicles

§ 4–107. Stolen, converted, recovered and unclaimed vehicles.

(a) Every Sheriff, Superintendent of police, Chief of police or other police officer in command of any Police department in any City, Village or Town of the State, shall, by the fastest means of communications available to his law enforcement agency, immediately report to the State Police, in Springfield, Illinois, the theft or recovery of any stolen or converted vehicle within his district or jurisdiction. The report shall give the date of theft, description of the vehicle including color, year of manufacture, manufacturer's trade name, manufacturer's series name, body style, vehicle identification number and license registration number, including the state in which the license was issued and the year of issuance, together with the name, residence address, business address, and telephone number of the owner. The report shall be routed by the originating law enforcement agency through the State Police District in which such agency is located.

(b) A registered owner or a lienholder may report the theft by conversion of a vehicle, to the State Police, or any other police department or Sheriff's office. Such report will be accepted as a report of theft and processed only if a formal complaint is on file and a warrant issued.

(c) An operator of a place of business for garaging, repairing, parking or storing vehicles for the public, in which a vehicle remains unclaimed, after being left for the purpose of garaging, repairing, parking or storage, for a period of 15 days, shall, within 5 days after the expiration of that period, report the vehicle as unclaimed to the municipal police when the vehicle is within the corporate limits of any City, Village or incorporated Town, or the County Sheriff, or State Police when the vehicle is outside the corporate limits of a City, Village or incorporated Town. This Section does not apply to any vehicle:

(1) removed to a place of storage by a law enforcement agency having jurisdiction, in accordance with Sections 4–201 and 4–203 of this Act; or

(2) left under a garaging, repairing, parking, or storage order signed by the owner, lessor, or other legally entitled person.

Failure to comply with this Section will result in the forfeiture of storage fees for that vehicle involved.

(d) The State Police shall keep a complete record of all reports filed under this Section of the Act. Upon receipt of such report, a careful search shall be made of the records of the office of the State Police, and where it is found that a vehicle reported recovered was stolen in a County, City, Village or Town other than the County, City, Village or Town in which it is recovered, the State Police shall immediately notify the Sheriff, Superintendent of police, Chief of police, or other police officer in command of the Sheriff's office or Police department of the County, City, Village or Town in which the vehicle was originally reported stolen, giving complete data as to the time and place of recovery.

(e) Notification of the theft or conversion of a vehicle will be furnished to the Secretary of State by the State Police. The Secretary of State shall place the proper information in the license registration and title registration files to indicate the theft or conversion of a motor vehicle or other vehicle. Notification of the recovery of a vehicle previously reported as a theft or a conversion will be furnished to the Secretary of State by the State Police. The Secretary of State shall remove the proper information from the license registration and title registration files that has previously indicated the theft or conversion of a vehicle. The Secretary of State shall suspend the registration of a vehicle upon receipt of a report from the State Police that such vehicle was stolen or converted.

(f) When the Secretary of State receives an application for a certificate of title or an application for registration of a vehicle and it is determined from the records of the office of the Secretary of State that such vehicle has been reported stolen or converted, the Secretary of State shall immediately notify the State Police and shall give the State Police the name and address of the person or firm titling or registering the vehicle, together with all other information contained in the application submitted by such person or firm.

(g) During the usual course of business the manufacturer of any vehicle shall place an original manufacturer's vehicle identification number on all such vehicles manufactured and on any part of such vehicles requiring an identification number.

(h) If a manufacturer's vehicle identification number is missing or has been removed, changed or mutilated on any vehicle, or any part of such vehicle requiring an identification number, the State Police shall restore, restamp or reaffix the vehicle identification number plate, or affix a new plate bearing the original manufacturer's vehicle identification number on each such vehicle and on all necessary parts of the vehicles. A vehicle identification number so affixed, restored, restamped, reaffixed or replaced is not falsified, altered or forged within the meaning of this Act.

(i) If a vehicle or part of any vehicle is found to have the manufacturer' s identification number removed, altered, defaced or destroyed, the vehicle or part shall be seized by any law enforcement agency having jurisdiction and held for the purpose of identification. In the event that the manufacturer's identification number of a vehicle or part cannot be identified, the vehicle or part shall be considered contraband, and no right of property shall exist in any person owning, leasing or possessing such property, unless the person owning, leasing or possessing the vehicle or part acquired such without knowledge that the manufacturer's vehicle identification number has been removed, altered, defaced, falsified or destroyed.

Either the seizing law enforcement agency or the State's Attorney of the county where the seizure occurred may make an application for an order of forfeiture to the circuit court in the county of seizure. The application for forfeiture shall be independent from any prosecution arising out of the seizure and is not subject to any final determination of such prosecution. The circuit court shall issue an order forfeiting the property to the seizing law enforcement agency if the court finds that the property did not at the time of seizure possess a valid manufacturer's identification number and that the original manufacturer's identification number cannot be ascertained. The seizing law enforcement agency may:

(1) retain the forfeited property for official use; or

(2) sell the forfeited property and distribute the proceeds in accordance with Section 4–211 of this Code, or dispose of the forfeited property in such manner as the law enforcement agency deems appropriate.

(i–1) If a motorcycle is seized under subsection (i), the motorcycle must be returned within 45 days of the date of seizure to the person from whom it was seized, unless (i) criminal charges are pending against that person or (ii) an application for an order of forfeiture has been submitted to the circuit in the county of seizure or (iii) the circuit court in the county of seizure has received from the seizing law enforcement agency and has granted a petition to extend, for a single 30 day period, the 45 days allowed for return of the motorcycle. Except as provided in subsection (i–2), a motorcycle returned to the person from whom it was seized must be returned in essentially the same condition it was in at the time of seizure.

(i–2) If any part or parts of a motorcycle seized under subsection (i) are found to be stolen and are removed, the seizing law enforcement agency is not required to replace the part or parts before returning the motorcycle to the person from whom it was seized.

(j) The State Police shall notify the Secretary of State each time a manufacturer's vehicle identification number is affixed, reaffixed, restored or restamped on any vehicle. The Secretary of State shall make the necessary changes or corrections in his records, after the proper applications and fees have been submitted, if applicable.

(k) Any vessel, vehicle or aircraft used with knowledge and consent of the owner in the commission of, or in the attempt to commit as defined in Section 8-4 of the Criminal Code of 1961,[1] an offense prohibited by Section 4-103 of this Chapter, including transporting of a stolen vehicle or stolen vehicle parts, shall be seized by any law enforcement agency. The seizing law enforcement agency may:

(1) return the vehicle to its owner if such vehicle is stolen; or

(2) confiscate the vehicle and retain it for any purpose which the law enforcement agency deems appropriate; or

(3) sell the vehicle at a public sale or dispose of the vehicle in such other manner as the law enforcement agency deems appropriate.

If the vehicle is sold at public sale, the proceeds of the sale shall be paid to the law enforcement agency.

The law enforcement agency shall not retain, sell or dispose of a vehicle under paragraphs (2) or (3) of this subsection (k) except upon an order of forfeiture issued by the circuit court. The circuit court may issue such order of forfeiture upon application of the law enforcement agency or State's Attorney of the county where the law enforcement agency has jurisdiction, or in the case of the Department of State Police or the Secretary of State, upon application of the Attorney General.

The court shall issue the order if the owner of the vehicle has been convicted of transporting stolen vehicles or stolen vehicle parts and the evidence establishes that the owner's vehicle has been used in the commission of such offense.

The provisions of subsection (k) of this Section shall not apply to any vessel, vehicle or aircraft, which has been leased, rented or loaned by its owner, if the owner did not have knowledge of and consent to the use of the vessel, vehicle or aircraft in the commission of, or in an attempt to commit, an offense prohibited by Section 4-103 of this Chapter.

P.A. 76-1586, § 4-107, eff. July 1, 1970. Amended by P.A. 77-65, § 1, eff. July 1, 1971; P.A. 78-858, § 1, eff. Jan. 1, 1974; P.A. 79-866, § 1, eff. Sept. 10, 1975; P.A. 83-830, § 1, eff. Sept. 24, 1983; P.A. 83-1473, § 1, eff. Jan. 1, 1985; P.A. 84-25, Art. IV, § 27, eff. July 18, 1985; P.A. 86-1275, § 1, eff. Jan. 1, 1991; P.A. 89-433, § 5, eff. Dec. 15, 1995; P.A. 92-443, § 5, eff. Jan. 1, 2002.

Formerly Ill.Rev.Stat.1991, ch. 95 ½, ¶ 4-107.

1 720 ILCS 5/8-4.

5/4-108. Violations of this Chapter

§ 4-108. Violations of this Chapter. (a) Any person who violates or aids or abets in the violation of any of the provisions of Section 4-102, 4-103, 4-104 or 4-105 shall be guilty of such offense and be subject to the same sentence as if he had committed the offense himself.

(b) Any person who is convicted of any offense under Chapter 4 of this Act,[1] in addition to any other fines or penalties provided therein, may be required to compensate the victim, if known, involved in the related offense, for any loss that the victim sustains to his person or property.

(c) The amount and method of payment of the compensation award shall be determined at the time of the conviction.

(d) For purposes of this Section, "victim" shall mean the owner or other legally entitled person.

P.A. 76-1586, § 4-108, eff. July 1, 1970. Amended by P.A. 77-2720, § 1, eff. Jan. 1, 1973; P.A. 82-695, § 1, eff. Jan. 1, 1982; P.A. 83-1473, § 1, eff. Jan. 1, 1985.

Formerly Ill.Rev.Stat.1991, ch. 95 ½, ¶ 4-108.

1 625 ILCS 5/4-100 et seq.

5/4-109. Motor Vehicle Theft Prevention Program

§ 4-109. Motor Vehicle Theft Prevention Program. The Secretary of State, in conjunction with the Motor Vehicle Theft Prevention Council, is hereby authorized to establish and operate a Motor Vehicle Theft Prevention Program as follows:

(a) Voluntary program participation.

(b) The registered owner of a motor vehicle interested in participating in the program shall sign an informed consent agreement designed by the Secretary of State under subsection (e) of this Section indicating that the motor vehicle registered to him is not normally operated between the hours of 1:00 a.m. and 5:00 a.m. The form and fee, if any, shall be submitted to the Secretary of State for processing.

(c) Upon processing the form, the Secretary of State shall issue to the registered owner a decal. The registered owner shall affix the decal in a conspicuous place on his motor vehicle as prescribed by the Secretary of State.

(d) Whenever any law enforcement officer shall see a motor vehicle displaying a decal issued under the provisions of subsection (c) of this Section being operated upon the public highways of this State between the hours of 1:00 a.m. and 5:00 a.m., the officer is authorized to stop that motor vehicle and to request the driver to produce a valid driver's license and motor vehicle registration card if required to be carried in the vehicle. Whenever the operator of a motor vehicle displaying a decal is unable to produce the documentation set forth in this Section, the police officer shall investigate further to determine if the person operating the motor vehicle is the registered owner or has the authorization of the owner to operate the vehicle.

(e) The Secretary of State, in consultation with the Director of the Department of State Police and Motor Vehicle Theft Prevention Council, shall design the manner and form of the informed consent agreement required under subsection (b) of this Section and the decal required under subsection (c) of this Section.

(f) The Secretary of State shall provide for the recording of registered owners of motor vehicles who participate in the program. The records shall be available to all law enforcement departments, agencies, and forces. The Secretary of State shall cooperate with and assist all law enforcement officers and other agencies in tracing or examining any questionable motor vehicles in order to determine the ownership of the motor vehicles.

(g) A fee not to exceed $10 may be charged for the informed consent form and decal provided under this Section. The fee, if any, shall be set by the Motor Vehicle Theft Prevention Council and shall be collected by the Secretary of State and deposited into the Motor Vehicle Theft Prevention Trust Fund.

(h) The Secretary of State, in consultation with the Director of the Department of State Police and the Motor Vehicle Theft Prevention Council shall promulgate rules and regulations to effectuate the purposes of this Section.

P.A. 76-1586, § 4-109, added by P.A. 88-128, § 5, eff. Jan. 1, 1994. Amended by P.A. 88-684, § 5, eff. Jan. 24, 1995.

ARTICLE II. ABANDONED, LOST, STOLEN OR UNCLAIMED VEHICLES

Section

5/4–200. § 4–200. Renumbered § 4–201 and amended by P.A. 78–858, § 1, eff. Jan. 1, 1974

5/4–201. Abandonment of vehicles prohibited

§ 4–201. Abandonment of vehicles prohibited.

(a) The abandonment of a vehicle or any part thereof on any highway in this State is unlawful and subject to penalties as set forth under Penalty Section 4–214 of this Chapter.

(b) The abandonment of a vehicle or any part thereof on private or public property, other than a highway, in view of the general public, anywhere in this State is unlawful except on property of the owner or bailee of such abandoned vehicle. A vehicle or any part thereof so abandoned on private property shall be authorized for removal, by a law enforcement agency having jurisdiction, after a waiting period of 7 days or more, or may be removed immediately if determined to be a hazardous dilapidated motor vehicle under Section 11–40–3.1 of the Illinois Municipal Code.[1] A violation of subsections (a) or (b) of this Section is subject to penalties as set forth under Section 4–214 of this Chapter.

(c) A towing service may begin to process an unclaimed vehicle as abandoned by requesting a record search by the Secretary of State up to 10 days after the date of the tow, or any later date acceptable to the Secretary of State. This subsection (c) shall not apply to vehicles towed by order or authorization of a law enforcement agency.

P.A. 76–1586, § 4–200, added by P.A. 76–1437, § 1, eff. July 1, 1970. Renumbered § 4–201 and amended by P.A. 78–858, § 1, eff. Jan. 1, 1974. Amended by P.A. 81–653, § 2, eff. Sept. 14, 1979; P.A. 86–460, § 2, eff. Jan. 1, 1990; P.A. 90–330, § 5, eff. Aug. 8, 1997.

Formerly Ill.Rev.Stat.1991, ch. 95 ½, ¶ 4–201.

[1] 65 ILCS 5/11–40–3.1.

5/4–202. Abandoned, lost, stolen or unclaimed vehicle—Notification to law enforcement agencies

§ 4–202. Abandoned, lost, stolen or unclaimed vehicle—Notification to law enforcement agencies. When an abandoned, lost, stolen or unclaimed vehicle comes into the temporary possession or custody of a person in this State, not the owner of the vehicle, such person shall immediately notify the municipal police when the vehicle is within the corporate limits of any city, village or town having a duly authorized police department, or the State Police or the county sheriff when the vehicle is outside the corporate limits of a city, village or town. Upon receipt of such notification, the municipal police, State Police or county sheriff will authorize a towing service to remove and take possession of the abandoned, lost, stolen or unclaimed vehicle. The towing service will safely keep the towed vehicle and its contents, maintain a record of the tow as set forth in Section 4–204 for law enforcement agencies, until the vehicle is claimed by the owner or any other person legally entitled to possession thereof or until it is disposed of as provided in this Chapter.

P.A. 76–1586, § 4–201, eff. July 1, 1970. Amended by P.A. 76–1437, § 1, eff. July 1, 1970. Renumbered § 4–202 and amended by P.A. 78–858, § 1, eff. Jan. 1, 1974.

Formerly Ill.Rev.Stat.1991, ch. 95 ½, ¶ 4–202.

5/4–203. Removal of motor vehicles or other vehicles; Towing or hauling away

§ 4–203. Removal of motor vehicles or other vehicles; Towing or hauling away.

(a) When a vehicle is abandoned, or left unattended, on a toll highway, interstate highway, or expressway for 2 hours or more, its removal by a towing service may be authorized by a law enforcement agency having jurisdiction.

(b) When a vehicle is abandoned on a highway in an urban district 10 hours or more, its removal by a towing service may be authorized by a law enforcement agency having jurisdiction.

(c) When a vehicle is abandoned or left unattended on a highway other than a toll highway, interstate highway, or expressway, outside of an urban district for 24 hours or more, its removal by a towing service may be authorized by a law enforcement agency having jurisdiction.

(d) When an abandoned, unattended, wrecked, burned or partially dismantled vehicle is creating a traffic hazard because of its position in relation to the highway or its physical appearance is causing the impeding of traffic, its immediate removal from the highway or private property adjacent to the highway by a towing service may be authorized by a law enforcement agency having jurisdiction.

(e) Whenever a peace officer reasonably believes that a person under arrest for a violation of Section 11–501 of this Code or a similar provision of a local ordinance is likely, upon release, to commit a subsequent violation of Section 11–501, or a similar provision of a local ordinance, the arresting officer shall have the vehicle which the person was operating at the time of the arrest impounded for a period of not more than 12 hours after the time of arrest. However, such vehicle may be released by the arresting law enforcement agency prior to the end of the impoundment period if:

(1) the vehicle was not owned by the person under arrest, and the lawful owner requesting such release pos-

sesses a valid operator's license, proof of ownership, and would not, as determined by the arresting law enforcement agency, indicate a lack of ability to operate a motor vehicle in a safe manner, or who would otherwise, by operating such motor vehicle, be in violation of this Code; or

(2) the vehicle is owned by the person under arrest, and the person under arrest gives permission to another person to operate such vehicle, provided however, that the other person possesses a valid operator's license and would not, as determined by the arresting law enforcement agency, indicate a lack of ability to operate a motor vehicle in a safe manner or who would otherwise, by operating such motor vehicle, be in violation of this Code.

(e–5) Whenever a registered owner of a vehicle is taken into custody for operating the vehicle in violation of Section 11–501 of this Code or a similar provision of a local ordinance or Section 6–303 of this Code, a law enforcement officer may have the vehicle immediately impounded for a period not less than:

(1) 24 hours for a second violation of Section 11–501 of this Code or a similar provision of a local ordinance or Section 6–303 of this Code or a combination of these offenses; or

(2) 48 hours for a third violation of Section 11–501 of this Code or a similar provision of a local ordinance or Section 6–303 of this Code or a combination of these offenses.

The vehicle may be released sooner if the vehicle is owned by the person under arrest and the person under arrest gives permission to another person to operate the vehicle and that other person possesses a valid operator's license and would not, as determined by the arresting law enforcement agency, indicate a lack of ability to operate a motor vehicle in a safe manner or would otherwise, by operating the motor vehicle, be in violation of this Code.

(f) Except as provided in Chapter 18a of this Code,[1] the owner or lessor of privately owned real property within this State, or any person authorized by such owner or lessor, or any law enforcement agency in the case of publicly owned real property may cause any motor vehicle abandoned or left unattended upon such property without permission to be removed by a towing service without liability for the costs of removal, transportation or storage or damage caused by such removal, transportation or storage. The towing or removal of any vehicle from private property without the consent of the registered owner or other legally authorized person in control of the vehicle is subject to compliance with the following conditions and restrictions:

1. Any towed or removed vehicle must be stored at the site of the towing service's place of business. The site must be open during business hours, and for the purpose of redemption of vehicles, during the time that the person or firm towing such vehicle is open for towing purposes.

2. The towing service shall within 30 minutes of completion of such towing or removal, notify the law enforcement agency having jurisdiction of such towing or removal, and the make, model, color and license plate number of the vehicle, and shall obtain and record the name of the person at the law enforcement agency to whom such information was reported.

3. If the registered owner or legally authorized person entitled to possession of the vehicle shall arrive at the scene prior to actual removal or towing of the vehicle, the vehicle shall be disconnected from the tow truck and that person shall be allowed to remove the vehicle without interference, upon the payment of a reasonable service fee of not more than one half the posted rate of the towing service as provided in paragraph 6 of this subsection, for which a receipt shall be given.

4. The rebate or payment of money or any other valuable consideration from the towing service or its owners, managers or employees to the owners or operators of the premises from which the vehicles are towed or removed, for the privilege of removing or towing those vehicles, is prohibited. Any individual who violates this paragraph shall be guilty of a Class A misdemeanor.

5. Except for property appurtenant to and obviously a part of a single family residence, and except for instances where notice is personally given to the owner or other legally authorized person in control of the vehicle that the area in which that vehicle is parked is reserved or otherwise unavailable to unauthorized vehicles and they are subject to being removed at the owner or operator's expense, any property owner or lessor, prior to towing or removing any vehicle from private property without the consent of the owner or other legally authorized person in control of that vehicle, must post a notice meeting the following requirements:

a. The notice must be prominently placed at each driveway access or curb cut allowing vehicular access to the property within 5 feet from the public right-of-way line. If there are no curbs or access barriers, the sign must be posted not less than one sign each 100 feet of lot frontage.

b. The notice must indicate clearly, in not less than 2 inch high light-reflective letters on a contrasting background, that unauthorized vehicles will be towed away at the owner's expense.

c. The notice must also provide the name and current telephone number of the towing service towing or removing the vehicle.

d. The sign structure containing the required notices must be permanently installed with the bottom of the sign not less than 4 feet above ground level, and must be continuously maintained on the property for not less than 24 hours prior to the towing or removing of any vehicle.

6. Any towing service that tows or removes vehicles and proposes to require the owner, operator, or person in control of the vehicle to pay the costs of towing and storage prior to redemption of the vehicle must file and keep on record with the local law enforcement agency a complete copy of the current rates to be charged for such services, and post at the storage site an identical rate schedule and any written contracts with property owners, lessors, or persons in control of property which authorize them to remove vehicles as provided in this Section.

7. No person shall engage in the removal of vehicles from private property as described in this Section without filing a notice of intent in each community where he intends to do such removal, and such notice shall be filed at least 7 days before commencing such towing.

8. No removal of a vehicle from private property shall be done except upon express written instructions of the owners or persons in charge of the private property upon which the vehicle is said to be trespassing.

9. Vehicle entry for the purpose of removal shall be allowed with reasonable care on the part of the person or firm towing the vehicle. Such person or firm shall be liable for any damages occasioned to the vehicle if such entry is not in accordance with the standards of reasonable care.

10. When a vehicle has been towed or removed pursuant to this Section, it must be released to its owner or custodian within one half hour after requested, if such request is made during business hours. Any vehicle owner or custodian or agent shall have the right to inspect the vehicle before accepting its return, and no release or waiver of any kind which would release the towing service from liability for damages incurred during the towing and storage may be required from any vehicle owner or other legally authorized person as a condition of release of the vehicle. A detailed, signed receipt showing the legal name of the towing service must be given to the person paying towing or storage charges at the time of payment, whether requested or not.

This Section shall not apply to law enforcement, firefighting, rescue, ambulance, or other emergency vehicles which are marked as such or to property owned by any governmental entity.

When an authorized person improperly causes a motor vehicle to be removed, such person shall be liable to the owner or lessee of the vehicle for the cost or removal, transportation and storage, any damages resulting from the removal, transportation and storage, attorney's fee and court costs.

Any towing or storage charges accrued shall be payable by the use of any major credit card, in addition to being payable in cash.

11. Towing companies shall also provide insurance coverage for areas where vehicles towed under the provisions of this Chapter will be impounded or otherwise stored, and shall adequately cover loss by fire, theft or other risks.

Any person who fails to comply with the conditions and restrictions of this subsection shall be guilty of a Class C misdemeanor and shall be fined not less than $100 nor more than $500.

(g) When a vehicle is determined to be a hazardous dilapidated motor vehicle pursuant to Section 11-40-3.1 of the Illinois Municipal Code,[2] its removal and impoundment by a towing service may be authorized by a law enforcement agency with appropriate jurisdiction.

When a vehicle removal from either public or private property is authorized by a law enforcement agency, the owner of the vehicle shall be responsible for all towing and storage charges.

Vehicles removed from public or private property and stored by a commercial vehicle relocator or any other towing service in compliance with this Section and Sections 4-201 and 4-202 of this Code, shall be subject to a possessor lien for services pursuant to "An Act concerning liens for labor, services, skill or materials furnished upon or storage furnished for chattels", filed July 24, 1941, as amended, and the provisions of Section 1 of that Act relating to notice and implied consent shall be deemed satisfied by compliance with Section 18a-302 and subsection (6) of Section 18a-300. In no event shall such lien be greater than the rate or rates established in accordance with subsection (6) of Section 18a-200 of this Code. In no event shall such lien be increased or altered to reflect any charge for services or materials rendered in addition to those authorized by this Act. Every such lien shall be payable by use of any major credit card, in addition to being payable in cash.

P.A. 76-1586, § 4-202, eff. July 1, 1970. Amended by P.A. 76-1437, § 1, eff. July 1, 1970. Renumbered § 4-203 and amended by 78-858, § 1, eff. Jan. 1, 1974. Amended by P.A. 83-879, § 2, eff. July 1, 1984; P.A. 84-1311, § 1, eff. Aug. 27, 1986; P.A. 85-963, § 1, eff. July 1, 1988; P.A. 85-1237, § 1, eff. Jan. 1, 1989; P.A. 86-460, § 2, eff. Jan. 1, 1990; P.A. 86-820, Art. III, § 3-35, eff. Sept. 7, 1989; P.A. 86-1028, Art. II, § 2-44, eff. Feb. 5, 1990; P.A. 87-531, § 1, eff. Jan. 1, 1992; P.A. 90-738, § 5, eff. Jan. 1, 1999.

Formerly Ill.Rev.Stat.1991, ch. 95 ½, ¶ 4-203.

1 625 ILCS 5/18a-100 et seq.

2 65 ILCS 5/11-40-3.1.

5/4-204. Police tows; reports, release of vehicles, payment

§ 4-204. Police tows; reports, release of vehicles, payment.

When a vehicle is authorized to be towed away as provided in Section 4-202 or 4-203:

(a) The authorization, any hold order, and any release shall be in writing, or confirmed in writing, with a copy given to the towing service.

(b) The police headquarters or office of the law officer authorizing the towing shall keep and maintain a record of the vehicle towed, listing the color, year of manufacture, manufacturer's trade name, manufacturer's series name, body style. Vehicle Identification Number, license plate year and number and registration sticker year and number displayed on the vehicle. The record shall also include the date and hour of tow, location towed from, location towed to, reason for towing and the name of the officer authorizing the tow.

(c) The owner, operator, or other legally entitled person shall be responsible to the towing service for payment of applicable removal, towing, storage, and processing charges and collection costs associated with a vehicle towed or held under order or authorization of a law enforcement agency. If a vehicle towed or held under order or authorization of a law enforcement agency is seized by the ordering or authorizing agency or any other law enforcement or governmental agency and sold, any unpaid removal, towing, storage, and processing charges and collection costs shall be paid to the towing service from the proceeds of the sale. If applicable law provides that the proceeds are to be paid into the treasury of the appropriate civil jurisdiction, then any unpaid removal, towing, storage, and processing charges and collection costs shall be paid to the towing service from the treasury of the civil jurisdiction. That payment shall not, however, exceed the amount of proceeds from the sale, with the balance to be paid by the owner, operator, or other legally entitled person.

(d) Upon delivery of a written release order to the towing service, a vehicle subject to a hold order shall be released to the owner, operator, or other legally entitled person upon proof of ownership or other entitlement and upon payment of applicable removal, towing, storage, and processing charges and collection costs.

P.A. 76-1586, § 4-203, eff. July 1, 1970. Amended by P.A. 76-1437, § 1, eff. July 1, 1970. Renumbered § 4-204 and amended by P.A. 78-858, § 1, eff. Jan. 1, 1974. Amended by P.A. 80-230, § 1, eff. Oct. 1, 1977; P.A. 89-433, § 5, eff. Dec. 15, 1995.

Formerly Ill.Rev.Stat.1991, ch. 95 ½, ¶ 4-204.

5/4-205. Record searches

§ 4-205. Record searches.

(a) When a law enforcement agency authorizing the impounding of a vehicle does not know the identity of the registered owner, lienholder or other legally entitled person, that law enforcement agency will cause the vehicle registration records of the State of Illinois to be searched by the Secretary of State for the purpose of obtaining the required ownership information.

(b) The law enforcement agency authorizing the impounding of a vehicle will cause the stolen motor vehicle files of the State Police to be searched by a directed communication to the State Police for stolen or wanted information on the vehicle. When the State Police files are searched with negative results, the information contained in the National Crime Information Center (NCIC) files will be searched by the State Police. The information determined from these record searches will be returned to the requesting law enforcement agency for that agency's use in sending a notification by certified mail to the registered owner, lienholder and other legally entitled persons advising where the vehicle is held, requesting a disposition be made and setting forth public sale information. Notification shall be sent no later than 10 business days after the date the law enforcement agency impounds or authorizes the impounding of a vehicle, provided that if the law enforcement agency is unable to determine the identity of the registered owner, lienholder or other person legally entitled to ownership of the impounded vehicle within a 10 business day period after impoundment, then notification shall be sent no later than 2 days after the date the identity of the registered owner, lienholder or other person legally entitled to ownership of the impounded vehicle is determined. Exceptions to a notification by certified mail to the registered owner, lienholder and other legally entitled persons are set forth in Section 4–209 of this Code.

(c) When ownership information is needed for a towing service to give notification as required under this Code, the towing service may cause the vehicle registration records of the State of Illinois to be searched by the Secretary of State.

The written request of a towing service, in the form and containing the information prescribed by the Secretary of State by rule, may be transmitted to the Secretary of State in person, by U.S. mail or other delivery service, by facsimile transmission, or by other means the Secretary of State deems acceptable.

The Secretary of State shall provide the required information, or a statement that the information was not found in the vehicle registration records of the State, by U.S. mail or other delivery service, facsimile transmission, as requested by the towing service, or by other means acceptable to the Secretary of State.

(d) The Secretary of State may prescribe standards and procedures for submission of requests for record searches and replies via computer link.

(e) Fees for services provided under this Section shall be in amounts prescribed by the Secretary of State under Section 3–821.1 of this Code. Payment may be made by the towing service using cash, any commonly accepted credit card, or any other means of payment deemed acceptable by the Secretary of State.

P.A. 76–1586, § 4–204, eff. July 1, 1970. Amended by P.A. 76–1437, § 1, eff. July 1, 1970. Renumbered § 4–205 and amended by P.A. 78–858, § 1, eff. Jan. 1, 1974. Amended by P.A. 82–363, § 1, eff. Jan. 1, 1982; P.A. 84–402, § 1, eff. Jan. 1, 1986; P.A. 86–947, § 2, eff. Nov. 13, 1989; P.A. 89–179, § 5, eff. Jan. 1, 1996; P.A. 89–433, § 5, eff. Dec. 15, 1995.

Formerly Ill.Rev.Stat.1991, ch. 95 ½, ¶ 4–205.

P.A. 89–433 incorporated the amendment by P.A. 89–179.

5/4–206. Identifying and tracing of vehicle ownership by Illinois State Police

§ 4–206. Identifying and tracing of vehicle ownership by Illinois State Police. When the registered owner, lienholder or other person legally entitled to the possession of a vehicle cannot be identified from the registration files of this State or from the registration files of a foreign state, if applicable, the law enforcement agency having custody of the vehicle shall notify the State Police, for the purpose of identifying the vehicle owner or other person legally entitled to the possession of the vehicle. The information obtained by the State Police will be immediately forwarded to the law enforcement agency having custody of the vehicle for notification purposes as set forth in Section 4–205 of this Code.

P.A. 76–1586, § 4–205, eff. July 1, 1970. Amended by P.A. 76–1437, § 1, eff. July 1, 1970. Renumbered § 4–206 and amended by P.A. 78–858, § 1, eff. Jan. 1, 1974. Amended by P.A. 82–363, § 1, eff. Jan. 1, 1982.

Formerly Ill.Rev.Stat.1991, ch. 95 ½, ¶ 4–206.

5/4–207. Reclaimed vehicles; expenses

§ 4–207. Reclaimed vehicles; expenses.

(a) Any time before a vehicle is sold at public sale or disposed of as provided in Section 4–208, the owner, lienholder or other person legally entitled to its possession may reclaim the vehicle by presenting to the law enforcement agency having custody of the vehicle proof of ownership or proof of the right to possession of the vehicle.

(b) No vehicle shall be released to the owner, lienholder, or other person under this Section until all towing, storage, and processing charges have been paid.

P.A. 76–1586, § 4–206, eff. July 1, 1970. Amended by P.A. 76–1437, § 1, eff. July 1, 1970. Renumbered § 4–207 and amended by P.A. 78–858, § 1, eff. Jan. 1, 1974. Amended by P.A. 82–363, § 1, eff. Jan. 1, 1982; P.A. 89–433, § 5, eff. Dec. 15, 1995.

Formerly Ill.Rev.Stat.1991, ch. 95 ½, ¶ 4–207.

5/4–208. Disposal of unclaimed vehicles

§ 4–208. Disposal of unclaimed vehicles.

(a) In cities having a population of more than 500,000, whenever an abandoned, lost, stolen or unclaimed vehicle, or vehicle determined to be a hazardous dilapidated motor vehicle pursuant to Section 11–40–3.1 of the Illinois Municipal Code,[1] remains unclaimed by the registered owner, lienholder or other legally entitled person for a period of 15 days after notice has been given under Sections 4–205 and 4–206 of this Code, the vehicle shall be disposed, pursuant to the provisions of the "Municipal purchasing act for cities of 500,000 or more population", to a person licensed as an automotive parts recycler, rebuilder or scrap processor under Chapter 5 of this Code.[2]

(b) Except as provided in Section 4–208 for cities with more than 500,000 inhabitants, when an abandoned, lost, stolen or unclaimed vehicle 7 years of age or newer remains unclaimed by the registered owner, lienholder or other legally entitled persons for a period of 30 days after notice has been given as provided in Sections 4–205 and 4–206 of this Code, the law enforcement agency or towing service having possession of the vehicle shall cause it to be sold at public auction to a person licensed as an automotive parts recycler, rebuilder or scrap processor under Chapter 5 of this Code or the towing operator which towed the vehicle. Notice of the time and place of the sale shall be posted in a conspicuous place for at least 10 days prior to the sale on the premises where the vehicle has been impounded. At least 10 days prior to the sale, the law enforcement agency where the vehicle is impounded, or the towing service where the vehicle is impounded, shall cause a notice of the time and place of the sale to be sent by certified mail to the registered owner, lienholder, or other legally entitled persons. Notice as provided in Sections 4-205 and 4-206 of this Code and as provided in this subsection (b) shall state the time and place of sale and shall contain a complete description of the vehicle to be sold and what steps must be taken by any legally entitled person to reclaim the vehicle.

(c) If an abandoned, lost, stolen, or unclaimed vehicle displays dealer plates, notice under this Section and Section 4-209 of this Code shall be sent to both the dealer and the registered owner, lienholder, or other legally entitled persons.

(d) In those instances where the certified notification specified in Sections 4-205 and 4-206 of this Code has been returned by the postal authorities to the law enforcement agency or towing service, the sending of a second certified notice will not be required.

P.A. 76-1586, § 4-207, eff. July 1, 1970. Amended by P.A. 76-1437, § 1, eff. July 1, 1970. Renumbered § 4-208 and amended by P.A. 78-858, § 1, eff. Jan. 1, 1974. Amended by P.A. 82-363, § 1, eff. Jan. 1, 1982; P.A. 83-1473, § 1, eff. Jan. 1, 1985; P.A. 84-1302, § 1, eff. Jan. 1, 1987; P.A. 84-1304, § 1, eff. Jan. 1, 1987; P.A. 86-460, § 2, eff. Jan. 1, 1990; P.A. 86-1260, § 1, eff. Jan. 1, 1991; P.A. 89-433, § 5, eff. Dec. 15, 1995; P.A. 90-330, § 5, eff. Aug. 8, 1997.

Formerly Ill.Rev.Stat.1991, ch. 95 ½, ¶ 4-208.

1 65 ILCS 5/11-40-3.1.

2 625 ILCS 5/5-100 et seq.

5/4-209. Disposal of unclaimed vehicles more than 7 years of age; disposal of abandoned or unclaimed vehicles without notice

§ 4-209. Disposal of unclaimed vehicles more than 7 years of age; disposal of abandoned or unclaimed vehicles without notice.

(a) When the identity of the registered owner, lienholder, or other legally entitled persons of an abandoned, lost, or unclaimed vehicle of 7 years of age or newer cannot be determined by any means provided for in this Chapter, the vehicle may be sold as provided in Section 4-208 without notice to any person whose identity cannot be determined.

(b) When an abandoned vehicle of more than 7 years of age is impounded as specified by this Chapter, or when any such vehicle is towed at the request or with the consent of the owner or operator and is subsequently abandoned, it will be kept in custody or storage for a minimum of 10 days for the purpose of determining the identity of the registered owner, lienholder, or other legally entitled persons and contacting the registered owner, lienholder, or other legally entitled persons by the U. S. Mail, public service or in person for a determination of disposition; and, an examination of the State Police stolen vehicle files for theft and wanted information. At the expiration of the 10 day period, without the benefit of disposition information being received from the registered owner, lienholder, or other legally entitled persons, the vehicle may be disposed of in either of the following ways:

(1) The law enforcement agency having jurisdiction will authorize the disposal of the vehicle as junk or salvage.

(2) The towing service may sell the vehicle in the manner provided in Section 4-208 of this Code, provided that this paragraph (2) shall not apply to vehicles towed by order or authorization of a law enforcement agency.

(c) A vehicle classified as an antique vehicle, custom vehicle, or street rod may however be sold to a person desiring to restore it.

P.A. 76-1586, § 4-208, eff. July 1, 1970. Amended by P.A. 78-738, § 1, eff. Jan. 1, 1974. Renumbered § 4-209 and amended by P.A. 78-858, § 1, eff. Jan. 1, 1974. Amended by P.A. 78-1205, § 1, eff. Sept. 5, 1974; P.A. 78-1297, § 58, eff. March 4, 1975; P.A. 81-653, § 2, eff. Sept. 14, 1979; P.A. 82-363, § 1, eff. Jan. 1, 1982; P.A. 83-449, § 1, eff. Jan. 1, 1984; P.A. 85-951, § 1, eff. July 1, 1988; P.A. 86-1260, § 1, eff. Jan. 1, 1991; P.A. 89-433, § 5, eff. Dec. 15, 1995; P.A. 92-668, § 5, eff. Jan. 1, 2003.

Formerly Ill.Rev.Stat.1991, ch. 95 ½, ¶ 4-209.

Validity

Provision for post-tow notice by U.S. mail to owner of impounded vehicle more than 7 years old has been held unconstitutional by the U.S. District Court, Northern District of Illinois, in the case of Kohn v. Mucia, N.D. Ill.1991, 776 F.Supp. 348. See Notes of Decisions.

5/4-209.1. Disposal of hazardous dilapidated motor vehicles

§ 4-209.1. Disposal of hazardous dilapidated motor vehicles. Any hazardous dilapidated motor vehicle impounded pursuant to the provisions of this Article and Section 11-40-3.1 of the Illinois Municipal Code,[1] whether impounded at a public facility or on the property of private towing service, shall be kept in custody for a period of 10 days for the purpose of determining the identity of the registered owner or lienholder and contacting such owner or lienholder, if known, by regular U.S. Mail. At the expiration of the 10-day period, without benefit of disposition information being received from the registered owner or lienholder, the law enforcement agency having jurisdiction will authorize the disposal of the vehicle as junk.

P.A. 76-1586, § 4-209.1, added by P.A. 86-460, § 2, eff. Jan. 1, 1990.

Formerly Ill.Rev.Stat.1991, ch. 95 ½, ¶ 4-209.1.

1 65 ILCS 5/11-40-3.1.

5/4-209.2. Collection of unpaid charges

§ 4-209.2. Collection of unpaid charges. In an action to collect towing, storage, and processing charges that remain unpaid after disposition of a vehicle towed or relocated under this Code, the towing service may recover reasonable collection costs.

P.A. 76-1586, § 4-209.2, added by P.A. 89-433, § 5, eff. Dec. 15, 1995.

5/4-210. Police reports after vehicle is reclaimed or disposed of

§ 4-210. Police reports after vehicle is reclaimed or disposed of. When a vehicle in the custody of a law enforcement agency is reclaimed by the registered owner, lienholder or other legally entitled person, or when the vehicle is sold at public sale or otherwise disposed of as provided in this Chapter, a report of the transaction will be maintained by that law enforcement agency for a period of one year from the date of the sale or disposal.

P.A. 76-1586, § 4-210, eff. July 1, 1970. Amended by P.A. 76-1437, § 1, eff. July 1, 1970; P.A. 78-858, § 1, eff. Jan. 1, 1974; P.A. 82-363, § 1, eff. Jan. 1, 1982.

Formerly Ill.Rev.Stat.1991, ch. 95 ½, ¶ 4-210.

5/4-211. Disposition of proceeds of sale of unclaimed vehicles

§ 4-211. Disposition of proceeds of sale of unclaimed vehicles. (a) When a vehicle located within the corporate limits of a city, village or town is authorized to be towed away by a law enforcement agency having jurisdiction and disposed of as set forth in this Chapter, the proceeds of the public sale or disposition after the deduction of towing, storage and processing charges shall be deposited in the treasury of such city, village or town.

(b) When a vehicle located outside the corporate limits of a city, village, or town is authorized to be towed away by a law enforcement agency having jurisdiction and disposed of as set forth in this Chapter, the proceeds of the public sale or disposition, after deducting towing, storage and processing costs shall be deposited in the county treasury of the county where the vehicle was located at the time of the tow.

(c) The provisions of this Section shall not apply to vehicles disposed of or sold at public sale under subsection (k) of Section 4-107 of this Code.

P.A. 76-1586, § 4-211, eff. July 1, 1970. Amended by P.A. 76-1437, § 1, eff. July 1, 1970; P.A. 83-830, § 1, eff. Sept. 24, 1983.

Formerly Ill.Rev.Stat.1991, ch. 95 ½, ¶ 4-211.

5/4-212. Ownership documents for vehicles after public sale—removal of liens

§ 4-212. Ownership documents for vehicles after public sale—removal of liens.

When an applicant for a salvage certificate or junking certificate under this Chapter presents to the Secretary of State proof that he has purchased or acquired a vehicle at a public sale as authorized by this Chapter and such fact is certified to by the law enforcement agency having jurisdiction over the public sale of a vehicle, the Secretary of State shall issue a salvage certificate or junking certificate for the vehicle upon receipt of the statutory fee and a properly executed application for a salvage certificate or junking certificate. The salvage certificate or junking certificate issued by the Secretary of State under this Section shall be free of any lien that existed against the vehicle prior to the time the vehicle was acquired by the applicant under this Chapter.

P.A. 76-1586, § 4-212, eff. July 1, 1970. Amended by P.A. 76-1437, § 1, eff. July 1, 1970; P.A. 78-858, § 1, eff. Jan. 1, 1974; P.A. 85-951, § 1, eff. July 1, 1988.

Formerly Ill.Rev.Stat.1991, ch. 95 ½, ¶ 4-212.

5/4-212.1. Department to perform duties related to abandoned, lost, stolen or unclaimed vehicles

§ 4-212.1. In cities with more than 500,000 inhabitants, the corporate authorities may, by ordinance, designate any department of municipal government to do any of the following:

(1) To perform any of the duties and functions specified for law enforcement agencies in subsection (a) of Section 4-205 and in Sections 4-201, 4-203, 4-204, 4-206, 4-207, 4-208, 4-209, 4-210, 4-211 and 4-212; and

(2) To authorize a towing service to remove and take possession of abandoned, lost, stolen or unclaimed vehicles, in the manner that municipal police may make such authorization pursuant to Section 4-202; and

(3) To send notifications as required under subsection (b) of Section 4-205.

P.A. 76-1586, § 4-212.1, added by P.A. 86-947, § 2, eff. Nov. 13, 1989.

Formerly Ill.Rev.Stat.1991, ch. 95 ½, ¶ 4-212.1.

5/4-213. Liability of law enforcement officers, agencies, and towing services

§ 4-213. Liability of law enforcement officers, agencies, and towing services.

(a) A law enforcement officer or agency, a department of municipal government designated under Section 4-212.1 or its officers or employees, or a towing service owner, operator, or employee shall not be held to answer or be liable for damages in any action brought by the registered owner, former registered owner, or his legal representative, lienholder or any other person legally entitled to the possession of a vehicle when the vehicle was processed and sold or disposed of as provided by this Chapter.

(b) A towing service, and any of its officers or employees, that removes or tows a vehicle as a result of being directed to do so by a law enforcement officer or agency or a department of municipal government or its officers or employees shall not be held to answer or be liable for injury to, loss of, or damages to any real or personal property that occurs in the course of the removal or towing of a vehicle or its contents on a limited access highway in a designated Incident Management Program that uses fast lane clearance techniques as defined by the Department of Transportation.

P.A. 76-1586, § 4-213, eff. July 1, 1970. Amended by P.A. 76-1437, § 1, eff. July 1, 1970; P.A. 78-858, § 1, eff. Jan. 1, 1974; P.A. 82-363, § 1, eff. Jan. 1, 1982; P.A. 86-947, § 2, eff. Nov. 13, 1989; P.A. 89-433, § 5, eff. Dec. 15, 1995.

Formerly Ill.Rev.Stat.1991, ch. 95 ½, ¶ 4-213.

5/4-214. Violations of section 4-201

§ 4-214. Violations of Section 4-201.

(a) Any person who violates Section 4-201 of this Code or who aids and abets in that violation:

(1) shall be subject to a mandatory fine of $200; and

(2) shall be required by the court to make a disposition on the abandoned or unclaimed vehicle and pay all towing, storage, and processing charges and collection costs pursuant to Section 4-203, subsections (a) and (e).

(b) When a vehicle is abandoned, it shall be presumed that the last registered owner is responsible for the abandonment and shall be liable for all towing, storage, and processing charges and collection costs, less any amounts realized in the disposal of the vehicle. The last registered owner's liability for storage fees may not exceed a maximum of 30 days' storage fees.

The presumption established under this subsection may be rebutted by a showing that, prior to the time of the tow:

(1) a report of vehicle theft was filed with respect to the vehicle; or

(2) the vehicle was sold or transferred and the last registered owner provides the towing service with the

correct identity and address of the new owner at the time of the sale or transfer.

If the presumption established under this subsection is rebutted, the person responsible for theft of the vehicle or to whom the vehicle was sold or transferred is liable for all towing, storage, and processing charges and collection costs.

P.A. 76-1586, § 4-214, added by P.A. 76-1437, § 1, eff. July 1, 1970. Amended by P.A. 77-2720, § 1, eff. Jan. 1, 1973; P.A. 85-963, § 1, eff. July 1, 1988; P.A. 86-460, § 2, eff. Jan. 1, 1990; P.A. 89-433, § 5, eff. Dec. 15, 1995.

Formerly Ill.Rev.Stat.1991, ch. 95 ½, ¶ 4-214.

5/4-214.1. Failure to pay fines, charges, and costs on an abandoned vehicle

§ 4-214.1. Failure to pay fines, charges, and costs on an abandoned vehicle.

(a) Whenever any resident of this State fails to pay any fine, charge, or cost imposed for a violation of Section 4-201 of this Code, or a similar provision of a local ordinance, the clerk may notify the Secretary of State, on a report prescribed by the Secretary, and the Secretary shall prohibit the renewal, reissue, or reinstatement of the resident's driving privileges until the fine, charge, or cost has been paid in full. The clerk shall provide notice to the driver, at the driver's last known address as shown on the court's records, stating that the action will be effective on the 46th day following the date of the above notice if payment is not received in full by the court of venue.

(b) Following receipt of the report from the clerk, the Secretary of State shall make the proper notation to the driver's file to prohibit the renewal, reissue, or reinstatement of the driver's driving privileges. Except as provided in subsection (d) of this Section, the notation shall not be removed from the driver's record until the driver satisfies the outstanding fine, charge, or cost and an appropriate notice on a form prescribed by the Secretary is received by the Secretary from the court of venue, stating that the fine, charge, or cost has been paid in full. Upon payment in full of a fine, charge, or court cost which has previously been reported under this Section as unpaid, the clerk of the court shall present the driver with a signed receipt containing the seal of the court indicating that the fine, charge, or cost has been paid in full, and shall forward immediately to the Secretary of State a notice stating that the fine, charge, or cost has been paid in full.

(c) Notwithstanding the receipt of a report from the clerk as prescribed in subsection (a), nothing in this Section is intended to place any responsibility upon the Secretary of State to provide independent notice to the driver of any potential action to disallow the renewal, reissue, or reinstatement of the driver's driving privileges.

(d) The Secretary of State shall renew, reissue, or reinstate a driver's driving privileges which were previously refused under this Section upon presentation of an original receipt which is signed by the clerk of the court and contains the seal of the court indicating that the fine, charge, or cost has been paid in full. The Secretary of State shall retain the receipt for his or her records.

P.A. 76-1586, § 4-214.1, added by P.A. 92-654, § 5, eff. Jan. 1, 2003.

5/4-215. Rebuilt vehicles; clean titles

§ 4-215. Rebuilt vehicles; clean titles. Persons licensed under Section 5-301 of this Code may obtain a certificate of title that does not bear the notation "REBUILT" from a certificate of purchase when the damage to the vehicle is 25% or less of its market value, there has been no structural damage to the vehicle, there is no history of a salvage certificate, and the vehicle has undergone a salvage inspection by the Secretary of State and a safety inspection under Section 13-101 of this Code. The application for a certificate of title shall contain an affirmation under penalty for perjury that the vehicle on the date of the application is not damaged in excess of 25% of its market value, has no structural damage, and has no history of salvage.

P.A. 76-1586, § 4-215, added by P.A. 89-433, § 5, eff. Dec. 15, 1995.

ARTICLE III. VEHICLE RECYCLING BOARD

Date Effective

Article 3 was added by P.A. 78-857, effective September 14, 1973.

5/4-300. Definitions

§ 4-300. Definitions. For the purposes of this Article, the following word shall have the meaning ascribed to it as follows:

Board. The Vehicle Recycling Board of the State of Illinois, acting directly or through its duly authorized officers and agents.

P.A. 76-1586, § 4-300, added by P.A. 78-857, § 1, eff. Sept. 14, 1973.

Formerly Ill.Rev.Stat.1991, ch. 95 ½, ¶ 4-300.

5/4-301. State policy

§ 4-301. State policy. The General Assembly finds that abandoned and derelict vehicles: constitute a safety hazard and a public nuisance; are detrimental to the health, safety and welfare of the general public by harboring disease, providing breeding places for vermin, inviting plundering, creating fire hazards, and presenting physical dangers to children and others; produce scenic blights which degrade the environment and adversely affect land values and the proper maintenance and continuing development of the State of Illinois and all of its subdivisions; represent a resource out of place and an energy loss to the Illinois economy, and require state and local governmental attention, in conjunction with any federal governmental attention, in order to assure the expeditious removal and recycling of these abandoned and derelict vehicles.

The General Assembly declares therefore, that it is the policy of the State of Illinois, to:

1. Prohibit the abandonment of vehicles and the retention of derelicts, and to enforce such prohibition by law while reminding vehicle owners of their own individual responsibility to dispose of such vehicles;

2. Encourage the development of procedures and techniques to facilitate the expeditious removal of abandoned and derelict vehicles from public or private premises;

3. Encourage the State of Illinois and all of its political subdivisions, in cooperation with the federal government and the private sector of our State, and in cooperation with other states of the United States, to recover and recycle the resource represented by abandoned and derelict vehicles to the fullest extent practicable.

P.A. 76-1586, § 4-301, added by P.A. 78-857, § 1, eff. Sept. 14, 1973. Amended by P.A. 81-653, § 2, eff. Sept. 14, 1979.

Formerly Ill.Rev.Stat.1991, ch. 95 ½, ¶ 4-301.

5/4-302. Vehicle Recycling Board

§ 4-302. Vehicle Recycling Board. There is hereby created the Vehicle Recycling Board of the State of Illinois composed of the Secretary of Transportation, the Director of State Police, the Director of Public Health, the Director of the Environmental Protection Agency, the Superintendent of State Troopers or their designated representatives. The Governor shall designate the Chairman and Secretary of the Board.

The Board shall appoint an advisory committee, of no less than 10 members, to include an official representative of the Office of the Secretary of State as designated by the Secretary; and other appropriate representatives from such sources as: statewide associations of city, county and township governing bodies; knowledgeable successful leaders from the auto recycling private sector; the State associations of chiefs of police, county sheriffs, police officers; and State agencies having a direct or indirect relationship with vehicle recycling.

P.A. 76-1586, § 4-302, added by P.A. 78-857, § 1, eff. Sept. 14, 1973. Amended by P.A. 81-653, § 2, eff. Sept. 14, 1979; P.A. 84-25, Art. IV, § 27, eff. July 18, 1985.

Formerly Ill.Rev.Stat.1991, ch. 95 ½, ¶ 4-302.

5/4-303. Tenure, vacancies and expenses

§ 4-303. Tenure, vacancies and expenses. State officers and their designated representatives on the Board and representatives of the State agencies serving on the advisory committee, shall serve without additional compensation and their necessary expenses shall be borne by the State office or agency represented. Members of the advisory committee shall be reimbursed for their necessary expenses in their attendance to meetings and functions as required by the Board.

The Board shall employ such personnel as deemed necessary by the Board to implement and administer this Act and any expenses incurred in its administration may be incurred and expended only within and pursuant to the appropriations made by the General Assembly.

The records of the Board shall be subject to audit by the Auditor General.

P.A. 76-1586, § 4-303, added by P.A. 78-857, § 1, eff. Sept. 14, 1973. Amended by P.A. 81-653, § 2, eff. Sept. 14, 1979.

Formerly Ill.Rev.Stat.1991, ch. 95 ½, ¶ 4-303.

5/4-304. Implementation and administration of policy

§ 4-304. Implementation and administration of policy. The Board shall consider and adopt such programs as are designed to implement and administer the policies hereinbefore expressed and within the appropriations provided for by the General Assembly.

In adopting such programs, the Board shall take into consideration the programs of the federal government in the same field, so as to assure full coordination therewith and that the State of Illinois does not duplicate federal actions and programs. The programs to be considered by the Board shall in addition be designed to:

1. Effect the efficient removal of abandoned vehicles from the highways, streets, roads, other public property, as well as from private property within Illinois.

2. Effect the efficient removal of abandoned and derelict vehicles from private property to be junked, salvaged, recycled, or reclaimed, to wrecking, recycling or salvaging facilities, or to a temporary impoundment or area collection center.

3. Effect efficient recycling or scrap processing of retired vehicles and the salvaging of usable parts.

4. Permit the restoration of antique and historic vehicles by private persons or agencies.

5. Work with other State agencies to effect the efficient and effective recycling of solid and liquid motor vehicle waste, including motor vehicle drain oil, derived in the recycling of a motor vehicle.

6. Recoup the costs of removal and disposal of abandoned and derelict vehicles from vehicle owners, land owners and persons who abandon or discard such vehicles and from other suitable sources.

7. Promote and publicize individual responsibility of vehicle owners for their personal disposal of unwanted and discarded vehicles and develop an effective promotional campaign to show owners how to properly dispose of such vehicles; and the legal consequences of not doing so.

8. Provide State coordination, expertise and assistance to all local units of government, as needed, seeking legislative remedy where appropriate regarding: vehicle detitling procedure; impoundment time periods; the legal restrictions unnecessarily delaying vehicle disposal; and, to promote and advance the technology, growth and development of the legitimate auto recycling industry to the end that this industry can effectively recycle all vehicles annually retired and accumulated in Illinois with a minimum of assistance from the State or its subdivisions.

The Board is empowered to negotiate and enter into reciprocal agreements with other states and State and federal agencies, in furtherance of the provisions of this Act, as amended; provided, however, that no such reciprocal agreement may be entered into without the approval and authorization of the State body legally required to approve such agreements.

The Board shall make rules, regulations and by-laws, not inconsistent with this Act or any other law of this State, as to its own organization and conduct and for the implementation and administration of this Act.

The Board is further empowered to enter into an agreement with any State agency represented on the Board, to carry out the administration of the abandoned and derelict vehicle abatement program of the Board, and to make such funds available as may be found necessary by the Board, as appropriated by the General Assembly.

P.A. 76-1586, § 4-304, added by P.A. 78-857, § 1, eff. Sept. 14, 1973. Amended by P.A. 81-653, § 2, eff. Sept. 14, 1979; P.A. 84-470, § 1, eff. Sept. 17, 1985; P.A. 90-655, § 153, eff. July 30, 1998; P.A. 91-357, § 231, eff. July 29, 1999.

Formerly Ill.Rev.Stat.1991, ch. 95 ½, ¶ 4-304.

5/4–305. Inventory, collection and disposal facilities

§ 4–305. Inventory, collection and disposal facilities. If not otherwise economically practicable, the Board may provide by contract with private persons or agencies, or with political subdivisions of the State of Illinois and all local governmental units of government, for the inventory, collection and disposal or any portion thereof, of abandoned and derelict vehicles to wrecking, salvage or recycling plants, or, provide facilities for the collection and proper disposal of any vehicle under the provisions of this Act, as amended.

The Board may further formulate a program, statewide or within prescribed areas, for the inventory and collection of abandoned and derelict vehicles and to provide for their junking, salvage or recycling. In all cases, the Board shall coordinate such program with each affected State agency, local governmental unit, and local law enforcement agencies.

The Board may further subsidize political subdivisions of this State, local governmental units and local law enforcement agencies for their costs, provable by audit and not otherwise recoverable from any proceeds derived from any sale of abandoned and derelict vehicles, in collecting, storing and disposing of such vehicles during a reimbursement period set by the Board.

Any expenditure of funds hereunder shall be subject to audit by the Auditor General, within the appropriations for this purpose by the General Assembly, and may be made only in the event that cost-analysis and program efficiency show that such reimbursement subsidy is justified. No owner of any abandoned or derelict vehicle shall in any way, receive any funds hereunder. This shall not, however, prohibit the Board from examining the strategy of paying owners of discarded vehicles a limited sum for delivering their vehicles to a collection point when scrap prices are depressed; and bringing emergency measures such as this to the attention of the General Assembly for its consideration at a later time.

P.A. 76–1586, § 4–305, added by P.A. 78–857, § 1, eff. Sept. 14, 1973. Amended by P.A. 81–653, § 2, eff. Sept. 14, 1979.

Formerly Ill.Rev.Stat.1991, ch. 95 ½, ¶ 4–305.

5/4–306. Federal aid

§ 4–306. Federal aid. The Board is authorized and empowered to do all things necessary and proper to fully cooperate with any agency of the United States in the administration of any federal act relating to abandoned and derelict vehicles or the recycling or scrapping of vehicles now in effect or hereafter enacted for the purpose of appropriation of funds for the payment to or toward the junking, salvaging, recycling or scrapping of retired and discarded vehicles.

Whenever federal funds are expended to provide for the payment to or toward the junking, salvaging, recycling or scrapping of such vehicles, the amount received as reimbursement therefor shall be paid into the fund or trust fund in the State Treasury from which such expenditure was made.

P.A. 76–1586, § 4–306, added by P.A. 78–857, § 1, eff. Sept. 14, 1973. Amended by P.A. 81–653, § 2, eff. Sept. 14, 1979.

Formerly Ill.Rev.Stat.1991, ch. 95 ½, ¶ 4–306.

5/4–307. Funding and fees

§ 4–307. Funding and fees. (a) The programs initiated by the Board shall be funded by appropriations by the General Assembly to the Board. In addition to any fees enacted by the General Assembly, the Board shall recommend additional and optional methods of financing such programs to the end that the programs shall become self-sufficient.

(b) In addition to any provisions made by the General Assembly, the Board shall recommend incentives to induce the junking of abandoned and derelict vehicles not suitable for rebuilding or restoring as antiques or historic vehicles. The Board may further recommend a subsidy to implement Section 4–305.

P.A. 76–1586, § 4–307, added by P.A. 78–857, § 1, eff. Sept. 14, 1973. Amended by P.A. 79–1107, § 2, eff. Sept. 26, 1975; P.A. 81–653, § 2, eff. Sept. 14, 1979; P.A. 84–470, § 1, eff. Sept. 17, 1985.

Formerly Ill.Rev.Stat.1991, ch. 95 ½, ¶ 4–307.

CHAPTER 5. DEALERS, TRANSPORTERS, WRECKERS AND REBUILDERS

Enactment

The Illinois Vehicle Code was enacted by P.A. 76–1586, effective July 1, 1970. The Code constitutes a consolidated recodification of various earlier laws and acts including the Illinois Motor Vehicle Law of 1957.

5/5–100. Definitions

§ 5–100. Definitions. For the purposes of this Chapter, the following words shall have the meanings ascribed to them as follows:

"Additional place of business" means a place owned or leased and occupied by the dealer in addition to its established place of business, at which the dealer conducts or intends to conduct business on a permanent or long term basis. The term does not include an area where an off site sale or exhibition is conducted. The Secretary of State shall adopt guidelines for the administration and enforcement of this definition by rule.

"Display exhibition" means a temporary display of vehicles by a dealer licensed under Section 5-101 or 5-102, at a location at which no vehicles are offered for sale, that is conducted at a place other than the dealer's established and additional places of business.

"Established place of business" means the place owned or leased and occupied by any person duly licensed or required to be licensed as a dealer for the purpose of engaging in selling, buying, bartering, displaying, exchanging or dealing in, on consignment or otherwise, vehicles and their essential parts and for such other ancillary purposes as may be permitted by the Secretary by rule. It shall include an office in which the dealer's records shall be separate and distinct from any other business or tenant which may occupy space in the same building except as provided in Section 5-101.1. This office shall not be located in a house trailer, residence, tent, temporary stand, temporary address, room or rooms in a hotel or rooming house, nor the premises occupied by a single or multiple unit residence. The established place of business of a scrap processor shall be the fixed location where the scrap processor maintains its principal place of business. The Secretary of State shall, by rule and regulation, adopt guidelines for the administration and enforcement of this definition, such as, but not limited to issues concerning the required hours of operation, describing where vehicles are displayed and offered for sale, where books and records are maintained and requirements for the fulfillment of warranties. A dealer may have an additional place of business as defined under this Section.

"Motor vehicle financing affiliate" means a business organization registered to do business in Illinois that, pursuant to a written contract with either (1) a single new or used motor vehicle dealer or (2) a single group of new or used motor vehicle dealers that share a common ownership within the group, purchases new or used motor vehicles on behalf of the dealer or group of dealers and then sells, transfers, or assigns those motor vehicles to the dealer or group of dealers. The motor vehicle financing affiliate must be incorporated or organized solely to purchase new or used vehicles on behalf of the new or used motor vehicle dealer or group of dealers with which it has contracted, shall not sell motor vehicles at retail, shall perform only those business functions related to the purchasing of motor vehicles and selling, transferring, or assigning those motor vehicles to the dealer or group of dealers. The motor vehicle financing affiliate must be licensed under the provisions of Section 5-101.1 and must not be licensed as a new or used motor vehicle dealer.

"Off site sale" means the temporary display and sale of vehicles, for a period of not more than 7 calendar days (excluding Sundays), by a dealer licensed under Section 5-101 or 5-102 at a place other than the dealer's established and additional places of business.

"Relevant market area", for a new vehicle dealer licensed under Section 5-101 and for a used vehicle dealer licensed under Section 5-102, means the area within 10 miles of the established or additional place of business of the dealer located in a county with a population of 300,000 or more, or within 15 miles if the established place of business is located in a county with a population of less than 300,000.

"Trade show exhibition" means a temporary display of vehicles, by dealers licensed under Section 5-101 or 5-102, or any other person as defined in subsection (c) of Section 5-102.1, at a location at which no vehicles are offered for sale that is conducted at a place other than the dealer's established and additional places of business. In order for a display exhibition to be considered a trade show exhibition, it must be participated in by at least 3 dealers, 2 of which must be licensed under Section 5-101 or 5-102; and a trade show exhibition of new vehicles shall only be participated in by licensed new vehicle dealers at least 2 of which must be licensed under Section 5-101.

P.A. 76-1586, § 5-100, eff. July 1, 1970. Amended by P.A. 77-1316, § 1, eff. Jan. 1, 1972; P.A. 77-2751, § 1, eff. Sept. 1, 1972; P.A. 78-255, § 61, eff. Oct. 1, 1973; P.A. 78-858, § 1, eff. Jan. 1, 1974; P.A. 78-1165, § 1, eff. Aug. 27, 1974; P.A. 78-1205, § 1, eff. Sept. 5, 1974; P.A. 78-1297, § 30, eff. March 4, 1975; P.A. 81-932, § 1, eff. Sept. 22, 1979; P.A. 83-1473, § 1, eff. Jan. 1, 1985; P.A. 84-1302, § 1, eff. Jan. 1 1987; P.A. 84-1304, § 1, eff. Jan. 1, 1987; P.A. 85-572, § 1, eff. Sept. 18, 1987; P.A. 85-1204, § 1, eff. Aug. 26, 1988; P.A. 86-444, § 1, eff. Jan. 1, 1990; P.A. 87-380, § 1, eff. July 1, 1992; P.A. 87-1249, § 1, eff. Dec. 24, 1992; P.A. 88-470, § 10, eff. Sept. 1, 1993; P.A. 88-588, § 5, eff. Jan. 1, 1995; P.A. 88-685, § 5, eff. Jan. 24, 1995; P.A. 89-235, Art. 2, § 2-120, eff. Aug. 4, 1995; P.A. 90-89, § 15, eff. Jan. 1, 1998; P.A. 91-415, § 5, eff. Jan. 1, 2000.

Formerly Ill.Rev.Stat.1991, ch. 95 ½, ¶ 5-100.

5/5-100-1. Findings and Purpose

§ 5-100-1. Findings and Purpose. The General Assembly finds that: (1) crimes involving the theft of vehicles and their parts have risen steadily over the past years, with a resulting loss of millions of dollars to the residents of this State; (2) essential to the criminal enterprise of vehicle theft operations is the ability of thieves to transfer or sell stolen vehicles or their parts through legitimate commercial channels, making them available for sale to the automotive industry; (3) vehicle dealers, scrap processors, automotive parts recyclers, repairers and rebuilders who comprise the vast majority of the persons engaged in the automotive business in this State are frequently exposed to pressures and influences from motor vehicle thieves; (4) elements of organized crime are constantly attempting to influence businessmen engaged in the sale and repair of motor vehicles so as to further their own criminal interests; and (5) close and strict government regulation of vehicle dealers, scrap processors, automotive parts recyclers, repairers and rebuilders will provide a system of tracking the flow of vehicles and their essential parts and therefore significantly reduce the numbers of vehicle-related thefts in this State. It is, therefore, the intent of the General Assembly to establish a system of mandatory licensing and record keeping which will prevent or reduce the transfer or sale of stolen vehicles or their parts within this State.

It further is the intent of the General Assembly that government agencies work in cooperation with vehicle dealers, scrap processors, automotive parts recyclers, repairers and rebuilders, utilizing their professional expertise in the development and execution of programs and strategies to reduce vehicle-related crime and maximize consumer protection while ensuring a healthy business climate for the legitimate automotive industry.

P.A. 76-1586, § 5-100-1, added by P.A. 82-984, § 1, eff. Jan. 1, 1983. Amended by P.A. 84-1302, § 1, eff. Jan. 1, 1987; P.A. 84-1304, § 1, eff. Jan. 1, 1987; P.A. 85-572, § 1, eff. Sept. 18, 1987.

Formerly Ill.Rev.Stat.1991, ch. 95 ½, ¶ 5-100-1.

ARTICLE I. DEALERS

Section

5/5-101. New vehicle dealers must be licensed

Text of section effective until June 1, 2003

§ 5-101. New vehicle dealers must be licensed.

(a) No person shall engage in this State in the business of selling or dealing in, on consignment or otherwise, new vehicles of any make, or act as an intermediary or agent or broker for any licensed dealer or vehicle purchaser other than as a salesperson, or represent or advertise that he is so engaged or intends to so engage in such business unless licensed to do so in writing by the Secretary of State under the provisions of this Section.

(b) An application for a new vehicle dealer's license shall be filed with the Secretary of State, duly verified by oath, on such form as the Secretary of State may by rule or regulation prescribe and shall contain:

1. The name and type of business organization of the applicant and his established and additional places of business, if any, in this State.

2. If the applicant is a corporation, a list of its officers, directors, and shareholders having a ten percent or greater ownership interest in the corporation, setting forth the residence address of each; if the applicant is a sole proprietorship, a partnership, an unincorporated association, a trust, or any similar form of business organization, the name and residence address of the proprietor or of each partner, member, officer, director, trustee, or manager.

3. The make or makes of new vehicles which the applicant will offer for sale at retail in this State.

4. The name of each manufacturer or franchised distributor, if any, of new vehicles with whom the applicant has contracted for the sale of such new vehicles. As evidence of this fact, the application shall be accompanied by a signed statement from each such manufacturer or franchised distributor. If the applicant is in the business of offering for sale new conversion vehicles, trucks or vans, except for trucks modified to serve a special purpose which includes but is not limited to the following vehicles: street sweepers, fertilizer spreaders, emergency vehicles, implements of husbandry or maintenance type vehicles, he must furnish evidence of a sales and service agreement from both the chassis manufacturer and second stage manufacturer.

5. A statement that the applicant has been approved for registration under the Retailers' Occupation Tax Act [1] by the Department of Revenue: Provided that this requirement does not apply to a dealer who is already licensed hereunder with the Secretary of State, and who is merely applying for a renewal of his license. As evidence of this fact, the application shall be accompanied by a certification from the Department of Revenue showing that that Department has approved the applicant for registration under the Retailers' Occupation Tax Act.

6. A statement that the applicant has complied with the appropriate liability insurance requirement. A Certificate of Insurance in a solvent company authorized to do business in the State of Illinois shall be included with each application covering each location at which he proposes to act as a new vehicle dealer. The policy must provide liability coverage in the minimum amounts of $100,000 for bodily injury to, or death of, any person, $300,000 for bodily injury to, or death of, two or more persons in any one accident, and $50,000 for damage to property. Such policy shall expire not sooner than December 31 of the year for which the license was issued or renewed. The expiration of the insurance policy shall not terminate the liability under the policy arising during the period for which the policy was filed. Trailer and mobile home dealers are exempt from this requirement.

7. (A) An application for a new motor vehicle dealer's license shall be accompanied by the following license fees:

$100 for applicant's established place of business, and $50 for each additional place of business, if any, to which the application pertains; but if the application is made after June 15 of any year, the license fee shall be $50 for applicant's established place of business plus $25 for each additional place of business, if any, to which the application pertains. License fees shall be returnable only in the event that the application is denied by the Secretary of State. All moneys received by the Secretary of State as license fees under this Section shall be deposited into the Motor Vehicle Review Board Fund and shall be used to administer the Motor Vehicle Review Board under the Motor Vehicle Franchise Act.[2]

(B) An application for a new vehicle dealer's license, other than for a new motor vehicle dealer's license, shall be accompanied by the following license fees:

$50 for applicant's established place of business, and $25 for each additional place of business, if any, to which the application pertains; but if the application is made after June 15 of any year, the license fee shall be $25 for applicant's established place of business plus $12.50 for each additional place of business, if any, to which the application pertains. License fees shall be returnable only in the event that the application is denied by the Secretary of State.

8. A statement that the applicant's officers, directors, shareholders having a 10% or greater ownership interest therein, proprietor, a partner, member, officer, director, trustee, manager or other principals in the business have not committed in the past 3 years any one violation as determined in any civil, criminal or administrative proceedings of any one of the following Acts:

(A) The Anti Theft Laws of the Illinois Vehicle Code; [3]

(B) The Certificate of Title Laws of the Illinois Vehicle Code; [4]

(C) The Offenses against Registration and Certificates of Title Laws of the Illinois Vehicle Code; [5]

(D) The Dealers, Transporters, Wreckers and Rebuilders Laws of the Illinois Vehicle Code; [6]

(E) Section 21-2 of the Criminal Code of 1961,[7] Criminal Trespass to Vehicles; or

(F) The Retailers' Occupation Tax Act.

9. A statement that the applicant's officers, directors, shareholders having a 10% or greater ownership interest therein, proprietor, partner, member, officer, director, trustee, manager or other principals in the business have not committed in any calendar year 3 or more violations, as determined in any civil, criminal or administrative proceedings, of any one or more of the following Acts:

(A) The Consumer Finance Act; [8]

(B) The Consumer Installment Loan Act; [9]

(C) The Retail Installment Sales Act; [10]

(D) The Motor Vehicle Retail Installment Sales Act; [11]

(E) The Interest Act; [12]

(F) The Illinois Wage Assignment Act; [13]

(G) Part 8 of Article XII of the Code of Civil Procedure; [14] or

(H) The Consumer Fraud Act.[15]

10. A bond or certificate of deposit in the amount of $20,000 for each location at which the applicant intends to act as a new vehicle dealer. The bond shall be for the term of the license, or its renewal, for which application is

made, and shall expire not sooner than December 31 of the year for which the license was issued or renewed. The bond shall run to the People of the State of Illinois, with surety by a bonding or insurance company authorized to do business in this State. It shall be conditioned upon the proper transmittal of all title and registration fees and taxes (excluding taxes under the Retailers' Occupation Tax Act) accepted by the applicant as a new vehicle dealer.

11. Such other information concerning the business of the applicant as the Secretary of State may by rule or regulation prescribe.

12. A statement that the applicant understands Chapter One through Chapter Five of this Code.

(c) Any change which renders no longer accurate any information contained in any application for a new vehicle dealer's license shall be amended within 30 days after the occurrence of such change on such form as the Secretary of State may prescribe by rule or regulation, accompanied by an amendatory fee of $2.

(d) Anything in this Chapter 5 to the contrary notwithstanding no person shall be licensed as a new vehicle dealer unless:

1. He is authorized by contract in writing between himself and the manufacturer or franchised distributor of such make of vehicle to so sell the same in this State, and

2. Such person shall maintain an established place of business as defined in this Act.

(e) The Secretary of State shall, within a reasonable time after receipt, examine an application submitted to him under this Section and unless he makes a determination that the application submitted to him does not conform with the requirements of this Section or that grounds exist for a denial of the application, under Section 5–501 of this Chapter, grant the applicant an original new vehicle dealer's license in writing for his established place of business and a supplemental license in writing for each additional place of business in such form as he may prescribe by rule or regulation which shall include the following:

1. The name of the person licensed;

2. If a corporation, the name and address of its officers or if a sole proprietorship, a partnership, an unincorporated association or any similar form of business organization, the name and address of the proprietor or of each partner, member, officer, director, trustee or manager;

3. In the case of an original license, the established place of business of the licensee;

4. In the case of a supplemental license, the established place of business of the licensee and the additional place of business to which such supplemental license pertains;

5. The make or makes of new vehicles which the licensee is licensed to sell.

(f) The appropriate instrument evidencing the license or a certified copy thereof, provided by the Secretary of State, shall be kept posted conspicuously in the established place of business of the licensee and in each additional place of business, if any, maintained by such licensee.

(g) Except as provided in subsection (h) hereof, all new vehicle dealer's licenses granted under this Section shall expire by operation of law on December 31 of the calendar year for which they are granted unless sooner revoked or cancelled under the provisions of Section 5–501 of this Chapter.

(h) A new vehicle dealer's license may be renewed upon application and payment of the fee required herein, and submission of proof of coverage under an approved bond under the "Retailers' Occupation Tax Act" or proof that applicant is not subject to such bonding requirements, as in the case of an original license, but in case an application for the renewal of an effective license is made during the month of December, the effective license shall remain in force until the application is granted or denied by the Secretary of State.

(i) All persons licensed as a new vehicle dealer are required to furnish each purchaser of a motor vehicle:

1. In the case of a new vehicle a manufacturer's statement of origin and in the case of a used motor vehicle a certificate of title, in either case properly assigned to the purchaser;

2. A statement verified under oath that all identifying numbers on the vehicle agree with those on the certificate of title or manufacturer's statement of origin;

3. A bill of sale properly executed on behalf of such person;

4. A copy of the Uniform Invoice-transaction reporting return referred to in Section 5–402 hereof;

5. In the case of a rebuilt vehicle, a copy of the Disclosure of Rebuilt Vehicle Status; and

6. In the case of a vehicle for which the warranty has been reinstated, a copy of the warranty.

(j) Except at the time of sale or repossession of the vehicle, no person licensed as a new vehicle dealer may issue any other person a newly created key to a vehicle unless the new vehicle dealer makes a copy of the driver's license or State identification card of the person requesting or obtaining the newly created key. The new vehicle dealer must retain the copy for 30 days.

A new vehicle dealer who violates this subsection (j) is guilty of a petty offense. Violation of this subsection (j) is not cause to suspend, revoke, cancel, or deny renewal of the new vehicle dealer's license.

This amendatory Act of 1983 shall be applicable to the 1984 registration year and thereafter.

P.A. 76–1586, § 5–101, eff. July 1, 1970. Amended by P.A. 77–2751, § 1, eff. Sept. 1, 1972; P.A. 81–759, § 6, eff. Sept. 16, 1979; P.A. 81–932, § 1, eff. Sept. 22, 1979; P.A. 82–783, Art. XI, § 140, eff. July 13, 1982; P.A. 83–765, § 1, eff. Sept. 23, 1983; P.A. 83–1473, § 1, eff. Jan. 1, 1985; P.A. 84–986, § 1, eff. Sept. 25, 1985; P.A. 85–340, § 2, eff. Sept. 10, 1987; P.A. 85–1396, § 2, eff. Sept. 2, 1988; P.A. 86–444, § 1, eff. Jan. 1, 1990; P.A. 86–971, § 1, eff. Jan. 1, 1991; P.A. 86–1028, Art. II, § 2–44, eff. Feb. 5, 1990; P.A. 86–1179, § 2, eff. Aug. 17, 1990; P.A. 87–380, § 1, eff. July 1, 1992; P.A. 87–435, Art. 2, § 2–19, eff. Sept. 10, 1991; P.A. 87–895, Art. 2, § 2–45, eff. Aug. 14, 1992; P.A. 88–158, § 5, eff. Jan. 1, 1994; P.A. 89–145, § 10, eff. July 14, 1995; P.A. 89–189, § 5, eff. Jan. 1, 1996; P.A. 89–433, § 5, eff. Dec. 15, 1995; P.A. 92–391, § 5, eff. Aug. 16, 2001.

Formerly Ill.Rev.Stat.1991, ch. 95 ½, ¶ 5–101.

[1] 35 ILCS 120/1 et seq.

[2] 815 ILCS 710/1 et seq.

[3] 625 ILCS 5/4–100 et seq.

[4] 625 ILCS 5/3–100 et seq.

[5] 625 ILCS 5/3–701 et seq.

[6] 625 ILCS 5/5–100 et seq.

[7] 720 ILCS 5/21–2.

[8] Former Ill.Rev.Stat. ch. 17, ¶ 5601 et seq. (repealed).

[9] 205 ILCS 670/1 et seq.

[10] 815 ILCS 405/1 et seq.

11 815 ILCS 375/1 et seq.
12 815 ILCS 205/0.01 et seq.
13 740 ILCS 170/.01 et seq.
14 735 ILCS 5/12-101 et seq.
15 815 ILCS 505/1 et seq.

For text of section effective June 1, 2003, see 625 ILCS 5/5-101, post

5/5-101. New vehicle dealers must be licensed

Text of section effective June 1, 2003

§ 5-101. New vehicle dealers must be licensed.

(a) No person shall engage in this State in the business of selling or dealing in, on consignment or otherwise, new vehicles of any make, or act as an intermediary or agent or broker for any licensed dealer or vehicle purchaser other than as a salesperson, or represent or advertise that he is so engaged or intends to so engage in such business unless licensed to do so in writing by the Secretary of State under the provisions of this Section.

(b) An application for a new vehicle dealer's license shall be filed with the Secretary of State, duly verified by oath, on such form as the Secretary of State may by rule or regulation prescribe and shall contain:

1. The name and type of business organization of the applicant and his established and additional places of business, if any, in this State.

2. If the applicant is a corporation, a list of its officers, directors, and shareholders having a ten percent or greater ownership interest in the corporation, setting forth the residence address of each; if the applicant is a sole proprietorship, a partnership, an unincorporated association, a trust, or any similar form of business organization, the name and residence address of the proprietor or of each partner, member, officer, director, trustee, or manager.

3. The make or makes of new vehicles which the applicant will offer for sale at retail in this State.

4. The name of each manufacturer or franchised distributor, if any, of new vehicles with whom the applicant has contracted for the sale of such new vehicles. As evidence of this fact, the application shall be accompanied by a signed statement from each such manufacturer or franchised distributor. If the applicant is in the business of offering for sale new conversion vehicles, trucks or vans, except for trucks modified to serve a special purpose which includes but is not limited to the following vehicles: street sweepers, fertilizer spreaders, emergency vehicles, implements of husbandry or maintenance type vehicles, he must furnish evidence of a sales and service agreement from both the chassis manufacturer and second stage manufacturer.

5. A statement that the applicant has been approved for registration under the Retailers' Occupation Tax Act [1] by the Department of Revenue: Provided that this requirement does not apply to a dealer who is already licensed hereunder with the Secretary of State, and who is merely applying for a renewal of his license. As evidence of this fact, the application shall be accompanied by a certification from the Department of Revenue showing that that Department has approved the applicant for registration under the Retailers' Occupation Tax Act.

6. A statement that the applicant has complied with the appropriate liability insurance requirement. A Certificate of Insurance in a solvent company authorized to do business in the State of Illinois shall be included with each application covering each location at which he proposes to act as a new vehicle dealer. The policy must provide liability coverage in the minimum amounts of $100,000 for bodily injury to, or death of, any person, $300,000 for bodily injury to, or death of, two or more persons in any one accident, and $50,000 for damage to property. Such policy shall expire not sooner than December 31 of the year for which the license was issued or renewed. The expiration of the insurance policy shall not terminate the liability under the policy arising during the period for which the policy was filed. Trailer and mobile home dealers are exempt from this requirement.

If the permitted user has a liability insurance policy that provides automobile liability insurance coverage of at least $100,000 for bodily injury to or the death of any person, $300,000 for bodily injury to or the death of any 2 or more persons in any one accident, and $50,000 for damage to property, then the permitted user's insurer shall be the primary insurer and the dealer's insurer shall be the secondary insurer. If the permitted user does not have a liability insurance policy that provides automobile liability insurance coverage of at least $100,000 for bodily injury to or the death of any person, $300,000 for bodily injury to or the death of any 2 or more persons in any one accident, and $50,000 for damage to property, or does not have any insurance at all, then the dealer's insurer shall be the primary insurer and the permitted user's insurer shall be the secondary insurer.

When a permitted user is "test driving" a new vehicle dealer's automobile, the new vehicle dealer's insurance shall be primary and the permitted user's insurance shall be secondary.

As used in this paragraph 6, a "permitted user" is a person who, with the permission of the new vehicle dealer or an employee of the new vehicle dealer, drives a vehicle owned and held for sale or lease by the new vehicle dealer which the person is considering to purchase or lease, in order to evaluate the performance, reliability, or condition of the vehicle. The term "permitted user" also includes a person who, with the permission of the new vehicle dealer, drives a vehicle owned or held for sale or lease by the new vehicle dealer for loaner purposes while the user's vehicle is being repaired or evaluated.

As used in this paragraph 6, "test driving" occurs when a permitted user who, with the permission of the new vehicle dealer or an employee of the new vehicle dealer, drives a vehicle owned and held for sale or lease by a new vehicle dealer that the person is considering to purchase or lease, in order to evaluate the performance, reliability, or condition of the vehicle.

As used in this paragraph 6, "loaner purposes" means when a person who, with the permission of the new vehicle dealer, drives a vehicle owned or held for sale or lease by the new vehicle dealer while the user's vehicle is being repaired or evaluated.

7. (A) An application for a new motor vehicle dealer's license shall be accompanied by the following license fees:

$100 for applicant's established place of business, and $50 for each additional place of business, if any, to which the application pertains; but if the application is made after June 15 of any year, the license fee shall be $50 for applicant's established place of business plus $25 for each additional place of business, if any, to which the application pertains. License fees shall be returnable only in the event that the application is denied by the Secretary of State. All moneys received by the Secretary of State as license fees under this Section shall be deposited into the Motor Vehicle Review Board Fund and shall be used to administer the Motor Vehicle Review Board under the Motor Vehicle Franchise Act.[2]

(B) An application for a new vehicle dealer's license, other than for a new motor vehicle dealer's license, shall be accompanied by the following license fees:

$50 for applicant's established place of business, and $25 for each additional place of business, if any, to which the application pertains; but if the application is made after June 15 of any year, the license fee shall be $25 for applicant's established place of business plus $12.50 for each additional place of business, if any, to which the application pertains. License fees shall be returnable only in the event that the application is denied by the Secretary of State.

8. A statement that the applicant's officers, directors, shareholders having a 10% or greater ownership interest therein, proprietor, a partner, member, officer, director, trustee, manager or other principals in the business have not committed in the past 3 years any one violation as determined in any civil, criminal or administrative proceedings of any one of the following Acts:

(A) The Anti Theft Laws of the Illinois Vehicle Code; [3]

(B) The Certificate of Title Laws of the Illinois Vehicle Code; [4]

(C) The Offenses against Registration and Certificates of Title Laws of the Illinois Vehicle Code; [5]

(D) The Dealers, Transporters, Wreckers and Rebuilders Laws of the Illinois Vehicle Code; [6]

(E) Section 21-2 of the Criminal Code of 1961,[7] Criminal Trespass to Vehicles; [7] or

(F) The Retailers' Occupation Tax Act.

9. A statement that the applicant's officers, directors, shareholders having a 10% or greater ownership interest therein, proprietor, partner, member, officer, director, trustee, manager or other principals in the business have not committed in any calendar year 3 or more violations, as determined in any civil, criminal or administrative proceedings, of any one or more of the following Acts:

(A) The Consumer Finance Act; [8]

(B) The Consumer Installment Loan Act; [9]

(C) The Retail Installment Sales Act; [10]

(D) The Motor Vehicle Retail Installment Sales Act; [11]

(E) The Interest Act; [12]

(F) The Illinois Wage Assignment Act; [13]

(G) Part 8 of Article XII of the Code of Civil Procedure; [14] or

(H) The Consumer Fraud Act.[15]

10. A bond or certificate of deposit in the amount of $20,000 for each location at which the applicant intends to act as a new vehicle dealer. The bond shall be for the term of the license, or its renewal, for which application is made, and shall expire not sooner than December 31 of the year for which the license was issued or renewed. The bond shall run to the People of the State of Illinois, with surety by a bonding or insurance company authorized to do business in this State. It shall be conditioned upon the proper transmittal of all title and registration fees and taxes (excluding taxes under the Retailers' Occupation Tax Act) accepted by the applicant as a new vehicle dealer.

11. Such other information concerning the business of the applicant as the Secretary of State may by rule or regulation prescribe.

12. A statement that the applicant understands Chapter One through Chapter Five of this Code.

(c) Any change which renders no longer accurate any information contained in any application for a new vehicle dealer's license shall be amended within 30 days after the occurrence of such change on such form as the Secretary of State may prescribe by rule or regulation, accompanied by an amendatory fee of $2.

(d) Anything in this Chapter 5 to the contrary notwithstanding no person shall be licensed as a new vehicle dealer unless:

1. He is authorized by contract in writing between himself and the manufacturer or franchised distributor of such make of vehicle to so sell the same in this State, and

2. Such person shall maintain an established place of business as defined in this Act.

(e) The Secretary of State shall, within a reasonable time after receipt, examine an application submitted to him under this Section and unless he makes a determination that the application submitted to him does not conform with the requirements of this Section or that grounds exist for a denial of the application, under Section 5-501 of this Chapter, grant the applicant an original new vehicle dealer's license in writing for his established place of business and a supplemental license in writing for each additional place of business in such form as he may prescribe by rule or regulation which shall include the following:

1. The name of the person licensed;

2. If a corporation, the name and address of its officers or if a sole proprietorship, a partnership, an unincorporated association or any similar form of business organization, the name and address of the proprietor or of each partner, member, officer, director, trustee or manager;

3. In the case of an original license, the established place of business of the licensee;

4. In the case of a supplemental license, the established place of business of the licensee and the additional place of business to which such supplemental license pertains;

5. The make or makes of new vehicles which the licensee is licensed to sell.

(f) The appropriate instrument evidencing the license or a certified copy thereof, provided by the Secretary of State, shall be kept posted conspicuously in the established place of business of the licensee and in each additional place of business, if any, maintained by such licensee.

(g) Except as provided in subsection (h) hereof, all new vehicle dealer's licenses granted under this Section shall expire by operation of law on December 31 of the calendar year for which they are granted unless sooner revoked or cancelled under the provisions of Section 5-501 of this Chapter.

(h) A new vehicle dealer's license may be renewed upon application and payment of the fee required herein, and submission of proof of coverage under an approved bond under the "Retailers' Occupation Tax Act" or proof that applicant is not subject to such bonding requirements, as in the case of an original license, but in case an application for the renewal of an effective license is made during the month of December, the effective license shall remain in force until the application is granted or denied by the Secretary of State.

(i) All persons licensed as a new vehicle dealer are required to furnish each purchaser of a motor vehicle:

1. In the case of a new vehicle a manufacturer's statement of origin and in the case of a used motor vehicle a certificate of title, in either case properly assigned to the purchaser;

2. A statement verified under oath that all identifying numbers on the vehicle agree with those on the certificate of title or manufacturer's statement of origin;

3. A bill of sale properly executed on behalf of such person;

4. A copy of the Uniform Invoice-transaction reporting return referred to in Section 5-402 hereof;

5. In the case of a rebuilt vehicle, a copy of the Disclosure of Rebuilt Vehicle Status; and

6. In the case of a vehicle for which the warranty has been reinstated, a copy of the warranty.

(j) Except at the time of sale or repossession of the vehicle, no person licensed as a new vehicle dealer may issue any other person a newly created key to a vehicle unless the new vehicle dealer makes a copy of the driver's license or State identification card of the person requesting or obtaining the newly created key. The new vehicle dealer must retain the copy for 30 days.

A new vehicle dealer who violates this subsection (j) is guilty of a petty offense. Violation of this subsection (j) is not cause to suspend, revoke, cancel, or deny renewal of the new vehicle dealer's license.

This amendatory Act of 1983 shall be applicable to the 1984 registration year and thereafter.

P.A. 76-1586, § 5-101, eff. July 1, 1970. Amended by P.A. 77-2751, § 1, eff. Sept. 1, 1972; P.A. 81-759, § 6, eff. Sept. 16, 1979; P.A. 81-932, § 1, eff. Sept. 22, 1979; P.A. 82-783, Art. XI, § 140, eff. July 13, 1982; P.A. 83-765, § 1, eff. Sept. 23, 1983; P.A. 83-1473, § 1, eff. Jan. 1, 1985; P.A. 84-986, § 1, eff. Sept. 25, 1985; P.A. 85-340, § 2, eff. Sept. 10, 1987; P.A. 85-1396, § 2, eff. Sept. 2, 1988; P.A. 86-444, § 1, eff. Jan. 1, 1990; P.A. 86-971, § 1, eff. Jan. 1, 1991; P.A. 86-1028, Art. II, § 2-44, eff. Feb. 5, 1990; P.A. 86-1179, § 2, eff. Aug. 17, 1990; P.A. 87-380, § 1, eff. July 1, 1992; P.A. 87-435, Art. 2, § 2-19, eff. Sept. 10, 1991; P.A. 87-895, Art. 2, § 2-45, eff. Aug. 14, 1992; P.A. 88-158, § 5, eff. Jan. 1, 1994; P.A. 89-145, § 10, eff. July 14, 1995; P.A. 89-189, § 5, eff. Jan. 1, 1996; P.A. 89-433, § 5, eff. Dec. 15, 1995; P.A. 92-391, § 5, eff. Aug. 16, 2001; P.A. 92-835, § 5, eff. June 1, 2003.

Formerly Ill.Rev.Stat.1991, ch. 95 ½, ¶ 5-101.

[1] 35 ILCS 120/1 et seq.

[2] 815 ILCS 710/1 et seq.

[3] 625 ILCS 5/4-100 et seq.

[4] 625 ILCS 5/3-100 et seq.

[5] 625 ILCS 5/3-701 et seq.

[6] 625 ILCS 5/5-100 et seq.

[7] 720 ILCS 5/21-2.

[8] Former Ill.Rev.Stat. ch. 17, ¶5601 et seq. (repealed).

[9] 205 ILCS 670/1 et seq.

[10] 815 ILCS 405/1 et seq.

[11] 815 ILCS 375/1 et seq.

[12] 815 ILCS 205/0.01 et seq.

[13] 740 ILCS 170/.01 et seq.

[14] 735 ILCS 5/12-801 et seq.

[15] 815 ILCS 505/1 et seq.

For text of section effective until June 1, 2003, see 625 ILCS 5/5-101, ante

P.A. 92-835 incorporated the amendment by P.A. 92-391.

5/5-101.1. Motor vehicle financing affiliates; licensing

§ 5-101.1. Motor vehicle financing affiliates; licensing.

(a) In this State no business shall engage in the business of a motor vehicle financing affiliate without a license to do so in writing from the Secretary of State.

(b) An application for a motor vehicle financing affiliate's license must be filed with the Secretary of State, duly verified by oath, on a form prescribed by the Secretary of State and shall contain all of the following:

(1) The name and type of business organization of the applicant and the applicant's established place of business and any additional places of business in this State.

(2) The name and address of the licensed new or used vehicle dealer to which the applicant will be selling, transferring, or assigning new or used motor vehicles pursuant to a written contract. If more than one dealer is on the application, the applicant shall state in writing the basis of common ownership among the dealers.

(3) A list of the business organization's officers, directors, members, and shareholders having a 10% or greater ownership interest in the business, providing the residential address for each person listed.

(4) If selling, transferring, or assigning new motor vehicles, the make or makes of new vehicles that it will sell, assign, or otherwise transfer to the contracting new motor vehicle dealer listed on the application pursuant to paragraph (2).

(5) The name of each manufacturer or franchised distributor, if any, of new vehicles with whom the applicant has contracted for the sale of new vehicles and a signed statement from each manufacturer or franchised distributor acknowledging the contract.

(6) A statement that the applicant has been approved for registration under the Retailers' Occupation Tax Act [1] by the Department of Revenue. This requirement does not apply to a motor vehicle financing affiliate that is already licensed with the Secretary of State and is applying for a renewal of its license.

(7) A statement that the applicant has complied with the appropriate liability insurance requirement and a Certificate of Insurance that shall not expire before December 31 of the year for which the license was issued or renewed with a minimum liability coverage of $100,000 for the bodily injury or death of any person, $300,000 for the bodily injury or death of 2 or more persons in any one accident, and $50,000 for damage to property. The expiration of the insurance policy shall not terminate the liability under the policy arising during the period for which the policy was filed. Trailer and mobile home dealers are exempt from the requirements of this paragraph. A motor vehicle financing affiliate is exempt from the requirements of this paragraph if it is covered by the insurance policy of the new or used dealer listed on the application pursuant to paragraph (2).

(8) A license fee of $1,000 for the applicant's established place of business and $250 for each additional place of business, if any, to which the application pertains. Howev-

er, if the application is made after June 15 of any year, the license fee shall be $500 for the applicant's established place of business and $125 for each additional place of business, if any, to which the application pertains. These license fees shall be returnable only in the event that the application is denied by the Secretary of State.

(9) A statement incorporating the requirements of paragraphs 8 and 9 of subsection (b) of Section 5-101.

(10) Any other information concerning the business of the applicant as the Secretary of State may prescribe.

(11) A statement that the applicant understands Chapter 1 through Chapter 5 of this Code. [2]

(c) Any change which renders no longer accurate any information contained in any application for a motor vehicle financing affiliate's license shall be amended within 30 days after the occurrence of the change on a form prescribed by the Secretary of State, accompanied by an amendatory fee of $2.

(d) If a new vehicle dealer is not listed on the application, pursuant to paragraph (2) of subsection (b), the motor vehicle financing affiliate shall not receive, possess, or transfer any new vehicle. If a new motor vehicle dealer is listed on the application, pursuant to paragraph (2) of subsection (b), the new motor vehicle dealer can only receive those new cars it is permitted to receive under its franchise agreement. If both a new and used motor vehicle dealer are listed on the application, pursuant to paragraph (2) of subsection (b), only the new motor vehicle dealer may receive new motor vehicles. If a used motor vehicle is listed on the application, pursuant to paragraph (2) of subsection (b), the used motor vehicle dealer shall not receive any new motor vehicles.

(e) The applicant and dealer provided pursuant to paragraph (2) of subsection (b) must be business organizations registered to conduct business in Illinois. Three-fourths of the dealer's board of directors must be members of the motor vehicle financing affiliate's board of directors, if applicable.

(f) Unless otherwise provided in this Chapter 5, no business organization registered to do business in Illinois shall be licensed as a motor vehicle financing affiliate unless:

(1) The motor vehicle financing affiliate shall only sell, transfer, or assign motor vehicles to the licensed new or used dealer listed on the application pursuant to paragraph (2) of subsection (b).

(2) The motor vehicle financing affiliate sells, transfers, or assigns to the new motor vehicle dealer listed on the application, if any, only those new motor vehicles the motor vehicle financing affiliate has received under the contract set forth in paragraph (5) of subsection (b).

(3) Any new vehicle dealer listed pursuant to paragraph (2) of subsection (b) has a franchise agreement that permits the dealer to receive motor vehicles from the motor vehicle franchise affiliate.

(4) The new or used motor vehicle dealer listed on the application pursuant to paragraph (2) of subsection (b) has one established place of business or supplemental places of business as referenced in subsection (g).

(g) The Secretary of State shall, within a reasonable time after receipt, examine an application submitted pursuant to this Section and, unless it is determined that the application does not conform with the requirements of this Section or that grounds exist for a denial of the application under Section 5–501, grant the applicant a motor vehicle financing affiliate license in writing for the applicant's established place of business and a supplemental license in writing for each additional place of business in a form prescribed by the Secretary, which shall include all of the following:

(1) The name of the business licensed;

(2) The name and address of its officers, directors, or members, as applicable;

(3) In the case of an original license, the established place of business of the licensee; and

(4) If applicable, the make or makes of new vehicles which the licensee is licensed to sell to the new motor vehicle dealer listed on the application pursuant to paragraph (2) of subsection (b).

(h) The appropriate instrument evidencing the license or a certified copy, provided by the Secretary of State, shall be kept posted conspicuously in the established place of business of the licensee.

(i) Except as provided in subsection (h), all motor vehicle financing affiliate's licenses granted under this Section shall expired by operation of law on December 31 of the calendar year for which they are granted, unless revoked or canceled at an earlier date pursuant to Section 5–501.

(j) A motor vehicle financing affiliate's license may be renewed upon application and payment of the required fee. However, when an application for renewal of a motor vehicle financing affiliate's license is made during the month of December, the effective license shall remain in force until the application is granted or denied by the Secretary of State.

(k) The contract a motor vehicle financing affiliate has with a manufacturer or franchised distributor, as provided in paragraph (5) of subsection (b), shall only permit the applicant to sell, transfer, or assign new motor vehicles to the new motor vehicle dealer listed on the application pursuant to paragraph (2) of subsection (b). The contract shall specifically prohibit the motor vehicle financing affiliate from selling motor vehicles at retail. This contract shall not be considered the granting of a franchise as defined in Section 2 of the Motor Vehicle Franchise Act. [3]

(*l*) When purchasing of a motor vehicle by a new or used motor vehicle dealer, all persons licensed as a motor vehicle financing affiliate are required to furnish all of the following:

(1) For a new vehicle, a manufacturer's statement of origin properly assigned to the purchasing dealer. For a used vehicle, a certificate of title properly assigned to the purchasing dealer.

(2) A statement verified under oath that all identifying numbers on the vehicle agree with those on the certificate of title or manufacturer's statement of origin.

(3) A bill of sale properly executed on behalf of the purchasing dealer.

(4) A copy of the Uniform Invoice-transaction report pursuant to Section 5–402.

(5) In the case of a rebuilt vehicle, a copy of the Disclosure of Rebuilt Vehicle Status pursuant to Section 5–104.3.

(6) In the case of a vehicle for which a warranty has been reinstated, a copy of the warranty.

(m) The motor vehicle financing affiliate shall use the established and supplemental place or places of business the new or used vehicle dealer listed on the application pursuant to paragraph (2) of subsection (b) as its established and supplemental place or places of business.

(n) The motor vehicle financing affiliate shall keep all books and records required by this Code with the books and records of the new or used vehicle dealer listed on the application pursuant to paragraph (2) of subsection (b). The motor vehicle financing affiliate may use the books and records of the new or used motor vehicle dealer listed on the application pursuant to paragraph (2) of subsection (b).

(*o*) Under no circumstances shall a motor vehicle financing affiliate sell, transfer, or assign a new vehicle to any place of business of a new motor vehicle dealer, unless that place of business is licensed under this Chapter to sell, assign, or otherwise transfer the make of the new motor vehicle transferred.

(p) All moneys received by the Secretary of State as license fees under this Section shall be deposited into the Motor Vehicle Review Board Fund and shall be used to administer the Motor Vehicle Review Board under the Motor Vehicle Franchise Act. [4]

(q) Except as otherwise provided in this Section, a motor vehicle financing affiliate shall comply with all provisions of this Code.

P.A. 76–1586, § 5–101.1, added by P.A. 91–415, § 5, eff. Jan. 1, 2000.

1 35 ILCS 120/1 et seq.

2 625 ILCS 5/1–100 et seq. through 5/5–100 et seq.

3 815 ILCS 710/2.

4 815 ILCS 710/1 et seq.

5/5–102. Used vehicle dealers must be licensed

Text of section effective until June 1, 2003

§ 5–102. Used vehicle dealers must be licensed.

(a) No person, other than a licensed new vehicle dealer, shall engage in the business of selling or dealing in, on consignment or otherwise, 5 or more used vehicles of any make during the year (except house trailers as authorized by paragraph (j) of this Section and rebuilt salvage vehicles sold by their rebuilders to persons licensed under this Chapter), or act as an intermediary, agent or broker for any licensed dealer or vehicle purchaser (other than as a salesperson) or represent or advertise that he is so engaged or intends to so engage in such business unless licensed to do so by the Secretary of State under the provisions of this Section.

(b) An application for a used vehicle dealer's license shall be filed with the Secretary of State, duly verified by oath, in such form as the Secretary of State may by rule or regulation prescribe and shall contain:

1. The name and type of business organization established and additional places of business, if any, in this State.

2. If the applicant is a corporation, a list of its officers, directors, and shareholders having a ten percent or greater ownership interest in the corporation, setting forth the residence address of each; if the applicant is a sole proprietorship, a partnership, an unincorporated association, a trust, or any similar form of business organization, the names and residence address of the proprietor or of each partner, member, officer, director, trustee or manager.

3. A statement that the applicant has been approved for registration under the Retailers' Occupation Tax Act [1] by the Department of Revenue. However, this requirement does not apply to a dealer who is already licensed hereunder with the Secretary of State, and who is merely applying for a renewal of his license. As evidence of this fact, the application shall be accompanied by a certification from the Department of Revenue showing that the Department has approved the applicant for registration under the Retailers' Occupation Tax Act.

4. A statement that the applicant has complied with the appropriate liability insurance requirement. A Certificate of Insurance in a solvent company authorized to do business in the State of Illinois shall be included with each application covering each location at which he proposes to act as a used vehicle dealer. The policy must provide liability coverage in the minimum amounts of $100,000 for bodily injury to, or death of, any person, $300,000 for bodily injury to, or death of, two or more persons in any one accident, and $50,000 for damage to property. Such policy shall expire not sooner than December 31 of the year for which the license was issued or renewed. The expiration of the insurance policy shall not terminate the liability under the policy arising during the period for which the policy was filed. Trailer and mobile home dealers are exempt from this requirement.

5. An application for a used vehicle dealer's license shall be accompanied by the following license fees:

$50 for applicant's established place of business, and $25 for each additional place of business, if any, to which the application pertains; however, if the application is made after June 15 of any year, the license fee shall be $25 for applicant's established place of business plus $12.50 for each additional place of business, if any, to which the application pertains. License fees shall be returnable only in the event that the application is denied by the Secretary of State.

6. A statement that the applicant's officers, directors, shareholders having a 10% or greater ownership interest therein, proprietor, partner, member, officer, director, trustee, manager or other principals in the business have not committed in the past 3 years any one violation as determined in any civil, criminal or administrative proceedings of any one of the following Acts:

(A) The Anti Theft Laws of the Illinois Vehicle Code; [2]

(B) The Certificate of Title Laws of the Illinois Vehicle Code; [3]

(C) The Offenses against Registration and Certificates of Title Laws of the Illinois Vehicle Code; [4]

(D) The Dealers, Transporters, Wreckers and Rebuilders Laws of the Illinois Vehicle Code; [5]

(E) Section 21–2 of the Illinois Criminal Code of 1961,[6] Criminal Trespass to Vehicles; or

(F) The Retailers' Occupation Tax Act.

7. A statement that the applicant's officers, directors, shareholders having a 10% or greater ownership interest therein, proprietor, partner, member, officer, director, trustee, manager or other principals in the business have not committed in any calendar year 3 or more violations, as determined in any civil or criminal or administrative proceedings, of any one or more of the following Acts:

(A) The Consumer Finance Act; [7]

(B) The Consumer Installment Loan Act; [8]

(C) The Retail Installment Sales Act; [9]

(D) The Motor Vehicle Retail Installment Sales Act; [10]

(E) The Interest Act; [11]

(F) The Illinois Wage Assignment Act; [12]

(G) Part 8 of Article XII of the Code of Civil Procedure; [13] or

(H) The Consumer Fraud Act.[14]

8. A bond or Certificate of Deposit in the amount of $20,000 for each location at which the applicant intends to

act as a used vehicle dealer. The bond shall be for the term of the license, or its renewal, for which application is made, and shall expire not sooner than December 31 of the year for which the license was issued or renewed. The bond shall run to the People of the State of Illinois, with surety by a bonding or insurance company authorized to do business in this State. It shall be conditioned upon the proper transmittal of all title and registration fees and taxes (excluding taxes under the Retailers' Occupation Tax Act) accepted by the applicant as a used vehicle dealer.

9. Such other information concerning the business of the applicant as the Secretary of State may by rule or regulation prescribe.

10. A statement that the applicant understands Chapter 1 through Chapter 5 of this Code.

(c) Any change which renders no longer accurate any information contained in any application for a used vehicle dealer's license shall be amended within 30 days after the occurrence of each change on such form as the Secretary of State may prescribe by rule or regulation, accompanied by an amendatory fee of $2.

(d) Anything in this Chapter to the contrary notwithstanding, no person shall be licensed as a used vehicle dealer unless such person maintains an established place of business as defined in this Chapter.

(e) The Secretary of State shall, within a reasonable time after receipt, examine an application submitted to him under this Section. Unless the Secretary makes a determination that the application submitted to him does not conform to this Section or that grounds exist for a denial of the application under Section 5-501 of this Chapter, he must grant the applicant an original used vehicle dealer's license in writing for his established place of business and a supplemental license in writing for each additional place of business in such form as he may prescribe by rule or regulation which shall include the following:

1. The name of the person licensed;

2. If a corporation, the name and address of its officers or if a sole proprietorship, a partnership, an unincorporated association or any similar form of business organization, the name and address of the proprietor or of each partner, member, officer, director, trustee or manager;

3. In case of an original license, the established place of business of the licensee;

4. In the case of a supplemental license, the established place of business of the licensee and the additional place of business to which such supplemental license pertains.

(f) The appropriate instrument evidencing the license or a certified copy thereof, provided by the Secretary of State shall be kept posted, conspicuously, in the established place of business of the licensee and in each additional place of business, if any, maintained by such licensee.

(g) Except as provided in subsection (h) of this Section, all used vehicle dealer's licenses granted under this Section expire by operation of law on December 31 of the calendar year for which they are granted unless sooner revoked or cancelled under Section 5-501 of this Chapter.

(h) A used vehicle dealer's license may be renewed upon application and payment of the fee required herein, and submission of proof of coverage by an approved bond under the "Retailers' Occupation Tax Act" or proof that applicant is not subject to such bonding requirements, as in the case of an original license, but in case an application for the renewal of an effective license is made during the month of December, the effective license shall remain in force until the application for renewal is granted or denied by the Secretary of State.

(i) All persons licensed as a used vehicle dealer are required to furnish each purchaser of a motor vehicle:

1. A certificate of title properly assigned to the purchaser;

2. A statement verified under oath that all identifying numbers on the vehicle agree with those on the certificate of title;

3. A bill of sale properly executed on behalf of such person;

4. A copy of the Uniform Invoice-transaction reporting return referred to in Section 5–402 of this Chapter;

5. In the case of a rebuilt vehicle, a copy of the Disclosure of Rebuilt Vehicle Status; and

6. In the case of a vehicle for which the warranty has been reinstated, a copy of the warranty.

(j) A real estate broker holding a valid certificate of registration issued pursuant to "The Real Estate Brokers and Salesmen License Act" [15] may engage in the business of selling or dealing in house trailers not his own without being licensed as a used vehicle dealer under this Section; however such broker shall maintain a record of the transaction including the following:

(1) the name and address of the buyer and seller,

(2) the date of sale,

(3) a description of the mobile home, including the vehicle identification number, make, model, and year, and

(4) the Illinois certificate of title number.

The foregoing records shall be available for inspection by any officer of the Secretary of State's Office at any reasonable hour.

(k) Except at the time of sale or repossession of the vehicle, no person licensed as a used vehicle dealer may issue any other person a newly created key to a vehicle unless the used vehicle dealer makes a copy of the driver's license or State identification card of the person requesting or obtaining the newly created key. The used vehicle dealer must retain the copy for 30 days.

A used vehicle dealer who violates this subsection (k) is guilty of a petty offense. Violation of this subsection (k) is not cause to suspend, revoke, cancel, or deny renewal of the used vehicle dealer's license.

P.A. 76–1586, § 5–102, eff. July 1, 1970. Amended by P.A. 77–2751, § 1, eff. Sept. 1, 1973; P.A. 81–932, § 1, eff. Sept. 22, 1979; P.A. 81–1458, § 1, eff. Sept. 8, 1980; P.A. 82–783, Art. XI, § 140, eff. July 13, 1982; P.A. 83–765, § 1, eff. Sept. 23, 1983; P.A. 83–1473, § 1, eff. Jan. 1, 1985; P.A. 84–986, § 1, eff. Sept. 25, 1985; P.A. 84–1302, § 1, eff. Jan. 1, 1987; P.A. 84–1304, § 1, eff. Jan. 1, 1987; P.A. 85–340, § 2, eff. Sept. 10, 1987; P.A. 85–1396, § 2, eff. Sept. 2, 1988; P.A. 86–444, § 1, eff. Jan. 1, 1990; P.A. 87–380, § 1, eff. July 1, 1992; P.A. 88–158, § 5, eff. Jan. 1, 1994; P.A. 89–189, § 5, eff. Jan. 1, 1996; P.A. 92–391, § 5, eff. Aug. 16, 2001.

Formerly Ill.Rev.Stat.1991, ch. 95 ½, ¶ 5–102.

[1] 35 ILCS 120/1 et seq.

[2] 625 ILCS 5/1–100 et seq.

[3] 625 ILCS 5/3–100 et seq.

[4] 625 ILCS 5/3–701 et seq.

[5] 625 ILCS 5/5–100 et seq.

[6] 720 ILCS 5/21–2.

[7] Former Ill.Rev.Stat. ch. 17, ¶ 5601 et seq. (repealed).

[8] 205 ILCS 670/1 et seq.

[9] 815 ILCS 405/1 et seq.

[10] 815 ILCS 375/1 et seq.

[11] 815 ILCS 205/0.01 et seq.

[12] 740 ILCS 170/.01 et seq.

[13] 735 ILCS 5/12–101 et seq.

[14] 815 ILCS 505/1 et seq.

[15] Former Ill.Rev.Stat. ch.111, ¶ 5701 et seq. (repealed; see, now, 225 ILCS 455/1 et seq.

For text of section effective June 1, 2003, see 625 ILCS 5/5–102, post

5/5–102. Used vehicle dealers must be licensed

Text of section effective June 1, 2003

§ 5–102. Used vehicle dealers must be licensed.

(a) No person, other than a licensed new vehicle dealer, shall engage in the business of selling or dealing in, on consignment or otherwise, 5 or more used vehicles of any make during the year (except house trailers as authorized by paragraph (j) of this Section and rebuilt salvage vehicles sold by their rebuilders to persons licensed under this Chapter), or act as an intermediary, agent or broker for any licensed dealer or vehicle purchaser (other than as a salesperson) or represent or advertise that he is so engaged or intends to so engage in such business unless licensed to do so by the Secretary of State under the provisions of this Section.

(b) An application for a used vehicle dealer's license shall be filed with the Secretary of State, duly verified by oath, in such form as the Secretary of State may by rule or regulation prescribe and shall contain:

1. The name and type of business organization established and additional places of business, if any, in this State.

2. If the applicant is a corporation, a list of its officers, directors, and shareholders having a ten percent or greater ownership interest in the corporation, setting forth the residence address of each; if the applicant is a sole proprietorship, a partnership, an unincorporated association, a trust, or any similar form of business organization, the names and residence address of the proprietor or of each partner, member, officer, director, trustee or manager.

3. A statement that the applicant has been approved for registration under the Retailers' Occupation Tax Act by the Department of Revenue. However, this requirement does not apply to a dealer who is already licensed hereunder with the Secretary of State, and who is merely applying for a renewal of his license. As evidence of this fact, the application shall be accompanied by a certification from the Department of Revenue showing that the Department has approved the applicant for registration under the Retailers' Occupation Tax Act.[1]

4. A statement that the applicant has complied with the appropriate liability insurance requirement. A Certificate of Insurance in a solvent company authorized to do business in the State of Illinois shall be included with each application covering each location at which he proposes to act as a used vehicle dealer. The policy must provide liability coverage in the minimum amounts of $100,000 for bodily injury to, or death of, any person, $300,000 for bodily injury to, or death of, two or more persons in any one accident, and $50,000 for damage to property. Such policy shall expire not sooner than December 31 of the year for which the license was issued or renewed. The expiration of the insurance policy shall not terminate the liability under the policy arising during the period for which the policy was filed. Trailer and mobile home dealers are exempt from this requirement.

If the permitted user has a liability insurance policy that provides automobile liability insurance coverage of at least $100,000 for bodily injury to or the death of any person, $300,000 for bodily injury to or the death of any 2 or more persons in any one accident, and $50,000 for damage to property, then the permitted user's insurer shall be the primary insurer and the dealer's insurer shall be the secondary insurer. If the permitted user does not have a liability insurance policy that provides automobile liability insurance coverage of at least $100,000 for bodily injury to or the death of any person, $300,000 for bodily injury to or the death of any 2 or more persons in any one accident, and $50,000 for damage to property, or does not have any insurance at all, then the dealer's insurer shall be the primary insurer and the permitted user's insurer shall be the secondary insurer.

When a permitted user is "test driving" a used vehicle dealer's automobile, the used vehicle dealer's insurance shall be primary and the permitted user's insurance shall be secondary.

As used in this paragraph 4, a "permitted user" is a person who, with the permission of the used vehicle dealer or an employee of the used vehicle dealer, drives a vehicle owned and held for sale or lease by the used vehicle dealer which the person is considering to purchase or lease, in order to evaluate the performance, reliability, or condition of the vehicle. The term "permitted user" also includes a person who, with the permission of the used vehicle dealer, drives a vehicle owned or held for sale or lease by the used vehicle dealer for loaner purposes while the user's vehicle is being repaired or evaluated.

As used in this paragraph 4, "test driving" occurs when a permitted user who, with the permission of the used vehicle dealer or an employee of the used vehicle dealer, drives a vehicle owned and held for sale or lease by a used vehicle dealer that the person is considering to purchase or lease, in order to evaluate the performance, reliability, or condition of the vehicle.

As used in this paragraph 4, "loaner purposes" means when a person who, with the permission of the used vehicle dealer, drives a vehicle owned or held for sale or lease by the used vehicle dealer while the user's vehicle is being repaired or evaluated.

5. An application for a used vehicle dealer's license shall be accompanied by the following license fees:

$50 for applicant's established place of business, and $25 for each additional place of business, if any, to which the application pertains; however, if the application is made after June 15 of any year, the license fee shall be $25 for applicant's established place of business plus $12.50 for each additional place of business, if any, to which the application pertains. License fees shall be returnable only in the event that the application is denied by the Secretary of State.

6. A statement that the applicant's officers, directors, shareholders having a 10% or greater ownership interest therein, proprietor, partner, member, officer, director, trustee, manager or other principals in the business have not committed in the past 3 years any one violation as determined in any civil, criminal or administrative proceedings of any one of the following Acts:

(A) The Anti Theft Laws of the Illinois Vehicle Code; [2]

(B) The Certificate of Title Laws of the Illinois Vehicle Code; [3]

(C) The Offenses against Registration and Certificates of Title Laws of the Illinois Vehicle Code; [4]

(D) The Dealers, Transporters, Wreckers and Rebuilders Laws of the Illinois Vehicle Code; [5]

(E) Section 21–2 of the Illinois Criminal Code of 1961, [6] Criminal Trespass to Vehicles; or

(F) The Retailers' Occupation Tax Act.

7. A statement that the applicant's officers, directors, shareholders having a 10% or greater ownership interest therein, proprietor, partner, member, officer, director, trustee, manager or other principals in the business have not committed in any calendar year 3 or more violations, as determined in any civil or criminal or administrative proceedings, of any one or more of the following Acts:

(A) The Consumer Finance Act; [7]

(B) The Consumer Installment Loan Act; [8]

(C) The Retail Installment Sales Act; [9]

(D) The Motor Vehicle Retail Installment Sales Act; [10]

(E) The Interest Act; [11]

(F) The Illinois Wage Assignment Act; [12]

(G) Part 8 of Article XII of the Code of Civil Procedure; [13] or

(H) The Consumer Fraud Act.[14]

8. A bond or Certificate of Deposit in the amount of $20,000 for each location at which the applicant intends to act as a used vehicle dealer. The bond shall be for the term of the license, or its renewal, for which application is made, and shall expire not sooner than December 31 of the year for which the license was issued or renewed. The bond shall run to the People of the State of Illinois, with surety by a bonding or insurance company authorized to do business in this State. It shall be conditioned upon the proper transmittal of all title and registration fees and taxes (excluding taxes under the Retailers' Occupation Tax Act) accepted by the applicant as a used vehicle dealer.

9. Such other information concerning the business of the applicant as the Secretary of State may by rule or regulation prescribe.

10. A statement that the applicant understands Chapter 1 through Chapter 5 of this Code.[15]

(c) Any change which renders no longer accurate any information contained in any application for a used vehicle dealer's license shall be amended within 30 days after the occurrence of each change on such form as the Secretary of State may prescribe by rule or regulation, accompanied by an amendatory fee of $2.

(d) Anything in this Chapter to the contrary notwithstanding, no person shall be licensed as a used vehicle dealer unless such person maintains an established place of business as defined in this Chapter.

(e) The Secretary of State shall, within a reasonable time after receipt, examine an application submitted to him under this Section. Unless the Secretary makes a determination that the application submitted to him does not conform to this Section or that grounds exist for a denial of the application under Section 5–501 of this Chapter, he must grant the applicant an original used vehicle dealer's license in writing for his established place of business and a supplemental license in writing for each additional place of business in such form as he may prescribe by rule or regulation which shall include the following:

1. The name of the person licensed;

2. If a corporation, the name and address of its officers or if a sole proprietorship, a partnership, an unincorporated association or any similar form of business organization, the name and address of the proprietor or of each partner, member, officer, director, trustee or manager;

3. In case of an original license, the established place of business of the licensee;

4. In the case of a supplemental license, the established place of business of the licensee and the additional place of business to which such supplemental license pertains.

(f) The appropriate instrument evidencing the license or a certified copy thereof, provided by the Secretary of State shall be kept posted, conspicuously, in the established place of business of the licensee and in each additional place of business, if any, maintained by such licensee.

(g) Except as provided in subsection (h) of this Section, all used vehicle dealer's licenses granted under this Section expire by operation of law on December 31 of the calendar year for which they are granted unless sooner revoked or cancelled under Section 5–501 of this Chapter.

(h) A used vehicle dealer's license may be renewed upon application and payment of the fee required herein, and submission of proof of coverage by an approved bond under the "Retailers' Occupation Tax Act" or proof that applicant is not subject to such bonding requirements, as in the case of an original license, but in case an application for the renewal of an effective license is made during the month of December, the effective license shall remain in force until the application for renewal is granted or denied by the Secretary of State.

(i) All persons licensed as a used vehicle dealer are required to furnish each purchaser of a motor vehicle:

1. A certificate of title properly assigned to the purchaser;

2. A statement verified under oath that all identifying numbers on the vehicle agree with those on the certificate of title;

3. A bill of sale properly executed on behalf of such person;

4. A copy of the Uniform Invoice-transaction reporting return referred to in Section 5–402 of this Chapter;

5. In the case of a rebuilt vehicle, a copy of the Disclosure of Rebuilt Vehicle Status; and

6. In the case of a vehicle for which the warranty has been reinstated, a copy of the warranty.

(j) A real estate broker holding a valid certificate of registration issued pursuant to "The Real Estate Brokers and Salesmen License Act" [16] may engage in the business of selling or dealing in house trailers not his own without being licensed as a used vehicle dealer under this Section; however such broker shall maintain a record of the transaction including the following:

(1) the name and address of the buyer and seller,

(2) the date of sale,

(3) a description of the mobile home, including the vehicle identification number, make, model, and year, and

(4) the Illinois certificate of title number. The foregoing records shall be available for inspection by any officer of the Secretary of State's Office at any reasonable hour.

(k) Except at the time of sale or repossession of the vehicle, no person licensed as a used vehicle dealer may issue any other person a newly created key to a vehicle unless the used vehicle dealer makes a copy of the driver's license or State identification card of the person requesting or obtaining the newly created key. The used vehicle dealer must retain the copy for 30 days.

A used vehicle dealer who violates this subsection (k) is guilty of a petty offense. Violation of this subsection (k) is not cause to suspend, revoke, cancel, or deny renewal of the used vehicle dealer's license.

P.A. 76-1586, § 5-102, eff. July 1, 1970. Amended by P.A. 77-2751, § 1, eff. Sept. 1, 1973; P.A. 81-932, § 1, eff. Sept. 22, 1979; P.A. 81-1458, § 1, eff. Sept. 8, 1980; P.A. 82-783, Art. XI, § 140, eff. July 13, 1982; P.A. 83-765, § 1, eff. Sept. 23, 1983; P.A. 83-1473, § 1, eff. Jan. 1, 1985; P.A. 84-986, § 1, eff. Sept. 25, 1985; P.A. 84-1302, § 1, eff. Jan. 1, 1987; P.A. 84-1304, § 1, eff. Jan. 1, 1987; P.A. 85-340, § 2, eff. Sept. 10, 1987; P.A. 85-1396, § 2, eff. Sept. 2, 1988; P.A. 86-444, § 1, eff. Jan. 1, 1990; P.A. 87-380, § 1, eff. July 1, 1992; P.A. 88-158, § 5, eff. Jan. 1, 1994; P.A. 89-189, § 5, eff. Jan. 1, 1996; P.A. 92-391, § 5, eff. Aug. 16, 2001; P.A. 92-835, § 5, eff. June 1, 2003.

Formerly Ill.Rev.Stat.1991, ch. 95 ½, ¶ 5-102.

1 35 ILCS 120/1 et seq.

2 625 ILCS 5/4-100 et seq.

3 625 ILCS 5/3-100 et seq.

4 625 ILCS 5/3-701 et seq.

5 625 ILCS 5/5-100 et seq.

6 720 ILCS 5/21-2.

7 Former Ill.Rev.Stat. ch. 17, ¶5601 et seq. (repealed).

8 205 ILCS 670/1 et seq.

9 815 ILCS 405/1 et seq.

10 815 ILCS 375/1 et seq.

11 815 ILCS 205/0.01 et seq.

12 740 ILCS 170/.01 et seq.

13 735 ILCS 5/12-801 et seq.

14 815 ILCS 505/1 et seq.

15 625 ILCS 5/1-100 et seq.

16 Former Ill.Rev.Stat. ch. 111, ¶5701 et seq. (repealed; see, now, 225 ILCS 455/1 et seq.).

For text of section effective until June 1, 2003, see 625 ILCS 5/5-102, ante

P.A. 92-835 incorporated the amendment by P.A. 92-391.

5/5-102.1. Permits for off site sales and exhibitions

§ 5-102.1. Permits for off site sales and exhibitions.

(a) A licensed new or used motor vehicle dealer licensed under Section 5-101 or 5-102 shall not engage in any off site sale without an off site sale permit issued by the Secretary under this Section.

The Secretary shall issue an off site sale permit to a dealer if:

(1) an application therefor is received by the Secretary prior to the beginning date of the proposed off site sale, accompanied by a fee of $25;

(2) the applicant is a licensed new vehicle dealer or used vehicle dealer in good standing; and

(3) the Secretary determines that the proposed off site sale will conform with the requirements imposed by law.

However, in no event shall an off site sale permit be issued to any licensed new or used vehicle dealer for any off site sale to be conducted outside that dealer's relevant market area, as that term is defined in this Chapter, except that this restriction shall not apply to off site sales of motor homes or recreational vehicles.

The provisions of this subsection shall not apply to self-contained motor homes, mini motor homes, van campers, and recreational trailers, including trailers designed and used to transport vessels or watercraft.

An off site sale permit does not authorize the sale of vehicles on a Sunday.

(b) Only a new or used vehicle dealer licensed under Section 5-101 or 5-102 may participate in a display exhibition and shall obtain a display exhibition permit issued by the Secretary under this Section.

The Secretary shall issue a display exhibition permit to a dealer if:

(1) an application therefor is received by the Secretary prior to the beginning date of the proposed exhibition, accompanied by a fee of $10;

(2) the applicant is a licensed new vehicle dealer or used vehicle dealer in good standing; and

(3) the Secretary determines that the proposed exhibition will conform with the requirements imposed by law.

A display exhibition permit shall be valid for a period of no longer than 30 days.

(c) A licensed new or used motor vehicle dealer under Section 5-101 or 5-102, or any other person as defined in this Section, may participate in a trade show exhibition and must obtain a trade show exhibition permit issued by the Secretary under this Section.

The Secretary shall issue a trade show exhibition permit if:

(1) an application is received by the Secretary before the beginning date of the proposed trade show exhibition, accompanied by a fee of $10;

(2) the applicant is a licensed new vehicle dealer or used vehicle dealer in good standing; and

(3) the Secretary determines that the proposed trade show exhibition shall conform with the requirements imposed by law.

A trade show exhibition permit shall be valid for a period of no longer than 30 days.

The provisions of this subsection shall not apply to self-contained motor homes, mini motor homes, van campers, and recreational trailers, including trailers designed and used to transport vessels or watercraft.

The term "any other person" shall mean new or used vehicle dealers licensed by other states; provided however, a trade show exhibition of new vehicles shall only be participated in by licensed new vehicle dealers, at least 2 of which must be licensed under Section 5-101.

(d) An Illinois or out-of-state licensed new or used trailer dealer, manufactured home dealer, motor home dealer, mini motor home dealer, or van camper dealer shall not engage in any off site sale or trade show exhibition without first acquiring a permit issued by the Secretary under this subsection. However, the provisions of this Section shall not apply to a licensed trailer dealer selling a mobile home or manufactured housing, as defined in the Illinois Manufactured Housing and Mobile Home Safety Act,[1] if the manufactured housing or mobile home has utilities permanently attached. The Secretary shall issue a permit to an Illinois dealer if:

(1) an application is received by the Secretary before the beginning date of the proposed off site sale or trade show exhibition, accompanied by a fee of $25;

(2) the applicant is a licensed new or used vehicle dealer in good standing; and

(3) the Secretary determines that the proposed off site sale or trade show exhibition will conform with the requirements imposed by law.

The Secretary shall issue a permit to an out-of-state dealer if the requirements of subdivisions (1), (2), and (3) of this subsection (d) are met and at least 2 licensed Illinois dealers will participate in the off site sale or trade show exhibition.

A permit issued pursuant to this subsection shall allow for the sale of vehicles at either an off site sale or at a trade show exhibition. The permit shall be valid for a period not to exceed 30 days.

(e) The Secretary of State may adopt rules regulating the conduct of off site sales and exhibitions, and governing the issuance and enforcement of the permits authorized under this Section.

P.A. 76–1586, § 5–102.1, added by P.A. 87–380, § 1, eff. July 1, 1992. Amended by P.A. 87–1249, § 1, eff. Dec. 24, 1992; P.A. 88–470, § 10, eff. Sept. 1, 1993; P.A. 88–588, § 5, eff. Jan. 1, 1995; P.A. 88–685, § 5, eff. Jan. 24, 1995; P.A. 89–235, Art. 2, § 2–120, eff. Aug. 4, 1995; P.A. 89–551, § 5, eff. Jan. 1, 1997; P.A. 90–718, § 5, eff. Jan. 1, 1999; P.A. 90–774, § 5, eff. Aug. 14, 1998; P.A. 91–357, § 231, eff. July 29, 1999.

Formerly Ill.Rev.Stat.1991, ch. 95 ½, ¶ 5–102.1.

[1] 430 ILCS 115/1 et seq.

5/5–103. Specifications of delivery and preparation obligations of vehicle dealers prior to delivery of new vehicles to retail buyers; inspection; applicability

§ 5–103. (a) Every new vehicle manufacturer shall specify the delivery and preparation obligations of its vehicle dealers prior to delivery of new vehicles to retail buyers. A copy of the delivery and preparation obligations of its dealers shall be filed with the Secretary of State by every vehicle manufacturer and shall constitute the vehicle dealer's only responsibility for product liability as between the dealer and the manufacturer. A manufacturer's product or warranty liability to the dealer shall extend to any mechanical, body or parts defect constituting a breach of any express or implied warranty of the manufacturer. The manufacturer shall reasonably compensate any authorized dealer who rectifies a defect which constitutes a breach of any express or implied warranty of the manufacturer and for preparation and delivery obligations. Every dealer shall perform the preparation and get ready services specified by the manufacturer to be performed prior to the delivery of the new vehicle to the buyer.

(b) The owner of the vehicle may cause the vehicle to be inspected according to this Section and have the original manufacturer's warranty reinstated if the vehicle is a theft recovery that has been salvaged and is recovered without structural damage or missing essential parts, excluding wheels, damage to the steering column, and radios provided the owner:

(1) Submits the vehicle to a franchised dealer for a complete inspection, including fluids, frame, essential parts, and other items deemed by the manufacturer as essential for verification of the condition of the vehicle at the time of recovery.

(2) Submits a copy of the police recovery report to the inspecting dealer.

(3) Paid the inspection fee charged by the franchised dealer.

The manufacturer shall reinstate the original manufacturer's warranty if a vehicle is certified by a franchised dealer as having complied with the provisions of this Section. The manufacturer shall, in addition to reinstating the warranty, provide the owner with a written statement indicating that the original manufacturer's warranty has been reinstated.

(c) Nothing in this Section shall affect a cause of action a buyer may have against a dealer or manufacturer under present applicable statutory or case law.

P.A. 76–1586, § 5–103, added by P.A. 77–1640, § 1, eff. Sept. 24, 1971. Amended by P.A. 77–2751, § 1, eff. Sept. 1, 1972; P.A. 78–255, § 61, eff. Oct. 1, 1973; P.A. 83–405, § 1, eff. Jan. 1, 1984; P.A. 89–189, § 5, eff. Jan. 1, 1996; P.A. 92–458, § 5, eff. Aug. 22, 2001.

Formerly Ill.Rev.Stat.1991, ch. 95 ½, ¶ 5–103.

5/5–104. Disclosure of miles per gallon in tests conducted by the U.S. Environmental Protection Agency

§ 5–104. (a) On and after January 1, 1976, each manufacturer of a 1976 or later model year vehicle of the first division manufactured for sale in this State, other than a motorcycle, shall clearly and conspicuously indicate, on the price listing affixed to the vehicle pursuant to the "Automobile Information Disclosure Act", (15 United States Code 1231 through 1233),[1] the following, with the appropriate gasoline mileage figure:

"In tests for fuel economy in city and highway driving conducted by the United States Environmental Protection Agency, this passenger vehicle obtained .... miles per gallon of gasoline."

P.A. 76–1586, § 5–104, added by P.A. 79–747, § 1, eff. Oct. 1, 1975.

Formerly Ill.Rev.Stat.1991, ch. 95 ½, ¶ 5–104.

[1] 15 U.S.C.A. § 1231 et seq.

5/5–104.1. Informational labels on pickup trucks; penalty

§ 5-104.1. Informational labels on pickup trucks; penalty. (1) Every manufacturer of second division vehicles having a gross vehicle weight rating of 8,500 pounds or less which are sold or offered for sale for use upon the public streets or highways within this State shall, prior to the delivery of the second division vehicle to an Illinois dealer, or on or prior to the introduction date of new models delivered to an Illinois dealer, securely affix to the windshield or side window of the second division vehicle a label upon which the manufacturer shall endorse clearly, distinctly and legibly true and correct entries disclosing information identical to and in the same manner as required on new first division vehicles. The label shall remain affixed to the second division vehicle until delivery of the second division vehicle to the ultimate purchaser. Any manufacturer who shall willfully fail to affix a proper label required by this Section or any person who shall willfully remove, alter or mutilate a label prior to delivery of the second division vehicle to the ultimate purchaser is guilty of a misdemeanor. This Section shall not apply to such second division vehicles for which the annual sales in Illinois of the previous model year were less than 200.

(2) This Section shall apply to second division vehicles having a gross vehicle weight rating of 8,500 pounds or less built after December 31, 1987.

P.A. 76-1586, § 5-104.1, added by P.A. 85-387, § 1, eff. Jan. 1, 1988.

Formerly Ill.Rev.Stat.1991, ch. 95 ½, ¶ 5-104.1.

5/5-104.2. Nonconforming vehicles; sale

§ 5-104.2. Nonconforming vehicles; sale.

(a) Every manufacturer shall be prohibited from reselling any motor vehicle that has been finally ordered, determined, or adjudicated as having a nonconformity under the New Vehicle Buyer Protection Act [1] or a similar law of any state, territory, or country, and that the manufacturer repurchased or replaced because of the nonconformity, unless the manufacturer has corrected the nonconformity and issues a disclosure statement prior to resale stating that the vehicle was repurchased or replaced under the New Vehicle Buyer Protection Act or similar law of any other state, territory, or country; identifying the nonconformity; and warranting that the nonconformity has been corrected. The disclosure statement must accompany the vehicle through the first retail purchase.

(b) "Nonconformity" refers to a new vehicle's failure to conform to all express warranties applicable to the vehicle, which failure substantially impairs the use, market value, or safety of the vehicle.

(c) The disclosure statement referred to in subsection (a) shall be in substantially the same form as below:

"IMPORTANT

Vehicle Identification Number (VIN): (Insert VIN Number); Year: (Insert Year); Make (Insert Make); Model: (Insert Model). This vehicle was previously sold as new. It was subsequently ordered as having a nonconformity by final decision of court proceeding or State run arbitration. It was subsequently repurchased by its manufacturer because it did not conform to the manufacturer's express warranty and the nonconformity was not cured within a reasonable time as provided by Illinois law. The following nonconformities have been corrected (a minimum of 5 numbered lines shall be provided to describe the nonconformity or nonconformities)."

The customer shall sign the disclosure statement. This disclosure language shall be in at least 8-point type.

P.A. 76-1586, § 5-104.2, added by P.A. 88-415, § 10, eff. Aug. 20, 1993.

1 815 ILCS 380/1 et seq.

5/5-104.3. Disclosure of rebuilt vehicle

§ 5-104.3. Disclosure of rebuilt vehicle.

(a) No person shall knowingly, with intent to defraud or deceive another, sell a vehicle for which a rebuilt title has been issued unless that vehicle is accompanied by a Disclosure of Rebuilt Vehicle Status form, properly signed and delivered to the buyer.

(b) The Secretary of State may by rule or regulation prescribe the format and information contained in the Disclosure of Rebuilt Vehicle Status form.

(c) A violation of subsection (a) of this Section is a Class A misdemeanor. A second or subsequent violation of subsection (a) of this Section is a Class 4 felony.

P.A. 76-1586, § 5-104.3, added by P.A. 89-189, § 5, eff. Jan. 1, 1996. Amended by P.A. 91-891, § 5, eff. July 6, 2000.

5/5-105. Investigation of licensee required

§ 5-105. Investigation of licensee required. Every person seeking a license under Chapter 5 of this Act, as part of the application process, authorizes an investigation to determine if the applicant has ever been convicted of a crime and if so, the disposition of those convictions. This authorization shall indicate the scope of the inquiry and the agencies which may be contacted. Upon this authorization the Secretary of State may request and receive information and assistance from any Federal, State or local governmental agency as part of the authorized investigation. The Department of State Police shall provide information concerning any criminal convictions and their disposition brought against the applicant upon request of the Secretary of State when the request is made in the form and manner required by the Department of State Police. The information derived from this investigation, including the source of this information, and any conclusions or recommendations derived from this information by the Secretary of State shall be provided to the applicant or his designee. Upon request to the Secretary of State prior to any final action by the Secretary of State on the application, no information obtained from such investigation may be placed in any automated information system. Any criminal convictions and their disposition information obtained by the Secretary of State shall be confidential and may not be transmitted outside the Office of the Secretary of State, except as required herein, and may not be transmitted to anyone within the Office of the Secretary of State except as needed for the purpose of evaluating the application. All criminal convictions and their disposition and information obtained by the Division of Investigation shall be destroyed no later than 60 days after the Division of Investigation has made a final ruling on the application, and all rights of appeal have expired and pending appeals have been completed. The only physical identity materials which the applicant can be required to provide the Secretary of State are photographs or fingerprints. Only information and standards which bear a reasonable and rational relation to the performance of a licensee shall be used by the Secretary of State. The Secretary of State shall adopt rules and regulations for the administration of this Section. Any employee of the Secretary of State who gives or causes to be given away any confidential information concerning any criminal convictions and their disposition of an applicant shall be guilty of a Class A misdemeanor.

P.A. 76-1586, § 5-105, added by P.A. 81-932, § 1, eff. Sept. 22, 1979. Amended by P.A. 84-25, Art. IV, § 27, eff. July 18, 1985.

Formerly Ill.Rev.Stat.1991, ch. 95 ½, ¶ 5-105.

5/5-106. Sales on Sunday

§ 5-106. No person may keep open, operate, or assist in keeping open or operating any established or additional place of business for the purpose of buying, selling, bartering, exchanging, or leasing for a period of 1 year or more, or offering for sale, barter, exchange, or lease for a period of 1 year or more, any motor vehicle, whether new or used, on the first day of the week, commonly called Sunday; provided, that this Section does not apply to the opening of an established or additional place of business on Sunday for the following purposes:

(1) to sell petroleum products, tires or repair parts and accessories;

(2) to operate and conduct a motor vehicle repair shop;

(3) to supply services for the washing, towing or wrecking of motor vehicles;

(4) to participate in a trade show exhibition or display exhibition by a dealer who has been granted a permit by the Secretary of State pursuant to Section 5-102.1 of this Article;

(5) to sell motorcycles, motor driven cycles, motorized pedalcycles when offered for sale by a dealer licensed under Sections 5-101 and 5-102 to sell only such motor vehicles;

(6) to offer for sale manufactured housing;

(7) to sell self-contained motor homes, mini motor homes, van campers and recreational trailers when offered for sale by a dealer at an established or additional place of business where only such vehicles are displayed or offered for sale. This exemption includes dealers with off site sales or trade show exhibition permits issued pursuant to subsection (d) of Section 5-102.1 of this Article.

P.A. 76-1586, § 5-106, added by P.A. 82-788, § 1, eff. Jan. 1, 1983. Amended by P.A. 84-818, § 1, eff. Sept. 22, 1985; P.A. 85-1374, § 1, eff. Jan. 1, 1989; P.A. 86-444, § 1, eff. Jan. 1, 1990; P.A. 89-551, § 5, eff. Jan. 1, 1997.

Formerly Ill.Rev.Stat.1991, ch. 95 ½, ¶ 5-106.

5/5-107. Bond exemption

§ 5-107. Bond exemption. The following persons shall be exempt from the bond required in Sections 5-101 and 5-102: (1) Any person who has been continuously licensed under Section 5-101 or 5-102 since calendar year 1983; (2) any licensee who as determined by the Secretary of State, has faithfully and continuously complied with conditions of the bond requirement for a period of 36 consecutive months.

This exemption shall continue for each licensee until such time as he may be determined by the Secretary of State to be delinquent or deficient in the transmittal of title and registration fees or taxes.

This amendatory Act of 1983 shall be applicable to the 1984 registration year and thereafter.

A person whose license is cancelled due to the voluntary surrender of such license, who applies for a new license for the same license year or one license year after the license year of the cancelled license, will remain exempt under paragraph (1) above if the only break in the continuous licensure is caused by the cancellation due to the voluntary surrender of the license.

P.A. 76-1586, § 5-107, added by P.A. 83-765, § 1, eff. Sept. 23, 1983. Amended by P.A. 85-572, § 1, eff. Sept. 18, 1987; P.A. 85-1209, Art. III, § 3-60, eff. Aug. 30, 1988; P.A. 88-158, § 5, eff. Jan. 1, 1994; P.A. 88-520, § 5, eff. Nov. 16, 1993.

Formerly Ill.Rev.Stat.1991, ch. 95 ½, ¶ 5-107.

P.A. 88-520 incorporated the amendment by P.A. 88-158.

5/5-108. Vehicle Referral and Marketing Services

§ 5-108. Vehicle Referral and Marketing Services. Nothing in this Code shall be construed to prohibit a credit union, as defined in the Illinois Credit Union Act,[1] a bank, as defined in the Illinois Banking Act,[2] or any firm, copartnership, association or corporation from advertising the sale of motor vehicles by licensed dealers or advertising motor vehicle purchase opportunities from licensed dealers, from referring potential purchasers of motor vehicles to licensed dealers, or from soliciting purchasers of motor vehicles for licensed dealers. However, any motor vehicle sale resulting from those activities may only be consummated by a dealer licensed under Section 5-101 or 5-102 of this Code.

P.A. 76-1586, § 5-108, added by P.A. 87-380, § 1, eff. July 1, 1992.

Formerly Ill.Rev.Stat.1991, ch. 95 ½, ¶ 5-108.

[1] 205 ILCS 305/1 et seq.

[2] 205 ILCS 5/1 et seq.

5/5-109. Manufacturers and Distributors; Fees

§ 5-109. Manufacturers and Distributors; Fees.

(a) "Manufacturer" means any person who manufactures or assembles new motor vehicles either within or without of this State.

(b) "Distributor" means any person who distributes or sells new motor vehicles to new vehicle dealers, or who maintains distributor representatives in this State, and who is not a manufacturer.

(c) Each manufacturer and distributor doing business in this State shall pay an annual fee of $1500 to the Secretary of State.

P.A. 76-1586, § 5-109, added by P.A. 89-145, § 10, eff. July 14, 1995. Amended by P.A. 89-433, § 5, eff. Dec. 15, 1995.

ARTICLE II. TRANSPORTERS

Section

5/5-201. Transporters must apply for in-transit plates

§ 5-201. Transporters must apply for in-transit plates. (a) No person shall engage in this State in the business as a transporter until such person shall apply for and receive from the Secretary of State a generally distinctive set of two "in-transit license plates" for any vehicle so transported by him.

(b) An application for a generally distinctive number under this Article shall be filed with the Secretary of State, duly verified by oath and in such form as the Secretary of State may by rule or regulation prescribe and shall contain the name and business address of such person, the certificate, registration or permit number issued by the Illinois Commerce Commission and such other information concerning the business of the applicant as the Secretary of State may by rule or regulation prescribe. If the applicant does not hold a certificate, registration or permit from the Illinois Commerce Commission to so transport, such application shall be denied.

(c) An application for a generally distinctive set of two "in-transit license plates" shall be accompanied by the prescribed fee. Upon the payment of such license fee, such application shall be filed and recorded in the office of the Secretary of State. Thereupon the Secretary of State shall assign and issue to such person a generally distinctive number and without any further expense to him shall deliver to such person at his business address a certificate of registration in such form as the Secretary of State may prescribe and one set of two "in-transit license plates" with a number corresponding to the number of such certificate of registration. Such in-transit plates shall be used by such person only on vehicles transported, but not owned, by him.

(d) Except as provided in sub-section (3) hereof, all certificates of registration and "in-transit plates" granted under this Section shall expire by operation of law on December 31 of the calendar year for which they are granted unless sooner revoked under the provisions of Section 5–501 of this Chapter.

(e) A certificate of registration under this Article may be renewed upon application and payment of the fee required herein as in the case of an original application, provided, however, that in case an application for renewal of an effective registration is made during the month of December, such existing registration shall remain in force until such application for renewal is granted by the Secretary of State.

(f) Any person registered as a transporter under the Article may make application for additional duplicate sets of "in-transit plates" on such form as the Secretary of State may by rule or regulation prescribe, from time to time to obtain as many duplicate sets of "in-transit plates" as he may desire upon payment of the prescribed fee for each set. Such duplicate plates shall bear the number of that person's original certificate of registration.

(g) In case of loss or destruction of one license plate issued to a transporter under this Section, such transporter may obtain a duplicate of the same by filing an affidavit to that effect with the Secretary of State, accompanied by the prescribed fee.

(h) An original "in-transit plate" or a duplicate shall be attached to the front and rear of each vehicle so transported in this State; provided, that if one such vehicle is towing another such vehicle, one plate or duplicate plate shall be attached to the front of the towing vehicle and one such plate to the rear of the rearmost towed vehicle.

(i) Anything in this Chapter to the contrary notwithstanding, the provisions of this Section shall not apply to a nonresident engaged in such business and using the public highways of this State if he has an "in-transit plate" or license from the State, foreign country or province, territory or federal district of which he is a resident and such State, country, province, territory or district grants a like exemption to residents of this State.

P.A. 76–1586, § 5–201, eff. July 1, 1970.

Formerly Ill.Rev.Stat.1991, ch. 95 ½, ¶ 5–201.

5/5–202. Tow or Wrecker operators must register tow or wrecker vehicles

§ 5–202. Tow or Wrecker operators must register tow or wrecker vehicles. (a) No person in this State shall engage in the business of operating a tow truck or wrecker or operate a tow or wrecker vehicle until such person shall register any vehicle to be used for such purpose and apply for and receive from the Secretary of State a generally distinctive set of 3 "tow truck" plates for any towing or wrecker vehicle operated by him.

(b) An application for registration for a generally distinctive set of 3 "tow truck" plates under this Article shall be filed with the Secretary of State, duly verified by oath and in such form as the Secretary of State may by rule or regulation prescribe and shall contain the name and business address of such person, the vehicle identification number of the vehicle for which such application is made, proof of insurance as set forth in paragraph (d) of Section 12–606 of this Code, and such other information concerning the business of the applicant as the Secretary of State may by rule or regulation prescribe.

(c) The application for registration and a generally distinctive set of 3 "tow truck" plates shall be accompanied by the prescribed fee. Upon payment of such fee, such registration and application shall be filed and recorded in the office of the Secretary of State. Thereupon the Secretary of State shall assign and issue to such person a generally distinctive number for each vehicle and without further expense to him shall deliver to such person at his place of business address one set of 3 "tow truck" plates. Such "tow truck" plates shall be used by such person only on the vehicle for which application was made and the vehicle being towed, and are not transferable.

(d) All "tow truck" plates granted under this Section shall expire by operation of law on December 31 of the calendar year for which they are granted unless sooner revoked under the provisions of Section 5–501 of this Chapter.

(e) One "tow truck" plate shall be attached to the front and rear of each registered vehicle, and one "tow truck" plate shall be attached to the rear of the vehicle being towed unless the towed vehicle displays a valid registration plate visible from the rear while being towed, so that the numbers and letter on the plate are clearly visible to any person following the vehicle being towed. However, illumination of the rear plate required by subsection (c) of Section 12–201 of this Code shall not apply to the third plate displayed on the towed vehicle. In addition, the vehicle registration plates assigned to the vehicle being towed shall be displayed as provided in Section 3–413 of this Code.

P.A. 76–1586, § 5–202, added by P.A. 83–1473, § 1, eff. Jan. 1, 1985. Amended by P.A. 86–444, § 1, eff. Jan. 1, 1990; P.A. 86–565, § 1, eff. Jan. 1, 1990; P.A. 86–1028, Art. II, § 2–44, eff. Feb. 5, 1990.

Formerly Ill.Rev.Stat.1991, ch. 95 ½, ¶ 5–202.

P.A. 86–1028, the First 1990 Revisory Act, provides in Art. II, for the revision and renumbering of certain Sections of Acts which have been added or amended by more than one Act of the 86th General Assembly; repeals certain Sections that have been both amended and repealed in the 86th General Assembly and incorporates amendments into successor laws; corrects errors, revises cross-references and deletes obsolete text in such sections contained in P.A. 86–1 through P.A. 86–1009.

5/5–207. Licensing of towing services as dealers

§ 5–207. Licensing of towing services as dealers. Any towing service that sells or disposes of 5 or more vehicles in a calendar year to anyone other than a person licensed under Chapter 5 of this Code must also be licensed under Section 5–102 of this Chapter.

P.A. 76–1586, § 5–207, added by P.A. 89–433, § 5, eff. Dec. 15, 1995.

ARTICLE III. USED PARTS DEALERS, SCRAP PROCESSORS, AUTOMOTIVE PARTS RECYCLERS AND REBUILDERS

Article III heading which formerly read "Used Parts Dealers, Wreckers and Rebuilders" was amended by P.A. 78–1205, § 2, eff. Sept. 5, 1974.

Section

5/5-301. Automotive parts recyclers, scrap processors, repairers and rebuilders must be licensed

§ 5-301. Automotive parts recyclers, scrap processors, repairers and rebuilders must be licensed.

(a) No person in this State shall, except as an incident to the servicing of vehicles, carry on or conduct the business of a automotive parts recyclers, a scrap processor, a repairer, or a rebuilder, unless licensed to do so in writing by the Secretary of State under this Section. No person shall rebuild a salvage vehicle unless such person is licensed as a rebuilder by the Secretary of State under this Section. Each license shall be applied for and issued separately, except that a license issued to a new vehicle dealer under Section 5-101 of this Code shall also be deemed to be a repairer license.

(b) Any application filed with the Secretary of State, shall be duly verified by oath, in such form as the Secretary of State may by rule or regulation prescribe and shall contain:

1. The name and type of business organization of the applicant and his principal or additional places of business, if any, in this State.

2. The kind or kinds of business enumerated in subsection (a) of this Section to be conducted at each location.

3. If the applicant is a corporation, a list of its officers, directors, and shareholders having a ten percent or greater ownership interest in the corporation, setting forth the residence address of each; if the applicant is a sole proprietorship, a partnership, an unincorporated association, a trust, or any similar form of business organization, the names and residence address of the proprietor or of each partner, member, officer, director, trustee or manager.

4. A statement that the applicant's officers, directors, shareholders having a ten percent or greater ownership interest therein, proprietor, partner, member, officer, director, trustee, manager, or other principals in the business have not committed in the past three years any one violation as determined in any civil or criminal or administrative proceedings of any one of the following Acts:

(a) The Anti Theft Laws of the Illinois Vehicle Code;[1]

(b) The "Certificate of Title Laws" of the Illinois Vehicle Code;[2]

(c) The "Offenses against Registration and Certificates of Title Laws" of the Illinois Vehicle Code;[3]

(d) The "Dealers, Transporters, Wreckers and Rebuilders Laws" of the Illinois Vehicle Code;[4]

(e) Section 21-2 of the Criminal Code of 1961,[5] Criminal Trespass to Vehicles; or

(f) The Retailers Occupation Tax Act.[6]

5. A statement that the applicant's officers, directors, shareholders having a ten percent or greater ownership interest therein, proprietor, partner, member, officer, director, trustee, manager or other principals in the business have not committed in any calendar year 3 or more violations, as determined in any civil or criminal or administrative proceedings, of any one or more of the following Acts:

(a) The Consumer Finance Act;[7]

(b) The Consumer Installment Loan Act;[8]

(c) The Retail Installment Sales Act;[9]

(d) The Motor Vehicle Retail Installment Sales Act;[10]

(e) The Interest Act;[11]

(f) The Illinois Wage Assignment Act;[12]

(g) Part 8 of Article XII of the Code of Civil Procedure;[13] or

(h) The Consumer Fraud Act.[14]

6. An application for a license shall be accompanied by the following fees: $50 for applicant's established place of business; $25 for each additional place of business, if any, to which the application pertains; provided, however, that if such an application is made after June 15 of any year, the license fee shall be $25 for applicant's established place of business plus $12.50 for each additional place of business, if any, to which the application pertains. License fees shall be returnable only in the event that such application shall be denied by the Secretary of State.

7. A statement that the applicant understands Chapter 1 through Chapter 5 of this Code.[15]

8. A statement that the applicant shall comply with subsection (e) of this Section.

(c) Any change which renders no longer accurate any information contained in any application for a license filed with the Secretary of State shall be amended within 30 days after the occurrence of such change on such form as the Secretary of State may prescribe by rule or regulation, accompanied by an amendatory fee of $2.

(d) Anything in this chapter to the contrary, notwithstanding, no person shall be licensed under this Section unless such person shall maintain an established place of business as defined in this Chapter.

(e) The Secretary of State shall within a reasonable time after receipt thereof, examine an application submitted to him under this Section and unless he makes a determination that the application submitted to him does not conform with the requirements of this Section or that grounds exist for a denial of the application, as prescribed in Section 5-501 of this Chapter, grant the applicant an original license as applied for in writing for his established place of business and a supplemental license in writing for each additional place of business in such form as he may prescribe by rule or regulation which shall include the following:

1. The name of the person licensed;

2. If a corporation, the name and address of its officers or if a sole proprietorship, a partnership, an unincorporated association or any similar form of business organization, the name and address of the proprietor or of each partner, member, officer, director, trustee or manager;

3. A designation of the kind or kinds of business enumerated in subsection (a) of this Section to be conducted at each location;

4. In the case of an original license, the established place of business of the licensee;

5. In the case of a supplemental license, the established place of business of the licensee and the additional place of business to which such supplemental license pertains.

(f) The appropriate instrument evidencing the license or a certified copy thereof, provided by the Secretary of State shall be kept, posted, conspicuously in the established place of business of the licensee and in each additional place of business, if any, maintained by such licensee. The licensee also shall post conspicuously in the established place of business and in each additional place of business a notice which states that such business is required to be licensed by the Secretary of State under Section 5-301, and which provides the license number of the business and the license expiration date. This notice also shall advise the consumer that any complaints as to the quality of service may be brought to the attention of the Attorney General. The information required on this notice also shall be printed conspicuously on all estimates and receipts for work by the licensee subject to this Section. The Secretary of State shall prescribe the specific format of this notice.

(g) Except as provided in subsection (h) hereof, licenses granted under this Section shall expire by operation of law on December 31 of the calendar year for which they are granted unless sooner revoked or cancelled under the provisions of Section 5-501 of this Chapter.

(h) Any license granted under this Section may be renewed upon application and payment of the fee required herein as in the case of an original license, provided, however, that in case an application for the renewal of an effective license is made during the month of December, such effective license shall remain in force until such application is granted or denied by the Secretary of State.

(i) All automotive repairers and rebuilders shall, in addition to the requirements of subsections (a) through (h) of this Section, meet the following licensing requirements:

1. Provide proof that the property on which first time applicants plan to do business is in compliance with local zoning laws and regulations, and a listing of zoning classification;

2. Provide proof that the applicant for a repairer's license complies with the proper workers' compensation rate code or classification, and listing the code of classification for that industry;

3. Provide proof that the applicant for a rebuilder's license complies with the proper workers' compensation rate code or classification for the repair industry or the auto parts recycling industry and listing the code of classification;

4. Provide proof that the applicant has obtained or applied for a hazardous waste generator number, and listing the actual number if available or certificate of exemption;

5. Provide proof that applicant has proper liability insurance, and listing the name of the insurer and the policy number; and

6. Provide proof that the applicant has obtained or applied for the proper State sales tax classification and federal identification tax number, and listing the actual numbers if available.

(j) All automotive parts recyclers shall, in addition to the requirements of subsections (a) through (h) of this Section, meet the following licensing requirements:

1. A statement that the applicant purchases 5 vehicles per year or has 5 hulks or chassis in stock;

2. Provide proof that the property on which all first time applicants will do business does comply to the proper local zoning laws in existence, and a listing of zoning classifications;

3. Provide proof that applicant complies with the proper workers' compensation rate code or classification, and listing the code of classification; and

4. Provide proof that applicant has obtained or applied for the proper State sales tax classification and federal identification tax number, and listing the actual numbers if available.

P.A. 76-1586, § 5-301, eff. July 1, 1970. Amended by P.A. 77-643, § 1, eff. Aug. 4, 1971; P.A. 78-858, § 1, eff. Jan. 1, 1974; P.A. 78-1205, § 1, eff. Sept. 5, 1974; P.A. 78-1297, § 58, eff. March 4, 1975; P.A. 81-932, § 1, eff. Sept. 22, 1979; P.A. 82-783, Art. XI, § 140, eff. July 13, 1982; P.A. 83-1473, § 1, eff. Jan. 1, 1985; P.A. 84-680, § 2, eff. Jan. 1, 1986; P.A. 84-1302, § 1, eff. Jan. 1, 1987; P.A. 84-1304, § 1, eff. Jan. 1, 1987; P.A. 85-1396, § 2, eff. Sept. 2, 1988; P.A. 86-295, § 1, eff. Aug. 30, 1989; P.A. 86-444, § 1, eff. Jan. 1, 1990; P.A. 86-1028, Art. II, § 2-44, eff. Feb. 5, 1990; P.A. 87-682, § 1, eff. Jan. 1, 1992; P.A. 89-189, § 5, eff. Jan. 1, 1996.

Formerly Ill.Rev.Stat.1991, ch. 95 ½, ¶ 5-301.

[1] 625 ILCS 5/4-100 et seq.

[2] 625 ILCS 5/3-100 et seq.

[3] 625 ILCS 5/3-701 et seq.

[4] 625 ILCS 5/5-100 et seq.

[5] 720 ILCS 5/21-2.

[6] 35 ILCS 120/1 et seq.

[7] Former Ill.Rev.Stat. ch. 17, ¶ 5601 et seq. (repealed).

[8] 205 ILCS 670/1 et seq.

[9] 815 ILCS 405/1 et seq.

[10] 815 ILCS 375/1 et seq.

[11] 815 ILCS 205/0.01 et seq.

[12] 740 ILCS 170/.01 et seq.

[13] 735 ILCS 5/12-801 et seq.

[14] 815 ILCS 505/1 et seq.

[15] 625 ILCS 5/1-100 et seq. to 5/5-100 et seq.

5/5-302. Out-of-state salvage vehicle buyer must be licensed

§ 5-302. Out-of-state salvage vehicle buyer must be licensed. (a) No person in this State shall sell or offer at auction salvage vehicles to a nonresident who has not been issued an out-of-state salvage vehicle buyer's ID card from the Secretary of State under this Section. To qualify for this ID card, the applicant shall submit with the application an out-of-state dealer license which is issued by the applicant's state and is substantially equivalent to that of a rebuilder, automotive parts recycler or scrap processor, as licensed under this Code.

(b) Any application filed with the Secretary of State, shall be duly verified by oath, in such form as the Secretary of State may by rule or regulation prescribe.

(c) An application for an out-of-state ID card shall be accompanied by a fee of $100; provided however, that if an application is made after June 15 of any year, the ID card fee shall be $50. Any fees shall be returnable only in the event that such application is denied by the Secretary of State.

(d) The Secretary of State shall within a reasonable time after receipt thereof, examine an application submitted to him under this Section and unless he makes a determination that the application submitted to him does not conform with the requirements of this Section or that grounds exist for a denial of the application, as prescribed in Section 5-501 of this Chapter, grant the applicant an out-of-state salvage vehicle buyer's ID card.

(e) Except as provided in subsection (f) of this Section, licenses granted under this Section shall expire by operation of law on December 31 of the calendar year for which they are granted unless revoked or cancelled under the provisions of Section 5-501 of this Chapter.

(f) Any license granted under this Section may be renewed upon application and payment of the fee required for an original license, provided however, that where an application for the renewal of a license is made during the month of December, the license in effect at the time of application for renewal shall remain in force until such application is granted or denied by the Secretary of State.

(g) An out-of-state salvage vehicle buyer shall be subject to the inspection of records pertaining to the acquisition of salvage vehicles in this State in accordance with this Code and such rules as the Secretary of State may promulgate.

(h) Beginning July 1, 1988, the application filed with the Secretary of State shall also contain:

1. The name and type of business organization of the applicant and his principal or other places of business;

2. If the applicant is a corporation, a list of its officers, directors, and shareholders having a 10% or greater ownership interest in the corporation, setting forth the residence address of each; if the applicant is a sole proprietorship, a partnership, an unincorporated association, a trust, or any similar form of business organization, the names and residence address of the proprietor, or of each partner, member, officer, director, trustee or manager;

3. A statement that the applicant's officers, directors, shareholders having a 10% or greater ownership interest therein, proprietor, partner, member, officer, director, trustee, manager, or other principals in the business have not committed in the past 3 years any one violation as determined in any civil or criminal or administrative proceedings of any one of the following Acts:

(A) The "Anti Theft Laws" of the Illinois Vehicle Code; [1]

(B) The "Certificate of Title Laws" of the Illinois Vehicle Code; [2]

(C) The "Offenses against Registration and Certificates of Title Laws" of the Illinois Vehicle Code; [3]

(D) The "Dealers, Transporters, Wreckers and Rebuilders Laws" of the Illinois Vehicle Code; [4]

(E) Section 21-2 of the Criminal Code of 1961,[5] Criminal Trespass to Vehicles; or

(F) The "Retailers Occupation Tax Act"; [6]

4. A statement that the applicant's officers, directors, shareholders having a 10% or greater ownership interest therein, proprietor, partner, member, officer, director, trustee, manager or other principals in the business have not committed in any calendar year 3 or more violations, as determined in any civil or criminal or administrative proceedings, of any one or more of the following Acts:

(A) The "Consumer Finance Act"; [7]

(B) The "Consumer Installment Loan Act"; [8]

(C) The "Retail Installment Sales Act"; [9]

(D) The "Motor Vehicle Retail Installment Sales Act"; [10]

(E) "An Act in relation to the rate of interest and other charges in connection with sales on credit and the lending of money", approved May 24, 1879, as amended; [11]

(F) "An Act to promote the welfare of wage earners by regulating the assignment of wages, and prescribing a penalty for the violation thereof", approved July 1, 1935, as amended; [12]

(G) Part 8 of Article XII of the Code of Civil Procedure; [13] or

(H) The "Consumer Fraud Act"; [14] and

5. A statement that the applicant understands Chapters 1 through 5 of this Code.[15]

(i) Any change which renders no longer accurate any information contained in any application for a license filed with the Secretary of State shall be amended within 30 days after the occurrence of such change on such form as the Secretary of State may prescribe by rule or regulation, accompanied by an amendatory fee of $2.

P.A. 76-1586, § 5-302, added by P.A. 85-572, § 1, eff. Sept. 18, 1987. Amended by P.A. 85-1396, § 2, eff. Sept. 2, 1988; P.A. 86-444, § 1, eff. Jan. 1, 1990.

Formerly Ill.Rev.Stat.1991, ch. 95 ½, ¶ 5-302.

1 625 ILCS 5/4-100 et seq.

2 625 ILCS 5/3-100 et seq.

3 625 ILCS 5/3-701 et seq.

4 625 ILCS 5/5-100 et seq.

5 720 ILCS 5/21-2.

6 35 ILCS 120/1 et seq.

7 Former Ill.Rev.Stat. ch. 17, ¶ 5601 et seq. (repealed).

8 205 ILCS 670/1 et seq.

9 815 ILCS 405/1 et seq.

10 815 ILCS 375/1 et seq.

11 815 ILCS 205/1 et seq.

12 740 ILCS 170/.01 et seq.

13 735 ILCS 5/12-801 et seq.

14 815 ILCS 505/1 et seq.

15 625 ILCS 5/1-100 et seq. to 5/5-100 et seq.

ARTICLE IV. RECORDS REQUIRED TO BE KEPT

Section

5/5-401 to 5/5-401.1. §§ 5-401 to 5-401.1. Repealed by P.A. 83-1473, § 2, eff. Jan. 1, 1985

5/5-401.2. Licensees required to keep records and make inspections

§ 5-401.2. Licensees required to keep records and make inspections.

(a) Every person licensed or required to be licensed under Section 5-101, 5-101.1, 5-102, 5-301 or 5-302 of this Code, shall, with the exception of scrap processors, maintain for 3 years, in a form as the Secretary of State may by rule or regulation prescribe, at his established place of business, additional place of business, or principal place of business if licensed under Section 5-302, the following records relating to the acquisition or disposition of vehicles and their essential parts possessed in this State, brought into this State from another state, territory or country, or sold or transferred to another person in this State or in another state, territory, or country.

(1) The following records pertaining to new or used vehicles shall be kept:

(A) the year, make, model, style and color of the vehicle;

(B) the vehicle's manufacturer's identification number or, if applicable, the Secretary of State or Illinois Department of State Police identification number;

(C) the date of acquisition of the vehicle;

(D) the name and address of the person from whom the vehicle was acquired and, if that person is a dealer, the Illinois or out-of-state dealer license number of such person;

(E) the signature of the person making the inspection of a used vehicle as required under subsection (d) of this Section, if applicable;

(F) the purchase price of the vehicle, if applicable;

(G) the date of the disposition of the vehicle;

(H) the name and address of the person to whom any vehicle was disposed, and if that person is a dealer, the Illinois or out-of-State dealer's license number of that dealer;

(I) the uniform invoice number reflecting the disposition of the vehicle, if applicable; and

(J) The sale price of the vehicle, if applicable.

(2) (A) The following records pertaining to used essential parts other than quarter panels and transmissions of vehicles of the first division shall be kept:

(i) the year, make, model, color and type of such part;

(ii) the vehicle's manufacturer's identification number, derivative number, or, if applicable, the Secretary of State or Illinois Department of State Police identification number of such part;

(iii) the date of the acquisition of each part;

(iv) the name and address of the person from whom the part was acquired and, if that person is a dealer, the Illinois or out-of-state dealer license number of such person; if the essential part being acquired is from a person other than a dealer, the licensee shall verify and record that person's identity by recording the identification numbers from at least two sources of identification, one of which shall be a drivers license or State identification card;

(v) the uniform invoice number or out-of-state bill of sale number reflecting the acquisition of such part;

(vi) the stock number assigned to the essential part by the licensee, if applicable;

(vii) the date of the disposition of such part;

(viii) the name and address of the person to whom such part was disposed of and, if that person is a dealer, the Illinois or out-of-state dealer license number of that person;

(ix) the uniform invoice number reflecting the disposition of such part.

(B) Inspections of all essential parts shall be conducted in accordance with Section 5-402.1.

(C) A separate entry containing all of the information required to be recorded in subparagraph (A) of paragraph (2) of subsection (a) of this Section shall be made for each separate essential part. Separate entries shall be made regardless of whether the part was a large purchase acquisition. In addition, a separate entry shall be made for each part acquired for immediate sale or transfer, or for placement into the overall inventory or stock to be disposed of at a later time, or for use on a vehicle to be materially altered by the licensee, or acquired for any other purpose or reason. Failure to make a separate entry for each essential part acquired or disposed of, or a failure to record any of the specific information required to be recorded concerning the acquisition or disposition of each essential part as set forth in subparagraph (A) of paragraph (2) of subsection (a) shall constitute a failure to keep records.

(D) The vehicle's manufacturer's identification number or Secretary of State or Illinois Department of State Police identification number for the essential part shall be ascertained and recorded even if such part is acquired from a person or dealer located in a State, territory, or country which does not require that such information be recorded. If the vehicle's manufacturer's identification number or Secretary of State or Illinois Department of State Police identification number for an essential part cannot be obtained, that part shall not be acquired by the licensee or any of his agents or employees. If such part or parts were physically acquired by the licensee or any of his agents or employees while the licensee or agent or employee was outside this State, that licensee or agent or employee was outside the State, that licensee, agent or employee shall not bring such essential part into this State or cause it to be brought into this State. The acquisition or disposition of an essential part by a licensee without the recording of the vehicle identification number or Secretary of State identification number for such part or the transportation into the State by the licensee or his agent or employee of such part or parts shall constitute a failure to keep records.

(E) The records of essential parts required to be kept by this Section shall apply to all hulks, chassis, frames or cowls, regardless of the age of those essential parts. The records required to be kept by this Section for essential parts other than hulks, chassis, frames or cowls, shall apply only to those essential parts which are 6 model years of age or newer. In determining the model year of such an essential part it may be presumed that the identification number of the vehicle from which the essential part came or the identification number affixed to the essential part itself acquired by the licensee denotes the model year of that essential part. This presumption, however, shall not apply if the gross appearance of the essential part does not correspond to the year, make or model of either the identification number of the vehicle from which the essential part is alleged to have come or the identification number which is affixed to the essential part itself. To determine whether an essential part is 6 years of age or newer within this paragraph, the model year of the essential part shall be subtracted from the calendar year in which the essential part is acquired or disposed of by the licensee. If the remainder is 6 or less, the record of the acquisition or disposition of that essential part shall be kept as required by this Section.

(F) The requirements of paragraph (2) of subsection (a) of this Section shall not apply to the disposition of an essential part other than a cowl which has been damaged or altered to a state in which it can no longer be returned to a usable condition and which is being sold or transferred to a scrap processor or for delivery to a scrap processor.

(3) the following records for vehicles on which junking certificates are obtained shall be kept:

(A) the year, make, model, style and color of the vehicle;

(B) the vehicle's manufacturer's identification number or, if applicable, the Secretary of State or Illinois Department of State Police identification number;

(C) the date the vehicle was acquired;

(D) the name and address of the person from whom the vehicle was acquired and, if that person is a dealer, the

Illinois or out-of-state dealer license number of that person;

(E) the certificate of title number or salvage certificate number for the vehicle, if applicable;

(F) the junking certificate number obtained by the licensee; this entry shall be recorded at the close of business of the fifth business day after receiving the junking certificate;

(G) the name and address of the person to whom the junking certificate has been assigned, if applicable, and if that person is a dealer, the Illinois or out-of-state dealer license number of that dealer;

(H) if the vehicle or any part of the vehicle is dismantled for its parts to be disposed of in any way, or if such parts are to be used by the licensee to materially alter a vehicle, those essential parts shall be recorded and the entries required by paragraph (2) of subsection (a) shall be made.

(4) The following records for rebuilt vehicles shall be kept:

(A) the year, make, model, style and color of the vehicle;

(B) the vehicle's manufacturer's identification number of the vehicle or, if applicable, the Secretary of State or Illinois Department of State Police identification number;

(C) the date the vehicle was acquired;

(D) the name and address of the person from whom the vehicle was acquired, and if that person is a dealer, the Illinois or out-of-state dealer license number of that person;

(E) the salvage certificate number for the vehicle;

(F) the newly issued certificate of title number for the vehicle;

(G) the date of disposition of the vehicle;

(H) the name and address of the person to whom the vehicle was disposed, and if a dealer, the Illinois or out-of-state dealer license number of that dealer;

(I) The sale price of the vehicle.

(a-1) A person licensed or required to be licensed under Section 5-101 or Section 5-102 of this Code who issues temporary registration permits as permitted by this Code and by rule must electronically file the registration with the Secretary and must maintain records of the registration in the manner prescribed by the Secretary.

(b) A failure to make separate entries for each vehicle acquired, disposed of, or assigned, or a failure to record any of the specific information required to be recorded concerning the acquisition or disposition of each vehicle as set forth in paragraphs (1), (3) and (4) of subsection (a) shall constitute a failure to keep records.

(c) All entries relating to the acquisition of a vehicle or essential part required by subsection (a) of this Section shall be recorded no later than the close of business on the seventh calendar day following such acquisition. All entries relating to the disposition of a vehicle or an essential part shall be made at the time of such disposition. If the vehicle or essential part was disposed of on the same day as its acquisition or the day thereafter, the entries relating to the acquisition of the vehicle or essential part shall be made at the time of the disposition of the vehicle or essential part. Failure to make the entries required in or at the times prescribed by this subsection following the acquisition or disposition of such vehicle or essential part shall constitute a failure to keep records.

(d) Every person licensed or required to be licensed shall, before accepting delivery of a used vehicle, inspect the vehicle to determine whether the manufacturer's public vehicle identification number has been defaced, destroyed, falsified, removed, altered, or tampered with in any way. If the person making the inspection determines that the manufacturer's public vehicle identification number has been altered, removed, defaced, destroyed, falsified or tampered with he shall not acquire that vehicle but instead shall promptly notify law enforcement authorities of his finding.

(e) The information required to be kept in subsection (a) of this Section shall be kept in a manner prescribed by rule or regulation of the Secretary of State.

(f) Every person licensed or required to be licensed shall have in his possession a separate certificate of title, salvage certificate, junking certificate, certificate of purchase, uniform invoice, out-of-state bill of sale or other acceptable documentary evidence of his right to the possession of every vehicle or essential part.

(g) Every person licensed or required to be licensed as a transporter under Section 5-201 shall maintain for 3 years, in such form as the Secretary of State may by rule or regulation prescribe, at his principal place of business a record of every vehicle transported by him, including numbers of or other marks of identification thereof, the names and addresses of persons from whom and to whom the vehicle was delivered and the dates of delivery.

(h) No later than 15 days prior to going out of business, selling the business, or transferring the ownership of the business, the licensee shall notify the Secretary of State that he is going out of business or that he is transferring the ownership of the business. Failure to notify under this paragraph shall constitute a failure to keep records.

(i) (Blank).

(j) A person who knowingly fails to comply with the provisions of this Section or knowingly fails to obey, observe, or comply with any order of the Secretary or any law enforcement agency issued in accordance with this Section is guilty of a Class B misdemeanor for the first violation and a Class A misdemeanor for the second and subsequent violations. Each violation constitutes a separate and distinct offense and a separate count may be brought in the same indictment or information for each vehicle or each essential part of a vehicle for which a record was not kept as required by this Section.

(k) Any person convicted of failing to keep the records required by this Section with intent to conceal the identity or origin of a vehicle or its essential parts or with intent to defraud the public in the transfer or sale of vehicles or their essential parts is guilty of a Class 2 felony. Each violation constitutes a separate and distinct offense and a separate count may be brought in the same indictment or information for each vehicle or essential part of a vehicle for which a record was not kept as required by this Section.

(*l*) A person may not be criminally charged with or convicted of both a knowing failure to comply with this Section and a knowing failure to comply with any order, if both offenses involve the same record keeping violation.

(m) The Secretary shall adopt rules necessary for implementation of this Section, which may include the imposition of administrative fines.

P.A. 76-1586, § 5-401.2, added by P.A. 83-1473, § 1, eff. Jan. 1, 1985. Amended by P.A. 83-1528, Art. II, § 24, eff. Jan. 17, 1985; P.A. 84-25, Art. IV, § 27, eff. July 18, 1985; P.A. 84-1105, § 1, eff. Dec. 10, 1985; P.A. 84-1302, § 1, eff. Jan. 1, 1987; P.A. 84-1304, § 1, eff. Jan. 1, 1987; P.A. 85-572, § 1, eff. Sept. 18, 1987; P.A. 85-1209, Art. III, § 3-60, eff. Aug. 30, 1988; P.A. 85-1396, § 2, eff. Sept. 2, 1988; P.A. 85-1440, Art. II, § 2-25, eff. Feb. 1, 1989; P.A. 86-444, § 1, eff.

Jan. 1, 1990; P.A. 86-1179, § 2, eff. Aug. 17, 1990; P.A. 86-1209, § 1, eff. Jan. 1, 1991; P.A. 89-189, § 5, eff. Jan. 1, 1996; P.A. 89-235, Art. 2, § 2-120, eff. Aug. 4, 1995; P.A. 91-415, § 5, eff. Jan. 1, 2000; P.A. 92-773, § 5, eff. Aug. 6, 2002.

Formerly Ill.Rev.Stat.1991, ch. 95 ½, ¶ 5-401.2.

Validity

The Supreme Court of Illinois has held that the provision making the known failure to maintain records of the acquisition and disposition of vehicles a Class 2 felony an unconstitutional violation of due process in the case of People v. Wright, 194 Ill.2d 1, 740 N.E.2d 755, 251 Ill.Dec. 469 (2000), rehearing denied (Nov. 27, 2000).

5/5-401.3. Scrap processors required to keep records

§ 5-401.3. Scrap processors required to keep records. (a) Every person licensed or required to be licensed as a scrap processor pursuant to Section 5-301 of this Chapter shall maintain for 3 years, at his established place of business, the following records relating to the acquisition of a vehicle, junk vehicle, or vehicle cowl which has been acquired for the purpose of processing into a form other than a vehicle, junk vehicle or vehicle cowl which is possessed in the State or brought into this State from another state, territory or country. No scrap metal processor shall sell a vehicle or essential part, as such, except for engines, transmissions, and powertrains, unless licensed to do so under another provision of this Code. A scrap processor who is additionally licensed as an automotive parts recycler shall not be subject to the record keeping requirements for a scrap processor when acting as an automotive parts recycler.

(1) For a vehicle, junk vehicle, or vehicle cowl acquired from a person who is licensed under this Chapter, the scrap processor shall record the name and address of the person, and the Illinois or out-of-state dealer license number of such person on the scrap processor's weight ticket at the time of the acquisition. The person disposing of the vehicle, junk vehicle, or vehicle cowl shall furnish the scrap processor with documentary proof of ownership of the vehicle, junk vehicle, or vehicle cowl in one of the following forms: a Certificate of Title, a Salvage Certificate, a Junking Certificate, a Secretary of State Junking Manifest, a Uniform Invoice, a Certificate of Purchase, or other similar documentary proof of ownership. The scrap processor shall not acquire a vehicle, junk vehicle or vehicle cowl without obtaining one of the aforementioned documentary proofs of ownership.

(2) For a vehicle, junk vehicle or vehicle cowl acquired from a person who is not licensed under this Chapter, the scrap processor shall verify and record that person's identity by recording the identification of such person from at least 2 sources of identification, one of which shall be a driver's license or State Identification Card, on the scrap processor's weight ticket at the time of the acquisition. The person disposing of the vehicle, junk vehicle, or vehicle cowl shall furnish the scrap processor with documentary proof of ownership of the vehicle, junk vehicle, or vehicle cowl in one of the following forms: a Certificate of Title, a Salvage Certificate, a Junking Certificate, a Secretary of State Junking Manifest, a Certificate of Purchase, or other similar documentary proof of ownership. The scrap processor shall not acquire a vehicle, junk vehicle or vehicle cowl without obtaining one of the aforementioned documentary proofs of ownership.

(3) In addition to the other information required on the scrap processor's weight ticket, a scrap processor who at the time of acquisition of a vehicle, junk vehicle, or vehicle cowl is furnished a Certificate of Title, Salvage Certificate or Certificate of Purchase shall record the vehicle Identification Number on the weight ticket or affix a copy of the Certificate of Title, Salvage Certificate or Certificate of Purchase to the weight ticket and the identification of the person acquiring the information on the behalf of the scrap processor.

(4) The scrap processor shall maintain a copy of a Junk Vehicle Notification relating to any Certificate of Title, Salvage Certificate, Certificate of Purchase or similarly acceptable out-of-state document surrendered to the Secretary of State pursuant to the provisions of Section 3-117.2 of this Code.

(b) Any licensee who knowingly fails to record any of the specific information required to be recorded on the weight ticket or who knowingly fails to acquire and maintain for 3 years documentary proof of ownership in one of the prescribed forms shall be guilty of a Class A misdemeanor and subject to a fine not to exceed $1,000. Each violation shall constitute a separate and distinct offense and a separate count may be brought in the same complaint for each violation. Any licensee who commits a second violation of this Section within two years of a previous conviction of a violation of this Section shall be guilty of a Class 4 felony.

(c) It shall be an affirmative defense to an offense brought under paragraph (b) of this Section that the licensee or person required to be licensed both reasonably and in good faith relied on information appearing on a Certificate of Title, a Salvage Certificate, a Junking Certificate, a Secretary of State Manifest, a Secretary of State's Uniform Invoice, a Certificate of Purchase, or other documentary proof of ownership prepared under Section 3-117.1(a) of this Code, relating to the transaction for which the required record was not kept which was supplied to the licensee by another licensee or out-of-state dealer.

(d) No later than 15 days prior to going out of business, selling the business, or transferring the ownership of the business, the scrap processor shall notify the Secretary of that fact. Failure to so notify the Secretary of State shall constitute a failure to keep records under this Section.

(e) Evidence derived directly or indirectly from the keeping of records required to be kept under this Section shall not be admissible in a prosecution of the licensee for an alleged violation of Section 4-102(a)(3) of this Code.

P.A. 76-1586, § 5-401.3, added by P.A. 83-1473, § 1, eff. Jan. 1, 1985. Amended by P.A. 84-1302, § 1, eff. Jan. 1, 1987; P.A. 84-1304, § 1, eff. Jan. 1, 1987; P.A. 85-1204, § 1, eff. Aug. 26, 1988; P.A. 86-444, § 1, eff. Jan. 1, 1990; P.A. 90-89, § 15, eff. Jan. 1, 1998.

Formerly Ill.Rev.Stat.1991, ch. 95 ½, ¶ 5-401.3.

5/5-402. Use of Department of Revenue Uniform Invoice for vehicle

§ 5-402. Use of Department of Revenue Uniform Invoice for vehicle. Every person licensed as a new vehicle dealer, or as a used vehicle dealer, or as a motor vehicle financing affiliate shall issue a Uniform Invoice with respect to each transaction wherein he disposes of a vehicle, except that where, in the same transaction, a vehicle dealer transfers more than one vehicle to another vehicle dealer for the purpose of resale, such seller for resale may issue one Uniform Invoice to the purchaser covering all the vehicles involved in that transaction and may report the transfer of all the vehicles involved in that transaction to the Department on the same Uniform Invoice-transaction reporting return form. Every person licensed as a rebuilder shall likewise issue a Uniform Invoice with respect to each transaction wherein he disposes of a rebuilt or restored vehicle. Such Uniform Invoice shall be the same document as the transaction reporting return referred to in Section 3 of the Retailers' Occupation Tax Act.[1] Such Uniform Invoice shall contain complete financial details of the transaction in such form as shall be prescribed by the Department of Revenue. Such Uniform Invoice shall include an affidavit by both the seller and the buyer that any trade-in title has been properly assigned from the buyer to the seller and that all information on the Uniform Invoice-transaction reporting return is true and accurate.

P.A. 76-1586, § 5-402, eff. July 1, 1970. Amended by P.A. 78-858, § 1, eff. Jan. 1, 1974; P.A. 83-1473, § 1, eff. Jan. 1, 1985; P.A. 85-1396, § 2, eff. Sept. 2, 1988; P.A. 91-415, § 5, eff. Jan. 1, 2000.

Formerly Ill.Rev.Stat.1991, ch. 95 ½, ¶ 5-402.

1 35 ILCS 120/3.

5/5-402.1. Use of Secretary of State Uniform Invoice for Essential Parts

§ 5-402.1. Use of Secretary of State Uniform Invoice for Essential Parts.

(a) Except for scrap processors, every person licensed or required to be licensed under Section 5-101, 5-101.1, 5-102 or 5-301 of this Code shall issue, in a form the Secretary of State may by rule or regulation prescribe, a Uniform Invoice, which may also act as a bill of sale, made out in triplicate with respect to each transaction in which he disposes of an essential part other than quarter panels and transmissions of vehicles of the first division. Such Invoice shall be made out at the time of the disposition of the essential part. If the licensee disposes of several essential parts in the same transaction, the licensee may issue one Uniform Invoice covering all essential parts disposed of in that transaction.

(b) The following information shall be contained on the Uniform Invoice:

(1) the business name, address and dealer license number of the person disposing of the essential part;

(2) the name and address of the person acquiring the essential part, and if that person is a dealer, the Illinois or out-of-state dealer license number of that dealer;

(3) the date of the disposition of the essential part;

(4) the year, make, model, color and description of each essential part disposed of by the person;

(5) the manufacturer's vehicle identification number, Secretary of State identification number or Illinois Department of State Police identification number, for each essential part disposed of by the person;

(6) the printed name and legible signature of the person or agent disposing of the essential part; and

(7) if the person is a dealer the printed name and legible signature of the dealer or his agent or employee accepting delivery of the essential part.

(c) Except for scrap processors, and except as set forth in subsection (d) of this Section, whenever a person licensed or required to be licensed by Section 5-101, 5-101.1, 5-102, or 5-301 accepts delivery of an essential part, other than quarter panels and transmissions of vehicles of the first division, that person shall, at the time of the acceptance or delivery, comply with the following procedures:

(1) Before acquiring or accepting delivery of any essential part, the licensee or his authorized agent or employee shall inspect the part to determine whether the vehicle identification number, Secretary of State identification number, Illinois Department of State Police identification number, or identification plate or sticker attached to or stamped on any part being acquired or delivered has been removed, falsified, altered, defaced, destroyed, or tampered with. If the licensee or his agent or employee determines that the vehicle identification number, Secretary of State identification number. Illinois Department of State Police identification number, identification plate or identification sticker containing an identification number, or Federal Certificate label of an essential part has been removed, falsified, altered, defaced, destroyed or tampered with, the licensee or agent shall not accept or receive that part.

If that part was physically acquired by or delivered to a licensee or his agent or employee while that licensee, agent or employee was outside this State, that licensee or agent or employee shall not bring that essential part into this State or cause it to be brought into this State.

(2) If the person disposing of or delivering the essential part to the licensee is a licensed in-state or out-of-state dealer, the licensee or his agent or employee, after inspecting the essential part as required by paragraph (1) of this subsection (c), shall examine the Uniform Invoice, or bill of sale, as the case may be, to ensure that it contains all the information required to be provided by persons disposing of essential parts as set forth in subsection (b) of this Section. If the Uniform Invoice or bill of sale does not contain all the information required to be listed by subsection (b) of this Section, the dealer disposing of or delivering such part or his agent or employee shall record such additional information or other needed modifications on the Uniform Invoice or bill of sale or, if needed, an attachment thereto. The dealer or his agent or employee delivering the essential part shall initial all additions or modifications to the Uniform Invoice or bill of sale and legibly print his name at the bottom of each document containing his initials. If the transaction involves a bill of sale rather than a Uniform Invoice, the licensee or his agent or employee accepting delivery of or acquiring the essential part shall affix his printed name and legible signature on the space on the bill of sale provided for his signature or, if no space is provided, on the back of the bill of sale. If the dealer or his agent or employee disposing of or delivering the essential part cannot or does not provide all the information required by subsection (b) of this Section, the licensee or his agent or employee shall not accept or receive any essential part for which that required information is not provided. If such essential part for which the information required is not fully provided was physically acquired while the licensee or his agent or employee was outside this State, the licensee or his agent or employee shall not bring that essential part into this State or cause it to be brought into this State.

(3) If the person disposing of the essential part is not a licensed dealer, the licensee or his agent or employee shall, after inspecting the essential part as required by paragraph (1) of subsection (c) of this Section verify the identity of the person disposing of the essential part by examining 2 sources of identification, one of which shall be either a driver's license or state identification card. The licensee or his agent or employee shall then prepare a Uniform Invoice listing all the information required to be provided by subsection (b) of this Section. In the space on the Uniform Invoice provided for the dealer license num-

ber of the person disposing of the part, the licensee or his agent or employee shall list the numbers taken from the documents of identification provided by the person disposing of the part. The person disposing of the part shall affix his printed name and legible signature on the space on the Uniform Invoice provided for the person disposing of the essential part and the licensee or his agent or employee acquiring the part shall affix his printed name and legible signature on the space provided on the Uniform Invoice for the person acquiring the essential part. If the person disposing of the essential part cannot or does not provide all the information required to be provided by this paragraph, or does not present 2 satisfactory forms of identification, the licensee or his agent or employee shall not acquire that essential part.

(d) If an essential part other than quarter panels and transmissions of vehicles of the first division was delivered by a licensed commercial delivery service delivering such part on behalf of a licensed dealer, the person required to comply with subsection (c) of this Section may conduct the inspection of that part required by paragraph (1) of subsection (c) and examination of the Uniform Invoice or bill of sale required by paragraph (2) of subsection (c) of this Section immediately after the acceptance of the part.

(1) If the inspection of the essential part pursuant to paragraph (1) of subsection (c) reveals that the vehicle identification number, Secretary of State identification number, Illinois Department of State Police identification number, identification plate or sticker containing an identification number, or Federal Certificate label of an essential part has been removed, falsified, altered, defaced, destroyed or tampered with, the licensee or his agent shall immediately record such fact on the Uniform Invoice or bill of sale, assign the part an inventory or stock number, place such inventory or stock number on both the essential part and the Uniform Invoice or bill of sale, and record the date of the inspection of the part on the Uniform Invoice or bill of sale. The licensee shall, within 7 days of such inspection, return such part to the dealer from whom it was acquired.

(2) If the examination of the Uniform Invoice or bill of sale pursuant to paragraph (2) of subsection (c) reveals that any of the information required to be listed by subsection (b) of this Section is missing, the licensee or person required to be licensed shall immediately assign a stock or inventory number to such part, place such stock or inventory number on both the essential part and the Uniform Invoice or bill of sale, and record the date of examination on the Uniform Invoice or bill of sale. The licensee or person required to be licensed shall acquire the information missing from the Uniform Invoice or bill of sale within 7 days of the examination of such Uniform Invoice or bill of sale. Such information may be received by telephone conversation with the dealer from whom the part was acquired. If the dealer provides the missing information the licensee shall record such information on the Uniform Invoice or bill of sale along with the name of the person providing the information. If the dealer does not provide the required information within the aforementioned 7 day period, the licensee shall return the part to that dealer.

(e) Except for scrap processors, all persons licensed or required to be licensed who acquire or dispose of essential parts other than quarter panels and transmissions of vehicles of the first division shall retain a copy of the Uniform Invoice required to be made by subsections (a), (b) and (c) of this Section for a period of 3 years.

(f) Except for scrap processors, any person licensed or required to be licensed under Sections 5-101, 5-102 or 5-301 who knowingly fails to record on a Uniform Invoice any of the information or entries required to be recorded by subsections (a), (b) and (c) of this Section, or who knowingly places false entries or other misleading information on such Uniform Invoice, or who knowingly fails to retain for 3 years a copy of a Uniform Invoice reflecting transactions required to be recorded by subsections (a), (b) and (c) of this Section, or who knowingly acquires or disposes of essential parts without receiving, issuing, or executing a Uniform Invoice reflecting that transaction as required by subsections (a), (b) and (c) of this Section, or who brings or causes to be brought into this State essential parts for which the information required to be recorded on a Uniform Invoice is not recorded as prohibited by subsection (c) of this Section, or who knowingly fails to comply with the provisions of this Section in any other manner shall be guilty of a Class 2 felony. Each violation shall constitute a separate and distinct offense and a separate count may be brought in the same indictment or information for each essential part for which a record was not kept as required by this Section or for which the person failed to comply with other provisions of this Section.

(g) The records required to be kept by this Section may be examined by a person or persons making a lawful inspection of the licensee's premises pursuant to Section 5-403.

(h) The records required to be kept by this Section shall be retained by the licensee at his principal place of business for a period of 7 years.

(i) The requirements of this Section shall not apply to the disposition of an essential part other than a cowl which has been damaged or altered to a state in which it can no longer be returned to a usable condition and which is being sold or transferred to a scrap processor or for delivery to a scrap processor.

P.A. 76-1586, § 5-402.1, added by P.A. 83-1473, § 1, eff. Jan. 1, 1985. Amended by P.A. 84-25, Art. IV, § 27, eff. July 18, 1985; P.A. 84-1302, § 1, eff. Jan. 1, 1987; P.A. 84-1304, § 1, eff. Jan. 1, 1987; P.A. 85-1204, § 1, eff. Aug. 26, 1988; P.A. 85-1396, § 2, eff. Sept. 2, 1988; P.A. 85-1440, Art. II, § 2-25, eff. Feb. 1, 1989; P.A. 86-1179, § 2, eff. Aug. 17, 1990; P.A. 86-1209, § 1, eff. Jan. 1, 1991; P.A. 86-1475, Art. 2, § 2-25, eff. Jan. 10, 1991; P.A. 91-415, § 5, eff. Jan. 1, 2000.

Formerly Ill.Rev.Stat.1991, ch. 95 ½, ¶ 5-402.1.

5/5-403. Inspection of records; notice; presence of licensee during inspection; duration; search warrants; public complaints

§ 5-403. (1) Authorized representatives of the Secretary of State including officers of the Secretary of State's Department of Police, other peace officers, and such other individuals as the Secretary may designate from time to time shall make inspections of individuals and facilities licensed or required to be licensed under Chapter 5 of the Illinois Vehicle Code for the purpose of reviewing records required to be maintained under Chapter 5 for accuracy and completeness and reviewing and examining the premises of the licensee's established or additional place of business for the purpose of determining the accuracy of the required records. Premises that may be inspected in order to determine the accuracy of the books and records required to be kept includes all premises used by the licensee to store vehicles and parts that are reflected by the required books and records.

(2) Persons having knowledge of or conducting inspections pursuant to this Chapter shall not in advance of such inspec-

tions knowingly notify a licensee or representative of a licensee of the contemplated inspection unless the Secretary or an individual designated by him for this purpose authorizes such notification. Any individual who, without authorization, knowingly violates this subparagraph shall be guilty of a Class A misdemeanor.

(3) The licensee or a representative of the licensee shall be entitled to be present during an inspection conducted pursuant to Chapter 5, however, the presence of the licensee or an authorized representative of the licensee is not a condition precedent to such an inspection.

(4) Inspection conducted pursuant to Chapter 5 may be initiated at any time that business is being conducted or work is being performed, whether or not open to the public or when the licensee or a representative of the licensee, other than a mere custodian or watchman, is present. The fact that a licensee or representative of the licensee leaves the licensed premises after an inspection has been initiated shall not require the termination of the inspection.

(5) Any inspection conducted pursuant to Chapter 5 shall not continue for more than 24 hours after initiation.

(6) In the event information comes to the attention of the individuals conducting an inspection that may give rise to the necessity of obtaining a search warrant, and in the event steps are initiated for the procurement of a search warrant, the individuals conducting such inspection may take all necessary steps to secure the premises under inspection until the warrant application is acted upon by a judicial officer.

(7) No more than 6 inspections of a premises may be conducted pursuant to Chapter 5 within any 6 month period except pursuant to a search warrant. Notwithstanding this limitation, nothing in this subparagraph shall be construed to limit the authority of law enforcement agents to respond to public complaints of violations of the Code. For the purpose of this subparagraph, a public complaint is one in which the complainant identifies himself or herself and sets forth, in writing, the specific basis for their complaint against the licensee.

(8) Nothing in this Section shall be construed to limit the authority of individuals by the Secretary pursuant to this Section to conduct searches of licensees pursuant to a duly issued and authorized search warrant.

(9) Any licensee who, having been informed by a person authorized to make inspections and examine records under this Section that he desires to inspect records and the licensee's premises as authorized by this Section, refuses either to produce for that person records required to be kept by this Chapter or to permit such authorized person to make an inspection of the premises in accordance with this Section shall subject the license to immediate suspension by the Secretary of State.

(10) Beginning July 1, 1988, any person licensed under 5–302 shall produce for inspection upon demand those records pertaining to the acquisition of salvage vehicles in this State. This inspection may be conducted at the principal offices of the Secretary of State.

P.A. 76–1586, § 5–403, added by P.A. 82–984, § 1, eff. Jan. 1, 1983. Amended by P.A. 83–1473, § 1, eff. Jan. 1, 1985; P.A. 85–572, § 1, eff. Sept. 18, 1987; P.A. 86–444, § 1, eff. Jan. 1, 1990.

Formerly Ill.Rev.Stat.1991, ch. 95 ½, ¶ 5–403.

5/5–403.1. Inventory System

§ 5–403.1. Inventory System.

(a) Every person licensed or required to be licensed under the provisions of Sections 5–101, 5–101.1, 5–102 and 5–301 of this Code shall, under rule and regulation prescribed by the Secretary of State, maintain an inventory system of all vehicles or essential parts in such a manner that a person making an inspection pursuant to the provisions of Section 5–403 of this Code can readily ascertain the identity of such vehicles or essential parts and readily locate such parts on the licensees premises.

(b) Failure to maintain an inventory system as required under this Section is a Class A misdemeanor.

(c) This Section does not apply to vehicles or essential parts which have been acquired by a scrap processor for processing into a form other than a vehicle or essential part.

P.A. 76–1586, § 5–403.1, added by P.A. 83–1473, § 1, eff. Jan. 1, 1985. Amended by P.A. 86–1209, § 1, eff. Jan. 1, 1991; P.A. 91–415, § 5, eff. Jan. 1, 2000.

Formerly Ill.Rev.Stat.1991, ch. 95 ½, ¶ 5–403.1.

5/5–404. § 5–404. Repealed by P.A. 86–1209, § 2, eff. Jan. 1, 1991

ARTICLE V. LICENSES—INJUNCTIONS

Article V heading which formerly read "Licenses" was amended by P.A. 78–1165, § 2, eff. Aug. 27, 1974.

Section

5/5–501. Denial, suspension or revocation or cancellation of a license

§ 5–501. Denial, suspension or revocation or cancellation of a license. (a) The license of a person issued under this Chapter may be denied, revoked or suspended if the Secretary of State finds that the applicant, or the officer, director, shareholder having a ten percent or greater ownership interest in the corporation, owner, partner, trustee, manager, employee or the licensee has:

1. Violated this Act;

2. Made any material misrepresentation to the Secretary of State in connection with an application for a license, junking certificate, salvage certificate, title or registration;

3. Committed a fraudulent act in connection with selling, bartering, exchanging, offering for sale or otherwise dealing in vehicles, chassis, essential parts, or vehicle shells;

4. As a new vehicle dealer has no contract with a manufacturer or enfranchised distributor to sell that new vehicle in this State;

5. Not maintained an established place of business as defined in this Code;

6. Failed to file or produce for the Secretary of State any application, report, document or other pertinent books, records, documents, letters, contracts, required to be filed or produced under this Code or any rule or regulation made by the Secretary of State pursuant to this Code;

7. Previously had, within 3 years, such a license denied, suspended, revoked, or cancelled under the provisions of subsection (c)(2) of this Section;

8. Has committed in any calendar year 3 or more violations, as determined in any civil or criminal proceeding, of any one or more of the following Acts:

a. the "Consumer Finance Act";[1]

b. the "Consumer Installment Loan Act";[2]

c. the "Retail Installment Sales Act";[3]

d. the "Motor Vehicle Retail Installment Sales Act";[4]

e. "An Act in relation to the rate of interest and other charges in connection with sales on credit and the lending of money", approved May 24, 1879, as amended;[5]

f. "An Act to promote the welfare of wage-earners by regulating the assignment of wages, and prescribing a penalty for the violation thereof", approved July 1, 1935, as amended;[6]

g. Part 8 of Article XII of the Code of Civil Procedure;[7] or

h. the "Consumer Fraud Act";[8]

9. Failed to pay any fees or taxes due under this Act, or has failed to transmit any fees or taxes received by him for transmittal by him to the Secretary of State or the State of Illinois;

10. Converted an abandoned vehicle;

11. Used a vehicle identification plate or number assigned to a vehicle other than the one to which originally assigned;

12. Violated the provisions of Chapter 5 of this Act, as amended;

13. Violated the provisions of Chapter 4 of this Act, as amended;

14. Violated the provisions of Chapter 3 of this Act, as amended;

15. Violated Section 21-2 of the Criminal Code of 1961,[9] Criminal Trespass to Vehicles;

16. Made or concealed a material fact in connection with his application for a license;

17. Acted in the capacity of a person licensed or acted as a licensee under this Chapter without having a license therefor;

18. Failed to pay, within 90 days after a final judgment, any fines assessed against the licensee pursuant to an action brought under Section 5-404.

(b) In addition to other grounds specified in this Chapter, the Secretary of State, on complaint of the Department of Revenue, shall refuse the issuance of renewal of a license, or suspend or revoke such license, for any of the following violations of the "Retailers' Occupation Tax Act":[10]

1. Failure to make a tax return;

2. The filing of a fraudulent return;

3. Failure to pay all or part of any tax or penalty finally determined to be due;

4. Failure to comply with the bonding requirements of the "Retailers' Occupation Tax Act".

(c) Cancellation of a license.

1. The license of a person issued under this Chapter may be cancelled by the Secretary of State prior to its expiration in any of the following situations:

A. When a license is voluntarily surrendered, by the licensed person; or

B. If the business enterprise is a sole proprietorship, which is not a franchised dealership, when the sole proprietor dies or is imprisoned for any period of time exceeding 30 days; or

C. If the license was issued to the wrong person or corporation, or contains an error on its face. If any person above whose license has been cancelled wishes to apply for another license, whether during the same license year or any other year, that person shall be treated as any other new applicant and the cancellation of the person's prior license shall not, in and of itself, be a bar to the issuance of a new license.

2. The license of a person issued under this Chapter may be cancelled without a hearing when the Secretary of State is notified that the applicant, or any officer, director, shareholder having a 10 per cent or greater ownership interest in the corporation, owner, partner, trustee, manager, employee or member of the applicant or the licensee has been convicted of any felony involving the selling, bartering, exchanging, offering for sale, or otherwise dealing in vehicles, chassis, essential parts, vehicle shells, or ownership documents relating to any of the above items.

P.A. 76-1586, § 5-501, eff. July 1, 1970. Amended by P.A. 77-643, § 1, eff. Aug. 4, 1971; P.A. 78-858, § 1, eff. Jan. 1, 1974; P.A. 81-932, § 1, eff. Sept. 22, 1979; P.A. 82-783, Art. XI, § 140, eff. July 13, 1982; P.A. 83-1473, § 1, eff. Jan. 1, 1985; P.A. 85-572, § 1, eff. Sept. 18, 1987; P.A. 85-1204, § 1, eff. Aug. 26, 1988; P.A. 85-1396, § 2, eff. Sept. 2, 1988; P.A. 86-820, Art. II, § 2-8, eff. Sept. 7, 1989.

Formerly Ill.Rev.Stat.1991, ch. 95 ½, ¶ 5-501.

1 Former Ill.Rev.Stat. ch. 17, ¶ 5601 et seq. (repealed).

2 205 ILCS 670/1 et seq.

3 815 ILCS 405/1 et seq.

4 815 ILCS 375/1 et seq.

5 815 ILCS 205/0.01 et seq.

6 740 ILCS 170/.01 et seq.

7 735 ILCS 5/12-801 et seq.

8 815 ILCS 505/1 et seq.

9 720 ILCS 5/21-2.

10 35 ILCS 120/1 et seq.

P.A. 86-820, the Second 1989 Revisory Act, provides in Art. II, for the nonsubstantive revision, renumbering, repeal or rerepeal of certain Acts both amended and repealed by Acts of the 85th General Assembly and, where successor laws have been enacted, incorporates such amendments into successor laws, and corrects errors, revises cross-references and deletes obsolete text in such sections contained in P.A. 85-1 through P.A. 85-1451.

5/5-502. Injunctions

§ 5-502. Injunctions. If any person operates in violation of any provision of this Chapter, or any rule, regulation, order or decision of the Secretary of State, or of any term, condition or limitation of any license, the Secretary of State, or any person injured thereby, or any interested person, may apply to the Circuit Court of the county in which such violation or some part thereof occurred, or in which the person complained of has his established or additional place of business or resides, to prevent such violation. The Court has jurisdiction to enforce obedience by injunction or other process restraining such person from further violation and enjoining upon him obedience.

P.A. 76-1586, § 5-502, added by P.A. 78-1165, § 1, eff. Aug. 27, 1974. Amended by P.A. 86-444, § 1, eff. Jan. 1, 1990.

Formerly Ill.Rev.Stat.1991, ch. 95 ½, ¶ 5-502.

5/5-503. Failure to obtain dealer's license, operation of a business with a suspended or revoked license

§ 5-503. Failure to obtain dealer's license, operation of a business with a suspended or revoked license. (a) Any person operating a business for which he is required to be licensed under Section 5-101, 5-102, 5-201 or 5-301 who fails to apply for such a license or licenses within 15 days after being informed in writing by the Secretary of State that he must obtain such a license or licenses is subject to a civil action brought by the Secretary of State for operating a business without a license in the circuit court in the county in which the business is located. If the person is found to be in violation of Section 5-101, 5-102, 5-201 or 5-301 by carrying on a business without being properly licensed, that person shall be fined $300 for each business day he conducted his business without such a license after the expiration of the 15 day period specified in this subsection (a).

(b) Any person who, having had his license or licenses issued under Section 5-101, 5-102, 5-201 or 5-301 suspended, revoked, cancelled or denied by the Secretary of State under Section 5-501, continues to operate business after the effective date of such revocation, suspension, cancellation or denial may be sued in a civil action by the Secretary of State in the county in which the established or additional place of such business is located. If such person is found by the court to have operated such a business after the license or licenses required for conducting such business have been suspended, revoked, cancelled or denied, that person shall be fined $500 for each day he conducted business thereafter.

P.A. 76-1586, § 5-503, added by P.A. 83-1473, § 1, eff. Jan. 1, 1985. Amended by P.A. 86-444, § 1, eff. Jan. 1, 1990.

Formerly Ill.Rev.Stat.1991, ch. 95 ½, ¶ 5-503.

5/5-504. Effect of revoked or denied license—Notification to prospective buyers—Rescinding of contracts

§ 5-504. Effect of revoked or denied license—Notification to prospective buyers—Rescinding of contracts. (a) No license shall be issued to any person to conduct the business of a new vehicle dealer, used vehicle dealer, scrap processor, automotive parts recycler, repairer, or rebuilder at a location or at property at which that person or any other person had his license as a new vehicle dealer, used vehicle dealer, scrap processor, automotive parts recycler, repairer, or rebuilder revoked or denied after a revocation or pending revocation within 2 months after such revocation or denial.

(b) A licensee who has been notified by the Secretary of State that the Secretary of State may take action to revoke the dealer's license or licenses of that licensee shall inform in writing any prospective buyer of his business of such possible action by the Secretary of State.

(c) If any person purchases or contracts to purchase a business required to be licensed by Section 5-101, 5-102, 5-201 or 5-301 without being informed in writing by the prior owner or owners that, at the time of the sale or making of contract to purchase, the prior owner or owners had been informed by the Secretary of State that the Secretary of State may be taking action to revoke the license or licenses of the prior owner or owners, the person who has purchased or contracted to purchase such business may, within one year after being informed that his application for a dealer's license at that location had been denied due to the revocation of the license or licenses of any prior owner or owners, rescind the purchase or contract to purchase such business or the property, both real and otherwise, at which the business is located.

(d) Notwithstanding the provisions of subsection (a) of this Section, the Secretary of State may issue a license to a person applying for a license as a new vehicle dealer, used vehicle dealer, scrap processor, automotive parts recycler, repairer or rebuilder if the Secretary of State, solely in his discretion, determines that a denial of the license under the circumstances would place extreme undue hardship upon the applicant.

No license shall be issued under this subsection to a person who is a spouse, offspring, sibling, parent, grandparent, grandchild, uncle or aunt, nephew or niece, cousin or in-law of the person whose license to do business at that location had been revoked or denied nor to a person who was an officer or employee of the business firm in relation to which the license was revoked or denied.

Notwithstanding the provisions of subsection (e) of Section 2-118 of this Code, the venue for judicial review of final acts or decisions under this subsection shall be the Circuit Court of Sangamon County.

P.A. 76-1586, § 5-504, added by P.A. 83-1473, § 1, eff. Jan. 1, 1985. Amended by P.A. 84-1302, § 1, eff. Jan. 1, 1987; P.A. 84-1304, § 1, eff. Jan. 1, 1987.

Formerly Ill.Rev.Stat.1991, ch. 95 ½, ¶ 5-504.

The amendments by P.A. 84-1302 and P.A. 84-1304 were identical.

ARTICLE VI. CREDIT OR CONDITIONAL SALES—INSURANCE

5/5-601. Credit or conditional sale of certain motor vehicles—Liability insurance status stamped on bill of sale

§ 5-601. Credit or conditional sale of certain motor vehicles—Liability insurance status stamped on bill of sale. Whenever, in connection with the credit sale of or conditional sale of a motor vehicle designed and used for the carrying of not more than 10 passengers, the agreement provides that all or any of the consideration to be paid by the buyer or conditional buyer may be paid more than 30 days after possession of such motor vehicle is transferred to such buyer or conditional buyer, and a policy of insurance which does not cover such buyer or conditional buyer for the risk of liability to the public arising out of the operation, use or maintenance of such motor vehicle, is issued in connection with such transaction, the seller or conditional seller shall stamp or have imprinted thereon a statement on the bill of sale at the time the transaction is consummated that no such coverage is included in such policy. Such statement shall be in the following form and shall be in bold type not less than one-half inch in height:

NO PUBLIC LIABILITY INSURANCE ISSUED WITH THIS TRANSACTION

P.A. 76-1586, § 5-601, eff. July 1, 1970.

Formerly Ill.Rev.Stat.1991, ch. 95 ½, ¶ 5-601.

5/5-602. Violations of this Article

§ 5-602. Whoever violates any of the provisions of this Article shall be guilty of a petty offense and shall be fined not more than $500.

P.A. 76-1586, § 5-602, eff. July 1, 1970. Amended by P.A. 77-2720, § 1, eff. Jan. 1, 1972.

Formerly Ill.Rev.Stat.1991, ch. 95 ½, ¶ 5-602.

ARTICLE VII. VEHICLE AUCTIONEERS

Section

Date Effective

Article 7 was added by P.A. 81-908, eff. Sept. 22, 1979.

5/5-700. Definitions

§ 5-700. Definitions. For the purposes of this Article, the following phrases have the meanings ascribed to them in this Section:

Place of business for a vehicle auctioneer. This means the place owned and regularly occupied by a vehicle auctioneer licensee, within or without the State, for the primary and principal purpose of keeping and maintaining the books and records required for the conduct of business, with the personnel available during normal business hours or an automatic telephone answering service during normal business hours. The additional place of business means that place within the State where the auction is held, which place of business shall contain the books and records required for said auction with personnel available during normal business hours. The Secretary of State shall be notified of the additional place of business at least 10 days before the auction.

Auctioning vehicles. This means arranging for and handling the sale of vehicles, not the property of the auctioneer, by auction to the highest bidder.

P.A. 76-1586, § 5-700, added by P.A. 81-908, § 1, eff. Sept. 22, 1979. Amended by P.A. 89-663, § 5, eff. Aug. 14, 1996.

Formerly Ill.Rev.Stat.1991, ch. 95 ½, ¶ 5-700.

5/5-701. Vehicle auctioneers to be licensed

§ 5-701. Vehicle auctioneers to be licensed. (a) No person, other than a licensed new vehicle dealer, a licensed used vehicle dealer, or municipality, shall engage in this State in the business of auctioning vehicles, for more than one owner, at auction or shall offer to sell, solicit or advertise the sale of a vehicle at auction without first acquiring a commercial vehicle auctioneer license from the Secretary of State under the provisions of this Section. A vehicle auction licensee shall be entitled thereunder to sell, solicit, and advertise the sale of used vehicles belonging to others at auction.

(b) An application for a vehicle auctioneer license shall be filed with the Secretary of State, duly verified by oath, in such form as the Secretary of State may by rule or regulation prescribe and shall contain:

1. The name and type of business organization established and the address of the place of business;

2. If the applicant is a corporation, a list of its officers and directors, setting forth the residence address of each; if the applicant is a sole proprietorship, a partnership, an unincorporated association, trust or any similar form of business organization, the names and residence addresses of the proprietor or of each partner, member, officer, director, trustee, manager and shareholder having 10% or greater ownership interest in the corporation;

3. A statement that the applicant has been approved for registration under the Retailers' Occupation Tax Act, approved June 28, 1933, as amended,[1] by the Department of Revenue. However, this requirement does not apply to licensee who is already licensed hereunder with the Secretary of State, and who is merely applying for a renewal of his license. As evidence of this fact, the application shall be accompanied by a certification from the Department of Revenue showing that the Department has approved the applicant for registration under the Retailers' Occupation Tax Act;

4. A statement that the applicant has complied with the bonding requirements of the "Retailers' Occupation Tax Act", approved June 28, 1933, as amended. As evidence of this fact, the application shall be accompanied by a certification from the Department of Revenue showing that the applicant is in compliance with the bonding requirements of the "Retailers' Occupation Tax Act" or that the applicant is not required to be bonded with the Department of Revenue under the "Retailers' Occupation Tax Act";

5. Such other information concerning the business of the applicant as the Secretary of State may by rule or regulation prescribe;

6. An application for a vehicle auctioneer license shall be accompanied by the following license fees: $50 for applicant's place of business plus $25 for each additional place of business, if any, to which the application pertains, provided, however, that if such an application is made after July 1 of any year, the license fee shall be $25 for applicant's place of business plus $12.50 for each additional place of business, if any, to which the application pertains. License fees shall be returnable only in the event that such application shall be denied by the Secretary of State.

7. A statement that the licensee has irrevocably consented to the appointment of the Secretary of State as its agent for service of process with the State of Illinois. Said service of process shall be accomplished as provided in Section 10-301 of the Illinois Vehicle Code.

(c) Any change which renders no longer accurate any information contained in any application for a vehicle auctioneer shall be amended within thirty days after the occurrence of each change on such form as the Secretary of State may prescribe by rule or regulation, accompanied by an amendatory fee of $2.

(d) Anything in this Chapter to the contrary notwithstanding, no person shall be licensed as a vehicle auctioneer unless such person shall maintain a place of business as defined in this Chapter.

(e) The Secretary of State shall, within a reasonable time after receipt, examine an application submitted to him under this Section. Unless the Secretary makes a determination that the application submitted to him does not conform to this Section or that grounds exist for a denial of the application under Section 5-501 of this Chapter, he must grant the applicant an original vehicle auctioneer license in writing for his place of business and a supplemental license in writing for each additional place of business, in such form as he may prescribe by rule or regulation which shall include the following:

1. The name of the person licensed;

2. If a corporation, the name and address of its officers or if a sole proprietorship, a partnership, an unincorporated association or any similar form of business organization, the

name and address of the proprietor or of each partner, member, officer, director, trustee or manager;

3. Complete address of the place of business of the licensee;

4. In the case of supplemental license, the place of business of the licensee and the place of business to which such supplemental license pertains.

(f) The appropriate instruments evidencing the license or a certified copy thereof, provided by the Secretary of State shall be kept posted, conspicuously, in the place of business of the licensee within the State and in each additional place of business, if any, maintained by such licensee.

(g) Except as provided in subsection (h) of this Section, all vehicle auctioneer licenses granted under this Section expire on December 31 of the calendar year for which they are granted unless sooner revoked under Section 5-501 of this Chapter.

(h) A vehicle auctioneer license may be renewed upon application and payment of the fee required herein, and submission of proof of coverage by an approved bond under the "Retailers' Occupation Tax Act" or proof that applicant is not subject to such bonding requirements, as in the case of an original license, but in case an application for the renewal of an effective license is made during the month of December, the effective license shall remain in force until the application for renewal is granted or denied by the Secretary of State.

(i) Each person licensed as a vehicle auctioneer or a licensed new or used car dealer when auctioning vehicles is required to furnish each purchaser of a motor vehicle the following:

1. A certificate of title properly assigned to the purchaser;

2. A statement verified under oath that all identifying numbers on the vehicle agree with those on the certificate of title;

3. A bill of sale properly executed on behalf of such person.

P.A. 76-1586, § 5-701, added by P.A. 81-908, § 1, eff. Sept. 22, 1979. Amended by P.A. 85-1396, § 2, eff. Sept. 1, 1988.

Formerly Ill.Rev.Stat.1991, ch. 95 ½, ¶ 5-701.

1 35 ILCS 120/1 et seq.

5/5-702. Salvage certificate vehicles; auction prohibition

§ 5-702. No person shall engage in the business of auctioning any vehicles for which a salvage certificate is required by law except to a bidder who is properly licensed as a rebuilder, automotive parts recycler, scrap processor or out-of-state salvage buyer, as required by Sections 5-301 and 5-302 of this Chapter.

P.A. 76-1586, § 5-702, added by P.A. 81-908, § 1, eff. Sept. 22, 1979. Amended by P.A. 85-572, § 1, eff. Sept. 18, 1987; P.A. 85-951, § 1, eff. July 1, 1988; P.A. 85-1209, Art. II, § 2-51, eff. Aug. 30, 1988; P.A. 89-663, § 5, eff. Aug. 14, 1996.

Formerly Ill.Rev.Stat.1991, ch. 95 ½, ¶ 5-702.

ARTICLE VIII. PENALTIES

Section

5/5-801. Penalties

§ 5-801. Penalties. Any person who violates any of the provisions of this Chapter, except as otherwise indicated, shall be guilty of a Class A misdemeanor. Any person who violates any provisions of Section 5-701 shall be guilty of a Class 3 felony.

P.A. 76-1586, § 5-801, eff. July 1, 1970. Amended by P.A. 77-2720, § 1, eff. Jan. 1, 1972; P.A. 83-1473, § 1, eff. Jan. 1, 1985.

Formerly Ill.Rev.Stat.1991, ch. 95 ½, ¶ 5-801.

5/5-802. Criminal offense

§ 5-802. The violation of any rule or regulation promulgated by the Office of the Secretary of State under this Chapter shall not in and of itself constitute a criminal offense.

P.A. 76-1586, § 5-802, added by P.A. 85-1204, § 1, eff. Aug. 26, 1988.

Formerly Ill.Rev.Stat.1991, ch. 95 ½, ¶ 5-802.

CHAPTER 6. THE ILLINOIS DRIVER LICENSING LAW

ARTICLE I. ISSUANCE OF LICENSES, EXPIRATION AND RENEWAL

Section

5/6-100. Definitions

§ 6-100. Definitions. For the purposes of this Chapter, the following words shall have the meanings ascribed to them:

(a) Application Process. The process of obtaining a driver's license, identification card, or permit. The process begins when a person enters a Secretary of State Driver Services facility and requests a driver's license, identification card or permit.

(b) Conviction. A final adjudication of guilty by a court of competent jurisdiction either after a bench trial, trial by jury, plea of guilty, order of forfeiture, or default.

(c) Identification Card. A document made or issued by or under the authority of the United States Government, the State of Illinois or any other state or political subdivision thereof, or any governmental or quasi-governmental organization that, when completed with information concerning the individual, is of a type intended or commonly accepted for the purpose of identifying the individual.

P.A. 76-1586, § 6-100, added by P.A. 78-663, § 1, eff. Jan. 1, 1974. Amended by P.A. 85-813, § 1, eff. Jan. 1, 1988; P.A. 89-283, § 10, eff. Jan. 1, 1996.

Formerly Ill.Rev.Stat.1991, ch. 95 ½, ¶ 6-100.

5/6-101. Drivers must have licenses or Permits

§ 6-101. Drivers must have licenses or Permits. (a) No person, except those expressly exempted by Section 6-102, shall drive any motor vehicle upon a highway in this State unless such person has a valid license or permit, or a restricted driving permit, issued under the provisions of this Act.

(b) No person shall drive a motor vehicle unless he holds a valid license or permit, or a restricted driving permit issued under the provisions of Section 6-205, 6-206, or 6-113 of this Act. Any person to whom a license is issued under the provisions of this Act must surrender to the Secretary of State all valid licenses or permits. No drivers license shall be issued to any person who holds a valid Foreign State license unless such person first surrenders to the Secretary of State any such valid Foreign State license.

(c) Any person licensed as a driver hereunder shall not be required by any city, village, incorporated town or other municipal corporation to obtain any other license to exercise the privilege thereby granted.

(d) In addition to other penalties imposed under this Section, any person in violation of this Section who is also in violation of Section 7-601 of this Code relating to mandatory insurance requirements shall have his or her motor vehicle immediately impounded by the arresting law enforcement officer. The motor vehicle may be released to any licensed driver upon a showing of proof of insurance for the motor vehicle that was impounded and the notarized written consent for the release by the vehicle owner.

P.A. 76-1586, § 6-101, eff. July 1, 1970. Amended by P.A. 86-549, § 1, eff. Jan. 1, 1990; P.A. 90-559, § 5, eff. June 1, 1998.

Formerly Ill.Rev.Stat.1991, ch. 95 ½, ¶ 6-101.

5/6-102. What persons are exempt

§ 6-102. What persons are exempt. The following persons are exempt from the requirements of Section 6-101 and are not required to have an Illinois drivers license or permit if one or more of the following qualifying exemptions are met and apply:

1. Any employee of the United States Government or any member of the Armed Forces of the United States, while operating a motor vehicle owned by or leased to the United States Government and being operated on official business need not be licensed;

2. A nonresident who has in his immediate possession a valid license issued to him in his home state or country may operate a motor vehicle for which he is licensed for the period during which he is in this State;

3. A nonresident and his spouse and children living with him who is a student at a college or university in Illinois who have a valid license issued by their home State.

4. A person operating a road machine temporarily upon a highway or operating a farm tractor between the home farm buildings and any adjacent or nearby farm land for the exclusive purpose of conducting farm operations need not be licensed as a driver.

5. A resident of this State who has been serving as a member of the Armed Forces of the United States outside the Continental limits of the United States, for a period of 45 days following his return to the continental limits of the United States.

6. A nonresident on active duty in the Armed Forces of the United States who has a valid license issued by his home state and such nonresident's spouse, and dependent children and living with parents, who have a valid license issued by their home state.

7. A nonresident who becomes a resident of this State, may for a period of the first 90 days of residence in Illinois operate any motor vehicle which he was qualified or licensed to drive by his home state or country so long as he has in his possession, a valid and current license issued to him by his home state or country. Upon expiration of such 90 day period, such new resident must comply with the provisions of this Act and apply for an Illinois license or permit.

8. An engineer, conductor, brakeman, or any other member of the crew of a locomotive or train being operated upon rails, including operation on a railroad crossing over a public street, road or highway. Such person is not required to display a driver's license to any law enforcement officer in connection with the operation of a locomotive or train within this State.

The provisions of this Section granting exemption to any nonresident shall be operative to the same extent that the laws of the State or country of such nonresident grant like exemption to residents of this State.

The Secretary of State may implement the exemption provisions of this Section by inclusion thereof in a reciprocity agreement, arrangement or declaration issued pursuant to this Act.

P.A. 76-1586, § 6-102, eff. July 1, 1970. Amended by P.A. 76-1905, § 1; P.A. 77-21, § 1, eff. April 27, 1971; P.A. 79-1141, § 1, eff. Jan. 1, 1976; P.A. 86-1258, § 1, eff. Jan. 1, 1991.

Formerly Ill.Rev.Stat.1991, ch. 95 ½, ¶ 6-102.

5/6-103. What persons shall not be licensed as drivers or granted permits

§ 6-103. What persons shall not be licensed as drivers or granted permits. The Secretary of State shall not issue, renew, or allow the retention of any driver's license nor issue any permit under this Code:

1. To any person, as a driver, who is under the age of 18 years except as provided in Section 6-107, and except that an instruction permit may be issued under paragraphs (a) and (b) of Section 6-105 to a child who is not less than 15 years of age if the child is enrolled in an approved driver education course as defined in Section 1-103 of this Code and requires an instruction permit to participate therein, except that an instruction permit may be issued under the provisions of Section 6-107.1 to a child who is 17 years and 9 months of age without the child having enrolled in an approved driver education course and except that an instruction permit may be issued to a child who is at least 15 years and 6 months of age, is enrolled in school, meets the educational requirements of the Driver Education Act,[1] and has passed examinations the Secretary of State in his or her discretion may prescribe;

2. To any person who is under the age of 18 as an operator of a motorcycle other than a motor driven cycle unless the person has, in addition to meeting the provisions of Section 6-107 of this Code, completed a motorcycle training course approved by the Illinois Department of Transportation and successfully completes the required Secretary of State's motorcycle driver's examination;

3. To any person, as a driver, whose driver's license or permit has been suspended, during the suspension, nor to any person whose driver's license or permit has been revoked, except as provided in Sections 6-205, 6-206, and 6-208;

4. To any person, as a driver, who is a user of alcohol or any other drug to a degree that renders the person incapable of safely driving a motor vehicle;

5. To any person, as a driver, who has previously been adjudged to be afflicted with or suffering from any mental or physical disability or disease and who has not at the time of application been restored to competency by the methods provided by law;

6. To any person, as a driver, who is required by the Secretary of State to submit an alcohol and drug evaluation or take an examination provided for in this Code unless the person has successfully passed the examination and submitted any required evaluation;

7. To any person who is required under the provisions of the laws of this State to deposit security or proof of financial responsibility and who has not deposited the security or proof;

8. To any person when the Secretary of State has good cause to believe that the person by reason of physical or mental disability would not be able to safely operate a motor vehicle upon the highways, unless the person shall furnish to the Secretary of State a verified written statement, acceptable to the Secretary of State, from a competent medical specialist to the effect that the operation of a motor vehicle by the person would not be inimical to the public safety;

9. To any person, as a driver, who is 69 years of age or older, unless the person has successfully complied with the provisions of Section 6-109;

10. To any person convicted, within 12 months of application for a license, of any of the sexual offenses enumerated in paragraph 2 of subsection (b) of Section 6-205;

11. To any person who is under the age of 21 years with a classification prohibited in paragraph (b) of Section 6-104 and to any person who is under the age of 18 years with a classification prohibited in paragraph (c) of Section 6-104;

12. To any person who has been either convicted of or adjudicated under the Juvenile Court Act of 1987[2] based upon a violation of the Cannabis Control Act[3] or the Illinois Controlled Substances Act[4] while that person was in actual physical control of a motor vehicle. For purposes of this Section, any person placed on probation under Section 10 of the Cannabis Control Act[5] or Section 410 of the Illinois Controlled Substances Act[6] shall not be considered convicted. Any person found guilty of this offense, while in actual physical control of a motor vehicle, shall have an entry made in the court record by the judge that this offense did occur while the person was in actual physical control of a motor vehicle and order the clerk of the court to report the violation to the Secretary of State as such. The Secretary of State shall not issue a new license or permit for a period of one year;

13. To any person who is under the age of 18 years and who has committed the offense of operating a motor vehicle without a valid license or permit in violation of Section 6-101

14. To any person who is 90 days or more delinquent in court ordered child support payments or has been adjudicated in arrears in an amount equal to 90 days' obligation or more and who has been found in contempt of court for failure to pay the support, subject to the requirements and procedures of Article VII of Chapter 7 of the Illinois Vehicle Code;[7] or

15. To any person released from a term of imprisonment for violating Section 9-3 of the Criminal Code of 1961[8] relating to reckless homicide within 24 months of release from a term of imprisonment.

The Secretary of State shall retain all conviction information, if the information is required to be held confidential under the Juvenile Court Act of 1987.

P.A. 76-1586, § 6-103, eff. July 1, 1970. Amended by P.A. 77-51, § 1, eff. July 1, 1971; P.A. 77-670, § 1, eff. Jan. 1, 1972; P.A. 77-2829, § 40, eff. Dec. 22, 1972; P.A. 78-255, § 61, eff. Oct. 1, 1973; P.A. 79-1141, § 1, eff. Jan. 1, 1976; P.A. 83-820, § 1, eff. Jan. 1, 1984; P.A. 85-951, § 1, eff. July 1, 1988; P.A. 86-1450, § 2, eff. July 1, 1991; P.A. 87-1114, § 1, eff. Sept. 15, 1992; P.A. 88-212, § 5, eff. Jan. 1, 1994; P.A. 90-369, § 5, eff. Jan. 1, 1998; P.A. 90-733, § 10, eff. Aug. 11, 1998; P.A. 92-343, § 5, eff. Jan. 1, 2002.

Formerly Ill.Rev.Stat.1991, ch. 95 ½, ¶ 6-103.

1 105 ILCS 5/27-24 et seq.

2 705 ILCS 405/1-1 et seq.

3 720 ILCS 550/1 et seq.

4 720 ILCS 570/100 et seq.

5 720 ILCS 550/10.

6 720 ILCS 570/410 et seq.

7 625 ILCS 5/7-700 et seq.

8 720 ILCS 5/9-3.

5/6-104. Classification of Driver—Special Restrictions

§ 6-104. Classification of Driver—Special Restrictions.

(a) A driver's license issued under the authority of this Act shall indicate the classification for which the applicant therefor has qualified by examination or by such other means that the Secretary of State shall prescribe. Driver's license classifications shall be prescribed by rule or regulation promulgated by the Secretary of State and such may specify classifications as to operation of motor vehicles of the first division, or of those of the second division, whether operated singly or in lawful combination, and whether for-hire or not-for-hire, and may specify such other classifications as the Secretary deems necessary.

No person shall operate a motor vehicle unless such person has a valid license with a proper classification to permit the operation of such vehicle, except that any person may operate a motorized pedalcycle if such person has a valid current Illinois driver's license, regardless of classification.

(b) No person who is under the age of 21 years or has had less than 1 year of driving experience shall drive: (1) in connection with the operation of any school, day camp, summer camp, or nursery school, any public or private motor vehicle for transporting children to or from any school, day camp, summer camp, or nursery school, or (2) any motor vehicle of the second division when in use for the transportation of persons for compensation.

(c) No person who is under the age of 18 years shall be issued a license for the purpose of transporting property for hire, or for the purpose of transporting persons for compensation in a motor vehicle of the first division.

(d) No person shall drive: (1) a school bus when transporting school children unless such person possesses a valid school bus driver permit or is accompanied and supervised, for the specific purpose of training prior to routine operation of a school bus, by a person who has held a valid school bus driver permit for at least one year; or (2) any other vehicle owned or operated by or for a public or private school, or a school operated by a religious institution, where such vehicle is being used over a regularly scheduled route for the transportation of persons enrolled as a student in grade 12 or below, in connection with any activity of the entities unless such person possesses a valid school bus driver permit.

(d-5) No person may drive a bus that has been chartered for the sole purpose of transporting students regularly enrolled in grade 12 or below to or from interscholastic athletic or interscholastic or school sponsored activities unless the person has a valid school bus driver permit in addition to any other permit or license that is required to operate that bus. This subsection (d-5) does not apply to any bus driver employed by a public transportation provider authorized to conduct local or interurban transportation of passengers when the bus is not traveling a specific school bus route but is on a regularly scheduled route for the transporting of other fare paying passengers.

(e) No person shall drive a religious organization bus unless such person has a valid and properly classified drivers license or a valid school bus driver permit.

(f) No person shall drive a motor vehicle for the purpose of providing transportation for the elderly in connection with the activities of any public or private organization unless such person has a valid and properly classified driver's license issued by the Secretary of State.

(g) No person shall drive a bus which meets the special requirements for school buses provided in Section 12-801, 12-802, 12-803 and 12-805 of this Code for the purpose of transporting persons 18 years of age or less in connection with any youth camp licensed under the Youth Camp Act [1] or any child care facility licensed under the Child Care Act of 1969 [2] unless such person possesses a valid school bus driver permit or is accompanied and supervised, for the specific purpose of training prior to routine operation of a school bus, by a person who has held a valid school bus driver permit for at least one year; however, a person who has a valid and properly classified driver's license issued by the Secretary of State may operate a school bus for the purpose of transporting persons 18 years of age or less in connection with any such youth camp or child care facility if the "SCHOOL BUS" signs are covered or concealed and the stop signal arm and flashing signal systems are not operable through normal controls.

P.A. 76-1586, § 6-104, eff. July 1, 1970. Amended by P.A. 76-1751, § 1; P.A. 78-499, § 1, eff. Aug. 30, 1973; P.A. 78-1244, § 1, eff. Sept. 5, 1974; P.A. 78-1297, § 58, eff. March 4, 1975; P.A. 79-798, § 1, eff. July 1, 1976; P.A. 79-1141, § 1, eff. Jan. 1, 1976; P.A. 79-1454, § 44, eff. Aug. 31, 1976; P.A. 80-262, § 1, eff. Aug. 20, 1977; P.A. 81-509, § 1, eff. Jan. 1, 1980; P.A. 82-532, § 1, eff. Jan. 1, 1982; P.A. 84-1311, § 2, eff. Aug. 27, 1986; P.A. 88-612, § 15, eff. July 1, 1995; P.A. 92-849, § 5, eff. Jan. 1, 2003.

Formerly Ill.Rev.Stat.1991, ch. 95 ½, ¶ 6-104.

[1] 210 ILCS 100/1 et seq.

[2] 225 ILCS 10/1 et seq.

5/6-105. Instruction permits and temporary licenses for persons 18 years of age or older

§ 6-105. Instruction permits and temporary licenses for persons 18 years of age or older.

(a) Except as provided in this Section, the Secretary of State upon receiving proper application and payment of the required fee may issue an instruction permit to any person 18 years of age or older who is not ineligible for a license under paragraphs 1, 3, 4, 5, 7, or 8 of Section 6-103, after the applicant has successfully passed such examination as the Secretary of State in his discretion may prescribe.

1. An instruction permit entitles the holder while having the permit in his immediate possession to drive a motor vehicle, excluding a motor driven cycle or motorcycle, upon the highways for a period of 12 months after the date of its issuance when accompanied by a licensed driver who is 21 years of age or older, who has had a valid driver's license classification to operate such vehicle for at least one year and has had one year of driving experience with such classification and who is occupying a seat beside the driver.

2. A 12 month instruction permit for a motor driven cycle or motorcycle may be issued to a person 18 years of age or more, and entitles the holder to drive upon the highways during daylight under the direct supervision of a licensed motor driven cycle operator or motorcycle operator with the same or greater classification, who is 21 years of age or older and who has at least one year of driving experience.

3. (Blank).

(b) (Blank).

(c) The Secretary of State may issue a temporary driver's license to an applicant for a license permitting the operation of a motor vehicle while the Secretary is completing an investigation and determination of all facts relative to such applicant's eligibility to receive such license, or for any other reason prescribed by rule or regulation promulgated by the Secretary of State. Such permit must be in the applicant's immediate possession while operating a motor vehicle, and it shall be invalid when the applicant's driver's license has been issued or for good cause has been refused. In each case the Secretary of State may issue the temporary driver's license for such period as appropriate but in no event for longer than 90 days.

P.A. 76–1586, § 6–105, eff. July 1, 1970. Amended by P.A. 76–1906, § 1; P.A. 76–2153, § 1, eff. July 1, 1970; P.A. 77–670, § 1, eff. Jan. 1, 1972; P.A. 77–2805, § 1, eff. Oct. 1, 1972; P.A. 78–255, § 61, eff. Oct. 1, 1973; P.A. 79–1141, § 1, eff. Jan. 1, 1976; P.A. 83–820, § 1, eff. Jan. 1, 1984; P.A. 85–522, § 1, eff. Jan. 1, 1988; P.A. 90–369, § 5, eff. Jan. 1, 1998.

Formerly Ill.Rev.Stat.1991, ch. 95 ½, ¶ 6–105.

5/6–106. Application for license or instruction permit

§ 6–106. Application for license or instruction permit.

(a) Every application for any permit or license authorized to be issued under this Act shall be made upon a form furnished by the Secretary of State. Every application shall be accompanied by the proper fee and payment of such fee shall entitle the applicant to not more than 3 attempts to pass the examination within a period of 1 year after the date of application.

(b) Every application shall state the name, social security number, zip code, date of birth, sex, and residence address of the applicant; briefly describe the applicant; state whether the applicant has theretofore been licensed as a driver, and, if so, when and by what state or country, and whether any such license has ever been cancelled, suspended, revoked or refused, and, if so, the date and reason for such cancellation, suspension, revocation or refusal; shall include an affirmation by the applicant that all information set forth is true and correct; and shall bear the applicant's signature. The application form may also require the statement of such additional relevant information as the Secretary of State shall deem necessary to determine the applicant's competency and eligibility. The Secretary of State may in his discretion substitute a federal tax number in lieu of a social security number, or he may instead assign an additional distinctive number in lieu thereof, where an applicant is prohibited by bona fide religious convictions from applying or is exempt from applying for a social security number. The Secretary of State shall, however, determine which religious orders or sects have such bona fide religious convictions. The Secretary of State may, in his discretion, by rule or regulation, provide that an application for a drivers license or permit may include a suitable photograph of the applicant in the form prescribed by the Secretary, and he may further provide that each drivers license shall include a photograph of the driver. The Secretary of State may utilize a photograph process or system most suitable to deter alteration or improper reproduction of a drivers license and to prevent substitution of another photo thereon.

(c) The application form shall include a notice to the applicant of the registration obligations of sex offenders under the Sex Offender Registration Act.[1] The notice shall be provided in a form and manner prescribed by the Secretary of State. For purposes of this subsection (c), "sex offender" has the meaning ascribed to it in Section 2 of the Sex Offender Registration Act.[2]

(d) Any male United States citizen or immigrant who applies for any permit or license authorized to be issued under this Act or for a renewal of any permit or license, and who is at least 18 years of age but less than 26 years of age, must be registered in compliance with the requirements of the federal Military Selective Service Act.[3] The Secretary of State must forward in an electronic format the necessary personal information regarding the applicants identified in this subsection (d) to the Selective Service System. The applicant's signature on the application serves as an indication that the applicant either has already registered with the Selective Service System or that he is authorizing the Secretary to forward to the Selective Service System the necessary information for registration. The Secretary must notify the applicant at the time of application that his signature constitutes consent to registration with the Selective Service System, if he is not already registered.

P.A. 76–1586, § 6–106, eff. July 1, 1970. Amended by P.A. 77–105, § 1, eff. Jan. 1, 1972; P.A. 78–197, § 1, eff. Jan. 1, 1974; P.A. 78–663, § 1, eff. Jan. 1, 1974; P.A. 78–1297, § 30, eff. March 4, 1975; P.A. 86–503, § 1, eff. Sept. 1, 1989; P.A. 87–233, § 1, eff. Jan. 1, 1992; P.A. 89–8, Art. 20, § 20–15, eff. Jan. 1, 1996; P.A. 90–191, § 10, eff. Jan. 1, 1998; P.A. 92–117, § 5, eff. Jan. 1, 2002.

Formerly Ill.Rev.Stat.1991, ch. 95 ½, ¶ 6–106.

1 730 ILCS 150/1 et seq.

2 730 ILCS 150/2.

3 50 App. U.S.C.A. §451 et seq.

5/6–106.1. School bus driver permit

§ 6–106.1. School bus driver permit.

(a) The Secretary of State shall issue a school bus driver permit to those applicants who have met all the requirements of the application and screening process under this Section to insure the welfare and safety of children who are transported on school buses throughout the State of Illinois. Applicants shall obtain the proper application required by the Secretary of State from their prospective or current employer and submit the completed application to the prospective or current employer along with the necessary fingerprint submission as required by the Department of State Police to conduct fingerprint based criminal background checks on current and future information available in the state system and current information available through the Federal Bureau of Investigation's system. Applicants who have completed the fingerprinting requirements shall not be subjected to the fingerprinting process when applying for subsequent permits or submitting proof of successful completion of the annual refresher course. Individuals who on the effective date of this Act possess a valid school bus driver permit that has been previously issued by the appropriate Regional School Superintendent are not subject to the fingerprinting provisions of this Section as long as the permit remains valid and does not lapse. The applicant shall be required to pay all related application and fingerprinting fees as established by rule including, but not limited to, the amounts established by the Department of State Police and the Federal Bureau of Investigation to process fingerprint based criminal background investigations. All fees paid for fingerprint processing services under this Section shall be deposited into the State Police Services Fund for the cost incurred in processing the fingerprint based criminal background investigations. All other fees paid under this Section shall be deposited into the Road Fund for the purpose of defraying the costs of the Secretary of State in administering this Section. All applicants must:

1. be 21 years of age or older;

2. possess a valid and properly classified driver's license issued by the Secretary of State;

3. possess a valid driver's license, which has not been revoked, suspended, or canceled for 3 years immediately prior to the date of application, or have not had his or her commercial motor vehicle driving privileges disqualified within the 3 years immediately prior to the date of application;

4. successfully pass a written test, administered by the Secretary of State, on school bus operation, school bus safety, and special traffic laws relating to school buses and submit to a review of the applicant's driving habits by the Secretary of State at the time the written test is given;

5. demonstrate ability to exercise reasonable care in the operation of school buses in accordance with rules promulgated by the Secretary of State;

6. demonstrate physical fitness to operate school buses by submitting the results of a medical examination, including tests for drug use for each applicant not subject to such testing pursuant to federal law, conducted by a licensed physician, an advanced practice nurse who has a written collaborative agreement with a collaborating physician which authorizes him or her to perform medical examinations, or a physician assistant who has been delegated the performance of medical examinations by his or her supervising physician within 90 days of the date of application according to standards promulgated by the Secretary of State;

7. affirm under penalties of perjury that he or she has not made a false statement or knowingly concealed a material fact in any application for permit;

8. have completed an initial classroom course, including first aid procedures, in school bus driver safety as promulgated by the Secretary of State; and after satisfactory completion of said initial course an annual refresher course; such courses and the agency or organization conducting such courses shall be approved by the Secretary of State; failure to complete the annual refresher course, shall result in cancellation of the permit until such course is completed;

9. not have been convicted of 2 or more serious traffic offenses, as defined by rule, within one year prior to the date of application that may endanger the life or safety of any of the driver's passengers within the duration of the permit period;

10. not have been convicted of reckless driving, driving while intoxicated, or reckless homicide resulting from the operation of a motor vehicle within 3 years of the date of application;

11. not have been convicted of committing or attempting to commit any one or more of the following offenses: (i) those offenses defined in Sections 9–1, 9–1.2, 9–2, 9–2.1, 9–3, 9–3.2, 9–3.3, 10–1, 10–2, 10–3.1, 10–4, 10–5, 10–6, 10–7, 11–6, 11–9, 11–9.1, 11–14, 11–15, 11–15.1, 11–16, 11–17, 11–18, 11–19, 11–19.1, 11–19.2, 11–20, 11–20.1, 11–21, 11–22, 12–3.1, 12–4.1, 12–4.2, 12–4.3, 12–4.4, 12–4.5, 12–6, 12–6.2, 12–7.1, 12–7.3, 12–7.4, 12–11, 12–13, 12–14, 12–14.1, 12–15, 12–16, 12–16.2, 12–21.5, 12–21.6, 12–33, 18–1, 18–2, 18–3, 18–4, 18–5, 20–1, 20–1.1, 20–2, 24–1, 24–1.1, 24–1.2, 24–3.3, 31A–1, 31A–1.1, and 33A–2, and in subsection (a) and subsection (b), clause (1), of Section 12–4 of the Criminal Code of 1961; [1] (ii) those offenses defined in the Cannabis Control Act [2] except those offenses defined in subsections (a) and (b) of Section 4, and subsection (a) of Section 5 of the Cannabis Control Act; [3] (iii) those offenses defined in the Illinois Controlled Substances Act; [4] (iv) any offense committed or attempted in any other state or against the laws of the United States, which if committed or attempted in this State would be punishable as one or more of the foregoing offenses; (v) the offenses defined in Section 4.1 and 5.1 of the Wrongs to Children Act [5] and (vi) those offenses defined in Section 6–16 of the Liquor Control Act of 1934; [6]

12. not have been repeatedly involved as a driver in motor vehicle collisions or been repeatedly convicted of offenses against laws and ordinances regulating the movement of traffic, to a degree which indicates lack of ability to exercise ordinary and reasonable care in the safe operation of a motor vehicle or disrespect for the traffic laws and the safety of other persons upon the highway;

13. not have, through the unlawful operation of a motor vehicle, caused an accident resulting in the death of any person; and

14. not have, within the last 5 years, been adjudged to be afflicted with or suffering from any mental disability or disease.

(b) A school bus driver permit shall be valid for a period specified by the Secretary of State as set forth by rule. It shall be renewable upon compliance with subsection (a) of this Section.

(c) A school bus driver permit shall contain the holder's driver's license number, name, address, zip code, social security number and date of birth, a brief description of the holder and a space for signature. The Secretary of State may require a suitable photograph of the holder.

(d) The employer shall be responsible for conducting a pre-employment interview with prospective school bus driver candidates, distributing school bus driver applications and medical forms to be completed by the applicant, and submitting the applicant's fingerprint cards to the Department of State Police that are required for the criminal background investigations. The employer shall certify in writing to the Secretary of State that all pre-employment conditions have been successfully completed including the successful completion of an Illinois specific criminal background investigation through the Department of State Police and the submission of necessary fingerprints to the Federal Bureau of Investigation for criminal history information available through the Federal Bureau of Investigation system. The applicant shall present the certification to the Secretary of State at the time of submitting the school bus driver permit application.

(e) Permits shall initially be provisional upon receiving certification from the employer that all pre-employment conditions have been successfully completed, and upon successful completion of all training and examination requirements for the classification of the vehicle to be operated, the Secretary of State shall provisionally issue a School Bus Driver Permit. The permit shall remain in a provisional status pending the completion of the Federal Bureau of Investigation's criminal background investigation based upon fingerprinting specimens submitted to the Federal Bureau of Investigation by the Department of State Police. The Federal Bureau of Investigation shall report the findings directly to the Secretary of State. The Secretary of State shall remove the bus driver permit from provisional status upon the applicant's successful completion of the Federal Bureau of Investigation's criminal background investigation.

(f) A school bus driver permit holder shall notify the employer and the Secretary of State if he or she is convicted in another state of an offense that would make him or her ineligible for a permit under subsection (a) of this Section. The written notification shall be made within 5 days of the entry of the conviction. Failure of the permit holder to provide the notification is punishable as a petty offense for a first violation and a Class B misdemeanor for a second or subsequent violation.

(g) Cancellation; suspension; notice and procedure.

(1) The Secretary of State shall cancel a school bus driver permit of an applicant whose criminal background

investigation discloses that he or she is not in compliance with the provisions of subsection (a) of this Section.

(2) The Secretary of State shall cancel a school bus driver permit when he or she receives notice that the permit holder fails to comply with any provision of this Section or any rule promulgated for the administration of this Section.

(3) The Secretary of State shall cancel a school bus driver permit if the permit holder's restricted commercial or commercial driving privileges are withdrawn or otherwise invalidated.

(4) The Secretary of State may not issue a school bus driver permit for a period of 3 years to an applicant who fails to obtain a negative result on a drug test as required in item 6 of subsection (a) of this Section or under federal law.

(5) The Secretary of State shall forthwith suspend a school bus driver permit for a period of 3 years upon receiving notice that the holder has failed to obtain a negative result on a drug test as required in item 6 of subsection (a) of this Section or under federal law.

The Secretary of State shall notify the State Superintendent of Education and the permit holder's prospective or current employer that the applicant has (1) has failed a criminal background investigation or (2) is no longer eligible for a school bus driver permit; and of the related cancellation of the applicant's provisional school bus driver permit. The cancellation shall remain in effect pending the outcome of a hearing pursuant to Section 2–118 of this Code. The scope of the hearing shall be limited to the issuance criteria contained in subsection (a) of this Section. A petition requesting a hearing shall be submitted to the Secretary of State and shall contain the reason the individual feels he or she is entitled to a school bus driver permit. The permit holder's employer shall notify in writing to the Secretary of State that the employer has certified the removal of the offending school bus driver from service prior to the start of that school bus driver's next workshift. An employing school board that fails to remove the offending school bus driver from service is subject to the penalties defined in Section 3–14.23 of the School Code.[7] A school bus contractor who violates a provision of this Section is subject to the penalties defined in Section 6–106.11.

All valid school bus driver permits issued under this Section prior to January 1, 1995, shall remain effective until their expiration date unless otherwise invalidated.

P.A. 76–1586, § 6–106.1, added by P.A. 78–1244, § 1, eff. Sept. 5, 1974. Amended by P.A. 79–845, § 1, eff. Jan. 1, 1976; P.A. 79–1399, § 1, eff. Oct. 1, 1976; P.A. 80–506, § 1, eff. Oct. 1, 1977; P.A. 81–509, § 1, eff. Jan. 1, 1980; P.A. 81–1508, § 8, eff. Sept. 25, 1980; P.A. 83–831, § 1, eff. Jan. 1, 1984; P.A. 83–1067, § 19, eff. July 1, 1984; P.A. 83–1286, § 1, eff. Aug. 31, 1984; P.A. 83–1362, Art. II, § 99, eff. Sept. 11, 1984; P.A. 84–1450, § 7, eff. July 1, 1987; P.A. 86–508, § 1, eff. Jan. 1, 1990; P.A. 86–578, § 1, eff. Jan. 1, 1990; P.A. 86–1028, Art. II, § 2–44, eff. Feb. 5, 1990; P.A. 86–1465, § 1, eff. April 1, 1992; P.A. 87–526, § 2, eff. Sept. 16, 1991; P.A. 87–895, Art. 3, § 3–52, eff. Aug. 14, 1992; P.A. 88–612, § 15, eff. July 1, 1995; P.A. 89–71, § 5, eff. Jan. 1, 1996; P.A. 89–120, § 10, eff. July 7, 1995; P.A. 89–375, § 3, eff. Aug. 18, 1995; P.A. 89–428, Art. 2, § 250, eff. Dec. 13, 1995; P.A. 89–462, Art. 2, § 250, eff. May 29, 1996; P.A. 89–626, Art. 2, § 2–66, eff. Aug. 9, 1996; P.A. 90–191, § 10, eff. Jan. 1, 1998; P.A. 91–500, § 5, eff. Aug. 13, 1999; P.A. 92–703, § 10, eff. July 19, 2002.

Formerly Ill.Rev.Stat.1991, ch. 95 ½, ¶ 6–106.1.

[1] 720 ILCS 5/9–1 et seq.

[2] 720 ILCS 550/1 et seq.

[3] 720 ILCS 550/5.

[4] 720 ILCS 570/100 et seq.

[5] 720 ILCS 150/4.1 and 150/5.1.

[6] 235 ILCS 556161–16.

[7] 105 ILCS 5/3–14.23.

For saving clause, construction and application of P.A. 83–1067, see note following 720 ILCS 5/12–12.

P.A. 89–428 was held by the Illinois Supreme Court to be in violation of the single subject requirement of subsection (d) of Section 8 of Article IV of the Illinois Constitution in the case of Johnson v. Edgar, 1997, 176 Ill.2d 499, 680 N.E.2d 1372, 224 Ill.Dec. 1. Public Act 89–462 reenacted the amendment of this text by P.A. 89–428.

5/6–106.1a. Cancellation of school bus driver permit; trace of alcohol

§ 6–106.1a. Cancellation of school bus driver permit; trace of alcohol.

(a) A person who has been issued a school bus driver permit by the Secretary of State in accordance with Section 6–106.1 of this Code and who drives or is in actual physical control of a school bus or any other vehicle owned or operated by or for a public or private school, or a school operated by a religious institution, when the vehicle is being used over a regularly scheduled route for the transportation of persons enrolled as students in grade 12 or below, in connection with any activity of the entities listed, upon the public highways of this State shall be deemed to have given consent to a chemical test or tests of blood, breath, or urine for the purpose of determining the alcohol content of the person's blood if arrested, as evidenced by the issuance of a Uniform Traffic Ticket for any violation of this Code or a similar provision of a local ordinance, if a police officer has probable cause to believe that the driver has consumed any amount of an alcoholic beverage based upon evidence of the driver's physical condition or other first hand knowledge of the police officer. The test or tests shall be administered at the direction of the arresting officer. The law enforcement agency employing the officer shall designate which of the aforesaid tests shall be administered. A urine test may be administered even after a blood or breath test or both has been administered.

(b) A person who is dead, unconscious, or who is otherwise in a condition rendering that person incapable of refusal, shall be deemed not to have withdrawn the consent provided by paragraph (a) of this Section and the test or tests may be administered subject to the following provisions:

(1) Chemical analysis of the person's blood, urine, breath, or other substance, to be considered valid under the provisions of this Section, shall have been performed according to standards promulgated by the Department of State Police by an individual possessing a valid permit issued by the Department of State Police for this purpose. The Director of State Police is authorized to approve satisfactory techniques or methods, to ascertain the qualifications and competence of individuals to conduct analyses, to issue permits that shall be subject to termination or revocation at the direction of the Department of State Police, and to certify the accuracy of breath testing equipment. The Department of State Police shall prescribe rules as necessary.

(2) When a person submits to a blood test at the request of a law enforcement officer under the provisions of this Section, only a physician authorized to practice medicine, a registered nurse, or other qualified person trained in veni-

puncture and acting under the direction of a licensed physician may withdraw blood for the purpose of determining the alcohol content. This limitation does not apply to the taking of breath or urine specimens.

(3) The person tested may have a physician, qualified technician, chemist, registered nurse, or other qualified person of his or her own choosing administer a chemical test or tests in addition to any test or tests administered at the direction of a law enforcement officer. The test administered at the request of the person may be admissible into evidence at a hearing conducted in accordance with Section 2–118 of this Code. The failure or inability to obtain an additional test by a person shall not preclude the consideration of the previously performed chemical test.

(4) Upon a request of the person who submits to a chemical test or tests at the request of a law enforcement officer, full information concerning the test or tests shall be made available to the person or that person's attorney by the requesting law enforcement agency within 72 hours of receipt of the test result.

(5) Alcohol concentration means either grams of alcohol per 100 milliliters of blood or grams of alcohol per 210 liters of breath.

(6) If a driver is receiving medical treatment as a result of a motor vehicle accident, a physician licensed to practice medicine, registered nurse, or other qualified person trained in venipuncture and acting under the direction of a licensed physician shall withdraw blood for testing purposes to ascertain the presence of alcohol upon the specific request of a law enforcement officer. However, that testing shall not be performed until, in the opinion of the medical personnel on scene, the withdrawal can be made without interfering with or endangering the well-being of the patient.

(c) A person requested to submit to a test as provided in this Section shall be warned by the law enforcement officer requesting the test that a refusal to submit to the test, or submission to the test resulting in an alcohol concentration of more than 0.00, may result in the loss of that person's privilege to possess a school bus driver permit. The loss of the individual's privilege to possess a school bus driver permit shall be imposed in accordance with Section 6–106.1b of this Code.

(d) If the person refuses testing or submits to a test that discloses an alcohol concentration of more than 0.00, the law enforcement officer shall immediately submit a sworn report to the Secretary of State on a form prescribed by the Secretary of State certifying that the test or tests were requested under subsection (a) and the person refused to submit to a test or tests or submitted to testing which disclosed an alcohol concentration of more than 0.00. The law enforcement officer shall submit the same sworn report when a person who has been issued a school bus driver permit and who was operating a school bus or any other vehicle owned or operated by or for a public or private school, or a school operated by a religious institution, when the vehicle is being used over a regularly scheduled route for the transportation of persons enrolled as students in grade 12 or below, in connection with any activity of the entities listed, submits to testing under Section 11–501.1 of this Code and the testing discloses an alcohol concentration of more than 0.00 and less than the alcohol concentration at which driving or being in actual physical control of a motor vehicle is prohibited under paragraph (1) of subsection (a) of Section 11–501.

Upon receipt of the sworn report of a law enforcement officer, the Secretary of State shall enter the school bus driver permit sanction on the individual's driving record and the sanction shall be effective on the 46th day following the date notice of the sanction was given to the person.

The law enforcement officer submitting the sworn report shall serve immediate notice of this school bus driver permit sanction on the person and the sanction shall be effective on the 46th day following the date notice was given.

In cases where the blood alcohol concentration of more than 0.00 is established by a subsequent analysis of blood or urine, the police officer or arresting agency shall give notice as provided in this Section or by deposit in the United States mail of that notice in an envelope with postage prepaid and addressed to that person at his or her last known address and the loss of the school bus driver permit shall be effective on the 46th day following the date notice was given.

Upon receipt of the sworn report of a law enforcement officer, the Secretary of State shall also give notice of the school bus driver permit sanction to the driver and the driver's current employer by mailing a notice of the effective date of the sanction to the individual. However, shall the sworn report be defective by not containing sufficient information or be completed in error, the notice of the school bus driver permit sanction may not be mailed to the person or his current employer or entered to the driving record, but rather the sworn report shall be returned to the issuing law enforcement agency.

(e) A driver may contest this school bus driver permit sanction by requesting an administrative hearing with the Secretary of State in accordance with Section 2–118 of this Code. An individual whose blood alcohol concentration is shown to be more than 0.00 is not subject to this Section if he or she consumed alcohol in the performance of a religious service or ceremony. An individual whose blood alcohol concentration is shown to be more than 0.00 shall not be subject to this Section if the individual's blood alcohol concentration resulted only from ingestion of the prescribed or recommended dosage of medicine that contained alcohol. The petition for that hearing shall not stay or delay the effective date of the impending suspension. The scope of this hearing shall be limited to the issues of:

(1) whether the police officer had probable cause to believe that the person was driving or in actual physical control of a school bus or any other vehicle owned or operated by or for a public or private school, or a school operated by a religious institution, when the vehicle is being used over a regularly scheduled route for the transportation of persons enrolled as students in grade 12 or below, in connection with any activity of the entities listed, upon the public highways of the State and the police officer had reason to believe that the person was in violation of any provision of this Code or a similar provision of a local ordinance; and

(2) whether the person was issued a Uniform Traffic Ticket for any violation of this Code or a similar provision of a local ordinance; and

(3) whether the police officer had probable cause to believe that the driver had consumed any amount of an alcoholic beverage based upon the driver's physical actions or other first-hand knowledge of the police officer; and

(4) whether the person, after being advised by the officer that the privilege to possess a school bus driver permit would be canceled if the person refused to submit to and complete the test or tests, did refuse to submit to or complete the test or tests to determine the person's alcohol concentration; and

(5) whether the person, after being advised by the officer that the privileges to possess a school bus driver permit would be canceled if the person submits to a chemical test or tests and the test or tests disclose an alcohol concentration of more than 0.00 and the person did submit to and complete the test or tests that determined an alcohol concentration of more than 0.00; and

(6) whether the test result of an alcohol concentration of more than 0.00 was based upon the person's consumption of alcohol in the performance of a religious service or ceremony; and

(7) whether the test result of an alcohol concentration of more than 0.00 was based upon the person's consumption of alcohol through ingestion of the prescribed or recommended dosage of medicine.

The Secretary of State may adopt administrative rules setting forth circumstances under which the holder of a school bus driver permit is not required to appear in person at the hearing.

Provided that the petitioner may subpoena the officer, the hearing may be conducted upon a review of the law enforcement officer's own official reports. Failure of the officer to answer the subpoena shall be grounds for a continuance if, in the hearing officer's discretion, the continuance is appropriate. At the conclusion of the hearing held under Section 2–118 of this Code, the Secretary of State may rescind, continue, or modify the school bus driver permit sanction.

(f) The results of any chemical testing performed in accordance with subsection (a) of this Section are not admissible in any civil or criminal proceeding, except that the results of the testing may be considered at a hearing held under Section 2–118 of this Code. However, the results of the testing may not be used to impose driver's license sanctions under Section 11–501.1 of this Code. A law enforcement officer may, however, pursue a statutory summary suspension of driving privileges under Section 11–501.1 of this Code if other physical evidence or first hand knowledge forms the basis of that suspension.

(g) This Section applies only to drivers who have been issued a school bus driver permit in accordance with Section 6–106.1 of this Code at the time of the issuance of the Uniform Traffic Ticket for a violation of this Code or a similar provision of a local ordinance, and a chemical test request is made under this Section.

(h) The action of the Secretary of State in suspending, revoking, canceling, or denying any license, permit, registration, or certificate of title shall be subject to judicial review in the Circuit Court of Sangamon County or in the Circuit Court of Cook County, and the provisions of the Administrative Review Law [1] and its rules are hereby adopted and shall apply to and govern every action for the judicial review of final acts or decisions of the Secretary of State under this Section.

P.A. 76–1586, § 6–106.1a, added by P.A. 90–107, § 5, eff. Jan. 1, 1998. Amended by P.A. 91–124, § 5, eff. July 16, 1999; P.A. 91–828, § 5, eff. Jan. 1, 2001.

[1] 735 ILCS 5/3–101 et seq.

P.A. 91–828 incorporated the amendment by P.A. 91–124.

5/6–106.1b. Loss of school bus driver permit privileges; failure or refusal to submit to chemical testing

§ 6–106.1b. Loss of school bus driver permit privileges; failure or refusal to submit to chemical testing. Unless the loss of school bus driver permit privileges based upon consumption of alcohol by an individual who has been issued a school bus driver permit in accordance with Section 6–106.1 of this Code or refusal to submit to testing has been rescinded by the Secretary of State in accordance with subsection (c) of Section 6–206 of this Code, a person whose privilege to possess a school bus driver permit has been canceled under Section 6–106.1a is not eligible for restoration of the privilege until the expiration of 3 years from the effective date of the cancellation for a person who has refused or failed to complete a test or tests to determine blood alcohol concentration or has submitted to testing with a blood alcohol concentration of more than 0.00.

P.A. 76–1586, § 6–106.1b, added by P.A. 90–107, § 5, eff. Jan. 1, 1998. Amended by P.A. 91–124, § 5, eff. July 16, 1999.

5/6–106.2. Religious organization bus driver

§ 6–106.2. Religious organization bus driver. A religious organization bus driver shall meet the following requirements:

1. is 21 years of age or older;

2. has a valid and properly classified driver's license issued by the Secretary of State;

3. has held a valid driver's license, not necessarily of the same classification, for 3 years prior to the date of application;

4. has demonstrated an ability to exercise reasonable care in the safe operation of religious organization buses in accordance with such standards as the Secretary of State prescribes including a driving test in a religious organization bus; and

5. has not been convicted of any of the following offenses within 3 years of the date of application: Sections 11–401 (leaving the scene of a traffic accident involving death or personal injury), 11–501 (driving under the influence), 11–503 (reckless driving) and 11–504 (drag racing) of this Code, or Sections 9–3 (manslaughter or reckless homicide) and 12–5 (reckless conduct arising from the use of a motor vehicle) of the Criminal Code of 1961.[1]

P.A. 76–1586, § 6–106.2, added by P.A. 79–798, § 1, eff. July 1, 1976. Amended by P.A. 82–532, § 1, eff. Jan. 1, 1982; P.A. 83–831, § 1, eff. Jan. 1, 1984; P.A. 84–641, § 1, eff. Sept. 20, 1985.

Formerly Ill.Rev.Stat.1991, ch. 95 ½, ¶ 6–106.2.

[1] 720 ILCS 5/9–3 and 5/12–5.

5/6–106.3. Senior citizen transportation—driver

§ 6–106.3. Senior citizen transportation—driver. A driver of a vehicle operated solely for the purpose of providing transportation for the elderly in connection with the activities of any public or private organization shall meet the following requirements:

(1) is 21 years of age or older;

(2) has a valid and properly classified driver's license issued by the Secretary of State;

(3) has had a valid driver's license, not necessarily of the same classification, for 3 years prior to the date of application;

(4) has demonstrated his ability to exercise reasonable care in the safe operation of a motor vehicle which will be utilized to transport persons in accordance with such standards as the Secretary of State prescribes including a driving test in such motor vehicle; and

(5) has not been convicted of any of the following offenses within 3 years of the date of application: Sections 11–401

(leaving the scene of a traffic accident involving death or personal injury), 11–501 (driving under the influence), 11–503 (reckless driving) and 11–504 (drag racing) of this Code, or Sections 9–3 (manslaughter or reckless homicide) and 12–5 (reckless conduct arising from the use of a motor vehicle) of the Criminal Code of 1961.[1]

P.A. 76–1586, § 6–106.3, added by P.A. 82–532, § 1, eff. Jan. 1, 1982. Amended by P.A. 84–641, § 1, eff. Sept. 20, 1985.

Formerly Ill.Rev.Stat.1991, ch. 95 ½, ¶ 6–106.3.

1 720 ILCS 5/9–3 and 5/12–5.

5/6–106.4. For-profit ridesharing arrangement—driver

§ 6–106.4. For-profit ridesharing arrangement—driver. No person may drive a commuter van while it is being used for a for-profit ridesharing arrangement unless such person:

(1) is 21 years of age or older;

(2) has a valid and properly classified driver's license issued by the Secretary of State;

(3) has held a valid driver's license, not necessarily of the same classification, for 3 years prior to the date of application;

(4) has demonstrated his ability to exercise reasonable care in the safe operation of commuter vans used in for-profit ridesharing arrangements in accordance with such standards as the Secretary of State may prescribe, which standards may require a driving test in a commuter van; and

(5) has not been convicted of any of the following offenses within 3 years of the date of application: Sections 11–401 (leaving the scene of a traffic accident involving death or personal injury), 11–501 (driving under the influence), 11–503 (reckless driving) and 11–504 (drag racing) of this Code, or Sections 9–3 (manslaughter or reckless homicide) and 12–5 (reckless conduct arising from the use of a motor vehicle) of the Criminal Code of 1961.[1]

P.A. 76–1586, § 6–106.4, added by P.A. 83–1091, § 1, eff. July 1, 1984. Amended by P.A. 84–641, § 1, eff. Sept. 20, 1985.

Formerly Ill.Rev.Stat.1991, ch. 95 ½, ¶ 6–106.4.

1 720 ILCS 5/9–3 and 5/12–5.

5/6–106.11. Violations; penalties

§ 6–106.11. (a) Any individual, corporation, partnership or association, who through contractual arrangements with a school district transports students, teachers or other personnel of that district for compensation, shall not permit any person to operate a school bus pursuant to that contract if the driver has not complied with the provisions of Sections 6–106.1 of this Code or such other rules or regulations that the Secretary of State may prescribe for the classification, restriction or licensing of school bus drivers.

(b) A violation of this Section is a business offense and shall subject the offender to a fine of no less than $1,000 nor more than $10,000 for a first offense, no less than $1,500 nor more than $15,000 for a second offense, and no less than $2,000 nor more than $20,000 for a third or subsequent offense. In addition to any fines imposed under this subsection, any offender who has been convicted three times under the provisions of subsection (a) shall, upon a fourth or subsequent conviction be prohibited from transporting or contracting to transport students, teachers or other personnel of a school district for a period of five years beginning with the date of conviction of such fourth or subsequent conviction.

P.A. 76–1586, § 6–106.11, added by P.A. 83–1286, § 1, eff. Aug. 31, 1984.

Formerly Ill.Rev.Stat.1991, ch. 95 ½, ¶ 6–106.11.

5/6–107. Graduated license

§ 6–107. Graduated license.

(a) The purpose of the Graduated Licensing Program is to develop safe and mature driving habits in young, inexperienced drivers and reduce or prevent motor vehicle accidents, fatalities, and injuries by:

(1) providing for an increase in the time of practice period before granting permission to obtain a driver's license;

(2) strengthening driver licensing and testing standards for persons under the age of 21 years;

(3) sanctioning driving privileges of drivers under age 21 who have committed serious traffic violations or other specified offenses; and

(4) setting stricter standards to promote the public's health and safety.

(b) The application of any person under the age of 18 years, and not legally emancipated by marriage, for a drivers license or permit to operate a motor vehicle issued under the laws of this State, shall be accompanied by the written consent of either parent of the applicant; otherwise by the guardian having custody of the applicant, or in the event there is no parent or guardian, then by another responsible adult.

No graduated driver's license shall be issued to any applicant under 18 years of age, unless the applicant has:

(1) Held a valid instruction permit for a minimum of 3 months.

(2) Passed an approved driver education course and submits proof of having passed the course as may be required.

(3) Certification by the parent, legal guardian, or responsible adult that the applicant has had a minimum of 25 hours of behind-the-wheel practice time and is sufficiently prepared and able to safely operate a motor vehicle.

(c) No graduated driver's license or permit shall be issued to any applicant under 18 years of age who has committed the offense of operating a motor vehicle without a valid license or permit in violation of Section 6–101 of this Code and no graduated driver's license or permit shall be issued to any applicant under 18 years of age who has committed an offense that would otherwise result in a mandatory revocation of a license or permit as provided in Section 6–205 of this Code or who has been either convicted of or adjudicated a delinquent based upon a violation of the Cannabis Control Act [1] or the Illinois Controlled Substances Act,[2] while that individual was in actual physical control of a motor vehicle. For purposes of this Section, any person placed on probation under Section 10 of the Cannabis Control Act [3] or Section 410 of the Illinois Controlled Substances Act [4] shall not be considered convicted. Any person found guilty of this offense, while in actual physical control of a motor vehicle, shall have an entry made in the court record by the judge that this offense did occur while the person was in actual physical control of a motor vehicle and order the clerk of the court to report the violation to the Secretary of State as such.

(d) No graduated driver's license shall be issued for 6 months to any applicant under the age of 18 years who has been convicted of any offense defined as a serious traffic violation in this Code or a similar provision of a local ordinance.

(e) No graduated driver's license holder under the age of 18 years shall operate any motor vehicle, except a motor driven cycle or motorcycle, with more than one passenger in the front seat of the motor vehicle and no more passengers in the back seats than the number of available seat safety belts as set forth in Section 12-603 of this Code.

(f) No graduated driver's license holder under the age of 18 shall operate a motor vehicle unless each driver and front or back seat passenger under the age of 18 is wearing a properly adjusted and fastened seat safety belt.

P.A. 76-1586, § 6-107, eff. July 1, 1970. Amended by P.A. 77-51, § 1, eff. July 1, 1971; P.A. 77-2805, § 1, eff. Oct. 1, 1972; P.A. 78-255, § 61, eff. Oct. 1, 1973; P.A. 80-359, § 1, eff. Oct. 1, 1977; P.A. 86-1450, § 2, eff. July 1, 1991; P.A. 88-197, § 5, eff. Aug. 5, 1993; P.A. 90-369, § 5, eff. Jan. 1, 1998.

Formerly Ill.Rev.Stat.1991, ch. 95 ½, ¶ 6-107.

[1] 720 ILCS 550/1 et seq.

[2] 720 ILCS 570/100 et seq.

[3] 720 ILCS 550/10.

[4] 720 ILCS 570/410.

5/6-107.1. Instruction permit for a minor.

§ 6-107.1. Instruction permit for a minor.

(a) The Secretary of State, upon receiving proper application and payment of the required fee, may issue an instruction permit to any person under the age of 18 years who is not ineligible for a license under paragraphs 1, 3, 4, 5, 7, or 8 of Section 6-103, after the applicant has successfully passed such examination as the Secretary of State in his discretion may prescribe.

(1) An instruction permit issued under this Section shall be valid for a period of 24 months after the date of its issuance and shall be restricted, by the Secretary of State, to the operation of a motor vehicle by the minor only when accompanied by the adult instructor of a driver education program during enrollment in the program or when practicing with a parent, legal guardian, family member, or a person in loco parentis who is 21 years of age or more, has a license classification to operate such vehicle and at least one year of driving experience, and who is occupying a seat beside the driver.

(2) A 24 month instruction permit for a motor driven cycle may be issued to a person 16 or 17 years of age and entitles the holder to drive upon the highways during daylight under direct supervision of a licensed motor driven cycle operator or motorcycle operator 21 years of age or older who has a license classification to operate such motor driven cycle or motorcycle and at least one year of driving experience.

(3) A 24 month instruction permit for a motorcycle other than a motor driven cycle may be issued to a person 16 or 17 years of age in accordance with the provisions of paragraph 2 of Section 6-103 and entitles a holder to drive upon the highways during daylight under the direct supervision of a licensed motorcycle operator 21 years of age or older who has at least one year of driving experience.

(b) An instruction permit issued under this Section when issued to a person under the age of 17 years shall, as a matter of law, be invalid for the operation of any motor vehicle during the same time the child is prohibited from being on any street or highway under the provisions of the Child Curfew Act.[1]

(c) Any person under the age of 16 years who possesses an instruction permit and whose driving privileges have been suspended or revoked under the provisions of this Code shall not be granted a Family Financial Responsibility Driving Permit or a Restricted Driving Permit.

P.A. 76-1586, § 6-107.1, added by P.A. 90-369, § 5, eff. Jan. 1, 1998.

[1] 720 ILCS 555/0.01 et seq.

5/6-107.2. Rules for graduated licenses

§ 6-107.2. Rules for graduated licenses. The Secretary of State, using the authority to license motor vehicle operators, may adopt such rules as may be necessary to establish standards, policies, and procedures for graduated licenses.

P.A. 76-1586, § 6-107.2, added by P.A. 90-369, § 5, eff. Jan. 1, 1998.

5/6-107.3. Distinct nature of driver's license dependent on age

§ 6-107.3. Distinct nature of driver's license dependent on age. The Secretary of State shall provide that each graduated driver's license and each regular driver's license issued to individuals under 21 years of age shall be of a distinct nature from those driver's licenses issued to individuals 21 years of age and older. The colors designated for the graduated driver's license and regular driver's license shall be at the discretion of the Secretary of State.

P.A. 76-1586, § 6-107.3, added by P.A. 90-369, § 5, eff. Jan. 1, 1998.

5/6-108. Cancellation of license issued to minor

§ 6-108. Cancellation of license issued to minor.

(a) The Secretary of State shall cancel the license or permit of any minor under the age of 18 years in any of the following events:

1. Upon the verified written request of the person who consented to the application of the minor that the license or permit be cancelled;

2. Upon receipt of satisfactory evidence of the death of the person who consented to the application of the minor;

3. Upon receipt of satisfactory evidence that the person who consented to the application of a minor no longer has legal custody of the minor.

After cancellation, the Secretary of State shall not issue a new license or permit until the applicant meets the provisions of Section 6-107 of this Code.

(b) The Secretary of State shall cancel the license or permit of any person under the age of 18 years if he or she is convicted of violating the Cannabis Control Act[1] or the Illinois Controlled Substances Act[2] while that person was in actual physical control of a motor vehicle. For purposes of this Section, any person placed on probation under Section 10 of the Cannabis Control Act[3] or Section 410 of the Illinois Controlled Substances Act[4] shall not be considered convicted. Any person found guilty of this offense, while in actual physical control of a motor vehicle, shall have an entry made in the court record by the judge that this offense did occur while the person was in actual physical control of a motor vehicle and order the clerk of the court to report the violation to the Secretary of State as such. After the cancellation, the Secretary of State shall not issue a new license or permit for a period of one year after the date of cancellation or until the minor attains the age of 18 years, whichever is longer. However, upon application, the Secretary of State may, if satisfied that the person applying will not endanger the public safety, or welfare, issue a restricted driving permit granting the privilege of driving a motor vehicle between the person's residence and person's place of employment or within the scope of the person's employment related duties, or to allow transportation for the person or a household member of the person's family for the receipt of necessary medical care or, if the professional evaluation indicates, provide transportation for the petitioner for alcohol remedial or rehabilitative activity, or for the person to attend classes, as a student, in an accredited educational institution; if the person is able to demonstrate that no alternative means of transportation is reasonably available; provided that the Secretary's discretion shall be limited to cases where undue hardship would result from a failure to issue such restricted driving permit. In each case the Secretary of State may issue a restricted driving permit for a period as he deems appropriate, except that the permit shall expire within one year from the date of issuance. A restricted driving permit issued hereunder shall be subject to cancellation, revocation, and suspension by the Secretary of State in like manner and for like cause as a driver's license issued hereunder may be cancelled, revoked, or suspended; except that a conviction upon one or more offenses against laws or ordinances regulating the movement of traffic shall be deemed sufficient cause for the revocation, suspension, or cancellation of a restricted driving permit. The Secretary of State may, as a condition to the issuance of a restricted driving permit, require the applicant to participate in a driver remedial or rehabilitative program. Thereafter, upon reapplication for a license as provided in Section 6–106 of this Code or a permit as provided in Section 6–105 of this Code and upon payment of the appropriate application fee, the Secretary of State shall issue the applicant a license as provided in Section 6–106 of this Code or shall issue the applicant a permit as provided in Section 6–105.

P.A. 76–1586, § 6–108, eff. July 1, 1970. Amended by P.A. 77–2805, § 1, eff. Oct. 1, 1972; P.A. 86–1450, § 2, eff. July 1, 1991; P.A. 87–1114, § 1, eff. Sept. 15, 1992.

Formerly Ill.Rev.Stat.1991, ch. 95 ½, ¶ 6–108.

1 720 ILCS 550/1 et seq.

2 720 ILCS 570/100 et seq.

3 720 ILCS 550/10.

4 720 ILCS 570/410.

5/6–108.1. Notice to Secretary; denial of license; persons under 18

§ 6–108.1. Notice to Secretary; denial of license; persons under 18.

(a) The State's Attorney must notify the Secretary of the charges pending against any person younger than 18 years of age who has been charged with a violation of this Code or the Criminal Code of 1961 [1] arising out of an accident in which the person was involved as a driver and that caused the death of or a type A injury to another person. A "type A injury" includes severely bleeding wounds, distorted extremities, and injuries that require the injured party to be carried from the scene. The State's Attorney must notify the Secretary on a form prescribed by the Secretary.

(b) The Secretary, upon receiving notification from the State's Attorney, may deny any driver's license to any person younger than 18 years of age against whom the charges are pending.

(c) The State's Attorney must notify the Secretary of the final disposition of the case of any person who has been denied a driver's license under subsection (b).

(d) The Secretary must adopt rules for implementing this Section.

P.A. 76–1586, § 6–108.1, added by P.A. 92–137, § 5, eff. July 24, 2001.

1 720 ILCS 5/1–1 et seq.

5/6–109. Examination of Applicants

§ 6–109. Examination of Applicants.

(a) The Secretary of State shall examine every applicant for a driver's license or permit who has not been previously licensed as a driver under the laws of this State or any other state or country, or any applicant for renewal of such driver's license or permit when such license or permit has been expired for more than one year. The Secretary of State shall, subject to the provisions of paragraph (c), examine every licensed driver at least every 8 years, and may examine or re-examine any other applicant or licensed driver, provided that during the years 1984 through 1991 those drivers issued a license for 3 years may be re-examined not less than every 7 years or more than every 10 years.

The Secretary of State shall require the testing of the eyesight of any driver's license or permit applicant who has not been previously licensed as a driver under the laws of this State and shall promulgate rules and regulations to provide for the orderly administration of all the provisions of this Section.

(b) Except as provided for those applicants in paragraph (c), such examination shall include a test of the applicant's eyesight, his ability to read and understand official traffic control devices, his knowledge of safe driving practices and the traffic laws of this State, and may include an actual demonstration of the applicant's ability to exercise ordinary and reasonable control of the operation of a motor vehicle, and such further physical and mental examination as the Secretary of State finds necessary to determine the applicant's fitness to operate a motor vehicle safely on the highways, except the examination of an applicant 75 years of age or older shall include an actual demonstration of the applicant's ability to exercise ordinary and reasonable control of the operation of a motor vehicle. All portions of written and verbal examinations under this Section, excepting where the English language appears on facsimiles of road signs, may be given in the Spanish language and, at the discretion of the Secretary of State, in any other language as well as in English upon request of the examinee. Deaf persons who are otherwise qualified are not prohibited from being issued a license, other than a commercial driver's license, under this Code.

(c) Re-examination for those applicants who at the time of renewing their driver's license possess a driving record devoid of any convictions of traffic violations or evidence of committing an offense for which mandatory revocation would be required upon conviction pursuant to Section 6–205 at the time of renewal shall be in a manner prescribed by the Secretary in order to determine an applicant's ability to safely operate a motor vehicle, except that every applicant for the renewal of a driver's license who is 75 years of age or older must prove, by an actual demonstration, the applicant's ability to exercise reasonable care in the safe operation of a motor vehicle.

(d) In the event the applicant is not ineligible under the provisions of Section 6–103 to receive a driver's license, the Secretary of State shall make provision for giving an examination, either in the county where the applicant resides or at a place adjacent thereto reasonably convenient to the applicant, within not more than 30 days from the date said application is received.

P.A. 76-1586, § 6-109, eff. July 1, 1970. Amended by P.A. 76-1750, § 1; P.A. 77-1774, § 1, eff. July 1, 1972; P.A. 78-738, § 1, eff. Jan. 1, 1974; P.A. 79-1141, § 1, eff. Jan. 1, 1976; P.A. 82-628, § 1, eff. July 1, 1982; P.A. 83-56, § 1, eff. Jan. 1, 1984; P.A. 83-239, § 1, eff. Jan. 1, 1984; P.A. 83-1362, Art. II, § 99, eff. Sept. 11, 1984; P.A. 83-1458, § 1, eff. Sept. 17, 1984; P.A. 86-467, § 1, eff. Aug. 31, 1989; P.A. 89-569, § 10, eff. Jan. 1, 1997; P.A. 91-350, § 5, eff. July 29, 1999.

Formerly Ill.Rev.Stat.1991, ch. 95 ½, ¶ 6-109.

5/6-110. Licenses issued to drivers

§ 6-110. Licenses issued to drivers.

(a) The Secretary of State shall issue to every qualifying applicant a driver's license as applied for, which license shall bear a distinguishing number assigned to the licensee, the name, social security number, zip code, date of birth, address, and a brief description of the licensee, and a space where the licensee may write his usual signature.

If the licensee is less than 17 years of age, the license shall, as a matter of law, be invalid for the operation of any motor vehicle during any time the licensee is prohibited from being on any street or highway under the provisions of the Child Curfew Act. [1]

Licenses issued shall also indicate the classification and the restrictions under Section 6-104 of this Code.

In lieu of the social security number, the Secretary may in his discretion substitute a federal tax number or other distinctive number.

A driver's license issued may, in the discretion of the Secretary, include a suitable photograph of a type prescribed by the Secretary.

(b) The Secretary of State shall provide a format on the reverse of each driver's license issued which the licensee may use to execute a document of gift conforming to the provisions of the Uniform Anatomical Gift Act. [2] The format shall allow the licensee to indicate the gift intended, whether specific organs, any organ, or the entire body, and shall accommodate the signatures of the donor and 2 witnesses. The Secretary shall also inform each applicant or licensee of this format, describe the procedure for its execution, and may offer the necessary witnesses; provided that in so doing, the Secretary shall advise the applicant or licensee that he or she is under no compulsion to execute a document of gift. A brochure explaining this method of executing an anatomical gift document shall be given to each applicant or licensee. The brochure shall advise the applicant or licensee that he or she is under no compulsion to execute a document of gift, and that he or she may wish to consult with family, friends or clergy before doing so. The Secretary of State may undertake additional efforts, including education and awareness activities, to promote organ and tissue donation.

(c) The Secretary of State shall designate on each driver's license issued a space where the licensee may place a sticker or decal of the uniform size as the Secretary may specify, which sticker or decal may indicate in appropriate language that the owner of the license carries an Emergency Medical Information Card.

The sticker may be provided by any person, hospital, school, medical group, or association interested in assisting in implementing the Emergency Medical Information Card, but shall meet the specifications as the Secretary may by rule or regulation require.

(d) The Secretary of State shall designate on each driver's license issued a space where the licensee may indicate his blood type and RH factor.

(e) The Secretary of State shall provide that each original or renewal driver's license issued to a licensee under 21 years of age shall be of a distinct nature from those driver's licenses issued to individuals 21 years of age and older. The color designated for driver's licenses for licensees under 21 years of age shall be at the discretion of the Secretary of State.

(e-1) The Secretary shall provide that each driver's license issued to a person under the age of 21 displays the date upon which the person becomes 18 years of age and the date upon which the person becomes 21 years of age.

(f) The Secretary of State shall inform all Illinois licensed commercial motor vehicle operators of the requirements of the Uniform Commercial Driver License Act, Article V of this Chapter, and shall make provisions to insure that all drivers, seeking to obtain a commercial driver's license, be afforded an opportunity prior to April 1, 1992, to obtain the license. The Secretary is authorized to extend driver's license expiration dates, and assign specific times, dates and locations where these commercial driver's tests shall be conducted. Any applicant, regardless of the current expiration date of the applicant's driver's license, may be subject to any assignment by the Secretary. Failure to comply with the Secretary's assignment may result in the applicant's forfeiture of an opportunity to receive a commercial driver's license prior to April 1, 1992.

(g) The Secretary of State shall designate on a driver's license issued, a space where the licensee may indicate that he or she has drafted a living will in accordance with the Illinois Living Will Act [3] or a durable power of attorney for health care in accordance with the Illinois Power of Attorney Act. [4]

(g-1) The Secretary of State, in his or her discretion, may designate on each driver's license issued a space where the licensee may place a sticker or decal, issued by the Secretary of State, of uniform size as the Secretary may specify, that shall indicate in appropriate language that the owner of the license has renewed his or her driver's license.

(h) A person who acts in good faith in accordance with the terms of this Section is not liable for damages in any civil action or subject to prosecution in any criminal proceeding for his or her act.

P.A. 76-1586, § 6-110, eff. July 1, 1970. Amended by P.A. 77-105, § 1, eff. Jan. 1, 1972; P.A. 78-197, § 1, eff. Jan. 1, 1974; P.A. 79-158, § 1, eff. July 9, 1975; P.A. 79-416, § 1, eff. Aug. 14, 1975; P.A. 79-1454, § 44, eff. Aug. 31, 1976; P.A. 80-516, § 1, eff. Jan. 1, 1978; P.A. 80-534, § 1, eff. Jan. 1, 1978; P.A. 80-1364, § 36, eff. Aug. 13, 1978; P.A. 82-278, § 1, eff. July 1, 1982; P.A. 84-270, § 1, eff. Jan. 1, 1986; P.A. 84-1409, § 7, eff. Jan. 1, 1987; P.A. 85-192, § 1, eff. Aug. 21, 1987; P.A. 86-845, § 1, eff. April 1, 1990; P.A. 87-590, § 1, eff. Jan. 1, 1992; P.A. 88-78, § 20, eff. July 9, 1993; P.A. 88-393, § 5, eff. Jan. 1, 1994; P.A. 88-670, Art. 2, § 2-59, eff. Dec. 2, 1994; P.A. 89-569, § 10, eff. Jan. 1, 1997; P.A. 90-191, § 10, eff. Jan. 1, 1998; P.A. 91-357, § 231, eff. July 29, 1999; P.A. 92-689, § 5, eff. Jan. 1, 2003.

Formerly Ill.Rev.Stat.1991, ch. 95 ½, ¶ 6-110.

[1] 720 ILCS 555/0.01 et seq.

[2] 755 ILCS 50/1 et seq.

[3] 755 ILCS 35/1 et seq.

[4] 755 ILCS 45/1-1 et seq.

5/6-110.1. Confidentiality of captured photographs or images

§ 6-110.1. Confidentiality of captured photographs or images. The Secretary of State shall maintain a file on or contract to file all photographs and signatures obtained in the process of issuing a driver's license, permit, or identification card. The photographs and signatures shall be confidential and shall not be disclosed except to the following persons:

(1) the individual upon written request;

(2) officers and employees of the Secretary of State who have a need to have access to the stored images for purposes of issuing and controlling driver's licenses, permits, or identification cards;

(3) law enforcement officials for a lawful civil or criminal law enforcement investigation; or

(4) other entities that the Secretary may exempt by rule.

P.A. 76-1586, § 6-110.1, added by P.A. 90-191, § 10, eff. Jan. 1, 1998. Amended by P.A. 92-16, § 85, eff. June 28, 2001.

5/6-111. § 6-111. Repealed by P.A. 76-1906, § 2, eff. July 1, 1970

5/6-112. License and permits to be carried and exhibited on demand

§ 6-112. License and permits to be carried and exhibited on demand. Every licensee or permittee shall have his drivers license or permit in his immediate possession at all times when operating a motor vehicle and, for the purpose of indicating compliance with this requirement, shall display such license or permit if it is in his possession upon demand made, when in uniform or displaying a badge or other sign of authority, by a member of the State Police, a sheriff or other police officer or designated agent of the Secretary of State. However, no person charged with violating this Section shall be convicted if he produces in court satisfactory evidence that a drivers license was theretofor issued to him and was valid at the time of his arrest.

For the purposes of this section, "display" means the manual surrender of his license certificate into the hands of the demanding officer for his inspection thereof.

P.A. 76-1586, § 6-112, eff. July 1, 1970. Amended by P.A. 76-1749, § 1, eff. July 1, 1970.

Formerly Ill.Rev.Stat.1991, ch. 95 ½, ¶ 6-112.

5/6-113. Restricted licenses and permits

§ 6-113. Restricted licenses and permits.

(a) The Secretary of State upon issuing a drivers license or permit shall have the authority whenever good cause appears to impose restrictions suitable to the licensee's driving ability with respect to the type of, or special mechanical control devices required on, a motor vehicle which the licensee may operate or such other restrictions applicable to the licensee as the Secretary of State may determine to be appropriate to assure the safe operation of a motor vehicle by the licensee.

(b) The Secretary of State may either issue a special restricted license or permit or may set forth such restrictions upon the usual license or permit form.

(c) The Secretary of State may issue a probationary license to a person whose driving privileges have been suspended pursuant to subsection (d) of this Section or subsections (a)(2), (a)(19) and (a)(20) of Section 6-206 of this Code. The Secretary of State shall promulgate rules pursuant to The Illinois Administrative Procedure Act,[1] setting forth the conditions and criteria for the issuance and cancellation of probationary licenses.

(d) The Secretary of State may upon receiving satisfactory evidence of any violation of the restrictions of such license or permit suspend, revoke or cancel the same without preliminary hearing, but the licensee or permittee shall be entitled to a hearing as in the case of a suspension or revocation.

(e) It is unlawful for any person to operate a motor vehicle in any manner in violation of the restrictions imposed on a restricted license or permit issued to him.

(f) Whenever the holder of a restricted driving permit is issued a citation for any of the following offenses including similar local ordinances, the restricted driving permit is immediately invalidated:

1. Reckless homicide resulting from the operation of a motor vehicle;

2. Violation of Section 11-501 of this Act relating to the operation of a motor vehicle while under the influence of intoxicating liquor or narcotic drugs;

3. Violation of Section 11-401 of this Act relating to the offense of leaving the scene of a traffic accident involving death or injury; or

4. Violation of Section 11-504 of this Act relating to the offense of drag racing;

The police officer issuing the citation shall confiscate the restricted driving permit and forward it, along with the citation, to the Clerk of the Circuit Court of the county in which the citation was issued.

(g) The Secretary of State may issue a special restricted license for a period of 12 months to individuals using vision aid arrangements other than standard eyeglasses or contact lenses, allowing the operation of a motor vehicle during nighttime hours. The Secretary of State shall adopt rules defining the terms and conditions by which the individual may obtain and renew this special restricted license. At a minimum, all drivers must meet the following requirements:

1. Possess a valid driver's license and have operated a motor vehicle during daylight hours for a period of 12 months using vision aid arrangements other than standard eyeglasses or contact lenses.

2. Have a driving record that does not include any traffic accidents that occurred during nighttime hours, for which the driver has been found to be at fault, during the 12 months before he or she applied for the special restricted license.

3. Successfully complete a road test administered during nighttime hours.

At a minimum, all drivers renewing this license must meet the following requirements:

1. Successfully complete a road test administered during nighttime hours.

2. Have a driving record that does not include any traffic accidents that occurred during nighttime hours, for which the driver has been found to be at fault, during the 12 months before he or she applied for the special restricted license.

(h) Any driver issued a special restricted license as defined in subsection (g) whose privilege to drive during nighttime hours has been suspended due to an accident occurring during nighttime hours may request a hearing as provided in Section 2-118 of this Code to contest that suspension. If it is determined that the accident for which the driver was at fault was not influenced by the driver's use of vision aid arrangements other than standard eyeglasses or contact lenses, the Secretary may reinstate that driver's privilege to drive during nighttime hours.

P.A. 76-1586, § 6-113, eff. July 1, 1970. Amended by P.A. 77-2830, Art. 73, § 1, eff. Jan. 1, 1973; P.A. 80-911, § 1, eff. Oct. 1, 1977; P.A. 81-1400, § 1, eff. Aug. 25, 1980; P.A. 84-510, § 1, eff. Jan. 1, 1986; P.A. 84-793, § 2, eff. Jan. 1, 1986; P.A. 84-1308, Art. II, § 96, eff. Aug. 25, 1986; P.A. 84-1450, § 7, eff. July 1, 1987; P.A. 85-293, Art. II, § 13, eff. Sept. 8, 1987; P.A. 85-813, § 1, eff. Jan. 1, 1988; P.A. 86-549, § 1, eff. Jan. 1, 1990; P.A. 92-274, § 5, eff. Jan. 1, 2002.

Formerly Ill.Rev.Stat.1991, ch. 95 ½, ¶ 6-113.

1 5 ILCS 100/1-1 et seq.

5/6-114. Duplicate and corrected licenses and permits

§ 6-114. Duplicate and corrected licenses and permits. In the event that a drivers license or permit issued under the provisions of this Act is lost or destroyed, the person to whom the same was issued may upon application and payment of the required fee obtain a duplicate or substitute thereof, upon furnishing evidence satisfactory to the Secretary of State that such permit or license has been lost or destroyed and if such applicant is not then ineligible under Section 6-103 of this Act. Any person to whom has been issued a drivers license or permit under the provisions of this Act and who desires to obtain a corrected permit or license to indicate a change of name or address or to correct a statement appearing upon the original permit or license may upon application and payment of the required fee obtain a corrected permit or license. The original permit or license must accompany the application for correction or evidence must be furnished satisfactory to the Secretary of State that such permit or license has been lost or destroyed.

P.A. 76-1586, § 6-114, eff. July 1, 1970.

Formerly Ill.Rev.Stat.1991, ch. 95 ½, ¶ 6-114.

5/6-115. Expiration of driver's license

§ 6-115. Expiration of driver's license.

(a) Except as provided elsewhere in this Section, every driver's license issued under the provisions of this Code shall expire 4 years from the date of its issuance, or at such later date, as the Secretary of State may by proper rule and regulation designate, not to exceed 12 calendar months; in the event that an applicant for renewal of a driver's license fails to apply prior to the expiration date of the previous driver's license, the renewal driver's license shall expire 4 years from the expiration date of the previous driver's license, or at such later date as the Secretary of State may by proper rule and regulation designate, not to exceed 12 calendar months.

The Secretary of State may, however, issue to a person not previously licensed as a driver in Illinois a driver's license which will expire not less than 4 years nor more than 5 years from date of issuance, except as provided elsewhere in this Section.

The Secretary of State is authorized to issue driver's licenses during the years 1984 through 1987 which shall expire not less than 3 years nor more than 5 years from the date of issuance, except as provided elsewhere in this Section, for the purpose of converting all driver's licenses issued under this Code to a 4 year expiration. Provided that all original driver's licenses, except as provided elsewhere in this Section, shall expire not less than 4 years nor more than 5 years from the date of issuance.

(b) Before the expiration of a driver's license, except those licenses expiring on the individual's 21st birthday, or 3 months after the individual's 21st birthday, the holder thereof may apply for a renewal thereof, subject to all the provisions of Section 6-103, and the Secretary of State may require an examination of the applicant. A licensee whose driver's license expires on his 21st birthday, or 3 months after his 21st birthday, may not apply for a renewal of his driving privileges until he reaches the age of 21.

(c) The Secretary of State shall, 30 days prior to the expiration of a driver's license, forward to each person whose license is to expire a notification of the expiration of said license which may be presented at the time of renewal of said license.

There may be included with such notification information explaining the anatomical gift and Emergency Medical Information Card provisions of Section 6-110. The format and text of such information shall be prescribed by the Secretary.

There shall be included with such notification, for a period of 4 years beginning January 1, 2000 information regarding the Illinois Adoption Registry and Medical Information Exchange established in Section 18.1 of the Adoption Act.[1]

(d) The Secretary may defer the expiration of the driver's license of a licensee, spouse, and dependent children who are living with such licensee while on active duty, serving in the Armed Forces of the United States outside of the State of Illinois, and 45 days thereafter, upon such terms and conditions as the Secretary may prescribe.

(e) The Secretary of State may decline to process a renewal of a driver's license of any person who has not paid any fee or tax due under this Code and is not paid upon reasonable notice and demand.

(f) The Secretary shall provide that each original or renewal driver's license issued to a licensee under 21 years of age shall expire 3 months after the licensee's 21st birthday. Persons whose current driver's licenses expire on their 21st birthday on or after January 1, 1986 shall not renew their driver's license before their 21st birthday, and their current driver's license will be extended for an additional term of 3 months beyond their 21st birthday. Thereafter, the expiration and term of the driver's license shall be governed by subsection (a) hereof.

(g) The Secretary shall provide that each original or renewal driver's license issued to a licensee 81 years of age through age 86 shall expire 2 years from the date of issuance, or at such later date as the Secretary may by rule and regulation designate, not to exceed an additional 12 calendar months. The Secretary shall also provide that each original or renewal driver's license issued to a licensee 87 years of age or older shall expire 12 months from the date of issuance, or at such later date as the Secretary may by rule and regulation designate, not to exceed an additional 12 calendar months.

(h) The Secretary of State shall provide that each special restricted driver's license issued under subsection (g) of Section 6-113 of this Code shall expire 12 months from the date of issuance. The Secretary shall adopt rules defining renewal requirements.

P.A. 76-1586, § 6-115, eff. July 1, 1970. Amended by P.A. 76-1904, § 1; P.A. 77-642, § 1, eff. Aug. 4, 1971; P.A. 79-1141, § 1, eff. Jan. 1, 1976; P.A. 82-278, § 1, eff. July 1, 1982; P.A. 83-239, § 1, eff. Jan. 1, 1984; P.A. 84-270, § 1, eff. Jan. 1, 1986; P.A. 86-467, § 2, eff. Jan. 1, 1990; P.A. 91-417, § 7, eff. Jan. 1, 2000; P.A. 92-274, § 5, eff. Jan. 1, 2002.

Formerly Ill.Rev.Stat.1991, ch. 95 ½, ¶ 6-115.

1 750 ILCS 50/18.1.

5/6–116. Notice of change of address or name

§ 6–116. Notice of change of address or name. Whenever any person after applying for or receiving a drivers license or permit moves from the address named in such application or on the license or permit issued to him or when the name of a licensee or permittee is changed by marriage or otherwise such person shall within 10 days thereafter notify the Drivers Services Department of the Secretary of State's Office in writing of his old and new addresses or of such former and new names and of the number of any license or permit then held by him. Such person may obtain a corrected license or permit as provided in Section 6–114.

P.A. 76–1586, § 6–116, eff. July 1, 1970. Amended by P.A. 79–1141, § 1, eff. Jan. 1, 1976.

Formerly Ill.Rev.Stat.1991, ch. 95 ½, ¶ 6–116.

5/6–116.5. Driver's duty to report medical condition

§ 6–116.5. Driver's duty to report medical condition. Every driver shall report to the Secretary any medical condition, as defined by the Driver's License Medical Review Law of 1992,[1] that is likely to cause loss of consciousness or any loss of ability to safely operate a motor vehicle within 10 days of the driver becoming aware of the condition. The Secretary, in conjunction with the Driver's License Medical Advisory Board, shall determine by administrative rule the temporary conditions not required to be reported under the provisions of this Section. All information furnished to the Secretary under the provisions of this Section shall be deemed confidential and for the privileged use of the Secretary in accordance with the provisions of subsection (j) of Section 2–123 of this Code.

P.A. 76–1586, § 6–116.5, added by P.A. 89–584, § 5, eff. July 31, 1996.

[1] 625 ILCS 5/6–900 et seq.

5/6–117. Records to be kept by the Secretary of State

§ 6–117. Records to be kept by the Secretary of State.

(a) The Secretary of State shall file every application for a license or permit accepted under this Chapter, and shall maintain suitable indexes thereof. The records of the Secretary of State shall indicate the action taken with respect to such applications.

(b) The Secretary of State shall maintain appropriate records of all licenses and permits refused, cancelled, revoked or suspended and of the revocation and suspension of driving privileges of persons not licensed under this Chapter, and such records shall note the reasons for such action.

(c) The Secretary of State shall maintain appropriate records of convictions reported under this Chapter. Records of conviction may be maintained in a computer processible medium.

(d) The Secretary of State may also maintain appropriate records of any accident reports received.

(e) The Secretary of State shall also maintain appropriate records of any disposition of supervision or records relative to a driver's referral to a driver remedial or rehabilitative program, as required by the Secretary of State or the courts. Such records shall only be available for use by the Secretary, law enforcement agencies, the courts, and the affected driver or, upon proper verification, such affected driver's attorney.

(f) The Secretary of State shall also maintain or contract to maintain appropriate records of all photographs and signatures obtained in the process of issuing any driver's license, permit, or identification card. The record shall be confidential and shall not be disclosed except to those entities listed under Section 6–110.1 of this Code.

P.A. 76–1586, § 6–117, eff. July 1, 1970. Amended by P.A. 82–311, § 1, eff. Jan. 1, 1982; P.A. 84–596, § 1, eff. Jan. 1, 1986; P.A. 85–1396, § 2, eff. Sept. 2, 1988; P.A. 90–191, § 10, eff. Jan. 1, 1998; P.A. 92–458, § 5, eff. Aug. 22, 2001.

Formerly Ill.Rev.Stat.1991, ch. 95 ½, ¶ 6–117.

5/6–118. Fees

§ 6–118. Fees.

(a) The fee for licenses and permits under this Article is as follows:

Original driver's license	$10
Original or renewal driver's license issued to 18, 19 and 20 year olds	5
All driver's licenses for persons age 69 through age 80	5
All driver's licenses for persons age 81 through age 86	2
All driver's licenses for persons age 87 or older	0
Renewal driver's license (except for applicants ages 18, 19 and 20 or age 69 and older)	10
Original instruction permit issued to persons (except those age 69 and older) who do not hold or have not previously held an Illinois instruction permit or driver's license	20
Instruction permit issued to any person holding an Illinois driver's license who wishes a change in classifications, other than at the time of renewal	5
Any instruction permit issued to a person age 69 and older	5
Instruction permit issued to any person, under age 69, not currently holding a valid Illinois driver's license or instruction permit but who has previously been issued either document in Illinois	10
Restricted driving permit	8
Duplicate or corrected driver's license or permit	5
Duplicate or corrected restricted driving permit	5
Original or renewal M or L endorsement	5

SPECIAL FEES FOR COMMERCIAL DRIVER'S LICENSE

The fees for commercial driver licenses and permits under Article V [1] shall be as follows:

Commercial driver's license: $6 for the CDLIS/AAMVAnet Fund (Commercial Driver's License Information System/American Association of Motor Vehicle Administrators network Trust Fund); $20 for the Motor Carrier Safety Inspection Fund; $10 for the driver's license; and $24 for the CDL:	$60
Renewal commercial driver's license: $6 for the CDLIS/AAMVAnet Trust Fund; $20 for the Motor Carrier Safety Inspection Fund; $10 for the driver's license; and $24 for the CDL:	$60
Commercial driver instruction permit issued to any person holding a valid Illinois driver's license for the purpose of changing to a CDL classification: $6 for the CDLIS/AAMVAnet Trust Fund; $20 for the Motor Carrier Safety Inspection Fund; and $24 for the CDL classification	$50

Commercial driver instruction permit issued to any person holding a valid Illinois CDL for the purpose of making a change in a classification, endorsement or restriction $5
CDL duplicate or corrected license $5

In order to ensure the proper implementation of the Uniform Commercial Driver License Act,[2] Article V of this Chapter, the Secretary of State is empowered to pro-rate the $24 fee for the commercial driver's license proportionate to the expiration date of the applicant's Illinois driver's license.

The fee for any duplicate license or permit shall be waived for any person age 60 or older who presents the Secretary of State's office with a police report showing that his license or permit was stolen.

No additional fee shall be charged for a driver's license, or for a commercial driver's license, when issued to the holder of an instruction permit for the same classification or type of license who becomes eligible for such license.

(b) Any person whose license or privilege to operate a motor vehicle in this State has been suspended or revoked under any provision of Chapter 6, Chapter 11, or Section 7–702 of the Family Financial Responsibility Law of this Code,[3] shall in addition to any other fees required by this Code, pay a reinstatement fee as follows:

Summary suspension under Section 11–501.1 .... $60
Other suspension $30
Revocation $60

However, any person whose license or privilege to operate a motor vehicle in this State has been suspended or revoked for a second or subsequent time for a violation of Section 11–501 or 11–501.1 of this Code or a similar provision of a local ordinance or a similar out-of-state offense or Section 9–3 of the Criminal Code of 1961[4] and each suspension or revocation was for a violation of Section 11–501 or 11–501.1 of this Code or a similar provision of a local ordinance or a similar out of state offense or Section 9–3 of the Criminal Code of 1961 shall pay, in addition to any other fees required by this Code, a reinstatement fee as follows:

Summary suspension under Section 11–501.1 .... $250
Revocation $250

(c) All fees collected under the provisions of this Chapter 6 shall be paid into the Road Fund in the State Treasury except as follows:

1. The following amounts shall be paid into the Driver Education Fund:

(A) $16 of the $20 fee for an original driver's instruction permit;

(B) $5 of the $10 fee for an original driver's license;

(C) $5 of the $10 fee for a 4 year renewal driver's license; and

(D) $4 of the $8 fee for a restricted driving permit.

2. $30 of the $60 fee for reinstatement of a license summarily suspended under Section 11–501.1 shall be deposited into the Drunk and Drugged Driving Prevention Fund. However, for a person whose license or privilege to operate a motor vehicle in this State has been suspended or revoked for a second or subsequent time for a violation of Section 11–501 or 11–501.1 of this Code or Section 9–3 of the Criminal Code of 1961, $190 of the $250 fee for reinstatement of a license summarily suspended under Section 11–501.1, and $190 of the $250 fee for reinstatement of a revoked license shall be deposited into the Drunk and Drugged Driving Prevention Fund.

3. $6 of such original or renewal fee for a commercial driver's license and $6 of the commercial driver instruction permit fee when such permit is issued to any person holding a valid Illinois driver's license, shall be paid into the CDLIS/AAMVAnet Trust Fund.

4. The fee for reinstatement of a license suspended under the Family Financial Responsibility Law[5] shall be paid into the Family Responsibility Fund.

5. The $5 fee for each original or renewal M or L endorsement shall be deposited into the Cycle Rider Safety Training Fund.

6. $20 of any original or renewal fee for a commercial driver's license or commercial driver instruction permit shall be paid into the Motor Carrier Safety Inspection Fund.

P.A. 76–1586, § 6–118, eff. July 1, 1970. Amended by P.A. 78–820, § 1, eff. Jan. 1, 1974; P.A. 81–462, § 1, eff. Jan. 1, 1980; P.A. 81–844, § 1, eff. Jan. 1, 1980; P.A. 81–1509, Art. I, § 57, eff. Sept. 26, 1980; P.A. 82–617, § 1, eff. Jan. 1, 1982; P.A. 83–148, § 1, eff. Aug. 29, 1983; P.A. 83–239, § 1, eff. Jan. 1, 1984; P.A. 83–1362, Art. II, § 99, eff. Sept. 11, 1984; P.A. 84–270, § 1, eff. Jan. 1, 1986; P.A. 84–272, § 7, eff. Jan. 1, 1986; P.A. 84–1308, Art. II, § 96, eff. Aug. 25, 1986; P.A. 84–1394, § 5, eff. Sept. 18, 1986; P.A. 85–1304, § 1, eff. Jan. 1, 1989; P.A. 86–467, § 2, eff. Jan. 1, 1990; P.A. 86–525, § 1, eff. Jan. 1, 1990; P.A. 86–845, § 1, eff. April 1, 1990; P.A. 86–1028, Art. II, § 2–44, eff. Feb. 5, 1990; P.A. 89–92, § 10, eff. July 1, 1996; P.A. 90–622, § 5, eff. March 1, 1999; P.A. 90–738, § 5, eff. Jan. 1, 1999; P.A. 91–357, § 231, eff. July 29, 1999; P.A. 91–537, § 10, eff. Aug. 13, 1999; P.A. 92–458, § 5, eff. Aug. 22, 2001.

Formerly Ill.Rev.Stat.1991, ch. 95 ½, ¶ 6–118.

[1] 625 ILCS 5/5–100 et seq.

[2] 625 ILCS 5/6–500 et seq.

[3] 625 ILCS 5/6–100 et seq., 5/11–100 et seq., or 5/7–702.

[4] 720 ILCS 5/9–3.

[5] 625 ILCS 5/7–701 et seq.

5/6–119. When fees returnable—Drivers license

§ 6–119. When fees returnable—Drivers license. (a) Whenever any application to the Secretary of State is accompanied by any fee as required by law and such application is refused or rejected, said fee shall be returned to said applicant.

(b) Whenever the Secretary of State through error collects any fee not required to be paid hereunder, the same shall be refunded to the person paying the same upon application therefor made within 6 months after the date of such payment.

(c) Whenever a person dies after making application for a drivers license or permit under this Article, application for a refund of the drivers license or permit may be made if the person dies prior to the effective date for which application has been made, and if the drivers license or permit has never been used. The Secretary of State shall refund the drivers license or permit fees upon receipt within 3 months after the application for a drivers license or permit of an application for refund accompanied with the drivers license or permit and proof of death of the applicant.

(d) Any application for refund received after the times specified in this Section shall be denied and the applicant in order to receive a refund must apply to the Court of Claims.

P.A. 76–1586, § 6–119, eff. July 1, 1970. Amended by P.A. 78–756, § 1, eff. Oct. 1, 1973.

Formerly Ill.Rev.Stat.1991, ch. 95 ½, ¶ 6–119.

5/6-120. Inter-agency agreement for information

§ 6-120. Inter-agency agreement for information. Notwithstanding any other provision of this Code, the Secretary of State shall enter into an inter-agency agreement with the Department of Children and Family Services to establish a procedure by which employees of the Department of Children and Family Services may have immediate access to driver's license records maintained by the Secretary of State if the Department of Children and Family Services determines the information is necessary to perform its duties under the Abused and Neglected Child Reporting Act,[1] the Child Care Act of 1969,[2] and the Children and Family Services Act.[3]

P.A. 76-1586, § 6-120, added by P.A. 88-614, § 108, eff. Sept. 7, 1994.

[1] 325 ILCS 5/1 et seq.

[2] 225 ILCS 10/1 et seq.

[3] 20 ILCS 505/1 et seq.

ARTICLE II. CANCELLATION, SUSPENSION, OR REVOCATION OF LICENSES AND PERMITS

Section

5/6-201. Authority to cancel licenses and permits

§ 6-201. Authority to cancel licenses and permits.

(a) The Secretary of State is authorized to cancel any license or permit upon determining that the holder thereof:

1. was not entitled to the issuance thereof hereunder; or

2. failed to give the required or correct information in his application; or

3. failed to pay any fees, civil penalties owed to the Illinois Commerce Commission, or taxes due under this Act and upon reasonable notice and demand; or

4. committed any fraud in the making of such application; or

5. is ineligible therefor under the provisions of Section 6-103 of this Act, as amended; or

6. has refused or neglected to submit an alcohol, drug, and intoxicating compound evaluation or to submit to examination or re-examination as required under this Act; or

7. has been convicted of violating the Cannabis Control Act,[1] the Illinois Controlled Substances Act,[2] or the Use of Intoxicating Compounds Act [3] while that individual was in actual physical control of a motor vehicle. For purposes of this Section, any person placed on probation under Section 10 of the Cannabis Control Act [4] or Section 410 of the Illinois Controlled Substances Act [5] shall not be considered convicted. Any person found guilty of this offense, while in actual physical control of a motor vehicle, shall have an entry made in the court record by the judge that this offense did occur while the person was in actual physical control of a motor vehicle and order the clerk of the court to report the violation to the Secretary of State as such. After the cancellation, the Secretary of State shall not issue a new license or permit for a period of one year after the date of cancellation. However, upon application, the Secretary of State may, if satisfied that the person applying will not endanger the public safety, or welfare, issue a restricted driving permit granting the privilege of driving a motor vehicle between the person's residence and person's place of employment or within the scope of the person's employment related duties, or to allow transportation for the person or a household member of the person's family for the receipt of necessary medical care or, if the professional evaluation indicates, provide transportation for the petitioner for alcohol remedial or rehabilitative activity, or for the person to attend classes, as a student, in an accredited educational institution; if the person is able to demonstrate that no alternative means of transportation is reasonably available; provided that the Secretary's discretion shall be limited to cases where undue hardship would result from a failure to issue such restricted driving permit. In each case the Secretary of State may issue such restricted driving permit for such period as he deems appropriate, except that such permit shall expire within one year from the date of issuance. A restricted driving permit issued hereunder shall be subject to cancellation, revocation and suspension by the Secretary of State in like manner and for like cause as a driver's license issued hereunder may be cancelled, revoked or suspended; except that a conviction upon one or more offenses against laws or ordinances regulating the movement of traffic shall be deemed sufficient cause for the revocation, suspension or cancellation of a restricted driving permit. The Secretary of State may, as a condition to the issuance of a restricted driving permit, require the applicant to participate in a driver remedial or rehabilitative program; or

8. failed to submit a report as required by Section 6-116.5 of this Code.

(b) Upon such cancellation the licensee or permittee must surrender the license or permit so cancelled to the Secretary of State.

(c) Except as provided in Sections 6–206.1 and 7–702.1, the Secretary of State shall have exclusive authority to grant, issue, deny, cancel, suspend and revoke driving privileges, drivers' licenses and restricted driving permits.

P.A. 76–1586, § 6–201, eff. July 1, 1970. Amended by P.A. 77–642, § 1, eff. Aug. 4, 1971; P.A. 79–1141, § 1, eff. Jan. 1, 1976; P.A. 84–272, § 7, eff. Jan. 1, 1986; P.A. 86–1450, § 2, eff. July 1, 1991; P.A. 88–212, § 5, eff. Jan. 1, 1994; P.A. 88–415, § 10, eff. Aug. 20, 1993; P.A. 88–670, Art. 2, § 2–59, eff. Dec. 2, 1994; P.A. 89–92, § 10, eff. July 1, 1996; P.A. 89–584, § 5, eff. July 31, 1996; P.A. 90–779, § 5, eff. Jan. 1, 1999.

Formerly Ill.Rev.Stat.1991, ch. 95 ½, ¶ 6–201.

1 720 ILCS 550/1 et seq.

2 720 ILCS 570/100 et seq.

3 720 ILCS 690/0.01 et seq.

4 720 ILCS 550/10.

5 720 ILCS 570/410.

5/6–202. Non-residents and unlicensed persons—Revocation and suspension—Reporting convictions

§ 6–202. Non-residents and unlicensed persons—Revocation and suspension—Reporting convictions. (a) The privilege of driving a motor vehicle on highways of this State given to a nonresident hereunder and the privilege which an unlicensed person might have to obtain a license under this Act shall be subject to suspension or revocation by the Secretary of State in like manner and for like cause as a drivers license issued hereunder may be suspended or revoked.

(b) The Secretary of State is authorized, upon receiving a report of the conviction in this State of a nonresident driver of a motor vehicle of any offense under the laws of this State relating to operation, custody or ownership of motor vehicles, to forward a copy or abstract of such report to the motor vehicle administrator of the State wherein the person so convicted is a resident.

(c) When a nonresident's operating privilege is suspended or revoked, the Secretary of State shall forward a certified copy of the record of such action to the motor vehicle administrator in the State where such person resides.

(d) This section is subject to the provisions of the Driver License Compact.[1]

P.A. 76–1586, § 6–202, eff. July 1, 1970. Amended by P.A. 76–1752, § 1, eff. July 1, 1970.

Formerly Ill.Rev.Stat.1991, ch. 95 ½, ¶ 6–202.

1 625 ILCS 5/6–700 et seq.

5/6–203. Suspending or revoking license or privilege upon conviction in another state

§ 6–203. Suspending or revoking license or privilege upon conviction in another state. The Secretary of State is authorized to suspend or revoke the license of any resident of this State or the privilege of a nonresident to drive a motor vehicle in this State upon receiving notice of the conviction of such person in another State of an offense therein which, if committed in this State would be grounds for the suspension or revocation of the license of a driver.

This Section is subject to the provisions of the Driver License Compact.[1]

P.A. 76–1586, § 6–203, eff. July 1, 1970.

Formerly Ill.Rev.Stat.1991, ch. 95 ½, ¶ 6–203.

1 625 ILCS 5/6–700 et seq.

5/6–203.1. Suspension of driving privileges; persons arrested in another state

§ 6–203.1. (a) The Secretary of State is authorized to suspend the driving privileges of persons arrested in another state for driving under the influence of alcohol, other drug or drugs, or intoxicating compound or compounds, or any combination thereof, or a similar provision, and who has refused to submit to a chemical test or tests under the provisions of implied consent.

(b) When a driving privilege has been suspended for a refusal as provided in paragraph (a) and the person is subsequently convicted of the underlying charge, for the same incident, any period served on suspension shall be credited toward the minimum period of revocation of driving privileges imposed pursuant to Section 6–206.

P.A. 76–1586, § 6–203.1, added by P.A. 84–272, § 7, eff. Jan. 1, 1986. Amended by P.A. 84–1394, § 5, eff. Sept. 18, 1986; P.A. 90–779, § 5, eff. Jan. 1, 1999.

Formerly Ill.Rev.Stat.1991, ch. 95 ½, ¶ 6–203.1.

5/6–204. When Court to forward License and Reports

§ 6–204. When Court to forward License and Reports.

(a) For the purpose of providing to the Secretary of State the records essential to the performance of the Secretary's duties under this Code to cancel, revoke or suspend the driver's license and privilege to drive motor vehicles of certain minors adjudicated truant minors in need of supervision, addicted, or delinquent and of persons found guilty of the criminal offenses or traffic violations which this Code recognizes as evidence relating to unfitness to safely operate motor vehicles, the following duties are imposed upon public officials:

(1) Whenever any person is convicted of any offense for which this Code makes mandatory the cancellation or revocation of the driver's license or permit of such person by the Secretary of State, the judge of the court in which such conviction is had shall require the surrender to the clerk of the court of all driver's licenses or permits then held by the person so convicted, and the clerk of the court shall, within 10 days thereafter, forward the same, together with a report of such conviction, to the Secretary.

(2) Whenever any person is convicted of any offense under this Code or similar offenses under a municipal ordinance, other than regulations governing standing, parking or weights of vehicles, and excepting the following enumerated Sections of this Code: Sections 11–1406 (obstruction to driver's view or control), 11–1407 (improper opening of door into traffic), 11–1410 (coasting on downgrade), 11–1411 (following fire apparatus), 11–1419.01 (Motor Fuel Tax I.D. Card), 12–101 (driving vehicle which is in unsafe condition or improperly equipped), 12–201(a) (daytime lights on motorcycles), 12–202 (clearance, identification and side marker lamps), 12–204 (lamp or flag on projecting load), 12–205 (failure to display the safety lights required), 12–401 (restrictions as to tire equipment), 12–502 (mirrors), 12–503 (windshields must be unobstructed and equipped with wipers), 12–601 (horns and warning devices), 12–602 (mufflers, prevention of noise or smoke), 12–603 (seat safety belts), 12–702 (certain vehicles to carry flares or other warning devices), 12–703 (vehicles for oiling roads operated on highways), 12–710 (splash guards and replacements), 13–101 (safety tests), 15–101 (size, weight and load), 15–102 (width), 15–103 (height), 15–104 (name and address on second division vehicles), 15–107 (length of vehicle), 15–109.1 (cover or tarpaulin), 15–111 (weights),

15–112 (weights), 15–301 (weights), 15–316 (weights), 15–318 (weights), and also excepting the following enumerated Sections of the Chicago Municipal Code: Sections 27–245 (following fire apparatus), 27–254 (obstruction of traffic), 27–258 (driving vehicle which is in unsafe condition), 27–259 (coasting on downgrade), 27–264 (use of horns and signal devices), 27–265 (obstruction to driver's view or driver mechanism), 27–267 (dimming of headlights), 27–268 (unattended motor vehicle), 27–272 (illegal funeral procession), 27–273 (funeral procession on boulevard), 27–275 (driving freight hauling vehicles on boulevard), 27–276 (stopping and standing of buses or taxicabs), 27–277 (cruising of public passenger vehicles), 27–305 (parallel parking), 27–306 (diagonal parking), 27–307 (parking not to obstruct traffic), 27–308 (stopping, standing or parking regulated), 27–311 (parking regulations), 27–312 (parking regulations), 27–313 (parking regulations), 27–314 (parking regulations), 27–315 (parking regulations), 27–316 (parking regulations), 27–317 (parking regulations), 27–318 (parking regulations), 27–319 (parking regulations), 27–320 (parking regulations), 27–321 (parking regulations), 27–322 (parking regulations), 27–324 (loading and unloading at an angle), 27–333 (wheel and axle loads), 27–334 (load restrictions in the downtown district), 27–335 (load restrictions in residential areas), 27–338 (width of vehicles), 27–339 (height of vehicles), 27–340 (length of vehicles), 27–352 (reflectors on trailers), 27–353 (mufflers), 27–354 (display of plates), 27–355 (display of city vehicle tax sticker), 27–357 (identification of vehicles), 27–358 (projecting of loads), and also excepting the following enumerated paragraphs of Section 2–201 of the Rules and Regulations of the Illinois State Toll Highway Authority: (*l*) (driving unsafe vehicle on tollway), (m) (vehicles transporting dangerous cargo not properly indicated), it shall be the duty of the clerk of the court in which such conviction is had within 10 days thereafter to forward to the Secretary of State a report of the conviction and the court may recommend the suspension of the driver's license or permit of the person so convicted.

The reporting requirements of this subsection shall apply to all violations stated in paragraphs (1) and (2) of this subsection when the individual has been adjudicated under the Juvenile Court Act [1] or the Juvenile Court Act of 1987.[2] Such reporting requirements shall also apply to individuals adjudicated under the Juvenile Court Act or the Juvenile Court Act of 1987 who have committed a violation of Section 11–501 of this Code, or similar provision of a local ordinance, or Section 9–3 of the Criminal Code of 1961, as amended,[3] relating to the offense of reckless homicide. The reporting requirements of this subsection shall also apply to a truant minor in need of supervision, an addicted minor, or a delinquent minor and whose driver's license and privilege to drive a motor vehicle has been ordered suspended for such times as determined by the Court, but only until he or she attains 18 years of age. It shall be the duty of the clerk of the court in which adjudication is had within 10 days thereafter to forward to the Secretary of State a report of the adjudication and the court order requiring the Secretary of State to suspend the minor's driver's license and driving privilege for such time as determined by the Court, but only until he or she attains the age of 18 years. All juvenile court dispositions reported to the Secretary of State under this provision shall be processed by the Secretary of State as if the cases had been adjudicated in traffic or criminal court. However, information reported relative to the offense of reckless homicide, or Section 11–501 of this Code, or a similar provision of a local ordinance, shall be privileged and available only to the Secretary of State, courts, and police officers.

(3) Whenever an order is entered vacating the forfeiture of any bail, security or bond given to secure appearance for any offense under this Code or similar offenses under municipal ordinance, it shall be the duty of the clerk of the court in which such vacation was had or the judge of such court if such court has no clerk, within 10 days thereafter to forward to the Secretary of State a report of the vacation.

(4) A report of any disposition of court supervision for a violation of Sections 6–303, 11–401, 11–501 or a similar provision of a local ordinance, 11–503 and 11–504 shall be forwarded to the Secretary of State. A report of any disposition of court supervision for a violation of an offense defined as a serious traffic violation in this Code or a similar provision of a local ordinance committed by a person under the age of 21 years shall be forwarded to the Secretary of State.

(5) Reports of conviction under this Code and sentencing hearings under the Juvenile Court Act of 1987 in an electronic format or a computer processible medium shall be forwarded to the Secretary of State via the Supreme Court in the form and format required by the Illinois Supreme Court and established by a written agreement between the Supreme Court and the Secretary of State. In counties with a population over 300,000, instead of forwarding reports to the Supreme Court, reports of conviction under this Code and sentencing hearings under the Juvenile Court Act of 1987 in an electronic format or a computer processible medium may be forwarded to the Secretary of State by the Circuit Court Clerk in a form and format required by the Secretary of State and established by written agreement between the Circuit Court Clerk and the Secretary of State. Failure to forward the reports of conviction or sentencing hearing under the Juvenile Court Act of 1987 as required by this Section shall be deemed an omission of duty and it shall be the duty of the several State's Attorneys to enforce the requirements of this Section.

(b) Whenever a restricted driving permit is forwarded to a court, as a result of confiscation by a police officer pursuant to the authority in Section 6–113(f), it shall be the duty of the clerk, or judge, if the court has no clerk, to forward such restricted driving permit and a facsimile of the officer's citation to the Secretary of State as expeditiously as practicable.

(c) For the purposes of this Code, a forfeiture of bail or collateral deposited to secure a defendant's appearance in court when forfeiture has not been vacated, or the failure of a defendant to appear for trial after depositing his driver's license in lieu of other bail, shall be equivalent to a conviction.

(d) For the purpose of providing the Secretary of State with records necessary to properly monitor and assess driver performance and assist the courts in the proper disposition of repeat traffic law offenders, the clerk of the court shall forward to the Secretary of State, on a form prescribed by the Secretary, records of a driver's participation in a driver remedial or rehabilitative program which was required, through a court order or court supervision, in relation to the driver's arrest for a violation of Section 11–501 of this Code or a similar provision of a local ordinance. The clerk of the court shall also forward to the Secretary, either on paper or in an electronic format or a computer processible medium as required under paragraph (5) of subsection (a) of this Section, any disposition of court supervision for any traffic violation, excluding those offenses listed in paragraph (2) of subsection (a) of this Section. These reports shall be sent within 10 days after disposition, or, if the driver is referred to a driver remedial or rehabilitative program, within 10 days of the driver's referral to that program. These reports received by the Secretary of State, including those required to be forwarded under paragraph (a)(4), shall be privileged information, available only (i) to the affected driver and (ii) for use by the courts, police officers, prosecuting authorities, and the Secretary of State.

P.A. 76-1586, § 6-204, eff. July 1, 1970. Amended by P.A. 76-2154, § 1, eff. July 1, 1970; P.A. 77-38, § 1, eff. Jan. 1, 1972; P.A. 81-348, § 1, eff. Jan. 1, 1980; P.A. 81-804, § 1, eff. Sept. 19, 1979; P.A. 81-840, § 41, eff. Sept. 19, 1979; P.A. 81-1400, § 1, eff. Aug. 25, 1980; P.A. 81-1509, Art. I, § 57, eff. Sept. 26, 1980; P.A. 82-311, § 1, eff. Jan. 1, 1982; P.A. 83-208, § 1, eff. Jan. 1, 1984; P.A. 84-272, § 7, eff. Jan. 1, 1986; P.A. 84-596, § 1, eff. Jan. 1, 1986; P.A. 84-1308, Art. II, § 96, eff. Aug. 25, 1986; P.A. 84-1394, § 5, eff. Sept. 18, 1986; P.A. 84-1395, § 11, eff. Jan. 1, 1987; P.A. 85-293, Art. II, § 13, eff. Sept. 8, 1987; P.A. 85-981, Art. III, § 2, eff. Dec. 16, 1987; P.A. 85-1209, Art. II, § 2-51, eff. Aug. 30, 1988; P.A. 85-1396, § 2, eff. Sept. 2, 1988; P.A. 85-1440, Art. II, § 2-54, eff. Feb. 1, 1989; P.A. 86-1450, § 2, eff. July 1, 1991; P.A. 88-415, § 10, eff. Aug. 20, 1993; P.A. 90-369, § 5, eff. Jan. 1, 1998; P.A. 90-590, Art. 3001, § 3001-5, eff. Jan. 1, 1999; P.A. 91-357, § 231, eff. July 29, 1999; P.A. 91-716, § 5, eff. Oct. 1, 2000; P.A. 92-458, § 5, eff. Aug. 22, 2001.

Formerly Ill.Rev.Stat.1991, ch. 95 ½, ¶ 6-204.

[1] Former Ill.Rev.Stat. ch. 37, ¶ 701-1 (repealed).

[2] 705 ILCS 405/1-1 et seq.

[3] 720 ILCS 5/9-3.

5/6-205. Mandatory revocation of license or permit; Hardship cases

§ 6-205. Mandatory revocation of license or permit; Hardship cases.

(a) Except as provided in this Section, the Secretary of State shall immediately revoke the license, permit, or driving privileges of any driver upon receiving a report of the driver's conviction of any of the following offenses:

1. Reckless homicide resulting from the operation of a motor vehicle;

2. Violation of Section 11-501 of this Code or a similar provision of a local ordinance relating to the offense of operating or being in physical control of a vehicle while under the influence of alcohol, other drug or drugs, intoxicating compound or compounds, or any combination thereof;

3. Any felony under the laws of any State or the federal government in the commission of which a motor vehicle was used;

4. Violation of Section 11-401 of this Code relating to the offense of leaving the scene of a traffic accident involving death or personal injury;

5. Perjury or the making of a false affidavit or statement under oath to the Secretary of State under this Code or under any other law relating to the ownership or operation of motor vehicles;

6. Conviction upon 3 charges of violation of Section 11-503 of this Code relating to the offense of reckless driving committed within a period of 12 months;

7. Conviction of any offense defined in Section 4-102 of this Code;

8. Violation of Section 11-504 of this Code relating to the offense of drag racing;

9. Violation of Chapters 8 and 9 of this Code; [1]

10. Violation of Section 12-5 of the Criminal Code of 1961 [2] arising from the use of a motor vehicle;

11. Violation of Section 11-204.1 of this Code relating to aggravated fleeing or attempting to elude a police officer;

12. Violation of paragraph (1) of subsection (b) of Section 6-507, or a similar law of any other state, relating to the unlawful operation of a commercial motor vehicle;

13. Violation of paragraph (a) of Section 11-502 of this Code or a similar provision of a local ordinance if the driver has been previously convicted of a violation of that Section or a similar provision of a local ordinance and the driver was less than 21 years of age at the time of the offense.

(b) The Secretary of State shall also immediately revoke the license or permit of any driver in the following situations:

1. Of any minor upon receiving the notice provided for in Section 5-901 of the Juvenile Court Act of 1987 [3] that the minor has been adjudicated under that Act [4] as having committed an offense relating to motor vehicles prescribed in Section 4-103 of this Code;

2. Of any person when any other law of this State requires either the revocation or suspension of a license or permit.

(c) Whenever a person is convicted of any of the offenses enumerated in this Section, the court may recommend and the Secretary of State in his discretion, without regard to whether the recommendation is made by the court may, upon application, issue to the person a restricted driving permit granting the privilege of driving a motor vehicle between the petitioner's residence and petitioner's place of employment or within the scope of the petitioner's employment related duties, or to allow transportation for the petitioner or a household member of the petitioner's family for the receipt of necessary medical care or, if the professional evaluation indicates, provide transportation for the petitioner for alcohol remedial or rehabilitative activity, or for the petitioner to attend classes, as a student, in an accredited educational institution; if the petitioner is able to demonstrate that no alternative means of transportation is reasonably available and the petitioner will not endanger the public safety or welfare; provided that the Secretary's discretion shall be limited to cases where undue hardship would result from a failure to issue the restricted driving permit.

If a person's license or permit has been revoked or suspended due to 2 or more convictions of violating Section 11-501 of this Code or a similar provision of a local ordinance or a similar out-of-state offense, arising out of separate occurrences, that person, if issued a restricted driving permit, may not operate a vehicle unless it has been equipped with an ignition interlock device as defined in Section 1-129.1.

If a person's license or permit has been revoked or suspended 2 or more times within a 10 year period due to a single conviction of violating Section 11-501 of this Code or a similar provision of a local ordinance or a similar out-of-state offense, and a statutory summary suspension under Section 11-501.1, or 2 or more statutory summary suspensions, or combination of 2 offenses, or of an offense and a statutory summary suspension, arising out of separate occurrences, that person, if issued a restricted driving permit, may not operate a vehicle unless it has been equipped with an ignition interlock device as defined in Section 1–129.1. The person must pay to the Secretary of State DUI Administration Fund an amount not to exceed $20 per month. The Secretary shall establish by rule the amount and the procedures, terms, and conditions relating to these fees. If the restricted driving permit was issued for employment purposes, then this provision does not apply to the operation of an occupational vehicle owned or leased by that person's employer. In each case the Secretary of State may issue a restricted driving permit for a period he deems appropriate, except that the permit shall expire within one year from the date of issuance. The Secretary may not, however, issue a restricted driving permit to any person whose current revocation is the result of a second or subsequent conviction for a violation of Section 11–501 of this Code or a similar provision of a local ordinance relating to the offense of operating or being in physical control of a motor vehicle while under the influence of alcohol, other drug or drugs, intoxicating compound or compounds, or any similar out-of-state offense, or any combination thereof, until the expiration of at least one year from the date of the revocation. A restricted driving permit issued under this Section shall be subject to cancellation, revocation, and suspension by the Secretary of State in like manner and for like cause as a driver's license issued under this Code may be cancelled, revoked, or suspended; except that a conviction upon one or more offenses against laws or ordinances regulating the movement of traffic shall be deemed sufficient cause for the revocation, suspension, or cancellation of a restricted driving permit. The Secretary of State may, as a condition to the issuance of a restricted driving permit, require the applicant to participate in a designated driver remedial or rehabilitative program. The Secretary of State is authorized to cancel a restricted driving permit if the permit holder does not successfully complete the program. However, if an individual's driving privileges have been revoked in accordance with paragraph 13 of subsection (a) of this Section, no restricted driving permit shall be issued until the individual has served 6 months of the revocation period.

(d) Whenever a person under the age of 21 is convicted under Section 11–501 of this Code or a similar provision of a local ordinance, the Secretary of State shall revoke the driving privileges of that person. One year after the date of revocation, and upon application, the Secretary of State may, if satisfied that the person applying will not endanger the public safety or welfare, issue a restricted driving permit granting the privilege of driving a motor vehicle only between the hours of 5 a.m. and 9 p.m. or as otherwise provided by this Section for a period of one year. After this one year period, and upon reapplication for a license as provided in Section 6–106, upon payment of the appropriate reinstatement fee provided under paragraph (b) of Section 6–118, the Secretary of State, in his discretion, may issue the applicant a license, or extend the restricted driving permit as many times as the Secretary of State deems appropriate, by additional periods of not more than 12 months each, until the applicant attains 21 years of age.

If a person's license or permit has been revoked or suspended due to 2 or more convictions of violating Section 11–501 of this Code or a similar provision of a local ordinance or a similar out-of-state offense, arising out of separate occurrences, that person, if issued a restricted driving permit, may not operate a vehicle unless it has been equipped with an ignition interlock device as defined in Section 1–129.1.

If a person's license or permit has been revoked or suspended 2 or more times within a 10 year period due to a single conviction of violating Section 11–501 of this Code or a similar provision of a local ordinance or a similar out-of-state offense, and a statutory summary suspension under Section 11–501.1, or 2 or more statutory summary suspensions, or combination of 2 offenses, or of an offense and a statutory summary suspension, arising out of separate occurrences, that person, if issued a restricted driving permit, may not operate a vehicle unless it has been equipped with an ignition interlock device as defined in Section 1–129.1. The person must pay to the Secretary of State DUI Administration Fund an amount not to exceed $20 per month. The Secretary shall establish by rule the amount and the procedures, terms, and conditions relating to these fees. If the restricted driving permit was issued for employment purposes, then this provision does not apply to the operation of an occupational vehicle owned or leased by that person's employer. A restricted driving permit issued under this Section shall be subject to cancellation, revocation, and suspension by the Secretary of State in like manner and for like cause as a driver's license issued under this Code may be cancelled, revoked, or suspended; except that a conviction upon one or more offenses against laws or ordinances regulating the movement of traffic shall be deemed sufficient cause for the revocation, suspension, or cancellation of a restricted driving permit. The revocation periods contained in this subparagraph shall apply to similar out-of-state convictions.

(e) This Section is subject to the provisions of the Driver License Compact.[5]

(f) Any revocation imposed upon any person under subsections 2 and 3 of paragraph (b) that is in effect on December 31, 1988 shall be converted to a suspension for a like period of time.

(g) The Secretary of State shall not issue a restricted driving permit to a person under the age of 16 years whose driving privileges have been revoked under any provisions of this Code.

(h) The Secretary of State shall require the use of ignition interlock devices on all vehicles owned by an individual who has been convicted of a second or subsequent offense under Section 11–501 of this Code or a similar provision of a local ordinance. The Secretary shall establish by rule and regulation the procedures for certification and use of the interlock system.

(i) The Secretary of State may not issue a restricted driving permit for a period of one year after a second or subsequent revocation of driving privileges under clause (a)(2) of this Section; however, one year after the date of a second or subsequent revocation of driving privileges under clause (a)(2) of this Section, the Secretary of State may, upon application, issue a restricted driving permit under the terms and conditions of subsection (c).

P.A. 76–1586, § 6–205, eff. July 1, 1970. Amended by P.A. 76–2155, § 1, eff. July 1, 1970; P.A. 78–663, § 1, eff. Jan. 1, 1974; P.A. 81–1400, § 1, eff. Aug. 25, 1980; P.A. 82–311, § 1, eff. Jan. 1, 1982; P.A. 83–1067, § 19, eff. July 1, 1984; P.A. 83–1326, § 1, eff. July 1, 1985; P.A. 84–1381, § 2, eff. Sept. 12, 1986; P.A. 84–1394, § 5, eff. Sept. 18, 1986; P.A. 84–1450, § 7, eff. July 1, 1987; P.A. 85–293, Art. II, § 13, eff. Sept. 8, 1987; P.A. 85–876, § 1, eff. Nov. 6, 1987; P.A. 85–951, § 1, eff. July 1, 1988; P.A. 85–1209, Art. II, § 2–51, eff. Aug. 30, 1988; P.A. 85–1259, § 3, eff. Jan. 1, 1989; P.A. 85–1440, Art. II, § 2–24, eff. Feb. 1, 1989; P.A. 86–845, § 1, eff. April 1, 1990; P.A. 86–929, § 2, eff. Sept. 21, 1989; P.A. 86–1028, Art. II, § 2–44, eff. Feb. 5, 1990; P.A. 87–1114, § 1, eff. Sept. 15, 1992; P.A. 88–209, § 5, eff. Jan. 1, 1994; P.A. 89–156, § 5, eff. Jan. 1, 1996; P.A. 89–245, § 5, eff. Jan. 1, 1996; P.A. 89–626, Art. 2, § 2–66, eff. Aug. 9, 1996; P.A. 90–369, § 5, eff. Jan. 1, 1998; P.A. 90–590, Art. 2001, § 2001–7, eff. Jan. 1, 1999; P.A. 90–611, § 5, eff. Jan. 1, 1999; P.A. 90–779, § 5, eff. Jan. 1, 1999; P.A. 91-357, § 231, eff. July 29, 1999; P.A. 92-248, § 5, eff. Aug. 3, 2001; P.A. 92-418, § 10, eff. Aug. 17, 2001; P.A. 92-651, § 77, eff. July 11, 2002; P.A. 92-834, § 5, eff. Aug. 22, 2002.

Formerly Ill.Rev.Stat.1991, ch. 95 ½, ¶ 6-205.

1 625 ILCS 5/8-101 et seq.

2 720 ILCS 5/12-5.

3 705 ILCS 405/5-901.

4 705 ILCS 405/1-1 et seq.

5 625 ILCS 5/6-700 et seq.

P.A. 92-651, the First 2002 General Revisory Act, amended various Acts to delete obsolete text, to correct patent and technical errors, to revise cross references, to resolve multiple actions in the 91st and 92nd General Assemblies and to make certain technical corrections in P.A. 91-937 through P.A. 92-520.

P.A. 92-834 incorporated the amendments by P.A. 92-248 and P.A. 92-418.

5/6-205.1. § 6-205.1. Repealed by P.A. 92-458, § 15, eff. Aug. 22, 2001

5/6-206. Discretionary authority to suspend or revoke license or permit; Right to a hearing.

Text of section as amended by P.A. 92-651 and P.A. 92-804, effective January 1, 2003

§ 6-206. Discretionary authority to suspend or revoke license or permit; Right to a hearing.

(a) The Secretary of State is authorized to suspend or revoke the driving privileges of any person without preliminary hearing upon a showing of the person's records or other sufficient evidence that the person:

1. Has committed an offense for which mandatory revocation of a driver's license or permit is required upon conviction;

2. Has been convicted of not less than 3 offenses against traffic regulations governing the movement of vehicles committed within any 12 month period. No revocation or suspension shall be entered more than 6 months after the date of last conviction;

3. Has been repeatedly involved as a driver in motor vehicle collisions or has been repeatedly convicted of offenses against laws and ordinances regulating the movement of traffic, to a degree that indicates lack of ability to exercise ordinary and reasonable care in the safe operation of a motor vehicle or disrespect for the traffic laws and the safety of other persons upon the highway;

4. Has by the unlawful operation of a motor vehicle caused or contributed to an accident resulting in death or injury requiring immediate professional treatment in a medical facility or doctor's office to any person, except that any suspension or revocation imposed by the Secretary of State under the provisions of this subsection shall start no later than 6 months after being convicted of violating a law or ordinance regulating the movement of traffic, which violation is related to the accident, or shall start not more than one year after the date of the accident, whichever date occurs later;

5. Has permitted an unlawful or fraudulent use of a driver's license, identification card, or permit;

6. Has been lawfully convicted of an offense or offenses in another state, including the authorization contained in Section 6-203.1, which if committed within this State would be grounds for suspension or revocation;

7. Has refused or failed to submit to an examination provided for by Section 6-207 or has failed to pass the examination;

8. Is ineligible for a driver's license or permit under the provisions of Section 6-103;

9. Has made a false statement or knowingly concealed a material fact or has used false information or identification in any application for a license, identification card, or permit;

10. Has possessed, displayed, or attempted to fraudulently use any license, identification card, or permit not issued to the person;

11. Has operated a motor vehicle upon a highway of this State when the person's driving privilege or privilege to obtain a driver's license or permit was revoked or suspended unless the operation was authorized by a judicial driving permit, probationary license to drive, or a restricted driving permit issued under this Code;

12. Has submitted to any portion of the application process for another person or has obtained the services of another person to submit to any portion of the application process for the purpose of obtaining a license, identification card, or permit for some other person;

13. Has operated a motor vehicle upon a highway of this State when the person's driver's license or permit was invalid under the provisions of Sections 6-107.1 and 6-110;

14. Has committed a violation of Section 6-301, 6-301.1, or 6-301.2 of this Act, or Section 14, 14A, or 14B of the Illinois Identification Card Act; [1]

15. Has been convicted of violating Section 21-2 of the Criminal Code of 1961 [2] relating to criminal trespass to vehicles in which case, the suspension shall be for one year;

16. Has been convicted of violating Section 11-204 of this Code relating to fleeing from a police officer;

17. Has refused to submit to a test, or tests, as required under Section 11-501.1 of this Code and the person has not sought a hearing as provided for in Section 11-501.1;

18. Has, since issuance of a driver's license or permit, been adjudged to be afflicted with or suffering from any mental disability or disease;

19. Has committed a violation of paragraph (a) or (b) of Section 6-101 relating to driving without a driver's license;

20. Has been convicted of violating Section 6-104 relating to classification of driver's license;

21. Has been convicted of violating Section 11-402 of this Code relating to leaving the scene of an accident resulting in damage to a vehicle in excess of $1,000, in which case the suspension shall be for one year;

22. Has used a motor vehicle in violating paragraph (3), (4), (7), or (9) of subsection (a) of Section 24-1 of the Criminal Code of 1961 [3] relating to unlawful use of weapons, in which case the suspension shall be for one year;

23. Has, as a driver, been convicted of committing a violation of paragraph (a) of Section 11-502 of this Code for a second or subsequent time within one year of a similar violation;

24. Has been convicted by a court-martial or punished by non-judicial punishment by military authorities of the

United States at a military installation in Illinois of or for a traffic related offense that is the same as or similar to an offense specified under Section 6-205 or 6-206 of this Code;

25. Has permitted any form of identification to be used by another in the application process in order to obtain or attempt to obtain a license, identification card, or permit;

26. Has altered or attempted to alter a license or has possessed an altered license, identification card, or permit;

27. Has violated Section 6-16 of the Liquor Control Act of 1934; [4]

28. Has been convicted of the illegal possession, while operating or in actual physical control, as a driver, of a motor vehicle, of any controlled substance prohibited under the Illinois Controlled Substances Act [5] or any cannabis prohibited under the provisions of the Cannabis Control Act, [6] in which case the person's driving privileges shall be suspended for one year, and any driver who is convicted of a second or subsequent offense, within 5 years of a previous conviction, for the illegal possession, while operating or in actual physical control, as a driver, of a motor vehicle, of any controlled substance prohibited under the provisions of the Illinois Controlled Substances Act or any cannabis prohibited under the Cannabis Control Act shall be suspended for 5 years. Any defendant found guilty of this offense while operating a motor vehicle, shall have an entry made in the court record by the presiding judge that this offense did occur while the defendant was operating a motor vehicle and order the clerk of the court to report the violation to the Secretary of State;

29. Has been convicted of the following offenses that were committed while the person was operating or in actual physical control, as a driver, of a motor vehicle: criminal sexual assault, predatory criminal sexual assault of a child, aggravated criminal sexual assault, criminal sexual abuse, aggravated criminal sexual abuse, juvenile pimping, soliciting for a juvenile prostitute and the manufacture, sale or delivery of controlled substances or instruments used for illegal drug use or abuse in which case the driver's driving privileges shall be suspended for one year;

30. Has been convicted a second or subsequent time for any combination of the offenses named in paragraph 29 of this subsection, in which case the person's driving privileges shall be suspended for 5 years;

31. Has refused to submit to a test as required by Section 11-501.6 or has submitted to a test resulting in an alcohol concentration of 0.08 or more or any amount of a drug, substance, or compound resulting from the unlawful use or consumption of cannabis as listed in the Cannabis Control Act, a controlled substance as listed in the Illinois Controlled Substances Act, or an intoxicating compound as listed in the Use of Intoxicating Compounds Act, [7] in which case the penalty shall be as prescribed in Section 6-208.1;

32. Has been convicted of Section 24-1.2 of the Criminal Code of 1961 [8] relating to the aggravated discharge of a firearm if the offender was located in a motor vehicle at the time the firearm was discharged, in which case the suspension shall be for 3 years;

33. Has as a driver, who was less than 21 years of age on the date of the offense, been convicted a first time of a violation of paragraph (a) of Section 11-502 of this Code or a similar provision of a local ordinance;

34. Has committed a violation of Section 11-1301.5 of this Code;

35. Has committed a violation of Section 11-1301.6 of this Code;

36. Is under the age of 21 years at the time of arrest and has been convicted of not less than 2 offenses against traffic regulations governing the movement of vehicles committed within any 24 month period. No revocation or suspension shall be entered more than 6 months after the date of last conviction;

37. Has committed a violation of subsection (c) of Section 11-907 of this Code; or

38. Has been convicted of a violation of Section 6-20 of the Liquor Control Act of 1934 or a similar provision of a local ordinance.

For purposes of paragraphs 5, 9, 10, 12, 14, 19, 25, 26, and 27 of this subsection, license means any driver's license, any traffic ticket issued when the person's driver's license is deposited in lieu of bail, a suspension notice issued by the Secretary of State, a duplicate or corrected driver's license, a probationary driver's license or a temporary driver's license.

(b) If any conviction forming the basis of a suspension or revocation authorized under this Section is appealed, the Secretary of State may rescind or withhold the entry of the order of suspension or revocation, as the case may be, provided that a certified copy of a stay order of a court is filed with the Secretary of State. If the conviction is affirmed on appeal, the date of the conviction shall relate back to the time the original judgment of conviction was entered and the 6 month limitation prescribed shall not apply.

(c) 1. Upon suspending or revoking the driver's license or permit of any person as authorized in this Section, the Secretary of State shall immediately notify the person in writing of the revocation or suspension. The notice to be deposited in the United States mail, postage prepaid, to the last known address of the person.

2. If the Secretary of State suspends the driver's license of a person under subsection 2 of paragraph (a) of this Section, a person's privilege to operate a vehicle as an occupation shall not be suspended, provided an affidavit is properly completed, the appropriate fee received, and a permit issued prior to the effective date of the suspension, unless 5 offenses were committed, at least 2 of which occurred while operating a commercial vehicle in connection with the driver's regular occupation. All other driving privileges shall be suspended by the Secretary of State. Any driver prior to operating a vehicle for occupational purposes only must submit the affidavit on forms to be provided by the Secretary of State setting forth the facts of the person's occupation. The affidavit shall also state the number of offenses committed while operating a vehicle in connection with the driver's regular occupation. The affidavit shall be accompanied by the driver's license. Upon receipt of a properly completed affidavit, the Secretary of State shall issue the driver a permit to operate a vehicle in connection with the driver's regular occupation only. Unless the permit is issued by the Secretary of State prior to the date of suspension, the privilege to drive any motor vehicle shall be suspended as set forth in the notice that was mailed under this Section. If an affidavit is received subsequent to the effective date of this suspension, a permit may be issued for the remainder of the suspension period.

The provisions of this subparagraph shall not apply to any driver required to obtain a commercial driver's license under Section 6-507 during the period of a disqualification of commercial driving privileges under Section 6-514.

Any person who falsely states any fact in the affidavit required herein shall be guilty of perjury under Section 6-

302 and upon conviction thereof shall have all driving privileges revoked without further rights.

3. At the conclusion of a hearing under Section 2-118 of this Code, the Secretary of State shall either rescind or continue an order of revocation or shall substitute an order of suspension; or, good cause appearing therefor, rescind, continue, change, or extend the order of suspension. If the Secretary of State does not rescind the order, the Secretary may upon application, to relieve undue hardship, issue a restricted driving permit granting the privilege of driving a motor vehicle between the petitioner's residence and petitioner's place of employment or within the scope of his employment related duties, or to allow transportation for the petitioner, or a household member of the petitioner's family, to receive necessary medical care and if the professional evaluation indicates, provide transportation for alcohol remedial or rehabilitative activity, or for the petitioner to attend classes, as a student, in an accredited educational institution; if the petitioner is able to demonstrate that no alternative means of transportation is reasonably available and the petitioner will not endanger the public safety or welfare.

If a person's license or permit has been revoked or suspended due to 2 or more convictions of violating Section 11-501 of this Code or a similar provision of a local ordinance or a similar out-of-state offense, arising out of separate occurrences, that person, if issued a restricted driving permit, may not operate a vehicle unless it has been equipped with an ignition interlock device as defined in Section 1-129.1.

If a person's license or permit has been revoked or suspended 2 or more times within a 10 year period due to a single conviction of violating Section 11-501 of this Code or a similar provision of a local ordinance or a similar out-of-state offense, and a statutory summary suspension under Section 11-501.1, or 2 or more statutory summary suspensions, or combination of 2 offenses, or of an offense and a statutory summary suspension, arising out of separate occurrences, that person, if issued a restricted driving permit, may not operate a vehicle unless it has been equipped with an ignition interlock device as defined in Section 1-129.1. The person must pay to the Secretary of State DUI Administration Fund an amount not to exceed $20 per month. The Secretary shall establish by rule the amount and the procedures, terms, and conditions relating to these fees. If the restricted driving permit was issued for employment purposes, then this provision does not apply to the operation of an occupational vehicle owned or leased by that person's employer. In each case the Secretary may issue a restricted driving permit for a period deemed appropriate, except that all permits shall expire within one year from the date of issuance. The Secretary may not, however, issue a restricted driving permit to any person whose current revocation is the result of a second or subsequent conviction for a violation of Section 11-501 of this Code or a similar provision of a local ordinance relating to the offense of operating or being in physical control of a motor vehicle while under the influence of alcohol, other drug or drugs, intoxicating compound or compounds, or any similar out-of-state offense, or any combination of those offenses, until the expiration of at least one year from the date of the revocation. A restricted driving permit issued under this Section shall be subject to cancellation, revocation, and suspension by the Secretary of State in like manner and for like cause as a driver's license issued under this Code may be cancelled, revoked, or suspended; except that a conviction upon one or more offenses against laws or ordinances regulating the movement of traffic shall be deemed sufficient cause for the revocation, suspension, or cancellation of a restricted driving permit. The Secretary of State may, as a condition to the issuance of a restricted driving permit, require the applicant to participate in a designated driver remedial or rehabilitative program. The Secretary of State is authorized to cancel a restricted driving permit if the permit holder does not successfully complete the program.

(c-5) The Secretary of State may, as a condition of the reissuance of a driver's license or permit to an applicant whose driver's license or permit has been suspended before he or she reached the age of 18 years pursuant to any of the provisions of this Section, require the applicant to participate in a driver remedial education course and be retested under Section 6-109 of this Code.

(d) This Section is subject to the provisions of the Drivers License Compact.

(e) The Secretary of State shall not issue a restricted driving permit to a person under the age of 16 years whose driving privileges have been suspended or revoked under any provisions of this Code.

P.A. 76-1586, § 6-206, eff. July 1, 1970. Amended by P.A. 76-2156, § 1, eff. July 1, 1970; P.A. 77-2739, § 1, eff. Oct. 1, 1972; P.A. 78-663, § 1, eff. Jan. 1, 1974; P.A. 79-1141, § 1, eff. Jan. 1, 1976; P.A. 81-1400, § 1, eff. Aug. 25, 1980; P.A. 82-141, § 1, eff. Jan. 1, 1982; P.A. 82-311, § 1, eff. Jan. 1, 1982; P.A. 82-783, Art. III, § 37, eff. July 13, 1982; P.A. 83-466, § 1, eff. Sept. 17, 1983; P.A. 83-905, § 1, eff. Jan. 1, 1984; P.A. 83-1362, Art. II, § 99, eff. Sept. 11, 1984; P.A. 84-112, § 1, eff. July 25, 1985; P.A. 84-272, § 7, eff. Jan. 1, 1986; P.A. 84-300, § 1, eff. Sept. 13, 1985; P.A. 84-551, § 50, eff. Sept. 18, 1985; P.A. 84-772, § 1, eff. Jan. 1, 1986; P.A. 84-1308, Art. II, § 96, eff. Aug. 25, 1986; P.A. 84-1394, § 5, eff. Sept. 18, 1986; P.A. 85-813, § 1, eff. Jan. 1, 1988; P.A. 85-1259, § 3, eff. Jan. 1, 1989; P.A. 86-879, § 1, eff. Jan. 1, 1990; P.A. 86-929, § 2, eff. Sept. 21, 1989; P.A. 86-947, § 2, eff. Jan. 1, 1991; P.A. 86-1019, § 7, eff. July 1, 1990; P.A. 86-1475, Art. 2, § 2-25, eff. Jan. 10, 1991; P.A. 87-233, § 1, eff. Jan. 1, 1992; P.A. 87-929, § 1, eff. Jan. 1, 1993; P.A. 87-1114, § 1, eff. Sept. 15, 1992; P.A. 88-45, Art. II, § 2-54, eff. July 6, 1993; P.A. 88-209, § 5, eff. Jan. 1, 1994; P.A. 88-211, § 5, eff. Jan. 1, 1994; P.A. 88-670, Art. 2, § 2-59, eff. Dec. 2, 1994; P.A. 89-283, § 10, eff. Jan. 1, 1996; P.A. 89-428, Art. 2, § 250, eff. Dec. 13, 1995; P.A. 89-462, Art. 2, § 250, eff. May 29, 1996; P.A. 90-43, § 5, eff. July 2, 1997; P.A. 90-106, § 5, eff. Jan. 1, 1998; P.A. 90-369, § 5, eff. Jan. 1, 1998; P.A. 90-655, § 153, eff. July 30, 1998; P.A. 92-283, § 5, eff. Jan. 1, 2002; P.A. 92-418, § 10, eff. Aug. 17, 2001; P.A. 92-458, § 5, eff. Aug. 22, 2001; P.A. 92-651, § 77, eff. July 11, 2002; P.A. 92-804, § 10, eff. Jan. 1, 2003.

Formerly Ill.Rev.Stat.1991, ch. 95 ½, ¶ 6-206.

[1] 15 ILSC 335/14, 335/14A, or 335/14B.

[2] 720 ILSC 5/21-2.

[3] 720 ILSC 5/24-1.

[4] 235 ILSC 5/6-16.

[5] 720 ILSC 570/100 et seq.

[6] 720 ILSC 550/1 et seq.

[7] 720 ILSC 690/0.01 et seq.

[8] 720 ILSC 5/24-1.2.

For text of section as amended by P.A. 92-651 and P.A. 92-814, effective January 1, 2003, see 625 ILCS 5/6-206, post

For final legislative action, see note following 625 ILCS 5/6-206, post

P.A. 89-428 was held by the Illinois Supreme Court to be in violation of the single subject requirement of subsection (d) of Section 8 of Article IV of the Illinois Constitution in the case of Johnson v. Edgar, 1997, 176 Ill.2d 499, 680 N.E.2d 1372, 224 Ill.Dec. 1. Public Act 89-462 reenacted the amendment of this text by P.A. 89-428.

P.A. 92-283, in subsec. (a), inserted par. 37 relating to violations of Section 11-907(c); and made nonsubstantive changes.

P.A. 92-418, in subsec. (c)3, inserted the second paragraph; and in the third paragraph, inserted the first four and the sixth sentences.

P.A. 92-458, in subsec. (a)31, inserted "or an intoxicating compound as listed in the use of Intoxicating Compounds Act," and made nonsubstantive changes; in subsec. (c-5), deleted "under the age of 18 years" preceding "whose driver's license" and inserted "before he or she reached the age of 18 years".

P.A. 92-651, the First 2002 General Revisory Act, amended various Acts to delete obsolete text, to correct patent and technical errors, to revise cross references, to resolve multiple actions in the 91st and 92nd General Assemblies and to make certain technical corrections in P.A. 91-937 through P.A. 92-520.

P.A. 92-804 incorporated the amendments by P.A. 92-283, 92-418, and 92-458.

See 5 ILCS 70/6 as to the effect of (1) more than one amendment of a section at the same session of the General Assembly or (2) two or more acts relating to the same subject matter enacted by the same General Assembly.

5/6-206. Discretionary authority to suspend or revoke license or permit; Right to a hearing.

Text of section as amended by P.A. 92-651 and P.A. 92-814, effective January 1, 2003

§ 6-206. Discretionary authority to suspend or revoke license or permit; Right to a hearing.

(a) The Secretary of State is authorized to suspend or revoke the driving privileges of any person without preliminary hearing upon a showing of the person's records or other sufficient evidence that the person:

1. Has committed an offense for which mandatory revocation of a driver's license or permit is required upon conviction;

2. Has been convicted of not less than 3 offenses against traffic regulations governing the movement of vehicles committed within any 12 month period. No revocation or suspension shall be entered more than 6 months after the date of last conviction;

3. Has been repeatedly involved as a driver in motor vehicle collisions or has been repeatedly convicted of offenses against laws and ordinances regulating the movement of traffic, to a degree that indicates lack of ability to exercise ordinary and reasonable care in the safe operation of a motor vehicle or disrespect for the traffic laws and the safety of other persons upon the highway;

4. Has by the unlawful operation of a motor vehicle caused or contributed to an accident resulting in death or injury requiring immediate professional treatment in a medical facility or doctor's office to any person, except that any suspension or revocation imposed by the Secretary of State under the provisions of this subsection shall start no later than 6 months after being convicted of violating a law or ordinance regulating the movement of traffic, which violation is related to the accident, or shall start not more than one year after the date of the accident, whichever date occurs later;

5. Has permitted an unlawful or fraudulent use of a driver's license, identification card, or permit;

6. Has been lawfully convicted of an offense or offenses in another state, including the authorization contained in Section 6-203.1, which if committed within this State would be grounds for suspension or revocation;

7. Has refused or failed to submit to an examination provided for by Section 6-207 or has failed to pass the examination;

8. Is ineligible for a driver's license or permit under the provisions of Section 6-103;

9. Has made a false statement or knowingly concealed a material fact or has used false information or identification in any application for a license, identification card, or permit;

10. Has possessed, displayed, or attempted to fraudulently use any license, identification card, or permit not issued to the person;

11. Has operated a motor vehicle upon a highway of this State when the person's driving privilege or privilege to obtain a driver's license or permit was revoked or suspended unless the operation was authorized by a judicial driving permit, probationary license to drive, or a restricted driving permit issued under this Code;

12. Has submitted to any portion of the application process for another person or has obtained the services of another person to submit to any portion of the application process for the purpose of obtaining a license, identification card, or permit for some other person;

13. Has operated a motor vehicle upon a highway of this State when the person's driver's license or permit was invalid under the provisions of Sections 6-107.1 and 6-110;

14. Has committed a violation of Section 6-301, 6-301.1, or 6-301.2 of this Act, or Section 14, 14A, or 14B of the Illinois Identification Card Act; [1]

15. Has been convicted of violating Section 21-2 of the Criminal Code of 1961 [2] relating to criminal trespass to vehicles in which case, the suspension shall be for one year;

16. Has been convicted of violating Section 11-204 of this Code relating to fleeing from a police officer;

17. Has refused to submit to a test, or tests, as required under Section 11-501.1 of this Code and the person has not sought a hearing as provided for in Section 11-501.1;

18. Has, since issuance of a driver's license or permit, been adjudged to be afflicted with or suffering from any mental disability or disease;

19. Has committed a violation of paragraph (a) or (b) of Section 6-101 relating to driving without a driver's license;

20. Has been convicted of violating Section 6-104 relating to classification of driver's license;

21. Has been convicted of violating Section 11-402 of this Code relating to leaving the scene of an accident resulting in damage to a vehicle in excess of $1,000, in which case the suspension shall be for one year;

22. Has used a motor vehicle in violating paragraph (3), (4), (7), or (9) of subsection (a) of Section 24-1 of the Criminal Code of 1961 [3] relating to unlawful use of weapons, in which case the suspension shall be for one year;

23. Has, as a driver, been convicted of committing a violation of paragraph (a) of Section 11-502 of this Code for a second or subsequent time within one year of a similar violation;

24. Has been convicted by a court-martial or punished by non-judicial punishment by military authorities of the

United States at a military installation in Illinois of or for a traffic related offense that is the same as or similar to an offense specified under Section 6–205 or 6–206 of this Code;

25. Has permitted any form of identification to be used by another in the application process in order to obtain or attempt to obtain a license, identification card, or permit;

26. Has altered or attempted to alter a license or has possessed an altered license, identification card, or permit;

27. Has violated Section 6–16 of the Liquor Control Act of 1934; [4]

28. Has been convicted of the illegal possession, while operating or in actual physical control, as a driver, of a motor vehicle, of any controlled substance prohibited under the Illinois Controlled Substances Act [5] or any cannabis prohibited under the provisions of the Cannabis Control Act, [6] in which case the person's driving privileges shall be suspended for one year, and any driver who is convicted of a second or subsequent offense, within 5 years of a previous conviction, for the illegal possession, while operating or in actual physical control, as a driver, of a motor vehicle, of any controlled substance prohibited under the provisions of the Illinois Controlled Substances Act or any cannabis prohibited under the Cannabis Control Act shall be suspended for 5 years. Any defendant found guilty of this offense while operating a motor vehicle, shall have an entry made in the court record by the presiding judge that this offense did occur while the defendant was operating a motor vehicle and order the clerk of the court to report the violation to the Secretary of State;

29. Has been convicted of the following offenses that were committed while the person was operating or in actual physical control, as a driver, of a motor vehicle: criminal sexual assault, predatory criminal sexual assault of a child, aggravated criminal sexual assault, criminal sexual abuse, aggravated criminal sexual abuse, juvenile pimping, soliciting for a juvenile prostitute and the manufacture, sale or delivery of controlled substances or instruments used for illegal drug use or abuse in which case the driver's driving privileges shall be suspended for one year;

30. Has been convicted a second or subsequent time for any combination of the offenses named in paragraph 29 of this subsection, in which case the person's driving privileges shall be suspended for 5 years;

31. Has refused to submit to a test as required by Section 11–501.6 or has submitted to a test resulting in an alcohol concentration of 0.08 or more or any amount of a drug, substance, or compound resulting from the unlawful use or consumption of cannabis as listed in the Cannabis Control Act, a controlled substance as listed in the Illinois Controlled Substances Act, or an intoxicating compound as listed in the Use of Intoxicating Compounds Act, [7] in which case the penalty shall be as prescribed in Section 6–208.1;

32. Has been convicted of Section 24–1.2 of the Criminal Code of 1961 [8] relating to the aggravated discharge of a firearm if the offender was located in a motor vehicle at the time the firearm was discharged, in which case the suspension shall be for 3 years;

33. Has as a driver, who was less than 21 years of age on the date of the offense, been convicted a first time of a violation of paragraph (a) of Section 11–502 of this Code or a similar provision of a local ordinance;

34. Has committed a violation of Section 11–1301.5 of this Code;

35. Has committed a violation of Section 11–1301.6 of this Code;

36. Is under the age of 21 years at the time of arrest and has been convicted of not less than 2 offenses against traffic regulations governing the movement of vehicles committed within any 24 month period. No revocation or suspension shall be entered more than 6 months after the date of last conviction;

37. Has committed a violation of subsection (c) of Section 11–907 of this Code; or

38. Has committed a second or subsequent violation of Section 11–1201 of this Code.

For purposes of paragraphs 5, 9, 10, 12, 14, 19, 25, 26, and 27 of this subsection, license means any driver's license, any traffic ticket issued when the person's driver's license is deposited in lieu of bail, a suspension notice issued by the Secretary of State, a duplicate or corrected driver's license, a probationary driver's license or a temporary driver's license.

(b) If any conviction forming the basis of a suspension or revocation authorized under this Section is appealed, the Secretary of State may rescind or withhold the entry of the order of suspension or revocation, as the case may be, provided that a certified copy of a stay order of a court is filed with the Secretary of State. If the conviction is affirmed on appeal, the date of the conviction shall relate back to the time the original judgment of conviction was entered and the 6 month limitation prescribed shall not apply.

(c) 1. Upon suspending or revoking the driver's license or permit of any person as authorized in this Section, the Secretary of State shall immediately notify the person in writing of the revocation or suspension. The notice to be deposited in the United States mail, postage prepaid, to the last known address of the person.

2. If the Secretary of State suspends the driver's license of a person under subsection 2 of paragraph (a) of this Section, a person's privilege to operate a vehicle as an occupation shall not be suspended, provided an affidavit is properly completed, the appropriate fee received, and a permit issued prior to the effective date of the suspension, unless 5 offenses were committed, at least 2 of which occurred while operating a commercial vehicle in connection with the driver's regular occupation. All other driving privileges shall be suspended by the Secretary of State. Any driver prior to operating a vehicle for occupational purposes only must submit the affidavit on forms to be provided by the Secretary of State setting forth the facts of the person's occupation. The affidavit shall also state the number of offenses committed while operating a vehicle in connection with the driver's regular occupation. The affidavit shall be accompanied by the driver's license. Upon receipt of a properly completed affidavit, the Secretary of State shall issue the driver a permit to operate a vehicle in connection with the driver's regular occupation only. Unless the permit is issued by the Secretary of State prior to the date of suspension, the privilege to drive any motor vehicle shall be suspended as set forth in the notice that was mailed under this Section. If an affidavit is received subsequent to the effective date of this suspension, a permit may be issued for the remainder of the suspension period.

The provisions of this subparagraph shall not apply to any driver required to obtain a commercial driver's license under Section 6–507 during the period of a disqualification of commercial driving privileges under Section 6–514.

Any person who falsely states any fact in the affidavit required herein shall be guilty of perjury under Section 6–302 and upon conviction thereof shall have all driving privileges revoked without further rights.

3. At the conclusion of a hearing under Section 2-118 of this Code, the Secretary of State shall either rescind or continue an order of revocation or shall substitute an order of suspension; or, good cause appearing therefor, rescind, continue, change, or extend the order of suspension. If the Secretary of State does not rescind the order, the Secretary may upon application, to relieve undue hardship, issue a restricted driving permit granting the privilege of driving a motor vehicle between the petitioner's residence and petitioner's place of employment or within the scope of his employment related duties, or to allow transportation for the petitioner, or a household member of the petitioner's family, to receive necessary medical care and if the professional evaluation indicates, provide transportation for alcohol remedial or rehabilitative activity, or for the petitioner to attend classes, as a student, in an accredited educational institution; if the petitioner is able to demonstrate that no alternative means of transportation is reasonably available and the petitioner will not endanger the public safety or welfare.

If a person's license or permit has been revoked or suspended due to 2 or more convictions of violating Section 11-501 of this Code or a similar provision of a local ordinance or a similar out-of-state offense, arising out of separate occurrences, that person, if issued a restricted driving permit, may not operate a vehicle unless it has been equipped with an ignition interlock device as defined in Section 1-129.1.

If a person's license or permit has been revoked or suspended 2 or more times within a 10 year period due to a single conviction of violating Section 11-501 of this Code or a similar provision of a local ordinance or a similar out-of-state offense, and a statutory summary suspension under Section 11-501.1, or 2 or more statutory summary suspensions, or combination of 2 offenses, or of an offense and a statutory summary suspension, arising out of separate occurrences, that person, if issued a restricted driving permit, may not operate a vehicle unless it has been equipped with an ignition interlock device as defined in Section 1-129.1. The person must pay to the Secretary of State DUI Administration Fund an amount not to exceed $20 per month. The Secretary shall establish by rule the amount and the procedures, terms, and conditions relating to these fees. If the restricted driving permit was issued for employment purposes, then this provision does not apply to the operation of an occupational vehicle owned or leased by that person's employer. In each case the Secretary may issue a restricted driving permit for a period deemed appropriate, except that all permits shall expire within one year from the date of issuance. The Secretary may not, however, issue a restricted driving permit to any person whose current revocation is the result of a second or subsequent conviction for a violation of Section 11-501 of this Code or a similar provision of a local ordinance relating to the offense of operating or being in physical control of a motor vehicle while under the influence of alcohol, other drug or drugs, intoxicating compound or compounds, or any similar out-of-state offense, or any combination of those offenses, until the expiration of at least one year from the date of the revocation. A restricted driving permit issued under this Section shall be subject to cancellation, revocation, and suspension by the Secretary of State in like manner and for like cause as a driver's license issued under this Code may be cancelled, revoked, or suspended; except that a conviction upon one or more offenses against laws or ordinances regulating the movement of traffic shall be deemed sufficient cause for the revocation, suspension, or cancellation of a restricted driving permit. The Secretary of State may, as a condition to the issuance of a restricted driving permit, require the applicant to participate in a designated driver remedial or rehabilitative program. The Secretary of State is authorized to cancel a restricted driving permit if the permit holder does not successfully complete the program.

(c-5) The Secretary of State may, as a condition of the reissuance of a driver's license or permit to an applicant whose driver's license or permit has been suspended before he or she reached the age of 18 years pursuant to any of the provisions of this Section, require the applicant to participate in a driver remedial education course and be retested under Section 6-109 of this Code.

(d) This Section is subject to the provisions of the Drivers License Compact.

(e) The Secretary of State shall not issue a restricted driving permit to a person under the age of 16 years whose driving privileges have been suspended or revoked under any provisions of this Code.

P.A. 76-1586, § 6-206, eff. July 1, 1970. Amended by P.A. 76-2156, § 1, eff. July 1, 1970; P.A. 77-2739, § 1, eff. Oct. 1, 1972; P.A. 78-663, § 1, eff. Jan. 1, 1974; P.A. 79-1141, § 1, eff. Jan. 1, 1976; P.A. 81-1400, § 1, eff. Aug. 25, 1980; P.A. 82-141, § 1, eff. Jan. 1, 1982; P.A. 82-311, § 1, eff. Jan. 1, 1982; P.A. 82-783, Art. III, § 37, eff. July 13, 1982; P.A. 83-466, § 1, eff. Sept. 17, 1983; P.A. 83-905, § 1, eff. Jan. 1, 1984; P.A. 83-1362, Art. II, § 99, eff. Sept. 11, 1984; P.A. 84-112, § 1, eff. July 25, 1985; P.A. 84-272, § 7, eff. Jan. 1, 1986; P.A. 84-300, § 1, eff. Sept. 13, 1985; P.A. 84-551, § 50, eff. Sept. 18, 1985; P.A. 84-772, § 1, eff. Jan. 1, 1986; P.A. 84-1308, Art. II, § 96, eff. Aug. 25, 1986; P.A. 84-1394, § 5, eff. Sept. 18, 1986; P.A. 85-813, § 1, eff. Jan. 1, 1988; P.A. 85-1259, § 3, eff. Jan. 1, 1989; P.A. 86-879, § 1, eff. Jan. 1, 1990; P.A. 86-929, § 2, eff. Sept. 21, 1989; P.A. 86-947, § 2, eff. Jan. 1, 1991; P.A. 86-1019, § 7, eff. July 1, 1990; P.A. 86-1475, Art. 2, § 2-25, eff. Jan. 10, 1991; P.A. 87-233, § 1, eff. Jan. 1, 1992; P.A. 87-929, § 1, eff. Jan. 1, 1993; P.A. 87-1114, § 1, eff. Sept. 15, 1992; P.A. 88-45, Art. II, § 2-54, eff. July 6, 1993; P.A. 88-209, § 5, eff. Jan. 1, 1994; P.A. 88-211, § 5, eff. Jan. 1, 1994; P.A. 88-670, Art. 2, § 2-59, eff. Dec. 2, 1994; P.A. 89-283, § 10, eff. Jan. 1, 1996; P.A. 89-428, Art. 2, § 250, eff. Dec. 13, 1995; P.A. 89-462, Art. 2, § 250, eff. May 29, 1996; P.A. 90-43, § 5, eff. July 2, 1997; P.A. 90-106, § 5, eff. Jan. 1, 1998; P.A. 90-369, § 5, eff. Jan. 1, 1998; P.A. 90-655, § 153, eff. July 30, 1998; P.A. 92-283, § 5, eff. Jan. 1, 2002; P.A. 92-418, § 10, eff. Aug. 17, 2001; P.A. 92-458, § 5, eff. Aug. 22, 2001; P.A. 92-651, § 77, eff. July 11, 2002; P.A. 92-814, § 5, eff. Jan. 1, 2003.

Formerly Ill.Rev.Stat.1991, ch. 95 ½, ¶ 6-206.

[1] 15 ILCS 335/14, 335/14A, or 335/14B.

[2] 720 ILCS 5/21-2.

[3] 720 ILCS 5/24.1.

[4] 235 ILCS 5/6-16.

[5] 720 ILCS 570/100 et seq.

[6] 720 ILCS 550/1 et seq.

[7] 720 ILSC 690/0.01 et seq.

[8] 720 ILSC 5/24-1.2.

For text of section as amended by P.A. 92-651 and P.A. 92-804, effective January 1, 2003, see 625 ILCS 5/6-206, ante

P.A. 89-428 was held by the Illinois Supreme Court to be in violation of the single subject requirement of subsection (d) of Section 8 of Article IV of the Illinois Constitution in the case of Johnson v. Edgar, 1997, 176 Ill.2d 499, 680 N.E.2d 1372, 224 Ill.Dec. 1. Public Act 89-462 reenacted the amendment of this text by P.A. 89-428.

P.A. 92–651, the First 2002 General Revisory Act, amended various Acts to delete obsolete text, to correct patent and technical errors, to revise cross references, to resolve multiple actions in the 91st and 92nd General Assemblies and to make certain technical corrections in P.A. 91–937 through P.A. 92–520.

P.A. 92–814 incorporated the amendments by P.A. 92–283, 92–418, and 92–458.

Final legislative action, 92nd General Assembly:

P.A. 92–651—May 14, 2002

P.A. 92–804—May 23, 2002

P.A. 92–814—May 31, 2002

See 5 ILCS 70/6 as to the effect of (1) more than one amendment of a section at the same session of the General Assembly or (2) two or more acts relating to the same subject matter enacted by the same General Assembly.

5/6–206.1. Judicial Driving Permit

§ 6–206.1. Judicial Driving Permit. Declaration of Policy. It is hereby declared a policy of the State of Illinois that the driver who is impaired by alcohol, other drug or drugs, or intoxicating compound or compounds is a threat to the public safety and welfare. Therefore, to provide a deterrent to such practice and to remove problem drivers from the highway, a statutory summary driver's license suspension is appropriate. It is also recognized that driving is a privilege and therefore, that in some cases the granting of limited driving privileges, where consistent with public safety, is warranted during the period of suspension in the form of a judicial driving permit to drive for the purpose of employment, receiving drug treatment or medical care, and educational pursuits, where no alternative means of transportation is available.

The following procedures shall apply whenever a first offender is arrested for any offense as defined in Section 11–501 or a similar provision of a local ordinance:

(a) Subsequent to a notification of a statutory summary suspension of driving privileges as provided in Section 11–501.1, the first offender as defined in Section 11–500 may petition the circuit court of venue for a Judicial Driving Permit, hereinafter referred as a JDP, to relieve undue hardship. The court may issue a court order, pursuant to the criteria contained in this Section, directing the Secretary of State to issue such a JDP to the petitioner. A JDP shall not become effective prior to the 31st day of the original statutory summary suspension and shall always be subject to the following criteria:

1. If ordered for the purposes of employment, the JDP shall be only for the purpose of providing the petitioner the privilege of driving a motor vehicle between the petitioner's residence and the petitioner's place of employment and return; or within the scope of the petitioner's employment related duties, shall be effective only during and limited to those specific times and routes actually required to commute or perform the petitioner's employment related duties.

2. The court, by a court order, may also direct the Secretary of State to issue a JDP to allow transportation for the petitioner, or a household member of the petitioner's family, to receive alcohol, drug, or intoxicating compound treatment or medical care, if the petitioner is able to demonstrate that no alternative means of transportation is reasonably available. Such JDP shall be effective only during the specific times actually required to commute.

3. The court, by a court order, may also direct the Secretary of State to issue a JDP to allow transportation by the petitioner for educational purposes upon demonstrating that there are no alternative means of transportation reasonably available to accomplish those educational purposes. Such JDP shall be only for the purpose of providing transportation to and from the petitioner's residence and the petitioner's place of educational activity, and only during the specific times and routes actually required to commute or perform the petitioner's educational requirement.

4. The Court shall not issue an order granting a JDP to:

(i) Any person unless and until the court, after considering the results of a current professional evaluation of the person's alcohol or other drug use by an agency pursuant to Section 15–10 of the Alcoholism and Other Drug Abuse and Dependency Act [1] and other appropriate investigation of the person, is satisfied that granting the privilege of driving a motor vehicle on the highways will not endanger the public safety or welfare.

(ii) Any person who has been convicted of reckless homicide within the previous 5 years.

(iii) Any person whose privilege to operate a motor vehicle was invalid at the time of arrest for the current violation of Section 11–501, or a similar provision of a local ordinance, except in cases where the cause for a driver's license suspension has been removed at the time a JDP is effective. In any case, should the Secretary of State enter a suspension or revocation of driving privileges pursuant to the provisions of this Code while the JDP is in effect or pending, the Secretary shall take the prescribed action and provide a notice to the person and the court ordering the issuance of the JDP that all driving privileges, including those provided by the issuance of the JDP, have been withdrawn.

(iv) Any person under the age of 18 years.

(b) Prior to ordering the issuance of a JDP the Court should consider at least, but not be limited to, the following issues:

1. Whether the person is employed and no other means of commuting to the place of employment is available or that the person must drive as a condition of employment. The employer shall certify the hours of employment and the need and parameters necessary for driving as a condition to employment.

2. Whether the person must drive to secure alcohol or other medical treatment for himself or a family member.

3. Whether the person must drive for educational purposes. The educational institution shall certify the person's enrollment in and academic schedule at the institution.

4. Whether the person has been repeatedly convicted of traffic violations or involved in motor vehicle accidents to a degree which indicates disrespect for public safety.

5. Whether the person has been convicted of a traffic violation in connection with a traffic accident resulting in the death of any person within the last 5 years.

6. Whether the person is likely to obey the limited provisions of the JDP.

7. Whether the person has any additional traffic violations pending in any court.

For purposes of this Section, programs conducting professional evaluations of a person's alcohol, other drug, or intoxicating compound use must report, to the court of venue, using a form prescribed by the Secretary of State. A copy of such evaluations shall be sent to the Secretary of State by the court. However, the evaluation information shall be privileged and only available to courts and to the Secretary of State, but shall not be admissible in the subsequent trial on the underlying charge.

(c) The scope of any court order issued for a JDP under this Section shall be limited to the operation of a motor vehicle as provided for in subsection (a) of this Section and shall specify the petitioner's residence, place of employment or location of educational institution, and the scope of job related duties, if relevant. The JDP shall also specify days of the week and specific hours of the day when the petitioner is able to exercise the limited privilege of operating a motor vehicle. If the Petitioner, who has been granted a JDP, is issued a citation for a traffic related offense, including operating a motor vehicle outside the limitations prescribed in the JDP or a violation of Section 6–303, or is convicted of any such an offense during the term of the JDP, the court shall consider cancellation of the limited driving permit. In any case, if the Petitioner commits an offense, as defined in Section 11–501, or a similar provision of a local ordinance, as evidenced by the issuance of a Uniform Traffic Ticket, the JDP shall be forwarded by the court of venue to the court ordering the issuance of the JDP, for cancellation. The court shall notify the Secretary of State of any such cancellation.

(d) The Secretary of State shall, upon receiving a court order from the court of venue, issue a JDP to a successful Petitioner under this Section. Such court order form shall also contain a notification, which shall be sent to the Secretary of State, providing the name, driver's license number and legal address of the successful petitioner, and the full and detailed description of the limitations of the JDP. This information shall be available only to the courts, police officers, and the Secretary of State, except during the actual period the JDP is valid, during which time it shall be a public record. The Secretary of State shall design and furnish to the courts an official court order form to be used by the courts when directing the Secretary of State to issue a JDP.

Any submitted court order that contains insufficient data or fails to comply with this Code shall not be utilized for JDP issuance or entered to the driver record but shall be returned to the issuing court indicating why the JDP cannot be so entered. A notice of this action shall also be sent to the JDP petitioner by the Secretary of State.

(e) The circuit court of venue may conduct the judicial hearing, as provided in Section 2–118.1, and the JDP hearing provided in this Section, concurrently. Such concurrent hearing shall proceed in the court in the same manner as in other civil proceedings.

(f) The circuit court of venue may, as a condition of the issuance of a JDP, prohibit the person from operating a motor vehicle not equipped with an ignition interlock device.

P.A. 76–1586, § 6–206.1, added by P.A. 84–272, § 7, eff. Jan. 1, 1986. Amended by P.A. 84–1394, § 5, eff. Sept. 18, 1986; P.A. 85–965, Art. XII, § 5, eff. July 1, 1988; P.A. 86–929, § 2, eff. Sept. 21, 1989; P.A. 88–670, Art. 3, § 3–80, eff. Dec. 2, 1994; P.A. 90–369, § 5, eff. Jan. 1, 1998; P.A. 90–779, § 5, eff. Jan. 1, 1999; P.A. 91–127, § 5, eff. Jan. 1, 2000.

Formerly Ill.Rev.Stat.1991, ch. 95 ½, ¶ 6–206.1.

[1] 20 ILCS 30/15–10.

5/6–206.2. Violations relating to an ignition interlock device

§ 6–206.2. Violations relating to an ignition interlock device.

(a) It is unlawful for any person whose driving privilege is restricted by being prohibited from operating a motor vehicle not equipped with an ignition interlock device to request or solicit any other person to blow into an ignition interlock device or to start a motor vehicle equipped with the device for the purpose of providing the person so restricted with an operable motor vehicle.

(b) It is unlawful to blow into an ignition interlock device or to start a motor vehicle equipped with the device for the purpose of providing an operable motor vehicle to a person whose driving privilege is restricted by being prohibited from operating a motor vehicle not equipped with an ignition interlock device.

(c) It is unlawful to tamper with, or circumvent the operation of, an ignition interlock device.

(d) Except as provided in subsection (c)(17) of Section 5–6–3.1 of the Unified Code of Corrections [1] or by rule, no person shall knowingly rent, lease, or lend a motor vehicle to a person known to have his or her driving privilege restricted by being prohibited from operating a vehicle not equipped with an ignition interlock device, unless the vehicle is equipped with a functioning ignition interlock device. Any person whose driving privilege is so restricted shall notify any person intending to rent, lease, or loan a motor vehicle to the restricted person of the driving restriction imposed upon him or her.

A person convicted of a violation of this subsection shall be punished by imprisonment for not more than 6 months or by a fine of not more than $5,000, or both.

(e) If a person prohibited under paragraph (2) or paragraph (3) of subsection (c–4) of Section 11–501 from driving any vehicle not equipped with an ignition interlock device nevertheless is convicted of driving a vehicle that is not equipped with the device, that person is prohibited from driving any vehicle not equipped with an ignition interlock device for an additional period of time equal to the initial time period that the person was required to use an ignition interlock device.

P.A. 76–1586, § 6–206.2, added by P.A. 91–127, § 5, eff. Jan. 1, 2000. Amended by P.A. 92–418, § 10, eff. Aug. 17, 2001.

[1] 730 ILCS 5/5–6–3.1.

5/6–207. Secretary of State may require reexamination or reissuance of a license

§ 6–207. Secretary of State may require reexamination or reissuance of a license.

(a) The Secretary of State, having good cause to believe that a licensed driver or person holding a permit or applying for a license or license renewal is incompetent or otherwise not qualified to hold a license or permit, may upon written notice of at least 5 days to the person require the person to submit to an examination as prescribed by the Secretary.

Refusal or neglect of the person to submit an alcohol, drug, or intoxicating compound evaluation or submit to or failure to successfully complete the examination is grounds for suspension of the person's license or permit under Section 6–206 of this Act or cancellation of his license or permit under Section 6–201 of this Act.

(b) The Secretary of State, having issued a driver's license or permit in error, may upon written notice of at least 5 days to the person, require the person to appear at a Driver Services facility to have the license or permit error corrected and a new license or permit issued.

Refusal or neglect of the person to appear is grounds for cancellation of the person's license or permit under Section 6–201 of this Act.

P.A. 76–1586, § 6–207, eff. July 1, 1970. Amended by P.A. 87–1114, § 1, eff. Sept. 15, 1992; P.A. 88–212, § 5, eff. Jan. 1, 1994; P.A. 90–779, § 5, eff. Jan. 1, 1999.

Formerly Ill.Rev.Stat.1991, ch. 95 ½, ¶ 6–207.

5/6–208. Period of Suspension—Application After Revocation

§ 6–208. Period of Suspension—Application After Revocation.

(a) Except as otherwise provided by this Code or any other law of this State, the Secretary of State shall not suspend a driver's license, permit or privilege to drive a motor vehicle on the highways for a period of more than one year.

(b) Any person whose license, permit or privilege to drive a motor vehicle on the highways has been revoked shall not be entitled to have such license, permit or privilege renewed or restored. However, such person may, except as provided under subsection (d) of Section 6–205, make application for a license pursuant to Section 6–106 (i) if the revocation was for a cause which has been removed or (ii) as provided in the following subparagraphs:

1. Except as provided in subparagraphs 2, 3, and 4, the person may make application for a license after the expiration of one year from the effective date of the revocation or, in the case of a violation of paragraph (b) of Section 11–401 of this Code or a similar provision of a local ordinance, after the expiration of 3 years from the effective date of the revocation or, in the case of a violation of Section 9–3 of the Criminal Code of 1961[1] relating to the offense of reckless homicide, after the expiration of 2 years from the effective date of the revocation or after the expiration of 24 months from the date of release from a period of imprisonment as provided in Section 6–103 of this Code, whichever is later.

2. If such person is convicted of committing a second violation within a 20 year period of:

(A) Section 11–501 of this Code, or a similar provision of a local ordinance; or

(B) Paragraph (b) of Section 11–401 of this Code, or a similar provision of a local ordinance; or

(C) Section 9–3 of the Criminal Code of 1961, as amended, relating to the offense of reckless homicide; or

(D) any combination of the above offenses committed at different instances;

then such person may not make application for a license until after the expiration of 5 years from the effective date of the most recent revocation. The 20 year period shall be computed by using the dates the offenses were committed and shall also include similar out-of-state offenses.

3. However, except as provided in subparagraph 4, if such person is convicted of committing a third, or subsequent, violation or any combination of the above offenses, including similar out-of-state offenses, contained in subparagraph 2, then such person may not make application for a license until after the expiration of 10 years from the effective date of the most recent revocation.

4. The person may not make application for a license if the person is convicted of committing a fourth or subsequent violation of Section 11–501 of this Code or a similar provision of a local ordinance, Section 11–401 of this Code, Section 9–3 of the Criminal Code of 1961, or a combination of these offenses or similar provisions of local ordinances or similar out-of-state offenses.

Notwithstanding any other provision of this Code, all persons referred to in this paragraph (b) may not have their privileges restored until the Secretary receives payment of the required reinstatement fee pursuant to subsection (b) of Section 6–118.

In no event shall the Secretary issue such license unless and until such person has had a hearing pursuant to this Code and the appropriate administrative rules and the Secretary is satisfied, after a review or investigation of such person, that to grant the privilege of driving a motor vehicle on the highways will not endanger the public safety or welfare.

(c) If a person prohibited under paragraph (2) or paragraph (3) of subsection (c–4) of Section 11–501 from driving any vehicle not equipped with an ignition interlock device nevertheless is convicted of driving a vehicle that is not equipped with the device, that person is prohibited from driving any vehicle not equipped with an ignition interlock device for an additional period of time equal to the initial time period that the person was required to use an ignition interlock device.

P.A. 76–1586, § 6–208, eff. July 1, 1970. Amended by P.A. 81–462, § 1, eff. Jan. 1, 1980; P.A. 84–1381, § 2, eff. Sept. 12, 1986; P.A. 85–303, § 1, eff. Jan. 1, 1988; P.A. 85–951, § 1, eff. July 1, 1988; P.A. 85–1209, Art. II, § 2–51, eff. Aug. 30, 1988; P.A. 89–156, § 5, eff. Jan. 1, 1996; P.A. 90–543, § 5, eff. Dec. 1, 1997; P.A. 90–738, § 5, eff. Jan. 1, 1999; P.A. 91–357, § 231, eff. July 29, 1999; P.A. 92–343, § 5, eff. Jan. 1, 2002; P.A. 92–418, § 10, eff. Aug. 17, 2001; P.A. 92–458, § 5, eff. Aug. 22, 2001; P.A. 92–651, § 77, eff. July 11, 2002.

Formerly Ill.Rev.Stat.1991, ch. 95 ½, ¶ 6–208.

[1] 720 ILCS 5/9–3.

P.A. 92–651, the First 2002 General Revisory Act, amended various Acts to delete obsolete text, to correct patent and technical errors, to revise cross references, to resolve multiple actions in the 91st and 92nd General Assemblies and to make certain technical corrections in P.A. 91–937 through P.A. 92–520.

5/6–208.1. Period of statutory summary alcohol, other drug, or intoxicating compound related suspension

§ 6–208.1. Period of statutory summary alcohol, other drug, or intoxicating compound related suspension.

(a) Unless the statutory summary suspension has been rescinded, any person whose privilege to drive a motor vehicle on the public highways has been summarily suspended, pursuant to Section 11-501.1, shall not be eligible for restoration of the privilege until the expiration of:

1. Six months from the effective date of the statutory summary suspension for a refusal or failure to complete a test or tests to determine the alcohol, drug, or intoxicating compound concentration, pursuant to Section 11-501.1; or

2. Three months from the effective date of the statutory summary suspension imposed following the person's submission to a chemical test which disclosed an alcohol concentration of 0.08 or more, or any amount of a drug, substance, or intoxicating compound in such person's breath, blood, or urine resulting from the unlawful use or consumption of cannabis listed in the Cannabis Control Act,[1] a controlled substance listed in the Illinois Controlled Substances Act,[2] or an intoxicating compound listed in the Use of Intoxicating Compounds Act,[3] pursuant to Section 11-501.1; or

3. Three years from the effective date of the statutory summary suspension for any person other than a first offender who refuses or fails to complete a test or tests to determine the alcohol, drug, or intoxicating compound concentration pursuant to Section 11-501.1; or

4. One year from the effective date of the summary suspension imposed for any person other than a first offender following submission to a chemical test which disclosed an alcohol concentration of 0.08 or more pursuant to Section 11-501.1 or any amount of a drug, substance or compound in such person's blood or urine resulting from the unlawful use or consumption of cannabis listed in the Cannabis Control Act, a controlled substance listed in the Illinois Controlled Substances Act, or an intoxicating compound listed in the Use of Intoxicating Compounds Act.

(b) Following a statutory summary suspension of the privilege to drive a motor vehicle under Section 11-501.1, full driving privileges shall be restored unless the person is otherwise disqualified by this Code. If the court has reason to believe that the person's driving privilege should not be restored, the court shall notify the Secretary of State prior to the expiration of the statutory summary suspension so appropriate action may be taken pursuant to this Code.

(c) Full driving privileges may not be restored until all applicable reinstatement fees, as provided by this Code, have been paid to the Secretary of State and the appropriate entry made to the driver's record.

(d) Where a driving privilege has been summarily suspended under Section 11-501.1 and the person is subsequently convicted of violating Section 11-501, or a similar provision of a local ordinance, for the same incident, any period served on statutory summary suspension shall be credited toward the minimum period of revocation of driving privileges imposed pursuant to Section 6-205.

(e) Following a statutory summary suspension of driving privileges pursuant to Section 11-501.1, for a first offender, the circuit court may, after at least 30 days from the effective date of the statutory summary suspension, issue a judicial driving permit as provided in Section 6-206.1.

(f) Subsequent to an arrest of a first offender, for any offense as defined in Section 11-501 or a similar provision of a local ordinance, following a statutory summary suspension of driving privileges pursuant to Section 11-501.1, for a first offender, the circuit court may issue a court order directing the Secretary of State to issue a judicial driving permit as provided in Section 6-206.1. However, this JDP shall not be effective prior to the 31st day of the statutory summary suspension.

(g) Following a statutory summary suspension of driving privileges pursuant to Section 11-501.1 where the person was not a first offender, as defined in Section 11-500, the Secretary of State may not issue a restricted driving permit.

(h) (Blank).

P.A. 76-1586, § 6-208.1, added by P.A. 84-272, § 7, eff. Jan. 1, 1986. Amended by P.A. 84-1394, § 5, eff. Sept. 18, 1986; P.A. 86-929, § 2, eff. Sept. 21, 1989; P.A. 86-1019, § 7, eff. July 1, 1990; P.A. 87-461, § 1, eff. Jan. 1, 1992; P.A. 88-415, § 10, eff. Aug. 20, 1993; P.A. 89-203, § 20, eff. July 21, 1995; P.A. 90-43, § 5, eff. July 2, 1997; P.A. 90-738, § 5, eff. Jan. 1, 1999; P.A. 90-779, § 5, eff. Jan. 1, 1999; P.A. 91-357, § 231, eff. July 29, 1999; P.A. 92-248, § 5, eff. Aug. 3, 2001.

Formerly Ill.Rev.Stat.1991, ch. 95 ½, ¶ 6-208.1.

[1] 720 ILCS 550/1 et seq.

[2] 35 ILCS 570/1 et seq.

[3] 720 ILCS 690/0.01 et seq.

Validity

On November 18, 1999, the Supreme Court of Illinois held that P.A. 89-203 violated the single-subject rule of the Illinois Constitution in the case of People v. Wooters, 1999, 243 Ill.Dec. 33, 188 Ill.2d 500, 722 N.E.2d 1102.

5/6-208.2. Restoration of driving privileges; persons under age 21

§ 6-208.2. Restoration of driving privileges; persons under age 21.

(a) Unless the suspension based upon consumption of alcohol by a minor or refusal to submit to testing has been rescinded by the Secretary of State in accordance with item (c)(3) of Section 6-206 of this Code, a person whose privilege to drive a motor vehicle on the public highways has been suspended under Section 11-501.8 is not eligible for restoration of the privilege until the expiration of:

1. Six months from the effective date of the suspension for a refusal or failure to complete a test or tests to determine the alcohol concentration under Section 11-501.8;

2. Three months from the effective date of the suspension imposed following the person's submission to a chemical test which disclosed an alcohol concentration greater than 0.00 under Section 11-501.8;

3. Two years from the effective date of the suspension for a person who has been previously suspended under Section 11-501.8 and who refuses or fails to complete a test or tests to determine the alcohol concentration under Section 11-501.8; or

4. One year from the effective date of the suspension imposed for a person who has been previously suspended under Section 11-501.8 following submission to a chemical test that disclosed an alcohol concentration greater than 0.00 under Section 11-501.8.

(b) Following a suspension of the privilege to drive a motor vehicle under Section 11-501.8, full driving privileges shall be restored unless the person is otherwise disqualified by this Code.

(c) Full driving privileges may not be restored until all applicable reinstatement fees, as provided by this Code, have been paid to the Secretary of State and the appropriate entry made to the driver's record. The Secretary of State may also, as a condition of the reissuance of a driver's license or permit to an individual under the age of 18 years whose driving privileges have been suspended pursuant to Section 11–501.8, require the applicant to participate in a driver remedial education course and be retested under Section 6–109.

(d) Where a driving privilege has been suspended under Section 11–501.8 and the person is subsequently convicted of violating Section 11–501, or a similar provision of a local ordinance, for the same incident, any period served on that suspension shall be credited toward the minimum period of revocation of driving privileges imposed under Section 6–205.

(e) Following a suspension of driving privileges under Section 11–501.8 for a person who has not had his or her driving privileges previously suspended under that Section, the Secretary of State may issue a restricted driving permit after at least 30 days from the effective date of the suspension.

(f) Following a second or subsequent suspension of driving privileges under Section 11–501.8, the Secretary of State may issue a restricted driving permit after at least 12 months from the effective date of the suspension.

(g) (Blank).

(h) Any restricted driving permit considered under this Section is subject to the provisions of item (e) of Section 11–501.8.

P.A. 76–1586, § 6–208.2, added by P.A. 88–588, § 5, eff. Jan. 1, 1995. Amended by P.A. 90–774, § 5, eff. Aug. 14, 1998; P.A. 92–248, § 5, eff. Aug. 3, 2001.

5/6–209. Notice of cancellation, suspension or revocation—Surrender and return of license

§ 6–209. Notice of cancellation, suspension or revocation—Surrender and return of license. The Secretary of State upon cancelling, suspending or revoking a license or permit shall immediately notify the holder thereof in writing and shall require that such license or permit shall be surrendered to and retained by the Secretary of State. However, upon payment of the reinstatement fee set out in subsection (g) of Section 6–118 at the end of any period of suspension of a license the licensee, if not ineligible for some other reason, shall be entitled to reinstatement of driving privileges and the return of his license if it has not then expired; or, in case it has expired, to apply for a new license.

P.A. 76–1586, § 6–209, eff. July 1, 1970. Amended by P.A. 81–462, § 1, eff. Jan. 1, 1980.

Formerly Ill.Rev.Stat.1991, ch. 95 ½, ¶ 6–209.

5/6–210. No operation under foreign license during suspension or revocation in this State

§ 6–210. No operation under foreign license during suspension or revocation in this State.

Any resident or nonresident whose drivers license or permit or privilege to operate a motor vehicle in this State has been suspended or revoked as provided in this Act shall not operate a motor vehicle in this State:

(1) during the period of such suspension, except as permitted by a restricted driving permit issued under the provisions of Section 6–206 of this Act; or

(2) after such revocation until a license is obtained when and as permitted under this Act, except as permitted by a restricted driving permit issued under the provisions of Section 6–205 of this Act.

P.A. 76–1586, § 6–210, eff. July 1, 1970. Amended by P.A. 92–16, § 85, eff. June 28, 2001.

Formerly Ill.Rev.Stat.1991, ch. 95 ½, ¶ 6–210.

5/6–211. Secretary of State to administer act—Notices required

§ 6–211. Secretary of State to administer act—Notices required. (a) The Secretary of State shall administer the provisions of this Chapter and may make and enforce rules and regulations relating to its administration.

(b) The Secretary of State shall either provide or prescribe suitable forms requisite or deemed necessary by him for the purposes of this Chapter.

(c) Whenever under the provisions of this Chapter the Secretary of State is required to give notice to any person such notice shall be deemed to have been served either when personally delivered or when deposited in the United States mail, in a sealed envelope, with postage prepaid, addressed to the party affected thereby at his last known residence or place of business.

P.A. 76–1586, § 6–211, eff. July 1, 1970.

Formerly Ill.Rev.Stat.1991, ch. 95 ½, ¶ 6–211.

5/6–212. Court Review

§ 6–212. Court Review. The provisions of the Administrative Review Law, and all amendments and modifications thereof,[1] and the rules adopted pursuant thereto, shall apply to and govern all proceedings for the judicial review of final administrative decisions of the Secretary of State hereunder.

P.A. 76–1586, § 6–212, eff. July 1, 1970. Amended by P.A. 82–783, Art. XI, § 140, eff. July 13, 1982.

Formerly Ill.Rev.Stat.1991, ch. 95 ½, ¶ 6–212.

1 735 ILCS 5/3–101 et seq.

ARTICLE III. VIOLATION OF LICENSE PROVISIONS

Section

5/6–301. Unlawful use of license or permit

§ 6–301. Unlawful use of license or permit.

(a) It is a violation of this Section for any person:

1. To display or cause to be displayed or have in his possession any cancelled, revoked or suspended license or permit;

2. To lend his license or permit to any other person or knowingly allow the use thereof by another;

3. To display or represent as his own any license or permit issued to another;

4. To fail or refuse to surrender to the Secretary of State or his agent or any peace officer upon his lawful demand, any license or permit, which has been suspended, revoked or cancelled;

5. To allow any unlawful use of a license or permit issued to him;

6. To submit to an examination or to obtain the services of another person to submit to an examination for the purpose of obtaining a drivers license or permit for some other person.

(b) Sentence.

1. Any person convicted of a violation of this Section shall be guilty of a Class A misdemeanor and shall be sentenced to a minimum fine of $500 or 50 hours of community service, preferably at an alcohol abuse prevention program, if available.

2. Any person convicted of a second or subsequent violation of this Section shall be guilty of a Class 4 felony.

3. In addition to any other sentence imposed under paragraph 1 or 2 of this subsection (b), a person convicted of a violation of paragraph 6 of subsection (a) shall be imprisoned for not less than 7 days.

(c) This Section does not prohibit any lawfully authorized investigative, protective, law enforcement or other activity of any agency of the United States, State of Illinois or any other state or political subdivision thereof.

(d) This Section does not apply to licenses and permits invalidated under Section 6–301.3 of this Code.

P.A. 76–1586, § 6–301, eff. July 1, 1970. Amended by P.A. 77–2830, Art. 73, § 1, eff. Jan. 1, 1973; P.A. 80–911, § 1, eff. Oct. 1, 1977; P.A. 81–306, § 1, eff. Aug. 30, 1979; P.A. 86–503, § 1, eff. Sept. 1, 1989; P.A. 88–197, § 5, eff. Aug. 5, 1993; P.A. 88–210, § 10, eff. Jan. 1, 1994; P.A. 88–670, Art. 2, § 2–59, eff. Dec. 2, 1994; P.A. 92–647, § 5, eff. Jan. 1, 2003; P.A. 92–883, § 5, eff. Jan. 13, 2003.

Formerly Ill.Rev.Stat.1991, ch. 95 ½, ¶ 6–301.

P.A. 88–670, Article 2, of the First 1994 General Revisory Act, resolved multiple actions in the 88th General Assembly and made certain technical corrections in P.A. 88–1 through P.A. 88–538.

P.A. 92–883 incorporated the amendment by P.A. 92–647.

5/6–301.1. Fictitious or unlawfully altered driver's license or permit

§ 6–301.1. Fictitious or unlawfully altered driver's license or permit.

(a) As used in this Section:

1. "A fictitious driver's license or permit" means any issued license or permit for which a computerized number and file have been created by the Secretary of State or other official driver's license agency in another jurisdiction which contains false information concerning the identity of the individual issued the license or permit;

2. "False information" means any information concerning the name, sex, date of birth, social security number or any photograph that falsifies all or in part the actual identity of the individual issued the license or permit;

3. "An unlawfully altered driver's license or permit" means any issued license or permit for which a computerized number and file have been created by the Secretary of State or other official driver's license agency in another jurisdiction which has been physically altered or changed in such a manner that false information appears upon the license or permit;

4. "A document capable of defrauding another" includes, but is not limited to, any document by which any right, obligation or power with reference to any person or property may be created, transferred, altered or terminated;

5. "An identification document" means any document made or issued by or under the authority of the United States Government, the State of Illinois or any other state or political subdivision thereof, or any other governmental or quasi-governmental organization which, when completed with information concerning the individual, is of a type intended or commonly accepted for the purpose of identification of an individual;

6. "Common carrier" means any public or private provider of transportation, whether by land, air, or water.

(b) It is a violation of this Section for any person:

1. To knowingly possess any fictitious or unlawfully altered driver's license or permit;

2. To knowingly possess, display or cause to be displayed any fictitious or unlawfully altered driver's license or permit for the purpose of obtaining any account, credit, credit card or debit card from a bank, financial institution or retail mercantile establishment;

3. To knowingly possess any fictitious or unlawfully altered driver's license or permit with the intent to commit a theft, deception or credit or debit card fraud in violation of any law of this State or any law of any other jurisdiction;

4. To knowingly possess any fictitious or unlawfully altered driver's license or permit with the intent to commit any other violation of any law of this State or any law of any other jurisdiction for which a sentence to a term of imprisonment in a penitentiary for one year or more is provided;

5. To knowingly possess any fictitious or unlawfully altered driver's license or permit while in possession without authority of any document, instrument or device capable of defrauding another;

6. To knowingly possess any fictitious or unlawfully altered driver's license or permit with the intent to use the license or permit to acquire any other identification document;

7. To knowingly issue or assist in the issuance of any fictitious driver's license or permit;

8. To knowingly alter or attempt to alter any driver's license or permit;

9. To knowingly manufacture, possess, transfer or provide any identification document whether real or fictitious for the purpose of obtaining a fictitious driver's license or permit;

10. To knowingly use any fictitious or unlawfully altered driver's license or permit to purchase or attempt to purchase any ticket for a common carrier or to board or attempt to board any common carrier;

11. To knowingly possess any fictitious or unlawfully altered driver's license or permit if the person has at the time a different driver's license issued by the Illinois Secretary of State or other official driver's license agency in another jurisdiction that is suspended or revoked.

(c) Sentence.

1. Any person convicted of a violation of paragraph 1 of subsection (b) of this Section shall be guilty of a Class A misdemeanor and shall be sentenced to minimum fine of $500 or 50 hours of community service, preferably at an alcohol abuse prevention program, if available. A person convicted of a second or subsequent violation shall be guilty of a Class 4 felony.

2. Any person convicted of a violation of paragraph 3 of subsection (b) of this Section who at the time of arrest had in his possession two or more fictitious or unlawfully altered driver's licenses or permits shall be guilty of a Class 4 felony.

3. Any person convicted of a violation of any of paragraphs 2 through 11 of subsection (b) of this Section shall be guilty of a Class 4 felony. A person convicted of a second or subsequent violation shall be guilty of a Class 3 felony.

(d) This Section does not prohibit any lawfully authorized investigative, protective, law enforcement or other activity of any agency of the United States, State of Illinois or any other state or political subdivision thereof.

P.A. 76–1586, § 6–301.1, added by P.A. 81–306, § 1, eff. Aug. 30, 1979. Amended by P.A. 86–503, § 1, eff. Sept. 1, 1989; P.A. 86–551, § 1, eff. Jan. 1, 1990; P.A. 86–1028, Art. II, § 2–44, eff. Feb. 5, 1990; P.A. 88–210, § 10, eff. Jan. 1, 1994; P.A. 92–673, § 5, eff. Jan. 1, 2003.

Formerly Ill.Rev.Stat.1991, ch. 95 ½, ¶ 6–301.1.

5/6–301.2. Fraudulent driver's license or permit

§ 6–301.2. Fraudulent driver's license or permit.

(a) (Blank).

(b) It is a violation of this Section for any person:

1. To knowingly possess any fraudulent driver's license or permit;

2. To knowingly possess, display or cause to be displayed any fraudulent driver's license or permit for the purpose of obtaining any account, credit, credit card or debit card from a bank, financial institution or retail mercantile establishment;

3. To knowingly possess any fraudulent driver's license or permit with the intent to commit a theft, deception or credit or debit card fraud in violation of any law of this State or any law of any other jurisdiction;

4. To knowingly possess any fraudulent driver's license or permit with the intent to commit any other violation of any laws of this State or any law of any other jurisdiction for which a sentence to a term of imprisonment in a penitentiary for one year or more is provided;

5. To knowingly possess any fraudulent driver's license or permit while in unauthorized possession of any document, instrument or device capable of defrauding another;

6. To knowingly possess any fraudulent driver's license or permit with the intent to use the license or permit to acquire any other identification document;

7. To knowingly possess without authority any driver's license-making or permit-making implement;

8. To knowingly possess any stolen driver's license-making or permit- making implement;

9. To knowingly duplicate, manufacture, sell or transfer any fraudulent driver's license or permit;

10. To advertise or distribute any information or materials that promote the selling, giving, or furnishing of a fraudulent driver's license or permit;

11. To knowingly use any fraudulent driver's license or permit to purchase or attempt to purchase any ticket for a common carrier or to board or attempt to board any common carrier. As used in this Section, "common carrier" means any public or private provider of transportation, whether by land, air, or water;

12. To knowingly possess any fraudulent driver's license or permit if the person has at the time a different driver's license issued by the Secretary of State or another official driver's license agency in another jurisdiction that is suspended or revoked.

(c) Sentence.

1. Any person convicted of a violation of paragraph 1 of subsection (b) of this Section shall be guilty of a Class 4 felony and shall be sentenced to a minimum fine of $500 or 50 hours of community service, preferably at an alcohol abuse prevention program, if available.

2. Any person convicted of a violation of any of paragraphs 2 through 9 or paragraph 11 or 12 of subsection (b) of this Section shall be guilty of a Class 4 felony. A person convicted of a second or subsequent violation shall be guilty of a Class 3 felony.

3. Any person convicted of a violation of paragraph 10 of subsection (b) of this Section shall be guilty of a Class B misdemeanor.

(d) This Section does not prohibit any lawfully authorized investigative, protective, law enforcement or other activity of any agency of the United States, State of Illinois or any other state or political subdivision thereof.

(e) The Secretary may request the Attorney General to seek a restraining order in the circuit court against any person who violates this Section by advertising fraudulent driver's licenses or permits.

P.A. 76–1586, § 6–301.2, added by P.A. 86–503, § 1, eff. Sept. 1, 1989. Amended by P.A. 86–1028, Art. II, § 2–44, eff. Feb. 5, 1990; P.A. 88–210, § 10, eff. Jan. 1, 1994; P.A. 89–283, § 10, eff. Jan. 1, 1996; P.A. 90–89, § 15, eff. Jan. 1, 1998; P.A. 90–191, § 10, eff. Jan. 1, 1998; P.A. 90–655, § 153, eff. July 30, 1998; P.A. 92–673, § 5, eff. Jan. 1, 2003.

Formerly Ill.Rev.Stat.1991, ch. 95 ½, ¶ 6–301.2.

P.A. 90–655, the First 1998 General Revisory Act, amended various Acts to delete obsolete text, to correct patent and technical errors, to revise cross references, to resolve multiple actions in the 89th and 90th General Assemblies and to make certain technical corrections in P.A. 89–708 through P.A. 90–566.

5/6-301.3. Invalidation of a driver's license or permit

§ 6-301.3. Invalidation of a driver's license or permit.

(a) The Secretary of State may invalidate a driver's license or permit when:

(1) when the holder voluntarily surrenders the license or permit and declares his or her intention to do so in writing to the Secretary;

(2) when the Secretary receives a certified court order indicating the holder is to refrain from driving;

(3) upon the death of the holder; or

(4) as the Secretary deems appropriate by administrative rule.

(b) A driver's license or permit invalidated under this Section shall nullify the holder's driving privileges. If a license is invalidated under subdivision (a)(3) of this Section, the actual license or permit may be released to a relative of the decedent; provided, the actual license or permit bears a readily identifiable designation evidencing invalidation as prescribed by the Secretary.

P.A. 76-1586, § 6-301.3, added by P.A. 88-197, § 5, eff. Aug. 5, 1993 Amended by P.A. 91-357, § 231, eff. July 29, 1999.

5/6-302. Making false application or affidavit—Perjury

§ 6-302. Making false application or affidavit—Perjury.

(a) It is a violation of this Section for any person:

1. To display or present any document for the purpose of making application for a driver's license or permit knowing that such document contains false information concerning the identity of the applicant;

2. To accept or allow to be accepted any document displayed or presented for the purpose of making application for a driver's license or permit knowing that such document contains false information concerning the identity of the applicant;

3. To knowingly make any false affidavit or swear or affirm falsely to any matter or thing required by the terms of this Act to be sworn to or affirmed.

(b) Sentence.

1. Any person convicted of a violation of this Section shall be guilty of a Class 4 felony.

2. Any person convicted of a second or subsequent violation of this Section shall be guilty of a Class 3 felony.

(c) This Section does not prohibit any lawfully authorized investigative, protective, law enforcement or other activity of any agency of the United States, State of Illinois or any other state or political subdivision thereof.

P.A. 76-1586, § 6-302, eff. July 1, 1970. Amended by P.A. 86-503, § 1, eff. Sept. 1, 1989.

Formerly Ill.Rev.Stat.1991, ch. 95 ½, ¶ 6-302.

5/6-303. Driving while driver's license, permit or privilege to operate a motor vehicle is suspended or revoked

§ 6-303. Driving while driver's license, permit or privilege to operate a motor vehicle is suspended or revoked.

(a) Any person who drives or is in actual physical control of a motor vehicle on any highway of this State at a time when such person's driver's license, permit or privilege to do so or the privilege to obtain a driver's license or permit is revoked or suspended as provided by this Code or the law of another state, except as may be specifically allowed by a judicial driving permit, family financial responsibility driving permit, probationary license to drive, or a restricted driving permit issued pursuant to this Code or under the law of another state, shall be guilty of a Class A misdemeanor.

(b) The Secretary of State upon receiving a report of the conviction of any violation indicating a person was operating a motor vehicle during the time when said person's driver's license, permit or privilege was suspended by the Secretary, by the appropriate authority of another state, or pursuant to Section 11-501.1; except as may be specifically allowed by a probationary license to drive, judicial driving permit or restricted driving permit issued pursuant to this Code or the law of another state; shall extend the suspension for the same period of time as the originally imposed suspension; however, if the period of suspension has then expired, the Secretary shall be authorized to suspend said person's driving privileges for the same period of time as the originally imposed suspension; and if the conviction was upon a charge which indicated that a vehicle was operated during the time when the person's driver's license, permit or privilege was revoked; except as may be allowed by a restricted driving permit issued pursuant to this Code or the law of another state; the Secretary shall not issue a driver's license for an additional period of one year from the date of such conviction indicating such person was operating a vehicle during such period of revocation.

(c) Any person convicted of violating this Section shall serve a minimum term of imprisonment of 10 consecutive days or 30 days of community service when the person's driving privilege was revoked or suspended as a result of:

(1) a violation of Section 11-501 of this Code or a similar provision of a local ordinance relating to the offense of operating or being in physical control of a vehicle while under the influence of alcohol, any other drug or any combination thereof; or

(2) a violation of paragraph (b) of Section 11-401 of this Code or a similar provision of a local ordinance relating to the offense of leaving the scene of a motor vehicle accident involving personal injury or death; or

(3) a violation of Section 9-3 of the Criminal Code of 1961,[1] as amended, relating to the offense of reckless homicide; or

(4) a statutory summary suspension under Section 11-501.1 of this Code.

Such sentence of imprisonment or community service shall not be subject to suspension in order to reduce such sentence.

(c-1) Except as provided in subsection (d), any person convicted of a second violation of this Section shall be ordered by the court to serve a minimum of 100 hours of community service.

(c-2) In addition to other penalties imposed under this Section, the court may impose on any person convicted a fourth time of violating this Section any of the following:

(1) Seizure of the license plates of the person's vehicle.

(2) Immobilization of the person's vehicle for a period of time to be determined by the court.

(d) Any person convicted of a second violation of this Section shall be guilty of a Class 4 felony and shall serve a minimum term of imprisonment of 30 days or 300 hours of community service, as determined by the court, if the revocation or suspension was for a violation of Section 11-401 or 11-501 of this Code, or a similar out-of-state offense, or a similar provision of a local ordinance, a violation of Section 9-

3 of the Criminal Code of 1961, relating to the offense of reckless homicide, or a similar out-of-state offense, or a statutory summary suspension under Section 11–501.1 of this Code.

(d–1) Except as provided in subsection (d–2) and subsection (d–3), any person convicted of a third or subsequent violation of this Section shall serve a minimum term of imprisonment of 30 days or 300 hours of community service, as determined by the court.

(d–2) Any person convicted of a third violation of this Section is guilty of a Class 4 felony and must serve a minimum term of imprisonment of 30 days if the revocation or suspension was for a violation of Section 11–401 or 11–501 of this Code, or a similar out-of-state offense, or a similar provision of a local ordinance, a violation of Section 9–3 of the Criminal Code of 1961, relating to the offense of reckless homicide, or a similar out-of-state offense, or a statutory summary suspension under Section 11–501. 1 of this Code.

(d–3) Any person convicted of a fourth or subsequent violation of this Section is guilty of a Class 4 felony and must serve a minimum term of imprisonment of 180 days if the revocation or suspension was for a violation of Section 11–401 or 11–501 of this Code, or a similar out-of-state offense, or a similar provision of a local ordinance, a violation of Section 9–3 of the Criminal Code of 1961, relating to the offense of reckless homicide, or a similar out-of-state offense, or a statutory summary suspension under Section 11–501.1 of this Code.

(e) Any person in violation of this Section who is also in violation of Section 7–601 of this Code relating to mandatory insurance requirements, in addition to other penalties imposed under this Section, shall have his or her motor vehicle immediately impounded by the arresting law enforcement officer. The motor vehicle may be released to any licensed driver upon a showing of proof of insurance for the vehicle that was impounded and the notarized written consent for the release by the vehicle owner.

(f) For any prosecution under this Section, a certified copy of the driving abstract of the defendant shall be admitted as proof of any prior conviction.

(g) The motor vehicle used in a violation of this Section is subject to seizure and forfeiture as provided in Sections 36–1 and 36–2 of the Criminal Code of 1961 if the person's driving privilege was revoked or suspended as a result of a violation listed in paragraph (1), (2), or (3) of subsection (c) of this Section or as a result of a summary suspension as provided in paragraph (4) of subsection (c) of this Section.

P.A. 76–1586, § 6–303, eff. July 1, 1970. Amended by P.A. 77–2720, § 1, eff. Jan. 1, 1973; P.A. 80–1462, § 1, eff. Jan. 1, 1979; P.A. 83–206, § 2, eff. Jan. 1, 1984; P.A. 84–272, § 7, eff. Jan. 1, 1986; P.A. 84–1394, § 5, eff. Sept. 18, 1986; P.A. 88–383, § 5, eff. Jan. 1, 1994; P.A. 88–680, Art. 20, § 20–900, eff. Jan. 1, 1995; P.A. 89–8, Art. 1, § 1–5, eff. March 21, 1995; P.A. 89–92, § 10, eff. July 1, 1996; P.A. 89–156, § 5, eff. Jan. 1, 1996; P.A. 89–626, Art. 2, § 2–66, eff. Aug. 9, 1996; P.A. 90–400, § 5, eff. Aug. 15, 1997; P.A. 90–738, § 5, eff. Jan. 1, 1999; Re-enacted by P.A; 91–692, Art. 20, § 20–900, eff. April 13, 2000. Amended by P.A. 92–340, § 5, eff. Aug. 10, 2001; P.A. 92–688, § 5, eff. July 16, 2002.

Formerly Ill.Rev.Stat.1991, ch. 95 ½, ¶ 6–303.

[1] 720 ILCS 5/9–3.

Validity

The Supreme Court of Illinois held that P.A. 88–680 violated the single-subject rule of the Illinois Constitution in the case of People v. Cervantes, 1999, 243 Ill.Dec. 233, 189 Ill.2d 80, 723 N.E.2d 265; P.A. 91–692 re-enacted this section as contained in P.A. 88–680, including subsequent amendments in order "to remove any question as to the validity or content of those provisions."

Section 1 of P.A. 91–692, approved and eff. April 13, 2000, provides: "Purpose.

"(1) The General Assembly finds and declares that:

"(i) Public Act 88–680, effective January 1, 1995, contained provisions amending the Illinois Vehicle Code. Public Act 88–680 also contained other provisions.

"(ii) In addition, Public Act 88–680 was entitled "AN ACT to create a Safe Neighborhoods Law". (A) Article 5 was entitled JUVENILE JUSTICE and amended the Juvenile Court Act of 1987. (B) Article 15 was entitled GANGS and amended various provisions of the Criminal Code of 1961 and the Unified Code of Corrections. (C) Article 20 was entitled ALCOHOL ABUSE and amended various provisions of the Illinois Vehicle Code. (D) Article 25 was entitled DRUG ABUSE and amended the Cannabis Control Act and the Illinois Controlled Substances Act. (E) Article 30 was entitled FIREARMS and amended the Criminal Code of 1961 and the Code of Criminal Procedure of 1963. (F) Article 35 amended the Criminal Code of 1961, the Rights of Crime Victims and Witnesses Act, and the Unified Code of Corrections. (G) Article 40 amended the Criminal Code of 1961 to increase the penalty for compelling organization membership of persons. (H) Article 45 created the Secure Residential Youth Care Facility Licensing Act and amended the State Finance Act, the Juvenile Court Act of 1987, the Unified Code of Corrections, and the Private Correctional Facility Moratorium Act. (I) Article 50 amended the WIC Vendor Management Act, the Firearm Owners Identification Card Act, the Juvenile Court Act of 1987, the Criminal Code of 1961, the Wrongs to Children Act, and the Unified Code of Corrections.

"(iii) On December 2, 1999, the Illinois Supreme Court, in People v. Cervantes, Docket No. 87229, ruled that Public Act 88–680 violates the single subject clause of the Illinois Constitution (Article IV, Section 8 (d)) and was unconstitutional in its entirety.

"(iv) The provisions of Public Act 88–680 amending the Illinois Vehicle Code are of vital concern to the people of this State and legislative action concerning those provisions of Public Act 88–680 is necessary.

"(2) It is the purpose of this Act to re-enact the provisions of Public Act 88–680 amending the Illinois Vehicle Code, including subsequent amendments. This re-enactment is intended to remove any question as to the validity or content of those provisions.

"(3) This Act re-enacts various provisions of Public Act 88–680 amending the Illinois Vehicle Code, including subsequent amendments, to remove any question as to the validity or content of those provisions; it is not intended to supersede any other Public Act that amends the text of the Sections as set forth in this Act. The material is shown as existing text (i.e., without underscoring)."

P.A. 92–688 incorporated the amendment by P.A. 92–340.

5/6–304. Permitting unauthorized person to drive

§ 6–304. Permitting unauthorized person to drive. No person shall cause, authorize or knowingly permit a motor vehicle owned by him or under his control to be driven upon any highway by any person who is not authorized hereunder or in violation of any of the provisions of this Act.

P.A. 76–1586, § 6–304, eff. July 1, 1970.

Formerly Ill.Rev.Stat.1991, ch. 95 ½, ¶ 6–304.

5/6–304.1. Permitting a driver under the influence to operate a motor vehicle

§ 6–304.1. Permitting a driver under the influence to operate a motor vehicle. No person shall knowingly cause, authorize, or permit a motor vehicle owned by, or under the control of, such person to be driven or operated upon a highway by anyone who is under the influence of alcohol, other drugs, or combination thereof. This provision shall not apply to a spouse of the person who owns or has control of, or a co-owner of, a motor vehicle or to a bailee for hire.

Any person convicted of violating this Section shall be guilty of a Class A misdemeanor.

P.A. 76–1586, § 6–304.1, added by P.A. 84–272, § 7, eff. Jan. 1, 1986. Amended by P.A. 84–1394, § 5, eff. Sept. 18, 1986.
Formerly Ill.Rev.Stat.1991, ch. 95 ½, ¶ 6–304.1.

5/6–305. Renting motor vehicle to another

§ 6–305. Renting motor vehicle to another.

(a) No person shall rent a motor vehicle to any other person unless the latter person, or a driver designated by a nondriver with disabilities and meeting any minimum age and driver's record requirements that are uniformly applied by the person renting a motor vehicle, is then duly licensed hereunder or, in the case of a nonresident, then duly licensed under the laws of the State or country of his residence unless the State or country of his residence does not require that a driver be licensed.

(b) No person shall rent a motor vehicle to another until he has inspected the drivers license of the person to whom the vehicle is to be rented, or by whom it is to be driven, and compared and verified the signature thereon with the signature of such person written in his presence unless, in the case of a nonresident, the State or country wherein the nonresident resides does not require that a driver be licensed.

(c) No person shall rent a motorcycle to another unless the latter person is then duly licensed hereunder as a motorcycle operator, and in the case of a nonresident, then duly licensed under the laws of the State or country of his residence, unless the State or country of his residence does not require that a driver be licensed.

(d) (Blank).

(e) (Blank).

(f) Any person who rents a motor vehicle to another shall only advertise, quote, and charge a rental rate that includes the entire amount except taxes and a mileage charge, if any, which a renter must pay to hire or lease the vehicle for the period of time to which the rental rate applies. Such person shall not charge in addition to the rental rate, taxes, and mileage charge, if any, any fee which must be paid by the renter as a condition of hiring or leasing the vehicle, such as, but not limited to, required fuel or airport surcharges, nor any fee for transporting the renter to the location where the rented vehicle will be delivered to the renter. In addition to the rental rate, taxes, and mileage charge, if any, such person may charge for an item or service provided in connection with a particular rental transaction if the renter can avoid incurring the charge by choosing not to obtain or utilize the optional item or service. Items and services for which such person may impose an additional charge include, but are not limited to, optional insurance and accessories requested by the renter, service charges incident to the renter's optional return of the vehicle to a location other than the location where the vehicle was hired or leased, and charges for refueling the vehicle at the conclusion of the rental transaction in the event the renter did not return the vehicle with as much fuel as was in the fuel tank at the beginning of the rental.

(g) Every person renting a motor vehicle to another shall keep a record of the registration number of the motor vehicle so rented, the name and address of the person to whom the vehicle is rented, the number of the license, if any, of said latter person, and the date and place when and where the license, if any, was issued. Such record shall be open to inspection by any police officer or designated agent of the Secretary of State.

(h) A person licensed as a new car dealer under Section 5–101 of this Code shall not be subject to the provisions of this Section regarding the rental of private passenger motor vehicles when providing, free of charge, temporary substitute vehicles for customers to operate during a period when a customer's vehicle, which is either leased or owned by that customer, is being repaired, serviced, replaced or otherwise made unavailable to the customer in accordance with an agreement with the licensed new car dealer or vehicle manufacturer, so long as the customer orally or in writing is made aware that the temporary substitute vehicle will be covered by his or her insurance policy and the customer shall only be liable to the extent of any amount deductible from such insurance coverage in accordance with the terms of the policy.

(i) This Section, except the requirements of subsection (g), also applies to rental agreements of 30 continuous days or less involving a motor vehicle that was delivered by an out of State person or business to a renter in this State.

(j) A public airport may, if approved by its local government corporate authorities or its airport authority, impose a customer facility charge upon customers of rental car companies for the purposes of financing, designing, constructing, operating, and maintaining consolidated car rental facilities and common use transportation equipment and facilities, which are used to transport the customer, connecting consolidated car rental facilities with other airport facilities.

Notwithstanding subsection (f) of this Section, the customer facility charge shall be collected by the rental car company as a separate charge, and clearly indicated as a separate charge on the rental agreement and invoice. Facility charges shall be immediately deposited into a trust account for the benefit of the airport and remitted at the direction of the airport, but not more often than once per month. The charge shall be uniformly calculated on a per-contract or per-day basis. Facility charges imposed by the airport may not exceed the reasonable costs of financing, designing, constructing, operating, and maintaining the consolidated car rental facilities and common use transportation equipment and facilities and may not be used for any other purpose.

Notwithstanding any other provision of law, the charges collected under this Section are not subject to retailer occupation, sales, use, or transaction taxes.

(k) When a rental car company states a rental rate in any of its rate advertisements, its proprietary computer reservation systems, or its in-person quotations intended to apply to an airport rental, a company that collects from its customers a customer facility charge for that rental under subsection (j) shall do all of the following:

(1) Clearly and conspicuously disclose in any radio, television, or other electronic media advertisements the existence and amount of the charge if the advertisement is intended for rentals at an airport imposing the charge or, if the advertisement covers an area with multiple airports with different charges, a range of amounts of customer facility charges if the advertisement is intended for rentals at an airport imposing the charge.

(2) Clearly and conspicuously disclose in any print rate advertising the existence and amount of the charge if the advertisement is intended for rentals at an airport imposing the charge or, if the print rate advertisement covers an area with multiple airports with different charges, a range of amounts of customer facility charges if the advertise-

ment is intended for rentals at an airport imposing the charge.

(3) Clearly and conspicuously disclose the existence and amount of the charge in any telephonic, in-person, or computer-transmitted quotation from the rental car company's proprietary computer reservation system at the time of making an initial quotation of a rental rate if the quotation is made by a rental car company location at an airport imposing the charge and at the time of making a reservation of a rental car if the reservation is made by a rental car company location at an airport imposing the charge.

(4) Clearly and conspicuously display the charge in any proprietary computer-assisted reservation or transaction directly between the rental car company and the customer, shown or referenced on the same page on the computer screen viewed by the customer as the displayed rental rate and in a print size not smaller than the print size of the rental rate.

(5) Clearly and conspicuously disclose and separately identify the existence and amount of the charge on its rental agreement.

(6) A rental car company that collects from its customers a customer facility charge under subsection (j) and engages in a practice which does not comply with subsections (f), (j), and (k) commits an unlawful practice within the meaning of the Consumer Fraud and Deceptive Business Practices Act.[1]

P.A. 76-1586, § 6-305, eff. July 1, 1970. Amended by P.A. 85-1374, § 1, eff. Jan. 1, 1989; P.A. 86-779, § 1, eff. July 1, 1990; P.A. 86-880, § 1, eff. Jan. 1, 1990; P.A. 87-1220, § 1, eff. July 1, 1993; P.A. 88-661, § 27, eff. Sept. 16, 1994; P.A. 89-248, § 5, eff. Aug. 4, 1995; P.A. 90-113, § 900, eff. July 14, 1997; P.A. 92-426, § 5, eff. Jan. 1, 2002.

Formerly Ill.Rev.Stat.1991, ch. 95 ½, ¶ 6-305.

[1] 815 ILCS 505/1 et seq.

5/6-305.1. Unlawful subleasing of a motor vehicle

§ 6-305.1. Unlawful subleasing of a motor vehicle. (a) It is unlawful for any person who is not a party to a lease contract, conditional sale contract, or security agreement which transfers any right or interest in a motor vehicle to:

(1) obtain or exercise control over a motor vehicle and then sell, transfer, assign, or lease the motor vehicle to another person without first obtaining written authorization from the secured creditor, lessor, or lienholder for the sale, transfer, assignment, or lease if he receives compensation or other consideration for the sale, transfer, assignment, or lease of the motor vehicle; or

(2) assist, cause, or arrange the actual or purported sale, transfer, assignment, or lease of a motor vehicle to another person without first obtaining written authorization from the secured creditor, lessor, or lienholder for the sale, transfer, assignment, or lease if he receives compensation or other consideration for assisting, causing, or arranging the sale, transfer, assignment, or lease of the motor vehicle.

(3) this subsection shall not apply to any employee acting upon request of his employer.

(b) Any person who violates the provisions of this Section is guilty of a Class A misdemeanor.

(c) Notwithstanding any other remedy or relief to which a person is entitled, anyone suffering damage as a result of a violation of this Section may bring an action to recover or obtain actual damages, equitable relief, including, but not limited to, an injunction or restitution of money and property, reasonable attorney's fees and costs, and any other relief the court deems proper.

P.A. 76-1586, § 6-305.1, added by P.A. 86-748, § 1, eff. July 1, 1990.

Formerly Ill.Rev.Stat.1991, ch. 95 ½, ¶ 6-305.1.

5/6-305.2. Limited liability for damage

§ 6-305.2. Limited liability for damage.

(a) Damage to private passenger vehicle. A person who rents a motor vehicle to another may hold the renter liable to the extent permitted under subsections (b) through (d) for physical or mechanical damage to the rented motor vehicle that occurs during the time the motor vehicle is under the rental agreement.

(b) Limits on liability. The total liability of a renter under subsection (a) for damage to a motor vehicle may not exceed all of the following:

(1) The lesser of:

(A) Actual and reasonable costs that the person who rents a motor vehicle to another incurred to repair the motor vehicle or that the rental company would have incurred if the motor vehicle had been repaired, which shall reflect any discounts, price reductions, or adjustments available to the rental company; or

(B) The fair market value of that motor vehicle immediately before the damage occurred, as determined in the customary market for the retail sale of that motor vehicle; and

(2) Actual and reasonable costs incurred by the loss due to theft of the rental motor vehicle up to $2,000; provided, however, that if it is established that the renter or an authorized driver failed to exercise ordinary care while in possession of the vehicle or that the renter or an authorized driver committed or aided and abetted the commission of the theft, then the damages shall be the actual and reasonable costs of the rental vehicle up to its fair market value, as determined by the customary market for the sale of that vehicle.

For purposes of this subsection (b), for the period prior to June 1, 1998, the maximum amount that may be recovered from an authorized driver shall not exceed $6,000; for the period beginning June 1, 1998 through May 31, 1999, the maximum recovery shall not exceed $7,500; and for the period beginning June 1, 1999 through May 31, 2000, the maximum recovery shall not exceed $9,000. Beginning June 1, 2000, and annually each June 1 thereafter, the maximum amount that may be recovered from an authorized driver shall be increased by $500 above the maximum recovery allowed immediately prior to June 1 of that year.

(c) Multiple recoveries prohibited. Any person who rents a motor vehicle to another may not hold the renter liable for any amounts that the rental company recovers from any other party.

(d) Repair estimates. A person who rents a motor vehicle to another may not collect or attempt to collect the amount described in subsection (b) unless the rental company obtains an estimate from a repair company or an appraiser in the business of providing such appraisals on the costs of repairing the motor vehicle, makes a copy of the estimate available upon request to the renter who may be liable under subsection (a), or the insurer of the renter, and submits a copy of the estimate with any claim to collect the amount described in subsection (b).

(e) Duty to mitigate. A claim against a renter resulting from damage or loss to a rental vehicle must be reasonably and rationally related to the actual loss incurred. A rental company shall mitigate damages where possible and shall not assert or collect any claim for physical damage which exceeds the actual costs of the repair, including all discounts or price reductions.

(f) No rental company shall require a deposit or an advance charge against the credit card of a renter, in any form, for damages to a vehicle which is in the renter's possession, custody, or control. No rental company shall require any payment for damage to the rental vehicle, upon the renter's return of the vehicle in a damaged condition, until after the cost of the damage to the vehicle and liability therefor is agreed to between the rental company and renter or is determined pursuant to law.

(g) If insurance coverage exists under the renter's personal insurance policy and the coverage is confirmed during regular business hours, the renter may require that the rental company must submit any claims to the renter's personal insurance carrier as the renter's agent. The rental company shall not make any written or oral representations that it will not present claims or negotiate with the renter's insurance carrier. For purposes of this Section, confirmation of coverage includes telephone confirmation from insurance company representatives during regular business hours. After confirmation of coverage, the amount of claim shall be resolved between the insurance carrier and the rental company.

P.A. 76–1586, § 6–305.2, added by P.A. 90–113, § 900, eff. July 14, 1997.

5/6–306. § 6–306. Repealed by P.A. 83–385, § 2, eff. Jan. 1, 1984

5/6–306.1. § 6–306.1. Repealed by P.A. 85–876, § 3, eff. Nov. 6, 1987

Section 4 of P.A. 85–876, veto overridden Nov. 6, 1987, provided:

"Sections 2 and 3 of this Act shall apply only to violations of a municipality's vehicular standing and parking regulations which occur on or after the effective date of this Act."

5/6–306.2. § 6–306.2. Repealed by P.A. 84–1231, § 2, eff. July 28, 1986

5/6–306.3. License as bail

§ 6–306.3. License as bail.

(a) Except as provided in Section 6–306.4 of this Code, any person arrested and charged with violation of Section 3–701, 3–707, or 3–710, or of any violation of Chapters 11 or 12 of this Code,[1] except the provisions of Sections 3–708, 11–401, 11–501, 11–503 or 11–504 of this Code shall have the option of depositing his valid driver's license issued under this Code with the officer demanding bail in lieu of any other security for his appearance in court in answer to any such charge.

(b) However, a uniform bail schedule and regulations adopted pursuant to Supreme Court Rule or Order may require that a driver's license issued under this Code must be deposited, in addition to appropriate cash deposit, where persons arrested and charged with violating Sections 3–708, 11–401, 11–501, 11–503 or 11–504 of this Code elect to take advantage of the uniform schedule establishing the amount of bail in such cases.

(c) When a license is deposited as security in lieu of or in addition to bail, the judge, court clerk, or other official accepting such deposit shall issue to the licensee a receipt for such license upon a form approved or provided by the Secretary of State.

(d) If the licensee whose license has been deposited as security for bail does not appear in court in compliance with the time and place for hearing as notified in such receipt, or the continued date thereof, if any has been ordered by the court, the court shall continue the case for a minimum of 30 days and require a notice of the continued court date be sent to the licensee at his last known address. The clerk of such court shall notify the licensee of the court's order. If the licensee does not appear in and surrender on the continued court date, or within such period, satisfy the court that his appearance in and surrender to the court is impossible and without any fault on his part, the court shall enter an order of failure to appear to answer such charge after depositing license in lieu of bail. The clerk of such court shall notify the Secretary of State of the court's order.

The Secretary of State, when notified by the clerk of such court that an order of failure to appear to answer such charge after depositing license in lieu of bail has been entered, shall immediately suspend the driver's license of such licensee without a hearing and shall not remove such suspension, nor issue any hardship license or privilege to such licensee thereafter until notified by such court that the licensee has appeared and answered the charges placed against him.

(e) 1. Any Illinois resident who has executed a written promise to comply with Section 6–306.2 of this Code, in effect until July 28, 1986, shall continue to be suspended until he or she complies with the terms and conditions of the written promise.

2. The Secretary of State, when notified by the clerk of such court that an order of failure to appear to answer a charge after promising to appear has been entered, shall immediately suspend the driver's license of such licensee without a hearing and shall not remove such suspension, nor issue a hardship license or privilege to such licensee thereafter until notified by such court that the licensee has appeared and answered the charges placed against him.

P.A. 76–1586, § 6–306.3, added by P.A. 84–1231, § 1, eff. July 28, 1986. Amended by P.A. 85–992, § 1, eff. Jan. 5, 1988; P.A. 86–149, § 2, eff. Aug. 11, 1989; P.A. 88–315, § 5, eff. Jan. 1, 1994; P.A. 88–415, § 10, eff. Aug. 20, 1993; P.A. 88–670, Art. 2, § 2–59, eff. Dec. 2, 1994.

Formerly Ill.Rev.Stat.1991, ch. 95 ½, ¶ 6–306.3.

1 625 ILCS 5/11–100 et seq. or 625 ILCS 5/12–100 et seq.

P.A. 88–670, Article 2, of the First 1994 General Revisory Act, resolved multiple actions in the 88th General Assembly and made certain technical corrections in P.A. 88–1 through P.A. 88–538.

5/6–306.4. Procedures for residents of other states

§ 6–306.4. Procedures for residents of other states. (a) Except as provided in paragraph (b) of this Section, any resident of another state which is a member of the Nonresident Violator Compact of 1977,[1] who is cited by a police officer for violating a traffic law or ordinance, shall have the option of (1) being taken without unnecessary delay before a court of jurisdiction or (2) executing a written promise to comply with the terms of the citation by signing at least one copy of a Uniform Traffic Ticket prepared by the police officer. The police officer may refuse to permit a nonresident violator to execute a written promise to comply with the terms of the citation if the nonresident violator cannot furnish satisfactory evidence of identity or if the officer has probable cause to believe the nonresident violator cited will disregard the written promise to comply with the citation.

If the person cited is a resident of another State which is not a member of the Nonresident Violator Compact of 1977, then the rules established by the Supreme Court for bail bond and appearance procedures apply.

(b) Any person cited for violating the following provisions of this Code or a similar provision of local ordinances shall be governed by the bail provisions of the Illinois Supreme Court Rules when it is not practical or feasible to take the person before a judge to have bail set or to avoid undue delay because of the hour or circumstances: Section 3-101, Section 3-702, Sections 3-707, 3-708 or 3-710, Chapter 4,[2] Chapter 5,[3] Section 6-101, Section 6-104, Section 6-113, Section 6-301, Section 6-303, Section 8-115, Section 11-204, Section 11-310, Section 11-311, Section 11-312, Section 11-401, Section 11-402, Section 11-403, Section 11-404, Section 11-409, Section 11-501, Section 11-503, Section 11-504, Section 11-601, when more than 30 m.p.h. over the posted limit, Section 11-1006, Section 11-1414, Section 15-102, Section 15-103, Section 15-107, Section 15-111, paragraph (f) of Section 15-112 or paragraph (j) of Section 15-301.

(c) If the person fails to comply with the executed written promise to comply with the original terms of the citation as indicated in paragraph (a) of this Section, the court shall continue the case for a minimum of 30 days and require that a notice of the continued court date be sent to the last known address of such person. If the person does not appear or otherwise satisfy the court on or before the continued court date, the court shall enter an order of failure to appear to answer such charge. The clerk of such court shall notify the Secretary of State of the court's order within 21 days.

(d) Upon receiving such notice, the Secretary of State shall comply with the provisions of Section 6-803 of this Code.

P.A. 76-1586, § 6-306.4, added by P.A. 84-1231, § 1, eff. July 28, 1986. Amended by P.A. 85-424, § 1, eff. Jan. 1, 1988; P.A. 86-149, § 2, eff. Aug. 11, 1989.

Formerly Ill.Rev.Stat.1991, ch. 95 ½, ¶ 6-306.4.

1 625 ILCS 5/6-800 et seq.

2 625 ILCS 5/4-100 et seq.

3 625 ILCS 5/5-100 et seq.

5/6-306.5. Failure to pay fine or penalty for standing, parking, or compliance violations; suspension of driving privileges

§ 6-306.5. Failure to pay fine or penalty for standing, parking, or compliance violations; suspension of driving privileges.

(a) Upon receipt of a certified report, as prescribed by subsection (c) of this Section, from any municipality stating that the owner of a registered vehicle has failed to pay any fine or penalty due and owing as a result of 10 or more violations of a municipality's vehicular standing, parking, or compliance regulations established by ordinance pursuant to Section 11-208.3 of this Code, the Secretary of State shall suspend the driving privileges of such person in accordance with the procedures set forth in this Section. The Secretary shall also suspend the driving privileges of an owner of a registered vehicle upon receipt of a certified report, as prescribed by subsection (f) of this Section, from any municipality stating that such person has failed to satisfy any fines or penalties imposed by final judgments for 10 or more violations of local standing, parking, or compliance regulations after exhaustion of judicial review procedures.

(b) Following receipt of the certified report of the municipality as specified in this Section, the Secretary of State shall notify the person whose name appears on the certified report that the person's drivers license will be suspended at the end of a specified period of time unless the Secretary of State is presented with a notice from the municipality certifying that the fine or penalty due and owing the municipality has been paid or that inclusion of that person's name on the certified report was in error. The Secretary's notice shall state in substance the information contained in the municipality's certified report to the Secretary, and shall be effective as specified by subsection (c) of Section 6-211 of this Code.

(c) The report of the appropriate municipal official notifying the Secretary of State of unpaid fines or penalties pursuant to this Section shall be certified and shall contain the following:

(1) The name, last known address and drivers license number of the person who failed to pay the fine or penalty and the registration number of any vehicle known to be registered to such person in this State.

(2) The name of the municipality making the report pursuant to this Section.

(3) A statement that the municipality sent a notice of impending drivers license suspension as prescribed by ordinance enacted pursuant to Section 11-208.3, to the person named in the report at the address recorded with the Secretary of State; the date on which such notice was sent; and the address to which such notice was sent. In a municipality with a population of 1,000,000 or more, the report shall also include a statement that the alleged violator's State vehicle registration number and vehicle make are correct as they appear on the citations.

(d) Any municipality making a certified report to the Secretary of State pursuant to this Section shall notify the Secretary of State, in a form prescribed by the Secretary, whenever a person named in the certified report has paid the previously reported fine or penalty or whenever the municipality determines that the original report was in error. A certified copy of such notification shall also be given upon request and at no additional charge to the person named therein. Upon receipt of the municipality's notification or presentation of a certified copy of such notification, the Secretary of State shall terminate the suspension.

(e) Any municipality making a certified report to the Secretary of State pursuant to this Section shall also by ordinance establish procedures for persons to challenge the accuracy of the certified report. The ordinance shall also state the grounds for such a challenge, which may be limited to (1) the person not having been the owner or lessee of the vehicle or vehicles receiving 10 or more standing, parking, or compliance violation notices on the date or dates such notices were issued; and (2) the person having already paid the fine or penalty for the 10 or more violations indicated on the certified report.

(f) Any municipality, other than a municipality establishing vehicular standing, parking, and compliance regulations pursuant to Section 11-208.3, may also cause a suspension of a person's drivers license pursuant to this Section. Such municipality may invoke this sanction by making a certified report to the Secretary of State upon a person's failure to satisfy any fine or penalty imposed by final judgment for 10 or more violations of local standing, parking, or compliance regulations after exhaustion of judicial review procedures, but only if:

(1) the municipality complies with the provisions of this Section in all respects except in regard to enacting an ordinance pursuant to Section 11-208.3;

(2) the municipality has sent a notice of impending drivers license suspension as prescribed by an ordinance enacted pursuant to subsection (g) of this Section; and

(3) in municipalities with a population of 1,000,000 or more, the municipality has verified that the alleged violator's State vehicle registration number and vehicle make are correct as they appear on the citations.

(g) Any municipality, other than a municipality establishing standing, parking, and compliance regulations pursuant to Section 11-208.3, may provide by ordinance for the sending of a notice of impending drivers license suspension to the person who has failed to satisfy any fine or penalty imposed by final judgment for 10 or more violations of local standing, parking, or compliance regulations after exhaustion of judicial review procedures. An ordinance so providing shall specify that the notice sent to the person liable for any fine or penalty shall state that failure to pay the fine or penalty owing within 45 days of the notice's date will result in the municipality notifying the Secretary of State that the person's drivers license is eligible for suspension pursuant to this Section. The notice of impending drivers license suspension shall be sent by first class United States mail, postage prepaid, to the address recorded with the Secretary of State.

(h) An administrative hearing to contest an impending suspension or a suspension made pursuant to this Section may be had upon filing a written request with the Secretary of State. The filing fee for this hearing shall be $20, to be paid at the time the request is made. A municipality which files a certified report with the Secretary of State pursuant to this Section shall reimburse the Secretary for all reasonable costs incurred by the Secretary as a result of the filing of the report, including but not limited to the costs of providing the notice required pursuant to subsection (b) and the costs incurred by the Secretary in any hearing conducted with respect to the report pursuant to this subsection and any appeal from such a hearing.

(i) The provisions of this Section shall apply on and after January 1, 1988.

(j) For purposes of this Section, the term "compliance violation" is defined as in Section 11-208.3.

P.A. 76-1586, § 6-306.5, added by P.A. 85-876, § 2, eff. Nov. 6, 1987. Amended by P.A. 89-190, § 5, eff. Jan. 1, 1996; P.A. 90-145, § 15, eff. Jan. 1, 1998; P.A. 90-481, § 30, eff. Aug. 17, 1997.

Formerly Ill.Rev.Stat.1991, ch. 95 ½, ¶ 6-306.5.

Section 4 of P.A. 85-876, veto overridden Nov. 6, 1987, provided:

"Sections 2 and 3 of this Act shall apply only to violations of a municipality's vehicular standing and parking regulations which occur on or after the effective date of this Act."

The amendments by P.A. 90-145 and P.A. 90-481 were identical.

5/6-306.6. Failure to pay traffic fines, penalties, and court costs

§ 6-306.6. Failure to pay traffic fines, penalties, and court costs.

(a) Whenever any resident of this State fails to pay any traffic fine, penalty, and cost imposed for a violation of this Code, or similar provision of local ordinance, the clerk may notify the Secretary of State, on a report prescribed by the Secretary, and the Secretary shall prohibit the renewal, reissue or reinstatement of such resident's driving privileges until such fine, penalty, and cost have been paid in full. The clerk shall provide notice to the driver, at the driver's last known address as shown on the court's records, stating that such action will be effective on the 46th day following the date of the above notice if payment is not received in full by the court of venue.

(b) Following receipt of the report from the clerk, the Secretary of State shall make the proper notation to the driver's file to prohibit the renewal, reissue or reinstatement of such driver's driving privileges. Except as provided in paragraph (2) of subsection (d) of this Section, such notation shall not be removed from the driver's record until the driver satisfies the outstanding fine, penalty, and cost and an appropriate notice on a form prescribed by the Secretary is received by the Secretary from the court of venue, stating that such fine, penalty, and cost has been paid in full. Upon payment in full of a traffic fine, penalty, and court cost which has previously been reported under this Section as unpaid, the clerk of the court shall present the driver with a signed receipt containing the seal of the court indicating that such fine, penalty, and cost have been paid in full, and shall forward forthwith to the Secretary of State a notice stating that the fine, penalty, and cost have been paid in full.

(c) The provisions of this Section shall be limited to a single action per arrest and as a post conviction measure only. Fines, penalty, and costs to be collected subsequent to orders of court supervision, or other available court diversions are not applicable to this Section. A driver making a partial payment of any outstanding fine, penalty, and cost is not a sufficient basis for the clerk to notify the Secretary for any subsequent action pursuant to this Section.

(d)(1) Notwithstanding the receipt of a report from the clerk as prescribed in subsection (a), nothing in this Section is intended to place any responsibility upon the Secretary of State to provide independent notice to the driver of any potential action to disallow the renewal, reissue or reinstatement of such driver's driving privileges. (2) The Secretary of State shall renew, reissue or reinstate a driver's driving privileges which were previously refused pursuant to this Section upon presentation of an original receipt which is signed by the clerk of the court and contains the seal of the court indicating that the fine, penalty, and cost have been paid in full. The Secretary of State shall retain such receipt for his records.

P.A. 76-1586, § 6-306.6, added by P.A. 86-609, § 1, eff. July 1, 1991. Amended by P.A. 89-71, § 5, eff. Jan. 1, 1996.

Formerly Ill.Rev.Stat.1991, ch. 95 ½, ¶ 6-306.6.

5/6-306.7. Failure to satisfy fines or penalties for toll violations or evasions; suspension of driving privileges

§ 6-306.7. Failure to satisfy fines or penalties for toll violations or evasions; suspension of driving privileges.

(a) Upon receipt of a certified report, as prescribed by subsection (c) of this Section, from the Authority stating that the owner of a registered vehicle has failed to satisfy any fine or penalty resulting from a final order issued by the Authority relating directly or indirectly to 5 or more toll violations, toll evasions, or both, the Secretary of State shall suspend the driving privileges of the person in accordance with the procedures set forth in this Section.

(b) Following receipt of the certified report of the Authority as specified in the Section, the Secretary of State shall notify the person whose name appears on the certified report that the person's driver's license will be suspended at the end of a specified period unless the Secretary of State is presented with a notice from the Authority certifying that the fines or penalties owing the Authority have been satisfied or that inclusion of that person's name on the certified report was in error. The Secretary's notice shall state in substance the information contained in the Authority's certified report to the Secretary, and shall be effective as specified by subsection (c) of Section 6-211 of this Code.

(c) The report from the Authority notifying the Secretary of unsatisfied fines or penalties pursuant to this Section shall be certified and shall contain the following:

(1) The name, last known address, and driver's license number of the person who failed to satisfy the fines or penalties and the registration number of any vehicle known to be registered in this State to that person.

(2) A statement that the Authority sent a notice of impending suspension of the person's driver's license, vehicle registration, or both, as prescribed by rules enacted pursuant to subsection (a-5) of Section 10 of the Toll Highway Act, [1] to the person named in the report at the address recorded with the Secretary of State; the date on which the notice was sent; and the address to which the notice was sent.

(d) The Authority, after making a certified report to the Secretary pursuant to this Section, shall notify the Secretary, on a form prescribed by the Secretary, whenever a person named in the certified report has satisfied the previously reported fines or penalties or whenever the Authority determines that the original report was in error. A certified copy of the notification shall also be given upon request and at no additional charge to the person named therein. Upon receipt of the Authority's notification or presentation of a certified copy of the notification, the Secretary shall terminate the suspension.

(e) The Authority shall, by rule, establish procedures for persons to challenge the accuracy of the certified report made pursuant to this Section. The rule shall also provide the grounds for a challenge, which may be limited to:

(1) the person not having been the owner or lessee of the vehicle or vehicles receiving 5 or more toll violations or toll evasion notices on the date or dates the notices were issued; or

(2) the person having already satisfied the fines or penalties for the 5 or more toll violations or toll evasions indicated on the certified report.

(f) All notices sent by the Authority to persons involved in administrative adjudications, hearings, and final orders issued pursuant to rules implementing subsection (a-5) of Section 10 of the Toll Highway Act shall state that failure to satisfy any fine or penalty imposed by the Authority shall result in the Secretary of State suspending the driving privileges, vehicle registration, or both, of the person failing to satisfy the fines or penalties imposed by the Authority.

(g) A person may request an administrative hearing to contest an impending suspension or a suspension made pursuant to this Section upon filing a written request with the Secretary. The filing fee for this hearing is $20, to be paid at the time of the request. The Authority shall reimburse the Secretary for all reasonable costs incurred by the Secretary as a result of the filing of a certified report pursuant to this Section, including, but not limited to, the costs of providing notice required pursuant to subsection (b) and the costs incurred by the Secretary in any hearing conducted with respect to the report pursuant to this subsection and any appeal from that hearing.

(h) The Secretary and the Authority may promulgate rules to enable them to carry out their duties under this Section.

(i) The Authority shall cooperate with the Secretary in the administration of this Section and shall provide the Secretary with any information the Secretary may deem necessary for these purposes, including regular and timely access to toll violation enforcement records.

The Secretary shall cooperate with the Authority in the administration of this Section and shall provide the Authority with any information the Authority may deem necessary for the purposes of this Section, including regular and timely access to vehicle registration records. Section 2-123 of this Code shall not apply to the provision of this information, but the Secretary shall be reimbursed for the cost of providing this information.

(j) For purposes of this Section, the term "Authority" means the Illinois State Toll Highway Authority.

P.A. 76-1586, § 6-306.7, added by P.A. 91-277, § 5, eff. Jan. 1, 2000.

[1] 605 ILCS 10/10.

5/6-307. Injunctions

§ 6-307. Injunctions. If any person operates in violation of any provision of this Chapter, or any rule, regulation, order or decision of the Secretary of State, or of any term, condition or limitation of any license, the Secretary of State, or any person injured thereby, or any interested person, may apply to the Circuit Court of the county in which such violation or some part thereof occurred, or in which the person complained of has his place of business or resides, to prevent such violation. The Court has jurisdiction to enforce obedience by injunction or other process restraining such person from further violation and enjoining upon him obedience.

P.A. 76-1586, § 6-307, added by P.A. 81-306, § 1, eff. Aug. 30, 1979.

Formerly Ill.Rev.Stat.1991, ch. 95 ½, ¶ 6-307.

ARTICLE IV. COMMERCIAL DRIVER TRAINING SCHOOLS

Section

5/6-401. Driver training schools—License required

§ 6-401. Driver training schools—License required. No person, firm, association, partnership or corporation shall operate a driver training school or engage in the business of giving instruction for hire or for a fee in the driving of motor vehicles or in the preparation of an applicant for examination given by the Secretary of State for a drivers license or permit, unless a license therefor has been issued by the Secretary.

This section shall not apply to public schools or to educational institutions in which driving instruction is part of the curriculum or to employers giving instruction to their employees.

P.A. 76-1586, § 6-401, eff. July 1, 1970.

Formerly Ill.Rev.Stat.1991, ch. 95 ½, ¶ 6-401.

5/6-402. Qualifications of driver training schools

§ 6-402. Qualifications of driver training schools. In order to qualify for a license to operate a driver training school, each applicant must:

(a) be of good moral character;

(b) be at least 21 years of age;

(c) maintain an established place of business open to the public which meets the requirements of Section 6-403 through 6-407;

(d) maintain bodily injury and property damage liability insurance on motor vehicles while used in driving instruction, insuring the liability of the driving school, the driving instructors and any person taking instruction in at least the following amounts: $50,000 for bodily injury to or death of one person in any one accident and, subject to said limit for one person, $100,000 for bodily injury to or death of 2 or more persons in any one accident and the amount of $10,000 for damage to property of others in any one accident. Evidence of such insurance coverage in the form of a certificate from the insurance carrier shall be filed with the Secretary of State, and such certificate shall stipulate that the insurance shall not be cancelled except upon 10 days prior written notice to the Secretary of State. The decal showing evidence of insurance shall be affixed to the windshield of the vehicle;

(e) provide a continuous surety company bond in the principal sum of $10,000 for the protection of the contractual rights of students in such form as will meet with the approval of the Secretary of State and written by a company authorized to do business in this State. However, the aggregate liability of the surety for all breaches of the condition of the bond in no event shall exceed the principal sum of $10,000. The surety on any such bond may cancel such bond on giving 30 days notice thereof in writing to the Secretary of State and shall be relieved of liability for any breach of any conditions of the bond which occurs after the effective date of cancellation;

(f) have the equipment necessary to the giving of proper instruction in the operation of motor vehicles;

(g) have and use a business telephone listing for all business purposes; and

(h) pay to the Secretary of State an application fee of $250.

No license shall be issued under this Section to a person who is a spouse, offspring, sibling, parent, grandparent, grandchild, uncle or aunt, nephew or niece, cousin, or in-law of the person whose license to do business at that location has been revoked or denied or to a person who was an officer or employee of a business firm that has had its license revoked or denied, unless the Secretary of State is satisfied the application was submitted in good faith and not for the purpose or effect of defeating the intent of this Code.

P.A. 76-1586, § 6-402, eff. July 1, 1970. Amended by P.A. 76-1838, § 1, eff. July 1, 1970; P.A. 87-829, § 1, eff. Jan. 17, 1992; P.A. 87-832, § 3, eff. Jan. 17, 1992; P.A. 87-895, Art. 2, § 2-45, eff. Aug. 14, 1992.

Formerly Ill.Rev.Stat.1991, ch. 95 ½, ¶ 6-402.

P.A. 87-895, the First 1992 General Revisory Act, provides in Article 2 for the revision and renumbering of certain Sections of Acts which have been added or amended by more than one Act of the 87th General Assembly; incorporates amendments to repealed Acts into successor laws passed by the same General Assembly; corrects errors, revises cross-references and deletes obsolete text in such Sections contained in Public Acts through P.A. 87-855.

5/6-403. Established place of business

§ 6-403. Established place of business. The established place of business of each driver training school must be owned or leased by the driver training school and regularly occupied and primarily used by that driver training school for the business of selling and giving driving instructions for hire or for a fee, and the business of preparing members of the public for examination given by the Secretary of State for a drivers license.

P.A. 76-1586, § 6-403, eff. July 1, 1970.

Formerly Ill.Rev.Stat.1991, ch. 95 ½, ¶ 6-403.

5/6-404. Location of schools

§ 6-404. Location of schools. The established place of business of each driver training school must be located in a district which is zoned for business or commercial purposes. The driver training school office must have a permanent sign clearly readable from the street, from a distance of no less than 100 feet, with the name of the driving school upon it.

P.A. 76-1586, § 6-404, eff. July 1, 1970. Amended by P.A. 76-1753, § 1, eff. July 1, 1970.

Formerly Ill.Rev.Stat.1991, ch. 95 ½, ¶ 6-404.

5/6-405. Restrictions of locations

§ 6-405. Restrictions of locations. The established place of business, or branch office, branch class room or advertised address of any driver training school shall not consist of or include a house trailer, residence, tent, temporary stand, temporary address, office space, a room or rooms in a hotel, rooming house or apartment house, or premises occupied by a single or multiple unit dwelling house or telephone answering service.

P.A. 76-1586, § 6-405, eff. July 1, 1970.

Formerly Ill.Rev.Stat.1991, ch. 95 ½, ¶ 6-405.

5/6-406. Required facilities

§ 6-406. Required facilities. (a) The established place of business of each driver training school must consist of at least the following permanent facilities:

(1) An office facility;

(2) A class room facility.

(b) The main class room facility of each driver training school must be reasonably accessible to the main office facility of the driver training school.

(c) All class room facilities must have adequate lighting, heating, ventilation, and must comply with all state, and local laws relating to public health, safety and sanitation.

(d) The main office facility and branch office facility of each driver training school must contain sufficient space, equipment, records and personnel to carry on the business of the driver training school. The main office facility must be specifically devoted to driver training school business.

(e) A driver training school which as an established place of business and a main office facility, may operate a branch office or a branch class room provided that all the requirements for the main office or main class room are met and that such branch office bears the same name and is operated as a part of the same business entity as the main office facility.

(f) No driver training school may share any main or branch facility or facilities with any other driver training school.

P.A. 76-1586, § 6-406, eff. July 1, 1970.

Formerly Ill.Rev.Stat.1991, ch. 95 ½, ¶ 6-406.

5/6-407. Locations and state facilities

§ 6-407. Locations and state facilities. No office or place of business of a driver training school shall be established within 1,500 feet of any building used as an office by any department of the Secretary of State having to do with the administration of any laws relating to motor vehicles, nor may any driving school solicit or advertise for business within 1,500 feet of any building used as an office by the Secretary of State having to do with the administration of any laws relating to motor vehicles.

P.A. 76-1586, § 6-407, eff. July 1, 1970.

Formerly Ill.Rev.Stat.1991, ch. 95 ½, ¶ 6-407.

5/6-408. Records

§ 6-408. Records. All driver training schools licensed by the Secretary of State must maintain a permanent record of instructions given to each student. The record must contain the name of the school and the name of the student, the number of all licenses or permits held by the student, the type and date of instruction given, whether class room or behind the wheel, and the signature of the instructor.

All permanent student instruction records must be kept on file in the main office of each driver training school for a period of 3 calendar years after the student has ceased taking instruction at or with the school.

The records should show the fees and charges of the school and also the record should show the course content and instructions given to each student.

P.A. 76-1586, § 6-408, eff. July 1, 1970. Amended by P.A. 76-1754, § 1, eff. July 1, 1970.

Formerly Ill.Rev.Stat.1991, ch. 95 ½, ¶ 6-408.

5/6-408.5 Courses for students or high school dropouts; limitation

§ 6-408.5. Courses for students or high school dropouts; limitation. (a) No driver training school or driving training instructor licensed under this Act may request a certificate of completion from the Secretary of State as provided in Section 6-411 for any person who is enrolled as a student in any public or non-public secondary school at the time such instruction is to be provided, or who was so enrolled during the semester last ended if that instruction is to be provided between semesters or during the summer after the regular school term ends, unless that student has received a passing grade in at least 8 courses during the 2 semesters last ending prior to requesting a certificate of completion from the Secretary of State for the student.

(b) No driver training school or driving training instructor licensed under this Act may request a certificate of completion from the Secretary of State as provided in Section 6-411 for any person who has dropped out of school and has not yet attained the age of 18 years unless the driver training school or driving training instructor has: 1) obtained written documentation verifying the dropout's enrollment in a GED or alternative education program or has obtained a copy of the dropout's GED certificate; 2) obtained verification that the student prior to dropping out had received a passing grade in at least 8 courses during the 2 previous semesters last ending prior to requesting a certificate of completion; or 3) obtained written consent from the dropout's parents or guardians and the regional superintendent.

(c) Students shall be informed of the eligibility requirements of this Act in writing at the time of registration.

(d) The superintendent of schools of the school district in which the student resides and attends school or in which the student resides at the time he or she drops out of school (with respect to a public high school student or a dropout from the public high school) or the chief school administrator (with respect to a student who attends a non-public high school or a dropout from a non-public high school) may waive the requirements of this Section if the superintendent or chief school administrator, as the case may be, deems it to be in the best interests of the student or dropout. Before requesting a certificate of completion from the Secretary of State for any person who is enrolled as a student in any public or non-public secondary school or who was so enrolled in the semester last ending prior to the request for a certificate of completion from the Secretary of State or who is of high school age, the driver training school shall determine from the school district in which that person resides or resided at the time of dropping out of school, or from the chief administrator of the non-public high school attended or last attended by such person, as the case may be, that such person is not ineligible to receive a certificate of completion under this Section.

(e) By January 1, 1997, the Secretary of State, in cooperation with the State Board of Education, shall complete, and submit to the General Assembly, a report that examines the impact of this Section and other changes made by Public Act 88-188.

P.A. 76-1586, § 6-408.5, added by P.A. 88-188, § 10, eff. Jan. 1, 1994. Amended by P.A. 88-628, § 10, eff. Sept. 9, 1994.

5/6-409. Display of license

§ 6-409. Display of license. Each driver training school must display at a prominent place in its main office all of the following:

(a) The State license issued to the school;

(b) The names and addresses and State instructors licenses of all instructors employed by the school;

(c) The address of all branch offices and branch class rooms.

P.A. 76-1586, § 6-409, eff. July 1, 1970.

Formerly Ill.Rev.Stat.1991, ch. 95 ½, ¶ 6-409.

5/6-410. Vehicle inspections

§ 6-410. Vehicle inspections. The Department of Transportation shall provide for the inspection of all motor vehicles used for driver training, and shall issue a safety inspection sticker provided:

(a) The motor vehicle has been inspected by the Department and found to be in safe mechanical condition;

(b) The motor vehicle is equipped with dual control brakes and a mirror on each side of the motor vehicle so located as to reflect to the driver a view of the highway for a distance of at least 200 feet to the rear of such motor vehicle; and

(c) The motor vehicle is equipped with a sign or signs visible from the front and the rear in letters no less than 2 inches tall, listing the full name of the driver training school which has registered and insured the motor vehicle.

P.A. 76-1586, § 6-410, eff. July 1, 1970. Amended by P.A. 77-170, § 1, eff. Jan. 1, 1972; P.A. 85-951, § 1, eff. July 1, 1988.

Formerly Ill.Rev.Stat.1991, ch. 95 ½, ¶ 6-410.

5/6-411. Qualifications of Driver Training Instructors

§ 6-411. Qualifications of Driver Training Instructors. In order to qualify for a license as an instructor for a driving school, an applicant must:

(a) Be of good moral character;

(b) Authorize an investigation to determine if the applicant has ever been convicted of a crime and if so, the disposition of those convictions; this authorization shall indicate the scope of the inquiry and the agencies which may be contacted. Upon this authorization the Secretary of State may request and receive information and assistance from any federal, state or local governmental agency as part of the authorized investigation. The Department of State Police shall provide information concerning any criminal convictions, and their disposition, brought against the applicant upon request of the Secretary of State when the request is made in the form and manner required by the Department of State Police. The information derived from this investigation including the source of this information, and any conclusions or recommendations derived from this information by the Secretary of State shall be provided to the applicant, or his designee, upon request to the Secretary of State, prior to any final action by the Secretary of State on the application. No information obtained from such investigation may be placed in any automated information system. Any criminal convictions and their disposition information obtained by the Secretary of State shall be confidential and may not be transmitted outside the Office of the Secretary of State, except as required herein, and may not be transmitted to anyone within the Office of the Secretary of State except as needed for the purpose of evaluating the applicant. The only physical identity materials which the applicant can be required to provide the Secretary of State are photographs or fingerprints; these shall be returned to the applicant upon request to the Secretary of State, after the investigation has been completed and no copy of these materials may be kept by the Secretary of State or any agency to which such identity materials were transmitted. Only information and standards which bear a reasonable and rational relation to the performance of a driver training instructor shall be used by the Secretary of State. Any employee of the Secretary of State who gives or causes to be given away any confidential information concerning any criminal charges and their disposition of an applicant shall be guilty of a Class A misdemeanor unless release of such information is authorized by this Section;

(c) Pass such examination as the Secretary of State shall require on (1) traffic laws, (2) safe driving practices, (3) operation of motor vehicles, and (4) qualifications of teacher;

(d) Be physically able to operate safely a motor vehicle and to train others in the operation of motor vehicles. An instructors license application must be accompanied by a medical examination report completed by a competent physician licensed to practice in the State of Illinois;

(e) Hold a valid Illinois drivers license;

(f) Have graduated from an accredited high school after at least 4 years of high school education or the equivalent; and

(g) Pay to the Secretary of State an application and license fee of $35.

If a driver training school class room instructor teaches an approved driver education course, as defined in Section 1-103 of this Code, to students under 18 years of age, he or she shall furnish to the Secretary of State a certificate issued by the State Board of Education that the said instructor is qualified and meets the minimum educational standards for teaching driver education courses in the local public or parochial school systems, except that no State Board of Education certification shall be required of any instructor who teaches exclusively in a commercial driving school. On and after July 1, 1986, the existing rules and regulations of the State Board of Education concerning commercial driving schools shall continue to remain in effect but shall be administered by the Secretary of State until such time as the Secretary of State shall amend or repeal the rules in accordance with The Illinois Administrative Procedure Act.[1] Upon request, the Secretary of State shall issue a certificate of completion to a student under 18 years of age who has completed an approved driver education course at a commercial driving school.

P.A. 76-1586, § 6-411, eff. July 1, 1970. Amended by P.A. 80-1447, § 1, eff. Sept. 15, 1978; P.A. 81-1508, § 8, eff. Sept. 25, 1980; P.A. 81-1509, Art. II, § 71, eff. Sept. 26, 1980; P.A. 81-1550, Art. I, § 22, eff. Jan. 8, 1981; P.A. 84-25, Art. IV, § 27, eff. July 18, 1985; P.A. 84-863, § 1, eff. July 1, 1986; P.A. 84-1308, Art. II, § 96, eff. Aug. 25, 1986; P.A. 87-829, § 1, eff. Jan. 17, 1992; P.A. 87-832, § 3, eff. Jan. 17, 1992.

Formerly Ill.Rev.Stat.1991, ch. 95 ½, ¶ 6-411.

1 5 ILCS 100/1-1 et seq.

The amendments by P.A. 87-829 and P.A. 87-832 were identical.

5/6-412. Issuance of licenses to driver training schools and driver training instructors

§ 6-412. Issuance of licenses to driver training schools and driver training instructors. The Secretary of State shall issue a license certificate to each applicant to conduct a driver training school or to each driver training instructor when the Secretary of State is satisfied that such person has met the qualifications required under this Act.

P.A. 76-1586, § 6-412, eff. July 1, 1970.

Formerly Ill.Rev.Stat.1991, ch. 95 ½, ¶ 6-412.

5/6-413. Expiration of Licenses

§ 6-413. Expiration of Licenses. All outstanding licenses issued to any driver training school or driver training instructor under this Act shall expire by operation of law 12 months from the date of issuance, unless sooner cancelled, suspended or revoked under the provisions of Section 6-420.

P.A. 76-1586, § 6-413, eff. July 1, 1970. Amended by P.A 87-829, § 1, eff. Jan. 17, 1992; P.A. 87-832, § 3, eff. Jan. 17, 1992.

Formerly Ill.Rev.Stat.1991, ch. 95 ½, ¶ 6-413.

The amendments by P.A. 87-829 and P.A. 87-832 were identical.

5/6-414. Renewal of Licenses

§ 6-414. Renewal of Licenses. The license of each driver training school may be renewed subject to the same conditions as the original license, and upon the payment of an annual renewal license fee of $250.

P.A. 76-1586, § 6-414, eff. July 1, 1970. Amended by P.A. 87-829, § 1, eff. Jan. 17, 1992; P.A. 87-832, § 3, eff. Jan. 17, 1992.

Formerly Ill.Rev.Stat.1991, ch. 95 ½, ¶ 6-414.

The amendments by P.A. 87-829 and P.A. 87-832 were identical.

5/6-415. Renewal Fee

§ 6-415. Renewal Fee. The license of each driver training instructor may be renewed subject to the same conditions of the original license, and upon the payment of annual renewal license fee of $35.

P.A. 76-1586, § 6-415, eff. July 1, 1970. Amended by P.A. 87-829, § 1, eff. Jan. 17, 1992; P.A. 87-832, § 3, eff. Jan. 17, 1992.

Formerly Ill.Rev.Stat.1991, ch. 95 ½, ¶ 6-415.

5/6-416. Licenses: Form and Filing

§ 6-416. Licenses: Form and Filing. All applications for renewal of a driver training school license or driver training instructor's license shall be on a form prescribed by the Secretary, and must be filed with the Secretary not less than 15 days preceding the expiration date of the license to be renewed.

P.A. 76-1586, § 6-416, eff. July 1, 1970. Amended by P.A. 87-829, § 1, eff. Jan. 17, 1992; P.A. 87-832, § 3, eff. Jan. 17, 1992.

Formerly Ill.Rev.Stat.1991, ch. 95 ½, ¶ 6-416.

The amendments by P.A. 87-829 and P.A. 87-832 were identical.

5/6-417. Instructor's license

§ 6-417. Instructor's license. Each driver training instructor's license shall authorize the licensee to instruct only at or for the driver training school indicated on the license. The Secretary shall not issue a driver training instructor's license to any individual who is licensed to instruct at or for another driver training school.

P.A. 76-1586, § 6-417, eff. July 1, 1970.

Formerly Ill.Rev.Stat.1991, ch. 95 ½, ¶ 6-417.

5/6-418. Instructor's records

§ 6-418. Instructor's records. Every licensee shall keep a record showing the name and address of each person given instruction and the instruction permit or driver's license number of every person given instruction in the driving of a motor vehicle, and shall show the particular type of instruction given and how much time was devoted to each such type of instruction. Such records shall be open to the inspection of the Secretary or his representatives at all reasonable times, but shall be for the confidential use of the Secretary.

P.A. 76-1586, § 6-418, eff. July 1, 1970.

Formerly Ill.Rev.Stat.1991, ch. 95 ½, ¶ 6-418.

5/6-419. Rules and regulations

§ 6-419. Rules and regulations. The Secretary is authorized to prescribe by rule standards for the eligibility, conduct and operation of driver training schools, and instructors and to adopt other reasonable rules and regulations necessary to carry out the provisions of this Act.

P.A. 76-1586, § 6-419, eff. July 1, 1970.

Formerly Ill.Rev.Stat.1991, ch. 95 ½, ¶ 6-419.

5/6-420. Denial, Cancellation, Suspension, Revocation and Failure to Renew License

§ 6-420. Denial, Cancellation, Suspension, Revocation and Failure to Renew License. The Secretary may deny, cancel, suspend or revoke, or refuse to renew any driver training school license or any driver training instructor license:

(1) When the Secretary is satisfied that the licensee fails to meet the requirements to receive or hold a license under this Code;

(2) Whenever the licensee fails to keep the records required by this Code;

(3) Whenever the licensee permits fraud or engages in fraudulent practices either with reference to a student or the Secretary, or induces or countenances fraud or fraudulent practices on the part of any applicant for a driver's license or permit;

(4) Whenever the licensee fails to comply with any provision of this Code or any rule of the Secretary made pursuant thereto;

(5) Whenever the licensee represents himself as an agent or employee of the Secretary or uses advertising designed to lead or which would reasonably have the effect of leading persons to believe that such licensee is in fact an employee or representative of the Secretary;

(6) Whenever the licensee or any employee or agent of the licensee solicits driver training or instruction in an office of any department of the Secretary of State having to do with the administration of any law relating to motor vehicles, or within 1,500 feet of any such office;

(7) Whenever the licensee is convicted of driving while under the influence of alcohol, other drugs, or a combination thereof; leaving the scene of an accident; reckless homicide or reckless driving; or

(8) Whenever a driver training school advertises that a driver's license is guaranteed upon completion of the course of instruction.

P.A. 76-1586, § 6-420, eff. July 1, 1970. Amended by P.A. 85-951, § 1, eff. July 1, 1988.

Formerly Ill.Rev.Stat.1991, ch. 95 ½, ¶ 6-420.

5/6-421. Judicial Review

§ 6-421. Judicial Review. The action of the Secretary in cancelling, suspending, revoking or denying any license under this Act shall be subject to judicial review in the Circuit Court of Sangamon County or the Circuit Court of Cook County, and the provisions of the Administrative Review Law, and all amendments and modifications thereto,[1] and the rules adopted pursuant thereto, are hereby adopted and shall apply to and govern every action for judicial review of the final acts or decisions of the Secretary under this Act. P.A. 76-1586, § 6-421, eff. July 1, 1970. Amended by P.A. 82-783, Art. XI, § 140, eff. July 13, 1982.

Formerly Ill.Rev.Stat.1991, ch. 95 ½, ¶ 6-421.

1 735 ILCS 5/3-101 et seq.

5/6-422. Prior law and licenses thereunder

§ 6-422. Prior law and licenses thereunder. This Act shall not affect the validity of any outstanding license issued to any driver training school or driver training instructor by the Secretary of State under any prior law, nor shall this Act affect the validity or legality of any contract, agreement or undertaking entered into by any driver training school or driver training instructor, or any person, firm, corporation, partnership or association based on those provisions of any prior law.

P.A. 76–1586, § 6–422, eff. July 1, 1970.

Formerly Ill.Rev.Stat.1991, ch. 95 ½, ¶ 6–422.

5/6–423. Deposit of fees

§ 6–423. Deposit of fees. Fees collected under this Article shall be deposited in the Road Fund.

P.A. 76–1586, § 6–423, eff. July 1, 1970.

Formerly Ill.Rev.Stat.1991, ch. 95 ½, ¶ 6–423.

5/6–424. Injunctions

§ 6–424. Injunctions. If any person operates in violation of any provision of this Article, or any rule, regulation, order, or decision of the Secretary of State established under this Article, or in violation of any term, condition or limitation of any license issued under this Article, the Secretary of State, or any other person injured as a result, or any interested person, may apply to the circuit court of the county where the violation or some part occurred, or where the person complained of has an established or additional place of business or resides, to prevent the violation. The court may enforce compliance by injunction or other process restraining the person from further violation and compliance.

P.A. 76–1586, § 6–424, added by P.A. 87–829, § 1, eff. Jan. 17, 1992; P.A. 87–832, § 3, eff. Jan. 17, 1992.

Formerly Ill.Rev.Stat.1991, ch. 95 ½, ¶ 6–424.

P.A. 87–829 and P.A. 87–832 added identical versions of this section.

ARTICLE V. UNIFORM COMMERCIAL DRIVER'S LICENSE ACT

Date Effective

Article VI was added by P.A. 85–630, § 1, eff. Sept. 20, 1987, and editorially renumbered as Art. V.

P.A. 86–620, Art. III, § 3–36, eff. Sept. 7, 1989, renumbered the Article.

Section

Section

5/6–500. Definitions of words and phrases

§ 6–500. Definitions of words and phrases. Notwithstanding the definitions set forth elsewhere in this Code, for purposes of the Uniform Commercial Driver's License Act (UCDLA),[1] the words and phrases listed below have the meanings ascribed to them as follows:

(1) Alcohol. "Alcohol" means any substance containing any form of alcohol, including but not limited to ethanol, methanol, propanol, and isopropanol.

(2) Alcohol concentration. "Alcohol concentration" means:

(A) the number of grams of alcohol per 210 liters of breath; or

(B) the number of grams of alcohol per 100 milliliters of blood; or

(C) the number of grams of alcohol per 67 milliliters of urine.

Alcohol tests administered within 2 hours of the driver being "stopped or detained" shall be considered that driver's "alcohol concentration" for the purposes of enforcing this UCDLA.

(3) (Blank).

(4) (Blank).

(5) (Blank).

(6) Commercial Motor Vehicle.

(A) "Commercial motor vehicle" means a motor vehicle, except those referred to in subdivision (B), designed to transport passengers or property if:

(i) the vehicle has a GVWR of 26,001 pounds or more or such a lesser GVWR as subsequently determined by federal regulations or the Secretary of State; or any combination of vehicles with a GCWR of 26,001 pounds or more, provided the GVWR of any vehicle or vehicles being towed is 10,001 pounds or more; or

(ii) the vehicle is designed to transport 16 or more persons; or

(iii) the vehicle is transporting hazardous materials and is required to be placarded in accordance with 49 C.F.R. Part 172, subpart F.

(B) Pursuant to the interpretation of the Commercial Motor Vehicle Safety Act of 1986[2] by the Federal Highway Administration, the definition of "commercial motor vehicle" does not include:

(i) recreational vehicles, when operated primarily for personal use;

(ii) United States Department of Defense vehicles being operated by non-civilian personnel. This includes any operator on active military duty; members of the Reserves; National Guard; personnel on part-time training; and National Guard military technicians (civilians who are required to wear military uniforms and are subject to the Code of Military Justice); or

(iii) firefighting and other emergency equipment with audible and visual signals, owned or operated by or for a governmental entity, which is necessary to the preservation of life or property or the execution of emergency governmental functions which are normally not subject to general traffic rules and regulations.

(7) Controlled Substance. "Controlled substance" shall have the same meaning as defined in Section 102 of the Illinois Controlled Substances Act,[3] and shall also include cannabis as defined in Section 3 of the Cannabis Control Act.[4]

(8) Conviction. "Conviction" means an unvacated adjudication of guilt or a determination that a person has violated or failed to comply with the law in a court of original jurisdiction or an authorized administrative tribunal; an unvacated forfeiture of bail or collateral deposited to secure the person's appearance in court; the payment of a fine or court cost regardless of whether the imposition of sentence is deferred and ultimately a judgment dismissing the underlying charge is entered; or a violation of a condition of release without bail, regardless of whether or not the penalty is rebated, suspended or probated.

(9) (Blank).

(10) (Blank).

(11) (Blank).

(12) (Blank).

(13) Driver. "Driver" means any person who drives, operates, or is in physical control of a commercial motor vehicle, or who is required to hold a CDL.

(14) Employee. "Employee" means a person who is employed as a commercial motor vehicle driver. A person who is self-employed as a commercial motor vehicle driver must comply with the requirements of this UCDLA pertaining to employees. An owner-operator on a long-term lease shall be considered an employee.

(15) Employer. "Employer" means a person (including the United States, a State or a local authority) who owns or leases a commercial motor vehicle or assigns employees to operate such a vehicle. A person who is self-employed as a commercial motor vehicle driver must comply with the requirements of this UCDLA.

(16) (Blank).

(17) Foreign jurisdiction. "Foreign jurisdiction" means a sovereign jurisdiction that does not fall within the definition of "State".

(18) (Blank).

(19) (Blank).

(20) Hazardous Material. Upon a finding by the United States Secretary of Transportation, in his or her discretion, under 49 App. U.S.C. 5103(a), that the transportation of a particular quantity and form of material in commerce may pose an unreasonable risk to health and safety or property, he or she shall designate the quantity and form of material or group or class of the materials as a hazardous material. The materials so designated may include but are not limited to explosives, radioactive materials, etiologic agents, flammable liquids or solids, combustible liquids or solids, poisons, oxidizing or corrosive materials, and compressed gases.

(21) Long-term lease. "Long-term lease" means a lease of a commercial motor vehicle by the owner-lessor to a lessee, for a period of more than 29 days.

(22) Motor Vehicle. "Motor vehicle" means every vehicle which is self-propelled, and every vehicle which is propelled by electric power obtained from over head trolley wires but not operated upon rails, except vehicles moved solely by human power and motorized wheel chairs.

(23) Non-resident CDL. "Non-resident CDL" means a commercial driver's license issued by a state to an individual who is domiciled in a foreign jurisdiction.

(24) (Blank).

(25) (Blank).

(25.5) Railroad-Highway Grade Crossing Violation. "Railroad-highway grade crossing violation" means a violation, while operating a commercial motor vehicle, of any of the following:

(A) Section 11-1201, 11-1202, or 11-1425 of this Code.

(B) Any other similar law or local ordinance of any state relating to railroad-highway grade crossing.

(26) Serious Traffic Violation. "Serious traffic violation" means:

(A) a conviction when operating a commercial motor vehicle of:

(i) a violation relating to excessive speeding, involving a single speeding charge of 15 miles per hour or more above the legal speed limit; or

(ii) a violation relating to reckless driving; or

(iii) a violation of any State law or local ordinance relating to motor vehicle traffic control (other than parking violations) arising in connection with a fatal traffic accident; or

(iv) a violation of Section 6-501, relating to having multiple driver's licenses; or

(v) a violation of paragraph (a) of Section 6-507, relating to the requirement to have a valid CDL; or

(vi) a violation relating to improper or erratic traffic lane changes; or

(vii) a violation relating to following another vehicle too closely; or

(B) any other similar violation of a law or local ordinance of any state relating to motor vehicle traffic control, other than a parking violation, which the Secretary of State determines by administrative rule to be serious.

(27) State. "State" means a state of the United States, the District of Columbia and any province or territory of Canada.

(28) (Blank).

(29) (Blank).

(30) (Blank).

(31) (Blank).

P.A. 76-1586, § 6-500, added by P.A. 85-630, § 1, eff. Sept. 20, 1987. Amended by P.A. 85-1396, § 2, eff. Sept. 2, 1988; P.A. 86-845, § 1, eff. April 1, 1990; P.A. 87-829, § 1, eff. Jan. 17, 1992; P.A. 87-832, § 3, eff. Jan. 17, 1992; P.A. 89-179, § 5, eff. Jan. 1, 1996; P.A. 89-571, § 5, eff. July 26, 1996; P.A. 90-89, § 15, eff. Jan. 1, 1998; P.A. 92-249, § 5, eff. Jan. 1, 2002; P.A. 92-651, § 77, eff. July 11, 2002; P.A. 92-834, § 5, eff. Aug. 22, 2002.

Formerly Ill.Rev.Stat.1991, ch. 95 ½, ¶ 6-500.

[1] 625 ILCS 5/6-500 et seq.

[2] 49 App. U.S.C.A. § 2701 et seq. (repealed).

[3] 720 ILCS 570/102.

[4] 720 ILCS 550/3.

See 5 ILCS 70/6 as to the effect of (1) more than one amendment of a section at the same session of the General Assembly or (2) two or more acts relating to the same subject matter enacted by the same General Assembly.

P.A. 92-834 incorporated the amendment by P.A. 92-249.

5/6-500.1. Short title

§ 6-500.1. Short title. This Article may be cited as the Uniform Commercial Driver's License Act or "UCDLA".

P.A. 76-1586, § 6-500.1, added by P.A. 86-845, § 1, eff. April 1, 1990.

Formerly Ill.Rev.Stat.1991, ch. 95 ½, ¶ 6-500.1.

5/6-500.2. Statement of intent and purpose

§ 6-500.2. Statement of intent and purpose. The purpose of this UCDLA is to implement the federal Commercial Motor Vehicle Safety Act of 1986 (CMVSA) (Title XII of Pub. Law 99-570) and reduce or prevent commercial motor vehicle accidents, fatalities and injuries by:

(a) permitting commercial drivers to hold only one driver's license;

(b) disqualifying commercial drivers who have committed certain serious traffic violations, or other specified offenses; and

(c) strengthening commercial driver licensing and testing standards.

This UCDLA is remedial in nature and should be liberally construed to promote the public's health, safety and welfare. To the extent that this UCDLA conflicts with any other provisions of this Code, the UCDLA shall prevail. Where this UCDLA is silent, the other general provisions of this Code shall apply.

P.A. 76-1586, § 6-500.2, added by P.A. 86-845, § 1, eff. April 1, 1990.

Formerly Ill.Rev.Stat.1991, ch. 95 ½, ¶ 6-500.2.

5/6-501. Commercial drivers—permitted only one driver's license

§ 6-501. Commercial drivers—permitted only one driver's license. No person who drives a commercial motor vehicle, on the highways, shall have more than one driver's license, except during the 10-day period beginning on the date such person is issued a CDL.

Any person convicted of violating this Section shall be guilty of a Class A misdemeanor.

P.A. 76-1586, § 6-501, added by P.A. 85-630, § 1, eff. Sept. 20, 1987. Amended by P.A. 86-845, § 1, eff. April 1, 1990.

Formerly Ill.Rev.Stat.1991, ch. 95 ½, ¶ 6-501.

5/6-502. Commercial motor vehicle drivers—reporting of traffic violations to the Secretary of State

§ 6-502. Commercial motor vehicle drivers—reporting of traffic violations to the Secretary of State. When required by the Commercial Motor Vehicle Safety Act of 1986, [1] every person who has been issued an Illinois non-resident CDL or who is a domiciliary of this State and drives a commercial motor vehicle in violation of a law or local ordinance of any State relating to motor vehicle traffic control (other than parking violations) in any other state, shall notify the Secretary of State, on a form and in a manner prescribed by the Secretary, of such violation within 30 days after the date such person has been convicted of such offense.

P.A. 76-1586, § 6-502, added by P.A. 85-630, § 1, eff. Sept. 20, 1987. Amended by P.A. 86-845, § 1, eff. April 1, 1990.

Formerly Ill.Rev.Stat.1991, ch. 95 ½, ¶ 6-502.

[1] 49 App. U.S.C.A. § 2701.

5/6-503. Commercial motor vehicle drivers—reporting of traffic violations to employer

§ 6-503. Commercial motor vehicle drivers—reporting of traffic violations to employer. Every person who is a domiciliary of this State or who has been issued an Illinois non-resident CDL and drives a commercial motor vehicle in violation of a law or local ordinance of any State relating to motor vehicle traffic control (other than parking violations) in this or any other state, shall notify such person's employer of such violation within 30 days after the date such person is convicted of such offense.

In the event such person is a "common carrier of property by motor vehicle", as defined in Section 18c-1104 of this Code, such person shall notify the principal lessor of such within 30 days after the date such person is convicted of the violation. However, if such person is an independent contractor or owner operator, such report shall be kept at the principal place of business and available during normal office hours for inspection and auditing purposes by an authorized agency.

P.A. 76-1586, § 6-503, added by P.A. 85-630, § 1, eff. Sept. 20, 1987. Amended by P.A. 85-1396, § 2, eff. Sept. 2, 1988; P.A. 86-845, § 1, eff. April 1, 1990.

Formerly Ill.Rev.Stat.1991, ch. 95 ½, ¶ 6-503.

5/6-504. Commercial motor vehicle drivers—other reporting requirements

§ 6-504. Commercial motor vehicle drivers—other reporting requirements. All drivers of commercial motor vehicles licensed or domiciled in Illinois:

(1) who have their driving privileges suspended, revoked or cancelled by any state; or

(2) who lose their privilege to operate a commercial motor vehicle in any state for any period; or

(3) who are disqualified from driving a commercial motor vehicle for any period; or

(4) who are placed "out-of-service" pursuant to Section 6-515;

shall notify: (i) their employer of such suspension, revocation, cancellation, lost right, disqualification, or "out-of-service" action before the end of the business day following the day the driver received notice of such action; and within 30 days after the effective date of such action.

(ii) the Secretary of State of any such out-of-state suspension, revocation, cancellation, lost right, disqualification, or "out-of-service" action within 30 days after the effective date of such action.

P.A. 76-1586, § 6-504, added by P.A. 85-630, § 1, eff. Sept. 20, 1987. Amended by P.A. 85-1396, § 2, eff. Sept. 2, 1988; P.A. 86-845, § 1, eff. April 1, 1990.

Formerly Ill.Rev.Stat.1991, ch. 95 ½, ¶ 6-504.

5/6–505. Commercial motor vehicle driver—duty to report certain previous employment to potential employer

§ 6–505. Commercial motor vehicle driver—duty to report certain previous employment to potential employer. Each person who applies for employment as a driver of a commercial motor vehicle, with any employer, shall notify such potential employer at the time of such application of any and all previous employment for the last 10 years, as a driver of a commercial motor vehicle including, but not necessarily limited to, the dates between which the applicant drove for each employer, the reason for leaving each such employment and the information contained in the notification requirements of Section 6–504.

P.A. 76–1586, § 6–505, added by P.A. 85–630, § 1, eff. Sept. 20, 1987. Amended by P.A. 86–845, § 1, eff. April 1, 1990.

Formerly Ill.Rev.Stat.1991, ch. 95 ½, ¶ 6–505.

5/6–506. Commercial motor vehicle driver—employer/owner responsibilities

§ 6–506. Commercial motor vehicle driver—employer/owner responsibilities.

(a) No employer or commercial motor vehicle owner shall knowingly allow, permit, or authorize an employee to drive a commercial motor vehicle on the highways during any period in which such employee:

(1) has a driver's license suspended, revoked or cancelled by any state; or

(2) has lost the privilege to drive a commercial motor vehicle in any state; or

(3) has been disqualified from driving a commercial motor vehicle; or

(4) has more than one driver's license, except as provided by this UCDLA; or

(5) is subject to or in violation of an "out-of-service" order.

(b) No employer or commercial motor vehicle owner shall knowingly allow, permit, authorize, or require a driver to operate a commercial motor vehicle in violation of any law or regulation pertaining to railroad-highway grade crossings.

(c) Any employer convicted of violating subsection (a) of this Section, whether individually or in connection with one or more other persons, or as principal agent, or accessory, shall be guilty of a Class A misdemeanor.

P.A. 76–1586, § 6–506, added by P.A. 85–630, § 1, eff. Sept. 20, 1987. Amended by P.A. 86–845, § 1, eff. April 1, 1990; P.A. 92–249, § 5, eff. Jan. 1, 2002; P.A. 92–834, § 5, eff. Aug. 22, 2002.

Formerly Ill.Rev.Stat.1991, ch. 95 ½, ¶ 6–506.

P.A. 92–834 incorporated the amendment by P.A. 92–249.

5/6–507. Commercial Driver's License (CDL) Required

§ 6–507. Commercial Driver's License (CDL) Required.

(a) Except as expressly permitted by this UCDLA,[1] or when driving pursuant to the issuance of a commercial driver instruction permit and accompanied by the holder of a CDL valid for the vehicle being driven; no person shall drive a commercial motor vehicle on the highways unless the person has been issued, and is in the immediate possession of, a CDL bearing all applicable endorsements valid for type or classification of the commercial vehicle being driven.

(b) Except as otherwise provided by this Code, no person may drive a commercial motor vehicle on the highways while such person's driving privilege, license or permit is:

(1) Suspended, revoked, cancelled, or subject to disqualification. Any person convicted of violating this provision or a similar provision of this or any other state shall have their driving privileges revoked under paragraph 12 of subsection (a) of Section 6–205 of this Code.

(2) Subject to or in violation of an "out-of-service" order. Any person who has been issued a CDL and is convicted of violating this provision or a similar provision of any other state shall be disqualified from operating a commercial motor vehicle under subsection (i) of Section 6–514 of this Code.

(3) Subject to or in violation of an "out of service" order and while transporting passengers or hazardous materials. Any person who has been issued a CDL and is convicted of violating this provision or a similar provision of this or any other state shall be disqualified from operating a commercial motor vehicle under subsection (i) of Section 6–514 of this Code.

(c) Pursuant to the options provided to the States by FHWA Docket No. MC–88–8, the driver of any motor vehicle controlled or operated by or for a farmer is waived from the requirements of this Section, when such motor vehicle is being used to transport: agricultural products; implements of husbandry; or farm supplies; as long as such movement is not over 150 air miles from the originating farm. This waiver does not apply to the driver of any motor vehicle being used in a common or contract carrier type operation. However, for those drivers of any truck-tractor semitrailer combination or combinations registered under subsection (c) of Section 3–815 of this Code, this waiver shall apply only when the driver is a farmer or a member of the farmer's family and the driver is 21 years of age or more and has successfully completed any tests the Secretary of State deems necessary.

In addition, the farmer or a member of the farmer's family who operates a truck-tractor semitrailer combination or combinations pursuant to this waiver shall be granted all of the rights and shall be subject to all of the duties and restrictions with respect to Sections 6–514 and 6–515 of this Code applicable to the driver who possesses a commercial driver's license issued under this Code, except that the driver shall not be subject to any additional duties or restrictions contained in Part 382 of the Federal Motor Carrier Safety Regulations that are not otherwise imposed under Section 6–514 or 6–515 of this Code.

For purposes of this subsection (c), a member of the farmer's family is a natural or in-law spouse, child, parent, or sibling.

(c–5) An employee of a township or road district with a population of less than 3,000 operating a vehicle within the boundaries of the township or road district for the purpose of removing snow or ice from a roadway by plowing, sanding, or salting is waived from the requirements of this Section when the employee is needed to operate the vehicle because the employee of the township or road district who ordinarily operates the vehicle and who has a commercial driver's license is unable to operate the vehicle or is in need of additional assistance due to a snow emergency.

(d) Any person convicted of violating this Section, shall be guilty of a Class A misdemeanor.

(e) Any person convicted of violating paragraph (b) of this Section, shall have all driving privileges revoked by the Secretary of State.

(f) This Section shall not apply to:

(1) A person who currently holds a valid Illinois driver's license, for the type of vehicle being operated, until the expiration of such license or April 1, 1992, whichever is earlier; or

(2) A non-Illinois domiciliary who is properly licensed in another State, until April 1, 1992. A non-Illinois domiciliary, if such domiciliary is properly licensed in another State or foreign jurisdiction, until April 1, 1992.

P.A. 76-1586, § 6-507, added by P.A. 86-845, § 1, eff. April 1, 1990. Amended by P.A. 89-245, § 5, eff. Jan. 1, 1996; P.A. 89-658, § 5, eff. Oct. 1, 1996; P.A. 90-386, § 5, eff. Aug. 15, 1997; P.A. 90-655, § 153, eff. July 30, 1998.

Formerly Ill.Rev.Stat.1991, ch. 95 ½, ¶ 6-507.

1 625 ILCS 5/6-500 et seq.

P.A. 90-655, the First 1998 General Revisory Act, amended various Acts to delete obsolete text, to correct patent and technical errors, to revise cross references, to resolve multiple actions in the 89th and 90th General Assemblies and to make certain technical corrections in P.A. 89-708 through P.A. 90-566.

5/6-508. Commercial Driver's License (CDL)—qualification standards

§ 6-508. Commercial Driver's License (CDL)—qualification standards.

(a) Testing.

(1) General. No person shall be issued an original or renewal CDL unless that person is domiciled in this State. The Secretary shall cause to be administered such tests as the Secretary deems necessary to meet the requirements of 49 C.F.R. Part 383, subparts G and H.

(2) Third party testing. The Secretary of state may authorize a "third party tester", pursuant to 49 C.F.R. Part 383.75, to administer the skills test or tests specified by Federal Highway Administration pursuant to the Commercial Motor Vehicle Safety Act of 1986 [1] and any appropriate federal rule.

(b) Waiver of Skills Test. The Secretary of State may waive the skills test specified in this Section for a commercial driver license applicant who meets the requirements of 49 C.F.R. Part 383.77.

(c) Limitations on issuance of a CDL. A CDL, or a commercial driver instruction permit, shall not be issued to a person while the person is subject to a disqualification from driving a commercial motor vehicle, or unless otherwise permitted by this Code, while the person's driver's license is suspended, revoked or cancelled in any state, or any territory or province of Canada; nor may a CDL be issued to a person who has a CDL issued by any other state, or foreign jurisdiction, unless the person first surrenders all such licenses. No CDL shall be issued to or renewed for a person who does not meet the requirement of 49 CFR 391.41(b)(11). The requirement may be met with the aid of a hearing aid.

(d) Commercial driver instruction permit. A commercial driver instruction permit may be issued to any person holding a valid Illinois driver's license if such person successfully passes such tests as the Secretary determines to be necessary. A commercial driver instruction permit shall not be issued to a person who does not meet the requirements of 49 CFR 391.41 (b)(11), except for the renewal of a commercial driver instruction permit for a person who possesses a commercial instruction permit prior to the effective date of this amendatory Act of 1999.

P.A. 76-1586, § 6-508, added by P.A. 86-845, § 1, eff. April 1, 1990. Amended by P.A. 91-350, § 5, eff. July 29, 1999.

Formerly Ill.Rev.Stat.1991, ch. 95 ½, ¶ 6-508.

1 49 U.S.C.A. § 2701 et seq. (repealed).

5/6-509. Non-resident commercial driver's license

§ 6-509. Non-resident commercial driver's license. The Secretary of State may issue a non-resident CDL to a domiciliary of a foreign jurisdiction if the United States Secretary of Transportation has determined that the commercial motor vehicle testing and licensing standards, in that foreign jurisdiction, do not meet the testing standards established in 49 C.F.R. Part 383. The word "Non-resident" must appear on the face of the non-resident CDL. An applicant must surrender any non-resident CDL, license or permit issued by any other state.

P.A. 76-1586, § 6-509, added by P.A. 86-845, § 1, eff. April 1, 1990.

Formerly Ill.Rev.Stat.1991, ch. 95 ½, ¶ 6-509.

5/6-510. Application for Commercial Driver's License (CDL)

§ 6-510. Application for Commercial Driver's License (CDL). (a) The application for a CDL or commercial driver instruction permit, must include, but not necessarily be limited to, the following:

(1) the full name and current Illinois domiciliary address (unless the application is for a Non-resident CDL) of the applicant;

(2) a physical description of the applicant including sex, height, weight, color of eyes and hair color;

(3) date of birth;

(4) the applicant's social security number or other identifying number acceptable to the Secretary of State;

(5) the applicant's signature;

(6) certifications required by 49 C.F.R. Part 383.71; and

(7) any other information required by the Secretary of State.

P.A. 76-1586, § 6-510, added by P.A. 86-845, § 1, eff. April 1, 1990.

Formerly Ill.Rev.Stat.1991, ch. 95 ½, ¶ 6-510.

5/6-511. Change of name or domiciliary address

§ 6-511. Change of name or domiciliary address. All persons to whom a CDL has been issued, must notify the Driver Services Department of the Secretary of State's Office within 10 days of any name change or change in domiciliary address. In addition, such person shall make application for a corrected CDL within 30 days of any such change.

P.A. 76-1586, § 6-511, added by P.A. 86-845, § 1, eff. April 1, 1990.

Formerly Ill.Rev.Stat.1991, ch. 95 ½, ¶ 6-511.

5/6-512. Unlawful operation of a commercial motor vehicle pursuant to a non-Illinois issued CDL

§ 6-512. Unlawful operation of a commercial motor vehicle pursuant to a non-Illinois issued CDL. No person, after becoming a domiciliary of this State for 30 days or more, shall drive a commercial motor vehicle on the highways of this State pursuant to the authority of a CDL issued by any other State or foreign jurisdiction.

P.A. 76-1586, § 6-512, added by P.A. 86-845, § 1, eff. April 1, 1990.

Formerly Ill.Rev.Stat.1991, ch. 95 ½, ¶ 6-512.

5/6-513. Commercial Driver's License or CDL

§ 6-513. Commercial Driver's License or CDL. The content of the CDL shall include, but not necessarily be limited to the following:

(a) A CDL shall be distinctly marked "Commercial Driver's License" or "CDL". It must include, but not necessarily be limited to, the following information:

(1) the name and the Illinois domiciliary address (unless it is a Non-resident CDL) of the person to whom the CDL is issued;

(2) the person's color photograph;

(3) a physical description of the person including sex, height, and may include weight, color of eyes and hair color;

(4) date of birth;

(5) a CDL or file number assigned by the Secretary of State;

(6) it also may include the applicant's Social Security Number pursuant to Section 6-106;

(7) the person's signature;

(8) the class or type of commercial vehicle or vehicles which the person is authorized to drive together with any endorsements or restrictions;

(9) the name of the issuing state; and

(10) the issuance and expiration dates of the CDL.

(b) Applicant Record Check.

Prior to the issuance of a CDL, the Secretary of State shall obtain and review the applicant's driving record as required by the CMVSA and the United States Secretary of Transportation.

(c) Notification of Commercial Driver's License (CDL) Issuance.

Within 10 days after issuing a CDL, the Secretary of State must notify the Commercial Driver License Information System of that fact, and provide all information required to ensure identification of the person.

(d) Renewal.

Every person applying for a renewal of a CDL must complete the appropriate application form required by this Code and any other test deemed necessary by the Secretary.

P.A. 76-1586, § 6-513, added by P.A. 86-845, § 1, eff. April 1, 1990. Amended by P.A. 87-829, § 1, eff. Jan. 17, 1992; P.A. 87-832, § 3, eff. Jan. 17, 1992.

Formerly Ill.Rev.Stat.1991, ch. 95 ½, ¶ 6-513.

The amendments by P.A. 87-829 and P.A. 87-832 were identical.

5/6-514. Commercial Driver's License (CDL)—Disqualifications

§ 6-514. Commercial Driver's License (CDL)—Disqualifications.

(a) A person shall be disqualified from driving a commercial motor vehicle for a period of not less than 12 months for the first violation of:

(1) Refusing to submit to or failure to complete a test or tests to determine the driver's blood concentration of alcohol, other drug, or both, while driving a commercial motor vehicle; or

(2) Operating a commercial motor vehicle while the alcohol concentration of the person's blood, breath or urine is at least 0.04, or any amount of a drug, substance, or compound in the person's blood or urine resulting from the unlawful use or consumption of cannabis listed in the Cannabis Control Act [1] or a controlled substance listed in the Illinois Controlled Substances Act [2] as indicated by a police officer's sworn report or other verified evidence; or

(3) Conviction for a first violation of:

(i) Driving a commercial motor vehicle while under the influence of alcohol, or any other drug, or combination of drugs to a degree which renders such person incapable of safely driving; or

(ii) Knowingly and wilfully leaving the scene of an accident while operating a commercial motor vehicle; or

(iii) Driving a commercial motor vehicle while committing any felony.

If any of the above violations or refusals occurred while transporting hazardous material(s) required to be placarded, the person shall be disqualified for a period of not less than 3 years.

(b) A person is disqualified for life for a second conviction of any of the offenses specified in paragraph (a), or any combination of those offenses, arising from 2 or more separate incidents.

(c) A person is disqualified from driving a commercial motor vehicle for life who uses a commercial motor vehicle in the commission of any felony involving the manufacture, distribution, or dispensing of a controlled substance, or possession with intent to manufacture, distribute or dispense a controlled substance.

(d) The Secretary of State may, when the United States Secretary of Transportation so authorizes, issue regulations in which a disqualification for life under paragraph (b) may be reduced to a period of not less than 10 years. If a reinstated driver is subsequently convicted of another disqualifying offense, as specified in subsection (a) of this Section, he or she shall be permanently disqualified for life and shall be ineligible to again apply for a reduction of the lifetime disqualification.

(e) A person is disqualified from driving a commercial motor vehicle for a period of not less than 2 months if convicted of 2 serious traffic violations, committed in a commercial motor vehicle, arising from separate incidents, occurring within a 3 year period. However, a person will be disqualified from driving a commercial motor vehicle for a period of not less than 4 months if convicted of 3 serious traffic violations, committed in a commercial motor vehicle, arising from separate incidents, occurring within a 3 year period.

(f) Notwithstanding any other provision of this Code, any driver disqualified from operating a commercial motor vehicle, pursuant to this UCDLA, shall not be eligible for restoration of commercial driving privileges during any such period of disqualification.

(g) After suspending, revoking, or cancelling a commercial driver's license, the Secretary of State must update the driver's records to reflect such action within 10 days. After suspending or revoking the driving privilege of any person who has been issued a CDL or commercial driver instruction permit from another jurisdiction, the Secretary shall originate notification to such issuing jurisdiction within 10 days.

(h) The "disqualifications" referred to in this Section shall not be imposed upon any commercial motor vehicle driver, by the Secretary of State, unless the prohibited action(s) occurred after March 31, 1992.

(i) A person is disqualified from driving a commercial motor vehicle in accordance with the following:

(1) For 6 months upon a first conviction of paragraph (2) of subsection (b) of Section 6–507 of this Code.

(2) For one year upon a second conviction of paragraph (2) of subsection (b) of Section 6–507 of this Code within a 10–year period.

(3) For 3 years upon a third or subsequent conviction of paragraph (2) of subsection (b) of Section 6–507 of this Code within a 10–year period.

(4) For one year upon a first conviction of paragraph (3) of subsection (b) of Section 6–507 of this Code.

(5) For 3 years upon a second conviction of paragraph (3) of subsection (b) of Section 6–507 of this Code within a 10–year period.

(6) For 5 years upon a third or subsequent conviction of paragraph (3) of subsection (b) of Section 6–507 of this Code within a 10–year period.

(j) Disqualification for railroad-highway grade crossing violation.

(1) General rule. A driver who is convicted of a violation of a federal, State, or local law or regulation pertaining to one of the following 6 offenses at a railroad-highway grade crossing must be disqualified from operating a commercial motor vehicle for the period of time specified in paragraph (2) of this subsection (j) if the offense was committed while operating a commercial motor vehicle:

(i) For drivers who are not required to always stop, failing to slow down and check that the tracks are clear of an approaching train, as described in subsection (a–5) of Section 11–1201 of this Code;

(ii) For drivers who are not required to always stop, failing to stop before reaching the crossing, if the tracks are not clear, as described in subsection (a) of Section 11–1201 of this Code;

(iii) For drivers who are always required to stop, failing to stop before driving onto the crossing, as described in Section 11–1202 of this Code;

(iv) For all drivers, failing to have sufficient space to drive completely through the crossing without stopping, as described in subsection (b) of Section 11–1425 of this Code;

(v) For all drivers, failing to obey a traffic control device or the directions of an enforcement official at the crossing, as described in subdivision (a)2 of Section 11–1201 of this Code;

(vi) For all drivers, failing to negotiate a crossing because of insufficient undercarriage clearance, as described in subsection (d–1) of Section 11–1201 of this Code.

(2) Duration of disqualification for railroad-highway grade crossing violation.

(i) First violation. A driver must be disqualified from operating a commercial motor vehicle for not less than 60 days if the driver is convicted of a violation described in paragraph (1) of this subsection (j) and, in the three-year period preceding the conviction, the driver had no convictions for a violation described in paragraph (1) of this subsection (j).

(ii) Second violation. A driver must be disqualified from operating a commercial motor vehicle for not less than 120 days if the driver is convicted of a violation described in paragraph (1) of this subsection (j) and, in the three-year period preceding the conviction, the driver had one other conviction for a violation described in paragraph (1) of this subsection (j) that was committed in a separate incident.

(iii) Third or subsequent violation. A driver must be disqualified from operating a commercial motor vehicle for not less than one year if the driver is convicted of a violation described in paragraph (1) of this subsection (j) and, in the three-year period preceding the conviction, the driver had 2 or more other convictions for violations described in paragraph (1) of this subsection (j) that were committed in separate incidents.

P.A. 76–1586, § 6–514, added by P.A. 86–845, § 1, eff. April 1, 1990. Amended by P.A. 88–212, § 5, eff. Jan. 1, 1994; P.A. 89–245, § 5, eff. Jan. 1, 1996; P.A. 90–422, § 5, eff. Jan. 1, 1998; P.A. 92–249, § 5, eff. Jan. 1, 2002; P.A. 92–834, § 5, eff. Aug. 22, 2002.

Formerly Ill.Rev.Stat.1991, ch. 95 ½, ¶ 6–514.

1 720 ILCS 550/1 et seq.

2 720 ILCS 570/100 et seq.

P.A. 92–834 incorporated the amendment by P.A. 92–249.

5/6–515. Prohibitions against a person driving a commercial motor vehicle while having any alcohol, other drug, or both in such person's system

§ 6–515. Prohibitions against a person driving a commercial motor vehicle while having any alcohol, other drug, or both in such person's system.

(a) Notwithstanding any other provisions of this Code, a person shall not drive a commercial motor vehicle while having any alcohol, other drug, or both in such person's system.

(b) A person who drives a commercial motor vehicle while having any alcohol, other drug, or both, in such person's system or who refuses to submit to or fails to complete an alcohol or other drug test or tests pursuant to Section 6–517, as evidenced by the issuance of a Sworn Report by a police officer, must be placed "out-of-service" for at least 24 hours.

(c) The police officer shall provide the Secretary of State with a copy of all Sworn Reports issued pursuant to this UCDLA.

(d) The "out-of-service" referred to in this Section shall not be entered to the record of any Illinois commercial motor vehicle driver, by the Secretary of State, unless the prohibited action or actions occurred after March 31, 1992.

P.A. 76–1586, § 6–515, added by P.A. 86–845, § 1, eff. April 1, 1990. Amended by P.A. 88–212, § 5, eff. Jan. 1, 1994.

Formerly Ill.Rev.Stat.1991, ch. 95 ½, ¶ 6–515.

5/6–516. Implied consent requirements for commercial motor vehicle drivers

§ 6–516. Implied consent requirements for commercial motor vehicle drivers.

(a) Effective April 1, 1992, any person who drives a commercial motor vehicle upon the highways is hereby deemed to have given consent to submit to a test or tests, subject to the provisions of Section 11–501.2 of this Code, of such person's breath, blood or urine for the purpose of determining the presence of alcohol, or other drugs, in such person's system.

(b) A test or tests may be administered at the direction of a law enforcement officer, who after stopping or detaining the commercial motor vehicle driver, has probable cause to believe that driver was driving a commercial motor vehicle while having alcohol or any amount of a drug, substance, or compound resulting from the unlawful use or consumption of cannabis listed in the Cannabis Control Act [1] or a controlled substance listed in the Illinois Controlled Substances Act [2] in such driver's system.

(c) Effective April 1, 1992, any person who operates a school bus at the time of an accident involving the school bus is hereby deemed to have given consent to submit to a test or tests to be administered at the direction of a law enforcement officer, subject to the provisions of Section 11–501.2 of this Code, of the driver's breath, blood or urine for the purpose of determining the presence of alcohol, or other drugs, in the person's system.

P.A. 76–1586, § 6–516, added by P.A. 86–845, § 1, eff. April 1, 1990. Amended by P.A. 86–1465, § 1, eff. April 1, 1992; P.A. 88–212, § 5, eff. Jan. 1, 1994.

Formerly Ill.Rev.Stat.1991, ch. 95 ½, ¶ 6–516.

[1] 720 ILCS 550/1 et seq.

[2] 720 ILCS 570/100 et seq.

5/6–517. Commercial driver; implied consent warnings

§ 6–517. Commercial driver; implied consent warnings.

(a) Any person driving a commercial motor vehicle who is requested by a police officer, pursuant to Section 6–516, to submit to a chemical test or tests to determine the alcohol concentration or any amount of a drug, substance, or compound resulting from the unlawful use or consumption of cannabis listed in the Cannabis Control Act [1] or a controlled substance listed in the Illinois Controlled Substances Act [2] in such person's system, must be warned by the police officer requesting the test or tests that a refusal to submit to the test or tests will result in that person being immediately placed out-of-service for a period of 24 hours and being disqualified from operating a commercial motor vehicle for a period of not less than 12 months; the person shall also be warned that if such person submits to testing which discloses an alcohol concentration of greater than 0.00 but less than 0.04 or any amount of a drug, substance, or compound in such person's blood or urine resulting from the unlawful use or consumption of cannabis listed in the Cannabis Control Act or a controlled substance listed in the Illinois Controlled Substances Act, such person shall be placed immediately out-of-service for a period of 24 hours; if the person submits to testing which discloses an alcohol concentration of 0.04 or more or any amount of a drug, substance, or compound in such person's blood or urine resulting from the unlawful use or consumption of cannabis listed in the Cannabis Control Act or a controlled substance listed in the Illinois Controlled Substances Act, such person shall be placed immediately out-of-service and disqualified from driving a commercial motor vehicle for a period of at least 12 months; also the person shall be warned that if such testing discloses an alcohol concentration of 0.08, or more or any amount of a drug, substance, or compound in such person's blood or urine resulting from the unlawful use or consumption of cannabis listed in the Cannabis Control Act or a controlled substance listed in the Illinois Controlled Substances Act, in addition to the person being immediately placed out-of-service and disqualified for 12 months as provided in this UCDLA, the results of such testing shall also be admissible in prosecutions for violations of Section 11–501 of this Code, or similar violations of local ordinances, however, such results shall not be used to impose any driving sanctions pursuant to Section 11–501.1 of this Code.

The person shall also be warned that any disqualification imposed pursuant to this Section, shall be for life for any such offense or refusal, or combination thereof; including a conviction for violating Section 11–501 while driving a commercial motor vehicle, or similar provisions of local ordinances, committed a second time involving separate incidents.

(b) If the person refuses or fails to complete testing, or submits to a test which discloses an alcohol concentration of at least 0.04, or any amount of a drug, substance, or compound in such person's blood or urine resulting from the unlawful use or consumption of cannabis listed in the Cannabis Control Act or a controlled substance listed in the Illinois Controlled Substances Act, the law enforcement officer must submit a Sworn Report to the Secretary of State, in a form prescribed by the Secretary, certifying that the test or tests was requested pursuant to paragraph (a); that the person was warned, as provided in paragraph (a) and that such person refused to submit to or failed to complete testing, or submitted to a test which disclosed an alcohol concentration of 0.04 or more, or any amount of a drug, substance, or compound in such person's blood or urine resulting from the unlawful use or consumption of cannabis listed in the Cannabis Control Act or a controlled substance listed in the Illinois Controlled Substances Act.

(c) The police officer submitting the Sworn Report under this Section shall serve notice of the CDL disqualification on the person and such CDL disqualification shall be effective as provided in paragraph (d). In cases where the blood alcohol concentration of 0.04 or more, or any amount of a drug, substance, or compound in such person's blood or urine resulting from the unlawful use or consumption of cannabis listed in the Cannabis Control Act or a controlled substance listed in the Illinois Controlled Substances Act, is established by subsequent analysis of blood or urine collected at the time of the request, the police officer shall give notice as provided in this Section or by deposit in the United States mail of such notice as provided in this Section or by deposit in the United States mail of such notice in an envelope with postage prepaid and addressed to such person's domiciliary address as shown on the Sworn Report and the CDL disqualification shall begin as provided in paragraph (d).

(d) The CDL disqualification referred to in this Section shall take effect on the 46th day following the date the Sworn Report was given to the affected person.

(e) Upon receipt of the Sworn Report from the police officer, the Secretary of State shall disqualify the person from driving any commercial motor vehicle and shall confirm the CDL disqualification by mailing the notice of the effective date to the person. However, should the Sworn Report be defective by not containing sufficient information or be completed in error, the confirmation of the CDL disqualification shall not be mailed to the affected person or entered into the record, instead the Sworn Report shall be forwarded to the issuing agency identifying any such defect.

P.A. 76–1586, § 6–517, added by P.A. 86–845, § 1, eff. April 1, 1990. Amended by P.A. 88–212, § 5, eff. Jan. 1, 1994; P.A. 90–43, § 5, eff. July 2, 1997; P.A. 91–357, § 231, eff. July 29, 1999.

Formerly Ill.Rev.Stat.1991, ch. 95 ½, ¶ 6–517.

[1] 720 ILCS 550/1 et seq.

[2] 570 ILCS 570/100 et seq.

5/6–518. Notification of Traffic Convictions

§ 6–518. Notification of Traffic Convictions. Within 10 days after receiving a report of an Illinois conviction, or other verified evidence, of any driver who has been issued a CDL by another State, for a violation of any law or local ordinance of this State, relating to motor vehicle traffic control, other than parking violations, committed in a commercial motor vehicle, the Secretary of State must notify the driver licensing authority which issued such CDL of said conviction.

P.A. 76-1586, § 6-518, added by P.A. 86-845, § 1, eff. April 1, 1990.

Formerly Ill.Rev.Stat.1991, ch. 95 ½, ¶ 6-518.

5/6-519. Driving Record Information To Be Furnished

§ 6-519. Driving Record Information To Be Furnished. Notwithstanding any other provision of law to the contrary, the Secretary of State shall furnish full information regarding a commercial driver's driving record to the driver licensing administrator of any other State requesting such information; and any other entity or person authorized to receive such information pursuant to Section 2-123 of this Code.

P.A. 76-1586, § 6-519, added by P.A. 86-845, § 1, eff. April 1, 1990.

Formerly Ill.Rev.Stat.1991, ch. 95 ½, ¶ 6-519.

5/6-520. CDL disqualification or out-of-service order; hearing

§ 6-520. CDL disqualification or out-of-service order; hearing.

(a) A disqualification of commercial driving privileges by the Secretary of State, pursuant to this UCDLA, shall not become effective until the person is notified in writing, by the Secretary, of the impending disqualification and advised that a CDL hearing may be requested.

(b) Upon receipt of the notice of a CDL disqualification not based upon a conviction, an out-of-service order, or notification that a CDL disqualification is forthcoming, the person may make a written petition in a form, approved by the Secretary of State, for a CDL hearing. Such petition must state the grounds upon which the person seeks to have the CDL disqualification rescinded or the out-of-service order removed from the person's driving record. Within 10 days after the receipt of such petition, it shall be reviewed by the Director of the Department of Administrative Hearings, Office of the Secretary of State, or by an appointed designee. If it is determined that the petition on its face does not state grounds upon which the relief may be based, the petition for a CDL hearing shall be denied and the disqualification shall become effective as if no petition had been filed and the out-of-service order shall be sustained. If such petition is so denied, the person may submit another petition.

(c) The scope of a CDL hearing, for any disqualification imposed pursuant to paragraphs (1) and (2) of subsection (a) of Section 6-514 shall be limited to the following issues:

1. Whether the person was operating a commercial motor vehicle;

2. Whether, after making the initial stop, the police officer had probable cause to issue a Sworn Report;

3. Whether the person was verbally warned of the ensuing consequences prior to submitting to any type of chemical test or tests to determine such person's blood concentration of alcohol, other drug, or both; and

4. Whether the person did refuse to submit to or failed to complete the chemical testing or did submit to such test or tests and such test or tests disclosed an alcohol concentration of at least 0.04 or any amount of a drug, substance, or compound resulting from the unlawful use or consumption of cannabis listed in the Cannabis Control Act[1] or a controlled substance listed in the Illinois Controlled Substances Act[2] in the person's system;

5. Whether the person was warned that if the test or tests disclosed an alcohol concentration of 0.08 or more or any amount of a drug, substance, or compound resulting from the unlawful use or consumption of cannabis listed in the Cannabis Control Act or a controlled substance listed in the Illinois Controlled Substances Act, such results could be admissible in a subsequent prosecution under Section 11-501 of this Code or similar provision of local ordinances; and

6. Whether such results could not be used to impose any driver's license sanctions pursuant to Section 11-501.1.

Upon the conclusion of the above CDL hearing, the CDL disqualification imposed shall either be sustained or rescinded.

(d) The scope of a CDL hearing for any out-of-service sanction, imposed pursuant to Section 6-515, shall be limited to the following issues:

1. Whether the person was driving a commercial motor vehicle;

2. Whether, while driving such commercial motor vehicle, the person had alcohol or any amount of a drug, substance, or compound resulting from the unlawful use or consumption of cannabis listed in the Cannabis Control Act or a controlled substance listed in the Illinois Controlled Substances Act in such person's system; or

3. Whether the person was verbally warned of the ensuing consequences prior to being asked to submit to any type of chemical test or tests to determine such person's alcohol, other drug, or both, concentration; and

4. Whether, after being so warned, the person did refuse to submit to or failed to complete such chemical test or tests or did submit to such test or tests and such test or tests disclosed an alcohol concentration greater than 0.00 or any amount of a drug, substance, or compound resulting from the unlawful use or consumption of cannabis listed in the Cannabis Control Act or a controlled substance listed in the Illinois Controlled Substances Act.

Upon the conclusion of the above CDL hearing, the out-of-service sanction shall either be sustained or removed from the person's driving record.

(e) If any person petitions for a hearing relating to any CDL disqualification based upon a conviction, as defined in this UCDLA, said hearing shall not be conducted as a CDL hearing, but shall be conducted as any other driver's license hearing, whether formal or informal, as promulgated in the rules and regulations of the Secretary.

(f) Any evidence of alcohol or other drug consumption, for the purposes of this UCDLA, shall be sufficient probable cause for requesting the driver to submit to a chemical test or tests to determine the presence of alcohol, other drug, or both in the person's system and the subsequent issuance of an out-of-service order or a Sworn Report by a police officer.

(g) For the purposes of this UCDLA, a CDL "hearing" shall mean a hearing before the Office of the Secretary of State in accordance with Section 2-118 of this Code, for the purpose of resolving differences or disputes specifically related to the scope of the issues identified in this Section. These proceedings will be a matter of record and a final appealable order issued. The petition for a CDL hearing shall not stay or delay the effective date of the impending disqualification.

(h) The CDL hearing may be conducted upon a review of the police officer's own official reports; provided however, that the petitioner may subpoena the officer. Failure of the officer to answer the subpoena shall be grounds for a continuance.

P.A. 76–1586, § 6–520, added by P.A. 86–845, § 1, eff. April 1, 1990. Amended by P.A. 87–829, § 1, eff. Jan. 17, 1992; P.A. 87–832, § 3, eff. Jan. 17, 1992; P.A. 87–895, Art. 2, § 2–45, eff. Aug. 14, 1992; P.A. 88–212, § 5, eff. Jan. 1, 1994; P.A. 88–670, Art. 3, § 3–80, eff. Dec. 2, 1994; P.A. 90–43, § 5, eff. July 2, 1997; P.A. 91–357, § 231, eff. July 29, 1999.

Formerly Ill.Rev.Stat.1991, ch. 95 ½, ¶ 6–520.

1 720 ILCS 550/100 et seq.

2 720 ILCS 570/100 et seq.

5/6–521. Rulemaking Authority

§ 6–521. Rulemaking Authority.

(a) The Secretary of State, using the authority to license motor vehicle operators under this Code, may adopt such rules and regulations as may be necessary to establish standards, policies and procedures for the licensing of commercial motor vehicle drivers in order to meet the requirements of the Commercial Motor Vehicle Act of 1986 (CMVSA);[1] subsequent federal rulemaking under 49 C.F.R. Part 383; and administrative and policy decisions of the U.S. Secretary of Transportation and the Federal Highway Administration. The Secretary may, as provided in the CMVSA, establish stricter requirements for the licensing of commercial motor vehicle drivers than those established by the federal government.

(b) By January 1, 1994, the Secretary of State shall establish rules and regulations for the issuance of a restricted commercial driver's license for farm-related service industries consistent with federal guidelines. The restricted license shall be available for a seasonal period or periods not to exceed a total of 180 days in any 12 month period.

(c) By July 1, 1995, the Secretary of State shall establish rules and regulations, to be consistent with federal guidelines, for the issuance and cancellation or withdrawal of a restricted commercial driver's license that is limited to the operation of a school bus. A driver whose restricted commercial driver's license has been cancelled or withdrawn may contest the sanction by requesting a hearing pursuant to Section 2–118 of this Code. The cancellation or withdrawal of the restricted commercial driver's license shall remain in effect pending the outcome of that hearing.

(d) By July 1, 1995, the Secretary of State shall establish rules and regulations for the issuance and cancellation of a School Bus Driver's Permit. The permit shall be required for the operation of a school bus as provided in subsection (c), a non-restricted CDL with passenger endorsement, or a properly classified driver's license. The permit will establish that the school bus driver has met all the requirements of the application and screening process established by Section 6–106.1 of this Code.

P.A. 76–1586, § 6–521, added by P.A. 86–845, § 1, eff. April 1, 1990. Amended by P.A. 88–450, § 5, eff. Aug. 20, 1993; P.A. 88–612, § 15, eff. July 1, 1995.

Formerly Ill.Rev.Stat.1991, ch. 95 ½, ¶ 6–521.

1 49 App. U.S.C.A. § 2701.

P.A. 88–612 incorporated the amendment by P.A. 88–450.

5/6–522. Authority to Enter Agreements

§ 6–522. Authority to Enter Agreements. The Secretary of State may enter into or make agreements, arrangements, or declarations to carry out the provisions of this UCDLA.

P.A. 76–1586, § 6–522, added by P.A. 86–845, § 1, eff. April 1, 1990.

Formerly Ill.Rev.Stat.1991, ch. 95 ½, ¶ 6–522.

5/6–523. Reciprocity

§ 6–523. Reciprocity. (a) Notwithstanding any law to the contrary, a person may drive a commercial motor vehicle in this State if such person has a valid commercial driver's license or CDL instruction permit issued by another State or foreign jurisdiction as long as such person has not been an established domiciliary of this State for 30 days or more.

(b) The Secretary of State shall give out of state convictions full faith and credit and treat them for sanctioning purposes, under this UCDLA, just as if they occurred in this State.

P.A. 76–1586, § 6–523, added by P.A. 86–845, § 1, eff. April 1, 1990.

Formerly Ill.Rev.Stat.1991, ch. 95 ½, ¶ 6–523.

5/6–524. Penalties

§ 6–524. Penalties.

(a) Every person convicted of violating any provision of this UCDLA for which another penalty is not provided shall for a first offense be guilty of a petty offense; and for a second conviction for any offense committed within 3 years of any previous offense, shall be guilty of a Class B misdemeanor.

(b) Any person convicted of violating subsection (b) of Section 6–506 of this Code shall be subject to a civil penalty of not more than $10,000.

P.A. 76–1586, § 6–524, added by P.A. 86–845, § 1, eff. April 1, 1990. Amended by P.A. 92–249, § 5, eff. Jan. 1, 2002.

Formerly Ill.Rev.Stat.1991, ch. 95 ½, ¶ 6–524.

5/6–525. Severability

§ 6–525. Severability. The provisions of this UCLDA shall be severable and if any phrase, clause, sentence or provision of this UCLDA is declared to be contrary to the Constitutions of this State, or of the United States, such unconstitutionality shall not affect the validity of the remainder of this UCDLA.

P.A. 76–1586, § 6–525, added by P.A. 86–845, § 1, eff. April 1, 1990.

Formerly Ill.Rev.Stat.1991, ch. 95 ½, ¶ 6–525.

ARTICLE VI. PENALTIES

Section

5/6–601. Penalties

Text of section as amended by P.A. 92–622 and P.A. 92–883

§ 6–601. Penalties.

(a) It is a petty offense for any person to violate any of the provisions of this Chapter unless such violation is by this Code or other law of this State declared to be a misdemeanor or a felony.

(b) General penalties. Unless another penalty is in this Code or other laws of this State, every person convicted of a petty offense for the violation of any provision of this Chapter shall be punished by a fine of not more than $500.

(c) Unlicensed driving. Except as hereinafter provided a violation of Section 6-101 shall be:

1. A Class A misdemeanor if the person failed to obtain a driver's license or permit after expiration of a period of revocation.

2. A Class B misdemeanor if the person has been issued a driver's license or permit, which has expired, and if the period of expiration is greater than one year; or if the person has never been issued a driver's license or permit, or is not qualified to obtain a driver's license or permit because of his age.

If a licensee under this Code is convicted of violating Section 6-101 for operating a motor vehicle during a time when such licensee's driver's license was invalid under the provisions of Section 6-110, then conviction under such circumstances shall be punishable by a fine of not more than $25.

If a licensee under this Code is convicted of violating Section 6-303 for operating a motor vehicle during a time when such licensee's driver's license was suspended under the provisions of Section 6-306.3, then such act shall be a petty offense (provided the licensee has answered the charge which was the basis of the suspension under Section 6-306.3), and there shall be imposed no additional like period of suspension as provided in paragraph (b) of Section 6-303.

P.A. 76-1586, § 6-601, eff. July 1, 1970. Amended by P.A. 76-2157, § 1, eff. July 1, 1970; P.A. 77-2720, § 1, eff. Jan. 1, 1973; P.A. 80-911, § 1, eff. Oct. 1, 1977; P.A. 80-1462, § 1, eff. Jan. 1, 1979; P.A. 83-385, § 1, eff. Jan. 1, 1984; P.A. 84-1231, § 1, eff. July 28, 1986; P.A. 85-992, § 1, eff. Jan. 5, 1988; P.A. 92-622, § 5, eff. Jan. 1, 2003; P.A. 92-883, § 5, eff. Jan. 13, 2003.

Formerly Ill.Rev.Stat.1991, ch. 95 ½, ¶ 6-601.

For text of section as amended by P.A. 92-647 and P.A. 92-883, see 625 ILCS 5/6-601, post

P.A. 92-883 incorporated the amendment by P.A. 92-622.

5/6-601. Penalties

Text of Section as amended by P.A. 92-647 and P.A. 92-883

§ 6-601. Penalties.

(a) It is a petty offense for any person to violate any of the provisions of this Chapter unless such violation is by this Code or other law of this State declared to be a misdemeanor or a felony.

(b) General penalties. Unless another penalty is in this Code or other laws of this State, every person convicted of a petty offense for the violation of any provision of this Chapter shall be punished by a fine of not more than $500.

(c) Unlicensed driving. Except as hereinafter provided a violation of Section 6-101 shall be:

1. A Class A misdemeanor if the person failed to obtain a driver's license or permit after expiration of a period of revocation.

2. A Class B misdemeanor if the person has been issued a driver's license or permit, which has expired, and if the period of expiration is greater than one year; or if the person has never been issued a driver's license or permit, or is not qualified to obtain a driver's license or permit because of his age.

If a licensee under this Code is convicted of violating Section 6-101 for operating a motor vehicle during a time when such licensee's driver's license was invalid under the provisions of Section 6-110, then conviction under such circumstances shall be punishable by a fine of not more than $25.

If a licensee under this Code is convicted of violating Section 6-303 for operating a motor vehicle during a time when such licensee's driver's license was suspended under the provisions of Section 6-306.3, then such act shall be a petty offense (provided the licensee has answered the charge which was the basis of the suspension under Section 6-306.3), and there shall be imposed no additional like period of suspension as provided in paragraph (b) of Section 6-303.

P.A. 76-1586, § 6-601, eff. July 1, 1970. Amended by P.A. 76-2157, § 1, eff. July 1, 1970; P.A. 77-2720, § 1, eff. Jan. 1, 1973; P.A. 80-911, § 1, eff. Oct. 1, 1977; P.A. 80-1462, § 1, eff. Jan. 1, 1979; P.A. 83-385, § 1, eff. Jan. 1, 1984; P.A. 84-1231, § 1, eff. July 28, 1986; P.A. 85-992, § 1, eff. Jan. 5, 1988; P.A. 92-622, § 5, eff. Jan. 1, 2003; P.A. 92-647, § 5, eff. Jan. 1, 2003; P.A. 92-883, § 5, eff. Jan. 13, 2003.

Formerly Ill.Rev.Stat.1991, ch. 95 ½, ¶ 6-601.

For text of section as amended by P.A. 92-622 and P.A. 92-883, see 625 ILCS 5/6-601, ante

P.A. 92-883 incorporated the amendment by P.A. 92-647.

See 5 ILCS 70/6 as to the effect of (1) more than one amendment of a section at the same session of the General Assembly or (2) two or more acts relating to the same subject matter enacted by the same General Assembly.

ARTICLE VII. DRIVER LICENSE COMPACT

Date Effective

Article VII was added by P.A. 76-1615, § 1, effective July 1, 1970.

Section

5/6-700. Definitions

§ 6-700. Definitions. As used in this compact:

(a) "State" means a state, territory or possession of the United States, the District of Columbia, or the Commonwealth of Puerto Rico.

(b) "Home state" means the state which has issued and has the power to suspend or revoke the use of the license or permit to operate a motor vehicle.

(c) "Conviction" means a conviction of any offense related to the use or operation of a motor vehicle which is prohibited by state law, municipal ordinance or administrative rule or regulation, or a forfeiture of bail, bond or other security deposited to secure appearance by a person charged with having committed any such offense, and which conviction or forfeiture is required to be reported to the licensing authority.

P.A. 76-1586, § 6-700, added by P.A. 76-1615, § 1, eff. July 1, 1970.

Formerly Ill.Rev.Stat.1991, ch. 95 ½, ¶ 6-700.

5/6-701. Findings and declaration of policy

§ 6-701. Findings and declaration of policy.

(a) The party states find that:

1. The safety of their streets and highways is materially affected by the degree of compliance with state laws and local ordinances relating to the operation of motor vehicles.

2. Violation of such a law or ordinance is evidence that the violator engages in conduct which is likely to endanger the safety of persons and property.

3. The continuance in force of a license to drive is predicated upon compliance with laws and ordinances relating to the operation of motor vehicles, in whichever jurisdiction the vehicle is operated.

(b) It is the policy of each of the party states to:

1. Promote compliance with the laws, ordinances and administrative rules and regulations relating to the operation of motor vehicles by their operators in each of the jurisdictions where such operators drive motor vehicles.

2. Make the reciprocal recognition of licenses to drive and eligibility therefor more just and equitable by considering the over-all compliance with motor vehicle laws, ordinances and administrative rules and regulations as a condition precedent to the continuance or issuance of any license by reason of which the licensee is authorized or permitted to operate a motor vehicle in any of the party states.

P.A. 76-1586, § 6-701, added by P.A. 76-1615, § 1, eff. July 1, 1970.

Formerly Ill.Rev.Stat.1991, ch. 95 ½, ¶ 6-701.

5/6-702. Reports of conviction

§ 6-702. Reports of conviction. The licensing authority of a party state shall report each conviction of a person from another party state occurring within its jurisdiction to the licensing authority of the home state of the licensee. Such report shall clearly identify the person convicted; describe the violation specifying the section of the statute, code or ordinance violated; identify the court in which action was taken; indicate whether a plea of guilty or not guilty was entered, or the conviction was a result of the forfeiture of bail, bond or other security; and shall include any special findings made in connection therewith.

P.A. 76-1586, § 6-702, added by P.A. 76-1615, § 1, eff. July 1, 1970.

Formerly Ill.Rev.Stat.1991, ch. 95 ½, ¶ 6-702.

5/6-703. Effect of conviction

§ 6-703. Effect of conviction. (a) The licensing authority in the home state, for the purposes of suspension, revocation or limitation of the license to operate a motor vehicle, shall give the same effect to the conduct reported, pursuant to Section 6-702, as it would if such conduct had occurred in the home state, in the case of convictions for:

1. Manslaughter or negligent homicide resulting from the operation of a motor vehicle;

2. Driving a motor vehicle while under the influence of intoxicating liquor or a narcotic drug, or under the influence of any other drug to a degree which renders the driver incapable of safely driving a motor vehicle;

3. Any felony in the commission of which a motor vehicle is used;

4. Failure to stop and render aid in the event of a motor vehicle accident resulting in the death or personal injury of another.

(b) As to other convictions, reported pursuant to Section 6-702, the licensing authority in the home state shall give such effect to the conduct as is provided by the laws of the home state.

(c) If the laws of a party state do not provide for offenses or violations denominated or described in precisely the words employed in paragraph (a) of this Section, such party state shall construe the denominations and descriptions appearing in paragraph (a) hereof as being applicable to and identifying those offenses or violations of a substantially similar nature, and the laws of such party state shall contain such provision as may be necessary to ensure that full force and effect is given to this Section.

P.A. 76-1586, § 6-703, added by P.A. 76-1615, § 1, eff. July 1, 1970.

Formerly Ill.Rev.Stat.1991, ch. 95 ½, ¶ 6-703.

5/6-704. Applications for new licenses

§ 6-704. Applications for new licenses. Upon application for a license to drive, the licensing authority in a party state shall ascertain whether the applicant has ever held, or is the holder of a license to drive issued by any other party state. The licensing authority in the state where application is made shall not issue a license to drive to the applicant if:

1. The applicant has held such a license, but the same has been suspended by reason, in whole or in part, of a violation and if such suspension period has not terminated.

2. The applicant has held such a license, but the same has been revoked by reason, in whole or in part, of a violation and if such revocation has not terminated, except that after the expiration of one year from the date the license was revoked, such person may make application for a new license if permitted by law. The licensing authority may refuse to issue a license to any such applicant if, after investigation, the licensing authority determines that it will not be safe to grant to such person the privilege of driving a motor vehicle on the public highways.

3. The applicant is the holder of a license to drive issued by another party state and currently in force unless the applicant surrenders such license.

P.A. 76-1586, § 6-704, added by P.A. 76-1615, § 1, eff. July 1, 1970.

Formerly Ill.Rev.Stat.1991, ch. 95 ½, ¶ 6-704.

5/6-705. Applicability of other laws

§ 6-705. Applicability of other laws. Except as expressly required by provisions of this compact, nothing contained herein shall be construed to affect the right of any party state to apply any of its other laws relating to the licenses to drive to any person or circumstance, nor to invalidate or prevent any driver license agreement or other cooperative arrangement between a party state and a nonparty state.

P.A. 76-1586, § 6-705, added by P.A. 76-1615, § 1, eff. July 1, 1970.

Formerly Ill.Rev.Stat.1991, ch. 95 ½, ¶ 6-705.

5/6-706. Compact administrator and interchange of information

§ 6-706. Compact administrator and interchange of information. (a) The head of the licensing authority of each party state shall be administrator of this compact for his state. The administrators, acting jointly, shall have the power to formulate all necessary and proper procedures for the exchange of information under this compact.

(b) The administrator of each party state shall furnish to the administrator of each other party state any information or documents reasonably necessary to facilitate the administration of this compact.

P.A. 76-1586, § 6–706, added by P.A. 76-1615, § 1, eff. July 1, 1970.

Formerly Ill.Rev.Stat.1991, ch. 95 ½, ¶ 6–706.

5/6–707. Entry into force and withdrawal

§ 6–707. Entry into force and withdrawal. (a) This compact shall enter into force and become effective as to any state when it has enacted the same into law.

(b) Any party state may withdraw from this compact by enacting a statute repealing the same, but no such withdrawal shall take effect until 6 months after the executive head of the withdrawing state has given notice of the withdrawal to the executive heads of all other party states. No withdrawal shall affect the validity or applicability by the licensing authorities of states remaining party to the compact of any report of conviction occurring prior to the withdrawal.

P.A. 76-1586, § 6–707, added by P.A. 76-1615, § 1, eff. July 1, 1970.

Formerly Ill.Rev.Stat.1991, ch. 95 ½, ¶ 6–707.

5/6–708. Construction and Severability

§ 6–708. Construction and Severability. (a) This compact shall be liberally construed so as to effectuate the purposes thereof. The provisions of this compact shall be severable and if any phrase, clause, sentence or provision of this compact is declared to be contrary to the constitution of any party state or of the United States or the applicability thereof to any government, agency, person or circumstance is held invalid, the validity of the remainder of this compact and the applicability thereof to any government, agency, person or circumstance shall not be affected thereby. If this compact shall be held contrary to the constitution of any state party thereto, the compact shall remain in full force and effect as to the remaining states and in full force and effect as to the state affected as to all severable matters.

(b) As used in the compact, the term "licensing authority" with reference to this state, means the Secretary of State. The Secretary of State shall furnish to the appropriate authorities of any other party state any information or documents reasonably necessary to facilitate the administration of Sections 6–702, 6–703 and 6–704 of the compact.

(c) The compact administrator provided for in Section 6–706 of the compact shall not be entitled to any additional compensation on account of his service as such administrator, but shall be entitled to expenses incurred in connection with his duties and responsibilities as such administrator, in the same manner as for expenses incurred in connection with any other duties or responsibilities of his office or employment.

(d) As used in the compact, with reference to this state, the term "executive head" shall mean the Governor.

(e) The phrase "manslaughter or negligent homicide," as used in subparagraph (1) of paragraph (a) of Section 6–703 of the compact includes the offense of reckless homicide as defined in Section 9–3 of the "Criminal Code of 1961," as heretofore or hereafter amended,[1] or in any predecessor statute, as well as the offenses of second degree murder and involuntary manslaughter.

The offense described in subparagraph (2) of paragraph (a) of Section 6–703 of the compact includes any violation of Section 11–501 of this Code or any similar provision of a local ordinance.

The offense described in subparagraph (4) of paragraph (a) of Section 6–703 of the compact includes any violation of paragraph (a) of Section 11–401 of this Code.

P.A. 76-1586, § 6–708, added by P.A. 76-1615, § 1, eff. July 1, 1970. Amended by P.A. 84–1450, § 7, eff. July 1, 1987; P.A. 85–951, § 1, eff. July 1, 1988.

Formerly Ill.Rev.Stat.1991, ch. 95 ½, ¶ 6–708.

[1] 720 ILCS 5/9–3.

ARTICLE VIII. NONRESIDENT VIOLATOR COMPACT

Date Effective

Article VIII was added by P.A. 83–385, § 1, eff. Jan. 1, 1984.

Section

5/6–800. Enactment

§ 6–800. The Nonresident Violator Compact, hereinafter referred to as the Compact, is hereby enacted into law and entered into with all other jurisdictions legally joining therein.

P.A. 76-1586, § 6–800, added by P.A. 83–385, § 1, eff. Jan. 1, 1984.

Formerly Ill.Rev.Stat.1991, ch. 95 ½, ¶ 6–800.

5/6–801. Findings, Declaration of Policy and Purpose

§ 6–801. Findings, Declaration of Policy and Purpose. (a) The party jurisdictions find that:

1. In most instances, a motorist who is cited for a traffic violation in a jurisdiction other than the motorist's home jurisdiction:

(i) Must post collateral or bond to secure appearance for trial at a later date; or

(ii) If unable to post collateral or bond, is taken into custody until the collateral or bond is posted; or

(iii) Is taken directly to court for immediate disposition.

2. A motorist receiving a traffic citation in the motorist's home jurisdiction is permitted, except for certain violations, to accept the citation from the officer at the scene of the violation, voluntarily deposit a valid driver's license and immediately continue after promising or being instructed to comply with the terms of the citation.

3. The purpose of the practices described in subsections 1 and 2 of paragraph (a) is to ensure compliance with the terms of a traffic citation by the motorist who, if permitted to continue after receiving the traffic citation, could return to the motorist's home jurisdiction and disregard any duty under the terms of the traffic citation.

4. The practice described in subsection 1 of paragraph (a) causes unnecessary inconvenience and, at times, a hardship for the motorist who is unable at the time to post collateral, furnish a bond, stand trial, or pay the fine, and thus is compelled to remain in custody until some arrangement can be made.

5. The deposit of a driver's license as a bail bond, as described in subsection 2 of paragraph (a), is viewed with disfavor.

6. The practices described herein consume an undue amount of law enforcement time.

(b) It is the policy of the party jurisdictions to:

1. Seek compliance with the laws, ordinances, and administrative rules and regulations relating to the operation of motor vehicles in each of the jurisdictions.

2. Allow a motorist to accept a traffic citation for certain violations and proceed without delay whether or not the motorist is a resident of the jurisdiction in which the citation was issued.

3. Extend cooperation to its fullest extent among the jurisdictions for obtaining compliance with the terms of a traffic citation issued in one jurisdiction to a resident of another jurisdiction.

4. Maximize effective utilization of law enforcement personnel and assist court systems in the efficient disposition of traffic violations.

(c) The purpose of the Compact is to:

1. Provide a means through which the party jurisdictions may participate in a reciprocal program to effectuate the policies enumerated in paragraph (b) above in a uniform and orderly manner.

2. Provide for the fair and impartial treatment of traffic violators operating within party jurisdictions in recognition of the motorist's right of due process and the sovereign status of a party jurisdiction.

P.A. 76–1586, § 6–801, added by P.A. 83–385, § 1, eff. Jan. 1, 1984.

Formerly Ill.Rev.Stat.1991, ch. 95 ½, ¶ 6–801.

5/6–802. Definitions

§ 6–802. Definitions. In the Nonresident Violator Compact, the following words have the meanings indicated, unless the context requires otherwise.

1. "Citation" means any summons, ticket, or other official document issued by a police officer for a traffic violation containing an order which requires the motorist to respond.

2. "Collateral" means any cash or other security deposited to secure an appearance for trial, following the issuance by a police officer of a citation for a traffic violation.

3. "Court" means a court of law or traffic tribunal.

4. "Driver's license" means any license or privilege to operate a motor vehicle issued under the laws of this State.

5. "Home Jurisdiction" means the jurisdiction that issued the driver's license of the traffic violator.

6. "Issuing jurisdiction" means the jurisdiction in which the traffic citation was issued to the motorist.

7. "Jurisdiction" means a state, territory, or possession of the United States, the District of Columbia, or the Commonwealth of Puerto Rico.

8. "Motorist" means a driver of a motor vehicle operating in a party jurisdiction.

9. "Personal recognizance" means an agreement by a motorist made at the time of issuance of the traffic citation that such motorist will comply with the terms of that traffic citation.

10. "Police officer" means every officer authorized to make arrests and issue citations for traffic violations.

11. "Secretary" means the Illinois Secretary of State.

12. "Terms of the citation" means those options expressly stated upon the citation.

P.A. 76–1586, § 6–802, added by P.A. 83–385, § 1, eff. Jan. 1, 1984.

Formerly Ill.Rev.Stat.1991, ch. 95 ½, ¶ 6–802.

5/6–803. Procedure for Issuing Jurisdiction

§ 6–803. Procedure for Issuing Jurisdiction. (a) When issuing a citation for a traffic violation, a police officer shall issue the citation to a motorist who possesses a valid driver's license issued by a party jurisdiction and shall not, subject to the exceptions noted in Section 6–306.4 of this Code and paragraph (b) of this Section, require the motorist to post collateral to secure appearance, if the officer receives the motorist's personal recognizance to comply with the terms of the citation.

(b) Personal recognizance is acceptable only if not prohibited by law. If mandatory appearance is required, it must take place according to law, following issuance of the citation.

(c) Upon failure of a motorist to comply with the terms of a traffic citation, the appropriate official shall report the failure to comply, in a manner prescribed by the Secretary, to the licensing authority of the jurisdiction in which the traffic citation was issued. The report shall be made in accordance with procedures specified by the Secretary and shall contain information as specified by the Secretary as minimum requirements for effective processing by the home jurisdiction.

(d) Upon receipt of the report, the Secretary shall transmit to the licensing authority in the home jurisdiction of the motorist the information in a form and content as contained in the Compact Manual.

(e) The Secretary may not, except as provided under Section 6–306.4 of this Code, suspend the privileges of a motorist for whom a report has been transmitted, under the terms of this Compact, to another member jurisdiction.

(f) The Secretary shall not transmit a report on any violation if the date of transmission is more than 6 months after the date on which the traffic citation was issued.

(g) The Secretary shall not transmit a report on any violation where the date of issuance of the citation predates the most recent of the effective dates of entry for the two jurisdictions affected.

P.A. 76–1586, § 6–803, added by P.A. 83–385, § 1, eff. Jan. 1, 1984. Amended by P.A. 84–1231, § 1, eff. July 28, 1986.

Formerly Ill.Rev.Stat.1991, ch. 95 ½, ¶ 6–803.

5/6–804. Procedure for Home Jurisdiction

§ 6–804. Procedure for Home Jurisdiction. (a) Upon receipt of a report of a failure to comply from the Secretary, the licensing authority of the home jurisdiction shall notify the motorist and initiate a suspension action in accordance with the home jurisdiction's procedures to suspend the motorist's driver's license until satisfactory evidence of compliance with the terms of the traffic citation has been furnished to the Secretary. Due process safeguards will be accorded.

(b) The Secretary shall maintain a record of actions taken and make reports to issuing jurisdictions as provided in the Compact Manual.

P.A. 76-1586, § 6-804, added by P.A. 83-385, § 1, eff. Jan. 1, 1984.

Formerly Ill.Rev.Stat.1991, ch. 95 ½, ¶ 6-804.

5/6-805. Applicability of Other Laws

§ 6-805. Applicability of Other Laws. Except as expressly required by provisions of this Compact, nothing contained herein shall be construed to affect the right of any party jurisdiction to apply any of its other laws relating to licenses to drive to any person or circumstance, or to invalidate or prevent any driver license agreement or other cooperative agreement between a party jurisdiction and a nonparty jurisdiction.

P.A. 76-1586, § 6-805, added by P.A. 83-385, § 1, eff. Jan. 1, 1984.

Formerly Ill.Rev.Stat.1991, ch. 95 ½, ¶ 6-805.

5/6-806. Compact Administrator Procedures

§ 6-806. Compact Administrator Procedures. (a) For the purpose of administering the provisions of this Compact and to serve as a governing body for the resolution of all matters relating to the operation of this Compact, a Board of Compact Administrators is established. The Board shall be composed of one representative from each party jurisdiction to be known as the Compact Administrator. The Compact Administrator shall be appointed by the Secretary and will serve and be subject to removal in accordance with the laws of the jurisdiction represented. A Compact Administrator may provide for the discharge of duties and the performance of the functions as a Board Member to an alternate. An alternate may not be entitled to serve unless written identification notice has been given to the Board.

(b) Each member of the Board of Compact Administrators shall be entitled to one vote. No action of the Board shall be binding unless taken at a meeting at which a majority of the total number of votes on the Board are cast in favor. Action by the Board shall be only at a meeting at which a majority of the party jurisdictions are represented.

(c) The Board shall elect annually, from its membership, a Chairman and Vice Chairman.

(d) The Board shall adopt bylaws, not inconsistent with the provisions of this Compact or the laws of a party jurisdiction, for the conduct of its business and shall have the power to amend and rescind its bylaws.

(e) The Board may accept, for any of its purposes and functions under this Compact, any and all donations, grants of money, equipment, supplies, materials and services, conditional or otherwise, from any jurisdiction, the United States, or any other governmental agency, and may receive, utilize and dispose of the same.

(f) The Board may contract with, or accept services or personnel from, any governmental or intergovernmental agency, person, firm, or corporation, or any private nonprofit organization or institution.

(g) The Board shall formulate all necessary procedures and develop uniform forms and documents for administering the provisions of this Compact. All procedures and forms adopted pursuant to Board action shall be contained in the Compact Manual.

P.A. 76-1586, § 6-806, added by P.A. 83-385, § 1, eff. Jan. 1, 1984.

Formerly Ill.Rev.Stat.1991, ch. 95 ½, ¶ 6-806.

5/6-807. Entry into Compact and Withdrawal

§ 6-807. Entry into Compact and Withdrawal. (a) This Compact shall become effective when it has been adopted by at least 2 jurisdictions.

(b) Entry into the Compact shall be made by a Resolution of Ratification executed by the Secretary and submitted to the Chairman of the Board.

1. The resolution shall be in a form and content as provided in the Compact Manual and shall include statements that in substance are as follows:

(i) A citation of the authority by which the jurisdiction is empowered to become a party to this Compact.

(ii) Agreement to comply with the terms and provisions of the Compact.

(iii) That Compact entry is with all jurisdictions then party to the Compact and with any jurisdiction that legally becomes a party to the Compact.

2. The effective date of entry shall be specified by the Secretary, but it shall not be before July 1, 1984 nor fewer than 60 days after notice has been given by the Chairman of the Board of Compact Administrators or by the American Association of Motor Vehicle Administrators that each party jurisdiction has received the Secretary's resolution.

A withdrawal shall not take effect until 90 days after notice of withdrawal is given. The notice shall be directed to the Compact Administrator of each member jurisdiction. No withdrawal shall affect the validity of this Compact as to the remaining party jurisdictions.

P.A. 76-1586, § 6-807, added by P.A. 83-385, § 1, eff. Jan. 1, 1984.

Formerly Ill.Rev.Stat.1991, ch. 95 ½, ¶ 6-807.

5/6-808. Exceptions

§ 6-808. Exceptions. The provisions of this Compact shall not apply to parking or standing violations, highway weight limit violations, or to violations of law governing the transportation of hazardous materials.

P.A. 76-1586, § 6-808, added by P.A. 83-385, § 1, eff. Jan. 1, 1984.

Formerly Ill.Rev.Stat.1991, ch. 95 ½, ¶ 6-808.

5/6-809. Amendments to the Compact

§ 6-809. Amendments to the Compact. (a) This Compact may be amended from time to time. Amendments shall be presented in resolution form to the Chairman of the Board of Compact Administrators and may be initiated by one or more party jurisdictions.

(b) Adoption of an amendment shall require endorsement of all party jurisdictions and shall become effective 30 days after the date of the last endorsement.

(c) Failure of a party jurisdiction to respond to the Compact Chairman within 12 days after receipt of the proposed amendment shall constitute endorsement.

P.A. 76-1586, § 6-809, added by P.A. 83-385, § 1, eff. Jan. 1, 1984.

Formerly Ill.Rev.Stat.1991, ch. 95 ½, ¶ 6-809.

5/6-810. Construction

§ 6-810. Construction. This Compact shall be liberally construed so as to effectuate the purposes stated herein.

If this Compact shall be held contrary to the Constitution of any jurisdiction party thereto, the Compact shall remain in full force and effect as to the remaining jurisdictions.

P.A. 76-1586, § 6-810, added by P.A. 83-385, § 1, eff. Jan. 1, 1984.

Formerly Ill.Rev.Stat.1991, ch. 95 ½, ¶ 6-810.

ARTICLE IX. DRIVER'S LICENSE MEDICAL REVIEW LAW OF 1992

Date Effective

Article IX was added by P.A. 87-1249, § 1, eff. Dec. 24, 1992.

5/6-900. Short title

§ 6-900. Short title. This Article may be cited as the Driver's License Medical Review Law of 1992.

P.A. 76-1586, § 6-900, added by P.A. 87-1249, § 1, eff. Dec. 24, 1992.

Formerly Ill.Rev.Stat., ch. 95½, ¶ 6-900.

5/6-901. Definitions

§ 6-901. Definitions. For the purposes of this Article:

"Board" means the Driver's License Medical Advisory Board.

"Medical examiner" or "medical practitioner" means any person licensed to practice medicine in all its branches in the State of Illinois.

P.A. 76-1586, § 6-901, added by P.A. 87-1249, § 1, eff. Dec. 24, 1992. Amended by P.A. 90-89, § 15, eff. Jan. 1, 1998; P.A. 92-703, § 10, eff. July 19, 2002.

Formerly Ill.Rev.Stat., ch. 95½, ¶ 6-901.

5/6-902. Driver's License Medical Advisory Board; membership; terms; compensation; meetings

§ 6-902. Driver's License Medical Advisory Board; membership; terms; compensation; meetings.

(a) There is established within the Office of the Secretary of State a Driver's License Medical Advisory Board consisting of at least 9 members appointed by the Secretary. Members' terms of service shall be set by the Secretary at his or her discretion. The members of the Board shall receive compensation from the Secretary at a rate per day designated by the Secretary for each day required for transacting business of the Board and shall be reimbursed for expenses reasonably incurred in the performance of their duties. The Secretary may also call in allied medical personnel to advise and consult with the Board. The Secretary shall select one of the members to act as Chairperson.

(b) The Board, or any of its subdivisions, may meet at any place within the State and shall meet at the call of the Secretary as frequently as he or she deems necessary in order to properly discharge the functions prescribed by this Act.

P.A. 76-1586, § 6-902, added by P.A. 87-1249, § 1, eff. Dec. 24, 1992.

Formerly Ill.Rev.Stat., ch. 95½, ¶ 6-902.

5/6-903. Standard for determining medical limitation; records

§ 6-903. Standard for determining medical limitation; records.

(a) The Secretary in cooperation with the Board shall establish standards for determining the degree to which a person's medical condition constitutes a limitation to the person's ability to operate a motor vehicle or causes the person to be a driving hazard.

(b) The standards may include, but need not be limited to, the following:

(1) Physical disorders characterized by momentary or prolonged lapses of consciousness or control.

(2) Disorders and impairments affecting the cardiovascular functions.

(3) Musculoskeletal disabilities and disorders affecting musculoskeletal functions.

(4) Vision and disorders affecting vision.

(5) The use of or dependence upon alcohol or drugs.

(6) The extent to which compensatory aids and devices may be utilized.

(7) Conditions or disorders that medically impair a person's mental health.

P.A. 76-1586, § 6-903, added by P.A. 87-1249, § 1, eff. Dec. 24, 1992.

Formerly Ill.Rev.Stat., ch. 95½, ¶ 6-903.

5/6-904. Referral of cases by the Secretary

§ 6-904. Referral of cases by the Secretary. The Secretary shall, when he or she has good cause to believe an individual by reason of a medical limitation would not be able to operate a motor vehicle safely, refer a case to the Board for consideration.

P.A. 76-1586, § 6-904, added by P.A. 87-1249, § 1, eff. Dec. 24, 1992.

Formerly Ill.Rev.Stat., ch. 95½, ¶ 6-904.

5/6-905. Medical evaluations of individuals under review; scope of driving privileges; report to the Secretary

§ 6-905. Medical evaluations of individuals under review; scope of driving privileges; report to the Secretary.

(a) Within the scope of the case request, as sent by the Secretary, a function of the Board shall be to make medical evaluations of the individual under review and determine what medical conditions exist that may impair the individual's ability to operate a motor vehicle safely.

(b) Based on the medical evaluations and determination under subsection (a) and in accordance with established standards, the Board shall, among other things, indicate the scope of driving privileges that would enable the individual under review to operate a motor vehicle safely, including the extent to which compensatory aids and devices must be used and the need for ongoing review or evaluation.

(c) The findings, determination, and recommendations of the Board or its subdivisions shall be forwarded to the Secretary who shall then take the action in accordance with the Board's recommendation.

P.A. 76–1586, § 6–905, added by P.A. 87–1249, § 1, eff. Dec. 24, 1992.

Formerly Ill.Rev.Stat., ch. 95½, ¶ 6–905.

5/6–906. Request for a hearing

§ 6–906. Request for a hearing.

(a) After utilizing all possible review by the Board under this Act or any regulation promulgated by the Secretary, any person who has their driver's license restricted or canceled or is otherwise denied a license has a right to request a hearing under Section 2–118 of this Code. The request for a hearing shall be in writing.

(b) The Secretary shall prescribe by rule and regulation the procedures to be followed at the hearing.

P.A. 76–1586, § 6–906, added by P.A. 87–1249, § 1, eff. Dec. 24, 1992.

Formerly Ill.Rev.Stat., ch. 95½, ¶ 6–906.

5/6–907. Cooperation required of person under review

§ 6–907. Cooperation required of person under review.

(a) In making an inquiry or conducting a hearing the Secretary or Board may require the person under review to:

(1) Submit to a medical examination by a medical examiner of the person's choice who is acceptable to the Secretary or Board.

(2) Submit to a medical examination by an impartial medical examiner after the person has submitted information from that person's own medical examiner.

(3) Consent to make available to the Secretary or Board all medical records pertaining to the reported conditions that may be necessary to aid the Board in formulating its findings and recommendations.

(b) Any person under review who refuses to submit to an examination or to consent to provide information, or both, shall as a matter of law be considered unqualified to operate a motor vehicle until the individual complies with the Secretary's or Board's request and the Board is able to make its findings and recommendations, at which time the findings and recommendations shall control.

(c) The results of any examination ordered or conducted by the Secretary or the Board shall be made available to the individual under review.

P.A. 76–1586, § 6–907, added by P.A. 87–1249, § 1, eff. Dec. 24, 1992.

Formerly Ill.Rev.Stat., ch. 95½, ¶ 6–907.

5/6–908. Confidential information

§ 6–908. Confidential information. As provided in subsection (j) of Section 2–123 of this Code, all information furnished to the Secretary or Board, the results of all examinations made at their direction, and all medical findings of the Board shall be confidential and for the sole use of the Board and the Secretary which may have access to the same for the purposes as set forth in this Act. No confidential information may be open to public inspection or the contents disclosed to anyone, except the person under review and then only to the extent necessary to comply with a request for discovery during the hearing process, unless so directed by a court of competent jurisdiction.

P.A. 76–1586, § 6–908, added by P.A. 87–1249, § 1, eff. Dec. 24, 1992.

Formerly Ill.Rev.Stat., ch. 95½, ¶ 6–908.

5/6–909. Rules and regulations; review under Administrative Review Law

§ 6–909. Rules and regulations; review under Administrative Review Law. The Secretary, in cooperation with the Board, shall administer and enforce this Act and shall have the power to make and institute reasonable rules and regulations as necessary to carry out the provisions of this Act.

P.A. 76–1586, § 6–909, added by P.A. 87–1249, § 1, eff. Dec. 24, 1992.

Formerly Ill.Rev.Stat., ch. 95½, ¶ 6–909.

5/6–910. Liability of persons for information supplied to Board or Secretary

§ 6–910. Liability of persons for information supplied to Board or Secretary. No member of the Board, medical practitioner, clinic, hospital, or mental institution, whether public or private, shall be liable or subject to criminal or civil action for any opinions, findings, or recommendations, or for any information supplied to the Secretary or the Board regarding persons under review, or for reports required by this Act, except for willful and wanton misconduct.

P.A. 76–1586, § 6–910, added by P.A. 87–1249, § 1, eff. Dec. 24, 1992.

Formerly Ill.Rev.Stat., ch. 95½, ¶ 6–910.

5/6–911. Information submitted by medical practitioners; police officers; State's attorneys; or members of the judiciary

§ 6–911. Information submitted by medical practitioners; police officers; State's attorneys; or members of the judiciary. Any qualified medical practitioner, commissioned police officer, State's attorney, or member of the judiciary acting in his or her official capacity may submit information to the Secretary relative to the medical condition of a person, including suspected chronic alcoholism or habitual use of narcotics or dangerous drugs, if the condition interferes with the person's ability to operate a motor vehicle safely. Persons reporting under this Section shall enjoy the same immunities granted members of the Board under Section 6–910.

P.A. 76–1586, § 6–911, added by P.A. 87–1249, § 1, eff. Dec. 24, 1992.

Formerly Ill.Rev.Stat., ch. 95½, ¶ 6–911.

5/6-912. Severability

§ 6-912. Severability. The provisions of this Article are severable under Section 1.31 of the Statute on Statutes.[1]

P.A. 76-1586, § 6-912, added by P.A. 87-1249, § 1, eff. Dec. 24, 1992.

Formerly Ill.Rev.Stat., ch. 95½, ¶ 6-912.

1 5 ILCS 70/1.31.

CHAPTER 7. ILLINOIS SAFETY AND FAMILY FINANCIAL RESPONSIBILITY LAW

Enactment

The Illinois Vehicle Code was enacted by P.A. 76-1586, effective July 1, 1970. The Code constitutes a consolidated recodification of various earlier laws and acts including the Illinois Motor Vehicle Law of 1957.

ARTICLE I. ADMINISTRATION

Section

5/7-100. Definition of words and phrases

§ 7-100. Definition of words and phrases. Notwithstanding the definitions set forth in Chapter 1,[1] for the purposes of this Chapter, the following words shall have the following meanings ascribed to them:

Administrator. The Department of Transportation.

Arrearage. The total amount of unpaid support obligations.

Authenticated document. A document from a court which contains a court stamp, showing it is filed with the court, or notarized, or is certified by the custodian of the original.

Compliance with a court order of support. The support obligor is no more than an amount equal to 90 days obligation in arrears in making payments in full for current support, or in making periodic payments on a support arrearage as determined by a court.

Court order of support. A judgment order for the support of dependent children issued by a court of this State, including a judgment of dissolution of marriage.

Driver's license. A license or permit to operate a motor vehicle in the State, including the privilege of a person to drive a motor vehicle whether or not the person holds a valid license or permit.

Family financial responsibility driving permit. A permit granting limited driving privileges for employment or medical purposes following a suspension of driving privileges under the Family Financial Responsibility Law.[2] This permit is valid only after the entry of a court order granting the permit and issuance of the permit by the Secretary of State's Office. An individual's driving privileges must be valid except for the family financial responsibility suspension in order for this permit to be issued. In order to be valid, the permit must be in the immediate possession of the driver to whom it is issued.

Judgment. A final judgment of any court of competent jurisdiction of any State, against a person as defendant for damages on account of bodily injury to or death of any person or damages to property resulting from the operation of any motor vehicle.

Obligor. The individual who owes a duty to make payments under a court order of support.

Obligee. The individual or other legal entity to whom a duty of support is owed through a court order of support or the individual's legal representatives.

P.A. 76-1586, § 7-100, eff. July 1, 1970, added by P.A. 76-2473, § 1, eff. July 1, 1971. Amended by P.A. 77-42, § 1, eff. July 1, 1971; P.A. 77-1910, § 1, eff. July 1, 1972; P.A. 78-255, § 61, eff. Oct. 1, 1973; P.A. 83-831, § 1, eff. Jan. 1, 1984; P.A. 84-797, § 1, eff. Jan. 1, 1986; P.A. 86-500, § 1, eff. Jan. 1, 1990; P.A. 89-92, § 10, eff. July 1, 1996; P.A. 90-89, § 15, eff. Jan. 1, 1998.

Formerly Ill.Rev.Stat.1991, ch. 95 ½, ¶ 7-100.

1 625 ILCS 5/1-100 et seq.

2 625 ILCS 5/7-701 et seq.

5/7-101. Administration of Illinois Safety and Family Financial Responsibility Law

§ 7-101. Administration of Illinois Safety and Family Financial Responsibility Law.[1] The Secretary of State and the Department, within the scope of their respective duties and powers under this Code, shall administer and enforce this Chapter and may make rules and regulations necessary for its administration and shall provide for hearings upon request of persons aggrieved by orders or acts of the Secretary of State, and the Department under this Section. However, the Secretary of State and the clerks of the circuit courts, within the scope of their respective duties and powers under this Code, shall administer and enforce Article VII of this Chapter.

P.A. 76-1586, § 7-101, eff. July 1, 1970. Amended by P.A. 76-2473, § 1, eff. July 1, 1971; P.A. 77-42, § 1, eff. July 1, 1971; P.A. 77-1910, § 1, eff. July 1, 1972; P.A. 78-255, § 61, eff. Oct. 1, 1973; P.A. 83-831, § 1, eff. Jan. 1, 1984; P.A. 89-92, § 10, eff. July 1, 1996.

Formerly Ill.Rev.Stat.1991, ch. 95 ½, ¶ 7-101.

1 625 ILCS 5/7-100 et seq.

5/7-102. Court Review

§ 7-102. Court Review. The provisions of the Administrative Review Law,[1] and all amendments and modifications thereof, and the rules adopted pursuant thereto, shall apply to and govern all proceedings for the judicial review of final administrative decisions of the Administrator or the Secretary of State hereunder.

P.A. 76-1586, § 7-102, eff. July 1, 1970. Amended by P.A. 76-2473, § 1, eff. July 1, 1971; P.A. 77-42, § 1, eff. July 1, 1971; P.A. 82-783, Art. XI, § 140, eff. July 13, 1982; P.A. 90-89, § 15, eff. Jan. 1, 1998.

Formerly Ill.Rev.Stat.1991, ch. 95 ½, ¶ 7-102.

1 735 ILCS 5/3-101 et seq.

ARTICLE II. SECURITY FOLLOWING ACCIDENT

Section

5/7-201. Application of Article II

§ 7-201. Application of Article II. The Administrator as soon as practicable after the receipt of the report, required to be filed under Sections 11-406 and 11-410, of a motor vehicle accident occurring within this State and that has resulted in bodily injury or death of any person or that damage to the property of any one person in excess of $500 was sustained, shall determine:

1. Whether Section 7-202 of this Code requires the deposit of security by or on behalf of any person who was the operator or owner of any motor vehicle in any manner involved in the accident and;

2. What amount of security shall be sufficient to satisfy any potential judgment or judgments for money damages resulting from the accident as may be recovered against the operator or owner, which amount shall in no event be less than $500.

P.A. 76-1586, § 7-201, eff. July 1, 1970. Amended by P.A. 76-1616, § 1, eff. July 1, 1970; P.A. 76-2473, § 1, eff. July 1, 1971; P.A. 77-42, § 1, eff. July 1, 1971; P.A. 77-327, § 1, eff. July 22, 1971; P.A. 77-1910, § 1, eff. July 1, 1972; P.A. 78-255, § 61, eff. Oct. 1, 1973; P.A. 84-797, § 1, eff. Jan. 1, 1986; P.A. 87-829, § 1, eff. Jan. 17, 1992.

Formerly Ill.Rev.Stat.1991, ch. 95 ½, ¶ 7-201.

5/7-201.1. Request for missing report or missing information

§ 7-201.1. If the Administrator has not received a report required to be filed under Sections 11-406 and 11-410, or if the information contained in a report is insufficient, the Administrator shall send to the person required to file the report a written request for the missing report or the missing information. The Administrator shall send such request no later than 45 days after the accident or 7 days after receiving information that such accident has occurred, whichever is later.

If the request is sent to a driver involved in an accident, the request or an attachment thereto shall contain in bold print a warning that failure to comply with the request within 15 days may result in the suspension of the driver's license.

P.A. 76-1586, § 7-201.1, eff. July 1, 1970. Amended by P.A. 76-2473, § 1, eff. July 1, 1971; P.A. 77-42, § 1, eff. July 1, 1971; P.A. 77-1910, § 1, eff. July 1, 1972; P.A. 78-255, § 61, eff. Oct. 1, 1973; P.A. 84-797, § 1, eff. Jan. 1, 1986.

Formerly Ill.Rev.Stat.1991, ch. 95 ½, ¶ 7-201.1.

5/7-201.2. Accident information; certification to Secretary of State; notice to persons whose names are certified

§ 7-201.2. The Administrator, within 30 days after compiling sufficient information on a motor vehicle accident, shall certify to the Secretary of State the name of each owner and the name of each operator of any vehicle involved in the accident, his determination that security is required under this Code, and the amount of the security. The Administrator also shall supply to the Secretary of State a copy of any accident report requested by the Secretary.

The Administrator shall send a copy of the certification to each person whose name is certified. The copy, or an attachment thereto, shall contain in bold print an explanation that, because the person did not furnish the Department of Transportation with evidence that he or she is insured or otherwise able to pay for damages resulting from the accident, the person's name has been forwarded to the Secretary of State for possible suspension of his or her driver's license.

P.A. 76-1586, § 7-201.2, added by P.A. 84-797, § 1, eff. Jan. 1, 1986.

Formerly Ill.Rev.Stat.1991, ch. 95 ½, ¶ 7-201.2.

5/7-201.3. Administrator to itemize potential claims

§ 7-201.3. Administrator to itemize potential claims. The Administrator shall send by mail to the person required to deposit security an itemization of each potential claim of personal injury or property damage and the name and address of each potential claimant within the knowledge of the Administrator and upon which the determination of the amount of security is based.

P.A. 76-1586, § 7-201.3, added by P.A. 84-797, § 1, eff. Jan. 1, 1986.

Formerly Ill.Rev.Stat.1991, ch. 95 ½, ¶ 7-201.3.

5/7-202. Exceptions to requirements of security

§ 7-202. Exceptions to requirements of security. (a) The requirements as to security and suspension as provided by Sections 7-201 and 7-205 shall not apply:

1. To the driver or owner if such owner had in effect at the time of such motor vehicle accident a liability policy covering such driver and owner with respect to the vehicle involved in such motor vehicle accident;

2. To the driver, if not the owner of such vehicle, if there was in effect at the time of such motor vehicle accident a liability policy or bond with respect to the operation of motor vehicles not owned by the driver;

3. To the driver or owner if the liability of such driver or owner for damages resulting from such motor vehicle accident is covered by any other form of liability insurance policy or bond;

4. To the driver or owner, if such owner is qualified as a self-insurer as provided in Section 7-502;

5. To the owner if such owner at the time of such motor vehicle accident was in compliance with Section 8-101 or Section 9-101;

6. To the driver or owner if such owner at the time of such motor vehicle accident was in compliance with the Federal Revised Interstate Commerce Act (P.L. 95-473), as now or hereafter amended;[1]

7. To the owner if the vehicle involved in such motor vehicle accident was owned by the United States, this State or any political sub-division of this State, any municipality therein, or any local Mass Transit District;

8. To the driver or the owner of a vehicle involved in a motor vehicle accident wherein no injury or damage was caused to the person or property of any one other than such driver or owner;

9. To the driver or the owner of a vehicle which at the time of the motor vehicle accident was parked, unless such vehicle was parked at a place where parking was at the time of the accident prohibited under any applicable law or ordinance;

10. To the owner of a vehicle if at the time of the motor vehicle accident the vehicle was being operated without his permission, express or implied, or was parked by a person who had been operating such motor vehicle without such permission;

11. To the driver, if not the owner, of a commercial motor vehicle on which there was no liability policy or bond with respect to the operation of such vehicle in effect at the time of the motor vehicle accident when the driver was operating the vehicle in the course of the driver's employment and had no actual knowledge of such lack of a liability policy or bond prior to the motor vehicle accident.

(b) If at the time of the motor vehicle accident, an owner or driver is covered by a motor vehicle liability policy or bond meeting the requirements of this Code, such owner or driver shall be exempt from suspension under Section 7-205 as to that motor vehicle accident, if the company issuing the policy or bond has failed, and such policy or bond was not effective at the time of the motor vehicle accident or any time thereafter, provided, that the owner or driver had no knowledge of the company's failure prior to the motor vehicle accident, and such owner or driver has secured within 30 days after learning of such failure another liability policy or bond meeting the requirements of the Code relating to future occurrences or motor vehicle accidents.

As used in this paragraph, the words "failed" or "failure" mean that the company has suspended operations by order of a court.

P.A. 76-1586, § 7-202, eff. July 1, 1970. Amended by P.A. 76-1616, § 1, eff. July 1, 1970; P.A. 76-2473, § 1, eff. July 1, 1971; P.A. 77-42, § 1, eff. July 1, 1971; P.A. 80-593, § 1, eff. Oct. 1, 1977; P.A. 81-1269, § .01, eff. June 30, 1980; P.A. 83-333, § 50, eff. Sept. 14, 1983; P.A. 83-831, § 1, eff. Jan. 1, 1984; P.A. 83-1362, Art. II, § 99, eff. Sept. 11, 1984; P.A. 85-293, Art. III, § 21, eff. Sept. 8, 1987.

Formerly Ill.Rev.Stat.1991, ch. 95 ½, ¶ 7-202.

1 49 U.S.C.A. § 10101 et seq.

5/7-203. Requirements as to policy or bond

§ 7-203. Requirements as to policy or bond. No such policy or bond referred to in Section 7-202 shall be effective under this Section unless issued by an insurance company or surety company authorized to do business in this State, except that if such motor vehicle was not registered in this State, or was a motor vehicle which was registered elsewhere than in this State at the effective date of the policy or bond, or the most recent renewal thereof, such policy or bond shall not be effective under this Section unless the insurance company or surety company, if not authorized to do business in this State, shall execute a power of attorney authorizing the Secretary of State to accept service on its behalf of notice or process in any action upon such policy or bond arising out of such motor vehicle accident. However, every such policy or bond is subject, if the motor vehicle accident has resulted in bodily injury or death, to a limit, exclusive of interest and costs, of not less than $20,000 because of bodily injury to or death of any one person in any one motor vehicle accident and, subject to said limit for one person, to a limit of not less than $40,000 because of bodily injury to or death of 2 or more persons in any one motor vehicle accident, and, if the motor vehicle accident has resulted in injury to or destruction of property, to a limit of not less than $15,000 because of injury to or destruction of property of others in any one motor vehicle accident.

Upon receipt of a written motor vehicle accident report from the Administrator the insurance company or surety company named in such notice shall notify the Administrator within such time and in such manner as the Administrator may require, in case such policy or bond was not in effect at the time of such motor vehicle accident.

P.A. 76-1586, § 7-203, eff. July 1, 1970. Amended by P.A. 76-2473, § 1, eff. July 1, 1971; P.A. 77-42, § 1, eff. July 1, 1971; P.A. 81-1202, § 2, eff. March 1, 1980; P.A. 83-831, § 1, eff. Jan. 1, 1984; P.A. 85-730, § 1, eff. Jan. 1, 1988.

Formerly Ill.Rev.Stat.1991, ch. 95 ½, ¶ 7-203.

5/7-204. Form and amount of security—Definition

§ 7-204. Form and amount of security—Definition. (A) Any security required to be deposited under this Act shall be in the form as the Secretary of State may require by administrative rule, and in the amounts as the Administrator may determine to be sufficient to satisfy any judgment or judgments for damages against an operator or owner but in no case in excess of the limits specified in Section 7-203 of this Act in reference to the acceptable limits of a policy or bond nor for an amount less than $500.

(B) The person depositing security shall specify in writing the person or persons on whose behalf the deposit is made and, while at any time the deposit is in the custody of the Secretary of State or State Treasurer, the person depositing it may, in writing, amend the specification of the person or persons on whose behalf the deposit is made to include an additional person or persons; provided, however, that a single deposit of security shall be applicable only on behalf of persons, required to furnish security because of the same accident.

(C) Within 10 days after any security required under the provisions of this Article is deposited with the Secretary of State, the Secretary shall send notice of the security deposit to the following, if known:

1. To each owner and operator of any vehicle involved in the accident that sustained damage in excess of $500;

2. To any person who sustained damage to personal or real property in excess of $500;

3. To any person who was injured as a result of the accident; and

4. To the estate of any person killed as a result of the accident.

P.A. 76-1586, § 7-204, eff. July 1, 1970. Amended by P.A. 76-1617, § 1, eff. July 1, 1970; P.A. 76-2473, § 1, eff. July 1, 1971; P.A. 77-42, § 1, eff. July 1, 1971; P.A. 77-327, § 1, eff. July 22, 1971; P.A. 77-1910, § 1, eff. July 1, 1972; P.A. 78-255, § 61, eff. Oct. 1, 1973; P.A. 84-300, § 1, eff. Sept. 13, 1985; P.A. 84-570, § 1, eff. Jan. 1, 1986; P.A. 84-1308, Art. II, § 96, eff. Aug. 25, 1986; P.A. 87-829, § 1, eff. Jan. 17, 1992.

Formerly Ill.Rev.Stat.1991, ch. 95 ½, ¶ 7-204.

5/7-205. Failure to deposit security—Hearings and suspensions

§ 7-205. Failure to deposit security—Hearings and suspensions. The Secretary of State, within 15 days after receipt of the determination of the Administrator that a deposit of security is required under this Code, shall review all reports, documents and other pertinent evidence in his possession, and make a preliminary finding as to whether or not there is reasonable possibility of a civil judgment being entered in a court of proper jurisdiction against the person so certified by the Administrator under this Code.

(a) Upon a preliminary finding that there is such a reasonable possibility, the Secretary of State shall notify such person by mail that his driving privileges, driver's license or registration will be suspended 45 days after the date of the mailing of the notice unless the person can prove to the satisfaction of the Secretary of State that he has deposited or has had deposited and filed on his behalf the security required under this Code or, within 15 days of the mailing of such notice, requests a formal hearing to determine whether his driving privileges, driver's license or registration should be suspended or whether the Secretary should enter an order of exoneration, and that such hearing shall be scheduled within 45 days after the mailing of such notice in accordance with the rules and regulations of the Secretary of State.

(b) Upon a preliminary finding that there is not such a reasonable possibility, the Secretary of State may elect to take no further action.

(c) In the event an order of suspension so entered applies to a nonresident owner or driver, then the privilege of driving or using a motor vehicle within the territorial limits of this State shall be so suspended.

P.A. 76-1586, § 7-205, eff. July 1, 1970. Amended by P.A. 76-1864, § 1, eff. July 1, 1970; P.A. 76-2473, § 1, eff. July 1, 1970; P.A. 77-42, § 1, eff. July 1, 1971; P.A. 77-327, § 1, eff. July 22, 1971; P.A. 77-1910, § 1, eff. July 1, 1972; P.A. 78-255, § 61, eff. Oct. 1, 1973; P.A. 83-831, § 1, eff. Jan. 1, 1984; P.A. 83-1081, § 1, eff. July 1, 1984; P.A. 83-1362, Art. II, § 99, eff. Sept. 11, 1984; P.A. 84-797, § 1, eff. Jan. 1, 1986.

Formerly Ill.Rev.Stat.1991, ch. 95 ½, ¶ 7-205.

5/7-206. Release from liability

§ 7-206. Release from liability. (a) A person shall be relieved from the requirement for deposit of security required by Section 7-201 in the event there shall be filed with the Secretary of State satisfactory evidence that the person who would otherwise be required to deposit security has been released from liability.

(b) A covenant not to sue shall relieve the parties thereto as to each other from the security requirements of this Article.

P.A. 76-1586, § 7-206, eff. July 1, 1970. Amended by P.A. 83-831, § 1, eff. Jan. 1, 1984.

Formerly Ill.Rev.Stat.1991, ch. 95 ½, ¶ 7-206.

5/7-207. Adjudication of non-liability

§ 7-207. Adjudication of non-liability. A person shall be relieved from the requirement for deposit of security, required by Section 7-201 of this Act, in the event there shall be filed with the Secretary of State evidence satisfactory of a final adjudication of non-liability.

P.A. 76-1586, § 7-207, eff. July 1, 1970. Amended by P.A. 77-327, § 1, eff. July 22, 1971.

Formerly Ill.Rev.Stat.1991, ch. 95 ½, ¶ 7-207.

5/7-208. Agreements for payment of damages

§ 7-208. Agreements for payment of damages. (a) Any 2 or more of the persons involved in a motor vehicle accident subject to the provisions of Section 7-201 or their authorized representatives, may at any time enter into a written agreement for the payment of an agreed amount in installments, with respect to all claims for injuries or damages resulting from the motor vehicle accident.

(b) The Secretary of State, to the extent provided by any such written agreement properly filed with him, shall not require the deposit of security and shall terminate any prior order of suspension, or, if security has previously been deposited, the Secretary of State shall immediately return such security to the depositor or an appropriate personal representative.

(c) In the event of a default in any payment under such agreement and upon notice of such default the Secretary of State shall forthwith suspend the driver's license and registration, or nonresident's operating privileges, of such person in default which shall not be restored unless and until:

1. Such person deposits and thereafter maintains security as required under Section 7-201 in such amount as the Secretary of State may then determine,

2. Two years have elapsed since the acceptance of the notice of default by the Secretary of State and during such period no action upon such agreement has been instituted in any court having jurisdiction, or

3. The person enters into a second written agreement for the payment of an agreed amount in installments with respect to all claims for injuries or damages resulting from the motor vehicle accident.

P.A. 76-1586, § 7-208, eff. July 1, 1970. Amended by P.A. 77-327, § 1, eff. July 22, 1971; P.A. 83-831, § 1, eff. Jan. 1, 1984; P.A. 84-300, § 1, eff. Sept. 13, 1985; P.A. 85-321, § 1, eff. Jan. 1, 1988; P.A. 90-774, § 5, eff. Aug. 14, 1998.

Formerly Ill.Rev.Stat.1991, ch. 95 ½, ¶ 7-208.

5/7-209. Payment upon judgment

§ 7-209. Payment upon judgment. The payment of a judgment arising out of a motor vehicle accident or the payment upon such judgment of an amount equal to the maximum amount which could be required for deposit under this Article shall for the purposes of this Code be deemed satisfied.

P.A. 76-1586, § 7-209, eff. July 1, 1970. Amended by P.A. 83-831, § 1, eff. Jan. 1, 1984.

Formerly Ill.Rev.Stat.1991, ch. 95 ½, ¶ 7-209.

5/7-210. Termination of security requirement

§ 7-210. Termination of security requirement. The Secretary of State, if satisfied as to the existence of any fact which under Sections 7-206, 7-207, 7-208, or 7-209 would entitle a person to be relieved from the security requirements of this Article, shall not require the deposit of security by the person so relieved from such requirement and shall terminate any prior order of suspension in respect to such person, or if security has previously been deposited by such person, the Secretary of State shall immediately return such deposit to such person.

P.A. 76-1586, § 7-210, eff. July 1, 1970.

Formerly Ill.Rev.Stat.1991, ch. 95 ½, ¶ 7-210.

5/7-211. Duration of suspension

§ 7-211. Duration of suspension.

(a) Unless a suspension is terminated under other provisions of this Code, the driver's license or registration and nonresident's operating privilege suspended as provided in Section 7-205 shall remain suspended and shall not be renewed nor shall any license or registration be issued to the person until:

1. The person deposits or there shall be deposited and filed on the person's behalf the security required under Section 7-201;

2. Two years have elapsed following the date the driver's license and registrations were suspended and evidence satisfactory to the Secretary of State that during the period no action for damages arising out of a motor vehicle accident has been properly filed;

3. Receipt of proper notice that the person has filed bankruptcy which would include all claims for personal injury and property damage resulting from the accident; or

4. After the expiration of 5 years from the date of the accident, the Secretary of State has not received documentation that any action at law for damages arising out of the motor vehicle accident has been filed against the person.

An affidavit that no action at law for damages arising out of the motor vehicle accident has been filed against the applicant, or if filed that it is not still pending shall be prima facie evidence of that fact. The Secretary of State may take whatever steps are necessary to verify the statement set forth in the applicant's affidavit.

(b) The driver's license or registration and nonresident's operating privileges suspended as provided in Section 7-205 shall also remain suspended and shall not be renewed nor shall any license or registration be issued to the person until the person gives proof of his or her financial responsibility in the future as provided in Section 1-164.5. The proof is to be maintained by the person in a manner satisfactory to the Secretary of State for a period of 3 years after the date the proof is first filed.

P.A. 76-1586, § 7-211, eff. July 1, 1970. Amended by P.A. 77-327, § 1, eff. July 22, 1971; P.A. 83-831, § 1, eff. Jan. 1, 1984; P.A. 84-832, Art. III, § 11, eff. Sept. 23, 1985; P.A. 85-321, § 1, eff. Jan. 1, 1988; P.A. 86-549, § 1, eff. Jan. 1, 1990; P.A. 87-1114, § 1, eff. Sept. 15, 1992; P.A. 90-264, § 5, eff. Jan. 1, 1998; P.A. 91-80, § 5, eff. July 9, 1999.

Formerly Ill.Rev.Stat.1991, ch. 95 ½, ¶ 7-211.

5/7-212. Authority of Administrator and Secretary of State to decrease amount of security

§ 7-212. Authority of Administrator and Secretary of State to decrease amount of security. The Administrator may reduce the amount of security ordered in any case within one year after the date of the accident, but in no event for an amount less than $500, if, in the judgment of the Administrator the amount ordered is excessive, or may revoke or rescind its order requiring the deposit of security in any case within one year after the date of the accident if, in the judgment of the Administrator, the provisions of Sections 7-202 and 7-203 excuse or exempt the operator or owner from the requirement of the deposit. In case the security originally ordered has been deposited the excess of the reduced amount ordered shall be returned to the depositor or his personal representative forthwith, notwithstanding the provisions of Section 7-214. The Secretary of State likewise shall have authority granted to the Administrator to reduce the amount of security ordered by the Administrator.

P.A. 76-1586, § 7-212, eff. July 1, 1970. Amended by P.A. 76-2473, § 1, eff. July 1, 1971; P.A. 77-42, § 1, eff. July 1, 1971; P.A. 77-1910, § 1, eff. July 1, 1972; P.A. 78-255, § 61, eff. Oct. 1, 1973; P.A. 87-829, § 1, eff. Jan. 17, 1992.

Formerly Ill.Rev.Stat.1991, ch. 95 ½, ¶ 7-212.

5/7-213. Custody of security

§ 7-213. Custody of security. Security deposited in compliance with the requirements of this Article shall be placed by the Secretary of State in the custody of the State Treasurer.

P.A. 76-1586, § 7-213, eff. July 1, 1970. Amended by P.A. 83-831, § 1, eff. Jan. 1, 1984.

Formerly Ill.Rev.Stat.1991, ch. 95 ½, ¶ 7-213.

5/7-214. Disposition of Security

§ 7-214. Disposition of Security.

Such security shall be applicable only to the payment of a judgment or judgments, rendered against the person or persons on whose behalf the deposit was made, for damages arising out of the accident in question, in an action at law, begun not later than two years after the later of (i) the date the driver's license and registration were suspended following the accident or (ii) the date of any default in any payment under an installment agreement for payment of damages, and such deposit or any balance thereof shall be returned to the depositor or his personal representative when evidence satisfactory to the Secretary of State has been filed with him:

1. that there has been a release from liability, or a final adjudication of non-liability; or

2. a duly acknowledged written agreement in accordance with Section 7-208 of this Act; or

3. whenever after the expiration of two years after the later of (i) the date the driver's license and registration were suspended following the accident or (ii) the date of any default in any payment under an installment agreement for payment of damages, the Secretary of State shall be given reasonable evidence that there is no such action pending and no judgment rendered in such action left unpaid.

P.A. 76-1586, § 7-214, eff. July 1, 1970. Amended by P.A. 90-774, § 5, eff. Aug. 14, 1998.

Formerly Ill.Rev.Stat.1991, ch. 95 ½, ¶ 7-214.

5/7-215. Matters not to be evidence in civil suits

§ 7-215. Matters not to be evidence in civil suits. Any action taken pursuant to this Chapter, or the Rules and Regulations adopted hereunder, or findings of the Administrator or the Secretary of State upon which such action is based, or the security filed as provided in this Article shall not be referred to in any way, nor shall it be any evidence of the negligence or due care of either party, at the trial of any civil action to recover damages.

P.A. 76-1586, § 7-215, eff. July 1, 1970. Amended by P.A. 76-2473, § 1, eff. July 1, 1971; P.A. 77-42, § 1, eff. July 1, 1971; P.A. 77-979, § 1, eff. Jan. 1, 1972; P.A. 77-1910, § 1, eff. July 1, 1972; P.A. 78-255, § 61, eff. Oct. 1, 1973; P.A. 83-831, § 1, eff. Jan. 1, 1984.

Formerly Ill.Rev.Stat.1991, ch. 95 ½, ¶ 7-215.

5/7-216. Reciprocity—Residents and nonresidents—Licensing of nonresidents

§ 7-216. Reciprocity—Residents and nonresidents—Licensing of nonresidents. (a) When a nonresident's operating privilege is suspended pursuant to Section 7-205 the Secretary of State shall transmit a certified copy of the record of such action to the official in charge of the issuance of driver's license and registration certificates in the state in which such nonresident resides, if the law of such other state provides for action in relation thereto similar to that provided for in paragraph (b).

(b) Upon receipt of such certification that the operating privilege of a resident of this State has been suspended or revoked in any such other state pursuant to a law providing for its suspension or revocation for failure to deposit security for the payment of judgments arising out of a motor vehicle accident, or for failure to deposit security under circumstances which would require the Secretary of State to suspend a nonresident's operating privilege had the motor vehicle accident occurred in this State, the Secretary of State shall suspend the driver's license of such resident and all other registrations. Such suspension shall continue until such resident furnishes evidence of compliance with the law of such other state relating to the deposit of such security.

(c) In case the operator or the owner of a motor vehicle involved in a motor vehicle accident within this State has no driver's license or registration, such operator shall not be allowed a driver's license or registration until the operator has complied with the requirements of Sections 7-201 thru 7-216 to the same extent that would be necessary if, at the time of the motor vehicle accident, such operator had held a license and registration.

P.A. 76-1586, § 7-216, eff. July 1, 1970. Amended by P.A. 83-831, § 1, eff. Jan. 1, 1984.

Formerly Ill.Rev.Stat.1991, ch. 95 ½, ¶ 7-216.

ARTICLE III. PROOF OF FINANCIAL RESPONSIBILITY FOR THE FUTURE

Section

Section

5/7-301. Application of Article III

§ 7-301. Application of Article III. The provisions of this Article requiring the deposit of proof of financial responsibility for the future, subject to certain exemptions, shall apply with respect to persons whose driver's license or driving privileges have been revoked as provided by this Code, or who have failed to pay judgments amounting to $500 or more as defined in Section 7-303.

P.A. 76-1586, § 7-301, eff. July 1, 1970. Amended by P.A. 83-831, § 1, eff. Jan. 1, 1984; P.A. 86-549, § 1, eff. Jan. 1, 1990; P.A. 87-829, § 1, eff. Jan. 17, 1992.

Formerly Ill.Rev.Stat.1991, ch. 95 ½, ¶ 7-301.

5/7-302. § 7-302. Repealed by P.A. 90-89, § 20, eff. Jan. 1, 1998

5/7-303. Suspension of driver's licenses, registration certificates, license plates and registration stickers for failure to satisfy judgment

§ 7-303. Suspension of driver's licenses, registration certificates, license plates and registration stickers for failure to satisfy judgment. (a) The Secretary of State shall, except as provided in paragraph (d), suspend the driver's license issued to any person upon receiving an authenticated report as hereinafter provided for in Section 7-307 that such person has failed for a period of 30 days to satisfy any final judgment in amounts as hereinafter stated, and shall also suspend all registration certificates, license plates and registration stickers issued to the person named as the judgment debtor in any such authenticated report.

(b) The term "judgment" shall mean: A final judgment of any court of competent jurisdiction of any State, against a person as defendant for damages on account of bodily injury to or death of any person or damages to property resulting from the operation, on and after July 12, 1938, of any motor vehicle.

(c) The term "State" shall mean: Any State, Territory, or possession of the United States, the District of Columbia, or any province of the Dominion of Canada.

(d) The Secretary of State shall not suspend the driver's license, registration certificates, registration stickers or license plates of the judgment debtor, nor shall such judgment debtor be subject to the suspension provisions of Sections 7-308 and 7-309 if all the following conditions are met:

1. At the time of the motor vehicle accident which gave rise to the unsatisfied judgment the judgment debtor was covered by a motor vehicle liability policy or bond meeting the requirements of this Chapter;

2. The insurance company which issued the policy or bond has failed and has suspended operations by order of a court;

3. The judgment debtor had no knowledge of the insurance company's failure prior to the motor vehicle accident;

4. Within 30 days after learning of the insurance company's failure the judgment debtor secured another liability policy or bond meeting the requirements of this Article relating to future occurrences or accidents;

5. The insurance company which issued the motor vehicle liability policy or bond that covered the judgment debtor at the time of the motor vehicle accident is unable to satisfy the judgment in the amounts specified in Section 7-311;

6. The judgment debtor presents to the Secretary of State such certified documents or other proofs as the Secretary of State may require that all of the conditions set forth in this Section have been met.

P.A. 76-1586, § 7-303, eff. July 1, 1970. Amended by P.A. 79-1358, § 43, eff. Oct. 1, 1976; P.A. 80-230, § 1, eff. Oct. 1, 1977; P.A. 83-831, § 1, eff. Jan. 1, 1984; P.A. 85-321, § 1, eff. Jan. 1, 1988.

Formerly Ill.Rev.Stat.1991, ch. 95 ½, ¶ 7-303.

5/7-304. Proof required

§ 7-304. Proof required. Upon the revocation of a driver's license of any person as provided in Section 6-113, 6-205 or 6-206, the Secretary of State shall suspend any and all of the registration certificates, license plates and registration stickers issued for any motor vehicle registered in the name of such person as owner except that the Secretary shall not suspend such evidences of registration in the event such owner has previously given or shall immediately give the Secretary and thereafter maintain for a period of 3 years, proof of financial responsibility in the manner hereinafter specified in this Article with respect to each and every motor vehicle owned and registered by such person.

P.A. 76-1586, § 7-304, eff. July 1, 1970. Amended by P.A. 80-230, § 1, eff. Oct. 1, 1977; P.A. 83-831, § 1, eff. Jan. 1, 1984.

Formerly Ill.Rev.Stat.1991, ch. 95 ½, ¶ 7-304.

5/7-305. Suspension until proof furnished

§ 7-305. Suspension until proof furnished. The suspension of such certificates of registration, license plates and registration stickers of such person as provided for in Section 7-304 shall remain in effect and the Secretary of State shall not issue to any such person any new or renewal of driver's license and shall not register or re-register in the name of such person any motor vehicle until permitted under this Article and not then unless and until said person gives proof of his financial responsibility in the future, as defined in this Code, such proof to be maintained by said person in a manner satisfactory to the Secretary of State for a period of 3 years after the date such proof is first filed.

P.A. 76-1586, § 7-305, eff. July 1, 1970. Amended by P.A. 80-230, § 1, eff. Oct. 1, 1977; P.A. 83-831, § 1, eff. Jan. 1, 1984; P.A. 84-112, § 1, eff. July 25, 1985; P.A. 90-89, § 15, eff. Jan. 1, 1998.

Formerly Ill.Rev.Stat.1991, ch. 95 ½, ¶ 7-305.

5/7-306. Action in respect to an unlicensed driver

§ 7-306. Action in respect to an unlicensed driver. Whenever any person who is not a resident of this State has been convicted of an offense which would require the revocation of the driver's license of a resident, such nonresident shall not operate any motor vehicle in this State nor shall any motor vehicle owned by such nonresident be operated within this State by any person, and the Secretary of State shall not issue to such nonresident any driver's license and shall not register any motor vehicle owned by such nonresident unless and until such nonresident shall give proof of financial responsibility.

P.A. 76-1586, § 7-306, eff. July 1, 1970. Amended by P.A. 83-831, § 1, eff. Jan. 1, 1984.

Formerly Ill.Rev.Stat.1991, ch. 95 ½, ¶ 7-306.

5/7-307. Courts to report nonpayments of judgment

§ 7-307. Courts to report nonpayments of judgment. The clerk of a court, or the judge of a court which has no clerk shall forward to the Secretary of State, on a form prescribed by the Secretary, a certified record of any judgment for damages, the rendering and nonpayment of which judgment required the suspension of the driver's license and registrations in the name of the judgment debtor hereunder, such record to be forwarded to the Secretary of State upon request by the plaintiff after the expiration of 30 days after such judgment has become final and when such judgment has not been stayed or satisfied within the amounts specified in this Article as shown by the records of the Court.

P.A. 76-1586, § 7-307, eff. July 1, 1970. Amended by P.A. 80-849, § 1, eff. Oct. 1, 1977; P.A. 83-831, § 1, eff. Jan. 1, 1984; P.A. 86-549, § 1, eff. Jan. 1, 1990.

Formerly Ill.Rev.Stat.1991, ch. 95 ½, ¶ 7-307.

5/7-308. Action in respect to nonresident for nonpayment of judgment

§ 7-308. Action in respect to nonresident for nonpayment of judgment. (a) If a person, whose failure to satisfy a judgment within 30 days after the same became final would require a suspension or revocation hereunder in respect to a resident, shall not be a resident of this State, such nonresident shall not operate any motor vehicle in this State, nor shall any motor vehicle owned by such nonresident be operated in this State by any person and the Secretary of State shall not issue to such nonresident a driver's license and shall not register any motor vehicle owned by such nonresident unless and until such nonresident shall give proof of financial responsibility and shall satisfy any such judgment as required with respect to a resident of this State.

(b) The Secretary of State shall forward to the Motor Vehicle Commissioner or state officer performing the functions of a Commissioner in the state, foreign country, or province of the Dominion of Canada in which a judgment debtor resides, a certified record of any unsatisfied judgment rendered against such nonresident which requires suspension of such nonresident's driving privileges in this State.

P.A. 76-1586, § 7-308, eff. July 1, 1970. Amended by P.A. 83-831, § 1, eff. Jan. 1, 1984.

Formerly Ill.Rev.Stat.1991, ch. 95 ½, ¶ 7-308.

5/7-309. Suspension to continue until judgments paid and proof given

§ 7-309. Suspension to continue until judgments paid and proof given.

(a) The suspension of such driver's license, license plates and registration stickers shall remain in effect and no other vehicle shall be registered in the name of such judgment debtor, nor any new license issued to such person (including any such person not previously licensed), unless and until the

Secretary of State receives authenticated documentation that such judgment is satisfied, or dormant as provided for in Section 12–108 of the Code of Civil Procedure, as now or hereafter amended,[1] or stayed by court order, and the judgment debtor gives proof of financial responsibility, as hereinafter provided. The Secretary of State may terminate the suspension of such person's driver's license, license plates and registration stickers and no proof of financial responsibility shall be required on any existing suspensions under this Article which are more than 20 years old.

(b) Whenever, after one judgment is satisfied and proof of financial responsibility is given as herein required, another such judgment is rendered against the judgment debtor for any motor vehicle accident occurring prior to the date of the giving of said proof and such person fails to satisfy the latter judgment within the amounts specified herein within 30 days after the same becomes final, then the Secretary of State shall again suspend the driver's license of such judgment debtor and shall again suspend the registration of any vehicle registered in the name of such judgment debtor as owner. Such driver's license and registration shall not be renewed nor shall a driver's license and registration of any vehicle be issued to such judgment debtor while such latter judgment remains in effect and unsatisfied within the amount specified herein.

P.A. 76–1586, § 7–309, eff. July 1, 1970. Amended by P.A. 80–230, § 1, eff. Oct. 1, 1977; P.A. 83–831, § 1, eff. Jan. 1, 1984; P.A. 84–112, § 1, eff. July 25, 1985; P.A. 86–500, § 1, eff. Jan. 1, 1990; P.A. 90–655, § 153, eff. July 30, 1998.

Formerly Ill.Rev.Stat.1991, ch. 95 ½, ¶ 7–309.

1 735 ILCS 5/12–108.

5/7–310. Petition for discharge filed in bankruptcy

§ 7–310. Petition for discharge filed in bankruptcy. A petition for discharge filed in bankruptcy following the rendering of any judgment shall relieve the judgment debtor from any of the requirements of this Chapter 7.

A petition for discharge filed in bankruptcy of the owner or lessee of a commercial vehicle by whom the judgment debtor is employed at the time of the motor vehicle accident that gives rise to the judgment also shall relieve the judgment debtor so employed from any of the requirements of this Chapter 7 if the discharge of the owner or lessee follows the rendering of the judgment and if the judgment debtor so employed was operating the commercial vehicle in connection with his regular employment or occupation at the time of the accident. This amendatory act of 1985 applies to all cases irrespective of whether the accident giving rise to the suspension of license or registration occurred before, on, or after its effective date.

P.A. 76–1586, § 7–310, eff. July 1, 1970. Amended by P.A. 78–233, § 1, eff. Aug. 6, 1973; P.A. 83–368, § 1, eff. Jan. 1, 1984; P.A. 84–406, § 1, eff. Jan. 1, 1986; P.A. 86–549, § 1, eff. Jan. 1, 1990; P.A. 87–1114, § 1, eff. Sept. 15, 1992.

Formerly Ill.Rev.Stat.1991, ch. 95 ½, ¶ 7–310.

5/7–311. Payments sufficient to satisfy requirements

§ 7–311. Payments sufficient to satisfy requirements. (a) Judgments herein referred to arising out of motor vehicle accidents occurring on or after January 1, 1956, shall for the purpose of this Chapter be deemed satisfied:

1. When $20,000 has been credited upon any judgment or judgments rendered in excess of that amount for bodily injury to or the death of one person as the result of any one motor vehicle accident; or

2. When, subject to said limit of $20,000 as to any one person, the sum of $40,000 has been credited upon any judgment or judgments rendered in excess of that amount for bodily injury to or the death of more than one person as the result of any one motor vehicle accident; or

3. When $15,000 has been credited upon any judgment or judgments, rendered in excess of that amount for damages to property of others as a result of any one motor vehicle accident.

(b) Credit for such amounts shall be deemed a satisfaction of any such judgment or judgments in excess of said amounts only for the purposes of this Chapter.

(c) Whenever payment has been made in settlement of any claim for bodily injury, death or property damage arising from a motor vehicle accident resulting in injury, death or property damage to two or more persons in such accident, any such payment shall be credited in reduction of the amounts provided for in this Section.

P.A. 76–1586, § 7–311, eff. July 1, 1970. Amended by P.A. 81–1202, § 2, eff. March 1, 1980; P.A. 83–831, § 1, eff. Jan. 1, 1984; P.A. 85–730, § 1, eff. Jan. 1, 1988.

Formerly Ill.Rev.Stat.1991, ch. 95 ½, ¶ 7–311.

5/7–312. Installment payment

§ 7–312. Installment payment. (a) A judgment debtor upon 5 days notice to the judgment creditor may apply to the trial court in which the judgment was entered for the privilege of paying such judgment in installments and the court in its discretion and without prejudice to any other judicial remedies which the judgment creditor may have may so[1] order, fixing the amounts and times of payment of the installments.

(b) The Secretary of State shall not suspend the driver's license, registration or nonresident's operating privilege, and any suspended driver's license or registration following nonpayment of a final judgment shall be restored when the judgment debtor gives proof of financial responsibility and when the judgment debtor obtains an order from the trial court permitting the payment of such judgment in installments and while the payment of any such installment is not in default.

P.A. 76–1586, § 7–312, eff. July 1, 1970. Amended by P.A. 83–345, § 52, eff. Sept. 14, 1983; P.A. 83–831, § 1, eff. Jan. 1, 1984; P.A. 83–1362, Art. II, § 99, eff. Sept. 11, 1984.

Formerly Ill.Rev.Stat.1991, ch. 95 ½, ¶ 7–312.

1 So in enrolled bill.

P.A. 83–1362, Art. II, the 1984 Revisory Act provided in § 0.1:

"This Article provides for the nonsubstantive revision or renumbering or repeal of Sections of Acts necessitated by the amendment, addition or repeal of Sections by two or more Public Acts of the 83rd General Assembly, which multiple action was not resolved by one of the Acts of the 83rd General Assembly affecting the particular Section."

5/7–313. Suspension required upon breach of agreement

§ 7–313. Suspension required upon breach of agreement. In the event the judgment debtor fails to pay any installments as permitted by the order of the court upon notice of such default, the Secretary of State, upon receipt of a court order, shall forthwith suspend the driver's license, registration certificate, license plates, registration stickers or nonresident's operating privilege of the judgment debtor until said judgment is satisfied as provided in Section 7–311 or a second installment payment plan is accepted as provided in Section 7-312.

P.A. 76-1586, § 7-313, eff. July 1, 1970. Amended by P.A. 80-230, § 1, eff. Oct. 1, 1977; P.A. 80-1185, § 1, eff. March 8, 1978; P.A. 83-831, § 1, eff. Jan. 1, 1984; P.A. 85-321, § 1, eff. Jan. 1, 1988; P.A. 90-774, § 5, eff. Aug. 14, 1998.

Formerly Ill.Rev.Stat.1991, ch. 95 ½, ¶ 7-313.

5/7-314. Alternate methods of giving proof

§ 7-314. Alternate methods of giving proof. Proof of financial responsibility when required under this Article may be given by filing with the Secretary of State:

1. A certificate of insurance as provided in Section 7-315 or Section 7-316;
2. A bond as provided in Section 7-320; or
3. A deposit of securities as provided in Section 7-323.

P.A. 76-1586, § 7-314, eff. July 1, 1970. Amended by P.A. 83-831, § 1, eff. Jan. 1, 1984.

Formerly Ill.Rev.Stat.1991, ch. 95 ½, ¶ 7-314.

5/7-315. A certificate of insurance proof

§ 7-315. A certificate of insurance proof. (a) Proof of financial responsibility may be made by filing with the Secretary of State the written certificate of any insurance carrier duly authorized to do business in this State, certifying that it has issued to or for the benefit of the person furnishing such proof and named as the insured in a motor vehicle liability policy, a motor vehicle liability policy or policies or in certain events an operator's policy meeting the requirements of this Code and that said policy or policies are then in full force and effect.

(b) Such certificate or certificates shall give the dates of issuance and expiration of such policy or policies and certify that the same shall not be canceled unless 15 days' prior written notice thereof be given to the Secretary of State and shall explicitly describe all motor vehicles covered thereby unless the policy or policies are issued to a person who is not the owner of a motor vehicle.

(c) The Secretary of State shall not accept any certificate or certificates unless the same shall cover all motor vehicles then registered in this State in the name of the person furnishing such proof as owner and an additional certificate or certificates shall be required as a condition precedent to the subsequent registration of any motor vehicle or motor vehicles in the name of the person giving such proof as owner.

P.A. 76-1586, § 7-315, eff. July 1, 1970. Amended by P.A. 83-831, § 1, eff. Jan. 1, 1984; P.A. 90-774, § 5, eff. Aug. 14, 1998.

Formerly Ill.Rev.Stat.1991, ch. 95 ½, ¶ 7-315.

5/7-316. Certificate furnished by nonresident as proof

§ 7-316. Certificate furnished by nonresident as proof. Any nonresident owner of a motor vehicle not registered in this State may give proof of financial responsibility by filing with the Secretary of State a certificate or certificates of an insurance carrier authorized to transact business in the state or province of the Dominion of Canada in which the motor vehicle or motor vehicles described in such certificate are registered, or if such nonresident does not own a motor vehicle then in the state or province of the Dominion of Canada in which the insured resides, and otherwise conforming to the provisions of this Code, and the Secretary of State shall accept the same if such carrier shall:

1. Execute a power of attorney authorizing the Secretary of State to accept service on its behalf of notice of process in any action arising out of a motor vehicle accident in this State;
2. Duly adopt a resolution which shall be binding upon it declaring that its policies shall be deemed to be varied to comply with the laws of this State relating to the terms of motor vehicle liability policies as required by Section 7-317; and
3. Agree to accept as final and binding any final judgment duly rendered in any action arising out of a motor vehicle accident in any court of competent jurisdiction in this State.

P.A. 76-1586, § 7-316, eff. July 1, 1970. Amended by P.A. 83-831, § 1, eff. Jan. 1, 1984.

Formerly Ill.Rev.Stat.1991, ch. 95 ½, ¶ 7-316.

5/7-317. "Motor vehicle liability policy" defined

§ 7-317. "Motor vehicle liability policy" defined. (a) **Certification.**—A "motor vehicle liability policy", as that term is used in this Act, means an "owner's policy" or an "operator's policy" of liability insurance, certified as provided in Section 7-315 or Section 7-316 as proof of financial responsibility for the future, and issued, except as otherwise provided in Section 7-316, by an insurance carrier duly authorized to transact business in this State, to or for the benefit of the person named therein as insured.

(b) **Owner's Policy.**—Such owner's policy of liability insurance:

1. Shall designate by explicit description or by appropriate reference, all motor vehicles with respect to which coverage is thereby intended to be granted;
2. Shall insure the person named therein and any other person using or responsible for the use of such motor vehicle or vehicles with the express or implied permission of the insured;
3. Shall insure every named insured and any other person using or responsible for the use of any motor vehicle owned by the named insured and used by such other person with the express or implied permission of the named insured on account of the maintenance, use or operation of any motor vehicle owned by the named insured, within the continental limits of the United States or the Dominion of Canada against loss from liability imposed by law arising from such maintenance, use or operation, to the extent and aggregate amount, exclusive of interest and cost, with respect to each motor vehicle, of $20,000 for bodily injury to or death of one person as a result of any one accident and, subject to such limit as to one person, the amount of $40,000 for bodily injury to or death of all persons as a result of any one accident and the amount of $15,000 for damage to property of others as a result of any one accident.

(c) **Operator's Policy.**—When an operator's policy is required, it shall insure the person named therein as insured against the liability imposed by law upon the insured for bodily injury to or death of any person or damage to property to the amounts and limits above set forth and growing out of the use or operation by the insured within the continental limits of the United States or the Dominion of Canada of any motor vehicle not owned by him.

(d) **Required Statements in Policies.**—Every motor vehicle liability policy must specify the name and address of the insured, the coverage afforded by the policy, the premium charged therefor, the policy period, and the limits of liability, and shall contain an agreement that the insurance thereunder is provided in accordance with the coverage defined in this Act, as respects bodily injury and death or property damage or both, and is subject to all the provisions of this Act.

(e) **Policy Need Not Insure Workers' Compensation.**—Any liability policy or policies issued hereunder need not cover any liability of the insured assumed by or imposed upon the insured under any workers' compensation law nor any liability for damage to property in charge of the insured or the insured's employees.

(f) **Provisions Incorporated in Policy.**—Every motor vehicle liability policy is subject to the following provisions which need not be contained therein:

1. The liability of the insurance carrier under any such policy shall become absolute whenever loss or damage covered by the policy occurs and the satisfaction by the insured of a final judgment for such loss or damage shall not be a condition precedent to the right or obligation of the carrier to make payment on account of such loss or damage.

2. No such policy may be cancelled or annulled as respects any loss or damage, by any agreement between the carrier and the insured after the insured has become responsible for such loss or damage, and any such cancellation or annulment shall be void.

3. The insurance carrier shall, however, have the right to settle any claim covered by the policy, and if such settlement is made in good faith, the amount thereof shall be deductible from the limits of liability specified in the policy.

4. The policy, the written application therefor, if any, and any rider or endorsement which shall not conflict with the provisions of this Act shall constitute the entire contract between the parties.

(g) **Excess or Additional Coverage.**—Any motor vehicle liability policy may, however, grant any lawful coverage in excess of or in addition to the coverage herein specified or contain any agreements, provisions, or stipulations not in conflict with the provisions of this Act and not otherwise contrary to law.

(h) **Reimbursement Provision Permitted.**—The policy may provide that the insured, or any other person covered by the policy shall reimburse the insurance carrier for payment made on account of any loss or damage claim or suit involving a breach of the terms, provisions or conditions of the policy; and further, if the policy shall provide for limits in excess of the limits specified in this Act, the insurance carrier may plead against any plaintiff, with respect to the amount of such excess limits of liability, any defense which it may be entitled to plead against the insured.

(i) **Proration of Insurance Permitted.**—The policy may provide for the pro-rating of the insurance thereunder with other applicable valid and collectible insurance.

(j) **Binders.**—Any binder pending the issuance of any policy, which binder contains or by reference includes the provisions hereunder shall be sufficient proof of ability to respond in damages.

(k) **Copy of Policy to Be Filed with Department of Insurance—Approval.**—A copy of the form of every motor vehicle liability policy which is to be used to meet the requirements of this Act must be filed, by the company offering such policy, with the Department of Insurance, which shall approve or disapprove the policy within 30 days of its filing. If the Department approves the policy in writing within such 30 day period or fails to take action for 30 days, the form of policy shall be deemed approved as filed. If within the 30 days the Department disapproves the form of policy filed upon the ground that it does not comply with the requirements of this Act, the Department shall give written notice of its decision and its reasons therefor to the carrier and the policy shall not be accepted as proof of financial responsibility under this Act.

(*l*) **Insurance Carrier Required to File Certificate.**—An insurance carrier who has issued a motor vehicle liability policy or policies or an operator's policy meeting the requirements of this Act shall, upon the request of the insured therein, deliver to the insured for filing, or at the request of the insured, shall file direct, with the Secretary of State a certificate, as required by this Act, which shows that such policy or policies have been issued. No insurance carrier may require the payment of any extra fee or surcharge, in addition to the insurance premium, for the execution, delivery or filing of such certificate.

(m) **Proof When Made By Endorsement.**—Any motor vehicle liability policy which by endorsement contains the provisions required hereunder shall be sufficient proof of ability to respond in damages.

P.A. 76-1586, § 7-317, eff. July 1, 1970. Amended by P.A. 77-1337, § 1, eff. Aug. 27, 1971; P.A. 80-1495, § 36, eff. Jan. 8, 1979; P.A. 81-992, § 1, eff. Jan. 1, 1980; P.A. 81-1202, § 2, eff. March 1, 1980; P.A. 81-1509, Art. I, § 57, eff. Sept. 26, 1980; P.A. 85-730, § 1, eff. Jan. 1, 1988.

Formerly Ill.Rev.Stat.1991, ch. 95 ½, ¶ 7-317.

5/7-318. Notice of Cancellation or Termination of Certified Policy

§ 7-318. Notice of Cancellation or Termination of Certified Policy. When an insurance carrier has certified a motor vehicle liability policy or policies under this Act, it shall notify the Secretary of State of any cancellation by mailing a written notice at least 15 days prior to cancellation of such policy and the policy shall continue in full force and effect until the date of cancellation specified in such notice or until its expiration, except that such a policy subsequently procured and certified shall, on the effective date of its certification, terminate the insurance previously certified with respect to any vehicle designated in both certificates.

P.A. 76-1586, § 7-318, eff. July 1, 1970. Amended by P.A. 86-549, § 1, eff. Jan. 1, 1990.

Formerly Ill.Rev.Stat.1991, ch. 95 ½, ¶ 7-318.

5/7-319. This Act not to affect other policies

§ 7-319. This Act not to affect other policies. Sections 7-301 through 7-329, each inclusive, of this Act shall not be held to apply to or affect bonds or policies of automobile insurance against liability which may now or hereafter be required by any other provision of this Act and such bonds or policies, if endorsed to conform to the requirements of this Act, shall be accepted as proof of financial responsibility when required under this Act. This Act shall not be held to apply to or affect policies insuring solely the insured named in the policy against liability resulting from the maintenance, operation or use by persons in the insured's employ or in his behalf of motor vehicles not owned by the insured.

P.A. 76-1586, § 7-319, eff. July 1, 1970.

Formerly Ill.Rev.Stat.1991, ch. 95 ½, ¶ 7-319.

5/7-320. Bond as Proof

§ 7-320. Bond as Proof. A person required to give proof of financial responsibility may file with the Secretary of State a bond, executed by the person giving such proof and by a surety company, duly authorized to transact business within the State; or by the person, giving such proof and by 2 individual sureties, each owning real estate within this State and having an equity therein in the amount of such bond, which real estate shall be scheduled therein.

1. The Secretary of State shall not accept any such real estate bond unless it is first approved by a judge of a court.

2. The Secretary of State shall not accept any such bond unless it is conditioned for payment in amounts and under the same circumstances as would be required in a motor vehicle liability policy furnished by the person giving such proof under this Act.

3. No such bond shall be cancelled unless 10 days' prior written notice is given to the Secretary of State, but cancellation of such bond shall not prevent recovery thereon with respect to any right or cause of action arising prior to the date of cancellation.

4. The principal and sureties of every such real estate bond shall execute and deliver an original and one copy of the bond and schedule and in addition, when the real property or any part thereof, listed or described in the schedule, shall lie in more than one county, then as many extra copies as there are counties in which the real property, or any part thereof, shall lie, to the judge to whom such bond is presented for approval, who shall, if he approved the bond, endorse upon the original and each copy of the bond the date of the approval thereof; and the clerk of the court shall immediately file one of the copies with the recorder in each county in which is situated any of the non-registered real property so scheduled.

5. If any of the lands so scheduled shall have been registered under "An Act concerning land titles", approved May 1, 1897,[1] as amended, the clerk of the court in which the bond is approved shall immediately file with the registrar of titles in and for each county in which any of the registered land so scheduled is situated, a notice stating that such land has been so scheduled, and the registrar shall thereupon enter a memorial of such fact upon the record.

6. The clerk of the court in which the bond is approved shall endorse upon the original of each such real estate bond approved the date upon which he or she filed a copy of such bond with the recorder in each county in which is situated any of the non-registered real property so scheduled or the notice with the registrar of titles in and for each county in which any of the registered land scheduled is situated and shall deliver such original bond to the principal thereon. P.A. 76-1586, § 7-320, eff. July 1, 1970. Amended by P.A. 83-345, § 52, eff. Sept. 14, 1983; P.A. 83-358, § 67, eff. Sept. 14, 1983; P.A. 83-1362, Art. II, § 99, eff. Sept. 11, 1984.

Formerly Ill.Rev.Stat.1991, ch. 95 ½, ¶ 7-320.

1 765 ILCS 35/1 et seq.

P.A. 83-1362, Art. II, the 1984 Revisory Act provided in § 0.1:

"This Article provides for the nonsubstantive revision or renumbering or repeal of Sections of Acts necessitated by the amendment, addition or repeal of Sections by two or more Public Acts of the 83rd General Assembly, which multiple action was not resolved by one of the Acts of the 83rd General Assembly affecting the particular Section."

5/7-321. When Bond Shall Constitute a Lien

§ 7-321. When Bond Shall Constitute a Lien. Such bond shall constitute a lien upon the unregistered real estate so scheduled of any surety from the time when a copy of such bond is filed in the office of the recorder in and for the county in which such non-registered real property so scheduled is situated, and such bond shall be a lien upon all registered real property listed or described in the accompanying schedule from the time when notice, as aforesaid, is filed in the office of the registrar of titles in and for the county in which such registered real estate so scheduled is situated. Such lien shall exist in favor of the People of the State of Illinois for the use of any holder of a final judgment against the principal on such bond upon a liability covered by the conditions of such bond.

P.A. 76-1586, § 7-321, eff. July 1, 1970. Amended by P.A. 80-1495, § 36, eff. Jan. 8, 1979; P.A. 83-358, § 67, eff. Sept. 14, 1983.

Formerly Ill.Rev.Stat.1991, ch. 95 ½, ¶ 7-321.

5/7-322. Action on bond

§ 7-322. Action on bond. If a judgment is rendered against the principal of any such surety or real estate bond upon a liability covered by the conditions of such bond and such judgment is not satisfied within thirty (30) days after it becomes final, then the judgment creditor may, for his own use and benefit, and at his sole expense, bring an action or actions in the name of the State against the company or persons who executed such bond including an action or proceeding to foreclose any lien that may exist upon the real estate of a person who has executed such bond, which action shall be brought in like manner and subject to all the provisions of law applicable to an action to foreclose a mortgage upon real estate.

P.A. 76-1586, § 7-322, eff. July 1, 1970.

Formerly Ill.Rev.Stat.1991, ch. 95 ½, ¶ 7-322.

5/7-323. Money or securities as proof

§ 7-323. Money or securities as proof. A person may give proof of financial responsibility by delivering to the Secretary of State a receipt of the State Treasurer showing the deposit with said State Treasurer of money in amount or securities endorsed in blank by the owner thereof and approved by said State Treasurer and of a market value in a total amount as would be required for coverage in a motor vehicle liability policy furnished by the person giving such proof under this Act. Such securities shall be of the type which may legally be purchased as investments of trust funds by trustees.

P.A. 76-1586, § 7-323, eff. July 1, 1970.

Formerly Ill.Rev.Stat.1991, ch. 95 ½, ¶ 7-323.

5/7-324. Application of deposit

§ 7-324. Application of deposit. All money or securities so deposited shall be subject to execution to satisfy any judgment mentioned in this Act but shall not otherwise be subject to attachment or execution. The State Treasurer shall not accept any such deposit or issue a certificate therefor, and the Secretary of State shall not accept such certificate unless accompanied by evidence that there are no unsatisfied judgments against the depositor registered in the county where the depositor resides.

P.A. 76-1586, § 7-324, eff. July 1, 1970.

Formerly Ill.Rev.Stat.1991, ch. 95 ½, ¶ 7-324.

5/7-325. Owner may give proof for others

§ 7-325. Owner may give proof for others. Whenever the Secretary of State determines that any person required to give proof under this Article by reason of a revocation is not the owner of a motor vehicle but was, at the time of such conviction a driver in the employ of an owner of a motor vehicle, or a member of the immediate family or household of the owner of a motor vehicle, the Secretary of State shall accept proof of financial responsibility given by such owner in lieu of proof given by such other person so long as such other person is operating a motor vehicle for which the owner has given proof as herein provided.

P.A. 76-1586, § 7-325, eff. July 1, 1970. Amended by P.A. 83-831, § 1, eff. Jan. 1, 1984.

Formerly Ill.Rev.Stat.1991, ch. 95 ½, ¶ 7-325.

5/7-326. Substitution of proof

§ 7-326. Substitution of proof. The Secretary of State shall cancel any bond or return any certificate of insurance, or the Secretary of State shall direct and the State Treasurer shall return any money or securities to the person entitled thereto, upon the substitution and acceptance of other adequate proof of financial responsibility pursuant to this Article.

P.A. 76-1586, § 7-326, eff. July 1, 1970. Amended by P.A. 83-831, § 1, eff. Jan. 1, 1984.

Formerly Ill.Rev.Stat.1991, ch. 95 ½, ¶ 7-326.

5/7-327. Other proof may be required

§ 7-327. Other proof may be required. Whenever any evidence of proof of ability to respond in damages filed under the provisions of this Article no longer fulfills the purpose for which required, the Secretary of State shall, for the purposes of this Chapter, require other evidence of ability to respond in damages as required by this Article, and the driver's license, registration certificates, license plates and registration stickers involved shall be suspended by the Secretary of State pending such proof.

P.A. 76-1586, § 7-327, eff. July 1, 1970. Amended by P.A. 80-230, § 1, eff. Oct. 1, 1977; P.A. 83-831, § 1, eff. Jan. 1, 1984.

Formerly Ill.Rev.Stat.1991, ch. 95 ½, ¶ 7-327.

5/7-328. Duration of proof—When proof may be canceled or returned

§ 7-328. Duration of proof—When proof may be canceled or returned. The Secretary of State shall upon request cancel any bond or return any certificate of insurance, or the Secretary of State shall direct and the State Treasurer shall return to the person entitled thereto any money or securities, deposited pursuant to this Chapter as proof of financial responsibility or waive the requirements of filing proof of financial responsibility in any of the following events:

1. In the event of the death of the person on whose behalf such proof was filed, or the permanent incapacity of such person to operate a motor vehicle;

2. In the event the person who has given proof of financial responsibility surrenders such person's driver's license, registration certificates, license plates and registration stickers, but the Secretary of State shall not release such proof in the event any action for damages upon a liability referred to in this Article is then pending or any judgment upon any such liability is then outstanding and unsatisfied or in the event the Secretary of State has received notice that such person has, within the period of 3 months immediately preceding, been involved as a driver in any motor vehicle accident. An affidavit of the applicant of the nonexistence of such facts shall be sufficient evidence thereof in the absence of evidence to the contrary in the records of the Secretary of State. Any person who has not completed the required 3 year period of proof of financial responsibility pursuant to Section 7-304, and to whom proof has been surrendered as provided in this paragraph applies for a driver's license or the registration of a motor vehicle shall have the application denied unless the applicant re-establishes such proof for the remainder of such period.

3. In the event that proof of financial responsibility has been deposited voluntarily, at any time upon request of the person entitled thereto, provided that the person on whose behalf such proof was given has not, during the period between the date of the original deposit thereof and the date of such request, been convicted of any offense for which revocation is mandatory as provided in Section 6-205; provided, further, that no action for damages is pending against such person on whose behalf such proof of financial responsibility was furnished and no judgment against such person is outstanding and unsatisfied in respect to bodily injury, or in respect to damage to property resulting from the ownership, maintenance, use or operation hereafter of a motor vehicle. An affidavit of the applicant under this Section shall be sufficient evidence of the facts in the absence of evidence to the contrary in the records of the Secretary of State.

P.A. 76-1586, § 7-328, eff. July 1, 1970. Amended by P.A. 80-230, § 1, eff. Oct. 1, 1977; P.A. 83-831, § 1, eff. Jan. 1, 1984; P.A. 85-321, § 1, eff. Jan. 1, 1988.

Formerly Ill.Rev.Stat.1991, ch. 95 ½, ¶ 7-328.

5/7-329. Proof of financial responsibility made voluntarily

§ 7-329. Proof of financial responsibility made voluntarily. 1. Proof of financial responsibility may be voluntarily by or on behalf of any person. The privilege of operation of any motor vehicle within this State by such person shall not be suspended or withdrawn under the provisions of this Article if such proof of financial responsibility has been voluntarily filed or deposited prior to the offense or accident out of which any conviction, judgment, or order arises and if such proof, at the date of such conviction, judgment, or order, is valid and sufficient for the requirements of this Code.

2. If the Secretary of State receives record of any conviction or judgment against such person which, in the absence of such proof of financial responsibility would have caused the suspension of the driver's license of such person, the Secretary of State shall forthwith notify the insurer or surety of such person of the conviction or judgment so reported.

P.A. 76-1586, § 7-329, eff. July 1, 1970. Amended by P.A. 83-831, § 1, eff. Jan. 1, 1984.

Formerly Ill.Rev.Stat.1991, ch. 95 ½, ¶ 7-329.

ARTICLE IV. VIOLATIONS OF PROVISIONS OF FINANCIAL RESPONSIBILITY ACT

Section

5/7-401. Transfer of registration to defeat purposes of act prohibited

§ 7-401. Transfer of registration to defeat purposes of act prohibited. (a) If an owner's registration has been suspended hereunder, such registration shall not be transferred nor the vehicle in respect to which such registration was issued be registered in any other name until the Secretary of State is satisfied that such transfer of registration is proposed in good faith and not for the purpose or with the effect of defeating the purposes of this act.

(b) Nothing in this section shall in any wise affect the rights of any conditional vendor, chattel mortgagee or lessor of such a vehicle registered in the name of another as owner who becomes subject to the provisions of this act.

(c) The Secretary of State shall suspend the registration of any vehicle transferred in violation of the provisions of this section.

P.A. 76-1586, § 7-401, eff. July 1, 1970.

Formerly Ill.Rev.Stat.1991, ch. 95 ½, ¶ 7-401.

5/7-402. Surrender of license to drive and registration

§ 7-402. Surrender of license to drive and registration. Except as otherwise provided in this Code or Article V of the Supreme Court Rules, any person whose license to drive has been suspended shall immediately return to the Secretary of State any driver's license, instruction permit, restricted driving permit or other evidence of driving privileges held by such person. Any driving authorization document issued under Section 6-206.1 or 11-501.1 of this Code shall be returned to the issuing court for proper processing. Any person whose vehicle registration has been suspended shall, upon the request of the Secretary, immediately return to the Secretary any license plates or other evidences of registration held by such person.

The Secretary is authorized to take possession of any license to drive, registration certificate, registration sticker or license plates upon the suspension thereof under the provisions of this Code or to direct any law enforcement officer to take possession thereof and to return the same to the Secretary.

Any person willfully failing to comply with this Section is guilty of a Class A misdemeanor and shall be punished as provided in Section 9-110 of this Code.

P.A. 76-1586, § 7-402, eff. July 1, 1970. Amended by P.A. 77-2830, Art. 73, § 1, eff. Jan. 1, 1973; P.A. 80-230, § 1, eff. Oct. 1, 1977; P.A. 80-1185, § 1, eff. March 8, 1978; P.A. 85-1201, § 1, eff. July 1, 1989; P.A. 91-357, § 231, eff. July 29, 1999.

Formerly Ill.Rev.Stat.1991, ch. 95 ½, ¶ 7-402.

5/7-403. Forged proof

§ 7-403. Forged proof. Any person who shall forge, or, without authority, sign any evidence of proof of financial responsibility for the future, or who files or offers for filing any such evidence of proof knowing or having reason to believe that it is forged or signed without authority, shall be guilty of a Class A misdemeanor.

P.A. 76-1586, § 7-403, eff. July 1, 1970. Amended by P.A. 77-2720, § 1, eff. Jan. 1, 1973.

Formerly Ill.Rev.Stat.1991, ch. 95 ½, ¶ 7-403.

ARTICLE V. MISCELLANEOUS PROVISIONS RELATING TO FINANCIAL RESPONSIBILITY

5/7-501. Assigned Risk Plans

§ 7-501. Assigned Risk Plans. If, on or before January 1, 1946, every insurance carrier authorized to write automobile bodily injury liability insurance in this State shall not subscribe to an assigned risk plan approved by the Director of Insurance, providing that no carrier may withdraw therefrom after approval of the Director, the Director of Insurance shall, when he finds that an application for bodily injury or property damage insurance by a risk, which may become subject to this Act or is a local public entity subject to the Local Governmental and Governmental Employees Tort Immunity Act, [1] and in good faith is entitled to such insurance, has been rejected by 3 insurance carriers, designate an insurance carrier which shall be obligated to issue forthwith its usual form of policy providing such insurance for such risk. The Director shall make equitable distribution of such assignments among insurance carriers proportionate, so far as practicable, by premiums to the respective net direct automobile bodily injury premium writings of the carriers authorized to do business in this State. The Director of Insurance shall establish rules and regulations for the administration of the provisions of this Section.

If any carrier refuses or neglects to comply with the provisions of this Section or with any lawful order or ruling made by the Director of Insurance pursuant to this Section, the Director may, after notice and hearing, suspend the license of such carrier to transact any insurance business in this State until such carrier shall have complied with such order. The provisions of the Administrative Review Law, [2] and all amendments and modifications thereof, and the rules adopted pursuant thereto, shall apply to and govern all proceedings for the judicial review of final administrative decisions of the Director of Insurance hereunder.

P.A. 76-1586, § 7-501, eff. July 1, 1970. Amended by P.A. 80-824, § 1, eff. Oct. 1, 1977; P.A. 82-783, Art. XI, § 140, eff. July 13, 1982; P.A. 90-89, § 15, eff. Jan. 1, 1998; P.A. 92-651, § 77, eff. July 11, 2002.

Formerly Ill.Rev.Stat.1991, ch. 95 ½, ¶ 7-501.

1 745 ILCS 10/1-101 et seq.

2 735 ILCS 5/3-101 et seq.

5/7-502. Self-insurers

§ 7-502. Self-insurers. Any person in whose name more than 25 motor vehicles are registered may qualify as a self-insurer by obtaining a certificate of self-insurance issued by the Director of the Department of Insurance as provided in this Section.

The Director may, in his discretion, upon the application of such a person, issue a certificate of self-insurance when he is satisfied that such person is possessed and will continue to be possessed of ability to pay judgment obtained against such person.

Upon not less than 5 days' notice, and a hearing pursuant to such notice, the Director may upon reasonable grounds cancel a certificate of self-insurance. Failure to pay any judgment against any person covered by such certificate of self-insurance and arising out of any accident in which a motor vehicle covered by such certificate of self-insurance has been involved within 30 days after such judgment shall have become final shall constitute a reasonable ground for the cancellation of a certificate of self-insurance.

P.A. 76–1586, § 7–502, eff. July 1, 1970. Amended by P.A. 77–2743, § 1, eff. July 1, 1972; P.A. 82–138, § 1, eff. Jan. 1, 1982.

Formerly Ill.Rev.Stat.1991, ch. 95 ½, ¶ 7–502.

5/7–503. Unclaimed security deposits

§ 7–503. Unclaimed security deposits. During July, annually, the Secretary shall compile a list of all securities on deposit, pursuant to this Article, for more than 3 years and concerning which he has received no notice as to the pendency of any judicial proceeding that could affect the disposition thereof. Thereupon, he shall promptly send a notice by certified mail to the last known address of each depositor advising him that his deposit will be subject to escheat to the State of Illinois if not claimed within 30 days after the mailing date of such notice. At the expiration of such time, the Secretary of State shall file with the State Treasurer an order directing the transfer of such deposit to the general revenue fund in the State Treasury. Upon receipt of such order, the State Treasurer shall make such transfer, after converting to cash any other type of security. Thereafter any person having a legal claim against such deposit may enforce it by appropriate proceedings in the Court of Claims subject to the limitations prescribed for such Court. At the expiration of such limitation period such deposit shall escheat to the State of Illinois.

P.A. 76–1586, § 7–503, eff. July 1, 1970.

Formerly Ill.Rev.Stat.1991, ch. 95 ½, ¶ 7–503.

5/7–504. Emergency telephone system outages; reimbursement

§ 7–504. Emergency telephone system outages; reimbursement. Any person who negligently causes a motor vehicle accident that causes an emergency telephone system outage must reimburse the public safety agency that provides personnel to answer calls or to maintain or operate an emergency telephone system during the outage for the agency's costs associated with answering calls or maintaining or operating the system during the outage. For the purposes of this Section, "public safety agency" means the same as in Section 2.02 of the Emergency Telephone System Act.

P.A. 76–1586, § 7–504, added by P.A. 92–149, § 10, eff. Jan. 1, 2002.

ARTICLE VI. MANDATORY INSURANCE

Date Effective

Article VI was added by P.A. 85–1201, § 1, eff. July 1, 1989.

Section

5/7–601. Required liability insurance policy

§ 7–601. Required liability insurance policy.

(a) No person shall operate, register or maintain registration of, and no owner shall permit another person to operate, register or maintain registration of, a motor vehicle designed to be used on a public highway unless the motor vehicle is covered by a liability insurance policy.

The insurance policy shall be issued in amounts no less than the minimum amounts set for bodily injury or death and for destruction of property under Section 7–203 of this Code, and shall be issued in accordance with the requirements of Sections 143a and 143a–2 of the Illinois Insurance Code, as amended. [1] No insurer other than an insurer authorized to do business in this State shall issue a policy pursuant to this Section for any vehicle subject to registration under this Code. Nothing herein shall deprive an insurer of any policy defense available at common law.

(b) The following vehicles are exempt from the requirements of this Section:

(1) vehicles subject to the provisions of Chapters 8 or 18a, [2] Article III [3] or Section 7–609 of Chapter 7, or Sections 12–606 or 12–707.01 of Chapter 12 of this Code;

(2) vehicles required to file proof of liability insurance with the Illinois Commerce Commission;

(3) vehicles covered by a certificate of self-insurance under Section 7–502 of this Code;

(4) vehicles owned by the United States, the State of Illinois, or any political subdivision, municipality or local mass transit district;

(5) implements of husbandry;

(6) other vehicles complying with laws which require them to be insured in amounts meeting or exceeding the minimum amounts required under this Section; and

(7) inoperable or stored vehicles that are not operated, as defined by rules and regulations of the Secretary.

(c) Every employee of a State agency, as that term is defined in the Illinois State Auditing Act, [4] who is assigned a specific vehicle owned or leased by the State on an ongoing basis shall provide the certification described in this Section annually to the director or chief executive officer of his or her agency.

The certification shall affirm that the employee is duly licensed to drive the assigned vehicle and that (i) the employee has liability insurance coverage extending to the employee when the assigned vehicle is used for other than official State business, or (ii) the employee has filed a bond with the Secretary of State as proof of financial responsibility, in an amount equal to, or in excess of the requirements stated within this Section. Upon request of the agency director or chief executive officer, the employee shall present evidence to support the certification.

The certification shall be provided during the period July 1 through July 31 of each calendar year, or within 30 days of any new assignment of a vehicle on an ongoing basis, whichever is later.

The employee's authorization to use the assigned vehicle shall automatically be rescinded upon:

(1) the revocation or suspension of the license required to drive the assigned vehicle;

(2) the cancellation or termination for any reason of the automobile liability insurance coverage as required in item (c) (i); or

(3) the termination of the bond filed with the Secretary of State.

All State employees providing the required certification shall immediately notify the agency director or chief executive officer in the event any of these actions occur.

All peace officers employed by a State agency who are primarily responsible for prevention and detection of crime and the enforcement of the criminal, traffic, or highway laws of this State, and prohibited by agency rule or policy to use an assigned vehicle owned or leased by the State for regular personal or off-duty use, are exempt from the requirements of this Section.

P.A. 76-1586, § 7-601, added by P.A. 85-1201, § 1, eff. July 1, 1989. Amended by P.A. 86-149, § 2, eff. Aug. 11, 1989; P.A. 86-880, § 1, eff. Jan. 1, 1990; P.A. 86-1028, Art. II, § 2-44, eff. Feb. 5, 1990; P.A. 88-315, § 5, eff. Jan. 1, 1994; P.A. 89-669, § 10, eff. Jan. 1, 1997; P.A. 91-661, § 5, eff. Dec. 22, 1999.

Formerly Ill.Rev.Stat.1991, ch. 95 ½, ¶ 7-601.

[1] 215 ILCS 5/143a and 143a-2.

[2] 625 ILCS 5/8-101 et seq. or 5/18a-100 et seq.

[3] 625 ILCS 5/7-301 et seq.

[4] 30 ILCS 5/1-1 et seq.

5/7-602. Insurance card

§ 7-602. Insurance card. Every operator of a motor vehicle subject to Section 7-601 of this Code shall carry within the vehicle evidence of insurance. The evidence shall be legible and sufficient to demonstrate that the motor vehicle currently is covered by a liability insurance policy as required under Section 7-601 of this Code and may include, but is not limited to, the following:

(a) an insurance card provided by the insurer under this Section;

(b) the combination of proof of purchase of the motor vehicle within the previous 60 days and a current insurance card issued for the motor vehicle replaced by such purchase;

(c) the current declarations page of a liability insurance policy;

(d) a liability insurance binder, certificate of liability insurance or receipt for payment to an insurer or its authorized representative for a liability insurance premium, provided such document contains all information the Secretary of State by rule and regulation may require;

(e) a current rental agreement;

(f) registration plates, registration sticker or other evidence of registration issued by the Secretary only upon submission of proof of liability insurance pursuant to this Code;

(g) a certificate, decal, or other document or device issued by a governmental agency for a motor vehicle indicating the vehicle is insured for liability pursuant to law.

An insurance card shall be provided for each motor vehicle insured by the insurer issuing the liability insurance policy.

The form, contents and manner of issuance of the insurance card shall be prescribed by rules and regulations of the Secretary of State. The insurance card shall display an effective date and an expiration date covering a period of time not to exceed 12 months. The insurance card shall contain the following disclaimer: "Examine policy exclusions carefully. This form does not constitute any part of your insurance policy." If the insurance policy represented by the insurance card does not cover any driver operating the motor vehicle with the owner's permission, or the owner when operating a motor vehicle other than the vehicle for which the policy is issued, the insurance card shall contain a warning of such limitations in the coverage provided by the policy.

No insurer shall issue a card, similar in appearance, form and content to the insurance card required under this Section, in connection with an insurance policy that does not provide the liability insurance coverage required under Section 7-601 of this Code.

The evidence of insurance shall be displayed upon request made by any law enforcement officer wearing a uniform or displaying a badge or other sign of authority. Any person who fails or refuses to comply with such request is in violation of Section 3-707 of this Code. Any person who displays evidence of insurance, knowing there is no valid liability insurance in effect on the motor vehicle as required under Section 7-601 of this Code or knowing the evidence of insurance is illegally altered, counterfeit or otherwise invalid, is in violation of Section 3-710 of this Code.

"Display" means the manual surrender of the evidence of insurance into the hands of the law enforcement officer, court, or officer of the court making the request for the officer's, court's, or officer of the court's inspection thereof.

P.A. 76-1586, § 7-602, added by P.A. 85-1201, § 1, eff. July 1, 1989. Amended by P.A. 86-149, § 2, eff. Aug. 11, 1989; P.A. 88-315, § 5, eff. Jan. 1, 1994; P.A. 89-565, § 5, eff. July 26, 1996.

Formerly Ill.Rev.Stat.1991, ch. 95 ½, ¶ 7-602.

5/7-603. Illegal insurance cards—penalty

§ 7-603. Illegal insurance cards—penalty. No person shall alter an invalid insurance card to make it appear valid. No person knowingly shall make, sell or otherwise make available an invalid or counterfeit insurance card.

Any person convicted of a violation of this Section is guilty of a Class 4 felony.

P.A. 76-1586, § 7-603, added by P.A. 85-1201, § 1, eff. July 1, 1989.

Formerly Ill.Rev.Stat.1991, ch. 95 ½, ¶ 7-603.

5/7-604. Verification of liability insurance policy

§ 7-604. Verification of liability insurance policy.

(a) The Secretary of State may select random samples of registrations of motor vehicles subject to Section 7-601 of this Code, or owners thereof, for the purpose of verifying whether or not the motor vehicles are insured.

In addition to such general random samples of motor vehicle registrations, the Secretary may select for verification other random samples, including, but not limited to registrations of motor vehicles owned by persons:

(1) whose motor vehicle registrations during the preceding 4 years have been suspended pursuant to Section 7-606 or 7-607 of this Code;

(2) who during the preceding 4 years have been convicted of violating Section 3-707, 3-708 or 3-710 of this Code while operating vehicles owned by other persons;

(3) whose driving privileges have been suspended during the preceding 4 years;

(4) who during the preceding 4 years acquired ownership of motor vehicles while the registrations of such vehicles under the previous owners were suspended pursuant to Section 7-606 or 7-607 of this Code; or

(5) who during the preceding 4 years have received a disposition of supervision under subsection (c) of Section

5–6–1 of the Unified Code of Corrections [1] for a violation of Section 3–707, 3–708, or 3–710 of this Code.

(b) Upon receiving certification from the Department of Transportation under Section 7–201.2 of this Code of the name of an owner or operator of any motor vehicle involved in an accident, the Secretary may verify whether or not at the time of the accident such motor vehicle was covered by a liability insurance policy in accordance with Section 7–601 of this Code.

(c) In preparation for selection of random samples and their verification, the Secretary may send to owners of randomly selected motor vehicles, or to randomly selected motor vehicle owners, requests for information about their motor vehicles and liability insurance coverage. The request shall require the owner to state whether or not the motor vehicle was insured on the verification date stated in the Secretary's request and the request may require, but is not limited to, a statement by the owner of the names and addresses of insurers, policy numbers, and expiration dates of insurance coverage.

(d) Within 30 days after the Secretary mails a request, the owner to whom it is sent shall furnish the requested information to the Secretary above the owner's signed affirmation that such information is true and correct. Proof of insurance in effect on the verification date, as prescribed by the Secretary, may be considered by the Secretary to be a satisfactory response to the request for information.

Any owner whose response indicates that his or her vehicle was not covered by a liability insurance policy in accordance with Section 7–601 of this Code shall be deemed to have registered or maintained registration of a motor vehicle in violation of that Section. Any owner who fails to respond to such a request shall be deemed to have registered or maintained registration of a motor vehicle in violation of Section 7–601 of this Code.

(e) If the owner responds to the request for information by asserting that his or her vehicle was covered by a liability insurance policy on the verification date stated in the Secretary's request, the Secretary may conduct a verification of the response by furnishing necessary information to the insurer named in the response. The insurer shall within 45 days inform the Secretary whether or not on the verification date stated the motor vehicle was insured by the insurer in accordance with Section 7–601 of this Code. The Secretary may by rule and regulation prescribe the procedures for verification.

(f) No random sample selected under this Section shall be categorized on the basis of race, color, religion, sex, national origin, ancestry, age, marital status, physical or mental disability, economic status or geography.

P.A. 76–1586, § 7–604, added by P.A. 85–1201, § 1, eff. July 1, 1989. Amended by P.A. 86–149, § 2, eff. Aug. 11, 1989; P.A. 88–315, § 5, eff. Jan. 1, 1994; P.A. 88–685, § 5, eff. Jan. 24, 1995; P.A. 92–458, § 5, eff. Aug. 22, 2001.

Formerly Ill.Rev.Stat.1991, ch. 95 ½, ¶ 7–604.

[1] 730 ILCS 5/5–6–1.

5/7–605. Uninsured motor vehicles—notice

§ 7–605. Uninsured motor vehicles—notice. If the Secretary determines that an owner has registered or maintained the registration of a motor vehicle without a liability insurance policy in accordance with Section 7–601 of this Code, the Secretary shall notify the owner that such owner's vehicle registration shall be suspended 45 days after the date of the mailing of the notice unless the owner within 30 days furnishes proof of insurance in effect on the verification date, as prescribed by the Secretary.

P.A. 76–1586, § 7–605, added by P.A. 85–1201, § 1, eff. July 1, 1989. Amended by P.A. 86–149, § 2, eff. Aug. 11, 1989.

Formerly Ill.Rev.Stat.1991, ch. 95 ½, ¶ 7–605.

5/7–606. Uninsured motor vehicles—suspension and reinstatement

§ 7–606. Uninsured motor vehicles—suspension and reinstatement. The Secretary shall suspend the vehicle registration of any motor vehicle determined by the Secretary to be in violation of Section 7–601 of this Code, including any motor vehicle operated in violation of Section 3–707, 3–708 or 3–710 of this Code by an operator other than the owner of the vehicle. Neither the fact that, subsequent to the date of verification or conviction, the owner acquired the required liability insurance policy nor the fact that the owner terminated ownership of the motor vehicle shall have any bearing upon the Secretary's decision to suspend.

The Secretary is authorized to suspend the registration of any motor vehicle registered in this State upon receiving notice of the conviction of the operator of the motor vehicle in another State of an offense which, if committed in this State, would constitute a violation of Section 7–601 of this Code.

Until it is terminated, the suspension shall remain in force after the registration is renewed or a new registration is acquired for the motor vehicle. The suspension also shall apply to any motor vehicle to which the owner transfers the registration.

In the case of a first violation, the Secretary shall terminate the suspension upon payment by the owner of a reinstatement fee of $100 and submission of proof of insurance as prescribed by the Secretary.

In the case of a second or subsequent violation by a person having ownership interest in a motor vehicle or vehicles within the preceding 4 years, or a violation of Section 3–708 of this Code, the Secretary shall terminate the suspension 4 months after its effective date upon payment by the owner of a reinstatement fee of $100 and submission of proof of insurance as prescribed by the Secretary.

All fees collected under this Section shall be deposited into the Road Fund of the State treasury.

P.A. 76–1586, § 7–606, added by P.A. 85–1201, § 1, eff. July 1, 1989. Amended by P.A. 86–149, § 2, eff. Aug. 11, 1989; P.A. 88–315, § 5, eff. Jan. 1, 1994.

Formerly Ill.Rev.Stat.1991, ch. 95 ½, ¶ 7–606.

5/7–607. Submission of false proof—penalty

§ 7–607. Submission of false proof—penalty. If the Secretary determines that the proof of insurance submitted by a motor vehicle owner under Section 7–604, 7–605 or 7–606 of this Code is false, the Secretary shall suspend the owner's vehicle registration. The Secretary shall terminate the suspension 6 months after its effective date upon payment by the owner of a reinstatement fee of $200 and submission of proof of insurance as prescribed by the Secretary.

All fees collected under this Section shall be deposited into the Road Fund of the State treasury.

P.A. 76–1586, § 7–607, added by P.A. 85–1201, § 1, eff. July 1, 1989.

Formerly Ill.Rev.Stat.1991, ch. 95 ½, ¶ 7–607.

5/7-608. Verification—limitation

§ 7-608. Verification—limitation. No verification procedure established under this Code shall include individual inspections of vehicles on a highway solely for the purpose of verifying the existence of an insurance policy. No law enforcement officer shall stop a vehicle solely for the purpose of verifying the existence of a valid insurance policy.

P.A. 76-1586, § 7-608, added by P.A. 85-1201, § 1, eff. July 1, 1989. Amended by P.A. 86-149, § 2, eff. Aug. 11, 1989.

Formerly Ill.Rev.Stat.1991, ch. 95 ½, ¶ 7-608.

5/7-609. Exemption for certain religious organizations

§ 7-609. Exemption for certain religious organizations. (a) Pursuant to the following minimum criteria, the Secretary may exempt from the provisions of Section 7-601 of this Code motor vehicles owned by a religious organization or its members:

(1) The religious organization and its members hold a bona fide conviction that the acquisition of insurance is contrary to their religious beliefs.

(2) The religious organization and its members submit to the Secretary evidence that historically, over a period of time not less than two years, they have paid or, by agreement with the other party or parties involved, are paying in a timely manner for all damages for which they were or are liable.

(3) The religious organization has filed with the Secretary a current, irrevocable letter of credit, valid for a period of 12 months and issued in accordance with this Section and Article 5 of the Uniform Commercial Code, approved July 31, 1961, as amended,[1] by a financial institution chartered by an agency of State or federal government. The Secretary of State by rule and regulation shall establish the minimum amount of credit required.

(4) The religious organization and its members meet other requirements which the Secretary by rule and regulation may prescribe.

(b) Upon accepting a letter of credit from a religious organization, the Secretary shall issue a certificate of exemption for each motor vehicle covered. The certificate of exemption shall serve as evidence of insurance in accordance with Section 7-602 of this Code.

Not less than 30 days before a current letter of credit expires, or by agreement between the issuer and customer is revoked, the religious organization shall file with the Secretary a new letter of credit. If a new letter of credit is not on file with the Secretary at the time the current letter of credit expires or is revoked, the exemption of the religious organization and its members shall expire and their certificates of exemption shall become invalid.

(c) If credit is used to the extent that the remaining amount of credit does not meet the minimum requirements of this Section, and the issuer declines to reinstate the used portion of the credit or issue a new letter of credit, the issuer immediately shall send written notice to the customer and the Secretary that the current letter of credit on file with the Secretary no longer meets the minimum requirements of the law.

If, within 30 days of receiving the notice, the Secretary has not received and accepted a new letter of credit from the customer, the exemption of that religious organization and its members shall expire and their certificates of exemption shall become invalid.

(d) Upon the request of the plaintiff, if a person, known by the court to be covered by a current letter of credit issued pursuant to this Section, fails to pay a judgment for damages within 30 days after the judgment has become final, the clerk of the court within 10 days shall forward to the Secretary a report of the person's failure to pay. The report shall indicate that the person is covered by a letter of credit and, if known by the court, the names of the issuer and the customer.

Upon receiving the report from the court, the Secretary shall notify the religious organization that, unless the payment is made, 30 days after the date of the mailing of the notice the exemption of the religious organization and its members shall be terminated and their certificates of exemption shall become invalid. If within the 30 days the religious organization does not submit evidence that the payment has been made, or furnish valid reasons why the payment has been delayed or not made, the Secretary shall terminate the exemptions.

(e) The Secretary is authorized to promulgate rules and regulations necessary for the administration of the provisions of this Section.

P.A. 76-1586, § 7-609, added by P.A. 86-149, § 2, eff. Aug. 11, 1989.

Formerly Ill.Rev.Stat.1991, ch. 95 ½, ¶ 7-609.

[1] 810 ILCS 5/5-101 et seq.

5/7-610. Immunity

§ 7-610. Immunity. No state or local governmental unit and no government official or employee acting in the course of his or her official duties in the administration or enforcement of Section 7-601 and related provisions of this Code shall be liable for any damages, brought directly or indirectly by the injured party or a third party, except for damages resulting from willful and wanton misconduct or gross negligence on the part of the governmental unit, official or employee.

P.A. 76-1586, § 7-610, added by P.A. 86-149, § 2, eff. Aug. 11, 1989.

Formerly Ill.Rev.Stat.1991, ch. 95 ½, ¶ 7-610.

5/7-611. § 7-611. Repealed by P.A. 88-315, § 10, eff. Jan. 1, 1994

ARTICLE VII. FAMILY FINANCIAL RESPONSIBILITY LAW

Date Effective

Article VII was added by P.A. 89-92, § 10, eff. July 1, 1996.

Section

5/7–701. Findings and purpose

§ 7–701. Findings and purpose. The General Assembly finds that the timely receipt of adequate financial support has the effect of reducing poverty and State expenditures for welfare dependency among children, and that the timely payment of adequate child support demonstrates financial responsibility. Further, the General Assembly finds that the State has a compelling interest in ensuring that drivers within the State demonstrate financial responsibility, including family financial responsibility, in order to safely own and operate a motor vehicle. To this end, the Secretary of State is authorized to establish systems to suspend driver's licenses for failure to comply with court orders of support.

P.A. 76–1586, § 7–701, added by P.A. 89–92, § 10, eff. July 1, 1996. Amended by P.A. 91–613, § 945, eff. July 1, 2000.

5/7–702. Suspension of driver's license for failure to pay child support

§ 7–702. Suspension of driver's license for failure to pay child support.

(a) The Secretary of State shall suspend the driver's license issued to an obligor upon receiving an authenticated report provided for in subsection (a) of Section 7–703, that the person is 90 days or more delinquent in court ordered child support payments or has been adjudicated in arrears in an amount equal to 90 days obligation or more, and has been found in contempt by the court for failure to pay the support.

(b) The Secretary of State shall suspend the driver's license issued to an obligor upon receiving an authenticated document provided for in subsection (b) of Section 7–703, that the person has been adjudicated in arrears in court ordered child support payments in an amount equal to 90 days obligation or more, but has not been held in contempt of court, and that the court has ordered that the person's driving privileges be suspended. The obligor's driver's license shall be suspended until such time as the Secretary of State receives authenticated documentation that the obligor is in compliance with the court order of support. When the obligor complies with the court ordered child support payments, the circuit court shall report the obligor's compliance with the court order of support to the Secretary of State, on a form prescribed by the Secretary of State, and shall order that the obligor's driver's license be reinstated.

P.A. 76–1586, § 7–702, added by P.A. 89–92, § 10, eff. July 1, 1996. Amended by P.A. 91–613, § 945, eff. July 1, 2000.

5/7–702.1. Family financial responsibility driving permits

§ 7–702.1. Family financial responsibility driving permits. Following the entry of an order that an obligor has been found in contempt by the court for failure to pay court ordered child support payments or upon a motion by the obligor who is subject to having his or her driver's license suspended pursuant to subsection (b) of Section 7–703, the court may enter an order directing the Secretary of State to issue a family financial responsibility driving permit for the purpose of providing the obligor the privilege of operating a motor vehicle between the obligor's residence and place of employment, or within the scope of employment related duties; or for the purpose of providing transportation for the obligor or a household member to receive alcohol treatment, other drug treatment, or medical care. The court may enter an order directing the issuance of a permit only if the obligor has proven to the satisfaction of the court that no alternative means of transportation are reasonably available for the above stated purposes. No permit shall be issued to a person under the age of 16 years who possesses an instruction permit.

Upon entry of an order granting the issuance of a permit to an obligor, the court shall report this finding to the Secretary of State on a form prescribed by the Secretary. This form shall state whether the permit has been granted for employment or medical purposes and the specific days and hours for which limited driving privileges have been granted.

The family financial responsibility driving permit shall be subject to cancellation, invalidation, suspension, and revocation by the Secretary of State in the same manner and for the same reasons as a driver's license may be cancelled, invalidated, suspended, or revoked.

The Secretary of State shall, upon receipt of a certified court order from the court of jurisdiction, issue a family financial responsibility driving permit. In order for this permit to be issued, an individual's driving privileges must be valid except for the family financial responsibility suspension. This permit shall be valid only for employment and medical purposes as set forth above. The permit shall state the days and hours for which limited driving privileges have been granted.

Any submitted court order that contains insufficient data or fails to comply with any provision of this Code shall not be used for issuance of the permit or entered to the individual's driving record but shall be returned to the court of jurisdiction indicating why the permit cannot be issued at that time. The Secretary of State shall also send notice of the return of the court order to the individual requesting the permit.

P.A. 76–1586, § 7–702.1, added by P.A. 89–92, § 10, eff. July 1, 1996. Amended by P.A. 90–369, § 5, eff. Jan. 1, 1998; P.A. 91–613, § 945, eff. July 1, 2000.

5/7–702.2. Written agreement to pay past-due support

§ 7–702.2. Written agreement to pay past-due support.

(a) An obligor who is presently unable to pay all past-due support and is subject to having his or her license suspended pursuant to subsection (b) of Section 7–703 may come into compliance with the court order for support by executing a written payment agreement that is approved by the court and by complying with that agreement. A condition of a written payment agreement must be that the obligor pay the current child support when due. Before a written payment agreement is executed, the obligor shall:

(1) Disclose fully to the court in writing, on a form prescribed by the court, the obligor's financial circumstances, including income from all sources, assets, liabilities, and work history for the past year; and

(2) Provide documentation to the court concerning the obligor's financial circumstances, including copies of the most recent State and federal income tax returns, both personal and business; a copy of a recent pay stub representative of current income; and copies of other records that show the obligor's income and the present level of assets held by the obligor.

(b) After full disclosure, the court may determine the obligor's ability to pay past-due support and may approve a written payment agreement consistent with the obligor's ability to pay, not to exceed the court-ordered support.

P.A. 76-1586, § 7-702.2, added by P.A. 91-613, § 945, eff. July 1, 2000.

5/7-703. Courts to report non-payment of court ordered support

§ 7-703. Courts to report non-payment of court ordered support.

(a) The clerk of the circuit court, as provided in subsection (b) of Section 505 of the Illinois Marriage and Dissolution of Marriage Act [1] or as provided in Section 15 of the Illinois Parentage Act of 1984, [2] shall forward to the Secretary of State, on a form prescribed by the Secretary, an authenticated document certifying the court's order suspending the driving privileges of the obligor. For any such certification, the clerk of the court shall charge the obligor a fee of $5 as provided in the Clerks of Courts Act.[3]

(b) If an obligor has been adjudicated in arrears in court ordered child support payments in an amount equal to 90 days obligation or more but has not been held in contempt of court, the circuit court may order that the obligor's driving privileges be suspended. If the circuit court orders that the obligor's driving privileges be suspended, it shall forward to the Secretary of State, on a form prescribed by the Secretary, an authenticated document certifying the court's order suspending the driving privileges of the obligor. The authenticated document shall be forwarded to the Secretary of State by the court no later than 45 days after entry of the order suspending the obligor's driving privileges.

P.A. 76-1586, § 7-703, added by P.A. 89-92, § 10, eff. July 1, 1996. Amended by P.A. 89-626, Art. 3, § 3-37, eff. Aug. 9, 1996; P.A. 91-613, § 945, eff. July 1, 2000.

[1] 750 ILCS 5/505.

[2] 750 ILCS 45/15.

[3] 705 ILCS 105/0.01 et seq.

5/7-704. Suspension to continue until compliance with court order of support

§ 7-704. Suspension to continue until compliance with court order of support.

(a) The suspension of a driver's license shall remain in effect unless and until the Secretary of State receives authenticated documentation that the obligor is in compliance with a court order of support or that the order has been stayed by a subsequent order of the court. Full driving privileges shall not be issued by the Secretary of State until notification of compliance has been received from the court. The circuit clerks shall report the obligor's compliance with a court order of support to the Secretary of State, on a form prescribed by the Secretary.

(b) Whenever, after one suspension of an individual's driver's license for failure to pay child support, another order of non-payment is entered against the obligor and the person fails to come into compliance with the court order of support, then the Secretary shall again suspend the driver's license of the individual and that suspension shall not be removed unless the obligor is in full compliance with the court order of support and has made full payment on all arrearages.

P.A. 76-1586, § 7-704, added by P.A. 89-92, § 10, eff. July 1, 1996.

5/7-705. Notice

§ 7-705. Notice. The Secretary of State, prior to suspending a driver's license under this Chapter, shall serve written notice upon an obligor that the individual's driver's license will be suspended in 60 days from the date on the notice unless the obligor satisfies the court order of support and the circuit clerk notifies the Secretary of State of this compliance.

P.A. 76-1586, § 7-705, added by P.A. 89-92, § 10, eff. July 1, 1996.

5/7-705.1. Notice of noncompliance with support order

§ 7-705.1. Notice of noncompliance with support order. Before forwarding to the Secretary of State the authenticated document under subsection (b) of Section 7-703, the circuit court must serve notice upon the obligor of its intention to suspend the obligor's driver's license for being adjudicated in arrears in court ordered child support payments in an amount equal to 90 days obligation. The notice must inform the obligor that:

(a) If the obligor is presently unable to pay all past-due support, the obligor may come into compliance with the support order by executing a written payment agreement with the court, as provided in Section 7-702.2, and by complying with that agreement;

(b) The obligor may contest the issue of compliance at a hearing;

(c) A request for a hearing must be made in writing and must be received by the clerk of the circuit court;

(d) If the obligor does not request a hearing to contest the issue of compliance within 45 days after the notice of noncompliance is mailed, the court may order that the obligor's driver's license be suspended as provided for in subsection (b) of Section 7-703;

(e) If the circuit court certifies the obligor to the Secretary of State for noncompliance with an order of support, the Secretary of State must suspend any driver's license or instruction permit the obligor holds and the obligor's right to apply for or obtain a driver's license or instruction permit until the obligor comes into compliance with the order of support;

(f) If the obligor files a motion to modify support with the court or requests the court to modify a support obligation, the circuit court shall stay action to certify the obligor to the Secretary of State for noncompliance with an order of support; and

(g) The obligor may comply with an order of support by doing all of the following:

(1) Paying the current support;

(2) Paying all past-due support or, if unable to pay all past-due support and a periodic payment for past-due support has not been ordered by the court, by making periodic payments in accordance with a written payment agreement approved by the court; and

(3) Meeting the obligor's health insurance obligation.

The notice must include the address and telephone number of the clerk of the circuit court. The clerk of the circuit court shall attach a copy of the obligor's order of support to the notice. The notice must be served by certified mail, return receipt requested, by service in hand, or as specified in the Code of Civil Procedure. [1]

P.A. 76-1586, § 7-705.1, added by P.A. 91-613, § 945, eff. July 1, 2000.

[1] 735 ILCS 5/1-101 et seq.

5/7-706. Administrative hearing

§ 7-706. Administrative hearing. A driver may contest this driver's license sanction by requesting an administrative hearing in accordance with Section 2-118 of this Code. If a written request for this hearing is received prior to the effective date of the suspension, the suspension shall be stayed. If a stay of the suspension is granted, it shall remain in effect until a hearing decision is entered. At the conclusion of this hearing, the Secretary of State may rescind or impose the driver's license suspension. If the suspension is upheld, it shall become effective 10 days from the date the hearing decision is entered. If the decision is to rescind the suspension, no suspension of driving privileges shall be entered. The scope of this hearing shall be limited to the following issues:

(a) Whether the driver is the obligor covered by the court order of support.

(b) Whether the authenticated document of a court order of support indicates that the obligor is 90 days or more delinquent or has been adjudicated in arrears in an amount equal to 90 days obligation or more and has been found in contempt of court for failure to pay child support.

(c) Whether a superseding authenticated document of any court order of support has been entered.

P.A. 76-1586, § 7-706, added by P.A. 89-92, § 10, eff. July 1, 1996.

5/7-706.1. Hearing for compliance with support order

§ 7-706.1. Hearing for compliance with support order.

(a) An obligor may request in writing to the clerk of the circuit court a hearing to contest the claim of noncompliance with an order of support and his or her subsequent driver's license suspension under subsection (b) of Section 7-702.

(b) If a written request for a hearing is received by the clerk of the circuit court, the clerk of the circuit court shall set the hearing before the circuit court.

(c) Upon the obligor's written request, the court must set a date for a hearing and afford the obligor an opportunity for a hearing as early as practical.

(d) The scope of this hearing is limited to the following issues:

(1) Whether the obligor is required to pay child support under an order of support.

(2) Whether the obligor has been adjudicated in arrears in court ordered child support payments in an amount equal to 90 days obligation or more.

(3) Any additional issues raised by the obligor, including the reasonableness of a payment agreement in light of the obligor's current financial circumstances, to be preserved for appeal.

(e) All hearings and hearing procedures shall comply with requirements of the Illinois Constitution and the United States Constitution, so that no person is deprived of due process of law nor denied equal protection of the laws. All hearings shall be held before a judge of the circuit court in the county in which the support order has been entered. Appropriate records of the hearings shall be kept. Where a transcript of the hearing is taken, the person requesting the hearing shall have the opportunity to order a copy of the transcript at his or her own expense.

(f) The action of the circuit court resulting in the suspension of any driver's license shall be a final judgment for purposes of appellate review.

P.A. 76-1586, § 7-706.1, added by P.A. 91-613, § 945, eff. July 1, 2000.

5/7-707. Payment of reinstatement fee

§ 7-707. Payment of reinstatement fee. When an obligor receives notice from the Secretary of State that the suspension of driving privileges has been terminated based upon receipt of notification from the circuit clerk of the obligor's compliance with a court order of support, the obligor shall pay a $30 reinstatement fee to the Secretary of State as set forth in Section 6-118 of this Code. The fee shall be deposited into the Family Responsibility Fund. In accordance with subsection (e) of Section 6-115 of this Code, the Secretary of State may decline to process a renewal of a driver's license of a person who has not paid this fee.

P.A. 76-1586, § 7-707, added by P.A. 89-92, § 10, eff. July 1, 1996. Amended by P.A. 92-16, § 85, eff. June 28, 2001.

5/7-708. Rules

§ 7-708. Rules. The Secretary of State, using the authority to license motor vehicle operators, may adopt such rules as may be necessary to establish standards, policies, and procedures for the suspension of driver's licenses for non-compliance with a court order of support.

P.A. 76-1586, § 7-708, added by P.A. 89-92, § 10, eff. July 1, 1996.

CHAPTER 8. MOTOR VEHICLES USED FOR TRANSPORTATION OF PASSENGERS

Section

Enactment

The Illinois Vehicle Code was enacted by P.A. 76-1586, effective July 1, 1970. The Code constitutes a consolidated recodification of various earlier laws and acts including the Illinois Motor Vehicle Law of 1957.

5/8-101. Proof of financial responsibility—Persons who operate motor vehicles in transportation of passengers for hire

§ 8-101. Proof of financial responsibility—Persons who operate motor vehicles in transportation of passengers for hire. It is unlawful for any person, firm or corporation to operate any motor vehicle along or upon any public street or highway in any incorporated city, town or village in this State for the carriage of passengers for hire, accepting and discharging all such persons as may offer themselves for transportation unless such person, firm or corporation has given, and there is in full force and effect and on file with the Secretary of State of Illinois, proof of financial responsibility provided in this Act. In addition this Section shall also apply to persons, firms or corporations who are in the business of providing transportation services for minors to or from educational or recreational facilities, except that this Section shall not apply to public utilities subject to regulation under "An Act concerning public utilities," approved June 29, 1921, as amended,[1] or to school buses which are operated by public or parochial schools and are engaged solely in the transportation of the pupils who attend such schools. This Section also applies to a contract carrier transporting employees in the course of their employment on a highway of this State in a vehicle designed to carry 15 or fewer passengers. This Section shall not apply to any person participating in a ridesharing arrangement or operating a commuter van, but only during the performance of activities authorized by the Ridesharing Arrangements Act.[2]

If the person operating such motor vehicle is not the owner, then proof of financial responsibility filed hereunder must provide that the owner is primarily liable.

P.A. 76-1586, § 8-101, eff. July 1, 1970. Amended by P.A. 77-2743, § 1, eff. July 1, 1972; P.A. 82-656, § 7, eff. Jan. 1, 1982; P.A. 92-108, § 5, eff. Jan. 1, 2002.

1 220 ILCS 5/1-101 et seq.

2 625 ILCS 30/1 et seq.

5/8-101.1. Proof of financial responsibility—Persons who operate medical transport vehicles

§ 8-101.1. Proof of financial responsibility—Persons who operate medical transport vehicles. It is unlawful for any person, firm or corporation, other than a unit of local government, to operate any medical transport vehicle along or upon any public street or highway in any incorporated city, town or village in this State unless such person, firm or corporation has given, and there is in full force and effect and on file with the Secretary of State, proof of financial responsibility provided in this Code.

If the person operating such motor vehicle is not the owner, then proof of financial responsibility filed hereunder must provide that the owner is primarily liable.

P.A. 76-1586, § 8-101.1, added by P.A. 82-433, § 1, eff. Sept. 8, 1981. Amended by P.A. 82-949, § 1, eff. Jan. 1, 1983.

Formerly Ill.Rev.Stat.1991, ch. 95 ½, ¶ 8-101.1.

Section 3 of P.A. 82-433 approved Sept. 8, 1981, provided:

"This Act takes effect upon its becoming a law, except that the provisions relating to safety tests and proof of financial responsibility for medical transport vehicles apply only to applications for and the issuance of registration plates which are required to be displayed on January 1, 1982 or thereafter."

5/8-102. Alternate methods of giving proof

§ 8-102. Alternate methods of giving proof. Proof of financial responsibility, when required under Section 8-101 or 8-101.1, may be given by filing with the Secretary of State one of the following:

1. A bond as provided in Section 8-103;

2. An insurance policy or other proof of insurance in a form to be prescribed by the Secretary as provided in Section 8-108;

3. A certificate of self-insurance issued by the Director;

4. A certificate of self-insurance issued to the Regional Transportation Authority by the Director naming municipal or non-municipal public carriers included therein;

5. A certificate of coverage issued by an intergovernmental risk management association evidencing coverages which meet or exceed the amounts required under this Code.

P.A. 76-1586, § 8-102, eff. July 1, 1970. Amended by P.A. 77-2743, § 1; P.A. 81-1269, § .01, eff. June 30, 1980; P.A. 82-138, § 1, eff. Jan. 1, 1982; P.A. 82-433, § 1, eff. Sept. 8, 1981; P.A. 82-783, Art. III, § 37, eff. July 13, 1982; P.A. 86-444, § 1, eff. Jan. 1, 1990.

Formerly Ill.Rev.Stat.1991, ch. 95 ½, ¶ 8-102.

Section 2 of P.A. 77-2743 provided:

"This amendatory Act shall take effect on July 1, 1972, as to motor vehicles registered on a fiscal year basis and January 1, 1973 as to motor vehicles registered on a calendar year basis."

Section 3 of P.A. 82-433 approved Sept. 8, 1981, provided:

"This Act takes effect upon its becoming a law, except that the provisions relating to safety tests and proof of financial responsibility for medical transport vehicles apply only to applications for and the issuance of registration plates which are required to be displayed on January 1, 1982 or thereafter."

5/8-103. Bond as proof of financial responsibility

§ 8-103. Bond as proof of financial responsibility. 1. A bond of the owner of motor vehicles, subject to the provisions of Section 8-101 or 8-101.1, with a solvent and responsible surety company authorized to do business under the laws of this State as surety thereon; or

2. A bond of such owner, with one or more personal sureties, owning real estate in the State of Illinois, of the value in the aggregate of $250,000 over and above all encumbrances, when approved by the Secretary of State shall be proof of financial responsibility as required by Section 8-101 or 8-101.1.

3. The bond shall not be approved unless accompanied by affidavits of the personal sureties, attached, stating the location, legal description, market value, nature and amount of encumbrances (if any), and the value above all encumbrances of such real estate scheduled to qualify on such bond, and not then unless all requirements for such bond as provided for by this Code have been met.

P.A. 76-1586, § 8-103, eff. July 1, 1970. Amended by P.A. 77-2743, § 1, eff. July 1, 1972; P.A. 82-433, § 1, eff. Sept. 8, 1981; P.A. 82-949, § 1, eff. Jan. 1, 1983.

Formerly Ill.Rev.Stat.1991, ch. 95 ½, ¶ 8-103.

Section 2 of P.A. 77-2743 provided:

"This amendatory Act shall take effect on July 1, 1972, as to motor vehicles registered on a fiscal year basis and January 1, 1973 as to motor vehicles registered on a calendar year basis."

Section 3 of P.A. 82-433 approved Sept. 8, 1981, provided:

"This Act takes effect upon its becoming a law, except that the provisions relating to safety tests and proof of financial responsibility for medical transport vehicles apply only to applications for and the

issuance of registration plates which are required to be displayed on January 1, 1982 or thereafter."

P.A. 82–949 incorporated the amendment by P.A. 82–433.

5/8–104. Requirements of bond

§ 8–104. Requirements of bond. 1. A surety bond or real estate bond filed as proof as provided in Section 8–103 shall be in the sum of $250,000 for each motor vehicle operated by the owner providing the motor vehicle is subject to Section 8–101 or 8–101.1.

2. The surety of real estate bond shall provide for the payment of each judgment by the owner of the motor vehicle (giving its manufacturer's name and number and state license number) within 30 days after it becomes final, provided each judgment shall have been rendered against such owner or any person operating the motor vehicle with the owner's express or implied consent, for any injury to or death of any person or for damage to property other than such motor vehicle, resulting from the negligence of such owner, his agent, or any person operating the motor vehicle with his express or implied consent, provided that the maximum payment required of the surety or sureties, on all judgments recovered against an owner hereunder, shall not exceed the sum of $250,000 for each motor vehicle operated, under Section 8–101 or 8–101.1.

P.A. 76–1586, § 8–104, eff. July 1, 1970. Amended by P.A. 77–2743, § 1, eff. July 1, 1972; P.A. 82–433, § 1, eff. Sept. 8, 1981; P.A. 82–949, § 1, eff. Jan. 1, 1983.

Formerly Ill.Rev.Stat.1991, ch. 95 ½, ¶ 8–104.

Section 2 of P.A. 77–2743 provided:

"This amendatory Act shall take effect on July 1, 1972, as to motor vehicles registered on a fiscal year basis and January 1, 1973 as to motor vehicles registered on a calendar year basis."

Section 3 of P.A. 82–433 approved Sept. 8, 1981, provided:

"This Act takes effect upon its becoming a law, except that the provisions relating to safety tests and proof of financial responsibility for medical transport vehicles apply only to applications for and the issuance of registration plates which are required to be displayed on January 1, 1982 or thereafter."

P.A. 82–949 incorporated the amendment by P.A. 82–433.

5/8–105. Action on bond

§ 8–105. Action on bond. The surety bond shall, by its terms, inure to the benefit of the person recovering any such judgment, and shall provide that an action may be brought in any court of competent jurisdiction upon such bond by the owner of any such judgment; and such bond, for the full amount thereof shall, by its terms, be a lien for the benefit of the beneficiaries of said bond on such real estate so scheduled, and shall be recorded in the office of the recorder in each county in which such real estate is located.

P.A. 76–1586, § 8–105, eff. July 1, 1970. Amended by P.A. 83–358, § 67, eff. Sept. 14, 1983.

Formerly Ill.Rev.Stat.1991, ch. 95 ½, ¶ 8–105.

Validity

Provision of 1923 motor vehicle law that surety bond of owner of motor vehicle used for transportation of passengers becomes a lien on real estate scheduled in the bond, without providing for discharge of the lien, which is continued in this Section, has been held unconstitutional by the Illinois Supreme Court in the case of Weksler v. Collins, 317 Ill. 132, 147 N.E. 797 (1925).

5/8–106. Withdrawal by sureties from bond—Notice

§ 8–106. Withdrawal by sureties from bond—Notice. Any surety or sureties may withdraw from any such bond by serving ten days previous notice in writing upon such owner and the Secretary of State, either personally or by registered mail, whereupon it shall be the duty of such owner to file another bond or insurance policy in accordance with the provisions of this Act. Upon the expiration of said ten days, the Secretary of State shall mark said bond "withdrawn", with the date such withdrawal became effective, and thereupon the liability of the sureties on such bond shall cease as to any injury or damages sustained after the date such withdrawal became effective.

P.A. 76–1586, § 8–106, eff. July 1, 1970. Amended by P.A. 80–1495, § 36, eff. Jan. 8, 1979.

Formerly Ill.Rev.Stat.1991, ch. 95 ½, ¶ 8–106.

5/8–107. Authority to require replacement of bond

§ 8–107. Authority to require replacement of bond. If, at any time, in the judgment of the Secretary of State, said bond is not sufficient for any good cause, he may require the owner of such motor vehicle who filed the same to replace said bond with another good and sufficient bond or insurance policy, in accordance with the provisions of this Act, and upon such replacement, the liability of the surety or sureties on such prior bond shall cease as to any injury or damage sustained after such replacement.

P.A. 76–1586, § 8–107, eff. July 1, 1970. Amended by P.A. 80–1495, § 36, eff. Jan. 8, 1979.

Formerly Ill.Rev.Stat.1991, ch. 95 ½, ¶ 8–107.

5/8–108. Insurance policy as bond

§ 8–108. Insurance policy as bond. A policy of insurance in a solvent and responsible company authorized to do business in the State of Illinois, and having admitted net assets of not less than $300,000 insuring the owner, his agent or any person operating the motor vehicle with the owner's express or implied consent against liability for any injury to or death of any person or for damage to property other than the motor vehicle resulting from the negligence of such owner, his agent or any person operating the vehicle with his express or implied consent, when accepted by the Secretary of State, shall be proof of financial responsibility as required by Section 8–101 or 8–101.1.

P.A. 76–1586, § 8–108, eff. July 1, 1970. Amended by P.A. 82–433, § 1, eff. Sept. 8, 1981.

Formerly Ill.Rev.Stat.1991, ch. 95 ½, ¶ 8–108.

Section 3 of P.A. 82–433 approved Sept. 8, 1981, provided:

"This Act takes effect upon its becoming a law, except that the provisions relating to safety tests and proof of financial responsibility for medical transport vehicles apply only to applications for and the issuance of registration plates which are required to be displayed on January 1, 1982 or thereafter."

5/8–109. Requirements of policy

§ 8–109. Requirements of policy. 1. The policy of insurance may cover one or more motor vehicles and for each such vehicle shall insure such owner against liability upon the owner to a minimum amount of $250,000 for bodily injury to, or death of, any person, and $50,000 for damage to property, provided that the maximum payment required of such company on all judgments recovered against an owner hereunder shall not exceed the sum of $300,000 for each motor vehicle operated under the provisions of this Section.

2. The policy of insurance shall provide for payment and satisfaction of any judgment within 30 days after it becomes final rendered against the owner or any person operating the motor vehicle with the owner's express or implied consent for such injury, death or damage to property other than the motor vehicle, and shall provide that suit may be brought in any court of competent jurisdiction upon such insurance policy by the owner of any such judgment.

3. The insurance policy shall contain a description of each motor vehicle, giving the manufacturer's name and number and state license number.

P.A. 76-1586, § 8-109, eff. July 1, 1970. Amended by P.A. 79-1141, § 1, eff. Jan. 1, 1976; P.A. 82-433, § 1, eff. Sept. 8, 1981; P.A. 82-949, § 1, eff. Jan. 1, 1983.

Formerly Ill.Rev.Stat.1991, ch. 95 ½, ¶ 8-109.

Section 3 of P.A. 82-433 approved Sept. 8, 1981, provided:

"This Act takes effect upon its becoming a law, except that the provisions relating to safety tests and proof of financial responsibility for medical transport vehicles apply only to applications for and the issuance of registration plates which are required to be displayed on January 1, 1982 or thereafter."

P.A. 82-949 recognized the amendment by P.A. 82-433.

5/8-110. Cancellation of insurance policy—Notice

§ 8-110. Cancellation of insurance policy—Notice. 1. In the event said policy of insurance be cancelled by the issuing company, or the authority of said issuing company to do business in the State of Illinois be revoked, the Secretary of State shall require the owner who filed the same either to furnish a bond or to replace said policy with another policy according to the provisions of this Act.

2. Said policy of insurance shall also contain a provision that the same cannot be cancelled by the company issuing it without giving ten days notice in writing of such cancellation to the owner and the Secretary of State, either personally or by registered mail.

3. Whenever the issuing company gives such notice of cancellation, the Secretary of State shall, at the expiration of said ten days, mark said insurance policy "Withdrawn" with the date such withdrawal became effective, and thereupon the liability of such company on said policy shall cease as to any injury or damage sustained after the date such withdrawal becomes effective.

P.A. 76-1586, § 8-110, eff. July 1, 1970.

Formerly Ill.Rev.Stat.1991, ch. 95 ½, ¶ 8-110.

5/8-111. Proof required after cancellation

§ 8-111. Proof required after cancellation. If, at any time, in the judgment of the Secretary of State, said policy of insurance is not sufficient for any good cause, he may require the owner of such motor vehicle who filed the same, to replace said policy of insurance with another good and sufficient bond or insurance policy, in accordance with the provisions of this Act, and upon such replacement, the liability of the company on said insurance policy shall cease as to any injury or damage sustained after such replacement.

P.A. 76-1586, § 8-111, eff. July 1, 1970.

Formerly Ill.Rev.Stat.1991, ch. 95 ½, ¶ 8-111.

5/8-112. When bond on policy to expire

§ 8-112. When bond on policy to expire. All bonds and policies of insurance filed with the Secretary of State, under this Act, shall expire not sooner than the 31st day of December as to a vehicle registered on a calendar year basis and not sooner than the 30th day of June as to a vehicle registered on a fiscal year basis in each year, provided, that the expiration of same shall not terminate liabilities upon such bonds and policies of insurance arising during the period for which the bonds and policies of insurance were filed.

P.A. 76-1586, § 8-112, eff. July 1, 1970. Amended by P.A. 77-99, § 1, eff. Jan. 1, 1972.

Formerly Ill.Rev.Stat.1991, ch. 95 ½, ¶ 8-112.

5/8-113. Secretary of State to suspend registration certificates, registration plates and registration sticker when bond or policy cancelled or withdrawn

§ 8-113. Secretary of State to suspend registration certificates, registration plates and registration sticker when bond or policy cancelled or withdrawn. In the event that a bond or policy of insurance is cancelled or withdrawn with respect to a vehicle or vehicles, subject to the provisions of Section 8-101 or 8-101.1, for which the bond or policy of insurance was issued, then the Secretary of State immediately shall suspend the registration certificates, registration plates and registration sticker or stickers of the owner, with respect to such motor vehicle or vehicles, and said registration certificates, registration plates and registration sticker or stickers shall remain suspended and no registration shall be permitted or renewed unless and until the owner of the motor vehicle shall have filed proof of financial responsibility as provided by Section 8-101 or 8-101.1.

P.A. 76-1586, § 8-113, eff. July 1, 1970. Amended by P.A. 80-230, § 1, eff. Oct. 1, 1977; P.A. 80-1185, § 1, eff. March 8, 1978; P.A. 82-433, § 1, eff. Sept. 8, 1981.

Formerly Ill.Rev.Stat.1991, ch. 95 ½, ¶ 8-113.

Section 3 of P.A. 82-433 approved Sept. 8, 1981, provided:

"This Act takes effect upon its becoming a law, except that the provisions relating to safety tests and proof of financial responsibility for medical transport vehicles apply only to applications for and the issuance of registration plates which are required to be displayed on January 1, 1982 or thereafter."

5/8-114. Issuance of license upon proof of financial responsibility

§ 8-114. Issuance of license upon proof of financial responsibility. The Secretary of State shall issue to each person who has in effect proof of financial responsibility as required by Section 8-101 or 8-101.1, a certificate for each motor vehicle operated by such person and included within the proof of financial responsibility. Each certificate shall specify the Illinois registration plate and registration sticker number of the vehicle, a statement that proof of financial responsibility has been filed, and the period for which the certificate was issued.

P.A. 76-1586, § 8-114, eff. July 1, 1970. Amended by P.A. 80-230, § 1, eff. Oct. 1, 1977; P.A. 82-433, § 1, eff. Sept. 8, 1981.

Formerly Ill.Rev.Stat.1991, ch. 95 ½, ¶ 8-114.

Section 3 of P.A. 82-433 approved Sept. 8, 1981, provided:

"This Act takes effect upon its becoming a law, except that the provisions relating to safety tests and proof of financial responsibility for medical transport vehicles apply only to applications for and the issuance of registration plates which are required to be displayed on January 1, 1982 or thereafter."

5/8-115. Display of certificate—Enforcement

§ 8-115. Display of certificate—Enforcement. The certificate issued pursuant to Section 8-114 shall be displayed upon a window of the motor vehicle for which it was issued, in such manner as to be visible to the passengers carried therein. This Section and Section 8-114 shall be enforced by the State Police, the Secretary of State, and other police officers.

P.A. 76-1586, § 8-115, eff. July 1, 1970. Amended by P.A. 82-433, § 1, eff. Sept. 8, 1981.

Formerly Ill.Rev.Stat.1991, ch. 95 ½, ¶ 8-115.

Section 3 of P.A. 82-433 approved Sept. 8, 1981, provided:

"This Act takes effect upon its becoming a law, except that the provisions relating to safety tests and proof of financial responsibility for medical transport vehicles apply only to applications for and the issuance of registration plates which are required to be displayed on January 1, 1982 or thereafter."

5/8-116. Failure to comply with provisions; punishment

§ 8-116. Any person who fails to comply with the provisions of this Chapter, or who fails to obey, observe or comply with any order of the Secretary of State or any law enforcement agency issued in accordance with the provisions of this Chapter is guilty of a Class A misdemeanor.

P.A. 76-1586, § 8-116, added by P.A. 77-2838, § 1, eff. Jan. 3, 1973.

Formerly Ill.Rev.Stat.1991, ch. 95 ½, ¶ 8-116.

CHAPTER 9. OWNERS OF FOR-RENT VEHICLES FOR-HIRE

Section

Enactment

The Illinois Vehicle Code was enacted by P.A. 76-1586, effective July 1, 1970. The Code constitutes a consolidated recodification of various earlier laws and acts including the Illinois Motor Vehicle Law of 1957.

5/9-101. Owner of for-rent motor vehicle to give proof of financial responsibility

§ 9-101. Owner of for-rent motor vehicle to give proof of financial responsibility. For purposes of this Chapter, "for rent" means any transfer of the possession of or right to possession of a motor vehicle to a user for a valuable consideration for a period of less than one year, and "to lease" means any transfer of the possession of or right to possession of a motor vehicle to a user for a period of one year or more. It is unlawful for the owner of any motor vehicle to engage in the business, or to hold himself out to the public generally as being engaged in the business of renting out such motor vehicle to be operated by the customer, unless the owner has given, and there is in full force and effect and on file with the Secretary of State proof of financial responsibility as hereinafter provided. The delivery of a vehicle owned by an out of State person or business to a renter in this State shall constitute engaging in the rental business in this State for purposes of this Section.

All owners of motor vehicles which are leased for a period of one year or more are not required to provide proof of insurance as required under this chapter, but instead must comply with Section 7-601 of this Code and obtain vehicle insurance in amounts no less than the minimum amount set for bodily injury or death and for destruction of property pursuant to Section 7-203 of this Code.

P.A. 76-1586, § 9-101, eff. July 1, 1970. Amended by P.A. 86-880, § 1, eff. Jan. 1, 1990; P.A. 87-1220, § 1, eff. July 1, 1993.

Formerly Ill.Rev.Stat.1991, ch. 95 ½, ¶ 9-101.

5/9-102. Alternate methods of giving proof of financial responsibility

§ 9-102. Alternate methods of giving proof of financial responsibility. Proof of financial responsibility when required under Section 9-101 may be given by the following methods. By filing with the Secretary of State:

1. A bond as provided in Section 9-103.
2. An insurance policy or other proof of insurance in a form to be prescribed by the Secretary as provided in Section 9-105.
3. A certificate of self insurance issued by the Director.

P.A. 76-1586, § 9-102, eff. July 1, 1970. Amended by P.A. 77-736, § 1, eff. Aug. 12, 1971; P.A. 77-2743, § 1; P.A. 78-255, § 61, eff. Oct. 1, 1973; P.A. 82-138, § 1, eff. Jan. 1, 1982; P.A. 86-444, § 1, eff. Jan. 1, 1990.

Formerly Ill.Rev.Stat.1991, ch. 95 ½, ¶ 9-102.

5/9-103. Bond as proof—requirements

§ 9-103. Bond as proof—requirements. A motor vehicle liability bond, conditioned that the owner of the motor vehicle will pay any judgment within 30 days after it becomes final, recovered against the customer and the owner of the motor vehicle or against any person operating the motor vehicle with the customer's and the owner's express or implied consent for damage to property other than to the rented motor vehicle, or for an injury to, or for the death of any person including an occupant of the rented motor vehicle, resulting from the operation of the motor vehicle, provided, however, every such bond is in the penal sum of $100,000.

The bond shall be executed by a solvent and responsible surety company authorized to do business in the State of Illinois, or by one or more personal sureties to be approved by the Secretary of State.

The personal sureties shall own real estate in the State of Illinois of the aggregate value of $100,000, over and above all encumbrances, and each of the personal sureties shall make an affidavit concerning the property which he schedules for the purpose of qualifying as surety, stating the location, legal description, market value, and the amount and nature of any encumbrances.

P.A. 76-1586, § 9-103, eff. July 1, 1970. Amended by P.A. 76-1718, § 1; P.A. 77-2743, § 1, eff. July 1, 1972; P.A. 83-566, § 1, eff. Jan. 1, 1984; P.A. 86-444, § 1, eff. Jan. 1, 1990.

Formerly Ill.Rev.Stat.1991, ch. 95 ½, ¶ 9-103.

Section 2 of P.A. 77-2743 provided:

"This amendatory Act shall take effect on July 1, 1972, as to motor vehicles registered on a fiscal year basis and January 1, 1973 as to motor vehicles registered on a calendar year basis."

5/9-104. Withdrawal of sureties—Notice

§ 9-104. Withdrawal of sureties—Notice. Any surety may withdraw from the bond by serving ten days previous notice in writing, either personally or by registered mail, upon the owner of the motor vehicle, and upon the Secretary of State, whereupon it shall be the duty of such owner to file another bond or insurance policy, in accordance with the provisions of this Act. Upon the expiration of the ten days, the Secretary of State shall mark the bond "Cancelled".

P.A. 76-1586, § 9-104, eff. July 1, 1970.

Formerly Ill.Rev.Stat.1991, ch. 95 ½, ¶ 9-104.

5/9-105. Insurance policy as proof—requirements

§ 9-105. Insurance policy as proof—requirements. A motor vehicle liability policy in a solvent and responsible company, authorized to do business in the State of Illinois, providing that the insurance carrier will pay any judgment within 30 days after it becomes final, recovered against the customer or against any person operating the motor vehicle with the customer's express or implied consent, for damage to property other than to the rented motor vehicles, or for an injury to or for the death of any person, including an occupant of the rented motor vehicle, resulting from the operation of the motor vehicle shall serve as proof of financial responsibility; provided however, every such policy provides insurance insuring the operator of the rented motor vehicle against liability upon such insured to a minimum amount of $50,000 because of bodily injury to, or death of any one person or damage to property and $100,000 because of bodily injury to or death of 2 or more persons in any one motor vehicle accident.

P.A. 76-1586, § 9-105, eff. July 1, 1970. Amended by P.A. 76-1718, § 1; P.A. 77-2743, § 1; P.A. 85-1374, § 1, eff. Jan. 1, 1989; P.A. 86-880, § 1, eff. Jan. 1, 1990.

Formerly Ill.Rev.Stat.1991, ch. 95 ½, ¶ 9-105.

Section 2 of P.A. 77-2743 provided:

"This amendatory Act shall take effect on July 1, 1972, as to motor vehicles registered on a fiscal year basis and January 1, 1973 as to motor vehicles registered on a calendar year basis."

5/9-106. Cancellation of policy—Notices

§ 9-106. Cancellation of policy—Notices. The policy shall provide that the insurance carrier may cancel it by serving 10 days' previous notice in writing, either personally or by registered mail, upon the owner of the motor vehicle and upon the Secretary of State. Whenever any such policy shall be so cancelled, the Secretary of State shall mark same "Cancelled" and shall require such owner either to furnish a bond or a new policy of insurance, in accordance with this Act.

All policies filed with the Secretary of State shall expire not sooner than the 31st day of December as to vehicles registered on a calendar year nor sooner than the 30th day of June as to vehicles registered on a fiscal year.

P.A. 76-1586, § 9-106, eff. July 1, 1970. Amended by P.A. 77-99, § 1, eff. Jan. 1, 1972.

Formerly Ill.Rev.Stat.1991, ch. 95 ½, ¶ 9-106.

5/9-107. Authority to require replacement of bond

§ 9-107. Authority to require replacement of bond. If, at any time, in the judgment of the Secretary of State, the liability policy filed hereunder, is not sufficient for any good cause, he may require the owner of such motor vehicle who filed the same to replace, within fifteen (15) days from the date of notice given, said policy with another good and sufficient liability policy or bond, in accordance with the provisions of this Act. At the time of replacement or at the expiration of the fifteen (15) day period, as the case may be, the Secretary of State shall mark the policy "Cancelled."

Upon the cancellation of any liability policy hereunder the liabilities on said policy shall thereupon cease as to any future damage or injury.

P.A. 76-1586, § 9-107, eff. July 1, 1970.

Formerly Ill.Rev.Stat.1991, ch. 95 ½, ¶ 9-107.

5/9-108. Application for approval of insurance policy or bond required

§ 9-108. Application for approval of insurance policy or bond required. Every person desiring to engage in the business of renting out a motor vehicle, to be operated by the customer, shall file with the Secretary of State, an application for the approval of the Secretary of State of the insurance policy or bond tendered under the provisions of this Act, by such person, and if the Secretary of State shall determine that such insurance policy or bond complies with the provisions of this Act, he shall accept such insurance policy or bond, and shall thereupon issue to such applicant a certificate setting forth the fact that the applicant has, in respect to the vehicle described therein, complied with the provisions of this Act.

P.A. 76-1586, § 9-108, eff. July 1, 1970.

Formerly Ill.Rev.Stat.1991, ch. 95 ½, ¶ 9-108.

5/9-109. Secretary of State to cancel certificate and to suspend license plates and registration stickers when bond or policy cancelled or withdrawn

§ 9-109. Secretary of State to cancel certificate and to suspend license plates and registration stickers when bond or policy cancelled or withdrawn. (a) If any insurance policy or bond filed hereunder shall for any reason become inoperative, the Secretary of State shall forthwith cancel the certificate of compliance with the owner and it shall be unlawful for the owner to rent out the motor vehicle, covered by said certificate, until a policy or bond meeting the requirements of this Act is filed with the Secretary of State and a certificate has been issued by him as provided by Section 9-108.

(b) The Secretary of State shall also suspend the registration certificate, license plates and registration sticker or stickers of the owner, with respect to the motor vehicle for which the insurance policy or bond had been issued, and said registration certificates, license plates and registration sticker or stickers shall remain suspended and no registration shall be permitted or renewed unless and until the owner of said motor vehicle shall have complied with the provisions of this Act.

P.A. 76-1586, § 9-109, eff. July 1, 1970. Amended by P.A. 80-230, § 1, eff. Oct. 1, 1977; P.A. 80-1185, § 1, eff. March 8, 1978.

Formerly Ill.Rev.Stat.1991, ch. 95 ½, ¶ 9-109.

5/9-110. Penalties for violations of this Act

§ 9-110. Penalties for violations of this Act. Any person who fails to comply with the provisions of this Chapter, or who fails to obey, observe or comply with any order of the

Secretary of State, in accordance with the provisions of this Chapter, is guilty of a Class A misdemeanor.

P.A. 76-1586, § 9-110, eff. July 1, 1970. Amended by P.A. 77-2720, § 1, eff. Jan. 1, 1972.

Formerly Ill.Rev.Stat.1991, ch. 95 ½, ¶ 9-110.

CHAPTER 10. CIVIL LIABILITY

Enactment

The Illinois Vehicle Code was enacted by P.A. 76-1586, effective July 1, 1970. The Code constitutes a consolidated recodification of various earlier laws and acts including the Illinois Motor Vehicle Law of 1957.

ARTICLE I. LIABILITY OF COUNTIES, MUNICIPALITIES AND OTHER PUBLIC CORPORATIONS

5/10-101. Insurance

§ 10-101. Insurance. (a) Any public entity or corporation may insure against the liability imposed by law and may insure persons who are legally entitled to recover damages from owners and operators of uninsured motor vehicles and hit-and-run motor vehicles because of bodily injury, sickness or disease including death incurred while using a motor vehicle of such public entity or corporation with any insurance carrier duly authorized to transact business in this State and the premium for such insurance shall be a proper charge against the general fund or any applicable special fund of such entity or corporation.

(b) Every employee of the State, who operates for purposes of State business a vehicle not owned, leased or controlled by the State shall procure insurance in the limit of the amounts of liability not less than the amounts required in Section 7-203 of this Act. The State may provide such insurance for the benefit of, and without cost to, such employees and may include such coverage in a plan of self-insurance under Section 405-105 of the Department of Central Management Services Law (20 ILCS 405/405-105). The State may also obtain uninsured or hit-and-run vehicle coverage, as defined in Section 143a of the "Illinois Insurance Code".[1] Any public liability insurance furnished by the State under this Section shall be under the policy or policies contracted for or under a self-insurance plan implemented by the Department of Central Management Services pursuant to Section 405-105 of the Department of Central Management Services Law (20 ILCS 405/405-105), the costs for procuring such insurance to be charged, collected and received as provided in that Section 25-105.

P.A. 76-1586, § 10-101, eff. July 1, 1970. Amended by P.A. 77-472, § 1, eff. July 27, 1971; P.A. 77-473, § 1, eff. July 27, 1971; P.A. 77-2829, § 40, eff. Dec. 22, 1972; P.A. 78-255, § 61, eff. Oct. 1, 1973; P.A. 79-352, § 1, eff. Aug. 7, 1975; P.A. 79-1331, § 4, eff. July 28, 1976; P.A. 80-57, § 16, eff. July 1, 1977; P.A. 82-413, § 2, eff. Sept. 4, 1981; P.A. 82-789, Art. I, § 24, eff. July 13, 1982; P.A. 91-239, Art. 5, § 5-530, eff. Jan. 1, 2000.

Formerly Ill.Rev.Stat.1991, ch. 95 ½, ¶ 10-101.

[1] 215 ILCS 5/143a.

ARTICLE II. LIABILITY TO GUESTS

Caption to article II amended by P.A. 76-2158, eff. July 1, 1970. The caption formerly read, "Imputing Negligence to Guests."

5/10-201. Liability for bodily injury to or death of guest

§ 10-201. Liability for bodily injury to or death of guest. No person riding in or upon a motor vehicle or motorcycle as a guest without payment for such ride and who has solicited such ride in violation of Subsection (a) of Section 11-1006 of this Act, nor his personal representative in the event of the death of such guest, shall have a cause of action for damages against the driver or operator of such motor vehicle or motorcycle, or its owner or his employee or agent for injury, death or loss, in case of accident, unless such accident has been caused by the willful and wanton misconduct of the driver or operator of such motor vehicle or motorcycle or its owner or his employee or agent and unless such willful and wanton misconduct contributed to the injury, death or loss for which the action is brought.

Nothing contained in this section relieves a motor vehicle or motorcycle carrier of passengers for hire of responsibility for injury or death sustained by any passenger for hire.

This amendatory Act of 1971 shall apply only to causes of action arising from accidents occurring after its effective date.

P.A. 76-1586, § 10-201, eff. July 1, 1970. Amended by P.A. 77-1482, § 1, eff. Jan. 1, 1972.

Formerly Ill.Rev.Stat.1991, ch. 95 ½, ¶ 10-201.

5/10-202. Liability of employer in regard to ridesharing

§ 10-202. Liability of employer in regard to ridesharing. (a) An employer shall not be liable for injuries to passengers and other persons resulting from the operation or use of a passenger car or commuter van in a ridesharing arrangement which is not owned, leased, contracted for or driven by the employer, and for which the employer has not paid wages to an employee for services rendered in driving the vehicle, provided, that wages shall not include a portion of the fares collected by the driver and shall not include expenses for gasoline or passenger car or commuter van repairs.

(b) An employer shall not be liable for injuries to passengers and other persons because he provides information, incentives or otherwise encourages his employees to participate in ridesharing arrangements.

P.A. 76-1586, § 10-202, added by P.A. 81-1452, § 1, eff. Jan. 1, 1981. Amended by P.A. 83-1091, § 1, eff. July 1, 1984.

Formerly Ill.Rev.Stat.1991, ch. 95 ½, ¶ 10-202.

ARTICLE III. PROCESS ON NON-RESIDENT

5/10-301. Service of process on non-resident

§ 10-301. Service of process on non-resident.

(a) The use and operation by any person or his duly authorized agent or employee of a vehicle over or upon the highways of the State of Illinois, shall be deemed an appointment by such person of the Secretary of State to be his true and lawful attorney upon whom may be served all legal process in any action or proceeding against him, growing out of such use or resulting in damage or loss to person or property, and the use or operation shall be signification of his agreement that such process against him which is so served, shall be of the same legal force and validity as though served upon him personally if such person is a non-resident of this State or at the time a cause of action arises is a resident of this State but subsequently becomes a non-resident of this State, or in the event the vehicle is owned by a non-resident and is being operated over and upon the highways of this State with the owner's express or implied permission.

(b) Service of such process shall be made by serving a copy upon the Secretary of State or any employee in his office designated by him to accept such service for him, or by filing such copy in his office, together with an affidavit of compliance from the plaintiff instituting the action, suit, or proceeding, which states that this Section is applicable to the proceeding and that the plaintiff has complied with the requirements of this Section, and a fee of $5 and such service shall be sufficient service upon the person, if notice of such service and a copy of the process are, within 10 days thereafter, sent by registered mail by the plaintiff to the defendant, at the last known address of the defendant, and the plaintiff's affidavit of compliance herewith is appended to the summons.

(c) The court in which the action is pending may order such continuances as may be necessary to afford the defendant reasonable opportunity to defend the action. The fee of $5 paid by the plaintiff to the Secretary of State at the time of the service shall be taxed as his cost, if he prevails in the action.

(d) The Secretary of State shall keep a record of all such processes, which shall show the day and hour of such service.

(e) When a final judgment is entered against any non-resident defendant who has not received notice and a copy of the process by registered mail, required to be sent to him as above provided, and such person, his heirs, legatees, executor, administrator or other legal representatives, as the case may require, shall within one year after the written notice given to him of such judgment, or within 5 years after such judgment, if no such notice has been given, as stated above, appear and petition the court to be heard regarding such judgment, and shall pay such costs as the court may deem reasonable in that behalf, the person so petitioning the court may appear and answer the plaintiff's allegations, and thereupon such proceeding shall be had as if the defendant had appeared in due time and no judgment had been entered. If it appears upon the hearing that such judgment ought not to have been entered against the defendant, the judgment may be set aside, altered or amended as shall appear just; otherwise, it shall be ordered that the judgment stands confirmed against the defendant. The judgment shall, after 5 years from the entry thereof, if not set aside in the manner stated above, be deemed and adjudged confirmed against such defendant, and all persons claiming under him by virtue of any act done subsequent to the commencement of such action, and at the end of the 5 years, the court may enter such further orders as shall be required for the enforcement of the judgment.

(f) Any person instituting any action, suit, or proceeding who uses this Section to effect service of process shall be liable for the attorney's fees and costs of the defendant if the court finds that the person instituting the action knew or should have known that this Section is not applicable for effecting service in such action.

P.A. 76-1586, § 10-301, eff. July 1, 1970. Amended by P.A. 77-100, § 1, eff. Jan. 1, 1972; P.A. 84-549, § 20, eff. Sept. 18, 1985; P.A. 85-412, § 1, eff. Jan. 1, 1988; P.A. 91-357, § 231, eff. July 29, 1999.

Formerly Ill.Rev.Stat.1991, ch. 95 ½, ¶ 10-301.

CHAPTER 11. RULES OF THE ROAD

Enactment

The Illinois Vehicle Code was enacted by P.A. 76-1586, effective July 1, 1970. The Code constitutes a consolidated recodification of various earlier laws and acts including the Uniform Act Regulating Traffic on Highways, 1935.

ARTICLE I. SPECIAL DEFINITIONS

Section
5/11-100. Definition of Administrator.

5/11-100. Definition of Administrator

§ 11-100. Definition of Administrator. For the purposes of this Chapter, "Administrator" means the Administrator of the Illinois Safety and Family Financial Responsibility Law in Chapter 7 of this Code.[1]

P.A. 76-1586, § 11-100, eff. July 1, 1970. Amended by P.A. 76-1618, § 1, eff. July 1, 1970; P.A. 77-42, § 1, eff. July 1, 1971; P.A. 77-170, § 1, eff. Jan. 1, 1972; P.A. 77-1910, § 1, eff. July 1, 1972; P.A. 78-255, § 61, eff. Oct. 1, 1973; P.A. 83-1473, § 3, eff. Jan. 1, 1985; P.A. 89-92, § 10, eff. July 1, 1996; P.A. 90-89, § 15, eff. Jan. 1, 1998.

Formerly Ill.Rev.Stat.1991, ch. 95 ½, ¶ 11-100.

[1] 625 ILCS 5/7-100 et seq.

ARTICLE II. OBEDIENCE TO AND EFFECT OF TRAFFIC LAWS

Section
5/11-201. Provisions of act refer to vehicles upon the highways—Exceptions.
5/11-202. Required obedience to traffic laws.
5/11-203. Obedience to police officers.
5/11-204. Fleeing or attempting to elude police officer.
5/11-204.1. Aggravated fleeing or attempt to elude a police officer.
5/11-205. Public officers and employees to obey Act—Exceptions.
5/11-206. Traffic laws apply to persons riding animals or driving animal-drawn vehicles.
5/11-207. Provisions of this Chapter uniform throughout State.
5/11-208. Powers of local authorities.
5/11-208.1. Uniformity.
5/11-208.2. Limitation on home rule units.
5/11-208.2. Limitation on home rule units.

5/11-201. Provisions of act refer to vehicles upon the highways—Exceptions

§ 11-201. Provisions of act refer to vehicles upon the highways—Exceptions. The provisions of this Chapter relating to the operation of vehicles refer exclusively to the operation of vehicles upon highways except:

1. Where a different place is specifically referred to in a given section.

2. The provisions of Articles IV and V of this Chapter shall apply upon highways and elsewhere throughout the State.

P.A. 76-1586, § 11-201, eff. July 1, 1970.

Formerly Ill.Rev.Stat.1991, ch. 95 ½, ¶ 11-201.

5/11-202. Required obedience to traffic laws

§ 11-202. Required obedience to traffic laws. It is unlawful and, unless otherwise declared in this Chapter with respect to particular offenses, it is a petty offense for any person to do any act forbidden or fail to perform any Act required in this Chapter.

P.A. 76-1586, § 11-202, eff. July 1, 1970. Amended by P.A. 77-2830, Art. 73, § 1, eff. Jan. 1, 1973; P.A. 80-911, § 1, eff. Oct. 1, 1977.

Formerly Ill.Rev.Stat.1991, ch. 95 ½, ¶ 11-202.

5/11-203. Obedience to police officers

§ 11-203. Obedience to police officers. No person shall wilfully fail or refuse to comply with any lawful order or direction of any police officer, fireman, or school crossing guard invested by law with authority to direct, control, or regulate traffic. Any person convicted of violating this Section is guilty of a petty offense and shall be subject to a mandatory fine of $150.

P.A. 76-1586, § 11-203, eff. July 1, 1970. Amended by P.A. 84-873, § 1, eff. Jan. 1, 1986; P.A. 90-749, § 5, eff. Jan. 1, 1999.

Formerly Ill.Rev.Stat.1991, ch. 95 ½, ¶ 11-203.

5/11-204. Fleeing or attempting to elude police officer

§ 11-204. Fleeing or attempting to elude police officer. (a) Any driver or operator of a motor vehicle who, having been given a visual or audible signal by a peace officer directing such driver or operator to bring his vehicle to a stop, wilfully fails or refuses to obey such direction, increases his speed, extinguishes his lights, or otherwise flees or attempts to elude the officer, is guilty of a Class A misdemeanor. The signal given by the peace officer may be by hand, voice, siren, red or blue light. Provided, the officer giving such signal shall be in police uniform, and, if driving a vehicle, such vehicle shall display illuminated oscillating, rotating or flashing red or blue lights which when used in conjunction with an audible horn or siren would indicate the vehicle to be an official police vehicle. Such requirement shall not preclude the use of amber or white oscillating, rotating or flashing lights in conjunction with red or blue oscillating, rotating or flashing lights as required in Section 12-215 of Chapter 12.

(b) Upon receiving notice of such conviction the Secretary of State shall suspend the drivers license of the person so convicted for a period of not more than 6 months for a first conviction and not more than 12 months for a second conviction.

(c) A third or subsequent violation of this Section is a Class 4 felony.

P.A. 76-1586, § 11-204, eff. July 1, 1970. Amended by P.A. 77-2720, § 1, eff. Jan. 1, 1972; P.A. 85-830, § 1, eff. Sept. 24, 1987; P.A. 90-134, § 5, eff. July 22, 1997.

Formerly Ill.Rev.Stat.1991, ch. 95 ½, ¶ 11-204.

5/11-204.1. Aggravated fleeing or attempt to elude a police officer

§ 11-204.1. Aggravated fleeing or attempt to elude a police officer.

(a) The offense of aggravated fleeing or attempting to elude a police officer is committed by any driver or operator of a motor vehicle who flees or attempts to elude a police officer, after being given a visual or audible signal by a police officer in the manner prescribed in subsection (a) of Section 11-204 of this Code, and such flight or attempt to elude:

(1) is at a rate of speed at least 21 miles per hour over the legal speed limit;

(2) causes bodily injury to any individual; or

(3) causes damage in excess of $300 to property.

(b) Any person convicted of a first violation of this Section shall be guilty of a Class 4 felony. Upon notice of such a conviction the Secretary of State shall forthwith revoke the driver's license of the person so convicted, as provided in Section 6-205 of this Code. Any person convicted of a second or subsequent violation of this Section shall be guilty of a Class 3 felony, and upon notice of such a conviction the Secretary of State shall forthwith revoke the driver's license of the person convicted, as provided in Section 6-205 of the Code.

(c) The motor vehicle used in a violation of this Section is subject to seizure and forfeiture as provided in Sections 36-1 and 36-2 of the Criminal Code of 1961.[1]

P.A. 76-1586, § 11-204.1, added by P.A. 83-1326, § 1, eff. July 1, 1985. Amended by P.A. 88-679, § 15, eff. July 1, 1995; P.A. 90-134, § 5, eff. July 22, 1997.

Formerly Ill.Rev.Stat.1991, ch. 95 ½, ¶ 11-204.1.

[1] 720 ILCS 5/36-1 and 5/36-2.

5/11-205. Public officers and employees to obey Act—Exceptions

§ 11-205. Public officers and employees to obey Act—Exceptions.

(a) The provisions of this Chapter applicable to the drivers of vehicles upon the highways shall apply to the drivers of all vehicles owned or operated by the United States, this State or any county, city, town, district or any other political subdivision of the State, except as provided in this Section and subject to such specific exceptions as set forth in this Chapter with reference to authorized emergency vehicles.

(b) The driver of an authorized emergency vehicle, when responding to an emergency call or when in the pursuit of an actual or suspected violator of the law or when responding to but not upon returning from a fire alarm, may exercise the privileges set forth in this Section, but subject to the conditions herein stated.

(c) The driver of an authorized emergency vehicle may:

1. Park or stand, irrespective of the provisions of this Chapter;

2. Proceed past a red or stop signal or stop sign, but only after slowing down as may be required and necessary for safe operation;

3. Exceed the maximum speed limits so long as he does not endanger life or property;

4. Disregard regulations governing direction of movement or turning in specified directions.

(d) The exceptions herein granted to an authorized emergency vehicle, other than a police vehicle, shall apply only when the vehicle is making use of either an audible signal when in motion or visual signals meeting the requirements of Section 12-215 of this Act.

(e) The foregoing provisions do not relieve the driver of an authorized emergency vehicle from the duty of driving with due regard for the safety of all persons, nor do such provisions protect the driver from the consequences of his reckless disregard for the safety of others.

(f) Unless specifically made applicable, the provisions of this Chapter, except those contained in Section 11-204 and Articles IV and V of this Chapter,[1] shall not apply to persons, motor vehicles and equipment while actually engaged in work upon a highway but shall apply to such persons and vehicles when traveling to or from such work.

P.A. 76-1586, § 11-205, eff. July 1, 1970. Amended by P.A. 76-1737, § 1; P.A. 76-1997, § 1, eff. July 1, 1970; P.A. 78-510, § 1, eff. Oct. 1, 1973; P.A. 79-1069, § 1, eff. Jan. 1, 1976; P.A. 89-710, § 15, eff. Feb. 14, 1997; P.A. 90-257, § 5, eff. July 30, 1997.

Formerly Ill.Rev.Stat.1991, ch. 95 ½, ¶ 11-205.

[1] 625 ILCS 5/11-401 et seq. and 5/11-500 et seq.

5/11-206. Traffic laws apply to persons riding animals or driving animal-drawn vehicles

§ 11-206. Traffic laws apply to persons riding animals or driving animal-drawn vehicles. Every person riding an animal or driving any animal-drawn vehicle upon a roadway shall be granted all of the rights and shall be subject to all of the duties applicable to the driver of a vehicle by this chapter, except those provisions of this chapter which by their very nature can have no application.

P.A. 76-1586, § 11-206, eff. July 1, 1970. Amended by P.A. 78-850, Art. II, § 1, eff. July 1, 1974; P.A. 79-858, § 1, eff. Jan. 1, 1976.

Formerly Ill.Rev.Stat.1991, ch. 95 ½, ¶ 11-206.

5/11-207. Provisions of this Chapter uniform throughout State

§ 11-207. Provisions of this Chapter uniform throughout State. The provisions of this Chapter shall be applicable and uniform throughout this State and in all political subdivisions and municipalities therein, and no local authority shall enact or enforce any ordinance rule or regulation in conflict with the provisions of this Chapter unless expressly authorized herein. Local authorities may, however, adopt additional traffic regulations which are not in conflict with the provisions of this Chapter, but such regulations shall not be effective until signs giving reasonable notice thereof are posted.

P.A. 76-1586, § 11-207, eff. July 1, 1970. Amended by P.A. 85-532, § 1, eff. Jan. 1, 1988; P.A. 92-651, § 77, eff. July 11, 2002.

Formerly Ill.Rev.Stat.1991, ch. 95 ½, ¶ 11-207.

5/11-208. Powers of local authorities

§ 11-208. Powers of local authorities.

(a) The provisions of this Code shall not be deemed to prevent local authorities with respect to streets and highways under their jurisdiction and within the reasonable exercise of the police power from:

1. Regulating the standing or parking of vehicles, except as limited by Section 11-1306 of this Act;

2. Regulating traffic by means of police officers or traffic control signals;

3. Regulating or prohibiting processions or assemblages on the highways;

4. Designating particular highways as one-way highways and requiring that all vehicles thereon be moved in one specific direction;

5. Regulating the speed of vehicles in public parks subject to the limitations set forth in Section 11-604;

6. Designating any highway as a through highway, as authorized in Section 11-302, and requiring that all vehicles stop before entering or crossing the same or designating any intersection as a stop intersection or a yield right-of-way intersection and requiring all vehicles to stop or yield the right-of-way at one or more entrances to such intersections;

7. Restricting the use of highways as authorized in Chapter 15;

8. Regulating the operation of bicycles and requiring the registration and licensing of same, including the requirement of a registration fee;

9. Regulating or prohibiting the turning of vehicles or specified types of vehicles at intersections;

10. Altering the speed limits as authorized in Section 11-604;

11. Prohibiting U-turns;

12. Prohibiting pedestrian crossings at other than designated and marked crosswalks or at intersections;

13. Prohibiting parking during snow removal operation;

14. Imposing fines in accordance with Section 11-1301.3 as penalties for use of any parking place reserved for persons with disabilities, as defined by Section 1-159.1, or disabled veterans by any person using a motor vehicle not bearing registration plates specified in Section 11-1301.1 or a special decal or device as defined in Section 11-1301.2 as evidence that the vehicle is operated by or for a person with disabilities or disabled veteran;

15. Adopting such other traffic regulations as are specifically authorized by this Code; or

16. Enforcing the provisions of subsection (f) of Section 3-413 of this Code or a similar local ordinance.

(b) No ordinance or regulation enacted under subsections 1, 4, 5, 6, 7, 9, 10, 11 or 13 of paragraph (a) shall be effective until signs giving reasonable notice of such local traffic regulations are posted.

(c) The provisions of this Code shall not prevent any municipality having a population of 500,000 or more inhabitants from prohibiting any person from driving or operating any motor vehicle upon the roadways of such municipality with headlamps on high beam or bright.

(d) The provisions of this Code shall not be deemed to prevent local authorities within the reasonable exercise of their police power from prohibiting, on private property, the unauthorized use of parking spaces reserved for persons with disabilities.

(e) No unit of local government, including a home rule unit, may enact or enforce an ordinance that applies only to motorcycles if the principal purpose for that ordinance is to restrict the access of motorcycles to any highway or portion of a highway for which federal or State funds have been used for the planning, design, construction, or maintenance of that highway. No unit of local government, including a home rule unit, may enact an ordinance requiring motorcycle users to wear protective headgear. Nothing in this subsection (e) shall affect the authority of a unit of local government to regulate motorcycles for traffic control purposes or in accordance with Section 12-602 of this Code. No unit of local government, including a home rule unit, may regulate motorcycles in a manner inconsistent with this Code. This subsection (e) is a limitation under subsection (i) of Section 6 of Article VII of the Illinois Constitution on the concurrent exercise by home rule units of powers and functions exercised by the State.

P.A. 76-1586, § 11-208, eff. July 1, 1970. Amended by P.A. 81-176, § 1, eff. Jan. 1, 1980; P.A. 83-831, § 1, eff. Jan. 1, 1984; P.A. 83-1058, § 1, eff. July 1, 1984; P.A. 83-1110, § 2, eff. May 25, 1984; P.A. 83-1316, § 1, eff. Jan. 1, 1985; P.A. 83-1362, Art. II, § 99, eff. Sept. 11, 1984; P.A. 83-1528, Art. II, § 24, eff. Jan. 17, 1985; P.A. 85-532, § 1, eff. Jan. 1, 1988; P.A. 88-685, § 5, eff. Jan. 24, 1995; P.A. 90-106, § 5, eff. Jan. 1, 1998; P.A. 90-513, § 5, eff. Aug. 22, 1997; P.A. 90-655, § 153, eff. July 30, 1998; P.A. 91-519, § 5, eff. Jan. 1, 2000.

Formerly Ill.Rev.Stat.1991, ch. 95 ½, ¶ 11-208.

5/11-208.1. Uniformity

§ 11-208.1. Uniformity. The provisions of this Chapter of this Act, as amended, and the rules and regulations promulgated thereunder by any State Officer, Office, Agency, Department or Commission, shall be applicable and uniformly applied and enforced throughout this State, in all other political subdivisions and in all units of local government.

P.A. 76-1586, § 11-208.1, added by P.A. 77-706, § 1, eff. Aug. 12, 1971.

Formerly Ill.Rev.Stat.1991, ch. 95 ½, ¶ 11-208.1.

5/11-208.2. Limitation on home rule units

Text of section effective until June 1, 2003

§ 11-208.2. Limitation on home rule units. The provisions of this Chapter of this Act limit the authority of home rule units to adopt local police regulations inconsistent herewith except pursuant to Sections 11-208 and 11-209 of this Chapter of this Act.

P.A. 76-1586, § 11-208.2, added by P.A. 77-706, § 1, eff. Aug. 12, 1971.

Formerly Ill.Rev.Stat.1991, ch. 95 ½, ¶ 11-208.2.

For text of section effective June 1, 2003, see 625 ILCS 5/11-208.2, post

5/11-208.2. Limitation on home rule units

Text of section effective June 1, 2003

§ 11-208.2. Limitation on home rule units.

The provisions of this Chapter of this Act limit the authority of home rule units to adopt local police regulations inconsistent herewith except pursuant to Sections 11-208, 11-209, 11-1005.1, 11-1412.1, and 11-1412.2 of this Chapter of this Act.

P.A. 76-1586, § 11-208.2, added by P.A. 77-706, § 1, eff. Aug. 12, 1971. Amended by P.A. 92-868, § 5, eff. June 1, 2003.

Formerly Ill.Rev.Stat.1991, ch. 95 ½, ¶ 11-208.2.

For text of section effective until June 1, 2003, see 625 ILCS 5/11-208.2, ante

5/11-208.3. Administrative adjudication of violations of traffic regulations concerning the standing, parking, or condition of vehicles

§ 11-208.3. Administrative adjudication of violations of traffic regulations concerning the standing, parking, or condition of vehicles.

(a) Any municipality may provide by ordinance for a system of administrative adjudication of vehicular standing and parking violations and vehicle compliance violations as defined in this subsection. The administrative system shall have as its purpose the fair and efficient enforcement of municipal regulations through the administrative adjudication of violations of municipal ordinances regulating the standing and parking of vehicles, the condition and use of vehicle equipment, and the display of municipal wheel tax licenses within the municipality's borders. The administrative system shall only have authority to adjudicate civil offenses carrying fines not in excess of $250 that occur after the effective date of the ordinance adopting such a system under this Section. For purposes of this Section, "compliance violation" means a violation of a municipal regulation governing the condition or use of equipment on a vehicle or governing the display of a municipal wheel tax license.

(b) Any ordinance establishing a system of administrative adjudication under this Section shall provide for:

(1) A traffic compliance administrator authorized to adopt, distribute and process parking and compliance violation notices and other notices required by this Section, collect money paid as fines and penalties for violation of parking and compliance ordinances, and operate an administrative adjudication system. The traffic compliance administrator also may make a certified report to the Secretary of State under Section 6-306.5.

(2) A parking, standing, or compliance violation notice that shall specify the date, time, and place of violation of a parking, standing, or compliance regulation; the particular regulation violated; the fine and any penalty that may be assessed for late payment, when so provided by ordinance; the vehicle make and state registration number; and the

identification number of the person issuing the notice. With regard to municipalities with a population of 1 million or more, it shall be grounds for dismissal of a parking violation if the State registration number or vehicle make specified is incorrect. The violation notice shall state that the payment of the indicated fine, and of any applicable penalty for late payment, shall operate as a final disposition of the violation. The notice also shall contain information as to the availability of a hearing in which the violation may be contested on its merits. The violation notice shall specify the time and manner in which a hearing may be had.

(3) Service of the parking, standing, or compliance violation notice by affixing the original or a facsimile of the notice to an unlawfully parked vehicle or by handing the notice to the operator of a vehicle if he or she is present. A person authorized by ordinance to issue and serve parking, standing, and compliance violation notices shall certify as to the correctness of the facts entered on the violation notice by signing his or her name to the notice at the time of service or in the case of a notice produced by a computerized device, by signing a single certificate to be kept by the traffic compliance administrator attesting to the correctness of all notices produced by the device while it was under his or her control. The original or a facsimile of the violation notice or, in the case of a notice produced by a computerized device, a printed record generated by the device showing the facts entered on the notice, shall be retained by the traffic compliance administrator, and shall be a record kept in the ordinary course of business. A parking, standing, or compliance violation notice issued, signed and served in accordance with this Section, a copy of the notice, or the computer generated record shall be prima facie correct and shall be prima facie evidence of the correctness of the facts shown on the notice. The notice, copy, or computer generated record shall be admissible in any subsequent administrative or legal proceedings.

(4) An opportunity for a hearing for the registered owner of the vehicle cited in the parking, standing, or compliance violation notice in which the owner may contest the merits of the alleged violation, and during which formal or technical rules of evidence shall not apply; provided, however, that under Section 11–1306 of this Code the lessee of a vehicle cited in the violation notice likewise shall be provided an opportunity for a hearing of the same kind afforded the registered owner. The hearings shall be recorded, and the person conducting the hearing on behalf of the traffic compliance administrator shall be empowered to administer oaths and to secure by subpoena both the attendance and testimony of witnesses and the production of relevant books and papers. Persons appearing at a hearing under this Section may be represented by counsel at their expense. The ordinance may also provide for internal administrative review following the decision of the hearing officer.

(5) Service of additional notices, sent by first class United States mail, postage prepaid, to the address of the registered owner of the cited vehicle as recorded with the Secretary of State or, under Section 11–1306 of this Code, to the lessee of the cited vehicle at the last address known to the lessor of the cited vehicle at the time of lease. The service shall be deemed complete as of the date of deposit in the United States mail. The notices shall be in the following sequence and shall include but not be limited to the information specified herein:

(i) A second notice of violation. This notice shall specify the date and location of the violation cited in the parking, standing, or compliance violation notice, the particular regulation violated, the vehicle make and state registration number, the fine and any penalty that may be assessed for late payment when so provided by ordinance, the availability of a hearing in which the violation may be contested on its merits, and the time and manner in which the hearing may be had. The notice of violation shall also state that failure either to pay the indicated fine and any applicable penalty, or to appear at a hearing on the merits in the time and manner specified, will result in a final determination of violation liability for the cited violation in the amount of the fine or penalty indicated, and that, upon the occurrence of a final determination of violation liability for the failure, and the exhaustion of, or failure to exhaust, available administrative or judicial procedures for review, any unpaid fine or penalty will constitute a debt due and owing the municipality.

(ii) A notice of final determination of parking, standing, or compliance violation liability. This notice shall be sent following a final determination of parking, standing, or compliance violation liability and the conclusion of judicial review procedures taken under this Section. The notice shall state that the unpaid fine or penalty is a debt due and owing the municipality. The notice shall contain warnings that failure to pay any fine or penalty due and owing the municipality within the time specified may result in the municipality's filing of a petition in the Circuit Court to have the unpaid fine or penalty rendered a judgment as provided by this Section, or may result in suspension of the person's drivers license for failure to pay fines or penalties for 10 or more parking violations under Section 6–306.5.

(6) A Notice of impending drivers license suspension. This notice shall be sent to the person liable for any fine or penalty that remains due and owing on 10 or more parking violations. The notice shall state that failure to pay the fine or penalty owing within 45 days of the notice's date will result in the municipality notifying the Secretary of State that the person is eligible for initiation of suspension proceedings under Section 6–306.5 of this Code. The notice shall also state that the person may obtain a photostatic copy of an original ticket imposing a fine or penalty by sending a self addressed, stamped envelope to the municipality along with a request for the photostatic copy. The notice of impending drivers license suspension shall be sent by first class United States mail, postage prepaid, to the address recorded with the Secretary of State.

(7) Final determinations of violation liability. A final determination of violation liability shall occur following failure to pay the fine or penalty after a hearing officer's determination of violation liability and the exhaustion of or failure to exhaust any administrative review procedures provided by ordinance. Where a person fails to appear at a hearing to contest the alleged violation in the time and manner specified in a prior mailed notice, the hearing officer's determination of violation liability shall become final: (A) upon denial of a timely petition to set aside that determination, or (B) upon expiration of the period for filing the petition without a filing having been made.

(8) A petition to set aside a determination of parking, standing, or compliance violation liability that may be filed by a person owing an unpaid fine or penalty. The petition shall be filed with and ruled upon by the traffic compliance administrator in the manner and within the time specified by ordinance. The grounds for the petition may be limited to: (A) the person not having been the owner or lessee of

the cited vehicle on the date the violation notice was issued, (B) the person having already paid the fine or penalty for the violation in question, and (C) excusable failure to appear at or request a new date for a hearing. With regard to municipalities with a population of 1 million or more, it shall be grounds for dismissal of a parking violation if the State registration number or vehicle make specified is incorrect. After the determination of parking, standing, or compliance violation liability has been set aside upon a showing of just cause, the registered owner shall be provided with a hearing on the merits for that violation.

(9) Procedures for non-residents. Procedures by which persons who are not residents of the municipality may contest the merits of the alleged violation without attending a hearing.

(10) A schedule of civil fines for violations of vehicular standing, parking, and compliance regulations enacted by ordinance pursuant to this Section, and a schedule of penalties for late payment of the fines, provided, however, that the total amount of the fine and penalty for any one violation shall not exceed $250.

(11) Other provisions as are necessary and proper to carry into effect the powers granted and purposes stated in this Section.

(c) Any municipality establishing vehicular standing, parking, and compliance regulations under this Section may also provide by ordinance for a program of vehicle immobilization for the purpose of facilitating enforcement of those regulations. The program of vehicle immobilization shall provide for immobilizing any eligible vehicle upon the public way by presence of a restraint in a manner to prevent operation of the vehicle. Any ordinance establishing a program of vehicle immobilization under this Section shall provide:

(1) Criteria for the designation of vehicles eligible for immobilization. A vehicle shall be eligible for immobilization when the registered owner of the vehicle has accumulated the number of unpaid final determinations of parking, standing, or compliance violation liability as determined by ordinance.

(2) A notice of impending vehicle immobilization and a right to a hearing to challenge the validity of the notice by disproving liability for the unpaid final determinations of parking, standing, or compliance violation liability listed on the notice.

(3) The right to a prompt hearing after a vehicle has been immobilized or subsequently towed without payment of the outstanding fines and penalties on parking, standing, or compliance violations for which final determinations have been issued. An order issued after the hearing is a final administrative decision within the meaning of Section 3–101 of the Code of Civil Procedure.[1]

(4) A post immobilization and post-towing notice advising the registered owner of the vehicle of the right to a hearing to challenge the validity of the impoundment.

(d) Judicial review of final determinations of parking, standing, and compliance violations and final administrative decisions issued after hearings regarding vehicle immobilization and impoundment made under this Section shall be subject to the provisions of the Administrative Review Law.[2]

(e) Any fine, penalty, or part of any fine or any penalty remaining unpaid after the exhaustion of, or the failure to exhaust, administrative remedies created under this Section and the conclusion of any judicial review procedures shall be a debt due and owing the municipality and, as such, may be collected in accordance with applicable law. Payment in full of any fine or penalty resulting from a standing, parking, or compliance violation shall constitute a final disposition of that violation.

(f) After the expiration of the period within which judicial review may be sought for a final determination of parking, standing, or compliance violation, the municipality may commence a proceeding in the Circuit Court for purposes of obtaining a judgment on the final determination of violation. Nothing in this Section shall prevent a municipality from consolidating multiple final determinations of parking, standing, or compliance violation against a person in a proceeding. Upon commencement of the action, the municipality shall file a certified copy of the final determination of parking, standing, or compliance violation, which shall be accompanied by a certification that recites facts sufficient to show that the final determination of violation was issued in accordance with this Section and the applicable municipal ordinance. Service of the summons and a copy of the petition may be by any method provided by Section 2–203 of the Code of Civil Procedure[3] or by certified mail, return receipt requested, provided that the total amount of fines and penalties for final determinations of parking, standing, or compliance violations does not exceed $2500. If the court is satisfied that the final determination of parking, standing, or compliance violation was entered in accordance with the requirements of this Section and the applicable municipal ordinance, and that the registered owner or the lessee, as the case may be, had an opportunity for an administrative hearing and for judicial review as provided in this Section, the court shall render judgment in favor of the municipality and against the registered owner or the lessee for the amount indicated in the final determination of parking, standing, or compliance violation, plus costs. The judgment shall have the same effect and may be enforced in the same manner as other judgments for the recovery of money.

P.A. 76–1586, § 11–208.3, added by P.A. 85–876, § 2, eff. Nov. 6, 1987. Amended by P.A. 86–947, § 2, eff. Nov. 13, 1989; P.A. 87–181, § 1, eff. Sept. 3, 1991; P.A. 88–415, § 10, eff. Aug. 20, 1993; P.A. 88–437, § 5, eff. Jan. 1, 1994; P.A. 88–670, Art. 2, § 2–59, eff. Dec. 2, 1994; P.A. 89–190, § 5, eff. Jan. 1, 1996; P.A. 92–695, § 10, eff. Jan. 1, 2003.

[1] 735 ILCS 5/3–101.

[2] 735 ILCS 5/3–101 et seq.

[3] 735 ILCS 5/2–203.

5/11–208.4. § 11–208.4. Repealed effective Dec. 31, 1994

5/11–209. Powers of municipalities and counties—Contract with school boards, hospitals, churches, condominium complex unit owners' associations, and commercial and industrial facility, shopping center, and apartment complex owners for regulation of traffic

§ 11–209. Powers of municipalities and counties—Contract with school boards, hospitals, churches, condominium complex unit owners' associations, and commercial and industrial facility, shopping center, and apartment complex owners for regulation of traffic.

(a) The corporate authorities of any municipality or the county board of any county, and a school board, hospital, church, condominium complex unit owners' association, or owner of any commercial and industrial facility, shopping center, or apartment complex which controls a parking area located within the limits of the municipality, or outside the limits of the municipality and within the boundaries of the county, may, by contract, empower the municipality or county to regulate the parking of automobiles and the traffic at such parking area. Such contract shall empower the municipality or county to accomplish all or any part of the following:

1. The erection of stop signs, flashing signals, person with disabilities parking area signs or yield signs at specified locations in a parking area and the adoption of appropriate regulations thereto pertaining, or the designation of any intersection in the parking area as a stop intersection or as a yield intersection and the ordering of like signs or signals at one or more entrances to such intersection, subject to the provisions of this Chapter.

2. The prohibition or regulation of the turning of vehicles or specified types of vehicles at intersections or other designated locations in the parking area.

3. The regulation of a crossing of any roadway in the parking area by pedestrians.

4. The designation of any separate roadway in the parking area for one-way traffic.

5. The establishment and regulation of loading zones.

6. The prohibition, regulation, restriction or limitation of the stopping, standing or parking of vehicles in specified areas of the parking area.

7. The designation of safety zones in the parking area and fire lanes.

8. Providing for the removal and storage of vehicles parked or abandoned in the parking area during snowstorms, floods, fires, or other public emergencies, or found unattended in the parking area, (a) where they constitute an obstruction to traffic, or (b) where stopping, standing or parking is prohibited, and for the payment of reasonable charges for such removal and storage by the owner or operator of any such vehicle.

9. Providing that the cost of planning, installation, maintenance and enforcement of parking and traffic regulations pursuant to any contract entered into under the authority of this paragraph (a) of this Section be borne by the municipality or county, or by the school board, hospital, church, property owner, apartment complex owner, or condominium complex unit owners' association, or that a percentage of the cost be shared by the parties to the contract.

10. Causing the installation of parking meters on the parking area and establishing whether the expense of installing said parking meters and maintenance thereof shall be that of the municipality or county, or that of the school board, hospital, church, condominium complex unit owners' association, shopping center or apartment complex owner. All moneys obtained from such parking meters as may be installed on any parking area shall belong to the municipality or county.

11. Causing the installation of parking signs in accordance with Section 11–301 in areas of the parking lots covered by this Section and where desired by the person contracting with the appropriate authority listed in paragraph (a) of this Section, indicating that such parking spaces are reserved for persons with disabilities.

12. Contracting for such additional reasonable rules and regulations with respect to traffic and parking in a parking area as local conditions may require for the safety and convenience of the public or of the users of the parking area.

(b) No contract entered into pursuant to this Section shall exceed a period of 20 years. No lessee of a shopping center or apartment complex shall enter into such a contract for a longer period of time than the length of his lease.

(c) Any contract entered into pursuant to this Section shall be recorded in the office of the recorder in the county in which the parking area is located, and no regulation made pursuant to the contract shall be effective or enforceable until 3 days after the contract is so recorded.

(d) At such time as parking and traffic regulations have been established at any parking area pursuant to the contract as provided for in this Section, then it shall be a petty offense for any person to do any act forbidden or to fail to perform any act required by such parking or traffic regulation. If the violation is the parking in a parking space reserved for persons with disabilities under paragraph (11) of this Section, by a person without special registration plates issued to a person with disabilities, as defined by Section 1–159.1, pursuant to Section 3–616 of this Code, or to a disabled veteran pursuant to Section 3–609 of this Code, the local police of the contracting corporate municipal authorities shall issue a parking ticket to such parking violator and issue a fine in accordance with Section 11–1301.3.

(e) The term "shopping center", as used in this Section, means premises having one or more stores or business establishments in connection with which there is provided on privately-owned property near or contiguous thereto an area, or areas, of land used by the public as the means of access to and egress from the stores and business establishments on such premises and for the parking of motor vehicles of customers and patrons of such stores and business establishments on such premises.

(f) The term "parking area", as used in this Section, means an area, or areas, of land near or contiguous to a school, church, or hospital building, shopping center, apartment complex, or condominium complex, but not the public highways or alleys, and used by the public as the means of access to and egress from such buildings and the stores and business establishments at a shopping center and for the parking of motor vehicles.

(g) The terms "owner", "property owner", "shopping center owner", and "apartment complex owner", as used in this Section, mean the actual legal owner of the shopping center parking area or apartment complex, the trust officer of a banking institution having the right to manage and control such property, or a person having the legal right, through lease or otherwise, to manage or control the property.

(g–5) The term "condominium complex unit owners' association", as used in this Section, means a "unit owners' association" as defined in Section 2 of the Condominium Property Act.[1]

(h) The term "fire lane", as used in this Section, means travel lanes for the fire fighting equipment upon which there shall be no standing or parking of any motor vehicle at any time so that fire fighting equipment can move freely thereon.

(i) The term "apartment complex", as used in this Section, means premises having one or more apartments in connection with which there is provided on privately-owned property near or contiguous thereto an area, or areas, of land used by occupants of such apartments or their guests as a means of access to and egress from such apartments or for the parking of motor vehicles of such occupants or their guests.

(j) The term "condominium complex", as used in this Section, means the units, common elements, and limited common elements that are located on the parcels, as those terms are defined in Section 2 of the Condominium Property Act.

(k) The term "commercial and industrial facility", as used in this Section, means a premises containing one or more commercial and industrial facility establishments in connection with which there is provided on privately-owned property near or contiguous to the premises an area or areas of land used by the public as the means of access to and egress from the commercial and industrial facility establishment on the premises and for the parking of motor vehicles of customers, patrons, and employees of the commercial and industrial facility establishment on the premises.

(*l*) The provisions of this Section shall not be deemed to prevent local authorities from enforcing, on private property, local ordinances imposing fines, in accordance with Section 11-1301.3, as penalties for use of any parking place reserved for persons with disabilities, as defined by Section 1-159.1, or disabled veterans by any person using a motor vehicle not bearing registration plates specified in Section 11-1301.1 or a special decal or device as defined in Section 11-1301.2 as evidence that the vehicle is operated by or for a person with disabilities or disabled veteran.

This amendatory Act of 1972 is not a prohibition upon the contractual and associational powers granted by Article VII, Section 10 of the Illinois Constitution.

P.A. 76-1586, § 11-209, eff. July 1, 1970. Amended by P.A. 77-1191, § 1, eff. Aug. 9, 1971; P.A. 77-2298, § 1, eff. Oct. 1, 1972; P.A. 77-2720, § 1, eff. Jan. 1, 1973; P.A. 78-255, § 26, eff. Oct. 1, 1973; P.A. 81-171, § 1, eff. Jan. 1, 1980; P.A. 83-358, § 67, eff. Sept. 14, 1983; P.A. 83-1058, § 1, eff. July 1, 1984; P.A. 83-1316, § 1, eff. Jan. 1, 1985; P.A. 83-1362, Art. II, § 99, eff. Sept. 11, 1984; P.A. 86-1179, § 2, eff. Aug. 17, 1990; P.A. 88-685, § 5, eff. Jan. 24, 1995; P.A. 89-551, § 5, eff. Jan. 1, 1997; P.A. 90-106, § 5, eff. Jan. 1, 1998; P.A. 90-145, § 15, eff. Jan. 1, 1998; P.A. 90-481, § 30, eff. Aug. 17, 1997; P.A. 90-655, § 153, eff. July 30, 1998.

Formerly Ill.Rev.Stat.1991, ch. 95 ½, ¶ 11-209.

1 765 ILCS 605/2.

P.A. 90-655, the First 1998 General Revisory Act, amended various Acts to delete obsolete text, to correct patent and technical errors, to revise cross references, to resolve multiple actions in the 89th and 90th General Assemblies and to make certain technical corrections in P.A. 89-708 through P.A. 90-566.

5/11-209.1. Powers of local authorities—enforcing the provisions of this Code on private streets and roads

§ 11-209.1. Powers of local authorities—enforcing the provisions of this Code on private streets and roads. (a) Any person or board of directors owning, operating or representing a residential subdivision, development, apartment house or apartment project, containing a minimum of 10 apartments or single family residences may file a written request, with the appropriate local authority wherein such property is situated, requesting their law enforcement agency enforce the provisions of this Code on all private streets or roads open to or used by the tenants, owners, employees or the public for the purposes of vehicular traffic by permission of such person or board of directors and not as a matter of public right. Notwithstanding Section 1-126 and Section 1-201 of this Code, if the local authority grants such request by the adoption of an enabling ordinance then all such private streets or roads shall be considered "highways" only for the enforcement purposes of this Code.

(b) All regulations adopted and traffic control devices employed by a local authority in the enforcement of this Code on such streets or roads within any private area, pursuant to this Section, shall be consistent with the provisions of this Code and shall conform to the Illinois Manual on Uniform Traffic Control Devices.

A local authority may require that any person who files a request for the installation of traffic signs pay for the cost of such traffic signs. Such traffic signs shall be in conformity with Section 11-604 of this Code.

(c) Any person or board of directors which has filed such a request under this Section, may rescind that request by filing with the appropriate local authority a written request for such rescission. Upon receipt of the written request, the local authority shall subsequently repeal the original enabling ordinance. Such repeal shall not take effect until the first day of January following any such action by the local authorities. However, no such rescission request may be filed within 12 months of the date of the original written request.

(d) The filing of a written request or the adoption of the enabling ordinance under this Section in no way constitutes a dedication to public use of any street, road, driveway, trail, terrace, bridle path, parkway, parking area, or other roadway open to or used by vehicular traffic, nor does it prevent such person or board of directors, as owners of such property, from requiring additional regulations than those specified by the local authorities or otherwise regulating such use as may seem best to such person or board of directors as long as they do not conflict with the powers granted to local authorities under Section 11-208 of this Code.

(e) This amendatory act of 1972 is not a prohibition upon the contractual and associational powers granted by Article VII, Section 10 of the Illinois Constitution.

P.A. 76-1586, § 11-209.1, added by P.A. 77-2296, § 1, eff. Oct. 1, 1972. Amended by P.A. 83-1473, § 3, eff. Jan. 1, 1985; P.A. 84-986, § 1, eff. Sept. 25, 1985; P.A. 86-521, § 1, eff. Sept. 1, 1989.

Formerly Ill.Rev.Stat.1991, ch. 95 ½, ¶ 11-209.1.

5/11-210. This Chapter not to interfere with rights of owners of real property with reference thereto

§ 11-210. This Chapter not to interfere with rights of owners of real property with reference thereto. Nothing in this Chapter shall be construed to prevent the owner of real property used by the public for purposes of vehicular travel by permission of the owner and not as matter of right from prohibiting such use, or from requiring other or different or additional conditions than those specified in this Chapter, or otherwise regulating such use as may seem best to such owner.

P.A. 76-1586, § 11-210, eff. July 1, 1970.

Formerly Ill.Rev.Stat.1991, ch. 95 ½, ¶ 11-210.

5/11-211. Local laws

§ 11-211. Local laws. No owner of a motor vehicle shall be limited as to speed upon any public place, at any time when the same is or may hereafter be opened to the use of persons having or using other vehicles, nor be required to comply with other provisions or conditions as to the use of such motor vehicles except as in this Chapter provided, and except as is provided in this Act.

P.A. 76-1586, § 11-211, eff. July 1, 1970. Amended by P.A. 77-1344, § 1, eff. Aug. 27, 1971.

Formerly Ill.Rev.Stat.1991, ch. 95 ½, ¶ 11-211.

ARTICLE III. TRAFFIC SIGNS, SIGNALS AND MARKINGS

5/11–301. Department to adopt sign manual

§ 11–301. Department to adopt sign manual.

(a) The Department shall adopt a State manual and specifications for a uniform system of traffic-control devices consistent with this Chapter for use upon highways within this State. Such manual shall include the adoption of the R 7–8 sign adopted by the United States Department of Transportation to designate the reservation of parking facilities for a person with disabilities. Non-conforming signs in use prior to January 1, 1985 shall not constitute a violation during their useful lives, which shall not be extended by other means than normal maintenance. The manual shall also specify insofar as practicable the minimum warrants justifying the use of the various traffic control devices. Such uniform system shall correlate with and, where not inconsistent with Illinois highway conditions, conform to the system set forth in the most recent edition of the national manual on Uniform Traffic Control Devices for Streets and Highways.

(b) Signs adopted by the Department to designate the reservation of parking facilities for a person with disabilities shall also exhibit, in a manner determined by the Department, the words "$100 Fine".

(c) If the amount of a fine is changed, the Department shall change the design of the signs to indicate the current amount of the fine.

P.A. 76–1586, § 11–301, eff. July 1, 1970. Amended by P.A. 76–2159, § 1, eff. July 1, 1970; P.A. 83–1316, § 1, eff. Jan. 1, 1985; P.A. 85–484, § 1, eff. Jan. 1, 1988; P.A. 88–685, § 5, eff. Jan. 24, 1995; P.A. 89–533, § 5, eff. Jan. 1, 1997.

Formerly Ill.Rev.Stat.1991, ch. 95 ½, ¶ 11–301.

5/11–301.1. Person with disabilities sign

§ 11–301.1. Beginning July 1, 1988, all signs erected and used to designate the reservation of parking facilities for a person with disabilities shall be in a form and manner prescribed under Section 11–301 of this Code, and all parking spaces reserved for a person with disabilities, except those reserving on-street parking areas, shall be at least 16 feet wide. Non-conforming signs in use prior to July 1, 1988 shall not constitute a violation during their useful lives, which shall not be extended by means other than normal maintenance. Beginning October 1, 1992, all parking spaces reserved for a person with disabilities, except those reserving on-street parking areas, shall be at least 16 feet wide.

P.A. 76–1586, § 11–301.1, added by P.A. 85–484, § 1, eff. Jan. 1, 1988. Amended by P.A. 87–562, § 1, eff. Jan. 1, 1992; P.A. 88–685, § 5, eff. Jan. 24, 1995.

Formerly Ill.Rev.Stat.1991, ch. 95 ½, ¶ 11–301.1.

5/11–302. Authority to designate through highway and stop and yield intersections

§ 11–302. Authority to designate through highway and stop and yield intersections. (a) The Department with reference to State highways under its jurisdiction, local authorities and road district highway commissioners with reference to other highways under their jurisdiction may designate through highways and erect stop signs or yield signs at specified entrances thereto, or may designate any intersection as a stop intersection or as a yield intersection and erect stop signs or yield signs at one or more entrances to such intersection. Designation of through highways and stop or yield intersections and the erection of stop signs or yield signs on township or road district roads are subject to the written approval of the county engineer or superintendent of highways.

(b) Every stop sign and yield sign shall conform to the State Manual and Specifications and shall be located as near as practicable to the nearest line of the crosswalk on the near side of the intersection or, if there is no crosswalk, then as close as practicable to the nearest line of the intersecting roadway.

(c) The Department may in its discretion and when traffic conditions warrant such action give preference to traffic upon any of the State highways under its jurisdiction over traffic crossing or entering such highway by erecting appropriate traffic control devices.

P.A. 76–1586, § 11–302, eff. July 1, 1970. Amended by P.A. 87–217, § 4, eff. Jan. 1, 1992.

Formerly Ill.Rev.Stat.1991, ch. 95 ½, ¶ 11–302.

5/11–303. The Department to place signs on all State highways

§ 11–303. The Department to place signs on all State highways.

(a) The Department shall place and maintain such traffic-control devices, conforming to its manual and specifications on all highways under its jurisdiction as it shall deem necessary to indicate and to carry out the provisions of this Chapter or to regulate, warn or guide traffic.

(b) No local authority shall place or maintain any traffic-control device upon any highway under the jurisdiction of the Department except by the latter's permission.

(c) The Department shall erect and maintain guide, warning and direction signs upon highways in cities, towns and villages of which portions or lanes of such highways are under the control and jurisdiction of the Department or for which the Department has maintenance responsibility.

(d) Nothing in this Chapter shall divest the corporate authorities of park districts of power to prohibit or restrict the use of highways under their jurisdiction by certain types or weights of motor vehicles or the power of cities, villages, incorporated towns and park districts to designate highways for one-way traffic or the power of such municipal corporations to erect and maintain appropriate signs respecting such uses.

(e) Nothing in this Section shall prohibit a municipality, township, or county from erecting signs as required under the Illinois Adopt-A-Highway Act.[1]

P.A. 76-1586, § 11-303, eff. July 1, 1970. Amended by P.A. 80-1495, § 36, eff. Jan. 8, 1979; P.A. 87-1118, § 90, eff. Sept. 16, 1992.

Formerly Ill.Rev.Stat.1991, ch. 95 ½, ¶ 11-303.

1 605 ILCS 120/1 et seq.

5/11-304. Local traffic-control devices; tourist oriented businesses signs

§ 11-304. Local traffic-control devices; tourist oriented businesses signs.

Local authorities and road district highway commissioners in their respective maintenance jurisdiction shall place and maintain such traffic-control devices upon highways under their maintenance jurisdiction as are required to indicate and carry out the provisions of this Chapter, and local traffic ordinances or to regulate, warn, or guide traffic. All such traffic control devices shall conform to the State Manual and Specifications and shall be justified by traffic warrants stated in the Manual. Placement of traffic-control devices on township or road district roads also shall be subject to the written approval of the county engineer or superintendent of highways.

Local authorities and road district highway commissioners in their respective maintenance jurisdictions shall have the authority to install signs, in conformance with the State Manual and specifications, alerting motorists of the tourist oriented businesses available on roads under local jurisdiction in rural areas as may be required to guide motorists to the businesses. The local authorities and road district highway commissioners shall also have the authority to sell or lease space on these signs to the owners or operators of the businesses.

P.A. 76-1586, § 11-304, eff. July 1, 1970. Amended by P.A. 87-217, § 4, eff. Jan. 1, 1992; P.A. 90-519, § 5, eff. June 1, 1998.

Formerly Ill.Rev.Stat.1991, ch. 95 ½, ¶ 11-304.

5/11-305. Obedience to and required traffic-control devices

§ 11-305. Obedience to and required traffic-control devices. (a) The driver of any vehicle shall obey the instructions of any official traffic-control device applicable thereto placed or held in accordance with the provisions of this Act, unless otherwise directed by a police officer, subject to the exceptions granted the driver of an authorized emergency vehicle in this Act.

(b) It is unlawful for any person to leave the roadway and travel across private property to avoid an official traffic control device.

(c) No provision of this Act for which official traffic-control devices are required shall be enforced against an alleged violator if at the time and place of the alleged violation an official device is not in proper position and sufficiently legible to be seen by an ordinarily observant person. Whenever a particular section does not state that official traffic-control devices are required, such section shall be effective even though no devices are erected or in place.

(d) Whenever any official traffic-control device is placed or held in position approximately conforming to the requirements of this Act and purports to conform to the lawful requirements pertaining to such device, such device shall be presumed to have been so placed or held by the official act or direction of lawful authority, and comply with the requirements of this Act, unless the contrary shall be established by competent evidence.

(e) The driver of a vehicle approaching a traffic control signal on which no signal light facing such vehicle is illuminated shall stop before entering the intersection in accordance with rules applicable in making a stop at a stop sign.

P.A. 76-1586, § 11-305, eff. July 1, 1970. Amended by P.A. 76-2160, § 1, eff. July 1, 1970; P.A. 79-1069, § 1, eff. Jan. 1, 1976; P.A. 80-267, § 1, eff. Oct. 1, 1977; P.A. 84-873, § 1, eff. Jan. 1, 1986.

Formerly Ill.Rev.Stat.1991, ch. 95 ½, ¶ 11-305.

5/11-306. Traffic-control signal legend

§ 11-306. Traffic-control signal legend. Whenever traffic is controlled by traffic-control signals exhibiting different colored lights or color lighted arrows, successively one at a time or in combination, only the colors green, red and yellow shall be used, except for special pedestrian signals carrying a word legend, and the lights shall indicate and apply to drivers of vehicles and pedestrians as follows:

(a) Green indication.

1. Vehicular traffic facing a circular green signal may proceed straight through or turn right or left unless a sign at such place prohibits either such turn. Vehicular traffic, including vehicles turning right or left, shall yield the right of way to other vehicles and to pedestrians lawfully within the intersection or an adjacent crosswalk at the time such signal is exhibited.

2. Vehicular traffic facing a green arrow signal, shown alone or in combination with another indication, may cautiously enter the intersection only to make the movement indicated by such arrow, or such other movement as is permitted by other indications shown at the same time. Such vehicular traffic shall yield the right of way to pedestrians lawfully within an adjacent crosswalk and to other traffic lawfully using the intersection.

3. Unless otherwise directed by a pedestrian-control signal, as provided in Section 11-307, pedestrians facing any green signal, except when the sole green signal is a turn arrow, may proceed across the roadway within any marked or unmarked crosswalk.

(b) Steady yellow indication.

1. Vehicular traffic facing a steady circular yellow or yellow arrow signal is thereby warned that the related green movement is being terminated or that a red indication will be exhibited immediately thereafter.

2. Pedestrians facing a steady circular yellow or yellow arrow signal, unless otherwise directed by a pedestrian-control signal as provided in Section 11-307, are thereby advised that there is insufficient time to cross the roadway before a red indication is shown and no pedestrian shall then start to cross the roadway.

(c) Steady red indication.

1. Except as provided in paragraph 3 of this subsection (c), vehicular traffic facing a steady circular red signal alone shall stop at a clearly marked stop line, but if there is no such stop line, before entering the crosswalk on the near side of the intersection, or if there is no such crosswalk, then before entering the intersection, and shall remain standing until an indication to proceed is shown.

2. Except as provided in paragraph 3 of this subsection (c), vehicular traffic facing a steady red arrow signal shall not enter the intersection to make the movement indicated by the arrow and, unless entering the intersection to make a movement permitted by another signal, shall stop at a clearly marked stop line, but if there is no such stop line, before entering the crosswalk on the near side of the intersection, or if there is no such crosswalk, then before entering the intersection, and shall remain standing until an indication permitting the movement indicated by such red arrow is shown.

3. Except when a sign is in place prohibiting a turn and local authorities by ordinance or State authorities by rule or regulation prohibit any such turn, vehicular traffic facing any steady red signal may cautiously enter the intersection to turn right, or to turn left from a one-way street into a one-way street, after stopping as required by paragraph 1 or paragraph 2 of this subsection. After stopping, the driver shall yield the right of way to any vehicle in the intersection or approaching on another roadway so closely as to constitute an immediate hazard during the time such driver is moving across or within the intersection or junction or roadways. Such driver shall yield the right of way to pedestrians within the intersection or an adjacent crosswalk.

4. Unless otherwise directed by a pedestrian-control signal as provided in Section 11-307, pedestrians facing a steady circular red or red arrow signal alone shall not enter the roadway.

5. A municipality with a population of 1,000,000 or more may enact an ordinance that provides for the use of an automated red light enforcement system to enforce violations of this subsection (c) that result in or involve a motor vehicle accident, leaving the scene of a motor vehicle accident, or reckless driving that results in bodily injury.

This paragraph 5 is subject to prosecutorial discretion that is consistent with applicable law.

(d) In the event an official traffic control signal is erected and maintained at a place other than an intersection, the provisions of this Section shall be applicable except as to provisions which by their nature can have no application. Any stop required shall be at a traffic sign or a marking on the pavement indicating where the stop shall be made or, in the absence of such sign or marking, the stop shall be made at the signal.

(e) The motorman of any streetcar shall obey the above signals as applicable to vehicles.

P.A. 76-1586, § 11-306, eff. July 1, 1970. Amended by P.A. 76-1737, § 1; P.A. 78-24, § 1, eff. Jan. 1, 1974; P.A. 79-1069, § 1, eff. Jan. 1, 1976; P.A. 81-861, § 1, eff. Jan. 1, 1980; P.A. 81-1509, Art. II, § 71, eff. Sept. 26, 1980; P.A. 84-873, § 1, eff. Jan. 1, 1986; P.A. 90-86, § 5, eff. July 10, 1997; P.A. 91-357, § 231, eff. July 29, 1999.

Formerly Ill.Rev.Stat.1991, ch. 95 ½, ¶ 11-306.

5/11-307. Pedestrian-control signals

§ 11-307. Pedestrian-control signals. Whenever special pedestrian-control signals exhibiting the words "Walk" or "Don't Walk" or the illuminated symbols of a walking person or an upraised palm are in place such signals shall indicate as follows:

(a) Walk or walking person symbol. Pedestrians facing such signal may proceed across the roadway in the direction of the signal, and shall be given the right of way by the drivers of all vehicles.

(b) Don't Walk or upraised palm symbol. No pedestrian shall start to cross the roadway in the direction of such signal, but any pedestrian who has partly completed his crossing on the Walk signal or walking person symbol shall proceed to a sidewalk or safety island while the "Don't Walk" signal or upraised palm symbol is illuminated, steady, or flashing.

P.A. 76-1586, § 11-307, eff. July 1, 1970. Amended by P.A. 79-1069, § 1, eff. Jan. 1, 1976; P.A. 81-553, § 1, eff. Jan. 1, 1980.

Formerly Ill.Rev.Stat.1991, ch. 95 ½, ¶ 11-307.

5/11-308. Lane-control signals

§ 11-308. Lane-control signals. Whenever lane-control signals are used in conjunction with official signs, they shall have the following meanings:

(a) Downward-pointing green arrow. A driver facing this indication is permitted to drive in the lane over which the arrow signal is located. Otherwise he shall obey all other traffic controls present and follow normal safe driving practices.

(b) Red X symbol. A driver facing this indication shall not drive in the lane over which the signal is located, and this indication shall modify accordingly the meaning of all other traffic controls present. Otherwise he shall obey all other traffic controls and follow normal safe driving practices.

(c) Yellow X (steady). A driver facing this indication should prepare to vacate the lane over which the signal is located, in a safe manner to avoid, if possible, occupying that lane when a steady red X is displayed.

(d) Flashing yellow arrow. A driver facing this indication may use the lane only for the purpose of approaching and making a left turn.

P.A. 76-1586, § 11-308, eff. July 1, 1970. Amended by P.A. 76-2161, § 1, eff. July 1, 1970; P.A. 81-552, § 1, eff. Jan. 1, 1980.

Formerly Ill.Rev.Stat.1991, ch. 95 ½, ¶ 11-308.

5/11-309. Flashing signals

§ 11-309. Flashing signals. Whenever an illuminated flashing red or yellow signal is used in conjunction with a traffic control device it shall require obedience by vehicular traffic as follows:

1. Flashing red (stop signal). When a red lens is illuminated with rapid intermittent flashes, drivers of vehicles shall stop at a clearly marked stop line, but if none, before entering the crosswalk on the near side of the intersection, or if none, then at a point nearest the intersecting roadway where the driver has a view of approaching traffic on the intersecting roadway before entering the intersection and the right to proceed shall be subject to the rules applicable after making a stop at a stop sign.

2. Flashing yellow (caution signal). When a yellow lens is illuminated with rapid intermittent flashes, drivers of vehicles may proceed through the intersection or past such signal only with caution.

3. This section does not apply at railroad grade crossings. Conduct of drivers of vehicles approaching railroad grade crossings shall be governed by Section 11-1201 of this Act.

P.A. 76-1586, § 11-309, eff. July 1, 1970. Amended by P.A. 76-1737, § 1; P.A. 76-2162, § 1, eff. July 1, 1970.

Formerly Ill.Rev.Stat.1991, ch. 95 ½, ¶ 11-309.

5/11-310. Display of Unauthorized Signs, Signals or Markings

§ 11-310. Display of Unauthorized Signs, Signals or Markings.

(a) No person shall place, maintain or display upon or in view of any highway any unauthorized sign, signal, marking, or device which purports to be or is an imitation of or resembles an official traffic-control device or railroad sign or signal, or which attempts to direct the movement of traffic, or which hides from view or interferes with the movement of traffic or the effectiveness of an official traffic-control device or any railroad sign or signal.

(b) No person shall place or maintain nor shall any public authority permit upon any highway any traffic sign or signal bearing thereon any commercial advertising.

(c) Every such prohibited sign, signal or marking is hereby declared to be a public nuisance and the authority having jurisdiction over the highway is hereby empowered to remove the same or cause it to be removed without notice.

(d) No person shall sell or offer for sale any traffic control device to be used on any street or highway in this State which does not conform to the requirements of this Chapter.

(e) This Section shall not be deemed to prohibit the erection upon private property adjacent to highways of signs giving useful directional information and of a type that cannot be mistaken for official signs.

(f) This Section shall not be deemed to prohibit the erection of Illinois Adopt-A-Highway signs by municipalities, townships, or counties as provided in the Illinois Adopt-A-Highway Act.[1]

(g) Any person failing to comply with this Section shall be guilty of a Class A misdemeanor.

P.A. 76-1586, § 11-310, eff. July 1, 1970. Amended by P.A. 77-49, § 1, eff. Jan. 1, 1972; P.A. 77-732, § 1, eff. Aug. 12, 1971; P.A. 77-2829, § 40, eff. Dec. 22, 1972; P.A. 78-255, § 61, eff. Oct. 1, 1973; P.A. 79-1069, § 1, eff. Jan. 1, 1976; P.A. 80-911, § 1, eff. Oct. 1, 1977; P.A. 81-1509, Art. II, § 71, eff. Sept. 26, 1980; P.A. 87-1118, § 90, eff. Sept. 16, 1992.

Formerly Ill.Rev.Stat.1991, ch. 95 ½, ¶ 11-310.

[1] 605 ILCS 120/1 et seq.

5/11-311. Interference with official traffic-control devices or railroad signs or signals

§ 11-311. Interference with official traffic-control devices or railroad signs or signals. No person shall without lawful authority attempt to or in fact alter, deface, injure, knock down, or remove any official traffic-control device, or any railroad sign or signal or any inscription, shield, or insignia thereon, or any other part thereof.

Every person who is convicted of a violation of this Section shall be guilty of a Class A misdemeanor, punishable by a fine of at least $250 in addition to any other penalties which may be imposed.

P.A. 76-1586, § 11-311, eff. July 1, 1970. Amended by P.A. 80-911, § 1, eff. Oct. 1, 1977; P.A. 83-672, § 1, eff. Jan. 1, 1984.

Formerly Ill.Rev.Stat.1991, ch. 95 ½, ¶ 11-311.

5/11-312. Unlawful Use or Damage to Highways, Appurtenances and Structures

§ 11-312. Unlawful Use or Damage to Highways, Appurtenances and Structures. It shall be unlawful for any person to wilfully injure or damage any public highway or street or any bridge or culvert, or to wilfully damage, injure or remove any sign, signpost, or structure upon or used or constructed in connection with any public highway or street for the protection thereof or for protection or regulation of traffic thereon by any wilfully unusual, improper or unreasonable use thereof, or by wilfully careless driving or use of any vehicle thereon, or by the wilful mutilation, defacing, destruction or removal thereof.

Every person who is convicted of a violation of this Section shall be guilty of a Class A misdemeanor, punishable by a fine of at least $250 in addition to any other penalty which may be imposed.

P.A. 76-1586, § 11-312, eff. July 1, 1970. Amended by P.A. 80-911, § 1, eff. Oct. 1, 1977; P.A. 81-1509, Art. II, § 71, eff. Sept. 26, 1980; P.A. 83-672, § 1, eff. Jan. 1, 1984.

Formerly Ill.Rev.Stat.1991, ch. 95 ½, ¶ 11-312.

5/11-313. Unlawful possession of highway sign or marker

§ 11-313. Unlawful possession of highway sign or marker. The Department and local authorities, with reference to traffic control signs, signals, or markers owned by the Department or local authority, are authorized to indicate the ownership of the signs, signals, or markers in letters not less than ⅜ inch or more than ¾ inch in height, by use of a metal stamp, etching, or other permanent means and, except for employees of the Department or local authorities, police officers, contractors and their employees engaged in a highway construction contract or work on the highway approved by the Department or local authority, it is unlawful for any person to possess such sign, signal, or marker so identified.

P.A. 76-1586, § 11-313, added by P.A. 77-1230, § 1, eff. Aug. 24, 1971. Amended by P.A. 77-2830, Art. 73, § 1, eff. Jan. 1, 1973; P.A. 80-526, § 1, eff. Oct. 1, 1977; P.A. 80-911, § 1, eff. Oct. 1, 1977; P.A. 80-1364, § 36, eff. Aug. 13, 1978; P.A. 91-512, § 5, eff. Aug. 13, 1999.

Formerly Ill.Rev.Stat.1991, ch. 95 ½, ¶ 11-313.

ARTICLE IV. ACCIDENTS

Section

5/11-401. Motor vehicle accidents involving death or personal injuries

§ 11-401. Motor vehicle accidents involving death or personal injuries.

(a) The driver of any vehicle involved in a motor vehicle accident resulting in personal injury to or death of any person shall immediately stop such vehicle at the scene of such accident, or as close thereto as possible and shall then forthwith return to, and in every event shall remain at the scene of the accident until the requirements of Section 11-403 have been fulfilled. Every such stop shall be made without obstructing traffic more than is necessary.

(b) Any person who has failed to stop or to comply with the requirements of paragraph (a) shall, as soon as possible but in no case later than one hour after such motor vehicle accident, or, if hospitalized and incapacitated from reporting at any time during such period, as soon as possible but in no case later than one hour after being discharged from the hospital, report the place of the accident, the date, the approximate time, the driver's name and address, the registration number of the vehicle driven, and the names of all other occupants of such vehicle, at a police station or sheriff's office near the place where such accident occurred. No report made as required under this paragraph shall be used, directly or indirectly, as a basis for the prosecution of any violation of paragraph (a).

For purposes of this Section, personal injury shall mean any injury requiring immediate professional treatment in a medical facility or doctor's office.

(c) Any person failing to comply with paragraph (a) shall be guilty of a Class A misdemeanor.

(d) Any person failing to comply with paragraph (b) is guilty of a Class 4 felony if the motor vehicle accident does not result in the death of any person. Any person failing to comply with paragraph (b) when the accident results in the death of any person is guilty of a Class 2 felony, for which the person, if sentenced to a term of imprisonment, shall be sentenced to a term of not less than 3 years and not more than 14 years.

(e) The Secretary of State shall revoke the driving privilege of any person convicted of a violation of this Section.

P.A. 76-1586, § 11-401, eff. July 1, 1970. Amended by P.A. 77-2720, § 1, eff. Jan. 1, 1973; P.A. 82-141, § 1, eff. Jan. 1, 1982; P.A. 83-831, § 1, eff. Jan. 1, 1984; P.A. 84-272, § 7, eff. Jan. 1, 1986; P.A. 90-543, § 5, eff. Dec. 1, 1997.

Formerly Ill.Rev.Stat.1991, ch. 95 ½, ¶ 11-401.

5/11-402. Motor vehicle accident involving damage to vehicle

§ 11-402. Motor vehicle accident involving damage to vehicle. (a) The driver of any vehicle involved in a motor vehicle accident resulting only in damage to a vehicle which is driven or attended by any person shall immediately stop such vehicle at the scene of such motor vehicle accident or as close thereto as possible, but shall forthwith return to and in every event shall remain at the scene of such motor vehicle accident until the requirements of Section 11-403 have been fulfilled. Every such stop shall be made without obstructing traffic more than is necessary.

Any person failing to comply with this Section shall be guilty of a Class A misdemeanor.

(b) Upon conviction of a violation of this Section, the court shall make a finding as to whether the damage to a vehicle is in excess of $1,000, and in such case a statement of this finding shall be reported to the Secretary of State with the report of conviction as required by Section 6-204 of this Code. Upon receipt of such report of conviction and statement of finding that the damage to a vehicle is in excess of $1,000, the Secretary of State shall suspend the driver's license or any nonresident's driving privilege.

P.A. 76-1586, § 11-402, eff. July 1, 1970. Amended by P.A. 80-911, § 1, eff. Oct. 1, 1977; P.A. 82-141, § 1, eff. Jan. 1, 1982; P.A. 83-831, § 1, eff. Jan. 1, 1984.

Formerly Ill.Rev.Stat.1991, ch. 95 ½, ¶ 11-402.

5/11-403. Duty to give information and render aid

§ 11-403. Duty to give information and render aid. The driver of any vehicle involved in a motor vehicle accident resulting in injury to or death of any person or damage to any vehicle which is driven or attended by any person shall give the driver's name, address, registration number and owner of the vehicle the driver is operating and shall upon request and if available exhibit such driver's license to the person struck or the driver or occupant of or person attending any vehicle collided with and shall render to any person injured in such accident reasonable assistance, including the carrying or the making of arrangements for the carrying of such person to a physician, surgeon or hospital for medical or surgical treatment, if it is apparent that such treatment is necessary or if such carrying is requested by the injured person.

If none of the persons entitled to information pursuant to this Section is in condition to receive and understand such information and no police officer is present, such driver after rendering reasonable assistance shall forthwith report such motor vehicle accident at the nearest office of a duly authorized police authority, disclosing the information required by this Section.

Any person failing to comply with this Section shall be guilty of a Class A misdemeanor.

P.A. 76-1586, § 11-403, eff. July 1, 1970. Amended by P.A. 80-911, § 1, eff. Oct. 1, 1977; P.A. 83-831, § 1, eff. Jan. 1, 1984.

Formerly Ill.Rev.Stat.1991, ch. 95 ½, ¶ 11-403.

5/11-404. Duty upon damaging unattended vehicle or other property

§ 11-404. Duty upon damaging unattended vehicle or other property. The driver of any vehicle which collides with or is involved in a motor vehicle accident with any vehicle which is unattended, or other property, resulting in any damage to such other vehicle or property shall immediately stop and shall then and there either locate and notify the operator or owner of such vehicle or other property of the driver's name, address, registration number and owner of the vehicle the driver was operating or shall attach securely in a conspicuous place on or in the vehicle or other property struck a written notice giving the driver's name, address, registration number and owner of the vehicle the driver was driving and shall without unnecessary delay notify the nearest office of a duly authorized police authority and shall make a written report of such accident when and as required in Section 11-406. Every such stop shall be made without obstructing traffic more than is necessary.

Any person failing to comply with this Section shall be guilty of a Class A misdemeanor.

P.A. 76-1586, § 11-404, eff. July 1, 1970. Amended by P.A. 76-1737, § 1; P.A. 80-911, § 1, eff. Oct. 1, 1977; P.A. 83-831, § 1, eff. Jan. 1, 1984.

Formerly Ill.Rev.Stat.1991, ch. 95 ½, ¶ 11-404.

5/11-405. § 11-405. Repealed by P.A. 76-1738, § 2

5/11-406. Duty to report accident

§ 11-406. Duty to report accident. (a) The driver of a vehicle that is in any manner involved in an accident within this State, resulting in injury to or death of any person, or in which damage to the property of any one person, including himself, in excess of $500 is sustained, shall, as soon as possible but not later than 10 days after the accident, forward a written report of the accident to the Administrator.

(b) Whenever a school bus is involved in an accident in this State, caused by a collision, a sudden stop or otherwise, resulting in any property damage, personal injury or death and whenever an accident occurs within 50 feet of a school bus in this State resulting in personal injury to or the death of any person while awaiting or preparing to board the bus or immediately after exiting the bus, the driver shall as soon as possible but not later than 10 days after the accident, forward a written report to the Department of Transportation. If a report is also required under Subsection (a) of this Section, that report and the report required by this Subsection shall be submitted on a single form.

(c) The Administrator may require any driver, occupant or owner of a vehicle involved in an accident of which report must be made as provided in this Section or Section 11-410 of this Chapter to file supplemental reports whenever the original report is insufficient in the opinion of the Secretary of State or the Administrator, and may require witnesses of the accident to submit written reports to the Administrator. The report may include photographs, charts, sketches, and graphs.

(d) Should the Administrator learn through other reports of accidents required by law of the occurrence of an accident reportable under this Article and the driver, owner, or witness has not reported as required under Subsections (a), (b) or (c) of this Section or Section 11-410, within the time specified, the person is not relieved of the responsibility and the Administrator shall notify the person by first class mail directed to his last known address of his legal obligation. However, the notification is not a condition precedent to impose the penalty for failure to report as provided in Subsection (e).

(e) The Secretary of State shall suspend the driver's license or any non-resident's driving privilege of any person who fails or neglects to make report of a traffic accident as required or as required by any other law of this State.

P.A. 76-1586, § 11-406, eff. July 1, 1970. Amended by P.A. 76-2473, § 1, eff. July 1, 1971; P.A. 77-42, § 1, eff. July 1, 1971; P.A. 77-1910, § 1, eff. July 1, 1972; P.A. 78-255, § 61, eff. Oct. 1, 1973; P.A. 78-1244, § 1, eff. Sept. 5, 1974; P.A. 78-1297, § 58, eff. March 4, 1975; P.A. 80-746, § 1, eff. Oct. 1, 1977; P.A. 87-829, § 1, eff. Jan. 17, 1992.

Formerly Ill.Rev.Stat.1991, ch. 95 ½, ¶ 11-406.

5/11-407. Immediate notice of accident

§ 11-407. Immediate notice of accident. (a) The driver of a vehicle which is in any manner involved in an accident described in Section 11-406 of this Chapter shall, if no police officer is present, give notice of the accident by the fastest available means of communication to the local police department if such accident occurs within a municipality or otherwise to the nearest office of the county sheriff or nearest headquarters of the Illinois State Police.

(b) Whenever the driver of a vehicle is physically incapable of giving immediate notice of an accident as required in Subsection (a) and there was another occupant in the vehicle at the time of the accident capable of doing so, that occupant must give notice as required in Subsection (a).

P.A. 76-1586, § 11-407, eff. July 1, 1970. Amended by P.A. 76-2163, § 1, eff. July 1, 1970.

Formerly Ill.Rev.Stat.1991, ch. 95 ½, ¶ 11-407.

5/11-408. Police to report motor vehicle accident investigations

§ 11-408. Police to report motor vehicle accident investigations.

(a) Every law enforcement officer who investigates a motor vehicle accident for which a report is required by this Article or who prepares a written report as a result of an investigation either at the time and scene of such motor vehicle accident or thereafter by interviewing participants or witnesses shall forward a written report of such motor vehicle accident to the Administrator on forms provided by the Administrator under Section 11-411 within 10 days after investigation of the motor vehicle accident, or within such other time as is prescribed by the Administrator. Such written reports required to be forwarded by law enforcement officers and the information contained therein are privileged as to the Secretary of State and the Department and, in the case of second division vehicles operated under certificate of convenience and necessity issued by the Illinois Commerce Commission, to the Commission, but shall not be held confidential by the reporting law enforcement officer or agency. The Secretary of State may also disclose notations of accident involvement maintained on individual driving records. However, the Administrator or the Secretary of State may require a supplemental written report from the reporting law enforcement officer and such supplemental report shall be for the privileged use of the Secretary of State and the Department and shall be held confidential.

(b) The Department at its discretion may require a supplemental written report from the reporting law enforcement officer on a form supplied by the Department to be submitted directly to the Department. Such supplemental report may be used only for accident studies and statistical or analytical purposes, and shall be for the privileged use of the Department and shall be held confidential.

(c) The Department at its discretion may also provide for in-depth investigations of a motor vehicle accident by individuals or special investigation groups, including but not limited to police officers, photographers, engineers, doctors, mechanics, and as a result of the investigation may require the submission of written reports, photographs, charts, sketches, graphs, or a combination of all. Such individual written reports, photographs, charts, sketches, or graphs may be used only for accident studies and statistical or analytical purposes, shall be for the privileged use of the Department and held confidential, and shall not be used in any trial, civil or criminal.

(d) On and after July 1, 1997, law enforcement officers who have reason to suspect that the motor vehicle accident was the result of a driver's loss of consciousness due to a medical condition, as defined by the Driver's License Medical Review Law of 1992,[1] or the result of any medical condition that impaired the driver's ability to safely operate a motor vehicle shall notify the Secretary of this determination. The Secretary, in conjunction with the Driver's License Medical Advisory Board, shall determine by administrative rule the temporary conditions not required to be reported under the provisions of this Section. The Secretary shall, in conjunction with the Illinois State Police and representatives of local and county law enforcement agencies, promulgate any rules necessary and develop the procedures and documents that may be required to obtain written, electronic, or other agreed upon methods of notification to implement the provisions of this Section.

(e) Law enforcement officers reporting under the provisions of subsection (d) of this Section shall enjoy the same immunities granted members of the Driver's License Medical Advisory Board under Section 6-910 of this Code.

(f) All information furnished to the Secretary under subsection (d) of this Section shall be deemed confidential and for the privileged use of the Secretary in accordance with the provisions of subsection (j) of Section 2-123 of this Code.

P.A. 76-1586, § 11-408, eff. July 1, 1970. Amended by P.A. 76-2473, § 1, eff. July 1, 1971; P.A. 77-42, § 1, eff. July 1, 1971; P.A. 77-1910, § 1, eff. July 1, 1972; P.A. 78-255, § 61, eff. Oct. 1, 1973; P.A. 79-865, § 1, eff. Jan. 1, 1976; P.A. 83-831, § 1, eff. Jan. 1, 1984; P.A. 89-503, § 10, eff. July 1, 1996; P.A. 89-584, § 5, eff. July 31, 1996; P.A. 90-14, Art. 2, § 2-225, eff. July 1, 1997.

Formerly Ill.Rev.Stat.1991, ch. 95 ½, ¶ 11-408.

[1] 625 ILCS 5/6-900 et seq.

P.A. 90-14, Article 2, of the First 1997 General Revisory Act, resolved multiple actions in the 89th General Assembly and made certain technical corrections in P.A. 89-443 through P.A. 89-707.

5/11-409. False motor vehicle accident reports or notices

§ 11-409. False motor vehicle accident reports or notices. Any person who provides information in an oral or written report required by this Code with knowledge or reason to believe that such information is false shall be guilty of a Class C misdemeanor.

P.A. 76-1586, § 11-409, eff. July 1, 1970. Amended by P.A. 77-2720, § 1, eff. Jan. 2, 1972; P.A. 80-911, § 1, eff. Oct. 1, 1977; P.A. 81-1509, Art. II, § 71, eff. Sept. 26, 1980; P.A. 83-831, § 1, eff. Jan. 1, 1984.

Formerly Ill.Rev.Stat.1991, ch. 95 ½, ¶ 11-409.

5/11-410. When driver fails to report a motor vehicle accident

§ 11-410. When driver fails to report a motor vehicle accident. Whenever the driver of a vehicle is physically incapable of making a required written accident report and if there was another occupant in the vehicle at the time of the motor vehicle accident capable of making a written report, such occupant shall make or cause to be made such written report. If said driver fails for any reason to make such report, the owner of the vehicle involved in such motor vehicle accident, shall, as soon as practicable, make said report to the Administrator.

P.A. 76-1586, § 11-410, eff. July 1, 1970. Amended by P.A. 76-2473, § 1, eff. July 1, 1971; P.A. 77-42, § 1, eff. July 1, 1971; P.A. 83-831, § 1, eff. Jan. 1, 1984.

Formerly Ill.Rev.Stat.1991, ch. 95 ½, ¶ 11-410.

5/11-411. Accident report forms

§ 11-411. Accident report forms. (a) The Administrator must prepare and upon request supply to police departments, sheriffs and other appropriate agencies or individuals, forms for written accident reports as required hereunder, suitable with respect to the persons required to make such reports and the purposes to be served. The written reports must call for sufficiently detailed information to disclose with reference to a vehicle accident the cause, conditions then existing, and the persons and vehicles involved or any other data concerning such accident that may be required for a complete analysis of all related circumstances and events leading to the accident or subsequent to the occurrence.

(b) Every accident report required to be made in writing must be made on an appropriate form approved or provided by the Administrator and must contain all the information required therein unless that information is not available.

(c) Should special accident studies be required by the Administrator, the Administrator may provide the supplemental forms for the special studies.

P.A. 76-1586, § 11-411, eff. July 1, 1970. Amended by P.A. 76-2473, § 1, eff. July 1, 1971; P.A. 77-42, § 1, eff. July 1, 1971; P.A. 77-1910, § 1, eff. July 1, 1972; P.A. 78-255, § 61, eff. Oct. 1, 1973.

Formerly Ill.Rev.Stat.1991, ch. 95 ½, ¶ 11-411.

5/11-412. Motor vehicle accident reports confidential

§ 11-412. Motor vehicle accident reports confidential. All required written motor vehicle accident reports and supplemental reports shall be without prejudice to the individual so reporting and shall be for the confidential use of the Department and the Secretary of State and, in the case of second division vehicles operated under certificate of convenience and necessity issued by the Illinois Commerce Commission, of the Commission, except that the Administrator or the Secretary of State or the Commission may disclose the identity of a person involved in a motor vehicle accident when such identity is not otherwise known or when such person denies his presence at such motor vehicle accident and the Department shall disclose the identity of the insurance carrier, if any, upon demand. The Secretary of State may also disclose notations of accident involvement maintained on individual driving records. The Department may furnish copies of its written accident reports to federal and State agencies that are engaged in highway safety research and studies. Reports furnished to any agency other than the Secretary of State or the Illinois Commerce Commission may be used only for statistical or analytical purposes and shall be held confidential by that agency. No such written report shall be used as evidence in any trial, civil or criminal, arising out of a motor vehicle accident, except that the Administrator shall furnish upon demand of any person who has, or claims to have, made such a written report, or upon demand of any court, a certificate showing that a specified written accident report has or has not been made to the Administrator solely to prove a compliance or a failure to comply with the requirement that such a written report be made to the Administrator.

The Department of Transportation at its discretion may provide for in-depth investigations of accidents involving Department employees. A written report describing the preventability of such an accident may be prepared to enhance the safety of Department employees. Such reports and any opinions expressed in the review of the accident as to the preventability of the accident shall be for the privileged use of the Department and held confidential and shall not be obtainable or used in any civil or criminal proceeding.

P.A. 76-1586, § 11-412, eff. July 1, 1970. Amended by P.A. 76-2473, § 1, eff. July 1, 1971; P.A. 77-42, § 1, eff. July 1, 1971; P.A. 77-330, § 1, eff. July 22, 1971; P.A. 77-1910, § 1, eff. July 1, 1972; P.A. 78-255, § 61, eff. Oct. 1, 1973; P.A. 79-865, § 1, eff. Jan. 1, 1976; P.A. 82-523, § 1, eff. Jan. 1, 1982; P.A. 83-831, § 1, eff. Jan. 1, 1984; P.A. 86-564, § 1, eff. Jan. 1, 1990; P.A. 89-503, § 10, eff. July 1, 1996.

Formerly Ill.Rev.Stat.1991, ch. 95 ½, ¶ 11-412.

5/11-413. Coroners to report

§ 11-413. Coroners to report. All coroners shall on or before the 10th day of each month report in writing to the Administrator the death of any person within their respective jurisdiction, during the preceding calendar month, as the result of a traffic accident giving the time and place of the accident and the circumstances relating thereto.

P.A. 76-1586, § 11-413, eff. July 1, 1970. Amended by P.A. 76-2473, § 1, eff. July 1, 1971; P.A. 77-42, § 1, eff. July 1, 1971; P.A. 83-831, § 1, eff. Jan. 1, 1984.

Formerly Ill.Rev.Stat.1991, ch. 95 ½, ¶ 11-413.

5/11-414. Department to tabulate and analyze motor vehicle accident reports

§ 11-414. Department to tabulate and analyze motor vehicle accident reports. The Department shall tabulate and may analyze all written motor vehicle accident reports received in compliance with this Code and shall publish annually or at more frequent intervals statistical information based thereon as to the number and circumstances of traffic accidents. The Department:

1. shall submit a report of school bus accidents and accidents resulting in personal injury to or the death of any person within 50 feet of a school bus while awaiting or preparing to board the bus or immediately after exiting the bus to the National Highway Safety Advisory Committee annually or as requested by the Committee;

2. shall compile, maintain, and make available to the public statistical information relating to traffic accidents involving medical transport vehicles;

3. may conduct special investigations of motor vehicle accidents and may solicit supplementary reports from drivers, owners, police departments, sheriffs, coroners, or any other individual. Failure of any individual to submit a supplementary report subjects such individual to the same penalties for failure to report as designated under Section 11-406.

P.A. 76-1586, § 11-414, eff. July 1, 1970. Amended by P.A. 76-2473, § 1, eff. July 1, 1971; P.A. 78-1244, § 1, eff. Sept. 5, 1974; P.A. 82-433, § 1, eff. Sept. 8, 1981; P.A. 83-831, § 1, eff. Jan. 1, 1984.

Formerly Ill.Rev.Stat.1991, ch. 95 ½, ¶ 11-414.

Section 3 of P.A. 82-433 approved Sept. 8, 1981, provided:

"This Act takes effect upon its becoming a law, except that the provisions relating to safety tests and proof of financial responsibility for medical transport vehicles apply only to applications for and the issuance of registration plates which are required to be displayed on January 1, 1982 or thereafter."

5/11-415. Municipalities may require traffic accident reports

§ 11-415. Municipalities may require traffic accident reports. Municipalities may by ordinance require that the driver or owner of a vehicle involved in a traffic accident file with the designated municipal office a written report of such accident. All such reports shall be for the confidential use of the municipal office and subject to the provisions of Section 11-412.

P.A. 76-1586, § 11-415, eff. July 1, 1970. Amended by P.A. 76-2164, § 1, eff. July 1, 1970; P.A. 83-831, § 1, eff. Jan. 1, 1984.

Formerly Ill.Rev.Stat.1991, ch. 95 ½, ¶ 11-415.

5/11-416. Furnishing copies—Fees

§ 11-416. Furnishing copies—Fees. The Department of State Police may furnish copies of an Illinois State Police Traffic Accident Report that has been investigated by the State Police and shall be paid a fee of $5 for each such copy, or in the case of an accident which was investigated by an accident reconstruction officer or accident reconstruction team, a fee of $20 shall be paid.

Other State law enforcement agencies or law enforcement agencies of local authorities may furnish copies of traffic accident reports prepared by such agencies and may receive a fee not to exceed $5 for each copy or in the case of an accident which was investigated by an accident reconstruction officer or accident reconstruction team, the State or local law enforcement agency may receive a fee not to exceed $20.

Any written accident report required or requested to be furnished the Administrator shall be provided without cost or fee charges authorized under this Section or any other provision of law.

P.A. 76-1586, § 11-416, eff. July 1, 1970. Amended by P.A. 76-2743, § 1, eff. July 1, 1971; P.A. 77-534, § 1, eff. July 31, 1971; P.A. 83-310, § 1, eff. Sept. 14, 1983; P.A. 84-25, Art. IV, § 27, eff. July 18, 1985; P.A. 84-1044, § 1, eff. July 1, 1986; P.A. 84-1308, Art. II, § 96, eff. Aug. 25, 1986; P.A. 90-89, § 15, eff. Jan. 1, 1998.

Formerly Ill.Rev.Stat.1991, ch. 95 ½, ¶ 11-416.

ARTICLE V. DRIVING WHILE INTOXICATED, TRANSPORTING ALCOHOLIC LIQUOR, AND RECKLESS DRIVING

Section

5/11-500. Definitions

§ 11-500. Definitions. For the purposes of interpreting Sections 6-206.1 and 6-208.1 of this Code, "first offender" shall mean any person who has not had a previous conviction or court assigned supervision for violating Section 11-501, or a similar provision of a local ordinance, or a conviction in any other state for a violation of driving while under the influence or a similar offense where the cause of action is the same or substantially similar to this Code or any person who has not had a driver's license suspension for violating Section 11-501.1 within 5 years prior to the date of the current offense, except in cases where the driver submitted to chemical testing resulting in an alcohol concentration of 0.08 or more, or any amount of a drug, substance, or compound in such person's blood or urine resulting from the unlawful use or consumption of cannabis listed in the Cannabis Control Act,[1] a controlled substance listed in the Illinois Controlled Substances Act,[2] or an intoxicating compound listed in the Use of Intoxicating Compounds Act[3] and was subsequently found not guilty of violating Section 11-501, or a similar provision of a local ordinance.

P.A. 76-1586, § 11-500, added by P.A. 84-272, § 7, eff. Jan. 1, 1986. Amended by P.A. 86-929, § 2, eff. Sept. 21, 1989; P.A. 86-1019, § 7, eff. July 1, 1990; P.A. 86-1475, Art. 2, § 2-25, eff. Jan. 10, 1991; P.A. 90-43, § 5, eff. July 2, 1997; P.A. 90-779, § 5, eff. Jan. 1, 1999.

Formerly Ill.Rev.Stat.1991, ch. 95 ½, ¶ 11-500.

1 720 ILCS 550/1 et seq.

2 720 ILCS 570/100 et seq.

3 720 ILCS 690/0.01 et seq.

P.A. 90-779 incorporated the amendment by P.A. 90-43.

5/11-500.1. Immunity

§ 11-500.1. Immunity.

(a) A person authorized under this Article to withdraw blood or collect urine shall not be civilly liable for damages when the person, in good faith, withdraws blood or collects urine for evidentiary purposes under this Code, upon the request of a law enforcement officer, unless the act is performed in a willful and wanton manner.

(b) As used in this Section, "willful and wanton manner" means a course of action that shows an actual or deliberate intention to cause harm or which, if not intentional, shows an utter indifference to or conscious disregard for the health or safety of another.

P.A. 76-1586, § 11-500.1, added by P.A. 89-689, § 70, eff. Dec. 31, 1996.

5/11-501. Driving while under the influence of alcohol, other drug or drugs, intoxicating compound or compounds or any combination thereof

§ 11-501. Driving while under the influence of alcohol, other drug or drugs, intoxicating compound or compounds or any combination thereof.

(a) A person shall not drive or be in actual physical control of any vehicle within this State while:

(1) the alcohol concentration in the person's blood or breath is 0.08 or more based on the definition of blood and breath units in Section 11-501.2;

(2) under the influence of alcohol;

(3) under the influence of any intoxicating compound or combination of intoxicating compounds to a degree that renders the person incapable of driving safely;

(4) under the influence of any other drug or combination of drugs to a degree that renders the person incapable of safely driving;

(5) under the combined influence of alcohol, other drug or drugs, or intoxicating compound or compounds to a degree that renders the person incapable of safely driving; or

(6) there is any amount of a drug, substance, or compound in the person's breath, blood, or urine resulting from the unlawful use or consumption of cannabis listed in the Cannabis Control Act,[1] a controlled substance listed in the Illinois Controlled Substances Act,[2] or an intoxicating compound listed in the Use of Intoxicating Compounds Act.[3]

(b) The fact that any person charged with violating this Section is or has been legally entitled to use alcohol, other drug or drugs, or intoxicating compound or compounds, or any combination thereof, shall not constitute a defense against any charge of violating this Section.

(c) Except as provided under paragraphs (c-3), (c-4), and (d) of this Section, every person convicted of violating this Section or a similar provision of a local ordinance, shall be guilty of a Class A misdemeanor and, in addition to any other criminal or administrative action, for any second conviction of violating this Section or a similar provision of a law of another state or local ordinance committed within 5 years of a previous violation of this Section or a similar provision of a local ordinance shall be mandatorily sentenced to a minimum of 5 days of imprisonment or assigned to a minimum of 30 days of community service as may be determined by the court. Every person convicted of violating this Section or a similar provision of a local ordinance shall be subject to an additional mandatory minimum fine of $500 and an additional mandatory 5 days of community service in a program benefiting children if the person committed a violation of paragraph (a) or a similar provision of a local ordinance while transporting a person under age 16. Every person convicted a second time for violating this Section or a similar provision of a local ordinance within 5 years of a previous violation of this Section or a similar provision of a law of another state or local ordinance shall be subject to an additional mandatory minimum fine of $500 and an additional 10 days of mandatory community service in a program benefiting children if the current offense was committed while transporting a person under age 16. The imprisonment or assignment under this subsection shall not be subject to suspension nor shall the person be eligible for probation in order to reduce the sentence or assignment.

(c-1) (1) A person who violates this Section during a period in which his or her driving privileges are revoked or suspended, where the revocation or suspension was for a violation of this Section, Section 11-501.1, paragraph (b) of Section 11-401, or Section 9-3 of the Criminal Code of 1961[4] is guilty of a Class 4 felony.

(2) A person who violates this Section a third time during a period in which his or her driving privileges are revoked or suspended where the revocation or suspension was for a violation of this Section, Section 11-501. 1, paragraph (b) of Section 11-401, or Section 9-3 of the Criminal Code of 1961 is guilty of a Class 3 felony.

(3) A person who violates this Section a fourth or subsequent time during a period in which his or her driving privileges are revoked or suspended where the revocation or suspension was for a violation of this Section, Section 11-501.1, paragraph (b) of Section 11-401, or Section 9-3 of the Criminal Code of 1961 is guilty of a Class 2 felony.

(c-2) (Blank).

(c-3) Every person convicted of violating this Section or a similar provision of a local ordinance who had a child under age 16 in the vehicle at the time of the offense shall have his or her punishment under this Act enhanced by 2 days of imprisonment for a first offense, 10 days of imprisonment for a second offense, 30 days of imprisonment for a third offense, and 90 days of imprisonment for a fourth or subsequent offense, in addition to the fine and community service required under subsection (c) and the possible imprisonment required under subsection (d). The imprisonment or assignment under this subsection shall not be subject to suspension nor shall the person be eligible for probation in order to reduce the sentence or assignment.

(c-4) When a person is convicted of violating Section 11-501 of this Code or a similar provision of a local ordinance, the following penalties apply when his or her blood, breath, or urine was .16 or more based on the definition of blood, breath, or urine units in Section 11-501.2 or when that person is convicted of violating this Section while transporting a child under the age of 16:

(1) A person who is convicted of violating subsection (a) of Section 11-501 of this Code a first time, in addition to any other penalty that may be imposed under subsection (c), is subject to a mandatory minimum of 100 hours of community service and a minimum fine of $500.

(2) A person who is convicted of violating subsection (a) of Section 11-501 of this Code a second time within 10 years, in addition to any other penalty that may be imposed under subsection (c), is subject to a mandatory minimum of 2 days of imprisonment and a minimum fine of $1,250.

(3) A person who is convicted of violating subsection (a) of Section 11-501 of this Code a third time within 20 years is guilty of a Class 4 felony and, in addition to any other penalty that may be imposed under subsection (c), is subject to a mandatory minimum of 90 days of imprisonment and a minimum fine of $2,500.

(4) A person who is convicted of violating this subsection (c-4) a fourth or subsequent time is guilty of a Class 2 felony and, in addition to any other penalty that may be imposed under subsection (c), is not eligible for a sentence of probation or conditional discharge and is subject to a minimum fine of $2,500.

(d) (1) Every person convicted of committing a violation of this Section shall be guilty of aggravated driving under the influence of alcohol, other drug or drugs, or intoxicating compound or compounds, or any combination thereof if:

(A) the person committed a violation of this Section, or a similar provision of a law of another state or a local ordinance when the cause of action is the same as or substantially similar to this Section, for the third or subsequent time;

(B) the person committed a violation of paragraph (a) while driving a school bus with children on board;

(C) the person in committing a violation of paragraph (a) was involved in a motor vehicle accident that resulted in great bodily harm or permanent disability or disfigurement to another, when the violation was a proximate cause of the injuries;

(D) the person committed a violation of paragraph (a) for a second time and has been previously convicted of violating Section 9-3 of the Criminal Code of 1961 relating to reckless homicide in which the person was determined to have been under the influence of alcohol, other drug or drugs, or intoxicating compound or compounds as an element of the offense or the person has previously been convicted under subparagraph (C) of this paragraph (1); or

(E) the person, in committing a violation of paragraph (a) while driving at any speed in a school speed zone at a time when a speed limit of 20 miles per hour was in effect under subsection (a) of Section 11-605 of this Code, was involved in a motor vehicle accident that resulted in bodily harm, other than great bodily harm or permanent disability or disfigurement, to another person, when the violation of paragraph (a) was a proximate cause of the bodily harm.

(2) Aggravated driving under the influence of alcohol, other drug or drugs, or intoxicating compound or compounds, or any combination thereof is a Class 4 felony. For a violation of subparagraph (C) of paragraph (1) of this subsection (d), the defendant, if sentenced to a term of imprisonment, shall be sentenced to not less than one year nor more than 12 years. For any prosecution under this subsection (d), a certified copy of the driving abstract of the defendant shall be admitted as proof of any prior conviction.

(e) After a finding of guilt and prior to any final sentencing, or an order for supervision, for an offense based upon an arrest for a violation of this Section or a similar provision of a local ordinance, individuals shall be required to undergo a professional evaluation to determine if an alcohol, drug, or intoxicating compound abuse problem exists and the extent of the problem, and undergo the imposition of treatment as appropriate. Programs conducting these evaluations shall be licensed by the Department of Human Services. The cost of any professional evaluation shall be paid for by the individual required to undergo the professional evaluation.

(f) Every person found guilty of violating this Section, whose operation of a motor vehicle while in violation of this Section proximately caused any incident resulting in an appropriate emergency response, shall be liable for the expense of an emergency response as provided under Section 5-5-3 of the Unified Code of Corrections.[5]

(g) The Secretary of State shall revoke the driving privileges of any person convicted under this Section or a similar provision of a local ordinance.

(h) Every person sentenced under paragraph (2) or (3) of subsection (c-1) of this Section or subsection (d) of this Section and who receives a term of probation or conditional discharge shall be required to serve a minimum term of either 60 days community service or 10 days of imprisonment as a condition of the probation or conditional discharge. This mandatory minimum term of imprisonment or assignment of community service shall not be suspended and shall not be subject to reduction by the court.

(i) The Secretary of State shall require the use of ignition interlock devices on all vehicles owned by an individual who has been convicted of a second or subsequent offense of this Section or a similar provision of a local ordinance. The Secretary shall establish by rule and regulation the procedures for certification and use of the interlock system.

(j) In addition to any other penalties and liabilities, a person who is found guilty of or pleads guilty to violating this Section, including any person placed on court supervision for violating this Section, shall be fined $100, payable to the circuit clerk, who shall distribute the money to the law enforcement agency that made the arrest. If the person has been previously convicted of violating this Section or a similar provision of a local ordinance, the fine shall be $200. In the event that more than one agency is responsible for the arrest, the $100 or $200 shall be shared equally. Any moneys received by a law enforcement agency under this subsection (j) shall be used to purchase law enforcement equipment that will assist in the prevention of alcohol related criminal violence throughout the State. This shall include, but is not limited to, in-car video cameras, radar and laser speed detection devices, and alcohol breath testers. Any moneys received by the Department of State Police under this subsection (j) shall be deposited into the State Police DUI Fund and shall be used to purchase law enforcement equipment that will assist in the prevention of alcohol related criminal violence throughout the State.

P.A. 76–1586, § 11–501, eff. July 1, 1970. Amended by P.A. 76–1738, § 1; P.A. 77–575, § 1, eff. July 31, 1971; P.A. 77–2720, § 1, eff. Jan. 1, 1973; P.A. 78–255, § 61, eff. Oct. 1, 1973; P.A. 80–1495, § 36, eff. Jan. 8, 1979; P.A. 82–221, § 3, eff. Jan. 1, 1982; P.A. 82–311, § 1, eff. Jan. 1, 1982; P.A. 82–783, Art. III, § 37, eff. July 13, 1982; P.A. 83–204, § 2, eff. Jan. 1, 1984; P.A. 83–1281, § 1, eff. July 1, 1985; P.A. 84–272, § 7, eff. Jan. 1, 1986; P.A. 84–899, § 1, eff. Jan. 1, 1986; P.A. 84–916, § 2, eff. Jan. 1, 1986; P.A. 84–1308, Art. II, § 96, eff. Aug. 25, 1986; P.A. 84–1394, § 5, eff. Sept. 18, 1986; P.A. 85–303, § 1, eff. Jan. 1, 1988; P.A. 86–581, § 2, eff. Jan. 1, 1990; P.A. 86–1019, § 7, eff. July 1, 1990; P.A. 86–1475, Art. 2, § 2–25, eff. Jan. 10, 1991; P.A. 87–274, § 2, eff. Jan. 1, 1992; P.A. 87–1073, § 2, eff. Jan. 1, 1993; P.A. 87–1074, § 2, eff. Jan. 1, 1993; P.A. 87–1075, § 2, eff. Jan. 1, 1993; P.A. 87–1198, § 6, eff. Sept. 25, 1992; P.A. 87–1222, § 1, eff. July 1, 1993; P.A. 88–45, Art. II, § 2–54, eff. July 6, 1993; P.A. 88–238, § 5, eff. Jan. 1, 1994; P.A. 88–433, § 1, eff. Jan. 1, 1994; P.A. 88–670, Art. 2, § 2–59, eff. Dec. 2, 1994; P.A. 88–680, Art. 20, § 20–900, eff. Jan. 1, 1995; P.A. 89–8, Art. 1, § 1–5, eff. March 21, 1995; P.A. 89–156, § 5, eff. Jan. 1, 1996; P.A. 89–203, § 25, eff. July 21, 1995; P.A. 89–507, Art. 90, § 90C–31, eff. July 1, 1997; P.A. 89–626, Art. 2, § 2–66, eff. Aug. 9, 1996; P.A. 90–43, § 5, eff. July 2, 1997; P.A. 90–400, § 5, eff. Aug. 15, 1997; P.A. 90–611, § 5, eff. Jan. 1, 1999; P.A. 90–655, § 153, eff. July 30, 1998; P.A. 90–738, § 5, eff. Jan. 1, 1999; P.A. 90–779, § 5, eff. Jan. 1, 1999; P.A. 91–126, § 5, eff. July 16, 1999; P.A. 91–357, § 231, eff. July 29, 1999. Re-enacted by P.A. 91–692, Art. 20, § 20–900, eff. April 13, 2000. Amended by P.A. 91–822, § 10, eff. June 13, 2000; P.A. 92–248, § 5, eff. Aug. 3, 2001; P.A. 92–418, § 10, eff. Aug. 17, 2001; P.A. 92–420, § 5, eff. Aug. 17, 2001; P.A. 92–429, § 5, eff. Jan. 1, 2002; P.A. 92–431, § 10, eff. Jan. 1, 2002; P.A. 92–651, § 77, eff. July 11, 2002.

Formerly Ill.Rev.Stat.1991, ch. 95 ½, ¶ 11–501.

1 720 ILCS 550/1 et seq.

2 35 ILCS 570/1 et seq.

3 720 ILCS 690/0.01 et seq.

4 720 ILCS 5/11–501, 5/1–401, 5/9–3.

5 730 ILCS 5/5–5–3.

Validity

The Supreme Court of Illinois held that P.A. 88–680 violated the single-subject rule of the Illinois Constitution in the case of People v. Cervantes, 1999, 243 Ill.Dec. 233, 189 Ill.2d 80, 723 N.E.2d 265; P.A. 91–692 re-enacted this section as contained in P.A. 88–680, including subsequent amendments in order "to remove any question as to the validity or content of those provisions."

On November 18, 1999, the Supreme Court of Illinois held that P.A. 89–203 violated the single-subject rule of the Illinois Constitution in the case of People v. Wooters, 1999, 243 Ill.Dec. 33, 188 Ill.2d 500, 722 N.E.2d 1102.

For purpose of P.A. 91–692, see Historical and Statutory Notes following 625 ILCS 5/6–303.

P.A. 92–651, the First 2002 General Revisory Act, amended various Acts to delete obsolete text, to correct patent and technical errors, to revise cross references, to resolve multiple actions in the 91st and 92nd General Assemblies and to make certain technical corrections in P.A. 91–937 through P.A. 92–520.

See 5 ILCS 70/6 as to the effect of (1) more than one amendment of a section at the same session of the General Assembly or (2) two or more acts relating to the same subject matter enacted by the same General Assembly.

5/11–501.1. Suspension of drivers license; statutory summary alcohol, other drug or drugs, or intoxicating compound or compounds related suspension; implied consent

§ 11–501.1. Suspension of drivers license; statutory summary alcohol, other drug or drugs, or intoxicating compound or compounds related suspension; implied consent.

(a) Any person who drives or is in actual physical control of a motor vehicle upon the public highways of this State shall be deemed to have given consent, subject to the provisions of Section 11–501.2, to a chemical test or tests of blood, breath, or urine for the purpose of determining the content of alcohol, other drug or drugs, or intoxicating compound or compounds or any combination thereof in the person's blood if arrested, as evidenced by the issuance of a Uniform Traffic Ticket, for any offense as defined in Section 11–501 or a similar provision of a local ordinance. The test or tests shall be administered at the direction of the arresting officer. The law enforcement agency employing the officer shall designate which of the aforesaid tests shall be administered. A urine test may be administered even after a blood or breath test or both has been administered. For purposes of this Section, an Illinois law enforcement officer of this State who is investigating the person for any offense defined in Section 11–501 may travel into an adjoining state, where the person has been transported for medical care, to complete an investigation and to request that the person submit to the test or tests set forth in this Section. The requirements of this Section that the person be arrested are inapplicable, but the officer shall issue the person a Uniform Traffic Ticket for an offense as defined in Section 11–501 or a similar provision of a local ordinance prior to requesting that the person submit to the test or tests. The issuance of the Uniform Traffic Ticket shall not constitute an arrest, but shall be for the purpose of notifying the person that he or she is subject to the provisions of this Section and of the officer's belief of the existence of probable cause to arrest. Upon returning to this State, the officer shall file the Uniform Traffic Ticket with the Circuit Clerk of the county where the offense was committed, and shall seek the issuance of an arrest warrant or a summons for the person.

(b) Any person who is dead, unconscious, or who is otherwise in a condition rendering the person incapable of refusal, shall be deemed not to have withdrawn the consent provided by paragraph (a) of this Section and the test or tests may be administered, subject to the provisions of Section 11–501.2.

(c) A person requested to submit to a test as provided above shall be warned by the law enforcement officer requesting the test that a refusal to submit to the test will result in the statutory summary suspension of the person's privilege to operate a motor vehicle as provided in Section 6–208.1 of this Code. The person shall also be warned by the law enforcement officer that if the person submits to the test or tests provided in paragraph (a) of this Section and the alcohol concentration in the person's blood or breath is 0.08 or greater, or any amount of a drug, substance, or compound resulting from the unlawful use or consumption of cannabis as covered by the Cannabis Control Act,[1] a controlled substance listed in the Illinois Controlled Substances Act,[2] or an intoxicating compound listed in the Use of Intoxicating Compounds Act [3] is detected in the person's blood or urine, a statutory summary suspension of the person's privilege to operate a motor vehicle, as provided in Sections 6–208.1 and 11–501.1 of this Code, will be imposed.

A person who is under the age of 21 at the time the person is requested to submit to a test as provided above shall, in addition to the warnings provided for in this Section, be further warned by the law enforcement officer requesting the test that if the person submits to the test or tests provided in paragraph (a) of this Section and the alcohol concentration in the person's blood or breath is greater than 0.00 and less than 0.08, a suspension of the person's privilege to operate a motor vehicle, as provided under Sections 6–208.2 and 11–501.8 of this Code, will be imposed. The results of this test shall be admissible in a civil or criminal action or proceeding arising from an arrest for an offense as defined in Section 11–501 of this Code or a similar provision of a local ordinance or pursuant to Section 11–501.4 in prosecutions for reckless homicide brought under the Criminal Code of 1961.[4] These test results, however, shall be admissible only in actions or proceedings directly related to the incident upon which the test request was made.

(d) If the person refuses testing or submits to a test that discloses an alcohol concentration of 0.08 or more, or any amount of a drug, substance, or intoxicating compound in the person's breath, blood, or urine resulting from the unlawful use or consumption of cannabis listed in the Cannabis Control Act, a controlled substance listed in the Illinois Controlled Substances Act, or an intoxicating compound listed in the Use of Intoxicating Compounds Act, the law enforcement officer shall immediately submit a sworn report to the circuit court of venue and the Secretary of State, certifying that the test or tests was or were requested under paragraph (a) and the person refused to submit to a test, or tests, or submitted to testing that disclosed an alcohol concentration of 0.08 or more.

(e) Upon receipt of the sworn report of a law enforcement officer submitted under paragraph (d), the Secretary of State shall enter the statutory summary suspension for the periods specified in Section 6–208.1, and effective as provided in paragraph (g).

If the person is a first offender as defined in Section 11–500 of this Code, and is not convicted of a violation of Section 11–501 of this Code or a similar provision of a local ordinance, then reports received by the Secretary of State under this Section shall, except during the actual time the Statutory Summary Suspension is in effect, be privileged information and for use only by the courts, police officers, prosecuting authorities or the Secretary of State.

(f) The law enforcement officer submitting the sworn report under paragraph (d) shall serve immediate notice of the statutory summary suspension on the person and the suspension shall be effective as provided in paragraph (g). In cases where the blood alcohol concentration of 0.08 or greater or any amount of a drug, substance, or compound resulting from the unlawful use or consumption of cannabis as covered by the Cannabis Control Act, a controlled substance listed in the Illinois Controlled Substances Act, or an intoxicating compound listed in the Use of Intoxicating Compounds Act is established by a subsequent analysis of blood or urine collected at the time of arrest, the arresting officer or arresting agency shall give notice as provided in this Section or by deposit in the United States mail of the notice in an envelope with postage prepaid and addressed to the person at his address as shown on the Uniform Traffic Ticket and the statutory summary suspension shall begin as provided in paragraph (g). The officer shall confiscate any Illinois driver's license or permit on the person at the time of arrest. If the person has a valid driver's license or permit, the officer shall issue the person a receipt, in a form prescribed by the Secretary of State, that will allow that person to drive during the periods provided for in paragraph (g). The officer shall immediately forward the driver's license or permit to the circuit court of venue along with the sworn report provided for in paragraph (d).

(g) The statutory summary suspension referred to in this Section shall take effect on the 46th day following the date the notice of the statutory summary suspension was given to the person.

(h) The following procedure shall apply whenever a person is arrested for any offense as defined in Section 11–501 or a similar provision of a local ordinance:

Upon receipt of the sworn report from the law enforcement officer, the Secretary of State shall confirm the statutory summary suspension by mailing a notice of the effective date of the suspension to the person and the court of venue. However, should the sworn report be defective by not containing sufficient information or be completed in error, the confirmation of the statutory summary suspension shall not be mailed to the person or entered to the record; instead, the sworn report shall be forwarded to the court of venue with a copy returned to the issuing agency identifying any defect.

P.A. 76–1586, § 11–501.1, added by P.A. 77–1800, § 1, eff. July 1, 1971. Amended by P.A. 77–1881, § 1, eff. July 1, 1972; P.A. 77–1884, § 1, eff. June 30, 1972; P.A. 78–255, § 27, eff. Oct. 1, 1973; P.A. 79–1363, § 12, eff. Oct. 1, 1976;

P.A. 82–221, § 3, eff. Jan. 1, 1982; P.A. 82–311, § 1, eff. Jan. 1, 1982; P.A. 82–783, Art. III, § 37, eff. July 13, 1982; P.A. 84–272, § 7, eff. Jan. 1, 1986; P.A. 84–1394, § 5, eff. Sept. 18, 1986; P.A. 86–929, § 2, eff. Sept. 21, 1989; P.A. 86–1019, § 7, eff. July 1, 1990; P.A. 86–1475, Art. 2, § 2–25, eff. Jan. 10, 1991; P.A. 87–1221, § 1, eff. July 1, 1993; P.A. 88–169, § 1, eff. Jan. 1, 1994; P.A. 88–588, § 5, eff. Jan. 1, 1995; P.A. 90–43, § 5, eff. July 2, 1997; P.A. 90–779, § 5, eff. Jan. 1, 1999; P.A. 91–357, § 231, eff. July 29, 1999.

Formerly Ill.Rev.Stat.1991, ch. 95 ½, ¶ 11–501.1.

1 720 ILCS 550/1 et seq.

2 720 ILCS 570/100 et seq.

3 720 ILCS 690/0.01 et seq.

4 720 ILCS 5/1–1 et seq.

5/11–501.2. Chemical and other tests

§ 11–501.2. Chemical and other tests.

(a) Upon the trial of any civil or criminal action or proceeding arising out of an arrest for an offense as defined in Section 11–501 or a similar local ordinance or proceedings pursuant to Section 2–118.1, evidence of the concentration of alcohol, other drug or drugs, or intoxicating compound or compounds, or any combination thereof in a person's blood or breath at the time alleged, as determined by analysis of the person's blood, urine, breath or other bodily substance, shall be admissible. Where such test is made the following provisions shall apply:

1. Chemical analyses of the person's blood, urine, breath or other bodily substance to be considered valid under the provisions of this Section shall have been performed according to standards promulgated by the Department of State Police by a licensed physician, registered nurse, trained phlebotomist acting under the direction of a licensed physician, certified paramedic, or other individual possessing a valid permit issued by that Department for this purpose. The Director of State Police is authorized to approve satisfactory techniques or methods, to ascertain the qualifications and competence of individuals to conduct such analyses, to issue permits which shall be subject to termination or revocation at the discretion of that Department and to certify the accuracy of breath testing equipment. The Department of State Police shall prescribe regulations as necessary to implement this Section.

2. When a person in this State shall submit to a blood test at the request of a law enforcement officer under the provisions of Section 11–501.1, only a physician authorized to practice medicine, a registered nurse, trained phlebotomist, or certified paramedic, or other qualified person approved by the Department of State Police may withdraw blood for the purpose of determining the alcohol, drug, or alcohol and drug content therein. This limitation shall not apply to the taking of breath or urine specimens.

When a blood test of a person who has been taken to an adjoining state for medical treatment is requested by an Illinois law enforcement officer, the blood may be withdrawn only by a physician authorized to practice medicine in the adjoining state, a registered nurse, a trained phlebotomist acting under the direction of the physician, or certified paramedic. The law enforcement officer requesting the test shall take custody of the blood sample, and the blood sample shall be analyzed by a laboratory certified by the Department of State Police for that purpose.

3. The person tested may have a physician, or a qualified technician, chemist, registered nurse, or other qualified person of their own choosing administer a chemical test or tests in addition to any administered at the direction of a law enforcement officer. The failure or inability to obtain an additional test by a person shall not preclude the admission of evidence relating to the test or tests taken at the direction of a law enforcement officer.

4. Upon the request of the person who shall submit to a chemical test or tests at the request of a law enforcement officer, full information concerning the test or tests shall be made available to the person or such person's attorney.

5. Alcohol concentration shall mean either grams of alcohol per 100 milliliters of blood or grams of alcohol per 210 liters of breath.

(b) Upon the trial of any civil or criminal action or proceeding arising out of acts alleged to have been committed by any person while driving or in actual physical control of a vehicle while under the influence of alcohol, the concentration of alcohol in the person's blood or breath at the time alleged as shown by analysis of the person's blood, urine, breath, or other bodily substance shall give rise to the following presumptions:

1. If there was at that time an alcohol concentration of 0.05 or less, it shall be presumed that the person was not under the influence of alcohol.

2. If there was at that time an alcohol concentration in excess of 0.05 but less than 0.08, such facts shall not give rise to any presumption that the person was or was not under the influence of alcohol, but such fact may be considered with other competent evidence in determining whether the person was under the influence of alcohol.

3. If there was at that time an alcohol concentration of 0.08 or more, it shall be presumed that the person was under the influence of alcohol.

4. The foregoing provisions of this Section shall not be construed as limiting the introduction of any other relevant evidence bearing upon the question whether the person was under the influence of alcohol.

(c) 1. If a person under arrest refuses to submit to a chemical test under the provisions of Section 11–501.1, evidence of refusal shall be admissible in any civil or criminal action or proceeding arising out of acts alleged to have been committed while the person under the influence of alcohol, other drug or drugs, or intoxicating compound or compounds, or any combination thereof was driving or in actual physical control of a motor vehicle.

2. Notwithstanding any ability to refuse under this Code to submit to these tests or any ability to revoke the implied consent to these tests, if a law enforcement officer has probable cause to believe that a motor vehicle driven by or in actual physical control of a person under the influence of alcohol, other drug or drugs, or intoxicating compound or compounds, or any combination thereof has caused the death or personal injury to another, that person shall submit, upon the request of a law enforcement officer, to a chemical test or tests of his or her blood, breath or urine for the purpose of determining the alcohol content thereof or the presence of any other drug or combination of both.

This provision does not affect the applicability of or imposition of driver's license sanctions under Section 11–501.1 of this Code.

3. For purposes of this Section, a personal injury includes any Type A injury as indicated on the traffic accident report completed by a law enforcement officer that requires immediate professional attention in either a doctor's office or a medical facility. A Type A injury

includes severe bleeding wounds, distorted extremities, and injuries that require the injured party to be carried from the scene.

P.A. 76–1586, § 11–501.2, added by P.A. 82–311, § 1, eff. Jan. 1, 1982. Amended by P.A. 84–25, Art. IV, § 27, July 18, 1985; P.A. 86–929, § 2, eff. Sept. 21, 1989; P.A. 87–1221, § 1, eff. July 1, 1993; P.A. 88–632, § 5, eff. Jan. 1, 1995; P.A. 90–43, § 5, eff. July 2, 1997; P.A. 90–779, § 5, eff. Jan. 1, 1999; P.A. 91–828, § 5, eff. Jan. 1, 2001.

Formerly Ill.Rev.Stat.1991, ch. 95 ½, ¶ 11–501.2.

5/11–501.3. § 11–501.3. Repealed by P.A. 84–1394, § 7, eff. Sept. 18, 1986

5/11–501.4. Admissibility of chemical tests of blood conducted in the regular course of providing emergency medical treatment

§ 11–501.4. Admissibility of chemical tests of blood conducted in the regular course of providing emergency medical treatment.

(a) Notwithstanding any other provision of law, the results of blood tests performed for the purpose of determining the content of alcohol, other drug or drugs, or intoxicating compound or compounds, or any combination thereof, of an individual's blood conducted upon persons receiving medical treatment in a hospital emergency room are admissible in evidence as a business record exception to the hearsay rule only in prosecutions for any violation of Section 11–501 of this Code or a similar provision of a local ordinance, or in prosecutions for reckless homicide brought under the Criminal Code of 1961,[1] when each of the following criteria are met:

(1) the chemical tests performed upon an individual's blood were ordered in the regular course of providing emergency medical treatment and not at the request of law enforcement authorities;

(2) the chemical tests performed upon an individual's blood were performed by the laboratory routinely used by the hospital; and

(3) results of chemical tests performed upon an individual's blood are admissible into evidence regardless of the time that the records were prepared.

(b) The confidentiality provisions of law pertaining to medical records and medical treatment shall not be applicable with regard to chemical tests performed upon an individual's blood under the provisions of this Section in prosecutions as specified in subsection (a) of this Section. No person shall be liable for civil damages as a result of the evidentiary use of chemical testing of an individual's blood test results under this Section, or as a result of that person's testimony made available under this Section.

P.A. 76–1586, § 11–501.4, added by P.A. 85–992, § 1, eff. Jan. 5, 1988. Amended by P.A. 88–212, § 5, eff. Jan. 1, 1994; P.A. 88–523, § 5, eff. July 1, 1994; P.A. 88–632, § 5, eff. Jan. 1, 1995; P.A. 88–670, Art. 2, § 2–59, eff. Dec. 2, 1994; P.A. 90–779, § 5, eff. Jan. 1, 1999.

Formerly Ill.Rev.Stat.1991, ch. 95 ½, ¶ 11–501.4.

[1] 720 ILCS 5/1–1 et seq.

Another § 11–501.4 was renumbered as § 11–501.5.

5/11–501.4–1. Reporting of test results of blood or urine conducted in the regular course of providing emergency medical treatment

§ 11–501.4–1. Reporting of test results of blood or urine conducted in the regular course of providing emergency medical treatment.

(a) Notwithstanding any other provision of law, the results of blood or urine tests performed for the purpose of determining the content of alcohol, other drug or drugs, or intoxicating compound or compounds, or any combination thereof, in an individual's blood or urine conducted upon persons receiving medical treatment in a hospital emergency room for injuries resulting from a motor vehicle accident shall be disclosed to the Department of State Police or local law enforcement agencies of jurisdiction, upon request. Such blood or urine tests are admissible in evidence as a business record exception to the hearsay rule only in prosecutions for any violation of Section 11–501 of this Code or a similar provision of a local ordinance, or in prosecutions for reckless homicide brought under the Criminal Code of 1961.[1]

(b) The confidentiality provisions of law pertaining to medical records and medical treatment shall not be applicable with regard to tests performed upon an individual's blood or urine under the provisions of subsection (a) of this Section. No person shall be liable for civil damages or professional discipline as a result of the disclosure or reporting of the tests or the evidentiary use of an individual's blood or urine test results under this Section or Section 11–501.4 or as a result of that person's testimony made available under this Section or Section 11–501.4, except for willful or wanton misconduct.

P.A. 76–1586, § 11–501.4–1, added by P.A. 89–517, § 10, eff. Jan. 1, 1997. Amended by P.A. 90–779, § 5, eff. Jan. 1, 1999; P.A. 91–125, § 5, eff. Jan. 1, 2000.

[1] 720 ILCS 5/1–1 et seq.

5/11–501.5. Preliminary Breath Screening Test

§ 11–501.5. Preliminary Breath Screening Test.

(a) If a law enforcement officer has reasonable suspicion to believe that a person is violating or has violated Section 11–501 or a similar provision of a local ordinance, the officer, prior to an arrest, may request the person to provide a sample of his or her breath for a preliminary breath screening test using a portable device approved by the Department of State Police. The person may refuse the test. The results of this preliminary breath screening test may be used by the law enforcement officer for the purpose of assisting with the determination of whether to require a chemical test as authorized under Sections 11–501.1 and 11–501.2, and the appropriate type of test to request. Any chemical test authorized under Sections 11–501.1 and 11–501.2 may be requested by the officer regardless of the result of the preliminary breath screening test, if probable cause for an arrest exists. The result of a preliminary breath screening test may be used by the defendant as evidence in any administrative or court proceeding involving a violation of Section 11–501 or 11–501.1.

(b) The Department of State Police shall create a pilot program to establish the effectiveness of pupillometer technology (the measurement of the pupil's reaction to light) as a noninvasive technique to detect and measure possible impairment of any person who drives or is in actual physical control of a motor vehicle resulting from the suspected usage of alcohol, other drug or drugs, intoxicating compound or compounds or any combination thereof. This technology shall also be used to detect fatigue levels of the operator of a Commercial Motor Vehicle as defined in Section 6–500(6), pursuant to Section 18b–105 (Part 395–Hours of Service of Drivers) of the Illinois Vehicle Code. A State Police officer may request that the operator of a commercial motor vehicle have his or her eyes examined or tested with a pupillometer device. The person may refuse the examination or test. The State Police officer shall have the device readily available to limit undue delays.

If a State Police officer has reasonable suspicion to believe that a person is violating or has violated Section 11–501, the officer may use the pupillometer technology, when available. The officer, prior to an arrest, may request the person to have his or her eyes examined or tested with a pupillometer device. The person may refuse the examination or test. The results of this examination or test may be used by the officer for the purpose of assisting with the determination of whether to require a chemical test as authorized under Sections 11–501.1 and 11–501.2 and the appropriate type of test to request. Any chemical test authorized under Sections 11–501. 1 and 11–501.2 may be requested by the officer regardless of the result of the pupillometer examination or test, if probable cause for an arrest exists. The result of the examination or test may be used by the defendant as evidence in any administrative or court proceeding involving a violation of 11–501 or 11–501.1.

The pilot program shall last for a period of 18 months and involve the testing of 15 pupillometer devices. Within 90 days of the completion of the pilot project, the Department of State Police shall file a report with the President of the Senate and Speaker of the House evaluating the project.

P.A. 76–1586, § 11–501.4, added by P.A. 85–485, § 1, eff. Jan. 1, 1988. Renumbered § 11–501.5 and amended by P.A. 85–1209, Art. II, § 2–51, eff. Aug. 30, 1988. Amended by P.A. 86–1019, § 7, eff. July 1, 1990; P.A. 88–169, § 1, eff. Jan. 1, 1994; P.A. 91–828, § 5, eff. Jan. 1, 2001; P.A. 91–881, § 5, eff. June 30, 2000; P.A. 92–16, § 85, eff. June 28, 2001.

Formerly Ill.Rev.Stat.1991, ch. 95 ½, ¶ 11–501.5.

5/11–501.6. Driver involvement in personal injury or fatal motor vehicle accident—chemical test

§ 11–501.6. Driver involvement in personal injury or fatal motor vehicle accident—chemical test.

(a) Any person who drives or is in actual control of a motor vehicle upon the public highways of this State and who has been involved in a personal injury or fatal motor vehicle accident, shall be deemed to have given consent to a breath test using a portable device as approved by the Department of State Police or to a chemical test or tests of blood, breath, or urine for the purpose of determining the content of alcohol, other drug or drugs, or intoxicating compound or compounds of such person's blood if arrested as evidenced by the issuance of a Uniform Traffic Ticket for any violation of the Illinois Vehicle Code [1] or a similar provision of a local ordinance, with the exception of equipment violations contained in Chapter 12 of this Code, or similar provisions of local ordinances. The test or tests shall be administered at the direction of the arresting officer. The law enforcement agency employing the officer shall designate which of the aforesaid tests shall be administered. A urine test may be administered even after a blood or breath test or both has been administered. Compliance with this Section does not relieve such person from the requirements of Section 11–501.1 of this Code.

(b) Any person who is dead, unconscious or who is otherwise in a condition rendering such person incapable of refusal shall be deemed not to have withdrawn the consent provided by subsection (a) of this Section. In addition, if a driver of a vehicle is receiving medical treatment as a result of a motor vehicle accident, any physician licensed to practice medicine, registered nurse or a phlebotomist acting under the direction of a licensed physician shall withdraw blood for testing purposes to ascertain the presence of alcohol, other drug or drugs, or intoxicating compound or compounds, upon the specific request of a law enforcement officer. However, no such testing shall be performed until, in the opinion of the medical personnel on scene, the withdrawal can be made without interfering with or endangering the well-being of the patient.

(c) A person requested to submit to a test as provided above shall be warned by the law enforcement officer requesting the test that a refusal to submit to the test, or submission to the test resulting in an alcohol concentration of 0.08 or more, or any amount of a drug, substance, or intoxicating compound resulting from the unlawful use or consumption of cannabis, as covered by the Cannabis Control Act, [2] a controlled substance listed in the Illinois Controlled Substances Act, [3] or an intoxicating compound listed in the Use of Intoxicating Compounds Act [4] as detected in such person's blood or urine, may result in the suspension of such person's privilege to operate a motor vehicle. The length of the suspension shall be the same as outlined in Section 6–208.1 of this Code regarding statutory summary suspensions.

(d) If the person refuses testing or submits to a test which discloses an alcohol concentration of 0.08 or more, or any amount of a drug, substance, or intoxicating compound in such person's blood or urine resulting from the unlawful use or consumption of cannabis listed in the Cannabis Control Act, a controlled substance listed in the Illinois Controlled Substances Act, or an intoxicating compound listed in the Use of Intoxicating Compounds Act, the law enforcement officer shall immediately submit a sworn report to the Secretary of State on a form prescribed by the Secretary, certifying that the test or tests were requested pursuant to subsection (a) and the person refused to submit to a test or tests or submitted to testing which disclosed an alcohol concentration of 0.08 or more, or any amount of a drug, substance, or intoxicating compound in such person's blood or urine, resulting from the unlawful use or consumption of cannabis listed in the Cannabis Control Act, a controlled substance listed in the Illinois Controlled Substances Act, or an intoxicating compound listed in the Use of Intoxicating Compounds Act.

Upon receipt of the sworn report of a law enforcement officer, the Secretary shall enter the suspension to the individual's driving record and the suspension shall be effective on the 46th day following the date notice of the suspension was given to the person.

The law enforcement officer submitting the sworn report shall serve immediate notice of this suspension on the person and such suspension shall be effective on the 46th day following the date notice was given.

In cases where the blood alcohol concentration of 0.08 or more, or any amount of a drug, substance, or intoxicating compound resulting from the unlawful use or consumption of cannabis as listed in the Cannabis Control Act, a controlled substance listed in the Illinois Controlled Substances Act, or an intoxicating compound listed in the Use of Intoxicating Compounds Act, is established by a subsequent analysis of blood or urine collected at the time of arrest, the arresting officer shall give notice as provided in this Section or by deposit in the United States mail of such notice in an envelope with postage prepaid and addressed to such person at his address as shown on the Uniform Traffic Ticket and the suspension shall be effective on the 46th day following the date notice was given.

Upon receipt of the sworn report of a law enforcement officer, the Secretary shall also give notice of the suspension to the driver by mailing a notice of the effective date of the suspension to the individual. However, should the sworn report be defective by not containing sufficient information or be completed in error, the notice of the suspension shall not be mailed to the person or entered to the driving record, but rather the sworn report shall be returned to the issuing law enforcement agency.

(e) A driver may contest this suspension of his driving privileges by requesting an administrative hearing with the Secretary in accordance with Section 2-118 of this Code. At the conclusion of a hearing held under Section 2-118 of this Code, the Secretary may rescind, continue, or modify the order of suspension. If the Secretary does not rescind the order, a restricted driving permit may be granted by the Secretary upon application being made and good cause shown. A restricted driving permit may be granted to relieve undue hardship to allow driving for employment, educational, and medical purposes as outlined in Section 6-206 of this Code. The provisions of Section 6-206 of this Code shall apply.

(f) (Blank).

(g) For the purposes of this Section, a personal injury shall include any type A injury as indicated on the traffic accident report completed by a law enforcement officer that requires immediate professional attention in either a doctor's office or a medical facility. A type A injury shall include severely bleeding wounds, distorted extremities, and injuries that require the injured party to be carried from the scene.

P.A. 76-1586, § 11-501.6, added by P.A. 86-947, § 2, eff. Jan. 1, 1991. Amended by P.A. 86-1275, § 1, eff. Jan. 1, 1991; P.A. 88-211, § 5, eff. Jan. 1, 1994; P.A. 90-43, § 5, eff. July 2, 1997; P.A. 90-779, § 5, eff. Jan. 1, 1999; P.A. 91-357, § 231, eff. July 29, 1999; P.A. 91-828, § 5, eff. Jan. 1, 2001.

Formerly Ill.Rev.Stat.1991, ch. 95 ½, ¶ 11-501.6.

1 625 ILCS 5/1-100 et seq.

2 720 ILCS 550/1 et seq.

3 720 ILCS 570/100 et seq.

4 720 ILCS 690/0.01 et seq.

Validity

The Illinois Supreme Court has held in the case of King v. Ryan, 153 Ill.2d 449, 607 N.E.2d 154, 180 Ill.Dec. 260 (1992) that implied consent for drug and alcohol testing of driver who is believed to have caused an accident involving death or personal injury pursuant to this Section is an unconstitutional violation of the 4th Amendment to the U.S. Constitution and Article I, § 6 of the Illinois Constitution.

P.A. 91-828 incorporated the amendment by P.A. 91-357.

5/11-501.7. Youthful Intoxicated Drivers' Visitation Program

§ 11-501.7. (a) As a condition of probation or discharge of a person convicted of a violation of Section 11-501 of this Code, who was less than 21 years of age at the time of the offense, or a person adjudicated delinquent pursuant to the Juvenile Court Act,[1] for violation of Section 11-501 of this Code, the Court may order the offender to participate in the Youthful Intoxicated Drivers' Visitation Program. The Program shall consist of a supervised visitation as provided by this Section by the person to at least one of the following, to the extent that personnel and facilities are available:

(1) A State or private rehabilitation facility that cares for victims of motor vehicle accidents involving persons under the influence of alcohol.

(2) A facility which cares for advanced alcoholics to observe persons in the terminal stages of alcoholism, under the supervision of appropriately licensed medical personnel.

(3) If approved by the coroner of the county where the person resides, the county coroner's office or the county morgue to observe appropriate victims of motor vehicle accidents involving persons under the influence of alcohol, under the supervision of the coroner or deputy coroner.

(b) The Program shall be operated by the appropriate probation authorities of the courts of the various circuits. The youthful offender ordered to participate in the Program shall bear all costs associated with participation in the Program. A parent or guardian of the offender may assume the obligation of the offender to pay the costs of the Program. The court may waive the requirement that the offender pay the costs of participation in the Program upon a finding of indigency.

(c) As used in this Section, "appropriate victims" means victims whose condition is determined by the visit supervisor to demonstrate the results of motor vehicle accidents involving persons under the influence of alcohol without being excessively gruesome or traumatic to the observer.

(d) Any visitation shall include, before any observation of victims or disabled persons, a comprehensive counseling session with the visitation supervisor at which the supervisor shall explain and discuss the experiences which may be encountered during the visitation in order to ascertain whether the visitation is appropriate.

P.A. 76-1586, § 11-501.7, added by P.A. 86-1242, § 1, eff. Jan. 1, 1991.

Formerly Ill.Rev.Stat.1991, ch. 95 ½, ¶ 11-501.7.

1 705 ILCS 405/1-1 et seq.

5/11-501.8. Suspension of driver's license; persons under age 21

§ 11-501.8. Suspension of driver's license; persons under age 21.

(a) A person who is less than 21 years of age and who drives or is in actual physical control of a motor vehicle upon the public highways of this State shall be deemed to have given consent to a chemical test or tests of blood, breath, or urine for the purpose of determining the alcohol content of the person's blood if arrested, as evidenced by the issuance of a Uniform Traffic Ticket for any violation of the Illinois Vehicle Code[1] or a similar provision of a local ordinance, if a police officer has probable cause to believe that the driver has consumed any amount of an alcoholic beverage based upon evidence of the driver's physical condition or other first hand knowledge of the police officer. The test or tests shall be administered at the direction of the arresting officer. The law enforcement agency employing the officer shall designate which of the aforesaid tests shall be administered. A urine test may be administered even after a blood or breath test or both has been administered.

(b) A person who is dead, unconscious, or who is otherwise in a condition rendering that person incapable of refusal, shall be deemed not to have withdrawn the consent provided by paragraph (a) of this Section and the test or tests may be administered subject to the following provisions:

(i) Chemical analysis of the person's blood, urine, breath, or other bodily substance, to be considered valid under the provisions of this Section, shall have been performed according to standards promulgated by the Department of State Police by an individual possessing a valid permit issued by that Department for this purpose. The Director of State Police is authorized to approve satisfactory techniques or methods, to ascertain the qualifications and competence of individuals to conduct analyses, to issue permits that shall be subject to termination or revocation at the direction of that Department, and to certify the accuracy of breath testing equipment. The Department of State Police shall prescribe regulations as necessary.

(ii) When a person submits to a blood test at the request of a law enforcement officer under the provisions of this Section, only a physician authorized to practice medicine, a registered nurse, or other qualified person trained in venipuncture and acting under the direction of a licensed physician may withdraw blood for the purpose of determining the alcohol content therein. This limitation does not apply to the taking of breath or urine specimens.

(iii) The person tested may have a physician, qualified technician, chemist, registered nurse, or other qualified person of his or her own choosing administer a chemical test or tests in addition to any test or tests administered at the direction of a law enforcement officer. The failure or inability to obtain an additional test by a person shall not preclude the consideration of the previously performed chemical test.

(iv) Upon a request of the person who submits to a chemical test or tests at the request of a law enforcement officer, full information concerning the test or tests shall be made available to the person or that person's attorney.

(v) Alcohol concentration means either grams of alcohol per 100 milliliters of blood or grams of alcohol per 210 liters of breath.

(vi) If a driver is receiving medical treatment as a result of a motor vehicle accident, a physician licensed to practice medicine, registered nurse, or other qualified person trained in venipuncture and acting under the direction of a licensed physician shall withdraw blood for testing purposes to ascertain the presence of alcohol upon the specific request of a law enforcement officer. However, that testing shall not be performed until, in the opinion of the medical personnel on scene, the withdrawal can be made without interfering with or endangering the well-being of the patient.

(c) A person requested to submit to a test as provided above shall be warned by the law enforcement officer requesting the test that a refusal to submit to the test, or submission to the test resulting in an alcohol concentration of more than 0.00, may result in the loss of that person's privilege to operate a motor vehicle. The loss of driving privileges shall be imposed in accordance with Section 6–208.2 of this Code.

(d) If the person refuses testing or submits to a test that discloses an alcohol concentration of more than 0.00, the law enforcement officer shall immediately submit a sworn report to the Secretary of State on a form prescribed by the Secretary of State, certifying that the test or tests were requested under subsection (a) and the person refused to submit to a test or tests or submitted to testing which disclosed an alcohol concentration of more than 0.00. The law enforcement officer shall submit the same sworn report when a person under the age of 21 submits to testing under Section 11–501.1 of this Code and the testing discloses an alcohol concentration of more than 0.00 and less than 0.08.

Upon receipt of the sworn report of a law enforcement officer, the Secretary of State shall enter the driver's license sanction on the individual's driving record and the sanctions shall be effective on the 46th day following the date notice of the sanction was given to the person. If this sanction is the individual's first driver's license suspension under this Section, reports received by the Secretary of State under this Section shall, except during the time the suspension is in effect, be privileged information and for use only by the courts, police officers, prosecuting authorities, the Secretary of State, or the individual personally.

The law enforcement officer submitting the sworn report shall serve immediate notice of this driver's license sanction on the person and the sanction shall be effective on the 46th day following the date notice was given.

In cases where the blood alcohol concentration of more than 0.00 is established by a subsequent analysis of blood or urine, the police officer or arresting agency shall give notice as provided in this Section or by deposit in the United States mail of that notice in an envelope with postage prepaid and addressed to that person at his last known address and the loss of driving privileges shall be effective on the 46th day following the date notice was given.

Upon receipt of the sworn report of a law enforcement officer, the Secretary of State shall also give notice of the driver's license sanction to the driver by mailing a notice of the effective date of the sanction to the individual. However, should the sworn report be defective by not containing sufficient information or be completed in error, the notice of the driver's license sanction may not be mailed to the person or entered to the driving record, but rather the sworn report shall be returned to the issuing law enforcement agency.

(e) A driver may contest this driver's license sanction by requesting an administrative hearing with the Secretary of State in accordance with Section 2–118 of this Code. An individual whose blood alcohol concentration is shown to be more than 0.00 is not subject to this Section if he or she consumed alcohol in the performance of a religious service or ceremony. An individual whose blood alcohol concentration is shown to be more than 0.00 shall not be subject to this Section if the individual's blood alcohol concentration resulted only from ingestion of the prescribed or recommended dosage of medicine that contained alcohol. The petition for that hearing shall not stay or delay the effective date of the impending suspension. The scope of this hearing shall be limited to the issues of:

(1) whether the police officer had probable cause to believe that the person was driving or in actual physical control of a motor vehicle upon the public highways of the State and the police officer had reason to believe that the person was in violation of any provision of the Illinois Vehicle Code or a similar provision of a local ordinance; and

(2) whether the person was issued a Uniform Traffic Ticket for any violation of the Illinois Vehicle Code or a similar provision of a local ordinance; and

(3) whether the police officer had probable cause to believe that the driver had consumed any amount of an alcoholic beverage based upon the driver's physical actions or other first-hand knowledge of the police officer; and

(4) whether the person, after being advised by the officer that the privilege to operate a motor vehicle would be

suspended if the person refused to submit to and complete the test or tests, did refuse to submit to or complete the test or tests to determine the person's alcohol concentration; and

(5) whether the person, after being advised by the officer that the privileges to operate a motor vehicle would be suspended if the person submits to a chemical test or tests and the test or tests disclose an alcohol concentration of more than 0.00, did submit to and complete the test or tests that determined an alcohol concentration of more than 0.00; and

(6) whether the test result of an alcohol concentration of more than 0.00 was based upon the person's consumption of alcohol in the performance of a religious service or ceremony; and

(7) whether the test result of an alcohol concentration of more than 0.00 was based upon the person's consumption of alcohol through ingestion of the prescribed or recommended dosage of medicine.

Provided that the petitioner may subpoena the officer, the hearing may be conducted upon a review of the law enforcement officer's own official reports. Failure of the officer to answer the subpoena shall be grounds for a continuance if, in the hearing officer's discretion, the continuance is appropriate. At the conclusion of the hearing held under Section 2–118 of this Code, the Secretary of State may rescind, continue, or modify the driver's license sanction. If the Secretary of State does not rescind the sanction, a restricted driving permit may be granted by the Secretary of State upon application being made and good cause shown. A restricted driving permit may be granted to relieve undue hardship by allowing driving for employment, educational, and medical purposes as outlined in item (3) of part (c) of Section 6–206 of this Code. The provisions of item (3) of part (c) of Section 6–206 of this Code shall apply. The Secretary of State shall promulgate rules providing for participation in an alcohol education and awareness program or activity, a drug education and awareness program or activity, or both as a condition to the issuance of a restricted driving permit for suspensions imposed under this Section.

(f) The results of any chemical testing performed in accordance with subsection (a) of this Section are not admissible in any civil or criminal proceeding, except that the results of the testing may be considered at a hearing held under Section 2–118 of this Code. However, the results of the testing may not be used to impose driver's license sanctions under Section 11–501.1 of this Code. A law enforcement officer may, however, pursue a statutory summary suspension of driving privileges under Section 11–501.1 of this Code if other physical evidence or first hand knowledge forms the basis of that suspension.

(g) This Section applies only to drivers who are under age 21 at the time of the issuance of a Uniform Traffic Ticket for a violation of the Illinois Vehicle Code or a similar provision of a local ordinance, and a chemical test request is made under this Section.

(h) The action of the Secretary of State in suspending, revoking, or denying any license, permit, registration, or certificate of title shall be subject to judicial review in the Circuit Court of Sangamon County or in the Circuit Court of Cook County, and the provisions of the Administrative Review Law [2] and its rules are hereby adopted and shall apply to and govern every action for the judicial review of final acts or decisions of the Secretary of State under this Section.

P.A. 76–1586, § 11–501.8, added by P.A. 88–588, § 5, eff. Jan. 1, 1995. Amended by P.A. 90–43, § 5, eff. July 2, 1997; P.A. 91–357, § 231, eff. July 29, 1999; P.A. 91–828, § 5, eff. Jan. 1, 2001.

[1] 625 ILCS 5/1–100 et seq.

[2] 735 ILCS 5/3–101 et seq.

P.A. 91–828 incorporated the amendment by P.A. 91–357.

5/11–502. Transportation or possession of alcoholic liquor in a motor vehicle

§ 11–502. Transportation or possession of alcoholic liquor in a motor vehicle. (a) Except as provided in paragraph (c), no driver may transport, carry, possess or have any alcoholic liquor within the passenger area of any motor vehicle upon a highway in this State except in the original container and with the seal unbroken.

(b) Except as provided in paragraph (c), no passenger may carry, possess or have any alcoholic liquor within any passenger area of any motor vehicle upon a highway in this State except in the original container and with the seal unbroken.

(c) This Section shall not apply to the passengers in a limousine when it is being used for purposes for which a limousine is ordinarily used, the passengers on a chartered bus when it is being used for purposes for which chartered buses are ordinarily used or on a motor home or mini motor home as defined in Section 1–145.01 of this Code. However, the driver of any such vehicle is prohibited from consuming or having any alcoholic liquor in or about the driver's area. Any evidence of alcoholic consumption by the driver shall be prima facie evidence of such driver's failure to obey this Section. For the purposes of this Section, a limousine is a motor vehicle of the first division with the passenger compartment enclosed by a partition or dividing window used in the for-hire transportation of passengers and operated by an individual in possession of a valid Illinois driver's license of the appropriate classification pursuant to Section 6–104 of this Code.

(d) The exemption applicable to chartered buses under paragraph (c) does not apply to any chartered bus being used for school purposes.

(e) Any driver who is convicted of violating subsection (a) of this Section for a second or subsequent time within one year of a similar conviction shall be subject to suspension of driving privileges as provided, in paragraph 23 of subsection (a) of Section 6–206 of this Code.

(f) Any driver, who is less than 21 years of age at the date of the offense and who is convicted of violating subsection (a) of this Section or a similar provision of a local ordinance, shall be subject to the loss of driving privileges as provided in paragraph 13 of subsection (a) of Section 6–205 of this Code and paragraph 33 of subsection (a) of Section 6–206 of this Code.

P.A. 76–1586, § 11–502, eff. July 1, 1970. Amended by P.A. 77–680, § 1, eff. Aug. 9, 1971; P.A. 77–2720, § 1, eff. Jan. 1, 1973; P.A. 78–255, § 28, eff. Oct. 1, 1973; P.A. 80–911, § 1, eff. Oct. 1, 1977; P.A. 80–1463, § 1, eff. Jan. 1, 1979; P.A. 83–205, § 1, eff. Jan. 1, 1984; P.A. 84–272, § 7, eff. Jan. 1, 1986; P.A. 85–951, § 1, eff. July 1, 1988; P.A. 86–747, § 1, eff. Jan. 1, 1990; P.A. 88–209, § 5, eff. Jan. 1, 1994.

Formerly Ill.Rev.Stat.1991, ch. 95 ½, ¶ 11–502.

5/11–503. Reckless driving; aggravated reckless driving

§ 11–503. Reckless driving; aggravated reckless driving. (a) Any person who drives any vehicle with a willful or wanton disregard for the safety of persons or property is guilty of reckless driving.

(b) Every person convicted of reckless driving shall be guilty of a Class A misdemeanor, except as provided under subsection (c) of this Section.

(c) Every person convicted of committing a violation of subsection (a) shall be guilty of aggravated reckless driving if the violation results in great bodily harm or permanent disability or disfigurement to another. Aggravated reckless driving is a Class 4 felony.

P.A. 76-1586, § 11-503, eff. July 1, 1970. Amended by P.A. 77-2720, § 1, eff. Jan. 1, 1973; P.A. 80-911, § 1, eff. Oct. 1, 1977; P.A. 86-581, § 2, eff. Jan. 1, 1990; P.A. 88-679, § 15, eff. July 1, 1995.

Formerly Ill.Rev.Stat.1991, ch. 95 ½, ¶ 11-503.

5/11-504. Drag racing

§ 11-504. Drag racing. Any person who, as an operator of a motor vehicle, is convicted of being a participant in drag racing shall be guilty of a Class C misdemeanor, and the driver's license of such person shall be revoked in the manner provided by Section 6-205.

"Drag racing" means the act of 2 or more individuals competing or racing on any street or highway in this State in a situation in which one of the motor vehicles is beside or to the rear of a motor vehicle operated by a competing driver and the one driver attempts to prevent the competing driver from passing or overtaking, either by acceleration or maneuver, or one or more individuals competing in a race against time on any street or highway in this State.

P.A. 76-1586, § 11-504, eff. July 1, 1970. Amended by P.A. 77-2720, § 1, eff. Jan. 1, 1973; P.A. 80-911, § 1, eff. Oct. 1, 1977; P.A. 83-831, § 1, eff. Jan. 1, 1984.

Formerly Ill.Rev.Stat.1991, ch. 95 ½, ¶ 11-504.

5/11-505. Squealing or screeching

§ 11-505. No person shall operate any motor vehicle in such a manner as to cause or allow to be emitted squealing, screeching or other such noise from the vehicle's tires due to rapid acceleration or excessive speed around corners or other such reason.

This Section shall not apply to the following conditions:

(a) an authorized emergency vehicle, when responding to an emergency call or when in the pursuit of an actual or suspected violator; nor

(b) the emergency operation of a motor vehicle when avoiding imminent danger; nor

(c) any raceway, racing facility or other public event, not part of a highway, sanctioned by the appropriate governmental authority.

P.A. 76-1586, § 11-505, added by P.A. 86-664, § 1, eff. Sept. 1, 1989.

Formerly Ill.Rev.Stat.1991, ch. 95 ½, ¶ 11-505.

ARTICLE VI. SPEED RESTRICTIONS

5/11-601. General speed restrictions

§ 11-601. General speed restrictions.

(a) No vehicle may be driven upon any highway of this State at a speed which is greater than is reasonable and proper with regard to traffic conditions and the use of the highway, or endangers the safety of any person or property. The fact that the speed of a vehicle does not exceed the applicable maximum speed limit does not relieve the driver from the duty to decrease speed when approaching and crossing an intersection, approaching and going around a curve, when approaching a hill crest, when traveling upon any narrow or winding roadway, or when special hazard exists with respect to pedestrians or other traffic or by reason of weather or highway conditions. Speed must be decreased as may be necessary to avoid colliding with any person or vehicle on or entering the highway in compliance with legal requirements and the duty of all persons to use due care.

(b) No person may drive a vehicle upon any highway of this State at a speed which is greater than the applicable statutory maximum speed limit established by paragraphs (c), (d), (e), (f) or (g) of this Section, by Section 11-605 or by a regulation or ordinance made under this Chapter.

(c) Unless some other speed restriction is established under this Chapter, the maximum speed limit in an urban district for all vehicles is:

1. 30 miles per hour; and
2. 15 miles per hour in an alley.

(d) Unless some other speed restriction is established under this Chapter, the maximum speed limit outside an urban district for any vehicle of the first division or a second division vehicle designed or used for the carrying of a gross weight of 8,000 pounds or less (including the weight of the vehicle and maximum load) is (1) 65 miles per hour (i) for all highways under the jurisdiction of the Illinois State Toll Highway Authority and (ii) for all or part of highways that are designated by the Department, have at least 4 lanes of traffic, and have a separation between the roadways moving in opposite directions and (2) 55 miles per hour for all other highways, roads, and streets.

(e) Unless some lesser speed restriction is established under this Chapter, the maximum speed limit outside an urban district for a second division vehicle designed or used for the carrying of a gross weight of 8,001 pounds or more (including the weight of the vehicle and maximum load) is 55 miles per hour.

(f) Unless some other speed restriction is established under this Chapter, the maximum speed limit outside an urban district for a bus is:

1. 65 miles per hour upon any highway which has at least 4 lanes of traffic and of which the roadways for traffic moving in opposite directions are separated by a strip of ground which is not surfaced or suitable for vehicular traffic, except that the maximum speed limit for a bus on

all highways, roads, or streets not under the jurisdiction of the Department or the Illinois State Toll Highway Authority is 55 miles per hour; and

2. 60 miles per hour on any other highway, except that the maximum speed limit for a bus on all highways, roads, or streets not under the jurisdiction of the Department or the Illinois State Toll Highway Authority is 55 miles per hour.

(g) Unless some other speed restriction is established under this Chapter, the maximum speed limit outside an urban district for a house car, camper, private living coach, vehicles licensed as recreational vehicles, and any vehicle towing any other vehicle is 55 miles per hour or the posted speed limit, whichever is less.

P.A. 76–1586, § 11–601, eff. July 1, 1970. Amended by P.A. 77–66, § 1, eff. July 1, 1971; P.A. 78–954, § 1, eff. Feb. 25, 1974; P.A. 79–267, § 1, eff. July 14, 1975; P.A. 84–730, § 1, eff. July 1, 1986; P.A. 89–444, § 5, eff. Jan. 25, 1996; P.A. 89–551, § 5, eff. Jan. 1, 1997.

Formerly Ill.Rev.Stat.1991, ch. 95 ½, ¶ 11–601.

P.A. 89–551 incorporated the amendment by P.A. 89–444.

5/11–601.5. Driving 40 miles per hour or more in excess of applicable limit

§ 11–601.5. Driving 40 miles per hour or more in excess of applicable limit. A person who drives a vehicle upon any highway of this State at a speed that is 40 miles per hour or more in excess of the applicable maximum speed limit established under this Chapter or a local ordinance commits a Class A misdemeanor.

P.A. 76–1586, § 11–601.5, added by P.A. 91–469, § 5, eff. Jan. 1, 2000.

5/11–602. Alteration of limits by Department

§ 11–602. Alteration of limits by Department. Whenever the Department determines, upon the basis of an engineering and traffic investigation concerning any highway for which the Department has maintenance responsibility, that a maximum speed limit prescribed in Section 11–601 of this Chapter is greater or less than is reasonable or safe with respect to the conditions found to exist at any intersection or other place on such highway or along any part or zone thereof, the Department shall determine and declare a reasonable and safe absolute maximum speed limit applicable to such intersection or place, or along such part or zone. However, such limit shall not exceed 65 miles per hour, or 55 miles per hour for a second division vehicle designed or used for the carrying of a gross weight of 8,001 pounds or more (including the weight of the vehicle and maximum load), on a highway or street which is especially designed for through traffic and to, from, or over which owners of or persons having an interest in abutting property or other persons have no right or easement, or only a limited right or easement, of access, crossing, light, air, or view, and shall not exceed 55 miles per hour on any other highway. A limit so determined and declared becomes effective, and suspends the applicability of the limit prescribed in Section 11–601 of this Chapter, when appropriate signs giving notice of the limit are erected at such intersection or other place, or along such part or zone of the highway. Electronic speed-detecting devices shall not be used within 500 feet beyond any such sign in the direction of travel; if so used in violation hereof, evidence obtained thereby shall be inadmissible in any prosecution for speeding. However, nothing in this Section prohibits the use of such electronic speed-detecting devices within 500 feet of a sign within a special school speed zone indicating such zone, conforming to the requirements of Section 11–605 of this Act, nor shall evidence obtained thereby be inadmissible in any prosecution for speeding provided the use of such device shall apply only to the enforcement of the speed limit in such special school speed zone.

P.A. 76–1586, § 11–602, eff. July 1, 1970. Amended by P.A. 77–101, § 1, eff. Jan. 1, 1972; P.A. 78–954, § 1, eff. Feb. 5, 1974; P.A. 79–267, § 1, eff. July 14, 1975; P.A. 89–444, § 5, eff. Jan. 25, 1996; P.A. 89–551, § 5, eff. Jan. 1, 1997.

Formerly Ill.Rev.Stat.1991, ch. 95 ½, ¶ 11–602.

P.A. 89–551 incorporated the amendment by P.A. 89–444.

5/11–603. Alteration of limits by Toll Highway Authority

§ 11–603. Alteration of limits by Toll Highway Authority. Whenever the Illinois State Toll Highway Authority determines, upon the basis of an engineering and traffic investigation concerning a toll highway under its jurisdiction, that a maximum speed limit prescribed in Section 11–601 of this Chapter is greater or less than is reasonable or safe with respect to conditions found to exist at any place or along any part or zone of such highway, the Authority shall determine and declare by regulation a reasonable and safe absolute maximum speed limit at such place or along such part or zone, not exceeding 65 miles per hour. A limit so determined and declared becomes effective, and suspends the application of the limit prescribed in Section 11–601 of this Chapter, when (a) the Department concurs in writing with the Authority's regulation, and (b) appropriate signs giving notice of the limit are erected at such place or along such part or zone of the highway. Electronic speed-detecting devices shall not be used within 500 feet beyond any such sign in the direction of travel; if so used in violation hereof, evidence obtained thereby shall be inadmissible in any prosecution for speeding.

P.A. 76–1586, § 11–603, eff. July 1, 1970. Amended by P.A. 77–643, § 1, eff. Aug. 4, 1971; P.A. 78–954, § 1, eff. Feb. 25, 1974; P.A. 79–267, § 1, eff. July 14, 1975; P.A. 89–444, § 5, eff. Jan. 25, 1996.

Formerly Ill.Rev.Stat.1991, ch. 95 ½, ¶ 11–603.

5/11–604. Alteration of limits by local authorities

§ 11–604. Alteration of limits by local authorities. Subject to the limitations set forth in this Section, the county board of a county may establish absolute maximum speed limits on all county highways, township roads and district roads as defined in the Illinois Highway Code,[1] except those under the jurisdiction of the Department or of the Illinois State Toll Highway Authority, as described in Sections 11–602 and 11–603 of this Chapter; and any park district, city, village, or incorporated town may establish absolute maximum speed limits on all streets which are within its corporate limits and which are not under the jurisdiction of the Department or of such Authority, and for which the county or a highway commissioner of such county does not have maintenance responsibility.

Whenever any such park district, city, village, or incorporated town determines, upon the basis of an engineering or traffic investigation concerning a highway or street on which it is authorized by this Section to establish speed limits, that a maximum speed limit prescribed in Section 11–601 of this Chapter is greater or less than is reasonable or safe with respect to the conditions found to exist at any place or along any part or zone of such highway or street, the local authority or park district shall determine and declare by ordinance a reasonable and safe absolute maximum speed limit at such place or along such part or zone, which:

(1) Decreases the limit within an urban district, but not to less than 20 miles per hour; or

(2) Increases the limit within an urban district, but not to more than 55 miles per hour; or

(3) Decreases the limit outside of an urban district, but not to less than 35 miles per hour, except as otherwise provided in subparagraph 4 of this paragraph; or

(4) Decreases the limit within a residence district, but not to less than 25 miles per hour, except as otherwise provided in subparagraph 1 of this paragraph.

The park district, city, village, or incorporated town may make such limit applicable at all times or only during certain specified times. Not more than 6 such alterations shall be made per mile along a highway or street; and the difference in limit between adjacent altered speed zones shall not be more than 10 miles per hour.

A limit so determined and declared by a park district, city, village, or incorporated town becomes effective, and suspends the application of the limit prescribed in Section 11–601 of this Chapter, when appropriate signs giving notice of the limit are erected at the proper place or along the proper part or zone of the highway or street. Electronic speed-detecting devices shall not be used within 500 feet beyond any such sign in the direction of travel; if so used in violation of this Section evidence obtained thereby shall be inadmissible in any prosecution for speeding. However, nothing in this Section prohibits the use of such electronic speed-detecting devices within 500 feet of a sign within a special school speed zone indicating such zone, conforming to the requirements of Section 11–605 of this Act, nor shall evidence obtained thereby be inadmissible in any prosecution for speeding provided the use of such device shall apply only to the enforcement of the speed limit in such special school speed zone. A county engineer or superintendent of highways may submit to the Department for approval, a county policy for establishing altered speed zones on township and county highways based upon engineering and traffic investigations.

Whenever the county board of a county determines that a maximum speed limit is greater or less than is reasonable or safe with respect to the conditions found to exist at any place or along any part or zone of the highway or road, the county board shall determine and declare by ordinance a reasonable and safe absolute maximum speed limit at that place or along that part or zone. However, the maximum speed limit shall not exceed 55 miles per hour. The limit becomes effective, and suspends the application of the limit prescribed in Section 11–601 of this Chapter, when appropriate signs giving notice of the limit are erected at the proper place or along the proper part of the zone of the highway. Electronic speed-detecting devices shall not be used within 500 feet beyond any such sign in the direction of travel; if so used in violation of this Section, evidence obtained thereby shall be inadmissible in any prosecution for speeding. However, nothing in this Section prohibits the use of such electronic speed-detecting devices within 500 feet of a sign within a special school speed zone indicating such zone, conforming to the requirements of Section 11–605 of this Act, nor shall evidence obtained thereby be inadmissible in any prosecution for speeding provided the use of such device shall apply only to the enforcement of the speed limit in such special school speed zone.

P.A. 76–1586, § 11–604, eff. July 1, 1970. Amended by P.A. 77–50, § 1, eff. Jan. 1, 1972; P.A. 77–101, § 1, eff. Jan. 1, 1972; P.A. 77–643, § 1, eff. Aug. 4, 1971; P.A. 77–2829, § 40, eff. Dec. 22, 1972; P.A. 78–255, § 61, eff. Oct. 1, 1973; P.A. 78–954, § 1, eff. Feb. 25, 1974; P.A. 78–1297, § 58, eff. March 4, 1975; P.A. 79–267, § 1, eff. July 14, 1975; P.A. 80–693, § 1, eff. Oct. 1, 1977; P.A. 81–875, § 1, eff. Jan. 1, 1980; P.A. 85–547, § 1, eff. Jan. 1, 1988; P.A. 87–217, § 4, eff. Jan. 1, 1992; P.A. 89–444, § 5, eff. Jan. 25, 1996.

Formerly Ill.Rev.Stat.1991, ch. 95 ½, ¶ 11–604.

1 605 ILCS 5/1–101 et seq.

5/11–605. Special speed limit while passing schools or while traveling through highway construction or maintenance zones

§ 11–605. Special speed limit while passing schools or while traveling through highway construction or maintenance zones.

(a) For the purpose of this Section, "school" means the following entities:

(1) A public or private primary or secondary school.

(2) A primary or secondary school operated by a religious institution.

(3) A public, private, or religious nursery school.

On a school day when school children are present and so close thereto that a potential hazard exists because of the close proximity of the motorized traffic, no person shall drive a motor vehicle at a speed in excess of 20 miles per hour while passing a school zone or while traveling on a roadway on public school property or upon any public thoroughfare where children pass going to and from school.

For the purpose of this Section a school day shall begin at seven ante meridian and shall conclude at four post meridian.

This Section shall not be applicable unless appropriate signs are posted upon streets and highways under their respective jurisdiction and maintained by the Department, township, county, park district, city, village or incorporated town wherein the school zone is located. With regard to the special speed limit while passing schools, such signs shall give proper due warning that a school zone is being approached and shall indicate the school zone and the maximum speed limit in effect during school days when school children are present.

(b) No person shall operate a motor vehicle in a construction or maintenance zone at a speed in excess of the posted speed limit when workers are present and so close to the moving traffic that a potential hazard exists because of the motorized traffic.

(c) Nothing in this Chapter shall prohibit the use of electronic speed-detecting devices within 500 feet of signs within a special school speed zone or a construction or maintenance zone indicating such zone, as defined in this Section, nor shall evidence obtained thereby be inadmissible in any prosecution for speeding provided the use of such device shall apply only to the enforcement of the speed limit in such special school speed zone or a construction or maintenance zone.

(d) For the purpose of this Section, a construction or maintenance zone is an area in which the Department, Toll Highway Authority, or local agency has determined that the preexisting established speed limit through a highway construction or maintenance project is greater than is reasonable or safe with respect to the conditions expected to exist in the construction or maintenance zone and has posted a lower speed limit with a highway construction or maintenance zone special speed limit sign.

Highway construction or maintenance zone special speed limit signs shall be of a design approved by the Department. The signs shall give proper due warning that a construction or maintenance zone is being approached and shall indicate the maximum speed limit in effect. The signs shall also state the amount of the minimum fine for a violation when workers are present.

(e) A first violation of this Section is a petty offense with a minimum fine of $150. A second or subsequent violation of this Section is a petty offense with a minimum fine of $300.

(f) When a fine for a violation of subsection (a) is $150 or greater, the person who violates subsection (a) shall be charged an additional $50 to be paid to the unit school district where the violation occurred for school safety purposes. If the violation occurred in a dual school district, $25 of the surcharge shall be paid to the elementary school district for school safety purposes and $25 of the surcharge shall be paid to the high school district for school safety purposes. Notwithstanding any other provision of law, the entire $50 surcharge shall be paid to the appropriate school district or districts.

For purposes of this subsection (f), "school safety purposes" includes the costs associated with school zone safety education and the purchase, installation, and maintenance of caution lights which are mounted on school speed zone signs.

(g) When a fine for a violation of subsection (b) is $150 or greater, the person who violates subsection (b) shall be charged an additional $50. The $50 surcharge shall be deposited into the Transportation Safety Highway Hire-back Fund.

(h) The Transportation Safety Highway Hire-back Fund is created as a special fund in the State treasury. Subject to appropriation by the General Assembly and approval by the Secretary, the Secretary of Transportation shall use all moneys in the Transportation Safety Highway Hire-back Fund to hire off-duty Department of State Police officers to monitor construction or maintenance zones.

P.A. 76–1586, § 11–605, eff. July 1, 1970. Amended by P.A. 77–101, § 1, eff. Jan. 1, 1972; P.A. 82–124, § 1, eff. Jan. 1, 1982; P.A. 89–251, § 5, eff. Jan. 1, 1996; P.A. 89–559, § 5, eff. Jan. 1, 1997; P.A. 91–531, § 5, eff. Jan. 1, 2000; P.A. 92–242, § 5, eff. Jan. 1, 2002; P.A. 92–619, § 10, eff. Jan. 1, 2003; P.A. 92–780, § 5, eff. Aug. 6, 2002.

Formerly Ill.Rev.Stat.1991, ch. 95 ½, ¶ 11–605.

P.A. 92–619 incorporated the amendment by P.A. 92–242.

P.A. 92–780 incorporated the amendment by P.A. 92–242.

See 5 ILCS 70/6 as to the effect of (1) more than one amendment of a section at the same session of the General Assembly or (2) two or more acts relating to the same subject matter enacted by the same General Assembly.

5/11–606. Minimum speed regulation

§ 11–606. Minimum speed regulation. (a) No person shall drive a motor vehicle at such a slow speed as to impede or block the normal and reasonable movement of traffic except when reduced speed is necessary for safe operation of his vehicle or in compliance with law.

(b) Whenever the Department, The Illinois State Toll Highway Authority, or a local authority described in Section 11–604 of this Chapter determines, upon the basis of an engineering and traffic investigation concerning a highway or street under its jurisdiction that slow vehicle speeds along any part or zone of such highway or street consistently impede the normal and reasonable movement of traffic, the Department, the Toll Highway Authority, or local authority (as appropriate) may determine and declare by proper regulation or ordinance a minimum speed limit below which no person shall drive except when necessary for safe operation of his vehicle or in compliance with law. A limit so determined and declared becomes effective when appropriate signs giving notice of the limit are erected along such part or zone of the highway or street.

P.A. 76–1586, § 11–606, eff. July 1, 1970. Amended by P.A. 81–840, § 41, eff. Sept. 19, 1979.

Formerly Ill.Rev.Stat.1991, ch. 95 ½, ¶ 11–606.

5/11–607. § 11–607. Repealed by P.A. 78–253, § 2, eff. Oct. 1, 1973

5/11–608. Special speed limitation on elevated structures

§ 11–608. Special speed limitation on elevated structures. (a) No person shall drive a vehicle over any bridge or other elevated structure constituting a part of a highway at a speed which is greater than the maximum speed which can be maintained with safety to such bridge or structure, when such structure is sign posted as provided in this Section.

(b) The Department upon request from any local authority shall, or upon its own initiative may, conduct an investigation of any bridge or other elevated structure constituting a part of a highway, and if it shall thereupon find that such structure cannot with safety to itself withstand vehicles traveling at the speed otherwise permissible under this Chapter, the Department shall determine and declare the maximum speed of vehicles which such structure can safely withstand, and shall cause or permit suitable signs stating such maximum speed to be erected and maintained before each end of such structure.

(c) Upon the trial of any person charged with a violation of this Section, proof of the determination of the maximum speed by the Department and the existence of such signs is conclusive evidence of the maximum speed which can be maintained with safety to such bridge or structure.

P.A. 76–1586, § 11–608, eff. July 1, 1970.

Formerly Ill.Rev.Stat.1991, ch. 95 ½, ¶ 11–608.

5/11–609. § 11–609. Repealed by P.A. 76–2165, § 1, eff. July 1, 1970

5/11–610. Charging violations and rule in civil actions

§ 11–610. Charging violations and rule in civil actions. (a) In every charge of violation of any speed regulation in this article the complaint, and also the summons or notice to appear, shall specify the speed at which the defendant is alleged to have driven and the maximum speed applicable within the district or at the location.

(b) The provision of this article declaring maximum speed limitations shall not be construed to relieve the plaintiff in any action from the burden of proving negligence on the part of the defendant as the proximate cause of an accident.

P.A. 76–1586, § 11–610, eff. July 1, 1970. Amended by P.A. 79–1069, § 1, eff. Jan. 1, 1976.

Formerly Ill.Rev.Stat.1991, ch. 95 ½, ¶ 11–610.

5/11–611. Maximum attainable operating speed

§ 11–611. No person shall drive or operate any motor vehicle on any street or highway in this State where the minimum allowable speed on that street or highway, as posted, is greater than the maximum attainable operating speed of the vehicle. Maximum attainable operating speed shall be determined by the manufacturer of the vehicle and clearly published in the manual of specifications and operation, or it shall be determined by applicable rule and regulation promulgated by the Secretary of State.

P.A. 76-1586, § 11-611, added by P.A. 79-700, § 1, eff. Oct. 1, 1975.

Formerly Ill.Rev.Stat.1991, ch. 95 ½, ¶ 11-611.

ARTICLE VII. DRIVING ON RIGHT SIDE OF ROADWAY—OVERTAKING AND PASSING, ETC.

Section

5/11-701. Drive on right side of roadway—Exceptions

§ 11-701. Drive on right side of roadway—Exceptions. (a) Upon all roadways of sufficient width a vehicle shall be driven upon the right half of the roadway, except as follows:

1. When overtaking and passing another vehicle proceeding in the same direction under the rules governing such movements;

2. When an obstruction exists making it necessary to drive to the left of the center of the roadway; provided, any person so doing shall yield the right-of-way to all vehicles traveling in the proper direction upon the unobstructed portion of the roadway within such distance as to constitute an immediate hazard;

3. Upon a roadway divided into three marked lanes for traffic under the rules applicable thereon;

4. Upon a roadway restricted to one way traffic;

5. Whenever there is a single track paved road on one side of the public highway and 2 vehicles meet thereon, the driver on whose right is the wider shoulder shall give the right-of-way on such pavement to the other vehicle.

(b) Upon all roadways any vehicle proceeding at less than the normal speed of traffic at the time and place and under the conditions then existing shall be driven in the right-hand lane available for traffic, or as close as practicable to the right hand curb or edge of the roadway, except when overtaking and passing another vehicle proceeding in the same direction or when preparing for a left turn at an intersection or into a private road or driveway.

(c) Upon any roadway having 4 or more lanes for moving traffic and providing for 2-way movement of traffic, no vehicle shall be driven to the left of the center line of the roadway, except when authorized by official traffic-control devices designating certain lanes to the left side of the center of the roadway for use by traffic not otherwise permitted to use such lanes, or except as permitted under Subsection (a)2. However, this Subsection shall not be construed as prohibiting the crossing of the center line in making a left turn into or from an alley, private road or driveway.

P.A. 76-1586, § 11-701, eff. July 1, 1970. Amended by P.A. 76-1739, § 1; P.A. 76-2166, § 1, eff. July 1, 1970; P.A. 77-1344, § 1, eff. Aug. 27, 1971.

Formerly Ill.Rev.Stat.1991, ch. 95 ½, ¶ 11-701.

5/11-702. Passing vehicles proceeding in opposite directions

§ 11-702. Passing vehicles proceeding in opposite directions. Drivers of vehicles proceeding in opposite directions shall pass each other to the right, and upon roadways having width for not more than one line of traffic in each direction each driver shall give to the other at least one-half of the main-traveled portion of the roadway as nearly as possible.

P.A. 76-1586, § 11-702, eff. July 1, 1970. Amended by P.A. 79-1069, § 1, eff. Jan. 1, 1976.

Formerly Ill.Rev.Stat.1991, ch. 95 ½, ¶ 11-702.

5/11-703. Overtaking a vehicle on the left

§ 11-703. Overtaking a vehicle on the left. The following rules govern the overtaking and passing of vehicles proceeding in the same direction, subject to those limitations, exceptions, and special rules otherwise stated in this Chapter:

(a) The driver of a vehicle overtaking another vehicle proceeding in the same direction shall pass to the left thereof at a safe distance and shall not again drive to the right side of the roadway until safely clear of the overtaken vehicle. In no event shall such movement be made by driving off the pavement or the main traveled portion of the roadway.

(b) Except when overtaking and passing on the right is permitted, the driver of an overtaken vehicle shall give way to the right in favor of the overtaking vehicle on audible signal and shall not increase the speed of his vehicle until completely passed by the overtaking vehicle.

(c) The driver of a 2 wheeled vehicle may not, in passing upon the left of any vehicle proceeding in the same direction, pass upon the right of any vehicle proceeding in the same direction unless there is an unobstructed lane of traffic available to permit such passing maneuver safely.

P.A. 76-1586, § 11-703, eff. July 1, 1970.

Formerly Ill.Rev.Stat.1991, ch. 95 ½, ¶ 11-703.

5/11-704. When overtaking on the right is permitted

§ 11-704. When overtaking on the right is permitted. (a) The driver of a vehicle with 3 or more wheels may overtake and pass upon the right of another vehicle only under the following conditions:

1. When the vehicle overtaken is making or about to make a left turn;

2. Upon a roadway with unobstructed pavement of sufficient width for two or more lines of vehicles moving lawfully in the direction being traveled by the overtaking vehicle.

3. Upon a one-way street, or upon any roadway on which traffic is restricted to one direction of movement, where the roadway is free from obstructions and of sufficient width for 2 or more lines of moving vehicles.

(b) The driver of a 2 wheeled vehicle may not pass upon the right of any other vehicle proceeding in the same direction unless the unobstructed pavement to the right of the vehicle being passed is of a width of not less than 8 feet.

(c) The driver of a vehicle may overtake and pass another vehicle upon the right only under conditions permitting such movement in safety. Such movement shall not be made by driving off the roadway.

P.A. 76-1586, § 11-704, eff. July 1, 1970. Amended by P.A. 84-873, § 1, eff. Jan. 1, 1986.

Formerly Ill.Rev.Stat.1991, ch. 95 ½, ¶ 11-704.

5/11-705. Limitations on overtaking on the left

§ 11-705. Limitations on overtaking on the left. No vehicle shall be driven to the left side of the center of the roadway in overtaking and passing another vehicle proceeding in the same direction unless authorized by the provisions of this Chapter and unless such left side is clearly visible and is free of oncoming traffic for a sufficient distance ahead to permit such overtaking and passing to be completely made without interfering with the safe operation of any vehicle approaching from the opposite direction or any vehicle overtaken. In every event the overtaking vehicle must return to an authorized lane of travel as soon as practicable and in the event the passing movement involves the use of a lane authorized for vehicles approaching from the opposite direction, before coming within 200 feet of any vehicle approaching from the opposite direction.

P.A. 76-1586, § 11-705, eff. July 1, 1970.

Formerly Ill.Rev.Stat.1991, ch. 95 ½, ¶ 11-705.

5/11-706. Further limitations on driving to the left of center of roadway

§ 11-706. Further limitations on driving to the left of center of roadway. (a) No vehicle shall be driven on the left side of the roadway under the following conditions:

1. When approaching or upon the crest of a grade or a curve in the highway where the driver's view is obstructed within such distance as to create a hazard in the event another vehicle might approach from the opposite direction.

2. When approaching within 100 feet of or traversing any intersection or railroad grade crossing.

3. When the view is obstructed upon approaching within 100 feet of any bridge, viaduct or tunnel.

(b) The limitations in sub-paragraphs 1, 2 and 3 do not apply upon a one-way roadway nor upon a roadway with unobstructed pavement of sufficient width for 2 or more lanes of moving traffic in each direction nor to the driver of a vehicle turning left into or from an alley, private road or driveway when such movements can be made with safety.

P.A. 76-1586, § 11-706, eff. July 1, 1970. Amended by P.A. 76-1739, § 1; P.A. 79-1069, § 1, eff. Jan. 1, 1976.

Formerly Ill.Rev.Stat.1991, ch. 95 ½, ¶ 11-706.

5/11-707. No-passing zones

§ 11-707. No-passing zones. (a) The Department and local authorities are authorized to determine those portions of any highway under their respective jurisdictions where overtaking and passing or driving on the left of the roadway would be especially hazardous and may by appropriate signs or markings on the roadway indicate the beginning and end of such zones. Upon request of a local school board, the Department or local authority which has jurisdiction over the roadway in question, shall determine whether a hazardous situation exists at a particular location and warrants a no-passing zone. If the Department or local authority determines that a no-passing zone is warranted, the school board and the Department or local authority shall share equally the cost of designating the no-passing zone by signs and markings. When such signs or markings are in place and clearly visible to an ordinarily observant person every driver of a vehicle shall obey the directions thereof.

(b) Where signs or markings are in place to define a no-passing zone as set forth in paragraph (a) no driver may at any time drive on the left side of the roadway within the no-passing zone or on the left side of any pavement striping designed to mark such no-passing zone throughout its length.

(c) This Section does not apply under the conditions described in Section 11-701(a)2, nor to the driver of a vehicle turning left into or from an alley, private road or driveway. The pavement striping designed to mark the no-passing zone may be crossed from the left hand lane for the purpose of completing a pass that was begun prior to the beginning of the zone in the driver's direction of travel.

(d) Special speed limit areas required under Section 11-605 of this Code in unincorporated areas only shall also be no-passing zones.

P.A. 76-1586, § 11-707, eff. July 1, 1970. Amended by P.A. 76-1739, § 1; P.A. 79-918, § 1, eff. Oct. 1, 1975; P.A. 79-1068, § 1, eff. Jan. 1, 1976; P.A. 79-1454, § 44, eff. Aug. 31, 1976; P.A. 86-471, § 1, eff. July 1, 1990.

Formerly Ill.Rev.Stat.1991, ch. 95 ½, ¶ 11-707.

5/11-708. One-way roadways and rotary traffic islands

§ 11-708. One-way roadways and rotary traffic islands. (a) The Department and local authorities, with respect to highways under their respective jurisdictions, may designate any highway, roadway, part of a roadway or specific lanes upon which vehicular traffic shall proceed in one direction at all or such times as shall be indicated by official traffic control devices.

(b) Upon a roadway so designated for one-way traffic, a vehicle shall be driven only in the direction designated at all or such times as shall be indicated by official traffic control devices.

(c) A vehicle passing around a rotary traffic island must be driven only to the right of such island.

(d) Whenever any highway has been divided into 2 or more roadways by leaving an intervening space or by a physical barrier or a clearly indicated dividing section so constructed as to impede vehicular traffic, every vehicle must be driven only upon the right-hand roadway unless directed or permitted to use another roadway by official traffic-control devices or police officers. No vehicle may be driven over, across, or within any such dividing space, barrier, or section, except through an opening in the physical barrier, or dividing section, or space, or at a cross-over or intersection as established by public authority.

(e) The driver of a vehicle may turn left across a paved noncurbed dividing space unless prohibited by an official traffic-control device.

P.A. 76-1586, § 11-708, eff. July 1, 1970. Amended by P.A. 76-1739, § 1; P.A. 84-873, § 1, eff. Jan. 1, 1986.

Formerly Ill.Rev.Stat.1991, ch. 95 ½, ¶ 11-708.

5/11-709. Driving on roadways laned for traffic

§ 11-709. Driving on roadways laned for traffic. Whenever any roadway has been divided into 2 or more clearly marked lanes for traffic the following rules in addition to all others consistent herewith shall apply.

(a) A vehicle shall be driven as nearly as practicable entirely within a single lane and shall not be moved from such lane until the driver has first ascertained that such movement can be made with safety.

(b) Upon a roadway which is divided into 3 lanes and provides for two-way movement of traffic, a vehicle shall not be driven in the center lane except when overtaking and passing another vehicle traveling in the same direction when such center lane is clear of traffic within a safe distance, or in preparation for making a left turn or where such center lane is at the time allocated exclusively to traffic moving in the same direction that the vehicle is proceeding and such allocation is designated by official traffic control devices.

(c) Official traffic control devices may be erected directing specific traffic to use a designated lane or designating those lanes to be used by traffic moving in a particular direction regardless of the center of the roadway and drivers of vehicles shall obey the directions of every such device. On multi-lane controlled access highways with 3 or more lanes in one direction or on any multi-laned highway with 2 or more lanes in one direction, the Department may designate lanes of traffic to be used by different types of motor vehicles. Drivers must obey lane designation signing except when it is necessary to use a different lane to make a turning maneuver.

(d) Official traffic control devices may be installed prohibiting the changing of lanes on sections of roadway and drivers of vehicles shall obey the directions of every such device.

P.A. 76–1586, § 11–709, eff. July 1, 1970. Amended by P.A. 77–67, § 1, eff. July 1, 1971; P.A. 84–1311, § 1, eff. Aug. 27, 1986.

Formerly Ill.Rev.Stat.1991, ch. 95 ½, ¶ 11–709.

5/11–709.1. Driving on shoulder

§ 11–709.1. (a) Vehicles shall be driven on a roadway, and shall only be driven on the shoulder for the purpose of stopping or accelerating from a stop while merging into traffic. It shall be a violation of this Section if while merging into traffic and while on the shoulder, the vehicle passes any other vehicle on the roadway adjacent to it.

(b) This Section shall not apply to any authorized emergency vehicle, or to any service vehicle while engaged in maintenance of the highway or related work.

P.A. 76–1586, § 11–709.1, added by P.A. 86–664, § 1, eff. Sept. 1, 1989.

Formerly Ill.Rev.Stat.1991, ch. 95 ½, ¶ 11–709.1.

5/11–710. Following too closely

§ 11–710. Following too closely. (a) The driver of a motor vehicle shall not follow another vehicle more closely than is reasonable and prudent, having due regard for the speed of such vehicles and the traffic upon and the condition of the highway.

(b) The driver of any truck or motor vehicle drawing another vehicle when traveling upon a roadway outside of a business or residence district and which is following another truck or motor vehicle drawing another vehicle shall, whenever conditions permit, leave sufficient space so that an overtaking vehicle may enter and occupy such space without danger, except that this shall not prevent a truck or motor vehicle drawing another vehicle from overtaking and passing any vehicle or combination of vehicles.

(c) Motor vehicles being driven upon any roadway outside of a business or residence district in a caravan or motorcade whether or not towing other vehicles shall be so operated as to allow sufficient space between each such vehicle or combination of vehicles so as to enable any other vehicle to enter and occupy such space without danger. This provision shall not apply to funeral processions.

P.A. 76–1586, § 11–710, eff. July 1, 1970. Amended by P.A. 79–1069, § 1, eff. Jan. 1, 1976.

Formerly Ill.Rev.Stat.1991, ch. 95 ½, ¶ 11–710.

5/11–711. Restrictions on use of controlled access highway

§ 11–711. Restrictions on use of controlled access highway. (a) No person may drive a vehicle onto or from any controlled access highway except at entrances and exits established by public authority.

(b) The Department with respect to any controlled access highway under its jurisdiction may prohibit the use of any such highways by pedestrians (except in authorized areas or facilities), bicycles, farm tractors, implements of husbandry, funeral processions, and any vehicle unable to maintain the minimum speed for which the highway is posted, or other non-motorized traffic or by any person operating a motor driven cycle. The Department may also prohibit the use of such highway to school buses picking up and discharging children and mail delivery vehicles picking up or delivering mail. The Department shall erect and maintain official signs on the controlled access highway on which such prohibitions are applicable and when so erected no person may disobey the restrictions stated on such sign.

P.A. 76–1586, § 11–711, eff. July 1, 1970.

Formerly Ill.Rev.Stat.1991, ch. 95 ½, ¶ 11–711.

ARTICLE VIII. TURNING AND STARTING AND SIGNALS ON STOPPING AND TURNING

Section

5/11–801. Required position and method of turning

§ 11–801. Required position and method of turning. (a) The driver of a vehicle intending to turn at an intersection shall do so as follows:

(1) Both the approach for a right turn and a right turn shall be made as close as practical to the right-hand curb or edge of the roadway.

(2) The driver of a vehicle intending to turn left at any intersection shall approach the intersection in the extreme left-hand lane lawfully available to traffic moving in the direction of travel of such vehicle, and after entering the intersection, the left turn shall be made so as to leave the intersection in a lane lawfully available to traffic moving in such direction upon the roadway being entered. Whenever practicable the left turn shall be made in that portion of the intersection to the left of the center of the intersection.

(3) The Department and local authorities in their respective jurisdictions may cause official traffic control devices to be placed within or adjacent to intersections and thereby require and direct that a different course from that specified in this Section be traveled by vehicles turning at an intersection, and when such devices are so placed no driver of a vehicle shall turn a vehicle at an intersection other than as directed and required by such devices.

(b) Two-way left turn lanes. Where a special lane for making left turns by drivers proceeding in opposite directions has been indicated by official traffic-control devices:

(1) A left turn shall not be made from any other lane.

(2) A vehicle shall not be driven in the lane except when preparing for or making a left turn from or into the roadway or when preparing for or making a U turn when otherwise permitted by law.

(c) When a motor vehicle and a mass transit bus are traveling in the same direction on the same multi-laned highway, street or road, the operator of the motor vehicle overtaking such bus, which is stopped at an intersection on the right side of the roadway to receive or discharge passengers, shall pass to the left of the bus at a safe distance and shall not turn to the right in front of the bus at that intersection.

P.A. 76-1586, § 11-801, eff. July 1, 1970. Amended by P.A. 76-1739, § 1; P.A. 81-860, § 1, eff. Jan. 1, 1980; P.A. 84-873, § 1, eff. Jan. 1, 1986; P.A. 85-786, § 1, eff. Jan. 1, 1988.

Formerly Ill.Rev.Stat.1991, ch. 95 ½, ¶ 11-801.

5/11-802. Limitations on U turns

§ 11-802. Limitations on U turns. (a) The driver of any vehicle shall not turn such vehicle so as to proceed in the opposite direction unless such movement can be made in safety and without interfering with other traffic.

(b) No vehicle shall be turned so as to proceed in the opposite direction upon any curve, or upon the approach to or near the crest of a grade, where such vehicle cannot be seen by the driver of any other vehicle approaching from either direction within 500 feet.

P.A. 76-1586, § 11-802, eff. July 1, 1970. Amended by P.A. 79-1068, § 1, eff. Jan. 1, 1976; P.A. 82-783, Art. IV, § 25, eff. July 13, 1982.

Formerly Ill.Rev.Stat.1991, ch. 95 ½, ¶ 11-802.

5/11-803. Starting parked vehicle

§ 11-803. Starting parked vehicle. No person shall start a vehicle which is stopped, standing, or parked unless and until such movement can be made with reasonable safety.

P.A. 76-1586, § 11-803, eff. July 1, 1970.

Formerly Ill.Rev.Stat.1991, ch. 95 ½, ¶ 11-803.

5/11-804. When signal required

§ 11-804. When signal required. (a) No person may turn a vehicle at an intersection unless the vehicle is in proper position upon the roadway as required in Section 11-801 or turn a vehicle to enter a private road or driveway, or otherwise turn a vehicle from a direct course or move right or left upon a roadway unless and until such movement can be made with reasonable safety. No person may so turn any vehicle without giving an appropriate signal in the manner hereinafter provided.

(b) A signal of intention to turn right or left when required must be given continuously during not less than the last 100 feet traveled by the vehicle before turning within a business or residence district, and such signal must be given continuously during not less than the last 200 feet traveled by the vehicle before turning outside a business or residence district.

(c) No person may stop or suddenly decrease the speed of a vehicle without first giving an appropriate signal in the manner provided in this Chapter to the driver of any vehicle immediately to the rear when there is opportunity to give such a signal.

(d) The electric turn signal device required in Section 12-208 of this Act must be used to indicate an intention to turn, change lanes or start from a parallel parked position but must not be flashed on one side only on a parked or disabled vehicle or flashed as a courtesy or "do pass" signal to operators of other vehicles approaching from the rear. However, such signal devices may be flashed simultaneously on both sides of a motor vehicle to indicate the presence of a vehicular traffic hazard requiring unusual care in approaching, overtaking and passing.

P.A. 76-1586, § 11-804, eff. July 1, 1970. Amended by P.A. 76-2167, § 1, eff. July 1, 1970; P.A. 78-510, § 1, eff. Oct. 1, 1973; P.A. 78-738, § 1, eff. Jan. 1, 1974; P.A. 78-1297, § 58, eff. March 4, 1975.

Formerly Ill.Rev.Stat.1991, ch. 95 ½, ¶ 11-804.

5/11-805. Signal by hand or arm or signal device

§ 11-805. Signal by hand or arm or signal device. Any stop or turn signal when required herein shall be given either by means of the hand and arm or by an electric turn signal device conforming to the requirements provided in Section 12-208 of this act.

P.A. 76-1586, § 11-805, eff. July 1, 1970. Amended by P.A. 79-1069, § 1, eff. Jan. 1, 1976.

Formerly Ill.Rev.Stat.1991, ch. 95 ½, ¶ 11-805.

5/11-806. Method of giving hand and arm signals

§ 11-806. Method of giving hand and arm signals. All signals herein required given by hand and arm shall be given from the left side of the vehicle in the following manner and such signals shall indicate as follows:

1. Left turn—Hand and arm extended horizontally.
2. Right turn—Hand and arm extended upward.
3. Stop or decrease of speed—Hand and arm extended downward.

P.A. 76-1586, § 11-806, eff. July 1, 1970.

Formerly Ill.Rev.Stat.1991, ch. 95 ½, ¶ 11-806.

ARTICLE IX. RIGHT-OF-WAY

Section

5/11-901. Vehicles approaching or entering intersection

§ 11-901. Vehicles approaching or entering intersection. (a) When 2 vehicles approach or enter an intersection from different roadways at approximately the same time, the driver of the vehicle on the left must yield the right-of-way to the vehicle on the right.

(b) The right-of-way rule declared in paragraph (a) of this Section is modified at through highways and otherwise as stated in this Chapter.

P.A. 76-1586, § 11-901, eff. July 1, 1970. Amended by P.A. 76-1739, § 1, eff. Oct. 6, 1969.

Formerly Ill.Rev.Stat.1991, ch. 95 ½, ¶ 11-901.

5/11-901.01. Vehicles approaching or entering a "T" intersection

§ 11-901.01. Vehicles approaching or entering a "T" intersection. The driver of a vehicle approaching the intersection of a highway from a highway which terminates at the intersection, not otherwise regulated by this Act or controlled by traffic control signs or signals, shall stop, yield, and grant the privilege of immediate use of the intersection to another vehicle which has entered the intersection from the non-terminating highway or is approaching the intersection on the non-terminating highway in such proximity as to constitute a hazard and after stopping may proceed when the driver may safely enter the intersection without interference or collision with the traffic using the non-terminating highway.

P.A. 76-1586, § 11-901.01, added by P.A. 81-860, § 1, eff. Jan. 1, 1980.

Formerly Ill.Rev.Stat.1991, ch. 95 ½, ¶ 11-901.01.

5/11-902. Vehicle turning left

§ 11-902. Vehicle turning left. The driver of a vehicle intending to turn to the left within an intersection or into an alley, private road, or driveway shall yield the right-of-way to any vehicle approaching from the opposite direction which is so close as to constitute an immediate hazard, but said driver, having so yielded may proceed at such time as a safe interval occurs.

P.A. 76-1586, § 11-902, eff. July 1, 1970.

Formerly Ill.Rev.Stat.1991, ch. 95 ½, ¶ 11-902.

5/11-903. Vehicles entering stop crosswalk

§ 11-903. Vehicles entering stop crosswalk. Where stop signs or flashing red signals are in place at an intersection or flashing red signals are in place at a plainly marked crosswalk between intersections, drivers of vehicles shall stop before entering the nearest crosswalk and pedestrians within or entering the crosswalk at either edge of the roadway shall have the right-of-way over vehicles so stopped. Drivers of vehicles having so yielded the right-of-way to pedestrians entering or within the nearest crosswalk at an intersection shall also yield the right-of-way to pedestrians within any other crosswalk at the intersection.

P.A. 76-1586, § 11-903, eff. July 1, 1970.

Formerly Ill.Rev.Stat.1991, ch. 95 ½, ¶ 11-903.

5/11-904. Vehicle entering stop or yield intersection

§ 11-904. Vehicle entering stop or yield intersection. (a) Preferential right-of-way at an intersection may be indicated by stop or yield signs as authorized in Section 11-302 of this Chapter.

(b) Except when directed to proceed by a police officer or traffic-control signal, every driver of a vehicle approaching a stop intersection indicated by a stop sign shall stop at a clearly marked stop line, but if none, before entering the crosswalk on the near side of the intersection, or if none, then at the point nearest the intersecting roadway where the driver has a view of approaching traffic on the intersecting roadway before entering the intersection. After having stopped, the driver shall yield the right-of-way to any vehicle which has entered the intersection from another roadway or which is approaching so closely on the roadway as to constitute an immediate hazard during the time when the driver is moving across or within the intersection, but said driver having so yielded may proceed at such time as a safe interval occurs.

(c) The driver of a vehicle approaching a yield sign shall in obedience to such sign slow down to a speed reasonable for the existing conditions and, if required for safety to stop, shall stop at a clearly marked stop line, but if none, before entering the crosswalk on the near side of the intersection, or if none, then at the point nearest the intersecting roadway where the driver has a view of approaching traffic on the intersecting roadway. After slowing or stopping, the driver shall yield the right-of-way to any vehicle in the intersection or approaching on another roadway so closely as to constitute an immediate hazard during the time such driver is moving across or within the intersection.

(d) If a driver is involved in a collision at an intersection or interferes with the movement of other vehicles after driving past a yield right-of-way sign, such collision or interference shall be deemed prima facie evidence of the driver's failure to yield right-of-way.

P.A. 76-1586, § 11-904, eff. July 1, 1970. Amended by P.A. 76-1739, § 1, eff. Oct. 6, 1969.

Formerly Ill.Rev.Stat.1991, ch. 95 ½, ¶ 11-904.

5/11-905. Merging traffic

§ 11-905. Merging traffic. Notwithstanding the right of way provision in Sec. 11-901 of this Act, at an intersection where traffic lanes are provided for merging traffic the driver of each vehicle on the converging roadways is required to adjust his vehicular speed and lateral position so as to avoid a collision with another vehicle.

P.A. 76-1586, § 11-905, eff. July 1, 1970. Amended by P.A. 81-860, § 1, eff. Jan. 1, 1980.

Formerly Ill.Rev.Stat.1991, ch. 95 ½, ¶ 11-905.

5/11-906. Vehicle entering highway from private road or driveway

§ 11-906. Vehicle entering highway from private road or driveway. The driver of a vehicle about to enter or cross a highway from an alley, building, private road or driveway shall yield the right-of-way to all vehicles approaching on the highway to be entered.

P.A. 76-1586, § 11-906, eff. July 1, 1970. Amended by P.A. 76-1739, § 1, eff. Oct. 6, 1969.

Formerly Ill.Rev.Stat.1991, ch. 95 ½, ¶ 11-906.

5/11-907. Operation of vehicles and streetcars on approach of authorized emergency vehicles.

Text of section effective until June 1, 2003

(a) Upon the immediate approach of an authorized emergency vehicle making use of audible and visual signals meeting the requirements of this Code or a police vehicle properly and lawfully making use of an audible or visual signal,

(1) the driver of every other vehicle shall yield the right-of-way and shall immediately drive to a position parallel to, and as close as possible to, the right-hand edge or curb of the highway clear of any intersection and shall, if necessary to permit the safe passage of the emergency vehicle, stop and remain in such position until the authorized emergency vehicle has passed, unless otherwise directed by a police officer and

(2) the operator of every streetcar shall immediately stop such car clear of any intersection and keep it in such position until the authorized emergency vehicle has passed, unless otherwise directed by a police officer.

(b) This Section shall not operate to relieve the driver of an authorized emergency vehicle from the duty to drive with due regard for the safety of all persons using the highway.

(c) Upon approaching a stationary authorized emergency vehicle, when the authorized emergency vehicle is giving a signal by displaying alternately flashing red, red and white, blue, or red and blue lights or amber or yellow warning lights, a person who drives an approaching vehicle shall:

(1) proceeding with due caution, yield the right-of-way by making a lane change into a lane not adjacent to that of the authorized emergency vehicle, if possible with due regard to safety and traffic conditions, if on a highway having at least 4 lanes with not less than 2 lanes proceeding in the same direction as the approaching vehicle; or

(2) proceeding with due caution, reduce the speed of the vehicle, maintaining a safe speed for road conditions, if changing lanes would be impossible or unsafe.

As used in this subsection (c), "authorized emergency vehicle" includes any vehicle authorized by law to be equipped with oscillating, rotating, or flashing lights under Section 12-215 of this Code, while the owner or operator of the vehicle is engaged in his or her official duties.

(d) A person who violates subsection (c) of this Section commits a business offense punishable by a fine of not more than $10,000. It is a factor in aggravation if the person committed the offense while in violation of Section 11-501 of this Code.

(e) If a violation of subsection (c) of this Section results in damage to the property of another person, in addition to any other penalty imposed, the person's driving privileges shall be suspended for a fixed period of not less than 90 days and not more than one year.

(f) If a violation of subsection (c) of this Section results in injury to another person, in addition to any other penalty imposed, the person's driving privileges shall be suspended for a fixed period of not less than 180 days and not more than 2 years.

(g) If a violation of subsection (c) of this Section results in the death of another person, in addition to any other penalty imposed, the person's driving privileges shall be suspended for 2 years.

(h) The Secretary of State shall, upon receiving a record of a judgment entered against a person under subsection (c) of this Section:

(1) suspend the person's driving privileges for the mandatory period; or

(2) extend the period of an existing suspension by the appropriate mandatory period.

P.A. 76-1586, § 11-907, eff. July 1, 1970. Amended by P.A. 83-781, § 1, eff. Jan. 1, 1984; P.A. 92-283, § 5, eff. Jan. 1, 2002.

Formerly Ill.Rev.Stat.1991, ch. 95 ½, ¶ 11-907.

For text of section effective June 1, 2003, see 625 ILCS 5/11-907, post

5/11-907. Operation of vehicles and streetcars on approach of authorized emergency vehicles.

Text of section effective June 1, 2003

§ 11-907. Operation of vehicles and streetcars on approach of authorized emergency vehicles.

(a) Upon the immediate approach of an authorized emergency vehicle making use of audible and visual signals meeting the requirements of this Code or a police vehicle properly and lawfully making use of an audible or visual signal,

(1) the driver of every other vehicle shall yield the right-of-way and shall immediately drive to a position parallel to, and as close as possible to, the right-hand edge or curb of the highway clear of any intersection and shall, if necessary to permit the safe passage of the emergency vehicle, stop and remain in such position until the authorized emergency vehicle has passed, unless otherwise directed by a police officer and

(2) the operator of every streetcar shall immediately stop such car clear of any intersection and keep it in such position until the authorized emergency vehicle has passed, unless otherwise directed by a police officer.

(b) This Section shall not operate to relieve the driver of an authorized emergency vehicle from the duty to drive with due regard for the safety of all persons using the highway.

(c) Upon approaching a stationary authorized emergency vehicle, when the authorized emergency vehicle is giving a signal by displaying alternately flashing red, red and white, blue, or red and blue lights or amber or yellow warning lights, a person who drives an approaching vehicle shall:

(1) proceeding with due caution, yield the right-of-way by making a lane change into a lane not adjacent to that of the authorized emergency vehicle, if possible with due regard to safety and traffic conditions, if on a highway having at least 4 lanes with not less than 2 lanes proceeding in the same direction as the approaching vehicle; or

(2) proceeding with due caution, reduce the speed of the vehicle, maintaining a safe speed for road conditions, if changing lanes would be impossible or unsafe.

As used in this subsection (c), "authorized emergency vehicle" includes any vehicle authorized by law to be equipped with oscillating, rotating, or flashing lights under Section 12-215 of this Code, while the owner or operator of the vehicle is engaged in his or her official duties.

(d) A person who violates subsection (c) of this Section commits a business offense punishable by a fine of not more than $10,000. A person charged with the offense must appear in court to answer the charges. It is a factor in aggravation if the person committed the offense while in violation of Section 11-501 of this Code.

(e) If a violation of subsection (c) of this Section results in damage to the property of another person, in addition to any other penalty imposed, the person's driving privileges shall be suspended for a fixed period of not less than 90 days and not more than one year.

(f) If a violation of subsection (c) of this Section results in injury to another person, in addition to any other penalty imposed, the person's driving privileges shall be suspended for a fixed period of not less than 180 days and not more than 2 years.

(g) If a violation of subsection (c) of this Section results in the death of another person, in addition to any other penalty imposed, the person's driving privileges shall be suspended for 2 years.

(h) The Secretary of State shall, upon receiving a record of a judgment entered against a person under subsection (c) of this Section:

(1) suspend the person's driving privileges for the mandatory period; or

(2) extend the period of an existing suspension by the appropriate mandatory period.

P.A. 76–1586, § 11–907, eff. July 1, 1970. Amended by P.A. 83–781, § 1, eff. Jan. 1, 1984; P.A. 92–283, § 5, eff. Jan. 1, 2002; P.A. 92–872, § 5, eff. June 1, 2003.

Formerly Ill.Rev.Stat.1991, ch. 95 ½, ¶ 11–907.

For text of section effective until June 1, 2003, see 625 ILCS 5/11–907, ante

5/11–908. Vehicle approaching highway construction or maintenance area

Text of section effective until June 1, 2003

§ 11–908. Vehicle approaching highway construction or maintenance area. (a) The driver of a vehicle shall yield the right of way to any authorized vehicle or pedestrian actually engaged in work upon a highway within any highway construction or maintenance area indicated by official traffic-control devices.

(b) The driver of a vehicle shall yield the right of way to any authorized vehicle obviously and actually engaged in work upon a highway whenever the vehicle engaged in construction or maintenance work displays flashing lights as provided in Section 12–215 of this Act.

(c) The driver of a vehicle shall stop if signaled to do so by a flagger or a traffic control signal and remain in such position until signaled to proceed. If a driver of a vehicle fails to stop when signaled to do so by a flagger, the flagger is authorized to report such offense to the State's Attorney or authorized prosecutor.

P.A. 76–1586, § 11–908, added by P.A. 81–312, § 1, eff. Jan. 1, 1980. Amended by P.A. 84–873, § 1, eff. Jan. 1, 1986; P.A. 86–611, § 1, eff. Sept. 1, 1989.

Formerly Ill.Rev.Stat.1991, ch. 95 ½, ¶ 11–908.

For text of section effective June 1, 2003, see 625 ILCS 5/11–908, post

5/11–908. Vehicle approaching or entering a highway construction or maintenance area or zone

Text of section effective June 1, 2003

§ 11–908. Vehicle approaching or entering a highway construction or maintenance area or zone.

(a) The driver of a vehicle shall yield the right of way to any authorized vehicle or pedestrian actually engaged in work upon a highway within any highway construction or maintenance area indicated by official traffic-control devices.

(a–1) Upon entering a construction or maintenance zone when workers are present, a person who drives a vehicle shall:

(1) proceeding with due caution, make a lane change into a lane not adjacent to that of the workers present, if possible with due regard to safety and traffic conditions, if on a highway having at least 4 lanes with not less than 2 lanes proceeding in the same direction as the approaching vehicle; or

(2) proceeding with due caution, reduce the speed of the vehicle, maintaining a safe speed for road conditions, if changing lanes would be impossible or unsafe.

(a–2) A person who violates subsection (a–1) of this Section commits a business offense punishable by a fine of not more than $10,000. A person charged with the offense must appear in court to answer the charges. It is a factor in aggravation if the person committed the offense while in violation of Section 11–501 of this Code.

(a–3) If a violation of subsection (a–1) of this Section results in damage to the property of another person, in addition to any other penalty imposed, the person's driving privileges shall be suspended for a fixed period of not less than 90 days and not more than one year.

(a–4) If a violation of subsection (a–1) of this Section results in injury to another person, in addition to any other penalty imposed, the person's driving privileges shall be suspended for a fixed period of not less than 180 days and not more than 2 years.

(a–5) If a violation of subsection (a–1) of this Section results in the death of another person, in addition to any other penalty imposed, the person's driving privileges shall be suspended for 2 years.

(a–6) The Secretary of State shall, upon receiving a record of a judgment entered against a person under subsection (a–1) of this Section:

(1) suspend the person's driving privileges for the mandatory period; or

(2) extend the period of an existing suspension by the appropriate mandatory period.

(b) The driver of a vehicle shall yield the right of way to any authorized vehicle obviously and actually engaged in work upon a highway whenever the vehicle engaged in construction or maintenance work displays flashing lights as provided in Section 12–215 of this Act.

(c) The driver of a vehicle shall stop if signaled to do so by a flagger or a traffic control signal and remain in such position until signaled to proceed. If a driver of a vehicle fails to stop when signaled to do so by a flagger, the flagger is authorized to report such offense to the State's Attorney or authorized prosecutor. The penalties imposed for a violation of this subsection (c) shall be in addition to any penalties imposed for a violation of subsection (a–1).

P.A. 76–1586, § 11–908, added by P.A. 81–312, § 1, eff. Jan. 1, 1980. Amended by P.A. 84–873, § 1, eff. Jan. 1, 1986; P.A. 86–611, § 1, eff. Sept. 1, 1989; P.A. 92–872, § 5, eff. June 1, 2003.

Formerly Ill.Rev.Stat.1991, ch. 95 ½, ¶ 11–908.

For text of section effective until June 1, 2003, see 625 ILCS 5/11–908, ante

ARTICLE X. PEDESTRIANS' RIGHTS AND DUTIES

5/11-1001. Pedestrian obedience to traffic control devices and traffic regulations

§ 11-1001. Pedestrian obedience to traffic control devices and traffic regulations.

(a) A pedestrian shall obey the instructions of any official traffic control device specifically applicable to him, unless otherwise directed by a police officer.

(b) Pedestrians shall be subject to traffic and pedestrian control signals provided in Sections 11-306 and 11-307 of this Chapter, but at all other places pedestrians shall be accorded the privileges and shall be subject to the restrictions stated in this Article.

P.A. 76-1586, § 11-1001, eff. July 1, 1970. Amended by P.A. 76-1734, § 1, eff. Oct. 6, 1969.

Formerly Ill.Rev.Stat.1991, ch. 95 ½, ¶ 11-1001.

5/11-1002. Pedestrians' right-of-way at crosswalks

§ 11-1002. Pedestrians' right-of-way at crosswalks. (a) When traffic control signals are not in place or not in operation the driver of a vehicle shall yield the right-of-way, slowing down or stopping if need be to so yield, to a pedestrian crossing the roadway within a crosswalk when the pedestrian is upon the half of the roadway upon which the vehicle is traveling, or when the pedestrian is approaching so closely from the opposite half of the roadway as to be in danger.

(b) No pedestrian shall suddenly leave a curb or other place of safety and walk or run into the path of a moving vehicle which is so close as to constitute an immediate hazard.

(c) Paragraph (a) shall not apply under the condition stated in Section 11-1003(b).

(d) Whenever any vehicle is stopped at a marked crosswalk or at any unmarked crosswalk at an intersection to permit a pedestrian to cross the roadway, the driver of any other vehicle approaching from the rear shall not overtake and pass such stopped vehicle.

(e) Whenever stop signs or flashing red signals are in place at an intersection or at a plainly marked crosswalk between intersections, drivers shall yield right-of-way to pedestrians as set forth in Section 11-904 of this Chapter.

P.A. 76-1586, § 11-1002, eff. July 1, 1970. Amended by P.A. 76-2168, § 1, eff. July 1, 1970; P.A. 77-329, § 1, eff. Jan. 1, 1972; P.A. 79-857, § 1, eff. Jan. 1, 1976.

Formerly Ill.Rev.Stat.1991, ch. 95 ½, ¶ 11-1002.

5/11-1003. Crossing at other than crosswalks

§ 11-1003. Crossing at other than crosswalks.

(a) Every pedestrian crossing a roadway at any point other than within a marked crosswalk or within an unmarked crosswalk at an intersection shall yield the right-of-way to all vehicles upon the roadway.

(b) Any pedestrian crossing a roadway at a point where a pedestrian tunnel or overhead pedestrian crossing has been provided shall yield the right-of-way to all vehicles upon the roadway.

(c) Between adjacent intersections at which traffic-control signals are in operation pedestrians shall not cross at any place except in a marked crosswalk.

(d) No pedestrian shall cross a roadway intersection diagonally unless authorized by official traffic-control devices; and, when authorized to cross diagonally, pedestrians shall cross only in accordance with the official traffic-control devices pertaining to such crossing movements.

(e) Pedestrians with disabilities may cross a roadway at any point other than within a marked crosswalk or within an unmarked crosswalk where the intersection is physically inaccessible to them but they shall yield the right-of-way to all vehicles upon the roadway.

P.A. 76-1586, § 11-1003, eff. July 1, 1970. Amended by P.A. 76-2169, § 1, eff. July 1, 1970; P.A. 79-857, § 1, eff. Jan. 1, 1976; P.A. 80-1495, § 36, eff. Jan. 8, 1979; P.A. 88-685, § 5, eff. Jan. 24, 1995.

Formerly Ill.Rev.Stat.1991, ch. 95 ½, ¶ 11-1003.

5/11-1003.1. Drivers to exercise due care

§ 11-1003.1. Drivers to exercise due care. Notwithstanding other provisions of this Code or the provisions of any local ordinance, every driver of a vehicle shall exercise due care to avoid colliding with any pedestrian, or any person operating a bicycle or other device propelled by human power and shall give warning by sounding the horn when necessary and shall exercise proper precaution upon observing any child or any obviously confused, incapacitated or intoxicated person.

P.A. 76-1586, § 11-1003.1, added by P.A. 79-857, § 2, eff. Jan. 1, 1976. Amended by P.A. 82-132, § 1, eff. Jan. 1, 1982.

Formerly Ill.Rev.Stat.1991, ch. 95 ½, ¶ 11-1003.1.

5/11-1004. Pedestrian with disabilities; right-of-way

§ 11-1004. Pedestrian with disabilities; right-of-way. The driver of a vehicle shall yield the right-of-way to any pedestrian with clearly visible disabilities.

P.A. 76-1586, § 11-1004, eff. July 1, 1970. Amended by P.A. 79-857, § 1, eff. Jan. 1, 1976; P.A. 82-222, § 5, eff. Jan. 1, 1982; P.A. 83-93, § 5, eff. Jan. 1, 1984; P.A. 88-685, § 5, eff. Jan. 24, 1995.

Formerly Ill.Rev.Stat.1991, ch. 95 ½, ¶ 11-1004.

5/11–1004.1. Motorized wheelchairs

§ 11–1004.1. Motorized wheelchairs. Every person operating a motorized wheelchair upon a sidewalk or roadway shall be granted all the rights and shall be subject to all the duties applicable to a pedestrian.

P.A. 76–1586, § 11–1004.1, added by P.A. 84–672, § 1, eff. Sept. 20, 1985.

Formerly Ill.Rev.Stat.1991, ch. 95 ½, ¶ 11–1004.1.

5/11–1005. Pedestrians to use right half of crosswalks

§ 11–1005. Pedestrians to use right half of crosswalks. Pedestrians shall move, whenever practicable, upon the right half of crosswalks.

P.A. 76–1586, § 11–1005, eff. July 1, 1970.

Formerly Ill.Rev.Stat.1991, ch. 95 ½, ¶ 11–1005.

5/11–1005.1. Electric personal assistive mobility devices

Text of section added effective June 1, 2003

§ 11–1005.1. Electric personal assistive mobility devices. Every person operating an electric personal assistive mobility device upon a sidewalk or roadway has all the rights and is subject to all the duties applicable to a pedestrian. Nothing in this Section shall be deemed to limit or preempt the authority of any home rule or non-home rule unit of local government from regulating or prohibiting the use of electric personal assistive mobility devices.

P.A. 76–1586, § 11–1005.1, added by P.A. 92–868, § 5, eff. June 1, 2003.

5/11–1006. Pedestrians soliciting rides or business

§ 11–1006. Pedestrians soliciting rides or business. (a) No person shall stand in a roadway for the purpose of soliciting a ride from the driver of any vehicle.

(b) No person shall stand on a highway for the purpose of soliciting employment or business from the occupant of any vehicle.

(c) No person shall stand on a highway for the purpose of soliciting contributions from the occupant of any vehicle except within a municipality when expressly permitted by municipal ordinance. The local municipality, city, village, or other local governmental entity in which the solicitation takes place shall determine by ordinance where and when solicitations may take place based on the safety of the solicitors and the safety of motorists. The decision shall also take into account the orderly flow of traffic and may not allow interference with the operation of official traffic control devices. The soliciting agency shall be:

1. registered with the Attorney General as a charitable organization as provided by "An Act to regulate solicitation and collection of funds for charitable purposes, providing for violations thereof, and making an appropriation therefor", approved July 26, 1963, as amended;[1]

2. engaged in a Statewide fund raising activity; and

3. liable for any injuries to any person or property during the solicitation which is causally related to an act of ordinary negligence of the soliciting agent.

Any person engaged in the act of solicitation shall be 16 years of age or more and shall be wearing a high visibility vest.

(d) No person shall stand on or in the proximity of a highway for the purpose of soliciting the watching or guarding of any vehicle while parked or about to be parked on a highway.

(e) Every person who is convicted of a violation of this Section shall be guilty of a Class A misdemeanor.

P.A. 76–1586, § 11–1006, eff. July 1, 1970. Amended by P.A. 76–1734, § 1; P.A. 79–857, § 1, eff. Jan. 1, 1976; P.A. 80–911, § 1, eff. Oct. 1, 1977; P.A. 81–29, § 1, eff. Jan. 1, 1980; P.A. 88–589, § 10, eff. Aug. 14, 1994.

Formerly Ill.Rev.Stat.1991, ch. 95 ½, ¶ 11–1006.

1 225 ILCS 460/1 et seq.

5/11–1007. Pedestrians walking on highways

§ 11–1007. Pedestrians walking on highways. (a) Where a sidewalk is provided and its use is practicable, it shall be unlawful for any pedestrian to walk along and upon an adjacent roadway.

(b) Where a sidewalk is not available, any pedestrian walking along and upon a highway shall walk only on a shoulder, as far as practicable from the edge of the roadway.

(c) Where neither a sidewalk nor a shoulder is available, any pedestrian walking along and upon a highway shall walk as near as practicable to an outside edge of a roadway, and, if on a two-way roadway, shall walk only on the left side of the roadway.

(d) Except as otherwise provided in this Chapter, any pedestrian upon a roadway shall yield the right-of-way to all vehicles upon the roadway.

P.A. 76–1586, § 11–1007, eff. July 1, 1970. Amended by P.A. 79–857, § 1, eff. Jan. 1, 1976.

Formerly Ill.Rev.Stat.1991, ch. 95 ½, ¶ 11–1007.

5/11–1007.1. § 11–1007.1. Repealed by P.A. 77–329, § 2, eff. Jan. 1, 1972

5/11–1008. Right-of-way on sidewalks

§ 11–1008. Right-of-way on sidewalks. The driver of a vehicle shall yield the right-of-way to any pedestrian on a sidewalk.

P.A. 76–1586, § 11–1008, added by P.A. 79–857, § 2, eff. Jan. 1, 1976.

Formerly Ill.Rev.Stat.1991, ch. 95 ½, ¶ 11–1008.

5/11–1009. Pedestrians yield to authorized emergency vehicles

§ 11–1009. Pedestrians yield to authorized emergency vehicles. Upon the immediate approach of an authorized emergency vehicle making use of an audible signal and visual signals meeting the requirements of Section 12–217 of this Chapter, or of a police vehicle properly and lawfully making use of an audible signal only, every pedestrian shall yield the right-of-way to the authorized emergency vehicle.

P.A. 76–1586, § 11–1009, added by P.A. 79–857, § 2, eff. Jan. 1, 1976.

Formerly Ill.Rev.Stat.1991, ch. 95 ½, ¶ 11–1009.

5/11–1010. Pedestrians under influence of alcohol or drugs

§ 11–1010. Pedestrians under influence of alcohol or drugs. A pedestrian who is under the influence of alcohol or any drug to a degree which renders himself a hazard shall not walk or be upon a highway except on a sidewalk.

P.A. 76–1586, § 11–1010, added by P.A. 79–857, § 2, eff. Jan. 1, 1976.

Formerly Ill.Rev.Stat.1991, ch. 95 ½, ¶ 11–1010.

5/11-1011. Bridge and railroad signals

§ 11-1011. Bridge and railroad signals.

(a) No pedestrian shall enter or remain upon any bridge or approach thereto beyond the bridge signal, gate, or barrier after a bridge operation signal indication has been given.

(b) No pedestrian shall pass through, around, over, or under any crossing gate or barrier at a railroad grade crossing or bridge while such gate or barrier is closed or is being opened or closed.

(c) No pedestrian shall enter, remain upon or traverse over a railroad grade crossing or pedestrian walkway crossing a railroad track when an audible bell or clearly visible electric or mechanical signal device is operational giving warning of the presence, approach, passage, or departure of a railroad train.

(d) A violation of any part of this Section is a petty offense for which a $250 fine shall be imposed for a first violation, and a $500 fine shall be imposed for a second or subsequent violation. The court may impose 25 hours of community service in place of the $250 fine for a first violation.

(e) Local authorities shall impose fines as established in subsection (d) for pedestrians who fail to obey signals indicating the presence, approach, passage, or departure of a train.

P.A. 76-1586, § 11-1011, added by P.A. 79-857, § 2, eff. Jan. 1, 1976. Amended by P.A. 86-429, § 1, eff. Jan. 1, 1990; P.A. 86-1028, Art. III, § 3-29, eff. Feb. 5, 1990; P.A. 89-186, § 5, eff. Jan. 1, 1996; P.A. 89-658, § 5, eff. Jan. 1, 1997; P.A. 92-814, § 5, eff. Jan. 1, 2003.

Formerly Ill.Rev.Stat.1991, ch. 95 ½, ¶ 11-1011.

P.A. 89-658 incorporated the amendment by P.A. 89-186.

ARTICLE XI. STREET CARS AND SAFETY ZONES

Section

5/11-1101. Passing street car on left

§ 11-1101. Passing street car on left. (a) The driver of a vehicle shall not overtake and pass upon the left nor drive upon the left side of any street car proceeding in the same direction, whether such street car is actually in motion or temporarily at rest, except:

1. When so directed by a police officer;

2. When upon a one-way street; or

3. When upon a street where the tracks are so located as to prevent compliance with the section.

(b) The driver of any vehicle when permitted to overtake and pass upon the left of a street car which has stopped for the purpose of receiving or discharging any passenger shall reduce speed and may proceed only upon exercising due caution for pedestrians and shall accord pedestrians the right-of-way when required by other Sections of this Chapter.

P.A. 76-1586, § 11-1101, eff. July 1, 1970.

Formerly Ill.Rev.Stat.1991, ch. 95 ½, ¶ 11-1101.

5/11-1102. Passing street car on right

§ 11-1102. Passing street car on right. The driver of a vehicle overtaking upon the right any street car stopped or about to stop for the purpose of receiving or discharging any passenger shall stop such vehicle at least ten feet to the rear of the nearest running board or door of such street car and thereupon remain standing until all passengers have boarded such car or upon alighting have reached a place of safety, except that where a safety zone has been established a vehicle need not be brought to a stop before passing any such street car but may proceed past such car at a speed not greater than is reasonable and proper and with due caution for the safety of pedestrians.

P.A. 76-1586, § 11-1102, eff. July 1, 1970.

Formerly Ill.Rev.Stat.1991, ch. 95 ½, ¶ 11-1102.

5/11-1103. Driving on street car tracks

§ 11-1103. Driving on street car tracks. (a) The driver of any vehicle proceeding upon any street car track in front of a street car upon a street shall remove such vehicle from the track as soon as practical after signal from the operator of said street car.

(b) The driver of a vehicle upon overtaking and passing a street car shall not turn in front of such street car so as to interfere with or impede its movement.

P.A. 76-1586, § 11-1103, eff. July 1, 1970.

Formerly Ill.Rev.Stat.1991, ch. 95 ½, ¶ 11-1103.

5/11-1104. Driving through safety zone prohibited

§ 11-1104. Driving through safety zone prohibited. No vehicle shall at any time be driven through or within a safety zone.

P.A. 76-1586, § 11-1104, eff. July 1, 1970.

Formerly Ill.Rev.Stat.1991, ch. 95 ½, ¶ 11-1104.

ARTICLE XII. SPECIAL STOPS REQUIRED

Section

5/11-1201. Obedience to signal indicating approach of train

§ 11-1201. Obedience to signal indicating approach of train.

(a) Whenever any person driving a vehicle approaches a railroad grade crossing where the driver is not always required to stop, the person must exercise due care and caution as the existence of a railroad track across a highway is a warning of danger, and under any of the circumstances stated in this Section, the driver shall stop within 50 feet but not less than 15 feet from the nearest rail of the railroad and shall not proceed until the tracks are clear and he or she can do so safely. The foregoing requirements shall apply when:

1. A clearly visible electric or mechanical signal device gives warning of the immediate approach of a railroad train;

2. A crossing gate is lowered or a human flagman gives or continues to give a signal of the approach or passage of a railroad train;

3. A railroad train approaching a highway crossing emits a warning signal and such railroad train, by reason of its speed or nearness to such crossing, is an immediate hazard;

4. An approaching railroad train is plainly visible and is in hazardous proximity to such crossing;

5. A railroad train is approaching so closely that an immediate hazard is created.

(a-5) Whenever a person driving a vehicle approaches a railroad grade crossing where the driver is not always required to stop but must slow down, the person must exercise due care and caution as the existence of a railroad track across a highway is a warning of danger, and under any of the circumstances stated in this Section, the driver shall slow down within 50 feet but not less than 15 feet from the nearest rail of the railroad and shall not proceed until he or she checks that the tracks are clear of an approaching train.

(b) No person shall drive any vehicle through, around or under any crossing gate or barrier at a railroad crossing while such gate or barrier is closed or is being opened or closed.

(c) The Department, and local authorities with the approval of the Department, are hereby authorized to designate particularly dangerous highway grade crossings of railroads and to erect stop signs thereat. When such stop signs are erected the driver of any vehicle shall stop within 50 feet but not less than 15 feet from the nearest rail of such railroad and shall proceed only upon exercising due care.

(d) At any railroad grade crossing provided with railroad crossbuck signs, without automatic, electric, or mechanical signal devices, crossing gates, or a human flagman giving a signal of the approach or passage of a train, the driver of a vehicle shall in obedience to the railroad crossbuck sign, yield the right-of-way and slow down to a speed reasonable for the existing conditions and shall stop, if required for safety, at a clearly marked stopped line, or if no stop line, within 50 feet but not less than 15 feet from the nearest rail of the railroad and shall not proceed until he or she can do so safely. If a driver is involved in a collision at a railroad crossing or interferes with the movement of a train after driving past the railroad crossbuck sign, the collision or interference is prima facie evidence of the driver's failure to yield right-of-way.

(d-1) No person shall, while driving a commercial motor vehicle, fail to negotiate a railroad-highway grade railroad crossing because of insufficient undercarriage clearance.

(d-5) (Blank.)

(e) It is unlawful to violate any part of this Section.

(1) A violation of this Section is a petty offense for which a fine of $250 shall be imposed for a first violation, and a fine of $500 shall be imposed for a second or subsequent violation. The court may impose 25 hours of community service in place of the $250 fine for the first violation.

(2) For a second or subsequent violation, the Secretary of State may suspend the driving privileges of the offender for a minimum of 6 months.

(f) Corporate authorities of municipal corporations regulating operators of vehicles that fail to obey signals indicating the presence, approach, passage, or departure of a train shall impose fines as established in subsection (e) of this Section.

P.A. 76-1586, § 11-1201, eff. July 1, 1970. Amended by P.A. 76-2170, § 1, eff. July 1, 1970; P.A. 79-1069, § 1, eff. Jan. 1, 1976; P.A. 89-186, § 5, eff. Jan. 1, 1996; P.A. 89-658, § 5, eff. Jan. 1, 1997; P.A. 92-245, § 5, eff. Aug. 3, 2001; P.A. 92-249, § 5, eff. Jan. 1, 2002; P.A. 92-651, § 77, eff. July 11, 2002; P.A. 92-814, § 5, eff. Jan. 1, 2003; P.A. 92-834, § 5, eff. Aug. 22, 2002.

Formerly Ill.Rev.Stat.1991, ch. 95 ½, ¶ 11-1201.

P.A. 92-814 incorporated the amendments by P.A. 92-245 and 92-249.

P.A. 92-834 incorporated the amendments by P.A. 92-245 and P.A. 92-249.

See 5 ILCS 70/6 as to the effect of (1) more than one amendment of a section at the same session of the General Assembly of (2) two or more acts relating to the same subject matter enacted by the same General Assembly

5/11-1201.1. Automated Railroad Crossing Enforcement System

§ 11-1201.1. Automated Railroad Crossing Enforcement System.

(a) For the purposes of this Section, an automated railroad grade crossing enforcement system is a system operated by a law enforcement agency that records a driver's response to automatic, electrical or mechanical signal devices and crossing gates. The system shall be designed to obtain a clear photograph or other recorded image of the vehicle, vehicle operator and the vehicle registration plate of a vehicle in violation of Section 11-1201. The photograph or other recorded image shall also display the time, date and location of the violation.

(b) Commencing on January 1, 1996, the Illinois Commerce Commission and the Commuter Rail Board of the Regional Transportation Authority shall, in cooperation with local law enforcement agencies, establish a 5 year pilot program within a county with a population of between 750,000 and 1,000,000 using an automated railroad grade crossing enforcement system. The Commission shall determine the 3 railroad grade crossings within that county that pose the greatest threat to human life based upon the number of accidents and fatalities at the crossings during the past 5 years and with approval of the local law enforcement agency equip the crossings with an automated railroad grade crossing enforcement system.

(b-1) Commencing on July 20, 2001 (the effective date of Public Act 92-98) , the Illinois Commerce Commission and the Commuter Rail Board may, in cooperation with the local law enforcement agency, establish in a county with a population of between 750,000 and 1,000,000 a 2 year pilot program using an automated railroad grade crossing enforcement system. This pilot program may be established at a railroad grade crossing designated by local authorities. No State moneys may be expended on the automated railroad grade crossing enforcement system established under this pilot program.

(c) For each violation of Section 11-1201 recorded by an automatic railroad grade crossing system, the local law enforcement agency having jurisdiction shall issue a written Uniform Traffic Citation of the violation to the registered owner of the vehicle as the alleged violator. The Uniform Traffic Citation shall be delivered to the registered owner of the vehicle, by mail, within 30 days of the violation. The Uniform Traffic Citation shall include the name and address of vehicle owner, the vehicle registration number, the offense charged, the time, date, and location of the violation, the first available court date and that the basis of the citation is the photograph or other recorded image from the automated railroad grade crossing enforcement system.

(d) The Uniform Traffic Citation issued to the registered owner of the vehicle shall be accompanied by a written notice, the contents of which is set forth in subsection (d–1) of this Section, explaining how the registered owner of the vehicle can elect to proceed by either paying the fine or challenging the issuance of the Uniform Traffic Citation.

(d–1) The written notice explaining the alleged violator's rights and obligations must include the following text:

"You have been served with the accompanying Uniform Traffic Citation and cited with having violated Section 11–1201 of the Illinois Vehicle Code. You can elect to proceed by:

1. Paying the fine; or

2. Challenging the issuance of the Uniform Traffic Citation in court; or

3. If you were not the operator of the vehicle at the time of the alleged offense, notifying in writing the local law enforcement agency that issued the Uniform Traffic Citation of the number of the Uniform Traffic Citation received and the name and address of the person operating the vehicle at the time of the alleged offense. If you fail to so notify in writing the local law enforcement agency of the name and address of the operator of the vehicle at the time of the alleged offense, you may be presumed to have been the operator of the vehicle at the time of the alleged offense."

(d–2) If the registered owner of the vehicle was not the operator of the vehicle at the time of the alleged offense, and if the registered owner notifies the local law enforcement agency having jurisdiction of the name and address of the operator of the vehicle at the time of the alleged offense, the local law enforcement agency having jurisdiction shall then issue a written Uniform Traffic Citation to the person alleged by the registered owner to have been the operator of the vehicle at the time of the alleged offense. If the registered owner fails to notify in writing the local law enforcement agency having jurisdiction of the name and address of the operator of the vehicle at the time of the alleged offense, the registered owner may be presumed to have been the operator of the vehicle at the time of the alleged offense.

(e) Evidence.

(i) A certificate alleging that a violation of Section 11–1201 occurred, sworn to or affirmed by a duly authorized agency, based on inspection of recorded images produced by an automated railroad crossing enforcement system are evidence of the facts contained in the certificate and are admissible in any proceeding alleging a violation under this Section.

(ii) Photographs or recorded images made by an automatic railroad grade crossing enforcement system are confidential and shall be made available only to the alleged violator and governmental and law enforcement agencies for purposes of adjudicating a violation of Section 11–1201 of the Illinois Vehicle Code. However, any photograph or other recorded image evidencing a violation of Section 11–1201 shall be admissible in any proceeding resulting from the issuance of the Uniform Traffic Citation when there is reasonable and sufficient proof of the accuracy of the camera or electronic instrument recording the image. There is a rebuttable presumption that the photograph or recorded image is accurate if the camera or electronic recording instrument was in good working order at the beginning and the end of the day of the alleged offense.

(f) Rail crossings equipped with an automatic railroad grade crossing enforcement system shall be posted with a sign visible to approaching traffic stating that the railroad grade crossing is being monitored, that citations will be issued, and the amount of the fine for violation.

(g) Except as provided in subsection (b–1), the cost of the installation and maintenance of each automatic railroad grade crossing enforcement system shall be paid from the Grade Crossing Protection Fund if the rail line is not owned by Commuter Rail Board of the Regional Transportation Authority. Except as provided in subsection (b–1), if the rail line is owned by the Commuter Rail Board of the Regional Transportation Authority, the costs of the installation and maintenance shall be paid from the Regional Transportation Authority's portion of the Public Transportation Fund.

(h) The Illinois Commerce Commission shall issue a report to the General Assembly at the conclusion of the 5 year pilot program established under subsection (b) on the effectiveness of the automatic railroad grade crossing enforcement system.

(i) If any part or parts of this Section are held by a court of competent jurisdiction to be unconstitutional, the unconstitutionality shall not affect the validity of the remaining parts of this Section. The General Assembly hereby declares that it would have passed the remaining parts of this Section if it had known that the other part or parts of this Section would be declared unconstitutional.

(j) Penalty.

(i) A violation of this Section is a petty offense for which a fine of $250 shall be imposed for a first violation, and a fine of $500 shall be imposed for a second or subsequent violation. The court may impose 25 hours of community service in place of the $250 fine for the first violation.

(ii) For a second or subsequent violation, the Secretary of State may suspend the registration of the motor vehicle for a period of at least 6 months.

P.A. 76–1586, § 1201.1, added by P.A. 89–454, § 10, eff. May 17, 1996. Renumbered § 11–1201.1 and amended by P.A. 90–14, Art. 2, § 2–225, eff. July 1, 1997. Amended by P.A. 92–98, § 5, eff. July 18, 2001; P.A. 92–245, § 5, eff. Aug. 3, 2001; P.A. 92–651, § 77, eff. July 11, 2002; P.A. 92–814, § 5, eff. Jan. 1, 2003.

P.A. 92–651, the First 2002 General Revisory Act, amended various Acts to delete obsolete text, to correct patent and technical errors, to revise cross references, to resolve multiple actions in the 91st and 92nd General Assemblies and to make certain technical corrections in P.A. 91–937 through P.A. 92–520.

P.A. 92–814 incorporated the amendments by P.A. 92–98 and 92–245.

See 5 ILCS 70/6 as to the effect of (1) more than one amendment of a section at the same session of the General Assembly or (2) two or more acts relating to the same subject matter enacted by the same General Assembly.

5/11-1202. Certain vehicles must stop at all railroad grade crossings

§ 11-1202. Certain vehicles must stop at all railroad grade crossings. (a) The driver of any of the following vehicles shall, before crossing a railroad track or tracks at grade, stop such vehicle within 50 feet but not less than 15 feet from the nearest rail and, while so stopped, shall listen and look for the approach of a train and shall not proceed until such movement can be made with safety:

1. Any second division vehicle carrying passengers for hire;

2. Any bus that meets all of the special requirements for school buses in Sections 12-801, 12-803, and 12-805 of this Code ;

3. Any other vehicle which is required by Federal or State law to be placarded when carrying as a cargo or part of a cargo hazardous material as defined in the "Illinois Hazardous Materials Transportation Act".[1] After stopping as required in this Section, the driver shall proceed only in a gear not requiring a change of gears during the crossing, and the driver shall not shift gears while crossing the track or tracks.

(b) This Section shall not apply:

1. At any railroad grade crossing where traffic is controlled by a police officer or flagperson;

2. At any railroad grade crossing controlled by a functioning traffic-control signal transmitting a green indication which, under law, permits the vehicle to proceed across the railroad tracks without slowing or stopping, except that subsection (a) shall apply to any school bus;

3. At any streetcar grade crossing within a business or residence district; or

4. At any abandoned, industrial or spur track railroad grade crossing designated as exempt by the Illinois Commerce Commission and marked with an official sign as authorized in the State Manual on Uniform Traffic Control Devices for Streets and Highways.

P.A. 76-1586, § 11-1202, eff. July 1, 1970. Amended by P.A. 76-2171, § 1, eff. July 1, 1970; P.A. 79-1069, § 1, eff. Jan. 1, 1976; P.A. 80-506, § 1, eff. Oct. 1, 1977; P.A. 81-805, § 1, eff. Jan. 1, 1980; P.A. 83-905, § 1, eff. Jan. 1, 1984; P.A. 84-1246, § 1, eff. July 29, 1986; P.A. 86-499, § 1, eff. Jan. 1, 1990; P.A. 89-658, § 5, eff. Jan. 1, 1997.

Formerly Ill.Rev.Stat.1991, ch. 95 ½, ¶ 11-1202.

[1] 430 ILCS 30/1 et seq.

5/11-1203. Moving heavy equipment at railroad grade crossing

§ 11-1203. Moving heavy equipment at railroad grade crossing. (a) No person shall operate or move any crawler-type tractor, power shovel, derrick, roller, or any equipment or structure having a normal operating speed of 10 or less miles per hour, or, for such equipment with 18 feet or less distance between two adjacent axles, having a vertical body or load clearance of less than 9 inches above a level surface, or, for such equipment with more than 18 feet between two adjacent axles, having a vertical body or load clearance of less than ½ inch per foot of distance between such adjacent axles above a level surface upon or across any tracks at a railroad grade crossing without first complying with this Section.

(b) Notice of any such intended crossing shall be given to a superintendent of such railroad and a reasonable time be given to such railroad to provide proper protection at such crossing.

(c) Before making any such crossing the person operating or moving any such vehicle or equipment shall first stop the same not less than 15 feet nor more than 50 feet from the nearest rail of such railway and while so stopped shall listen and look in both directions along such track for any approaching train and for signals indicating the approach of a train, and shall not proceed until the crossing can be made safely.

(d) No such crossing shall be made when warning is given by automatic signal or crossing gates or a flagman or otherwise of the immediate approach of a railroad train or car.

P.A. 76-1586, § 11-1203, eff. July 1, 1970. Amended by P.A. 76-2172, § 1, eff. July 1, 1970.

Formerly Ill.Rev.Stat.1991, ch. 95 ½, ¶ 11-1203.

5/11-1204. Stop and yield signs

§ 11-1204. Stop and yield signs. (a) Preferential right-of-way at an intersection may be indicated by stop signs or yield signs as authorized in Section 11-302 of this Act.

(b) Except when directed to proceed by a police officer or traffic control signal, every driver of a vehicle and every motorman of a streetcar approaching a stop intersection indicated by a stop sign shall stop before entering the crosswalk on the near side of the intersection or, in the event there is no crosswalk, shall stop at a clearly marked stop line, but if none, then at the point nearest the intersection roadway where the driver has a view of approaching traffic on the intersecting roadway before entering the intersection.

(c) The driver of a vehicle approaching a yield sign if required for safety to stop shall stop before entering the crosswalk on the near side of the intersection or, in the event there is no crosswalk, at a clearly marked stop line, but if none, then at the point nearest the intersecting roadway where the driver has a view of approaching traffic on the intersecting roadway.

P.A. 76-1586, § 11-1204, eff. July 1, 1970.

Formerly Ill.Rev.Stat.1991, ch. 95 ½, ¶ 11-1204.

5/11-1205. Emerging from alley, building, private road or driveway

§ 11-1205. Emerging from alley, building, private road or driveway. The driver of a vehicle emerging from an alley, building, private road or driveway within an urban area shall stop such vehicle immediately prior to driving into the sidewalk area extending across such alley, building entrance, road or driveway, or in the event there is no sidewalk area, shall stop at the point nearest the street to be entered where the driver has a view of approaching traffic thereon, and shall yield the right-of-way to any pedestrian as may be necessary to avoid collision, and upon entering the roadway shall yield the right-of-way to all vehicles approaching on such roadway.

P.A. 76-1586, § 11-1205, eff. July 1, 1970. Amended by P.A. 76-1735, § 1; P.A. 77-1344, § 1, eff. Aug. 27, 1971.

Formerly Ill.Rev.Stat.1991, ch. 95 ½, ¶ 11-1205.

ARTICLE XIII. STOPPING, STANDING, AND PARKING

5/11-1301. Stopping, standing or parking outside of business or residence district

§ 11-1301. Stopping, standing or parking outside of business or residence district.

(a) Outside a business or residence district, no person shall stop, park or leave standing any vehicle, whether attended or unattended, upon the roadway when it is practicable to stop, park or so leave such vehicle off the roadway, but in every event an unobstructed width of the highway opposite a standing vehicle shall be left for the free passage of other vehicles and a clear view of such stopped vehicle shall be available from a distance of 200 feet in each direction upon such highway.

(b) The Department with respect to highways under its jurisdiction or for the maintenance of which it is responsible may place signs prohibiting or restricting the stopping, standing or parking of vehicles on any highway where in its opinion such stopping, standing or parking is dangerous to those using the highway or where the stopping, standing or parking of vehicles would unduly interfere with the free movement of traffic thereon. Any such regulations adopted by the Department regarding the stopping, standing or parking of vehicles upon any specific street, streets or highways become effective at the time of the erection of appropriate signs indicating such regulations. Any such signs may be erected either by the Department or by a local authority with the approval of the Department.

(c) This Section, Section 11-1303 and Section 11-1304 shall not apply to the driver of any vehicle which is disabled in such manner and to such extent that it is impossible to avoid stopping and temporarily leaving the vehicle in such position.

(d) Any second division vehicle used exclusively for the collection of garbage, refuse, or recyclable material may stop or stand on the road in a business, rural, or residential district for the sole purpose of collecting garbage, refuse, or recyclable material. The vehicle, in addition to having its hazard lights lighted at all times that it is engaged in stopping or standing, shall also use its amber oscillating, rotating, or flashing light or lights as authorized under paragraph 12 of subsection (b) of Section 12-215, if so equipped.

P.A. 76-1586, § 11-1301, eff. July 1, 1970. Amended by P.A. 76-2173, § 1, eff. July 1, 1970; P.A. 79-1069, § 1, eff. Jan. 1, 1976; P.A. 91-869, § 5, eff. Jan. 1, 2001.

Formerly Ill.Rev.Stat.1991, ch. 95 ½, ¶ 11-1301.

5/11-1301.1. Persons with disabilities—Parking privileges—Exemptions

§ 11-1301.1. Persons with disabilities—Parking privileges—Exemptions. A motor vehicle bearing registration plates issued to a person with disabilities, as defined by Section 1-159.1, pursuant to Section 3-616 or to a disabled veteran pursuant to Section 3-609 or a special decal or device issued pursuant to Section 3-616 or pursuant to Section 11-1301.2 of this Code or a motor vehicle registered in another jurisdiction, state, district, territory or foreign country upon which is displayed a registration plate, special decal or device issued by the other jurisdiction designating the vehicle is operated by or for a person with disabilities shall be exempt from the payment of parking meter fees and exempt from any statute or ordinance imposing time limitations on parking, except limitations of one-half hour or less, on any street or highway zone, or any parking lot or parking place which are owned, leased or owned and leased by a municipality or a municipal parking utility; and shall be recognized by state and local authorities as a valid license plate or parking device and shall receive the same parking privileges as residents of this State; but, such vehicle shall be subject to the laws which prohibit parking in "no stopping" and "no standing" zones in front of or near fire hydrants, driveways, public building entrances and exits, bus stops and loading areas, and is prohibited from parking where the motor vehicle constitutes a traffic hazard, whereby such motor vehicle shall be moved at the instruction and request of a law enforcement officer to a location designated by the officer. Any motor vehicle bearing registration plates or a special decal or device specified in this Section or in Section 3-616 of this Code or such parking device as specifically authorized in Section 11-1301.2 as evidence that the vehicle is operated by or for a person with disabilities or disabled veteran may park, in addition to any other lawful place, in any parking place specifically reserved for such vehicles by the posting of an official sign as provided under Section 11-301. Parking privileges granted by this Section are strictly limited to the person to whom the special registration plates, special decal or device were issued and to qualified operators acting under his express direction while the person with disabilities is present. A person to whom privileges were granted shall, at the request of a police officer or any other person invested by law with authority to direct, control, or regulate traffic, present an identification card with a picture as verification that the person is the person to whom the special registration plates, special decal or device was issued.

Such parking privileges granted by this Section are also extended to motor vehicles of not-for-profit organizations used for the transportation of persons with disabilities when such motor vehicles display the decal or device issued pursuant to Section 11-1301.2 of this Code.

No person shall use any area for the parking of any motor vehicle pursuant to Section 11-1303 of this Code or where an official sign controlling such area expressly prohibits parking at any time or during certain hours.

P.A. 76-1586, § 11-1301.1, added by P.A. 79-974, § 1, eff. Oct. 1, 1975. Amended by P.A. 81-171, § 1, eff. Jan. 1, 1980; P.A. 81-176, § 1, eff. Jan. 1, 1980; P.A. 81-1509, Art. 1, § 57, eff. Sept. 26, 1980; P.A. 83-1058, § 1, eff. July 1, 1984; P.A. 83-1316, § 1, eff. Jan. 1, 1985; P.A. 84-980, § 1, eff. Sept. 25, 1985; P.A. 86-539, § 1, eff. Jan. 1, 1990; P.A. 88-685, § 5, eff. Jan. 24, 1995; P.A. 90-106, § 5, eff. Jan. 1, 1998.

Formerly Ill.Rev.Stat.1991, ch. 95 ½, ¶ 11-1301.1.

5/11-1301.2. Special decals for a person with disabilities parking

§ 11-1301.2. Special decals for a person with disabilities parking.

(a) The Secretary of State shall provide for, by administrative rules, the design, size, color, and placement of a person with disabilities motorist decal or device and shall provide for, by administrative rules, the content and form of an application for a person with disabilities motorist decal or device, which shall be used by local authorities in the issuance thereof to a person with temporary disabilities, provided that the decal or device is valid for no more than 90 days, subject to renewal for like periods based upon continued disability, and further provided that the decal or device clearly sets forth the date that the decal or device expires. The application shall include the requirement of an Illinois Identification Card number or a State of Illinois driver's license number. This decal or device shall be the property of such person with disabilities and may be used by that person to designate and identify a vehicle not owned or displaying a registration plate as provided in Sections 3-609 and 3-616 of this Act to designate when the vehicle is being used to transport said person or persons with disabilities, and thus is entitled to enjoy all the privileges that would be afforded a person with disabilities licensed vehicle. Person with disabilities decals or devices issued and displayed pursuant to this Section shall be recognized and honored by all local authorities regardless of which local authority issued such decal or device.

The decal or device shall be issued only upon a showing by adequate documentation that the person for whose benefit the decal or device is to be used has a temporary disability as defined in Section 1-159.1 of this Code.

(b) The local governing authorities shall be responsible for the provision of such decal or device, its issuance and designated placement within the vehicle. The cost of such decal or device shall be at the discretion of such local governing authority.

(c) The Secretary of State may, pursuant to Section 3-616(c), issue a person with disabilities parking decal or device to a person with disabilities as defined by Section 1-159.1. Any person with disabilities parking decal or device issued by the Secretary of State shall be registered to that person with disabilities in the form to be prescribed by the Secretary of State. The person with disabilities parking decal or device shall not display that person's address. One additional decal or device may be issued to an applicant upon his or her written request and with the approval of the Secretary of State. The written request must include a justification of the need for the additional decal or device.

(d) Replacement decals or devices may be issued for lost, stolen, or destroyed decals upon application and payment of a $10 fee. The replacement fee may be waived for individuals that have claimed and received a grant under the Senior Citizens and Disabled Persons Property Tax Relief and Pharmaceutical Assistance Act.[1]

P.A. 76-1586, § 11-1301.2, added by P.A. 81-171, § 1, eff. Jan. 1, 1980. Amended by P.A. 82-1011, § 2, eff. Sept. 17, 1982; P.A. 83-1058, § 1, eff. July 1, 1984; P.A. 83-1421, § 10, eff. July 1, 1985; P.A. 85-484, § 1, eff. Jan. 1, 1988; P.A. 88-685, § 5, eff. Jan. 24, 1995; P.A. 90-106, § 5, eff. Jan. 1, 1998; P.A. 92-411, § 5, eff. Jan. 1, 2002.

Formerly Ill.Rev.Stat.1991, ch. 95 ½, ¶ 11-1301.2.

1 320 ILCS 25/1 et seq.

Another § 11-1301.2 was renumbered § 11-1301.3.

5/11-1301.3. Unauthorized use of parking places reserved for persons with disabilities

§ 11-1301.3. Unauthorized use of parking places reserved for persons with disabilities.

(a) It shall be prohibited to park any motor vehicle which is not properly displaying registration plates or decals issued to a person with disabilities, as defined by Section 1-159.1, pursuant to Sections 3-616, 11-1301.1 or 11-1301.2, or to a disabled veteran pursuant to Section 3-609 of this Act, as evidence that the vehicle is operated by or for a person with disabilities or disabled veteran, in any parking place, including any private or public offstreet parking facility, specifically reserved, by the posting of an official sign as designated under Section 11-301, for motor vehicles displaying such registration plates. It shall be prohibited to park any motor vehicle in a designated access aisle adjacent to any parking place specifically reserved for persons with disabilities, by the posting of an official sign as designated under Section 11-301, for motor vehicles displaying such registration plates. When using the parking privileges for persons with disabilities, the parking decal or device must be displayed properly in the vehicle where it is clearly visible to law enforcement personnel, either hanging from the rearview mirror or placed on the dashboard of the vehicle in clear view. An individual with a vehicle properly displaying a person with disabilities license plate or parking decal or device issued to a disabled person under Sections 3-616, 11-1301.1, or 11-1301.2 is in violation of this Section if the person is not the authorized holder of a person with disabilities license plate or parking decal or device and is not transporting the authorized holder of a person with disabilities license plate or parking decal or device to or from the parking location and the person uses the person with disabilities license plate or parking decal or device to exercise any privileges granted through the person with disabilities license plates or parking decals or devices under this Code. Any motor vehicle properly displaying a person with disabilities license plate or a person with disabilities parking decal or device containing the International symbol of access issued to persons with disabilities by any local authority, state, district, territory or foreign country shall be recognized by State and local authorities as a valid license plate or device and receive the same parking privileges as residents of this State.

(b) Any person or local authority owning or operating any public or private offstreet parking facility may, after notifying the police or sheriff's department, remove or cause to be removed to the nearest garage or other place of safety any vehicle parked within a stall or space reserved for use by a person with disabilities which does not display person with disabilities registration plates or a special decal or device as required under this Section.

(c) Any person found guilty of violating the provisions of this Section shall be fined $100 in addition to any costs or charges connected with the removal or storage of any motor vehicle authorized under this Section; but municipalities by ordinance may impose a fine up to $200 and shall display signs indicating the fine imposed. If the amount of the fine is subsequently changed, the municipality shall change the sign to indicate the current amount of the fine. It shall not be a defense to a charge under this Section that the sign posted pursuant to this Section does not comply with the technical requirements of Section 11-301, Department regulations, or local ordinance if a reasonable person would be made aware by the sign or notice on or near the parking place that the place is reserved for a person with disabilities.

(d) Local authorities shall impose fines as established in subsection (c) for violations of this Section.

(e) As used in this Section, "authorized holder" means an individual issued a person with disabilities license plate under Section 3-616 of this Code or an individual issued a person with disabilities parking decal or device under Section 11-1301.2 of this Code.

P.A. 76-1586, § 11-1301.2, added by P.A. 81-176, § 1, eff. Jan. 1, 1980. Renumbered § 11-1301.3 and amended by P.A. 81-1509, Art. I, § 57, eff. Sept. 26, 1980. Amended by P.A. 82-226, § 1, eff. Jan. 1, 1982; P.A. 83-1058, § 1, eff. July 1, 1984; P.A. 83-1316, § 1, eff. Jan. 1, 1985; P.A. 86-539, § 1, eff. Jan. 1, 1990; P.A. 88-685, § 5, eff. Jan. 24, 1995; P.A. 89-275, § 5, eff. Jan. 1, 1996; P.A. 89-533, § 5, eff. Jan. 1, 1997; P.A. 89-626, Art. 2, § 2-66, eff. Aug. 9, 1996; P.A. 90-106, § 5, eff. Jan. 1, 1998; P.A. 91-427, § 5, eff. Aug. 6, 1999; P.A. 92-411, § 5, eff. Jan. 1, 2002; P.A. 92-637, § 5, eff. Jan. 1, 2003.

Formerly Ill.Rev.Stat.1991, ch. 95 ½, ¶ 11-1301.3.

P.A. 92-637 incorporated the amendment by P.A. 92-411.

5/11-1301.4. Reciprocal agreements with other jurisdictions

§ 11-1301.4. Reciprocal agreements with other jurisdictions. The Secretary of State, or his designee, may enter into agreements with other jurisdictions, including foreign jurisdictions, on behalf of this State relating to the extension of parking privileges by such jurisdictions to permanently disabled residents of this State who display a special license plate or parking device that contains the International symbol of access on his or her motor vehicle, and to recognize such plates or devices issued by such other jurisdictions. This State shall grant the same parking privileges which are granted to disabled residents of this State to any non-resident whose motor vehicle is licensed in another state, district, territory or foreign country if such vehicle displays the International symbol of access or a distinguishing insignia on license plates or parking device issued in accordance with the laws of the non-resident's state, district, territory or foreign country.

P.A. 76-1586, § 11-1301.4, added by P.A. 84-868, § 1, eff. Sept. 23, 1985. Amended by P.A. 86-539, § 1, eff. Jan. 1, 1990.

Formerly Ill.Rev.Stat.1991, ch. 95 ½, ¶ 11-1301.4.

5/11-1301.5. Fictitious or unlawfully altered person with disabilities license plate or parking decal or device

§ 11-1301.5. Fictitious or unlawfully altered person with disabilities license plate or parking decal or device.

(a) As used in this Section:

"Fictitious person with disabilities license plate or parking decal or device" means any issued person with disabilities license plate or parking decal or device that has been issued by the Secretary of State or an authorized unit of local government that was issued based upon false information contained on the required application.

"False information" means any incorrect or inaccurate information concerning the name, date of birth, social security number, driver's license number, physician certification, or any other information required on the application for a person with disabilities license plate or parking permit or device that falsifies the content of the application.

"Unlawfully altered person with disabilities license plate or parking permit or device" means any person with disabilities license plate or parking permit or device issued by the Secretary of State or an authorized unit of local government that has been physically altered or changed in such manner that false information appears on the license plate or parking decal or device.

"Authorized holder" means an individual issued a person with disabilities license plate under Section 3-616 of this Code or an individual issued a person with disabilities parking decal or device under Section 11-1301.2 of this Code.

(b) It is a violation of this Section for any person:

(1) to knowingly possess any fictitious or unlawfully altered person with disabilities license plate or parking decal or device;

(2) to knowingly issue or assist in the issuance of, by the Secretary of State or unit of local government, any fictitious person with disabilities license plate or parking decal or device;

(3) to knowingly alter any person with disabilities license plate or parking decal or device;

(4) to knowingly manufacture, possess, transfer, or provide any documentation used in the application process whether real or fictitious, for the purpose of obtaining a fictitious person with disabilities license plate or parking decal or device;

(5) to knowingly provide any false information to the Secretary of State or a unit of local government in order to obtain a person with disabilities license plate or parking decal or device; or

(6) to knowingly transfer a person with disabilities license plate or parking decal or device for the purpose of exercising the privileges granted to an authorized holder of a person with disabilities license plate or parking decal or device under this Code in the absence of the authorized holder.

(c) Sentence.

(1) Any person convicted of a violation of this Section shall be guilty of a Class A misdemeanor.

(2) Any person who commits a violation of this Section may have his or her driving privileges suspended or revoked by the Secretary of State for a period of time determined by the Secretary of State.

(3) Any police officer may seize the parking decal or device from any person who commits a violation of this Section. Any police officer may seize the person with disabilities license plate upon authorization from the Secretary of State. Any police officer may request that the Secretary of State revoke the parking decal or device or the person with disabilities license plate of any person who commits a violation of this Section.

P.A. 76-1586, § 11-1301.5, added by P.A. 90-106, § 5, eff. Jan. 1, 1998. Amended by P.A. 90-655, § 153, eff. July 30, 1998; P.A. 92-411, § 5, eff. Jan. 1, 2002.

Another § 11–1301.5, relating to appointed volunteers and contracted entities for policing disabled person parking violations, was renumbered § 11–1301.7 by P.A. 90–655, § 153.

5/11–1301.6. Fraudulent person with disabilities license plate or parking decal or device

§ 11–1301.6. Fraudulent person with disabilities license plate or parking decal or device.

(a) As used in this Section:

"Fraudulent person with disabilities license plate or parking decal or device" means any person with disabilities license plate or parking decal or device that purports to be an official person with disabilities license plate or parking decal or device and that has not been issued by the Secretary of State or an authorized unit of local government.

"Person with disabilities license plate or parking decal or device-making implement" means any implement specially designed or primarily used in the manufacture, assembly, or authentication of a person with disabilities license plate or parking decal or device issued by the Secretary of State or a unit of local government.

(b) It is a violation of this Section for any person:

(1) to knowingly possess any fraudulent person with disabilities license plate or parking decal;

(2) to knowingly possess without authority any person with disabilities license plate or parking decal or device-making implement;

(3) to knowingly duplicate, manufacture, sell, or transfer any fraudulent or stolen person with disabilities license plate or parking decal or device;

(4) to knowingly assist in the duplication, manufacturing, selling, or transferring of any fraudulent or stolen person with disabilities license plate or parking decal or device; or

(5) to advertise or distribute a fraudulent person with disabilities license plate or parking decal or device.

(c) Sentence.

(1) Any person convicted of a violation of this Section shall be guilty of a Class 4 felony.

(2) Any person who commits a violation of this Section may have his or her driving privileges suspended or revoked by the Secretary of State for a period of time determined by the Secretary of State.

(3) Any police officer may seize the parking decal or device from any person who commits a violation of this Section. Any police officer may seize the person with disabilities license plate upon authorization from the Secretary of State. Any police officer may request that the Secretary of State revoke the parking decal or device or the person with disabilities license plate of any person who commits a violation of this Section.

P.A. 76–1586, § 11–1301.6, added by P.A. 90–106, § 5, eff. Jan. 1, 1998. Amended by P.A. 92–411, § 5, eff. Jan. 1, 2002.

5/11–1301.7. Appointed volunteers and contracted entities; disabled person parking violations

§ 11–1301.7. Appointed volunteers and contracted entities; disabled person parking violations.

(a) The chief of police of a municipality and the sheriff of a county authorized to enforce parking laws may appoint volunteers or contract with public or private entities to issue parking violation notices for violations of Section 11–1301.3 or ordinances dealing with parking privileges for persons with disabilities. Volunteers appointed under this Section and any employees of public or private entities that the chief of police or sheriff has contracted with under this Section who are issuing these parking violation notices must be at least 21 years of age. The chief of police or sheriff appointing the volunteers or contracting with public or private entities may establish any other qualifications that he or she deems desirable.

(b) The chief of police or sheriff appointing volunteers under this Section shall provide training to the volunteers before authorizing them to issue parking violation notices.

(c) A parking violation notice issued by a volunteer appointed under this Section or by a public or private entity that the chief of police or sheriff has contracted with under this Section shall have the same force and effect as a parking violation notice issued by a police officer for the same offense.

(d) All funds collected as a result of the payment of the parking violation notices issued under this Section shall go to the municipality or county where the notice is issued.

(e) An appointed volunteer or private or public entity under contract pursuant to this Section is not liable for his or her or its act or omission in the execution or enforcement of laws or ordinances if acting within the scope of the appointment or contract authorized by this Section, unless the act or omission constitutes willful and wanton conduct.

(f) Except as otherwise provided by statute, a local government, a chief of police, sheriff, or employee of a police department or sheriff, as such and acting within the scope of his or her employment, is not liable for an injury caused by the act or omission of an appointed volunteer or private or public entity under contract pursuant to this Section. No local government, chief of police, sheriff, or an employee of a local government, police department or sheriff shall be liable for any actions regarding the supervision or direction, or the failure to supervise and direct, an appointed volunteer or private or public entity under contract pursuant to this Section unless the act or omission constitutes willful and wanton conduct.

(g) An appointed volunteer or private or public entity under contract pursuant to this Section shall assume all liability for and hold the property owner and his agents and employees harmless from any and all claims of action resulting from the work of the appointed volunteer or public or private entity.

P.A. 76–1586, § 11–1301.5, added by P.A. 90–181, § 5, eff. July 23, 1997. Renumbered § 11–1301.7 and amended by P.A. 90–655, § 153, eff. July 30, 1998.

P.A. 90–655, the First 1998 General Revisory Act, amended various Acts to delete obsolete text, to correct patent and technical errors, to revise cross references, to resolve multiple actions in the 89th and 90th General Assemblies and to make certain technical corrections in P.A. 89–708 through P.A. 90–566.

5/11–1302. Officers authorized to remove vehicles

§ 11–1302. Officers authorized to remove vehicles. (a) Whenever any police officer finds a vehicle in violation of any of the provisions of Section 11–1301 such officer is hereby authorized to move such vehicle, or require the driver or other person in charge of the vehicle to move the same, to a position off the roadway.

(b) Any police officer is hereby authorized to remove or cause to be removed to a place of safety any unattended vehicle illegally left standing upon any highway, bridge, causeway, or in a tunnel, in such a position or under such circumstances as to obstruct the normal movement of traffic.

Whenever the Department finds an abandoned or disabled vehicle standing upon the paved or main-traveled part of a highway, which vehicle is or may be expected to interrupt the free flow of traffic on the highway or interfere with the maintenance of the highway, the Department is authorized to move the vehicle to a position off the paved or improved or main-traveled part of the highway.

(c) Any police officer is hereby authorized to remove or cause to be removed to the nearest garage or other place of safety any vehicle found upon a highway when:

1. Report has been made that such vehicle has been stolen or taken without the consent of its owner, or

2. The person or persons in charge of such vehicle are unable to provide for its custody or removal, or

3. When the person driving or in control of such vehicle is arrested for an alleged offense for which the officer is required by law to take the person arrested before a proper magistrate without unnecessary delay.

P.A. 76–1586, § 11–1302, eff. July 1, 1970. Amended by P.A. 76–1735, § 1; P.A. 79–1069, § 1, eff. Jan. 1, 1976.

Formerly Ill.Rev.Stat.1991, ch. 95 ½, ¶ 11–1302.

5/11–1303. Stopping, standing or parking prohibited in specified places

§ 11–1303. Stopping, standing or parking prohibited in specified places.

(a) Except when necessary to avoid conflict with other traffic, or in compliance with law or the directions of a police officer or official traffic-control device, no person shall:

1. Stop, stand or park a vehicle:

a. On the roadway side of any vehicle stopped or parked at the edge or curb of a street;

b. On a sidewalk;

c. Within an intersection;

d. On a crosswalk;

e. Between a safety zone and the adjacent curb or within 30 feet of points on the curb immediately opposite the ends of a safety zone, unless a different length is indicated by signs or markings;

f. Alongside or opposite any street excavation or obstruction when stopping, standing or parking would obstruct traffic;

g. Upon any bridge or other elevated structure upon a highway or within a highway tunnel;

h. On any railroad tracks. A violation of any part of this subparagraph h. shall result in a mandatory fine of $500 or 50 hours of community service.

i. At any place where official signs prohibit stopping;

j. On any controlled-access highway;

k. In the area between roadways of a divided highway, including crossovers;

l. In a public parking area if the vehicle does not display a current annual registration sticker or current temporary permit pending registration.

2. Stand or park a vehicle, whether occupied or not, except momentarily to pick up or discharge passengers:

a. In front of a public or private driveway;

b. Within 15 feet of a fire hydrant;

c. Within 20 feet of a crosswalk at an intersection;

d. Within 30 feet upon the approach to any flashing signal, stop sign, yield sign, or traffic control signal located at the side of a roadway;

e. Within 20 feet of the driveway entrance to any fire station and on the side of a street opposite the entrance to any fire station within 75 feet of such entrance (when properly sign-posted);

f. At any place where official signs prohibit standing.

3. Park a vehicle, whether occupied or not, except temporarily for the purpose of and while actually engaged in loading or unloading property or passengers:

a. Within 50 feet of the nearest rail of a railroad crossing;

b. At any place where official signs prohibit parking.

(b) No person shall move a vehicle not lawfully under his control into any such prohibited area or away from a curb such distance as is unlawful.

P.A. 76–1586, § 11–1303, eff. July 1, 1970. Amended by P.A. 77–1345, § 1, eff. Aug. 27, 1971; P.A. 79–1069, § 1, eff. Jan. 1, 1976; P.A. 89–245, § 5, eff. Jan. 1, 1996; P.A. 89–658, § 5, eff. Jan. 1, 1997.

Formerly Ill.Rev.Stat.1991, ch. 95 ½, ¶ 11–1303.

P.A. 89–658 incorporated the amendment by P.A. 89–245.

5/11–1304. Additional parking regulations

§ 11–1304. Additional parking regulations. (a) Except as otherwise provided in this section, every vehicle stopped or parked upon a two-way roadway shall be so stopped or parked with the right-hand wheels parallel to and within 12 inches of the right-hand curb or as close as practicable to the right edge of the right-hand shoulder.

(b) Except when otherwise provided by local ordinance, every vehicle stopped or parked upon a one-way roadway shall be so stopped or parked parallel to the curb or edge of the roadway, in the direction of authorized traffic movement, with its right-hand wheels within 12 inches of the right-hand curb or as close as practicable to the right edge of the right-hand shoulder, or with its left-hand wheels within 12 inches of the left-hand curb or as close as practicable to the left edge of the left-hand shoulder.

(c) Local authorities may permit angle parking on any roadway, except that angle parking shall not be permitted on any federal-aid or State highway unless the Department has determined that the roadway is of sufficient width to permit angle parking without interfering with the free movement of traffic.

(d) The Department with respect to highways under its jurisdiction may place signs prohibiting, limiting, or restricting the stopping, standing or parking of vehicles on any highway where in its opinion such stopping, standing or parking is dangerous to those using the highway or where the stopping, standing or parking of vehicles would unduly interfere with the free movement of traffic thereon. No person shall stop, stand or park any vehicle in violation of the restrictions indicated by such devices.

P.A. 76–1586, § 11–1304, eff. July 1, 1970. Amended by P.A. 79–801, § 1, eff. Oct. 1, 1975; P.A. 79–1069, § 1, eff. Jan. 1, 1976; P.A. 79–1454, § 44, eff. Aug. 31, 1976.

Formerly Ill.Rev.Stat.1991, ch. 95 ½, ¶ 11–1304.

5/11–1304.5. Parking of vehicle with expired registration

§ 11–1304.5. Parking of vehicle with expired registration. No person may stop, park, or leave standing upon a public street, highway, or roadway a vehicle upon which is displayed an Illinois registration plate or plates or registration sticker after the termination of the registration period for which the registration plate or plates or registration sticker was issued or after the expiration date set under Section 3-414 or 3-414.1 of this Code.

P.A. 76-1586, § 11-1304.5, added by P.A. 91-487, § 5, eff. Jan. 1, 2000.

5/11-1305. Lessors of visitor vehicles—Duty upon receiving notice of violation of this Article or local parking regulation

§ 11-1305. Lessors of visitor vehicles—Duty upon receiving notice of violation of this Article or local parking regulation. Every person in whose name a vehicle is registered pursuant to law and who leases such vehicle to others, after receiving written notice of a violation of this Article or a parking regulation of a local authority involving such vehicle, shall upon request provide such police officers as have authority of the offense, and the court having jurisdiction thereof, with a written statement of the name and address of the lessee at the time of such offense and the identifying number upon the registration plates and registration sticker or stickers of such vehicle.

P.A. 76-1586, § 11-1305, eff. July 1, 1970. Amended by P.A. 77-2720, § 1, eff. Jan. 1, 1973; P.A. 80-230, § 1, eff. Oct. 1, 1977; P.A. 80-911, § 1, eff. Oct. 1, 1977; P.A. 80-1185, § 1, eff. March 8, 1978.

Formerly Ill.Rev.Stat.1991, ch. 95 ½, ¶ 11-1305.

See 5 ILCS 70/6 as to the effect of (1) more than one amendment of a section at the same session of the General Assembly or (2) two or more acts relating to the same subject matter enacted by the same General Assembly.

5/11-1306. Parking liability of lessor

§ 11-1306. Parking liability of lessor. No person who is the lessor of a vehicle pursuant to a written lease agreement shall be liable for the violation of any parking or standing regulation of this Act, or of a local authority, involving such vehicle during the period of the lease; provided that upon the request of the appropriate authority received within 120 days after the violation occurred, the lessor provides within 60 days after such receipt the name and address of the lessee. The drivers license number of a lessee may be subsequently individually requested by the appropriate authority if needed for enforcement of the Act.

P.A. 76-1586, § 11-1306, added by P.A. 83-1110, § 2, eff. May 25, 1984. Amended by P.A. 84-354, § 1, eff. Sept. 14, 1985.

Formerly Ill.Rev.Stat.1991, ch. 95 ½, ¶ 11-1306.

ARTICLE XIV. MISCELLANEOUS LAWS

5/11-1401. Unattended motor vehicles

§ 11-1401. Unattended motor vehicles. No person driving or in charge of a motor vehicle shall permit it to stand unattended without first stopping the engine, locking the ignition, removing the key from the ignition, effectively setting the brake thereon and, when standing upon any perceptible grade, turning the front wheels to the curb or side of the highway.

P.A. 76-1586, § 11-1401, eff. July 1, 1970. Amended by P.A. 76-2174, § 1, eff. July 1, 1970; P.A. 79-1069, § 1, eff. Jan. 1, 1976.

Formerly Ill.Rev.Stat.1991, ch. 95 ½, ¶ 11-1401.

5/11-1402. Limitations on backing

§ 11-1402. Limitations on backing. (a) The driver of a vehicle shall not back the same unless such movement can be made with safety and without interfering with other traffic.

(b) The driver of a vehicle shall not back the same upon any shoulder or roadway of any controlled-access highway.

P.A. 76-1586, § 11-1402, eff. July 1, 1970. Amended by P.A. 79-1069, § 1, eff. Jan. 1, 1976.

Formerly Ill.Rev.Stat.1991, ch. 95 ½, ¶ 11-1402.

5/11-1403. Riding on motorcycles

§ 11-1403. Riding on motorcycles. (a) A person operating a motorcycle shall ride only upon the permanent and regular seat attached thereto, and such operator shall not carry any other person nor shall any other person ride on a motorcycle unless such motorcycle is designed to carry more than one person, in which event a passenger may ride upon the permanent and regular seat if designed for 2 persons, or upon another seat firmly attached to the motorcycle at the rear or side of the operator.

(b) A person shall ride upon a motorcycle only while sitting astride the seat, facing forward, with one leg on each side of the motorcycle.

(c) No person shall operate any motorcycle with handlebars higher than the height of the shoulders of the operator when the operator is seated in the normal driving position astride that portion of the seat or saddle occupied by the operator.

P.A. 76-1586, § 11-1403, eff. July 1, 1970. Amended by P.A. 84-602, § 1, eff. Jan. 1, 1986.

Formerly Ill.Rev.Stat.1991, ch. 95 ½, ¶ 11-1403.

5/11-1403.1. Riding on motorized pedalcycles

§ 11-1403.1. Riding on motorized pedalcycles. (a) The operator of a motorized pedalcycle shall ride only astride the permanent and regular seat attached thereto, and shall not permit 2 persons to ride thereon at the same time, unless the motorized pedalcycle is designed to carry 2 persons; any motorized pedalcycle designed for 2 persons must be equipped with a passenger seat and footrests for use of a passenger.

(b) The provisions of Article XV shall be applicable to the operation of motorized pedalcycles, except for those provisions which by their nature can have no application to motorized pedalcycles.

P.A. 76-1586, § 11-403.1, added by P.A. 80-262, § 1, eff. Aug. 20, 1977. Renumbered § 11-1403.1 and amended by P.A. 82-783, Art. IV, § 25, eff. July 13, 1982. Amended by P.A. 84-602, § 1, eff. Jan. 1, 1986; P.A. 85-830, § 1, eff. Sept. 24, 1987.

Formerly Ill.Rev.Stat.1991, ch. 95 ½, ¶ 11-1403.1.

5/11-1403.2. Operation on one wheel

§ 11-1403.2. No person shall operate a motorcycle, motor driven cycle, or motorized pedalcycle on one wheel.

P.A. 76-1586, § 11-1403.2, added by P.A. 81-844, § 1, eff. Jan. 1, 1980. Amended by P.A. 85-830, § 1, eff. Sept. 24, 1987.

Formerly Ill.Rev.Stat.1991, ch. 95 ½, ¶ 11-1403.2.

5/11-1403.3. Intercom helmets

§ 11-1403.3. Intercom helmets. Any driver of a vehicle defined in Section 1-145.001, 1-147, or 1-148.2 of this Code may use a helmet equipped with an electronic intercom system permitting 2-way vocal communication with drivers of any such vehicles or passengers on such vehicles.

P.A. 76-1586, § 11-1403.3, added by P.A. 85-273, § 1, eff. Jan. 1, 1988. Amended by P.A. 90-89, § 15, eff. Jan. 1, 1998.

Formerly Ill.Rev.Stat.1991, ch. 95 ½, ¶ 11-1403.3.

5/11-1404. Special equipment for persons riding motorcycles, motor driven cycles or motorized pedalcycles

§ 11-1404. Special equipment for persons riding motorcycles, motor driven cycles or motorized pedalcycles.

(a) The operator of a motorcycle, motor driven cycle or motorized pedalcycle and every passenger thereon shall be protected by glasses, goggles or a transparent shield.

(b) For the purposes of this Section, glasses, goggles, and transparent shields are defined as follows:

"Glasses" means ordinary eye pieces such as spectacles or sunglasses worn before the eye, made of shatter-resistant material. Shatter-resistant material, as used in this Section, means material so manufactured, fabricated, or created that it substantially prevents shattering or flying when struck or broken.

"Goggles" means a device worn before the eyes, the predominant function of which is protecting the eyes without obstructing peripheral vision. Goggles shall provide protection from the front and sides, and may or may not form a complete seal with the face.

"Transparent shield" means a windshield attached to the front of a motorcycle that extends above the eyes when an operator is seated in the normal, upright riding position, made of shatter-resistant material, or a shatter-resistant protective face shield that covers the wearer's eyes and face at least to a point approximately to the tip of the nose.

(c) Contact lenses are not acceptable eye protection devices.

P.A. 76-1586, § 11-1404, eff. July 1, 1970. Amended by P.A. 76-2175, § 1, eff. July 1, 1970; P.A. 78-748, § 1, eff. Jan. 1, 1974; P.A. 85-830, § 1, eff. Sept. 24, 1987; P.A. 89-271, § 5, eff. Jan. 1, 1996.

Formerly Ill.Rev.Stat.1991, ch. 95 ½, ¶ 11-1404.

5/11-1405. Required equipment on motorcycles

§ 11-1405. Required equipment on motorcycles. Any motorcycle carrying a passenger, other than in a sidecar or enclosed cab, shall be equipped with footrests for such passenger.

P.A. 76-1586, § 11-1405, eff. July 1, 1970. Amended by P.A. 76-1736, § 1; P.A. 81-804, § 1, eff. Sept. 19, 1979; P.A. 84-602, § 1, eff. Jan. 1, 1986.

Formerly Ill.Rev.Stat.1991, ch. 95 ½, ¶ 11-1405.

5/11-1406. Obstruction of driver's view or driving mechanism

§ 11-1406. Obstruction of driver's view or driving mechanism. (a) No person shall drive a vehicle when it is so loaded, or when there are in the front seat such a number of persons, exceeding three, as to obstruct the view of the driver to the front or sides of the vehicle or as to interfere with the driver's control over the driving mechanism of the vehicle.

(b) No passenger in a vehicle or streetcar shall ride in such position as to interfere with the driver's or motorman's view ahead or to the sides, or to interfere with his control over the driving mechanism of the vehicle or streetcar.

(c) No passenger on a school bus may ride or stand in a position as to interfere with the driver's view ahead or to the side or to the rear, or to interfere with his control of the driving mechanism of the bus.

P.A. 76-1586, § 11-1406, eff. July 1, 1970. Amended by P.A. 78-499, § 1, eff. Aug. 30, 1973; P.A. 79-1069, § 1, eff. Jan. 1, 1976.

Formerly Ill.Rev.Stat.1991, ch. 95 ½, ¶ 11-1406.

5/11-1407. Opening and closing vehicle doors

§ 11-1407. Opening and closing vehicle doors. No person shall open the door of a vehicle on the side available to moving traffic unless and until it is reasonably safe to do so, and can be done without interfering with the movement of other traffic, nor shall any person leave a door open on the side of a vehicle available to moving traffic for a period of time longer than necessary to load or unload passengers.

P.A. 76-1586, § 11-1407, eff. July 1, 1970. Amended by P.A. 79-1069, § 1, eff. Jan. 1, 1976.

Formerly Ill.Rev.Stat.1991, ch. 95 ½, ¶ 11-1407.

5/11-1408. Riding in house trailers

§ 11-1408. Riding in house trailers. No person or persons shall occupy a house trailer, travel trailer while it is being towed upon a public highway.

P.A. 76-1586, § 11-1408, eff. July 1, 1970. Amended by P.A. 81-969, § 1, eff. Jan. 1, 1980.

Formerly Ill.Rev.Stat.1991, ch. 95 ½, ¶ 11-1408.

Section 3 of P.A. 81-969, approved Sept. 22, 1979, provided:

"This amendatory Act takes effect at the start of the 1981 registration year."

5/11-1409. Driving on mountain highways

§ 11-1409. Driving on mountain highways. The driver of a motor vehicle traveling through defiles or canyons or on mountain highways shall hold such motor vehicle under control and as near the right-hand edge of the roadway as reasonably possible and, except when driving entirely to the right of the center of the roadway, shall give audible warning with the horn of such motor vehicle upon approaching any curve where the view is obstructed within a distance of 200 feet along the highway.

P.A. 76-1586, § 11-1409, eff. July 1, 1970. Amended by P.A. 79-1069, § 1, eff. Jan. 1, 1976.

Formerly Ill.Rev.Stat.1991, ch. 95 ½, ¶ 11-1409.

5/11-1410. Coasting prohibited

§ 11-1410. Coasting prohibited. (a) The driver of any motor vehicle when traveling upon a down grade shall not coast with the gears or transmission of such vehicle in neutral.

(b) The driver of a truck or bus when traveling upon a down grade shall not coast with the clutch disengaged.

P.A. 76-1586, § 11-1410, eff. July 1, 1970. Amended by P.A. 76-1736, § 1; P.A. 79-1069, § 1, eff. Jan. 1, 1976.

Formerly Ill.Rev.Stat.1991, ch. 95 ½, ¶ 11-1410.

5/11-1411. Following fire apparatus prohibited

§ 11-1411. Following fire apparatus prohibited. The driver of any vehicle other than one on official business shall not follow any fire apparatus traveling in response to a fire alarm closer than 500 feet or stop such vehicle within 500 feet of any fire apparatus stopped in answer to a fire alarm.

P.A. 76-1586, § 11-1411, eff. July 1, 1970. Amended by P.A. 79-1069, § 1, eff. Jan. 1, 1976.

Formerly Ill.Rev.Stat.1991, ch. 95 ½, ¶ 11-1411.

5/11-1412. Crossing fire hose

§ 11-1412. Crossing fire hose. No vehicle shall be driven over any unprotected hose of a fire department when laid down on any street, private road or driveway to be used at any fire or alarm of fire, without the consent of the fire department official in command.

P.A. 76-1586, § 11-1412, eff. July 1, 1970. Amended by P.A. 76-1736, § 1, eff. Oct. 6, 1969.

Formerly Ill.Rev.Stat.1991, ch. 95 ½, ¶ 11-1412.

5/11-1412.1. Driving upon sidewalk

Text of section effective until June 1, 2003

§ 11-1412.1. Driving upon sidewalk. No person shall drive any vehicle upon a sidewalk or sidewalk area except upon a permanent or duly authorized temporary driveway. This Section does not apply to any vehicle moved exclusively by human power nor to any motorized wheelchair.

P.A. 76-1586, § 11-1412.1, added by P.A. 76-1736, § 1. Amended by P.A. 79-1069, § 1, eff. Jan. 1, 1976; P.A. 84-672, § 1, eff. Sept. 20, 1985.

Formerly Ill.Rev.Stat.1991, ch. 95 ½, ¶ 11-1412.1.

For text of section effective June 1, 2003, see 625 ILCS 5/11-1412.1, post

5/11-1412.1. Driving upon sidewalk

Text of section effective June 1, 2003

§ 11-1412.1. Driving upon sidewalk. No person shall drive any vehicle upon a sidewalk or sidewalk area except upon a permanent or duly authorized temporary driveway. This Section does not apply to any vehicle moved exclusively by human power, to any electric personal assistive mobility device, nor to any motorized wheelchair. Nothing in this Section shall be deemed to limit or preempt the authority of any home rule or non-home rule unit of local government from regulating or prohibiting the use of electric personal assistive mobility devices.

P.A. 76-1586, § 11-1412.1, added by P.A. 76-1736, § 1. Amended by P.A. 79-1069, § 1, eff. Jan. 1, 1976; P.A. 84-672, § 1, eff. Sept. 20, 1985; P.A. 92-868, § 5, eff. June 1, 2003.

Formerly Ill.Rev.Stat.1991, ch. 95 ½, ¶ 11-1412.1.

For text of section effective until June 1, 2003, see 625 ILCS 5/11-1412.1, ante

5/11-1412.2. Operating an electric personal assistive mobility device on a public sidewalk

Text of section added effective June 1, 2003

§ 11-1412.2. Operating an electric personal assistive mobility device on a public sidewalk. A person may not operate an electric personal assistive mobility device upon a public sidewalk at a speed greater than 8 miles per hour. Nothing in this Section shall be deemed to limit or preempt the authority of any home rule or non-home rule unit of local government from regulating or prohibiting the use of electric personal assistive mobility devices.

P.A. 76–1586, § 11–1412.2, added by P.A. 92–868, § 5, eff. June 1, 2003.

5/11-1413. Depositing material on highway prohibited

§ 11–1413. Depositing material on highway prohibited.

(a) No person shall throw, spill or deposit upon any highway any bottle, glass, nails, tacks, wire, cans, or any litter (as defined in Section 3 of the Litter Control Act).[1]

(b) Any person who violates subsection (a) upon any highway shall immediately remove such material or cause it to be removed.

(c) Any person removing a wrecked or damaged vehicle from a highway shall remove any glass or other debris, except any hazardous substance as defined in Section 3.215 of the Environmental Protection Act,[2] hazardous waste as defined in Section 3.220 of the Environmental Protection Act,[3] and potentially infectious medical waste as defined in Section 3.360 of the Environmental Protection Act,[4] dropped upon the highway from such vehicle.

P.A. 76–1586, § 11–1413, eff. July 1, 1970. Amended by P.A. 79–1069, § 1, eff. Jan. 1, 1976; P.A. 86–664, § 1, eff. Sept. 1, 1989; P.A. 87–190, § 1, eff. Jan. 1, 1992; P.A. 88–415, § 10, eff. Aug. 20, 1993; P.A. 88–670, Art. 3, § 3–80, eff. Dec. 2, 1994; P.A. 92–574, § 70, eff. June 26, 2002.

Formerly Ill.Rev.Stat.1991, ch. 95½, ¶ 11–1413.

1 415 ILCS 105/3.

2 415 ILCS 5/3.215.

3 415 ILCS 5/3.220.

4 415 ILCS 5/3.360.

P.A. 88–670, Article 3, of the First 1994 General Revisory Act, amended various Acts to delete obsolete text, to correct patent and technical errors, and to revise cross references.

5/11-1414. Approaching, overtaking, and passing school bus

§ 11–1414. Approaching, overtaking, and passing school bus.

(a) The driver of a vehicle shall stop such vehicle before meeting or overtaking, from either direction, any school bus stopped for the purpose of receiving or discharging pupils on a highway, on a roadway on school property, or upon a private road within an area that is covered by a contract or agreement executed pursuant to Section 11–209.1 of this Code. Such stop is required before reaching the school bus when there is in operation on the school bus the visual signals as specified in Sections 12–803 and 12–805 of this Code. The driver of the vehicle shall not proceed until the school bus resumes motion or the driver of the vehicle is signaled by the school bus driver to proceed or the visual signals are no longer actuated.

(b) The stop signal arm required by Section 12–803 of this Code shall be extended after the school bus has come to a complete stop for the purpose of loading or discharging pupils and shall be closed before the school bus is placed in motion again. The stop signal arm shall not be extended at any other time.

(c) The alternately flashing red signal lamps of an 8–lamp flashing signal system required by Section 12–805 of this Code shall be actuated after the school bus has come to a complete stop for the purpose of loading or discharging pupils and shall be turned off before the school bus is placed in motion again. The red signal lamps shall not be actuated at any other time except as provided in paragraph (d) of this Section.

(d) The alternately flashing amber signal lamps of an 8–lamp flashing signal system required by Section 12–805 of this Code shall be actuated continuously during not less than the last 100 feet traveled by the school bus before stopping for the purpose of loading or discharging pupils within an urban area and during not less than the last 200 feet traveled by the school bus outside an urban area. The amber signal lamps shall remain actuated until the school bus is stopped. The amber signal lamps shall not be actuated at any other time.

(e) The driver of a vehicle upon a highway having 4 or more lanes which permits at least 2 lanes of traffic to travel in opposite directions need not stop such vehicle upon meeting a school bus which is stopped in the opposing roadway; and need not stop such vehicle when driving upon a controlled access highway when passing a school bus traveling in either direction that is stopped in a loading zone adjacent to the surfaced or improved part of the controlled access highway where pedestrians are not permitted to cross.

(f) Beginning with the effective date of this amendatory Act of 1985, the Secretary of State shall suspend for a period of 3 months the driving privileges of any person convicted of a violation of subsection (a) of this Section or a similar provision of a local ordinance; the Secretary shall suspend for a period of one year the driving privileges of any person convicted of a second or subsequent violation of subsection (a) of this Section or a similar provision of a local ordinance if the second or subsequent violation occurs within 5 years of a prior conviction for the same offense. In addition to the suspensions authorized by this Section, any person convicted of violating this Section or a similar provision of a local ordinance shall be subject to a mandatory fine of $150 or, upon a second or subsequent violation, $500. The Secretary may also grant, for the duration of any suspension issued under this subsection, a restricted driving permit granting the privilege of driving a motor vehicle between the driver's residence and place of employment or within other proper limits that the Secretary of State shall find necessary to avoid any undue hardship. A restricted driving permit issued hereunder shall be subject to cancellation, revocation and suspension by the Secretary of State in like manner and for like cause as a driver's license may be cancelled, revoked or suspended; except that a conviction upon one or more offenses against laws or ordinances regulating the movement of traffic shall be deemed sufficient cause for the revocation, suspension or cancellation of the restricted driving permit. The Secretary of State may, as a condition to the issuance of a restricted driving permit, require the applicant to participate in a designated driver remedial or rehabilitative program. Any conviction for a violation of this subsection shall be included as an offense for the purposes of determining suspension action under any other provision of this Code, provided however, that the penalties provided under this subsection shall be imposed unless those penalties imposed under other applicable provisions are greater.

The owner of any vehicle alleged to have violated paragraph (a) of this Section shall, upon appropriate demand by the State's Attorney or other authorized prosecutor acting in response to a signed complaint, provide a written statement or deposition identifying the operator of the vehicle if such operator was not the owner at the time of the alleged violation. Failure to supply such information shall be construed to be the same as a violation of paragraph (a) and shall be subject to the same penalties herein provided. In the event the owner has assigned control for the use of the vehicle to another, the person to whom control was assigned shall comply with the provisions of this paragraph and be subject to the same penalties as herein provided.

P.A. 76-1586, § 11-1414, eff. July 1, 1970. Amended by P.A. 76-1723, § 1; P.A. 78-510, § 1, eff. Oct. 1, 1973; P.A. 78-738, § 1, eff. Jan. 1, 1974; P.A. 78-1244, § 1, eff. Sept. 5, 1974; P.A. 78-1297, § 58, eff. March 4, 1975; P.A. 79-63, § 1, eff. June 26, 1975; P.A. 80-506, § 1, eff. Oct. 1, 1977; P.A. 82-648, § 1, eff. July 1, 1982; P.A. 83-905, § 1, eff. Jan. 1, 1984; P.A. 84-112, § 1, eff. July 25, 1985; P.A. 89-210, § 5, eff. Aug. 2, 1995; P.A. 91-260, § 5, eff. Jan. 1, 2000.

Formerly Ill.Rev.Stat.1991, ch. 95 ½, ¶ 11-1414.

5/11-1414.1. School transportation of students

§ 11-1414.1. School transportation of students.

(a) Every student enrolled in grade 12 or below in any entity listed in paragraph (a) of Section 1-182 of this Code who is transported in a second division motor vehicle owned or operated by or for that entity, in connection with any official activity of such entity, must be transported in a school bus or a bus described in subparagraph (1) of paragraph (b) of Section 1-182.

(b) This Section shall not apply to any second division vehicle being used by such entity in a parade, homecoming or similar school activity, nor to a motor vehicle designed for the transportation of not less than 7 nor more than 16 persons while that vehicle is being operated by or for a public or private primary or secondary school, including any primary or secondary school operated by a religious institution, for the purpose of transporting not more than 15 students to and from interscholastic athletic or other interscholastic or school sponsored activities.

P.A. 76-1586, § 11-1414.1, added by P.A. 83-299, § 1, eff. Jan. 1, 1984. Amended by P.A. 89-132, § 10, eff. July 14, 1995.

Formerly Ill.Rev.Stat.1991, ch. 95 ½, ¶ 11-1414.1.

5/11-1415. School buses stopping, loading and discharging passengers on one-way roadways on highways having 4 or more lanes

§ 11-1415. School buses stopping, loading and discharging passengers on one-way roadways on highways having 4 or more lanes. (a) A school bus traveling on a one-way roadway or a highway having 4 or more lanes for vehicular traffic shall stop for the loading or discharging of passengers only on the right side of the highway. If the highway has 4 or more lanes and permits traffic to operate in both directions, the school bus shall load or discharge only those passengers whose residences are located to the right of the highway. The routes of school buses shall be so arranged that no child shall be required to cross a highway of 4 or more lanes to board a school bus or to reach such child's residence after leaving the school bus. A school child in an urban area shall cross a highway only at a crossing for pedestrians, except as provided in paragraph (b) of this Section.

(b) With respect to school children crossing a highway at other than a pedestrian crossing, this Section shall not apply when children are escorted or controlled by competent persons designated by the school authorities or by police officers.

P.A. 76-1586, § 11-1415, eff. July 1, 1970. Amended by P.A. 83-905, § 1, eff. Jan. 1, 1984.

Formerly Ill.Rev.Stat.1991, ch. 95½, ¶ 11-1415.

5/11-1416. Obstructing person in highways

§ 11-1416. Obstructing person in highways. No person shall wilfully and unnecessarily hinder, obstruct or delay, or wilfully and unnecessarily attempt to delay, hinder or obstruct any other person in lawfully driving or traveling along or upon any highway within this State or offer for barter or sale merchandise on said highway so as to interfere with the effective movement of traffic.

P.A. 76-1586, § 11-1416, eff. July 1, 1970. Amended by P.A. 77-2830, Art. 73, § 1, eff. Jan. 1, 1973; P.A. 78-494, § 1, eff. Oct. 1, 1973; P.A. 80-911, § 1, eff. Oct. 1, 1977.

Formerly Ill.Rev.Stat.1991, ch. 95 ½, ¶ 11-1416.

5/11-1417. Travel regulated

§ 11-1417. Travel regulated. It shall be unlawful for any person to drive or cause to be driven a vehicle of any description in or upon any portion of the highway immediately after the same has been dragged and before such portion of the highway shall have partially dried out or frozen; provided, that nothing in this Section shall apply in those instances where it is impossible to drive with safety at one side of said dragged portion of the road, or where a vehicle does not make a rut on such dragged portion of the road, injurious to the work accomplished by use of the road drag or where a vehicle does not make a rut nearer than nine (9) feet from the center of the dragged portion of the road.

P.A. 76-1586, § 11-1417, eff. July 1, 1970.

Formerly Ill.Rev.Stat.1991, ch. 95 ½, ¶ 11-1417.

5/11-1418. Farm tractor operation regulated

§ 11-1418. Farm tractor operation regulated.

No person shall operate a farm tractor on a highway unless the tractor is being used as an implement of husbandry in connection with farming operations.

For the purpose of this Section, use of a farm tractor as an implement of husbandry in connection with farming operations shall be deemed to include use of the tractor in connection with the transportation of agricultural products and of farm machinery, equipment and supplies as well as transportation of the implement of husbandry from its place of purchase to its place of storage, in connection with the obtaining of repairs of the implement of husbandry, and the towing of a registered truck not more than 8,000 pounds for use as return transportation after the tractor is left at the place of work or repair.

P.A. 76-1586, § 11-1418, eff. July 1, 1970. Amended by P.A. 77-631, § 1, eff. Aug. 4, 1971; P.A. 87-1028, § 1, eff. Jan. 1, 1993.

Formerly Ill.Rev.Stat.1991, ch. 95 ½, ¶ 11-1418.

5/11-1419. Operation of motor vehicles—Duration—Exceptions

§ 11-1419. Operation of motor vehicles—Duration—Exceptions. It is unlawful for any owner to require, permit or allow any operator of any of his motor vehicles of the second division to operate any such motor vehicle for a longer period than 10 hours following 8 consecutive hours off-duty or drive for any period after having been on duty 15 hours following 8 consecutive hours off-duty, or to be or remain on duty more than 60 hours in any 7 consecutive days, and whenever any such operator has operated such motor vehicle for 10 hours following 8 consecutive hours off-duty or has been on duty 15 hours following 8 consecutive hours off-duty, he or she shall be relieved and not required, permitted or allowed again to operate any such motor vehicle until he or she has had at least 8 consecutive hours off-duty. The Department of State Police shall fix by general rule or temporary order the circumstances and regulations under which in case of emergency or unusual temporary demands for transportation any such operator may be permitted to operate any such motor vehicle or to stay on duty for longer periods of time than set by this Section.

The provisions of this Section shall not apply to any public utility in the operation of any motor vehicle not for hire in case of emergency or in case of unusual temporary necessity for transportation of persons or property or safeguarding of vehicles and their loads, nor shall such provisions apply to operation of any motor vehicle as a part of the agricultural operations of canning, packing or freezing establishments engaged in the growing and processing of perishable fruits and vegetables, including the hauling of such products between fields and such canning, packing or freezing establishments and between such establishments, nor shall such provisions apply to operation of any motor vehicle being used for transportation of construction materials or equipment to, on or from construction sites within a radius of 50 miles of such construction sites, nor to driver sales persons operating within a radius of 50 miles of their principal place of business.

P.A. 76-1586, § 11-1419, eff. July 1, 1970. Amended by P.A. 76-2176, § 1, eff. July 1, 1970; P.A. 84-25, Art. IV, § 27, eff. July 18, 1985; P.A. 84-551, § 50, eff. Sept. 18, 1985; P.A. 84-1308, Art. II, § 96, eff. Aug. 25, 1986.

Formerly Ill.Rev.Stat.1991, ch. 95 ½, ¶ 11-1419.

Article II of P.A. 84-1308, the First 84th General Assembly Combining Revisory Act, provides for the nonsubstantive revision or renumbering or repeal of Sections of Acts necessitated by the amendment, addition or repeal of Sections by two or more Public Acts of the 84th General Assembly, which multiple action was not resolved by one of the Acts of the 84th General Assembly affecting the particular Section and makes technical corrections in Acts amended by the 84th General Assembly.

5/11-1419.01. Operating without a valid single trip permit

§ 11-1419.01. Operating without a valid single trip permit. If a single trip permit is required by Section 13a.5 of the Motor Fuel Tax Law,[1] a motor carrier shall not operate in Illinois without a single trip permit issued by the Department of Revenue or its agents.

If a commercial motor vehicle is found operating in Illinois without displaying a required valid single trip permit, the operator is guilty of a petty offense as provided in Section 13a.6 of the Motor Fuel Tax Law.[2]

P.A. 76-1586, § 11-1419.01, added by P.A. 81-348, § 1, eff. Jan. 1, 1980. Amended by P.A. 88-669, Art. 90, § 90-9.5, eff. Nov. 29, 1994; P.A. 89-399, § 35, eff. Aug. 20, 1995.

Formerly Ill.Rev.Stat.1991, ch. 95 ½, ¶ 11-1419.01.

[1] 35 ILCS 505/13a.5.

[2] 35 ILCS 505/13a.6.

5/11-1419.02. Failure to display a valid motor fuel use tax license

§ 11-1419.02. Failure to display a valid motor fuel use tax license.

(a) If required by Section 13a.4 of the Motor Fuel Tax Law,[1] every valid motor fuel use tax license, or an authorized reproduction, shall at all times be carried in the cab of the vehicle. The operator shall display the license or reproduction upon demand of a police officer or agent of the Department of Revenue. An operator who fails to display a valid motor fuel use tax license is guilty of a petty offense as provided in Section 13a.6 of the Motor Fuel Tax Law.[2]

(b) As used in this Section:

"Display" means the manual surrender of the motor fuel use tax license into the hands of the demanding officer or agent for inspection.

"Motor fuel use tax license" means a motor fuel use tax license issued by the Department of Revenue or by any member jurisdiction under the International Fuel Tax Agreement, or a valid 30 day International Fuel Tax Agreement temporary permit.

P.A. 76-1586, § 11-1419.02, added by P.A. 83-1426, § 1, eff. Jan. 1, 1985. Amended by P.A. 84-1076, § 1, eff. July 1, 1986; P.A. 85-340, § 2, eff. Sept. 10, 1987; P.A. 88-669, Art. 90, § 90-9.5, eff. Nov. 29, 1994; P.A. 89-399, § 35, eff. Aug. 20, 1995.

Formerly Ill.Rev.Stat.1991, ch. 95 ½, ¶ 11-1419.02.

[1] 35 ILCS 505/13a.4.

[2] 35 ILCS 505/13a.6.

5/11-1419.03. Failure to Display Valid External Motor Fuel Use Tax Decals

§ 11-1419.03. Failure to Display Valid External Motor Fuel Use Tax Decals.

(a) Except as provided in the Motor Fuel Tax Law,[1] a motor carrier shall not operate or cause to be operated a commercial motor vehicle upon the highways of this State unless there is properly affixed to that commercial vehicle 2 valid external motor use tax decals required by Section 13a.4 of the Motor Fuel Tax Law.[2] An operator who operates a commercial motor vehicle without 2 properly displayed valid external motor fuel use tax decals is guilty of a petty offense as provided in Section 13a.6 of the Motor Fuel Tax Law.[3] A valid 30-day International Fuel Tax Agreement temporary permit may be displayed instead of decals during the temporary period specified on the permit.

(b) As used in this Section:

"Properly displayed" means 2 motor fuel use tax decals, one placed on each side of the exterior of the cab. In the case of transporters, manufacturers, dealers, or driveaway operations, the decals need not be permanently affixed but may be temporarily displayed in a visible manner on the exterior sides of the cab.

"Commercial motor vehicle" means a motor vehicle used, designed, or maintained for the transportation of people or property and either having 2 axles and a gross vehicle weight or registered gross vehicle weight exceeding 26,000 pounds or 11,793 kilograms, or having 3 or more axles regardless of weight, or that is used in combination, when the weight of the combination exceeds 26,000 pounds or 11,793 kilograms gross vehicle weight or registered gross vehicle weight except for motor vehicles operated by this State or the United States, recreational vehicles, school buses, and commercial motor vehicles operated solely within this State for which all motor fuel is purchased within this State.

"Motor carrier" means any person who operates or causes to be operated any commercial motor vehicle on any highway within this State.

P.A. 76-1586, § 11-1419.03, added by P.A. 88-669, Art. 90, § 90-9.5, eff. Nov. 29, 1994. Amended by P.A. 89-399, § 35, eff. Aug. 20, 1995.

1 35 ILCS 505/1 et seq.

2 35 ILCS 505/13a.4.

3 35 ILCS 505/13a.6.

5/11-1419.04. Failure to carry a manifest

§ 11-1419.04. Failure to carry a manifest. Any person who acts as a motor carrier and who fails to carry a manifest as provided in Section 5.5 of the Motor Fuel Tax Law[1] is guilty of a Class A misdemeanor. For each subsequent offense, the person is guilty of a Class 4 felony.

P.A. 76-1586, § 11-1419.04, added by P.A. 89-399, § 35, eff. Aug. 20, 1995.

1 35 ILCS 505/5.5.

5/11-1419.05. Operation of commercial motor vehicle with revoked motor fuel use tax license

§ 11-1419.05. A motor carrier shall not operate or cause to be operated a commercial motor vehicle upon the highways of this State with a revoked motor fuel use tax license. Any person who operates a commercial motor vehicle with a revoked motor fuel use tax license is guilty of a petty offense as provided in Section 13a.6 of the Motor Fuel Tax Law.[1] When a commercial motor vehicle is found to be operating in Illinois with a revoked motor fuel use tax license, the vehicle shall be placed out of service and not allowed to operate in Illinois until the motor fuel use tax license is reinstated.

P.A. 76-1586, § 11-1419.05, added by P.A. 91-173, § 15, eff. Jan. 1, 2000.

1 35 ILCS 505/13a.6.

5/11-1420. Funeral processions

§ 11-1420. Funeral processions.

(a) Funeral processions have the right-of-way at intersections when vehicles comprising such procession have their headlights lighted, subject to the following conditions and exceptions:

1. Operators of vehicles in a funeral procession shall yield the right-of-way upon the approach of an authorized emergency vehicle giving an audible or visible signal;

2. Operators of vehicles in a funeral procession shall yield the right-of-way when directed to do so by a traffic officer;

3. The operator of the leading vehicle in a funeral procession shall comply with stop signs and traffic control signals but when the leading vehicle has proceeded across an intersection in accordance with such signal or after stopping as required by the stop sign, all vehicles in such procession may proceed without stopping, regardless of the sign or signal and the leading vehicle and the vehicles in procession shall proceed with due caution.

(b) The operator of a vehicle not in the funeral procession shall not drive his vehicle in the funeral procession except when authorized to do so by a traffic officer or when such vehicle is an authorized emergency vehicle giving audible or visible signal.

(c) Operators of vehicles not a part of a funeral procession may not form a procession or convoy and have their headlights lighted for the purpose of securing the right-of-way granted by this Section to funeral processions.

(d) The operator of a vehicle not in a funeral procession may overtake and pass the vehicles in such procession if such overtaking and passing can be accomplished without causing a traffic hazard or interfering with such procession.

(e) The lead vehicle in the funeral procession may be equipped with a flashing amber light which may be used only when such vehicle is used as a lead vehicle in such procession. Vehicles comprising a funeral procession may utilize funeral pennants or flags or windshield stickers or flashing hazard warning signal flashers to identify the individual vehicles in such a procession.

P.A. 76-1586, § 11-1420, eff. July 1, 1970. Amended by P.A. 90-58, § 5, eff. Jan. 1, 1998.

Formerly Ill.Rev.Stat.1991, ch. 95 ½, ¶ 11-1420.

5/11-1421. Conditions for operating ambulances and rescue vehicles

§ 11-1421. Conditions for operating ambulances and rescue vehicles.

(a) No person shall operate an ambulance or rescue vehicle in a manner not conforming to the motor vehicle laws and regulations of this State or of any political subdivision of this State as such laws and regulations apply to motor vehicles in general, unless in compliance with the following conditions:

1. The person operating the ambulance shall be either responding to a bona fide emergency call or specifically directed by a licensed physician to disregard traffic laws in operating the ambulance during and for the purpose of the specific trip or journey that is involved;

2. The ambulance or rescue vehicle shall be equipped with a siren producing an audible signal of an intensity of 100 decibels at a distance of 50 feet from the siren, and with a lamp or lamps emitting an oscillating, rotating or flashing red beam directed in part toward the front of the vehicle, and these lamps shall have sufficient intensity to be visible at 500 feet in normal sunlight, and in addition to other lighting requirements, excluding those vehicles operated in counties with a population in excess of 2,000,000, may also operate with a lamp or lamps emitting an oscillating, rotating, or flashing green light;

3. The aforesaid siren and lamp or lamps shall be in operation at all times when it is reasonably necessary to warn pedestrians and other drivers of the approach thereof during such trip or journey;

4. Whenever the ambulance or rescue vehicle is operated at a speed in excess of 40 miles per hour, the ambulance or rescue vehicle shall be operated in complete conformance with every other motor vehicle law and regulation of this State and of the political subdivision in which the ambulance or rescue vehicle is operated, relating to the operation of motor vehicles, as such provision applies to motor vehicles in general, except laws and regulations pertaining to compliance with official traffic-control devices or to vehicular operation upon the right half of the roadway; and

5. The ambulance shall display registration plates identifying the vehicle as an ambulance.

(b) The foregoing provisions do not relieve the driver of an ambulance or rescue vehicle from the duty of driving with due regard for the safety of all persons, nor do such provisions protect the driver from the consequences resulting from the reckless disregard for the safety of others.

P.A. 76-1586, § 11-1421, eff. July 1, 1970. Amended by P.A. 82-433, § 1, eff. Sept. 8, 1981; P.A. 83-831, § 1, eff. Jan. 1, 1984; P.A. 88-517, § 10, eff. Nov. 16, 1993.

Formerly Ill.Rev.Stat.1991, ch. 95 ½, ¶ 11-1421.

Section 3 of P.A. 82-433 approved Sept. 8, 1981, provided:

"This Act takes effect upon its becoming a law, except that the provisions relating to safety tests and proof of financial responsibility for medical transport vehicles apply only to applications for and the issuance of registration plates which are required to be displayed on January 1, 1982 or thereafter."

5/11-1422. Illegal operation of an ambulance or rescue vehicle—Penalty

§ 11-1422. Illegal operation of an ambulance or rescue vehicle—Penalty. A person who operates an ambulance or rescue vehicle in violation of Section 11-1421 shall be subject to the penalty prescribed by the applicable law, or regulation or ordinance of this State or any political subdivision thereof.

P.A. 76-1586, § 11-1422, eff. July 1, 1970. Amended by P.A. 83-831, § 1, eff. Jan. 1, 1984.

Formerly Ill.Rev.Stat.1991, ch. 95 ½, ¶ 11-1422.

5/11-1423. Passengers boarding or exiting a school bus

§ 11-1423. Passengers boarding or exiting a school bus. (a) At all pick-up points where it is necessary for a school bus passenger to cross the roadway to board the bus, the school bus driver shall signal the awaiting passenger when it is safe to cross the roadway ahead of the bus.

(b) At all discharge points where it is necessary for a school bus passenger to cross the roadway, the school bus driver shall direct the passenger to a point approximately 10 feet in front of the bus on the shoulder and shall then signal the passenger when it is safe to cross the roadway.

P.A. 76-1586, § 11-1423, added by P.A. 78-1244, § 1, eff. Sept. 5, 1974.

Formerly Ill.Rev.Stat.1991, ch. 95 ½, ¶ 11-1423.

5/11-1424. Operation of religious organization bus

§ 11-1424. Operation of a religious organization bus. (a) No religious organization bus may be operated on any street or highway unless all passengers, except for supervisory personnel, are seated in seats permanently mounted to the vehicle, and the aisle of the bus is kept clean and open.

(b) No religious organization bus may be operated on any street or highway while carrying more than the manufacturer's rated passenger capacity for such bus, or at a gross weight in excess of the chassis manufacturer's gross vehicle weight rating (GVWR) or gross axle weight rating (GAWR), or in excess of the weight load ratings of the tires on such bus. For Buses or tires on which the manufacturer has not shown such ratings, by a label, embossment, molding or equivalent means, the Department shall provide, or assist in obtaining, the necessary ratings and may publish such ratings.

(c) In loading or unloading passengers, the religious organization bus driver shall stop the bus out of the lane of moving traffic at any bus stop, officially designated as such by government authorities or in a parking lane on the pavement of the highway or on the shoulder off of the highway, if wide enough to permit the safe loading or unloading of passengers. If, however, there is no such bus stop, parking lane or shoulder within 50 feet of the residence or temporary residence of the passenger transported or to be transported by the bus or within 50 feet of the religious facility, the driver may stop the bus on the pavement of the highway after activating unison amber warning lights for not less than 200 feet before the bus is brought to a stop and while passengers are being loaded or unloaded, or if the bus is equipped as a school bus and meets the requirements of Article VIII of this Act,[1] by complying with the subsections (b), (c) and (d) of Section 11-1414.

(d) At all pickup points where it is necessary for a religious organization bus passenger under the age of 12 years to cross the roadway to board the bus, a responsible supervisor on the bus shall personally escort the awaiting passenger when it is safe to cross the roadway ahead of the bus.

(e) At all discharge points where it is necessary for a religious organization bus passenger under the age of 12 to cross the roadway, a responsible supervisor on the bus shall personally escort the passenger to a point approximately 10 feet in front of the bus on the shoulder and then, when it is safe to cross the roadway, across the roadway to a place of safety.

(f) If a school bus is used by a religious organization bus for the purposes specified in subsection (a) of Section 1-111.1a and activates the visual signals as required by subsections (b), (c) and (d) of Section 11-1414 when picking up or discharging passengers, compliance with subsections (d) and (e) of this Section is optional.

P.A. 76-1586, § 11-1424, added by P.A. 79-798, § 1, eff. July 1, 1976. Amended by P.A. 80-506, § 1, eff. Oct. 1, 1977; P.A. 90-89, § 15, eff. Jan. 1, 1998.

Formerly Ill.Rev.Stat.1991, ch. 95 ½, ¶ 11-1424.

[1] 625 ILCS 5/6-800 et seq.

Another § 11-1424, relating to stop when traffic obstructed, was renumbered as § 11-1425 by P.A. 79-1454, § 44.

5/11-1425. Stop when traffic obstructed

§ 11-1425. Stop when traffic obstructed.

(a) No driver shall enter an intersection or a marked crosswalk or drive onto any railroad grade crossing unless there is sufficient space on the other side of the intersection, crosswalk or railroad grade crossing to accommodate the vehicle he is operating without obstructing the passage of other vehicles, pedestrians or railroad trains notwithstanding any traffic-control signal indication to proceed.

(b) No driver shall enter a highway rail grade crossing unless there is sufficient space on the other side of the highway rail grade crossing to accommodate the vehicle being operated without obstructing the passage of a train or other railroad equipment using the rails, notwithstanding any traffic-control signal indication to proceed. Any person found in violation of subsection (b) shall be subject to a mandatory fine of $500 or 50 hours of community service.

(c) Local authorities shall impose fines as established in subsection (b) for persons found in violation of this Section or any similar local ordinance.

P.A. 76-1586, § 11-1424, added by P.A. 79-1068, § 1, eff. Jan. 1, 1976. Renumbered § 11-1425 and amended by P.A. 79-1454, § 44, eff. Aug. 31, 1976. Amended by P.A. 91-532, § 5, eff. Jan. 1, 2000.

Formerly Ill.Rev.Stat.1991, ch. 95 ½, ¶ 11-1425.

5/11-1426. Operation of all-terrain vehicles and off-highway motorcycles on streets, roads and highways

§ 11-1426. Operation of all-terrain vehicles and off-highway motorcycles on streets, roads and highways.

(a) Except as provided under this Section, it shall be unlawful for any person to drive or operate any all-terrain vehicle or off-highway motorcycle upon any street, highway or roadway in this State.

(b) Except as provided under subsection (c) of this Section, all-terrain vehicles and off-highway motorcycles may make a direct crossing provided:

(1) The crossing is made at an angle of approximately 90 degrees to the direction of the street, road or highway and at a place where no obstruction prevents a quick and safe crossing; and

(2) The all-terrain vehicle or off-highway motorcycle is brought to a complete stop before attempting a crossing; and

(3) The operator of the all-terrain vehicle or off-highway motorcycle yields the right of way to all pedestrian and vehicular traffic which constitutes a hazard; and

(4) That when crossing a divided highway, the crossing is made only at an intersection of the highway with another public street, road, or highway; and

(5) That when accessing township roadways in counties which contain a tract of the Shawnee National Forest, the accessing complies with rules promulgated by the Department of Natural Resources to govern the accessing.

(c) No person operating an all-terrain vehicle or off-highway motorcycle shall make a direct crossing upon or across any tollroad, interstate highway, or controlled access highway in this State.

(d) The corporate authorities of a county, road district, township, city, village, or incorporated town may adopt ordinances or resolutions allowing all-terrain vehicles and off-highway motorcycles to be operated on roadways under their jurisdiction, designated by signs as may be prescribed by the Department, when it is necessary to cross a bridge or culvert or when it is impracticable to gain immediate access to an area adjacent to a highway where an all-terrain vehicle or off-highway motorcycle is to be operated. The crossing shall be made in the same direction as traffic.

(e) The corporate authorities of a county, road district, township, city, village, or incorporated town may adopt ordinances or resolutions designating one or more specific public highways or streets under their jurisdiction as egress and ingress routes for the use of all-terrain vehicles and off-highway motorcycles. Operation of all-terrain vehicles and off-highway motorcycles on the routes shall be in the same direction as traffic. Corporate authorities acting under the authority of this subsection (e) shall erect and maintain signs, as may be prescribed by the Department, giving proper notice of the designation.

P.A. 76–1586, § 11–1426, added by P.A. 85–830, § 1, eff. Sept. 24, 1987. Amended by P.A. 86–1091, § 1, eff. July 13, 1990; P.A. 89–445, § 9A–87, eff. Feb. 7, 1996; P.A. 90–287, § 100, eff. Jan. 1, 1998.

Formerly Ill.Rev.Stat.1991, ch. 95 ½, ¶ 11–1426.

5/11–1427. Illegal operation of an all-terrain vehicle or off-highway motorcycle

§ 11–1427. Illegal operation of an all-terrain vehicle or off-highway motorcycle. It is unlawful for any person to drive or operate any all-terrain vehicle or off-highway motorcycle in the following ways:

(a) Careless Operation. No person shall operate any all-terrain vehicle or off-highway motorcycle in a careless or heedless manner so as to be grossly indifferent to the person or property of other persons, or at a rate of speed greater than will permit him in the exercise of reasonable care to bring the all-terrain vehicle or off-highway motorcycle to a stop within the assured clear distance ahead.

(b) Reckless Operation. No person shall operate any all-terrain vehicle or off-highway motorcycle in such a manner as to endanger the life, limb or property of any person.

(c) Within any nature preserve as defined in Section 3.11 of the Illinois Natural Areas Preservation Act.[1]

(d) On the tracks or right of way of an operating railroad.

(e) In any tree nursery or planting in a manner which damages or destroys growing stock, or creates a substantial risk thereto.

(f) On private property, without the written or verbal consent of the owner or lessee thereof. Any person operating an all-terrain vehicle or off-highway motorcycle upon lands of another shall stop and identify himself upon the request of the landowner or his duly authorized representative, and, if requested to do so by the landowner shall promptly remove the all-terrain vehicle or off-highway motorcycle from the premises.

(g) Notwithstanding any other law to the contrary, an owner, lessee, or occupant of premises owes no duty of care to keep the premises safe for entry or use by others for use by an all-terrain vehicle or off-highway motorcycle, or to give warning of any condition, use, structure or activity on such premises. This subsection does not apply where permission to drive or operate an all-terrain vehicle or off-highway motorcycle is given for a valuable consideration other than to this State, any political subdivision or municipality of this State, or any landowner who is paid with funds from the Off-Highway Vehicle Trails Fund. In the case of land leased to the State or a subdivision of the State, any consideration received is not valuable consideration within the meaning of this Section.

Nothing in this subsection limits in any way liability which otherwise exists for willful or malicious failure to guard or warn against a dangerous condition, use, structure, or activity.

(h) On publicly owned lands unless such lands are designated for use by all-terrain vehicles or off-highway motorcycles. For publicly owned lands to be designated for use by all-terrain vehicles or off-highway motorcycles a public hearing shall be conducted by the governmental entity that has jurisdiction over the proposed land prior to the designation.

Nothing in this subsection limits in any way liability which otherwise exists for willful or malicious failure to guard or warn against a dangerous condition, use, structure, or activity.

(h–1) At a rate of speed too fast for conditions, and the fact that the speed of the all-terrain vehicle or off-highway motorcycle does not exceed the applicable maximum speed limit allowed does not relieve the driver from the duty to decrease speed as may be necessary to avoid colliding with any person, vehicle, or object within legal requirements and the duty of all persons to use due care.

(h–2) On the frozen surface of public waters of this State within 100 feet of a person, including a skater, not in or upon an all-terrain vehicle or off-highway motorcycle; within 100 feet of a person engaged in fishing, except at the minimum speed required to maintain forward movement of the all-terrain vehicle or off-highway motorcycle; on an area which has been cleared of snow for skating purposes unless the area is necessary for access to the frozen waters of this State.

(h–3) Within 100 feet of a dwelling between midnight and 6 a.m. at a speed greater than the minimum required to maintain forward movement of the all-terrain vehicle or off-highway motorcycle. This subdivision (h-5) does not apply on private property where verbal or written consent of the owner or lessee has been granted to drive or operate an all-terrain vehicle or off-highway motorcycle upon the private property or frozen waters of this State.

(i) Other Prohibitions.

(1) No person, except persons permitted by law, shall operate or ride any all-terrain vehicle or off-highway motorcycle with any firearm in his or her possession unless he or she is in compliance with Section 2.33 of the Wildlife Code.[2]

(2) No person shall operate any all-terrain vehicle or off-highway motorcycle emitting pollutants in violation of standards established pursuant to the Environmental Protection Act.[3]

(3) No person shall deposit from an all-terrain vehicle or off-highway motorcycle on the snow, ice or ground surface, trash, glass, garbage, insoluble material, or other offensive matter.

P.A. 76-1586, § 11.1427, added by P.A. 86-1091, § 1, eff. July 13, 1990. Renumbered § 11-1427 and amended by P.A. 90-14, Art. 2, § 2-225, eff. July 1, 1997. Amended by P.A. 90-287, § 100, eff. Jan. 1, 1998.

Formerly Ill.Rev.Stat.1991, ch. 95 ½, ¶ 11-1427.

[1] 525 ILCS 30/3.11.

[2] 520 ILCS 5/2.33.

[3] 415 ILCS 5/1 et seq.

P.A. 90-14, Article 2, of the First 1997 General Revisory Act, resolved multiple actions in the 89th General Assembly and made certain technical corrections in P.A. 89-443 through P.A. 89-707.

5/11-1427.1. Operation of an all-terrain vehicle or off-highway motorcycle on ice

§ 11-1427.1. Operation of an all-terrain vehicle or off-highway motorcycle on ice. All-terrain vehicles and off-highway motorcycles may be operated on the frozen waters of this State subject to the provisions of this Section and the rules of the Department of Natural Resources.

P.A. 76-1586, § 11-1427.1, added by P.A. 90-287, § 100, eff. Jan. 1, 1998.

5/11-1427.2. Special all-terrain vehicle or off-highway motorcycle event

§ 11-1427.2. Special all-terrain vehicle or off-highway motorcycle event. Nothing contained in Section 11-1426, 11-1427, or 11-1427.1 shall be construed to prohibit any local authority of this State from designating a special all-terrain vehicle or off-highway motorcycle event. In such case the provisions of Sections 11-1426, 11-1427, and 11-1427.1 shall not apply to areas or highways under the jurisdiction of that local authority.

P.A. 76-1586, § 11-1427.2, added by P.A. 90-287, § 100, eff. Jan. 1, 1998.

5/11-1427.3. Rules for all-terrain vehicles and off-highway motorcycles

§ 11-1427.3. Rules for all-terrain vehicles and off-highway motorcycles. The Department of Natural Resources shall adopt rules to implement and administer the provisions of Sections 11-1426, 11-1427, 11-1427.1, and 11-1427.2.

P.A. 76-1586, § 11-1427.3, added by P.A. 90-287, § 100, eff. Jan. 1, 1998.

5/11-1427.4. Signal from officer to stop

§ 11-1427.4. Signal from officer to stop. An all-terrain vehicle or off-highway motorcycle operator, after having received a visual or audible signal from a law enforcement officer to come to a stop, may not:

(1) operate an all-terrain vehicle or off-highway motorcycle in willful or wanton disregard of the signal to stop;

(2) interfere with or endanger the law enforcement officer or another person or vehicle; or

(3) increase speed or attempt to flee or elude the officer.

P.A. 76-1586, § 11-1427.4, added by P.A. 90-287, § 100, eff. Jan. 1, 1998.

5/11-1428. Operation of golf carts on streets, roads and highways

§ 11-1428. Operation of golf carts on streets, roads and highways.

(a) Except as otherwise provided in this Section, it shall be unlawful for any person to drive or operate any golf cart upon any street, highway or roadway in this State.

(b) Except as provided under subsection (c) of this Section, golf carts may make a direct crossing over a street, highway or roadway that runs through a golf course provided:

(1) The crossing is made at an interchange approved by the local unit of government and at a place where no obstruction prevents a quick and safe crossing; and

(2) The golf cart is brought to a complete stop before attempting a crossing; and

(3) The operator of the golf cart yields the right of way to all pedestrian and vehicular traffic which constitutes a hazard; and

(4) There is no tunnel or overpass ramp provided for the golf cart to cross through the golf course.

(c) No person operating a golf cart shall make a direct crossing upon or across any highway under the jurisdiction of the State, tollroad, interstate highway, or controlled access highway in this State.

(d) For purposes of this Section, "golf cart" means a vehicle specifically designed and intended for the purposes of transporting one or more persons and their golf clubs or maintenance equipment while engaged in the playing of golf, supervising the play of golf, or maintaining the condition of the grounds on a public or private golf course.

(e) Subject to subsection (b), a municipality, township, county, or other unit of local government may authorize, by ordinance or resolution, the operation of golf carts on roadways under their respective jurisdictions. The Department may authorize the operation of golf carts on the roadways under its jurisdiction.

Before permitting the operation of golf carts on its roadway, a municipality, township, county, other unit of local government, or the Department must consider the volume, speed, and character of traffic on the roadway and determine whether golf carts may safely travel on or cross the roadway. Upon determining that golf carts may safely operate on a roadway and the adoption of an ordinance or resolution by a municipality, township, county or other unit of local government, or authorization by the Department, appropriate signs shall be posted.

If a roadway is under the jurisdiction of more than one unit of government, golf carts may not be operated on the roadway unless each unit of government agrees and takes action as provided in this subsection.

No golf cart may be operated on a roadway unless, at a minimum, it has the following: brakes, a steering apparatus, tires, a rearview mirror, red reflectorized warning devices in the front and rear, a slow moving emblem (as required of other vehicles in Section 12-709) on the rear of the golf cart, a headlight that emits a white light visible from a distance of 500 feet to the front, a tail lamp that emits a red light visible from at least 100 feet from the rear, brake lights, and turn signals. When operated on a roadway, a golf cart shall have its headlight and tail lamps lighted as required by Section 12-201.

(f) A person who drives or is in actual physical control of a golf cart on a roadway while under the influence is subject to Section 11-500 through 11-502.

P.A. 76-1586, § 11-1428, added by P.A. 87-847, § 105, eff. July 1, 1992. Amended by P.A. 90-683, § 5, eff. Jan. 1, 1999.

Formerly Ill.Rev.Stat.1991, ch. 95 ½, ¶ 11-1428.

ARTICLE XV. BICYCLES

5/11-1501. Application of rules

§ 11-1501. Application of rules. (a) It is unlawful for any person to do any act forbidden or fail to perform any act required in Article XV of Chapter 11 of this Code.

(b) The parent of any child and the guardian of any ward shall not authorize or knowingly permit any such child or ward to violate any of the provisions of this Code.

P.A. 76-1586, § 11-1501, added by P.A. 79-858, § 1, eff. Jan. 1, 1976. Amended by P.A. 80-911, § 1, eff. Oct. 1, 1977; P.A. 82-132, § 1, eff. Jan. 1, 1982.

Formerly Ill.Rev.Stat.1991, ch. 95 ½, ¶ 11-1501.

5/11-1502. Traffic laws apply to persons riding bicycles

§ 11-1502. Traffic laws apply to persons riding bicycles. Every person riding a bicycle upon a highway shall be granted all of the rights and shall be subject to all of the duties applicable to the driver of a vehicle by this Code, except as to special regulations in this Article XV and except as to those provisions of this Code which by their nature can have no application.

P.A. 76-1586, § 11-1502, added by P.A. 79-858, § 1, eff. Jan. 1, 1976. Amended by P.A. 82-132, § 1, eff. Jan. 1, 1982.

Formerly Ill.Rev.Stat.1991, ch. 95 ½, ¶ 11-1502.

5/11-1503. Riding on bicycles

§ 11-1503. Riding on bicycles. (a) A person propelling a bicycle shall not ride other than upon or astride a permanent and regular seat attached thereto.

(b) No bicycle shall be used to carry more persons at one time than the number for which it is designed and equipped, except that an adult rider may carry a child securely attached to his person in a back pack or sling.

P.A. 76-1586, § 11-1503, added by P.A. 79-858, § 1, eff. Jan. 1, 1976. Amended by P.A. 82-132, § 1, eff. Jan. 1, 1982.

Formerly Ill.Rev.Stat.1991, ch. 95 ½, ¶ 11-1503.

5/11-1504. Clinging to vehicles

§ 11-1504. Clinging to vehicles. No person riding upon any bicycle, coaster, roller skates, sled or toy vehicle shall attach the same or himself to any vehicle upon a roadway.

P.A. 76-1586, § 11-1504, added by P.A. 79-858, § 1, eff. Jan. 1, 1976. Amended by P.A. 82-132, § 1, eff. Jan. 1, 1982.

Formerly Ill.Rev.Stat.1991, ch. 95 ½, ¶ 11-1504.

5/11-1505. Position of bicycles and motorized pedal cycles on roadways—Riding on roadways and bicycle paths

§ 11-1505. Position of bicycles and motorized pedal cycles on roadways—Riding on roadways and bicycle paths. (a) Any person operating a bicycle or motorized pedal cycle upon a roadway at less than the normal speed of traffic at the time and place and under the conditions then existing shall ride as close as practicable to the right-hand curb or edge of the roadway except under the following situations:

1. When overtaking and passing another bicycle, motorized pedal cycle or vehicle proceeding in the same direction; or

2. When preparing for a left turn at an intersection or into a private road or driveway; or

3. When reasonably necessary to avoid conditions including, but not limited to, fixed or moving objects, parked or moving vehicles, bicycles, motorized pedal cycles, pedestrians, animals, surface hazards, or substandard width lanes that make it unsafe to continue along the right-hand curb or edge. For purposes of this subsection, a "substandard width lane" means a lane that is too narrow for a bicycle or motorized pedal cycle and a vehicle to travel safely side by side within the lane.

(b) Any person operating a bicycle or motorized pedal cycle upon a one-way highway with two or more marked traffic lanes may ride as near the left-hand curb or edge of such roadway as practicable.

P.A. 76-1586, § 11-1505, added by P.A. 79-858, § 1, eff. Jan. 1, 1976. Amended by P.A. 82-132, § 1, eff. Jan. 1, 1982; P.A. 83-549, § 1, eff. Jan. 1, 1984.

Formerly Ill.Rev.Stat.1991, ch. 95 ½, ¶ 11-1505.

5/11-1505.1. Riding bicycles or motorized pedal cycles on roadways

§ 11-1505.1. Persons riding bicycles or motorized pedal cycles upon a roadway shall not ride more than 2 abreast, except on paths or parts of roadways set aside for their exclusive use. Persons riding 2 abreast shall not impede the normal and reasonable movement of traffic and, on a laned roadway, shall ride within a single lane subject to the provisions of Section 11-1505.

P.A. 76-1586, § 11-1505.1, added by P.A. 83-549, § 1, eff. Jan. 1, 1984.

Formerly Ill.Rev.Stat.1991, ch. 95 ½, ¶ 11-1505.1.

5/11-1506. Carrying articles

§ 11-1506. Carrying articles. No person operating a bicycle shall carry any package, bundle or article which prevents the use of both hands in the control and operation of the bicycle. A person operating a bicycle shall keep at least one hand on the handlebars at all times.

P.A. 76-1586, § 11-1506, added by P.A. 79-858, § 1, eff. Jan. 1, 1976. Amended by P.A. 82-132, § 1, eff. Jan. 1, 1982.

Formerly Ill.Rev.Stat.1991, ch. 95 ½, ¶ 11-1506.

5/11-1507. Lamps and other equipment on bicycles

§ 11-1507. Lamps and other equipment on bicycles. (a) Every bicycle when in use at nighttime shall be equipped with a lamp on the front which shall emit a white light visible from a distance of at least 500 feet to the front and with a red reflector on the rear of a type approved by the Department which shall be visible from all distances from 100 feet to 600 feet to the rear when directly in front of lawful lower beams of headlamps on a motor vehicle. A lamp emitting a red light visible from a distance of 500 feet to the rear may be used in addition to the red reflector.

(b) A bicycle shall not be equipped with nor shall any person use upon a bicycle any siren.

(c) Every bicycle shall be equipped with a brake which will adequately control movement of and stop and hold such bicycle.

(d) No person shall sell a new bicycle or pedal for use on a bicycle that is not equipped with a reflex reflector conforming to specifications prescribed by the Department, on each pedal, visible from the front and rear of the bicycle during darkness from a distance of 200 feet.

(e) No person shall sell or offer for sale a new bicycle that is not equipped with side reflectors. Such reflectors shall be visible from each side of the bicycle from a distance of 500 feet and shall be essentially colorless or red to the rear of the center of the bicycle and essentially colorless or amber to the front of the center of the bicycle provided. The requirements of this paragraph may be met by reflective materials which shall be at least $\frac{3}{16}$ of an inch wide on each side of each tire or rim to indicate as clearly as possible the continuous circular shape and size of the tires or rims of such bicycle and which reflective materials may be of the same color on both the front and rear tire or rim. Such reflectors shall conform to specifications prescribed by the Department.

(f) No person shall sell or offer for sale a new bicycle that is not equipped with an essentially colorless front-facing reflector.

P.A. 76-1586, § 11-1507, added by P.A. 79-858, § 1, eff. Jan. 1, 1976. Amended by P.A. 80-506, § 1, eff. Oct. 1, 1977; P.A. 82-132, § 1, eff. Jan. 1, 1982.

Formerly Ill.Rev.Stat.1991, ch. 95 ½, ¶ 11-1507.

5/11-1507.1. Lamps on motorized pedalcycles

§ 11-1507.1. Lamps on motorized pedalcycles. Every motorized pedalcycle, when in use at nighttime, shall be equipped with a lamp on the front which shall emit a white light visible from a distance of at least 500 feet to the front, and with a red reflector on the rear of a type approved by the Department which shall be visible from all distances from 100 feet to 600 feet to the rear when in front of lawful, low-powered beams of head lamps on a motor vehicle. A lamp emitting a red light visible from a distance of 500 feet to the rear may be used in addition to the red reflector.

P.A. 76-1586, § 11-1507.1, added by P.A. 80-262, § 1, eff. Aug. 20, 1977.

Formerly Ill.Rev.Stat.1991, ch. 95 ½, ¶ 11-1507.1.

5/11-1508. Bicycle identifying number

§ 11-1508. Bicycle identifying number. A person engaged in the business of selling bicycles at retail shall not sell any bicycle unless the bicycle has an identifying number permanently stamped or cast on its frame.

P.A. 76-1586, § 11-1508, added by 82-132, § 1, eff. Jan. 1, 1982.

Formerly Ill.Rev.Stat.1991, ch. 95 ½, ¶ 11-1508.

5/11-1509. Inspecting bicycles

§ 11-1509. Inspecting bicycles. A uniformed police officer may at any time upon reasonable cause to believe that a bicycle is unsafe or not equipped as required by law, or that its equipment is not in proper adjustment or repair, require the person riding the bicycle to stop and submit the bicycle to an inspection and such test with reference thereto as may be appropriate.

P.A. 76-1586, § 11-1509, added by P.A. 82-132, § 1, eff. Jan. 1, 1982.

Formerly Ill.Rev.Stat.1991, ch. 95 ½, ¶ 11-1509.

5/11-1510. Left Turns

§ 11-1510. Left Turns. (a) A person riding a bicycle or motorized pedalcycle intending to turn left shall follow a course described in Section 11-801 or in paragraph (b) of this Section.

(b) A person riding a bicycle or motorized pedalcycle intending to turn left shall approach the turn as close as practicable to the right curb or edge of the roadway. After proceeding across the intersecting roadway to the far corner of the curb or intersection of the roadway edges, the bicyclist or motorized pedalcycle driver shall stop, as much as practicable out of the way of traffic. After stopping the person shall yield to any traffic proceeding in either direction along the roadway such person had been using. After yielding, the bicycle or motorized pedalcycle driver shall comply with any official traffic control device or police officer regulating traffic on the highway along which he intends to proceed, and the bicyclist or motorized pedalcycle driver may proceed in the new direction.

(c) Notwithstanding the foregoing provisions, the Department and local authorities in their respective jurisdictions may cause official traffic-control devices to be placed and thereby require and direct that a specific course be traveled by turning bicycles and motorized pedalcycles, and when such devices are so placed, no person shall turn a bicycle or motorized pedalcycle other than as directed and required by such devices.

P.A. 76-1586, § 11-1510, added by P.A. 82-132, § 1, eff. Jan. 1, 1982. Amended by P.A. 85-951, § 1, eff. July 1, 1988.

Formerly Ill.Rev.Stat.1991, ch. 95 ½, ¶ 11-1510.

5/11–1511. Turn and stop signals

§ 11–1511. Turn and stop signals. (a) Except as provided in this Section, a person riding a bicycle shall comply with Section 11–804.

(b) A signal of intention to turn right or left when required shall be given during not less than the last 100 feet traveled by the bicycle before turning, and shall be given while the bicycle is stopped waiting to turn. A signal by hand and arm need not be given continuously if the hand is needed in the control or operation of the bicycle.

P.A. 76–1586, § 11–1511, added by P.A. 82–132, § 1, eff. Jan. 1, 1982.

Formerly Ill.Rev.Stat.1991, ch. 95 ½, ¶ 11–1511.

5/11–1512. Bicycles on sidewalks

§ 11–1512. Bicycles on sidewalks. (a) A person propelling a bicycle upon and along a sidewalk, or across a roadway upon and along a crosswalk, shall yield the right of way to any pedestrian and shall give audible signal before overtaking and passing such pedestrian.

(b) A person shall not ride a bicycle upon and along a sidewalk, or across a roadway upon and along a crosswalk, where such use of bicycles is prohibited by official traffic-control devices.

(c) A person propelling a bicycle upon and along a sidewalk, or across a roadway upon and along a crosswalk, shall have all the rights and duties applicable to a pedestrian under the same circumstances.

P.A. 76–1586, § 11–1512, added by P.A. 82–132, § 1, eff. Jan. 1, 1982.

Formerly Ill.Rev.Stat.1991, ch. 95 ½, ¶ 11–1512.

5/11–1513. Bicycle parking

§ 11–1513. Bicycle parking. (a) A person may park a bicycle on a sidewalk unless prohibited or restricted by an official traffic-control device.

(b) A bicycle parked on a sidewalk shall not impede the normal and reasonable movement of pedestrian or other traffic.

(c) A bicycle may be parked on the roadway at any angle to the curb or edge of the roadway at any location where parking is allowed.

(d) A bicycle may be parked on the roadway abreast of another bicycle or bicycles near the side of the roadway at any location where parking is allowed.

(e) A person shall not park a bicycle on a roadway in such a manner as to obstruct the movement of a legally parked motor vehicle.

(f) In all other respects, bicycles parked anywhere on a highway shall conform with the provisions of this Code regulating the parking of vehicles.

P.A. 76–1586, § 11–1513, added by P.A. 82–132, § 1, eff. Jan. 1, 1982.

Formerly Ill.Rev.Stat.1991, ch. 95 ½, ¶ 11–1513.

5/11–1514. Bicycle racing

§ 11–1514. Bicycle racing. (a) Bicycle racing on a highway shall not be unlawful when a racing event has been approved by State or local authorities on any highway under their respective jurisdictions. Approval of bicycle highway racing events shall be granted only under conditions which assure reasonable safety for all race participants, spectators and other highway users, and which prevent unreasonable interference with traffic flow which would seriously inconvenience other highway users.

(b) By agreement with the approving authority, participants, in an approved bicycle highway racing event may be exempted from compliance with any traffic laws otherwise applicable thereto, provided that traffic control is adequate to assure the safety of all highway users.

P.A. 76–1586, § 11–1514, added by P.A. 82–132, § 1, eff. Jan. 1, 1982.

Formerly Ill.Rev.Stat.1991, ch. 95 ½, ¶ 11–1514.

5/11–1515. Operation of a commercial bicycle messenger service; insurance coverage

§ 11–1515. No person, firm, or corporation shall operate a commercial bicycle messenger service in a city with a population of more than 2,000,000 unless the bicycles used are covered by a liability insurance policy at the expense of the person, firm, or corporation. The insurance policy shall be issued in amounts no less than the minimum amounts set for bodily injury or death and for destruction of property under Section 7–203 of this Code. No insurer other than an insurer authorized to do business in this State shall issue a policy under this Section.

P.A. 76–1586, § 11–1515, added by P.A. 87–1203, § 1, eff. Sept. 25, 1992.

Formerly Ill.Rev.Stat., ch. 95½, ¶ 11–1515.

CHAPTER 12. EQUIPMENT OF VEHICLES

Enactment

The Illinois Vehicle Code was enacted by P.A. 76–1586, effective July 1, 1970. The Code constitutes a consolidated recodification of various earlier laws and acts including the Uniform Act Regulating Traffic on Highways.

Chapter 12 was amended, divided into Articles 1 to 7 and resectioned by P.A. 77–37, effective January 1, 1972.

ARTICLE I. GENERAL PROVISIONS

Section

5/12–100. § 12–100. Repealed by P.A. 90–89, § 20, eff. Jan. 1, 1998

5/12–101. Scope and effect of equipment requirements

§ 12–101. Scope and effect of equipment requirements. (a) It is unlawful for any person to drive or move or for the owner to cause or knowingly permit to be driven or moved on any highway any vehicle or combination of vehicles which is in such unsafe condition as to endanger any person or property, or which does not contain those parts or is not at all times equipped with such lamps and other equipment in proper condition and adjustment as required in this Chapter 12, or which is equipped in any manner in violation of this Code, or for any person to do any act forbidden or fail to perform any act required under this Chapter 12.

(b) The provisions of this Chapter 12 with respect to equipment on vehicles shall not apply to implements of husbandry, road machinery, road rollers, or farm tractors or to farm-wagon type trailers having a fertilizer spreader attachment permanently mounted thereon, having a gross weight of not to exceed 36,000 pounds and used only for the transportation of bulk fertilizer or to farm-wagon type tank trailers of not to exceed 2,000 gallons capacity, used during the liquid fertilizer season as field-storage "nurse tanks" supplying the fertilizer to a field applicator and moved on highways only for bringing the fertilizer from a local source of supply to farm or field or from one farm or field to another.

P.A. 76-1586, § 12-101, eff. July 1, 1970. Amended by P.A. 77-37, § 1, eff. Jan. 1, 1972; P.A. 81-327, § 1, eff. Jan. 1, 1980; P.A. 82-523, § 1, eff. Jan. 1, 1982.

Formerly Ill.Rev.Stat.1991, ch. 95 ½, ¶ 12-101.

ARTICLE II. LIGHTS AND LAMPS

Section

5/12-201. When lighted lamps are required

§ 12-201. When lighted lamps are required.

(a) When operated upon any highway in this State, every motorcycle shall at all times exhibit at least one lighted lamp, showing a white light visible for at least 500 feet in the direction the motorcycle is proceeding. However, in lieu of such lighted lamp, a motorcycle may be equipped with and use a means of modulating the upper beam of the head lamp between high and a lower brightness. No such head lamp shall be modulated, except to otherwise comply with this Code, during times when lighted lamps are required for other motor vehicles.

(b) All other motor vehicles shall exhibit at least 2 lighted head lamps, with at least one on each side of the front of the vehicle, which satisfy United States Department of Transportation requirements, showing white lights, including that emitted by high intensity discharge (HID) lamps, or lights of a yellow or amber tint, during the period from sunset to sunrise, at times when rain, snow, fog, or other atmospheric conditions require the use of windshield wipers, and at any other times when, due to insufficient light or unfavorable atmospheric conditions, persons and vehicles on the highway are not clearly discernible at a distance of 1000 feet. Parking lamps may be used in addition to but not in lieu of such head lamps. Every motor vehicle, trailer, or semi-trailer shall also exhibit at least 2 lighted lamps, commonly known as tail lamps, which shall be mounted on the left rear and right rear of the vehicle so as to throw a red light visible for at least 500 feet in the reverse direction, except that a truck tractor or road tractor manufactured before January 1, 1968 and all motorcycles need be equipped with only one such tail lamp.

(c) Either a tail lamp or a separate lamp shall be so constructed and placed as to illuminate with a white light a rear registration plate when required and render it clearly legible from a distance of 50 feet to the rear. Any tail lamp or tail lamps, together with any separate lamp or lamps for illuminating a rear registration plate, shall be so wired as to be lighted whenever the head lamps or auxiliary driving lamps are lighted.

(d) A person shall install only head lamps that satisfy United States Department of Transportation regulations and show white light, including that emitted by HID lamps, or light of a yellow or amber tint for use by a motor vehicle.

(e) For purposes of this Section, a custom vehicle or street rod is considered to be in compliance with all vehicle lamp requirements if it has passed the approved safety inspection provided for in Section 3-804.1 or 3-804.2.

P.A. 76-1586, § 12-102, eff. July 1, 1970. Amended by P.A. 76-2177, § 1, eff. July 1, 1970. Renumbered § 12-201 by P.A. 77-37, § 1, eff. Jan. 1, 1972. Amended by P.A. 81-804, § 1, eff. Sept. 19, 1979; P.A. 83-331, § 1, eff. Jan. 1, 1984; P.A. 88-147, § 5, eff. Jan. 1, 1994; P.A. 91-130, § 5, eff. Jan. 1, 2000; P.A. 91-135, § 5, eff. Jan. 1, 2000; P.A. 92-16, § 85, eff. June 28, 2001; P.A. 92-668, § 5, eff. Jan. 1, 2003.

Formerly Ill.Rev.Stat.1991, ch. 95 ½, ¶ 12-201.

P.A. 92-668 incorporated the amendment by P.A. 92-16.

5/12-202. Clearance, identification and side marker lamps

§ 12-202. Clearance, identification and side marker lamps. (a) Every motor vehicle of the second division, the length of which together with any trailer or trailers in tow thereof, is more than 25 feet or the width of which is more than 80 inches exclusive of mirrors, bumpers and other required safety devices, while being operated on the highways of this State during the period from sunset to sunrise, shall display on the front of the vehicle 2 yellow or amber lights, one on each upper front corner of the vehicle, which shall be plainly visible at a distance of at least 500 feet; also on the rear thereof in a horizontal line, 3 red lights plainly visible at a distance of not less than 500 feet; also on the front of the body of that vehicle near the lower left hand corner one yellow or amber tinted reflector, and near the lower right hand corner one yellow or amber tinted reflector; also red reflectors on the rear of the body of that vehicle, not more than 12 inches from the lower left and right hand corners. All motor vehicles of the second division more than 20 feet long, and all trailers and semitrailers, except trailers and semitrailers having a gross weight of 3,000 pounds or less including the weight of the trailer and maximum load, while being operated on the highways of this State during the period from sunset to sunrise, shall display on each side of the vehicle at approximately the one-third points of the length of the same, at a height not exceeding 5 feet above the surface of the road, and reflecting on a line approximately at right angles to the center line of the vehicle, 2 amber tinted reflectors. After January, 1974, all new motor vehicles of the second division more than 20 feet long, and all trailers and semitrailers except trailers and semitrailers having a gross weight of 3,000 pounds or less including the weight of the trailer and maximum load sold as new in this State, while being operated on the highways of this State during period from sunset to sunrise, shall display on each side of the vehicle, not more than 12 inches from the front, one amber tinted reflector, and not more than 12 inches from the rear one red reflector at a height not exceeding 5 feet above the surface of the road, and reflecting on a line approximately at right angles to the center line of the vehicle, approved by the Department.

(b) Every trailer and semitrailer having a gross weight of 3,000 pounds or less including the weight of the trailer and maximum load, towed either by a motor vehicle of the first division or a motor vehicle of the second division shall be equipped with 2 red reflectors, which will be visible when hit by headlight beams 300 feet away at night, on the rear of the body of such trailer, not more than 12 inches from the lower left hand and lower right hand corners.

(c) Every vehicle designated in paragraph (a) or (b) of this Section that is manufactured after December 31, 1973, shall, at the places and times specified in paragraph (a) or (b) of this Section, display reflectors and clearance, identification, and side marker lamps in conformance with the specifications prescribed by the Department.

P.A. 76–1586, § 12–103, eff. July 1, 1970. Amended by P.A. 76–1725, § 1, eff. July 1, 1970; P.A. 76–1997, § 1, eff. July 1, 1970. Renumbered § 12–202 by P.A. 77–37, § 1, eff. Jan. 1, 1972. Amended by P.A. 78–748, § 1, eff. Jan. 1, 1974; P.A. 78–501, § 1, eff. Oct. 1, 1973; P.A. 78–1297, § 30, eff. March 4, 1975.

Formerly Ill.Rev.Stat.1991, ch. 95 ½, ¶ 12–202.

5/12–203. Lamps on parked vehicles

§ 12–203. Lamps on parked vehicles. (a) During the period from sunset to sunrise every motorcycle or motor vehicle which is standing on any highway shall display a parking light on the front and at the rear of the same. However, any city, village or incorporated town may by ordinance, under rules and regulations it may prescribe, designate any part or parts of any street, or other highway under their jurisdiction, as parking places in which motorcycles and motor vehicles may be parked without having their lamps lighted, as otherwise required by this Section.

(b) Any lighted driving lamps upon a parked vehicle shall be depressed or dimmed.

P.A. 76–1586, § 12–104, eff. July 1, 1970. Renumbered § 12–203 by P.A. 77–37, § 1, eff. Jan. 1, 1972.

Formerly Ill.Rev.Stat.1991, ch. 95 ½, ¶ 12–203.

5/12–204. Lamp or flag on projecting load

§ 12–204. Lamp or flag on projecting load. Whenever the load upon any vehicle extends to the rear 4 feet, or more beyond the bed or body of such vehicle there shall be displayed at the extreme rear end of the load, at the times specified in Section 12–201 hereof, a red light or lantern plainly visible from a distance of at least 500 feet to the sides and rear. The red light or lantern required under this Section shall be in addition to the red rear light required upon every vehicle. At any other time there shall be displayed at the extreme rear end of such load a red flag or cloth not less than 12 inches square.

P.A. 76–1586, § 12–105, eff. July 1, 1970. Renumbered § 12–204 by P.A. 77–37, § 1, eff. Jan. 1, 1972.

Formerly Ill.Rev.Stat.1991, ch. 95 ½, ¶ 12–204.

5/12–205. Lamps on other vehicles and equipment

§ 12–205. Lamps on other vehicles and equipment. Every vehicle, including animal drawn vehicles, referred to in paragraph (b) of Section 12–101, not specifically required by the provisions of this Article to be equipped with lamps or other lighting devices, shall at all times specified in Section 12–201 of this Act be equipped with at least 2 lamps on the power or towing unit, displaying a white light visible from a distance of not less than 1,000 feet to the front of such vehicle and shall also be equipped with 2 lamps each displaying a red light visible from a distance of not less than 1,000 feet to the rear of such vehicle.

Where the towed unit or any load thereon partially or totally obscures the 2 lamps displaying red light to the rear of the towing unit, the rearmost towed unit shall be equipped with 2 lamps displaying red light visible from a distance of not less than 1,000 feet to the rear of such towed unit which are positioned in such a manner as to not obstruct the visibility of the red light to any vehicle operator approaching from the rear of such vehicle or combination of vehicles.

Where the 2 lamps displaying red light are not obscured by the towed unit or its load, then either towing unit or towed unit, or both, may be equipped with the 2 lamps displaying red light as required.

The preceding paragraph does not apply to antique vehicles, custom vehicles, or street rods. An antique vehicle shall be equipped with lamps of the same type originally installed by the manufacturer as original equipment and in working order.

P.A. 76–1586, § 12–106. Amended by P.A. 76–1627, § 1, eff. Dec. 1, 1970; P.A. 76–2178, § 1, eff. July 1, 1970. Renumbered § 12–205 by P.A. 77–37, § 1, eff. Jan. 1, 1972. Amended by P.A. 85–830, § 1, eff. Sept. 24, 1987; P.A. 92–668, § 5, eff. Jan. 1, 2003.

Formerly Ill.Rev.Stat.1991, ch. 95 ½, ¶ 12–205.

5/12–205.1. Implements of husbandry or slow-moving vehicles—Display of amber signal lamp

§ 12–205.1. Implements of husbandry or slow-moving vehicles—Display of amber signal lamp. Every animal drawn vehicle, farm tractor, implement of husbandry and special mobile equipment, except when used for road construction or maintenance within the limits of a construction or maintenance project where traffic control devices are used in compliance with the applicable provisions of the manual and specifications adopted under Section 11–301 of the Illinois Vehicle Code, when operated on a highway during a time when lighted lamps are required by Section 12–201 of this Chapter, shall display to the rear at least one flashing amber signal lamp mounted as high as practicable and of sufficient intensity to be visible for a distance of at least 500 feet in normal sunlight; provided, that only the rearmost vehicle of a combination of vehicles coupled together need display such lamp. The flashing amber signal lamp may be operated lighted during daylight hours when other lamps are not required to be lighted when vehicles authorized in this Section are operated on a highway. Implements of husbandry manufactured on or after January 1, 2003 and operated on public roads between sunset and sunrise shall display markings and lighting that meet or exceed the design, performance, and mounting specifications adopted by the American Society of Agricultural Engineers and published by that body as ASAE S279.11 APR01.

P.A. 76–1586, § 12–205.1, added by P.A. 78–253, § 1, eff. Oct. 1, 1973. Amended by P.A. 84–285, § 1, eff. Jan. 1, 1986; P.A. 91–505, § 5, eff. Jan. 1, 2000; P.A. 92–820, § 5, eff. Aug. 21, 2002.

Formerly Ill.Rev.Stat.1991, ch. 95 ½, ¶ 12–205.1.

5/12–206. § 12–206. Repealed by P.A. 79–858, § 2, eff. Jan. 1, 1976

5/12–207. Spot lamps and auxiliary driving lamps

§ 12–207. Spot lamps and auxiliary driving lamps.

(a) Any motor vehicle may be equipped with not to exceed one spot lamp and every lighted spot lamp shall be so aimed and used upon approaching another vehicle that no part of the high-intensity portion of the beam will be directed to the left of the prolongation of the extreme left side of the vehicle nor more than 100 feet ahead of the vehicle.

(b) Any motor vehicle may be equipped with not to exceed three auxiliary driving lamps mounted on the front at a height not less than 12 inches nor more than 42 inches above the level surface upon which the vehicle stands.

(c) The restrictions of subsections 12–207 (a) and 12–207 (b) of this Act shall not apply to authorized emergency vehicles or equipment used for snow and ice removal operations if owned or operated by or for any governmental body.

(d) The minimum and maximum height restrictions prescribed in subsection (b) of Section 12–207 shall not apply to privately owned motor vehicles on which a snow plow is mounted, while in transit between or during snow and ice removal operations. This exemption shall apply only during the period from November 15 through April 1, and only when the snow plow blade, commonly referred to as a "moldboard", is properly and securely affixed to the front of the motor vehicle.

P.A. 76–1586, § 12–108, eff. July 1, 1970. Renumbered § 12–207 by P.A. 77–37 § 1, eff. Jan. 1, 1972. Amended by P.A. 77–63, § 1, eff. July 1, 1971; P.A. 77–2829, § 40, eff. Dec. 22, 1972; P.A. 78–255, § 61, eff. Oct. 1, 1973; P.A. 78–510, § 1, eff. Oct. 1, 1973; P.A. 78–1297, § 58, eff. March 4, 1975; P.A. 84–677, § 1, eff. Jan. 1, 1986; P.A. 85–1010, § 1, eff. March 2, 1988.

Formerly Ill.Rev.Stat.1991, ch. 95 ½, ¶ 12–207.

5/12–208. Signal lamps and signal devices

§ 12–208. Signal lamps and signal devices.

(a) Every vehicle other than an antique vehicle displaying an antique plate operated in this State shall be equipped with a stop lamp or lamps on the rear of the vehicle which shall display a red or amber light visible from a distance of not less than 500 feet to the rear in normal sunlight and which shall be actuated upon application of the service (foot) brake, and which may but need not be incorporated with other rear lamps. During times when lighted lamps are not required, an antique vehicle may be equipped with a stop lamp or lamps on the rear of such vehicle of the same type originally installed by the manufacturer as original equipment and in working order. However, at all other times, such antique vehicle must be equipped with stop lamps meeting the requirements of Section 12–208 of this Act.

(b) Every motor vehicle other than an antique vehicle displaying an antique plate shall be equipped with an electric turn signal device which shall indicate the intention of the driver to turn to the right or to the left in the form of flashing lights located at and showing to the front and rear of the vehicle on the side of the vehicle toward which the turn is to be made. The lamps showing to the front shall be mounted on the same level and as widely spaced laterally as practicable and, when signaling, shall emit a white or amber light, or any shade of light between white and amber. The lamps showing to the rear shall be mounted on the same level and as widely spaced laterally as practicable and, when signaling, shall emit a red or amber light. An antique vehicle shall be equipped with a turn signal device of the same type originally installed by the manufacturer as original equipment and in working order.

(c) Every trailer and semitrailer shall be equipped with an electric turn signal device which indicates the intention of the driver in the power unit to turn to the right or to the left in the form of flashing red or amber lights located at the rear of the vehicle on the side toward which the turn is to be made and mounted on the same level and as widely spaced laterally as practicable.

(d) Turn signal lamps must be visible from a distance of not less than 300 feet in normal sunlight.

(e) Motorcycles and motor-driven cycles need not be equipped with electric turn signals. Antique vehicles need not be equipped with turn signals unless such were installed by the manufacturer as original equipment.

(f) For purposes of this Section, a custom vehicle or street rod is considered to be in compliance with all signal lamp and signal device requirements if it has passed the approved safety inspection provided for in Section 3–804.1 or 3–804.2.

P.A. 76–1586, § 12–109. Amended by P.A. 76–1627, § 1, eff. Dec. 1, 1970; P.A. 76–2179, § 1, eff. July 1, 1970. Renumbered § 12–208 by P.A. 77–37, § 1, eff. Jan. 1, 1972. Amended by P.A. 92–668, § 5, eff. Jan. 1, 2003.

Formerly Ill.Rev.Stat.1991, ch. 95 ½, ¶ 12–208.

5/12–209. Additional lighting equipment

§ 12–209. Additional lighting equipment. (a) Any motor vehicle may be equipped with not more than 2 side cowl or fender lamps which shall emit an amber or white light without glare.

(b) Any motor vehicle may be equipped with not more than one running board courtesy lamp on each side thereof which shall emit a white or amber light without glare.

(c) Any motor vehicle may be equipped with one or more back-up lamps either separately or in combination with other lamps; but any such back-up lamp or lamps shall not be lighted when the motor vehicle is in forward motion.

P.A. 76–1586, § 12–110, eff. July 1, 1970. Amended by P.A. 76–2180, § 1, eff. July 1, 1970. Renumbered § 12–209 by P.A. 77–37, § 1, eff. Jan. 1, 1972.

Formerly Ill.Rev.Stat.1991, ch. 95 ½, ¶ 12–209.

5/12–210. Use of head lamps and auxiliary driving lamps

§ 12–210. Use of head lamps and auxiliary driving lamps. (a) Whenever the driver of any vehicle equipped with an electric driving head lamp, driving head lamps, auxiliary driving lamp or auxiliary driving lamps is within 500 feet of another vehicle approaching from the opposite direction, the driver shall dim or drop such head lamp or head lamps and shall extinguish all auxiliary driving lamps.

(b) The driver of any vehicle equipped with an electric driving head lamp, head lamps, auxiliary driving lamp or auxiliary driving lamps shall dim or drop such head lamp or head lamps and shall extinguish all auxiliary driving lamps when there is another vehicle traveling in the same direction less than 300 feet to the front of him.

(c) No vehicle shall have the lighting system modified to allow more than 2 electric head lamps to be lighted while operating in the dimmed or dropped position.

(d) Nothing in this Section shall prohibit the use of auxiliary driving lamps, commonly referred to as "fog" lamps, when used in conjunction with head lamps, if such auxiliary driving lamps are adjusted and so aimed that the glaring rays are not projected into the eyes of drivers of oncoming vehicles.

P.A. 76–1586, § 12–111, eff. July 1, 1970. Renumbered § 12–210 by P.A. 77–37, § 1, eff. Jan. 1, 1972. Amended by P.A. 85–830, § 1, eff. Sept. 24, 1987; P.A. 85–1144, § 1, eff. July 29, 1988.

Formerly Ill.Rev.Stat.1991, ch. 95 ½, ¶ 12–210.

P.A. 85–1144 incorporated the amendment by P.A. 85–830.

5/12–211. Number of driving lamps required or permitted

§ 12–211. Number of driving lamps required or permitted. (a) At all times specified in Section 12–201, at least 2 lighted driving lamps shall be displayed, one on each side of the front of every motor vehicle other than a motorcycle, except when such vehicle is parked subject to the regulations governing lights on parked vehicles.

(b) Whenever a motor vehicle equipped with driving lamps as herein required is also equipped with any auxiliary driving lamps or a spot lamp or any other lamp on the front thereof, not more than a total of 4 of any such lamps on the front of a vehicle shall be lighted at any one time when upon a highway.

P.A. 76–1586, § 12–112, eff. July 1, 1970. Amended by P.A. 76–2181, § 1, eff. July 1, 1970. Renumbered § 12–211 by P.A. 77–37, § 1, eff. Jan. 1, 1972. Amended by P.A. 86–1236, § 1, eff. Jan. 1, 1991.

Formerly Ill.Rev.Stat.1991, ch. 95 ½, ¶ 12–211.

5/12–212. Special restrictions on lamps

§ 12–212. Special restrictions on lamps. (a) No person shall drive or move any vehicle or equipment upon any highway with any lamp or device on the vehicle or equipment displaying a red light visible from directly in front of the vehicle or equipment except as otherwise provided in this Act.

(b) Subject to the restrictions of this Act, flashing lights are prohibited on motor vehicles except as a means for indicating a right or left turn as provided in Section 12–208 or the presence of a vehicular traffic hazard requiring unusual care as expressly provided in Sections 11–804 or 12–215.

(c) Unless otherwise expressly authorized by this Code, all other lighting or combination of lighting on any vehicle shall be prohibited.

P.A. 76–1586, § 12–113, eff. July 1, 1970. Renumbered § 12–212 by P.A. 77–37, § 1, eff. Jan. 1, 1972. Amended by P.A. 81–879, § 1, eff. Sept. 21, 1979; P.A. 86–664, § 1, eff. Sept. 1, 1989.

Formerly Ill.Rev.Stat.1991, ch. 95 ½, ¶ 12–212.

5/12–213. § 12–213. Repealed by P.A. 78–1244, § 4, eff. Sept. 5, 1974

5/12–214. Special lighting equipment on rural mail delivery vehicles

§ 12–214. Special lighting equipment on rural mail delivery vehicles. If a rural mail delivery vehicle is equipped with special signal lamps, there shall be displayed to the front 2 such alternately flashing amber lamps located at the same level and mounted as high and as widely spaced laterally as practicable and to the rear 2 alternately flashing amber lamps located at the same level and mounted as high and as widely spaced laterally as practicable. Such lamps shall be of sufficient intensity to be visible at 500 feet in normal sunlight and shall be controlled so that they will only be used to indicate to other traffic that a stop is being made for the purpose of picking up or delivering U. S. mail.

P.A. 76–1586, § 12–115, eff. July 1, 1970. Renumbered § 12–214 by P.A. 77–37, § 1, eff. Jan. 1, 1972.

Formerly Ill.Rev.Stat.1991, ch. 95 ½, ¶ 12–214.

5/12–214.1. Tow trucks meeting federal motor carrier safety requirements; lighting and signalling equipment

§ 12–214.1. Tow trucks meeting federal motor carrier safety requirements; lighting and signalling equipment. Any tow truck that meets the requirements of the Federal Motor Carrier Safety Regulations of the United States Department of Transportation, regarding lighting and signalling equipment required on commercial motor vehicles, shall be deemed to comply with the provisions of this Chapter regarding required lighting and signalling equipment.

P.A. 76–1586, § 12–214.1, added by P.A. 89–433, § 5, eff. Dec. 15, 1995.

5/12–215. Oscillating, rotating or flashing lights on motor vehicles

Text of section effective until June 1, 2003

§ 12–215. Oscillating, rotating or flashing lights on motor vehicles. Except as otherwise provided in this Code:

(a) The use of red or white oscillating, rotating or flashing lights, whether lighted or unlighted, is prohibited except on:

1. Law enforcement vehicles of State, Federal or local authorities;

2. A vehicle operated by a police officer or county coroner and designated or authorized by local authorities, in writing, as a law enforcement vehicle; however, such designation or authorization must be carried in the vehicle;

3. Vehicles of local fire departments and State or federal firefighting vehicles;

4. Vehicles which are designed and used exclusively as ambulances or rescue vehicles; furthermore, such lights shall not be lighted except when responding to an emergency call for and while actually conveying the sick or injured;

5. Tow trucks licensed in a state that requires such lights; furthermore, such lights shall not be lighted on any such tow truck while the tow truck is operating in the State of Illinois;

6. Vehicles of the Illinois Emergency Management Agency, and vehicles of the Department of Nuclear Safety; and

7. Vehicles operated by a local or county emergency management services agency as defined in the Illinois Emergency Management Agency Act.

(b) The use of amber oscillating, rotating or flashing lights, whether lighted or unlighted, is prohibited except on:

1. Second division vehicles designed and used for towing or hoisting vehicles; furthermore, such lights shall not be lighted except as required in this paragraph 1; such lights shall be lighted when such vehicles are actually being used at the scene of an accident or disablement; if the towing vehicle is equipped with a flat bed that supports all wheels of the vehicle being transported, the lights shall not be lighted while the vehicle is engaged in towing on a highway; if the towing vehicle is not equipped with a flat bed that supports all wheels of a vehicle being transported, the lights shall be lighted while the towing vehicle is engaged in towing on a highway during all times when the use of headlights is required under Section 12-201 of this Code;

2. Motor vehicles or equipment of the State of Illinois, local authorities and contractors; furthermore, such lights shall not be lighted except while such vehicles are engaged in maintenance or construction operations within the limits of construction projects;

3. Vehicles or equipment used by engineering or survey crews; furthermore, such lights shall not be lighted except while such vehicles are actually engaged in work on a highway;

4. Vehicles of public utilities, municipalities, or other construction, maintenance or automotive service vehicles except that such lights shall be lighted only as a means for indicating the presence of a vehicular traffic hazard requiring unusual care in approaching, overtaking or passing while such vehicles are engaged in maintenance, service or construction on a highway;

5. Oversized vehicle or load; however, such lights shall only be lighted when moving under permit issued by the Department under Section 15-301 of this Code;

6. The front and rear of motorized equipment owned and operated by the State of Illinois or any political subdivision thereof, which is designed and used for removal of snow and ice from highways;

7. Fleet safety vehicles registered in another state, furthermore, such lights shall not be lighted except as provided for in Section 12-212 of this Code;

8. Such other vehicles as may be authorized by local authorities;

9. Law enforcement vehicles of State or local authorities when used in combination with red oscillating, rotating or flashing lights;

9.5. Propane delivery trucks;

10. Vehicles used for collecting or delivering mail for the United States Postal Service provided that such lights shall not be lighted except when such vehicles are actually being used for such purposes;

11. Any vehicle displaying a slow-moving vehicle emblem as provided in Section 12-205.1;

12. All trucks equipped with self-compactors or roll-off hoists and roll- on containers for garbage or refuse hauling. Such lights shall not be lighted except when such vehicles are actually being used for such purposes;

13. Vehicles used by a security company, alarm responder, or control agency; and

14. Security vehicles of the Department of Human Services; however, the lights shall not be lighted except when being used for security related purposes under the direction of the superintendent of the facility where the vehicle is located.

(c) The use of blue oscillating, rotating or flashing lights, whether lighted or unlighted, is prohibited except on:

1. Rescue squad vehicles not owned by a fire department and vehicles owned or fully operated by a:

voluntary firefighter;

paid firefighter;

part-paid firefighter;

call firefighter;

member of the board of trustees of a fire protection district;

paid or unpaid member of a rescue squad;

paid or unpaid member of a voluntary ambulance unit; or

paid or unpaid members of a local or county emergency management services agency as defined in the Illinois Emergency Management Agency Act,[1] designated or authorized by local authorities, in writing, and carrying that designation or authorization in the vehicle.

However, such lights are not to be lighted except when responding to a bona fide emergency.

2. Police department vehicles in cities having a population of 500,000 or more inhabitants.

3. Law enforcement vehicles of State or local authorities when used in combination with red oscillating, rotating or flashing lights.

4. Vehicles of local fire departments and State or federal firefighting vehicles when used in combination with red oscillating, rotating or flashing lights.

5. Vehicles which are designed and used exclusively as ambulances or rescue vehicles when used in combination with red oscillating, rotating or flashing lights; furthermore, such lights shall not be lighted except when responding to an emergency call.

6. Vehicles that are equipped and used exclusively as organ transport vehicles when used in combination with red oscillating, rotating, or flashing lights; furthermore, these lights shall only be lighted when the transportation is declared an emergency by a member of the transplant team or a representative of the organ procurement organization.

7. Vehicles of the Illinois Emergency Management Agency and vehicles of the Department of Nuclear Safety, when used in combination with red oscillating, rotating, or flashing lights.

8. Vehicles operated by a local or county emergency management services agency as defined in the Illinois Emergency Management Agency Act, when used in combination with red oscillating, rotating, or flashing lights.

(c-1) In addition to the blue oscillating, rotating, or flashing lights permitted under subsection (c), and notwithstanding subsection (a), a vehicle operated by a voluntary firefighter may be equipped with flashing white headlights and blue grill lights, which may be used only in responding to an emergency call.

(c-2) In addition to the blue oscillating, rotating, or flashing lights permitted under subsection (c), and notwithstanding subsection (a), a vehicle operated by a paid or unpaid member of a local or county emergency management services agency as defined in the Illinois Emergency Management

Agency Act, may be equipped with white oscillating, rotating, or flashing lights to be used in combination with blue oscillating, rotating, or flashing lights, if authorization by local authorities is in writing and carried in the vehicle.

(d) The use of a combination of amber and white oscillating, rotating or flashing lights, whether lighted or unlighted, is prohibited, except motor vehicles or equipment of the State of Illinois, local authorities and contractors may be so equipped; furthermore, such lights shall not be lighted except while such vehicles are engaged in highway maintenance or construction operations within the limits of highway construction projects.

(e) All oscillating, rotating or flashing lights referred to in this Section shall be of sufficient intensity, when illuminated, to be visible at 500 feet in normal sunlight.

(f) Nothing in this Section shall prohibit a manufacturer of oscillating, rotating or flashing lights or his representative from temporarily mounting such lights on a vehicle for demonstration purposes only.

(g) Any person violating the provisions of subsections (a), (b), (c) or (d) of this Section who without lawful authority stops or detains or attempts to stop or detain another person shall be guilty of a Class 4 felony.

(h) Except as provided in subsection (g) above, any person violating the provisions of subsections (a) or (c) of this Section shall be guilty of a Class A misdemeanor.

P.A. 76-1586, § 12-116, eff. July 1, 1970. Amended by P.A. 76-2182, § 1, eff. July 1, 1970. Renumbered § 12-215 by P.A. 77-37, § 1, eff. Jan. 1, 1972. Amended by P.A. 77-103, § 1, eff. Jan. 1, 1972; P.A. 77-2829, § 40, eff. Dec. 22, 1972; P.A. 78-255, § 61, eff. Oct. 1, 1973; P.A. 78-509, § 1, eff. Jan. 1, 1974; P.A. 78-1203, § 1, eff. Sept. 5, 1974; P.A. 78-1297, § 58, eff. March 4, 1975; P.A. 79-537, § 1, eff. Oct. 1, 1975; P.A. 79-870, § 1, eff. Oct. 1, 1975; P.A. 79-916, § 1, eff. Oct. 1, 1975; P.A. 79-1454, § 44, eff. Aug. 31, 1976; P.A. 80-1013, § 1, eff. Oct. 1, 1977; P.A. 81-1509, Art. II, § 71, eff. Sept. 26, 1980; P.A. 83-769, § 1, eff. Jan. 1, 1984; P.A. 84-256, § 1, eff. Jan. 1, 1986; P.A. 84-285, § 1, eff. Jan. 1, 1986; P.A. 84-1105, § 1, eff. Dec. 10, 1985; P.A. 84-1231, § 1, eff. July 28, 1986; P.A. 84-1308, Art. II, § 96, eff. Aug. 25, 1986; P.A. 84-1438, Art. II, § 30, eff. Dec. 22, 1986; P.A. 85-586, § 1, eff. Sept. 20, 1987; P.A. 85-1368, § 1, eff. Jan. 1, 1989; P.A. 86-611, § 1, eff. Sept. 1, 1989; P.A. 87-531, § 1, eff. Jan. 1, 1992; P.A. 88-58, § 5, eff. Jan. 1, 1994; P.A. 88-341, § 1, eff. Jan. 1, 1994; P.A. 88-670, Art. 2, § 2-59, eff. Dec. 2, 1994; P.A. 89-433, § 5, eff. Dec. 15, 1995; P.A. 89-507, Art. 90, § 90D-84, eff. July 1, 1997; P.A. 90-330, § 5, eff. Aug. 8, 1997; P.A. 90-347, § 5, eff. Jan. 1, 1998; P.A. 90-655, § 153, eff. July 30, 1998; P.A. 91-357, § 231, eff. July 29, 1999; P.A. 92-138, § 5, eff. July 24, 2001; P.A. 92-407, § 5, eff. Aug. 17, 2001; P.A. 92-651, § 77, eff. July 11, 2002; P.A. 92-782, § 5, eff. Aug. 6, 2002; P.A. 92-820, § 5, eff. Aug. 21, 2002.

Formerly Ill.Rev.Stat.1991, ch. 95 ½, ¶ 12-215.

[1] 20 ILCS 3305/1 et seq.

For text of section effective June 1, 2003, see 625 ILCS 5/12-215, post

P.A. 92-651, the First 2002 General Revisory Act, amended various Acts to delete obsolete text, to correct patent and technical errors, to revise cross references, to resolve multiple actions in the 91st and 92nd General Assemblies and to make certain technical corrections in P.A. 91-937 through P.A. 92-520.

P.A. 92-782 incorporated the amendments by P.A. 92-138 and P.A. 92-407.

P.A. 92-820 incorporated the amendments by P.A. 92-138 and P.A. 92-407.

5/12-215. Oscillating, rotating or flashing lights on motor vehicles

Text of section effective June 1, 2003

§ 12-215. Oscillating, rotating or flashing lights on motor vehicles. Except as otherwise provided in this Code:

(a) The use of red or white oscillating, rotating or flashing lights, whether lighted or unlighted, is prohibited except on:

1. Law enforcement vehicles of State, Federal or local authorities;

2. A vehicle operated by a police officer or county coroner and designated or authorized by local authorities, in writing, as a law enforcement vehicle; however, such designation or authorization must be carried in the vehicle;

3. Vehicles of local fire departments and State or federal firefighting vehicles;

4. Vehicles which are designed and used exclusively as ambulances or rescue vehicles; furthermore, such lights shall not be lighted except when responding to an emergency call for and while actually conveying the sick or injured;

5. Tow trucks licensed in a state that requires such lights; furthermore, such lights shall not be lighted on any such tow truck while the tow truck is operating in the State of Illinois;

6. Vehicles of the Illinois Emergency Management Agency, and vehicles of the Department of Nuclear Safety; and

7. Vehicles operated by a local or county emergency management services agency as defined in the Illinois Emergency Management Agency Act.

(b) The use of amber oscillating, rotating or flashing lights, whether lighted or unlighted, is prohibited except on:

1. Second division vehicles designed and used for towing or hoisting vehicles; furthermore, such lights shall not be lighted except as required in this paragraph 1; such lights shall be lighted when such vehicles are actually being used at the scene of an accident or disablement; if the towing vehicle is equipped with a flat bed that supports all wheels of the vehicle being transported, the lights shall not be lighted while the vehicle is engaged in towing on a highway; if the towing vehicle is not equipped with a flat bed that supports all wheels of a vehicle being transported, the lights shall be lighted while the towing vehicle is engaged in towing on a highway during all times when the use of headlights is required under Section 12-201 of this Code;

2. Motor vehicles or equipment of the State of Illinois, local authorities and contractors; furthermore, such lights shall not be lighted except while such vehicles are engaged in maintenance or construction operations within the limits of construction projects;

3. Vehicles or equipment used by engineering or survey crews; furthermore, such lights shall not be lighted except while such vehicles are actually engaged in work on a highway;

4. Vehicles of public utilities, municipalities, or other construction, maintenance or automotive service vehicles except that such lights shall be lighted only as a means for indicating the presence of a vehicular traffic hazard requiring unusual care in approaching, overtaking or passing

while such vehicles are engaged in maintenance, service or construction on a highway;

5. Oversized vehicle or load; however, such lights shall only be lighted when moving under permit issued by the Department under Section 15-301 of this Code;

6. The front and rear of motorized equipment owned and operated by the State of Illinois or any political subdivision thereof, which is designed and used for removal of snow and ice from highways;

7. Fleet safety vehicles registered in another state, furthermore, such lights shall not be lighted except as provided for in Section 12-212 of this Code;

8. Such other vehicles as may be authorized by local authorities;

9. Law enforcement vehicles of State or local authorities when used in combination with red oscillating, rotating or flashing lights;

9.5. Propane delivery trucks;

10. Vehicles used for collecting or delivering mail for the United States Postal Service provided that such lights shall not be lighted except when such vehicles are actually being used for such purposes;

11. Any vehicle displaying a slow-moving vehicle emblem as provided in Section 12-205.1;

12. All trucks equipped with self-compactors or roll-off hoists and roll- on containers for garbage or refuse hauling. Such lights shall not be lighted except when such vehicles are actually being used for such purposes;

13. Vehicles used by a security company, alarm responder, or control agency;

14. Security vehicles of the Department of Human Services; however, the lights shall not be lighted except when being used for security related purposes under the direction of the superintendent of the facility where the vehicle is located; and

15. Vehicles of union representatives, except that the lights shall be lighted only while the vehicle is within the limits of a construction project or while the vehicle is parked alongside any roadway.

(c) The use of blue oscillating, rotating or flashing lights, whether lighted or unlighted, is prohibited except on:

1. Rescue squad vehicles not owned by a fire department and vehicles owned or fully operated by a:

voluntary firefighter;

paid firefighter;

part-paid firefighter;

call firefighter;

member of the board of trustees of a fire protection district;

paid or unpaid member of a rescue squad;

paid or unpaid member of a voluntary ambulance unit; or

paid or unpaid members of a local or county emergency management services agency as defined in the Illinois Emergency Management Agency Act,[1] designated or authorized by local authorities, in writing, and carrying that designation or authorization in the vehicle.

However, such lights are not to be lighted except when responding to a bona fide emergency.

2. Police department vehicles in cities having a population of 500,000 or more inhabitants.

3. Law enforcement vehicles of State or local authorities when used in combination with red oscillating, rotating or flashing lights.

4. Vehicles of local fire departments and State or federal firefighting vehicles when used in combination with red oscillating, rotating or flashing lights.

5. Vehicles which are designed and used exclusively as ambulances or rescue vehicles when used in combination with red oscillating, rotating or flashing lights; furthermore, such lights shall not be lighted except when responding to an emergency call.

6. Vehicles that are equipped and used exclusively as organ transport vehicles when used in combination with red oscillating, rotating, or flashing lights; furthermore, these lights shall only be lighted when the transportation is declared an emergency by a member of the transplant team or a representative of the organ procurement organization.

7. Vehicles of the Illinois Emergency Management Agency and vehicles of the Department of Nuclear Safety, when used in combination with red oscillating, rotating, or flashing lights.

8. Vehicles operated by a local or county emergency management services agency as defined in the Illinois Emergency Management Agency Act, when used in combination with red oscillating, rotating, or flashing lights.

(c-1) In addition to the blue oscillating, rotating, or flashing lights permitted under subsection (c), and notwithstanding subsection (a), a vehicle operated by a voluntary firefighter, a voluntary member of a rescue squad, or a member of a voluntary ambulance unit may be equipped with flashing white headlights and blue grill lights, which may be used only in responding to an emergency call.

(c-2) In addition to the blue oscillating, rotating, or flashing lights permitted under subsection (c), and notwithstanding subsection (a), a vehicle operated by a paid or unpaid member of a local or county emergency management services agency as defined in the Illinois Emergency Management Agency Act, may be equipped with white oscillating, rotating, or flashing lights to be used in combination with blue oscillating, rotating, or flashing lights, if authorization by local authorities is in writing and carried in the vehicle.

(d) The use of a combination of amber and white oscillating, rotating or flashing lights, whether lighted or unlighted, is prohibited, except motor vehicles or equipment of the State of Illinois, local authorities, contractors, and union representatives may be so equipped; furthermore, such lights shall not be lighted on vehicles of the State of Illinois, local authorities, and contractors except while such vehicles are engaged in highway maintenance or construction operations within the limits of highway construction projects, and shall not be lighted on the vehicles of union representatives except when those vehicles are within the limits of a construction project.

(e) All oscillating, rotating or flashing lights referred to in this Section shall be of sufficient intensity, when illuminated, to be visible at 500 feet in normal sunlight.

(f) Nothing in this Section shall prohibit a manufacturer of oscillating, rotating or flashing lights or his representative from temporarily mounting such lights on a vehicle for demonstration purposes only.

(g) Any person violating the provisions of subsections (a), (b), (c) or (d) of this Section who without lawful authority stops or detains or attempts to stop or detain another person shall be guilty of a Class 4 felony.

(h) Except as provided in subsection (g) above, any person violating the provisions of subsections (a) or (c) of this Section shall be guilty of a Class A misdemeanor.

P.A. 76-1586, § 12-116, eff. July 1, 1970. Amended by P.A. 76-2182, § 1, eff. July 1, 1970. Renumbered § 12-215 by P.A. 77-37, § 1, eff. Jan. 1, 1972. Amended by P.A. 77-103, § 1, eff. Jan. 1, 1972; P.A. 77-2829, § 40, eff. Dec. 22, 1972; P.A. 78-255, § 61, eff. Oct. 1, 1973; P.A. 78-509, § 1, eff. Jan. 1, 1974; P.A. 78-1203, § 1, eff. Sept. 5, 1974; P.A. 78-1297, § 58, eff. March 4, 1975; P.A. 79-537, § 1, eff. Oct. 1, 1975; P.A. 79-870, § 1, eff. Oct. 1, 1975; P.A. 79-916, § 1, eff. Oct. 1, 1975; P.A. 79-1454, § 44, eff. Aug. 31, 1976; P.A. 80-1013, § 1, eff. Oct. 1, 1977; P.A. 81-1509, Art. II, § 71, eff. Sept. 26, 1980; P.A. 83-769, § 1, eff. Jan. 1, 1984; P.A. 84-256, § 1, eff. Jan. 1, 1986; P.A. 84-285, § 1, eff. Jan. 1, 1986; P.A. 84-1105, § 1, eff. Dec. 10, 1985; P.A. 84-1231, § 1, eff. July 28, 1986; P.A. 84-1308, Art. II, § 96, eff. Aug. 25, 1986; P.A. 84-1438, Art. II, § 30, eff. Dec. 22, 1986; P.A. 85-586, § 1, eff. Sept. 20, 1987; P.A. 85-1368, § 1, eff. Jan. 1, 1989; P.A. 86-611, § 1, eff. Sept. 1, 1989; P.A. 87-531, § 1, eff. Jan. 1, 1992; P.A. 88-58, § 5, eff. Jan. 1, 1994; P.A. 88-341, § 1, eff. Jan. 1, 1994; P.A. 88-670, Art. 2, § 2-59, eff. Dec. 2, 1994; P.A. 89-433, § 5, eff. Dec. 15, 1995; P.A. 89-507, Art. 90, § 90D-84, eff. July 1, 1997; P.A. 90-330, § 5, eff. Aug. 8, 1997; P.A. 90-347, § 5, eff. Jan. 1, 1998; P.A. 90-655, § 153, eff. July 30, 1998; P.A. 91-357, § 231, eff. July 29, 1999; P.A. 92-138, § 5, eff. July 24, 2001; P.A. 92-407, § 5, eff. Aug. 17, 2001; P.A. 92-651, § 77, eff. July 11, 2002; P.A. 92-782, § 5, eff. Aug. 6, 2002; P.A. 92-820, § 5, eff. Aug. 21, 2002; P.A. 92-872, § 5, eff. June 1, 2003.

Formerly Ill.Rev.Stat.1991, ch. 95 ½, ¶ 12-215.

1 20 ILCS 3305/1 et seq.

For text of section effective until June 1, 2003, see 625 ILCS 5/12-215, ante

P.A. 92-407 inserted subpar. (c-1).

P.A. 92-651, the First 2002 General Revisory Act, amended various Acts to delete obsolete text, to correct patent and technical errors, to revise cross references, to resolve multiple actions in the 91st and 92nd General Assemblies and to make certain technical corrections in P.A. 91-937 through P.A. 92-520.

P.A. 92-782 incorporated the amendments by P.A. 92-138 and P.A. 92-407.

P.A. 92-820 incorporated the amendments by P.A. 92-138 and P.A. 92-407.

See 5 ILCS 70/6 as to the effect of (1) more than one amendment of a section at the same session of the General Assembly or (2) two or more acts relating to the same subject matter enacted by the same General Assembly.

5/12-216. Operation of oscillating, rotating or flashing lights

§ 12-216. Operation of oscillating, rotating or flashing lights. Oscillating, rotating or flashing lights located on or within police vehicles in this State shall be lighted whenever a police officer is in pursuit of a violator of a traffic law or regulation.

P.A. 76-1586, § 12-117, eff. July 1, 1970. Renumbered § 12-216 by P.A. 77-37, § 1, eff. Jan. 1, 1972. Amended by P.A. 85-830, § 1, eff. Sept. 24, 1987.

Formerly Ill.Rev.Stat.1991, ch. 95 ½, ¶ 12-216.

5/12-217. Special lighting equipment for interstate transportation authority

§ 12-217. Special lighting equipment for interstate transportation authority. (a) Notwithstanding any other provisions of this Chapter, an interstate transportation authority, as defined in this Section, in addition to headlights and other required or authorized lighting, may affix to the top front of its buses, 2 sets of lights, each containing up to 5 stationary lights, of different colors, including the colors white, yellow, blue, green and purple, and excepting, however, the color red. Such lights shall be located symmetrically above the windshield with one set of lights on each side of the headsign and may reflect an intensity of up to 64 candlepower each. Provided further however, that normally no more than 3 of such colored lights on each set of lights may be on or displayed at any one time. Such lights shall be stationary only, and shall not be oscillating, rotating, or flashing. The lights shall be displayed only on the top front of such buses, lighted in various combinations to indicate the route, the destination, and the express or local nature of the service.

(b) As used herein, the term "interstate transportation authority" shall mean any body, agency, entity, or political subdivision created by compact between Illinois and another state, which is a body corporate and politic, and which operates a public mass transportation or transit system.

P.A. 76-1586, § 12-217, added by P.A. 85-1144, § 1, eff. July 29, 1988.

Formerly Ill.Rev.Stat.1991, ch. 95 ½, ¶ 12-217.

ARTICLE III. BRAKES

5/12-301. Brakes

§ 12-301. Brakes.

(a) Brake equipment required.

1. Every motor vehicle, other than a motor-driven cycle and an antique vehicle displaying an antique plate, when operated upon a highway shall be equipped with brakes adequate to control the movement of and to stop and hold such vehicle, including 2 separate means of applying the brakes, each of which means shall be effective to apply the brakes to at least one wheel on a motorcycle and at least 2 wheels on all other first division and second division vehicles. If these 2 separate means of applying the brakes are connected in any way, they shall be so constructed that failure of any one part of the operating mechanism shall not leave the motor vehicle without brakes.

2. Every motor-driven cycle when operated upon a highway shall be equipped with at least one brake which may be operated by hand or foot.

3. Every antique vehicle shall be equipped with the brakes of the same type originally installed by the manufacturer as original equipment and in working order.

4. Every trailer or semitrailer of a gross weight of over 3,000 pounds, when operated upon a highway must be equipped with brakes adequate to control the movement of, to stop and to hold such vehicle, and designed so as to be operable by the driver of the towing vehicle from its cab. Such brakes must be so designed and connected that

in case of an accidental breakaway of a towed vehicle over 5,000 pounds, the brakes are automatically applied.

5. Every motor vehicle, trailer, pole trailer or semitrailer, sold in this State or operated upon the highways shall be equipped with service brakes upon all wheels of every such vehicle, except any motor-driven cycle, and except that any trailer, pole trailer or semitrailer 3,000 pounds gross weight or less need not be equipped with brakes, and except that any trailer or semitrailer with gross weight over 3,000 pounds but under 5,001 pounds need be equipped with brakes on only one wheel on each side of the vehicle. Any motor vehicle and truck tractor having 3 or more axles and manufactured prior to July 25, 1980 need not have brakes on the front wheels, except when such vehicles are equipped with at least 2 steerable axles, the wheels of one such axle need not be equipped with brakes. However, a vehicle that is more than 30 years of age and which is driven on the highways only in going to and returning from an antique auto show or for servicing or for a demonstration need be equipped with 2 wheel brakes only.

(b) Performance ability of brakes.

1. The service brakes upon any motor vehicle or combination of vehicles operating on a level surface shall be adequate to stop such vehicle or vehicles when traveling 20 miles per hour within a distance of 30 feet when upon dry asphalt or concrete pavement surface free from loose material.

2. Under the above conditions the hand brake shall be adequate to stop such vehicle or vehicles, except any motorcycle, within a distance of 55 feet and the hand brake shall be adequate to hold such vehicle or vehicles stationary on any grade upon which operated.

3. Under the above conditions the service brakes upon an antique vehicle shall be adequate to stop the vehicle within a distance of 40 feet and the hand brake adequate to stop the vehicle within a distance of 55 feet.

4. All braking distances specified in this Section apply to all vehicles mentioned, whether such vehicles are unloaded or are loaded to the maximum capacity permitted under this Act.

5. All brakes shall be maintained in good working order and shall be so adjusted as to operate as equally as practicable with respect to the wheels on opposite sides of the vehicle.

6. Brake assembly requirements for mobile homes shall be the standards required by the United States Department of Housing and Urban Development adopted under Title VI of the Housing and Community Development Act of 1974.[1]

(c) For purposes of this Section, a custom vehicle or street rod is considered to be in compliance with all brake equipment requirements if it has passed the approved vehicle safety inspection provided for in Section 3–804.1 or 3–804.2.

P.A. 76–1586, § 12–118, eff. July 1, 1970. Amended by P.A. 76–1627, § 1, eff. July 1, 1970; P.A. 76–1997, § 1, eff. July 1, 1970. Renumbered § 12–301 by P.A. 77–37, § 1, eff. Jan. 1, 1972. Amended by P.A. 77–217, § 1, eff. Jan. 1, 1972; P.A. 77–2829, § 40, eff. Dec. 22, 1972; P.A. 78–255, § 61, eff. Oct. 1, 1973; P.A. 80–1038, § 1, eff. Sept. 27, 1977; P.A. 86–447, § 2, eff. Aug. 30, 1989; P.A. 86–1340, § 1, eff. July 1, 1990; P.A. 92–668, § 5, eff. Jan. 1, 2003.

Formerly Ill.Rev.Stat.1991, ch. 95 ½, ¶ 12–301.

[1] 42 U.S.C.A. § 5401 et seq.

P.A. 86–1340 incorporated the amendment by P.A. 86–447.

5/12–302. Brake fluid

§ 12–302. Brake fluid. No person shall sell, offer for sale or distribute brake fluid for use on motor vehicles for repair purposes unless such fluid conforms to specifications prescribed by the Department.

P.A. 76–1586, § 12–119, eff. July 1, 1970. Renumbered § 12–302 by P.A. 77–37, § 1, eff. Jan. 1, 1972. Amended by P.A. 77–2830, Art. 73, § 1, eff. Jan. 1, 1973; P.A. 78–748, § 1, eff. Jan. 1, 1974.

Formerly Ill.Rev.Stat.1991, ch. 95 ½, ¶ 12–302.

ARTICLE IV. TIRES

Section

5/12–401. Restriction as to tire equipment

§ 12–401. Restriction as to tire equipment. No metal tired vehicle, including tractors, motor vehicles of the second division, traction engines and other similar vehicles, shall be operated over any improved highway of this State, if such vehicle has on the periphery of any of the road wheels any block, stud, flange, cleat, ridge, lug or any projection of metal or wood which projects radially beyond the tread or traffic surface of the tire. This prohibition does not apply to pneumatic tires with metal studs used on vehicles operated by rural letter carriers who are employed or enjoy a contract with the United States Postal Service for the purpose of delivering mail if such vehicle is actually used for such purpose during operations between November 15 of any year and April 1 of the following year, or to motor vehicles displaying a person with disabilities or disabled veteran license plate whose owner resides in an unincorporated area located upon a county or township highway or road and possesses a valid driver's license and operates the vehicle with such tires only during the period heretofore described, or to tracked type motor vehicles when that part of the vehicle coming in contact with the road surface does not contain any projections of any kind likely to injure the surface of the road; however, tractors, traction engines, and similar vehicles may be operated which have upon their road wheels V-shaped, diagonal or other cleats arranged in such a manner as to be continuously in contact with the road surface, provided that the gross weight upon such wheels per inch of width of such cleats in contact with the road surface, when measured in the direction of the axle of the vehicle, does not exceed 800 pounds.

All motor vehicles and all other vehicles in tow thereof, or thereunto attached, operating upon any roadway, shall have tires of rubber or some material of equal resiliency. Solid tires shall be considered defective and shall not be permitted to be used if the rubber or other material has been worn or otherwise reduced to a thickness of less than three-fourths of an undue vibration when the vehicle is in motion or to cause undue concentration of the wheel load on the surface of the road. The requirements of this Section do not apply to agricultural tractors or traction engines or to agricultural machinery, including wagons being used for agricultural purposes in tow thereof, or to road rollers or road building machinery operated at a speed not in excess of 10 miles per hour. All motor vehicles of the second division, operating upon any roadway shall have pneumatic tires, unless exempted herein.

Nothing in this Section shall be deemed to prohibit the use of tire chains of reasonable proportion upon any vehicle when required for safety because of snow, ice or other conditions tending to cause a vehicle to skid.

P.A. 76-1586, § 12-124, eff. July 1, 1970. Amended by P.A. 76-2184, § 1, eff. July 1, 1970. Renumbered § 12-401 by P.A. 77-37, § 1, eff. Jan. 1, 1972. Amended by P.A. 78-381, § 1, eff. Oct. 1, 1973; P.A. 79-466, § 1, eff. Aug. 21, 1975; P.A. 83-213, § 1, eff. Jan. 1, 1984; P.A. 83-888, § 1, eff. Nov. 2, 1983; P.A. 83-1362, Art. II, § 99, eff. Sept. 11, 1984; P.A. 88-685, § 5, eff. Jan. 24, 1995.

Formerly Ill.Rev.Stat.1991, ch. 95 ½, ¶ 12-401.

5/12-402. Sale or lease of siped or regrooved pneumatic tire

§ 12-402. Sale or lease of siped or regrooved pneumatic tire. No person or organization shall sell or lease or offer for sale or lease, for use on a highway, any pneumatic tire, either original tread or retread, on which the tread is siped or regrooved to a depth equal to or deeper than the molded groove depth, unless the tire was constructed or retreaded with sufficient tread material and type of labels to permit such siping or regrooving. Such labels and siping or regrooving shall be in compliance with Part 569 of Title 49 of the Code of Federal Regulations, and after siping or regrooving the tire shall conform to that Part.

For the purpose of this Article, siped shall mean cut without removing material, and regrooved shall mean the tread groove pattern is renewed, or a new pattern generated, or both, without additional tread material being added.

P.A. 76-1586, § 12-134, eff. July 1, 1970. Renumbered § 12-402 by P.A. 77-37, § 1, eff. Jan. 1, 1972. Amended by P.A. 83-213, § 1, eff. Jan. 1, 1984.

Formerly Ill.Rev.Stat.1991, ch. 95 ½, ¶ 12-402.

5/12-403. Sale or lease of retreaded or "recapped" pneumatic tire

§ 12-403. Sale or lease of retreaded or "recapped" pneumatic tire. No person or organization shall sell or lease or offer for sale or lease, for use on a highway, any pneumatic tire produced or rebuilt by a process in which tread material is attached to a used tire, unless the tire, tread material, labelling and certification, before and after processing, conform to Part 571.117 of Title 49 of the Code of Federal Regulations.

P.A. 76-1586, § 12-135, eff. July 1, 1970. Renumbered § 12-403 by P.A. 77-37, § 1, eff. Jan. 1, 1972. Amended by P.A. 83-213, § 1, eff. Jan. 1, 1984.

Formerly Ill.Rev.Stat.1991, ch. 95 ½, ¶ 12-403.

5/12-404. Sale or lease of pneumatic tire without marking

§ 12-404. Sale or lease of pneumatic tire without marking. No person or organization shall sell or lease or offer for sale or lease, for use on a highway, any pneumatic tire that does not bear the special marking required by this Section.

(a) Regrooved or siped tire. In addition to the identification, labelling and certification required under Section 12-402, either the word "regrooved" or the word "siped" shall be branded on each side of a pneumatic tire on which the tread is either regrooved or siped, as the case may be. In the case of a tire that is both regrooved and siped, the word "regrooved" alone on each side shall suffice, although both words may appear on each side. Each branding shall be conspicuous but shall be sized, located and applied so as not to weaken or damage the tire or otherwise degrade the performance of the tire or shorten its useful life.

(b) Retreaded tire. In addition to the labelling, identification, certification and other marking required under Section 12-403, the word "retreaded" shall be branded or molded into or onto each side of a pneumatic tire that has been retreaded or "recapped". Each molding or branding shall be conspicuous but shall be sized, located and applied so as not to weaken or damage the tire or otherwise degrade the performance of the tire or shorten its useful life.

(c) New tire. The labelling, identification, certification and other marking required by Part 571.109 of Title 49 of the Code of Federal Regulations shall appear on each new pneumatic tire intended for use on a passenger car other than a multipurpose passenger vehicle. The labelling, identification, certification and other marking required by Part 571.119 of Title 49 of the Code of Federal Regulations shall appear on each new pneumatic tire intended for use on either a multipurpose passenger vehicle or other type of vehicle that is not a passenger car.

P.A. 76-1586, § 12-136, eff. July 1, 1970. Renumbered § 12-404 by P.A. 77-37, § 1, eff. Jan. 1, 1972. Amended by P.A. 83-213, § 1, eff. Jan. 1, 1984.

Formerly Ill.Rev.Stat.1991, ch. 95 ½, ¶ 12-404.

5/12-405. Operating condition of pneumatic tires

§ 12-405. Operating condition of pneumatic tires. **(a) Definition.** The term "spare tire" as used in this Section 12-405 means any new, used or specially constructed tire that is either carried or installed for short term emergency use.

(b) Promulgated Rules. The Department shall promulgate rules concerning unsafe operating conditions of pneumatic tires. The rules shall be enforced by police officers by visual inspection of tires, including visual comparison with simple measuring scales or gauges. The rules shall include precepts and standards for determining unsafe conditions, including the determination of an effective depth of tread groove, and shall be based upon, to the extent that it is reasonable and practical, all provisions set forth in paragraph (d) of this Section.

(c) Use of Unsafe Tire. 1. No person or organization shall place, drive or move, or cause or allow to be placed, driven or moved, on a highway of this State, any vehicle equipped with one or more pneumatic tires deemed to be unsafe under a provision of paragraph (d) of this Section or a rule promulgated under paragraph (b) of this Section.

2. Exemptions. Any restriction stated in this paragraph (c) shall not apply:

(i) To a tire on a damaged, disabled, abandoned, or other unsafe or unwanted vehicle being legally towed, pushed or otherwise transferred to a repair, relocation, storage, salvage, junking, or other collection site;

(ii) To a tire on a racing or other competitive vehicle being legally moved or transported, not under its own power, to a lawful competition site or to a bona fide testing site; or

(iii) To a spare tire either carried or in short term emergency use for only such distance or time as is reasonably necessary to accomplish the repair or replacement of the damaged or unsafe tire for which the spare was substituted.

(d) Criteria for Unsafe Pneumatic Tires. A pneumatic tire shall be deemed to be unsafe if it has:

1. Any part of a ply or cord exposed;

2. A tread or sidewall crack, cut, snag, or other surface interruption deep enough to expose a ply or cord;

3. Any bulge, knot, or separation;

4. Tread wear indicators flush with the tread outer surface in any 2 or more adjacent tread grooves at 3 locations approximately equally spaced around the circumference of the tire;

5. A depth of tread groove less than $\frac{2}{32}$ of an inch or less than $\frac{1}{32}$ of an inch if on a motorcycle or truckster, measured in any 2 or more adjacent tread grooves at 3 locations approximately equally spaced around the circumference of the tire, at least one of which, in the judgment of the inspecting officer, is a location at which the tread is thinnest, providing that any measurement over a tie bar, tread wear indicator, hump or fillet is excluded;

6. A depth of tread groove less than $\frac{4}{32}$ of an inch at any one location and the tire is mounted on the front wheel of a motor vehicle subject to the provisions of Chapter 18B of this Code, provided that any measurement over a tie bar, tread wear indicator, hump or fillet is excluded;

7. A marking which indicates that the tire is not intended for use on a public highway;

8. Been regrooved or recut below the bottom of an original tread groove, except in the case of a special "regroovable" tire that was manufactured or retreaded with thick undertread, identified and regrooved in compliance with the applicable federal standard in Title 49 of the Code of Federal Regulations, and in compliance with each applicable Section of this Code; or

9. Other condition, marking or lack of marking that may be reasonably demonstrated to identify the tire as unsuitable for highway use, including inflation, load, speed or installation condition seriously incompatible with the tire size, construction, or other pertinent marking or feature.

(e) Sale, Lease or Installation of Pneumatic Tires. 1. No person or organization shall sell, lease, or offer for sale or lease, or mount, install, or cause or allow to be mounted or installed, for use on a highway, any pneumatic tire deemed to be unsafe under paragraph (d) of this Section or under a rule promulgated under paragraph (b) of this Section. Except as provided in paragraph (c) of this Section, any person or organization offering a vehicle for sale or lease shall, prior to its being placed, driven or moved on a highway, correct any unsafe tire condition.

2. No person or organization shall sell, lease, or offer for sale or lease, for highway use, any pneumatic tire, or any vehicle equipped with a pneumatic tire, which has a depth of tread groove less than $\frac{3}{32}$ of an inch; except a pneumatic tire on a motorcycle or truckster may have a depth of tire groove of not less than $\frac{2}{32}$ of an inch. Groove depth shall not be measured where a tie bar, tread wear indicator, hump or fillet is located.

(f) Compliance and Enforcement. Any police officer, upon reasonable cause to believe that a person or organization has acted or is acting in violation of any provision of this Section, shall require the driver, owner, or other appropriate custodian to submit the tire or tires to an inspection. When so required, the owner or other appropriate custodian shall allow the tire inspection and the driver of a vehicle or combination of vehicles shall stop at a designated location and allow the tire or tires to be inspected or shall move the vehicle or combination to a location that is reasonably convenient and is suitable for such inspection.

P.A. 76-1586, § 12-405, added by P.A. 77-2770, § 1, eff. Jan. 1, 1973. Amended by P.A. 83-213, § 1, eff. Jan. 1, 1984.

Formerly Ill.Rev.Stat.1991, ch. 95 ½, ¶ 12-405.

5/12-406. § 12-406. Repealed by P.A. 80-911, § 2, eff. Oct. 1, 1977

5/12-407. Rules and regulations

§ 12-407. Rules and regulations. The Department may promulgate rules and regulations to clarify or specify the requirements of this Article IV.

P.A. 76-1586, § 12-407, added by P.A. 83-213, § 1, eff. Jan. 1, 1984.

Formerly Ill.Rev.Stat.1991, ch. 95 ½, ¶ 12-407.

ARTICLE V. GLASS, WINDSHIELDS AND MIRRORS

Section

5/12-500. § 12-500. Repealed by P.A. 90-89, § 20, eff. Jan. 1, 1998

5/12-501. Windshields and safety glazing material in motor vehicles

§ 12-501. Windshields and safety glazing material in motor vehicles.

(a) Every motor vehicle operated upon the highways of this State shall be equipped with a front windshield which complies with those standards as established pursuant to this Section and Section 12-503 of this Code. This subsection shall not apply to motor vehicles designed and used exclusively for off-highway use, motorcycles, motor-driven cycles, motorized pedalcycles, nor to motor vehicles registered as antique vehicles, custom vehicles, or street rods when the original design of such vehicles did not include front windshields.

(b) No person shall knowingly sell any 1936 or later model motor vehicle unless such vehicle is equipped with safety glazing material conforming to specifications prescribed by the Department wherever glazing material is used in doors, windows and windshields. Regulations promulgated by the Department specifying standards for safety glazing material on windshields shall, as a minimum, conform with those applicable Federal Motor Vehicles Safety Standards (49 CFR 571.205). These provisions apply to all motor vehicles of the first and second division but with respect to trucks, including truck tractors, the requirements as to safety glazing material apply to all glazing material used in doors, windows and windshields in the drivers' compartments of such vehicles.

(c) It is unlawful for the owner or any other person knowingly to install or cause to be installed in any motor vehicle any glazing material other than safety glazing material conforming to the specifications prescribed by the Department.

P.A. 76-1586, § 12-126, eff. July 1, 1970. Resectioned in part § 12-501 by P.A. 77-37, § 1, eff. Jan. 1, 1972. Amended by P.A. 78-748, § 1, eff. Jan. 1, 1974; P.A. 85-1144, § 1, eff. July 29, 1988; P.A. 92-668, § 5, eff. Jan. 1, 2003.

Formerly Ill.Rev.Stat.1991, ch. 95 ½, ¶ 12-501.

5/12-502. Mirrors

§ 12-502. Mirrors. Every motor vehicle, operated singly or when towing another vehicle, shall be equipped with a mirror so located as to reflect to the driver a view of the highway for a distance of at least 200 feet to the rear of such motor vehicle.

P.A. 76-1586, § 12-122, eff. July 1, 1970. Renumbered § 12-502 by P.A. 77-37, § 1, eff. Jan. 1, 1972. Amended by P.A. 82-122, § 1, eff. Jan. 1, 1982.

Formerly Ill.Rev.Stat.1991, ch. 95 ½, ¶ 12-502.

5/12-503. Windshields must be unobstructed and equipped with wipers

§ 12-503. Windshields must be unobstructed and equipped with wipers.

(a) No person shall drive a motor vehicle with any sign, poster, window application, reflective material, nonreflective material or tinted film upon the front windshield, sidewings or side windows immediately adjacent to each side of the driver. A nonreflective tinted film may be used along the uppermost portion of the windshield if such material does not extend more than 6 inches down from the top of the windshield. Nothing in this Section shall create a cause of action on behalf of a buyer against a dealer or manufacturer who sells a motor vehicle with a window which is in violation of this Section.

(b) Nothing contained in this Section shall prohibit the use of nonreflective, smoked or tinted glass, nonreflective film, perforated window screen or other decorative window application on windows to the rear of the driver's seat, except that any motor vehicle with a window to the rear of the driver's seat treated in this manner shall be equipped with a side mirror on each side of the motor vehicle which are in conformance with Section 12-502.

(c) No person shall drive a motor vehicle with any objects placed or suspended between the driver and the front windshield, rear window, side wings or side windows immediately adjacent to each side of the driver which materially obstructs the driver's view.

(d) Every motor vehicle, except motorcycles, shall be equipped with a device, controlled by the driver, for cleaning rain, snow, moisture or other obstructions from the windshield; and no person shall drive a motor vehicle with snow, ice, moisture or other material on any of the windows or mirrors, which materially obstructs the driver's clear view of the highway.

(e) No person shall drive a motor vehicle when the windshield, side or rear windows are in such defective condition or repair as to materially impair the driver's view to the front, side or rear. A vehicle equipped with a side mirror on each side of the vehicle which are in conformance with Section 12-502 will be deemed to be in compliance in the event the rear window of the vehicle is materially obscured.

(f) Paragraphs (a) and (b) of this Section shall not apply to:

(1) motor vehicles manufactured prior to January 1, 1982; or

(2) to those motor vehicles properly registered in another jurisdiction.

(g) Paragraph (a) of this Section shall not apply to any motor vehicle with a window treatment, including but not limited to a window application, reflective material, nonreflective material, or tinted film, applied or affixed to the motor vehicle for the purposes set forth in item (1) or (2) before the effective date of this amendatory Act of 1997 and:

(1) that is owned and operated by a person afflicted with or suffering from a medical illness, ailment, or disease which would require that person to be shielded from the direct rays of the sun; or

(2) that is used in transporting a person when the person resides at the same address as the registered owner of the vehicle and the person is afflicted with or suffering from a medical illness, ailment or disease which would require the person to be shielded from the direct rays of the sun;

It must be certified by a physician licensed to practice medicine in Illinois that such person owning and operating or being transported in a motor vehicle is afflicted with or suffers from such illness, ailment, or disease and such certification must be carried in the motor vehicle at all times. The certification shall be legible and shall contain the date of issuance, the name, address and signature of the attending physician, and the name, address, and medical condition of the person requiring exemption. The information on the certificate for a window treatment applied or affixed before the effective date of this amendatory Act of 1997 must remain current and shall be renewed annually by the attending physician, but in no event shall a certificate issued for purposes of this subsection be valid on or after January 1, 2008. The person shall also submit a copy of the certification to the Secretary of State. The Secretary of State may forward notice of certification to law enforcement agencies.

This subsection shall not be construed to authorize window treatments applied or affixed on or after the effective date of this amendatory Act of 1997.

The exemption provided by this subsection (g) shall not apply to any motor vehicle on and after January 1, 2008.

(h) Paragraph (a) of this Section shall not apply to motor vehicle stickers or other certificates issued by State or local authorities which are required to be displayed upon motor vehicle windows to evidence compliance with requirements concerning motor vehicles.

(i) Those motor vehicles exempted under paragraph (f)(1) of this Section shall not cause their windows to be treated as described in paragraph (a) after January 1, 1993.

(j) A person found guilty of violating paragraphs (a), (b), or (i) of this Section shall be guilty of a petty offense and fined no less than $50 nor more than $500. A second or subsequent violation of paragraphs (a), (b), or (i) of this Section shall be treated as a Class C misdemeanor and the violator fined no less than $100 nor more than $500. Any person convicted under paragraphs (a), (b), or (i) of this Section shall be ordered to alter any nonconforming windows into compliance with this Section.

P.A. 76-1586, § 12-123, eff. July 1, 1970. Amended by P.A. 76-1997, § 1, eff. July 1, 1970. Renumbered § 12-503 and amended by P.A. 77-37, § 1, eff. Jan. 1, 1972. Amended by P.A. 78-462, § 1, eff. Jan. 1, 1974; P.A. 82-122, § 1, eff. Jan. 1, 1982; P.A. 85-1144, § 1, eff. July 29, 1988; P.A. 86-488, § 1, eff. Jan. 1, 1990; P.A. 87-1203, § 1, eff. Sept. 25, 1992; P.A. 88-52, § 5, eff. July 7, 1993; P.A. 90-389, § 5, eff. Jan. 1, 1998.

Formerly Ill.Rev.Stat.1991, ch. 95 ½, ¶ 12-503.

ARTICLE VI. MISCELLANEOUS REQUIREMENTS

Section

5/12-600. § 12-600. Repealed by P.A. 90-89, § 20, eff. Jan. 1, 1998

5/12-601. Horns and warning devices

§ 12-601. Horns and warning devices.

(a) Every motor vehicle when operated upon a highway shall be equipped with a horn in good working order and capable of emitting sound audible under normal conditions from a distance of not less than 200 feet, but no horn or other warning device shall emit an unreasonable loud or harsh sound or a whistle. The driver of a motor vehicle shall when reasonably necessary to insure safe operation give audible warning with his horn but shall not otherwise use such horn when upon a highway.

(b) No vehicle shall be equipped with nor shall any person use upon a vehicle any siren, whistle, or bell, except as otherwise permitted in this section. Any authorized emergency vehicle or organ transport vehicle as defined in Chapter 1 of this Act [1] may be equipped with a siren, whistle, or bell, capable of emitting sound audible under normal conditions from a distance of not less than 500 feet, but such siren, whistle or bell, shall not be used except when such vehicle is operated in response to an emergency call or in the immediate pursuit of an actual or suspected violator of the law in either of which events the driver of such vehicle shall sound such siren, whistle or bell, when necessary to warn pedestrians and other drivers of the approach thereof.

(c) Trackless trolley coaches, as defined by Section 1-206 of this Code, and replica trolleys, as defined by Section 1-171.04 of this Code, may be equipped with a bell or bells in lieu of a horn, and may, in addition to the requirements of paragraph (a) of this Section, use a bell or bells for the purpose of indicating arrival or departure at designated stops during the hours of scheduled operation.

P.A. 76-1586, § 12-120. Renumbered § 12-601 by P.A. 77-37, § 1, eff. Jan. 1, 1972. Amended by P.A. 79-858, § 1, eff. Jan. 1, 1976; P.A. 89-345, § 10, eff. Jan. 1, 1996; P.A. 89-687, § 5, eff. June 1, 1997; P.A. 90-347, § 5, eff. Jan. 1, 1998; P.A. 90-655, § 153, eff. July 30, 1998.

Formerly Ill.Rev.Stat.1991, ch. 95 ½, ¶ 12-601.

[1] 625 ILCS 5/1-100 et seq.

P.A. 90-655, the First 1998 General Revisory Act, amended various Acts to delete obsolete text, to correct patent and technical errors, to revise cross references, to resolve multiple actions in the 89th and 90th General Assemblies and to make certain technical corrections in P.A. 89-708 through P.A. 90-566.

5/12-602. Mufflers, prevention of noise

§ 12-602. Mufflers, prevention of noise. Every motor vehicle driven or operated upon the highways of this State shall at all times be equipped with an adequate muffler or exhaust system in constant operation and properly maintained to prevent any excessive or unusual noise. No such muffler or exhaust system shall be equipped with a cutout, bypass or similar device. No person shall modify the exhaust system of a motor vehicle in a manner which will amplify or increase the noise of such vehicle above that emitted by the muffler originally installed on the vehicle, and such original muffler shall comply with all the requirements of this Section.

P.A. 76-1586, § 12-121, eff. July 1, 1970. Amended by P.A. 76-2183, § 1, eff. July 1, 1970. Resectioned in part § 12-602 by P.A. 77-37, § 1, eff. Jan. 1, 1972.

Formerly Ill.Rev.Stat.1991, ch. 95 ½, ¶ 12-602.

5/12-603. Seat safety belts

§ 12-603. Seat safety belts.

(a) No person shall sell any 1965 or later model motor vehicle of the first division unless the front seat of such motor vehicle is equipped with 2 sets of seat safety belts. Motorcycles are exempted from the provisions of this Section.

(b) No person shall operate any 1965 or later model motor vehicle of the first division that is titled or licensed by the Secretary of State unless the front seat of such motor vehicle is equipped with 2 sets of seat safety belts.

(b-5) No person under the age of 18 years shall operate any motor vehicle, except a motor driven cycle or motorcycle, with more than one passenger in the front seat of the motor vehicle and no more passengers in the back seats than the number of available seat safety belts, except that each driver under the age of 18 years operating a second division vehicle having a gross vehicle weight rating of 8,000 pounds or less that contains only a front seat may operate the vehicle with more than one passenger in the front seat, provided that each passenger is wearing a properly adjusted and fastened seat safety belt.

(c) (Blank).

(d) The Department shall establish performance specifications for seat safety belts and for the attachment and installation thereof.

P.A. 76-1586, § 12-127, eff. July 1, 1970. Amended by P.A. 76-2185, § 1, eff. July 1, 1970. Renumbered § 12-603 by P.A. 77-37, § 1, eff. Jan. 1, 1972. Amended by P.A. 78-748, § 1, eff. Jan. 1, 1974; P.A. 89-120, § 10, eff. July 7, 1995; P.A. 90-89, § 15, eff. Jan. 1, 1998; P.A. 90-369, § 5, eff. Jan. 1, 1998; P.A. 90-655, § 153, eff. July 30, 1998.

Formerly Ill.Rev.Stat.1991, ch. 95 ½, ¶ 12-603.

P.A. 90-655, the First 1998 General Revisory Act, amended various Acts to delete obsolete text, to correct patent and technical errors, to revise cross references, to resolve multiple actions in the 89th and 90th General Assemblies and to make certain technical corrections in P.A. 89-708 through P.A. 90-566.

5/12–603.1. Driver and passenger required to use safety belts, exceptions and penalty

§ 12–603.1. Driver and passenger required to use safety belts, exceptions and penalty.

(a) Each driver and front seat passenger of a motor vehicle operated on a street or highway in this State shall wear a properly adjusted and fastened seat safety belt; except that, a child less than 6 years of age shall be protected as required pursuant to the Child Passenger Protection Act.[1] Each driver under the age of 18 years and each of the driver's passengers under the age of 18 years of a motor vehicle operated on a street or highway in this State shall wear a properly adjusted and fastened seat safety belt. Each driver of a motor vehicle transporting a child 6 years of age or more, but less than 16 years of age, in the front seat of the motor vehicle shall secure the child in a properly adjusted and fastened seat safety belt.

(b) Paragraph (a) shall not apply to any of the following:

1. A driver or passenger frequently stopping and leaving the vehicle or delivering property from the vehicle, if the speed of the vehicle between stops does not exceed 15 miles per hour.

2. A driver or passenger possessing a written statement from a physician that such person is unable, for medical or physical reasons, to wear a seat safety belt.

3. A driver or passenger possessing an official certificate or license endorsement issued by the appropriate agency in another state or country indicating that the driver is unable for medical, physical, or other valid reasons to wear a seat safety belt.

4. A driver operating a motor vehicle in reverse.

5. A motor vehicle with a model year prior to 1965.

6. A motorcycle or motor driven cycle.

7. A motorized pedalcycle.

8. A motor vehicle which is not required to be equipped with seat safety belts under federal law.

9. A motor vehicle operated by a rural letter carrier of the United States postal service while performing duties as a rural letter carrier.

(c) Failure to wear a seat safety belt in violation of this Section shall not be considered evidence of negligence, shall not limit the liability of an insurer, and shall not diminish any recovery for damages arising out of the ownership, maintenance, or operation of a motor vehicle.

(d) A violation of this Section shall be a petty offense and subject to a fine not to exceed $25.

(e) No motor vehicle, or driver or passenger of such vehicle, shall be stopped or searched by any law enforcement officer solely on the basis of a violation or suspected violation of this Section.

P.A. 76–1586, § 12–603.1, added by P.A. 83–1507, § 1, eff. July 1, 1985. Amended by P.A. 85–291, § 2, eff. Jan. 1, 1988; P.A. 90–369, § 5, eff. Jan. 1, 1998.

Formerly Ill.Rev.Stat.1991, ch. 95 ½, ¶ 12–603.1.

[1] 625 ILCS 25/1 et seq.

5/12–604. Television receivers

§ 12–604. Television receivers.

(a) No motor vehicle operated on the highways of this State shall be equipped with television broadcast receiver equipment so located that the viewer or screen is visible from the driver's seat.

(b) A visual display device permitted under this Section shall be attached to the vehicle in a manner that meets all applicable federal motor vehicle dash safety standards.

(c) This section does not prohibit the use of television-type receiving equipment used exclusively for safety or traffic engineering studies.

P.A. 76–1586, § 12–138, eff. July 1, 1970. Renumbered § 12–604 by P.A. 77–37, § 1, eff. Jan. 1, 1972. Amended by P.A. 77–1344, § 1, eff. Aug. 27, 1971; P.A. 77–2829, § 40, eff. Dec. 22, 1972; P.A. 78–255, § 61, eff. Oct. 1, 1973; P.A. 88–415, § 10, eff. Aug. 20, 1993.

Formerly Ill.Rev.Stat.1991, ch. 95 ½, ¶ 12–604.

5/12–605. Taxicabs—Bullet proof shields

§ 12–605. Taxicabs—Bullet proof shields. In municipalities with 1,000,000 or more population, any taxicab manufactured, owned or operated after September 1, 1970, and regularly operated in such a municipality must have a bullet proof shield completely separating the driver's seat from the back seat.

P.A. 76–1586, § 12–605, added by P.A. 77–37, § 1, eff. Jan. 1, 1972. Amended by P.A. 77–2720, § 1, eff. Jan. 1, 1973; P.A. 78–255, § 61, eff. Oct. 1, 1973; P.A. 80–911, § 1, eff. Oct. 1, 1977.

Formerly Ill.Rev.Stat.1991, ch. 95 ½, ¶ 12–605.

5/12–605.1. Buses; two-way radios

§ 12–605.1. (a) On or after two years from the effective date of this Act, no bus which was first placed in service after July 1, 1969, or which has undergone complete renovation and restoration since July 1, 1969 shall be operated as a part of any local mass transit system in this State unless the vehicle is equipped with radio facilities permitting two-way vocal communications between the bus and a local transit control office. This Section does not apply to buses used for charter service, school buses, intrastate carriers while not providing transportation services pursuant to contracts with any local mass transit system, private non-profit carriers receiving assistance under Section 16(b)2 of the Urban Mass Transportation Act of 1964 as amended,[1] carriers receiving assistance pursuant to Article III of the Downstate Public Transportation Act,[2] or interstate carriers and buses owned by a private local mass transit system;

(b) A local mass transit system operating a bus not in compliance with the requirements of subsection (a) shall not be in violation of that subsection, provided that the bus is brought into compliance within a reasonable time (in no event to exceed 1 week) following written notification to the mass transit system of the fact that the bus is not in compliance.

P.A. 76–1586, § 12–605.1, added by P.A. 81–1184, § 1, eff. July 1, 1980. Amended by P.A. 90–89, § 15, eff. Jan. 1, 1998.

Formerly Ill.Rev.Stat.1991, ch. 95 ½, ¶ 12–605.1.

[1] 49 U.S.C.A. § 1601 et seq. (repealed; see, now, 49 U.S.C.A. § 5301 et seq.)

[2] 30 ILCS 740/3–1 et seq.

5/12–605.2. Consumption of food or drink on bus

§ 12–605.2. Beginning 30 days after the effective date of this amendatory Act of 1988, no person shall consume any food or drink, excluding any medicine, upon any bus operated as a part of any local mass transit system in this State. This Section does not apply to buses used for charter service, school buses, intrastate carriers while not providing transportation services pursuant to contracts with any local mass transit system, and private non-profit carriers.

Persons found guilty of violating this Section shall be fined $100.

P.A. 76-1586, § 12-605.2, added by P.A. 85-1364, § 1, eff. Jan. 1, 1989. Amended by P.A. 90-89, § 15, eff. Jan. 1, 1998.

Formerly Ill.Rev.Stat.1991, ch. 95 ½, ¶ 12-605.2.

5/12-606. Tow-trucks; identification; equipment; insurance

§ 12-606. Tow-trucks; identification; equipment; insurance.

(a) Every tow-truck, except those owned by governmental agencies, shall have displayed on each side thereof, a sign with letters not less than 2 inches in height, contrasting in color to that of the background, stating the full legal name, complete address (including street address and city), and telephone number of the owner or operator thereof. This information shall be permanently affixed to the sides of the tow truck.

(b) Every tow-truck shall be equipped with:

(1) One or more brooms and shovels;

(2) One or more trash cans of at least 5 gallon capacity; and

(3) One fire extinguisher. This extinguisher shall be either:

(i) of the dry chemical or carbon dioxide type with an aggregate rating of at least 4-B, C units, and bearing the approval of a laboratory qualified by the Division of Fire Prevention for this purpose; or

(ii) One that meets the requirements of the Federal Motor Carrier Safety Regulations of the United States Department of Transportation for fire extinguishers on commercial motor vehicles.

(c) Every owner or operator and driver of a tow-truck shall comply with Section 11-1413 of this Act and shall remove or cause to be removed all glass and debris, except any (i) hazardous substance as defined in Section 3.215 of the Environmental Protection Act,[1] (ii) hazardous waste as defined in Section 3.220 of the Environmental Protection Act,[2] and (iii) medical samples or waste, including but not limited to any blood samples, used syringes, other used medical supplies, or any other potentially infectious medical waste as defined in Section 3.360 of the Environmental Protection Act,[3] deposited upon any street or highway by the disabled vehicle being serviced, and shall in addition, spread dirt or sand or oil absorbent upon that portion of any street or highway where oil or grease has been deposited by the disabled vehicle being serviced.

(d) Every tow-truck operator shall in addition file an indemnity bond, insurance policy, or other proof of insurance in a form to be prescribed by the Secretary for: garagekeepers liability insurance, in an amount no less than a combined single limit of $500,000, and truck (auto) liability insurance in an amount no less than a combined single limit of $500,000, on hook coverage or garagekeepers coverage in an amount of no less than $25,000 which shall indemnify or insure the tow-truck operator for the following:

(1) Bodily injury or damage to the property of others.

(2) Damage to any vehicle towed by the tower.

(3) In case of theft, loss of, or damage to any vehicle stored, garagekeepers legal liability coverage in an amount of no less than $25,000.

(4) In case of injury to or occupational illness of the tow truck driver or helper, workers compensation insurance meeting the minimum requirements of the Workers' Compensation Act.[4]

Any such bond or policy shall be issued only by a bonding or insuring firm authorized to do business as such in the State of Illinois, and a certificate of such bond or policy shall be carried in the cab of each tow-truck.

(e) The bond or policy required in subsection (d) shall provide that the insurance carrier may cancel it by serving previous notice, as required by Sections 143.14 and 143.16 of the Illinois Insurance Code,[5] in writing, either personally or by registered mail, upon the owner or operator of the motor vehicle and upon the Secretary of State. Whenever any such bond or policy shall be so cancelled, the Secretary of State shall mark the policy "Cancelled" and shall require such owner or operator either to furnish a new bond or policy, in accordance with this Act.

P.A. 76-1586, § 12-606, added by P.A. 78-324, § 1, eff. Jan. 1, 1974. Amended by P.A. 83-1473, § 1, eff. Jan. 1, 1985; P.A. 85-1396, § 2, eff. Sept. 2, 1988; P.A. 86-444, § 1, eff. Jan. 1, 1990; P.A. 86-563, § 1, eff. Jan. 1, 1990; P.A. 86-1028, Art. II, § 2-44, eff. Feb. 5, 1990; P.A. 87-190, § 1, eff. Jan. 1, 1992; P.A. 87-757, § 3, eff. Oct. 3, 1991; P.A. 87-895, Art. 2, § 2-45, eff. Aug. 14, 1992; P.A. 88-415, § 10, eff. Aug. 20, 1993; P.A. 88-670, Art. 3, § 3-80, eff. Dec. 2, 1994; P.A. 89-433, § 5, eff. Dec. 15, 1995; P.A. 92-574, § 70, eff. June 26, 2002.

Formerly Ill.Rev.Stat.1991, ch. 95 ½, ¶ 12-606.

1 415 ILCS 5/3.215.

2 415 ILCS 5/3.220.

3 415 ILCS 5/3.360.

4 820 ILCS 305/1 et seq.

5 215 ILCS 5561143.14 and 5/143.16.

Another § 12-606 was added by P.A. 78-436; see § 12-608, post.

5/12-607. Suspension System

§ 12-607. Suspension System.

(a) It shall be unlawful to operate a motor vehicle on any highway of this State when the suspension system has been modified from the original manufactured design by lifting the body from the chassis in excess of 3 inches or to cause the horizontal line from the front to the rear bumper to vary over 3 inches in height when measured from a level surface of the highway to the lower edge of the bumper, except that it is unlawful to operate a street rod or custom vehicle when the suspension system has been modified from the original manufactured design so that the horizontal line from the front to the rear bumper varies over 7 inches in height when measured from a level surface of the highway to the lower edge of the bumper.

(b) Nothing in this Section shall prevent the installation of manufactured heavy duty equipment to include shock absorbers and overload springs, nor shall anything contained in this Section prevent a person to operate a motor vehicle on any highway of this State with normal wear of the suspension system if normal wear does not affect the control or safe operation of the vehicle. This Section shall not apply to motor vehicles designed or modified primarily for off-highway racing purposes while such vehicles are in tow or to motorcycles or motor driven cycles.

P.A. 76-1586, § 12-607, added by P.A. 78-436, § 1, eff. Jan. 1, 1974. Amended by P.A. 92-668, § 5, eff. Jan. 1, 2003.

Formerly Ill.Rev.Stat.1991, ch. 95 ½, ¶ 12-607.

5/12–607.1. Frame and floor height

§ 12–607.1. Frame and floor height. (a) No person shall operate upon a highway a first division vehicle which has a clearance between the frame and ground in excess of 22 inches. The lowest portion of the body floor shall not be more than 4 inches above the top of the frame. No such vehicle shall be modified to cause the vehicle body or chassis to come in contact with the ground, expose the fuel tank to damage from collision or cause the wheels to come in contact with the body under normal operation.

(b) No person shall operate upon a highway a second division vehicle which has a clearance between the frame and ground which is in excess of the limits specified within this subsection for its gross vehicle weight rating (GVWR) category. For the purpose of this section, GVWR means the manufacturer's gross vehicle weight rating whether or not the vehicle is modified by the use of parts not originally installed by the manufacturer. The stacking or attaching of vehicle frames (one frame on top of or beneath another frame) is prohibited. No portion of the body floor shall be raised above the frame.

(1) The frame height of second division vehicles, whose GVWR is under 4,500 pounds, shall be no more than 24 inches.

(2) The frame height of second division vehicles, whose GVWR is more than 4,500 pounds and less than 7,500 pounds, shall be no more than 26 inches.

(3) The frame height of second division vehicles, whose GVWR is more than 7,500 pounds and less than 10,000 pounds, shall be no more than 28 inches.

(c) Under subsections (a) or (b) of this Section, measurements shall be made when a vehicle is unladen on a level surface at the lowest point from the bottom of the original vehicle manufacturer's longitudinal frame rail between the front axle and second axle on the vehicle.

(d) This Section does not apply to specially designed or modified motor vehicles when operated off the highways. Such motor vehicles may be transported upon the highway only by use of a trailer or semitrailer. The specially designed or modified motor vehicle may also be transported upon another vehicle, providing that the entire weight of the specifically designed or modified vehicle is resting upon the transporting vehicle.

(e) Any violation of this Section is a Class C misdemeanor. A second conviction under this Section shall be punished with a fine of not less than $500. An officer making an arrest under this Section shall order the vehicle driver to remove the vehicle from the highway. A person convicted under this Section shall be ordered to bring his vehicle into compliance with this Section.

P.A. 76–1586, § 12–607.1, added by P.A. 86–498, § 1, eff. Jan. 1, 1990. Amended by P.A. 90–89, § 15, eff. Jan. 1, 1998.

Formerly Ill.Rev.Stat.1991, ch. 95 ½, ¶ 12–607.1.

5/12–608. Bumpers

§ 12–608. Bumpers.

(a) It shall be unlawful to operate any motor vehicle with a gross vehicle weight rating of 9,000 pounds or less or any motor vehicle registered as a recreational vehicle under this Code on any highway of this State unless such motor vehicle is equipped with both a front and rear bumper.

Except as indicated below, maximum bumper heights of such motor vehicles shall be determined by weight category of gross vehicle weight rating (GVWR) measured from a level surface to the highest point of the bottom of the bumper when the vehicle is unloaded and the tires are inflated to the manufacturer's recommended pressure.

Maximum bumper heights are as follows:

	Maximum Front Bumper height	Maximum Rear Bumper Height
All motor vehicles of the first division except multipurpose passenger vehicles:	22 inches	22 inches
Multipurpose passenger vehicles and all other motor vehicles:		
4,500 lbs. and under GVWR	24 inches	26 inches
4,501 lbs. through 7,500 lbs. GVWR	27 inches	29 inches
7,501 lbs. through 9,000 lbs. GVWR	28 inches	30 inches

For any vehicle with bumpers or attaching components which have been modified or altered from the original manufacturer's design in order to conform with the maximum bumper requirements of this section, the bumper height shall be measured from a level surface to the bottom of the vehicle frame rail at the most forward and rearward points of the frame rail. The bumper on any vehicle so modified or altered shall be at least 4.5 inches in vertical height and extend no less than the width of the respective wheel tracks outermost distance.

However, nothing in this Section shall prevent the installation of bumper guards.

(b) This Section shall not apply to street rods, custom vehicles, motor vehicles designed or modified primarily for off-highway purposes while such vehicles are in tow or to motorcycles or motor driven cycles, nor to motor vehicles registered as antique vehicles when the original design of such antique vehicles did not include bumpers. The provisions of this Section shall not apply to any motor vehicle driven during the first 1000 recorded miles of that vehicle, when such vehicle is owned or operated by a manufacturer, dealer or transporter displaying a special plate or plates as described in Chapter 3 of this Code while such vehicle is (1) being delivered from the manufacturing or assembly plant directly to the purchasing dealer or distributor, or from one dealership or distributor to another; (2) being moved by the most direct route from one location to another for the purpose of installing special bodies or equipment; or (3) being driven for purposes of demonstration by a prospective buyer with the dealer or his agent present in the cab of the vehicle during the demonstration.

The dealer shall, prior to the receipt of any deposit made or any contract signed by the buyer to secure the purchase of a vehicle, inform such buyer, by written statement signed by the purchaser to indicate acknowledgement of the contents thereof, of the legal requirements of this Section regarding front and rear bumpers if such vehicle is not to be equipped with bumpers at the time of delivery.

(c) Any violation of this Section is a Class C misdemeanor. A second conviction under this Section shall be punishable with a fine of not less than $500. An officer making an arrest under this Section shall order the vehicle driver to remove the vehicle from the highway. A person convicted under this Section shall be ordered to bring his vehicle into compliance with this Section.

P.A. 76–1586, § 12–606, added by P.A. 78–436, § 1, eff. Jan. 1, 1974. Renumbered § 12–608 and amended by P.A. 78–1297, § 30, eff. March 4, 1975. Amended by P.A. 83–838, § 1, eff. Jan. 1, 1984; P.A. 83–1386, § 1, eff. Jan. 1, 1985; P.A. 86–498, § 1, eff. Jan. 1, 1990; P.A. 92–668, § 5, eff. Jan. 1, 2003.

Formerly Ill.Rev.Stat.1991, ch. 95 ½, ¶ 12–608.

5/12–609. Disposal of motor vehicles bearing police markings

§ 12–609. No official or employee of the State or any political subdivision thereof shall sell, trade or otherwise dispose of any motor vehicle bearing equipment, markings, or other indicia of police authority unless, prior to delivery of the vehicle, the equipment and markings have been sufficiently altered or obliterated to remove the appearance of such authority.

P.A. 76–1586, § 12–609, added by P.A. 79–544, § 1, eff. Oct. 1, 1975. Amended by P.A. 79–1454, § 44, eff. Aug. 31, 1976.

Formerly Ill.Rev.Stat.1991, ch. 95 ½, ¶ 12–609.

Another § 12–609 was renumbered as § 12–610 by P.A. 85–273, § 1, eff. Jan. 1, 1988.

5/12–610. Headset receivers

§ 12–610. Headset receivers.

(a) Except as provided under Section 11–1403.3, no driver of a motor vehicle on the highways of this State shall wear headset receivers while driving.

(b) This Section does not prohibit the use of a headset type receiving equipment used exclusively for safety or traffic engineering studies, by law enforcement personnel on duty, or emergency medical services and fire service personnel.

(c) This Section does not prohibit the use of any single sided headset type receiving and transmitting equipment designed to be used in or on one ear which is used exclusively for providing two-way radio vocal communications by an individual in possession of a current and valid novice class or higher amateur radio license issued by the Federal Communications Commission and an amateur radio operator special registration plate issued under Section 3–607 of this Code.

(d) This Section does not prohibit the use of a single-sided headset or earpiece with a cellular or other mobile telephone.

P.A. 76–1586, § 12–609, added by P.A. 80–361, § 1, eff. Aug. 26, 1977. Renumbered § 12–610 and amended by P.A. 85–273, § 1, eff. Jan. 1, 1988; P.A. 85–293, Art. III, § 21, eff. Sept. 8, 1987. Amended by P.A. 86–1193, § 1, eff. Aug. 29, 1990; P.A. 89–551, § 5, eff. Jan. 1, 1997; P.A. 92–152, § 5, eff. July 25, 2001.

Formerly Ill.Rev.Stat.1991, ch. 95 ½, ¶ 12–610.

5/12–610.5. Tinted registration plate covers

§ 12–610.5. Tinted registration plate covers.

(a) It shall be unlawful to operate any motor vehicle that is equipped with tinted plastic or tinted glass registration plate covers.

(b) A violation of this Section or a similar provision of a local ordinance shall be an offense against laws and ordinances regulating the movement of traffic.

P.A. 76–1586, § 12–610.5, added by P.A. 89–245, § 5, eff. Jan. 1, 1996.

5/12–611. Sound amplification systems

§ 12–611. No driver of any motor vehicle within this State shall operate or permit operation of any sound amplification system which can be heard outside the vehicle from 75 or more feet when the vehicle is being operated upon a highway, unless such system is being operated to request assistance or warn of a hazardous situation.

This Section does not apply to authorized emergency vehicles.

Any violation of the provisions of this Section shall be a petty offense punishable by a fine not to exceed $50.

P.A. 76–1586, § 12–611, added by P.A. 86–1240, § 1, eff. Jan. 1, 1991. Amended by P.A. 91–919, § 5, eff. Jan. 1, 2001.

Formerly Ill.Rev.Stat.1991, ch. 95 ½, ¶ 12–611.

Validity

The Supreme Court of Illinois has held that this section violates the First Amendment's free speech guarantee in the case of People v. Jones, 1999, 188 Ill.2d 352, 242 Ill.Dec. 267, 721 N.E.2d 546. P.A. 91–919 amended this section to delete the exception for vehicles engaged in advertising.

5/12–612. False or secret compartment in a motor vehicle

§ 12–612. False or secret compartment in a motor vehicle.

(a) Offenses. It is unlawful for any person to own or operate any motor vehicle he or she knows to contain a false or secret compartment. It is unlawful for any person to knowingly install, create, build, or fabricate in any motor vehicle a false or secret compartment.

(b) Definitions. For purposes of this Section, a "false or secret compartment" means any enclosure that is intended and designed to be used to conceal, hide, and prevent discovery by law enforcement officers of the false or secret compartment, or its contents, and which is integrated into a vehicle. For purpose of this Section, a person's intention to use a false or secret compartment to conceal the contents of the compartment from a law enforcement officer may be inferred from factors including, but not limited to, the discovery of a person, firearm, controlled substance, or other contraband within the false or secret compartment, or from the discovery of evidence of the previous placement of a person, firearm, controlled substance, or other contraband within the false or secret compartment.

(c) Forfeiture. Any motor vehicle containing a false or secret compartment, as well as any items within that compartment, shall be subject to seizure by the Department of State Police or by any municipal or other local law enforcement agency within whose jurisdiction that property is found as provided in Sections 36–1 and 36–2 of the Criminal Code of 1961 (720 ILCS 5/36–1 and 5/36–2).

(d) Sentence. A violation of this Section is a Class C misdemeanor.

P.A. 76–1586, § 12–612, added by P.A. 91–359, § 5, eff. Jan. 1, 2000.

ARTICLE VII. SPECIAL REQUIREMENTS FOR VEHICLES OF THE SECOND DIVISION

Section

5/12-701. Tractors, traction engines and motor trucks—Operation on highways—Turning on highways during farming operations—Violations

§ 12-701. Tractors, traction engines and motor trucks—Operation on highways—Turning on highways during farming operations—Violations. No tractor, traction engine, motor truck or other similar vehicle shall be operated across, over or along any public highway of this State which has been oil-treated, if any such vehicle has on the periphery of any of the road wheels any block, stud, flange, cleat, ridge, lug, or any projection of metal or wood which projects radially beyond the tread or traffic surface of the tire; except that this prohibition shall not apply to tractors or traction engines equipped with what is known as crawler type tractors, when the same does not contain any projections of any kind likely to injure the surface of the road, nor to tractors, traction engines and similar vehicles which have upon their road wheels V-shaped, diagonal or other cleats arranged in such a manner as to be continuously in contact with the road surface. In no event shall the oil mat surface of any oil-treated public road be used as an area or space for turning any tractor or other farm machinery in carrying on or performing any farming operations upon the adjacent land. Provided, that nothing in this Section contained shall prohibit the operation of tractors, traction engines or motor trucks across any oil-treated road in order to reach adjacent lands or the operation of any such vehicles upon the treated portion of such oil-treated roads if there is no untreated portion thereof over which they may be operated or the operation of any such vehicles on oil-treated roads if in passing along said road they travel over the portion of said road which does not constitute the oil mat surface created by said oil treatment or the use of flexible tire chains on any tractor, traction engine, motor truck or other similar vehicle being operated upon any such oil-treated road.

It is unlawful for any person to operate any tractor, traction engine, motor truck or other similar vehicle over and along any public highway of this State, which has been oil-treated, in violation of the provisions of this Section.

P.A. 76-1586, § 12-125, eff. July 1, 1970. Renumbered § 12-701 by P.A. 77-37, § 1, eff. Jan. 1, 1972. Amended by P.A. 77-2720, § 1, eff. Jan. 1, 1973; P.A. 78-255, § 61, eff. Oct. 1, 1973; P.A. 80-911, § 1, eff. Oct. 1, 1977.

Formerly Ill.Rev.Stat.1991, ch. 95 ½, ¶ 12-701.

5/12-702. Certain vehicles to carry flares or other warning devices

§ 12-702. Certain vehicles to carry flares or other warning devices.

(a) No person shall operate any motor vehicle of the second division weighing more than 8,000 pounds or any vehicle of the second division weighing 8,000 pounds or less towing a trailer or any motor vehicle towing a house trailer upon any highway outside an urban district at any time unless there is carried in such vehicle the following equipment, except as provided in paragraph (b) of this Section:

1. At least 3 liquid-burning flares, or 3 red electric lanterns or 3 portable red emergency reflectors, each of which is capable of being seen and distinguished at a distance of not less than 500 feet when lighted lamps are required, provided that emergency reflectors meeting the requirements of Federal Motor Vehicle Safety Standard No. 125 shall be deemed acceptable as regards visibility and color; and

2. At least 3 red-burning 15-minute fusees unless red electric lanterns or portable red emergency reflectors are carried; and

3. At least 2 red-cloth flags, not less than 12 inches square, with standards to support flags or in lieu thereof, 2 portable emergency reflectors meeting the requirements of Federal Motor Vehicle Safety Standard No. 125.

(b) No person shall operate at the time and under the conditions stated in paragraph (a) of this Section any motor vehicle used for the transportation of explosives, any cargo tank truck used for the transportation of flammable liquids or compressed gases or any motor vehicle using compressed gas as a fuel unless there is carried in such vehicle 3 red electric lanterns or 3 portable red emergency reflectors meeting the requirements of paragraph (a) of this Section, and such vehicle shall not carry any flares, fusees or signals produced by flame.

(c) Whenever any motor vehicle of the second division weighing more than 8,000 pounds or any vehicle of the second division weighing 8,000 pounds or less towing a trailer or any motor vehicle towing a house trailer is disabled upon the roadway of any highway or the shoulder thereof outside an urban district or on any controlled access highway within an urban district at any time when lighted lamps are required, the driver of such vehicle shall display the following warning devices upon the highway during the time the vehicle is so disabled, except as provided in paragraph (d) of this Section:

1. A lighted fusee, a lighted red electric lantern or a portable red emergency reflector shall be immediately placed at the traffic side of the vehicle in the direction of the nearest approaching traffic. However, the driver of such vehicle upon learning of the disability may simultaneously flash the 2 front and 2 rear turn signals as a vehicular traffic warning and continue such flashing until the portable signals have been placed as required by this Section and during the time such portable emergency signals are being picked up for storage prior to the movement of the vehicle.

2. As soon thereafter as possible, but in any event within the burning period of the fusee (15 minutes), the driver shall place 3 liquid-burning flares, or 3 lighted red electric lanterns or 3 portable red emergency reflectors on

the roadway or shoulder of the highway in the following order:

One approximately 100 feet from the disabled vehicle in the center of the lane or shoulder occupied by such vehicle and toward traffic approaching in that lane; and

One approximately 100 feet in the opposite direction from the disabled vehicle and in the center of the traffic lane or shoulder occupied by such vehicle; and

One at the traffic side of the disabled vehicle not less than 10 feet to the rear or forward thereof in the direction of the nearest approaching traffic. If a lighted red electric lantern or a portable red emergency reflector has been placed at the traffic side of the vehicle in accordance with paragraph (c)(1) of this Section, it may be used for this purpose.

(d) Whenever any vehicle referred to in this Section is disabled within 500 feet of a curve, hill crest or other obstruction to view, the warning signal in that direction shall be so placed as to afford ample warning to other users of the highway, but in no case less than 100 feet nor more than 500 feet from the disabled vehicle.

(e) Whenever any vehicle of a type referred to in this Section is disabled upon any roadway or shoulder of a divided highway during the time that lighted lamps are required, the appropriate warning devices prescribed in paragraph (a)(1) and (2) of this Section shall be placed as follows:

One at a distance of approximately 200 feet from the vehicle in the center of the lane or shoulder occupied by the stopped vehicle and in the direction of traffic approaching in that lane; and

One at a distance of approximately 100 feet from the vehicle in the center of the lane or shoulder occupied by the vehicle and in the direction of traffic approaching in that lane; and

One at the traffic side of the vehicle and approximately 10 feet from the vehicle in the direction of the nearest approaching traffic.

(f) Whenever any vehicle of a type referred to in this Section is disabled upon the roadway of any highway or the shoulder thereof outside an urban district or on any controlled access highway within an urban district at any time when the display of fusees, flares, red electric lanterns or portable red emergency reflectors are not required, the driver of the vehicle shall display 2 red-cloth flags or 2 portable emergency reflectors meeting the requirements of Federal Motor Vehicle Safety Standard No. 125 upon the roadway or shoulder in the lane of traffic occupied by the disabled vehicle in the following order:

One at a distance of approximately 100 feet in advance of the vehicle; and

One at a distance of approximately 100 feet in the rear of the vehicle.

(g) Whenever any vehicle of a type referred to in this Section is disabled upon any roadway or shoulder of a divided highway during the time that lighted lamps are not required, the driver of such vehicle shall display 2 red-cloth flags or 2 portable emergency reflectors meeting the requirements of Federal Motor Vehicle Safety Standard No. 125 upon the roadway or shoulder in the center of the lane of traffic occupied by the disabled vehicle in the following order:

One at a distance of approximately 200 feet to the rear of the vehicle; and

One at a distance of approximately 100 feet to the rear of the vehicle.

(h) Whenever any motor vehicle used for the transportation of explosives, or any cargo tank truck used for the transportation of any flammable liquid or compressed flammable gas or any motor vehicle using compressed gas as a fuel is disabled upon a highway of this State at any time or place mentioned in paragraph (c) of this Section, the driver of such vehicle shall immediately display 3 red electric lanterns or portable red emergency reflectors placed in the following order:

One at the traffic side of the vehicle and approximately 10 feet from the vehicle in the direction of the nearest approaching traffic; and

One at a distance of approximately 100 feet to the front of the disabled vehicle in the center of the lane of traffic or shoulder occupied by such vehicle; and

One at a distance of approximately 100 feet to the rear of the disabled vehicle in the center of the lane of traffic or shoulder occupied by such vehicle. Flares, fusees or signals produced by flame shall not be used as warning devices for disabled vehicles of the type mentioned in this paragraph.

(i) The flares, fusees, red electric lanterns, portable red emergency reflectors and flags to be displayed as required in this Section shall conform with the requirements of paragraphs (a) and (b) of this Section applicable thereto.

P.A. 76–1586, § 12–128, eff. July 1, 1970. Amended by P.A. 76–1725, § 1, eff. July 1, 1970; P.A. 76–2187, § 1, eff. July 1, 1970. Renumbered § 12–702 by P.A. 77–37, § 1, eff. Jan. 1, 1972. Amended by P.A. 78–280, § 1, eff. Jan. 1, 1974; P.A. 78–693, § 1, eff. Jan. 1, 1974; P.A. 78–1297, § 30, eff. March 4, 1975; P.A. 89–687, § 5, eff. June 1, 1997.

Formerly Ill.Rev.Stat.1991, ch. 95 ½, ¶ 12–702.

5/12–703. Road oil vehicles—Dripping on certain highways forbidden

§ 12–703. Road oil vehicles—Dripping on certain highways forbidden. No person shall operate, on a durable all-weather highway of a type other than gravel or crushed stone, any vehicle used for the purpose of applying road oil, liquid asphalt or similar material to road surfaces unless such vehicle is so equipped as to absolutely prevent such material from dripping on such highway, nor shall such material be allowed to drip on any such highway.

P.A. 76–1586, § 12–129, eff. July 1, 1970. Renumbered § 12–703 by P.A. 77–37, § 1, eff. Jan. 1, 1972.

Formerly Ill.Rev.Stat.1991, ch. 95 ½, ¶ 12–703.

5/12–704, 5/12–704.1. §§ 12–704, 12–704.1. Repealed by P.A. 88–415, § 15, eff. Aug. 20, 1993

5/12–704.3. Motor vehicles using alternate fuels; markings

§ 12–704.3. Motor vehicles using alternate fuels; markings. Notwithstanding any other regulation or requirement, every motor vehicle using liquefied petroleum gas or compressed natural gas must be marked in accordance with guidelines established by the National Fire Protection Association's (NFPA) standards for the Storage and Handling of Liquefied Petroleum Gases and for Compressed Natural Gas Vehicular Fuel Systems and published by that body as NFPA 58 and NFPA 52 dated February 10, 1992 and August 14, 1992, respectively.

The sign or decal shall be maintained in good legible condition. A sign or decal that is deteriorated or defaced so as to impair its legibility, quick recognition, or meaning shall be replaced by a new sign or decal.

P.A. 76-1586, § 12-704.3, added by P.A. 83-1027, § 2, eff. July 1, 1984. Amended by P.A. 88-415, § 10, eff. Aug. 20, 1993.

Formerly Ill.Rev.Stat.1991, ch. 95 ½, ¶ 12-704.3.

5/12-705. § 12-705. Repealed by P.A. 88-415, § 15, eff. Aug. 20, 1993

5/12-706. Fire apparatus—Safety belts

§ 12-706. Fire apparatus—Safety belts. No fire apparatus equipped to carry firemen on the outside of such vehicle on the sides, or rear, or both, shall be operated without first installing on the fire apparatus on the sides and rear thereof a sufficient number of safety belts and safety belt connections to protect the maximum number of firemen who can occupy the sides and rear of such apparatus while responding to alarms of fire. The municipality shall cause inspection of such safety equipment at least semi-annually.

P.A. 76-1586, § 12-139, added by P.A. 76-2190, § 1, eff. July 1, 1970. Renumbered § 12-706 by P.A. 77-37, § 1, eff. Jan. 1, 1972.

Formerly Ill.Rev.Stat.1991, ch. 95 ½, ¶ 12-706.

5/12-707. Vehicle passenger capacity

§ 12-707. Vehicle passenger capacity. No school bus, commuter van or motor vehicle owned by or used for hire by and in connection with the operation of private or public schools, day camps, summer camps or nursery schools or in charter operations, and no commuter van or passenger car used for a for-profit ridesharing arrangement, shall be operated if it is occupied by more passengers than recommended by the manufacturer thereof if the vehicle is manufactured as a passenger vehicle; if the vehicle is manufactured for use other than passenger, then it shall not accommodate more passengers than provided for by the manufacturer in passenger vehicles of like style or rating.

P.A. 76-1586, § 12-133, eff. July 1, 1970. Renumbered § 12-707 by P.A. 77-37, § 1, eff. Jan. 1, 1972. Amended by P.A. 78-499, § 1, eff. Aug. 30, 1973; P.A. 80-529, § 1, eff. Jan. 1, 1979; P.A. 81-509, § 1, eff. Jan. 1, 1980; P.A. 83-1091, § 1, eff. July 1, 1984.

Formerly Ill.Rev.Stat.1991, ch. 95 ½, ¶ 12-707.

5/12-707.01. Liability insurance

§ 12-707.01. Liability insurance. No school bus, commuter van or motor vehicle owned by or used for hire by and in connection with the operation of private or public schools, day camps, summer camps or nursery schools, and no commuter van or passenger car used for a for-profit ridesharing arrangement, shall be operated for such purposes unless the owner thereof shall carry a minimum of personal injury liability insurance in the amount of $25,000 for any one person in any one accident, and subject to the limit for one person, $100,000 for two or more persons injured by reason of the operation of the vehicle in any one accident.

P.A. 76-1586, § 12-707.01, added by P.A. 81-509, § 1, eff. Jan. 1, 1980. Amended by P.A. 83-1091, § 1, eff. July 1, 1984.

Formerly Ill.Rev.Stat.1991, ch. 95 ½, ¶ 12-707.01.

5/12-708. Operator protective frames on tractor-mower combinations

§ 12-708. Operator protective frames on tractor-mower combinations. No tractor unit over 16 engine horsepower designed for mowing or tractor-mower combination unit over 16 engine horsepower owned or leased by the Department, a municipal corporation or political subdivision shall be operated for the purpose of mowing vegetation on highway right-of-way unless the tractor of such unit is equipped with an operator protective frame conforming to the specifications prescribed by regulations under the United States Occupational Safety and Health Act of 1970, as amended,[1] and with a seat safety belt.

The operator protective frame may be incorporated into a cab which design shall conform to the specifications established by the United States Occupational Safety and Health Act of 1970, as amended.[1]

The seat safety belt must meet the requirements provided in Section 12-603 of this Act.

P.A. 76-1586, § 12-140, added by P.A. 76-2191, § 1, eff. July 1, 1970. Renumbered § 12-708 and amended by P.A. 77-37, § 1, eff. Jan. 1, 1972. Amended by P.A. 77-157, § 1, eff. Jan. 1, 1972; P.A. 77-202, § 1, eff. Jan. 1, 1972; P.A. 77-2829, § 40, eff. Dec. 22, 1972; P.A. 78-255, § 61, eff. Oct. 1, 1973; P.A. 78-748, § 1, eff. Jan. 1, 1974; P.A. 78-1297, § 58, eff. March 4, 1975; P.A. 81-435, § 1, eff. Jan. 1, 1980.

Formerly Ill.Rev.Stat.1991, ch. 95 ½, ¶ 12-708.

1 29 U.S.C.A. § 651 et seq.

5/12-709. Slow-moving vehicle emblem

§ 12-709. Slow-moving vehicle emblem.

(a) Every animal drawn vehicle, farm tractor, implement of husbandry and special mobile equipment, when operated on a highway must display a slow-moving vehicle emblem mounted on the rear except as provided in paragraph (b) of this Section. Special mobile equipment is exempt when operated within the limits of a construction or maintenance project where traffic control devices are used in compliance with the applicable provisions of the manual and specifications adopted under Section 11-301 of the "Illinois Vehicle Code".

(b) Every vehicle or unit described in paragraph (a) of this Section when operated in combination on a highway must display a slow-moving vehicle emblem as follows:

1. Where the towed unit or any load thereon partially or totally obscures the slow-moving vehicle emblem on the towing unit, the towed unit shall be equipped with a slow-moving vehicle emblem. In such cases the towing unit need not display the emblem.

2. Where the slow-moving vehicle emblem on the towing unit is not obscured by the towed unit or its load, then either or both may be equipped with the required emblem but it shall be sufficient if either displays it.

3. A registered truck towed behind a farm tractor in conformity with the provisions of Section 11-1418 of the "Illinois Vehicle Code" must display a slow-moving vehicle emblem in the manner provided in paragraph (c) while being towed on a highway if the emblem on the towing vehicle is partially or totally obscured.

(c) The slow-moving vehicle emblem required by paragraphs (a) and (b) of this Section must meet or exceed the specifications and mounting requirements established by the Department. Such specifications and mounting requirements shall, on and before August 31, 2004, be based on the specifications adopted by the American Society of Agricultural Engineers and published by that body as ASAE S 276.2 dated March, 1968 or as ASAE S 276.5. On and after September 1, 2004, the specifications and mounting requirements shall be based on the specifications adopted by the American Society of Agricultural Engineers and published by that body as ASAE S 276.5 NOV 97. No advertising or other marking shall appear upon the emblem except that specified by the American Society of Agricultural Engineers to identify the standard to which the material complies. Each original package containing a slow-moving vehicle emblem shall display a notice on the outside of the package stating that such emblem shall only be used for the purposes stated in subsections (a) and (b).

(d) A slow-moving vehicle emblem is intended as a safety identification device and shall not be displayed on any vehicle nor displayed in any manner other than as described in paragraphs (a), (b) and (c) of this Section. A violation of this subsection (d) is a petty offense punishable by a fine of $25 for the first offense and $75 for a second or subsequent offense within one year of the first offense.

P.A. 76–1586, § 12–141 added by P.A. 76–2192, § 1, eff. July 1, 1970. Renumbered § 12–709 by P.A. 77–37, § 1, eff. Jan. 1, 1972. Amended by P.A. 78–253, § 1, eff. Oct. 1, 1973; P.A. 78–748, § 1, eff. Jan. 1, 1974; P.A. 78–1297, § 58, eff. March 4, 1975; P.A. 86–1259, § 1, eff. Jan. 1, 1991; P.A. 91–505, § 5, eff. Jan. 1, 2000; P.A. 92–72, § 5, eff. Jan. 1, 2002.

Formerly Ill.Rev.Stat.1991, ch. 95 ½, ¶ 12–709.

5/12–710. Rear fender splash guards

§ 12–710. Rear fender splash guards. It is unlawful for any person to operate any vehicle of the second division, except a truck tractor, to which this Section is applicable upon any highway of this State unless such vehicle is equipped with rear fender splash guards of either the contour type or the flap type which comply with the specifications provided in this Section for the type of splash guards used on the vehicle, and which are so attached as to prevent the splashing of mud or water upon the windshield of other motor vehicles.

(a) Specifications for contour type splash guards. When contour type rear fender splash guards are used, they shall contour the wheel in such a manner that the relationship of the inside surface of any such splash guard to the tread surface of the tire or wheel shall be relatively parallel, both laterally and across the wheel, at least throughout the top 90 degrees of the rear 180 degrees of the wheel surface; provided however, on vehicles which have a clearance of less than 5 inches between the top of the tire or wheel and that part of the body of the vehicle directly above the tire or wheel when the vehicle is loaded to maximum legal capacity, the curved portion of the splash guard need only extend from a point directly behind the center of the rear axle and to the rear of the wheel surface upwards to within at least 2 inches of the bottom line of the body when the vehicle is loaded to maximum legal capacity. There shall be a downward extension of the curved surface which shall end not more than 12 inches from the ground when the vehicle is loaded to maximum legal capacity. This downward extension shall be part of the curved surface or attached directly to such curved surface, but it need not contour the wheel. Such contour type splash guards shall be wide enough to cover the full tread width of the tire or tires being protected and shall be installed not more than 6 inches from the tread surface of the tire or wheel when the vehicle is loaded to maximum legal capacity. The splash guard shall have a lip or flange on its outside edge to minimize side throw and splash. The lip or flange shall extend toward the center of the wheel, and shall be perpendicular to and extend not less than 2 inches below the inside or bottom surface line or plane of the guard. Such contour type splash guards may be constructed of either a rigid or flexible material, but shall be attached in such a manner that, regardless of movement either by the splash guards or the vehicle, the splash guards will retain their general parallel relationship to the tread surface of the tire or wheel under all ordinary operating conditions.

(b) Specifications for flap type splash guards. When flap type splash guards are used, they shall be wide enough to cover the full tread width of the tire or tires being protected; shall be so installed that they extend from the underside of the vehicle in a vertical plane behind the rear wheels to within 12 inches of the ground, when the vehicle is loaded to maximum legal capacity; shall be so constructed and attached so that when the vehicle is in forward motion such splash guard will not deviate or move backward from the vertical plane by an angle of more than 30 degrees measured from the vertical plane and so that when the forward motion of the vehicle causes such splash guard to deviate from the vertical plane, the bottom of such flap type splash guard will not be more than 15 inches from the ground, when the vehicle is loaded to maximum legal capacity. Such flap type splash guard may be constructed of either a rigid or flexible material.

(c) Exemptions. This Section shall not apply to vehicles the construction or design of which does not require such splash guards, nor to vehicles in-transit and capable only of using temporary splash guards prescribed by the Department, nor to pole trailers.

P.A. 76–1586, § 12–130. Renumbered § 12–710 by P.A. 77–37, § 1, eff. Jan. 1, 1972. Amended by P.A. 77–36, § 1, eff. July 1, 1971; P.A. 77–2829, § 40, eff. Dec. 22, 1972; P.A. 78–255, § 61, eff. Oct. 1, 1973; P.A. 78–748, § 1, eff. Jan. 1, 1974; P.A. 78–1297, § 58, eff. March 4, 1975; P.A. 85–830, § 1, eff. Sept. 24, 1987; P.A. 85–1010, § 1, eff. March 2, 1988; P.A. 89–117, § 10, eff. July 7, 1995.

Formerly Ill.Rev.Stat.1991, ch. 95 ½, ¶ 12–710.

P.A. 85–1010 recognized the amendment by P.A. 85–830.

5/12–711. Trucks equipped with self-compactors or roll-off hoists and roll-on containers for garbage or refuse hauls; audible warning signal

§ 12–711. Commencing January 1, 1987, all trucks equipped with self-compactors or roll-off hoists and roll-on containers for garbage or refuse hauls shall, before operating on any public or private highway, alley or parking area of this State, be equipped with an operably working external audible warning signal device that meets the standard of American National Standards Institute, SAE J994b, Type A, B or C, which is activated when the vehicle is operated in reverse or when top-hinged tailgates are open.

P.A. 76–1586, § 12–711, added by P.A. 84–813, § 1, eff. Sept. 22, 1985.

Formerly Ill.Rev.Stat.1991, ch. 95 ½, ¶ 12–711.

5/12–712. Construction equipment to display company name

§ 12–712. Construction equipment to display company name.

(a) Construction equipment that is capable of being self propelled or any construction equipment capable of being towed shall display on the side of the equipment the name of the company for which it is employed. The name shall be in letters at least 2 inches tall and one-half inch wide. This Section shall not apply to any motor vehicle upon which is affixed the insignia required under Section 18c-4701 of the Illinois Commercial Transportation Law.[1]

(b) Any person convicted of violating this Section shall be guilty of a petty offense and subject to a fine not to exceed $100.

P.A. 76-1586, § 12-712, added by P.A. 87-1160, § 1, eff. Jan. 1, 1993. Amended by P.A. 88-45, Art. II, § 2-54, eff. July 6, 1993.

Formerly Ill.Rev.Stat., ch. 95½, ¶ 12-712.

[1] 625 ILCS 5/18c-4701.

Former § 12-712, prohibiting the possession and use of radar detection devices, was renumbered § 12-714 by P.A. 88-45, Art. II, § 2-54.

P.A. 88-45, Article II, of the First 1993 General Revisory Act, resolved multiple actions in the 87th General Assembly and made certain technical corrections in P.A. 87-895 through P.A. 87-1280.

5/12-713. Commercial trucks used by construction contractors or subcontractors to display company name

§ 12-713. Commercial trucks used by construction contractors or subcontractors to display company name.

(a) Every second division vehicle operating commercially in this State that is used by a construction contractor or subcontractor shall display on the side of the vehicle or its trailer the name of the company for which it is employed. The name shall be in letters at least 2 inches tall and one-half inch wide. This Section shall not apply to any motor vehicle upon which is affixed the insignia required under Section 18c-4701 of the Illinois Commercial Transportation Law.[1]

(b) Any person convicted of violating this Section shall be guilty of a petty offense and subject to a fine not to exceed $100.

P.A. 76-1586, § 12-713, added by P.A. 87-1160, § 1, eff. Jan. 1, 1993. Amended by P.A. 88-45, Art. II, § 2-54, eff. July 6, 1993.

Formerly Ill.Rev.Stat., ch. 95½, ¶ 12-713.

[1] 625 ILCS 5/18c-4701.

Former § 12-713, prohibiting the possession and use of radar jamming devices, was renumbered § 12-715 by P.A. 88-45, Art. II, § 2-54.

P.A. 88-45, Article II, of the First 1993 General Revisory Act, resolved multiple actions in the 87th General Assembly and made certain technical corrections in P.A. 87-895 through P.A. 87-1280.

5/12-714. Possession and use of radar detection devices prohibited

§ 12-714. Possession and use of radar detection devices prohibited.

(a) No person shall operate or be in actual physical control of a commercial motor vehicle as defined in Section 6-500(6) of this Code while the motor vehicle is equipped with any instrument designed to detect the presence of police radar for the purpose of monitoring vehicular speed.

(b) Notwithstanding subsection (a) of this Section, a person operating a commercial motor vehicle as defined in Section 6-500(6) of this Code, who possesses within the vehicle a radar detecting device that is contained in a locked opaque box or similar container, or that is not in the passenger compartment of the vehicle, and that is not in operation, shall not be in violation of subsection (a) of this Section.

Any person found guilty of violating this Section shall be guilty of a petty offense. A minimum fine of $50 shall be imposed for a first offense and a minimum fine of $100 for a second or subsequent offense.

(c) The radar detection device or mechanism shall be seized by the law enforcement officer at the time of the violation if the offender has previously been convicted of violating this Section. This Section shall not be construed to authorize the permanent forfeiture to the State of any radar detection device or mechanism. Any such device or mechanism shall be taken and held for the period when needed as evidence. When no longer needed for evidence, the defendant may petition the court for the return of the device or mechanism; provided the defendant shall prove to the court by a preponderance of the evidence that the device or mechanism will be used only for a legitimate and lawful purpose.

(d) No commercial motor vehicle, or driver of such vehicle, shall be stopped or searched by any law enforcement officer solely on the basis of a violation or suspected violation of this Section.

P.A. 76-1586, § 12-712, added by P.A. 87-1202, § 1, eff. Jan. 1, 1993. Renumbered § 12-714 and amended by P.A. 88-45, Art. II, § 2-54, eff. July 6, 1993. Amended by P.A. 90-89, § 15, eff. Jan. 1, 1998.

Formerly Ill.Rev.Stat., ch. 95½, ¶ 12-712.

5/12-715. Possession and use of radar jamming devices prohibited

§ 12-715. Possession and use of radar jamming devices prohibited.

(a) No person shall operate or be in actual physical control of a commercial motor vehicle as defined in Section 6-500(6) of this Code while the motor vehicle is equipped with any instrument designed to interfere with microwaves or lasers at frequencies used by police radar for the purpose of monitoring vehicular speed.

(b) Notwithstanding subsection (a) of this Section, a person operating a commercial motor vehicle as defined in Section 6-500(6) of this Code, who possesses within the vehicle a radar or laser jamming device that is contained in a locked opaque box or similar container, or that is not in the passenger compartment of the vehicle, and that is not in operation, shall not be in violation of subsection (a) of this Section.

Any person found guilty of violating this Section shall be guilty of a petty offense. A minimum fine of $50 shall be imposed for a first offense and a minimum fine of $100 for a second or subsequent offense.

(c) The radar or laser jamming device or mechanism shall be seized by the law enforcement officer at the time of the violation. This Section shall not be construed to authorize the permanent forfeiture to the State of any radar or laser jamming device or mechanism. Any such device or mechanism shall be taken and held for the period when needed as evidence. When no longer needed for evidence, the defendant may petition the court for the return of the device or mechanism; provided the defendant shall prove to the court by a preponderance of the evidence that the device or mechanism will be used only for a legitimate and lawful purpose.

(d) No commercial motor vehicle, or driver of such vehicle, shall be stopped or searched by any law enforcement officer solely on the basis of a violation or suspected violation of this Section.

P.A. 76-1586, § 12-713, added by P.A. 87-1202, § 1, eff. Jan. 1, 1993. Renumbered § 12-715 and amended by P.A. 88-45, Art. II, § 2-54, eff. July 6, 1993. Amended by P.A. 90-89, § 15, eff. Jan. 1, 1998; P.A. 91-243, § 5, eff. Jan. 1, 2000.

Formerly Ill.Rev.Stat., ch. 95½, ¶ 12-713.

ARTICLE VIII. SPECIAL REQUIREMENTS FOR SCHOOL BUSES

Date Effective

Article VIII, consisting of Sections 12–800 to 12–812, was added by P.A. 78–1244, eff. Sept. 5, 1974.

Section

5/12–800. § 12–800. Repealed by P.A. 90–89, § 20, eff. Jan. 1, 1998

5/12–801. Color

§ 12–801. Color. The exterior of each school bus shall be national school bus glossy yellow except as follows:

The rooftop may be white.

The fenders of school buses manufactured before January 1, 1976, may be black.

Body trim, rub rails, lettering other than on a stop signal arm and bumpers on a Type I school bus shall be glossy black.

Lettering on a stop signal arm shall be white on a red background.

Bumpers on a Type II school bus may be glossy black or a bright, light or colorless finish.

The hood and upper cowl may be lusterless black or lusterless school bus yellow.

Grilles on the front, lamp trim and hubcaps may be a bright finish.

The name or emblem of a manufacturer may be colorless or any color.

The exterior paint of any school bus shall match the central value, hue and chroma set forth in rules promulgated by the Department.

P.A. 76–1586, § 12–801, added by P.A. 78–1244, § 1, eff. Sept. 5, 1974. Amended by P.A. 79–845, § 1, eff. Jan. 1, 1976; P.A. 80–1495, § 36, eff. Jan. 8, 1979; P.A. 81–740, § 1, eff. Jan. 1, 1980; P.A. 88–415, § 10, eff. Aug. 20, 1993; P.A. 89–433, § 5, eff. Dec. 15, 1995.

Formerly Ill.Rev.Stat.1991, ch. 95 ½, ¶ 12–801.

5/12–802. Identification

§ 12–802. Identification. Each school bus shall have the sign "SCHOOL BUS" painted on both the front and rear of the bus as high as practicable in letters at least 8 inches high. The vehicle weight and the vehicle maximum passenger capacity recommended by the manufacturer of the bus, which shall be based upon provision for 13 inches of seating space for each passenger exclusive of the driver, shall be painted on the body to the left of the service door in letters at least 2 inches high. The name of the owner or the entity for which the school bus is operated or both shall be painted in a contrasting color on both sides, centered as high as practicable below the window line, in letters at least 4 inches high. A school bus identification number shall be painted as high as practicable on both the front and rear of the bus in letters at least 4 inches high. Decals may be used instead of painting.

P.A. 76–1586, § 12–802, added by P.A. 78–1244, § 1, eff. Sept. 5, 1974. Amended by P.A. 79–63, § 1, eff. June 26, 1975; P.A. 79–845, § 1, eff. Jan. 1, 1976; P.A. 79–1454, § 44, eff. Aug. 31, 1976; P.A. 82–111, § 1, eff. Aug. 6, 1981.

Formerly Ill.Rev.Stat.1991, ch. 95 ½, ¶ 12–802.

5/12–803. Stop signal arm

§ 12–803. (a) Each school bus shall be equipped with a stop signal arm on the driver's side of the school bus that may be operated either manually or mechanically. For each school bus manufactured on and after September 1, 1992, the stop signal arm shall be an octagon shaped semaphore that conforms to 49 C.F.R. 571.131, "SCHOOL BUS PEDESTRIAN SAFETY DEVICES", S5.1 through S5.5.

(b) Each school bus manufactured prior to September 1, 1992 shall be equipped with a stop signal arm that conforms to standards promulgated by the Department.

P.A. 76–1586, § 12–803, added by P.A. 78–1244, § 1, eff. Sept. 5, 1974. Amended by P.A. 79–63, § 1, eff. June 26, 1975; P.A. 79–845, § 1, eff. Jan. 1, 1976; P.A. 79–1454, § 44, eff. Aug. 31, 1976; P.A. 83–299, § 1, eff. Jan. 1, 1984; P.A. 88–415, § 10, eff. Aug. 20, 1993.

Formerly Ill.Rev.Stat.1991, ch. 95 ½, ¶ 12–803.

5/12–804. Other vehicles—Color, stop signal arm and identification

§ 12–804. Other vehicles—Color, stop signal arm and identification. No vehicle other than a school bus shall be identified with the sign "SCHOOL BUS", shall be equipped with a stop signal arm, shall be equipped with a strobe lamp or shall be equipped with a warning lamp system as described in Section 12–805 of this Act. No commuter van or bus other than a school bus shall be painted national school bus glossy yellow or a color that closely resembles national school bus glossy yellow.

P.A. 76–1586, § 12–804, added by P.A. 78–1244, § 1, eff. Sept. 5, 1974. Amended by P.A. 79–63, § 1, eff. June 26,

1975; P.A. 81-509, § 1, eff. Jan. 1, 1980; P.A. 81-740, § 1, eff. Jan. 1, 1980; P.A. 81-1509, Art. I, § 57, eff. Sept. 26, 1980.

Formerly Ill.Rev.Stat.1991, ch. 95 ½, ¶ 12-804.

Art. I, § 1 of P.A. 81-1509 provided in part:

"This Article provides for the nonsubstantive revision or renumbering or repeal of Sections of Acts necessitated by the amendment, addition or repeal of Sections by two or more Public Acts of the 81st General Assembly, through Public Act 81-1224, which multiple action was not resolved by one of the Acts affecting the particular Section."

5/12-805. Special lighting equipment

§ 12-805. Special lighting equipment. Each school bus purchased as a new vehicle after December 31, 1975 shall be equipped with an 8-lamp flashing signal system. Until December 31, 1978, all other school buses shall be equipped with either a 4-lamp or an 8-lamp flashing signal system. After December 31, 1978, all school buses shall be equipped with an 8-lamp flashing signal system.

A 4-lamp flashing signal system shall have 2 alternately flashing red lamps mounted as high and as widely spaced laterally on the same level as practicable at the front of the school bus and 2 such lamps mounted in the same manner at the rear.

An 8-lamp flashing signal system shall have, in addition to a 4-lamp system, 4 alternately flashing amber lamps. Each amber lamp shall be mounted next to a red lamp and at the same level but closer to the centerline of the school bus.

Each signal lamp shall be a sealed beam at least 5½ inches in diameter and shall have sufficient intensity to be visible at 500 feet in normal sunlight. Both the 4-lamp and 8-lamp system shall be actuated only by means of a manual switch. There shall be a device for indicating to the driver that the system is operating properly or is inoperative.

P.A. 76-1586, § 12-805, added by P.A. 78-1244, § 1, eff. Sept. 5, 1974. Amended by P.A. 79-1400, § 1, eff. Oct. 1, 1976.

Formerly Ill.Rev.Stat.1991, ch. 95 ½, ¶ 12-805.

5/12-806. Identification, stop signal arms and special lighting when not used as a school bus

§ 12-806. Identification, stop signal arms and special lighting when not used as a school bus. Except as provided in Section 12-806a, whenever a school bus is operated for the purpose of transporting passengers other than persons in connection with an activity of the school or religious organization which owns the school bus or for which the school bus is operated, the "SCHOOL BUS" signs shall be covered or concealed and the stop signal arm and flashing signal system shall not be operable through normal controls.

P.A. 76-1586, § 12-806, added by P.A. 78-1244, § 1, eff. Sept. 5, 1974. Amended by P.A. 79-798, § 1, eff. July 1, 1976; P.A. 84-1311, § 2, eff. Aug. 27, 1986.

Formerly Ill.Rev.Stat.1991, ch. 95 ½, ¶ 12-806.

5/12-806a. Identification, stop signal arms and special lighting on school buses used in connection with a youth camp, child care facility, or community based rehabilitation facility

§ 12-806a. Identification, stop signal arms and special lighting on school buses used in connection with a youth camp, child care facility, or community based rehabilitation facility.

(a) Subject to the conditions in Subsection (c), a bus which meets any of the special requirements for school buses in Section 12-801, 12-802, 12-803 and 12-805 of this Code may be used for the purpose of transporting persons 18 years of age or less in connection with any of the following facilities:

(i) any youth camp licensed under the Youth Camp Act; [1] and

(ii) any child care facility licensed under the Child Care Act of 1969.[2]

(b) Subject to the conditions in subsection (c), a bus which meets any of the special requirements for school buses in Sections 12-801, 12-802, 12-803 and 12-805 of this Code may be used for the purpose of transporting persons recognized as clients of a community based rehabilitation facility which is accredited by the Commission on Accreditation of Rehabilitation Facilities of Tucson, Arizona, and which is under a contractual agreement with the Department of Human Services.

(c) A bus used for transportation as provided in subsection (a) or (b) shall either (i) meet all of the special requirements for school buses in Section 12-801, 12-802, 12-803 and 12-805 or (ii) shall have the "SCHOOL BUS" signs covered or concealed and the stop signal arm and flashing signal system rendered inoperable through normal means. A bus which meets all of the special requirements for school buses in Section 12-801, 12-802, 12-803 and 12-805 shall be operated by a person who has a valid and properly classified driver's license issued by the Secretary of State and who possesses a valid school bus driver permit or is accompanied and supervised, for the specific purpose of training prior to routine operation of a school bus, by a person who has held a valid school bus driver permit for at least one year. A bus which has had the "SCHOOL BUS" signs covered or concealed and the stop signal arm and flashing signal system rendered inoperable through normal means may be operated by a person who has a valid and properly classified driver's license issued by the Secretary of State.

P.A. 76-1586, § 12-806a, added by P.A. 84-1311, § 2, eff. Aug. 27, 1986. Amended by P.A. 85-815, § 1, eff. Jan. 1, 1988; P.A. 89-507, Art. 90, § 90D-84, eff. July 1, 1997.

Formerly Ill.Rev.Stat.1991, ch. 95 ½, ¶ 12-806a.

[1] 210 ILCS 100/1 et seq.

[2] 225 ILCS 10/1 et seq.

5/12-807. Seat belt for driver

§ 12-807. Seat belt for driver. Each school bus shall be equipped with a retractable lap belt assembly for the driver's seat. No school bus shall be operated unless the driver has properly restrained himself with the lap belt assembly.

P.A. 76-1586, § 12-807, added by P.A. 78-1244, § 1, eff. Sept. 5, 1974.

Formerly Ill.Rev.Stat.1991, ch. 95 ½, ¶ 12-807.

5/12-807.1. Seat back height

§ 12-807.1. Seat back height. No Type I school bus manufactured after June 30, 1987 shall be sold for use as, or purchased for use as, or used as a school bus within this State unless such bus is equipped with passenger seat backs having a seat back height of 28 inches installed by the original bus body manufacturer.

P.A. 76-1586, § 12-807.1, added by P.A. 84-1334, § 2, eff. Sept. 9, 1986. Amended by P.A. 85-1010, § 1, eff. March 2, 1988.

Formerly Ill.Rev.Stat.1991, ch. 95 ½, ¶ 12-807.1.

5/12-807.2. Crossing control arms

§ 12-807.2. Crossing control arms.

(a) No Type I or Type II school bus may be operated or used as a school bus within this State after December 31, 1999 unless that bus is equipped with a crossing control arm on the front of the bus that conforms to equipment and installation standards that the Department of Transportation shall promulgate for purposes of this subsection.

(b) If a Type I or Type II school bus is manufactured after December 31, 1997, that bus shall not be sold for use as, or purchased for the use as, or used as a school bus within this State unless that bus is equipped with a crossing control arm that is installed on the front of the bus by the original bus body manufacturer and that conforms to equipment and installation standards that the Department shall promulgate for purposes of this subsection.

(c) A crossing control arm meeting standards promulgated by the Department under this Section shall be designed to swing out from the front of a school bus when the bus stops and opens its doors while school children enter or exit the bus, as prescribed in rules promulgated by the State Board of Education.

(d) This Section does not apply to the temporary operation in this State of a school bus that is legally registered in another state and is displaying valid registration plates of that state if (i) the bus is not operated in Illinois on a regular basis, and (ii) the bus is being operated in Illinois in connection with a cultural, tourist, athletic, or similar activity that is sponsored by one or more schools located outside of Illinois for the benefit of their enrolled students who are being transported to or from that activity.

P.A. 76-1586, § 12-807.2, added by P.A. 90-108, § 15, eff. July 14, 1997.

5/12-808. Fire extinguisher

§ 12-808. Fire extinguisher. Each school bus shall be equipped with at least one dry chemical gauge type fire extinguisher mounted in the extinguisher manufacturer's automobile type bracket in a position readily accessible to the driver.

P.A. 76-1586, § 12-808, added by P.A. 78-1244, § 1, eff. Sept. 5, 1974.

Formerly Ill.Rev.Stat.1991, ch. 95 ½, ¶ 12-808.

5/12-809. First aid kit

§ 12-809. First aid kit. Each school bus shall be equipped with a first aid kit mounted in full view of and readily accessible to the driver.

P.A. 76-1586, § 12-809, added by P.A. 78-1244, § 1, eff. Sept. 5, 1974.

Formerly Ill.Rev.Stat.1991, ch. 95 ½, ¶ 12-809.

5/12-810. Restraining devices for passengers who are persons with disabilities

§ 12-810. Restraining devices for passengers who are persons with disabilities.

Each school bus which is operated for transporting passengers who are persons with disabilities shall be equipped with an appropriate restraining or safety device for each such passenger.

P.A. 76-1586, § 12-810, added by P.A. 78-1244, § 1, eff. Sept. 5, 1974. Amended by P.A. 88-685, § 5, eff. Jan. 24, 1995.

Formerly Ill.Rev.Stat.1991, ch. 95 ½, ¶ 12-810.

5/12-811. Amber 3 bar clearance light

§ 12-811. Amber 3 bar clearance light. Each Type I school bus shall be equipped with an amber 3 bar clearance light on the front of the bus. The light shall be illuminated at all times when the bus is being operated between sunset and sunrise and in conditions of reduced visibility.

P.A. 76-1586, § 12-811, added by P.A. 78-1244, § 1, eff. Sept. 5, 1974. Amended by P.A. 79-63, § 1, eff. June 26, 1975.

Formerly Ill.Rev.Stat.1991, ch. 95 ½, ¶ 12-811.

5/12-812. Rules and regulations

§ 12-812. Rules and regulations.

(a) The Department may promulgate rules and regulations to more completely specify the equipment requirements of this Article.

(b) All rules, regulations and standards promulgated from time to time by the State Board of Education and the Department for the safety and construction of school buses shall be applicable to every motor vehicle in this State defined as a school bus under Section 1-182.

P.A. 76-1586, § 12-812, added by P.A. 78-1244, § 1, eff. Sept. 5, 1974. Amended by P.A. 81-1508, § 8, eff. Sept. 25, 1980.

Formerly Ill.Rev.Stat.1991, ch. 95 ½, ¶ 12-812.

5/12-812.1. Alternate fuels; use; rules and regulations

§ 12-812.1. (a) The Department shall adopt and promulgate rules and regulations governing the use of liquefied petroleum gases, compressed natural gases and liquefied natural gases as a propellant fuel in school buses. Such rules and regulations shall include the installation, maintenance and operation of such equipment installed on school buses and shall be based on the generally accepted standards of safety as recommended by the National Fire Protection Association.

(b) All school buses using liquefied petroleum gases, compressed natural gases or liquefied natural gases as a propellant fuel must conform to and obey any rule or regulation lawfully adopted by the Department.

P.A. 76-1586, § 12-812.1, added by P.A. 83-1027, § 2, eff. July 1, 1984.

Formerly Ill.Rev.Stat.1991, ch. 95 ½, ¶ 12-812.1.

5/12-813. § 12-813. Repealed by P.A. 80-506, § 2, eff. Oct. 1, 1977

5/12-813.1. Operation of a school bus while using a cellular radio telecommunication device

§ 12-813.1. Operation of a school bus while using a cellular radio telecommunication device.

(a) In this Section:

"School bus driver" means a person operating a school bus who has a valid school bus driver permit as required under Sections 6-104 and 6-106.1 of this Code.

"Cellular radio telecommunication device" means a device capable of sending or receiving telephone communications without an access line for service and which requires the operator to dial numbers manually. It does not, however, include citizens band radios or citizens band radio hybrids.

"Using a cellular radio telecommunication device" means talking or listening to or dialing a cellular radio telecommunication device.

To "operate" means to have the vehicle in motion while it contains one or more passengers.

(b) A school bus driver may not operate a school bus while using a cellular radio telecommunication device.

(c) This Section does not apply:

(1) To the use of a cellular radio telecommunication device for the purpose of communicating with any of the following regarding an emergency situation:

(A) an emergency response operator;

(B) a hospital;

(C) a physician's office or health clinic;

(D) an ambulance service;

(E) a fire department, fire district, or fire company; or

(F) a police department.

(2) To the use of a cellular radio telecommunication device to call for assistance in the event that there is a mechanical breakdown or other mechanical problem that impairs the safe operation of the bus.

(3) To the use of a cellular radio telecommunication device that has a digital two-way radio service capability owned and operated by the school district, when that device is being used as a digital two-way radio.

(4) When the school bus is parked.

(d) A school bus driver who violates this Section is guilty of a petty offense punishable by a fine of not less than $100 and not more than $250.

P.A. 76–1586, § 12–813.1, added by P.A. 92–730, § 5, eff. Jan. 1, 2003.

5/12–814. § 12–814. Repealed by P.A. 81–509, § 2, eff. Jan. 1, 1980

5/12–815. Strobe lamp on school bus

§ 12–815. Strobe lamp on school bus.

(a) A school bus manufactured prior to January 1, 2000 may be equipped with one strobe lamp that will emit 60 to 120 flashes per minute of white or bluish-white light visible to a motorist approaching the bus from any direction. A school bus manufactured on or after January 1, 2000 shall be equipped with one strobe lamp that will emit 60 to 120 flashes per minute of white or bluish-white light visible to a motorist approaching the bus from any direction. The lamp shall be of sufficient brightness to be visible in normal sunlight when viewed directly from a distance of at least one mile.

(b) The strobe lamp shall be mounted on the rooftop of the bus with the light generating element in the lamp located equidistant from each side and either at or behind the center of the rooftop. The maximum height of the element above the rooftop shall not exceed 1/30 of its distance from the rear of the rooftop. If the structure of the strobe lamp obscures the light generating element, the element shall be deemed to be in the center of the lamp with a maximum height 1/4 inch less than the maximum height of the strobe lamp unless otherwise indicated in rules and regulations promulgated by the Department. The Department may promulgate rules and regulations to govern measurements, glare, effectiveness and protection of strobe lamps on school buses, including higher strobe lamps than authorized in this paragraph.

(c) The strobe lamp may be lighted only when the school bus is actually being used as a school bus and:

1. is stopping or stopped for loading or discharging pupils on a highway outside an urban area; or

2. is bearing one or more pupils and is either stopped or, in the interest of safety, is moving very slowly at a speed:

(i) less than the posted minimum speed limit, or

(ii) less than 30 miles per hour on a highway outside an urban area.

P.A. 76–1586, § 12–815, added by P.A. 81–879, § 1, eff. Sept. 21, 1979. Amended by P.A. 87–768, § 2, eff. Oct. 10, 1991; P.A. 91–168, § 5, eff. Jan. 1, 2000; P.A. 91–679, § 5, eff. Jan. 26, 2000.

Formerly Ill.Rev.Stat.1991, ch. 95 ½, ¶ 12–815.

P.A. 91–679 incorporated the amendment by P.A. 91–168.

5/12–815.1. Emergency exits identification

§ 12–815.1. Emergency exits identification. On and after August 1, 2000, all emergency exits of a school bus shall be outlined around the perimeter of the exit with a minimum one inch wide yellow reflective tape or decal. This yellow reflective tape or decal shall be placed on the exterior surface of the school bus.

P.A. 76–1586, § 12–815.1, added by P.A. 91–168, § 5, eff. Jan. 1, 2000. Amended by P.A. 91–785, § 5, eff. June 9, 2000.

5/12–820. Nursery school buses

§ 12–820. Nursery school buses. The Department of Transportation, after conducting a Public Hearing, may, by regulation, modify and supplement the requirements pertaining to seat dimensions, spacing and height from the floor and to other safety features in the interior of a school bus used to transport preschool children, when such modification or supplementing will enhance the safety of the bus when transporting such children.

P.A. 76–1586, § 12–820, added by P.A. 79–845, § 1, eff. Jan. 1, 1976. Amended by P.A. 82–523, § 1, eff. Jan. 1, 1982; P.A. 85–828, § 7, eff. Jan. 1, 1988.

Formerly Ill.Rev.Stat.1991, ch. 95 ½, ¶ 12–820.

ARTICLE IX. SPECIAL REQUIREMENTS FOR RELIGIOUS ORGANIZATION BUSES

Section

5/12–900. Color and markings

§ 12–900. Color and markings. Each religious organization bus may be of any color and have any markings designating its purpose other than those required for school buses under Article VIII of this Act.

P.A. 76–1586, § 12–900, added by P.A. 79–798, § 1, eff. July 1, 1976.

Formerly Ill.Rev.Stat.1991, ch. 95 ½, ¶ 12–900.

5/12–901. Special lighting equipment

§ 12–901. Special lighting equipment. Any religious organization bus may be equipped with a 4-lamp flashing signal system having unison flashing amber lamps, 2 at the front and 2 at the rear of the bus, mounted as high and as widely spaced laterally on the same level as is practicable. If such equipment is installed, (a) each lamp must be a sealed beam at least 5½ inches in diameter and have sufficient intensity to be visible at 500 feet in normal sunlight, (b) the system shall be actuated only by means of a manual switch, and (c) there shall be a device for indicating to the driver that the system is operating properly or is inoperative.

P.A. 76-1586, § 12-901, added by P.A. 79-798, § 1, eff. July 1, 1976.

Formerly Ill.Rev.Stat.1991, ch. 95 ½, ¶ 12-901.

5/12-902. Rules and regulations

§ 12-902. Rules and regulations. The Department of Transportation may promulgate rules and regulations to more completely specify the equipment requirements for every motor vehicle defined as a religious organization bus under Section 1-111.1a.

P.A. 76-1586, § 12-902, added by P.A. 79-798, § 1, eff. July 1, 1976. Amended by P.A. 90-89, § 15, eff. Jan. 1, 1998.

Formerly Ill.Rev.Stat.1991, ch. 95 ½, ¶ 12-902.

CHAPTER 13. INSPECTION OF VEHICLES

Section

Enactment

The Illinois Vehicle Code was enacted by P.A. 76-1586, effective July 1, 1970. The Code constitutes a consolidated recodification of various earlier laws and acts including the Uniform Act Regulating Traffic on Highways.

5/13-100. § 13-100. Repealed by P.A. 90-89, § 20, eff. Jan. 1, 1998

5/13-100.1. Definitions

§ 13-100.1. Definitions. As used in this Chapter, "affected areas" means the counties of Cook, DuPage, Lake, Kane, McHenry, Will, Madison, St. Clair, and Monroe and the townships of Aux Sable and Goose Lake in Grundy County and the township of Oswego in Kendall County.

P.A. 76-1586, § 13-100.1, added by P.A. 91-254, § 10, eff. July 1, 2000.

5/13-101. Submission to safety test; Certificate of safety

§ 13-101. Submission to safety test; Certificate of safety. To promote the safety of the general public, every owner of a second division vehicle, medical transport vehicle, tow truck, or contract carrier transporting employees in the course of their employment on a highway of this State in a vehicle designed to carry 15 or fewer passengers shall, before operating the vehicle upon the highways of Illinois, submit it to a "safety test" and secure a certificate of safety furnished by the Department as set forth in Section 13-109. Each second division motor vehicle that pulls or draws a trailer, semitrailer or pole trailer, with a gross weight of more than 8,000 lbs or is registered for a gross weight of more than 8,000 lbs, motor bus, religious organization bus, school bus, senior citizen transportation vehicle, and limousine shall be subject to inspection by the Department and the Department is authorized to establish rules and regulations for the implementation of such inspections.

The owners of each salvage vehicle shall submit it to a "safety test" and secure a certificate of safety furnished by the Department prior to its salvage vehicle inspection pursuant to Section 3-308 of this Code.

However, none of the provisions of Chapter 13 requiring safety tests or a certificate of safety shall apply to:

(a) farm tractors, machinery and implements, wagons, wagon-trailers or like farm vehicles used primarily in agricultural pursuits;

(b) vehicles other than school buses, tow trucks and medical transport vehicles owned or operated by a municipal corporation or political subdivision having a population of 1,000,000 or more inhabitants and which are subject to safety tests imposed by local ordinance or resolution;

(c) a semitrailer or trailer having a gross weight of 5,000 pounds or less including vehicle weight and maximum load;

(d) recreational vehicles;

(e) vehicles registered as and displaying Illinois antique vehicle plates;

(f) house trailers equipped and used for living quarters;

(g) vehicles registered as and displaying Illinois permanently mounted equipment plates or similar vehicles eligible therefor but registered as governmental vehicles provided that if said vehicle is reclassified from a permanently mounted equipment plate so as to lose the exemption of not requiring a certificate of safety, such vehicle must be safety tested within 30 days of the reclassification;

(h) vehicles owned or operated by a manufacturer, dealer or transporter displaying a special plate or plates as described in Chapter 3 of this Code while such vehicle is being delivered from the manufacturing or assembly plant directly to the purchasing dealership or distributor, or being temporarily road driven for quality control testing, or from one dealer or distributor to another, or are being moved by the most direct route from one location to another for the purpose of installing special bodies or equipment, or driven for purposes of demonstration by a prospective buyer with the dealer or his agent present in the cab of the vehicle during the demonstration;

(i) pole trailers and auxiliary axles;

(j) special mobile equipment;

(k) vehicles properly registered in another State pursuant to law and displaying a valid registration plate;

(*l*) water-well boring apparatuses or rigs;

(m) any vehicle which is owned and operated by the federal government and externally displays evidence of such ownership; and

(n) second division vehicles registered for a gross weight of 8,000 pounds or less, except when such second division motor vehicles pull or draw a trailer, semi-trailer or pole trailer having a gross weight of or registered for a gross weight of more than 8,000 pounds; motor buses; religious organization buses; school buses; senior citizen transportation vehicles; medical transport vehicles and tow trucks.

The safety test shall include the testing and inspection of brakes, lights, horns, reflectors, rear vision mirrors, mufflers, safety chains, windshields and windshield wipers, warning flags and flares, frame, axle, cab and body, or cab or body, wheels, steering apparatus, and other safety devices and appliances required by this Code and such other safety tests as the Department may by rule or regulation require, for second division vehicles, school buses, medical transport vehicles, tow trucks, vehicles designed to carry 15 or fewer passengers operated by a contract carrier transporting employees in the course of their employment on a highway of this State, trailers, and semitrailers subject to inspection.

For tow trucks, the safety test and inspection shall also include the inspection of winch mountings, body panels, body mounts, wheel lift swivel points, and sling straps, and other tests and inspections the Department by rule requires for tow trucks.

For trucks, truck tractors, trailers, semi-trailers, and buses, the safety test shall be conducted in accordance with the Minimum Periodic Inspection Standards promulgated by the Federal Highway Administration of the U.S. Department of Transportation and contained in Appendix G to Subchapter B of Chapter III of Title 49 of the Code of Federal Regulations. Those standards, as now in effect, are made a part of this Code, in the same manner as though they were set out in full in this Code.

The passing of the safety test shall not be a bar at any time to prosecution for operating a second division vehicle, medical transport vehicle, or vehicle designed to carry 15 or fewer passengers operated by a contract carrier as provided in this Section which is unsafe as determined by the standards prescribed in this Code.

P.A. 76-1586, § 13-101, eff. July 1, 1970. Amended by P.A. 77-157, § 1, eff. Jan. 1, 1972; P.A. 77-170, § 1, eff. Jan. 1, 1972; P.A. 77-1633, § 1, eff. Sept. 23, 1972; P.A. 77-1688, § 1, eff. July 1, 1972; P.A. 77-2170, § 1, eff. Aug. 2, 1972; P.A. 78-255, § 61, eff. Oct. 1, 1973; P.A. 78-1244, § 1, eff. Sept. 5, 1974; P.A. 78-1297, § 58, eff. March 4, 1975; P.A. 79-798, § 1, eff. July 1, 1976; P.A. 79-865, § 1, eff. Jan. 1, 1976; P.A. 79-1454, § 44, eff. Aug. 31, 1976; P.A. 80-606, § 1, eff. Oct. 1, 1977; P.A. 80-1018, § 1, eff. Oct. 1, 1977; P.A. 80-1364, § 36, eff. Aug. 13, 1978; P.A. 81-1554, § 1, eff. Jan. 13, 1981; P.A. 82-433, § 1, eff. Sept. 8, 1981; P.A. 82-573, § 1, eff. Sept. 24, 1981; P.A. 82-783, Art. III, § 37, eff. July 13, 1982; P.A. 82-957, § 1, eff. Jan. 1, 1983; P.A. 83-315, § 1, eff. Jan. 1, 1984; P.A. 83-497, § 1, eff. Jan. 1, 1984; P.A. 83-831, § 1, eff. Jan. 1, 1984; P.A. 83-1260, § 1, eff. Aug. 16, 1984; P.A. 83-1362, Art. II, § 99, eff. Sept. 11, 1984; P.A. 84-832, Art. II, § 10, eff. Sept. 23, 1985; P.A. 84-1060, § 1, eff. July 1, 1986; P.A. 85-572, § 1, eff. Sept. 18, 1987; P.A. 86-408, § 1, eff. Jan. 1, 1990; P.A. 86-447, § 2, eff. Aug. 30, 1989; P.A. 86-1028, Art. II, § 2-44, eff. Feb. 5, 1990; P.A. 87-1111, § 1, eff. Sept. 15, 1992; P.A. 89-433, § 5, eff. Dec. 15, 1995; P.A. 92-108, § 5, eff. Jan. 1, 2002.

Formerly Ill.Rev.Stat.1991, ch. 95 ½, ¶ 13-101.

Section 3 of P.A. 82-433 approved Sept. 8, 1981, provided:

"This Act takes effect upon its becoming a law, except that the provisions relating to safety tests and proof of financial responsibility for medical transport vehicles apply only to applications for and the issuance of registration plates which are required to be displayed on January 1, 1982 or thereafter."

5/13-101.1. Senior citizen transportation vehicle

§ 13-101.1. Senior citizen transportation vehicle. Any vehicle of 12 or more passengers used in the transportation of senior citizens shall bear placards on both sides indicating it is being used for such purposes. The placards may be permanently or temporarily affixed to the vehicle. The size of the letters must be at least 2 inches high and the stroke of the brush must be at least ½ inch wide. Any such vehicle used for such purposes shall be subject to the inspections provided for vehicles of the second division and its operation shall be governed according to the requirements of this Code.

P.A. 76-1586, § 13-101.1, added by P.A. 82-957, § 1, eff. Jan. 1, 1983.

Formerly Ill.Rev.Stat.1991, ch. 95 ½, ¶ 13-101.1.

5/13-102. Tests and investigations

§ 13-102. Tests and investigations. The Department shall conduct tests and make investigations to determine the kind and type of equipment necessary to test the brakes, lights, frame, wheels, steering apparatus, including camber and caster of the axle, and toe-in and tracking of the wheels, and all other devices and appliances referred to in this Act; and shall make public its findings and furnish upon request a list of the various testing devices approved by it.

P.A. 76-1586, § 13-102, eff. July 1, 1970. Amended by P.A. 77-157, § 1, eff. Jan. 1, 1972; P.A. 77-170, § 1, eff. Jan. 1, 1972; P.A. 77-2829, § 40, eff. Dec. 22, 1972; P.A. 78-255, § 61, eff. Oct. 1, 1973; P.A. 78-1244, § 1, eff. Sept. 5, 1974; P.A. 78-1297, § 58, eff. March 4, 1975.

Formerly Ill.Rev.Stat.1991, ch. 95 ½, ¶ 13-102.

5/13-102.1. Diesel powered vehicle emission inspection report

§ 13-102.1. Diesel powered vehicle emission inspection report. Beginning July 1, 2000, the Department of Transportation and the Department of State Police shall each conduct an annual study concerned with the results of emission inspections for diesel powered vehicles registered for a gross weight of more than 16,000 pounds or having a gross vehicle weight rating of more than 16,000 pounds. The studies shall be reported to the General Assembly by June 30, 2001, and every June 30 thereafter. The studies shall also be sent to the Illinois Environmental Protection Agency for its use in environmental matters.

The studies shall include, but not be limited to, the following information:

(a) the number of diesel powered vehicles that were inspected for emission compliance by the respective departments pursuant to this Chapter 13 during the previous year;

(b) the number of diesel powered vehicles that failed and passed the emission inspections conducted by the respective departments required pursuant to this Chapter 13 during the previous year; and

(c) the number of diesel powered vehicles that failed the emission inspections conducted by the respective departments pursuant to this Chapter 13 more than once in the previous year.

P.A. 76-1586, § 13-102.1, added by P.A. 91-254, § 10, eff. July 1, 2000. Amended by P.A. 91-865, § 5, eff. July 1, 2000.

5/13-103. Official testing stations—Fee—Permit—Bond

§ 13-103. Official testing stations—Fee—Permit—Bond. Upon the payment of a fee of $10 and the filing of an application by the proprietor of any vehicle service station or public or private garage upon forms furnished by the Department, accompanied by proof of experience, training and ability of the operator of the testing equipment, together with proof of installation of approved testing equipment as defined in Section 13-102 and the giving of a bond conditioned upon faithful observance of this Section and of rules and regulations issued by the Department in the amount of $1,000 with security approved by the Department, the Department shall issue a permit to the proprietor of such vehicle service station or garage to operate an Official Testing Station. Such permit shall expire 12 months following its issuance, but may be renewed annually by complying with the requirements set forth in this Section and upon the payment of a renewal fee of $10. Proprietors of official testing stations for which permits have been issued prior to the effective date of this Act may renew such permits for the renewal fee of $10 on the expiration of each 12 months following issuance of such permits, by complying with the requirements set forth in this Section. However, any city, village or incorporated town shall upon application to the Department and without payment of any fee or filing of any bond, but upon proof of experience, training and ability of the operator of the testing equipment, and proof of the installation of approved testing equipment as defined in Section 13-102, be issued a permit to operate such testing station as an Official Testing Station under this Act. The permit so issued shall at all times be displayed in a prominent place in the vehicle service station, garage or municipal testing station which is licensed as an Official Testing Station under this Act. No person or vehicle service station, garage or municipal testing station shall in any manner claim or represent himself or itself to be an official testing station unless a permit has been issued to him or it as provided in this Section.

Any person or municipality who or which has received a permit under this Section may test his or its own second division vehicles and issue certificates of safety and conduct emission inspections of his or its own second division vehicles in accordance with the requirements of Section 13-109.1 with respect to any such second division vehicles owned, operated or controlled by him or it.

Each such permit issued by the Department shall state on its face the location of the official testing station to be operated under the permit and safety tests shall be made only at such location. However, the Department may, upon application, authorize a change in the location of the official testing station and the removal of the testing equipment to the new location. Upon approval of such application, the Department shall issue an endorsement which the applicant shall affix to his permit. Such endorsement constitutes authority for the applicant to make such change in location and to remove his testing equipment at the times and to the places stated in the endorsement.

P.A. 76-1586, § 13-103, eff. July 1, 1970. Amended by P.A. 76-1620, § 1, eff. July 1, 1970; P.A. 77-157, § 1, eff. Jan. 1, 1972; P.A. 77-170, § 1, eff. Jan. 1, 1972; P.A. 77-2829, § 40, eff. Dec. 22, 1972; P.A. 78-255, § 61, eff. Oct. 1, 1973; P.A. 80-606, § 1, eff. Oct. 1, 1977; P.A. 91-254, § 10, eff. July 1, 2000.

Formerly Ill.Rev.Stat.1991, ch. 95 ½, ¶ 13-103.

5/13-103.1. Annual certification of safety testers—Fee—Renewal

§ 13-103.1. Annual certification of safety testers—Fee—Renewal. Only certified safety testers are authorized to perform safety tests and affix Certificates of Safety to vehicles. The Department shall annually certify those safety testers who have met its requirements. Safety testers' certificates shall expire 12 months following the date of issue, but may be renewed annually by complying with the requirements as established by the Department.

P.A. 76-1586, § 13-103.1, added by P.A. 80-606, § 1, eff. Oct. 1, 1977.

Formerly Ill.Rev.Stat.1991, ch. 95 ½, ¶ 13-103.1.

5/13-103.2. Reclassification of nonconforming station

§ 13-103.2. Reclassification of nonconforming station. The Department may not change the administrative classification of a nonconforming official testing station from its present classification to a less favorable classification upon a change in ownership of the station, if (1) the nonconforming official testing station has held its present administrative classification since July 1, 1972, and (2) the station meets all requirements for its present classification, other than the requirement of having an exit door in direct line with the safety test equipment and (3) the station is located in a county with no other class "A" or class "C" official testing station.

P.A. 76-1586, § 13-103.2, added by P.A. 84-1422, § 1, eff. Sept. 24, 1986.

Formerly Ill.Rev.Stat.1991, ch. 95 ½, ¶ 13-103.2.

5/13-104. Obtaining or issuing a certificate of safety without proper test—Suspension or revocation of license

§ 13-104. Obtaining or issuing a certificate of safety without proper test—Suspension or revocation of license. Any motor vehicle owner, driver or operator who accepts, obtains or attempts to obtain a certificate of safety without securing a test, or by a test which is known by him to have been improperly made, shall be guilty of a petty offense and shall be fined not less than $5.00 nor more than $100.00 for the first such certificate so accepted or obtained, or attempted to be obtained; and for the second such certificate obtained or attempted to be obtained, not less than $25.00 nor more than $200.00; and for each certificate after the second certificate, obtained or attempted to be obtained, not less than $100.00 nor more than $300.00. The same penalties shall apply to official testing station operators who issue certificates of safety in violation of this Chapter.

When a license is suspended, the suspension shall be for not less than 30 nor more than 180 days. When a license is revoked, the owner of the station cannot make an application for a new license within the period of twelve months after the date of the revocation and then, upon his making an application, the Department of Transportation shall consider this record in deciding whether or not to grant the license. P.A. 76-1586, § 13-104, eff. July 1, 1970. Amended by P.A. 77-157, § 1, eff. Jan. 1, 1972; P.A. 77-170, § 1, eff. Jan. 1, 1972; P.A. 77-2720, § 1, eff. Jan. 1, 1973; P.A. 78-255, § 61, eff. Oct. 1, 1973.

Formerly Ill.Rev.Stat.1991, ch. 95 ½, ¶ 13-104.

5/13-105. Inspection of official testing stations

§ 13-105. Inspection of official testing stations. Employees specifically authorized by the Department so to do shall inspect all "Official Testing Stations" at frequent intervals. Such employees shall have access to all records relating to tests and work done or parts sold as a result of such tests, to ascertain whether or not tests are properly, fairly and honestly made, and may examine the owner of the official testing station or any officer or employee thereof under oath. The Department shall conduct periodic nonscheduled inspection on owners premises of vehicles owned and operated by licensed "Independent Official Testing Stations."

P.A. 76-1586, § 13-105, eff. July 1, 1970. Amended by P.A. 77-157, § 1, eff. Jan. 1, 1972; P.A. 77-170, § 1, eff. Jan. 1, 1972; P.A. 77-2829, § 40, eff. Dec. 22, 1972; P.A. 78-255, § 61, eff. Oct. 1, 1973; P.A. 86-447, § 2, eff. Aug. 30, 1989.

Formerly Ill.Rev.Stat.1991, ch. 95 ½, ¶ 13-105.

5/13-106. Rates and charges by official testing stations—Schedule to be filed

§ 13-106. Rates and charges by official testing stations-Schedule to be filed. Every operator of an official testing station shall file with the Department, in the manner prescribed by the Department, a schedule of all rates and charges made by him for performing the tests provided for in Section 13-101 and Section 13-109.1. Such rate or charge shall include an amount to reimburse the operator of the official testing station for the purchase from the Department of the certificate of safety required by this chapter, not to exceed that fee paid to the Department by the operator authorized by this chapter. Such rates and charges shall be just and reasonable and the Department upon its own initiative or upon complaint of any person or corporation may require the testing station operator to appear for a hearing and prove that the rates so filed are just and reasonable. A "just and reasonable" rate or charge, for the purposes of this Section, means a rate or charge which is the same, or nearly the same, as the prevailing rate or charge for the same or similar tests made in the community where the station is located. No operator may change this schedule of rates and charges until the proposed changes are filed with and approved by the Department. No license may be issued to any official testing station unless the applicant has filed with the Department a proposed schedule of rates and charges and unless such rates and charges have been approved by the Department. No operator of an official testing station shall charge more or less than the rates so filed with and approved by the Department.

P.A. 76-1586, § 13-106, eff. July 1, 1970. Amended by P.A. 77-157, § 1, eff. Jan. 1, 1972; P.A. 77-170, § 1, eff. Jan. 1, 1972; P.A. 77-2829, § 40, eff. Dec. 22, 1972; P.A. 78-255, § 61, eff. Oct. 1, 1973; P.A. 80-606, § 1, eff. Oct. 1, 1977; P.A. 91-254, § 10, eff. July 1, 2000.

Formerly Ill.Rev.Stat.1991, ch. 95 ½, ¶ 13-106.

5/13-107. Investigation of complaints against official testing stations

§ 13-107. Investigation of complaints against official testing stations. The Department shall, upon its own motion, or upon charges made in writing verified under oath, investigate complaints that an official testing station is willfully falsifying records or tests, either for the purpose of selling parts or services not actually required, or for the purpose of issuing a certificate of safety for a vehicle designed to carry 15 or fewer passengers operated by a contract carrier transporting employees in the course of their employment on a highway of this State, second division vehicle, or medical transport vehicle that is not in safe mechanical condition as determined by the standards of this Chapter in violation of the provisions of this Chapter or of the rules and regulations issued by the Department.

The Secretary of Transportation, for the purpose of more effectively carrying out the provisions of Chapter 13, may appoint such a number of inspectors as he may deem necessary. Such inspectors shall inspect and investigate applicants for official testing station permits and investigate and report violations. With respect to enforcement of the provisions of this Chapter 13, such inspectors shall have and may exercise throughout the State all the powers of police officers.

The Secretary must authorize to each inspector and to any other employee of the Department exercising the powers of a peace officer a distinct badge that, on its face, (i) clearly states that the badge is authorized by the Department and (ii) contains a unique identifying number. No other badge shall be authorized by the Department.

P.A. 76-1586, § 13-107, eff. July 1, 1970. Amended by P.A. 76-2193, § 1, eff. July 1, 1970; P.A. 77-157, § 1, eff. Jan. 1, 1972; P.A. 77-170, § 1, eff. Jan. 1, 1972; P.A. 77-2829, § 40, eff. Dec. 22, 1972; P.A. 78-255, § 61, eff. Oct. 1, 1973; P.A. 82-433, § 1, eff. Sept. 8, 1981; P.A. 91-883, § 105, eff. Jan. 1, 2001; P.A. 92-108, § 5, eff. Jan. 1, 2002.

Formerly Ill.Rev.Stat.1991, ch. 95 ½, ¶ 13-107.

Section 3 of P.A. 82-433 approved Sept. 8, 1981, provided:

"This Act takes effect upon its becoming a law, except that the provisions relating to safety tests and proof of financial responsibility for medical transport vehicles apply only to applications for and the issuance of registration plates which are required to be displayed on January 1, 1982 or thereafter."

5/13-108. Hearing on complaint against official testing station—Suspension or revocation of permit

§ 13-108. Hearing on complaint against official testing station—Suspension or revocation of permit. If it appears to the Department, either through its own investigation or upon charges verified under oath, that any of the provisions of this Chapter or the rules and regulations of the Department, are being violated, the Department, shall after notice to the person, firm or corporation charged with such violation, conduct a hearing. At least 10 days prior to the date of such hearing the Department shall cause to be served upon the person, firm or corporation charged with such violation, a copy of such charge or charges by registered mail or by the personal service thereof, together with a notice specifying the time and place of such hearing. At the time and place specified in such notice the person, firm or corporation charged with such violation shall be given an opportunity to appear in person or by counsel and to be heard by the Secretary of Transportation or an officer or employee of the Department designated in writing by him to conduct such hearing. If it appears from the hearing that such person, firm or corporation is guilty of the charge preferred against him or it, the Secretary of Transportation may order the permit suspended or revoked, and the bond forfeited. Any such revocation or suspension shall not be a bar to subsequent arrest and prosecution for violation of this Chapter.

P.A. 76–1586, § 13–108, eff. July 1, 1970. Amended by P.A. 77–157, § 1, eff. Jan. 1, 1972; P.A. 77–170, § 1, eff. Jan. 1, 1972; P.A. 77–2829, § 40, eff. Dec. 22, 1972; P.A. 78–255, § 61, eff. Oct. 1, 1973.

Formerly Ill.Rev.Stat.1991, ch. 95 ½, ¶ 13–108.

5/13–109. Safety test prior to application for license—Subsequent tests—Repairs—Retest

§ 13–109. Safety test prior to application for license—Subsequent tests—Repairs—Retest.

(a) Except as otherwise provided in Chapter 13, each second division vehicle and medical transport vehicle, except those vehicles other than school buses or medical transport vehicles owned or operated by a municipal corporation or political subdivision having a population of 1,000,000 or more inhabitants which are subjected to safety tests imposed by local ordinance or resolution, operated in whole or in part over the highways of this State, and each vehicle designed to carry 15 or fewer passengers operated by a contract carrier transporting employees in the course of their employment on a highway of this State, shall be subjected to the safety test provided for in Chapter 13 of this Code. Tests shall be conducted at an official testing station within 6 months prior to the application for registration as provided for in this Code. Subsequently each vehicle shall be subject to tests at least every 6 months, and in the case of school buses at least every 6 months or 10,000 miles whichever occurs first, and according to schedules established by rules and regulations promulgated by the Department. Any component subject to regular inspection which is damaged in a reportable accident must be reinspected before the bus is returned to service.

(b) The Department shall also conduct periodic nonscheduled inspections of school buses, of buses registered as charitable vehicles and of religious organization buses. If such inspection reveals that a vehicle is not in substantial compliance with the rules promulgated by the Department, the Department shall remove the Certificate of Safety from the vehicle, and shall place the vehicle out-of-service. A bright orange, triangular decal shall be placed on an out-of-service vehicle where the Certificate of Safety has been removed. The vehicle must pass a safety test at an official testing station before it is again placed in service.

(c) If the violation is not substantial a bright yellow, triangular sticker shall be placed next to the Certificate of Safety at the time the nonscheduled inspection is made. The Department shall reinspect the vehicle after 3 working days to determine that the violation has been corrected and remove the yellow, triangular decal. If the violation is not corrected within 3 working days, the Department shall place the vehicle out-of-service in accordance with procedures in subsection (b).

(d) If a violation is not substantial and does not directly affect the safe operation of the vehicle, the Department shall issue a warning notice requiring correction of the violation. Such correction shall be accomplished as soon as practicable and a report of the correction shall be made to the Department within 30 days in a manner established by the Department. If the Department has not been advised that the corrections have been made, and the violations still exist, the Department shall place the vehicle out-of-service in accordance with procedures in subsection (b).

(e) The Department is authorized to promulgate regulations to implement its program of nonscheduled inspections. Causing or allowing the operation of an out-of-service vehicle with passengers or unauthorized removal of an out-of-service sticker is a Class 3 felony. Causing or allowing the operation of a vehicle with a 3–day sticker for longer than 3 days with the sticker attached or the unauthorized removal of a 3–day sticker is a Class C misdemeanor.

(f) If a second division vehicle, medical transport vehicle, or vehicle operated by a contract carrier as provided in subsection (a) of this Section is in safe mechanical condition, as determined pursuant to Chapter 13, the operator of the official testing station must at once issue to the second division vehicle or medical transport vehicle a certificate of safety, in the form and manner prescribed by the Department, which shall be affixed to the vehicle by the certified safety tester who performed the safety tests. The owner of the second division vehicle or medical transport vehicle or the contract carrier shall at all times display the Certificate of Safety on the second division vehicle, medical transport vehicle, or vehicle operated by a contract carrier in the manner prescribed by the Department.

(g) If a test shows that a second division vehicle, medical transport vehicle, or vehicle operated by a contract carrier is not in safe mechanical condition as provided in this Section, it shall not be operated on the highways until it has been repaired and submitted to a retest at an official testing station. If the owner or contract carrier submits the vehicle to a retest at a different official testing station from that where it failed to pass the first test, he shall present to the operator of the second station the report of the original test, and shall notify the Department in writing, giving the name and address of the original testing station and the defects which prevented the issuance of a Certificate of Safety, and the name and address of the second official testing station making the retest.

P.A. 76–1586, § 13–109, eff. July 1, 1970. Amended by P.A. 77–157, § 1, eff. Jan. 1, 1972; P.A. 77–170, § 1, eff. Jan. 1, 1972; P.A. 77–2170, § 1, eff. Aug. 2, 1972; P.A. 78–255, § 61, eff. Oct. 1, 1973; P.A. 78–1244, § 1, eff. Sept. 5, 1974; P.A. 78–1297, § 58, eff. March 4, 1975; P.A. 79–63, § 1, eff. June 26, 1975; P.A. 79–798, § 1, eff. July 1, 1976; P.A. 79–1454, § 44, eff. Aug. 31, 1976; P.A. 80–606, § 1, eff. Oct. 1, 1977; P.A. 82–433, § 1, eff. Sept. 8, 1981; P.A. 86–447, § 2, eff. Aug. 30, 1989; P.A. 86–1223, § 1, eff. Jan. 1, 1991; P.A. 92–108, § 5, eff. Jan. 1, 2002.

Formerly Ill.Rev.Stat.1991, ch. 95 ½, ¶ 13–109.

Section 3 of P.A. 82–433 approved Sept. 8, 1981, provided:

"This Act takes effect upon its becoming a law, except that the provisions relating to safety tests and proof of financial responsibility for medical transport vehicles apply only to applications for and the issuance of registration plates which are required to be displayed on January 1, 1982 or thereafter."

5/13–109.1. Annual and nonscheduled emission inspection tests; standards; penalties; funds

§ 13–109.1. Annual and nonscheduled emission inspection tests; standards; penalties; funds.

(a) For each diesel powered vehicle that (i) is registered for a gross weight of more than 16,000 pounds, (ii) is registered within an affected area, and (iii) is a 2 year or older model year, an annual emission inspection test shall be conducted at an official testing station certified by the Illinois Department of Transportation to perform diesel emission inspections pursuant to the standards set forth in subsection (b) of this Section. This annual emission inspection test may be conducted in conjunction with a semi-annual safety test.

(a–5) Beginning October 1, 2000, the Department of State Police is authorized to perform nonscheduled emission inspections for cause, at any place within an affected area, of any diesel powered vehicles that are operated on the roadways of this State, and are registered for a gross weight of more than 16,000 pounds or have a gross vehicle weight rating of more than 16,000 pounds. The inspections shall adhere to the procedures and standards set forth in subsection (b). These nonscheduled emission inspections shall be conducted by the Department of State Police at weigh stations, roadside, or other safe and reasonable locations within an affected area. Before any person may inspect a diesel vehicle under this Section, he or she must receive adequate training and certification for diesel emission inspections by the Department of State Police. The Department of State Police shall adopt rules for the training and certification of persons who conduct emission inspections under this Section.

(b) Diesel emission inspections conducted under this Chapter 13 shall be conducted in accordance with the Society of Automotive Engineers Recommended Practice J1667 "Snap-Acceleration Smoke Test Procedure for Heavy–Duty Diesel Powered Vehicles" and the cutpoint standards set forth in the United States Environmental Protection Agency guidance document "Guidance to States on Smoke Opacity Cutpoints to be used with the SAE J1667 In–Use Smoke Test Procedure". Those procedures and standards, as now in effect, are made a part of this Code, in the same manner as though they were set out in full in this Code.

Notwithstanding the above cutpoint standards, for motor vehicles that are model years 1973 and older, until December 31, 2002, the level of peak smoke opacity shall not exceed 70 percent. Beginning January 1, 2003, for motor vehicles that are model years 1973 and older, the level of peak smoke opacity shall not exceed 55 percent.

(c) If the annual emission inspection under subsection (a) reveals that the vehicle is not in compliance with the diesel emission standards set forth in subsection (b) of this Section, the operator of the official testing station shall issue a warning notice requiring correction of the violation. The correction shall be made and the vehicle submitted to an emissions retest at an official testing station certified by the Department to perform diesel emission inspections within 30 days from the issuance of the warning notice requiring correction of the violation.

If, within 30 days from the issuance of the warning notice, the vehicle is not in compliance with the diesel emission standards set forth in subsection (b) as determined by an emissions retest at an official testing station, the operator of the official testing station or the Department shall place the vehicle out-of-service in accordance with the rules promulgated by the Department. Operating a vehicle that has been placed out-of-service under this subsection (c) is a petty offense punishable by a $1,000 fine. The vehicle must pass a diesel emission inspection at an official testing station before it is again placed in service. The Secretary of State, Department of State Police, and other law enforcement officers shall enforce this Section. No emergency vehicle, as defined in Section 1–105, may be placed out-of-service pursuant to this Section.

The Department or an official testing station may issue a certificate of waiver subsequent to a reinspection of a vehicle that failed the emissions inspection. Certificate of waiver shall be issued upon determination that documented proof demonstrates that emissions repair costs for the noncompliant vehicle of at least $3,000 have been spent in an effort to achieve compliance with the emission standards set forth in subsection (b). The Department of Transportation shall adopt rules for the implementation of this subsection including standards of documented proof as well as the criteria by which a waiver shall be granted.

(c–5) If a nonscheduled inspection reveals that the vehicle is not in compliance with the diesel emission standards set forth in subsection (b), the operator of the vehicle is guilty of a petty offense punishable by a $400 fine, and a State Police officer shall issue a citation for a violation of the standards. A third or subsequent violation within one year of the first violation is a petty offense punishable by a $1,000 fine. An operator who receives a citation under this subsection shall not, within 30 days of the initial citation, receive a second or subsequent citation for operating the same vehicle in violation of the emission standards set forth in subsection (b).

(d) There is hereby created within the State Treasury a special fund to be known as the Diesel Emissions Testing Fund, constituted from the fines collected pursuant to subsections (c) and (c–5) of this Section. Subject to appropriation, moneys from the Diesel Emissions Testing Fund shall be available, as a supplement to moneys appropriated from the General Revenue Fund, to the Department of Transportation and the Department of State Police for their implementation of the diesel emission inspection requirements under this Chapter 13. All moneys received from fines imposed under this Section shall be paid into the Diesel Emissions Testing Fund. All citations issued pursuant to this Section shall be considered non-moving violations. The Department of Transportation and the Department of State Police are authorized to promulgate rules to implement their responsibilities under this Section.

P.A. 76–1586, § 13–109.1, added by P.A. 91–254, § 10, eff. July 1, 2000. Amended by P.A. 91–865, § 5, eff. July 1, 2000.

5/13–109.2. Pollution Control Board diesel emission standards and tests

§ 13–109.2. Pollution Control Board diesel emission standards and tests. Within 8 months of the effective date of this amendatory Act of the 91st General Assembly, the Pollution Control Board shall amend its heavy-duty diesel smoke opacity standards and test procedures to be consistent with the procedures and standards set forth in Section 13–109.1.

P.A. 76–1586, § 13–109.2, added by P.A. 91–254, § 10, eff. July 1, 2000.

5/13–109.3. Exemption from diesel emissions inspections

§ 13–109.3. Exemption from diesel emissions inspections. Second division vehicles being operated on plates issued pursuant to subsection (c) of Section 3–815 are exempt from the diesel emissions inspection requirements set forth in this Chapter.

P.A. 76–1586, § 13–109.3, added by P.A. 91–254, § 10, eff. July 1, 2000.

5/13–110. Certificate of safety

§ 13–110. Certificate of safety. (a) Certificates of Safety shall be in contrasting colors, with a number on the face of the Certificate indicating the month of the next inspection period the vehicle is subject to inspection. Certificates for school buses shall also indicate the mileage at which the school bus shall be subject to inspection if it occurs before the next regular inspection period. The colors of Certificates of Safety shall be prescribed by the Department.

(b) Certificates of Safety, which remain the property of the State of Illinois, will be provided to Official Testing Stations by the Department at the fee of $1 each. Certificates of Safety which remain unused at the end of each inspection period will be redeemed for the same amount in a manner prescribed by the Department.

(c) Nothing in this Chapter shall be construed as a suggestion or direction to any owner to require him to have any repairs made or any work done by any official testing station, but all tests must be made at an official testing station to secure the issuance of a certificate of safety, and no certificate of safety issued by any other than an official testing station shall be deemed a compliance with this Chapter.

P.A. 76–1586, § 13–110, eff. July 1, 1970. Amended by P.A. 80–606, § 1, eff. Oct. 1, 1977; P.A. 83–311, § 1, eff. Jan. 1, 1984.

Formerly Ill.Rev.Stat.1991, ch. 95 ½, ¶ 13–110.

5/13–111. Operation without certificate of safety attached; Effective date of certificate

§ 13–111. Operation without certificate of safety attached; Effective date of certificate.

(a) Except as provided for in Chapter 13, no person shall operate any vehicle required to be inspected by this Chapter upon the highways of this State unless there is affixed to that vehicle a certificate of safety then in effect. The Secretary of State, State Police, and other police officers shall enforce this Section. The Department shall determine the expiration date of the certificate of safety.

The certificates, all forms and records, reports of tests and retests, and the full procedure and methods of making the tests and retests, shall be in the form prescribed by the Department.

(b) Every person convicted of violating this Section is guilty of a Class C misdemeanor.

P.A. 76–1586, § 13–111, eff. July 1, 1970. Amended by P.A. 77–157, § 1, eff. Jan. 1, 1972; P.A. 77–170, § 1, eff. Jan. 1, 1972; P.A. 77–2170, § 1, eff. Aug. 2, 1972; P.A. 78–255, § 61, eff. Oct. 1, 1973; P.A. 81–1554, § 1, eff. Jan. 13, 1981; P.A. 82–433, § 1, eff. Sept. 8, 1981; P.A. 83–12, § 1, eff. Jan. 1, 1984; P.A. 88–415, § 10, eff. Aug. 20, 1993.

Formerly Ill.Rev.Stat.1991, ch. 95 ½, ¶ 13–111.

Section 3 of P.A. 82–433 approved Sept. 8, 1981, provided:

"This Act takes effect upon its becoming a law, except that the provisions relating to safety tests and proof of financial responsibility for medical transport vehicles apply only to applications for and the issuance of registration plates which are required to be displayed on January 1, 1982 or thereafter."

Section 4 of P.A. 83–12, approved July 1, 1983, provided:

"Effective date. This Act takes effect as provided in this Section.

"The amendments to those portions of Sections 3–815(a), 3–818 and 3–819(b) of 'The Illinois Vehicle Code' in Section 1 of this Act which create the 'X', 'Z', 'MX', 'MZ', 'MM' and 'TN' registration classifications and the fees and taxes imposed for those classifications, the amendments to Sections 2–119, 3–401 and 3–802 of 'The Illinois Vehicle Code' in Section 1 of this Act, and the amendments to Chapter 15 of 'The Illinois Vehicle Code' in Section 1 of this Act take effect July 1, 1983.

"The remaining amendments to 'The Illinois Vehicle Code' in Section 1 of this Act take effect July 1, 1983 and apply beginning with the 1985 registration year, except that the amendments to Sections 3–813 through 3–816 and Section 3–819 apply beginning with the 1984 registration year for those vehicles registered on a calendar year basis only.

"The amendments to Chapters 13 and 18 of 'The Illinois Vehicle Code' in Section 1 of this Act take effect January 1, 1984.

"Section 2 of this Act takes effect on the first day of the next succeeding month which commences at least 30 days after the date on which this Act becomes law.

"Section 3 of this Act takes effect July 1, 1983.

"Section 3.1 of this Act takes effect January 1, 1984.

"This Section 4 takes effect upon its becoming a law."

5/13–112. Exemption from local tests

§ 13–112. Exemption from local tests. Any second division vehicle or limousine displaying a certificate of safety issued under this Chapter is exempt from any test required by ordinance or otherwise in any city, village or incorporated town in this State.

P.A. 76–1586, § 13–101, eff. July 1, 1970. Amended by P.A. 77–157, § 1, eff. Jan. 1, 1972; P.A. 77–170, § 1, eff. Jan. 1, 1972; P.A. 77–1633, § 1, eff. Sept. 23, 1972; P.A. 77–1688, § 1, eff. July 1, 1972; P.A. 77–2170, § 1, eff. Aug. 2, 1972; P.A. 78–255, § 61, eff. Oct. 1, 1973; P.A. 78–1244, § 1, eff. Sept. 5, 1974; P.A. 78–1297, § 58, eff. March 4, 1975; P.A. 79–798, § 1, eff. July 1, 1976; P.A. 79–865, § 1, eff. Jan. 1, 1976; P.A. 79–1454, § 44, eff. Aug. 31, 1976; P.A. 80–606, § 1, eff. Oct. 1, 1977; P.A. 80–1018, § 1, eff. Oct. 1, 1977; P.A. 80–1364, § 36, eff. Aug. 13, 1978; P.A. 81–1554, § 1, eff. Jan. 13, 1981; P.A. 82–433, § 1, eff. Sept. 8, 1981; P.A. 82–573, § 1, eff. Sept. 24, 1981; P.A. 82–783, Art. III, § 37, eff. July 13, 1982; P.A. 82–957, § 1, eff. Jan. 1, 1983; P.A. 83–315, § 1, eff. Jan. 1, 1984; P.A. 83–497, § 1, eff. Jan. 1, 1984; P.A. 83–831, § 1, eff. Jan. 1, 1984; P.A. 83–1260, § 1, eff. Aug. 16, 1984; P.A. 83–1362, Art. II, § 99, eff. Sept. 11, 1984; P.A. 84–832, Art. II, § 10, eff. Sept. 23, 1985; P.A. 84–1060, § 1, eff. July 1, 1986; P.A. 85–572, § 1, eff. Sept. 18, 1987; P.A. 86–408, § 1, eff. Jan. 1, 1990; P.A. 86–447, § 2, eff. Aug. 30, 1989; P.A. 86–1028, Art. II, § 2–44, eff. Feb. 5, 1990; P.A. 87–1111, § 1, eff. Sept. 15, 1992.

Formerly Ill.Rev.Stat.1991, ch. 95 ½, ¶ 13–112.

5/13–113. Sale or exchange of used vehicle without certificate of safety

§ 13–113. Sale or exchange of used vehicle without certificate of safety. No person engaged in the business of buying, selling or exchanging motor vehicles shall sell, transfer or exchange any used second division vehicle or medical transport vehicle unless it has been tested and a currently valid certificate of safety has been issued therefor: Provided, that such person engaged in the business of buying, selling or exchanging motor vehicles may sell, transfer or exchange any used second division vehicle or medical transport vehicle without a valid certificate of safety if the sale, transfer or exchange is for the purpose of restoring or repairing such vehicle to a condition in which it can pass the test for a certificate of safety, or for the purpose of junking. Provided, however, that the used second division vehicle or medical transport vehicle is not moved under its own power to the location in which it will be restored, repaired or junked.

P.A. 76–1586, § 13–113, eff. July 1, 1970. Amended by P.A. 81–694, § 1, eff. Sept. 16, 1979; P.A. 82–433, § 1, eff. Sept. 8, 1981.

Formerly Ill.Rev.Stat.1991, ch. 95 ½, ¶ 13–113.

Section 3 of P.A. 82–433 approved Sept. 8, 1981, provided:

"This Act takes effect upon its becoming a law, except that the provisions relating to safety tests and proof of financial responsibility for medical transport vehicles apply only to applications for and the issuance of registration plates which are required to be displayed on January 1, 1982 or thereafter."

5/13–114. Interstate carriers of property

§ 13–114. Interstate carriers of property. Any vehicle registered in Illinois and operated by an interstate carrier of property shall be exempt from the provisions of this Chapter provided such carrier has registered with the Bureau of Motor Carrier Safety of the Federal Highway Administration as an interstate motor carrier of property and has been assigned a federal census number by such Bureau. An interstate carrier of property, however, is not exempt from the provisions of Section 13–111(b) of this Chapter.

Any vehicle registered in Illinois and operated by a private interstate carrier of property shall be exempt from the provisions of this Chapter, except the provisions of Section 13–111(b), provided it:

1. is registered with the Bureau of Motor Carrier Safety of the Federal Highway Administration, and
2. carries in the motor vehicle documentation issued by the Bureau of Motor Carrier Safety of the Federal Highway Administration displaying the federal census number assigned, and
3. displays on the sides of the motor vehicle the census number, which must be no less than 2 inches high, with a brush stroke no less than ¼ inch wide in a contrasting color.

Notwithstanding any other provision of this Section, each diesel powered vehicle that is registered for a gross weight of more than 16,000 pounds or has a gross vehicle weight rating of more than 16,000 pounds and that is operated by an interstate carrier of property or a private interstate carrier of property within the affected area is subject only to the provisions of this Chapter that pertain to nonscheduled diesel emission inspections.

P.A. 76–1586, § 13–114, eff. July 1, 1970. Amended by P.A. 76–1725, § 1, eff. July 1, 1970; P.A. 77–43, § 1, eff. Jan. 1, 1972; P.A. 78–498, § 1, eff. Oct. 1, 1973; P.A. 81–1554, § 1, eff. Jan. 13, 1981; P.A. 83–12, § 1, eff. Jan. 1, 1984; P.A. 85–560, § 1, eff. Sept. 18, 1987; P.A. 85–1407, § 2, eff. Sept. 22, 1988; P.A. 91–254, § 10, eff. July 1, 2000; P.A. 91–865, § 5, eff. July 1, 2000.

Formerly Ill.Rev.Stat.1991, ch. 95 ½, ¶ 13–114.

Section 4 of P.A. 83–12, approved July 1, 1983, provided:

"Effective date. This Act takes effect as provided in this Section.

"The amendments to those portions of Sections 3–815(a), 3–818 and 3–819(b) of 'The Illinois Vehicle Code' in Section 1 of this Act which create the 'X', 'Z', 'MX', 'MZ', 'MM' and 'TN' registration classifications and the fees and taxes imposed for those classifications, the amendments to Sections 2–119, 3–401 and 3–802 of 'The Illinois Vehicle Code' in Section 1 of this Act, and the amendments to Chapter 15 of 'The Illinois Vehicle Code' in Section 1 of this Act take effect July 1, 1983.

"The remaining amendments to 'The Illinois Vehicle Code' in Section 1 of this Act take effect July 1, 1983 and apply beginning with the 1985 registration year, except that the amendments to Sections 3–813 through 3–816 and Section 3–819 apply beginning with the 1984 registration year for those vehicles registered on a calendar year basis only.

"The amendments to Chapters 13 and 18 of 'The Illinois Vehicle Code' in Section 1 of this Act take effect January 1, 1984.

"Section 2 of this Act takes effect on the first day of the next succeeding month which commences at least 30 days after the date on which this Act becomes law.

"Section 3 of this Act takes effect July 1, 1983.

"Section 3.1 of this Act takes effect January 1, 1984.

"This Section 4 takes effect upon its becoming a law."

P.A. 91–865 incorporated the amendment by P.A. 91–254.

5/13–115. School buses—pretrip inspections

§ 13–115. School buses—pretrip inspections.

Each day that a school bus is operated the driver shall conduct a pretrip inspection of the mechanical and safety equipment on the bus as prescribed by rule or regulation of the Department. A person other than the driver may perform portions of the pretrip inspection as prescribed by rule of the Department.

P.A. 76–1586, § 13–115, added by P.A. 78–1244, § 1, eff. Sept. 5, 1974. Amended by P.A. 89–658, § 5, eff. Jan. 1, 1997.

Formerly Ill.Rev.Stat.1991, ch. 95 ½, ¶ 13–115.

5/13–116. Deposit of funds

§ 13–116. All funds collected by the Department under this Chapter shall be deposited in the road fund in the State Treasury.

P.A. 76–1586, § 13–116, added by P.A. 80–606, § 1, eff. Oct. 1, 1977.

Formerly Ill.Rev.Stat.1991, ch. 95 ½, ¶ 13–116.

5/13–116.1. Emission inspection funding

§ 13–116.1. Emission inspection funding. The Department of Transportation shall be reimbursed for all expenses related to the training, equipment, recordkeeping, and conducting of diesel powered emission inspections pursuant to this Chapter 13 when that testing is conducted within the affected areas, subject to appropriation, from the General Revenue Fund and the Diesel Emissions Testing Fund. No moneys from any funds other than the General Revenue Fund and the Diesel Emissions Testing Fund shall be appropriated for diesel emission inspections under this Chapter 13.

P.A. 76–1586, § 13–116.1, added by P.A. 91–254, § 10, eff. July 1, 2000.

5/13–117. Home rule

§ 13–117. Home rule. A unit of local government within the affected areas, including home rule units, shall not require or conduct a diesel emission inspection program that does not meet or exceed the standards of the diesel emission inspections provided for in this Chapter 13. A unit of local government within the affected areas, including home rule units, must affirmatively comply with the diesel emission inspection requirements of this Chapter 13. This Section is a limitation under subsection (i) of Section 6 of Article VII of the Illinois Constitution on the concurrent exercise by home rule units of powers and functions exercised by the State.

P.A. 76–1586, § 13–117, added by P.A. 91–254, § 10, eff. July 1, 2000.

CHAPTER 13A. EMISSION INSPECTION

Section
5/13A-101 to 5/13A-115. Repealed.

Enactment and Repeal

Chapter 13A was added by P.A. 83-1477, § 1, eff. Sept. 24, 1984, and was repealed eff. Jan. 1, 2003, pursuant to 625 ILCS 5/13A-115, as amended by P.A. 92-682.

5/13A-101 to 5/13A-115. §§ 13A-101 to 13A-115. Repealed eff. Jan. 1, 2003

CHAPTER 13B. EMISSION INSPECTION

Enactment

Chapter 13B was added by P.A. 88-533, § 15, eff. Jan. 1, 1994

5/13B-1. Short title

§ 13B-1. Short title. This Chapter may be cited as the Vehicle Emissions Inspection Law of 1995.

P.A. 76-1586, § 13B-1, added by P.A. 88-533, § 15, eff. Jan. 18, 1994.

5/13B-5. Definitions

§ 13B-5. Definitions. For the purposes of this Chapter:

"Affected counties" means Cook County; DuPage County; Lake County; those parts of Kane County that are not included within any of the following ZIP code areas, as designated by the U.S. Postal Service on the effective date of this amendatory Act of 1994: 60109, 60119, 60135, 60140, 60142, 60144, 60147, 60151, 60152, 60178, 60182, 60511, 60520, 60545, and 60554; those parts of Kendall County that are not included within any of the following ZIP code areas, as designated by the U.S. Postal Service on the effective date of this amendatory Act of 1994: 60447, 60512, 60536, 60537, 60541, those parts of 60543 that are not within the census defined urbanized area, 60545, and 60560; those parts of McHenry County that are not included within any of the following ZIP code areas, as designated by the U.S. Postal Service on the effective date of this amendatory Act of 1994: 60001, 60033, 60034, 60071, 60072, 60097, 60098, 60142, 60152, and 60180; those parts of Will County that are not included within any of the following ZIP code areas, as designated by the U.S. Postal Service on the effective date of this amendatory Act of 1994: 60401, 60407, 60408, 60410, 60416, 60418, 60421, 60442, 60447, 60468, 60481, 60935 and 60950; those parts of Madison County that are not included within any of the following ZIP code areas, as designated by the U.S. Postal Service on the effective date of this amendatory Act of 1994: 62001, 62012, 62021, 62026, 62046, 62058, 62061, 62067, 62074, 62088, 62097, 62249, 62275, and 62281; those parts of Monroe County that are not included within any of the following ZIP code areas, as designated by the U.S. Postal Service on the effective date of this amendatory Act of 1994: 62244, 62248, 62256, 62261, 62276, 62278, 62279, 62295, and 62298; and those parts of St. Clair County that are not included within any of the following ZIP code areas, as designated by the U.S. Postal Service on the effective date of this amendatory Act of 1994: 62224, 62243, 62248, 62254, 62255, 62257, 62258, 62260, 62264, 62265, 62269, 62278, 62282, 62285, 62289, and 62298.

"Board" means the Illinois Pollution Control Board.

"Claim evaluation center" means an automotive diagnostic facility that meets the standards prescribed by the Agency for performing examinations of vehicle emissions inspection damage claims.

"Contractor" means the vehicle emissions test contractor for Official Inspection Stations described in Section 13B-45.

"Inspection area" means Cook County, DuPage County, Lake County and those portions of Kane, Kendall, Madison, McHenry, Monroe, Will, and St. Clair Counties included in the definition of "affected counties".

"Owner" means the registered owner of the vehicle, as indicated on the vehicle's registration. In the case of an unregistered vehicle, "owner" has the meaning set forth in Section 1-155 of this Code.

"Program" means the vehicle emission inspection program established under this Chapter.

"Resident" includes natural persons, foreign and domestic corporations, partnerships, associations, and all other commercial and governmental entities. For the purpose of determining residence, the owner of a vehicle shall be presumed to reside at the address indicated on the vehicle's registration. A governmental entity, including the federal government and its agencies, and any unit of local government or school district, any part of which is located within an affected county, shall be deemed a resident of an affected county for the purpose of any vehicle that is owned by the governmental entity and regularly operated in an affected county.

"Registration" of a vehicle means its registration under Article IV of Chapter 3 of this Code.[1]

P.A. 76-1586, § 13B-5, added by P.A. 88-533, § 15, eff. Jan. 18, 1994. Amended by P.A. 90-89, § 15, eff. Jan. 1, 1998; P.A. 92-821, § 5, eff. Aug. 21, 2002.

[1] 625 ILCS 5/3-400 et seq.

5/13B-10. Program

§ 13B-10. Program.

(a) The Agency shall establish a program to begin January 1, 1995, to reduce the emission of pollutants by motor vehicles. At a minimum, this program shall provide for all of the following:

(1) The inspection of certain motor vehicles every 2 years, as required under Section 13B-15.

(2) The establishment and operation of official inspection stations.

(3) The designation of official test equipment and testing procedures.

(4) The training and supervision of inspectors and other personnel.

(5) Procedures to assure the correct operation, maintenance and calibration of test equipment.

(6) Procedures for certifying test results and for reporting and maintaining relevant data and records.

(b) The Agency shall provide for the operation of a sufficient number of official inspection stations to prevent undue difficulty in obtaining the inspections required under this Chapter. In the event that the Agency operates inspection stations or contracts with one or more parties to operate inspection stations on its behalf, the Agency shall endeavor to: (i) locate the stations so that the owners of vehicles subject to inspection reside within 12 miles of an official inspection station; and (ii) have sufficient inspection capacity at the stations so that the usual wait before the start of an inspection does not exceed 20 minutes.

P.A. 76-1586, § 13B-10, added by P.A. 88-533, § 15, eff. Jan. 18, 1994.

5/13B-15. Inspections

§ 13B-15. Inspections.

(a) Beginning with the implementation of the program required by this Chapter, every motor vehicle that is owned by a resident of an affected county, other than a vehicle that is exempt under subsection (f) or (g), is subject to inspection under the program.

The Agency shall send notice of the assigned inspection month, at least 15 days before the beginning of the assigned month, to the owner of each vehicle subject to the program. For a vehicle that was subject to inspection before the effective date of this amendatory Act of 1994 and for which an initial inspection sticker or initial inspection certificate has already been issued, the month to be assigned by the Agency for that vehicle shall not be earlier than the current assigned month, unless so requested by the owner. If the assigned month is later than the current assigned month, the Agency shall issue either a corrected inspection sticker or corrected certificate for that vehicle.

Initial emission inspection stickers or initial inspection certificates, as the case may be, expire on the last day of the third month following the month assigned by the Agency for the first inspection of the vehicle. Renewal inspection stickers or certificates expire on the last day of the third month following the month assigned for inspection in the year in which the vehicle's next inspection is required.

The Agency or its agent may issue an interim emission inspection sticker or certificate for any vehicle subject to inspection that does not have a currently valid emission inspection sticker or certificate at the time the Agency is notified by the Secretary of State of its registration by a new owner, and for which an initial emission inspection sticker or certificate has already been issued. Interim emission inspection stickers or certificates expire no later than the last day of the sixth complete calendar month after the date the Agency issued the interim emission inspection sticker or certificate.

The owner of each vehicle subject to inspection shall obtain an emission inspection sticker or certificate for the vehicle in accordance with this subsection. Before the expiration of the emission inspection sticker or certificate, the owner shall have the vehicle inspected and, upon demonstration of compliance, obtain a renewal emission inspection sticker or certificate. A renewal emission inspection sticker or certificate shall not be issued more than 5 months before the expiration date of the previous inspection sticker or certificate.

(b) Except as provided in subsection (c), vehicles shall be inspected every 2 years on a schedule that begins either in the second, fourth, or later calendar year after the vehicle model year. The beginning test schedule shall be set by the Agency and shall be consistent with the State's requirements for emission reductions as determined by the applicable United States Environmental Protection Agency vehicle emissions estimation model and applicable guidance and rules.

(c) A vehicle may be inspected out of its 2-year inspection schedule when a new owner acquires the vehicle and it should have been, but was not, in compliance with this Act when the vehicle was acquired by the new owner.

(d) The owner of a vehicle subject to inspection shall have the vehicle inspected and obtain and display on the vehicle or carry within the vehicle, in a manner specified by the Agency, a valid unexpired emission inspection sticker or certificate in the manner specified by the Agency.

Any person who violates this subsection (d) is guilty of a petty offense, except that a third or subsequent violation within one year of the first violation is a Class C misdemeanor. The fine imposed for a violation of this subsection shall be not less than $50 if the violation occurred within 60 days following the date by which a new or renewal emission inspection sticker or certificate was required to be obtained for the vehicle, and not less than $300 if the violation occurred more than 60 days after that date.

(e) (1) For a $20 fee, to be paid into the Vehicle Inspection Fund, the Agency shall inspect:

(A) Vehicles operated on federal installations within an affected county, pursuant to Title 40, Section 51.356 of the Code of Federal Regulations.

(B) Federally owned vehicles operated in affected counties.

(2) For a fee of $20, to be paid into the Vehicle Inspection Fund, the Agency may inspect:

(A) Vehicles registered in and subject to emission inspections requirements of another state.

(B) Vehicles presented for inspection on a voluntary basis.

Any fees collected under this subsection shall not offset normally appropriated Motor Fuel Tax Funds.

(f) The following vehicles are not subject to inspection:

(1) Vehicles not subject to registration under Article IV of Chapter 3 of this Code,[1] other than vehicles owned by the federal government.

(2) Motorcycles, motor driven cycles, and motorized pedalcycles.

(3) Farm vehicles and implements of husbandry.

(4) Implements of warfare owned by the State or federal government.

(5) Antique vehicles, custom vehicles, street rods, and vehicles of model year 1967 or before.

(6) Vehicles operated exclusively for parade or ceremonial purposes by any veterans, fraternal, or civic organization, organized on a not-for-profit basis.

(7) Vehicles for which a Junking Certificate has been issued by the Secretary of State under Section 3-117 of this Code.

(8) Diesel powered vehicles, and vehicles that are powered exclusively by electricity.

(9) Vehicles operated exclusively in organized amateur or professional sporting activities, as defined in the Environmental Protection Act.[2]

(10) Vehicles registered in, subject to, and in compliance with the emission inspection requirements of another state.

The Agency may issue temporary or permanent exemption stickers or certificates for vehicles temporarily or permanently exempt from inspection under this subsection (f). An exemption sticker or certificate does not need to be displayed.

(g) According to criteria the Agency may adopt, a motor vehicle may be exempted from the inspection requirements of this Section by the Agency on the basis of an Agency determination that the vehicle is located and primarily used outside of the affected counties or in other jurisdictions where vehicle emission inspections are not required. The Agency may issue an annual exemption sticker or certificate without inspection for any vehicle exempted from inspection under this subsection.

(h) Any owner or lessee of a fleet of 15 or more motor vehicles which are subject to inspection under this Section may apply to the Agency for a permit to establish and operate a Private Official Inspection Station.

(i) Pursuant to Title 40, Section 51.371 of the Code of Federal Regulations, the Agency shall establish a program of on-road testing of in-use vehicles through the use of remote sensing devices. The Agency shall evaluate the emission performance of 0.5% of the subject fleet or 20,000 vehicles, whichever is less. Under no circumstances shall on-road testing include any sort of roadblock or roadside pullover or cause any type of traffic delay.

If, during the course of on-road inspections, a vehicle is found to exceed the on-road emissions standards established for the model year and type of vehicle, the Agency shall send a notice to the vehicle owner. The notice shall document the occurrence and results of on-road exceedances. The notice of a second on-road exceedance shall indicate that the vehicle has been reassigned and is subject to an out-of-cycle follow-up inspection at an official inspection station. In no case shall the Agency send a notice of an on-road exceedance to the owner of a vehicle that was found to exceed the on-road emission standards established for the model year and type of vehicle if the vehicle is registered outside of the affected counties.

P.A. 76-1586, § 13B-15, added by P.A. 88-533, § 15, eff. Jan. 18, 1994. Amended by P.A. 90-475, § 10, eff. Aug. 17, 1997; P.A. 92-668, § 5, eff. Jan. 1, 2003.

[1] 625 ILCS 5/3-400 et seq.

[2] 415 ILCS 5/1 et seq.

5/13B-20. Rules and standards

§ 13B-20. Rules and standards.

(a) The Agency shall propose standards necessary to achieve reductions in the emission of hydrocarbons, carbon monoxide, and oxides of nitrogen from motor vehicles subject to inspection under this Chapter. Within 120 days after the Agency proposes these standards, the Board shall adopt rules establishing standards for the emission of hydrocarbons, carbon monoxide, and oxides of nitrogen from motor vehicles subject to inspection under this Chapter. These rules may be amended from time to time pursuant to Agency proposals. The Board shall set standards necessary to achieve the reductions in vehicle hydrocarbons, carbon monoxide, and oxides of nitrogen emissions, as determined by the applicable vehicle emission estimation model and rules developed by the United States Environmental Protection Agency, required by the federal Clean Air Act.[1] A predetermined rate of failure shall not be used in determining standards necessary to achieve the reductions in vehicle hydrocarbons, carbon monoxide and oxides of nitrogen emissions. The emission standards established by the Board for vehicles of model year 1981 or later shall be identical in substance, as defined in Section 7.2(a) of the Environmental Protection Act,[2] to the emission standards promulgated by the United States Environmental Protection Agency.

If the Administrator of the United States Environmental Protection Agency finds that oxides of nitrogen emission reductions are not beneficial under Title 40, Section 51.351(d) of the Code of Federal Regulations, the Board shall not adopt rules establishing such standards for the emission of oxides of nitrogen under this Chapter. Any rules establishing these standards that have already been adopted before the findings by the United States Environmental Protection Agency shall be repealed by the Board by preemptory rulemaking under the Illinois Administrative Procedure Act [3] upon petition by the Agency.

Except as otherwise provided in this subsection, subsection (b) of Section 27 of the Environmental Protection Act [4] and the rulemaking provisions of the Illinois Administrative Procedure Act shall not apply to rules adopted by the Board under this subsection. Challenges to the validity of rules adopted by the Board under this subsection (a) may only be brought by filing a petition for review in the Appellate Court under Section 29 of the Environmental Protection Act within 35 days after the rule is filed with the Secretary of State.

(b) The Agency shall establish, and may from time to time amend, procedures designed to implement this Chapter.

P.A. 76-1586, § 13B-20, added by P.A. 88-533, § 15, eff. Jan. 18, 1994.

[1] 42 U.S.C.A. § 7401 et seq.

[2] 415 ILCS 5/7.2.

[3] 5 ILCS 100/1-1 et seq.

[4] 415 ILCS 5/27.

5/13B-25. Performance of inspections

§ 13B-25. Performance of inspections.

(a) The inspection of vehicles required under this Chapter shall be performed only: (i) by inspectors who have been certified by the Agency after successfully completing a course of training and successfully passing a written test; (ii) at official inspection stations or official on-road inspection sites established under this Chapter; and (iii) with equipment that has been approved by the Agency for these inspections.

(b) Except as provided in subsections (c) and (d), the inspection shall consist of (i) a loaded mode exhaust gas analysis; (ii) an evaporative system integrity test; (iii) an on-board computer diagnostic system check; and (iv) a verification that all required emission-related recall repairs have been made under Title 40, Section 51.370 of the Code of Federal Regulations; and may also include an evaporative system purge test. The owner of the vehicle or the owner's agent shall be entitled to an emission inspection certificate issued by an inspector only if all required tests are passed at the time of the inspection.

(c) A steady-state idle exhaust gas analysis may be substituted for the loaded mode exhaust gas analysis and the evaporative purge system test in the following cases:

(1) On any vehicle of model year 1980 or older.

(2) On any heavy duty vehicle with a manufacturer gross vehicle weight rating in excess of 8,500 pounds.

(3) On any vehicle for which loaded mode testing is not possible due to vehicle design or configuration.

(d) The procedures contained in subsections (d)(1) and (d)(2) of this Section shall be followed on model year 1996 and newer vehicles equipped with OBD on-board computer diagnostic equipment, as required.

(1) Beginning on July 1, 2002, and continuing through December 31, 2003, such vehicles shall be given a complete on-board diagnostic test consistent with the requirements of paragraphs (d)(1)(A) through (d)(1)(D) of this Section.

(A) If the vehicle meets the standards set for the complete on-board computer diagnostic test, neither the loaded mode exhaust gas analysis nor the idle exhaust gas analysis shall be performed; however, all other elements of the test contained in subsection (b) of this Section shall be performed.

(B) If, however, the vehicle fails to meet the standard for the complete on-board computer diagnostic test, it shall be given the loaded mode exhaust gas analysis or the idle exhaust gas analysis, as required, and all other elements of the test contained in subsection (b) of this Section, unless the owner of the vehicle chooses to avoid the loaded mode exhaust gas analysis or idle exhaust gas analysis and proceed directly under paragraph (d)(1)(C) of this Section. For those vehicles that fail to meet the standard for the complete on-board computer diagnostic test, the owner of the vehicle must be informed that he or she has the option to have the vehicle tested using the less stringent loaded mode exhaust gas analysis or the idle exhaust gas analysis, as appropriate, for one test cycle.

(C) If the vehicle fails to meet the standard for the complete on-board computer diagnostic test and the standard for the loaded mode exhaust gas analysis or the idle exhaust gas analysis, as required, or the owner of the vehicle has chosen to avoid the loaded mode exhaust gas analysis or idle exhaust gas analysis and proceed directly under this paragraph, the vehicle must be repaired to pass either the complete on-board computer diagnostic test or the loaded mode exhaust gas analysis or idle exhaust gas analysis, as required, and all other elements of the test contained in subsection (b) of this Section.

(D) The on-board computer diagnostic test shall not be a required element of the inspection mandated by this Section for such vehicles for which on-board computer diagnostic testing is not possible due to the vehicle's originally certified design or its design as modified in accordance with federal law and regulations, or for vehicles with known on-board diagnostic communications or software problems, as determined by the Agency. In such cases, all other elements of the inspection required under this Section shall be performed on such vehicles, including the exhaust gas analysis as specified in subsection (b) of this Section.

By April 15, 2003, the Agency shall submit to the General Assembly a report detailing the effectiveness of the use of the on-board computer diagnostic test. The report shall include the number of failures, the reason for each failure, the number of vehicle damage complaints, and the average wait time at the test stations.

(2) Beginning on January 1, 2004, such vehicles shall be given a complete on-board diagnostic test consistent with the requirements of paragraphs (d)(2)(A) and (d)(2)(B) of this Section.

(A) The loaded mode exhaust gas analysis specified in subsection (b) of this Section shall not be performed on such vehicles for which the on-board computer diagnostic test specified in subsection (h) of this Section can be performed. All other elements of the inspection required for such vehicles shall be performed in accordance with the provisions of this Section.

(B) The on-board computer diagnostic test shall not be a required element of the inspection mandated by this Section for such vehicles for which on-board computer diagnostic testing is not possible due to the vehicle's originally certified design or its design as modified in accordance with federal law and regulations, or for vehicles with known on-board diagnostic communications or software problems, as determined by the Agency. In such cases, all other elements of the inspection required under this Section shall be performed on such vehicles, including the exhaust gas analysis as specified in subsection (b) of this Section.

(e) The exhaust gas analysis shall consist of a test of an exhaust gas sample to determine whether the quantities of exhaust gas pollutants emitted by the vehicle meet the standards set for vehicles of that type under Section 13B–20. A vehicle shall be deemed to have passed this portion of the inspection if the evaluation of the exhaust gas sample indicates that the quantities of exhaust gas pollutants emitted by the vehicle do not exceed the standards set for vehicles of that type under Section 13B–20 or an inspector certifies that the vehicle qualifies for a waiver of the exhaust gas pollutant standards under Section 13B–30.

(f) The evaporative system integrity test shall consist of a procedure to determine if leaks exist in all or a portion of the vehicle fuel evaporation emission control system. A vehicle shall be deemed to have passed this test if it meets the criteria that the Board may adopt for an evaporative system integrity test.

(g) The evaporative system purge test shall consist of a procedure to verify the purging of vapors stored in the evaporative canister. A vehicle shall be deemed to have passed this test if it meets the criteria that the Board may adopt for an evaporative system purge test.

(h) The on-board computer diagnostic test shall consist of accessing the vehicle's on-board computer system, if so equipped, and reading any stored diagnostic codes that may be present. The vehicle shall be deemed to have passed this test if the codes observed did not exceed standards set for vehicles of that type under Section 13B–20.

P.A. 76–1586, § 13B–25, added by P.A. 88–533, § 15, eff. Jan. 18, 1994. Amended by P.A. 90–475, § 10, eff. Aug. 17, 1997; P.A. 92–682, § 5, eff. July 16, 2002.

5/13B–30. Waivers

§ 13B–30. Waivers.

(a) The Agency shall certify that a vehicle that has failed a vehicle emission retest qualifies for a waiver of the emission inspection standards if the following criteria are met:

(1) The vehicle has received all repairs and adjustments for which it is eligible under any emission performance warranty provided under Section 207 of the federal Clean Air Act.[1]

(2) The Agency determines by normal inspection procedures that the vehicle's emission control devices are present and appear to be properly connected and operating.

(3) Consistent with Title 40, Section 51.360 of the Code of Federal Regulations, for vehicles required to be tested

under this Chapter, a minimum expenditure of at least $450 in emission-related repairs exclusive of tampering-related repairs have been made.

(4) Repairs for vehicles of model year 1981 and later are conducted by a recognized repair technician.

(5) Evidence of repair is presented consisting of either signed and dated receipts identifying the vehicle and describing the work performed and amount charged for eligible emission-related repairs, or an affidavit executed by the person performing the eligible emission related repairs.

(6) The repairs have resulted in an improvement in vehicle emissions as determined by comparison of initial and final retest results.

(b) The Agency may issue an emission inspection certificate to vehicles failing a transient loaded mode emission retest if a complete documented physical and functional diagnosis and inspection shows that no additional emission-related repairs are needed. This diagnostic inspection must be performed by the Agency or its designated agent and shall be available only to motorists whose vehicle was repaired by a recognized repair technician.

(c) The Agency may extend the emission inspection certificate expiration date by one year upon receipt of a petition by the vehicle owner that needed repairs cannot be made due to economic hardship. Consistent with Title 40, Section 51.360 of the Code of Federal Regulations, this extension may be granted more than once during the life of the vehicle.

(d) The Agency shall propose procedures, practices, and performance requirements for operation of vehicle scrappage programs by any person that wants to receive credits for certain emissions reductions from these vehicles. The proposal shall include the method of vehicle selection, testing of vehicle emissions, documentation of annual vehicle miles traveled, determination of emissions, and determination of emissions reductions credits. Any applicable guidance available from the United States Environmental Protection Agency regarding these programs shall also be considered by the Agency. Within 180 days after the Agency files this proposal, the Board shall adopt rules for vehicle scrappage programs. Subsection (b) of Section 27 of the Environmental Protection Act [2] and the rulemaking provisions of the Illinois Administrative Procedure Act [3] shall not apply to rules adopted by the Board under this subsection (d).

(e) The Agency may adopt procedures to purchase vehicles for scrap that are unable to meet emission inspection standards and for which motorists provide a signed estimate from a recognized repair technician that the cost of emission-related repairs is expected to exceed an amount equal to one-half of the current minimum expenditure required in item (3) of subsection (a) of this Section. If the Agency adopts such procedures, they must be included in the vehicle scrappage programs in subsection (d). Such procedures shall require the Agency to arrange for private sector funding for the purchase of at least 90% of the vehicles which will be purchased for scrap.

(f) The Agency may issue an emission inspection certificate for vehicles subject to inspection under this Chapter that are located and primarily used in an area subject to the vehicle emission inspection requirements of another state. Emission inspection certificates shall be issued under this subsection only upon receipt by the Agency of evidence that the vehicle has been inspected and is in compliance with the emission inspection requirements and standards applicable in the state or local jurisdiction where the vehicle is being used.

P.A. 76-1586, § 13B-30, added by P.A. 88-533, § 15, eff. Jan. 18, 1994. Amended by P.A. 90-475, § 10, eff. Aug. 17, 1997.

[1] 42 U.S.C.A. § 7541.

[2] 415 ILCS 5/27.

[3] 5 ILCS 100/1-1 et seq.

5/13B-35. Inquiries

§ 13B-35. Inquiries. The Agency shall develop a means of responding to inquiries from inspectors and members of the public concerning the program, including (i) when inspections are required, (ii) what kind of inspections are required, (iii) whether emission inspection stickers or certificates previously required for a vehicle have been obtained, and (iv) the procedures for resolving disputes concerning inspections.

P.A. 76-1586, § 13B-35, added by P.A. 88-533, § 15, eff. Jan. 18, 1994.

5/13B-40. Grievance and damage claim requirements and procedures

§ 13B-40. Grievance and damage claim requirements and procedures.

(a) Emissions inspection and waiver denial grievance procedures. Any person aggrieved by a decision regarding the failure of an emissions test or the denial of a waiver may file a petition with the Agency within 30 days after the decision was made, and the Agency shall thereupon investigate the matter. Within 45 days after its receipt of the petition, the Agency shall submit to the petitioner and any affected inspector or station its written determination of the correctness or incorrectness of the decision complained of. The written determination shall include a statement of the facts relied upon and the legal and technical issues decided by the Agency in making its determination, and may also include an order directing the inspector (i) to issue an emission inspection certificate for the vehicle effective on such date as the Agency may specify, (ii) to reinspect the vehicle, (iii) to apply the standards that the Agency has determined to be applicable, or (iv) to take any other action that the Agency deems to be appropriate. In conducting the investigation, the Agency may require the petitioner to present the vehicle for inspection by the Agency or its designated agent. The written determination of the Agency shall be subject to review in circuit court in accordance with the provisions of the Administrative Review Law,[1] except that no challenge to the validity of a rule adopted by the Board under subsection (a) of Section 13B-20 shall be heard by the circuit court if the challenge could have been raised in a timely petition for review under Section 13B-20.

(b) Vehicle damage claim requirements and procedures.

(1) The contractor shall make vehicle damage claim forms authorized by the Agency available for vehicle owners in sufficient quantities at all official inspection stations.

(2) Notice of the vehicle damage claim procedures and the vehicle owner's rights in relation to a vehicle damage claim shall be conspicuously posted at all official inspection stations.

(3) If a vehicle owner believes that his or her vehicle was damaged by an act or omission of the contractor during or as a result of an emissions inspection performed on or after August 1, 2002, the owner may initiate resolution of the damage claim under this subsection by complying with the following:

(A) Within 30 days of the date of the vehicle emissions inspection that allegedly caused the vehicle damage, the vehicle owner shall submit a vehicle damage claim to the contractor at the Official Inspection Station at which the vehicle damage allegedly occurred.

(B) Within 30 days of filing the claim, the owner shall submit to the contractor any relevant information relating to the owner's claim for vehicle damage, including but not limited to evaluations conducted by a claims evaluation center or automotive repair shop meeting standards prescribed by the Agency.

(4) The contractor shall promptly notify the Agency of each vehicle damage claim received by the contractor under subdivision (b)(3) and shall forward to the Agency any additional information provided by the owner.

(5) Within 60 days after the filing of a vehicle damage claim, the contractor shall notify the vehicle owner of its proposed resolution of the damage claim.

(6) Within 30 days after receiving the contractor's proposed resolution of the damage claim, the owner may petition the Agency for a review of the adequacy and completeness of the contractor's proposed resolution. The petition shall be in a form specified by the Agency.

(7) Upon receiving a petition for review, the Agency shall request the contractor to deliver to the Agency a copy of the contractor's proposed resolution of the damage claim, together with all documents, videotapes, and information relevant to the damage claim and the proposed resolution. The contractor shall provide the requested materials to the Agency within 15 days of receiving the Agency's request.

(8) Within 30 days after receiving the relevant materials from the contractor, the Agency shall review the materials and determine whether the contractor's proposed resolution of the damage claim is adequate and complete. The Agency may deem the proposed resolution of the damage claim to be adequate and complete. If the Agency does not deem the proposed resolution of the damage claim to be adequate and complete, it may request the contractor to further investigate and evaluate the damage claim and resubmit its proposed resolution of the claim. The contractor shall then have 30 days to respond in writing to the Agency with the results of its further evaluation of the damage claim and its proposed resolution.

(9) The Agency shall notify the vehicle owner in writing of the result of its review of the adequacy and completeness of the contractor's proposed resolution of the damage claim. Copies of all correspondence between the Agency and the contractor relating to the damage claim shall also be sent to the vehicle owner.

(10) If, after the Agency's review, the vehicle owner still does not agree with all or a portion of the proposed resolution of the damage claim by the contractor, the vehicle owner may further pursue the damage claim through the binding arbitration process established by the contractor and accepted by the Agency, or in circuit court.

(11) The Agency's review of the adequacy and completeness of the contractor's proposed resolution of a damage claim is not binding upon the vehicle owner or the contractor and does not affect the rights of the vehicle owner or the contractor under law. The Agency's review of the adequacy and completeness of the contractor's proposed resolution of a damage claim is not a final action subject to administrative review and is not subject to review by the Pollution Control Board or otherwise appealable.

P.A. 76-1586, § 13B-40, added by P.A. 88-533, § 15, eff. Jan. 18, 1994. Amended by P.A. 92-821, § 5, eff. Aug. 21, 2002.

[1] 735 ILCS 5/13-101 et seq.

5/13B-45. Contracts

§ 13B-45. Contracts.

(a) The Agency may enter into contracts with one or more responsible parties to construct and operate official inspection stations, provide and maintain approved test equipment, administer tests, certify results, issue emission inspection stickers or certificates, maintain records, train personnel, or provide information to the public concerning the program.

These contracts (i) shall be subject to the Illinois Purchasing Act,[1] (ii) may be for a term of up to 9 years, (iii) shall be in writing, and (iv) shall not take effect until a copy of the contract is filed with the State Comptroller.

(b) In preparing its proposals for bidding by potential contractors, the Agency shall endeavor to include provisions relating to the following factors:

(1) The demonstrated financial responsibility of the potential contractor.

(2) The specialized experience and technical competence of the potential contractor in connection with the type of services required and the complexity of the project.

(3) The potential contractor's past record of performance on contracts with the Agency, with other government agencies or public bodies, and with private industry, including such items as cost, quality of work, and ability to meet schedules.

(4) The capacity of the potential contractor to perform the work within the time limitations.

(5) The familiarity of the potential contractor with the types of problems applicable to the project.

(6) The potential contractor's proposed method to accomplish the work required including, where appropriate, any demonstrated capability of exploring and developing innovative or advanced techniques and methods.

(7) Avoidance of personal and organizational conflicts of interest prohibited under federal, State, or local law.

(8) The potential contractor's present and prior involvement in the community and in the State of Illinois.

(c) Any contract for the operation of one or more official inspection stations shall include a provision that the contractor shall not perform emission-related repairs or adjustments to vehicles, other than to the contractor's own vehicles, necessary to enable vehicles to pass Illinois emission inspections.

P.A. 76-1586, § 13B-45, added by P.A. 88-533, § 15, eff. Jan. 18, 1994.

[1] 30 ILCS 505/1 et seq.

5/13B-50. Costs

§ 13B-50. Costs.

(a) Except as otherwise provided in subsection (e) of Section 13B-15, no fee shall be charged to motor vehicle owners for obtaining inspections required under this Chapter. The Vehicle Inspection Fund, which is a fund created in the State treasury for the purpose of receiving moneys from the Motor Fuel Tax Fund and other sources, shall be used, subject to appropriation, for the payment of the costs of the program, including reimbursement of those agencies of the State that incur expenses in the administration or enforcement of the program. The Vehicle Inspection Fund shall continue in existence notwithstanding the repeal of Chapter 13A.[1] Any money in the Vehicle Inspection Fund on January 1, 1995, shall be used for the purposes set forth in this Chapter.

(b) The Agency may acquire, own, maintain, operate, sell, lease and otherwise transfer real and personal property and interests in real and personal property for the purpose of creating or operating inspection stations and for any other purpose relating to the administration of this Chapter, and may use money from the Vehicle Inspection Fund for these purposes.

P.A. 76-1586, § 13B-50, added by P.A. 88-533, § 15, eff. Jan. 18, 1994.

[1] 625 ILCS 5/13A-101 et seq.

5/13B-55. Enforcement

§ 13B-55. Enforcement.

(a) The Agency shall cooperate in the enforcement of this Chapter by (i) identifying probable violations through computer matching of vehicle registration records and inspection records; (ii) sending one notice to each suspected violator identified through such matching, stating that registration and inspection records indicate that the vehicle owner has not complied with this Chapter; (iii) directing the vehicle owner to notify the Agency or the Secretary of State if he or she has ceased to own the vehicle or has changed residence; and (iv) advising the vehicle owner of the consequences of violating this Chapter.

The Agency shall cooperate with the Secretary of State in the administration of this Chapter and the related provisions of Chapter 3,[1] and shall provide the Secretary of State with such information as the Secretary of State may deem necessary for these purposes, including regular and timely access to vehicle inspection records. The Agency shall be reimbursed for the cost of providing this information.

The Secretary of State shall cooperate with the Agency in the administration of this Chapter and shall provide the Agency with such information as the Agency may deem necessary for the purposes of this Chapter, including regular and timely access to vehicle registration records. Section 2-123 of this Code shall not apply to the provision of this information, but the Secretary of State shall be reimbursed for the cost of providing the information.

(b) The Secretary of State shall suspend either the driving privileges or the vehicle registration, or both, of any vehicle owner who has not complied with this Chapter, if (i) the vehicle owner failed to satisfactorily respond to the one notice sent by the Agency under subsection (a), and (ii) the Secretary of State has mailed the vehicle owner a notice that the suspension will be imposed if the owner does not comply within a stated period, and the Secretary of State has not received satisfactory evidence of compliance within that period. The Secretary of State shall send this notice only after receiving a statement from the Agency that the vehicle owner has failed to comply with this Section. Notice shall be effective as specified in subsection (c) of Section 6-211 of this Code.

A suspension under this subsection shall not be terminated until satisfactory proof of compliance has been submitted to the Secretary of State. No driver's license or permit, or renewal of a license or permit, may be issued to a person whose driving privileges have been suspended under this Section until the suspension has been terminated. No vehicle registration or registration plate that has been suspended under this Section may be reinstated or renewed, or transferred by the owner to any other vehicle, until the suspension has been terminated.

The filing fee for an administrative hearing to contest a suspension made under this Section shall be $20, to be paid by the vehicle owner at the time written request for the hearing is made to the Secretary of State.

The Secretary of State may promulgate rules to enable him or her to carry out his or her duties under this Chapter.

P.A. 76-1586, § 13B-55, added by P.A. 88-533, § 15, eff. Jan. 18, 1994.

[1] 625 ILCS 5/3-100 et seq.

5/13B-60. Other offenses

§ 13B-60. Other offenses.

(a) Any person who knowingly displays an emission inspection sticker or exemption sticker on any vehicle other than the one for which the sticker was lawfully issued in accordance with the provisions of this Chapter, or duplicates, alters, uses, possesses, issues, or distributes any emission inspection sticker, exemption sticker, inspection certificate, or facsimile thereof, except in accordance with the provisions of this Chapter and the rules and regulations adopted hereunder, is guilty of a Class C misdemeanor.

(b) A vehicle owner shall pay a monetary fine equivalent to the test fee plus the applicable waiver repair expenditure for the continued operation of a noncomplying vehicle beyond 4 months past the expiration of the vehicle emission inspection certificate. Any fines collected under this Section shall be divided equally between the local jurisdiction issuing the citation and the Vehicle Inspection Fund.

P.A. 76-1586, § 13B-60, added by P.A. 88-533, § 15, eff. Jan. 18, 1994.

5/13B-70. Legislative intent

§ 13B-70. Legislative intent. It is the intent of the General Assembly that, to the greatest extent possible, there be continuity in the operation of the Vehicle Emissions Inspection Programs under this Chapter and Chapter 13A[1] during the transition phase when certain affected counties become subject to the program under this Chapter instead of the program under Chapter 13A.

P.A. 76-1586, § 13B-70, added by P.A. 88-533, § 15, eff. Jan. 18, 1994.

[1] 625 ILCS 5/13A-101 et seq.

5/13B-75. Home rule

§ 13B-75. Home rule. Pursuant to subsections (h) and (i) of Section 6 of Article VII of the Illinois Constitution, the exercise by a home rule unit of any power which is inconsistent with this Chapter is hereby specifically denied and preempted, and the vehicle emission inspection program created by this Chapter is hereby declared to be the subject of exclusive State jurisdiction.

P.A. 76-1586, § 13B-75, added by P.A. 88-533, § 15, eff. Jan. 18, 1994.

CHAPTER 14. VEHICLE EQUIPMENT SAFETY COMPACT

5/14-101 to 5/14-110. §§ 14-101 to 14-110. Repealed by P.A. 83-821, § 2, eff. Sept. 24, 1983

CHAPTER 15. SIZE, WEIGHT, AND LOAD PERMITS

Enactment

The Illinois Vehicle Code was enacted by P.A. 76–1586, effective July 1, 1970. The Code constitutes a consolidated recodification of various earlier laws and acts including the Uniform Act Regulating Traffic on Highways.

5/15–100. § 15–100. Repealed by P.A. 90–89, § 20, eff. Jan. 1, 1998

ARTICLE I. SIZE, WEIGHT AND LOAD

5/15–101. Scope and effect of Chapter 15

§ 15–101. Scope and effect of Chapter 15. (a) It is unlawful for any person to drive or move on, upon or across or for the owner to cause or knowingly permit to be driven or moved on, upon or across any highway any vehicle or vehicles of a size and weight exceeding the limitations stated in this Chapter or otherwise in violation of this Chapter, and the maximum size and weight of vehicles herein specified shall be lawful throughout this State, and local authorities shall have no power or authority to alter such limitations except as express authority may be granted in this Chapter.

(b) The provisions of this Chapter governing size, weight and load do not apply to fire apparatus or equipment for snow and ice removal operations owned or operated by any governmental body, or to implements of husbandry, as defined in Chapter 1 of this Code,[1] temporarily operated or towed in a combination upon a highway provided such combination does not consist of more than 3 vehicles or, in the case of hauling fresh, perishable fruits or vegetables from farm to the point of first processing, not more than 3 wagons being towed by an implement of husbandry, or to a vehicle operated under the terms of a special permit issued hereunder.

P.A. 76–1586, § 15–101, eff. July 1, 1970. Amended by P.A. 76–1694, § 1; P.A. 76–2194, § 1, eff. July 1, 1970; P.A. 83–831, § 1, eff. Jan. 1, 1984; P.A. 92–417, § 5, eff. Jan. 1, 2002.

Formerly Ill.Rev.Stat.1991, ch. 95 ½, ¶ 15–101.

1 625 ILCS 5/1–101 et seq.

5/15–102. Width of Vehicles

§ 15–102. Width of Vehicles.

(a) On Class III and non-designated State and local highways, the total outside width of any vehicle or load thereon shall not exceed 8 feet.

(b) Except during those times when, due to insufficient light or unfavorable atmospheric conditions, persons and vehicles on the highway are not clearly discernible at a distance of 1000 feet, the following vehicles may exceed the 8 feet limitation during the period from a half hour before sunrise to a half hour after sunset:

(1) Loads of hay, straw or other similar farm products provided that the load is not more than 12 feet wide.

(2) Implements of husbandry being transported on another vehicle and the transporting vehicle while loaded.

The following requirements apply to the transportation on another vehicle of an implement of husbandry wider than 8 feet 6 inches on the National System of Interstate and Defense Highways or other highways in the system of State highways:

(A) The driver of a vehicle transporting an implement of husbandry that exceeds 8 feet 6 inches in width shall obey all traffic laws and shall check the roadways prior to making a movement in order to ensure that adequate clearance is available for the movement. It is prima facie evidence that the driver of a vehicle transporting an implement of husbandry has failed to check the roadway prior to making a movement if the vehicle is involved in a collision with a bridge, overpass, fixed structure, or properly placed traffic control device or if the vehicle blocks traffic due to its inability to proceed because of a bridge, overpass, fixed structure, or properly placed traffic control device.

(B) Flags shall be displayed so as to wave freely at the extremities of overwidth objects and at the extreme ends of all protrusions, projections, and overhangs. All flags shall be clean, bright red flags with no advertising, wording, emblem, or insignia inscribed upon them and at least 18 inches square.

(C) "OVERSIZE LOAD" signs are mandatory on the front and rear of all vehicles with loads over 10 feet wide. These signs must have 12–inch high black letters with a 2–inch stroke on a yellow sign that is 7 feet wide by 18 inches high.

(D) One civilian escort vehicle is required for a load that exceeds 14 feet 6 inches in width and 2 civilian escort vehicles are required for a load that exceeds 16 feet in width on the National System of Interstate and Defense Highways or other highways in the system of State highways.

(E) The requirements for a civilian escort vehicle and driver are as follows:

(1) The civilian escort vehicle shall be a passenger car or a second division vehicle not exceeding a gross vehicle weight of 8,000 pounds that is designed to afford clear and unobstructed vision to both front and rear.

(2) The escort vehicle driver must be properly licensed to operate the vehicle.

(3) While in use, the escort vehicle must be equipped with illuminated rotating, oscillating, or flashing amber lights or flashing amber strobe lights mounted on top that are of sufficient intensity to be visible at 500 feet in normal sunlight.

(4) "OVERSIZE LOAD" signs are mandatory on all escort vehicles. The sign on an escort vehicle shall

have 8–inch high black letters on a yellow sign that is 5 feet wide by 12 inches high.

(5) When only one escort vehicle is required and it is operating on a two-lane highway, the escort vehicle shall travel approximately 300 feet ahead of the load. The rotating, oscillating, or flashing lights or flashing amber strobe lights and an "OVERSIZE LOAD" sign shall be displayed on the escort vehicle and shall be visible from the front. When only one escort vehicle is required and it is operating on a multilane divided highway, the escort vehicle shall travel approximately 300 feet behind the load and the sign and lights shall be visible from the rear.

(6) When 2 escort vehicles are required, one escort shall travel approximately 300 feet ahead of the load and the second escort shall travel approximately 300 feet behind the load. The rotating, oscillating, or flashing lights or flashing amber strobe lights and an "OVERSIZE LOAD" sign shall be displayed on the escort vehicles and shall be visible from the front on the lead escort and from the rear on the trailing escort.

(7) When traveling within the corporate limits of a municipality, the escort vehicle shall maintain a reasonable and proper distance from the oversize load, consistent with existing traffic conditions.

(8) A separate escort shall be provided for each load hauled.

(9) The driver of an escort vehicle shall obey all traffic laws.

(10) The escort vehicle must be in safe operational condition.

(11) The driver of the escort vehicle must be in radio contact with the driver of the vehicle carrying the oversize load.

(F) A transport vehicle while under load of more than 8 feet 6 inches in width must be equipped with an illuminated rotating, oscillating, or flashing amber light or lights or a flashing amber strobe light or lights mounted on the top of the cab that are of sufficient intensity to be visible at 500 feet in normal sunlight. If the load on the transport vehicle blocks the visibility of the amber lighting from the rear of the vehicle, the vehicle must also be equipped with an illuminated rotating, oscillating, or flashing amber light or lights or a flashing amber strobe light or lights mounted on the rear of the load that are of sufficient intensity to be visible at 500 feet in normal sunlight.

(G) When a flashing amber light is required on the transport vehicle under load and it is operating on a two-lane highway, the transport vehicle shall display to the rear at least one rotating, oscillating, or flashing light or a flashing amber strobe light and an "OVERSIZE LOAD" sign. When a flashing amber light is required on the transport vehicle under load and it is operating on a multilane divided highway, the sign and light shall be visible from the rear.

(H) Maximum speed shall be 45 miles per hour on all such moves or 5 miles per hour above the posted minimum speed limit, whichever is greater, but the vehicle shall not at any time exceed the posted maximum speed limit.

(3) Portable buildings designed and used for agricultural and livestock raising operations that are not more than 14 feet wide and with not more than a 1 foot overhang along the left side of the hauling vehicle. However, the buildings shall not be transported more than 10 miles and not on any route that is part of the National System of Interstate and Defense Highways.

All buildings when being transported shall display at least 2 red cloth flags, not less than 12 inches square, mounted as high as practicable on the left and right side of the building.

A State Police escort shall be required if it is necessary for this load to use part of the left lane when crossing any 2 laned State highway bridge.

(c) Vehicles propelled by electric power obtained from overhead trolley wires operated wholly within the corporate limits of a municipality are also exempt from the width limitation.

(d) Exemptions are also granted to vehicles designed for the carrying of more than 10 persons under the following conditions:

(1) (Blank);

(2) When operated within any public transportation service with the approval of local authorities or an appropriate public body authorized by law to provide public transportation. Any vehicle so operated may be 8 feet 6 inches in width; or

(3) When a county engineer or superintendent of highways, after giving due consideration to the mass transportation needs of the area and to the width and condition of the road, has determined that the operation of buses wider than 8 feet will not pose an undue safety hazard on a particular county or township road segment, he or she may authorize buses not to exceed 8 feet 6 inches in width on any highway under that engineer's or superintendent's jurisdiction.

(e) A vehicle and load traveling upon the National System of Interstate and Defense Highways or any other highway in the system of State highways that has been designated as a Class I or Class II highway by the Department, or any street or highway designated by local authorities or road district commissioners, may have a total outside width of 8 feet 6 inches, provided that certain safety devices that the Department determines as necessary for the safe and efficient operation of motor vehicles shall not be included in the calculation of width.

(e–1) A vehicle and load more than 8 feet wide but not exceeding 8 feet 6 inches in width is allowed access according to the following:

(1) A vehicle and load not exceeding 73,280 pounds in weight is allowed access from any State designated highway onto any county, township, or municipal highway for a distance of 5 highway miles for the purpose of loading and unloading, provided:

(A) The vehicle and load does not exceed 65 feet overall length.

(B) There is no sign prohibiting that access.

(C) The route is not being used as a thoroughfare between State designated highways.

(2) A vehicle and load not exceeding 73,280 pounds in weight is allowed access from any State designated highway onto any county or township highway for a distance of 5 highway miles or onto any municipal highway for a distance of one highway mile for the purpose of food, fuel, repairs, and rest, provided:

(A) The vehicle and load does not exceed 65 feet overall length.

(B) There is no sign prohibiting that access.

(C) The route is not being used as a thoroughfare between State designated highways.

(3) A vehicle and load not exceeding 80,000 pounds in weight is allowed access from a Class I highway onto any street or highway for a distance of one highway mile for the purpose of loading, unloading, food, fuel, repairs, and rest, provided there is no sign prohibiting that access.

(4) A vehicle and load not exceeding 80,000 pounds in weight is allowed access from a Class I or Class II highway onto any State highway or any locally designated highway for a distance of 5 highway miles for the purpose of loading, unloading, food, fuel, repairs, and rest.

(5) A trailer or semi-trailer not exceeding 28 feet 6 inches in length, that was originally in combination with a truck tractor, shall have unlimited access to points of loading and unloading.

(6) All household goods carriers shall have unlimited access to points of loading and unloading.

Section 5–35 of the Illinois Administrative Procedure Act [1] relating to procedures for rulemaking shall not apply to the designation of highways under this paragraph (e).

(f) Mirrors required by Section 12–502 of this Code and other safety devices identified by the Department may project up to 14 inches beyond each side of a bus and up to 6 inches beyond each side of any other vehicle, and that projection shall not be deemed a violation of the width restrictions of this Section.

(g) Any person who is convicted of violating this Section is subject to the penalty as provided in paragraph (b) of Section 15–113.

P.A. 76–1586, § 15–102, eff. July 1, 1970. Amended by P.A. 76–2195, § 1, eff. July 1, 1970; P.A. 77–123, § 1, eff. Jan. 1, 1972; P.A. 78–510, § 1, eff. Oct. 1, 1973; P.A. 80–574, § 1, eff. Oct. 1, 1977; P.A. 80–1173, § 1, eff. July 1, 1978; P.A. 80–1364, § 36, eff. Aug. 13, 1978; P.A. 83–12, § 1, eff. July 1, 1983; P.A. 83–848, § 1, eff. Jan. 1, 1984; P.A. 83–1362, Art. II, § 99, eff. Sept. 11, 1984; P.A. 84–691, § 1, eff. Jan. 1, 1986; P.A. 86–1236, § 1, eff. Jan. 1, 1991; P.A. 87–217, § 4, eff. Jan. 1, 1992; P.A. 87–1160, § 1, eff. Jan. 1, 1993; P.A. 87–1203, § 1, eff. Sept. 25, 1992; P.A. 88–45, Art. II, § 2–54, eff. July 6, 1993; P.A. 88–476, § 2, eff. July 1, 1994; P.A. 88–517, § 10, eff. Nov. 16, 1993; P.A. 88–589, § 10, eff. Aug. 14, 1994; P.A. 88–670, Art. 2, § 2–59, eff. Dec. 2, 1994; P.A. 88–675, § 5, eff. Dec. 14, 1994; P.A. 88–684, § 5, eff. Jan. 24, 1995; P.A. 89–551, § 5, eff. Jan. 1, 1997; P.A. 89–658, § 5, eff. Jan. 1, 1997; P.A. 90–14, Art. 2, § 2–225, eff. July 1, 1997; P.A. 91–780, § 5, eff. June 9, 2000; P.A. 92–417, § 5, eff. Jan. 1, 2002.

Formerly Ill.Rev.Stat.1991, ch. 95 ½, ¶ 15–102.

1 5 ILCS 100/5–35.

Section 4 of P.A. 83–12, approved July 1, 1983, provided:

"Effective date. This Act takes effect as provided in this Section.

"The amendments to those portions of Sections 3–815(a), 3–818 and 3–819(b) of 'The Illinois Vehicle Code' in Section 1 of this Act which create the 'X', 'Z', 'MX', 'MZ', 'MM' and 'TN' registration classifications and the fees and taxes imposed for those classifications, the amendments to Sections 2–119, 3–401 and 3–802 of 'The Illinois Vehicle Code' in Section 1 of this Act, and the amendments to Chapter 15 of 'The Illinois Vehicle Code' in Section 1 of this Act take effect July 1, 1983.

"The remaining amendments to 'The Illinois Vehicle Code' in Section 1 of this Act take effect July 1, 1983 and apply beginning with the 1985 registration year, except that the amendments to Sections 3–813 through 3–816 and Section 3–819 apply beginning with the 1984 registration year for those vehicles registered on a calendar year basis only.

"The amendments to Chapters 13 and 18 of 'The Illinois Vehicle Code' in Section 1 of this Act take effect January 1, 1984.

"Section 2 of this Act takes effect on the first day of the next succeeding month which commences at least 30 days after the date on which this Act becomes law.

"Section 3 of this Act takes effect July 1, 1983.

"Section 3.1 of this Act takes effect January 1, 1984.

"This Section 4 takes effect upon its becoming a law."

5/15–103. Height of vehicles

§ 15–103. Height of vehicles. The height of a vehicle from the under side of the tire to the top of the vehicle, inclusive of load, shall not exceed 13 feet, 6 inches on any highway in the State.

A person convicted of violating this Section is subject to the penalty provided in paragraph (b) of Section 15–113.

P.A. 76–1586, § 15–103, eff. July 1, 1970. Amended by P.A. 83–831, § 1, eff. Jan. 1, 1984; P.A. 92–417, § 5, eff. Jan. 1, 2002.

Formerly Ill.Rev.Stat.1991, ch. 95 ½, ¶ 15–103.

5/15–104. § 15–104. Repealed by P.A. 83–527, § 1, eff. Sept. 17, 1983

5/15–105. Projecting loads on passenger vehicles

§ 15–105. Projecting loads on passenger vehicles. No passenger-type vehicle shall be operated on any highway with any load carried thereon extending beyond the line of the fenders on the left side of such vehicle nor extending more than 6 inches beyond the line of the fenders on the right side thereof.

P.A. 76–1586, § 15–105, eff. July 1, 1970.

Formerly Ill.Rev.Stat.1991, ch. 95 ½, ¶ 15–105.

5/15–106. Protruding members of vehicles

§ 15–106. Protruding members of vehicles.

No vehicle with boom, arm, drill rig or other protruding component shall be operated upon any highway in this State unless such protruding component is fastened so as to prevent shifting, bouncing or moving in any manner.

P.A. 76–1586, § 15–106, eff. July 1, 1970. Amended by P.A. 92–417, § 5, eff. Jan. 1, 2002.

Formerly Ill.Rev.Stat.1991, ch. 95 ½, ¶ 15–106.

5/15–107. Length of vehicles

§ 15–107. Length of vehicles.

(a) The maximum length of a single vehicle on any highway of this State may not exceed 42 feet except the following:

(1) Semitrailers.

(2) Charter or regulated route buses may be up to 45 feet in length, not including energy absorbing bumpers.

(a–1) A motor home as defined in Section 1–145.01 may be up to 45 feet in length, not including energy absorbing bumpers. The length limitations described in this subsection (a–1) shall be exclusive of energy-absorbing bumpers and rear view mirrors.

(b) On all non-State highways, the maximum length of vehicles in combinations is as follows:

(1) A truck tractor in combination with a semitrailer may not exceed 55 feet overall dimension.

(2) A truck tractor-semitrailer-trailer may not exceed 60 feet overall dimension.

(3) Combinations specially designed to transport motor vehicles or boats may not exceed 60 feet overall dimension.

Vehicles operating during daylight hours when transporting poles, pipes, machinery, or other objects of a structural nature that cannot readily be dismembered are exempt from length limitations, provided that no object may exceed 80 feet in length and the overall dimension of the vehicle including the load may not exceed 100 feet. This exemption does not apply to operation on a Saturday, Sunday, or legal holiday. Legal holidays referred to in this Section are the days on which the following traditional holidays are celebrated: New Year's Day; Memorial Day; Independence Day; Labor Day; Thanksgiving Day; and Christmas Day.

Vehicles and loads operated by a public utility while en route to make emergency repairs to public service facilities or properties are exempt from length limitations, provided that during night operations every vehicle and its load must be equipped with a sufficient number of clearance lamps on both sides and marker lamps on the extreme ends of any projecting load to clearly mark the dimensions of the load.

A tow truck in combination with a disabled vehicle or combination of disabled vehicles, as provided in paragraph (6) of subsection (c) of this Section, is exempt from length limitations.

All other combinations not listed in this subsection (b) may not exceed 60 feet overall dimension.

(c) Combinations of vehicles may not exceed a total of 2 vehicles except the following:

(1) A truck tractor semitrailer may draw one trailer.

(2) A truck tractor semitrailer may draw one converter dolly.

(3) A truck tractor semitrailer may draw one vehicle that is defined in Chapter 1 [1] as special mobile equipment, provided the overall dimension does not exceed 60 feet.

(4) A truck in transit may draw 3 trucks in transit coupled together by the triple saddlemount method.

(5) Recreational vehicles consisting of 3 vehicles, provided the following:

(A) The total overall dimension does not exceed 60 feet.

(B) The towing vehicle is a properly registered vehicle capable of towing another vehicle using a fifth-wheel type assembly.

(C) The second vehicle in the combination of vehicles is a recreational vehicle that is towed by a fifth-wheel assembly. This vehicle must be properly registered and must be equipped with brakes, regardless of weight.

(D) The third vehicle must be the lightest of the 3 vehicles and be a trailer or semitrailer designed or used for transporting a boat, all-terrain vehicle, personal watercraft, or motorcycle.

(E) The towed vehicles may be only for the use of the operator of the towing vehicle.

(F) All vehicles must be properly equipped with operating brakes and safety equipment required by this Code, except the additional brake requirement in subdivision (C) of this subparagraph (5).

(6) A tow truck in combination with a disabled vehicle or combination of disabled vehicles, provided the towing vehicle:

(A) Is specifically designed as a tow truck having a gross vehicle weight rating of at least 18,000 pounds and equipped with air brakes, provided that air brakes are required only if the towing vehicle is towing a vehicle, semitrailer, or tractor-trailer combination that is equipped with air brakes. For the purpose of this subsection, gross vehicle weight rating, or GVWR, means the value specified by the manufacturer as the loaded weight of the tow truck.

(B) Is equipped with flashing, rotating, or oscillating amber lights, visible for at least 500 feet in all directions.

(C) Is capable of utilizing the lighting and braking systems of the disabled vehicle or combination of vehicles.

(D) Does not engage a tow exceeding 50 highway miles from the initial point of wreck or disablement to a place of repair. Any additional movement of the vehicles may occur only upon issuance of authorization for that movement under the provisions of Sections 15-301 through 15-319 of this Code.

The Department may by rule or regulation prescribe additional requirements regarding length limitations for a tow truck towing another vehicle.

For purposes of this Section, a tow-dolly that merely serves as substitute wheels for another legally licensed vehicle is considered part of the licensed vehicle and not a separate vehicle.

(d) On Class I highways there are no overall length limitations on motor vehicles operating in combinations provided:

(1) The length of a semitrailer, unladen or with load, in combination with a truck tractor may not exceed 53 feet.

(2) The distance between the kingpin and the center of the rear axle of a semitrailer longer than 48 feet, in combination with a truck tractor, may not exceed 45 feet 6 inches.

(3) The length of a semitrailer or trailer, unladen or with load, operated in a truck tractor-semitrailer-trailer combination, may not exceed 28 feet 6 inches.

(4) Maxi-cube combinations, as defined in Chapter 1, may not exceed 65 feet overall dimension.

(5) Combinations of vehicles specifically designed to transport motor vehicles or boats may not exceed 65 feet overall dimension. The length limitation is inclusive of front and rear bumpers but exclusive of the overhang of the transported vehicles, as provided in paragraph (i) of this Section.

(6) Stinger steered semitrailer vehicles as defined in Chapter 1, specifically designed to transport motor vehicles or boats, may not exceed 75 feet overall dimension. The length limitation is inclusive of front and rear bumpers but exclusive of the overhang of the transported vehicles, as provided in paragraph (i) of this Section.

(7) A truck in transit transporting 3 trucks coupled together by the triple saddlemount method may not exceed 75 feet overall dimension.

Vehicles operating during daylight hours when transporting poles, pipes, machinery, or other objects of a structural nature that cannot readily be dismembered are exempt from length limitations, provided that no object may exceed 80 feet in length and the overall dimension of the vehicle including the load may not exceed 100 feet. This exemption does not apply to operation on a Saturday, Sunday, or legal holiday. Legal holidays referred to in this Section are the days on which the following traditional holidays are celebrated: New Year's Day; Memorial Day; Independence Day; Labor Day; Thanksgiving Day; and Christmas Day.

Vehicles and loads operated by a public utility while en route to make emergency repairs to public service facilities or properties are exempt from length limitations, provided that during night operations every vehicle and its load must be equipped with a sufficient number of clearance lamps on both sides and marker lamps on the extreme ends of any projecting load to clearly mark the dimensions of the load.

A tow truck in combination with a disabled vehicle or combination of disabled vehicles, as provided in paragraph (6) of subsection (c) of this Section, is exempt from length limitations.

The length limitations described in this paragraph (d) shall be exclusive of safety and energy conservation devices, such as bumpers, refrigeration units or air compressors and other devices, that the Department may interpret as necessary for safe and efficient operation; except that no device excluded under this paragraph shall have by its design or use the capability to carry cargo.

Section 5–35 of the Illinois Administrative Procedure Act[2] relating to procedures for rulemaking shall not apply to the designation of highways under this paragraph (d).

(e) On Class II highways there are no overall length limitations on motor vehicles operating in combinations, provided:

(1) The length of a semitrailer, unladen or with load, in combination with a truck tractor, may not exceed 53 feet overall dimension.

(2) The distance between the kingpin and the center of the rear axle of a semitrailer longer than 48 feet, in combination with a truck tractor, may not exceed 45 feet 6 inches.

(3) A truck tractor-semitrailer-trailer combination may not exceed 65 feet in dimension from front axle to rear axle.

(4) The length of a semitrailer or trailer, unladen or with load, operated in a truck tractor-semitrailer-trailer combination, may not exceed 28 feet 6 inches.

(5) Maxi–cube combinations, as defined in Chapter 1, may not exceed 65 feet overall dimension.

(6) A combination of vehicles, specifically designed to transport motor vehicles or boats, may not exceed 65 feet overall dimension. The length limitation is inclusive of front and rear bumpers but exclusive of the overhang of the transported vehicles, as provided in paragraph (i) of this Section.

(7) Stinger steered semitrailer vehicles, as defined in Chapter 1, specifically designed to transport motor vehicles or boats, may not exceed 75 feet overall dimension. The length limitation is inclusive of front and rear bumpers but exclusive of the overhang of the transported vehicles, as provided in paragraph (i) of this Section.

(8) A truck in transit transporting 3 trucks coupled together by the triple saddlemount method may not exceed 75 feet overall dimension.

Vehicles operating during daylight hours when transporting poles, pipes, machinery, or other objects of a structural nature that cannot readily be dismembered are exempt from length limitations, provided that no object may exceed 80 feet in length and the overall dimension of the vehicle including the load may not exceed 100 feet. This exemption does not apply to operation on a Saturday, Sunday, or legal holiday. Legal holidays referred to in this Section are the days on which the following traditional holidays are celebrated: New Year's Day; Memorial Day; Independence Day; Labor Day; Thanksgiving Day; and Christmas Day.

Vehicles and loads operated by a public utility while en route to make emergency repairs to public service facilities or properties are exempt from length limitations, provided that during night operations every vehicle and its load must be equipped with a sufficient number of clearance lamps on both sides and marker lamps on the extreme ends of any projecting load to clearly mark the dimensions of the load.

A tow truck in combination with a disabled vehicle or combination of disabled vehicles, as provided in paragraph (6) of subsection (c) of this Section, is exempt from length limitations.

Local authorities and road district commissioners, with respect to streets and highways under their jurisdiction, may also by ordinance or resolution allow length limitations of this subsection (e).

The length limitations described in this paragraph (e) shall be exclusive of safety and energy conservation devices, such as bumpers, refrigeration units or air compressors and other devices, that the Department may interpret as necessary for safe and efficient operation; except that no device excluded under this paragraph shall have by its design or use the capability to carry cargo.

(e–1) Combinations of vehicles not exceeding 65 feet overall length are allowed access as follows:

(1) From any State designated highway onto any county, township, or municipal highway for a distance of 5 highway miles for the purpose of loading and unloading, provided:

(A) The vehicle does not exceed 73,280 pounds in gross weight and 8 feet 6 inches in width.

(B) There is no sign prohibiting that access.

(C) The route is not being used as a thoroughfare between State designated highways.

(2) From any State designated highway onto any county or township highway for a distance of 5 highway miles or onto any municipal highway for a distance of one highway mile for the purpose of food, fuel, repairs, and rest, provided:

(A) The vehicle does not exceed 73,280 pounds in gross weight and 8 feet 6 inches in width.

(B) There is no sign prohibiting that access.

(C) The route is not being used as a thoroughfare between State designated highways.

(e–2) Except as provided in subsection (e–3), combinations of vehicles over 65 feet in length, with no overall length limitation except as provided in subsections (d) and (e) of this Section, are allowed access as follows:

(1) From a Class I highway onto any street or highway for a distance of one highway mile for the purpose of loading, unloading, food, fuel, repairs, and rest, provided there is no sign prohibiting that access.

(2) From a Class I or Class II highway onto any State highway or any locally designated highway for a distance of 5 highway miles for the purpose of loading, unloading, food, fuel, repairs, and rest.

(e–3) Combinations of vehicles over 65 feet in length operated by household goods carriers, with no overall length limitations except as provided in subsections (d) and (e) of this Section, have unlimited access to points of loading and unloading.

Section 5–35 of the Illinois Administrative Procedure Act relating to procedures for rulemaking shall not apply to the designation of highways under this paragraph (e).

(f) On Class III and other non-designated State highways, the length limitations for vehicles in combination are as follows:

(1) Truck tractor-semitrailer combinations, must comply with either a maximum 55 feet overall wheel base or a maximum 65 feet extreme overall dimension.

(2) Semitrailers, unladen or with load, may not exceed 53 feet overall dimension.

(3) No truck tractor-semitrailer-trailer combination may exceed 60 feet extreme overall dimension.

(4) The distance between the kingpin and the center axle of a semitrailer longer than 48 feet, in combination with a truck tractor, may not exceed 42 feet 6 inches.

(g) Length limitations in the preceding subsections of this Section 15–107 do not apply to the following:

(1) Vehicles operated in the daytime, except on Saturdays, Sundays, or legal holidays, when transporting poles, pipe, machinery, or other objects of a structural nature that cannot readily be dismembered, provided the overall length of vehicle and load may not exceed 100 feet and no object exceeding 80 feet in length may be transported unless a permit has been obtained as authorized in Section 15–301.

(2) Vehicles and loads operated by a public utility while en route to make emergency repairs to public service facilities or properties, but during night operation every vehicle and its load must be equipped with a sufficient number of clearance lamps on both sides and marker lamps upon the extreme ends of any projecting load to clearly mark the dimensions of the load.

(3) A tow truck in combination with a disabled vehicle or combination of disabled vehicles, provided the towing vehicle meets the following conditions:

(A) It is specifically designed as a tow truck having a gross vehicle weight rating of at least 18,000 pounds and equipped with air brakes, provided that air brakes are required only if the towing vehicle is towing a vehicle, semitrailer, or tractor-trailer combination that is equipped with air brakes.

(B) It is equipped with flashing, rotating, or oscillating amber lights, visible for at least 500 feet in all directions.

(C) It is capable of utilizing the lighting and braking systems of the disabled vehicle or combination of vehicles.

(D) It does not engage in a tow exceeding 50 miles from the initial point of wreck or disablement.

The Department may by rule or regulation prescribe additional requirements regarding length limitations for a tow truck towing another vehicle.

For the purpose of this subsection, gross vehicle weight rating, or GVWR, shall mean the value specified by the manufacturer as the loaded weight of the tow truck. Legal holidays referred to in this Section shall be specified as the day on which the following traditional holidays are celebrated:

New Year's Day;

Memorial Day;

Independence Day;

Labor Day;

Thanksgiving Day; and

Christmas Day.

(h) The load upon any vehicle operated alone, or the load upon the front vehicle of a combination of vehicles, shall not extend more than 3 feet beyond the front wheels of the vehicle or the front bumper of the vehicle if it is equipped with a front bumper. The provisions of this subsection (h) shall not apply to any vehicle or combination of vehicles specifically designed for the collection and transportation of waste, garbage, or recyclable materials during the vehicle's operation in the course of collecting garbage, waste, or recyclable materials if the vehicle is traveling at a speed not in excess of 15 miles per hour during the vehicle's operation and in the course of collecting garbage, waste, or recyclable materials. However, in no instance shall the load extend more than 7 feet beyond the front wheels of the vehicle or the front bumper of the vehicle if it is equipped with a front bumper.

(i) The load upon the front vehicle of a combination of vehicles specifically designed to transport motor vehicles shall not extend more than 3 feet beyond the foremost part of the transporting vehicle and the load upon the rear transporting vehicle shall not extend more than 4 feet beyond the rear of the bed or body of the vehicle. This paragraph shall only be applicable upon highways designated in paragraphs (d) and (e) of this Section.

(j) Articulated vehicles comprised of 2 sections, neither of which exceeds a length of 42 feet, designed for the carrying of more than 10 persons, may be up to 60 feet in length, not including energy absorbing bumpers, provided that the vehicles are:

1. operated by or for any public body or motor carrier authorized by law to provide public transportation services; or

2. operated in local public transportation service by any other person and the municipality in which the service is to be provided approved the operation of the vehicle.

(j–1) (Blank).

(k) Any person who is convicted of violating this Section is subject to the penalty as provided in paragraph (b) of Section 15–113.

(*l*) (Blank).

P.A. 76–1586, § 15–107, eff. July 1, 1970. Amended by P.A. 76–2196, § 1, eff. July 1, 1970; P.A. 77–58, § 1, eff. July 1, 1971; P.A. 77–1344, § 1, eff. Aug. 27, 1971; P.A. 77–2637, § 1, eff. Oct. 1, 1972; P.A. 77–2829, §§ 40, 67, eff. Dec. 22, 1972; P.A. 78–255, § 29, eff. Oct. 1, 1973; P.A. 78–486, § 1, eff. Jan. 1, 1974; P.A. 78–1297, § 58, eff. March 4, 1975; P.A. 81–967, § 1, eff. Jan. 1, 1980; P.A. 82–198, § 1, eff. Jan. 1, 1982; P.A. 82–573, § 1, eff. Sept. 24, 1981; P.A. 82–649, § 1, eff. July 1, 1982; P.A. 82–783, Art. III, § 37, eff. July 13, 1982; P.A. 83–12, § 1, eff. July 1, 1983; P.A. 83–475, § 1, eff. Jan. 1, 1984; P.A. 83–781, § 1, eff. Jan. 1, 1984; P.A. 83–953, § 1, eff. Dec. 2, 1983; P.A. 83–1362, Art. II, § 99, eff. Sept. 11, 1984; P.A. 84–1061, § 1, eff. July 1, 1986; P.A. 85–505, § 1, eff. Sept. 18, 1987; P.A. 85–562, § 1, eff. Sept. 18, 1987; P.A. 85–830, § 1, eff. Sept. 24, 1987; P.A. 85–1209, Art. II, § 2–51, eff. Aug. 30, 1988; P.A. 85–1345, § 1, eff. Aug. 31, 1988; P.A. 85–1440, Art. II, § 2–54, eff. Feb. 1, 1989; P.A. 86–419, § 1, eff. Aug. 30, 1989; P.A. 86–447, § 2, eff. Aug. 30, 1989; P.A. 86–589, § 1, eff. Jan. 1, 1990; P.A. 86–1028, Art. II, § 2–44, eff. Feb. 5, 1990; P.A. 87–1203, § 1, eff. Sept. 25, 1992; P.A. 88–45, Art. III, § 3–128, eff. July 6, 1993; P.A. 88–384, § 5, eff. Jan. 1, 1994; P.A. 88–670, Art. 2, § 2–59, eff. Dec. 2, 1994; P.A. 89–219, § 5, eff. Jan. 1, 1996; P.A. 89–434, § 5, eff. June 1, 1996; P.A. 89–626, Art. 2, § 2–66, eff. Aug. 9, 1996; P.A. 90–89, § 15, eff. Jan. 1, 1998; P.A. 90–147, § 5, eff. July 23, 1997; P.A. 90–407, § 5, eff. Aug. 15, 1997; P.A.

90–655, § 153, eff. July 30, 1998; P.A. 92–417, § 5, eff. Jan. 1, 2002; P.A. 92–766, § 5, eff. Jan. 1, 2003; P.A. 92–883, § 5, eff. Jan. 13, 2003.

Formerly Ill.Rev.Stat.1991, ch. 95 ½, ¶ 15–107.

1 625 ILCS 5/1–101 et seq.

2 5 ILCS 100/5–35.

Section 4 of P.A. 83–12, approved July 1, 1983, provided:

"Effective date. This Act takes effect as provided in this Section.

"The amendments to those portions of Sections 3–815(a), 3–818 and 3–819(b) of 'The Illinois Vehicle Code' in Section 1 of this Act which create the 'X', 'Z', 'MX', 'MZ', 'MM' and 'TN' registration classifications and the fees and taxes imposed for those classifications, the amendments to Sections 2–119, 3–401 and 3–802 of 'The Illinois Vehicle Code' in Section 1 of this Act, and the amendments to Chapter 15 of 'The Illinois Vehicle Code' in Section 1 of this Act take effect July 1, 1983.

"The remaining amendments to 'The Illinois Vehicle Code' in Section 1 of this Act take effect July 1, 1983 and apply beginning with the 1985 registration year, except that the amendments to Sections 3–813 through 3–816 and Section 3–819 apply beginning with the 1984 registration year for those vehicles registered on a calendar year basis only.

"The amendments to Chapters 13 and 18 of 'The Illinois Vehicle Code' in Section 1 of this Act take effect January 1, 1984.

"Section 2 of this Act takes effect on the first day of the next succeeding month which commences at least 30 days after the date on which this Act becomes law.

"Section 3 of this Act takes effect July 1, 1983.

"Section 3.1 of this Act takes effect January 1, 1984.

"This Section 4 takes effect upon its becoming a law."

P.A. 92–766 incorporated the amendment by P.A. 92–417.

P.A. 92–883 incorporated the amendments by P.A. 92–417 and P.A. 92–766.

5/15–108. Planking edge of a pavement

§ 15–108. Planking edge of a pavement. No tractor, traction engine or other metal tired vehicle, weighing more than 4 tons, including the weight of the vehicle and its load, shall drive up onto, off or over the edge of any paved public highway in this State, without protecting such edge by putting down solid planks or other suitable device to prevent such vehicle from breaking off the edges or corners of such pavement.

P.A. 76–1586, § 15–108, eff. July 1, 1970. Amended by P.A. 90–655, § 153, eff. July 30, 1998.

Formerly Ill.Rev.Stat.1991, ch. 95 ½, ¶ 15–108.

5/15–109. Spilling loads on highways prohibited

§ 15–109. Spilling loads on highways prohibited. (a) No vehicle shall be driven or moved on any highway unless such vehicle is so constructed or loaded as to prevent any of its load from dropping, shifting, leaking or otherwise escaping therefrom, except that sand may be dropped for the purpose of securing traction, or water or other substance may be sprinkled on a roadway in cleaning or maintaining such roadway.

(b) No person shall operate on any highway any vehicle with any load unless said load and any covering thereon is securely fastened so as to prevent said covering or load from becoming loose, detached, or in any manner a hazard to other users of the highway.

(c) The Department shall adopt such rules and regulations it deems appropriate which require the securing of steel rolls and other objects on flatbed trucks so as to prevent injury to users of highways and damage to property. Any person who operates a flatbed truck on any highway in violation of the rules and regulations promulgated by the Department under this subsection shall be guilty of a Class A misdemeanor.

P.A. 76–1586, § 15–109, eff. July 1, 1970. Amended by P.A. 82–231, § 1, eff. Jan. 1, 1982.

Formerly Ill.Rev.Stat.1991, ch. 95 ½, ¶ 15–109.

5/15–109.1. Covers or tarpaulins required for certain loads

§ 15–109.1. Covers or tarpaulins required for certain loads.

(a) No person shall operate or cause to be operated, on a highway, any second division vehicle loaded with dirt, aggregate, garbage, refuse, or other similar material, when any portion of the load is falling, sifting, blowing, dropping or in any way escaping from the vehicle.

(b) No person shall operate or cause to be operated, on a highway, any second division vehicle having a gross vehicle weight rating of 8,000 pounds or more loaded with dirt, aggregate, garbage, refuse, or other similar material in or on any part of the vehicle other than in the cargo area. In addition, no person shall operate on any highway, such vehicle unless the tailgate on the vehicle is in good repair and operating condition and closes securely so as to prevent any load, residue, or other material from escaping.

(c) This Section shall not apply to the operation of highway maintenance vehicles engaged in removing snow and ice from the roadway, nor to implements of husbandry or other farm vehicles while transporting agricultural products to or from the original place of production.

(d) For the purpose of this Section "aggregate" shall include all ores, minerals, sand, gravel, shale, coal, clay, limestone or any other ore or mineral which may be mined.

(e) Notwithstanding any other penalty, whenever a police officer determines that the operator of a vehicle is in violation of this Section, as evidenced by the issuance of a citation for a violation of Section 15–109.1 of this Code, or where a police officer determines that a dangerous condition exists whereby any portion of the load may fall, sift, blow, drop, or in any way escape or fall from the vehicle, the police officer shall require the operator to stop the vehicle in a suitable place and keep such vehicle stationary until the load has either been reduced, secured, or covered with a cover or tarpaulin of sufficient size to prevent any further violation of this Section.

(f) Any violation of the provisions of this Section shall be a petty offense punishable by a fine not to exceed $250.

P.A. 76–1586, § 15–109.1, added by P.A. 84–226, § 1, eff. Jan. 1, 1986. Amended by P.A. 91–858, § 5, eff. Jan. 1, 2001.

Formerly Ill.Rev.Stat.1991, ch. 95 ½, ¶ 15–109.1.

5/15–110. Towed vehicles

§ 15–110. Towed vehicles. (a) When one vehicle is towing another, the drawbar or other connection shall be of sufficient strength to pull all the weight towed thereby and the drawbar or other connection shall not exceed 15 feet from one vehicle to the other, except for the connection between any 2 vehicles transporting poles, pipes, machinery or other objects of structural nature which cannot readily be dismembered.

(b) Outside a business, residential or suburban district or on any controlled access highway, no vehicle other than a pole trailer or a semitrailer which is being towed by a truck tractor and is connected by the means of a fifth wheel shall be towed on a roadway except by a drawbar and each such vehicle so towed shall, in addition, be coupled with 2 safety chains or cables to the towing vehicle. Such chains or cables shall be of sufficient size and strength to prevent the towed vehicle parting from the drawing vehicle in case the drawbar should break or become disengaged.

(c) The provisions of this section shall not apply to any second division vehicle owned, operated or controlled by any person who is registered with the Bureau of Motor Carrier Safety of the Federal Highway Administration and has complied with the federal safety provisions of the Bureau of Motor Carrier Safety of the Federal Highway Administration and the rules and regulations of the Bureau.

P.A. 76-1586, § 15-110, eff. July 1, 1970. Amended by P.A. 77-22, § 1, eff. July 1, 1971.

Formerly Ill.Rev.Stat.1991, ch. 95 ½, ¶ 15-110.

5/15-111. Wheel and axle loads and gross weights

§ 15-111. Wheel and axle loads and gross weights.

(a) On non-designated highways, no vehicle or combination of vehicles equipped with pneumatic tires may be operated, unladen or with load, when the total weight transmitted to the road surface exceeds 18,000 pounds on a single axle or 32,000 pounds on a tandem axle with no axle within the tandem exceeding 18,000 pounds except:

(1) when a different limit is established and posted in accordance with Section 15-316 of this Code;

(2) vehicles for which the Department of Transportation and local authorities issue overweight permits under authority of Section 15-301 of this Code;

(3) tow trucks subject to the conditions provided in subsection (d) may not exceed 24,000 pounds on a single rear axle or 44,000 pounds on a tandem rear axle;

(4) any single axle of a 2-axle truck weighing 36,000 pounds or less and not a part of a combination of vehicles, shall not exceed 20,000 pounds;

(5) any single axle of a 2-axle truck equipped with a personnel lift or digger derrick, weighing 36,000 pounds or less, owned and operated by a public utility, shall not exceed 20,000 pounds;

(6) any single axle of a 2-axle truck specially equipped with a front loading compactor used exclusively for garbage, refuse, or recycling may not exceed 20,000 pounds per axle, provided that the gross weight of the vehicle does not exceed 40,000 pounds;

(7) a truck, not in combination and specially equipped with a selfcompactor or an industrial roll-off hoist and roll-off container, used exclusively for garbage or refuse operations may, when laden, transmit upon the road surface the following maximum weights: 22,000 pounds on a single axle; 40,000 pounds on a tandem axle;

(8) a truck, not in combination and used exclusively for the collection of rendering materials, may, when laden, transmit upon the road surface the following maximum weights: 22,000 pounds on a single axle; 40,000 pounds on a tandem axle;

(9) tandem axles on a 3-axle truck registered as a Special Hauling Vehicle, manufactured prior to or in the model year of 2004 and first registered in Illinois prior to January 1, 2005, with a distance greater than 72 inches but not more than 96 inches between any series of 2 axles, is allowed a combined weight on the series not to exceed 36,000 pounds and neither axle of the series may exceed 18,000 pounds. Any vehicle of this type manufactured after the model year of 2004 or first registered in Illinois after December 31, 2004 may not exceed a combined weight of 32,000 pounds through the series of 2 axles and neither axle of the series may exceed 18,000 pounds;

(10) tandem axles on a 4-axle truck mixer, whose fourth axle is a road surface engaging mixer trailing axle, registered as a Special Hauling Vehicle, used exclusively for the mixing and transportation of concrete and manufactured prior to or in the model year of 2004 and first registered in Illinois prior to January 1, 2005, with a distance greater than 72 inches but not more than 96 inches between any series of 2 axles, is allowed a combined weight on the series not to exceed 36,000 pounds and neither axle of the series may exceed 18,000 pounds. Any vehicle of this type manufactured after the model year of 2004 or first registered in Illinois after December 31, 2004 may not exceed a combined weight of 32,000 pounds through the series of 2 axles and neither axle of the series may exceed 18,000 pounds;

(11) 4-axle vehicles or a 5 or more axle combination of vehicles: The weight transmitted upon the road surface through any series of 3 axles whose centers are more than 96 inches apart, measured between extreme axles in the series, may not exceed those allowed in the table contained in subsection (f) of this Section. No axle or tandem axle of the series may exceed the maximum weight permitted under this Section for a single or tandem axle.

No vehicle or combination of vehicles equipped with other than pneumatic tires may be operated, unladen or with load, upon the highways of this State when the gross weight on the road surface through any wheel exceeds 800 pounds per inch width of tire tread or when the gross weight on the road surface through any axle exceeds 16,000 pounds.

(b) On non-designated highways, the gross weight of vehicles and combination of vehicles including the weight of the vehicle or combination and its maximum load shall be subject to the foregoing limitations and further shall not exceed the following gross weights dependent upon the number of axles and distance between extreme axles of the vehicle or combination measured longitudinally to the nearest foot.

VEHICLES HAVING 2 AXLES .... 36,000 pounds

VEHICLES OR COMBINATIONS HAVING 3 AXLES

With Tandem Axles Minimum distance to nearest foot between extreme axles	Maximum Gross Weight (pounds)	With or Without Tandem Axles Minimum distance to nearest foot between extreme axles	Maximum Gross Weight (pounds)
10 feet	41,000	16 feet	46,000
11	42,000	17	47,000
12	43,000	18	47,500
13	44,000	19	48,000
14	44,500	20	49,000
15	45,000	21 feet or more	50,000

VEHICLES OR COMBINATIONS HAVING 4 AXLES

Minimum distance to nearest foot between extreme axles	Maximum Gross Weight (pounds)	Minimum distance to nearest foot between extreme axles	Maximum Gross Weight (pounds)
15 feet	50,000	26 feet	57,500

Minimum distance to nearest foot between extreme axles	Maximum Gross Weight (pounds)	Minimum distance to nearest foot between extreme axles	Maximum Gross Weight (pounds)
16	50,500	27	58,000
17	51,500	28	58,500
18	52,000	29	59,500
19	52,500	30	60,000
20	53,500	31	60,500
21	54,000	32	61,500
22	54,500	33	62,000
23	55,500	34	62,500
24	56,000	35	63,500
25	56,500	36 feet or more	64,000

A vehicle not in a combination having more than 4 axles may not exceed the weight in the table in this subsection (b) for 4 axles measured between the extreme axles of the vehicle.

COMBINATIONS HAVING 5 OR MORE AXLES

Minimum distance to nearest foot between extreme axles	Maximum Gross Weight (pounds)
42 feet or less	72,000
43	73,000
44 feet or more	73,280

VEHICLES OPERATING ON CRAWLER TYPE TRACKS . . . . 40,000 pounds

TRUCKS EQUIPPED WITH SELFCOMPACTORS OR ROLL–OFF HOISTS AND ROLL–OFF CONTAINERS FOR GARBAGE OR REFUSE HAULS ONLY AND TRUCKS USED FOR THE COLLECTION OF RENDERING MATERIALS

On Highway Not Part of National System of Interstate and Defense Highways

with 2 axles	36,000 pounds
with 3 axles	54,000 pounds

TWO AXLE TRUCKS EQUIPPED WITH A FRONT LOADING COMPACTOR USED EXCLUSIVELY FOR THE COLLECTION OF GARBAGE, REFUSE, OR RECYCLING

with 2 axles	40,000 pounds

(c) Cities having a population of more than 50,000 may permit by ordinance axle loads on 2 axle motor vehicles 33 ½ % above those provided for herein, but the increase shall not become effective until the city has officially notified the Department of the passage of the ordinance and shall not apply to those vehicles when outside of the limits of the city, nor shall the gross weight of any 2 axle motor vehicle operating over any street of the city exceed 40,000 pounds.

(d) Weight limitations shall not apply to vehicles (including loads) operated by a public utility when transporting equipment required for emergency repair of public utility facilities or properties or water wells.

A combination of vehicles, including a tow truck and a disabled vehicle or disabled combination of vehicles, that exceeds the weight restriction imposed by this Code, may be operated on a public highway in this State provided that neither the disabled vehicle nor any vehicle being towed nor the tow truck itself shall exceed the weight limitations permitted under this Chapter. During the towing operation, neither the tow truck nor the vehicle combination shall exceed 24,000 pounds on a single rear axle and 44,000 pounds on a tandem rear axle, provided the towing vehicle:

(1) is specifically designed as a tow truck having a gross vehicle weight rating of at least 18,000 pounds and is equipped with air brakes, provided that air brakes are required only if the towing vehicle is towing a vehicle, semitrailer, or tractor-trailer combination that is equipped with air brakes;

(2) is equipped with flashing, rotating, or oscillating amber lights, visible for at least 500 feet in all directions;

(3) is capable of utilizing the lighting and braking systems of the disabled vehicle or combination of vehicles; and

(4) does not engage in a tow exceeding 20 miles from the initial point of wreck or disablement. Any additional movement of the vehicles may occur only upon issuance of authorization for that movement under the provisions of Sections 15–301 through 15–319 of this Code.

Gross weight limits shall not apply to the combination of the tow truck and vehicles being towed. The tow truck license plate must cover the operating empty weight of the tow truck only. The weight of each vehicle being towed shall be covered by a valid license plate issued to the owner or operator of the vehicle being towed and displayed on that vehicle. If no valid plate issued to the owner or operator of that vehicle is displayed on that vehicle, or the plate displayed on that vehicle does not cover the weight of the vehicle, the weight of the vehicle shall be covered by the third tow truck plate issued to the owner or operator of the tow truck and temporarily affixed to the vehicle being towed.

The Department may by rule or regulation prescribe additional requirements. However, nothing in this Code shall prohibit a tow truck under instructions of a police officer from legally clearing a disabled vehicle, that may be in violation of weight limitations of this Chapter, from the roadway to the berm or shoulder of the highway. If in the opinion of the police officer that location is unsafe, the officer is authorized to have the disabled vehicle towed to the nearest place of safety.

For the purpose of this subsection, gross vehicle weight rating, or GVWR, shall mean the value specified by the manufacturer as the loaded weight of the tow truck.

(e) No vehicle or combination of vehicles equipped with pneumatic tires shall be operated, unladen or with load, upon the highways of this State in violation of the provisions of any permit issued under the provisions of Sections 15–301 through 15–319 of this Chapter.

(f) On designated Class I, II, or III highways and the National System of Interstate and Defense Highways, no vehicle or combination of vehicles with pneumatic tires may be operated, unladen or with load, when the total weight on the road surface exceeds the following: 20,000 pounds on a single axle; 34,000 pounds on a tandem axle with no axle within the tandem exceeding 20,000 pounds; 80,000 pounds gross weight for vehicle combinations of 5 or more axles; or a total weight on a group of 2 or more consecutive axles in excess of that weight produced by the application of the following formula: W = 500 times the sum of (LN divided by N–1) + 12N + 36, where "W" equals overall total weight on any group of 2 or more consecutive axles to the nearest 500 pounds, "L" equals the distance measured to the nearest foot between extremes of any group of 2 or more consecutive axles, and "N" equals the number of axles in the group under consideration.

The above formula when expressed in tabular form results in allowable loads as follows:

Distance measured to the nearest foot between the extremes of any group of 2 or more consecutive axles	Maximum weight in pounds of any group of 2 or more consecutive axles				
feet	2 axles	3 axles	4 axles	5 axles	6 axles
4	34,000				
5	34,000				
6	34,000				
7	34,000				
8	38,000*	42,000			
9	39,000	42,500			
10	40,000	43,500			
11		44,000			
12		45,000	50,000		
13		45,500	50,500		
14		46,500	51,500		
15		47,000	52,000		
16		48,000	52,500	58,000	
17		48,500	53,500	58,500	
18		49,500	54,000	59,000	
19		50,000	54,500	60,000	
20		51,000	55,500	60,500	66,000
21		51,500	56,000	61,000	66,500
22		52,500	56,500	61,500	67,000
23		53,000	57,500	62,500	68,000
24		54,000	58,000	63,000	68,500
25		54,500	58,500	63,500	69,000
26		55,500	59,500	64,000	69,500
27		56,000	60,000	65,000	70,000
28		57,000	60,500	65,500	71,000
29		57,500	61,500	66,000	71,500
30		58,500	62,000	66,500	72,000
31		59,000	62,500	67,500	72,500
32		60,000	63,500	68,000	73,000
33			64,000	68,500	74,000
34			64,500	69,000	74,500
35			65,500	70,000	75,000
36			66,000	70,500	75,500
37			66,500	71,000	76,000
38			67,500	72,000	77,000
39			68,000	72,500	77,500
40			68,500	73,000	78,000
41			69,500	73,500	78,500
42			70,000	74,000	79,000
43			70,500	75,000	80,000
44			71,500	75,500	
45			72,000	76,000	
46			72,500	76,500	
47			73,500	77,500	
48			74,000	78,000	
49			74,500	78,500	
50			75,500	79,000	
51			76,000	80,000	
52			76,500		
53			77,500		
54			78,000		
55			78,500		
56			79,500		
57			80,000		

* If the distance between 2 axles is 96 inches or less, the 2 axles are tandem axles and the maximum total weight may not exceed 34,000 pounds, notwithstanding the higher limit resulting from the application of the formula.

Vehicles not in a combination having more than 4 axles may not exceed the weight in the table in this subsection (f) for 4 axles measured between the extreme axles of the vehicle.

Vehicles in a combination having more than 6 axles may not exceed the weight in the table in this subsection (f) for 6 axles measured between the extreme axles of the combination.

Local authorities and road district highway commissioners, with respect to streets and highways under their jurisdiction, without additional fees, may also by ordinance or resolution allow the weight limitations of this subsection, provided the maximum gross weight on any one axle shall not exceed 20,000 pounds and the maximum total weight on any tandem axle shall not exceed 34,000 pounds, on designated highways when appropriate regulatory signs giving notice are erected upon the street or highway or portion of any street or highway affected by the ordinance or resolution.

The following are exceptions to the above formula:

(1) Two consecutive sets of tandem axles may carry a total weight of 34,000 pounds each if the overall distance between the first and last axles of the consecutive sets of tandem axles is 36 feet or more.

(2) Vehicles for which a different limit is established and posted in accordance with Section 15–316 of this Code.

(3) Vehicles for which the Department of Transportation and local authorities issue overweight permits under authority of Section 15–301 of this Code. These vehicles are not subject to the bridge formula.

(4) Tow trucks subject to the conditions provided in subsection (d) may not exceed 24,000 pounds on a single rear axle or 44,000 pounds on a tandem rear axle.

(5) A tandem axle on a 3–axle truck registered as a Special Hauling Vehicle, manufactured prior to or in the model year of 2004, and registered in Illinois prior to January 1, 2005, with a distance between 2 axles in a series greater than 72 inches but not more than 96 inches may not exceed a total weight of 36,000 pounds and neither axle of the series may exceed 18,000 pounds.

(6) A truck not in combination, equipped with a self compactor or an industrial roll-off hoist and roll-off container, used exclusively for garbage or refuse operations, may, when laden, transmit upon the road surface, except when on part of the National System of Interstate and Defense Highways, the following maximum weights: 22,000 pounds on a single axle; 40,000 pounds on a tandem axle; 36,000 pounds gross weight on a 2–axle vehicle; 54,000 pounds gross weight on a 3–axle vehicle. This vehicle is not subject to the bridge formula.

(7) Combinations of vehicles, registered as Special Hauling Vehicles that include a semitrailer manufactured prior to or in the model year of 2004, and registered in Illinois prior to January 1, 2005, having 5 axles with a distance of 42 feet or less between extreme axles, may not exceed the following maximum weights: 18,000 pounds on a single axle; 32,000 pounds on a tandem axle; and 72,000 pounds gross weight. This combination of vehicles is not subject to the bridge formula. For all those combinations of vehicles that include a semitrailer manufactured after the effective date of this amendatory Act of the 92nd General Assembly, the overall distance between the first and last axles of the 2 sets of tandems must be 18 feet 6 inches or more. Any combination of vehicles that has had its cargo container replaced in its entirety after December 31, 2004 may not exceed the weights allowed by the bridge formula.

No vehicle or combination of vehicles equipped with other than pneumatic tires may be operated, unladen or with load, upon the highways of this State when the gross weight on the road surface through any wheel exceeds 800 pounds per inch width of tire tread or when the gross weight on the road surface through any axle exceeds 16,000 pounds.

(f-1) A vehicle and load not exceeding 73,280 pounds is allowed access as follows:

(1) From any State designated highway onto any county, township, or municipal highway for a distance of 5 highway miles for the purpose of loading and unloading, provided:

(A) The vehicle and load does not exceed 8 feet 6 inches in width and 65 feet overall length.

(B) There is no sign prohibiting that access.

(C) The route is not being used as a thoroughfare between State designated highways.

(2) From any State designated highway onto any county or township highway for a distance of 5 highway miles, or any municipal highway for a distance of one highway mile for the purpose of food, fuel, repairs, and rest, provided:

(A) The vehicle and load does not exceed 8 feet 6 inches in width and 65 feet overall length.

(B) There is no sign prohibiting that access.

(C) The route is not being used as a thoroughfare between State designated highways.

(f-2) A vehicle and load greater than 73,280 pounds in weight but not exceeding 80,000 pounds is allowed access as follows:

(1) From a Class I highway onto any street or highway for a distance of one highway mile for the purpose of loading, unloading, food, fuel, repairs, and rest, provided there is no sign prohibiting that access.

(2) From a Class I, II, or III highway onto any State highway or any local designated highway for a distance of 5 highway miles for the purpose of loading, unloading, food, fuel, repairs, and rest.

Section 5-35 of the Illinois Administrative Procedure Act [1] relating to procedures for rulemaking shall not apply to the designation of highways under this subsection.

(g) No person shall operate a vehicle or combination of vehicles over a bridge or other elevated structure constituting part of a highway with a gross weight that is greater than the maximum weight permitted by the Department, when the structure is sign posted as provided in this Section.

(h) The Department upon request from any local authority shall, or upon its own initiative may, conduct an investigation of any bridge or other elevated structure constituting a part of a highway, and if it finds that the structure cannot with safety to itself withstand the weight of vehicles otherwise permissible under this Code the Department shall determine and declare the maximum weight of vehicles that the structures can withstand, and shall cause or permit suitable signs stating maximum weight to be erected and maintained before each end of the structure. No person shall operate a vehicle or combination of vehicles over any structure with a gross weight that is greater than the posted maximum weight.

(i) Upon the trial of any person charged with a violation of subsections (g) or (h) of this Section, proof of the determination of the maximum allowable weight by the Department and the existence of the signs, constitutes conclusive evidence of the maximum weight that can be maintained with safety to the bridge or structure.

P.A. 76-1586, § 15-111, eff. July 1, 1970. Amended by P.A. 76-2197, § 1, eff. July 1, 1970; P.A. 77-643, § 1, eff. Aug. 4, 1971; P.A. 77-1226, § 1, eff. Aug. 24, 1971; P.A. 77-1418, § 1, eff. Jan. 1, 1972; P.A. 77-2829, § 40, eff. Dec. 22, 1972; P.A. 78-255, § 61, eff. Oct. 1, 1973; P.A. 78-324, § 1, eff. Jan. 1, 1974; P.A. 78-1297, § 58, eff. March 4, 1975; P.A. 79-628, § 1, eff. Aug. 28, 1975; P.A. 83-12, § 1, eff. July 1, 1983; P.A. 83-953, § 1, eff. Dec. 2, 1983; P.A. 83-1478, § 1, eff. Jan. 1, 1985; P.A. 84-598, § 1, eff. Jan. 1, 1986; P.A. 84-1007, § 1, eff. Oct. 31, 1985; P.A. 84-1061, § 1, eff. July 1, 1986; P.A. 84-1308, Art. II, § 96, eff. Aug. 25, 1986; P.A. 84-1311, § 1, eff. Aug. 27, 1986; P.A. 84-1330, § 1, eff. Sept. 9, 1986; P.A. 84-1438, Art. II, § 30, eff. Dec. 22, 1986; P.A. 85-561, § 1, eff. Sept. 18, 1987; P.A. 85-563, § 1, eff. Sept. 18, 1987; P.A. 85-678, § 1, eff. July 1, 1989; P.A. 85-757, § 1, eff. Sept. 23, 1987; P.A. 85-1209, Art. II, § 2-51, eff. Aug. 30, 1988; P.A. 85-1345, § 1, eff. Aug. 31, 1988; P.A. 85-1440, Art. II, § 2-25, eff. Feb. 1, 1989; P.A. 86-409, § 1, eff. Aug. 30, 1989; P.A. 86-519, § 1, eff. Sept. 1, 1989; P.A. 86-1005, § 3, eff. Dec. 28, 1989; P.A. 86-1028, Art. II, § 2-44, eff. Feb. 5, 1990; P.A. 86-1236, § 1, eff. Jan. 1, 1991; P.A. 87-1203, § 1, eff. Sept. 25, 1992; P.A. 87-1249, § 1, eff. Dec. 24, 1992; P.A. 88-45, Art. III, § 3-128, eff. July 6, 1993; P.A. 88-385, § 5, eff. Jan. 1, 1994; P.A. 88-403, § 5, eff. Jan. 1, 1994; P.A. 88-476, § 2, eff. July 1, 1994; P.A. 88-670, Art. 2, § 2-59, eff. Dec. 2, 1994; P.A. 89-117, § 10, eff. July 7, 1995; P.A. 89-433, § 5, eff. Dec. 15, 1995; P.A. 90-89, § 15, eff. Jan. 1, 1998; P.A. 90-330, § 5, eff. Aug. 8, 1997; P.A. 90-655, § 153, eff. July 30, 1998; P.A. 92-417, § 5, eff. Jan. 1, 2002.

Formerly Ill.Rev.Stat.1991, ch. 95 ½, ¶ 15-111.

[1] 5 ILCS 100/5-35.

Effective date and application of P.A. 83-12, see note under 625 ILCS 5/2-119.

5/15-112. Officers to weigh vehicles and require removal of excess loads

§ 15-112. Officers to weigh vehicles and require removal of excess loads.

(a) Any police officer having reason to believe that the weight of a vehicle and load is unlawful shall require the driver to stop and submit to a weighing of the same either by means of a portable or stationary scales that have been tested and approved at a frequency prescribed by the Illinois Department of Agriculture, or for those scales operated by the State, when such tests are requested by the Department of State Police, whichever is more frequent. If such scales are not available at the place where such vehicle is stopped, the police officer shall require that such vehicle be driven to the nearest available scale that has been tested and approved pursuant to this Section by the Illinois Department of Agriculture. Notwithstanding any provisions of the Weights and Measures Act [1] or the United States Department of Commerce NIST handbook 44, multi or single draft weighing is an acceptable method of weighing by law enforcement for determining a violation of Chapter 3 or 15 of this Code.[2] Law enforcement is exempt from the requirements of commercial weighing established in NIST handbook 44.

Within 18 months after the effective date of this amendatory Act of the 91st General Assembly, all municipal and county officers, technicians, and employees who set up and operate portable scales for wheel load or axle load or both and issue citations based on the use of portable scales for wheel load or axle load or both and who have not successfully completed initial classroom and field training regarding the set up and operation of portable scales, shall attend and successfully complete initial classroom and field training administered by the Illinois Law Enforcement Training Standards Board.

(b) Whenever an officer, upon weighing a vehicle and the load, determines that the weight is unlawful, such officer shall require the driver to stop the vehicle in a suitable place and remain standing until such portion of the load is removed as may be necessary to reduce the weight of the vehicle to the limit permitted under this Chapter, or to the limit permitted under the terms of a permit issued pursuant to Sections 15–301 through 15–318 and shall forthwith arrest the driver or owner. All material so unloaded shall be cared for by the owner or operator of the vehicle at the risk of such owner or operator; however, whenever a 3 or 4 axle vehicle with a tandem axle dimension greater than 72 inches, but less than 96 inches and registered as a Special Hauling Vehicle is transporting asphalt or concrete in the plastic state that exceeds axle weight or gross weight limits by less than 4,000 pounds, the owner or operator of the vehicle shall accept the arrest ticket or tickets for the alleged violations under this Section and proceed without shifting or reducing the load being transported or may shift or reduce the load under the provisions of subsection (d) or (e) of this Section, when applicable. Any fine imposed following an overweight violation by a vehicle registered as a Special Hauling Vehicle transporting asphalt or concrete in the plastic state shall be paid as provided in subsection 4 of paragraph (a) of Section 16–105 of this Code.

(c) The Department of Transportation may, at the request of the Department of State Police, erect appropriate regulatory signs on any State highway directing second division vehicles to a scale. The Department of Transportation may also, at the direction of any State Police officer, erect portable regulating signs on any highway directing second division vehicles to a portable scale. Every such vehicle, pursuant to such sign, shall stop and be weighed.

(d) Whenever any axle load of a vehicle exceeds the axle or tandem axle weight limits permitted by paragraph (a) or (f) of Section 15–111 by 2000 pounds or less, the owner or operator of the vehicle must shift or remove the excess so as to comply with paragraph (a) or (f) of Section 15–111. No overweight arrest ticket shall be issued to the owner or operator of the vehicle by any officer if the excess weight is shifted or removed as required by this paragraph.

(e) Whenever the gross weight of a vehicle with a registered gross weight of 73,280 pounds or less exceeds the weight limits of paragraph (b) or (f) of Section 15–111 of this Chapter by 2000 pounds or less, the owner or operator of the vehicle must remove the excess. Whenever the gross weight of a vehicle with a registered gross weight of 73,281 pounds or more exceeds the weight limits of paragraph (b) or (f) of Section 15–111 by 1,000 pounds or less or 2,000 pounds or less if weighed on wheel load weighers, the owner or operator of the vehicle must remove the excess. In either case no arrest ticket for any overweight violation of this Code shall be issued to the owner or operator of the vehicle by any officer if the excess weight is removed as required by this paragraph. A person who has been granted a special permit under Section 15–301 of this Code shall not be granted a tolerance on wheel load weighers.

(f) Whenever an axle load of a vehicle exceeds axle weight limits allowed by the provisions of a permit an arrest ticket shall be issued, but the owner or operator of the vehicle may shift the load so as to comply with the provisions of the permit. Where such shifting of a load to comply with the permit is accomplished, the owner or operator of the vehicle may then proceed.

(g) Any driver of a vehicle who refuses to stop and submit his vehicle and load to weighing after being directed to do so by an officer or removes or causes the removal of the load or part of it prior to weighing is guilty of a business offense and shall be fined not less than $500 nor more than $2,000.

P.A. 76–1586, § 15–112, eff. July 1, 1970. Amended by P.A. 76–2198, § 1, eff. July 1, 1970; P.A. 77–77, § 1, eff. July 1, 1971; P.A. 77–170, § 1, eff. Jan. 1, 1972; P.A. 77–1225, § 1, eff. Aug. 24, 1971; P.A. 77–2720, § 1, eff. Jan. 1, 1973; P.A. 77–2830, Art. 73, § 1, eff. Jan. 1, 1973; P.A. 78–255, § 61, eff. Oct. 1, 1973; P.A. 81–942, § 1, eff. Jan. 1, 1980; P.A. 83–12, § 1, eff. July 1, 1983; P.A. 83–953, § 1, eff. Dec. 2, 1983; P.A. 84–25, Art. IV, § 27, eff. July 18, 1985; P.A. 85–830, § 1, eff. Sept. 24, 1987; P.A. 86–849, § 1, eff. Sept. 7, 1989; P.A. 88–403, § 5, eff. Jan. 1, 1994; P.A. 88–476, § 2, eff. July 1, 1994; P.A. 88–535, § 25, eff. Jan. 26, 1994; P.A. 91–129, § 10, eff. July 16, 1999; P.A. 92–417, § 5, eff. Jan. 1, 2002.

Formerly Ill.Rev.Stat.1991, ch. 95 ½, ¶ 15–112.

1 225 ILCS 470/1 et seq.

2 625 ILCS 5/1–100 or 5/15–100 et seq.

Section 4 of P.A. 83–12, approved July 1, 1983, provided:

"Effective date. This Act takes effect as provided in this Section.

"The amendments to those portions of Sections 3–815(a), 3–818 and 3–819(b) of 'The Illinois Vehicle Code' in Section 1 of this Act which create the 'X', 'Z', 'MX', 'MZ', 'MM' and 'TN' registration classifications and the fees and taxes imposed for those classifications, the amendments to Sections 2–119, 3–401 and 3–802 of 'The Illinois Vehicle Code' in Section 1 of this Act, and the amendments to Chapter 15 of 'The Illinois Vehicle Code' in Section 1 of this Act take effect July 1, 1983.

"The remaining amendments to 'The Illinois Vehicle Code' in Section 1 of this Act take effect July 1, 1983 and apply beginning with the 1985 registration year, except that the amendments to Sections 3–813 through 3–816 and Section 3–819 apply beginning with the 1984 registration year for those vehicles registered on a calendar year basis only.

"The amendments to Chapters 13 and 18 of 'The Illinois Vehicle Code' in Section 1 of this Act take effect January 1, 1984.

"Section 2 of this Act takes effect on the first day of the next succeeding month which commences at least 30 days after the date on which this Act becomes law.

"Section 3 of this Act takes effect July 1, 1983.

"Section 3.1 of this Act takes effect January 1, 1984.

"This Section 4 takes effect upon its becoming a law."

5/15–113. Violations; Penalties

§ 15–113. Violations; Penalties.

(a) Whenever any vehicle is operated in violation of the provisions of Section 15–111 or subsection (d) of Section 3–401, the owner or driver of such vehicle shall be deemed guilty of such violation and either the owner or the driver of such vehicle may be prosecuted for such violation. Any person charged with a violation of any of these provisions who pleads not guilty shall be present in court for the trial on the charge. Any person, firm or corporation convicted of any violation of Section 15–111 including, but not limited to, a maximum axle or gross limit specified on a regulatory sign posted in accordance with paragraph (g) or (h) of Section 15–111, shall be fined according to the following schedule:

Up to and including	2000 pounds overweight	=	$50
from 2001 through	2500 pounds overweight	=	the fine is $135
from 2501 through	3000 pounds overweight	=	the fine is $165
from 3001 through	3500 pounds overweight	=	the fine is $260
from 3501 through	4000 pounds overweight	=	the fine is $300
from 4001 through	4500 pounds overweight	=	the fine is $425
from 4501 through	5000 pounds overweight	=	the fine is $475
from 5001 or more pounds	overweight	=	the fine shall be computed by assessing $750 for the first 5000 pounds overweight and $75 for each additional increment of 500 pounds overweight or fraction thereof.

In addition any person, firm or corporation convicted of 4 or more violations of Section 15–111 within any 12 month period shall be fined an additional amount of $2500 for the fourth and each subsequent conviction within the 12 month period. Provided, however, that with regard to a firm or corporation, a fourth or subsequent conviction shall mean a fourth or subsequent conviction attributable to any one employee-driver.

(b) Whenever any vehicle is operated in violation of the provisions of Sections 15–102, 15–103 or 15–107, the owner or driver of such vehicle shall be deemed guilty of such violation and either may be prosecuted for such violation. Any person, firm or corporation convicted of any violation of Sections 15–102, 15–103 or 15–107 shall be fined for the first or second conviction an amount equal to not less than $50 nor more than $500, and for the third and subsequent convictions by the same person, firm or corporation within a period of one year after the date of the first offense, not less than $500 nor more than $1,000.

P.A. 76–1586, § 15–113, eff. July 1, 1970. Amended by P.A. 81–199, § 1, eff. Jan. 1, 1980; P.A. 81–942, § 1, eff. Jan. 1, 1980; P.A. 81–1509, Art. I, § 57, eff. Sept. 26, 1980; P.A. 83–12, § 1, eff. July 1, 1983; P.A. 83–838, § 1, eff. Jan. 1, 1984; P.A. 83–953, § 1, eff. Dec. 2, 1983; P.A. 86–664, § 1, eff. Sept. 1, 1989; P.A. 88–476, § 2, eff. July 1, 1994; P.A. 89–117, § 10, eff. July 7, 1995; P.A. 89–245, § 5, eff. Jan. 1, 1996.

Formerly Ill.Rev.Stat.1991, ch. 95 ½, ¶ 15–113.

Section 4 of P.A. 83–12, approved July 1, 1983, provided:

"Effective date. This Act takes effect as provided in this Section.

"The amendments to those portions of Sections 3–815(a), 3–818 and 3–819(b) of 'The Illinois Vehicle Code' in Section 1 of this Act which create the 'X', 'Z', 'MX', 'MZ', 'MM' and 'TN' registration classifications and the fees and taxes imposed for those classifications, the amendments to Sections 2–119, 3–401 and 3–802 of 'The Illinois Vehicle Code' in Section 1 of this Act, and the amendments to Chapter 15 of 'The Illinois Vehicle Code' in Section 1 of this Act take effect July 1, 1983.

"The remaining amendments to 'The Illinois Vehicle Code' in Section 1 of this Act take effect July 1, 1983 and apply beginning with the 1985 registration year, except that the amendments to Sections 3–813 through 3–816 and Section 3–819 apply beginning with the 1984 registration year for those vehicles registered on a calendar year basis only.

"The amendments to Chapters 13 and 18 of 'The Illinois Vehicle Code' in Section 1 of this Act take effect January 1, 1984.

"Section 2 of this Act takes effect on the first day of the next succeeding month which commences at least 30 days after the date on which this Act becomes law.

"Section 3 of this Act takes effect July 1, 1983.

"Section 3.1 of this Act takes effect January 1, 1984.

"This Section 4 takes effect upon its becoming a law."

The amendments by P.A. 89–117 and P.A. 89–245 were identical.

5/15–113.1. Violations—Sentence of permit moves

§ 15–113.1. Violations—Sentence of permit moves. Whenever any vehicle is operated in violation of the provisions of a permit issued under the provisions of Sections 15–301 through 15–319 of this Chapter by operating under a fraudulent permit or under a permit not specifically covering the move, the owner or driver of such vehicle shall be deemed guilty of a business offense and either the owner or the driver of such vehicle may be prosecuted for such violation. When any person, firm or corporation is convicted of such violation, the permit shall be null and void and such person, firm or corporation shall be fined in an amount not less than 10 cents per pound for each pound the gross weight of the vehicle exceeds the gross weight of such vehicles allowable under Section 15–111 of this Chapter.

Penalties for violations of this section shall be in addition to any penalties imposed for violation of Section 15–301(j) of this Chapter.

P.A. 76–1586, § 15–113.1, added by P.A. 77–1224, § 1, eff. Aug. 24, 1971. Amended by P.A. 77–2830, Art. 73, § 1, eff. Jan. 1, 1973.

Formerly Ill.Rev.Stat.1991, ch. 95 ½, ¶ 15–113.1.

5/15–113.2. Violations—Sentence of permit moves exceeding axle weights

§ 15–113.2. Violations—Sentence of permit moves exceeding axle weights. Whenever any vehicle is operated in violation of the provisions of a permit issued under the provisions of Sections 15–301 through 15–319 of this Chapter by operating with axle weights in excess of those authorized in such permit, the owner or driver of such vehicle shall be deemed guilty of a business offense and either the owner or the driver of such vehicle may be prosecuted for such violation. Any person, firm or corporation convicted of such violation shall be fined in an amount not less than 2 cents nor more than 5 cents per pound for each pound of excess weight on such axle or tandem axle in excess of the weight authorized in the permit when the excess is 1,000 pounds or less; not less than 5 cents nor more than 10 cents per pound for each pound of excess weight when the excess exceeds 1,000 pounds and is 2,000 pounds or less; not less than 10 cents nor more than 15 cents per pound for each pound of excess weight when the excess exceeds 2,000 pounds and is 3,000 pounds or less; and not less than 15 cents nor more than 20 cents per pound for each pound of excess weight when the excess exceeds 3,000 pounds.

Penalties for violations of this section shall be in addition to any penalties imposed for violation of Section 15–301(j) of this Chapter.

P.A. 76–1586, § 15–113.2, added by P.A. 77–1224, § 1, eff. Aug. 24, 1971. Amended by P.A. 77–2830, Art. 73, § 1, eff. Jan. 1, 1973; P.A. 81–199, § 1, eff. Jan. 1, 1980.

Formerly Ill.Rev.Stat.1991, ch. 95 ½, ¶ 15–113.2.

5/15–113.3. Violations—Sentence of permit moves exceeding gross weight

§ 15–113.3. Violations—Sentence of permit moves exceeding gross weight. Whenever any vehicle is operated in violation of the provisions of a permit issued under the provisions of Sections 15–301 through 15–319 of this Chapter by operating with the gross weight in excess of that authorized in such permit, the owner or driver of such vehicle shall be deemed guilty of a business offense and either the owner or the driver of such vehicle may be prosecuted for such violation. Any person, firm or corporation convicted of such violation shall be fined in an amount not less than 2 cents nor more than 5 cents per pound for each pound of excess weight in excess of the gross weight authorized in the permit when the excess is 1,000 pounds or less; not less than 4 cents nor more than 7 cents per pound for each pound of excess weight when the excess exceeds 1,000 pounds and is 2,000 pounds or less; not less than 7 cents nor more than 10 cents per pound for each pound of excess weight when the excess exceeds 2,000 pounds and is 3,000 pounds or less; not less than 10 cents nor more than 15 cents per pound for each pound of excess weight when the excess exceeds 3,000 pounds and is 4,000 pounds or less; not less than 15 cents nor more than 20 cents per pound for each pound of excess weight when the excess exceeds 4,000 pounds and is 5,000 pounds or less; and not less than 17 cents nor more than 25 cents per pound for each pound of excess weight when the excess exceeds 5,000 pounds.

Penalties for violations of this section shall be in addition to any penalties imposed for violation of Section 15-301(j) of this Chapter.

P.A. 76-1586, § 15-113.3, added by P.A. 77-1224, § 1, eff. Aug. 24, 1971. Amended by P.A. 77-2830, Art. 73, § 1, eff. Jan. 1, 1973.

Formerly Ill.Rev.Stat.1991, ch. 95 ½, ¶ 15-113.3.

5/15-114. Pushing of disabled vehicles

§ 15-114. Pushing of disabled vehicles. It is unlawful under any circumstances for any vehicle to push any other vehicle on or along any highway outside an urban area in this State, except in an extreme emergency and then the vehicle shall not be pushed farther than is reasonably necessary to remove it from the roadway or from the immediate hazard that exists.

P.A. 76-1586, § 15-114, added by P.A. 78-486, § 1, eff. Jan. 1, 1974.

Formerly Ill.Rev.Stat.1991, ch. 95 ½, ¶ 15-114.

5/15-115. Report; operation of larger vehicles; consumption of diesel fuel by first and second division vehicles

§ 15-115. By July 1, 1985, and every 3 years thereafter, the Department of Transportation shall publish and deliver to the Governor and the General Assembly a report which assesses the damage done to public highways in the State of Illinois by virtue of the increased lengths, widths and weight loads allowed under this amendatory Act of 1983 and which determines whether the proceeds of the taxes imposed by the addition of Section 2(c) to "The Motor Fuel Tax Law" [1] in Section 2 of this amendatory Act of 1983 and the proceeds of the fees and taxes paid by the owners of vehicles classified in the "X", "Z", "MX" and "MZ" classifications under the amendments to Sections 3-815(a) and 3-818 in Section 1 of this amendatory Act of 1983 are sufficient to cover the costs of permitting the operation of such larger vehicles. The report shall also assess the consumption of diesel fuel by first and second division motor vehicles.

P.A. 76-1586, § 15-115, added by P.A. 83-12, § 1, eff. July 1, 1983.

Formerly Ill.Rev.Stat.1991, ch. 95 ½, ¶ 15-115.

[1] 35 ILCS 505/2.

ARTICLE II. VEHICLES EXCEEDING WEIGHT LIMITS

Section

5/15-201. Vehicles exceeding prescribed weight limits—Preventing use of highway by

§ 15-201. Vehicles exceeding prescribed weight limits—Preventing use of highway by. The Department of State Police is directed to institute and maintain a program designed to prevent the use of public highways by vehicles which exceed the maximum weights allowed by Section 15-111 of this Act or which exceeds the maximum weights allowed as evidenced by the license plates attached to such vehicle and which license is required by this Act.

P.A. 76-1586, § 15-201, eff. July 1, 1970. Amended by P.A. 77-1057, § 1, eff. Aug. 17, 1971; P.A. 84-25, Art. IV, § 27, eff. July 18, 1985.

Formerly Ill.Rev.Stat.1991, ch. 95 ½, ¶ 15-201.

5/15-202. Enforcement

§ 15-202. Enforcement. Such program shall make provision for an intensive campaign by the State Police to apprehend any violators of the acts above mentioned, and at all times to maintain a vigilant watch for possible violators of such acts.

P.A. 76-1586, § 15-202, eff. July 1, 1970. Amended by P.A. 77-506, § 1, eff. Jan. 1, 1972.

Formerly Ill.Rev.Stat.1991, ch. 95 ½, ¶ 15-202.

5/15-203. Records of violations

§ 15-203. Records of violations. The Department of State Police shall maintain records of the number of violators of such acts apprehended and the number of convictions obtained. A resume of such records shall be included in the Department's annual report to the Governor; and the Department shall also present such resume to each regular session of the General Assembly.

The requirement for reporting to the General Assembly shall be satisfied by filing copies of the report with the Speaker, the Minority Leader and the Clerk of the House of Representatives and the President, the Minority Leader and the Secretary of the Senate and the Legislative Research Unit, as required by Section 3.1 of "An Act to revise the law in relation to the General Assembly", approved February 25, 1874, as amended,[1] and filing such additional copies with the State Government Report Distribution Center for the General Assembly as is required under paragraph (t) of Section 7 of the State Library Act.[2]

P.A. 76-1586, § 15-203, eff. July 1, 1970. Amended by P.A. 77-1058, § 1, eff. Aug. 17, 1971; P.A. 83-784, § 51, eff. Jan. 1, 1984; P.A. 84-25, Art. IV, § 27, eff. July 18, 1985; P.A. 84-1438, Art. III, § 46, eff. Dec. 22, 1986.

Formerly Ill.Rev.Stat.1991, ch. 95 ½, ¶ 15-203.

[1] 25 ILCS 5/3.1.

[2] 15 ILCS 320/7.

5/15-204 to 5/15-211. §§ 15-204 to 15-211. Repealed by P.A. 77-506, § 2, eff. Jan. 1, 1972

ARTICLE III. PERMITS

Section

5/15-301. Permits for excess size and weight

§ 15-301. Permits for excess size and weight.

(a) The Department with respect to highways under its jurisdiction and local authorities with respect to highways under their jurisdiction may, in their discretion, upon application and good cause being shown therefor, issue a special permit authorizing the applicant to operate or move a vehicle or combination of vehicles of a size or weight of vehicle or load exceeding the maximum specified in this Act or otherwise not in conformity with this Act upon any highway under the jurisdiction of the party granting such permit and for the maintenance of which the party is responsible. Applications and permits other than those in written or printed form may only be accepted from and issued to the company or individual making the movement. Except for an application to move directly across a highway, it shall be the duty of the applicant to establish in the application that the load to be moved by such vehicle or combination is composed of a single nondivisible object that cannot reasonably be dismantled or disassembled. For the purpose of over length movements, more than one object may be carried side by side as long as the height, width, and weight laws are not exceeded and the cause for the over length is not due to multiple objects. For the purpose of over height movements, more than one object may be carried as long as the cause for the over height is not due to multiple objects and the length, width, and weight laws are not exceeded. For the purpose of an over width movement, more than one object may be carried as long as the cause for the over width is not due to multiple objects and length, height, and weight laws are not exceeded. No state or local agency shall authorize the issuance of excess size or weight permits for vehicles and loads that are divisible and that can be carried, when divided, within the existing size or weight maximums specified in this Chapter. Any excess size or weight permit issued in violation of the provisions of this Section shall be void at issue and any movement made thereunder shall not be authorized under the terms of the void permit. In any prosecution for a violation of this Chapter when the authorization of an excess size or weight permit is at issue, it is the burden of the defendant to establish that the permit was valid because the load to be moved could not reasonably be dismantled or disassembled, or was otherwise nondivisible.

(b) The application for any such permit shall: (1) state whether such permit is requested for a single trip or for limited continuous operation; (2) state if the applicant is an authorized carrier under the Illinois Motor Carrier of Property Law, if so, his certificate, registration or permit number issued by the Illinois Commerce Commission; (3) specifically describe and identify the vehicle or vehicles and load to be operated or moved except that for vehicles or vehicle combinations registered by the Department as provided in Section 15-319 of this Chapter, only the Illinois Department of Transportation's (IDT) registration number or classification need be given; (4) state the routing requested including the points of origin and destination, and may identify and include a request for routing to the nearest certified scale in accordance with the Department's rules and regulations, provided the applicant has approval to travel on local roads; and (5) state if the vehicles or loads are being transported for hire. No permits for the movement of a vehicle or load for hire shall be issued to any applicant who is required under the Illinois Motor Carrier of Property Law to have a certificate, registration or permit and does not have such certificate, registration or permit.

(c) The Department or local authority when not inconsistent with traffic safety is authorized to issue or withhold such permit at its discretion; or, if such permit is issued at its discretion to prescribe the route or routes to be traveled, to limit the number of trips, to establish seasonal or other time limitations within which the vehicles described may be operated on the highways indicated, or otherwise to limit or prescribe conditions of operations of such vehicle or vehicles, when necessary to assure against undue damage to the road foundations, surfaces or structures, and may require such undertaking or other security as may be deemed necessary to compensate for any injury to any roadway or road structure. The Department shall maintain a daily record of each permit issued along with the fee and the stipulated dimensions, weights, conditions and restrictions authorized and this record shall be presumed correct in any case of questions or dispute. The Department shall install an automatic device for recording applications received and permits issued by telephone. In making application by telephone, the Department and applicant waive all objections to the recording of the conversation.

(d) The Department shall, upon application in writing from any local authority, issue an annual permit authorizing the local authority to move oversize highway construction, transportation, utility and maintenance equipment over roads under the jurisdiction of the Department. The permit shall be applicable only to equipment and vehicles owned by or registered in the name of the local authority, and no fee shall be charged for the issuance of such permits.

(e) As an exception to paragraph (a) of this Section, the Department and local authorities, with respect to highways under their respective jurisdictions, in their discretion and upon application in writing may issue a special permit for limited continuous operation, authorizing the applicant to move loads of sweet corn, soybeans, corn, wheat, milo, other small grains and ensilage during the harvest season only on a 2 axle single vehicle registered by the Secretary of State with axle loads not to exceed 35% above those provided in Section 15-111. Permits may be issued for a period not to exceed 40 days and moves may be made of a distance not to exceed 25 miles from a field to a specified processing plant over any highway except the National System of Interstate and Defense Highways. All such vehicles shall be operated in the daytime except when weather or crop conditions require emergency operation at night, but with respect to such night operation, every such vehicle with load shall be equipped with flashing amber lights as specified under Section 12-215. Upon a declaration by the Governor that an emergency harvest situation exists, a special permit issued by the Department under this Section shall not be required from September 1 through December 31 during harvest season emergencies, provided that the weight does not exceed 20% above the limits provided in Section 15-111. All other restrictions that apply to permits issued under this Section shall apply during the declared time period. With respect to highways under the jurisdiction of local authorities, the local authorities may, at their discretion, waive special permit requirements during harvest season emergencies. This permit exemption shall apply to all vehicles eligible to obtain permits under this Section, including commercial vehicles in use during the declared time period.

(f) The form and content of the permit shall be determined by the Department with respect to highways under its jurisdiction and by local authorities with respect to highways under their jurisdiction. Every permit shall be in written form and carried in the vehicle or combination of vehicles to which it refers and shall be open to inspection by any police officer or authorized agent of any authority granting the permit and no person shall violate any of the terms or conditions of such special permit. Violation of the terms and conditions of the permit shall not be deemed a revocation of the permit; however, any vehicle and load found to be off the route prescribed in the permit shall be held to be operating without a permit. Any off route vehicle and load shall be required to obtain a new permit or permits, as necessary, to authorize the movement back onto the original permit routing. No rule or regulation, nor anything herein shall be construed to authorize any police officer, court, or authorized agent of any authority granting the permit to remove the permit from the possession of the permittee unless the permittee is charged with a fraudulent permit violation as provided in paragraph (i). However, upon arrest for an offense of violation of permit, operating without a permit when the vehicle is off route, or any size or weight offense under this Chapter when the permittee plans to raise the issuance of the permit as a defense, the permittee, or his agent, must produce the permit at any court hearing concerning the alleged offense.

If the permit designates and includes a routing to a certified scale, the permitee, while enroute to the designated scale, shall be deemed in compliance with the weight provisions of the permit provided the axle or gross weights do not exceed any of the permitted limits by more than the following amounts:

Single axle	2000 pounds
Tandem axle	3000 pounds
Gross	5000 pounds

(g) The Department is authorized to adopt, amend, and to make available to interested persons a policy concerning reasonable rules, limitations and conditions or provisions of operation upon highways under its jurisdiction in addition to those contained in this Section for the movement by special permit of vehicles, combinations, or loads which cannot reasonably be dismantled or disassembled, including manufactured and modular home sections and portions thereof. All rules, limitations and conditions or provisions adopted in the policy shall have due regard for the safety of the traveling public and the protection of the highway system and shall have been promulgated in conformity with the provisions of the Illinois Administrative Procedure Act.[1] The requirements of the policy for flagmen and escort vehicles shall be the same for all moves of comparable size and weight. When escort vehicles are required, they shall meet the following requirements:

(1) All operators shall be 18 years of age or over and properly licensed to operate the vehicle.

(2) Vehicles escorting oversized loads more than 12-feet wide must be equipped with a rotating or flashing amber light mounted on top as specified under Section 12-215.

The Department shall establish reasonable rules and regulations regarding liability insurance or self insurance for vehicles with oversized loads promulgated under The Illinois Administrative Procedure Act. Police vehicles may be required for escort under circumstances as required by rules and regulations of the Department.

(h) Violation of any rule, limitation or condition or provision of any permit issued in accordance with the provisions of this Section shall not render the entire permit null and void but the violator shall be deemed guilty of violation of permit and guilty of exceeding any size, weight or load limitations in excess of those authorized by the permit. The prescribed route or routes on the permit are not mere rules, limitations, conditions, or provisions of the permit, but are also the sole extent of the authorization granted by the permit. If a vehicle and load are found to be off the route or routes prescribed by any permit authorizing movement, the vehicle and load are operating without a permit. Any off route movement shall be subject to the size and weight maximums, under the applicable provisions of this Chapter, as determined by the type or class highway upon which the vehicle and load are being operated.

(i) Whenever any vehicle is operated or movement made under a fraudulent permit the permit shall be void, and the person, firm, or corporation to whom such permit was granted, the driver of such vehicle in addition to the person who issued such permit and any accessory, shall be guilty of fraud and either one or all persons may be prosecuted for such violation. Any person, firm, or corporation committing such violation shall be guilty of a Class 4 felony and the Department shall not issue permits to the person, firm or corporation convicted of such violation for a period of one year after the date of conviction. Penalties for violations of this Section shall be in addition to any penalties imposed for violation of other Sections of this Act.

(j) Whenever any vehicle is operated or movement made in violation of a permit issued in accordance with this Section, the person to whom such permit was granted, or the driver of such vehicle, is guilty of such violation and either, but not both, persons may be prosecuted for such violation as stated in this subsection (j). Any person, firm or corporation convicted of such violation shall be guilty of a petty offense and shall be fined for the first offense, not less than $50 nor more than $200 and, for the second offense by the same person, firm or corporation within a period of one year, not less than $200 nor more than $300 and, for the third offense by the same person, firm or corporation within a period of one year after the date of the first offense, not less than $300 nor more than $500 and the Department shall not issue permits to the person, firm or corporation convicted of a third offense during a period of one year after the date of conviction for such third offense.

(k) Whenever any vehicle is operated on local roads under permits for excess width or length issued by local authorities, such vehicle may be moved upon a State highway for a distance not to exceed one-half mile without a permit for the purpose of crossing the State highway.

(*l*) Notwithstanding any other provision of this Section, the Department, with respect to highways under its jurisdiction, and local authorities, with respect to highways under their jurisdiction, may at their discretion authorize the movement of a vehicle in violation of any size or weight requirement, or both, that would not ordinarily be eligible for a permit, when there is a showing of extreme necessity that the vehicle and load should be moved without unnecessary delay.

For the purpose of this subsection, showing of extreme necessity shall be limited to the following: shipments of livestock, hazardous materials, liquid concrete being hauled in a mobile cement mixer, or hot asphalt.

(m) Penalties for violations of this Section shall be in addition to any penalties imposed for violating any other Section of this Code.

(n) The Department with respect to highways under its jurisdiction and local authorities with respect to highways under their jurisdiction, in their discretion and upon application in writing, may issue a special permit for continuous limited operation, authorizing the applicant to operate a tow-truck that exceeds the weight limits provided for in subsection (d) of Section 15-111, provided:

(1) no rear single axle of the tow-truck exceeds 26,000 pounds;

(2) no rear tandem axle of the tow-truck exceeds 50,000 pounds;

(3) neither the disabled vehicle nor the disabled combination of vehicles exceed the weight restrictions imposed by this Chapter 15, or the weight limits imposed under a permit issued by the Department prior to hookup;

(4) the tow-truck prior to hookup does not exceed the weight restrictions imposed by this Chapter 15;

(5) during the tow operation the tow-truck does not violate any weight restriction sign;

(6) the tow-truck is equipped with flashing, rotating, or oscillating amber lights, visible for at least 500 feet in all directions;

(7) the tow-truck is specifically designed and licensed as a tow-truck;

(8) the tow-truck has a gross vehicle weight rating of sufficient capacity to safely handle the load;

(9) the tow-truck is equipped with air brakes;

(10) the tow-truck is capable of utilizing the lighting and braking systems of the disabled vehicle or combination of vehicles;

(11) the tow distance of the tow does not exceed 50 miles from the point of disablement to a place of repair or safekeeping;

(12) the permit issued to the tow-truck is carried in the tow-truck and exhibited on demand by a police officer; and

(13) the movement shall be valid only on state routes approved by the Department.

P.A. 76-1586, § 15-301, eff. July 1, 1970. Amended by P.A. 76-2202, § 1, eff. July 1, 1970; P.A. 77-1223, § 1, eff. Aug. 24, 1971; P.A. 77-2720, § 1, eff. Jan. 1, 1973; P.A. 78-255, § 61, eff. Oct. 1, 1973; P.A. 78-692, § 1, eff. Oct. 1, 1973; P.A. 78-802, § 1, eff. Oct. 1, 1973; P.A. 78-1297, § 30, eff. March 4, 1975; P.A. 81-199, § 1, eff. Jan. 1, 1980; P.A. 82-783, Art. XI, § 140, eff. July 13, 1982; P.A. 84-986, § 1, eff. Sept. 25, 1985; P.A. 86-1232, § 1, eff. Jan. 1, 1991; P.A. 88-291, § 5, eff. Aug. 11, 1993; P.A. 88-476, § 2, eff. July 1, 1994; P.A. 88-670, Art. 2, § 2-59, eff. Dec. 2, 1994; P.A. 90-89, § 15, eff. Jan. 1, 1998; P.A. 90-228, § 5, eff. July 25, 1997; P.A. 90-655, § 153, eff. July 30, 1998; P.A. 90-676, § 5, eff. July 31, 1998; P.A. 91-569, § 5, eff. Jan. 1, 2000.

Formerly Ill.Rev.Stat.1991, ch. 95 ½, ¶ 15-301.

[1] 5 ILCS 100/1-1 et seq.

5/15-302. Fees for special permits

§ 15-302. Fees for special permits. The Department with respect to highways under its jurisdiction shall collect a fee from the applicant for the issuance of a permit to operate or move a vehicle or combination of vehicles or load as authorized in Section 15-301. The charge for each permit shall consist of:

1. a service charge for special handling of a permit when requested by an applicant;

2. fees for any dimension, axle weight or gross weight in excess of the maximum size or weight specified in this Chapter; and

3. additional fees for special investigations as in Section 15-311 and special police escort as in Section 15-312 when required.

With respect to overweight fees, the charge shall be sufficient to compensate in part for the cost of the extra wear and tear on the mileage of highways over which the load is to be moved. With respect to over-dimension permits, the fee shall be sufficient to compensate in part for the special privilege of transporting oversize vehicle or vehicle combination and load and to compensate in part for the economic loss of operators of vehicles in regular operation due to inconvenience occasioned by the oversize movements.

Fees to be paid by the applicant are to be at the rates specified in this Chapter. In determining the fees in Section 15-306 and paragraph (f) of Section 15-307, all weights shall be to the next highest 1,000 pounds and all distances shall be determined from the Illinois Official Highway Map.

For repeated moves of like objects which cannot be dismantled or disassembled and which are monolithically structured for permanent use in the transported form, the fees specified in Sections 15-305, 15-306 and 15-307 for other than the first move shall be reduced by $4 provided the objects are to be moved from the same origin to the same destination, the number of trips will not be less than 5, the trips will be completed within 30 days, and all applications are submitted at one time. Round trip permits shall be the same as a single trip permit except the fee shall be computed based upon the total distance traveled, and shall be for the same vehicle, vehicle combination or like load traveling both directions over the same route, provided a description including make and model of the equipment being transported is furnished to the Department, except that a vehicle combination registered by the Department as provided in Section 15-319 may be one of the same class. Limited continuous operation permits are to be valid for a period of 90 days or one year, and shall be for the same vehicle, vehicle combination or like load.

P.A. 76-1586, § 15-302, eff. July 1, 1970. Amended by P.A. 76-2203, § 1, eff. July 1, 1970; P.A. 81-199, § 1, eff. Jan. 1, 1980; P.A. 83-831, § 1, eff. Jan. 1, 1984; P.A. 84-566, § 1, eff. Jan. 1, 1986; P.A. 89-219, § 5, eff. Jan. 1, 1996; P.A. 91-357, § 231, eff. July 29, 1999.

Formerly Ill.Rev.Stat.1991, ch. 95 ½, ¶ 15-302.

5/15-303. Transmission fees

§ 15-303. Transmission Fees. When special transmission of permits is requested by an applicant, a service charge in an amount sufficient to defray the cost shall be charged.

P.A. 76-1586, § 15-303, eff. July 1, 1970. Amended by P.A. 76-2204, § 1, eff. July 1, 1970; P.A. 81-199, § 1, eff. Jan. 1, 1980.

Formerly Ill.Rev.Stat.1991, ch. 95 ½, ¶ 15-303.

5/15-303.1. § 15-303.1. Repealed by P.A. 81-199, § 2, eff. Jan. 1, 1980

5/15-304. Fees for house trailer combinations, or a unit carrying roof or floor trusses

§ 15-304. Fees for house trailer combinations, or a unit carrying roof or floor trusses. Fees for special permits to move a house trailer, oversize storage building, modular home section, or a unit carrying roof or floor trusses in combination with a towing vehicle shall be paid by the applicant to the Department at the following rates:

	Single Trip	90 Day Limited Continuous Operation	Annual Limited Continuous Operation
(a) Maximum overall width of 10 feet or less; maximum overall height of 14 feet 6 inches or less; or maximum overall length, including the towing vehicle, of 70 feet or less:		$100.00	$400.00
For the first 90 miles	$12.00		
From 90 miles to 180 miles	$15.00		
From 180 miles to 270 miles	$18.00		
For more than 270 miles	$21.00		
(b) Maximum overall width of 12 feet or less, plus an additional 2 inch overhang on each side to allow for eaves, drip edges or guttering that is at least 9 feet above the surface of the pavement; maximum overall height of 14 feet 6 inches or less; or maximum overall length, including the towing vehicle, of 115 feet or less:		$150.00	$600.00
For the first 90 miles	$15.00		
From 90 miles to 180 miles	$20.00		
From 180 miles to 270 miles	$25.00		
For more than 270 miles	$30.00		

(c) Maximum overall width of 14 feet or less; maximum overall height of 15 feet or less; maximum overall length, including the towing vehicle, of 115 feet or less;

	Single Trip	90 Day Limited Continuous Operation	Annual Limited Continuous Operation
		$250.00	$1000.00
For the first 90 miles	$25.00		
From 90 miles to 180 miles	$30.00		
From 180 miles to 270 miles	$35.00		
For more than 270 miles	$40.00		

(d) Maximum overall width of 14 feet 4 inches or less, maximum overall height of 15 feet or less; or maximum overall length, including the towing vehicle, of 115 feet or less:

	Single Trip	90 Day Limited Continuous Operation	Annual Limited Continuous Operation
		$250.00	$1000.00
For the first 90 miles	$30.00		
From 90 miles to 180 miles	$40.00		
From 180 miles to 270 miles	$50.00		
From 270 miles or more	$60.00		

(e) Maximum overall width of 16 feet or less provided that a tolerance in width of up to 3 inches will be allowed for house trailer combinations; or maximum overall height of 15 feet or less; or maximum overall length, including the towing vehicle of 115 feet or less:

	Single Trip Only	90 Day Limited Continuous Operation	Annual Limited Continuous Operation
For the first 90 miles	$30.00	$250.00	$1000.00
From 90 miles to 180 miles	$40.00		
From 180 miles to 270 miles	$50.00		
From 270 miles or more	$60.00		

P.A. 76-1586, § 15-304, eff. July 1, 1970. Amended by P.A. 76-2206, § 1, eff. July 1, 1970; P.A. 78-802, § 1, eff. Oct. 1, 1973; P.A. 81-199, § 1, eff. Jan. 1, 1980; P.A. 83-821, § 1, eff. Sept. 24, 1983; P.A. 86-1223, § 1, eff. Jan. 1, 1991; P.A. 87-140, § 1, eff. Aug. 16, 1991; P.A. 88-517, § 10, eff. Nov. 16, 1993; P.A. 89-219, § 5, eff. Jan. 1, 1996; P.A. 90-148, § 5, eff. July 23, 1997.

Formerly Ill.Rev.Stat.1991, ch. 95 ½, ¶ 15-304.

5/15-305. Fees for legal weight but overdimension vehicles, combinations, and loads, other than house trailer combinations

§ 15-305. Fees for legal weight but overdimension Vehicles, Combinations, and Loads, other than House Trailer Combinations. Fees for special permits to move overdimension vehicles, combinations, and loads, other than house trailer combinations, shall be paid by the applicant to the Department at the following rates:

	Single Trip	90 Day Limited Continuous Operation	Annual Limited Continuous Operation
(a) Overall width of 10 feet or less, overall height of 14 feet 6 inches or less, and overall length of 70 feet or less		$100.00	$ 400.00
For the first 90 miles	$ 12.00		
From 90 miles to 180 miles	15.00		
From 180 miles to 270 miles	18.00		
For more than 270 miles	$ 21.00		
(b) Overall width of 12 feet or less, overall height of 14 feet 6 inches or less, and overall length of 85 feet or less		$150.00	$ 600.00
For the first 90 miles	$ 15.00		
From 90 miles to 180 miles	$ 20.00		
From 180 miles to 270 miles	$ 25.00		
For more than 270 miles	$ 30.00		
(c) Overall width of 14 feet or less, overall height of 15 feet or less, and overall length of 100 feet or less		Single Trip Only	
For the first 90 miles	$ 25.00		
From 90 miles to 180 miles	$ 30.00		
From 180 miles to 270 miles	$ 35.00		
For more than 270 miles	$ 40.00		
(d) Overall width of 18 feet or less (authorized only under special conditions and for limited distances), overall height of 16 feet or less, and overall length of 120 feet or less		Single Trip Only	
For the first 90 miles	$ 30.00		
From 90 miles to 180 miles	$ 40.00		
From 180 miles to 270 miles	$ 50.00		
For more than 270 miles	$ 60.00		
(e) Overall width of more than 18 feet (authorized only under special conditions and for limited distances), overall height more than 16 feet, and overall length more than 120 feet		Single Trip Only	
For the first 90 miles	$ 50.00		
From 90 miles to 180 miles	$ 75.00		
From 180 miles to 270 miles	$100.00		
For more than 270 miles	$125.00		

Permits issued under this Section shall be for a vehicle, or vehicle combination and load not exceeding legal weights; and, in the case of the limited continuous operation, shall be for the same vehicle, vehicle combination or like load.

Escort requirements shall be as prescribed in the Department's Rules and Regulations. Fees for the State Police vehicle escort, when required, shall be in addition to the permit fees.

P.A. 76–1586, § 15–305, eff. July 1, 1970. Amended by P.A. 78–270, § 1, eff. Aug. 13, 1973; P.A. 81–199, § 1, eff. Jan. 1, 1980; P.A. 89–219, § 5, eff. Jan. 1, 1996.

Formerly Ill.Rev.Stat.1991, ch. 95 ½, ¶ 15–305.

5/15–306. Fees for Overweight–Axle Loads

§ 15–306. Fees for Overweight–Axle Loads. Fees for special permits to move legal gross weight vehicles, combinations of vehicles and loads with overweight-axle loads shall be paid by the applicant to the Department as follows:

For each overweight single axle or tandem axle group, the flat rate fees herein scheduled for increments of 45 miles or fraction thereof including issuance fee predicated upon an 18,000 pound single axle equivalency.

18,000 Pound Single Axle Equivalency Fees

Axle weight in excess	2–Axle Single Axle	3–Axle Tandem	Tandem Tandem
1–6000 lbs.	$ 5	$ 5	$ 5
6001–11,000 lbs.	8	7	6
11,001–17,000 lbs.	not permitted	8	7
17,001–22,000 lbs.	not permitted	not permitted	9
22,001–29,000 lbs.	not permitted	not permitted	11

P.A. 76–1586, § 15–306, eff. July 1, 1970. Amended by P.A. 81–199, § 1, eff. Jan. 1, 1980; P.A. 90–676, § 5, eff. July 31, 1998.

Formerly Ill.Rev.Stat.1991, ch. 95 ½, ¶ 15–306.

5/15–307. Fees for Overweight–Gross Loads

§ 15–307. Fees for Overweight–Gross Loads. Fees for special permits to move vehicles, combinations of vehicles and loads with overweight-gross loads shall be paid at the flat rate fees established in this Section for weights in excess of legal gross weights, by the applicant to the Department.

(a) With respect to fees for overweight-gross loads listed in this Section and for overweight-axle loads listed in Section 15–306, one fee only shall be charged, whichever is the greater, but not for both.

(b) In lieu of the fees stated in this Section and Section 15–306, with respect to combinations of vehicles consisting of a 3–axle truck tractor with a tandem axle composed of 2 consecutive axles drawing a semitrailer, or other vehicle approved by the Department, equipped with a tandem axle composed of 3 consecutive axles, weighing over 73,280 pounds but not more than 88,000 pounds gross weight, the fees shall be at the following rates:

Distance	Rate
For the first 45 miles	$10
From 45 miles to 90 miles	12.50
From 90 miles to 135 miles	15.00
From 135 miles to 180 miles	17.50
From 180 miles to 225 miles	20.00
For each additional 45 miles or part thereof in excess of the rate for 225 miles, an additional	2.50

For such combinations weighing over 88,000 pounds but not more than 100,000 pounds gross weight, the fees shall be at the following rates:

Distance	Rate
For the first 45 miles	15
From 45 miles to 90 miles	25
From 90 miles to 135 miles	35
From 135 miles to 180 miles	45
From 180 miles to 225 miles	55
For each additional 45 miles or part thereof in excess of the rate for 225 miles, an additional	10

For such combination weighing over 100,000 pounds but not more than 110,000 pounds gross weight, the fees shall be at the following rates:

Distance	Rate
For the first 45 miles	$20
From 45 miles to 90 miles	32.50
From 90 miles to 135 miles	45
From 135 miles to 180 miles	57.50
From 180 miles to 225 miles	70

Distance	Rate
For each additional 45 miles or part thereof in excess of the rate for 225 miles an additional	12.50

For such combinations weighing over 110,000 pounds but not more than 120,000 pounds gross weight, the fees shall be at the following rates:

Distance	Rate
For the first 45 miles	$30
From 46 miles to 90 miles	55
From 90 miles to 135 miles	80
From 135 miles to 180 miles	105
From 180 miles to 225 miles	130
For each additional 45 miles or part thereof in excess of the rate for 225 miles an additional	25

Payment of overweight fees for the above combinations also shall include fees for overwidth dimensions of 4 feet or less, overheight and overlength. Any overwidth in excess of 4 feet shall be charged an additional fee of $15.

(c) In lieu of the fees stated in this Section and Section 15-306 of this Chapter, with respect to combinations of vehicles consisting of a 3-axle truck tractor with a tandem axle composed of 2 consecutive axles drawing a semitrailer, or other vehicle approved by the Department, equipped with a tandem axle composed of 2 consecutive axles, weighing over 73,280 pounds but not more than 88,000 pounds gross weight, the fees shall be at the following rates:

Distance	Rate
For the first 45 miles	$20
From 45 miles to 90 miles	32.50
From 90 miles to 135 miles	45
From 135 miles to 180 miles	57.50
From 180 miles to 225 miles	70
For each additional 60 miles or part thereof in excess of the rate for 225 miles an additional	12.50

For such combination weighing over 88,000 pounds but not more than 100,000 pounds gross weight, the fees shall be at the following rates:

Distance	Rate
For the first 45 miles	$30
From 46 miles to 90 miles	55
From 90 miles to 135 miles	80
From 135 miles to 180 miles	105
From 180 miles to 225 miles	130
For each additional 45 miles or part thereof in excess of the rate for 225 miles an additional	25

Payment of overweight fees for the above combinations also shall include fees for overwidth dimension of 4 feet or less, overheight and overlength. Any overwidth in excess of 4 feet shall be charged an additional overwidth fee of $15.

(d) In lieu of the fees stated in this Section and in Section 15-306 of this Chapter, with respect to a 3 (or more) axle mobile crane or water well-drilling vehicle consisting of a single axle and a tandem axle or 2 tandem axle groups composed of 2 consecutive axles each, with a distance of extreme axles not less than 18 feet, weighing not more than 60,000 pounds gross with no single axle weighing more than 21,000 pounds, or any tandem axle group to exceed 40,000 pounds, the fees shall be at the following rates:

Distance	Rate
For the first 45 miles	$12.50
For each additional 45 miles or portion thereof	9.00

For such vehicles weighing over 60,000 pounds but not more than 68,000 pounds with no single axle weighing more than 21,000 pounds and no tandem axle group exceeding 48,000 pounds, the fees shall be at the following rates:

Distance	Rate
For the first 45 miles	$20
For each additional 45 miles or portion thereof	12.50

Payment of overweight fees for the above vehicle shall include overwidth dimension of 4 feet or less, overheight and overlength. Any overwidth in excess of 4 feet shall be charged an additional overwidth fee of $15.

(e) In lieu of the fees stated in this Section and in Section 15-306 of this Chapter, with respect to a 4 (or more) axle mobile crane or water well drilling vehicle consisting of 2 sets of tandem axles composed of 2 or more consecutive axles each with a distance between extreme axles of not less than 23 feet weighing not more than 72,000 pounds with axle weights on one set of tandem axles not more than 34,000 pounds, and weight in the other set of tandem axles not to exceed 40,000 pounds, the fees shall be at the following rates:

Distance	Rate
For the first 45 miles	$15
For each additional 45 miles or portion thereof	10

For such vehicles weighing over 72,000 pounds but not more than 76,000 pounds with axle weights on either set of tandem axles not more than 44,000 pounds, the fees shall be at the following rates:

Distance	Rate
For the first 45 miles	$20
For each additional 45 miles or portion thereof	12.50

Payment of overweight fees for the above vehicle shall include overwidth dimension of 4 feet or less, overheight and overlength. Any overwidth in excess of 4 feet shall be charged an additional fee of $15.

(f) In lieu of fees stated in this Section and in Section 15-306 of this Chapter, with respect to a two axle mobile crane or water well-drilling vehicle consisting of 2 single axles weighing not more than 48,000 pounds with no single axle weighing more than 25,000 pounds, the fees shall be at the following rates:

Distance	Rate
For the first 45 miles	$15
For each additional 45 miles or portion thereof	10

For such vehicles weighing over 48,000 pounds but not more than 54,000 pounds with no single axle weighing more than 28,000 pounds, the fees shall be at the following rates:

Distance	Rate
For the first 45 miles	$20
For each additional 45 miles or portion thereof	12.50

Payment of overweight fees for the above vehicle shall include overwidth dimension of 4 feet or less, overheight and overlength. Any overwidth in excess of 4 feet shall be charged an additional overwidth fee of $15.

(g) Fees for special permits to move vehicles, combinations of vehicles, and loads with overweight gross loads not included in the fee categories shall be paid by the applicant to the Department at the rate of $50 plus 3.5 cents per ton-mile in excess of legal weight.

With respect to fees for overweight gross loads not included in the schedules specified in paragraphs (a) through (e) of Section 15-307 and for overweight axle loads listed in Section 15-306, one fee only shall be charged, whichever is the greater, but not both. An additional fee in accordance with the schedule set forth in Section 15-305 shall be charged for each overdimension.

P.A. 76-1586, § 15-307, eff. July 1, 1970. Amended by P.A. 76-2207, § 1, eff. July 1, 1970; P.A. 77-1221, § 1, eff. Aug. 24, 1971; P.A. 78-1165, § 1, eff. Aug. 27, 1974; P.A. 81-199, § 1, eff. Jan. 1, 1980; P.A. 82-783, Art. IV, § 25, eff. July 13, 1982; P.A. 84-566, § 1, eff. Jan. 1, 1986; P.A. 90-228, § 5, eff. July 25, 1997; P.A. 90-676, § 5, eff. July 31, 1998.

Formerly Ill.Rev.Stat.1991, ch. 95 ½, ¶ 15-307.

P.A. 90-676 incorporated the amendment by P.A. 90-228.

5/15-308. Fees for overweight trucks hauling sweet corn

§ 15-308. Fees for overweight trucks hauling sweet corn. Fees for special permits for two axle truck with gross axle load not to exceed 35 percent in excess of the legal axle load to be used for hauling sweet corn and ensilage, for a period of 40 days only during harvest season; limited continuous operation permit only, $10.

P.A. 76-1586, § 15-308, eff. July 1, 1970.

Formerly Ill.Rev.Stat.1991, ch. 95 ½, ¶ 15-308.

5/15-308.1. Fees for moving oversize or overweight equipment to the site of rail derailments

§ 15-308.1. Fees for moving oversize or overweight equipment to the site of rail derailments. Fees for permits to move oversize or overweight equipment to the sites of train derailments shall include all equipment otherwise eligible to obtain single trip permits under normal situations. The permit shall be valid for a period of one year and can be used at any time for movement to the site of a train derailment during an emergency. The amount of the fee shall be $500.

P.A. 76-1586, § 15-308.1, added by P.A. 90-273, § 65, eff. July 30, 1997.

5/15-308.2. Fees for special permits for tow-trucks

§ 15-308.2. Fees for special permits for tow-trucks. The fee for a special permit to operate a tow-truck pursuant to subsection (n) of Section 15-301 is $500 quarterly and $2,000 annually.

P.A. 76-1586, § 15-308.2, added by P.A. 91-569, § 5, eff. Jan. 1, 2000.

5/15-309. Fees for moves directly across highway

§ 15-309. Fees for moves directly across highway. Fees for special permits for vehicles or vehicle combinations exceeding the legal sizes and weights specified in this Chapter either empty or hauling material directly across a highway making repeated moves in the course of industrial operations, for a period of 6 months; limited continuous operation permit only, $15.

P.A. 76-1586, § 15-309, eff. July 1, 1970. Amended by P.A. 81-199, § 1, eff. Jan. 1, 1980.

Formerly Ill.Rev.Stat.1991, ch. 95 ½, ¶ 15-309.

5/15-310. Fees for buildings and special moves

§ 15-310. Fees for buildings and special moves. Fees for special permits for moving buildings or large machines.

(a) When moved on house moving equipment or on own trucks or tracks fees will be based on maximum overall dimensions, plus engineering investigation and police escort fees when required; single trip only.

(b) When moved on a vehicle or vehicle combination applicable overdimension and overweight fees shall apply; single trip only.

P.A. 76-1586, § 15-310, eff. July 1, 1970.

Formerly Ill.Rev.Stat.1991, ch. 95 ½, ¶ 15-310.

5/15-311. Fees for Engineering Inspections or Field Investigations

§ 15-311. Fees for Engineering Inspections or Field Investigations. Engineering inspections or field investigations will be made by the Department and the following fees shall be paid by the applicant: for normal field investigations, or for special engineering investigations requiring assessment of work to be done on the highway and final inspection, $40 per hour.

P.A. 76-1586, § 15-311, eff. July 1, 1970. Amended by P.A. 81-199, § 1, eff. Jan. 1, 1980; P.A. 84-566, § 1, eff. Jan. 1, 1986.

Formerly Ill.Rev.Stat.1991, ch. 95 ½, ¶ 15-311.

5/15-312. Fees for Police Escort

§ 15-312. Fees for Police Escort. When State Police escorts are required by the Department for the safety of the motoring public, the following fees shall be paid by the applicant to the Department: $40 per hour per vehicle based upon pre-estimated time of movement to be agreed upon between Department and applicant. Minimum fee $80 per vehicle.

P.A. 76-1586, § 15-312, eff. July 1, 1970. Amended by P.A. 81-199, § 1, eff. Jan. 1, 1980; P.A. 84-566, § 1, eff. Jan. 1, 1986.

Formerly Ill.Rev.Stat.1991, ch. 95 ½, ¶ 15-312.

5/15-313. Supplemental permit fee

§ 15-313. Supplemental permit fee. The Department shall collect a fee of $5 and other applicable fees to cover the cost of processing an application for supplemental special permit. This fee shall be charged for each supplemental special permit issued. In addition, if the supplemental permit provides for an increase in size or weight or both over that specified in the original special permit, additional fees shall be charged as provided in Sections 15-303 through 15-312 as applicable, to correct for the increase.

P.A. 76-1586, § 15-313, eff. July 1, 1970. Amended by P.A. 81-199, § 1, eff. Jan. 1, 1980.

Formerly Ill.Rev.Stat.1991, ch. 95 ½, ¶ 15-313.

5/15-314. Payment of Fees

§ 15-314. Payment of Fees. The Department shall prescribe the time and method of payment of all appropriate fees authorized by Section 15-302 through 15-313.

The Department may, at its discretion, establish credit accounts with billing to be made at intervals not exceeding one month.

Failure to pay invoices in full within a period of 30 days after the billing date shall be sufficient cause for the Department to withhold issuance of any further permits or credit to the individual, company, or subsidiary firm.

The Department is authorized to charge a service fee of $3 for a check returned for any reason. All money received by the Department under the provisions of this Section shall be deposited in the Road Fund. No refund shall be made to applicant following issuance of a permit if move is not completed.

P.A. 76-1586, § 15-314, eff. July 1, 1970. Amended by P.A. 81-199, § 1, eff. Jan. 1, 1980.

Formerly Ill.Rev.Stat.1991, ch. 95 ½, ¶ 15-314.

5/15-315. Exemptions to requirement of fees

§ 15-315. Exemptions to requirement of fees. (a) The requirements as to fees authorized by Sections 15-302 through 15-314 shall not apply to the owner of the vehicle or vehicle combination if owned by the United States, this State, or any political subdivision of this State, or any municipality therein.

(b) The provisions of Sections 15-302 through 15-314 requiring fees for a permit shall not modify, alter or in any manner affect either the provisions of Section 15-301, or the policy of the Department adopted for the administration of this Chapter.

P.A. 76-1586, § 15-315, eff. July 1, 1970. Amended by P.A. 83-831, § 1, eff. Jan. 1, 1984.

Formerly Ill.Rev.Stat.1991, ch. 95 ½, ¶ 15-315.

5/15-316. When the Department, local authority or road district highway commissioner may restrict right to use highways

§ 15-316. When the Department, local authority or road district highway commissioner may restrict right to use highways.

(a) Local authorities and road district highway commissioners with respect to highways under their jurisdiction may by ordinance or resolution prohibit the operation of vehicles upon any such highway or impose restrictions as to the weight of vehicles to be operated upon any such highway, for a total period of not to exceed 90 days in any one calendar year, whenever any said highway by reason of deterioration, rain, snow, or other climate conditions will be seriously damaged or destroyed unless the use of vehicles thereon is prohibited or the permissible weights thereof reduced.

(b) The local authority or road district highway commissioner enacting any such ordinance or resolution shall erect or cause to be erected and maintained signs designating the provision of the ordinance or resolution at each end of that portion of any highway affected thereby, and the ordinance or resolution shall not be effective unless and until such signs are erected and maintained.

(c) Local authorities and road district highway commissioners with respect to highways under their jurisdiction may also, by ordinance or resolution, prohibit the operation of trucks or other commercial vehicles, or may impose limitations as the weight thereof, on designated highways, which prohibitions and limitations shall be designated by appropriate signs placed on such highways.

(c-1) (Blank).

(d) The Department shall likewise have authority as hereinbefore granted to local authorities and road district highway commissioners to determine by resolution and to impose restrictions as to the weight of vehicles operated upon any highway under the jurisdiction of said department, and such restrictions shall be effective when signs giving notice thereof are erected upon the highway or portion of any highway affected by such resolution.

(d-1) (Blank).

(d-2) (Blank).

(e) When any vehicle is operated in violation of this Section, the owner or driver of the vehicle shall be deemed guilty of a violation and either the owner or the driver of the vehicle may be prosecuted for the violation. Any person, firm, or corporation convicted of violating this Section shall be fined $50 for any weight exceeding the posted limit up to the axle or gross weight limit allowed a vehicle as provided for in subsections (a) or (b) of Section 15-111 and $75 per every 500 pounds or fraction thereof for any weight exceeding that which is provided for in subsections (a) or (b) of Section 15-111.

(f) A municipality is authorized to enforce a county weight limit ordinance applying to county highways within its corporate limits and is entitled to the proceeds of any fines collected from the enforcement.

P.A. 76-1586, § 15-316, eff. July 1, 1970. Amended by P.A. 81-540, § 1, eff. Jan. 1, 1980; P.A. 86-447, § 2, eff. Aug. 30, 1989; P.A. 87-1203, § 1, eff. Sept. 25, 1992; P.A. 88-384, § 5, eff. Jan. 1, 1994; P.A. 89-117, § 10, eff. July 7, 1995; P.A. 89-687, § 5, eff. June 1, 1997; P.A. 90-211, § 5, eff. Jan. 1, 1998; P.A. 92-417, § 5, eff. Jan. 1, 2002.

Formerly Ill.Rev.Stat.1991, ch. 95 ½, ¶ 15-316.

5/15-317. Special weight limitation on elevated structures

§ 15-317. Special weight limitation on elevated structures. (a) No person shall operate a vehicle or combination of vehicles over a bridge or other elevated structure constituting a part of a highway with a gross weight which is greater than the maximum weight permitted by the Department, when such structure is sign posted as provided in this Section.

(b) The Department upon request from any local authority shall, or upon its own initiative may, conduct an investigation of any bridge or other elevated structure constituting a part of a highway, and if it finds that such structure cannot with safety to itself withstand the weight of vehicles otherwise permissible under this Chapter the Department shall determine and declare the maximum weight of vehicles which such structure can withstand, and shall cause or permit suitable signs stating maximum weight to be erected and maintained before each end of such structure.

(c) Upon the trial of any person charged with a violation of this Section, proof of the determination of the maximum allowable weight by the Department and the existence of the signs, constitutes conclusive evidence of the maximum weight which can be maintained with safety to such bridge or structure.

P.A. 76-1586, § 15-317, eff. July 1, 1970.

Formerly Ill.Rev.Stat.1991, ch. 95 ½, ¶ 15-317.

5/15-318. Liability if highway or structure damaged

§ 15-318. Liability if highway or structure damaged. (a) Any person driving any vehicle, object or contrivance upon any highway or highway structure is liable for all damage which the highway or structure may sustain as a result of any illegal operation, driving or moving of such vehicle, object or contrivance, or as a result of operating, driving, or moving any vehicle, object, or contrivance exceeding the maximum dimensions or weighing in excess of the maximum weight specified in this Chapter but authorized by a special permit issued as provided in this Chapter. The measure of liability is the cost of repairing a facility partially damaged or the depreciated replacement cost of a facility damaged beyond repair together with all other expenses incurred by the authorities in control of the highway or highway structure in providing a temporary detour, including a temporary structure, to serve the needs of traffic during the period of repair or replacement of the damaged highway or highway structure.

(b) Whenever such driver is not the owner of such vehicle, object, or contrivance, but is so operating, driving, or moving the same with the express or implied permission of such owner, then the owner and driver are jointly and severally liable to the extent provided in paragraph (a) of this Section.

(c) Recovery may be had in a civil action brought by the authorities in control of such highway or highway structure.

P.A. 76-1586, § 15-318, eff. July 1, 1970. Amended by P.A. 81-199, § 1, eff. Jan. 1, 1980.

Formerly Ill.Rev.Stat.1991, ch. 95 ½, ¶ 15-318.

5/15-319. Special registration of vehicles by department

§ 15-319. Special registration of vehicles by department. (a) Applicants for special permits authorized in Section 15-301 may apply to the Department for an Illinois Department of Transportation (IDT) registration number and classification identification label issued for the purpose of identifying and classifying vehicles or combinations of vehicles that may be operated or moved by special permit. Applications shall be made on a form provided by the Department and certified to be true.

(b) For a fee of $5 and following an analysis of data submitted by the applicant, the Department may, at its discretion, issue an Illinois Department of Transportation (IDT) registration number and classification identification label. The label shall be issued for a period of not to exceed 2 years or for a lesser period of time in conformance with rules to be established by the Department and to be valid must be displayed in a conspicuous place on the outside of a vehicle as designated by the Department. The label, all forms, records, rules, procedures, methods of analysis, and classification shall be in the form or as prescribed in rules promulgated by the Department.

(c) All monies received by the Department under the provisions of this Section shall be deposited in the Road Fund. Vehicle classification shall be for identification purposes and shall not alter or in any manner affect either the provisions of Section 15-301 or the policy adopted by the Department for the administration thereof.

P.A. 76-1586, § 15-319, eff. July 1, 1970, added by P.A. 76-2208, § 1, eff. July 1, 1970. Amended by P.A. 81-199, § 1, eff. Jan. 1, 1980; P.A. 83-831, § 1, eff. Jan. 1, 1984.

Formerly Ill.Rev.Stat.1991, ch. 95 ½, ¶ 15-319.

CHAPTER 16. ENFORCEMENT, PENALTIES AND DISPOSITION OF FINES AND FORFEITURES, AND CRIMINAL CASES

Enactment

The Illinois Vehicle Code was enacted by P.A. 76-1586, effective July 1, 1970. The Code constitutes a consolidated recodification of various earlier laws and acts including the Uniform Act Regulating Traffic on Highways.

ARTICLE I. ENFORCEMENT, PENALTIES AND DISPOSITION OF FINES AND FORFEITURES

5/16-101. Applicability

§ 16-101. Applicability. The provisions of this Chapter shall be applicable to the enforcement of this entire Code, except where another penalty is set forth in a specific Chapter which is applicable to that Chapter or a designated part or Section thereof.

P.A. 76-1586, § 16-101, eff. July 1, 1970. Amended by P.A. 82-695, § 2, eff. July 1, 1982; P.A. 82-1011, § 2, eff. Sept. 17, 1982.

Formerly Ill.Rev.Stat.1991, ch. 95 ½, ¶ 16-101.

P.A. 82-1011 recognized the amendment by P.A. 82-695.

5/16-102. Arrests—Investigations—Prosecutions

§ 16-102. Arrests—Investigations—Prosecutions. The State Police shall patrol the public highways and make arrests for violation of the provisions of this Act.

The Secretary of State, through the investigators provided for in this Act shall investigate and report violations of the provisions of this Act in relation to the equipment and operation of vehicles as provided for in Section 2-115 and for such purposes these investigators have and may exercise throughout the State all of the powers of police officers.

The State's Attorney of the county in which the violation occurs shall prosecute all violations except when the violation occurs within the corporate limits of a municipality, the municipal attorney may prosecute if written permission to do so is obtained from the State's Attorney.

P.A. 76-1586, § 16-102, eff. July 1, 1970. Amended by P.A. 76-1863, § 1, eff. July 1, 1970; P.A. 78-885, § 1, eff. Jan. 1, 1974; P.A. 83-341, § 5, eff. Sept. 14, 1983.

Formerly Ill.Rev.Stat.1991, ch. 95 ½, ¶ 16-102.

5/16-102.5. Enforcement by municipality

§ 16-102.5. Enforcement by municipality.

(a) If a municipality adopts an ordinance similar to subsection (f) of Section 3-413 or Section 11-1304.5 of this Code, any person that a municipality designates to enforce ordinances regulating the standing or parking of vehicles shall have the authority to enforce the provisions of subsection (f) of Section 3-413 or Section 11-1304.5 of this Code or the similar local ordinance. However, the authority to enforce subsection (f) of Section 3-413 or Section 11-1304.5 of this Code or a similar local ordinance shall not be given to an appointed volunteer or private or public entity under contract to enforce person with disabilities parking laws.

(b) To enforce the provisions of subsection (f) of Section 3-413 or Section 11-1304.5 of this Code or a similar local ordinance, a municipality shall impose a fine not exceeding $25.

P.A. 76-1586, § 16-102.5, added by P.A. 90-513, § 5, eff. Aug. 22, 1997. Amended by P.A. 90-655, § 153, eff. July 30, 1998; P.A. 91-487, § 5, eff. Jan. 1, 2000.

5/16-103. Arrest outside county where violation committed

§ 16-103. Arrest outside county where violation committed. Whenever a defendant is arrested upon a warrant charging a violation of this Act in a county other than that in which such warrant was issued, the arresting officer, immediately upon the request of the defendant, shall take such defendant before a circuit judge or associate circuit judge in the county in which the arrest was made who shall admit the defendant to bail for his appearance before the court named in the warrant. On taking such bail the circuit judge or associate circuit judge shall certify such fact on the warrant and deliver the warrant and undertaking of bail or other security, or the drivers license of such defendant if deposited, under the law relating to such licenses, in lieu of such security, to the officer having charge of the defendant. Such officer shall then immediately discharge the defendant from arrest and without delay deliver such warrant and such undertaking of bail, or other security or drivers license to the court before which the defendant is required to appear.

P.A. 76-1586, § 16-103, eff. July 1, 1970. Amended by P.A. 77-1280, § 1, eff. Aug. 24, 1971.

Formerly Ill.Rev.Stat.1991, ch. 95 ½, ¶ 16-103.

5/16-104. Penalties

§ 16-104. Penalties. Every person convicted of a violation of any provision of this Code for which another penalty is not provided shall, for a first or second conviction thereof, be guilty of a petty offense and, for a third or subsequent conviction within one year after the first conviction, be guilty of a Class C misdemeanor.

P.A. 76-1586, § 16-104, eff. July 1, 1970. Amended by P.A. 77-493, § 1, eff. July 28, 1971; P.A. 77-2720, § 1, eff. Jan. 1, 1973; P.A. 78-255, § 61, eff. Oct. 1, 1973; P.A. 80-911, § 1, eff. Oct. 1, 1977; P.A. 91-357, § 231, eff. July 29, 1999.

Formerly Ill.Rev.Stat.1991, ch. 95 ½, ¶ 16-104.

5/16-104a. Additional penalty for certain violations

§ 16-104a. Additional penalty for certain violations. There is added to every fine imposed upon conviction of an offense reportable to the Secretary of State under the provisions of subdivision (a) (2) of Section 6-204 of this Act an additional penalty of $4 for each $40, or fraction thereof, of fine imposed. Each such additional penalty received shall be remitted within one month to the State Treasurer to be deposited into the Drivers Education Fund, unless the additional penalty is subject to disbursement by the circuit clerk under Section 27.5 of the Clerks of Courts Act. [1] Such additional amounts shall be assessed by the court and shall be collected by the Clerk of the Circuit Court in addition to the fine and costs in the case. Such additional penalty shall not be considered a part of the fine for purposes of any reduction made in the fine for time served either before or after sentencing. Not later than March 1 of each year the Clerk of the Circuit Court shall submit to the State Comptroller a report of the amount of funds remitted by him to the State Treasurer under this Section during the preceding calendar year. Except as otherwise provided by Supreme Court Rules, if a court in sentencing an offender levies a gross amount for fine, costs, fees and penalties, the amount of the additional penalty provided for herein shall be computed on the amount remaining after deducting from the gross amount levied all fees of the Circuit Clerk, the State's Attorney and the Sheriff. After deducting from the gross amount levied the fees and additional penalty provided for herein, less any other additional penalties provided by law, the clerk shall remit the net balance remaining to the entity authorized by law to receive the fine imposed in the case. For purposes of this Section "fees of the Circuit Clerk" shall include, if applicable, the fee provided for under Section 27.3a of the Clerks of Courts Act [2] and the fee, if applicable, payable to the county in which the violation occurred pursuant to Section 5-1101 of the Counties Code. [3]

When bail is forfeited for failure to appear in connection with an offense reportable to the Secretary of State under subdivision (a) (2) of Section 6-204 of this Act, and no fine is imposed ex parte, $4 of every $40 cash deposit, or fraction thereof, given to secure appearance shall be remitted within one month to the State Treasurer to be deposited into the Drivers Education Fund, unless the bail is subject to disbursement by the circuit clerk under Section 27.5 of the Clerks of Courts Act.

P.A. 76-1586, § 16-104a, added by P.A. 82-695, § 2, eff. July 1, 1982. Amended by P.A. 84-1313, § 7, eff. Aug. 28, 1986; P.A. 85-757, § 1, eff. Sept. 23, 1987; P.A. 86-1475, Art. 3, § 3-42, eff. Jan. 10, 1991; P.A. 87-670, § 6, eff. Jan. 1, 1992; P.A. 91-716, § 5, eff. Oct. 1, 2000.

Formerly Ill.Rev.Stat.1991, ch. 95 ½, ¶ 16-104a.

[1] 705 ILCS 105/27.5.

[2] 705 ILCS 105/27.3a.

[3] 55 ILCS 5/5-1101.

5/16-104b. Amounts for Trauma Center Fund

§ 16-104b. Amounts for Trauma Center Fund. In counties that have elected not to distribute moneys under the disbursement formulas in Sections 27.5 and 27.6 of the Clerks of Courts Act,[1] the Circuit Clerk of the County, when collecting fees, fines, costs, additional penalties, bail balances assessed or forfeited, and any other amount imposed upon a conviction of or an order of supervision for a violation of laws or ordinances regulating the movement of traffic that amounts to $55 or more, shall remit $5 of the total amount collected, less 2 ½% of the $5 to help defray the administrative costs incurred by the Clerk, except that upon a conviction or order of supervision for driving under the influence of alcohol or drugs the Clerk shall remit $105 of the total amount collected ($5 for a traffic violation that amounts to $55 or more and an additional fee of $100 to be collected by the Circuit Clerk for a conviction or order of supervision for driving under the influence of alcohol or drugs), less the 2 ½ %, within 60 days to the State Treasurer to be deposited into the Trauma Center Fund. Of the amounts deposited into the Trauma Center Fund under this Section, 50% shall be disbursed to the Department of Public Health and 50% shall be disbursed to the Department of Public Aid. Not later than March 1 of each year the Circuit Clerk shall submit a report of the amount of funds remitted to the State Treasurer under this Section during the preceding calendar year.

P.A. 76–1586, § 16–104b, added by P.A. 87–1229, § 3, eff. Jan. 1, 1993. Amended by P.A. 88–667, § 15, eff. Sept. 16, 1994; P.A. 89–105, § 10, eff. Jan. 1, 1996; P.A. 92–431, § 10, eff. Jan. 1, 2002.

Formerly Ill.Rev.Stat., ch. 95½, ¶ 16–104b.

1 705 ILCS 105/27.5 and 105/27.6.

5/16–105. Disposition of fines and forfeitures

§ 16–105. Disposition of fines and forfeitures.

(a) Except as provided in Section 16–104a of this Act and except for those amounts required to be paid into the Traffic and Criminal Conviction Surcharge Fund in the State Treasury pursuant to Section 9.1 of the Illinois Police Training Act [1] and Section 5–9–1 of the Unified Code of Corrections [2] and except those amounts subject to disbursement by the circuit clerk under Section 27.5 of the Clerks of Courts Act,[3] fines and penalties recovered under the provisions of Chapters 11 through 16 [4] inclusive of this Code shall be paid and used as follows:

1. For offenses committed upon a highway within the limits of a city, village, or incorporated town or under the jurisdiction of any park district, to the treasurer of the particular city, village, incorporated town or park district, if the violator was arrested by the authorities of the city, village, incorporated town or park district, provided the police officers and officials of cities, villages, incorporated towns and park districts shall seasonably prosecute for all fines and penalties under this Code. If the violation is prosecuted by the authorities of the county, any fines or penalties recovered shall be paid to the county treasurer. Provided further that if the violator was arrested by the State Police, fines and penalties recovered under the provisions of paragraph (a) of Section 15–113 of this Code or paragraph (e) of Section 15–316 of this Code shall be paid over to the Department of State Police which shall thereupon remit the amount of the fines and penalties so received to the State Treasurer who shall deposit the amount so remitted in the special fund in the State treasury known as the Road Fund except that if the violation is prosecuted by the State's Attorney, 10% of the fine or penalty recovered shall be paid to the State's Attorney as a fee of his office and the balance shall be paid over to the Department of State Police for remittance to and deposit by the State Treasurer as hereinabove provided.

2. Except as provided in paragraph 4, for offenses committed upon any highway outside the limits of a city, village, incorporated town or park district, to the county treasurer of the county where the offense was committed except if such offense was committed on a highway maintained by or under the supervision of a township, township district, or a road district to the Treasurer thereof for deposit in the road and bridge fund of such township or other district; Provided, that fines and penalties recovered under the provisions of paragraph (a) of Section 15–113, paragraph (d) of Section 3–401, or paragraph (e) of Section 15–316 of this Code shall be paid over to the Department of State Police which shall thereupon remit the amount of the fines and penalties so received to the State Treasurer who shall deposit the amount so remitted in the special fund in the State treasury known as the Road Fund except that if the violation is prosecuted by the State's Attorney, 10% of the fine or penalty recovered shall be paid to the State's Attorney as a fee of his office and the balance shall be paid over to the Department of State Police for remittance to and deposit by the State Treasurer as hereinabove provided.

3. Notwithstanding subsections 1 and 2 of this paragraph, for violations of overweight and overload limits found in Sections 15–101 through 15–203 of this Code, which are committed upon the highways belonging to the Illinois State Toll Highway Authority, fines and penalties shall be paid over to the Illinois State Toll Highway Authority for deposit with the State Treasurer into that special fund known as the Illinois State Toll Highway Authority Fund, except that if the violation is prosecuted by the State's Attorney, 10% of the fine or penalty recovered shall be paid to the State's Attorney as a fee of his office and the balance shall be paid over to the Illinois State Toll Highway Authority for remittance to and deposit by the State Treasurer as hereinabove provided.

4. With regard to violations of overweight and overload limits found in Sections 15–101 through 15–203 of this Code committed by operators of vehicles registered as Special Hauling Vehicles, for offenses committed upon a highway within the limits of a city, village, or incorporated town or under the jurisdiction of any park district, all fines and penalties shall be paid over or retained as required in paragraph 1. However, with regard to the above offenses committed by operators of vehicles registered as Special Hauling Vehicles upon any highway outside the limits of a city, village, incorporated town or park district, fines and penalties shall be paid over or retained by the entity having jurisdiction over the road or highway upon which the offense occurred, except that if the violation is prosecuted by the State's Attorney, 10% of the fine or penalty recovered shall be paid to the State's Attorney as a fee of his office.

(b) Failure, refusal or neglect on the part of any judicial or other officer or employee receiving or having custody of any such fine or forfeiture either before or after a deposit with the proper official as defined in paragraph (a) of this Section, shall constitute misconduct in office and shall be grounds for removal therefrom.

P.A. 76–1586, § 16–105, eff. July 1, 1970. Amended by P.A. 76–2209, § 1, eff. July 1, 1970; P.A. 81–1468, § 1, eff. Sept. 9, 1980; P.A. 82–604, § 1, eff. Jan. 1, 1982; P.A. 82–695, § 2, eff. July 1, 1982; P.A. 82–739, § 4, eff. Jan. 1, 1982; P.A. 82–783, Art. III, § 37, eff. July 13, 1982; P.A. 84–25, Art. IV, § 27, eff. July 18, 1985; P.A. 87–670, § 6, eff. Jan. 1, 1992; P.A. 88–403, § 5, eff. Jan. 1, 1994; P.A. 88–476, § 2, eff. July 1, 1994; P.A. 88–535, § 25, eff. Jan. 26, 1994; P.A. 89–117, § 10, eff. July 7, 1995.

Formerly Ill.Rev.Stat.1991, ch. 95 ½, ¶ 16–105.

1 50 ILCS 705/9.1.

2 730 ILCS 5/5–9–1.

3 705 ILCS 105/27.5.

4 625 ILCS 5/11–101 et seq. to 5/16–101 et seq.

5/16-105.5. Payment to municipality

§ 16-105.5. Payment to municipality. All revenues derived from the issuance of citations for violations of subsection (f) of Section 3-413 of this Code or a similar local ordinance that are required to be paid to a municipality under this Code shall be deposited into the general fund of the municipality.

P.A. 76-1586, § 16-105.5, added by P.A. 90-513, § 5, eff. Aug. 22, 1997.

5/16-106. Notice to accused concerning multiple court appearances

§ 16-106. For offenses committed under the provisions of this Act or the ordinances of any municipality, park district or county which involve the regulation of the ownership, use or operation of vehicles, the police officers and officials of such municipalities and park districts, and sheriffs shall, when issuing a traffic ticket, other citation, or Notice to Appear in lieu of either, in counties other than Cook, also issue written notice to the accused in substantially the following form:

AVOID MULTIPLE COURT APPEARANCES

If you intend to plead "not guilty" to this charge, or if, in addition, you intend to demand a trial by jury, so notify the clerk of the court at least 5 days (excluding Saturdays, Sundays or holidays) before the day set for your appearance. A new appearance date will be set, and arrangements will be made to have the arresting officer present on that new date. Failure to notify the clerk of either your intention to plead "not guilty" or your intention to demand a jury trial, may result in your having to return to court, if you plead "not guilty" on the date originally set for your court appearance. Upon timely receipt of notice that the accused intends to plead "not guilty", the clerk shall set a new appearance date not less than 7 days nor more than 49 days after the original appearance date set by the arresting officer, and notify all parties of the new date and the time for appearance. If the accused fails to notify the clerk as provided above, the arresting officer's failure to appear on the date originally set for appearance may, in counties other than Cook, be considered good cause for a continuance.

P.A. 76-1586, § 16-106, added by P.A. 78-273, § 1, eff. Oct. 1, 1973. Amended by P.A. 81-781, § 1, eff. Jan. 1, 1980.

Formerly Ill.Rev.Stat.1991, ch. 95 ½, ¶ 16-106.

5/16-106.5. Pilot project; notice of violation to owner

§ 16-106.5. Pilot project; notice of violation to owner.

(a) A pilot project is created that shall be in operation from January 1, 2002 through December 31, 2003 in the counties of DuPage, Kendall, and Sangamon. Under the pilot project, when a traffic citation is issued for a violation of this Code to a person who is under the age of 18 years, who is a resident of the county in which the traffic citation was issued, and who is not the registered owner of the vehicle named in the traffic citation, the circuit clerk of the county in which the traffic citation was issued shall, within 10 days after the traffic citation is filed with the circuit clerk, send notice of the issuance of the traffic citation to the registered owner of the vehicle. The notice must include:

(1) the date and time the violation was alleged to have been committed;

(2) the location where the violation was alleged to have been committed;

(3) the name of the person cited for committing the alleged violation;

(4) the violation alleged to have been committed; and

(5) the date and time of any required court appearance by the person cited for committing the alleged violation.

(b) On or before March 31, 2004, the Department of State Police shall report to the General Assembly on the effectiveness of the pilot project.

P.A. 76-1586, § 16-106.5, added by P.A. 92-344, § 5, eff. Aug. 10, 2001.

5/16-107. Appearance of parent or guardian of minor in certain court proceedings—Judicial discretion

§ 16-107. Appearance of parent or guardian of minor in certain court proceedings—Judicial discretion. (a) Whenever an unemancipated minor is required to appear in court pursuant to a citation for violation of any Section or any subsection of any Section of this Act specified in subsection (b) of this Section, the court may require that a parent or guardian of the minor accompany the minor and appear before the court with the minor, unless, in the discretion of the court, such appearance would be unreasonably burdensome under the circumstances.

(b) This Section shall apply whenever an unemancipated minor is charged with violation of any of the following Sections and subsections of this Act:

1) Sections 3-701, 3-702 and 3-703;

2) Sections 4-102, 4-103, 4-104 and 4-105;

3) Section 6-101, subsections (a), (b) and (c) of Section 6-104, and Sections 6-113, 6-301, 6-302, 6-303 and 6-304;

4) Sections 11-203 and 11-204, subsection (b) of Section 11-305, Sections 11-311, 11-312, 11-401, 11-402, 11-403, 11-404, 11-407, 11-409, 11-501, 11-502, 11-503 and 11-504, subsection (b) of Section 11-601, Sections 11-704, 11-707, 11-1007, 11-1403, 11-1404 and subsection (a) of Section 11-1414.

P.A. 76-1586, § 16-107, added by P.A. 80-646, § 1, eff. Oct. 1, 1977.

Formerly Ill.Rev.Stat.1991, ch. 95 ½, ¶ 16-107.

5/16-108. Claims of diplomatic immunity

§ 16-108. Claims of diplomatic immunity.

(a) This Section applies only to an individual that displays to a police officer a driver's license issued by the U.S. Department of State or that otherwise claims immunities or privileges under Title 22, Chapter 6 of the United States Code with respect to the individual's violation of Section 9-3 or Section 9-3.2 of the Criminal Code of 1961 [1] or his or her violation of a traffic regulation governing the movement of vehicles under this Code or a similar provision of a local ordinance.

(b) If a driver subject to this Section is stopped by a police officer that has probable cause to believe that the driver has committed a violation described in subsection (a) of this Section, the police officer shall:

(1) As soon as practicable contact the U.S. Department of State office in order to verify the driver's status and immunity, if any;

(2) Record all relevant information from any driver's license or identification card, including a driver's license or identification card issued by the U.S. Department of State; and

(3) Within 5 workdays after the date of the stop, forward the following to the Secretary of State of Illinois:

(A) A vehicle accident report, if the driver was involved in a vehicle accident;

(B) If a citation or charge was issued to the driver, a copy of the citation or charge; and

(C) If a citation or charge was not issued to the driver, a written report of the incident.

(c) Upon receiving material submitted under paragraph (3) of subsection (b) of this Section, the Secretary of State shall:

(1) File each vehicle accident report, citation or charge, and incident report received;

(2) Keep convenient records or make suitable notations showing each:

(A) Conviction;

(B) Disposition of court supervision for any violation of Section 11-501 of this Code; and

(C) Vehicle accident; and

(3) Send a copy of each document and record described in paragraph (2) of this subsection (c) to the Bureau of Diplomatic Security, Office of Foreign Missions, of the U.S. Department of State.

(d) This Section does not prohibit or limit the application of any law to a criminal or motor vehicle violation by an individual who has or claims immunities or privileges under Title 22, Chapter 6 of the United States Code.

P.A. 76-1586, § 16-108, added by P.A. 92-160, § 5, eff. July 25, 2001.

[1] 720 ILCS 5/9-3 or 5/9-3.2.

ARTICLE II. PARTIES IN CRIMINAL CASES

5/16-201. Parties to a crime

§ 16-201. Parties to a crime. Every person who commits, attempts to commit, conspires to commit, or aids, or abets in the commission of any act declared to be a crime, whether individually or in connection with one or more other persons or as principal, agent or accessory, shall be guilty of such offense, and every person who falsely, fraudulently, forcibly, or wilfully induces, causes, coerces, requires, permits, or directs another to violate any provision of this Act is likewise guilty of such offense.

P.A. 76-1586, § 16-201, eff. July 1, 1970.

Formerly Ill.Rev.Stat.1991, ch. 95 ½, ¶ 16-201.

5/16-202. Offenses by persons owning or controlling vehicles

§ 16-202. Offenses by persons owning or controlling vehicles. It is unlawful for the owner, or any other person, employing or otherwise directing the driver of any vehicle to require or knowingly to permit the operation of such vehicle upon a highway in any manner contrary to law.

P.A. 76-1586, § 16-202, eff. July 1, 1970.

Formerly Ill.Rev.Stat.1991, ch. 95 ½, ¶ 16-202.

CHAPTER 17. ILLINOIS HIGHWAY SAFETY LAW

Enactment

The Illinois Vehicle Code was enacted by P.A. 76-1586, effective July 1, 1970. The Code constitutes a consolidated recodification of various earlier laws and acts including the Illinois Motor Vehicle Law of 1957.

5/17-101. Powers and duties of Governor

§ 17-101. Powers and duties of Governor.

The Governor, in addition to other duties and responsibilities conferred upon him by the constitution and laws of this State is empowered to contract and to do all other things necessary in behalf of this State to secure the full benefits available to this State under the Federal Highway Safety Act of 1966, as amended,[1] and in so doing, to cooperate with Federal and State agencies, agencies private and public, interested organizations, and with individuals, to effectuate the purposes of that enactment, and any and all subsequent amendments thereto. The Governor is the official of this State having the ultimate responsibility for dealing with the Federal Government with respect to programs and activities pursuant to the National Highway Safety Act of 1966 and any amendments thereto. To that end he shall coordinate the activities of the Secretary of State and the State Board of Education and of any and all departments and agencies of this State and its subdivisions, relating thereto.

P.A. 76-1586, § 17-101, eff. July 1, 1970. Amended by P.A. 81-1508, § 8, eff. Sept. 25, 1980.

Formerly Ill.Rev.Stat.1991, ch. 95 ½, ¶ 17-101.

[1] 23 U.S.C.A. § 401 et seq.

5/17-102 to 5/17-105. §§ 17-102 to 17-105. Repealed by P.A. 82-523, § 2, eff. Jan. 1, 1982

CHAPTER 18. ILLINOIS MOTOR CARRIER OF PROPERTY LAW

5/18-100 to 5/18-903. §§ 18-100 to 18-903. Repealed by P.A. 81-501, § 2, eff. Jan. 1, 1980; P.A. 84-796, § 21, eff. Jan. 1, 1986; P.A. 84-1308, Art. II, § 97, eff. Aug. 25, 1986

Article II of P.A. 84-1308, the First 84th General Assembly Combining Revisory Act, provides for the nonsubstantive revision or renumbering or repeal of Sections of Acts necessitated by the amendment, addition or repeal of Sections by two or more Public Acts of the 84th General Assembly, which multiple action was not resolved by one of the Acts of the 84th General Assembly affecting the particular Section and makes technical corrections in Acts amended by the 84th General Assembly.

CHAPTER 18a. ILLINOIS COMMERCIAL RELOCATION OF TRESPASSING VEHICLES LAW

Enactment

Chapter 18a was added by P.A. 80-1459, § 2, effective January 1, 1979

ARTICLE I. DEFINITIONS, POLICY AND JURISDICTION

5/18a–100. Definitions

§ 18a–100. Definitions. As used in this Chapter: (1) "Commercial vehicle relocator" or "relocator" means any person or entity engaged in the business of removing trespassing vehicles from private property by means of towing or otherwise, and thereafter relocating and storing such vehicles;

(2) "Commission" means the Illinois Commerce Commission;

(3) "Operator" means any person who, as an employee of a commercial vehicle relocator, removes trespassing vehicles from private property by means of towing or otherwise. This term includes the driver of any vehicle used in removing a trespassing vehicle from private property, as well as any person other than the driver who assists in the removal of a trespassing vehicle from private property;

(4) "Operator's employment permit" means a license issued to an operator in accordance with Sections 18a–403 or 18a–405 of this Chapter;

(5) "Relocator's license" means a license issued to a commercial vehicle relocator in accordance with Sections 18a–400 or 18a–401 of this Chapter;

(6) "Dispatcher" means any person who, as an employee or agent of a commercial vehicle relocator, dispatches vehicles to or from locations from which operators perform removal activities; and

(7) "Dispatcher's employment permit" means a license issued to a dispatcher in accordance with Sections 18a–407 or 18a–408 of this Chapter.

P.A. 76–1586, § 18a–100, added by P.A. 80–1459, § 2, eff. Jan. 1, 1979. Amended by P.A. 82–616, § 1, eff. Jan. 1, 1982; P.A. 85–923, § 1, eff. Dec. 1, 1987.

Formerly Ill.Rev.Stat.1991, ch. 95 ½, ¶ 18a–100.

5/18a–101. Declaration of policy and delegation of jurisdiction

§ 18a–101. Declaration of policy and delegation of jurisdiction. It is hereby declared to be the policy of the State of Illinois to supervise and regulate the commercial removal of trespassing vehicles from private property, and the subsequent relocation and storage of such vehicles in such manner as to fairly distribute rights and responsibilities among vehicle owners, private property owners and commercial vehicle relocators, and for this purpose the power and authority to administer and to enforce the provisions of this Chapter shall be vested in the Illinois Commerce Commission.

P.A. 76–1586, § 18a–101, added by P.A. 80–1459, § 2, eff. Jan. 1, 1979.

Formerly Ill.Rev.Stat.1991, ch. 95 ½, ¶ 18a–101.

5/18a–102. Local regulation

§ 18a–102. Local regulation. Nothing contained in this Chapter shall be construed to infringe upon the right of non-home rule units of local government to regulate the commercial relocation of vehicles in a manner consistent with, or in addition to, State or federal laws or regulations. Nothing in this Chapter shall constitute a limitation on the authority of any home rule unit; however, the provisions of this Chapter shall remain in full force and effect in home rule units notwithstanding any applicable ordinances of home rule units.

P.A. 76–1586, § 18a–102, added by P.A. 80–1459, § 2, eff. Jan. 1, 1979.

Formerly Ill.Rev.Stat.1991, ch. 95 ½, ¶ 18a–102.

5/18a–103. Review

§ 18a–103. Review. A person aggrieved by an order of the Commission under this Chapter is entitled, in addition to any other remedy, to a review thereof by the Circuit Court in accordance with the Administrative Review Law, as amended.[1]

P.A. 76–1586, § 18a–103, added by P.A. 80–1459, § 2, eff. Jan. 1, 1979. Amended by P.A. 82–783, Art. XI, § 140, eff. July 13, 1982.

Formerly Ill.Rev.Stat.1991, ch. 95 ½, ¶ 18a–103.

[1] 735 ILCS 5/3–101 et seq.

5/18a–104. Towing performed pursuant to police order

§ 18a–104. Towing performed pursuant to police order. Nothing contained in this Chapter shall be construed to regulate or otherwise affect towing performed by any relocator pursuant to the order of a law enforcement official or agency in accordance with Sections 4–201 through 4–214 of the Illinois Vehicle Code.

P.A. 76–1586, § 18a–104, added by P.A. 80–1459, § 2, eff. Jan. 1, 1979.

Formerly Ill.Rev.Stat.1991, ch. 95 ½, ¶ 18a–104.

5/18a–105. Exemptions

§ 18a–105. Exemptions. This Chapter shall not apply to the relocation of:

(1) Vehicles registered for a gross weight in excess of 10,000 pounds, or if the vehicle is not registered, with a gross weight in excess of 10,000 pounds including vehicle weight and maximum load; or

(2) Motorcycles.

Such relocation shall be governed by the provisions of Section 4–203 of this Code.

P.A. 76–1586, § 18a–105, added by P.A. 85–923, § 1, eff. Dec. 1, 1987.

Formerly Ill.Rev.Stat.1991, ch. 95 ½, ¶ 18a–105.

ARTICLE II. DUTIES AND POWERS

5/18a-200. General powers and duties of Commission

§ 18a-200. General powers and duties of Commission. The Commission shall:

(1) Regulate commercial vehicle relocators and their employees or agents in accordance with this Chapter and to that end may establish reasonable requirements with respect to proper service and practices relating thereto;

(2) Require the maintenance of uniform systems of accounts, records and the preservation thereof;

(3) Require that all drivers and other personnel used in relocation be employees of a licensed relocator;

(4) Regulate equipment leasing to and by relocators;

(5) Adopt reasonable and proper rules covering the exercise of powers conferred upon it by this Chapter, and reasonable rules governing investigations, hearings and proceedings under this Chapter;

(6) Set reasonable rates for the commercial towing or removal of trespassing vehicles from private property. The rates shall not exceed the mean average of the 5 highest rates for police tows within the territory to which this Chapter applies that are performed under Sections 4-201 and 4-214 of this Code and that are of record at hearing; provided that the Commission shall not re-calculate the maximum specified herein if the order containing the previous calculation was entered within one calendar year of the date on which the new order is entered. Set reasonable rates for the storage, for periods in excess of 24 hours, of the vehicles in connection with the towing or removal; however, no relocator shall impose charges for storage for the first 24 hours after towing or removal. Set reasonable rates for other services provided by relocators, provided that the rates shall not be charged to the owner or operator of a relocated vehicle. Any fee charged by a relocator for the use of a credit card that is used to pay for any service rendered by the relocator shall be included in the total amount that shall not exceed the maximum reasonable rate established by the Commission. The Commission shall require a relocator to refund any amount charged in excess of the reasonable rate established by the Commission, including any fee for the use of a credit card;

(7) Investigate and maintain current files of the criminal records, if any, of all relocators and their employees and of all applicants for relocator's license, operator's licenses and dispatcher's licenses;

(8) Issue relocator's licenses, dispatcher's employment permits, and operator's employment permits in accordance with Article IV of this Chapter; [1]

(9) Establish fitness standards for applicants seeking relocator licensees and holders of relocator licenses;

(10) Upon verified complaint in writing by any person, organization or body politic, or upon its own initiative may, investigate whether any commercial vehicle relocator, operator, dispatcher, or person otherwise required to comply with any provision of this Chapter or any rule promulgated hereunder, has failed to comply with any provision or rule;

(11) Whenever the Commission receives notice from the Secretary of State that any domestic or foreign corporation regulated under this Chapter has not paid a franchise tax, license fee or penalty required under the Business Corporation Act of 1983,[2] institute proceedings for the revocation of the license or right to engage in any business required under this Chapter or the suspension thereof until such time as the delinquent franchise tax, license fee or penalty is paid.

P.A. 76-1586, § 18a-200, added by P.A. 80-1459, § 2, eff. Jan. 1, 1979. Amended by P.A. 81-332, § 2, eff. Jan. 1, 1980; P.A. 81-333, § 1, eff. Jan. 1, 1980; P.A. 82-616, § 1, eff. Jan. 1, 1982; P.A. 83-1295, § 1, eff. July 1, 1985; P.A. 83-1362, Art. IV, § 15, eff. Sept. 11, 1984; P.A. 83-1528, Art. II, § 24, eff. Jan. 17, 1985; P.A. 84-796, § 1, eff. Jan. 1, 1986; P.A. 85-923, § 1, eff. Dec. 1, 1987; P.A. 86-492, § 1, eff. Sept. 1, 1989; P.A. 88-448, § 1, eff. Aug. 20, 1993.

Formerly Ill.Rev.Stat.1991, ch. 95 ½, ¶ 18a-200.

1 625 ILCS 5/18a-400 et seq.

2 805 ILCS 5/1.01 et seq.

5/18a-201. Additional officers and employees

§ 18a-201. Additional officers and employees. The Commission, for the purpose of more effectively carrying out the provisions of this Chapter, shall obtain pursuant to the provisions of the "Personnel Code" [1] such officers and employees as it may deem necessary to carry out the provisions of this Chapter or to perform the duties and exercise the powers conferred by law upon the Commission.

P.A. 76-1586, § 18a-201, added by P.A. 80-1459, § 2, eff. Jan. 1, 1979.

Formerly Ill.Rev.Stat.1991, ch. 95 ½, ¶ 18a-201.

1 20 ILCS 415/1 et seq.

ARTICLE III. REQUIREMENTS AND PROHIBITIONS

5/18a-300. Commercial vehicle relocators—Unlawful practices

§ 18a-300. Commercial vehicle relocators—Unlawful practices. It shall be unlawful for any commercial vehicle relocator:

(1) To operate in any county in which this Chapter is applicable without a valid, current relocator's license as provided in Article IV of this Chapter; [1]

(2) To employ as an operator, or otherwise so use the services of, any person who does not have at the commencement of employment or service, or at any time during the course of employment or service, a valid, current operator's employment permit, or temporary operator's employment permit issued in accordance with Sections 18a-403 or 18a-405 of this Chapter; or to fail to notify the Commission, in writing, of any known criminal conviction of any employee occurring at any time before or during the course of employment or service;

(3) To employ as a dispatcher, or otherwise so use the services of, any person who does not have at the commencement of employment or service, or at any time during the course of employment or service, a valid, current dispatcher's or operator's employment permit or temporary dispatcher's or operator's employment permit issued in accordance with Sections 18a–403 or 18a–407 of this Chapter; or to fail to notify the Commission, in writing, of any known criminal conviction of any employee occurring at any time before or during the course of employment or service;

(4) To operate upon the highways of this State any vehicle used in connection with any commercial vehicle relocation service unless:

(A) There is painted or firmly affixed to the vehicle on both sides of the vehicle in a color or colors vividly contrasting to the color of the vehicle the name, address and telephone number of the relocator. The Commission shall prescribe reasonable rules and regulations pertaining to insignia to be painted or firmly affixed to vehicles and shall waive the requirements of the address on any vehicle in cases where the operator of a vehicle has painted or otherwise firmly affixed to the vehicle a seal or trade mark that clearly identifies the operator of the vehicle; and

(B) There is carried in the power unit of the vehicle a certified copy of the currently effective relocator's license and operator's employment permit. Copies may be photographed, photocopied, or reproduced or printed by any other legible and durable process. Any person guilty of not causing to be displayed a copy of his relocator's license and operator's employment permit may in any hearing concerning the violation be excused from the payment of the penalty hereinafter provided upon a showing that the license was issued by the Commission, but was subsequently lost or destroyed;

(5) To operate upon the highways of this State any vehicle used in connection with any commercial vehicle relocation service that bears the name or address and telephone number of any person or entity other than the relocator by which it is owned or to which it is leased;

(6) To advertise in any newspaper, book, list, classified directory or other publication unless there is contained in the advertisement the license number of the relocator;

(7) To remove any vehicle from private property without having first obtained the written authorization of the property owner or other person in lawful possession or control of the property, his authorized agent, or an authorized law enforcement officer. The authorization may be on a contractual basis covering a period of time or limited to a specific removal;

(8) To charge the private property owner, who requested that an unauthorized vehicle be removed from his property, with the costs of removing the vehicle contrary to any terms that may be a part of the contract between the property owner and the commercial relocator. Nothing in this paragraph shall prevent a relocator from assessing, collecting, or receiving from the property owner, lessee, or their agents any fee prescribed by the Commission;

(9) To remove a vehicle when the owner or operator of the vehicle is present or arrives at the vehicle location at any time prior to the completion of removal, and is willing and able to remove the vehicle immediately;

(10) To remove any vehicle from property on which signs are required and on which there are not posted appropriate signs under Section 18a–302;

(11) To fail to notify law enforcement authorities in the jurisdiction in which the trespassing vehicle was removed within one hour of the removal. Notification shall include a complete description of the vehicle, registration numbers if possible, the locations from which and to which the vehicle was removed, the time of removal, and any other information required by regulation, statute or ordinance;

(12) To impose any charge other than in accordance with the rates set by the Commission as provided in paragraph (6) of Section 18a–200 of this Chapter;

(13) To fail, in the office or location at which relocated vehicles are routinely returned to their owners, to prominently post the name, address and telephone number of the nearest office of the Commission to which inquiries or complaints may be sent;

(13.1) To fail to distribute to each owner or operator of a relocated vehicle, in written form as prescribed by Commission rule or regulation, the relevant statutes, regulations and ordinances governing commercial vehicle relocators, including, in at least 12 point boldface type, the name, address and telephone number of the nearest office of the Commission to which inquiries or complaints may be sent;

(14) To remove any vehicle, otherwise in accordance with this Chapter, more than 15 air miles from its location when towed from a location in an unincorporated area of a county or more than 10 air miles from its location when towed from any other location;

(15) To fail to make a telephone number available to the police department of any municipality in which a relocator operates at which the relocator or an employee of the relocator may be contacted at any time during the hours in which the relocator is engaged in the towing of vehicles, or advertised as engaged in the towing of vehicles, for the purpose of effectuating the release of a towed vehicle; or to fail to include the telephone number in any advertisement of the relocator's services published or otherwise appearing on or after the effective date of this amendatory Act; or to fail to have an employee available at any time on the premises owned or controlled by the relocator for the purposes of arranging for the immediate release of the vehicle.

Apart from any other penalty or liability authorized under this Act, if after a reasonable effort, the owner of the vehicle is unable to make telephone contact with the relocator for a period of one hour from his initial attempt during any time period in which the relocator is required to respond at the number, all fees for towing, storage, or otherwise are to be waived. Proof of 3 attempted phone calls to the number provided to the police department by an officer or employee of the department on behalf of the vehicle owner within the space of one hour, at least 2 of which are separated by 45 minutes, shall be deemed sufficient proof of the owner's reasonable effort to make contact with the vehicle relocator. Failure of the relocator to respond to the phone calls is not a criminal violation of this Chapter;

(16) To use equipment which the relocator does not own, except in compliance with Section 18a–306 of this Chapter and Commission regulations. No equipment can be leased to more than one relocator at any time. Equipment leases shall be filed with the Commission. If equipment is leased to one relocator, it cannot thereafter be leased to another relocator until a written cancellation of lease is properly filed with the Commission;

(17) To use drivers or other personnel who are not employees or contractors of the relocator;

(18) To fail to refund any amount charged in excess of the reasonable rate established by the Commission;

(19) To violate any other provision of this Chapter, or of Commission regulations or orders adopted under this Chapter.

P.A. 76-1586, § 18a-300, added by P.A. 80-1459, § 2, eff. Jan. 1, 1979. Amended by P.A. 80-1495, § 36, eff. Jan. 8, 1979; P.A. 81-332, § 2, eff. Jan. 1, 1980; P.A. 81-333, § 1, eff. Jan. 1, 1980; P.A. 81-990, § 1, eff. Jan. 1, 1980; P.A. 81-1509, Art. I, § 57, eff. Sept. 26, 1980; P.A. 82-616, § 1, eff. Jan. 1, 1982; P.A. 83-879, § 2, eff. July 1, 1984; P.A. 85-923, § 1, eff. Dec. 1, 1987; P.A. 86-1272, § 1, eff. Jan. 1, 1991; P.A. 88-448, § 1, eff. Aug. 20, 1993.

Formerly Ill.Rev.Stat.1991, ch. 95 ½, ¶ 18a-300.

[1] 625 ILCS 5/18a-400 et seq.

5/18a-301. Commercial vehicle relocators—Security requirements

§ 18a-301. Commercial vehicle relocators—Security requirements. Every commercial vehicle relocator shall file with the Commission and have in effect an indemnity bond or insurance policy or certificates of bonds or insurance in lieu thereof which shall indemnify or insure the relocator for its liability: (1) for injury to person, in an amount not less than $100,000 to any one person and $300,000 for any one accident; (2) in case of damage to property other than a vehicle being removed, in an amount not less than $50,000 for any one accident; and (3) in case of damage to any vehicle relocated or stored by the relocator, in an amount not less than $15,000 per vehicle. Any such bond or policy shall be issued by a bonding or insurance firm authorized to do business as such in the State of Illinois. All certificates or indemnity bonds or insurance filed with the Commission must show the coverage effective continuously until cancelled, and the Commission may require such evidence of continued validity as it deems necessary.

P.A. 76-1586, § 18a-301, added by P.A. 80-1459, § 2, eff. Jan. 1, 1979. Amended by P.A. 85-1396, § 2, eff. Sept. 2, 1988.

Formerly Ill.Rev.Stat.1991, ch. 95 ½, ¶ 18a-301.

5/18a-302. Owner or other person in lawful possession or control of private property—Right to employ relocation service

§ 18a-302. Owner or other person in lawful possession or control of private property—Right to employ relocation service. It shall be unlawful for an owner or other person in lawful possession or control of private property to remove or employ a commercial relocator to remove an unauthorized vehicle from such property unless written notice is provided to the effect that such vehicles will be removed, including the name, address and telephone number of the appropriate commercial vehicle relocator, if any. Such notice shall consist of a sign, posted in a conspicuous place in the affected area, of a size at least 24 inches in height by 36 inches in width. Such sign shall be at least 4 feet from the ground but less than 8 feet from the ground and shall be either illuminated or painted with reflective paint, or both. Such sign shall state the amount of towing charges to which the person parking may be subject. This provision shall not be construed as prohibiting any unit of local government from imposing additional or greater notice requirements.

No express notice shall be required under this Section upon residential property which, paying due regard to the circumstances and the surrounding area, is clearly reserved or intended exclusively for the use or occupation of residents or their vehicles.

P.A. 76-1586, § 18a-302, added by P.A. 80-1459, § 2, eff. Jan. 1, 1979. Amended by P.A. 81-332, § 2, eff. Jan. 1, 1980.

Formerly Ill.Rev.Stat.1991, ch. 95 ½, ¶ 18a-302.

5/18a-303. Civil and Criminal liability

§ 18a-303. Civil and Criminal liability. Nothing in this Chapter shall be construed to limit or alter the vehicle owner's civil or criminal liability for trespass. Nothing in this Chapter shall be construed to limit or alter the civil or criminal liability of any person or entity for any act or omission. All penalties accruing under this Law shall be cumulative of each other and a suit for recovery of one penalty shall not bar or affect the recovery of another penalty.

P.A. 76-1586, § 18a-303, added by P.A. 80-1459, § 2, eff. Jan. 1, 1979. Amended by P.A. 82-616, § 1, eff. Jan. 1, 1982; P.A. 85-923, § 1, eff. Dec. 1, 1987.

Formerly Ill.Rev.Stat.1991, ch. 95 ½, ¶ 18a-303.

5/18a-304. Operators—Unlawful Practices

§ 18a-304. Operators—Unlawful Practices. It shall be unlawful for any operator:

(1) To act as an operator without a valid, current operator's employment permit.

(2) To violate any other provision of this Chapter, or of Commission regulations or orders adopted under this Chapter.

P.A. 76-1586, § 18a-304, added by P.A. 85-923, § 1, eff. Dec. 1, 1987.

Formerly Ill.Rev.Stat.1991, ch. 95 ½, ¶ 18a-304.

5/18a-305. Aiding and abetting

§ 18a-305. Aiding and abetting. It shall be unlawful for any person to aid or abet in any violation of this Chapter, or of Commission regulations or orders adopted under this Chapter.

P.A. 76-1586, § 18a-305, added by P.A. 85-923, § 1, eff. Dec. 1, 1987.

Formerly Ill.Rev.Stat.1991, ch. 95 ½, ¶ 18a-305.

5/18a-306. Equipment Leasing

§ 18a-306. Equipment Leasing. Provisions in Section 18c-4103 of the Illinois Commercial Transportation Law, as amended,[1] shall likewise govern equipment leasing by relocators except to the extent as otherwise provided in this Law.

P.A. 76-1586, § 18a-306, added by P.A. 85-923, § 1, eff. Dec. 1, 1987.

Formerly Ill.Rev.Stat.1991, ch. 95 ½, ¶ 18a-306.

[1] 625 ILCS 5/18c-4103.

5/18a-307. Enforcement

§ 18a-307. Enforcement. Provisions in Article VII of subchapter 1 of the Illinois Commercial Transportation Law,[1] governing enforcement of the Illinois Commercial Transportation Law, shall likewise govern the enforcement of this Chapter.

P.A. 76-1586, § 18a-307, added by P.A. 85-923, § 1, eff. Dec. 1, 1987.

Formerly Ill.Rev.Stat.1991, ch. 95 ½, ¶ 18a-307.

[1] 625 ILCS 5/18c-1701 et seq.

ARTICLE IV. LICENSES

Section

5/18a-400. Relocator's licenses—Applications, original determinations

§ 18a-400. Relocator's licenses—Applications, original determinations. (a) Each application for a license to operate as a commercial vehicle relocator shall be made in writing to the Commission, shall be verified under oath, shall be in such form and contain such information as the Commission may by regulation require, and shall be accompanied by the required application fee and proof of security.

(b) Upon the filing of such application, the Commission shall, within a reasonable time, fix a time and place for public hearing thereon. At least 10 days before the hearing, the Commission shall notify the applicant and all parties of record to such proceeding of the time and place of such hearing, by mailing a notice thereof to each such party to the address of such party shown in the records of such proceeding. Any person having an interest in the subject matter may appear at the hearing in support of or in objection to the application.

(c) The applicant shall publish a notice on a form prescribed by the Commission covering the filing of such application at least 10 days prior to the time of the initial hearing in (i) the official newspaper selected by the Department of Finance of the State of Illinois pursuant to Section 4 of the Illinois Purchasing Act,[1] and (ii) a secular newspaper of general circulation and published in the county in the State of Illinois, wherein the applicant or applicants propose to maintain their principal office and place of business within the State of Illinois. The Commission may by regulation or otherwise order applicants to give such further notice as it deems required. The Commission may give additional notice of the filing of such application as it may deem reasonable and proper as prescribed in its rules. The Director of the Department of Finance of the State of Illinois for the purposes hereof shall over his or her signature as such Director annually and immediately upon selecting the official newspaper certify to the Illinois Commerce Commission the name and address of said newspaper, together with the date of expiration of the period of one year for which said newspaper was so selected and the Commission shall filemark each such certification as of the date it receives the same and shall keep an official file of said certifications of said Director conveniently available at its office in Springfield, Illinois; provided, however, that in any and all events and for all purposes of this Section and this Chapter, should the aforesaid Director for any reason fail to make said certification annually, the newspaper set forth in the certification aforesaid of said Director filemarked by the Commission as of the most recent date shall be the official newspaper in which publication is required hereby. In case publication is required hereby in a newspaper published in a particular county and no newspaper is so published, then and in that case publication shall be made in a newspaper published in the closest county thereto which meets the circulation requirements of this Section.

(d) The Commission shall issue a relocator's license to any qualified applicant therefor after hearing, pursuant to an application filed, if it is found that the applicant is fit, willing and able properly to perform the service proposed and to conform to provisions of this Chapter and the requirements, rules and regulations of the Commission thereunder; otherwise such application shall be denied. The order of the Commission granting or denying a relocator's license shall set forth the specific findings of fact on which such order is based. Notwithstanding any other provision of this Chapter no such license shall be issued to any person who has failed to pay any registration fee or any tax due from such person to the State of Illinois for the privilege of operating any motor vehicle on the public highways in the State of Illinois.

(e) Operation over the public highways of this State conducted pursuant to a relocator's license shall be in conformity with all of the laws of this State pertaining to motor vehicle operation over such public highways.

(f) No relocator's license shall confer any proprietary or property rights in the use of the public highways.

P.A. 76-1586, § 18a-400, added by P.A. 80-1459, § 2, eff. Jan. 1, 1979.

Formerly Ill.Rev.Stat.1991, ch. 95 ½, ¶ 18a-400.

[1] 30 ILCS 505/4.

5/18a-401. Relocator's licenses—Expiration and renewal

§ 18a-401. Relocator's licenses—Expiration and renewal. All relocator's licenses shall expire 2 years from the date of issuance by the Commission. The Commission may temporarily extend the duration of a license for the pendency of a renewal application until formally approved or denied. Upon filing, no earlier than 90 days nor later than 45 days prior to such expiration, of written application for renewal, verified under oath, in such form and containing such information as the Commission shall by regulation require, and accompanied by the required application fee and proof of security, the Commission shall, unless it has received information of cause not to do so, renew the license. If the Commission has information of cause not to renew such license, it shall so notify the applicant, and shall hold a hearing as provided for in Section 18a-400. The Commission may at any time during the term of the license make inquiry into the management, conduct of business, or otherwise to determine that the provisions of this Chapter 18A and the regulations of the Commission promulgated thereunder are being observed.

P.A. 76-1586, § 18a-401, added by P.A. 80-1459, § 2, eff. Jan. 1, 1979. Amended by P.A. 82-616, § 1, eff. Jan. 1, 1982.

Formerly Ill.Rev.Stat.1991, ch. 95 ½, ¶ 18a-401.

5/18a-402. Relocator's license—Transfer

§ 18a-402. Relocator's license—Transfer. A relocator's license is not transferable.

P.A. 76-1586, § 18a-402, added by P.A. 80-1459, § 2, eff. Jan. 1, 1979.

Formerly Ill.Rev.Stat.1991, ch. 95 ½, ¶ 18a-402.

5/18a-403. Operator's or dispatcher's employment permits—Applications, original determinations

§ 18a-403. Operator's or dispatcher's employment permits—Applications, original determinations. (1) Each application for an operator's or dispatcher's employment permit shall be made in writing to the Commission, shall be acknowledged before a notary public, shall be in such form and shall contain such information as the Commission may by regulation require, and shall be accompanied by the required application fee and proof, in a form prescribed by the Commission, that the operator applicant has a valid driver's license issued by the Secretary of State.

(2) Upon the filing of such application, the Commission shall conduct an investigation of the criminal record, if any, of the applicant. The Commission shall, within 3 working days, issue to any new applicant for an employment permit a provisional operator's or dispatcher's employment permit unless the Commission finds that the applicant has committed an offense for which the permit could be revoked under Section 18a-404 of this Chapter. This provisional employment permit shall be valid for a period of 1 year unless suspended or revoked by order of the Commission. At the end of 1 year, the provisional permit shall automatically become permanent unless the permit was revoked by order of the Commission during the preceding year. The permanent permit shall remain valid unless suspended or revoked by order of the Commission under this law.

(3) The permit shall identify the operator or dispatcher by name and address, and shall identify the relocator by which the operator or dispatcher will be employed by name, address and relocator's permit number. The permit shall be valid only when the operator or dispatcher is employed by the relocator identified thereon.

Operation over the public highways of this State conducted pursuant to an operator's license issued under the provisions of this Section shall be in conformity with all the laws of this State pertaining to motor vehicle operation over such public highways.

P.A. 76-1586, § 18a-403, added by P.A. 80-1459, § 2, eff. Jan. 1, 1979. Amended by P.A. 82-616, § 1, eff. Jan. 1, 1982; P.A. 85-923, § 1, eff. Dec. 1, 1987.

Formerly Ill.Rev.Stat.1991, ch. 95 ½, ¶ 18a-403.

5/18a-404. Operator's and dispatcher's employment permits—Revocation

§ 18a-404. Operator's and dispatcher's employment permits—Revocation. (1) The Commission shall suspend or revoke the permit of an operator if it finds that:

(a) The operator or dispatcher made a false statement on the application for an operator's or dispatcher's employment permit;

(b) The operator's or dispatcher's driver's license issued by the Secretary of State has been suspended or revoked; or

(c) The operator or dispatcher has been convicted, during the preceding 5 years, of any criminal offense of the State of Illinois or any other jurisdiction involving any of the following, and the holder does not make a compelling showing that he is nevertheless fit to hold an operator's license:

(i) Bodily injury or attempt to inflict bodily injury to another;

(ii) Theft of property or attempted theft of property; or

(iii) Sexual assault or attempted sexual assault of any kind.

(2) The Commission, upon notification and verification of any conviction described in this Section, of any person to whom license has been issued, occurring within the 5 years prior to such issuance or any time thereafter, shall immediately suspend the employment permit of such person, and issue an order setting forth the grounds for revocation. The person and his employer shall be notified of such suspension. Such person shall not thereafter be employed by a relocator until a final order is issued by the Commission either reinstating the employment permit, upon a finding that the reinstatement of an employment permit to the person constitutes no threat to the public safety, or revoking the employment permit.

(3) If the employment permit is revoked, the person shall not thereafter be employed by a relocator until he obtains an employment permit license under Article IV of this Chapter.

P.A. 76-1586, § 18a-404, added by P.A. 80-1459, § 2, eff. Jan. 1, 1979. Amended by P.A. 82-616, § 1, eff. Jan. 1, 1982; P.A. 85-923, § 1, eff. Dec. 1, 1987.

Formerly Ill.Rev.Stat.1991, ch. 95 ½, ¶ 18a-404.

5/18a-405. Operator's employment permits—Expiration and renewal

§ 18a-405. Operator's employment permits—Expiration and renewal. All operator's employment permits shall expire 2 years from the date of issuance by the Commission. The Commission may temporarily extend the duration of an employment permit for the pendency of a renewal application until formally approved or denied. Upon filing, no earlier than 90 nor later than 45 days prior to such expiration, of written application for renewal, acknowledged before a notary public, in such form and containing such information as the Commission shall by regulation require, and accompanied by the required fee and proof of possession of a valid driver's license issued by the Secretary of State, the Commission shall, unless it has received information of cause not to do so, renew the applicant's operator's employment permit. If the Commission does not renew such employment permit, it shall issue an order setting forth the grounds for denial. The Commission may at any time during the term of the employment permit make inquiry into the conduct of the permittee to determine that the provisions of this Chapter 18A and the regulations of the Commission promulgated thereunder are being adhered to.

P.A. 76-1586, § 18a-405, added by P.A. 80-1459, § 2, eff. Jan. 1, 1979. Amended by P.A. 82-616, § 1, eff. Jan. 1, 1982; P.A. 85-923, § 1, eff. Dec. 1, 1987.

Formerly Ill.Rev.Stat.1991, ch. 95 ½, ¶ 18a-405.

5/18a-406. Operator's employment permits—Transfer

§ 18a-406. Operator's employment permits—Transfer. An operator's employment permit is not transferrable to another operator or to another relocator.

P.A. 76-1586, § 18a-406, added by P.A. 80-1459, § 2, eff. Jan. 1, 1979. Amended by P.A. 85-923, § 1, eff. Dec. 1, 1987.

Formerly Ill.Rev.Stat.1991, ch. 95 ½, ¶ 18a-406.

5/18a-407. Dispatcher's employment permits, expiration and renewal

§ 18a-407. Dispatcher's employment permits, expiration and renewal. All dispatcher's employment permits shall expire 2 years from the date of issuance by the Commission. The Commission may temporarily extend the duration of an employment permit for the pendency of a renewal application until formally approved or denied. Upon filing, no earlier than 90 nor later than 45 days prior to such expiration, of written application for renewal, acknowledged before a notary public, in such form and containing such information as the Commission shall by regulation require, and accompanied by the required fee, the Commission shall, unless it has received information of cause not to do so, renew the applicant's dispatcher's employment permit. If the Commission does not renew such employment permit, it shall issue an order setting forth the grounds for denial. The Commission may at any time during the term of the employment permit make inquiry into the conduct of the permittee to determine that the provisions of this Chapter 18A and the regulations of the Commission promulgated thereunder are being observed.

P.A. 76–1586, § 18a–407, added by P.A. 82–616, § 1, eff. Jan. 1, 1982. Amended by P.A. 85–923, § 1, eff. Dec. 1, 1987.

Formerly Ill.Rev.Stat.1991, ch. 95 ½, ¶ 18a–407.

5/18a–408. Dispatcher's employment permit—Transfer

§ 18a–408. Dispatcher's employment permit—Transfer. A dispatcher's employment permit is not transferable to another dispatcher or to another relocator.

P.A. 76–1586, § 18a–408, added by P.A. 82–616, § 1, eff. Jan. 1, 1982. Amended by P.A. 85–923, § 1, eff. Dec. 1, 1987.

Formerly Ill.Rev.Stat.1991, ch. 95 ½, ¶ 18a–408.

ARTICLE V. RATES AND CHARGES—LIENS

Section

5/18a–500. Posting of rates

§ 18a–500. Posting of rates. Every commercial vehicle relocator shall print and keep open to the public, all authorized rates and charges for towing, otherwise moving, and storing vehicles in connection with removal of unauthorized vehicles from private property. Such rates and charges shall be clearly stated in terms of lawful money of the United States, and shall be posted in such form and manner, and shall contain such information as the Commission shall by regulation prescribe.

P.A. 76–1586, § 18a–500, added by P.A. 80–1459, § 2, eff. Jan. 1, 1979.

Formerly Ill.Rev.Stat.1991, ch. 95 ½, ¶ 18a–500.

5/18a–501. Liens against relocated vehicles

§ 18a–501. Liens against relocated vehicles. Unauthorized vehicles removed and stored by a commercial vehicle relocator in compliance with this Chapter shall be subject to a possessory lien for services pursuant to the Labor and Storage Lien (Small Amount) Act [1], and the provisions of Section 1 of that Act [2] relating to notice and implied consent shall be deemed satisfied by compliance with Section 18a–302 and item (10) of Section 18a–300. In no event shall such lien be greater than the rate or rates established in accordance with item (6) of Section 18a–200. In no event shall such lien be increased or altered to reflect any charge for services or materials rendered in addition to those authorized by this Act. Every such lien shall be payable by use of any major credit card, in addition to being payable in cash. Upon receipt of a properly signed credit card receipt, a relocator shall become a holder in due course, and neither the holder of the credit card nor the company which issued the credit card may thereafter refuse to remit payment in the amount shown on the credit card receipt minus the ordinary charge assessed by the credit card company for processing the charge. The Commission may adopt regulations governing acceptance of credit cards by a relocator.

P.A. 76–1586, § 18a–501, added by P.A. 80–1459, § 2, eff. Jan. 1, 1979. Amended by P.A. 85–923, § 1, eff. Dec. 1, 1987; P.A. 91–357, § 231, eff. July 29, 1999.

Formerly Ill.Rev.Stat.1991, ch. 95 ½, ¶ 18a–501.

1 770 ILCS 50/0.01 et seq.

2 770 ILCS 50/1.

ARTICLE VI. FEES

Section

5/18a–600. Relocator's license

§ 18a–600. Relocator's license. Each application for a license to operate as a commercial vehicle relocator, or for a renewal of such license, shall be accompanied by a filing fee in the amount provided or prescribed by the Commission.

P.A. 76–1586, § 18a–600, added by P.A. 80–1459, § 2, eff. Jan. 1, 1979. Amended by P.A. 82–616, § 1, eff. Jan. 1, 1982; P.A. 85–923, § 1, eff. Dec. 1, 1987.

Formerly Ill.Rev.Stat.1991, ch. 95 ½, ¶ 18a–600.

5/18a–601. Operator's or dispatcher's employment permit

§ 18a–601. Operator's or dispatcher's employment permit. Each application for dispatcher's or an operator's employment permit shall be accompanied by a filing fee in the amount provided or prescribed by the Commission. Each application for renewal of an operator's or dispatcher's employment permit shall be accompanied by a filing fee in the amount provided herein or prescribed by the Commission.

P.A. 76–1586, § 18a–601, added by P.A. 80–1459, § 2, eff. Jan. 1, 1979. Amended by P.A. 82–616, § 1, eff. Jan. 1, 1982; P.A. 85–923, § 1, eff. Dec. 1, 1987; P.A. 85–1209, Art. III, § 3–60, eff. Aug. 30, 1988.

Formerly Ill.Rev.Stat.1991, ch. 95 ½, ¶ 18a–601.

5/18a–602. Establishment and Adjustment of Fees

§ 18a–602. Establishment and Adjustment of Fees.

(1) General Provisions. The Commission may exercise any and all powers with respect to establishment and adjustment of fees with respect to commercial vehicle relocators which it may exercise with respect to motor carriers under subsections (2), (3) and (4) of Section 18c–1501 of the Illinois Commercial Transportation Law.

(2) Initial fees. The Commission shall set initial fees by rulemaking in accordance with Section 5–50 of the Illinois Administrative Procedure Act.[1] Initial fees shall be set and take effect within 60 days after December 1, 1987. Such fees

shall remain in effect until adjusted by the Commission in accordance with subsection (1) of this Section.

P.A. 76–1586, § 18a–602, added by P.A. 80–1459, § 2, eff. Jan. 1, 1979. Amended by P.A. 84–796, § 1, eff. Jan. 1, 1986; P.A. 85–923, § 1, eff. Dec. 1, 1987; P.A. 88–45, Art. III, § 3–128, eff. July 6, 1993.

Formerly Ill.Rev.Stat.1991, ch. 95 ½, ¶ 18a–602.

[1] 5 ILCS 100/5–50.

5/18a–603. Disposition of funds

§ 18a–603. Disposition of funds. All fees and fines collected by the Commission under this Chapter shall be paid into the Transportation Regulatory Fund in the State Treasury. The money in that fund shall be used to defray the expenses of the administration of this Chapter and for the purposes specified in Section 18c–1601 of this Code.

P.A. 76–1586, § 18a–603, added by P.A. 85–923, § 1, eff. Dec. 1, 1987.

Formerly Ill.Rev.Stat.1991, ch. 95 ½, ¶ 18a–603.

ARTICLE VII. COUNTIES COVERED

5/18a–700. Counties covered

§ 18a–700. Counties covered. (a) The provisions of this Chapter apply to all the activities of relocators and operators in any counties of 1,000,000 or more and in any county of less than 1,000,000 which adopts regulation under this Chapter as provided in this Section.

(b) Any operation of a relocator or operator involving the removal or storage of a given vehicle which takes place in any part in a regulated county shall subject all the activities of the relocator and operator involving that vehicle to regulation under this Chapter, except operations which take place entirely within the territory of a city, village or incorporated town excluded from this Chapter under paragraph (d).

(c) Any county of under 1,000,000 may elect to be covered under this Chapter by the adoption of a resolution by the County Board, approved by a majority of its members, providing that the county shall be subject to this Chapter. The county clerk shall certify to the Commission that the County Board has adopted the resolution. The Commission shall certify to such County Board an effective date for the applicability of this Chapter in such county. Such effective date shall be no earlier than 30 days from certification to the County Board nor later than 6 months from such certification or the beginning of the next fiscal year, whichever is last.

(d) Cities, villages and incorporated towns in counties to which the provisions of this Chapter apply may, by resolution adopted by a majority of the members of the corporate authorities and filed with the County Clerk of such county and with the Illinois Commerce Commission, choose to be excluded from the provisions of this Chapter. Upon the filing of such resolution, the provisions of this Chapter shall not be applicable to operations of relocators or operators which take place entirely within the territory of such city, village or incorporated town.

P.A. 76–1586, § 18a–700, added by P.A. 80–1459, § 2, eff. Jan. 1, 1979. Amended by P.A. 80–1495, § 36, eff. Jan. 8, 1979; P.A. 86–492, § 1, eff. Sept. 1, 1989.

Formerly Ill.Rev.Stat.1991, ch. 95 ½, ¶ 18a–700.

CHAPTER 18b. MOTOR CARRIER SAFETY REGULATIONS

Enactment

Chapter 18b was added by P.A. 82–657, § 1, effective January 1, 1982

ARTICLE I. FEDERAL MOTOR CARRIER SAFETY REGULATIONS

5/18b–100. Short Title

§ 18b–100. Short Title. This Chapter shall be known and may be cited as "The Illinois Motor Carrier Safety Law".

P.A. 76–1586, § 18b–100, added by P.A. 82–657, § 1, eff. Jan. 1, 1982. Amended by P.A. 82–887, § 1, eff. Aug. 2, 1982; P.A. 83–12, § 1, eff. Jan. 1, 1984; P.A. 83–542, § 1, eff. Jan. 1, 1984; P.A. 83–1362, Art. II, § 99, eff. Sept. 11, 1984; P.A. 84–1246, § 1, eff. July 29, 1986; P.A. 85–1144, § 1, eff. July 29, 1988; P.A. 86–611, § 1, eff. Sept. 1, 1989.

Formerly Ill.Rev.Stat.1991, ch. 95 ½, ¶ 18b–100.

Section 4 of P.A. 83–12, approved July 1, 1983, provided:

"Effective date. This Act takes effect as provided in this Section.

"The amendments to those portions of Sections 3–815(a), 3–818 and 3–819(b) of 'The Illinois Vehicle Code' in Section 1 of this Act which create the 'X', 'Z', 'MX', 'MZ', 'MM' and 'TN' registration classifications and the fees and taxes imposed for those classifications, the amendments to Sections 2–119, 3–401 and 3–802 of 'The Illinois Vehicle Code' in Section 1 of this Act, and the amendments to Chapter 15 of 'The Illinois Vehicle Code' in Section 1 of this Act take effect July 1, 1983.

"The remaining amendments to 'The Illinois Vehicle Code' in Section 1 of this Act take effect July 1, 1983 and apply beginning with the 1985 registration year, except that the amendments to Sections 3–813 through 3–816 and Section 3–819 apply beginning with the 1984 registration year for those vehicles registered on a calendar year basis only.

"The amendments to Chapters 13 and 18 of 'The Illinois Vehicle Code' in Section 1 of this Act take effect January 1, 1984.

"Section 2 of this Act takes effect on the first day of the next succeeding month which commences at least 30 days after the date on which this Act becomes law.

"Section 3 of this Act takes effect July 1, 1983.

"Section 3.1 of this Act takes effect January 1, 1984.

"This Section 4 takes effect upon its becoming a law."

5/18b–101. Definitions

§ 18b–101. Definitions. Unless the context otherwise clearly requires, as used in this Chapter:

"Commercial motor vehicle" means any self propelled or towed vehicle used on public highways in interstate and intrastate commerce to transport passengers or property when the vehicle has a gross vehicle weight, a gross vehicle weight rating, a gross combination weight, or a gross combination weight rating of 10,001 or more pounds; or the vehicle is designed to transport more than 15 passengers, including the driver; or the vehicle is designed to carry 15 or fewer passengers and is operated by a contract carrier transporting employees in the course of their employment on a highway of this State; or the vehicle is used in the transportation of hazardous materials in a quantity requiring placarding under the Illinois Hazardous Materials Transportation Act.[1] This definition shall not include farm machinery, fertilizer spreaders, and other special agricultural movement equipment described in Section 3–809 nor implements of husbandry as defined in Section 1–130;

"Officer" means Illinois State Police Officer;

"Person" means any natural person or individual, governmental body, firm, association, partnership, copartnership, joint venture, company, corporation, joint stock company, trust, estate or any other legal entity or their legal representative, agent or assigns.

P.A. 76–1586, § 18b–101, added by P.A. 86–611, § 1, eff. Sept. 1, 1989. Amended by P.A. 87–829, § 1, eff. Jan. 17, 1992; P.A. 90–89, § 15, eff. Jan. 1, 1998; P.A. 91–179, § 5, eff. Jan. 1, 2000; P.A. 92–108, § 5, eff. Jan. 1, 2002.

Formerly Ill.Rev.Stat.1991, ch. 95 ½, ¶ 18b–101.

1 430 ILCS 30/1 et seq.

5/18b–102. Authority of Department

§ 18b–102. Authority of Department. To the extent necessary to administer this Chapter, the Department is authorized to:

(a) Adopt by reference all or any portion of the Federal Motor Carrier Safety Regulations of the United States Department of Transportation, as they are now or hereafter amended.

(b) Conduct investigations; make reports; issue subpoenas; conduct hearings; require the production of relevant documents, records and property; take depositions; and, in conjunction with the Illinois State Police, conduct directly or indirectly research, development, demonstrations and training activities.

(c) Authorize any officer or Department employee to enter upon, inspect and examine at reasonable times and in a reasonable manner, the records and properties of persons to the extent such records and properties relate to the transportation by motor vehicle of persons or property.

(d) Conduct a continuing review of all aspects of the transportation of persons and property by motor vehicle in order to determine and recommend appropriate steps to assure safe transportation by motor vehicle in Illinois.

(e) Administer and enforce the provisions of this Chapter and any rules and regulations issued under this Chapter. Only the Illinois State Police shall be authorized to stop and inspect any commercial motor vehicle or driver at any time for the purpose of determining compliance with the provisions of this Chapter or rules and regulations issued under this Chapter.

P.A.76–1586, § 18b–102, added by P.A. 86–611, § 1, eff. Sept. 1, 1989. Amended by P.A. 87–829, § 1, eff. Jan. 17, 1992; P.A. 90–89, § 15, eff. Jan. 1, 1998.

Formerly Ill.Rev.Stat.1991, ch. 95 ½, ¶ 18b–102.

5/18b–103. Compliance with this Chapter

§ 18b–103. Compliance with this Chapter. Transportation by motor vehicle of persons or property in commerce that is not in compliance with this Chapter or any rules and regulations issued under this Act is prohibited.

P.A. 76–1586, § 18b–103, added by P.A. 86–611, § 1, eff. Sept. 1, 1989.

Formerly Ill.Rev.Stat.1991, ch. 95 ½, ¶ 18b–103.

5/18b–103.1. Obedience to Police Officer

§ 18b–103.1. Obedience to Police Officer.

(a) No person shall willfully fail or refuse to comply with any lawful order or direction of any officer authorized by law to enforce this Chapter and to perform vehicle and driver motor carrier safety inspections under this Chapter. Lawful orders or directions shall include providing documentation and answering questions necessary to determine compliance with the provisions of this Chapter. The driver or owner shall assist the officer, as needed, during the course of any such inspection.

(b) Any person who violates this Section shall be guilty of a Class C misdemeanor offense.

P.A. 76–1586, § 18b–103.1, added by P.A. 87–768, § 2, eff. Oct. 10, 1991. Amended by P.A. 88–476, § 2, eff. July 1, 1994.

Formerly Ill.Rev.Stat.1991, ch. 95 ½, ¶ 18b–103.1.

5/18b–104. Cooperation with State Agencies—Records and Data—Availability

§ 18b–104. Cooperation with State Agencies—Records and Data—Availability. The Department shall cooperate with other State agencies regulating transportation by motor vehicles and may enter into interagency agreements for the purpose of sharing data. The Department shall enter into an interagency agreement with the Illinois State Police for the purpose of enforcing any provisions of this Chapter and the rules and regulations issued under this Chapter.

P.A. 76–1586, § 18b–104, added by P.A. 86–611, § 1, eff. Sept. 1, 1989.

Formerly Ill.Rev.Stat.1991, ch. 95 ½, ¶ 18b–104.

5/18b–105. Rules and Regulations

§ 18b–105. Rules and Regulations.

(a) The Department is authorized to make and adopt reasonable rules and regulations and orders consistent with law necessary to carry out the provisions of this Chapter.

(b) The following parts of Title 49 of the Code of Federal Regulations, as now in effect, are hereby adopted by reference as though they were set out in full:

Part 383—Commercial Driver's License Standards, Requirements, and Penalties;

Part 385—Safety Fitness Procedures;

Part 390—Federal Motor Carrier Safety Regulations: General;

Part 391—Qualifications of Drivers;

Part 392—Driving of Motor Vehicles;

Part 393—Parts and Accessories Necessary for Safe Operation;

Part 395—Hours of Service of Drivers, except as provided in Section 18b–106.1; and

Part 396—Inspection, Repair and Maintenance.

(b–5) Individuals who meet the requirements set forth in the definition of "medical examiner" in Section 390.5 of Part 390 of Title 49 of the Code of Federal Regulations may act as medical examiners in accordance with Part 391 of Title 49 of the Code of Federal Regulations.

(c) The following parts and Sections of the Federal Motor Carrier Safety Regulations shall not apply to those intrastate carriers, drivers or vehicles subject to subsection (b).

(1) Section 393.93 of Part 393 for those vehicles manufactured before June 30, 1972.

(2) Section 393.86 of Part 393 for those vehicles which are registered as farm trucks under subsection (c) of Section 3–815 of this Code.

(3) (Blank).

(4) (Blank).

(5) Paragraph (b)(1) of Section 391.11 of Part 391.

(6) All of Part 395 for all agricultural movements as defined in Chapter 1, between the period of February 1 through November 30 each year, and all farm to market agricultural transportation as defined in Chapter 1 and for grain hauling operations within a radius of 200 air miles of the normal work reporting location.

(7) Paragraphs (b)(3) (insulin dependent diabetic) and (b)(10) (minimum visual acuity) of Section 391.41 of part 391, but only for any driver who immediately prior to July 29, 1986 was eligible and licensed to operate a motor vehicle subject to this Section and was engaged in operating such vehicles, and who was disqualified on July 29, 1986 by the adoption of Part 391 by reason of the application of paragraphs (b)(3) and (b)(10) of Section 391.41 with respect to a physical condition existing at that time unless such driver has a record of accidents which would indicate a lack of ability to operate a motor vehicle in a safe manner.

(d) Intrastate carriers subject to the recording provisions of Section 395.8 of Part 395 of the Federal Motor Carrier Safety Regulations shall be exempt as established under paragraph (1) of Section 395.8; provided, however, for the purpose of this Code, drivers shall operate within a 150 air-mile radius of the normal work reporting location to qualify for exempt status.

(e) Regulations adopted by the Department subsequent to those adopted under subsection (b) hereof shall be identical in substance to the Federal Motor Carrier Safety Regulations of the United States Department of Transportation and adopted in accordance with the procedures for rulemaking in Section 5–35 of the Illinois Administrative Procedure Act.[1]

P.A. 76–1586, § 18b–105, added by P.A. 86–611, § 1, eff. Sept. 1, 1989. Amended by P.A. 87–829, § 1, eff. Jan. 17, 1992; P.A. 88–45, Art. III, § 3–128, eff. July 6, 1993; P.A. 88–476, § 2, eff. July 1, 1994; P.A. 90–89, § 15, eff. Jan. 1, 1998; P.A. 90–228, § 5, eff. July 25, 1997; P.A. 90–655, § 153, eff. July 30, 1998; P.A. 91–179, § 5, eff. Jan. 1, 2000; P.A. 92–108, § 5, eff. Jan. 1, 2002; P.A. 92–249, § 5, eff. Jan. 1, 2002; P.A. 92–651, § 77, eff. July 11, 2002; P.A. 92–703, § 10, eff. July 19, 2002.

Formerly Ill.Rev.Stat.1991, ch. 95 ½, ¶ 18b–105.

[1] 5 ILCS 100/5–35.

P.A. 92–651, the First 2002 General Revisory Act, amended various Acts to delete obsolete text, to correct patent and technical errors, to revise cross references, to resolve multiple actions in the 91st and 92nd General Assemblies and to make certain technical corrections in P.A. 91–937 through P.A. 92–520.

See 5 ILCS 70/6 as to the effect of (1) more than one amendment of a section at the same session of the General Assembly or (2) two or more acts relating to the same subject matter enacted by the same General Assembly.

5/18b–106. Application of Chapter and Regulations

§ 18b–106. Application of Chapter and Regulations. Except as expressly specified within this Chapter, this Chapter and the rules and regulations issued under this Chapter shall be applicable to all persons employing drivers, drivers and commercial motor vehicles which transport property or passengers in interstate or intrastate commerce.

P.A. 76–1586, § 18b–106, added by P.A. 86–611, § 1, eff. Sept. 1, 1989. Amended by P.A. 87–829, § 1, eff. Jan. 17, 1992.

Formerly Ill.Rev.Stat.1991, ch. 95½, ¶ 18b–106.

5/18b–106.1. Hours of service of drivers employed by contract carriers transporting employees in the course of their employment

§ 18b–106.1. Hours of service of drivers employed by contract carriers transporting employees in the course of their employment. A contract carrier shall limit the hours of service by a driver transporting employees in the course of their employment on a road or highway of this State in a vehicle designed to carry 15 or fewer passengers to 12 hours of vehicle operation per day, 15 hours of on-duty service per day, and 70 hours of on-duty service in 7 consecutive days. The contract carrier shall require a driver who has 12 hours of vehicle operation per day or 15 hours of on-duty service per day to have at least 8 consecutive hours off duty before operating a vehicle again.

P.A. 76–1586, § 18b–106.1, added by P.A. 92–108, § 5, eff. Jan. 1, 2002.

5/18b–107. Violations—Civil penalties

§ 18b–107. Violations—Civil penalties.

Except as provided in Section 18b–108, any person who is determined by the Department after reasonable notice and opportunity for a fair and impartial hearing to have committed an act in violation of this Chapter or any rule or regulation issued under this Chapter is liable to the State for a civil penalty. Such person is subject to a civil penalty of not more than $5,000 for such violation, except that a person committing a railroad-highway grade crossing violation is subject to a civil penalty of not more than $10,000, and, if any such violation is a continuing one, each day of violation constitutes a separate offense. The amount of any such penalty shall be assessed by the Department by a written notice. In determining the amount of such penalty, the Department shall take into account the nature, circumstances, extent and gravity of the violation and, with respect to a person found to have committed such violation, the degree of culpability, history or prior offenses, ability to pay, effect on ability to continue to do business and such other matters as justice may require.

Such civil penalty is recoverable in an action brought by the State's Attorney or the Attorney General on behalf of the State in the circuit court or, prior to referral to the State's Attorney or the Attorney General, such civil penalty may be compromised by the Department. The amount of such penalty when finally determined (or agreed upon in compromise), may be deducted from any sums owed by the State to the person charged. All civil penalties collected under this subsection shall be deposited in the Road Fund.

P.A. 76–1586, § 18b–107, added by P.A. 86–611, § 1, eff. Sept. 1, 1989. Amended by P.A. 86–1236, § 1, eff. Jan. 1, 1991; P.A. 92–249, § 5, eff. Jan. 1, 2002.

Formerly Ill.Rev.Stat.1991, ch. 95 ½, ¶ 18b–107.

5/18b–108. Violations; Criminal penalties

§ 18b–108. Violations; Criminal penalties.

(a) The provisions of Chapter 16 [1] shall be applicable to acts committed by a driver of a motor vehicle that violate this Chapter or any rule or regulation issued under this Chapter.

(b) Any driver who willfully violates any provision of this Chapter or any rule or regulation issued under this Chapter is guilty of a Class 4 felony. In addition to any other penalties prescribed by law, the maximum fine for each offense is $10,000. Such violation shall be prosecuted by the State's Attorney or the Attorney General.

(c) Any person, other than a driver, who willfully violates or causes another to violate any provision of this Chapter or any rule or regulation issued under this Chapter is guilty of a Class 3 felony. In addition to any other penalties prescribed by law, the maximum fine for each offense is $25,000. Such violation shall be prosecuted at the request of the Department by the State's Attorney or the Attorney General.

P.A. 76–1586, § 18b–108, added by P.A. 86–611, § 1, eff. Sept. 1, 1989. Amended by P.A. 86–1236, § 1, eff. Jan. 1, 1991; P.A. 88–476, § 2, eff. July 1, 1994; P.A. 89–179, § 5, eff. Jan. 1, 1996.

Formerly Ill.Rev.Stat.1991, ch. 95 ½, ¶ 18b–108.

[1] 625 ILCS 5/16–101 et seq.

5/18b–109. Enforcement of Rules and Regulations

§ 18b–109. Enforcement of Rules and Regulations. Only the Illinois State Police shall enforce the rules and regulations issued under this Chapter against drivers. The Department and the Illinois State Police shall enforce the rules and regulations issued under this Chapter against persons other than drivers.

P.A. 76–1586, § 18b–109, added by P.A. 86–611, § 1, eff. Sept. 1, 1989.

Formerly Ill.Rev.Stat.1991, ch. 95 ½, ¶ 18b–109.

5/18b–110. Conflict With Other Laws

§ 18b–110. Conflict With Other Laws. This Chapter is not intended to affect any State law or ordinance of a local authority now in effect or intrude upon the duties and responsibilities of any State or local officer with respect to matters related to the subject to this Chapter, but in the case of any conflict with other State laws or ordinance of local authorities relating to the transportation of persons or property by highway, the provisions of this Chapter shall control.

P.A. 76–1586, § 18b–110, added by P.A. 86–611, § 1, eff. Sept. 1, 1989.

Formerly Ill.Rev.Stat.1991, ch. 95 ½, ¶ 18b–110.

5/18b–111. Review Under Administrative Review Law

§ 18b–111. Review Under Administrative Review Law. All administrative decisions of the Department under this Chapter shall be subject to judicial review under the Administrative Review Law, as now or hereafter amended.[1]

P.A. 76–1586, § 18b–111, added by P.A. 86–611, § 1, eff. Sept. 1, 1989. Amended by P.A. 90–89, § 15, eff. Jan. 1, 1998.

Formerly Ill.Rev.Stat.1991, ch. 95 ½, ¶ 18b–111.

[1] 735 ILCS 5/3–101 et seq.

5/18b–112. Intermodal trailer, chassis, and safety

§ 18b–112. Intermodal trailer, chassis, and safety.

(a) Definitions. For purposes of this Section:

"Department" means the Department of State Police.

"Equipment interchange agreement" means a written document executed by the intermodal equipment provider and operator at the time the equipment is interchanged by the provider to the operator.

"Equipment provider" is the owner of an intermodal trailer, chassis, or container. This includes any forwarding company, water carrier, steamship line, railroad, vehicle equipment leasing company, and their subsidiary or affiliated companies owning the equipment.

"Federal motor carrier safety regulations" means regulations promulgated by the United States Department of Transportation governing the condition and maintenance of commercial motor vehicles contained in Title 49 of the United States Code of Federal Regulations on the day of enactment of this Act or as amended or revised by the United States Department of Transportation thereafter.

"Interchange" means the act of providing a vehicle to a motor carrier by an equipment provider for the purpose of transporting the vehicle for loading or unloading by another party or the repositioning of the vehicle for the benefit of the equipment provider. "Interchange" does not include the leasing of the vehicle by a motor carrier from an owner-operator pursuant to subpart B of Part 376 of Title 49 of the Code of Federal Regulations or the leasing of a vehicle to a motor carrier for use in the motor carrier's over-the-road freight hauling operations.

"Operator" means a motor carrier or driver of a commercial motor vehicle.

"Vehicle" means an intermodal trailer, chassis, or container.

(b) Responsibility of equipment provider. An equipment provider shall not interchange or offer for interchange a vehicle with an operator for use on a highway which vehicle is in violation of the requirements contained in the federal motor carrier safety regulations. It is the responsibility of the equipment provider to inspect and, if a vehicle at the time of inspection does not comply with all federal motor carrier safety regulation requirements, perform the necessary repairs on, all vehicles prior to interchange or offering for interchange.

(c) Duty of inspection by the operator. Before interchanging a vehicle with an operator, an equipment provider must provide the operator the opportunity and facilities to perform a visual inspection of the equipment. The operator must determine if it complies with the provisions of the federal motor carrier safety regulation capable of being determined from an inspection. If the operator determines that the vehicle does not comply with the provisions of the federal motor carrier safety regulations, the equipment provider shall immediately perform the necessary repairs to the vehicle so that it complies with the federal motor carrier safety regulations or shall immediately provide the operator with another vehicle.

(d) Presumption of defect prior to interchange.

(1) If as a result of a roadside inspection by the Department, any of the defects listed in paragraph (2) are discovered, a rebuttable presumption existed at the time of the interchange. If a summons or complaint is issued to the operator, the operator may seek relief pursuant to paragraph (3).

(2) A rebuttable presumption exists that the following defects were present at the time of the interchange:

(A) There is a defect with the brake drum when:

(I) the drum cracks;

(II) the lining is loose or missing; or

(III) the lining is saturated with oil.

(B) There is a defect of inoperative brakes when:

(I) there is no movement of any components;

(II) there are missing, broken, or loose components; or

(III) there are mismatched components.

(C) There is a defect with the air lines and tubing when:

(I) there is a bulge and swelling;

(II) there is an audible air leak; or

(III) there are air lines broken,cracked, or crimped.

(D) There is a defect with the reservoir tank when there is any separation of original attachment points.

(E) There is a defect with the frames when:

(I) there is any cracked, loose, sagging, or broken frame members which measure one and one-half inch in web or one inch or longer in bottom flange or any crack extending from web radius into bottom flange; or

(II) there is any condition which causes moving parts to come in contact with the frame.

(F) There is an electrical defect when wires are chaffed.

(G) There is a defect with the wheel assembly when:

(I) there is low or no oil;

(II) there is oil leakage on brake components;

(III) there are lug nuts that are loose or missing; or

(IV) the wheel bearings are not properly maintained.

(H) There is a defect with the tires when:

(I) there is improper inflation;

(II) there is tire separation from the casing; or

(III) there are exposed plys or belting material.

(I) There is defect with rim cracks when:

(I) there is any circumferential crack, except a manufactured crack; or

(II) there is a lock or side ring cracked, bent, broken, sprung, improperly seated, or mismatched.

(J) There is a defect with the suspension when:

(I) there are spring assembly leaves broken, missing, or separated; or

(II) there are spring hanger, u-bolts, or axle positioning components cracked, broken loose, or missing.

(K) There is a defect with the chassis locking pins when there is any twist lock or fitting for securement that is sprung, broken, or improperly latched.

(3) If an operator receives a citation for a violation due to a defect in any equipment specified in subsection (d)(2), the equipment provider shall reimburse the operator for any:

(A) fines and costs, including court costs and reasonable attorneys fees, incurred as a result of the citation; and

(B) costs incurred by the operator to repair the defects specified in the citation, including any towing costs incurred.

The equipment provider shall reimburse the operator within 30 days of the final court action. If the equipment provider fails to reimburse the operator within 30 days, the operator has a civil cause of action against the equipment provider.

(e) Fines and penalties. Any person violating the provisions of this Section shall be fined no less than $50 and no more than $500 for each violation.

(f) Obligation of motor carrier. Nothing in Section is intended to eliminate the responsibility and obligation of a motor carrier and operator to maintain and operate vehicles in accordance with the federal motor carrier safety regulations and applicable State and local laws and regulations.

(g) This Section shall not be applied, construed, or implemented in any manner inconsistent with, or in conflict with, any provision of the federal motor carrier safety regulations.

P.A. 76–1586, § 18b–112, added by P.A. 91–662, § 5, eff. July 1, 2000.

CHAPTER 18c. ILLINOIS COMMERCIAL TRANSPORTATION LAW

Enactment

Chapter 18c was added by P.A. 84–796, § 1, eff. Jan. 1, 1986.

SUB–CHAPTER 1. GENERAL PROVISIONS

ARTICLE I. SHORT TITLE, LEGISLATIVE INTENT, STATE TRANSPORTATION POLICY, AND DEFINITIONS

ARTICLE II. JURISDICTION AND POWER OF THE COMMISSION

ARTICLE I. SHORT TITLE, LEGISLATIVE INTENT, STATE TRANSPORTATION POLICY, AND DEFINITIONS

5/18c-1101. Short Title

§ 18c-1101. Short Title. This Chapter shall be known and may be cited as the "Illinois Commercial Transportation Law".

P.A. 76-1586, § 18c-1101, added by P.A. 84-796, § 1, eff. Jan. 1, 1986.

Formerly Ill.Rev.Stat.1991, ch. 95 ½, ¶ 18c-1101.

5/18c-1102. Legislative Intent

§ 18c-1102. Legislative Intent. The General Assembly finds that:

(a) a comprehensive recodification of existing transportation regulatory statutes is needed to delete obsolete provisions and facilitate a coordinated approach to regulation of motor carriers, rail carriers, and brokers;

(b) the accelerating pace of change in the transportation industry, as an outgrowth of changing economic conditions and federal legislation, necessitates the streamlining of regulatory procedures to allow for prompt action to protect the interests of the people of the State of Illinois; and

(c) an increasing incidence of unlawful activity by unlicensed carriers and others has rendered existing enforcement mechanisms inadequate.

Where the language of any provision in this Chapter is substantially similar to the language in the predecessor statute, the legislative intent expressed in this Chapter shall be the same as the legislative intent embodied in the predecessor statute as construed by the courts of this State and, where appropriate, reports of the Illinois Motor Vehicle Laws Commission.

P.A. 76-1586, § 18c-1102, added by P.A. 84-796, § 1, eff. Jan. 1, 1986. Amended by P.A. 89-42, § 10, eff. Jan. 1, 1996; P.A. 91-357, § 231, eff. July 29, 1999.

Formerly Ill.Rev.Stat.1991, ch. 95 ½, ¶ 18c-1102.

5/18c-1103. State Transportation Policy

§ 18c-1103. State Transportation Policy. It is hereby declared to be the policy of the State of Illinois to actively supervise and regulate commercial transportation of persons and property within this state. This policy shall be carried out in such manner as to: (a) promote adequate, economical, efficient and responsive commercial transportation service, with adequate revenues to carriers and reasonable rates to the public, and without discrimination; (b) recognize and preserve the inherent advantages of, and foster sound economic conditions in, the several modes of commercial transportation in the public interest; (c) develop and preserve a commercial transportation system properly supportive of the broad economic development goals of the State of Illinois; (d) create economic and employment opportunities in commercial transportation and affected industries through economic growth and development; (e) encourage fair wages and safe and suitable working conditions in the transportation industry; (f) protect the public safety through administration of a program of safety standards and insurance; (g) insure a stable and well-coordinated transportation system for shippers, carriers and the public; and (h) cooperate with the federal government, the several states, and with the organizations representing states and commercial transportation service providers and consumers.

P.A. 76-1586, § 18c-1103, added by P.A. 84-796, § 1, eff. Jan. 1, 1986.

Formerly Ill.Rev.Stat.1991, ch. 95 ½, ¶ 18c-1103.

5/18c-1104. Definitions

§ 18c-1104. Definitions. The following terms, when used in this Chapter, have the hereinafter designated meanings unless their context clearly indicates otherwise:

(1) "Broker" means any person other than a motor carrier of property, that arranges, offers to arrange, or holds itself out, by solicitation, advertisement, or otherwise, as arranging or offering to arrange for-hire transportation of property or other service in connection therewith by a motor carrier of

property which holds or is required to hold a license issued by the Commission.

(2) "Carrier" means any motor carrier or rail carrier other than a private carrier.

(3) "Certificate" means a certificate of public convenience and necessity issued under this Chapter to common carriers of household goods.

(4) "Commission" means the Illinois Commerce Commission.

(5) "Commission regulations and orders" means rules and regulations adopted and orders or decisions issued by the Commission pursuant to this Chapter; any certificate, permit, broker's license or other license or registration issued pursuant to such rules, regulations, orders and decisions; and all terms, conditions, or limitations thereof.

(6) (Blank).

(7) (Blank).

(8) (Blank).

(9) "Discrimination" means undue discrimination in the context of the particular mode of transportation involved.

(10) "Farm crossing" means a crossing used for agricultural and livestock purposes only.

(11) "For-hire" means for compensation or hire, regardless of the form of compensation and whether compensation is direct or indirect.

(12) "Freight forwarder" means any person other than a motor carrier, rail carrier, or common carrier by pipeline which holds itself out as a common carrier to provide transportation of property, for compensation or hire, which, in the rendition of its services:

(a) Undertakes responsibility for the consolidation (where applicable), transportation, break-bulk (where applicable), and distribution of such property from the point of receipt to the point of delivery; and

(b) Utilizes, for the transportation of such property, the services of one or more motor carriers or rail carriers.

(13) "Hazardous material" means any substance or material in a quantity and form determined by the federal Office of Hazardous Materials and the Federal Railroad Administration to be capable of posing an unreasonable risk to health, safety, or property when transported in commerce.

(13.1) "Household goods" means:

(A) Personal effects and property used or to be used in a dwelling when a part of the equipment or supply of such dwelling; except that this subdivision (13.1) shall not be construed to include property moving from a factory or store, except such property as the householder has purchased with intent to use in his or her dwelling and that is transported at the request of, and the transportation charges paid to the carrier by, the householder;

(B) Furniture, fixtures, equipment, and the property of stores, offices, museums, institutions, hospitals, or other establishments, when a part of the stock, equipment, or supply of such stores, offices, museums, institutions, hospitals, or other establishments; except that this subdivision (13.1) shall not be construed to include the stock-in-trade of any establishment, whether consignor or consignee, other than used furniture and used fixtures, except when transported as an incident to the moving of the establishment, or a portion thereof, from one location to another; and

(C) Articles, including, but not limited to, objects of art, displays, and exhibits, which, because of their unusual nature or value, require the specialized handling and equipment usually employed in moving household goods; except that this subdivision (13.1) shall not be construed to include any article, whether crated or uncrated, that does not, because of its unusual nature or value, require the specialized handling and equipment usually employed in moving household goods.

(13.2) "Household goods carrier" means a motor carrier of property authorized to transport household goods.

(13.3) "Household goods common carrier" means any household goods carrier engaged in transportation for the general public over regular or irregular routes. Household goods common carriers may also be referred to as "common carriers of household goods".

(13.4) "Household goods contract carrier" means any household goods carrier engaged in transportation under contract with a limited number of shippers (that shall not be freight forwarders, shippers' agents or brokers) that either (a) assigns motor vehicles for a continuing period of time to the exclusive use of the shipper or shippers served, or (b) furnishes transportation service designed to meet the distinct need of the shipper or shippers served. Household goods contract carriers may also be referred to as "contract carriers of household goods".

(14) "Interstate carrier" means any person engaged in the for-hire transportation of persons or property in interstate or foreign commerce in this State, whether or not such transportation is pursuant to authority issued to it by the Interstate Commerce Commission.

(15) "Intrastate carrier" means any person engaged in the for-hire transportation of persons or property in intrastate commerce in this State.

(16) "Interstate commerce" means commerce between a point in the State of Illinois and a point outside the State of Illinois, or between points outside the State of Illinois when such commerce moves through Illinois, or between points in Illinois moving through another state in a bona fide operation that is either exempt from federal regulation or moves under a certificate or permit issued by the Interstate Commerce Commission authorizing interstate transportation, whether such commerce moves wholly by motor vehicle or partly by motor vehicle and partly by any other regulated means of transportation where the commodity does not come to rest or change its identity during the movement, and includes commerce originating or terminating in a foreign country moving through the State of Illinois.

(17) "Intrastate commerce" means commerce moving wholly between points within the State of Illinois, whether such commerce moves wholly by one transportation mode or partly by one mode and partly by any other mode of transportation.

(18) "License" means any certificate, permit, broker's license, or other license issued under this Chapter. For purposes of Article III of Sub-chapter 4 of this Chapter,[1] "license" does not include a "public carrier certificate".

(19) "Motor carrier" means any person engaged in the transportation of property or passengers, or both, for hire, over the public roads of this State, by motor vehicle. Motor carriers engaged in the transportation of property are referred to as "motor carriers of property"; motor carriers engaged in the transportation of passengers are referred to as "motor carriers of passengers" or "bus companies".

(20) "Motor vehicle" means any vehicle, truck, trucktractor, trailer or semitrailer propelled or drawn by mechanical power and used upon the highways of the State in the transportation of property or passengers.

(21) "Non-relocation towing" means the:

(a) For-hire transportation of vehicles by use of wrecker or towing equipment, other than the removal of trespassing vehicles from private property subject to the provisions of Chapter 18a of this Code,[2] and other than transportation exempted by Section 18c–4102; and

(b) For-hire towing of wheeled property other than vehicles.

(22) "Notice" means with regard to all proceedings except enforcement proceedings instituted on the motion of the Commission, and except for interstate motor carrier registrations, public notice by publication in the official state newspaper, unless otherwise provided in this Chapter.

(23) "Official state newspaper" means the newspaper designated and certified to the Commission annually by the Director of Central Management Services of the State of Illinois, or, if said Director fails to certify to the Commission the name and address of the official newspaper selected by the Director prior to expiration of the previous certification, the newspaper designated in the most recent certification.

(24) "Party" means any person admitted as a party to a Commission proceeding or seeking and entitled as a matter of right to admission as a party to a Commission proceeding.

(25) "Permit" means a permit issued under this Chapter to contract carriers of property by motor vehicle.

(26) "Person" means any natural person or legal entity, whether such entity is a proprietorship, partnership, corporation, association, or other entity, and, where a provision concerns the acts or omissions of a person, includes the partners, officers, employees, and agents of the person, as well as any trustees, assignees, receivers, or personal representatives of the person.

(27) "Private carrier by motor vehicle" means any person engaged in the transportation of property or passengers by motor vehicle other than for hire, whether the person is the owner, lessee or bailee of the lading or otherwise, when the transportation is for the purpose of sale, lease, or bailment and in furtherance of the person's primary business, other than transportation. "Private carriers by motor vehicle" may be referred to as "private carriers". Ownership, lease or bailment of the lading is not sufficient proof of a private carrier operation if the carrier is, in fact, engaged in the transportation of property for-hire.

(27.1) "Public carrier" means a motor carrier of property, other than a household goods carrier.

(27.2) "Public carrier certificate" means a certificate issued to a motor carrier to transport property, other than household goods, in intrastate commerce. The issuance of a public carrier certificate shall not be subject to the provisions of Article I of Sub-chapter 2 of this Chapter.[3]

(28) "Public convenience and necessity" shall be construed to have the same meaning under this Chapter as it was construed by the courts to have under the Illinois Motor Carrier of Property Law,[4] with respect to motor carriers of property, and the Public Utilities Act [5] with respect to motor carriers of passengers and rail carriers.

(29) "Public interest" shall be construed to have the same meaning under this Chapter as it was construed by the courts to have under the Illinois Motor Carrier of Property Law.

(30) "Rail carrier" means any person engaged in the transportation of property or passengers for hire by railroad, together with all employees or agents of such person or entity, and all property used, controlled, or owned by such person or entity.

(31) "Railroad" means track and associated structures, including bridges, tunnels, switches, spurs, terminals and other facilities, and equipment, including engines, freight cars, passenger cars, cabooses, and other equipment, used in the transportation of property or passengers by rail.

(32) "Rail yard" means a system of parallel tracks, crossovers and switches where cars are switched and made up into trains, and where cars, locomotives, and other rolling stock are kept when not in use or awaiting repairs. A "rail yard" may also be referred to as a "yard".

(33) "Rate" means every individual or joint rate, fare, toll, or charge of any carrier or carriers, any provisions relating to application thereof, and any tariff or schedule containing rates and provisions. The term "tariff" refers to a publication or document containing motor common carrier rates and provisions or rates and provisions applicable via rail carrier under contracts established pursuant to 49 U.S. Code 10713. The term "schedule" refers to a publication or document containing motor contract carrier rates and provisions.

(34) "Registration" means a registration issued to an interstate carrier.

(35) "Shipper" means the consignor or consignee.

(36) "Terminal area" means, in addition to the area within the corporate boundary of an incorporated city, village, municipality, or community center, the area (whether incorporated or unincorporated) within 10 air miles of the corporate limits of the base city, village, municipality, or community center, including all of any city, village or municipality which lies within such area.

(37) "Transfer" means the sale, lease, consolidation, merger, acquisition or change of control, or other transfer of a license, in whole or in part.

(38) "Transportation" means the actual movement of property or passengers by motor vehicle (without regard to ownership of vehicles or equipment used in providing transportation service) or rail together with loading, unloading, and any other accessorial or ancillary service provided by the carrier in connection with movement by motor vehicle or rail, which is performed by or on behalf of the carriers, its employees or agents, or under the authority or direction of the carrier or under the apparent authority or direction and with the knowledge of the carrier. Transportation of property by motor vehicle includes driveaway or towaway delivery service.

(39) "Towing" means the pushing, towing, or drawing of wheeled property by means of a crane, hoist, towbar, towline, or auxiliary axle.

(40) "Wrecker or towing equipment" means tow trucks or auxiliary axles, when used in relation to towing accidentally wrecked or disabled vehicles; and roll-back carriers or trailers, when used in relation to transporting accidentally wrecked or disabled vehicles. Wrecker or towing equipment does not include car carriers or trailers other than roll-back car carriers or trailers.

P.A. 76–1586, § 18c–1104, added by P.A. 84–796, § 1, eff. Jan. 1, 1986. Amended by P.A. 84–1025, § 2, eff. Jan. 1, 1986; P.A. 84–1311, § 1, eff. Aug. 27, 1986; P.A. 85–553, § 2, eff. Sept. 18, 1987; P.A. 85–963, § 1, eff. July 1, 1988; P.A. 85–1209, Art. II, § 2–51, eff. Aug. 30, 1988; P.A. 89–42, § 10, eff. Jan. 1, 1996; P.A. 89–444, § 5, eff. Jan. 25, 1996; P.A. 90–14, Art. 2, § 2–225, eff. July 1, 1997.

Formerly Ill.Rev.Stat.1991, ch. 95 ½, ¶ 18c–1104.

1 625 ILCS 5/18c–4301 et seq.

2 625 ILCS 5/18a–100 et seq.

3 625 ILCS 5/18c–2101 et seq.

4 625 ILCS 5/18–101 et seq. (repealed).

5 220 ILCS 5/1–101 et seq.

P.A. 90–14, Article 2, of the First 1997 General Revisory Act, resolved multiple actions in the 89th General Assembly and made certain technical corrections in P.A. 89–443 through P.A. 89–707.

ARTICLE II. JURISDICTION AND POWER OF THE COMMISSION

5/18c–1201. Jurisdiction

§ 18c–1201. Jurisdiction. The jurisdiction of the Commission under this Chapter shall extend to for-hire transportation by motor carrier and rail carrier, the activities of brokers, and to other activities specifically enumerated herein, within the State of Illinois, and except as otherwise provided elsewhere in this Chapter shall extend only to intrastate commerce.

P.A. 76–1586, § 18c–1201, added by P.A. 84–796, § 1, eff. Jan. 1, 1986. Amended by P.A. 89–42, § 10, eff. Jan. 1, 1996.

Formerly Ill.Rev.Stat.1991, ch. 95 ½, ¶ 18c–1201.

5/18c–1202. Enumeration of Powers

§ 18c–1202. Enumeration of Powers. The Commission shall have the power to:

(1) Administer and enforce provisions of this Chapter;

(2) Regulate the entry, exit, and services of carriers; as to public carriers, this power is limited to matters relating to insurance and safety standards;

(3) Regulate rates and practices of household goods carriers, rail carriers, passenger carriers, and common carriers by pipeline;

(4) Establish and maintain systems of accounting as well as reporting and record-keeping requirements for household goods carriers, rail carriers, passenger carriers, and common carriers by pipeline;

(5) Establish and maintain systems for the classification of carriers, commodities and services;

(6) Regulate practices, terms and conditions relating to the leasing of equipment and to the interchange of equipment among carriers; as to public carriers, this power is limited to matters relating to insurance and safety standards;

(7) Protect the public safety through insurance and safety standards;

(8) Regulate brokers in accordance with provisions of this Chapter;

(9) Adopt appropriate regulations setting forth the standards and procedures by which it will administer and enforce this Chapter, with such regulations being uniform for all modes of transportation or different for the different modes as will, in the opinion of the Commission, best effectuate the purposes of this Chapter;

(10) Conduct hearings and investigations, on its own motion or the motion of a person;

(11) Adjudicate disputes, hear complaints or other petitions for relief, and settle such matters by stipulation or agreement;

(12) Create special procedures for the receipt and handling of consumer complaints;

(13) Issue certificates describing the extent to which a person is exempt under the provisions of this Chapter;

(14) Construe this Chapter, Commission regulations and orders, except that the rule of ejusdem generis shall not be applicable in the construction or interpretation of any license, certificate or permit originally issued under the Illinois Motor Carrier of Property Law and now governed by subchapter 4 of this Chapter [1] or issued under subchapter 4 of this Chapter prior to July 1, 1989;

(15) Employ such persons as are needed to administer and enforce this Chapter, in such capacities as they are needed, whether as hearings examiners, special examiners, enforcement officers, investigators, or otherwise;

(16) Create advisory committees made up of representatives of the various transportation modes, shippers, receivers, or other members of the public;

(17) Initiate and participate in proceedings in the federal or State courts, and in proceedings before federal or other State agencies, to the extent necessary to effectuate the purposes of this Chapter, provided that participation in specific proceedings is directed, in writing, by the Commission;

(18) Direct any telecommunications carrier to disconnect the telephone number published in any commercial listing of any household goods carrier that does not have a valid license issued by the Commission.

P.A. 76–1586, § 18c–1202, added by P.A. 84–796, § 1, eff. Jan. 1, 1986. Amended by P.A. 85–553, § 2, eff. Sept. 18, 1987; P.A. 86–1005, § 3, eff. Dec. 28, 1989; P.A. 89–444, § 5, eff. Jan. 25, 1996.

Formerly Ill.Rev.Stat.1991, ch. 95 ½, ¶ 18c–1202.

1 Former Ill.Rev.Stat. ch. 95½, ¶ 18–100 et seq. (repealed; see, now, 625 ILCS 5/18c–4101 et seq.).

5/18c–1203. Initial Decisions

§ 18c–1203. Initial Decisions. (1) Delegation of Authority. (a) General Delegation. The power to make an initial decision in all matters under this Chapter and Chapter 18a [1] which are interlocutory or which are not the subject of an active controversy between parties, except in motor carrier of property licensing cases and cases assigned for hearing, is delegated to one or more staff members who shall be designated by the Commission. (b) Delegation to Examiners. The power to make initial decisions shall be vested in the examiner, in all cases assigned for hearing, except in household goods carrier licensing cases.

(2) Form of Decisions. Decisions under this Section shall be by letter notice or directive, signed by the person authorized to make the initial decision. Such notice or directive shall be effective and enforceable in the same manner as an order of the Commission.

(3) Appeal of Initial Decisions. All initial decisions rendered under this Section may be appealed to the Commission. Appeal of interlocutory decisions by an examiner in a case assigned for hearing shall be in accordance with the Commission's Rules of Practice. Appeal of other initial decisions shall be by motion for reconsideration in accordance with Section 18c–2110 of this Chapter.

(4) Enforcement. An initial decision which has not been administratively appealed or the administrative appeal of which has been denied shall be effective and enforceable in the same manner as an order of the Commission.

P.A. 76–1586, § 18c–1203, added by P.A. 85–553, § 2, eff. Sept. 18, 1987. Amended by P.A. 89–444, § 5, eff. Jan. 25, 1996.

Formerly Ill.Rev.Stat.1991, ch. 95 ½, ¶ 18c–1203.

1 625 ILCS 5/18a–100 et seq.

5/18c–1204. Transportation Division

§ 18c–1204. Transportation Division.

(1) Establishment. There shall be established within the staff of the Commission a Transportation Division in which

primary staff responsibility for the administration and enforcement of this Chapter and Chapter 18a shall be vested. The Transportation Division shall be headed by a division manager responsible to the executive director.

(2) Structure. The Transportation Division shall consist of 4 programs and 2 offices. The 4 programs shall be Compliance, Review and Examination, Docketing and Processing, and Rail Safety. Each program shall be headed by a program director and responsible to the division manager, except that in the Compliance Program the 3 staff supervisors shall each be responsible to the division manager. The 2 offices shall be the Office of Transportation Counsel and the Office of the Division Manager. The Office of Transportation Counsel shall be headed by a Chief Counsel responsible to the Division Manager. The Division Manager shall coordinate the activities and responsibilities of the Office of Transportation Counsel with the executive director and the personal assistant serving as staff counsel to the executive director in the office of the executive director, and with the Commission.

(a) The Compliance Program.

(i) The Compliance Program shall consist of a police staff, a rate auditing staff, and a civil penalties staff. These staffs shall be headed by a Chief of Police, a Supervisor of Tariffs and Audits, and a Supervisor of Civil Penalties, respectively.

(ii) The police staff shall be divided into districts with a field office in each district. Each district shall be headed by a working supervisor responsible to the Chief of Police. All staff responsibility for enforcement of this Chapter, except with regard to rail safety, shall be vested in the Compliance Program.

(b) The Review and Examination Program.

(i) Staff responsibility for review of all nonhearing matters under this Chapter and Chapter 18a and examination of all matters assigned for hearing under this Chapter and Chapter 18a shall be vested in the Review and Examination Program, except as otherwise provided in Section 18c–1204b.

(ii) Hearing examiners in the program shall have responsibility for developing a full, complete and impartial record on all issues to be decided in a proceeding; recommending disposition of the issues or making an initial decision on them, as provided in this Chapter; and setting forth in writing the basis for their recommendations or initial decisions. The program director shall be the chief hearing examiner for matters under this Chapter and Chapter 18a with responsibility to insure consistency of recommendations and initial decisions.

(c) The Processing and Docketing Program. All staff responsibility for docketing and processing filings, accounting of receipts and expenditures, issuing, file maintenance and other processing functions under this Chapter and Chapter 18a shall be vested in the Processing Program.

(d) The Rail Safety Program. Staff responsibility for administration and enforcement of the rail safety provisions of this Chapter shall be vested in the Rail Safety Program.

(e) The Office of Transportation Counsel.

(i) All Commission staff responsibility for provision of legal services in connection with any matter under this Chapter, excepting any matter under subchapters 7 and 8 of this Chapter, or in connection with any matter under Chapter 18a shall, except with regard to functions vested in the review and examination program under paragraph (b) of this subsection, be vested exclusively in the Office of Transportation Counsel.

(ii) The Office of Transportation Counsel shall, when directed through the division manager to do so, represent the Commission or Commission staff in administrative or judicial proceedings and render staff advisory opinions to the executive director and the Commission.

(f) Levels of Administration. No additional levels of administration, supervision or authority shall be superimposed, or remain superimposed, between levels prescribed under this Section, and no organizational units may be created within the Transportation Division except as prescribed under this Section.

(3) Additional functions. Staff functions relating to rule-making, policy recommendations and advisory committees under this Chapter and Chapter 18a shall be vested in the Transportation Division.

The staff shall prepare and distribute to the General Assembly, in April of each year, a report on railway accidents in Illinois which involve hazardous materials. The report shall include the location, substance involved, amounts involved, and the suspected reason for each accident. The report shall also reveal the rail line and point of origin of the hazardous material involved in each accident.

P.A. 76–1586, § 18c–1204, added by P.A. 85–553, § 2, eff. Sept. 18, 1987. Amended by P.A. 86–1005, § 3, eff. Dec. 28, 1989; P.A. 86–1166, § 1, eff. Aug. 10, 1990; P.A. 88–415, § 10, eff. Aug. 20, 1993.

Formerly Ill.Rev.Stat.1991, ch. 95 ½, ¶ 18c–1204.

5/18c–1204a. Docketing Procedures

§ 18c–1204a. Docketing Procedures. (1) Mandatory Docketing Requirement. All pleadings filed with the Commission under this Chapter and Chapter 18a shall be docketed in a timely manner.

(2) Staff Objections. If staff believes a pleading filed with the Commission under this Chapter and Chapter 18a to be defective in any respect, it may file its objection with the Commission in writing, provided a copy of the objection is simultaneously served on the person who filed the pleading and 15 days are allowed for the filing of a reply. The Commission may, if it finds that the pleading is defective, either dismiss the proceeding or permit amendment of the pleading, provided that intervenors are permitted adequate time after amendment to prepare for continuation of the proceeding.

P.A. 76–1586, § 18c–1204a, added by P.A. 85–553, § 2, eff. Sept. 18, 1987.

Formerly Ill.Rev.Stat.1991, ch. 95 ½, ¶ 18c–1204a.

5/18c–1204b. Certification of Records

§ 18c–1204b. Certification of Records. Copies of all official documents and orders filed or deposited according to the law in the office of the Commission under this Chapter or Chapter 18a, certified by the director of the processing and docketing program to be true copies of the originals, under the official seal of the Commission, shall be evidence in like manner as the originals.

P.A. 76–1586, § 18c–1204b, added by P.A. 85–553, § 2, eff. Sept. 18, 1987.

Formerly Ill.Rev.Stat.1991, ch. 95 ½, ¶ 18c–1204b.

5/18c–1204c. Independent Review of Decisions on Administrative Appeal

§ 18c–1204c. Independent Review of Decisions on Administrative Appeal. (1) Requirement of Independent Review. Except as otherwise provided in subsection (3) of this Section:

(a) Review of Staff Decisions. No decision made by other than the Commission shall be reviewed on administrative appeal by the person or board which made the decision, unless the appeal requests review by the person or board which made the decision.

(b) Review of Commission or Employee Board Decisions. No decision made by the Commission or an employee board shall be reviewed on administrative appeal by the person or board which made the formal recommendation pursuant to which the decision was made, unless the appeal requests review by the person or board which made the formal recommendation.

(2) Independent Review Board. (a) Establishment of an Independent Review Board. The Commission shall establish an Independent Review Board which shall review motions for rehearing and reconsideration which do not request review by the person or board which made the decision or the formal recommendation pursuant to which the decision was made.

(b) Composition of the Independent Review Board. The Board shall consist of 3 members appointed by the Commission, one of whom shall be designated as the chairman. The Commission shall appoint the members from Commission staff whose expenses may be allocated to the Transportation Regulatory Fund under Section 18c–1603. If the Transportation Division is not represented on the Board by a voting member, the Commission shall appoint a nonvoting member from the Transportation Division.

(c) Functions of the Independent Review Board. The Board shall review all motions presented to it under this Section. The Board may, in its discretion, review the record of the proceeding and hear oral argument by the parties. The Board shall recommend a decision by the Commission. If a Board member dissents from the recommendation, any dissenting opinion supplied by the member shall be attached.

(3) Applicability of Section. The provisions of this Section shall not apply to any matter arising under Subchapter 7 of this Chapter.

P.A. 76–1586, § 18c–1204c, added by P.A. 85–553, § 2, eff. Sept. 18, 1987. Amended by P.A. 86–1005, § 3, eff. Dec. 28, 1989.

Formerly Ill.Rev.Stat.1991, ch. 95 ½, ¶ 18c–1204c.

5/18c–1204d. Staff participation

§ 18c–1204d. Staff participation. (1) General Provisions. Except as otherwise provided in this Section, Commission staff participation in the administration or enforcement of this Law in a supervisory, advisory, or other capacity shall be limited to personnel whose expenses are, in whole or in part, allocable to the Transportation Regulatory Fund.

(2) Exceptions. The provisions of subsection (1) of this Section shall not apply to:

(a) Staff of the office of chairman and commissioners serving as personal assistants or clerical support to the members;

(b) Members of the Independent Review Board serving on the effective date of this amendatory Act of 1989, while serving in their current capacities; or

(c) Commission staff other than the staff of the office of chairman and commissioners participating in proceedings involving subchapters 5, 6, 7 or 8 of this Chapter.

P.A. 76–1586, § 18c–1204d, added by P.A. 86–1005, § 3, eff. Dec. 28, 1989.

Formerly Ill.Rev.Stat.1991, ch. 95 ½, ¶ 18c–1204d.

5/18c–1204e. Communications with the Office of Chairman and Commissioners

§ 18c–1204e. Communications with the Office of Chairman and Commissioners. (1) The chairman, members and executive director shall jointly adopt and adhere to written procedures concerning communication with staff of the Transportation Division to insure that:

(a) Communications from the members or staff of the office of chairman and commissioners which do not require substantial work from staff shall be transmitted to the manager of the Transportation Division; and

(b) Communications from the members or staff of the office of chairman and commissioners which do require substantial work from staff shall be transmitted to the executive director.

(2) The executive director shall establish written procedures, which staff other than staff of the office of chairman and commissioners shall adhere to, in regard to communications of such staff to the chairman, members or staff of the office of chairman and commissioners.

P.A. 76–1586, § 18c–1204e, added by P.A. 86–1005, § 3, eff. Dec. 28, 1989.

Formerly Ill.Rev.Stat.1991, ch. 95 ½, ¶ 18c–1204e.

5/18c–1205. Qualifications of Transportation Compliance Program Staff

§ 18c–1205. Qualifications of Transportation Compliance Program Staff.

(1) General provisions. The manager of the Transportation Division shall establish and adhere to written professional standards and procedures for the employment, education and training, performance and dismissal of all nonclerical compliance program personnel. Such standards and procedures shall include:

(a) Merit standards and procedures, and education requirements, applicable to State troopers, and training requirements at least equivalent to that received from a police training school approved by the Illinois Law Enforcement Training Standards Board, together with such additional qualifications as are needed under this Chapter, for all nonclerical field operations personnel;

(b) Successful completion of an accredited accounting or transportation-related education program, or at least 4 years experience in motor carrier rate analysis or auditing, plus such additional qualifications as are needed under this Chapter, for all nonclerical rate auditing personnel; and

(c) Successful completion of an accredited legal or paralegal education program, or equivalent administrative law experience, plus such additional qualifications as are needed under this Chapter, for all nonclerical civil penalties program personnel.

(2) Merit Selection Committee. Standards and procedures under this Section for police shall include the establishment of one or more merit selection committees, each composed of one Commission employee and no fewer than 3, nor more than 5, persons who are not employed by the Commission, each of whom shall from time to time be designated by

the division manager, subject to the approval of the Commission. The division manager shall submit a list of candidates to the committee or subcommittee thereof for its consideration. The committee or subcommittee thereof shall interview each candidate on the list and rate those interviewed as "most qualified", "qualified", or "not qualified". The committee shall recommend candidates rated "most qualified" and "qualified" to the division manager. In filling positions to which this Section applies, the division manager shall first offer the position to persons rated "most qualified". If all persons rated "most qualified" have been offered the position and each failed to accept the offer within the time specified by the division manager in the offer, the position may be offered to a person rated "qualified". Only persons rated "most qualified" or "qualified" shall be offered positions within the Compliance Program.

(3) The Commission shall authorize to each employee of the Commission exercising the powers of a peace officer a distinct badge that, on its face, (i) clearly states the badge is authorized by the Commission and (ii) contains a unique identifying number. No other badge shall be authorized by the Commission.

P.A. 76-1586, § 18c-1205, added by P.A. 85-553, § 2, eff. Sept. 18, 1987. Amended by P.A. 86-1005, § 3, eff. Dec. 28, 1989; P.A. 88-415, § 10, eff. Aug. 20, 1993; P.A. 89-444, § 5, eff. Jan. 25, 1996; P.A. 91-357, § 231, eff. July 29, 1999; P.A. 91-883, § 105, eff. Jan. 1, 2001.

Formerly Ill.Rev.Stat.1991, ch. 95 ½, ¶ 18c-1205.

P.A. 91-883 incorporated the amendment by P.A. 91-357.

ARTICLE III. EMPLOYEE BOARDS

5/18c-1301. Employee Boards Generally

§ 18c-1301. Employee Boards Generally. The Commission may, except as expressly provided in this Section, delegate one or more of its functions under this Chapter to Transportation Employee Boards. The Commission shall reserve to itself the function of making transportation policy. The Board shall be subject, in its deliberations, to all restraints which would govern the Commission if such functions had not been delegated to a Board, and to such other restraints as the Commission may by regulation prescribe. All decisions delegated to an Employee Board shall be appealable to the Commission.

P.A. 76-1586, § 18c-1301, added by P.A. 84-796, § 1, eff. Jan. 1, 1986.

Formerly Ill.Rev.Stat.1991, ch. 95 ½, ¶ 18c-1301.

5/18c-1302. Members of Employee Boards

§ 18c-1302. Members of Employee Boards. (1) Appointment of Members. Each board shall have 3 members. Members of employee boards established under provisions of this Article shall be appointed by the Commission. When any member is unable to act upon any matter before a Board because of absence, conflict, or other cause, and a qualified alternate appointed by the Commission is available, such alternate shall be called upon to serve on the Board. If no qualified alternate is available, the Chairman of the Commission may designate another qualified employee to serve temporarily until a member appointed by the Commission is available to serve.

(2) Qualification of Members. The Commission or its Chairman may, subject to limitations set forth in this Section, appoint any manager, section chief, examiner, attorney, or other qualified professional employee to serve on an Employee Board, either as a regular member or as an alternate member. No Employee Board member shall participate in any decision in which such person has a pecuniary or other direct interest. No 3 sitting members of an Employee Board shall be employed in the same division of the Commission.

P.A. 76-1586, § 18c-1302, added by P.A. 84-796, § 1, eff. Jan. 1, 1986. Amended by P.A. 86-1166, § 1, eff. Aug. 10, 1990.

Formerly Ill.Rev.Stat.1991, ch. 95 ½, ¶ 18c-1302.

5/18c-1303. Conduct of Employee Board Proceedings

§ 18c-1303. Conduct of Employee Board Proceedings. A majority of an Employee Board shall constitute a quorum for the transaction of business. Decisions on matters before an Employee Board shall be by majority vote of members present. Any party may appear before an Employee Board and be heard, in person or by representative, to the extent such party would be permitted to appear and be heard before the Commission itself. Each meeting of an Employee Board shall be a public meeting. Every vote and official act of an Employee Board shall be entered of record, and such records shall be made public on request.

P.A. 76-1586, § 18c-1303, added by P.A. 84-796, § 1, eff. Jan. 1, 1986.

Formerly Ill.Rev.Stat.1991, ch. 95 ½, ¶ 18c-1303.

5/18c-1304. Orders of Employee Boards

§ 18c-1304. Orders of Employee Boards. Employee Board orders shall be served, in writing, on all parties to the proceeding in which the order is entered. Such orders shall contain, in addition to the decision of the Board, a statement of findings, conclusions, or other reasons therefore. Employee Board decisions and orders shall have the same force and effect, and may be made, issued, and evidenced in the same manner, as if the decision had been made and the order issued by the Commission itself. The filing of a timely motion for reconsideration shall, unless otherwise provided by the Commission, stay the effect of an Employee Board order pending reconsideration.

P.A. 76-1586, § 18c-1304, added by P.A. 84-796, § 1, eff. Jan. 1, 1986.

Formerly Ill.Rev.Stat.1991, ch. 95 ½, ¶ 18c-1304.

ARTICLE IV. MODIFICATION OF STANDARDS AND PROCEDURES

5/18c-1401. Modification of Standards and Procedures in Response to Preemptive Federal Legislation

§ 18c-1401. Modification of Standards and Procedures in Response to Preemptive Federal Legislation. The Commission may, except with regard to licensing and ratemaking standards for motor carriers of property or passengers, conform its standards and procedures to the standards and procedures in a valid, preemptive federal statute where the provisions of this Chapter are in conflict with and would otherwise be preempted by such statute, any other provision of this Chapter notwithstanding.

P.A. 76-1586, § 18c-1401, added by P.A. 84-796, § 1, eff. Jan. 1, 1986.

Formerly Ill.Rev.Stat.1991, ch. 95 ½, ¶ 18c-1401.

5/18c–1402. Interim Rulemaking

§ 18c–1402. Interim Rulemaking. The Commission may, by publishing interim rules in the official state newspaper and simultaneously initiating rulemaking proceedings in accordance with the Administrative Procedure Act: [1]

(1) Modify its standards and procedures in accordance with Section 18c–1401 of this Chapter; or

(2) Modify its procedures in accordance with this Chapter in response to other circumstances impacting on the jurisdiction of the Commission in the field of transportation which are not of the Commission's own making but which necessitate adoption or amendment of regulations prior to the completion of normal rulemaking proceedings pursuant to the Illinois Administrative Procedure Act. Nothing in this subsection shall be construed to permit modification of licensing or ratemaking standards for motor carriers of property or passengers.

Such interim rules shall remain in effect only until regulations are adopted in accordance with the Administrative Procedure Act.

P.A. 76–1586, § 18c–1402, added by P.A. 84–796, § 1, eff. Jan. 1, 1986.

Formerly Ill.Rev.Stat.1991, ch. 95 ½, ¶ 18c–1402.

[1] 5 ILCS 100/1–1 et seq.

ARTICLE V. FEES AND TAXES

5/18c–1501. Franchise, Franchise Renewal, Filing and Other Fees for Motor Carriers of Property

§ 18c–1501. Franchise, Franchise Renewal, Filing and Other Fees for Motor Carriers of Property. (1) Franchise, Franchise Renewal, Filing, and Other Fee Levels in Effect Absent Commission Regulations Prescribing Different Fee Levels. The levels of franchise, franchise renewal, filing, and other fees for motor carriers of property in effect, absent Commission regulations prescribing different fee levels, shall be:

(a) Franchise and franchise renewal fees: $19 for each motor vehicle operated by a motor carrier of property in intrastate commerce, and $2 for each motor vehicle operated by a motor carrier of property in interstate commerce.

(b) Filing fees: $100 for each application seeking a Commission license or other authority, the reinstatement of a cancelled license or authority, or authority to establish a rate, other than by special permission, excluding both released rate applications and rate filings which may be investigated or suspended but which require no prior authorization for filing; $25 for each released rate application and each application to register as an interstate carrier; $15 for each application seeking special permission in regard to rates; and $15 for each equipment lease.

(2) Adjustment of Fee Levels. The Commission may, by rulemaking in accordance with provisions of The Illinois Administrative Procedure Act,[1] adjust franchise, franchise renewal, filing, and other fees for motor carriers of property by increasing or decreasing them from levels in effect absent Commission regulations prescribing different fee levels. Franchise and franchise renewal fees prescribed by the Commission for motor carriers of property shall not exceed:

(a) $50 for each motor vehicle operated by a household goods carrier in intrastate commerce;

(a–5) $5 for each motor vehicle operated by a public carrier in intrastate commerce; and

(b) $7 for each motor vehicle operated by a motor carrier of property in interstate commerce.

(3) Late–Filing Fees.

(a) Commission to Prescribe Late–Filing Fees. The Commission may prescribe fees for the late filing of proof of insurance, operating reports, franchise or franchise renewal fee applications, or other documents required to be filed on a periodic basis with the Commission.

(b) Late-filing Fees to Accrue Automatically. Late-filing fees shall accrue automatically from the filing deadline set forth in Commission regulations, and all persons or entities required to make such filings shall be on notice of such deadlines.

(c) Maximum Fees. Late-filing fees prescribed by the Commission shall not exceed $100 for an initial period, plus $10 for each day after the expiration of the initial period. The Commission may provide for waiver of all or part of late-filing fees accrued under this subsection on a showing of good cause.

(d) Effect of Failure to Make Timely Filings and Pay Late–Filing Fees. Failure of a person to file proof of continuous insurance coverage or to make other periodic filings required under Commission regulations shall make licenses and registrations held by the person subject to revocation or suspension. The licenses or registrations cannot thereafter be returned to good standing until after payment of all late-filing fees accrued and not waived under this subsection.

(4) Payment of Fees.

(a) Franchise and Franchise Renewal Fees. Franchise and franchise renewal fees for motor carriers of property shall be due and payable on or before the 31st day of December of the calendar year preceding the calendar year for which the fees are owing, unless otherwise provided in Commission regulations.

(b) Filing and Other Fees. Filing and other fees (including late-filing fees) shall be due and payable on the date of filing, or on such other date as is set forth in Commission regulations.

(5) When Fees Returnable.

(a) Whenever an application to the Illinois Commerce Commission is accompanied by any fee as required by law and such application is refused or rejected, said fee shall be returned to said applicant.

(b) The Illinois Commerce Commission may reduce by interlineation the amount of any personal check or corporate check or company check drawn on the account of and delivered by any person for payment of a fee required by the Illinois Commerce Commission.

(c) Any check altered pursuant to above shall be endorsed by the Illinois Commerce Commission as follows: "This check is warranted to subsequent holders and to the drawee to be in the amount $____."

(d) All applications to the Illinois Commerce Commission requiring fee payment upon reprinting shall contain the following authorization statement: "My signature authorizes the Illinois Commerce Commission to lower the amount of check if fee submitted exceeds correct amount."

P.A. 76–1586, § 18c–1501, added by P.A. 84–796, § 1, eff. Jan. 1, 1986. Amended by P.A. 85–553, § 2, eff. Sept. 18, 1987; P.A. 86–1005, § 3, eff. Dec. 28, 1989; P.A. 89–444, § 5, eff. Jan. 25, 1996.

Formerly Ill.Rev.Stat.1991, ch. 95 ½, ¶ 18c–1501.

[1] 5 ILCS 100/1–1 et seq.

5/18c-1502. Gross Receipts Taxes For Motor Carriers of Passengers and Rail Carriers

§ 18c-1502. Gross Receipts Taxes For Motor Carriers of Passengers and Rail Carriers. Each motor carrier of passengers and rail carrier shall pay to the Commission, in accordance with Sections 2-202, 3-120 and 3-121 of "The Public Utilities Act", as amended,[1] a gross receipts tax in the amount provided herein.

The amount of the tax for motor carriers of passengers shall be prescribed by the Commission by rulemaking in accordance with provisions of The Illinois Administrative Procedure Act,[2] and shall not exceed 0.1% of the carrier's gross Illinois intrastate revenues for each calendar year.

The amount of the tax for rail carriers shall be 0.15% of the carrier's gross Illinois intrastate revenues for each calendar year.

P.A. 76-1586, § 18c-1502, added by P.A. 84-796, § 1, eff. Jan. 1, 1986. Amended by P.A. 84-1025, § 2, eff. Jan. 1, 1986; P.A. 85-6, § 1, eff. June 30, 1987; P.A. 85-553, § 2, eff. Sept. 18, 1987; P.A. 85-1209, Art. II, § 2-51, eff. Aug. 30, 1988; P.A. 89-42, § 10, eff. Jan. 1, 1996; P.A. 89-699, § 15, eff. Jan. 16, 1997.

Formerly Ill.Rev.Stat.1991, ch. 95 ½, ¶ 18c-1502.

[1] 220 ILCS 5/2-202, 5/3-120, and 5/3-121.

[2] 5 ILCS 100/1-1 et seq.

P.A. 89-699 incorporated the amendment by P.A. 89-42.

5/18c-1502.05. Route Mileage Fee for Rail Carriers

§ 18c-1502.05. Route Mileage Fee for Rail Carriers. Beginning with calendar year 1997, every rail carrier shall pay to the Commission for each calendar year a route mileage fee of $37 for each route mile of railroad right of way owned by the rail carrier in Illinois. The fee shall be based on the number of route miles as of January 1 of the year for which the fee is due, and the payment of the route mileage fee shall be due by February 1 of each calendar year.

P.A. 76-1586, § 18c-1502.05, added by P.A. 89-699, § 15, eff. Jan. 16, 1997.

5/18c-1502.10. Railroad-Highway Grade Crossing and Grade Separation Fee

§ 18c-1502.10. Railroad-Highway Grade Crossing and Grade Separation Fee. Beginning with calendar year 1997, every rail carrier shall pay to the Commission for each calendar year a fee of $23 for each location at which the rail carrier's track crosses a public road, highway, or street, whether the crossing be at grade, by overhead structure, or by subway. The fee shall be based on the number of the crossings as of January 1 of each calendar year, and the fee shall be due by February 1 of each calendar year.

P.A. 76-1586, § 18c-1502.10, added by P.A. 89-699, § 15, eff. Jan. 16, 1997.

5/18c-1503. Legislative Intent

§ 18c-1503. Legislative Intent. It is the intent of the Legislature that the exercise of powers under Sections 18c-1501 and 18c-1502 of this Chapter shall not diminish revenues to the Commission, and that any surplus or deficit of revenues in the Transportation Regulatory Fund, together with any projected changes in the cost of administering and enforcing this Chapter, should be considered in establishing or adjusting fees and taxes in succeeding years. The Commission shall administer fees and taxes under this Chapter in such a manner as to insure that any surplus generated or accumulated in the Transportation Regulatory Fund does not exceed the surplus accumulated in the Motor Vehicle Fund during fiscal year 1984, and shall adjust the level of such fees and taxes to insure compliance with this provision.

P.A. 76-1586, § 18c-1503, added by P.A. 84-796, § 1, eff. Jan. 1, 1986.

Formerly Ill.Rev.Stat.1991, ch. 95 ½, ¶ 18c-1503.

5/18c-1504. Reciprocity

§ 18c-1504. Reciprocity. The Commission may enter into agreements with agencies in other jurisdictions for the reciprocal waiver of motor carrier fees or taxes administered by the Commission, and may revoke such agreements where another jurisdiction does not extend reciprocal treatment to carriers based in the State of Illinois. The Commission may, in addition, and notwithstanding any other provision of this Chapter, prescribe fees for carriers based in jurisdictions other than the State of Illinois equal to fees charged to Illinois carriers by such other jurisdictions.

P.A. 76-1586, § 18c-1504, added by P.A. 84-796, § 1, eff. Jan. 1, 1986.

Formerly Ill.Rev.Stat.1991, ch. 95 ½, ¶ 18c-1504.

5/18c-1505. Proration of Fees

§ 18c-1505. Proration of Fees. The Commission may prorate fees and levies provided in this Chapter throughout the calendar year.

P.A. 76-1586, § 18c-1505, added by P.A. 84-796, § 1, eff. Jan. 1, 1986.

Formerly Ill.Rev.Stat.1991, ch. 95 ½, ¶ 18c-1505.

ARTICLE VI. TRANSPORTATION REGULATORY FUND

5/18c-1601. Deposit of Monies into the Transportation Regulatory Fund

§ 18c-1601. Deposit of Monies into the Transportation Regulatory Fund.

(1) Deposit of Fees, Taxes, and Monies Other Than Criminal Fines. All fees, penalties (other than criminal penalties) or monies collected in settlement of enforcement proceedings, taxes, and other monies collected under this Chapter or which are transferred, appropriated or reimbursed to the Commission for the purpose of administering and enforcing this Chapter, shall be promptly paid into a special fund in the State treasury known as the Transportation Regulatory Fund.

(2) Accounting for Monies Received. The Commission shall account separately for the receipt of monies from the following classes:

(a) motor carriers of property (other than carriers engaged in nonrelocation towing);

(b) rail carriers; and

(c) other monies.

The Commission may account separately with regard to groups of persons within the foregoing classes.

(3) Deposit of criminal fines. Criminal fines collected under this Chapter from motor carriers of property or persons or entities found to have aided or abetted motor carriers of property or passengers in violation of this Chapter shall be disposed of in accordance with Section 16-105 of this Code. Other criminal fines collected under this Chapter

shall be deposited into the Transportation Regulatory Fund in accordance with subsection (1) of this Section.

(4) (Blank).

P.A. 76-1586, § 18c-1601, added by P.A. 84-796, § 1, eff. Jan. 1, 1986. Amended by P.A. 85-7, § 1, eff. June 30, 1987; P.A. 85-553, § 2, eff. Sept. 18, 1987; P.A. 85-1209, Art. II, § 2-51, eff. Aug. 30, 1988; P.A. 87-838, § 155, eff. Jan. 24, 1992; P.A. 90-372, Art. 10, § 10-125, eff. July 1, 1998.

Formerly Ill.Rev.Stat.1991, ch. 95 ½, ¶ 18c-1601.

5/18c-1602. Appropriations from the Transportation Regulatory Fund

§ 18c-1602. Appropriations from the Transportation Regulatory Fund. (1) Appropriation of Monies. Appropriations from the Transportation Regulatory Fund shall be separately identified both in the Commission's appropriations request and the Act by which appropriations from the Fund are made.

(2) Authorization of Staff Positions. Authorized staff positions to be funded with monies appropriated from the Transportation Regulatory Fund shall be separately identified in the Commission's appropriations request.

(3) Appropriations and Authorizations Not Transferable. Appropriations from the Transportation Regulatory Fund shall be used only for the administration and enforcement of this Chapter and Chapter 18a. Such appropriations and authorized headcount may be transferred within the Transportation Regulatory Fund, but may not be transferred to any other fund.

P.A. 76-1586, § 18c-1602, added by P.A. 85-553, § 2, eff. Sept. 18, 1987.

Formerly Ill.Rev.Stat.1991, ch. 95 ½, ¶ 18c-1602.

5/18c-1603. Expenditures from the Transportation Regulatory Fund

§ 18c-1603. Expenditures from the Transportation Regulatory Fund. (1) Authorization of Expenditures from the Fund. Monies deposited in the Transportation Regulatory Fund shall be expended only for the administration and enforcement of this Chapter and Chapter 18a.

(2) Allocation of Expenses to the Fund. (a) Expenses Allocated Entirely to the Transportation Regulatory Fund. All expenses of the Transportation Division shall be allocated to the Transportation Regulatory Fund, provided that they were:

(i) Incurred by and for staff employed within the Transportation Division and accountable, directly or through a program director or staff supervisor, to the Transportation Division manager;

(ii) Incurred exclusively in the administration and enforcement of this Chapter and Chapter 18a; and

(iii) Authorized by the Transportation Division manager.

(b) Expenses Partially Allocated to the Transportation Regulatory Fund. A portion of expenses for the following persons and activities may be allocated to the Transportation Regulatory Fund:

(i) The Executive Director, his deputies and personal assistants, and their clerical support;

(ii) The legislative liaison activities of the Office of Legislative Affairs, its constituent elements and successors;

(iii) The activities of the Administrative Services Division on the effective date of this amendatory Act of 1987, exclusive of the Chief Clerk's office;

(iv) The payroll expenses of Commissioners' assistants;

(v) The internal auditor; and

(vi) The in-state travel expenses of the Commissioners to and from the offices of the Commission.

(c) Allocation Methodology for Expenses Other Than Administrative Services Division and Commissioners' Assistants. The portion of total expenses (other than Administrative Services Division and commissioners' assistants' expenses) allocated to the Transportation Regulatory Fund under paragraph (b) of this subsection shall be the lessor of:

(i) The portion of staff time spent exclusively on administration and enforcement of this Chapter and Chapter 18a, as shown by a time study updated at least once each 6 months; and

(ii) The percentage of total authorized Commission staff for the fiscal year which is employed in Transportation Division (based on the average for the fiscal year).

(d) Allocation Methodology for Expenses of Administration Services Division. The portion of expenses for Administrative Services Division allocated to the Transportation Regulatory Fund under paragraph (b) of this subsection shall not exceed:

(i) The portion allocable under paragraph (c) of this subsection, for staff payroll expenses; and

(ii) The portion used exclusively in the administration and enforcement of this Chapter and Chapter 18a, for other than staff payroll expenses.

(e) Allocation methodology for Commissioners' Assistants Expenses. Five percent of the payroll expenses of commissioners' assistants may be allocated to the Transportation Regulatory Fund.

(f) Expenses not allocable to the Transportation Regulatory Fund. No expenses shall be allocated to or paid from the Transportation Regulatory Fund except as expressly authorized in paragraphs (a) through (e) of this subsection. In particular, no expenses shall be allocated to the Fund which were incurred by or in relation to the following persons and activities:

(i) Commissioners' travel, except as otherwise provided in paragraphs (b) and (c) of this subsection;

(ii) Commissioners' assistants except as otherwise provided in paragraphs (b) and (e) of this subsection;

(iii) The Policy Analysis and Research Division, its constituent elements and successors;

(iv) The Chief Clerk's office, its constituent elements and successors;

(v) The Hearing Examiners Division, its constituent elements and successors, and any hearing examiners or hearings conducted, in whole or in part, outside the Transportation Division;

(vi) The Public Affairs Group, its constituent elements and successors;

(vii) The Office of General Counsel, its constituent elements and successors, including but not limited to the Office of Public Utility Counsel and any legal staff in the office of the executive director, but not including the personal assistant serving as staff counsel to the executive director as provided in Section 18c-1204(2) and the Office of Transportation Counsel; and

(viii) Any other expenses or portion thereof not expressly authorized in this subsection to be allocated to the Fund.

The constituent elements of the foregoing shall, for purposes of this Section, be their constituent elements on the effective date of this amendatory Act of 1987.

(3) Allocation of Expenses Within the Fund. (a) Monies deposited in the Transportation Regulatory Fund shall be expended only in the regulation of that class of persons as defined in subsection (2) of Section 18c-1601 of this Chapter from or in relation to which the monies were received.

(b) Expenses incurred exclusively in relation to one class shall be allocated to that class and no other.

(c) A portion of each expense incurred in relation to more than one class may be allocated to each of the involved classes based on time study or actual use, provided that the portion allocated to any class shall not exceed the maximum specified in paragraph (d) of this subsection.

(d) Total expenses allocated to any one class under paragraph (c) of this subsection shall not exceed the amount which bears the same percentage relationship to expenses allocated to that class under paragraph (b) of this subsection ((c) divided by (b)) as total expenses allocated to all classes under paragraph (b) bear to total expenses allocated to all classes under paragraph (c) ((c) divided by (b)).

(4) Effective Date of Section. The Commission shall have 180 calendar days from the effective date of this amendatory Act of 1987 to comply fully with this Section.

P.A. 76-1586, § 18c-1603, added by P.A. 85-553, § 2, eff. Sept. 18, 1987. Amended by P.A. 86-1005, § 3, eff. Dec. 28, 1989.

Formerly Ill.Rev.Stat.1991, ch. 95 ½, ¶ 18c-1603.

5/18c-1604. Annual Report of Expenditures

§ 18c-1604. Annual Report of Expenditures. The Commission shall, within 60 calendar days after the end of each fiscal year, submit to the Governor and the General Assembly a report of the following for such fiscal year:

(1) All monies deposited in the Transportation Regulatory Fund, showing the total and subtotals by class as defined in subsection (2) of Section 18c-1601 of this Chapter;

(2) All expenditures from the Transportation Regulatory Fund, showing the total and the sub-totals by class as defined in subsection (2) of Section 18c-1601 of this Chapter;

(3) A listing and description by function of all staff positions actually funded, in whole or in part, at any time during the fiscal year, from the Transportation Regulatory Fund; and

(4) The methods used to allocate expenses between the Transportation Regulatory Fund and other funds, and between classes within the Transportation Regulatory Fund.

P.A. 76-1586, § 18c-1604, added by P.A. 85-553, § 2, eff. Sept. 18, 1987.

Formerly Ill.Rev.Stat.1991, ch. 95 ½, ¶ 18c-1604.

ARTICLE VII. VIOLATIONS OF THE LAW

5/18c-1701. Violations Defined

§ 18c-1701. Violations Defined. Each person who fails to comply, in whole or in part, with any provision of this Chapter, Commission regulations or orders shall have committed a violation of this Chapter. Likewise, any person who aids or abets another in such failure to comply shall have committed a violation of this Chapter. The agent of a carrier shall not be found to have aided or abetted in violation of this Chapter where the act of the agent was required by this Chapter, Commission regulations or orders. The act or omission of any officer, employee, or agent within the scope of such person's office, employment or agency shall be deemed the act or omission of the business entity; such entity shall be named as the party defendant or respondent and the officer, employee, or agent shall not be held liable. Failure to comply with more than one provision of this Chapter or regulations or orders hereunder shall constitute multiple violations. Each day's continuance of a violation shall constitute a separate violation.

P.A. 76-1586, § 18c-1701, added by P.A. 84-796, § 1, eff. Jan. 1, 1986.

Formerly Ill.Rev.Stat.1991, ch. 95 ½, ¶ 18c-1701.

5/18c-1702. Responsibility for Enforcement

§ 18c-1702. Responsibility for Enforcement. It shall be the duty of the Commission and of the State Police and the Secretary of State to conduct investigations, make arrests, and take any other action necessary for the enforcement of this Chapter.

P.A. 76-1586, § 18c-1702, added by P.A. 84-796, § 1, eff. Jan. 1, 1986.

Formerly Ill.Rev.Stat.1991, ch. 95 ½, ¶ 18c-1702.

5/18c-1703. Investigations and Arrests

§ 18c-1703. Investigations and Arrests. (1) Enforcement Officers and Investigators. Enforcement officers and investigators appointed by the Commission shall have, and may exercise throughout the state, all the powers of police officers when enforcing provisions of this Chapter, subject to the regulations and orders of the Commission.

(2) Investigations.

(a) General Provisions. The Commission, through its employees, shall conduct such investigations as are necessary for the enforcement of this Chapter.

(b) Examination, Audit and Production of Records. Authorized employees of the Commission shall have the power at any and all times to examine, audit, or demand production of all accounts, books, records, memoranda, and other papers in the possession or control of a license or registration holder, its employees or agents. In addition, every person other than a license or registration holder and every officer, employee or agent of such person shall permit every authorized employee of the Commission, upon administrative subpoena issued by the Chairman or his designee or the Attorney General, to inspect and copy any accounts, books, records, memoranda, letters, checks, vouchers, telegrams, documents, or other papers in its possession or control which the Commission deems necessary to the proper conduct of an investigation to determine whether provisions of this Chapter, Commission regulations or orders, have been violated.

(c) Inspection of Equipment and Facilities. Authorized employees of the Commission shall have the power at all times to inspect the equipment, facilities, and other property of the licensee in the possession or control of a carrier or broker, its employees or agents.

(d) Special Investigations. The Commission may also conduct special investigations as necessary for the enforcement of this Chapter. Where such person is found by the Commission to have violated this Chapter, and where the Commission imposes a sanction for such violation under Section 18c-1704 of this Chapter, the Commission may impose on such person an assessment of reasonable expenses incurred by the Commission in the investigation and subsequent proceeding. Such assessment shall not exceed a fee of $100 per work day or $50 per half work day, per employee, for the payroll costs of the Commission staff, plus actual transportation (in accordance with applicable state employee travel expense reimbursement regulations) and all other actual expenses incurred in the special investigation and subsequent proceeding.

(3) Arrests and Citations. The Commission shall make arrests and issue notices of civil violations where necessary for the enforcement of this Chapter. No rail carrier employee shall be arrested for violation of this Chapter. No person operating a motor vehicle in violation of the licensing or safety provisions of this Chapter shall be permitted to transport property or passengers beyond the point of arrest unless, in the opinion of the officer making the arrest, it is necessary to transport the property or passengers to another location to insure their safety or to preserve or tend cargo carried in the vehicle.

P.A. 76–1586, § 18c–1703, added by P.A. 84–796, § 1, eff. Jan. 1, 1986. Amended by P.A. 85–553, § 2, eff. Sept. 18, 1987.

Formerly Ill.Rev.Stat.1991, ch. 95 ½, ¶ 18c–1703.

5/18c-1704. Sanctions

§ 18c–1704. Sanctions. Each violation of this Chapter shall subject the violator to the following sanctions, except as otherwise provided elsewhere in this Chapter. Sanctions provided for in this Section may be imposed by the Commission only in compliance with the notice and hearing requirements of Section 18c–2102 of this Chapter.

(1) Criminal Misdemeanor Penalties. Each violation of this Chapter shall constitute a Class C misdemeanor.

(2) Civil Penalties. The Commission may assess, against any person found by it to have violated this Chapter, a civil penalty not greater than $1,000 nor less than $100 per violation. The penalty assessed by the Commission shall reflect the number and severity of violations found to have been committed. Penalties assessed by the Commission shall be enforced by any court having venue in enforcement cases under this Chapter.

(3) Cease and Desist Orders. The Commission may, where a person is found after hearing to have violated this Chapter, Commission regulations or orders, and justice requires, order the person to cease and desist from further or from any future violations. A cease and desist order may be entered on the Commission's own motion or by agreement between the parties. Orders and agreements under this Section shall be valid and enforceable for the period stated therein, not to exceed 2 years from the date the order or agreement is approved by the Commission, unless the parties stipulate otherwise. Such orders and agreements shall be enforceable in any court of this State having venue and jurisdiction in enforcement actions under this Chapter. Failure to comply with a Commission cease and desist order shall constitute a violation of this Chapter separate and apart from any underlying violations.

(4) Stipulated Settlements.

(a) General Provisions. The Commission may accept a reasonable monetary settlement, suspension or revocation of a license or registration, or any other reasonable terms stipulated between the respondent and staff, with or without a finding of violations.

(b) Presumption of Reasonableness. Such stipulations shall be presumed reasonable. Unless the terms of a stipulation exceed such parameters as the Commission may establish, this presumption is rebuttable only by evidence of record at hearing.

(c) Parameters. Parameters for settlement shall be based on type of violation; severity, as measured by revenues from unlawful activities; and number of violations. Minimum settlement amounts may be established.

(d) Orders. Orders suspending proposed settlements shall cite reasons for suspension which are specific to the case. Orders rejecting proposed settlements shall recite the grounds on which the settlements are found to be unreasonable and describe the evidence which supports such findings.

(5) Injunctive Relief. Any court with jurisdiction and venue for purposes of enforcing this Chapter shall have the power to enjoin any person from committing violations of this Chapter. Suit for penalties shall not be a prerequisite to injunctive relief. No bond shall be required when injunctive relief is granted at the request of the Commission.

(6) Suspension or Revocation of Licenses and Registrations.

(a) Availability of Suspension and Revocation as Sanctions. Violation of this Chapter by a motor carrier of property or passengers shall, in addition to other sanctions provided herein, subject the violator to suspension or revocation of any or all Commission licenses and registrations. The Commission may impose the sanctions of suspension and revocation. Where the violation is failure of a motor carrier of property or passengers to have in effect and file proof of continuous insurance coverage in accordance with this Chapter, Commission regulations and orders, the license or registration or both may be suspended by telephonic or telegraphic directive, confirmed by certified or registered mail or personal service, pending final disposition of revocation proceedings.

(b) Suspension Pending Adjudication. Where the violation is failure of a motor carrier of property to pay a franchise or franchise renewal fee, the license or registration or both may be suspended by certified or registered mail or personally served directive, pending final disposition of revocation proceedings.

(c) Special Revocation Procedures.

(i) Notice. The Commission shall serve notice upon all persons who have failed to pay a franchise tax, license fee, or penalty required under the Business Corporation Act of 1983,[1] or who have failed to comply with this Chapter, Commission regulations and orders, regarding the filing of proof of continuous insurance or bond coverage, the payment of periodic fees, the filing of periodic reports, the payment of civil penalties, or the filing of rates to the full extent of a carrier's authority. The notice shall advise such person of the apparent violations and state that, unless the Commission receives a written request for hearing or extension of time within 30 days from the date the notice is served, the person's license or registration will be revoked by operation of law without further action by the Commission.

(ii) Extensions of Time. The Commission may grant one extension of time not exceeding 60 days where the extension will not endanger the public.

(iii) Request for Hearing. If a timely written request for hearing is received, no further action shall be taken until the requirements of Section 18c–2102 of this Chapter have been satisfied.

(iv) Revocation by Operation of Law. If, at the expiration of the applicable time period, the person has not complied with the pertinent requirements, and a written request for hearing has not been received, the person will be deemed to have waived hearing and the license or registration shall be revoked by operation of law without further action by the Commission as if the Commission has served an order on the date following expiration revoking the license or registration.

(7) Probation. The Commission may probate the imposition of any of the sanctions set forth in this Section.

P.A. 76-1586, § 18c-1704, added by P.A. 84-796, § 1, eff. Jan. 1, 1986. Amended by P.A. 85-553, § 2, eff. Sept. 18, 1987; P.A. 86-1286, § 1, eff. Sept. 6, 1990; P.A. 88-415, § 10, eff. Aug. 20, 1993.

Formerly Ill.Rev.Stat.1991, ch. 95 ½, ¶ 18c-1704.

1 805 ILCS 5/1.01 et seq.

5/18c-1705. Expedited Enforcement Procedures

§ 18c-1705. Expedited Enforcement Procedures. The Commission shall, within 60 days from the effective date of this amendatory Act of 1987, implement expedited administrative enforcement procedures.

(a) Initiation of Administrative Enforcement Proceedings. The Transportation Division Manager or his designee shall have the power to issue, or refuse to issue, a notice or citation instituting an administrative enforcement proceeding.

(b) Settlement of Enforcement Proceedings by Stipulation.

(i) Power to Negotiate Settlements. The Transportation Division Manager or his designee shall have the power to negotiate and sign proposed settlements of enforcement proceedings by written stipulation.

(ii) Review and Acceptance of Stipulations. The Commission shall provide for any appropriate and necessary review of proposed settlements within 30 days after a stipulation is signed by the parties. Unless a stipulation is suspended for review by order of the Commission served within 30 calendar days after it was signed by the parties, it shall be deemed accepted by operation of law. A stipulation which has been suspended for review shall likewise be deemed accepted by operation of law unless it is rejected by order of the Commission served within 45 days after it was suspended. A stipulation which is deemed accepted under this sub-paragraph shall become effective and shall be enforceable in the same manner as an order of the Commission.

(iii) Administrative Appeal of Settlements. Administrative appeal of a stipulation which has been approved by order of the Commission or by operation of law shall be by motion for rehearing or reconsideration in accordance with Section 18c-2110 of this Chapter. The right to administratively appeal a settlement may be waived by written stipulation.

P.A. 76-1586, § 18c-1705, added by P.A. 85-553, § 2, eff. Sept. 18, 1987. Amended by P.A. 86-1005, § 3, eff. Dec. 28, 1989; P.A. 86-1166, § 1, eff. Aug. 10, 1990; P.A. 91-357, § 231, eff. July 29, 1999.

Formerly Ill.Rev.Stat.1991, ch. 95 ½, ¶ 18c-1705.

ARTICLE VIII. SERVICE OF NOTICES, ORDERS AND PROCESS

5/18c-1801. Persons Who May Be Served

§ 18c-1801. Persons Who May be Served. It shall be the responsibility of each person subject to the licensing or ratemaking provisions of this Chapter to keep on file with the Commission the name of a person upon whom notices, orders, or process in administrative or judicial proceedings under this Chapter may be served, together with a current address within the State of Illinois at which such person may be served. The Commission shall maintain a file of such "agents for service of process." Service of any Commission notice, order, or process on the agent for service of process at the address shown in the file shall be conclusively presumed to be service on the carrier, broker, or other person. If a person fails to make the filing required herein, the person may be served at the most current address in other records of the Commission, or at the address on file with the Secretary of State for service of process, and the same conclusive presumption shall apply.

P.A. 76-1586, § 18c-1801, added by P.A. 84-796, § 1, eff. Jan. 1, 1986.

Formerly Ill.Rev.Stat.1991, ch. 95 ½, ¶ 18c-1801.

5/18c-1802. Time of Service

§ 18c-1802. Time of Service. Notices, orders, process and other correspondence of the Commission shall be deemed served at the time they are deposited in the United States mail or delivered to a commercial delivery service or delivered in person by an employee or agent of the Commission. Notices, orders, process and other correspondence shall be deemed served on the Commission at the time of receipt.

P.A. 76-1586, § 18c-1802, added by P.A. 84-796, § 1, eff. Jan. 1, 1986.

Formerly Ill.Rev.Stat.1991, ch. 95 ½, ¶ 18c-1802.

SUB-CHAPTER 2. PROCEEDINGS BEFORE THE COMMISSION AND THE COURTS

ARTICLE I. ADMINISTRATIVE PROCEEDINGS BEFORE THE COMMISSION

ARTICLE II. JUDICIAL REVIEW PROCEEDINGS

ARTICLE III. ADMINISTRATIVE AND JUDICIAL ENFORCEMENT PROCEEDINGS

ARTICLE I. ADMINISTRATIVE PROCEEDINGS BEFORE THE COMMISSION

5/18c–2101. Hearings in household goods carrier licensing cases

§ 18c–2101. Hearings in household goods carrier licensing cases. (1) Hearing required. The Commission shall issue orders in household goods carrier licensing cases only after notice and hearing in accordance with the rules of practice applicable to proceedings under this Chapter.

(2) Hearing not required. Hearing shall be required in household goods carrier licensing cases, except as provided in Sections 18c–2107 and 18c–4306 of this Chapter.

P.A. 76–1586, § 18c–2101, added by P.A. 84–796, § 1, eff. Jan. 1, 1986. Amended by P.A. 85–553, § 2, eff. Sept. 18, 1987; P.A. 89–444, § 5, eff. Jan. 25, 1996.

Formerly Ill.Rev.Stat.1991, ch. 95 ½, ¶ 18c–2101.

5/18c–2102. Hearings in other than household goods carrier authority cases

§ 18c–2102. Hearings in other than household goods carrier authority cases. (1) Hearing required. Except as otherwise provided in subsection (2) of this Section, and in Section 18c–2108 of this Chapter the Commission shall, in other than household goods carrier authority cases, issue orders granting authority or other relief, prescribing rates, imposing sanctions, or directing that a person take, continue to take, refrain from taking or cease and desist from continuing to take any action, only after notice and hearing in accordance with the rules of practice applicable to proceedings under this Chapter.

(2) Hearing not required. Except as otherwise provided in Section 18c–2108 of this Chapter, the Commission may, in other than household goods carrier authority cases, conduct its review and issue orders without hearing, the taking of evidence, or the making of a record where action taken in the order:

(a) Was not opposed in a timely pleading addressed to the Commission;

(b) Was opposed in a timely pleading, but such opposition was later withdrawn or the parties in opposition waived further hearing and taking of evidence;

(c) Was taken on an emergency temporary or interim basis in accordance with Section 18c–2108 of this Chapter; or

(d) Is interlocutory in nature.

(3) Section not applicable to household goods carrier authority cases. Nothing in this Section shall have application to any household goods carrier authority case.

P.A. 76–1586, § 18c–2102, added by P.A. 84–796, § 1, eff. Jan. 1, 1986. Amended by P.A. 89–444, § 5, eff. Jan. 25, 1996.

Formerly Ill.Rev.Stat.1991, ch. 95 ½, ¶ 18c–2102.

5/18c–2103. Rules of Practice

§ 18c–2103. Rules of Practice. (1) General Provisions. The Commission shall adopt General and Special rules of practice to govern administrative proceedings under this Chapter. Such rules shall be designed to effectuate the purposes of this Chapter. Rules of practice heretofore issued by the Commission shall be the rules of practice applicable under this Chapter unless changed, repealed, or supplemented by the Commission.

(2) Verification of Pleadings. Unless otherwise expressly provided therein, the signature on any pleading, document, or other paper filed with the Commission on which a verification or oath is required under applicable statutes or regulations shall constitute the verification or oath of the signatory and no further verification or oath shall be required. False verification or oath shall be a violation of this Chapter.

P.A. 76–1586, § 18c–2103, added by P.A. 84–796, § 1, eff. Jan. 1, 1986.

Formerly Ill.Rev.Stat.1991, ch. 95 ½, ¶ 18c–2103.

5/18c–2104. Rules of Evidence

§ 18c–2104. Rules of Evidence. The rules of evidence which apply in civil cases before the circuit courts of this State shall, except as otherwise provided herein, apply to proceedings before the Commission under this Chapter. Evidence not admissible under the rules of evidence applicable in civil courts may be admitted if it is of a type commonly relied upon by prudent persons in the conduct of their affairs. Objections must be made at hearing to preserve them on appeal. Evidence may be received orally or in writing.

P.A. 76–1586, § 18c–2104, added by P.A. 84–796, § 1, eff. Jan. 1, 1986.

Formerly Ill.Rev.Stat.1991, ch. 95 ½, ¶ 18c–2104.

5/18c–2105. Discovery

§ 18c–2105. Discovery. (1) Discovery Generally. Any party may utilize written interrogatories, depositions, requests for discovery or inspection of documents or property and other discovery tools commonly utilized in civil actions in the circuit courts in the State of Illinois in the manner contemplated by the Code of Civil Procedure[1] and the Rules of the Supreme Court of Illinois; except that discovery must be completed by the 30th day after the party filed its petition for leave to intervene, unless the period of discovery is extended by agreement of the parties or by the Commission. The Chairman or a hearing examiner may, at any time, on his own motion or at the request of a party, issue such rulings denying, limiting, conditioning, or regulating discovery as justice requires, and may supervise all or part of any discovery procedure. Parties to proceedings before the Commission are encouraged to clarify and resolve issues where possible through the use of pre-hearing discovery. However, discovery order should be calculated to lessen the time and expense required to reach an informed resolution of the issues.

(2) Subpoenas. The Chairman or a hearing examiner may, for good cause, issue a subpoena directing a person to appear and testify, and to produce records, documents, or other papers, at a time and place set forth in the subpoena, in connection with a proceeding before the Commission. Service of the subpoena shall be in the same manner as a subpoena issued by a court. The Commission may, on its own motion or the motion of a person served with a subpoena, quash the subpoena, in whole or in part.

(3) Appeal from Discovery and Subpoenas. A person served with a discovery request or subpoena may appeal such interlocutory matter to the Commission. Such appeals shall set forth grounds for seeking to quash or limit the scope of the discovery or subpoena, as well as the specific relief sought, and must be filed within 10 days after service of the discovery or subpoena. If discovery is stayed by the Commission, the person served shall be excused from compliance with the discovery order or subpoena until a decision on its appeal is made by the Commission.

(4) Assessment and Payment of Discovery Costs. The Commission may assess the costs of discovery, including fees for witness attendance and travel, against the party by which discovery was requested. Where a subpoena is issued on the Commission's own motion, fees for witness attendance and travel shall be paid by the Commission on request. Witness fees shall be the same as for a circuit court proceeding. Deposits to insure payment of costs and fees may be required.

(5) Enforcement of Discovery Procedures. The Commission may, where a person has failed to comply with or permit discovery authorized hereunder, determine any or all issues within the scope of the discovery or subpoena adverse to such person without further evidence. The Commission may, in addition, assess civil penalties under Article VII of Subchapter 1 of this Chapter for such violator for contempt and may assess the costs of enforcement, both before the Commission and before the court, against the violator.

P.A. 76–1586, § 18c–2105, added by P.A. 84–796, § 1, eff. Jan. 1, 1986.

Formerly Ill.Rev.Stat.1991, ch. 95 ½, ¶ 18c–2105.

1 735 ILCS 5/1–101 et seq.

5/18c–2106. Standing

§ 18c–2106. Standing. (1) General Provisions. Each person with an administratively cognizable interest in a proceeding before the Commission shall, upon compliance with procedural rules adopted by the Commission for such proceedings, be entitled to appear and participate as a party to the proceeding. The Commission may, in addition, grant leave to appear and participate on such terms as it may prescribe, where to do so would assist the Commission in reaching an informed and just decision in the proceeding.

(2) Definition of Administratively Cognizable Interest. The following persons or entities shall be deemed to have an administratively cognizable interest in proceedings under this Chapter:

(a) Licensing Proceedings. A person shall be deemed to have an administratively cognizable interest in a proceeding in which an application for a new, amended, or extended intrastate license is under consideration only if:

(i) The person possesses a license authorizing all or part of the service for which authority is sought, such license is in good standing, and the person has transported or actively solicited traffic or both within the scope of the application during the 12 month period immediately preceding initiation of the proceeding; or

(ii) The proceeding involves an application for a household goods carrier license and the person is an organization representing employees of a household goods carrier .

(b) Rate Proceedings. A person shall be deemed to have an administratively cognizable interest in a proceeding in which new or amended rates are under consideration only if the person is:

(i) A carrier authorized to transport traffic such as would be subject to or affected by the rates;

(ii) A shipper or receiver of traffic such as would be subject to or affected by the rates;

(iii) An association of two or more carriers, acting at the request of and on behalf of one or more carriers authorized to transport traffic such as would be subject to or affected by the rates; or an association of two or more shippers or receivers acting at the request of and on behalf of one or more shippers or receivers of such traffic; or

(iv) An organization representing employees of a household goods carrier.

(c) Proceedings to Transfer a License. A person shall be deemed to have an administratively cognizable interest in a proceeding to transfer an intrastate license only if the person:

(i) Has an ownership interest in or control of the license which is the subject of the proceeding;

(ii) Would, if the proposed transfer is approved, acquire ownership or control of the license which is the subject of the proceeding;

(iii) Possesses a license authorizing all or part of the service authorized by the license sought to be transferred, such license is in good standing, and the person or entity has transported or actively solicited traffic within the scope of the license sought to be transported during the 12 months period immediately preceding initiation of the proceeding;

(iv) Would be directly affected by the transfer; or

(v) Is an organization representing employees of a household goods carrier.

(d) Complaint and Enforcement Proceedings. A person shall be deemed to have an administratively cognizable interest in a complaint proceeding if the person:

(i) Has an ownership interest in or control of the license which is the subject of the proceeding;

(ii) Would be directly and adversely affected by failure to grant relief sought in the complaint or enforcement action and such adverse effect is contrary to the purposes of this Chapter; or

(iii) Is an organization representing employees of a household goods carrier of property.

(e) All Proceedings. Notwithstanding the provisions of subsections (2)(a) through (2)(d) of this Section, a person shall be deemed to have an administratively cognizable interest in a proceeding other than a complaint proceeding if the person:

(i) Filed the pleading pursuant to which the proceeding was initiated; or

(ii) Is an organization representing employees of a household goods carrier.

P.A. 76–1586, § 18c–2106, added by P.A. 84–796, § 1, eff. Jan. 1, 1986. Amended by P.A. 85–553, § 2, eff. Sept. 18, 1987; P.A. 89–444, § 5, eff. Jan. 25, 1996.

Formerly Ill.Rev.Stat.1991, ch. 95 ½, ¶ 18c–2106.

5/18c–2107. Orders in household goods carrier authority proceedings

§ 18c–2107. Orders in household goods carrier authority proceedings. (1) Emergency Proceedings Orders. The Commission may, on request, and upon a finding that urgent and immediate public need requires emergency temporary action, issue orders granting emergency temporary relief in household goods carrier authority proceedings. The Commission shall promptly post notice of any such request at a prominent location at the Commission offices in Springfield and Chicago, and where action affecting a specific named person is requested shall promptly notify the person by telephone or telegram. Such orders may be issued without hearing and shall remain in effect pending notice and hearing in accordance with subsection (1) of Section 18c–2101 of this Chapter, but shall not remain in effect for a period exceeding 45 days from issuance, and shall not be renewed or extended. Any person in opposition to such relief shall be entitled, on request, to an oral hearing on the request for emergency temporary relief. The filing or granting of a request for an oral hearing shall not, unless the Commission so provides, stay the issuance or effect of any emergency temporary order under this subsection.

(2) Interim orders. The Commission may, on request, issue interim orders for temporary authority in household goods carrier authority proceedings making temporary disposition of issues in a proceeding after notice and review of verified supporting statements. Such orders shall remain in effect pending final disposition in accordance with Section 18c–2101 of this Chapter unless otherwise provided in the interim order or the interim order is modified or rescinded by the Commission. Any person in opposition to such relief shall be entitled, on request, to an oral hearing on the request for temporary relief. The filing or granting of such a request for an oral hearing shall not, unless the Commission so provides, stay the issuance or effect of any interim order under this subsection. A request for oral hearing on a request for interim relief shall, unless otherwise specified by the party making the request for oral hearing, be construed as a request for oral hearing on the application for permanent relief as well.

(3) Final Orders. Final orders shall be issued in household goods carrier of property authority proceedings only after an oral hearing.

P.A. 76–1586, § 18c–2107, added by P.A. 84–796, § 1, eff. Jan. 1, 1986. Amended by P.A. 89–444, § 5, eff. Jan. 25, 1996.

Formerly Ill.Rev.Stat.1991, ch. 95 ½, ¶ 18c–2107.

5/18c–2108. Orders in other than household goods carrier authority and enforcement proceedings

§ 18c–2108. Orders in other than household goods carriers authority and enforcement proceedings.

(1) Emergency Orders. The Commission may, on request, and upon a finding that urgent and immediate public need requires emergency temporary action, issue orders granting emergency temporary relief in other than household goods carrier authority or enforcement cases. The Commission shall promptly post notice of any such request at a prominent location at the Commission offices in Springfield and Chicago, and where action affecting a specific named person is requested shall promptly notify the person by telephone or telegram. Such orders may be issued without hearing and shall remain in effect pending notice and hearing in accordance with subsection (1) of Section 18c–2101 of this Chapter, but shall not remain in effect for a period exceeding 45 days from issuance, and shall not be renewed or extended. Any person in opposition to such relief shall be entitled, on request, to an oral hearing on the request for emergency temporary relief. The filing or granting of such request for oral hearing shall not, unless the Commission so provides, stay the issuance or effect of any emergency temporary order under this subsection.

(2) Interim Orders. The Commission may, on request, issue interim orders making temporary disposition of issues in a proceeding, other than a household goods carrier authority or enforcement proceeding, after notice and hearing on written submissions. Such orders shall remain in effect pending final disposition in accordance with Section 18c–2102 of this Chapter unless otherwise provided in the interim order or the interim order is modified or rescinded by the Commission. Any person in opposition to such relief shall be entitled, on request, to an oral hearing on the request for temporary relief. The filing or granting of such a request for oral hearing shall not, unless the Commission so provides, stay the issuance or effect of any interim order under this subsection. A request for oral hearing on a request for temporary relief shall, unless otherwise specified by the party making the request for oral hearing, be construed as a request for oral hearing on the application for permanent relief as well.

(3) Final orders. Any party to a proceeding before the Commission shall be entitled, on timely written request, to an oral hearing prior to issuance of a final order in the proceeding. Where the Commission has issued an interim order and no timely request for oral hearing has been filed or is pending, the Commission may issue a final order without oral hearing, except in household goods carrier authority proceedings.

(4) Section not applicable to household goods carrier authority proceedings. Nothing in this Section shall have application to any household goods carrier authority proceeding.

P.A. 76–1586, § 18c–2108, added by P.A. 84–796, § 1, eff. Jan. 1, 1986. Amended by P.A. 89–444, § 5, eff. Jan. 25, 1996; P.A. 92–651, § 77, eff. July 11, 2002.

Formerly Ill.Rev.Stat.1991, ch. 95 ½, ¶ 18c–2108.

5/18c–2109. Prompt Final Disposition of Proceedings

§ 18c–2109. Prompt Final Disposition of Proceedings. The Commission shall consider matters properly before it in the most expeditious manner possible, and in no case shall the final order resolving matters in a proceeding be entered later than the 90th day following the close of oral hearing. Proceedings may be reassigned in order to expedite consideration and disposition.

P.A. 76–1586, § 18c–2109, added by P.A. 84–796, § 1, eff. Jan. 1, 1986. Amended by P.A. 85–553, § 2, eff. Sept. 18, 1987.

Formerly Ill.Rev.Stat.1991, ch. 95 ½, ¶ 18c–2109.

5/18c–2110. Reconsideration, Rehearing and Reopening of Proceedings

§ 18c–2110. Reconsideration, Rehearing and Reopening of Proceedings. (1) Motions for Rehearing or Reconsideration.

(a) Who May File Motions. Any party of record to an administrative proceeding before the Commission may file a motion administratively appealing the action or inaction of the Commission, Employee Board, or Commission staff.

(b) Relief Which May Be Sought. A motion may request modification or rescission of a Commission or Employee Board order, or of the action or inaction of the Commission, Employee Board, or Commission staff; the Commission or Employee Board may likewise request such relief.

(c) To Whom Motions May Be Addressed. If the order appealed is a nonfinal order of an Employee Board, the motion may be addressed to the Board or to the Commission; otherwise, the motion must be addressed to the Commission.

(d) Deadline For Filing Motions. The motion must be filed within 30 days after service of the order, or of the action or inaction appealed, unless the time for filing a motion is extended by the Commission in writing.

(e) Style and Contents of Motions. The motion must set forth specific grounds for modification or rescission of the order. Appeals from orders issued by the Commission, or from the action or inaction of the Commission shall be styled "motions for rehearing;" appeals from orders of an Employee Board, or from the action or inaction of Employee Board or staff, shall be styled "motions for reconsideration."

(f) Grant or Denial of Motions. The Commission may grant or deny such motions, in whole or in part. If the Commission grants such a motion a new order shall be issued within 180 days after service of the order granting the motion unless the order granting the motion also disposed of the issues in the proceeding and is therefore a final, appealable order. If the Commission fails to act on any such motion within 45 days after it is filed, or up to 90 days if the period for acting on the motion has been extended by the Commission in writing, the motion shall be deemed to have been denied by operation of law.

(g) Appeals of Rulings by Hearing Examiners. Notwithstanding any other provision of this Section, interlocutory appeals of rulings by hearing examiners shall be as provided by the Commission's Rules of Practice; no other appeals of action or inaction by a hearing examiner may be taken.

(2) Motions to Reopen. The Commission may, at any time after notice to the parties and the public, reopen a proceeding to consider clarification, modification, or rescission of its order. Reopening may be on the Commission's own motion or on the motion of any interested person. Upon a finding of clerical or technical error the Commission may modify or rescind its order in the proceeding. The Commission may not, on reopening, impair the vested rights of any person.

P.A. 76–1586, § 18c–2110, added by P.A. 84–796, § 1, eff. Jan. 1, 1986. Amended by P.A. 84–1025, § 2, eff. Jan. 1, 1986; P.A. 85–553, § 2, eff. Sept. 18, 1987.

Formerly Ill.Rev.Stat.1991, ch. 95 ½, ¶ 18c–2110.

ARTICLE II. JUDICIAL REVIEW PROCEEDINGS

5/18c–2201. Availability of Judicial Review

§ 18c–2201. Availability of Judicial Review. (1) Standing to Seek Judicial Review. No person shall have standing to seek judicial review of a Commission action unless such person shall have an administratively cognizable interest in the order, be aggrieved by it, and have exhausted its administrative remedies. A person admitted as a party to an administrative proceeding shall be presumed to have an administratively cognizable interest in orders issued in the proceeding for purposes of standing to seek judicial review.

(2) Exhaustion of Administrative Remedies. A person shall be deemed to have exhausted its administrative remedies only if:

(a) The person participated as a party to the proceeding before the Commission, or filed a timely pleading seeking to participate as a party and was entitled as matter of right to participate as a party;

(b) The person filed a timely motion for reconsideration or rehearing which was denied by the Commission or by operation of law, unless the Commission expressly waived the filing of such a motion; and

(c) The action of which judicial review is sought is, in all respects, a final order of the Commission.

(3) Deadline for Filing Petitions for Judicial Review. A petition for judicial review must be filed within 35 days after the order of the Commission becomes final.

(4) Remedy Exclusive. Judicial review as provided for under this Article shall be exclusive of all other remedies at law or equity in regard to review of Commission actions, regulations or orders.

P.A. 76–1586, § 18c–2201, added by P.A. 84–796, § 1, eff. Jan. 1, 1986. Amended by P.A. 84–1025, § 2, eff. Jan. 1, 1986.

Formerly Ill.Rev.Stat.1991, ch. 95 ½, ¶ 18c–2201.

5/18c–2202. Scope of Judicial Review

§ 18c–2202. Scope of Judicial Review. (1) Issues on Review. The reviewing court shall be limited in its review to whether:

(a) The Commission's order is against the manifest weight of evidence in the record before the Commission;

(b) The order is contrary to provisions of this Chapter or Commission regulations;

(c) The order is an abuse of discretion;

(d) The order is beyond the jurisdiction of the Commission; or

(e) The order denies constitutional rights of the person seeking judicial review.

(2) Record on Review. In reviewing an order of the Commission, the court shall be limited to issues of fact or law presented to the Commission in either a motion for reconsideration or a motion for rehearing, and to:

(a) Evidence in the record before the Commission;

(b) Evidence offered but erroneously excluded by the Commission from the record; and

(c) Evidence of procedural irregularities which could not, with reasonable diligence, have been offered, either at the administrative hearing or in the motion for reconsideration or rehearing.

P.A. 76–1586, § 18c–2202, added by P.A. 84–796, § 1, eff. Jan. 1, 1986.

Formerly Ill.Rev.Stat.1991, ch. 95 ½, ¶ 18c–2202.

5/18c–2203. Submission of the Administrative Record

§ 18c–2203. Submission of the Administrative Record. It shall be the responsibility of the Commission to submit to the court certified copies of the record before the Commission. The record submitted must be complete in all respects unless all parties have, by written stipulation, agreed to deletion of materials not relevant to the issues raised in the petition for judicial review. The cost of preparing certified copies of the record may be assessed, in whole or in part, to the party seeking judicial review, and failure to pay such costs shall be grounds for dismissal in accordance with the Illinois Administrative Review Law.[1]

P.A. 76–1586, § 18c–2203, added by P.A. 84–796, § 1, eff. Jan. 1, 1986.

Formerly Ill.Rev.Stat.1991, ch. 95 ½, ¶ 18c–2203.

[1] 735 ILCS 5/3–101 et seq.

5/18c–2204. Relief

§ 18c–2204. Relief. The reviewing court may grant relief in accordance with provisions of the Illinois Administrative Review Law.[1]

P.A. 76–1586, § 18c–2204, added by P.A. 84–796, § 1, eff. Jan. 1, 1986.

Formerly Ill.Rev.Stat.1991, ch. 95 ½, ¶ 18c–2204.

[1] 735 ILCS 5/3–101 et seq.

5/18c–2205. Stay of Action Pending Judicial Review

§ 18c–2205. Stay of Action Pending Judicial Review. (1) Commission Orders Not Stayed by Filing of Appeal. The filing or pendency of a petition for judicial review shall not of itself stay, suspend, restrain or enjoin the operation of a rule, regulation, order or decision of the Commission.

(2) Power of Court to Stay Commission Orders. During the pendency of a petition for judicial review the reviewing court in its discretion may, except as provided in this subsection, stay, suspend, restrain or enjoin, in whole or in part, the operation of a Commission regulation or order. No order staying, suspending, restraining or enjoining a Commission regulation or order shall be made by the court except upon 3 days' actual notice to the Commission and the Attorney General and after hearing. Where the Commission action relates to enforcement of this Chapter, the reviewing court shall not stay, suspend, restrain or enjoin the action of the Commission for a period longer than 180 days from the filing of the appeal; unless at the expiration of the initial 180 day period, the court finds that continuation is necessary for the informed and just resolution of the issues; and unless the court does continue the stay, suspension, restraint, or injunction in effect for one or more definite periods of time not to exceed 180 days each.

(3) Bond Required. In case an action, regulation or order of the Commission is stayed, suspended, restrained, or enjoined, the order of the court shall not become effective until a bond shall first have been executed and filed with and approved by the court, except as otherwise provided in this paragraph. Where the order under review does not relate to enforcement of this law, the court may, for good cause, waive the requirement of a bond.

P.A. 76–1586, § 18c–2205, added by P.A. 84–796, § 1, eff. Jan. 1, 1986.

Formerly Ill.Rev.Stat.1991, ch. 95 ½, ¶ 18c–2205.

5/18c–2206. Application of Illinois Administrative Review Law

§ 18c–2206. Application of the Illinois Administrative Review Law.[1] Where this Article is silent, proceedings for judicial review of a Commission action, regulation or order shall be governed by provisions of the Administrative Review Law.

P.A. 76–1586, § 18c–2206, added by P.A. 84–796, § 1, eff. Jan. 1, 1986.

Formerly Ill.Rev.Stat.1991, ch. 95 ½, ¶ 18c–2206.

[1] 735 ILCS 5/3–101 et seq.

ARTICLE III. ADMINISTRATIVE AND JUDICIAL ENFORCEMENT PROCEEDINGS

5/18c–2301. Initiation of Proceedings

§ 18c–2301. Initiation of Proceedings. The Commission may initiate either administrative or judicial proceedings, or both, to enforce provisions of this Chapter, and Commission regulations and orders. In addition, any interested person may apply to a circuit court, which has jurisdiction and venue as set out in this Chapter, for injunctive relief to enforce provisions of Sub-Chapter 4 of this Chapter, and Commission regulations and orders issued pursuant to Sub-Chapter 4.

P.A. 76–1586, § 18c–2301, added by P.A. 84–796, § 1, eff. Jan. 1, 1986.

Formerly Ill.Rev.Stat.1991, ch. 95 ½, ¶ 18c–2301.

5/18c–2302. Governing Procedures

§ 18c–2302. Governing Procedures. Administrative enforcement proceedings initiated hereunder shall be governed by the Commission's rules of practice. Judicial enforcement proceedings initiated hereunder shall be governed by the rules of procedure applicable in the courts of this State.

P.A. 76–1586, § 18c–2302, added by P.A. 84–796, § 1, eff. Jan. 1, 1986.

Formerly Ill.Rev.Stat.1991, ch. 95 ½, ¶ 18c–2302.

ARTICLE IV. VENUE AND JURISDICTION

5/18c–2401. Venue and Jurisdiction in Actions for Judicial Review

§ 18c–2401. Venue and Jurisdiction in Actions for Judicial Review. (1) Venue. Actions for judicial review under this Chapter may be filed in the circuit courts of Sangamon or Cook Counties.

(2) Jurisdiction. Jurisdiction in actions for judicial review under this Chapter shall be vested in the circuit courts of Sangamon and Cook Counties.

P.A. 76–1586, § 18c–2401, added by P.A. 84–796, § 1, eff. Jan. 1, 1986.

Formerly Ill.Rev.Stat.1991, ch. 95 ½, ¶ 18c–2401.

5/18c–2402. Venue and Jurisdiction in Actions to Enforce this Chapter

§ 18c–2402. Venue and Jurisdiction in Actions to Enforce this Chapter.

(a) Venue in Suits for Criminal Misdemeanor Penalties. Actions in which criminal misdemeanor penalties are sought may be brought in the county where any part of the subject matter is located, or part of the violation(s) occurred, or the arrest was made, and venue shall lie in that county; the case may be transferred to another county only with the approval of the court and the agreement of the parties.

(b) Venue in Actions Other Than Suits for Criminal Penalties. Actions to enforce this Chapter, Commission regulations and orders, other than suits for criminal misdemeanor penalties, may be brought in the circuit courts of any county in which any part of the subject matter is located, or any part of the violation(s) occurred; the case may be transferred to another county only with the approval of the court and the agreement of the parties.

P.A. 76–1586, § 18c–2402, added by P.A. 84–796, § 1, eff. Jan. 1, 1986. Amended by P.A. 85–553, § 2, eff. Sept. 18, 1987; P.A. 91–357, § 231, eff. July 29, 1999.

Formerly Ill.Rev.Stat.1991, ch. 95 ½, ¶ 18c–2402.

SUB–CHAPTER 3. SUBSTANTIVE PROVISIONS APPLICABLE TO MORE THAN ONE TRANSPORTATION MODE

ARTICLE I. LICENSING

Section

ARTICLE II. RATEMAKING

ARTICLE III. OTHER PROVISIONS COMMON TO ALL TRANSPORTATION MODES

ARTICLE I. LICENSING

5/18c–3101. Terms, Conditions, and Limitations

§ 18c–3101. Terms, Conditions, and Limitations. The Commission may attach to the exercise of rights under any license or other authorization issued or granted by it such terms, conditions, and limitations as will protect the public interest and effectuate the purposes of this Chapter.

P.A. 76–1586, § 18c–3101, added by P.A. 84–796, § 1, eff. Jan. 1, 1986.

Formerly Ill.Rev.Stat.1991, ch. 95 ½, ¶ 18c–3101.

5/18c–3102. Geographical Restrictions

§ 18c–3102. Geographical Restrictions. A prima facie determination whether transportation is within the geographical scope of a license may be made by reference to a copy of the official state highway map and the distance scale shown thereon. Such a determination may be rebutted by a showing, based on a municipal ordinance; other official document; or commercially published map, chart or other competent evidence; that the geographical scope of the license is other than as represented on the official state highway map.

P.A. 76–1586, § 18c–3102, added by P.A. 84–796, § 1, eff. Jan. 1, 1986.

Formerly Ill.Rev.Stat.1991, ch. 95 ½, ¶ 18c–3102.

ARTICLE II. RATEMAKING

5/18c–3201. Prohibition of transportation services in the absence of effective rates

§ 18c–3201. Prohibition of transportation services in the absence of effective rates. No common carrier by pipeline, household goods carrier, rail carrier, or passenger carrier shall render service until such carrier has in effect a tariff or schedule of rates applicable to such service in compliance with this Chapter. Likewise, no such carrier shall render service under a license issued by the Commission if the Commission has suspended or cancelled the tariff or schedule of rates previously in effect and applicable to such service, or if the tariff or schedule is, by action of a party thereto or by its own terms, no longer effective.

P.A. 76–1586, § 18c–3201, added by P.A. 84–796, § 1, eff. Jan. 1, 1986. Amended by P.A. 89–444, § 5, eff. Jan. 25, 1996.

Formerly Ill.Rev.Stat.1991, ch. 95 ½, ¶ 18c–3201.

5/18c–3202. Effective Dates of New or Amended Rates

§ 18c–3202. Effective Dates of New or Amended Rates. The Commission shall prescribe the periods of notice which must elapse between the filing of a proposed rate and its proposed effective date. In no case shall the Commission prescribe a notice period greater than 30 days or the period established by a valid, preemptive federal statute.

P.A. 76–1586, § 18c–3202, added by P.A. 84–796, § 1, eff. Jan. 1, 1986. Amended by P.A. 85–553, § 2, eff. Sept. 18, 1987.

Formerly Ill.Rev.Stat.1991, ch. 95 ½, ¶ 18c–3202.

5/18c–3203. Filing, publishing and posting of tariffs and schedules

§ 18c–3203. Filing, publishing and posting of tariffs and schedules.

(1) General requirement of filing, publication and posting. Each common carrier of household goods or passengers shall file, publish, and make available for public inspection its current tariffs (other than rail contract rate tariffs). Copies of such tariffs shall be provided by the carrier to any member of the public on request and at a reasonable cost. Each contract carrier of household goods shall file its current schedule of rates and provisions.

(2) Tariff and schedule specifications. Tariffs and schedules filed in accordance with this subsection shall be in such form and contain such information as the Commission may specify. The Commission may, by special permission for good cause shown, grant permission to deviate from its tariff and schedule regulations.

(3) Rejection of tariffs and schedules. The Commission may, at any time prior to the effective date of a tariff or schedule, reject or suspend a tariff or schedule which does not conform to its specifications or which on its face is in violation of this Chapter, Commission regulations or orders.

(4) Right of independent action. Each carrier subject to this Chapter shall have the individual right to publish, file, and post any rate for transportation provided by such carrier or in connection with any other carrier. No carrier shall be a member of any bureau, tariff publishing agency, or other organization which, directly or indirectly, prohibits such carrier from publishing and filing any rate or which requires

that such rate be published or filed by the bureau, publishing agency, or other organization.

P.A. 76–1586, § 18c–3203, added by P.A. 84–796, § 1, eff. Jan. 1, 1986. Amended by P.A. 85–553, § 2, eff. Sept. 18, 1987; P.A. 89–444, § 5, eff. Jan. 25, 1996; P.A. 90–655, § 153, eff. July 30, 1998.

Formerly Ill.Rev.Stat.1991, ch. 95 ½, ¶ 18c–3203.

5/18c–3204. Rate Proceedings

§ 18c–3204. Rate Proceedings.

(1) Initiation of proceedings. The Commission may initiate a proceeding to investigate or prescribe tariffs or schedules on its own motion or on complaint.

(2) Suspension of tariffs and schedules.

(a) Suspension of tariffs. The Commission may suspend a tariff, in whole or in part, during the pendency of a proceeding to consider the reasonableness of the tariff, or to consider whether the tariff is discriminatory, or to consider whether the tariff otherwise violates provisions of this Chapter, Commission regulations or orders, provided the order of suspension is issued prior to the effective date of the tariff. The suspension shall remain in effect for the period allowed under this Chapter unless the Commission order provides for a shorter period of suspension. At the end of the statutory suspension period the suspension may be extended by agreement of the parties; otherwise, the tariff shall go into effect. The statutory suspension period is:

(i) Seven months for public carriers and household goods common carriers;

(ii) One hundred and twenty days for motor carriers of passengers; and

(iii) Five months for rail carriers, unless the period is extended for an additional 3 months in accordance with provisions of the Interstate Commerce Act.[1]

(b) Suspension of schedules. The Commission may suspend a household goods contract carrier schedule, in whole or in part, during the pendency of a proceeding to consider whether the schedule violates provisions of this Chapter, Commission regulations or orders, provided the order of suspension is issued prior to the effective date of the schedule. The suspension shall remain in effect for 7 months unless the Commission order provides for a shorter period of suspension. At the end of this period, the suspension may be extended by agreement of the parties; otherwise, the schedule shall go into effect.

(c) Burden of proof in investigation proceedings. The burden of proof in an investigation proceeding shall be on the proponent of the rate unless otherwise provided in a valid preemptive federal statute which governs the rate.

(3) Prescription of tariffs and schedules. The Commission may prescribe tariffs where it has determined, in accordance with Section 18c–2102 of this Chapter, that a tariff published by a carrier is unreasonable, discriminatory, or otherwise in violation of this Chapter, Commission regulations or orders. The Commission may prescribe schedules where it has determined, after hearing, that a schedule filed by a carrier is in violation of this Chapter, Commission regulations or orders.

(4) Relief. The Commission may, where it finds a tariff or schedule to be in violation of this Chapter, its regulations or orders, or finds rates or provisions in a tariff unjust, unreasonable, or discriminatory, and in accordance with Section 18c–2102 of this Chapter, direct the carrier to:

(a) Publish and file a supplement cancelling the tariff or file notice of cancellation of the schedule, in whole or in part;

(b) Publish and file a new tariff or file a new schedule containing rates and provisions prescribed by the Commission; and

(c) Repay any overcharges or collect any undercharges, and, except with regard to household goods carriers, pay reparations.

P.A. 76–1586, § 18c–3204, added by P.A. 84–796, § 1, eff. Jan. 1, 1986. Amended by P.A. 85–553, § 2, eff. Sept. 18, 1987; P.A. 89–42, § 10, eff. Jan. 1, 1996; P.A. 89–444, § 5, eff. Jan. 25, 1996; P.A. 90–14, Art. 2, § 2–225, eff. July 1, 1997.

Formerly Ill.Rev.Stat.1991, ch. 95 ½, ¶ 18c–3204.

[1] 49 U.S.C.A. § 10101 et seq.

P.A. 90–14, Article 2, of the First 1997 General Revisory Act, resolved multiple actions in the 89th General Assembly and made certain technical corrections in P.A. 89–443 through P.A. 89–707.

5/18c–3205. Ratemaking Standards

§ 18c–3205. Ratemaking Standards. (1) Reasonableness. Rates for household goods common carrier service must be just, reasonable, and not discriminatory.

(2) Factors to be Considered. The Commission shall, in exercising its ratemaking powers consider, among other factors, the inherent advantages of transportation by a particular class of carriers, the public need for and interest in adequate and efficient transportation service, at rates consistent with provision of such service, and the revenue needs of carriers under honest, economical and efficient management.

(3) Factors Not Considered. The Commission shall not, in exercising its ratemaking powers, consider the value of any operating authority held by a carrier, or the value of any goodwill or earning power connected with operations of the carrier.

P.A. 76–1586, § 18c–3205, added by P.A. 84–796, § 1, eff. Jan. 1, 1986. Amended by P.A. 89–444, § 5, eff. Jan. 25, 1996.

Formerly Ill.Rev.Stat.1991, ch. 95 ½, ¶ 18c–3205.

5/18c–3206. Charges to conform to tariffs or schedules and orders of the commission

§ 18c–3206. Charges to conform to tariffs or schedules and orders of the Commission. (1) Overcharges and undercharges prohibited. No common or contract household goods or passenger carrier shall offer, advertise, charge, demand, collect, or receive, in any manner, a greater, lesser, or different compensation for transportation or for any service in connection therewith than the rates and charges specified in tariffs or schedules on file with the Commission and in effect at the time the transportation or any other service is rendered; nor shall any such carrier offer, advertise, charge, demand, collect, or receive any compensation for transportation or for any other service rendered in connection therewith where there is not in effect at the time a lawfully applicable tariff or schedule. Likewise, no such carrier shall refund or remit, in any manner or by any device, whether directly or indirectly, or through any agent or otherwise, or pursuant to Commission order, any portion of the rates or charges specified in tariffs or schedules on file with the Commission and in effect at the time; nor shall any such carrier extend to any person any discount, value, privilege, or facilities for transportation or any service rendered in connection therewith, except as are specified in tariffs or schedules on file with the Commission and in effect at the time.

(2) Repayment of overcharges, collection of undercharges and reparations.

(a) Repayment of overcharges and payment of reparations. The Commission may, in accordance with Section 18c–2101 of this Chapter, order any carrier to pay to one or more shippers the amount by which the carrier received compensation greater than the rates and charges specified in tariffs or schedules in effect at the time the carrier rendered the transportation or other service in connection therewith. The Commission may likewise, in accordance with Section 18c–2101 of this Chapter, order any carrier other than a household goods carrier to pay to one or more shippers the amount by which the carrier received compensation greater than reasonable rates and charges as determined by the Commission.

(b) Collection of undercharges. The Commission may, in accordance to Section 18c–2101 of this Chapter, order any carrier to make all reasonable efforts to collect from one or more shippers the difference between amounts collected and the amount of compensation specified in tariffs or schedules in effect at the time the transportation or other service in connection therewith was rendered.

P.A. 76–1586, § 18c–3206, added by P.A. 84–796, § 1, eff. Jan. 1, 1986. Amended by P.A. 89–444, § 5, eff. Jan. 25, 1996.

Formerly Ill.Rev.Stat.1991, ch. 95 ½, ¶ 18c–3206.

5/18c–3207. Zones of Rate Flexibility

§ 18c–3207. Zones of Rate Flexibility. (1) Zone for Motor Carriers of Passengers. Notwithstanding any other provisions of this Sub-chapter, the Commission may not investigate, suspend, revise, or revoke any single-line rate proposed by a motor carrier of passengers, or joint rate proposed by one or more such companies, applicable to any transportation on the grounds that such rate is unreasonably high or low if:

(a) The rate was published in accordance with provisions of this Chapter, Commission regulations and orders;

(b) The Commission was properly notified that the carrier or carriers wish to have the rate considered pursuant to this subsection; and

(c) The net of all increases and decreases, during the calendar year in which the rate is to become effective, is not more than 25%.

(2) Zone for Rail Carriers. Notwithstanding any other provision of this Sub-chapter the Commission may not investigate, suspend, revise, or revoke any rate proposed by a rail carrier on the grounds that such rate is unreasonably high or low if:

(a) The rate was published in accordance with provisions of this Chapter and Commission regulations;

(b) Commission was properly notified that the carrier wished to have the rate to be considered pursuant to this subsection; and

(c) The net of all increases and decreases, during the calendar year in which the rate is to become effective, is not more than the amount specified under 49 U.S. Code 10707a and 10708.

(3) Commission to Adopt Regulations. The Commission may adopt regulations specifying procedures for determining whether a rate published by a carrier falls within the zone of rate flexibility.

P.A. 76–1586, § 18c–3207, added by P.A. 84–796, § 1, eff. Jan. 1, 1986.

Formerly Ill.Rev.Stat.1991, ch. 95 ½, ¶ 18c–3207.

5/18c–3208. Joint rates and routes

§ 18c–3208. Joint rates and routes. (1) Establishment by carriers. Two or more common carriers of household goods or passengers may establish through routes and joint rates, provided that the rates, and divisions and practices relating thereto, are just, reasonable, and not discriminatory.

(2) Establishment by the Commission. The Commission may, on its own motion or on petition or complaint, where 2 or more carriers have failed to establish through routes, joint rates, or divisions and practices relating thereto, establish such routes, rates, divisions and practices. The Commission shall take such action only after notice and hearing to consider whether any proposed routes, rates, divisions and practices are just, reasonable and not discriminatory, whether any carrier has a reasonable objection to establishment of such routes, rates, divisions and practices, and whether such objections can be satisfied by imposing reasonable terms and conditions on the application of such routes, rates, divisions and practices. The provisions of this subsection shall have no application to household goods carriers.

P.A. 76–1586, § 18c–3208, added by P.A. 84–796, § 1, eff. Jan. 1, 1986. Amended by P.A. 89–444, § 5, eff. Jan. 25, 1996.

Formerly Ill.Rev.Stat.1991, ch. 95 ½, ¶ 18c–3208.

5/18c–3209. Charges Not Part of Direct Transportation Cost

§ 18c–3209. Charges Not Part of Direct Transportation Cost. Any agreement, arrangement, or device, or part thereof, which, as a condition to the provision of transportation service, requires or permits any carrier, shipper, or receiver to pay a charge to any person, where such charge is not part of the direct cost of transportation service, shall be void.

P.A. 76–1586, § 18c–3209, added by P.A. 84–796, § 1, eff. Jan. 1, 1986. Amended by P.A. 85–553, § 2, eff. Sept. 18, 1987.

Formerly Ill.Rev.Stat.1991, ch. 95 ½, ¶ 18c–3209.

5/18c–3210. Presentation of freight bills, payment of freight charges, and extension of credit

§ 18c–3210. Presentation of freight bills, payment of freight charges, and extension of credit. Except as otherwise provided in this Chapter, this Section is applicable only to household goods carriers. (1) Presentation of freight bills. Freight bills shall be presented to the person responsible for payment of freight charges not later than the 7th day following delivery of the freight.

(2) Payment required before delivery or relinquishment of possession. Except as provided in subsection (3) of this Section, no common carrier shall deliver or relinquish possession of a shipment transported by it until all freight charges for such shipment under lawfully applicable rates have been paid to the carrier. Where credit has been extended in accordance with this Section, and all freight charges on the shipment under lawfully applicable rates have not been paid before expiration of the period for which credit has been extended, the carrier shall cease delivering or relinquishing

possession of the shipment and may decline to transport future shipments until all such charges have been paid.

(3) Exception: Delivery or relinquishment of possession before payment. A carrier may deliver or relinquish possession of a shipment transported by it in advance of payment of all freight charges on the shipment under lawfully applicable rates if the carrier has, in accordance with this Section, extended credit to the person responsible for payment of freight charges.

(4) Extension of credit. Credit, if extended by a carrier, must be extended without discrimination. Credit for payment of freight charges shown on the initial freight bill shall be for a period not to exceed 30 days, beginning on the later of the date of delivery or the date on which the freight bill is presented. If freight charges shown on the initial freight bill are paid and the carrier subsequently presents a supplemental freight bill, the carrier may extend credit in the amount of freight charges shown on the supplemental freight bill for an additional period not to exceed 15 days, beginning on the date on which the supplemental freight bill is presented.

(5) Commission regulation of credit terms. The Commission may regulate the extension and terms of credit extended by carriers under this Section, and no credit shall be extended except in accordance with such regulations.

(6) Use of U.S. Postal Service for presentation of bills or payment of charges. Where the United States Postal Service is used for the presentation of freight bills or payment of freight charges, the date of mailing, as indicated by the postmark, shall be the date of presentation or payment.

(7) Calculation of times for extension of credit. Time periods of extension of credit under this Section shall commence at midnight on the date of the event (delivery or presentation of freight bill). The initial 7 day period shall not include Saturdays, Sundays, or legal holidays.

P.A. 76–1586, § 18c–3210, added by P.A. 84–796, § 1, eff. Jan. 1, 1986. Amended by P.A. 85–553, § 2, eff. Sept. 18, 1987; P.A. 89–444, § 5, eff. Jan. 25, 1996.

Formerly Ill.Rev.Stat.1991, ch. 95 ½, ¶ 18c–3210.

5/18c–3211. Free or Reduced Rate Carriage

§ 18c–3211. Free or Reduced Rate Carriage. Nothing in this Chapter shall prevent a carrier from establishing reduced rate or free carriage rates applicable to transportation provided for the United States, the State of Illinois, or any municipality or subdivision of this State, where it is required by law that the carrier providing such transportation be selected by competitive bid. Such rates shall be filed in the form and manner required by the Commission.

P.A. 76–1586, § 18c–3211, added by P.A. 84–796, § 1, eff. Jan. 1, 1986.

Formerly Ill.Rev.Stat.1991, ch. 95 ½, ¶ 18c–3211.

5/18c–3212. Statute of Limitations for Freight Charges

§ 18c–3212. Statute of Limitations for Freight Charges. (1) Collection Actions. Actions to collect freight charges under lawfully applicable rates must be instituted within 3 years after rendition of the service.

(2) Reparations or Overcharge Proceedings. Petitions seeking reparations or repayment of overcharges must be filed with the Commission within 3 years after rendition of the service, and any action seeking judicial enforcement of a Commission order awarding reparations must be instituted within 1 year after issuance of such order. Where an action seeking judicial review of a Commission order awarding reparations is filed, the time preceding final adjudication of the action shall be excluded in computing the time for instituting the action seeking judicial enforcement of the Commission order.

P.A. 76–1586, § 18c–3212, added by P.A. 84–796, § 1, eff. Jan. 1, 1986.

Formerly Ill.Rev.Stat.1991, ch. 95 ½, ¶ 18c–3212.

5/18c–3213. Application of Rate Regulations to Exempt Traffic

§ 18c–3213. Application of Rate Regulations to Exempt Traffic. Notwithstanding any other provision of this Chapter to the contrary, the provisions of this Article shall not apply to traffic which is altogether exempt from Commission jurisdiction under this Chapter or a valid, preemptive federal statute.

P.A. 76–1586, § 18c–3213, added by P.A. 84–796, § 1, eff. Jan. 1, 1986.

Formerly Ill.Rev.Stat.1991, ch. 95 ½, ¶ 18c–3213.

ARTICLE III. OTHER PROVISIONS COMMON TO ALL TRANSPORTATION MODES

5/18c–3301. Certain Third Party Payments Prohibited

§ 18c–3301. Certain Third Party Payments Prohibited. Whenever a shipper or receiver of property requires that any person who owns or operates a motor vehicle transporting property in intrastate commerce under the provisions of this Chapter be assisted in the loading or unloading of such vehicle, the shipper or receiver shall be responsible for providing such assistance or shall compensate the owner or operator for all costs associated with securing and compensating the person or persons providing such assistance. It shall be unlawful to coerce or attempt to coerce any person providing transportation of property by motor vehicle for-hire in intrastate commerce to employ or pay one or more persons to load or unload any part of such property onto or from such vehicle, except that this subsection shall not be construed as making unlawful any activity which is not unlawful under the National Labor Relations Act[1] or any other acts governing labor practices.

P.A. 76–1586, § 18c–3301, added by P.A. 84–796, § 1, eff. Jan. 1, 1986.

Formerly Ill.Rev.Stat.1991, ch. 95 ½, ¶ 18c–3301.

[1] 29 U.S.C.A. § 151 et seq.

5/18c–3302. Prohibition against discrimination

§ 18c–3302. Prohibition against discrimination. It shall be unlawful for any household goods carrier, rail carrier, common carrier by pipeline, or passenger carrier to discriminate by giving or causing to be given any unreasonable preference or advantage to any person or traffic, or to subject any such person or traffic to unreasonable prejudice or disadvantage.

P.A. 76–1586, § 18c–3302, added by P.A. 84–796, § 1, eff. Jan. 1, 1986. Amended by P.A. 89–444, § 5, eff. Jan. 25, 1996.

Formerly Ill.Rev.Stat.1991, ch. 95 ½, ¶ 18c–3302.

5/18c–3303. Failure to Reject or Suspend, or to Invoke Sanctions, Not to be Construed as Acceptance

§ 18c–3303. Failure to Reject or Suspend, or to Invoke Sanctions, Not to be Construed as Acceptance. Failure of the Commission to reject or suspend any rate, contract, application, or other document filed with it, or to initiate enforcement proceedings or invoke sanctions against any person for action or violation of this Chapter, Commission regulations or orders, shall not be construed in any proceeding of either any administrative or judicial nature as authorization or acceptance of such document or action, or any portion thereof. Nothing in this Section shall be construed to affect the date on which a rate or tariff is lawfully in effect.

P.A. 76–1586, § 18c–3303, added by P.A. 84–796, § 1, eff. Jan. 1, 1986.

Formerly Ill.Rev.Stat.1991, ch. 95 ½, ¶ 18c–3303.

5/18c–3304. Records and accounts

§ 18c–3304. Records and accounts. Each household goods carrier, rail carrier, common carrier by pipeline, and passenger carrier shall:

(1) Keep written accounts and records of its revenues, expenses, contracts, and other activities subject to regulation under this Chapter in accordance with regulations prescribed by the Commission;

(2) Maintain, for a period of 3 years, copies of all accounts and records required by Commission regulations; and

(3) Make such accounts and records available for inspection, on request, by any authorized employee of the Commission.

Accounts and records kept pursuant to this Section shall be kept at an office in the State of Illinois unless the Commission shall have authorized maintenance at a location outside of the State.

P.A. 76–1586, § 18c–3304, added by P.A. 84–796, § 1, eff. Jan. 1, 1986. Amended by P.A. 89–444, § 5, eff. Jan. 25, 1996.

Formerly Ill.Rev.Stat.1991, ch. 95 ½, ¶ 18c–3304.

SUB–CHAPTER 4. MOTOR CARRIERS OF PROPERTY

ARTICLE I. GENERAL PROVISIONS GOVERNING MOTOR CARRIERS OF PROPERTY

ARTICLE I. GENERAL PROVISIONS GOVERNING MOTOR CARRIERS OF PROPERTY

5/18c–4101. Scope of Commission Jurisdiction

§ 18c–4101. Scope of Commission Jurisdiction. Except as provided in Section 18c–4102 of this Chapter, the jurisdiction of the Commission shall extend to all motor carriers of property operating within the State of Illinois.

P.A. 76-1586, § 18c-4101, added by P.A. 84-796, § 1, eff. Jan. 1, 1986.

Formerly Ill.Rev.Stat.1991, ch. 95 ½, ¶ 18c-4101.

5/18c-4102. Exemptions from Commission Jurisdiction

§ 18c-4102. Exemptions from Commission Jurisdiction. The provisions of this chapter shall not apply to transportation, by motor vehicle:

(a) of mail exclusively for the United States Postal Service;

(b) of agricultural commodities, farm supplies, and other commodities for sale by farm supply retail outlets, by an agricultural cooperative association as defined in the Illinois "Agricultural Co-Operative Act" as amended; [1]

(c) of farm or dairy products, livestock, poultry, fruits and agricultural products, by the producer thereof or by a producer on behalf of other producers from farm to a farm, market, warehouse, dairy or shipping terminal, for which no monetary compensation is paid or received;

(d) of livestock from farm to a farm market, farm to farm, or farm market to a farm as long as the vehicle is not registered for a gross vehicle weight that exceeds 28,000 pounds or a truck and trailer with a registered combined gross vehicle weight that does not exceed 28,000 pounds;

(e) by farm tractors and any other motorized, self-propelled machinery used in the production of agricultural commodities on a farm, where the transportation is provided by the owner of the machinery or another farmer as an incident to the business of farming;

(f) consisting of towing performed by any towing service pursuant to the written order of a law enforcement official or agency in accordance with Sections 4-201 through 4-214 of The Illinois Vehicle Code;

(g) of trespassing motor vehicles by a licensed commercial vehicle relocator;

(h) of newspapers being delivered to residential subscribers or to persons who will deliver the newspapers to residential subscribers;

(i) of waste having no commercial value to a disposal site for disposal;

(j) where the transportation is incidental to and within the scope of the person's primary business purpose, and the primary business is other than transportation;

(k) consisting of emergency transportation of a wrecked or disabled vehicle. Further movements to an additional place of repair or storage are not exempt under this subsection. Emergency transportation of wrecked or disabled vehicles shall include the transportation, pursuant to written authorization of law enforcement official if the owner is unavailable or unable to make the request, of wrecked or disabled vehicles which might otherwise constitute a public safety hazard along a street or highway, and transportation of wrecked or disabled vehicles in other bona fide emergency situations;

(*l*) consisting of transportation by a tow truck or rollback car carrier equipped as a tow truck of a motor vehicle when requested by the owner;

(m) of waste from the facilities of the generator of the waste to a recognized recycling or waste processing facility when the generator receives no direct or indirect compensation from anyone for the waste and when the transportation is by garbage trucks with self contained compacting devices, roll off trucks with containers, or vehicles or containers specially designed and used to receive separated recyclables, and when the transportation is an interim step toward recycling, reclamation, reuse, or disposal; and

(n) of potable water for human and livestock consumption transported in containers of 1,600 gallons or less. This subsection does not apply to vehicles transporting more than one container.

P.A. 76-1586, § 18c-4102, added by P.A. 84-796, § 1, eff. Jan. 1, 1986. Amended by P.A. 84-1308, Art. II, § 98, eff. Aug. 25, 1986; P.A. 85-553, § 2, eff. Sept. 18, 1987; P.A. 85-963, § 1, eff. July 1, 1988; P.A. 85-1209, Art. II, § 2-51, eff. Aug. 30, 1988; P.A. 86-564, § 1, eff. Jan. 1, 1990; P.A. 87-465, § 1, eff. Sept. 13, 1991; P.A. 87-531, § 1, eff. Jan. 1, 1992; P.A. 87-727, § 110, eff. Sept. 23, 1991; P.A. 87-768, § 2, eff. Oct. 10, 1991; P.A. 87-895, Art. 2, § 2-45, eff. Aug. 14, 1992; P.A. 87-1203, § 1, eff. Sept. 25, 1992; P.A. 87-1249, § 1, eff. Dec. 24, 1992.

Formerly Ill.Rev.Stat.1991, ch. 95 ½, ¶ 18c-4102.

[1] 805 ILCS 315/1 et seq.

P.A. 87-895, the First 1992 General Revisory Act, provides in Article 2 for the revision and renumbering of certain Sections of Acts which have been added or amended by more than one Act of the 87th General Assembly; incorporates amendments to repealed Acts into successor laws passed by the same General Assembly; corrects errors, revises cross-references and deletes obsolete text in such Sections contained in Public Acts through P.A. 87-855.

P.A. 87-1249 incorporated the amendments by P.A. 87-465, P.A. 87-531, P.A. 87-727, P.A. 87-768 and P.A. 87-1203 and included the amendment by P.A. 87-895.

5/18c-4103. Leasing

§ 18c-4103. Leasing. (1) Prohibition Against Single-Source Leasing. No private carrier shall lease any motor vehicle with driver, nor shall any person lease a motor vehicle with driver to any private carrier. Likewise, no person shall lease any motor vehicle to any private carrier and either:

(a) Procure or exercise control over drivers of such vehicles, directly or indirectly; or

(b) Be responsible for or hold itself out to be responsible for driver's wages, payroll, unemployment compensation, social security tax, income withholding tax or any other taxes or payments normally due by reason of the employer-employee relationship, or any other compensation to drivers.

The provision of motor vehicles with drivers shall constitute motor carrier operations subject to the licensing, ratemaking, and other jurisdiction of the Commission under this Chapter.

(2) Exclusive Use of Household Goods Contract Carrier Vehicles. The prohibition against single source leasing in subsection (1) of this Section shall not prohibit a household goods contract carrier from providing motor vehicles, with drivers, for exclusive use by a private carrier where:

(a) The private carrier is a contracting shipper;

(b) Operations conducted with such motor vehicles are within the scope of the household goods contract carrier's authority;

(c) The household goods contract carrier exercises direct supervision and control of such motor vehicles and drivers; and

(d) The lease does not have the effect of circumventing rate or other provisions of this Chapter, Commission regulations and orders.

This subsection shall apply regardless of whether the household goods contract carrier's permit expressly provides for the lease of vehicles, with drivers, to contracting shippers.

(3) Equipment Leasing.

(a) Requirements for Content, Filing, and Carrying of Leases. The Commission may prescribe requirements for the leasing of equipment, with driver, and of equipment without driver, to or by a motor carrier of property; provided that such regulations shall not encompass the leasing of equipment, without drivers, from a bona fide equipment leasing company to a motor carrier of property. Such leases shall be in writing, constitute the complete and exclusive statement of terms between the parties, specify the compensation for the lease and the duration of the lease, be signed by the parties thereto, be filed with the Commission, and be carried in each motor vehicle covered thereby, provided, however, that the Commission may exempt from the foregoing requirements leases between parties, all of whom hold public carrier certificates issued by the Commission. The provisions of this paragraph shall not apply to the interchange of equipment or drivers between carriers for use wholly within a county having a population of more than 1,000,000 inhabitants.

(b) Direction and Control of Leased Equipment. It shall be the responsibility of the license holder to exercise full direction and control of all equipment and personnel used in its operations. Equipment used in its operations must be owned by or under lease to the carrier.

P.A. 76–1586, § 18c–4103, added by P.A. 84–796, § 1, eff. Jan. 1, 1986. Amended by P.A. 85–553, § 2, eff. Sept. 18, 1987; P.A. 89–444, § 5, eff. Jan. 25, 1996.

Formerly Ill.Rev.Stat.1991, ch. 95 ½, ¶ 18c–4103.

5/18c–4104. Unlawful Operations

§ 18c–4104. Unlawful Operations. (1) Prohibition. Except as provided in Article I of this Sub-chapter, and subject to the provisions stated herein, it shall be unlawful for any person to:

(a) Operate as an intrastate motor carrier of property without a license from the Commission; or as an interstate motor carrier of property without a registration from the Commission.

(b) Operate as an intrastate household goods carrier in excess of the scope of a license issued to it by the Commission in regard to any of the following:

1. hauling unauthorized commodities;
2. operating outside authorized territory; or
3. violating other restrictions.

(c) Operate, as an intrastate motor carrier of property, any motor vehicle which does not carry a copy of a valid, current license issued by the Commission to such carrier; or operate, as an interstate motor carrier of property, any motor vehicle which does not carry a copy of a valid, current registration issued by the Commission to such carrier; or fail to produce such copy on request; provided that an authorized interstate motor carrier of property shall be exempted from the requirement that a copy of its registration be carried in each motor vehicle.

(d) Operate, as an intrastate household goods carrier, any motor vehicle not owned by the carrier, or operate as an intrastate public carrier, any motor vehicle not owned by the carrier or another intrastate public carrier, for which a valid lease is not on file in compliance with Section 18c–4103 of this Chapter, Commission regulations and orders.

(e) Operate, as an intrastate household goods carrier, any motor vehicle not owned by the carrier, or operate as an intrastate public carrier, any motor vehicle not owned by the carrier or another intrastate public carrier, which does not carry an executed copy of the lease required in paragraph (d) of this subsection; or fail to produce such copy on request.

(f) Operate, as an intrastate motor carrier of property, any motor vehicle for which the carrier has not executed a prescribed intrastate cab card, with current Illinois intrastate identifier printed thereon; or, as an interstate motor carrier of property, any motor vehicle for which the carrier has not executed a prescribed interstate cab card, with current Illinois interstate identifier affixed or printed thereon.

(g) Operate, as an intrastate motor carrier of property, any motor vehicle which does not carry the properly executed intrastate cab card, with current Illinois intrastate identifier printed thereon; or, as an interstate motor carrier of property, any motor vehicle which does not carry the properly executed interstate cab card, with current Illinois interstate identifier affixed or printed thereon.

(h) Operate, as an intrastate or interstate motor carrier of property, any motor vehicle which is not identified or is not properly identified in compliance with Section 18c–4701 of this Chapter, Commission regulations and orders.

(i) Operate, as an intrastate motor carrier of property, in violation of transfer requirements in Section 18c–4307 of this Chapter.

(j) Provide, as an intrastate household goods carrier, service at rates other than those contained in lawfully applicable tariffs or schedules for such service.

(k) Otherwise operate as a motor carrier of property in violation of any provision of this Chapter, Commission regulations and orders, or any other law of this State.

(*l*) Aid or abet any other person in a violation of this Chapter, Commission regulations or orders, by soliciting, receiving, or compensating service from a person not authorized to provide such service, or at other than lawful rates for such service, or otherwise.

(2) Provisos.

(a) Presentation of Documents at Hearing as Defense. Presentation, at hearing, of a copy of a current license or registration issued by the Commission to the carrier which was valid on the date the violation occurred shall, if no concurrent violations of this Chapter, Commission regulations or orders are found, excuse the carrier from any penalties under paragraph (c) of subsection (1) of this Section. Presentation, at hearing, of an executed copy of the current lease in the form prescribed by and on file with the Commission shall, if no concurrent violations of this Chapter, Commission regulations or orders are found, excuse the carrier from penalties under paragraph (d) of subsection (1) of this Section. Presentation, at hearing, of the required intrastate or interstate cab card, with the required Illinois intrastate or interstate identifier affixed or printed thereon, if valid on the date the violation occurred, and if no concurrent violations are found, shall excuse the carrier from penalties under paragraph (g) of subsection (1) of this Section.

(b) Lease Form Prescribed by the Commission. A lease shall, for purposes of paragraph (d) of subsection (1) of this Section, be deemed to be in the form prescribed by the Commission if it contains all provisions called for in the

Commission-prescribed lease and does not contain any provisions inconsistent therewith.

P.A. 76–1586, § 18c–4104, added by P.A. 84–796, § 1, eff. Jan. 1, 1986. Amended by P.A. 85–553, § 2, eff. Sept. 18, 1987; P.A. 89–444, § 5, eff. Jan. 25, 1996.

Formerly Ill.Rev.Stat.1991, ch. 95 ½, ¶ 18c–4104.

ARTICLE II. LICENSING

5/18c–4201. Licensing cases

§ 18c–4201. Licensing cases. (1) Scope of Section. The provisions of this Chapter relating to household goods carrier licensing apply to applications:

(a) For a license authorizing a carrier to operate as an intrastate household goods carrier;

(b) To transfer a certificate, permit, or license or to change the name on a certificate, permit, or license; and

(c) To convert household goods contract carrier authority to household goods common carrier authority.

(2) Form and content of household goods carrier licensing applications. Household goods carrier licensing applications shall be on such forms and contain such information as may be prescribed by the Commission, be verified under oath, and shall be accompanied by the required filing fee.

(3) Public notice of applications.

(a) Review of applications prior to publication. The Commission may provide for preliminary review of each application to determine if it is complete, if it gives adequate notice, and if the authority requested is unenforceably vague or otherwise contrary to the provisions of this Chapter.

(b) Authorization to submit application for publication. If the Commission determines after review that the application is defective in any respect, it shall promptly notify the applicant. No application shall be submitted to the official newspaper for publication until after it has been approved for publication, if the Commission has provided for preliminary review. If the Commission does not find that the application is defective, or if it finds that any defects have been removed by amendment, the applicant shall be permitted to submit the application to the official newspaper for publication. The Commission shall complete its review and notify the applicant within 15 days after filing of the application.

(c) Additional notice prescribed by the Commission. The Commission may direct applicant to give such further notice in connection with its application as the Commission deems necessary. The Commission may, itself, give such additional notice as it deems necessary.

(4) Hearing on licensing applications.

(a) Participation at hearing. Any person having standing to participate under this Chapter may appear and participate in a hearing before the Commission to the extent of its standing, provided that the person has complied with Commission regulations concerning the filing of petitions for leave to intervene and like pleadings. Petitions for leave to intervene must be filed within 15 days after publication, unless the Commission provides for filing at a later date. The Commission may permit additional persons to appear and participate, on such terms as the Commission shall prescribe, where such participation is deemed necessary to an informed and just resolution of the issues in the proceeding. No shipper representative shall be permitted to testify in support of an application for a motor common carrier certificate or a motor contract carrier permit on the issue of need for service unless:

(i) A supporting statement was filed on behalf of the shipper at least 10 days prior to the date of testimony; and

(ii) If the supporting statement was not filed with the application, the statement was served on all parties of record at least 10 days prior to the date of testimony.

(b) Setting, notice, and hearing. Notwithstanding any contrary provisions in Section 18c–2101 of this Chapter, a hearing shall be held on each licensing application to determine that the requirements of this Chapter have been satisfied, except as otherwise provided in Section 18c–4306 of this Chapter. The Commission shall set the hearing at a time not less than 15 days after publication in the official newspaper. The Commission shall serve notice of hearing on each party of record.

(c) Issuance of orders after hearing. The Commission may issue summary orders in cases where the licensing application was not opposed in a timely pleading addressed to the Commission, or was opposed in a timely pleading but such opposition was later withdrawn or the parties in opposition waived all right to other than a summary order. Summary orders shall be issued within 10 days after the close of oral hearing or such other period as the Commission may prescribe. Where a party requests, in a properly filed motion for reconsideration or rehearing, a detailed statement of findings and conclusions, the Commission shall vacate the summary order and issue a new order in accordance with Sub-chapters 1 and 2 of this Chapter.[1] Otherwise, orders shall be issued in accordance with provisions of Sub-chapters 1 and 2 of this Chapter.

P.A. 76–1586, § 18c–4201, added by P.A. 84–796, § 1, eff. Jan. 1, 1986. Amended by P.A. 85–553, § 2, eff. Sept. 18, 1987; P.A. 89–444, § 5, eff. Jan. 25, 1996.

Formerly Ill.Rev.Stat.1991, ch. 95 ½, ¶ 18c–4201.

1 625 ILCS 5/18–1101 et seq. and 5/18c–2101 et seq.

5/18c–4202. Household goods common carrier certificates

§ 18c–4202. Household goods common carrier certificates. (1) Prerequisite to operation as a household goods common carrier. No person shall operate as a household goods common carrier unless such person possesses a common carrier of household goods certificate issued by the Commission and in good standing.

(2) Requirements for issuance. The Commission shall grant an application for a common carrier of household goods certificate, in whole or in part, to the extent that it finds that the application was properly filed; a public need for the service exists; the applicant is fit, willing and able to provide the service in compliance with this Chapter, Commission regulations or orders; and the public convenience and necessity requires issuance of the certificate. Otherwise, the application shall be denied. The burden of proving that the requirements for issuance of a common carrier of household goods certificate have been met shall be borne by the applicant.

(3) Duties and practices of household goods common carriers. Household goods common carriers shall provide safe and adequate transportation service to the general public within the scope of their authorities and in compliance with this Chapter, Commission regulations and orders. Such service shall be at reasonable rates and without discrimination.

P.A. 76–1586, § 18c–4202, added by P.A. 84–796, § 1, eff. Jan. 1, 1986. Amended by P.A. 89–444, § 5, eff. Jan. 25, 1996.

Formerly Ill.Rev.Stat.1991, ch. 95 ½, ¶ 18c–4202.

5/18c-4203. Household goods contract carrier permits

§ 18c-4203. Household goods contract carrier permits. (1) Prerequisite to operation as a household goods contract carrier. No person shall operate as a household goods contract carrier of property unless such person possesses a household goods contract carrier permit issued by the Commission and in good standing.

(2) Requirements for issuance.

(a) General requirements. The Commission shall grant an application for a household goods contract carrier permit, in whole or in part, to the extent that it finds that the application was properly filed; supporting shippers need the proposed service; the applicant is fit, willing and able to provide the service in compliance with this Chapter, Commission regulations and orders; and issuance of the permit will be consistent with the public interest. Otherwise, the application shall be denied. The burden of proving that the requirements for issuance of a household goods contract carrier permit have been met shall be borne by the applicant.

(b) Conversion to household goods common carrier authority. The Commission may, at the request of the holder, authorize the conversion of household goods contract carrier authority to household goods common carrier authority, subject to the same terms, conditions, limitations, and regulations as other household goods common carriers.

(c) Cancellation and non-renewal of contracts. Cancellation or non-renewal of a contract, or failure to keep on file with the Commission a copy of a valid contract, shall render a permit void with regard to the involved shipper.

(3) Duties and practices of household goods contract carriers.

(a) Services. Household goods contract carriers shall provide safe and adequate transportation service to their contracting shippers within the scope of their authorities and contracts and in compliance with this Chapter, Commission regulations and orders.

(b) Contracts. Each household goods contract carrier shall file with the Commission a copy of each contract executed under authority of its permit, and shall provide no service except in accordance with contracts on file with the Commission. The Commission may, at any time, reject contracts filed with it which do not comply with the provisions of this Chapter, Commission regulations and orders.

P.A. 76-1586, § 18c-4203, added by P.A. 84-796, § 1, eff. Jan. 1, 1986. Amended by P.A. 89-444, § 5, eff. Jan. 25, 1996.

Formerly Ill.Rev.Stat.1991, ch. 95 ½, ¶ 18c-4203.

5/18c-4204. Standards to be considered in issuing common and contract household goods carrier licenses

§ 18c-4204. Standards to be considered in issuing common and contract household goods carrier licenses. The Commission shall exercise its discretion in regard to issuance of common carrier of household goods or contract carrier of household goods licenses in accordance with standards enumerated in this Section. (1) Standards relevant to both common and contract household goods carrier licenses. In determining whether to issue a common carrier of household goods certificate or a contract carrier of household goods permit under Sections 18c-4202 and 18c-4203 of this Chapter, the Commission shall consider, in addition to other standards enumerated in this Chapter:

(a) The characteristics of the supporting shipper or shippers transportation needs, including the total volume of shipments, the amounts handled by existing authorized carriers and others, the amounts which would be tendered to the applicant, the nature and location of points where traffic would be picked up and delivered, and any special transportation needs of the supporting shipper or shippers or their receiver or receivers;

(b) The existing authorized carriers' services, including the adequacy of such services and the effect which issuance of a new certificate or permit would have on such services;

(c) The proposed service, and whether it would meet the needs of the supporting shipper or shippers;

(d) Any evidence bearing on the fitness, willingness, or ability of the applicant, including but not limited to any past history of violations of this Chapter, Commission regulations or orders, whether or not such violations were the subject of an enforcement proceeding; and

(e) The effect which issuing the certificate or permit would have on the development, maintenance and preservation of the highways of this State for commercial and other public use.

(2) Additional standards relevant to household goods contract carrier licenses. In determining whether to issue a household goods contract carrier permit under Section 18c-4203 of this Chapter, the Commission shall consider, in addition to standards enumerated in subsection (1) of this Section or elsewhere in this Sub-chapter:

(a) Whether the proposed service is contract carrier service; and

(b) The effect which failure to issue the permit would have on the supporting shipper or shippers.

(3) Standards not relevant to either household goods common or household goods contract carrier licenses. In determining whether to issue a household goods common carrier certificate or a household goods contract carrier permit under Sections 18c-4202 and 18c-4203 of this Chapter, the Commission shall not consider:

(a) The mere preference of the supporting shipper or shippers or their receiver or receivers for the applicant's service; or

(b) Any illegal operations of the applicant as evidence of shipper need or the inadequacy of existing carriers' services.

P.A. 76-1586, § 18c-4204, added by P.A. 84-796, § 1, eff. Jan. 1, 1986. Amended by P.A. 85-553, § 2, eff. Sept. 18, 1987; P.A. 86-1005, § 3, eff. Dec. 28, 1989; P.A. 89-444, § 5, eff. Jan. 25, 1996.

Formerly Ill.Rev.Stat.1991, ch. 95 ½, ¶ 18c-4204.

5/18c-4204a. Fitness standards

§ 18c-4204a. Fitness standards. (1) Establishment of administrative standards. The Commission shall, within 180 days from the effective date of this amendatory Act of 1987, adopt and implement standards for determining fitness to hold or continue to hold a household goods carrier license.

(2) Statutory standards. A person shall not be considered fit for purposes of this Section unless the record shows that, at the time of hearing, the person:

(a) Is aware of its obligations under this Chapter, Commission regulations and orders, and other provisions of The Illinois Vehicle Code; [1]

(b) Has substantially complied with applicable statutes and regulations; and

(c) Possesses the equipment, facilities, financial resources, knowledge and experience to provide the proposed service and meet the needs of supporting shippers, in compliance with applicable statutes and regulations, on a long-term basis.

(3) Burden of proof in application proceedings. (a) Temporary authority. Each applicant for temporary household goods carrier authority shall have the burden of making a prima facie showing of fitness. The Commission may, in its discretion, deny an application for temporary household goods authority where the applicant's fitness is controverted by specific allegations, under oath, by an intervenor.

(b) Permanent authority. Each applicant for permanent household goods authority shall have the burden of proving its fitness by clear and convincing evidence.

(c) Findings. The order granting permanent household goods authority shall contain specific findings, with citation to the record, on each aspect of fitness.

(4) Revocation proceedings. If the record in a revocation proceeding shows that a licensee is no longer fit to hold a household goods carrier license, the Commission shall suspend or revoke the license. When a license is suspended under this Section, the holder shall have 6 months in which to demonstrate, by clear and convincing evidence, that its fitness has been restored. Unless the Commission finds that such a demonstration has been made, the license shall be revoked. A license revoked under this Section shall not be reinstated.

P.A. 76-1586, § 18c-4204a, added by P.A. 85-553, § 2, eff. Sept. 18, 1987. Amended by P.A. 89-444, § 5, eff. Jan. 25, 1996.

Formerly Ill.Rev.Stat.1991, ch. 95 ½, ¶ 18c-4204a.

1 625 ILCS 5/1-100 et seq.

5/18c-4205. § 18c-4205. Repealed by P.A. 85-553, § 3, eff. Sept. 18, 1987

5/18c-4206. Dual operations

§ 18c-4206. Dual operations. (1) Dual common/contract operations. No person shall hold both a household goods common carrier certificate and a household goods contract carrier permit unless the Commission determines, or has determined, that both licenses may be held consistent with the public interest and authorizes such dual licensing. Issuance of household goods contract carrier authority after the effective date of this amendatory Act of 1995 to a person that already holds household goods common carrier authority, or vice versa, shall be rebuttably presumed inconsistent with the public interest if the two authorities would be duplicative, in whole or in part.

(2) Merger of duplicative operating rights. The Commission may, except as otherwise provided in this subsection, order that duplicative operating rights, whether household goods common carrier or household goods contract carrier or both, be merged into a single license and may impose such requirements upon operations under such license as will promote the public interest and effectuate the purposes of this Chapter. The power of the Commission to order merger shall not extend to duplicative operating rights in existence on the effective date of this Chapter.

P.A. 76-1586, § 18c-4206, added by P.A. 84-796, § 1, eff. Jan. 1, 1986. Amended by P.A. 89-444, § 5, eff. Jan. 25, 1996.

Formerly Ill.Rev.Stat.1991, ch. 95 ½, ¶ 18c-4206.

5/18c-4207. Cessation of service under a license

§ 18c-4207. Cessation of service under a license. No household goods carrier shall abandon, discontinue, or suspend any service that it is authorized to provide pursuant to a license issued by the Commission without authorization by the Commission. If the Commission finds good cause for the abandonment, discontinuance, or suspension, it may approve same. If the Commission finds that a household goods carrier has abandoned, discontinued, or suspended service without authorization, it may revoke the carrier's license.

P.A. 76-1586, § 18c-4207, added by P.A. 84-796, § 1, eff. Jan. 1, 1986. Amended by P.A. 89-444, § 5, eff. Jan. 25, 1996.

Formerly Ill.Rev.Stat.1991, ch. 95 ½, ¶ 18c-4207.

ARTICLE III. TRANSFER OF LICENSES

5/18c-4301. Power of Commission to Approve Transfers

§ 18c-4301. Power of Commission to Approve Transfers. A license issued under this Sub-chapter may be transferred, with Commission approval, under the conditions specified in this Article and in accordance with such rules and regulations as the Commission may prescribe.

P.A. 76-1586, § 18c-4301, added by P.A. 84-796, § 1, eff. Jan. 1, 1986.

Formerly Ill.Rev.Stat.1991, ch. 95 ½, ¶ 18c-4301.

5/18c-4302. Types of Transfers Which May be Approved

§ 18c-4302. Types of Transfers Which May be Approved. It is lawful, with prior authorization from the Commission, for:

(1) Two or more motor carriers of property to consolidate or merge their properties into one business entity for the ownership, management, or operation of the properties theretofore in separate ownership;

(2) A motor carrier of property, or two or more such carriers jointly, to purchase, lease or contract to operate the properties of another such carrier;

(3) A motor carrier of property, or two or more such carriers jointly, to acquire control of another such carrier through ownership of its stock or otherwise;

(4) A person not a motor carrier of property, to acquire control of one or more such motor carriers through ownership of its or their stock or otherwise;

(5) A person not a motor carrier of property and which has control of one or more such carriers to acquire control of another carrier through ownership of its stock or otherwise; or

(6) A person to acquire possession, ownership, or control, by means of the sale or other conveyance of a license issued by the Commission to another person.

P.A. 76-1586, § 18c-4302, added by P.A. 84-796, § 1, eff. Jan. 1, 1986.

Formerly Ill.Rev.Stat.1991, ch. 95 ½, ¶ 18c-4302.

5/18c-4303. Applications for Approval

§ 18c-4303. Applications for Approval. Applications for approval of the transfer of a license shall be on forms prescribed by the Commission and shall, where possible, be accompanied by a copy of the written contract executed by parties to the proposed transfer. The contract must state that it:

(1) Is expressly conditioned on approval of the transfer by the Commission;

(2) Is a complete and exclusive statement of the rights of the parties in regard to the proposed transfer; and

(3) Cannot be amended without notice to and approval by the Commission. The application shall also be accompanied by an abstract of shipments performed by the transferor within the last year prior to the date of the contract showing the date of each shipment, the identification number of the shipment, the origin and destination of the shipment, and a description of the commodity shipped.

The application shall not be docketed until a contract and abstract have been filed. Where the contract cannot be signed because of some operation of law, the Commission may waive the signature of the transferor, but not the filing of the written contract.

P.A. 76-1586, § 18c-4303, added by P.A. 84-796, § 1, eff. Jan. 1, 1986.

Formerly Ill.Rev.Stat.1991, ch. 95 ½, ¶ 18c-4303.

5/18c-4304. Standard for Review of Applications

§ 18c-4304. Standard for Review of Applications. The Commission may approve a proposed transfer if it finds that:

(1) The license to be transferred is in good standing and has not been abandoned, discontinued, or suspended, in whole or in part;

(2) The proposed transferee is fit, willing, and able to provide service for which the license was issued, and to do so in compliance with provisions of this Chapter, Commission regulations and orders; and

(3) The transfer would be consistent with the public interest and the state transportation policy.

The Commission may approve or disapprove a transfer, in whole or in part, and may subject the transfer to such terms and conditions as will protect the public interest and effectuate the purposes of this Chapter.

P.A. 76-1586, § 18c-4304, added by P.A. 84-796, § 1, eff. Jan. 1, 1986.

Formerly Ill.Rev.Stat.1991, ch. 95 ½, ¶ 18c-4304.

5/18c-4305. Abandonment, Discontinuance, or Suspension of Service Under a License to be Transferred

§ 18c-4305. Abandonment, Discontinuance, or Suspension of Service Under a License to be Transferred. In determining whether the proposed transferor has abandoned, discontinued or suspended service without authorization, the Commission shall only consider the operations of the transferring party performed within the last 2 years prior to the date on which the contract between transferor and transferee was executed, or the date the application was filed.

P.A. 76-1586, § 18c-4305, added by P.A. 84-796, § 1, eff. Jan. 1, 1986.

Formerly Ill.Rev.Stat.1991, ch. 95 ½, ¶ 18c-4305.

5/18c-4306. Expedited Transfer Procedures

§ 18c-4306. Expedited Transfer Procedures.

(1) The Commission may provide for the transfer of a license, without notice and hearing, and without the necessity of making the findings specified above, when such transfer or control is to:

(a) A member or members of the transferor's immediate family;

(b) A corporation, the stock of which is wholly owned by the transferor or members of his immediate family or a member or members of the transferor partnership;

(c) A member or members of a partnership of which the transferor is a partner;

(d) A stockholder or stockholders of the transferor corporation or of a corporation wholly owned by the transferor or the transferor's immediate family;

(e) The heirs of a person who dies intestate or the legatees of a testator, upon order of the probate court having jurisdiction;

(f) The heirs or legatees of the transferor pursuant to the Probate Act of 1975, as amended;[1]

(g) A corporation, more than 50% of the stock of which is controlled by the stockholders of the transferor corporation; or

(h) A corporation, all of the stock of which is controlled by a member or members of the immediate family of the stockholder or stockholders of the transferor corporation.

(2) When a transfer of a license may be accomplished on an expedited basis without notice and hearing through 2 or more transactions of the type described in subsection (a), and they do, in fact, represent a single, contemporaneous transaction, then the Commission shall allow the transfer to be made as a single transaction in a single application. However, it shall be the applicants' burden to demonstrate that they are entitled to this treatment of their application by setting forth each of the individual qualifying transactions under subsection (1) with the same detail and specificity as if each individual application were filed.

P.A. 76-1586, § 18c-4306, added by P.A. 84-796, § 1, eff. Jan. 1, 1986. Amended by P.A. 85-553, § 2, eff. Sept. 18, 1987; P.A. 88-415, § 10, eff. Aug. 20, 1993.

Formerly Ill.Rev.Stat.1991, ch. 95 ½, ¶ 18c-4306.

[1] 755 ILCS 5/1-1 et seq.

5/18c-4307. Unapproved Transfers

§ 18c-4307. Unapproved Transfers. (1) Unapproved Transfers Prohibited. Except as provided in this Article, no person may enter into a transaction to accomplish or effectuate, or participate in accomplishing or effectuating, the ownership, control or management of any one or more motor carriers, however such result is attained, whether directly or indirectly by use of common directors, officers, or stockholders, a holding or investment company, a voting trust, or in any other manner, and regardless of whether or not the carrier received compensation or value from the transaction. Nor shall any person continue to maintain control or management accomplished or effectuated in violation of this Article. The words "control or management," when used in this Article, shall be construed to include the power to exercise control or management.

(2) Direct Supervision and Control by License Holder Required. The holder of a motor carrier license shall exercise direct supervision and control over all operations conducted with vehicles registered under its license or utilized in conducting operations under its license. The holder may be called upon to demonstrate that it is exercising direct supervision and control. Failure to exercise active supervision and control shall constitute the unauthorized transfer of operating rights in violation of this Chapter. Where an unauthorized transfer occurs, both the transferor and transferee shall have committed violations of this Chapter. Nothing contained herein shall prevent the holder from exercising such supervision and control through a manager or other

bona fide employee of the holder. Elements to be considered in evaluating whether supervision and control is being exercised include solicitation; public identification; billing; collecting; dispatching drivers and equipment; hiring; evaluation and firing of drivers and other personnel; liability for cargo loss or damage; and responsibility for payment of carrier expenses.

P.A. 76-1586, § 18c-4307, added by P.A. 84-796, § 1, eff. Jan. 1, 1986. Amended by P.A. 85-553, § 2, eff. Sept. 18, 1987.

Formerly Ill.Rev.Stat.1991, ch. 95 ½, ¶ 18c-4307.

5/18c-4308. Enforcement of Transfer Requirements

§ 18c-4308. Enforcement of Transfer Requirements. The Commission may, on its own motion or on complaint, investigate and determine whether violations of this Article have occurred. When the Commission determines that a carrier or other person is violating the provisions of this Article it shall by order require the carrier or other person to take whatever action is necessary to prevent continuance of the violation, and may, in addition, impose sanctions as provided in this Chapter.

P.A. 76-1586, § 18c-4308, added by P.A. 84-796, § 1, eff. Jan. 1, 1986.

Formerly Ill.Rev.Stat.1991, ch. 95 ½, ¶ 18c-4308.

5/18c-4309. Temporary Suspension and Transfer

§ 18c-4309. Temporary Suspension and Transfer. Periods during which a license is temporarily suspended by order of the Commission shall not be considered as part of the 1-year period for which an abstract of shipments must be provided for application to transfer a license pursuant to Section 18c-4303 of this Chapter, or for the 2-year period used to determine whether a proposed transferor has abandoned, discontinued or suspended service without Commission authorization pursuant to Section 18c-4305 of this Chapter. This Section shall apply to all temporary suspension applications filed, and all temporary suspensions granted, on or after January 1, 1986.

P.A. 76-1586, § 18c-4309, added by P.A. 85-553, § 2, eff. Sept. 18, 1987.

Formerly Ill.Rev.Stat.1991, ch. 95 ½, ¶ 18c-4309.

ARTICLE IV. RATE FILINGS AND REGISTRATION OF INTRASTATE PUBLIC CARRIERS AND EQUIPMENT AND REGISTRATION OF INTERSTATE CARRIERS AND EQUIPMENT

5/18c-4401. Registration required

§ 18c-4401. Registration required. (1) General provisions. No intrastate public carrier and no interstate motor carrier of property shall operate over the public roads of this State without a registration issued pursuant to this Article and in effect at the time operations are conducted.

(2) Interstate intercorporate hauling and single-source leasing. Persons or entities engaged in interstate compensated intercorporate hauling, and interstate private carriers which lease equipment, with drivers, are interstate carriers for purposes of this Article notwithstanding any other provision of this Chapter. However, the Commission may:

(a) Exempt such carriers from the requirements of this Article;

(b) Subject any such exemption to such reasonable terms and conditions as the Commission deems necessary to effectuate the purposes of this Chapter; and

(c) Revoke any exemption granted hereunder if it deems revocation necessary to effectuate the purposes of this Chapter.

P.A. 76-1586, § 18c-4401, added by P.A. 84-796, § 1, eff. Jan. 1, 1986. Amended by P.A. 85-553, § 2, eff. Sept. 18, 1987; P.A. 89-444, § 5, eff. Jan. 25, 1996.

Formerly Ill.Rev.Stat.1991, ch. 95 ½, ¶ 18c-4401.

5/18c-4402. Registration Standards

§ 18c-4402. Registration Standards. The Commission shall not issue a registration until after the carrier has:

(1) Properly filed an application for registration; and

(2) Complied with Commission regulations and orders regarding:

(a) Application, franchise, franchise renewal, and other fees and levies; and

(b) Proof of insurance.

P.A. 76-1586, § 18c-4402, added by P.A. 84-796, § 1, eff. Jan. 1, 1986. Amended by P.A. 85-553, § 2, eff. Sept. 18, 1987.

Formerly Ill.Rev.Stat.1991, ch. 95 ½, ¶ 18c-4402.

5/18c-4403. Issuance of registrations

§ 18c-4403. Issuance of registrations. The Commission may issue registrations to any qualified applicant authorizing bona fide intrastate public carrier or interstate operations, if it is found that the applicant is fit, willing, and able to provide service in conformity with the requirements of this Chapter, Commission regulations and orders.

P.A. 76-1586, § 18c-4403, added by P.A. 84-796, § 1, eff. Jan. 1, 1986. Amended by P.A. 89-444, § 5, eff. Jan. 25, 1996.

Formerly Ill.Rev.Stat.1991, ch. 95 ½, ¶ 18c-4403.

5/18c-4404. Revocation of Registrations

§ 18c-4404. Revocation of Registrations. The Commission may revoke any registration if it determines that the carrier has failed to comply with this Chapter, Commission regulations or orders, or with any other statute or regulation of this State relating to the privilege of operating motor vehicles over the public roads of the State.

P.A. 76-1586, § 18c-4404, added by P.A. 84-796, § 1, eff. Jan. 1, 1986.

Formerly Ill.Rev.Stat.1991, ch. 95 ½, ¶ 18c-4404.

5/18c-4405. Intrastate public carrier rate filings

§ 18c-4405. Intrastate public carrier rate filings. Public carriers that voluntarily file rates under an agreement approved by the Commission under Section 18c-4502 of this Chapter are subject to all provisions of Sub-chapter 3, Article II,[1] and Section 18c-4501 of this Chapter 18c.

[1] 625 ILCS 5/18c-3201 et seq.

P.A. 76-1586, § 18c-4405, added by P.A. 89-444, § 5, eff. Jan. 25, 1996.

ARTICLE V. RATEMAKING

5/18c-4501. Jurisdiction and power of the Commission

§ 18c-4501. Jurisdiction and power of the Commission. (1) Power to set rates. The Commission shall have jurisdiction and power to set the maximum or minimum, or maximum and minimum, lawful rates for intrastate service by common carriers of household goods, to set the minimum lawful rates for contract carriers of household goods, and to prescribe the form and content of tariffs and schedules containing such rates.

(2) Power to Establish Ratemaking Procedures. The Commission may establish procedures for the filing, publication, investigation, suspension and prescription of rates. The Commission may provide that rates for particular services will go into effect unless suspended by the Commission, or may require that rates for such services be approved by the Commission before going into effect.

P.A. 76-1586, § 18c-4501, added by P.A. 84-796, § 1, eff. Jan. 1, 1986. Amended by P.A. 89-444, § 5, eff. Jan. 25, 1996.

Formerly Ill.Rev.Stat.1991, ch. 95 ½, ¶ 18c-4501.

5/18c-4502. Collective Ratemaking

§ 18c-4502. Collective Ratemaking. (1) Application for Approval. Any carrier party to an agreement between or among 2 or more carriers relating to rates, fares, classifications, divisions, allowances, or charges (including charges between carriers and compensation paid or received for the use of facilities and equipment), or rules and regulations pertaining thereto, or procedures for the joint consideration, initiation or establishment thereof, whether such conference, bureau, committee, or other organization be a "for-profit" or "not-for-profit" corporate entity or whether or not such conference, bureau, committee or other organization is or will be controlled by other businesses may, under such rules and regulations as the Commission may prescribe, apply to the Commission for approval of the agreement, and the Commission shall by order approve any such agreement, if approval thereof is not prohibited by subsection (3), (4), or (5) of this Section, if it finds that, by reason of furtherance of the State transportation policy declared in Section 18c-1103 of this Chapter, the relief provided in subsection (8) should apply with respect to the making and carrying out of such agreement; otherwise the application shall be denied. The approval of the Commission shall be granted only upon such terms and conditions as the Commission may prescribe as necessary to enable it to grant its approval in accordance with the standard above set forth in this paragraph.

(2) Accounts, Reporting, and Internal Procedures. Each conference, bureau, committee, or other organization established or continued pursuant to any agreement approved by the Commission under the provisions of this Section shall maintain such accounts, records, files and memoranda and shall submit to the Commission such reports, as may be prescribed by the Commission, and all such accounts, records, files, and memoranda shall be subject to inspection by the Commission or its duly authorized representatives. Any conference, bureau committee, or other organization described in subsection (1) of this Section shall cause to be published notice of the final disposition of any action taken by such entity together with a concise statement of the reasons therefore. The Commission shall withhold approval of any agreement under this Section unless the agreement specifies a reasonable period of time within which proposals by parties to the agreement will be finally acted upon by the conference, bureau, committee, or other organization.

(3) Matters Which May Be the Subject of Agreements Approved By the Commission. The Commission shall not approve under this Section any agreement between or among carriers of different classes unless it finds that such agreement is of the character described in subsection (1) of this Section and is limited to matters relating to transportation under joint rates or over through routes. For purposes of this paragraph carriers by railroad and express companies are carriers of one class; carriers by motor vehicle are carriers of one class and carriers by water are carriers of one class.

(4) Non-Applicability of Section to Transfers. The Commission shall not approve under this Section any agreement which it finds is an agreement with respect to a pooling, division, or other matter or transaction, to which Section 18c-4302 of this Chapter is applicable.

(5) Independent Action. The Commission shall not approve under this Section any agreement which establishes a procedure for the determination of any matter through joint consideration unless it finds that under the agreement there is accorded to each party the free and unrestrained right to take independent action either before or after any determination arrived at through such procedures. The Commission shall not find that each party has a free and unrestrained right to take independent action if the conference, bureau, committee, or other organization is granted by the agreement any right to engage in proceedings before the Commission or before any court regarding any action taken by a party to an agreement authorized by this Section, or by any other party providing or seeking authority to provide transportation services.

(6) Investigation of Activities. The Commission is authorized, upon complaint or upon its own initiative without complaint, to investigate and determine whether any agreement previously approved by it under this Section, or terms and conditions upon which such approval was granted, is not or are not in conformity with the standard, set forth in subsection (1), or whether any such terms and conditions are not necessary for purposes of conformity with such standard, and, after such investigation, the Commission shall by order terminate or modify its approval of such agreement if it finds such action necessary to insure conformity with such standard, and shall modify the terms and conditions upon which such approval was granted to the extent it finds necessary to insure conformity with such standard or to the extent to which it finds such terms and conditions not necessary to insure such conformity. The effective date of any order terminating or modifying approval, or modifying terms and conditions, shall be postponed for such period as the Commission determines to be reasonably necessary to avoid undue hardship.

(7) Hearings and Orders. No order shall be entered under this Section except after interested parties have been afforded reasonable opportunity for hearing.

(8) Exemption From State Antitrust Laws. Parties to any agreement approved by the Commission under this Section and other persons are, if the approval of such agreement is not prohibited by subsection (3), (4), or (5), hereby relieved from the operation of the antitrust laws with respect to the making of such agreement, and with respect to the carrying out of such agreement in conformity with its provisions and in conformity with the terms and conditions prescribed by the Commission.

(9) Other Laws Not Affected. Any action of the Commission under this Section in approving an agreement, or in denying an application for such approval, or in terminating or modifying its approval of an agreement, or in prescribing the terms and conditions upon which its approval is to be granted, or in modifying such terms and conditions, shall be construed as having effect solely with reference to the appli-

cability of the relief provisions of paragraph subsection (8) of this Section.

P.A. 76–1586, § 18c–4502, added by P.A. 84–796, § 1, eff. Jan. 1, 1986.

Formerly Ill.Rev.Stat.1991, ch. 95 ½, ¶ 18c–4502.

5/18c–4503. Terminal Area Operations

§ 18c–4503. Terminal Area Operations.

(1) Exemption From Rate Regulation. Except as provided in subsection (2) of this Section, nothing contained in this Chapter shall be construed to require any carrier engaged in the transportation of property by motor vehicle between points wholly within a terminal area to comply with the provisions of this Chapter with respect to the filing, publishing, observance or enforcement of tariffs or schedules of rates with respect to transportation wholly within any such area.

(2) Application of Section. Notwithstanding any contrary provisions therein, the ratemaking provisions of subsection (1) of this Section shall have no application to transportation of household goods, as defined in Commission regulations, wholly within a county having a population of more than 1,000,000.

P.A. 76–1586, § 18c–4503, added by P.A. 85–553, § 2, eff. Sept. 18, 1987.

Formerly Ill.Rev.Stat.1991, ch. 95 ½, ¶ 18c–4503.

ARTICLE VI. CAB CARDS AND IDENTIFIERS

5/18c–4601. Cab Card and Identifier to be Carried and Displayed in Each Vehicle

§ 18c–4601. Cab Card and Identifier to be Carried and Displayed in Each Vehicle.

(1) General Provisions.

(a) Carrying Requirement. Each motor vehicle used in for-hire transportation upon the public roads of this State shall carry a current cab card together with an identifier issued by or under authority of the Commission. If the carrier is an intrastate motor carrier of property, the prescribed intrastate cab card and identifier shall be required; if the carrier is an interstate motor carrier of property, the prescribed interstate cab card and identifier shall be required.

(b) Execution and Presentation Requirement. Such cab card shall be properly executed by the carrier. The cab card, with an identifier affixed or printed thereon, shall be carried in the vehicle for which it was executed. The cab card and identifier shall be presented upon request to any authorized employee of the Commission or the State Police or Secretary of State.

(c) Deadlines for Execution, Carrying, and Presentation. Cab cards and identifiers shall be executed, carried, and presented no earlier than December 1 of the calendar year preceding the calendar year for which fees are owing, and no later than February 1 of the calendar year for which fees are owing, unless otherwise provided in Commission regulations and orders.

(2) Interstate Compensated Intercorporate Hauling and Single-Source Leasing. The provisions of subsection (1) of this Section apply to motor vehicles used in interstate compensated intercorporate hauling or which are leased, with drivers, to private carriers for use in interstate commerce, as well as to other motor vehicles used in for-hire transportation upon the public roads of this State. However, the Commission may:

(a) Exempt such carriers from the requirements of this Article;

(b) Subject any exemption to such reasonable terms and conditions as the Commission deems necessary to effectuate the purposes of this Chapter; and

(c) Revoke any exemption granted hereunder if it deems revocation necessary to effectuate the purposes of this Chapter.

P.A. 76–1586, § 18c–4601, added by P.A. 84–796, § 1, eff. Jan. 1, 1986. Amended by P.A. 85–553, § 2, eff. Sept. 18, 1987.

Formerly Ill.Rev.Stat.1991, ch. 95 ½, ¶ 18c–4601.

5/18c–4602. Commission to Prescribe Cab Cards and Identifiers

§ 18c–4602. Commission to Prescribe Cab Cards and Identifiers. The Commission shall prescribe the cab cards and identifiers required under Section 18c–4601 of this Chapter.

P.A. 76–1586, § 18c–4602, added by P.A. 84–796, § 1, eff. Jan. 1, 1986. Amended by P.A. 85–553, § 2, eff. Sept. 18, 1987.

Formerly Ill.Rev.Stat.1991, ch. 95 ½, ¶ 18c–4602.

5/18c–4603. Issuance of Cab Cards and Identifiers

§ 18c–4603. Issuance of Cab Cards and Identifiers. (1) Applications for Cards and Identifiers. Applications for cab cards and identifiers shall be on forms prescribed by the Commission and shall be accompanied by the per vehicle franchise or franchise renewal fee prescribed by the Commission.

(2) Expiration and Renewal of Cab Cards and Identifiers. Identifiers issued by or under authority of the Commission shall expire automatically on January 31 of each year, or on such other date as the Commission may prescribe. It shall be the responsibility of each carrier to insure that the cab cards and identifiers in its vehicles are current.

(3) Issuance of Cards and Identifiers. Applications and fees for cab cards and identifiers may be filed with, and cards or identifiers may be issued by, the Commission or its agent. The Commission shall issue intrastate cab cards and identifiers and interstate identifiers as proof of payment of franchise and franchise renewal fees by licensed intrastate and registered interstate carriers. Upon payment of the intrastate fee by a licensed intrastate motor carrier of property, the Commission shall issue a current Illinois cab card with identifier printed thereon. Upon payment of the interstate fee by a registered interstate motor carrier of property, the Commission shall issue a current Illinois interstate identifier which the carrier shall affix to the interstate cab card.

P.A. 76–1586, § 18c–4603, added by P.A. 84–796, § 1, eff. Jan. 1, 1986. Amended by P.A. 85–553, § 2, eff. Sept. 18, 1987.

Formerly Ill.Rev.Stat.1991, ch. 95 ½, ¶ 18c–4603.

5/18c–4604. Enforcement

§ 18c–4604. Enforcement. It shall be a violation of this Chapter, separate and apart from any other violation, for a person to:

(1) Operate a vehicle without a current, executed cab card and identifier as required by this Article;

(2) Transfer a cab card and identifier to a vehicle other than the vehicle for which it was originally executed, except in accordance with Commission regulations;

(3) Use a cab card and identifier issued to another carrier or permit the use of a cab card by another carrier except in accordance with Commission regulations; or

(4) Fail to present a cab card and identifier as required by this Article.

P.A. 76–1586, § 18c–4604, added by P.A. 84–796, § 1, eff. Jan. 1, 1986. Amended by P.A. 85–553, § 2, eff. Sept. 18, 1987.

Formerly Ill.Rev.Stat.1991, ch. 95 ½, ¶ 18c–4604.

ARTICLE VII. IDENTIFICATION OF CARRIERS

5/18c–4701. Insignia on Vehicles

§ 18c–4701. Insignia on Vehicles.

(1) General Requirements to be Prescribed by Commission. Except as otherwise provided in this Section, no intrastate carrier shall operate any motor vehicle upon the public roads of this State unless there is painted or affixed to both sides of the cab or power unit, in accordance with such specifications as the Commission may prescribe, the trade name of the carrier as it appears on the carrier's license or the carrier's recognized logo, together with the license and registration number of the carrier. Likewise, no interstate carrier shall operate any motor vehicle upon the public roads of this State unless there is painted or affixed to both sides of the cab or power unit, in accordance with such specifications as the Commission may prescribe, the registration or authority number of the carrier.

(2) Use of ICC–Prescribed Identification. Identifying information prescribed by the Interstate Commerce Commission may be used in satisfaction of requirements established under this Section, including special orders granting a petition for waiver of Sections 1057.22(a) and 1057.22(c)(2) and (4), as they relate to equipment receipts, of the Lease and Interchange of Vehicle Regulations (49 CFR 1057), in lieu of numbers or symbols prescribed by the Commission.

(3) Identification of Trip Lessees. Notwithstanding any other provision of this Section to the contrary, a motor vehicle trip leased in accordance with this Chapter, Commission regulations and orders shall not be required to bear the name and license number of the lessee if:

(a) the motor vehicle bears the name and license or registration number of the lessor in accordance with subsection (1) of this Section, Commission regulations and orders;

(b) the lessor and lessee are commonly-owned; and

(c) the vehicle carries a photocopy of a letter signed by the lessor, on file with the Commission, stating that the lessor and lessee are commonly-owned.

(4) Rules not superseded. The authority of the Illinois Commerce Commission to regulate the identification of motor vehicles of intrastate and interstate carriers, engaged in the transportation of hazardous materials, shall not supersede or replace the rules and regulations of the Illinois Department of Transportation and Federal Motor Carrier Safety regulations Part 390.21, as relates now or hereafter to the markings and identification of such vehicles.

(5) Identification on vehicles under 9,000 pounds gross vehicle weight (GVW). Vehicles with a gross vehicle weight (GVW) less than 9,000 pounds may, in lieu of identification required under subsection (1) of this Section display the trade name of the carrier as it appears on the carrier's license or the carrier's recognized logo, together with the license and registration number of the carrier in such manner as to be clearly legible and visible from both sides of the vehicle at a distance of 25 feet, when the vehicle is not in motion, and in accordance with such specifications as the Commission may prescribe.

P.A. 76–1586, § 18c–4701, added by P.A. 84–796, § 1, eff. Jan. 1, 1986. Amended by P.A. 85–553, § 2, eff. Sept. 18, 1987; P.A. 85–786, § 1, eff. Jan. 1, 1988; P.A. 85–809, § 1, eff. Sept. 24, 1987; P.A. 85–1209, Art. II, § 2–51, eff. Aug. 30, 1988; P.A. 85–1407, § 2, eff. Sept. 22, 1988; P.A. 85–1440, Art. II, § 2–54, eff. Feb. 1, 1989; P.A. 88–415, § 10, eff. Aug. 20, 1993; P.A. 91–357, § 231, eff. July 29, 1999.

Formerly Ill.Rev.Stat.1991, ch. 95 ½, ¶ 18c–4701.

5/18c–4702. Identification of Carrier in Advertising, Solicitation, and Other Documents

§ 18c–4702. Identification of Carrier in Advertising, Solicitation, and other Documents. No carrier shall use in any advertising, solicitation, correspondence, publication, or other document connected with its transportation service any name other than its name or trade name as it appears on the carrier's license or registration. Each advertisement, solicitation, correspondence, publication, or other document shall contain the carrier's license or registration number unless otherwise provided in Commission regulations or orders.

P.A. 76–1586, § 18c–4702, added by P.A. 84–796, § 1, eff. Jan. 1, 1986. Amended by P.A. 85–553, § 2, eff. Sept. 18, 1987.

Formerly Ill.Rev.Stat.1991, ch. 95 ½, ¶ 18c–4702.

ARTICLE VIII. BILLS OF LADING

5/18c–4801. Rights, Obligations and Liabilities

§ 18c–4801. Rights, Obligations, and Liabilities. The provisions of Sections 7–101, 7–102, 7–103, 7–104, 7–105, 7–301, 7–302, 7–303, 7–304, 7–305, 7–306, 7–307, 7–308, 7–309, 7–401, 7–402, 7–403, 7–404, 7–501, 7–502, 7–503, 7–504, 7–505, 7–506, 7–507, 7–508, 7–509, 7–601, 7–602, 7–603 of the "Uniform Commercial Code", as amended,[1] are adopted by reference to the extent that they relate to bills of lading and the intrastate transportation of property by a motor common carrier.

P.A. 76–1586, § 18c–4801, added by P.A. 84–796, § 1, eff. Jan. 1, 1986.

Formerly Ill.Rev.Stat.1991, ch. 95 ½, ¶ 18c–4801.

[1] 810 ILCS 5/7–101, 5/7–102, 5/7–103, 5/7–104, 5/7–105, 5/7–301, 5/7–302, 5/7–303, 5/7–304, 5/7–305, 5/7–306, 5/7–307, 5/7–308, 5/7–309, 5/7–401, 5/7–402, 5/7–403, 5/7–404, 5/7–501, 5/7–502, 5/7–503, 5/7–504, 5/7–505, 5/7–506, 5/7–507, 5/7–508, 5/7–509, 5/7–601, 5/7–602, 5/7–603.

5/18c–4802. Straight Bill of Lading

§ 18c–4802. Straight Bill of Lading. A bill in which it is stated that the goods are consigned or destined to a specific person is a straight bill.

P.A. 76–1586, § 18c–4802, added by P.A. 84–796, § 1, eff. Jan. 1, 1986.

Formerly Ill.Rev.Stat.1991, ch. 95 ½, ¶ 18c–4802.

5/18c–4803. Order Bill of Lading

§ 18c–4803. Order Bill of Lading. A bill of lading in which it is stated that the goods are consigned or destined to the order of any person named in such bill is an order bill of lading. Any provision in such a bill or in any notice, contract, regulation, or tariff that it is nonnegotiable shall be null and void unless upon its face and in writing such provision is agreed to by the shipper.

P.A. 76-1586, § 18c-4803, added by P.A. 84-796, § 1, eff. Jan. 1, 1986.

Formerly Ill.Rev.Stat.1991, ch. 95 ½, ¶ 18c-4803.

5/18c-4804. Limitation of Liability

§ 18c-4804. Limitation of Liability. The provisions of this Section respecting liability for full actual loss, damage or injury, notwithstanding subsection 2 of Section 7-309 of the "Uniform Commercial Code", as amended,[1] do not apply to property received for transportation concerning which the carrier is expressly authorized or required by order of the Commission to establish rates based on value declared in writing by the shipper or agreed upon by the shipper, in writing, as the released value of the property. Such declarations or agreements have no other effect than to limit liability to an amount not exceeding the value declared or released, and are not in violation of this Chapter. A tariff containing such rates shall contain specific reference to the Commission order authorizing them.

P.A. 76-1586, § 18c-4804, added by P.A. 84-796, § 1, eff. Jan. 1, 1986.

Formerly Ill.Rev.Stat.1991, ch. 95 ½, ¶ 18c-4804.

[1] 810 ILCS 5/7-309.

5/18c-4805. Other Remedies Available to Holder of Bill of Lading Not Preempted

§ 18c-4805. Other Remedies Available to Holder of Bill of Lading Not Preempted. This Article does not deprive any holder of a receipt or bill of lading of any remedy or right of action had under existing law.

P.A. 76-1586, § 18c-4805, added by P.A. 84-796, § 1, eff. Jan. 1, 1986.

Formerly Ill.Rev.Stat.1991, ch. 95 ½, ¶ 18c-4805.

5/18c-4806. Delivering Carrier Defined

§ 18c-4806. Delivering Carrier Defined. For the purposes of this Section the delivering carrier is the carrier performing transportation service to or nearest to the point of destination.

P.A. 76-1586, § 18c-4806, added by P.A. 84-796, § 1, eff. Jan. 1, 1986.

Formerly Ill.Rev.Stat.1991, ch. 95 ½, ¶ 18c-4806.

5/18c-4807. Bill of Lading or Similar Documentation Required

§ 18c-4807. Bill of Lading or Similar Documentation Required. (1) General Requirements. Except as provided in subsection (2) of this Section, every motor common carrier of property shall be required to issue a bill of lading and freight bill indicating the commodities transported, weight thereof (where freight charges are assessed by weight), the points of origin and destination of such commodities, the consignor and consignee, and the charge therefor. If the commodities are not delivered by the originating carrier, the bill of lading or freight bill shall indicate the point of interchange and the connecting carrier. This Section shall not apply to motor contract carriers of property.

(2) Exceptions.

(a) Simplified Documentation. The Commission may prescribe simplified documentation to be issued by classes of carriers where such requirements would be less burdensome and would effectuate the purposes of this Chapter. Simplified documentation shall be prescribed for the following classes of carriers:

(i) Motor common carriers of shipments composed of parcels weighing 100 pounds or less and not exceeding 200 pounds from one consignor to one consignee on one day;

(ii) Carriers of agricultural or dairy products, poultry, eggs, or fruits;

(iii) Aggregate carriers; and

(iv) Messenger carriers; and

(v) Such other classes as the Commission may, from time to time, determine.

(b) Supplementary Requirements. The Commission may adopt supplementary requirements for the issuance or carrying of documentation for household goods carriers or other carriers where large numbers of non-commercial shippers may be affected and such documentation is necessary to effectuate the purposes of this Chapter.

(c) Commodity descriptions for shipments weighing 10 pounds or less. Where a shipment weighs ten pounds or less, except when it contains dangerous articles or hazardous materials, the following may be used in lieu of a commodity description: "Parcel 10 Pounds or Under".

P.A. 76-1586, § 18c-4807, added by P.A. 84-796, § 1, eff. Jan. 1, 1986. Amended by P.A. 85-1407, § 2, eff. Sept. 22, 1988.

Formerly Ill.Rev.Stat.1991, ch. 95 ½, ¶ 18c-4807.

ARTICLE IX. SAFETY REGULATIONS FOR MOTOR CARRIERS OF PROPERTY: INSURANCE

5/18c-4901. Insurance Coverage as a Prerequisite to Operations

§ 18c-4901. Insurance Coverage as a Prerequisite to Operations. No motor carrier of property shall operate within this State unless it has on file with the Commission or its agent proof of continuous insurance or surety coverage in accordance with Commission regulations.

P.A. 76-1586, § 18c-4901, added by P.A. 84-796, § 1, eff. Jan. 1, 1986. Amended by P.A. 85-553, § 2, eff. Sept. 18, 1987.

Formerly Ill.Rev.Stat.1991, ch. 95 ½, ¶ 18c-4901.

5/18c-4902. Commission to Set Insurance Coverage Limits and Establish Procedures

§ 18c-4902. Commission to Set Insurance Coverage Limits and Establish Procedures. The Commission shall prescribe the amounts of insurance or surety coverage required as a minimum, the maximum allowable deductible limits, procedures for the filing and rejection or return of filings, and such other reasonable regulations regarding insurance or surety coverage as are necessary to protect the travelling and shipping or receiving public.

P.A. 76-1586, § 18c-4902, added by P.A. 84-796, § 1, eff. Jan. 1, 1986. Amended by P.A. 84-1025, § 2, eff. Jan. 1, 1986; P.A. 85-553, § 2, eff. Sept. 18, 1987.

Formerly Ill.Rev.Stat.1991, ch. 95 ½, ¶ 18c-4902.

5/18c-4903. Implied Terms of Insurance Coverage

§ 18c-4903. Implied Terms of Insurance Coverage. Each certificate or other proof of insurance or surety coverage shall have, as an implied term, that the insurance or surety coverage will remain in effect continuously until notice of cancellation is filed in accordance with Commission regulations, and that all motor vehicles operated by or under authority of the carrier will be covered, whether or not such vehicles have been reported to the insurance, surety, or other company. Filing proof of insurance with the Commission shall constitute acceptance of this implied term, and such acceptance may not thereafter be withdrawn except on withdrawal of all proof of insurance or surety coverage.

P.A. 76-1586, § 18c-4903, added by P.A. 84-796, § 1, eff. Jan. 1, 1986. Amended by P.A. 85-553, § 2, eff. Sept. 18, 1987.

Formerly Ill.Rev.Stat.1991, ch. 95 ½, ¶ 18c-4903.

5/18c-4904. Liability to Be Covered by Insurance

§ 18c-4904. Liability to Be Covered by Insurance. Insurance or surety under this Article shall cover the carrier's liability for injury to persons and damage to property other than cargo. Coverage shall, in the case of motor common carriers, also extend to cargo damage.

P.A. 76-1586, § 18c-4904, added by P.A. 84-796, § 1, eff. Jan. 1, 1986. Amended by P.A. 85-553, § 2, eff. Sept. 18, 1987.

Formerly Ill.Rev.Stat.1991, ch. 95 ½, ¶ 18c-4904.

5/18c-4905. Self-insurance

§ 18c-4905. Self-insurance. The Commission may exempt a carrier from the requirement of Sections 18c-4901, 18c-4902, 18c-4903, and 18c-4904 of this Chapter if it determines that the carrier has the financial ability to pay for any and all damages the liability for which would otherwise be assumed by an insurance or surety company under the referenced sections. Each carrier so exempted shall file periodic reports, at such intervals as the Commission shall specify, showing its continuing ability to act as a self-insurer. The Commission may rescind an exemption on 10 days' notice if rescission appears necessary to protect the public. Upon the granting or rescission of a self-insured status of a carrier by the Commission, the Commission shall immediately notify, in writing, the Illinois Department of Transportation of the name, address, and other pertinent information required by the Department of Transportation concerning the status of the carrier.

P.A. 76-1586, § 18c-4905, added by P.A. 84-796, § 1, eff. Jan. 1, 1986. Amended by P.A. 84-1246, § 1, eff. July 29, 1986.

Formerly Ill.Rev.Stat.1991, ch. 95 ½, ¶ 18c-4905.

SUB-CHAPTER 5. SPECIAL PROVISIONS APPLICABLE TO TRANSPORTATION OF PROPERTY OVER PUBLIC ROADS

ARTICLE I. BROKERS

ARTICLE II. RESOLUTION OF HOUSEHOLD GOODS DISPUTES

ARTICLE III. NON-RELOCATION TOWING

ARTICLE I. BROKERS

5/18c-5101. Unlawful Activities

§ 18c-5101. Unlawful Activities. It shall be unlawful for any person:

(1) To act as a broker without a license in good standing issued to it by the Commission;

(2) To act as a broker in violation of any provision of this Chapter, Commission regulations and orders, or any other law of this state;

(3) To act as a broker of any shipment which the person owns or in which the person has a beneficial interest;

(4) To act as a broker of any shipment over which the person is able to exercise control because the person acting as a broker owns or controls the shipper, the shipper owns or controls the person acting as a broker, or there is a common ownership or control of the two;

(5) Which is also a broker to act or represent itself as a shipper in dealing with a common or contract carrier of property by motor vehicle;

(6) To act as a broker in connection with transportation by a person other than an authorized common or contract carrier of property by motor vehicle, unless the carrier does not require authorization to transport the shipment;

(7) To act as a broker in connection with transportation at other than lawfully applicable rates for the motor carrier service;

(8) To act as a broker in any name other than that which appears on its Commission license;

(9) To act as a broker without fully disclosing its brokering status;

(10) To provide transportation service with regard to freight for which it was the broker;

(11) To receive any compensation for brokering services other than a fee assessed to the shipper or, alternatively, to the carrier, in addition to freight charges at lawfully applicable rates for the motor carrier service;

(12) To advertise, offer, or give anything of value to a shipper, consignor, or consignee, other than inexpensive promotional items; or

(13) Act as a broker of household goods.

P.A. 76-1586, § 18c-5101, added by P.A. 84-796, § 1, eff. Jan. 1, 1986.

Formerly Ill.Rev.Stat.1991, ch. 95 ½, ¶ 18c-5101.

5/18c-5102. Licensing of Brokers

§ 18c-5102. Licensing of Brokers. (1) Procedures for Issuing Brokers' Licenses. The Provisions of Article II of Sub-chapter 4 of this Chapter which govern the form and manner of filing of applications for authority, notice to be given to the public, and hearing, shall likewise govern the issuance of a brokers' license.

(2) Standards for Review of Brokers' License Applications. The Commission shall issue a license authorizing a person to act as a statewide broker of general commodities where:

(a) The person has properly filed an application on forms prescribed by the Commission;

(b) The person has remitted the filing fee prescribed by the Commission;

(c) The person has filed proof of bond or insurance as required by Commission regulations; and

(d) The Commission has determined that the person is fit, willing, and able to;

(i) Act as a statewide broker of general commodities as authorized by the license; and

(ii) Comply with provisions of this Chapter, Commission regulations and orders. Otherwise, the application shall be denied.

(3) Suspension or Revocation of Brokers' Licenses. If at any time the Commission determines after notice and hearing that the holder of a broker's license is not fit, willing, or able to continue to act as a broker, the Commission may suspend or revoke the license.

P.A. 76-1586, § 18c-5102, added by P.A. 84-796, § 1, eff. Jan. 1, 1986.

Formerly Ill.Rev.Stat.1991, ch. 95 ½, ¶ 18c-5102.

5/18c-5103. The Fitness Standard

§ 18c-5103. The Fitness Standard. A person shall be rebuttably presumed unfit to act or to continue to act as a broker if:

(1) The person has violated any provision of this Chapter, Commission regulations or orders, or any other law governing its activities as a broker;

(2) The person has violated any fiduciary or other obligation with regard to transmittal of monies, bills, or other matters entrusted to it as broker; or

(3) The person is applying for a broker's license and any other person the ownership, management, or control of which is or was in substantial identity with the applicant has committed an act of the type described in (1) or (2), above. The Commission may consider any relevant facts in determining whether a person is fit to act or to continue to act as a broker, or whether any presumption which arises under this Section has been rebutted.

P.A. 76-1586, § 18c-5103, added by P.A. 84-796, § 1, eff. Jan. 1, 1986.

Formerly Ill.Rev.Stat.1991, ch. 95 ½, ¶ 18c-5103.

5/18c-5104. Transfer of Brokers' Licenses

§ 18c-5104. Transfer of Brokers' Licenses. (1) Transfer of Brokers' Licenses Permitted. A broker's license may be transferred, with Commission approval, under the conditions specified in this Section and in accordance with such regulations as the Commission may prescribe.

(2) Procedures for Transferring Brokers' Licenses. The provisions of Article III of the Sub-chapter 4 of this Chapter that define a transfer and which govern the form and manner of filing of applications for approval of the transfer of a motor carrier of property license, notice to be given to the public, and hearing, shall likewise govern the transfer of a broker's license.

(3) Standards for Review of Transfer Applications. The Commission shall grant an application for authority to transfer a broker's license where:

(a) The application was properly filed on forms prescribed by the Commission;

(b) The person has remitted the filing fee prescribed by the Commission; and

(c) The transferee is fit, willing, and able under the terms of Section 18c-5103 of this Chapter.

Otherwise, the application shall be denied.

P.A. 76-1586, § 18c-5104, added by P.A. 84-796, § 1, eff. Jan. 1, 1986.

Formerly Ill.Rev.Stat.1991, ch. 95 ½, ¶ 18c-5104.

5/18c-5105. Bonds and Insurance

§ 18c-5105. Bonds and Insurance. The Commission may prescribe for brokers such requirements regarding bonds, insurance, and the terms of coverage thereof, as the Commission determines are needed to protect carriers, shippers, consignors, and consignees of freight with respect to which brokering service is provided. Unless otherwise provided by the Commission, such requirements shall be the same as are applicable to property brokers under the Interstate Commerce Act [1] and regulations adopted thereunder.

P.A. 76-1586, § 18c-5105, added by P.A. 84-796, § 1, eff. Jan. 1, 1986.

Formerly Ill.Rev.Stat.1991, ch. 95 ½, ¶ 18c-5105.

[1] 49 U.S.C.A. § 10101 et seq.

5/18c-5106. Records of Brokers

§ 18c-5106. Records of Brokers. (1) Records to be Kept by Brokers. A broker shall keep a record of each transaction which shows:

(a) The name, address, and license number of the motor carrier or carriers;

(b) The name and address of the shipper, consignor, and consignee;

(c) The Bill of Lading or freight bill number;

(d) The amount of compensation received by the broker for brokering service, and the identity of the payor;

(e) A description of any non-brokering service provided in connection with each shipment or other activity, the amount of compensation received for such non-brokering service, and the identity of the payor;

(f) The amount of any freight charges collected by the broker, the date on which such charges were paid over to the carrier, and the amount of payment to the carrier; and

(g) Any other information which the Commission may prescribe.

(2) Maintenance of Records. Records required to be kept under this Section shall be maintained at an office within the State of Illinois, unless maintenance of an office outside the State of Illinois is expressly authorized by the Commission,

and shall be maintained for a period of 3 years after the date on which the shipment was delivered.

(3) Accounting. Each broker which engages in other business shall maintain accounts so that the brokering portion of its business or businesses is segregated from its other activities.

P.A. 76–1586, § 18c–5106, added by P.A. 84–796, § 1, eff. Jan. 1, 1986.

Formerly Ill.Rev.Stat.1991, ch. 95 ½, ¶ 18c–5106.

5/18c–5107. Brokers and Motor Carrier Applications

§ 18c–5107. Brokers and Motor Carrier Applications. A Broker shall not have standing to support any application for motor carrier of property authority.

P.A. 76–1586, § 18c–5107, added by P.A. 84–796, § 1, eff. Jan. 1, 1986.

Formerly Ill.Rev.Stat.1991, ch. 95 ½, ¶ 18c–5107.

ARTICLE II. RESOLUTION OF HOUSEHOLD GOODS DISPUTES

5/18c–5201. Application of Article

§ 18c–5201. Application of Article. The provisions of this Article apply to the collect-on-delivery transportation of household goods for non-commercial use where:

(1) The dispute relates to the propriety of charges for services rendered or loss of or damage to lading from the loading, unloading, or transportation thereof;

(2) The movement to which the dispute relates was between points in the State of Illinois; or

(3) Either the movement was made under authority issued by the Commission or the movement was such that it could have been lawfully made only under authority issued by the Commission.

P.A. 76–1586, § 18c–5201, added by P.A. 84–796, § 1, eff. Jan. 1, 1986.

Formerly Ill.Rev.Stat.1991, ch. 95 ½, ¶ 18c–5201.

5/18c–5202. Commission to prescribe dispute resolution procedure

§ 18c–5202. Commission to prescribe dispute resolution procedures. (1) Within 180 days after the effective date of this amendatory Act of 1995, the Commission shall propose rules specifying the procedures by which disputes between carriers and shippers to which this Sub-chapter is applicable will be resolved. Upon adoption, the rules will be applicable to all household goods carriers.

(2) Standards for dispute resolution procedures. The rules adopted by the Commission shall be calculated to provide for the objective, expeditious, and inexpensive resolution of household goods disputes, and shall include, without limitation, provisions dealing with: the location of any required hearings; required notifications; whether participation in a dispute resolution procedure is mandatory; and how the fees and costs of the procedures shall be distributed. To the extent authorized by Commission rules, procedures adopted under this Article may specify that dispute resolution services will be provided by the Commission, and in accordance with procedural rules adopted by the Commission.

(3) Grounds for Resolution of Household Goods Disputes. A dispute under this Article shall be resolved adverse to the carrier if:

(a) The carrier assessed a rate not contained in a lawfully applicable tariff or tariffs for such services;

(b) The carrier failed to fully apprise the shipper, prior to execution of any contract or contract amendment covering the services, of the lawful rates and charges for such services;

(c) Damages to lading occurred during the loading, transportation, or unloading of the shipments, or rendition of any accessorial service by the carrier, its employees or agents, without regard to negligence or fault, and the shipper did not elect in writing to assume liability for all or part of such damages.

P.A. 76–1586, § 18c–5202, added by P.A. 84–796, § 1, eff. Jan. 1, 1986. Amended by P.A. 89–444, § 5, eff. Jan. 25, 1996.

Formerly Ill.Rev.Stat.1991, ch. 95 ½, ¶ 18c–5202.

5/18c–5203. Award of Attorney Fees

§ 18c–5203. Award of Attorneys Fees. (1) Award to Complaining Shipper. In any court action to resolve a dispute within the scope of this Article, the court shall award reasonable attorney's fees to the complaining shipper if:

(a) The shipper submitted a claim to the carrier within 120 days after delivery of the shipment is completed;

(b) The shipper prevailed in the court action; and

(c) Either:

(i) No certified private dispute resolution procedure was available for use by the shipper at the time the court action was initiated; or

(ii) (Blank).

(iii) The court action was to enforce a timely decision rendered under the dispute resolution procedures specified by the Commission under this amendatory Act of 1995.

(2) Award to carrier. In any court action to resolve a dispute within the scope of this Article, the court may award reasonable attorney's fees to the carrier if the shipper brought the action in bad faith after submitting the dispute for resolution under the dispute resolution procedures specified by the Commission.

P.A. 76–1586, § 18c–5203, added by P.A. 84–796, § 1, eff. Jan. 1, 1986. Amended by P.A. 89–444, § 5, eff. Jan. 25, 1996.

Formerly Ill.Rev.Stat.1991, ch. 95 ½, ¶ 18c–5203.

5/18c–5204. Investigation of Practices of Household Goods Carriers

§ 18c–5204. Investigation of Practices of Household Goods Carriers. The Commission may, on its own motion or on complaint, conduct an investigation to determine whether a household goods carrier has, with or without the license required under Sub-chapter 4 of this Chapter,[1] engaged in a pattern or practice of underestimating freight charges for household goods shipments, or has otherwise violated provisions of this Chapter, Commission regulations or orders, and may invoke any or all sanctions provided for in Article VII of Sub-chapter 1 of this Chapter[2] against the carrier if such a pattern or practice, or any other violation, is found to have occurred.

P.A. 76–1586, § 18c–5204, added by P.A. 84–796, § 1, eff. Jan. 1, 1986. Amended by P.A. 90–89, § 15, eff. Jan. 1, 1998.

Formerly Ill.Rev.Stat.1991, ch. 95 ½, ¶ 18c–5204.

1 625 ILCS 5/18c–4101 et seq.

2 625 ILCS 5/18c–1701 et seq.

5/18c–5205. Applicability of Article

§ 18c–5205. Applicability of Article. This Article applies to disputes arising from transactions which occur at least 180 days after the effective date of this amendatory Act of 1985.

P.A. 76–1586, § 18c–5205, added by P.A. 84–796, § 1, eff. Jan. 1, 1986.

Formerly Ill.Rev.Stat.1991, ch. 95 ½, ¶ 18c–5205.

ARTICLE III. NON–RELOCATION TOWING

Enactment

Article III was added by P.A. 84–1311, § 1, eff. Aug. 27, 1986.

5/18c–5301. Application of Article

§ 18c–5301. Application of Article. The provisions of this Article shall apply to non-relocation towing. Where the provisions of this Article conflict with any other provisions in this Chapter, the provisions of this Article shall govern.

P.A. 76–1586, § 18c–5301, added by P.A. 84–1311, § 1, eff. Aug. 27, 1986.

Formerly Ill.Rev.Stat.1991, ch. 95 ½, ¶ 18c–5301.

5/18c–5302. Commission to Adopt Special Rules

§ 18c–5302. Commission to Adopt Special Rules.

(1) General Provisions. The Commission shall, within 180 days after the effective date of this Article, have finally adopted special forms and regulations applicable to non-relocation towing. Such regulations shall encompass definitions of terms, licensing, ratemaking, record-keeping, insurance or surety coverage, fees, and such other provisions as are necessary to effectuate the purposes of this Article. Such regulations shall be consistent with the provisions of this Article and shall implement such provisions with regard to non-relocation towing in a manner which recognizes the special circumstances and conditions which pertain to non-relocation towing as distinguished from other forms of motor carriage of property.

(2) Towing at Owner's Request. The Commission shall, within 60 days from July 1, 1988, adopt rules in accordance with Section 5–50 of the Illinois Administrative Procedure Act [1] which implement the provisions of this Chapter dealing with the exemption of non-relocation towing at the request of the vehicle owner.

P.A. 76–1586, § 18c–5302, added by P.A. 84–1311, § 1, eff. Aug. 27, 1986. Amended by P.A. 85–963, § 1, eff. July 1, 1988; P.A. 88–45, Art. III, § 3–128, eff. July 6, 1993.

Formerly Ill.Rev.Stat.1991, ch. 95 ½, ¶ 18c–5302.

[1] 5 ILCS 100/5–50.

5/18c–5303. Fitness Test

§ 18c–5303. The Fitness Test.

(1) Prima Facie Evidence of Applicant Fitness in Licensing Cases. Applicants for non-relocation towing licenses may establish a prima facie showing of fitness by the following evidence:

(a) A summary statement of net worth;

(b) A listing of applicant's drivers and any persons who assist or supervise drivers;

(c) A description of equipment to be used in providing service under the license;

(d) A statement that the applicant has not:

(i) Been convicted, during the 2 years immediately preceding the filing of the application, of a felony involving theft of property, violence to persons, or criminal damage to property; or

(ii) Been convicted, during the year immediately preceding the filing of the application, of safety violations on 3 or more occasions in which its vehicle or vehicles were taken out of service, or which otherwise show the applicant to be unfit;

(e) A statement that the applicant does not and will not employ or lease any driver, or any person who will assist or supervise drivers, who has been convicted, during the applicable time frames, of the foregoing violations;

(f) A statement that the applicant does not and will not employ or lease any driver who does not hold a valid classified driver's license to operate a tow truck;

(g) A statement that the applicant is familiar with and will comply with the provisions of this Chapter, Commission regulations and orders; and

(h) Proof of insurance in compliance with Commission regulations and orders.

(2) Prima Facie Evidence of Licensee Fitness in Enforcement Cases. The respondent in a proceeding to consider whether to suspend or revoke a license authorizing non-relocation towing or to impose other sanctions on grounds of unfitness may establish a prima facie showing of fitness in the manner provided in subsection (1) of this Section.

(3) Rebuttal of Prima Facie Showing of Fitness. A prima facie showing of applicant or licensee fitness may be rebutted by other evidence of record, either from the applicant or otherwise.

P.A. 76–1586, § 18c–5303, added by P.A. 84–1311, § 1, eff. Aug. 27, 1986.

Formerly Ill.Rev.Stat.1991, ch. 95 ½, ¶ 18c–5303.

5/18c–5304. Public Need/Public Convenience and Necessity Test

§ 18c–5304. The Public Need/Public Convenience and Necessity Test. Applicants for non-relocation towing licenses may establish, and other parties may rebut, a prima facie showing of public need/public convenience and necessity by the following evidence:

(1) Existing Towing Companies.

(a) Evidentiary Standard. Any person engaged in non-relocation towing between July 1, 1985 and January 1, 1986 may establish a prima facie showing of public convenience and necessity to the extent of such operations by submitting a statement:

(i) Affirming that the person was engaged in non-relocation during the foregoing time period; and

(ii) Describing its operations during such period.

(b) Extent of Existing Operations. The extent of the applicant's operations shall be presumed to encompass non-relocation towing within the following territory, unless otherwise shown on the record:

(i) Movements within a 50 mile radius of the applicant's principal place of business in Illinois; and

(ii) Movements from points within the foregoing radius to points in Illinois, and vice versa.

(c) Deadline for Filing Applications. Applications under this subsection must be filed within 9 months after the effective date of this amendatory Act of 1986, or by July 1, 1987, whichever is later.

(2) New Towing Companies and Extension of Existing Company Operations. Applications for non-relocation towing

licenses need not be supported by shippers intending to use the carrier's service if other evidence of public need/public convenience and necessity is offered by carrier witnesses, non-carrier witnesses from other than shippers intending to use the carrier's service, or others.

(3) Rebuttal of Prima Facie Showing of Public Need/Public Convenience and Necessity. A prima facie showing of public need/public convenience and necessity may be rebutted by other evidence of record, either from the applicant or otherwise.

P.A. 76–1586, § 18c–5304, added by P.A. 84–1311, § 1, eff. Aug. 27, 1986.

Formerly Ill.Rev.Stat.1991, ch. 95 ½, ¶ 18c–5304.

5/18c–5305. Hearings in Non-Relocation Towing Authority Cases

§ 18c–5305. Hearings in Non-Relocation Towing Authority Cases.

(1) Hearings on Fitness Required. Hearings on applications for non-relocation towing licenses shall be governed by the provisions of Section 18c–2101 of this Code, with regard to the issue of fitness; and by the provisions of subsection (2) of Section 18c–2102 of this Code, with regard to the issue of public need/public convenience and necessity. Hearings in other non-relocation towing cases shall be governed by the provisions of Section 18c–2102 of this Code.

(2) Setting and Conduct of Licensing Hearings.

(a) Regional Hearings. Hearings on applications for non-relocation towing licenses shall be consolidated and conducted regionally for the convenience of the parties. Where practicable:

(i) Hearings shall be conducted at a location not more than 50 miles from the principal place of the applicant's business;

(ii) The Commission shall schedule joint hearings at each regional location.

(b) Scheduling of Hearings. Hearings on applications for non-relocation towing licenses shall be scheduled and concluded so as to minimize inconvenience to the parties. Where practicable, hearings on an application shall be concluded in a single day, unless:

(i) Continuance is required for the applicant to produce evidence of its fitness; or

(ii) A petition for leave to intervene in opposition is properly filed and granted.

P.A. 76–1586, § 18c–5305, added by P.A. 84–1311, § 1, eff. Aug. 27, 1986.

Formerly Ill.Rev.Stat.1991, ch. 95 ½, ¶ 18c–5305.

5/18c–5306. Denial, Suspension or Revocation of Licenses

§ 18c–5306. Denial, Suspension, or Revocation of Licenses. If, at any time during or after adjudication of a non-relocation towing license application, there exists an issue with regard to the fitness of the applicant, the Commission may suspend any temporary license granted to the applicant. If the applicant is not shown to be fit, the Commission shall revoke the temporary license and deny the application for a permanent license. If, at any time subsequent to the grant of a permanent license, the holder is determined to be unfit, the Commission shall suspend or revoke the license. Suspension or revocation shall be after notice and hearing, absent waiver of same by respondent, as provided for other than motor carrier of property authority cases under Section 18c–2102 of this Code.

P.A. 76–1586, § 18c–5306, added by P.A. 84–1311, § 1, eff. Aug. 27, 1986.

Formerly Ill.Rev.Stat.1991, ch. 95 ½, ¶ 18c–5306.

5/18c–5307. False Statements by Applicant

§ 18c–5307. False Statements by Applicant. Any false statement of a material fact by an applicant shall be grounds for denial or revocation of a license.

P.A. 76–1586, § 18c–5307, added by P.A. 84–1311, § 1, eff. Aug. 27, 1986.

Formerly Ill.Rev.Stat.1991, ch. 95 ½, ¶ 18c–5307.

5/18c–5308. Intervention in Opposition to Non-Relocation Towing Applications

§ 18c–5308. Intervention in Opposition to Non-Relocation Towing Applications.

(1) Filing Fee for Petitions for Leave to Intervene in Opposition. The Commission shall prescribe a filing fee of not less than $100 for each petition for leave to intervene in opposition in a non-relocation towing authority case.

(2) Standing to Participate and Intervene. Any person with evidence relating to the fitness of an applicant for a non-relocation towing license may be permitted, at the discretion of the examiner, to present such evidence at hearing. The provisions of paragraph (a) of subsection (2) of Section 18c–2106 of this Code shall not apply to persons filing petitions for leave to intervene in opposition to non-relocation towing license applications, unless the issue of public need/public convenience and necessity is controverted by such persons at hearing.

P.A. 76–1586, § 18c–5308, added by P.A. 84–1311, § 1, eff. Aug. 27, 1986.

Formerly Ill.Rev.Stat.1991, ch. 95 ½, ¶ 18c–5308.

5/18c–5309. Ratemaking

§ 18c–5309. Ratemaking. Unless otherwise specified in the tariff, rates applicable to non-relocation towing shall be the maximum rates which may be charged by carriers participating in the tariff for such service.

P.A. 76–1586, § 18c–5309, added by P.A. 84–1311, § 1, eff. Aug. 27, 1986.

Formerly Ill.Rev.Stat.1991, ch. 95 ½, ¶ 18c–5309.

5/18c–5310. Insurance

§ 18c–5310. Insurance.

(1) Implied Garagekeeper's Liability. The filing of a form E certificate of insurance shall constitute a representation by the insurance company that the underlying insurance policy includes, with regard to non-relocation towing, liability for damage to vehicles in the custody of the non-relocation towing company, whether in transit or otherwise, in an amount not less than the amount of cargo insurance required under Commission regulations and orders, unless otherwise specified by the insurance company on the form E certificate of liability insurance.

(2) Filing Proof of Cargo Insurance. Except where the form E certificate of liability insurance indicates, in accordance with subsection (1) of this Section, that garagekeeper's liability is not covered by the underlying policy of insurance,

a non-relocation towing company shall not be required to file proof of cargo insurance for the transportation of vehicles.

P.A. 76–1586, § 18c–5310, added by P.A. 84–1311, § 1, eff. Aug. 27, 1986.

Formerly Ill.Rev.Stat.1991, ch. 95 ½, ¶ 18c–5310.

SUB–CHAPTER 6. MOTOR CARRIERS OF PASSENGERS

ARTICLE I. GENERAL PROVISIONS GOVERNING MOTOR CARRIERS OF PASSENGERS

ARTICLE I. GENERAL PROVISIONS GOVERNING MOTOR CARRIERS OF PASSENGERS

5/18c–6101. Scope of Commission Jurisdiction

§ 18c–6101. Scope of Commission Jurisdiction. Except as provided in Section 18c–6102 of this Chapter, the jurisdiction of the Commission shall extend to all motor carriers of passengers operating within the State of Illinois.

P.A. 76–1586, § 18c–6101, added by P.A. 84–796, § 1, eff. Jan. 1, 1986.

Formerly Ill.Rev.Stat.1991, ch. 95 ½, ¶ 18c–6101.

5/18c–6102. Exemptions From Commission Jurisdiction

§ 18c–6102. Exemptions From Commission Jurisdiction. The provisions of this Sub-chapter shall not, except as provided in Section 18c–6501 of this Chapter, apply to:

(1) carriers owned by any political subdivision, school district, institution of higher education, or municipality, and operated either by such political subdivision, institution of higher education, or municipality or its lessee or agent;

(2) commuter vans as defined in this Code;

(3) carriers transporting passengers without fixed routes or schedules and charging on a time or distance basis, including taxicabs, charter operations, and contract bus operations;

(4) carriers transporting passengers with fixed routes and schedules and charging on a per passenger fixed charge basis and which do not include an airport as a point to be served on the route, in whole or in part;

(5) transportation in vehicles with a manufacturer's rated seating capacity of less than 8 persons, including the driver;

(6) transportation subject to the Ridesharing Arrangements Act; [1]

(7) commuter buses offering short-haul for-hire regularly scheduled passenger transportation service within metropolitan and suburban areas, over regular routes with fixed schedules, and utilized primarily by passengers using reduced-fare, multiple-ride, or commutation tickets during morning and evening peak periods in travelling to and from their places of employment; and

(8) those persons owning and operating school buses, as defined in this Code, and regulated by other provisions of this Code.

P.A. 76–1586, § 18c–6102, added by P.A. 84–796, § 1, eff. Jan. 1, 1986. Amended by P.A. 84–1025, § 2, eff. Jan. 1, 1986; P.A. 84–1246, § 1, eff. July 29, 1986; P.A. 85–809, § 1, eff. Sept. 24, 1987; P.A. 90–407, § 5, eff. Aug. 15, 1997; P.A. 91–357, § 231, eff. July 29, 1999.

Formerly Ill.Rev.Stat.1991, ch. 95 ½, ¶ 18c–6102.

[1] 625 ILCS 30/1 et seq.

5/18c–6103. Unlawful Operations

§ 18c–6103. Unlawful Operations. Except as provided in Article I of this Sub-chapter, and subject to the provisions stated herein, no person shall:

(1) Operate as a motor carrier of passengers unless the person possesses a valid license authorizing such operations.

(2) Provide service at rates other than those contained in lawfully applicable tariffs for such service;

(3) Otherwise operate as a motor carrier of passengers in violation of any provision of this Chapter, Commission regulations and orders, or any other law of this state; or

(4) Aid or abet any other person in a violation of this Chapter, Commission regulations or orders, by soliciting or receiving, or by compensating service from a person not authorized to provide such service, or at other than lawful rates for such service, or otherwise.

P.A. 76–1586, § 18c–6103, added by P.A. 84–796, § 1, eff. Jan. 1, 1986.

Formerly Ill.Rev.Stat.1991, ch. 95 ½, ¶ 18c–6103.

ARTICLE II. LICENSING

5/18c–6201. Requirements for Issuance of Licenses

§ 18c–6201. Requirements for Issuance of Licenses. (1) General Requirements. Except as provided in subsection (2) of this Section, the Commission shall grant an application for a motor carrier of passengers license, in whole or in part, to the extent that it finds that the application was properly filed, a need for the proposed service exists, the applicant if fit, willing, and able to provide the service in compliance with this Chapter, Commission regulations and orders, absent a showing that issuance of the license would be inconsistent with the public interest. Otherwise, the application shall be denied. In determining whether issuance of a motor carrier of passengers license would be inconsistent with the public interest, the Commission shall consider:

(a) The value of competition which would result from issuance to the travelling public;

(b) The effect of issuance on motor carrier of passengers service to small communities;

(c) The effect of issuance on the ability of any other carrier to provide a substantial portion of the passenger service such carrier provides over its entire system, except that diversion of revenue or traffic from a carrier in and of itself shall not be sufficient to support a finding that issuance of the license would impair the ability of the other carrier to provide a substantial portion of the passenger service such carrier provides over its entire system; and

(d) Any other factor relevant to the public interest.

(2) Motor Carriers of Passengers Providing Service to or from Airports. The Commission shall grant an application for a motor carrier of passengers license authorizing service along any route where an airport is a point to be served on the route, in whole or in part, to the extent that it finds that the application was properly filed, a need for the proposed service exists, the applicant is fit, willing, and able to provide the service in compliance with this Chapter, Commission regulations and orders, and the public convenience and necessity requires issuance of the license. Otherwise, the application shall be denied. The provisions of this subsection shall be construed to impose the same entry requirements as were previously applicable under Section 55 of "An Act concerning public utilities", approved June 29, 1921, as amended.[1]

P.A. 76–1586, § 18c–6201, added by P.A. 84–796, § 1, eff. Jan. 1, 1986. Amended by P.A. 85–553, § 2, eff. Sept. 18, 1987.

Formerly Ill.Rev.Stat.1991, ch. 95 ½, ¶ 18c–6201.

[1] Former Ill.Rev.Stat. ch. 111⅔, ¶ 55 (repealed; see, now 220 ILCS 5/8–302).

5/18c–6202. Other Provisions Relating to Licensing and Registration

§ 18c–6202. Other Provisions Relating to Licensing and Registration. Provisions in Articles II, III, and IV of Subchapter 4 of this Chapter, governing the suspension, revocation, and transfer of motor carrier of property licenses, the registration of interstate motor carriers of property shall likewise govern motor carriers of passengers as if all references therein were to motor carriers of passengers.

P.A. 76–1586, § 18c–6202, added by P.A. 84–796, § 1, eff. Jan. 1, 1986. Amended by P.A. 85–553, § 2, eff. Sept. 18, 1987.

Formerly Ill.Rev.Stat.1991, ch. 95 ½, ¶ 18c–6202.

ARTICLE III. ADDITION, CHANGE, REDUCTION, OR DISCONTINUANCE OF SCHEDULED MOTOR BUS SERVICE

5/18c–6301. General Provisions

§ 18c–6301. General Provisions. No motor common carrier of passengers shall add to, change, reduce, or discontinue service to any point along a route over which the carrier is authorized to provide intrastate service, except in accordance with the provisions of this Article.

P.A. 76–1586, § 18c–6301, added by P.A. 84–796, § 1, eff. Jan. 1, 1986. Amended by P.A. 85–553, § 2, eff. Sept. 18, 1987.

Formerly Ill.Rev.Stat.1991, ch. 95 ½, ¶ 18c–6301.

5/18c–6302. Definitions

§ 18c–6302. Definitions. The following terms, when used in this Article, shall have the hereinafter designated meanings.

(1) "Addition" to service means the institution of new scheduled service.

(2) "Change" in service means a change in the time or times of scheduled service which does not constitute a reduction or discontinuance of service.

(3) "Reduction" of service means any reduction in the level of scheduled service which does not constitute discontinuance of the carrier's service.

(4) "Discontinuance" of service means total discontinuance of service to any point along a route over which the carrier is authorized to provide service or reduction in the level of service to any such point to less than one round trip per weekday (Monday through Friday).

P.A. 76–1586, § 18c–6302, added by P.A. 84–796, § 1, eff. Jan. 1, 1986. Amended by P.A. 90–655, § 153, eff. July 30, 1998.

Formerly Ill.Rev.Stat.1991, ch. 95 ½, ¶ 18c–6302.

5/18c–6303. Schedule Changes and Reductions in Service

§ 18c–6303. Schedule Changes and Reductions in Service. Any motor common carrier of passengers may add to, change, or reduce the level of its service to any point along a route over which the carrier is authorized to provide service, provided that the addition, change or reduction does not constitute discontinuance of service to any point along a route over which the carrier is authorized to serve, after the carrier has served notice in accordance with Commission regulations adopted pursuant to this Article, and without prior authorization.

P.A. 76–1586, § 18c–6303, added by P.A. 84–796, § 1, eff. Jan. 1, 1986.

Formerly Ill.Rev.Stat.1991, ch. 95 ½, ¶ 18c–6303.

5/18c–6304. Discontinuances

§ 18c–6304. Discontinuances. No motor common carrier of passengers shall discontinue service to any point along a route over which the carrier is authorized to provide service except in accordance with provisions of Section 18c–6305 of this Chapter.

P.A. 76–1586, § 18c–6304, added by P.A. 84–796, § 1, eff. Jan. 1, 1986.

Formerly Ill.Rev.Stat.1991, ch. 95 ½, ¶ 18c–6304.

5/18c–6305. Prior Notice and Petition for Authorization

§ 18c–6305. Prior Notice and Petition for Authorization. (1) Annual and Amended Lists of Points Under Consideration for Discontinuance. By March of each calendar year, each motor carrier of passengers shall submit to the Commission a list of routes and points which it is authorized to serve which the carrier has under consideration for discontinuance within the following 12 months. A carrier may amend its list on the 1st day of each subsequent month.

(2) Notice of Intent to Discontinue. Not less than 30 days after a point appears on a list of points under consideration for discontinuance, the carrier may serve on the Commission the carrier's Notice of Intent to discontinue service. Such notice shall be for the purpose of alerting the Commission

and allowing a period of time during which alternatives to discontinuance, or alternative service, may be explored.

(3) Petitions to Discontinue. Not less than 60 nor more than 90 days after the filing of a Notice of Intent to discontinue, the carrier may formally propose discontinuance by filing in accordance with such requirements as to form and content as the Commission may prescribe. The Commission may investigate the proposal, and may suspend the discontinuance pending the outcome of the investigation for a period not to exceed 90 days from the date the proposal is filed. The Commission shall determine, after considering the public need for service, revenues (both those which have been received and those which might be received, by subsidy or otherwise) and variable costs associated with the service, and the availability of reasonable alternative transportation service whether the public convenience and necessity requires continuation of the service proposed to be discontinued. If the Commission determines that the public convenience and necessity requires continuation, it shall so order; otherwise, the proceeding shall be dismissed.

(4) Waiver or Notice. Prior notice requirements under this Section may be waived for good cause or where the carrier has made substantial compliance with such prior notice requirements or compliance is not necessary to effectuate the purposes of this Chapter.

P.A. 76-1586, § 18c-6305, added by P.A. 84-796, § 1, eff. Jan. 1, 1986.

Formerly Ill.Rev.Stat.1991, ch. 95 ½, ¶ 18c-6305.

ARTICLE IV. RATEMAKING

5/18c-6401. Ratemaking

§ 18c-6401. Ratemaking. The Commission may exercise, with respect to rate regulation of motor carriers of passengers, any and all power which it may exercise with respect to rate regulation of motor carriers of property. Motor carriers of passengers shall be in all respects subject to provisions of this Chapter governing ratemaking for motor carriers of property, except as provided in 49 U.S. Code 11501(e).

P.A. 76-1586, § 18c-6401, added by P.A. 84-796, § 1, eff. Jan. 1, 1986.

Formerly Ill.Rev.Stat.1991, ch. 95 ½, ¶ 18c-6401.

ARTICLE V. SAFETY REQUIREMENTS FOR MOTOR CARRIERS OF PASSENGERS

5/18c-6501. Hours of Service for Drivers

§ 18c-6501. Hours of Service for Drivers. No motor carrier of passengers shall operate any vehicle with a manufacturer's rated seating capacity of more than 8 persons, including the driver, except in compliance with federal hours of service regulations codified at 49 Code of Federal Regulations Part 395, Hours of Service of Drivers, as amended.

P.A. 76-1586, § 18c-6501, added by P.A. 84-796, § 1, eff. Jan. 1, 1986.

Formerly Ill.Rev.Stat.1991, ch. 95 ½, ¶ 18c-6501.

5/18c-6502. Report and Investigations of Accidents

§ 18c-6502. Report and Investigation of Accidents. (1) Reports. Every motor carrier of passengers shall report to the Commission, by the speediest means possible, whether telephone, telegraph, or otherwise, every accident involving its equipment which resulted in loss of life to any person. In addition to reports required to be filed with the Department of Transportation, under Article IV of Chapter 11 and Chapter 7 of this Code,[1] such carrier shall file a written report with the Commission, in accordance with regulations adopted hereunder, of any accident which results in injury or loss of life to any employee, or damage to the person or property of any member of the public. The Commission and the Department of Transportation may adopt, by reference, such state or federal reporting requirements as will effectuate the purposes of this Section and promote uniformity in bus accident reporting.

(2) Investigations. The Commission and the Department of Transportation may investigate any bus accident reported to it or of which it acquires knowledge independent of reports made by motor carriers of passengers, and shall have the power to enter such orders and adopt such regulations as will minimize the risk of future accidents.

P.A. 76-1586, § 18c-6502, added by P.A. 84-796, § 1, eff. Jan. 1, 1986. Amended by P.A. 84-1246, § 1, eff. July 29, 1986.

Formerly Ill.Rev.Stat.1991, ch. 95 ½, ¶ 18c-6502.

[1] 625 ILCS 5/11-401 et seq. and 5/7-100 et seq.

5/18c-6503. Insurance

§ 18c-6503. Insurance. The provisions of Article IX of Subchapter 4 of this Chapter regarding insurance for motor carriers of property shall apply to motor carriers of passengers subject to the jurisdiction of the Commission under this Subchapter as if all references in Article IX were to motor carriers of passengers.

P.A. 76-1586, § 18c-6503, added by P.A. 84-1025, § 2, eff. Jan. 1, 1986.

Formerly Ill.Rev.Stat.1991, ch. 95 ½, ¶ 18c-6503.

SUB-CHAPTER 7. RAIL CARRIERS

ARTICLE I. JURISDICTION OVER RAIL CARRIERS

ARTICLE II. REGISTRATION AND SERVICES OF RAIL CARRIERS

ARTICLE III. RATEMAKING

ARTICLE IV. SAFETY REQUIREMENTS FOR RAIL CARRIERS

ARTICLE V. MISCELLANEOUS PROVISIONS

ARTICLE I. JURISDICTION OVER RAIL CARRIERS

5/18c-7101. Jurisdiction Over Rail Carriers

§ 18c-7101. Jurisdiction Over Rail Carriers. The jurisdiction of the Commission under this Sub-chapter shall be exclusive and shall extend to all intrastate and interstate rail carrier operations within this State, except to the extent that its jurisdiction is preempted by valid provisions of the Staggers Rail Act of 1980 [1] or other valid federal statute, regulation, or order.

P.A. 76-1586, § 18c-7101, added by P.A. 84-796, § 1, eff. Jan. 1, 1986. Amended by P.A. 85-406, § 1, eff. Sept. 15, 1987.

Formerly Ill.Rev.Stat.1991, ch. 95 ½, ¶ 18c-7101.

[1] 49 U.S.C.A. § 10101 et seq.

ARTICLE II. REGISTRATION AND SERVICES OF RAIL CARRIERS

5/18c-7201. Registration as a Rail Carrier

§ 18c-7201. Registration as a Rail Carrier. (1) General Provisions. Except as provided in subsection (2) of this Section, no person shall operate as a rail carrier, and no person shall begin or continue construction of any track or other facilities, other than the repair or replacement of existing plant, for use in operations as a rail carrier unless such person has registered with the Commission as a rail carrier.

(2) Exceptions. Each rail carrier operating within the State of Illinois on the effective date of this Chapter shall automatically be deemed, as of that date, to have registered as a rail carrier for purposes of this Section. Such constructive registration shall expire on the 180th day after the effective date of this amendatory Act of 1985.

P.A. 76-1586, § 18c-7201, added by P.A. 84-796, § 1, eff. Jan. 1, 1986.

Formerly Ill.Rev.Stat.1991, ch. 95 ½, ¶ 18c-7201.

5/18c-7202. Duties and Obligations of Rail Carriers

§ 18c-7202. Duties and Obligations of Rail Carriers. Each rail carrier shall provide adequate service to the public at reasonable rates and without discrimination.

P.A. 76-1586, § 18c-7202, added by P.A. 84-796, § 1, eff. Jan. 1, 1986.

Formerly Ill.Rev.Stat.1991, ch. 95 ½, ¶ 18c-7202.

5/18c-7203. § 18c-7203. Repealed by P.A. 90-257, § 10, eff. July 30, 1997

ARTICLE III. RATEMAKING

5/18c-7301, 5/18c-7302. §§ 18c-7301, 18c-7302. Repealed by P.A. 90-257, § 10, eff. July 30, 1997

ARTICLE IV. SAFETY REQUIREMENTS FOR RAIL CARRIERS

5/18c-7401. Safety Requirements for Track, Facilities, and Equipment

§ 18c-7401. Safety Requirements for Track, Facilities, and Equipment.

(1) General Requirements. Each rail carrier shall, consistent with rules, orders, and regulations of the Federal Railroad Administration, construct, maintain, and operate all of its equipment, track, and other property in this State in such a manner as to pose no undue risk to its employees or the person or property of any member of the public.

(2) Adoption of Federal Standards. The track safety standards and accident/incident standards promulgated by the Federal Railroad Administration shall be safety standards of the Commission. The Commission may, in addition, adopt by reference in its regulations other federal railroad safety standards, whether contained in federal statutes or in regulations adopted pursuant to such statutes.

(3) Railroad Crossings. No public road, highway, or street shall hereafter be constructed across the track of any rail carrier at grade, nor shall the track of any rail carrier be constructed across a public road, highway or street at grade, without having first secured the permission of the Commission; provided, that this Section shall not apply to the replacement of lawfully existing roads, highways and tracks. No public pedestrian bridge or subway shall be constructed across the track of any rail carrier without having first secured the permission of the Commission. The Commission shall have the right to refuse its permission or to grant it upon such terms and conditions as it may prescribe. The Commission shall have power to determine and prescribe the manner, including the particular point of crossing, and the terms of installation, operation, maintenance, use and protection of each such crossing.

The Commission shall also have power, after a hearing, to require major alteration of or to abolish any crossing, heretofore or hereafter established, when in its opinion, the public safety requires such alteration or abolition, and, except in cities, villages and incorporated towns of 1,000,000 or more inhabitants, to vacate and close that part of the highway on such crossing altered or abolished and cause barricades to be erected across such highway in such manner as to prevent the use of such crossing as a highway, when, in the opinion of the Commission, the public convenience served by the crossing in question is not such as to justify the further retention thereof; or to require a separation of grades, at railroad-highway grade crossings; or to require a separation of grades at any proposed crossing where a proposed public highway may cross the tracks of any rail carrier or carriers; and to prescribe, after a hearing of the parties, the terms upon which such separations shall be made and the proportion in which the expense of the alteration or abolition of such crossings or the separation of such grades, having regard to the benefits, if any, accruing to the rail carrier or any party in interest, shall be divided between the rail carrier or carriers affected, or between such carrier or carriers and the State, county, municipality or other public authority in interest. However, a public hearing by the Commission to abolish a crossing shall not be required when the public highway authority in interest vacates the highway. In such instance the rail carrier, following notification to the Commission and the highway authority, shall remove any grade crossing warning devices and the grade crossing surface.

The Commission shall also have power by its order to require the reconstruction, minor alteration, minor relocation or improvement of any crossing (including the necessary highway approaches thereto) of any railroad across any highway or public road, pedestrian bridge, or pedestrian subway, whether such crossing be at grade or by overhead structure or by subway, whenever the Commission finds after a hearing or without a hearing as otherwise provided in this paragraph that such reconstruction, alteration, relocation or improvement is necessary to preserve or promote the safety or convenience of the public or of the employees or passengers of such rail carrier or carriers. By its original order or supplemental orders in such case, the Commission may direct such reconstruction, alteration, relocation, or improvement to be made in such manner and upon such terms and conditions as may be reasonable and necessary and may apportion the cost of such reconstruction, alteration, relocation or improvement and the subsequent maintenance thereof, having regard to the benefits, if any, accruing to the railroad or any party in interest, between the rail carrier or carriers and public utilities affected, or between such carrier or carriers and public utilities and the State, county, municipality or other public authority in interest. The cost to be so apportioned shall include the cost of changes or alterations in the equipment of public utilities affected as well as the cost of the relocation, diversion or establishment of any public highway, made necessary by such reconstruction, alteration, relocation or improvement of said crossing. A hearing shall not be required in those instances when the Commission enters an order confirming a written stipulation in which the Commission, the public highway authority or other public authority in interest, the rail carrier or carriers affected, and in instances involving the use of the Grade Crossing Protection Fund, the Illinois Department of Transportation, agree on the reconstruction, alteration, relocation, or improvement and the subsequent maintenance thereof and the division of costs of such changes of any grade crossing (including the necessary highway approaches thereto) of any railroad across any highway, pedestrian bridge, or pedestrian subway.

Every rail carrier operating in the State of Illinois shall construct and maintain every highway crossing over its tracks within the State so that the roadway at the intersection shall be as flush with the rails as superelevated curves will allow, and, unless otherwise ordered by the Commission, shall construct and maintain the approaches thereto at a grade of not more than 5% within the right of way for a distance of not less the 6 feet on each side of the centerline of such tracks; provided, that the grades at the approaches may be maintained in excess of 5% only when authorized by the Commission.

Every rail carrier operating within this State shall remove from its right of way at all railroad-highway grade crossings within the State, such brush, shrubbery, and trees as is reasonably practical for a distance of not less than 500 feet in either direction from each grade crossing. The Commission shall have power, upon its own motion, or upon complaint, and after having made proper investigation, to require the installation of adequate and appropriate luminous reflective warning signs, luminous flashing signals, crossing gates illuminated at night, or other protective devices in order to promote and safeguard the health and safety of the public. Luminous flashing signal or crossing gate devices installed at grade crossings, which have been approved by the Commission, shall be deemed adequate and appropriate. The Commission shall have authority to determine the number, type, and location of such signs, signals, gates, or other protective devices which, however, shall conform as near as may be with generally recognized national standards, and the Commission shall have authority to prescribe the division of the cost of the installation and subsequent maintenance of such signs, signals, gates, or other protective devices between the rail carrier or carriers, the public highway authority or other public authority in interest, and in instances involving the use of the Grade Crossing Protection Fund, the Illinois Department of Transportation.

No railroad may change or modify the warning device system at a railroad-highway grade crossing, including warning systems interconnected with highway traffic control signals, without having first received the approval of the Commission. The Commission shall have the further power, upon application, upon its own motion, or upon complaint and after having made proper investigation, to require the interconnection of grade crossing warning devices with traffic control signals at highway intersections located at or near railroad crossings within the distances described by the State Manual on Uniform Traffic Control Devices adopted pursuant to Section 11–301 of this Code. In addition, State and local authorities may not install, remove, modernize, or otherwise modify traffic control signals at a highway intersection that is interconnected or proposed to be interconnected with grade crossing warning devices when the change affects the number, type, or location of traffic control devices on the track approach leg or legs of the intersection or the timing of the railroad preemption sequence of operation until the Commission has approved the installation, removal, modernization, or modification. Commission approval shall be limited to consideration of issues directly affecting the public safety at the railroad-highway grade crossing. The electrical circuit devices, alternate warning devices, and preemption sequences shall conform as nearly as possible, considering the particular characteristics of the crossing and intersection area, to the State manual adopted by the Illinois Department of Transportation pursuant to Section 11–301 of this Code and such federal standards as are made applicable by subsection (2) of this Section. In order to carry out this authority, the Commission shall have the authority to determine the number, type, and location of traffic control devices on the track approach leg or legs of the intersection and the timing of the railroad preemption sequence of operation. The Commission shall prescribe the division of costs for installation and maintenance of all devices required by this paragraph between the railroad or railroads and the highway authority in interest and in instances involving the use of the Grade Crossing Protection Fund or a State highway, the Illinois Department of Transportation.

Any person who unlawfully or maliciously removes, throws down, damages or defaces any sign, signal, gate or other protective device, located at or near any public grade crossing, shall be guilty of a petty offense and fined not less than $50 nor more than $200 for each offense. In addition to fines levied under the provisions of this Section a person adjudged guilty hereunder may also be directed to make restitution for the costs of repair or replacement, or both, necessitated by his misconduct.

It is the public policy of the State of Illinois to enhance public safety by establishing safe grade crossings. In order to implement this policy, the Illinois Commerce Commission is directed to conduct public hearings and to adopt specific criteria by July 1, 1994, that shall be adhered to by the Illinois Commerce Commission in determining if a grade crossing should be opened or abolished. The following factors shall be considered by the Illinois Commerce Commission in developing the specific criteria for opening and abolishing grade crossings:

(a) timetable speed of passenger trains;

(b) distance to an alternate crossing;

(c) accident history for the last 5 years;

(d) number of vehicular traffic and posted speed limits;

(e) number of freight trains and their timetable speeds;

(f) the type of warning device present at the grade crossing;

(g) alignments of the roadway and railroad, and the angle of intersection of those alignments;

(h) use of the grade crossing by trucks carrying hazardous materials, vehicles carrying passengers for hire, and school buses; and

(i) use of the grade crossing by emergency vehicles.

The Illinois Commerce Commission, upon petition to open or abolish a grade crossing, shall enter an order opening or abolishing the crossing if it meets the specific criteria adopted by the Commission.

Except as otherwise provided in this subsection (3), in no instance shall a grade crossing be permanently closed without public hearing first being held and notice of such hearing being published in an area newspaper of local general circulation.

(4) Freight Trains—Radio Communications. The Commission shall after hearing and order require that every main line railroad freight train operating on main tracks outside of yard limits within this State shall be equipped with a radio communication system. The Commission after notice and hearing may grant exemptions from the requirements of this Section as to secondary and branch lines.

(5) Railroad Bridges and Trestles—Walkway and Handrail. In cases in which the Commission finds the same to be practical and necessary for safety of railroad employees, bridges and trestles, over and upon which railroad trains are operated, shall include as a part thereof, a safe and suitable walkway and handrail on one side only of such bridge or trestle, and such handrail shall be located at the outer edge of the walkway and shall provide a clearance of not less than 8 feet, 6 inches, from the center line of the nearest track, measured at right angles thereto.

(6) Packages Containing Articles for First Aid to Injured on Trains. All rail carriers shall provide a package containing the articles prescribed by the Commission, on each train or engine, for first aid to persons who may be injured in the course of the operation of such trains.

(7) Abandoned Bridges, Crossings, and Other Rail Plant. The Commission shall have authority, after notice and hearing, to order:

(a) The removal of any abandoned railroad tracks from roads, streets or other thoroughfares in this State; and

(b) The removal of abandoned overhead railroad structures crossing highways, waterways, or railroads.

The Commission may equitably apportion the cost of such actions between the rail carrier or carriers, public utilities, and the State, county, municipality, township, road district, or other public authority in interest.

(8) Railroad–Highway Bridge Clearance. A vertical clearance of not less than 23 feet above the top of rail shall be provided for all new or reconstructed highway bridges constructed over a railroad track. The Commission may permit a lesser clearance if it determines that the 23 foot clearance standard cannot be justified based on engineering, operational, and economic conditions.

P.A. 76–1586, § 18c–7401, added by P.A. 84–796, § 1, eff. Jan. 1, 1986. Amended by P.A. 88–296, § 5, eff. Jan. 1, 1994; P.A. 89–699, § 15, eff. Jan. 16, 1997; P.A. 90–691, § 10, eff. Jan. 1, 1999; P.A. 91–725, § 10, eff. June 2, 2000.

Formerly Ill.Rev.Stat.1991, ch. 95 ½, ¶ 18c–7401.

5/18c–7402. Safety Requirements for Railroad Operations

§ 18c–7402. Safety Requirements for Railroad Operations.

(1) Obstruction of Crossings.

(a) Obstruction of Emergency Vehicles. Every railroad shall be operated in such a manner as to minimize obstruction of emergency vehicles at crossings. Where such obstruction occurs and the train crew is aware of the obstruction, the train crew shall immediately take any action, consistent with safe operating procedure, necessary to remove the obstruction. In the Chicago and St. Louis switching districts, every railroad dispatcher or other person responsible for the movement of railroad equipment in a specific area who receives notification that railroad equipment is obstructing the movement of an emergency vehicle at any crossing within such area shall immediately notify the train crew through use of existing communication facilities. Upon notification, the train crew shall take immediate action in accordance with this paragraph.

(b) Obstruction of Highway at Grade Crossing Prohibited. It is unlawful for a rail carrier to permit any train, railroad car or engine to obstruct public travel at a railroad-highway grade crossing for a period in excess of 10 minutes, except where such train or railroad car is continuously moving or cannot be moved by reason of circumstances over which the rail carrier has no reasonable control.

In a county with a population of greater than 1,000,000, as determined by the most recent federal census, during the hours of 7:00 a.m. through 9:00 a. m. and 4:00 p.m. through 6:00 p.m. it is unlawful for a rail carrier to permit any single train or railroad car to obstruct public travel at a railroad-highway grade crossing in excess of a total of 10 minutes during a 30 minute period, except where the train or railroad car cannot be moved by reason or circumstances over which the rail carrier has no reasonable control. Under no circumstances will a moving train be stopped for the purposes of issuing a citation related to this Section.

However, no employee acting under the rules or orders of the rail carrier or its supervisory personnel may be prosecuted for a violation of this subsection (b).

(c) Punishment for Obstruction of Grade Crossing. Any rail carrier violating paragraph (b) of this subsection shall be guilty of a petty offense and fined not less than $200 nor more than $500 if the duration of the obstruction is in excess of 10 minutes but no longer than 15 minutes. If the duration of the obstruction exceeds 15 minutes the violation shall be a business offense and the following fines shall be imposed: if the duration of the obstruction is in excess of 15 minutes but no longer than 20 minutes, the fine shall be $500; if the duration of the obstruction is in excess of 20 minutes but no longer than 25 minutes, the fine shall be $700; if the duration of the obstruction is in excess of 25 minutes, but no longer than 30 minutes, the fine shall be $900; if the duration of the obstruction is in excess of 30 minutes but no longer than 35 minutes, the fine shall be $1,000; if the duration of the obstruction is in excess of 35 minutes, the fine shall be $1,000 plus an additional $500 for each 5 minutes of obstruction in excess of 25 minutes of obstruction.

(2) Other Operational Requirements.

(a) Bell and Whistle-Crossings. Every rail carrier shall cause a bell, and a whistle or horn to be placed and kept on each locomotive, and shall cause the same to be rung or sounded by the engineer or fireman, at the distance of a least 1,320 feet, from the place where the railroad crosses or intersects any public highway, and shall be kept ringing or sounding until the highway is reached; provided that at crossings where the Commission shall by order direct, only after a hearing has been held to determine the public is reasonably and sufficiently protected, the rail carrier may be excused from giving warning provided by this paragraph.

(a–5) The requirements of paragraph (a) of this subsection (2) regarding ringing a bell and sounding a whistle or horn do not apply at a railroad crossing that has a permanently installed automated audible warning device authorized by the Commission under Section 18c–7402.1 that sounds automatically when an approaching train is at least 1,320 feet from the crossing and that keeps sounding until the lead locomotive has crossed the highway. The engineer or fireman may ring the bell or sound the whistle or horn at a railroad crossing that has a permanently installed audible warning device.

(b) Speed Limits. Each rail carrier shall operate its trains in compliance with speed limits set by the Commission. The Commission may set train speed limits only where such limits are necessitated by extraordinary circumstances effecting the public safety, and shall maintain such train speed limits in effect only for such time as the extraordinary circumstances prevail.

The Commission and the Department of Transportation shall conduct a study of the relation between train speeds and railroad-highway grade crossing safety. The Commission shall report the findings of the study to the General Assembly no later than January 5, 1997.

(c) Special Speed Limit; Pilot Project. The Commission and the Board of the Commuter Rail Division of the Regional Transportation Authority shall conduct a pilot project in the Village of Fox River Grove, the site of the fatal school bus accident at a railroad crossing on October 25, 1995, in order to improve railroad crossing safety. For this project, the Commission is directed to set the maximum train speed limit for Regional Transportation Authority trains at 50 miles per hour at intersections on that portion of the intrastate rail line located in the Village of Fox River Grove. If the Regional Transportation Authority deliberately fails to comply with this maximum speed limit, then any entity, governmental or otherwise, that provides capital or operational funds to the Regional Transportation Authority shall appropriately reduce or eliminate that funding. The Commission shall report to the Governor and the General Assembly on the results of this pilot project in January 1999, January 2000, and January 2001. The Commission shall also submit a final report on the pilot project to the Governor and the General Assembly in January 2001. The provisions of this subsection (c), other than this sentence, are inoperative after February 1, 2001.

(3) Report and Investigation of Rail Accidents.

(a) Reports. Every rail carrier shall report to the Commission, by the speediest means possible, whether telephone, telegraph, or otherwise, every accident involving its equipment, track, or other property which resulted in loss of life to any person. In addition, such carriers shall file a written report with the Commission. Reports submitted under this paragraph shall be strictly confidential, shall be specifically prohibited from disclosure, and shall not be admissible in any administrative or judicial proceeding relating to the accidents reported.

(b) Investigations. The Commission may investigate all railroad accidents reported to it or of which it acquires knowledge independent of reports made by rail carriers, and shall have the power, consistent with standards and procedures established under the Federal Railroad Safety Act, as amended,[1] to enter such temporary orders as will minimize the risk of future accidents pending notice, hearing, and final action by the Commission.

P.A. 76–1586, § 18c–7402, added by P.A. 84–796, § 1, eff. Jan. 1, 1986. Amended by P.A. 85–1144, § 1, eff. July 29, 1988; P.A. 89–699, § 15, eff. Jan. 16, 1997; P.A. 90–187, § 5, eff. Jan. 1, 1998; P.A. 91–675, § 5, eff. June 1, 2000; P.A. 92–284, § 5, eff. Aug. 9, 2001.

Formerly Ill.Rev.Stat.1991, ch. 95 ½, ¶ 18c–7402.

1 45 U.S.C.A. § 421 et seq.

5/18c–7402.1. Pilot projects; automated audible warning devices

§ 18c–7402.1. Pilot projects; automated audible warning devices.

(a) The General Assembly finds and declares that, for the communities of the State that are traversed by railroads, there is a growing need to mitigate train horn noise without compromising the safety of the public. Therefore, after applications are filed and approved by the Commission, the Commission shall authorize pilot projects in the counties of Cook, DuPage, Lake, and Will to test the utility and safety of stationary automated audible warning devices as an alternative to trains having to sound their horns as they approach highway-rail crossings.

(b) In light of the pending proposed ruling by the Federal Railroad Administration on the use of locomotive horns at all highway-rail crossings across the nation, it is in the best interest of the State for the Commission to expedite the pilot projects in order to contribute data to the federal rulemaking process regarding the possible inclusion of stationary automated warning devices in the counties of Cook, DuPage, Lake, and Will as a safety measure option to the proposed federal rule.

(c) The Commission shall adopt rules for implementing the pilot projects in the counties of Cook, DuPage, Lake, and Will.

P.A. 76–1586, § 18c–7402.1, added by P.A. 92–284, § 5, eff. Aug. 9, 2001.

5/18c–7402.5. § 18c–7402.5. Repealed effective Feb. 1, 2001

5/18c–7403. Enforcement and Waiver of Safety Requirements

§ 18c–7403. Enforcement and Waiver of Safety Requirements. (1) Enforcement. Except with regard to grade crossing obstructions under Section 18c–7402 of this Chapter and trespass on railroad rights of way and yards under

Section 18c-7503 of this Chapter, jurisdiction to initiate actions to enforce provisions of this Chapter is vested exclusively in the Commission. Where a valid federal statute, regulation, or order sets forth procedures or sanctions for violation of safety standards, and such procedures or sanctions are preemptive of state law, the Commission shall exercise its enforcement jurisdiction under this Article in accordance therewith. Otherwise, the provisions of this Chapter regarding enforcement procedures and sanctions shall apply.

(2) Waiver. The Commission may waive any of the safety requirements under this Article if continued adherence to the requirement or requirements is not required for the safety of railroad employees or the public.

P.A. 76-1586, § 18c-7403, added by P.A. 84-796, § 1, eff. Jan. 1, 1986. Amended by P.A. 90-257, § 5, eff. July 30, 1997.

Formerly Ill.Rev.Stat.1991, ch. 95 ½, ¶ 18c-7403.

5/18c-7404. Transportation of Hazardous Materials by Rail Carriers

§ 18c-7404. Transportation of Hazardous Materials by Rail Carriers. (1) Commission to Regulate Hazardous Materials Transportation by Rail Carrier.

(a) Powers of the Commission. The Commission is authorized to regulate the transportation of hazardous materials by rail carrier by:

(i) Adopting by reference the hazardous materials regulations of the Office of Hazardous Materials Transportation and the Federal Railroad Administration of the United States Department of Transportation, as amended;

(ii) Conducting investigations, issuing subpoenas, taking depositions, requiring the production of relevant documents, records and property, and conducting hearings in aid of such investigations;

(iii) Conducting a continuing review of all aspects of hazardous materials transportation by rail carrier to determine and recommend actions necessary to insure safe transportation of such materials;

(iv) Undertaking, directly or indirectly, research, development, demonstration and training activities;

(v) Cooperating with other State agencies and enter into interagency agreements; and

(vi) Entering upon, inspecting and examining the records and properties relating to the transportation of hazardous materials by rail, including all portions of any facility used in the loading, unloading, and actual movement of such materials, or in the storage of such materials incidental to actual movement by rail;

(vii) Stopping and inspecting trains, at reasonable times and locations and in a reasonable manner, or taking any other action necessary to administer or enforce the provisions of this Section.

(b) Scope of Section. The provisions of this Section apply generally to the transportation of hazardous materials by rail carrier within the State of Illinois, but do not apply to:

(i) Natural gas pipelines;

(ii) Transportation of firearms or ammunition for personal use or in commerce; or

(iii) Transportation exempted by the Commission where the exemption granted by the Commission is:

(A) Coextensive with an exemption granted by the Office of Hazardous Materials and the Federal Railroad Administration; or

(B) Otherwise exempt under statutes or regulations governing similar transportation in interstate commerce.

(c) Rail Carriers to Comply with Commission Regulations. No person shall transport hazardous materials by rail carrier except in compliance with this Section, Commission regulations and orders.

(2) Enforcement.

(a) Criminal Penalties. Any person who willfully violates the provisions of this Section, Commission regulations or orders shall have committed a class 3 felony and be subject to criminal penalties in an amount not to exceed $25,000.

(b) Civil Penalties. Any person who knowingly violates the provisions of this Section, Commission regulations or orders shall also be subject to civil penalties in an amount not to exceed $10,000.

(c) Injunctive Relief. The Commission may petition any circuit court with venue and jurisdiction to enforce this Chapter to enjoin actions which it has reason to believe may pose an imminent hazard, and to issue such other orders as will eliminate or ameliorate the imminent hazard. As used in this Section, "imminent hazard" means a substantial likelihood that death, serious illness, or severe personal injury will occur prior to the time during which an administrative proceeding to abate the danger could normally be completed.

(3) Commission to Adopt Regulations. The Commission may adopt regulations governing the transportation of hazardous materials by rail carrier where:

(a) The risk created by such transportation is susceptible to control by regulation;

(b) State regulation would be more effective in controlling the risk than federal regulation; and

(c) The regulations adopted by the Commission are not inconsistent with federal regulations.

P.A. 76-1586, § 18c-7404, added by P.A. 84-796, § 1, eff. Jan. 1, 1986. Amended by P.A. 85-815, § 1, eff. Jan. 1, 1988.

Formerly Ill.Rev.Stat.1991, ch. 95 ½, ¶ 18c-7404.

5/18c-7405. Accident counseling

§ 18c-7405. Accident counseling.

(a) Every Class I rail carrier, according to federal regulations, operating in this State must establish a counseling or trauma program and provide or make available counseling or other critical incident stress debriefing services to each member of an operating crew directly involved in an accident that results in loss of life or serious bodily injury on its railway or right-of-way.

(b) Each Class I rail carrier, according to federal regulations, operating in this State must file its counseling or trauma program with the processing section of the Transportation Division of the Illinois Commerce Commission, whose sole responsibility under this Section shall be to receive the program and make it available for public inspection.

P.A. 76-1586, § 18c-7405, added by P.A. 91-729, § 5, eff. Jan. 1, 2001.

ARTICLE V. MISCELLANEOUS PROVISIONS

5/18c-7501. Eminent Domain

§ 18c-7501. Eminent Domain. If any rail carrier shall be unable to agree with the owner for the purchase of any real estate required for the purposes of its incorporation, or the transaction of its business, or for its depots, station buildings, machine and repair shops, or for right of way or any other lawful purpose connected with or necessary to the building, operating or running of such rail carrier, such may acquire such title in the manner that may be now or hereafter provided for by the law of eminent domain.

A rail carrier may exercise quick take powers of eminent domain as provided in Article VII of the Code of Civil Procedure, as now or hereafter amended,[1] when all of the following conditions are met: (1) the complaint for condemnation is filed within one year of the effective date of this amendatory Act of 1988; (2) the purpose of the condemnation proceeding is to acquire land for the construction of an industrial harbor railroad port; and (3) the total amount of land to be acquired for that purpose is less than 75 acres and is adjacent to the Illinois River.

P.A. 76-1586, § 18c-7501, added by P.A. 84-796, § 1, eff. Jan. 1, 1986. Amended by P.A. 85-1159, § 2-3, eff. Aug. 4, 1988.

Formerly Ill.Rev.Stat.1991, ch. 95 ½, ¶ 18c-7501.

[1] 735 ILCS 5/7-101 et seq.

5/18c-7502. Malicious removal of or damage to railroad property or freight

§ 18c-7502. Malicious removal of or damage to railroad property or freight.

(a) Malicious removal of or damage to railroad property or freight.

A person is guilty of an offense if he or she is found to have:

(i) removed, taken, stolen, changed, added to, taken from, or in any manner changed, defaced, or interfered with any of the parts or attachments of any locomotive or car, or any plant or property used in or in connection with the operation of any railroad carrier, locomotive, car, or train, or shoots, throws, or drops any object onto or at any train, locomotive, or car;

(ii) willfully and with intent to permanently deprive the owner thereof, taken or removed railroad freight from any freight car, including a boxcar, container, or flatbed; or

(iii) bought or received any of the railroad freight described in item (ii), having reason to know that such freight was stolen.

(b) Penalties.

(1) If the railroad property damage does not exceed $500 and no bodily injury occurs to another as a result of a violation of this Section, the person shall be guilty of a Class A misdemeanor. Upon being found in violation of item (i) of subsection (a), the person shall, in addition to such other sanctions as may be deemed appropriate by the court, be subject to pay the railroad carrier involved the cost to repair any railroad property damaged, and to perform community service for not less than 30 hours or more than 120 hours. If community service is not available in the jurisdiction where the offense was committed, that person shall be subject to pay a fine of not less than $150 or more than $1,000, or imprisonment for not less than 5 days or more than 1 year, or both. If railroad property damage exceeds $500 or bodily injury occurs to another as a result of a violation of this Section, the person shall be guilty of a Class 4 felony. Upon being found in violation of item (i) of subsection (a), the person shall, in addition to such other sanctions as may be deemed appropriate by the court, be subject to pay the railroad carrier involved for the cost to repair any railroad property damaged, and shall be fined not less than $1,000, nor more than $25,000, or imprisonment for not less than 1 year, or more than 3 years, or both. If serious bodily injury or death occurs to another as a result of a violation of item (i) of subsection (a), the person shall be guilty of a Class 2 felony and shall, in addition to such sanctions as may be deemed appropriate by the court, be subject to pay the railroad carrier involved the cost to repair any railroad property damaged, and shall be fined not less than $5,000 nor more than $25,000, or imprisonment for not less than 3 years nor more than 7 years, or both. If any such action is malicious and is the cause of wrecking any train, locomotive, or car in this State whereby the life of any person is lost, the person found guilty thereof shall be liable for first degree murder and the person shall be subject to pay the railroad carrier involved the cost to repair any railroad property damaged.

(2) Upon being found in violation of item (ii) or (iii), the person shall be guilty of a Class 4 felony. In addition to such other sanctions as may be deemed appropriate by the court, the person shall be subject to pay the railroad carrier involved for the cost to repair any railroad property damaged, and shall be fined not less than $1,000, nor more than $25,000, or imprisoned for not less than 1 year nor more than 3 years.

(3) Local authorities shall impose fines as established in this subsection (b) for persons found in violation of this Section or any similar local ordinance.

(c) Definitions. As used in this Section:

"Bodily injury" means:

(i) a cut, abrasion, bruise, bump, or disfigurement;

(ii) physical pain;

(iii) illness;

(iv) impairment of the function of a bodily member, organ, or mental faculty; or

(v) any other injury to the body, no matter how temporary.

"Railroad" means any form of nonhighway ground transportation that runs on rails or electromagnetic guideways, including:

(i) commuter or other short-haul railroad passenger service in a metropolitan or urban area; and

(ii) high-speed ground transportation systems that connect metropolitan areas, but does not include rapid transit operations in an urban area that are not connected to the general railroad system of transportation.

"Railroad carrier" means a person providing railroad transportation.

"Railroad property" means all tangible property owned, leased, or operated by a railroad carrier including a right of way, track, bridge, yard, shop, station, tunnel, viaduct, trestle, depot, warehouse, terminal, or any other structure, appurtenance, or equipment owned, leased, or used in the operation of any railroad carrier including trains, locomotives, engines, railroad cars, work equipment, rolling stock, or safety devices. "Railroad property" does not include a railroad carrier's administrative buildings or offices, office equipment, or intangible property such as software or other information.

"Right of way" means the track or roadbed owned, leased, or operated by a rail carrier that is located on either side of its tracks and that is readily recognizable to a reasonable person as being railroad property or is reasonably identified as such by fencing or appropriate signs.

"Yard" means a system of parallel tracks, crossovers, and switches where railroad cars are switched and made up into

trains, and where railroad cars, locomotives, and other rolling stock is kept when not in use or when awaiting repair.

"Serious bodily injury" means bodily injury that involves:

(i) a substantial risk of death;

(ii) extreme physical pain;

(iii) protracted and obvious disfigurement; or

(iv) protracted loss or impairment of the function of a bodily member, organ, or mental faculty.

P.A. 76–1586, § 18c–7502, added by P.A. 84–796, § 1, eff. Jan. 1, 1986. Amended by P.A. 85–293, Art. III, § 21, eff. Sept. 8, 1987; P.A. 90–691, § 10, eff. Jan. 1, 1999; P.A. 91–532, § 5, eff. Jan. 1, 2000.

Formerly Ill.Rev.Stat.1991, ch. 95 ½, ¶ 18c–7502.

5/18c–7503. Trespassing on railroad property

§ 18c–7503. Trespassing on railroad property.

(1) Trespassing on railroad property prohibited.

(a) General prohibition. Except as otherwise provided in paragraph (b) of this subsection, no person may:

(i) walk, ride, drive or be upon or along the right of way or rail yard of a rail carrier within the State, at a place other than a public crossing;

(ii) enter or be upon any railroad property;

(iii) without lawful authority or the railroad carrier's consent, ride on the outside of a train or inside a passenger car, locomotive, or freight car, including a box car, flatbed, or container;

(iv) willfully lead or contrive any animal to go upon the railroad's rights of way for any reason other than to pass over such rights of way at a marked public crossing; or

(v) throw or cause to be thrown on to the railroad's rights of way any waste paper, ashes, household waste, glass, metal, tires, refuse, or rubbish.

(b) Exceptions. This subsection shall not apply to:

(i) fare paying passengers on trains or employees of a rail carrier;

(ii) railroad employees and an authorized representative of rail carrier employees, while performing required duties in accordance with reasonable rail carrier company guidelines;

(iii) a person going upon the right of way or into the rail yard to save human life or to remove an object that a reasonable person would believe poses an imminent threat to human life or limb;

(iv) a person being on the station grounds or in the depot of the rail carrier for the purpose of transacting business;

(v) a person, his family, or his employees or agents going across a farm crossing, as defined in this Chapter, for the purpose of crossing from one part to another part of a farm he owns or leases, where the farm lies on both sides of the right of way;

(vi) a person having written permission from the rail carrier to go upon the right of way or into the rail yard;

(vii) representatives of local, State, and federal governmental agencies in performance of their official duties; and

(viii) a person having written permission from the rail carrier to go in or be upon railroad property.

(2) Penalties.

(a) Any person found in violation of item (i), (ii), (iii) or (iv) of paragraph (a) of subsection (1) shall be guilty of a Class C misdemeanor for a first offense. In addition to such other sanctions as may be deemed appropriate by the court, the person shall be subject to a mandatory fine of not less than $150 or more than $500, or to imprisonment for not less than 5 days nor more than 30 days, or both. For each subsequent offense, the person shall be guilty of a Class A misdemeanor. In addition to such sanctions as may be deemed appropriate by the court, the person shall be subject to a mandatory fine of not less than $500 nor more than $1,000, or to imprisonment for not less than 10 days or more than one year, or both.

(b) Any person found in violation of item (v) of paragraph (a) of subsection (1) shall be guilty of an offense and in addition to such sanctions as may be deemed appropriate by the court shall be subject to a fine of not less than $100 nor more than $500, or community service of not less than 8 hours nor more than 50 hours, or both. If damage to any railroad property or bodily injury occurs to another as a result of a violation of item (v) of paragraph (a) of subsection (1), that person shall be charged with the offense of Malicious Removal of or Damage to Railroad Property or Freight pursuant to Section 18c–7502.

(c) Local authorities shall impose fines as established in paragraphs (a) and (b) of this subsection (2) for persons found in violation of this Section or any similar local ordinance.

(3) Definitions. For purposes of this Section:

"Passenger" means a person who is traveling by train with lawful authority and who does not participate in the train's operation. The term "passenger" does not include stowaways.

"Railroad" means any form of nonhighway ground transportation that runs on rails or electromagnetic guideways, including:

(i) commuter or other short-haul railroad passenger service in a metropolitan or urban area; and

(ii) high-speed ground transportation systems that connect metropolitan areas; but does not include rapid transit operations in an urban area that are not connected to the general railroad system of transportation.

"Railroad carrier" means a person providing railroad transportation.

"Railroad property" means all tangible property owned, leased, or operated by a railroad carrier including a right of way, track, bridge, yard, shop, station, tunnel, viaduct, trestle, depot, warehouse, terminal, or any other structure, appurtenance, or equipment owned, leased, or used in the operation of any railroad carrier including trains, locomotives, engines, railroad cars, work equipment, rolling stock, or safety devices. "Railroad property" does not include a railroad carrier's administrative buildings or offices, office equipment, or intangible property such as software or other information.

"Right of way" means the track or roadbed owned, leased, or operated by a rail carrier which is located on either side of its tracks and which is readily recognizable to a reasonable person as being railroad property or is reasonably identified as such by fencing or appropriate signs.

"Yard" means a system of parallel tracks, crossovers, and switches where railroad cars are switched and made up into

trains, and where railroad cars, locomotives, and other rolling stock is kept when not in use or when awaiting repair.

P.A. 76-1586, § 18c-7503, added by P.A. 84-796, § 1, eff. Jan. 1, 1986. Amended by P.A. 90-655, § 153, eff. July 30, 1998; P.A. 90-691, § 10, eff. Jan. 1, 1999; P.A. 91-532, § 5, eff. Jan. 1, 2000.

Formerly Ill.Rev.Stat.1991, ch. 95 ½, ¶ 18c-7503.

5/18c-7504. Construction of Fences, Farm Crossings, and Damages

§ 18c-7504. Construction of Fences, Farm Crossings, and Damages. (1) Fencing. Every rail carrier shall, within 6 months after any part of its line is open for use, erect and thereafter maintain fences on both sides of its road or so much thereof as is open for use, suitable and sufficient to prevent cattle, horses, sheep, hogs or other livestock from getting on such railroad, provided that the other 3 sides of the property are enclosed, except at the crossings of public roads and highways, and within such portion of cities and incorporated towns and villages as are or may be hereafter laid out and platted into lots and blocks, with gates at the farm crossings of such railroad, which farm crossings shall be constructed by such rail carrier when and where the same may become necessary, for the use of the proprietors of the lands adjoining such railroad; and when such fences are not made as aforesaid, or when such fences are not kept in good repair, such rail carrier shall be liable for all damages which may be done by the agents, engines or cars of such rail carrier, to such cattle, horses, sheep, hogs or other livestock thereof, and reasonable attorney's fees in any court wherein suit is brought for such damages, or to which the same may be appealed; but where such fences have been duly made and kept in good repair, such rail carrier shall not be liable for any such damages, unless negligently or willfully done.

(2) Enforcement. If the rail carrier, after being notified, shall refuse to build or repair such fence, gates, or farm crossings, in accordance with the provisions of this Section, the owner or occupant of the land required to be fenced shall be entitled to an order from any court of competent jurisdiction requiring the rail carrier to build or repair such fence, gates, or farm crossing and may recover interest at one percent per month of the cost of such building or repair, from the time the crossing or repair was requested, as damage in the circuit court, together with costs to be taxed by the court.

P.A. 76-1586, § 18c-7504, added by P.A. 84-796, § 1, eff. Jan. 1, 1986.

Formerly Ill.Rev.Stat.1991, ch. 95 ½, ¶ 18c-7504.

SUB-CHAPTER 8. COMMON CARRIERS BY PIPELINE

ARTICLE I. JURISDICTION AND POWER OVER COMMON CARRIERS BY PIPELINE

ARTICLE II. LICENSING AND RATEMAKING

ARTICLE III. SAFETY REGULATION

ARTICLE IV. MISCELLANEOUS PROVISIONS

ARTICLE I. JURISDICTION AND POWER OVER COMMON CARRIERS BY PIPELINE

5/18c-8101. § 18c-8101. Repealed by P.A. 89-42, § 15, eff. Jan. 1, 1996

ARTICLE II. LICENSING AND RATEMAKING

5/18c-8201. § 18c-8201. Repealed by P.A. 89-42, § 15, eff. Jan. 1, 1996

ARTICLE III. SAFETY REGULATION

5/18c-8301. § 18c-8301. Repealed by P.A. 89-42, § 15, eff. Jan. 1, 1996

ARTICLE IV. MISCELLANEOUS PROVISIONS

5/18c-8401. § 18c-8401. Repealed by P.A. 89-42, § 15, eff. Jan. 1, 1996

SUB-CHAPTER 9. MISCELLANEOUS PROVISIONS OF LAW

ARTICLE I. REMEDIES CUMULATIVE

ARTICLE II. GRANDFATHER PROVISIONS

ARTICLE I. REMEDIES CUMULATIVE

5/18c-9101. Remedies Cumulative

§ 18c-9101. Remedies Cumulative. Rights and remedies under this Chapter shall be cumulative of each other and of rights and remedies under other provisions of law, except as otherwise expressly provided herein. Exercise of one right or remedy under this Chapter shall not waive or bar exercise of any other, and imposition of one sanction under this Chapter shall not be a bar to imposition of any other sanction provided for in this Chapter.

P.A. 76-1586, § 18c-9101, added by P.A. 84-796, § 1, eff. Jan. 1, 1986.

Formerly Ill.Rev.Stat.1991, ch. 95 ½, ¶ 18c-9101.

ARTICLE II. GRANDFATHER PROVISIONS

5/18c-9201. Grandfather Clause

§ 18c-9201. Grandfather Clause. Except as otherwise expressly provided in this Chapter, valid regulations adopted, licenses, registrations, certifications and other authorizations issued or recognized, rates established or recognized, and forms promulgated or utilized under Acts or parts of Acts repealed by this Act shall have the same force and effect as if adopted, issued, established, or recognized under this Chapter.

P.A. 76-1586, § 18c-9201, added by P.A. 84-796, § 1, eff. Jan. 1, 1986. Amended by P.A. 85-553, § 2, eff. Sept. 18, 1987.

Formerly Ill.Rev.Stat.1991, ch. 95 ½, ¶ 18c-9201.

CHAPTER 19. ILLINOIS VEHICLE LAWS COMMISSION

5/19-101 to 5/19-104. §§ 19-101 to 19-104. Repealed by P.A. 83-1257, Art. 12, § 12-18, eff. Sept. 30, 1984

CHAPTER 20. MISCELLANEOUS PROVISIONS, EFFECT OF ACT AND REPEAL OF NAMED ACTS

Enactment

The Illinois Vehicle Code was enacted by P.A. 76-1586, effective July 1, 1970. The Code constitutes a consolidated recodification of various earlier laws and acts including the Illinois Motor Vehicle Law of 1957.

ARTICLE I. DISTRIBUTION OF FEES AND TAXES

5/20-101. Moneys derived from registration, operation and use of automobiles and from fuel taxes—Use

§ 20-101. Moneys derived from registration, operation and use of automobiles and from fuel taxes—Use. From and after the effective date of this Act, no public moneys derived from fees, excises or license taxes relating to registration, operation and use of vehicles on public highways or to fuels used for the propulsion of such vehicles, shall be appropriated or expended other than for costs of administering the laws imposing such fees, excises and license taxes, statutory refunds and adjustments allowed thereunder, administrative costs of the Department of Transportation, payment of debts and liabilities incurred in construction and reconstruction of public highways and bridges, acquisition of rights-of-way for, and the cost of construction, reconstruction, maintenance, repair and operation of public highways and bridges under the direction and supervision of the State, political subdivision or municipality collecting such moneys, and the costs for patrolling and policing the public highways (by the State, political subdivision or municipality collecting such money) for enforcement of traffic laws; provided, that such moneys may be used for the retirement of and interest on bonds heretofore issued for purposes other than the construction of public highways or bridges but not to a greater extent, nor a greater length of time, than is provided in acts theretofore adopted and now in force. Further the separation of grades of such highways with railroads and costs associated with protection of at-grade highway and railroad crossings shall also be permissible.

P.A. 76-1586, § 20-101, eff. July 1, 1970. Amended by P.A. 81-3, 2nd Sp.Sess., § 4, eff. Sept. 19, 1979.

Formerly Ill.Rev.Stat.1991, ch. 95 ½, ¶ 20-101.

ARTICLE II. EFFECT OF ACT

5/20-201. Effect of headings

§ 20-201. Effect of headings. Chapter, Article and Section headings contained herein shall not be deemed to govern, limit, modify or in any manner affect the scope, meaning or intent of the provisions of any Chapter, Article or Section hereof.

P.A. 76-1586, § 20-201, eff. July 1, 1970.

Formerly Ill.Rev.Stat.1991, ch. 95 ½, ¶ 20-201.

5/20-201.1. Gender

§ 20-201.1. Gender. When used in this Code, words importing the masculine may be applied to females and vice versa.

P.A. 76-1586, § 20-201.1, added by P.A. 82-123, § 1, eff. Jan. 1, 1982.

Formerly Ill.Rev.Stat.1991, ch. 95 ½, ¶ 20-201.1.

5/20-201.2. Number

§ 20-201.2. Number. When used in this Code, words importing the singular may extend and be applied to several persons or things, and words importing the plural number may include singular.

P.A. 76-1586, § 20-201.2, added by P.A. 82-123, § 1, eff. Jan. 1, 1982.

Formerly Ill.Rev.Stat.1991, ch. 95 ½, ¶ 20-201.2.

5/20-201.3. Tense

§ 20-201.3. Tense. When used in this Code, words importing the present tense may include the future and vice versa.

P.A. 76-1586, § 20-201.3, added by P.A. 82-123, § 1, eff. Jan. 1, 1982.

Formerly Ill.Rev.Stat.1991, ch. 95 ½, ¶ 20-201.3.

5/20-202. Act not retroactive

§ 20-202. Act not retroactive. This Act shall not have a retroactive effect and shall not apply to any traffic accident, to a cause of action arising out of a traffic accident or judgment arising therefrom, or to any violation of the laws of this State, occurring prior to the effective date of this Act.

P.A. 76-1586, § 20-202, eff. July 1, 1970.

Formerly Ill.Rev.Stat.1991, ch. 95 ½, ¶ 20-202.

5/20-203. Constitutionality

§ 20-203. Constitutionality. If any part or parts of this Act shall be held to be unconstitutional, such unconstitutionality shall not affect the validity of the remaining parts of this Act. The legislature hereby declares that it would have passed the remaining parts of this Act if it had known that such part or parts thereof would be declared unconstitutional.

P.A. 76-1586, § 20-203, eff. July 1, 1970.

Formerly Ill.Rev.Stat.1991, ch. 95 ½, ¶ 20-203.

5/20–204. Adoption by municipality by reference of all or part of Code

§ 20–204. The corporate authorities of a municipality may adopt all or any portion of this Illinois Vehicle Code by reference.

P.A. 76–1586, § 20–204, added by P.A. 78–738, § 1, eff. Jan. 1, 1974.

Formerly Ill.Rev.Stat.1991, ch. 95 ½, ¶ 20–204.

ARTICLE III. REPEAL OF NAMED ACTS

5/20–301. Repeal

§ 20–301. Repeal. The following acts are repealed:

(a) The "Illinois Vehicle Law", approved July 11, 1957, as amended.[1]

(b) "AN ACT in relation to motor vehicles and to repeal a certain act therein named", approved June 30, 1919, as amended.[2]

(c) "AN ACT in relation to the issuance of insurance policies in connection with certain transactions involving motor vehicles, and providing a penalty for the violation thereof", approved July 7, 1955, as amended.[3]

(d) "AN ACT providing for the use of public money derived from fees, excises, and license taxes relating to registration, operation and use of vehicles on public highways, and fuels used for the propulsion of such vehicles", approved July 21, 1947, as amended.[4]

(e) The "Uniform Act Regulating Traffic on Highways", approved July 9, 1935, as amended.[5]

(f) "AN ACT in relation to the prevention of the use of public highways by vehicles exceeding prescribed weight limits", approved August 6, 1949, as amended.[6]

(g) "AN ACT relating to the operation of ambulances", approved July 25, 1963.[7]

(h) "AN ACT to prevent the overloading of motor vehicles used in transporting children", approved July 22, 1959, as amended.[8]

(i) "AN ACT in relation to the sale of certain tires for use on motor vehicles", approved July 9, 1955, as amended.[9]

(j) The "Illinois Motor Carrier of Property Act", approved July 7, 1953, as amended.[10]

(k) "AN ACT to create a Motor Vehicle Laws Commission, to define its powers and duties, and to make an appropriation therefor", approved June 21, 1951, as amended.[11]

(*l*) "AN ACT to authorize the Department of Public Safety to furnish copies of traffic accident reports and be paid a fee therefor", approved April 17, 1967.[12]

(m) "AN ACT relating to the powers and duties of the Governor in connection with the Federal Highway Safety Act of 1966", approved August 18, 1967.[13]

(n) "AN ACT enacting and entering into the Driver Licenses Compact", approved August 19, 1963, as amended.[14]

(*o*) "AN ACT to adopt the Vehicle Equipment Safety Compact and to provide for the administration thereof", approved August 19, 1963.[15]

P.A. 76–1586, § 20–301, eff. July 1, 1970. Amended by P.A. 85–293, Art. III, § 21, eff. Sept. 8, 1987.

Formerly Ill.Rev.Stat.1991, ch. 95 ½, ¶ 20–301.

1 Former Ill.Rev.Stat. ch. 95½, ¶ 1 et seq. (repealed; see, now, 625 ILCS 5/1–101 et seq.).

2 Former Ill.Rev.Stat. ch. 95½, ¶ 1 et seq. (repealed; see, now, 625 ILCS 5/1–101 et seq.).

3 Former Ill.Rev.Stat. ch. 95½, ¶¶ 58p and 58q (repealed; see, now, 625 ILCS 5/5–601, 5/5–602).

4 Former Ill.Rev.Stat. ch. 95½, ¶ 73a (repealed; see, now, 625 ILCS 5/20–101).

5 Former Ill.Rev.Stat. ch. 95½, ¶ 98 et seq. (repealed).

6 Former Ill.Rev.Stat. ch. 95½, ¶ 239.1 et seq. (repealed; see, now, 625 ILCS 5/15–201 et seq.).

7 Former Ill.Rev.Stat. ch. 95½, ¶¶ 239.4 and 239.5 (repealed; see, now, 625 ILCS 5/11–1421, 5/11–1422).

8 Former Ill.Rev.Stat. ch. 95½, ¶ 239.21 et seq. (repealed).

9 Former Ill.Rev.Stat. ch. 95½, ¶ 239.21 et seq. (repealed; see, now, 625 ILCS 5/12–402).

10 Former Ill.Rev.Stat. ch. 95½, ¶ 282.1 et seq. (repealed).

11 Former Ill.Rev.Stat. ch. 95½, ¶ 401 et seq. (repealed).

12 Former Ill.Rev.Stat. ch. 95½, ¶ 411 (repealed; see, now, 625 ILCS 5/11–416).

13 Former Ill.Rev.Stat. ch. 95½, ¶ 421 (repealed; see, now, 625 ILCS 5/17–101).

14 Former Ill.Rev.Stat. ch. 95½, ¶ 501 et seq. (repealed; see, now, 625 ILCS 5/6-700 et seq.).

15 Former Ill.Rev.Stat. ch. 95½, ¶ 551 et seq. (repealed; see, now 625 ILCS 5/1-218).

ARTICLE IV. SAVINGS CLAUSE AND EFFECTIVE DATE

5/20–401. Saving provisions

§ 20–401. Saving provisions. The repeal of any Act by this Chapter shall not affect any right accrued or liability incurred under said repealed Act to the effective date hereof.

The provisions of this Act, insofar as they are the same or substantially the same as those of any prior Act, shall be construed as a continuation of said prior Act. Any license, permit, certificate, registration, registration plate, registration sticker, bond, policy of insurance or other instrument or document issued or filed or any deposit made under any such prior Act and still in effect on the effective date of this Act shall, except as otherwise specifically provided in this Act, be deemed the equivalent of a license, permit, certificate, registration, registration plate, registration sticker, bond, policy of insurance, or other instrument or document issued or filed or any deposit made under this Act, and shall continue in effect until its expiration or until suspended, revoked, cancelled or forfeited under this Act.

Furthermore, when any section of any of the various laws or acts repealed by this Act is amended by an Amendatory Act of the 76th General Assembly, and such amended section becomes law prior to the effective date of this Act, then it is the intent of the General Assembly that the corresponding section of this Code and Act be construed so as to give effect to such amendment as if it were made a part of this Code. Should, however, any such Amendatory Act amend a definition of a word or phrase in an act repealed by this Act, and such becomes law prior to the effective date of this Act, it is the further intent of the General Assembly that the corresponding section of this Code specifically defining such word or phrase be construed so as to give effect to such amendment, and if not specifically defined, that the corresponding section of Chapter 1 of this Code be construed so as to give effect to such amendment. In the event that a new section is added to an act repealed by this Act by an Act of the 76th General Assembly, it is the further intent of the General Assembly that this Code be construed as if such were made a part of this Code.

P.A. 76-1586, § 20-401, eff. July 1, 1970. Amended by P.A. 80-230, § 1, eff. Oct. 1, 1977.

Formerly Ill.Rev.Stat.1991, ch. 95 ½, ¶ 20-401.

5/20-402. Effective Date

§ 20-402. Effective Date. This Act is effective July 1, 1970.

P.A. 76-1586, § 20-402, eff. July 1, 1970.

Formerly Ill.Rev.Stat.1991, ch. 95 ½, ¶ 20-402.

ACT 10. MOTOR VEHICLE THEFT REPORTING ACT

CHAPTER 20. MISCELLANEOUS PROVISIONS, EFFECT OF ACT AND REPEAL OF NAMED ACTS

Section

10/1. Short title

§ 1. Short title. This Act may be cited as the Motor Vehicle Theft Reporting Act.

P.A. 88-566, § 1, eff. Jan. 1, 1995.

Title of Act:

An Act concerning motor vehicle theft. P.A. 88-566, approved Aug. 5, 1994, eff. Jan. 1, 1995.

10/5. Definitions

§ 5. Definitions.

"Motor vehicle repair station" means a place where the business of performing repair work on motor vehicles is conducted.

"Repair work" includes without limitation diagnosis, maintenance, alteration, adjustment, installation, or replacement of a part, component, or accessory for a motor vehicle.

P.A. 88-566, § 5, eff. Jan. 1, 1995.

10/10. Theft of motor vehicle; report to police

§ 10. Theft of motor vehicle; report to police. If a motor vehicle in the possession of a motor vehicle repair station is stolen, the operator of the motor vehicle repair station shall, immediately upon discovering the theft, report the theft to the police department or sheriff's department of the jurisdiction in which the motor vehicle repair station is located. As soon as possible after reporting the theft to the police department or sheriff's department, the operator of the motor vehicle repair station shall notify the customer whose motor vehicle was stolen of the theft.

P.A. 88-566, § 10, eff. Jan. 1, 1995.

10/15. Penalty

§ 15. Penalty. A person who violates Section 10 of this Act is guilty of a business offense and shall be fined not less than $501 and not more than $1,000.

P.A. 88-566, § 15, eff. Jan. 1, 1995.

ACT 15. CHINA AFFAIRS COUNCIL ACT

Section

15/0.01. Short title

§ 0.01. Short title. This Act may be cited as the China Affairs Council Act.

P.A. 82-676, § 0.01, added by P.A. 86-1324, § 57, eff. Sept. 6, 1990.

Formerly Ill.Rev.Stat.1991, ch. 1, ¶ 6000.

Title of Act:

An Act relating to the Coordination Council for North American Affairs of the Republic of China. P.A. 82-676, veto overridden and eff. Oct. 29, 1981.

15/1. Coordination Council for North American affairs; rights, privileges and immunities

§ 1. Every official or employee of an office of the Coordination Council for North American Affairs located in Illinois shall have the same rights, privileges and immunities enjoyed by officials and employees of any office of the Republic of China on Taiwan located in Illinois prior to January 1, 1979, including applying for and displaying special Illinois registration plates, registration stickers and cards as provided in Section 3-615 of the Illinois Vehicle Code.[1]

P.A. 82-676, § 1, eff. Oct. 29, 1981.

Formerly Ill.Rev.Stat.1991, ch. 1, ¶ 6001.

[1] 625 ILCS 5/3-615.

ACT 20. CHAUFFEUR PROTECTION ACT

Section

20/0.01. Short title

§ 0.01. Short title. This Act may be cited as the Chauffeur Protection Act.

Laws 1913, p. 334, § 0.01, added by P.A. 86-1324, § 461, eff. Sept. 6, 1990.

Formerly Ill.Rev.Stat.1991, ch. 48, ¶ 88.9.

Title of Act:

An Act to protect chauffeurs in their employment from dust, wind, and inclement weather. Laws 1913, p. 334, approved June 27, 1913, eff. July 1, 1913.

20/1. Shield and hood on delivery trucks and automobiles

§ 1. Every person or corporation owning, operating or controlling automobiles or auto trucks used for the delivery of merchandise, produce or freight, shall keep upon the front of the said automobiles or auto trucks a shield and hood as an inclosure to protect chauffeurs from wind, dust and inclement weather.

Laws 1913, p. 334, § 1, eff. July 1, 1913.

Formerly Ill.Rev.Stat.1991, ch. 48, ¶ 89.

20/2. Penalty for violation

§ 2. Every person or corporation owning, operating or controlling an automobile or auto truck who shall neglect or refuse to comply with the provisions of section 1 of this act upon conviction shall be guilty of a petty offense and fined not less than $10 nor more than $50 for each and every day and for each and every automobile or auto truck used and operated in violation of section 1 of this act.

Laws 1913, p. 334, § 2, eff. July 1, 1913. Amended by P.A. 77–2427, § 1, eff. Jan. 1, 1973.

Formerly Ill.Rev.Stat.1991, ch. 48, ¶ 90.

ACT 25. CHILD PASSENGER PROTECTION ACT

Section

25/1. Title and citation

§ 1. Title and citation. This Act shall be known and may be cited as the "Child Passenger Protection Act".

P.A. 83–8, § 1, eff. July 1, 1983.

Formerly Ill.Rev.Stat.1991, ch. 95 ½, ¶ 1101.

Title of Act:

An Act to protect children who are passengers in motor vehicles, as well as the motoring public in general. P.A. 83–8, approved June 27, 1983, eff. July 1, 1983.

25/2. Legislative Finding—Purpose

§ 2. Legislative Finding—Purpose. The General Assembly finds that a substantial number of passengers under the age of 6 years riding in motor vehicles, which are most frequently operated by a parent, annually die or sustain serious physical injury as a direct result of not being placed in a child passenger restraint system. The General Assembly further finds that the safety of the motoring public is seriously threatened as indicated by the significant number of traffic accidents annually caused, directly or indirectly, by driver distraction or other impairment of driving ability induced by the movement or actions of unrestrained passengers under the age of 6 years.

It is the purpose of this Act to further protect the health, safety and welfare of motor vehicle passengers under the age of 6 years and the motoring public through the proper utilization of approved child restraint systems.

P.A. 83–8, § 2, eff. July 1, 1983.

Formerly Ill.Rev.Stat.1991, ch. 95 ½, ¶ 1102.

25/3. Definitions

§ 3. Definitions. The terms "highway", "motor vehicle", "owner", "police officer", "recreational vehicle", "roadway", and "street" as used in this Act, unless the context otherwise requires, have the meaning ascribed to them in The Illinois Vehicle Code, as now or hereafter amended.[1] For the purpose of this Act, "motor vehicle" does not include motorcycles.

P.A. 83–8, § 3, eff. July 1, 1983.

Formerly Ill.Rev.Stat.1991, ch. 95 ½, ¶ 1103.

[1] 625 ILCS 5/1–100 et seq.

25/4. Transporting child under age of 4; restraint system

§ 4. When any person is transporting a child in this State under the age of 4 years in a non-commercial motor vehicle of the first division, a motor vehicle of the second division with a gross vehicle weight rating of 9,000 pounds or less, or a recreational vehicle on the roadways, streets or highways of this State, such person shall be responsible for providing for the protection of such child by properly securing him or her in a child restraint system. The parent or legal guardian of a child under the age of 4 years shall provide a child restraint system to any person who transports his or her child. Any person who transports the child of another shall not be in violation of this Section unless a child restraint system was provided by the parent or legal guardian but not used to transport the child.

For purposes of this Section and Section 4a, "child restraint system" means any device which meets the standards of the United States Department of Transportation designed to restrain, seat or position children.

P.A. 83–8, § 4, eff. July 1, 1983. Amended by P.A. 85–1209, Art. III, § 3–62, eff. Aug. 30, 1988; P.A. 86–1241, § 1, eff. Jan. 1, 1991; P.A. 88–17, § 5, eff. Jan. 1, 1994.

Formerly Ill.Rev.Stat.1991, ch. 95 ½, ¶ 1104.

25/4a. Children 4 years of age or older but under age of 16; restraint system or seat belts

§ 4a. Every person, when transporting a child 4 years of age or older but under the age of 16, as provided in Section 4 of this Act, shall be responsible for securing that child in either a child restraint system or seat belts.

P.A. 83–8, § 4a, eff. July 1, 1983. Amended by P.A. 86–1241, § 1, eff. Jan. 1, 1991; P.A. 88–17, § 5, eff. Jan. 1, 1994; P.A. 92–171, § 5, eff. Jan. 1, 2002.

Formerly Ill.Rev.Stat.1991, ch. 95 ½, ¶ 1104a.

25/4b. Children 6 years of age or older but under the age of 18; seat belts

§ 4b. Children 6 years of age or older but under the age of 18; seat belts. Every person under the age of 18 years, when transporting a child 6 years of age or older but under the age of 18 years, as provided in Section 4 of this Act, shall be responsible for securing that child in a properly adjusted and fastened seat safety belt.

P.A. 83–8, § 4b, added by P.A. 90–369, § 10, eff. Jan. 1, 1998.

25/5. Failure to secure or properly secure child; negligence; admissibility in trial

§ 5. In no event shall a person's failure to secure a child under 6 years of age in an approved child restraint system or properly secure such child, if age 4 or 5, in a seat belt constitute contributory negligence or be admissible as evidence in the trial of any civil action.

P.A. 83–8, § 5, eff. July 1, 1983. Amended by P.A. 86–1241, § 1, eff. Jan. 1, 1991.

Formerly Ill.Rev.Stat.1991, ch. 95 ½, ¶ 1105.

25/6. Violations; fines

§ 6. A violation of this Act is a petty offense punishable by a fine of not more than $50 waived upon proof of possession of an approved child restraint system as defined under this Act. A subsequent violation of this Act is a petty offense punishable by a fine of not more than $100.

P.A. 83–8, § 6, eff. July 1, 1983. Amended by P.A. 92–173, § 5, eff. Jan. 1, 2002.

Formerly Ill.Rev.Stat.1991, ch. 95 ½, ¶ 1106.

25/7. Arrests—Prosecutions

§ 7. Arrests—Prosecutions. The State Police shall patrol the public highways and make arrests for a violation of this Act. Police officers shall make arrests for violations of this Act occurring upon the highway within the limits of a county, city, village, or unincorporated town or park district.

The State's Attorney of the county in which the violation of this Act occurs shall prosecute all violations except when the violation occurs within the corporate limits of a municipality, the municipal attorney may prosecute if written permission to do so is obtained from the State's Attorney.

The provisions of this Act shall not apply to a child passenger with a physical disability of such a nature as to prevent appropriate restraint in a seat, provided that the disability is duly certified by a physician who shall state the nature of the disability, as well as the reason the restraint is inappropriate. No physician shall be liable, and no cause of action may be brought for personal injuries resulting from the exercise of good faith judgment in making certifications under this provision.

P.A. 83–8, § 7, eff. July 1, 1983. Amended by P.A. 85–1277, § 1, eff. Aug. 30, 1988; P.A. 88–685, § 10, eff. Jan. 24, 1995.

Formerly Ill.Rev.Stat.1991, ch. 95 ½, ¶ 1107.

25/8. Repealer

§ 8. The "Child Passenger Restraint Act", enacted by the 82nd General Assembly, is repealed.

P.A. 83–8, § 8, eff. July 1, 1983.

Formerly Ill.Rev.Stat.1991, ch. 95 ½, ¶ 1108.

25/9. Effective date

§ 9. This Act takes effect July 1, 1983.

P.A. 83–8, § 9, eff. July 1, 1983.

Formerly Ill.Rev.Stat.1991, ch. 95 ½, ¶ 1109.

ACT 27. RENTER'S FINANCIAL RESPONSIBILITY AND PROTECTION ACT

Section

Section

27/1. Short title

§ 1. Short title. This Act may be cited as the Renter's Financial Responsibility and Protection Act.

P.A. 90–113, § 1, eff. July 14, 1997.

Title of Act:

An Act concerning rental vehicles. P.A. 90–113, approved and eff. July 14, 1997.

27/5. Legislative findings

§ 5. Legislative findings. The General Assembly finds and declares the following:

(a) Amendments enacted in 1988 which limit negligent drivers' liability for damage to vehicles rented from motor vehicle rental companies to $200 have had the unintended, anti-consumer effect of unfairly transferring most of the costs of liability for renters' negligence to car rental companies.

(b) This transfer of liability from negligent renters has forced Illinois rental companies and dealers to experience significant financial losses in the form of actual costs to repair, service, and replace vehicles and loss of economic opportunity by being deprived of the rental use of damaged or destroyed rental cars; as a result, many Illinois vehicle rental companies in Illinois have been forced to close because of the current amendments, and high risk to capital threatens to close existing companies; economic losses have also resulted in Illinois renters paying daily and weekly vehicle rental rates almost two-fold higher than renters in other states, including those states surrounding Illinois.

(c) As the vast majority of renters in Illinois are non-Illinois residents, the increased damage costs of rental car companies and dealers are absorbed and paid by all Illinois consumers and business.

(d) The current law also threatens the public safety of all Illinois citizens as it has contributed to an almost three-fold increase in driver accident and fatality rates in Illinois.

P.A. 90–113, § 5, eff. July 14, 1997.

27/10. Definitions

§ 10. Definitions. As used in this Act:

"Rental Company" means a person or entity that rents private passenger vehicles to the public for 30 days or less.

"Renter" means a person or entity that obtains the use of a private passenger vehicle from a rental company under terms of a rental agreement.

"Rental Agreement" means an agreement for 30 days or less setting forth the terms and conditions governing the use of a private passenger vehicle provided by a rental company.

"Authorized Driver" means: the renter; the renter's spouse if the spouse is a licensed driver and satisfies the rental company's minimum age requirement; the renter's employer, employee, or co-worker if that person is a licensed driver, satisfies the rental company's minimum age requirement, and at the time of the rental is engaged in a business activity with the renter; any person who is expressly listed by the rental company on the rental agreement as an authorized driver; and any person driving directly to a medical or police facility under circumstances reasonably believed to constitute an emergency and who is a licensed driver.

"Damage Waiver" means a rental company's agreement not to hold an authorized driver liable for all or a part of any damage to or loss of a rented vehicle for which the renter may be liable pursuant to Section 6–305.2. "Damage Waiver" shall encompass within its meaning other similar terms used by rental companies, such as "Collision Damage Waiver", "Loss Damage Waiver", "Physical Damage Waiver", and the like.

P.A. 90–113, § 10, eff. July 14, 1997.

27/15. Prohibited practices

§ 15. Prohibited practices.

(a) A rental company may not sell a damage waiver unless the renter agrees to the damage waiver in writing at or prior to the time the rental agreement is executed.

(b) A rental company may not void a damage waiver except for one or more of the following reasons:

(1) Damage or loss while the rental vehicle is used to carry persons or property for a charge or fee.

(2) Damage or loss during an organized or agreed upon racing or speed contest or demonstration or pushing or pulling activity in which the rental vehicle is actively involved.

(3) Damage or loss that could reasonably be expected from an intentional or criminal act of the driver other than a traffic infraction.

(4) Damage or loss to any rental vehicle resulting from any auto business operation, including but not limited to repairing, servicing, testing, washing, parking, storing, or selling of automobiles.

(5) Damage or loss occurring to a rental vehicle if the rental contract is based on fraudulent or material misrepresentation by the renter.

(6) Damage or loss arising out of the use of the rental vehicle outside the continental United States when such use is specifically prohibited in the rental agreement.

(7) Damage or loss occurring while the rental vehicle is operated by a driver not permitted under the rental agreement.

(c) A rental company shall not charge more than $9 per full or partial 24 hour rental day for a collision damage waiver if the manufacturer's suggested retail price of the rental vehicle type is not greater than $30,000. A rental company shall not charge more than $12 per full or partial 24 hour rental day for a collision damage waiver if the manufacturer's suggested retail price of the rental vehicle type is greater than $30,000. On January 1, 2000, the maximum charges in this subsection (c) shall be increased to $9.50 and $12.50, respectively, and shall be subsequently increased to $10 and $13 on January 1, 2001 and $10.50 and $13.50 on January 1, 2002.

P.A. 90–113, § 15, eff. July 14, 1997.

27/20. Disclosure notice and advertising requirements

§ 20. Disclosure notice and advertising requirements.

(a) Each renter who purchases a damage waiver that is not included in the base rental shall be provided the following disclosure notice:

NOTICE: This contract offers, for an additional charge, a collision damage waiver to cover your financial responsibility for damage to the rental vehicle. The purchase of a collision damage waiver is optional and may be declined. You are advised to carefully consider whether to sign this waiver if you have rental vehicle collision coverage provided by your credit card or collision insurance on your own vehicle. Before deciding whether to purchase the collision damage waiver, you may wish to determine whether your own vehicle insurance affords you coverage for damage to the rental vehicle and the amount of deductible under your own insurance coverage.

(b) The disclosure notice required in subsection (a) shall be made on the face of the rental agreement either by stamp, label, or as part of the written contract, shall be set apart in boldface type and in no smaller print than 10 point type, and shall include a space for the renter to acknowledge his or her receipt of the notice. The contract shall also include in boldface type and in no smaller print than 10 point type, in simple and readable language, any other conditions and exclusions applicable to the collision damage waiver.

(c) Any rental company who states or permits to be stated the rental cost of a rental motor vehicle in any advertisement shall state conspicuously, in plain language and in conjunction with the advertised rental cost of the vehicle, the daily rate of the applicable collision damage waiver, that the rate constitutes an additional daily charge to the renter, that the collision damage waiver is optional, and that prospective renters should examine their automobile insurance policies for rental vehicle coverage.

(1) When a written advertisement, including all print media, contains the statement of the rental cost of a vehicle, the disclosure required by this subsection shall be printed in type no less than 10 point type.

(2) When the video presentation of a television advertisement contains the written statement of the rental cost of a vehicle, the depiction of the disclosure required by this subsection shall be no less than one-third the size of the depiction of the rental cost.

(3) When a radio advertisement or the audio presentation of a television advertisement contains the statement of the rental cost of the vehicle, the oral statement of the rental cost shall be immediately accompanied by an oral statement of the disclosure required by this subsection.

(d) Any rental company that makes any oral statement, excluding telephonic communications, or written statement of the rental cost of a vehicle shall disclose, in plain language and in conjunction with that statement, the daily rate of the applicable collision damage waiver and that the rate constitutes an additional daily charge to the renter.

(e) Any rental company that offers the collision damage waiver option to a renter shall inform the renter in posted signs or in pamphlets, written in plain language, of all of the information described in Sections 15 through 20. The requirements of this subsection shall be deemed to be satisfied if the rental company places the pamphlets or posted signs prominently and conspicuously where the posted signs and pamphlets may be easily seen or reached by renters.

P.A. 90–113, § 20, eff. July 14, 1997.

27/25. Mandatory charges

§ 25. Mandatory charges.

(a) As used in this Section, "mandatory charge" means any charge, surcharge, or fee in addition to the base rental rate for an item or service provided in connection with the rental transaction that the renter does not have the option of avoiding or declining and that is not otherwise imposed by law.

(b) A rental agreement containing any mandatory charge shall prominently display and fully disclose the charge separately on the face of the agreement.

(c) A mandatory charge shall also be prominently displayed and fully disclosed in all price advertising, price displays, price quotes, and price offers, including displays in computerized reservation systems.

(d) Notwithstanding the foregoing, a rental company may not impose or require the purchase of a damage waiver as a mandatory charge.

P.A. 90–113, § 25, eff. July 14, 1997.

27/999. Effective date

§ 999. Effective date. This Act takes effect upon becoming law.

P.A. 90–113, § 999, eff. July 14, 1997.

ACT 30. RIDESHARING ARRANGEMENTS ACT

Section

30/1. Short title

§ 1. This Act shall be known and may be cited as the Ridesharing Arrangements Act.

P.A. 82–656, § 1, eff. Jan. 1, 1982.

Formerly Ill.Rev.Stat.1991, ch. 95 ½, ¶ 901.

Title of Act:

An Act in relation to ridesharing and amending a certain Act in connection therewith. P.A. 82–656, approved Sept. 25, 1981, eff. Jan. 1, 1982.

30/2. Definitions

§ 2. (a) "Ridesharing arrangement" means the transportation by motor vehicle of not more than 16 persons (including the driver):

(1) for purposes incidental to another purpose of the driver, for which no fee is charged or paid except to reimburse the driver or owner of the vehicle for his operating expenses on a nonprofit basis; or

(2) when such persons are travelling between their homes and their places of employment, or places reasonably convenient thereto, for which (i) no fee is charged or paid except to reimburse the driver or owner of the vehicle for his operating expenses on a nonprofit basis, or (ii) a fee is charged in accordance with the provisions of Section 6 of this Act.

(b) "For-profit ridesharing arrangement" means a ridesharing arrangement for which a fee is charged in accordance with Section 6 of this Act.

P.A. 82–656, § 2, eff. Jan. 1, 1982. Amended by P.A. 83–1091, § 2, eff. July 1, 1984.

Formerly Ill.Rev.Stat.1991, ch. 95 ½, ¶ 902.

30/3. Commerce commission; regulation; exemption

§ 3. No ridesharing arrangement, whether or not a fee is charged, shall be subject to regulation by the Illinois Commerce Commission.

P.A. 82–656, § 3, eff. Jan. 1, 1982. Amended by P.A. 83–1091, § 2, eff. July 1, 1984.

Formerly Ill.Rev.Stat.1991, ch. 95 ½, ¶ 903.

30/4. Vehicle code; compliance

§ 4. Persons participating in a ridesharing arrangement are not thereby relieved of compliance with The Illinois Safety Responsibility Law contained in Chapter 7 of The Illinois Vehicle Code.[1]

P.A. 82–656, § 4, eff. Jan. 1, 1982. Amended by P.A. 83–1091, § 2, eff. July 1, 1984.

Formerly Ill.Rev.Stat.1991, ch. 95 ½, ¶ 904.

[1] 625 ILCS 5/7–100 et seq.

30/5. Local government regulation; licenses; fares

§ 5. No unit of local government, whether or not it is a home rule unit, may:

(1) license or regulate ridesharing arrangements;

(2) impose any tax or fee upon the owner or operator of a motor vehicle because of its use in a ridesharing arrangement;

(3) prohibit or regulate the charging of fees for ridesharing arrangements in accordance with Section 6 of this Act.

This Act is declared to be a denial and limitation of the powers of home rule units pursuant to paragraph (g) of Section 6 of Article VII of the Illinois Constitution.

P.A. 82–656, § 5, eff. Jan. 1, 1982. Amended by P.A. 83–1091, § 2, eff. July 1, 1984.

Formerly Ill.Rev.Stat.1991, ch. 95 ½, ¶ 905.

30/6. Commercial vehicles; application of law

§ 6. (a) The operator of a ridesharing arrangement may charge his or her passengers a fee in excess of the amount required to reimburse the operator for his or her expenses, if:

(1) the operator makes no more than 2 round trips per day in the course of operating any ridesharing arrangement;

(2) any passenger so charged is a person whom the operator has agreed to transport in advance of such person presenting himself or herself at the pickup point; and

(3) the operator complies with Sections 6–106.4, 12–707 and 12–707.01 of the Illinois Vehicle Code.[1]

(b) A for-profit ridesharing arrangement may, but need not, be organized as a sole proprietorship, or as any other appropriate form of business entity.

P.A. 82–656, § 6, eff. Jan. 1, 1982. Amended by P.A. 83–1091, § 2, eff. July 1, 1984; P.A. 91–357, § 232, eff. July 29, 1999.

Formerly Ill.Rev.Stat.1991, ch. 95 ½, ¶ 906.

[1] 625 ILCS 5/6–106.4, 5/12–707 and 5/12–707.01.

ACT 32. EMPLOYEE COMMUTE OPTIONS ACT

32/1 to 32/99. §§ 1 to 99. Repealed by P.A. 89–493, § 45, eff. Jan. 1, 1997

Section 75 provided:

"Repealer. If Section 182(d)(1)(B) of the Clean Air Act is repealed or the United States Environmental Protection Agency determines that Section 182(d)(1)(B) no longer applies to any area in Illinois, this Act is repealed."

ACT 33. VOLUNTARY EMPLOYEE COMMUTE OPTIONS EMISSION REDUCTION CREDIT ACT

Section

33/1. Short title

§ 1. Short title. This Act may be cited as the Voluntary Employee Commute Options Emission Reduction Credit Act.

P.A. 89–493, § 1, eff. Jan. 1, 1997.

Title of Act:

An Act to create the Voluntary Employee Commute Options Emission Reduction Credit Act and to repeal the Employee Commute Options Act, amending named Acts. P.A. 89–493, approved June 21, 1996, eff. Jan. 1, 1997.

33/5. Purpose

§ 5. Purpose. It is the purpose of this Act to provide owners with the opportunity to implement voluntary employee commute options programs. These programs would enable the owners to obtain emission reductions that are creditable toward the level of emission reductions required under the federal Clean Air Act Amendments of 1990 [1] for the post–1996 period, including emission reductions required under Section 9.8 of the Environmental Protection Act.[2]

P.A. 89–493, § 5, eff. Jan. 1, 1997.

[1] 42 U.S.C.A. § 7401 et seq.

[2] 415 ILCS 5/9.8.

33/10. Definitions

§ 10. Definitions. For purposes of this Act:

"Agency" means the Environmental Protection Agency.

"Department" means the Illinois Department of Transportation.

"Owners" means employers in the Chicago, Illinois ozone nonattainment area who operate stationary sources that are subject to emission reduction requirements for the post–1996 period under the Clean Air Act Amendments of 1990.[1]

P.A. 89–493, § 10, eff. Jan. 1, 1997.

[1] 42 U.S.C.A. § 7401 et seq.

33/15. Voluntary Employee Commute Options Program

§ 15. Voluntary Employee Commute Options Program. Owners may implement voluntary programs to encourage the use of carpooling, mass transit, vanpooling, telecommuting, compressed work weeks, clean fuel vehicles, and other measures that either reduce the number of commuting trips by their employees or reduce the emissions associated with those commuting trips for the purpose of creating emission reduction credits that may be used by the owners of stationary sources to satisfy the post–1996 emission reduction requirements under the Clean Air Act Amendments of 1990.[1]

P.A. 89–493, § 15, eff. Jan. 1, 1997.

[1] 42 U.S.C.A. § 7401 et seq.

33/20. Submission of programs and awarding of credits

§ 20. Submission of programs and awarding of credits. Owners may submit voluntary programs as described in Section 15 to the Department for approval. The Department, after consultation with the Agency, shall determine the appropriate emission reduction credit to be awarded to owners who carry out their programs and to be used by the owners of stationary sources to satisfy the post–1996 emission reduction requirements under the Clean Air Act Amendments of 1990.[1] Emission reduction credits shall not be awarded to owners for programs that are required under the Clean Air Act or the Environmental Protection Act [2] or that are substantially the same as an owner's employees' existing level of use of employee commute options programs. The Department shall adjust credits to avoid duplicating the credits the State takes for similar transportation demand management practices under the applicable State Implementation Plan. Credits may be revoked for failure to achieve the reductions called for in the owner's voluntary program.

P.A. 89–493, § 20, eff. Jan. 1, 1997.

[1] 42 U.S.C.A. § 7401 et seq.

[2] 415 ILCS 5/1 et seq.

33/25. Voluntary compliance

§ 25. Voluntary compliance. Within 30 days after the effective date of this amendatory Act of 1996, the State of Illinois shall notify the United States Environmental Protection Agency to remove the mandated Employee Commute Options requirement from the State Implementation Plan for ozone. The State of Illinois shall also notify the United States Environmental Protection Agency that emissions reductions achieved from voluntary implementation of the Voluntary Employee Commute Options Emission Reduction Credit Act by an owner are creditable toward the level of emission reductions required under other post–1996 stationary source emission reduction programs.

P.A. 89–493, § 25, eff. Jan. 1, 1997.

33/30. Rules

§ 30. Rules. The Department is authorized to adopt rules that may be necessary to accomplish the purposes of this Act.

P.A. 89–493, § 30, eff. Jan. 1, 1997.

33/35. Review under Administrative Review Law; venue

§ 35. Review under Administrative Review Law; [1] venue. An owner who does not agree with the credit awarded for his or her program, whose program is disapproved, or whose credit is revoked may seek relief under the Administrative Review Law, as amended now or hereafter, and the rules adopted pursuant to that Law.

Those proceedings for judicial review of final administrative decisions of the Department under this Act shall be commenced in the Appellate Court in the District in which the party applying for review resides, but if the party is not a resident of this State, the venue shall be the Fourth Appellate District.

P.A. 89–493, § 35, eff. Jan. 1, 1997.

1 735 ILCS 5/3–101 et seq.

33/40. Repealer

§ 40. The State Finance Act is amended by repealing Section 5.354.[1]

P.A. 89–493, § 40, eff. Jan. 1, 1997.

1 30 ILCS 105/5.354 (repealed).

33/45. Repealer

§ 45. The Employee Commute Options Act [1] is repealed.

P.A. 89–493, § 45, eff. Jan. 1, 1997.

1 625 ILCS 32/1 et seq. (repealed).

ACT 35. CYCLE RIDER SAFETY TRAINING ACT

Section

35/1. Short title

§ 1. This Act shall be known and may be cited as the "Cycle Rider Safety Training Act". It is the policy of this State to promote safety for persons and property connected with the use and operation of motorcycles, motor driven cycles and motorized pedalcycles.

P.A. 82–649, § 1, eff. Jan. 1, 1982. Amended by P.A. 85–183, Art. X, § 10–1, eff. Aug. 30, 1989; P.A. 86–1005, § 4, eff. Dec. 28, 1989.

Formerly Ill.Rev.Stat.1991, ch. 95 ½, ¶ 801.

Title of Act:

An Act to create the "Cycle Rider Safety Training Act" and to amend Sections 2–119 and 3–806 of "The Illinois Vehicle Code", approved September 29, 1969, as amended, and to add Section 5.92 to "An Act in relation to State finance", approved June 10, 1911, as amended. P.A. 82–649, approved Sept. 25, 1981, eff. Jan. 1, 1982.

35/2. Definitions

§ 2. As used in this Act, the terms specified in Sections 2.01 through 2.06 have the meanings ascribed to them in those Sections unless the context clearly requires a different meaning.

P.A. 82–649, § 1, eff. Jan. 1, 1982.

Formerly Ill.Rev.Stat.1991, ch. 95 ½, ¶ 802.

35/2.01. "Cycle"

§ 2.01. "Cycle" means a motorcycle, motor driven cycle or motorized pedalcycle, as defined in The Illinois Vehicle Code [1].

P.A. 82–649, § 1, eff. Jan. 1, 1982. Amended by P.A. 85–183, Art. X, § 10–1, eff. Aug. 30, 1989; P.A. 86–1005, § 4, eff. Dec. 28, 1989.

Formerly Ill.Rev.Stat.1991, ch. 95 ½, ¶ 802.01.

1 625 ILCS 5/1–100 et seq.

35/2.02. "Cycle Rider"

§ 2.02. "Cycle Rider" means every person who rides and is in actual physical control of a cycle.

P.A. 82–649, § 1, eff. Jan. 1, 1982.

Formerly Ill.Rev.Stat.1991, ch. 95 ½, ¶ 802.02.

35/2.03. "Cycle Rider Safety Training Courses"

§ 2.03. "Cycle Rider Safety Training Courses" and "Courses" mean courses of instruction in the use and operation of cycles, including instruction in the safe on-road operation of cycles, the rules of the road and the laws of this State relating to motor vehicles, which courses meet the minimum requirements of this Act and the rules and regulations issued hereunder by the Department and which have been approved by the Department as meeting such requirements.

P.A. 82–649, § 1, eff. Jan. 1, 1982.

Formerly Ill.Rev.Stat.1991, ch. 95 ½, ¶ 802.03.

35/2.04. "Department"

§ 2.04. "Department" means the Illinois Department of Transportation.

P.A. 82–649, § 1, eff. Jan. 1, 1982.

Formerly Ill.Rev.Stat.1991, ch. 95 ½, ¶ 802.04.

35/2.05. "Driver's License"

§ 2.05. "Driver's License" means any license or permit to operate a motor vehicle under the laws of this State.

P.A. 82–649, § 1, eff. Jan. 1, 1982.

Formerly Ill.Rev.Stat.1991, ch. 95 ½, ¶ 802.05.

35/2.06. "Person"

§ 2.06. "Person" means every person, firm, partnership or corporation.

P.A. 82–649, § 1, eff. Jan. 1, 1982.

Formerly Ill.Rev.Stat.1991, ch. 95 ½, ¶ 802.06.

35/3. Powers and duties; department

§ 3. The Department shall have the power, duty and authority to administer this Act.

P.A. 82–649, § 1, eff. Jan. 1, 1982.

Formerly Ill.Rev.Stat.1991, ch. 95 ½, ¶ 803.

35/4. Regional centers; organization; curriculum

§ 4. Any State or community college, State university or community agency designated by the Department may organize a Regional Cycle Rider Safety Training Center and may offer cycle rider safety training courses through such Training Centers which it operates. The curriculum and accreditation for the courses, and the geographic areas in which each Training Center may offer the courses, shall be provided for by rules and regulations of the Department. Instructors of such courses shall meet the qualification and certification requirements of the regulations of the Department and the college, university or community agency offering the program and may be employed on a calendar year rather than a school year basis. Such courses shall be open to all residents of the State who hold a currently valid driver's license and who have reached their 16th birthday without regard to whether such person is enrolled in any other course offered by said State or community college, State university or community agency. Such courses may be offered throughout the calendar year. The courses may be offered as credit or noncredit courses, but no fee shall be charged except for a nominal registration fee which shall be refunded upon completion of the course.

P.A. 82–649, § 1, eff. Jan. 1, 1982. Amended by P.A. 85–183, Art. X, § 10–1, eff. Aug. 30, 1989; P.A. 86–1005, § 4, eff. Dec. 28, 1989.

Formerly Ill.Rev.Stat.1991, ch. 95 ½, ¶ 804.

35/5. Rules and regulations

§ 5. The Department may promulgate rules and regulations not inconsistent with the provisions of the Cycle Rider Safety Training Act for the administration of the Cycle Rider Safety Training Act.

P.A. 82–649, § 1, eff. Jan. 1, 1982.

Formerly Ill.Rev.Stat.1991, ch. 95 ½, ¶ 805.

35/6. Cycle Rider Safety Training Fund; deposits

§ 6. To finance the Cycle Rider Safety Training program and to pay the costs thereof, the Secretary of State will hereafter deposit with the State Treasurer an amount equal to each annual fee and each reduced fee, for the registration of each motorcycle, motor driven cycle and motorized pedalcycle processed by the Office of the Secretary of State during the preceding quarter as required in subsection (d) of Section 2–119 of the Illinois Vehicle Code,[1] which amount the State Comptroller shall transfer quarterly to a trust fund outside of the State treasury to be known as the Cycle Rider Safety Training Fund, which is hereby created. In addition, the Department may accept any federal, State, or private moneys for deposit into the Fund and shall be used by the Department only for the expenses of the Department in administering the provisions of this Act, for funding of contracts with approved Regional Cycle Rider Safety Training Centers for the conduct of courses, or for any purpose related or incident thereto and connected therewith.

P.A. 82–649, § 1, eff. Jan. 1, 1982. Amended by P.A. 85–183, Art. X, § 10–1, eff. Aug. 30, 1989; P.A. 86–1005, § 4, eff. Dec. 28, 1989; P.A. 87–838, § 165, eff. Jan. 24, 1992; P.A. 87–1217, § 1, eff. Jan. 1, 1993.

Formerly Ill.Rev.Stat.1991, ch. 95 ½, ¶ 806.

1 625 ILCS 5/2–119.

P.A. 87–1217 incorporated the amendment by P.A. 87–838.

35/7. Contracts; safety training courses

§ 7. The Department is authorized to and shall award contracts out of appropriations to the Department from "The Cycle Rider Safety Training Fund" to qualifying Regional Cycle Rider Safety Training Centers for the conduct of approved Cycle Rider Safety Training courses.

P.A. 82–649, § 1, eff. Jan. 1, 1982.

Formerly Ill.Rev.Stat.1991, ch. 95 ½, ¶ 807.

ACT 40. SNOWMOBILE REGISTRATION AND SAFETY ACT

Article

ARTICLE I. DEFINITIONS—APPLICATION—JURISDICTION

Section

40/1–1. Title and declaration of intent

§ 1–1. Title and declaration of intent. This Act shall be known and may be cited as the "Snowmobile Registration and Safety Act". It is the policy of this State to promote safety for persons and property in and connected with the use, operation and equipment of snowmobiles and to promote uniformity of laws relating thereto.

P.A. 77–1312, § 1–1, eff. Aug. 27, 1971.

Formerly Ill.Rev.Stat.1991, ch. 95 ½, ¶ 601–1.

Title of Act:

An Act for the registration of snowmobiles, providing for regulations pertaining to the operation thereof, and providing penalties for the violations thereof. P.A. 77–1312, approved and eff. Aug. 27, 1971.

40/1–2. Definitions

§ 1–2. Definitions. As used in this Act, the terms specified in Sections 1–2.01 through 1–2.20 [1] have the meanings ascribed to them in those Sections unless the context clearly requires a different meaning.

P.A. 77–1312, § 1–2, eff. Aug. 27, 1971. Resectioned §§ 1–2, 1–2.01 to 1–2.15 and amended by P.A. 78–856, § 1, eff. Sept. 14, 1973.

Formerly Ill.Rev.Stat.1991, ch. 95 ½, ¶ 601-2.

1 625 ILCS 40/1-2.01 to 40/1-2.15; no §§ 1-2.16 to 1-2.20 in enrolled bill.

40/1-2.01. Cowling

§ 1-2.01. "Cowling" means the forward portions of a snowmobile surrounding the motor and clutch assembly.

P.A. 77-1312, § 1-2, eff. Aug. 27, 1971. Resectioned in part § 1-2.01 by P.A. 78-856, § 1, eff. July 1, 1974.

Formerly Ill.Rev.Stat.1991, ch. 95 ½, ¶ 601-2.01.

40/1-2.02. Dealer

§ 1-2.02. "Dealer" means a person, partnership, or corporation engaged in the business of manufacturing, selling, or leasing snowmobiles at wholesale or retail.

P.A. 77-1312, § 1-2, eff. Aug. 27, 1971. Resectioned in part § 1-2.02 by P.A. 78-856, § 1, eff. July 1, 1974.

Formerly Ill.Rev.Stat.1991, ch. 95 ½, ¶ 601-2.02.

40/1-2.03. Dangerous drug

§ 1-2.03. "Dangerous drug" means any drug defined as a depressant or stimulant substance in the "Illinois Controlled Substances Act" [1] and cannabis as defined in the "Cannabis Control Act" [2].

P.A. 77-1312, § 1-2, eff. Aug. 27, 1971. Resectioned in part § 1-2.03 and amended by P.A. 78-856, § 1, eff. July 1, 1974.

Formerly Ill.Rev.Stat.1991, ch. 95 ½, ¶ 601-2.03.

1 720 ILCS 570/100 et seq.

2 720 ILCS 550/1 et seq.

40/1-2.04. Department

§ 1-2.04. "Department" means the Department of Natural Resources.

P.A. 77-1312, § 1-2, eff. Aug. 27, 1971. Resectioned in part § 1-2.04 by P.A. 78-856, § 1, eff. July 1, 1974. Amended by P.A. 89-445, § 9A-88, eff. Feb. 7, 1996.

Formerly Ill.Rev.Stat.1991, ch. 95 ½, ¶ 601-2.04.

40/1-2.05. Highway; state highway; Interstate highway; controlled access highway; tollroad

§ 1-2.05. (a) "Highway" means the entire width between the boundary lines of every way publicly maintained when any part thereof is open to the use of the public for purposes of vehicular travel.

(b) "State highway" means State highways as defined in the Illinois Highway Code.[1]

(c) "Interstate highway" means any highway which now is, or shall hereafter be a part of the national system of interstate and defense highways within this State.

(d) "Controlled access highway" means every highway, street or roadway in respect to which owners or occupants of abutting lands and other persons have no legal right of access to or from the same except at such points only and in such manner as may be determined by the public authority having jurisdiction over such highway, street or roadway.

(e) "Tollroad" means all highways under the jurisdiction of the Illinois State Toll Highway Authority.

P.A. 77-1312, § 1-2, eff. Aug. 27, 1971. Resectioned in part § 1-2.05 by P.A. 78-856, § 1, eff. Sept. 14, 1973. Amended by P.A. 83-789, § 1, eff. Jan. 1, 1984.

Formerly Ill.Rev.Stat.1991, ch. 95 ½, ¶ 601-2.05.

1 605 ILCS 5/1-101 et seq.

40/1-2.06. Intoxicating Beverage

§ 1-2.06. "Intoxicating Beverage" means any beverage enumerated in the "Liquor Control Act".[1]

P.A. 77-1312, § 1-2, eff. Aug. 27, 1971. Resectioned in part § 1-2.06 by P.A. 78-856, § 1, eff. Sept. 14, 1973.

Formerly Ill.Rev.Stat.1991, ch. 95 ½, ¶ 601-2.06.

1 235 ILCS 5/1-1 et seq.

40/1-2.07. Local Authority

§ 1-2.07. "Local Authority" means every county, municipal, and other local board or body having authority to adopt local police regulations under the Constitution and laws of this State.

P.A. 77-1312, § 1-2, eff. Aug. 27, 1971. Resectioned in part § 1-2.07 by P.A. 78-856, § 1, eff. Sept. 14, 1973.

Formerly Ill.Rev.Stat.1991, ch. 95 ½, ¶ 601-2.07.

40/1-2.08. Narcotic drug

§ 1-2.08. "Narcotic drug" means any substance defined as a narcotic drug in the "Illinois Controlled Substances Act.[1] ".

P.A. 77-1312, § 1-2, eff. Aug. 27, 1971. Resectioned in part § 1-2.08 and amended by P.A. 78-856, § 1, eff. Sept. 14, 1973.

Formerly Ill.Rev.Stat.1991, ch. 95 ½, ¶ 601-2.08.

1 720 ILCS 570/100 et seq.

40/1-2.09. Operate

§ 1-2.09. "Operate" means to ride in or on, other than as a passenger, use or control the operation of a snowmobile in any manner, whether or not the snowmobile is under way.

P.A. 77-1312, § 1-2, eff. Aug. 27, 1971. Resectioned in part § 1-2.09 by P.A. 78-856, § 1, eff. Sept. 14, 1973.

Formerly Ill.Rev.Stat.1991, ch. 95 ½, ¶ 601-2.09.

40/1-2.10. Operator

§ 1-2.10. "Operator" means every person who operates or is in actual physical control of a snowmobile.

P.A. 77-1312, § 1-2, eff. Aug. 27, 1971. Resectioned in part § 1-2.10 by P.A. 78-856, § 1, eff. Sept. 14, 1973.

Formerly Ill.Rev.Stat.1991, ch. 95 ½, ¶ 601-2.10.

40/1-2.11. Owner

§ 1-2.11. "Owner" means a person, other than a lien holder, having title to a snowmobile. The term includes a person entitled to the use or possession of a snowmobile subject to an interest in another person, reserved or created by agreement and securing payment or performance of an obligation, but the term excludes a lessee under a lease not intended as security.

P.A. 77-1312, § 1-2, eff. Aug. 27, 1971. Resectioned in part § 1-2.11 by P.A. 78-856, § 1, eff. Sept. 14, 1973.

Formerly Ill.Rev.Stat.1991, ch. 95 ½, ¶ 601-2.11.

40/1-2.12. Person

§ 1-2.12. "Person" means an individual, partnership, firm, corporation, association, or other entity.

P.A. 77-1312, § 1-2, eff. Aug. 27, 1971. Resectioned in part § 1-2.12 by P.A. 78-856, § 1, eff. Sept. 14, 1973.

Formerly Ill.Rev.Stat.1991, ch. 95 ½, ¶ 601-2.12.

40/1-2.13. Register

§ 1-2.13. "Register" means the act of assigning a registration number to a snowmobile.

P.A. 77-1312, § 1-2, eff. Aug. 27, 1971. Resectioned in part § 1-2.13 by P.A. 78-856, § 1, eff. Sept. 14, 1973.

Formerly Ill.Rev.Stat.1991, ch. 95 ½, ¶ 601-2.13.

40/1-2.14. Roadway

§ 1-2.14. "Roadway" means that portion of a highway improved, designed or ordinarily used for vehicular travel, exclusive of the berm or shoulder. In the event a highway includes 2 or more separate roadways the term "roadway" as used in this Act refers to any such roadway separately but not to all such roadways collectively.

P.A. 77-1312, § 1-2, eff. Aug. 27, 1971. Resectioned in part § 1.14 by P.A. 78-856, § 1, eff. Sept. 14, 1973. Renumbered § 1-2.14 and amended by P.A. 79-885, § 1, eff. Oct. 1, 1975.

Formerly Ill.Rev.Stat.1991, ch. 95 ½, ¶ 601-2.14.

40/1-2.15. Snowmobile

§ 1-2.15. "Snowmobile" means a self-propelled device designed for travel on snow or ice or natural terrain steered by skis or runners, and supported in part by skis, belts, or cleats.

P.A. 77-1312, § 1-2, eff. Aug. 27, 1971. Resectioned in part § 1-2.15 by P.A. 78-856, § 1, eff. Sept. 14, 1973.

Formerly Ill.Rev.Stat.1991, ch. 95 ½, ¶ 601-2.15.

40/1-3. Application and jurisdiction

§ 1-3. Application and jurisdiction. The Department shall, for purposes of this Act, have the power, duty, and authority to administer and enforce all statutes, rules and regulations, except as otherwise provided by statute, relating to the operation and use of snowmobiles within the state.

P.A. 77-1312, § 1-3, eff. Aug. 27, 1971.

Formerly Ill.Rev.Stat.1991, ch. 95 ½, ¶ 601-3.

ARTICLE II. ENFORCEMENT—INSPECTION—PROSECUTIONS

40/2-1. Enforcement

§ 2-1. Enforcement. It is the duty of all Conservation Police Officers and all sheriffs, deputy sheriffs, and other police officers to arrest any person detected in violation of any of the provisions of this Act. It is further the duty of all such officers to make prompt investigation of any violation of the provisions of this Act reported by any other person, and to cause a complaint to be filed before the circuit court if there seems just ground for such complaint and evidence procurable to support the same.

P.A. 77-1312, § 2-1, eff. Aug. 27, 1971. Amended by P.A. 79-885, § 1, eff. Oct. 1, 1975.

Formerly Ill.Rev.Stat.1991, ch. 95 ½, ¶ 602-1.

40/2-2. Inspection

§ 2-2. Inspection. Agents of the Department or other duly authorized police officers may stop and inspect any snowmobile at any time for the purpose of determining if the provisions of this Act are being complied with. If the inspecting officer or agent discovers any violation of the provisions of this Act, he must issue a summons to the operator of such snowmobile requiring that the operator appear before the circuit court for the county within which the offense was committed.

Every snowmobile subject to this Act, if under way and upon being hailed by a designated law enforcement officer, must stop immediately.

P.A. 77-1312, § 2-2, eff. Aug. 27, 1971.

Formerly Ill.Rev.Stat.1991, ch. 95 ½, ¶ 602-2.

40/2-3. Prosecutions

§ 2-3. Prosecutions. All prosecutions under this Act shall be brought in the name and by the authority of the People of the State of Illinois before the circuit court having jurisdiction under the law relative to the enforcement of the provisions hereof. It is the duty of all State's Attorneys to enforce this Act in their respective counties and to prosecute all persons charged with violating the provisions hereof.

P.A. 77-1312, § 2-3, eff. Aug. 27, 1971.

Formerly Ill.Rev.Stat.1991, ch. 95 ½, ¶ 602-3.

40/2-4. Resistance to officers

§ 2-4. Resistance to officers. It is unlawful for any person to resist or obstruct any officer or employee of the Department in the discharge of his duties under this Act.

P.A. 77-1312, § 2-4, eff. Aug. 27, 1971.

Formerly Ill.Rev.Stat.1991, ch. 95 ½, ¶ 602-4.

40/2-5. False representation

§ 2-5. False representation. It is unlawful for any person to represent himself falsely to be an officer or employee of the Department or to assume to act as such without having been duly appointed and employed as such.

P.A. 77-1312, § 2-5, eff. Aug. 27, 1971.

Formerly Ill.Rev.Stat.1991, ch. 95 ½, ¶ 602-5.

ARTICLE III. REGISTRATION OF SNOWMOBILES

40/3-1. Operation of Unnumbered Snowmobiles

§ 3-1. Operation of Unnumbered Snowmobiles. Except as hereinafter provided, no person shall, after the effective date of this Act, operate any snowmobile within this State unless such snowmobile has been registered and numbered in accordance with the provisions of this Article, and unless

(1) the certificate of number awarded to such snowmobile is in full force and effect.

P.A. 77-1312, § 3-1, eff. Aug. 27, 1971. Amended by P.A. 81-702, § 1, eff. Jan. 1, 1981.

Formerly Ill.Rev.Stat.1991, ch. 95 ½, ¶ 603-1.

40/3-2. Identification Number Application

§ 3-2. Identification Number Application. The owner of each snowmobile requiring numbering by this State shall file an application for number with the Department on forms approved by it. The application shall be signed by the owner of the snowmobile and shall be accompanied by a fee of $18. When a snowmobile dealer sells a snowmobile the dealer shall, at the time of sale, require the buyer to complete an application for the registration certificate, collect the required fee and mail the application and fee to the Department no later than 14 days after the date of sale. Combination application-receipt forms shall be provided by the Department and the dealer shall furnish the buyer with the completed receipt showing that application for registration has been made. This completed receipt shall be in the possession of the user of the snowmobile until the registration certificate is received. No snowmobile dealer may charge an additional fee to the buyer for performing this service required under this subsection. However, no purchaser exempted under Section 3-11 of this Act shall be charged any fee or be subject to the other requirements of this Section. The application form shall so state in clear language the requirements of this Section and the penalty for violation near the place on the application form provided for indicating the intention to register in another jurisdiction. Each dealer shall maintain, for one year, a record in a form prescribed by the Department for each snowmobile sold. These records shall be open to inspection by the Department. Upon receipt of the application in approved form the Department shall enter the same upon the records of its office and issue to the applicant a certificate of number stating the number awarded to the snowmobile and the name and address of the owner.

P.A. 77-1312, § 3-2, eff. Aug. 27, 1971. Amended by P.A. 81-702, § 1, eff. Jan. 1, 1981; P.A. 82-195, § 1, eff. April 1, 1982; P.A. 84-151, § 2, eff. Jan. 1, 1986; P.A. 84-973, § 2, eff. Jan. 1, 1986; P.A. 92-174, § 5, eff. July 26, 2001.

Formerly Ill.Rev.Stat.1991, ch. 95 ½, ¶ 603-2.

40/3-3. Identification Number Display

§ 3-3. Identification Number Display. The Department shall issue to the snowmobile owner two registration expiration decals with the number awarded to that snowmobile imprinted upon the decals. The owner shall apply these decals on each side of the cowling of such snowmobile. The certificate of number shall be pocket size and shall be available at all times for inspection on the snowmobile for which issued, whenever such snowmobile is in operation.

P.A. 77-1312, § 3-3, eff. Aug. 27, 1971. Amended by P.A. 81-702, § 1, eff. Jan. 1, 1981; P.A. 81-1509, Art. II, § 73, eff. Sept. 26, 1980.

Formerly Ill.Rev.Stat.1991, ch. 95 ½, ¶ 603-3.

40/3-4. Destruction, sale, transfer or abandonment

§ 3-4. Destruction, sale, transfer or abandonment. The owner of any snowmobile shall within 15 days notify the Department if such snowmobile is destroyed or abandoned, or is sold or transferred either wholly or in part to another person or persons. In all such cases, the notice shall be accompanied by a surrender of the certificate of number. When the surrender of the certificate is by reason of the snowmobile being destroyed or abandoned, the Department shall cancel the certificate and enter such fact in its records. The Department shall be notified in writing of any change of address. Should the owner desire a new certificate of number, showing the new address, he shall surrender his old certificate and notify the Department of the new address, remitting one dollar to cover the issuance of a new certificate of number. If the surrender is by reason of a sale or transfer either wholly or in part to another person or persons, the owner surrendering the certificate shall state to the Department, under oath, the name of the purchaser or transferee.

P.A. 77-1312, § 3-4, eff. Aug. 27, 1971.

Formerly Ill.Rev.Stat.1991, ch. 95 ½, ¶ 603-4.

40/3-5. Transfer of Identification Number

§ 3-5. Transfer of Identification Number. The purchaser of a snowmobile shall, within 15 days after acquiring same, make application to the Department for the transfer to him of the certificate of number issued to the snowmobile, giving his name, his address and the number of the snowmobile. The purchaser shall apply for a transfer-renewal for a fee of $18 for approximately 3 years. All transfers will bear September 30 expiration dates in the calendar year of expiration. Upon receipt of the application and fee, the Department shall transfer the certificate of number issued to the snowmobile to the new owner. Unless the application is made and fee paid within 30 days, the snowmobile shall be deemed to be without certificate of number and it shall be unlawful for any person to operate the snowmobile until the certificate is issued.

P.A. 77-1312, § 3-5, eff. Aug. 27, 1971. Amended by P.A. 82-195, § 1, eff. April 1, 1982; P.A. 84-151, § 2, eff. Jan. 1, 1986; P.A. 84-973, § 2, eff. Jan. 1, 1986; P.A. 87-1109, § 2, eff. April 1, 1993; P.A. 92-174, § 5, eff. July 26, 2001.

Formerly Ill.Rev.Stat.1991, ch. 95 ½, ¶ 603-5.

40/3-6. Loss of certificate

§ 3-6. Loss of certificate. Should a certificate of number or registration expiration decal become lost, destroyed, or mutilated beyond legibility, the owner of the snowmobile shall make application to the Department for the replacement of the certificate or decal, giving his name, address, and the number of his snowmobile and shall at the same time pay to the Department a fee of $1.

P.A. 77-1312, § 3-6, eff. Aug. 27, 1971.

Formerly Ill.Rev.Stat.1991, ch. 95 ½, ¶ 603-6.

40/3-7. Department Records

§ 3-7. Department Records. All records of the Department made or kept under this Article shall be public records.

P.A. 77-1312, § 3-7, eff. Aug. 27, 1971. Amended by P.A. 79-885, § 1, eff. Oct. 1, 1975.

Formerly Ill.Rev.Stat.1991, ch. 95 ½, ¶ 603-7.

40/3-8. Certificate of Number

§ 3-8. Certificate of Number. Every certificate of number awarded under this Act shall continue in full force and effect for approximately 3 years unless sooner terminated or discontinued in accordance with this Act. All new certificates issued will bear September 30 expiration dates in the calendar year 3 years after the issuing date. Provided however, that the Department may, for purposes of implementing this Section, adopt rules for phasing in the issuance of new certificates and provide for 1, 2 or 3 year expiration dates and pro-rated payments or charges for each registration.

All certificates shall be renewed for 3 years from the nearest September 30 for a fee of $18. All certificates will be considered invalid after October 15 of the year of expiration. All certificates expiring in a given year shall be renewed between April 1 and September 30 of that year, in order to allow sufficient time for processing.

The Department shall issue "registration expiration decals" with all new certificates of number, all certificates of number transferred and renewed, and all certificates of number renewed. The decals issued for each year shall be of a different and distinct color from the decals of each year currently displayed. The decals shall be affixed to each side of the cowling of the snowmobile in the manner prescribed by the rules and regulations of the Department. The Department shall fix a day and month of the year on which certificates of number due to expire shall lapse and no longer be of any force and effect unless renewed pursuant to this Act.

No number or registration expiration decal, except a sticker or number which may be required by a political subdivision, municipality, or state, other than the registration expiration decal issued to a snowmobile or granted reciprocity pursuant to this Act, shall be painted, attached, or otherwise displayed on either side of the cowling of such snowmobile.

A dealer engaged in the manufacture, sale, or leasing of snowmobiles required to be numbered hereunder, upon application to the Department upon forms prescribed by it, may obtain certificates of number for use in the testing or demonstrating of such snowmobiles upon payment of $18 for each registration. Certificates of number so issued may be used by the applicant in the testing or demonstrating of snowmobiles by temporary placement of the registration expiration decals assigned by such certificates on the snowmobile so tested or demonstrated.

P.A. 77-1312, § 3-8, eff. Aug. 27, 1971. Amended by P.A. 78-856, § 1, eff. July 1, 1974; P.A. 82-195, § 1, eff. April 1, 1982; P.A. 84-151, § 2, eff. Jan. 1, 1986; P.A. 84-973, § 2, eff. Jan. 1, 1986; P.A. 92-174, § 5, eff. July 26, 2001.

Formerly Ill.Rev.Stat.1991, ch. 95 ½, ¶ 603-8.

40/3-9. Registration List

§ 3-9. Registration List.

A snowmobile registration list may be furnished for official use at no charge only to such federal, state, county and municipal enforcement agencies as may require such data. A snowmobile registration list may be furnished, at the cost of reproduction, to statewide not-for-profit Illinois snowmobile organizations for use only with educational programs.

P.A. 77-1312, § 3-9, eff. Aug. 27, 1971. Amended by P.A. 92-174, § 5, eff. July 26, 2001.

Formerly Ill.Rev.Stat.1991, ch. 95 ½, ¶ 603-9.

40/3-10. Penalty

§ 3-10. Penalty. No person shall at any time falsely alter or change in any manner the certificate of number issued under the provisions hereof, or falsify any record required by this Act, or counterfeit any form of license provided for by this Act.

P.A. 77-1312, § 3-10, eff. Aug. 27, 1971.

Formerly Ill.Rev.Stat.1991, ch. 95 ½, ¶ 603-10.

40/3-11. Exception from numbering provisions of this Act

§ 3-11. Exception from numbering provisions of this Act. A snowmobile shall not be required to be numbered under this Act if it is:

A. Owned and used by the United States, another state, or a political subdivision thereof, but such snowmobiles shall display the name of the owner on the cowling thereof.

B. Covered by a valid registration or license of another state, province or country which is the domicile of the owner of the snowmobile and is not operated within this State on more than 30 consecutive days in any calendar year.

C. Owned and operated on lands owned by the owner or operator or on lands to which he has a contractual right other than as a member of a club or association, provided the snowmobile is not operated elsewhere within the state.

D. Used only on international or national competition circuits in events for which written permission has been obtained by the sponsoring or sanctioning body from the governmental unit having jurisdiction over the location of any event held in this State.

E. Owned by persons domiciled in Illinois but used entirely in another jurisdiction when such owner has complied with the provisions of Section 3-2 of this Act.

F. Designed for use by small children primarily as a toy and used only on private property and not on any public use trail.

P.A. 77-1312, § 3-11, eff. Aug. 27, 1971. Amended by P.A. 78-856, § 1, eff. July 1, 1974; P.A. 81-702, § 1, eff. Jan. 1, 1981; P.A. 92-174, § 5, eff. July 26, 2001.

Formerly Ill.Rev.Stat.1991, ch. 95 ½, ¶ 603-11.

ARTICLE IV. SNOWMOBILE EQUIPMENT

Section

40/4-1. Equipment

§ 4-1. Equipment. All snowmobiles operating within the State of Illinois shall be equipped with:

A. At least one white head-lamp having a minimum candlepower of sufficient intensity to exhibit a white light plainly visible from a distance of at least 500 feet ahead during hours of darkness under normal atmospheric conditions. If a snowmobile is equipped with a single beam lamp, such lamp shall be so aimed that when the vehicle is loaded none of the high intensity portion of the light, at a distance of 25 feet in front of the vehicle, projects higher than the level of the center of the lamp from which it originates.

B. At least one red tail lamp having a minimum candlepower of sufficient intensity to exhibit a red light plainly visible from a distance of five hundred feet to the rear during hours of darkness under normal atmospheric conditions.

C. A brake system in good mechanical condition.

D. Reflective material of a minimum area of 16 square inches mounted on each side of the cowling. Identifying numbers may be included in computing the required 16 square inch area.

E. Adequate sound suppression equipment. No snowmobile manufactured after June 1, 1972, shall be sold or offered for sale, unless it is equipped with sound suppression devices that limit total machine noise in accordance with noise pollution standards established pursuant to the Environmental Protection Act.[1]

P.A. 77-1312, § 4-1, eff. Aug. 27, 1971. Amended by P.A. 82-417, § 1, eff. Sept. 4, 1981.

Formerly Ill.Rev.Stat.1991, ch. 95 ½, ¶ 604-1.

1 415 ILCS 5/1 et seq.

40/4-2. Inspection and testing

§ 4-2. Inspection and testing. The Department may adopt rules and regulations with respect to the inspection of snowmobiles and the testing of machine noise.

P.A. 77-1312, § 4-2, eff. Aug. 27, 1971.

Formerly Ill.Rev.Stat.1991, ch. 95 ½, ¶ 604-2.

40/4-3. Sale prohibited

§ 4-3. Sale prohibited. No person shall have for sale, sell, or offer for sale in this State any snowmobile which fails to comply with Section 4-1, or which does not comply with the specifications for such equipment required by the rules and regulations of the Department after the effective date of such rules and regulations.

P.A. 77-1312, § 4-3, eff. Aug. 27, 1971.

Formerly Ill.Rev.Stat.1991, ch. 95 ½, ¶ 604-3.

40/4-4. Racing machines

§ 4-4. Racing machines. Snowmobiles used only on international or national competition circuits in events for which written permission has been obtained by the sponsoring or sanctioning body from the governmental unit having jurisdiction over the location of any event held in this State are exempt from the provisions of this Article.

P.A. 77-1312, § 4-4, eff. Aug. 27, 1971. Amended by P.A. 78-856, § 1, eff. Sept. 14, 1973.

Formerly Ill.Rev.Stat.1991, ch. 95 ½, ¶ 604-4.

ARTICLE V. CONTROL PROVISIONS

Section

40/5-1. Operation Generally

§ 5-1. Operation Generally. It is unlawful for any person to drive or operate any snowmobile in the following ways:

A. At a rate of speed too fast for conditions and the fact that the speed of the snowmobile does not exceed the applicable maximum speed limit allowed does not relieve the driver from the duty to decrease speed as may be necessary to avoid colliding with any person or vehicle or object within legal requirements and the duty of all persons to use due care.

B. In a careless, reckless, or negligent manner.

C. (Blank)

D. At any time without at least one lighted headlamp and one lighted tail lamp on the snowmobile.

E. Within any nature preserve.

F. On the tracks or right of way of an operating railroad.

G. In any tree nursery or planting in a manner which damages or destroys growing stock, or creates a substantial risk thereto.

H. On private property, without the written or verbal consent of the owner or lessee thereof. Any person operating a snowmobile upon lands of another shall stop and identify himself upon the request of the landowner or his duly authorized representative, and, if requested to do so by the landowner shall promptly remove the snowmobile from the premises.

I. Notwithstanding any other law to the contrary, an owner, lessee, or occupant of premises owes no duty of care to keep the premises safe for entry or use by others for snowmobiling, or to give warning of any condition, use, structure or activity on such premises. This subsection does not apply where permission to snowmobile is given for a valuable consideration other than to this State, any political subdivision or municipality thereof, or any landowner who is paid with funds from the Snowmobile Trail Establishment Fund. In the case of land leased to the State or a subdivision thereof, any consideration received is not valuable consideration within the meaning of this section. Nothing in this section limits in any way liability which otherwise exists for willful or malicious failure to guard or warn against a dangerous condition, use, structure, or activity.

J. Notwithstanding any other law to the contrary, an owner, lessee or occupant of premises who gives permission to another to snowmobile upon such premises does not thereby extend any assurance that the premises are safe for such purpose, or assume responsibility for or incur liability for any injury to person or property caused by any act or omission of persons to whom the permission to snowmobile is granted. This subsection shall not apply where permission to snowmobile is given for a valuable consideration other than to this State, any political subdivision or municipality thereof, or any landowner who is paid with funds from the Snowmobile Trail Establishment Fund. In the case of land leased to the State or a subdivision thereof, any consideration received is not valuable consideration within the meaning of this section. Nothing in this section limits in any way liability which otherwise exists for willful or malicious failure to guard or warn against a dangerous condition, use, structure, or activity.

K. On the frozen surface of public waters of this State within 100 feet of a person, including a skater not in or upon a snowmobile; within 100 feet of a person engaged in fishing, except at the minimum speed required to maintain forward movement of the snowmobile; on an area which has been cleared of snow for skating purposes unless the area is necessary for access to the frozen waters of this State.

L. Within 100 feet of a dwelling between midnight and 6 a.m. at a speed greater than the minimum required to maintain forward movement of the snowmobile. This provision would not apply on private property where verbal or written consent of the owner or lessee has been granted to snowmobile upon such private property or frozen waters of this State.

M. Notwithstanding any other law to the contrary, any owner, lessee or occupant of premises or any person or association who, with the permission of the owner of the premises, places, maintains or displays a sign, signal, marking or device to give warning of any unsafe condition on the premises for snowmobiling shall not be liable for any personal injuries allegedly caused by his or her acts or omissions in providing such warning unless the alleged misconduct was willful or malicious. This subsection shall not apply where the owner, occupant or lessee of the premises grants express permission for snowmobiling in exchange for valuable consideration. However, this subsection will apply where such consideration is given to such owner, occupant or lessee by the State or one of its political subdivisions.

N. Notwithstanding any other law or Section of this Act to the contrary, the State and any political subdivision or municipality thereof owes no duty of care to keep the premises safe for entry or use by others for snowmobiling or to guard against or give warnings of any condition, use, structure or activity on property in which the State and any political subdivision or municipality thereof has any interest.

P.A. 77-1312, § 5-1, eff. Aug. 27, 1971. Amended by P.A. 78-856, § 1, eff. July 1, 1974; P.A. 81-701, § 1, eff. Jan. 1, 1980; P.A. 81-915, § 1, eff. Jan. 1, 1980; P.A. 81-1509, Art. I, § 58, eff. Sept. 26, 1980; P.A. 82-195, § 1, eff. April 1, 1982; P.A. 82-993, § 1, eff. Sept. 10, 1982; P.A. 83-1044, § 1, eff. Jan. 5, 1984; P.A. 84-151, § 2, eff. Jan. 1, 1986; P.A. 84-973, § 2, eff. Jan. 1, 1986; P.A. 89-55, § 5, eff. Jan. 1, 1996.

Formerly Ill.Rev.Stat.1991, ch. 95 ½, ¶ 605-1.

40/5-2. Operation on Highways

§ 5-2. Operation on Highways. It is unlawful for any person to drive or operate any snowmobile on a highway in this State except as follows:

A. On highways other than tollways, interstate highways and fully or limited access-controlled highways snowmobiles may make a direct crossing provided:

(1) the crossing is made at an angle of approximately 90 degrees to the direction of the highway and at a place where no obstruction prevents a quick and safe crossing; and

(2) the snowmobile is brought to a complete stop before crossing a roadway; and

(3) the operator yields the right of way to all oncoming traffic which constitutes a hazard.

B. On highways other than tollways, interstate highways and fully or limited access-controlled highways snowmobiles may be operated not less than 10 feet from the roadway and in the same direction as traffic. On such highways, other than State highways, the corporate authorities of a city, village or incorporated town may adopt ordinances providing for variance from the 10-foot separation requirement of this subsection, including ordinances permitting the operation of snowmobiles upon the roadways of such highways, other than State highways, within city, village or town limits. In addition, the corporate authorities of any unit of local government with jurisdiction over such highways may adopt ordinances authorizing the operation of snowmobiles within 10 feet of the roadway to avoid obstructions or hazardous terrain. Other than for State highways, corporate authorities of a city, village or incorporated town may adopt ordinances providing for trails, including the designation of the roadways of highways referred to in this paragraph as snowmobile trails, and regulating snowmobile operation within city, village or town limits.

C. On highways other than tollways, interstate highways and fully or limited access-controlled highways snowmobiles may be operated on roadways when it is necessary to cross a bridge or culvert or when it is impracticable to gain immediate access to an area adjacent to a highway where a snowmobile is to be operated.

D. Corporate authorities of a city, village or incorporated town may by ordinance designate 1 or more specific public highways or streets within their jurisdiction as egress and ingress routes for the use of snowmobiles. In the event that such public highways or streets are under the jurisdiction of the State of Illinois, express written consent of the Illinois Department of Transportation shall be required. Corporate authorities acting under the authority of this paragraph D shall erect and maintain signs giving proper notice thereof.

E. Snowmobiles may be lawfully driven or operated upon those highways where posted with signs giving proper notice and erected and maintained by the township road commissioner. A township or township road commissioner shall not be liable for any personal injuries caused as a result of the operation of a snowmobile on such highways. For purposes of this paragraph E, "highways" are defined as township roads pursuant to Section 2-205 of the Illinois Highway Code.[1]

P.A. 77-1312, § 5-2, eff. Aug. 27, 1971. Amended by P.A. 79-885, § 1, eff. Oct. 1, 1975; P.A. 81-828, § 1, eff. Jan. 1, 1980; P.A. 82-195, § 1, eff. April 1, 1982; P.A. 82-347, § 1, eff. Jan. 1, 1982; P.A. 82-377, § 1, eff. Sept. 2, 1981; P.A. 82-464, § 1, eff. Sept. 15, 1981; P.A. 82-783, Art. III, § 38, eff. July 13, 1982; P.A. 83-789, § 1, eff. Jan. 1, 1983; P.A. 84-151, § 2, eff. Jan. 1, 1986; P.A. 84-973, § 2, eff. Jan. 1, 1986; P.A. 91-357, § 233, eff. July 29, 1999.

Formerly Ill.Rev.Stat.1991, ch. 95 ½, ¶ 605-2.

[1] 605 ILCS 5/2-205.

40/5-3. Youthful Operators

§ 5-3. Youthful Operators.

A. No person under 10 years of age may operate a snowmobile, other than machines designed for use by small children primarily as a toy and used only on private property and not on any public use trail.

B. Persons at least 10 and less than 12 years of age may operate a snowmobile only if they are either accompanied on the snowmobile by a parent or guardian or a person at least 18 years of age designated by a parent or guardian.

C. Persons at least 12 and less than 16 years of age may operate a snowmobile only if they are either accompanied on the snowmobile by a parent or guardian or a person at least 16 years of age designated by a parent or guardian, or such operator is in possession of a certificate issued by the Department authorizing the holder to operate snowmobiles.

D. Any person who operates a snowmobile on a highway as provided in Section 5-2 shall (1) possess a valid motor vehicle driver's license; or (2) possess a safety certificate as provided for in this Section. Any such person less than 16 years of age shall also be under the immediate supervision of a parent or guardian or a person at least 18 years of age designated by the parent or guardian.

E. Violations of this Section done with the knowledge of a parent or guardian shall be deemed a violation by the parent or guardian and punishable under Article X of this Act.

F. The department shall establish a program of instruction on snowmobile laws, regulations, safety and related subjects. It is unlawful for any person under 16 years of age to operate a snowmobile on a public highway in this State.

The program shall be conducted by instructors certified by the department. The department may procure liability insurance coverage for certified instructors for work within the scope of their duties under this section. Persons satisfactorily completing this program shall receive certification from the department. The department may charge each person who enrolls in the course an instruction fee of $2.50. If a fee is authorized by the department, the department shall authorize instructors conducting such courses meeting standards established by it to retain $1 of the fee to defray expenses incurred locally to operate the program. The remaining $1.50 of the fee shall be retained by the department to defray a part of its expenses incurred to operate the safety and accident reporting program. A person over the age of 12 years but under the age of 16 years who holds a valid certificate issued by another state or province of the Dominion of Canada need not obtain a certificate from the department if the course content of the program in such other state or province substantially meets that established by the department under this section. A certificate issued by the Department, or by another State or a province of the Dominion of Canada, shall not constitute a valid motor vehicle operator's license for the purpose of this Section.

P.A. 77-1312, § 5-3, eff. Aug. 27, 1971. Amended by P.A. 79-1058, § 1, eff. Oct. 1, 1975; P.A. 84-151, § 2, eff. Jan. 1, 1986; P.A. 84-973, § 2, eff. Jan. 1, 1986; P.A. 85-293, Art. III, § 22, eff. Sept. 8, 1987; P.A. 92-174, § 5, eff. July 26, 2001.

Formerly Ill.Rev.Stat.1991, ch. 95 ½, ¶ 605-3.

40/5-4. Operation on Ice

§ 5-4. Operation on Ice.

Snowmobiles may be operated on the frozen waters of this State subject to the provisions of Section 5-1 and the rules and regulations of the Department.

P.A. 77-1312, § 5-4, eff. Aug. 27, 1971. Amended by P.A. 89-55, § 5, eff. Jan. 1, 1996.

Formerly Ill.Rev.Stat.1991, ch. 95 ½, ¶ 605-4.

40/5-5. Special events

§ 5-5. Special events. Nothing contained in this Article shall be construed to prohibit any local authority of this State from designating a special snowmobile event. In such case the provisions of this article shall not apply to areas or highways under the jurisdiction of that local authority.

P.A. 77-1312, § 5-5, eff. Aug. 27, 1971.

Formerly Ill.Rev.Stat.1991, ch. 95 ½, ¶ 605-5.

40/5-6. Other Prohibition

§ 5-6. Other Prohibition. A. No person, except persons permitted by law, shall operate or ride any snowmobile with any firearm in his possession unless it is unloaded and enclosed in a carrying case, or any bow unless it is unstrung in a carrying case.

B. No person shall operate any snowmobile emitting pollutants in accordance with standards established pursuant to the Environmental Protection Act.[1]

C. No person shall deposit from a snowmobile on the snow, ice, or ground surface, trash, glass, garbage, insoluble material, or other offensive matter.

D. No person shall use a snowmobile to take, pursue or intentionally harass or disturb wildlife as defined in Section 1.2t of the Wildlife Code, except such restriction shall not apply to any person acting to protect livestock from predatory animals.

P.A. 77-1312, § 5-6, eff. Aug. 12, 1971. Amended by P.A. 82-629, § 2, eff. Sept. 24, 1981.

Formerly Ill.Rev.Stat.1991, ch. 95 ½, ¶ 605-6.

[1] 415 ILCS 5/1 et seq.

40/5-7. Operating a snowmobile while under the influence of alcohol or other drug; criminal penalties; suspension of operating privileges

§ 5-7. Operating a snowmobile while under the influence of alcohol or other drug; criminal penalties; suspension of operating privileges.

(a) A person may not operate a snowmobile within this State while:

1. The alcohol concentration in that person's blood or breath is a concentration at which driving a motor vehicle is prohibited under subdivision (1) of subsection (a) of Section 11-501 of the Illinois Vehicle Code;[1]

2. The person is under the influence of alcohol;

3. The person is under the influence of any other drug or combination of drugs to a degree that renders that person incapable of safely operating a snowmobile;

4. The person is under the combined influence of alcohol and any other drug or drugs to a degree that renders that person incapable of safely operating a snowmobile; or

5. There is any amount of a drug, substance, or compound in that person's blood or urine resulting from the unlawful use or consumption of cannabis listed in the Cannabis Control Act,[2] or controlled substance listed in the Illinois Controlled Substances Act.[3]

(b) The fact that a person charged with violating this Section is or has been legally entitled to use alcohol or other drugs does not constitute a defense against a charge of violating this Section.

(c) Every person convicted of violating this Section or a similar provision of a local ordinance is guilty of a Class A misdemeanor, except as otherwise provided in this Section.

(d) Every person convicted of violating this Section is guilty of a Class 4 felony if:

1. The person has a previous conviction under this Section; or

2. The offense results in personal injury where a person other than the operator suffers great bodily harm or permanent disability or disfigurement, when the violation was a proximate cause of the injuries. A person guilty of a Class 4 felony under this paragraph 2, if sentenced to a term of imprisonment, shall be sentenced to not less than one year nor more than 12 years.

(e) Every person convicted of violating this Section is guilty of a Class 2 felony if the offense results in the death of a person. A person guilty of a Class 2 felony under this subsection (e), if sentenced to a term of imprisonment, shall be sentenced to a term of not less than 3 years and not more than 14 years.

(f) In addition to any criminal penalties imposed, the Department of Conservation shall suspend the snowmobile operation privileges of a person convicted of a misdemeanor under this Section for a period of one year or for a period of

5 years if the person is convicted of a felony under this Section.

P.A. 77-1312, § 5-7, added by P.A. 89-55, § 5, eff. Jan. 1, 1996. Amended by P.A. 90-215, § 5, eff. Jan. 1, 1998; P.A. 92-615, § 5, eff. Jan. 1, 2003.

[1] 625 ILCS 5/11-501.

[2] 720 ILCS 550/1 et seq.

[3] 720 ILCS 570/100 et seq.

40/5-7.1. Implied consent

§ 5-7.1. Implied consent.

(a) A person who operates a snowmobile in this State is deemed to have given consent to a chemical test or tests of blood, breath, or urine for the purpose of determining the alcohol or other drug content of that person's blood if arrested for a violation of Section 5-7. The test or tests shall be administered at the direction of the arresting officer. The law enforcement agency employing the officer shall designate which tests shall be administered. A urine test may be administered even after a blood or breath test or both has been administered.

(b) A person who is dead, unconscious, or who is otherwise in a condition rendering that person incapable of refusal, is deemed not to have withdrawn the consent provided in subsection (a).

(c) A person requested to submit to a test as provided in this Section shall be verbally advised by the law enforcement officer requesting the test that a refusal to submit to the test will result in suspension of that person's privilege to operate a snowmobile for a minimum of 2 years.

(d) Following this warning, if a person under arrest refuses upon the request of a law enforcement officer to submit to a test designated by the officer, no test may be given, but the law enforcement officer shall file with the clerk of the circuit court for the county in which the arrest was made, a sworn statement naming the person refusing to take and complete the test or tests requested under the provisions of this Section. The sworn statement shall identify the arrested person, the person's current residence address and shall specify that a refusal by that person to take the test or tests was made. The sworn statement shall include a statement that the officer had reasonable cause to believe the person was operating the snowmobile within this State while under the influence of alcohol or other drug and that test or tests were requested as an incident to and following the lawful arrest for an offense as defined in Section 5-7 or a similar provision of a local ordinance, and that the person, after being arrested for an offense arising out of acts alleged to have been committed while operating a snowmobile, refused to submit to and complete a test or tests as requested by the law enforcement officer.

(e) The clerk shall notify the person in writing that the person's privilege to operate a snowmobile will be suspended for a minimum of 2 years unless, within 28 days from the date of mailing of the notice, that person requests a hearing in writing.

If the person desires a hearing, the person shall file a complaint in the circuit court in the county where that person was arrested within 28 days from the date of mailing of the notice. The hearing shall proceed in the court in the same manner as other civil proceedings. The hearing shall cover only the following issues: (1) whether the person was placed under arrest for an offense as defined in Section 5-7 or a similar provision of a local ordinance as evidenced by the issuance of a uniform citation; (2) whether the arresting officer had reasonable grounds to believe that the person was operating a snowmobile while under the influence of alcohol or other drug; and (3) whether that person refused to submit and complete the test or tests upon the request of the law enforcement officer. Whether the person was informed that the person's privilege to operate a snowmobile would be suspended if that person refused to submit to the test or tests may not be an issue in the hearing.

If the court finds against the person on the issues before the court, the clerk shall immediately notify the Department of Conservation of the court's decision, and the Department shall suspend the snowmobile operation privileges of that person for at least 2 years.

(f) If the person fails to request a hearing in writing within 28 days of the date of mailing of the notice, the clerk shall immediately notify the Department of Conservation that no request for a hearing was received within the statutory time period, and the Department shall suspend the snowmobile operation privileges of that person for at least 2 years.

(g) A person must submit to each test offered by the law enforcement officer in order to comply with implied consent provisions of this Section.

(h) The provision of Section 11-501.2 of the Illinois Vehicle Code [1] concerning the certification and use of chemical tests applies to the use of those tests under this Section.

P.A. 77-1312, § 5-7.1, added by P.A. 89-55, § 5, eff. Jan. 1, 1996.

[1] 625 ILCS 5/11-501.2.

40/5-7.2. Chemical and other tests

§ 5-7.2. Chemical and other tests.

(a) Upon the trial of a civil or criminal action or proceeding arising out of acts alleged to have been committed while under the influence of alcohol, the concentration of alcohol in the person's blood or breath at the time alleged as shown by analysis of the person's blood, urine, breath, or other bodily substance gives rise to the presumptions specified in subdivisions 1, 2, and 3 of subsection (b) of Section 11-501.2 of the Illinois Vehicle Code.[1]

(b) The provisions of subsection (a) shall not be construed as limiting the introduction of any other relevant evidence bearing upon the question whether the person was under the influence of alcohol.

(c) If a person under arrest refuses to submit to a chemical test under the provisions of Section 5-7.1, evidence of refusal is admissible in a civil or criminal action or proceeding arising out of acts alleged to have been committed while the person under the influence of alcohol or other drugs was operating a snowmobile.

P.A. 77-1312, § 5-7.2, added by P.A. 89-55, § 5, eff. Jan. 1, 1996. Amended by P.A. 90-215, § 5, eff. Jan. 1, 1998.

[1] 625 ILCS 5/11-501.2.

40/5-7.3. Supervision of operator; notification; 6 hour operating limitation

§ 5-7.3. Supervision of operator; notification; 6 hour operating limitation.

(a) The owner of a snowmobile or person given supervisory authority over a snowmobile, may not knowingly permit a snowmobile to be operated by a person under the influence of alcohol or other drug.

(b) Whenever a person is convicted of a violation of Section 5-7, the court shall notify the Office of Law Enforcement of the Department with the records essential for the performance of the Department's duties to monitor and enforce an order of suspension or revocation concerning the person's privilege to operate a snowmobile.

(c) A person who has been arrested and charged with violating Section 5-7 may not operate a snowmobile within this State for a period of 6 hours after that person's arrest.

P.A. 77-1312, § 5-7.3, added by P.A. 89-55, § 5, eff. Jan. 1, 1996.

40/5-7.4. Admissibility of blood alcohol tests

§ 5-7.4. Admissibility of blood alcohol tests.

(a) Notwithstanding any other provision of law, the written results of blood alcohol tests conducted upon persons receiving medical treatment in a hospital emergency room are admissible in evidence as a business record exception to the hearsay rule only in prosecutions for a violation of Section 5-7 of this Act or a similar provision of a local ordinance or in prosecutions for reckless homicide brought under the Criminal Code of 1961.[1] The results of the tests are admissible only when each of the following criteria are met:

1. The blood alcohol tests were ordered by a physician on duty at the hospital emergency room and were performed in the regular course of providing emergency medical treatment in order to assist the physician in diagnosis or treatment;

2. The blood alcohol tests were performed by the hospital's own laboratory; and

3. The written results of the blood alcohol tests were received and considered by the physician on duty at the hospital emergency room to assist that physician in diagnosis or treatment.

(b) The confidentiality provisions of law pertaining to medical records and medical treatment are not applicable with regard to blood alcohol tests performed under the provisions of this Section in prosecutions as specified in subsection (a) of this Section. No person shall be liable for civil damages as a result of the evidentiary use of blood alcohol tests results under this Section or as a result of that person's testimony made available under this Section.

P.A. 77-1312, § 40/5-7.4, added by P.A. 89-55, § 5, eff. Jan. 1, 1996. Renumbered § 5-7.4 and amended by P.A. 89-626, Art. 3, § 3-38, eff. Aug. 9, 1996.

[1] 720 ILCS 5/1-1 et seq.

40/5-7.5. Preliminary breath screening test

§ 5-7.5. Preliminary breath screening test. If a law enforcement officer has probable cause to believe that a person is violating or has violated Section 5-7 or a similar provision of a local ordinance, the officer, before an arrest, may request the person to provide a sample of his or her breath for a preliminary breath screening test using a portable device approved by the Department of State Police. The results of this preliminary breath screening test may be used by the law enforcement officer for the purpose of assisting with the determination of whether to require a chemical test, as authorized under Sections 5-7.1 and 5-7.2 and the appropriate type of test to request. Any chemical test authorized under Sections 5-7.1 and 5-7.2 may be requested by the officer regardless of the result of the preliminary breath screening test if probable cause for an arrest exists. The result of a preliminary breath screening test may be used by the defendant as evidence in an administrative or court proceeding involving a violation of Section 5-7 or 5-7.1.

P.A. 77-1312, § 40/5-7.5, added by P.A. 89-55, § 5, eff. Jan. 1, 1996. Renumbered § 5-7.5 and amended by P.A. 89-626, Art. 3, § 3-38, eff. Aug. 9, 1996. Amended by P.A. 91-828, § 10, eff. Jan. 1, 2001.

ARTICLE VI. ACCIDENT REPORTS—OPERATOR'S RESPONSIBILITY—TRANSMITTAL OF INFORMATION

Section

40/6-1. Collisions, accidents, and casualties; reports

§ 6-1. Collisions, accidents, and casualties; reports.

A. The operator of a snowmobile involved in a collision, accident, or other casualty, shall render to other persons affected by this collision, accident, or other casualty such assistance as may be practicable and as may be necessary in order to save them from or minimize any danger caused by the collision, accident, or other casualty, and also shall give his name, address, and identification of his snowmobile to any person injured and to the owner of any property damaged in the collision, accident, or other casualty.

B. In the case of collision, accident, or other casualty involving the operation of a snowmobile, the operator thereof, if the collision, accident, or other casualty results in death or injury to a person or damage to property in excess of $750, shall file with the Department a full description of the collision, accident, or other casualty, including such information as the Department may, by regulation, require. Reports of such accidents must be filed with the Department on a Department Accident Report form within 5 days.

C. Reports of accidents resulting in personal injury, wherein a person is incapacitated for a period exceeding 72 hours, must be filed with the Department on a Department Accident Report form within 5 days. Accidents which result in loss of life shall be reported to the Department on a Department form within 48 hours.

D. All required accident reports and supplemental reports are without prejudice to the individual so reporting, and are for the confidential use of the Department, except that the Department may disclose the identity of a person involved in an accident when such identity is not otherwise known or when such person denies his presence at such accident. No such report may be used as evidence in any trial, civil or criminal, arising out of an accident, except that the Department must furnish upon demand of any person who has or claims to have made such a report, or upon demand of any court, a certificate showing that a specified accident report has or has not been made to the Department, solely to prove a compliance or a failure to comply with the requirements that such a report be made to the Department.

P.A. 77-1312, § 6-1, eff. Aug. 27, 1971. Amended by P.A. 92-174, § 5, eff. July 26, 2001.

Formerly Ill.Rev.Stat.1991, ch. 95 ½, ¶ 606-1.

40/6-2. Owner's and operator's responsibility

§ 6-2. Owner's and operator's responsibility. The owner and any operator of a snowmobile are jointly and severally liable for any injury or damage occasioned by the operation of such snowmobile.

P.A. 77–1312, § 6–2, eff. Aug. 27, 1971.

Formerly Ill.Rev.Stat.1991, ch. 95 ½, ¶ 606–2.

ARTICLE VII. LOCAL REGULATION

40/7–1. Local ordinances

§ 7–1. Local ordinances. This Act and other applicable laws of this State govern the operation, equipment, numbering and all other matters relating thereto whenever any snowmobile is operated within this State; but this Act does not prevent the adoption of any ordinance or local law by any political subdivision of the State relating to the operation and equipment of snowmobiles which is not inconsistent with this Act, amendments hereto or regulations issued hereunder. Such ordinances or local laws shall be operative only so long as they continue to be not inconsistent with this Act, amendments hereto or regulations issued hereunder. However, this Act is not a limit upon any home rule unit.

P.A. 77–1312, § 7–1, eff. Aug. 27, 1971. Amended by P.A. 78–856, § 1, eff. Sept. 14, 1973.

Formerly Ill.Rev.Stat.1991, ch. 95 ½, ¶ 607–1.

ARTICLE VIII. FILING OF REGULATIONS

40/8–1. Rules and regulations, filing

§ 8–1. Rules and regulations, filing. The implementation and administration of the provisions of this Act shall be by rules and regulations adopted by the Department of Natural Resources. A copy of the rules and regulations adopted pursuant to this Act, and of any amendments thereto, shall be filed in the office of the Department and in the office of the Secretary of State. Rules and regulations shall be published by the Department in a convenient form.

P.A. 77–1312, § 8–1, eff. Aug. 27, 1971. Amended by P.A. 84–151, § 2, eff. Jan. 1, 1986; P.A. 84–973, § 2, eff. Jan. 1, 1986; P.A. 89–445, § 9A–88, eff. Feb. 7, 1996.

Formerly Ill.Rev.Stat.1991, ch. 95 ½, ¶ 608–1.

ARTICLE IX. SNOWMOBILE REGISTRATION AND SAFETY ACT REVENUES

40/9–1. Special fund

§ 9–1. Special fund. Except as provided in Section 9–2, all revenues received under this Act, including registration fees, fines, bond forfeitures or other income of whatever kind or nature shall be deposited in the State Treasury in "The State Boating Act Fund". Appropriations of revenue received as a result of this Act from "The State Boating Act Fund" shall be made only to the Department for administering the registration of snowmobiles, snowmobile safety, snowmobile safety education and enforcement provisions of this Act or for any purpose related or connected thereto, including the construction, maintenance, and rehabilitation of snowmobile recreation areas or any other facilities for the use of snowmobiles, including plans and specifications, engineering surveys and supervision and land acquisition where necessary, and including the disbursement of funds to political subdivisions upon written application to and subsequent approval by the Department for construction, maintenance, and rehabilitation of snowmobile recreation areas or any other facilities for the use of snowmobiles, including plans and specifications, engineering surveys and supervision and land acquisition where necessary.

P.A. 77–1312, § 9–1, eff. Aug. 27, 1971. Amended by P.A. 78–856, § 1, eff. July 1, 1974; P.A. 82–195, § 1, eff. April 1, 1982.

Formerly Ill.Rev.Stat.1991, ch. 95 ½, ¶ 609–1.

40/9–2. Special fund

§ 9–2. Special fund. There is created a special fund in the State Treasury to be known as the Snowmobile Trail Establishment Fund. Thirty-three percent of each new, transfer-renewal and renewal registration fee collected under Sections 3–2, 3–5 and 3–8 of this Act shall be deposited in the fund. The fund shall be administered by the Department and shall be used for disbursement, upon written application to and subsequent approval by the Department, to nonprofit snowmobile clubs and organizations for construction, maintenance, and rehabilitation of snowmobile trails and areas for the use of snowmobiles, including plans and specifications, engineering surveys and supervision where necessary. The Department shall promulgate such rules or regulations as it deems necessary for the administration of the fund.

P.A. 77–1312, § 9–2, added by P.A. 82–195, § 1, eff. April 1, 1982. Amended by P.A. 82–993, § 1, eff. Sept. 10, 1982; P.A. 85–153, § 1, eff. Aug. 14, 1987; P.A. 92–174, § 5, eff. July 26, 2001.

Formerly Ill.Rev.Stat.1991, ch. 95 ½, ¶ 609–2.

ARTICLE X. PENALTIES

40/10–1. Violations

§ 10–1. Violations.

(a) Except as otherwise provided in this Act, a person who violates any of the provisions of this Act is guilty of a Class C misdemeanor.

(b) A person who violates subsection (B) of Section 5–1 of this Act is guilty of a Class B misdemeanor.

(c) A person who violates Section 2–4 or Section 5–7.3 of this Act is guilty of a Class A misdemeanor.

P.A. 77–1312, § 10–1, eff. Aug. 27, 1971. Amended by P.A. 77–2779, § 1, eff. Jan. 1, 1973; P.A. 78–255, § 61, eff. Oct. 1, 1973; P.A. 82–629, § 2, eff. Sept. 24, 1981; P.A. 84–151, § 2, eff. Jan. 1, 1986; P.A. 84–973, § 2, eff. Jan. 1, 1986; P.A. 89–55, § 5, eff. Jan. 1, 1996.

Formerly Ill.Rev.Stat.1991, ch. 95 ½, ¶ 610–1.

40/10–2. Denial of operating privilege

§ 10–2. Denial of operating privilege. A person who is convicted of a violation of subsection (B) of Section 5–1 or Section 5–7 of this Act, in addition to other penalties authorized in this Act, may in the discretion of the court be refused the privilege to operate a snowmobile in this State for a period of one year or more.

P.A. 77-1312, § 10-2, added by P.A. 89-55, § 5, eff. Jan. 1, 1996.

40/10-3. Unlawful operation of a snowmobile

§ 10-3. Unlawful operation of a snowmobile. A person who operates a snowmobile during the period when he or she is denied the privilege to operate a snowmobile is guilty of a Class A misdemeanor.

P.A. 77-1312, § 10-3, added by P.A. 89-55, § 5, eff. Jan. 1, 1996.

ARTICLE XI. PARTIAL INVALIDITY

40/11-1. Invalid provisions and applications; effect

§ 11-1. If any provision of this Act, or the application of such provision to any persons, body or circumstances shall be held invalid, the remainder of this Act, or the application of such provision to persons, bodies or circumstances other than those as to which it shall have been held invalid, shall not be affected thereby.

P.A. 77-1312, § 11-1, eff. Aug. 27, 1971.

Formerly Ill.Rev.Stat.1991, ch. 95 ½, ¶ 611-1.

ARTICLE XII. APPROPRIATION

40/12.1. § 12.1. Repealed by P.A. 81-371, eff. Jan. 1, 1980

ACT 45. BOAT REGISTRATION AND SAFETY ACT

ARTICLE I. DEFINITIONS—APPLICATION—JURISDICTION

45/1-1. Title and declaration of intent

§ 1-1. Title and declaration of intent. This Act shall be known and may be cited as the "Boat Registration and Safety Act." It is the policy of this State to promote safety for persons and property in and connected with the use, operation and equipment of vessels and to promote uniformity of laws relating thereto.

Laws 1959, p. 1473, Art. I, § 1. Amended by Laws 1967, p. 2217, § 1. Renumbered § 1-1 and amended by P.A. 82-783, Art. VII, § 2, eff. July 13, 1982.

Formerly Ill.Rev.Stat.1991, ch. 95 ½, ¶ 311-1.

Title of Act:

An Act for the registration of boats, providing for regulations pertaining to the operation thereof, providing penalties for the violation thereof, and repealing certain Acts herein named. Laws 1959, p. 1473, approved July 17, 1959, eff. March 1, 1960.

45/1-2. Definitions

§ 1-2. Definitions. As used in this Act, unless the context clearly requires a different meaning:

"Vessel" or "Watercraft" means every description of watercraft used or capable of being used as a means of transportation on water, except a seaplane on the water, innertube, air mattress or similar device, and boats used for concession rides in artificial bodies of water designed and used exclusively for such concessions.

"Motorboat" means any vessel propelled by machinery, whether or not such machinery is the principal source of propulsion, but does not include a vessel which has a valid marine document issued by the Bureau of Customs of the United States Government or any Federal agency successor thereto.

"Sailboat" means any watercraft propelled by sail or canvas, including sailboards. For the purposes of this Act, any watercraft propelled by both sail or canvas and machinery of any sort shall be deemed a motorboat when being so propelled.

"Airboat" means any boat (but not including airplanes or hydroplanes) propelled by machinery applying force against the air rather than the water as a means of propulsion.

"Lifeboat" means a small boat kept on board a larger boat for use in emergency.

"Owner" means a person, other than lien holder, having title to a motorboat. The term includes a person entitled to the use or possession of a motorboat subject to an interest in another person, reserved or created by agreement and securing payment of performance of an obligation, but the term excludes a lessee under a lease not intended as security.

"Waters of this State" means any water within the jurisdiction of this State.

"Person" means an individual, partnership, firm, corporation, association, or other entity.

"Operate" means to navigate or otherwise use a motorboat or vessel.

"Department" means the Department of Natural Resources.

"Competent" means capable of assisting a skier in case of injury or accident.

"Personal flotation device" or "PFD" means a device that is approved by the Commandant, U.S. Coast Guard, under Part 160 of Title 46 of the Code of Federal Regulations.

"Recreational boat" means any vessel manufactured or used primarily for noncommercial use; or leased, rented or chartered to another for noncommercial use.

"Personal watercraft" means a vessel that uses an inboard motor powering a water jet pump as its primary source of motor power and that is designed to be operated by a person sitting, standing, or kneeling on the vessel, rather than the conventional manner of sitting or standing inside the vessel, and includes vessels that are similar in appearance and operation but are powered by an outboard or propeller drive motor.

"Specialty prop-craft" means a vessel that is similar in appearance and operation to a personal watercraft but that is powered by an outboard or propeller driven motor.

"Underway" applies to a vessel or watercraft at all times except when it is moored at a dock or anchorage area.

"Use" applies to all vessels on the waters of this State, whether moored or underway.

Laws 1959, p. 1473, Art. I, § 2. Amended by Laws 1967, p. 2217, § 1; P.A. 79-470, § 1, eff. Oct. 1, 1975. Renumbered § 1-2 and amended by P.A. 82-783, Art. VII, § 2, eff. July 13, 1982. Amended by P.A. 84-973, § 1, eff. Jan. 1, 1986; P.A. 85-149, § 1, eff. Jan. 1, 1988; P.A. 87-798, § 4, eff. Dec. 16, 1991; P.A. 89-445, § 9A-89, eff. Feb. 7, 1996.

Formerly Ill.Rev.Stat.1991, ch. 95 ½, ¶ 311-2.

45/1-3. Application and jurisdiction

§ 1-3. Application and jurisdiction. The Department shall, for the purposes of this Act, have full and complete jurisdiction of all waters within the boundaries of the State of Illinois, subject only to the paramount authority of the Federal Government with reference to the navigation of such stream or streams and further subject to such powers as may be granted to political subdivisions of the State. Wherever the provisions of this Act conflict with the laws and regulations of the Federal Government, the laws and regulations of the Federal Government shall take precedence.

Laws 1959, p. 1473, Art. I, § 3. Amended by Laws 1961, p. 3349, § 1. Renumbered § 1-3 and amended by P.A. 82-783, Art. VII, § 2, eff. July 13, 1982.

Formerly Ill.Rev.Stat.1991, ch. 95 ½, ¶ 311-3.

45/1-4. Rules

§ 1-4. The Department is authorized to issue administrative rules for carrying out, administering and enforcing the provisions of this Act. The administrative rules shall be promulgated in accordance with The Illinois Administrative Procedure Act.[1]

Such rules, after becoming effective, shall be enforced in the same manner as are any other provisions of this Act and violators thereof are subject to the penalties set out in this Act.

Laws 1959, p. 1473, Art. I, § 1-4, added by P.A. 85-149, § 1, eff. Jan. 1, 1988.

Formerly Ill.Rev.Stat.1991, ch. 95 ½, ¶ 311-4.

1 5 ILCS 100/1-1 et seq.

45/1-5. Reciprocal agreements

§ 1-5. The Department is authorized to cooperate with and to enter into reciprocal agreements with the appropriate departments of the federal government and other departments or agencies of other states for carrying out, administering, and enforcing the provisions of this Act.

Laws 1959, p. 1473, Art. I, § 1-5, added by P.A. 85-149, § 1, eff. Jan. 1, 1988.

Formerly Ill.Rev.Stat.1991, ch. 95 ½, ¶ 311-5.

ARTICLE II. ENFORCEMENT—INSPECTION—PROSECUTIONS

Section

45/2-1. Enforcement

§ 2-1. Enforcement. It is the duty of all Conservation Police Officers and other employees of the Department designated by the Director to enforce this Act, and all sheriffs, deputy sheriffs and other police officers to arrest any person detected in violation of any of the provisions of this Act. It is further the duty of all such officers to make prompt investigation of any violation of the provisions of this Act reported by any other person, and to cause a complaint to be filed before the circuit court if there seems just ground for such complaint and evidence procurable to support the same.

Laws 1959, p. 1473, Art. II, § 1. Amended by Laws 1965, p. 332, § 1; Laws 1965, p. 338, § 1; Laws 1967, p. 3943, § 1; P.A. 79-470, § 1, eff. Oct. 1, 1975. Renumbered § 2-1 and amended by P.A. 82-783, Art. VII, § 2, eff. July 13, 1982.

Formerly Ill.Rev.Stat.1991, ch. 95 ½, ¶ 312-1.

45/2-2. Inspection

§ 2-2. Inspection.

(a) Agents of the Department or other duly authorized police officers may board and inspect any boat at any time for the purpose of determining if this Act is being complied with. If the boarding officer or agent discovers any violation of this Act, he may issue a summons to the operator of the boat requiring that the operator appear before the circuit court for the county within which the offense was committed.

(b) Every vessel subject to this Act, if under way and upon being hailed by a designated law enforcement officer, must stop immediately and lay to.

(c) Agents of the Department and other duly authorized police officers may enforce all federal laws and regulations which have been mutually agreed upon by the federal and state governments and are applicable to the operation of watercraft on navigable waters and federal impoundments where concurrent jurisdiction exists between the federal and state governments.

(d) Agents of the Department and other duly authorized police officers may seize and impound, at the owner's or operator's expense, any watercraft involved in a boating accident or a violation of Section 3A-21, 5-1, 5-2, or 5-16 of this Act.

Laws 1959, p. 1473, Art. II, § 2. Amended by Laws 1963, p. 66, § 1; Laws 1965, p. 332, § 1; Laws 1967, p. 1054, § 1; Laws 1967, p. 2217, § 1; Laws 1968, p. 311, § 1, eff. July 1, 1969; P.A. 79-470, § 1, eff. Oct. 1, 1975. Renumbered § 2-2 and amended by P.A. 82-783, Art. VII, § 2, eff. July 13, 1982. Amended by P.A. 87-798, § 4, eff. Dec. 16, 1991; P.A. 88-670, Art. 3, § 3-81, eff. Dec. 2, 1994.

Formerly Ill.Rev.Stat.1991, ch. 95 ½, ¶ 312-2.

45/2-3. Prosecutions

§ 2-3. Prosecutions. All prosecutions under the provisions of this Act shall be brought in the name and by the authority of the People of the State of Illinois before the circuit court having jurisdiction under the law relative to the enforcement of the provisions hereof. It is the duty of all State's Attorneys to enforce the provisions of this Act in their respective counties, and to prosecute all persons charged with violating the provisions hereof.

Laws 1959, p. 1473, Art. II, § 3. Amended by Laws 1965, p. 332, § 1; Laws 1965, p. 627, § 1; Laws 1967, p. 3944, § 1. Renumbered § 2-3 and amended by P.A. 82-783, Art. VII, § 2, eff. July 13, 1982.

Formerly Ill.Rev.Stat.1991, ch. 95 ½, ¶ 312-3.

45/2-4. Resistance to officers

§ 2-4. Resistance to officers.

(a) It is unlawful for any person to resist or obstruct any officer or employee of the Department in the discharge of his duties under the provisions hereof.

(b) It is unlawful for the operator of a watercraft, having been given a signal by a conservation police officer, sheriff, deputy sheriff, or other police officer directing the operator of the watercraft to bring the watercraft to a stop, to willfully fail or refuse to obey the direction, to increase speed, to extinguish lights, or otherwise flee or attempt to elude the officer. The signal given by the officer may be by hand, voice, sign, siren, or blue or red light.

Laws 1959, p. 1473, Art. II, § 4, added by Laws 1963, p. 2012, § 1. Renumbered § 2-4 and amended by P.A. 82-783, Art. VII, § 2, eff. July 13, 1982. Amended by P.A. 88-524, § 1, eff. July 1, 1994.

Formerly Ill.Rev.Stat.1991, ch. 95 ½, ¶ 312-4.

45/2-5. False representation

§ 2-5. False representation. It is unlawful for any person to represent himself falsely to be an officer or employee of the Department or to assume to act as such without having been duly appointed and employed as such.

Laws 1959, p. 1473, Art. II, § 5, added by Laws 1963, p. 2012, § 1. Renumbered § 2-5 and amended by P.A. 82-783, Art. VII, § 2, eff. July 13, 1982.

Formerly Ill.Rev.Stat.1991, ch. 95 ½, ¶ 312-5.

ARTICLE III. REGISTRATION OF MOTORBOATS AND SAILBOATS OVER 12 FEET IN LENGTH

Section

Article III heading was amended by Laws 1967, p. 2217 and P.A. 76-1495, § 1.

45/3-1. Unlawful operation of unnumbered watercraft

§ 3-1. Unlawful operation of unnumbered watercraft. Every watercraft other than sailboards, on waters within the jurisdiction of this State shall be numbered. No person may operate or give permission for the operation of any such watercraft on such waters unless the watercraft is numbered in accordance with this Act, or in accordance with applicable Federal law, or in accordance with a Federally-approved numbering system of another State, and unless (1) the certificate of number awarded to such watercraft is in full force and effect, and (2) the identifying number set forth in the certificate of number is displayed on each side of the bow of such watercraft.

Laws 1959, p. 1473, Art. III, § 1. Amended by Laws 1967, p. 2217, § 1. Renumbered § 3-1 and amended by P.A. 82-783, Art. VII, § 2, eff. July 13, 1982. Amended by P.A. 84-973, § 1, eff. Jan. 1, 1986; P.A. 85-149, § 1, eff. Jan. 1, 1988.

Formerly Ill.Rev.Stat.1991, ch. 95 ½, ¶ 313-1.

45/3-2. Identification number application

§ 3-2. Identification number application. The owner of each watercraft requiring numbering by this State shall file an application for number with the Department on forms approved by it. The application shall be signed by the owner of the watercraft and shall be accompanied by a fee as follows:

A. Class A (all canoes and kayaks) .... $ 6
B. Class 1 (all watercraft less than 16 feet in length, except canoes and kayaks) $15
C. Class 2 (all watercraft 16 feet or more but less than 26 feet in length except canoes and kayaks) $20
D. Class 3 (all watercraft 26 feet or more but less than 40 feet in length) $25
E. Class 4 (all watercraft 40 feet in length or more) $30

Upon receipt of the application in approved form, and when satisfied that no tax imposed pursuant to the "Municipal Use Tax Act" [1] or the "County Use Tax Act" [2] is owed, or that such tax has been paid, the Department shall enter the same upon the records of its office and issue to the applicant a certificate of number stating the number awarded to the watercraft and the name and address of the owner.

Laws 1959, p. 1473, Art. III, § 2. Amended by Laws 1961, p. 3349, § 1; Laws 1963, p. 66, § 1; Laws 1963, p. 2012, § 1; Laws 1965, p. 332, § 1; Laws 1965, p. 1818, § 1; Laws 1967, p. 1054, § 1; Laws 1967, p. 2217, § 1; Laws 1968, p. 312, § 1, eff. July 1, 1969; P.A. 78-1142, § 5, eff. Aug. 26, 1974. Renumbered § 3-2 and amended by P.A. 82-783, Art. VII, § 2, eff. July 13, 1982. Amended by P.A. 84-973, § 1, eff. Jan. 1, 1986; P.A. 85-149, § 1, eff. Jan. 1, 1988; P.A. 88-91, § 125, eff. July 14, 1993.

Formerly Ill.Rev.Stat.1991, ch. 95 ½, ¶ 313-2.

[1] 65 ILCS 5/8-11-6 et seq.

[2] 35 ILCS 105/1 et seq.

45/3–3. Identification number display

§ 3-3. Identification number display. A. The owner shall paint on or attach to both sides of the bow (front) of a watercraft the identification number, which shall be of block characters at least 3 inches in height. The figures shall read from left to right, be of contrasting color to their background, and be maintained in a legible condition. No other number shall be displayed on the bow of the boat. In affixing the number to the boat, a space or a hyphen shall be provided between the IL and the number and another space or hyphen between the number and the letters which follow. On vessels of unconventional design or constructed so that it is impractical or impossible to display identification numbers in a prominent position on the forward half of their hulls or permanent substructures, numbers may be displayed in brackets or fixtures firmly attached to the vessel. Exact positioning of the numbers in brackets or protruding fixtures shall be discretionary with vessel owners, providing the numbers are placed on the forward half of the vessel and meet the standard requirements for legibility, size, style and contrast with the background.

B. A watercraft already covered by a number in full force and effect which has been awarded to it pursuant to Federal law is exempt from number display as prescribed by this Section.

C. All non-powered canoes and kayaks are exempt from number display as prescribed by this Section.

Laws 1959, p. 1473, Art. III, § 2. Amended by Laws 1961, p. 3349, § 1; Laws 1963, p. 66, § 1; Laws 1963, p. 2012, § 1; Laws 1965, p. 332, § 1; Laws 1965, p. 1818, § 1. Resectioned § 3 and amended by Laws 1967, p. 2217, § 1. Amended by Laws 1968, p. 312, § 1, eff. July 1, 1969. Renumbered § 3–3 and amended by P.A. 82–783, Art. VII, § 2, eff. July 13, 1982. Amended by P.A. 85–149, § 1, eff. Jan. 1, 1988; P.A. 85–1328, § 1, eff. Aug. 31, 1988; P.A. 87–391, § 1, eff. Jan. 1, 1992.

Formerly Ill.Rev.Stat.1991, ch. 95 ½, ¶ 313–3.

45/3–4. Destruction, sale, transfer or abandonment

§ 3-4. Destruction, sale, transfer or abandonment. The owner of any watercraft shall within 15 days notify the Department if the watercraft is destroyed or abandoned, or is sold or transferred either wholly or in part to another person or persons. In sale or transfer cases, the notice shall be accompanied by a surrender of the certificate of number. In destruction or abandonment cases, the notice shall be accompanied by a surrender of the certificate of title. When the surrender of the certificate is by reason of the watercraft being destroyed or abandoned, the Department shall cancel the certificate and enter such fact in its records. The Department shall be notified in writing of any change of address. Should the owner desire a new certificate of number, showing the new address, he shall surrender his old certificate and notify the Department of the new address, remitting $1 to cover the issuance of a new certificate of number. If the surrender is by reason of a sale or transfer either wholly or in part to another person or persons, the owner surrendering the certificate shall state to the Department, under oath, the name of the purchaser or transferee.

Laws 1959, p. 1473, Art. III, § 2. Amended by Laws 1961, p. 3349, § 1; Laws 1963, p. 66, § 1; Laws 1963, p. 2012, § 1; Laws 1965, p. 332, § 1; Laws 1965, p. 1818, § 1. Resectioned § 4 and amended by Laws 1967, p. 2217, § 1. Amended by Laws 1968, p. 312, § 1, eff. July 1, 1969. Renumbered § 3–4 and amended by P.A. 82–783, Art. VII, § 2, eff. July 13, 1982. Amended by P.A. 84–973, § 1, eff. Jan. 1, 1986; P.A. 85–149, § 1, eff. Jan. 1, 1988.

Formerly Ill.Rev.Stat.1991, ch. 95 ½, ¶ 313–4.

45/3–5. Transfer of Identification Number

§ 3–5. Transfer of Identification Number. The purchaser of a watercraft shall, within 15 days after acquiring same, make application to the Department for transfer to him of the certificate of number issued to the watercraft giving his name, address and the number of the boat. The purchaser shall apply for a transfer-renewal for a fee as prescribed under Section 3–2 of this Act for approximately 3 years. All transfers will bear June 30 expiration dates in the calendar year of expiration. Upon receipt of the application and fee, together with proof that any tax imposed under the Municipal Use Tax Act [1] or County Use Tax Act [2] has been paid or that no such tax is owed, the Department shall transfer the certificate of number issued to the watercraft to the new owner.

Unless the application is made and fee paid, and proof of payment of municipal use tax or county use tax or nonliability therefor is made, within 30 days, the watercraft shall be deemed to be without certificate of number and it shall be unlawful for any person to operate the watercraft until the certificate is issued.

Laws 1959, p. 1473, Art. III, § 2. Amended by Laws 1961, p. 3349, § 1; Laws 1963, p. 66, § 1; Laws 1963, p. 2012, § 1; Laws 1965, p. 332, § 1; Laws 1965, p. 1818, § 1. Resectioned § 5 and amended by Laws 1967, p. 2217, § 1. Amended by Laws 1968, p. 312, § 1, eff. July 1, 1969; P.A. 76–1495, § 1, eff. Sept. 22, 1969; P.A. 78–1142, § 5, eff. Aug. 26, 1974. Renumbered § 3–5 and amended by P.A. 82–783, Art. VII, § 2, eff. July 13, 1982. Amended by P.A. 84–973, § 1, eff. Jan. 1, 1986; P.A. 85–149, § 1, eff. Jan. 1, 1988; P.A. 87–1109, § 1, eff. Jan. 1, 1993.

Formerly Ill.Rev.Stat.1991, ch. 95 ½, ¶ 313–5.

[1] 65 ILCS 5/8–11–6.

[2] Former Ill.Rev.Stat. ch. 34, ¶ 409.10 (repealed).

45/3–6. Conformity with United States Government

§ 3–6. Conformity with United States Government. In the event that an agency of the United States Government has in force an over-all system of identification numbering for watercraft within the United States, the numbering system employed pursuant to this Act by the Department shall be in conformity therewith.

Laws 1959, p. 1473, Art. III, § 2. Amended by Laws 1961, p. 3349, § 1; Laws 1963, p. 66, § 1; Laws 1963, p. 2012, § 1; Laws 1965, p. 332, § 1; Laws 1965, p. 1818, § 1. Resectioned § 6 and amended by Laws 1967, p. 2217, § 1. Amended by Laws 1968, p. 312, § 1, eff. July 1, 1969. Renumbered § 3–6 and amended by P.A. 82–783, Art. VII, § 2, eff. July 13, 1982. Amended by P.A. 85–149, § 1, eff. Jan. 1, 1988.

Formerly Ill.Rev.Stat.1991, ch. 95 ½, ¶ 313–6.

45/3–7. Loss of certificate

§ 3-7. Loss of certificate. Should a certificate of number or registration expiration decal become lost, destroyed, or mutilated beyond legibility, the owner of the watercraft shall make application to the Department for the replacement of the certificate or decal, giving his name, address, and the number of his boat and shall at the same time pay to the Department a fee of $1.

Laws 1959, p. 1473, Art. III, § 2. Amended by Laws 1961, p. 3349, § 1; Laws 1963, p. 66, § 1; Laws 1963, p. 2012, § 1; Laws 1965, p. 332, § 1; Laws 1965, p. 1818, § 1. Resectioned § 7 and amended by Laws 1967, p. 2217, § 1. Amended by Laws 1968, p. 312, § 1, eff. July 1, 1969. Renumbered § 3-7 and amended by P.A. 82-783, Art. VII, § 2, eff. July 13, 1982. Amended by P.A. 85-149, § 1, eff. Jan. 1, 1988.

Formerly Ill.Rev.Stat.1991, ch. 95 ½, ¶ 313-7.

45/3-8. Department records

§ 3-8. Department records. All records of the Department made or kept pursuant to this Article shall be public records.

Laws 1959, p. 1473, Art. III, § 2. Amended by Laws 1961, p. 3349, § 1; Laws 1963, p. 66, § 1; Laws 1963, p. 2012, § 1; Laws 1965, p. 332, § 1; Laws 1965, p. 1818, § 1. Resectioned § 8 and amended by Laws 1967, p. 2217, § 1. Amended by Laws 1968, p. 312, § 1, eff. July 1, 1969; P.A. 79-470, § 1, eff. Oct. 1, 1975. Renumbered § 3-8 and amended by P.A. 82-783, Art. VII, § 2, eff. July 13, 1982. Amended by P.A. 86-1088, § 1, eff. July 13, 1990.

Formerly Ill.Rev.Stat.1991, ch. 95 ½, ¶ 313-8.

45/3-9. Certificate of Number

§ 3-9. Certificate of Number. Every certificate of number awarded pursuant to this Act shall continue in full force and effect for approximately 3 years unless sooner terminated or discontinued in accordance with this Act. All new certificates issued will bear June 30 expiration dates in the calendar year 3 years after the issuing date. Provided however, that the Department may, for purposes of implementing this Section, adopt rules for phasing in the issuance of new certificates and provide for 1, 2 or 3 year expiration dates and pro-rated payments or charges for each registration.

All certificates shall be renewed for 3 years from the nearest June 30 for a fee as prescribed in Section 3-2 of this Act. All certificates will be invalid after July 15 of the year of expiration. All certificates expiring in a given year shall be renewed between January 1 and June 30 of that year, in order to allow sufficient time for processing.

The Department shall issue "registration expiration decals" with all new certificates of number, all certificates of number transferred and renewed and all certificates of number renewed. The decals issued for each year shall be of a different and distinct color from the decals of each other year currently displayed. The decals shall be affixed to each side of the bow of the watercraft, except for federally documented vessels, in the manner prescribed by the rules and regulations of the Department. Federally documented vessels shall have decals affixed to the watercraft on each side of the federally documented name of the vessel in the manner prescribed by the rules and regulations of the Department.

The Department shall fix a day and month of the year on which certificates of number due to expire shall lapse and no longer be of any force and effect unless renewed pursuant to this Act.

No number or registration expiration decal other than the number awarded or the registration expiration decal issued to a watercraft or granted reciprocity pursuant to this Act shall be painted, attached, or otherwise displayed on either side of the bow of such watercraft. A person engaged in the operation of a licensed boat livery shall pay a fee as prescribed under Section 3-2 of this Act for each watercraft used in the livery operation.

A person engaged in the manufacture or sale of watercraft of a type otherwise required to be numbered hereunder, upon application to the Department upon forms prescribed by it, may obtain certificates of number for use in the testing or demonstrating of such watercraft upon payment of $10 for each registration. Certificates of number so issued may be used by the applicant in the testing or demonstrating of watercraft by temporary placement of the numbers assigned by such certificates on the watercraft so tested or demonstrated.

Laws 1959, p. 1473, Art. III, § 2. Amended by Laws 1961, p. 3349, § 1; Laws 1963, p. 66, § 1; Laws 1963, p. 2012, § 1; Laws 1965, p. 332, § 1; Laws 1965, p. 1818, § 1. Resectioned § 9 and amended by Laws 1967, p. 2217, § 1. Amended by Laws 1968, p. 312, § 1, eff. July 1, 1969; P.A. 76-1495, § 1, eff. Sept. 22, 1969. Renumbered § 3-9 and amended by P.A. 82-783, Art. VII, § 2, eff. July 13, 1982. Amended by P.A. 84-973, § 1, eff. Jan. 1, 1986; P.A. 85-149, § 1, eff. Jan. 1, 1988; P.A. 87-798, § 4, eff. Dec. 16, 1991.

Formerly Ill.Rev.Stat.1991, ch. 95 ½, ¶ 313-9.

45/3-10. Registration list

§ 3-10. Registration list. A boat registration list may be furnished for official use at no charge only to such federal, state, county and municipal enforcement agencies as may require such data.

Laws 1959, p. 1473, Art. III, § 2. Amended by Laws 1961, p. 3349, § 1; Laws 1963, p. 66, § 1; Laws 1963, p. 2012, § 1; Laws 1965, p. 332, § 1; Laws 1965, p. 1818, § 1. Resectioned § 10 and amended by Laws 1967, p. 2217, § 1. Amended by Laws 1968, p. 312, § 1, eff. July 1, 1969. Renumbered § 3-10 and amended by P.A. 82-783, Art. VII, § 2, eff. July 13, 1982.

Formerly Ill.Rev.Stat.1991, ch. 95 ½, ¶ 313-10.

45/3-11. Penalty

§ 3-11. Penalty. No person shall at any time falsely alter or change in any manner a certificate of number issued under the provisions hereof, or falsify any record required by this Act, or counterfeit any form of license provided for by this Act.

Laws 1959, p. 1473, Art. III, § 2. Amended by Laws 1961, p. 3349, § 1; Laws 1963, p. 66, § 1; Laws 1963, p. 2012, § 1; Laws 1965, p. 332, § 1; Laws 1965, p. 1818, § 1. Resectioned § 11 and amended by Laws 1967, p. 2217, § 1. Amended by Laws 1968, p. 312, § 1, eff. July 1, 1969. Renumbered § 3-11 and amended by P.A. 82-783, Art. VII, § 2, eff. July 13, 1982.

Formerly Ill.Rev.Stat.1991, ch. 95 ½, ¶ 313-11.

45/3-12. Exemption from numbering provisions of this Act

§ 3-12. Exemption from numbering provisions of this Act. A watercraft shall not be required to be numbered under this Act if it is:

A. A watercraft which has a valid marine document issued by the United States Coast Guard, provided the owner of any such vessel used upon the waters of this State for more than 60 days in any calendar year shall be required to comply with the registration requirements of Section 3-9 of this Act.

B. Already covered by a number in full force and effect which has been awarded to it pursuant to Federal law or a

Federally-approved numbering system of another State, if such boat will not be within this State for a period in excess of 60 consecutive days.

C. A watercraft from a country other than the United States temporarily using the waters of this State.

D. A watercraft whose owner is the United States, a State or a subdivision thereof, and used solely for official purposes and clearly identifiable.

E. A vessel used exclusively as a ship's lifeboat.

F. A watercraft belonging to a class of boats which has been exempted from numbering by the Department after such agency has found that an agency of the Federal Government has a numbering system applicable to the class of watercraft to which the watercraft in question belongs and would be exempt from numbering if it were subject to the Federal law.

G. Watercraft while competing in any race approved by the Department under the provisions of Section 5–15 of this Act or if the watercraft is designed and intended solely for racing while engaged in navigation that is incidental to preparation of the watercraft for the race. Preparation of the watercraft for the race may be accomplished only after obtaining the written authorization of the Department.

H. Non-powered, owned and operated on water completely impounded on land belonging to the owner of the watercraft. This Section does not apply to water controlled by a club or association.

I. A canoe or kayak which is owned by an organization which is organized and conducted on a not-for-profit basis with no personal profit inuring to anyone as a result of the operation.

Laws 1959, p. 1473, Art. III, § 3. Amended by Laws 1961, p. 3349, § 1; Laws 1963, p. 66, § 1; Laws 1963, p. 2012, § 1; Laws 1965, p. 332, § 1; Laws 1965, p. 1818, § 1. Renumbered § 12 and amended by Laws 1967, p. 2217, § 1. Amended by P.A. 79–470, § 1, eff. Oct. 1, 1975. Renumbered § 3–12 and amended by P.A. 82–783, Art. VII, § 2, eff. July 13, 1982. Amended by P.A. 85–149, § 1, eff. Jan. 1, 1988; P.A. 85–1323, § 1, eff. Aug. 31, 1988; P.A. 88–524, § 1, eff. July 1, 1994.

Formerly Ill.Rev.Stat.1991, ch. 95 ½, ¶ 313–12.

45/3–13. Hull identification numbers

§ 3–13. Hull identification numbers. Any watercraft manufactured after the effective date of this amendatory Act shall have a hull identification number carved, burned, stamped, embossed, or otherwise permanently affixed to the outboard side of the transom or, if there is no transom, to the outermost starboard side at the end of the hull that bears the rudder or other steering mechanism, above the water line in such a way that alteration, removal, or replacement would be obvious and evident. Any individual who manufactures any watercraft, either for private or public use, shall apply to the Department of Natural Resources for issuance of a Hull Identification Number and shall affix such number to watercraft as required by the rules and regulations of the Department.

Laws 1959, p. 1473, Art. III, § 13, added by P.A. 79–470, § 1, eff. Oct. 1, 1975. Renumbered § 3–13 and amended by P.A. 82–783, Art. VII, § 2, eff. July 13, 1982. Amended by P.A. 89–445, § 9A–89, eff. Feb. 7, 1996.

Formerly Ill.Rev.Stat.1991, ch. 95 ½, ¶ 313–13.

45/3–14. Historical watercraft identification plaque

§ 3–14. A. The Department may issue a historical watercraft identification plaque for a boat that is (1) at least 25 years of age and (2) powered by the boat's original type of power plant. Such a boat shall be known as a "heritage watercraft".

B. An application for such a plaque shall be on a form prescribed by the Department and shall be accompanied by a $25.00 fee. The heritage watercraft identification plaque shall be designed by the Department and shall be nonexpiring.

C. When prominently displayed on the boat, a heritage watercraft identification plaque shall entitle the boat owner to apply to participate in parades, shows, and special events. The heritage watercraft plaque does not in itself qualify a boat for recreational use.

Laws 1959, p. 1473, Art. III, § 14, added by P.A. 82–109, § 1, eff. Jan. 1, 1982. Renumbered § 3–14 and amended by P.A. 82–783, Art. VII, § 2, eff. July 13, 1982.

Formerly Ill.Rev.Stat.1991, ch. 95 ½, ¶ 313–14.

ARTICLE IIIA. CERTIFICATE OF TITLE—MOTORBOATS AND SAILBOATS OVER 12 FEET IN LENGTH

Section

Enactment

Article IIIA was added by P.A. 81–1199, eff. Jan. 1, 1981.

45/3A–1. Certificate of title required

§ 3A–1. Certificate of title required.

(a) Every owner of a watercraft required to be numbered by this State and for which no certificate of title has been issued by the Department of Natural Resources shall make application to the Department of Natural Resources for a certificate of title either before or at the same time he next applies for issuance, transfer or renewal of a certificate of number. All watercraft already covered by a number in full force and effect which has been awarded to it pursuant to Federal law is exempt from titling requirements in this Act.

(b) The Department shall not issue, transfer or renew a certificate of number unless a certificate of title has been issued by the Department of Natural Resources or an application for a certificate of title has been delivered to the Department.

Laws 1959, p. 1473, Art. III, § 3A-1, added by P.A. 81-1199, § 1, eff. Jan. 1, 1981. Amended by P.A. 85-149, § 1, eff. Jan. 1, 1988; P.A. 89-445, § 9A-89, eff. Feb. 7, 1996.

Formerly Ill.Rev.Stat.1991, ch. 95 ½, ¶ 313A-1.

45/3A-2. Voluntary titling

§ 3A-2. Voluntary titling. The owner of any watercraft exempt from Section 3A-1(a) of this Act may apply to the Department of Natural Resources for a certificate of title by filing an application accompanied by the prescribed fee. Any owner exempt from this Act who obtains a certificate of title must also obtain a certificate of number as prescribed in Section 3-9 of this Act.

Laws 1959, p. 1473, Art. III, § 3A-2, added by P.A. 81-1199, § 1, eff. Jan. 1, 1981. Amended by P.A. 89-445, § 9A-89, eff. Feb. 7, 1996; P.A. 91-357, § 234, eff. July 29, 1999.

Formerly Ill.Rev.Stat.1991, ch. 95 ½, ¶ 313A-2.

45/3A-3. Application for first certificate of title

§ 3A-3. Application for first certificate of title.

(a) The application for the first certificate of title in this State must be made by the owner to the Department of Natural Resources on the form prescribed and must contain:

1. The name, residence and mail address of the owner;

2. A description of the watercraft so far as the following data exists: Its make, model, year of manufacture, manufacturer's serial number or builder's hull number, length and principal material used in construction;

3. The date of purchase by applicant, the name and address of the person from whom the watercraft was acquired and the names and addresses of any lienholders in the order of their priority and the dates of their security agreements; and

4. Any further information the Department of Natural Resources reasonably requires to identify the watercraft and to enable the Department to determine whether the owner is entitled to a certificate of title and the existence or nonexistence of security interests in the watercraft.

(b) If the application refers to a watercraft purchased from a dealer, it must contain the name and address of any lienholder holding a security interest created or reserved at the time of the sale and the date of his security agreement and be signed by the dealer as well as the owner, and the dealer must within 15 days mail or deliver the application to the Department of Natural Resources.

(c) If the application refers to a watercraft last previously registered in another State or country, the application must contain or be accompanied by:

1. Any certificate of title issued by the other State or country; and

2. Any other information and documents the Department of Natural Resources reasonably requires to establish ownership and the existence or nonexistence of security interests.

Laws 1959, p. 1473, Art. III, § 3A-3, added by P.A. 81-1199, § 1, eff. Jan. 1, 1981. Amended by P.A. 85-149, § 1, eff. Jan. 1, 1988; P.A. 89-445, § 9A-89, eff. Feb. 7, 1996; P.A. 91-357, § 234, eff. July 29, 1999.

Formerly Ill.Rev.Stat.1991, ch. 95 ½, ¶ 313A-3.

45/3A-4. Examination of records

§ 3A-4. Examination of records. The Department of Natural Resources, upon receiving application for a first certificate of title, shall check the identifying description of the watercraft shown in the application against the records required to be maintained by Section 3A-5 of this Article and against the record of stolen and converted watercraft required to be maintained by Section 3A-6 of this Article.

Laws 1959, p. 1473, Art. III, § 3A-4, added by P.A. 81-1199, § 1, eff. Jan. 1, 1981. Amended by P.A. 85-149, § 1, eff. Jan. 1, 1988; P.A. 89-445, § 9A-89, eff. Feb. 7, 1996.

Formerly Ill.Rev.Stat.1991, ch. 95 ½, ¶ 313A-4.

45/3A-5. Certificate of title—Issuance—Records

§ 3A-5. Certificate of title—Issuance—Records.

(a) The Department of Natural Resources shall file each application received and, when satisfied as to its genuineness and regularity, and that no tax imposed by the "Use Tax Act" [1] is owed as evidenced by the receipt for payment or determination of exemption from the Department of Revenue provided for in Section 3A-3 of this Article, and that the applicant is entitled to the issuance of a certificate of title, shall issue a certificate of title.

(b) The Department of Natural Resources shall maintain a record of all certificates of title issued under a distinctive title number assigned to the watercraft and, in the discretion of the Department, in any other method determined.

Laws 1959, p. 1473, Art. III, § 3A-5, added by P.A. 81-1199, § 1, eff. Jan. 1, 1981. Amended by P.A. 85-149, § 1, eff. Jan. 1, 1988; P.A. 89-445, § 9A-89, eff. Feb. 7, 1996.

Formerly Ill.Rev.Stat.1991, ch. 95 ½, ¶ 313A-5.

[1] 35 ILCS 105/1 et seq.

45/3A-6. Stolen and recovered watercraft

§ 3A-6. Stolen and recovered watercraft.

(a) Every sheriff, superintendent of police, chief of police or other police officer in command of any police department in any city, village or town of the State shall, by the fastest means of communications available to his or her law enforcement agency, immediately report to the Department of State Police the theft or recovery of any stolen or converted watercraft within his or her district or jurisdiction. The report shall give the date of theft, description of the watercraft including color, manufacturer's trade name, manufacturer's series name, identification number and registration number, including the state in which the registration number was issued, together with the name, residence address, business address, and telephone number of the owner. The report shall be routed by the originating law enforcement agency through the State Police in a form and manner prescribed by the Department of State Police.

(b) A registered owner or a lienholder may report the theft by conversion of a watercraft to the Department of State Police or any other police department or sheriff's office. The report will be accepted as a report of theft and processed only if a formal complaint is on file and a warrant issued.

(c) The Department of State Police shall keep a complete record of all reports filed under this Section. Upon receipt of the report, a careful search shall be made of the records of the Department of State Police, and where it is found that a watercraft reported recovered was stolen in a county, city, village or town other than the county, city, village or town in which it is recovered, the recovering agency shall notify the reporting agency of the recovery in a form and manner prescribed by the Department of State Police.

(d) Notification of the theft of a watercraft will be furnished to the Department of Natural Resources by the Department of State Police. The Department of Natural Resources shall place the proper information in the title registration files and in the certificate of number files to indicate the theft of a watercraft. Notification of the recovery of a watercraft previously reported as a theft or a conversion will be furnished to the Department of Natural Resources by the Department of State Police. The Department of Natural Resources shall remove the proper information from the certificate of number and title registration files that has previously indicated the theft of a watercraft. The Department of Natural Resources shall suspend the certificate of number of a watercraft upon receipt of a report that the watercraft was stolen.

(e) When the Department of Natural Resources receives an application for a certificate of title or an application for a certificate of number of a watercraft and it is determined from the records that the watercraft has been reported stolen, the Department of Natural Resources, Division of Law Enforcement, shall immediately notify the State Police and shall give the State Police the name and address of the person or firm titling or registering the watercraft, together with all other information contained in the application submitted by the person or firm.

Laws 1959, p. 1473, Art. III, § 3A-6, added by P.A. 81-1199, § 1, eff. Jan. 1, 1981. Amended by P.A. 84-25, Art. IV, § 28, eff. July 18, 1985; P.A. 85-149, § 1, eff. Jan. 1, 1988; P.A. 85-1042, § 3, eff. July 13, 1988; P.A. 87-803, § 1, eff. July 1, 1992; P.A. 89-445, § 9A-89, eff. Feb. 7, 1996.

Formerly Ill.Rev.Stat.1991, ch. 95 ½, ¶ 313A-6.

45/3A-7. Contents and effect

§ 3A-7. Contents and effect.

(a) Each certificate of title issued by the Department of Natural Resources shall contain:

1. The date issued;
2. The name and address of the owner;
3. The names and addresses of any lienholders, in the order of priority as shown on the application or, if the application is based on a certificate of title, as shown on the certificate;
4. The title number assigned to the watercraft;
5. A description of the watercraft including, so far as the following data exists: its make, model, year of manufacture, registration number, and manufacturer's serial number or, if none, the builder's hull number, length, purchase date, and the principal material used in construction;
6. Any other data the Department of Natural Resources prescribes.

(b) The certificate of title shall contain forms for assignment and warranty of title by the owner, and for assignment and warranty of title by a dealer, and may contain forms for applications for a certificate of title by a transferee, the naming of a lienholder and the assignment or release of the security interest of a lienholder.

(c) A certificate of title issued by the Department of Natural Resources is prima facie evidence of the facts appearing on it.

(d) A certificate of title is not subject to garnishment, attachment, execution or other judicial process, but this subsection does not prevent a lawful levy upon the watercraft.

(e) Any certificate of title issued by the Department of Natural Resources is subject to a lien in favor of the State of Illinois for any fees or taxes required to be paid under this Act and as have not been paid, as provided for in this Act.

Laws 1959, p. 1473, Art. III, § 3A-7, added by P.A. 81-1199, § 1, eff. Jan. 1, 1981. Amended by P.A. 89-445, § 9A-89, eff. Feb. 7, 1996.

Formerly Ill.Rev.Stat.1991, ch. 95 ½, ¶ 313A-7.

45/3A-8. Presumption of tenancy

§ 3A-8. Presumption of tenancy. When a certificate of title is made out to a husband and wife with the marital relationship shown on the certificate, it shall be presumed that the title is held as joint tenants with right of survivorship.

Laws 1959, p. 1473, Art. III, § 3A-8, added by P.A. 81-1199, § 1, eff. Jan. 1, 1981.

Formerly Ill.Rev.Stat.1991, ch. 95 ½, ¶ 313A-8.

45/3A-9. Delivery

§ 3A-9. Delivery. The certificate of title shall be mailed to the first lienholder named in it or, if none, to the owner.

Laws 1959, p. 1473, Art. III, § 3A-9, added by P.A. 81-1199, § 1, eff. Jan. 1, 1981.

Formerly Ill.Rev.Stat.1991, ch. 95 ½, ¶ 313A-9.

45/3A-10. Refusing certificate of title

§ 3A-10. Refusing certificate of title. The Department of Natural Resources shall refuse issuance of a certificate of title if any required fee is not paid or if he has reasonable grounds to believe that:

(a) The applicant is not the owner of the watercraft;

(b) The application contains a false or fraudulent statement; or

(c) The applicant fails to furnish required information or documents or any additional information the Department of Natural Resources reasonably requires;

(d) The applicant has not paid any fees or taxes due under this Act and have not been paid upon reasonable notice and demand.

Laws 1959, p. 1473, Art. III, § 3A-10, added by P.A. 81-1199, § 1, eff. Jan. 1, 1981. Amended by P.A. 89-445, § 9A-89, eff. Feb. 7, 1996.

Formerly Ill.Rev.Stat.1991, ch. 95 ½, ¶ 313A-10.

45/3A-11. Lost, stolen or mutilated certificates

§ 3A-11. Lost, stolen or mutilated certificates.

(a) If a certificate of title is lost, stolen, mutilated or destroyed or becomes illegible, the first lienholder or, if none, the owner or legal representative of the owner named in the certificate, as shown by the records of the Department of Natural Resources, shall promptly make application for and may obtain a duplicate upon furnishing information satisfactory to the Department of Natural Resources. The duplicate certificate of title shall contain the legend "This is a duplicate certificate and may be subject to the rights of a person under the original certificate." It shall be mailed to the first lienholder named in it or, if none, to the owner.

(b) The Department of Natural Resources shall not issue a duplicate certificate of title to any person within 15 days after the issuance of an original certificate of title to such person.

(c) A person recovering an original certificate of title for which a duplicate has been issued shall promptly surrender the original certificate to the Department of Natural Resources.

Laws 1959, p. 1473, Art. III, § 3A-11, added by P.A. 81-1199, § 1, eff. Jan. 1, 1981. Amended by P.A. 89-445, § 9A-89, eff. Feb. 7, 1996.

Formerly Ill.Rev.Stat.1991, ch. 95 ½, ¶ 313A-11.

45/3A-12. Transfer

§ 3A-12. Transfer.

(a) If an owner transfers his interest in a watercraft other than by the creation of a security interest, he shall, at the time of the delivery, execute an assignment and warranty of title to the transferee in the space provided therefor on the certificate or as the Department of Natural Resources prescribes and cause the certificate and assignment to be mailed or delivered to the transferee or to the Department of Natural Resources.

(b) Except as provided in Section 3A-14 of this Article, the transferee shall, promptly and within 15 days after delivery to him of the watercraft and the assigned title, execute the application for a new certificate of title in the space provided therefor on the certificate or as the Department of Natural Resources prescribes, and cause the certificate and application to be mailed or delivered to the Department of Natural Resources.

(c) Upon request of the owner or transferee, a lienholder in possession of the certificate of title shall, unless the transfer was a breach of his security agreement, either deliver the certificate to the transferee for delivery to the Department of Natural Resources or, upon receipt from the transferee of the owner's assignment, the transferee's application for a new certificate and the required fee, mail or deliver them to the Department of Natural Resources . The delivery of the certificate does not affect the rights of the lienholder under his security agreement.

(d) If a security interest is reserved or created at the time of the transfer, the certificate of title shall be retained by or delivered to the person who becomes the lienholder, and the parties shall comply with the provisions of Section 3B-3 of Article IIIB.[1]

(e) Except as provided in Section 3A-14 of this Article and as between the parties, a transfer by an owner is not effective until the provisions of this Section and Section 3A-16 of this Article have been complied with; however, an owner who has delivered possession of the watercraft to the transferee and has complied with the provisions of this Section and Section 3A-16 of this Article requiring action by him as not liable as owner for any damages thereafter resulting from operation of the watercraft.

(f) The Department of Natural Resources may decline to process any application for a transfer of an interest in a watercraft if any fees or taxes due under this Act from the transferor or the transferee have not been paid upon reasonable notice and demand.

Laws 1959, p. 1473, Art. III, § 3A-12, added by P.A. 81-1199, § 1, eff. Jan. 1, 1981. Amended by P.A. 85-149, § 1, eff. Jan. 1, 1988; P.A. 89-445, § 9A-89, eff. Feb. 7, 1996.

Formerly Ill.Rev.Stat.1991, ch. 95 ½, ¶ 313A-12.

[1] 625 ILCS 45/3B-1 et seq.

45/3A-13. Transfer to or from dealer—Manufacturer's or Importer's Certificate

§ 3A-13. Transfer to or from dealer—Manufacturer's or Importer's Certificate. (a) No dealer shall purchase or acquire a new watercraft without obtaining from the seller thereof a manufacturer's or importer's certificate.

(b) No manufacturer, importer, dealer or other person shall sell or otherwise dispose of a new watercraft to a dealer for purposes of display and resale, without delivering to such dealer a manufacturer's or importer's certificate.

Laws 1959, p. 1473, Art. III, § 3A-13, added by P.A. 81-1199, § 1, eff. Jan. 1, 1981.

Formerly Ill.Rev.Stat.1991, ch. 95 ½, ¶ 313A-13.

45/3A-14. Transfer to or from dealer—Records

§ 3A-14. Transfer to or from dealer—Records.

(a) If a dealer buys a watercraft and holds it for resale and procures the certificate of title from the owner or the lienholder within 10 days after delivery to him of the watercraft he need not send the certificate to the Department of Natural Resources but, upon transferring the watercraft to another person other than by the creation of a security interest, shall promptly and within 15 days execute the assignment and warranty of title by a dealer, showing the names and addresses of the transferee and of any lienholder holding a security interest created or reserved at the time of the resale and the date of his security agreement, in the spaces provided therefor on the certificate or as the Department of Natural Resources prescribes, and mail or deliver the certificate to the Department with the transferee's application for a new certificate.

(b) Every dealer shall maintain for 3 years a record in the form the Department of Natural Resources prescribes of every watercraft bought, sold or exchanged by him, or received by him for sale or exchange, which shall be open to inspection by a representative of the Department of Natural Resources or peace officer during reasonable business hours.

(c) The Department of Natural Resources may decline to process any application for a transfer of an interest in a watercraft if any fees or taxes due under this Act from the transferor or the transferee have not been paid upon reasonable notice and demand.

Laws 1959, p. 1473, Art. III, § 3A-14, added by P.A. 81-1199, § 1, eff. Jan. 1, 1981. Amended by P.A. 85-149, § 1, eff. Jan. 1, 1988; P.A. 89-445, § 9A-89, eff. Feb. 7, 1996.

Formerly Ill.Rev.Stat.1991, ch. 95 ½, ¶ 313A-14.

45/3A-15. Transfer by operation of law

§ 3A-15. Transfer by operation of law.

(a) If the interest of an owner in a watercraft passes to another other than by voluntary transfer, the transferee shall, except as provided in subsection (b), promptly mail or deliver within 15 days to the Department of Natural Resources the last certificate of title, if available, proof of the transfer, and his or her application for a new certificate in the form the Department prescribes. It shall be unlawful for any person having possession of a certificate of title for a watercraft by reason of his or her having a lien or encumbrance on such watercraft, to fail or refuse to deliver such certificate to the owner, upon the satisfaction or discharge of the lien or encumbrance, indicated upon such certificate of title.

(b) If the interest of an owner in a watercraft passes to another under the provisions of the Small Estates provisions of the Probate Act of 1975, as amended,[1] the transferee shall promptly mail or deliver to the Department of Natural Resources, within 120 days, the last certificate of title, if available, the documentation required under the provisions of the Probate Act of 1975, as amended, and an application for certificate of title. The transfer may be to the transferee or to the nominee of the transferee.

(c) If the interest of an owner in a watercraft passes to another under other provisions of the Probate Act of 1975, as amended, and the transfer is made by an executor, administrator, or guardian for a disabled person, such transferee shall promptly mail or deliver to the Department of Natural Resources, the last certificate of title, if available, and a certified copy of the letters testamentary, letters of administration or letters of guardianship, as the case may be, and an application for certificate of title. Such application shall be made before the estate is closed. The transfer may be to the transferee or to the nominee of the transferee.

(d) If the interest of an owner in joint tenancy passes to the other joint tenant with survivorship rights as provided by law, the transferee shall promptly mail or deliver to the Department of Natural Resources, the last certificate of title, if available, proof of death of the one joint tenant and survivorship of the surviving joint tenant, and an application for certificate of title. Such application shall be made within 120 days after the death of the joint tenant. The transfer may be to the transferee or to the nominee of the transferee.

(e) If the interest of the owner is terminated or the watercraft is sold under a security agreement by a lienholder named in the certificate of title, the transferee shall promptly mail or deliver within 15 days to the Department of Natural Resources the last certificate of title, his or her application for a new certificate in the form the Department prescribes, and an affidavit made by or on behalf of the lienholder that the watercraft was repossessed and that the interest of the owner was lawfully terminated or sold pursuant to the terms of the security agreement. In all cases wherein a lienholder has found it necessary to repossess a watercraft and desires to obtain certificate of title for such watercraft in the name of such lienholder, the Department of Natural Resources shall not issue a certificate of title to such lienholder unless the person from whom such watercraft has been repossessed, is shown to be the last registered owner of such watercraft and such lienholder establishes to the satisfaction of the Department that he or she is entitled to such certificate of title.

(f) A person holding a certificate of title whose interest in the watercraft has been extinguished or transferred other than by voluntary transfer shall mail or deliver the certificate within 15 days upon request of the Department of Natural Resources. The delivery of the certificate pursuant to the request of the Department of Natural Resources does not affect the rights of the person surrendering the certificate, and the action of the Department in issuing a new certificate of title as provided herein is not conclusive upon the rights of an owner or lienholder named in the old certificate.

(g) The Department of Natural Resources may decline to process any application for a transfer of an interest hereunder if any fees or taxes due under this Act from the transferor or the transferee have not been paid upon reasonable notice and demand.

(h) The Department of Natural Resources shall not be held civilly or criminally liable to any person because any purported transferor may not have had the power or authority to make a transfer of any interest in any watercraft.

Laws 1959, p. 1473, Art. III, § 3A–15, added by P.A. 81–1199, § 1, eff. Jan. 1, 1981. Amended by P.A. 83–706, § 42, eff. Sept. 23, 1983; P.A. 85–149, § 1, eff. Jan. 1, 1988; P.A. 89–445, § 9A–89, eff. Feb. 7, 1996.

Formerly Ill.Rev.Stat.1991, ch. 95 ½, ¶ 313A–15.

[1] 755 ILCS 5/1–1 et seq.

45/3A–16. Fees

§ 3A-16. Fees. Fees shall be paid according to the following schedule:

Certificate of title	$7
Duplicate certificate of title	5
Corrected certificate of title	5
Search	5

Laws 1959, p. 1473, Art. III, § 3A–16, added by P.A. 81–1199, § 1, eff. Jan. 1, 1981. Amended by P.A. 85–149, § 1, eff. Jan. 1, 1988.

Formerly Ill.Rev.Stat.1991, ch. 95 ½, ¶ 313A–16.

45/3A–17. Transfer of watercraft

§ 3A–17. Transfer of watercraft. A transferor of a watercraft other than a dealer transferring a new watercraft, shall deliver to the transferee at the time of delivery of possession of the watercraft the properly assigned certificate of title.

Laws 1959, p. 1473, Art. III, § 3A–17, added by P.A. 81–1199, § 1, eff. Jan. 1, 1981. Amended by P.A. 85–149, § 1, eff. Jan. 1, 1988.

Formerly Ill.Rev.Stat.1991, ch. 95 ½, ¶ 313A–17.

45/3A–18. Transfer or surrender of certificate of title

§ 3A–18. Transfer or surrender of certificate of title.

(a) The Department of Natural Resources, upon receipt of a properly assigned certificate of title, with an application for a new certificate of title, the required fee and any other documents required by law, shall issue a new certificate of title in the name of the transferee as owner and mail it to the first lienholder named in it or, if none, to the owner.

(b) The Department of Natural Resources, upon receipt of an application for a new certificate of title by a transferee other than by voluntary transfer, with proof of the transfer, the required fee and any other documents required by law, shall issue a new certificate of title in the name of the transferee as owner. If the outstanding certificate of title is not delivered to him, the Department shall make demand therefor from the holder thereof.

(c) The Department of Natural Resources shall file and retain for 4 years every surrendered Illinois certificate of title, the file to be maintained so as to permit the tracing of title of the watercraft designated therein.

Laws 1959, p. 1473, Art. III, § 3A–18, added by P.A. 81–1199, § 1, eff. Jan. 1, 1981. Amended by P.A. 89–445, § 9A–89, eff. Feb. 7, 1996.

Formerly Ill.Rev.Stat.1991, ch. 95 ½, ¶ 313A–18.

45/3A–19. Scrapping, junking or destroying a watercraft

§ 3A–19. Scrapping, junking or destroying a watercraft. An owner who scraps, junks or destroys a watercraft, or a person who purchases a watercraft as scrap or as a watercraft to be junked or destroyed shall immediately cause the certificate of title to be mailed or delivered to the Department of Natural Resources, and a certificate of title shall not again be issued for such watercraft. Upon receipt of the certificate of title, the Department shall cancel the certificate.

Laws 1959, p. 1473, Art. III, § 3A-19, added by P.A. 81-1199, § 1, eff. Jan. 1, 1981. Amended by P.A. 85-149, § 1, eff. Jan. 1, 1988; P.A. 89-445, § 9A-89, eff. Feb. 7, 1996.

Formerly Ill.Rev.Stat.1991, ch. 95 ½, ¶ 313A-19.

45/3A-20. Offenses relating to titling; misdemeanors

§ 3A-20. Offenses relating to titling; misdemeanors. Violation of any of the following provisions shall constitute a Class A misdemeanor:

(a) No person shall operate in this State a watercraft for which a certificate of title is required without having such certificate of title.

(b) No person shall sell, transfer or otherwise dispose of a watercraft without delivering to the purchaser or transferee a certificate of title, or a manufacturer's or importer's certificate, assigned to such purchaser or transferee as required by this Act.

(c) No person shall fail to surrender to the Department of Natural Resources any certificate of title upon cancellation of the same by the Department for any valid reason set forth in this Act or regulations adopted pursuant thereto.

Laws 1959, p. 1473, Art. III, § 3A-20, added by P.A. 81-1199, § 1, eff. Jan. 1, 1981. Amended by P.A. 85-149, § 1, eff. Jan. 1, 1988; P.A. 88-524, § 1, eff. July 1, 1994; P.A. 89-445, § 9A-89, eff. Feb. 7, 1996.

Formerly Ill.Rev.Stat.1991, ch. 95 ½, ¶ 313A-20.

45/3A-21. Offenses relating to titling; felonies

§ 3A-21. Offenses relating to titling; felonies. Violation of any of the following provisions shall constitute a Class 2 felony:

(a) No person shall alter, forge or counterfeit any certificate of title or a manufacturer's or importer's certificate to a watercraft.

(b) No person shall alter or falsify any assignment of a certificate of title, or an assignment or cancellation of a security interest on a certificate of title to a watercraft.

(c) No person shall hold or use a certificate of title to a watercraft nor hold or use any assignment or cancellation of a security interest on a certificate of title to a watercraft, knowing it to have been altered, forged, counterfeited or falsified.

(d) No person shall use a false or fictitious name or address, or make any material false statement, or conceal any material fact, in an application for a certificate of title, or in a bill of sale or sworn statement of ownership.

(e) No person shall procure or attempt to procure a certificate of title to a watercraft, or pass or attempt to pass a certificate of title or any assignment thereof to a watercraft, knowing or having reason to believe that such watercraft has been stolen.

(f) No person shall have possession of, buy, receive, sell or offer to sell, or otherwise dispose of a watercraft on which the manufacturer's or assigned serial number of the watercraft has been destroyed, removed, covered, altered, or defaced, knowing of such destruction, removal, covering, alteration or defacement of such manufacturer's or assigned serial number.

(g) No person shall destroy, remove, cover, alter or deface the manufacturer's or assigned serial number on any watercraft.

(h) No person shall possess, buy, sell, exchange or give away, or offer to buy, sell, exchange, or give away the certificate of title to any watercraft which is a junk or salvage.

Laws 1959, p. 1473, Art. III, § 3A-21, added by P.A. 81-1199, § 1, eff. Jan. 1, 1981. Amended by P.A. 81-1509, Art. II, § 72, eff. Sept. 26, 1980; P.A. 85-149, § 1, eff. Jan. 1, 1988; P.A. 88-524, § 1, eff. July 1, 1994.

Formerly Ill.Rev.Stat.1991, ch. 95 ½, ¶ 313A-21.

45/3A-22. § 3A-22. Repealed by P.A. 85-149, § 2, eff. Jan. 1, 1988

ARTICLE IIIB. SECURITY INTERESTS

Section

Enactment

Article IIIB was added by P.A. 81-1199, § 1, eff. Jan. 1, 1981.

45/3B-1. Excepted liens and security interests

§ 3B-1. Excepted liens and security interests. This Article does not apply to or affect:

(a) A lien given by statute or rule of law to a supplier of services or materials for the watercraft;

(b) A lien given by the statute to the United States, this State or any political subdivision of this State.

(c) A security interest in a watercraft created by a manufacturer or dealer who holds the watercraft for sale, but a buyer in the ordinary course of trade from the manufacturer or dealer takes free of the security interest.

Laws 1959, p. 1473, Art. III, § 3B-1, added by P.A. 81-1199, § 1, eff. Jan. 1, 1981.

Formerly Ill.Rev.Stat.1991, ch. 95 ½, ¶ 313B-1.

45/3B-2. Perfection of security interest

§ 3B-2. Perfection of security interest.

(a) Unless excepted by Section 3B-1, a security interest in a watercraft of a type for which a certificate of title is required is not valid against subsequent transferees or lienholders of the watercraft unless perfected as provided in this Act.

(b) A security interest is perfected by the delivery to the Department of Natural Resources of the existing certificate of title, if any, an application for a certificate of title containing the name and address of the lienholder and the date of his security agreement and the required fee. It is perfected as of the time of its creation if the delivery is completed within 21 days thereafter, otherwise as of the time of the delivery.

(c) If a watercraft is subject to a security interest when brought into this State, the validity of the security interest is determined by the law of the jurisdiction where the watercraft was when the security interest attached, subject to the following:

1. If the parties understood at the time the security interest attached that the watercraft would be kept in this State and it was brought into this State within 30 days thereafter for purposes other than transportation through this State, the validity of the security interest in this State is determined by the law of this State.

2. If the security interest was perfected under the law of the jurisdiction where the watercraft was when the security interest attached, the following rules apply:

(A) If the name of the lienholder is shown on an existing certificate of title issued by that jurisdiction, his security interest continues perfected in this State.

(B) If the name of the lienholder is not shown on an existing certificate of title issued by that jurisdiction, a security interest may be perfected by the lienholder delivering to the Department of Natural Resources the prescribed notice and by payment of the required fee. Such security interest is perfected as of the time of delivery of the prescribed notice and payment of the required fee.

3. If the security interest was not perfected under the law of the jurisdiction where the watercraft was when the security interest attached, it may be perfected in this State; in that case perfection dates from the time of perfection in this State.

4. A security interest may be perfected under paragraph 3 of this subsection either as provided in subsection (b) or by the lienholder delivering to the Department of Natural Resources a notice of security interest in the form the Department prescribes and the required fee.

Laws 1959, p. 1473, Art. III, § 3B–2, added by P.A. 81–1199, § 1, eff. Jan. 1, 1981. Amended by P.A. 85–149, § 1, eff. Jan. 1, 1988; P.A. 89–445, § 9A–89, eff. Feb. 7, 1996.

Formerly Ill.Rev.Stat.1991, ch. 95 ½, ¶ 313B–2.

45/3B-3. Security interest

§ 3B–3. Security interest. If an owner creates a security interest in a watercraft:

(a) The owner shall immediately execute the application, in the space provided therefor on the certificate of title or on a separate form the Department of Natural Resources prescribes, to name the lienholder on the certificate, showing the name and address of the lienholder and the date of his security agreement, and cause the certificate, application and the required fee to be delivered to the lienholder.

(b) The lienholder shall immediately cause the certificate, application and the required fee to be mailed or delivered to the Department of Natural Resources.

(c) Upon request of the owner or subordinate lienholder, a lienholder in possession of the certificate of title shall either mail or deliver the certificate to the subordinate lienholder for delivery to the Department of Natural Resources or, upon receipt from the subordinate lienholder of the owner's application and the required fee, mail or deliver them to the Department of Natural Resources with the certificate. The delivery of the certificate does not affect the rights of the first lienholder under his security agreement.

(d) Upon receipt of the certificate of title, application and the required fee, the Department of Natural Resources shall either endorse on the certificate or issue a new certificate containing the name and address of the new lienholder, and mail the certificate to the first lienholder named in it.

Laws 1959, p. 1473, Art. III, § 3B–3, added by P.A. 81–1199, § 1, eff. Jan. 1, 1981. Amended by P.A. 89–445, § 9A–89, eff. Feb. 7, 1996.

Formerly Ill.Rev.Stat.1991, ch. 95 ½, ¶ 313B–3.

45/3B-4. Assignment by lienholder

§ 3B–4. Assignment by lienholder. (a) A lienholder may assign, absolutely or otherwise, his security interest in the watercraft to a person other than the owner without affecting the interest of the owner or the validity of the security interest, but any person without notice of the assignment is protected in dealing with the lienholder as the holder of the security interest and the lienholder remains liable for any obligations as lienholder until the assignee is named as lienholder on the certificate.

(b) The assignee may, but need not to perfect the assignment, have the certificate of title endorsed or issued with the assignee named as lienholder, upon delivering to the Department of Natural Resources the certificate and an assignment by the lienholder named in the certificate in the form the Department prescribes.

Laws 1959, p. 1473, Art. III, § 3B–4, added by P.A. 81–1199, § 1, eff. Jan. 1, 1981. Amended by P.A. 89–445, § 9A–89, eff. Feb. 7, 1996.

Formerly Ill.Rev.Stat.1991, ch. 95 ½, ¶ 313B–4.

45/3B-5. Release of security interest

§ 3B–5. Release of security interest.

(a) Upon the satisfaction of a security interest in a watercraft for which the certificate of title is in the possession of the lienholder, he shall, within 10 days after demand and, in any event, within 30 days, execute a release of his security interest, and mail or deliver the certificate and release to the next lienholder named therein, or, if none, to the owner or any person who delivers to the lienholder an authorization from the owner to receive the certificate. The owner, other than a dealer holding the watercraft for resale, shall promptly cause the certificate and release to be mailed or delivered to the Department of Natural Resources, which shall release the lienholder's rights on the certificate or issue a new certificate.

(b) Upon the satisfaction of a security interest in a watercraft for which the certificate of title is in the possession of a prior lienholder, the lienholder whose security interest is satisfied shall within 10 days after demand and, in any event, within 30 days execute a release and deliver the release to the owner or any person who delivers to the lienholder an authorization from the owner to receive it. The lienholder in possession of the certificate of title shall either deliver the certificate to the owner, or the person authorized by him, for delivery to the Department of Natural Resources, or, upon receipt of the release, mail or deliver the certificate and release to the Department, which shall release the subordinate lienholder's rights on the certificate or issue a new certificate.

Laws 1959, p. 1473, Art. III, § 3B–5, added by P.A. 81–1199, § 1, eff. Jan. 1, 1981. Amended by P.A. 89–445, § 9A–89, eff. Feb. 7, 1996.

Formerly Ill.Rev.Stat.1991, ch. 95 ½, ¶ 313B–5.

45/3B-6. Duty of lienholder

§ 3B–6. Duty of lienholder. A lienholder named in a certificate of title shall, upon written request of the owner or of another lienholder named on the certificate, disclose any pertinent information as to his security agreement and the indebtedness secured by it.

Laws 1959, p. 1473, Art. III, § 3B-6, added by P.A. 81-1199, § 1, eff. Jan. 1, 1981.

Formerly Ill.Rev.Stat.1991, ch. 95 ½, ¶ 313B-6.

45/3B-7. Exclusiveness of procedure

§ 3B-7. Exclusiveness of procedure. The method provided in this Act of perfecting and giving notice of security interests subject to this Act is exclusive. Security interests subject to this Act are hereby exempted from the provisions of law which otherwise require or relate to the recording or filing of instruments creating or evidencing security interests in watercraft including chattel mortgages and conditional sale agreements.

Laws 1959, p. 1473, Art. III, § 3B-7, added by P.A. 81-1199, § 1, eff. Jan. 1, 1981. Amended by P.A. 85-149, § 1, eff. Jan. 1, 1988.

Formerly Ill.Rev.Stat.1991, ch. 95 ½, ¶ 313B-7.

45/3B-8. Suspension or revocation of certificates

§ 3B-8. Suspension or revocation of certificates.

(a) The Department of Natural Resources may suspend or revoke a certificate of title, upon notice and reasonable opportunity to be heard, when authorized by any other provision of law or if he finds:

1. The certificate of title was fraudulently procured or erroneously issued, or

2. The watercraft has been scrapped, dismantled or destroyed.

(b) Suspension or revocation of a certificate of title does not, in itself, affect the validity of a security interest noted on it.

(c) When the Department of Natural Resources suspends or revokes a certificate of title, the owner or person in possession of it shall, immediately upon receiving notice of the suspension or revocation, mail or deliver the certificate to the Department.

(d) The Department of Natural Resources may seize and impound any certificate of title which has been suspended or revoked.

Laws 1959, p. 1473, Art. III, § 3B-8, added by P.A. 81-1199, § 1, eff. Jan. 1, 1981. Amended by P.A. 89-445, § 9A-89, eff. Feb. 7, 1996.

Formerly Ill.Rev.Stat.1991, ch. 95 ½, ¶ 313B-8.

45/3B-9. Powers of Department of Natural Resources

§ 3B-9. Powers of Department of Natural Resources.

(a) The Department of Natural Resources shall prescribe and provide suitable forms of applications, certificates of title, notices of security interests, and all other notices and forms necessary to carry out the provisions of this Article and Article IIIA.[1]

(b) The Department of Natural Resources may:

1. Make necessary investigations to procure information required to carry out the provisions of this Article and Article IIIA;

2. Assign a new identifying number to a watercraft if it has none, or its identifying number is destroyed or obliterated, and shall either issue a new certificate of title showing the new identifying number or make an appropriate endorsement on the original certificate.

Laws 1959, p. 1473, Art. III, § 3B-9, added by P.A. 81-1199, § 1, eff. Jan. 1, 1981. Amended by P.A. 89-445, § 9A-89, eff. Feb. 7, 1996.

Formerly Ill.Rev.Stat.1991, ch. 95 ½, ¶ 313B-9.

1 625 ILCS 45/3A-1 et seq.

45/3B-10. Court Review

§ 3B-10. Court review. A person aggrieved by an act or omission to act of the Department of Natural Resources under this Article or Article IIIA [1] is also entitled to a review thereof by the Circuit Court of Sangamon County in accordance with the Administrative Review Law, as amended.[2]

Laws 1959, p. 1473, Art. III, § 3B-10, added by P.A. 81-1199, § 1, eff. Jan. 1, 1981. Amended by P.A. 82-783, Art. XI, § 141, eff. July 13, 1982; P.A. 89-445, § 9A-89, eff. Feb. 7, 1996.

Formerly Ill.Rev.Stat.1991, ch. 95 ½, ¶ 313B-10.

1 625 ILCS 45/3A-1 et seq.

2 735 ILCS 5/3-101 et seq.

ARTICLE IIIC. LOST AND ABANDONED WATERCRAFT

Section

Enactment

Article IIIC was added by P.A. 84-646, § 1, eff. Jan. 1, 1986.

45/3C-1. Abandonment of watercraft prohibited

§ 3C-1. Abandonment of watercraft prohibited. (a) The abandonment of a watercraft or any part thereof on any waters in this State is unlawful and subject to penalties as set forth under Section 3C-14.

(b) The abandonment of a watercraft or any part thereof on private or public property, other than a waterway, in view of the general public, anywhere in this State is unlawful except on property of the owner or bailee of such abandoned watercraft.

Laws 1959, p. 1473, Art. IIIC, § 3C-1, added by P.A. 84-646, § 1, eff. Jan. 1, 1986.

Formerly Ill.Rev.Stat.1991, ch. 95 ½, ¶ 313C-1.

45/3C-2. Notification to law enforcement agencies

§ 3C-2. Notification to law enforcement agencies. When an abandoned, lost, stolen or unclaimed watercraft comes into the temporary possession or custody of a person in this

State, not the owner of the watercraft, such person shall immediately notify the municipal police when the watercraft is within the corporate limits of any city, village or town having a duly authorized police department, or the State Police, Conservation Police or the county sheriff when the watercraft is outside the corporate limits of a city, village or town. Upon receipt of such notification, the municipal police, State Police, Conservation Police, or county sheriff will authorize a towing service to remove and take possession of the abandoned, lost, stolen or unclaimed watercraft. The towing service will safely keep the towed watercraft and its contents, and maintain a record of the tow as set forth in Section 3C-4 for law enforcement agencies, until the watercraft is claimed by the owner or any other person legally entitled to possession thereof or until it is disposed of as provided in this Article.

Laws 1959, p. 1473, Art. IIIC, § 3C-2, added by P.A. 84-646, § 1, eff. Jan. 1, 1986.

Formerly Ill.Rev.Stat.1991, ch. 95 ½, ¶ 313C-2.

45/3C-3. Removal of watercraft

§ 3C-3. Removal of watercraft. (a) When a watercraft is abandoned on any waters of this State for 24 hours or more, its removal by a towing service may be authorized by a law enforcement agency having jurisdiction.

(b) When an abandoned, unattended, wrecked, burned or partially dismantled watercraft is creating a traffic or navigational hazard because of its position in relation to the waterway or because its physical appearance is impeding traffic or navigation, its immediate removal from the waterway by a towing service may be authorized by a law enforcement agency having jurisdiction.

(c) When a watercraft removal from either public or private property is authorized by a law enforcement agency, the owner of the watercraft will be responsible for all towing costs. Watercraft removed from public or private property and stored by a commercial relocator or any other towing service shall be subject to a possessory lien for services pursuant to "An Act concerning liens for labor, services, skills or materials furnished upon or storage furnished for chattels", filed July 24, 1941, as amended,[1] and the provisions of Section 1 of that Act[2] relating to notice and implied consent shall be deemed satisfied. In no event shall such lien be greater than the rates established by that Act. In no event shall such lien be increased or altered to reflect any charge for services or materials rendered in addition to those authorized by this Article. Every such lien shall be payable in cash.

Laws 1959, p. 1473, Art. IIIC, § 3C-3, added by P.A. 84-646, § 1, eff. Jan. 1, 1986.

Formerly Ill.Rev.Stat.1991, ch. 95 ½, ¶ 313C-3.

[1] 770 ILCS 50/0.01 et seq.

[2] 770 ILCS 50/1.

45/3C-4. Reports on towed watercraft

§ 3C-4. Reports on towed watercraft. When a watercraft is authorized to be towed away as provided in Section 3C-2, the police headquarters or office of the law enforcement officer authorizing the towing shall keep and maintain a record of the watercraft towed, listing the color, manufacturer's trade name, manufacturer's series name, hull type, hull material, hull identification number, and registration number displayed on the watercraft. The record shall also include the date and hour of tow, location towed from, location towed to, and reason for towing and the name of the officer authorizing the tow.

Laws 1959, p. 1473, Art. IIIC, § 3C-4, added by P.A. 84-646, § 1, eff. Jan. 1, 1986.

Formerly Ill.Rev.Stat.1991, ch. 95 ½, ¶ 313C-4.

45/3C-5. Record searches

§ 3C-5. Record searches. When a law enforcement agency authorizing the impounding of a watercraft does not know the identity of the registered owner, lienholder or other legally entitled person, that law enforcement agency will cause the watercraft registration records of the State of Illinois to be searched by the Department of Natural Resources for the purpose of obtaining the required ownership information. The law enforcement agency authorizing the impounding of a watercraft will cause the stolen watercraft files of the State Police to be searched by a directed communication to the State Police for stolen or wanted information on the watercraft. When the State Police files are searched with negative results, the information contained in the National Crime Information Center (NCIC) files will be searched by the State Police. The information determined from these record searches will be returned to the requesting law enforcement agency for that agency's use in sending a notification by certified mail to the registered owner, lienholder and other legally entitled persons advising where the watercraft is held, requesting that a disposition be made and setting forth public sale information. Notification shall be sent no later than 10 days after the date the law enforcement agency impounds or authorizes the impounding of a watercraft, provided that if the law enforcement agency is unable to determine the identity of the registered owner, lienholder or other person legally entitled to ownership of the impounded watercraft within a 10 day period after impoundment, then notification shall be sent no later than 2 days after the date the identity of the registered owner, lienholder or other person legally entitled to ownership of the impounded watercraft is determined. Exceptions to a notification by certified mail to the registered owner, lienholder and other legally entitled persons are set forth in Section 3C-9.

Laws 1959, p. 1473, Art. IIIC, § 3C-5, added by P.A. 84-646, § 1, eff. Jan. 1, 1986. Amended by P.A. 85-149, § 1, eff. Jan. 1, 1988; P.A. 89-445, § 9A-89, eff. Feb. 7, 1996.

Formerly Ill.Rev.Stat.1991, ch. 95 ½, ¶ 313C-5.

45/3C-6. Identifying and tracing of watercraft ownership by the Department of Natural Resources

§ 3C-6. Identifying and tracing of watercraft ownership by the Department of Natural Resources. When the registered owner, lienholder or other person legally entitled to the possession of a watercraft cannot be identified from the registration files of this State or from the registration files of a foreign state, if applicable, the law enforcement agency having custody of the watercraft shall notify the Department of Natural Resources, for the purpose of identifying the watercraft owner or other person legally entitled to the possession of the watercraft. The information obtained by the Department of Natural Resources will be immediately forwarded to the law enforcement agency having custody of the watercraft for notification purposes as set forth in Section 3C-5.

Laws 1959, p. 1473, Art. IIIC, § 3C-6, added by P.A. 84-646, § 1, eff. Jan. 1, 1986. Amended by P.A. 89-445, § 9A-89, eff. Feb. 7, 1996.

Formerly Ill.Rev.Stat.1991, ch. 95 ½, ¶ 313C-6.

45/3C-7. Reclaimed watercraft

§ 3C-7. Reclaimed watercraft. Any time before a watercraft is sold at public sale or disposed of as provided in Section 3C-8, the owner, lienholder or other person legally entitled to its possession may reclaim the watercraft by presenting to the law enforcement agency having custody of the watercraft proof of ownership or proof of the right to possession of the watercraft. No watercraft shall be released to the owner, lienholder or other person under this Section until all towing and storage charges have been paid.

Laws 1959, p. 1473, Art. IIIC, § 3C-7, added by P.A. 84-646, § 1, eff. Jan. 1, 1986.

Formerly Ill.Rev.Stat.1991, ch. 95 ½, ¶ 313C-7.

45/3C-8. Disposal of unclaimed watercraft

§ 3C-8. Disposal of unclaimed watercraft. (a) In cities having a population of more than 500,000 inhabitants, whenever an abandoned, lost, stolen or unclaimed watercraft or other watercraft remains unclaimed by the registered owner, lienholder or other legally entitled person for a period of 15 days after notice has been given as provided in Sections 3C-5 and 3C-6, the watercraft may be disposed of as provided in the "Municipal purchasing act for cities of 500,000 or more population".[1]

(b) Except as provided in subsection (a), when an abandoned, lost, stolen or unclaimed watercraft 7 years of age or newer remains unclaimed by the registered owner, lienholder or other person legally entitled to its possession for a period of 30 days after notice has been given as provided in Sections 3C-5 and 3C-6, the law enforcement agency or towing service having possession of the watercraft shall cause it to be sold at public sale to the highest bidder. Notice of the time and place of the sale shall be posted in a conspicuous place for at least 10 days prior to the sale, on the premises where the watercraft has been impounded. At least 10 days prior to the sale, the law enforcement agency where the watercraft is impounded, or the towing service where the watercraft is impounded, shall cause a notice of the time and place of the sale to be sent by certified mail to the registered owner, lienholder and other persons known by the law enforcement agency or towing service to be legally entitled to the possession of the watercraft. Such notice shall contain a complete description of the watercraft to be sold and what steps must be taken by any legally entitled person to reclaim the watercraft. In those instances where the certified notification specified in Sections 3C-5 and 3C-6 has been returned by the postal authorities to the law enforcement agency or towing service due to the addressee having moved, or being unknown at the address obtained from the registration records of this State, the sending of a second certified notice will not be required.

Laws 1959, p. 1473, Art. IIIC, § 3C-8, added by P.A. 84-646, § 1, eff. Jan. 1, 1986.

Formerly Ill.Rev.Stat.1991, ch. 95 ½, ¶ 313C-8.

[1] 65 ILCS 5/8-10-1 et seq.

45/3C-9. Disposal of unclaimed watercraft without notice

§ 3C-9. Disposal of unclaimed watercraft without notice.

(a) When the identity of the registered owner, lienholder and other person legally entitled to the possession of an abandoned, lost or unclaimed watercraft of 7 years of age or newer cannot be determined by any means provided for in this Article, the watercraft may be sold as provided in Section 3C-8 without notice to any person whose identity cannot be determined.

(b) When an abandoned watercraft of more than 7 years of age is impounded as specified by this Article, it will be kept in custody for a minimum of 10 days for the purpose of determining the identity of the registered owner and lienholder, contacting the registered owner and lienholder for a determination of disposition, and an examination of the State Police stolen watercraft files for the theft and wanted information. At the expiration of the 10 day period, if disposition information has not been received from the registered owner or the lienholder, the law enforcement agency having jurisdiction will authorize the disposal of the watercraft as junk.

However if, in the opinion of the police officer processing the watercraft, it has a value of $200 or more and can be restored to safe operating condition, the law enforcement agency may authorize its purchase for salvage and the Department of Natural Resources may issue a certificate of title. A watercraft classified as a historical watercraft may be sold to a person desiring to restore it.

Laws 1959, p. 1473, Art. IIIC, § 3C-9, added by P.A. 84-646, § 1, eff. Jan. 1, 1986. Amended by P.A. 89-445, § 9A-89, eff. Feb. 7, 1996.

Formerly Ill.Rev.Stat.1991, ch. 95 ½, ¶ 313C-9.

45/3C-10. Police reports

§ 3C-10. Police reports. When a watercraft in the custody of a law enforcement agency is reclaimed by the registered owner, lienholder or other legally entitled person, or when the watercraft is sold at public sale or otherwise disposed of as provided in this Article, a report of the transaction will be maintained by the law enforcement agency for a period of one year from the date of the sale or disposal.

Laws 1959, p. 1473, Art. IIIC, § 3C-10, added by P.A. 84-646, § 1, eff. Jan. 1, 1986.

Formerly Ill.Rev.Stat.1991, ch. 95 ½, ¶ 313C-10.

45/3C-11. Disposition of proceeds

§ 3C-11. Disposition of proceeds. (a) When a watercraft located within the corporate limits of a city, village or town is towed away by a law enforcement agency having jurisdiction and disposed of as set forth in this Article, the proceeds of the public sale or disposition, after the deduction of towing, storage and processing charges, shall be deposited in the treasury of such city, village or town.

(b) When a watercraft located outside the corporate limits of any city, village or town is towed away by a law enforcement agency having jurisdiction and disposed of as set forth in this Article, the proceeds of the public sale or disposition, after deducting towing, storage and processing costs, shall be deposited in the county treasury of the county where the watercraft was located at the time of the tow.

Laws 1959, p. 1473, Art. IIIC, § 3C-11, added by P.A. 84-646, § 1, eff. Jan. 1, 1986.

Formerly Ill.Rev.Stat.1991, ch. 95 ½, ¶ 313C-11.

45/3C-12. Titling watercraft

§ 3C-12. Titling watercraft. When an applicant for a certificate of title presents to the Department of Natural Resources proof that he has purchased or acquired a watercraft at a public sale as authorized by this Article and such fact is certified by the law enforcement agency having jurisdiction over the public sale of the watercraft, the Department shall issue a certificate of title for the watercraft upon receipt of the statutory fee and a properly executed application for a certificate of title. The title issued by the Department under this Section shall be free of any lien that existed against the watercraft prior to the time the watercraft was acquired by the applicant under this Article.

Laws 1959, p. 1473, Art. IIIC, § 3C–12, added by P.A. 84–646, § 1, eff. Jan. 1, 1986. Amended by P.A. 89–445, § 9A–89, eff. Feb. 7, 1996.

Formerly Ill.Rev.Stat.1991, ch. 95 ½, ¶ 313C–12.

45/3C–13. Liability

§ 3C–13. Liability. A law enforcement officer or agency, towing service owner, operator or employee shall not be held liable for damages in any action brought by the registered owner, former registered owner or his legal representative, lienholder or any other person legally entitled to the possession of a watercraft when the watercraft was processed and sold or disposed of as provided by this Article.

Laws 1959, p. 1473, Art. IIIC, § 3C–13, added by P.A. 84–646, § 1, eff. Jan. 1, 1986.

Formerly Ill.Rev.Stat.1991, ch. 95 ½, ¶ 313C–13.

45/3C–14. Violations

§ 3C–14. Violations. Any person who violates or aids and abets in the violation of Section 3C–1 of this Act is guilty of a petty offense, and may be required by the court to make a disposition on the abandoned or unclaimed watercraft.

Laws 1959, p. 1473, Art. IIIC, § 3C 14, added by P.A. 84–646, § 1, eff. Jan. 1, 1986.

Formerly Ill.Rev.Stat.1991, ch. 95 ½, ¶ 313C–14.

ARTICLE IV. MOTORBOAT EQUIPMENT

Section

45/4–1. Personal flotation devices

§ 4–1. Personal flotation devices.

A. No person may operate a watercraft unless at least one U.S. Coast Guard approved PFD of the following types or their equivalent is on board for each person: Type I, Type II or Type III.

B. No person may operate a personal watercraft or specialty prop-craft unless each person aboard is wearing a Type I, Type II, Type III or Type V PFD approved by the United States Coast Guard.

C. No person may operate a watercraft 16 feet or more in length, except a canoe or kayak, unless at least one Type IV U.S. Coast Guard approved PFD or its equivalent is on board in addition to the PFD's required in paragraph A of this Section.

D. A U.S. Coast Guard approved Type V personal flotation device may be carried in lieu of the Type I, II, III or IV personal flotation device required in this Section, if the Type V personal flotation device is approved for the activity in which it is being used.

E. When assisting a person on waterskis, aquaplane or similar device, there must be one U.S. Coast Guard approved PFD on board the watercraft for each person being assisted or towed or worn by the person being assisted or towed.

F. No person may operate a watercraft unless each device required by this Section is:

1. Readily accessible;
2. In serviceable condition;
3. Of the appropriate size for the person for whom it is intended; and
4. Legibly marked with the U.S. Coast Guard approval number.

G. Approved personal flotation devices are defined as follows:

Type I—A Type I personal flotation device is an approved device designed to turn an unconscious person in the water from a face downward position to a vertical or slightly backward position and to have more than 20 pounds of buoyancy.

Type II—A Type II personal flotation device is an approved device designed to turn an unconscious person in the water from a face downward position to a vertical or slightly backward position and to have at least 15½ pounds of buoyancy.

Type III—A Type III personal flotation device is an approved device designed to keep a conscious person in a vertical or slightly backward position and to have at least 15½ pounds of buoyancy.

Type IV—A Type IV personal flotation device is an approved device designed to be thrown to a person in the water and not worn. It is designed to have at least 16½ pounds of buoyancy.

Type V—A Type V personal flotation device is an approved device for restricted use and is acceptable only when used in the activity for which it is approved.

H. The provisions of subsections A through G of this Section shall not apply to sailboats.

I. No person may operate a watercraft under 26 feet in length unless a Type I, Type II, Type III, or Type V personal flotation device is being properly worn by each person under the age of 13 on board the watercraft at all times in which the watercraft is underway; however, this requirement shall not apply to persons who are below decks or in totally enclosed cabin spaces. The provisions of this subsection I shall not apply to a person operating a watercraft on private property.

Laws 1959, p. 1473, Art. IV, § 1. Amended by Laws 1965, p. 332, § 1; Laws 1967, p. 2217, § 1; P.A. 79–470, § 1, eff. Oct. 1, 1975; P.A. 80–560, § 1, eff. Oct. 1, 1977; P.A. 80–1495, § 37, eff. Jan. 8, 1979. Renumbered § 4–1 and amended by P.A. 82–783, Art. VII, § 2, eff. July 13, 1982. Amended by P.A. 85–149, § 1, eff. Jan. 1, 1988; P.A. 87–798, § 4, eff. Dec. 16, 1991; P.A. 87–391, § 1, eff. Jan. 1, 1992; P.A. 87–895, Art. 2, § 2–46, eff. Aug. 14, 1992; P.A. 90–411, § 5, eff. Jan. 1, 1998.

Formerly Ill.Rev.Stat.1991, ch. 95 ½, ¶ 314–1.

45/4–2. Lights

§ 4–2. Lights.

A. It is unlawful to operate any vessel less than 39 feet in length unless the following lights are carried and displayed when underway from sunset to sunrise:

1. A bright, white light after to show all around the horizon, visible for a distance of 2 miles. The word "visible" as used herein means visible on a dark night with clear atmosphere.

2. A combination light in the forepart of the boat lower than the white light after, showing green to starboard and red to port, so fixed as to throw a light from dead ahead to 2 points abaft the beam on their respective sides and visible for a distance of not less than 1 mile.

3. Lights under International Rules may be shown as an alternative to the above requirements.

B. Watercraft propelled by muscular power when underway shall carry on board from sunset to sunrise, but not fixed to any part of the boat, a lantern or flashlight capable of showing a white light visible all around the horizon at a distance of 2 miles or more, and shall display such lantern in sufficient time to avoid collision with another watercraft.

C. Every vessel 39 feet or more in length shall carry and display when underway such additional or alternate lights as shall be required by the U.S. Coast Guard for watercraft of equivalent length and type.

D. Sailboats equipped with motors and being propelled partly or solely by such motors shall carry and display the same lights required for motorboats of the same class. Sailboats being propelled entirely by sail between sunset and sunrise shall have lighted the combination running light, and a white light visible aft only. Sailboats 26 feet or more in length, equipped with motors but being propelled entirely by sail between sunset and sunrise, shall have lighted the colored side lights suitably screened, but not the white lights prescribed for motorboats.

E. Dinghies, tenders and other watercraft, whose principal function is as an auxiliary to other larger watercraft, when so operating need carry only a flashlight visible to other craft in the area, anything in this section to the contrary notwithstanding.

F. Vessels at anchor between the hours of sunset and sunrise, except those in a "Special Anchorage Area", shall display such anchor lights as shall be required by the U.S. Coast Guard for watercraft of equivalent length and type.

G. Watercraft operated manually or by motor which are located on bodies of water where motors of over 7½ horsepower are prohibited must be equipped during the hours between sunset and sunrise with a lantern or flashlight which is capable of showing a beam for 2 miles, anything in this Section to the contrary notwithstanding.

Laws 1959, p. 1473, Art. IV, § 2. Amended by Laws 1961, p. 3349, § 1; Laws 1963, p. 2012, § 1; Laws 1965, p. 332, § 1; Laws 1967, p. 2217, § 1. Renumbered § 4-2 and amended by P.A. 82-783, Art. VII, § 2, eff. July 13, 1982. Amended by P.A. 88-524, § 1, eff. July 1, 1994.

Formerly Ill.Rev.Stat.1991, ch. 95 ½, ¶ 314-2.

45/4-3. Mufflers

§ 4-3. Mufflers. A. All motorboats shall be equipped and maintained with an effective muffler or underwater exhaust system. For the purpose of this Section, an effective muffler or underwater exhaust system is one that does not produce sound levels that create excessive or unusual noise, or sound levels that are in excess of 90 decibels when subjected to a stationary sound level test as prescribed by the Society of Automotive Engineers in its procedure J2005.

B. No person may operate a motorboat on the waters of this State in a manner to exceed a noise level of 75 decibels measured as specified in the Society of Automotive Engineers in its procedure J1970 from any point on the shoreline, or from any point on the water within 20 feet of of the shoreline, of the body of water on which the motorboat is being operated.

C. No person may manufacture or offer for sale any motorboat for use on the waters of this State if that motorboat cannot be operated in compliance with the sound levels in subsections A and B above.

D. The provisions of this Section shall apply to all public waters over which the State has jurisdiction.

E. This Section does not apply to:

(1) a motorboat tuning up for or participating in official trials for a sanctioned race or regatta conducted as authorized by the appropriate unit of government, or

(2) a motorboat being operated by a boat or marine engine manufacturer for the purpose of testing or development as authorized by the appropriate unit of government.

F. Any person violating subsection A or B of this Section shall be required to:

(1) install an effective muffler system on the motorboat in violation;

(2) pass the sound level test prescribed by the Society of Automotive Engineers in its procedure J2005 before putting the motorboat back into use; and

(3) be subject to a Class B misdemeanor for the first offense and a Class A misdemeanor for any subsequent offense occurring within 3 years of the date of the most recent offense.

G. Any person violating subsection C of this Section shall be required to:

(1) install an effective muffler system on the motorboat in violation;

(2) pass the sound level test prescribed by the Society of Automotive Engineers in its procedure J2005 before putting the motorboat back into use; and

(3) be subject to a Class A misdemeanor for the first offense and a Class 4 felony for any subsequent offense.

H. Any person who operates any motorboat upon the waters of this State shall be deemed to have given consent to the test or tests as may be prescribed in this Section or by the Department to determine if the motorboat is in compliance with the provisions of this Section.

Laws 1959, p. 1473, Art. IV, § 3. Renumbered § 4-3 and amended by 82-783, Art. VII, § 2, eff. July 13, 1982. Amended by P.A. 87-391, § 1, eff. Jan. 1, 1992; P.A. 87-422, § 1, eff. Jan. 1, 1992; P.A. 87-895, Art. 2, § 2-46, eff. Aug. 14, 1992.

Formerly Ill.Rev.Stat.1991, ch. 95 ½, ¶ 314-3.

P.A. 87-895, the First 1992 General Revisory Act, provides in Article 2 for the revision and renumbering of certain Sections of Acts which have been added or amended by more than one Act of the 87th General Assembly; incorporates amendments to repealed Acts into successor laws passed by the same General Assembly; corrects errors, revises cross-references and deletes obsolete text in such Sections contained in Public Acts through P.A. 87-855.

45/4-4. Whistles

§ 4-4. Whistles. It is unlawful to operate a motorboat without a mouth, hand or power operated whistle, horn or other appliance, capable of producing a blast of 2 seconds or more duration and audible for at least one-half mile.

Laws 1959, p. 1473, Art. IV, § 4. Amended by Laws 1967, p. 2217, § 1; P.A. 79-470, § 1, eff. Oct. 1, 1975. Renumbered § 4-4 and amended by P.A. 82-783, Art. VII, § 2, eff. July 13, 1982.

Formerly Ill.Rev.Stat.1991, ch. 95 ½, ¶ 314-4.

45/4-5. Fire extinguisher

§ 4-5. Fire extinguisher. It is unlawful to operate a motorboat equipped with an internal combustion engine anywhere in this State without at least one U. S. Coast Guard approved fire extinguisher, so placed as to be readily accessible and in such condition as to be ready for immediate and effective use.

Laws 1959, p. 1473, Art. IV, § 5. Amended by Laws 1967, p. 2217, § 1; P.A. 79-470, § 1, eff. Oct. 1, 1975. Renumbered § 4-5 and amended by P.A. 82-783, Art. VII, § 2, eff. July 13, 1982. Amended by P.A. 85-149, § 1, eff. Jan. 1, 1988.

Formerly Ill.Rev.Stat.1991, ch. 95 ½, ¶ 314-5.

45/4-6. Carburetor arrestors

§ 4-6. Carburetor arrestors. Carburetors on all engines of motorboats other than those propelled by a detachable outboard motor shall be fitted with or protected by a U. S. Coast Guard approved device for arresting backfire.

Laws 1959, p. 1473, Art. IV, § 6. Renumbered § 4-6 and amended by P.A. 82-783, Art. VII, § 2, eff. July 13, 1982.

Formerly Ill.Rev.Stat.1991, ch. 95 ½, ¶ 314-6.

45/4-7. Ventilators

§ 4-7. Ventilators. Except for open boats, all motorboats which use fuel having a flashpoint of 110 degrees Fahrenheit or less shall have at least 2 ventilator ducts, fitted with cowls or their equivalent, for the efficient removal of explosive or flammable gases from the bilges of every engine and fuel tank compartment. There shall be at least one exhaust duct installed so as to extend from the open atmosphere to the lower portion of the bilge and at least one intake duct installed so as to extend to a point at least midway to the bilge or at least below the level of the carburetor air intake. The cowls shall be located and trimmed for maximum effectiveness and in such a manner so as to prevent displaced fumes from being recirculated.

Laws 1959, p. 1473, Art. IV, § 7. Amended by Laws 1967, p. 2217, § 1. Renumbered § 4-7 and amended by P.A. 82-783, Art. VII, § 2, eff. July 13, 1982.

Formerly Ill.Rev.Stat.1991, ch. 95 ½, ¶ 314-7.

45/4-8. Sirens and flashing lights

§ 4-8. Sirens and flashing lights.

(a) Except as provided in this Section, it shall be unlawful for any person to use a watercraft equipped with a siren or any red or blue oscillating, rotating, or flashing light. The use of a siren or light in violation of this Section shall constitute a public nuisance subject to confiscation and disposal as determined by a court of competent jurisdiction.

(b) Any authorized emergency watercraft described in subsection (c) or (d) may be equipped with a siren, but the siren shall not be used except when the watercraft is operating in response to an emergency call or in the immediate pursuit of an actual or suspected violator of the law.

(c) The use of blue oscillating, rotating, or flashing lights, whether lighted or unlighted, is prohibited except on law enforcement watercraft of State, federal, or local authorities.

(d) The use of red oscillating, rotating, or flashing lights, whether lighted or unlighted, is prohibited except on fire, rescue, or other emergency watercraft as authorized by State, federal, or local authorities having jurisdiction, provided the watercraft are clearly identifiable as such; the lights shall not be lighted except when responding to an emergency call or while actually engaged in a hazardous situation.

(e) The use of any other color of oscillating, rotating, or flashing lights, whether lighted or unlighted, is prohibited except as authorized by the Department.

Laws 1959, p. 1473, Art. IV, § 8. Renumbered § 4-8 and amended by P.A. 82-783, Art. VII, § 2, eff. July 13, 1982. Amended by P.A. 88-524, § 1, eff. July 1, 1994.

Formerly Ill.Rev.Stat.1991, ch. 95 ½, ¶ 314-8.

45/4-9. Sealing of marine heads

§ 4-9. Sealing of marine heads. No marine head (toilet) on any watercraft used upon waters of this State may be so constructed and operated as to permit the discharge of any sewage into the waters directly or indirectly.

Laws 1959, p. 1473, Art. IV, § 9, added by Laws 1967, p. 2217, § 1. Renumbered § 4-9 and amended by P.A. 82-783, Art. VII, § 2, eff. July 13, 1982. Amended by P.A. 88-524, § 1, eff. July 1, 1994.

Formerly Ill.Rev.Stat.1991, ch. 95 ½, ¶ 314-9.

45/4-10. Battery Covers

§ 4-10. Battery Covers. Every motorboat equipped with storage batteries shall be provided with suitable supports and secured against shifting with the motion of the boat. Such storage batteries shall be equipped with non-conductive shielding means to prevent accidental shorting of battery terminals.

Laws 1959, p. 1473, Art. IV, § 10, added by P.A. 76-1495, § 1, eff. Sept. 22, 1969. Renumbered § 4-10 and amended by P.A. 82-783, Art. VII, § 2, eff. July 13, 1982.

Formerly Ill.Rev.Stat.1991, ch. 95 ½, ¶ 314-10.

45/4-11. Lanyard cut-off switch

§ 4-11. Lanyard cut-off switch. No person may operate any motor boat, including personal watercraft or specialty prop-craft, which is equipped with a lanyard type engine cut-off switch unless such lanyard is properly attached to his or her person, clothing or worn PFD, as appropriate for the specific vessel.

Laws 1959, p. 1473, Art. IV, § 4-11, added by P.A. 87-798, § 4, eff. Dec. 16, 1991.

Formerly Ill.Rev.Stat.1991, ch. 95 ½, ¶ 314-11.

45/4-12. Visual distress signals

§ 4-12. Visual distress signals. It is unlawful to operate any watercraft on the waters of Lake Michigan without having onboard visual distress signals as required and approved by the U.S. Coast Guard, so placed as to be readily accessible and in such condition as to be ready for immediate and effective use.

Laws 1959, p. 1473, Art. IV, § 4-12, added by P.A. 88-524, § 1, eff. July 1, 1994.

ARTICLE V. OPERATION OF MOTORBOATS

45/5-1. Careless operation

§ 5-1. Careless operation. No person shall operate any watercraft in a careless or heedless manner so as to endanger any person or property or at a rate of speed greater than will permit him in the exercise of reasonable care to bring the watercraft to a stop within the assured clear distance ahead.

Laws 1959, p. 1473, Art. V, § 1. Renumbered § 5-1 and amended by P.A. 82-783, Art. VII, § 2, eff. July 13, 1982. Amended by P.A. 85-149, § 1, eff. Jan. 1, 1988.

Formerly Ill.Rev.Stat.1991, ch. 95 ½, ¶ 315-1.

45/5-2. Reckless operation

§ 5-2. Reckless operation. No person shall operate any watercraft, specialty prop-craft, personal watercraft or manipulate any water skis, aquaplane, or similar device in such a manner as to willfully or wantonly endanger the life, limb or property of any person, to weave through congested traffic, to jump the wake of another vessel unreasonably or unnecessarily close to the other vessel or when visibility around the other vessel is obstructed, to wait until the last possible moment to swerve to avoid collision, or operate any watercraft so as to approach or pass another watercraft in such a manner or at such a rate of speed as to create a hazardous wake or wash.

Laws 1959, p. 1473, Art. V, § 2. Amended by P.A. 79-875, § 1, eff. Oct. 1, 1975. Renumbered § 5-2 and amended by P.A. 82-783, Art. VII, § 2, eff. July 13, 1982. Amended by P.A. 85-149, § 1, eff. Jan. 1, 1988; P.A. 87-798, § 4, eff. Dec. 16, 1991.

Formerly Ill.Rev.Stat.1991, ch. 95 ½, ¶ 315-2.

45/5-2.1. § 5-2.1. Repealed by P.A. 80-268, § 1, eff. Jan. 1, 1978

45/5-3. Interference with navigation

§ 5-3. Interference with navigation. No person shall operate any watercraft in a manner which unreasonably or unnecessarily interferes with other watercraft or with the free and proper navigation of the waterways of the State. Anchoring under bridges or in heavily traveled channels constitutes such interference if unreasonable under the prevailing circumstances.

Laws 1959, p. 1473, Art. V, § 3. Amended by Laws 1961, p. 3349, § 1. Renumbered § 5-3 and amended by P.A. 82-783, Art. VII, § 2, eff. July 13, 1982.

Formerly Ill.Rev.Stat.1991, ch. 95 ½, ¶ 315-3.

45/5-4. Overloading

§ 5-4. Overloading. A. No motorboat may be loaded with passengers or cargo beyond its safe carrying capacity taking into consideration weather and other existing operating conditions.

B. Capacity plates. (1) Every vessel less than 26 feet in length, designed to carry 2 or more persons and to be propelled by machinery as its principal source of power or designed to be propelled by oars shall, if manufactured or offered for sale in this State, have affixed permanently thereto by the manufacturer a capacity plate as required by this Section. As used in this Section, "manufacture" means to construct or assemble a vessel or alter a vessel in such manner as to change its weight capacity.

(2) A capacity plate shall bear the following information permanently marked thereon in such manner as to be clearly visible and legible from the position designed or normally intended to be occupied by the operator of the vessel when under way:

a. For all vessels designed for or represented by the manufacturer as being suitable for use with outboard motor:

1. The total weight of persons, motor, gear and other articles placed aboard which the vessel is capable of carrying with safety under normal conditions.

2. The recommended number of persons commensurate with the weight capacity of the vessel and the presumed weight in pounds of each such person. In no instance may such presumed weight per person be less than 150 pounds.

3. Clear notice that the information appearing on the capacity plate is applicable under normal conditions and that the weight of the outboard motor and associated equipment is considered to be part of total weight capacity.

4. The maximum horsepower of the motor the vessel is designed or intended to accommodate.

b. For all other vessels to which this Section applies:

1. The total weight of persons, gear and other articles placed aboard which the vessel is capable of carrying with safety under normal conditions.

2. The recommended number of persons commensurate with the weight capacity of the vessel and the presumed weight in pounds of each such person. In no instance shall such presumed weight per person be less than 150 pounds.

3. Clear notice that the information appearing on the capacity plate is applicable under normal conditions.

(3) The information relating to maximum capacity required to appear on capacity plates by Subsection B(2) of this Section shall be determined in accordance with such methods and formulas as shall be prescribed by rule or regulation adopted by the Department. In prescribing such methods and formulas, the Department shall be guided by and give due regard to the necessity for uniformity in methods and formulas lawful for use in determining small vessel capacity in the several states and to any methods and formulas which may be recognized or recommended by the United States Coast Guard or any agency successor thereto.

(4) Any vessel to which this Section applies, not having a capacity plate meeting the requirements of law affixed thereto by the manufacturer thereof, may have such affixed by any other person in accordance with such rules and regulations as the Department may prescribe and may thereafter be offered for sale in this State, but no action taken pursuant to this Section, or in the manner described herein, shall relieve any manufacturer from liability for failure to comply with the requirements of this Section.

(5) The information appearing on a capacity plate shall be deemed to warrant that the manufacturer, or the person affixing the capacity plate is permitted by Subsection B(4) of this Section, as the case may be, has correctly and faithfully employed a method and formula for the calculation of maximum weight capacity prescribed by the Department and that the information appearing on the capacity plate with respect to maximum weight capacity and recommended number of persons is the result of the application of such method and formula, and with respect to information concerning horsepower limitations, that such information is not a deliberate or negligent misrepresentation.

(6) If any vessel required by this Section to have a capacity plate affixed thereto is of such design or construction as to make it impracticable or undesirable to affix such plate, the manufacturer, or other person having the responsibility for affixing the plate, may represent such impracticability or undesirability to the Department in writing. Upon determination by the Department that such representation has merit and that a proper and effective substitute for the capacity plate which will serve the same purpose is feasible, the Department may authorize such alternative compliance and such alternative compliance shall thereafter be deemed compliance with the capacity plate requirements of this Section.

(7) The Department may by rules or regulations exempt from the requirements of this Section vessels which it finds to be of such unconventional design or construction that the information required on capacity plates would not assist in promoting safety or is not reasonably obtainable.

(8) The Department is authorized to issue and amend rules and regulations to carry out the purposes of this Section.

Failure to affix a proper capacity plate shall constitute a separate violation of this subsection B for each vessel with respect to which such failure occurs.

Laws 1959, p. 1473, Art. V, § 4. Amended by Laws 1967, p. 707, § 1, eff. Jan. 1, 1968. Renumbered § 5-4 and amended by P.A. 82-783, Art. VII, § 2, eff. July 13, 1982.

Formerly Ill.Rev.Stat.1991, ch. 95 ½, ¶ 315-4.

45/5-5. Incapacity of operator

§ 5-5. Incapacity of operator. The owner of any motorboat or any person having such in charge or in control shall not authorize or knowingly permit the same to be operated by any person who by reason of physical or mental disability is incapable of operating such motorboat under the prevailing circumstances.

Laws 1959, p. 1473, Art. V, § 5. Renumbered § 5-5 and amended by P.A. 82-783, Art. VII, § 2, eff. July 13, 1982.

Formerly Ill.Rev.Stat.1991, ch. 95 ½, ¶ 315-5.

45/5-6. Overpowering

§ 5-6. Overpowering. No motorboat shall be equipped with any motor or other propulsion machinery beyond its safe power capacity taking into consideration the type and construction of such motorboat and other existing operating conditions.

Laws 1959, p. 1473, Art. V, § 6. Renumbered § 5-6 and amended by P.A. 82-783, Art. VII, § 2, eff. July 13, 1982.

Formerly Ill.Rev.Stat.1991, ch. 95 ½, ¶ 315-6.

45/5-7. Restricted areas

§ 5-7. Restricted areas. No person shall operate a watercraft within a water area that has been clearly marked by buoys or some other distinguishing device as a bathing, fishing, swimming or otherwise restricted area by the Department or a political subdivision of the State or by an owner or lessee of property in accordance with his or her rights to the use of the property, except in the manner prescribed by the buoys or other distinguishing devices. This Section shall not apply in the case of an emergency, or to patrol or rescue craft.

No person shall operate a watercraft within 150 feet of a public launching ramp owned, operated or maintained by the Department or a political subdivision of the State at greater than a "No Wake" speed as defined in Section 5-12 of this Act. Posting of the areas by the Department or a political subdivision of the State is not required.

The Department and other political subdivisions of the State may, within their discretion and after issuing an administrative rule in accordance with the Illinois Administrative Procedure Act, [1] designate certain areas by proper signs to be bathing, fishing, swimming or otherwise restricted areas, or eliminate, alter or otherwise modify existing areas. The Department or a political subdivision of the State shall further have the authority in order to fully carry out the provisions of this Act to place signs, beacons and buoys in designated areas controlling the flow of traffic.

It shall be unlawful for any person to deface, move, obliterate, tear down, or destroy, in whole or in part, or attempt to deface, move, obliterate, tear down or destroy any buoys or signs posted pursuant to the provisions of this Act, except as authorized by the Department.

Laws 1959, p. 1473, Art. V, § 7. Amended by Laws 1961, p. 3349, § 1; Laws 1963, p. 2012, § 1. Renumbered § 5-7 and amended by P.A. 82-783, Art. VII, § 2, eff. July 13, 1982. Amended by P.A. 85-149, § 1, eff. Jan. 1, 1988; P.A. 87-803, § 1, eff. July 1, 1992; P.A. 92-651, § 78, eff. July 11, 2002.

Formerly Ill.Rev.Stat.1991, ch. 95 ½, ¶ 315-7.

[1] 5 ILCS 100/1-1 et seq.

45/5-8 to 45/5-11. §§ 5-8 to 5-11. Repealed by P.A. 85-149, § 2, eff. Jan. 1, 1988

45/5-11a. § 5-11a. Renumbered as § 5-16a by P.A. 88-670, Art. 3, § 3-81, eff. Dec. 2, 1994

45/5-11b. § 5-11b. Renumbered as § 5-16b by P.A. 88-670, Art. 3, § 3-81, eff. Dec. 2, 1994

45/5-12. Wake; posted areas

§ 5-12. A wake is defined as a movement of the water created by a boat underway great enough to disturb a boat at rest, but under no circumstances shall a boat underway exceed 5 miles per hour while in a posted "No Wake" area. "No Wake" areas shall be clearly posted with buoys or appropriate signs except as provided in Section 5-7 of this

Act. All buoys or signs posting "No Wake" areas shall meet the specifications as prescribed by the United States Coast Guard or the Illinois Department of Natural Resources.

Laws 1959, p. 1473, Art. V, § 7.5, added by P.A. 79–470, § 1, eff. Oct. 1, 1975. Renumbered § 5–12 and amended by P.A. 82–783, Art. VII, § 2, eff. July 13, 1982. Amended by P.A. 87–803, § 1, eff. July 1, 1992; P.A. 89–445, § 9A–89, eff. Feb. 7, 1996.

Formerly Ill.Rev.Stat.1991, ch. 95 ½, ¶ 315–7.5.

45/5-13. Traffic rules

§ 5–13. Traffic rules. **A. Passing.** When 2 boats are approaching each other "head on" or nearly so (so as to involve risk of collision), each boat must bear to the right and pass the other boat on its left side.

B. Crossing. When boats approach each other obliquely or at right angles, the boat approaching on the right side has the right of way.

C. Overtaking. One boat may overtake another on either side but must grant right of way to the overtaken boat.

D. Sailboats and Rowboats. When a motorboat is approaching a boat propelled solely by sails or oars, the motorboat must yield the right of way to the sailboat or rowboat except, when a large craft is navigating in a confined channel, the large craft has the right of way over a boat propelled solely by oars or sails.

Laws 1959, p. 1473, Art. V, § 8. Amended by Laws 1967, p. 2217, § 1. Renumbered § 5–13 and amended by P.A. 82–783, Art. VII, § 2, eff. July 13, 1982.

Formerly Ill.Rev.Stat.1991, ch. 95 ½, ¶ 315–8.

45/5-14. Water Skiing

§ 5–14. Water Skiing. A. No person may operate a motorboat that has in tow or is otherwise assisting a person on water skis, an aquaplane, or a similar contrivance in or upon any waterway, unless the motorboat has a capacity of at least 3 persons and is occupied by at least 2 competent persons.

B. No person may operate a motorboat having in tow or otherwise be assisting a person on water skis, aquaplane or similar contrivance from the period of one-half hour after sunset to one-half hour before sunrise. This paragraph B does not apply to motorboats used in duly authorized water ski tournaments, competitions, exhibitions or trials therefor where adequate lighting is provided.

C. All persons operating a motorboat having in tow or otherwise assisting a person on water skis, aquaplane or similar contrivance, must be careful and prudent in their operation and keep at a reasonable distance from persons and property so as not to endanger the life or property of any person.

D. No person may operate or manipulate any vessel, tow rope or other device by which the direction or location of water skis, aquaplane, or similar device may be affected or controlled in such a way as to cause the water skis, aquaplane, or similar device, or any persons thereon to collide with or strike against any person or object, except ski jumps, buoys and like objects normally used in competitive or recreational skiing.

Laws 1959, p. 1473, Art. V, § 9. Amended by Laws 1961, p. 3349, § 1; Laws 1967, p. 2217, § 1; P.A. 76–1495, § 1, eff. Sept. 22, 1969. Renumbered § 5–14 and amended by P.A. 82–783, Art. VII, § 2, eff. July 13, 1982. Amended by P.A. 90–412, § 5, eff. Jan. 1, 1998.

Formerly Ill.Rev.Stat.1991, ch. 95 ½, ¶ 315–9.

45/5-15. Regattas and races

§ 5–15. Regattas and races. A. The Department may authorize the holding of regattas, motorboat or other boat races on any waters of this State. It shall adopt and may, from time to time, amend regulations concerning the safety of motorboats and other vessels and persons thereon, either observers or participants. Whenever a regatta, motorboat or other boat race is proposed to be held, the person in charge thereof, shall, at least 30 days prior thereto, file an application with the Department for permission to hold such regatta, motorboat or other boat race. The application shall set forth the date, time and location where it is proposed to hold such regatta, motorboat or other boat race and it shall not be conducted without authorization of the Department in writing.

B. When a regatta, motorboat or other boat race authorized or proposed to be authorized under subsection A of this Section is to be held on a body of water owned and operated by a unit of local government, the unit of local government may schedule those events, but only after adopting an ordinance providing for such scheduling and filing it with the Department.

C. The provisions of this Section do not exempt any person from compliance with applicable Federal law or regulation, but nothing contained herein may be construed to require the securing of a State permit pursuant to this Section if a permit therefor has been obtained from an authorized agency of the United States.

Laws 1959, p. 1473, Art. V, § 10. Amended by Laws 1967, p. 2217, § 1. Renumbered § 5–15 and amended by P.A. 82–783, Art. VII, § 2, eff. July 13, 1982. Amended by P.A. 84–559, § 1, eff. Jan. 1, 1986.

Formerly Ill.Rev.Stat.1991, ch. 95 ½, ¶ 315–10.

45/5-16. Operating a watercraft under the influence of alcohol, other drug, or combination thereof

§ 5–16. Operating a watercraft under the influence of alcohol, other drug, or combination thereof.

(A) 1. A person shall not operate any watercraft within this State while:

(a) The alcohol concentration in such person's blood or breath is a concentration at which driving a motor vehicle is prohibited under subdivision (1) of subsection (a) of Section 11–501 of the Illinois Vehicle Code; [1]

(b) Under the influence of alcohol;

(c) Under the influence of any other drug or combination of drugs to a degree which renders such person incapable of safely operating any watercraft;

(d) Under the combined influence of alcohol and any other drug or drugs to a degree which renders such person incapable of safely operating a watercraft; or

(e) There is any amount of a drug, substance, or compound in the person's blood or urine resulting from the unlawful use or consumption of cannabis as defined in the Cannabis Control Act [2] or a controlled substance listed in the Illinois Controlled Substances Act.[3]

2. The fact that any person charged with violating this Section is or has been legally entitled to use alcohol, or other drugs, or any combination of both, shall not constitute a defense against any charge of violating this Section.

3. Every person convicted of violating this Section shall be guilty of a Class A misdemeanor, except as otherwise provided in this Section.

4. Every person convicted of violating this Section shall be guilty of a Class 4 felony if:

(a) He has a previous conviction under this Section; or

(b) The offense results in personal injury where a person other than the operator suffers great bodily harm or permanent disability or disfigurement, when the violation was a proximate cause of the injuries. A person guilty of a Class 4 felony under this subparagraph (b), if sentenced to a term of imprisonment, shall be sentenced to a term of not less than one year nor more than 12 years.

5. Every person convicted of violating this Section shall be guilty of a Class 2 felony if the offense results in the death of a person. A person guilty of a Class 2 felony under this paragraph 5, if sentenced to a term of imprisonment, shall be sentenced to a term of not less than 3 years and not more than 14 years.

6. (a) In addition to any criminal penalties imposed, the Department of Natural Resources shall suspend the watercraft operation privileges of any person convicted of a misdemeanor under this Section for a period of one year.

(b) In addition to any criminal penalties imposed, the Department of Natural Resources shall suspend the watercraft operation privileges of any person convicted of a felony under this Section for a period of 3 years.

(B) 1. Any person who operates any watercraft upon the waters of this State shall be deemed to have given consent to a chemical test or tests of blood, breath or urine for the purpose of determining the alcohol, other drug, or combination thereof content of such person's blood if arrested for any offense of subsection (A) above. The test or tests shall be administered at the direction of the arresting officer.

2. Any person who is dead, unconscious or who is otherwise in a condition rendering such person incapable of refusal, shall be deemed not to have withdrawn the consent provided above.

3. A person requested to submit to a test as provided above shall be verbally advised by the law enforcement officer requesting the test that a refusal to submit to the test will result in suspension of such person's privilege to operate a watercraft. Following this warning, if a person under arrest refuses upon the request of a law enforcement officer to submit to a test designated by the officer, none shall be given, but the law enforcement officer shall file with the clerk of the circuit court for the county in which the arrest was made, a sworn statement naming the person refusing to take and complete the test or tests requested under the provisions of this Section. Such sworn statement shall identify the arrested person, such person's current residence address and shall specify that a refusal by such person to take the test or tests was made. Such sworn statement shall include a statement that the arresting officer had reasonable cause to believe the person was operating the watercraft within this State while under the influence of alcohol, other drug, or combination thereof and that such test or tests were made as an incident to and following the lawful arrest for an offense as defined in this Section or a similar provision of a local ordinance, and that the person after being arrested for an offense arising out of acts alleged to have been committed while so operating a watercraft refused to submit to and complete a test or tests as requested by the law enforcement officer.

The clerk shall thereupon notify such person in writing that the person's privilege to operate a watercraft will be suspended unless, within 28 days from the date of mailing of the notice, such person shall request in writing a hearing thereon; if the person desires a hearing, such person shall file a complaint in the circuit court for and in the county in which such person was arrested for such hearing. Such hearing shall proceed in the court in the same manner as other civil proceedings, shall cover only the issues of whether the person was placed under arrest for an offense as defined in this Section or a similar provision of a local ordinance as evidenced by the issuance of a uniform citation; whether the arresting officer had reasonable grounds to believe that such person was operating a watercraft while under the influence of alcohol, other drug, or combination thereof; and whether such person refused to submit and complete the test or tests upon the request of the law enforcement officer. Whether the person was informed that such person's privilege to operate a watercraft would be suspended if such person refused to submit to the test or tests shall not be an issue.

If the court finds against the person on the issues before the court, the clerk shall immediately notify the Department of Natural Resources of the court's decision, and the Department shall suspend the watercraft operation privileges of the person for at least 2 years.

4. A person must submit to each test offered by the law enforcement officer in order to comply with the implied consent provisions of this Section.

5. The provisions of Section 11-501.2 of the Illinois Vehicle Code, [4] as amended, concerning the certification and use of chemical tests apply to the use of such tests under this Section.

(C) Upon the trial of any civil or criminal action or proceeding arising out of acts alleged to have been committed by any person while operating a watercraft while under the influence of alcohol, the concentration of alcohol in the person's blood or breath at the time alleged as shown by analysis of a person's blood, urine, breath, or other bodily substance shall give rise to the presumptions specified in subdivisions 1, 2, and 3 of subsection (b) of Section 11-501.2 of the Illinois Vehicle Code. The foregoing provisions of this subsection (C) shall not be construed as limiting the introduction of any other relevant evidence bearing upon the question whether the person was under the influence of alcohol.

(D) If a person under arrest refuses to submit to a chemical test under the provisions of this Section, evidence of refusal shall be admissible in any civil or criminal action or proceeding arising out of acts alleged to have been committed while the person under the influence of alcohol, or other drugs, or combination of both was operating a watercraft.

(E) The owner of any watercraft or any person given supervisory authority over a watercraft, may not knowingly permit a watercraft to be operated by any person under the influence of alcohol, other drug, or combination thereof.

(F) Whenever any person is convicted of a violation of this Section, the court shall notify the Division of Law Enforcement of the Department of Natural Resources, to provide the Department with the records essential for the performance of the Department's duties to monitor and enforce any order of suspension or revocation concerning the privilege to operate a watercraft.

(G) No person who has been arrested and charged for violating paragraph 1 of subsection (A) of this Section shall operate any watercraft within this State for a period of 6 hours after such arrest.

Laws 1959, p. 1473, Art. V, § 11. Amended by Laws 1967, p. 2217, § 1. Renumbered § 5-16 and amended by P.A. 82-

783, Art. VII, § 2, eff. July 13, 1982. Amended by P.A. 84-515, § 1, eff. Jan. 1, 1986; P.A. 85-147, § 1, eff. Jan. 1, 1988; P.A. 85-1328, § 1, eff. Aug. 31, 1988; P.A. 86-535, § 1, eff. Jan. 1, 1990; P.A. 88-175, § 1, eff. Jan. 1, 1994; P.A. 88-670, Art. 2, § 2-60, eff. Dec. 2, 1994; P.A. 89-445, § 9A-89, eff. Feb. 7, 1996; P.A. 90-215, § 10, eff. Jan. 1, 1998; P.A. 90-655, § 154, eff. July 30, 1998; P.A. 92-615, § 10, eff. Jan. 1, 2003.

Formerly Ill.Rev.Stat.1991, ch. 95 ½, ¶ 315-11.

1 625 ILCS 5/11-501.

2 720 ILCS 550/1 et seq.

3 720 ILCS 570/100 et seq.

4 625 ILCS 5/11-501.2.

Another § 5-16, relating to unlawful operation of a personal watercraft or a specialty prop craft at night, was renumbered § 5-20 by P.A. 88-670, Art. 2, § 2-60.

P.A. 90-655, the First 1998 General Revisory Act, amended various Acts to delete obsolete text, to correct patent and technical errors, to revise cross references, to resolve multiple actions in the 89th and 90th General Assemblies and to make certain technical corrections in P.A. 89-708 through P.A. 90-566.

45/5-16a. Admissibility of written blood alcohol test results conducted in the regular course of providing emergency medical treatment

§ 5-16a. Admissibility of written blood alcohol test results conducted in the regular course of providing emergency medical treatment.

(a) Notwithstanding any other provision of law, the written results of blood alcohol tests conducted upon persons receiving medical treatment in a hospital emergency room are admissible in evidence as a business record exception to the hearsay rule only in prosecutions for any violation of Section 5-16 of this Act or a similar provision of a local ordinance or in prosecutions for reckless homicide brought under the Criminal Code of 1961,[1] when each of the following criteria are met:

(1) the blood alcohol tests were ordered by a physician on duty at the hospital emergency room and were performed in the regular course of providing emergency medical treatment in order to assist the physician in diagnosis or treatment;

(2) the blood alcohol tests were performed by the hospital's own laboratory; and

(3) the written results of the blood alcohol tests were received and considered by the physician on duty at the hospital emergency room to assist that physician in diagnosis or treatment.

(b) The confidentiality provisions of law pertaining to medical records and medical treatment shall not be applicable with regard to blood alcohol tests performed under the provisions of this Section in prosecutions as specified in subsection (a) of this Section. No person shall be liable for civil damages as a result of the evidentiary use of blood alcohol test results under this Section or as a result of that person's testimony made available under this Section.

Laws 1959, p. 1473, Art. V, § 5-11a, added by P.A. 87-803, § 1, eff. July 1, 1992. Renumbered § 5-16a and amended by P.A. 88-670, Art. 3, § 3-81, eff. Dec. 2, 1994.

Formerly Ill.Rev.Stat.1991, ch. 95 ½, ¶ 315-11a.

1 720 ILCS 5/1-1 et seq.

45/5-16b. Preliminary breath screening test

§ 5-16b. Preliminary breath screening test. If a law enforcement officer has reasonable suspicion to believe that a person is violating or has violated Section 5-16 or a similar provision of a local ordinance, the officer, prior to an arrest, may request the person to provide a sample of his or her breath for a preliminary breath screening test using a portable device approved by the Department of State Police. The results of this preliminary breath screening test may be used by the law enforcement officer for the purpose of assisting with the determination of whether to require a chemical test as authorized under Section 5-16 and the appropriate type of test to request. Any chemical test authorized under Section 5-16 may be requested by the officer regardless of the result of the preliminary breath screening test if probable cause for an arrest exists. The result of a preliminary breath screening test may be used by the defendant as evidence in any administrative or court proceeding involving a violation of Section 5-16.

Laws 1959, p. 1473, Art. V, § 5-11b, added by P.A. 87-803, § 1, eff. July 1, 1992. Renumbered § 5-16b and amended by P.A. 88-670, Art. 3, § 3-81, eff. Dec. 2, 1994. Amended by P.A. 90-215, § 10, eff. Jan. 1, 1998; P.A. 91-828, § 15, eff. Jan. 1, 2001.

Formerly Ill.Rev.Stat.1991, ch. 95 ½, ¶ 315-11b.

45/5-17. Uniform waterway marking system

§ 5-17. The Department is authorized and empowered to establish a system of regulatory aids on the waters of the State in accordance with United States Coast Guard specifications and as recommended by the Coast Guard as a uniform waterway marking system.

Laws 1959, p. 1473, Art. V, § 12, added by Laws 1965, p. 332, § 1. Renumbered § 5-17 and amended by P.A. 82-783, Art. VII, § 2, eff. July 13, 1982.

Formerly Ill.Rev.Stat.1991, ch. 95 ½, ¶ 315-12.

45/5-18. Age of operators; limitations; certificates

§ 5-18. No person under 10 years of age may operate a motorboat. Persons at least 10 years of age and less than 12 years of age may operate a motorboat only if they are accompanied on the motorboat and under the direct control of a parent or guardian or a person at least 18 years of age designated by a parent or guardian. Persons at least 12 years of age and less than 18 years of age may operate a motorboat only if they are accompanied on the motorboat and under the direct control of a parent or guardian or a person at least 18 years of age designated by a parent or guardian, or such motorboat operator is in possession of a Boating Safety Certificate issued by the Department of Natural Resources, Division of Law Enforcement, authorizing the holder to operate motorboats.

Violations of this Section done with the knowledge of a parent or guardian shall be deemed a violation by the parent or guardian and punishable under Section 11A-1-6.

The Department of Natural Resources, Division of Law Enforcement, shall establish a program of instruction on boating safety, laws, regulations and administrative laws, and any other subject matter which might be related to the subject of general boat safety. The program shall be conducted by instructors certified by the Department of Natural Resources, Division of Law Enforcement. The course of instruction for persons certified to teach boating safety shall be not less than 8 hours in length, and the Department shall have the authority to revoke the certification of any instructor who has demonstrated his inability to conduct courses on the subject matter. Students satisfactorily completing a program of not less than 8 hours in length shall receive a certificate of safety from the Department of Natural Resources, Division of Law Enforcement. The Department may cooperate with schools, private clubs and other organizations in offering boating safety courses throughout the State of Illinois.

The Department shall issue certificates of boating safety to persons 10 years of age or older successfully completing the prescribed course of instruction and passing such tests as may be prescribed by the Department. The Department may charge each person who enrolls in a course of instruction a fee not to exceed $5. If a fee is authorized by the Department, the Department shall authorize instructors conducting such courses meeting standards established by it to charge for the rental of facilities or for the cost of materials utilized in the course. Fees retained by the Department shall be utilized to defray a part of its expenses to operate the safety and accident reporting programs of the Department.

A person over the age of 12 years who holds a valid certificate issued by another state, a province of the Dominion of Canada, the United States Coast Guard Auxiliary or the United States Power Squadron need not obtain a certificate from the Department if the course content of the program in such other state, province or organization substantially meets that established by the Department under this Section. A certificate issued by the Department or by another state, province of the Dominion of Canada or approved organization shall not constitute an operator's license, but shall certify only that the student has successfully passed a course in boating safety instruction.

The Department of Natural Resources, Division of Law Enforcement, shall implement and enforce the provisions of this Section.

Laws 1959, p. 1473, Art. V, § 13, added by P.A. 80-268, § 2, eff. Jan. 1, 1978. Renumbered § 5-18 and amended by P.A. 82-783, Art. VII, § 2, eff. July 13, 1982. Amended by P.A. 87-798, § 4, eff. Dec. 16, 1991; P.A. 89-445, § 9A-89, eff. Feb. 7, 1996; P.A. 91-357, § 234, eff. July 29, 1999.

Formerly Ill.Rev.Stat.1991, ch. 95 ½, ¶ 315-13.

45/5-19. Skin diving

§ 5-19. Skin diving.

(A) 1. No person may engage in underwater diving or swimming with the use of swimming fins or skin diving in waters other than marked swimming areas or within 150 feet of shoreline.

2. No person may engage in underwater diving or swimming with the use of self-contained underwater breathing apparatus in waters other than marked swimming areas, unless the location of such diving or swimming is distinctly marked by a diver's flag, not less than 12 inches high and 15 inches long, displaying one diagonal white stripe 3 inches wide on a red background, and of a height above the water so as to be clearly apparent at a distance of 100 yards under normal conditions, and so designed and displayed as to be visible from any point on the horizon.

3. Except in case of emergency, anyone engaging in such diving or swimming shall not rise to the surface outside of a radius of 50 feet from such flag.

4. No person engaged in such diving or swimming shall interfere with the operation of anyone fishing, nor engage in such diving or swimming in established traffic lanes; nor shall any person acting alone, or with another, intentionally or unintentionally block or obstruct any boat in any manner from proceeding to its destination where a reasonable alternative is unavailable. A reasonable alternative route is available when the otherwise unobstructed boat can proceed to its destination without reducing its lawful speed, by passing to the right or to the left of a marked diving operation.

(B) An alternate flag recognized and approved by the United States Coast Guard may be substituted for the flag required in subsection (A)2 of this Section.

(C) No watercraft shall be operated within 150 feet of a diving flag except for watercraft directly associated with that diving activity.

Laws 1959, p. 1473, Art. V, § 5-14, added by P.A. 85-149, § 1, eff. Jan. 1, 1988. Amended by P.A. 85-1209, Art. III, § 3-61, eff. Aug. 30, 1988. Renumbered § 5-19 and amended by P.A. 87-895, Art. 3, § 3-53, eff. Aug. 14, 1992. Amended by P.A. 90-655, § 154, eff. July 30, 1998.

Formerly Ill.Rev.Stat.1991, ch. 95½, ¶ 315-14.

45/5-20. Unlawful operation at night

§ 5-20. Unlawful operation at night. Beginning July 1, 1994, no person shall operate a personal watercraft or a specialty prop craft between the hours of sunset and sunrise.

Laws 1959, p. 1473, Art. V, § 5-16, added by P.A. 88-524, § 1, eff. July 1, 1994. Renumbered § 5-20 and amended by P.A. 88-670, Art. 2, § 2-60, eff. Dec. 2, 1994.

P.A. 88-670, Article 2, of the First 1994 General Revisory Act, resolved multiple actions in the 88th General Assembly and made certain technical corrections in P.A. 88-1 through P.A. 88-538.

45/5-21. Passenger location

§ 5-21. Passenger location. No person operating a motorboat shall allow a person in the motorboat to ride or sit on the gunwales, tops of seat backs, or on the decking over the bow or stern of the motorboat while the motorboat is underway, unless the person is inboard of guards or rails provided on the motorboat to prevent passengers from being lost overboard.

Nothing in this Section shall be construed to prohibit entry upon the decking over the bow or stern of the motorboat for the purpose of anchoring, mooring, or casting off or some other necessary purpose nor to prohibit customary practices while lawfully engaged in commercial fishing under the provisions of the Fish and Aquatic Life Code [1] or hunting and trapping under the provisions of the Wildlife Code.[2]

The provisions of this Section shall not apply to the driver of the boat, a person while fishing or to a person on private property.

Laws 1959, p. 1473, Art. V, § 5-21, added by P.A. 90-412, § 5, eff. Jan. 1, 1998.

[1] 515 ILCS 5/1 et seq.

[2] 520 ILCS 5/1 et seq.

ARTICLE VI. ACCIDENT REPORTS—OPERATOR'S RESPONSIBILITY—TRANSMITTAL OF INFORMATION

Section

45/6-1. Collisions, accidents, and casualties; reports

§ 6-1. Collisions, accidents, and casualties; reports.

A. The operator of a vessel involved in a collision, accident, or other casualty, so far as he can without serious danger to his own vessel, crew, passengers and guests, if any, shall render to other persons affected by the collision, accident, or other casualty assistance as may be practicable and as may be necessary in order to save them from or minimize any danger caused by the collision, accident, or other casualty, and also shall give his name, address, and identification of his vessel to any person injured and to the owner of any property damaged in the collision, accident, or other casualty.

B. In the case of collision, accident, or other casualty involving a vessel, the operator, if the collision, accident, or other casualty results in death or injury to a person or damage to property in excess of $500, shall file with the Department a full description of the collision, accident, or other casualty, including information as the Department may by regulation require. Reports of the accidents must be filed with the Department on a Department Accident Report form within 5 days.

C. Reports of accidents resulting in personal injury, where a person is incapacitated for a period exceeding 72 hours, must be filed with the Department on a Department Accident Report form within 5 days. Accidents that result in loss of life shall be reported to the Department on a Department form within 48 hours.

D. All required accident reports and supplemental reports are without prejudice to the individual reporting, and are for the confidential use of the Department, except that the Department may disclose the identity of a person involved in an accident when the identity is not otherwise known or when the person denies his presence at the accident. No report may be used as evidence in any trial, civil or criminal, arising out of an accident, except that the Department must furnish upon demand of any person who has or claims to have made a report or upon demand of any court a certificate showing that a specified accident report has or has not been made to the Department solely to prove a compliance or a failure to comply with the requirements that a report be made to the Department.

E. (1) Every coroner or medical examiner shall on or before the 10th day of each month report in writing to the Department the circumstances surrounding the death of any person that has occurred as the result of a boating accident within the examiner's jurisdiction during the preceding calendar month.

(2) Within 6 hours after a death resulting from a boating accident, but in any case not more than 12 hours after the occurrence of the boating accident, a blood specimen of at least 10 cc shall be withdrawn from the body of the decedent by the coroner or medical examiner or by a qualified person at the direction of the physician. All morticians shall obtain a release from the coroner or medical examiner prior to proceeding with embalming any body coming under the scope of this Section. The blood so drawn shall be forwarded to a laboratory approved by the Department of State Police for analysis of the alcoholic content of the blood specimen. The coroner or medical examiner causing the blood to be withdrawn shall be notified of the results of each analysis made and shall forward the results of each analysis to the Department. The Department shall keep a record of all examinations to be used for statistical purposes only. The cumulative results of the examinations, without identifying the individuals involved, shall be disseminated and made public by the Department.

Laws 1959, p. 1473, Art. VI, § 1. Amended by Laws 1967, p. 2217, § 1. Renumbered § 6-1 and amended by P.A. 82-783, Art. VII, § 2, eff. July 13, 1982. Amended by P.A. 84-515, § 1, eff. Jan. 1, 1986; P.A. 85-149, § 1, eff. Jan. 1, 1988; P.A. 87-803, § 1, eff. July 1, 1992; P.A. 91-828, § 15, eff. Jan. 1, 2001.

Formerly Ill.Rev.Stat.1991, ch. 95 ½, ¶ 316-1.

45/6-2. Operator's responsibility

§ 6-2. Operator's responsibility. The operator of a watercraft is liable for any injury or damage occasioned by the negligent operation of such watercraft, whether such negligence consists of a violation of the provisions of the Statutes of this State, or in the failure to observe such ordinary care in such operation as the rules of the common law require.

Laws 1959, p. 1473, Art. VI, § 2. Renumbered § 6-2 and amended by P.A. 82-783, Art. VII, § 2, eff. July 13, 1982.

Formerly Ill.Rev.Stat.1991, ch. 95 ½, ¶ 316-2.

45/6-3. Transmittal of information

§ 6-3. Transmittal of information. In accordance with any request duly made by an authorized official or agency of the United States, any information compiled or otherwise available to the Department pursuant to subsection (B) of Section 6-1 [1] shall be transmitted to such official or agency of the United States.

Laws 1959, p. 1473, Art. VI, § 3. Renumbered § 6-3 and amended by P.A. 82-783, Art. VII, § 2, eff. July 13, 1982.

Formerly Ill.Rev.Stat.1991, ch. 95 ½, ¶ 316-3.

1 625 ILCS 45/6-1.

ARTICLE VII. BUSINESS OF BOAT RENTAL SERVICE

45/7-1. License

§ 7-1. On and after March 1, 1960 it shall be unlawful for any person to engage in the business of operating a boat or boats carrying passengers for hire, or renting a boat or boats for hire without first having obtained a license so to do from the Department. Such license shall be renewable each year on March 1st, shall be good only for one year or portion of a year to March 1st, and it shall be unlawful for such person to so engage in such business without having a valid license currently then in force.

Laws 1959, p. 1473, Art. VII, § 1. Renumbered § 7-1 and amended by P.A. 82-783, Art. VII, § 2, eff. July 13, 1982. Amended by P.A. 85-149, § 1, eff. Jan. 1, 1988.

Formerly Ill.Rev.Stat.1991, ch. 95 ½, ¶ 317-1.

45/7-2. License fee

§ 7-2. License fee. The fee for a license to operate a boat for carrying passengers for hire shall be $50 for each boat. The fee for a license for engaging in the business of renting boats for hire shall be $30, plus an annual fee for each boat rented or offered for rent of $1 for each boat less than 16 feet in length; $2 for each boat 16 feet or over and less than 26 feet in length; and $8 for each boat 26 feet or over in length. No boat shall, after March 1, 1960, be rented or offered for rent until such license has been granted and the boat marked as hereinafter provided.

Laws 1959, p. 1473, Art. VII, § 2. Renumbered § 7-2 and amended by P.A. 82-783, Art. VII, § 2, eff. July 13, 1982. Amended by P.A. 85-149, § 1, eff. Jan. 1, 1988.

Formerly Ill.Rev.Stat.1991, ch. 95 ½, ¶ 317-2.

45/7-3. Rules and regulations

§ 7-3. Rules and regulations. The Department is hereby empowered, and it shall be their duty, to prescribe methods of inspection to determine the weight capacity for each boat carrying passengers for hire, or for rent, and to satisfy the Department that such boat is of a suitable structure for the service in which it is to be employed, and is in a condition to warrant the belief that it may be used in navigation with safety to life and property.

Laws 1959, p. 1473, Art. VII, § 3. Renumbered § 7-3 and amended by P.A. 82-783, Art. VII, § 2, eff. July 13, 1982. Amended by P.A. 85-149, § 1, eff. Jan. 1, 1988.

Formerly Ill.Rev.Stat.1991, ch. 95 ½, ¶ 317-3.

45/7-4. Weight capacity of boats; determination

§ 7-4. In order to authorize the maximum number of pounds of weight for boats less than 16 feet in length, the Department shall have their cubic foot capacity accurately determined, divide this number by twelve, and multiply the quotient by 150 pounds. The Department shall determine the basis for computing the weight capacity of boats 16 feet or over and less than 45 feet in length.

Laws 1959, p. 1473, Art. VII, § 4. Renumbered § 7-4 and amended by P.A. 82-783, Art. VII, § 2, eff. July 13, 1982.

Formerly Ill.Rev.Stat.1991, ch. 95 ½, ¶ 317-4.

45/7-5. Compliance with standards, rules and regulations

§ 7-5. It shall be the duty of the Department to see that all of such boats comply with the standards prescribed in this Act and the rules and regulations of the Department.

Laws 1959, p. 1473, Art. VII, § 5. Renumbered § 7-5 and amended by P.A. 82-783, Art. VII, § 2, eff. July 13, 1982. Amended by P.A. 85-149, § 1, eff. Jan. 1, 1988.

Formerly Ill.Rev.Stat.1991, ch. 95 ½, ¶ 317-5.

45/7-6. Non-compliance; notice to owner; rectification of defective conditions

§ 7-6. Whenever, it shall be found that any boat does not comply with the standards of this Act and the rules and regulations of the Department, it shall thereupon be the duty of the Department to notify the owner, proprietor or agent in charge of any such boat, the respect in which the boat fails to comply, and to demand that such defective conditions be rectified prior to further use of such boat.

Laws 1959, p. 1473, Art. VII, § 6. Renumbered § 7-6 and amended by P.A. 82-783, Art. VII, § 2, eff. July 13, 1982. Amended by P.A. 85-149, § 1, eff. Jan. 1, 1988.

Formerly Ill.Rev.Stat.1991, ch. 95 ½, ¶ 317-6.

45/7-7. Display of license or tags

§ 7-7. The Department shall furnish to the licensee an appropriate license which shall be prominently displayed in his place of business, or upon the boat if only one boat is involved. In addition to said license the Department shall also furnish to such licensee a durable tag or disc for each boat so licensed with such markings as the Department shall deem necessary, which tag or disc must be affixed to some prominent place at the bow of said boat plainly visible to the public. The licensee shall also cause to be painted on the after quarter of the boat the number of pounds of weight authorized to be carried therein, and no licensee or his agent shall knowingly permit more than that number of pounds of weight or number of persons to occupy said boat at any one given time.

Laws 1959, p. 1473, Art. VII, § 7. Renumbered § 7-7 and amended by P.A. 82-783, Art. VII, § 2, eff. July 13, 1982.

Formerly Ill.Rev.Stat.1991, ch. 95 ½, ¶ 317-7.

45/7-8. Equipment

§ 7-8. Equipment. Neither the owner of a boat livery, nor his agent or employee shall permit any watercraft to depart from his premises unless it has been provided, either by owner or renter, with the equipment required pursuant to Article IV of this Act and any rules and regulations made pursuant thereto.

Laws 1959, p. 1473, Art. VII, § 8. Renumbered § 7-8 and amended by P.A. 82-783, Art. VII, § 2, eff. July 13, 1982. Amended by P.A. 87-198, § 1, eff. Jan. 1, 1992.

Formerly Ill.Rev.Stat.1991, ch. 95 ½, ¶ 317-8.

45/7-9. Registration

§ 7-9. It shall be the responsibility of the owner of a boat livery, or his agent or employee, to determine that all watercraft are properly registered as required pursuant to Article III of this Act.

Laws 1959, p. 1473, Art. VII, § 9, added by Laws 1961, p. 3349, § 1. Renumbered § 7-9 and amended by P.A. 82-783, Art. VII, § 2, eff. July 13, 1982. Amended by P.A. 86-1340, § 2, eff. Sept. 7, 1990; P.A. 87-198, § 1, eff. Jan. 1, 1992.

Formerly Ill.Rev.Stat.1991, ch. 95 ½, ¶ 317-9.

45/7-10. Unlawful rental of personal watercraft or specialty prop-craft

§ 7-10. Unlawful rental of personal watercraft or specialty prop-craft.

(a) A livery shall not lease, hire or rent a personal watercraft or a specialty prop-craft to, or for operation by, any person who is under 16 years of age.

(b) Any person convicted of violating this Section is guilty of a Class A misdemeanor.

Laws 1959, p. 1473, Art. VII, § 7-10, added by P.A. 87-798, § 4, eff. Dec. 16, 1991. Amended by P.A. 90-412, § 5, eff. Jan. 1, 1998.

Formerly Ill.Rev.Stat.1991, ch. 95 ½, ¶ 317-10.

ARTICLE VIII. LOCAL REGULATION

Section

45/8-1. Local ordinances

§ 8-1. Local ordinances. The provisions of this Act, and of other applicable laws of this State shall govern the operation, equipment, numbering and all other matters relating thereto whenever any vessel shall be operated on the waters of this State, or when any activity regulated by this Act shall take place thereon; but nothing in this Act shall be construed to prevent the adoption of any ordinance or local law by any political subdivision of the State relating to operation and equipment of vessels the provisions of which are not inconsistent with the provisions of this Act, amendments thereto or regulations issued thereunder: Provided, that such ordinances or local laws shall be operative only so long as and to the extent that they continue to be not inconsistent with the provisions of this Act, amendments thereto or regulations issued thereunder.

Laws 1959, p. 1473, Art. VIII, § 1. Renumbered § 8-1 and amended by P.A. 82-783, Art. VII, § 2, eff. July 13, 1982.

Formerly Ill.Rev.Stat.1991, ch. 95 ½, ¶ 318-1.

45/8-2. Special rules—Application

§ 8-2. Special rules—Application. Any subdivision of this State may, at any time, but only after public notice, make formal application to the Department for special rules and regulations with reference to the operation of vessels on any waters within its territorial limits and shall set forth therein the reasons which make such special rules or regulations necessary or appropriate.

Laws 1959, p. 1473, Art. VIII, § 2. Renumbered § 8-2 and amended by P.A. 82-783, Art. VII, § 2, eff. July 13, 1982.

Formerly Ill.Rev.Stat.1991, ch. 95 ½, ¶ 318-2.

45/8-3. Special rules—Power

§ 8-3. Special rules—Power. The Department is hereby authorized to make special rules and regulations with reference to the operation of vessels on any waters within the territorial limits of any subdivision of this State.

Laws 1959, p. 1473, Art. VIII, § 3. Renumbered § 8-3 and amended by P.A. 82-783, Art. VII, § 2, eff. July 13, 1982.

Formerly Ill.Rev.Stat.1991, ch. 95 ½, ¶ 318-3.

ARTICLE IX. FILING OF REGULATIONS

Section

45/9-1. Rules and regulations, filing

§ 9-1. Rules and regulations, filing. The implementation and administration of the provisions of this Act shall be by rules and regulations adopted by the Department of Natural Resources. A copy of the rules and regulations adopted pursuant to this Act, and of any amendments thereto, shall be filed in the office of the Department and in the office of the Secretary of State. Rules and regulations shall be published by the Department in a convenient form.

Laws 1959, p. 1473, Art. IX, § 1. Renumbered § 9-1 and amended by P.A. 82-783, Art. VII, § 2, eff. July 13, 1982. Amended by P.A. 84-973, § 1, eff. Jan. 1, 1986; P.A. 89-445, § 9A-89, eff. Feb. 7, 1996.

Formerly Ill.Rev.Stat.1991, ch. 95 ½, ¶ 319-1.

ARTICLE X. THE STATE BOATING ACT FUND

Section

45/10-1. Special fund

§ 10-1. Special fund. All revenue received under the provisions of this Act, including registration fees, fines, or other income of any kind or nature, shall be deposited in the State Treasury and shall be set apart in a special fund to be known as the State Boating Act Fund, except that revenue from fines resulting from citations written by a county sheriff or his deputy shall be deposited in a county fund in the county where the citation was written. Appropriations from the State Boating Act Fund, excepting those revenues received as a result of the Snowmobile Registration and Safety Act,[1] shall be made to the Department, and shall be used for the expenses of the Department in administering the registration, boat safety, boat safety education, and enforcement provisions of this Act or for any purpose related or incident thereto and connected therewith, including the construction and improvement of boating facilities, such as access areas, launching sites, harbor facilities, lakes, and marinas, including plans and specifications, engineering surveys, and supervision and land acquisition where necessary. In addition to the foregoing, appropriations from the State Boating Act Fund, other than revenues received as a result of the Snowmobile Registration and Safety Act, may be made to the Department of Natural Resources to pay operational expenses for recreational boating facilities at McHenry Lock and Dam in McHenry County and Sinnissippi Dam in Whiteside County.

Laws 1959, p. 1473, Art. X, § 1. Amended by Laws 1963, p. 2598, § 1; P.A. 77-1314, § 1, eff. Aug. 27, 1971. Renumbered § 10-1 and amended by P.A. 82-783, Art. VII, § 2, eff. July 13, 1982. Amended by P.A. 83-971, § 1, eff. Dec. 2, 1983; P.A. 87-1109, § 1, eff. Jan. 1, 1993; P.A. 89-445, § 9E-46, eff. Feb. 7, 1996.

Formerly Ill.Rev.Stat.1991, ch. 95 ½, ¶ 320-1.

[1] 325 ILCS 40/1-1 et seq.

45/10-2. Snowmobile Registration and Safety Act Revenues

§ 10-2. Snowmobile Registration and Safety Act Revenues. All revenue received under the provisions of the "Snowmobile Registration and Safety Act",[1] including registration fees, fines, or other income of whatsoever kind or nature, shall be deposited in the State Treasury in "The State Boating Act Fund". Appropriations of such revenue shall be made only to the Department for administering the registration of snowmobiles, snowmobile safety, snowmobile safety education and enforcement provisions of the "Snowmobile Registration and Safety Act" or for any purpose related or connected thereto, including the construction, maintenance, and rehabilitation of snowmobile recreation areas or any other facilities for the use of snowmobiles, including plans and specifications, engineering surveys and supervision and land acquisition where necessary.

Laws 1959, p. 1473, Art. X, § 2, added by P.A. 77-1314, § 1, eff. Aug. 27, 1971. Renumbered § 10-2 and amended by P.A. 82-783, Art. VII, § 2, eff. July 13, 1982.

Formerly Ill.Rev.Stat.1991, ch. 95 ½, ¶ 320-2.

[1] 625 ILCS 40/1-1 et seq.

ARTICLE XI. PENALTIES

45/11-1 to 45/11-9. §§ 11-1 to 11-9. Repealed by P.A. 85-149, § 2, eff. Jan. 1, 1988

ARTICLE XIA. PENALTIES

Section

Enactment

Article XIA was added by P.A. 85-149, § 1, eff. Jan. 1, 1988.

45/11A-1. Violations; punishment

§ 11A-1. Except as otherwise provided in this Act, any person who violates any of the provisions of this Act shall be guilty of a petty offense.

Laws 1959, p. 1473, Art. XIA, § 11A-1, added by P.A. 85-149, § 1, eff. Jan. 1, 1988.

Formerly Ill.Rev.Stat.1991, ch. 95 ½, ¶ 321A-1.

45/11A-2. Violations of sections 3A-3, 3A-13, 3A-14, 3A-20 or 3A-21

§ 11A-2. A. Any person who violates Section 3A-3, 3A-13, 3A-14, or 3A-20 is guilty of a Class A misdemeanor.

B. Any person who violates Section 3A-21 is guilty of a Class 2 felony.

Laws 1959, p. 1473, Art. XIA, § 11A-2, added by P.A. 85-149, § 1, eff. Jan. 1, 1988. Amended by P.A. 88-524, § 1, eff. July 1, 1994.

Formerly Ill.Rev.Stat.1991, ch. 95 ½, ¶ 321A-2.

45/11A-3. Violations of sections 5-1 or 5-2

§ 11A-3. Any person who violates any of the provisions of Section 5-1 or 5-2 of this Act is guilty of a Class B misdemeanor.

Laws 1959, p. 1473, Art. XIA, § 11A-3, added by P.A. 85-149, § 1, eff. Jan. 1, 1988.

Formerly Ill.Rev.Stat.1991, ch. 95 ½, ¶ 321A-3.

45/11A-4. Additional penalties

§ 11A-4. Any person who is convicted of a violation of Sections 5-1, 5-2 or 11A-5 of this Act, in addition to any other penalties authorized in this Act, may in the discretion of the court be refused the privilege of operating any watercraft on any of the waterways of this State for a period of not less than one year.

Laws 1959, p. 1473, Art. XIA, § 11A-4, added by P.A. 85-149, § 1, eff. Jan. 1, 1988.

Formerly Ill.Rev.Stat.1991, ch. 95 ½, ¶ 321A-4.

45/11A-5. Operation of watercraft during period when privilege is denied

§ 11A-5. Any person who operates any watercraft during the period when he is denied the privilege to so operate is guilty of a Class A misdemeanor.

Laws 1959, p. 1473, Art. XIA, § 11A-5, added by P.A. 85-149, § 1, eff. Jan. 1, 1988.

Formerly Ill.Rev.Stat.1991, ch. 95 ½, ¶ 321A-5.

45/11A-6. Violations of section 2-4

§ 11A-6. Any person who violates any provision of Section 2-4 is guilty of a Class A misdemeanor.

Laws 1959, p. 1473, Art. XIA, § 11A-6, added by P.A. 85-149, § 1, eff. Jan. 1, 1988.

Formerly Ill.Rev.Stat.1991, ch. 95 ½, ¶ 321A-6.

ARTICLE XII. PARTIAL INVALIDITY

Section

45/12-1. Effect

§ 12-1. If any provision of this Act, or the application of such provision to any persons, body or circumstances shall be held invalid, the remainder of this Act, or the application of such provision to persons, bodies or circumstances other than those as to which it shall have been held invalid, shall not be affected thereby.

Laws 1959, p. 1473, Art. XII, § 1. Renumbered § 12-1 and amended by P.A. 82-783, Art. VII, § 2, eff. July 13, 1982.

Formerly Ill.Rev.Stat.1991, ch. 95 ½, ¶ 322-1.

ARTICLE XIII. EFFECTIVE DATE

Section

45/13-1. Effective date

§ 13-1. This Act takes effect on March 1, 1960.

Laws 1959, p. 1473, Art. XIII, § 1. Renumbered § 13-1 and amended by P.A. 82-783, Art. VII, § 2, eff. July 13, 1982.

Formerly Ill.Rev.Stat.1991, ch. 95 ½, ¶ 323-1.

ARTICLE XIV. REPEAL

Section

45/1. Repeal

§ 1. "An Act regulating Motorboats" approved July 15, 1941, as amended, and "An Act regulating the Operation of Motorboats", approved July 18, 1947,[1] are repealed.

Laws 1959, p. 1473, Art. XIV, § 1.

Formerly Ill.Rev.Stat.1991, ch. 95 ½, ¶ 324-1.

[1] Former Ill.Rev.Stat. ch. 95½, ¶¶ 283 to 303 (repealed).

ACT 50. PUBLIC CONVEYANCE NOTICE ACT

Section

50/0.01. Short title

§ 0.01. Short title. This Act may be cited as the Public Conveyance Notice Act.

Laws 1967, p. 2850, § 0.01, added by P.A. 86–1324, § 674, eff. Sept. 6, 1990.

Formerly Ill.Rev.Stat.1991, ch. 100, ¶ 30.

Title of Act:

An Act to require displaying of notices in conveyances used for the transportation of the public for hire in relation to aggravated assault and aggravated battery against a driver, operator, employee or passenger. Laws 1967, p. 2850, approved and eff. Aug. 11, 1967.

50/1. Form and contents of notice

§ 1. A notice shall be prominently displayed in each vehicle or conveyance used for the transportation of the public for hire which must state substantially the following: Any person who assaults or harms an individual whom he knows to be a driver, operator, employee or passenger of a transportation facility or system engaged in the business of transportation for hire and who is then performing in such capacity or using such public transportation as a passenger, if such individual is assaulted, commits a Class A misdemeanor, or if such individual is harmed, commits a Class 3 felony.

Laws 1967, p. 2850, § 1, eff. Aug. 11, 1967. Amended by P.A. 77–2830, Art. 74, § 1, eff. Jan. 1, 1973.

Formerly Ill.Rev.Stat.1991, ch. 100, ¶ 31.

INDEX

References are to Chapter, Act and Section

†

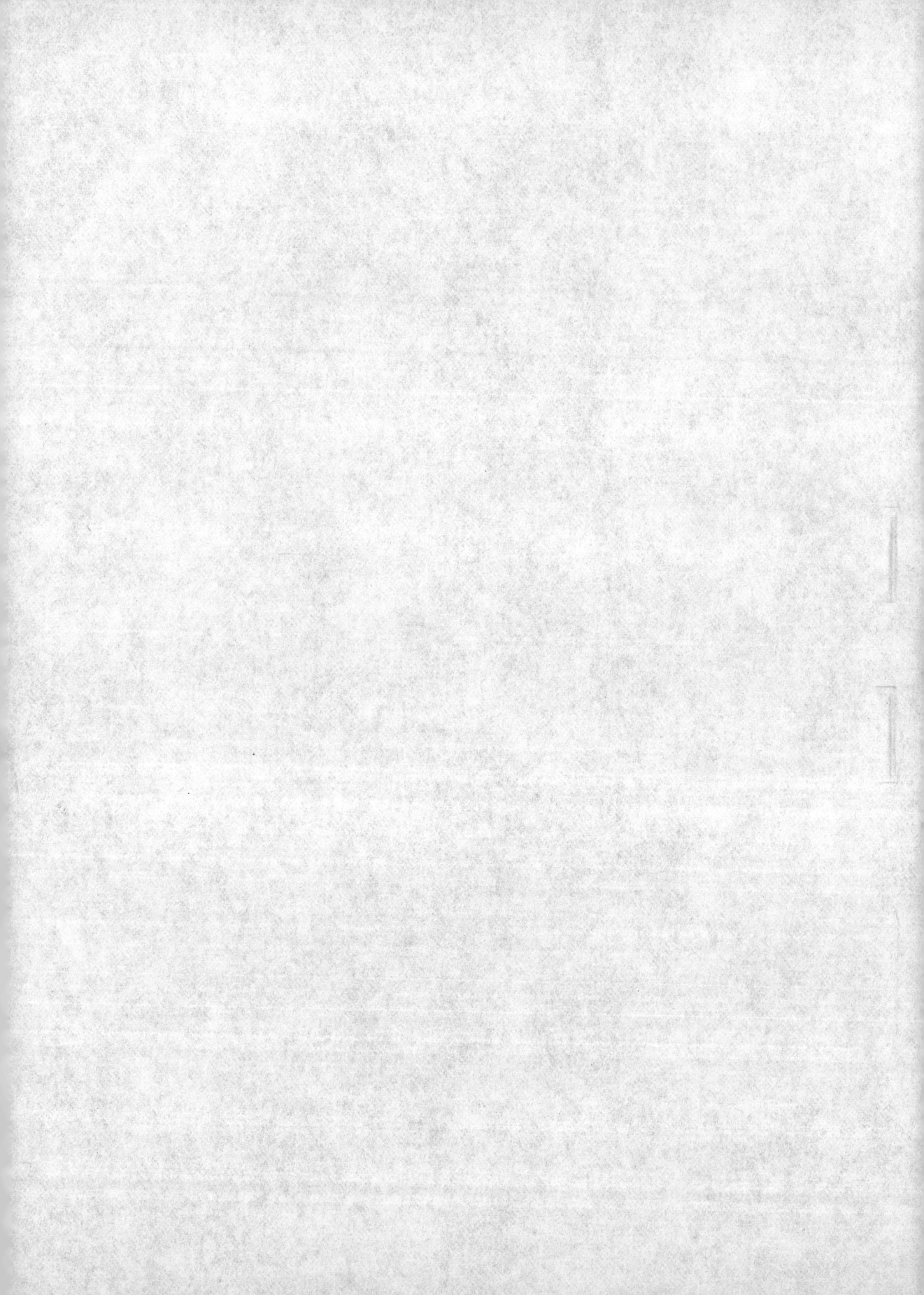